GAINS...
STALLI...

AGE, WEIGHT & DISTANCE TABLE

Timeform's scale of weight-for-age for the flat

Dist	Age	Jan 1-16	Jan 17-31	Feb 1-16	Feb 17-28	Mar 1-16	Mar 17-31	Apr 1-16	Apr 17-30	May 1-16	May 17-31	June 1-16	June 17-30
5f	4	10-0	10-0	10-0	10-0	10-0	10-0	10-0	10-0	10-0	10-0	10-0	10-0
	3	9—5	9—5	9—6	9—7	9—7	9—8	9—8	9—9	9—9	9—10	9-10	9-11
	2						8—0	8—1	8—3	8—4	8—5	8—6	8—7
6f	4	10-0	10-0	10-0	10-0	10-0	10-0	10-0	10-0	10-0	10-0	10-0	10-0
	3	9—2	9—3	9—4	9—5	9—5	9—6	9—7	9—7	9—8	9—8	9—9	9—9
	2									8—0	8—2	8—3	8—4
7f	4	9-13	9-13	10-0	10-0	10-0	10-0	10-0	10-0	10-0	10-0	10-0	10-0
	3	9—0	9—1	9—2	9—3	9—4	9—4	9—5	9—6	9—6	9—7	9—8	9—8
	2											7-13	8—1
1m	4	9-13	9-13	9-13	9-13	10-0	10-0	10-0	10-0	10-0	10-0	10-0	10-0
	3	8—12	8-13	9—0	9—1	9—2	9—2	9—3	9—4	9—5	9—5	9—6	9—7
	2												
9f	4	9-12	9-12	9-12	9-13	9-13	9-13	9-13	10-0	10-0	10-0	10-0	10-0
	3	8—10	8—11	8—12	8-13	9—0	9—1	9—2	9—2	9—3	9—4	9—5	9—5
	2												
1¼m	4	9-11	9-12	9-12	9-12	9-13	9-13	9-13	9-13	9-13	9-13	10-0	10-0
	3	8—8	8—9	8—10	8—11	8—12	8-13	9—0	9—1	9—2	9—2	9—3	9—4
	2												
11f	4	9-10	9-11	9-11	9-12	9-12	9-12	9-13	9-13	9-13	9-13	9-13	10-0
	3	8—6	8—7	8—8	8—9	8-10	8—11	8-12	8-13	9—0	9—1	9—2	9—2
1½m	4	9-10	9-10	9-10	9-11	9-11	9-12	9-12	9-12	9-13	9-13	9-13	9-13
	3	8—4	8—5	8—6	8—7	8—8	8—9	8-10	8—11	8-12	8-13	9—0	9—1
13f	4	9—9	9—9	9-10	9-10	9-11	9-11	9-11	9-12	9-12	9-12	9-13	9-13
	3	8—2	8—3	8—4	8—5	8—7	8—8	8—9	8-10	8-11	8-12	8-13	9—0
1¾m	4	9—8	9—8	9—9	9—9	9-10	9-10	9-11	9-11	9-12	9-12	9-12	9-13
	3	8—0	8—2	8—3	8—4	8—5	8—6	8—7	8—8	8—9	8-10	8-11	8-12
15f	4	9—7	9—8	9—8	9—9	9—9	9—10	9-10	9-11	9-11	9-11	9-12	9-12
	3	7-13	8—0	8—1	8—2	8—4	8—5	8—6	8—7	8—8	8—9	8-10	8-11
2m	4	9—6	9—7	9—7	9—8	9—9	9—9	9-10	9-10	9-11	9-11	9-11	9-12
	3	7-11	7-12	7-13	8—1	8—2	8—3	8—4	8—5	8—6	8—7	8—8	8—9
2¼m	4	9—5	9—5	9—6	9—7	9—7	9—8	9—9	9—9	9-10	9-10	9-10	9-11
	3	7—8	7—9	7-11	7-12	7-13	8—0	8—2	8—3	8—4	8—5	8—6	8—7
2½m	4	9—3	9—4	9—5	9—6	9—6	9—7	9—7	9—8	9—9	9—9	9-10	9-10
	3	7—5	7—7	7—8	7—9	7-11	7-12	7-13	8—1	8—2	8—3	8—4	8—5

For 5-y-o's and older, use 10-0 in all cases
Race distances in the above tables are shown only at 1 furlong intervals.
For races over odd distances, the nearest distance shown in the table should be used:
thus for races of 1m to 1m 109 yards, use the table weights for 1m;
for 1m 110 yards to 1m 219 yards use the 9f table

**The age, weight and distance table covering July to December
appears on the end paper at the back of the book**

RACEHORSES OF 2001

Price £70.00

A TIMEFORM PUBLICATION

CONTENTS

The age, weight and distance tables, for use in applying the ratings in races involving horses of different ages, appear on the end papers at the front and back of the book

Compiled and produced by

G. Greetham (Director), C. S. Williams (Managing Editor & Handicapper), P. Morrell (Essays & Editor), S. D. Rowlands (Handicapper & Editor), J. Ingles (Essays & Editor for pedigrees & 'Top Horses Abroad'), G. J. North, M. J. Taylor (Handicappers), R. J. C. Austen, J. Early, G. J. McGibbon, E. K. Wilkinson (Essays), S. Boow, R. J. O'Brien, J. A. Todd (Short Commentaries), G. Crowther, M. Hall, D. Holdsworth, G. Johnstone, W. Muncaster, A-M. Stevens, R. Todd, C. Wright (Production)

© **Portway Press Limited 2002**　　　　　　ISBN 1 901570 29 0

Racehorses of 2001

Introduction

'In the context of life as a whole, racing is a triviality . . . it's only a piddling little pond really.' The words of Timeform's founder Phil Bull—usually expressed pithily as 'racing is the great triviality'—were never more appropriate than in 2001. The year was dominated by the most devastating terrorist act in history: the coordinated crashing of hijacked passenger airliners on September 11th into the twin towers of the World Trade Center in New York, killing thousands, and the Pentagon in Washington. A disbelieving global audience watched man's inhumanity to man live on TV as a second plane hit the Trade Center minutes after the first. The events were the catalyst for crisis, among the most trivial consequences being the cancellation of sports fixtures such as the Ryder Cup. If sport is essentially irrelevant, however, it can still play its part at such times. It was another colourful figure from racing history, 'I've Gotta Horse' Prince Monolulu, who preferred the view that betting on horses was a powerful agent for world peace. 'Horse racing will stop wars because as soon as a man backs a winner, he becomes a capitalist!' Whether the organisers of the Breeders' Cup, America's international racing showcase, were influenced by similar thoughts or not, their determination to press on with arrangements for the meeting on October 27th reflected great credit on them. Staged as 'the re-birth of international sport in our country,' the Breeders' Cup went ahead in New York at Belmont Park where, before September 11th, the

A period of silence is observed at the opening of the St Leger meeting after the horrific events in America

roof of the grandstand offered a view in the distance of the twin towers of the World Trade Center. The absence of most of the Arab owners, including the Maktoum family which pledged $5m to a relief fund, served as another stark reminder that the world was still potentially on the brink of turmoil.

Leaving aside any wider symbolic significance of the latest Breeders' Cup day, the meeting proved particularly successful for the European challengers. The eagerly-promoted Breeders' Cup clash between Europe's top three-year-old **Galileo** and the leader of North America's classic generation Point Given (who has a short commentary in this Annual along with a number of other top international performers) had already been thwarted when the latter was retired through injury at the end of August. Galileo, winner of the Derby and the Irish Derby as well as the King George VI and Queen Elizabeth Stakes, was unplaced in the Breeders' Cup Classic on dirt, but Europe won three other races. Galileo's stable-companion **Johannesburg** crowned a fine season by winning the Breeders' Cup Juvenile on dirt and **Fantastic Light**, whose rivalry with Galileo was a feature of the European season, won the Breeders' Cup Turf and was retired with record earnings for a horse in Europe of over £4m. **Banks Hill** was a most impressive winner of the Filly & Mare Turf, her stable, incidentally, the only one among the Europeans to reject using the diuretic drug lasix (a subject discussed in the essay). Europe's Horse of the Year **Sakhee**, the wide-margin winner of the International at York and the Prix de l'Arc at Longchamp, was just touched off by the previous year's winner Tiznow in the Breeders' Cup Classic. The timing of the Breeders' Cup meeting, incidentally, did not please the organisers of Champions Day at Newmarket, the highlight of which, in the absence of Sakhee, was a fourth win in succession by his 'substitute' **Nayef** in the Champion Stakes. The Breeders' Cup came only a week after Champions Day, which it is also set to do in the next three years. Sakhee's performance at York was the best seen on a British racecourse all year and his six-length winning margin in the Arc, climax of a card in which all the pattern events were Group 1s, equalled the record held by Ribot and Sea Bird II.

The playing of 'God Save The Queen' after Sakhee's triumph in the Arc seemed a little incongruous given that the American-bred winner was owned and trained by Arabs and ridden by an Italian. The cosmopolitan nature of British racing makes claims of 'British' victories sound hollow on occasions, but it is nonetheless interesting to record that British-trained horses picked up £10,474,893 abroad in prize-money in 2001, just ahead of the International Racing Bureau's figure for the previous year and the third-highest annual total after those of 1996 and 1997. The international aspect of racing nowadays was again illustrated by figures showing that the number of challengers sent from leading racing countries to compete on foreign soil topped eight hundred for

Sakhee's demolition of his rivals in the Juddmonte International at York was the best performance seen on a British racecourse in 2001

Galileo (No.9) and Fantastic Light—their first clash in Britain's most prestigious all-aged championship, the King George VI and Queen Elizabeth Diamond Stakes

the first time; the number crossing to other continents for major races also reached an all-time high of two hundred and sixteen. American sorties abroad continue to be limited, focussing almost exclusively on Japan, Hong Kong and the United Arab Emirates where **Captain Steve** became the third American-trained winner of the world's richest race, the Dubai World Cup. The progress made by the Dubai World Cup meeting in its short history is outlined in the essay on Captain Steve and also under **Express Tour**, winner of the UAE Derby, the richest Derby in the world.

The overseas victories of **Morshdi** (Derby Italiano and Grosser Preis von Baden) and **Endless Hall** (International Cup, Singapore) helped Michael Jarvis and Luca Cumani to finish second and third respectively in the British trainers' table of overseas earnings, behind Saeed bin Suroor, who finished with total earnings on foreign soil from his Newmarket base of £3,805,010, a new record for a British-based trainer (the IRB excluded £728,363 won in place money in Hong Kong by **Tobougg**, **China Visit** and **Ekraar**, on the grounds that the Godolphin string had then returned to Dubai). One of bin Suroor's biggest earners **Kutub**, who completed a four-timer in the Singapore Gold Cup, a

The 'return match'—rounding the home turn in the Irish Champion, Galileo's pacemaker is about to be swallowed up as Fantastic Light slips through on the inside of Give The Slip (white cap); Galileo (dark colours) has to challenge three-wide

handicap, after two Group 1 wins in Germany and one in Italy, never even ran in Britain, his campaign emphasising the global ambitions of the Godolphin operation. Fantastic Light won the Emirates World Series, the brainchild of Godolphin's driving force Sheikh Mohammed, for the second successive year. The wide-ranging essay on Fantastic Light looks at the merits of the Series and at other methods of identifying and recognising racing's champions; Timeform also defends weight-for-age allowances, the desirability of which was called into question again in some quarters in the latest season. French-trained **Jim And Tonic** and the German-trained pair **Silvano** and **Proudwings** also provided notable examples in their own countries of horses whose greatest victories were achieved on foreign soil. **Super Tassa** gained a major overseas victory for Italy when winning the Yorkshire Oaks, but Italy's comparative weakness as a racing nation is highlighted in the essay on the top miler **Slickly**, another Godolphin horse aimed almost exclusively at big prizes abroad. There were no Japanese runners in Europe in 2001 but important successes at the Dubai World Cup meeting and in Hong Kong further emphasised that nation's arrival as a formidable force in international racing. 'Top Horses Abroad' at the back of this Annual reviews the year in each of the leading racing countries and includes Timeform ratings for their top performers.

Britain's Group 1 races were dominated by the stables of Godolphin and Ballydoyle which won fifteen of the twenty-seven between them. Aidan

O'Brien became the first overseas-based trainer to win the trainers' championship on the Flat in Britain since Vincent O'Brien in 1977. After landing the Epsom classic double with Galileo and **Imagine**, Aidan O'Brien went on to win record first-three prize-money of £3,245,024 for a champion trainer in Britain, on the way achieving eight more Group 1 victories, including those of champion sprinter **Mozart** in the July Cup and the Nunthorpe and **Milan** in the St Leger. O'Brien's world-wide total of Group/Grade 1s by the end of the year was twenty-three, a new record. Stable-jockey Michael Kinane was on seventeen of them, one more than Frankie Dettori managed in 2001, the latter's total including the Irish Oaks and Nassau Stakes on **Lailani** for Ed Dunlop and the Prix Marcel Boussac on **Sulk** for John Gosden, in addition to thirteen of the fourteen Group/Grade 1s won by Saeed bin Suroor (supposed

Aidan O'Brien, the first overseas-based trainer to be champion in Britain since 1977

pacemaker **Summoner** in the Queen Elizabeth II Stakes being the one which escaped him). Among the Group 1 victories that Kinane missed for Ballydoyle were those on **Black Minnaloushe**, successful in the St James's Palace Stakes after winning the Irish Two Thousand Guineas, in which O'Brien saddled the first three, a feat he repeated with his two-year-olds in the Dewhurst and the Criterium de Saint-Cloud. The Ballydoyle two-year-old colts maintained a virtual stranglehold on the top races in Europe, winning nine of the ten Group 1s in their age group open to them. Half of the twenty-two two-year-olds rated

110 or higher in this Annual were trained by O'Brien, headed by Breeders' Cup Juvenile winner Johannesburg (whose essay looks at the qualities that might be needed for a Kentucky Derby bid). **Rock of Gibraltar** completed the Grand Criterium/Dewhurst double and also won the Gimcrack. The impressive victory of Godolphin's **Dubai Destination** over Rock of Gibraltar in the Champagne Stakes at Doncaster and the promise of French-trained **Shaanmer** should have tempered winter talk of Ballydoyle's sweeping all before it again in the 2002 classics (the stable won seven in 2001, three each in Britain and Ireland and one in France). The last northern-trained classic winner was Mister Baileys in the 1994 Two Thousand Guineas and his trainer Mark Johnston, who reached a century of winners in Britain for the eighth successive year, had a notably promising set of juveniles in the latest season, including **Fight Your Corner**, **Bandari** and the highly-thought-of **Love Regardless**. The highest rated two-year-old colt trained in Britain, **Captain Rio**, was also trained in Yorkshire, providing the small stable of Richard Whitaker with its biggest victory. Ballydoyle and Godolphin were overshadowed in the juvenile fillies' department by the Mick Channon-trained **Queen's Logic**, the best juvenile filly seen out in Britain for over a decade, and the very promising **Gossamer**, trained by Luca Cumani for owner-breeder Gerald Leigh who donated all the prize-money won by his horses in 2001 to the charity CancerBACUP.

The previous season's champion trainer Sir Michael Stoute divided O'Brien and bin Suroor in the end-of-season table. He was the only other trainer to win more than one Group 1 event in Britain during the year, taking the Two Thousand Guineas with **Golan** and the Lockinge and the Eclipse with **Medicean**. Freemason Lodge might have housed the Oaks winner had the

Champion jockey Kieren Fallon and trainer Sir Michael Stoute after the Musidora Stakes at York

The Gold Cup runners pass the packed Royal Ascot stands; Persian Punch (in second) and Royal Rebel (disputing third on the outside) go on to fight out one of the finishes of the season

Queen's **Flight of Fancy** enjoyed better luck in running. Her Majesty will be pinning her classic hopes in her Golden Jubilee year in 2002 on the promising Stoute-trained colt **Right Approach**, and champion jockey Kieren Fallon appears to be doing the same given his enthusiasm for the colt (as reported in the essay). Fallon will not, however, be retained by the Stoute stable in 2002. The period leading up to the announcement of the decision not to renew the champion jockey's contract—after only two seasons at the Freemason Lodge/ Beech Hurst complex—produced more rumours than the stereotypical ladies' coffee morning, a statement released by Stoute finally clarifying that not all his owners wished to use Fallon though 'his association with the stable will continue with those that do.' The latest chapter in Fallon's eventful career should not rule out the prospect of a fourth jockeys' championship in 2002. His main rival for the title in the latest season, Kevin Darley, rode as a freelance, as he did when taking the title in 2000 when Fallon was sidelined for the rest of that season after being badly injured at Royal Ascot. Fallon was written off by some during a somewhat hesitant comeback in the spring but he ended the year with one hundred and sixty-six winners, four more than Darley. The main beneficiary of Fallon's enforced absence during the second half of 2000 was Irish-based Johnny Murtagh who formed a good association with the Stoute stable, riding numerous Group 1 winners including **Kalanisi** for the Aga Khan, for whom he also won the Derby, Irish Derby and Prix de l'Arc on Sinndar. The Aga Khan's fortunes in the latest season contrasted starkly with the previous season, as the essay on Kalanisi reveals. Another of racing's major figures, trainer Henry Cecil, also had a season he will wish to forget, the essay on **Wellbeing** containing a selection of facts and figures to illustrate the point. Murtagh, on the other hand, was always in demand at the big meetings and in the major races and again highlighted his prowess, his five victories at Royal Ascot—a meeting being extended from four days to five in Jubilee year— including the Gold Cup on **Royal Rebel** who just held off **Persian Punch** in one of the finishes of the season. The revival of the Gold Cup in recent seasons is discussed in Royal Rebel's essay. **Vinnie Roe**, the first three-year-old to complete the Irish St Leger/Prix Royal-Oak double since 1979, looks sure to provide tough opposition for the likes of Royal Rebel and Persian Punch in the major staying events in 2002.

Royal Rebel's Gold Cup victory provided some light relief for his owner Peter Savill, chairman of the British Horseracing Board, who was embroiled in negotiations to resurrect a media rights deal with the Go Racing consortium. Forty-nine courses had finally signed up with Go Racing in May (ten small tracks having opted to go with GG-Media), but the deal brokered through the

Racecourse Association was scuppered by the BHB in mid-June when it refused to grant the consortium a licence covering pre-race data, such as runners, riders and weights. The BHB had been under growing pressure from some owners and trainers, among them the president of the Racehorse Owners' Association who accused racing of 'selling its soul'. Peter Savill joined the criticism, labelling the way that the media deal had been negotiated by the Racecourse Association as 'amateurish', and the BHB directors voted 6-5 against granting Go Racing a data licence. After intensive 'on-off' renegotiations during Royal Ascot week, the long-running saga was finally concluded in the early hours of Friday morning. Go Racing—which later changed its trade name to attheraces—signed a contract said to be worth £307m to racing over ten years, plus £80m for marketing.

Royal Rebel's owner Peter Savill had plenty of other things on his mind at Royal Ascot

The BHB's position was considerably strengthened, responsibility for contracts for pictures in betting shops being transferred to the BHB from the RCA, and half the income from future projects developed through any new technology (plans also included a joint venture on a new 'superbet') going directly to the BHB. At the same time, the BHB also secured near industry-wide agreement on plans for the future funding of racing, based on a commercial arrangement for beaming pictures into betting shops and providing pre-race data; the Government had imposed a deadline for racing's agreement on a new funding plan before going ahead with its own plans to disband the Levy Board, in the process ridding itself of statutory responsibilities for racing.

If the renegotiated rights deal and agreement on the plan for future funding represented a triumph for the BHB, there still remained the big question of how the BHB would fare in negotiations with the bookmakers. The bookmakers had secured a major victory of their own when their campaign for the replacement of betting tax charged to punters with a tax on bookmakers' gross profits was successful. The Government adopted the radical idea as a solution to the migration of credit betting to 'tax-free' offshore operators. The betting tax was abolished on October 6th, the leading bookmakers agreeing to stop deductions from punters. So much for Benjamin Franklin's saying that only two things in life are certain, death and taxes. For punters, it seemed a case of one down and one to go—though whether punters will really be any better off in the long run remains to be seen. The BHB played no part in the campaign to abolish betting tax and never supported it publicly, but it wasn't long before it made clear its intention to secure some of the bookmakers' anticipated 'tax

savings'. The yield from the levy of over £60m, added to the fees paid for live television coverage into betting shops, was bringing in around £75m for racing. The BHB announced that it would want the equivalent of two and a half per cent of betting turnover—estimated to be worth over £150m—in the post-Levy Board era. Bookmakers, through the newly-formed Confederation of Bookmakers Associations, hinted that they might agree to pay around ten per cent of their gross profits, estimated at around £120m. With the BHB's database copyright case against Hills referred to the European Court of Justice (the Court of Appeal overturned a High Court injunction against Hills in July), the Office of Fair Trading also began to look into claims that the BHB's demands breached competition law, the consequences of

Saturday October 6th—the first day of a new era for off-course punters

the BHB and the Racecourse Association pooling their rights to sell them to broadcasters and bookmakers coming under particular scrutiny. The investigation was later extended to embrace the contract of attheraces with the forty-nine tracks. With the BHB in the dock accused of exploiting a monopoly position, the talks on the levy agreement for 2002 ended in acrimonious disarray, leaving the Government legally obliged to determine the outcome. What is believed will be the final levy scheme, ending in March 2003, was eventually set at around 9% of bookmakers' gross profits from British horseracing, which could, in theory, yield between £90m to £105m (to be offset against any higher sums from a commercial agreement), making it the biggest-ever projected year-on-year increase in the levy. Parliament was told that gross profits were, in the Government's opinion, 'the fairest and most reliable indication of the bookmakers' capacity to pay.' An independent report commissioned by the Government into racing was used by Culture Secretary Tessa Jowell in her determination of the levy settlement. The report, by consultants Organisation Consulting Partnership, concluded: 'The arguments that a large increase is needed in payments to racing are difficult to assess but are in our view far from self-evident . . . we do not believe that it has been demonstrated that the needs of racing cannot be accommodated within this rise in other income [including the £27m+ each year from the attheraces media deal].' The bookmakers reportedly offered £90m during the Levy Board negotiations, plus £20m for pictures (nothing for data), pending determination in the European Court about whether the BHB owns and has the right to sell pre-race data, and pending any findings of the Office of Fair Trading. Throughout the negotiations, the bookmakers insisted that any levy deal went hand in hand with an agreement on rights to pictures and pre-race data, agreeing the one without the other regarded as weakening their bargaining position. Over the last few days of negotiations, the BHB was said to have reduced its demands—though still insisting on payment based on turnover rather than gross profits—but agreement could not be reached.

The publicly-owned Tote, set to be transferred to racing interests by the Government around the same time that the Levy Board is wound up, caused something of a furore when, like all the other leading bookmakers, it too rejected the data and picture charges proposed by the BHB. The move was widely portrayed as 'stabbing racing in the back' and the Tote's chairman Peter Jones became the subject of what looked suspiciously like an orchestrated smear campaign in sections of the media. Replying to one vitriolic attack in a national newspaper, the Tote's chief executive John Heaton stated categorically that the Tote had made its decision based purely on the statutory requirements to 'operate a profitable and successful business.' The Tote's profits go back into racing but Heaton pointed out that it was 'not controlled by the BHB or its chairman, and if we accepted their terms merely because they demanded it, we would be in breach of our responsibilities.' A snapshot of the first three months of tax-free betting, based on data provided by a study of 340 independent betting offices, showed that betting turnover increased by almost 50%, but bookmakers' margins fell from 22% to 14% and gross profits by 7% (at the clear expense of the Treasury compared to the days of betting duty). Regardless of whether this sample proves an accurate pointer to the long term, it does at least help to explain why the bookmakers have strongly resisted BHB demands so far.

The newly-appointed Sports Minister, Richard Caborn, warned both sides that they had to start 'living in the new era', rather than relying on Government ministers or the courts to sort out their differences. 'I wasn't aware of the deep antagonism between the racing and betting industries until I got involved, but the industry's future health depends on the two sides acting in a concerted way.' Clear enough, but will either side take any notice? If no general agreement on pictures and data is forthcoming, a significant section of British racing—which accounts for around 70% of betting shop turnover—will be unavailable from May onwards to betting shops not signed up with the BHB (likely to include all the major chains). Their customers will instead be faced with betting on a mixed diet of terrestrial televised racing, racing from the ten GG-Media courses (only two of which stage Flat racing), and from South Africa and Ireland, plus a plethora of greyhound racing and 'numbers' betting. The BHB's brinkmanship paid off in the Go Racing renegotiations, but whether it will do so with the bookmakers remains to be seen. If the demands made by the BHB are, indeed, excessive, they can be met only by means of new deductions, declared or hidden, which would meet with strong disapproval from punters' champions and from the Government, or, alternatively, from a reduction in bookmakers' gross profits, which would, in turn, hit the Government's coffers. The current bickering between 'racing' and 'betting'—which should be working together to increase the sport's attraction—has been likened to fighting over the deckchairs on the Titanic. The ship has not struck the iceberg yet, but it is approaching at a rapid rate of knots. Almost everyone, it seems, can see the dangers but no-one appears able to plot a course to safety.

The ranks of Europe's owner-breeders were hit particularly hard in 2001 with the deaths of Prince Fahd Salman, Daniel Wildenstein, Dick Hollingsworth and Lord Carnarvon. Prince Fahd's dark green silks were carried most famously by Generous and he also owned Ramruma, Ibn Bey, Bint Pasha, Knight's Baroness, Zoman and many others; he bred Mozart, the latest champion sprinter who was sold as a yearling for 340,000 guineas. Daniel Wildenstein, who won the Prix de l'Arc de Triomphe four times, had the runner-up in the latest season in **Aquarelliste**, whose essay includes details of her owner's extensive racing achievements. Dick Hollingsworth produced a string of high-class horses over a period of nearly half a century, many of their names—including Oaks winner Bireme and Gold Cup and stayers' triple crown winner Longboat—having nautical connections (many of his best horses were descended from Felucca, who took her name from a small boat). Lord Carnarvon, whose part in the abrupt dismissal of the Queen's trainer Dick Hern in 1989 made him unpopular,

John Reid on his last big winner, Boreal in the Deutsches Derby

certainly deserves to be judged more kindly by history in at least one aspect. As the architect of the pattern system, an achievement discussed in the essay on Fantastic Light, Lord Carnarvon changed the face of the sport. He was a successful owner-breeder in his own right, his colours carried by such as Tamerlane, Little Wolf, Roseate Tern, Niche, Lyric Fantasy and Lemon Souffle. Among those who retired during the season were jockeys John Reid and stalwart lightweights John Lowe and Nicky Carlisle. John Reid won the Arc (Tony Bin) and the King George twice (Ile de Bourbon and Swain), as well as English classics on On The House, Dr Devious, Las Meninas and Nedawi. Reid, whose career is reviewed further in the essay on Kutub, was also joint president of the Jockeys' Association and has been succeeded by Kevin Darley.

More horses than ever—nearly 9,700—are dealt with individually in *Racehorses of 2001*, and that is without counting the many others listed in the complete Timeform Irish Handicap and the 'Top Horses Abroad' section. The horses highlighted in bold in this introduction are among those who are the subject of essays. They include the redoubtable **Madame Jones**. She equalled the record for the most handicap wins in a year on the Flat in Britain, running twice as many times as almost any other horse during the year, and she fully deserves her place among the performers who contributed most to British racing in 2001.

February 2002

HORSE OF THE YEAR
BEST OLDER MALE
BEST MIDDLE-DISTANCE HORSE
RATED AT 136

SAKHEE

BEST TWO-YEAR-OLD FILLY RATED AT 125
QUEEN'S LOGIC

BEST TWO-YEAR-OLD COLT RATED AT 127
JOHANNESBURG

BEST THREE-YEAR-OLD FILLY RATED AT 128
BANKS HILL

BEST THREE-YEAR-OLD COLT RATED AT 134
GALILEO

BEST OLDER FEMALE RATED AT 121
PIPALONG

BEST SPRINTER RATED AT 131
MOZART

BEST MILERS RATED AT 128
MEDICEAN
SLICKLY

BEST STAYER RATED AT 129
MILAN

BEST PERFORMANCE IN A HANDICAP IN BRITAIN
TILLERMAN
ran to 121
when third in Tote International Stakes at Ascot

BEST PERFORMANCES ON ALL-WEATHER IN BRITAIN
CRETAN GIFT
ran to 112
when third in the Tote Scoop6 Handicap at Wolverhampton
DANCING MYSTERY
ran to 112
when second in the Ladbroke Handicap at Wolverhampton

THE TIMEFORM 'TOP HUNDRED'

Here are listed the 'Top 100' two-year-olds, three-year-olds and older horses in the annual. Fillies and mares are denoted by (f).

2-YEAR-OLDS
127	Johannesburg
125	Queen's Logic (f)
122	Captain Rio
119p	Dubai Destination
118	Rock of Gibraltar
118	Zipping
116p	Act One
116p	Hawk Wing
115p	High Chaparral
115	Landseer
114p	Ballingarry
114p	Fight Your Corner
114p	Gossamer (f)
114p	Tendulkar
113p	Bandari
113	Castle Gandolfo
113	Guys And Dolls
113	Meshaheer
112p	Saddad
112	Mutinyonthebounty
111	Black Sam Bellamy
110p	Della Francesca
110	Where Or When
109p	Danseuse d'Etoile (f)
109p	Henri Lebasque
109p	Shaanmer
109p	Tholjanah
109	Firebreak
109	Naheef
109	Sophisticat (f)
109	Sulk (f)
108p	Summertime Legacy (f)
108	Berk The Jerk
108	Leggy Lou (f)
108	Prism
108	Rashbag
108	Sholokhov
107p	Comfy
107p	Maryinsky (f)
107p	Playapart
107+	Redback
107	Acclamation
107	Mister Cosmi
107	Parasol
107	Rapscallion
107	Scottish River
107	Silent Honor (f)
107	Sparkling Water
106p	Quarter Moon (f)
106p	Revealing (f)
106	Camp David
106	Samhari
106	Stonemason
106	Ya Hajar (f)
105p	Kazzia (f)

105p	King of Happiness
105p	Savannah Bay
105	Asheer
105	Dominica (f)
105	Swing Wing
104p	Bragadino
104p	Dress To Thrill (f)
104p	Esloob (f)
104p	Half Glance (f)
104p	Kriskova
104	Distant Valley (f)
104	Doc Holiday
104	Lahinch (f)
104	Prince Dayjur
104	Resplendent Cee
104	Shah Jehan
103P	Right Approach
103p	Bestam
103p	Coshocton
103p	Hills of Gold
103p	Leo's Luckyman
103p	On The Nile (f)
103p	Protectress (f)
103p	Saranac Lake (f)
103	Advance Party
103	Anna Walhaan
103	Misterah (f)
103	Rum Charger (f)
103	Sundari (f)
103	Whitbarrow
102p	Forty On Line (f)
102p	Fraulein (f)
102p	Kournakova (f)
102p	Mount Joy
102p	Snowfire (f)
102p	Swiss Lake (f)
102	Bright And Clear (f)
102	Diaghilev
102	Falcon Hill
102	Ho Choi
102	Irony
102	Lady High Havens (f)
102	Loweswater
102	Mr Sandancer
102	Wiseman's Ferry

3-YEAR-OLDS
134	Galileo
134	Point Given
131	Jungle Pocket
131	Mozart
130	Kurofune
129	Milan
129	Nayef
128	Banks Hill (f)
128	Storming Home

126	Vinnie Roe
125	Golan
125	Noverre
125	Sagacity
125	Tobougg
124	Grandera
123p	Carnival Dancer
123	Aquarelliste (f)
123	Black Minnaloushe
123	Morshdi
122	E Dubai
122	Hawkeye
122	Lailani (f)
121	Boreal
121	Diamilina (f)
121	Do The Honours (f)
121	Express Tour
121	Mr Combustible
121	No Excuse Needed
121	Olden Times
121	Street Cry
120p	Alexius
120	Anabaa Blue
120	Double Honour
120	King Charlemagne
120	Perfect Sunday
120	Sabiango
120	Vahorimix
119p	Equerry
119	Asian Heights
119	Chichicastenango
119	Clearing
119	Demophilos
119	Dilshaan
119	Imagine (f)
119	Masterful
119	Tamburlaine
118	Celtic Silence
118	Denon
118	Frenchmans Bay
118	Munir
118	Orientor
118	Royal Dragon
118	Wareed
117p	Foreign Affairs
117	Alleluia (f)
117	Chancellor
117	Danehurst (f)
117	Indian Creek
117	Iron Mask
117	Maille Pistol
117	Mare Nostrum (f)
117	Mizzen Mast
117	Mugharreb
116p	High Pitched
116	Aghnoyoh

14

116 Ameerat (f)
116 Beekeeper
116 Bosham Mill
116 Capal Garmon
116 Independence (f)
116 Keltos
116 King of Tara
116 Minardi
116 Nadia (f)
116 Noroit
116 Snowstorm
116 Volata
116 Zollner
115 Choc Ice (f)
115 Dietrich (f)
115 Golden Apples (f)
115 Golden Wells
115 Hill Country
115 Malhub
115 Momentum
115 Mot Juste (f)
115 Muwakleh (f)
115 Okawango
115 Poussin
115 Priors Lodge
115 Pugin
115 Putra Sandhurst
115 Qaatef
115 Theatre Script
115 The Trader
115 Visorhill
115 Walking Around
114 Bonnard
114 Crystal Music (f)
114 Dandoun
114 Flight of Fancy (f)
114 Head In The Clouds (f)
114 Jessica's Dream (f)
114 Karsavina (f)
114 King's Ironbridge
114 Mediterranean
114 Rose Gypsy (f)
114 Sunny Glenn
114 Time Away (f)

OLDER HORSES
136 Sakhee
134 Fantastic Light
133 Tiznow
130 Agnes Digital
130 Captain Steve
129 Hightori
129 Kalanisi
128 Medicean
128 Slickly
128 T M Opera O
127 Golden Snake
127 Observatory
127 Stay Gold
126 Nuclear Debate
126 Silvano
125 Ekraar

124 Jim And Tonic
124 Millenary
124 Mirio
124 Persian Punch
123 Kutub
123 Mount Abu
123 Mubtaker
123 Tough Speed
123§ Royal Rebel
122 Best of The Bests
122 China Visit
122 Mutamam
122 Water Jump
121 Bach
121 Distant Music
121 Endless Hall
121 Generic
121 Germinis
121 Give The Slip
121 Harmonic Way
121 Little Rock
121 Paolini
121 Pipalong (f)
121 Samum
121 Sandmason
121 Solo Mio
121 State Shinto
121 Tillerman
121 Wellbeing
120+ Misraah
120 Anzillero
120 Bahamian Pirate
120 Holding Court
120 Mutafaweq
120 Right Wing
120 San Sebastian
120 Swallow Flight
120 Zindabad
119 Arkadian Hero
119 Banyumanik
119 Belenus
119 Boreas
119 Cape Town
119 Cassandra Go (f)
119 Daliapour
119 Jardines Lookout
119 Marienbard
119 Superior Premium
119 Terre A Terre (f)
119 Three Points
119 Warningford
118 Akbar
118 Albarahin
118 Border Arrow
118 Danger Over
118 Festival of Light
118 Idaho Quest
118 Imperial Beauty (f)
118 Island House
118 Muakaad
118 Proudwings (f)
118 Romantic Affair

118 Shibboleth
118 Subiaco
118 Summoner
118 Super Tassa (f)
118 The Whistling Teal
118 Valley Chapel
118 Yavana's Pace
118§ Valentino
117 Bishops Court
117 Broche
117 Caitano
117 Compton Bolter
117 Dano-Mast
117 Egyptband (f)
117 First Magnitude
117 Mahfooth
117 Nice One Clare (f)
117 Nicobar
117 Rainbow High
117 Repertory
117 Sagittarius
117 Slew The Red
117 Speedmaster
117 St Expedit
117d Rushcutter Bay

2001 STATISTICS

The following tables show the leading owners, trainers, jockeys, sires of winners and horses on the Flat in Britain during 2001 (Jan 1–Dec 31). The prize-money statistics, compiled by *Timeform*, relate to first-three prize money and win-money. Win money was traditionally used to decide the trainers' championship until, in 1994, the BHB and the National Trainers' Federation established a championship decided by total prize-money as determined by *Racing Post*. The jockeys' championship has traditionally been decided by the number of winners ridden during the year, though since 1997 the Jockeys' Association has recognised a championship that runs for the turf season (Mar–Nov).

OWNERS (1,2,3 earnings)	Horses	Indiv'l Wnrs	Races Won	Runs	%	Stakes £
1 Godolphin	41	21	24	84	28.5	1,852,815
2 Mr Hamdan Al Maktoum	153	74	108	510	21.1	1,701,829
3 Mrs John Magnier & Mr M. Tabor	17	7	8	36	22.2	1,437,622
4 Mr M. Tabor & Mrs John Magnier	22	9	13	51	25.4	1,261,533
5 Mr K. Abdulla	113	54	71	353	20.1	985,925
6 Maktoum Al Maktoum	69	32	49	225	21.7	829,835
7 Cheveley Park Stud	49	28	38	163	23.3	719,046
8 Sheikh Mohammed	55	32	42	152	27.6	533,712
9 Lord Weinstock	12	5	5	26	19.2	478,610
10 Sheikh Ahmed Al Maktoum	54	24	30	199	15.0	399,283
11 Mr J. C. Smith	29	8	13	149	8.7	361,025
12 Mr Jaber Abdullah	9	4	9	25	36.0	238,353

OWNERS (win-money, £½m+)	Horses	Indiv'l Wnrs	Races Won	Runs	%	Stakes £
1 Mrs John Magnier & Mr M. Tabor	17	7	8	36	22.2	1,328,009
2 Mr Hamdan Al Maktoum	153	74	108	510	21.1	1,198,984
3 Godolphin	41	21	24	84	28.5	1,108,786
4 Mr M. Tabor & Mrs John Magnier	22	9	13	51	25.4	974,406
5 Mr K. Abdulla	113	54	71	353	20.1	727,970
6 Cheveley Park Stud	49	28	38	163	23.3	634,016
7 Maktoum Al Maktoum	69	32	49	225	21.7	551,781

TRAINERS (1,2,3 earnings)	Horses	Indiv'l Wnrs	Races Won	Runs	%	Stakes £
1 A. P. O'Brien, Ireland	49	14	20	99	20.2	3,245,024
2 Sir Michael Stoute	137	62	75	397	18.8	1,967,583
3 Saeed bin Suroor	41	21	24	84	28.5	1,852,815
4 M. Johnston	148	72	116	771	15.0	1,731,836
5 B. W. Hills	164	78	107	722	14.8	1,459,810
6 R. Hannon	212	80	110	1180	9.3	1,314,464
7 J. L. Dunlop	174	78	107	646	16.5	1,227,210
8 M. P. Tregoning	60	30	53	219	24.2	957,202
9 M. R. Channon	136	51	67	804	8.3	853,140
10 E. A. L. Dunlop	110	48	74	445	16.6	812,068
11 H. R. A. Cecil	88	38	48	256	18.7	736,365
12 T. D. Easterby	132	42	73	804	9.0	732,972

TRAINERS (win-money, £1m+)	Horses	*Indiv'l* Wnrs	*Races* Won	Runs	%	*Stakes* £
1 A. P. O'Brien, Ireland	49	14	20	99	20.2	2,679,994
2 M. Johnston	148	72	116	771	15.0	1,338,490
3 Sir Michael Stoute	137	62	75	397	18.8	1,262,499
4 Saeed bin Suroor	41	21	24	84	28.5	1,108,786

TRAINERS (with 100+ winners)	Horses	*Indiv'l* Wnrs	*Races* Won	2nd	3rd	Runs	%
1 M. Johnston	148	72	116	90	78	771	15.0
2 R. Hannon	212	80	110	109	112	1180	9.3
3 B. W. Hills	164	78	107	97	90	722	14.8
3 J. L. Dunlop	174	78	107	84	73	646	16.5

JOCKEYS (by winners)	1st	2nd	3rd	Unpl	*Total* Mts	%
1 K. Fallon	166	127	112	583	988	16.8
2 K. Darley	162	121	115	587	985	16.4
3 Pat Eddery	121	82	77	513	793	15.2
4 T. Quinn	116	125	87	449	777	14.9
5 J. P. Spencer	112	90	62	437	701	15.9
6 D. Holland	105	66	72	386	629	16.6
7 G. Duffield	95	60	70	553	778	12.2
8 L. Dettori	94	64	44	197	399	23.5
9 R. Hughes	90	60	70	364	584	15.4
10 S. Sanders	83	74	51	453	661	12.5
11 F. Norton	82	78	69	589	818	10.0
12 S. Drowne	80	98	85	698	961	8.3

Note: K. Fallon rode all his winners during the turf season (Mar 22-Nov 10)

JOCKEYS (1,2,3 earnings, £1m+)	*Races* Won	Rides	%	*Stakes* £
1 M. J. Kinane	26	162	16.0	2,937,704
2 K. Fallon	166	988	16.8	2,852,557
3 L. Dettori	94	399	23.5	2,782,830
4 K. Darley	162	985	16.4	2,296,396
5 T. Quinn	116	777	14.9	1,811,207
6 Pat Eddery	121	793	15.2	1,739,022
7 R. Hills	79	446	17.7	1,522,767
8 J. P. Spencer	112	701	15.9	1,280,175
9 D. Holland	105	629	16.6	1,212,053
10 R. Hughes	90	584	15.4	1,206,291
11 M. Hills	58	487	11.9	1,027,612

JOCKEYS (win-money, £1m+)	*Races* Won	Rides	%	*Stakes* £
1 M. J. Kinane	26	162	16.0	2,437,927
2 K. Fallon	166	988	16.8	2,019,890
3 L. Dettori	94	399	23.5	1,820,203
4 K. Darley	162	985	16.4	1,705,896
5 R. Hills	79	446	17.7	1,088,026
6 Pat Eddery	121	793	15.2	1,008,610

APPRENTICES (by winners)	1st	2nd	3rd	Unpl	Total Mts	%
1 C. Catlin	71	69	60	658	858	8.2
2 I. Mongan	67	74	64	522	727	9.2
3 K. Dalgleish	65	52	58	537	712	9.1
4 G. Gibbons	54	40	57	354	505	10.6

SIRES OF WINNERS (1,2,3 earnings)	Races Won	Runs	%	Stakes £
1 Sadler's Wells (by Northern Dancer)	48	316	15.1	2,716,201
2 Danehill (by Danzig)	51	340	15.0	1,292,099
3 Machiavellian (by Mr Prospector)	40	282	14.1	1,058,216
4 Indian Ridge (by Ahonoora)	66	549	12.0	958,632
5 Rahy (by Blushing Groom)	7	54	12.9	623,220
6 Grand Lodge (by Chief's Crown)	32	264	12.1	622,641
7 Inchinor (by Ahonoora)	46	458	10.0	610,998
8 Selkirk (by Sharpen Up)	51	405	12.5	563,536
9 Rainbow Quest (by Blushing Groom)	36	241	14.9	546,894
10 Spectrum (by Rainbow Quest)	19	195	9.7	524,042
11 Caerleon (by Nijinsky)	32	219	14.6	521,243
12 Polar Falcon (by Nureyev)	63	442	14.2	501,940

SIRES OF WINNERS (win-money)	Horses	Indiv'l Wnrs	Races Won	Stakes £
1 Sadler's Wells (by Northern Dancer)	105	35	48	2,334,407
2 Danehill (by Danzig)	85	38	51	970,445
3 Machiavellian (by Mr Prospector)	55	26	40	719,848
4 Indian Ridge (by Ahonoora)	90	43	66	629,243
5 Inchinor (by Ahonoora)	70	26	46	474,842
6 Grand Lodge (by Chief's Crown)	56	23	32	442,605
7 Gulch (by Mr Prospector)	28	10	16	421,638
8 Royal Applause (by Waajib)	43	19	25	416,536
9 Rainbow Quest (by Blushing Groom)	56	27	36	413,788
10 Selkirk (by Sharpen Up)	73	34	51	377,415
11 Polar Falcon (by Nureyev)	81	38	63	356,612
12 Lahib (by Riverman)	42	21	31	355,773

LEADING HORSES (1,2,3 earnings)	Races Won	Runs	Stakes £
1 Galileo 3 b.c. Sadler's Wells – Urban Sea	2	2	1,015,000
2 Golan 3 b.c. Spectrum – Highland Gift	1	2	394,000
3 Medicean 4 ch.c. Machiavellian – Mystic Goddess	3	4	359,100
4 Nayef 3 b.c. Gulch – Height of Fashion	4	7	352,140
5 Fantastic Light 5 b.h. Rahy – Jood	1	2	310,000
6 Milan 3 b.c. Sadler's Wells – Kithanga	2	3	309,000
7 Noverre 3 b.c. Rahy – Danseur Fabuleux	1	3	290,400
8 Mozart 3 b.c. Danehill – Victoria Cross	3	3	282,700
9 Sakhee 4 b.c. Bahri – Thawakib	2	2	275,429
10 Sir George Turner 2 ch.c. Nashwan – Ingozi	2	4	211,810
11 Imagine 3 b.f. Sadler's Wells – Doff The Derby	1	1	211,700
12 Rock of Gibraltar 2 b.c. Danehill – Offshore Boom	2	4	211,500

EXPLANATORY NOTES

'Racehorses of 2001' deals individually, in alphabetical sequence, with every horse that ran on the Flat in Britain in 2001 (including on the all-weather tracks), plus many foreign-trained horses that did not race here. For each of these horses is given (1) its age, colour and sex, (2) its breeding, and, where this information has not been given in a previous Racehorses Annual, a family outline, (3) a form summary giving its Timeform rating at the end of the previous year, followed by the details of all its performances during the past year, (4) a Timeform rating, or ratings, of its merit in 2001 (which appears in the margin), (5) a Timeform commentary on its racing or general characteristics as a racehorse, with some suggestions, perhaps, regarding its prospects for 2002, and (6) the name of the trainer in whose charge it was on the last occasion it ran. For each two-year-old the foaling date is also given.

The book is published with a twofold purpose. Firstly, it is intended to have permanent value as a review of the exploits and achievements of the more notable of the Flat-racing thoroughbreds in 2001. Thus, while the commentaries upon the vast majority of the horses are, of necessity, in note form, the best horses are more critically examined. The text is illustrated by half-tone portraits of the most notable horses (where these are available) and photographs of the major races. Secondly, the book is designed to help the punter to analyse races, and the notes which follow contain instructions for using the data. The attention of foreign buyers of British bloodstock, and others who are concerned with Timeform Ratings as a measure of absolute racing class in terms of a standard scale, is particularly drawn to the section headed 'The Level of the Ratings'.

TIMEFORM RATINGS

The Timeform Rating of a horse is simply the merit of the horse expressed in pounds and is arrived at by careful examination of its running against other horses using a scale of weight for distance beaten which, without going into the complexities, ranges from around 3 lb a length at five furlongs and 2 lb a length at a mile and a quarter to 1 lb at two miles. Timeform maintains a 'running' handicap of all horses in training throughout the season.

THE LEVEL OF THE RATINGS

At the close of each season the ratings of all the horses that have raced are re-examined, and, if necessary, the general level of the handicap is adjusted so that all the ratings are kept at the same standard level from year to year. Some of the ratings may, therefore, be different from those in the final issue of the 2001 Timeform Black Book series.

RATINGS AND WEIGHT-FOR-AGE

The reader has, in the ratings in this book, a universal handicap embracing all the horses in training it is possible to weigh up, ranging from tip-top performers, with ratings from 130 to 145, through categories such as high-class, very smart, smart, useful, fairly useful, fair and modest, down to the poorest, rated around the 20 mark. All the ratings are at weight-for-age, so that equal ratings mean horses of equal merit: perhaps it would be clearer if we said that the universal rating handicap is really not a single handicap, but four handicaps side by side: one for two-year-olds, one for three-year-olds, one for four-year-olds and one for older horses. Thus, a three-year-old rated, for argument's sake, at 117 is deemed to be identical in point of 'merit' with a four-year-old also rated at 117: but for them to have equal chances in, say, a mile race in May, the three-year-old would need to be receiving 9 lb from the four-year-old, which is the weight difference specified by the Age, Weight and Distance Tables on the end papers at the front and back of the book.

USING THE RATINGS

In using Timeform Ratings with a view to discovering which horses in any race have the best chances at the weights, we have two distinct cases, according to whether the horses taking part are of the same age or of different ages. Here is the procedure in each case:-

A. Horses of the Same Age

If the horses all carry the same weight there are no adjustments to be made, and the horses with the highest ratings have the best chances. If the horses carry different weights, jot down their ratings, and to the rating of each horse add one point for every pound the horse is set to carry less than 10 st, or subtract one point for every pound it has to carry more than 10 st. When the ratings have been adjusted in this way the highest resultant figure indicates the horse with the best chance at the weights.

Example (any distance: any week of the season)

2 Reflect (9-6)	.... Rating 119	.... add 8	....	127
2 Saturn Moon (9-4)	.... Rating 113	.... add 10	....	123
2 Ardesco (8-11)	.... Rating 107	.... add 17	....	124
2 Eastern Law (8-7)	.... Rating 108	.... add 21	....	129
2 Velma (8-2)	.... Rating 100	.... add 26	....	126
2 Iron Street (7-7)	.... Rating 92	.... add 35	....	127

Eastern Law (129) has the best chance strictly on form;
Reflect (127) and Iron Street (127) are the next best

B. Horses of Different Ages

Take no notice of the weight any horse receives from any other. Instead, consult the Age, Weight and Distance Tables printed on the end papers at the front and back of the book. Treat each horse separately, and compare the weight it has to carry with the weight prescribed for it in the tables, according to the age of the horse, the distance of the race and the time of the year. Then, add one point to the rating for each pound the horse has to carry less than the weight given in the tables: or, subtract one point from the rating for every pound it has to carry more than the weight prescribed by the tables. The highest resultant figure indicates the horse most favoured by the weights.

Example (1½ miles on June 30th)

(Table Weights: 5-y-o 10-0; 4-y-o 9-13; 3-y-o 9-1)

6 Bay Pearl (10-2)	.... Rating 115	.... subtract 2	113
4 Elshabeeba (9-9)	.... Rating 114	.... add 4	118
6 Regal Charge (9-5)	.... Rating 115	.... add 9	124
3 Inclination (9-2)	.... Rating 120	.... subtract 1	119
4 Great Bangle (8-11)	.... Rating 101	.... add 16	117
3 Water Moss (8-7)	.... Rating 108	.... add 8	116

Regal Charge (124) has the best chance at the weights,
with 5 lb in hand of Inclination

TURF AND ARTIFICIAL SURFACE

When a horse has raced on turf and on an artificial surface and its form on one is significantly different from the other, the two ratings are given, the artificial one set out below the turf preceded by 'a'.

Thus with BLUE SHARK 47
a55

the top figure, 47, is the rating to be used in turf races, and the one below, a55, is for use in races on an artificial surface. Where there is only one rating, that is to be used for both turf and on artificial surfaces.

NOTE ON RIDERS' ALLOWANCES

For the purposes of rating calculations it should, in general, be assumed that the allowance a rider is able to claim is nullified by his or her inexperience. Therefore, the *weight adjustments to the ratings should be calculated on the weight allotted by the handicapper, or determined by the conditions of the race*, and no extra addition should be made to a rating because the horse's rider claims an allowance. This is the general routine procedure; but of course, after the usual adjustments have been made, the quality of jockeyship is still an important factor to be considered when deciding between horses with similar chances.

WEIGHING UP A RACE

The ratings tell you which horses in a particular race are most favoured by the weights; but complete analysis demands that the racing character of each horse, as set out in the commentary upon it, is also studied carefully to see if there is any reason why the horse might be expected not to run up to its rating or indeed might improve on it. It counts for little that a horse is thrown in at the weights if it has no pretensions whatever to staying the distance, or is unable to act on the prevailing going.

These two matters, suitability of distance and going, are no doubt the most important points to be considered. But there are others. For example, the ability of a horse to accommodate itself to the conformation of the track. Then there is the matter of temperament and behaviour: nobody would be in a hurry to take a short price about a horse with whom it is always an even chance whether it will give its running.

A few minutes spent checking up on these matters in the commentaries upon the horses concerned will sometimes put a very different complexion on a race from that which is put upon it by the ratings alone. We repeat, therefore, that the correct way to use Timeform, or this annual volume, in the analysis of individual races is, first to use the ratings to discover which horses are most favoured by the weights, and second, to check through the comments on the horse to discover what factors other than weight might also affect the outcome of the race.

THE FORM SUMMARIES

The form summary enclosed in the brackets lists each horse's performances on the Flat during the past year in chronological sequence, showing, for each race, the distance, the state of the going and the horse's placing at the finish.

The distance of each race is given in furlongs, fractional distances being expressed in the decimal notation to the nearest tenth of a furlong. The prefix 'a' signifies a race on an artificial surface (except for 'f' for fibresand at Southwell and Wolverhampton, and 'e' for equitrack at Lingfield prior to the change in surface there, in November 2001, to 'p' for polytrack).

The going is symbolised as follows: f=firm (turf) or fast (artificial surface); m=good to firm; g=good (turf) or standard (artificial surface); d=good to soft/dead; s=soft (turf) or slow, sloppy, muddy or wet (artificial surface); v=heavy.

Placings are indicated, up to sixth place, by the use of superior figures, an asterisk being used to denote a win.

Thus [2001 81: 10s* 12f³ 11.7g f11g² Sep 7] signifies that the horse was rated 81 the previous year (if there is no rating it indicates that the horse did not appear in 'Racehorses' for that year). In 2001 it ran four times, winning over 10 furlongs on soft going first time out, then finishing third over 12 furlongs on firm going, then out of the first six over 11.7 furlongs on good going, then second over 11 furlongs on standard going on a fibresand track. The date of its last run was September 7.

Included in the pedigree details are the highest Timeform Annual ratings during their racing careers of the sires, dams and sires of dams of all horses, where the information is available.

Where sale prices are considered relevant F denotes the price as a foal, Y the price as a yearling, 2-y-o as a two-year-old, and so on. These are given in guineas unless prefixed by IR (Irish guineas), $ (American dollars) or accompanied by francs (French francs). Other currencies are converted approximately into guineas or pounds sterling at the prevailing exchange rate. Sales mentioned towards the end of the commentaries refer to those after the horse's final outing. The symbol € appears for the first time in stallion fees, denoting the new common European currency, the euro.

THE RATING SYMBOLS

The following symbols, attached to the ratings, are to be interpreted as stated:-

p   likely to improve.

P   capable of *much* better form.

+   the horse may be better than we have rated it.

d   the horse appears to have deteriorated, and might no longer be capable of running to the rating given.

§   unreliable (for temperamental or other reasons).

§§   so temperamentally unsatisfactory as not to be worth a rating.

?   the horse's rating is suspect. If used without a rating the symbol implies that the horse can't be assessed with confidence, or, if used in the in-season Timeform publications, that the horse is out of form.

RACEHORSES OF 2001

Horse	Commentary	Rating

AAHGOWANGOWAN (IRE)   2 b.f. (Apr 14) Tagula (IRE) 116 – Cabcharge **75**
Princess (IRE) 64 (Rambo Dancer (CAN) 107) [2001 5.7g 5m 6m* 6s⁴ 6v² 6s* 5g* f6g
5.1s² 5g* Nov 7] IR 12,500Y: sturdy filly: poor mover: fourth foal: sister to a 2-y-o 5f
winner in Italy and half-sister to 9f (in Switzerland) and 1½m winner Luz Bay (by
Tenby): dam 2-y-o 5f winner: fair performer: won seller at Ripon in August, nurseries at
Brighton and Newmarket (on consecutive days) in October and seller at Musselburgh
(despite swerving right final 1f) in November: will prove best at 5f/6f: acts on good to
firm and heavy ground, not disgraced on fibresand: tough and reliable. *M. R. Channon*

AA-YOUKNOWNOTHING   5 b.g. Superpower 113 – Bad Payer 72 (Tanfirion **63**
110) [2001 73, a77: f6g f5g f5g⁴ f5g⁶ f5g* e5g f5g f5s Dec 27] tall, angular gelding:
modest performer: won seller at Wolverhampton in March: best at 5f: acts on soft going,
good to firm and fibresand/equitrack: blinkered/visored/tongue tied: tries to dominate:
often looks none too keen. *Miss J. F. Craze*

ABAJANY   7 b.g. Akarad (FR) 130 – Miss Ivory Coast (USA) (Sir Ivor 135) [2001 78: **75**
10f 9m 8.3d 8m² 8f⁵ 8m 8m 8.2s⁵ 8.3m 8d⁶ 8m 8.5g² 8g* 10.2d³ 8s p8g Dec 4] sturdy
gelding: fair handicapper: won 30-runner event at Redcar in October: effective at 1m/
1¼m: acts on firm and soft going: tried visored: tends to wander in front and usually held
up. *M. R. Channon*

ABBAJABBA   5 b.g. Barrys Gamble 102 – Bo' Babbity 75 (Strong Gale 116) [2001 **104 +**
86: 6v⁵ 5s² 6s² 6g 6m³ 5.6m 6m 6d* Oct 13] quite good-topped gelding: has a round
action: useful handicapper: 20/1, better than ever when winning 23-runner race at York
in October comfortably by ¾ length from Polar Kingdom, short of room before
quickening well: length third to Antonio Canova in Great St Wilfrid Handicap at Ripon
on fifth start: best at 5f/6f: has done all winning on good ground or softer: waited with.
C. W. Fairhurst

ABBEY BRIDGE (USA)   3 b.f. Irish River (FR) 131 – Francisco Road (USA) **73**
(Strawberry Road (AUS) 128) [2001 7m³ 6m* 7g Jul 3] leggy filly: first foal: dam winner
in USA around 1m: won maiden at Redcar in June: last only subsequent start (reportedly
lost a shoe): should stay 1m: sent to USA. *J. Noseda*

ABBEY PARK (USA)   2 b. or br.f. (Mar 14) Known Fact (USA) 135 – Taylor Park **71**
(USA) (Sir Gaylord) [2001 6g⁴ 7.1f² f6g Oct 23] half-sister to several winners, including
1m winner Anghaam (by Diesis) and 1½m winner Howjal (by Conquistador Cielo), both
fairly useful: dam won up to 7f in USA, including minor stakes: fair maiden: took strong
hold when second at Chepstow, best effort: soon beaten at Wolverhampton final start: not
sure to stay beyond 7f. *J. W. Hills*

*Coral Eurobet Sprint Trophy (Handicap), York—a career-best effort from Abbajabba,
who beats Polar Kingdom (right), Seven No Trumps and the blinkered Lago di Varano*

ABBOT 3 b.g. Bishop of Cashel 122 – Gifted (Shareef Dancer (USA) 135) [2001 –p: **80**
8.2v 11.1s³ 11.8g⁶ 12f⁶ 16.2m⁵ 11.6m⁶ Jul 16] very big gelding: fairly useful maiden:
stays 1½m, possibly not 2m: acts on firm going: blinkered final start: joined C. Mann and
won on hurdling debut in November. *B. J. Meehan*

ABBY GOA (IRE) 3 b.f. Dr Devious (IRE) 127 – Spring Reel (Mill Reef (USA) 141) **–**
[2001 67: 7.5f 5f 9m 10m Sep 6] strong filly: fair maiden at 2 yrs: well held in 2001: tried
blinkered. *M. W. Easterby*

ABERCORN (IRE) 2 b.g. (Mar 19) Woodborough (USA) 112 – Ravensdale Rose **–**
(IRE) (Henbit (USA) 130) [2001 7.1g 7m 7.1m 10s Oct 15] IR 14,000F, 38,000Y: small-
lish, well-made gelding: fifth foal: half-brother to 3 winners, including 3-y-o Mamore
Gap and 9f winner Floorso'theforest (by Forest Wind): dam ran twice in Ireland at 2 yrs:
well beaten in maidens/minor event: blinkered final start. *B. J. Meehan*

ABERCROMBIE 2 ch.c. (Apr 7) Dancing Spree (USA) – Coleford (USA) (Secreto **53 §**
(USA) 128) [2001 6m 7m² 6g 7g Jul 11] leggy colt: fourth foal: half-brother to a winner
up to 1m abroad by Faustus: dam, unraced, out of half-sister to Irish St Leger winner
Mashaallah: modest maiden: easily best effort when second in seller at Yarmouth: should
stay at least 1m: visored/blinkered all starts: not an easy ride: probably temperamental:
sent to Kuwait. *C. A. Dwyer*

ABERKEEN 6 ch.g. Keen 116 – Miss Aboyne 64 (Lochnager 132) [2001 74: 7d⁶ f7g⁶ **53**
f8g³ f7g⁵ f8g 7d f7g³ f8g Dec 17] workmanlike gelding: modest handicapper: left
M. Dods 500 gns after sixth start: stays 8.5f: acts on firm going, good to soft and fibresand: visored once: held up. *Jedd O'Keeffe*

ABERTHATCH (FR) 2 b.f. (Mar 25) Thatching 131 – Academy Angel (FR) (Royal **68**
Academy (USA) 130) [2001 7d 7v² 7d Nov 3] 40,000 francs F, 90,000 francs Y: lengthy
filly: second foal: dam, ran 3 times in France, out of half-sister to high-class French 1½m
performer Altayan: best effort in maidens (modest form) when second of 5 at Newcastle:
will stay at least 1m: raced only on ground softer than good. *M. J. Ryan*

A BIT SPECIAL 3 b.f. Rahy (USA) 115 – Speedybird (IRE) 71 (Danehill (USA) 126) **82**
[2001 66p: 7g² 9.9m² 7g* Jun 19] lengthy, useful-looking filly: fairly useful form: landed
odds in maiden at Thirsk in June: should stay 1m+: sent to USA. *H. R. A. Cecil*

ABLE AYR 4 ch.g. Formidable (USA) 125 – Ayr Classic (Local Suitor (USA) 128) **63 d**
[2001 72d: 6d⁴ 6m⁴ 6m³ 5g² 6d⁴ 5m 5d 6g 6d 6g 6g⁵ 6f 5d 6v Oct 16] small, lengthy
gelding: modest handicapper, on downgrade: effective at 5f/6f: acts on any turf going:
tried blinkered/visored: sometimes slowly away, and often gets well behind: sold 1,000
gns, sent to Denmark. *J. S. Goldie*

ABLE BAKER CHARLIE (IRE) 2 b.g. (Apr 16) Sri Pekan (USA) 117 – Lavez- **73 p**
zola (IRE) (Salmon Leap (USA) 131) [2001 7.5s³ 7d³ Oct 3] 15,000Y: strong, attractive
gelding: fifth foal: brother to Italian winner around 1m (including at 2 yrs) Lampugnano
and half-brother to fairly useful 6f (at 2 yrs) to 1¼m winner Lady Angharad (by
Tenby): dam Italian 7f to 1¼m winner: fair form when third in maidens at Beverley and
Newcastle, slowly away and not knocked about when beaten 4 lengths by Short Respite
in latter (gelded after): should stay 1¼m: type to progress. *J. R. Fanshawe*

ABLE MILLENIUM (IRE) 5 ch.g. Be My Guest (USA) 126 – Miami Life (Miami **57 d**
Springs 121) [2001 55d: e7g⁶ f8s e10g 8s* 8.1g 10f³ 10.1g 9.7m 10g 8f 9.9s f11g⁵ f12s
p10g Dec 29] lengthy, sparely-made gelding: modest handicapper: won at Pontefract in
May: below form after: stays 8.5f: acts on fibresand and soft going: tried blinkered,
visored after third start in 2001. *Mrs Lydia Pearce*

ABLE NATIVE (IRE) 4 b.f. Thatching 131 – Native Joy (IRE) 76 (Be My Native **–**
(USA) 122) [2001 69: 14.1v f14g⁵ f16g May 21] modest handicapper: stays 1¾m: acts on **a59**
heavy going and all-weather: often blinkered. *G. M. Moore*

ABLE PETE 5 b.g. Formidable (USA) 125 – An Empress (USA) (Affirmed (USA)) **–**
[2001 26, a44: f11g³ f12g³ f12g³ f12g² 11.9s f12g⁴ f14g 11.9g f14.8g⁵ f14.8s⁴ Sep 6] poor **a40**
handicapper: stays 1½m: acts on fibresand and good to firm going: tried tongue tied.
A. G. Newcombe

ABLE SEAMAN (USA) 4 b. or br.g. Northern Flagship (USA) 96 – Love At Dawn **–**
(USA) (Grey Dawn II 132) [2001 65: e16g³ f16.2g² f16s* e16s⁴ Feb 17] big gelding: fair **a68**
handicapper: won at Southwell in February: stays 2m: acts on soft going, good to firm
and equitrack/fibresand: effective visored/blinkered. *C. E. Brittain*

A B MY BOY 3 ch.g. Young Ern 120 – Whitstar 93 (Whitstead 125) [2001 –: 11.5f **–**
8.2f 7v f8g Nov 19] little form: tried blinkered. *J. R. Best*

ABOVE BOARD 6 b.g. Night Shift (USA) – Bundled Up (USA) (Sharpen Up 127) –
[2001 –, a59: f6g f7g f6f f5g f6g⁵ f7g³ f6g f8g f5g f6s Dec 15] smallish, robust gelding: **a43**
poor maiden: stays 7f: acts on fibresand: tried blinkered/tongue tied. *R. F. Marvin*

ABOVE THE CUT (USA) 9 ch.g. Topsider (USA) – Placer Queen (Habitat 134) –
[2001 f12g p16g Dec 4] one-time fairly useful 7f winner: well held both Flat outings
since 1996: tried blinkered. *C. P. Morlock*

ABRACADABJAR 3 b.g. Royal Abjar (USA) 121 – Celt Song (IRE) (Unfuwain **51**
(USA) 131) [2001 64?: e8g² 10m 8.2g⁵ 7.1f 10g⁵ f8.5g Oct 20] short-backed gelding: **a59**
modest maiden handicapper: stays 1¼m: acts on firm ground and equitrack: blinkered
final 2 starts: has been slowly away: held up: inconsistent: sold 400 gns. *G. A. Butler*

ABRAXAS 3 b.c. Emperor Jones (USA) 119 – Snipe Hall 93 (Crofthall 110) [2001 **56**
e5g² 6g 6g 6m 5m⁴ Jul 11] 23,000Y: first foal: dam, 2-y-o 5f/6f winner, half-sister to dam **a63**
of smart sprinter Atraf: modest maiden: should stay 6f: acts on equitrack. *J. Akehurst*

ABSENT FRIENDS 4 b.g. Rock City 120 – Green Supreme (Primo Dominie 121) **82**
[2001 68: 6s⁵ 5m² 5m* 5f³ 5m³ 5m 5m Jul 13] strong, lengthy gelding: fairly useful
handicapper: won at Redcar in May: best at 5f: acts on firm going, probably on soft: tends
to be slowly away, very much so final 2 starts. *J. Balding*

ABSINTHER 4 b.g. Presidium 124 – Heavenly Queen (Scottish Reel 123) [2001 62, **66**
a68: f9.4s² f12g f8g 8.1m⁴ 9m 10g⁵ 11.5f² 10.5s² 12m* 12g 14v f12g Oct 22] good-
bodied gelding: fair handicapper: left E. Alston after reappearance: won at Folkestone in
August: effective at 1m to 1½m: acts on fibresand, firm and soft ground: visored once:
usually held up. *M. R. Bosley*

ABSOLUTE CHARMER (IRE) 2 ch.f. (Mar 12) Entrepreneur 123 – Diavolina **77**
(USA) (Lear Fan (USA) 130) [2001 6m² 7m⁴ 8m⁴ Sep 11] closely related to useful French
1¼m/1½m winner Go Boldly (by Sadler's Wells) and half-sister to several winners,
including useful 6f (at 2 yrs) to 1m (in USA) winner Polish Spring (by Polish Precedent):
dam, French 1¼m winner, from good family: fair form when in frame in maidens: will
stay 1¼m: raced only on good to firm ground. *R. Charlton*

ABSOLUTE FANTASY 5 b.m. Beveled (USA) – Sharp Venita 84 (Sharp Edge 123) **80**
[2001 72+: e6g⁶ 5m³ 6m 5.3f² 5m³ 5m* 5d* 5.1m 5m 5.1g⁴ 5m² 5m² 5g 5s⁴ 5g² f5g* f5g⁶
Dec 8] lengthy mare: fairly useful handicapper: won at Goodwood in June, Haydock in
July and Wolverhampton in November: best at 5f: acts on equitrack/fibresand, firm and
soft going: blinkered: sometimes slowly away/edges left/finds little. *E. A. Wheeler*

ABSOLUTELYMARVELOS 2 b.g. (Apr 15) Royal Applause 124 – Snipe Hall 93 –
(Crofthall 110) [2001 5.1f⁶ 6m 5m f7g⁶ Aug 18] 35,000Y: second foal: dam, 2-y-o 5f/6f
winner, half-sister to dam of smart sprinter Atraf: little form in maidens. *N. Tinkler*

ABSOLUTE UTOPIA (USA) 8 b.g. Mr Prospector (USA) – Magic Gleam (USA) **67**
122 (Danzig (USA)) [2001 10f⁶ 12m 9.9m 12g 12m⁵ p10g⁵ p10g* Dec 28] tall gelding:
hobdayed/had soft palate operation early in career: fair performer: won apprentice
handicap at Lingfield in December: stays 1½m: acts on firm going, good to soft and
polytrack: blinkered fifth outing: held up. *N. E. Berry*

ABUELOS 2 b.g. (Feb 13) Sabrehill (USA) 120 – Miss Oasis 54 (Green Desert (USA) **56**
127) [2001 6f 6s 6v Oct 26] 8,000F, 16,000Y: smallish, well-made gelding: fifth foal:
half-brother to 1½m seller winner Keen Waters (by Keen): dam twice-raced half-sister to
smart sprinter Sizzling Melody: modest form, not knocked about, in maidens: gelded
afterwards: will probably stay 1m: slowly away/edged right second start. *S. Dow*

ABYSSINIAN WOLF 3 ch.g. Dr Devious (IRE) 127 – Guilty Secret (IRE) 109 (Kris **93**
135) [2001 –p: 12g³ 12m 12m* 13.3m³ 14s 14g Oct 6] big, good-topped gelding: fairly
useful handicapper: made all at Newmarket in June: good third at Newbury next time:
should stay at least 1¾m: acts on good to firm going. *J. R. Fanshawe*

ACADEMIC ACCURACY 3 b.f. Environment Friend 128 – Branitska (Mummy's **66 d**
Pet 125) [2001 70: 7d 8m² 8f³ 8m⁴ 9.7m⁴ 8.5f⁶ 8m 8.1g⁶ 10s Oct 3] leggy, lengthy
filly: fair performer: well below form after fourth start: stays 1m: raced mainly on good
going or firmer: usually races prominently: sold 2,000 gns. *R. Hannon*

ACADEMIC GOLD (IRE) 3 ch.g. Royal Academy (USA) 130 – Penultimate **73**
(USA) (Roberto (USA) 131) [2001 72: f8g² 8m f8g 12m 12m Aug 27] big, rangy gelding: fair
form: well below par after reappearance: should stay 1¼m: acts on fibresand: tongue tied
final outing: withdrawn after refusing to enter stall once in 2001. *K. R. Burke*

25

ACADEMIC RECORD 3 b.g. Royal Academy (USA) 130 – Bala Monaafis (IRE) **49** (In The Wings 128) [2001 55: e10g⁶ f9.4g e10s³ f11g 9.9m² 9.9m f11g⁶ 12m 11.1m* 10m Jun 22] poor performer: won claimer at Hamilton in June: stays 11f: acts on all-weather, best turf efforts on good to firm going: usually blinkered: has run in snatches/found little: sold 3,000 gns in July, then little form over hurdles. *K. R. Burke*

ACCEPTING 4 b.c. Mtoto 134 – D'Azy 91 (Persian Bold 123) [2001 83: 14.1g³ **89** 13.9m 16m* 16.1f 16.1g³ 15.9d² 16.2s 16g Nov 7] sturdy colt: fairly useful handicapper: won at Musselburgh in June: stays 2m: acts on good to firm and good to soft going (well held on soft): sometimes hangs. *J. Mackie*

ACCESS DENIED (FR) 2 b.c. (Jan 28) Revoque (IRE) 122 – Forentia 89 (Formid- **95** able (USA) 125) [2001 6f² 6s* 6d⁴ Oct 13] 60,000F, 2,500,000 francs Y: good-bodied colt: second foal: dam, 2-y-o 5f winner, half-sister to smart Prix Morny and Middle Park Stakes winner Bahamian Bounty out of smart sprinter Clarentia: fairly useful form: won maiden at Pontefract in September easily by 6 lengths: respectable fourth to Prism in listed race at York: should stay 7f: acts on firm and soft going. *D. R. Loder*

ACCLAMATION 2 b.c. (Apr 26) Royal Applause 124 – Princess Athena 119 **107** (Ahonoora 122) [2001 5s² 5m* 5g² 5.2m* 6m* Sep 12] 33,000Y: lengthy, unfurnished colt: eighth foal: half-brother to 3 winners, including useful 6f/7f winner Waypoint (by Cadeaux Genereux): dam, best at 5f, won Queen Mary Stakes but better at 3/4 yrs: useful peformer: won maiden at Sandown in June, minor event at Newbury in August and £200000 St Leger Yearling Stakes at Doncaster in September: beat Old Blue Eyes by 2½ lengths in 22-runner race for last-named, tracking pace before quickening clear final 1f: likely to prove best at 5f/6f: acts on good to firm ground, shaped well on soft. *L. G. Cottrell*

ACCYSTAN 6 ch.g. Efisio 120 – Amia (CAN) (Nijinsky (CAN) 138) [2001 –, a60: **–** f12s f12g 11.1d 10f 14.1g Jun 16] quite good-topped gelding: no form in 2001: tried blinkered. *A. Crook*

ACE-MA-VAHRA 3 b.f. Savahra Sound 111 – Asmarina 50 (Ascendant 96) [2001 **52** f7g⁵ f6g f7g² f7g² 7.5m⁵ 10m 7v f7g² f8g⁵ Dec 17] leggy filly: second foal: dam, 9.4f winner, half-sister to useful performer up to 1m First Maite: modest maiden: probably stays 1m: acts on fibresand. *S. R. Bowring*

ACE OF TRUMPS 5 ch.g. First Trump 118 – Elle Reef (Shareef Dancer (USA) 135) **66** [2001 56, a–: 9v³ 10s³ 8d² 8s 9.2d³ 9.1m⁵ 8.3d⁴ 8m² 10f 9f 9.2g* 8f⁶ 9.2m 9.2d³ 9f⁶ 9.2d* **a–** 8.3s* 10g* 9.2g 9.1m³ 8.3m⁴ 10v⁶ Oct 15] small, sturdy gelding: fair performer: won seller, claimer (left J. Hetherton) and selling handicap at Hamilton and handicap at Ayr in summer: effective at 1m to 11f: acts on any turf going, no show on fibresand: blinkered/ visored earlier in career: tongue tied: usually races up with pace: game. *Miss L. A. Perratt*

A CHEF TOO FAR 8 b.g. Be My Chief 122 – Epithet 105 (Mill Reef (USA) **–** 141) [2001 f16s Feb 9] one-time fair 7f winner. *R. G. Frost*

ACHILLES SKY 5 b.g. Hadeer 118 – Diva Madonna 85 (Chief Singer 131) [2001 **70** 74: 10s 14.1v 12s 11.6g² 11.9f* 12g 12m⁶ f12g Oct 9] strong, close-coupled gelding: fair performer: won minor event at Brighton (ladies) in June: stays easy 1½m: acts on firm and good to soft going: sometimes visored/blinkered: has broken blood vessels: made running final 5 starts: sold 4,000 gns, sent to Switzerland. *Jamie Poulton*

ACHILLES SPIRIT (IRE) 3 b.g. Deploy 131 – Scenic Spirit (IRE) (Scenic 128) **84** [2001 74: 10d 10d* 10.9d² 12.3m² 12m² 13.9m 11m Sep 26] fairly useful performer: won minor event at Pontefract in July: should stay beyond 1½m: acts on good to firm and good to soft ground, well beaten on soft. *J. A. Osborne*

ACHILLES SUN 3 b.g. Deploy 131 – Tsungani 64 (Cure The Blues (USA)) [2001 **59** 60: 11m 12m 10.4m 10.1g 11.9s² 11.6v Oct 29] close-coupled gelding: modest maiden: stays 11f: acts on fibresand, soft and good to firm ground: has looked none too keen. *Jamie Poulton*

ACHILLES WINGS (USA) 5 b.g. Irish River (FR) 131 – Shirley Valentine 104 **68** (Shirley Heights 130) [2001 77: 10.9g⁴ 10d⁴ 14.1m 12.1s⁴ f12g⁴ f14.8s⁶ 14.1d⁵ Oct 3] **a56** small, sparely-made gelding: fair maiden: stays 1¾m: acts on equitrack and soft going, probably on fibresand. *Miss K. M. George*

ACID TEST 6 ch.g. Sharpo 132 – Clunk Click 72 (Star Appeal 133) [2001 70, a58: **–** e8g² e8g⁶ f8g f8s⁵ Feb 9] good-bodied gelding: modest handicapper: reportedly finished **a59** lame final start: stays 1m: acts on firm going, good to soft and fibresand/equitrack: tried visored/blinkered. *M. A. Buckley*

£200000 St Leger Yearling Stakes, Doncaster—Acclamation shows further improvement to land the huge prize ahead of Old Blue Eyes and Captain Rio

ACONITE 2 b.f. (Apr 25) Primo Dominie 121 – Laugharne (Known Fact (USA) 135) **52** [2001 7g⁶ f6s⁶ p6g Dec 28] 13,000F: half-sister to several winners, including useful sprinter Power Lake (by Formidable) and fairly useful 6f winner Lough Erne (by Never So Bold): dam ran once: modest form in maidens: marginally best effort when patiently-ridden eighth at Lingfield final outing: should prove best at 5f/6f. *C. N. Allen*

ACORAZADO (IRE) 2 b.g. (Feb 6) Petorius 117 – Jaldi (IRE) 75 (Nordico (USA)) **79 p** [2001 6d³ 5.1s* Oct 30] IR 4,000F, IR 5,700Y: quite good-topped gelding: has scope: fourth foal: half-brother to fairly useful Irish 6f winner who stayed 1m Spokane (by Indian Ridge): dam 7f winner: odds on, confirmed promise when winning maiden at Nottingham by 3 lengths from White Cliffs, disputing lead and asserting from over 1f out: subsequently gelded: will prove best at 5f/6f: likely to improve further. *S. P. C. Woods*

ACORN CATCHER 3 b.f. Emarati (USA) 74 – Anytime Baby 56 (Bairn (USA) 126) **–** [2001 55, a67: e5s⁶ f5g f5g² f5g Dec 1] modest performer: left B. Palling after third start: **a52** best at 5f/easy 6f: acts on good to firm ground and fibresand: visored once: sometimes gives trouble stalls: not one to trust implicitly. *M. Wigham*

ACQUITTAL (IRE) 9 b.g. Danehill (USA) 126 – Perfect Alibi (Law Society (USA) **45 §** 130) [2001 37§: 10.5g⁶ 14.1f² 14.1g⁶ 12.3m³ 12.1m 14.1m³ 13.8g⁵ 12g* 14m³ 12m 12.3d Aug 31] poor handicapper: won amateur event at Catterick in August: stays 1¾m: races mainly on good ground or firmer: blinkered once, usually visored: ungenuine. *P. L. Clinton*

ACTION JACKSON 9 ch.g. Hadeer 118 – Water Woo (USA) 102 (Tom Rolfe) **27** [2001 33: f11s⁵ e13g³ e13s f16g e10g⁵ 11.9f⁵ 14.1g 10g 10m Aug 18] close-coupled gelding: bad handicapper: stays 1¾m: unraced on heavy ground/polytrack, acts on any other: sometimes tongue tied: blinkered final 5 starts. *A. W. Carroll*

ACTIVIST 3 ch.g. Diesis 133 – Shicklah (USA) 106 (The Minstrel (CAN) 135) [2001 **75** –p: 8m 7.1g⁴ 11.5g² 12.4g² 12m⁴ Aug 30] fair maiden: better at 1½m than shorter: acts on good to firm going. *M. L. W. Bell*

ACTIVITY (IRE) 2 ch.c. (Apr 16) Pennekamp (USA) 130 – Actoris (USA) (Diesis **76 p** 133) [2001 7g Oct 4] quite good-topped colt: first foal: dam, useful French 1m winner, out of half-sister to smart miler Sensation, herself out of Breeders' Cup Juvenile Fillies' winner Outstandingly: 10/1, never-dangerous tenth of 21 to Millennium Dragon in maiden at Newmarket: should do better. *D. R. Loder*

ACT ONE 2 gr.c. (Apr 19) In The Wings 128 – Summer Sonnet (Baillamont (USA) **116 p** 124) [2001 8d* 8s* 8s* Nov 3]
    The programme of French two-year-old pattern races underwent some radical changes for the 2001 season, one of the main ones being the creation of a new Group 1 event, the Criterium International, run over a mile at Saint-Cloud in early-November. The new race was staged to fill the gap left by the Grand Criterium, France's most important two-year-old contest, which had had its distance reduced from a mile to seven furlongs. The existing Group 1 seven-furlong event for two-year-olds, the Prix de la Salamandre, run at Longchamp in September, was scrapped altogether.
    The main reason for the changes was the contrasting fortunes in recent years of the Prix de la Salamandre and Grand Criterium as guides to the classics and other

27

Criterium International, Saint-Cloud—Act One ends Aidan O'Brien's 2001 domination of Group 1 two-year-old contests for colts, beating Landseer (rail), Guys And Dolls and Mutinyonthebounty

big races. Although both Group 1 in status, the Grand Criterium had traditionally enjoyed the greater prestige, something reflected in its prize-money allocation, which was more than twice that of the Prix de la Salamandre in 2000. But the Salamandre repeatedly upstaged the Grand Criterium through the 'nineties, with the likes of Zafonic, Pennekamp, Aljabr and Giant's Causeway all going on to further Group 1 success as three-year-olds. The Grand Criterium's record in the same period was woeful; Hector Protector, who also won the Salamandre in 1990, was the last Grand Criterium winner to go on to win a classic, while the 1999 winner Ciro (who was awarded the race) has been the only subsequent winner to score in Group 1 company again at three. The last winner of the Grand Criterium as a mile event, Okawango, failed to win a race of any description as a three-year-old in the latest season, a fate that also befell Lost World, Goldmark (who did not run), Loup Solitaire and Way of Light among Grand Criterium winners of the 'nineties. The French racing authorities, also concerned that their top two-year-old contest attracted just three runners in Ciro's year (and only one of them trained in France), therefore came to the view that seven furlongs rather than a mile was the optimum distance for their most prestigious juvenile event, though, rather than dispense with tradition entirely, they decided to keep the name Grand Criterium.

There was, though, still room in the French two-year-old programme for a Group 1 contest open to colts over a mile (the fillies' Prix Marcel Boussac over a mile was left untouched), hence the creation of the Criterium International. Whether or not its title was an acceptance of the regular plundering of the top French juvenile prizes by Ballydoyle and British yards, an international field was certainly what the authorities got, so much so that only one French-trained horse took his chance in a field of six. In fact, French-trained two-year-olds were outnumbered in all five of their Group 1 contests in 2001, the dearth of good French two-year-olds being a subject taken up in the essay on the only other one to have earned a rating above 110, Zipping.

There was some irony therefore in French-trained Act One beating off his two rivals from Britain, the Paul Cole-trained Prix La Rochette winner Guys And Dolls and the Clive Brittain-trained York maiden runner-up Halawellfin Hala, and a trio of colts from Ballydoyle—Coventry Stakes winner Landseer, the Royal Lodge winner Mutinyonthebounty and the twice-raced maiden Diaghilev—who had been charged with maintaining Aidan O'Brien's stranglehold on the season's Group 1 races for two-year-old colts. But Act One had already marked himself out as a really promising colt by winning both his starts, a newcomers race at Chantilly in September and the Prix Thomas Bryon run over the same course and distance as the

28

Criterium International in October. Act One won the Thomas Bryon readily by three lengths from Rouvres, leading approaching the final furlong before going clear without coming under maximum pressure. Act One's winning margin was only half a length in the Criterium International but he always looked like holding the challenge of Landseer, after tracking the pace-setter Halawellfin Hala and then being shaken up to lead under two furlongs out. Guys And Dolls was a further three quarters of a length back in third followed by the two other O'Brien colts.

Act One (gr.c. Apr 19, 1999)	In The Wings (b 1986)	Sadler's Wells (b 1981)	Northern Dancer / Fairy Bridge
		High Hawk (b 1980)	Shirley Heights / Sunbittern
	Summer Sonnet (gr 1991)	Baillamont (b 1982)	Blushing Groom / Lodeve
		Noesis (gr 1986)	Persepolis / Proskona

Act One has already done his bit to maintain his dam's record at stud. He is the third foal out of Summer Sonnet, whose first two foals are both useful fillies by Caerleon. Four-year-old Summer Solstice won twice in France for Jonathan Pease at three, notably a listed race over an extended twelve furlongs at Deauville, before winning a nine-furlong allowance at Gulfstream early in the latest season for Christophe Clement. Her year-younger sister Summer Symphony, trained by Luca Cumani, looked to have a bright future after running second in the Fillies' Mile but was restricted to just one outing in the Sun Chariot Stakes in the latest season. Summer Sonnet, who won a minor event over a mile and a half at Evry for Act One's connections, proved a bargain buy as a future broodmare at just 70,000 francs as a yearling. She comes from an excellent family, her grandam being the high-class six- and seven-furlong filly Proskona, herself half-sister to the dam of Bosra Sham,

Mr Gerald Leigh's "Act One"

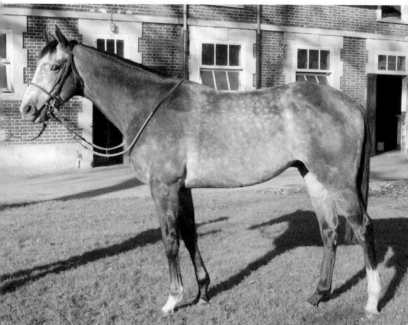

Hector Protector and Shanghai, who all won classics in either Britain or France. Summer Sonnet's dam Noesis won at around a mile and a quarter in France and has also bred a runner-up in the Japanese version of the One Thousand Guineas, Ibuki Perceive.

Act One looks more likely at this stage to contest the Prix du Jockey Club than the Derby; with further improvement almost certain, he is one to look out for in the French trials in the spring. He will be well suited by the step up from a mile, and looks sure to stay a mile and a half. He has raced only on ground softer than good so far. *J. E. Pease, France*

ADALEEL 2 b.c. (Mar 2) Polar Falcon (USA) 126 – Ameerat Jumaira (USA) 64 (Alydar (USA)) [2001 7m 7.9d 7s Oct 25] good-topped colt: has scope: fifth foal: half-brother to 1¼m winner in Italy by In The Wings and 1m to 1½m winner in Scandinavia by Caerleon: dam, maiden who stayed 1¼m, half-sister to Zilzal from family of Polish Precedent and Culture Vulture: only a little sign of ability in maidens: looks type to do better. *A. C. Stewart* — **p**

ADALPOUR (IRE) 3 b.g. Kayhasi 130 – Adalya (IRE) (Darshaan 133) [2001 9.9d³ 10v Oct 8] second foal: half-brother to fairly useful 7.5f winner Adawar (by Perugino): dam lightly-raced sister to disqualified Oaks winner Aliysa: better effort in maidens when 5¼ lengths third at Goodwood in September: will be suited by 1½m: sold 8,000 gns, and gelded. *Sir Michael Stoute* — **68**

ADAMAS (IRE) 4 b.f. Fairy King (USA) – Corynida (USA) (Alleged (USA) 138) [2001 75: 9.9f 12g 9f⁵ 10.3m⁶ 10m 10.2g⁴ 6f⁴ 7m 6v Oct 16] good-quartered filly: modest handicapper, on downgrade: has form at 6f and stays 1½m: acts on firm going, below form on softer than good. *Andrew Turnell* — **64 d**

ADAMATIC (IRE) 10 b.g. Henbit (USA) 130 – Arpal Magic (Master Owen) [2001 16f Jul 9] rear half chaser: tailed off on Flat debut. *R. Allan* — **–**

ADAMS ALE 2 b.f. (Apr 7) Mistertopogigo (IRE) 118 – Knayton Lass 94 (Presidium 124) [2001 5g 5f Aug 29] leggy filly: third living foal: dam 5f (at 2 yrs)/6f winner: well held in maidens. *J. M. Jefferson* — **–**

ADANTINO 2 b.c. (Apr 14) Glory of Dancer 121 – Sweet Whisper 63 (Petong 126) [2001 6.1g 7.1f 5.7g Oct 1] 5,500F, 13,000Y: third foal: half-brother to 2 winning sprinters, notably useful 5f (including at 2 yrs)/6f winner Blue Velvet (by Formidable): dam 5f/6f winner at 2 yrs: modest form in maidens: likely to prove best at 7f/1m. *B. R. Millman* — **60**

A DAY ON THE DUB 8 b.g. Presidium 124 – Border Mouse (Border Chief 101) [2001 57: 9v* 11s 8m² 10.1m³ 10f 10.1m 11.1s 12m⁵ 11.1g 16.1f⁵ 12s Oct 20] strong gelding: modest performer: won selling handicap at Musselburgh in March: effective at 1m to 1½m: acts on any turf going/fibresand: often slowly away/held up. *D. Eddy* — **53**

ADDEYLL 2 ch.c. (Feb 15) Efisio 120 – Rohita (IRE) 94 (Waajib 121) [2001 6m² 6m* 6.3g⁵ 6g² 6d² 7d⁵ Oct 13] 130,000Y: small, sturdy colt: fourth foal: brother to useful 5f (at 2 yrs) and 7f winner Kalindi: dam 2-y-o 5f/6f winner: fairly useful performer: won maiden at Ayr in June: best efforts when fifth of 8 to Johannesburg in Anglesey Stakes at the Curragh and neck second of 10 to Inishowen in minor event at Doncaster next 2 starts: stays 6f: acts on good to firm ground, possibly unsuited by good to soft: races up with pace. *M. R. Channon* — **88**

ADDITION 5 b.m. Dilum (USA) 115 – Cedar Lady (Telsmoss 91) [2001 58: 6m 8m⁴ 7g 7.1g 7g⁴ 7.1f Sep 18] poor handicapper: barely stays 1m: acts on firm and good to soft going. *R. J. Hodges* — **49**

ADDO (IRE) 2 b.f. (Jan 25) Mujadil (USA) 119 – Miss Siham (IRE) 59 (Green Forest (USA) 134) [2001 5m⁴ 6.3d⁶ 5f* 5.2m 5f 5d³ 5g f6g Oct 22] IR 22,000Y: smallish, sturdy filly: second foal: dam 5f (including at 2 yrs) winner: fair performer: won maiden at Beverley in July: well held in nurseries last 2 starts: likely to prove best at 5f/6f: acts on firm and good to soft ground: sold 5,500 gns. *G. C. Bravery* — **77**

ADELPHI BOY (IRE) 5 ch.g. Ballad Rock 122 – Toda 53 (Absalom 128) [2001 78, a103: f7g f8.5g f7g⁵ 8.5s 10.3m 8.5m⁶ 8m⁶ 10.1m 5g 7g 7m 12m² 12d 9g⁶ f8g f12g⁶ Dec 10] workmanlike gelding: poor mover: one-time useful handicapper on all-weather: fair performer on turf: effective at 7f to easy 1½m: acts on fibresand/equitrack, soft and good to firm going: sometimes slowly away: on downgrade. *M. C. Chapman* — **67 a96 d**

ADELPHI THEATRE (USA)   4 b.g. Sadler's Wells (USA) 132 – Truly Bound   **93**
(USA) (In Reality) [2001 75: 11.6g 9.7m* 12g⁴ 12s Sep 30] good-topped gelding: brother
to useful Irish 1m (at 2 yrs) to 1¾m winner Yeoman's Point and half-brother to several
winners, including useful Irish 1996 2-y-o 7f winner Shell Ginger (by Woodman): dam
US Grade 2 winner over 7f at 2 yrs who stayed at least 9f, from very good middle-distance
family: fairly useful performer: trained by A. O'Brien in Ireland in 1999/2000: won
minor event at Folkestone in July: good fourth at Kempton next start, much better effort
in handicaps after: stays 1½m: acts on good to firm going, possibly not on soft: blinkered
(ran creditably) once: fairly useful hurdler. *R. Rowe*

ADEPT   2 b.f. (Feb 18) Efisio 120 – Prancing 98 (Prince Sabo 123) [2001 5.1s³ 6.1v³   **71**
5d⁶ Oct 9] quite good-topped filly: second foal: dam, 2-y-o 5f winner who stayed 1m,
half-sister to 1993 Middle Park winner First Trump: fair form when third in maidens at
Chepstow and Nottingham: only sixth (second race in less than a week) final start: should
stay 7f: raced only on going softer than good: sold 7,000 gns. *Sir Mark Prescott*

ADIEMUS   3 b.c. Green Desert (USA) 127 – Anodyne 100 (Dominion 123) [2001 7f⁴   **87**
6v³ 8.3v* p8g² Dec 4] 40,000Y: seventh foal: brother to 8.5f winner Desert Mirage,
closely related to 6f winner Tondyne (by Owington) and half-brother to several winners,
including 6f (at 2 yrs) and 7f winner Pharmacy (by Mtoto): dam 6f winner, including at 2
yrs: won maiden at Windsor in November despite wandering markedly: easily best effort
when second to Devolution in handicap at Lingfield next time: stays 1m: acts on heavy
ground and polytrack. *J. Noseda*

ADILABAD (USA)   4 b.c. Gulch (USA) – Adaiyka (IRE) 110 (Doyoun 124) [2001   **116**
118: 10v⁵ 10.3f* 10m³ 12f⁴ 10m⁴ 10m* Aug 25] tall, quite attractive colt: good walker:
smart performer: won listed race at Chester in May by short head from Island House
(rider on runner-up dropped hands) and Technology Facility Management PLC Winter
Hill Stakes at Windsor (repeated success of 2000, beating Askham by a neck) in August:
pulled hard but still ran respectably when fourth to Sandmason in steadily-run Hardwicke
Stakes at Royal Ascot on fourth outing: best form at 1¼m: acts on firm and good to soft

H.H. Aga Khan's "Adilabad"

going (lost 20 lengths at tape start on heavy): usually held up, but led/disputed at Windsor: sent to Saudi Arabia. *Sir Michael Stoute*

ADJAWAR (IRE)   3 b.g. Ashkalani (IRE) 128 – Adjriyna 82 (Top Ville 129) [2001 **99**
–p: 6.9v 8.2v³ 11.6d* 11.9d 12m² 11.9g 10.3d Aug 31] useful handicapper: won at
Windsor in May: easily best effort when 1½ lengths second to Arrive at Salisbury in June,
pair clear: looked none too resolute when visored final 2 starts (coltish and fractious in
paddock penultimate one): stays 1½m: acts on good to firm and good to soft ground:
tongue tied final 3 starts: sold 14,000 gns, joined C. Dwyer and gelded. *Sir Michael Stoute*

ADJIRAM (IRE)   5 b.g. Be My Guest (USA) 126 – Adjriyna 82 (Top Ville 129) [2001 **–**
–: 7f 10.3m⁴ 8.3g 12g Aug 23] well-made gelding: fair 11f winner in France in 1999: well
beaten on Flat in Britain. *D. C. O'Brien*

ADJUDICATOR (IRE)   3 br.g. Barathea (IRE) 127 – Mnaafa (IRE) 70 (Darshaan **67 d**
133) [2001 f7g³ 7.1m 6m⁴ f8.5g f6s⁶ Dec 21] 24,000F, 8,000Y, 26,000 2-y-o: third foal:
half-brother to fairly useful 1998 2-y-o 6f winner (probably stayed 1m) Island Hero (by
Polar Falcon): dam, 1¼m winner who stayed 1½m, from family of Alderbrook and 3-y-o
Hawkeye: fair form on debut when third to Japan in maiden at Southwell: nowhere near
that form after, leaving P. Cole 700 gns after penultimate start: should stay 1m: carried
head awkwardly third outing. *Mrs K. Walton*

ADMIRALS FLAME (IRE)   10 b.g. Doulab (USA) 115 – Fan The Flame 69 (Grundy **48**
137) [2001 65: 8s 8g⁶ Jul 20] leggy gelding: one-time fairly useful handicapper: poor
form in 2001: best around 1m: won on firm going earlier in career, has gone well on softer
than good. *C. F. Wall*

ADMIRAL'S GUEST (IRE)   9 ch.g. Be My Guest (USA) 126 – Watership (USA) **–**
(Foolish Pleasure (USA)) [2001 f12g f12g Apr 30] little form on Flat: tried visored.
W. Clay

ADMIRALS PLACE (IRE)   5 ch.h. Perugino (USA) 84 – Royal Daughter (High **83**
Top 131) [2001 75, a78: e12g* e12g³ e12g⁵ 12s* 12v⁴ 12m³ 12.4m* 12g 12.3m Jul 21] **a81**
close-coupled horse: fairly useful handicapper: won at Lingfield in January, Kempton in
May and Newcastle in June: below form last 2 starts: stays 1½m: acts on fibresand/
equitrack, good to firm and heavy going (reportedly finished lame on firm early in
career): consistent. *H. J. Collingridge*

ADOBE   6 b.g. Green Desert (USA) 127 – Shamshir 116 (Kris 135) [2001 87, a68: f7g **90**
7.6f 8.1m⁴ 8f² 8m⁵ 8.1d⁵ 8f³ 9.1f⁵ 8m² 8.1g 8m 8m* 8.1g 8.3m³ 8m* 8.3g 8s 8d Oct 19] **a?**
small, stocky gelding: fairly useful handicapper: won at Thirsk and Ripon in August:
soundly beaten last 3 starts: effective at 7f to easy 9f: acts on fibresand, firm and good
to soft going, not on softer: used to wear tongue strap: usually waited with: tough.
W. M. Brisbourne

ADORARA (USA)   3 b. or br.f. Silver Hawk (USA) 123 – Adored Slew (USA) **75**
(Seattle Slew (USA)) [2001 10m* Jul 11] $270,000F, $825,000Y: second foal: dam,
French 1m winner who stayed 1½m (second in Prix Minerve) and later won in USA at 4
yrs, granddaughter of champion US older mare Straight Deal: 7/2, won maiden at
Kempton on debut by ½ length from Khazayin, dictating steady pace and running on
well: has left Godolphin. *Saeed bin Suroor*

ADRIANA   4 b.f. Tragic Role (USA) – Beatle Song 70 (Song 132) [2001 50: f9.4s f8g **43 +**
11.9m 10m 9.7m⁶ 10g 11.5g² 12s 10s p12g p7g⁵ Dec 19] poor performer: stays 11.5f:
acts on firm ground and polytrack: blinkered final start (ran well): has wandered.
C. E. Brittain

ADROCK BOY   2 b.g. (Feb 11) Rock City 120 – Riva La Belle § (Ron's Victory **68**
(USA) 129) [2001 5.1s² 5s⁴ 5m 6d³ Jul 19] 2,800Y, resold 3,600Y: workmanlike gelding:
second foal: dam, temperamental maiden, half-sister to useful 2-y-o 5f/6f winner Amigo
Sucio: fair maiden: best effort when never-nearer third in nursery at Leicester: should stay
7f: acts on soft ground: has been slowly away: possibly temperamental. *M. W. Easterby*

ADS-SIXTY-FIVE   4 b.g. Casteddu 111 – Come On Lucy 43 (Reesh 117) [2001 **–**
11.6m 10.2s f9.4g Aug 18] first living foal: dam lightly-raced maiden: well held in sellers.
D. J. Wintle

ADSTONE BLAZE   2 ch.f. (Feb 1) Selkirk (USA) 129 – Galine 91 (Most Welcome **55**
131) [2001 6m 6m 6g 8.2m f8.5g⁴ Oct 9] 14,000Y: leggy, lengthy filly: first foal: dam,
5f (including at 2 yrs)/6f winner, out of half-sister to top-class French middle-distance
performer Le Marmot: modest maiden: settled better than previously and showed

improved form at Wolverhampton final start: should stay 1¼m: acts on fibresand. *J. G. Smyth-Osbourne*

ADVANCE PARTY (IRE)   2 b.c. (Mar 14) Mujadil (USA) 119 – Battle Queen 85   **103** (Kind of Hush 118) [2001 6m* 6d* 6g 7d⁴ 7v³ Oct 26] 17,000Y: small colt: good walker: half-brother to several winners, including 4-y-o Celebration Town and 5f (at 2 yrs)/6f winner Avondale Girl (both by Case Law): dam best at 6f/7f: useful performer: won minor event at Windsor in August and 22-runner sales race at Doncaster (slowly away) in September: best effort when about 2 lengths third of 9 finishers to Rapscallion in Horris Hill Stakes at Newbury final start, no extra final 100 yds: stays 7f: acts on heavy and good to firm going: sold 70,000 gns, sent to Norway. *J. Noseda*

ADWEB   3 b.f. Muhtarram (USA) 125 – What A Present (Pharly (FR) 130) [2001 70:   **81** 5m* 5m² 5.2m 5g⁴ 6m² 6g 5g 5.1d Oct 25] tall, angular filly: poor mover: fairly useful handicapper: won at Sandown in July: mostly at least respectably efforts after: will prove best at 5f/6f: acts on soft and good to firm going: sometimes slowly away. *J. Cullinan*

AEGEAN DAISY   2 ch.f. (Mar 12) Bal Harbour 113 – Dizzydaisy 57 (Sharpo 132)   **68 d** [2001 5m⁵ 6m⁴ 6g 6m² 5m⁶ 6g 6.1m⁴ 6s 5.7d⁵ p7g p8g f7g p7g Dec 12] third foal: closely related to 1½m winner Aegean Sunrise (by Deploy) and half-sister to fairly useful 1998 2-y-o 5f winner Aegean Flame (by Anshan): dam maiden who stayed 6f: fair maiden: became disappointing, leaving R. Hannon after third start, K. Ivory after ninth: stays 6f: acts on good to firm ground: tried blinkered: has run in snatches/flashed tail/hung left: ungenuine. *R. M. Flower*

AEGEAN DREAM (IRE)   5 b.m. Royal Academy (USA) 130 – L'Ideale (USA)   **97** (Alysheba (USA)) [2001 92+: 12m⁶ 10m⁶ 10m³ 12g⁶ 11m³ 10.1g* 10.1g² 10f⁶ 10.3s* Nov 9] small mare: useful performer: won handicap at Epsom (beat Danakil by 1½ lengths) in August and weak minor event at Doncaster in November: best around 1¼m: best form on good going or firmer: travels strongly, and best held up: consistent. *R. Hannon*

AEGEAN FLOWER   4 b.g. Robellino (USA) 127 – Bercheba (Bellypha 130) [2001   **–** 51: 7d 8.1m 7g Aug 11] workmanlike gelding: maiden: well beaten in 2001: tried blinkered. *R. M. Flower*

AEGEAN GLORY   5 b.m. Shareef Dancer (USA) 135 – Sayulita 67 (Habitat 134)   **–** [2001 10.2s Aug 9] rather leggy mare: modest maiden at 3 yrs: well beaten in seller in 2001. *J. G. M. O'Shea*

AEGEAN HEIGHTS   3 b.c. Ezzoud (IRE) 126 – Perdicula (IRE) (Persian Heights   **68 ?** 129) [2001 10.1m³ 10.1s⁶ 11.5g⁶ Sep 5] 24,000Y: second foal: dam, German winner around 1¼m at 4 yrs, half-sister to High-Rise: fair form: seemingly best effort in maidens when sixth to Prompt Payment at Lingfield final start: stayed 11.5f: dead. *R. Hannon*

AEGEAN SUNRISE   3 ch.g. Deploy 131 – Dizzydaisy 57 (Sharpo 132) [2001 55:   **48** e8g f8g e12g* 14.4m 12f 12m 11.9g⁵ f16g 14.1m⁴ 12m 11.9m 16g Sep 5] modest on   **a59** all-weather, poor on turf: won maiden at Lingfield in February: below form final 3 starts: probably stays 2m: acts on all-weather and good to firm ground: tried blinkered. *R. M. Flower*

AEGEAN WIND   4 b.g. Dolphin Street (FR) 125 – Perdicula (IRE) (Persian Heights   **–** 129) [2001 64: 12s 16.2m Jun 18] lengthy, unfurnished gelding: modest maiden at 3 yrs: no show in 2001. *D. R. C. Elsworth*

AESKULAP (GER)   4 b.c. Acatenango (GER) 127 – Aerope (Celestial Storm (USA)   **115** 132) [2001 110: 10.5s⁶ 12v² 11m⁴ 11g* 12g 12d⁶ 12v⁴ a10.5g Nov 24] third foal: dam German 1¼m and 11f winner: smart performer: successful in maiden at Cologne, handicap at Dusseldorf and national listed race at Hanover at 3 yrs, when also second in Deutsches St Leger at Dortmund: won Idee Hansa-Preis at Hamburg in June: ran creditably when sixth to Morshdi in Grosser Preis von Baden and fourth to Kutub in Preis von Europa at Cologne last 2 starts in Germany: soundly beaten in Japan Cup Dirt at Tokyo final start: stays 1¾m: acts on heavy ground. *H. Blume, Germany*

AFAAN (IRE)   8 ch.h. Cadeaux Genereux 131 – Rawaabe (USA) 87 (Nureyev (USA)   **109 ?** 131) [2001 97: f5g f6g f5g³ f5g⁴ 5s³ 5f⁶ 5g 5m⁵ 5m² 5.2m* 6d³ 5.1g 5g⁵ 5m⁵ 5.6m 5s 5g   **a90** Oct 4] big horse: poor mover: useful performer: seemed to excel when ¾-length second to Dietrich in King George Stakes at Goodwood in August: won handicap at Newbury later in month by length from Annette Vallon: creditable efforts after on next 3 starts only: best at 5f: acts on firm going, soft and fibresand/equitrack: effective blinkered/visored or not: often bandaged: sometimes hangs/finds little: often a front runner. *R. F. Marvin*

AFEEF (USA) 2 br.c. (Jan 30) Dayjur (USA) 137 – Jah (USA) (Relaunch (USA)) **68**
[2001 8d 7s⁵ Oct 31] good-topped colt: second foal: dam, US stakes winner at 8.5f to 11f,
out of Breeders' Cup Juvenile Fillies second Sweet Roberta: tongue tied, fair form in
maidens at Newmarket and Yarmouth: likely to prove best up to 1m. *E. A. L. Dunlop*

AFFAIRE D'AMOUR 2 ch.f. (Mar 27) Hernando (FR) 127 – Entente Cordiale **50 p**
(USA) (Affirmed (USA)) [2001 7d 7s³ 7g Nov 5] leggy, quite good-topped filly: fourth
foal: sister to useful 1¼m winner Bien Entendu and 3-y-o Foreign Affairs, and half-sister
to a winner up to 9.5f in Italy by Northern Park: dam once-raced half-sister to smart
middle-distance performer Pegnitz: modest form, not knocked about, in maidens: should
be well suited by 1¼m+: type to do well in handicaps. *Sir Mark Prescott*

AFFAIRE ROYALE (IRE) 3 b.f. Royal Academy (USA) 130 – Fleet Amour (USA) **95**
(Afleet (CAN)) [2001 7m* 8g 7m 7d⁴ Sep 4] tall, lengthy, useful-looking filly: has plenty
of scope: second foal: dam, ran 4 times in USA, closely related to US Grade 1 1m winner
Quiet American: useful form: won maiden at Yarmouth in June on debut: best effort when
ninth to Proudwings in Falmouth Stakes at Newmarket month later (edged markedly left):
only respectable effort in listed race at Goodwood next time: stays 1m: acts on good to
firm going, possibly not on good to soft. *J. R. Fanshawe*

AFFARATI 3 b.g. Emarati (USA) 74 – Affairiste (IRE) (Simply Great (FR) 122) [2001 **73 d**
71: 7v³ 7.1d 8v⁵ 8g 8g⁵ 9.9m 10.3f⁶ 7g 8s 7m⁴ 8.5s f6g 7s Oct 16] smallish, strong
gelding: has a fluent action: fair handicapper: mostly well below best after third start: best
at 7f/1m: acts on heavy and good to firm ground: has raced too freely/wandered: sold
2,100 gns, sent to Denmark. *J. L. Eyre*

AFFRAY (USA) 2 b.c. (Feb 1) Affirmed (USA) – Wee Miss Bee (USA) (Shelter Half **83**
(USA)) [2001 8g² 8.3g⁴ 8.2d* Sep 21] $75,000Y, $160,000Y: rangy, angular colt: first
foal: dam won 13 races in USA and third in Grade 3 9f event: fairly useful form:
confirmed debut promise (runner-up to Bestam at Newmarket) when winning 17-runner
maiden at Nottingham by neck from Always, leading 3f out and battling on well: will stay
at least 1¼m. *M. Johnston*

AFKAAR (USA) 3 b.f. Unbridled (USA) 128 – Barakat 93 (Bustino 136) [2001 **68**
10.2g² Oct 1] fifth foal: half-sister to several winners, including useful 1¼m performer
Ta Awun (by Housebuster) and fairly useful performer up to 1½m Mumaris (by Capote):
dam, winner around 1¾m, half-sister to Ibn Bey and Roseate Tern from family of
Teleprompter: 9 lengths second of 16 to Najah in maiden at Bath, travelling smoothly
long way, only outing: visits Aljabr. *A. C. Stewart*

AFRICA (IRE) 4 b.f. Namaqualand (USA) – Tannerrun (IRE) 65 (Runnett 125) [2001 **–**
51, a63: f12g⁵ f14.8g* f16.2g⁶ 16f 14.1m Jul 28] sturdy filly: modest performer: won **a51**
seller at Wolverhampton in February: barely stays 2m: acts on fibresand and firm going,
well held on softer than good: blinkered once: has been slowly away. *A. Streeter*

AFRICAN DAWN 3 b.c. Spectrum (IRE) 126 – Lamu Lady (IRE) 70 (Lomond (USA) **79**
128) [2001 10f³ 10g⁶ p12g* f14g f14g² Dec 14] leggy colt: fourth foal: half-brother to
fairly useful 8.5f to 1¼m winner Thekryaati (by Indian Ridge) and 1¼m winner Much
Ado (by Mujtahid): dam, 2-y-o 7f winner who stayed 1¼m, closely related to high-class
miler The Noble Player: fair performer: won maiden at Lingfield in November: running
well when hampered and unseated rider close home next start, and good effort final one:
stays 1¾m: acts on fibresand/polytrack: has started slowly. *J. H. M. Gosden*

AFRICAN SAHARA (USA) 2 br.c. (Mar 10) El Gran Senor (USA) 136 – Able **78**
Money (USA) (Distinctive (USA)) [2001 6g⁴ 7m⁶ 6s⁴ Sep 27] $45,000Y: rather leggy,
useful-looking colt: half-brother to several winners, including fairly useful 1½m/1½m
winner Abel Prospect (by Mr Prospector) and a winner up to 6f in USA by Jade Hunter:
dam US Grade 1 9f winner: fair form in maidens: fourth at Newmarket and Pontefract:
bred to stay at least 1m: tongue tied all starts. *E. A. L. Dunlop*

AFTERJACKO (IRE) 5 ch.g. Seattle Dancer (USA) 119 – Shilka (Soviet Star **–**
(USA) 128) [2001 107: 16d Nov 2] big, lengthy gelding: useful handicapper at 4 yrs:
soundly beaten only run on Flat in 2001: best around 1¾m: yet to race on soft/heavy
going, acts on any other: has been bandaged in front: edgy type, and withdrawn having
broken out of stall once: usually held up. *D. R. C. Elsworth*

AFTER SHOCK (IRE) 3 ch.g. Grand Lodge (USA) 125 – Fancy Boots (IRE) 62 **77 ?**
(Salt Dome (USA)) [2001 81: 6.5v 5g⁶ 6g⁴ 6m 7s f6s* Dec 15] IR 10,000Y: second foal:
dam, Irish maiden, half-sister to dams of dual Breeders' Cup Mile winner Da Hoss and
Prix Morny winner Tagula: fair performer: nowhere near best when winning maiden at

Southwell in December: should stay 7f: acts on fibresand and good to soft ground. *G. Stack, Ireland*

AGENT MULDER   7 b.g. Kylian (USA) – Precious Caroline (IRE) 60 (The Noble **–** Player (USA) 126) [2001 74, a–: 6m f5g 5.2v Oct 26] angular gelding: one-time fairly useful performer: well held in 2001: was usually blinkered: dead. *P. D. Cundell*

AGHNOYOH (GER)   3 ch.c. Local Suitor (USA) 128 – Aghniyah (USA) 76 **116** (Lyphard (USA) 132) [2001 7.5s* 7.5g* 7.5d2 8v4 8v* 8.5v3 8m3 8g* 10g4 8m3 8s* Sep 22] third reported foal: half-brother to 2 winners, including French 1m/9f winner Abela (by Persian Bold): dam 2-y-o 7f winner out of smart 7f/1m winner Goodbye Shelley: smart performer: trained by G. Sybrecht in Germany first 4 starts at 2 yrs: won maiden and minor event at Cagnes-sur-Mer in January/February, listed race at Saint-Cloud in March, Prix de la Jonchere at Chantilly (made all, held on gamely by ½ length from Domedriver) in June and Grosse Karstadt-Meile (by length from Pardus) at Cologne in September: stays 1m: acts on good to firm and heavy ground: tough and genuine: sold 3.3m francs in October. *T. Clout, France*

AGILE DANCER (IRE)   3 ch.f. Eagle Eyed (USA) 111 – Be Nimble (Wattlefield **–** 117) [2001 40: e8g Jan 17] poor maiden at 2 yrs: blinkered, well held only run in 2001: seems to stay 1m: acts on firm going and equitrack. *N. A. Graham*

AGINCOURT WARRIOR   2 b.c. (Feb 5) Distant Relative 128 – Careful (IRE) 59 **70 p** (Distinctly North (USA) 115) [2001 p6g* Dec 28] second foal: dam, maiden best at 6f at 2 yrs, should have stayed further: 9/2, won 14-runner maiden at Lingfield by length from Cressex Katie, leading well over 2f out and running on having initially seemed bit green: should improve. *J. M. P. Eustace*

AGITANDO (IRE)   5 b.g. Tenby 125 – Crown Rose (Dara Monarch 128) [2001 10m **88 d** 12m3 11.9d 12m 10.3g 8g 10s 11.7d5 Oct 25] lengthy gelding: useful at 3 yrs: generally disappointing at 5 yrs: stays 1½m: yet to race on heavy going, acts on any other: visored sixth and seventh starts: reportedly lost action third start: sold 9,000 gns, joined B. de Haan. *R. Charlton*

AGLOW   2 b.f. (Apr 3) Spinning World (USA) 130 – Flame Valley (USA) 112 (Gulch **90 p** (USA)) [2001 7g2 8m* 8d4 Nov 3] first foal: dam, best around 1¼m, out of useful sister to Prix de la Salamandre winner Common Grounds: fairly useful form: landed odds cosily in maiden at Leicester in September: good fourth, beaten about 4 lengths by Sundrenched, in listed race at Newmarket: should stay 1¼m: likely to do better still. *Sir Michael Stoute*

AGNES DIGITAL (USA)   4 ch.c. Crafty Prospector (USA) – Chancey Squaw **130** (USA) (Chief's Crown (USA)) [2001 118: 8f3 7f 8f a9g* a8f* 10d* 10m* Dec 16] first foal: dam, 1m winner in USA, half-sister to several useful winners, including 1999 Royal Lodge winner Royal Kingdom, out of half-sister to Blushing Groom: top-class colt: won Mile Championship at Kyoto in 2000: in excellent form late in 2001, winning stakes races at Funabashi and Morioka, Tenno Sho (Autumn) at Tokyo (best effort, by length from T M Opera O) and Hong Kong Cup at Sha Tin: held on by head from rallying Tobougg after leading over 1f out for final win: effective at 1m to 1¼m: acts on firm and good to soft ground, and on dirt. *T. Shirai, Japan*

AGNES FOR RANSOM (USA)   3 b. or br.f. Red Ransom (USA) – Golden Rhyme **73** 87 (Dom Racine (FR) 121) [2001 –p: 8.3s2 9.9m5 10.1g 11.7g 11.9m 11.5g 12g5 10v 10s Oct 30] leggy, close-coupled filly: fair maiden handicapper: probably stays 1½m: acts on soft ground, possibly not on good to firm: blinkered final 3 starts: none too consistent. *J. L. Dunlop*

AGO   3 ch.f. Rudimentary (USA) 118 – Amidst 86 (Midyan (USA) 124) [2001 –: 7m **71** 8m 8f 8m* Jul 27] lengthy filly: modest performer: won handicap at Salisbury in July: will stay further than 1m: raced only on firm/good to firm ground: sold 3,500 gns in October. *R. F. Johnson Houghton*

AGOSTINI   2 b.g. (Mar 21) Octagonal (NZ) – Majestic Image 86 (Niniski (USA) 125) **62** [2001 7m 8m4 6m6 7.9s Oct 11] 40,000Y: smallish, sparely-made gelding: fifth foal: half-brother to 3 winners, including smart German winner up to 2m Montalban (by Mondrian) and 4-y-o Mbele: dam 1¾m/2m winner: modest maiden: should be suited by 1½m+: acts on good to firm going, possibly not soft. *T. D. Easterby*

AGRIPPINA   4 b.f. Timeless Times (USA) 99 – Boadicea's Chariot (Commanche Run **83** 133) [2001 96: 7d 7v5 8d5 6s6 p7g f7g Dec 11] smallish, good-topped filly: unimpressive mover: only fairly useful form on balance in 2001: stays 7f: acts on soft and good to firm going: has raced freely. *A. Bailey*

AGUILA LOCO (IRE)   2 ch.g. (Apr 14) Eagle Eyed (USA) 111 – Go Likecrazy 51   **60**
(Dowsing (USA) 124) [2001 5s 5d³ 5.1f 5d⁴ 5m⁴ 6g 5d³ 5s⁴ f5g⁵ f5g³ f5g⁶ Dec 17] IR
7,500F, 10,000Y: smallish gelding: third foal: dam 2-y-o 5f/6f winner: modest maiden:
seems best at 5f: acts on firm going, good to soft and fibresand: blinkered (raced freely)
eighth start: has swished tail: races prominently. *E. J. Alston*

AHOUOD   5 b.m. Merdon Melody 98 – Balidilemma 77 (Balidar 133) [2001 53d: p12g   **– §**
Nov 13] maiden handicapper: blinkered, pulled up lame only 5-y-o start: unreliable.
P. S. McEntee

AHRAAR (USA)   3 b.c. Gulch (USA) – Saffaanh (USA) 87 (Shareef Dancer (USA)   **106**
135) [2001 73P: 8m 8.1d⁴ 9.9m³ 10g* 12.3m* 12m* 12g² 12s Sep 30] smallish, quite
attractive colt: fluent mover: useful performer: won maiden and handicap at Ripon then
minor event at Beverley, all in August: very good second to High Pitched at Doncaster,
much better effort in handicaps after: stays 1½m: acts on good to firm going, seemingly
not on soft: blinkered third start. *M. P. Tregoning*

AILINCALA (IRE)   3 b.f. Pursuit of Love 124 – Diabaig 76 (Precocious 126) [2001   **66**
63: 8d⁴ 7f⁴ 7m⁴ 6m 8.1m² 10g⁶ 8g² 7m⁴ 8s Sep 24] lengthy, quite attractive filly: modest
maiden handicapper: best around 1m: acts on firm and good to soft going: sometimes
slowly away (went sharply left and unseated leaving stall on debut). *C. F. Wall*

AINTNECESSARILYSO   3 ch.g. So Factual (USA) 120 – Ovideo 58 (Domynsky   **78**
110) [2001 71: 6g 5.7m 5.1m* 7m 5m* 6g⁴ 6f² 6m⁴ 5g⁶ 5g Sep 2] workmanlike gelding:
has quick action: fair performer: won claimer at Bath in June and handicap at Kempton in
July: mostly creditable efforts after: best at 5f/6f: yet to race on heavy ground, acts on any
other: ran poorly in blinkers once at 2 yrs: hung/looked hard ride for 7-lb claimer on
reappearance, stumbled and almost unseated leaving stall next time: has looked ill at ease
at Epsom/Goodwood: sold 8,000 gns. *D. R. C. Elsworth*

AIRA FORCE (USA)   4 ch.g. Dehere (USA) 111 – Cinnamon Splendor (USA) (Trem-   **58**
polino (USA) 135) [2001 83: 6g 7d⁵ 6m⁴ 7.1g f7g² f8s Dec 21] small, sturdy gelding:
fairly useful handicapper at best, just modest nowadays: stays 7f: acts on fibresand,
equitrack and good to firm going, possibly not on soft. *A. G. Newcombe*

AIR MAIL   4 b.g. Night Shift (USA) – Wizardry 83 (Shirley Heights 130) [2001 66,   **73**
a90: f5g² f6s⁴ f6g* f7s² f6s f6g³ f7g² f8.5g² f7g² f8.5g⁶ f7g³ 5.1f 6f³ 7m 6d 6m 6v⁵   **a100**
5s⁴ f5g⁵ p7g f6g⁵ f5s³ Dec 15] leggy gelding: useful on all-weather, fair on turf: won
handicap at Southwell in January: effective at 5f to easy 8.5f: acts on fibresand/equitrack
and any turf going: tried blinkered/visored at 3 yrs: usually races prominently: tough and
consistent. *Mrs N. Macauley*

AIR MARSHALL (IRE)   4 ch.g. In The Wings 128 – Troyanna 109 (Troy 137) [2001   **–**
121: 12g May 4] lengthy gelding: very smart performer at 3 yrs, winning Great Voltigeur
Stakes at York and beaten ¾ length by Millenary in St Leger at Doncaster: tailed off
after slipping in early stages of Jockey Club Stakes at Newmarket only outing at 4 yrs:
subsequently gelded, joined J. Hammond in France but didn't race there, then sent to
N. Henderson: effective at 1½m to 14.6f: acts on firm going, probably on soft: has run
well when sweating: held up. *Sir Michael Stoute*

AIR OF ESTEEM   5 b.g. Forzando 122 – Shadow Bird 70 (Martinmas 128) [2001   **71 d**
76: f8g² f8g f8g⁶ 10v⁵ 8s 8.3d f7g f8g f8.5g² f9.4g³ f8g Dec 17] smallish gelding: fair
handicapper: below best after second start: stays 9.4f: acts on fibresand/equitrack, good
to soft and good to firm going: visored once: often held up. *P. C. Haslam*

AISLE   4 b.g. Arazi (USA) 135 – Chancel (USA) 60 (Al Nasr (FR) 126) [2001 64?: f6g⁶   **52**
f8g f6g⁶ f7g² f6g⁴ f6f⁶ f6g⁴ f7g³ 8.1g f7g² 7m 6.1f⁶ f6g⁶ 6m 6m 7v 8d f6g f7g⁵ f8.5s³
Dec 26] small gelding: modest handicapper: effective at 6f/7f: acts on soft ground and
fibresand: usually blinkered: sometimes tongue tied earlier in career: tends to carry head
awkwardly/edge left. *S. R. Bowring*

AISLING'S DREAM (IRE)   2 ch.f. (Apr 15) Desert King (IRE) 129 – Daftiyna   **50**
(IRE) 74 (Darshaan 133) [2001 5f⁶ 6m 7m 5.1f Sep 18] IR 15,000Y: fourth foal: dam,
placed up to 9f in Ireland, daughter of very smart Irish sprinter Dafayna, herself half-
sister to Doyoun: modest maiden: easily best effort third start: should stay 1m: unseated
rider to post, bolted and withdrawn fourth intended outing. *S. Kirk*

AIWAI (IRE)   4 b.c. Thatching 131 – Peach Melba 96 (So Blessed 130) [2001 e8g f7g   **–**
f6g f11g Mar 26] fairly useful maiden at 2 yrs: little show at 4 yrs. *G. C. H. Chung*

AIX EN PROVENCE (USA)   6 b.g. Geiger Counter (USA) – Low Hill (Rousillon   **–**
(USA) 133) [2001 52, a–: 7m May 30] one-time useful performer, very lightly raced
nowadays. *C. A. Dwyer*

AJEEL (IRE)   2 b.c. (Feb 17) Green Desert (USA) 127 – Samheh (USA) 62 (Private   **67 p**
Account (USA)) [2001 6d 6d⁶ Nov 2] big, strong, rangy colt: fluent mover: third foal:
half-brother to fairly useful 1999 2-y-o 7f winner Marah (by Machiavellian): dam,
maiden who stayed 1¼m, out of US Grade 1 7f (at 2 yrs) and 9f winner Lucky Lucky
Lucky: some promise in Newmarket maidens, fair form when keeping-on sixth of 20 to
Feet So Fast second start: will stay at least 7f: type to do better. *J. L. Dunlop*

AJNAD (IRE)   7 b.g. Efisio 120 – Lotte Lenta (Gorytus (USA) 132) [2001 61, a69: f5g   **–**
Dec 14] deep-bodied gelding: fair handicapper on all-weather, modest on turf in 2000: off
13 months, reportedly finished lame only 7-y-o outing: sometimes blinkered/visored: has
been tongue tied. *R. F. Marvin*

AJWAA (IRE)   3 ch.c. Mujtahid (USA) 118 – Nouvelle Star (AUS) (Luskin Star   **78**
(AUS)) [2001 95+: 6m 6g Aug 6] angular colt: won maiden at Newmarket at 2 yrs: below
form both starts in 2001, seeming less than co-operative in visor final one: may prove best
at 5f/6f: acts on soft going: sold 14,000 gns in October. *M. P. Tregoning*

AKALIM   8 b.g. Petong 126 – Tiszta Sharok 81 (Song 132) [2001 60: 7.1g 7.1g Sep   **51**
13] good-topped gelding: modest handicapper: best at 6f/7f: acts on fibresand/equitrack,
probably on any turf going: tried blinkered/visored. *L. G. Cottrell*

AKATIB (IRE)   3 b.f. Lahib (USA) 129 – Daltak (Night Shift (USA)) [2001 –: 8.2f   **–**
f8g f7g⁵ 7g⁵ Jul 18] small, stocky filly: well held in varied company. *B. S. Rothwell*

AKBAR (IRE)   5 b. or br.h. Doyoun 124 – Akishka (Nishapour (FR) 125) [2001 102:   **118**
a10g⁴ f12f 14m* 12m² 13.9m* 14g³ 12.4v³ 12s³ Nov 10] smart performer, better than
ever at 5 yrs: won handicaps at Goodwood in May and York (listed contest, comfortably

Foster's Silver Cup Rated Stakes (Handicap), York—
Akbar records a convincing success from Maniatis (rail) and Bay of Islands (visor)

by 2½ lengths from Maniatis) in July: short-headed by stable-companion Takamaka Bay in Duke of Edinburgh Handicap at Royal Ascot in between, and also ran well when 2¼ lengths third to Shamaiel in listed event at Goodwood sixth start: should stay 2m: acts on good to firm going, has won on soft: usually races prominently: genuine. *M. Johnston*

AKEBONO (IRE) 5 ch.g. Case Law 113 – Elanmatina (IRE) 77 (Burslem 123) [2001 **52** 65: p7g f9.4g p7g⁴ Dec 28] winning handicapper: off 13 months, only modest at 5 yrs: stays 7f: acts on polytrack, heavy and firm going: effective blinkered or not. *P. Burgoyne*

AKEED (USA) 4 ch.c. Affirmed (USA) – Victorious Lil (CAN) (Vice Regent (CAN)) – [2001 –: 7d Apr 18] strong, lengthy colt: useful form at 2 yrs: little form since. *P. F. I. Cole*

AKEESHA 2 b.f. (Apr 27) Mukaddamah (USA) 125 – Butterwick Belle (IRE) 64 **57** (Distinctly North (USA) 115) [2001 6m 6m 6m* 5s⁵ f6s Sep 6] 1,200Y: second foal: dam, maiden who should have stayed beyond 6f, out of half-sister to smart 1½m performer Pencader: modest performer: won seller at Redcar in August: well held in nurseries last 2 starts: bred to stay 1m: acts on good to firm ground: has reportedly had trouble with joints. *R. A. Fahey*

AKER WOOD 3 b.f. Bin Ajwaad (IRE) 119 – Wannaplantatree 72 (Niniski (USA) **77** 125) [2001 73: 10s³ 10s² 10.9m* 12m⁴ 10m 10m 10m⁴ 10.1m² 10.1g² f12g f8.5g⁶ Nov 3] **a65** leggy, plain filly: fair performer: won maiden at Ayr in May: good efforts when in frame in handicaps after: should stay 1½m: acts on soft and good to firm going, possibly on fibresand: usually races prominently. *A. P. Jarvis*

AKHIRA 4 b.f. Emperor Jones (USA) 119 – Fakhira (IRE) 83 (Jareer (USA) 115) [2001 **76** 64: f8g³ f8g 7f² 6.9m³ 7f 7g* 7m 7g⁴ Aug 9] leggy filly: fair handicapper: won at Yarmouth in July: stays easy 1m: acts on fibresand, soft and firm going: races prominently. *S. P. C. Woods*

AKINA (NZ) 10 b.g. Ivory Hunter (USA) – Wairoa Belle (NZ) (Bold Venture (NZ)) – [2001 16v Oct 26] New Zealand-bred gelding: won twice at 1m on Flat and twice over hurdles in native country: yet to win over jumps in Britain (stays 23f), and well held on Flat debut in Britain. *J. Neville*

AL AALI 3 b.c. Lahib (USA) 129 – Maraatib (IRE) 93 (Green Desert (USA) 127) **92 p** [2001 6g 7g* 7g* Aug 4] good-bodied, quite attractive colt: fifth foal: half-brother to 3 winners, including useful 5f (including in France) and 6f winner Khasayl (by Lycius) and 1m (at 2 yrs) and 1¼m winner Nebl (by Persian Bold): dam 5f (including at 2 yrs) and 6f winner: progressive form: won maiden at Thirsk in June and handicap at Newmarket (beat Kameynn by 1½ lengths, always travelling strongly and needing only to be pushed out once gap appeared) in August: not short of speed, but should stay 1m: should make useful colt if all is well. *J. L. Dunlop*

ALABAMA WURLEY 4 b.f. Environment Friend 128 – Logarithm (King of Spain – 121) [2001 47: 6m 5f 6m 6.1m 6g 6s Sep 24] lengthy, dipped-backed filly: little form at 4 yrs: tried visored. *J. Balding*

ALABAMY SOUND (IRE) 5 ch.m. Superlative 118 – Salt Peanuts (IRE) (Salt Dome – (USA)) [2001 44, a31: 7m 7.6m 7m Jul 24] no form in 2001: tried visored. *K. A. Morgan*

ALABANG 10 ch.g. Valiyar 129 – Seleter (Hotfoot 126) [2001 f11g² e16g* e12g⁵ **77** e16s⁵ f16g* Apr 9] quite good-topped gelding: fair handicapper: won at Lingfield in January and (having left C. Egerton) Southwell in April: effective at 11f to 2m: acts on firm ground and fibresand/equitrack: sometimes slowly away: held up. *C. G. Cox*

ALAFZAR (IRE) 3 b.c. Green Desert (USA) 127 – Alasana (IRE) (Darshaan 133) **71** [2001 8d 8.1v 8d⁴ Oct 8] lengthy, good sort: third living foal: dam, French 1m/9f winner, half-sister to high-class French 1½m performer Altayan: fair form: best effort when 10 lengths fourth to Sea Star in maiden at Pontefract: raced only at 1m on ground softer than good: sold 11,000 gns. *Sir Michael Stoute*

ALAGAZAM 3 ch.g. Alhijaz 122 – Maziere 45 (Mazilier (USA) 107) [2001 55: 11.6g **37** 8m 11.6m⁶ 15m 16.4g Aug 23] workmanlike gelding: poor maiden: stays 11.6f: yet to race on extremes of going. *B. I. Case*

ALAKANANDA 3 br.f. Hernando (FR) 127 – Alouette 105 (Darshaan 133) [2001 71: **92** 12m³ 11.6v⁴ 11.7d* 11.6v* 12.5v Nov 19] fairly useful performer: won maiden at Bath and handicap at Windsor (by 4 lengths after going clear around halfway), both in October: not discredited in listed race at Maisons-Laffitte final start: should stay beyond 1½m: acts on heavy ground, probably on good to firm: blinkered last 3 outings. *Sir Mark Prescott*

ALAMEIN (USA) 8 ch.g. Roi Danzig (USA) – Pollination 100 (Pentotal) [2001 48§: **41 §** f8g 10s 9.2d 11.1d 12.4m 10m² 10.1m⁶ 11.9m⁵ 12.4g 8.9m 10.3m Sep 12] big, work-manlike gelding: poor performer: effective at 1m/easy 1¼m: acts on firm ground, good to soft and fibresand/equitrack: sometimes blinkered: tongue tied: unreliable. *W. Storey*

ALAM (USA) 2 b.c. (Mar 28) Silver Hawk (USA) 123 – Ghashtah (USA) (Nijinsky **77 P** (CAN) 138) [2001 7d⁵ Sep 4] sixth foal: half-brother to 1998 2-y-o 1m Nafis (by Kingmambo): dam unraced sister to Seattle Dancer, close relative of Lomond and half-sister to Seattle Slew: 20/1, very much caught the eye when fifth of 15 to Samhari in maiden at Yarmouth, poorly placed when race began in earnest then running on strongly without being knocked about, giving impression would have gone close had run started sooner: will stay 1¼m: open to considerable improvement, and sure to win races. *E. A. L. Dunlop*

ALAN'S PRINCE (IRE) 3 b.c. Anita's Prince 126 – Fandangerina (USA) (Grey **–** Dawn II 132) [2001 f6g Jul 27] IR 8,000Y, 5,000 2-y-o: brother to useful 1999 2-y-o 6f winner Trinculo and half-brother to several winners, including useful 7f (at 2 yrs) to 1½m winner Ocean Air (by Elegant Air): dam won up to 1m in USA: 20/1, well held in Southwell maiden. *B. Palling*

ALASHA (IRE) 2 ch.f. (Apr 4) Barathea (IRE) 127 – Alasana (IRE) (Darshaan 133) **89 p** [2001 7f³ 7m* Sep 6] good-bodied filly: fourth foal: dam, French 1m/9f winner, half-sister to high-class French 1½m performer Altayan: 2/1, confirmed promise to win 13-runner maiden at Salisbury by head from Pretty Clear, getting on top last 50 yds: will stay 1¼m: useful filly in the making. *Sir Michael Stoute*

ALASTAIR SMELLIE 5 ch.g. Sabrehill (USA) 120 – Reel Foyle (USA) 77 (Irish **67 §** River (FR) 131) [2001 88d: f6g 6g f6g 6g³ 5f⁴ 5m 6.1v 6v Oct 16] good-topped gelding: has a quick action: fair handicapper: effective at 5f to 7f: acts on firm and soft going: visored last 6 starts: sometimes mulish to post/slowly away: flashes tail/looks awkward ride: refused to race second start: unreliable. *D. Nicholls*

AL AWAALAH 4 b.f. Mukaddamah (USA) 125 – Zippy Zoe 46 (Rousillon (USA) **50** 133) [2001 52: f9.4g⁴ f8g⁴ 8.2f⁶ 8m³ 8f 8.3g 9m Jul 11] modest maiden: barely stays 9.4f: acts on good to firm going, soft and fibresand. *M. Salaman*

ALAWAR 4 ch.c. Wolfhound (USA) 126 – Ghassanah 73 (Pas de Seul 133) [2001 59: **44** 8.2s 8m 7.5f⁶ f8g⁶ Jul 2] poor maiden handicapper: effective at 7f/easy 1m: acts on soft and firm going, probably on fibresand: blinkered final 2 starts: tongue tied: sold 2,000 gns. *C. G. Cox*

ALAZAN 6 ch.g. Risk Me (FR) 127 – Gunnard 62 (Gunner B 126) [2001 –: f12g 11.8f **–** 8.3m 7.6m 7d 8m Aug 12] of little account: dead. *W. de Best-Turner*

AL AZHAR 7 b.g. Alzao (USA) 117 – Upend 120 (Main Reef 126) [2001 85: 9v⁶ 10s² **79** 10.3m⁵ 10g 12g² 11.4g⁶ 10s³ 14g 12g⁴ 13.1v 10g f14g Nov 26] well-made gelding: has reportedly had knee trouble: fair handicapper nowadays: stays 1½m: yet to race on firm going, acts on any other turf (some promise on fibresand final start): sometimes starts slowly: held up. *M. Dods*

ALBADOU 3 ch.c. Wolfhound (USA) 126 – Ameerat Jumaira (USA) 64 (Alydar **76** (USA)) [2001 6.9v² 8.3g⁵ 8.1d⁵ 7.5g Dec 27] good-bodied colt: fourth foal: half-brother to an Italian 1¼m winner by In The Wings and a 1m to 1½m winner in Scandinavia by Caerleon: dam, maiden who stayed 1¼m, half-sister to Zilzal from family of Polish Precedent and Culture Vulture: fair maiden: left M. Tregoning before final outing: stays 1m. *D. J. Selvaratnam, UAE*

ALBANIA 2 ch.c. (Jan 30) Selkirk (USA) 129 – Elaine's Honor (USA) (Chief's Crown **75** (USA)) [2001 5.2d⁵ 5g³ 5.1m³ 5.1f* 6m⁴ 7g 7m Aug 23] 82,000Y: good-topped colt: fourth foal: brother to 3-y-o Ishaam and half-brother to useful 1999 2-y-o 5f winner Areydha (by Cadeaux Genereux) and a 1m winner in Japan by Indian Ridge: dam, French winner around 8.5f (including at 2 yrs), half-sister to useful 1987 French 2-y-o Savannah's Honor, later winner up to 1½m in USA: fair performer: won maiden at Chester in June: bit below form in nurseries last 2 starts: will need to settle better to stay 7f: acts on firm and good to soft ground: visored final start. *M. R. Channon*

ALBANOVA 2 gr.f. (Feb 16) Alzao (USA) 117 – Alouette 105 (Darshaan 133) [2001 **75 P** 7.1v* Sep 29] fourth foal: sister to very smart 7f (at 2 yrs) and 1¼m (dual Champion Stakes) winner Alborada and half-sister to 3-y-o Alakananda: dam, Irish 1m (at 2 yrs) and 1½m winner, half-sister to very smart 1¼m filly Last Second and 3-y-o Alleluia: 5/1, overcame greenness to win 9-runner maiden at Haydock by 1¾ lengths from Benny The

Vice, slowly away and in rear before finally getting hang of things final 2f and leading last 50 yds despite edging left: will stay at least 1¼m: open to plenty of improvement, and should win more races. *Sir Mark Prescott*

ALBARAHIN (USA) 6 b.h. Silver Hawk (USA) 123 – My Dear Lady (USA) (Mr **118** Prospector (USA)) [2001 118: 8s² 9d² 8.1v⁴ 10d² 10g* 10.9m* 9.8d* 10d Oct 20] strong, deep-girthed horse: smart performer: reportedly fractured leg early in 1998: as good as ever in 2001, winning minor event at Newmarket in August, listed race at Ayr (beat Esyoueffcee by 4 lengths) in September and Prix Dollar Fouquet's Barriere at Longchamp (beat Chancellor a head) in October, rallying typically tenaciously in gaining first pattern-race success in last-named: appeared to act as pacemaker for Nayef in Dubai Champion Stakes at Newmarket final start: was effective at 1m (given a test) to 11f: acted on heavy and good to firm ground: was effective ridden from front/held up: most game, genuine and consistent: a credit to his stable: stud in South Africa. *M. P. Tregoning*

ALBASHOOSH 3 b.g. Cadeaux Genereux 131 – Annona (USA) 72 (Diesis 133) **84** [2001 76: 10d 7.9g⁵ 8.1m 8g⁶ 7.1s* 7.6m⁵ 7d² Sep 4] quite good-topped gelding: fairly useful performer: won maiden at Chepstow in August: stays 1m: acts on soft and good to firm going: blinkered third start, visored fifth and sixth, racing freely each occasion: sold 21,000 gns. *E. A. L. Dunlop*

ALBEMARLE STREET 2 b.f. (Feb 17) Alhaarth (IRE) 126 – Pigeon Hole (Green **59** Desert (USA) 127) [2001 6.1m⁵ 7m⁵ 7m 6s 6s Oct 5] 22,000Y: second foal: dam lightly-raced half-sister to 1000 Guineas second Niche: modest maiden: well held last 3 starts: should stay 1m: acts on good to firm ground, possibly not soft: tried blinkered: sold 1,200 gns, sent to Sweden. *J. A. Osborne*

ALBERICH (IRE) 6 b.g. Night Shift (USA) – Tetradonna (IRE) 102 (Teenoso (USA) **75 +** 135) [2001 95: f12s* Dec 26] sturdy gelding: good mover: useful performer at best: has reportedly had knee problem: off 19 months, won maiden at Wolverhampton (sold 7,000 gns) in December very easily: probably best at 1½m/13f: acts on equitrack, fibre-sand and firm ground, probably on heavy: sometimes hangs: usually races up with pace. *M. Johnston*

ALBERKINNIE 6 b.m. Ron's Victory (USA) 129 – Trojan Desert 97 (Troy 137) **46 §** [2001 51§, a32§: f9.4s f12g f11g f8f f8g⁵ 10v³ 10g⁵ 10v 10.1m 11.8m 10g⁵ 10.5s 9.9m 8f **a23 §** 10.4s 12d Nov 2] sturdy mare: poor handicapper: stays 1½m: acts on heavy going, good to firm and fibresand/equitrack: not one to trust. *John A. Harris*

ALBERO (IRE) 2 b.g. (Apr 21) Priolo (USA) 127 – Woody's Colours (USA) (Caro **49** 133) [2001 6m 7.1d 7m² 7m⁵ 8s f8.5g 8.3v p8g² p7g Dec 12] IR 7,500F, IR 4,000Y, 6,500 2-y-o: fourth foal: half-brother to 2 winners in Italy, including a 5f to 1m winner by Ballad Rock: dam Irish 7f winner: poor maiden: second in sellers: stays 1m: acts on good to firm ground and polytrack: blinkered last 3 starts. *P. R. Chamings*

ALBERT'S LAD 3 br.g. Alhijaz 122 – Nikiya (IRE) (Lead On Time (USA) 123) **–** [2001 f7g f5g f6g f12g Apr 17] 600F: second foal: dam placed around 9f in France: no sign of ability on fibresand. *M. W. Easterby*

ALBERT THE BEAR 8 b.g. Puissance 110 – Florentynna Bay 61 (Aragon 118) **53** [2001 62, a–: 6v⁴ 7.1m 6m 6m 6d² 6g⁵ 6m⁶ 5f 5.7m⁶ 6g 5d 6d 6g 6v³ Oct 16] tall gelding: **a–** modest nowadays: effective at 6f/7f: acts on any turf going, no show on fibresand: tried blinkered, visored nowadays: usually races prominently: none too consistent. *A. Berry*

ALBUHERA (IRE) 3 b.g. Desert Style (IRE) 121 – Morning Welcome (IRE) (Be My **112** Guest (USA) 126) [2001 79p: 8d² 9.9g³ 7m 8m* 8m 10m* 10.4g³ 8.9m⁴ 10f* 9g 9d Oct 19] lengthy, good sort: developed into a smart performer: won minor event at Ayr in May and handicaps at Newmarket and Newbury in July/September, beating Kirovski by 3 lengths in Courage Best Stakes for last success: poor efforts last 2 starts: will probably stay beyond 1¼m: yet to race on heavy going, acts on any other: genuine. *M. Johnston*

ALBUNDY (IRE) 2 b.g. (Mar 17) Alzao (USA) 117 – Grove Daffodil (IRE) 83 (Salt **–** Dome (USA)) [2001 6g 7m 5s Oct 5] strong gelding: fourth foal: half-brother to Irish 1½m winner Galtip Flyer (by Be My Chief): dam 2-y-o 7f winner who was probably suited by middle distances: no encouragement in maidens: looked reluctant in blinkers final start. *M. H. Tompkins*

ALBURACK 3 b.g. Rock City 120 – Suzannah's Song (Song 132) [2001 –: f7g 8v **42** 6.1d 5.3f 5.1m 10g 10m Aug 29] leggy gelding: poor maiden: stays 6f: tried blinkered. *G. G. Margarson*

Prix Dollar Fouquet's Barriere, Longchamp—a pulsating finish as Albarahin gains a deserved first pattern-race success; Chancellor (rail) is narrowly held with King of Tara back in third

ALCAYDE 6 ch.g. Alhijaz 122 – Lucky Flinders 77 (Free State 125) [2001 61: 14.1s⁵ **65** 14.1v⁶ 17.2f* 17.2g⁸ 18m³ 16m⁶ 21m⁴ 17.1g⁵ 16g⁴ 16d³ Sep 27] good-bodied gelding: fluent mover: fair handicapper: won at Bath in May and June: stays 21f: acts on any ground: often soon off bridle. *J. Akehurst*

ALCAZAR (IRE) 6 b.g. Alzao (USA) 117 – Sahara Breeze 85 (Ela-Mana-Mou 132) **110** [2001 14m* Sep 22] smart performer: trained by J. Dunlop at 3 yrs, winning 4 races, including listed event: missed next 2 seasons reportedly due to broken pelvis and injured tendon: 25/1, returned almost as good as ever to win handicap at Newmarket in September by 3 lengths from Serge Lifar, quickening to lead over 1f out then drawing clear despite edging right: stays 1¾m: acts on soft and good to firm going: has been bandaged. *H. Morrison*

ALCONBURY 3 b.c. Green Desert (USA) 127 – Allegra 73 (Niniski (USA) 125) **70 d** [2001 f6g* f6g f8.5g⁴ 7s⁵ 7g 8.5g 9.5m 7g 6d Oct 29] seventh foal: half-brother to 2 winners by Selkirk, including fairly useful 1996 2-y-o 6f winner All Is Fair: dam, 1½m winner, half-sister to Last Second and to dam of Alborada, both very smart 1¼m fillies: fair performer at best: won maiden at Southwell in January: left Sir Mark Prescott 16,000 gns and off 6 months after third start: seemingly flattered next time and no form after: should prove best short of 1m: acts on fibresand. *Patrick J. Flynn, Ireland*

ALCONLEIGH 6 ch.g. Pursuit of Love 124 – Serotina (IRE) 73 (Mtoto 134) [2001 –: **41** 5m 8m 8m⁴ 8.5m Jun 6] strong, lengthy gelding: lightly raced and only poor form since 1999: probably best at 7f/1m: acts on firm and soft ground: blinkered once: has had tongue tied: has been slowly away. *B. Ellison*

ALDAFRA 2 b.f. (Mar 20) Spectrum (IRE) 126 – Abeyr 106 (Unfuwain (USA) 131) **91** [2001 6f⁵ 6.1m* 7g⁶ 6m³ 6m 7d Oct 2] strong filly: second foal: half-sister to 3-y-o Raheibb: dam 7f/1m winner: fairly useful performer: won maiden at Nottingham in July: easily best effort when third in minor event at Salisbury: should stay 7f: acts on good to firm ground. *M. R. Channon*

ALDEBARAN (USA) 3 b.c. Mr Prospector (USA) – Chimes of Freedom (USA) 121 **110** (Private Account (USA)) [2001 105p: 8m² 8m² 7m² 7.3m² 10.3d² 8g³ 8f* 9d³ Nov 25] leggy, attractive colt: smart performer: placed all starts in Britain in 2001, including when runner-up to Dandoun in listed race at Kempton, to Mozart in Jersey Stakes at Royal Ascot (beaten a neck) and to Lagudin in minor event at Doncaster on second, third and fifth starts and when 1½ lengths third to Beckett in listed race at Newmarket (final start for H. Cecil): won non-graded handicap at Belmont in October and creditable third to Denon in Hollywood Derby following month: stays 10.3f: acts on firm and good to soft going: most consistent. *R. J. Frankel, USA*

ALDENHAM (IRE) 4 b.f. Namaqualand (USA) – Lamp of Phoebus (USA) (Sunshine **–** Forever (USA)) [2001 7m Jun 12] first foal: dam twice-raced half-sister to smart French performer up to 10.5f Accommodating: well beaten in claimer at Salisbury. *Andrew Reid*

ALDORA   2 ch.f. (Apr 12) Magic Ring (IRE) 115 – Sharp Top 62 (Sharpo 132) [2001   **83**
7f 6d³ 5d* Oct 30] leggy filly: sixth foal: half-sister to 4-y-o Polar Red, fairly useful
9f/1¼m winner Top Jem (by Damister) and 1998 2-y-o 6f winner Hi Nicky (by High
Kicker): dam 1½m and 2m winner at 4 yrs: fairly useful form in maidens: third of 22 to
Hiddendale at Newmarket before landing odds easily at Redcar: should stay 7f: heavily
bandaged all round on debut. *M. J. Ryan*

ALDWYCH   3 ch.c. In The Wings 128 – Arderelle (FR) 80 (Pharly (FR) 130) [2001   **113**
102p: 10.2d* 10.4m⁴ 10m² 12f⁵ 10m² 10d Aug 18] lengthy colt: has a short action: smart
performer: won minor event at Bath in May: creditable efforts next 4 starts, including
when fourth in Dante Stakes at York and second in listed races at Newmarket (beaten
neck by Potemkin) and Newbury (beaten 3 lengths by Sakhee): blinkered, bumped
leaving stall and never dangerous in Secretariat Stakes at Arlington final start: effective
at 1¼m/1½m: acts on firm and good to soft going: carries head awkwardly: seems
faint-hearted. *R. Charlton*

ALDWYCH ARROW (IRE)   6 ch.g. Rainbows For Life (CAN) – Shygate (Shy   **41**
Groom (USA)) [2001 47, a57: f12g² 14.1v 12.3g³ 12g³ f14g f12s⁴ Dec 27] smallish,   **a55**
sturdy gelding: modest handicapper on all-weather, seems on turf: effective at 1½m to 2m:
has form on firm going, but all wins on good or softer (also acts on fibresand): blinkered
once. *M. A. Buckley*

ALEGRANZA (IRE)   3 b.f. Lake Coniston (IRE) 131 – Angelic Sounds (IRE) (The   **106**
Noble Player (USA) 126) [2001 –p: 5.8m² 5m* 5g⁵ 5m² 5g⁵ 5.2f Sep 22] lightly-made,
angular filly: third foal: half-sister to useful 1999 2-y-o 5f winner Seraphina and 10.8f
winner who stays 1½m Harp Player (both by Pips Pride): dam, Irish 2-y-o 5f winner,
half-sister to 4-y-o Mount Abu: useful performer: won minor event at Tipperary in May
by 7 lengths from Ishiguro: best effort when ½-length second to Misraah in listed race at
Sandown in July, making most: best at 5f: acts on good to firm ground. *Declan Gillespie,
Ireland*

ALEGRIA   5 b.m. Night Shift (USA) – High Habit 79 (Slip Anchor 136) [2001 94: 5m   **86 d**
f6g 5.2m³ 5.1f⁴ 6m⁴ 5m⁴ 5m⁶ 6m³ 6g⁴ 5.1g³ 7g 5m 6m 6s Sep 30] good-topped mare:
fairly useful performer, seems on downgrade: best at 5f/6f: acts on firm ground, seemingly not on softer than good: effective blinkered/visored or not: has had tongue tied.
J. M. P. Eustace

ALESSANDRO SEVERO   2 gr.c. (May 9) Brief Truce (USA) 126 – Altaia (FR) 90   **79**
(Sicyos (USA) 126) [2001 7.5s³ 6d⁶ 7d² f8.5g⁵ Oct 9] 1,800F, 10,000Y: leggy, unfurnished colt: sixth foal: half-brother to German 6f winner Royal Hussar (by Efisio) and
1994 2-y-o 7f winner Silver Tzar (by Dominion): dam 6f/7f winner: fair maiden: will stay
at least 1m: raced only on going softer than good on turf, well below form on fibresand.
N. P. Littmoden

ALEXANDER ACADEMY (USA)   2 b. or br.f. (Feb 23) Royal Academy (USA)   **70**
130 – Fantastic Bid (USA) (Auction Ring (USA) 123) [2001 6m 6d³ 6m⁶ p5g⁴ Nov 13]
$30,000F, IR 40,000Y: tall, strong filly: sixth foal: half-sister to 7f winner Fantastic
Dance (by Imperial Ballet): dam, French 1m winner, half-sister to smart performer up to
1½m Germano: fair maiden: below form after third at Goodwood: should stay 7f: started
slowly final outing. *R. Hannon*

ALEXANDER ALLSTARS (IRE)   2 ch.f. (Jan 3) Petardia 113 – Katherine Gorge   **85 ?**
(USA) (Hansel (USA)) [2001 f5g⁵ 5d 6f³ a5.5g* a8g* 8d Dec 9] IR 8,000Y: first foal:
dam unraced daughter of useful sprinter Katies First, herself out of Irish 1000 Guineas
winner Katies: poor form for T. Easterby first 3 starts (subsequently sold 3,400 gns):
much improved afterwards, winning minor events at Mijas in August and September and
seventh in listed race at Toulouse: stays 1m: acts on sand and soft ground. *E. Olgado,
Spain*

ALEXANDER STAR (IRE)   3 b. or br.f. Inzar (USA) 112 – Business Centre (IRE)   **68**
58 (Digamist (USA) 110) [2001 53: 6m² 6m⁵ 8.3g 6g² 6m 6v Oct 8] fair maiden: sold
from J. Toller 9,000 gns after second start: should stay beyond 6f: acts on good to firm
going. *Miss D. A. McHale*

ALEXANDER THREE D (IRE)   2 b.f. (May 6) Pennekamp (USA) 130 – Loon   **101 p**
(FR) (Kaldoun (FR) 122) [2001 7g 7m³ 8.1g² 8.1g⁴ 7.9s² 10d* Nov 3] IR 35,000Y: tall,
unfurnished filly: half-sister to several winners, including French/US winner up to 1¼m
La Piaf (by Fabulous Dancer), second in Grade 3 8.5f event, and 3-y-o Golden Apples:
dam French 1m (at 2 yrs) to 1½m winner: useful performer: clearly best effort when
winning listed event at Newmarket on final start by 4 lengths from Dusky Warbler,

leading over 1f out: will stay 1½m: acts on soft ground: has raced freely and edged left: should make a smart 3-y-o. *B. W. Hills*

ALEXANDRA S (IRE)   3 b.f. Sadler's Wells (USA) 132 – Heaven Only Knows – (High Top 131) [2001 12v⁴ 12g May 6] 130,000F: eighth foal: sister to very smart Irish 1¼m winner/Irish Derby second Glyndebourne, closely related to 3 winners in Italy and half-sister to a winner there by Alzao: dam, maiden who stayed 1½m, half-sister to Breeders' Cup Turf winner Northern Spur from family of Salsabil (both by Sadler's Wells): little promise in maidens at Folkestone and Salisbury (pulled up after jockey sensed something amiss but later reported to have been sound): joined L. Cumani after, then sold 120,000 gns in December. *P. F. I. Cole*

ALEXIUS (IRE)   3 b.c. Rainbow Quest (USA) 134 – Alexandrie (USA) 114 (Val de L'Orne (FR) 133) [2001 10m* 12m* Jul 31]   **120 p**

The performance of Alexius in the latest edition of the Peugeot Gordon Stakes at Goodwood in July seems destined to feature in the 'What happened next?' section of BBC TV's popular programme *A Question of Sport*. Once-raced Alexius dwelt, leaving the stalls a good ten lengths behind the others, and those who had backed him at 7/1 could have been forgiven for tearing up their betting slips. The Gordon Stakes, run over a mile and a half, is recognised as one of the most significant trials for the St Leger, and a fairly good field for the latest renewal included, in betting order, the Lingfield Derby Trial winner and Derby sixth Perfect Sunday, the Predominate Stakes second and third Wareed and Snowstorm (runner-up since in the King Edward VII Stakes at Royal Ascot) and Nayef, the winter favourite for the Derby who had been given a break since disappointing in the spring. Alexius shared fourth favouritism with Nayef on the strength of upsetting the odds laid on Lingfield Derby Trial runner-up and Derby eighth Putra Sandhurst in an eight-runner maiden over a mile and a quarter on the last day of the three-day July meeting. Alexius lost some ground at the start at Newmarket but connections could not have been prepared for his unexplained tardiness at Goodwood. Patiently handled by Kieren Fallon, Alexius was allowed time to find his stride and he was back in touch with the main body of the field approaching the four-furlong marker. In the space of the next two furlongs or so he passed nine of his rivals until only the 14/1-shot Demophilos stood between Alexius and victory. The pair engaged in a sustained duel over the final two furlongs before Alexius, keeping on really strongly, finally edged ahead to win by a neck, with Nayef a length and a half away third, the principals clear of fourth-placed Snowstorm.

For all his many successes, Sir Michael Stoute has yet to win the St Leger, but, after the Gordon Stakes, Alexius looked to give him a major chance. The horse was promoted to favouritism in the ante-post betting, though he had dropped to third favourite by St Leger week behind Mr Combustible and Milan, respectively successful in the Geoffrey Freer and the Great Voltigeur in the weeks after Alexius

Peugeot Gordon Stakes, Goodwood—after losing many lengths at the start, Alexius keeps on really strongly to get the better of Demophilos (left); Nayef is third and Snowstorm fourth

had won at Goodwood. Stoute has won every other British classic at least once but the St Leger still eludes him following the eleventh-hour withdrawal of Alexius with a tendon injury. The horse's owner Sheikh Mohammed subsequently transferred Alexius to Dubai for the winter and, if the horse recovers, he will be returned to race in Britain under the Godolphin banner.

The very well bred Alexius was reportedly too backward to race as a two-year-old, which probably accounts for his 'slipping through the net' at that stage. However, his loss to Godolphin proved nowhere near so great as that most famous example, another Stoute inmate, Singspiel, who was passed over at the end of his three-year-old season by Sheikh Mohammed and his advisers in favour of stable-companion Annus Mirabilis. Stoute was said to have been 'non-committal' when asked for his views about the relative prospects of that pair. While Annus Mirabilis was a very smart performer over the next two seasons, Singspiel built up a tremendous record in the big international races, carrying Sheikh Mohammed's colours, and retired with record total earnings for a European-trained horse of over £3.5m. Alexius had his debut as a three-year-old delayed by a cyst on his back, and, still green in the paddock (swishing his tail repeatedly) and on the way to post before the Gordon Stakes, he remains inexperienced and clearly open to further improvement if his temperament allows. With that proviso, he is certainly capable of winning more good races if he recovers fully from his injury. The Gordon Stakes form was franked when runner-up Demophilos went on to fill the same position behind the impressive Milan in the St Leger; the Gordon Stakes third Nayef went unbeaten through his next four races.

The attractive, good-topped Alexius, a 320,000-guinea yearling, is by Rainbow Quest, who is generally an influence for stamina—his offspring include two Gordon Stakes winners, dead-heater Nedawi and Millenary, who went on to St

Sheikh Mohammed's "Alexius"

Alexius (IRE)
(b.c. 1998)

	Rainbow Quest (USA) (b 1981)	Blushing Groom (ch 1974)	Red God
			Runaway Bride
		I Will Follow (b 1975)	Herbager
			Where You Lead
	Alexandrie (USA) (b 1980)	Val de L'Orne (b 1972)	Val de Loir
			Aglae
		Apachee (b 1975)	Sir Gaylord
			Americaine

Leger success. The dam Alexandrie, who started favourite for the Oaks on her only outing over a mile and a half, showed smart form at up to an extended mile and a quarter (at which trip she won the Prix Cleopatre). Alexandrie's numerous winners include two pattern-winning brothers to Alexius, the smart mile and a quarter to mile and a half winner King Alex and the smart Japanese performer at up to eleven furlongs Admire Kaiser, who notched his biggest success to date over nine furlongs in the Group 3 Epsom Cup in June. Alexandrie has bred five pattern winners in all, the two others being Animatrice (by Alleged) and Poliglote (by Sadler's Wells), both of whom were placed in classics at a mile and a half, the former in the Oaks and the latter in the Prix du Jockey Club. This is also the family of Derby winnner Quest For Fame (a grandson of Alexius' third dam Americaine), he too by Rainbow Quest. If Alexius remains in training he will stay at least a mile and three quarters. Both his outings so far have been on good to firm going. *Sir Michael Stoute*

ALFALFA 3 b.g. Rudimentary (USA) 118 – Zalfa (Luthier 126) [2001 –: 8.1v[2] 10g 8m **45 ?**
8.2s[5] Aug 6] strong, short-backed gelding: poor maiden: stays 1m, probably not 1¼m: acts on heavy going, tailed off on good to firm. *G. B. Balding*

ALFANO (IRE) 3 b.g. Priolo (USA) 127 – Sartigila 67 (Efisio 120) [2001 65: 10s 9s **70 +**
11.6g 11.5m[6] 10.9d* 12g[4] 12m 11m[4] 10v 8d[2] 8d* Nov 2] fair handicapper: won at Warwick in July and Newmarket (24-runner apprentice race) in November: effective at 1m to 1½m: acts on good to firm and good to soft ground: effective visored or not: has worn tongue strap. *P. Mitchell*

ALFIE LEE (IRE) 4 ch.g. Case Law 113 – Nordic Living (IRE) 53 (Nordico (USA)) **75 d**
[2001 87: f6g f6g f7g f6g e6g f5g[4] 5m 5m Jun 15] compact, well-made gelding: un-impressive mover: fair performer: below par after second start in 2001: raced mainly at 5f/6f: acts on good to firm going and fibresand: blinkered once: has worn tongue strap: sold 800 gns in October. *C. N. Allen*

AL GHABRAA 4 ch.f. Pursuit of Love 124 – Tenderetta (Tender King 123) [2001 75: **62 §**
f12g[2] f14.8g[6] f9.4g f8g* f8g f8g[5] 8f 7.5m 8g 10m[4] 7.5m 8d[6] 6g[2] 7.1m[6] 6g[3] 7g[6] 6m 6f f7s[3] **a68 §**
f8.5s[3] Dec 26] fair handicapper: won at Southwell (second start since leaving J. Hills) in April: effective at 6f to 9.4f: acts on firm going and fibresand: blinkered (reluctant to race) eighth start, usually visored after: has had tongue tied: has been early to post/mounted on track: one to treat with caution. *D. Shaw*

ALGUNAS VECES 2 b.g. (Apr 9) Timeless Times (USA) 99 – Nuthatch (IRE) 36 **69**
(Thatching 131) [2001 5v[5] f5g* 5m[6] 6d[4] 5m[2] 5m 5f 7m f6g[3] f7g[4] Nov 30] 3,300Y: lengthy gelding: second foal: dam, maiden, should have stayed 1m: fair performer: won maiden at Southwell in April: some creditable efforts subsequently, leaving T. D. Barron after ninth start: stays easy 7f: acts on fibresand and good to firm ground: blinkered (below form) seventh start: sometimes hangs right. *R. Wilman*

ALHESN (USA) 6 b. or br.g. Woodman (USA) 126 – Deceit Princess (CAN) (Vice **39**
Regent (CAN)) [2001 –, a76: f16g[2] f16.2s[2] f16.2s* e16g f16.2g[3] f16.2g* f16g[4] f16g[5] **a64**
17.2f 14.1m 16.4m[6] 16m Jul 30] angular gelding: modest handicapper on all-weather, poor on turf: won at Wolverhampton in January and March: should stay beyond 2m: acts on fibresand/equitrack, raced mainly on good going or firmer on turf: tried visored/tongue tied in 1999: sometimes slowly away: tends to be soon off bridle: sold 2,000 gns in October. *C. N. Allen*

ALHITRATE 3 ch.f. Alhijaz 122 – Infiltrate (IRE) (Bering 136) [2001 8.2d 10m 10m **–**
12f 12g Aug 4] 4,000Y: first foal: dam, French maiden who stayed 1m, sister to smart French miler Trojan Sea: no sign of ability, leaving Mrs L. Pearce before final start. *C. A. Dwyer*

ALHUWBILL 6 b.g. Full Extent (USA) 113 – Hale Lane 59 (Comedy Star (USA) **35**
121) [2001 42: 8m[5] 7m 7m 8m 7m 8f 10m 8.3v Nov 8] smallish, good-topped gelding: poor maiden: stays 1m: acts on good to firm ground: tried blinkered. *J. J. Bridger*

ALIABAD (IRE) 6 b. or br.g. Doyoun 124 – Alannya (FR) (Relko 136) [2001 –: f12g⁶ **43** f14.8s⁴ e16g f14.8g² f16.2g³ f14g⁴ f12g² f14g* f14g* 17.2g³ 16.2f⁵ 18m Jul 5] modest **a53** performer: won handicap at Southwell in May and claimer there (left D. Haydn Jones) in June: stays 17f: acts on fibresand and firm going: tried visored/blinkered: has run in snatches. *J. G. M. O'Shea*

ALI CAN (IRE) 2 b.c. (Mar 5) Ali-Royal (IRE) 127 – Desert Native 42 (Formidable **51** (USA) 125) [2001 7m 6g⁵ Aug 8] 4,200F, 5,500Y: first foal: dam, maiden who stayed 7f, half-sister to useful Italian sprinter Desert Vert: modest form in maidens at Lingfield and Leicester, not knocked about in latter: bred to prove best up to 1m. *A. P. Jarvis*

ALI D 3 b.c. Alhijaz 122 – Doppio 62 (Dublin Taxi) [2001 6m 7g⁴ 5f⁵ 7g³ 8m 10d³ Sep **66** 21] 5,000Y: sturdy, quite attractive colt: half-brother to 3 winners, including 6f winner Wandering Stranger (by Petong) and 6f (including at 2 yrs)/7f winner Thordis (by Mazilier): dam, 2-y-o 5f winner, out of sister to high-class sprinter Runnett: fair maiden: stays 1¼m: acts on good to soft ground. *A. B. Mulholland*

ALIGATOU 2 b.c. (Feb 26) Distant Relative 128 – Follow The Stars 86 (Sparkler 130) **78 d** [2001 7.1s³ 7.1m⁶ 7m 7.5s 7.1g f8g⁵ f8.5g⁶ Oct 9] 17,000Y: sturdy colt: half-brother to numerous winners, including useful 5f (at 2 yrs) to 1¼m winner Brigante di Cielo (by Robellino) and fairly useful 5f (at 2 yrs)/6f winner Montserrat (by Aragon): dam 8.5f and 1¼m winner: fair maiden: disappointing after debut: should stay 1m: blinkered final start. *C. E. Brittain*

ALI GEE GEE (IRE) 2 b.g. (Mar 28) Desert Style (IRE) 121 – Molvina (ITY) (Final **37** Straw 127) [2001 6m Aug 11] IR 3,000F, IR 5,200Y: third foal: dam, ran once in Italy at 2 yrs, half-sister to useful 1997 Irish 2-y-o 5f winner Danyross (later winner in USA): 33/1, eleventh of 18 in Redcar seller. *J. L. Eyre*

AL IHSAS (IRE) 3 b.f. Danehill (USA) 126 – Simaat (USA) 72 (Mr Prospector **99** (USA)) [2001 97: 7m* 7m* 7m 7m⁴ 5d Sep 13] strong, angular filly: good mover: has a scar on near-hind quarter: useful performer: reportedly suffered from colic after final 2-y-o start: successful in maiden at Goodwood in May and minor event at Leicester (3/1-on) in June: best effort when 1¾ lengths fourth to Mauri Moon in listed race at Goodwood: stayed 7f: acted on good to firm going: visored/tongue tied final start: visits Rahy. *J. H. M. Gosden*

ALIJO 3 b.f. Alhijaz 122 – Hen Night (Mummy's Game 120) [2001 7s May 3] fourth **–** foal: dam unraced: 50/1, well held in maiden at Redcar. *J. Balding*

ALI OOP 4 b.g. Shareef Dancer (USA) 135 – Happydrome (Ahonoora 122) [2001 –: **–** 9d 10s 14m May 21] sturdy gelding: no sign of ability: tried blinkered. *J. D. Bethell*

ALI PASHA 2 b.g. (Feb 14) Ali-Royal (IRE) 127 – Edge of Darkness 62 (Vaigly Great **49** 127) [2001 6f 6.1m 6.1m Jul 27] 11,000F, 25,000Y: fourth foal: half-brother to 3-y-o Joint Instruction and 5-y-o Salford Flyer: dam 1¼m to 2m winner: poor maiden: should be suited by 1m+. *D. W. P. Arbuthnot*

ALI ROSE 3 b.f. Cigar 68 – Hurricane Rose (Windjammer (USA)) [2001 8.2v 7s 8.2s **47** f8g³ f9.4s⁶ Dec 27] sister to a 5f to 6.5f winner in Italy: dam maiden: poor maiden: likely to prove best up to 1m: acts on fibresand. *H. Morrison*

ALITHINI (IRE) 3 b.f. Darshaan 133 – Quiet Counsel (IRE) 81 (Law Society (USA) **75** 130) [2001 10d 10.5s⁴ 12d Nov 18] 150,000Y: strong, lengthy filly: second foal: dam, lightly-raced 1m winner in Ireland, half-sister to Yorkshire Oaks winner Key Change (by Darshaan): best effort in maidens/minor event on debut (final one for J. Noseda): should be suited by 1½m+: sent to France. *H-A. Pantall, France*

ALIZARIN (IRE) 2 b.f. (Apr 20) Tagula (IRE) 116 – Persian Empress (IRE) 51 **62** (Persian Bold 123) [2001 6m³ 6g⁴ 7g Aug 17] IR 19,000Y: half-sister to several winners, including 3-y-o Scotty's Future and 4-y-o Rhodamine: dam, maiden who ran only at 2 yrs, stayed 7f: modest form when third in maiden at Hamilton: disappointing in similar events after: should stay at least 7f. *J. L. Eyre*

ALJARD (USA) 3 ch.c. Gilded Time (USA) – Diaspora (USA) (Vice Regent (CAN)) **59** [2001 8m 9m³ 8.2f⁴ 10m 8.1s Sep 7] $140,000F: lengthy colt: fifth foal: half-brother to winners in USA by Carson City (6f) and Valiant Nature (8.5f): dam winner in USA up to 7f and placed in minor stakes: modest maiden: left E. Dunlop after third start and no form in handicaps after: barely stays 9f: acts on firm going. *D. W. Barker*

ALJAZ 11 b.g. Al Nasr (FR) 126 – Santa Linda (USA) (Sir Ivor 135) [2001 –, a66d: **–** f6g* f5g f6s f6g⁴ f7g f6g f6f f6g⁶ f5g⁶ f5g f6g Jul 2] poor nowadays: won claimer at **a52**

Southwell in January: best at 5f/6f: acts on fibresand/equitrack: blinkered once, usually visored in 2001. *Mrs N. Macauley*

ALJAZIR 4 b.g. Alhijaz 122 – Duxyana (IRE) (Cyrano de Bergerac 120) [2001 60d: f6s⁵ f5g⁴ f6g⁴ f6g³ f6g⁶ f5g⁶ 5d 6m 7.1f Jun 18] workmanlike gelding: disappointing maiden: best at 6f/7f: acts on fibresand, heavy and good to firm going: often blinkered/visored: has wandered/carried head high. *E. J. Alston* **56 d**

ALJOHONCHA 3 b.f. Bigstone (IRE) 126 – Ibda 67 (Mtoto 134) [2001 –: f7g f6g 8d 7m Jul 23] no sign of ability, including visored. *C. N. Kellett* **–**

ALJOMAR 2 b.g. (Mar 23) College Chapel 122 – Running For You (FR) (Pampabird 124) [2001 f5g⁶ f5g f5g⁵ 7m 7g⁵ 6m 8m 6d f8.5g⁴ f6g Nov 12] leggy, unfurnished gelding: fifth foal: half-brother to several winners, including 6-y-o Sing For Me and winners abroad by Shalford and Kahyasi: dam French 1m winner: modest maiden: stays 8.5f: acts on fibresand, best turf effort on good ground. *R. Hollinshead* **55**

ALKA INTERNATIONAL 9 b.g. Northern State (USA) 91 – Cachucha (Gay Fandango (USA) 132) [2001 11.9s⁵ Apr 12] workmanlike gelding: lightly-raced maiden on Flat: fair hurdler. *Mrs P. Townsley* **–**

ALKATEB 9 ch.g. Rock City 120 – Corley Moor 97 (Habitat 134) [2001 f11g⁵ 13.3f 12m 13.1d⁴ Aug 19] big, workmanlike gelding: unimpressive mover: modest form in 2001: stays 13f: acts on any going: tried blinkered/visored. *A. E. Jones* **51**

AL-KING SLAYER 4 b.c. Batshoof 122 – Top Sovereign (High Top 131) [2001 71: e7g³ f8.5g Feb 13] fair maiden, lightly raced: should stay 1m: acts on soft ground and equitrack, no show on fibresand. *T. P. McGovern* **66**

ALL BUSINESS 2 b.f. (Feb 11) Entrepreneur 123 – Belle Esprit (Warning 136) [2001 7s³ Nov 9] first foal: dam, unraced sister to smart performer up to 1¼m Torch Rouge, from family of Opera House and Kayf Tara: 9/1 and very green, close third to Ballet Score in maiden at Doncaster, nearest at finish: will be suited by 1m+: sure to improve. *J. Noseda* **79 p**

ALLEGEDLY RED 2 ch.f. (Mar 18) Sabrehill (USA) 120 – Tendency 77 (Ballad Rock 122) [2001 10d f8g Nov 30] sturdy filly: sixth foal: half-sister to fairly useful 6f to 8.7f winner Le Sport and to 7f winner Dowdency (both by Dowsing): dam 6f winner at 4 yrs: well held in maidens at Pontefract (missed break) and Southwell. *Mrs A. Duffield* **–**

ALLEGRESSE (IRE) 4 b.f. Alzao (USA) 117 – Millie Musique (Miller's Mate 116) [2001 73: 13.1m⁶ May 21] rather sparely-made filly: disappointing maiden: well held only 3-y-o start: blinkered once. *H. Candy* **–**

ALLELUIA 3 b.f. Caerleon (USA) 132 – Alruccaba 83 (Crystal Palace (FR) 132) [2001 58: 10f* 10m* 12.3m² 12.1g* 15.4m* 16g* 18d* 18d⁶ Oct 20] **117**

With the benefit of hindsight, 'may do better in handicaps'—the tailpiece on Alleluia in *Racehorses of 2000* after three modest efforts—might look like a case of serious understatement, if not misjudgement. Alleluia's stable has a reputation for producing three-year-olds who seem to spring from nowhere to run up a sequence, and a casual glance at Alleluia's form figures in her second season—six wins from eight outings—might suggest her record was a product mainly of her trainer's skilful placing. A closer look puts a different complexion on things. Alleluia's three outings at two came within eighteen days in back-end maidens at Leicester, Newcastle and Windsor and qualified her for a handicap mark. In none of these races, however, did Alleluia finish closer than nine and a half lengths to the winner, and it was hard to detect much potential, even though she patently wasn't fully wound up. Furthermore, the smallish, close-coupled Alleluia didn't possess the physical scope usually associated with horses from her stable and had a less than impressive short, round action.

Alleluia failed to develop physically over the winter and actually didn't take in a handicap until her fifth start, beginning her three-year-old career in lowly minor events and being workmanlike at best in winning a race for apprentices at Nottingham on her reappearance in June. She followed up at Ripon ten days later, without having to show improved form to do so, and seemingly had her limitations exposed when beaten in a similar event at Chester in July. Picking up the winning thread in another minor race at Chepstow, Alleluia graduated to handicap company at Folkestone at the end of July, her BHB mark of 78 looking plenty high enough at the time. The Folkestone handicap, though, provided Alleluia with her first opportunity at around two miles. She relished the step up in trip, winning with her rider easing up and looking to have excellent prospects of following up if turned out quickly under a penalty. In fact, it was nearly a month before Alleluia was seen out again, and she confirmed that staying was her game when picking up another ordinary two-mile handicap at Thirsk at the end of August.

A Cesarewitch entry was made for Alleluia in the same week that she won at Thirsk and the weights for that event were already published when—somewhat surprisingly —Alleluia appeared in the line-up for the GNER Doncaster Cup at the St Leger meeting. Her trainer has since said that the aim was simply to 'try to get some black type by finishing third', his research having revealed that the Doncaster Cup attracts the smallest average field of any pattern or listed race in Britain run at two miles or further. Ironically, the latest running attracted the first double-figure field for the Doncaster Cup since 1990. Three-year-olds rarely contest the race nowadays, and none had been successful since Weld in 1989, but Alleluia, who had only 7-11, was one of a trio in the line-up, including the Goodwood Cup runner-up Double Honour, who started favourite. With neither of the stable's retained riders, George Duffield (who rode Double Honour) and Seb Sanders, able to do the weight, the mount on 14/1-shot Alleluia went to leading apprentice Jamie Mackay, who had ridden the filly to her first two victories but couldn't draw his 3-lb allowance because of the status of the race. In the race itself Alleluia made smooth progress to lead over two furlongs out and galloped on strongly to resist the renewed challenge of Goodwood Cup third Rainbow High by three quarters of a length. Third place, two and a half lengths further back, went to another three-year-old, 20/1-shot Bosham Mill, who showed improved form given his first chance beyond two miles; Double Honour managed only seventh of eleven. Alleluia's first place was confirmed after a stewards' inquiry into interference between her and the runner-up shortly after she had taken the lead. Alleluia drifted left across Rainbow High, who was forced to check, but Rainbow High was under strong pressure at the time and the stewards could not be sure the result had been affected. They did, however, impose a three-day suspension on Mackay for careless riding, a rare black mark in a fine season for the eighteen-year-old, who, time and again, looked a top jockey in the making.

Alleluia showed something in the region of 20 lb improvement in the Doncaster Cup on her previous form and, as a result, looked the proverbial 'handicap good thing' in the Cesarewitch, for which she collected a 7-lb penalty. The filly's owners apparently had doubts about her contesting the race and were said to favour a tilt at the Jockey Club Cup instead on the same day. In the end, though, Alleluia ran in the handicap, for which she started 7/2 favourite in a field of thirty-one. Everything seemed to be going to plan when she was ridden into a narrow lead over two furlongs out, but she could find no extra and eventually faded into sixth, beaten over six lengths by the winner Distant Prospect. Alleluia was lame walking away after the race and was found to have suffered a fracture to the sesamoid bone in a hind leg.

GNER Doncaster Cup—Alleluia (right) shows plenty of improvement, resisting Rainbow High's renewed challenge and providing a big winner for promising apprentice Jamie Mackay; Bosham Mill is third

Mrs Sonia Rogers' "Alleluia"

		Caerleon (USA) (b 1980)	Nijinsky (b 1967)	Northern Dancer
Alleluia (b.f. 1998)				Flaming Page
			Foreseer (b or br 1969)	Round Table
				Regal Gleam
		Alruccaba (br or gr 1983)	Crystal Palace (gr 1974)	Caro
				Hermieres
			Allara (gr 1973)	Zeddaan
				Nucciolina

That Alleluia should prove at her best over long distances could hardly have been predicted from her pedigree. Her sire Caerleon is not so strong an influence for stamina as such as Niniski, Darshaan and Slip Anchor, all of whom have sired winners out of the ex-Aga Khan filly Alruccaba, who gained her only win in a six-furlong maiden at Brighton as a two-year-old. Niniski was responsible for two of Alruccaba's seven winning fillies to date, Allegra and Ballymac Girl, successful respectively at a mile and a half and at up to a mile and seven furlongs. The Darshaan fillies Arrikala and Alouette were more distinguished, both contesting the Irish Oaks (Arrikala was an unlucky third) and winning at up to a mile and three quarters and a mile and a half respectively. Alouette became the dam of dual Champion Stakes winner Alborada, while another daughter of Darshaan out of Alruccaba, the lightly-raced Jude, is the dam of Moyglare Stud Stakes winner Quarter Moon. The best offspring produced by Alruccaba herself is the Nassau Stakes and Sun Chariot Stakes winner Last Second (by Alzao), who was never tried over as far as a mile and a half. The other winning filly out of Alruccaba is the fair handicapper Alexandrine (by Nashwan), successful at up to thirteen furlongs. Alleluia, who acted on firm and good to soft going, should make an interesting addition to the broodmare bands of her joint owner-breeders Kirsten Rausing and Sonia Rogers, owners of the Lanwades Stud and Airlie Stud respectively. Alleluia begins her stud career with a visit to Galileo. *Sir Mark Prescott*

ALLENBY   2 b.c. (May 9) Inchinor 119 – Lady Lydia 66 (Ela-Mana-Mou 132) [2001   **89 p** 7g⁶ 7s* 7v* Oct 27] 18,000Y: lengthy colt: third foal: half-brother to 4-y-o Lucky Judge: dam 11f winner: fairly useful form: won maiden at Leicester and nursery at Doncaster (beat Offa's Dyke by 1¾ lengths, off bridle early but strong run to win going away), both in October: should stay 1¼m: raced only on good ground or softer: capable of better still. *R. Hannon*

ALLERTON BOY   2 ch.g. (Apr 30) Beveled (USA) – Darakah 78 (Doulab (USA)   **67** 115) [2001 5.1g⁵ 5.1g² 5.1f Sep 18] 2,500Y: sixth foal: half-brother to 5-y-o Bodfari Signet and 4-y-o Mobo-Baco: dam 5f (at 2 yrs) to 1m winner: fair maiden: second at Chepstow, best effort: will stay at least 6f. *R. J. Hodges*

ALLEZ MOUSSON   3 b.g. Hernando (FR) 127 – Rynechra 102 (Blakeney 126)   **85** [2001 10s³ 12.1d⁴ 12m⁴ 16.2m* 13.1d⁵ 16.2s² 15.9d 15m⁶ 17.5m* 16.1d³ 17.1d* 18s⁶ 16g 16.5s² Nov 10] 16,000Y: tall, leggy gelding: closely related to smart 1m (at 2 yrs) to 14.6f (Park Hill) winner Coigach (by Niniski) and half-brother to 3 winners, including smart 1¼m to 13f winner Applecross (by Glint of Gold), dam of Invermark and Craig-steel: dam 1½m winner: fairly useful handicapper: won at Chepstow in July, Ayr in September and Pontefract in October: gelded after final outing: will stay beyond 17.5f: acts on soft and good to firm going: tried blinkered: often soon off bridle. *A. Bailey*

ALL GOOD THINGS (IRE)   4 b.c. Marju (IRE) 127 – Garah 107 (Ajdal (USA)   **59** 130) [2001 67: e12g⁶ e8g 10m 9m 8d 12m* 12m 11.5f Jul 25] modest handicapper: won at Folkestone in June: best at 1¼m/1½m: acts on soft going, good to firm and fibresand/equitrack: has had tongue tied. *R. Ingram*

ALL GRAIN   3 b.f. Polish Precedent (USA) 131 – Mill Line 71 (Mill Reef (USA) 141)   **102** [2001 57P: 9.9s³ 12.6m* 11.9d³ 12g Sep 28] smallish, angular filly: useful performer: won maiden at Warwick in June: best effort when 6 lengths third to Sacred Song in Lancashire Oaks at Haydock in July, every chance 2f out: tubed before final outing (edgy/moved short to post, reportedly finished distressed): should stay 1¾m. *Sir Michael Stoute*

ALL I ASK   3 b.c. Spectrum (IRE) 126 – Christine Daae 74 (Sadler's Wells (USA)   **70** 132) [2001 8m³ 8.2d⁴ Sep 21] half-brother to several winners, including smart sprinter To The Roof (by Thatching) and useful 5f (at 2 yrs) and 1m winner Risque Lady (by Kenmare): dam 1¼m winner: fair form in maidens at Salisbury and Nottingham (still seemed in need of experience when 2¾ lengths fourth to Magnusson, wandering and not knocked about as he kept on). *P. W. Harris*

ALL IN ALL   2 ch.f. (Apr 21) Halling (USA) 133 – Alligram (USA) 61 (Alysheba   **74** (USA)) [2001 7g 8d Nov 3] leggy, unfurnished filly: fifth foal: half-sister to very smart 1m/1¼m winner Kissogram (by Caerleon): dam lightly-raced daughter of top-class miler Milligram: better effort (fair form) when 10 lengths ninth of 13 to Sundrenched in listed race at Newmarket, racing freely: looked none too keen on debut. *L. M. Cumani*

ALLINJIM (IRE)   2 b.c. (Mar 30) Turtle Island (IRE) 123 – Bounayya (USA) (Al   **69** Nasr (FR) 126) [2001 7g 6m 6m⁴ 8.3v² Oct 8] IR 3,500F, IR 4,800Y, 16,000 2-y-o: good-bodied colt: fifth foal: half-brother to 2 winners, including Italian winner up to 11f Il Sorpasso (by Nordico): dam unraced sister to very smart French filly up to 10.5f Bint Alnasr: fair maiden: best effort when second in nursery at Windsor: should stay at least 1¼m: acts on heavy going, probably on good to firm. *J. A. Glover*

ALLOTROPE (IRE)   6 b.g. Nashwan (USA) 135 – Graphite (USA) 80 (Mr Pros-   **–** pector (USA)) [2001 –: 17.1f 16f 14.4d 16m 17.1g 18f⁶ Sep 20] workmanlike gelding: no longer of much account: tried blinkered. *Mrs M. Reveley*

ALL POINTS NORTH (IRE)   2 b.g. (May 16) Distinctly North (USA) 115 – Win-   **54** scarlet North (Garland Knight 92) [2001 5.1s⁵ 5d 5f⁵ 7m 8m Sep 11] 3,200Y: angular, unfurnished gelding: brother to 5-y-o Gypsy and half-brother to a winner in Belgium by Le Johnstan: dam unraced half-sister to very smart sprinter Willy Willy: modest maiden: should stay at least 6f: went sharply right leaving stalls second start. *M. W. Easterby*

ALL SMILES 3 ch.f. Halling (USA) 133 – Fairy Flax (IRE) 97 (Dancing Brave **41**
(USA) 140) [2001 8.2d 6g f6g Nov 21] 58,000Y: fifth foal: half-sister to 3 winners,
including fairly useful 1¼m winner Fairywings (by Kris) and 7-y-o Caution: dam, 6f
winner, half-sister to smart performer up to 9f Hoy: best effort in maidens (poor form) on
second start: should stay at least 7f. *Mrs J. R. Ramsden*

ALLTHEDOTCOMS 3 ch.g. Elmaamul (USA) 125 – North Wind (IRE) 101 **57**
(Lomond (USA) 128) [2001 48: 8.2m 12g 10g² 10g⁵ 8.5s² 8g Oct 1] modest maiden
handicapper: effective at 8.5f (given a test) to 1¼m: acts on soft going, possibly not on
firmer than good: sold 5,000 gns. *N. A. Callaghan*

ALL THE WAY (IRE) 5 b.h. Shirley Heights 130 – Future Past (USA) (Super Con- **115**
corde (USA) 128) [2001 114: 10g* 12g⁶ Feb 25] leggy, angular horse: has a quick action:
smart performer: won prestige race at Nad Al Sheba in February by ¾ length from River's
Curtain: below-form sixth to Give The Slip in Dubai City of Gold there later in month:
effective at 1¼m to 14.6f: raced only on good/good to firm going: blinkered final 4-y-o
start: races up with pace: genuine: joined P. Rudkin in UAE. *Saeed bin Suroor*

ALL TRUMPS 2 b.g. (Apr 27) First Trump 118 – So Bold (Never So Bold 135) [2001 **64**
8.2s p8g p10g⁶ Dec 4] sixth living foal: closely related to 9-y-o Stoppes Brow: dam
lightly raced: modest form in maidens: stays 1¼m: slowly away second start. *G. L. Moore*

ALLUDE (IRE) 2 b.c. (Mar 10) Darshaan 133 – Ahliyat (USA) 55 (Irish River (FR) **76**
131) [2001 8g⁵ 8d Oct 2] unfurnished colt: first foal: dam, 8.5f winner, half-sister to 3-y-o
Artillery (by Darshaan) out of half-sister to disqualified Oaks winner Aliysa (also by
Darshaan): fair form in maidens at Newmarket: seventh of 21 to Hathaal on second
occasion: will stay at least 1¼m. *N. P. Littmoden*

AL MAALI (IRE) 2 b.c. (Mar 17) Polar Falcon (USA) 126 – Amwag (USA) 106 (El **82**
Gran Senor (USA) 136) [2001 6g² 6.1d² Sep 21] rather leggy, useful-looking colt: has a
short action: fourth foal: half-brother to 7-y-o Irsal and Irish 1¼m winner Sawarim (both
by Nashwan): dam, 7f/1m winner, half-sister to smart middle-distance stayer Istidaad:
runner-up in maidens at Lingfield and Nottingham (sweating and edgy), fairly useful
form when beaten ½ length by Helen Bradley in latter: should stay 7f. *A. C. Stewart*

AL MABROOK (IRE) 6 b.g. Rainbows For Life (CAN) – Sky Lover (Ela-Mana- **–**
Mou 132) [2001 57, a65: f8g f8s⁵ f11s f8s f9.4g³ f8g f8g³ 9v f11g 8.3d f11g⁴ f9.4g⁶ **a49**
f11g⁴ Dec 17] leggy gelding: poor performer: stays 11f: acts on fibresand/equitrack, very
best turf efforts on good/good to firm going: sometimes blinkered: none too reliable.
K. A. Ryan

ALMASHROUK (IRE) 4 b.c. Common Grounds 118 – Red Note (Rusticaro (FR) **59**
124) [2001 73d: 5g⁵ 5g⁵ 5m⁵ f6s 8m Sep 26] lengthy colt: modest maiden: probably stays
7f: acts on good to soft going: tried blinkered. *Miss Gay Kelleway*

ALMAYDAN 3 b.c. Marju (IRE) 127 – Cunning 118 (Bustino 136) [2001 60p: 10m³ **78**
12d² f12g³ Nov 26] fair maiden: left S. R. Bowring 6,000 gns after reappearance: stays
1½m: acts on good to soft going: carried head awkwardly last 2 starts. *R. Lee*

ALMIDDINA (IRE) 4 b.f. Selkirk (USA) 129 – Arbela (IRE) (Persian Bold 123) **87**
[2001 78: 8.1m 7m⁵ 7m* 7m² 7m³ 7f 7g Oct 6] leggy filly: fairly useful performer:
won minor event at Redcar in June and handicap at Newbury in July: effective at 7f/1m:
acts on any going: sold 20,000 gns, sent to USA. *R. Charlton*

ALMINSTAR 5 b.m. Minshaanshu Amad (USA) 91§ – Joytime (John de Coombe **–**
122) [2001 –: e13g 8.1m Jul 25] of little account nowadays. *Mrs L. Richards*

ALMNADIA (IRE) 2 b.f. (Apr 23) Alhaarth (IRE) 126 – Mnaafa (IRE) 70 (Darshaan **–**
133) [2001 6.1v 6g 6v Nov 8] 20,000 2-y-o: well-made filly: fourth foal: half-sister to
fairly useful 1998 2-y-o 6f winner Island Hero (by Polar Falcon): dam, 1¼m winner, from
family of Alderbrook and 3-y-o Hawkeye: well held in maidens. *G. A. Butler*

ALMOHAD 6 ch.g. Belmez (USA) 131 – Anna Paola (GER) (Prince Ippi (GER)) **–**
[2001 f11g 10g 10.1g 12g 10.1v Oct 24] of little account nowadays: tried blinkered/
visored. *Dr J. D. Scargill*

AL MOHALLAB (FR) 2 b.c. (Mar 14) Marju (IRE) 127 – Deyaajeer (USA) 64 **97 p**
(Dayjur (USA) 137) [2001 7m³ 7f* Sep 22] lengthy, attractive colt: has scope: third
foal: dam once-raced half-sister to Nashwan, Nayef and Unfuwain: evens, confirmed
considerable promise of debut when beating Kaieteur by 1½ lengths in 18-runner maiden
at Newbury, making all: will probably stay 1m: should make a smart 3-y-o. *B. W. Hills*

AL MOUGHAZEL (USA) 2 b.c. (Apr 3) Royal Academy (USA) 130 – Wild **100**
Vintage (USA) (Alysheba (USA)) [2001 6m* 7.2m* 8d⁴ Oct 13] 50,000Y: tall, good sort:
fourth foal: dam, French 1¼m winner, half-sister to very smart French miler In Extremis
and Prix Marcel Boussac winner (stayed 1½m) Juvenia: useful form: won maiden at
Newmarket in June and minor event at Ayr (idled) in September: good fourth of 8, beaten
under 7 lengths by Fight Your Corner, in listed event at Ascot: should stay 1¼m: yet to
race on extremes of going. *J. W. Payne*

AL MUALLIM (USA) 7 b.g. Theatrical 128 – Gerri N Jo Go (USA) (Top Command **89**
(USA)) [2001 103: 6v 6s 7g⁵ 6m⁵ 7m 7f² 7m⁶ 6m* 6f* 7g⁴ 6g* 6g* Sep 15] compact
gelding: fairly useful nowadays: won claimers at Kempton (2) and Epsom (2) between
July and September: best at 6f/7f: acts on firm and soft going: usually tongue tied: has
been edgy in paddock/slowly away/edged right: free-going sort: best held up. *D. Nicholls*

ALNAHAAM (IRE) 3 ch.c. Hamas (IRE) 125§ – Abir 73 (Soviet Star (USA) 128) **88**
[2001 87: 7m* 8.1m 8m⁵ 7g Aug 11] strong, lengthy colt: fairly useful performer: made
all in maiden at Doncaster in May, despite hanging left: below form in handicaps after:
should stay 1m: raced only on good/good to firm going: sent to UAE. *B. Hanbury*

ALOWMDAH (USA) 3 b.c. Gone West (USA) – Halholah (USA) 65 (Secreto (USA) **79**
128) [2001 79p: 8.5s⁵ 10.3f* 9m 12f 9.9m⁵ 10m² 8f Nov 4] strong, good sort: fair
performer: won maiden at Chester in May: left B. Hanbury and off 3½ months before
final start: stays 1¼m: acts on firm going: has been slowly away. *D. C. Peitz, USA*

ALPEN WOLF (IRE) 6 ch.g. Wolfhound (USA) 126 – Oatfield 69 (Great Nephew **85**
126) [2001 94: 6s 6m⁶ 6m 5.7g⁶ 6m⁵ 6f² 7m 7m 6g 7g 5.7m p7g⁶ p7g p7g Dec 29] sturdy, **a73**
rather dipped-backed gelding: fairly useful handicapper on turf, fair on all-weather: races
mainly at 6f/7f nowadays: acts on polytrack, best on going firmer than good on turf: tried
visored/blinkered: usually races prominently. *W. R. Muir*

ALPHACALL 3 b.f. Forzando 122 – Second Call 67 (Kind of Hush 118) [2001 48: 9s **53**
9.9m⁴ 12m 10g⁴ 10m⁶ 8.2f² 8f 8m⁵ 8.2m² 8.2s⁴ Aug 6] angular filly: modest maiden:
should stay 1½m: acts on firm going: blinkered fourth to eighth starts: has looked none
too easy ride: sold 4,000 gns. *T. D. Easterby*

ALPHAEUS 3 b.g. Sillery (USA) 122 – Aethra (USA) 89 (Trempolino (USA) 135) **106 +**
[2001 89p: 10g* 10g* 9g Oct 6] tall, good-topped gelding: has plenty of scope: useful
handicapper, lightly raced: made all at Newmarket twice in July, beating Askham by 2
lengths on first occasion and Staging Post by comfortable 1¼ lengths on second: co-
favourite, disappointing when mid-field in Cambridgeshire there final start: stays 1¼m:
acts on fibresand, raced only on good/good to firm going on turf: sent to Saudi Arabia.
Sir Mark Prescott

ALPHA HEIGHTS (IRE) 4 b.f. Namaqualand (USA) – Mnaafa (IRE) 70 (Dar- **41**
shaan 133) [2001 –: f6g f8s f8.5g 8m 9.1v 11d³ f12g² f14g⁶ f14g³ f11s⁵ Dec 21] poor
maiden: stays 1¾m: acts on good to firm going, good to soft and fibresand. *D. W. Barker*

ALPHA ROSE 4 ch.f. Inchinor 119 – Philgwyn 66 (Milford 119) [2001 86: 12d⁵ 11.7d **78**
14.4m⁴ 12m 10.3m³ 11.9m³ 10g³ 11.9m² f12g 12d² Nov 2] lengthy filly: only fair in
2001: best at 1½m/1¾m: acts on firm going, soft and equitrack. *M. L. W. Bell*

ALPHONSE (IRE) 3 b.g. Common Grounds 118 – Windini (Windjammer (USA)) **–**
[2001 10.4m 9m Sep 6] IR 42,000Y: brother to fairly useful Irish 1m winner Crystal
Wind, later winner in Italy, and half-brother to several winners, including fairly useful
Irish 6f winner who stayed 1m Faydini (by Fayruz): dam unraced: tailed off in maidens.
D. Nicholls

ALPINE HIDEAWAY (IRE) 8 b.g. Tirol 127 – Arbour (USA) 76 (Graustark) [2001 **55**
–: f16g 10s 8s⁴ 9m 8.5m⁵ 8m³ 8m 8m 9.9m 8.5g⁵ 10.3m Sep 12] modest performer:
trained on reappearance by K. Ryan: probably best around 1m: acts on any turf going and
fibresand: blinkered twice earlier in career. *J. S. Wainwright*

ALPINE LOVE (IRE) 2 ch.f. (Mar 8) Pursuit of Love 124 – Alpina (USA) 69 (El **–**
Prado (IRE) 119) [2001 8s Sep 30] IR 3,000Y: first foal: dam lightly-raced half-sister to
dam of Rodrigo de Triano: 25/1, tailed off in maiden at Brighton. *E. J. O'Neill*

ALPINE RACER (IRE) 2 b.g. (Apr 9) Lake Coniston (IRE) 131 – Cut No Ice 97 **64**
(Great Nephew 126) [2001 8s⁶ 8.2s 8.3v² Nov 8] IR 12,000F, IR 26,000Y: leggy, rather
unfurnished gelding: half-brother to several winners, including Polish Derby winner
Country Club (by Suave Dancer) and 5f (at 2 yrs)/6f winner Subzero (by Thatching):
dam 1m (in France)/1¼m winner: modest form in maiden/sellers: likely to stay 1¼m:
blinkered (looked less than keen) final start. *B. J. Meehan*

ALQABAS (IRE)   3 b.g. Nashwan (USA) 135 – Harayir (USA) 119 (Gulch (USA))   **71 d**
[2001 10d 10m⁴ 10g⁵ 12m 12g 16v Oct 17] smallish gelding: second foal: brother to
4-y-o Moonjaz: dam, 6f (Lowther Stakes) to 1m (1000 Guineas) winner, granddaughter
of Irish Oaks winner Give Thanks: fair maiden at best: left M. Tregoning 5,000 gns after
third start: well held subsequently, looking difficult ride: stays 1¼m: tried blinkered.
M. R. Ewer-Hoad

ALQAWAASER (USA)   4 b. or br.g. Dayjur (USA) 137 – Alghuzaylah 90 (Habitat   –
134) [2001 68: 8m 13.3g 10g 8m Jul 4] good-bodied gelding: fair maiden at 3 yrs: well
held in 2001: blinkered last 2 starts (also tongue tied final one). *J. G. Portman*

ALRAFID (IRE)   2 ch.c. (Mar 24) Halling (USA) 133 – Ginger Tree (USA) 86   **78**
(Dayjur (USA) 137) [2001 6s 7s² Oct 16] rather unfurnished colt: has a round action:
second foal: half-brother to fairly useful 2000 2-y-o 7f winner Hotaaff (by Arazi): dam,
2-y-o 6f winner, out of North American Grade 1 1¼m/1½m winner Carotene: much better
effort in maidens (fair form) when neck second of 19 to Allenby at Leicester, leading over
1f out until close home: should stay 1m. *A. C. Stewart*

ALRIDA (IRE)   2 b.g. (Apr 6) Ali-Royal (IRE) 127 – Ride Bold (USA) (J O Tobin   **78**
(USA) 130) [2001 6m⁵ 6m 7m⁴ 7.1g⁶ 8.5g³ 10v³ 8s³ Oct 22] 28,000F, 50,000Y: half-
brother to 3 winners, notably smart Irish 5f (including at 2 yrs)/6f winner Petite Fantasy
(by Mansooj): dam unraced half-sister to smart French performer up to 1¼m Vidor: fair
maiden: good efforts in nurseries last 2 starts, slowly away each time: shapes as if will
stay beyond 1¼m: acts on heavy and good to firm going: looked ungenuine second start
(gelded after). *W. Jarvis*

ALRISHA (IRE)   4 b.f. Persian Bold 123 – Rifaya (IRE) (Lashkari 128) [2001 90p: **88**
14.1g 16m 14s 14.1m* 16.1g³ 14.8m³ 21m 16m⁴ Sep 12] angular filly: fairly useful
handicapper: won at Salisbury in June: should stay beyond 2m: acts on good to firm
ground, possibly not on softer than good. *D. R. C. Elsworth*

ALSAHIB (USA)   8 b.g. Slew O' Gold (USA) – Khwlah (USA) 99 (Best Turn (USA))   –
[2001 e16g* f16.2g³ f16.2g* f16.2g² f16g⁶ 14.1s f14g⁶ f16g f14g* f16.2g² f12g² f16.2g⁴   **a74 d**
f16g⁶ f14.8g⁶ f14.8s² f14g f14.8s² f12s⁴ Dec 26] big gelding: fair performer on all-
weather in first half of season, winning seller at Lingfield, handicap at Wolverhampton
and claimer at Southwell: stays 2m: acts on fibresand/equitrack: tried blinkered/visored/
tongue tied: probably best with strong handling. *W. R. Muir*

ALSALEET (USA)   3 ch.c. Mr Prospector (USA) – Bint Salsabil (USA) 110 (Nash-   **69 +**
wan (USA) 135) [2001 9f⁴ 7g⁴ a7f* a7f Nov 23] first foal: dam, 6f (at 2 yrs, also won 7f
Rockfel Stakes) to 1¼m winner, daughter of Salsabil from very good family: fair form
when fourth in maidens at Lingfield and Newmarket (tongue tied) in the summer, then
left Saeed bin Suroor: won similar event at Belmont in October by a neck: well held in
allowance race at Aqueduct only subsequent outing: stays 7f: acts on dirt: visored/
blinkered all starts. *M. A. Hennig, USA*

AL'S ALIBI   8 b.g. Alzao (USA) 117 – Lady Kris (IRE) (Kris 135) [2001 68: f12s³   **52**
f12g f12g* f14g⁴ f12g⁵ f12s⁵ f12s³ Dec 27] smallish, sturdy gelding: modest performer:
won seller at Wolverhampton in February: best around 1½m: acts on good to firm going,
soft and fibresand. *W. R. Muir*

ALSANUTTER   2 b.f. (Jan 26) Royal Applause 124 – Andbell (Trojan Fen 118) [2001   –
f6g Oct 9] 3,000Y: eighth foal: half-sister to 4-y-o Willoughby's Boy and a winner in
Norway by Mango Express: dam of little account: last in claimer at Wolverhampton.
Mrs C. A. Dunnett

AL'S FELLA (IRE)   6 br.g. Alzao (USA) 117 – Crystal Cross (USA) 88 (Roberto   –
(USA) 131) [2001 f12g⁵ Jun 29] sparely-made gelding: well beaten only Flat start in
2001: sometimes blinkered/tongue tied. *Miss K. M. George*

ALSHADIYAH (USA)   3 gr.f. Danzig (USA) – Shadayid (USA) 122 (Shadeed   **102**
(USA) 135) [2001 95p: 7d³ 6g² 6g⁴ 6g 7d² Sep 13] strong, lengthy, attractive filly: useful
performer: in frame in 2001 in Fred Darling at Newbury, minor event at Yarmouth,
handicap at Newmarket (good fourth to Flying Millie) and listed race at Doncaster
(equal-second to Nice One Clare, beaten ½ length, forced to switch wide to challenge):
stayed 7f: acted on firm and good to soft going: raced freely: visits Kingmambo.
J. L. Dunlop

AL'S ME TRAINER   3 b.g. Emarati (USA) 74 – Ray of Hope 53 (Rainbow Quest   **70**
(USA) 134) [2001 60: 6g 6g f6g* 5g* 5.1d⁴ f6g Sep 22] quite good-topped gelding: fair
performer: won maiden at Southwell in July and handicap at Thirsk in August: reportedly

broke blood vessel final start: effective at 5f/6f: acts on fibresand and good to soft going: visored last 4 starts: slowly away penultimate outing: usually races up with pace. *A. Dickman*

ALSYATI   3 ch.g. Salse (USA) 128 – Rubbiyati 56 (Cadeaux Genereux 131) [2001 65:   **70**
7v⁶ 8s⁵ 10.2f² 9s⁶ 11.5m⁵ 10d 10.1s Aug 31] quite attractive gelding: fair maiden: stays 11.5f: acts on firm ground, below form on soft: blinkered last 2 starts: probably one to treat with some caution. *C. E. Brittain*

ALTAY   4 b.g. Erins Isle 121 – Aliuska (IRE) 70 (Fijar Tango (FR) 127) [2001 67: 8.3m⁵   **68**
8m⁴ 9.9f* f9.4s Dec 27] tall gelding: has a round action: fair handicapper: won at Beverley in June, despite briefly veering left under pressure: off 6 months afterwards: probably best around 1¼m: acts on firm going, probably on soft. *R. A. Fahey*

AL TOWD (USA)   4 b.c. Kingmambo (USA) 125 – Toujours Elle (USA) (Lyphard   **78**
(USA) 132) [2001 92: 10.1s 13.9m 14m 20m⁵ 16.4m⁶ 17.2m Jul 15] big, rangy colt: has a rather round action: fair handicapper nowadays: stays 2½m: acts on good to firm and good to soft going: sold 10,000 gns in October. *S. Dow*

ALUNISSAGE (USA)   3 b.c. Rainbow Quest (USA) 134 – Moonshell (IRE) 117   **112**
(Sadler's Wells (USA) 132) [2001 9.9m² 12m² 14m* 14.1m² 14.6g⁶ Sep 15] attractive colt: first foal: dam, 1m (at 2 yrs) and 1½m (Oaks) winner, sister to 4-y-o Hatha Anna and half-sister to smart performer up to 15f Ocean of Storms: smart performer: won maiden at Lingfield in August by 15 lengths: excellent neck second to stable-companion Hatha Anna in minor event at Salisbury next time, dictating pace and rallying: respectable 14 lengths sixth to Milan in St Leger at Doncaster final start: will be suited by 2m: raced only on good/good to firm going: visored last 3 starts: hung left first 2 outings. *Saeed bin Suroor*

ALUNITE (USA)   3 b.c. Red Ransom (USA) – Allusion (USA) (Mr Prospector   **105**
(USA)) [2001 104p: 8f* 9f² Sep 22] strong, good-topped colt: has plenty of scope: half-brother to several winners, including graded stakes-placed winners in USA by Devil's Bag and Topsider: dam 7f/8.5f minor stakes winner in USA: trained only 2-y-o start by A. Fabre in France: made all in maiden at Thirsk in June: rather on edge and sweating quite profusely, again showed useful form when neck second of 7 to Gryffindor in minor event at Newbury: stays 9f: acts on firm going. *Saeed bin Suroor*

ALVARO (IRE)   4 ch.g. Priolo (USA) 127 – Gezalle (Shareef Dancer (USA) 135)   **?**
[2001 60d, a–: 10.1m 12.4m⁴ 10g 10m 5g Aug 6] strong gelding: little form in 2001: blinkered once. *M. C. Chapman*

ALWAYS   2 b.c. (May 1) Dynaformer (USA) – Love And Affection (USA) (Exclusive   **82**
Era (USA)) [2001 7g⁴ 7m³ 8.2d² 10d⁶ Nov 2] 85,000Y: tall, useful-looking colt: has scope: sixth living foal: half-brother to 3-y-o Londoner and several winners in USA: dam, 5f to 1m winner (second in Grade 1 6f event at 2 yrs), closely related to very smart 1¼m performer Zoman: fairly useful maiden: best effort when neck second to Affray at Nottingham: stays 1m, possibly not 1¼m: flashed tail/found little second start. *J. L. Dunlop*

ALWAYS DARING   2 b.f. (May 2) Atraf 116 – Steamy Windows § (Dominion 123)   **64**
[2001 5m² 5m⁵ 5f² 5m⁴ 5m⁶ 7m⁴ 7d⁴ Oct 9] rather unfurnished filly: fifth foal: half-sister to winners abroad by Superlative and Casteddu: dam, ungenuine maiden, sister to smart 1986 2-y-o sprinter Dominion Royale: modest maiden: creditable efforts in nurseries last 3 starts: stays 7f: acts on firm and good to soft going: has wandered under pressure. *K. R. Burke*

ALYPORTENT   7 b.g. Warning 136 – Alilisa (USA) (Alydar (USA)) [2001 –: f16g   **–**
Jan 5] little form: tried visored. *N. Bycroft*

ALZOLA (IRE)   4 b.f. Alzao (USA) 117 – Polistatic 53 (Free State 125) [2001 7m   **57**
8.3d 8.3v⁴ p10g³ p10g⁴ Dec 19] small, compact filly: modest maiden: bred to stay beyond 1¼m: acts on polytrack: very slowly away second outing. *C. A. Horgan*

AMACITA   3 b.f. Shareef Dancer (USA) 135 – Kina (USA) (Bering 136) [2001 49:   **69 d**
8.3s⁴ 10g 11.8f² 14m 10.9g 11.6m 12.1s 11.7m⁴ 10d Oct 15] neat filly: fair maiden: below best after third start: probably best around 1½m: acts on firm ground: visored (pulled too hard) final outing: hung quite badly left turning for home at Windsor sixth start. *Miss E. C. Lavelle*

AMADEUS (AUS)   4 ch.g. Brief Truce (USA) 126 – Amazaan (NZ) (Zamazaan (FR)   **?**
126) [2001 7g⁵ f9.4g Dec 8] ex-Australian gelding: winner of one of his 9 starts in native country, namely handicap in 2000: behind on British debut second start: stays 10.3f: raced only on good ground or softer on turf. *J. M. Bradley*

AMAMACKEMMUSH (IRE)   3 b.g. General Monash (USA) 107 – Paganina (FR)   **51**
(Galetto (FR) 118) [2001 65: f5s f5g f5g⁶ f5g⁴ 6.1v³ f5g⁶ f6g 6m⁵ 6f⁴ 5f 5f 6m f6g Jul 12]   **a36**
leggy gelding: modest maiden handicapper on turf, poor on all-weather: stays easy 6f:
acts on firm going and fibresand: blinkered last 2 starts (pulled too hard on penultimate):
usually races prominently. *K. A. Ryan*

AMANDARI (FR)   5 ch.g. Petit Loup (USA) 123 – Baby Sitting (FR) (Son of Silver   **–**
123) [2001 12v 12.3s 8.1m f14g Jun 8] won claimer at Fontainebleau for J. Bertran de
Balanda in 1999: little show since, trained in France in 2000: stays 15.5f: raced mainly on
good ground or softer: has been blinkered, including for win. *A. Berry*

AMANDOLO (IRE)   2 ch.c. (Feb 24) Grand Lodge (USA) 125 – Marqueterie (USA)   **–**
(Well Decorated (USA)) [2001 6f⁵ 7.1d 6d 7.2v Oct 15]   IR 8,000F, 24,000Y: quite
attractive colt: half-brother to several winners, including fairly useful Irish 1m winner
Antiquity (by Treasure Kay): dam no worthwhile form: well beaten in minor event/
maidens: left M. Quinn after second start. *A. Bailey*

AMARANTH (IRE)   5 b.g. Mujadil (USA) 119 – Zoes Delight (IRE) (Hatim (USA)   **96**
121) [2001 97, a89: f8.5g⁴ 8v 6m⁴ 5m 6m 7f* 7m 6g³ 7f 6g⁵ 7d⁶ 6m 7d 7s 7d* 7s f7g⁵   **a99**
p7g³ p7g* f7g³ p8g* p7g Dec 29] tall, quite good-topped gelding: useful performer: won
handicap in June and minor event in October, both at Newcastle, and minor events at
Lingfield in November and December: stays easy 8.5f: acts on firm going, soft and
all-weather: tongue tied: has sweated: usually races prominently: genuine. *J. L. Eyre*

AMARETTO EXPRESS (IRE)   2 b.g. (May 7) Blues Traveller (IRE) 59 – Cap-   **53**
puchino (IRE) 59 (Roi Danzig (USA)) [2001 6.1g f8.5s⁵ 7.1m p8g Nov 24] 9,500Y:
useful-looking gelding: fourth foal: brother to useful 1999 2-y-o 7f winner Blue Bolivar
and half-brother to 3-y-o Cayman Expresso: dam 7f winner: modest maiden: will prove
best up to 1m: hung badly left on debut. *B. J. Meehan*

AMARO   5 b.m. Emarati (USA) 74 – Redcross Miss 64 (Tower Walk 130) [2001 44:   **37**
f7g⁵ Jan 4] poor maiden: seems to stay 7f: acts on fibresand/equitrack and good to firm
going. *J. L. Harris*

AMARONE   3 b.g. Young Ern 120 – Tendresse (IRE) 60 (Tender King 123) [2001 –:   **27**
7s 10f⁵ 7m f7g⁴ f8g Jul 20] smallish, strong gelding: poor maiden: barely stays 1¼m: acts   **a41**
on firm going and fibresand: blinkered/visored. *M. J. Ryan*

AMAZED   4 ch.f. Clantime 101 – Indigo 86 (Primo Dominie 121) [2001 58: 5g 5g   **–**
Jul 28] good-topped filly: modest maiden at 3 yrs: well held in 2001: visored final start.
Mrs J. R. Ramsden

AMBASSADOR LADY (IRE)   3 b.f. General Monash (USA) 107 – La Fandango   **43**
(IRE) 51 (Taufan (USA) 119) [2001 –: 6f f6g 6m 7m⁴ 6m Aug 30] poor maiden handicapper: should stay 1m: acts on good to firm going. *A. G. Newcombe*

AMBER BROWN   5 b.m. Thowra (FR) – High Velocity 53 (Frimley Park 109) [2001   **65**
67: f6g⁶ e7g² f6g e8g e7s* e8g e7g⁴ e7g³ 6.1v⁶ 7m³ 7m 7m 6g f8g p7g⁴ Dec 28]
workmanlike mare: fair performer: won minor event at Lingfield in February: stays 7f:
acts on all-weather: usually blinkered: has started slowly. *K. T. Ivory*

AMBER FORT   8 gr.g. Indian Ridge 123 – Lammastide 93 (Martinmas 128) [2001   **76**
77, a55: 7.1v 7m 7s* 7f⁴ 7m 7f 7m 7d⁶ 7m 7.5m⁴ 7m³ 7g⁶ 7.5s 7s 7d³ 8s Nov 9] tall   **a–**
gelding: fair handicapper: won at Salisbury in May: best at 7f/1m: acts on any going
(though all wins on good going or softer): blinkered/visored: not an easy ride (flashes tail/
tends to wander): best waited with. *J. M. Bradley*

AMBER ROSE (IRE)   3 ch.f. Royal Academy (USA) 130 – La Fille de Cirque 49   **66**
(Cadeaux Genereux 131) [2001 72: 6m 9.9m³ 8.3g⁴ 9g⁶ f8g Oct 18] leggy, rather sparely-
made filly: has a quick action: fair maiden: stays 1¼m: raced only on good going or
firmer on turf: has worn tongue tie. *M. Johnston*

AMBER'S BLUFF   2 b.f. (Feb 7) Mind Games 121 – Amber Mill 96 (Doulab (USA)   **80 p**
115) [2001 6g² Sep 7] 35,000Y: tall filly: has scope: sixth foal: half-sister to 1997 2-y-o
5f winner Salamanca (by Paris House): dam sprinter: 16/1, promising ½-length second of
19 to Ringmoor Down in maiden at Kempton, soon in rear after slow start but finishing
strongly: sure to improve and win a race or 2. *A. C. Stewart*

AMBERSONG   3 ch.g. Hernando (FR) 127 – Stygian (USA) 73 (Irish River (FR) 131)   **74 d**
[2001 58: 6g⁵ 7.1m 8g² 8.1f 8.1m 8d 8.5g Sep 19] strong, angular gelding: fair maiden
handicapper: well held last 3 starts: stays 1m: best efforts on good going (tailed off on
heavy). *J. W. Hills*

AMBER TIDE (IRE) 3 ch.f. Pursuit of Love 124 – Tochar Ban (USA) 83 (Assert **75**
134) [2001 69: 6.1d³ 8m 8.2f³ 8m⁴ 8.5d⁴ 8g² 8f² 10m² 9.2g⁴ Sep 3] strong, well-made
filly: unimpressive mover: fair maiden: reportedly finished lame final start: stays 1¼m:
unraced on heavy going, acts on any other: has run well when sweating/edgy: reliable.
M. L. W. Bell

AMBITIOUS 6 b.m. Ardkinglass 114 – Ayodhya (IRE) (Astronef 116) [2001 96: 5m **98**
5g⁵ 5m³ 5f² 5g 5m³ 5g 6g 6d³ 5g 5.6m 6m 5v⁶ f5g Nov 21] lengthy mare: useful handi- **a?**
capper on turf, fairly useful at best on all-weather: best effort when head second to Smart
Predator at Doncaster in July: effective at 5f/sharp 6f: probably acts on any turf going and
all-weather: visored/blinkered early in 1999: has been bandaged in front/worn crossed
noseband: sometimes early to post: has been slowly away. *K. T. Ivory*

AMBITIOUS ALLIANCE (IRE) 2 b.g. (May 10) General Monash (USA) 107 – **–**
Northern Amber (Shack (USA) 118) [2001 5.1v⁵ f5g⁶ 5.7f 6d 5d 7f Jul 25] workmanlike
gelding: half-brother to 5f (including at 2 yrs) winner Minizen Music (by Anita's Prince)
and 6f winner Karseam (by Mon Tresor), later winner abroad: dam lightly raced: poor
maiden: tried blinkered. *M. Quinn*

AMBRY 4 b.g. Machiavellian (USA) 123 – Alkaffeyeh (IRE) (Sadler's Wells (USA) **74 §**
132) [2001 87§: f16g³ 14.1g² 16.4m³ 16v⁶ Oct 17] fourth foal: brother to useful UAE 5f/
6f winner (also 6f winner in Britain at 2 yrs) Kharir and useful winner up to 1½m in
Ireland Mudaa-Eb and half-brother to smart 1½m/1¾m winner (stayed 2¼m) Ta-Lim (by
Ela-Mana-Mou): dam unraced sister to smart 1½m performer Larrocha and half-sister to
Ardross: fair maiden: bought from K. Prendergast in Ireland 23,000 gns after final 3-y-o
start: stays 2m: acts on fibresand and heavy going, probably on good to firm: tried
blinkered, including last 2 starts: looks none too genuine. *G. L. Moore*

AMBUSHED (IRE) 5 b.g. Indian Ridge 123 – Surprise Move (IRE) (Simply Great **68**
(FR) 122) [2001 64, a45: 8.3d⁵ 9.1m* 8.3d 8m⁵ 6m⁶ 9f⁴ 9f⁴ 9.2m 9.1d Aug 3] fair
handicapper: won at Ayr in May: stays 9f: acts on fibresand and any turf going: tried
blinkered earlier in career: usually races up with pace. *P. Monteith*

AMEERAT 3 b.f. Mark of Esteem (IRE) 137 – Walimu (IRE) 82 (Top Ville 129) **116**
[2001 102p: 8g* 8f⁵ 8m 8g Oct 6]
    For a race run in May, the latest One Thousand Guineas has a very end-of-
career look to it for far too many of its participants. For a significant number, it
proved the fast lane to retirement or obscurity. Muwakleh was the first to succumb,
retired within twenty-four hours after fracturing a knee; Dora Carrington also never
ran again, and others might as well have joined her. Sir Michael Stoute, who looked
to have such a strong hand for the classic over the winter, failed to get Regal Rose
to the track at all as a three-year-old, while his fillies which did make the Guineas
line-up, Karasta and Enthused, were both retired after two fifteen starts proved
miserable failures. Between them after the Guineas, the entire fifteen-runner field
mustered only one win of note, Toroca's Group 3 Premio Sergio Cumani, and only
two other victories of any kind, in Autumnal's minor event and, at 8/1-on, Arhaaff's
maiden. One day before Toroca's Italian victory in mid-October, Ameerat, the
Guineas winner, joined the ranks of those that had been retired. She had had three
races after her classic win and failed to make the frame in any of them. Amazingly,
in the footsteps of Sleepytime, Cape Verdi, Wince and Lahan, she became the fifth
consecutive filly who failed to win again after classic triumph at Newmarket in
the spring.
    It seemed to be a build-down rather than a build-up for the latest One
Thousand. The two major trials, the Fred Darling Stakes and the Nell Gwyn, were
won by Rolly Polly and Lil's Jessy, neither of whom held a Guineas entry. The
beaten horses were hardly bursting with promise either, even in the imaginations of
their own connections, as come Guineas day, the Fred Darling had only one
representative, in Ashlinn who had finished sixth of ten, and so did the Nell Gwyn,
in Autumnal who had come eighth of fourteen. The ante-post favourite for the
classic before the trials was Regal Rose, shortly to be struck out of all betting.
Henry Cecil's Autumn Rhythm had been a major market mover in the ante-post
lists, but when she reappeared it was to finish only sixth in the Feilden Stakes, after
which she was transferred to the States. Just over a fortnight later, on Guineas day
itself, John Gosden, trainer of the Fillies' Mile winner Crystal Music, reported that
'she works very much like a filly who needs a mile and a quarter or a mile and a

half,' while Stoute commented pithily of his dual challenge that 'we are running them both because we feel they are ready to have a race.'

Ameerat was having her first race of the season in the Guineas, and the same was true of no fewer than eight of the fourteen other runners. In Ameerat's case it was reported that she had been slow to come to hand in the wet spring. Of the minority that had enjoyed a previous outing in 2001, the pick appeared to be Godolphin's Muwakleh, a sister to the Dubai World Cup winner Almutawakel who had not run as a two-year-old but had won two starts on the dirt at Nad Al Sheba, most recently the UAE 1000 Guineas by five and a half lengths. From France, Criquette Head-Maarek sent the Prix Imprudence winner Stunning, while, from Ireland, Aidan O'Brien was represented by Toroca, runner-up to Regal Rose in the Cheveley Park and then winner of a maiden in April. Among the seasonal debutantes, Karasta had won the May Hill and been runner-up in the Marcel Boussac, Enthused had won the Princess Margaret Stakes and the Lowther, Dora Carrington the Cherry Hinton and Sayedah the Rockfel. Ameerat had been second in the May Hill and sixth in the Rockfel, hampered on both occasions but also notably edgy before the Rockfel Stakes.

Karasta was sent off favourite at 9/2, followed in the betting by Crystal Music at 5/1, Enthused backed from 12/1 to 6/1, and Muwakleh at 13/2; Toroca was 10/1 and Ameerat 11/1. Chief feature of this field in the parade ring was the strikingly massive Karasta, but Ameerat also took the eye as a grand-looking filly with plenty of scope. Karasta could hardly have made her presence felt less in the actual race though, a race in which barely a handful ever figured with a serious chance and the favourite, fighting for her head early on, trailed throughout.

Sagitta 1000 Guineas Stakes, Newmarket—Ameerat provides trainer Michael Jarvis with his first classic success in Britain; runner-up Muwakleh suffers a career-ending injury, whilst Toroca (left) and Crystal Music fill the frame

Ameerat meanwhile disputed third place as Muwakleh made the running at a sound pace, and she had moved into second, with a length and a half to make up, at the two-furlong marker. Thereafter, Ameerat reduced the deficit by fractions before getting her head in front inside the last half furlong to win by a neck. Crystal Music was the only other runner to hint at a challenge, but she faded inside the final furlong and was caught by Toroca, who finished a length and three quarters behind the runner-up. Fifth-placed Enthused was clear of the remainder.

The 2001 Guineas form was solid but unspectacular, by our reckoning marginally worse than that of Wince and Lahan in the two previous editions, a little better than that of Sayyedati and Las Meninas early in the 'nineties. Trainer Michael Jarvis has had plenty of big-race victories with horses such as Carroll House, Petong, Beldale Flutter and Holding Court, but, in his thirty-fourth year with a licence, Ameerat gave him his first British classic winner. His previous best was back in 1970 when Meadowville was beaten a length by Nijinsky in the St Leger. Meadowville was also runner-up in the Irish Derby and Irish St Leger. Jockey Philip Robinson, who won the One Thousand with Pebbles, the Irish One Thousand with Katies and the St Leger with Bob's Return, has enjoyed a renaissance of late and was adding Ameerat's victory to the multiple successes of Crimplene a year earlier.

Ameerat, contrastingly, made a negligible contribution to the remainder of the season. Three and a half lengths fifth to Banks Hill in the Coronation Stakes was respectable and connections blamed the firm ground (it had been good at Newmarket). The going was, by our reckoning, good to firm when, at 16/1, she trailed in eighth of ten in the Sussex Stakes at Goodwood, dropping right away in the last two furlongs, and confidence in her seemed to have disappeared by the time

Sheikh Ahmed Al Maktoum's "Ameerat"

that she made her final appearance in the Sun Chariot Stakes two months later. Back over the same course and distance of her greatest triumph, and back on good ground again, she was sent off at 11/1 and finished seventh of sixteen behind Independence. Prior to the Sun Chariot it was reported that connections feared she had a wind problem and that 'she was making a lot of noise after her last race.' As far as race-goers were concerned, Ameerat finished with a whimper.

Ameerat (b.f. 1998)	Mark of Esteem (IRE) (b 1993)	Darshaan (br 1981)	Shirley Heights / Delsy
		Homage (b 1989)	Ajdal / Home Love
	Walimu (IRE) (b 1989)	Top Ville (b 1976)	High Top / Sega Ville
		Summer Impressions (ch 1980)	Lyphard / Roussalka

Ameerat's sire Mark of Esteem made his way down the Rowley Mile to classic glory in a photo-finish with Even Top and Bijou d'Inde five years earlier. Ameerat is therefore from his first crop, conceived at a fee of £20,000. Mark of Esteem's win over Bosra Sham in the Queen Elizabeth II Stakes, part of Frankie Dettori's 'Magnificent Seven', was the top-rated performance of that year and the best by any miler in the 'nineties. A classic winner at the first attempt is a fine start at stud. Ameerat is easily the best performer in Britain or Ireland from Mark of Esteem's first crop, but he was also represented by the smart French filly Spring Oak. Ameerat is from a family imbued with success at the top level. Her dam and grandam may not be that familiar, but her third dam is Roussalka, who, having missed the Guineas following a flop in the Nell Gwyn, made amends with easy wins in the Coronation Stakes and Nassau Stakes and won the Nassau again as a four-year-old. Roussalka is also a half-sister to fillies' triple crown winner Oh So Sharp (who was put down in the autumn after suffering from laminitis) and a sister to Our Home, who was beaten a neck in the One Thousand Guineas in 1980. One grandson of Oh So Sharp is the St Leger winner Shantou. Roussalka's daughter Summer Impressions gained her only win at Cagnes-sur-Mer as a four-year-old, over a mile in an amateur riders race, which makes her very much a poor relation seeing as Roussalka also produced high-class sprinter Gayane and Sun Chariot Stakes winner Ristna. Summer Impressions has had five winners, the best of whom was probably Ameerat's dam Walimu, a fairly useful three-year-old winner over a mile, a mile and a quarter and a mile and a half. Her three foals before Ameerat include Elbarree (by Green Desert), a winner in Britain (over both a mile and seven furlongs, showing fairly useful form) and in the UAE, and Walmooh (by In The Wings), who got off the mark as a five-year-old in the UAE in 2001.
Ameerat is a tall, quite good-topped filly with a fluent, round action. A smart performer on Guineas day, she was best at a mile and put up her best effort on good ground. She was rather a flighty sort on occasions and raced freely in the Coronation Stakes. She begins her stud career with a visit to Seeking The Gold. *M. A. Jarvis*

AMELIA (IRE) 3 b.f. General Monash (USA) 107 – Rose Tint (IRE) (Salse (USA) 128) [2001 88: 6d 5s 6g 5g 6.1m 8d f6g f8g p6g Dec 29] neat filly: has a short action: fairly useful at 2 yrs: disappointing in 2001: effective at 5f/6f: acts on good to firm ground, good to soft and fibresand: races prominently: edgy sort: has hung under pressure. *J. Cullinan*   **77 d**

AMEN CORNER (USA) 3 ch.g. Mt Livermore (USA) – For All Seasons (USA) (Crafty Prospector (USA)) [2001 73, a80: f6g e6g 8.5f⁵ Jul 7] well-made gelding: fairly useful on all-weather, fair on turf: below form in 2001: seems best at 6f/7f: acts on fibresand and firm ground, possibly not on softer than good: inconsistent: sold 10,000 gns in July, sent to USA. *M. Johnston*   **64**

AMERICA CALLING (USA) 3 b.f. Quiet American (USA) – Allison's Dance (USA) (Storm Bird (CAN) 134) [2001 81: e6g⁵ 6s⁵ 5g³ 5m⁶ 6.1f* 6m³ 5g Oct 6] $110,000Y: neat filly: half-sister to several winners, including fairly useful 1m winner Distinctive Dance (by Distinctive Pro) and French 1m/1¼m winner Danse Polonaise (by Halo): dam, won up to 1m in USA, from very good family: fairly useful performer: **81**

trained by K. Prendergast in Ireland at 2 yrs: blinkered, won handicap at Chepstow in September: best at 6f: acts on firm and soft ground: has had tongue tied. *G. A. Butler*

AMERICAN COUSIN   6 b.g. Distant Relative 128 – Zelda (USA) (Sharpen Up 127) **77**
[2001 64: 5v⁵ 5v⁴ f6g 6.1d⁴ 5m 5m⁶ 5m* 6m² 5m⁵ 5f 5m* 5m 6g 5m 6m 5d 5s Sep 24] **a?**
sturdy gelding: fair handicapper: won at Musselburgh in June and York in July: effective
at 5f/6f: acts on heavy and good to firm going: blinkered twice earlier in career:
sometimes slowly away. *D. Nicholls*

AMEZOLA   5 gr.g. Northern Park (USA) 107 – Yamamah 54 (Siberian Express (USA) **49**
125) [2001 –: 14.1v 10m 16m 14.1d 14.1d 16g 16d 14.1s⁶ Oct 31] quite good-topped
gelding: poor handicapper nowadays: left Mrs A. Perrett after reappearance: stays 1¾m:
probably best on going softer than good (acts on heavy): blinkered once: has had tongue
tied: sometimes slowly away. *J. C. McConnochie*

AMIABLA (IRE)   2 gr.f. (Feb 24) Dr Devious (IRE) 127 – Safkana (IRE) 78 (Doyoun **60**
124) [2001 7g⁴ 7m Jul 20] 20,000Y: leggy, rather unfurnished filly: third foal: half-sister
to 2 winners abroad, including Spanish 1m and 10.5f winner Barakana (by Barathea):
dam, Irish 1m winner, half-sister to smart performer up to 1m Speedfit Too: better effort
in maidens (modest form) when fourth of 6 at Yarmouth. *C. E. Brittain*

AMICABLE (IRE)   3 b.c. Common Grounds 118 – Bahia Laura (FR) (Bellypha 130) **108**
[2001 89: 7v³ 7.6f* 8g 7m² 8m 8g⁴ 8g⁴ 7d Oct 20] tall, quite good-topped colt: useful
performer: won maiden at Doncaster in March and handicap at Chester in May: ran
creditably when ½-length second to Jentzen in listed race at Epsom and seventh in
Britannia Handicap at Royal Ascot on fourth/fifth starts: effective at 7f/1m: acts on any
going: sent to USA. *B. W. Hills*

AMIGO (IRE)   3 b.c. Spectrum (IRE) 126 – Eleanor Antoinette (IRE) (Double **54**
Schwartz 128) [2001 67: 8g 9m 10.1g 10d p10g Nov 28] modest maiden handicapper:
will stay 1½m: acts on soft going and fibresand: blinkered (slowly away/raced freely)
final start. *P. Mitchell*

AMINGTON LADY   3 ch.f. Superlative 118 – Amington Lass 70 (Cree Song 99) **–**
[2001 5g Aug 23] first foal: dam 5f winner: 33/1, pulled up after 2f in maiden at Folkestone: dead. *P. D. Evans*

AMIR ZAMAN   3 ch.g. Salse (USA) 128 – Colorvista (Shirley Heights 130) [2001 **73**
59p: 8.2s⁴ 8d 11m⁴ 11.4g⁶ 16.2m³ 14.1m* Jul 24] big, strong, lengthy gelding: has scope:
fair performer: won maiden handicap at Yarmouth in July: probably stays 2m: acts on
good to firm ground: gelded after final start. *J. W. Payne*

AMI'S ANGEL (IRE)   3 b.f. Fayruz 116 – Khunasira (FR) (Nishapour (FR) 125) **–**
[2001 75: f5g f5g f5g 6m 7m 6m 8m Sep 10] unfurnished filly: fair at 2 yrs: disappointing
in 2001: should stay 7f: acts on firm and good to soft ground: blinkered penultimate start.
A. G. Newcombe

AMJAD   4 ch.g. Cadeaux Genereux 131 – Babita 107 (Habitat 134) [2001 75: f8g* **75 d**
f9.4g⁶ 8s f12g⁴ 8.3d³ 9g Aug 24] lengthy, useful-looking gelding: fair performer: well
below form after winning handicap at Southwell in January: stays 1m, not 1½m: acts on
fibresand and firm going: tried blinkered/visored: won over hurdles in December.
P. C. Haslam

AMNESTY   2 ch.g. (Jun 2) Salse (USA) 128 – Amaranthus (Shirley Heights 130) **63**
[2001 6m 6.1m 7s⁵ Oct 3] 2,500Y: lengthy gelding: sixth foal: half-brother to fairly useful
7.5f winner Acidanthera (by Alzao): dam unraced daughter of smart sprinter Amaranda:
modest maiden: should stay 1m. *H. Candy*

AMONG EQUALS   4 b.g. Sadler's Wells (USA) 132 – Epicure's Garden (USA) 102 **84**
(Affirmed (USA)) [2001 90: 13.1m⁶ 16.2s Sep 29] fairly useful performer: won maiden
at Listowel as 3-y-o (sold from D. Weld, Ireland 40,000 gns after final start): better effort
in 2001 on reappearance: stays 13f: acts on heavy and good to firm going: blinkered last
2 starts at 3 yrs. *M. Meade*

AMONG WOMEN   3 b.f. Common Grounds 118 – Key West (FR) (Highest Honor **67**
(FR) 124) [2001 66: 8s⁴ 8.3s⁶ 8m⁴ 9m 8m 7d³ 8.3g 10.1g 8s⁴ f8.5g³ f8.5g f9.4g f7g⁴ f6s **a62**
Dec 26] leggy, workmanlike filly: fair on turf, modest on all-weather: won claimer at
Lingfield (final start for N. Callaghan) in July: left J. Best after penultimate start: effective
at 7f to 8.5f: acts on fibresand, possibly best on going softer than good on turf (though has
form on good to firm). *K. R. Burke*

AMORAS (IRE)   4 b.f. Hamas (IRE) 125§ – Red Lory 87 (Bay Express 132) [2001 **78**
78: 7m² 7.1d³ 8m 8.3m⁵ 7d⁴ p8g³ p8g p10g² Dec 12] good-bodied filly: fair handicapper:
stays 1¼m: acts on any turf going and polytrack. *J. W. Hills*

AMOROUS SARITA   3 b.f. Pursuit of Love 124 – Hug Me 96 (Shareef Dancer **56**
(USA) 135) [2001 –: 8g 6.9m 6m⁴ 6.1s 6f 5.2v Oct 26] quite good-topped filly: modest
maiden: should stay beyond 6f: acts on good to firm going: has wandered. *P. W. Harris*

AMOURE KING (IRE)   2 b.c. (Feb 15) Desert King (IRE) 129 – Ange Rouge (Priolo **69**
(USA) 127) [2001 7m 7.1m⁵ 6v Oct 8] 23,000F, IR 175,000Y: rather leggy colt: first foal:
dam, French 1¼m winner, half-sister to useful French/Italian 1m/1¼m performer Ardane
(by Danehill, sire of Desert King): fair maiden: will stay 1m: well beaten on heavy going:
sent to USA. *B. W. Hills*

AMOUR SANS FIN (FR)   2 b.c. (Apr 4) Kendor (FR) 122 – Nuit Sans Fin (FR) **91**
(Lead On Time (USA) 123) [2001 5g⁴ 6s* 8m³ 7d⁶ 8s 8d p7g Nov 13] 200,000 francs Y:
small, sturdy colt: second living foal: dam, ran once in France, half-sister to dam of useful
French 1m/1¼m performer The Mask: fairly useful performer: won maiden at Newbury
in May: out of depth fourth to sixth starts: not sure to stay beyond 1m: acts on soft and
good to firm ground: blinkered last 2 outings (slowly away final one). *B. J. Meehan*

AMPULLA   3 b.g. Primo Dominie 121 – Lead Them Lady (FR) (Lead On Time (USA) **48**
123) [2001 50: 6.1v 6g 5d 6m 5m 7.1g 6.1f Sep 18] poor maiden: should stay 7f.
G. B. Balding

AMRAK AJEEB (IRE)   9 b.h. Danehill (USA) 126 – Noble Dust (USA) (Dust **62 §**
Commander (USA)) [2001 81: 10s 10d 13.3g 11.9g⁴ 10m 12m 11.9g⁴ 11.5f⁴ 12.1s⁵ 9.9m
10m⁵ Sep 11] leggy, good-topped horse: modest performer nowadays: barely stays 1½m:
acts on firm and soft going: blinkered second and (very reluctant to race) third outings:
often slowly away: ungenuine. *R. J. Baker*

AMRITSAR   4 ch.c. Indian Ridge 123 – Trying For Gold (USA) 103 (Northern Baby **64**
(CAN) 127) [2001 81d: 10g 10g 10.1m Jul 8] angular colt: modest maiden handicapper:
best around 1¼m: acts on good to firm and good to soft ground. *P. Howling*

AMRON   14 b.g. Bold Owl 101 – Sweet Minuet (Setay 105) [2001 44d: 9.1m⁴ 8m⁶ 8m **31 d**
10.9f 10.1m 7d 10v Oct 15] sparely-made gelding: veteran handicapper: stays 1¼m: acts
on any going: usually held up. *A. Berry*

AMSARA (IRE)   5 b.m. Taufan (USA) 119 – Legend of Spain (USA) (Alleged (USA) **21**
138) [2001 27: f11g 13m 14.1g 12f 12.1d⁶ 12f 16g⁴ 16.2s³ Aug 16] tall mare: bad
handicapper: stays 2m: acts on soft going and fibresand: tried blinkered. *D. W. Chapman*

AMUSED   2 ch.f. (Feb 28) Prince Sabo 123 – Indigo 86 (Primo Dominie 121) [2001 **63 p**
5g⁵ Sep 19] short-backed filly: half-sister to several winning sprinters, notably smart pair
Astonished (by Weldnaas) and Bishops Court (by Clantime): dam 2-y-o 5f winner: 14/1,
backward and green, encouraging fifth of 18 to Marcus Aurelius in maiden at Beverley,
staying on from towards rear under hands and heels: sure to progress. *R. A. Fahey*

AMWELL STAR (USA)   3 gr.f. Silver Buck (USA) – Markham Fair (CAN) (Wood- **46**
man (USA) 126) [2001 –: f11g⁵ 11.6s 14.1d² 14.1m 11.9f 16.2m 16g⁴ 14.1s³ 16.4g⁴ 14.1s
12d² Nov 6] poor maiden handicapper: will stay beyond 2m: acts on soft ground: has
reared leaving stall (unseated when doing so second outing). *J. R. Jenkins*

AMY DEE   3 b.f. Be My Chief (USA) 122 – Baileys By Name 66 (Nomination 125) **28**
[2001 48: 6m 6g 8.2f 6m Jul 5] sturdy filly: bad maiden: tried blinkered: very slowly
away final outing. *N. Tinkler*

AMY G (IRE)   3 b.f. Common Grounds 118 – Queen Canute (IRE) (Ahonoora 122) **52**
[2001 45: 5g 5g² 6m³ 6g⁵ 7v f7g Nov 12] modest maiden: best efforts at 5f/6f: acts on **a?**
good to firm going: sold 800 gns. *N. Tinkler*

ANABAA BLUE   3 b.c. Anabaa (USA) 130 – Allez Les Trois (USA) 114 (River- **120**
man (USA) 131) [2001 10v* 11v* 10.5m² 12m* 12m 12m² 12s Oct 7]
   In the course of three months in 2001, Christophe Soumillon lost one job, as
second jockey to Andre Fabre, and found another, as first jockey to the Aga Khan.
And in between the two career moves, he picked up a useful outside ride in the Prix
du Jockey Club on Anabaa Blue. Soumillon's run-in with Fabre was apparently the
result of some poor timekeeping. 'Everyone has his faults,' said the jockey, 'and
one of mine is that from time to time I cannot get up early in the morning.'
Less-than-charitable onlookers might have included his fast-finishing second on

Vahorimix in the Poule d'Essai des Poulains in the same bracket. It may have been coincidental, but Soumillon did not ride for Fabre in any listed or pattern race after the Poulains. Soumillon's reluctance to rise with the birds, however, which provoked a public dressing-down from Monsieur Fabre the day before the Prix du Jockey Club, proved somewhat reminiscent of Graham Bradley's famous lie-in prior to the 1996 Champion Hurdle: on that occasion, blaming a broken alarm clock for his absence from an early-morning workout failed to prevent Bradley losing the ride on Alderbrook, who went on to finish second in the Champion, but did enable him to team up with Collier Bay, who won it.

Soumillon's opportunity for a swift riposte came in a fourteen-runner renewal of the Jockey Club which boasted the winners of all the major trials in France. Favourite Maille Pistol had run up his hat-trick in a listed race, the Prix Greffulhe and the Hocquart, winning by at least five lengths on each occasion; Fabre's sole runner Sagacity had been second in the Hocquart, beaten eight lengths; Chichicastenango had won the Lupin in a tight finish with Anabaa Blue and Milan; Okawango was stepping up from a mile after his fifth (later promoted to fourth) in the Poulains; Art Contemporain, Sensible, Doctorate and Musha Merr all arrived with last-time-out victories in either Group 3 or listed company, the last-named representing Godolphin; two further challengers from Britain were John Gosden's Sydenham, runner-up in a Bath maiden, and James Fanshawe's Grandera, who had gone close in the Dee Stakes. A sprint finish at Longchamp for the Lupin had seen Chichicastenango outpace Anabaa Blue soon after turning for home and just hang on as Anabaa Blue rallied. At Chantilly three weeks later, there was an extra furlong and a half, a stronger early pace and different riding tactics, and Anabaa Blue came out on top. Carlos Lerner, his trainer, told Soumillon beforehand that 'I have no interest in coming second', and the jockey responded with a most positive ride. Anabaa Blue was quickest out of the stalls but headed after a furlong or so as Maille Pistol, as expected, took up his usual position up front. Soumillon, who had been told to hold up Anabaa Blue in the Lupin, this time raced in second, and, switching off the rail entering the straight, was in a perfect position as the favourite faltered. Certainly, he was in a much better position than either Grandera, two lengths further back on the rail and about to be hampered, or Milan, even further back after a slow

Prix du Jockey Club, Chantilly—Anabaa Blue reverses Prix Lupin form with Chichicastenango (No.2); Grandera is a somewhat unlucky third

start. Both of those colts were running on well at the finish, but only for third and fifth places respectively. Chichicastenango made a strong challenge on the outside (followed by eventual fourth Okawango), and there could not have been more than a neck between him and Anabaa Blue over the last two furlongs before Anabaa Blue inched ahead in the last fifty yards to take his advantage at the winning post to half a length. After his Champion Hurdle triumph five years earlier, Graham Bradley had returned to the winner's enclosure with gesticulations in the manner, seemingly, of looking at his watch. Soumillon's reaction was to weep uncontrollably. It was the eve of his twentieth birthday, his final day as a teenager marking his first as a proven big-race jockey. He has been routinely described as clearly the best jockey prospect in France since Olivier Peslier, an opinion with which the Aga Khan is presumably in agreement. His first winner in the Aga Khan's colours came on Miliana in the Prix de Flore at Saint-Cloud in October.

Anabaa Blue provided a first classic triumph for the trainer Carlos Lerner. An Argentine who gained his first taste of racing in 1973 on a visit to the French stables of his celebrated compatriot Angel Penna, Lerner has had a trainer's licence in France since 1983 and for the first seventeen years was training mostly jumpers. In 1999, however, one of five two-year-olds in his charge was Volvoreta, who went on to win the Prix Vermeille and finish third in the 2000 Arc de Triomphe. It was reported that Lerner had a string of forty, including seventeen two-year-olds, for 2001.

Anabaa Blue's Prix du Jockey Club provided a first classic victory for his sire, as well as his trainer, and provided another chapter in a rapidly expanding run of success for his family on the dam's side. Anabaa Blue comes from the first crop of the Danzig stallion Anabaa, a crop that warranted enthusiastic comment twelve months ago, when he was the top French sire of two-year-olds at the first attempt and responsible for the Prix Marcel Boussac winner Amonita. A number of Anabaa's two-year-olds of 2000 failed to go on, indeed some would say that Amonita was one of them, but she did win a listed race (over seven furlongs) in the latest season, as did Messoeurs (over five) and Tarzan Cry (over a mile), and two Group 1 winners in his first crop has to be described as promising for their sire, even if the evidence is not quite there yet to support Alec Head's assertion in December 2000 that 'I have the best sire in the world.' Rouvres, from Anabaa's second crop, was second in the Prix Thomas Bryon in October. To recap briefly on a now famous story, Anabaa is the horse who entered Head's ownership for nothing, as a gift from Sheikh Maktoum Al Maktoum; Anabaa's life had been threatened by injury as a two-year-old, but, after it had originally been intended that he be kept as a teaser, he emerged as Europe's champion sprinter as a four-year-old.

		Danzig	Northern Dancer
	Anabaa (USA)	(b 1977)	Pas de Nom
	(b 1992)	Balbonella	Gay Mecene
Anabaa Blue		(b or br 1984)	Bamieres
(b.c. 1998)		Riverman	Never Bend
	Allez Les Trois (USA)	(b 1969)	River Lady
	(ch 1991)	Allegretta	Lombard
		(ch 1978)	Anatevka

Little more than a glance should be required at the distaff side of Anabaa Blue's pedigree to realise that he is extremely well connected—his grandam is Allegretta and the family is described in greater detail elsewhere in this Annual. Dam herself of an Arc winner in Urban Sea and a Two Thousand Guineas winner in King's Best, in the latest season Allegretta appeared as grandam not only of Anabaa Blue, but of German Group 1 winner Anzillero and of Derby, Irish Derby and King George winner Galileo. Anabaa Blue's dam, Allez Les Trois, was the third-best of Allegretta's offspring on the racecourse, winner of the Group 3 ten-and-a-half-furlong Prix de Flore and two other races as a three-year-old for Criquette Head; she was also beaten only about five lengths when eighth of nine in the Vermeille. Allez Les Trois' one foal prior to Anabaa Blue was Al Ishq (by Nureyev), who won one race over an extended mile in France, and she had a colt by Zafonic in 1999 and a filly by Indian Ridge in 2000.

2001 therefore saw Anabaa Blue's jockey, trainer, sire and dam's family all in the ascendancy, but what of Anabaa Blue himself? Up to and including the

Mr C. Mimouni's "Anabaa Blue"

French Derby, his story had seemed one of continuing progress. Small, according to his trainer, when bought for 650,000 francs at Deauville as a yearling, Anabaa Blue was a big, good-topped colt to our eyes as a three-year-old. Third in a new-comers race and a minor event over a mile as a juvenile, he was transformed during the winter and reappeared to make all in the first race of the Parisian season, a minor event at Maisons-Laffitte in March. Soumillon, who rode Anabaa Blue on his debut and in all his races of 2001, again made all on him in the Prix Noailles at Long-champ. It was a weak renewal but Anabaa Blue was undeniably impressive in scoring by six lengths, forging clear in a manner which left no doubt that he would be suited by the extra furlong of the Prix du Jockey Club, an impression backed up when he met his first defeat of the year in the Lupin. After the Jockey Club, though, Anabaa Blue did not win again. The closest he came was when going down by three quarters of a length to Golan in the Prix Niel, running as well as he has ever done, with Chichicastenango this time two lengths behind. Either side of that run, however, Anabaa Blue was put in his place in both the King George and the Arc, finishing seventh of twelve and ninth of seventeen. He was edgy and moved short to post before the King George, but the obvious explanation for defeat in both the King George and the Arc, if not quite for the magnitude of it, is that he was not good enough. This Annual has twenty-four other European-raced three-year-olds rated above him. The form of his Prix du Jockey Club win, which he improved on marginally in the Prix Niel, ranks among the lowest for a winner of the race in recent years, alongside that shown by Polytain, Celtic Arms and Ragmar. Anabaa Blue is better at a mile and a half than shorter distances, suited by bowling along at the front or close up, and he acts on heavy and good to firm ground. He is genuine and a grand battler, but the current evidence is that those qualities will not be enough to see him pass the post in front in top company as a four-year-old. *C. Lerner, France*

ANADA (FR)　3 b.f. Exit To Nowhere (USA) 122 – Anafi 95 (Slip Anchor 136) [2001 8d 8.2v⁴ 9.7m 12.1g² Jul 20] strong, angular filly: sixth foal: half-sister to 5-y-o Seliana and to 3 winners abroad, notably useful French performer up to 11.5f Vissinia (by Belmez): dam 1¼m and 1¾m winner: fair performer: best effort when second to Alleluia in Chepstow minor event: will be suited by further than 1½m. *L. M. Cumani*　**78**

ANADONIS　3 b.c. Anabaa (USA) 130 – Stiletta (Dancing Brave (USA) 140) [2001 7d³ 8.2s² Oct 30] big, good-topped colt: has plenty of scope: third living foal: dam unraced sister to Derby winner Commander In Chief and half-sister to Warning, Deploy, Dushyantor and Yashmak (by Danzig, sire of Anabaa): better effort in maidens (fairly useful form) when 2 lengths second to Island Light at Nottingham: stays 1m: should do better still. *H. R. A. Cecil*　**81 p**

ANALYSER (IRE)　3 ch.c. Royal Academy (USA) 130 – Mountain Ash 107 (Dominion 123) [2001 82: 7m 7.1m² 7m* 8m* 8m² 8g Aug 2] big, good-topped colt: useful handicapper: won at Newbury and Royal Ascot (Britannia Stakes, beat Ecclesiastical by 1¾ lengths) in June: good head second to Zucchero in Ladbroke Handicap at Newbury penultimate start: favourite, well below form in William Hill Mile at Goodwood final one: stays 1m: yet to race on extremes of going: visored after reappearance: tends to be soon off bridle/hang, and probably requires strong handling: sent to Saudi Arabia. *J. H. M. Gosden*　**105 +**

ANALYTICAL　5 b.g. Pursuit of Love 124 – Risha Flower 85 (Kris 135) [2001 66: 7m 7m² 7m Sep 11] fair performer, lightly raced: raced only at 7f/1m: yet to race on extremes of going: visored once. *R. Charlton*　**72**

ANALYZE (FR)　3 b.g. Anabaa (USA) 130 – Bramosia (Forzando 122) [2001 75: 9s 8.5s⁵ 7.1g 8d⁶ 10m³ 8.3g⁴ 9.9m⁶ 8m⁴ 10m* 10d³ 9.7m³ 10g⁴ 9.7g³ 10.1s 10m⁶ 10s 8d Oct 8] smallish, workmanlike gelding: fair performer: won handicap at Nottingham in July: unlikely to stay beyond 1¼m: yet to race on heavy going, probably acts on any other. *M. R. Channon*　**73**

ANASTASIA'S SHADOW　5 b.m. Theatrical Charmer 114 – Lamloum (IRE) (Vacarme (USA) 121) [2001 f8s 8f 8g 8d f9.4s Dec 27] leggy mare: first foal: dam, fourth at 6f in France, out of Irish Oaks winner Olwyn: had several trainers in France in 2000, winning handicaps at Chantilly and Deauville (final start for G. Nakouzi): well held for J. Piednoel later in year and in Britain in 2001, leaving H. Akbary after second outing and Ms A. Embiricos after penultimate one: stays 1¼m: raced mainly on good going or softer: tongue tied final start: has been slowly away. *T. T. Clement*　**–**

Britannia Stakes (Handicap), Royal Ascot—Analyser gives trainer John Gosden his fourth winner in the race in six years; Ecclesiastical (No.6) takes second with Muthaaber (No.14), Wannabe Around (far rail) and Top Dirham coming next

ANASTASIA VENTURE 4 b.f. Lion Cavern (USA) 117 – Our Shirley 84 (Shirley **48**
Heights 130) [2001 70d: 10g 9f 9m⁵ f8.5g⁶ Jul 12] sparely-made filly: disappointing
maiden: stays 1¼m: acts on good to firm going, good to soft and fibresand: visored once.
J. Akehurst

ANCIENT QUEST 8 b.g. Rainbow Quest (USA) 134 – Racquette 120 (Ballymore **64**
123) [2001 12.3g⁶ 14m⁶ 12.4m⁵ Jun 4] tall, workmanlike gelding: fairly useful handicapper for N. Callaghan in 1997: modest form on return from hurdling in 2001: should
stay at least 1¾m: acts on soft ground: blinkered last 2 starts. *T. D. Easterby*

AND BEYOND (IRE) 3 b.c. Darshaan 133 – Al Najah (USA) 96 (Topsider (USA)) **111**
[2001 12v* 12g⁵ 13.9m* 16.2m* 14.6g Sep 15] rangy, good-topped colt: good walker/
mover: brother to French 1¼m winner Shanjah and half-brother to several winners,
including useful 6f winner Tabook (by Cadeaux Genereux) and 5-y-o Direct Deal (by
Rainbow Quest): dam 8.5f winner: smart performer: won maiden at Musselburgh in
April, minor event at York in May and Queen's Vase at Royal Ascot (beat When In Rome
by a neck in bunch finish): only seventh in St Leger at Doncaster when next seen out: will
stay beyond 2m: yet to race on firm going, acts on any other: races prominently: genuine.
M. Johnston

ANDREW DOBLE 2 ch.c. (Apr 3) Sabrehill (USA) 120 – Verchinina 99 (Star **64 p**
Appeal 133) [2001 7g Aug 10] strong, well-made colt: brother to 5-y-o Inducement and
half-brother to several winners, including 1½m to 2m winner Golden Hadeer and 8-y-o
General Haven (both by Hadeer): dam 1m winner: 33/1 and green, seventh of 19 to
Grampian in maiden at Newmarket, not unduly punished having chased pace: will stay at
least 1m: should improve. *M. A. Jarvis*

ANDREYEV (IRE) 7 ch.g. Presidium 124 – Missish (Mummy's Pet 125) [2001 117: **99**
a6f 6f 6d⁶ 6m 5d 6v Oct 26] tall gelding: impresses in appearance: smart performer at
best, only useful in 2001: effective at 5f (given a test) to 7f: has form on good to firm
going, very best efforts on good or softer: blinkered last 4 starts in 1999, visored final one
in 2001: sometimes starts slowly/hangs left/flashes tail: sold 15,000 gns. *R. Hannon*

ANDROMACHE 2 ch.f. (Mar 23) Hector Protector (USA) 124 – South Sea Bubble **66 p**
(IRE) 75 (Bustino 136) [2001 6g⁶ 6g⁵ 8.2v Oct 4] rather leggy, lengthy filly: has scope:
second foal: dam, 1¼m winner, out of useful sprinter Night At Sea: fair form in maidens:
caught eye on final start, never dangerous under considerate handling: should be suited
by 1¼m/1½m: interesting type for handicaps. *L. M. Cumani*

ANDROMEDA (IRE) 2 b.f. (Mar 16) Barathea (IRE) 127 – Royal York 75 (Bustino **68 p**
136) [2001 7d Nov 3] leggy, unfurnished filly: first foal: dam, won at 1¼m/1½m, out of
half-sister to high-class performer up to 1½m Kirtling: 20/1, seventh of 21 in Newmarket
maiden won by Ballet Fame, making running: bred to be well suited by 1m+: should do
better. *J. Noseda*

Queen's Vase, Royal Ascot—
a blanket finish as And Beyond forges ahead of When In Rome (pale colours),
Aquarius (right), Year Two Thousand (striped sleeves) and Double Honour (rail)

ANDROMEDA'S WAY 3 b.f. Kris 135 – Titania's Way 91 (Fairy King (USA)) – [2001 60d: 10m Aug 22] close-coupled filly: has a quick action: disappointing maiden: has carried head awkwardly/shown signs of temperament: sent to Greece. *P. R. Chamings*

ANDY'S ELECTIVE 4 b.g. Democratic (USA) 101 – English Mint 66 (Jalmood (USA) 126) [2001 68: 7m 7f 7.6f³ 8.3g³ 8g 7g* 7g 8m Sep 24] fair handicapper: won at Folkestone in August: stays 1m: acts on firm and soft ground: usually visored: has wandered: often front runner. *J. R. Jenkins* **68**

ANEMOS (IRE) 6 ch.g. Be My Guest (USA) 126 – Frendly Persuasion (General Assembly (USA)) [2001 75, a83: f9.4s f9.4g e10g⁴ e10g⁵ 12.6d Jul 6] tall gelding: fair handicapper: form in 2001 only on third start: stays 1¼m: acts on equitrack, soft and good to firm going (probably on firm): tried blinkered. *Ian Williams* **75**

ANGEL HILL 6 ch.m. King's Signet (USA) 110 – Tawny 81 (Grey Ghost 98) [2001 68: 5s* 5m 7.5m 5f 6m 6g 6f 7m Sep 22] strong mare: fair handicapper: won at Redcar in May: effective at 5f (given a test) to 7.5f: acts on firm, soft going and fibresand: tried blinkered/visored, not in 2001: has been slowly away/raced freely: tends to hang right: none too consistent. *K. A. Ryan* **67**

ANGELICUS (IRE) 2 b.f. (Apr 28) Pennekamp (USA) 130 – Merry Devil (IRE) (Sadler's Wells (USA) 132) [2001 6g 5.1d Aug 19] IR 11,000Y: sixth foal: half-sister to useful UAE 7f to 9f winner Meshty (by Lahib) and a 2-y-o 7f/1m winner in Italy by Mujtahid: dam, ran once at 2 yrs, closely related to smart French winner up to 11f Lichine: well held in maidens. *J. S. Moore* –

ANGEL LANE 4 b.f. Merdon Melody 98 – Young Whip (Bold Owl 101) [2001 40: 8.3g 6.9m 8m f8g 8.1g³ 8.3m⁶ 10.9m 10m Sep 4] unfurnished filly: poor maiden: stays 1m: acts on good to firm going: has worn tongue tie. *A. W. Carroll* **39**

ANGELS VENTURE 5 ch.g. Unfuwain (USA) 131 – City of Angels (Woodman (USA) 126) [2001 78d: 12m* 12m 11.8g⁵ 12.3m⁶ p12g³ p13g Dec 29] close-coupled gelding: fair performer: dead-heated in handicap at Southwell in May: stays 1½m: acts on polytrack, soft and good to firm going: tried visored: often tongue tied: has hung left. *J. R. Jenkins* **78** **a75**

ANGELUS DOMINI (IRE) 2 b.f. (Apr 21) Blues Traveller (IRE) 119 – Lyphards Goddess (IRE) (Lyphard's Special (USA) 122) [2001 5.1m 6.1v f6g³ Oct 18] leggy, unfurnished filly: sixth foal: half-sister to 3 winners, including 5-y-o Route Sixty Six: dam, lightly-raced Irish maiden, half-sister to useful 1988 2-y-o 5f winner Petrillia: best effort in maidens (modest form) when third at Southwell: swerved violently left leaving stall and unseated rider second start. *B. A. McMahon* **62**

ANGELUS SUNSET (USA) 2 b.c. (Jan 29) Numerous (USA) – Angelic Note (USA) 90 (The Minstrel (CAN) 135) [2001 7.1g³ 8m 7d* 8v* 10v Nov 13] 42,000Y: good-topped colt: seventh foal: half-brother to 2 winners in USA, including minor stakes winner around 9f Grand Forks (by Quiet American): dam, 2-y-o 7f winner, half-sister to smart performer up to 9f Satin Flower, herself dam of Middle Park winner Lujain: useful performer: won minor events at Salisbury and Newbury (beat Caroline Silk 2 lengths in 3-runner race) in October: seemed to run creditably when ninth of 10 to Ballingarry in Criterium de Saint-Cloud final start, making most: likely to prove better at 1¼m/1½m than shorter: acts on heavy going. *B. J. Meehan* **101**

ANGIE MARINIE 5 b.m. Sabrehill (USA) 120 – Lambast 70 (Relkino 131) [2001 60, a–: 13.1m Aug 24] small mare: winning hurdler: tailed off only 5-y-o start on Flat. *C. J. Price* –

ANGIES QUEST 4 b.f. Inchinor 119 – Chanson d'Avril 54 (Chief Singer 131) [2001 73: e13g² f12g⁶ f12g f8s² f8.5s⁴ Dec 26] fair maiden in 2000: only poor on all-weather at 4 yrs: probably stays 13f: acts on fibresand/equitrack: tried tongue tied. *P. W. D'Arcy* **47**

ANGUS-G 9 br.g. Chief Singer 131 – Horton Line 89 (High Line 125) [2001 69: 10m* 10m² 12m⁴ 10.3f* 10m Jul 21] big, useful-looking gelding: impresses in appearance: good mover: fairly useful handicapper: won at Ayr in June and Doncaster in July: effective at 1¼m/1½m: acts on firm and good to soft going: held up, and tends to idle in front. *Mrs M. Reveley* **82**

ANIKITOS 3 ch.c. Nashwan (USA) 135 – Tamassos 67 (Dance In Time (CAN)) [2001 11s 12g⁵ 12g³ 12g* Jul 18] heavy-bodied colt: half-brother to several winners, notably very smart winner up to 1½m Posidonas (by Slip Anchor) and smart winner up to 1½m Carry The Flag (by Tenby): dam, 1¼m winner, half-sister to high-class 1¼m/1½m **90**

performer Ile de Chypre: fairly useful form: best effort in maidens (possibly needed previous races) when winning at Kempton by length from Faerie Realm, carried left then wandering before getting on top late on: stays 1½m. *Mrs A. J. Perrett*

ANIMAL CRACKER 3 gr.f. Primo Dominie 121 – Child Star (FR) 58 (Bellypha **58** 130) [2001 73: f5g 5.1s 6g 5s⁴ 6m 7s Oct 5] close-coupled, workmanlike filly: fair at 2 yrs: modest form at best in 2001, leaving D. Marks before penultimate start: should be suited by 6f+: acts on good to firm and good to soft going: has been edgy/given trouble at stalls. *Mrs Merrita Jones*

ANIMA MUNDI (IRE) 2 b.f. (Apr 14) Namaqualand (USA) – Dieci Anno (IRE) 72 **79** (Classic Music (USA)) [2001 5d⁶ 5s* 5m⁵ 5m 5g* 5.2m 5s² 6m³ 6m⁴ 7m⁵ Sep 22] IR 1,200F, IR 5,000Y: leggy filly: first foal: dam, Irish 5f winner, half-sister to useful 1998 2-y-o 6f/7f winner Smittenby: fair performer: won maiden at Redcar in May and minor event at Windsor in July: creditable fifth in sales race at Cork final start: stays easy 7f: acts on soft and good to firm ground: reliable: sent to USA. *Mrs P. N. Dutfield*

AN JOLIEN 4 b.f. Aragon 118 – Joli's Girl 79 (Mansingh (USA) 120) [2001 58d: 7m **–** f7g 8m 8.1m Jul 13] little form in 2001: tried blinkered. *M. J. Ryan*

ANKASAMEN 3 b.f. Muhtarram (USA) 125 – Arusha (IRE) 84 (Dance of Life **44** (USA)) [2001 –: 14.1d⁵ 11.5m⁵ May 26] poor maiden: may prove best around 1½m: sent to Kuwait. *M. L. W. Bell*

ANNABELLE 3 ch.f. Most Welcome 131 – Saluti Tutti 77 (Trojan Fen 118) [2001 7g **72** 8.3g⁵ 10d² 8.1s Sep 7] seventh foal: half-sister to winner up to 1m (5f/6f at 2 yrs) Mazeeka (by Glow) and 1m winner F-Zero (by Bin Ajwaad): dam sprint maiden: fair maiden: stays 1¼m: raced only on good going or softer. *C. F. Wall*

ANNADAWI 6 b.g. Sadler's Wells (USA) 132 – Prayers'n Promises (USA) (Foolish **83 d** Pleasure (USA)) [2001 89, a41: f11s 12v 10s⁴ 10s 12.3s⁴ 10.3f 12.3f 8.5m 12m 10.3f **a–** 10d⁴ 11.1d³ 12g 10.3d³ 10v⁶ 11.9s 10s 10d⁶ 10s Nov 5] quite good-topped gelding: fairly useful handicapper on turf at best, poor on all-weather: generally on downgrade in 2001: stays 1½m: acts on good to firm going, heavy and fibresand: tried blinkered/visored/ tongue tied: sometimes slowly away/looks none too keen: sold 6,600 gns. *C. N. Kellett*

ANNATTO (USA) 3 b. or br.f. Mister Baileys 123 – Miss Rossi (Artaius (USA) 129) **52** [2001 84: f8g⁵ 6s⁶ May 2] quite attractive filly: fairly useful maiden at 2 yrs: well below form in 2001, finding little on reappearance and blinkered (very edgy in preliminaries) next time: should stay 1m: acts on firm going, probably on good to soft: has moved short to post: carries head awkwardly: sold 27,000 gns in July, resold 27,000 gns in December. *I. A. Balding*

ANNA WALHAAN (IRE) 2 b.c. (Feb 3) Green Desert (USA) 127 – Queen's Music **103** (USA) 66 (Dixieland Band (USA)) [2001 6.1f* 6m³ 6g⁶ 7d Oct 2] 42,000F, 70,000Y: deep-bodied colt: second foal: dam, Irish 13f winner, half-sister to smart 6f to 8.5f winner Aim For The Top, from good family: useful performer: won maiden at Nottingham in June: best effort when just over a length third to Mister Cosmi in Richmond Stakes at Goodwood: behind in Gimcrack Stakes at York and valuable sales race at Newmarket last 2 starts: bred to stay 7f: acts on firm going, possibly not on good to soft. *M. R. Channon*

ANNE-LISE 3 ch.f. Inchinor 119 – Red Gloves 83 (Red God 128§) [2001 7d 8s 8.3d **53** 8.2g² 10m⁵ 8s 9d Oct 27] lengthy filly: half-sister to several winners, including 6-y-o Peaceful Sarah and fairly useful 6f and 1m winner Takdeer, both by Sharpo: dam, second at 6f/7f at 2 yrs, later won in Norway: modest maiden: stays 1¼m: acts on good to firm ground: looked less than keen fifth start. *D. J. S. Cosgrove*

ANNE'S BIRTHDAY 2 ch. or gr.f. (Mar 25) Emarati (USA) 74 – Kinraddie (Wuzo **55 §** (USA) 99) [2001 5f⁶ 6g⁶ 5s f6g f5g Nov 23] first foal: dam unraced: modest maiden: bred to stay at least 7f: blinkered final start: ungenuine. *M. G. Quinlan*

ANNE-SOPHIE 3 ch.f. First Trump 118 – Hardiprincess (Keen 116) [2001 43: 8.1g⁶ **65** 8m 10.1m* 10m* 11.5m² 10m⁴ 10g⁴ 10.1g⁵ f12g⁴ f9.4g* f9.4g Dec 1] angular filly: modest handicapper: won at Yarmouth and Windsor in June and at Wolverhampton in November: effective at 9.4f to 1½m: acts on fibresand, raced only on good/good to firm going on turf: consistent. *M. L. W. Bell*

ANNETTE VALLON (IRE) 4 b.f. Efisio 120 – Christine Daae 74 (Sadler's Wells **92** (USA) 132) [2001 92: 6g 5m 5.2m² 5.2f 5g⁴ Sep 1] big, strong, lengthy filly: fairly useful handicapper: in frame at Newbury (second to Afaan) and Sandown (fourth to Jessica's Dream) in summer: best at 5f: acts on good to firm and good to soft going. *P. W. Harris*

ANNE TUDOR (IRE)   2 b.f. (Feb 1) Anabaa (USA) 130 – Alikhlas 81 (Lahib (USA)   **77**
129) [2001 5.7g² 6g² Oct 19] IR 25,000F, IR 70,000Y: first foal: dam 1m winner: fair
form with runner-up in maidens at Bath and Redcar, beaten ¾ length by Wish in latter:
will probably stay 7f. *B. W. Hills*

ANNIE APPLE (IRE)   5 ch.m. Petardia 113 – Art Duo 86 (Artaius (USA) 129) [2001   **45**
59: f8g⁶ f8g f7g 7d⁶ 8f⁵ 8m 7s 8.1g f8g⁵ p10g Nov 28] leggy, quite good-topped mare: **a49**
poor nowadays: stays 1m: acts on firm going, soft and fibresand/equitrack: tried visored.
N. Hamilton

ANNIEGETYOURGUN (USA)   3 b.f. Gone West (USA) – Encorelle (FR) (Arctic   **82 ?**
Tern (USA) 126) [2001 8f² 8.1d⁴ Jul 21] sister to very smart German miler Royal Abjar
and useful 7f (at 2 yrs) and 1¼m (in UAE) winner Sunbeam Dance and half-sister to
several winners abroad: dam unraced sister to Prix de Diane winner Escaline: ran 3 times
for E. Harty in USA at 2 yrs: much better effort in maidens in 2001 when second to
Kafezah at Brighton: may prove best short of 1m: acts on firm ground. *E. A. L. Dunlop*

ANNIEGRAM   5 br.m. Petong 126 – Pinkerton's Pet (Dominion 123) [2001 5d 7.1f   **–**
Jun 18] first foal: dam once-raced sister to useful performer up to 9f Pinkerton's Pal: no
show in maiden/claimer at Musselburgh. *A. R. Dicken*

ANNIE RUAN   3 b.f. So Factual (USA) 120 – Sans Diablo (IRE) (Mac's Imp (USA)   **65**
116) [2001 67: f5g⁵ f6g 6m 5.1f 6m² 5g² 5m 5g 6.1d f6g p5g f5s⁴ Dec 15] fair maiden   **a61**
handicapper on turf, modest on all-weather: raced only at 5f/6f: acts on fibresand and firm
going: none too consistent. *D. Haydn Jones*

ANNIE'S SONG   3 b.f. Farfelu 103 – Arasong 76 (Aragon 118) [2001 65: 7v* 8s 6s   **69 d**
7.1g f7g 7v Oct 26] good-topped filly: fair performer: won handicap at Doncaster in
March: well held after, leaving M. Mullineaux and off 5 months before final start: stays
7f: acts on fibresand and heavy going: usually races prominently. *Mrs H. Dalton*

ANNIJAZ   4 b.f. Alhijaz 122 – Figment 75 (Posse (USA) 130) [2001 66: f8g⁴ f9.4g f7g   **67**
e8g⁴ e10g⁴ 7.1v 10g⁶ e10m² 10f 6.9m* 7g³ 7g⁴ 7.6g⁶ 8m 8s³ 6s⁴ p7g f7g* f8g f7s p7g   **a56**
Dec 28] sparely-made filly: fair on turf, modest on all-weather: won handicaps at
Folkestone in June and (having left J. Portman after fourteenth start) Wolverhampton in
December: probably best around 7f: acts on fibresand/equitrack and any turf going: held
up. *J. M. Bradley*

ANNIVERSARY   3 b.f. Salse (USA) 128 – Applecross 117 (Glint of Gold 128) [2001   **101**
12m* 14v³ 12d 16d³ Nov 2] tall, rangy filly: has scope: seventh foal: half-sister to several
winners, including 7-y-o Invermark and 7f (at 2 yrs) to 14.6f winner Craigsteel (by
Suave Dancer), both very smart: dam, 1¼m to 13.3f winner, second in Park Hill: useful
performer: overcame greenness to win maiden at Doncaster in August: blinkered, best
effort when 4 lengths third to Give Notice in listed rated stakes at Newmarket final start,
never far away: will stay beyond 2m: yet to race on firm going, acts on any other: ran
moodily third outing. *H. R. A. Cecil*

ANNIVERSARY GUEST (IRE)   2 b. or br.f. (Apr 20) Desert King (IRE) 129 – Poly-
nesian Goddess (IRE) (Salmon Leap (IRE) 131) [2001 7f 8.1g⁶ 8d Sep 4] IR 60,000Y:
sixth foal: half-sister to fairly useful 1997 2-y-o 6f winner Jay Gee (by Second Set), 1m
winner Sea Squirt (by Fourstars Allstar) and German 11f winner Casito (by Law Society):
dam third at 7f in Ireland: little form in maidens: sold 3,500 gns. *M. R. Channon*

ANNONCE (GER)   4 b.f. Daun (GER) – Alenka (GER) (Akari (GER)) [2001 –: e13g   **–**
f9.4g e12g Mar 7] of little account. *M. G. Quinlan*

ANN'S MILL   4 b.f. Pelder (IRE) 125 – Honey Mill 67 (Milford 119) [2001 48: f12s   **–**
7.6m 7.1d 7.1m 6g 7m Sep 4] leggy filly: no form in 2001: left J. S. Moore after reappearance. *N. E. Berry*

ANOOF   2 b.f. (Mar 19) Marju (IRE) 127 – Waqood (USA) 75 (Riverman (USA) 131)   **75**
[2001 7m⁵ 7s² 8v⁴ Oct 16] third foal: half-sister to 3-y-o Mutawaqed and UAE 6f winner
Rezif (by Machiavellian): dam, maiden who should have stayed 1½m, half-sister to
Lowther Stakes and 1000 Guineas winner Harayir: fair maiden: seemed barely to stay
testing 1m. *M. P. Tregoning*

ANOTHER ASPECT (IRE)   2 b.c. (Apr 16) Inzar (USA) 112 – The Aspecto Girl   **67**
(IRE) 53 (Petong 126) [2001 6.1m⁵ 6m 6.1m 7m 7m 6g³ 7g 7s⁴ 7s 8.2s* 8g 8.3v*
f8g f7g² p7g⁶ Dec 29] 9,000 2-y-o: fourth foal: brother to 3-y-o Cedar Tsar: dam maiden
half-sister to useful 7f to 1¼m performer Canaska Star: fair performer: won sellers at
Nottingham in October and Windsor (final start for M. Channon) in November: needs

good test at 1m and will stay at least 1¼m: acts on fibresand, goes well on soft/heavy going on turf. *J. Cullinan*

ANOTHER DIAMOND (IRE) 3 b.f. First Trump 118 – Rockin' Rosie 59 (Song **60** 132) [2001 55: 7g 7m⁶ 10.1m 10m 9.7m² 14.1m³ 13.1m 16v Oct 17] modest maiden handicapper: seems to stay 1¾m: acts on good to firm going. *P. Howling*

ANOTHER GLIMPSE 3 b.g. Rudimentary (USA) 118 – Running Glimpse (IRE) **–** 84 (Runnett 125) [2001 7m 8m 10g 11.6m Jun 25] strong, close-coupled gelding: third foal: dam, 5f (at 2 yrs)/6f winner, half-sister to smart 1¼m/1½m performer Captain Horatius: never dangerous in maidens/handicap: swished tail continuously in paddock second start. *Miss B. Sanders*

ANOTHER SECRET 3 b.f. Efisio 120 – Secrets of Honour (Belmez (USA) 131) **87** [2001 67: 8.3g 8d² 8f⁴ 9f 7s³ 8d* 10v Nov 8] sturdy filly: fairly useful handicapper: best effort when winning at Leicester in October: stays 1m: acts on soft going. *R. Hannon*

ANOTHER TIME 9 ch.g. Clantime 101 – Another Move 69 (Farm Walk 111) [2001 **83** 91: 10.3m 10m 9f⁶ 10m* 10.2g² 10m⁴ 10.1m³ 10.3m 10.1g⁶ 12m⁶ Sep 8] neat gelding: carries condition: poor mover: fairly useful handicapper: won at Ripon in June: best around 1¼m: acts on any turf going except heavy, well beaten only run on fibresand: held up, and best in truly-run race. *S. P. C. Woods*

ANOTHER VICTIM 7 ch.g. Beveled (USA) – Ragtime Rose (Ragstone 128) [2001 **58 +** 47: 6s 5m 6m² 5g* 5d⁴ 5m 6s 5v² Oct 24] leggy gelding: modest handicapper: won at Windsor in June: best at 5f/6f: acts on heavy and good to firm going: none too consistent. *M. R. Bosley*

ANSAR (IRE) 5 b.g. Kahyasi 130 – Anaza 100 (Darshaan 133) [2001 99: 10v⁵ 18.7f **95** 12g⁴ 12.3f⁵ 14m⁴ 16s Nov 11] sparely-made gelding: useful performer: only respectable efforts in handicaps most starts in 2001, including when eighth of 17 to Rainbow High in Chester Cup (also runner-up in race in 2000) on second start: stays 2¼m: acts on firm and soft going: blinkered (well held) on 4-y-o reappearance: smart and progressive hurdler, won Grade 2 event at Tipperary in October. *D. K. Weld, Ireland*

ANSELLAD (IRE) 4 b.g. Dancing Dissident (USA) 119 – Dutch Queen (Ahonoora **79 d** 122) [2001 86, a77: e6g² f6s e5g* e5g e6g⁴ 5s 5m 5.1f 5.7f Jun 1] leggy gelding: fair performer: won claimer at Lingfield (final start for A. Berry) in January: generally on downgrade afterwards: barely stays easy 6f: acts on firm going and fibresand/equitrack: visored final start: sold 2,400 gns. *Andrew Reid*

ANSELLMAN 11 gr.g. Absalom 128 – Grace Poole (Sallust 134) [2001 66: f5g 5.1d **61** 6g 5m⁶ 5d 5.1g³ 6g⁶ 5.1f³ Jul 26] sturdy gelding: carried condition: had a round action: useful performer at his peak, winner of 11 of his 128 races: only fair at best in final few seasons: was effective at 5f/6f: acted on any turf going and fibresand/equitrack: usually blinkered/visored: reportedly retired. *A. Berry*

ANSTAND 6 b.g. Anshan 119 – Pussy Foot 83 (Red Sunset 120) [2001 55d: e6s⁵ f7g* **71** f7g* e7g² f7g³ f7g* f7g² f7g a8f a6f Dec 13] tall, useful-looking gelding: fair handicapper: won at Southwell (amateurs) in February and Wolverhampton (twice) in March: left M. Saunders before penultimate outing: stays 7f: acts on fibresand, best on good/good to firm ground on turf: tried blinkered. *S. Seemar, UAE*

ANSWERED PROMISE (FR) 2 gr.g. (Feb 20) Highest Honor (FR) 124 – Answered **70 p** Prayer (Green Desert (USA) 127) [2001 7g 8.2s⁵ Nov 5] strong, short-backed gelding: second foal: half-brother to French 1m/10.5f winner Grateful Thanks (by Bering): dam, ran once in France, out of Oaks winner Jet Ski Lady: better effort in maidens (fair form) when fifth to Star Cross at Nottingham, held up and never on terms: should stay at least 1¼m: capable of better. *E. A. L. Dunlop*

ANTHONY MON AMOUR (USA) 6 b.g. Nicholas (USA) 111 – Reine de La Ciel **68** (USA) (Conquistador Cielo (USA)) [2001 78: 5v 6g 5m 5.3m³ 5f² 5g 5m 5m 5g⁶ 5g* 6m 5g 5d 5m 5s Sep 27] big, strong gelding: fair handicapper: won at Newcastle in July: best at 5f/6f: acts on fibresand, soft and firm going: tongue tied: has been slowly away: usually races prominently. *D. Nicholls*

ANTHONY ROYLE 3 ch.g. King's Signet (USA) 110 – La Thuile 46 (Statoblest **37** 120) [2001 –: f8.5g f6g f6g⁴ f6g³ f6g 7.1d f5g⁵ f5g 8m 7.5f 7.1f 6f 5m f6g⁵ 5g f6s Dec 15] **a49** sparely-made gelding: poor maiden: possibly best around 6f: acts on fibresand, firm and good to soft going: tried blinkered. *A. Berry*

ANTICIPATE 3 ch.c. Nashwan (USA) 135 – De Stael (USA) 93 (Nijinsky (CAN) **96** 138) [2001 8.1d³ 9.9m² 10g³ 11.9g² 11.7m* Sep 10] rangy, rather unfurnished colt: brother to 2 winners, notably very smart 9f to 1½m winner in Britain and USA Wandesta, closely related to very smart French 1½m winner De Quest and useful middle-distance stayer Source of Light (both by Rainbow Quest) and half-brother to 2 winners: dam, 2-y-o 6f winner, sister to Coronation Cup winner Quiet Fling: useful performer: best effort when winning maiden at Bath in September by 7 lengths from Lithgow Flash: will stay 1¾m: yet to race on extremes of going: sold 60,000 gns. *R. Charlton*

ANTICLES (FR) 4 ch.g. Barathea (IRE) 127 – Alexandra Fair (USA) 104 (Green **86** Dancer (USA) 132) [2001 99: 12v 8d 10.4g 10d³ 10.5d 11d² 12d⁴ 12.5v Oct 25] tall, good-topped gelding: fairly useful at 4 yrs: left I. Williams after fifth outing: stays 12.5f: acts on good to soft ground: visored fourth start. *R. Chotard, France*

ANTIPODES (USA) 3 gr.f. Pleasant Colony (USA) – La Grande Epoque (USA) 120 **76** (Lyphard (USA) 132) [2001 –: 8s³ 8.3d 9.9m⁴ 10m 10m Sep 10] angular filly: fair maiden: takes good hold, and may prove best around 1m: acts on soft and good to firm going: sent to USA. *J. L. Dunlop*

ANTONIA'S DILEMMA 3 ch.f. Primo Dominie 121 – Antonia's Folly 64 (Music **–** Boy 124) [2001 72: 5.1f 5f 5g 5g 5g Oct 6] fair winner at 2 yrs: disappointing in 2001: raced only at 5f: acts on firm ground: blinkered once. *A. Berry*

ANTONIO CANOVA 5 ch.g. Komaite (USA) – Joan's Venture (Beldale Flutter **99** (USA) 130) [2001 85: 6m* 6f⁴ 6g* 6m* 6m⁴ Sep 22] stocky gelding: useful handicapper, quite lightly raced: progressed again in 2001, winning at Kempton in May and New-market and Ripon (William Hill Great St Wilfrid Stakes, landed gamble in beating Banjo Bay ½ length, quickening well final 1f after runner-up got first run) in August: good fourth to Continent in Ayr Gold Cup final start: best at 5f/6f: acts on firm and good to soft going: genuine and reliable. *Bob Jones*

ANTONIO MARIANO (SWE) 10 b.g. Mango Express 106 – Mango Sampaquita **–** (SWE) (Colombian Friend (USA)) [2001 12m Jun 12] no form in 4 starts on Flat: fair handicap chaser. *Lady Herries*

ANTONY EBENEEZER 2 ch.c. (Apr 10) Hurricane Sky (AUS) – Captivating **51** (IRE) 63 (Wolfhound (USA) 126) [2001 6m 6.1m 7m 7s⁵ 7s f5g³ f5s⁴ p6g Dec 19] leggy, useful-looking colt: first foal: dam, maiden at 2 yrs, later had poor form up to 17f: modest maiden: stays 7f: acts on soft going, good to firm and fibresand: carried head awkwardly final start. *I. A. Wood*

ANYHOW (IRE) 4 b.f. Distant Relative 128 – Fast Chick 93 (Henbit (USA) 130) **68** [2001 75, a67: f7g f9.4s⁶ f8g f6g 6m⁴ 7m 7m⁶ 8.3m⁵ 9f* 8m 10v 8d Oct 15] angular filly: **a54** fair handicapper on turf, modest on all-weather: won at Lingfield in June: stays easy 9.4f: acts on fibresand and firm going, possibly not on softer than good: sometimes wanders: sold 2,000 gns. *Andrew Reid*

William Hill Great St Wilfrid Stakes (Handicap), Ripon—
a big gamble is landed as Antonio Canova quickens well to beat Banjo Bay (far rail);
Abbajabba (No.13), Jarn (centre), the grey Night Flight and Nineacres (far rail) are next home

ANYWHICHWAY 2 b.f. (Feb 10) Bijou d'Inde 127 – Risk The Witch (Risk Me (FR) **52** 127) [2001 6m 6.9m 6m 6s f6g 8.2s f8.5g p6g Nov 15] 3,000F: smallish, leggy filly: third **a43** foal: half-sister to a winner in Greece by Most Welcome: dam, of little account, half-sister to useful sprinter Cantoris: modest maiden on turf, poor on all-weather: stays 7f: acts on good to firm going and fibresand. *C. E. Brittain*

ANZILLERO (GER) 4 b.c. Law Society (USA) 130 – Anzille (GER) (Plugged **120** Nickle (USA)) [2001 107: 10.5s² 12v⁴ 11m³ 11g³ 12g* 12d 12s 10d Nov 18] approx. 12,500Y in Germany: quite attractive colt: fourth foal: half-brother to 3 winners in Germany, including 9f to 11f winner All Blade (by Sure Blade): dam, French maiden, half-sister to 2000 Guineas winner King's Best, Arc winner Urban Sea (dam of Galileo), and to dam of Prix du Jockey Club winner Anabaa Blue: very smart performer: won maiden and listed race at Cologne early at 3 yrs: improved form to win WGZ Bank-Deutschland Preis at Dusseldorf in July by 1¼ lengths from Sabiango: well beaten final 3 starts, in Prix de l'Arc de Triomphe at Longchamp (prominent long way) on penultimate one: stays 1½m: acts on heavy and good to firm ground. *D. Richardson, Germany*

A ONE (IRE) 2 b.g. (Apr 22) Alzao (USA) 117 – Anita's Contessa (IRE) 68 (Anita's **72** Prince 126) [2001 5.1d⁶ 6m³ 6g² 6.1m⁴ 6.1g⁵ 7d⁵ 7s Oct 20] IR 24,000Y: rather leggy gelding: first foal: dam, 6f/7f winner, sister to useful sprinter Carranita: fair maiden: creditable efforts most starts (gelded after final one): barely stays 7f: acts on good to soft going, probably on good to firm. *B. Palling*

APACHE POINT (IRE) 4 ch.g. Indian Ridge 123 – Ausherra (USA) 106 (Diesis **62** 133) [2001 –: 7s* 8.5m⁴ 8f 8f⁶ 8m 9.1d³ 8.5g 8m 8.1g⁵ 8f⁶ 8d² 8d⁵ Oct 30] rather leggy, unfurnished gelding: modest performer: won seller at Redcar in May: stays 9f: yet to race on heavy going, acts on any other: refused to go to start second intended outing: races freely. *N. Tinkler*

APADI (USA) 5 ch.g. Diesis 133 – Ixtapa (USA) (Chief's Crown (USA)) [2001 –: f8g **53** 12g 15.8m Sep 22] one-time fairly useful 5.5f winner: modest nowadays: left K.Bell after reappearance: seems to stay 2m. *M. C. Chapman*

APHELION 3 b.c. Superlative 118 – Starchy Cove 61 (Starch Reduced 112) [2001 **–** 7.1g f6g 7g Aug 12] fourth foal: dam 5f (at 2 yrs)/6f winner: well held in maidens/seller. *N. M. Babbage*

APOLLO RED 12 ch.g. Dominion 123 – Woolpack (Golden Fleece (USA) 133) [2001 –, a82: e6g e8g² e8g f6g⁶ e7g f6g⁴ 7d May 16] sturdy gelding: veteran performer, **a43** poor in 2001 (reportedly lame behind on reappearance): best at 7f/easy 1m: acts on firm going, good to soft and equitrack: visored earlier in career: usually races up with pace. *G. L. Moore*

APORTO 3 ch.g. Clantime 101 – Portvally (Import 127) [2001 53: f7g f8g 6.1v⁶ 8d⁵ **52** 8m 8m³ 7.5m⁵ 8f 7.5f 8m 8m⁴ 12g 9.9g 8m⁶ 10s Sep 24] rather leggy gelding: modest **a–** performer: probably stays 1¼m: possibly unsuited by firm going, seems to act on any other turf (no show on fibresand): often slowly away: usually held up. *D. W. Barker*

APPELLATION 3 b.c. Clantime 101 – Chablisse 69 (Radetzky 123) [2001 94p: 6d **86** 6g⁶ 6f² 7m 7m Dec 16] lengthy, rather unfurnished colt: fairly useful performer: best effort at 3 yrs when second to Night Haven in minor event at Leicester: left W. Jarvis before final outing (renamed Naughty Naughty): stays 6f, seemingly not 7f: yet to race on heavy ground, acts on any other. *P. W. Chapple-Hyam, Hong Kong*

APPIAN WAY 3 b.g. Shareef Dancer (USA) 135 – Ambassadress (USA) (Alleged **78** (USA) 138) [2001 7v³ 7s⁵ Apr 16] compact, attractive gelding: first foal: dam unraced half-sister to smart French sprinters La Grande Epoque and Crack Regiment: best effort in maidens when ¾-length third to Amicable at Doncaster: not sure to stay beyond 7f: sold 5,500 gns in July, sent to Malaysia. *J. Noseda*

APPLEACRE 2 b.f. (Apr 19) Polar Falcon (USA) 126 – Absaloute Service 96 **51** (Absalom 128) [2001 6.1v 7v Oct 26] strong, useful-looking filly: half-sister to several winners, including 3-y-o Serviceable and 1m and 9.4f winner Benjamins Law (by Mtoto): dam 2-y-o 5f winner: modest form in maidens at Nottingham and Doncaster (still green, unseated rider to post). *J. M. P. Eustace*

APPLE ZED 3 b.f. Catrail (USA) 123 – Mrs Croesus (USA) (Key To The Mint **51** (USA)) [2001 7.5m⁴ 6.9m² 8.3g 6m 7g 7.1g f8g² p6g Dec 19] half-sister to 4-y-o Lydia's Look and a winner in USA by Little Missouri: dam once-raced half-sister to very smart 1¼m performer Tamayaz: modest maiden: stays 1m: acts on fibresand and good to firm going. *G. C. Bravery*

APPROACHABLE (USA) 6 b. or br.g. Known Fact (USA) 135 – Western Approach – (USA) 115 (Gone West (USA)) [2001 –, a54: f12g⁴ f8g³ f9.4g³ f11g⁴ f11g⁶ 10.1m f11g⁶ **a57** 10m 8g f11g* f12g f12g² f11g² f11g f11g Dec 17] leggy gelding: modest handicapper: won claimer at Southwell in October: stays easy 1½m: acts on fibresand/equitrack, no form on turf: tried blinkered/visored early in career: often takes strong hold: has shown temperament. *K. A. Morgan*

APPROVAL 2 b.c. (Apr 24) Royal Applause 124 – Gentle Persuasion 95 (Bustino **95** 136) [2001 6m* 6m² 6g⁵ Sep 7] tall, lengthy colt: has plenty of scope: half-brother to several winners, including smart 5f (including at 2 yrs) to 7f winner Sharp Prod (by Sharpo), fairly useful 6f/7f winner Gracious Gift (by Cadeaux Genereux) and 1¼m winner Punkah (by Lear Fan): dam, 2-y-o 6f winner, stayed 1m: useful form: won maiden at Salisbury in July: neck second to Kulachi at Newbury, better effort in listed races after: not sure to stay beyond 6f: carried head high final start. *R. Hannon*

APRIL ACE 5 ch.g. First Trump 118 – Champ d'Avril 89 (Northfields (USA)) [2001 – –: 10f 8.1g Jul 6] big, lengthy gelding: modest handicapper at 3 yrs: little form since: tried visored. *R. J. Baker*

APRIL LEE 3 b.f. Superpower 113 – Petitesse 55 (Petong 126) [2001 70: f8g³ e7g⁶ **68** f8g⁵ f7g³ f7g 7.1g² f7g 7f² 7m³ 7m 8.1f 7m⁵ 7g 7f⁵ Aug 29] fair performer: best around 7f: acts on fibresand (possibly not on equitrack) and firm going, probably on soft: blinkered/visored after fifth start: usually races prominently: possibly none too resolute. *K. McAuliffe*

APRIL LOUISE 5 b.m. Meqdaam (USA) – California Dreamin (Slip Anchor 136) – [2001 9.9m Aug 26] first live foal: dam, no sign of ability, closely related to useful middle-distance stayer Misbelief: 16/1, well held in maiden at Beverley. *T. Wall*

APRIL'S COMAIT 4 br.f. Komaite (USA) – Sweet Caroline 62 (Squill (USA) 122) – § [2001 46§: 9.7m 7d Aug 26] workmanlike filly: temperamental maiden: sometimes blinkered. *T. T. Clement*

APRIL STAR 4 ch.f. Deploy 131 – Cabaret Artiste (Shareef Dancer (USA) 135) [2001 – –: 11.5g p12g Nov 13] lengthy filly: little form. *B. A. Pearce*

APRIL STOCK 6 ch.m. Beveled (USA) – Stockline (Capricorn Line 111) [2001 80: **95** 12s³ 11.7d* 12v* 13.9m 10d³ 12s p12g Nov 24] leggy mare: useful handicapper: better than ever in 2001: won at Bath (runner-up eased prematurely) and Newbury (beat Inching Closer 4 lengths) in May: off 4 months before good length third to Golden Wells at Ascot in October, twice short of room: only twelfth when joint-favourite for November Handicap next outing: effective at 1¼m (given good test), probably at 2m: raced mainly on good going or softer (well held on good to firm): often tongue tied. *G. A. Butler*

AQABA 2 b.f. (May 4) Lake Coniston (IRE) 131 – Sahara Breeze 85 (Ela-Mana-Mou **65** 132) [2001 6.1v² 6d Oct 12] leggy filly: seventh foal: half-sister to 3 winners, including 6-y-o Alcazar and French 1m (including Prix Marcel Boussac) winner Lady of Chad (by Last Tycoon), both smart: dam, maiden who stayed 1m, half-sister to Fillies' Mile winner Ivanka: better effort in maidens (fair form) when second to Foursome at Nottingham: should stay 1m. *S. Kirk*

AQUAE SULIS 2 ch.f. (Jan 23) Greensmith 121 – Stealthy 73 (Kind of Hush 118) – [2001 5s 6.1v 6v Oct 26] 4,500Y: good-bodied filly: sixth foal: half-sister to 4-y-o Stealthy Times and a 5f (at 2 yrs) to 7.5f winner in Italy by Presidium: dam 1m winner: little form in maidens/sales race. *W. M. Brisbourne*

AQUARELLISTE (FR) 3 b.f. Danehill (USA) 126 – Agathe (USA) 114 (Manila **123** (USA)) [2001 10s* 10g* 10.5m* 12m* 12s² Oct 7]

Daniel Wildenstein's death at the age of eighty-four in October marked the passing of one of the most successful owner-breeders of modern times. His horses won more than eighty Group 1 races or their equivalent from 1968 onwards and at least sixteen of the winners were rated 130 or above in *Racehorses*, a phenomenal achievement. The runners concerned, in order of merit, were: Peintre Celebre (137), Allez France (136), Sagace (135), All Along (134), Crow (134), Buckskin (133), Lianga (133), Pistolet Bleu (133), Flying Water (132), Broadway Dancer (131), Epervier Bleu (131), Pawneese (131), Faraway Son (130), Gravelines (130), Paulista (130) and Yelapa (130). Most of the best races in Europe fell to Wildenstein horses, the pick of them four Prix de l'Arc de Triomphes (Allez France, All Along, Sagace and Peintre Celebre—Sagace was also disqualified from first in the race), a

King George VI & Queen Elizabeth Stakes with Pawneese, British classics with Flying Water, Crow and Pawneese again, ten French classics, the Breeders' Cup Classic with Arcangues and the Breeders' Cup Mile with Steinlen. The final horse to join this select group was Aquarelliste, who developed into one of the best two middle-distance fillies in France and chased home Sakhee in the Prix de l'Arc de Triomphe. Unraced at two, Aquarelliste started her career in a nine-runner newcomers event at Longchamp in April, winning readily by three lengths. She added to her gains with a smooth success from four opponents in a listed race at Chantilly in May, by which time, along with forty-one other Wildenstein horses, she had changed stables from Andre Fabre to Elie Lellouche. Wildenstein's reputation, almost notoriety, for hiring and firing made good newspaper copy but has been exaggerated somewhat. True, trainers Peter Walwyn and Henry Cecil and jockeys Pat Eddery and Lester Piggott preceded Fabre, with whom the owner's son Alec said there had been 'a deterioration in communication', but five major disagreements in the space of thirty-three years hardly justifies some of the barbs aimed at Wildenstein. Significantly, he had horses in training with Cecil in the latest season, notably Rolly Polly, and Fabre had trained for him since 1987, Lellouche since 1990. This suggests rather more stability than some of the obituaries allowed. Wildenstein's racing interests were by no means confined to the Flat and his successes in other branches of the sport were covered in the essay on his top-class chaser Kotkijet in *Chasers & Hurdlers 2000/01*.

With two simple tasks successfully negotiated, Aquarelliste faced her first major test in the Prix de Diane Hermes at Chantilly again in June. Her eleven rivals were headed by five pattern winners, including British challenger Time Away, successful in the Musidora Stakes, the Prix Saint-Alary winner Nadia, and Spring Oak, who had won the Prix Cleopatre. For all her lack of experience and lack of top form Aquarelliste started a short-priced favourite and gave her supporters not a moment's worry. Held up on the rail, she made good ground round the field on the home turn and quickened impressively to cut down Nadia in the final furlong and go clear to win by a length and a half. Time Away was three quarters of a length away third. It is commonplace for French-trained fillies with pretensions to winning the Prix de l'Arc de Triomphe to be put away after the Diane and brought back in the Prix Vermeille at Longchamp in September. A summer break seems to work very well but, in some respects, it is a case of necessity being the mother of invention, since there are no Group 1 events restricted to fillies in France in late-July or August and only the Prix de Pomone, which is over nearly a mile and three quarters, among Group 2 events. Contesting the Irish Oaks or the open-aged Nassau Stakes and Yorkshire Oaks would be feasible but, for reasons best known to themselves, most French trainers seem reluctant to try their luck in Britain or Ireland nowadays.

Prix de Diane Hermes, Chantilly—
Aquarelliste quickens to beat front-running Nadia (left), with Time Away (black sash) third

Prix Vermeille - Hermitage Barriere, Longchamp—
Aquarelliste is confidently ridden and maintains her unbeaten record;
the grey Diamilina battles back well, with Mare Nostrum (right) and Mot Juste next

Prix de Diane winners Daryaba in 1999 and Egyptband in 2000, plus the runner-up to the latter, Volvoreta, all went straight to the Vermeille, and so did Aquarelliste, who started a short-priced favourite in a field of twelve. Second in the market was Diamilina, winner of the Prix de Malleret and Prix de la Nonette, ahead of Irish Oaks runner-up Mot Juste and Prix de Diane fifth Mare Nostrum. The remainder, including Oaks d'Italia winner Zanzibar and Inchiri from Britain and Karsavina and Lime Gardens from Ireland, started at over 20/1. Under a confident ride, Aquarelliste travelled strongly throughout, moved through easily to join Diamilina entering the closing stages and did not have to be hard ridden to get the better of the issue by a short neck. Mare Nostrum was two and a half lengths away third. This was an encouraging display so far as the Arc was concerned. The Arc took place over the course and distance three weeks later and Aquarelliste went off second favourite to Sakhee. The ground was soft, compared with good to firm for the Vermeille, but Aquarelliste had won on such a surface on her debut and it posed no problems for her. Sakhee did pose problems, however; he was in a different league as he stormed away up the straight. Aquarelliste, though, ran a fine race to be beaten six lengths into second despite not enjoying an entirely smooth passage, getting bumped a couple of times early on and finding herself poorly placed in relation to the winner when he hit top pace off the home turn. Aquarelliste was merely plugging on in the last fifty yards and cannot be regarded as in any way unlucky.

Immediately after the Prix de Diane, and again after the Vermeille, Alec Wildenstein claimed Aquarelliste was 'another Allez France'. She's a good performer without doubt, but the French, indeed European, middle-distance fillies were far from outstanding as a group and, on her form so far, Aquarelliste cannot hold a candle to her illustrious predecessor, who had to compete against another exceptional filly in Dahlia. The winner of thirteen of her twenty-one starts including Group 1 races in four successive seasons, Allez France was rated 126 at two, 132 at three, 136 at four and 132 at five in *Racehorses*. Like Aquarelliste, she finished second in the Prix de l'Arc de Triomphe after winning the Prix de Diane and Prix Vermeille in her classic campaign, but finishing two and a half lengths behind Rheingold was better form than finishing six lengths behind Sakhee. Aquarelliste has the chance to improve her already fine record as she stays in training, running in the name of Ecurie Wildenstein. As a big, strong, albeit rather plain filly, and a good walker, she looks the type to train on and have a say in the top races, especially at a mile and a half, over which trip her redoubtable turn of foot will always stand her in good stead. Whether she'll be capable of winning the Arc is a different matter entirely, though.

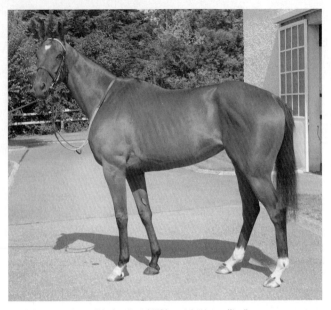

Exors of the late Daniel Wildenstein's "Aquarelliste"

Aquarelliste (FR) (b.f. 1998)	Danehill (USA) (b 1986)	Danzig (b 1977)	Northern Dancer
			Pas de Nom
		Razyana (b 1981)	His Majesty
			Spring Adieu
	Agathe (USA) (ch 1991)	Manila (b 1983)	Lyphard
			Dona Ysidra
		Albertine (b 1981)	Irish River
			Almyre

Judged by the record of her sire Danehill, Aquarelliste was no certainty to be suited by a mile and a half. Danehill does, however, get winners over all sorts of distances and there is no shortage of stamina on the dam's side. Agathe, another fairly plain-looking individual, was a smart filly who managed only two wins in three seasons, highlighted by the Prix de Psyche, but was placed in numerous pattern events, including when second in the Poule d'Essai des Pouliches and third in the Prix de Diane. Although never tried at a mile and a half, the way Agathe raced suggested the trip might have suited her since she wasn't blessed with abundant pace. Her dam Albertine showed smart form at up to a mile and a quarter and also foaled Arcangues, successful in the Prix d'Ispahan as well as the Breeders' Cup Classic, and the dam of One Thousand Guineas winner Cape Verdi. Albertine was a half-sister to high-class middle-distance stayer Ashmore and smart middle-distance filly Acoma, dam of a Group 2 winner from a family that served Wildenstein well. Agathe has produced one other winner, the Nashwan colt Aigle Royal, successful in a small race over a mile and a half at Maisons-Laffitte. In 1999 she foaled a filly by Sillery named Arme Ancienne, followed by a Nashwan colt called American Mystery. She was returned to Danehill in 2001. *E. Lellouche, France*

AQUARIUS (IRE)   3 b.g. Royal Academy (USA) 130 – Rafha 123 (Kris 135) [2001   **110**
77p: 11.1s* 12g⁴ 13.9m² 16.2m³ 15g⁴ 15d⁵ 15d⁶ Sep 9] smallish, angular gelding: smart
performer: won maiden at Kempton in April: in frame next 4 starts, including when close
third to And Beyond in Queen's Vase at Royal Ascot (best effort, weaved through late)
and fourth (dead-heated for second but demoted having hung right) to Roman Saddle in
Prix Berteux at Vichy: visored, below form in listed race at Deauville and Prix de Lutece
at Longchamp last 2 outings: stays 2m: acts on soft and good to firm ground: usually held
up. *J. L. Dunlop*

AQUILINE   3 ch.g. Sanglamore (USA) 126 – Fantasy Flyer (USA) (Lear Fan (USA)   **–**
130) [2001 10.4m⁶ Sep 2] 13,500 3-y-o: second foal: brother to 4-y-o Fantasy Park: dam
unraced daughter of Irish 1000 Guineas and Irish Oaks winner Godetia: 25/1, never
nearer in maiden at York. *John A. Harris*

ARAB GOLD   6 b.g. Presidium 124 – Parklands Belle 73 (Stanford 121§) [2001 45:   **–**
p7g f6s Dec 26] tall, leggy gelding: well held in 2001: sometimes blinkered/visored.
J. S. Moore

ARABIAN GOGGLES   2 ch.f. (Mar 14) Cosmonaut – Jarrettelle (All Systems Go   **–**
119) [2001 7m 8d 6v Oct 26] 2,000Y: fifth foal: half-sister to ungenuine 1998 2-y-o 5f
winner Yorkshire Grit (by Ardkinglass): dam unraced: little sign of ability in maidens.
H. S. Howe

ARABIAN MOON (IRE)   5 ch.h. Barathea (IRE) 127 – Excellent Alibi (USA)   **92**
(Exceller (USA) 129) [2001 98: e12g⁵ 12s 14m⁶ 13.3m² 16.1f 14.4m⁴ 13.3m⁴ Jul 21]   **a84**
leggy, quite good-topped horse: easy mover: fairly useful handicapper: short-head second
to Inching Closer at Newbury in June: barely stays 2m: acts on equitrack, best turf efforts
on good going or firmer: held up, and sometimes finds little. *S. Dow*

ARABIAN WATERS   3 b.f. Muhtarram (USA) 125 – Secret Waters 100 (Pharly (FR)   **60**
130) [2001 49: 8.3s⁵ 10g 11.8g⁵ 14.1s f12g⁶ Sep 22] fifth foal: half-sister to smart 1¼m
winner Gargalhada Final (by Sabrehill): dam 12.5f to 1¾m winner, half-sister to smart
dam of Tenby: modest maiden handicapper: probably stays 1½m: acts on soft ground.
R. F. Johnson Houghton

ARABIE   3 b.c. Polish Precedent (USA) 131 – Always Friendly 111 (High Line 125)   **103**
[2001 10d 10s⁴ 12m² 10g* 12f³ 10g⁶ 10.1d* Aug 26] lengthy, angular colt: second foal:
closely related to useful Italian 1m winner Dane Friendly (by Danehill): dam won Princess Royal Stakes and second in Prix Royal-Oak: useful performer: won handicap at
Windsor in June and minor event at Yarmouth (by 4 lengths from Blue Sugar) in August:
creditable efforts in between in handicaps at Royal Ascot (King George V Stakes, third to
Beekeeper) and Newmarket (sixth to Alphaeus): likely to prove best at 1¼m: acts on firm
and good to soft ground. *H. R. A. Cecil*

ARABIN   2 b.c. (Feb 25) Bin Ajwaad (IRE) 119 – Just Julia (Natroun (FR) 128) [2001   **58**
7f 7.1f Sep 18] leggy, quite good-topped colt: fifth foal: half-brother to fairly useful 1996
2-y-o 5f/6f winner Just Visiting (by Superlative): dam no worthwhile form: modest form
in maidens at Newbury and Chepstow, slowly away and tending to hang left both times.
K. O. Cunningham-Brown

ARACHINE   2 ch.g. (May 16) Indian Ridge 123 – Hill Hopper (IRE) 106 (Danehill   **– p**
(USA) 126) [2001 7s f7g⁵ 7d Nov 6] 22,000Y: third foal: half-brother to 3-y-o Sea Vixen
and 4-y-o Rainbow Hill: dam, 6f/7f (Criterion Stakes) winner, half-sister to smart
middle-distance performer Water Boatman: signs of ability, not knocked about, in
maidens: gelded after final start: free-going sort, not sure to stay beyond 7f: capable of
better. *Sir Mark Prescott*

ARAF   2 b.g. (Mar 2) Millkom 124 – Euphyllia 70 (Superpower 113) [2001 f7g f8g Nov   **–**
16] 1,800Y: second foal: dam 7f winner: well beaten in seller/claimer. *A. G. Newcombe*

ARAGANT (FR)   5 b. or br.g. Aragon 118 – Soolaimon (IRE) 71 (Shareef Dancer   **41**
(USA) 135) [2001 37: 10m⁶ 10d⁵ 10f 8m⁴ 7m Jul 23] poor maiden nowadays: stays 1¼m:
acts on good to firm and good to soft going: tried blinkered. *R. J. Hodges*

ARAGLIN   2 b.c. (Mar 8) Sadler's Wells (USA) 132 – River Cara (USA) 86 (Irish   **79**
River (FR) 131) [2001 7f 8d² 8s² 8s³ 7s⁴ f9.4g* f8.5s⁴ f8.5s Dec 27] useful-looking colt:
first foal: dam, French 2-y-o 1m winner, granddaughter of Musidora winner Fatah Flare:
fair performer: left J. Gosden 22,000 gns after fourth start: won maiden at Wolverhampton in November: poor efforts after: stays 9.4f: acts on fibresand and soft going:
blinkered fourth, fifth and final outings: sometimes looks ungenuine. *Miss S. J. Wilton*

Foster's Lager Northumberland Plate (Handicap), Newcastle—
Archduke Ferdinand holds off the strong challenge of Cover Up, providing trainer Paul Cole
with his third success in the race in five years

ARAJAMBO   2 b.f. (Feb 25) Aragon 118 – Jambo 68 (Rambo Dancer (CAN) 107)   **39**
[2001 f5g 6m⁴ 7.1f 6m 7d f7g Nov 17] 1,000Y: second foal: dam 7f (at 2 yrs) to 8.5f
winner: poor maiden: probably stays 7f: sent to Denmark. *J. R. Weymes*

ARANA   6 b.m. Noble Patriarch 115 – Pod's Daughter (IRE) 43 (Tender King 123)   **–**
[2001 –: 14.1m 8.2s 8.3v Nov 8] of no account. *W. de Best-Turner*

ARANUI (IRE)   4 b.g. Pursuit of Love 124 – Petite Rosanna 89 (Ile de Bourbon (USA)   **–**
133) [2001 ?: 9m 8d 9m Jul 1] poor maiden: was usually tongue tied: dead. *J. Gallagher*

ARAVONIAN   3 ch.f. Night Shift (USA) – Age of Reality (USA) 63 (Alleged (USA)   **82**
138) [2001 78: 8.3s 8.1g* 10g⁶ 8.3d³ 7g 8.1m² 8g 8.3m² 8.5g⁵ 8.2s Oct 30] fairly useful
performer: won maiden at Warwick in May: stays 1m: acts on soft and good to firm going:
often front runner: none too consistent. *R. Hannon*

ARAWAK PRINCE (IRE)   5 ch.g. College Chapel 122 – Alpine Symphony (North-   **59**
ern Dancer) [2001 –: e13s³ f16g f12g⁴ 8d⁵ 10m 14.1m f14.8g Nov 17] lengthy gelding:
formerly fairly useful, just modest nowadays: left D. Bridgwater after third start:
probably best at 1¼m/1½m: acts on equitrack, raced mainly on ground softer than good
on turf: tried blinkered/visored: has found little/flashed tail. *G. Prodromou*

ARBENIG (IRE)   6 b.m. Anita's Prince 126 – Out On Her Own (Superlative 118)   **60**
[2001 56: 10g² 10f³ 11.6g² 10.9m 10.3f 10g f12g Nov 23] neat mare: modest performer: **a–**
barely stays 11.5f: acts on firm going, soft and fibresand: often blinkered earlier in career:
races up with pace: none too consistent. *B. Palling*

ARBIE (CAN)   2 b.g. (Mar 28) Mountain Cat (USA) – Empress of Love (USA)   **59 p**
(Czaravich (USA)) [2001 5.2m 7m 8d Oct 3] $32,000F, $15,000Y, resold 24,000Y: strong
gelding: half-brother to several winners in USA, including sprinter by Black Tie Affair
and winner around 1m by Quiet American: dam, 6f and 1m winner in USA, second in
Grade 3 8.5f event at 5 yrs: modest form in maidens: short of room and considerably
handled final start: gelded afterwards: should stay beyond 1m: should do better. *C. F. Wall*

ARC EL CIEL (ARG)   3 b.c. Fitzcarraldo (ARG) – Ardoise (USA) (Diamond Pro-   **65**
spect (USA) 126) [2001 7m³ 7.1m⁴ 8.2d Sep 21] fifth foal: half-brother to winners in
Argentina by Lode and Mat-Boy: dam ran 3 times in USA: best effort in maidens when
third at Salisbury: bred to stay 1m (though raced too freely when tried final start).
B. R. Millman

ARC EN CIEL   3 b.g. Rainbow Quest (USA) 134 – Nadia Nerina (CAN) 82 (Northern   **80**
Dancer) [2001 72: 10.2d² 11.6d⁴ 11.4g 11.5m³ 12m* 11.7g* 13.1d 12g Sep 15] useful-

looking gelding: fairly useful handicapper: won at Thirsk in July and Bath in August: stays 1½m: acts on firm and good to soft going: visored (raced freely/found nothing) third start: sold 40,000 gns. *J. L. Dunlop*

ARCHDUKE FERDINAND (FR) 3 ch.g. Dernier Empereur (USA) 125 – Lady **111** Norcliffe (USA) (Norcliffe (CAN)) [2001 96: 10s³ 12.3f⁶ 13.9m³ 16.2m 16.1f* 13.9g 18d Oct 20] strong, close-coupled gelding: smart performer: sometimes quite highly tried on occasions (seventh in Queen's Vase at Royal Ascot) before successful handicap debut in Foster's Lager Northumberland Plate at Newcastle in June, getting first run to beat Cover Up by neck: raced too freely in Ebor and Cesarewitch last 2 starts: gelded afterwards: stays 2m: acts on firm and soft going: has worn crossed/dropped noseband. *P. F. I. Cole*

ARCHELLO (IRE) 7 b.m. Archway (IRE) 115 – Golden Room (African Sky 124) – [2001 61d: 5f f7g Jul 13] robust mare: well beaten in 2001: tried visored. *D. W. Barker*

ARCHER FOR FOUR (USA) 2 b. or br.g. (May 8) Royal Academy (USA) 130 – – Depelchin (USA) (Star de Naskra (USA)) [2001 6d 6g 5s Sep 7] $32,000F: strong gelding: fifth foal: half-brother to sprint winners in USA (including at 2 yrs) by Chromite and Creole Dancer: dam unraced: little form in maidens. *N. Tinkler*

ARCHIE BABE (IRE) 5 ch.g. Archway (IRE) 115 – Frensham Manor (Le Johnstan **71 §** 123) [2001 86§: 13s 12s 12.3f 14m 14g 10m⁵ 11.1d² 12.3m³ 10d⁵ Aug 8] workmanlike gelding: fair handicapper nowadays: effective at 1¼m/1½m: below form on firm going, acts on any other: unreliable. *J. J. Quinn*

ARCHIRONDEL 3 b.g. Bin Ajwaad (IRE) 119 – Penang Rose (NZ) (Kingdom Bay **60** (NZ)) [2001 –: 8.1v 10g* 10.9f⁶ 9f⁴ 10m* 9.7m* Jul 30] smallish gelding: modest handicapper: won at Redcar in June then Brighton (idled) and Folkestone in July, travelling strongly each time: effective at 9f/1¼m: acts on firm ground, possibly not on softer than good: genuine. *John Berry*

ARCHON (IRE) 4 ch.g. Archway (IRE) 115 – Lindas Delight 54 (Batshoof 122) **63** [2001 8d³ 8m 10m³ 12g p13g Dec 29] IR 10,000Y, IR 2,200 2-y-o: strong gelding: first foal: half-brother to 3-y-o Fromsong: dam 6f seller winner at 2 yrs (only season to race): modest maiden: seems to stay 13f: acts on polytrack: tongue tied first 4 starts. *Mrs P. N. Dutfield*

ARC (IRE) 7 b.g. Archway (IRE) 115 – Columbian Sand (IRE) (Salmon Leap (USA) **81** 131) [2001 77: f8.5s⁶ f8g f8.5g³ f8.5g² f8g⁵ f9.4g* f9.4g 8s 8m* 8m³ 8m 8m 9g* 10.3g 10g Oct 6] tall gelding: fairly useful performer: won handicap at Wolverhampton in March, minor event at Musselburgh in June and handicap at Newcastle in August: best at 1m to easy 1¼m: acts on heavy and good to firm going and fibresand: tried blinkered early in career. *G. M. Moore*

ARCTIC FALCON (IRE) 2 b.f. (Apr 18) Polar Falcon (USA) 126 – Chandni (IRE) **73** (Ahonoora 122) [2001 6g⁴ 5g⁴ 6.1g 6d Oct 18] rather angular filly: fifth foal: half-sister to fairly useful Irish 9f and 1½m winner Chanoud (by Ezzoud): dam, of no account, sister to smart 1m/1¼m performer Visto Si Stampi: fair performer: landed odds in maiden at Lingfield in August: respectable effort on second of 2 starts in nurseries after: will probably stay 7f. *R. Hannon*

ARCTIC FANCY (USA) 8 ch.g. Arctic Tern (USA) 126 – Fit And Fancy (USA) – (Vaguely Noble 140) [2001 f12f Mar 19] big, good-topped gelding: fairly useful handicapper at best: well beaten only Flat start since 6 yrs: sold 35,000 gns. *J. G. Smyth-Osbourne*

ARCTIC FLIGHT 3 ch.f. Polar Falcon (USA) 126 – Laugharne (Known Fact (USA) **71** 135) [2001 8.3g 8m 8.3g 7s⁵ 7m* Sep 11] 7,500Y: ninth foal: half-sister to several winners, including useful sprinter Power Lake (by Formidable) and fairly useful 6f winner who stayed 7f Lough Erne (by Never So Bold): dam ran once: fair performer: best effort when winning handicap at Leicester in September: should stay 1m. *P. W. Harris*

ARCTIC HIGH 4 b.f. Polar Falcon (USA) 126 – Oublier L'Ennui (FR) 79 (Bellman – (FR) 123) [2001 49, a62: f9.4s³ f8.5g³ f9.4g⁵ f8.5g⁵ f9.4g 6v f8.5f* Dec 5] modest on **a60** all-weather: left M. Saunders after fifth start: won maiden at Wolverhampton in December: effective at 1m/9f: acts on fibresand: has hung right: none too consistent. *I. A. Wood*

ARDANZA (IRE) 4 b.f. Hernando (FR) 127 – Arrastra 79 (Bustino 136) [2001 70: f8g f12g 7g 10.5s⁶ 12m Aug 29] fair maiden in 2000: no form in 2001, leaving Miss J. Feilden after third start: reportedly bled from nose once. *T. Stack, Ireland*

ARDENT 7 b.g. Aragon 118 – Forest of Arden (Tap On Wood 130) [2001 52: e10g⁴ 8f **39** 9m p10g Dec 29] well-made gelding: poor handicapper: best at 1m/1¼m: acts on equitrack, firm and good to soft going: blinkered once as 4-y-o: sometimes looks moody. *Miss B. Sanders*

ARDGOWAN 4 b.g. Ardkinglass 114 – Final Fling 49 (Last Tycoon 131) [2001 12v **37** 12g 16g 12m⁴ 9.2d 10.9d 9.2d Aug 15] leggy, lengthy gelding: first foal: dam, maiden who should have stayed beyond 1m, also second over hurdles: poor maiden: should stay 1¾m: visored fourth start. *Denys Smith*

ARELLA RABBIT 5 b.m. Presidium 124 – Musical Star 54 (Music Boy 124) [2001 f6g f6s⁶ f6g Feb 16] first foal: dam, maiden (form only at 6f), closely related to smart performer up to 1¼m Stella Grande: no form in maidens/claimer. *A. Smith*

ARETINO (IRE) 4 ch.g. Common Grounds 118 – Inonder 31 (Belfort (FR) 89) [2001 **89** 82: 6m 6m 7f² 7m² 7f* 7m³ 7m³ 7g⁵ Sep 5] strong, useful-looking gelding: fairly useful handicapper: won at Epsom in July: effective at 6f/7f: acts on firm and soft going: usually front runner. *P. W. Harris*

ARGAMIA (GER) 5 b.m. Orfano (GER) – Arkona (GER) 108 (Aspros (GER)) **63** [2001 f11g² f12g² f12g* e16g 14.1v⁴ f11g³ 14.1s* 16s³ 13.9m⁵ f14g 14.1d⁵ 16m f14.8g* 14v³ 11.9s⁵ 16v⁴ 12d f12s Dec 21] tall, angular mare: first foal: dam German 10.5f/11f (Preis der Diana) winner: modest performer: trained by H. Blume in Germany at 4 yrs: won handicaps at Wolverhampton (amateurs) and Nottingham in February/April and minor event at Wolverhampton in September: stays 2m: acts on fibresand, heavy and good to firm going: blinkered last 3 starts at 4 yrs: usually held up. *M. G. Quinlan*

ARGENT FACILE (IRE) 4 b.g. Midhish 109 – Rosinish (IRE) (Lomond (USA) **93 §** 128) [2001 94§: 6s 6g⁶ 5m⁴ 6m 6g* 6m 5m⁵ Jul 6] lengthy, quite attractive gelding: fairly useful performer: won minor event at Windsor in June: effective at 5f/easy 6f: acts on soft and good to firm going: well held only try in blinkers: has worn tongue strap: tends to carry head high/hang, and isn't a straightforward ride. *D. J. S. Cosgrove*

ARGOSTOLI 2 b.f. (Feb 17) Marju (IRE) 127 – Barque Bleue (USA) (Steinlen 127) **–** [2001 6m⁶ 8s⁴ 7g Oct 19] 11,000F, 22,000Y: smallish filly: second foal: dam unraced half-sister to very smart French performer up to 1m Bon Vent: well held in maidens/claimer. *P. C. Haslam*

ARGUE 2 b.c. (Jan 18) College Chapel 122 – Cache (Bustino 136) [2001 7g 7d f7g⁵ **55** Oct 22] 12,000F, 22,000Y: big, good-topped colt: has scope: fifth foal: half-brother to fairly useful 1½m and 14.7f winner Swan Hunter (by Sharrood) and 5-y-o Lunar Lord: dam lightly-raced close relative of useful middle-distance performer Black Monday: modest maiden: raced only in sellers: should stay 1m: sold 2,500 gns. *N. A. Callaghan*

ARHAAFF (IRE) 3 b.f. Danehill (USA) 126 – Mosaique Bleue (Shirley Heights 130) **101 +** [2001 75p: 7d² 8g⁶ 9.9m² 10.5m 8m* 10.2m⁴ Jul 27] lengthy, quite attractive filly: useful performer: landed odds in maiden at Newcastle in July: highly tried previous 3 starts, 7 lengths sixth to Ameerat in 1000 Guineas at Newmarket, head second to Foodbroker Fancy in listed race at Goodwood and 4½ lengths seventh (probably flattered) to Aquarelliste in Prix de Diane at Chantilly: not discredited when fourth to Sauterne in listed race at Chepstow final start, tending to hang in behind winner: seemed to stay 10.5f: acted on good to firm going: had gone right/left leaving stall: visits Unbridled's Song. *M. R. Channon*

ARIALA 4 b.f. Arazi (USA) 135 – Kashtala 102 (Lord Gayle (USA) 124) [2001 60?: **32** 14d 10s 9s⁴ 11.6g⁶ 11.9g Aug 9] small filly: poor maiden: left K. Burke before penultimate start: seems to stay 11.6f: yet to race on going firmer than good. *G. L. Moore*

ARISTAEUS 3 b.g. Mistertopogigo (IRE) 118 – Zealous (Hard Fought 125) [2001 –: **–** f7g f9.4s e10g 8.1v 9.9m 8f⁶ 7f Jun 5] little form: visored last 4 starts. *Mrs Lydia Pearce*

ARIZONA (IRE) 3 b.c. Sadler's Wells (USA) 132 – Marie de Beaujeu (FR) 108 **–** (Kenmare (FR) 125) [2001 8.2v 7.5m 10g⁶ 15.8g Aug 17] IR 36,000Y: strong colt: half-brother to several winners, notably smart German Derby winner All My Dreams (by Assert): dam, French 2-y-o 5.5f/6.5f winner, didn't train on: no form. *S. Gollings*

ARIZONA LADY 4 ch.f. Lion Cavern (USA) 117 – Unfuwaanah 74 (Unfuwain **65** (USA) 131) [2001 77+: f9.4s 12d 9.2m⁴ 10m 9.2m⁴ 9m 9f 9.9m 11.1g³ 8.5g 8.3m f12g⁵ f12g Nov 3] sturdy filly: fair handicapper: stays easy 11f: acts on firm going, good to soft and fibresand: blinkered once: none too consistent. *I. Semple*

ARJAY 3 b.g. Shaamit (IRE) 127 – Jenny's Call (Petong 126) [2001 84: 8v 10.5m⁶ **87** 10m⁶ 8m⁵ 9g⁴ 7.9m⁴ 7.2m* 7d Oct 13] tall, rather leggy gelding: fairly useful handicapper: best effort when winning at Ayr in September despite wandering: effective at 7f to 9f: yet to race on firm going, acts on any other. *Andrew Turnell*

ARJAYPEAR (IRE) 2 b.g. (Mar 30) Petardia 113 – Lila Pedigo (IRE) 62 (Classic **45** Secret (USA) 91) [2001 5s 5m f6g² 6g 6g Aug 8] IR 10,000Y: first foal: dam 6f (at 2 yrs) and 1¼m winner: poor maiden: left K. Ryan after third start: should stay 7f: acts on fibresand. *W. R. Muir*

ARKADIAN HERO (USA) 6 ch.h. Trempolino (USA) 135 – Careless Kitten **119** (USA) (Caro 133) [2001 123: 8.9g⁵ 8s⁶ 8m³ 7.3f 8g² Aug 28] strong, rangy, full-quartered horse: had a fluent action: very smart performer at best: won 3 pattern races, namely Mill Reef Stakes at Newbury at 2 yrs and Criterion Stakes at Newmarket and Hungerford Stakes at Newbury in 2000: placed in 2001 in Queen Anne Stakes at Royal Ascot (1¼ lengths third to Medicean) and Prix Quincey at Deauville (¾-length second to Ing Ing): showed similar form from 6f to 1m: raced mainly on good going or firmer: sometimes flashed tail/got on edge/was slowly away: often blanketed for stall entry: to stand at Longholes Stud, Newmarket, fee £3,000, Oct 1st. *L. M. Cumani*

ARKATME 3 b.g. Then Again 126 – Watheeqah (USA) 60 (Topsider (USA)) [2001 **62** f7g⁴ f7g⁶ f6g⁵ f5g⁵ f6g² 6d May 7] 6,200Y: good-topped gelding: second foal: dam 5f winner: modest maiden: best effort at 6f: acts on fibresand: sold 750 gns in October. *T. D. Barron*

ARMAGNAC 3 b.g. Young Ern 120 – Arianna Aldini (Habitat 134) [2001 85: 6d **96** 6.1f³ 6m⁶ 6m 6d² 6m* 6g⁴ 6g⁴ 6s 6m 6d⁶ Oct 13] tall, good-topped gelding: unimpressive mover: useful handicapper: won at Ripon in June: generally creditable efforts otherwise, notably when short-head second to Orientor in William Hill Trophy at York in June: raced only at 6f at 3 yrs, should be as effective back at 5f: acts on firm and soft going: has pulled hard. *M. A. Buckley*

ARMEN (FR) 4 b.g. Kaldoun (FR) 122 – Anna Edes (FR) (Fabulous Dancer (USA) **–** 124) [2001 81: 17.2f May 22] useful winner over hurdles: well held only run on Flat in 2001. *M. C. Pipe*

ARMENIA (IRE) 4 ch.f. Arazi (USA) 135 – Atlantic Flyer (USA) 98 (Storm Bird **–** (CAN) 134) [2001 61, a67d: f11g Jan 12] smallish filly: fair performer at best: well held only 4-y-o start. *A. G. Newcombe*

ARMIDA 3 b.f. Lycius (USA) 124 – Ma Petite Cherie (USA) 93 (Caro 133) [2001 –: **38** 12v⁴ 10s 7m 8f⁵ 10.1m 8m⁵ 10m⁵ Jun 29] strong, close-coupled filly: poor maiden: looks headstrong, and better form around 1m than further: form only on good going or firmer: blinkered last 2 starts: tongue tied last 5: sold 3,200 gns in July. *G. G. Margarson*

ARMS ACROSSTHESEA 2 b.g. (Mar 22) Namaqualand (USA) – Zolica 60 **63** (Beveled (USA)) [2001 5.1s 5m³ 6m* 6g³ 7.1f⁴ 7m⁴ f7g³ 7.5s⁵ 7m f6g Oct 9] 500Y: leggy gelding: third foal: half-brother to 1998 2-y-o 6f winner Claranna (by Local Suitor): dam ran twice at 2 yrs: modest performer: won claimer at Newcastle in May: ran creditably in nurseries next 4 starts: will stay at least 1m: acts on good to firm ground and fibresand: visored (below form) eighth/ninth appearances. *R. A. Fahey*

ARNBI DANCER 2 b.g. (May 21) Presidium 124 – Travel Myth 66§ (Bairn (USA) **51** 126) [2001 5f 5m 6m Aug 18] 1,500F, 3,800Y: good-topped gelding: has scope: sixth foal: brother to 1997 2-y-o 5f winner Lasham: dam, ungenuine maiden, stayed 1¼m: modest maiden: likely to prove best at 5f/6f: wandered final start. *P. C. Haslam*

ARNISTON LOVER 3 ch.g. Tigani 120 – Chelwood (Kala Shikari 125) [2001 6f 6m **–** Sep 8] 500Y: first foal: dam well beaten in maidens. *B. Ellison*

AROGANT PRINCE 4 ch.g. Aragon 118 – Versaillesprincess (Legend of France **59** (USA) 124) [2001 59: e5g e5g e5g⁶ e6g 5.3s⁵ 5v³ 5m 5m 5m³ 5.3f² 7m⁴ 7m 5m 6m 6m³ 7m 5m f5s* f5s Dec 27] smallish gelding: modest handicapper: left J. Bridger after ninth start and B. Hills prior to winning at Wolverhampton in December: best at 5f/6f: acts on any turf going and fibresand/equitrack: blinkered (well held) once. *I. Semple*

ARONA (IRE) 3 b.f. Spectrum (IRE) 126 – Divine Valse (FR) (Groom Dancer (USA) **–** 128) [2001 47: 12m 14.1m 11.1m⁶ Jun 13] angular filly: unimpressive mover: poor maiden: stays 7f: blinkered final start. *J. G. Given*

ARPEGGIO 6 b.g. Polar Falcon (USA) 126 – Hilly 96 (Town Crier 119) [2001 82: **86** f8g⁵ f7g* f7s⁵ f7s f8g 9v f7g⁶ f8g² 10m⁶ 8m⁶ 8g* 8s³ 8.1g 8.9d 8d³ Oct 18] **a81** good-topped gelding: has a quick action: fairly useful handicapper: won at Southwell in January and Newmarket in July: good effort final start: probably best at 7f/1m: acts on soft and good to firm going and fibresand: blinkered (below form) once: sometimes slowly away/looks less than keen. *D. Nicholls*

ARPELLO 4 b.f. Unfuwain (USA) 131 – Arpero 107 (Persian Bold 123) [2001 f9.4s⁵ **60** f12g* f11g* f14g² Feb 23] modest handicapper: won at Wolverhampton then Southwell in February: barely stays 1¾m: acts on fibresand: has idled/flicked tail. *Sir Mark Prescott*

ARRAN MIST 3 b.f. Alhijaz 122 – Saraswati 55 (Mansingh (USA) 120) [2001 55: **48** 6m 6m 6g f6g 5g 5g⁵ 5s² 5g 6d⁵ f6g Nov 16] angular filly: poor maiden: effective at 5f/6f: acts on soft and good to firm going, some promise first of 2 starts on fibresand. *D. W. Barker*

ARRIBILO (GER) 7 b.g. Top Ville 129 – Arborea (GER) (Priamos (GER) 123) [2001 **74 d** e12g⁶ 8s 10.3f 12m 11.5f⁴ 8d⁶ 10.1g⁶ 10g 12g 16g 10.9m Sep 17] quite good-topped ex-German gelding: winner of 5 starts in Germany, including handicap at Hanover in September 2000 on final outing for H. Horwart: fair form in Britain in 2001 only early on: best form at 1¼m/1½m: acts on heavy and good to firm ground: has been blinkered, not in Britain: has been very slowly away/looked none too keen. *G. M. McCourt*

ARRIVE 3 b.f. Kahyasi 130 – Kerali 88 (High Line 125) [2001 9.9s* 11.6g² 12m* **109** 14.8g* 13.5s Aug 5] rather leggy, quite attractive filly: sister to French 1993 2-y-o 5f to 8.5f winner Hasili (dam of high-class French miler Dansili and 3-y-o Banks Hill) and half-sister to several winners, including fairly useful 7f winner Sharp Tempo (by Sharpo) and 6f (at 2 yrs) to 1m (in France) winner Zerali (by Alzao): dam, 7f winner, half-sister to very smart sprinter So Factual: useful performer: won maiden in May and handicap in June, both at Salisbury, and listed race at Newmarket in July, beating Fair Question 4 lengths in last-named, easing into lead 2f out: disappointing in Prix de Pomone at Deauville final start, already looking beaten when squeezed out: stayed 15f: had won on soft ground, best efforts on good/good to firm: retired. *R. Charlton*

ART EXPERT (FR) 3 b.g. Pursuit of Love 124 – Celtic Wing (Midyan (USA) 124) **62** [2001 70: 8.2v f8g⁵ 10.9m⁵ 10g³ 10g⁵ 12.6f³ 18m⁵ 16g⁵ 10m⁵ f14g² f12g⁶ f14.8g f12g⁴ f14g Dec 14] sturdy, attractive gelding: modest maiden handicapper: left P. Cole after seventh start: stays 2¼m: acts on fibresand and any turf going: sometimes blinkered/visored: carries head high. *Mrs N. Macauley*

ARTFUL DANE (IRE) 9 b.g. Danehill (USA) 126 – Art Age (Artaius (USA) 129) **48 §** [2001 66§, a57§: 8.1m 8m⁶ 8.1m 8.1s 8m⁵ 8.1g Sep 13] good-quartered gelding: poor nowadays: best around 1m: acts on firm going, soft and equitrack: usually blinkered/visored: tries to dominate: unreliable. *C. G. Cox*

ARTHURS KINGDOM (IRE) 5 b.g. Roi Danzig (USA) – Merrie Moment (IRE) **–** (Taufan (USA) 119) [2001 62: 14m⁵ 16.2f Jul 7] tall, angular gelding: maiden handicapper: well held both 5-y-o starts: sometimes visored. *Miss Kate Milligan*

ARTHUR SYMONS 3 b.g. River Falls 113 – Anchor Inn 48 (Be My Guest (USA) **–** 126) [2001 5g 8.3g 6f f11g Oct 1] fifth foal: half-brother to 6f/7f winner Bargash (by Sharpo) and 4-y-o Mister McGoldrick: dam, 1¼m winner, from good family: well beaten in maidens/claimer: bolted before start second outing. *J. M. Jefferson*

ARTIE 2 b.g. (Mar 31) Whittingham (IRE) 104 – Calamanco 71 (Clantime 101) [2001 **83 p** 5v² 5.1f* 5f² 6d Sep 14] 3,000Y, resold 8,000Y: big, good-topped gelding: has scope: third foal: half-brother to 3-y-o Kingscross: dam, 5f winner, sister to useful sprinter Cape Merino: fairly useful form: won maiden at Chester (reportedly jarred muscle, off 4 months after) in May: heavily backed, beaten head in nursery at Musselburgh next time: poorly drawn final start: likely to prove best at 5f/6f: acts on any ground: looks type to do better at 3 yrs. *T. D. Easterby*

ARTIFACT 3 b.f. So Factual (USA) 120 – Ancient Secret (Warrshan (USA) 117) **–** [2001 f7g² f6g* f6s* f7g⁶ 8d 10g 8.1s 6.1d 8s f7g⁵ f9.4g⁶ f8g⁴ f8.5g³ f8.5g* f9.4g³ **a72** f8.5g f8g⁶ Dec 10] tall, lengthy filly: fair handicapper: won at Southwell and Wolverhampton in January and at latter track in November: stays 9.4f: acts on fibresand, no form on turf in 2001: has idled: held up. *J. A. Pickering*

ARTIFICE 3 b.f. Green Desert (USA) 127 – Reuval 102 (Sharpen Up 127) [2001 7m³ **80** 7m² 8m² 6m² 6m* 6m⁴ 6g Oct 5] sister to smart 7f/1m performer Ardkinglass and useful 7f winner Darnaway and half-sister to useful 1¼m winners Jura (by Rousillon), Pitcroy (by Unfuwain) and Kinlochewe (by Old Vic): dam best at 1m: fairly useful performer: won maiden at Thirsk in September: ran well in handicap next time: effective at 6f to 1m: raced mainly on good to firm going. *J. R. Fanshawe*

Melrose Rated Stakes (Handicap), York—Artillery (near side) makes up plenty of ground to deny Ovambo, with Harlestone Grey (centre) a close third

ARTILLERY (IRE)   3 b.c. Darshaan 133 – Alimana 74 (Akarad (FR) 130) [2001   **109 p**
10.2f³ 11.8m* 16.2m 13.9m* 14.1m³ Sep 6] 220,000F: rangy, quite attractive colt: sixth
foal: half-brother to several winners, including Irish 11f winner Alonsa (by Trempolino)
and 8.5f winner Ahliyat (by Irish River): dam, 2-y-o 9f winner on only start, half-sister
to disqualified Oaks winner Aliysa (by Darshaan): smart form: successful in maiden at
Leicester (tended to hang right) in June and Melrose Rated Stakes at York (by neck from
Ovambo, despite poor run through) in August: raced freely and well held in Queen's Vase
at Royal Ascot in between, and probably unsuited by false pace when only third to Hatha
Anna in minor event at Salisbury final start: should stay beyond 1¾m: raced only on
going firmer than good: joined Godolphin: type to go on again at 4 yrs. *Sir Michael Stoute*

ARTISTS RETREAT   2 ch.f. (Apr 10) Halling (USA) 133 – Jumairah Sunset 67 (Be   **63**
My Guest (USA) 126) [2001 5g 6m⁴ 6g 6.5g Sep 28] 14,500Y: tall, leggy filly: second
foal: dam, 7f winner, closely related to smart 1m/9f performer Fanaar: modest maiden:
should stay 1m: best effort on good to firm going. *D. J. S. ffrench Davis*

ARZAMAS   2 b.f. (Mar 25) Cadeaux Genereux 131 – Belle Argentine (FR) 113 (Fijar   **74 p**
Tango (FR) 127) [2001 6g² Jul 23] second foal: half-sister to 3-y-o Saaryeh: dam, French
1m winner (including at 2 yrs) and in frame in Poule d'Essai des Pouliches and Prix de
Diane, out of half-sister to top-class French middle-distance performer Lovely Dancer:
10/1, length second of 14 to Lady Lindsay in maiden at Warwick, always close up but
edging left: probably capable of better. *M. P. Tregoning*

ARZILLO   5 b.g. Forzando 122 – Titania's Dance (IRE) 61 (Fairy King (USA)) [2001   **–**
61?, a58: f7s⁴ f6s⁶ e7g 8.1s 7m Aug 30] small gelding: poor maiden handicapper: stays   **a44**
7f: acts on firm going and fibresand/equitrack, well beaten on softer than good: blinkered
twice at 4 yrs: has been slowly away/tended to hang. *J. M. Bradley*

ASAREER (USA)   3 b.f. Gone West (USA) – Leo's Lucky Lady (USA) (Seattle Slew   **60**
(USA)) [2001 71p: 10m 8g⁵ Jun 25] big, good-topped filly: fair form in Doncaster maiden
only 2-y-o start: below that level both runs in 2001: best efforts at 1m: visits Aljabr.
M. P. Tregoning

ASCARI   5 br.g. Presidium 124 – Ping Pong 65 (Petong 126) [2001 68: p10g³ Dec 22]   **60**
strong gelding: modest handicapper: effective at 1m/1¼m: acts on firm going, good to
soft and polytrack (some promise on fibresand): visored/blinkered once each: sometimes
races too freely. *W. Jarvis*

Mr Norman Cheng's "Ascension"

ASCENSION (IRE) 3 ch.f. Night Shift (USA) – Outeniqua (Bold Lad (IRE) 133) **110**
[2001 105: 8s* Aug 5] strong, well-made filly: has a quick action: smart performer: best
effort to win Prix d'Astarte at Deauville in August on only outing at 3 yrs by neck from
Just Special, leading well inside final 1f: should stay bit beyond 1m: acts on any going.
M. R. Channon

ASEELAH 2 b.f. (Mar 27) Nashwan (USA) 135 – Mawhiba (USA) 63 (Dayjur (USA) **72 p**
137) [2001 7g 8.2s³ Nov 5] first foal: dam once-raced half-sister to Derby winner Erhaab:
better effort in maidens (fair form) when third to Star Cross at Nottingham: will stay at
least 1¼m: probably capable of better. *J. L. Dunlop*

AS GOOD AS IT GETS 3 b.f. Alhijaz 122 – Iota 83 (Niniski (USA) 125) [2001 –: **–**
10s 9.9m 15.8m f12g f11s Dec 21] sparely-made filly: little form. *C. Smith*

ASH 3 b.f. Salse (USA) 128 – Thundercloud 70 (Electric 126) [2001 –p: 7d 7g 16.2m **–**
14.1d 12f Aug 29] close-coupled, useful-looking filly: well held in maidens/handicaps:
bred to be suited by 1¼m+: tried blinkered. *L. M. Cumani*

ASHAKA (IRE) 3 b.f. Mujtahid (USA) 118 – Ashkara (IRE) (Chief Singer 131) **67**
[2001 8f5 8.3g* 10m Aug 27] useful-looking filly: scratchy mover: second foal: half-
sister to French 8.5f winner Ashara (by Kahyasi): dam unraced half-sister to high-class
French miler Ashkalani out of half-sister to Prix du Cadran winner Shafaraz: easy winner
of maiden at Hamilton in July: favourite, well held in handicap next time: should stay
beyond 1m: sold 3,000 gns in December. *Sir Michael Stoute*

ASHANTIANA 2 ch.f. (May 8) Ashkalani (IRE) 128 – Fast Chick 93 (Henbit (USA) **55**
130) [2001 6g 8s4 f7g5 Oct 23] 6,500 2-y-o: half-sister to several winners, including smart

84

6f (at 2 yrs) and 1m winner Missile (by Rock City), later winner in Hong Kong, and 3-y-o Fast Foil: dam 9f to 1½m winner: modest maiden: will stay 1¼m: slowly away first 2 starts: sold 9,000 gns. *E. L. James*

ASHA'TH 2 b.c. (Mar 16) Barathea (IRE) 127 – Elrayahin 76 (Riverman (USA) 131) **83** [2001 7m 7g³ 7m² 8.1g 7s⁴ Oct 3] small, sturdy colt: first foal: dam, 2-y-o maiden who stayed 1m, out of half-sister to Dayjur: fairly useful maiden: short-headed by Fashionable Man at Newcastle: disappointing both subsequent outings: seems barely to stay 7f: acts on good to firm going: races prominently: sent to UAE. *M. P. Tregoning*

ASHDOWN EXPRESS (IRE) 2 ch.c. (Feb 4) Ashkalani (IRE) 128 – Indian **100** Express 61 (Indian Ridge 123) [2001 6.1f³ 7m* 7.5m* 8m² 8s 8d* Nov 2] IR 33,000F, IR 50,000Y: lengthy colt: third foal: half-brother to a winner around 1m in Germany by College Chapel: dam, 8.5f and 1¼m winner, sister to useful 6f/7f performer Cheyenne Spirit: useful performer: won maiden at Newcastle and minor event at Beverley in July and minor event at Newmarket (beat First Charter by ½ length) in November: has raced freely, and not sure to stay beyond 1m: acts on good to firm and good to soft ground: tends to wander. *S. P. C. Woods*

ASHEER 2 b.c. (Apr 13) Inchinor 119 – Shoshone (Be My Chief (USA) 122) [2001 **105** 5m³ 6d² 7g² 7.1g³ 8s⁴ Sep 29] 30,000F, 105,000Y: big, strong colt: has plenty of scope: second foal: dam, maiden who shaped like a stayer, half-sister to very smart 7f to 1¼m performer Lockton out of half-sister to high-class stayer Crash Course: useful performer: won maiden at Lingfield in July: best efforts when second to Comfy in listed race at York and fourth to Mutinyonthebounty in Royal Lodge Stakes at Ascot: should stay 1¼m: acts on soft going: tail swisher. *J. W. Payne*

ASHGAR SAYYAD (USA) 2 b.c. (Feb 3) Kingmambo (USA) 125 – Quelle Affaire **89** (USA) (Riverman (USA) 131) [2001 6s³ 6m² 7f³ 7m⁴ 7d⁴ Oct 2] 60,000Y: rather leggy, close-coupled colt: third foal: half-brother to winning 1999 2-y-o 5f winner Ma Yoram (by Dayjur): dam, French maiden, sister to smart 7f/1m performer Rami and half-sister to smart French sprinters Crack Regiment and La Grande Epoque: fairly useful maiden: in frame all starts: good fourth of 16 to Sir George Turner in valuable sales race at Newmarket final start: will probably stay 1m: acts on firm and soft ground. *M. R. Channon*

ASH HAB (USA) 3 b.c. A P Indy (USA) 131 – Histoire (FR) (Riverman (USA) 131) **71** [2001 63: 11.6s 14.1m 16m* 16.2f³ 12d 12d 8.5d Aug 5] rather leggy, slightly dipped-backed colt: fair performer: won 22-runner maiden handicap at Thirsk in June: left J. Dunlop 23,000 gns after next start: stays 2m: acts on firm ground: blinkered third, fourth and final outings. *Luke Comer, Ireland*

ASHKALANI STAR (IRE) 2 ch.g. (Apr 12) Ashkalani (IRE) 128 – Atacama **75** (Green Desert (USA) 127) [2001 5s 5m⁵ f7g* p7g Nov 13] IR 15,000Y: strong gelding: fifth foal: half-brother to useful 1997 2-y-o 6f winner Surveyor (by Lycius) and 1999 2-y-o 7f winner Tumbleweed Inca (by Ezzoud): dam unraced granddaughter of Oaks third The Dancer: fair performer: off 4 months, won maiden at Wolverhampton in October by 1¾ lengths from Chandler's Secret: seemed unsuited by track at Lingfield next time: will stay 1m: acts on fibresand: tongue tied. *M. Johnston*

ASHKELON 2 ch.c. (Feb 6) Ashkalani (IRE) 128 – Subtle Blush 60 (Nashwan (USA) **86 p** 135) [2001 7m* 7s Sep 24] 20,000Y: fourth living foal: dam, third at 1m from 3 starts, half-sister to high-class 7f to 9f performer Indian Lodge and very smart French middle-distance performer Sarhoob: overcame greenness (gave some trouble in stall) to win maiden at Salisbury in August by neck from Snow Leopard, leading final 1f despite edging right: seemed ill at ease on soft ground only start after: will stay 1m: likely to make a useful 3-y-o. *Mrs A. J. Perrett*

ASHLEIGH BAKER (IRE) 6 b. or br.m. Don't Forget Me 127 – Gayla Orchestra **61** (Lord Gayle (USA) 124) [2001 55: 14m⁶ 16.1f 14v 10v² 10.1v² 10g Nov 5] leggy, angular mare: modest handicapper: effective at 1¼m (given good test) to easy 2m: has won on good to firm going but best 6-y-o efforts on heavy, well held both starts on fibresand: twice blinkered in 1998: usually races prominently. *A. Bailey*

ASHLINN (IRE) 3 ch.f. Ashkalani (IRE) 128 – Always Far (USA) (Alydar (USA)) **86** [2001 82: 7d⁶ 8g 8m⁶ 7m³ 8f 7g 7.6d⁵ 7g 9.7g⁵ 7g² 7d 8s³ Oct 25] sturdy filly: has a quick action: fairly useful performer: stays 1m: acts on firm and soft going: usually blinkered/visored in 2001: has worn near-side pricker: usually races prominently. *R. Hannon*

ASH MOON (IRE) 3 ch.f. General Monash (USA) 107 – Jarmar Moon (Unfuwain **91** (USA) 131) [2001 92: 7d 6m 6d⁵ 6m a6g 7d² 7.1v 7g 6d 7s p10g² p10g Nov 24] lengthy, leggy filly: fairly useful performer: effective at 6f to easy 1¼m: acts on soft going, good to firm and polytrack/dirt: blinkered once: has been on toes/free to post: races prominently: inconsistent: sold 18,000 gns. *K. R. Burke*

ASHNAYA (FR)   3 b.f. Ashkalani (IRE) 128 – Upend 120 (Main Reef 126) [2001 –p: 10s⁴ 12g⁶ 14m 14.1s 16.2s⁵ 16g 16d² 16v* 17.1d 18s Oct 22] lengthy filly: fair handicapper: won at Nottingham in October: stays 2m: acts on heavy going: blinkered last 5 starts: sold 10,000 gns. *J. L. Dunlop*   **79**

ASHTON VALE   2 ch.c. (Jan 22) Ashkalani (IRE) 128 – My Valentina 84 (Royal Academy (USA) 130) [2001 p10g⁵ Dec 4] first foal: dam, 2-y-o 7f winner who stayed 1¼m, half-sister to smart sprinter Averti: 12/1, 10¾ lengths fifth to Playapart in maiden at Lingfield, taking good hold and leading briefly 2f out: should improve. *R. Hannon*   **65 p**

ASHTORETH (IRE)   2 ch.f. (Mar 15) Ashkalani (IRE) 128 – Sally Chase 101 (Sallust 134) [2001 6v p6g Dec 28] 17,000F: good-bodied filly: half-sister to several winners, notably smart 7f/1m winner Unanimous Vote (by Roi Danzig) and useful 1m/1¼m winner Super Sally (by Superlative): dam 2-y-o 5f/6f winner: better effort in maidens (modest form) when seventh at Lingfield on second outing. *Mrs A. J. Perrett*   **53**

ASHTREE BELLE   2 b.f. (Mar 15) Up And At 'em 109 – Paris Babe 94 (Teenoso (USA) 135) [2001 6m⁴ 5d³ f6g⁴ f6g* f6g⁵ p6g³ Dec 28] first foal: dam 6f winner: fair performer: won maiden at Wolverhampton (then left J. Smyth-Osbourne) in October: good third to Madame Maxine in nursery at Lingfield final start: likely to stay 7f: acts on fibresand/polytrack, good to firm and good to soft ground. *D. Haydn Jones*   **70**

ASHVILLE LAD   4 b.c. Bigstone (IRE) 126 – Hooray Lady 92 (Ahonoora 122) [2001 –: f6s⁴ f6g² f7g² f8g 8.1g 8.2f² 10g⁴ Jun 16] strong colt: modest maiden handicapper: stays 1¼m: acts on fibresand and firm going: usually blinkered/tongue tied. *B. A. McMahon*   **60**

Mr M. J. Dawson's "Askham"

ASIAN HEIGHTS 3 b.c. Hernando (FR) 127 – Miss Rinjani 83 (Shirley Heights 130) **119**
[2001 91p: 10v² 11m* May 22] useful-looking colt: has a quick action: half-brother to
4-y-o St Expedit: progressive form: won listed race at Goodwood in May by 1¾ lengths
from Wareed, missing break quite badly and running a little in snatches but finishing in
good style: ¾-length second to Chancellor in Classic Trial at Sandown on reappearance:
reportedly split a pastern on June 1 during final workout for Derby (was operated on and
had 2 screws inserted): will be suited by 1½m+: yet to race on firm going, acts on any
other: stays in training. *G. Wragg*

ASIAN PERSUASION (IRE) 2 gr.g. (Feb 5) Danehill Dancer (IRE) 117 – Kaitlin **65**
(IRE) (Salmon Leap (USA) 131) [2001 5m⁴ 6m Sep 2] IR 11,500Y: rather leggy,
workmanlike gelding: third foal: dam Irish 1½m and hurdles winner: slightly better effort
in maidens (fair form) when fourth at Folkestone: will probably stay 1m. *E. L. James*

ASKHAM (USA) 3 b.c. El Gran Senor (USA) 136 – Konvincha (USA) (Cormorant **112**
(USA)) [2001 86p: 8g² 8m* 10g² 9.9g* 10m² 9.9m² 8g Oct 4] good-topped colt: smart
performer: impressive winner of maiden at Ripon in June and valuable handicap at
Goodwood (by 3 lengths from Masterful) in August: good efforts when runner-up in
Winter Hill Stakes at Windsor (beaten neck by Adilabad) and 3-runner Select Stakes at
Goodwood (beaten 6 lengths by Nayef) next 2 starts, but well below form in listed event
at Newmarket final one: stays 1¼m: acts on good to firm going: has taken good hold/
worn crossed noseband. *L. M. Cumani*

ASPIRANT DANCER 6 b.g. Marju (IRE) 127 – Fairy Ballerina (Fairy King (USA)) **73**
[2001 69: 10m 15.9d³ 17.1d⁶ 13.8s* Oct 20] good-topped gelding: fair performer:
won minor event at Catterick (edged left) in October: probably stays 17f: has form on
good to firm going, goes very well on softer than good/fibresand: normally races
prominently: often claimer ridden: joined Mrs L. Wadham and useful winner over
hurdles. *M. L. W. Bell*

ASSAAF (IRE) 2 ch.c. (Feb 23) Night Shift (USA) – Wannabe 84 (Shirley Heights **100**
130) [2001 8.2g* 8m* 8d³ Oct 13] 170,000F: fourth foal: half-brother to smart 6f winner
(including Cheveley Park at 2 yrs) and 1000 Guineas runner-up Wannabe Grand (by
Danehill) and French 1m winner Masseera (by Alzao): dam, 1m and (in France) 1¼m
winner, half-sister to Cheveley Park runner-up Tanami: useful form: won minor events at
Nottingham in August and Salisbury (raced freely) in September: visored, waited with
when good 6½ lengths third of 8 to Fight Your Corner in listed event at Ascot: will stay
1¼m: acts on good to firm and good to soft ground. *D. R. Loder*

ASSAILABLE 7 b.g. Salse (USA) 128 – Unsuitable (Local Suitor (USA) 128) [2001 –
10f 8m Jul 4] sturdy gelding: well held in 2001. *P. Howling*

ASSURED GAMBLE 7 b.g. Rock Hopper 124 – Willowbank 66 (Gay Fandango –
(USA) 132) [2001 12.6d Jul 6] one-time fairly useful handicapper: no show only outing
since 5 yrs. *R. J. Baker*

ASSURED PHYSIQUE 4 b.g. Salse (USA) 128 – Metaphysique (FR) (Law Society –
(USA) 130) [2001 74d: 11.9f 12.1s 11.7m⁶ Sep 10] tall gelding: fair maiden at best: well
held in 2001: tried visored: has worn tongue strap. *R. J. Baker*

ASTAFORT (FR) 2 ch.g. (May 3) Kendor (FR) 122 – Tres Chic (USA) (Northern –
Fashion (USA) 114) [2001 8s³ Sep 27] 100,000 francs Y: strong, close-coupled gelding:
fifth foal: half-brother to French 9f winner Beauty Queen (by Exit To Nowhere): dam,
French 1¼m winner, also successful in USA: 20/1, well-beaten third of 4 in maiden at
Pontefract: sold 3,100 gns. *Mrs J. R. Ramsden*

ASTAIREDOTCOM (IRE) 3 b.f. Lake Coniston (IRE) 131 – Romantic Overture **51**
(USA) 73 (Stop The Music (USA)) [2001 53, a60: f6g f8g² f7g f7g⁵ f7g⁴ 6.1f Jun 25]
leggy filly: modest performer: barely stays 1m: acts on fibresand and soft going: tried
visored/blinkered at 2 yrs: inconsistent: sold 1,800 gns, sent to Israel. *K. R. Burke*

ASTER FIELDS (IRE) 3 b.f. Common Grounds 118 – North Telstar 104 (Sallust –
134) [2001 46: 6g 5g 5m 5g f5g Dec 14] sturdy filly: poor maiden handicapper: should
stay at least 6f: acts on soft ground. *D. Shaw*

AS TIME GOES BY 3 ch.g. Timeless Times (USA) 99 – Parfait Amour 73 (Clantime **34**
101) [2001 –: f7g 8.2v³ Mar 28] poor maiden: not sure to stay beyond 1m: acts on heavy
going. *B. S. Rothwell*

ASTLE (IRE) 3 ch.g. Spectrum (IRE) 126 – Very Sophisticated (USA) (Affirmed –
(USA)) [2001 f7g³ e6g² f7g* f8.5g* f8g² 8g 7.1m f8.5g⁶ f8g f8.5g f7s Dec 15] IR **a85 d**
30,000F, 18,000Y, 23,000 2-y-o: big gelding: has plenty of scope: half-brother to 3

winners, including fairly useful Irish 6f winner Hartstown Girl (by Common Grounds) and Irish 1m/1¼m winner Sir True Blue (by Bluebird): dam unraced: fairly useful performer: won maiden and handicap at Wolverhampton in February: no form after next start, leaving W. Jarvis 16,000 gns after seventh one: not sure to stay beyond 8.5f: acts on fibresand. *Mrs N. Macauley*

ASTONISHED   5 ch.g. Weldnaas (USA) 112 – Indigo 86 (Primo Dominie 121) [2001   **114** 118: 6d 5g 6m³ 5m 5m³ 6.1m⁴ 5.1g* 5d* 5g 5.5f⁶ Dec 17] big, good-topped gelding: good walker: smart performer: won 3 listed races in 2000 for J. Hammond in France: returned to former trainer in 2001, and won minor event at Nottingham (by head from Eastern Purple) in August and listed race at Doncaster (overcame trouble to beat Autumnal by head) in September: ran creditably otherwise when third, including in Duke of York Stakes behind Pipalong on third outing: sold from Mrs J. Ramsden 92,000 gns before final outing: effective at 5f/6f: acts on good to firm and good to soft going: blinkered/ visored last 5 starts (hung right penultimate one): held up. *S. Shulman, USA*

ASTON MARA   4 b.g. Bering 136 – Coigach 110 (Niniski (USA) 125) [2001 –: 14f⁵   **50** 16f⁴ Jul 2] neat gelding: fairly useful winner on 2-y-o debut: modest form at best since: stays 2m: acts on firm going: tried blinkered. *Mrs M. Reveley*

ASTORIA   2 ch.f. (May 2) Primo Dominie 121 – Ciboure 74 (Norwick (USA) 125)   **56** [2001 6m⁶ 6g 7.2m 7d 6d Nov 6] big, good-topped filly: has scope: seventh foal: half-sister to 3 winners, including 5-y-o Riberac and 4-y-o Cryfield: dam 6f (at 2 yrs) and 1m winner: modest maiden: well beaten in nurseries last 2 starts: stays 7f: acts on good to firm going. *M. Johnston*

ASTORMYDAYISCOMING   3 b.g. Alhaatmi – Valentine Song 63 (Pas de Seul   – 133) [2001 f9.4g 10d 10m 11.9s Sep 30] ninth living foal: dam 1m winner: little form. *Mrs A. L. M. King*

ASTRAC (IRE)   10 b.g. Nordico (USA) – Shirleen (Daring Display (USA) 129) [2001   **57** 60, a93: 6v 7.5f 6.1f 7.5f⁴ 7.1d* 7m⁴ f7g 7g f6g⁶ Oct 6] sturdy gelding: modest handi-   **a60** capper nowadays: won apprentice event at Warwick in July: stays 7f: acts on soft going, firm and fibresand: tried blinkered (well beaten). *Mrs A. L. M. King*

ASTRAL PRINCE   3 ch.g. Efisio 120 – Val d'Erica 119 (Ashmore (FR) 125) [2001   **70 §** 56+: 7d 9s f7g* 7.1m⁴ 7m 6m⁵ f7g 7d⁵ 6g f6g 7d p7g Dec 19] strong gelding: fair   **a79 §** performer: won handicap at Wolverhampton in May: should stay 1m: acts on fibresand and good to firm going: blinkered after second start: sweating profusely (respectable effort) fourth one: has taken good hold: not one to trust implicitly. *B. J. Meehan*

ASTROCHARM (IRE)   2 b.f. (Jan 17) Charnwood Forest (IRE) 125 – Charm The   **77** Stars (Roi Danzig (USA)) [2001 6m 6m 7m⁴ 7g* 6.5g 6d⁴ Oct 19] 6,800Y: leggy, unfurnished filly: has a round action: first foal: dam, ran twice, out of half-sister to Breeders' Cup Turf winner Northern Spur and high-class stayer Kneller: fair performer: won nursery at Lingfield in September: never-nearer fourth of 30 to Major Laugh in sales race at Newmarket final start: will stay 1m: acts on good to soft going. *M. H. Tompkins*

ASTROLOVE (IRE)   3 ch.f. Bigstone (IRE) 126 – Pizzazz 47 (Unfuwain (USA)   – 131) [2001 –: 14.1d 16m⁴ Jul 5] little form: tried blinkered. *M. H. Tompkins*

Ladbrokes Bunbury Cup (Handicap), Newmarket—Atavus quickens clear in fine style from Hand Chime (right), with Pays d'Amour (striped cap) third

ASWAN (IRE)   3 ch.c. Ashkalani (IRE) 128 – Ghariba 112 (Final Straw 127) [2001   **90**
8m[5] 8m[3] 8m* 8m* 8d Oct 18] 40,000F, 55,000Y: seventh foal: half-brother to 4 winners,
including useful Italian sprinter Reinaldo (by Green Desert) and fairly useful 6f to (in
USA) 1m winner Promptly (by Lead On Time): dam, won Nell Gwyn Stakes, half-sister
to smart performers Braashee (up to 2m) and Adam Smith (up to 1¼m): fairly useful
performer: won maiden at Newcastle in August and handicap at Kempton (by ¾ length
from Sky Dome) in September: well-beaten favourite in 30-runner handicap at Newmarket final start: will stay 1¼m: acts on good to firm going: sold 65,000 gns. *Sir Michael
Stoute*

ATACAT (IRE)   5 b.g. Catrail (USA) 123 – Atsuko (IRE) (Mtoto 134) [2001 96:   **53**
10.3m 10.4g 11.9d 10.5d 10.5g 10d 13.9d 10.1v 11d[6] 14.6s[5] Nov 9] leggy gelding: useful
winner for J. Oxx in Ireland in 2000: modest form at best in 2001: stays 9f: acts on good
to soft going. *Miss L. C. Siddall*

ATALL'S FLYER   3 b.f. Atall Atall 112 – Branston Kristy 55 (Hallgate 127) [2001 7s   **–**
7g 8f Sep 10] first foal: dam sprint maiden: well held in seller (very slowly away) then
maidens: tongue tied first 2 outings. *M. A. Barnes*

ATAMANA (IRE)   3 b.f. Lahib (USA) 129 – Dance Ahead 81 (Shareef Dancer (USA)   **82**
135) [2001 68: 8.1m* 8g[5] 7m Sep 6] fairly useful performer, lightly raced: won maiden at
Sandown in July by neck from Houseparty: failed to make expected progress in
handicaps after, slowly away in blinkers final start: stayed 1m: raced only on good/good
to firm going: visits Singspiel. *M. P. Tregoning*

ATARAMA (IRE)   2 b.f. (Feb 5) Sadler's Wells (USA) 132 – Regal Portrait (IRE) 57   **93 p**
(Royal Academy (USA) 130) [2001 7g 7g[2] 7d* 8d[3] Nov 3] 400,000Y: well-made filly:
third foal: half-sister to useful Italian sprinter King's Ivory (by Lake Coniston): dam,
lightly-raced maiden, half-sister to high-class 1988 2-y-o High Estate and Racing Post
Trophy/King George VI & Queen Elizabeth Diamond Stakes winner King's Theatre (by
Sadler's Wells): won maiden at Redcar (slowly away) in October: good third, beaten less
than 3 lengths by Sundrenched, in listed race at Newmarket: should stay at least 1¼m:
tends to take time to warm to task, and has wandered: should make a useful 3-y-o.
J. L. Dunlop

ATAVUS   4 b.c. Distant Relative 128 – Elysian 94 (Northfields (USA)) [2001 90: 8s 8g*   **109**
7m[2] 8m[4] 7m* 7m* 8g[4] 7.3f* 6s 7d Oct 20] sturdy colt: poor mover: useful performer:
better than ever in 2001: well ridden by claimer J. Mackay, won handicaps at Newmarket
(2, latter Ladbrokes Bunbury Cup by 3 lengths) and Ascot (Tote International Stakes by
short head from Nice One Clare) and Stan James Hungerford Stakes at Newbury (beat
Tamburlaine ¾ length having dictated steady pace) between May and August: best at 7f/
1m on good going or firmer: sometimes slowly away: has edged right under pressure:
races prominently: game: retained 180,000 gns after final start. *G. G. Margarson*

Tote International Stakes (Handicap), Ascot—
another big handicap goes to Atavus (noseband) and Jamie Mackay;
close behind them are Nice One Clare (stars) and Tillerman (left)

A TEEN 3 ch.c. Presidium 124 – Very Good (Noalto 120) [2001 56: e5g² e6g³ f5g e5g⁵ **56**
f5g⁶ 5m⁶ 6g 5m 5m 5m⁵ 5m p5g⁴ f5g p6g⁵ p6g Dec 29] modest maiden: possibly better at **a61**
5f than 6f: tried blinkered: acts on all-weather and good to firm going: has carried head
high: usually races prominently. *P. Howling*

AT'EM DONUT (IRE) 4 ch.g. Up And At 'em 109 – Florentink (USA) (The Minstrel **50**
(CAN) 135) [2001 f6g f5g 6s 6m f5g f6g 6.1m 7.1d 5g⁶ 5g⁵ 5.1d p6g f5g f5s² Dec 15]
workmanlike gelding: brother to 5-y-o Done And Dusted and half-brother to several
winners, including useful Irish 1½m performer/smart jumper Cheering News (by Shernazar): dam unraced: modest maiden: may prove best at 5f: acts on soft going and
fibresand: visored/blinkered ninth to twelfth starts: none too consistent. *C. N. Kellett*

ATHENIAN 2 b.g. (Apr 28) Distant Relative 128 – Confection (Formidable (USA) **68**
125) [2001 8d³ 7.9m 8d⁴ 8d 8g Nov 5] 12,000Y: leggy gelding: brother to useful performer up to 1¼m Anthelia, 5f/6f winner at 2 yrs, and to 7f (including at 2 yrs)/1m winner
Spaniard's Mount, and half-brother to winners by Bairn and Magic Ring: dam ran twice:
fair maiden: ran creditably in nurseries last 2 starts: should stay at least 1¼m: acts on
good to soft going. *D. Morris*

ATHLETIC SAM (IRE) 3 b.c. Definite Article 121 – No Hard Feelings (IRE) 86 **93**
(Alzao (USA) 117) [2001 –: f12g* Mar 22] big, rangy colt: has a round action: much
better effort in maidens when winning at Wolverhampton (made most to beat Serge Lifar
by 1¼ lengths) only 3-y-o start: should stay 1¾m. *T. G. Mills*

ATLANTIC ACE 4 b.g. First Trump 118 – Risalah (Marju (IRE) 127) [2001 75: f8g³ **95**
f9.4s 7m* 8m³ 7d* Oct 30] useful handicapper, lightly raced: won at Goodwood in June
and Redcar (by cosy 1¼ lengths from First Waltz) in October: effective at 7f/1m: acts on
good to firm going, heavy and fibresand: has gained all 3 wins when fresh: usually held
up. *B. Smart*

ATLANTIC EAGLE (USA) 3 b.g. Mt Livermore (USA) – Lyphdum (USA) (Lyp- **63**
hard (USA) 132) [2001 73: 8m 8m 9.1m⁴ 10g Jun 12] sturdy gelding: modest maiden:
stays 9f: yet to race on extremes of going: blinkered (reported by jockey to have felt
wrong behind) final start: sold 4,500 gns, sent to Kuwait. *M. Johnston*

ATLANTIC MYSTERY (IRE) 3 ch.f. Cadeaux Genereux 131 – Nottash (IRE) 74 **68**
(Royal Academy (USA) 130) [2001 65: 6m³ 7.1m 6f Jul 9] small, sparely-made filly: fair
maiden: stays 6f: acts on heavy and good to firm going, ran poorly on fibresand: sold
3,500 gns in July, sent to Bahrain. *M. Johnston*

ATLANTIC RHAPSODY (FR) 4 b.g. Machiavellian (USA) 123 – First Waltz (FR) **94 §**
117 (Green Dancer (USA) 132) [2001 109: 8v 8d 12.3s³ 12g 12f⁴ 10g 11.6g³ 10m⁴ 9.9m⁵
Jul 31] tall gelding: usually looks well: fairly useful performer: several creditable efforts
in 2001, including third in minor events at Ripon and Windsor: stays 1½m: acts on any
turf going and fibresand: won first outing in blinkers, below form in them twice since:
sometimes sweating/edgy/led to post/slowly away: difficult ride, and not one to trust.
M. Johnston

ATLANTIC VIKING (IRE) 6 b.g. Danehill (USA) 126 – Hi Bettina 96 (Henbit **90**
(USA) 130) [2001 88: 5m⁶ 5m* 5m⁶ 5f 5m⁵ 5m⁴ 6g 7d 5s³ 5m 5v Sep 29] well-made
gelding: fairly useful handicapper: won at Ripon in June: some creditable efforts after,
including fourth in valuable event at Ascot in July and third at Haydock in September:
best at 5f/6f: below form on heavy going, acts on any other: sometimes blinkered:
sometimes wanders: often races prominently. *D. Nicholls*

ATLANTIS PRINCE 3 ch.c. Tagula (IRE) 116 – Zoom Lens (IRE) 65 (Caerleon **109**
(USA) 132) [2001 111: a9f 10.5m⁵ 12f May 27] lengthy, useful-looking colt: useful
performer: game and genuine when trained in 2000 by S. Woods, unbeaten in 4 races,
notably Royal Lodge Stakes at Ascot: not discredited when 3 lengths last of 5 to Chichicastenango in Prix Lupin at Longchamp on second start: always behind in Derby Italiano
at Rome only subsequent outing: probably stays 10.5f: acts on soft and good to firm
going, well below form on dirt in UAE Derby on reappearance: usually front runner/races
prominently. *Saeed bin Suroor*

ATOMIC FLAIR (IRE) 2 ch.g. (Mar 11) Up And At 'em 109 – Gold Flair 93 (Tap **70**
On Wood 130) [2001 5.7f⁵ 7m³ 7g⁵ 6.1s 6.1m² 6.1m³ 7m⁴ f8.5g³ f8.5g⁴ Nov 3] IR 6,000F,
10,000Y: well-grown, close-coupled gelding: half-brother to several winners, including
4-y-o Atylan Boy and French 1½m winner Harlem Swing (by Night Shift): dam, middle-
distance maiden, sister to very smart middle-distance performer Nisnas: fair maiden:
gelded after final start: will stay 1¼m: acts on firm ground and fibresand, well held on
soft: consistent. *P. R. Chamings*

timeform.com Silver Salver (Handicap), Newmarket—
the grey A Touch of Frost stays on dourly to snatch the verdict from I Cried For You (No.10),
with Hand Chime (black braces) third and Karameg (checked cap) fourth

A TOUCH OF FROST 6 gr.m. Distant Relative 128 – Pharland (FR) (Bellypha 130) **97 +**
[2001 89: 7s⁵ 7.1m 7.1s⁶ 8m 7m³ 7m³ 7g* 7f* 7m⁵ 7d⁴ 7s 7d³ 7d³ Oct 20] workmanlike
mare: useful performer: won handicaps at Newmarket (timeform.com Silver Salver) and
Newbury in August: mostly at least respectable efforts otherwise, including in listed races
at Doncaster (over a length fourth to Nice One Clare) and Ascot (2½ lengths third to
Toffee Nosed) on tenth/twelfth outings: effective at 7f/1m: acts on firm and good to soft
going, probably on soft: blinkered: sometimes slowly away/races lazily. *G. G. Margarson*

ATRACTIVE GIRL 2 ch.f. (Apr 26) Atraf 116 – Harold's Girl (FR) (Northfields **49**
(USA)) [2001 5d⁵ f6g 6g 8.1g Sep 13] 6,000F, IR 8,000Y: half-sister to several winners,
including useful 7f/1m winner Jafn (by Sharpo): dam, 2-y-o 6f winner in France, also
won over jumps: poor maiden: best effort on debut: blinkered final start. *J. L. Spearing*

ATTACHE 3 ch.g. Wolfhound (USA) 126 – Royal Passion 78 (Ahonoora 122) [2001 **103**
104: 8d 10.3m* 10f⁵ 11.9d⁶ 10.5g⁵ 7.9m 8g⁶ 8f 10g 8d 8d Nov 3] lengthy gelding: useful
performer: won minor event at Doncaster in May by short head from Ennoblement:
creditable fifth to Freefourinternet in listed race at Ascot next time: left M. Johnston after
sixth start: never dangerous in handicaps at Newmarket last 3 outings: gelded afterwards:
stays 10.3f: yet to race on heavy going, acts on any other. *Mrs J. R. Ramsden*

ATTACKER (USA) 4 b.g. Defensive Play (USA) 118 – Bold Ballerina (Sadler's Wells **–**
(USA) 132) [2001 –: 10m⁵ 12m 10.5d⁵ 10.5g 12d Nov 6] lengthy gelding: little form.
Miss L. C. Siddall

ATTENTION SEEKER (USA) 4 b.f. Exbourne (USA) 125 – Popularity (USA) 58 **75 d**
(Blushing Groom (FR) 131) [2001 12s 12g 10m 12m⁶ 9m 10m⁶ 12g 11.9m⁴ 10s 11.9s
f9.4g⁶ f14.8g Dec 1] tall, leggy filly: third foal: half-sister to 1¾m winner Devilish Charm
(by Devil's Bag): dam, twice-raced maiden, half-sister to US Grade 1 1¼m/1½m winner
Vanlandingham and to dam of Distant Music: fair handicapper at best: trained in 2000 by
Mme C. Head-Maarek in France: well below form 4 of last 5 starts in 2001: barely stays
1½m: acts on good to firm going, not on softer than good: blinkered twice (also wore
hood second time): sometimes slowly away/pulls hard. *S. C. Williams*

ATTLEE (USA) 2 br. or b.g. (Jan 28) Atticus (USA) 121 – No Rego (USA) (Riverman **75**
(USA) 131) [2001 6m⁴ Jul 4] $130,000Y: second foal: half-brother to a sprint winner in
USA by Star de Naskra: dam, maiden in USA, out of smart performer up to 1½m Top
Hope: 20/1 and green, 5 lengths fourth of 8 to In Space in slowly-run maiden at Yar-
mouth: gelded afterwards. *E. A. L. Dunlop*

ATTO (IRE) 7 b.g. Mandalus 110 – Deep Cristina (Deep Run 119) [2001 –: 10.9g **–**
11.8d Jul 19] little sign of ability: sold 900 gns (in December). *J. S. King*

ATTORNEY 3 ch.g. Wolfhound (USA) 126 – Princess Sadie 86 (Shavian 125) [2001 **81**
81: 5.1s² 5d* 6m 5m³ 6m³ 6d⁶ 5.1m 5v f6g⁵ f6g⁵ f7g f5s Dec 15] tall, quite good-topped **a72**

91

gelding: fairly useful performer on turf, fair on all-weather: won maiden at Musselburgh in April: stays 6f: acts on soft and good to firm going, probably on fibresand: blinkered (ran as though something amiss) final start: has been on edge/sweating: races prominently. *M. A. Jarvis*

A TWO (IRE) 2 b.f. (Mar 27) Ali-Royal (IRE) 127 – Rainelle (Rainbow Quest (USA) 134) [2001 8.1g Aug 27] IR 1,800Y: second foal: dam, maiden, from family of smart performers up to 1m Inchmurrin and Inchinor: 50/1 and green, well beaten in maiden at Chepstow. *B. Palling* —

ATYLAN BOY (IRE) 4 b.g. Efisio 120 – Gold Flair 93 (Tap On Wood 130) [2001 72, a80: f7g* f7g³ Jan 15] leggy, close-coupled gelding: fair performer: won seller at Southwell in January: probably best around 7f: acts on all-weather and heavy going, possibly not on good to firm: usually blinkered/visored nowadays: sold 8,200 gns in January, sent to Kuwait. *B. J. Meehan* — a66

AUBRIETA (USA) 5 b.m. Dayjur (USA) 137 – Fennel 97 (Slew O' Gold (USA)) [2001 57, a65: f7g² e6g* f7s⁶ e7g³ f6g* e7s³ f7g⁵ f6g² f7g 5m² 5.2m⁶ 5g 6.1f 5.3f f6g f6g f5g⁴ p5g p5g⁵ f6g Dec 10] tall mare: modest performer: won claimers at Lingfield and Wolverhampton in January: left D. Haydn Jones after ninth start: effective at 5f to 8.5f: acts on good to firm going, good to soft and fibresand/equitrack: usually blinkered nowadays, has worn visor. *Andrew Reid* 55 a63

AUDACITY 5 b.g. Minshaanshu Amad (USA) 91§ – Glory Isle 60 (Hittite Glory 125) [2001 –: f12g² f11g f16g f14g³ 12.6f Jun 27] tall gelding: bad maiden: stays 1¾m: acts on fibresand: sometimes blinkered. *N. Hamilton* 25

AUDREY'S DILEMMA 2 b.f. (Feb 19) Piccolo 121 – Yesterday's Song (Shirley Heights 130) [2001 6s 7s⁵ 6d Nov 2] 9,000Y: first living foal: dam unraced daughter of sister to useful stayer Parting Moment: easily best effort in maidens (modest form) when fifth of 14 at Brighton: slowly away both other starts: should stay at least 1m. *S. Dow* 58

AUNT DORIS 4 b.f. Distant Relative 128 – Nevis 61 (Connaught 130) [2001 62: 5m 6g 6g 6g⁴ 6f 6v f6g⁴ f6g f5g f6g f6s Dec 21] poor handicapper: stays 6f: acts on good to firm going and fibresand: visored last 2 starts: none too consistent. *M. J. Polglase* 48 a39

AUNT HILDA 2 b.f. (Apr 10) Distant Relative 128 – Aloha Jane (USA) 57 (Hawaii) [2001 7m⁵ 7d Nov 3] small filly: seventh foal: sister to useful 7f/1m performer Aunty Jane and half-sister to 2 winners, including fairly useful 7f winner Asian Jane (by Persian Bold): dam 2m winner: fair form in maidens at Kempton and Newmarket: should stay 1m. *J. L. Dunlop* 65

AUNTIE DOT COM 2 ch.f. (Feb 9) Tagula (IRE) 116 – Jadebelle 66 (Beldale Flutter (USA) 130) [2001 f5g⁶ 5s* 6m³ 5m 6g⁶ 7.1f³ 7g Aug 4] lengthy filly: fourth reported foal: half-sister to useful 1997 2-y-o 5f/6f winner Prince Foley (by Greensmith): dam 2-y-o 6f winner who stayed 1½m: fair performer: won maiden at Pontefract in April: creditable efforts in nurseries fifth/sixth starts: should stay 1m: acts on soft and firm going: has been edgy/hung markedly right: usually races prominently. *W. G. M. Turner* 70

AUNT RUBY (USA) 3 ch.f. Rubiano (USA) – Redress (USA) 77 (Storm Cat (USA)) [2001 67: e8g⁴ e7g⁵ f7g* 8s 7m 8m 7m Jun 12] lengthy filly: modest performer: won seller at Southwell (left M. Bell 6,000 gns) in March: stays 1m: acts on fibresand, best turf efforts on good going. *T. P. McGovern* 52

AUNT SUSAN 3 b.f. Distant Relative 128 – Lawn Order 51 (Efisio 120) [2001 –: 8s f8g 11.7m Aug 24] close-coupled filly: no form: reportedly had breathing problem final start. *K. McAuliffe* —

AUNTY MARY 2 b.f. (Feb 11) Common Grounds 118 – Flirtation (Pursuit of Love 124) [2001 6m 5g* 5m 5m² 5m² 6g 5d Sep 25] 31,000Y: useful-looking filly: first foal: dam once-raced half-sister to French 1½m listed winner Carmita: fairly useful performer: won maiden at York in June: creditable second in nurseries on same track and at Thirsk: should stay 6f: acts on good to firm going. *T. D. Easterby* 82

AUNTY ROSE (IRE) 4 b.f. Caerleon (USA) 132 – Come On Rosi 77 (Valiyar 129) [2001 101: 9g⁶ 8m⁴ 8.5m³ 7d 8g 8s⁵ Oct 21] smallish, leggy filly: had quick action: useful performer: ran creditably in 2001 when in frame behind Sheppard's Watch in listed races at Goodwood and Epsom and when fifth to Toroca in Premio Sergio Cumani at Milan: stayed 8.5f: acted on soft and good to firm going: was often slowly away: stud. *J. L. Dunlop* 103

AURA OF GRACE (USA) 4 b. or br.f. Southern Halo (USA) – Avarice (USA) (Manila (USA)) [2001 80p: 10g² May 10] leggy, lengthy filly: fair performer, lightly 78 +

raced: second in Ripon handicap only 4-y-o start: unlikely to stay beyond 1¼m: acts on soft ground. *M. Johnston*

AURIFEROUS (USA) 2 b.c. (Apr 30) Seeking The Gold (USA) – Minigroom **66 p** (USA) (Mt Livermore (USA)) [2001 6g⁶ Jul 11] $200,000F, $440,000Y: rather leggy, quite good-topped colt: second foal: half-brother to a 2-y-o 5.5f winner in USA by Dehere: dam, winning sprinter in USA, out of sister to Prix de la Foret winner Septieme Ciel: 6/4-on, 10 lengths sixth of 7 to Esenin in minor event at Newmarket, leading over 2f out then folding tamely: wore crossed noseband: joined K. McLaughlin in UAE: should do better. *D. R. Loder*

AUTUMNAL (IRE) 3 b.f. Indian Ridge 123 – Please Believe Me 93 (Try My Best **104** (USA) 130) [2001 103: 7d 8g 6s⁴ 7m⁶ 6d 6m* 5d² 5.2f⁶ 5s Oct 7] good-topped filly: useful performer: won minor event at Newmarket in June by ¾ length from Magic of Love: good head second to Astonished in listed race at Doncaster next start: very stiff task in Prix de l'Abbaye de Longchamp final one: probably best at 5f/6f: acts on soft and good to firm going: blinkered fourth to sixth starts: has been bandaged: tends to be on toes. *B. J. Meehan*

AUTUMN FANTASY (USA) 2 b. or br.c. (May 7) Lear Fan (USA) 130 – Autumn **67 p** Glory (USA) (Graustark) [2001 8s⁶ Oct 31] half-brother to several winners, including smart French performer up to 15f Glorify (by Nijinsky), and to dam of very smart filly up to 10.5f Ryafan (by Lear Fan): dam, 6f to 9f winner in USA, sister to dam of US Grade 1 winners Brian's Time and Sunshine Forever: 12/1, not at all knocked about when sixth of 14 to Jawwala in maiden at Yarmouth: should be suited by 1¼m/1½m: will do better. *J. H. M. Gosden*

AUTUMN RAIN (USA) 4 br.g. Dynaformer (USA) – Edda (USA) (Ogygian (USA)) **78** [2001 78: 8d 7d p8g² Nov 13] big, strong gelding: fair performer, lightly raced: trained by L. Montague Hall on reappearance: effective at 7f/1m: acts on polytrack, raced mainly on good to soft/soft going on turf. *R. J. Frankel, USA*

AUTUMN RHYTHM 3 b.f. Hernando (FR) 127 – Fextal (USA) (Alleged (USA) **?** 138) [2001 99p: 9d⁶ 8.5s² 9f Oct 14] angular filly: poor walker: has a markedly round action: impressive winner of maiden at Yarmouth only 2-y-o start: reportedly bled from nose when disappointing in listed race at Newmarket on reappearance in April (final start for H. Cecil): off 5 months, better subsequent effort when second in allowance race at Belmont in September: should stay at least 1¼m: acts on heavy going: tongue tied both outings in Britain. *R. J. Frankel, USA*

AVALANCHE (FR) 4 gr.g. Highest Honor (FR) 124 – Fairy Gold 73 (Golden Fleece (USA) 133) [2001 66: 9.7v Apr 24] fair maiden at 3 yrs (left C. O'Brien in Ireland 30,000 gns after final start): well beaten only outing in 2001: stays 1m: acts on good to firm ground: has worn tongue strap. *J. R. Best*

AVANTI 5 gr.h. Reprimand 122 – Dolly Bevan 53 (Another Realm 118) [2001 –: f9.4g **–** 14.1m Jul 27] smallish, well-made horse: fair handicapper at 3 yrs: no form in 2001: seems to stay 1¾m: blinkered once. *Dr J. R. J. Naylor*

AVEBURY 5 b.g. Fairy King (USA) – Circle of Chalk (FR) 74 (Kris 135) [2001 f11g⁵ **66** 9d⁴ f11g 9m² 8m³ 9f³ 7.5m⁵ 7m³ 9g⁴ 8.3g⁶ f8.5g* f8.5s⁵ Dec 27] 54,000Y, 17,500 3-y-o: **a73 +** tall, leggy gelding: second foal: dam, French 1¼m winner, sister to useful French 1¼m winner From Beyond out of Coronation Stakes winner Magic of Life: fair handicapper: left T. Easterby 11,000 gns after eighth start: won maiden event at Wolverhampton in September: should prove best at 1m/1¼m: acts on firm going and fibresand: has been tongue tied: held up: has found little. *S. E. Kettlewell*

AVEIRO (IRE) 5 b.g. Darshaan 133 – Avila 76 (Ajdal (USA) 130) [2001 f9.4s⁵ e16g **54 +** e13g² f12g e13g² f16g³ 14.1s 11.9s³ 11.9f* 11.5m* 12m³ 14.1m⁵ 12m⁴ 11.6m 12m³ **a72 +** 16.2m f14g⁶ f16.2g* f14g* f16.2s* Dec 18] fair handicapper on all-weather, modest on turf: won at Brighton (selling maiden) and Yarmouth in May and Wolverhampton (twice) and Southwell in December: effective at 11.5f to 2m: acts on fibresand/equitrack, firm and soft ground: blinkered. *C. P. Morlock*

AVERHAM STAR 6 ch.g. Absalom 128 – Upper Sister (Upper Case (USA)) [2001 **–** 31: f7g 6s 6m May 26] small gelding: no form in 2001. *W. Clay*

AVERTED VIEW (USA) 4 ch.f. Distant View (USA) 126 – Averti (USA) 97 (Known **85** Fact (USA) 135) [2001 10m 10m³ 11.8m² 12d⁵ 10v Nov 8] good-topped filly: second foal: half-sister to useful French 6f to 1m winner (including at 2 yrs) Acerbic (by Lear Fan): dam, 6f and (at 2 yrs) 7f winner, half-sister to very smart performer up to 11f Defensive Play: fairly useful performer: trained in France by Mme C. Head-Maarek at 3 yrs, winning minor event at Bordeaux: ran creditably in 2001 when placed in handicaps: unlikely to stay beyond 1½m: acts on heavy and good to firm going: won in blinkers in France. *R. T. Phillips*

AVERY RING 3 b.g. Magic Ring (IRE) 115 – Thatcherella 80 (Thatching 131) [2001 66: f7g² f7g* f8.5g⁵ f7g 7s 7s 7m⁶ 7g⁵ 7m³ Aug 24] fair on all-weather, modest on turf: won maiden at Wolverhampton in February: stays 7f: acts on fibresand, best turf efforts on good going or firmer: sold 4,200 gns. *A. P. Jarvis* **58 a65**

AVORADO (IRE) 3 b.g. Royal Academy (USA) 130 – Voronova (IRE) 71 (Sadler's Wells (USA) 132) [2001 92: 10s 7s⁴ 7g* 6.3g* 9g² 8.5d 8m² 6d⁵ Oct 27] tall, attractive gelding: third foal: dam, lightly-raced maiden, half-sister to smart winner up to 10.5f Optimistic Lass (dam of high-class sprinter/miler Golden Opinion): smart performer: improved in 2001, winning handicaps at Leopardstown and the Curragh in June/July: ran well afterwards when second in valuable handicap at Leopardstown (beaten neck by Right Honorable) and listed race at Cork (beaten 3 lengths by Caumshinaun): stays 9f: acts on good to soft and good to firm ground: has been blinkered, including last 6 starts. *J. S. Bolger, Ireland* **113**

AWAKE 4 ch.g. First Trump 118 – Pluvial 90 (Habat 127) [2001 101: 6v 6d 5g 5.1f 5m 5f 5d 5v Oct 27] strong, smallish gelding: useful at 2/3 yrs when trained by M. Johnston: below best in 2001, leaving N. Littmoden and gelded after sixth start: probably best at 5f (given good test)/6f: acts on good to firm and heavy going: has been taken early to post. *D. Nicholls* **87**

AWAY WIN 3 b.f. Common Grounds 118 – Cafe Glace (Beldale Flutter (USA) 130) [2001 50: 6d 8.3g 7g Sep 3] no form at 3 yrs. *B. Palling* **–**

AYEM (IRE) 6 ch.g. Sharp Victor (USA) 114 – Morning Crown (USA) (Chief's Crown (USA)) [2001 11.9s May 3] close-coupled gelding: maiden: well held only 6-y-o start: sometimes tongue tied. *C. Weedon* **–**

AYZAL 2 br.f. (Feb 27) Zilzal (USA) 137 – Ayunli 81 (Chief Singer 131) [2001 5.2m* 5m* 6m² 6d³ Oct 19] tall, quite good-topped filly: fluent mover: second foal: dam 8.5f to 15.5f winner: fairly useful performer: won maiden at Yarmouth and minor event at Beverley in June: good placed efforts in 20-runner nursery at Ayr and 30-runner sales race at Newmarket (finished strongly into third behind Major Laugh) in the autumn: will be well suited by 7f+: sold 48,000 gns, sent to USA. *W. J. Haggas* **84**

AZILLION (IRE) 2 b.c. (Feb 2) Alzao (USA) 117 – Olivia (IRE) (Ela-Mana-Mou 132) [2001 7f 8.1g² p8g* Nov 15] 32,000F, 21,000Y: strong colt: second living foal: dam Irish 1¼m winner: fairly useful form: won maiden at Lingfield in November by 5 lengths from Murdinga, edging left: will be suited by 1¼m/1½m: sent to USA. *J. W. Hills* **87**

AZIZ PRESENTING (IRE) 3 br.f. Charnwood Forest (IRE) 125 – Khalatara (IRE) (Kalaglow 132) [2001 86: 6d Apr 19] lengthy, workmanlike filly: fairly useful winner at 2 yrs: well beaten only 3-y-o outing: should stay 7f: acts on firm and soft ground: has been edgy. *M. R. Channon* **–**

AZUR (IRE) 4 b.f. Brief Truce (USA) 126 – Bayadere (USA) 61 (Green Dancer (USA) 132) [2001 64: 9.9m 11.8f 9.9f 10m³ 10.2f* 10m* 10g4 10g⁵ 10m Sep 11] quite good-topped filly: fair handicapper: successful at Bath and Leicester in July/August: should stay 1½m: raced mainly on good going or firmer: tried visored: has started slowly. *Mrs A. L. M. King* **65**

AZZAN (USA) 5 b. or br.g. Gulch (USA) – Dixieland Dream (USA) (Dixieland Band (USA)) [2001 –§: 12s 16.2m May 26] temperamental maiden: tried blinkered/tongue tied. *T. Keddy* **– §**

B

BAARIDD 3 b.c. Halling (USA) 133 – Millstream (USA) 107 (Dayjur (USA) 137) [2001 104: 6m⁶ 6m 7m a6f 6g⁵ Dec 20] well-made, attractive colt: has a quick action: useful performer: best effort in 2001 when sixth to Volata in handicap at Haydock on reappearance: hampered in Cork And Orrery Stakes at Royal Ascot, then well held in Tote International Handicap on same course (final outing for M. Jarvis): not sure to stay beyond 7f: acts on good to firm and good to soft going: has been edgy/given trouble at stalls/taken fierce hold. *D. J. Selvaratnam, UAE* **105**

BABA AU RHUM (IRE) 9 b.g. Baba Karam 117 – Spring About (Hard Fought 125) [2001 59: 10.9m⁶ Jun 18] tall gelding: modest handicapper, lightly raced on Flat nowadays: stays 11f: acts on good to firm going, probably good to soft: sold 800 gns. *Ian Williams* — **64**

BABY BARRY 4 b.g. Komaite (USA) – Malcesine (IRE) 46 (Auction Ring (USA) 123) [2001 89: 7m³ 7m 6m 6g* 6g³ 6g* 6g 6g* 6g* 6g⁴ 6g Nov 5] good-topped gelding: fairly useful performer: won minor event at Pontefract in July and handicaps at Newcastle in August and Goodwood in September: effective at 5f, probably at easy 7f: acts on fibre-sand and firm going, possibly not on softer than good: visored last 7 starts in 2001, has been blinkered: sometimes hangs/looks awkward ride: often front runner. *Mrs G. S. Rees* — **83**

BABY BE 7 b.m. Bold Arrangement 127 – B Grade 59 (Lucky Wednesday 124) [2001 6s 6m 6m 7.5f 5f⁶ Jul 7] first foal: dam 6f winner who stayed 7f: well beaten in maidens/ handicap. *T. P. Tate* — **–**

BABY BUNTING 3 b.f. Wolfhound (USA) 126 – Flitteriss Park 62§ (Beldale Flutter (USA) 130) [2001 63: e5g⁶ 5m 6m⁶ 6g 5.3g³ 6m Aug 27] good-quartered filly: poor mover: modest maiden: should stay 7f: yet to race on extremes of going on turf. *M. L. W. Bell* — **61**

BABY MAYBE (USA) 3 b.f. Known Fact (USA) 135 – Bai Shun (USA) (Fappiano (USA)) [2001 –: 5s 5m⁵ 5g 6d 5m 5d 5m Aug 25] robust filly: little form: blinkered last 3 starts. *T. H. Caldwell* — **–**

BACCHANALIA (IRE) 2 b.f. (Feb 20) Blues Traveller (IRE) 119 – Daffodil Dale (IRE) 78 (Cyrano de Bergerac 120) [2001 7m 8.5m⁵ 7d* 7d Oct 9] IR 25,000Y: strong filly: first foal: dam, Irish 2-y-o 5f winner who stayed 1m, granddaughter of US Grade 1 2-y-o 6f winner Share The Fantasy: easily best effort (fair form) when winning maiden at Chester in September: said to have had a rotated vertebra when tailed off only subsequent start: not sure to stay beyond 7f. *J. L. Eyre* — **69**

BACCHUS 7 b.g. Prince Sabo 123 – Bonica 56 (Rousillon (USA) 133) [2001 81?, a73: 8v 10s 9.2d* 9.9m* 9m 10.3f 10.5g Jun 8] workmanlike gelding: fair performer: won claimer at Hamilton and ladies handicap at Beverley, both in May: ran badly after: stays 1¼m: acts on good to firm going, soft and fibresand: sometimes blinkered/visored (not last 5 starts): carries head high/sometimes reluctant: best left alone. *K. A. Ryan* — **70 §** **a– §**

BACCURA (IRE) 3 b.g. Dolphin Street (FR) 125 – Luzzara (IRE) (Tate Gallery (USA) 117) [2001 84: f7g f7g⁴ 8d 7g² 7.9g² 7m² 5g 7m Dec 16] sturdy, well-made gelding: useful handicapper: excellent efforts when runner-up in quite valuable events in May at Newmarket, York and Goodwood: left A. Jarvis and mid-division at Happy Valley and Sha Tin last 2 outings: stays 1m: acts on good to firm going and fibresand: sometimes starts slowly. *L. Fownes, Hong Kong* — **95**

BACHELORS PAD 7 b.g. Pursuit of Love 124 – Note Book 94 (Mummy's Pet 125) [2001 69: f16.2g⁴ f12s² f12g³ f12g² f12g f11g⁶ 10d² 12m³ 12.3d³ 10m f12g 12s Oct 20] leggy gelding: has plenty of knee action: moderate performer: effective at 1¼m (given a bit of a test) to 1¾m: possibly unsuited by firm going, acts on any other turf and on fibresand: tried blinkered: has shown signs of temperament: winning hurdler. *Miss S. J. Wilton* — **60** **a64**

BACH (IRE) 4 b.c. Caerleon (USA) 132 – Producer (USA) 130 (Nashua) [2001 111: 10g² 10.5g⁵ 8d² 10m 8g* 10m³ 8m 10s* 10g³ 8s⁴ 8f³ 10m Dec 16] — **121**

Just four of the previous year's three-year-olds trained at Ballydoyle were still there in the latest season, namely Bach, Mull of Kintyre, Shoal Creek and Van Dantzig, and only the first of those mentioned managed to enhance his reputation significantly. Neither the 1999 Gimcrack Stakes winner Mull of Kintyre nor Van Dantzig won a race, though at least the former returned from injury to show smart form once again; and while Shoal Creek did pick up another listed event in May he didn't need to improve much on what he'd shown at three to do so. Bach, on the other hand, had his first full season and showed himself a tough and genuine sort, developing into a very smart performer.

Bach, like Mull of Kintyre, was also returning from injury, after reportedly fracturing his pelvis when second in the Prix Jean Prat in June 2000 on only his fifth appearance—he'd won his first three starts, including the Chesham Stakes as a two-year-old, and finished second to Sinndar, beaten a head in receipt of 7 lb, in the Derby Trial at Leopardstown on his fourth. It soon became apparent that Bach's setback had done him no lasting harm, though it wasn't until his fifth outing that he

Budweiser Celebration Stakes, the Curragh—Bach passes the post clear of Maumee and Mastermind

managed to get off the mark for the season. That win came in a twelve-runner listed event, the Budweiser Celebration Stakes, for which he started favourite at the Curragh in July, and he won by one and a half lengths from Maumee. Six days later Bach was out again, and running better than he had ever done before to finish a very close third behind Medicean and Grandera in the Eclipse Stakes at Sandown, taking over nearly three furlongs out and sticking on well once headed a furlong out. More good efforts were to follow, including a half-length defeat of Jammaal in the five-runner Royal Whip Stakes at the Curragh in August which gave Bach his first pattern-race victory. Although never able to trouble Fantastic Light and Galileo in the Irish Champion Stakes at Leopardstown, Bach ran every bit as well as could be expected in finishing third, as he did when subsequently occupying the same position behind Val Royal and Forbidden Apple in the Breeders' Cup Mile at Belmont. Bach failed by a long way to do himself justice in the Hong Kong Cup in December on his final outing, finishing last of the fourteen runners, having chased the leader.

Bach (IRE) (b.c. 1997)	Caerleon (USA) (b 1980)	Nijinsky (b 1967)	Northern Dancer / Flaming Page
		Foreseer (b or br 1969)	Round Table / Regal Gleam
	Producer (USA) (br 1976)	Nashua (b 1952)	Nasrullah / Segula
		Marion (br 1961)	Tantieme / Magda

Bach, who cost IR 200,000 guineas as a yearling, is the twelfth foal of the top-class racemare Producer. Producer did finish second in the Irish Oaks, but she was better over shorter distances and won the Prix de la Foret over seven furlongs and the Prix de l'Opera over nine. Producer's five other winners include three useful performers, namely Irish sprinter Music And Dance (by Northern Dancer), Dancing Goddess (by Nijinsky), who won over as far as ten furlongs in Ireland but seemed best up to a mile and finished second in the Irish One Thousand Guineas, and Las Flores (by Sadler's Wells). The last-named stayed a mile and a half well and was placed in both the Lingfield Oaks Trial and Oaks d'Italia. Bach's grandam Marion, a twin, won three times at up to a mile in France and was then exported to the States, where two of her other offspring were stakes-winning fillies. Bach, a strong, good-quartered colt, is just as effective at a mile as he is at a mile and a quarter, and is capable of producing his form on both firm and soft ground. *A. P. O'Brien, Ireland*

BACK FROM HEAVEN (BEL) 2 b.f. (Feb 13) Septieme Ciel (USA) 123 – Green Gem (BEL) 91 (Pharly (FR) 130) [2001 7g 7g Sep 11] 24,000Y: first foal: dam, won at 6.5f to 7f (including in France), sister to useful French stayer Battle Green: little form in maidens. *S. C. Williams*

BACK PASS (USA) 3 b. or br.f. Quest For Fame 127 – Skiable (IRE) (Niniski (USA) **65**
125) [2001 55: 10m² 10.1f³ 14m³ 13.1m⁵ Sep 10] leggy, quite good-topped filly: fair
maiden: probably stays 13f: twice slowly away: sold 30,000 gns. *B. W. Hills*

BACKWOODS 8 ch.g. In The Wings 128 – Kates Cabin 96 (Habitat 134) [2001 –: **55**
10.9f 11.9m* 16g² 13.1d 16g⁶ 17.5m² 15.8d 18s³ Oct 22] heavy-topped gelding: has
reportedly had leg trouble: modest performer: creditable placed efforts in handicaps after: stays 2¼m: acts on soft going, good to firm and
fibresand: sometimes slowly away. *W. M. Brisbourne*

BADERNA 3 b.c. Rainbow Quest (USA) 134 – Baaderah (IRE) 102 (Cadeaux **–**
Genereux 131) [2001 –: 10.3v Mar 23] angular colt: no show in 2 maidens: pulled up,
reportedly distressed on reappearance. *M. R. Channon*

BADRINATH (IRE) 7 b.g. Imperial Frontier (USA) 112 – Badedra (Kings Lake **61**
(USA) 133) [2001 55§, a46§: e10g³ e10g* e8g e10g³ 10f* 9.9f² 8m 9.9f³ 10m⁶ 9.9m
p10g* Dec 29] quite good-topped gelding: fair performer: won handicap at Lingfield in
February, selling handicap at Leicester in May and, after 5-month break, seller at
Lingfield in December: stays 11.5f: acts on firm going, good to soft and all-weather: often
finds little, and best held up as long as possible. *H. J. Collingridge*

BAHAMAS (IRE) 4 b.g. Barathea (IRE) 127 – Rum Cay (USA) 75 (Our Native **67**
(USA)) [2001 82, a77: 12s 10v 11.6g 12d 14.1d f12g Dec 10] good-topped gelding: fair
handicapper in 2001: stays 1½m: acts on good to firm going, soft and fibresand:
blinkered: tends to wander/go in snatches: sold 6,400 gns. *J. A. B. Old*

BAHAMIAN HEIR (IRE) 2 b.c. (Jan 16) Lake Coniston (IRE) 131 – Bally Souza **45**
(IRE) 87 (Alzao (USA) 117) [2001 6m 7.9d f6g Oct 18] IR 23,000Y: lengthy colt: fluent
mover: first foal: dam, 11f/1½m winner, half-sister to useful miler A La Carte: poor form
in maidens: not knocked about last 2 starts: should be suited by at least 1m. *D. Nicholls*

BAHAMIAN MINSTREL 2 b.g. (Mar 2) Bahamian Bounty 116 – Penny Ghent **75**
(Dominion 123) [2001 5.1m 5g² 5.7g p5g⁵ f5s* f5s³ Dec 21] 3,000F, 8,000Y: neat
gelding: first foal: dam, ran 3 times, out of half-sister to high-class sprinter Double
Schwartz: fair performer: won nursery at Southwell in December: creditable third in
similar event there: will stay 6f: acts on fibresand. *Mrs L. Stubbs*

BAHAMIAN PIRATE (USA) 6 ch.g. Housebuster (USA) – Shining Through **120**
(USA) (Deputy Minister (CAN)) [2001 111: 6v 6d⁶ 5g⁶ 6m 6m 6f² 5m 6d* 6g³ 6s³
5s² 6d³ Oct 19]

    With his problems behind him, Bahamian Pirate has been able to show just
what he is capable of in the last two seasons, improving over three stones as he
progressed from fair handicapper to pattern-race performer. Bahamian Pirate was
unraced at two, had a couple of outings for Con Collins in Ireland and half a dozen
for his present trainer, including three on the fibresand at Southwell in his four-
year-old season, before managing to get his head in front. Subsequently gelded and
also operated on to have bone chips removed from his knees, Bahamian Pirate got
off the mark in a Ripon maiden in August 1999 on his return and picked up a
handicap at Carlisle the following May before suffering another setback. This was a
much more serious one. Thought at first to have colic, Bahamian Pirate was found
to have slipped his spleen and reportedly nearly died. It says much for Bahamian
Pirate's powers of recovery that he was back in action within two months and by the
end of the 2000 season had won four more races, including the Ayr Gold Cup
and a listed event at Newmarket.

    Handicaps were not on the agenda for Bahamian Pirate in the latest season
and it wasn't until his sixth start, at Newcastle at the end of June, that he made the
frame, when second in the Group 3 Chipchase Stakes. He gained his first, and what
turned out to be only, victory of the season on his eighth outing, in another Group 3,
the Phoenix Sprint Stakes at Leopardstown in August, winning by a short head
from One Won One. Bahamian Pirate showed even better form in defeat in his four
subsequent outings, particularly so in the last three. Indeed, he was unlucky not to
add a Group 2 race to his collection two outings after Leopardstown, flashing home
after having anything but a clear run when third to Nice One Clare and Orientor,
beaten a neck and a short head, in the Diadem Stakes at Ascot. Pipalong, a short
head away in fourth, was two and a half lengths behind Bahamian Pirate when
they met again in the Prix de l'Abbaye de Longchamp eight days later, the pair

Phoenix Sprint Stakes, Leopardstown—a British-trained winner for the sixth year running as Bahamian Pirate (near side) just comes out on top from One Won One

occupying the minor placings behind Imperial Beauty. Bahamian Pirate had every chance this time, keeping on well after chasing the leaders and going down by half a length. A Group 3 penalty meant that Bahamian Pirate faced a stiffish task when attempting to repeat his win of the previous year in the listed Bentinck Stakes at Newmarket on his final start, and in finishing third behind Danehurst and Orientor he ran right up to his best.

		Mt Livermore (ch 1981)	Blushing Groom / Flama Ardiente
	Housebuster (USA) (br 1987)	Big Dreams (b or br 1980)	Great Above / Dolphins Dream
Bahamian Pirate (USA) (ch.g. 1995)		Deputy Minister (b or br 1979)	Vice Regent / Mint Copy
	Shining Through (USA) (b 1989)	Solar (ch 1976)	Halo / Sex Appeal

Bahamian Pirate is by Housebuster, champion sprinter in the States at three and four. Bahamian Pirate is the second foal of Shining Through, an unraced daughter of the useful 1978 Irish two-year-old Solar, herself a half-sister to El Gran Senor and Try My Best. Shining Through's third foal, a colt by Crafty Prospector, is a winner in the USA. The sturdy Bahamian Pirate, who acts on firm and soft going, is very much a sprinter in appearance and does virtually all of his racing at five and six furlongs, though he probably needs testing conditions to be seen to best advantage at the former trip. *D. Nicholls*

BAHAMIAN RHAPSODY (IRE) 3 b.f. Fairy King (USA) – Lupescu 102 (Dixie- **76** land Band (USA)) [2001 10.5s³ 14g² 12f 12m⁵ 14.1m⁶ 10m 13.1m² 16d⁴ 16v² 16v⁵ f12g* Nov 26] big, angular filly: unimpressive mover: third foal: half-sister to 2m winner Junkanoo (by Generous) and Irish 7f winner Lindissima (by Green Desert): dam 9f/1¼m winner in Britain/USA who stayed 1½m: fair performer: left M. Channon after sixth start: won maiden at Southwell in November: barely stays 2m when conditions are testing: acts on heavy going, good to firm and fibresand. *S. P. C. Woods*

BAHIA 2 ch.f. (Jan 20) Grand Lodge (USA) 125 – Helens Dreamgirl 95 (Caerleon **59**
(USA) 132) [2001 8m⁶ 7.9d⁶ 8v⁶ 7s Nov 10] 17,000 2-y-o: sturdy filly: half-sister to
several winners, including fairly useful performer up to 1¼m Eastways (by Efisio), 5f
winner at 2 yrs, and middle-distance stayer House of Dreams (by Darshaan): dam 1¼m
winner: modest maiden: should stay 1¼m. *Bob Jones*

BAHIRAH 3 b.f. Ashkalani (IRE) 128 – Top of The League 85 (High Top 131) [2001 **71**
11.9m³ 12m⁴ 10m² 9.2m³ 10d f9.4g* Nov 27] 160,000Y: half-sister to numerous winners,
including Lancashire Oaks winner and Oaks second Noushkey (by Polish Precedent), 7f
winner at 2 yrs, and 7-y-o San Sebastian: dam, 2-y-o 7f winner who stayed 1¼m, from
good family: fair performer: blinkered, won maiden at Wolverhampton in November by
7 lengths: had form at 9f to 1½m: acted on good to firm going and fibresand: free-going
sort: had wandered: visits Polish Precedent. *M. A. Jarvis*

BAHRAIN (IRE) 5 ch.g. Lahib (USA) 129 – Twin Island (IRE) (Standaan (FR) 118) **63**
[2001 65: 7.1v 8.1g 8f* 8.1m 7.5m⁴ 8f 8.5f² 8m 7m 8d 7.5m f8.5g f8.5g f9.4g f7s p7g **a47**
Dec 19] stocky gelding: modest handicapper: won ladies race at Brighton in May: well
held last 7 starts: effective at 7f to 8.5f: acts on fibresand, firm and soft going: tried tongue
tied. *J. M. Bradley*

BAHRQUEEN (USA) 2 b.f. (Mar 18) Bahri (USA) 125 – April In Kentucky (USA) **86 p**
(Palace Music (USA) 129) [2001 7d³ Oct 15] IR 23,000Y: quite attractive filly: fourth
foal: half-sister to a winner in USA, including at 2 yrs, by Mr Greeley: dam, maiden, half-
sister to 3 smart French middle-distance performers, out of Arc runner-up Rescousse:
6/1, narrowly-beaten third of 20 to Opening Ceremony in maiden at Leicester, travelling
strongly and leading from over 2f out until close home without coming under undue
pressure: will stay at least 1m: sure to improve. *H. R. A. Cecil*

BAILEYS PRIZE (USA) 4 ch.g. Mister Baileys 123 – Mar Mar (USA) (Forever **84**
Casting (USA)) [2001 86: 10d⁴ 10m 10m⁴ 10m 11.8g 10g⁵ 10.4s³ 12s* Oct 20] robust
gelding: unimpressive mover: fairly useful performer: not at best after third start, but still
won apprentice claimer at Catterick in October: effective at 1¼m/1½m: acts on soft and
good to firm going: sold 12,000 gns. *M. Johnston*

BAILIEBOROUGH (IRE) 2 b.c. (Jan 14) Charnwood Forest (IRE) 125 – She- **80 p**
rannda (USA) (Trempolino (USA) 135) [2001 5g 6g* 6d⁴ 8d⁶ Oct 19] 13,500F, 33,000Y:
quite good-topped colt: first foal: dam unraced half-sister to useful French 1m and 10.5f
winner Sherema from family of high-class miler Sendawar: won maiden at Thirsk in
August: good fourth of 22 in sales race at Doncaster: tended to go in snatches when
running creditably in nursery at Newmarket final start: stays 1m: sweating slightly last 2
starts: likely to make useful 3-y-o. *T. D. Easterby*

BAISSE D'ARGENT (IRE) 5 b.g. Common Grounds 118 – Fabulous Pet (Some- –
thingfabulous (USA)) [2001 54: f16.2g Dec 8] leggy, useful-looking gelding: well held
only 5-y-o start: blinkered once. *D. J. S. Cosgrove*

BAJAN BLUE 3 b.f. Lycius (USA) 124 – Serotina (IRE) 73 (Mtoto 134) [2001 57?: **59**
12.6f 8f 11.6g* 12f Aug 1] close-coupled filly: modest performer: won selling handicap
at Windsor in July: stays 11.6f: sold 4,200 gns in August. *M. Johnston*

BAJAN BROKER (IRE) 4 br.f. Turtle Island (IRE) 123 – Foxrock (Ribero 126) **45**
[2001 63: 8.2v 8.2v 7s⁵ Oct 16] tall filly: poor maiden: stays 1¼m: acts on soft going: has
edged left. *E. Stanners*

BAJAN SUNSET (IRE) 4 ch.g. Mujtahid (USA) 118 – Dubai Lady 78 (Kris 135) **39**
[2001 53: f11g f12g³ f12g⁵ f11g⁵ 10f 10.9f Jun 22] long-backed, angular gelding: poor
maiden handicapper: stays 1½m: acts on firm going and fibresand: tried visored/tongue
tied. *J. D. Bethell*

BAKIRI (IRE) 3 b.c. Doyoun 124 – Bakiya (USA) 94 (Trempolino (USA) 135) [2001 **93**
8s⁴ 8s⁴ 8m* 8m 10g⁴ 9g² Aug 6] leggy colt: first foal: dam, 1½m winner, out of half-sister
to very smart performer up to 13.5f River Memories: won maiden at Kempton in May,
drifting right: good efforts in handicaps after: stays 1¼m: acts on soft
and good to firm ground: sold 30,000 gns. *Sir Michael Stoute*

BALADEUR (IRE) 3 b.g. Doyoun 124 – Singing Filly (Relkino 131) [2001 85?: 8v **73 d**
7.1g 8m 8.1v 8g 8s f7g f8.5g f8.5s Dec 26] IR 12,500F, IR 23,000Y: strong gelding:
fourth foal: half-brother to fairly useful Irish 6.5f winner Amahsan (by Nashamaa): dam
French 1m and 11f winner: fairly useful maiden winner for K. Prendergast in Ireland at 2
yrs: fair form on second start only in 2001: probably stays 7f: acts on heavy ground.
T. D. Barron

BALAKHERI (IRE) 2 b.c. (Mar 7) Theatrical 128 – Balanka (IRE) 116 (Alzao (USA) 117) [2001 7d 7s² 8.2s* Oct 30] third foal: dam, French 1m/1¼m winner, out of half-sister to dam of Prix du Jockey Club winner Bering: won maiden at Nottingham in October by 3 lengths from Pure Mischief, responding well to pressure and asserting final 1f: will be suited by 1¼m/1½m: raced only on ground softer than good: should make a smart 3-y-o. *Sir Michael Stoute* **96 p**

BALAKIREF 2 b.c. (Feb 7) Royal Applause 124 – Pluck 80 (Never So Bold 135) [2001 6g 6g⁵ 7g² 7s⁴ f7g* Nov 27] 25,000Y: third living foal: half-brother to Swedish winner up to 1¼m Cub Chief (by Be My Chief): dam, 5.7f (at 2 yrs) and 6f winner, out of half-sister to very smart sprinter Piccolo: fair performer: won maiden at Wolverhampton in November by ¾ length from Emigrate, edging left: stays 7f: acts on fibresand and soft going. *W. Jarvis* **76**

BALANOU 3 b. or br.f. Valanour (IRE) 125 – Batalya (BEL) (Boulou) [2001 56: e10g³ e8g⁵ f8g⁴ f9.4g* 10s³ 8.1g 10m* 10.1m² 10m⁶ 9.7m 10m² 10.1m³ 10m 12g f11g Oct 1] strong filly: modest handicapper: won at Wolverhampton in March and Brighton in June: stays 1¼m: acts on fibresand/equitrack, soft and good to firm going: usually races prominently. *S. C. Williams* **59**

BALDOUR (IRE) 2 b.c. (Mar 11) Green Desert (USA) 127 – Baldemara (FR) (Sanglamore (USA) 126) [2001 6g² 6m² Sep 1] good-topped colt: first foal: dam unraced half-sister to very smart French filly up to 1m Balbonella, herself dam of top-class sprinter Anabaa, high-class 1¼m performer Key of Luck and Poule d'Essai des Pouliches winner Always Loyal: reportedly threw a splint and was pin-fired in the spring: fairly useful form when runner-up in maidens at Yarmouth and Ripon, eased once held behind 6-length winner Captain Rio in latter: will probably stay 1m: likely to improve further. *E. A. L. Dunlop* **87 p**

BALI 3 br.f. Darshaan 133 – Bonne Ile 115 (Ile de Bourbon (USA) 133) [2001 8g 10m 10g² 11.9s⁴ Sep 30] rather leggy, angular filly: half-sister to fairly useful 1m and 1¼m winner Bonne Etoile and 1m winner Belle Ile (both by Diesis) and winner up to around 9f in USA by Gulch: dam middle-distance stayer, later Grade 1 1¼m winner in USA: fairly useful maiden: easily best effort when ½-length second at Pontefract in July: should stay 1½m: found little (softer ground) final start: sent to France. *Sir Michael Stoute* **82**

BALIDARE 4 b.f. King's Signet (USA) 110 – Baligay 84 (Balidar 133) [2001 –: 6m 6m 5m Sep 6] robust, lengthy filly: little form. *M. J. Weeden* **–**

BALI ROYAL 3 b.f. King's Signet (USA) 110 – Baligay 84 (Balidar 133) [2001 57: f5g⁴ 5.1v² 5d* f6g* 5d² 5.3f* 5m* 5.1m³ 5.1m* 5.1f² 5g* 5d⁶ 5v⁵ Oct 27] strong, good-quartered filly: useful handicapper: had a good year, winning at Musselburgh (unseated to post), Southwell, Brighton, Newcastle, Chester and Goodwood between April/August: will prove best at 5f/6f: acts on any turf going and fibresand: has been unruly stalls/withdrawn: has awkward head carriage: races prominently: tough and much improved. *J. M. Bradley* **97**

BALI-STAR 6 b.g. Alnasr Alwasheek 117 – Baligay 84 (Balidar 133) [2001 52: 6g³ 5g 5m 6m⁴ 5.1m⁵ 5m Sep 6] modest maiden handicapper: stays 6f: possibly unsuited by soft ground. *M. J. Weeden* **52 +**

BALLA D'AIRE (IRE) 6 b. or br.g. Balla Cove 119 – Silius (Junius (USA) 124) [2001 34: f12g Feb 27] disappointing maiden: tried blinkered. *C. N. Kellett* **–**

BALLADEER (IRE) 3 b.g. King's Theatre (IRE) 128 – Carousel Music 56 (On Your Mark 125) [2001 81: 8.1v* 10.4m 11.6g* 12f 14g⁵ 13.3m⁴ 14s⁴ 13.3f f12g* Oct 6] workmanlike gelding: fairly useful performer: won minor events at Warwick in April and Windsor in June, and handicap at Wolverhampton in October: stays 1¾m: acts on good to firm ground, heavy and fibresand: gelded after final start. *J. W. Hills* **91**

BALLADONIA 5 b.m. Primo Dominie 121 – Susquehanna Days (USA) 68 (Chief's Crown (USA)) [2001 98: 10g³ 10.1f² 10m⁵ Jul 21] smallish, leggy mare: useful performer: good efforts when placed in handicap at Sandown and listed event at Newcastle (head second to Tarfshi) in June: stiff task final outing: effective at 1¼m/1½m: acts on any going: usually races prominently: consistent. *Lady Herries* **103**

BALLARD CONNECTION 2 ch.f. (Apr 8) Danzig Connection (USA) – Ballard Lady (IRE) 53 (Ballad Rock 122) [2001 6.1v Oct 4] 3,000Y: strong filly: first foal: dam, 6f to 1m winner, out of half-sister to Chief Singer: 40/1 and backward, well beaten in maiden at Nottingham. *J. S. Wainwright* **–**

BALLET FAME (USA)   2 br.f. (May 10) Quest For Fame 127 – Bold Ballerina   **79 p**
(Sadler's Wells (USA) 132) [2001 7d* Nov 3] leggy, quite good-topped filly: fourth foal:
dam, second at 1m in France, half-sister to Lowther winner Kingscote out of smart
performer up to 1m Bold Fantasy: 10/1, won 21-runner maiden at Newmarket by ½
length from Unfaithful Thought, edging right before leading final 1f: should stay at least
1¼m: will improve. *B. W. Hills*

BALLET GIRL (USA)   2 b.f. (Jan 18) Theatrical 128 – Atelier (Warning 136) [2001   **70 p**
7d Nov 3] angular filly: second foal: dam, unraced, out of sister to Commander In Chief
and half-sister to Warning and Deploy: weak 11/2-shot, not at all knocked about once
unable to go with principals when eighth of 21 in Newmarket maiden: should be suited
by 1¼m+: sure to improve. *B. W. Hills*

BALLET HIGH (IRE)   8 b.g. Sadler's Wells (USA) 132 – Marie d'Argonne (FR)   **67**
104 (Jefferson 129) [2001 –: 13.3m⁶ 16.2m⁵ 18m Jul 7] tall, sparely-made gelding: fair
maiden on Flat, very lightly raced nowadays: stays 2m: acts on good to firm going (has
form on soft over hurdles): has high head carriage. *R. Dickin*

BALLET-K   7 ch.m. Gunner B 126 – Nicolene 91 (Nice Music 115) [2001 16.5s Nov   **–**
10] fairly useful at 5 yrs, winning handicap at Bath: well held only Flat outing since: stays
17f: useful staying hurdler. *J. Neville*

BALLET MASTER (USA)   5 ch.h. Kingmambo (USA) 125 – Danse Royale (IRE)   **83**
112 (Caerleon (USA) 132) [2001 –: f8g⁶ f7g* 7.6f⁶ 8g³ 8m⁴ 10.4m⁴ 10.3m 8m 7.9m   **a90**
10s⁵ 8.9d f8g² f7g* f8g p7g p8g Dec 28] strong horse: fairly useful handicapper: won at
Southwell in March and (having left M. W. Easterby after tenth start) at Wolverhampton
(by 5 lengths) in November: well held last 3 starts: effective at 7f to 10.4f: unraced on
heavy, probably acts on any other turf going and goes on fibresand: sometimes blinkered:
has pulled hard, and unseated to post fifth intended start. *J. D. Czerpak*

BALLET SCORE (IRE)   2 b.f. (Feb 17) Sadler's Wells (USA) 132 – Puzzled Look   **80 p**
(USA) (Gulch (USA)) [2001 7s* Nov 9] big, rangy filly: first foal: dam, minor stakes
sprint winner in USA, half-sister to smart performer in Britain and in USA up to 1½m
Winged Victory: 4/1 and fit, overcame greenness to win maiden at Doncaster (beat
Maranilla by short head), staying on well once getting hang of things to lead close home:
will stay at least 1m: open to improvement. *J. H. M. Gosden*

BALLETS RUSSES (IRE)   4 b.f. Marju (IRE) 127 – Elminya (IRE) (Sure Blade   **42**
(USA) 130) [2001 49d: 8m 11.5m⁶ 11.9m⁴ 10.1m⁴ 14.1d² 15.8g⁵ 14m⁵ 11.9m Aug 29]   **a?**
poor maiden handicapper: stays 15.8f: acts on good to firm and good to soft going: tried
visored: has given trouble start: often slowly away. *John Berry*

BALLET SUITE   3 b.f. Sadler's Wells (USA) 132 – Houseproud (USA) 115 (River-   **90**
man (USA) 131) [2001 9.9d³ 11.5m* Jun 1] sixth foal: half-sister to useful 1996 2-y-o 7f
winner Imperial President (by Known Fact), later winner in USA, and 1994 2-y-o 6f
winner Homely (by Mr Prospector): dam, French 5.5f (at 2 yrs) and 1m (Poule d'Essai
des Pouliches) winner: landed odds in 6-runner maiden at Yarmouth in June by 7 lengths
from Saabirr, quickening away in good style: slowly away/carried head high on
debut: stayed 11.5f: acted on good to firm going: dead. *H. R. A. Cecil*

BALL GAMES   3 b.g. Mind Games 121 – Deb's Ball 70 (Glenstal (USA) 118) [2001   **64**
63: 8v³ 8m⁵ 9.1m³ 7d 10d Oct 30] rather leggy, close-coupled gelding: modest maiden:
seems to stay 9f: acts on heavy and good to firm going. *D. Moffatt*

BALLINA LAD (IRE)   5 b.g. Mac's Imp (USA) 116 – Nationalartgallery (IRE) (Tate   **–**
Gallery (USA) 117) [2001 46: f6g f5g⁴ f6s f5g Jan 29] angular gelding: poor handicapper: **a43**
probably best at 5f/6f: acts on fibresand: blinkered twice. *D. Nicholls*

BALLINGARRY (IRE)   2 b.c. (Apr 13) Sadler's Wells (USA) 132 – Flamenco   **114 p**
Wave (USA) 103 (Desert Wine (USA)) [2001 7d⁶ 9v³ 8d* 10v* Nov 13]
    Only twice since it was awarded Group 1 status in 1987 has the Criterium
de Saint-Cloud not been won by a French-trained runner. On the first occasion, a
photo was needed to determine that Polaris Flight, trained by Peter Chapple-Hyam,
had prevailed, but in the latest edition it was clear some way from the finish that
the first prize of over £37,000 was destined for abroad. Or, to be more precise,
Ireland. Aidan O'Brien's representatives Ballingarry, Black Sam Bellamy and
Castle Gandolfo, who had all been prominent from the start in a steadily-run race,
occupied the first three places approaching the final furlong and were beginning
to draw away from the seven other runners. Ballingarry, having taken the lead

Criterium de Saint-Cloud—Aidan O'Brien completes a 1,2,3 in a Group 1 for the third time during the year as Ballingarry fends off Castle Gandolfo (near side) and Black Sam Bellamy (rail)

travelling well shortly after turning into the straight, was being strongly pressed by Castle Gandolfo at this point, but found plenty for pressure and was still running on well at the finish, where he had a length to spare over Castle Gandolfo with the same distance back to Black Sam Bellamy. It was the third time in the season that O'Brien runners had finished first, second and third in a Group 1 contest, an achievement, along with others, which is dealt with in greater detail in the essays on Black Minnaloushe and Johannesburg. Unlike Johannesburg, Ballingarry's light was hidden under a bushel for the great majority of the season. He had looked nothing out of the ordinary on his first two starts, but it was a very different story on his third. A one-mile maiden at Leopardstown at the end of October saw Ballingarry open his account by six lengths, and, while his winning margin fell eight lengths short of that recorded by his stable-companion Galileo on his debut in the equivalent race twelve months earlier, it was still an impressive performance. The step up to a mile and a quarter at Saint-Cloud showed Ballingarry to even better advantage, and the manner of his victory there suggests a mile and a half should be well within his compass.

	Sadler's Wells (USA) (b 1981)	Northern Dancer (b 1961)	Nearctic / Natalma
Ballingarry (IRE) (b.c. Apr 13, 1999)		Fairy Bridge (b 1975)	Bold Reason / Special
	Flamenco Wave (USA) (ch 1986)	Desert Wine (b 1980)	Damascus / Anne Campbell
		Armada Way (ch 1976)	Sadair / Hurry Call

A tilt at the Derby could also be on the cards for Ballingarry, and if he does get to Epsom we would expect him to give a much better account of himself there than his brother Aristotle did in the race in 2000. Aristotle, winner of the Racing Post Trophy, folded tamely in the straight to finish tenth, and it was later reported that he had been found to have cysts on his epiglottis. Subsequently sold to race in Singapore, Aristotle won over a mile and a quarter there in the latest season, racing under the name of Our Aristotle. A full sister to the pair, the three-year-old Kylemore, ran twice without success at two but still attracted a great deal of attention when she appeared at the December Sales in foal to Giant's Causeway, the bidding for her finally coming to a halt at 650,000 guineas. Their dam Flamenco Wave has produced several other winners, notably the high-class miler Starborough (by Soviet Star), successful in both the Prix Jean Prat and St James's Palace Stakes, and Spanish Falls (by Belmez), a useful performer who won the twelve-furlong Group 3 Prix de Royaumont. Flamenco Wave, a daughter of Armada Way who was one of the leading juvenile fillies in Canada in 1978, did well herself as a juvenile. She won both her starts that season, over six furlongs on soft ground, including the Moyglare Stud Stakes. However, she failed to train on and finished last on both her

Mrs John Magnier's "Ballingarry"

outings at three. There are no worries on that score where Ballingarry is concerned. Further improvement and further victories look assured for this promising colt, who so far has raced only on ground softer than good and acts on heavy. Incidentally, his posed portrait was taken very late in the year when he had gone in his coat. *A. P. O'Brien, Ireland*

BALLINGER RIDGE 2 b.g. (Feb 28) Sabrehill (USA) 120 – Branston Ridge (Indian Ridge 123) [2001 6m⁵ Aug 15] first foal: dam unraced from family of Branston Abby: 10/1, well-beaten fifth of 9 in maiden at Salisbury, slowly into stride. *B. Hanbury* —

BALLISTIC BOY 4 ch.g. First Trump 118 – Be Discreet (Junius (USA) 124) [2001 58: 10s Apr 10] leggy gelding: modest maiden at 3 yrs: well beaten only run on Flat in 2001: winning hurdler. *Jonjo O'Neill* —

BALL KING (IRE) 3 ch.c. Ball Park (NZ) – Firey Encounter (IRE) (Kris 135) [2001 74p: 7s⁵ 8m² 7.1g⁶ 5m⁴ 6m⁴ 7.6m Aug 22] rather sparely-made colt: fairly useful performer: apparently best effort when close fourth in handicap at Sandown fourth start: left G. Butler before final outing: seems effective at 5f (on stiff track) to 1m: acts on equitrack, good to firm and soft ground: sometimes tongue tied. *P. J. Makin* 83

BALLYBUNION (IRE) 2 ch.c. (Feb 12) Entrepreneur 123 – Clarentia 111 (Ballad Rock 122) [2001 6g 5s 6m* 6g* p7g Nov 13] 30,000F, IR 230,000Y: strong colt: seventh foal: half-brother to smart 1996 2-y-o 5f/6f (Prix Morny and Middle Park Stakes) winner Bahamian Bounty (by Cadeaux Genereux) and fairly useful 1995 2-y-o 5f winner 87 p

Forentia (by Formidable): dam sprinter: won maiden at Catterick in September and nursery at Newmarket (led final 1f and held Racing Bailey's by a head) in October: stays 6f, seemingly not quite 7f: acts on good to firm going: likely to make a useful 3-y-o handicapper. *P. F. I. Cole*

BALLYHURRY (USA) 4 b.g. Rubiano (USA) – Balakhna (FR) (Tyrant (USA)) –
[2001 76: 11f a9f 8.9d 10d Oct 30] $60,000F, 7,500 2-y-o: half-brother to several winners in France/USA, including 1987 Prix Robert Papin winner Balawaki (by Miswaki): dam, won up to 1m in France, half-sister to dam of Zieten and Blue Duster: fair performer at best: won handicaps at Tralee and Cork in August 2000 for D. Hanley in Ireland: well beaten since (trained by E. Charpy in UAE until after second 4-y-o start): stays 1¼m: best efforts on good going: tried blinkered, including for wins. *J. S. Goldie*

BALLYHURST (IRE) 2 b.g. (Mar 31) Charnwood Forest (IRE) 125 – La Belle Katherine (USA) (Lyphard (USA) 132) [2001 6m 5m⁶ 7.5f Jul 7] 12,000F, 17,000Y: tall, leggy gelding: good walker: second foal: half-brother to 6f winner Criss Cross (by Lahib): dam, ran twice in France, from family of high-class 6f/7f performer Russian Revival: no form in sellers/maiden: dead. *M. W. Easterby*

BALLYJAZZ 3 b.c. Alhijaz 122 – All The Girls (IRE) 49 (Alzao (USA) 117) [2001 **73**
f7g⁵ f8g³ f7g* 8f 8.5f Jun 13] 6,500Y: second foal: dam maiden who stayed 1m: fair form: won maiden at Southwell in January, carrying head awkwardly: left J. Osborne, then well held in claimers at Hollywood: stays 1m: acts on fibresand: blinkered final outing. *P. G. Aguirre, USA*

BALLYKISSANN 6 ch.g. Ballacashtal (CAN) – Mybella Ann (Anfield 117) [2001 –: –
f9.4s e7g e12g 11.9f May 23] big, lengthy gelding: no form on Flat in 2001: sometimes blinkered/visored. *J. C. Tuck*

BALLYMAGAN (IRE) 3 b.c. Charnwood Forest (IRE) 125 – Bold Miss (Bold Lad **78**
(IRE) 133) [2001 64p: f7g* f9.4s* f8.5g² Jan 25] fair performer: won maiden at Southwell and handicap at Wolverhampton in January: stays 9.4f: raced only on fibresand: sold 3,600 gns in July, sent to Italy. *B. W. Hills*

BALMACARA 2 b.f. (Mar 5) Lake Coniston (IRE) 131 – Diabaig 76 (Precocious **43**
126) [2001 6g 6.1m 5.7g Oct 1] 5,500Y: fourth foal: dam 1m winner: poor maiden. *Miss K. B. Boutflower*

BAMALKO (IRE) 2 b.c. (Mar 7) Royal Applause 124 – Shadowglow (Shaadi (USA) **87**
126) [2001 5m³ 5.1g² 5m² 6g⁵ f7g² 7g* 7g³ Sep 15] IR 40,000Y: well-made colt: good mover: second foal: half-brother to 4-y-o Holy Orders: dam, ran once in Ireland, half-sister to useful performers Alpenglow and Attitre: fairly useful performer: won nursery at Epsom in August: good third in similar event there final start: takes good hold, and will prove best up to 1m: acts on fibresand, raced only on good/good to firm ground on turf: races prominently. *B. W. Hills*

BANAADIR (USA) 3 b.f. Diesis 133 – Treble (USA) 118 (Riverman (USA) 131) **50**
[2001 10.5d 9.9m² 12.1g Sep 13] third living foal: half-sister to fairly useful 1¼m winner Faateq (by Caerleon): dam, French 9f (at 2 yrs) and 1¼m (Prix Saint-Alary) winner, out of half-sister to Triptych: modest form: stayed 1¼m: visits Grand Lodge. *J. L. Dunlop*

BANASAN (IRE) 3 b.c. Marju (IRE) 127 – Banaja (IRE) (Sadler's Wells (USA) 132) **96**
[2001 8.3g 10.2f⁵ 10g³ 10d* 12m⁴ Sep 8] fifth foal: half-brother to 3 winners, including useful 11f winner Baniyar (by Alzao) and Irish 2m winner Banjala (by Kahyasi): dam unraced half-sister to Arc second Behera: useful performer: won maiden at Windsor in June by short head from Eljohar and good fourth in handicap at Thirsk final start: will stay beyond 1½m: acts on good to firm and good to soft going: carries head high/tends to hang left: visored final 2 starts. *Sir Michael Stoute*

BANCO 2 b.g. (Feb 27) Efisio 120 – Peace Dance (Bikala 134) [2001 f7g Dec 14] fifth –
foal: half-brother to fairly useful 1¼m winner Polo (by Warning): dam unraced sister to Prix du Jockey Club winner Polytain: 20/1, very slowly away when well held in maiden at Southwell. *M. W. Easterby*

BANCO SUIVI (IRE) 4 b.f. Nashwan (USA) 135 – Pay The Bank 81 (High Top **86**
131) [2001 93: 12s 9g⁵ May 4] angular, workmanlike filly: fairly useful performer: not disgraced final outing in 2001: stays 1¾m: acts on any going: races prominently: has sweated/been on edge/raced freely. *B. W. Hills*

BANDANNA 4 gr.f. Bandmaster (USA) 97 – Gratclo 65 (Belfort (FR) 89) [2001 89: **90**
5s⁶ 6s⁵ 5.1f⁶ 5.7f² 6g² 5f 5.1m⁵ 6m⁵ 6g 5.7d⁴ 5g 6g 6.1d² 6g 5.1d⁴ 5v⁴ Oct 29] big, leggy,

close-coupled filly: fairly useful handicapper: effective at 5f/6f: acts on any turf going: usually held up. *R. J. Hodges*

BANDARELLO   3 b.f. Distant Relative 128 – Bangles 83 (Chilibang 120) [2001 53: **53** f6g³ f6g 5g⁵ 6g⁵ 5m⁴ 6d Oct 9] lengthy filly: poor mover: modest maiden: likely to prove best at 5f/6f. *John A. Harris*

BANDARI (IRE)   2 b.c. (Apr 29) Alhaarth (IRE) 126 – Miss Audimar (USA) (Mr **113 p** Leader (USA)) [2001 7.5g* 7.1g 8m* 8s* Oct 22]
        Trainers don't come much hungrier than Mark Johnston, so it must have been all the harder for him to starve himself of the opportunity of pattern-race success with some of his promising youngsters in the autumn. As Aidan O'Brien's juveniles set about the top table of races as if there was an 'all you can eat' sign on display, Johnston kept the likes of Bandari, Fight Your Corner, Legal Approach and Love Regardless nibbling at the bar snacks, resisting temptation with them, no doubt in the hope of greater rewards in the next season. The Racing Post Trophy at Doncaster, in particular, was the poorer as a result of Johnston's policy, drawing a field of just six, which included only Mount Joy, Redback and the 66/1-shot Mr Sandancer from outside the O'Brien camp. Bandari had put up a performance not far removed from that recorded by O'Brien's High Chapparal in winning at Doncaster when in action at Pontefract only five days beforehand. Bandari ran away with the listed Tote Bookmakers Silver Tankard Stakes over a mile, starting at 7/2 favourite in a field of twelve and making virtually all, being ridden out to beat Infinite Spirit by nine lengths. It was Bandari's third win from four starts, following a debut success in a maiden at Beverley in August and a convincing win in a minor event at Ayr in September. Bandari's one defeat came in between those wins when only seventh behind Redback in the Group 3 Solario Stakes at Sandown, a muddling contest in which several of the better horses failed to give their true running.

	Alhaarth (IRE) (b 1993)	Unfuwain (b 1985)	Northern Dancer Height of Fashion
Bandari (IRE)		Irish Valley (ch 1982)	Irish River Green Valley
(b.c. Apr 29, 1999)	Miss Audimar (USA) (b 1981)	Mr Leader (b 1966)	Hail To Reason Jolie Deja
		Quick Selection (ch 1972)	Viceregal Lachine

        Bandari looks sure to train on well and his form leaves him only a step or two away from being up to making a bold show in a classic. Whether the trip of the Guineas or the Derby will suit him better is open to debate on pedigree. The best previous foal of his dam Miss Audimar's many produce is Diaghilef (by Royal Academy), whom Johnston trained to win the King George V Handicap at Royal Ascot over a mile and a half and to be fifth in the Ebor. Miss Audimar's next best progeny before Bandari was Noora Park (by Ahonoora), a useful sprinter in Ireland who died at the end of her two-year-old career. Miss Audimar, who is a grand-daughter of Lachine, a smart filly for Sir Gordon Richards in the 'sixties, won at up to eleven furlongs in America, where she was also stakes-placed, and she is also responsible for the three-year-old Gold Standard (by Goldmark), a winner at a mile

Tote Bookmakers Silver Tankard Stakes, Pontefract—Bandari spreadeagles his field; the others are led home by Infinite Spirit

and three quarters in 2001. Bandari's sire Alhaarth finished fifth in the Derby and didn't race again over a mile and a half after disappointing when blinkered in the Irish Derby, winning three pattern races from a mile to almost a mile and a quarter subsequently. Bandari is from Alhaarth's first crop, which also includes the Cornwallis Stakes winner Dominica. The strong, angular Bandari is much more stoutly bred than Dominica on the dam's side, and shapes as though sure to stay beyond a mile. A powerful-looking galloper, he has yet to tackle ground firmer than good to firm and clearly coped well with soft at Pontefract. He has shown a tendency to swish his tail in the paddock, but so far has gone about his job with notable relish once racing. The IR 40,000 guineas he cost as a yearling already looks money well spent. *M. Johnston*

BANDBOX (IRE)   6 ch.g. Imperial Frontier (USA) 112 – Dublah (USA) (Private **74** Account (USA)) [2001 74: 7.1g 5.7m 6m³ 6m⁵ 5.7f² 6m⁶ 7m⁵ 6g² 6d⁴ 6m⁶ 6g 6m² 5.7d⁵ Aug 19] small gelding: fair performer: effective at 5f to 7f: acts on fibresand, firm and soft going: formerly effective in visor/blinkers/tongue tie, not tried in 2001. *M. Salaman*

BANDLER CHING (IRE)   4 b.g. Sri Pekan (USA) 117 – Stanerra's Wish (IRE) **70** (Caerleon (USA) 132) [2001 81: 9.9f 10g 9.9m 11.5g⁶ 10m⁴ 10m⁶ 8.5g 8s⁴ 9g Oct 19] angular gelding: tubed: fair handicapper: well below form last 3 starts: best around 1¼m: acts on good to firm going: tends to hang. *C. N. Allen*

BAND OF COLOUR (IRE)   3 b.f. Spectrum (IRE) 126 – Regal Scintilla 103 (King – of Spain 121) [2001 7.1s Aug 9] 14,000Y, 18,000 2-y-o: third foal: dam, 5f performer, won Prix d'Arenberg at 2 yrs: 8/1, always behind in maiden at Chepstow. *C. R. Egerton*

BAND SUBSTANCE   5 b.m. Bandmaster (USA) 97 – Bold Dancer (FR) (Bold – Arrangement 127) [2001 f12s Jan 22] first foal: dam ran once: tailed off in bumper early in 2000, and on only Flat outing. *A. T. Murphy*

BANGLED   4 ch.g. Beveled (USA) – Bangles 83 (Chilibang 120) [2001 49, a58: f6f* – f6g 6d 6m 6m f6g p7g Dec 12] deep-girthed gelding: modest handicapper: won at **a58 d** Southwell in March: showed nothing after: stays 6f: acts on fibresand and good to firm going: tried visored/tongue tied. *D. J. Coakley*

BANIYAR (IRE)   4 ch.c. Alzao (USA) 117 – Banaja (IRE) (Sadler's Wells (USA) – 132) [2001 105: 12m May 23] big, strong, rangy colt: fluent mover: useful form when fifth in King Edward VII Stakes at Royal Ascot in 2000: tailed off only run in 2001 (poorly to post): stays 1½m: sold only 3,500 gns in October. *Sir Michael Stoute*

BANJO BAY (IRE)   3 b.c. Common Grounds 118 – Thirlmere (Cadeaux Genereux **98** 131) [2001 62: 6s* 7.9g⁶ 7d* 8m² 7g 6m² 6m⁵ 7s Sep 29] close-coupled colt: useful performer: vastly improved, and won maiden at Pontefract in May and handicap at Leicester in June: some good efforts after, including second to Antonio Canova in Great St Wilfrid at Ripon sixth outing and fifth to Continent in Ayr Gold Cup penultimate start: effective at 6f to 1m: acts on soft and good to firm going: sometimes slowly away. *B. A. McMahon*

BANK ON HIM   6 b.g. Elmaamul (USA) 125 – Feather Flower 74 (Relkino 131) **53** [2001 –: f12g 10.1d 8.1g² 9.7d p10g³ p8g² p10g⁶ Dec 12] fair handicapper on all-weather, **a72** modest on turf: stays easy 1¼m: acts on good to firm going and all-weather: races freely: has hung left. *G. L. Moore*

BANKS HILL   3 b.f. Danehill (USA) 126 – Hasili (IRE) (Kahyasi 130) [2001 8v⁴ **128** 8m² 8m* 8f* 8d² 8d² 10f* Oct 27]

    The diuretic furosemide, traded under the brand name lasix and banned for runners in European races, is almost a standard medication in the States, based on the principle that its supposed efficiency in preventing horses bleeding internally must be an advantage. The majority of European trainers with runners in America habitually give lasix nowadays, presumably working on the theory that it might help in providing a level playing field against the home-trained opposition. At the Breeders' Cup at Belmont Park in October, the card showed ninety of the ninety-four contestants racing on lasix, including fifteen of the eighteen European challengers. The trainers concerned had to state that each runner was a 'confirmed bleeder', meaning the horse had been seen to have bled either endoscopically or visually from the nose after induced exercise on the gallops or on a racecourse. There needs to be only a trace of blood internally for the horse to be deemed a

Coronation Stakes, Royal Ascot—
Banks Hill becomes Andre Fabre's first winner in Britain for over three years, beating Crystal Music,
Tempting Fate (No.13), Lethals Lady and Guineas winner Ameerat (No.1)

'confirmed bleeder', and the bleeding needs to have happened only once. The assessment is based on a veterinarian's examination. Judged on this evidence, what purports to be a precisely regulated method for controlling which horses can run on the medication is in truth nothing but a sham. Did Galileo or Johannesburg bleed in any of their races? You wouldn't know it from the way they ran, which suggests any minor bleeding they experienced at work had no bearing on their ability to run to their best on the racecourse. If ninety out of ninety-four runners in the Breeders' Cup were 'confirmed bleeders' it is long odds on that the four others—Bella Bellucci in the Fillies Juvenile and the three Andre Fabre-trained contenders, Banks Hill and Spring Oak in the Filly & Mare Turf and Slew The Red in the Turf—could have been designated the same had their connections wished. If the American racing authorities hope to avoid looking ridiculous by systematically nodding and winking on this issue, they should either remove the current criterion for using lasix, clearly fatuous when a presumed hundred per cent of horses fulfil it, or introduce meaningful criteria by making eligibility depend upon a higher and more frequent level of bleeding. In the event, however, there's no proof that the medication actually helped any of the Europeans, including Johannesburg, Fantastic Light and Sakhee, but what can be said without reservation is that its absence did nothing whatever to harm the chances of Banks Hill, whose crushing victory was the easiest in any of the eight races on the day. Fabre's view, as quoted in the *Racing Post*, is informative: 'I'm against running horses on lasix because I'm sure it has some effect you can't assess, and that's bad for the horses. Ask the jockeys what they feel about lasix. It's a diuretic and if you take some yourself you will soon have the answer.' Perhaps Fabre's success—he has the best record of any European trainer in the Breeders' Cup, with three victories, four seconds and seven thirds—might encourage some of his colleagues on this side of the Atlantic to reassess their approach.

Banks Hill came to the Breeders' Cup with a record of three wins from seven starts, starting off with her only race at two, an autumn minor event at

Breeders' Cup Filly & Mare Turf, Belmont—Banks Hill proves well suited by the step up in trip
and nothing else comes close to matching her acceleration;
Spook Express (left) claims second with Spring Oak (star on cap) third

Maisons-Laffitte. She lost her first two starts on her return, finishing fourth in a listed race at Chantilly and runner-up to Rose Gypsy in the Poule d'Essai des Pouliches at Longchamp, where she had to be switched two furlongs out and only just failed to pass the winner. Two readily-achieved victories followed, in the Prix de Sandringham at Chantilly, where she beat the Pouliches third Lethals Lady by a length and a half, and the Coronation Stakes at Royal Ascot. Amonita was a late withdrawal but the twelve other runners for the Coronation included Rose Gypsy, One Thousand Guineas winner Ameerat, classic-placed fillies Crystal Music and Toroca, and Lethals Lady again. Banks Hill, who took the eye beforehand though a shade on edge, slammed them, racing in mid-division, taking a bit of time to find room off the home turn but settling the issue swiftly in the final furlong to score by a length and a half from Crystal Music with something in reserve. An impressive display, Fabre's first success in Britain since Xaar's Craven Stakes in 1998, and one which suggested Banks Hill would be worth pitching in against the colts. In the Prix Jacques le Marois at Deauville she might have been a bit unlucky, as she finished just over a length third (promoted to second) behind the disqualified Proudwings after being bumped inside the final furlong when delivering her challenge. In the Prix du Moulin de Longchamp, she was set plenty to do and could never get to all-the-way winner Slickly, who beat her by three lengths.

Banks Hill did not contest her next planned race, the Prix de l'Opera, because of the state of the ground—although she has won on heavy and acts on good to soft, her trainer is on the record as believing she is unsuited by testing conditions. Banks Hill certainly goes well on good to firm. The Prix de l'Opera, over a mile and a quarter, would have provided a useful test of her stamina, but the way she settled in her races, and finished strongly, indicated that the Breeders' Cup trip of a mile and a quarter (reduced from eleven furlongs in 2000) would not inconvenience her, particularly on such a sharp track, set inside the other turf course at Belmont. A strong European challenge in the field of twelve also included Lailani, Mot Juste, Crystal Music and Spring Oak, with the pick of the home team England's Legend (a near eight-length winner of the Beverly D at Arlington, then second to Lailani in the Flower Bowl Handicap and favourite this time), Spook Express, who has lately landed a Grade 2 race, Kalypso Katie, Starine and Volga. All of those except Spook Express had started their careers in Europe and she had begun hers in South Africa, emphasising the extent to which the top turf races in the States depend on imports and, in the autumn, foreign runners. Banks Hill put herself in line for an Eclipse Award with a devastating performance, travelling easily close behind the pace, breezing into the lead entering the straight and storming clear with a majestic show of acceleration to beat Spook Express by five and a half lengths.

Banks Hill (b.f. 1998)	Danehill (USA) (b 1986)	Danzig (b 1977)	Northern Dancer
			Pas de Nom
		Razyana (b 1981)	His Majesty
			Spring Adieu
	Hasili (IRE) (b 1991)	Kahyasi (b 1985)	Ile de Bourbon
			Kadissya
		Kerali (ch 1984)	High Line
			Sookera

Immediately after the race Fabre said that he would be looking at all the top mile and a half races for Banks Hill in 2002. With her sex allowance she will be a formidable opponent in any contest up to a mile and a quarter, though there have to be doubts about her effectiveness at the longer trip, even though she races in a relaxed manner. Danehill admittedly does get winners at a mile and a half—Aquarelliste is a case in point—but elements in Banks Hill's pedigree involve more influences for speed than the Arc runner-up's. She is a sister to Dansili, a high-class colt clearly best at a mile, and, although by Kahyasi, the dam Hasili won over five furlongs at two before proving she stayed a mile. The grandam Kerali was by a stayer in High Line but did not win beyond seven furlongs and is out of a winner of the Cheveley Park Stakes who also foaled good sprinters in Bold Fact and So Factual. Since foaling the strong, lengthy Banks Hill, Hasili has produced the two-year-old Green Desert filly Heat Haze, followed by another filly by Danehill and a colt by the same sire. *A. Fabre, France*

BANNERET (USA)   8 b.g. Imperial Falcon (CAN) – Dashing Partner 71 (Formidable   –
(USA) 125) [2001 –, a46: f12g f12g⁵ f14g May 25] good-bodied gelding: probably
temperamental nowadays: sometimes blinkered/visored. *A. G. Juckes*

BANNINGHAM BLIZ   3 ch.f. Inchinor 119 – Mary From Dunlow 49 (Nicholas Bill   50
125) [2001 47: f7g 6m⁵ 6m 6g⁶ 7.1m⁵ Jun 17] leggy filly: modest maiden: stays 7f: acts
on firm and good to soft going: visored/blinkered: edgy sort: has looked wayward.
D. Shaw

BANNISTER   3 ch.c. Inchinor 119 – Shall We Run 59 (Hotfoot 126) [2001 101: 8m⁵   96
6f 6m Jul 21] useful-looking colt: has a quick action: useful performer: won Gimcrack
Stakes at York at 2 yrs: form in 2001 only when fifth in listed race at Kempton on
reappearance: may prove best at 6f/7f: acts on good to firm going: blinkered final start:
tends to race freely: sold 16,000 gns in October. *R. Hannon*

BANSTEAD (USA)   3 b.c. Known Fact (USA) 135 – Rapid Raja (USA) (Darby Creek   –
Road (USA)) [2001 60: 7m May 11] twice raced: modest form only on debut. *T. G. Mills*

BANYUMANIK (IRE)   5 b.h. Perugino (USA) 84 – Bennetta (FR) (Top Ville 129)   119
[2001 115: 8s⁶ 8.8g* 8g⁴ 8m* 8m⁴ 8s Sep 22] smart performer: won Grosser Preis der
Dortmunder Wirtschaft at Dortmund (for second year running, by ½ length from Peppercorn) in June and Jaguar-Meile at Cologne (by 1¾ lengths from Late Night Out) in July:
well below form last 2 starts: best around 1m: acted on soft and good to firm going: took
good hold and usually led: to stand at Gestut Erftmuhle, Bergheim, Germany, fee €3,000.
M. Hofer, Germany

BAPTISMAL ROCK (IRE)   7 ch.g. Ballad Rock 122 – Flower From Heaven   51
(Baptism 119) [2001 51: f5g* f6g³ 5.3s 5.7f⁶ Jun 1] good-bodied gelding: poor mover:
modest handicapper: won at Southwell in March: best at 5f/6f: acts on fibresand/
equitrack, firm and good to soft going: has found little/carried head awkwardly: usually
races prominently. *A. G. Newcombe*

BARABASCHI   5 b.g. Elmaamul (USA) 125 – Hills' Presidium (Presidium 124) [2001   58
81: 8.3g 7m 8.3g 9.9m Aug 15] angular, unfurnished gelding: modest in 2001: stays 1m:
acts on any going: blinkered once as 3-y-o: sometimes flashes tail/hangs. *J. White*

BARALINKA (IRE)   2 b.f. (Feb 6) Barathea (IRE) 127 – Kalinka (IRE) 88 (Soviet   72 +
Star (USA) 128) [2001 p5g* f7g⁴ Nov 26] first foal: dam, 7f winner (at 2 yrs) who
probably stayed 1¼m, out of smart 7f and 1¼m winner Tralthee: won maiden at Lingfield
in November by 1½ lengths from Italian Mist: fourth in minor event at Southwell, no
extra late on: may prove best up to 7f. *P. F. I. Cole*

BARANOVA (IRE)   3 b.f. Caerleon (USA) 132 – Lacandona (USA) 71 (Septieme   95
Ciel (USA) 123) [2001 80p: 9.9m 12g⁴ 12f Jun 21] angular filly: useful form, lightly
raced (reportedly struck into final 2-y-o start): best effort in 2001 when fourth to Volga
in Prix de Royaumont at Saint-Cloud: well beaten in blinkers in Ribblesdale Stakes at
Royal Ascot only subsequent start: stayed 1½m: raced only on good ground or firmer:
sometimes made running: dead. *J. H. M. Gosden*

BARATHEA BLAZER   2 b.c. (Mar 8) Barathea (IRE) 127 – Empty Purse (Pennine   86 p
Walk 120) [2001 7d* 10s* Oct 15] 14,000Y: sturdy colt: sixth foal: half-brother to 3
winners, including 1m/1¼m winner Going For Broke (by Simply Great) and 1½m winner
Three White Sox (by Most Welcome): dam unraced: won maiden at Newcastle and minor
event at Leicester in October, beating Editor In Chief by 2½ lengths in latter: will stay
1½m: raced only on ground softer than good: likely to make useful 3-y-o. *P. W. Harris*

BARATHEASTAR   3 ch.f. Barathea (IRE) 127 – Sueboog (IRE) 109 (Darshaan 133)   79
[2001 84p: 8.3m³ 10m⁶ 7d² 8d⁶ 7g* 7v 7d⁶ p8g⁴ Nov 24] big, lengthy filly: shows
plenty of knee action: fair handicapper: won at Redcar in October: barely stays 1m: acts
on polytrack, best turf form on good/good to soft going: has been slowly away: free-going
sort: sold 65,000 gns. *C. E. Brittain*

BARATHIKI   3 gr.f. Barathea (IRE) 127 – Tagiki (IRE) (Doyoun 124) [2001 81: f6g⁵   70
7s 8.5g Sep 15] tall, useful-looking filly: fair handicapper: form in 2001 only on reappearance: off 4 months before final outing: stays 7f: acts on firm and soft going: blinkered
(raced too freely) once at 2 yrs. *P. F. I. Cole*

BARBA PAPA (IRE)   7 b.g. Mujadil (USA) 119 – Baby's Smile 68 (Shirley Heights   93
130) [2001 101: 12g 20m 18d Oct 20] smallish gelding: good mover: fairly useful
handicapper: successful in Ascot Stakes and third in Cesarewitch (tended to hang) at 6
yrs: no better than tenth in same races in 2001: stays 2½m: acts on firm and good to soft
ground: tongue tied: useful hurdler. *A. J. Martin, Ireland*

BARBASON 9 ch.g. Polish Precedent (USA) 131 – Barada (USA) (Damascus (USA)) **58**
[2001 73, a62: f9.4g e10g 10m⁵ 10d* 9m 8m 10.2s² 10g³ 8s Sep 30] compact gelding: **a–**
modest performer: won seller at Brighton in May: stays 1¼m: acts on firm ground, soft
and equitrack (below form on fibresand): has won in blinkers (not tried in 2001):
sometimes pulls hard/finds little: usually held up. *G. L. Moore*

BARBERELLO (IRE) 3 b.f. Bigstone (IRE) 126 – Missish (Mummy's Pet 125) **–**
[2001 –: 7m 6f 6m⁶ 6m 6g 7s Oct 5] no form: left Miss E. Lavelle after third outing.
G. C. Bravery

BARCELONA 4 b.c. Barathea (IRE) 127 – Pipitina 91 (Bustino 136) [2001 87: 14m⁵ **84 d**
16.4m 16m 14.4g 13.3f 14.1d³ Oct 3] sturdy colt: fairly useful handicapper, on downgrade: stays 1¾m: acts on soft and good to firm going: tongue tied: has hung under
pressure: often held up. *G. L. Moore*

BAREFOOTED FLYER (USA) 3 ch.f. Fly So Free (USA) 122 – Carmelita (USA) **67**
(Mogambo (USA)) [2001 56: 8v⁵ f7g² f7g² f7g⁶ 7.1m² 6m³ 6g³ 7g 7.1m 7m⁶ f7g 7g
Oct 19] big, leggy filly: fair handicapper: won at Southwell in April: below form final 5
starts: effective at 6f to easy 1m: acts on fibresand, good to firm and good to soft ground:
sold 3,000 gns. *T. D. Barron*

BARINGO (USA) 2 b.c. (Apr 13) Miswaki (USA) 124 – Galega (Sure Blade (USA) **66**
130) [2001 7f Jul 5] fifth foal: half-brother to 7-y-o Burning Truth: dam, French 9f
winner, half-sister to US Grade 3 11f winner Flaming Torch out of close relative to
Coronation Cup winner Quiet Fling: 9/1 and green, seventh of 11 to Laissezaller in
maiden at Newbury, outpaced from halfway. *R. Charlton*

BARITONE 7 b.g. Midyan (USA) 124 – Zinzi (Song 132) [2001 –, a50: f6g⁵ f7g f6s **38 +**
f5g⁶ f5g⁶ e7g f6g f5g² f6g* f6g³ f5g² f6g f5g* 5s⁵ f6g f6s⁶ Dec 15] close-coupled gelding: **a69**
fair performer on all-weather, poor on turf: left S. Kettlewell after sixth start: won minor
event at Southwell and handicap at Wolverhampton in summer: has form at 1m, probably
best at 5f/6f nowadays: acts on fibresand/equitrack and soft going: tried blinkered/
visored. *J. Balding*

BARKBY (IRE) 2 b.c. (Apr 28) Lahib (USA) 129 – Portree 82 (Slip Anchor 136) **50**
[2001 5f 6g 8g Aug 17] IR 28,000Y: tall, rather leggy colt: fifth foal: half-brother to 4-y-o
Sovereign State and 5-y-o Best Port: dam maiden half-sister to Park Hill winner Coigach
and to dam of very smart stayer Invermark: modest maiden: easily best effort on debut:
bred to be suited by at least 1¼m. *M. H. Tompkins*

BARKING MAD (USA) 3 b. or br.g. Dayjur (USA) 137 – Avian Assembly (USA) **95**
(General Assembly (USA)) [2001 98: 7d 10.3f May 10] sturdy, lengthy gelding: useful
performer: respectable seventh in European Free Handicap at Newmarket in April: never
a threat in listed Dee Stakes at Chester only subsequent outing: suffered injury to near-
fore and also gelded after: stays 7.5f: acts on firm going: pulled hard once at 2 yrs: edgy
sort: has been bandaged near-hind. *M. L. W. Bell*

BARMAN (USA) 2 ch.c. (May 15) Atticus (USA) 121 – Blue Tip (FR) 117 (Tip Moss **88 p**
(FR)) [2001 8.2s² Nov 5] $35,000Y: half-brother to several winners, including useful
French 1½m winner Bright Mountain (by Time For A Change): dam French 7.5f (at 2
yrs) to 10.5f (Prix Penelope) winner: 3/1 odds-on-favourite, 1½ lengths second to Five Stars in
maiden at Nottingham, carrying head awkwardly and caught near finish after taking good
hold and going clear over 3f out: should improve. *P. F. I. Cole*

BARNA WOODS (IRE) 2 b. or br.f. (Feb 18) Charnwood Forest (IRE) 125 – Bardia **50**
42 (Jalmood (USA) 126) [2001 5.3s 5m 6m 6m Jun 12] IR 4,600Y: second foal: dam
1¼m winner: modest maiden: looked wayward and reportedly finished lame final start:
should stay at least 1m. *S. Kirk*

BARNIE RUBBLE 5 ch.g. Pharly (FR) 130 – Sharp Fairy (Sharpo 132) [2001 67: **75**
7m² 7d⁴ 6m 7.6g 7d³ p7g* f9.4g⁵ p8g³ Dec 22] smallish, sturdy gelding: fair handicapper,
quite lightly raced: won at Lingfield in November: stays 1m, not 9.4f: acts on soft going,
good to firm and polytrack (probably on fibresand). *P. W. D'Arcy*

BARNINGHAM 3 b.g. Emperor Jones (USA) 119 – Lady Anchor (Slip Anchor 136) **64 d**
[2001 53: 12m⁵ 12m⁶ 14.1m⁴ 14f⁶ 16.2m 11.9g³ 12.1g f14g Oct 22] leggy gelding: fair
maiden handicapper: below par after third outing: seems to stay 1¾m: raced only on good
ground or firmer on turf: blinkered/visored: has pulled hard: sold 10,000 gns. *J. D. Bethell*

BAROLO 2 b.c. (May 10) Danehill (USA) 126 – Lydia Maria 70 (Dancing Brave **77 p**
(USA) 140) [2001 7f⁵ Aug 24] strong, close-coupled colt: sixth foal: half-brother to 3
winners, including useful 6f (at 2 yrs) and 10.4f winner Premier Bay (by Primo Dominie)
and 7f (at 2 yrs) and 1¾m winner Taufan Boy (by Taufan): dam, maiden who stayed

1¼m, sister to dam of smart sprinter Primo Valentino out of very smart middle-distance performer Connaught Bridge: 14/1 and burly, 7 lengths fifth of 12 to Savannah Bay in maiden at Newmarket: should stay at least 1m: should improve. *P. W. Harris*

BARON CROCODILE   3 b.g. Puissance 110 – Glow Again 78 (The Brianstan 128)   **65**
[2001 78: f6g 6.1f 5m 6.1f 6g 5d 5m⁶ 5f⁶ 5f⁴ 5g⁶ 5g² 5m 5m* 6g⁶ 6.1f³ 6s* 6d 5v 8g Nov 7] close-coupled gelding: fair performer: won claimers at Warwick in August and Leicester (final start for A. Berry) in September: best at 5f/6f: acts on any turf going: tried blinkered/visored: sometimes slowly away: carries head high: not one to trust implicitly. *Mrs Dianne Sayer*

BARON DE PICHON (IRE)   5 b.g. Perugino (USA) 84 – Ariadne 79 (Bustino 136)   **–**
[2001 –, a78: f8g⁶ f9.4s⁴ f8.5s³ f9.4s* f9.4g³ f8.5g³ f8.5g⁶ f9.4g² f12g* f12g² f12f   **a78**
f14g f12g 14.1s f14g⁶ f12g Dec 1] workmanlike gelding: fair performer: won claimer (left A. Reid) in January and handicap in March, both at Wolverhampton: effective at 8.5f to 1½m: acts on fibresand/equitrack, little form on turf: visored once as 2-y-o. *Miss S. J. Wilton*

BARRANTES   4 b.f. Distant Relative 128 – Try The Duchess 99 (Try My Best (USA)   **68**
130) [2001 10d 5m* 6f 5m Sep 26] 8,800F, 3,000Y: half-sister to several winners, including 1¼m/1½m winner Uncharted Waters (by Celestial Storm) and UAE 6f/7f winner The New Girl (by Primo Dominie): dam 2-y-o 6f winner: fair form: won maiden at Lingfield in July: stiff tasks in handicaps after: may prove best at 5f. *Miss S. West*

BARRESBO   7 br.g. Barrys Gamble 102 – Bo' Babbity 75 (Strong Gale 116) [2001   **45**
9v 13.1m 13m⁵ 16f⁴ 16f⁵ 12g Nov 7] strong, lengthy gelding: poor handicapper nowadays: missed 1999/2000 seasons: probably stays 2m: acts on firm and soft ground: tried visored/blinkered. *A. C. Whillans*

BARRETTSTOWN   6 ch.g. Cadeaux Genereux 131 – Sagar 74 (Habitat 134) [2001   **–**
71: 10g 10m 16g Sep 7] big, lengthy gelding: no form in 2001. *R. M. Stronge*

BARROSA   2 b.f. (Apr 23) Sabrehill (USA) 120 – Shehana (USA) 86 (The Minstrel   **51**
(CAN) 135) [2001 5g⁶ 6m⁵ 6.1g⁶ 7d 7.5m Aug 25] 10,000Y: leggy, rather unfurnished filly: seventh foal: closely related to 1m seller winner (including at 2 yrs) Blue Desert (by Elmaamul) and half-sister to 3 winners, including useful sprinter React (by Reprimand) and 1½m winner Legion of Honour (by Ahonoora): dam, 2-y-o 9f winner, seemed to stay 1½m: modest maiden: best efforts at 6f. *A. Berry*

BARRY ISLAND   2 b.c. (Apr 23) Turtle Island (IRE) 123 – Pine Ridge 80 (High Top   **78 p**
131) [2001 6m 8d p10g* Dec 4] 7,000Y: half-brother to several winners, including high-class 1m to 1½m performer In The Groove (by Night Shift) and 1½m winner Pineapple (by Superlative), latter dam of 6-y-o Harmonic Way: dam 1½m winner: best effort in maidens when winning at Lingfield by neck from Redisham, getting up close home: will stay 1½m: acts on polytrack: should improve. *D. R. C. Elsworth*

BARRYS DOUBLE   4 br.g. Barrys Gamble 102 – Pennine Star (IRE) 68 (Pennine   **40**
Walk 120) [2001 42: f7f³ f11g 7d 8f 8d³ 10f f8g p16g Dec 4] close-coupled gelding: poor   **a47**
maiden: best at 7f/1m: acts on fibresand, good to soft and good to firm going: tried visored/blinkered/tongue tied. *Jean-Rene Auvray*

BARSAYA   3 b.f. Wolfhound (USA) 126 – Zeffirella 88 (Known Fact (USA) 135)   **59**
[2001 8.3g 8m⁵ 8.3m 7d 7g 7g 7m 8g f8g³ f8.5g⁴ f8g Dec 17] 1,400Y: eighth foal: half-sister to useful Irish 1m (including at 2 yrs) winner Charillus (by Be My Chief) and to a winner abroad: dam 7f winner: modest maiden: stays 1m: acts on good to firm going and fibresand: blinkered last 4 starts (looked difficult ride last 2). *P. R. Chamings*

BARTON LEA (IRE)   4 b.f. Distinctly North (USA) 115 – La Mazya (IRE) (Mazaad   **29**
106) [2001 f12g³ f12g Mar 16] poor form, lightly raced: should stay beyond 1½m: raced only on fibresand. *R. A. Fahey*

BARTON MISS   4 ch.f. Whittingham (IRE) 104 – Miss Derby (USA) (Master Derby   **–**
(USA)) [2001 –: e7g Jan 31] of little account. *T. E. Powell*

BARTON SANDS (IRE)   4 b.c. Tenby 125 – Hetty Green (Bay Express 132) [2001   **86 +**
95: 10s 10g 8m⁵ Jun 27] neat, attractive colt: fairly useful handicapper, lightly raced: would have gone close with clear run at Salisbury final start: stays 1¼m: acts on firm and good to soft ground, well beaten on soft/heavy: sold 4,000 gns in October. *L. M. Cumani*

BARZAH (IRE)   2 b.f. (Apr 12) Darshaan 133 – Lepikha (USA) 72 (El Gran Senor   **93**
(USA) 136) [2001 6f* Jun 3] IR 300,000Y: quite attractive filly: second foal: dam, 2¼m winner, half-sister to Derby second Glacial Storm: 11/4 on, won 5-runner minor event at Pontefract by 7 lengths from Lady Netbetsports, soon disputing running and readily pulling clear from over 2f out: bred to be suited by 1¼m+. *Sir Michael Stoute*

BASBOUSATE NADIA   2 b.f. (Apr 28) Wolfhound (USA) 126 – Sarabah (IRE) 83   **92**
(Ela-Mana-Mou 132) [2001 6m⁶ 5m* 5g³ 5m 5.2m 6m 6m Sep 12] tall, good-topped
filly: sixth foal: closely related to 4 winners, including 3-y-o Saratov and 5-y-o Ice, and
half-sister to a useful 1m/9f winner in Germany by Shareef Dancer: dam, 1¼m winner,
half-sister to smart 7f/1m performer Gothenberg: fairly useful performer: won maiden at
Newcastle in June: good third in listed event at Sandown next start: shaped well in
Doncaster nursery final one: will need to settle to stay further than 6f: raced only on good/
good to firm going. *W. R. Muir*

BASE LINE   3 b.g. Rudimentary (USA) 118 – Hemline 77 (Sharpo 132) [2001 –: e8g   **45**
f8g⁵ e7g f8g* e10g* 10m 9.9m 8m f11g⁴ 12g 10.1s 10.1g 9.9d f9.4s² f9.4s⁵ Dec 27] leggy   **a54**
gelding: modest handicapper on all-weather, poor on turf: won at Southwell and Lingfield
in February: stays easy 1¼m: acts on fibresand/equitrack: sometimes takes strong hold.
R. M. Flower

BASINET   3 b.g. Alzao (USA) 117 – Valiancy 87 (Grundy 137) [2001 68: 7v 7d 8.2v   **63**
8m 7.5m 10m 8m* 8m² 8.5f⁴ 9g³ 10m⁶ f8.5g* f8.5g³ f9.4g⁴ Dec 8] strong, close-coupled,   **a73**
quite attractive gelding: fair handicapper on all-weather, modest on turf: won at Newcastle in June and Wolverhampton (sold from Mrs J. Ramsden 22,000 gns after) in
October: best around 1m: acts on fibresand, firm and good to soft ground: has been slowly
away/taken strong hold/carried head high. *J. J. Quinn*

BASSET   3 b.c. Salse (USA) 128 – Bempton 57 (Blakeney 126) [2001 8.3m⁶ 12.1g   **54**
p12g Nov 13] 8,200Y: half-brother to several winners, including very smart Princess
Royal Stakes winner Banket (by Glint of Gold), Ribblesdale Stakes winner Gull Nook
(by Mill Reef), herself dam of Pentire, and smart Ormonde Stakes winner Mr Pintips (by
Kris): dam, maiden, half-sister to Shirley Heights: some ability in maidens (very green on
debut, keeping on in mid-field when nearly falling next start, not knocked about final
one): should be suited by 1¼m+. *J. A. Osborne*

BATCHWORTH BREEZE   3 ch.f. Beveled (USA) – Batchworth Dancer 67 (Balla-   **–**
cashtal (CAN)) [2001 –: 6g 7m 7g Jul 21] little form: blinkered final start. *E. A. Wheeler*

BATCHWORTH LOCK   3 b.g. Beveled (USA) – Treasurebound 63 (Beldale Flutter   **46**
(USA) 130) [2001 44: 5.1f 7m Jun 12] tall, leggy, close-coupled gelding: poor maiden,
lightly raced: stays 7f: raced only on going firmer than good. *E. A. Wheeler*

BATHWICK BABE (IRE)   4 b.f. Sri Pekan (USA) 117 – Olean (Sadler's Wells   **66**
(USA) 132) [2001 71?, a63: 11.6g³ 11.9d⁴ 13.1m* 13.3g 12.1m 11.5m⁵ 17.2m 14.1m⁵ Jul   **a–**
27] fair performer: won handicap at Bath in May: stays 1¾m: acts on fibresand, good to
firm and good to soft going: reportedly in foal to Dr Fong. *E. J. O'Neill*

BATHWICK BRUCE (IRE)   3 b.g. College Chapel 122 – Naivity (IRE) 72 (Auction   **77**
Ring (USA) 123) [2001 7m⁶ 7m² 7.1s* 8d 7d Sep 27] IR 10,500F, 28,000Y: third foal:
brother to a 2-y-o 6f winner in Italy and half-brother to 6f (at 2 yrs) to 1m winner who
seems to stay 1½m Bernardo Bellotto (by High Estate): dam Irish 2-y-o 7f winner: fair
form in maidens, winning at Chepstow in August: disappointing in handicaps final 2
starts, reportedly felt lame but returned sound on latter occasion: should stay 1m.
B. R. Millman

BATHWICK DREAM   4 b.f. Tragic Role (USA) – Trina 37 (Malaspina 118) [2001   **40**
–: e12g⁵ f16.2s⁵ e16g² f14.8g³ f16.2g e16g* 16.2m 17.2g⁶ Jun 16] modest performer: **a53**
won apprentice event at Lingfield in March: stays 2m: acts on fibresand/equitrack: hung
badly right for win: front runner. *Dr J. R. J. Naylor*

BATOUTOFTHEBLUE   8 br.g. Batshoof 122 – Action Belle (Auction Ring (USA)   **–**
123) [2001 49, a–: f16s⁴ f16g³ f16g* 16v Mar 29] big gelding: poor walker: fair handi-   **a71**
capper on all-weather: won at Southwell in March: acts on fibresand: carries head awkw-
ered twice earlier in career: carries head awkwardly/often gets behind. *G. A. Swinbank*

BATSWING   6 b.g. Batshoof 122 – Magic Milly 60 (Simply Great (FR) 122) [2001 92:   **81**
11.9m 11.9d 10d 12s Nov 10] quite good-topped gelding: fairly useful performer: well
held in 2001: raced mainly over 1½m nowadays: acts on any going: tried blinkered at 2
yrs: can race lazily: usually held up. *B. Ellison*

BATTLE CRUISER (USA)   3 b.g. Sea Hero (USA) 124 – Wholey Ghost (USA)   **81**
(Rare Performer (USA)) [2001 70: 7g³ 7d 9f² 8g² 10m² 9m⁴ 8m 7.5g² 6g* 7s Nov 10]
$25,000F, IR 38,000Y: third foal: half-brother to winners abroad by Sunny's Halo and
Alydeed: dam unraced: fairly useful performer: many creditable efforts in handicaps
prior to winning maiden at Fairyhouse in October: sold from C. O'Brien in Ireland 26,000
gns before well held (soon under pressure) final start: was effective at 6f to 1¼m: acted
on firm ground: blinkered last 2 starts: dead. *Miss S. J. Wilton*

BATTLE GREEN LAD   4 b.g. Presidium 124 – Antouna (Clantime 101) [2001 –: f5g f5g 7s 5m Jun 9] no form: blinkered/tongue tied second start. *J. Balding* —

BATTLE LINE   2 b.g. (May 14) Brief Truce (USA) 126 – Forest Heights 81 (Slip Anchor 136) [2001 6f 6.1m 8g⁵ 8.2s 8.3v p7g⁴ Nov 20] second foal: dam, 1½m winner, out of half-sister to Yorkshire Oaks winner Magnificent Star: modest maiden: left E. Stanners after second start: probably stays 1m: acts on polytrack: blinkered last 2 outings (wandered on first occasion). *K. McAuliffe*   **56**

BATTLE WARNING   6 b.g. Warning 136 – Royal Ballet (IRE) (Sadler's Wells (USA) 132) [2001 59: f11g f12g⁶ f16g² f14g* f16g* f14g⁴ 14.1v⁵ f16g² f12g f12s Dec 15] well-made gelding: fair handicapper: won at Southwell in February and March (left M. Hammond after next start): seems better at 1¾m/2m than shorter: acts on good to firm going and fibresand. *A. Crook*   **73**

BATWINK   4 b.f. Batshoof 122 – Quick As A Wink (Glint of Gold 128) [2001 –: f12g⁵ f12g f12s Feb 9] lengthy filly: poor maiden handicapper: stays 1½m: acts on fibresand. *P. D. Cundell*   **30**

BAWSIAN   6 b.g. Persian Bold 123 – Bawaeth (USA) 72 (Blushing Groom (FR) 131) [2001 88: f11g 12s* 10v* 12s² 10.3f⁴ 11.9d 12.3m 9.9s⁴ 11.9g³ 12.3m⁵ 14s² 12g 12v 12s p12g f12g* f14.8g² f12s⁶ Dec 21] small, close-coupled gelding: fairly useful handicapper: won at Doncaster (apprentice race) and Nottingham in March and Wolverhampton in December: effective at 1¼m (given good test) to 1¾m: acts on fibresand (probably on equitrack/polytrack), probably ideally suited by good going or softer on turf nowadays: tongue tied after reappearance: can race lazily. *J. L. Eyre*   **94 a88**

BAXTERS HOLLY   3 b.f. Puissance 110 – Sveltissima 48 (Dunphy 124) [2001 12v 11.1d 12.1d⁶ 10.1m Jun 4] seems of little account. *I. Semple*   —

BAY BREEZE (IRE)   3 b.g. Pennekamp (USA) 130 – Prairie Neba (GER) (Nebos (GER) 129) [2001 10.2f 11.8m Jun 4] IR 5,000Y, resold 10,000Y: fourth reported living foal: half-brother to French/German 1¼m to 2m winner Prairie Champion (by Wassl) and useful French/German 7f to 1¼m winner Prairie Shadow (by Shaadi): dam won German St Leger and third in German Oaks: last in maidens at Bath and Leicester. *P. W. Harris*   —

BAY OF BENGAL (IRE)   5 ch.m. Persian Bold 123 – Adjamiya (USA) (Shahrastani (USA) 135) [2001 47: f8.5s f11g 10s 10d 10f 9.2m⁶ 8m 12f⁵ 8.3g³ 8d 8f 10m⁶ Jul 29] leggy mare: poor performer: probably stays 1½m: acts on firm and good to soft going, no form on fibresand: sometimes starts slowly. *J. S. Wainwright*   **36**

BAY OF DREAMS   2 ch.g. (Apr 25) Salse (USA) 128 – Cantico 58 (Green Dancer (USA) 132) [2001 7d p10g Dec 4] brother to smart 1m (at 2 yrs) to 14.6f winner Sausalito Bay and half-brother to 3 winners, including 7f winner Dauntess (by Formidable): dam, staying maiden, half-sister to very smart 1m to 1½m winner Calderina: well held in maidens at Newmarket and Lingfield. *I. A. Balding*   —

BAY OF ISLANDS   9 b.g. Jupiter Island 126 – Lawyer's Wave (USA) (Advocator) [2001 104: 16s 13.4f³ 16.1f 13.9m³ Jul 14] strong gelding: fluent mover: useful performer: won Northumberland Plate at Newcastle in 2000: creditable seventh in same race in 2001 on third outing: also creditable third in Ormonde Stakes at Chester in May and listed rated stakes at York (3 lengths behind Akbar) in July: reported in early-August to be suffering from suspensory trouble: effective at around 13f to 2m: acts on firm and good to soft going: usually visored nowadays: reliable. *D. Morris*   **104**

BAYONET   5 b.m. Then Again 126 – Lambay 88 (Lorenzaccio 130) [2001 61: 5.1d 5.7m 6g 6m⁵ 6m² 7g 6m³ 7g² 6m 7.1g² 6.1d Sep 21] deep-girthed mare: modest handicapper: stays 7f: acts on good to firm and good to soft going: blinkered twice at 3 yrs: none too consistent. *Jane Southcombe*   **62**

BAYRAMI   3 ch.f. Emarati (USA) 74 – Music Mistress (IRE) 55 (Classic Music (USA)) [2001 39: 5m 5.3f 7m Jul 28] poor maiden: left S. Kettlewell after second start. *R. E. Barr*   —

BAYTOWN GRACE   2 b.f. (Feb 7) Presidium 124 – Thalya (Crofthall 110) [2001 5d 5g f5g⁵ 6m 5.2g⁴ 6g⁴ 5m² f5g⁵ 6m 6m⁶ 6d⁶ Sep 4] 500Y: third foal: half-sister to 3-y-o Fairgame Man: dam unraced: poor maiden: in frame in sellers: best efforts at 5f: acts on good to firm going. *P. S. McEntee*   **42**

BAYTOWN RHAPSODY   4 b.f. Emperor Jones (USA) 119 – Sing A Rainbow (IRE) 68 (Rainbow Quest (USA) 134) [2001 62: f6g f7s f6g⁶ f6g f7g 6.1v³ 7m May 8] poor performer: best at 6f/7f: acts on fibresand and heavy going. *P. S. McEntee*   **43**

BAYTOWN ROBIN   2 ch.f. (Feb 18) Dancing Spree (USA) – Homebeforemidnight   –
(Fools Holme (USA)) [2001 5d 5g 6m 6f⁴ f8.5g Oct 20] 850Y: second foal: dam, lightly
raced on Flat/over hurdles, half-sister to smart sprinter Roman Prose: no form, including
in seller: tried blinkered. *P. S. McEntee*

B BEAUTIFUL (IRE)   2 ch.f. (Feb 1) Be My Guest (USA) 126 – Lady Donna 92   51
(Dominion 123) [2001 8.1v 6v 7f7g⁶ Nov 27] IR 160,000Y: unfurnished filly: closely
related to fairly useful 6f winner At Large (by Night Shift) and half-sister to 3 winners,
notably 1999 Phoenix Stakes winner Lavery (by Royal Academy): dam, 2-y-o 5f winner,
half-sister to 2000 Guineas winner Tirol: modest form in maidens. *M. L. W. Bell*

BEACH HUT (IRE)   3 b.g. Pennekamp (USA) 130 – Kates Cabin 96 (Habitat 134)   62
[2001 8g 7.9d⁶ 8f⁵ 10m 12g 10d Sep 21] 16,000Y: lengthy, angular, unfurnished gelding:
has a splayed action: half-brother to several winners, including fairly useful 6f winner
Madmun (by Cadeaux Genereux) and 1¼m to 2m winner Backwoods (by In The Wings):
dam 1m winner: probably stays 1¼m: blinkered (pulled too hard) final
start: sold 2,000 gns. *J. L. Dunlop*

BEACON HILL GEM   3 b.c. Mtoto 134 – Emeraude 84 (Kris 135) [2001 10s⁶ 10s   –
7.5m 9m Jun 23] good-topped colt: sixth living foal: half-brother to 6f (at 2 yrs)/7f winner
Green Jewel, later useful in USA, and a 11f winner in Italy (both by Environment Friend):
dam, 1m winner, half-sister to Irish St Leger winner Opale: little form: dead.
C. W. Fairhurst

BEADING   4 b.f. Polish Precedent (USA) 131 – Silver Braid (USA) 101 (Miswaki   82
(USA) 124) [2001 76: 8.3g 8m³ 7.1s⁵ 7m³ 8g³ 8m² 7m² 8s 7d Oct 13] strong, lengthy,
angular filly: fairly useful handicapper: effective at 7f/1m: acts on firm and soft going:
tongue tied: tends to race freely. *J. W. Hills*

BEADY (IRE)   2 b.g. (Mar 12) Eagle Eyed (USA) 111 – Tales of Wisdom 70 (Rousil-   73
lon (USA) 133) [2001 7m 8.5m⁴ 7.5g³ 8d Oct 19] IR 10,000F, 20,000Y: good-topped
gelding: fourth foal: half-brother to 8.5f (at 2 yrs) and 1½m winner Mystic Quest (by
Arcane): dam, 1½m winner, half-sister to Oaks d'Italia winner Bright Generation: fair
maiden: third at Beverley: soundly beaten in nursery final start (gelded after): stays 8.5f:
races freely, and has worn crossed noseband. *B. Smart*

BEANBOY   3 b.g. Clantime 101 – Lady Blues Singer (Chief Singer 131) [2001 –: 5m   46
7.5m f6g 6m² 5g 8d⁴ 6s 10f 7v 8d⁵ f7g Nov 23] leggy gelding: poor maiden: stays 1m: a35
acts on good to firm and good to soft going: tried visored. *Mrs S. Lamyman*

BEASLEY   2 b.g. (Feb 27) First Trump 118 – Le Shuttle 49 (Presidium 124) [2001 5m   48 §
6m 6.1f 7f⁴ Jul 4] 1,000F, 7,000Y, 13,000 2-y-o: first foal: dam, sprint maiden, out of
sister to very smart 5f performer Paris House: poor maiden: blinkered final start (gelded
after): ungenuine. *Miss Gay Kelleway*

BEAT THE RING (IRE)   3 br.g. Tagula (IRE) 116 – Pursue 78 (Auction Ring (USA)   –
123) [2001 –: f8g 7m Aug 8] little form. *G. Brown*

BEAUCHAMP MAGIC   6 b.g. Northern Park (USA) 107 – Beauchamp Buzz 85   57
(High Top 131) [2001 58: e16g³ f16.2s² f16.2s⁴ Jan 16] good-bodied gelding: modest
handicapper: stays 2m: acts on fibresand/equitrack and firm ground: tried blinkered/
visored/tongue tied, not since 1999: usually held up. *M. D. I. Usher*

BEAUCHAMP NYX   5 b.m. Northern Park (USA) 107 – Beauchamp Image 79   –
(Midyan (USA) 124) [2001 –: 13.1m May 21] of no account. *P. A. Pritchard*

BEAUCHAMP PILOT   3 ch.g. Inchinor 119 – Beauchamp Image 79 (Midyan (USA)   96 p
124) [2001 –p: 6m 5m³ 7g 8g* 8d* 7d* Nov 3] tall, rather leggy gelding: progressive
handicapper: won in big fields at Ascot, Redcar and Newmarket (useful form, beat Cork
Harbour by ¾ length in 26-runner race) in the autumn: effective at 7f/1m: acts on good to
soft going, showed promise only run on fibresand: waited with: should make a smart
4-y-o. *G. A. Butler*

BEAUCHAMP QUIZ   2 b. or gr.f. (Mar 15) Inchinor 119 – Beauchamp Jade 105   54 p
(Kalaglow 132) [2001 7d 6v p5g Nov 13] smallish, rather leggy filly: first foal: dam,
1½m winner, out of half-sister to very smart 1½m winner Beauchamp Hero: modest form
in maidens: likely to do better at 1m+. *G. A. Butler*

BEAUDACIOUS (IRE)   2 b.c. (May 28) Indian Ridge 123 – Marwell 133 (Habitat   58
134) [2001 6g 7.1s⁶ 6d Oct 12] IR 45,000Y: leggy, quite good-topped colt: brother to
useful 5f(including at 2 yrs) 6f winner Littlefeather and half-brother to several winners,
notably very smart miler Marling (by Lomond) and very smart sprinter/miler Caerwent
(by Caerleon): dam top-class sprinter: modest maiden: easily best effort on second start:
will probably stay 1m. *N. Tinkler*

BEAU DUCHESS (FR) 4 ch.f. Bering 136 – Turkish Coffee (FR) (Gay Mecene **43**
(USA) 128) [2001 63: 13.3g 11.6m² 12m 11.8d² 14.1m⁶ Aug 11] close-coupled, angular
filly: poor maiden: stays 1½m: acts on firm and good to soft going. *P. W. Harris*

BEAUFORT LADY (IRE) 2 b.f. (Apr 22) Alhaarth (IRE) 126 – Brentsville (USA) **74**
(Arctic Tern (USA) 126) [2001 5f⁶ 6d⁶ 7m² f8.5g⁵ 7s⁶ p8g Nov 20] IR 16,000Y: leggy **a–**
filly: half-sister to several winners, including 8-y-o Sylva Paradise and 3-y-o Vitesse:
dam, Irish 2-y-o 6f winner, half-sister to smart performer up to 1¼m Young Senor: fair
maiden: second at Redcar: should stay 1m: acts on good to firm ground, well beaten on
all-weather. *M. Johnston*

BEAU ROBERTO 7 b.g. Robellino (USA) 127 – Night Jar 102 (Night Shift (USA)) **–**
[2001 12m 12m Jun 2] small, strong gelding: shows knee action: fair handicapper in
1999: behind both runs since: tried blinkered earlier in career. *J. S. Goldie*

BEAU SAUVAGE 3 b.g. Wolfhound (USA) 126 – Maestrale (Top Ville 129) [2001 **58**
51: 6.1v 8.1v 8m 6m⁶ 8m⁶ 7.1g³ 8m* 8f⁶ 7.5f 8d⁴ 8f⁶ 6f³ 9.1m 7g³ Oct 19] lengthy
gelding: modest handicapper: won amateur event at Redcar in June: stays easy 1m: acts
on firm ground, no form on heavy/fibresand: blinkered last 4 starts: has been slowly
away: often front runner. *M. W. Easterby*

BEAUSEJOUR (USA) 3 ch.f. Diesis 133 – Libeccio (NZ) (Danzatore (CAN) 120) **54**
[2001 7g 7m 7m⁶ 10.9g f8.5g⁴ 10.1g⁶ f9.4s² f8.5g² 10s⁶ f8.5g Oct 20] rather sparely- **a58**
made filly: has fluent, round action: fourth foal: half-sister to fairly useful 8.5f winner
Hollow Haze (by Woodman): dam unraced out of half-sister to Generous and Imagine:
modest maiden handicapper: stays 9.4f: acts on good to firm ground and fibresand:
tongue tied final 5 starts: sold 6,500 gns. *J. W. Hills*

BEAUTEOUS (IRE) 2 ch.g. (Apr 16) Tagula (IRE) 116 – Beauty Appeal (USA) **72**
(Shadeed (USA) 135) [2001 6m 5m³ 7.1f* 7.5s⁶ 6m 6v Oct 26] 16,000Y: tall, quite
good-topped gelding: third foal: half-brother to 1999 2-y-o 5f winner Agua Caballo
(by Petorius): dam unraced: fair performer: below form after winning minor event at
Musselburgh in June: stays 7f: acts on firm ground: gelded after final start. *A. Berry*

BEAUTIFULTOMMORROW 2 ch.f. (Jan 10) Pursuit of Love 124 – Bella **52**
Domani (Cadeaux Genereux 131) [2001 f5g⁶ 7g 6m f7g p7g Nov 20] 6,000Y: small,
strong, angular filly: third foal: half-sister to a 1m/9f winner in Italy by Dolphin Street:
dam, Italian maiden, half-sister to high-class 1985 2-y-o up to 7f Nomination: modest
maiden: should stay 1m. *K. R. Burke*

BEAU TUDOR (IRE) 7 b.g. Aragon 118 – Sunley Silks 80 (Formidable (USA) 125) **–**
[2001 5m⁵ 6.1f 5f 5g 7g 6g Oct 19] workmanlike gelding: little form. *Miss L. C. Siddall*

BECKETT (IRE) 3 b.c. Fairy King (USA) – Groom Order (Groom Dancer (USA) **113**
128) [2001 116: 8m² 8g* 10d Oct 20] small, attractive colt: smart performer: successful
in National Stakes at the Curragh at 2 yrs: off 12 months before reappearance (reportedly
had muscle problems early in 2001): won listed race at Newmarket in October by ¾
length from Priors Lodge, dictating pace: below form (quickly beaten after disputing lead
to 2f out) in Dubai Champion Stakes there final start: was best at 7f/1m: acted on good to
firm and good to soft going: had worn crossed noseband: to stand at Tally-Ho Stud,
Ireland, fee €4,500, Oct 1st. *A. P. O'Brien, Ireland*

BECKON 5 ch.m. Beveled (USA) – Carolynchristensen 58 (Sweet Revenge 129) **50**
[2001 46, a59: e12g e10g 10d³ 10f 11.9f⁵ 11.5m² 10m* 11.6g 11.9g³ 10m² 11.5g⁵ Aug
30] leggy, lengthy mare: modest performer: won seller at Lingfield in July: stays easy
1½m: acts on equitrack (poor form on fibresand), best turf form on going firmer than
good: tried visored: sometimes slowly away/carries head high/hangs right. *B. R. Johnson*

BECKY SIMMONS 3 b.f. Mujadil (USA) 119 – Jolies Eaux 73 (Shirley Heights **78**
130) [2001 80: 6m* 7.1g² 7m 7d 5.7m f6g Oct 18] fair performer: won minor event at
Kempton in June: well below form final 2 starts: probably stays 7f: acts on firm going,
probably on good to soft: takes strong hold. *A. P. Jarvis*

BE DECISIVE 3 b.f. Diesis 133 – Robellino Miss (USA) (Robellino (USA) 127) **65**
[2001 7g⁵ 8d 8.2v* 8.2s Oct 30] leggy filly: fourth foal: sister to useful 1999 2-y-o 7f
winner who stayed 1m Decision Maid, closely related to winner up to 11f in France by
Trempolino and half-sister to useful 1998 2-y-o 6f winner who stayed 1m Chief Rebel
(by Chief's Crown): dam, won up to 9f in USA, out of close relative of high-class sprinter
Silver Fling: fair performer: won maiden at Nottingham in October: stiff task, well held
in handicap at same track final start: stays 1m: acts on heavy ground: sold 12,000 gns.
G. Wragg

King George V Stakes (Handicap), Royal Ascot—
Beekeeper shows smart form on just his fourth career start to deny the tenacious Tomasino,
with Arabie, Compton Commander (white cap) and Regatta Point (stars on sleeves) next to finish

BEDEVILLED 6 ch.g. Beveled (USA) – Putout 69 (Dowsing (USA) 124) [2001 75: **55**
f6g f5s⁶ 6m⁵ 6f² 5.1f 5m⁵ 5.5m⁵ 5.7g 5g⁴ 5m⁶ 5s Sep 24] close-coupled gelding: modest
performer: effective at 5f/6f: acts on firm going, soft and fibresand: tried blinkered/
visored: none too consistent. *P. D. Evans*

BEECHY BANK (IRE) 3 b.f. Shareef Dancer (USA) 135 – Neptunalia 70 (Slip **38**
Anchor 136) [2001 f8g 10.2g f7g⁶ Oct 20] 4,500Y: third foal: sister to 7f winner Jabuka:
dam, 1½m winner, half-sister to Dante winner/Derby fourth Glory of Dancer (by Shareef
Dancer): trained by Mrs M. Hambro on debut (off nearly 10 months after): blinkered, first
form in maidens at Wolverhampton final start. *R. T. Phillips*

BEE GEE 4 b.f. Beveled (USA) – Bunny Gee (Last Tycoon 131) [2001 42: f16g³ f11g² **42**
f11g³ f11g⁶ Apr 9] neat filly: poor performer: has form at 2m, at least as effective at
shorter: acts on fibresand/equitrack and turf going. *M. Blanshard*

BEE J GEE 3 b.g. Dilum (USA) 115 – Sound Check 62 (Formidable (USA) 125) **–**
[2001 64: 9m 11.6m f12g 8f Aug 14] modest maiden at 2 yrs: well held in handicaps in
2001. *Mrs Lydia Pearce*

BEEKEEPER 3 b.c. Rainbow Quest (USA) 134 – Chief Bee 89 (Chief's Crown **116**
(USA)) [2001 94p: 12m* 12f* 11.9g⁴ Aug 21] tall, close-coupled, attractive colt: fluent
mover: smart performer: won maiden at Thirsk in May and King George V Handicap at
Royal Ascot (much improved, by ½ length from Tomasino): changed hands privately
before good 3½ lengths fourth to Milan in Great Voltigeur Stakes at York (stayed on,
never a threat) 2 months later: will be suited by 1¾m+: acts on firm going: joined
Godolphin: type to win pattern races. *Sir Michael Stoute*

BEENABOUTABIT 3 b.f. Komaite (USA) – Tassagh Bridge (IRE) (Double **61**
Schwartz 128) [2001 68: 7m 6.1m 6m 6m⁵ 5m 6g 8.2s p7g Nov 20] angular filly: modest
maiden handicapper: stays 6f: tried visored: reportedly had breathing problem second
start, tongue tied after. *R. Ingram*

BEHAN 2 ch.g. (Mar 16) Rainbows For Life (CAN) – With Finesse (Be My Guest **58**
(USA) 126) [2001 p8g⁵ f9.4g⁴ f7s³ Dec 18] IR 2,200F, IR 1,800Y, 3,500 2-y-o: first
foal: dam unraced from family of Lowther winner Kingscote and 6-y-o Rainbow High:
best effort in sellers (modest form) when third in blinkers at Wolverhampton.
D. J. S. Cosgrove

BEL   3 b.f. Darshaan 133 – Jezebel Monroe (USA) 98 (Lyphard (USA) 132) [2001 12m³   **83 p**
11.7d³ 12d* Nov 6] fifth foal: half-sister to useful French 10.5f to 11.5f winner Leros (by
Exit To Nowhere): dam, 1¼m winner, closely related to 1999 Royal Lodge winner Royal
Kingdom and half-sister to dam of 4-y-o Agnes Digital: fairly useful form in maidens
first 2 starts, then comfortably landed odds at Catterick by neck from Amwell Star (didn't
have to run anywhere near previous form): stays 1½m: remains open to progress.
R. Charlton

B'ELANNA TORRES   2 b.f. (Mar 26) Entrepreneur 123 – Miss Kemble (Warning   **66**
136) [2001 5m³ 7d Oct 15] 500,000 francs Y: first foal: dam, ran once, half-sister to Irish
Oaks winner Princess Pati from family of high-class middle-distance performer Leggera:
better effort in maidens (fair form) when third at Salisbury: should be suited by 1m+.
W. R. Muir

BELENUS (GER)   5 ch.h. Lomitas 129 – Beaute (GER) (Lord Udo (GER)) [2001   **119**
10.5s* 10g* 11g 12g 12d³ 12m² Sep 8] smart performer: top 3-y-o in Germany in 1999
when wins included Deutsches Derby: injured in 2000: successful on return in minor
events at Bremen and Baden-Baden in May: very good effort when ½-length third to
Sabiango in Credit Suisse Private Banking Pokal at Cologne in August: below-form
second to King's Boy in Bosphorus Cup at Veliefendi final start: stayed 1½m: acted on
good to firm and good to soft going, probably on soft: blinkered last 2 outings: to stand at
Polish National Stud. *A. Wohler, Germany*

BELINDA   4 ch.f. Mizoram (USA) 105 – Mountain Dew (Pharly (FR) 130) [2001 53,   **53**
a63: 10g 10f⁴ 10g 10m f11g² f12g³ f12g² f11g f14.8g³ p10g f12s* Dec 27] modest   **a63**
handicapper: won at Wolverhampton in December: stays 1½m: acts on firm going and
fibresand: carries head awkwardly (reportedly blind in right eye). *K. Bell*

BELLA BEGUINE   2 b.f. (Mar 19) Komaite (USA) – On The Record 72 (Record   **–**
Token 128) [2001 5.1s Apr 16] 23,000Y: small, strong filly: seventh living foal:
half-sister to 3 winners, including fairly useful 6f/7f winner Sky Music (by Absalom) and
9-y-o Lago di Varano: dam 5f/6f winner: last in maiden at Nottingham. *A. Bailey*

BELLA CHICA (IRE)   2 b.f. (Mar 14) Bigstone (IRE) 126 – Just Like Annie (IRE)   **94**
65 (Mujadil (USA) 119) [2001 5.1f* 6f 5m* 6g* 6m⁴ 6g⁵ 6v⁶ Oct 27] IR 13,000Y: leggy,
lengthy filly: good mover: first foal: dam, Irish 5f winner, half-sister to smart 6f to 1m
(including at 2 yrs) performer Pipe Major: fairly useful performer: won minor events at
Nottingham and Ripon in June and 29-runner Tattersalls Breeders Stakes (by length from
Partytime) at the Curragh in August: good fourth to Misterah in listed event at Ayr: should
stay 7f: acts on firm ground, well below form on heavy: seemed unsuited by track at
Epsom second start. *J. A. Glover*

Tattersalls Breeders Stakes, the Curragh—
Bella Chica provides trainer Jeremy Glover with his most valuable win

BELLA FREGATA 2 ch.f. (Jan 27) Dancing Spree (USA) – Bella Bambola (IRE) 42 **49** (Tate Gallery (USA) 117) [2001 6m 7.9d Oct 12] quite good-topped filly: third foal: dam sprint maiden: poor form in maidens. *J. S. Wainwright*

BELLA PAVLINA 3 ch.f. Sure Blade (USA) 130 – Pab's Choice 61 (Telsmoss 91) **47** [2001 52: 8m⁴ 10.2m⁵ 8m 8m 10.2g Oct 1] poor maiden: stays 1m: acts on soft and good to firm going. *M. Blanshard*

BELLA PUPA 5 ch.m. Theatrical Charmer 114 – Louisa Anne 73 (Mummy's Pet 125) **–** [2001 11.9g Jun 7] workmanlike mare: of no account. *N. M. Babbage*

BELLAS GATE BOY 9 b.g. Doulab (USA) 115 – Celestial Air 96 (Rheingold 137) **– §** [2001 56§, a–§: f7g 8s 7m 10.1m May 30] leggy gelding: temperamental handicapper. *Mrs Lydia Pearce*

BELLBIT 6 b.m. Henbit (USA) 130 – Bell Cord (Beldale Flutter (USA) 130) [2001 **–** f6g May 3] fifth foal: dam French 5f (at 2 yrs) to 1m winner: well beaten in claimer. *R. Lee*

BELLBOTTOM 2 b.c. (Apr 8) Mtoto 134 – Satin Bell 99 (Midyan (USA) 124) [2001 **62** 7m⁶ 7f⁵ 7m 7s⁶ 7s Oct 25] second foal: dam 7f winner: modest maiden: should be suited by 1¼m/1½m: acts on firm going: sold 5,500 gns. *J. L. Dunlop*

BELLE D'ANJOU (FR) 4 b.f. Saint Cyrien (FR) 128 – Epsibelle (IRE) (Darshaan **82** 133) [2001 10.3f² 10.9m 11.6g³ 10.5s 10.2f* 12g* Sep 28] small, leggy filly: first foal: dam, French 1m to 1½m winner (also won over jumps), daughter of smart French/Belgian performer up to 15f Epsiba: fairly useful performer: won minor event at La Rochelle for H. Bidon in France in 2000: won handicaps at Chepstow and Ascot (amateur event) in September: effective at 1¼m/1½m: acts on firm going (has won on soft over hurdles): fairly useful hurdler. *M. C. Pipe*

BELLE OF THE BLUES (IRE) 2 b.f. (May 9) Blues Traveller (IRE) 119 – **–** Blackpool Belle 70 (The Brianstan 128) [2001 f6g f8s Dec 21] 9,000 2-y-o: half-sister to several winners, notably smart sprinter Croft Pool (by Crofthall): dam sprinter: well held in maidens at Southwell: slowly away on debut. *J. A. Glover*

BELLE OF THE MANOR (IRE) 3 b.f. Bluebird (USA) 125 – Pharsala (FR) **73** (Hello Gorgeous (USA) 128) [2001 6g 6m³ 6m³ 6m 10m² 10s⁶ 12d 10d² 10g² p12g² **a65** p10g³ f11g Dec 3] 750,000 francs Y: quite attractive filly: fifth reported foal: sister to Coventry Stakes winner Harbour Master and half-sister to 2 winners in France, including 1¼m winner Phardoun (by Kaldoun): dam French 1m winner: fair maiden: best at 1¼m: acts on good to firm going, good to soft and polytrack: blinkered (below form) twice: has started slowly/carried head high. *G. A. Butler*

BELLE ROUGE 3 b.f. Celtic Swing 138 – Gunner's Belle 69 (Gunner B 126) [2001 **56** –p: 10g 10.2m 12.1m⁵ 14m 16.2g⁴ Aug 27] workmanlike filly: modest maiden: stays 2m: acts on good to firm going. *M. Blanshard*

BELLINO EMPRESARIO (IRE) 3 b.g. Robellino (USA) 127 – The Last **29** Empress (IRE) 73 (Last Tycoon 131) [2001 43: e10g e10s⁵ e10g² f8g 10s 11.5m 11.5m³ **a49** 16.2g f11g* Dec 3] poor handicapper: off over 3 months, won at Southwell in December: stays 11f: acts on fibresand/equitrack and good to firm going: tried blinkered/visored/ tongue tied: often making running. *I. A. Wood*

BELLS BEACH (IRE) 3 ch.f. General Monash (USA) 107 – Clifton Beach (Auction **60** Ring (USA) 123) [2001 40: f5g⁴ f6g* f6g 5.3d* f6g² 5g³ 6m f6g Oct 1] strong, close-coupled filly: modest handicapper: won at Wolverhampton in March and Brighton in May: will prove best at 5f/6f: acts on fibresand and good to soft ground: sometimes slowly away. *A. G. Newcombe*

BELLS BOY'S 2 b.g. (Mar 25) Mind Games 121 – Millie's Lady (IRE) (Common **56** Grounds 118) [2001 5v 6m 5g Sep 19] 2,800Y, resold 19,000Y: workmanlike gelding: fourth living foal: brother to 3-y-o Milly's Lass: dam unraced: modest maiden: easily best effort on second start. *A. Dickman*

BELLS FOR MARLIN (USA) 2 b.f. (Feb 14) Marlin (USA) 124 – Bells For Thee **85** (USA) (Sette Bello (USA)) [2001 6m² 7g* 8s Sep 19] 50,000F, $47,000Y: tall, leggy filly: has scope: half-sister to several winners in USA, including Grade 3 9f/9.5f winner Shots Are Ringing (by Turkey Shoot): dam unraced: fairly useful filly: odds on, won maiden at Folkestone in August: seventh of 9 in Prix d'Aumale at Chantilly, eased once held: should stay 1¼m: sent to USA. *P. F. I. Cole*

BELSTANE BADGER (IRE) 3 b.f. Blues Traveller (IRE) 119 – Brigadina (Brig- **44** adier Gerard 144) [2001 44: 8m 7f⁶ 8d Oct 8] unfurnished filly: poor maiden, lightly raced: stays 7f: has worn crossed noseband. *I. Semple*

BELSTANE FOX (IRE) 3 ch.f. General Monash (USA) 107 – Countess Kildare **48**
(Dominion 123) [2001 31: 7m⁵ 6m⁵ 7.5m 7.1m 8m 7s* 7g 7.5m³ 8.3m 9.1v f7g f8.5g Dec
1] good-topped filly: poor performer: won seller at Ayr in July: stays 1m: acts on soft and
good to firm ground: sometimes slowly away: has carried head awkwardly. *I. Semple*

BELTANE 3 b.c. Magic Ring (IRE) 115 – Sally's Trust (IRE) 51 (Classic Secret (USA) **42**
91) [2001 –: 10s 8m 8.3m 7m* 7m 7.6g Sep 5] poor performer: won apprentice handicap
at Brighton in August: stays 7f: acts on good to firm ground. *W. de Best-Turner*

BELUGA BAY 2 b.g. (Apr 24) Millkom 124 – Bellyphax (Bellypha 130) [2001 6s* **69 p**
Oct 22] 5,000Y: sturdy gelding: half-brother to several winners, including 1994 2-y-o 6f
winner Belle Vue (by Petong) and fairly useful Irish 2000 2-y-o 7f winner Cedar du Liban
(by First Trump): dam unraced half-sister to very smart sprinter/US Grade 1 1m winner
Forzando: 7/1, won 10-runner maiden at Pontefract by head from Secreto Dreams,
leading 1f out: will probably stay 1m: should improve. *J. R. Fanshawe*

BE MY BUDDY 2 b.g. (Mar 26) Be My Chief (USA) 122 – Trull (Lomond (USA) **53**
128) [2001 8d 7s p8g Nov 15] 15,000F, 19,000Y: useful-looking gelding: half-brother to
several winners, including useful German performer up to 1m Indian Point (by Indian
Ridge) and 3-y-o Trillie: dam ran once: best effort in maidens (modest form) on second
start: left J. Smyth-Osbourne after: should stay at least 1m. *Lady Herries*

BE MY TINKER 3 ch.f. Be My Chief (USA) 122 – Tinkerbird 76 (Music Boy 124) **54 d**
[2001 59: e5g f7g⁴ f6g⁵ 5m 5.3f⁶ 8m⁵ 10g 6.1s 7m 10m³ Sep 1] lengthy filly: modest
maiden: best effort at 3 yrs on second outing: probably stays 1¼m: acts on fibresand and
firm going: blinkered fifth start. *G. Brown*

BEN BRITTEN 2 ch.g. (Mar 21) Sabrehill (USA) 120 – Golden Panda 77 (Music Boy **–**
124) [2001 7d 7s Oct 11] 4,500F, IR 10,000Y: good-bodied gelding: half-brother to 3
winners, including 1996 2-y-o 6f winner Pandiculation (by Statoblest): dam 1m winner:
burly, well beaten in maiden/minor event. *J. S. Wainwright*

BENBYAS 4 b.g. Rambo Dancer (CAN) 107 – Light The Way 72 (Nicholas Bill 125) **78**
[2001 62, a50: f8g⁶ 8s* 11s² 12.3g³ 12m² 10m² 10m f14g 10g Oct 6] sturdy, lengthy **a–**
gelding: fair performer: won minor event at Pontefract in April and handicap at Redcar in
May: below best last 3 starts: probably best at 1¼m/1½m: acts on heavy and good to
firm ground: sometimes visored/blinkered (usually not in 2001): fairly useful hurdler.
J. L. Eyre

BEND WAVY (IRE) 9 ch.g. Kefaah (USA) 124 – Prosodie (FR) (Relko 136) [2001 **–**
10.5s Sep 7] fairly useful handicapper in 1998: well beaten only run since: has had tongue
tied. *T. H. Caldwell*

BEN EAGLE (IRE) 2 ch.g. (Jan 8) Eagle Eyed (USA) 111 – Checkers (Habat 127) **56**
[2001 5m 6m 7.1m⁴ 7.1d 6.1s⁶ Aug 9] IR 3,000F, 3,200Y: half-brother to several winners,
including useful 7f/1m winner Belfry Green (by Doulab) and 5f winner Classic Pet (by
Petorius): dam placed at 1m/9.5f in Ireland: modest maiden: will stay 1m: acts on good to
firm ground. *B. R. Millman*

BENEDICTINE 3 b.c. Primo Dominie 121 – Benedicite (Lomond (USA) 128) [2001 **79**
79p: 6d⁵ 6s² 7m² 6g⁶ 6m* 6d Oct 3] strong, good-bodied colt: fair performer: won maiden
at Salisbury in July: effective at 6f/7f: acts on soft and good to firm going. *R. Hannon*

BEN EWAR 7 b.g. Old Vic 136 – Sunset Reef (Mill Reef (USA) 141) [2001 108: 12d⁵ **108 d**
12g⁶ 12m⁶ 12s p10g Dec 12] useful performer at best: creditable fifth to Dano-Mast in
Prix Jean de Chaudenay at Saint-Cloud in May: well below form after, leaving F. Doumen
in France before final start: stays 13f: acts on heavy and good to firm going: often breaks
blood vessels, and not one to rely on. *K. O. Cunningham-Brown*

BENJAMBO 3 b.g. Primo Dominie 121 – Young Lady (Young Generation 129) [2001 **–**
8g Jul 14] workmanlike gelding: sixth reported foal: half-brother to 1m to 1½m winner
Billaddie (by Touch of Grey): dam unraced: 66/1, tailed off in maiden at Ascot (slowly
away). *R. M. Flower*

BEN KENOBI 3 ch.g. Accondy (IRE) 79 – Nour El Sahar (USA) (Sagace (FR) 135) **–**
[2001 7s Oct 15] well-made gelding: sixth foal: closely related to a 2-y-o 6.5f winner by
Peking Opera and half-brother to a 10.5f winner by Chief Singer, both in Germany: dam
French 7.5f winner: 50/1, last of 18 in maiden at Leicester. *Mrs P. Ford*

BENNOCHY 4 ch.g. Factual (USA) 108 – Agreloui 59 (Tower Walk 130) [2001 55: **–**
f5g f6g 5v Apr 19] well held in 2001. *A. Berry*

BENNY THE VICE (USA) 2 ch.g. (Apr 30) Benny The Dip (USA) 127 – Vice On **72**
Ice (USA) (Vice Regent (CAN)) [2001 8f³ 8.2m⁵ 7.1v² 7.9s 8g Nov 5] $20,000F, IR

119

15,000Y: tall, rangy gelding: second foal: dam won 7 races in USA, including 9f minor stakes: fair maiden: second at Haydock: will be well suited by 1¼m+: acts on heavy going: carried head awkwardly final start (gelded afterwards). *M. Johnston*

BENTYHEATH LANE   4 b.g. Puissance 110 – Eye Sight 67 (Roscoe Blake 120) –
[2001 –: f12g 10.3s Mar 22] angular gelding: headstrong. *M. Mullineaux*

BENZOE (IRE)   11 b.g. Taufan (USA) 119 – Saintly Guest (What A Guest 119) [2001   **54**
62: 5m 7m 5d³ 5g 6m² 6m Aug 11] tall gelding: had a round action: useful handicapper at
best, winner of 11 of his 118 races for various trainers: modest in 2001: was effective at
5f/6f: acted on any going: blinkered/visored earlier in career and final start: sometimes
slowly away: difficult ride (though won for apprentice), and was possibly best on straight
track (won 6 times at Thirsk): reportedly retired. *K. A. Ryan*

BERGAMO   5 b.g. Robellino (USA) 127 – Pretty Thing 83 (Star Appeal 133) [2001   **60**
65: 12s 13s³ 14d* 16.2m⁵ 13.9m 14m² 12m⁶ 12.1m³ 12f⁴ 12.4m⁵ 14.1m⁴ f14.8g⁵   **a–**
f16.2s Dec 18] small, compact gelding: modest performer: won handicap
at Musselburgh in April: stays easy 2m: acts on firm and soft going: usually blinkered/
visored: sometimes looks less than keen. *B. Ellison*

BERGEN (IRE)   6 b.g. Ballad Rock 122 – Local Custom (IRE) (Be My Native (USA)   **62**
122) [2001 69: f7g f7g⁶ f7g³ f7g⁵ f7g⁵ f7g⁵ f6g f6g² 7s⁴ 6g 6f* 7m⁵ 5d⁵ 6m³ 6.1m³ f6s
Dec 21] quite good-topped gelding: modest performer: won seller at Brighton in May and
claimer at Hamilton in June: effective at 5f (given bit of test), barely at 8.5f: acts on
fibresand, firm and good to soft going: usually tongue tied. *D. Nicholls*

BERKELEY HALL   4 b.f. Saddlers' Hall (IRE) 126 – Serious Affair (Valiyar 129)   **56**
[2001 68, a–: 6.1d 6f 7f⁵ 7m³ 6f⁴ 6m² 6m² 6f² Sep 10] stocky filly: modest handicapper: **a–**
barely stays 7f: acts on firm going: sometimes blinkered. *B. Palling*

BERKELEYSQUARE BOY (IRE)   2 b.c. (May 13) Spectrum (IRE) 126 –   –
Galatrix 72 (Be My Guest (USA) 126) [2001 7m Sep 22] 48,000Y: well-made colt:
half-brother to 3-y-o Royal Millennium and a winner in Sweden by Persian Bold: dam,
1m winner, half-sister to Croco Rouge and to dam of Sleepytime, Ali-Royal and Taipan:
14/1, weakened from 2f out when behind in maiden at Newmarket: dead. *W. J. Haggas*

BERK THE JERK (IRE)   2 b.c. (Feb 10) Bahamian Bounty 116 – Pocket Book   **108**
(IRE) 60 (Reference Point 139) [2001 5s* 6m 5f³ 5g* 6g 5g³ 5d² Oct 13] 44,000F,
67,000Y: sturdy, lengthy colt: first living foal: dam, Irish maiden who stayed 1¼m,
half-sister to high-class 7f to 9f winner Indian Lodge and very smart French performer up
to 1½m Sarhoob: useful performer: won maiden at Windsor in April and listed race at
Sandown (final start for M. Tompkins) in July: good efforts last 2 starts when 2¾ lengths
third to Saddad in Flying Childers Stakes at Doncaster and 1¾ lengths second to
Dominica in Cornwallis Stakes at Ascot: likely to prove best at 5f/6f: acts on soft going:
sweating/edgy/wandered third start: reportedly sold, and joined D. Oughton in Hong
Kong. *P. W. D'Arcy*

BERNARDO BELLOTTO (IRE)   6 b.g. High Estate 127 – Naivity (IRE) 72   **41**
(Auction Ring (USA) 123) [2001 50: 8d f7g⁴ f9.4f Dec 5] smallish, workmanlike gelding:
has reportedly had wind operation: poor nowadays: seems to stay 1½m: acts on firm
going, soft, sand and fibresand: sometimes blinkered. *G. A. Swinbank*

BERNEEN   2 b.f. (Apr 19) Alzao (USA) 117 – Chickamauga (USA) (Wild Again   –
(USA)) [2001 f5g 7m 5m 6d Sep 4] 1,500F, 800Y: first foal: dam ran once: no promise:
visored in seller final start. *C. Smith*

BERRY BROOK   2 ch.f. (Mar 5) Magic Ring (IRE) 115 – Star Entry 67 (In The   **37**
Wings 128) [2001 6v p8g⁶ Nov 24] first foal: dam 9.7f winner: poor form in maiden/
seller. *E. A. Wheeler*

BERSAGLIO   6 ch.h. Rainbow Quest (USA) 134 – Escrime (USA) 92 (Sharpen Up   **53 §**
127) [2001 f12g⁴ f16g f12g Apr 27] big, rangy horse: modest maiden: stays 1¾m: acts on
firm going, good to soft and fibresand: visored/tongue tied in 2001: not to be trusted.
K. A. Morgan

BERTOLINI (USA)   5 b.h. Danzig (USA) – Aquilegia (USA) (Alydar (USA)) [2001   **114**
121: a6f³ 6m⁴ 5m⁵ Jun 19] strong, sturdy horse: had a powerful, round action: very smart
performer at best, successful in Free Handicap at Newmarket in 1999 (when also placed
in July Cup, Prix Maurice de Gheest and Sprint Cup at Haydock), but didn't win
subsequently: respectable efforts at 5 yrs in Dubai Golden Shaheen at Nad Al Sheba,
Duke of York Stakes (fourth to Pipalong) and King's Stand Stakes at Royal Ascot (fifth
to Cassandra Go): was effective at 5f to 7f: acted on firm and soft going, respectable

efforts on dirt: wore blinkers/visor: usually raced prominently: sometimes sweated/got edgy/on toes: reported to have met with slight setback after final start: to stand at Overbury Stud, Gloucestershire, fee £4,000, Oct 1st special live foal. *Saeed bin Suroor*

BERZOUD 4 b.f. Ezzoud (IRE) 126 – Bertie's Girl (Another Realm 118) [2001 69: **63** f11g e12g⁵ 8.3g 8m 10f* 11.5m* 11.5m⁴ 12d⁵ 12g⁶ 11.9m³ Aug 29] unfurnished filly: modest performer: won sellers at Brighton and Lingfield in June: better around 1¼m/ 1½m than shorter: acts on firm and soft going: visored fourth start. *J. R. Jenkins*

BESTAM 2 b.c. (Mar 18) Selkirk (USA) 129 – Showery 76 (Rainbow Quest (USA) **103 p** 134) [2001 7m⁴ 8g* 8d* 10d³ Nov 3] 200,000Y: rather leggy, unfurnished colt: third foal: dam 6f winner out of useful sprinter Anodyne: useful performer: won maiden in August and nursery (24-runner race, by 3½ lengths from McBain) in October, both at Newmarket: seemed not to stay when 6 lengths third to Alexander Three D in listed event there, travelling smoothly long way: stays 1m: acts on good to soft going: should still do better. *J. L. Dunlop*

BEST BOND 4 ch.g. Cadeaux Genereux 131 – My Darlingdaughter (Night Shift **58** (USA)) [2001 66: f6s e7g² e5g³ f5g⁴ e5g³ f6g⁵ 5.2m 6m² 8m⁵ 6.1f 7m 6f 6v⁶ f6g² f6g⁵ f7s² p6g* Dec 19] lengthy gelding: modest performer: won maiden at Lingfield in December: probably best at 6f/7f: acts on all-weather, good to firm and good to soft going: blinkered once, visored nowadays: has started slowly: not an easy ride. *N. P. Littmoden*

BEST EVER 4 ch.g. Rock City 120 – Better Still (IRE) (Glenstal (USA) 118) [2001 **52** 55: f6g 7m³ 10m 8f⁵ f7g Nov 23] compact, workmanlike gelding: modest maiden **a–** handicapper: barely stays 1¼m: acts on firm and good to soft going: none too consistent. *M. W. Easterby*

BEST GUEST (IRE) 3 b.c. Barathea (IRE) 127 – Common Rumpus (IRE) 87 **–** (Common Grounds 118) [2001 –: 8m 8.1g 9m 8.5d 10m 13.8s Oct 20] strong colt: little form. *G. G. Margarson*

BEST LEAD 2 b.c. (Mar 9) Distant Relative 128 – Bestemor 60 (Selkirk (USA) 129) **89** [2001 5m³ 5f² 5m* 5s⁴ 5.1g* 5m⁶ 6g Oct 6] leggy colt: first foal: dam maiden who stayed 1m: fairly useful performer: won maiden at Leicester and nursery at Chepstow in August: creditable sixth to Irish Vale in listed event at Ayr: likely to prove best at 5f/easy 6f: acts on firm and soft going: has carried head awkwardly/hung right under pressure: usually waited with: sold 6,000 gns. *G. A. Butler*

BESTMORTGAGE UK 4 b.f. Emperor Jones (USA) 119 – Lady Lustre 70 (On **–** Your Mark 125) [2001 f8s f5g 8.1m Jul 25] third foal: dam 1m winner: no sign of ability. *T. T. Clement*

BEST OF THE BESTS (IRE) 4 ch.c. Machiavellian (USA) 123 – Sueboog (IRE) **122** 109 (Darshaan 133) [2001 122: a9f* a10f 10d Oct 20] big, rangy colt: very smart performer: won listed event at Nad Al Sheba (beat Sobieski by 12 lengths) in February: well held in Dubai World Cup there following month (later found to have suffered ankle injury): off 7 months and sweating, only 10 lengths seventh to Nayef in Dubai Champion Stakes at Newmarket final start (tongue tied): stays 1¼m: yet to race on heavy going: acts on any other turf and on dirt: has been edgy: sometimes makes running (has taken good hold): bandaged behind in 2000. *Saeed bin Suroor*

BEST PORT (IRE) 5 b.g. Be My Guest (USA) 126 – Portree 82 (Slip Anchor 136) **64** [2001 42: 12.4d⁴ 14.1m³ 14.1f* 12.3m³ 16.2f* 16.2f⁵ 16m* 16m² Sep 30] lightly-made gelding: modest handicapper: won at Nottingham, Beverley and Redcar in the summer: effective at 1½m to 2m: acts on firm going, good to soft (probably on soft) and fibresand: usually held up: looked wayward earlier in career. *J. Parkes*

BE SWIFT 2 ch.g. (Feb 27) Millkom 124 – Conwy (Rock City 120) [2001 7d⁵ 8g 6m **53** Aug 15] 6,000Y: second foal: dam, no form, half-sister to smart Hong Kong performer up to 1¼m Keen Winner: modest maiden: should stay at least 1m: gelded after final start. *S. Dow*

BETHANIA 3 gr.f. Mark of Esteem (IRE) 137 – Anneli Rose 56 (Superlative 118) **70 d** [2001 –: 7m⁵ 7m³ 9m 8.5m³ 9.9d⁶ 8.3v⁵ p10g⁴ Dec 29] sturdy, close-coupled filly: fluent mover: fair maiden at best: stays easy 8.5f: acts on good to firm ground. *Mrs A. J. Perrett*

BETHESDA 4 gr.f. Distant Relative 128 – Anneli Rose 56 (Superlative 118) [2001 60: **89** 7m⁶ 6m* 5.7m* 6g Sep 19] rangy filly: fairly useful handicapper: won in big fields at Salisbury in August and Bath (beat Skylark by 5 lengths, soon in front) in September: went sharply left at stalls and never travelling well final start: raced mainly around 6f: acts on good to firm and good to soft going: blinkered last 3 starts: possibly has some temperament. *Mrs A. J. Perrett*

BETSMART GIRL   2 b.f. (Apr 12) Danzig Connection (USA) – Mira Lady (Henbit **42** (USA) 130) [2001 5m⁶ 6m f6g 6g⁶ f7g² 7.5f² 7.1f⁵ f7g⁵ 7.1s f7g Oct 1] 800Y: unfurnished **a45** filly: half-sister to several winners, including 1995 2-y-o 1m winner Eric's Bett (by Chilibang) and 1m winner Nuin Tara (by Petoski): dam winner in Germany: poor maiden: runner-up in sellers: stays 7.5f: acts on firm going and fibresand: tongue tied: sold 800 gns, sent to Denmark. *M. Dods*

BETTERGETGONE   2 b.f. (Apr 9) Bettergeton 97 – Impromptu Melody (IRE)   **–** (Mac's Imp (USA) 116) [2001 f5g f6g 5.1f 6f 6.1v f6g f5g Nov 16] 3,600Y: leggy filly: third foal: half-sister to winner in Holland by Suluk: dam no form: bad maiden: tried visored/blinkered. *Mrs N. Macauley*

BETTER MOMENT (IRE)   4 b.g. Turtle Island (IRE) 123 – Snoozeandyoulose **47** (IRE) 73 (Scenic 128) [2001 56: 10s² f12g² 14.1m⁶ Jul 28] small gelding: poor maiden: left J. FitzGerald after first start: stays 1½m: acts on fibresand, soft and good to firm ground: blinkered in 2001. *John Berry*

BETTER OFF   3 ch.g. Bettergeton 97 – Miami Pride 48 (Miami Springs 121) [2001   **–** 70: f6g² f7g* f7g² f6g² f7g⁴ f7g³ f7g² f8g f7g³ f6g* f6g³ 6s⁵ f6g 7d f7g⁵ f6g f7g f8.5g f7g **a77** f6g² Dec 17] fair handicapper: won at Wolverhampton in January and Southwell in April: best at 6f/7f: acts on fibresand (well held both starts on turf): sometimes races freely. *Mrs N. Macauley*

BETTER PAL   2 ch.g. (May 29) Prince Sabo 123 – Rattle Along 80 (Tap On Wood **65** 130) [2001 6.1d⁵ f6g 6s⁵ Nov 10] 2,000Y: good-bodied gelding: half-brother to several winners, including smart 6f to 1m performer Night Manoeuvres (by Night Shift) and fairly useful 1m winner Blot (by Warning): dam 1¼m winner: fair form when fifth in maidens at Nottingham and Doncaster: reportedly lost action in between: should stay 7f. *W. Jarvis*

BETTERTHEDEVILUNO   2 b.c. (Apr 18) Hector Protector (USA) 124 – **52** Aquaglow 84 (Caerleon (USA) 132) [2001 7f³ Jul 4] 10,500Y: half-brother to several winners, including 7f/1m winner Alpenglow (by Ezzoud) and 1m (at 2 yrs) to 1½m (in USA) winner Attitre (by Mtoto), both useful: dam 7f/1m winner: third of 5 in claimer at Brighton, racing freely: sold 800 gns. *E. J. O'Neill*

BETTINA BLUE (IRE)   4 b.f. Paris House 123 – Born To Fly (IRE) 57 (Last Tycoon   **–** 131) [2001 59d: e6g e8g⁶ e7g³ e7g f6g Feb 10] poor maiden: barely stays easy 7f: acts on **a39** firm ground, soft and equitrack: tends to race freely. *R. Ingram*

BETTY BATHWICK (IRE)   4 b.f. Common Grounds 118 – Tynaghmile (IRE) **58 d** (Lyphard's Special (USA) 122) [2001 66: 6s⁶ 7m 6d 6g f7g p7g Dec 12] modest performer, on downgrade: stays 6f: acts on soft ground. *J. Akehurst*

BETTY'S PRIDE   2 b.f. (Apr 11) Lion Cavern (USA) 117 – Final Verdict (IRE) (Law **80** Society (USA) 130) [2001 5d 5s⁵ 5m² 6g 5m³ 5s⁵ Oct 20] 9,500Y, 7,000 2-y-o: leggy, quite good-topped filly: sixth foal: half-sister to Irish 1997 2-y-o 7f winner First Encounter (by Alzao): dam, Irish maiden, sister to smart performers up to 1½m Newton's Law and Close Conflict: fairly useful maiden: easily best effort when third to Dominica at Musselburgh: likely to prove best at bare 5f: acts on good to firm ground, seemingly not on softer than good. *A. Berry*

BEVEL BLUE   3 b.g. Beveled (USA) – Blue Angel (Lord Gayle (USA) 124) [2001 **48** 48: 5m 5m 6.1s 7.1g Sep 13] poor maiden: stays 6f: acts on good to firm going. *G. B. Balding*

BEVELED LEGGINGS   2 b.f. (Mar 26) Beveled (USA) – Nahla (Wassl 125) [2001   **–** 5.1g 5.1d Aug 19] 700Y: first foal: dam, ran once on Flat, bumper winner: no sign of ability in seller/maiden. *Miss Jacqueline S. Doyle*

BEVERLEY MACCA   3 ch.f. Piccolo 121 – Kangra Valley 56 (Indian Ridge 123) **68** [2001 75: f5s f6g f5g² e5g* f5g² 5.1v 5.3f³ 5g 5g 5g f5g f5s f5s² Dec 18] small, compact **a73** filly: unimpressive mover: fair handicapper: won at Lingfield in March: best at 5f: acts on fibresand/equitrack, firm and good to soft going, possibly not on soft/heavy: sometimes edges right: usually makes running: difficult to predict. *A. Berry*

BE WARNED   10 b.g. Warning 136 – Sagar 74 (Habitat 134) [2001 66: f9.4s² f8s⁴ f12g* f11g* f12g⁵ f12g³ 8.1g f12g* f11g³ 12.6d f8.5g* f9.4g⁶ f8.5g⁶ f12s⁵ Dec 26] **a63** good-topped gelding: unimpressive mover: modest performer: won at Wolverhampton (selling handicap/claimer/handicap) and Southwell (seller) between January and October: effective at 8.5f to easy 1½m: acts on fibresand/equitrack, lightly raced and little form on turf nowadays: visored, used to be blinkered: often soon behind. *R. Brotherton*

BEYOND CALCULATION (USA)   7 ch.g. Geiger Counter (USA) – Placer Queen   **83**
(Habitat 134) [2001 76: f6g f6g e6g⁴ 5.7f³ 5.1f* 5d 5m 5.1m⁴ 5.7m² 5.5d 5m 5m 5.3g²   **a64**
5m³ 6m* 5g 5m⁶ 6d Oct 3] sturdy gelding: fairly useful handicapper on turf, modest on
all-weather: won at Chester in June and Redcar in September: effective at 5f/6f: acts on
fibresand/equitrack, firm and good to soft going: often races up with pace. *J. M. Bradley*

BEYOND THE CLOUDS (IRE)   5 b.g. Midhish 109 – Tongabezi (IRE) 75 (Sher-   **90**
nazar 131) [2001 74: 5v 5m* 5g* 5f³ 5g⁴ 5m 8g 5g 5m⁴ 5d⁵ 5s 5v 5s Nov 9] big gelding:
fairly useful handicapper: won at Beverley in May and Windsor in June: best at 5f: acts
on firm and good to soft going, not on soft/heavy: tried visored (not in 2001): races
prominently. *J. S. Wainwright*

BEZWELL PRINCE   2 ch.g. (Mar 27) Bluegrass Prince (IRE) 110 – Money Supply   **62**
(Brigadier Gerard 144) [2001 7g 7.1s⁶ 6d⁴ Oct 3] 6,500F, 10,000Y: strong gelding:
half-brother to several winners, including 7f (at 2 yrs) to 1½m winner Credit Squeeze (by
Superlative) and 1996 2-y-o 5.7f winner Silver Purse (by Interrex): dam unraced sister to
smart Irish 1m winner Senior Citizen: modest maiden: best effort when fourth at
Newcastle: should stay at least 1m. *N. Tinkler*

BEZWELL'S GUEST (IRE)   2 ch.c. (Mar 11) Be My Guest (USA) 126 – Fine   **55**
Project (IRE) 92 (Project Manager 111) [2001 5g³ 5f May 28] IR 8,000F, IR 12,000Y:
first foal: dam, Irish 5f (at 2 yrs) and 7f winner, from family of useful Irish 2-y-o's Eva
Luna (6f) and Cois Na Tine (up to 1m): modest form in maidens at Leicester: bred to stay
at least 1m. *R. M. Beckett*

BEZZA (IRE)   3 ch.f. Bob Back (USA) 124 – Lady Lord (IRE) (Coquelin (USA) 121)   **40**
[2001 –: 9.9m⁶ 10g 10g 14.1s Sep 4] close-coupled, plain filly: poor maiden: blinkered
final start: sold IR £6,500 (in December). *M. H. Tompkins*

BHUTAN (IRE)   6 b.g. Polish Patriot (USA) 128 – Bustinetta 89 (Bustino 136) [2001   **74**
77: 14d⁵ 12m³ 14.1m 16m² 12.1m 12f⁵ 12.4m 15.9m⁴ 12f² 15.8m⁶ 14.1g⁴ Oct 6] lengthy
gelding: fair performer: effective at 1½m to 17.5f: acts on any going: visored (below
form) fifth start: usually held up: tends to find little. *Mrs M. Reveley*

BIANCHI (USA)   3 b.f. Gulch (USA) – Northern Trick (USA) 131 (Northern Dancer)   **76**
[2001 64: 8.1g⁴ 8.3d² 10.3f² 12.3f³ 10d⁴ 11.9m⁴ 10m⁵ Sep 1] smallish, leggy filly: fair
maiden, generally disappointing: stays 1½m: acts on firm and good to soft going: sold
80,000 gns in December. *P. F. I. Cole*

BIBLE BOX (IRE)   3 b.f. Bin Ajwaad (IRE) 119 – Addie Pray (IRE) 68 (Great   **76**
Commotion (USA) 123) [2001 53: 8.3s² 8.2d⁴ 8m 7m* 7d³ 8m⁴ 8d Oct 15] fair
handicapper: won at Yarmouth in July: best at 7f/1m: best efforts on good to firm going.
Mrs Lydia Pearce

BIDDY   2 b.f. (Apr 2) Rock Hopper 124 – Wanda 74 (Taufan (USA) 119) [2001 7s⁶ 7g   **50**
8s Nov 9] small, compact filly: fourth living foal: dam 5f (including at 2 yrs)/6f winner:
best effort in maidens (modest form) at Redcar second start: rider suspended under
non-triers rule final one: should stay at least 1m: slowly away first 2 outings, swerved
leaving stall final one. *M. W. Easterby*

BID FOR FAME (USA)   4 b. or br.g. Quest For Fame 127 – Shroud (USA) (Vaguely   **89**
Noble 140) [2001 92: 12v 14m 10m⁵ 12m² 12m³ 12g² 12m 13.3m⁵ 12g 12g⁶ 12g Sep
28] leggy, lengthy, quite attractive gelding: has a quick, rather round action: fairly useful
handicapper: should stay beyond 13f: acts on good going or firmer: blinkered (ran
poorly) final start: has won when sweating. *T. G. Mills*

BID ME WELCOME   5 b.g. Alzao (USA) 117 – Blushing Barada (USA) 53   **–**
(Blushing Groom (FR) 131) [2001 86: 12s 12d 13.9m 17.1f 14.1f 14.6f⁶ 16.2f 16f Jul
22] angular gelding: fluent mover: fairly useful handicapper at 4 yrs: well held in 2001.
Mrs J. R. Ramsden

BID SPOTTER (IRE)   2 b.c. (Mar 2) Eagle Eyed (USA) 111 – Bebe Auction (IRE)   **62 d**
(Auction Ring (USA) 123) [2001 6m⁶ 6m f7g f7g f5s Dec 21] IR 5,000F, IR 13,000Y:
fourth foal: dam unraced: modest maiden: disappointing after debut (hung left): left
R. Hannon after third start. *M. C. Chapman*

BIFF-EM (IRE)   7 ch.g. Durgam (USA) – Flash The Gold (Ahonoora 122) [2001 44:   **35 d**
5m⁵ 6m 6g 5f⁵ 6g 7d⁵ 5s 6v Oct 16] rather leggy gelding: poor handicapper: effective at
5f to 7f: acts on any going: has run well for amateur/when sweating. *Miss L. A. Perratt*

BIG BERTHA   3 ch.f. Dancing Spree (USA) – Bertrade 75 (Homeboy 114) [2001   **59 ?**
8.2v³ 6v 8.3v Nov 8] half-sister to 5f (at 2 yrs) and 7f winner Winsome Wooster (by Primo
Dominie) and 7f to 1½m winner Homestead (by Indian Ridge): dam maiden who stayed

1¼m: seemingly best effort in maidens at Nottingham in October on debut: restless in stall/very slowly away next time: likely to stay 1¼m. *John Berry*

BIG BOPPER (IRE) 2 b.c. (Mar 23) Danehill Dancer (IRE) 117 – Apocalypse **69** (Auction Ring (USA) 123) [2001 6g⁶ 6m 7d⁴ 7s Oct 16] IR 12,000F, 35,000Y: tall, leggy, rather unfurnished colt: half-brother to 3 winners, including 5f winner Cellito (by Flash of Steel) and irresolute 5f (at 2 yrs) and 1m winner Lars Porsena (by Trojan Fen): dam, French 1m winner, from good family: fair maiden: best efforts last 2 starts: will probably stay 1m: acts on soft ground. *R. Hannon*

BIG FUTURE 4 b.c. Bigstone (IRE) 126 – Star of The Future (USA) 100 (El Gran **104** Senor (USA) 136) [2001 102: 7m 8m² 8.1g³ 8g 7.9m 8d² 9g 8f⁶ Dec 31] smallish, good-bodied colt: useful handicapper: best efforts in 2001 when second to Surprise Encounter in Hunt Cup at Royal Ascot and third to Desert Deer at Sandown on second/third starts: sold from Mrs A. Perrett 52,000 gns before final outing: better at 1m than 7f: acts on any going: races freely. *D. Vienna, USA*

BIGGLES (IRE) 4 b.g. Desert Style (IRE) 121 – Excruciating (CAN) (Bold Forbes **?** (USA)) [2001 62: 8.2v 11s a12g⁴ 11d³ a10.5g² a10.5g* a10g³ a12g⁴ Dec 16] modest form in maidens at 3 yrs: sold from A. Turnell 900 gns after second start: won handicap at Mijas in September: stays 1½m: acts on sand and good to soft ground: blinkered, tongue tied once. *P. Haley, Spain*

BIG ISSUE 4 b.g. First Trump 118 – Hollow Heart 89 (Wolver Hollow 126) [2001 –: **–** 7s⁶ May 3] seller winner at 2 yrs: well held both starts since. *A. Bailey*

BIG JOHN (IRE) 3 ch.c. Cadeaux Genereux 131 – India Atlanta (Ahonoora 122) **66** [2001 67: e7g 6s 7m* 6m 6.1f⁶ 8m 6f Aug 1] sparely-made colt: fair performer: won claimer at Brighton in May: left E. Dunlop before final 2 starts: stays 7f: acts on firm going. *Miss S. J. Wilton*

BIG MOMENT 3 ch.g. Be My Guest (USA) 126 – Petralona (USA) (Alleged (USA) **104 p** 138) [2001 86p: 10d⁴ 10.3f² 11m² 12f* 14g* 13.9m⁴ 14.6d³ 18d Oct 20] quite attractive, unfurnished gelding: has a short, round action: useful performer: won maiden at Doncaster in July and handicap at Goodwood in August: good efforts after in handicaps at York, Doncaster (unlucky in running when third to Darasim in Mallard Stakes) and Newmarket (set with plenty to do when seventh to Distant Prospect in Cesarewitch): gelded after: stays 2m+: acts on firm and good to soft going: type to make a smart 4-y-o, and win a good prize. *B. W. Hills*

BIG RED 8 ch.g. Left To Me – Backherorbust (Casino Boy 114) [2001 8.1d Jul 6] **–** tailed off on Flat debut. *Miss K. M. George*

BIGWIG (IRE) 8 ch.g. Thatching 131 – Sabaah (USA) 65 (Nureyev (USA) 131) **50** [2001 –: e16g² Jan 6] modest handicapper: lightly raced on Flat nowadays: barely stays easy 2m: acts on fibresand/equitrack: blinkered: possibly none too genuine. *G. L. Moore*

BIJAN (IRE) 3 b.f. Mukaddamah (USA) 125 – Alkariyh (USA) 79 (Alydar (USA)) **68** [2001 75: 7g 5m 7m 5.1g 6.1d 6m⁶ 6d 5.1d 6d f6g* f7g³ f7s⁶ f6s³ Dec 26] leggy filly: fair handicapper: won at Southwell in November: stays 7f: yet to race on extremes of going on turf, acts on fibresand: visored (ran poorly) once. *R. Hollinshead*

BIJOU BELLE 2 b.f. (Apr 8) Bijou d'Inde 127 – Primitive Gift 38 (Primitive Rising **–** (USA) 113) [2001 6f⁵ 6m 5s Oct 20] 9,500Y: tall filly: fifth foal: half-sister to 4-y-o La Sylphide and a sprint winner abroad by Then Again: dam lightly-raced maiden who virtually refused to race on final start: well beaten in minor events/maiden. *Mrs A. Duffield*

BIJOU BOUNTY 2 b.f. (Apr 29) Bijou d'Inde 127 – Kick The Boss (Robellino **–** (USA) 127) [2001 5.1s 7m Jun 23] 500Y, resold 650Y: leggy, plain filly: second foal: dam, unraced, from family of high-class stayer High Line: tailed off in sellers: blinkered final start. *A. Smith*

BIJOU STAR 2 b.c. (Apr 21) Bijou d'Inde 127 – Starisk 47 (Risk Me (FR) 127) [2001 **59** 7m⁶ 7.1m⁵ 7.9m 7s Oct 5] 17,000F, 14,000Y: workmanlike colt: fourth foal: half-brother to 2-y-o winners Shatin Beauty (5f in 1999, by Mistertopogigo) and Robber Red (6f in 1998, by Mon Tresor): dam maiden who should have stayed beyond 1m: modest maiden: best efforts first 2 starts: dead. *S. Kirk*

BILLADDIE 8 b.g. Touch of Grey 90 – Young Lady (Young Generation 129) [2001 –: **62** f12g⁵ f11g 12d⁶ 10g³ 10v 10m 12m 9.9m⁵ 10m² 12m⁶ 11.5f⁵ 12g* 10g 12m⁴ 12g Aug 26] **a65** leggy, angular gelding: fair handicapper: won at Newmarket in August: effective at 1¼m/

1½m: acts on any turf going and fibresand/equitrack: tried blinkered: has run well sweating: held up (tends to idle in front): none too consistent. *R. M. Flower*

BILLICHANG   5 b.h. Chilibang 120 – Swing O'The Kilt (Hotfoot 126) [2001 –, a62d: e10g⁶ e8g² e8g⁴ e10g Mar 28] strong horse: poor performer: effective at 1m to bare 1½m: acts on fibresand/equitrack and good to firm ground: often visored/blinkered. *P. Howling*   **– a44**

BILLIE H   3 ch.f. Cool Jazz 116 – Rachels Eden (Ring Bidder 88) [2001 54: f7g f8g² e8g³ e7g³ e7g² 7m² 8f 7g⁵ 7m⁴ 7m⁵ 7g f7g* 7d f8g⁴ f7g² f7g p7g Dec 12] strong, sturdy filly: modest performer: won seller at Wolverhampton in October: effective at 7f/1m: acts on firm going and fibresand/equitrack: usually blinkered: sometimes looks less than keen: untrustworthy. *C. E. Brittain*   **60 §**

BILLIE HOLIDAY   3 b.f. Fairy King (USA) – Raymouna (IRE) (High Top 131) [2001 7g 6g 6m⁶ 8.1d⁶ 7.6f 6m Aug 13] 80,000Y: lengthy, quite attractive filly: fifth foal: sister to winner in Greece and half-sister to smart Irish performers up to 1¼m Rayouni (by Zayyani) and Raiyoun (by Doyoun): dam, Irish 1m winner, half-sister to smart performer up to 1¾m Rayseka: well held in maidens/handicaps: should stay 1m: blinkered final start: sent to France. *B. J. Meehan*   **–**

BILLY BATHWICK (IRE)   4 ch.c. Fayruz 116 – Cut It Fine (USA) (Big Spruce (USA)) [2001 68: 8s 8m² 10g* 10g⁶ 10.1m 9d 9.7m 8m 8m 8s³ Sep 24] smallish, close-coupled colt: fair handicapper: won at Windsor in June: well below form after next start: stays 1¼m: acts on soft and good to firm ground, showed promise on fibresand: tried blinkered. *Dr J. R. J. Naylor*   **70**

BILLYJO (IRE)   3 b.g. Idris (IRE) 118 – Village Countess (IRE) (Reasonable (FR) 119) [2001 43: f8.5s⁶ f9.4s⁴ f8.5g f9.4g 9m 10m 7.5f f7g³ f8g 7d f12g 13.8m 6d⁶ f6g⁶ f8.5g f7g Nov 23] quite attractive gelding: poor maiden: barely stays 9.4f: acts on good to soft going and fibresand: tried blinkered/visored: has started slowly/looked less than keen. *Miss A. Stokell*   **33**

BINARY FILE (USA)   3 b.c. Nureyev (USA) 131 – Binary 109 (Rainbow Quest (USA) 134) [2001 7m* 8f* Jun 23] medium-sized, deep-girthed colt: has a round action: first foal: dam, French/US 9f/1¼m winner, sister to smart 1½m winner Bequeath and half-sister to smart 1¼m winner Bal Harbour: favourite, won maiden at Salisbury in June: much improved (smart performance) to follow up in 5-runner minor event at Ascot by ¾ length from Bourgainville, again quickening well from off false pace, pushed out: free-going sort who may prove best around 1m: stays in training. *J. H. M. Gosden*   **110**

Alfred Franks And Bartlett Sunglasses EBF Classified Stakes, Ascot—
Binary File impresses in a falsely-run race, beating Bourgainville (rail)

BINTALBAWADI (IRE)   3 b.f. Diesis 133 – Solar Star (USA) 93 (Lear Fan (USA) **67**
130) [2001 8m* Aug 30] 200,000Y: fifth foal: sister to useful French 1999 2-y-o 7f
winner Bintalreef and half-sister to fairly useful 1m winner Irish Light (by Irish River)
and winner in USA by Boundary: dam, 2-y-o 6f winner, half-sister to smart US 6f/7f
performer Gold Land from family of Soviet Line: 5/2, overcame greenness to win maiden
at Salisbury by short head from Spectina, going freely and edging ahead inside final 2f
despite hanging left: visits Green Desert. *M. P. Tregoning*

BINTANG TIMOR (USA)   7 ch.g. Mt Livermore (USA) – Frisky Kitten (USA) **75**
(Isopach (USA)) [2001 78, a75: f8g f8s 6.1v⁴ 7s⁴ 6m² 6g 6g 7m⁵ 7m 7m 8.3m 6g 7s⁵ 7d⁶ **a62**
7s⁵ p7g³ Nov 20] close-coupled gelding: unimpressive mover: fair handicapper: effective
at 6f to easy 1m: acts on any turf going and all-weather: sometimes slowly away: held up.
W. J. Musson

BINT HABIBI   4 b.f. Bin Ajwaad (IRE) 119 – High Stepping (IRE) (Taufan (USA) **71**
119) [2001 63: f9.4s* f9.4g³ f9.4g² f8.5g² Mar 8] angular filly: fair handicapper: won at
Wolverhampton in January: stays 9.4f: acts on fibresand, firm and soft going: visored
third start: has raced freely/wandered: consistent. *Mrs Lydia Pearce*

BINT ROYAL (IRE)   3 ch.f. Royal Abjar (USA) 121 – Living Legend (USA) **54**
(Septieme Ciel (USA) 123) [2001 64: e7g 6.1v 5m 5m 5m 6.1m² f6g³ 6m⁴ 5g 6m 5g³ 6m⁶
6g³ 5g³ 5g 6f⁴ p6g³ Dec 19] close-coupled, workmanlike filly: modest handicapper: stays
6f: acts on firm going, good to soft and fibresand/polytrack: blinkered/visored after fourth
start. *Miss V. Haigh*

BINT ST JAMES   6 b.m. Shareef Dancer (USA) 135 – St James's Antigua (IRE) 79 **–**
(Law Society (USA) 130) [2001 14.1m 12.6d 17.1g Aug 19] modest maiden handicapper
at 3 yrs: lightly raced on Flat nowadays. *W. Clay*

BIRCHWOOD SUN   11 b.g. Bluebird (USA) 125 – Shapely Test (USA) (Elocu- **50**
tionist (USA)) [2001 54: 7s⁵ 7d² 6m 6g² 6g³ Jul 20] compact gelding: poor mover: modest
performer: effective at 6f (given test) to 1m: acts on any going: used to be blinkered,
visored nowadays: comes from behind. *M. Dods*

BIRDIE   2 b.f. (Feb 25) Alhaarth (IRE) 126 – Fade (Persepolis (FR) 127) [2001 7f **82**
7.5g⁴ 7s² 8.3v² Nov 8] big, good-topped filly: has plenty of scope: half-sister to several
winners, including 1m/1¼m winner Fickle (by Danehill) and 1m winner Eve (by Rainbow Quest), both fairly useful, and useful French performer up to 13.5f Faru (by Mtoto):
dam unraced daughter of Cheshire/Lancashire Oaks winner One Over Parr: fairly useful
maiden: best effort when second in nursery at Windsor final start: will stay 1¼m: acts on
heavy going: edged right second outing: tail flasher. *M. L. W. Bell*

BIRDLIP HILL   2 br.f. (Apr 23) Prince Sabo 123 – Be My Bird 65 (Be My Chief **56**
(USA) 122) [2001 7.1f 7.1d³ 7m⁴ 8g 7m⁶ f7g* f7g⁴ f8g f8.5g Oct 20] 10,000Y: third foal:
half-sister to 4-y-o Timeless Chick: dam, third at 7f/8.5f at 2 yrs, half-sister to smart
performer up to 1¼m Stato One: modest performer: won seller at Wolverhampton in
September: should stay 1m: acts on fibresand, good to firm and good to soft going:
sometimes slowly away: sent to Norway. *A. Berry*

BIRDWATCHING   2 b.g. (Feb 21) Primo Dominie 121 – Area Girl 76 (Jareer (USA) **–**
115) [2001 7.5g 10d f9.4g Nov 17] 52,000Y: quite good-topped gelding: brother to fairly
useful 5f (including at 2 yrs)/6f winner Dominant Air, closely related to fairly useful 2000
2-y-o 5f/6f winner Clarion (by First Trump), later 1m winner abroad, and half-brother to
2 winners, including useful 6f (including at 2 yrs)/7f winner Flying Officer (by Efisio):
dam 2-y-o 5f winner: well held in maidens: pulled hard second start: slowly away final
one. *S. C. Williams*

BIRTHDAY BELLE   5 ch.m. Lycius (USA) 124 – Dance Festival 101 (Nureyev **–**
(USA) 131) [2001 8d 7.1m 6m 6m 7.1f 8f Jun 22] sixth foal: half-sister to several
winners, including useful 7.3f and 8.5f winner Allemande (by Nashwan) and fairly useful
Irish 1995 2-y-o 9f winner Matsuri (by Darshaan): dam, lightly-raced maiden, placed at
6f and 7f: fair form at 3 yrs in Ireland for J. Oxx: won maiden at Frankfurt and 2 handicaps
at Dusseldorf at 4 yrs for M. Hofer in Germany: well held in Britain in 2001: stays 8.5f:
acts on soft ground: has been blinkered/visored. *P. Monteith*

BIRTH OF THE BLUES   5 ch.g. Efisio 120 – Great Steps 88 (Vaigly Great 127) **52**
[2001 65d: e13s⁶ e16g 10m* 10f⁵ 11.5m⁵ 12m* 11.6g⁵ Aug 6] lengthy, angular
gelding: modest performer: won seller at Brighton in May and amateur handicap at
Salisbury in July: stays 1½m: acts on any ground: tried visored/blinkered at 4 yrs.
K. O. Cunningham-Brown

Vodafone 'Dash' Rated Stakes (Handicap), Epsom—Bishops Court bursts clear under Robert Winston to win the race for the second time; the battle for the places is between Ivory's Joy (No.7), Deep Space (hidden by winner), Repertory (spots on cap) and Proud Native (left)

BISHOP'S BLADE 4 b.g. Sure Blade (USA) 130 – Myrtilla (Beldale Flutter (USA) 130) [2001 –: 11.9f 14.1f 16.4m Jul 12] well held in maidens/handicaps. *J. S. King* —

BISHOPS COURT 7 ch.g. Clantime 101 – Indigo 86 (Primo Dominie 121) [2001 115: 5.1v³ 5m 5f* 5g 5m⁴ 5m³ 5.2f Sep 22] big, good-quartered gelding: usually looks really well: smart performer: back with former trainer, showed himself as good as ever when winning listed Vodafone 'Dash' Rated Stakes at Epsom (won same race in 1998) in June by 1¾ lengths from Ivory's Joy: in frame after in King George Stakes at Goodwood (fourth to Dietrich, might well have won with more luck) and Nunthorpe Stakes at York (good 2¾ lengths third to Mozart after being squeezed out at start): reportedly found to have sustained hairline fracture of pelvis final start: best form at 5f: acts on any turf going: tongue tied in 2000, bandaged in 2001: has edged left/idled: held up, and travels very strongly. *Mrs J. R. Ramsden* **117**

BISHOP'S SECRET 3 b.g. Bishop of Cashel 122 – Secret Rapture (USA) (Woodman (USA) 126) [2001 56: f7g³ f7s⁵ f7g f8g f7g f5g 6.1d f11g⁴ 10f f8g 8m 10.1g Aug 17] tall gelding: modest maiden at best: probably stays 11f: acts on fibresand, little form on turf: usually blinkered/visored: often looks none too keen. *Mrs N. Macauley* — § a61 d

BISHOPSTONE BELLE 4 b.f. Formidable (USA) 125 – Relatively Easy 70 (Relkino 131) [2001 f9.4g Feb 1] fifth foal: half-sister to 1993 2-y-o 5f and 1m winner Beats Working (by Aragon) and 2m winner Uplift (by Bustino): dam middle-distance stayer who also won over jumps: tailed off in maiden. *S. Mellor* —

BISHOPSTONE MAN 4 b.g. Piccolo 121 – Auntie Gladys 49 (Great Nephew 126) [2001 76: e7g⁴ e10g f8.5g f7g² f7g⁶ f7g⁵ f7g² e8g f8.5g⁴ 7m² f7g⁴ 7.6f⁴ 7.6m 7m⁶ 7.1g² 8s 6v Oct 8] well-made gelding: fair handicapper: left S. Mellor after thirteenth start: effective at 6f to 8.5f: acts on firm going, soft and fibresand/equitrack: usually visored of late: sometimes pulls hard. *H. Candy* **69** a65

BISHOP'S WING'S 3 br.f. Bishop of Cashel 122 – Butterfly Rose (USA) (Iron Ruler (USA)) [2001 48: f8.5g⁶ e7g 7m 7s f6g⁵ Jun 15] poor maiden at 2 yrs: well held in 2001. *P. R. Chamings* —

BISHOP'S WOOD (IRE) 2 b.c. (May 21) Charnwood Forest (IRE) 125 – Samriah (IRE) (Wassl 125) [2001 6m³ 6.9m* 8f Oct 12] 14,500Y, 15,000 2-y-o: fifth foal: half-brother to several winners, including fairly useful 1997 2-y-o 5f winner Baby Grand (by Mukaddamah) and 4-y-o Cedar Master: dam unraced: fair form when winning maiden at Folkestone in June: left M. Quinlan: blinkered, behind in non-graded event at Santa Anita final start: stays 7f. *R. Baffert, USA* **76**

BISHR 2 b.c. (Feb 16) Royal Applause 124 – Hawayah (IRE) 68 (Shareef Dancer (USA) 135) [2001 6f⁵ 7m⁵ 6m² Jul 31] 50,000F, 190,000Y: fifth foal: half-brother to 3 winners, including 3-y-o Showpiece and 7f winner Tee Cee (by Lion Cavern): dam 2-y-o 7f winner out of Nell Gwyn winner Ghariba, herself half-sister to smart middle-distance stayer Braashee: fairly useful maiden: tongue tied, beaten 4 lengths by Serieux at Good- **84**

wood final start: not sure to stay beyond 7f: raced only on going firmer than good. *M. P. Tregoning*

BISQUE 3 ch.f. Inchinor 119 – Biscay 67 (Unfuwain (USA) 131) [2001 51p: 8f² 8d 7m **61 d** 7g 8.1f Sep 18] angular, workmanlike filly: modest maiden: behind in handicaps final 3 starts: stays 1m: acts on firm going: sold 1,500 gns. *R. Charlton*

BISQUET-DE-BOUCHE 7 ch.m. Most Welcome 131 – Larive 80 (Blakeney 126) **36** [2001 –: f16.2s 18m* 17.1g Aug 19] shallow-girthed mare: poor performer, lightly raced: won maiden handicap at Chepstow in July: stays 2¼m: acts on good to firm ground. *A. W. Carroll*

BIT OF LUCK 2 ch.c. (May 10) First Trump 118 – Elle Reef (Shareef Dancer (USA) **93** 135) [2001 6m⁵ 6g² 7f² 7g² 7.5s* 8m² 8m² 8s⁵ Oct 22] 15,000F, 22,000Y: strong colt: fifth foal: brother to 5-y-o Ace of Trumps and half-brother to winners abroad by Aragon and Emperor Jones: dam unraced: fairly useful performer: won nursery at Beverley in August: good efforts in valuable nursery at Newcastle, minor event at Ayr and listed event at Pontefract (fifth to Bandari) last 3 starts: will stay 1¼m: acts on soft and good to firm going: game and reliable. *M. H. Tompkins*

BITTER SWEET 5 gr.m. Deploy 131 – Julia Flyte 91 (Drone (USA)) [2001 51d: 10g **58** 10g⁶ 8m⁶ 8.5f³ 9.7m* 9g 10.1d* 9.9m² 10m³ 10m⁵ 10m⁵ 10.2g² 10m⁵ 10.4m³ 10s Sep 30] modest handicapper: won at Folkestone and Epsom (apprentices) in July: creditable efforts most starts after: stays 1¼m: acts on firm and soft going: sometimes visored in 2000: has found little: held up. *J. L. Spearing*

BIYA (IRE) 9 ch.g. Shadeed (USA) 135 – Rosie Potts 83 (Shareef Dancer (USA) 135) **–** [2001 f8.5g e10g Mar 19] of little account nowadays. *D. McCain*

BLACK ARMY 6 b.g. Aragon 118 – Morgannwg (IRE) 86 (Simply Great (FR) 122) **59** [2001 65, a73: f5g f7g 5g 6m* 5.1f 6f⁶ 6f Jun 13] good-topped gelding: modest performer: won claimer at Doncaster in May (final run for K. Ryan): broke down final start: stays 6f: acts on fibresand and any turf going: sometimes blinkered. *Andrew Reid*

BLACKHEATH (IRE) 5 ch.g. Common Grounds 118 – Queen Caroline (USA) 67 **90 d** (Chief's Crown (USA)) [2001 80: 5m² 6m³ 6m³ 6m 5g 6m 5.7m 7f 7g Oct 6] barrel-shaped gelding: type to carry condition: fluent mover: fairly useful handicapper: well below form after third start: effective at 5f/6f: acts on firm going, probably on good to soft: tried blinkered: very slowly away fourth outing: sold 9,000 gns. *J. A. R. Toller*

BLACK ICE BOY (IRE) 10 b.g. Law Society (USA) 130 – Hogan's Sister (USA) **–** (Speak John) [2001 49, a–: 17.1s 21.6s⁶ 14.6s Nov 9] tall, workmanlike gelding: well held in 2001: usually blinkered/visored. *R. Bastiman*

BLACK KNIGHT 3 b. or br.g. Contract Law (USA) 108 – Another Move 69 (Farm **100** Walk 111) [2001 95: 8s³ 10.1s³ 10.3f⁴ 8m* 10f 8.1m⁵ Jul 6] quite attractive gelding: useful performer: mostly creditable efforts in 2001, and won minor event at Thirsk in May by neck from Palatial: in frame in listed races at Kempton and Chester on first/third starts: effective at 1m to 1¼m: acts on firm and soft going: front runner: sent to Hong Kong. *S. P. C. Woods*

BLACKMAIL (USA) 3 b.c. Twining (USA) 120 – Black Penny (USA) (Private **93 +** Account (USA)) [2001 6g* 8g 8g² 8.5d 10m 8d p7g p10g⁶ p10g⁴ Dec 12] second foal: half-brother to Poule d'Essai des Pouliches winner Bluemamba (by Kingmambo): dam placed at 1m in France, half-sister to Prix Morny winner Orpen: quite useful performer: won maiden at Naas in June: sold from J. Oxx in Ireland 17,000 gns after sixth start: seemed to run well when fourth to Reef Diver in minor event at Lingfield final one: stays 1¼m: acts on polytrack. *B. R. Johnson*

BLACK MINNALOUSHE (USA) 3 b.c. Storm Cat (USA) – Coral Dance (FR) **123** 111 (Green Dancer (USA) 132) [2001 104p: 7s³ 7g⁵ 8m⁶ 8g* 8m* 10m⁵ 8m³ 10.4g⁴ a10f Oct 27]

Depending on degrees of equanimity, the results of the Two Thousand and One Thousand Guineas in Ireland on the weekend of May 26th and 27th might have provided consolation or consternation for punters. On the one hand, if even Aidan O'Brien did not know which was the best of his Guineas prospects, how could punters be blamed for picking the wrong one? On the other, if even O'Brien did not know which was the best of his Guineas prospects, what hope had punters of getting it right? In the Irish Two Thousand, O'Brien fielded Minardi, the 2/1 favourite with stable jockey Mick Kinane on board, Freud at 9/1, Black Minnaloushe at 20/1 and

Mozart at 20/1. In the One Thousand, Kinane was on Toroca, the 11/2 second favourite, O'Brien also being responsible for Sequoyah at 14/1, Imagine 16/1, Bonheur 100/1 and Love Me True 100/1. Well, at least neither Bonheur nor Love Me True ran out winners. Twenty-four hours before Imagine led home the One Thousand Guineas field in the hands of Seamus Heffernan, Black Minnaloushe had completed his surprise turn in the colts' race with Johnny Murtagh.

To give O'Brien his due, providing the first three in a classic is probably achievement enough, without having also to name them in the right order. And this was what O'Brien achieved in the Irish Two Thousand. While stating that the feat was 'unusual, but by no means unique, in classic history,' the *Racing Post*'s redoubtable historian John Randall had to delve as far back as 1935 for an Irish precedent, when Jack Rogers trained the first three in the Two Thousand, and to 1918 for one in Britain when Alec Taylor did the same in the St Leger; James Croft was responsible for the first four home in the 1822 St Leger, as was Alduino Botti in the 1981 Oaks d'Italia. More recently, Andreas Schutz trained the first three in the Deutsches Derby in 2000, Saeed bin Suroor did likewise in the 1998 Eclipse and O'Brien served up his own second and third doses in the autumn of the latest season when Rock of Gibraltar, Landseer and Tendulkar almost dead-heated in the Dewhurst and Ballingarry, Castle Gandolfo and Black Sam Bellamy dominated the Criterium de Saint-Cloud.

Black Minnaloushe had been relegated to the ranks of an outsider for the Irish Guineas after three defeats from three starts in 2001. He had won a listed race as a two-year-old but was beaten, after a notably headstrong display, in a similar event on his reappearance at three. The idea that Black Minnaloushe might be contributing to his own downfall crystalised further when he ruined his chance with a very slow start in the Tetrarch Stakes, finishing last of five but beaten only about two lengths. In the Poule d'Essai des Poulains, Black Minnaloushe might again have impressed with his late run, had it not been that this proved good enough only for seventh of twelve. Beaten a good deal less than he had given away in the Tetrarch, and just four and a half lengths behind first-past-the-post Noverre in the Poulains, it is not too difficult to see—in hindsight at least—that Black Minnaloushe had a big race in him.

On the day of the Entenmann's Irish Two Thousand Guineas, things looked rather different, as amply illustrated by the betting. Another way of looking at these three defeats, however, was as three trials. Some coaching at the stalls had presumably been undertaken before the Poulains, while it was clear that a good

Entenmann's Irish 2000 Guineas, the Curragh—a 1,2,3 for Aidan O'Brien
as Black Minnaloushe (right) collars the tiring Mozart; favourite Minardi (blaze) has to settle for third

*St James's Palace Stakes, Royal Ascot—a thrilling climax to a competitive renewal
as Black Minnaloushe just shades Noverre (left); next home are Olden Times (epaulets),
and Vahorimix (second right) whilst No Excuse Needed (behind winner) suffers trouble in running*

pace at the Curragh would assist his rider in settling Black Minnaloushe; Jamie
Spencer also reported back from the Poulains that the horse had to be 'produced
late'. The last two factors hinted at the benefits of a pacemaker, and there could not
have been a much better one available in the Irish Two Thousand than the soon-
to-be champion sprinter Mozart. He too had failed in the Tetrarch, when third at
5/2-on, having been ridden with restraint. The Irish Two Thousand was the
beginning of Mozart's career as a trail-blazer, and he soon had a clear lead. Two and
a half furlongs out it was obvious that most of the field were going to have a great
deal of trouble catching him, indeed Black Minnaloushe, just beginning to emerge
from mid-division, was the only one of the pursuers still on the bridle. Ridden with
great confidence by Murtagh, Black Minnaloushe was shown the whip at the
furlong marker and had no difficulty moving past Minardi at the head of the chasing
bunch, though he still had six lengths to make up on Mozart. Mozart would have to
weaken dramatically, but weaken he did, allowing Black Minnaloushe to sweep
past fifty yards out. Minardi finished third and the rest included a below-form
Tamburlaine, runner-up in the Newmarket Two Thousand, in fifth.

After the Irish Guineas, Black Minnaloushe ran in five of the seven races
contested twelve months earlier by Giant's Causeway, Ballydoyle's 2000 standard-
bearer, also a son of Storm Cat. Comparisons were bound to be made, but whereas
Giant's Causeway won five of those seven races, Black Minnaloushe won one.
When the classic milers moved on to the St James's Palace Stakes at Royal Ascot,
Golan had been stepped up in trip and Mozart had been moved down, but all of the
other principals took their chance. Noverre and Vahorimix had been first and
second past the post in the Poulains, Olden Times had won the Prix Jean Prat,
Tamburlaine was trying again, Malhub and Dandoun were promising listed-race
winners, No Excuse Needed was highly regarded from the Stoute stable and two
outsiders, Keltos and Darwin, were thrown in for good measure in an eleven-runner
field. Black Minnaloushe and Minardi were there again and Kinane this time chose
Black Minnaloushe, before O'Brien asked him to ride Minardi instead. Minardi
started at 5/1, Black Minnaloushe at 8/1. It looked a highly competitive race beforehand, as the betting (with Noverre favourite at 9/2) clearly indicated, and highly
competitive it turned out to be. Two furlongs out there was no more than three
lengths covering the entire field, but Noverre was rushed up into the lead soon

afterwards. Vahorimix and Olden Times started to fight back and Black Minnaloushe, who had been switched very early on to race against the rail, was in danger of being blocked by the weakening Minardi. In the words of Johnny Murtagh 'One moment I was wondering what I was going to say to Aidan, the next we'd got out between Noverre and Olden Times and I knew he'd win. He stuck his head down, I gave him a couple of cracks and we were there.' Black Minnaloushe won by a neck and a head from Noverre and Olden Times.

After Royal Ascot, Black Minnaloushe ran in the Eclipse Stakes at Sandown, the Sussex Stakes at Goodwood and the International at York and could not find any further improvement. Fifth of eight in the Eclipse was a creditable effort, beaten around a length by Medicean, but three and a half lengths third to Noverre at Goodwood was not quite at that level and neither was Black Minnaloushe's fourth of eight to Sakhee at York. In early-October it was announced that Black Minnaloushe would be retired to Coolmore's American branch, the Ashford Stud in Kentucky, alongside Giant's Causeway, for one. This probably had some bearing on the subsequent confirmation that he would run in the Breeders' Cup Classic rather than the Mile, any achievement on dirt being bound to appeal to American breeders. It is unlikely that he increased his stud value in finishing tenth of thirteen, never threatening from mid-division. Black Minnaloushe had gone one better than Giant's Causeway in the Irish Two Thousand and emulated him in the St James's Palace, but after that his limitations were exposed.

Black Minnaloushe's fee, not announced prior to the Breeders' Cup, has now been set at 15,000 dollars. His sire Storm Cat currently commands the biggest stud fee in the world, and now earns nearly as much with reportedly thirty seconds work in the covering shed as he did in his entire career on the racecourse, 500,000 dollars (raised from 400,000 in 2001) as opposed to 570,610 in the whole of his career as a racehorse. Black Minnaloushe went through the sale-ring for 750,000 dollars as a foal. Contemporaries by Storm Cat bought by the Coolmore team at auction include the fairly useful maiden Norway (3,000,000 dollars) and King George Stakes winner Dietrich (2,000,000).

Black Minnaloushe (USA) (b.c. 1998)	Storm Cat (USA) (b or br 1983)	Storm Bird (b 1978)	Northern Dancer
			South Ocean
		Terlingua (ch 1976)	Secretariat
			Crimson Saint
	Coral Dance (FR) (b 1978)	Green Dancer (b 1972)	Nijinsky
			Green Valley
		Carvinia (br 1970)	Diatome
			Coraline

Black Minnaloushe is very well related, the previous six winners out of his dam Coral Dance including the good French and US middle-distance performer Nasr El Arab (by Al Nasr) and Two Thousand Guineas winner Pennekamp (by Bering). These two colts are their respective sire's best offspring. There was not much chance that, in Black Minnaloushe, Coral Dance would also produce the best colt by Storm Cat, but he is a lot better than the three-years-older filly Dancing Sea, the result of her first union with the stallion—she showed fair form at best in eight starts, including one on the all-weather at Lingfield. Coral Dance changed hands for just 77,000 dollars in 1993, one year before Pennekamp (a 40,000-dollar yearling) captured his first Group 1s, the Salamandre and the Dewhurst. Coral Dance herself won a maiden and was second in the Marcel Boussac as a two-year-old, was injured at three and won two allowance races in the USA at four. Her dam Carvinia was a useful winner at around a mile and a quarter in France and a half-sister to the high-class colt Carvin.

Black Minnaloushe, a good-topped, attractive colt, was effective at a mile to a mile and a quarter, and best with waiting tactics in a strongly-run race. All of his turf starts after those tactics were adopted came on good ground or good to firm. Connections never quite managed, however, to sort out some highly-strung tendencies in the preliminaries and Black Minnaloushe skipped the parade at York because of concerns that he might rear over. He wore a blanket for stall entry. A very smart performer, Black Minnaloushe was a dual Group 1 winner in a year when the three-year-old colts lacked a top-class miler. *A. P. O'Brien, Ireland*

BLACK SAM BELLAMY (IRE) 2 b.c. (Apr 21) Sadler's Wells (USA) 132 – **111**
Urban Sea (USA) 126 (Miswaki (USA) 124) [2001 8d³ 8d⁶ 10v³ Nov 13] big, strong,
close-coupled colt: has a round, choppy action: fourth foal: brother to 3-y-o Galileo and
half-brother to 1¼m winner Melikah (by Lammtarra) and Irish 1m (at 2 yrs) to 1½m
winner Urban Ocean (by Bering), both smart: dam, won Prix de l'Arc de Triomphe,
closely related to King's Best: third in maiden at Newmarket in October and Criterium
de Saint-Cloud in November: much improved (smart form) when beaten 2 lengths by
stable-companion Ballingarry in latter, staying on: will be suited by 1½m+: had 2
handlers on debut: wears crossed noseband: sure to win a race or 2. *A. P. O'Brien, Ireland*

BLACKS BOY (IRE) 2 b.g. (Mar 11) Fayruz 100 – Wolverstar 100 (Wolverlife 115) **84**
[2001 5v* 5m 5m⁴ 6d⁴ 6m⁶ Aug 12] IR 6,000F, IR 8,000Y: small, workmanlike gelding:
sixth foal: half-brother to Italian 2000 2-y-o 7.5f winner Weltronilla (by Ridgewood
Ben): dam Irish sprinter: fairly useful performer: won maiden at Ripon in April: good
fourth in minor event at Beverley and nursery at Leicester: will stay 7f: acts on good to
firm and heavy ground: sent to Macau. *J. J. Quinn*

BLACK SILVER 2 br.f. (Mar 24) Dilum (USA) 115 – Silver Charm (Dashing Blade **55**
117) [2001 5s³ 5.1d⁵ 5g f7g² f7g⁵ Oct 1] good-topped filly: second foal: half-sister to
3-y-o Zando's Charm: dam unraced sister to useful 9f/1¼m winner Dashiba from family
of Oscar Schindler: modest maiden: second in seller at Wolverhampton in August: stays 7f: acts on
fibresand, best turf effort on soft going: finished lame second start: races prominently:
sent to Sweden. *J. M. P. Eustace*

BLACKSMITH LANE 2 b.f. (May 19) Makbul 104 – Dutch Auntie (Prince Sabo **44**
123) [2001 6g 6m 5.3s⁴ Oct 3] lengthy filly: first foal: dam, lightly raced in bumpers/
over hurdles, half-sister to useful stayer Double Dutch: form only when fourth in seller at
Brighton: should stay at least 7f. *D. R. C. Elsworth*

BLACKTHORN 2 ch.c. (Mar 19) Deploy 131 – Balliasta (USA) (Lyphard (USA) **82**
132) [2001 6.9m⁴ 8g* 8f⁶ 8d 10s³ Oct 15] strong, compact colt: has a fluent, round action:
fifth living foal: half-brother to useful 7f (at 2 yrs) and 1m (in France) winner Kilting (by
Nashwan): dam, twice-raced French maiden, half-sister to high-class performer up to
1½m Sanglamore out of Ribblesdale winner Ballinderry: fairly useful performer: won
maiden at Newmarket in August: creditable third in minor event at Leicester: will stay
1½m: acts on soft going: sold 30,000 gns. *Mrs A. J. Perrett*

BLACK WEASEL (IRE) 6 br.g. Lahib (USA) 129 – Glowlamp (IRE) 93 (Glow **39**
(USA)) [2001 43, a46+: f16g⁵ f16.2g³ f16g² 17.1s⁴ 17.1m⁴ 16f³ 16f 17.2m Jul 15] strong **a44**
gelding: poor handicapper: stays 17.5f: acts on soft going, good to firm and fibresand:
tried blinkered/visored/tongue tied. *A. Bailey*

BLAGOVEST 2 b.c. (Mar 14) Singspiel (IRE) 133 – Tass (Soviet Star (USA) 128) **81**
[2001 7d⁶ 7s⁶ 7d Nov 3] 90,000F, 60,000Y: lengthy, good sort: fourth foal: half-brother to
2000 2-y-o 5f seller winner Syringa (by Lure): dam unraced half-sister to good middle-
distance colts Nomrood, Monastery and Alleging and to dam of 3-y-o Dilshaan:
improved with each start in maidens, fairly useful form when close seventh of 27 to
Prince Hector at Newmarket on final one: will stay 1¼m. *R. Charlton*

BLAIR (IRE) 4 b.g. Persian Bold 123 – Zara's Birthday (IRE) 71 (Waajib 121) [2001 **42**
33: 13m 16m 14.1m* 16g 14.1m 12d⁶ Sep 25] sparely-made gelding: poor handicapper:
won seller at Nottingham in July: stays 1¾m: acts on good to firm going, probably on
soft. *G. A. Swinbank*

BLAKESET 6 ch.g. Midyan (USA) 124 – Penset (Red Sunset 120) [2001 69, a106: **–**
f6s* a5.5f⁴ a8f⁶ a6f⁵ a7f Dec 27] sturdy gelding: useful performer on all-weather/dirt, fair **a108**
on turf in 2000: won handicap at Wolverhampton in January by a head from Effervescent
(final outing for T. D. Barron): respectable fourth in allowance race at Philadelphia Park
next time, then well held including in claimer (left M. Dickinson after third outing): best
at 6f/7f: acts on fibresand/equitrack/dirt, good to firm and good to soft going: has been
bandaged/tongue tied: best recent efforts when blinkered: races prominently: fell final
outing. *Katherine M. Voss, USA*

BLAKESHALL 2 ch.g. (Apr 25) Piccolo 121 – Corniche Quest (IRE) 74 (Salt Dome **54**
(USA)) [2001 5v 5.1s 5f⁶ 7g⁶ 5.2g* 5.8s⁵ Sep 9] workmanlike gelding: first foal: dam 5f
to 1m winner: modest performer: won seller at Yarmouth in June: left M. Channon, fifth
of 6 in minor event at Taby: best effort at 5f. *C. Bjorling, Sweden*

BLAKESHALL BOY 3 b.g. Piccolo 121 – Giggleswick Girl 67 (Full Extent (USA) **88**
113) [2001 78: 6d 6s 5m² 6s³ 5d* 6m 6m 5f 5m* 6g 5.1f³ 5g 5.2f 5g 5m⁴ 5g⁵ 5m⁵ 5g
5d Oct 13] rather leggy, quite attractive gelding: fairly useful handicapper: won at
Windsor in May and Newmarket in June: barely stays 6f: acts on firm and soft going:

reportedly had breathing problem thirteenth start: usually held up: tough and consistent. *M. R. Channon*

BLAKESHALL JOE   3 ch.g. Fraam 114 – Lorcanjo 36 (Hallgate 127) [2001 –: f7g   –
f8g f9.4s³ Jan 20] well held in sellers: blinkered at 3 yrs. *J. G. Given*

BLAYNEY DANCER   4 b.g. Contract Law (USA) 108 – Lady Poly (Dunbeath   –
(USA) 127) [2001 45: 12g 11.9s Oct 25] well held in 2001. *Jamie Poulton*

BLAZING BILLY   6 ch.g. Anshan 119 – Worthy Venture 76 (Northfields (USA))   –
[2001 –: 5.2m 6f Jun 13] little form: visored once. *C. A. Dwyer*

BLAZING SADDLES (IRE)   2 b.c. (Mar 20) Sadler's Wells (USA) 132 – Dalawara   **68 p**
(IRE) (Top Ville 129) [2001 8d Oct 19] 750,000 francs Y: rather leggy, workmanlike colt:
has a round action: sixth foal: brother to French 1½m winner Dal Segno and half-brother
to smart 1m (at 2 yrs) to 1½m winner who stayed 2½m Heron Island (by Shirley Heights):
dam French maiden half-sister to Darshaan and to dam of Daliapour (by Sadler's Wells):
25/1 and green, eleventh of 20 to Rawyaan in maiden at Newmarket: will stay at least
1½m: should do better. *I. A. Balding*

BLENHEIM TERRACE   8 b.g. Rambo Dancer (CAN) 107 – Boulevard Girl 80   **45**
(Nicholas Bill 125) [2001 45: 12.4m 10m 10f 12f² 11m 14.1m⁵ 12d⁵ Sep 25] sturdy
gelding: poor performer: stays 1¾m: acts on firm and good to soft ground. *W. H. Tinning*

BLESS   4 ch.f. Beveled (USA) – Ballystate 71 (Ballcashtal (CAN)) [2001 50, a42: e7g   **50**
e12s* e13g 11.9s Apr 12] modest handicapper: won at Lingfield in February: stays easy
1½m: acts on good to firm going and equitrack: tried in blinkers, usually visored
nowadays: has wandered. *M. Madgwick*

BLESSINGINDISGUISE   8 b.g. Kala Shikari 125 – Blowing Bubbles 72 (Native   **75**
Admiral (USA)) [2001 85: 5s 5v 5g 5m⁴ 5f* 5f 5m⁶ 5g 6m⁴ 5m⁴ 6m 5s⁵ 5d 5d 5s Nov 9]
strong gelding: fair handicapper: won at Newcastle in June: has form at 5f but very best
at 5f on good going or firmer: wears blinkers: often gives trouble at stalls. *M. W. Easterby*

BLEU D'ALTAIR (FR)   4 b.c. Green Tune (USA) 125 – Parannda 117 (Bold Lad   **115**
(IRE) 133) [2001 115: 10v² 10v⁶ 9.5g² 10g⁴ 10s Jul 18] smart performer: won listed races
at Longchamp and Marseille-Borely in 2000: creditable 1½ lengths second to Earlene in
Prix Exbury at Saint-Cloud in March: below form afterwards: best around 1¼m: raced
mainly on good ground or softer (acts on heavy): often makes running. *D. Smaga, France*

BLIND SPOT   3 ch.c. Inchinor 119 – High Tern 93 (High Line 125) [2001 –p: f11g   **60**
8.3g⁶ 8.2g* 8m 7.6f Jul 25] quite attractive colt: modest handicapper: won at Nottingham
in June: stayed 8.2f: acted on good to firm going, probably on soft: raced prominently:
dead. *E. A. L. Dunlop*

BLIXEN (USA)   3 b.f. Gone West (USA) – Danish (IRE) 117 (Danehill (USA) 126)   –
[2001 90p: 7m⁴ Jun 4] fairly useful form at 2 yrs for J. Oxx, winning maiden at the
Curragh and third in listed event there: disappointing in minor event at Leicester only run
in 2001: bred to stay 1m: has left Godolphin. *Saeed bin Suroor*

BLODWEN (USA)   3 b.f. Mister Baileys 123 – Ma Biche (USA) 125 (Key To The   **52**
Kingdom (USA)) [2001 7g 6m 6g 8.3d 8m 12m 10g 8d Nov 2] $52,000F: leggy, close-
coupled filly: half-sister to several winners, including useful 6f to 1m performer in
Britain/UAE Kassbaan (by Alydar) and fairly useful but unreliable 7f winner Desert
Symphony (by Mr Prospector): dam won Cheveley Park Stakes and 1000 Guineas:
modest maiden handicapper: probably stays 1½m: acts on good to firm going: tried
blinkered. *M. L. W. Bell*

BLOOMING LUCKY (IRE)   2 b.f. (Apr 20) Lucky Guest 109 – Persian Flower   –
(Persian Heights 129) [2001 f6g f6g f6g⁶ Dec 1] IR 6,200Y: third foal: half-sister to fairly
useful 1999 2-y-o 5f and 7f winner Flowington (by Owington): dam lightly raced: well
beaten in maidens. *J. A. Osborne*

BLOSSOM WHISPERS   4 b.f. Ezzoud (IRE) 126 – Springs Welcome 86 (Blakeney   **60**
126) [2001 71, a63: 11.9m 10g² f12g² f14g f14.8g⁵ f16.2g Nov 21] good-bodied filly:
modest maiden handicapper: stays 2m: acts on good to firm going and fibresand/
equitrack: blinkered final start. *C. A. Cyzer*

BLOWING AWAY (IRE)   7 b. or br.m. Last Tycoon 131 – Taken By Force (Persian   –
Bold 123) [2001 38, a31: f16g⁶ f14.8s⁵ f12g⁴ e10g⁵ e12g e10g⁶ 15.4v 10m 11.9f⁶ 11.6m   **a29**
Jun 11] leggy mare: bad performer: left J. Pearce after third start: stays 1¾m: probably
acts on any turf going and fibresand/equitrack: sometimes visored. *Julian Poulton*

BLUE AWAY (IRE)   3 b. or br.g. Blues Traveller (IRE) 119 – Lomond Heights (IRE)   **76**
(Lomond (USA) 128) [2001 –: f7g f11g³ 11.4g⁴ 12.6f* 16m* 16m⁵ 14.1d² Oct 3]

progressive handicapper: won at Warwick (maiden event) in June and Yarmouth in July: unlucky second at Salisbury final start: better form at 1¾m/2m than shorter: acts on firm and good to soft going, some promise on fibresand: hung left (reportedly had fibrillating heart) penultimate start. *C. F. Wall*

BLUEBERRY RHYME 2 b.g. (Apr 9) Alhijaz 122 – Irenic 64 (Mummy's Pet 125) **74**
[2001 6.1m 6.1g 5s⁵ 5g² 6d 5.1s⁴ Oct 30] 600F: good-topped gelding: brother to 5f winner Jazznic and half-brother to 3 winners, including 7.6f (at 2 yrs) to 11f winner Gentle Irony (by Mazilier): dam, 6f maiden, half-sister to very smart performer up to 9f Forzando: fair maiden: second in nursery at Newmarket: likely to prove best at 5f/easy 6f: acts on soft ground: visored (ran respectably) last 2 starts: looks a difficult ride. *P. J. Makin*

BLUE CASCADE (IRE) 2 b.g. (Apr 22) Royal Academy (USA) 130 – Blaine (USA) **–**
(Lyphard's Wish (FR) 124) [2001 7m 7.9d Oct 13] IR 72,000Y: rather leggy gelding: half-brother to several winners abroad, including St Blaine (by St Jovite), also 1m winner in Britain: dam, ran 4 times in North America, half-sister to dam of Croco Rouge from family of Ali-Royal and Sleepytime (both by Royal Academy): well held in maidens at York: sold 6,000 gns and gelded. *J. D. Bethell*

BLUE EYES 3 br.g. Imp Society (USA) – Morning Surprise 58 (Tragic Role (USA)) **56**
[2001 62p: f6g⁶ f5f* f5g f6g 5.2m 5f f5g Oct 18] modest performer: won seller at South-well in March: well held in handicaps subsequently (left A. Jarvis after fifth start): likely to prove best at 5f: acts on fibresand: blinkered final start: has edged left. *S. R. Bowring*

BLUE FOREST (IRE) 3 b.c. Charnwood Forest (IRE) 125 – Vian (USA) (Far Out **–**
East (USA)) [2001 75: f7g Jan 6] leggy colt: fair performer: won maiden at 2 yrs: broke leg on reappearance: should have stayed 1m: dead. *P. C. Haslam*

BLUE GOLD 4 b.c. Rainbow Quest (USA) 134 – Relatively Special 112 (Alzao **110**
(USA) 117) [2001 109: 9.9m⁴ 11.8d⁶ 10m* 12m⁵ 10m 10.1g³ 10.9m⁴ Sep 22] close-coupled, attractive colt: has a quick action: smart performer: won listed event at Kempton in June by 1¼ lengths from Nooshman: below form after: effective at 1¼m/1½m: acts on good to firm and good to soft going: usually patiently ridden: sold 38,000 gns in October. *R. Hannon*

BLUEGRASS 2 ch.c. (Feb 7) Bluegrass Prince (IRE) 110 – Seymour Ann (Krayyan **–**
117) [2001 7.1f 6v Oct 8] half-brother to several winners, including fairly useful 7f (at 2 yrs) and 1¼m winner Captain's Day (by Ballacashtal): dam unraced: well held in maidens. *M. Madgwick*

BLUEGRASS HOPPER 2 b.f. (Mar 20) Bluegrass Prince (IRE) 110 – Heavenly **– §**
State (Enchantment 115) [2001 5m 7f⁵ 6g Aug 10] fifth reported foal: dam unraced: tailed off, including in seller: tried visored: looks wayward. *M. Madgwick*

BLUE HAWAII (IRE) 4 ch.g. Up And At 'em 109 – Astral Way (Hotfoot 126) [2001 **–**
55d: f16g Jan 5] big, leggy gelding: disappointing maiden: tried tongue tied/blinkered. *S. R. Bowring*

BLUE HAWK (IRE) 4 ch.g. Prince of Birds (USA) 121 – Classic Queen (IRE) **55**
(Classic Secret (USA) 91) [2001 –: 16.2f² 15m f14.8g² 15.8g* 15.8m f12g² f14g f14.8g⁴ f12g f16.2f⁶ f16.2s Dec 18] neat gelding: modest handicapper: won at Catterick in August: effective 1½m to 2m: acts on firm ground and fibresand. *R. Hollinshead*

BLUE HOLLY (IRE) 4 b.f. Blues Traveller (IRE) 119 – Holly Bird (Runnett 125) **83**
[2001 80: 5s 5g 5.7m 5.7f⁴ 5m 5f 5m⁵ 6f 7d² 6f* 5.1g⁶ 5g* 5.2f 5.7d 5.1m² 5m* 5m 5s 6d 5s Oct 20] quite attractive filly: fairly useful performer: left J. M. Bradley for former trainer after ninth start: won handicaps at Lingfield in July and Leicester (ladies) and Folkestone in August: below form last 3 outings: effective at 5f/6f: acts on any going: usually blinkered, tried visored: sometimes slowly away: sold 8,000 gns. *J. S. Moore*

BLUE JAY WAY 3 b.g. Dr Devious (IRE) 127 – Skuld (Kris 135) [2001 7.5m 9m Jun **–**
10] IR 3,500Y, 1,800 2-y-o, resold 750 2-y-o: third living foal: half-brother to fairly useful 1½m winner Skimra (by Hernando): dam unraced half-sister to Petoski: soon tailed off in maidens. *J. S. Wainwright*

BLUE KITE 6 ch.g. Silver Kite (USA) 111 – Gold And Blue (IRE) (Bluebird (USA) **60 d**
125) [2001 68, a91: f6g f6g f7g³ f6g f7g f6g f7g f6g f6g* 6m 6f 7.6m 7m 6d f7g **a72 d**
Sep 8] stocky gelding: unimpressive mover: fair on turf, modest on all-weather in 2001 at best: won amateur claimer at Wolverhampton in May: left N. Littmoden after next start: best at 6f/easy 7f: acts on fibresand/equitrack, firm and soft going: tried tongue tied/blinkered/visored: sometimes slowly away: on the downgrade. *M. Mullineaux*

BLUE KNIGHT (IRE) 2 ch.c. (Jan 14) Bluebird (USA) 125 – Fer de Lance (IRE) **72 p**
(Diesis 133) [2001 6d 6d Oct 18] IR 30,000F, 25,000Y: strong, lengthy colt: second

foal: half-brother to 4-y-o Ferzao: dam unraced daughter of sister to smart sprinter Rustic Amber: still backward, much better effort in maidens (fair form) when ninth of 22 at Newmarket, not knocked about: likely to prove best up to 1m: should improve. *A. P. Jarvis*

BLUE LADY (IRE)   3 b.f. College Chapel 122 – Dancing Bluebell (IRE) 79   **45 d** (Bluebird (USA) 125) [2001 60: f6g² f6s f8g f8g⁶ 8.2v 8f⁶ f8g 8.2f 7.5m 10d f7g f6g f8g f8.5g f9.4f Dec 5] small filly: poor performer: well held after reappearance: stays 7f: acts on fibresand, good to firm and good to soft going: tends to be soon off bridle, and has hung right. *B. P. J. Baugh*

BLUE LAGOON   2 gr.g. (Mar 15) Lugana Beach 116 – Aimee Jane (USA) 76 (Our   – Native (USA)) [2001 5f 5m 7g Nov 5] 3,000Y, 3,800 2-y-o: strong gelding: seventh living foal: half-brother to 1998 2-y-o 6f winner Dispol Safa (by Safawan) and a winner up to 15f in Germany by Niniski: dam ungenuine 1½m winner, also successful over hurdles: well beaten in maidens/claimer. *N. Tinkler*

BLUE LEGEND (IRE)   4 b.f. Blues Traveller (IRE) 119 – Swoon Along (Dunphy   – 124) [2001 44: 8m 8.3g⁴ 8f 8f 12f⁶ 13d Aug 15] of little account nowadays. *B. Mactaggart*

BLUE LINE ANGEL   5 b.g. Cyrano de Bergerac 120 – Northern Line 92 (Camden   – Town 125) [2001 5m 8.2m Sep 10] modest for R. Fahey at 3 yrs: trained by H. Horwart in Germany at 4 yrs, winning maiden at Gelsenkirchen: well held on return to Britain. *John Berry*

BLUE LINE LADY (IRE)   4 b.f. Common Grounds 118 – Best Academy (USA)   – (Roberto (USA) 131) [2001 44: f7g f7g Apr 4] no form in 2001: tried blinkered. *K. A. Ryan*

BLUE MANTLE (IRE)   2 ch.f. (Apr 9) Barathea (IRE) 127 – Blue Wedding (USA)   **– p** (Irish River (FR) 131) [2001 8.1v 8.2v 8v⁶ Oct 16] big, strong filly: half-sister to several winners, including fairly useful Irish 9f winner Blending Element (by Great Commotion), later winner up to 11f in USA, and useful Italian performer up to 1½m Antoniocastiglione (by Pursuit of Love): dam French maiden: signs of ability in maidens: should be well suited by 1¼m+: type to do better in handicaps. *Sir Mark Prescott*

BLUE MOUNTAIN   4 ch.c. Elmaamul (USA) 125 – Glenfinlass (Lomond (USA)   **108** 128) [2001 108: 7g⁵ 8.3g³ 7.9m⁶ 8.5f 8m⁵ 8.1g 7m 8g 8d² 7g 7g Sep 19] strong, lengthy colt: useful performer: mostly creditable efforts in 2001, including fifth to Surprise Encounter in Hunt Cup at Royal Ascot fifth start, and 2½ lengths second to Duck Row in minor event at Bath ninth outing: effective at 6f to 1m: yet to race on soft/heavy going, acts on any other: waited with. *R. F. Johnson Houghton*

BLUE ORCHID   2 ch.f. (Feb 26) King's Signet (USA) 110 – Name That Tune 40   – (Fayruz 116) [2001 f5g Nov 17] 2,000Y: second foal: half-sister to 4-y-o Chorus: dam sprint maiden: 25/1, last in seller at Wolverhampton. *R. J. Hodges*

BLUE ORLEANS   3 b.g. Dancing Spree (USA) – Blues Player 70 (Jaazeiro (USA)   – 127) [2001 10s 10g 10.9f Jun 27] maiden: no form in 2001: tried blinkered: probably ungenuine. *A. G. Newcombe*

BLUE PLANET (IRE)   3 b.g. Bluebird (USA) 125 – Millie Musique (Miller's Mate   **88** 116) [2001 84p: 8m² 8m 8d⁶ 8f⁵ 10s³ Sep 27] big, good-topped gelding: fairly useful performer: probably stays 1¼m: yet to race on heavy ground, acts on any other: sold 25,000 gns, joined P. Murphy. *Sir Mark Prescott*

BLUE POOL   3 b.f. Saddlers' Hall (IRE) 126 – Blue Brocade 91 (Reform 132) [2001   **39** –p: 6.9v 14.1m 12f 12g Oct 4] sturdy filly: poor maiden: probably stays 1¾m: sold 1,600 gns (in December). *J. A. R. Toller*

BLUE REIGNS   3 b.c. Whittingham (IRE) 104 – Gold And Blue (IRE) (Bluebird   **93** (USA) 125) [2001 92p: 6m² 7m 6g⁶ 6g Aug 12] tall, useful-looking colt: has scope: usually takes the eye in appearance: has a quick action: fairly useful performer: good second to Vicious Dancer in valuable handicap at Lingfield in May: disappointing after, off 2 months and tubed following second start: likely to prove best at 5f/6f: acts on good to firm and good to soft ground. *N. P. Littmoden*

BLUE RIVER (IRE)   7 ch.g. River Falls 113 – Royal Resident 86 (Prince Regent   **49** (FR) 129) [2001 f12g² e13g Apr 3] strong, rangy gelding: fluent mover: useful performer at 3 yrs: poor form on first start for 3 years in seller at Wolverhampton in March: stays easy 1½m: acts on good to firm and good to soft ground, probably on fibresand. *T. G. Mills*

BLUE SAFARI (IRE)   2 b. or br.f. (Apr 28) Blues Traveller (IRE) 119 – Lady   **53**
Montekin (Montekin 125) [2001 6m 7m 7m⁵ 7s⁶ Aug 31] 10,500Y: tall, leggy filly: sixth
foal: half-sister to fairly useful 1998 2-y-o 5f winner Open Secret (by Mac's Imp) and
winners abroad by Classic Secret and Contract Law: dam, Irish maiden, third at 7f:
modest maiden: should stay 1m: looked none too keen third start. *R. Hannon*

BLUE SATIN (IRE)   4 b.f. Bluebird (USA) 125 – Cheviot Amble (IRE) 105 (Pennine
Walk 120) [2001 57: 10m May 25] IR 40,000Y: quite good-topped filly: third foal:
half-sister to smart 1m to 10.4f winner who stayed 1½m Amalia (by Danehill): dam Irish
6f to 1¼m winner who stayed 1½m: modest maiden: left D. Weld, Ireland after final 3-y-o
start: no show only run in 2001: tried blinkered. *K. A. Ryan*

BLUES BAND (IRE)   2 b. or br.f. (Mar 5) Blues Traveller (IRE) 119 – Davenport
Goddess (IRE) (Classic Secret (USA) 91) [2001 7f 8.1g Aug 27] IR 7,500Y: fourth foal:
half-sister to 4-y-o Ptah: dam unraced: well held in maidens. *R. Hannon*

BLUE SONG   3 b.f. Shaamit (IRE) 127 – November Song (Scorpio (FR) 127) [2001   **–**
10g f12g Dec 8] second foal: dam unraced: well held in maidens. *N. P. Littmoden*

BLUE STREAK (IRE)   4 ch.g. Bluebird (USA) 125 – Fleet Amour (USA) (Afleet   **61**
(CAN)) [2001 69: 10.3m 8m 10f⁵ 7m 8g³ 8m⁵ 10m 8g f9.4g⁵ p10g² Dec 29] tall, rangy   **a52 +**
gelding: modest maiden: stays 1¼m: acts on polytrack, firm and good to soft going:
visored once at 3 yrs: tongue tied last time. *K. Bell*

BLUE STREET   5 b.g. Deploy 131 – Kumzar (Hotfoot 126) [2001 63d, a45: 10m   **57**
12.1s* 14.1d* 16.1f 16d 12d Oct 8] small, sturdy gelding: modest handicapper on turf: **a–**
won at Chepstow and Yarmouth in August: ran poorly last 2 outings: should stay 2m: acts
on soft ground and fibresand: visored once: sold 4,500 gns, sent to Italy. *S. C. Williams*

BLUE STYLE (IRE)   5 ch.g. Bluebird (USA) 125 – Style For Life (IRE) (Law   **60**
Society (USA) 130) [2001 66d: 13d 10.9m⁶ 12.1m 10.1v Oct 24] lengthy gelding: has a
round action: modest handicapper: should stay at least 1¾m: acts on heavy going,
probably on good to firm: tried blinkered/tongue tied. *Miss L. A. Perratt*

BLUE SUGAR (USA)   4 ch.g. Shuailaan (USA) 122 – Chelsea My Love (USA)   **97**
(Opening Verse (USA) 126) [2001 100+: 10g⁶ 12f² 12m 10.4m 10m³ 10.1d² 10.1g* 9g
Oct 6] useful-looking gelding: fluent mover: useful performer: won minor event at
Epsom in September by head from Aegean Dream: sweating, well held in Cam-
bridgeshire at Newmarket final start: effective at 1¼m: raced once on heavy going, acts
on any other: visored (well beaten) fourth start/tongue tied sixth: sold 25,000 gns.
J. R. Fanshawe

BLUES WHISPERER (IRE)   4 b.g. Blues Traveller (IRE) 119 – Princess Roxanne   **–**
68 (Prince Tenderfoot (USA) 126) [2001 –: f12g Nov 26] no form. *B. R. Millman*

BLUE VELVET   4 gr.f. Formidable (USA) 125 – Sweet Whisper 63 (Petong 126)   **99 d**
[2001 98: 5.2d² 5.1d⁴ 5m³ 6g 6d 6.3g⁶ 5g 5g 6m 5v⁴ 5v 5s Oct 22] well-made filly: poor
mover: useful performer: gradually deteriorated after reappearance: effective at 5f to 7f:
acts on any turf going and fibresand/equitrack: often bandaged: swished tail/veered left
fourth start. *K. T. Ivory*

BLUEWATCH (IRE)   3 b.c. Bluebird (USA) 125 – Fire of London 78 (Shirley   **58**
Heights 130) [2001 8m⁶ 7g 7m⁶ 8d⁶ f9.4g Nov 27] 140,000Y: sturdy, medium-sized colt:
second foal: dam, second at 1¼m, sister to useful winner up to 1¼m Spitfire: modest
maiden: should stay beyond 1m: acts on good to firm and good to soft going: reportedly
had breathing problem final outing. *G. Wragg*

BLUNDELL LANE (IRE)   6 ch.g. Shalford (IRE) 124§ – Rathbawn Realm (Doulab   **72**
(USA) 115) [2001 80d, a–: f6g 5.3m⁵ 6m³ 6m* 7.1d³ 6g⁴ 5.2m 6g* 7m f6g p6g Dec 19]   **a58**
fair on turf, modest on all-weather: won minor event at Hamilton in July and handicap at
Newmarket in August: best at 5f/6f: acts on firm going, good to soft and fibresand:
sometimes visored/blinkered (not for wins): usually races prominently. *A. P. Jarvis*

BLUSHING GRENADIER (IRE)   9 ch.g. Salt Dome (USA) – La Duse 66 (Junius   **51**
(USA) 124) [2001 58, a63: f6s f6g 7s 6m f6g⁵ f5g f7g² f6g⁴ f7g 5g f7g³ f5g f7g⁵ f6g⁴ f7s   **a54**
Dec 18] leggy gelding: modest performer: races mainly at 6f/7f nowadays: acts on good
to firm ground, heavy and fibresand/equitrack: usually blinkered, has been visored:
usually races prominently. *S. R. Bowring*

BLUSHING PRINCE (IRE)   3 b.c. Priolo (USA) 127 – Eliade (IRE) 82 (Flash of   **?**
Steel 120) [2001 73p: f9.4s* e10g³ 9g 8g f9.4g² f9.4g⁶ f9.4g³ f12g Dec 8] fairly useful   **a81**
performer: won maiden at Wolverhampton in January: left J. Noseda 14,000 gns after

fifth start: stays 1¼m: acts on all-weather, well held on turf: sometimes tongue tied. *Mrs L. Stubbs*

BLUSHING QUEEN (IRE)   2 b.f. (Apr 22) Desert King (IRE) 129 – Phazania (Tap   **75** On Wood 130) [2001 6g 7g⁴ 8.1v f7g³ Oct 23] 25,000Y: good-bodied filly: half-sister to several winners, including 7-y-o Future Prospect: dam Irish 2-y-o 6f and 1m winner: fair form in maidens: stays 7f: acts on fibresand: visored (took strong hold) final start. *J. Noseda*

BLUSHING SPUR   3 b.g. Flying Spur (AUS) – Bogus John (CAN) (Blushing John   **60** (USA) 120) [2001 60, a69: f7g³ 6m 7.1g⁵ 6m⁶ f6g⁵ 6.1s⁶ 8.1s⁶ 7.5d f6g⁴ f6g* f6g* Dec 10]   **a83** tall gelding: fairly useful handicapper on all-weather, modest on turf: improved to win at Wolverhampton in November and Southwell in December: stays 7f: acts on fibresand and heavy going: often visored nowadays: sometimes slowly away. *D. Shaw*

BLUSIENKA (IRE)   4 b.f. Blues Traveller (IRE) 119 – Pudgy Poppet (Danehill   **–** (USA) 126) [2001 102: f7g Mar 8] unfurnished filly: one-time useful performer: well held only outing in 2001. *G. A. Butler*

BLYTHE PRINCESS   2 b.f. (May 17) Makbul 104 – Miss Petella (Dunphy 124) [2001   **52** f5g⁵ Apr 10] 7,000Y: half-sister to several winners, including fairly useful 7f (at 2 yrs) to 11.4f winner Traceability (by Puissance) and 7f winner Prince Consort (by Clantime): dam, of little account, half-sister to 1000 Guineas second Meis El-Reem: fifth of 14 in maiden at Southwell: dead. *K. A. Ryan*

BLYTHE SPIRIT   2 b.f. (Jan 31) Bahamian Bounty 116 – Lithe Spirit (IRE) 74 (Danc-   **68** ing Dissident (USA) 119) [2001 6m² 6m 6m Aug 18] 20,000Y: lengthy, unfurnished gelding: second foal: half-brother to 2000 2-y-o 6f winner Berezina (by Brief Truce): dam, maiden who stayed 1m, out of half-sister to smart 7f/1m performers Bog Trotter and Poteen: easily best effort in maidens (fair form) when second at Thirsk: bit seemed to slip next time: not knocked about final start: should stay 7f. *R. A. Fahey*

B MAJOR (IRE)   2 b.g. (Mar 26) Key of Luck (USA) 126 – Lingering Melody (IRE)   **78 p** 59 (Nordico (USA)) [2001 6d 6g p5g² p6g² f6s* Dec 15] IR 50,000Y: robust gelding: third foal: half-brother to 3-y-o Indian Prince and fairly useful 7f (including at 2 yrs) winner Rainbow Melody (by Rainbows For Life): dam, Irish maiden who stayed 1m, half-sister to very smart miler Alflora from family of Ardross: fair form: won maiden at Wolverhampton by 2 lengths from Givemethemoonlight: stays 6f: acts on fibresand/polytrack: should progress. *M. A. Jarvis*

BOADICEA   3 b.f. Celtic Swing 138 – Another Legend (USA) (Lyphard's Wish (FR)   **–** 124) [2001 7d 10s 8m May 30] IR 58,000F: unfurnished filly: first foal: dam US Grade 2 9f winner: fair form at 2 yrs in France when trained by Mme C. Head-Maarek, winning maiden at Divonne-Les-Bains: no show in handicaps/claimer in 2001, all but refusing to race final start: stays 8.5f: acts on soft ground. *Mrs J. R. Ramsden*

BOADICEA THE RED (IRE)   4 gr.f. Inchinor 119 – Kanika §§ (Be My Chief   **61** (USA) 122) [2001 58: f7g² f7s* f8g³ f7g³ 7.1m⁶ f7g 7m 6m* 6.1f³ 6f³ 6f 7m 6m⁴ 6g⁶ 6g³ Aug 9] leggy filly: modest performer: won maiden at Southwell in January and handicap at Doncaster in June: effective at 6f to 1m: acts on fibresand/equitrack, good to soft and firm going: effective visored or not: sometimes slowly away: tends to wander/find little/ flash final start: sold 6,000 gns in December. *B. S. Rothwell*

BOANERGES (IRE)   4 br.g. Caerleon (USA) 132 – Sea Siren 68 (Slip Anchor 136)   **89** [2001 83: 6s 5m³ 5m* 6m 5m⁵ 5m 5g 5g² 5m 6g 6m⁶ 6d 5s Oct 22] smallish, strong gelding: fairly useful handicapper: won at Musselburgh in June: some good efforts after, including sixth (first home on stand side) in Silver Cup at Ayr in September: effective at 5f/sharp 6f: acts on firm and good to soft going: visored once at 2 yrs: has been early to post (bolted and withdrawn once): usually held up. *R. Guest*

BOATER   7 b.g. Batshoof 122 – Velvet Beret (IRE) (Dominion 123) [2001 61§: 8.1m   **61 §** 10.9m⁴ Jun 18] well-made gelding: modest handicapper: best around 1¼m: acts on firm ground, soft and equitrack: blinkered once: ungenuine. *R. J. Baker*

BOBANVI   3 b.f. Timeless Times (USA) 99 – Bobanlyn (IRE) 76 (Dance of Life (USA))   **–** [2001 48: 10m 12m 12.4g 12.1d 16.2m 12.1s Aug 21] small filly: maiden handicapper: blinkered final start. *J. S. Wainwright*

BOBSLEIGH   2 b.g. (Mar 1) Robellino (USA) 127 – Do Run Run 75 (Commanche   **53** Run 133) [2001 7f 7m 8g⁶ Sep 7] leggy, useful-looking gelding: sixth foal: half-brother to 1997 2-y-o 6f winner Deeceebee (by Rudimentary): dam 1m winner: modest form in maidens: seemed to lose action on second start: should stay 1¼m. *Mrs A. J. Perrett*

*EDS Handicap, Epsom—Bogus Dreams is well ridden by John Reid; eventual second
Parisien Star (light star on cap) still has work to do, Riberac (dark sleeves) eventually finishing third*

BOCELLI (NZ)   5 b.g. Lord Ballina (AUS) – Sweet Vienna (NZ) (Dahar (USA) 125)   **116**
[2001 7d* 7g* 7g* 8g* 10m* 9g² 7.3f⁴ 8s 10g*ᵈⁱˢ 11g³ 10m Dec 16] big, lengthy ex-New
Zealand gelding: in excellent form after moving to Singapore, gaining most important
wins at Kranji in Emirates Singapore Derby (eighth consecutive win, by 2 lengths from
Our Aristotle) in June and Queen Elizabeth II Cup (by neck from Saddle Up, later disqualified after positive test) in October: not discredited last 2 starts when third to Kutub
in Singapore Gold Cup at same track and eighth to Agnes Digital in Hong Kong Cup at
Sha Tin: also ran twice in Britain in September, better effort when creditable fourth to
Welcome Friend in listed race at Newbury: stiffer task and possibly unsuited by soft going
in Queen Elizabeth II Stakes at Ascot next time: probably best at 1m/1¼m: acts on firm
and good to soft ground: usually blinkered. *P. Busuttin, Singapore*

BODFARI ANNA   5 br.m. Casteddu 111 – Lowrianna (IRE) 50 (Cyrano de Bergerac   **61 §**
120) [2001 63§, a46§: f7g 6g 7.1m⁴ 7m 7m* 7.5f 7f⁴ 7.1f 7.6m 7g 8.1g 8f⁶ 7m Sep 22]   **a– §**
leggy, unfurnished mare: had a round action: modest handicapper on turf, poor on all-
weather: won at Southwell in May: stayed easy 1m: acted on fibresand and any turf
ground: blinkered/visored: probably ungenuine: dead. *J. L. Eyre*

BODFARI KOMAITE   5 b.g. Komaite (USA) – Gypsy's Barn Rat 55 (Balliol 125)   **83**
[2001 81+: 5v 5d³ 5m 5m² 5.1f* 5d 5g 5.1d* 5.1d 5s Nov 9] workmanlike gelding: fairly
useful handicapper: successful at Chester in June and September: best at 5f: acts on firm
and good to soft going, probably on soft: blinkered last 6 starts: seemed reluctant leaving
stall sixth start: usually races up with pace: tends to wander. *M. W. Easterby*

BODFARI MILLENNIUM   3 b.g. Tragic Role (USA) – Petomania 34 (Petong 126)   **–**
[2001 –: f8g 8m 14.1m 16m Jun 27] poor maiden: tried blinkered: dead. *M. W. Easterby*

BODFARI PRIDE (IRE)   6 b.g. Pips Pride 117 – Renata's Ring (IRE) (Auction Ring   **87**
(USA) 123) [2001 85: 5s⁶ 5d² f6g² 5g⁵ 5m* f6g 5.1d 5s⁶ 6m 5.1d Sep 26] strong,
lengthy gelding: poor mover: fairly useful handicapper: won at Lingfield in May: below
form after: effective at 5f to easy 7.6f: acts on soft going, good to firm and fibresand.
D. Nicholls

BODFARI SIGNET   5 ch.g. King's Signet (USA) 110 – Darakah 78 (Doulab (USA)   **56 ?**
115) [2001 –: 12m³ 12f⁵ 9.9s Sep 25] leggy, lengthy gelding: modest performer at best:
stays 1½m: acts on soft and firm going: tried blinkered/visored/tongue tied: tends to find
little. *Mrs S. C. Bradburne*

BOGUS BALLET   2 ch.f. (Jan 20) Halling (USA) 133 – Classic Ballet (FR) 75   **–**
(Fabulous Dancer (USA) 124) [2001 7g Aug 4] 27,000Y: first foal: dam 1m and 1½m
winner: ran as if race needed when last of 9 in maiden at Newmarket. *M. L. W. Bell*

BOGUS DREAMS (IRE)   4 ch.c. Lahib (USA) 129 – Dreams Are Free (IRE) 71   **109**
(Caerleon (USA) 132) [2001 96: 10s⁶ 10g³ 10g³ 10.1m* 10.3f* 10m² 12g⁵ 10.1g² 9.9m⁵
Sep 26] angular colt: useful performer: won quite valuable handicap at Epsom (dictated
pace in beating Parisien Star by 1¾ lengths) in June and minor event at Doncaster (simple
task) in July: below form last 3 starts: seems best around 1¼m: acts on firm and soft
ground: often front runner. *S. P. C. Woods*

BOGUS PENNY (IRE)   3 b.f. Pennekamp (USA) 130 – Dreams Are Free (IRE) 71   **78**
(Caerleon (USA) 132) [2001 80: f8g³ 8.5s² 10.5m⁵ 9f² Jun 13] fair maiden: stays

9f, probably not 10.5f: acts on firm and soft going: sometimes takes good hold. *S. P. C. Woods*

BOHEMIAN SPIRIT (IRE)   3 b.g. Eagle Eyed (USA) 111 – Tuesday Morning   **54** (Sadler's Wells (USA) 132) [2001 58: f8.5g⁵ f9.4s f11g Oct 1] modest maiden: well held (after 6-month break) final 2 starts: should stay 1¼m: sold 500 gns. *P. G. Murphy*

BOILING POINT   5 b.m. Beveled (USA) – A Little Hot (Petong 126) [2001 –: e8g   **–** Jan 3] no form in maidens. *E. A. Wheeler*

BOIRA (USA)   3 b.f. Diesis 133 – Noblissima (IRE) 77 (Sadler's Wells (USA) 132)   **77** [2001 63: 7m² 8m² 8g⁴ 9m 7.6m³ 8d³ 8.2s⁶ Oct 30] quite good-topped filly: fair maiden: stays 9f: acts on good to firm ground, possibly not on softer than good: sent to France. *D. Morris*

BOISDALE (IRE)   3 b.c. Common Grounds 118 – Alstomeria 61 (Petoski 135) [2001   **77** 93: 7d 7g 7m 7d f7g Sep 8] workmanlike colt: fairly useful at 2 yrs: respectable efforts first 2 starts in 2001: should stay 1m: acts on soft ground: tongue tied final start. *J. A. R. Toller*

BOIS DE CITRON (USA)   3 b.f. Woodman (USA) 126 – Lemon Souffle 115 (Salse   **86** (USA) 128) [2001 88: 6f 5f⁵ 6g 6m 5.7d 6g 6s Nov 10] leggy filly: fairly useful performer: best at 5f: acts on firm going, probably on soft: has shown temperament. *R. Hannon*

BOLD AMUSEMENT   11 ch.g. Never So Bold 135 – Hysterical 68 (High Top 131)   **67** [2001 70: 10m 9.9f⁵ 9.2m⁵ 9.9m 10.1g² 10.9m* 11.9s 10.1v⁴ 11d* 10g Nov 5] strong gelding: fair performer: won amateur handicap at Ayr in September and claimer at Redcar in October: effective at 9f to 1½m: acts on firm and good to soft going, probably not on soft nowadays: tried blinkered earlier in career: sometimes races freely/wanders. *W. S. Cunningham*

BOLD ARISTOCRAT (IRE)   10 b.g. Bold Arrangement 127 – Wyn Mipet (Welsh   **–** Saint 126) [2001 –, a49: f5g f6g Feb 19] poor performer: best at 6f/7f: acts on fibresand,   **a33** lightly raced and no recent form on turf: tried blinkered. *R. Hollinshead*

BOLDBIRD   4 b.g. Puissance 110 – Plum Bold 83 (Be My Guest (USA) 126) [2001   **56** 50: e8g³ e10g 10f 8d f8g 8.1m² Jul 13] modest maiden: stays 1m: acts on fibresand/ equitrack and good to firm going: visored (ran well) final start. *D. J. Coakley*

BOLD CENTURY   4 b.g. Casteddu 111 – Bold Green (FR) (Green Dancer (USA)   **–** 132) [2001 64: e13g* e16s⁶ 10g May 8] modest performer: won maiden at Lingfield in   **a51** February: well beaten in handicaps final 2 outings: free-going sort, unlikely to stay beyond 13f: acts on fibresand/equitrack. *T. J. Naughton*

BOLD CLASSIC (IRE)   8 b.g. Persian Bold 123 – Bay Street 117 (Grundy 137)   **–** [2001 16.5m 16m Aug 12] tall gelding: fairly useful handicapper in 1996: well held on Flat-return (won over fences in August). *C. Grant*

BOLD DANCE   2 b.f. (Apr 30) Marju (IRE) 127 – Tropical Dance (USA) 93 (Thorn   **58 ?** Dance (USA) 107) [2001 6m 7g³ 7.1g⁴ 7.1s⁵ f7g Oct 1] smallish, quite good-topped filly: second foal: dam, 2-y-o 5f/6f winner, half-sister to smart US 1997 2-y-o performer up to 8.5f Johnbill: modest maiden: well held in seller final start: should stay 1m. *K. McAuliffe*

BOLD EFFORT (FR)   9 b.g. Bold Arrangement 127 – Malham Tarn (Riverman   **85 §** (USA) 131) [2001 87§: f6g e5g e6g 6g 5.1m⁵ 5.7f* 6m 5.7g 5m 8d 6g f6g⁴ 6d f6g p6g   **a69 §** p6g f5g Dec 19] good-quartered, dipped-backed gelding: poor mover: fairly useful handi- capper on turf, fair on all-weather: won at Bath in June: best at 5f/6f: acts on soft ground, firm and fibresand/equitrack: usually wears blinkers, has been visored: sometimes slowly away: none too reliable. *K. O. Cunningham-Brown*

BOLDER ALEXANDER (IRE)   4 b.g. Persian Bold 123 – Be Yourself (USA)   **41 ?** (Noalcoholic (FR) 128) [2001 –: 10.2f 11.5m³ 10f 14.1m 11.9g Aug 9] leggy gelding: poor performer: stays 11.5f: acts on firm going: sometimes blinkered. *F. Jordan*

BOLD EWAR (IRE)   4 ch.g. Persian Bold 123 – Hot Curry (USA) (Sharpen Up 127)   **82** [2001 84: f9.4g⁶ e8g² f8.5g³ 8v 8d 8m 7f* 7m f8g p7g f8.5s⁶ Dec 27] leggy, close-coupled gelding: easy mover: fairly useful handicapper: won at Brighton in June: well held after: effective at 7f to 1¼m: acts on fibresand/equitrack, firm and good to soft going: blinkered: sometimes carries head awkwardly: none too consistent. *C. E. Brittain*

BOLD KING   6 br.g. Anshan 119 – Spanish Heart 86 (King of Spain 121) [2001 102:   **99 d** 8s² 8.1m⁶ 8m 7m 8g 7g 7s 7.9d⁴ 7d f8g Nov 19] rangy gelding: useful handicapper: well below form after third start: effective at 7f/1m: acts on fibresand, best on going softer than good on turf: goes well fresh. *J. W. Hills*

BOLD LADY   2 b.f. (Feb 19) Never So Bold 135 – Perfect Lady (Petong 126) [2001   **44**
5.2g³ 6m 5m Aug 13] 900Y: first foal: dam, ran twice at 2 yrs, out of half-sister to smart
performer up to 1m Petardia: poor maiden: best effort on debut. *John Berry*

BOLD LIGHT   2 b.c. (Mar 25) Persian Bold 123 – Kind of Light 83 (Primo Dominie   **61 ?**
121) [2001 6d 7.5s⁵ 8g 7.5g Sep 19] 17,000Y: tall, workmanlike colt: first foal: dam 6f
and (at 2 yrs) 7f winner, out of sister to high-class sprinter Blue Cashmere: appeared to
show modest form second start: well held otherwise: should stay 1m: blinkered final
outing: sold 4,500 gns, sent to Norway. *T. D. Easterby*

BOLDLY CLIFF (BEL)   7 br.h. Never So Bold 135 – Miami Beach (Miami Springs   **66**
121) [2001 72: e5g⁶ 5v⁴ 5g⁵ 5.5g 5d 5g² 5d 5s 4v p5g Dec 22] fair performer: largely
below form in 2001, including at Lingfield: has won at 1m, but very speedy and probably
best at bare 5f: acts on equitrack, good to firm ground, heavy and dirt: often blinkered:
front runner. *Ecurie Denderland, Belgium*

BOLD MCLAUGHLAN   3 b.g. Mind Games 121 – Stoneydale 83 (Tickled Pink   **–**
114) [2001 58: 6g 6m 5f 5f 7d Jul 16] smallish gelding: maiden: no form in 2001: tried
blinkered. *J. S. Goldie*

BOLD PRECEDENT   4 b.g. Polish Precedent (USA) 131 – Shining Water (USA)   **63**
(Riverman (USA) 131) [2001 71: e12g 10f 9.9f 8m⁴ 8f 8g³ 10m 9.9m⁴ 10g 10.2f⁵ 10s
p13g Dec 29] angular gelding: modest handicapper: left P. Harris before final start: stays
1¼m: acts on good to firm going and equitrack, probably on fibresand, possibly not on
soft: usually visored: has been slowly away: sold 4,500 gns. *R. M. Stronge*

BOLD RAIDER   4 b.g. Rudimentary (USA) 118 – Spanish Heart 86 (King of Spain   **87**
121) [2001 77: 8.5s² 8m 7.5m⁴ 8.3d* 8f⁴ 8g² 8m⁶ 8.5g⁴ 8.1v⁵ 8d 8.2s² 10v² Nov 8]
tall, leggy gelding: fairly useful handicapper: won at Windsor in June: some good efforts
after, particularly last 2 starts: stays 1¼m: probably acts on any going: has carried head
awkwardly/found little. *I. A. Balding*

BOLD SABOTEUR   4 b.g. Prince Sabo 123 – Latest Flame (IRE) 66 (Last Tycoon   **–**
131) [2001 46: f7g 6f 6m Jun 29] tall, workmanlike gelding: of little account nowadays.
K. O. Cunningham-Brown

BOLD STATE   4 b.g. Never So Bold 135 – Multi-Sofft 30 (Northern State (USA) 91)   **71**
[2001 74: 7m 8m 8g⁵ 8.5m² 8.2m⁴ 8.5g 9.1m⁴ 8.3m f8g² Oct 22] leggy, quite good-topped
gelding: has quick action: fair handicapper: effective at 1m/9f: acts on firm going, good
to soft and fibresand: has worn visor/blinkers, including last 6 starts: often looks none too
keen: sold 11,000 gns. *M. H. Tompkins*

BOLD VIEW   3 b.g. Nalchik (USA) – Corvo Cutie (Rolfe (USA) 77) [2001 8v⁶ 10.3f⁶   **–**
10.5m f8g Jul 2] sparely-made, angular gelding: fourth foal: dam unraced: well held in
maidens/handicap. *M. Mullineaux*

BOLD WILLY   4 b.g. Never So Bold 135 – Indian Star 58 (Indian King (USA) 128)   **–**
[2001 –: 7m 7m 8m Jun 2] little form. *J. E. Long*

BOLEYN CASTLE (USA)   4 ch.g. River Special (USA) – Dance Skirt (CAN) (Cau-   **98 ?**
casus (USA) 127) [2001 95: 5.2f⁴ 5g* 5.6m 5s f5g Nov 21] strong, compact gelding:
useful handicapper: won at Epsom (possibly gained advantage when several rivals' stalls
failed to open on time) in August by length from Smart Predator: below that form after:
best at 5f: acts on firm and good to soft ground: has shown reluctance at stalls/been taken
early to post: often tries to dominate. *T. G. Mills*

BOLHAM LADY   3 b.f. Timeless Times (USA) 99 – Stratford Lady 48 (Touching   **–**
Wood (USA) 127) [2001 37: f7g⁶ f6g⁴ f5g* f6g⁶ 5.1v f5g³ 5m f6g⁴ f5g f5s Dec 27]   **a53**
compact filly: modest performer: won seller at Southwell in February: well below form
final 4 starts: best at 5f: acts on fibresand, well held on turf: blinkered. *J. Balding*

BOLINGBROKE CASTLE (IRE)   3 ch.g. Goldmark (USA) 113 – Ruby River   **–**
(Red God 128§) [2001 62: 7m 6g 8d 10g 8d Oct 8] lengthy, workmanlike gelding:
disappointing maiden: tried visored/tongue tied. *Miss J. A. Camacho*

BOLLIN EDWARD   2 b.c. (Apr 1) Timeless Times (USA) 99 – Bollin Harriet (Loch-   **79**
nager 132) [2001 5f³ 5m³ Jul 21] good-bodied colt: half-sister to several winners up to 7f,
including fairly useful sprinters Bollin Harry (by Domynsky) and Bollin Rita (by Rambo
Dancer): dam unraced: fair form in maidens at Beverley and Ripon: will prove best at 5f/
6f. *T. D. Easterby*

BOLLIN ERIC   2 b.c. (Feb 18) Shaamit (IRE) 127 – Bollin Zola 90 (Alzao (USA)   **95 p**
117) [2001 6m³ 7.1g² 8.5m* 8g² Sep 13] big, strong, useful-looking colt: has scope:

good walker: has a round action: half-brother to several winners, including smart sprinter Bollin Joanne (by Damister) and fairly useful 1m winner Bollin Terry (by Terimon): dam 5f (at 2 yrs) and 7.6f winner: useful form: won maiden at Beverley (in good style) in August and nursery at Doncaster in September: shade edgy, landed gamble by ¾ length from Hoax in 18-runner race in latter, staying on strongly to lead final 1f: should stay 1¼m: raced only on good ground or firmer: well regarded, and type to win a good prize at 3 yrs. *T. D. Easterby*

BOLLIN NELLIE 4 ch.f. Rock Hopper 124 – Bollin Magdalene 55 (Teenoso (USA) 135) [2001 73: 11.9m 12m* 12f⁶ 12.4m 12.3m⁶ 10.5g² 10m* 9m⁶ 10g³ 12d* Nov 2] **81** sparely-made, plain filly: fairly useful handicapper: won at Beverley in June, Ripon in August and Newmarket in November: effective at 1¼m/1½m: yet to race on heavy going, acts on any other: tough and reliable. *T. D. Easterby*

BOLLIN THOMAS 3 b.g. Alhijaz 122 – Bollin Magdalene 55 (Teenoso (USA) 135) **77** [2001 53: 12m 14.1m 12f* 12f* 11f⁵ 12m² 11.9d⁵ 12m² 12g³ 12d² 14.1g² Oct 19] close-coupled, workmanlike gelding: fair handicapper: won at Beverley in June and July: good efforts final 4 starts: effective at 1½m/1¾m: acts on firm and good to soft ground: consistent. *T. D. Easterby*

BOLSHOI BALLET 3 b.g. Dancing Spree (USA) – Broom Isle 74 (Damister (USA) **63** 123) [2001 73: 8d 8m 10.1m 12.3m 10g 10m⁶ 8.1m 8.3d³ 8.5s f8g² f8.5s⁵ Dec 26] quite good-topped gelding: modest maiden handicapper: barely stays 1¼m: acts on heavy going, good to firm and fibresand. *T. D. Barron*

BOLT FROM THE BLUE 5 b.g. Grand Lodge (USA) 125 – Lightning Legacy – (USA) 78 (Super Concorde (USA) 128) [2001 39: f16g³ f11g Mar 26] close-coupled **a30** gelding: poor maiden handicapper: stays 2m: acts on good to firm going, heavy and fibresand: blinkered (unruly to post) once as 3-y-o. *Don Enrico Incisa*

BOLTOUTOFTHEBLUE 2 ch.g. (Jan 29) Bluegrass Prince (IRE) 110 – Forget To **52** Remindme 51 (Forzando 122) [2001 7m⁶ 7m⁵ f8g 6v 10d Nov 2] 1,000Y: first foal: dam 7f winner: modest maiden: form only when fifth at Brighton: should be suited by at least 1m. *J. S. Moore*

BOLULA 2 b.f. (Feb 3) Tagula (IRE) 116 – Bollin Dorothy 73 (Rambo Dancer (CAN) **61** 107) [2001 5s⁶ 5s³ f6g 5g⁴ 7g Sep 15] strong, workmanlike filly: first foal: dam 7f winner: modest maiden: should stay at least 6f. *T. D. Easterby*

BOMB ALASKA 6 br.g. Polar Falcon (USA) 126 – So True 116 (So Blessed 130) **?** [2001 109: 8v 7.3m⁶ 7g 9g Oct 6] big, rangy gelding: one-time useful performer: disappointing nowadays (reportedly had wind operation after final 5-y-o start). *G. B. Balding*

BONAGUIL (USA) 4 b.g. Septieme Ciel (USA) 123 – Chateaubrook (USA) (Alleged **100** (USA) 138) [2001 103: 8.1v 10.4g⁶ 12m 11.9m⁵ 10g⁵ 12g⁵ 10f Sep 22] sparely-made gelding: useful handicapper: best effort in 2001 at York on second start: ran poorly, finding little, when well backed in valuable event at Newbury final outing: probably stays 1½m: acts on any turf going and equitrack: often held up: tends to wander. *C. F. Wall*

BON AMI (IRE) 5 b.g. Paris House 123 – Felin Special (Lyphard's Special (USA) **92 d** 122) [2001 94: 7s³ 6g² 7m 6f 6f 5g 6m 6g 6g 6g 7g 7.6g⁴ 8m Sep 24] rather leggy gelding: fluent mover: fairly useful handicapper: last won in 1998, and on the downgrade in 2001: stays 7.6f: acts on any going: tried blinkered/visored: sometimes edges left/carries head high. *K. T. Ivory*

BOND BOY 4 b.c. Piccolo 121 – Arabellajill 97 (Aragon (118) [2001 79: 5v³ 5.1d⁶ 6m⁴ **87** 6m⁴ 6g⁵ 6g² 6g 5s* 5g* 5s 5s* Nov 9] fairly useful performer: won handicap at Pontefract in September, minor event at Redcar in October and handicap at Doncaster in November: best at 5f (given bit of a test)/6f: acts on heavy and good to firm ground: consistent. *B. Smart*

BOND DIAMOND 4 gr.g. Prince Sabo 123 – Alsiba 68 (Northfields (USA)) [2001 **66 +** 59, a68: 8.3g 8f* 8m² 8d³ p8g Dec 22] fair handicapper: won apprentice race at Redcar in July: best at 7f/1m: acts on firm going, good to soft, fibresand and polytrack. *B. Smart*

BOND DOMINGO 2 b.g. (Jan 21) Mind Games 121 – Antonia's Folly 64 (Music **82 §** Boy 124) [2001 5.1v² 5.1s⁴ 5.1f⁴ 5m 6.1m 5g* 6d 6d f5g* f5g f5s Dec 21] 36,000Y: strong, well-made gelding: fourth foal: half-brother to fairly useful 1998 2-y-o 5f winner Zaragossa (by Paris House) and 3-y-o Antonia's Dilemma: dam 2f 5f winner: fairly useful performer: won nurseries at Hamilton in September and Southwell in November: best at 5f: acts on fibresand and heavy ground: usually blinkered: has hung markedly left: unreliable. *B. Smart*

BOND JOVI (IRE)   2 b.g. (Mar 9) Danehill Dancer (IRE) 117 – Vieux Carre (Pas de   **72**
Seul 133) [2001 5g⁶ 5m⁵ 6v⁴ 6d f6g² f6g* Nov 19] 18,000Y: smallish gelding: half-
brother to several winners, including 1996 2-y-o 5f to 7f winner Contravene (by Contract
Law) and 1m seller winner Amelia Jess (by Mac's Imp): dam, poor maiden, sometimes
appeared reluctant: fair performer: won maiden at Southwell: stays 6f: acts on heavy
ground and fibresand. *B. Smart*

BOND MILLENNIUM   3 ch.g. Piccolo 121 – Farmer's Pet 90 (Sharrood (USA)   **76**
124) [2001 53: f7g² e8g* 8.3s f8g 8.3g 8.2g* 8.1f⁵ 8.5f* 8.2m 10m² 9.2s² 9m⁴ 10.5v 10s   **a93**
10s⁶ f8g* p10g⁴ f9.4s⁵ Dec 15] sturdy gelding: fairly useful on all-weather, fair on turf:
won maiden at Lingfield and handicaps at Nottingham, Beverley and Southwell between
February and November: effective at 1m/1¼m: acts on all-weather, firm and soft going.
B. Smart

BOND MIRAGE   3 b.g. Primo Dominie 121 – Arabellajill 97 (Aragon 118) [2001 6m   **42**
7.1s 7.1m f7g f8.5g⁶ Dec 11] 13,500F, 21,000Y: third foal: half-brother to 4-y-o Bond
Boy and a 7f (at 2 yrs) to 1m winner in Italy by Pursuit of Love: dam 5f (at 2 yrs) and 6f
winner: poor maiden: stays 8.5f: acts on fibresand. *B. Smart*

BONDOSAN   5 b.g. Barathea (IRE) 127 – Fern 100 (Shirley Heights 130) [2001 f11g   **–**
Nov 30] fair form in 2 maidens at 3 yrs: behind in seller only run since. *J. F. Coupland*

BONDS GULLY (IRE)   5 b.h. Pips Pride 117 – Classic Ring (IRE) 50 (Auction Ring   **50**
(USA) 123) [2001 55, a66: 11.5m 10.1g 10.1d⁴ 10.1g 9.7d⁵ 9.9s f9.4g p10g f12g⁵ f12s
Dec 15] lengthy horse: modest maiden handicapper: stays 1½m: acts on firm going, soft
and fibresand/equitrack: tried blinkered/visored/tongue tied: has run in snatches. *Mrs
Lydia Pearce*

BONECRUSHER   2 b.c. (Mar 17) Revoque (IRE) 122 – Eurolink Mischief 84 (Be   **88**
My Chief (USA) 122) [2001 7m 7.1s* 7d Oct 3] third foal: half-brother to useful 6f/7f
winner (at 2 yrs) who stayed 1¼m Eurolink Raindance (by Alzao) and 3-y-o Eurolink
Sundance: dam 1½m winner: easily best effort (fairly useful form) when winning maiden
at Haydock in September by 3 lengths from Oakley Rambo: should stay 1¼m: acts on
soft ground. *J. L. Dunlop*

BONELLA (IRE)   3 gr.f. Eagle Eyed (USA) 111 – Mettlesome (Lomond (USA) 128)   **56**
[2001 –: 8m* 10m 8.2m 10s² Sep 30] tall filly: modest handicapper: won at Leicester in
August: ran well final outing: should stay 1½m: acts on soft and good to firm going. *Mrs
Lydia Pearce*

BON MARCHE   2 ch.f. (Apr 2) Definite Article 121 – Sabre Penny (IRE) (Sabrehill   **75**
(USA) 120) [2001 7.1m² 7m² 6m 7d* 8d 7v Oct 26] 800Y: lengthy, rather sparely-made
filly: first foal: dam unraced out of half-sister to Gorytus: fair performer: runner-up in
maidens prior to winning 21-runner nursery at Newmarket in October: well held last 2
starts: should stay 1m: acts on good to firm and good to soft ground. *A. P. Jarvis*

BONNARD (IRE)   3 b.c. Nureyev (USA) 131 – Utr (Mr Prospector (USA))   **114**
[2001 110: 10f³ 9g³ 10m² 8d⁵ 8g⁵ Aug 25] deep-bodied colt: smart performer: ran well
first 4 starts in 2001, including 3 lengths third to Chichicastenango in Grand Prix de
Paris at Longchamp on first occasion and 1½ lengths second to Muakaad in Meld Stakes
at the Curragh and sixth past post (beaten just over 2 lengths, promoted to fifth) behind
disqualified Proudwings in Prix Jacques le Marois at Deauville on last two: crossed
noseband and a little on edge, slowly away when below form in Celebration Mile at
Goodwood final outing: stays 1¼m: yet to race on heavy ground, acts on any other: very
upset in stall third 2-y-o start, blinkered (well below form) fifth one: sent to Saudi Arabia.
A. P. O'Brien, Ireland

BONNERS BAR   2 b.f. (May 22) Bluegrass Prince (IRE) 110 – Another Batchworth   **–**
72 (Beveled (USA)) [2001 5.1m p5g f5f Dec 5] first foal: dam, untrustworthy 5f/6f
winner, sister to 7-y-o Dancing Mystery: little sign of ability, including in seller. *E. A. Wheeler*

BONNIE FLORA   5 b.m. Then Again 126 – My Minnie 67 (Kind of Hush 118) [2001   **52**
69d: 11.7d⁶ 12s 12.1m 10.2f² 10m* 10m Aug 22] big, heavy-topped mare: modest handicapper: won at Brighton in August: stays 1½m: acts on firm going. *K. Bishop*

BONNIE LAD (IRE)   2 b.g. (Apr 19) Tagula (IRE) 116 – Sabonis (USA) 68 (The   **73**
Minstrel (CAN) 135) [2001 5.1f⁶ 6m⁵ 5.1f 5.1m⁶ 5g³ 6d Sep 14] 22,000Y: rather leggy,
useful-looking gelding: seventh foal: half-brother to fairly useful 2000 2-y-o 5f winner
Stregone (by Namaqualand) and 1997 2-y-o 1m winner who stayed 1½m Premium Quest
(by Forzando): dam 2-y-o 6f winner: fair maiden: likely to prove best at 5f/easy 6f: acts

on firm ground: raced too freely in blinkers fourth start: often slowly away: gelded after final outing. *A. Berry*

BONNIE MAITE   2 ch.f. (Apr 8) Komaite (USA) – Narbonne 60 (Rousillon (USA)   **58**
133) [2001 5.1m⁶ 5.7g Oct 1] first foal: dam 1m winner: better effort in maidens (modest form) when sixth at Nottingham: may prove best at 5f/6f. *P. D. Evans*

BONNYELLA   3 b.f. Phountzi (USA) 104 – Diavalezza (Connaught 130) [2001 38:   **38**
f12g 10d 8f 10f⁴ 10.9f⁴ 10m 16.2m⁵ 16.2g 13.8m Sep 22] angular, lightly-made filly: poor maiden: stays 11f, probably not 2m: acts on firm going: blinkered fourth to sixth starts: has looked none too genuine. *B. Palling*

BONNY RUAN   2 b.f. (May 14) So Factual (USA) 120 – Sans Diablo (IRE) (Mac's   **84**
Imp (USA) 116) [2001 5.1g* 5.1m* 5g⁵ 5.1m* 5g 6d Oct 19] tall, leggy filly: third foal: dam unraced: fairly useful performer: won maiden at Bath in June, minor event at Chepstow in July and nursery at Nottingham in September: may well prove best at 5f. *D. Haydn Jones*

BONTADINI   2 b.c. (Apr 25) Emarati (USA) 74 – Kintail 76 (Kris 135) [2001 7m Aug   **–**
13] 800Y: sixth foal: half-brother to 6f winner Invergordon (by Efisio), later winner in USA, and 4-y-o Ulshaw: dam runner-up on debut at 1¼m: no promise in maiden at Folkestone. *D. Morris*

BONVIVANT (GER)   4 ch.c. Sternkonig (IRE) 112 – Bonne Chance (GER) (Surumu   **115**
(GER)) [2001 107: 12v⁵ 11m* 11g 12g 12d 12v Sep 23] fifth foal: half-brother to German 1994 2-y-o 6f winner Bien Sur (by Zampano): dam German 1m and 11f winner: smart performer: best effort when beating below-form Samum (who gave 7 lb) a neck in Grosser Mercedes-Benz-Preis at Baden-Baden in May: failed to repeat that form: stays 1½m: acts on soft and good to firm ground: joined E. Pils. *H. Horwart, Germany*

BOOBALA (IRE)   2 b.f. (Apr 21) General Monash (USA) 107 – Best Swinger (IRE)   **78**
(Ela-Mana-Mou 132) [2001 6g 6m⁴ 5.1s* 5.2m 5g⁶ 6m Sep 12] IR 40,000Y: sixth foal: half-sister to 3 winners, notably useful 1999 2-y-o 7f winner Scarteen Fox (by Fox-hound), later 1m winner in Hong Kong under name of Best Light: dam Irish 7f winner: fair performer: won maiden at Chepstow in August: gave impression something amiss final start: should prove better at 6f than 5f: acts on soft and good to firm ground. *D. R. C. Elsworth*

BOO B PRIZE (USA)   2 b.g. (Apr 6) Prized (USA) – Sugar Hollow (USA) (Val de   **59**
L'Orne (FR) 133) [2001 6m⁶ 7s² 7d⁵ Oct 30] $13,000Y: tall, rather unfurnished gelding: has scope: half-brother to several winners, including very smart 1¼m winner Cruachan (by Lear Fan) and useful 1¼m/1½m winner Banbury (by Silver Hawk): dam unraced: modest maiden: well below form final start: should stay 1¼m: acts on soft and good to firm ground. *T. D. Barron*

BOOGARBAROO (IRE)   3 gr.g. Turtle Island (IRE) 123 – Lingdale Lass 60 (Petong   **60 ?**
126) [2001 7m⁴ 8.1m 8s Oct 3] 7,000F, 9,000Y, 1,100 3-y-o: fourth foal: half-brother to 6f (at 2 yrs) and 7f winner Blue Shadow and 5-y-o Malaah (both by Pips Pride): dam 2-y-o 6f winner: appeared to show modest form in maiden at Salisbury on debut in August: soundly beaten in similar events after: reportedly wrong behind final outing. *Julian Poulton*

BOOKS LAW   3 b.g. Contract Law (USA) 108 – In A Whirl (USA) 63 (Island Whirl   **–**
(USA)) [2001 7.1g 7.1s 7.1m Aug 27] third foal: dam 2-y-o 6f winner: well held in maidens. *J. M. Bradley*

BOOM OR BUST (IRE)   2 ch.g. (Apr 30) Entrepreneur 123 – Classic Affair (USA)   **61**
66 (Trempolino (USA) 135) [2001 5m⁵ 6.3d 7.1f⁴ 7m⁴ 8m⁶ 7d Oct 3] IR 16,000F, IR 9,000Y: close-coupled, quite good-topped gelding: second foal: dam, 2m winner, from family of Japan Cup winner Pay The Butler: modest maiden: should stay at least 1¼m: races prominently. *A. Berry*

BOOMSHADOW   4 ch.g. Imperial Frontier (USA) 112 – Marie de Sologne (Lashkari   **41 §**
128) [2001 32§: 12s 11d⁴ f11g f14g Dec 14] smallish gelding: poor maiden: seems to   **a– §**
stay 1½m: acts on fibresand, probably on heavy going: tried tongue tied: untrustworthy. *J. L. Eyre*

BOON COMPANION   2 b.g. (Mar 23) Sure Blade (USA) 130 – Pea Green 98 (Try   **–**
My Best (USA) 130) [2001 5m Aug 13] 15,000Y: half-brother to several winners, including 7-y-o The Green Grey and 4-y-o Sussex Lad: dam, 2-y-o 5f winner who probably stayed 1m, grandam of smart sprinter Sampower Star: well beaten in maiden at Folkestone. *John Berry*

BOP   4 b. or br.f. Darkwood Bay (USA) 82 – Call of The Night (IRE) 72 (Night Shift   **60 ?**
(USA)) [2001 –: f8g⁵ f8f e8g⁶ 9d² 8s e10m 8m 8f 9.2g² 10f Jul 9] strong filly: modest   **a43**
maiden at best on turf, poor on all-weather: should stay 1¼m: acts on fibresand and good
to soft going: visored eighth start: very slowly away fifth outing. *K. R. Burke*

BORDER ARROW   6 ch.g. Selkirk (USA) 129 – Nibbs Point (IRE) 107 (Sure Blade   **118**
(USA) 130) [2001 118: 10s* 10v² 10m* 10m* 10m 10d³ 12s² p10g⁶ Nov 24] big, lengthy
gelding: has a markedly round action: has reportedly had leg problems: smart performer,
lightly raced: won listed race at Kempton in April by head from Pawn Broker and Credit
Suisse First Boston Brigadier Gerard Stakes at Sandown in May by 2 lengths from
Compton Bolter: also ran creditably when second to Island House in Gordon Richards
Stakes at Sandown and to Boreas (beaten 8 lengths) in listed event at Doncaster: stays
1½m: acts on heavy and good to firm going, well below form on polytrack: effective
visored or not: tongue tied once: tends to sweat: often slowly away. *I. A. Balding*

BORDER ARTIST   2 ch.g. (Feb 8) Selkirk (USA) 129 – Aunt Tate (Tate Gallery   **69**
(USA) 117) [2001 6s⁶ 6m⁶ 7f⁵ 6m* 6m 6m Sep 12] well-made gelding: third foal:
half-brother to French 12.5f winner Devious Aunty (by Dr Devious): dam, ran twice, out
of smart French 1¼m winner Aunty: fair performer: won maiden at Windsor in July:
below form both starts after (gelded after final one): barely stays 7f: acts on soft and good
to firm ground. *M. Blanshard*

BORDER COMET   3 b.c. Selkirk (USA) 129 – Starlet 119 (Teenoso (USA) 135)   **98**
[2001 88p: 10g² 12f 10m* 9.9g⁶ 13.1m⁵ 12d Oct 2] good-topped colt: good mover: useful
performer: made all in maiden at Ascot in July: improved form in handicaps next 2 starts,
in second beaten 5 lengths behind Prairie Falcon having been clear 2f out: barely stays
13.1f: acts on good to firm going, seemingly not on good to soft: sold 50,000 gns. *Sir
Michael Stoute*

BORDER EDGE   3 b.g. Beveled (USA) – Seymour Ann (Krayyan 117) [2001 60d: **59**
f9.4s⁴ f8g² f9.4g² 8.2s f8g² 8.1g* 8.1s⁵ 7s 8d Oct 25] unfurnished gelding: fair   **a69**
handicapper on all-weather, modest on turf: won at Warwick in May: gelded and off 4
months before below form final 3 starts: probably best at 1m/9f: acts on fibresand, best
turf efforts on good going: visored: sometimes races freely. *K. McAuliffe*

BORDER GLEN   5 b.g. Selkirk (USA) 129 – Sulitelma (USA) 63 (The Minstrel   **50**
(CAN) 135) [2001 59, a69d: e7g⁶ e6g* e5g e6s* e6g² e6g⁴ e6g 6v 7m 5.7m 5m 6m 6m   **a66**
6f 6m 5m f6g p7g p5g³ p6g p6g Dec 19] big gelding: poor mover: fair handicapper on
all-weather, modest on turf: won at Lingfield in January and (apprentice event) February:
effective at 5f to easy 1m: acts on soft going, good to firm and all-weather: usually wears
blinkers/visor: races prominently: has wandered/flashed tail/found little. *J. J. Bridger*

BORDERLINE   4 ch.c. Polish Precedent (USA) 131 – Brecon Beacons (IRE) 71   **43**
(Shirley Heights 130) [2001 56: e12g⁶ f8.5s e10g⁴ e8g Jan 24] poor maiden: reportedly
lame final start: barely stays 1¼m: acts on equitrack: visored once at 3 yrs. *M. Quinn*

BORDER MARAUDER (IRE)   2 b.g. (Mar 30) Priolo (USA) 127 – Irrestible Lady   **72**
(IRE) 77 (Mtoto 134) [2001 8g f8.5g f9.4g³ p10g f8g² f8s⁵ Dec 21] IR 10,000F, IR
13,000Y: quite good-topped gelding: third foal: dam, Irish 1½m winner, granddaughter
of 1000 Guineas winner Full Dress II: fair maiden: placed at Wolverhampton and
Southwell: should stay 1¼m: acts on fibresand. *J. A. Osborne*

BORDER MINSTREL (IRE)   2 b. or br.f. (May 9) Sri Pekan (USA) 117 – Persian   **69 ?**
Song 45 (Persian Bold 123) [2001 5m 6g 6g* 5.2m 6m 6s Sep 24] angular filly: fifth foal:
sister to 4-y-o Zagaleta and half-sister to 3 winners, including smart 7f (at 2 yrs) to 1¼m

winner Mountain Song (by Tirol): dam, ran 3 times at 2 yrs, half-sister to high-class performer up to 1¼m Bold Arrangement: easily best effort in maidens when enterprisingly ridden to win at Windsor in August: no show in listed race/nurseries after: should stay at least 1m: visored final start. *B. J. Meehan*

BORDER PRINCE   5 ch.g. Selkirk (USA) 129 – Princess Oberon (IRE) 91 (Fairy King (USA)) [2001 e8s⁶ Feb 17] leggy, unfurnished gelding: fairly useful maiden in 1999: well held only run since. *I. A. Wood*   –

BORDER RUN   4 b.g. Missed Flight 123 – Edraianthus 78 (Windjammer (USA)) [2001 65, a–: 14.1v Mar 28] well-made gelding: fair maiden at 3 yrs: well beaten only run in 2001: blinkered twice. *M. Mullineaux*   –

BORDERS   5 b.g. Selkirk (USA) 129 – Pretty Poppy 67 (Song 132) [2001 5m* 5m³ 5s² 5m 5d Sep 13] big, well-made gelding: useful performer: missed 2000 (reportedly suffered from stress fractures in quarters and a problem with a hind joint): won minor event at Beverley in May prior to creditable placed efforts in listed race at Kempton (beaten 2 necks behind Emerald Peace) and minor event at Sandown (1¼-length second of 5 to Proud Native): down field in King George Stakes at Goodwood and listed event at Doncaster last 2 starts: best at 5f: acts on soft and good to firm going: has worn dropped noseband: front runner: sold only 8,000 gns. *H. Candy*   **106**

BORDERS BELLE (IRE)   3 b.f. Pursuit of Love 124 – Sheryl Lynn (Miller's Mate 116) [2001 80: 10d⁵ 12.3f³ 12m⁶ 11.9d⁴ 11.9d³ 11.9g* 11.9s² 12d 12v Oct 27] sturdy filly: fairly useful handicapper: won at York in August by neck from Warning Reef: good efforts on next 2 starts: stays 1½m: acts on firm and soft going: often held up: sold 32,000 gns. *J. D. Bethell*   **86**

BORDER SUBJECT   4 b.g. Selkirk (USA) 129 – Topicality (USA) (Topsider (USA)) [2001 96p: 7m* 8m 7m⁶ Jul 12] big, strong, good-topped gelding: useful handicapper: won at Lingfield in May by ½ length from Zucchero: creditable sixth to Atavus in Bunbury Cup at Newmarket final start: successful at 1m, but races freely and may prove best around 7f: yet to race on extremes of going: has worn tongue tie: sold only 11,000 gns in October, and gelded. *R. Charlton*   **106**

BOREAL (GER)   3 ch.c. Java Gold (USA) – Britannia (GER) (Tarim) [2001 10v* 11v² 10g³ 11g³ 12s* 12d² 12d² 12v Sep 23] fourth foal: half-brother to 2 winners by Acatenango, notably very smart Deutsches Derby winner Borgia, later placed in Arc and Breeders' Cup Turf: dam won up to 2m in Germany, including Deutsches St Leger: very smart performer: won maiden at Frankfurt in March and BMW Deutsches Derby at Hamburg (led over 1f out when beating Lierac by 1½ lengths) in July: runner-up in Credit Suisse Private Banking Pokal at Cologne (beaten ½ length by Sabiango) and Grosser Preis von Baden (went down by 1¼ lengths to Morshdi) next 2 starts: hampered and fell in early stages of Preis von Europa at Cologne final outing: stays 1½m: acts on heavy going. *P. Schiergen, Germany*   **121**

BOREAS   6 b.g. In The Wings 128 – Reamur 68 (Top Ville 129) [2001 119: 12g⁶ 12d³ 12s³ 12v 12s* Nov 10] leggy gelding: good mover, with a long stride: smart performer, lightly raced: won listed race at Doncaster in November (for second year running) by 8 lengths from Border Arrow: also ran well when 2¼ lengths third to Nayef in Cumberland   **119**

CIU Serlby Stakes, Doncaster—Boreas runs away with the race for the second year running; Border Arrow is second, ahead of Akbar (spots)

Lodge Stakes at Ascot third start: well beaten at Longchamp in between: effective at 1½m/1¾m: very best efforts on soft/heavy going. *L. M. Cumani*

BOREHILL JOKER 5 ch.g. Pure Melody (USA) 77 – Queen Matilda 44 (Castle — Keep 121) [2001 16v Oct 17] little form on Flat (fair winning hurdler): tried blinkered/visored/tongue tied. *W. G. M. Turner*

BORN SPECIAL 2 b.g. (Feb 25) Bluebird (USA) 125 – Dixie Eyes Blazing (USA) **54** 56 (Gone West (USA)) [2001 6g 6m 5d Sep 25] 12,000Y: has a round action: second foal: half-brother to 3-y-o Johnny Reb: dam, ran twice, from family of Zafonic, Reams of Verse and Elmaamul: modest maiden: likely to stay 1m. *P. C. Haslam*

BORN WILD (FR) 3 b.f. Exit To Nowhere (USA) 122 – Passerella (FR) (Brustolon — 117) [2001 –: 7g 8m 14.1m May 29] leggy filly: well held in maidens/handicap. *K. A. Ryan*

BOROFAN 5 b.g. Mon Tresor 113 – Musical Drive (Hotfoot 126) [2001 12v 5v 7s 7d — May 7] fourth foal: dam unraced: of little account. *M. Dods*

BORORA 2 gr.c. (Jan 20) Shareef Dancer (USA) 135 – Bustling Nelly 94 (Bustino **61 p** 136) [2001 p8g Nov 28] 15,000F, 30,000Y: brother to fairly useful 1½m winner Shareef and half-brother to several winners, notably very smart middle-distance stayer Busy Flight (by Pharly): dam, 1½m winner, half-sister to Further Flight: eighth of 12 in maiden at Lingfield, staying on after slow start: will be suited by 1¼m+: should improve. *I. A. Balding*

BOSHAM MILL 3 ch.g. Nashwan (USA) 135 – Mill On The Floss 117 (Mill Reef **116** (USA) 141) [2001 12d³ 12g⁴ 12s* 16.2m⁶ 14.8g⁴ 16g 18d³ 15.5s* Nov 2] 120,000Y: tall, close-coupled gelding: fluent mover: closely related to fairly useful 1¼m winner Arabis (by Arazi) and half-brother to several winners, including useful middle-distance performers Milly Ha Ha (by Dancing Brave) and Yeltsin (by Soviet Star): dam 7f (at 2 yrs) and 1½m winner: smart performer: won maiden and minor event at Salisbury in May and listed race at Maisons-Laffitte (by 2 lengths from Torrealta) in November: also very good 3¼ lengths third to Alleluia in Doncaster Cup penultimate start: stays 2¼m: acts on soft and good to firm going: usually sweating/on edge in preliminaries, and sometimes flashes tail/goes in snatches, including final start: gelded afterwards. *G. Wragg*

BOSRA BADGER 3 ch.g. Emarati (USA) 74 – Mrs McBadger 67 (Weldnaas (USA) **53** 112) [2001 59: 6m 6d⁶ 6f 6m⁶ 5m 6m 5.3m 6g⁴ 5g⁵ 5v 6d p6g Dec 19] modest maiden handicapper: barely stays 6f: raced mainly on good going or firmer, well held on softer than good/polytrack: effective visored: has been early to post/slowly away: withdrawn after bolting to post fifth intended outing: none too consistent. *Mrs L. C. Jewell*

BOSSARATI ROCK 3 b.f. Emarati (USA) 74 – La Bossette (IRE) 56 (Cyrano de — Bergerac 120) [2001 8.2d Sep 21] first living foal: dam sprint maiden in Ireland: tailed off in maiden at Nottingham. *A. G. Newcombe*

BOSSCAT 4 b.g. Presidium 124 – Belltina 41 (Belfort (FR) 89) [2001 54: f12g 10d Jul — 18] headstrong maiden: tried blinkered. *K. McAuliffe*

BOSS TWEED (IRE) 4 b.g. Persian Bold 123 – Betty Kenwood 39 (Dominion 123) **62** [2001 67: e10g* e12g⁴ f12g 10s⁵ f11g 9.2d⁵ Jul 19] leggy gelding: modest performer: won minor event at Lingfield in January: stays 1½m: acts on fibresand/equitrack and heavy ground: has had tongue tied: sometimes runs moodily. *Ronald Thompson*

BOSSY SPICE 4 br.f. Emperor Jones (USA) 119 – Million Heiress (Auction Ring — (USA) 123) [2001 –: 11.7d 11.9m⁶ 12.1m Jul 13] compact filly: of little account: dead. *N. M. Babbage*

BOTTELINO JOE (IRE) 4 b. or br.g. Bluebird (USA) 125 – My-O-My (IRE) 105 — (Waajib 121) [2001 53: e8s⁵ f7g e10g Mar 19] maiden: no form in 2001: tried blinkered. *M. S. Saunders*

BOUCHRA (IRE) 3 ch.f. Inchinor 119 – My Darlingdaughter (Night Shift (USA)) **75** [2001 73: f7s² 5d⁵ 6m 6s* 6d⁴ 9.2s 7.1v⁵ f6g² 6v 6g f7g f7g f6s Dec 15] fair performer: won maiden at Hamilton in July: has form at 1m, probably best at 6f/7f: acts on fibresand, soft and good to firm going: usually visored/blinkered: has been slowly away/raced freely: often makes running. *I. Semple*

BOULEVARD (IRE) 5 gr.g. Sadler's Wells (USA) 132 – Ispahan 87 (Rusticaro (FR) **86 §** 124) [2001 e12g⁶ 12v 16m² 13.3m 20m 16.2f² 16m 16s 12g 14d³ 12s⁶ Oct 18] good-topped gelding: brother to 2 winners, notably smart 10.5f Prix Lupin winner Cloudings, and half-brother to several winners: dam 6f (at 2 yrs) and 1m (in France) winner: fairly useful performer: won minor events at Compiegne and Deauville for A. Fabre in France at 3 yrs: left S. Kirk after eighth start in 2001: stays 2m: probably acts on any going: not one to trust (has refused to race several times over hurdles). *M. F. Morris, Ireland*

BOUNCING BOWDLER 3 b.g. Mujadil (USA) 119 – Prima Volta 80 (Primo **106** Dominie 121) [2001 104: 6m 6f 6m³ 6g 6g 7s* 6m⁴ 7.3f⁵ 6s⁵ 6d 6v 6s Nov 10] rather leggy, quite good-topped gelding: has a quick action: useful performer: won listed race at Epsom in August by ¾ length from Russian Rhapsody: in frame otherwise behind Invincible Spirit in similar event at Newbury and Boland Stakes at the Curragh: well held last 3 starts (gelded after final one): stays 7.3f: acts on firm and soft going: races up with pace. *M. Johnston*

BOUND 3 b.g. Kris 135 – Tender Moment (IRE) 78 (Caerleon (USA) 132) [2001 70, – a86: 10.2f⁶ May 22] big, workmanlike gelding: fairly useful on all-weather, fair on turf at 2 yrs: reportedly choked only 3-y-o start: should stay at least 1¼m: acts on fibresand and soft going, probably on good to firm: sold 2,800 gns and gelded. *B. W. Hills*

BOUND BY LAW (IRE) 2 b.f. (May 14) Dolphin Street (FR) 125 – Basovizza **72** (Statoblest 120) [2001 7g⁵ 8.1g 7g⁵ 7m 7g³ 7d² 8d³ 7d* Dec 24] first foal: dam Italian sprint winner out of sister to high-class sprinter Petong: fair performer: left L. Cumani after sixth start: won minor event at Naples in December: best form at 7f: acts on good to soft ground. *R. Brogi, Italy*

BOUND FOR PLEASURE (IRE) 5 gr.h. Barathea (IRE) 127 – Dazzlingly **88** Radiant 81 (Try My Best (USA) 130) [2001 99: 10f 10d Oct 13] big, strong horse: not a good walker/mover: lightly-raced handicapper: fairly useful form first outing in 2001: should stay 1½m: acts on any going: blinkered final 3-y-o start: wears tongue tie: has worn crossed noseband: sometimes slowly away: held up. *J. H. M. Gosden*

BOUNDLESS PROSPECT (USA) 2 b.c. (May 14) Boundary (USA) 117 – Cape **62 p** (USA) (Mr Prospector (USA)) [2001 p8g Nov 28] $39,000Y: fifth living foal: half-brother to 2 winners abroad, including French 1½m winner In Business (by Time For A Change): dam, unraced, out of half-sister to Canadian Grade 1 13f winner Great Neck: seventh of 12 in maiden at Lingfield, forced wide: should do better. *J. W. Hills*

BOUND TO PLEASE 6 b.g. Warrshan (USA) 117 – Hong Kong Girl 94 (Petong **50** 126) [2001 56, a76: f8g³ f8g* f7g² f7g 7.1v⁴ f8g f8g³ f7g p7g⁵ Dec 19] neat gelding: fair **a75** handicapper on all-weather, modest on turf: won at Southwell in February: stays 1m: acts on heavy ground, good to firm and fibresand (respectable effort on polytrack): usually races prominently: none too consistent. *P. J. Makin*

BOURGAINVILLE 3 b.c. Pivotal 124 – Petonica (IRE) 77 (Petoski 135) [2001 93p: **104** 9.9g⁵ 9m² 8f² 8m² 9.9g⁴ 8f³ 9g Oct 6] tall, close-coupled colt: usually looks well: has a long, rather round stride: useful performer: creditable efforts in 2001 when in frame, including minor event at Ascot (¾-length second to Binary File) on third outing and in handicaps at Goodwood and Newbury (2¼ lengths third to Indura) on fifth/sixth starts: stays 1¼m: raced mainly on good going or firmer: reliable. *I. A. Balding*

BOURGEOIS 4 ch.g. Sanglamore (USA) 126 – Bourbon Girl 116 (Ile de Bourbon – (USA) 133) [2001 105: 12.3s Apr 28] strong gelding: half-brother to several winners, including French 1¼m and 1½m winner Apogee (by Shirley Heights) and French 1½m and 14.5f winner Daring Miss (by Sadler's Wells), both smart: dam, 2-y-o 7f winner, second in Oaks and Irish Oaks: useful performer at best: won minor event at Maisons-Laffitte in 2000, when also creditable third of 5 in Prix du Lys at Chantilly (sold from Mme C. Head-Maarek in France 56,000 gns and gelded after final start): tailed off in minor event at Ripon only 4-y-o outing: stays 15f: acts on good to firm and good to soft ground, probably on soft: blinkered (ran creditably) final 3-y-o start. *T. D. Easterby*

BOWCLIFFE 10 b.g. Petoski 135 – Gwiffina 87 (Welsh Saint 126) [2001 73: 8s 8.3d **59 d** 8.3d 7m 8m⁵ 8m 8m 8f 8f 8.9m 10.3m Sep 12] good-topped gelding: modest nowadays: best at 1m/easy 1¼m: acts on fibresand, firm and soft going: tried blinkered/visored. *W. Storey*

BOWCLIFFE GRANGE (IRE) 9 b.g. Dominion Royale 112 – Cala-Vadella 110 – (Mummy's Pet 125) [2001 42d: f5g f5g f5g Mar 21] good-topped gelding: winning sprint handicapper: well beaten in 2001: tried blinkered. *D. W. Chapman*

BOWFELL 3 b.f. Alflora (IRE) 120 – April City 56 (Lidhame 109) [2001 58: 6m 6d – 6.1m 7s f5g p5g⁶ f6g f6s Dec 21] close-coupled filly: modest performer: well beaten in 2001: effective at 5f/6f: acts on soft and good to firm ground: tried visored/blinkered. *C. Smith*

BOWLAND PRINCE (USA) 3 gr.c. Rubiano (USA) – Lake Champlain 108 (Kings **46**
Lake (USA) 133) [2001 10m 10.5d 9m⁴ f9.4g Nov 27] $19,000Y, 14,000 2-y-o: half-
brother to several winners abroad: dam, Irish 1m/1¼m performer who later won in USA,
half-sister to dam of Theatrical: poor maiden. *E. J. Alston*

BOWLERS BOY 8 ch.g. Risk Me (FR) 127 – Snow Wonder (Music Boy 124) [2001 **68**
68: 5m 5d 5g⁴ 6g 6.1v² 5s 5v³ 6g 5s Nov 9] workmanlike gelding: fair handicapper:
effective at 5f (on stiff track) to 7f: acts on heavy and good to firm ground: tried blinkered:
comes from off pace: carries head high. *J. J. Quinn*

BOW PEEP (IRE) 6 b. or br.m. Shalford (IRE) 124§ – Gale Force Seven (Strong **–**
Gale 116) [2001 64: 5v Mar 29] leggy, useful-looking mare: modest handicapper: well
held only 6-y-o start: blinkered. *M. W. Easterby*

BOW STRADA 4 ch.g. Rainbow Quest (USA) 134 – La Strada (Niniski (USA) 125) **82 +**
[2001 –: 13.9m 16.2f 16d⁵ 13.9d* 12s Nov 10] leggy, quite attractive gelding: fairly
useful performer: best effort since 2 yrs when winning handicap at York in October: well
backed, faded after making running in November Handicap at Doncaster final start: stays
1¾m, but not short of speed: acts on good to soft going: sold 61,000 gns, joined P. Hobbs,
won twice over hurdles in December. *P. W. Harris*

BOX BUILDER 4 ch.g. Fraam 114 – Ena Olley (Le Moss 135) [2001 91: 14.1g 14m² **86**
13.3m 16.2m 13.3m 13.1m Aug 24] close-coupled, good-topped gelding: fairly useful
handicapper: generally disappointing at 4 yrs (reportedly had wind operation after third
outing): should stay beyond 2m: acts on soft and good to firm going: blinkered final start.
B. G. Powell

BOX CAR (IRE) 4 b.g. Blues Traveller (IRE) 119 – Racey Naskra (USA) 75 (Star de **48**
Naskra (USA)) [2001 70: 11.9f 16.5m 12.6d⁶ f8.5f⁴ Dec 5] poor maiden: left G. L. Moore
after reappearance: stays 12.6f: acts on fibresand and soft going: has worn sheepskin
cheek-pieces. *R. Wilman*

BOXER BILL 2 b.g. (Mar 27) Atraf 116 – Paper Maze 51 (Mazilier (USA) 107) [2001 **68**
5s⁶ e5g⁴ 5.3s⁵ 5.1d² 5m⁴ 6m² 5f² 5m 5g⁴ 5s⁶ Aug 19] 9,400Y: quite good-topped gelding:
first foal: dam, third at 5f on debut at 2 yrs, showed little afterwards: fair maiden: beaten
favourite 3 times: will prove best at 5f/easy 6f: acts on firm and soft going: tried visored:
usually races prominently: difficult ride: sent to Macau. *W. G. M. Turner*

BOX HILL WESTERN 2 b.c. (Apr 19) Lugana Beach 116 – Currer Bell (Belmez **49**
(USA) 131) [2001 6.9m 6.1m 5m Jul 30] 7,000Y: first foal: dam, showed some ability in
a bumper, well beaten only Flat start: poor maiden: dead. *R. Hannon*

BOY BAND (IRE) 3 b.g. Desert Style (IRE) 121 – Arab Scimetar (IRE) (Sure Blade **47**
(USA) 130) [2001 48: 8s⁶ 8.2s 7m⁵ 7s May 17] leggy, workmanlike gelding: poor
maiden: stays 1m: acts on soft going, probably on good to firm. *M. R. Channon*

BRADY BOYS (USA) 4 b.g. Cozzene (USA) – Elvia (USA) (Roberto (USA) 131) **54**
[2001 76: 6d 10m 8.3v³ Nov 8] strong, lengthy gelding: modest maiden in 2001: stays
1¼m: acts on heavy ground: blinkered on debut: has carried head high. *J. G. M. O'Shea*

BRAGADINO 2 b.c. (May 9) Zilzal (USA) 137 – Graecia Magna (USA) 109 (Private **104 p**
Account (USA)) [2001 7.1m* 7m² 8s⁶ Sep 29] close-coupled, quite good-topped colt:
half-brother to several winners, including 3-y-o Demophilos, and smart 7f/1m performer
Thourios (by Green Desert): dam 7f (at 2 yrs) and 1½m winner: useful form: landed odds
in maiden at Sandown in July: keeping-on 2 lengths second to Naheef in Vintage Stakes
at Goodwood following month: co-favourite, possibly unsuited by soft ground when only
sixth of 9 in Royal Lodge Stakes at Ascot: will probably stay 1¼m: remains capable of
better. *Sir Michael Stoute*

BRAIGO (IRE) 2 ch.f. (May 4) Woodborough (USA) 112 – Golden Form (Formid- **32**
able (USA) 125) [2001 6d p7g f6g f5s Dec 27] small, sturdy filly: half-sister to several
winners, including fairly useful 2000 2-y-o 5f/6f winner Soldier On (by General Monash)
and useful 7f (at 2 yrs) to 1¼m (in USA) winner Rug (by Persian Bold): dam Irish winner
around 9f (including at 2 yrs, and in listed race): poor maiden. *H. Morrison*

BRAINWAVE 3 b.f. Mind Games 121 – Thorner Lane 86 (Tina's Pet 121) [2001 59p: **72**
5.1s⁴ 6g 6m⁴ 6.1m 5.1g* 5.1g⁵ 5m* 5m Sep 6] sturdy filly: fair performer: won minor
event at Chepstow in July and handicap at Folkestone in August: broke leg final start: was
speedy and best at 5f: acted on good to firm going, probably on soft: dead. *H. Candy*

BRAMBLE 3 ch.g. Polar Falcon (USA) 126 – Sharpthorne (USA) 91 (Sharpen Up **65**
127) [2001 6d 6.1d 5.1f* 5m 5m 5g 5g 5g p5g Dec 22] well-made gelding: fifth foal:
closely related to fairly useful 1998 2-y-o 5f winner Thicket (by Wolfhound) and half-

brother to 2 sprint winners, including 6-y-o Cold Climate: dam 6f (including at 2 yrs) winner: fair performer: made all in maiden at Bath in May: left R. Charlton after next start: best efforts at 5f: acts on firm going: tongue tied fourth start: has been slowly away: hung left off home turn final outing. *Mrs L. Stubbs*

BRAMLEY DANCER   2 b.c. (May 1) Suave Dancer (USA) 136 – Hailgaf 61 (Raja Baba (USA)) [2001 p7g Dec 22] second reported foal: dam, maiden who stayed 1¼m, half-sister to useful performer up to 1½m Cameo Performance: 12/1, well beaten in minor event at Lingfield, slowly away. *J. Noseda* —

BRAM STOKER (IRE)   3 ch.c. General Monash (USA) 107 – Taniokey (Grundy 137) [2001 103: 7d⁴ 8g 6s⁶ 5g 8d 6d 5d³ Dec 21] sturdy, quite attractive colt: has a quick action: useful performer: not discredited when fourth to Clearing in European Free Handicap at Newmarket on reappearance, but well below form subsequently, leaving R. Hannon after third start: probably best at 6f: acts on good to firm and good to soft ground: blinkered fifth appearance. *A. Peraino, Italy*   **100 d**

BRAND NEW DAY (IRE)   3 b.c. Robellino (USA) 127 – Nawaji (USA) 45 (Trempolino (USA) 135) [2001 –: f8g e8g e7g f11g 10g 10m⁵ 13.8m Sep 22] smallish, workmanlike colt: little form: blinkered/visored first 4 starts. *D. W. P. Arbuthnot* —

BRANDON COURT (IRE)   10 b.g. Law Society (USA) 130 – Dance Date (IRE) (Sadler's Wells (USA) 132) [2001 f12g f11g 11.6g May 8] modest handicapper: well held on Flat in 2001. *I. A. Balding* —

BRANDON ROCK   4 b.g. Robellino (USA) 127 – The Kings Daughter 79 (Indian King (USA) 128) [2001 –: f7g f5g 6f 6m 7f 5m 8.1m Jul 25] good-topped gelding: no form in 2001, leaving N. Littmoden after second start: tried blinkered. *Julian Poulton* —

BRANDY COVE   4 b.g. Lugana Beach 116 – Tender Moment (IRE) 78 (Caerleon (USA) 132) [2001 74: f8g f8g³ f8.5g 8.2v 7g 7.5f p10g Dec 12] tall, quite attractive gelding: fair performer: well below form after second start in 2001 (gelded before final one): should stay 1¼m: acts on fibresand, best turf effort on soft going: has been slowly away. *B. Smart*   **a74**

BRANSTON GEM   3 br.f. So Factual (USA) 120 – Branston Jewel (IRE) 95 (Prince Sabo 123) [2001 59: 5f⁵ f5g 7.5m⁵ 8f Sep 20] poor maiden: probably stays easy 7f: acts on soft ground, good to firm and fibresand: sometimes slowly away: has raced freely. *M. Johnston*   **42**

BRANSTON LUCY   4 b.f. Prince Sabo 123 – Softly Spoken 87 (Mummy's Pet 125) [2001 65d: e6g Jan 3] modest performer: below form only start in 2001: tried in hood/blinkers. *J. Pearce* —

BRANSTON PICKLE   4 ch.g. Piccolo 121 – Indefinite Article (IRE) (Indian Ridge 123) [2001 69, a82: f5g⁶ f5g² f5s³ f5s⁵ f6g² e5g² f6g* f5g e5g⁵ f6g³ e5g⁵ f5g f6g f5g 5v 5m f5g³ 5m f5g² f5g f6g² f6s² f6g* f6g⁵ 5.1d f6g f5g⁴ f5g² f5g² f5s f5s³ f5s² p6g Dec 29] smallish gelding: fair on all-weather, modest on turf: won claimer in February and handicap in September, both at Wolverhampton: raced only at 5f/6f: acts on fibresand/equitrack and soft going: tried blinkered, often visored: has worn tongue tie: often races prominently: tough. *P. D. Evans*   **50 a77**

BRANSTON TIGER   2 b.c. (May 14) Mark of Esteem (IRE) 137 – Tuxford Hideaway 102 (Cawston's Clown 113) [2001 6.1f 7m² 7f² f7g³ Aug 18] rangy colt: half-brother to numerous winners, notably smart 5f (including at 2 yrs) to 7f winner Branston Abby (by Risk Me): dam sprinter: fair maiden: placed at Newcastle, Redcar and Wolverhampton: should stay 1m: acts on fibresand, raced only on ground firmer than good on turf. *M. Johnston*   **76**

BRASSIKA   2 ch.f. (Apr 3) Whittingham (IRE) 104 – Tough Nell (IRE) 61 (Archway (IRE) 115) [2001 5.3s⁴ 6m 5s Oct 5] first foal: dam, lightly-raced 2-y-o maiden, out of half-sister to smart French performer up to 11f Schwepperusschian: modest maiden: left G. L. Moore and off 4½ months before running poorly final start: should stay 7f. *S. Dow*   **64**

BRATBY (IRE)   5 b.g. Distinctly North (USA) 115 – Aridje 79 (Mummy's Pet 125) [2001 –: f7g f7g f6s f6g f7s f7g f5g f7f f16g Mar 26] no longer of much account. *M. C. Chapman* —

BRAVE BURT (IRE)   4 ch.g. Pips Pride 117 – Friendly Song 48 (Song 132) [2001 91: 6s 6g 5m 5g* 5g² 5g 5v Oct 27] good-topped gelding: useful handicapper, lightly raced: won at Newmarket in July by 2½ lengths from Our Fred: good second to Corridor Creeper at Ascot later in month: well held last 2 starts (reportedly lost action on   **95**

penultimate): speedy, and probably best at 5f: acts on firm going, probably on good to soft: often bandaged: races prominently: gelded after final start. *D. Nicholls*

BRAVE EDGE 10 b.g. Beveled (USA) – Daring Ditty (Daring March 116) [2001 91: – 5.2d 6m 6m May 26] good-topped gelding: one-time useful performer: on a long losing sequence, and well held in 2001. *R. Hannon*

BRAVE EMIR 2 b.g. (Mar 26) Emarati (USA) 74 – Hearten (Hittite Glory 125) [2001 **63** 5.2g 5m⁴ 5g f6g Oct 22] 16,000Y: half-brother to numerous winners, including smart sprinter Northern Goddess (by Night Shift) and 1m winner Racing Heart (by Pursuit of Love): dam unraced: modest maiden: easily best effort on second start: headstrong, and likely to prove best at 5f/6f: tongue tied final outing (gelded after). *J. W. Hills*

BRAVE GIRAFFE 2 b.c. (Mar 29) Distant Relative 128 – Prinia (Priolo (USA) 127) – [2001 6g 8d Oct 19] 6,000Y: leggy, quite attractive colt: first foal: dam, ran twice, out of half-sister to Oaks winner Intrepidity: well held in maidens. *Miss D. A. McHale*

BRAVE KNIGHT 4 b.g. Presidium 124 – Agnes Jane (Sweet Monday 122) [2001 49: **43** 10f 9.9m 10.1m 10.5d⁶ 9.9m 16m 8d³ 9.9m³ 10g 9.9s Sep 25] poor maiden: stays 1¼m: has looked temperamental. *N. Bycroft*

BRAVE SHAMAN (IRE) 2 b.c. (Apr 2) Common Grounds 118 – Indiana Bride – (IRE) (Indian Ridge 123) [2001 5m May 21] IR 3,200Y, 8,500 2-y-o: first foal: dam, unraced daughter of Poule d'Essai des Pouliches winner Ukraine Girl: 12/1, pulled up soon after start in maiden at Musselburgh: dead. *K. A. Ryan*

BRAVO 3 b. or br.g. Efisio 120 – Apache Squaw 54 (Be My Guest (USA) 126) [2001 –: **61** f7g f8g f8g³ 8d⁴ f9.4g⁶ 12.4g³ 12.4g⁶ 12.4m² 12.1g 12g⁶ Sep 19] workmanlike gelding: modest maiden handicapper: stays 1½m: acts on good to soft ground, good to firm and fibresand: has started slowly/carried head awkwardly: sold 12,000 gns. *C. W. Thornton*

BRAVURA 3 ch.g. Never So Bold 135 – Sylvan Song (Song 132) [2001 –: e7g* e7g⁴ **54** 7f 7.6f 7m 7.1m 7m f8g p7g⁵ p7g⁶ p7g p10g³ Dec 22] modest handicapper: won at **a62** Lingfield in March: stays easy 1¼m: acts on firm ground and equitrack/polytrack: tried blinkered: often slowly away. *G. L. Moore*

BRAZILIAN MOOD (IRE) 5 b.g. Doyoun 124 – Sea Mistress (Habitat 134) [2001 – 70: e10g 9.7v Apr 24] lightly-raced handicapper: no form in 2001: blinkered final start. *C. E. Brittain*

BREAKFAST BAY (IRE) 3 b. or br.f. Charnwood Forest (IRE) 125 – Diavolina **74** (USA) (Lear Fan (USA) 130) [2001 80: 7.1m 7.1m⁶ 8f⁴ 8m⁵ 8m 8.3m⁵ 7.1f Sep 18] strong, close-coupled filly: fair performer: stays 1m: acts on firm going, probably on good to soft: has started slowly/raced freely/shown signs of temperament: sold 13,000 gns. *R. Charlton*

City Index Rated Stakes (Handicap), Ascot—
eighth success of the year for Brevity, who holds off Trace Clip and Halmahera

BREAK THE GLASS (USA) 4 b. or br.g. Dynaformer (USA) – Greek Wedding –
(USA) (Blushing Groom (FR) 131) [2001 84: f9.4s⁶ f12g Feb 13] good-bodied gelding:
fairly useful maiden in 2000: well beaten both 4-y-o starts. *R. Ford*

BREAK THE RULES 9 b.g. Dominion 123 – Surf Bird (Shareef Dancer (USA) 135) –
[2001 –: f14g Mar 24] neat gelding: fair handicapper in 1998: lightly raced and well
beaten since: blinkered once. *A. G. Juckes*

BREATHLESS DREAMS (IRE) 4 ch.g. College Chapel 122 – Foston Bridge 68 **64**
(Relkino 131) [2001 –: 7m 5m 7m² 7m 5.1g⁶ f5g 7s Oct 16] big gelding: has a round
action: modest nowadays: left S. Kettlewell before final start: stays 7f: acts on good to
firm going, probably on soft: tried visored. *M. Wigham*

BRECONGILL LAD 9 b.g. Clantime 101 – Chikala 81 (Pitskelly 122) [2001 93+: **82 d**
6s 5.1f⁵ 5m 5m 5m⁴ 6m 5g 6m 5g³ 6f 5d 5m⁶ 5g 5g 5d⁴ Nov 6] tall, good-topped gelding:
fairly useful performer: on the downgrade in 2001, leaving D. Nicholls after sixth start:
effective at 5f/6f: acts on firm and soft going: tried blinkered/visored earlier in career: has
hung/carried head high/idled: usually held up. *Mrs M. Reveley*

BREMRIDGE (IRE) 4 ch.g. Ridgewood Ben 113 – Eimkar (Junius (USA) 124) –
[2001 –: f12g³ f8.5g Mar 8] fair maiden at 2 yrs: well held since. *G. Brown*

BRESSBEE (USA) 3 ch.c. Twining (USA) 120 – Bressay (USA) (Nureyev (USA) **79**
131) [2001 83: f8g² f7g* 9s⁶ 8g 7m f8g 8d f8g f9.4g f9.4f³ f9.4s* f9.4s³ f8.5s Dec 27]
$75,000F, IR 28,000Y: close-coupled, quite attractive colt: first foal: dam, 1¼m winner
in France and later successful in USA, granddaughter of Oaks third Britannia's Rule: fair
performer: trained at 2 yrs by L. Browne in Ireland: won maiden at Southwell in February
and handicap at Wolverhampton (made all) in December: stays 9.4f: acts on fibresand
and soft ground, probably on firm: visored last 3 starts. *K. R. Burke*

BREST (IRE) 2 b.f. (Apr 28) General Monash (USA) 107 – Armadillo (IRE) **76**
(Dominion 123) [2001 6m⁵ 5.7g* 6g 6g Oct 6] IR 1,300Y, resold IR 26,000Y: second
foal: dam, third up to 7f in Ireland, out of useful Irish sprinter Princess Seal: fair form:
won maiden at Bath in August: respectable eleventh of 29 in valuable sales race at the
Curragh next time: should stay 7f: sold 11,000 gns. *G. C. Bravery*

BREVITY 6 b.g. Tenby 125 – Rive (USA) (Riverman (USA) 131) [2001 62: f5g e6g⁶ **108**
f5g⁶ e7g⁶ 5.3s³ 5v⁶ 6v 6m* 6f* 6f* 7m* 7f² 6m* 6m* 6f 6f* 6m* 6g 6m 5g³ 6m 5.6m⁴
6m² Sep 22] big, strong gelding: useful performer: considerably better than ever in 2001:
thrived on racing, winning amateur minor event at Hamilton and handicaps (all bar one of
them for claimer P. Fitzsimons) at Brighton (2), Leicester, Epsom (2), Salisbury and
Ascot between May/July: some good efforts after, particularly last 2 starts when fourth to
Smokin Beau in Portland at Doncaster and neck second to Continent in Ayr Gold Cup:
effective at stiff 5f to easy 7f: acts on fibresand/equitrack, best turf efforts on good going
or firmer: has worn crossed noseband/tongue tie and been early to post: sometimes carries
head awkwardly: often makes running: tough and game: a great credit to connections.
J. M. Bradley

BREW 5 b.g. Primo Dominie 121 – Boozy 111 (Absalom 128) [2001 55d: 5m 5m 5m –
Sep 8] well-made gelding: maiden handicapper. *A. Berry*

BRIANS BAY 3 b.g. River Falls 113 – Petrina Bay 67 (Clantime 101) [2001 6m 7g⁵ –
f6g 5.1m 6.1s 8.5s 8s 10d 10v f8.5g Dec 11] 1,100Y: small, strong gelding: third foal:
dam, 5f winner, sister to useful sprinter Saint Express: little form: blinkered final start.
J. Gallagher

BRIDE'S BOUNTY 2 b.f. (Apr 12) Aragon 118 – Bride's Reprisal 87 (Dunbeath –
(USA) 127) [2001 5m 7s 7d Nov 6] 1,200Y: first foal: dam 2-y-o 5f winner: well beaten
in maidens. *E. W. Tuer*

BRIDEWELL (USA) 2 b.g. (Jan 29) Woodman (USA) 126 – La Alleged (USA) **84**
(Alleged (USA) 138) [2001 6m 8m 7.1v² 7.2v Oct 15] neat gelding: has a round action:
first foal: dam unraced half-sister to Breeders' Cup Juvenile Fillies winner Outstandingly
and to dam of smart Irish 6f/7f performer Bernstein: easily best effort in maidens (fairly
useful form) when second at Haydock, racing freely and leading from 2f out until close
home: ran as if something amiss final start: will probably stay 1m: acts on heavy ground:
sold 7,500 gns and gelded. *M. R. Channon*

BRIDGE STREET LAD 3 b.g. Puissance 110 – Bridge Street Lady 93 (Decoy Boy –
129) [2001 7.1m 6m 6v Oct 29] fifth reported living foal: half-brother to 5f winner
Windrush Boy (by Dowsing): dam sprinter: well held in maidens. *M. R. Bosley*

BRIDIE'S PRIDE 10 b.g. Alleging (USA) 120 – Miss Monte Carlo 75 (Reform 132) –
[2001 77, a–: 16v 16s 21.6s Apr 23] fair handicapper at best: well beaten at 10 yrs.
G. A. Ham

BRIEF CONTACT (IRE) 3 b.g. Brief Truce (USA) 126 – Incommunicado (IRE) **43**
(Sadler's Wells (USA) 132) [2001 38: 8.2v 10.1m[6] 9.9m 11.9f[6] 10.9g 8m Aug 30] poor
maiden: stays easy 1¼m: acts on good to firm going. *Jamie Poulton*

BRIEF KEY (IRE) 3 b.f. Brief Truce (USA) 126 – Latch Key Lady (USA) 48 –
(Tejano (USA)) [2001 –: f7g 7.5m 6m Jun 4] little form: left N. Tinkler after
reappearance. *Don Enrico Incisa*

BRIERY (IRE) 3 ch.f. Salse (USA) 128 – Wedgwood (USA) (Woodman (USA) 126) **66 +**
[2001 6g 7g* 7.6g[3] Sep 5] second foal: dam unraced daughter of Cheveley Park winner/
Irish 1000 Guineas second Woodstream: fair form: won maiden at Newcastle in August:
looked none too co-operative throughout final start: stays 7f. *W. J. Haggas*

BRIERY MEC 6 b.g. Ron's Victory (USA) 129 – Briery Fille 81 (Sayyaf 121) [2001 **65**
59: e12g[3] 9.9m 10f[3] 10.5g 10.1g[3] 10g* 11.5f 10m* 10m[4] 10.4m 10d p12g[4] p13g[6] Dec 29]
tall gelding: fair handicapper: won at Pontefract (ladies) in July and Windsor
(apprentices) in August: effective at 1¼m/easy 1½m: acts on soft going, good to firm and
polytrack/equitrack: has raced freely: often held up. *H. J. Collingridge*

BRIGADIER JONES (IRE) 2 br.g. (Apr 2) Emperor Jones (USA) 119 – Fight **100**
Right (FR) (Crystal Glitters (USA) 127) [2001 7d[4] f6g* a8.5f Dec 15] IR 8,700F, IR
8,200Y: rather leggy, quite good-topped gelding: half-brother to 3 winners in France,
including 1¼m/11f winner Royal Groom (by Al Nasr): dam French 2-y-o 1m winner:
confirmed promise when winning maiden at Southwell in October easily by 3 lengths
from Red Forest: left H. Akbary, 12½ lengths last of 8 behind Siphonic in Hollywood
Futurity: seems to stay 8.5f. *Kathy Walsh, USA*

BRIGADORE 2 b.c. (Jan 26) Magic Ring (IRE) 115 – Music Mistress (IRE) 55 **92**
(Classic Music (USA)) [2001 5v[6] 5d[2] 5d[4] 5d* 5m* 5m[2] 5m[5] 5.1m* 5m[3] 6m Sep 12]
5,000F, 3,200Y: close-coupled, good-quartered colt: second foal: dam, 2-y-o 5f winner
who stayed 7f, out of half-sister to smart sprinter Puissance: fairly useful performer: won
maiden and minor event at Newcastle in May: good 2½ lengths third to Whitbarrow in
Molecomb Stakes at Goodwood: likely to prove best at 5f: acts on good to firm and good
to soft going: races prominently: tough and consistent. *J. R. Weymes*

BRIGHT AND CLEAR 2 b.f. (Apr 24) Danehill (USA) 126 – Shining Water 111 **102**
(Kalaglow 132) [2001 7g[2] 7g* 7g[5] 7d Oct 20] good-topped filly: half-sister to numerous
winners, including high-class 7f (at 2 yrs) to 10.4f winner Tenby (by Caerleon) and smart
winner up to 1½m Bristol Channel (by Generous): dam won Solario Stakes and second in
Park Hill: useful form: won maiden at Newmarket in August despite edging left: very
good 1¾ lengths fifth of 17 to Quarter Moon in Moyglare Stud Stakes at the Curragh
following month: off 7 weeks before running poorly (possibly unsuited by softer ground)
in Rockfel Stakes at Newmarket: will stay at least 1m. *B. W. Hills*

BRIGHT EDGE 2 ch.f. (Feb 28) Danehill Dancer (IRE) 117 – Beveled Edge 60 **87**
(Beveled (USA)) [2001 5f[2] 6.1g* 6g* 6m[2] 7d[4] Aug 26] 4,000Y: tall, rather unfurnished
filly: third foal: dam 6f winner at 4 yrs: fairly useful performer: won maiden at Nottingham in June and minor event at Windsor in July: in frame in minor event at Windsor (hung
under pressure) and Prestige Stakes at Goodwood (fourth to Gossamer) last 2 starts: best
effort at 6f: acts on firm and good to soft ground. *B. Palling*

BRIGHTER FUTURE 2 b.f. (Feb 19) Night Shift (USA) – Welsh Mist 102 **56**
(Damister (USA) 123) [2001 5d 6d 6v Nov 8] 60,000Y: second foal: half-sister to 3-y-o
Early Morning Mist: dam 5f (including at 2 yrs)/6f winner: modest maiden: likely to
prove best at 5f/6f. *B. W. Hills*

BRIGHT HOPE (IRE) 5 b.m. Danehill (USA) 126 – Crystal Cross (USA) 88 **75**
(Roberto (USA) 131) [2001 –: 11.9d 10m[5] Jun 29] well-made mare: fairly useful winner
at 3 yrs: fair form at best since: stays 1¼m: acts on good to firm going. *P. W. Harris*

BRIGHT MIST 2 b.f. (Mar 24) Anita's Prince 126 – Out On Her Own (Superlative –
118) [2001 6.1v Oct 4] 3,200Y: rather leggy, quite good-topped filly: fourth reported live
foal: sister to 6-y-o Arbenig: dam Irish 2-y-o 6f winner: well held in maiden at
Nottingham. *B. Palling*

BRIGHT SMILE (IRE) 3 b.f. Caerleon (USA) 132 – Never So Fair 65 (Never So **83**
Bold 135) [2001 8d[4] 10.2m[2] 10m* 10.3v p10g Nov 13] sixth foal: closely related to smart
6f (at 2 yrs) to 9f (in USA) winner Circle of Gold and useful 1996 2-y-o 6f winner Crystal
Crossing (both by Royal Academy), and half-sister to 2 winners: dam ran 3 times: fairly

useful form: won maiden at Nottingham in July: not sure to stay much beyond 1¼m: acts on good to firm going. *J. H. M. Gosden*

BRIGHT SPANGLE (IRE) 2 ch.f. (Feb 13) General Monash (USA) 107 – No **67** Shame 56 (Formidable (USA) 125) [2001 5g⁶ f5g 6m² 7m 6.1m* 6d 7g Sep 15] strong, sturdy filly: first foal: dam, maiden who stayed 7f (ran only at 2 yrs), half-sister to 4-y-o Hunting Lion: fair performer: won maiden at Chepstow in July: below form in nurseries after: should stay 7f: acts on good to firm ground: edgy final start. *B. Palling*

BRIGHT SPARK (IRE) 4 b.g. Sri Pekan (USA) 117 – Exciting (Mill Reef (USA) **84** 141) [2001 8.2v⁴ 9d 6.9v* 10g 8m* 7s² 7g 10g⁶ Sep 8] IR 70,000Y: half-brother to several winners, notably very smart 6f (at 2 yrs) to 1m winner Almushtarak (by Fairy King): dam once-raced sister to smart stayer The Miller: fairly useful performer: made all in maiden at Folkestone in April and minor event at Musselburgh in June: stays 1m: acts on heavy and good to firm going: sold 22,000 gns, then gelded. *G. Wragg*

BRIG O'TURK 4 ch.g. Inchinor 119 – Sharmood (USA) (Sharpen Up 127) [2001 72: **53** 11.6m* 10m 10g 11.6g f12s Dec 26] leggy, close-coupled gelding: modest performer, lightly raced: won claimer at Windsor in June: left C. Mann and off 5 months before running badly final start: stays 11.6f: acts on good to firm and good to soft going: has raced freely/looked unenthusiastic. *J. S. Moore*

BRILLANO (FR) 2 b.f. (Feb 5) Desert King (IRE) 129 – Voliere (USA) (Arctic Tern **75 p** (USA) 126) [2001 7d 7v* Oct 24] 26,000F, 41,000Y: sturdy filly: fourth foal: half-sister to 2 winners in France by Alzao, including 1m/1¼m winner Voltage: dam, French 1m winner, out of half-sister to smart French performers up to 1m Vorias and Verria: better effort in maidens when winning 5-runner one at Newcastle in October by 3½ lengths from Aberthatch, leading halfway: will stay 1m: should improve. *Miss J. A. Camacho*

BRILLIANT BASIL (USA) 2 b.g. (Mar 15) Hazaam (USA) 113 – Speed Shift **80** (USA) (Foyt (USA)) [2001 f5g² f5g² Dec 17] 10,000 2-y-o: half-brother to 3 minor winners in USA: dam unraced: patiently ridden when second in maidens at Southwell, fairly useful form on first occasion: will stay 6f. *Mrs L. Stubbs*

BRILLIANT RED 8 b.g. Royal Academy (USA) 130 – Red Comes Up (USA) **103** (Blushing Groom (FR) 131) [2001 109: e10g 10s 8.1v⁵ 8m* 8f 8.1g⁴ 8g⁶ 8g 9m⁶ 8d³ 8d p10g p10g³ p10g³ Dec 12] tall, lengthy gelding: has a long stride: useful handicapper: won at Goodwood in May by ½ length from Calcutta, pair clear: respectable efforts at best after: effective at 1m/1¼m: acts on firm going, soft and all-weather: sometimes visored: often tongue tied: races up with pace. *Mrs L. Richards*

BRILLIANTRIO 3 ch.f. Selkirk (USA) 129 – Loucoum (FR) 93 (Iron Duke (FR) **71 +** 122) [2001 74: 8v 8g⁴ 9.9m⁵ 8m⁵ 8.5f³ 7.5f³ 7.5m⁵ 7.1m² Aug 22] big, workmanlike filly: fair performer: effective at 7f to 8.5f: acts on firm going: has been early/led to post: very unruly at stalls penultimate 2-y-o start: has raced freely/found little. *Miss J. A. Camacho*

BRILLYANT DANCER 3 b.f. Environment Friend 128 – Brillyant Glen (IRE) **47** (Glenstal (USA) 118) [2001 48: 7.5m⁶ 8m 8d 8f Sep 4] poor maiden: should stay 1¼m. *Mrs A. Duffield*

BRIMSTONE (IRE) 6 ch.g. Ballad Rock 122 – Blazing Glory (IRE) (Glow (USA)) **51** [2001 –: 5.2m⁴ 5m⁶ 5.7m 5s⁶ 6f² Sep 10] tall, good-topped gelding: one-time fairly useful performer, modest nowadays: probably best around 6f: acts on equitrack, best turf efforts on good going or firmer: visored nowadays: has been slowly away. *Mrs D. Haine*

BRING SWEETS 5 b.g. Sabrehill (USA) 120 – Che Gambe (USA) (Lyphard (USA) **94** 132) [2001 –: 12v³ Mar 24] fairly useful performer: creditable third to Lucido in minor event at Doncaster only 5-y-o start: stayed 1½m: went well on ground softer than good (acted on heavy): blinkered once at 3 yrs: dead. *B. Ellison*

BRIONEY (IRE) 4 ch.f. Barathea (IRE) 127 – La Vigie (King of Clubs 124) [2001 **–** 70+: f12g⁶ f12g f12g Jun 20] fair winner at 3 yrs: well held in 2001, leaving J. Gosden 4,000 gns before final outing: blinkered once: tongue tied. *J. A. Glover*

BRITTANY GIRL 3 b.f. Faustus (USA) 118 – Kimble Princess (Kala Shikari 125) **–** [2001 8.1m 8.2v f8.5g Nov 3] small filly: half-sister to 1995 2-y-o 5f winner Nellie North (by Northern State): dam ran twice at 2 yrs: no form in maidens. *J. W. Unett*

BROADWAY BANKER (FR) 2 b.c. (Mar 22) Broadway Flyer (USA) 121 – Hariti **58 ?** (IRE) 45 (Flash of Steel 120) [2001 8g⁵ 8g Oct 19] 3,800F, 145,000 francs Y: good-topped colt: has scope: fourth foal: dam thrice-raced granddaughter of 1000 Guineas winner Caergwrle: backward, modest form at best in maidens: will be suited by 1¼m+. *J. W. Hills*

BROADWAY LEGEND (IRE)   4 b.f. Caerleon (USA) 132 – Tetradonna (IRE) 102   –
(Teenoso (USA) 135) [2001 90: 10.3m 10.4m 10m Jun 7] tall, angular filly: fairly useful
performer at 3 yrs: little form in 2001. *J. W. Hills*

BROADWAY SCORE (USA)   3 b.c. Theatrical 128 – Brocaro (USA) (Mr Prospector   **80 p**
(USA)) [2001 8d⁶ 9g* Sep 2] quite attractive colt: eighth foal: brother to a 1m to 11f
winner in USA, and half-brother to winners up to 1m in USA by Dahar and Strawberry
Road: dam ran once in France: confirmed promise of debut nearly 5 months earlier
(having reportedly had training accident) when winning maiden at Sandown by ¾ length
from Weecandoo, never far away and leading just inside final 1f: reluctant at stalls: likely
to do better still, particularly at 1¼m+. *J. W. Hills*

BROCHE (USA)   4 b.c. Summer Squall (USA) – Ribbonwood (USA) 100 (Diesis   **107 +**
133) [2001 112: a8f⁴ a12f* a10f² a10f 10m⁶ 11.9s² Aug 18] strong, smallish, quite attrac-   **a117**
tive colt: smart performer: won handicap at Nad Al Sheba in January: very good ½-length
second to Hightori in Maktoum Challenge (Round III) there in March: creditable
½-length second to Yavana's Pace in minor event at Haydock final start: stays 1½m: acts
on dirt and soft going: tried visored (below form) in Dubai World Cup and Eclipse Stakes:
has been bandaged behind: has acted as pacemaker. *Saeed bin Suroor*

BROCKETEER   2 b.g. (Mar 9) Prince Sabo 123 – Mistral's Dancer (Shareef Dancer   –
(USA) 135) [2001 6g 5.7g 6s Oct 5] 13,500Y: seventh foal: brother to 7f winner Cruise
and half-brother to 2 winners, including 7-y-o Queen's Pageant: dam, maiden, best at 7f:
behind in maidens. *J. A. Osborne*

BROKEN BARRICADES (IRE)   2 gr.c. (Apr 12) Common Grounds 118 – Gratclo   **88 d**
65 (Belfort (FR) 89) [2001 6m³ 6m* 6m 7d 6d Oct 18] 50,000Y: close-coupled colt:
seventh foal: brother to useful 1996 2-y-o 6f (July Stakes) winner Rich Ground and
half-brother to 3 winners, including 4-y-o Bandanna: dam 6f (including at 2 yrs)/7f
winner: fairly useful performer: won maiden at Salisbury in August: ran badly last 2
starts: not sure to stay beyond 6f: yet to race on extremes of going. *B. W. Hills*

BROKE ROAD (IRE)   5 b.g. Deploy 131 – Shamaka 53 (Kris 135) [2001 –: 12m⁴   –
f16.2g Jul 12] angular gelding: no form since 1999: sometimes blinkered. *Mrs V. C. Ward*

BRONX BOMBER   3 ch.g. Prince Sabo 123 – Super Yankee (IRE) (Superlative 118)   **47**
[2001 6.9m⁴ 7g 6g 8g p6g Dec 19] first foal: dam unraced daughter of useful sprinter
Four-Legged-Friend: poor maiden: tongue tied final start. *Dr J. D. Scargill*

BROOKSBY WHORLTON (IRE)   7 b.g. Commanche Run 133 – Superlee (IRE)   –
(Le Moss) 135) [2001 14.1v 14.6s Nov 9] tall, good-topped gelding: second foal: dam
unraced: well beaten in minor events: winning hurdler. *R. Bastiman*

BROTHER JOE (NZ)   7 ch.g. Hula Town (NZ) – Olivia Rose (NZ) (Travolta (FR))   **111 +**
[2001 8.3g⁴ 16.2g² 16.1f⁶ 13.9g³ Aug 22] angular New Zealand-bred gelding: smart
performer: won 4 races up to 1m in native country, where second in St Leger: had little
luck in Northumberland Plate at Newcastle and Ebor at York last 2 starts in 2001, best
effort when 1¼ lengths third to Mediterranean in latter, forced to ease back a good dozen
places to get a run and finishing strongly: stays 2m, but not short of speed: acts on firm
and soft going: has his quirks: smart hurdler: type to win good prize on Flat. *P. J. Hobbs*

BROUGHTON KNOWS   4 b.g. Most Welcome 131 – Broughtons Pet (IRE) (Cyrano   **47**
de Bergerac 120) [2001 8.2v 6.9v 7m 8.3g 9.9s³ Sep 25] 2,000Y: tall gelding: second
foal: dam unraced: poor maiden: stays 1¼m: has been slowly away/carried head high.
W. J. Musson

BROUGHTON MAGIC (IRE)   6 ch.g. Archway (IRE) 115 – Magic Green (Magic   –
Mirror 105) [2001 47: f8g f8s* f9.4g f8.5g² May 19] modest handicapper, lightly raced: **a52**
won at Southwell in February: ran well in blinkers final start: best around 1m: acts on
fibresand. *W. J. Musson*

BROUGHTON MELODY   2 ch.f. (Jan 29) Alhijaz 122 – Broughton Singer (IRE)   –
61 (Common Grounds 118) [2001 7d 7s Nov 9] unfurnished filly: second foal: half-sister
to fairly useful 8.5f (at 2 yrs) and 9.7f winner Keltic Bard (by Emperor Jones): dam 9f
winner: well held in maidens. *W. J. Musson*

BROUGHTONS FLUSH   3 b.g. First Trump 118 – Glowing Reference (Reference   **48**
Point 139) [2001 55: f8g 10s f12g⁵ 11.6g f12g³ f12g² f14g Dec 14] poor maiden
handicapper: should stay 1¾m: acts on fibresand: sometimes slowly away. *W. J. Musson*

BROUGHTONS MILL   6 gr.g. Ron's Victory (USA) 129 – Sandra's Desire (Grey   –
Desire 115) [2001 47, a–: f12g 11.5m May 30] poor maiden at best: no form in 2001.
W. J. Musson

BROUGHTONS MOTTO   3 b.f. Mtoto 134 – Ice Chocolate (USA) 77 (Icecapade – (USA)) [2001 60: 10s 8.2v 7s f8.5g² f8.5g² f9.4s⁴ 8g 8d f8.5g³ f8.5g⁵ Nov 27] good- **a69** topped filly: fair handicapper on all-weather: should be suited by 1¼m+: acts on fibresand. *W. J. Musson*

BROUGHTON STORM   3 ch.g. Chaddleworth (IRE) 103 – Rainy Day Song 61 – (Persian Bold 123) [2001 –: e10g e8g f8g 8.2v⁵ 8.2s 10m 11.5m 10f Jun 1] little form: has worn tongue tie/blinkers. *W. J. Musson*

BROUGHTON ZEST   2 b.f. (Mar 30) Colonel Collins (USA) 122 – Broughtons – Relish (Nomination 125) [2001 6g 7m 6s 7d Oct 18] smallish filly: second foal: dam of no account: only a little sign of ability, including in seller. *W. J. Musson*

BROUGHTY CASTLE (IRE)   3 b.g. Inzar (USA) 112 – Heavenly Note 82 (Chief – Singer 131) [2001 10m 10.1g 11.9s Sep 30] 23,000Y: seventh foal: half-brother to 1996 2-y-o 5f winner Hil Rhapsody (by Anshan) and winner up to 9f in Germany by Magic Ring: dam 2-y-o 7.5f winner who probably stayed 1½m: well held in maidens. *B. J. Meehan*

BROWN EYES   2 b.f. (Jan 18) Danehill (USA) 126 – La Belle Otero (USA) 60 **86** (Nureyev (USA) 131) [2001 6f³ 7m* 7g Oct 6] 165,000Y: tall, rather leggy filly: has scope: first foal: dam, lightly-raced maiden, half-sister to US Grade 3 9f winner Summer Matinee: fairly useful performer: won maiden at Salisbury in August, making most: respectable tenth in listed event at Newmarket: will stay at least 1m. *B. W. Hills*

Sir Robert Ogden's "Brother Joe"

BROWN HOLLY 3 br.g. So Factual (USA) 120 – Scarlett Holly 81 (Red Sunset 120) –
[2001 –: 5.7m p6g Dec 19] well held in maidens. *H. E. Haynes*

BROWNING 6 b.g. Warrshan (USA) 117 – Mossy Rose 78 (King of Spain 121) [2001 **85**
67: e12g* e12g² 12m² 14.4m* 14m* 16f³ Sep 21] well-made gelding: fairly useful
handicapper on turf, fair on all-weather: better than ever in 2001, winning at Lingfield in
January and Kempton and Sandown in July: barely stays 2m: acts on firm going and
fibresand/equitrack: blinkered once at 5 yrs: takes good hold (has worn crossed
noseband): effective held up or ridden from front. *M. P. Tregoning*

BROWN MADDER (IRE) 2 ch.g. (Feb 7) Perugino (USA) 84 – El Pina (Be My **57**
Guest (USA) 126) [2001 5m⁴ 5m 5.6f 8m Sep 21] 14,000F, IR 22,000Y: big, close-
coupled gelding: half-brother to several winners, including useful 6f (at 2 yrs) to 1m
winner Mansion House (by Thatching) and 1½m winner Life Saver (by Commanche
Run), both in Ireland: dam unraced daughter of Princess Royal Stakes winner Aloft:
modest maiden: raced freely when last in nursery final start: bred to stay at least 7f: raced
only on ground firmer than good. *T. D. Easterby*

BROWNS DELIGHT 4 b.f. Runnett 125 – Fearless Princess (Tyrnavos 129) [2001 –
51: 10.9m 10.9m Sep 17] close-coupled filly: modest performer: no form at 4 yrs: tried
visored. *M. Tate*

BRUNNHILDE 3 ch.f. Wolfhound (USA) 126 – Vilanika (FR) 81 (Top Ville 129) **52**
[2001 61: 7s 10.9m 10.1m Jun 14] workmanlike filly: poor mover: modest maiden:
should stay beyond 1m: acts on soft ground. *John Berry*

BRYANO DE BERGERAC 2 b.c. (Feb 19) Cyrano de Bergerac 120 – Cow Pastures **82**
(Homing 130) [2001 5.1d 5f* 5d 5m Aug 2] 4,500Y, resold 5,500Y: sixth living foal:
half-brother to 2 winners, including 1994 2-y-o 7f seller winner Petindia (by Petong):
dam unraced: fairly useful form: won maiden at Lingfield in June: good eighth of 14 to
Whitbarrow in Molecomb Stakes at Goodwood final start: likely to prove best at sharp 5f:
acts on firm going. *M. D. I. Usher*

BUALADHBOS (IRE) 2 b.g. (Jan 30) Royal Applause 124 – Goodnight Girl (IRE) **61**
(Alzao (USA) 117) [2001 6m 6g 7.1d⁵ 7.1m⁶ Sep 17] 4,000F, 15,000Y: long-backed
gelding: fourth foal: half-brother to winners in Italy by Imp Society (5f to 7f) and
Namaqualand (1m/9f): dam, unraced, out of half-sister to Irish Oaks winner Regal
Exception: modest maiden: best effort in nursery final start: should stay 1m. *F. Jordan*

BUCKENHAM JEM 3 b.f. Wing Park 104 – Walk That Walk 61 (Hadeer 118) [2001 –
7m Aug 24] first foal: dam 2-y-o 5f winner: slowly away/pulled hard when well held in
claimer at Newmarket. *Mrs Lydia Pearce*

BUCKS 4 b.g. Slip Anchor 136 – Alligram (USA) 61 (Alysheba (USA)) [2001 14m² **86**
12g³ 14m⁴ 16v Oct 26] 140,000Y: quite good-topped gelding: third foal: half-brother
to very smart 1m/1¼m winner Kissogram (by Caerleon): dam lightly-raced daughter of
top-class miler Milligram: fairly useful maiden: best effort when 1½ lengths third to Turn
of A Century at Newmarket: stays 1½m: tailed off on heavy going. *Mrs A. J. Perrett*

BUDDELIEA 3 b.f. Pivotal 124 – Fernlea (USA) (Sir Ivor 135) [2001 54: f8g* e10g⁴ **75**
e10g² f11g² 9s 8m* 8m 7.1m6 8g² 7g 8f⁶ f8g f8.5g⁴ p10g p8g Dec 22] quite good-topped, **a69**
angular filly: fair performer: won maiden at Southwell in February and handicap at
Newcastle in May: has form at 11f, best efforts at 1m: acts on firm going and fibresand/
equitrack: visored (well held) final outing. *J. S. Moore*

BUDE 2 gr.g. (Apr 19) Environment Friend 128 – Gay Da Cheen (IRE) (Tenby 125) **63**
[2001 7.5s f9.4g⁵ f8s⁴ Dec 21] 5,000Y: rather leggy, quite good-topped gelding: first foal:
dam well beaten in sellers at 2 yrs: modest form in maidens: should stay 1¼m: acts on
fibresand. *S. A. Brookshaw*

BUDELLI (IRE) 4 b.g. Elbio 125 – Eves Temptation (IRE) (Glenstal (USA) 118) **90**
[2001 85: 6s⁶ 6m³ 6m⁵ 6f 6m⁵ 5m 6g² 6m² 6m 6g⁶ 6m² 5.7d⁶ 6m² 6g² 6d² 6d² 5s* 6g
Nov 5] strong gelding: fairly useful handicapper: won at Pontefract in October: stays
6f: acts on any going: visored (below form) once: has edged left: tough and consistent.
M. R. Channon

BUDOOR (IRE) 2 b.f. (Mar 26) Darshaan 133 – Haddeyah (USA) 68 (Dayjur (USA) **80 p**
137) [2001 8m³ 8.1v* Sep 29] rather lengthy filly: second foal: half-sister to 3-y-o
Makboola: dam, 6f winner only 2-y-o start, tailed off both outings at 3 yrs: favourite,
confirmed promise when winning maiden at Haydock in September by ½ length
from Dubai Belle, getting on top final 1f: will be suited by 1¼m+: open to further
improvement. *J. L. Dunlop*

BUENO VIDA (IRE) 2 b.c. (Apr 4) Petardia 113 – Pat Said No (IRE) 59 (Last **60** Tycoon 131) [2001 6g 7g 6d f8s³ p6g⁴ Dec 22] small colt: first foal: dam, second at 5f at 2 yrs, half-sister to useful stayer El Conquistador: modest maiden: barely stays 1m: blinkered last 2 starts, looking less than keen final one. *D. J. S. Cosgrove*

BUFFOON 2 ch.g. (Apr 15) Bijou d'Inde 127 – Jelabna (Jalmood (USA) 126) [2001 **56** 7m 7m⁴ f8.5s 8m 8s⁵ Oct 22] 9,200F, IR 11,000Y: leggy, close-coupled gelding: third foal: dam, ran once, half-sister to useful 6f to 1m performer Baaderah: modest maiden: should stay 1¼m: acts on soft and good to firm ground, well beaten on fibresand: sold 2,800 gns. *I. A. Balding*

BULA ROSE (IRE) 3 ch.f. Alphabatim (USA) 126 – Titled Dancer (IRE) (Where To **51** Dance (USA)) [2001 57: 8m 12m 12f 12f⁴ 14.4d Aug 8] modest performer: probably stays 1½m: seemed rather reluctant to race final start. *E. W. Tuer*

BULAWAYO 4 b.g. Prince Sabo 123 – Ra Ra Girl 77 (Shack (USA) 118) [2001 –, a70: **56** 6.1v 6f 7m⁴ 8d³ 7.5m 7.1f 7.5m 8.2g f8.5g⁶ f6g f6g⁴ f6g² Oct 20] strong, good-topped **a67** gelding: fair handicapper on all-weather, modest on turf: effective at 6f to 1m: acts on fibresand, good to firm and good to soft going. *B. A. McMahon*

BULLET 6 b.g. Alhijaz 122 – Beacon (High Top 131) [2001 12g 11.8s Oct 16] quite **–** attractive gelding: fair at 4 yrs: well held both 6-y-o starts. *M. C. Pipe*

BULLFIGHTER 2 b.g. (Mar 24) Makbul 104 – Bollin Victoria 51 (Jalmood (USA) **74** 126) [2001 5s f5g⁵ 5.3m⁴ 5.1m² 5m 5m⁵ 6s³ 5g² 5.1m 6m 6s f5g⁵ f6g f5s³ Dec 27] **a63** 24,000Y: neat gelding: fifth foal: half-brother to 2-y-o 5f winners Blushing Victoria (in 1997, by Weldnaas) and First Blood (in 1999, by Rambo Dancer), latter fairly useful, and to 3-y-o Lady Rock: dam, ran only at 2 yrs, third at 7f: fair maiden on turf, modest on all-weather: will prove best at 5f: acts on soft ground, good to firm and fibresand: tried blinkered: occasionally slowly away: usually races prominently. *N. P. Littmoden*

BULLSEFIA (USA) 3 gr.g. Holy Bull (USA) 134 – Yousefia (USA) 84 (Danzig **80** (USA)) [2001 82p: 7.1m* 7m⁵ 7.9m 7d Jul 23] strong, lengthy gelding: fairly useful performer: won maiden at Warwick in May: headstrong, and will need to settle better to stay beyond 7f: raced mainly on good to firm ground: sold 8,800 gns, sent to Singapore. *B. W. Hills*

BUNDY 5 b.g. Ezzoud (IRE) 126 – Sanctuary Cove (Habitat 134) [2001 73: 6m⁶ 6g 6m **67** 6m³ 6d² 6d 7m 6g⁵ 7.5s 6.1v⁵ 6v⁴ Oct 16] smallish, leggy gelding: fair performer: best at 6f/7f: acts on heavy and good to firm going, below form on fibresand: blinkered once at 3 yrs: often races prominently. *M. Dods*

BUNKUM 3 b.g. Robellino 127 – Spinning Mouse 65 (Bustino 136) [2001 –: **–** f12g* 11.8f 12.3m 14f⁵ Jul 5] quite good-topped gelding: modest performer: won **a59** handicap at Wolverhampton (flashed tail) in May: should stay beyond 1½m: acts on fibresand: visored final start: sold 8,000 gns. *M. L. W. Bell*

BUNTY 5 b.m. Presidium 124 – Shirlstar Investor (Some Hand 119) [2001 40: f8g f8g² **42** f9.4s³ f8s f8g 8.2v 7s⁵ 7m 6d 7m 6d 7.1m Jul 27] small, compact mare: poor performer: stays 1m: acts on firm going, soft and fibresand: none too consistent. *R. C. Spicer*

BURGUNDY 4 b.g. Lycius (USA) 124 – Decant 68 (Rousillon (USA) 133) [2001 102: **90** f8.5g⁶ 10g 8m 10m² 10g⁴ 10g⁵ 10m 10g⁵ 10d⁵ 8d p8g² Dec 22] smallish gelding: fairly useful performer: stays 1¼m: acts on equitrack/polytrack and good to firm ground: visored (ran well) last time: sometimes slowly away: has wandered/found nothing. *S. Dow*

BURJ AL ARAB 2 b.c. (Mar 2) Alderbrook 120 – Princess Moodyshoe 72 (Jalmood **81** (USA) 126) [2001 6g⁵ 8.1g⁵ 8d³ Oct 3] fourth foal: half-brother to useful 1999 2-y-o 5f to 1m winner Misbehave (by Reprimand): dam winner around 1½m and over hurdles: fairly useful maiden: best effort when staying-on fifth at Chepstow second start: will be suited by 1¼m+. *M. C. Pipe*

BURN BABY BURN (IRE) 2 b.f. (May 17) King's Theatre (IRE) 128 – Tropicaro **–** (FR) 116 (Caro 133) [2001 7s Nov 9] IR 47,000Y: leggy, plain filly: half-sister to 3 winners abroad, notably smart French winner up to 1¼m The Scout (by Kris): dam won Prix Marcel Boussac and stayed 1¼m: 25/1 and green, well held in maiden at Doncaster. *R. Hollinshead*

BURNING COST 11 br.m. Lochnager 132 – Sophie Avenue (Guillaume Tell (USA) **–** 121) [2001 8.1m⁶ Aug 1] of no account in recent years: dead. *R. E. Peacock*

BURNING IMPULSE 3 b.c. Cadeaux Genereux 131 – Isle of Flame (Shirley **93 p**
Heights 130) [2001 8m² 8f* 7g 8d* Oct 19] 82,000 2-y-o: third foal: half-brother to fairly
useful 1998 2-y-o 7f winner Eden (by Polish Precedent) and French 1m winner Aranda
(by Fairy King): dam unraced out of close relation to Middle Park winner Balla Cove:
fairly useful form: won maiden at Newcastle (easily) in September and 25-runner
handicap at Newmarket in October, latter by head from Thihn, travelling strongly and
battling on well: may prove best at 7f/1m: sold 120,000 gns, joined P. Webber: capable of
better still, and type to do well in useful handicaps in 2002. *J. Noseda*

BURNING SUN (USA) 2 b.c. (Jan 21) Danzig (USA) – Media Nox 98 (Lycius **76 p**
(USA) 124) [2001 7s⁵ Nov 9] good-topped colt: first foal: dam, 5f (in France at 2 yrs) to
1m (US Grade 2 event) winner, half-sister to smart French performer up to 1½m Bonash:
favourite but green and on toes, 4 lengths fifth of 14 to Ballet Score in maiden at
Doncaster, twice not clear run: sure to improve. *H. R. A. Cecil*

BURNING TRUTH (USA) 7 ch.g. Known Fact (USA) 135 – Galega (Sure Blade **65**
(USA) 130) [2001 69, a85: f11g⁴ f12g⁵* 10.3m⁶ 9.9f 8m 10.4m f8g⁵ f8g f9.4f⁴ f9.4s Dec **a78**
27] angular gelding: fluent mover: fair performer: won minor event at Wolverhampton in
March: in-and-out form after: effective at 1m, probably at easy 1½m: acts on firm going,
soft and fibresand/equitrack: usually held up. *Mrs A. Duffield*

BURRA SAHIB 5 b.g. First Trump 118 – Old Flower (Persian Bold 123) [2001 54: **–**
e16g⁵ 16g Sep 5] modest maiden at best, lightly raced. *J. Akehurst*

BURRY BRAVE 2 b.g. (Apr 8) Presidium 124 – Keep Mum 63 (Mummy's Pet 125) **51**
[2001 6d 6s⁶ 6d⁴ 7.1m 7m Sep 6] seventh foal: half-brother to 3 winners, including 1m
winner (stayed 1¾m) Seconds Away (by Hard Fought): dam, sprint maiden, best at 2 yrs:
form only when fourth to Fight Your Corner in falsely-run maiden at Newcastle: well
held in nurseries: should stay 7f. *J. S. Goldie*

BUSCADOR (USA) 2 ch.c. (Feb 9) Crafty Prospector (USA) – Fairway Flag (USA) **62**
(Fairway Phantom (USA)) [2001 7m 6.1m⁶ 7m⁶ 6g Sep 7] $40,000F, IR 33,000Y, 15,000
2-y-o: workmanlike colt: half-brother to several winners, including useful Hong Kong
performer up to 1m Michael's Choice (by Theatrical) and 1992 2-y-o 6f winner Astrac
Trio (by Timeless Moment): dam 2-y-o sprint winner in USA: modest maiden: will stay
1m: sold 1,550 gns. *E. L. James*

BUSHIE BILL 3 ch.g. Captain Webster 69 – Mistress Royal 74 (Royalty 130) [2001 **71**
12g 11.7d³ 12m 11.7d⁴ Oct 25] fifth reported living foal: dam winning stayer:
fair maiden: will stay 1¾m+: yet to race on extremes of going: has been slowly away.
P. R. Hedger

BUSTLE (USA) 3 ch.f. Chief Honcho (USA) – Parliament House (USA) (General **54**
Assembly (USA)) [2001 45: e5g 8m 16.4g³ 14.1s⁵ 15.8m Sep 22] modest maiden
handicapper: stays 2m: sold 5,700 gns (in December). *J. A. R. Toller*

BUSTLING RIO (IRE) 5 b.g. Up And At 'em 109 – Une Venitienne (FR) (Green **81**
Dancer (USA) 132) [2001 78: f16g² f16.2g* Jan 6] big, good-topped gelding: fairly
useful handicapper: won at Wolverhampton in January: stays 2¼m well: acts on
fibresand, best turf efforts on good going or firmer: held up, and tends to idle/hang in
front: promising hurdler/chaser. *P. C. Haslam*

BUSY BUSY BEE 4 gr.f. Batshoof 122 – Rectitude 99 (Runnymede 123) [2001 –, **–**
a57: f11g² f12g⁶ f9.4s* f9.4g⁵ f9.4g⁵ f8.5g f9.4g⁶ 9.7m 12.1g f9.4s 11d f12s Dec 26] **a53**
modest performer: won maiden at Wolverhampton in January: below form after next
start: effective at 9.4f to 1½m: form only on fibresand: blinkered/visored after second
start. *N. P. Littmoden*

BUTRINTO 7 ch.g. Anshan 119 – Bay Bay 101 (Bay Express 132) [2001 69, a63: e7g **66**
f8.5g* f8.5g⁴ e13g⁶ f8.5g³ 9m⁶ 8g 7m² 7g⁵ 8m* 7.6g⁴ 7s Sep 30] tall, strong gelding:
good mover: fair performer: won claimers at Wolverhampton in February and Brighton
in August: best at 7f to 9f: acts on fibresand/equitrack and any turf going: sometimes
blinkered/visored (not in 2001): often carries head high. *B. R. Johnson*

BUTTERMANS BAY 4 b.g. Muhtarram (USA) 125 – River Fantasy (USA) (Irish **–**
River (FR) 131) [2001 7s Apr 16] sturdy gelding: shows plenty of knee action: first foal:
dam, no worthwhile form, half-sister to Norfolk Stakes winner Romeo Romani: 33/1,
green and backward when well held in maiden at Kempton. *C. F. Wall*

BUTTERWICK CHIEF 4 b.g. Be My Chief (USA) 122 – Swift Return 79 (Double **– §**
Form 130) [2001 –§: 16s Oct 30] compact gelding: temperamental maiden. *R. A. Fahey*

BUYING A DREAM (IRE) 4 ch.g. Prince of Birds (USA) 121 – Cartagena Lady **55**
(IRE) (Prince Rupert (FR) 121) [2001 79: 10v 10s 8.1m 10f 10m⁶ 11.1s⁶ 12.3g 10.1g
10g² 10m⁴ 12d Oct 8] lengthy, quite good-topped gelding: modest handicapper: stays
1¼m: acts on good to firm and good to soft going: effective blinkered or not: none too
consistent. *Andrew Turnell*

BUZ KIRI (USA) 3 b.c. Gulch (USA) – White Corners (USA) (Caro 133) [2001 55p: **62**
11.6g³ 11.8f⁵ 14m² 16.2m² 15.8g⁶ 14.1s 16d f12g f16g Nov 12] smallish, sturdy colt: **a–**
modest maiden handicapper: better at 2m than shorter: acts on good to firm going, below
form on softer than good (had form on fibresand at 2 yrs): blinkered final start.
A. W. Carroll

B W LEADER 4 b.g. Owington 123 – Showery 76 (Rainbow Quest (USA) 134) [2001 **–**
–: f8g f7g f5s⁵ 5.3s Apr 12] little form: tried blinkered/tongue tied. *Miss D. A. McHale*

BY DEFINITION (IRE) 3 gr. or b.f. Definite Article 121 – Miss Goodbody (Castle **54**
Keep 121) [2001 –: 7s 8.1g 8f³ 8m³ 8m Jul 7] rather sparely-made filly: modest maiden
handicapper: stays 1m: acts on firm ground: sold 1,500 gns in October. *P. W. Harris*

BYLAW (USA) 3 b.f. Lear Fan (USA) 130 – Byre Bird (USA) (Diesis 133) [2001 78: **99**
8.3s⁴ 10g 13.1m² 12d* 12.3f² 13.3m² 14g⁶ 15d³ 18f³ Sep 20] quite good-topped filly:
shows knee action: useful performer: won handicap at Salisbury in June: some good
efforts after, including 3½ lengths third to Pushkin in listed race at Deauville penultimate
start: stays 15f: acts on any ground: seems best in blinkers: reluctant at stalls first 2
outings: races prominently. *J. H. M. Gosden*

BYO (IRE) 3 gr.c. Paris House 123 – Navan Royal (IRE) 61 (Dominion Royale 112) **88 d**
[2001 90: f5g e5g⁵ e5g⁴ 5.1s³ 5s⁵ 5.1f 6f⁴ 6g 5f 5m 5m 5.1m 5.7m⁶ 5.1f 6g 5g 5g⁶ 5g 5v⁶
6v⁵ 6d 6v Nov 8] smallish, workmanlike colt: fairly useful performer: on the downgrade
in 2001, leaving M. Quinn after fourteenth start: best at 5f: acts on equitrack and probably
any turf going. *G. M. McCourt*

C

CABALLE (USA) 4 ch.f. Opening Verse (USA) 126 – Attirance (FR) (Crowned **79**
Prince (USA) 128) [2001 79: 10g f8g⁴ 10m⁴ f12g² 16m² 16d⁵ 12d² Sep 3] strong, good
sort: good walker: fair performer: probably best at 1½m to 2m (at least when conditions
aren't testing): acts on fibresand, yet to race on extremes of going on turf: free-going sort:
joined N. Henderson, successful over hurdles in December. *S. P. C. Woods*

CABALLO NOBILE (USA) 2 b.f. (Mar 2) Kris S (USA) – Serene Nobility (USA) **–**
(His Majesty (USA)) [2001 6m 8d Oct 19] fifth foal: half-sister to 2 winners, including
smart 1998 2-y-o 6f to 1m (including Royal Lodge) winner Mutaahab (by Dixieland
Band): dam 6f to (minor stakes) 9f winner in USA: signs of a little ability in minor event/
maiden. *B. J. Meehan*

CABARET QUEST 5 ch.g. Pursuit of Love 124 – Cabaret Artiste (Shareef Dancer **50**
(USA) 135) [2001 52: 9m⁵ 8m⁶ 7.5f 8f 7.5f* 8.1m 8.5g Aug 15] strong gelding: modest
handicapper: ended long losing sequence in seller at Beverley in July: effective at 7.5f,
barely at 1¼m: acts on firm going, possibly not on softer than good: blinkered last 4 starts.
J. M. Bradley

CABO SALINAS (IRE) 3 b.g. Hamas (IRE) 125§ – Easter Heroine (IRE) 72 (Exactly **68**
Sharp (USA) 121) [2001 75: 6v 7g 7g⁶ 7d⁴ 10g⁵ 8.5s 10s⁴ 6m 7m 7s 6d⁵ p7g Dec 28] IR
18,000Y: first foal: half-brother to useful 2-y-o Doc Holiday: dam, Irish maiden who
stayed 1¼m, half-sister to useful sprinter Ocker: fair maiden at best: left K. Prendergast
in Ireland before final outing: probably best at 7f to 1¼m: acts on soft and good to firm
ground: blinkered (well held) once. *B. J. Curley*

CADEAUX CHER 7 ch.g. Cadeaux Genereux 131 – Home Truth 98 (Known Fact **94**
(USA) 135) [2001 88: 6v* 6g 6f² 6g 6f 6m 6g 6m 6g 6g 6g Oct 5] lengthy gelding: unimpressive mover: fairly useful handicapper: won at Doncaster in March: some creditable
efforts after: best around 6f: acts on any going: tried blinkered in 1998: wears bandages:
held up: sometimes hangs left. *B. W. Hills*

CAERDYDD FACH 5 b.m. Bluebird (USA) 125 – Waitingformargaret 78 (Kris 135) **42**
[2001 30, a–: 9.2d 10f⁶ 8m⁵ 10m⁶ 8m 10f³ 8f⁶ 9.1d 11.1d⁶ 9.9m 8.9m Sep 2] small mare: **a–**

poor maiden: seems to stay 11f: acts on firm and soft ground: tried visored: none too consistent. *A. B. Mulholland*

CAERNOMORE 3 b.g. Caerleon (USA) 132 – Nuryana 107 (Nureyev (USA) 131) **72** [2001 9g⁴ 9.9g³ 11.7d Oct 25] 10,000Y: brother to smart 1½m performer Mystic Knight, 1m winner at 2 yrs, and half-brother to several winners, notably very smart miler Rebecca Sharp (by Machiavellian): dam 1m winner out of half-sister to 1000 Guineas winner On The House: best effort in maidens when third at Goodwood: stays 1¼m: sold 6,000 gns, and gelded. *J. H. M. Gosden*

CAESAREAN HUNTER (USA) 2 ch.g. (Mar 15) Jade Hunter (USA) – Grey Fay – (USA) (Grey Dawn II 132) [2001 7f 8g 7s Oct 16] $21,000F, IR 40,000Y: big, workmanlike gelding: has scope: third foal: dam unraced half-sister to 1997 Solario Stakes winner Little Indian and useful 6f (at 2yrs) and 1¼m winner Mukaddar: little form in maidens: coltish/early to post last 2 starts (gelded after final one). *S. Kirk*

CAFE GRANDE (IRE) 3 b.g. Grand Lodge (USA) 125 – Olean (Sadler's Wells **87** (USA) 132) [2001 88p: 10.1s² 10.1g* Sep 15] lengthy, good sort: fairly useful form: probably unlucky in maiden at Epsom on reappearance, then landed odds in similar event there by 2 lengths from Silly Goose, taking while to work his way to front but always in control once asserting: gelded afterwards: will stay 1½m: yet to race on ground firmer than good: sent to Hong Kong. *M. A. Jarvis*

CAFETERIA BAY (USA) 3 ch.g. Sky Classic (CAN) – Go On Zen (USA) (Zen **94** (USA)) [2001 99: 9d 8m⁴ 8.1m 8.2g Dec 12] strong gelding: has scope: fairly useful performer: best effort at 3 yrs when fourth to Black Knight in minor event at Thirsk: gelded, then left K. Burke before final outing (renamed Great Dragon): will probably stay 1¼m: yet to race on extremes of going. *P. C. Kan, Hong Kong*

CAIR PARAVEL (IRE) 4 b. or br.c. Dolphin Street (FR) 125 – Queen's Ransom **89 d** (IRE) 70 (Last Tycoon 131) [2001 91?: 8s 8f⁴ 7m 8m 7d³ 7.1s 7d 7m 7v⁴ Oct 27] sturdy, good-quartered colt: has a quick action: fairly useful performer, on downgrade: best form at 7f/1m: acts on any turf going: sometimes blinkered/visored: sold 6,000 gns, sent to Norway. *R. Hannon*

CAITANO 7 b.h. Niniski (USA) 125 – Eversince (USA) (Foolish Pleasure (USA)) **117** [2001 119: 10g² 12g⁶ 10m 11g 12g⁵ 10d⁴ 10.2g 16d 12m Dec 16] tall, angular horse: smart performer: best efforts in 2001 when 5½ lengths second to Silvano in Singapore Cup at Kranji and sixth to Stay Gold in Dubai Sheema Classic at Nad Al Sheba in March: not discredited when fifth to Anzillero in Deutschland-Preis at Dusseldorf and seventh to Northerly in Cox Plate at Moonee Valley fifth/seventh outings: stays 1½m (didn't get 2m in Melbourne Cup): acts on heavy and good to firm going: usually blinkered: held up: often slowly away: has found little: tough (now raced in 11 countries). *A. Schutz, Germany*

CAITLAND 2 b.f. (Apr 12) Puissance 110 – Lorlanne (Bustino 136) [2001 5d⁵ 7g **51** 8.3s⁶ 8m⁵ 8v⁵ Oct 16] leggy, workmanlike filly: third foal: dam no form in 3 starts: modest maiden: will probably stay 1¼m: acts on heavy and good to firm ground: has been free to post/slowly away. *D. Moffatt*

CALA DI VOLPE (USA) 3 ch.c. (Jan 26) Mt Livermore (USA) – Frenchman's **91** Cove (IRE) (Caerleon (USA) 132) [2001 5d³ 5g³ 5f² 6g⁵ 7m* 7.1s* 7s Sep 30] $50,000Y: small, quite attractive colt: fourth foal: dam, French 2-y-o 1m winner who later won up to 1¼m in USA and third in Grade 3 event, half-sister to very smart performer up to 1¼m Splendid Moment from very good family: fairly useful performer: won nursery at Newbury and minor event at Sandown (edged right) in August: well held final start: will probably stay 1m: yet to race on heavy going, seems to act on any other: started slowly first 2 outings. *P. F. I. Cole*

CALAMINT 2 gr.g. (Jan 13) Kaldoun (FR) 122 – Coigach 110 (Niniski (USA) 125) **78 p** [2001 7g 7d 8.2s² Nov 5] close-coupled, good-topped gelding: unimpressive mover: third foal: half-brother to 4-y-o Aston Mara and 3-y-o Motto: dam 1m (at 2 yrs) to 14.6f (Park Hill) winner from good staying family: tongue tied, clearly best effort in maidens (fair form) when 3½ lengths second of 11 to Star Cross at Nottingham: gelded afterwards: will be suited by 1½m+: raced only on good ground or softer: probably capable of better still. *J. R. Fanshawe*

CALANDA 3 b.f. Aragon 118 – Henceforth 58 (Full of Hope 125) [2001 52: 7.1m 7m – 7m 7g 6m 8s Oct 3] poor maiden. *H. Candy*

CALATAGAN (IRE) 2 ch.g. (Mar 9) Danzig Connection (USA) – Calachuchi 74 **65** (Martinmas 128) [2001 7g⁶ 6d Oct 3] good-topped gelding: has scope: fifth foal: half-brother to 3 winners,including 1½m and 2m winner Quezon City (by Keen) and 3-y-o Cateel Bay: dam prolific winner from 7.5f to 12.4f: fair form on first of 2 starts in maidens at Newcastle: will stay 1¼m. *Miss J. A. Camacho*

CALCAVELLA 5 b.m. Pursuit of Love 124 – Brightside (IRE) 99 (Last Tycoon 131) **68** [2001 68: f8.5g⁵ 7m³ 7.5m⁵ 7.6f 7.1g Sep 13] workmanlike mare: fair maiden handicapper: should stay 1m: acts on firm and good to soft going: has been slowly away/raced freely. *M. Kettle*

CALCUTTA 5 b.h. Indian Ridge 123 – Echoing 93 (Formidable (USA) 125) [2001 **103** 100: 8v 7d⁴ 8m² 8.1m* 8m 8.1g 8m 8g 8g⁵ 7.9m⁵ 8g* 7g⁴ 8d⁵ Oct 19] smallish, sturdy horse: carries condition: useful handicapper: won at Sandown (by ½ length from Duke of Modena) in May and Doncaster (by 1¼ lengths from Red N' Socks) in September: best at 7f/1m: acts on firm and good to soft going: blinkered final 4-y-o start: sometimes swishes tail/looks less than keen, and best produced as late as possible. *B. W. Hills*

CALDIZ 4 b.g. Warning 136 – Segovia 95 (Groom Dancer (USA) 128) [2001 65d: f8g⁶ **35** f12g⁶ f12s f12g³ e13g f12g⁶ f16.2g⁵ Feb 22] poor maiden nowadays: stays 1½m: acts on fibresand: tongue tied. *Mrs A. L. M. King*

CALGARTH (IRE) 2 b.f. (Mar 9) Efisio 120 – Waypoint 95 (Cadeaux Genereux **54 p** 131) [2001 6s 6s f6g⁶ Oct 18] 24,000Y: rather leggy filly: first foal: dam, 6f/7f winner, out of smart 5f performer Princess Athena: modest form in maidens: best effort when sixth at Southwell: likely to prove best at 5f/6f: type to do better in handicaps. *W. J. Haggas*

CALIBAN (IRE) 3 ch.g. Rainbows For Life (CAN) – Amour Toujours (IRE) (Law **53** Society (USA) 130) [2001 53: e8g f9.4g² f11g* f12g⁴ f9.4g⁶ f11g* f12g Apr 17] lengthy gelding: modest performer: won handicap in February and seller in March, both at Southwell: stays 1½m: acts on fibresand and good to firm going: visored after reappearance: has been slowly away/raced freely: sold 5,400 gns. *N. P. Littmoden*

CALIWAG (IRE) 5 b.g. Lahib (USA) 129 – Mitsubishi Style (Try My Best (USA) **50 §** 130) [2001 65: f7g 6.9v³ 8g 7m 9m 8.3m 12m⁴ 11.6v p13g Nov 13] modest maiden: stays 1m: probably stays on any going: tried blinkered: not one to trust. *Jamie Poulton*

CALKO 4 ch.g. Timeless Times (USA) 99 – Jeethgaya (USA) 61 (Critique (USA) 126) **–** [2001 –, a67: f8s² f8g⁶ f8.5g f8g 10v f7g 9.2d f8g³ f8.5g f8s Dec 21] sturdy gelding: win- **a55 d** ning handicapper, on the downgrade: left T. D. Barron after fourth start, S. R. Bowring after sixth and Mrs H. Walton after seventh: stays 1m: acts on fibresand: usually blinkered/visored. *R. Wilman*

CALLDAT SEVENTEEN 5 b.g. Komaite (USA) – Westminster Waltz (Dance In **77** Time (CAN)) [2001 77§: f16.2g² f16g f14g⁴ f11g* f12g² f12s Dec 21] good-bodied gelding: fair performer: off 8½ months (reportedly fractured hock) before winning minor event at Southwell in November: stays easy 2m: acts on soft going, good to firm and fibresand/equitrack: twice reluctant at start at 4 yrs (refused to race on first occasion, visored on second): sometimes tongue tied/wears crossed noseband/led to post: not one to trust implicitly. *P. W. D'Arcy*

CALLING DOT COM (IRE) 3 ch.g. Halling (USA) 133 – Rawya (USA) 80 **65** (Woodman (USA) 126) [2001 –p: 6d 7m 7m f8.5f⁴ f9.4s⁴ p10g* Dec 29] tall, quite attractive gelding: fair performer: left Sir Michael Stoute after third start: blinkered, progressive form in blinkers final 3 starts, winning maiden at Lingfield in December by 5 lengths: stays 1¼m: acts on fibresand and polytrack: has been taken last and quietly to post: has reared leaving stalls/started very slowly. *N. P. Littmoden*

CALLING THE SHOTS 4 b.g. Democratic (USA) 101 – Two Shots (Dom Racine **62** (FR) 121) [2001 55: f8g⁵ f12g* f11s³ f16g f8g² f8g* f7g* f7g³ f8g⁴ f8g² 7m² 5m 6.1f 7m⁴ **a77** 6g⁵ 7m 5g f8g f6g⁴ f8g f6g³ f6g f7g³ f8g Dec 17] fair handicapper on all-weather, modest on turf: won at Southwell and Wolverhampton (2) in January/March: has won at easy 1½m, probably best at 6f to 1m: acts on firm going and fibresand: usually visored/ blinkered: sometimes tongue tied: has looked none too keen. *S. R. Bowring*

CALLISTO (IRE) 2 br.f. (Apr 27) Darshaan 133 – Moon Parade 73 (Welsh Pageant **– p** 132) [2001 7d 7d Nov 3] rather leggy filly: sister to 3-y-o Shaandar and half-sister to several winners, including smart 1¾m winner Rain Rider (by Fools Holme): dam, 1¼m winner, half-sister to Moon Madness and Sheriff's Star: behind in maidens at Leicester and Newmarket: likely to do better at 1½m+. *J. L. Dunlop*

CALL MY GUEST (IRE) 11 b.g. Be My Guest (USA) 126 – Overcall (Bustino **29** 136) [2001 f16.2g f16g⁶ Feb 16] bad maiden on Flat, lightly raced: probably stays 2m: acts on fibresand and heavy going: tried blinkered. *R. E. Peacock*

CALL THE MARK (IRE) 2 b.c. (Mar 15) Goldmark (USA) 113 – Shalerina (USA) **67**
(Shalford (IRE) 124§) [2001 8m⁵ 8d p8g⁶ p8g p7g³ Dec 29] IR 14,000Y: second foal:
half-brother to fairly useful Irish 2000 2-y-o 7f winner Calumet Spice (by Mujadil): dam,
well beaten both starts at 2 yrs, from family of Alydar: fair maiden: will probably stay
1¼m: best efforts on polytrack: tongue tied debut/penultimate start. *P. Mitchell*

CAL MAC 2 b.g. (Feb 11) Botanic (USA) – Shifting Mist 76 (Night Shift (USA)) **78**
[2001 6m 6f⁴ Sep 21] 3,000Y: has a quick action: fourth foal: dam 1¼m to 1¾m winner:
gelded after debut: much better effort (fair form) when 3½ lengths fourth of 23 to Farqad
in maiden at Newbury, finishing well: will stay at least 1m. *H. Morrison*

CAMARADERIE 5 b.g. Most Welcome 131 – Secret Valentine 71 (Wollow 132) **55**
[2001 51: 9s⁶ 8m* 8m⁴ 10.1m 8f* 8m⁵ 9g Aug 24] leggy, workmanlike gelding: modest
handicapper: won at Newcastle in June and Redcar (27-runner apprentice race) in July:
effective at 1m, has form over 1½m: probably acts on any turf going: blinkered after
reappearance: sometimes starts slowly. *Mrs M. Reveley*

CAMARET 2 b.f. (Feb 3) Danehill (USA) 126 – Armorique (IRE) (Top Ville 129) **79 p**
[2001 7d³ Oct 15] rather leggy, useful-looking filly: fifth foal: sister to 3-y-o Darwin:
dam, French 1½m winner, half-sister to several good middle-distance performers out of
Irish 1000 Guineas winner Arctique Royale: 12/1, narrowly-beaten third of 20 to Trojan
Princess in maiden at Leicester, keeping on well without being given hard time: should
stay 1m: sure to improve and win a race or 2. *J. H. M. Gosden*

CAMARGUE 3 ch.g. Pivotal 124 – Colonial Line (USA) 75 (Plenty Old (USA)) **44**
[2001 10s 10.2d 7m⁶ 8f⁶ 7.6f 6m⁶ Aug 16] 5,000Y, 4,000 2-y-o: half-brother to 2 winners
up to 1¼m, including useful Secretary of State (by Alzao): dam 5f winner: poor maiden:
probably stays 1m: blinkered after debut. *E. A. Wheeler*

CAMBERLEY (IRE) 4 b.c. Sri Pekan (USA) 117 – Nsx 74 (Roi Danzig (USA)) **98**
[2001 99+: 8m 7f⁵ 7m 7m 7g⁴ 7g⁶ 7d 7g⁵ 8g⁴ Oct 5] rangy colt: good mover: useful
performer: some creditable efforts in 2001: stays 7f: acts on firm and good to soft going:
blinkered last 3 starts: reportedly bled penultimate 3-y-o outing: has worn crossed noseband: free-going sort: best held up: none too resolute. *P. F. I. Cole*

CAMBIADO (IRE) 3 ch.g. Ashkalani (IRE) 128 – Changed Around (IRE) (Doulab **65**
(USA) 115) [2001 69p: 7.1v³ 7g Oct 19] rather leggy, angular gelding: fair maiden,
lightly raced: unlikely to stay beyond 7f: yet to race on firm going, seems to act on any
other: sold 6,500 gns. *J. R. Fanshawe*

CAMBIO (IRE) 3 b.g. Turtle Island (IRE) 123 – Motley (Rainbow Quest (USA) 134) **61**
[2001 7g⁵ 10m⁶ 8s⁴ 10d p12g p12g Nov 20] IR 27,000F, IR 48,000Y: angular, quite
good-topped gelding: fifth foal: half-brother to 2 winners, including fairly useful Irish
1996 2-y-o 6f winner Blushing Minstrel (by Nicholas): dam maiden daughter of Galtres
Stakes winner Sans Blague: modest maiden: left T. Easterby 2,400 gns after second start:
stays 1¼m: acts on soft ground: usually slowly away: visored final outing. *B. R. Johnson*

CAMEO COOLER 2 ch.c. (Mar 9) Inchinor 119 – Mystique Smile 78 (Music Boy **–**
124) [2001 6m 5m 7.2v Oct 15] 18,000Y: good-topped colt: first foal: dam, 2-y-o 5f
winner who failed to progress, half-sister to useful performer up to 1m Kaibo: no
encouragement in maidens. *Miss L. A. Perratt*

CAMMAEUS 2 ch.f. (May 7) Greensmith 121 – Pastelle 52 (Tate Gallery (USA) 117) **51 §**
[2001 5.3m⁶ 5.1g³ 5m³ 5.1g⁵ 5m⁶ 5.3s⁵ 5v² 5.7d f5g⁴ f5s⁶ Dec 27] 1,000Y: second living
foal: dam, maiden, best at 5f: modest maiden: raced mainly in sellers: likely to prove best
at 5f: acts on fibresand, good to firm and heavy going: sometimes slowly away/looks
irresolute: often forces pace. *J. Akehurst*

CAMP COMMANDER (IRE) 2 b.c. (Feb 24) Pennekamp (USA) 130 – Khalatara **69**
(IRE) (Kalaglow 132) [2001 5g⁶ 6f⁵ 6g 7s⁵ 6v f6g p8g³ p10g³ p8g² p7g² Dec 22] **a81**
16,500F, 16,000Y: good-topped colt: fourth foal: half-brother to 3-y-o Aziz Presenting
and a winner in Germany by Marju: dam unraced half-sister to smart middle-distance
performer Khariyda: fairly useful maiden on all-weather, fair on turf: ended year in good
form, including in nurseries: seems best at 7f/1m: acts on polytrack, firm and soft going:
tongue tied last 6 starts: reliable. *C. E. Brittain*

CAMP DAVID (USA) 2 b.c. (Apr 20) Deputy Minister (CAN) – Alamosa (Alydar **106**
(USA)) [2001 7d* 8d² 8v⁵ Oct 27] $1,000,000Y: compact colt: half-brother to
several winners, including US Grade 3 7f winner Trafalger (by Storm Bird), smart 7f (at
2 yrs)/1m winner who stayed 1½m Etizaaz (by Diesis) and 3-y-o Santolina: dam unraced
half-sister to Swain: useful form: won maiden at Naas in August: 7 lengths second to

Castle Gandolfo in Beresford Stakes at the Curragh: not discredited when fifth of 6 to High Chaparral in Racing Post Trophy at Doncaster, dictating pace: should stay 1¼m: raced only on ground softer than good: sent to USA. *A. P. O'Brien, Ireland*

CAMZO (USA) 3 ch.g. Diesis 133 – Cary Grove (USA) (Theatrical 128) [2001 –: 8s **73** e8g² 10d 10m⁵ 8.5m⁴ 10.4m⁵ 12g Sep 15] compact gelding: fair maiden: gelded after final start: stays 1¼m: acts on equitrack and good to firm ground: tends to get behind. *P. W. Harris*

CANADA 3 b.g. Ezzoud (IRE) 126 – Chancel (USA) 60 (Al Nasr (FR) 126) [2001 89: **105** 10g⁵ 10.4m 10m* 10.4d* 10m⁶ 9.9g 10.4g 11.9m³ 10g² Oct 5] rather leggy gelding: useful performer: won maiden at Ayr (made all) and handicap at York (hung left) in June: good ½-length second to Jokesmith in handicap at Newmarket final start: stays 10.4f: acts on heavy and good to firm going: visored (ran poorly) once: free-going sort: none too consistent: sold 52,000 gns, gelded and joined M. Pipe. *B. W. Hills*

CANADIAN CON (USA) 2 b. or br.c. (Apr 21) Foxhound (USA) 103 – Me And **77** Molly (USA) (Slewpy (USA)) [2001 6.9m⁶ 6.9m* 7d² 8m⁵ f7g³ f8.5s² f8.5s² Dec 27] **a83** $42,000F, 25,000Y: leggy, useful-looking colt: fifth foal: half-brother to 3 winners in USA, including one around 1m by Black Tie Affair: dam winner up to 9f in USA at 4/5 yrs: fairly useful on all-weather, fair on turf: won maiden at Folkestone in July: good second in Wolverhampton nursery final start: effective at 7f to 8.5f: acts on fibresand, good to firm and good to soft ground: blinkered fourth start/visored final 2: sometimes takes strong hold/wanders. *N. P. Littmoden*

CANBERRA (IRE) 2 b.c. (Feb 18) Sadler's Wells (USA) 132 – Rafina (USA) (Mr **99 p** Prospector (USA)) [2001 7g⁶ 8.5m* Sep 11] first foal: dam, placed up to around 1m in France, sister to very smart performer up to 1m Machiavellian, and half-sister to very smart 1m/1¼m performer Exit To Nowhere: better effort in maidens when winning 16-runner event at Galway in September by 6 lengths from Aqualina, leading 2f out and soon clear: will stay 1¼m: a smart prospect. *A. P. O'Brien, Ireland*

CANCUN CARIBE (IRE) 4 ch.g. Port Lucaya 118 – Miss Tuko (Good Times (ITY)) **74** [2001 71: 9.7v f9.4s 10s³ 10v² 10.4s f8.5g² p10g Dec 12] leggy gelding: fair performer: reportedly fractured a pastern after third 3-y-o start: stays 1¼m: acts on heavy going and fibresand: sometimes blinkered. *K. McAuliffe*

CANDICE (IRE) 3 br.f. Caerleon (USA) 132 – Criquette 104 (Shirley Heights 130) **97** [2001 101: 9.9m³ 12m 8.1g⁴ 10f² 10s⁵ 10d Oct 18] rather leggy, quite good-topped filly: useful performer: out of depth in Oaks at Epsom second start, but ran creditably in listed races most other ones, including when placed behind Foodbroker Fancy at Goodwood and Newbury: should stay 1½m: acts on firm and soft ground. *E. A. L. Dunlop*

CANDID 2 ch.f. (Mar 5) Lion Cavern (USA) 117 – Shady Deed (USA) 80 (Shadeed **76** (USA) 135) [2001 5s³ 6f⁴ 6g⁶ Sep 7] strong, rangy filly: has scope: third foal: dam 1m winner: fair maiden: off 2½ months before final start: should stay 1m. *B. J. Meehan*

CANDLERIGGS (IRE) 5 ch.g. Indian Ridge 123 – Ridge Pool (IRE) 74 (Bluebird **101** (USA) 125) [2001 100: 6g² 6m 5m³ 5m⁶ 6g 5.6m 6m 5g⁶ 6d Oct 13] smallish, sturdy, lengthy gelding: impresses in appearance: poor mover: useful performer: mostly creditable efforts in 2001, including ¾-length second to Yorkies Boy in handicap at York in May and sixth to Indian Prince in listed event at Newmarket penultimate start: best at 6f/ stiff 5f: acts on good to firm and good to soft ground: sold 40,000 gns. *E. A. L. Dunlop*

CANDOTHAT 3 b.g. Thatching 131 – Yo-Cando (IRE) 64 (Cyrano de Bergerac 120) **61 d** [2001 78: e5g⁶ 6f 5m 5.1m 5d 5.2v Oct 26] strong, compact gelding: good walker: fair at 2 yrs: below form in 2001: stays 6f: acts on good to firm going, possibly not on soft: visored last 2 starts. *P. W. Harris*

CANDOUR 2 b.f. (Mar 21) So Factual (USA) 120 – Outward's Gal 78 (Ashmore (FR) **–** 125) [2001 6d 7d Nov 3] 2,000Y: angular filly: half-sister to useful 5f (at 2 yrs) to 7.5f winner Abbey's Gal (by Efisio) and unreliable 1m winner Princess of Orange (by Master Willie): dam, maiden, should have stayed 1m: well held in Newmarket maidens. *Mrs D. Haine*

CANDY ANCHOR (FR) 2 b.f. (Mar 30) Slip Anchor 136 – Kandavu 87 (Safawan **41** 118) [2001 7m⁵ f7g 7.5g 7.5g Sep 19] 2,000Y: lengthy filly: second foal: dam, 5f winner, raced mainly in sellers. *J. G. Given*

CANFORD (IRE) 4 b.g. Caerleon (USA) 132 – Veronica (Persian Bold 123) [2001 **93** 97: 10s⁶ 10s² 12v 10m⁶ 10g 10.4g⁴ 14s 12g Sep 15] tall, good-topped gelding: fairly useful handicapper: effective at 1¼m, probably at 1¾m: acts on heavy ground, probably on good to firm: visored last 3 starts: usually leads: has carried head awkwardly/hung left: none too consistent: sold 21,000 gns. *W. Jarvis*

CANLIS 2 b.c. (Mar 15) Halling (USA) 133 – Fajjoura (IRE) 84 (Fairy King (USA)) – [2001 6d Oct 18] 31,000F, 36,000Y: unfurnished colt: has a quick action: third foal: half-brother to fairly useful 7f winner Wildflower (by Namaqualand): dam 2-y-o 5f winner: slowly away and always behind in Newmarket maiden. *B. W. Hills*

CANNY HILL 4 ch.g. Bold Arrangement 127 – Jersey Maid 82 (On Your Mark 125) – [2001 41, a58: 9v Mar 29] maiden: tailed off (visored) only 4-y-o start. *D. Moffatt*

CANOPY 3 b.f. Ezzoud (IRE) 126 – Zenith 88 (Shirley Heights 130) [2001 64p: 10m **66** 10m 8.1d³ 8m³ 9m⁴ 10s Sep 30] leggy, quite good-topped filly: fair maiden: probably stays 1¼m: acts on good to firm and good to soft going: has looked none too enthusiastic: sold 3,000 gns in December. *R. Hannon*

CANOVAS HEART 12 b.g. Balidar 133 – Worthy Venture 76 (Northfields (USA)) **67** [2001 –: 7m 6m 7g 5g* 5g Sep 2] neat gelding: has a quick action: one-time useful handicapper, just fair nowadays: won at Windsor in August: stays 7f: acts on firm ground, soft and fibresand: pulled up lame only 11-y-o start: usually races prominently. *Bob Jones*

CANOVAS KINGDOM 3 ch.g. Aragon 118 – Joan's Venture (Beldale Flutter (USA) **61** 130) [2001 40: 8d² 8.1g 7m 6m⁴ 6d³ Nov 2] strong, lengthy gelding: has a round action: modest maiden: seems effective at 6f to 1m: acts on good to firm and good to soft going: sweating and edgy (well beaten) final 2-y-o start. *Bob Jones*

CAN PAU 2 b.f. (Apr 18) Tragic Role (USA) – Distant Isle (IRE) (Bluebird (USA) **40** 125) [2001 5s 5g May 5] 12,000Y: well-grown, quite good-topped filly: third living foal: half-sister to 5-y-o Entropy: dam unraced: poor maiden. *K. A. Ryan*

CANTERLOUPE (IRE) 3 b.f. Wolfhound (USA) 126 – Missed Again 84 (High Top **94 p** 131) [2001 75p: 5m* 5m³ 5d³ Oct 13] quite good-topped filly: keen walker: useful performer, lightly raced: won minor event at Windsor in June: off 3½ months, best effort when 2¼ lengths third to Dancing Mystery in handicap at Ascot final start, missing break and plenty to do towards unfavoured stand side but finishing strongly: likely to prove best at 5f/6f: acts on good to firm and good to soft ground (raced too freely only start on heavy): should do better still. *P. J. Makin*

CANTGETYOURBREATH (IRE) 5 ch.g. College Chapel 122 – Cathy Garcia – (IRE) (Be My Guest (USA) 126) [2001 –: f7g f7g f6g 6m 8m Jun 4] no longer of much account. *B. P. J. Baugh*

CANTINA 7 b.m. Tina's Pet 121 – Real Claire (Dreams To Reality (USA) 113) [2001 **96** 103: 8g 7m 7f 7.1s 7f* 7f 7m⁵ 7.6d⁴ 7m 7.6m 6m Sep 21] leggy, good-topped mare: useful handicapper: won at Ayr in June: best around 7f: acts on firm going, good to soft and equitrack: often leads, and very best efforts on turning track. *A. Bailey*

CANTON VENTURE 9 ch.g. Arctic Tern (USA) 126 – Ski Michaela (USA) (Devil's – Bag (USA)) [2001 16.2m Aug 27] lengthy, angular gelding: formerly fairly useful handicapper: little recent form: tried blinkered/visored. *A. W. Carroll*

CAPA 4 gr.g. Salse (USA) 128 – Pippas Song 75 (Reference Point 139) [2001 80: 12d – 10g 16m May 30] lengthy, angular gelding: fairly useful maiden at best: has become disappointing: blinkered final start. *B. W. Hills*

CAPACOOSTIC 4 ch.f. Savahra Sound 111 – Cocked Hat Girl 47 (Ballacashtal **44** (CAN)) [2001 49, a–: f5g f6g f6g f7g f5g² 5s⁶ 7.5m⁵ 8g⁵ 6d f8g f5g³ 6d⁵ 6m⁵ 7v f6g Nov 16] angular filly: poor maiden: has form up to 1m, best recent efforts at 5f/6f: acts on good to firm going, soft and fibresand: sometimes blinkered: often claimer ridden. *S. R. Bowring*

CAPAL GARMON (IRE) 3 b.g. Caerleon (USA) 132 – Elevate 98 (Ela-Mana-Mou **116** 132) [2001 98p: 10.2d⁵ 16.2m 15.9g 15d² 15s² 14d* Oct 20] lengthy gelding: smart performer: good second at Longchamp in Prix de Lutece (went down by 2 lengths to Street Shaana) and Prix Hubert de Chaudenay (beaten 4 lengths by Wareed) prior to winning Jockey Club Cup at Newmarket by ½ length from Invermark, well ridden to the fore and keeping on willingly despite drifting left (distressed afterwards and needed oxygen): should stay beyond 2m: acts on soft and good to firm going: moved poorly to post second start: has been blanketed for stall entry. *J. H. M. Gosden*

CAPALLIN (IRE) 2 gr.f. (May 3) Desert Style (IRE) 121 – Rustic Lawn (Rusticaro **62** (FR) 124) [2001 6g f7g⁴ f8g* f8g⁶ Dec 3] half-sister to fairly useful 1m/1¼m winner Silver Groom (by Shy Groom): dam unraced half-sister to dam of very smart 1m/1¼m

164

performer Broken Hearted: modest form: won claimer at Southwell in November: respectable effort (slowly away) in nursery there final start: will stay 1¼m: acts on fibresand. *M. H. Tompkins*

CAPE COAST (IRE) 4 b.g. Common Grounds 118 – Strike It Rich (FR) (Rheingold 137) [2001 81, a64: e7g f7g⁶ e7g 7s⁶ 7m 6m⁵ 7f f6g p7g p6g p7g Dec 28] fair on turf, modest on all-weather: well held last 5 starts: best around 7f: acts on good to firm going, soft and fibresand: tried blinkered: none too consistent. *N. P. Littmoden* **67 a54**

CAPE COD (IRE) 3 b.f. Unfuwain (USA) 131 – Haboobti (Habitat 134) [2001 62: 8f 7m 9f Jul 4] modest maiden: may prove best up to 1m: acts on good to firm going, possibly on soft: sold 27,000 gns in July, resold 35,000 gns in December. *J. W. Hills* **61**

CAPE OF GOOD HOPE 3 ch.c. Inchinor 119 – Cape Merino 103 (Clantime 101) [2001 7d⁵ 7g* 8d⁴ Sep 14] 25,000Y: strong, well-made colt: first foal: dam 5f/6f winner, including at 2 yrs: progressive form: won maiden at Newmarket in May: 4¼ lengths fourth to Rumpold in minor event at Doncaster when next seen out: unlikely to stay beyond 1m: sent to Hong Kong. *D. R. C. Elsworth* **101**

CAPE SOCIETY 3 ch.f. Imp Society (USA) – La Noisette (Rock Hopper 124) [2001 –: 8.1g⁴ 8m 11.5m Jun 26] modest maiden: form only at 1m: dead. *J. G. Smyth-Osbourne* **63**

CAPE TOWN (IRE) 4 gr.c. Desert Style (IRE) 121 – Rossaldene 79 (Mummy's Pet 125) [2001 116: 7g* 8g* 8m⁶ Aug 1] leggy, useful-looking colt: smart performer: successful in small-field minor event at Yarmouth (beat Winning Venture 5 lengths) and listed race at Ascot (3 ran, by ½ length from Swallow Flight) in July: respectable sixth to Noverre in Sussex Stakes at Goodwood final start: raced only at 7f/1m: yet to race on heavy going, acts on any other: tends to edge left: consistent. *R. Hannon* **119**

CAPITAL ACCESS 2 b.g. (Feb 14) Efisio 120 – Thilda (IRE) (Roi Danzig (USA)) [2001 6s³ 6m⁶ 7g³ 6d Oct 12] 14,500F, 50,000Y: lengthy, well-made gelding: third foal: half-brother to winners abroad by Mango Express and Lotus Pool: dam unraced half-sister to useful 1m winner Yarn: tailed off in nursery final start (gelded after): not sure to stay 1m: acts on soft ground: blinkered last 2 starts: has wandered under pressure. *B. J. Meehan* **70**

CAPITAL BREEZE (IRE) 3 b.c. Shareef Dancer (USA) 135 – Crystal Land (Kris 135) [2001 8d 10v 8.3g 11.9s 10v Oct 29] 9,000Y, 13,000 2-y-o: good-topped, angular colt: sixth foal: half-brother to 9.4f winner Crystal Gold (by Arazi) and 1¼m winner King's Crown (by Lead On Time), both fairly useful: dam lightly-raced sister to Prix Saint-Alary winner Fitnah: no form: left D. Elsworth after second start. *G. L. Moore* **–**

CAPITAL LAD (IRE) 3 b.g. Charnwood Forest (IRE) 125 – Casla (Lomond (USA) 128) [2001 68?: 10v f11g⁵ 10f 11.5f 12d 8.2s Oct 30] rangy gelding: little form at 3 yrs: tried blinkered. *G. Brown* **–**

Jockey Club Cup, Newmarket—the only three-year-old in the field Capal Garmon prevails in a rousing finish from Invermark (right), Royal Rebel (second left) and the blinkered San Sebastian

CAPOSO (IRE) 3 gr.f. Common Grounds 118 – High Mare (FR) (Highest Honor (FR) **52**
124) [2001 56: 7m⁵ 6m 6m 5m 6m 5m Sep 8] small filly: poor maiden: possibly best at
6f/7f: blinkered penultimate start: sold 900 gns. *P. W. Harris*

CAPPELLINA (IRE) 4 b.f. College Chapel 122 – Santa Ana Wind (Busted 134) **–**
[2001 61, a54: f7g* f8.5s³ f7g Feb 22] modest performer: won maiden at Wolverhampton **a54**
in January: barely stays 8.5f: acts on firm going and fibresand. *P. G. Murphy*

CAPRICCIO (IRE) 4 gr.g. Robellino (USA) 127 – Yamamah 54 (Siberian Express **–**
(USA) 125) [2001 81: 16v Oct 26] fairly useful maiden at best: well held only 4-y-o start.
C. G. Cox

CAPRICHO (IRE) 4 gr.g. Lake Coniston (IRE) 131 – Star Spectacle (Spectacular Bid **96**
(USA)) [2001 104p: 6g⁴ 6m⁶ 6.1m² 7.6d⁶ 7s Sep 29] tall, leggy, useful-looking gelding:
useful handicapper: creditable efforts in 2001 only on first 2 starts, fourth at York in May
and sixth to Nice One Clare in Wokingham Handicap at Royal Ascot: best at 6f/7f: acts
on good to firm and good to soft going: has been bandaged hind-joints: has gone freely to
post: sold 17,000 gns. *W. J. Haggas*

CAPRIOLO (IRE) 5 ch.g. Priolo (USA) 127 – Carroll's Canyon (IRE) (Hatim **80**
(USA) 121) [2001 84: 12s 10m⁵ 12m 12m⁵ 12m 9.9m² 10m⁴ 12g⁵ 12d⁶ 9.9d³ 10.2d Oct
25] rather leggy gelding: fairly useful performer: effective at 1¼m/1½m: yet to race on
heavy going, acts on any other: visored once, often blinkered: races prominently: usually
carries head high: sometimes finishes weakly: sold 7,800 gns. *R. Hannon*

CAPTAIN BRADY (IRE) 6 ch.g. Soviet Lad (USA) – Eight Mile Rock 76 (Domin- **–**
ion 123) [2001 59: 10v 11d 8g Nov 7] lengthy, workmanlike gelding: modest handicapper
at best: no form in 2001: stays 11f: acts on good to firm going, heavy and fibresand:
blinkered once: usually front runner. *J. S. Goldie*

CAPTAIN CRUSOE 3 b.g. Selkirk (USA) 129 – Desert Girl (Green Desert (USA) **79**
127) [2001 –: 8m² 9m⁴ 9d Aug 26] strong gelding: fairly useful maiden: best effort when
second at Goodwood: will stay 1¼m+. *C. A. Horgan*

CAPTAIN GIBSON 3 b.g. Beveled (USA) – Little Egret 74 (Carwhite 127) [2001 **75 §**
79: 6d 6g 6g⁴ 6g 6d 6g 7g⁴ 7.1d⁴ 7s 6v 6v³ 7s Nov 10] strong, lengthy gelding: fair
handicapper: stays 7f: raced mainly on good going or softer: blinkered/visored after
second start: has been slowly away/raced freely: has unseated rider and bolted to post:
wayward, and one to treat with caution. *D. J. S. ffrench Davis*

CAPTAIN KOZANDO 3 b.g. Komaite (USA) – Times Zando 64 (Forzando 122) **60**
[2001 60: f6g* f7g⁵ f7g⁴ f7g⁴ 7.5f 6m 8.3m f7g 8v f6g Nov 16] rather angular, good- **a73**
quartered gelding: fair handicapper on all-weather, modest on turf: mostly disappointing
after winning at Southwell in January: effective at 6f, seemingly at 1m: acts on good to
firm going, heavy and fibresand: tends to start slowly: has wandered/found little.
P. C. Haslam

CAPTAIN MCCLOY (USA) 6 ch.g. Lively One (USA) – Fly Me First (USA) (Her- **43**
bager 136) [2001 51: 10f 10m 10m 8m 10.1d Jul 19] lengthy gelding: poor handicapper
nowadays: stays 10.5f, probably not 1½m: acts on firm and soft going: usually visored/
blinkered: often races prominently. *N. E. Berry*

CAPTAIN MILLER 5 b.g. Batshoof 122 – Miller's Gait 74§ (Mill Reef (USA) 141) **–**
[2001 86: 11.9s Oct 11] leggy gelding: fairly useful handicapper at 4 yrs: below form only
5-y-o start: stays 2m: acts on any going. *N. J. Henderson*

CAPTAIN RIO 2 ch.c. (Apr 11) Pivotal 124 – Beloved Visitor (USA) 83 **122**
(Miswaki (USA) 124) [2001 5g 6m* 6m³ 5m³ 6g* 6v* Oct 25]
  As the distribution of top quality yearlings tends to become more con-
centrated among the best-known stables it gets harder and harder for the smaller
yards to win major races on the Flat. All the more reason then to celebrate the
success of Richard Whitaker's Yorkshire yard with Captain Rio who put up the best
performance of the season by a British-trained two-year-old colt. The performance
which earned Captain Rio that plaudit—and gave his stable its first Group win—
came on his last appearance of the year, in the Group 2 Criterium de Maisons-
Laffitte over six furlongs (it was formerly seven) at the end of October. The
programme of top races in the European Flat season was drawing to a close and
Captain Rio's trouncing of a useful field didn't get the widespread recognition it
deserved—though it wasn't long before offers for the horse began to come in.
Encountering heavy ground for the first time, Captain Rio was a revelation,

travelling strongly on the bridle from the start and turning the Criterium into a one-horse race, having everything else in trouble soon after halfway and running right away from the field when pushed along with hands and heels over the final furlong or so. He was credited with an eight-length victory—the winning margin looked nearer six and three quarters—over the Fabre-trained War Zone, who reversed placings with the third and fourth Perrexa and Hothaifah from the Prix Eclipse over the same course and distance three weeks earlier. The two other British challengers for the Criterium, the useful pair Highdown and Doc Holiday (third in the Middle Park on his previous run) finished fifth and seventh respectively in the field of eleven. In terms of form, Captain Rio put up a very smart performance, bettered, in our estimation, during the year by only two other European-based two-year-olds, the Irish-trained Johannesburg and the outstanding filly Queen's Logic.

Whereas both Johannesburg and Queen's Logic went unbeaten through their two-year-old careers, Captain Rio did not hit the high spots until that tremendously impressive performance at Maisons-Laffitte. He made his debut, starting at 20/1, in the Roses Stakes at York's August meeting, taking the eye beforehand but proving too green to do himself justice, managing only seventh of eight after being slowly into his stride. He looked a good prospect when winning a Ripon maiden by six lengths on his second start, showing bags of speed and readily disposing of the odds-on Baldour, on the strength of which he started 5/2 favourite in a field of twenty-two for the very valuable St Leger Yearling Stakes at Doncaster. It was Captain Rio's third outing in as many weeks and he couldn't fend off Acclamation and Old Blue Eyes after making most in the stand-side group which dominated the finish. The strong, good-topped Captain Rio looked just the sort to train on and make up into an even better three-year-old, but there was seemingly no question of his being given a break or being 'put by' after Doncaster, nor after a somewhat

betabet Two-Year-Old Trophy, Redcar—jockey Dean McKeown,
who turned down the ride on I Cried For You in the Cambridgeshire on the same day,
collects this more valuable prize aboard Captain Rio; Old Blue Eyes is second

*Criterium de Maisons-Laffitte—Captain Rio is a revelation under much softer conditions,
putting up the best performance by a British-trained two-year-old colt all year; War Zone is second*

disappointing third when favourite for the Harry Rosebery Stakes at Ayr the
following week. Considering the speed he had been showing over six, Captain Rio
shouldn't have been troubled by the drop back to five furlongs in the Harry
Rosebery, but he couldn't find enough to get the better of Irish Vale and Master
Robbie in a close finish to a muddling race. It was back to six furlongs in the
betabet Two-Year-Old Trophy at Redcar at the beginning of October. The twenty-
five-runner field was packed with previous winners, and 16/1-shot Captain Rio
won a good renewal by a length and a quarter from Doncaster second Old Blue
Eyes, soon with the leaders and staying on strongly after going to the front just
inside the final two furlongs. The success was particularly sweet for Captain Rio's
jockey Dean McKeown, who turned down the winning ride on I Cried For You
in the Cambridgeshire on the same day (Captain Rio earned £105,908 at Redcar
compared to I Cried For You's £69,600 at Newmarket). Captain Rio's display
confirmed his toughness—it was his fifth outing in a little over six weeks—and
showed that he was still on the upgrade, clearly thriving on the programme mapped
out for him. He was declared again for the Rockingham Stakes at York a week after
Redcar, but suffered a slight foot injury when losing a shoe on the gallops. The
Criterium de Maisons-Laffitte, for which Captain Rio started favourite, took place
nineteen days after the betabet Two-Year-Old Trophy, the longest gap Captain Rio
had between any of his races.

Captain Rio (ch.c. Apr 11, 1999)	Pivotal (ch 1993)	Polar Falcon (b or br 1987)	Nureyev
			Marie d' Argonne
		Fearless Revival (ch 1987)	Cozzene
			Stufida
	Beloved Visitor (USA) (b 1988)	Miswaki (ch 1978)	Mr Prospector
			Hopespringseternal
		Abeesh (b 1982)	Nijinsky
			Lady Bugler

Captain Rio passed through the sale-ring three times before going into
training—fetching 23,000 guineas as a foal, 28,000 as a yearling (at the Doncaster
St Leger Yearling Sales) and 66,000 as a two-year-old at the Tattersalls Breeze-Up
Sales at Newmarket in April. Captain Rio's sire the King's Stand and Nunthorpe
winner Pivotal has made a fine start to his stud career, his first crop of three-
year-olds including Group/Grade 1 winners Silvester Lady (Preis der Diana) and
Golden Apples (Del Mar Oaks). That pair are unusual among Pivotal's offspring so
far in that they have been successful beyond a mile and Captain Rio is nine
furlongs, the Preis der Diana eleven furlongs). None of Pivotal's winners in Britain,
which include smart performers Red Carpet, Kyllachy and Needwood Blade, has
won at much beyond a mile and Captain Rio is unlikely to do so either. His dam
Beloved Visitor, a six-furlong winner as a two-year-old, bred two mile-and-a-half
winners before Captain Rio—One Pound (by Shareef Dancer) and Martial Arts (by
Arazi)—but Captain Rio's end-to-end style of racing is very much that of a sprinter
and it will be a surprise if he proves fully effective at much beyond six furlongs.
Although he has won on good to firm going, Captain Rio, who is named after Leeds
and England footballer Rio Ferdinand, clearly goes well on heavy, though, given
the rate at which he was progressing at the end of the latest season, it would be
dangerous to conclude that he will *need* soft or heavy ground to make a name
for himself at three. He looks likely to train on into one of the season's leading

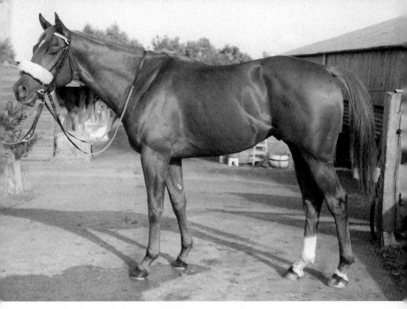

Mr D. Samuel's "Captain Rio"

sprinters. Plans at the time of writing are that he will start with a spring campaign on dirt in Dubai, taking in the Dubai Golden Shaheen, an all-aged six-furlong event at Nad Al Sheba on World Cup day. *R. M. Whitaker*

CAPTAIN RON (IRE) 5 b.g. Marju (IRE) 127 – Callas Star (Chief Singer 131) – [2001 11.9f⁶ 10.5g 18m Jun 24] little form. *P. D. Evans*

CAPTAIN SCOTT (IRE) 7 b.g. Polar Falcon (USA) 126 – Camera Girl (Kalaglow – 132) [2001 ?: 8v Mar 24] tall, lengthy gelding: formerly useful handicapper: very lightly raced nowadays. *G. A. Butler*

CAPTAIN SCOTTLAND 2 b.g. (May 3) Beveled (USA) – Little Egret 74 (Car- – white 127) [2001 7.1g 7f 6s Oct 5] 6,000Y: tall, leggy gelding: ninth foal: brother to 3-y-o Captain Gibson: dam Italian 1¼m/11f winner: behind in maidens. *D. J. S. ffrench Davis*

CAPTAIN'S FOLLY 3 b.f. Mind Games 121 – Miss Petella (Dunphy 124) [2001 35: – 5f Jul 22] small, sparely-made filly: poor maiden: should stay at least 6f. *J. S. Wainwright*

CAPTAIN'S LOG 6 b.g. Slip Anchor 136 – Cradle of Love (USA) 87 (Roberto **92** (USA) 131) [2001 87: 10d* 10.1m 10m⁴ 11.7m³ 10.1m* 10m 12g 10d 12d 10v Nov 8] leggy, rather lightly-made gelding: fairly useful performer: won minor events at Nottingham in May, Newcastle in July and Ayr in August: below form last 5 starts: best at 1¼m/1½m: acts on any ground: has run well when sweating: has started slowly/carried head high/raced freely: often held up. *M. L. W. Bell*

CAPTAIN STEVE (USA) 4 ch.c. Fly So Free (USA) 122 – Sparkling Delite **130** (USA) (Vice Regent (CAN)) [2001 127: a9f* a10f* a9f² a10f⁴ a8.5f³ a10f⁴ Aug 19]
The Dubai World Cup meeting goes from strength to strength and the day might not be too far distant when it comes close to justifying its billing as 'the Olympic Games of horseracing'. Thoroughbreds from sixteen countries contested the heavily-endowed six-race programme—the richest in the world—in March. All six races carried pattern status—it can't be long before officialdom catches up with

169

nearly everyone else in racing and recognises them all as Group 1—and there are said to be plans to introduce a second day. One of the main achievements of the Dubai World Cup—probably *the* main achievement—has been its success in tempting the Americans to send some of their best horses. American racing has traditionally been insular, in contrast to its more internationally-attuned European cousin, but the Dubai World Cup has hopefully paved the way for more leading American horses to be campaigned overseas in major international races.

The American challengers for the Dubai World Cup have generally proved very much at home on the artificial sand-based surface at Nad Al Sheba—more so than some of the best Europeans who have not managed to repeat their best turf form—and Captain Steve's victory in the latest edition gave the Americans their third victory in the short history of the event. An American one, two, three by Cigar, Soul of The Matter and L'Carriere in the inaugural running in 1996 was followed by a second and third (behind British-trained Singspiel) for Siphon and Sandpit and a second victory in 1998, when Kentucky Derby winner Silver Charm beat Swain narrowly. Silver Charm and the previous year's fourth Malek contested the Dubai World Cup again in 1999, when the Belmont Stakes winner Victory Gallop also took the field. Silver Charm was well below form but Malek and Victory Gallop came second and third behind surprise winner Almutawakel, who was generally reckoned only to be Godolphin's third string. The brilliant Dubai Millennium trounced his rivals in 2000 to give Godolphin and the United Arab Emirates a second victory, chased home by four of the five American challengers, Behrens, Public Purse, Puerto Madero and Ecton Park.

The American challengers had no runner of the calibre of Dubai Millennium to contend with in the latest edition of the Dubai World Cup, which carried total prize money of six million dollars, three million six hundred thousand of it (£2,509,714 at prevailing exchange rates) for the winner. The twelve runners were drawn from six countries, but none of the challengers from outside the United Arab Emirates had claims to being the best in their respective parts of the world. Captain Steve, third to Tiznow and Giant's Causeway in the Breeders' Cup Classic the previous year, and the Kentucky Derby and Belmont Stakes runner-up Aptitude represented North America. Along with Best of The Bests, who started 7/4 joint favourite with Captain Steve in the British betting, only Aptitude, French challenger Hightori and Godolphin's second-string Ekraar started at odds shorter than 22/1. Captain Steve arrived at Nad Al Sheba right at the top of his form, having put up the best performance of his career when beating Albert The Great, the pair ten and a half lengths clear, by a length and a quarter in the Donn Handicap at Gulfstream Park in February. Success in the Donn Handicap meant that Captain Steve had won Grade 1 events in America at two (Hollywood Futurity), three (Swaps Stakes) and four. He won the Dubai World Cup by three lengths, reeling in the long-time leader, the Japanese-trained mare To The Victory, in the home straight and running on strongly after taking the lead about a furlong out. To The Victory, who set a scorching pace, did well to hang on for second, half a length and a short head in front of Hightori and former Godolphin inmate State Shinto. Aptitude came sixth and the Godolphin representatives Ekraar, Best of The Bests and Broche seventh, eighth and tenth respectively. There was no British runner following the late withdrawal of Petrushka through injury.

Captain Steve provided his trainer Bob Baffert—'Winning here gives us Yanks the bragging rights for a year'—with his second Dubai World Cup winner, following Silver Charm, and his jockey Jerry Bailey with his third, following Cigar and Singspiel. The victories of Captain Steve and of Caller One in the Dubai Golden Shaheen helped the ten-strong American challenge to finish top of the day's prize-money table, ahead of the United Arab Emirates, Japan and France; a return of two fourths and a fifth for the British 'team' from fifteen runners—the biggest contingent after the United Arab Emirates—was a meagre return which yielded only sixth place in the table.

It was nearly three months before Captain Steve was seen out again, and, although he came a creditable second to Guided Tour at Churchill Downs on his return, he never recaptured his best form. He was beaten into fourth of five at odds on in the Hollywood Gold Cup at Hollywood Park in early-July and was below

Dubai World Cup, Nad Al Sheba—jockey Jerry Bailey wins the world's richest race for the third time aboard Captain Steve, beating the Japanese-trained To The Victory and Hightori

form again in two subsequent outings at Del Mar in California, on his last appearance managing only fourth of six behind Skimming in the Pacific Classic in August. Captain Steve was sold to Japanese interests in October for a reported five million dollars and will be standing at the Shizunai Stallion Station in 2002.

	Fly So Free (USA) (ch 1988)	Time For A Change (ch 1981)	Damascus / Resolver
Captain Steve (USA) (ch.c. 1997)		Free To Fly (b 1974)	Stevward / Dancing Lark
	Sparkling Delite (USA) (ch 1985)	Vice Regent (ch 1967)	Northern Dancer / Victoria Regina
		Sparkling Topaz (b 1974)	Jacinto / Alotoffun

Captain Steve provided his sire, the Breeders' Cup Juvenile winner Fly So Free, with his first Grade 1 winner. Fly So Free won twelve of his thirty-three races and was successful at up to nine furlongs, though showing his best form at shorter distances. Captain Steve's winning dam Sparkling Delite, a useful sprinter-miler, bred only two minor winners before Captain Steve, who fetched only 12,000 dollars as a foal before changing hands again as a yearling for 70,000 dollars; six months before Captain Steve's second sale, thirteen-year-old Sparkling Delite made only 7,000 dollars at Fasig-Tipton's Kentucky January Sale. Sparkling Delite was the best of four winning offspring out of Sparkling Topaz, who won five races and was twice placed in Grade 2 company over eight and a half furlongs as a four-year-old. Captain Steve, who usually raced prominently, was best at nine furlongs to a mile and a quarter and was campaigned exclusively on dirt (had won on sloppy going). He used to wear blinkers and had also worn a tongue tie. *R. Baffert, USA*

CAPTAIN VENTI   2 br.g. (Feb 25) Ventiquattrofogli (IRE) 118 – Lady Liza 69 (Air   **86** Trooper 115) [2001 5f 6d 6m* 7d* 7.5m³ 7.1s 7g⁴ 7m⁵ 6v³ Oct 26] 2,000Y: robust gelding: ninth foal: dam 1m winner: fairly useful performer: won maiden at Hamilton and nursery at Ayr in July: third of 22 in sales race at Doncaster final start: has pulled hard, but will stay 1m: acts on heavy and good to firm going. *J. J. Quinn*

171

CAQUI D'OR (IRE) 3 b.c. Danehill (USA) 126 – Ghaiya (USA) 110 (Alleged **90** (USA) 138) [2001 63p: 10s⁶ 12m* 12.3m² 14.1g* 14s* 14g Oct 6] sturdy, angular colt: fairly useful handicapper: won at Beverley (flashed tail under whip) in May, Nottingham in August and Haydock (beat Bawsian a head) in September: stays 1¾m: acts on soft and good to firm going. *J. L. Dunlop*

CARABOSSE 2 b.f. (Mar 3) Salse (USA) 128 – Ballet 61 (Sharrood (USA) 124) **51** [2001 6m 7.1m 6.1d 7s Oct 5] leggy, workmanlike filly: half-sister to several winners, notably 3-y-o Serge Lifar and 4-y-o Island Sound: dam, maiden, half-sister to May Hill winner Satinette: regressed after showing modest form on debut: bred to be suited by 1¼m+. *M. L. W. Bell*

CARADAYA 5 b.m. Presidium 124 – Caraniya 94 (Darshaan 133) [2001 12.3d⁴ 18f **–** Sep 20] angular mare: half-sister to useful Irish 7f (at 2 yrs) and 1¼m winner Cajarian and Irish 9f winner Caraiyma (both by Shahrastani): dam 1m (at 2 yrs) and 12.3f winner: no show in maiden at Chester and minor event at Pontefract. *W. M. Brisbourne*

CARADOC 6 ch.g. Bustino 136 – Hathaway (Connaught 130) [2001 11.9s Apr 12] **–** very lightly-raced maiden. *Mrs L. C. Jewell*

CARAFE 2 b.f. (Apr 26) Selkirk (USA) 129 – Caramba 114 (Belmez (USA) 131) [2001 **77 p** 6m⁴ Jul 27] rangy, good sort: has plenty of scope: very good walker: third foal: half-sister to 3-y-o Coyote: dam, 1m (Falmouth Stakes) and 1¼m (Nassau Stakes) winner, half-sister to smart performer up to 1m Lemon Souffle: 5/2 second favourite but very green, 7¾ lengths fourth of 5 to Ya Hajar in maiden at Ascot, drifting right from halfway and not knocked about: should do better. *Sir Michael Stoute*

CARBON COPY 3 ch.f. Pivotal 124 – Astolat (Rusticaro (FR) 124) [2001 73: 6.1d³ **77** 7.1m⁵ 7m² 7g 7m² 8.1m⁸ 8g Sep 28] tall, good sort: fair performer: won maiden at Warwick in September: stays 1m: acts on good to firm and good to soft going: blinkered last 4 starts: sold 18,000 gns, sent to USA. *W. J. Haggas*

CARD GAMES 4 b.f. First Trump 118 – Pericardia 60 (Petong 126) [2001 89: 6v 7s **–** 6d 7m 8.3g 8.1d Jun 9] lengthy filly: fairly useful handicapper at 3 yrs: well held in 2001, trained by S. Williams fourth/fifth starts: said to have suffered set-fast final one: has run well visored. *M. W. Easterby*

CARDINAL VENTURE (IRE) 3 b.g. Bishop of Cashel 122 – Phoenix Venture **91** (IRE) 69 (Thatching 131) [2001 62: 8s⁴ 8m² 8.1d 7m* 7.6f⁴ 8m³ 8g⁴ 7m 7d* 7d 7d Oct 20] tall, close-coupled gelding: fairly useful handicapper: won at Redcar in June and Doncaster (made all to beat Nashaab by ½ length) in September: probably best around 7f: acts on firm and good to soft ground. *K. A. Ryan*

CAREFULLY 3 ch.g. Caerleon (USA) 132 – Sabaah Elfull 75 (Kris 135) [2001 52: **51** e7g⁶ e7g⁵ f6g Mar 22] modest maiden: should be suited by at least 1m: acts on equitrack, raced only on good to firm going on turf. *N. A. Graham*

CAREL 3 b.c. Polish Precedent (USA) 131 – Castle Peak 90 (Darshaan 133) [2001 **78** 55p: 8.2v² 8m³ 10.5s⁵ Sep 8] fair maiden: should be suited by 1¼m/1½m: yet to race on firm going, probably acts on any other. *M. L. W. Bell*

CARENS HERO (IRE) 3 ch.g. Petardia 113 – Clear Glade (Vitiges (FR) 132) [2001 **73** 90: 7s 10g 8m² 7m³ 8f² 8.1m⁴ 8.2g⁵ 8.5m² 10d f8g f8.5g⁶ f9.4g Dec 11] strong gelding: **a61** fair performer on turf nowadays, modest on all-weather: left Mrs A. Perrett after sixth start: stays 8.5f: acts on fibresand, firm and soft going: tried blinkered once: reportedly bled from nose eighth start: free-going sort: usually races prominently: none too reliable. *R. Brotherton*

CAREQUICK 5 ch.m. Risk Me (FR) 127 – Miss Serlby 65 (Runnett 125) [2001 42: **–** 7v Oct 27] leggy, unfurnished mare: poor maiden at 4 yrs: well beaten only start in 2001: blinkered once at 3 yrs. *W. M. Brisbourne*

CARGO 2 b.g. (Feb 25) Emarati (USA) 74 – Portvasco 90 (Sharpo 132) [2001 5d 5f **59** 7m 6m⁴ 6m⁵ f6s* f6g⁵ 6d⁴ 6d Oct 30] 6,500F, 3,000Y: angular gelding: ninth foal: half-brother to 3 winners, including fairly useful 5f (at 2 yrs)/6f winner who stayed 1m Midwich Cuckoo (by Midyan): dam 6f winner: modest performer: won nursery at Wolverhampton in September: stays 6f: acts on fibresand, good to firm and soft going: sold 3,500 gns. *M. W. Easterby*

CARIBBEAN CORAL 2 ch.g. (Mar 15) Brief Truce (USA) 126 – Caribbean Star 81 **92** (Soviet Star (USA) 128) [2001 6m 6m* 6m⁵ 6m⁴ 6d Oct 13] 15,000Y: strong gelding: has scope: first foal: dam, 7f winner, half-sister to smart miler Caribbean Monarch: fairly useful performer: won maiden at Brighton in July: best effort when fifth to Acclamation in valuable sales race at Doncaster: not sure to stay much beyond 6f: acts on good to firm ground, ran poorly on good to soft: wandered under pressure penultimate start: gelded after final one. *C. F. Wall*

CARIB LADY (IRE)   2 b.f. (Feb 14) Sadler's Wells (USA) 132 – Belle Passe (Be My — p
Guest (USA) 126) [2001 8v Oct 26] IR 195,000Y: strong, well-made filly: seventh foal: closely related to smart Irish 6f to 1m performer Burden of Proof (by Fairy King), and half-sister to 4-y-o Noble Pasao and Italian winner up to 1¼m (including listed event) Revenger (by Persian Heights): dam ran once in Ireland: 6/1 and very green, well-held eighth of 11 in maiden at Doncaster, taking strong hold early and hanging badly left in straight: almost certainly capable better. *H. R. A. Cecil*

CARINAE (USA)   2 b.f. (Feb 22) Nureyev (USA) 131 – Turning Wheel (USA) 108   **99**
(Seeking The Gold (USA)) [2001 6m* 6m⁶ 6d² Oct 13] leggy, lightly-made filly: first foal: dam, 1¼m/11f winner in Britain/France, closely related to smart miler Ajfan and half-sister to smart performer up to 14.6f Minds Music: useful performer: won minor event at Newmarket in July: sixth to Queen's Logic in Lowther Stakes at York: improved on same course when 1½ lengths second to Prism in listed race: will probably stay 1m: sent to USA. *Sir Michael Stoute*

CARINA TOO (IRE)   2 b.f. (Apr 5) Entrepreneur 123 – Highly Respected (IRE) 57   —
(High Estate 127) [2001 7g Aug 2] IR 30,000F, IR 45,000Y: well-made filly: first foal: dam, maiden, closely related to smart Irish 6f performer Make No Mistake: 16/1, last in maiden at Goodwood: sold 3,000 gns. *M. A. Jarvis*

CARIOCA DREAM (USA)   3 b.f. Diesis 133 – Highland Ceilidh (IRE) 100 (Scottish   **77**
Reel 123) [2001 79p: 8s 12v* 11.8g⁵ 11.6v⁶ 12d 14.1s Nov 5] workmanlike filly: fair performer: won maiden at Folkestone in April: well below form last 3 starts: stays 1½m: raced only on good going or softer (acts on heavy). *W. J. Haggas*

CARK   3 b.g. Farfelu 103 – Precious Girl 76 (Precious Metal 106) [2001 57: 5m 5m 5m⁵   **73**
5f² 5d⁵ 5g² 5f⁴ 5g 5s³ 5g³ 5v² 5v³ 5v Oct 24] fair handicapper: best at 5f/6f: acts on any turf going: races prominently: has idled, and wanders under pressure, often markedly so: consistent. *M. Todhunter*

CARLOS GIRL (IRE)   2 b.f. (Mar 30) Sri Pekan (USA) 117 – Sliding (Formidable   **44**
(USA) 125) [2001 5.1m 6.1v Oct 4] 1,200 2-y-o: sparely-made filly: first foal: dam unraced half-sister to 2-y-o Rashbag and 3-y-o Suggestive: poor form in maidens: sent to Sweden. *B. A. McMahon*

CARLTON RODE   4 b.g. Carlton (GER) 116 – Alghabrah 70 (Lomond (USA) 128)   —
[2001 10m May 8] sixth foal: half-brother to a winner at up to 1¼m in Italy by Dominion: dam maiden who stayed 1m: slowly away in Brighton seller. *D. R. C. Elsworth*

CARLYS QUEST   7 ch.g. Primo Dominie 121 – Tuppy (USA) (Sharpen Up 127) [2001   **97**
96: 16s⁴ 16m³ 12m² 20m Jun 20] leggy gelding: useful performer: creditable efforts in 2001 when in frame: effective at 1½m to 2¼m: acts on any going: visored/blinkered/tongue tied: often off bridle early on/comes from behind: quirky, but is consistent. *J. Neville*

CARMOSINE (IRE)   3 b.g. Tagula (IRE) 116 – Adocentyn (USA) (Upper Nile   —
(USA)) [2001 f8g 8d⁶ 6m Sep 8] IR 7,000F, IR 7,000Y, 24,000 2-y-o: half-brother to 2 winners abroad: dam, ran once at 2 yrs, half-sister to US Grade 3 9f winner Father Hogan and smart 1982 2-y-o 6f/7f winner Northern Adventure: tongue tied, well beaten in maidens. *J. L. Eyre*

CARNAGE (IRE)   4 b.g. Catrail (USA) 123 – Caranina (USA) 85 (Caro 133) [2001   **60**
53: 6v⁶ 7s 8.1m³ 8g³ f14g* Dec 14] tall, leggy gelding: modest performer: off 4 months, having left Mrs P. N. Dutfield, won handicap at Southwell (all-weather debut) in December: stays 1¾m: acts on fibresand, soft and good to firm ground. *C. Drew*

CARNIVAL DANCER   3 b.c. Sadler's Wells (USA) 132 – Red Carnival (USA)   **123 p**
109 (Mr Prospector (USA)) [2001 86P: 7.9d* 8.1m² 10d* 10d⁵ Oct 20]
    Unlike his namesake, who went downhill rapidly after winning the 1959 Granville Stakes at Ascot and ended up doing the rounds in modest handicaps on the northern circuit, Carnival Dancer has made great strides and on only his fourth start showed very smart form when running out an impressive winner of the Sodexho Prestige Scottish Classic at Ayr. In very good hands and with further improvement likely, there's every reason to anticipate Carnival Dancer's enjoying further pattern-race success as a four-year-old.

Sodexho Prestige Scottish Classic, Ayr—
Carnival Dancer quickens impressively to account for the consistent Albarahin

The well-bred Carnival Dancer had very much caught the eye on his only outing at two, despite failing to land the odds in a minor event at Newmarket, and he wasted no time in getting off the mark in his second season, winning a maiden at York in June on his return easily. Although Carnival Dancer showed better form in finishing second in a minor event at Sandown on his next start, he gave the impression he wasn't at ease on the good to firm ground, taking time to warm to his task. Therefore, it came as no surprise to see him show further marked improvement back on good to soft and stepped up to a mile and a quarter in the Scottish Classic. The six-runner event looked to rest between the four southern-trained runners, Carnival Dancer the only three-year-old in a quartet made up of proven smart performers in Albarahin, Island House and Right Wing. The confidently-ridden Carnival Dancer was handily placed when the race began in earnest in the straight. Shaken up two furlongs out, he quickened in very good style to lead shortly after, then stormed clear, still looking to have plenty of running left in him as he passed the post three lengths clear of runner-up Albarahin, who had made the running.

Carnival Dancer and Albarahin, who went on to win his next three races including the Prix Dollar, met again three months later in the Champion Stakes at Newmarket. Carnival Dancer, who had two handlers in the paddock, looked in the pink of condition following his absence and again got the better of Albarahin though without managing to run up to his best. He finished fifth of twelve to the latter's stable-companion Nayef, beaten around six lengths, momentarily looking as though he'd get into the argument under two furlongs out but unable to sustain his effort. With Kieren Fallon opting for stable-companion No Excuse Needed, Carnival Dancer was ridden for the first time by Olivier Peslier, whose tactics reportedly didn't please connections, who said Peslier had ignored instructions and given the horse too much to do. They have a point, but on the day it probably didn't make a great deal of difference. Only a little improvement on his Ayr form would have seen Carnival Dancer involved in the finish, but as the least experienced runner in the field, it is only fair to make some allowances for him. Carnival Dancer looked a cracking prospect at Ayr, and he deserves another chance.

Carnival Dancer (b.c. 1998)	Sadler's Wells (USA) (b 1981)	Northern Dancer (b 1961)	Nearctic
			Natalma
		Fairy Bridge (b 1975)	Bold Reason
			Special
	Red Carnival (USA) (b 1992)	Mr Prospector (b 1970)	Raise A Native
			Gold Digger
		Seaside Attraction (b 1987)	Seattle Slew
			Kamar

Carnival Dancer is the first foal of Red Carnival, also owned by the Cheveley Park Stud and trained by Sir Michael Stoute. A 750,000-dollar yearling, Red Carnival won both her starts as a two-year-old, including the Cherry Hinton from Harayir, who went on to win the One Thousand Guineas. Red Carnival missed the Guineas after injuring her near-fore when third in the Nell Gwyn on her reappearance and ran only twice more, showing her best form when third to Harayir in the Challenge Stakes. A sister to Golden Attraction, a leading two-year-old filly in the States in 1995, and half-sister to the 1998 Florida Derby winner Cape Town, Red Carnival is a daughter of the Kentucky Oaks winner Seaside Attraction. Seaside Attraction is closely related to another Oaks winner, Gorgeous, who won the Hollywood version the same year as she won the Grade 1 Ashland Stakes and finished second in the Breeders' Cup Distaff; she is also a half-sister to the Queen's Plate winner and 1984 champion Canadian three-year-old Key To The Moon and the Stoute-trained Princess Margaret winner Hiaam. Both their dam Kamar and grandam Square Angel won the Canadian Oaks and were champions in Canada, and are now the grandams of Fantastic Light and Swain respectively. Hopefully, more will be seen of Carnival Dancer's year-younger half-brother Funfair (by Singspiel) who refused to enter the stalls on his intended debut at Newmarket in November. Red Carnival never raced, nor was she likely to have stayed, beyond a mile. Carnival Dancer, on the other hand, has shown better form at a mile and a quarter than at a mile and will probably stay a mile and a half. A strong colt, he has raced only on good to soft and soft going apart from at Sandown. *Sir Michael Stoute*

CARNOUSTIE (USA) 3 gr.f. Ezzoud (IRE) 126 – Sarba (USA) (Persepolis (FR) **79**
127) [2001 10s 10g^2 12.6m^2 11.9m^2 12g^4 9.9m* 10m Sep 21] $27,000F: lengthy, good-topped filly: second foal: dam won up to 2m in France, placed in Prix de Royallieu and Prix Gladiateur: fairly useful performer: made hard work of landing odds in maiden at Beverley in August: should stay 1¾m: acts on good to firm going: found little/carried head awkwardly final start: sold 11,000 gns. *M. A. Jarvis*

CAROLE'S DOVE 5 b.m. Manhal – Nimble Dove 62 (Starch Reduced 112) [2001 –: **–**
16s Oct 30] big, lengthy mare: no form. *C. J. Price*

CAROLINA SILK (IRE) 2 b.c. (Feb 14) Barathea (IRE) 127 – Bold Fashion (FR) **95 p**
(Nashwan (USA) 135) [2001 8g 8f^6 8v^2 Oct 26] 20,000F, 65,000Y: big, good sort: third foal: dam, French 10.5f winner, sister to useful French 1m/9f performer Irish Fashion: showed plenty of promise prior to 2 lengths second of 3 to Angelus Sunset in minor event at Newbury: acts on heavy going (carried head rather high and didn't stride out on firm): type to make a better 3-y-o, and should win races. *R. Hannon*

CAROLINE ISLAND (IRE) 2 b.f. (Feb 22) Catrail (USA) 123 – Pacific Grove 89 **89**
(Persian Bold 123) [2001 5g^6 7m^5 6m* Aug 1] 6,500F, 12,500Y: leggy filly: second foal: half-sister to fairly useful Irish 6f winner John Dorans Melody (by Bluebird): dam, 2-y-o 7f/1m winner, half-sister to useful French performer around 1¼m All Glory: much improved effort (fairly useful form) when beating Princess Petardia easily by 6 lengths in maiden at Leicester: not sure to stay much beyond 6f: sent to USA. *H. Morrison*

CAROLS CHOICE 4 ch.f. Emarati (USA) 74 – Lucky Song 91 (Lucky Wednesday **57**
124) [2001 62, a71: e5g^5 e6g^3 f6g^3 f5g^5 5.1d f6g^6 f5g 5g^2 5f^3 5g^4 5m f5s^2 f5g f5s^3 Dec **a67**
15] fair maiden handicapper on all-weather, modest on turf: effective at 5f/6f: acts on

fibresand/equitrack, firm and good to soft going: tried blinkered/visored: has swished tail: usually races prominently. *D. Haydn Jones*

CAROUSING 4 b.g. Selkirk (USA) 129 – Moon Carnival 94 (Be My Guest (USA) **88** 126) [2001 94d: 12s 13s 12d 12m* 10.3f 12.3f⁶ 16.1m* 16m³ 16.2g 16.1f 16g 12s f16.2f Dec 5] good-topped gelding: unimpressive mover: fairly useful handicapper: left R. Beckett after second start: successful at Musselburgh and Newcastle in May: well below form last 4 starts: stays 2m: acts on firm and soft going: tried blinkered at 3 yrs: has been slowly away: possibly none too genuine. *A. Bailey*

CARPET LADY (IRE) 3 b.f. Night Shift (USA) – Lucky Fountain (IRE) (Lafontaine **–** (USA) 117) [2001 70: 8d Jun 17] fair maiden: well held only 3-y-o start: should stay at least 7f: acts on good to firm ground. *Mrs P. N. Dutfield*

CARPET PRINCESS (IRE) 3 gr. or ro.f. Prince of Birds (USA) 121 – Krayyalei **54** (IRE) 94 (Krayyan 117) [2001 61?: 7s⁴ 10m 8.1m 8g 8g³ Oct 1] smallish, close-coupled filly: modest maiden: stays 1m: acts on soft and good to firm going: has gone left leaving stall/edged left. *Mrs P. N. Dutfield*

CARRACA (IRE) 3 b.g. Alzao (USA) 117 – Honey Bun 51 (Unfuwain (USA) 131) **58 §** [2001 –: 8.2v³ 9.9m 10g² 12.3f 10.5g 12d Oct 9] strong, good-bodied gelding: modest maiden: should stay 1½m: acts on heavy going: blinkered: downed tools fourth start, refused to race last 2: one to avoid: sold 1,300 gns. *J. D. Bethell*

CARRADALE 2 ch.f. (May 13) Pursuit of Love 124 – Rynavey 67 (Rousillon (USA) **73** 133) [2001 5f* 6d³ 6d³ Jul 23] fifth foal: half-sister to 1998 2-y-o 6f winner Dipple (later won in Norway up to 9f, by Komaite) and 1999 2-y-o 6f winner Zestril (by Zilzal): dam, middle-distance maiden, half-sister to smart winner up to 13f Applecross (dam of very smart performers Craigsteel and Invermark): fair form: won maiden at Musselburgh in June: third in 5-runner minor event at Haydock and in nursery at Ayr: will stay 1m. *Denys Smith*

CARRICK LADY (IRE) 3 ch.f. Fayruz 116 – Mantlepiece (IRE) (Common Grounds **40** 118) [2001 44: f7g³ f8g³ f8.5g 7m⁶ 8.5d 7m⁵ 10v Oct 29] small, compact filly: poor **a46** maiden: stays 1m: acts on soft going, good to firm and fibresand: blinkered once at 2 yrs. *G. P. Enright*

CARRIE CAN CAN 4 b.f. Green Tune (USA) 125 – Maidenhair (IRE) (Darshaan **–** 133) [2001 67, a73: f11s Jan 22] angular filly: fair handicapper at 3 yrs: below form only 4-y-o start. *J. G. Given*

CARRIE POOTER 5 b.m. Tragic Role (USA) – Ginny Binny 113 (Ahonoora 122) **95** [2001 87: f6s⁴ f6g⁸ f6g² Mar 10] workmanlike mare: useful handicapper, raced only on all-weather at 5 yrs: won at Wolverhampton in February: reportedly injured a joint final start: stays 7f: acts on fibresand and has form on any turf going: possibly best in blinkers nowadays. *T. D. Barron*

CARRINGTON DYNASTY 2 b.g. (May 11) Flockton's Own 98 – Starlite Night **–** (USA) 105 (Star de Naskra (USA)) [2001 5g 7m 6g p6g Dec 22] fifth reported living foal: dam 7f winner: no sign of ability, including in sellers. *M. Madgwick*

CARROZZINA 2 br.f. (Jan 20) Vettori (IRE) 119 – Doliouchka (Saumarez 132) [2001 **70** 7.1m* f8.5s³ Dec 15] unfurnished filly: first foal: dam, French 9f winner, half-sister to smart French sprinter Titus Livius: won maiden at Warwick in September in blanket finish, always well placed: well below that form in 4-runner minor event at Wolverhampton: should stay at least 1m. *J. G. Given*

CARSON DANCER (USA) 3 ch.f. Carson City (USA) – All Dance (USA) (North- **52 ?** ern Dancer) [2001 8.3d 8f⁶ 10m 8.5s Sep 25] $97,000F, $110,000Y: angular filly: closely related to winner in USA by Fappiano and half-sister to several winners, including 7f winner Shake Town (by Caro) and very smart hurdler Ruling (by Alleged): dam, French 1m winner, half-sister to Kentucky Derby winner Winning Colors: apparently modest form at best: said to have had breathing problem final start. *M. L. W. Bell*

CARTMEL PARK 5 ch.g. Skyliner 117 – Oh My Oh My (Ballacashtal (CAN)) [2001 **61 §** 84d, a87d; 5m 5m* 5m 5m f5g 5f Jul 9] tall, lengthy gelding: modest nowadays: won claimer at Newcastle (left M. Todhunter £5,000) in June: raced only at 5f: acts on firm going, soft and fibresand: effective visored/blinkered or not: has had tongue tied: quirky, unreliable sort who needs to dominate. *J. R. Weymes*

CARTOUCHE 7 gr.g. Terimon 124 – Emblazon 91 (Wolver Hollow 126) [2001 f16g **–** Apr 9] winning handicapper at 3 yrs: tailed off on only Flat outing since. *Miss H. M. Irving*

CARUSO'S 3 b.f. Be My Guest (USA) 126 – Courtisane (Persepolis (FR) 127) [2001 —
51: e8g f8g 6m 10m 9.9m 7.5m Aug 26] small, quite attractive filly: has a quick action:
modest maiden at 2 yrs: well beaten in 2001: best form at 5f: acts on firm ground, below
form on soft/all-weather. *E. J. O'Neill*

CARYS LYN 3 b.f. Awesome 73 – Reigning Royal (Tina's Pet 121) [2001 7g 8d Aug —
19] first foal: dam seemed of little account: well beaten in Leicester seller (very slowly
away) and Pontefract maiden. *D. Burchell*

CASA GRANDE (IRE) 3 b.f. Grand Lodge (USA) 125 – Sodium's Niece (North- **53**
fields (USA)) [2001 8.3g 8.1s⁵ 8s 10.9v² 14.1s Oct 31] IR 5,600F, IR 7,700Y: half-sister
to several winners, including useful 7f winner who stayed 1¼m Rickenbacker (by
Bluebird): dam third at 8.5f in Ireland at 2 yrs: modest maiden: probably stays 11f: raced
only on good going or softer: sold 800 gns. *R. Guest*

CASE STUDY (IRE) 2 ch.f. (Apr 19) Case Law 113 – Look Nonchalant (IRE) 61 **60**
(Fayruz 116) [2001 5d 5m* May 25] IR 2,200Y: lengthy, good-bodied filly: second living
foal: half-sister to fairly useful Irish 9f and 1½m winner Nonchalant (by Magical
Wonder): dam, Irish maiden, probably stayed 1m: modest form when winning claimer at
Haydock in May: should stay at least 6f. *Mrs P. N. Dutfield*

CASH 3 b.g. Bishop of Cashel 122 – Ballad Island 83 (Ballad Rock 122) [2001 –: 7.1d **66**
6.1v⁴ f6g⁴ f6g f6g* f6g⁵ f6g² f5g³ f6g² f5g* Dec 14] fair performer on all-weather, poor
on turf: won maiden at Southwell (after 3½-month break) in October and handicap there
in December: effective at 5f/6f: acts on heavy going and fibresand: races up with pace:
genuine. *M. Brittain*

CASHEL BAY (USA) 3 b.c. Nureyev (USA) 131 – Madame Premier (USA) (Raja **85**
Baba (USA)) [2001 85: 8s⁵ 8m⁴ 14g⁶ 8g 12f 8m 12g 9m⁵ 12g 12s 8.5d 10s Nov 11] leggy
colt: brother to 3 winners, including French sprinter Baba Thong and Irish 7f (at 2 yrs)
and 8.5f winner Moiseyev, both useful, closely related to smart French 6.5f (at 2 yrs) to
1m winner Northern Premier (by Northern Baby) and half-brother to several winners:
dam 2-y-o 5f stakes winner in USA: fairly useful performer: trained first three 2-y-o starts
by A. O'Brien, making all in maiden at Galway: only a few creditable efforts in 2001,
though often very highly tried (including in Irish 2000 Guineas, Derby and Irish Derby):
seems to stay 1¾m: acts on soft and good to firm going: usually blinkered. *Luke Comer,
Ireland*

CASHEL DANCER 2 b.f. (Mar 26) Bishop of Cashel 122 – Dancing Debut 83 (Polar **47**
Falcon (USA) 126) [2001 f6g 7.1m 7.1s⁴ 10d f8g Nov 19] 13,500F, 1,000Y: leggy,
angular filly: second foal: dam, maiden who stayed 1¼m, out of half-sister to 2000
Guineas winner Entrepreneur and Coronation Stakes winner Exclusive: poor maiden.
S. A. Brookshaw

CASHMERE 2 ch.f. (Feb 2) Barathea (IRE) 127 – Wanton 106 (Kris 135) [2001 6g **69 P**
Oct 6] strong, lengthy filly: has scope: half-sister to several winners, including Irish 1000
Guineas winner Classic Park (by Robellino) and useful 5f (at 2 yrs) and 9f (in UAE)
winner Magongo (by Be My Chief): dam, sprinter (best at 2 yrs), half-sister to smart
sprinter Easy Option: 33/1 and backward, shaped well when eighth of 17 to Scarlet
Ribbons in maiden at Newmarket, travelling strongly under restraint long way and
keeping on under considerate handling: bred to prove best up to 1m: type to do much
better at 3 yrs. *J. R. Fanshawe*

CASHMERE LADY 9 b.m. Hubbly Bubbly (USA) – Choir (High Top 131) [2001 **64**
70d: 10v* 9.9m 12m 12g Jul 20] big, strong mare: modest handicapper nowadays: won at
Nottingham in May: best at 1¼m (given a test) to 1½m: acts on any turf going and
fibresand: held up: none too consistent. *J. L. Eyre*

CASHNEEM (IRE) 3 b.g. Case Law 113 – Haanem 64 (Mtoto 134) [2001 83: 8d 7g **86**
7m³ 7.1m 6m* 7f Aug 1] strong gelding: fairly useful handicapper: won at Newbury in
July: headstrong, and likely to prove best around 6f: acts on good to firm ground,
probably on soft. *P. W. Harris*

CASING (IRE) 3 gr.f. Case Law 113 – Singhana (IRE) (Mouktar 129) [2001 7.1m **41**
6m⁵ 7g 6d Nov 2] third foal: dam Irish 1¾m winner: poor maiden. *F. Jordan*

CASPIAN SEA 2 ch.c. (Mar 11) Cadeaux Genereux 131 – Zilayah (USA) 79 (Zilzal —
(USA) 137) [2001 6m Jul 4] third foal: half-brother to fairly useful French 1m/9f winner
Billowing Sail (by Bering): dam, 2-y-o 7f winner, half-sister to smart French stayer
Molesnes and to dam of very smart French performer up to 7f Cherokee Rose: 20/1 and
green, seventh of 8 in maiden at Yarmouth: sent to UAE. *E. A. L. Dunlop*

CASSANDRA   5 b.m. Catrail (USA) 123 – Circo 77 (High Top 131) [2001 61: 10v⁴   **53**
10g* 12m 9.9f 10m 10.5g 10.1g 9.9s³ 10.4s Oct 11] deep-girthed mare: modest handicapper: won at Ripon in May: best around 1¼m: acts on soft and good to firm going: has
raced freely/looked bit wayward: thoroughly mulish in preliminaries sixth start: often
leads: none too consistent. *M. Brittain*

CASSANDRA GO (IRE)   5 gr.m. Indian Ridge 123 – Rahaam (USA) 91   **119**
(Secreto (USA) 128) [2001 110: 5g² 5f* 5m* 6m² Jul 12]
    The very smart and notably speedy Cassandra Go will not be seen again on
the racecourse, but, all being well, she should continue to make her mark on it for
many years yet through her offspring, possibly starting in 2004 when the Green
Desert foal she is carrying will be a two-year-old. An in-foal Cassandra Go was
better than ever as her career drew to a close, and had she continued after the July
Cup there was every chance she could have added to her six victories. The King
George Stakes at Goodwood, which she'd won in a thrilling finish the previous
year, would have provided her with one good opportunity to do so, while there was
also the option of taking her to Deauville. Unlike in Britain, where the time limit
is one hundred and twenty days, an in-foal mare can race in France at up to one
hundred and fifty days after she conceives.
    Adding another King George would not have enhanced Cassandra Go's
reputation significantly given what she had achieved in even more prestigious
events on her last three starts, the first two of those providing her with wins in
Group 2 races. A promising second to Rushcutter Bay in the Palace House Stakes
at Newmarket on her reappearance, Cassandra Go then contested the Tripleprint
Temple Stakes at Sandown and went off disputing favouritism with the previous
season's King's Stand and Nunthorpe winner Nuclear Debate. There wasn't much
between them at the finish but it was Cassandra Go who held on to win, with third
favourite Vision of Night splitting the pair. Whereas Nuclear Debate didn't receive
the best of rides, Cassandra Go was, as usual, handled with great expertise by
Michael Roberts, the filly's partner in all but the first of her seventeen races.
Roberts, despite being hampered by a saddle which reportedly had slipped shortly
after the stalls opened, soon had Cassandra Go disputing the lead and was quick to
maximise his chance. Sent on over a furlong out, Cassandra Go ran on gamely to
hold on by half a length.
    The first three in the Temple Stakes renewed rivalry in the King's Stand at
Royal Ascot, where the betting suggested that Nuclear Debate would turn the
tables. He started favourite at 11/4, with Cassandra Go next in the betting at 8/1
in a twenty-two-runner field which raced in two distinct groups through the early
stages. Those involved in the finish came from the stand-side bunch, with Cassandra Go, who travelled strongly just off the pace, quickly settling the issue after

Tripleprint Temple Stakes, Sandown—the in-foal Cassandra Go beats Vision of Night (second right),
Nuclear Debate (right) and Cotton House (rail)

King's Stand Stakes, Ascot—Cassandra Go takes the third pattern race of her career; fellow grey 50/1-shot Misty Eyed follows her home, ahead of 100/1-shot Funny Valentine (No.17)

being pushed ahead approaching the final furlong. At the line she had a length and a quarter to spare over Misty Eyed, who finished fast to take second ahead of another three-year-old Funny Valentine, with Vision of Night in fourth and Nuclear Debate only seventh. Although she had won over as far as seven furlongs earlier in her career, five furlongs was considered to be Cassandra Go's optimum trip, but her performance in the July Cup at Newmarket on her final outing left no room for doubt that she was equally effective at six. Like so many other sprinters during the season, Cassandra Go was unable to trouble Mozart, who beat her by three and a half lengths. However, she took care of the sixteen others in the field decisively enough, keeping on well in pursuit of the winner.

Cassandra Go (IRE) (gr.m. 1996)	Indian Ridge (ch 1985)	Ahonoora (ch 1975)	Lorenzaccio
			Helen Nichols
		Hillbrow (ch 1975)	Swing Easy
			Golden City
	Rahaam (USA) (gr 1987)	Secreto (b 1981)	Northern Dancer
			Betty's Secret
		Fager's Glory (gr 1976)	Mr Prospector
			Street's Glory

Cassandra Go, a lengthy, angular mare, cost 82,000 guineas as a foal and according to her owner, Trevor Stewart, was bought to pinhook. Sent to the yearling sales, the bidding was apparently well under way when Stewart decided he didn't want to sell after all and went to 200,000 guineas to buy her back. It was an inspired decision. Not only has Cassandra Go more than repaid her purchase price, but she is also going to prove a valuable addition to her owner's band of broodmares based at the Ballyhimikin Stud in Ireland.

A few months before Cassandra Go was first put up for sale, her half-brother Verglas (by Highest Honor) won the Coventry Stakes at Royal Ascot, and

179

he went on to finish runner-up in the Irish Two Thousand Guineas. Their dam Rahaam, a fairly useful seven-furlong winner who stayed a mile and a quarter, has produced four other winners, three of them useful. They include Cassandra Go's brother Grey Eminence, who has shown his best form at six furlongs, Verglas' brother Tortuguero, a winner twice at two in 2000 before being sold to race in the States, and Persian Secret (by Persian Heights). The last-named, successful at up to a mile in France, is the dam of the very smart French three-year-old Do The Honours. Cassandra Go's grandam, the unraced Fager's Glory, produced nine winners all told, notably the 1986 Prix Thomas Bryon winner Glory Forever. Cassandra Go reportedly had a wind operation in 1999, and was tongue tied on three occasions that year. She has raced in a crossed and dropped noseband. A genuine and consistent performer, Cassandra Go never encountered soft or heavy going but acted on any other. *G. Wragg*

CASSE-NOISETTE (IRE)   3 b.f. Brief Truce (USA) 126 – Highdrive (Ballymore – 123) [2001 7m 10m 7g 10g 7s 14.1s Oct 31] 10,500Y: half-sister to 3 winners, including smart sprinter Anzio (by Hatim) and fairly useful 1992 2-y-o 7f winner who probably stayed 1¼m Wynona (by Cyrano de Bergerac): dam well beaten: no form: tried blinkered: has been reluctant stalls/slowly away. *Miss Gay Kelleway*

CASSIRER (IRE)   2 ch.c. (Mar 17) Zafonic (USA) 130 – Oriane 109 (Nashwan   **89 p** (USA) 135) [2001 6m³ 6s² 7s* Oct 16] strong colt: first foal: dam, Irish 1m winner, half-sister to smart miler Killer Instinct (by Zafonic) out of smart half-sister to Irish Oaks winner Colorspin, herself dam of Opera House and Kayf Tara: progressive form in maidens: won 18-runner event at Leicester by ¾ length from Ridley, gamely getting on top final 1f: will stay 1m: acts on soft ground: should make a useful 3-y-o. *Sir Michael Stoute*

CASSIUS   3 b.g. Machiavellian (USA) 123 – Chain Dance 88 (Shareef Dancer (USA) – 135) [2001 73: 7g 10.3f 10g Jul 2] good-topped gelding: promising debut at 2 yrs but little form after, including visored: dead. *J. R. Fanshawe*

CASTA DIVA (IRE)   2 ch.f. (Feb 14) Case Law 113 – Casting Vote (USA) 54 (Monte-   **74** verdi 129) [2001 6m 6g³ 6g 7m* 7d⁶ Oct 2] IR 3,500Y: strong filly: fourth foal: sister to a winner up to 10.5f in Scandinavia and closely related to 8-y-o Mr Speaker: dam, maiden best at 1¼m, winning hurdler: fair performer: won maiden at Thirsk in September: good sixth in nursery at Newmarket: will stay 1m. *C. F. Wall*

CASTANET   2 b.f. (Apr 1) Pennekamp (USA) 130 – Addaya (IRE) (Persian Bold 123)   **78** [2001 6g² 5s Aug 16] 85,000Y: rangy, angular filly: third foal: half-sister to 3-y-o Priors Lodge: dam once-raced daughter of half-sister to smart 7f/1m performer Hadeer: shaped well when 5 lengths second to Guys And Dolls in maiden at Newmarket: reportedly upset at start when beaten at odds on 13 days later: should be suited by at least 7f: joined W. Haggas. *Sir Michael Stoute*

CASTAWAY QUEEN (IRE)   2 ch.f. (Mar 14) Selkirk (USA) 129 – Surfing 71   **68** (Grundy 137) [2001 6g² 6m 7m⁶ 7d Oct 2] IR 135,000Y: good-topped filly: half-sister to several winners, including useful 6f to 9.4f winner Mister Fire Eyes (by Petorius), later US Grade 3 1m winner, and a 1½m winner in France by Glow: dam, maiden who stayed 7f, half-sister to Middle Park winner Bassenthwaite: fair maiden: second at Windsor, best effort: should stay 1m. *W. R. Muir*

CAST IRON   2 b.g. (Jan 18) Efisio 120 – Misellina (FR) 57 (Polish Precedent (USA) – 131) [2001 6s f8g⁴ 8.2s f7g³ f6g² f5s* Dec 27] 17,000Y: first foal: dam temperamental   **a62** maiden who stayed 1m: modest performer: won seller at Wolverhampton: likely to prove best at 5f/6f: acts on fibresand, well beaten both starts on turf: blinkered last 2 starts: has edged left under pressure. *R. Guest*

CASTLEBAR   4 b.g. Formidable (USA) 125 – Nineteenth of May 86 (Homing 130) – [2001 57: f8.5g f8.5g f12g f9.4s Dec 27] modest winner at 3 yrs: well held in 2001, leaving K. Burke after penultimate start: tried blinkered. *I. A. Wood*

CASTLE BELLE   5 ch.m. King's Signet (USA) 110 – Castle Maid 38 (Castle Keep – 121) [2001 5.1f Jul 26] no form. *R. J. Hodges*

CASTLEBRIDGE   4 b.g. Batshoof 122 – Super Sisters (AUS) (Call Report (USA))   **49 §** [2001 78d: 10f 10.9m 10m 8.1m* 10.1d⁴ 7.1m 9.7m f12g 10g 10s* f11g f12f Dec 5]   **a– §** neat gelding: poor performer: won selling handicaps at Chepstow in July and Brighton in October: effective at 1m to 10.5f: acts on fibresand, good to firm and heavy going: usually visored/blinkered: needs to dominate: unreliable. *M. D. I. Usher*

CASTLE GANDOLFO (USA)   2 ch.c. (Feb 14) Gone West (USA) – Golden   **113**
Oriole (USA) (Northern Dancer) [2001 6s* 8d* 8v² 10v² Nov 13]
 At a time when Castel Gandolfo was in the public eye as the Pope's summer residence, there were no sightings of the Aidan O'Brien-trained Castle Gandolfo. The colt had provided his trainer with his second two-year-old winner of the season—Rock of Gibraltar was the first—when landing the odds in a six-furlong maiden at Cork in April, but was reportedly then given time to develop, missing the next five months. The break would appear to have served its purpose. Castle Gandolfo returned to show smart form in each of his three remaining races, winning the Group 3 Juddmonte Beresford Stakes at the Curragh and finishing second in two Group 1 events, the Racing Post Trophy and the Criterium de Saint-Cloud. O'Brien had trained the five previous winners of the Beresford but none had put up anything like so good a performance in the race as Castle Gandolfo. Seeming well suited by the step up to a mile, he stayed on strongly after taking up the running a furlong and a half out and drew seven lengths clear of his nearest pursuer, his stable-companion Camp David. Two of the stable's previous winners of the race had gone on to run well in the Racing Post Trophy at Doncaster, Saratoga Springs winning it in 1997 and Lermontov finishing second, to the O'Brien-trained Aristotle, two years later. Castle Gandolfo started at odds on to emulate the former, but suffered the same fate as the latter after looking the likely winner when improving steadily to lead over two furlongs out. Though keeping on strongly to draw well clear of the remainder, Castle Gandolfo was caught near the finish by stable-companion High Chaparral and beaten three quarters of a length. It was another O'Brien runner, Ballingarry, who came between Castle Gandolfo and victory at Saint-Cloud. Castle Gandolfo kept up a persistent challenge to Ballingarry after the latter took up the running early in the straight, but he could do no more close home and was beaten a length. On heavy ground, the distance of a mile and a quarter seemed plenty far enough for Castle Gandolfo, though he will prove fully effective at the trip under much less testing conditions.

		Mr Prospector (b 1970)	Raise A Native
			Gold Digger
Castle Gandolfo (USA)	Gone West (USA) (b 1984)	Secrettame (ch 1978)	Secretariat
(ch.c. Feb 14, 1999)			Tamerett
		Northern Dancer (b 1961)	Nearctic
	Golden Oriole (USA)		Natalma
	(ch 1983)	Sex Appeal (ch 1970)	Buckpasser
			Best In Show

 The rather leggy, close-coupled Castle Gandolfo is the tenth live foal of Golden Oriole and her fifth winner. Her other successful produce include a couple by Woodman, and therefore both closely related to Castle Gandolfo, notably Devonwood, who has shown smart form at up to a mile and three quarters in the States. The beautifully-bred Golden Oriole is a sister to El Gran Senor and Try My Best, and although not in the same league as that pair on the racecourse she did manage to win a minor event over six furlongs in Ireland at three. Their dam Sex Appeal, who didn't reach the racecourse, is a half-sister to three European pattern-race winners up to a mile, Malinowski, Monroe (the dam of Xaar) and Gielgud, and to Blush With Pride, who won four stakes races in North America. The next dam, Best In Show, was also a stakes winner in the States. Castle Gandolfo, who wears a crossed noseband, has raced only on ground softer than good so far, and he acts on heavy. *A. P. O'Brien, Ireland*

CASTLE RING   2 b.c. (Apr 30) Sri Pekan (USA) 117 – Understudy 60 (In The Wings   **61**
128) [2001 5.1f f6g⁵ 8s f8g Dec 3] close-coupled, useful-looking colt: first foal: dam, placed at 1¼m, half-sister to smart winner up to 1½m Pipsted: modest maiden: best effort third start: should stay beyond 1m: acts on soft ground, probably on fibresand. *R. Hollinshead*

CASTLE RIVER (USA)   2 b.g. (Mar 16) Irish River (FR) 131 – Castellina (USA)   **77 ?**
(Danzig Connection (USA)) [2001 7g⁶ f7g⁴ 6v Nov 8] second foal: dam, 8.5f winner in USA, half-sister to smart US Grade 1 1¼m winner Chelsey Flower: best effort (fair form) when sixth of 8 in minor event at Kempton: odds on, found little next time: raced freely final start: should stay at least 1m. *B. W. Hills*

CASTLESHANE (IRE) 4 b.g. Kris 135 – Ahbab (IRE) 81 (Ajdal (USA) 130) [2001   **83**
102: 10g 8.5m 10m³ 7m 10.3m⁴ 9.9s 12g⁶ 12g³ Sep 28] IR 22,000Y: big, strong gelding:
fairly useful handicapper: left K. Prendergast, Ireland, after final 3-y-o start: ran creditably in 2001 when in frame: effective at 1¼m/1½m: acts on heavy and good to firm
going: blinkered (raced freely) first 2 starts at 4 yrs: winning hurdler. *S. Gollings*

CASTLETOWN COUNT 9 b.g. Then Again 126 – Pepeke 78 (Mummy's Pet 125)   **–**
[2001 38: f16g Mar 26] lightly raced on Flat: blinkered only 9-y-o start. *M. W. Easterby*

CASTRATO 5 b.g. Rock City 120 – Vocalist 102 (Crooner 119) [2001 –: 14.1v May   **–**
1] no form. *B. N. Doran*

CATCANDO (IRE) 3 ch.c. Catrail (USA) 123 – Tongabezi (IRE) 75 (Shernazar 131)   **70**
[2001 8g 8m* 8m 8m Jun 21] IR 12,000Y, 9,000 2-y-o: quite attractive colt: third foal:
half-brother to 5-y-o Beyond The Clouds: dam Irish 2-y-o 7f winner: fair form: won
maiden at Bath in May: well held in handicaps after (said to have had breathing problem
next time): stays 1m: tongue tied first 3 outings. *C. N. Allen*

CATCH FIRE (IRE) 2 b.f. (Jan 28) Entrepreneur 123 – Lyric Theatre (USA) (Seeking   **65**
The Gold (USA)) [2001 6.1m 7g 7.1s² 8s 7g Oct 19] IR 30,000Y: smallish, good-topped
filly: first foal: dam unraced daughter of smart 2-y-o sprinter Lyric Fantasy (herself
closely related to Dewhurst winner In Command and half-sister to very smart sprinter
Royal Applause): easily best effort (fair form) when second in claimer at Haydock: not
sure to stay much beyond 7f: acts on soft ground: blinkered last 3 starts: has hung left/
found little: sold 1,000 gns, sent to Holland. *C. R. Egerton*

CATCHTHEBATCH 5 b.g. Beveled (USA) – Batchworth Dancer 67 (Ballacashtal   **51**
(CAN)) [2001 53: 5g 5.7f f5g² 5m³ 5f f5s³ 5m p5g² f5g⁴ f5g* Dec 14] fair handicapper   **a72**
on all-weather, modest on turf: won at Southwell in December: effective at 5f/easy 6f:
acts on all-weather and good to firm going: tried blinkered: forces pace nowadays (used
to be slowly away). *E. A. Wheeler*

CATCH THE CAT (IRE) 2 b.g. (Mar 4) Catrail (USA) 123 – Tongabezi (IRE) 75   **70 d**
(Shernazar 131) [2001 5s 5d² 5m³ 5m 5g 6d 6d Oct 12] IR 4,000F, IR 14,000Y: well-
made gelding: fourth foal: brother to 3-y-o Catcando and half-brother to 5-y-o Beyond
The Clouds: dam Irish 2-y-o 7f winner: fair maiden: disappointing after second at
Newmarket (off 4 months after next start): will stay 6f: acts on good to soft ground.
J. S. Wainwright

CATCH THE CHRON 3 b.f. Clantime 101 – Emerald Gulf (IRE) (Wassl 125) [2001   **43**
70: 5.1v 5v³ 6s 6m 6.1f f7g Jun 21] small, compact filly: fair at 2 yrs: just poor at best in
2001: should stay 7f: best efforts on going softer than good. *N. Tinkler*

CATCHY WORD 4 ch.c. Cadeaux Genereux 131 – Lora's Guest 99 (Be My Guest   **109**
(USA) 126) [2001 107: 10s⁴ 10.4g³ 10g* 10.1m 10m 10m 10.4g⁵ 8g Sep 15] close-
coupled, good-topped colt: useful handicapper: made all at Windsor (beat Ferzao by 1½
lengths) in June: best effort after when respectable fifth to The Whistling Teal at York
penultimate start: stays 1¼m: yet to race on heavy going, acts on any other: visored twice,
including penultimate outing: sent to USA. *E. A. L. Dunlop*

CATEEL BAY 3 ch.f. Most Welcome 131 – Calachuchi 74 (Martinmas 128) [2001   **48**
41p: f7g 8m f11g 8.1d* 9.1v Oct 16] unfurnished filly: poor performer: won maiden
claimer at Haydock in August: should stay beyond 1m: acts on good to soft going:
sometimes slowly away. *Miss J. A. Camacho*

CATERHAM COMMON 2 b.c. (Jan 20) Common Grounds 118 – Pennine Pink   **77**
(IRE) 72 (Pennine Walk 120) [2001 6m⁶ 7.2g⁴ 7.1f* 7.9s 6d f6g³ f8.5g³ f6g f8.5s⁴ Dec   **a60**
27] 22,000Y: smallish, sturdy colt: unimpressive mover: third foal: half-brother to 4-y-o
Never Diss Miss: dam 1m/1¼m winner: fair on turf, modest on all-weather: won maiden
at Chepstow in September: left B. Meehan after next start: third in claimers at Wolverhampton: should stay 1¼m: acts on firm going and fibresand. *D. W. Chapman*

CATOKI (USA) 8 b.h. Storm Cat (USA) – Matoki (USA) (Hail To Reason) [2001   **98**
107: 8v 7s* 8d 7.5g 8g³ 7d* 8.5v 8.5v⁶ p10g Nov 24] $260,000Y: brother to a winner in
USA and half-brother to several winners, notably very smart 1¼m performer Knifebox
(by Diesis): dam US 7f/8.3f winner: useful performer: won 3 times in listed company in
1999: bit below best in 2001, though won minor events at Bremen in June and Dresden
(for third year running) in September: tongue tied, behind in listed event at Lingfield
final start: raced mainly around 7f/1m: acts on heavy and good to firm going. *P. Lautner,
Germany*

CATSTREET (IRE) 3 b.g. Catrail (USA) 123 – Catherinofaragon (USA) (Chief's **a61** Crown (USA)) [2001 –p: f8.5s* e8g* e7g e8g e7g² f7g 7.6f f9.4g 7m Jul 4] rather leggy, quite attractive gelding: modest performer: won seller at Wolverhampton (for B. Hills) and apprentice handicap at Lingfield in January: effective at 7f to 8.5f: acts on all-weather, well beaten on turf: has had tongue tied: has been slowly away: withdrawn after getting very upset in stalls seventh intended start: usually races prominently: sold 1,600 gns, sent to Macau. *P. S. McEntee*

CAT'S WHISKERS 2 b.g. (Feb 9) Catrail (USA) 123 – Haut Volee (Top Ville 129) **70** [2001 5s 5m⁵ 5m 7m* 7g³ 8d Oct 19] 1,300F: rather leggy gelding: fourth foal: half-brother to German 11f winner La Peregrina (by Shirley Heights): dam German 2-y-o 6f and 1m winner: fair performer: won nursery at Redcar in September: should stay 1m: acts on good to firm ground. *M. W. Easterby*

CAUDA EQUINA 7 gr.g. Statoblest 120 – Sea Fret 96 (Habat 127) [2001 87: 5s⁴ **82** 7.1g⁵ 5.1m⁶ 5.7f⁵ 7f⁵ 5.7g³ 6d⁵ 6m 6f 5.2f 5.1m⁴ 5.7m Sep 10] good-topped gelding: unimpressive mover: fairly useful performer: effective at 5f to 7f: acts on any going: twice visored in 1998: has been slowly away: usually held up, and needs things to go his way: has won 7 times at Bath: tough. *M. R. Channon*

CAUGHNAWAGA (FR) 3 b.c. Indian Ridge 123 – Wakria (IRE) (Sadler's Wells **104** (USA) 132) [2001 91p: 7d³ 7g² 8g⁵ 9g² 10m⁴ 8d² 8g* 8v² 8v² Nov 20] strong, good sort: has plenty of scope: useful performer: won minor event at Bath (beat Gleaming Blade 2½ lengths) in October: mostly creditable efforts otherwise, including 2 lengths second to Al Namix in listed race at Saint-Cloud final outing (sold from H. Cecil 58,000 gns beforehand): effective at 1m/1¼m: acts on heavy and good to firm going: free-going sort who often makes running: consistent. *P. Mitchell*

CAUGHT IN THE RAIN 3 b.f. Spectrum (IRE) 126 – Captive Heart (Conquistador **66** Cielo (USA)) [2001 9m 9g² Sep 2] fourth living foal: half-sister to 15f winner Windfall (by Polish Precedent) and to 2 winners abroad, including a 7f/1m winner in France by Pursuit of Love: dam, maiden who was suited by 7f, half-sister to Irish Oaks winner Knight's Baroness: better effort in maidens when 6 lengths second to Morro Castle at Sandown, dropped out and staying on steadily: should be suited by 1¼m+: very slowly away on debut. *J. L. Dunlop*

CAUGHT SHORT (IRE) 2 ch.c. (Mar 18) Night Shift (USA) – Sharp Deposit **–** (Sharpo 132) [2001 6m 5g 5s Oct 5] 30,000F: fourth living foal: half-brother to 3 winners, including useful 1998 2-y-o 6f winner Rose of Mooncoin (by Brief Truce) and a winner up to 1m in Italy by Tenby: dam unraced: well held in maidens: sold 2,800 gns, sent to Sweden. *J. A. R. Toller*

CAUMSHINAUN (IRE) 4 ch.f. Indian Ridge 123 – Ridge Pool (IRE) 74 (Bluebird **114** (USA) 125) [2001 87: 6m* 7f³ 6g* 7f* 7g⁴ 8m* Aug 6] second foal: sister to 5-y-o Candleriggs: dam, Irish 6f winner, ran only at 2 yrs: smart performer: much improved in 2001, winning handicaps at Leopardstown and the Curragh (2) in May/June and listed race at Cork (led over 1f out and beat Avorado 3 lengths) in August: was effective at 6f to 1m: seemed to act on any going: blinkered: reportedly in foal to Mujadil. *D. K. Weld, Ireland*

CAUSED CONFUSION (USA) 6 b.g. Miswaki (USA) 124 – Reassert (USA) **–** (Assert 134) [2001 14v f12g Oct 9] no form. *G. Barnett*

CAUTION 7 b.m. Warning 136 – Fairy Flax (IRE) 97 (Dancing Brave (USA) 140) **60** [2001 63: f7g⁴ f8g⁴ 10v 10m⁶ 8g* 8g⁶ 8m⁵ 8d² 7.6m 7m 8g⁴ 7.5m 8m⁶ 8.5g Sep 19] small mare: modest handicapper: won at Redcar in June: probably stays 1¼m: acts on any turf going and fibresand: blinkered once in 1998: sometimes slowly away. *S. Gollings*

CAUTIOUS JOE 4 b.f. First Trump 118 – Jomel Amou (IRE) (Ela-Mana-Mou 132) **64** [2001 73: 10.3s 8s² 9.2m³ 8m 8d 8s* 8.1g 8d⁴ 10.1v⁵ 8d Oct 30] neat filly: modest handicapper: won at Ayr in July: best form at 1m: acts on any going: visored final start: none too consistent: sold 3,500 gns. *R. A. Fahey*

CAUVERY 3 ch.c. Exit To Nowhere (USA) 122 – Triple Zee (USA) (Zilzal (USA) **105** 137) [2001 103: 7d² 8g⁴ 7m⁵ 8.5f² 8m³ 8g⁵ 7m Dec 16] rangy, quite attractive colt: has a quick action: useful performer: mostly creditable efforts in 2001, including head second to Pulau Tioman in Diomed Stakes at Epsom and 1¾ lengths third of 4 to Late Night Out in listed race at Goodwood on fourth/fifth starts: left S. Woods and renamed Royal Majesty before final outing: stays 8.5f: acts on firm and good to soft going: tends to carry head awkwardly: often races prominently. *L. Fownes, Hong Kong*

CAVERNARA (IRE) 3 b.f. Lion Cavern (USA) 117 – Rainbow Ring (Rainbow Quest (USA) 134) [2001 71: f8.5g f9.4g Nov 17] angular filly: fair maiden: well held in 2001: should stay 1m: acts on fibresand. *T. D. Barron* —

CAVERSFIELD 6 ch.h. Tina's Pet 121 – Canoodle 66 (Warpath 113) [2001 43, a56: f8g³ f7g⁴ f8s* f7g⁶ f8s³ f8.5g f8g* f7g⁵ e8g f7g 8.3m 8.3d 7m p7g f8g⁵ f7s⁶ Dec 18] workmanlike horse: modest performer on all-weather: won claimers at Southwell in January (apprentice race) and March: stays 1m: acts on fibresand/equitrack, firm and soft going: below form in blinkers/visor. *J. M. Bradley* — a59

CAXTON LAD 4 b.g. Cyrano de Bergerac 120 – Urania 66 (Most Welcome 131) [2001 90: 5d 5s 5v 5.2v Oct 26] lightly-raced performer, fairly useful at best: best at 5f: acts on soft going and fibresand: visored penultimate start. *P. J. Makin* —

CAYMAN EXPRESSO (IRE) 3 b.f. Fayruz 116 – Cappuchino (IRE) 59 (Roi Danzig (USA)) [2001 77: 5g 6g³ 5.1f³ 6m 6m⁶ 5g⁴ 5g 5g* 5g Sep 19] leggy, close-coupled filly: has a quick action: fair performer: won maiden at Folkestone in August: stays 6f: raced only on good going or firmer. *R. Hannon* 79

CAYMAN LODGE (IRE) 2 b.f. (Feb 12) Grand Lodge (USA) 125 – Damezao (Alzao (USA) 117) [2001 6d⁵ 7m⁶ 7g 8.1v³ 7.9s Oct 11] 12,000F, 32,000Y: leggy, quite attractive filly: eighth foal: half-sister to 3 winners, including 4-y-o Clever Girl and 1993 2-y-o 6f winner and Nell Gwyn third Salvezza (by Superpower): dam unraced: fair maiden: will stay at least 1¼m: acts on heavy and good to firm going. *M. W. Easterby* 77

CAYMAN SOUND 2 b.f. (Mar 15) Turtle Island (IRE) 123 – Kukri (Kris 135) [2001 6s Sep 27] half-sister to several winners, including useful 1m winner Blessed Spirit (also won in USA, by Statoblest), 4-y-o Knocktopher Abbey and 3-y-o Manuka Too: dam unraced: 20/1, seventh of 10 to Eastern Image in maiden at Pontefract, swerving left stalls and never a threat: should stay 1m: should do better. *C. F. Wall* 54 p

CAYMAN SUNSET (IRE) 4 ch.f. Night Shift (USA) – Robinia (USA) 90 (Roberto (USA) 131) [2001 100: 9g* 10.4m⁴ 10.5g⁶ 8.5f⁴ 8g 9.9g⁴ 9s 9f³ 10g 8f Oct 7] strong filly: useful performer: won listed race at Newmarket in May by 1¾ lengths from Katy Nowaitee: generally respectable efforts at least after, including fourth to Lailani in Nassau Stakes at Goodwood and third to Diadella in Grade 2 handicap at Woodbine on sixth and eighth starts: stays 1¼m: acts on firm and soft going: flashes tail: free-going sort (saddle slipped penultimate outing). *E. A. L. Dunlop* 108

CD EUROPE (IRE) 3 ch.g. Royal Academy (USA) 130 – Woodland Orchid (IRE) 64 (Woodman (USA) 126) [2001 107: 8d⁴ 8g 8m⁶ 7g 7.1g² 8d³ Sep 14] lengthy gelding: carries little condition: useful performer: won Coventry Stakes at Royal Ascot at 2 yrs: creditable efforts in 2001 when 4½ lengths fourth to King's Ironbridge in Craven Stakes at Newmarket in April and 3¼ lengths third to Rumpold in minor event at Doncaster (carried head awkwardly under pressure) in September: stays 1m: acts on good to firm and good to soft going: reportedly had sinus problem third start: has taken good hold, including to post: gelded after final outing. *M. R. Channon* 104

CD FLYER (IRE) 4 ch.g. Grand Lodge (USA) 125 – Pretext (Polish Precedent (USA) 131) [2001 80+: 6d⁵ 5.7m⁵ 6g⁴ 6g⁴ 6g² 7f 6.1d⁴ 6v² 5v 6g 7s Nov 10] lengthy, angular gelding: good walker: fairly useful handicapper: probably best at 6f: acts on heavy and good to firm going: held up: consistent, but without a win since 1999. *M. R. Channon* 85

CEAD MILE FAILTE 6 ch.g. Most Welcome 131 – Avionne 59 (Derrylin 115) [2001 11.8d* 12.1s Aug 9] poor performer, lightly raced: won claimer at Leicester in July: stays 1½m: acts on firm and good to soft ground. *B. J. Llewellyn* 45

CEARNACH 3 b.g. Night Shift (USA) – High Matinee (Shirley Heights 130) [2001 65: e7g 8s f6g³ 7f⁶ 6m⁵ 6.1m⁴ 6.1m⁶ 5.1f 5.7g 6m⁶ 6g 6.1f f6g f6g f5g⁵ p6g Dec 19] fair maiden at best: left B. Meehan after ninth start: effective at 6f to 1m: acts on fibresand, soft and good to firm ground: tried blinkered/tongue tied: reportedly had breathing problem on reappearance: races prominently. *J. M. Bradley* 65 d

CEDAR FLAG (IRE) 7 br.g. Jareer (USA) 115 – Sasha Lea (Cawston's Clown 113) [2001 46, a50: f12s 10m 11.9g 12g Aug 23] winning handicapper: no form in 2001, leaving R. O'Sullivan after reappearance. *M. R. Ewer-Hoad* —

CEDAR GOLD (IRE) 3 ch.c. Rainbows For Life (CAN) – Miss Roberto (FR) (Don Roberto (USA)) [2001 9m⁵ Jun 22] IR 7,200F, 7,000Y: second foal: dam champion older mare in Spain/French 10.5f winner: 11½ lengths fifth to Momentum in Goodwood maiden, pulling hard in rear after slow start. *R. J. O'Sullivan* 50 ?

CEDAR HOOPS 3 b.c. Charnwood Forest (IRE) 125 – Zagreb Flyer (Old Vic 136) **55 ?**
[2001 7.1s⁶ 6m 7g Sep 11] 8,000F, 5,000Y: first foal: dam unraced half-sister to Oaks
d'Italia second Flying Girl out of half-sister to 2000 Guineas winner To-Agori-Mou:
seemingly best effort in maidens on second start: dead. *R. J. O'Sullivan*

CEDAR JENEVA 3 b.f. Muhtarram (USA) 125 – Soba Up 74 (Persian Heights 129) **34**
[2001 –: e10g⁴ e12g⁵ e6s e10g⁴ Mar 19] poor maiden: probably stays 1¼m: acts on
equitrack: blinkered first 3 starts. *R. J. O'Sullivan*

CEDAR MASTER (IRE) 4 b.g. Soviet Lad (USA) – Samriah (IRE) (Wassl 125) **78**
[2001 89: 8m 8m⁶ 9m p8g p10g p10g Dec 28] quite attractive gelding: fairly useful at 3 **a?**
yrs: just fair form at best in 2001: stays 1m: acts on good to soft going, probably
on soft (below form on polytrack): blinkered: sometimes soon off bridle: tends to hang.
R. J. O'Sullivan

CEDAR RANGERS (USA) 3 b.g. Anabaa (USA) 130 – Chelsea (USA) (Miswaki **55**
(USA) 124) [2001 76: 6m 6m 5m 5m 6g 7g 7s Aug 31] rather leggy gelding: fair 6f
winner at 2 yrs: just modest form at best in 2001. *R. J. O'Sullivan*

CEDAR TREBLE 3 b.c. Emperor Jones (USA) 119 – Tjakka (USA) (Little Missouri **44**
(USA)) [2001 47: 7s 8s 10f 7m 8d 12g⁵ Aug 17] leggy, close-coupled colt: poor maiden:
seems to stay 1½m. *R. J. O'Sullivan*

CEDAR TSAR (IRE) 3 b.c. Inzar (USA) 112 – The Aspecto Girl (IRE) 53 (Alzao **–**
(USA) 117) [2001 59d, a79d: f7g e6g f6s² f7g³ f6g⁴ f6f⁵ f6g⁶ f6g 6m 7m May 30] modest **a52**
nowadays: effective at 6f/7f: acts on firm going, good to soft and fibresand: tried
blinkered: has twice reportedly finished lame. *D. W. Chapman*

CEEPIO (IRE) 3 b.g. Pennekamp (USA) 130 – Boranwood (IRE) (Exhibitioner 111) **101 d**
[2001 101: 6s² 6m 6g 7m 7.1g⁵ 6g Sep 28] lengthy, good-topped gelding: has a quick
action: useful performer: creditable 1¼ lengths second to Zilch in minor event at
Newbury in May, but below form after: races freely, and best efforts at 6f: acts on soft and
good to firm ground: races prominently: gelded after final outing. *T. G. Mills*

CEILIDH JIG (IRE) 2 b.f. (May 11) General Monash (USA) 107 – Ringawoody **33**
102 (Auction Ring (USA) 123) [2001 5f 5f f7g 6m 8g 7g Oct 19] IR 7,000Y: small,
sparely-made filly: half-sister to several winners, including Irish 1989 2-y-o 6f winner
Blues Quartet (by Cure The Blues), later winner abroad, and Irish 1¼m winner Life
Dancing (by Dance of Life): dam won up to 1m in Ireland: poor maiden: stays 1m:
visored penultimate start. *J. J. Quinn*

CEINWEN 6 ch.m. Keen 116 – Drudwen (Sayf El Arab (USA) 127) [2001 –: 10.2g 7g **–**
Sep 5] no sign of ability. *A. W. Carroll*

CELEBRATION TOWN (IRE) 4 b. or br.g. Case Law 113 – Battle Queen 85 **94**
(Kind of Hush 118) [2001 103p: 7d 6g 8m 7.9m² 8g 8m⁵ 8g 8d 7d Nov 3] lengthy gelding:
unimpressive mover: useful handicapper at 3 yrs, winning 4 times: not so good in 2001,
and well beaten last 3 starts: probably best at 7f/1m: acts on good to firm and heavy going:
sometimes on toes: held up. *D. Morris*

CELEBRE BLU 4 b.g. Suave Dancer (USA) 136 – Taufan Blu (IRE) 97 (Taufan **68**
(USA) 119) [2001 67: 10s* 12.4d* 14m May 26] fair handicapper: won at Pontefract in
April and Newcastle (awarded race) in May: stays 12.5f: best efforts on good to soft/soft
going: has been slowly away. *J. Mackie*

CELERITY (IRE) 3 b.f. Fairy King (USA) – Three Terns (USA) (Arctic Tern (USA) **53**
126) [2001 44: f6g⁵ f7g⁴ f8g 8.2s³ 8.1v* f7g⁴ 8.1g 10.9m f8g 9.2m 10.4s 10.1v 7v⁴ 8d⁶ 8s
8v f8.5g f8s Dec 21] strong filly: modest handicapper: won at Warwick in April: below
form after next outing: stays 1m: acts on fibresand, best turf effort on heavy going:
inconsistent. *M. J. Polglase*

CELESTIAL POWER 3 b.f. Superpower 113 – Heavenly Queen (Scottish Reel **–**
123) [2001 –: 7.5f⁵ 7g⁶ 6.1m 6m Aug 4] smallish filly: little form. *A. Bailey*

CELESTIEN 2 ch.f. (Mar 22) Hurricane Sky (AUS) – Gate of Heaven 43 (Starry **73**
Night (USA)) [2001 7m⁴ 5g² 5g* 5m Aug 2] leggy filly: second foal: half-sister to 3-y-o
Thats All Jazz: dam maiden who stayed 7.5f: fair performer: won minor event at
Doncaster in July: appeared to break down in Molecomb Stakes at Goodwood only
subsequent start: seemed not to stay 7f: dead. *I. A. Wood*

CELLER WINE 2 b.g. (Apr 28) Lugana Beach 116 – Noble Canonire 58 (Gunner B **–**
126) [2001 f6g May 21] 3,000Y: first foal: dam 11f seller winner at 4 yrs: tailed off in
Southwell seller. *B. Palling*

CELLO SOLO   4 b.g. Piccolo 121 – Whirling Words 75 (Sparkler 130) [2001 68: 7s **54** 5m 7s Oct 16] leggy gelding: modest maiden: should stay 1m: has taken strong hold: sold 320 gns. *P. J. Makin*

CELOTTI (IRE)   3 b.f. Celtic Swing 138 – Zalotti (IRE) 84 (Polish Patriot (USA) **57 d** 128) [2001 72: 6g 7.1m 5f 5m 6m⁵ f5g 5f 6m 6s 6d 5v Oct 15] tall, rather unfurnished filly: unimpressive mover: modest handicapper at best in 2001: best at 5f/6f: acts on fibresand and good to firm going, possibly not on softer than good: has had tongue tied: sometimes slowly away: sold 800 gns. *R. Hollinshead*

CELTIC BALLET   2 b.f. (Mar 22) Celtic Swing 138 – Fairy Feet 78 (Sadler's Wells **85 p** (USA) 132) [2001 7m² 7.5g* 6.5g⁴ 7s* Oct 20] 6,000Y: lengthy, quite attractive filly: half-sister to several winners, including 5-y-o Fairtoto and useful 1½m/1¾m winner Aginor (by Slip Anchor): dam, second at 11f only start, half-sister to 1000 Guineas winner Fairy Footsteps and St Leger winner Light Cavalry: won maiden at Beverley in September and nursery at Catterick in October: fared best of those drawn on unfavoured stand side when fourth of 28 to Madame Boulangere in valuable sales race at Ascot in between: will stay at least 1¼m: acts on soft ground, shaped well on good to firm: carries head awkwardly: useful prospect, and should win more races. *M. A. Jarvis*

CELTIC EXIT (FR)   7 b.g. Exit To Nowhere (USA) 122 – Amour Celtique (North- **72 d** fields (USA)) [2001 84+: 7s 7g 7m 7.1s 7m 7g p7g Dec 19] winning handicapper, on downgrade: probably best at 7f/1m: acts on heavy going, probably on good to firm: blinkered final start: often tongue tied: has been slowly away. *I. A. Balding*

CELTIC H'ALO   3 b.f. Celtic Swing 138 – Alo Ez 100 (Alzao (USA) 117) [2001 f7g **57** 7s 8m 8g* f8.5g 8d Nov 2] good-bodied filly: sixth living foal: half-sister to 5-y-o Pleasant Mount and winning sprinters Alamode and 9-y-o Mousehole (both by Stato-blest): dam sprinter: modest performer: left Miss J. Camacho and off 4 months before winning apprentice handicap at Bath in October: likely to stay 1¼m. *R. Guest*

CELTIC ISLAND   3 b.f. Celtic Swing 138 – Chief Island 62 (Be My Chief (USA) **92** 122) [2001 94?: 8v² 10.2d³ 10.5m⁴ 9.9m⁵ 11.6g⁴ 12f 10.3m* 11.9s² 12v Oct 27] lengthy, angular filly: fairly useful performer: left W. Turner after fifth start: won minor event at Doncaster in September by neck from Chem's Truce: stays 1½m: acts on any going: has started slowly: often held up: consistent. *Mrs M. Reveley*

CELTIC MAID   2 b.f. (Mar 19) Celtic Swing 138 – Native Thatch (IRE) 47 (Thatching **76** 131) [2001 5d⁵ 5v* 5g³ 5.2s⁵ 5.1f⁶ Jun 30] leggy filly: second foal: sister to 3-y-o Celtic Thatcher: dam, maiden, probably best at 5f/6f: fair performer: won maiden at Warwick in April by 8 lengths: should stay 6f: probably acts on any going: joined Mrs M. Reveley. *W. G. M. Turner*

CELTIC MILL   3 b.g. Celtic Swing 138 – Madam Millie 99 (Milford 119) [2001 12g **78** 12m⁵ 10m 10g 8d* 8d² 8g 8d⁶ Oct 8] tall, leggy gelding: half-brother to 1½m winners Millie's Dream (by Petoski) and My Millie (by Midyan): dam sprinter: fair handicapper: won at Pontefract in August: best efforts at 1m on good to soft ground. *D. W. Barker*

CELTIC MISS   3 b.f. Celtic Swing 138 – Regent Miss (CAN) (Vice Regent (CAN)) **63** [2001 63: 11.6s 11.6g 10.5g³ 10.5v⁵ 15v⁴ Nov 25] rather angular filly: modest maiden: ran as though something amiss first 2 starts in 2001, then sold from J. Dunlop 17,000 gns: better efforts for new stable: seems to stay 15f: acts on heavy ground. *J. L. Dunlop*

CELTIC MISSION (USA)   3 ch.g. Cozzene (USA) – Norfolk Lavender (CAN) 80 **106** (Ascot Knight (CAN) 130) [2001 83p: f8.5g⁴ f12g⁶ 8v² 8.3s* 8g 7.9g⁴ 10g³ 10.1m 8m 10m⁵ 11.9d* 10.1m² 11.9d² 11m² 12.1m² 10.5v* 12d² 10.4d 11d* 12v⁶ Oct 27] angular gelding: developed into a useful handicapper: won at Windsor in April, Haydock in July and September and Naas (beat Per Amore by 2 lengths in valuable race) in October: also ran particularly well when 2 lengths second to High Pitched at Newmarket seventeenth start: stays 1½m: acts on heavy going, good to firm and fibresand: usually races prominently: tough and consistent: sold 78,000 gns. *M. Johnston*

CELTIC ROMANCE   2 b.f. (Mar 21) Celtic Swing 138 – Southern Sky 89 (Comedy **82** Star (USA) 121) [2001 5v² f5g 6m 5m* 6g² 6m 7m² 7g* 7d Oct 2] sparely-made filly: eighth living foal: half-sister to fairly useful 1993 2-y-o 6f winner Southern Ridge (by Indian Ridge) and 9-y-o Southern Dominion: dam 7f/1m winner: fairly useful performer: won claimer at Hamilton in June (left W. Turner after next start) and nursery at Doncaster in September: stays 7f: acts on good to firm and good going. *Mrs M. Reveley*

CELTIC ROVER   3 b.g. Celtic Swing 138 – Lady Sabo 69 (Prince Sabo 123) [2001 **– §** 5⅟₂s f7g 7g 5m 5d 5f 10m 8d Aug 8] plain gelding: fourth foal: dam 5f (at 2 yrs)/6f winner who stayed 1m: no form and temperamental: tried blinkered. *R. C. Spicer*

CELTIC SILENCE 3 b.c. Celtic Swing 138 – Smart 'n Noble (USA) (Smarten (USA)) **118**
[2001 106p: a9f⁴ 10.4m² May 16] big, useful-looking colt: has plenty of scope: smart
form: won both starts for M. Johnston at 2 yrs, including Chesham Stakes at Royal Ascot:
in frame in 2001 in UAE Derby at Nad Al Sheba (9½ lengths fourth to Express Tour)
in March and Dante Stakes at York (clearly best effort, ½-length second to Dilshaan,
dictating pace and edged out inside final 1f): reportedly found to be lame after work later
in May: will be well suited by 1½m: acts on dirt, raced only on good going or firmer on
turf: resolute galloper. *Saeed bin Suroor*

CELTIC STAR (IRE) 3 b.g. Celtic Swing 138 – Recherchee (Rainbow Quest (USA) **55**
134) [2001 8.3g 8s 10f⁴ 10m 8.1m 8g 8m⁶ Sep 10] 55,000F, 25,000Y: tall, unfurnished
gelding: fifth foal: half-brother to useful 5f (at 2 yrs) winner Recondite and
1¼m/1½m winner who stays 1¾m Freedom Quest (both by Polish Patriot): dam
unraced from family of 4-y-o Best of The Bests: modest maiden handicapper: should stay
at least 1¼m: visored final start: joined Nick Williams. *M. R. Channon*

CELTIC STYLE 2 b.c. (Mar 28) Celtic Swing 138 – Stylish Rose (IRE) 65 (Don't **88 p**
Forget Me 127) [2001 10d⁴ 8d² 8g* Nov 7] tall, leggy colt: first foal: dam won at 1m:
shaped promisingly prior to winning maiden at Musselburgh in November by 3
lengths from Ettrick Water: likely to prove suited at 1¼m+: should make a useful 3-y-o.
M. Johnston

CELTIC THATCHER 3 b.c. Celtic Swing 138 – Native Thatch (IRE) 47 (Thatching **63 +**
131) [2001 7m⁶ 8m⁶ 10.2m 8f f9.4g* f8.5g³ f9.4g⁶ f8.5g* f8g f9.4g³ p8g f8.5g* f8.5f* **a104**
p8g³ Dec 22] first foal: dam, maiden, probably best at 5f/6f: useful performer on all-
weather, modest on turf: won maiden (final start for W. Turner) in July, handicap in
October and minor event and handicap in December, all at Wolverhampton: beat Nose
The Trade by 4 lengths for final success: stays 9.4f: acts on fibresand and good to firm
going, ran respectably on polytrack: visored final 3 starts. *N. P. Littmoden*

CELTIC VENTURE 6 ch.g. Risk Me (FR) 127 – Celtic River (IRE) (Caerleon (USA) **68**
132) [2001 47, a36: e6g³ e6g⁴ f8.5s⁶ e6g³ e6s⁴ e6g⁴ 7f* 8m 7m* 7f³ Jul 4] good-topped **a56**
gelding: fair on turf, modest on all-weather: won claimer at sixth start: won claimer
at Lingfield (left Miss S. West £5,000) and apprentice handicap at Goodwood in June:
probably best at 7f: acts on firm going and equitrack. *K. T. Ivory*

CELTS DAWN 3 b.f. Celtic Swing 138 – Susie's Baby (Balidar 133) [2001 –: f8g⁶ **–**
6.1d 6g 6g 5g Sep 19] little form: left J. Smyth-Osbourne after second outing: has looked
no easy ride/raced freely/started slowly. *M. S. Saunders*

CENTAUR SPIRIT 4 b.g. Distant Relative 128 – Winnie Reckless (Local Suitor **–**
(USA) 128) [2001 58: 12.6d 10.9m Sep 17] leggy gelding: no form at 4 yrs. *A. Streeter*

CENTIMETRE 2 ch.g. (Mar 23) Inchinor 119 – Matisse 65 (Shareef Dancer (USA) **54**
135) [2001 6f 5m 7m⁴ 8m 8m 6d 7.9s Oct 11] 4,200F: leggy gelding: second foal: half-
brother to 4-y-o Grantley: dam maiden who stayed 1m: modest maiden: should stay 1m:
acts on good to firm going: tried blinkered: sent to Holland. *M. W. Easterby*

CENTURY CITY (IRE) 2 b.c. (Feb 17) Danzig (USA) – Alywow (CAN) 119 **96 p**
(Alysheba (USA)) [2001 7g³ 7d* Oct 19] IR 2,000,000Y: good-topped, attractive colt:
third foal: dam, champion 3-y-o filly in Canada who also finished second in 1½m
Rothmans International Stakes, out of half-sister to smart winner up to 13.4f Zilzal
Zamaan: shaped well when third of 21 to Millennium Dragon in maiden at Newmarket,
and won 6-runner minor event there later in October by 3 lengths from Lunar Sovereign,
staying on strongly to assert from over 1f out: will stay at least 1m: smart prospect,
sure to win more races. *A. P. O'Brien, Ireland*

CERALBI (IRE) 3 b.c. Goldmark (USA) 113 – Siwana (IRE) (Dom Racine (FR) 121) **80**
[2001 62: 9.9m* 11m² 10m* 12.4m 11m³ 12m 10.3v² Oct 26] lengthy colt: fair handicapper: won at Beverley in May and Pontefract in June: stays 1½m: probably acts on any
going. *R. Hollinshead*

CEREMONIAL 3 b.f. Lion Cavern (USA) 117 – Blessed Event 117 (Kings Lake **72**
(USA) 133) [2001 7m² f8g⁶ 8.2g* Aug 3] half-sister to several winners, including smart
8.5f to 1¼m winner Sacrament and useful 1¼m winner Auspicious (both by Shirley
Heights): dam, 1¼m winner, second in Yorkshire Oaks: fair form: won maiden at
Nottingham by ½ length from Dollar King, despite flashing tail: will probably stay 1¼m:
carried head high (seemed unsuited by surface) second start. *Sir Mark Prescott*

CEREUS (USA) 2 ch.c. (Mar 8) Gilded Time (USA) – Dayflower (USA) 108 **84 +**
(Majestic Light (USA)) [2001 7g⁵ 7.5g² 7d* 8g Sep 13] strong, deep-girthed colt: fourth

foal: half-brother to useful 6f (at 2 yrs) and 8.5f (in USA) winner Day Journey (by Dayjur): dam 7f (at 2 yrs) to 1¼m winner in Britain/USA: fairly useful form: won maiden at Chester in September, overcoming wide draw to make all: poorly drawn final start: will stay at least 1m: may be better than he's rated. *B. W. Hills*

CERTAIN JUSTICE (USA) 3 gr.c. Lit de Justice (USA) 125 – Pure Misk 55 **101** (Rainbow Quest (USA) 134) [2001 101: 6m³ 6m² 7g² 7s⁵ 6v Oct 26] rather leggy colt: useful performer: won both starts at 2 yrs (reportedly suffered hairline fracture of near fore and underwent surgery after second one): mostly creditable efforts in 2001, including when 4½ lengths fifth to Kayo in rated stakes at York: stays 7f: acts on soft and good to firm going: edgy and unseated leaving paddock third start. *P. F. I. Cole*

CERTAINLY SO 3 ch.f. So Factual (USA) 120 – Indubitable 87 (Sharpo 132) [2001 **48** 46: 8.3g 8.3g 8.3m Jul 16] poor maiden: should be suited by further than 1m. *G. B. Balding*

CERULEAN ROSE 2 ch.f. (May 13) Bluegrass Prince (IRE) 110 – Elegant Rose 72 **–** (Noalto 120) [2001 5m 6m Sep 2] workmanlike filly: fifth living foal: half-sister to useful sprinter Bowden Rose (by Dashing Blade): dam 6f winner: well beaten in maidens. *A. W. Carroll*

C'EST FANTASTIQUE (IRE) 4 b.f. Hernando (FR) 127 – Dolcezza (FR) (Lichine **63** (USA) 117) [2001 11.8d 12d 16g Nov 7] 130,000Y: fourth foal: half-sister to French 9.5f winner Dairen (by Kaldoun): dam unraced close relation of smart French performer up to 10.5f Caprarola: unraced at 2 yrs: won maiden at Hanover and handicap at Gelsenkirchen in 2000: left P. Rau in Germany after reappearance: modest form when tenth of 19 in handicap at Newmarket on first start in Britain: seems to stay 11.8f: raced only on good going or softer: made running last 2 starts. *E. J. O'Neill*

CEZZARO (IRE) 3 ch.g. Ashkalani (IRE) 128 – Sept Roses (USA) (Septieme Ciel **65** (USA) 123) [2001 78: 6v⁴ 7f 6m 7s 7.6g⁴ 8s⁵ 10v* 10s f9.4g⁵ f11g Nov 30] compact **a?** gelding: fluent mover: fair performer: left D. Nicholls after fourth start: won seller at Windsor (edged left) in October: stays 1¼m: acts on heavy and good to firm going, well below form on fibresand: visored twice. *W. R. Muir*

CHABIBI 2 br.f. (Mar 14) Mark of Esteem (IRE) 137 – Nunsharpa 87 (Sharpo 132) **65** [2001 5.1f 5f⁶ 5f⁵ 6d² 6m³ 7g 8s Sep 27] 10,000Y: leggy, quite good-topped filly: second foal: half-sister to 3-y-o Magnusson: dam, 7f winner, half-sister to smart 6f/7f performer Unblest: fair maiden: placed at Ayr and Thirsk: stays 7f, possibly not testing 1m: acts on firm and good to soft ground. *T. H. Caldwell*

CHABLIS 3 b.f. Kingmambo (USA) 125 – Nicer (IRE) 113 (Pennine Walk 120) [2001 **60** 7d⁶ 7g 8.1v³ 8d 8d p6g Nov 15] workmanlike filly: third foal: dam, 6f (at 2 yrs) and Irish 1000 Guineas winner, out of Musidora Stakes winner Everything Nice: modest maiden: not sure to stay much beyond 1m: raced only on good going or softer (acts on heavy), below form (blinkered) on polytrack. *P. F. I. Cole*

CHABROL (CAN) 8 b.g. El Gran Senor (USA) 136 – Off The Record (USA) (Chas **– §** Conerly (USA)) [2001 12m 10.1g 13.3f 16.5m⁴ 14.1m 14.1d Aug 8] leggy gelding: one to treat with caution nowadays. *Ms A. E. Embiricos*

CHAFAYA (IRE) 3 ch.f. Mark of Esteem (IRE) 137 – Matila (IRE) 98 (Persian Bold **87** 123) [2001 67: 7g* 8m³ 7m⁵ 7g* 7d 7g Oct 6] tall, lengthy filly: fairly useful performer: won maiden at Thirsk in May and handicap at Newmarket (made all) in August: was effective at 7f/1m: acted on good to firm going, probably on soft: visits Munir. *N. A. Graham*

CHAGALL 4 b.c. Fraam 114 – Pooka 65 (Dominion 123) [2001 109: 6d⁴ 6m⁶ 6s³ **111** 6.5g² 6m⁵ 6s² 7d Oct 20] small, strong colt: poor mover: smart performer: best efforts when second in Grosser Preis von Berlin at Hoppegarten (beaten neck by Swedish Shave) in July and listed race at Dortmund (beaten 1¼ lengths by Call Me Big): well beaten in Challenge Stakes at Newmarket final outing: effective at 6f to 1m: acts on soft and good to firm going: has been blinkered (not in 2001). *B. Hellier, Germany*

CHAHAYA TIMOR (IRE) 9 b.g. Slip Anchor 136 – Roxy Hart (High Top 131) **–** [2001 45: f14g⁶ f16.2g Jun 20] sturdy gelding: no form in 2001. *Miss S. J. Wilton*

CHAIRMAN BOBBY 3 ch.g. Clantime 101 – Formidable Liz 66 (Formidable **65** (USA) 125) [2001 57: f6g² 6g 5m² 5f 6m³ 6g 5m 5m⁶ 5.3m 5m Sep 8] modest maiden **a70** handicapper: left T. D. Barron after fifth start: effective at 5f/6f: acts on fibresand and good to firm going: has been early to post. *Jedd O'Keeffe*

CHAI-YO   11 b.g. Rakaposhi King 119 – Ballysax Lass (Main Reef 126) [2001 –: f12g³   **58**
f12g Feb 2] close-coupled gelding: useful hurdler on his day: lightly raced on Flat, and
just modest nowadays: seems to stay 1½m: acts on fibresand: free-going sort. *J. A. B. Old*

CHAKA ZULU   4 b.g. Muhtarram (USA) 125 – African Dance (USA) (El Gran Senor   **67**
(USA) 136) [2001 71: 11.5m 12m 9.9m 11.5g³ 12g³ 12m² 12g 12g Sep 28] sturdy gelding: fair performer: stays 1½m: acts on firm ground, well held only outing on fibresand:
visored twice: has worn tongue strap: usually held up: sold 4,800 gns. *W. J. Haggas*

CHAKRA   7 gr.g. Mystiko (USA) 124 – Maracuja (USA) (Riverman (USA) 131)   **57**
[2001 56, a43: e6s e8g 5.7m² 6f² 6m* 5.7g 5d 6m 5.1f⁵ 6g 6m⁶ 6s Sep 30] big gelding: **a–**
modest handicapper on turf, poor on all-weather: won at Goodwood in May: effective at
5f to easy 7f: acts on firm ground (not on softer than good) and fibresand/equitrack:
sometimes races away: usually held up. *M. S. Saunders*

CHALCEDONY   5 ch.g. Highest Honor (FR) 124 – Sweet Holland (USA) (Alydar   **–**
(USA)) [2001 56, a78d: 11.6g 14.1d Oct 3] tall, quite good-topped gelding: winning
handicapper: no form in 2001: tried blinkered. *G. L. Moore*

CHALFONT (IRE)   2 b.f. (May 3) Common Grounds 118 – Pirie (USA) (Green   **71 p**
Dancer (USA) 132) [2001 7m 6g³ Sep 3] first living foal: dam unraced half-sister to
useful 7f/1m winner Tregaron from good middle-distance family: much better effort in
maidens when close third to Commanding at Folkestone, still green and again racing
freely up with pace: should stay 1m: likely to do better. *H. Morrison*

CHALLENGER TWO (IRE)   6 b.g. Petorius 117 – Blue Elver (Kings Lake (USA)   **48**
133) [2001 83: f11g⁵ f11g f7g 7.5f 8m 7.5f Jul 6] fairly useful handicapper at best: left   **a63**
J. Muldoon in Ireland after final 5-y-o start: modest form in 2001, leaving Ferdy Murphy
after second outing: stayed 9f: acts on firm and soft ground, probably on fibresand: tried
blinkered/tongue tied: dead. *K. A. Ryan*

CHALLENOR   3 ch.g. Casteddu 111 – Expletive 77 (Shiny Tenth 120) [2001 –: 10m   **53**
8.1m 10g 7.5m² 7.1g f7g² f8.5g* f8.5g f7s Dec 18] close-coupled gelding: modest
performer: won maiden at Wolverhampton in November: stays 8.5f: acts on fibresand and
good to firm ground: visored (well held) final start. *N. P. Littmoden*

CHALOM (IRE)   3 b.g. Mujadil (USA) 119 – The Poachers Lady (IRE) (Salmon   **82**
Leap (USA) 131) [2001 72: 8.3s⁴ 10g⁶ 8.1m* 8.1s³ Aug 9] strong, lengthy gelding: fairly
useful handicapper: won at Chepstow in July: stays 1m: acts on soft and good to firm
ground: runs right final start: races freely. *B. J. Meehan*

CHAMLANG   3 b.f. Petong 126 – Makalu 79 (Godswalk (USA) 130) [2001 –: 6s 6m   **–**
f6g 7s Oct 5] workmanlike filly: little form. *N. A. Graham*

CHAMPAGNE KING   2 b.g. (Mar 2) Prince Sabo 123 – Champagne Season (USA)   **55**
54 (Vaguely Noble 140) [2001 7.9d 8d 8s Nov 9] lengthy, well-made gelding: fifth foal:
brother to useful 7f (at 2 yrs) to 1¼m winner Champagne Prince and half-brother to 7f
winners Bubbly and Festive (both by Rudimentary): dam ran twice at 2 yrs: best effort
in maidens (modest form) at Bath on second start: not sure to stay much beyond 1m.
P. W. Harris

CHAMPAGNE RIDER   5 b.g. Presidium 124 – Petitesse 55 (Petong 126) [2001 81:   **85**
f9.4g* f8.5g² 10s² 8d 10f⁶ 8.9d Oct 13] leggy, angular gelding: good walker: fairly useful
handicapper: won at Wolverhampton in February: good second next 2 starts (1¾ lengths
behind Gentleman Venture in Rosebery at Kempton on second occasion): effective at 7f
to 1¼m: acts on heavy going, good to firm and fibresand: blinkered once in 2000:
reportedly bled from nose fourth outing: has been early to post/worn crossed noseband/
carried head awkwardly. *K. McAuliffe*

CHAMPAIN SANDS (IRE)   2 b.c. (Mar 8) Green Desert (USA) 127 – Grecian   **70 p**
Bride (IRE) (Groom Dancer (USA) 128) [2001 7g Oct 4] IR 75,000Y: first foal: dam,
unraced close relative of smart 1¼m and 13f winner Multicoloured, out of half-sister to
Prix du Cadran winner Sought Out: 40/1, fourteenth of 21 to Millennium Dragon in
maiden at Newmarket, travelling well in rear, short of room and not knocked about: sure
to improve. *P. W. Harris*

CHAMPFIS   4 b.g. Efisio 120 – Champ d'Avril 89 (Northfields (USA)) [2001 73, a61:   **63**
7m f7g⁶ f6g² 7.1f³ 6m³ 9.2d 6v f6g³ f6g⁴ f7g f6g Dec 10] modest maiden: barely stays   **a55**
1m: acts on soft going, firm and fibresand: blinkered final start: races prominently: tends
to edge left. *W. M. Brisbourne*

CHAMPION LODGE (IRE)   4 b.g. Sri Pekan (USA) 117 – Legit (IRE) (Runnett   **87 +**
125) [2001 98: 7g 9g 8m 9g 8d³ 8d Nov 3] big, rangy gelding: fluent mover: fairly useful

handicapper: best effort in 2001 when fast-finishing third to Burning Impulse at Newmarket: retained 34,000 gns, then didn't get run of race when seventh of 30 on same course final start (gelded after): best form at 1m: acts on good to firm and good to soft going: visored after second start: sometimes slowly away: may yet show more like old form. *J. A. R. Toller*

CHANCELLOR (IRE) 3 ch.c. Halling (USA) 133 – Isticanna (USA) 96 (Far North **117** (CAN) 120) [2001 93p: 10v* 12f 10d² 11f⁵ 9.8d² 10d Oct 20] strong, lengthy colt: smart performer: won cantorindex.com Classic Trial at Sandown in April by ¾ length from Asian Heights, seeming to idle: never in the hunt in Derby at Epsom next time, but good efforts after when second in Prix Guillaume d'Ornano at Deauville (beaten length by Masterful) in August and Prix Dollar at Longchamp (beaten head by Albarahin) in October: well beaten in Champion Stakes at Newmarket final start: best around 1¼m: acts on heavy going, below form on firm. *B. W. Hills*

CHANCE REMARK (IRE) 3 ch.f. Goldmark (USA) 113 – Fair Chance (Young **42** Emperor 133) [2001 –: f8g f7g⁶ f7g⁶ 7d⁵ 8f⁴ 7.5m Jun 8] small filly: poor maiden: stays 1m. *A. Berry*

CHANCIT 2 b.f. (Apr 5) Piccolo 121 – Polly Worth 55 (Wolver Hollow 126) [2001 **71 d** 5.1d 5g² 6f⁴ 5.2m³ 6f³ 6m 5m 6m 7m² 7g⁶ 7m 8d 6g f8.5g⁵ f7g f8.5g Nov 27] 1,800Y, resold 9,000Y: angular filly: half-sister to 3 winners, including 1993 2-y-o 5f/6f winner Culsyth Flyer (by Nomination) and 1995 2-y-o 7f seller winner Sizzling Symphony (by Sizzling Melody): dam maiden who stayed 1m: fair maiden: mostly disappointing after second start: left M. Channon after fifth one: probably stays 1m: acts on firm and good to soft going. *Andrew Reid*

Mr W. J. Gredley's "Chancellor"

CHANDLER'S SECRET   2 ch.f. (Feb 9) So Factual (USA) 120 – Sheila's Secret   **60**
(IRE) 97 (Bluebird (USA) 125) [2001 f7g² f6s p7g Dec 22] 5,600F, 1,500Y: third foal:
half-sister to 3-y-o Olivia Grace and 4-y-o Our Fred: dam 5f winner (including at 2 yrs)
who stayed 6f: modest form when second in maiden at Wolverhampton: reared leaving
stall next time: bred to be best up to 1m. *C. N. Allen*

CHANDRIS   2 b.g. (May 14) Son Pardo 107 – Dash Cascade (Absalom 128) [2001   **60 p**
6m⁵ Sep 6] 5,000Y: quite good-topped gelding: fifth foal: closely related to 2 winners
abroad by Petong, including Swiss Toni (also 1m seller winner in Britain at 2 yrs), and
half-brother to 6f winner Red Typhoon (by Belfort): dam unraced: 14/1, 9 lengths fifth of
15 to Road To Justice in maiden at Redcar, late headway having been soon chased along:
should do better. *J. A. Glover*

CHANGE OF IMAGE   3 b.f. Spectrum (IRE) 126 – Reveuse du Soir (Vision (USA))   **65 p**
[2001 52: 7s 8m 10.1g 9.7d* Sep 3] modest performer: left J. Eustace after second start:
improved to win handicap at Folkestone in September: stays 1¼m: acts on good to soft
going, probably on good to firm: likely to progress further. *H. R. A. Cecil*

CHANGING GUARD (IRE)   2 b.g. (Apr 24) Royal Applause 124 – Milne's Way   **68**
83 (The Noble Player (USA) 126) [2001 5m 6s 7.1s⁵ f7g³ p8g Dec 12] IR 20,000Y:
half-brother to several winners, including 9-y-o That Man Again and 1¼m winner Who's
That Man (by Mystiko): dam 6f (at 2 yrs) to 1m winner: fair maiden: best effort when
third in nursery at Southwell: should stay 1m: acts on fibresand, probably on soft ground.
B. W. Hills

CHANSON   2 ch.f. (May 6) Bijou d'Inde 127 – Tiny Feet (Music Maestro 119) [2001   **–**
5g May 7] eighth reported living foal: dam ran once at 2 yrs: well beaten in maiden at
Warwick. *J. D. Czerpak*

CHANTAIGNE (IRE)   3 ch.f. General Monash (USA) 107 – Blue Vista (IRE)   **58 d**
(Pennine Walk 120) [2001 67: 7.6m³ 7g 6m 10.1v f9.4g f7g f8.5f⁶ Dec 5] tall, lengthy
filly: unimpressive mover: modest maiden: well below form after reappearance: not sure
to stay much beyond 1m: acts on soft and good to firm ground. *A. Bailey*

CHANTESSA SIOUX   3 b.f. Paley Prince (USA) 110 – Legendary Lady (Reprimand   **–**
122) [2001 6g 8m 6f 6m 7.1v Sep 28] 500Y: third foal: half-sister to 1998 2-y-o 6f winner
Helen's Stardust (by Ballacashtal): dam little form: no form. *M. D. I. Usher*

CHANTILLY GOLD (USA)   2 ch.f. (May 13) Mutakddim (USA) 112 – Bouffant   **66 d**
(USA) (Alydar (USA)) [2001 6m² 6m⁵ 6d⁴ 6d 6m 5g Sep 2] $6,500Y, 17,500 2-y-o:
unfurnished filly: half-sister to 3 winners, including fairly useful 7f to 1¼m winner Secret
Aly (by Secreto): dam, US 8.5f winner, half-sister to US Grade 1 1¼m winner Spit Curl:
fair maiden: ran badly last 3 starts: should stay 7f. *N. P. Littmoden*

CHANTILLY MYTH   2 b.f. (Apr 23) Sri Pekan (USA) 117 – Charolles 82 (Ajdal   **74**
(USA) 130) [2001 6m³ 5m 6m⁴ 6m* 6d Sep 14] 19,000Y: tall, workmanlike filly: half-
sister to 1998 2-y-o 5f winner Charlie Girl (by Puissance) and a winner around 11f in
Germany by Slip Anchor: dam, maiden who stayed 1m, half-sister to high-class French
performer around 1¼m Creator: fair performer: won maiden at Thirsk in July: will prove
best at 5f/6f. *T. D. Easterby*

CHANTRESS LORELEI   3 b.f. So Factual (USA) 120 – Sound of The Sea 91   **68**
(Windjammer (USA)) [2001 63: 6g 6m⁴ 7g³ 8.1m⁴ 8s Oct 3] sturdy filly: fair maiden:
best form at 6f/7f: yet to race on firm going, acts on any other: sold 6,800 gns, sent to
Holland. *Mrs A. J. Perrett*

CHAPARRO AMARGOSO (IRE)   8 b.g. Ela-Mana-Mou 132 – Champanera (Top   **–**
Ville 129) [2001 12g⁵ Jul 10] fairly useful bumper winner in 1997 and also winner over
fences: well beaten in maiden at Pontefract. *B. Ellison*

CHAPEAU   2 ch.f. (Feb 19) Zafonic (USA) 130 – Barboukh 95 (Night Shift (USA))   **– p**
[2001 7d Oct 15] strong filly: fifth foal: half-sister to smart French 1¼m winner Barbola
(by Diesis) and 4-y-o Tarboush: dam, 1m winner, out of half-sister to Old Vic: 25/1,
twelfth of 20 in maiden at Leicester, not given hard time once fading: should stay at least
1m: should do better. *D. R. C. Elsworth*

CHAPEL ORCHID   2 b.f. (Mar 7) College Chapel 122 – Royal Orchid (IRE) 74   **58 p**
(Shalford (IRE) 124§) [2001 6m Sep 2] 11,000Y: sturdy filly: first foal: dam, maiden who
stayed 7f, half-sister to 6-y-o Ho Leng out of half-sister to smart sprinter Mistertopogigo:
14/1, backward and very green to post, eighth of 23 to Sophies Symphony in maiden at
York, never nearer under considerate handling: sure to improve. *T. D. Easterby*

CHAPEL ROYALE (IRE) 4 gr.c. College Chapel 122 – Merci Royale (Fairy King **78** (USA)) [2001 85: 8s 8g⁴ 8.5m⁴ 8g⁵ 8m 8.3g 9.2d f8g f8g f8.5s Dec 27] tall colt: fair handicapper nowadays: effective at 7f, barely at 8.5f: acts on soft and good to firm going, well held on fibresand: has worn tongue tie. *D. Nicholls*

CHAPERONE 3 b.f. Shaamit (IRE) 127 – Loving Legacy 82 (Caerleon (USA) 132) **51** [2001 f8s⁵ f11g⁶ 12v 8m May 30] third foal: dam, disappointing maiden, out of useful 2-y-o 7f/1m performer Tender Loving Care: modest maiden: should stay beyond 1m: acts on fibresand: visored/tongue tied final start. *W. J. Haggas*

CHARANGO (USA) 4 b.c. Danzig (USA) – Nidd (USA) 112 (Known Fact (USA) **87** 135) [2001 f5g³ 5m* 5d 5m Sep 22] 13,000 3-y-o: small, strong colt: first foal: half-brother to younger winners in USA by Kris S and Distant View: dam, 5.5f (in USA) and 7f (including Prix de la Porte Maillot) winner, closely related to Breeders' Cup Classic winner Skywalker: fairly useful performer: made all in maiden at Ripon in August: probably improved again when tenth to Astonished in listed event at Doncaster next start: well held in handicap at Newmarket final one: speedy, and likely to prove best at 5f: sold 21,000 gns. *G. C. Bravery*

CHARENTE (USA) 3 ch.c. Hennessy (USA) 122 – Zalamalec (USA) (Septieme Ciel **–** (USA) 123) [2001 67: f9.4s⁶ e10s* f12g⁴ 10.3d f9.4g f8g p12g Nov 28] fair performer: **a73 d** won maiden at Lingfield in February: well beaten last 4 starts: stays 1¼m: acts on good to soft going, fibresand and equitrack: visored (ran poorly) final 2-y-o start. *P. G. Murphy*

CHARGE 5 gr.g. Petong 126 – Madam Petoski 61 (Petoski 135) [2001 64, a76: e6g⁶ **57** f5g e6g* e6s³ e6g f6g e6g* e6g* e5g 5m⁶ May 4] fair on all-weather, modest on turf: won **a68** handicap and 2 claimers at Lingfield in February/March: best at 5f/6f: acts on soft going, firm and equitrack, not at best on fibresand: blinkered twice: tongue tied. *K. R. Burke*

CHARITABLE (IRE) 3 b.f. Mujadil (USA) 119 – Verusa (IRE) (Petorius 117) [2001 **76** 79: f6g⁴ f7g³ e6g⁶ Jan 31] fair performer: stays 7f: raced only on all-weather: has had tongue tied. *J. A. Osborne*

CHARLATAN (IRE) 3 b.g. Charnwood Forest (IRE) 125 – Taajreh (IRE) 89 (Mtoto **–** 134) [2001 –: 8.3m 8m 10.1g 10d 14.1s Oct 31] no form. *Mrs C. A. Dunnett*

CHARLEM 4 br.f. Petardia 113 – La Neva (FR) (Arctic Tern (USA) 126) [2001 –, **–** a43: f8g f9.4s f8s f12s f8g Feb 23] tall, angular filly: no form in 2001: blinkered/visored. *D. Shaw*

CHARLES SPENCELAYH (IRE) 5 b.g. Tenby 125 – Legit (IRE) (Runnett 125) **92** [2001 a11.5d² 12f⁴ 13g⁴ 14g² 13.4d 12d⁶ 12g² Oct 4] fairly useful performer: trained by P. Cole at 2 yrs: won Norsk St Leger at Ovrevoll following season: respectable second of 27 to Tissifer in claimer at Newmarket (joined M. Pipe £12,000) final start: ran creditably in listed rated stakes at Chester 2 starts earlier: stays 1¾m: acts on fibresand, dirt and soft going. *Rune Haugen, Norway*

CHARLEY BATES (USA) 2 b. or br.g. (May 1) Benny The Dip (USA) 127 – Vouch **86** (USA) (Halo (USA)) [2001 7f² 8g² 8d⁴ Oct 2] $280,000Y: big, lengthy, good-topped gelding: has plenty of scope: fifth foal: half-brother to a winner in USA by Distant View: dam, won up to 9f in USA, out of sister to champion US filly Revidere: fairly useful form in maidens: runner-up at Newmarket and Kempton: visored, fourth of 21 to Hathaal at Newmarket: gelded after final start: will probably stay 1¼m: acts on firm and good to soft ground. *J. H. M. Gosden*

CHARLEY FARLEY 2 ch.c. (May 14) Bluegrass Prince (IRE) 110 – Miss Copyforce **55** (Aragon 118) [2001 6s 7s 6d p6g Dec 28] fourth foal: dam, little sign of ability, half-sister to smart 5f to 7f performer Jimmy Barnie: modest maiden: easily best effort at Brighton third start: should stay at least 7f. *E. A. Wheeler*

CHARLIE CHAP (IRE) 2 ch.c. (Mar 14) College Chapel 122 – Fable 37 (Absalom **89** 128) [2001 5m 5f* 5g* 6s² 5g⁴ 6m³ Sep 21] IR 12,000Y: strong colt: first foal: maiden who stayed 1m, granddaughter of Galtres Stakes winner Sans Blague: fairly useful performer: won minor events at Ayr in June and Hamilton in July: good third in nursery at Ayr: will stay 7f: acts on firm and soft going: sometimes slowly away: sold 14,000 gns, sent to Sweden. *Miss L. A. Perratt*

CHARLIE PARKES 3 ch.c. Pursuit of Love 124 – Lucky Parkes 108 (Full Extent **98** (USA) 113) [2001 97: 5m* 5m* 5m⁶ 5f.1m 6g 5m 5d⁶ Oct 18] strong, lengthy colt: useful performer: won maiden at Beverley in May: some creditable efforts in varied events after (though possibly flattered on occasions): best at 5f: acts on good to firm ground: races prominently: tends to edge left (seemed not to handle track at Epsom third start). *A. Berry*

CHARLIE SIMMONS (IRE)   3 ch.g. Forest Wind (USA) 111 – Ballinlee (IRE)   **68**
(Skyliner 117) [2001 8s 8m⁴ 8m² Jul 8] big gelding: second foal: brother to useful 7f
winner who stayed 1m Alfie Boy: dam unraced sister to smart sprinter Blyton Lad: fair
form in maidens, 2½ lengths second to Arhaaff at Newcastle final start: should prove best
up to 1m. *A. P. Jarvis*

CHARLIE'S QUEST   5 b.g. Kylian (USA) – Pleasure Quest (Efisio 120) [2001 –:   **33 ?**
e13s f16g⁵ 11.9f 10.2f⁴ Jun 1] poor maiden at best: blinkered/visored in 2001.
D. W. P. Arbuthnot

CHARLOTTEVALENTINA (IRE)   4 ch.f. Perugino (USA) 84 – The Top Diesis   **71 d**
(USA) (Diesis 133) [2001 80: 6f 6m 6g 6g Sep 15] workmanlike filly: fairly useful 3-y-o:
on downgrade in 2001: better at 6f than 5f: acts on good to firm going: visored once as
2-y-o. *R. Ingram*

CHARMANTE FEMME   3 b.f. Bin Ajwaad (IRE) 119 – Charmante Dame (FR)   **?**
(Bellypha 130) [2001 f9.4g f11g 11s 10.2m⁵ 10.9g 12.1s 11.7d Aug 19] 7,400Y: half-
sister to several winners, including useful 7f (in France at 2 yrs) to 1½m (in Ireland)
winner Sabrinsky (by Polish Precedent): dam, French 11f winner, out of sister to Dahlia:
form only on fourth start (appeared to run to 66, but probably flattered): sold 700 gns.
K. McAuliffe

CHARMAWAY   3 b.g. Charmer 123 – Dismiss 95 (Daring March 116) [2001 7d 8s   **73**
May 7] 3,000F: tall, rather leggy gelding: fifth foal: closely related to fairly useful 6f
(at 2 yrs) winner La Modiste (by Most Welcome) and half-brother to 7f winner
Mystery (by Mystiko): dam 1m/1¼m winner: well held in Greenham Stakes at Newbury
and maiden at Kempton. *C. E. Brittain*

CHARMED   3 ch.g. Savahra Sound 111 – Sweet And Lucky (Lucky Wednesday 124)   **42**
[2001 –: f8g f6g f12g e8g 7s 6.1v³ 7m 6d 6m 8m Jun 22] poor maiden: left N. Littmoden
after fourth start: stays 7f: acts on heavy going: visored last 6 outings: sometimes slowly
away. *M. J. Gingell*

CHARMER VENTURE   3 ch.f. Zilzal (USA) 137 – City of Angels (Woodman   **89**
(USA) 126) [2001 74p: e10g* 11.5g³ 12m 10.3m⁶ 9.7m⁴ Jul 30] angular filly: fairly
useful performer: easily won 4-runner maiden at Lingfield in April: 8¼ lengths last of 3
to Double Crossed in listed race at same course next start: well held after: should stay
1½m: acts on equitrack: sold 13,000 gns in December. *S. P. C. Woods*

CHARMING ADMIRAL (IRE)   8 b.g. Shareef Dancer (USA) 135 – Lilac Charm   **60**
87 (Bustino 136) [2001 60, a–: 17.1s⁵ 21.6s* f16g Nov 12] workmanlike gelding: carries   **a–**
plenty of condition: modest handicapper: won at Pontefract in April: off over 6 months
before well beaten final start: stays 2¾m: acts on fibresand and heavy ground, probably
on good to firm: usually visored/blinkered: has carried head high. *Mrs A. Duffield*

CHARMING LOTTE   4 b.f. Nicolotte 118 – Courtisane (Persepolis (FR) 127) [2001   **69**
72: 6.1v⁶ 6s⁶ 6v³ 6.1v* 6m³ 6.1d⁶ 6d³ 6d⁶ 6f 6f 6m 6g⁴ 6g 6.1d² 6.1v⁴ 6v² 7d Nov 6]
leggy, angular filly: fair performer: won seller at Pontefract in April and handicap at
Nottingham in May: left N. Tinkler after seventh start: best around 6f on ground softer
than good (acts on heavy): usually visored: has been slowly away: held up. *Don Enrico
Incisa*

CHARM OFFENSIVE   3 b.f. Zieten (USA) 118 – Shoag (USA) (Affirmed (USA))   **54**
[2001 7d* 7s⁶ 7.1g⁵ 8.2g⁴ 10g 8d⁵ 9.9g 7.5m⁴ 8.5s f8g f12s⁴ Dec 27] 42,000Y: tall,
angular filly: closely related to 5-y-o Lost Spirit and half-sister to several winners, including fairly useful 7f performer in Britain/UAE Showgi (by Topsider): dam once-raced
close relative of US Grade 1 1¼m winner Sisterhood: modest performer: won claimer at
Newcastle (left Mrs J. Ramsden) in May: below form in second half of year, leaving
K. Ryan before penultimate start: probably stays easy 1½m: acts on good to firm and
good to soft going, probably on fibresand. *S. R. Bowring*

CHARNWOOD BOY   3 b.g. Charnwood Forest (IRE) 125 – Jeanne Avril 99 (Music   **64**
Boy 124) [2001 6d 6m f6g² 5g 6g⁵ f6g a8g² Dec 6] 22,000F, 20,000Y: useful-looking
gelding: half-brother to several winners, including useful 5f/6f winner Mary Hinge (by
Dowsing) and fairly useful 6f/7f winner Dark Shot (by Rock City): dam, 6f (including at
2 yrs) winner, sister to Middle Park winner and 2000 Guineas second Mattaboy: modest
maiden: sold from W. Jarvis 4,000 gns before final start: probably stays 1m: acts on sand/
fibresand: visored final start in Britain. *M. Alvarez, Spain*

CHARNWOOD PRINCESS (IRE)   3 b.f. Charnwood Forest (IRE) 125 – Desert   **56**
Gift 69 (Green Desert (USA) 127) [2001 57: e5g³ e5g⁴ e6g e6g⁴ 6d May 21] modest

maiden: best at 5f/6f: acts on equitrack and fibresand: blinkered first 4 outings: has found little. *E. A. Wheeler*

CHARNWOOD STREET (IRE)   2 b.c. (Mar 21) Charnwood Forest (IRE) 125 –   **65 d**
La Vigie (King of Clubs 124) [2001 f6g f7g⁵ 7.1d⁴ 7g⁶ 8m 8g Nov 5] IR 34,000F, 24,000
2-y-o: fifth living foal: half-brother to Irish 9f winner City Imp (by Mac's Imp), 4-y-o
Brioney and a winner in Italy by Bluebird: dam, lightly raced in Ireland, half-sister to
dam of Middle Park winner Balla Cove: fair maiden: well below form in nurseries last
3 starts (visored final one): should stay 1m: acts on good to soft going and fibresand.
D. Shaw

CHARTER FLIGHT   5 b.g. Cosmonaut – Irene's Charter 72 (Persian Bold 123) [2001   **–**
–, a69: f12s* e12g Feb 21] tall, rangy gelding: fair performer on all-weather: won claimer   **a72**
at Southwell (left A. Newcombe 8,000 gns) in February: stays 1½m: acts on fibresand:
sold 1,400 gns. *K. R. Burke*

CHARTLEYS PRINCESS   3 b.f. Prince Sabo 123 – Ethel Knight (Thatch (USA)   **55**
136) [2001 59: e6g e6g³ 6m 6m³ 6m 6m 5f 6m p6g⁶ Dec 29] lengthy filly: modest maiden
handicapper: stays easy 6f: acts on firm ground and equitrack: visored/blinkered fourth to
seventh starts: often starts slowly: has found little. *K. R. Burke*

CHASE THE BLUES (IRE)   4 b.g. Blues Traveller (IRE) 119 – Highdrive (Bally-   **–**
more 123) [2001 ?: f8s Feb 9] no form. *H. Akbary*

CHASE THE GOLD   2 ch.c. (May 9) Greensmith 121 – Rainbow Chaser (IRE) 54   **46**
(Rainbow Quest (USA) 134) [2001 7.1d 6g 7m f8.5g f8.5g⁶ Nov 3] 850Y, resold 1,000Y:
third foal: dam 2m winner in Jersey: poor maiden: will stay 1½m: acts on fibresand.
J. G. Portman

CHATEAU NICOL   2 b.g. (May 18) Distant Relative 128 – Glensara (Petoski 135)   **76**
[2001 6m 6.1m* f6g* Aug 18] 2,800 2-y-o: second foal: half-brother to 3-y-o Skukusa:
dam unraced out of half-sister to smart middle-distance performer Water Boatman and
useful performer up to 7f Hill Hopper: fair performer: won maiden at Warwick and quite
valuable sales race at Wolverhampton (beat Tiger Feet by a neck) in August: will stay 7f:
reluctant stalls/slowly away on debut. *R. Guest*

CHATER FLAIR   4 b.g. Efisio 120 – Native Flair 87 (Be My Native (USA) 122)   **60**
[2001 66: f14g² f16.2s* f16g* f16s³ 16.2g 13.3m 14g 16g 16d f14g f12g³ f12g⁶ f16g⁴   **a75**
f14.8g Dec 1] rather leggy gelding: fair handicapper on all-weather, modest on turf: won
at Wolverhampton and Southwell in January: will stay beyond 2m: acts on fibresand and
good to soft going (probably on firm): blinkered/visored last 4 starts: has flashed tail.
W. R. Muir

CHAWENG BEACH   3 ro.f. Chaddleworth (IRE) 103 – Swallow Bay 54 (Penmarric   **53 d**
(USA) 111) [2001 68: 8.3m⁶ 7g 10s 7d Nov 2] just modest form at best in 2001: should
stay 1m: acts on firm and soft going, little show on all-weather. *S. Kirk*

CHEENEY BASIN (IRE)   3 ch.g. King's Signet (USA) 110 – Gratclo 65 (Belfort   **79**
(FR) 89) [2001 6g 6m³ 6d* 5s 6g f6g* f6g⁴ f6g⁴ Dec 17] 9,500Y: leggy gelding: sixth
foal: half-brother to 3 winning sprinters, including useful 1996 2-y-o 6f winner Rich
Ground (by Common Grounds) and 4-y-o Bandanna: dam seemed best at 7f: fair
performer: made all in maiden at Catterick in October and handicap at Southwell in
November: likely to prove best at 5f/6f: acts on fibresand and soft, probably on
good to firm: has wandered/looked less than keen. *M. Johnston*

CHEERFUL GROOM (IRE)   10 ch.g. Shy Groom (USA) – Carange (Known Fact   **–**
(USA) 135) [2001 –: f8s f8.5s⁶ f12g f8g f11g f11g f8g May 25] sturdy gelding: no longer
of much account. *Mrs H. L. Walton*

CHE GUEVARA   3 b.c. Machiavellian (USA) 123 – Girl From Ipanema 106 (Salse   **67**
(USA) 128) [2001 8d 8g 7.1m 10g³ 10g 8.3g⁶ 8m⁴ 8m f8.5g 7g Oct 19] strong, angular
colt: second foal: closely related to 4-y-o Ipanema Beach: dam 7f (at 2 yrs) and 1m winner
who stayed 10.5f: fair maiden handicapper: effective at 1m/1¼m: acts on good to firm
going: blinkered last 4 starts: has worn tongue strap: sold 10,000 gns. *J. W. Hills*

CHELSEA BLUE (ITY)   3 ch.f. Barathea (IRE) 127 – Indigo Blue (IRE) 56 (Bluebird   **71**
(USA) 125) [2001 7g⁵ 7g 6g⁴ 6.1m⁶ 6f³ 6g Aug 15] 62,000Y: big, strong filly: sixth
foal: half-sister to 6-y-o Ho Leng and 9f winner who stayed 1m Major Dundee (by
Distinctly North): dam, sprint maiden, half-sister to smart 5f performer Mistertopogigo:
fair maiden: will prove at least as effective at 5f as 6f: raced only on good going or firmer.
J. W. Payne

CHEMICALATTRACTION (IRE)   3 b.g. Definite Article 121 – Domino's Nurse   **78**
104 (Dom Racine (FR) 121) [2001 54: 8.5f⁵ 10g³ 12.1g* 10.5v² 12d* 16g Nov 7] sturdy,
good-bodied gelding: poor mover: fair handicapper: won at Hamilton in September and
Catterick (edged left) in October: pulled up lame final start: stays 1½m: has form on good
to firm going, best efforts on good or softer: has been slowly away. *R. A. Fahey*

CHEM'S TRUCE (IRE)   4 b.g. Brief Truce (USA) 126 – In The Rigging (USA) 78   **96**
(Topsider (USA)) [2001 85: 10.3m⁴ 10m* 10f³ 10.4m 10m⁴ 10g 10m 10.3m² 10f 9g
11.9s³ Oct 11] leggy, good-topped gelding: poor mover: useful performer: won 19-runner
handicap at Kempton in May: mostly only respectable efforts after: stays 1½m: acts on
soft and firm going: blinkered once as 3-y-o: has got worked up in preliminaries/raced
freely: usually held up: sold 60,000 gns. joined Miss V. Williams. *W. R. Muir*

CHERINE (IRE)   2 b.f. (Mar 20) Robellino (USA) 127 – Escrime (USA) 92 (Sharpen   **60 p**
Up 127) [2001 6g 7d Nov 3] good-topped filly: has scope: eighth foal: half-sister to 4-y-o
Luxor and a winner in Greece by Royal Academy: dam, 1m/1¼m winner, sister to Kris
and Diesis: green to post and modest form on first of 2 starts in Newmarket maidens:
likely to stay 1¼m: looks sort to do better. *M. A. Jarvis*

CHERISHED NUMBER   2 b.g. (Mar 29) King's Signet (USA) 110 – Pretty Average   **66**
40 (Skyliner 117) [2001 5m 7.2g⁶ 6m⁵ 6d⁶ 6v³ Oct 15] workmanlike gelding: second foal:
half-brother to a winner in Greece by Bold Arrangement: dam disqualified 6f winner: fair
maiden: good third in nursery at Ayr: should stay 7f: acts on heavy going, probably on
good to firm. *I. Semple*

CHERRYCOMBE-ROW   2 gr.f. (Mar 15) Classic Cliche (IRE) 128 – Key In The   **77**
Ring (Pyjama Hunt 126) [2001 6m 7m 7m² 8.3v⁶ 7v* Oct 26] 2,800Y: half-sister to
several winners abroad: dam unraced: fair performer: best effort when winning nursery at
Newbury in October, leading 3f out: should stay 1m: acts on heavy going, probably on
good to firm. *P. R. Hedger*

CHERRY HILLS (IRE)   2 b.f. (Jan 28) Anabaa (USA) 130 – Fernanda 95 (Be My   **–**
Chief (USA) 122) [2001 5g⁵ Jun 4] IR 220,000Y: first foal: dam, 6f (at 2 yrs) and 1m (in
France) winner, half-sister to smart performer up to 1m Chipaya: 2/1, fifth of 8 in minor
event at Windsor. *P. F. I. Cole*

CHESNUT RIPPLE   2 ch.f. (Mar 21) Cosmonaut – Shaft of Sunlight 58 (Sparkler   **66**
130) [2001 5m 7g³ 7.5m⁵ 7m 8m 7s⁴ 8g³ Nov 5] strong filly: half-sister to several
winners, including fairly useful 1m winner Green Power (by Green Desert) and 2¼m
winner Winter Lightning (by Dominion): dam maiden who stayed 1½m: fair maiden:
creditable efforts in nurseries last 4 starts: stays 1m: acts on soft and good to firm going:
has given trouble at stalls: has taken strong hold/hung left. *R. M. Whitaker*

CHESTINO   3 ch.c. Bustino 136 – Coir 'a' Ghaill 38 (Jalmood (USA) 126) [2001 10d   **–**
Apr 17] workmanlike colt: sixth foal: half-brother to a 1m winner in Italy by Piccolo: dam
maiden who stayed 15f: 50/1 and bandaged near-hind, eleventh of 20 to Curtain Time in
maiden at Newmarket: will be suited by 1½m+. *C. E. Brittain*

CHEVENING LODGE   3 ch.g. Eagle Eyed (USA) 111 – Meadmore Magic 68   **55**
(Mansingh (USA) 120) [2001 49, a73: e8g⁵ e10g⁶ e10g³ e7g³ f7g⁶ e8g 8m⁵ 11f⁶ 8.5m   **a68**
7.6g² 9.7d f6g f8g Oct 22] strong, close-coupled gelding: fair on all-weather, modest on
turf: best at 7f/1m: acts on good to soft and good to firm going, possibly better on equitrack than fibresand: blinkered/visored last 5 starts: races prominently: inconsistent.
K. R. Burke

CHEYENNE CHIEF   2 b.c. (Apr 2) Be My Chief (USA) 122 – Cartuccia (IRE)   **–**
(Doyoun 124) [2001 f5g May 21] 4,000Y: first foal: dam unraced half-sister to Derby/
Irish Derby second City Honours: ninth of 13 in Southwell maiden. *G. M. Moore*

CHEZ BONITO (IRE)   4 br.f. Persian Bold 123 – Tycoon Aly (IRE) 70 (Last Tycoon   **–**
131) [2001 49, a46: f16g 8m 9.7m⁵ Jun 29] lengthy filly: no form in 2001: left R. Wilman
after second start. *J. M. Bradley*

CHEZ FORET (IRE)   2 b.c. (Mar 31) Charnwood Forest (IRE) 125 – Ezilana (IRE)   **48**
(Shardari 134) [2001 7d 8.2d 8d f9.4g³ f8.5s Dec 27] 16,000F, 10,000Y: quite good-
topped colt: fourth foal: half-brother to 1999 Irish 2-y-o 7.7f winner Zuleika (by Lucky
Guest): dam natural half-sister to smart Irish performer up to 1½m Ebaziya, herself
dam of good horses at 1½m or more Enzeli, Ebadiyla and Edabiya: poor maiden: left
E. Dunlop after third start: tailed off in nursery final one: stays 9.4f: acts on fibresand.
C. N. Kellett

CHIANG MAI (IRE) 4 b.f. Sadler's Wells (USA) 132 – Eljazzi 92 (Artaius (USA) **113** 129) [2001 113: 12d² 12m⁴ Jun 10] close-coupled filly: smart performer: successful in Blandford Stakes at the Curragh in 2000, when trained by A. O'Brien in Ireland: better effort in France at 4 yrs when 2 lengths second to Dano-Mast in Prix Jean de Chaudenay at Saint-Cloud in May, making most: only fair fourth to Egyptband in Grand Prix de Chantilly only subsequent start: needs good test at 1½m and stays 15.5f: acts on soft going. *J. H. M. Gosden*

CHIANTI (IRE) 3 b.c. Danehill (USA) 126 – Sabaah (USA) 65 (Nureyev (USA) **109** 131) [2001 102: 8s 7m 10f² 10.1m* 10.5g² 12d⁴ 10d² Nov 2] attractive colt: has a quick, fluent action: useful performer: won minor event at Epsom in July by 2 lengths from Gold Academy: ran creditably otherwise when runner-up in listed race at Ascot (beaten neck by Freefourinternet), Rose of Lancaster Stakes at Haydock (beaten 5 lengths by Nayef) and listed event at Newmarket (short-headed by Lagudin): stays 1¼m: acts on firm and good to soft going, possibly not on soft: tongue tied after reappearance: sometimes bandaged in front: early to post/wears crossed noseband. *J. L. Dunlop*

CHIARO 4 b.f. Safawan 118 – Bold Dove (Never So Bold 135) [2001 –: f6g f7g Jan **–** 29] no sign of ability. *M. P. Muggeridge*

CHICAGO BLUES (IRE) 4 b.f. Blues Traveller (IRE) 119 – Flight of Pleasure **–** (USA) 74 (Roberto (USA) 131) [2001 f12g f8f f14g Jun 8] of little account nowadays. *A. G. Newcombe*

CHICAGO BULLS (IRE) 3 b.c. Darshaan 133 – Celestial Melody (USA) 75 (The **78** Minstrel (CAN) 135) [2001 84p: 12d⁴ 12g⁵ 11.8d³ 14.1s Sep 4] big, strong, good sort: fair maiden: reportedly struck into himself final start: stays 1½m: acts on soft going, yet to race on firmer than good: has carried head awkwardly: tends to race freely: joined A. King. *C. F. Wall*

CHICAGO SOX (IRE) 3 b.c. Grand Lodge (USA) 125 – Elle Meme (Ela-Mana- **67** Mou 132) [2001 7g 8.3m 7.5d 7d 7.5g² 8.5d Dec 8] approx 48,600Y in Italy: second foal: dam Irish maiden out of half-sister to Danzig: fair form in maidens at Milan at 2 yrs and Newmarket on reappearance: left C. Wall after next start (tongue tied): second in seller at Pisa, final outing for V. Valiani: stays 7.5f. *F. Ferramosca, Italy*

CHICANE (IRE) 3 ch.c. Mark of Esteem (IRE) 137 – Rapid Repeat (IRE) 95 (Exactly **–** Sharp (USA) 121) [2001 71p: 7s 6.9v Apr 24] big, strong colt: fair form only 2-y-o start: disappointing both runs in 2001: will stay at least 1¼m: raced only on going softer than good: slowly away first 2 starts (unseated before going behind stalls on debut): sold 3,500 gns. *L. M. Cumani*

CHICANERY (IRE) 4 b.g. Irish River (FR) 131 – Deceive 100 (Machiavellian **50 d** (USA) 123) [2001 –: f8g⁴ e7g⁶ 8.2v⁶ f8g 9s 8m 7d³ 7m⁶ 8d⁵ 7v f8g⁵ f9.4g Nov 27] disappointing maiden. *Mrs L. Stubbs*

CHICARA 3 ch.f. Beveled (USA) – Chili Lass (Chilibang 120) [2001 53: f7g f7g⁵ 8g **–** 5m Sep 11] modest maiden in 2000: no form at 3 yrs: tried visored. *John A. Harris*

CHICHICASTENANGO (FR) 3 gr.c. Smadoun (FR) 111 – Smala (FR) **119** (Antheus (USA) 122) [2001 106: 8v⁴ 10.5v³ 10.5m* 12m² 10f* 8d⁴ 12m³ Sep 16]
    Whilst the St Leger has never been short of sturdy defenders resisting pressure for change, France's long-distance 'classic' the Grand Prix de Paris was not so lucky. For over a century, the Grand Prix de Paris, run over one mile seven furlongs at the end of June, was one of the world's great races. Before 1965 it was worth more than the Prix du Jockey Club and was the climax to French racing's spring and summer season. It became a natural meeting point for horses who had contested the Derby at both Chantilly and Epsom, fulfilling one of the aims of its founders in 1863 to encourage cross-channel competition. But fashions change in racing, as in other activities, and the gradual trend away from staying events in the second half of the twentieth century saw the Grand Prix de Paris wilfully neglected by the French racing authorities. Sagaro won the 1974 running from Bustino, but over the next few years the race's value was halved and it went into sharp decline, its circumstances reduced to such an extent that by the mid-'eighties it was worth little more than a third of the value of the Prix du Jockey Club. The decline provided the excuse needed to scrap the race altogether in its traditional form. Though remaining restricted to three-year-olds, the Grand Prix de Paris became a mile and

a quarter race, an unwelcome step which added to the unhealthy dominance of middle-distance racing in the eyes of many.

In the fifteen runnings since its conversion in 1987, the Grand Prix de Paris has been won by subsequent Arc winners Saumarez, Subotica and Peintre Celebre. However, despite its prize money moving a long way back towards a level comparable with other big European races, the new Grand Prix has arguably failed to establish itself as an event of true international Group 1 quality. The first prize for the latest edition was boosted by sponsorship from Juddmonte to £166,205, but the race attracted challengers from only three different stables and had a meagre turnout of five. Adding insult to injury, the race had to be postponed for two days after Longchamp's original fixture was abandoned when angry punters sat down on the track to protest against surprise on-course industrial action which closed the French tote and stopped betting. The re-arranged card—which clashed with a scheduled jumping meeting at nearby Auteuil—went ahead without betting on or off course in front of a 'crowd' put at little more than a couple of hundred. Chichicastenango would have started a short-priced favourite for the Grand Prix de Paris, and he duly recorded a clear-cut victory, closing gradually in the straight and catching long-time leader Mizzen Mast inside the final furlong. Chichicastenango beat Mizzen Mast by a length and a half with Irish-trained Bonnard the same distance away third; the prevailing firm going and the fierce pace set by Mizzen Mast helped the winner to set a new time record for the course and distance. Regular readers will need no reminding that a course-record time in itself has no particular significance, usually indicating little more than that conditions were ideal for the setting of fast times. Chichicastenango won't be remembered as one of the best horses to win the Grand Prix de Paris but in the latest season he certainly proved himself a smart colt, as well as a tough and genuine one.

Chichicastenango won the Prix Thomas Bryon on his final start at two, but he looked exposed after seven races and, on his first two starts as a three-year-old, was beaten a fair way in a listed race at Saint-Cloud and in the Prix Greffulhe at Longchamp, one of the early Prix du Jockey Club trials. Victory at Longchamp in the Group 1 Prix Lupin, all out in a photo finish with Anabaa Blue and Milan, therefore came as a surprise. But when the same trio met again over further in the Prix du Jockey Club at Chantilly, Chichicastenango confirmed his improvement, going down by half a length after another good battle with Anabaa Blue over the

Prix Lupin, Longchamp—Chichicastenango leaves his earlier efforts a long way behind as he beats Anabaa Blue (No.5), Milan, Amiwain and Atlantis Prince

Juddmonte Grand Prix de Paris, Longchamp—Chichicastenango gets the better of Mizzen Mast (rail) to gain a second Group 1 victory; Bonnard is third

final furlong and a half, with Milan back in fifth. Chichicastenango further illustrated his versatility when far from discredited in fifth, dropped back to a mile, in the Prix Jacques le Marois at Deauville. His autumn target was the Arc, but, after a creditable, staying-on third to Golan and Anabaa Blue in the Prix Niel at Longchamp in September, his preparation was interrupted by tendonitis and he wasn't seen out again. He underwent a leg operation in October from which he was said over the winter to be making a good recovery. The plan is that he will stay in training.

			Kaldoun	Caro
Chichicastenango (FR) (gr.c. 1998)	Smadoun (FR) (gr 1990)		(gr 1975)	Katana
		Mossma (ch 1982)	Tip Moss
				Ticma
	Smala (FR) (ch 1993)	Antheus (b 1982)	Northern Dancer
			Apachee
		Small Partie (ch 1988)	Fabulous Dancer
			Summer Parties

The sturdy Chichicastenango, named after a town in the Guatemalan mountains famous with tourists for its colourful market, is from the first crop of the useful mile-and-a-half performer Smadoun, whose victories came at exotic-sounding venues such as Bordeaux Le Bouscat and Lyon Parilly. Smadoun won sixteen races in the French Provinces, including eight of listed status. Chichicastenango's successes should provide encouragement for any small breeder—the sire stood at a fee of only 6,000 francs when Chichicastenango's undistinguished dam Smala, whose only victory came in a claimer, visited him. Chichicastenango is Smala's first foal, her second being the fairly useful Faimara (by Homme de Loi), who has so far been placed in minor events at Saint-Cloud, Maisons-Laffitte and Longchamp. Chichicastenango seems effective at a mile to a mile and a half and probably acts on any going. He is usually held up. *P. H. Demercastel, France*

CHICKASAW TRAIL   3 ch.f. Be My Chief (USA) 122 – Maraschino 53 (Lycius (USA) 124) [2001 38: f7g⁴ f9.4s⁴ f8g 9.9m⁴ 8f³ 8m⁴ 9m⁵ 12f⁴ 10f² 8.1m⁴ 12m⁵ 12g⁴ 10m⁴ 8.1m 12d f9.4g f8g⁴ f7s⁵ Dec 15] small filly: modest maiden: effective at 1m to 1½m: acts on fibresand and firm going. *R. Hollinshead* **52 a46**

CHIEF CASHIER   6 b.g. Persian Bold 123 – Kentfield (Busted 134) [2001 85: 10.1s² 10.3f⁶ 10m⁴ 10m* 10g² 10g² 9.7m² 12m 10.1g 10v p10g p10g Dec 28] close-coupled gelding: fairly useful handicapper: won at Windsor in June: close second at Sandown next 2 starts, below form last 6: very best efforts around 1¼m: acts on firm and soft going: below form when sweating twice in 2000: usually races prominently. *G. B. Balding* **91**

CHIEF OF JUSTICE   4 b.c. Be My Chief (USA) 122 – Clare Court 89 (Glint of Gold 128) [2001 72, a80: f11g Jan 8] strong, useful-looking colt: fair handicapper at 3 yrs: well held only 4-y-o start. *D. Shaw* **–**

CHIEF WALLAH   5 b.g. Be My Chief (USA) 122 – Arusha (IRE) 84 (Dance of Life   **60**
(USA)) [2001 65: 14.4m⁶ 16.2m 18m Jul 7] tall, useful-looking gelding: modest maiden
handicapper: stays 17f: acts on firm going, possibly not on softer than good: blinkered
final start. *N. J. Henderson*

CHIEF WARDANCE   7 ch.g. Profilic 88 – Dolly Wardance (Warpath 113) [2001   **65**
53?: 12s⁴ 10s* 10s⁴ 10g 12m 10f⁵ Jun 3] big gelding: fair handicapper, lightly raced: won
apprentice race at Pontefract in April: effective at 1¼m (given test)/1½m: acts on soft
ground. *Mrs S. Lamyman*

CHILI PEPPER   4 b.f. Chilibang 120 – Game Germaine (Mummy's Game 120)   **–**
[2001 –, a57: f6g f7g f7g f8g 10g 5g f7g Dec 3] small, leggy filly: modest handicapper,   **a50 d**
on downgrade: stays 7f: acts on fibresand: tried blinkered. *A. Smith*

CHILLI   4 br.g. Most Welcome 131 – So Saucy 59 (Teenoso (USA) 135) [2001 54: 10f   **–**
10g 8d Aug 8] maiden: no form in 2001: tried visored/tongue tied. *K. Bell*

CHILLI BOY   3 gr.g. Belfort (FR) 89 – Con Carni (Blakeney 126) [2001 41: 6g 8m   **–**
Jun 11] no form at 3 yrs. *J. R. Turner*

CHILTERN BUCKS   2 ch.c. (Feb 11) Muhtarram (USA) 125 – Lavender Della (IRE)   **–**
66 (Shernazar 131) [2001 7.1m 7s Oct 16] small, sturdy colt: unimpressive mover: first
foal: dam, maiden who stayed 1½m, out of half-sister to very smart French middle-
distance stayer Hard To Sing: burly, well held in maidens. *J. A. R. Toller*

CHILWORTH (IRE)   4 ch.g. Shalford (IRE) 124§ – Close The Till (Formidable   **43 +**
(USA) 125) [2001 57: 7m 7f⁴ 7m Jun 15] sturdy gelding: poor maiden: best up to 7f:
acts on firm and good to soft going, well held on soft/heavy: often blinkered/visored.
T. M. Jones

CHIMES AT MIDNIGHT (USA)   4 b.c. Danzig (USA) – Surely Georgies (USA)   **108 §**
(Alleged (USA) 138) [2001 119§: 12m⁶ 20f 14d* 14g⁵ 12m 10g 14m⁶ 12s 10s Oct 29]
well-made colt: useful performer: won IAWS Curragh Cup in June by 2 lengths from
Mediterranean: well held otherwise in 2001, mostly in Group 1 events: finds 11f a
minimum and stays 14.6f: acts on firm and good to soft going: usually blinkered:
inconsistent. *Luke Comer, Ireland*

IAWS Curragh Cup, the Curragh—in a very slowly-run race,
the blinkered Chimes At Midnight leads again in the final furlong to account for Mediterranean,
Pillars of Society (No.5) and Ancelin

CHINA 3 b.f. Royal Academy (USA) 130 – One Way Street 119 (Habitat 134) [2001 **74**
10s 14.1g³ 14m² 15.9d⁴ 17.2g Oct 1] tall, lengthy filly: has scope: closely related to 2
winners, notably very smart French 6.5f (at 2 yrs) to 10.5f (including Grand Prix de Paris)
winner Grape Tree Road (by Caerleon) and half-sister to several winners, including 1¼m
to 15f winner Red Route (by Polish Precedent) and 2m Queen's Vase winner Windsor
Castle (by Generous), both smart: dam 1m to 1½m (Princess Royal Stakes) winner: fair
maiden: should stay beyond 2m: acts on good to firm and good to soft going: sold 180,000
gns. *H. R. A. Cecil*

CHINA CASTLE 8 b.g. Sayf El Arab (USA) 127 – Honey Plum 57 (Kind of Hush –
118) [2001 –, a93: f12s* f12g* f11g⁴ f12g² f14g² f11g* f11g* f12g* f14.8g² f12s* f12s* **a86**
Dec 21] good-topped gelding: fairly useful all-weather performer (has gained 23 of his
26 victories on fibresand): won 5 claimers at Wolverhampton/Southwell in 2001, and 2
handicaps at Southwell in December: best at 11f to 1¾m: acts on firm going, fibresand
and equitrack: usually held up: tough. *P. C. Haslam*

CHINA FAIN (IRE) 3 b.f. Emarati (USA) 74 – Oriental Air (IRE) 56 (Taufan (USA) **51**
119) [2001 –: f6g³ e7g f5g⁶ f6g 6d Oct 9] modest maiden: stays 6f: acts on fibresand:
visored in 2001: tried tongue tied: front runner: sold 1,000 gns. *K. McAuliffe*

CHINA RED (USA) 7 br.g. Red Ransom (USA) – Akamare (FR) (Akarad (FR) 130) **74**
[2001 76, a92: f7s e8g⁵ e10s f8.5g 10.3s⁴ 8s² 8.2s* 8.1d 8.1g 7.6d 8.1v 8d Oct 3] tall
gelding: has a fluent, round action: formerly useful handicapper, just fair nowadays: won
at Nottingham in April: effective at 7f, barely at 1¼m: probably acts on any turf going
and fibresand/equitrack: front runner, and seems best on a turning track. *J. J. Quinn*

CHINA VISIT (USA) 4 b.c. Red Ransom (USA) – Furajet (USA) 101 (The **122**
Minstrel (CAN) 135) [2001 120: a8f* a8f² a8f⁴ 8d² 8s* 7s² 8m³ Dec 16]
China Visit will be racing again in 2002, and, perhaps by the end of it, the
plural version of his name could be a more appropriate one. Having acquitted
himself well enough in finishing third in the Hong Kong Mile in December, there
must be every chance that China Visit will be back to contest the next running of
this Group 1 contest. China Visit, sent off at 12/1 in a fourteen-runner field, raced
prominently from the start at Sha Tin but couldn't quicken in the closing stages and
was passed by both Eishin Preston and Electronic Unicorn, finishing four lengths
behind the winner.

The latest season, in which China Visit ran seven times, was his busiest to
date. In his first two he had appeared only four times, each appearance in a different
country. The winner of a newcomers race at Deauville at two, he was successful in
the inaugural UAE Derby at Nad Al Sheba on his reappearance at three and then
failed to do himself justice in either the Kentucky Derby at Churchill Downs or the
St James's Palace Stakes at Royal Ascot, reportedly finishing lame in the last-
named. Nad Al Sheba was the scene of China Visit's return in the January of the
latest season and he ran three times there, winning a listed event, finishing a very
good short-head second to State Shinto in a minor event, but then a disappointing
fourth in the Godolphin Mile, before setting off again on his travels. Subsequently
off for almost six months, China Visit returned to run three good races back on
turf, finishing second to Tough Speed in the White Rose Park Stakes at Doncaster
and to Mount Abu in the Prix de la Foret at Longchamp. In between, he won at
Longchamp on Arc weekend, his victory in the six-runner Prix du Rond-Point -
Casino Barriere La Rochelle owing much to the ride he received and to that given
to favourite Jim And Tonic. Dettori set out to make all on China Visit and kept
enough in reserve to hold on by a length from Jim And Tonic, who was given a lot
to do.

			Roberto	Hail To Reason
	Red Ransom (USA)		(b 1969)	Bramalea
	(b 1987)	Arabia	Damascus
China Visit (USA)		(b 1977)	Christmas Wind
(b.c. 1997)		The Minstrel	Northern Dancer
	Furajet (USA)	(ch 1974)	Fleur
	(ch 1988)	Zummerudd	Habitat
		(b 1981)	Ampulla

China Visit is the fourth foal of Furajet, whose other winners are both by
Quiet American, namely poor hurdler The Nobleman and China Visit's three-year-

old stable-companion Dubai Visit, who has shown useful form at up to nine furlongs. Furajet, a useful and consistent five-furlong performer, finished in the frame in both the Queen Mary and King's Stand Stakes at Royal Ascot. She is closely related to the Two Thousand Guineas winner King of Kings and to that horse's sister, the Irish One Thousand Guineas second Amethyst; and also to the Prix Robert Papin winner General Monash, the leading first-season sire in Britain in 2000 by number of wins. Their dam Zummerudd was the third highest-priced yearling filly (at 240,000 guineas) sold in Britain in 1982, but flopped on the racecourse, and Furajet was her only notable success at stud before she was sold for only 36,000 dollars, carrying General Monash, at the age of ten. The next dam Ampulla won the Cherry Hinton and was a half-sister to some notable sprinters, including the Gimcrack and Middle Park winner Steel Heart. This is a speedy family and China Visit himself has stamina limitations, though he showed in the UAE Derby that he stays nine furlongs. A strong, good-topped, attractive colt, he acts on heavy and good to firm ground and also on dirt. *Saeed bin Suroor*

CHINESE CRACKER   3 b.g. King's Signet (USA) 110 – Heart Broken 78 (Bustino 136) [2001 10g⁵ Aug 6] third foal: dam 6f/7f winner: 50/1, always behind in Ripon maiden. *N. Tinkler*   –

CHINON (IRE)   2 b.f. (Mar 23) Entrepreneur 123 – Ivyanna (IRE) 112 (Reference Point 139) [2001 6g 8.3v Oct 29] 3,200,000 francs Y: sturdy filly: fourth living foal: half-sister to 3-y-o Snowflake: dam 1m (at 2 yrs in Ireland) and 1½m (Oaks d'Italia) winner: last in maidens. *B. J. Meehan*   –

CHIOMARA (IRE)   3 b.f. Namaqualand (USA) – Violet Crown (IRE) 93 (Kefaah (USA) 124) [2001 68: 10s f7g 6m 6.1m 7.1m Jul 27] IR 1,800F, IR 1,500Y: angular filly: second foal: dam, 1m winner at 2 yrs, half-sister to useful performer up to 8.5f Tough Guy (by Namaqualand): fair performer for J. Burns in Ireland at 2 yrs, winning claimer at Sligo: no form in 2001: should stay beyond 6.5f: acts on soft ground: tried blinkered. *F. Jordan*   –

CHISPA   3 b.f. Imperial Frontier (USA) 112 – Digamist Girl (IRE) (Digamist (USA) 110) [2001 82: f5s* f5s⁴ f6g² f6g⁴ f6g² 5s 5s* 5g⁶ 5m 5m 5f 6g f5g f6g f5s f6g Dec 17] lengthy filly: useful performer: won handicap in January and minor event in February, both at Southwell, and handicap at Epsom in April: well held last 6 starts: raced only at 5f/6f: acts on fibresand and soft going: tried blinkered: usually races prominently. *M. C. Chapman*   **94 d**

CHIU CHOW KID   3 b.g. Wolfhound (USA) 126 – Sakura Queen (IRE) 52 (Woodman (USA) 126) [2001 e6g³ 7.1d² 8.3g³ 8m 7m* 7.1m Jun 18] 12,500F: useful-looking gelding: fourth foal: brother to 1999 2-y-o 7f winner Seeking Utopia and half-brother to 2 winners by Shareef Dancer, including 1½m winner Reine Cerise: dam, maiden who stayed 1¼m, out of half-sister to Riverman: fair performer: won maiden at Yarmouth in June: barely stays 1m: showed promise on equitrack, yet to race on extremes of going on turf: somewhat headstrong, and seems best allowed to stride on (refused to settle final start): sent to Hong Kong, where renamed Sensible Mind. *S. P. C. Woods*   **77**

CHIVALRY   2 b.g. (Feb 14) Mark of Esteem (IRE) 137 – Gai Bulga 110 (Kris 135) [2001 6s⁵ 6s 6d⁶ Nov 2] 52,000Y: lengthy gelding: has scope: second living foal: half-brother to 1m winner Sword Arm (by Be My Guest): dam, best at 1¼m/1½m, out of Nassau Stakes winner Dancing Rocks: modest form in maidens: never-nearer sixth of 13 at Brighton final start, swishing tail: should do better at 1m+. *Sir Mark Prescott*   **61 p**

CHIVITE (IRE) 2 b.c. (Apr 4) Alhaarth (IRE) 126 – Laura Margaret (Persian Bold **67 p** 123) [2001 7f Aug 24] 45,000F, IR 290,000Y: well-made colt: half-brother to several winners abroad, including useful winner up to 2m in Scandinavia Account Express (by Roi Danzig): dam Italian 2-y-o 9.5f winner: 16/1 and green, took strong hold when tenth of 12 to Savannah Bay in maiden at Newmarket: should improve. *Mrs A. J. Perrett*

CHOC ICE (IRE) 3 b.f. Kahyasi 130 – Sherkiya (IRE) (Goldneyev (USA) 114) **115** [2001 106: 8v² 8m⁶ 10m³ 10.5m⁶ 12m⁴ 10d* 10m⁶ 8g⁵ 10g* 10m Dec 16] 250,000 francs Y: workmanlike filly: first foal: dam, unraced half-sister to very smart Irish 1¼m performer Shemaran (by Kahyasi), out of sister to Shergar: smart performer: successful in minor event at Deauville in August and (best effort) E. P. Taylor Stakes at Woodbine in September, latter by a neck from Volga, just holding on: respectable efforts otherwise in Prix Saint-Alary at Longchamp (1¾ lengths third to Nadia), Prix de Diane at Chantilly (3¾ lengths sixth behind Aquarelliste), Prix de Malleret at Saint-Cloud (3 lengths fourth to Diamilina) and Hong Kong Cup at Sha Tin (ninth to Agnes Digital): probably stays 1½m: has won on good to soft going, best efforts on good/good to firm. *R. Collet, France*

CHOCOLATE BOY (IRE) 2 b.c. (Apr 9) Dolphin Street (FR) 125 – Kawther (Tap **50** On Wood 130) [2001 6d 6m 6g Sep 11] IR 8,800Y, 5,000 2-y-o: half-brother to several winners, including 3-y-o Diamond Max and a winner up to 11f in Italy by Petardia: dam little sign of ability: modest maiden: should stay at least 7f. *T. P. McGovern*

CHOOKIE HEITON (IRE) 3 br.g. Fumo di Londra (IRE) 108 – Royal Wolff **103 +** (Prince Tenderfoot (USA) 126) [2001 60: 5d⁶ 6m³ 6m* 5f⁴ 6g* 6g⁶ 5d² Oct 18] strong, lengthy gelding: useful performer: progressed well in 2001, winning maiden at Redcar in May and minor event at Newcastle in August: very good ¾-length second to Smart Predator in handicap at Newmarket final start, taken off feet somewhat through early stages: effective at 5f/6f: yet to race on soft/heavy going, acts on any other: usually races prominently. *I. Semple*

CHORIST 2 ch.f. (Feb 11) Pivotal 124 – Choir Mistress (Chief Singer 131) [2001 8g – Oct 19] leggy, angular filly: fifth foal: half-sister to useful 1998 2-y-o 7f winner Choirgirl (by Unfuwain) and 7f (at 2 yrs) to 2m winner Operatic (by Goofalik): dam unraced half-sister to smart middle-distance performer Sacrament: 12/1, well held in maiden at Redcar. *W. J. Haggas*

CHORUS 4 b.f. Bandmaster (USA) 97 – Name That Tune 40 (Fayruz 116) [2001 80: **60** 5v 6g 5.1f 5s 7m 7.1g 6s² 5.1d 5.2v⁶ Oct 26] neat filly: modest nowadays: effective at 5f/ 6f: ran poorly on heavy, acts on any other turf going: tried blinkered, effective visored or not. *B. R. Millman*

CHORUS GIRL 3 ch.f. Dancing Spree (USA) – Better Still (IRE) (Glenstal (USA) – 118) [2001 42: f8.5s f9.4s Jan 20] quite attractive filly: poor maiden: probably stays 7f: acts on firm and soft going. *S. E. Kettlewell*

CHOTO MATE (IRE) 5 ch.g. Brief Truce (USA) 126 – Greatest Pleasure (Be My **87** Guest (USA) 126) [2001 95?: 7.6m² 8m⁶ 7.1g 8m 7m 7m 8d* 7g* 7d 7d* f7g f8.5g⁵ p7g* p7g Dec 29] useful-looking gelding: poor mover (reportedly suffered from knee chips at 3 yrs): fairly useful performer: won handicaps at Bath in August and Lingfield in September, claimer at Brighton in November and handicap at Lingfield in December: best at 7f/1m: acts on polytrack, firm and good to soft ground, well held on fibresand: has carried head high. *S. Kirk*

CHRIS'S LITTLE LAD (IRE) 4 ch.g. Hamas (IRE) 125§ – Jeema 102 (Thatch – (USA) 136) [2001 60: f11g Jul 2] modest maiden at 3 yrs: well beaten only 4-y-o start. *W. R. Muir*

CHRISTIANSTED (IRE) 6 ch.g. Soviet Lad (USA) – How True (Known Fact – (USA) 135) [2001 85: 15f⁶ 16.5m⁶ 16m 17.5m Sep 21] leggy gelding: fairly useful handicapper in 2000 for Ferdy Murphy: well beaten in 2001. *K. A. Ryan*

CHRISTMAS MORNING (IRE) 3 b.g. Brief Truce (USA) 126 – Maid O'Cannie **45** 72 (Efisio 120) [2001 46: 9m 8m 9m 6m⁶ 8.5f Jul 17] quite good-topped, close-coupled gelding: poor maiden handicapper: stays 9f: best efforts on good/good to firm going: tried blinkered. *M. W. Easterby*

CHRISTMAS TRUCE (IRE) 2 b.c. (Feb 17) Brief Truce (USA) 126 – Superflash **74** (Superlative 118) [2001 7g 8d 7.1s* 7.9s Oct 11] 5,000F, IR 7,600Y: good-topped colt: eighth foal: half-brother to 3 winners abroad, including a 2-y-o 6f winner in Italy by Common Grounds: dam unraced daughter of 1000 Guineas second Photo Flash: easily best effort (fair form) when winning claimer at Haydock in September: poorly drawn in nursery final start: should stay at least 1m: raced only on good going or softer. *M. H. Tompkins*

CHRISTOPHERSSISTER   4 br.f. Timeless Times (USA) 99 – Petite Elite 47   **37 §** (Anfield 117) [2001 60d: 5s 5m 5m f5g 5f 6m 6g⁵ 5g 6v f6g⁴ f6s³ Dec 21] plain filly: poor   **a46 §** nowadays: effective at 5f/6f: acts on fibresand, best turf runs on good going or firmer: tried blinkered: has had tongue tied: often starts slowly: inconsistent. *N. Bycroft*

CHRYSOLITE (IRE)   6 ch.g. Kris 135 – Alamiya (IRE) (Doyoun 124) [2001 –:   **41** f12g² f12g f9.4g⁴ e10g⁴ 10m May 8] well-made, attractive gelding: poor nowadays: stays 1½m: acts on fibresand/equitrack, good to firm and good to soft going: often blinkered/visored: tried tongue tied: reportedly broke blood vessel final start. *B. W. Hills*

CHUNKY O'BRIEN (IRE)   3 b.g. Cois Na Tine (IRE) 101 – Berenice (ITY)   **–** (Marouble 116) [2001 –: 8s f16.2g Dec 8] IR 8,000F: third foal: half-brother to 1999 2-y-o 6f winner Berenica (by College Chapel) and 6f (at 2 yrs) and 7f winner The Bomber Liston (by Perugino), both useful in Ireland, latter also winner around 1m in Italy: dam unraced: no form for J. Bolger in Ireland, leaving stable after reappearance (off a year beforehand): well beaten on all-weather debut at Wolverhampton final outing: blinkered penultimate start. *K. A. Ryan*

CHURCH FARM FLYER (IRE)   4 b.f. College Chapel 122 – Young Isabel (IRE)   **–** (Last Tycoon 131) [2001 58, a66: f9.4g f7g 8.2s p13g Dec 29] fair on all-weather at best, modest on turf: no show in 2001. *C. N. Allen*

CHURCHILL'S SHADOW (IRE)   7 b.g. Polish Precedent (USA) 131 – Shy   **–** Princess (USA) 117 (Irish River (FR) 131) [2001 –: e8g Mar 28] one-time modest handicapper: little form since 1999. *B. A. Pearce*

CHURCH MICE (IRE)   3 br.f. Petardia 113 – Negria (IRE) (Al Hareb (USA) 123)   **81** [2001 82: f7g 6s 6m* 6g⁵ 6g² 7d⁵ 6f 7d³ 6g Nov 5] good-quartered filly: fairly useful on turf: won handicap at Newcastle in June: effective at 6f/7f: acts on heavy ground, good to firm and had form on fibresand at 2 yrs: usually visored: has wandered/flashed tail. *W. H. Tinning*

CHURLISH CHARM   6 b.h. Niniski (USA) 125 – Blushing Storm (USA) 102 (Blush-   **110** ing Groom (FR) 131) [2001 118: 12s 16g⁵ 13.9g 16.4m⁶ 15.5d³ 15d⁶ Jun 27] good-bodied horse: smart performer in 2000: not so good in 2001, best effort when sixth to Solo Mio in Bonusprint Stakes (Henry II) at Sandown on third start: stays 2½m: acts on any going: visored last 3 starts: tends to wander: sold only 9,000 gns in October, joined J. Boyle. *R. Hannon*

CIELITO LINDO   3 b.f. Pursuit of Love 124 – Seal Indigo (IRE) 93 (Glenstal (USA)   **78** 118) [2001 84: 6m* 7.1m³ 6g 7m 6f Sep 20] good-quartered filly: fair performer: won maiden at Salisbury in July: below form last 2 starts: effective at 6f/easy 7f: acts on good to firm going: free going sort: sold 43,000 gns. *R. Hannon*

CILANTRO   4 b.g. Minshaanshu Amad (USA) 91§ – Laquette (Bairn (USA) 126)   **31** [2001 f8g 7f9g f11.9s⁶ f11g f14g 16m f12g⁶ f14.8s⁶ Sep 6] poor maiden handicapper: stays 1¾m: acts on soft going and fibresand: has carried head awkwardly. *A. G. Newcombe*

CINDESTI (IRE)   5 b.g. Barathea (IRE) 127 – Niamh Cinn Oir (IRE) (King of Clubs   **–** 124) [2001 –: f16.2s f16g Jan 29] probably of no account nowadays. *J. G. Given*

CINDRIER (IRE)   2 b.c. (Apr 12) Alhaarth (IRE) 126 – Fag End (IRE) 88 (Treasure   **69 d** Kay 114) [2001 f5g 5f 6m³ 7m⁵ 5m 6m 6d 7.5g f6g Oct 9] 18,000F, 12,000Y: leggy colt: first foal: dam 2-y-o 6f/7f winner: fair maiden: easily best effort when third at Brighton: likely to prove best at 5f/6f: acts on good to firm going: tongue tied last 2 starts. *G. C. Bravery*

CINEMA PARADISO   7 b.g. Polar Falcon (USA) 126 – Epure (Bellypha 130) [2001   **–** 8m Jun 17] tall gelding: fairly useful handicapper at 3 yrs: well held only Flat outing since. *N. G. Richards*

CIRCLE OF LIGHT   4 b.f. Anshan 119 – Cockatoo Island 99 (High Top 131) [2001   **84** 102: 7m 10.1d³ 12g Sep 28] useful-looking filly: useful performer at 3 yrs: well below best in 2001: best around 1¼m: acts on good to firm going: often wears net muzzle: often early to post: headstrong front runner. *P. W. D'Arcy*

CIRCLE OF WOLVES   3 ch.g. Wolfhound (USA) 126 – Misty Halo 93 (High Top   **–** 131) [2001 56: 8.2s⁵ 10.9m May 26] rather unfurnished gelding: maiden: well held both 3-y-o starts. *Bob Jones*

CIRCLET 3 ch.f. Lion Cavern (USA) 117 – Chiltern Court (USA) (Topsider (USA)) **74**
[2001 –: 8m* 7m 8f Jun 23] fair form when winning maiden at Bath in May: stiff tasks, no show in handicaps at Newmarket and Ascot (on toes, sweating and too free) after: stays 1m. *J. W. Hills*

CIRCUIT LIFE (IRE) 3 ch.g. Rainbows For Life (CAN) – Alicedale (USA) (Trem- –
polino (USA) 135) [2001 51: 8v 8.2s f5g 9.2d[6] 9.9m 10m 10.3f 11m[6] Jul 28] leggy gelding: poor maiden at 2 yrs, little form in 2001: tried blinkered/visored. *A. Berry*

CIRCUMSTANCE 3 ch.f. Beveled (USA) – Instant Pleasure (Bairn (USA) 126) –
[2001 f6g Jun 29] first foal: dam unraced sister to smart hurdler Batabanoo: tailed off in maiden at Southwell: withdrawn after breaking out of stall next intended start in August. *Andrew Reid*

CITRINE (IRE) 3 ch.f. Selkirk (USA) 129 – Classic Coral (USA) (Seattle Dancer **75**
(USA) 119) [2001 8.3d[6] 10m[6] 10f[4] 10.2g 14.1d 14.1g[6] 16v* 14.1s[2] Nov 5] tall, leggy filly: second foal: dam unraced out of half-sister to Yorkshire Cup winner Bright Finish and St Simon Stakes winner Shining Finish (both very smart): fair performer: won maiden handicap at Lingfield (idled) in October: stays 2m: probably acts on any going: visored (raced freely/wandered) final start. *C. F. Wall*

CITRUS MAGIC 4 b.g. Cosmonaut – Up All Night 56 (Green Desert (USA) 127) **59**
[2001 62, a67: 11.6g f16g[6] 14s[2] 16d[4] 16g 13.9d p12g f14g[3] f16.2g p13g Dec 29] modest maiden handicapper: stays 2m: acts on fibresand/equitrack, soft and good to firm going: blinkered last 4 starts: has carried head awkwardly: none too consistent. *K. Bell*

CITY BANK DUDLEY 4 b.g. Noble Patriarch 115 – Derry's Delight (Mufrij) [2001 – §
44, a–: f8g 6s Apr 10] small gelding: temperamental maiden: banned from Flat races from stalls. *N. Wilson*

CITY FAITH 2 b.f. (Mar 15) Glory of Dancer 121 – Broughtons Star (Belmez (USA) **83**
131) [2001 6g* 6d[4] 6d Oct 19] 600F: quite good-topped filly: first foal: dam unraced out of half-sister to smart King Edward VII Stakes winner Private Tender: fairly useful form: landed gamble in maiden at Lingfield in September: not well drawn when well held in sales race at Newmarket final start: bred to stay 1m. *G. C. Bravery*

CITY FLYER 4 br.g. Night Shift (USA) – Al Guswa 98 (Shernazar 131) [2001 63?: **48**
f8g[4] 10d 7m[4] f7g 10.1g[3] 10g 10g 10.2g f8g[3] f8g[2] Dec 17] leggy, good-topped gelding: **a57**
modest handicapper on all-weather, poor on turf: stays 1¼m: acts on good to firm going and fibresand: visored twice: has had tongue tied: has carried head awkwardly. *Miss J. Feilden*

CITY OF LONDON (IRE) 3 ch.c. Grand Lodge (USA) 125 – Penny Fan 58 **79**
(Nomination 125) [2001 52p: 6m 6.9m* 7f 7d[5] Sep 4] fair performer: won maiden at Folkestone (hung badly left under pressure) in July: likely to stay 1m: acts on firm going: free-going sort. *J. W. Payne*

CITY PLAYER 3 ch.c. Komaite (USA) – Blink Naskra (USA) (Naskra (USA)) [2001 **66**
78: e6g[3] Jan 6] good-topped colt: has scope: fair winner at 2 yrs: below form only 3-y-o start: should stay 7f: acts on fibresand, well held (on debut) only turf outing. *Sir Mark Prescott*

CITY REACH 5 b.g. Petong 126 – Azola (IRE) 63 (Alzao (USA) 117) [2001 64, **50**
a77+: 6m 5.7g 5.3f f7g[4] 6m p7g p8g[5] Dec 4] strong gelding: fair on all-weather, modest **a71**
on turf: stays easy 1m: acts on any turf going/all-weather: usually visored nowadays (not last 2 starts): has carried head awkwardly: held up. *P. J. Makin*

CLAIRE'S DANCER (IRE) 8 b.g. Classic Music (USA) – Midnight Patrol (Ash- –
more (FR) 125) [2001 17.1m Jun 11] fair winner at 3 yrs: well beaten only Flat outing since. *Andrew Turnell*

CLANBROAD 3 ch.c. Clantime 101 – Under The Wing 69 (Aragon 118) [2001 76: **74**
f6g e6g[6] f6g 6s 6s[4] 6m[6] 6m* 6m 6f 6m[3] 6.1m 6d f6g Oct 18] strong colt: poor mover: fair handicapper: won at Ripon in May: seems best around 6f: acts on firm going, soft and fibresand: visored final start: has started slowly: none too reliable: sold 6,000 gns. *K. R. Burke*

CLAN CHIEF 8 b.g. Clantime 101 – Mrs Meyrick 42 (Owen Dudley 121) [2001 65: **70 d**
5.7m* 5m[6] 5.7g 5.7f 5s 5.1d Oct 25] sparely-made gelding: fair handicapper: first win since 1996 at Bath in May: below form after: effective at 5f/easy 6f: acts on firm and good to soft going: blinkered once at 5 yrs: often races prominently: usually weak finisher. *M. Blanshard*

CLANDESTINE 5 b.m. Saddlers' Hall (IRE) 126 – Fleeting Affair 98 (Hotfoot 126) – [2001 21m Aug 1] tall, good-topped mare: useful winner at 3 yrs: well held only Flat outing since: should stay 1¾m: acts on good to soft ground (has form on good to firm over hurdles). *N. J. Henderson*

CLANSINGE 3 ch.f. Clantime 101 – North Pine (Import 127) [2001 55, a–: f6g 5d 6d 5m 7m 7m 6m Jun 27] modest 5f winner at 2 yrs: little form in 2001: tried blinkered/ tongue tied. *H. A. McWilliams*

CLARENDON (IRE) 5 ch.h. Forest Wind (USA) 111 – Sparkish (IRE) (Persian **79** Bold 123) [2001 88: 12d 12m⁴ May 26] tall, good-topped horse: only fair handicapper at 5 yrs: stays 1½m: yet to race on heavy going, acts on any other: blinkered once at 2 yrs: none too genuine. *P. J. Hobbs*

CLARETELLE (IRE) 3 ch.f. Ela-Mana-Mou 132 – Kutaisi (IRE) (Soviet Star **65** (USA) 128) [2001 8m² 9.9g Sep 19] IR 12,500F, IR 12,000Y: first foal: dam unraced out of smart 1m winner who stayed 1¼m Mamouna, herself out of half-sister to Poule d'Essai des Pouliches winner Masarika: better effort in maidens when 7 lengths second to Elsundus at Salisbury in August: should stay 1¼m. *D. R. C. Elsworth*

CLARICE STARLING 3 b.f. Saddlers' Hall (IRE) 126 – Uncharted Waters 68 **72** (Celestial Storm (USA) 132) [2001 11m⁴ 12m⁴ Jul 1] strong, good-topped filly: second foal: half-sister to 4-y-o Establishment: dam 1¼m/1½m winner: fair form in maidens at Goodwood (reportedly lame final start): should stay beyond 1½m. *C. A. Cyzer*

CLARINCH CLAYMORE 5 b.g. Sabrehill (USA) 120 – Salu 65 (Ardross 134) **72** [2001 64, a72: f14g* f12p² f14g 12.4d² 14g 12f f12g³ f12g⁵ Dec 10] smallish gelding: fair handicapper: first past post at Southwell in January and Newcastle (demoted after edging slightly left) in May: off 6 months before penultimate start: has won at 1¾m, probably best around 1½m: acts on heavy going, good to firm and fibresand: reportedly finished lame fourth start: genuine. *J. M. Jefferson*

CLASSIC AFFAIR (FR) 5 b.g. Always Fair (USA) 121 – Classic Storm 73 (Belfort – (FR) 89) [2001 f8.5g f12g 8m 16m Jun 27] sturdy gelding: little form. *Miss A. Stokell*

CLASSICAL WALTZ (IRE) 3 ch.f. In The Wings 128 – Fascination Waltz 83 (Shy **46** Groom (USA)) [2001 8f⁴ 7m⁵ 9m⁶ 10.2m 11.5m⁵ 11.6m 9.9d⁶ Oct 3] second foal: dam 6f winner: poor maiden handicapper, trained by M. Channon first 5 starts: should stay 1¼m: acts on good to firm going. *J. J. Sheehan*

CLASSIC BRIEF (IRE) 2 b.g. (Apr 29) Brief Truce (USA) 126 – Shprinza (Vitiges **79** (FR) 132) [2001 6m³ 7.1d² 7m* 7m² 7g² 8m⁴ Sep 10] IR 7,000Y: half-brother to numerous winners abroad, including useful German performer up to 1¼m Lucky Power (by Waajib): dam French 2-y-o 7f winner: fair performer: won maiden at Brighton in August: good second in nurseries after: should stay 1m: yet to race on extremes of going: sold 12,000 gns. *R. M. Beckett*

CLASSIC CALVADOS (FR) 2 b.c. (Apr 18) Thatching 131 – Mountain Stage **58 p** (IRE) (Pennine Walk 120) [2001 7g 7m Aug 27] 19,000Y: big, leggy colt: fifth foal: brother to fairly useful Irish 2000 2-y-o 5f winner Mountain Greenery and half-brother to a winner around 1m in Italy by Fayruz: dam, Irish 1¼m winner, also successful over hurdles: green, modest form in maidens at Newcastle, not knocked about on either occasion: will stay 1m: should do better. *T. D. Easterby*

CLASSIC COLOURS (USA) 8 ch.g. Blushing John (USA) 120 – All Agleam (USA) – § (Gleaming (USA)) [2001 –§: 11.7f 10d Sep 21] temperamental maiden. *G. H. Yardley*

CLASSIC CONKERS (IRE) 7 b.g. Conquering Hero (USA) 116 – Erck (Sun **58 §** Prince 128) [2001 51§, a–§: 12m³ 16.5m* 16.2m⁵ 12g² 12.3d² 12g 12g p16g⁴ Dec 4] **a56 §** sparely-made gelding: modest handicapper: grossly flattered when winning amateur race at Doncaster (allowed to set up massive early lead) in July by 22 lengths: stays 2m: acts on soft going, good to firm and polytrack: usually slowly away, sometimes markedly so: often looks far from keen. *Pat Mitchell*

CLASSIC DEFENCE (IRE) 8 b.g. Cyrano de Bergerac 120 – My Alanna (Dalsaan – 125) [2001 47, a–: 10d May 16] leggy gelding: one-time fair handicapper. *B. J. Llewellyn*

CLASSIC EAGLE 8 b.g. Unfuwain (USA) 131 – La Lutine 95 (My Swallow 134) **35 §** [2001 43§: 12m⁶ 12m 12.1m 12.1m 14.1d Aug 8] workmanlike gelding: poor handicapper: probably stays 2m: acts on good to soft and good to firm going, probably on fibresand: tried visored: often slowly away: refused to race final start. *Pat Mitchell*

Victor Chandler European Free Handicap, Newmarket—
ill-fated Clearing (right) masters Palace Affair, with Reel Buddy third

CLASSIC MANOEUVRE (USA) 6 ch.g. Sky Classic (CAN) – Maid of Honor   –
(USA) (Blushing Groom (FR) 131) [2001 e8g f11g Apr 9] leggy gelding: fair maiden at 3
yrs: no form since: tried visored. *J. M. Bradley*

CLASSIC MILLENNIUM 3 b.f. Midyan (USA) 124 – Classic Colleen (IRE) 79   **56**
(Sadler's Wells (USA) 132) [2001 45: 8m 11.5f 8m³ 10m⁴ 10m³ 10.1g 10g 8m 10d⁵ 8g
10s⁵ 11.8s³ 14.1s⁵ f11g³ p10g Dec 12] lightly-made filly: modest maiden: stays 1½m:
acts on polytrack/fibresand, soft and good to firm going: sometimes slowly away: has
pulled hard. *Pat Mitchell*

CLASS LEADER (USA) 2 b.c. (Jan 31) Honor Grades (USA) – Serena (SAF) (Jan   **95**
Ekels 122) [2001 6m* 7m² Jul 11] $230,000Y: quite attractive colt: sixth living foal:
half-brother to 3 winners, notably very smart performer up to 14.6f in Britain and USA
Broadway Flyer (by Theatrical), 1m winner at 2 yrs: dam won South African Oaks: useful
form when winning maiden at Newmarket in June by ¾ length from Funfair Wane,
always up with pace: again odds on, beaten 3 lengths by Kundooz in 4-runner minor event
at Doncaster, leading only briefly 2f out: should stay at least 1m. *D. R. Loder*

CLASS WAN 5 ch.m. Safawan 118 – Ayr Classic (Local Suitor (USA) 128) [2001 5v   –
5v Apr 19] angular mare: fair 5f/6f winner at 2 yrs: well beaten since. *J. S. Goldie*

CLASSY ACT 3 ch.f. Lycius (USA) 124 – Stripanoora (Ahonoora 122) [2001 76: 7v   **74 d**
7.6f 6m⁵ 7m⁵ 7f³ 6f⁵ 7d 6d⁶ 7s 7g 7v 8.2s Nov 5] leggy filly: fair performer, on downgrade: stays 7f: acts on firm and soft going: blinkered last 3 starts: inconsistent: sold 4,200
gns. *A. Berry*

CLASSY CLARE 3 b.f. Nicholas Bill 125 – Clare's Choice (Pragmatic 115) [2001   –
8f⁵ 8.5m 7.1s 7d Aug 26] good-topped filly: third foal: dam third in bumper on only start:
no form. *J. M. Bradley*

CLASSY CLEO (IRE) 6 b.m. Mujadil (USA) 119 – Sybaris 91 (Crowned Prince   –
(USA) 128) [2001 82, a97: f6s³ f6s⁶ f6g² f6g² 5v 6m f6g 6m 6f 5.1f Jun 6] neat mare: **a91**
unimpressive mover: fairly useful in first half of 2001: effective at 5f to easy 7f: acts on
fibresand/equitrack: often sweats/gets on toes: has been bandaged: good mount for
claimer: usually comes from off pace. *P. D. Evans*

CLAUDIUS TERTIUS 4 b.g. Rudimentary (USA) 118 – Sanctuary Cove (Habitat   –
134) [2001 56?: f12g f8g 7.5f 8f Jul 22] sturdy, good-quartered gelding: maiden: well
held in 2001: tried blinkered. *M. E. Sowersby*

CLEAR CRYSTAL 4 b.f. Zilzal (USA) 137 – Shoot Clear 111 (Bay Express 132)   –
[2001 44, a–: f9.4s f5g Feb 1] small filly: maiden handicapper: tried visored/blinkered/
tongue tied. *R. M. H. Cowell*

CLEARING   3 b.c. Zafonic (USA) 130 – Bright Spells (USA) (Alleged (USA) 138)   **119**
[2001 111: 7d* 8m² May 13] quite attractive colt: smart performer: won twice at 2 yrs,
including Vodafone Horris Hill Stakes at Newbury: improved again to justify favouritism
in Victor Chandler European Free Handicap at Newmarket in April by neck from Palace
Affair: beaten 2 heads behind Noverre and Vahorimix in Poule d'Essai des Poulains at
Longchamp following month (subsequently promoted to second), leading over 1f out
until well inside last: put down after reportedly shattering hind pastern in June: stayed
1m: acted on soft and good to firm going. *J. H. M. Gosden*

CLEAR PROSPECT (USA)   4 b.g. Virginia Rapids (USA) 122 – Cameo Perform-   –
ance (USA) 104 (Be My Guest (USA) 126) [2001 71: 10d 12m 16m Jun 27] strong,
lengthy, good sort: disappointing maiden. *M. A. Buckley*

CLEAR THOUGHT   2 br.f. (Jan 31) Mind Games 121 – Awham (USA) (Lear Fan   –
(USA) 130) [2001 7.9d 7d Nov 6] 10,000Y: quite good-topped filly: fifth foal: half-sister
to 1997 2-y-o 7f winner Suggest (by Midyan): dam unraced: soundly beaten in maidens.
A. P. Jarvis

CLEDLYN   3 b.g. Awesome 73 – Amany (IRE) 43 (Waajib 121) [2001 7g 8d Aug 19]   –
first foal: dam, maiden, should have stayed 1m: well held in seller at Leicester (slowly
away) and maiden at Pontefract. *D. Burchell*

CLEVER GIRL (IRE)   4 b.f. College Chapel 122 – Damezao (Alzao (USA) 117)   **72**
[2001 89d: 8.5m 7.5m 8d⁴ 8m* 8m* 8f 8.5f⁵ 8g 9d 8.1g 8f* 8.5g 8d a8g Nov 25]
tall, good-topped filly: fair performer: won handicap at Pontefract and handicap at
Newcastle in June and handicap at Musselburgh in September: sold from T. Easterby
7,500 gns before final start: stays 9f: acts on any going: blinkered twice in 2000: has worn
tongue tie: usually races prominently: none too consistent. *C. Bjorling, Spain*

CLICK-ON (IRE)   3 b.g. Danehill (USA) 126 – Bold Flawless (USA) 73 (Bold Bidder)   **75**
[2001 84p: e6g⁴ 7g² May 5] good-bodied gelding: fair form in 3 maidens, ½-length
second to Riverina at Thirsk final start (subsequently gelded): barely stays easy 7f: sent
to Hong Kong. *J. Noseda*

CLIFTON WOOD (IRE)   6 b.g. Paris House 123 – Millie's Lady (IRE) (Common   –
Grounds 118) [2001 –: f8g Jan 1] lengthy, workmanlike gelding: disappointing maiden:
tried blinkered/tongue tied. *J. Gallagher*

CLIMATE CONTROL (USA)   2 ch.f. (Jan 24) Mt Livermore (USA) – Descant   **60**
(USA) (Nureyev (USA) 131) [2001 6d⁵ Jul 7] second foal: dam unraced half-sister to
2000 Guineas winner Zafonic: 7/2 and green, 4 lengths last of 5 to Sandy Lady in minor
event at Haydock. *R. Charlton*

CLIMATE (IRE)   2 ch.c. (Feb 24) Catrail (USA) 123 – Burishki 49 (Chilibang 120)   **73**
[2001 6m² 6m³ 6f 6g 7v p8g⁴ p8g² Nov 28] 5,500F, IR 22,000Y: strong, compact colt: **a80**
fourth living foal: brother to a 1m winner in Spain and half-brother to a winner in Italy by
Indian Ridge: dam 6f winner, including at 2 yrs: fairly useful maiden on all-weather, fair
on turf: stays 1m: acts on good to firm going (well beaten on heavy) and polytrack:
wandered final outing. *R. Hannon*

CLIMBING ROSE (USA)   3 b.f. Quest For Fame 127 – Abeer (USA) 115 (Dewan   –
(USA)) [2001 69p: 7s 6m 6m⁵ 7v Oct 28] smallish, lengthy, unfurnished filly: fair form
final 2-y-o start: disappointing at 3 yrs, leaving R. Charlton 13,000 gns after third outing:
free-going sort, but should stay at least 1m: acts on heavy ground: has carried head
awkwardly. *A. L. T. Moore, Ireland*

CLIPPERTON   2 b.c. (Apr 16) Mister Baileys 123 – Theresita (GER) (Surumu   **67**
(GER)) [2001 6f⁵ Jun 14] 12,000F, 66,000Y: half-brother to several winners abroad,
including French 1¼m and 13f winner Tamana (by Northern Baby): dam, German 1¼m
winner, sister to German Derby winner Temporal: green, fifth of 7 in minor event at
Newbury: bred to be suited by at least 1m: retained 18,000 gns in October. *I. A. Balding*

CLIQUEY   2 b.g. (Feb 12) Muhtarram (USA) 125 – Meet Again (Lomond (USA) 128)   –
[2001 f8.5g Oct 9] 5,000F, 4,200Y: sixth foal: half-brother to fairly useful 1m winner
Cool Vibes (by Rock City) and 1¼m seller winner Today Tonite (by Adbass): dam fourth
at 6f at 2 yrs: 12/1, well beaten in maiden at Wolverhampton. *J. A. Osborne*

CLOONDESH   3 b.g. Forzando 122 – Shalati (FR) (High Line 125) [2001 47: 6.1v f8g   –
Apr 28] quite good-topped gelding: no form since debut. *R. A. Fahey*

CLOONE EXPRESS   2 ch.g. (Feb 20) Polar Falcon (USA) 126 – Simple Logic 73   **63**
(Aragon 118) [2001 6d 6v p7g Dec 12] 7,000Y: lengthy gelding: first foal: dam 2-y-o 6f

winner: modest maiden: raced freely and looked difficult ride in claimer at Lingfield final outing: should stay at least 7f. *N. A. Callaghan*

CLOPTON GREEN   4 b.g. Presidium 124 – Silkstone Lady (Puissance 110) [2001   **53**
57+: f6g* f6s e7g f6s² f6f f6g 7m p5g⁴ f6g p6g⁵ Dec 19] modest handicapper: won at Southwell in January: effective at 5f/6f: acts on fibresand/equitrack and good to soft going: usually blinkered in 2000: tried tongue tied. *J. W. Payne*

CLOTH OF GOLD   4 b.g. Barathea (IRE) 127 – Bustinetta 89 (Bustino 136) [2001   **64**
72: 12d⁴ Nov 6] leggy, quite attractive gelding: lightly-raced maiden: probably stays 1½m. *Lady Herries*

CLOUD DANCER   2 b. or br.f. (Apr 12) Bishop of Cashel 122 – Summer Pageant   **83 p**
81 (Chief's Crown (USA)) [2001 7m³ 6.1m* f6g² f7g² Nov 30] 4,000Y: leggy, rather unfurnished filly: half-sister to 5-y-o Join The Parade and French/Spanish winner around 11f Echalar (both by Elmaamul): dam 1½m winner out of half-sister to Sun Princess and Saddlers' Hall: fairly useful performer: won maiden at Warwick in September: ran well in nurseries at Southwell (forced wide first occasion/winner got first run on second) last 2 starts: should stay at least 1m: raced only on good to firm going on turf, acts on fibresand: open to improvement. *D. J. Coakley*

CLOUDY   3 b.f. Ashkalani (IRE) 128 – Shady Leaf (IRE) 56 (Glint of Gold 128) [2001   **69**
68: 10.2d 8.1g 7m⁴ 9m³ 8g f8.5g⁴ Nov 17] lengthy, useful-looking filly: fair maiden: left F. J. Houghton 5,000 gns after third outing: well below form last 3 starts: should prove best at 1m/1¼m: acts on good to firm going. *Mrs Lydia Pearce*

CLOWNIN AROUND   2 b.f. (Jan 29) Mistertopogigo (IRE) 118 – Pokey's Pet 56   **–**
(Uncle Pokey 116) [2001 f5g⁵ 6m Sep 20] 1,000Y: seventh foal: half-sister to 1995 2-y-o 7f seller winner Catwalk Girl (by Skyliner): dam 7f seller winner (including at 2 yrs): well beaten in seller (for B. Baugh) then maiden. *M. Mullineaux*

CLYTHA HILL LASS   2 ch.f. (May 14) Bluegrass Prince (IRE) 110 – Manhunt 70   **49**
(Posse (USA) 130) [2001 5.1g⁶ 5.7f 6.1m 5.1s⁵ Aug 9] 800Y: sixth foal: half-sister to 1993 2-y-o 7f winner Mokaite and 1m winner Whackford Squeers (both by Komaite): dam, maiden, probably stayed 7f: poor maiden: easily best effort on final start: should stay at least 6f. *J. M. Bradley*

COALITION   2 b.c. (May 9) Polish Precedent (USA) 131 – Selection Board 75 (Welsh   **54 p**
Pageant 132) [2001 7s f7g 7d f7g⁶ Nov 30] 25,000Y: rather leggy, good-topped colt: half-brother to several winners, including 1m winner (stayed 1½m) Star Selection (by Rainbow Quest) and 7f winner Cruinn A Bhord (by Inchinor), both raced: dam twice-raced sister to Teleprompter: modest form in maidens/nursery: again not knocked about final outing: likely to be suited by 1¼m+: should do better at 3 yrs. *Sir Mark Prescott*

COASTAL BLUFF   9 gr.g. Standaan (FR) 118 – Combattente (Reform 132) [2001   **94**
93: 5m 5m* 5f 5m 5m 5m Jul 31] tall, angular gelding: fairly useful handicapper: won at Haydock (well ridden from front by J. Fanning) in May by head from Mitcham: ran creditably after only on penultimate start: effective at 5f/6f: acts on soft and firm going: tried blinkered: has had wind operations/worn tongue strap, and is tubed: usually bandaged behind: best with strong handling. *N. P. Littmoden*

COCCOLONA (IRE)   3 b.f. Idris (IRE) 118 – Fair Siobahn (Petingo 135) [2001 54:   **59**
7m 7m 10m f8.5g⁵ f12g f11g* f12g⁶ f12g f14.8s Dec 15] modest performer: won claiming minor event at Southwell in October: stays 1½m: acts on fibresand, soft and good to firm going: has been slowly away. *D. Haydn Jones*

COCKNEY BOSS (IRE)   2 b.g. (Apr 17) General Monash (USA) 107 – Cockney   **–**
Ground (IRE) (Common Grounds 118) [2001 7m 6g Sep 7] IR 5,000Y, 14,000 2-y-o: tall gelding: third foal: half-brother to a winner in Italy by Fayruz: dam unraced: no sign of ability in maiden/sales race. *B. R. Millman*

COCO DE MER   4 ch.g. Prince Sabo 123 – Musica 82 (Primo Dominie 121) [2001   **50**
64d: e5g⁵ 5f 5s Sep 24] strong gelding: has a quick action: fairly useful at 2 yrs: modest form at best since, leaving Miss D. McHale after reappearance: best at 5f: best turf form on good going or firmer: edgy sort, and has shown signs of temperament. *T. Keddy*

COCO LOCO   4 b.f. Bin Ajwaad (IRE) 119 – Mainly Me 76 (Huntingdale 132) [2001   **98**
95: 16s² 18.7f 14.4m³ 16.1g⁵ Aug 10] tall, workmanlike filly: useful handicapper: ran well in 2001 when placed at Newbury and Kempton: should stay beyond 16.5f: has form on good to firm going, all wins on soft/heavy: hung/carried head awkwardly when running poorly final start. *Mrs Lydia Pearce*

COCONUT 5 b.g. Shirley Heights 130 – Magical Retreat (USA) 115 (Sir Ivor 135) – [2001 10d⁶ 12g 11.9g 17.1g Aug 19] no sign of ability. *W. Clay*

CO DOT UK 3 b.g. Distant Relative 128 – Cubist (IRE) 71 (Tate Gallery (USA) 117) **63** [2001 68: f7g f7g³ f7g² f7g³ e7g 8m 8m² 8m 7.1f² 7m f7g⁶ 8.2m⁶ 9.2d Aug 15] modest performer: left K. Ryan £5,000 after fourth start: effective at 6f to easy 1m: acts on any turf going and fibresand: usually blinkered: has been early to post/slowly away: often makes running: sold 650 gns. *T. D. Barron*

CODY 2 ch.c. (Jan 8) Zilzal (USA) 137 – Ibtihaj (USA) 97 (Raja Baba (USA)) [2001 – 5m 6v f7g Oct 23] 8,000Y: good-topped colt: half-brother to 3 winners, including fairly useful 1986 2-y-o 5f winner Abhaaj (by Kris), herself dam of useful sprinter Mubhij: dam, 2-y-o 5f winner, half-sister to Danzig: no form in minor event/maidens: pulled up final start. *R. Hannon*

COFFEE TIME (IRE) 2 b.f. (May 19) Efisio 120 – Petula 103 (Petong 126) [2001 **88 d** 5.1m⁵ 5m³ 5m 5.2m 5.1s² 5.2m⁴ 5g⁵ 5.1m² 5.7g⁴ 5s³ p5g⁴ p6g⁴ Nov 28] 17,000Y: quite good-topped filly: fourth foal: half-sister to 6f winner Etienne Lady (by Imperial Frontier), 5f (at 2 yrs)/6f winner Night Life (by Night Shift) and 3-y-o Middleton Grey: dam 2-y-o 5f/6f winner: fairly useful maiden: in frame 8 times, including in listed events at Beverley and Newbury on second and sixth starts: not so good after latter: likely to prove better at 6f than 5f: best turf efforts on good to firm ground, probably acts on polytrack: usually held up. *D. J. S. ffrench Davis*

COLD CLIMATE 6 b.g. Pursuit of Love 124 – Sharpthorne (USA) 91 (Sharpen Up **80** 127) [2001 65: 6g* 6d² 6m* 6g 6g⁶ Aug 10] lengthy gelding: fairly useful handicapper: much improved in first half of 2001, and won at Newbury and Redcar: probably best at 5f/6f: acts on heavy and good to firm going: has worn visor: usually comes from behind. *Bob Jones*

COLEY 4 ch.f. Pursuit of Love 124 – Cole Slaw (Absalom 128) [2001 47: e6g e6g Jan – 10] useful-looking filly: well beaten in 2001: often blinkered. *B. A. Pearce*

COLIN COOK 3 b.g. Presidium 124 – Horton Lady 46 (Midyan (USA) 124) [2001 –: – f6s Dec 15] no sign of ability. *Miss J. F. Craze*

COLLARD 3 ch.f. Wolfhound (USA) 126 – Collide 102 (High Line 125) [2001 68p: **79** 8.3d* 8.2f² 9m⁶ 12m⁶ 10v⁵ 11.7d Oct 25] workmanlike filly: fair performer: won maiden at Windsor in May: seems to stay 1¼m: probably acts on any turf going: sold 14,500 gns, joined M. Johnston. *H. Candy*

COLLECTIVITY 3 b.f. Dr Devious (IRE) 127 – Loch Quest (USA) (Lomond (USA) **38** 128) [2001 60: f9.4s³ 12.1g⁴ 16g⁶ 8m 13.1m 10s Oct 3] strong, lengthy filly: poor maiden nowadays: left B. Hills after reappearance and B. de Haan after third start: seems to stay 1½m: acts on equitrack and soft ground: looked uncooperative in blinkers final start. *J. S. Moore*

COLLEGE BLUE (IRE) 5 b.m. College Chapel 122 – Mitsubishi Centre (IRE) **45 §** (Thatching 131) [2001 64§: 6f³ 6m 10m 7d Jul 18] modest performer: below form in 2001: best at 5f/6f: acts on all-weather and firm going: tried blinkered/visored: inconsistent. *Miss S. West*

COLLEGE CITY (IRE) 2 b.g. (Apr 20) College Chapel 122 – Polish Crack (IRE) **44** (Polish Patriot (USA) 128) [2001 5s f5g 7.1f 8g⁵ 7.9m f8g Dec 10] IR 8,000Y: strong gelding: third foal: dam unraced half-sister to useful performer up to 7f Fair Crack: poor maiden: left T. Easterby after fifth start: stays 1m: blinkered third outing/visored final one. *S. J. Magnier*

COLLEGE DEAN (IRE) 5 ch.g. College Chapel 122 – Phyllode (Pharly (FR) 130) – [2001 –: 6g 7d 9.2d 8.3s Aug 21] of no account nowadays. *P. Monteith*

COLLEGE DELINQUENT (IRE) 2 br.g. (Mar 20) College Chapel 122 – St Cyr **73** Aty (IRE) (Ela-Mana-Mou 132) [2001 6f 7s Oct 16] IR 5,000F, IR 2,500Y: quite good-topped gelding: first foal: dam unraced half-sister to very smart sprinter Cyrano de Bergerac: better effort in maidens (fair form) when close seventh of 19 to Allenby at Leicester on second start: bred to prove best up to 7f: sent to France. *B. J. Meehan*

COLLEGE FACT 3 b.g. So Factual (USA) 120 – Starfida (Soviet Star (USA) 128) – [2001 –: f8g f6g 6m 6s 10d Oct 15] no form: tried visored/blinkered. *Mrs C. A. Dunnett*

COLLEGE HIPPIE 2 b.f. (Apr 29) Cosmonaut – Eccentric Dancer 47 (Rambo **65** Dancer (CAN) 107) [2001 5.1g⁵ f5g⁶ 5f² 5g³ 5.2m² 5.1g⁵ 5g⁶ 5.1m⁴ 5g⁴ Sep 19] plain, angular filly: second foal: dam maiden who stayed 9.4f: fair maiden: second at Beverley and Yarmouth (minor event): will prove best at 5f/6f: acts on firm ground. *J. F. Coupland*

COLLEGE KING (IRE)   5 b.g. College Chapel 122 – Genetta (Green Desert (USA) – 127) [2001 –: 8.2v 7d 7.5m 10.1g Aug 17] small, sturdy gelding: no form. *M. Brittain*

COLLEGE MAID (IRE)   4 b.f. College Chapel 122 – Maid of Mourne (Fairy King   85 (USA)) [2001 75: 7.1d 5v 5s 6d³ 6m 7m⁵ 6m³ 6d² 7f 5m 6s³ 5d* 6d² 5g⁵ 6g 6m³ 5g 6g⁵ 5s 5m 6m 5d³ 5d 7d³ 6v⁶ 7d Oct 30] sturdy filly: fairly useful handicapper: won at Ayr in July: mostly respectable efforts at least otherwise in 2001: effective at 5f (given a test) to 7f: possibly not at best on firm ground, acts on any other: has been mulish in paddock: has edged right: tough. *J. S. Goldie*

COLLEGE PRINCESS   7 b.m. Anshan 119 – Tinkers Fairy (Myjinski (USA)) [2001   – 34: f5g f5g e6g f5g e6g⁶ 8g 5f 6m Jul 4] little form in 2001: blinkered first 5 starts. *Mrs C. A. Dunnett*

COLLEGE QUEEN   3 b.f. Lugana Beach 116 – Eccentric Dancer 47 (Rambo Dancer   – (CAN) 107) [2001 57: f6g⁵ f6s Jan 18] maiden: well held both 3-y-o starts. *J. G. Given*

COLLEGE ROCK   4 ch.g. Rock Hopper 124 – Sea Aura 89 (Roi Soleil 125) [2001   79 68, a52: f8g 8.5s 8s² 8d* 8.1m⁴ 8.3g f8g f8g 8.1m³ 8.1m³ 10g⁶ 8d² 8m 8.2m 8s⁴ p8g Dec   a47 22] small, sturdy gelding: fair handicapper on turf, modest on all-weather: won at Brighton in May: probably best at 1m/9f: probably acts on any turf going and fibresand/ equitrack: visored nowadays: has given trouble in preliminaries. *R. Brotherton*

COLLEGE STAR   3 b.g. Lugana Beach 116 – Alis Princess (Sayf El Arab (USA)   – 127) [2001 41: 7m f8g⁶ f9.4g⁵ 7.5f 8f 10.1g 7.5m 8d f7g f7g f8g Nov 30] tall gelding: maiden: tried visored. *J. F. Coupland*

COLLIERS TREASURE   4 b.f. Manhal – Indian Treasure (IRE) (Treasure Kay   – 114) [2001 –: e12g Feb 3] well held in 2 maidens. *J. S. Moore*

COLLINE DE FEU   4 ch.f. Sabrehill (USA) 120 – Band of Fire (USA) (Chief's   – Crown (USA)) [2001 61: f16g f16s f14g⁶ 14.1s⁶ 14.1v f14g May 14] little form in 2001. *Mrs P. Sly*

COLNE VALLEY AMY   4 b.f. Mizoram (USA) 105 – Panchellita (USA) 78 (Pancho   56 Villa (USA)) [2001 76: 9m 9m 8.3g 10g 8g 8m⁵ p10g⁵ f8g⁵ Dec 10] tall filly: modest   a49 handicapper nowadays: left W. Musson after fifth start: best at 1m/bare 1¼m: acts on firm going, good to soft and polytrack: often makes running. *G. L. Moore*

COLOMBE D'OR   4 gr.g. Petong 126 – Deep Divide 74 (Nashwan (USA) 135) [2001   42 50§, a59d: f11g⁶ f7g³ f8g⁵ f8s⁴ f8g* f8.5g* f8g² 10.3s f11g f8g f8g³ 8m 8m f8g³ f8g 8g⁴   a60 10m f11g f8g Nov 26] workmanlike gelding: modest handicapper on all-weather, poor on turf: won at Southwell in February and Wolverhampton in March: has form at 1½m, probably best around 1m: acts on fibresand/equitrack and good to soft going: tried blinkered: used to look far from keen. *M. C. Chapman*

COLONEL COTTON (IRE)   2 b.g. (Feb 25) Royal Applause 124 – Cutpurse Moll   80 76 (Green Desert (USA) 127) [2001 6g 6g⁴ 6m⁶ 6.1d² 7s³ 6s² Nov 10] good-topped gelding: third foal: half-brother to 1999 2-y-o 7f seller winner Inch Pincher (by Inchinor): dam, 7f winner, out of useful 1m/1¼m winner Pretty Pol: fairly useful maiden: placed last 3 starts, including in nurseries: will prove best at 6f/7f: acts on soft going. *N. A. Callaghan*

COLONEL CUSTER   6 ch.g. Komaite (USA) – Mohican 75 (Great Nephew 126)   – § [2001 –§, a61§: f12g* f12g* f11s* f9.4g* f8.5s⁶ f12g⁴ f12g 10.9m f11g² f11g² 11.8d   a61 § f9.4s⁵ f12g f11g⁴ f12g⁵ f8g f11g* f12s⁶ Dec 27] tall, angular gelding: modest performer on all-weather: won 3 sellers and amateur handicap at Wolverhampton/Southwell in January and claimer at Southwell (apprentices) in December: stays 1½m: acts on fibresand: sometimes visored/blinkered: tends to wander/carry head awkwardly under pressure: none too trustworthy. *R. Brotherton*

COLONEL KOZANDO   2 b.c. (Feb 5) Komaite (USA) – Times Zando 64 (Forzando   57 ? 122) [2001 6d⁵ 7.1f⁵ 7.9m 7d Oct 3] 4,400Y, 12,500 2-y-o: strong, workmanlike colt: third foal: brother to 3-y-o Captain Kozando: dam 2-y-o 7f/1m winner: modest maiden: seemingly best effort on second start: stays 7f. *Mrs G. S. Rees*

COLONEL KURTZ (USA)   3 b.g. Slip Anchor 136 – Rustaka (USA) 68 (Riverman   – (USA) 131) [2001 –: 8m 10g 12.6f 12.1d Jul 19] big, leggy gelding: little form. *John Berry*

COLONEL MUSTARD   5 ch.g. Keen 116 – Juliet Bravo 61 (Glow (USA)) [2001   71 8m 10.3f 8m³ 8.3g 9.9m⁴ 10.3m 8m 8d⁵ f9.4g* f11g p10g f9.4s⁴ Dec 27] unfurnished gelding: has a long stride: fair handicapper: sold 8,000 gns and left J. Fanshawe after fourth start: won at Wolverhampton in November: stays 1¼m: acts on polytrack/fibresand and firm going: tried visored: has looked reluctant. *P. G. Murphy*

COLONEL SAM 5 b.g. Puissance 110 – Indian Summer 78 (Young Generation 129) **41 §**
[2001 46§: f6s f5g f6g f5g f5g 6m 5g⁵ 6m 5g⁵ Aug 8] strong, good-quartered gelding: poor maiden handicapper: effective at 5f to 7f: acts on firm going, good to soft and fibresand: visored once, sometimes blinkered: usually tongue tied at 4 yrs: refused to race once as 4-y-o: inconsistent. *S. R. Bowring*

COLONNADE 2 b.f. (Mar 27) Blushing Flame (USA) 109 – White Palace 80 (Shirley **51 p**
Heights 130) [2001 8d⁶ Oct 25] third foal: half-sister to 3-y-o Palatial: dam 1m winner: weak 14/1-shot, late headway after slow start when 14 lengths sixth of 15 to Kaieteur in maiden at Bath: sold 10,000 gns: should improve. *J. R. Fanshawe*

COLORADO FALLS (IRE) 3 b.g. Nashwan (USA) 135 – Ballet Shoes (IRE) 75 **93**
(Ela-Mana-Mou 132) [2001 11s³ 12g* May 18] IR 180,000Y: medium-sized, useful-looking gelding: fourth foal: closely related to 4-y-o Petrushka and half-brother to fairly useful Irish 7f winner Danse Classique (by Night Shift): dam, 5f winner, half-sister to Spectrum from family of 4-y-o Millenary: quite useful form: landed odds in 4-runner maiden at Newmarket in May, beating Year Two Thousand 1¼ lengths: should stay beyond 1½m: edged left under pressure both starts: sold 14,000 gns in October, joined P. Monteith and gelded. *H. R. A. Cecil*

COLOUR PURPLE 2 b.f. (Mar 17) Spectrum (IRE) 126 – Awtaar (USA) 67 **47**
(Lyphard (USA) 132) [2001 6g⁵ 7.5m 8m 7s Oct 25] 18,000Y: well-made filly: fourth foal: half-sister to useful 1½m/1¾m winner Sharp Stepper (by Selkirk) and 4-y-o Magical River: dam, disappointing maiden, out of half-sister to 1000 Guineas winner Fairy Footsteps and St Leger winner Light Cavalry: poor maiden. *C. E. Brittain*

COLOUR SERGEANT (USA) 3 ch.g. Candy Stripes (USA) 115 – Princess Afleet **55**
(USA) (Afleet (CAN)) [2001 65: f9.4g⁵ 5.1s 8g f7g 6m⁴ 7m⁴ 7m³ 7g 8.1d⁴ 9m⁵ 8g⁴ 7v **a60**
Oct 26] smallish, lengthy gelding: modest maiden: left M. Bell after seventh start: may prove best at 7f/1m: acts on fibresand and good to firm going: tried visored. *Don Enrico Incisa*

COLUMBINE (IRE) 3 b.f. Pivotal 124 – Heart of India (IRE) (Try My Best (USA) **82**
130) [2001 74: f6g 5m⁶ 5m 6m 5m⁵ 5m 5.1m⁴ 5m⁶ 5g² 6g⁴ 5.2d 6.1m⁶ 5g 6d³ f6g 5.1d²
Oct 25] lengthy, useful-looking filly: really good walker: fairly useful handicapper: best efforts at 5f: acts on firm and good to soft ground: blinkered final start: sold 10,000 gns. *A. Berry*

COLUMNA 5 gr.m. Deploy 131 – Copper Trader 53 (Faustus (USA) 118) [2001 –: **–**
f16g Jan 5] little form: tried blinkered. *M. D. I. Usher*

COLWAY RITZ 7 b.g. Rudimentary (USA) 118 – Million Heiress (Auction Ring **71**
(USA) 123) [2001 90: 8g 11.9m 10m 10m⁶ 10m³ 10m⁴ 12.4m⁶ 12g⁶ 10m⁵ 12m 10.1f⁶
Sep 10] big, strong gelding: good mover: fair handicapper: stays easy 1½m: acts on firm and good to soft going (possibly not on soft): tried blinkered: held up. *W. Storey*

COMANCHE QUEEN 4 ch.f. Totem (USA) 118 – Chess Mistress (USA) 59 (Run **51**
The Gantlet (USA)) [2001 –: 12m 16f³ 14f² 12f* 13.8g⁴ 11.1d 14m⁴ 12m 16f⁶ Sep 4]
close-coupled filly: modest handicapper: won selling event at Musselburgh in August: effective at 1½m to 2m: acts on firm ground: tried blinkered. *J. S. Wainwright*

COMBINED VENTURE (IRE) 5 b.h. Dolphin Street (FR) 125 – Centinela 67 **–**
(Caerleon (USA) 132) [2001 –: f11g Nov 30] no longer of any account. *J. A. Pickering*

COME ON MURGY 4 b.f. Weldnaas (USA) 112 – Forest Song 60 (Forzando 122) **37**
[2001 –, a49: f7g⁴ f7s² f9.4s⁴ f7s² f8.5s* f8g f9.4g f8.5g* f8f f8g³ f8g⁵ 7.1f⁵ f8.5g f8g **a55**
f7g Dec 3] leggy filly: modest handicapper on all-weather, poor on turf: won amateur events at Wolverhampton in January and March: stays 8.5f: acts on good to firm going, fibresand/equitrack: tried blinkered. *A. Bailey*

COMEOUTOFTHEFOG (IRE) 6 b.g. Mujadil (USA) 119 – Local Belle (Bally **38**
more 123) [2001 –, a61d: f9.4s f7g⁶ f6g 8.2v 8.1g 9.9d Oct 3] small gelding: poor nowadays: left Miss S. Wilton after reappearance: effective at 7f/1m: acts on fibresand/equitrack, best turf form on good going or firmer: tried blinkered. *R. J. Price*

COMEUPPANCE (IRE) 3 b.g. General Monash (USA) 107 – Press Reception **52**
(Beldale Flutter (USA) 130) [2001 45: 8.1g 6m² 6m 6m Aug 3] leggy gelding: modest maiden: stays 6f: acts on good to firm going, yet to race on softer than good. *J. G. Given*

COMEX FLYER (IRE) 4 ch.g. Prince of Birds (USA) 121 – Smashing Pet –
(Mummy's Pet 125) [2001 52: f8g 10s Apr 10] close-coupled, useful-looking gelding: no
form in 2001: tried blinkered: useful novice hurdler for P. Nicholls. *D. Nicholls*

COMFORTABLE CALL 3 ch.g. Nashwan (USA) 135 – High Standard 83 (Kris **74**
135) [2001 10s 10m³ 14g⁴ 14.1g² 14.1m³ 14f⁴ 14.1s Sep 4] strong gelding: second foal:
half-brother to useful 7f (at 2 yrs) to 1½m winner Summer Song (by Green Desert): dam,
2-y-o 1m winner who stayed 1½m, out of close relation to Nureyev: fair maiden: should
be suited by 2m: acts on good to firm going: sold 5,000 gns, then gelded. *E. A. L. Dunlop*

COMFY (USA) 2 b.c. (Jan 26) Lear Fan (USA) 130 – Souplesse (USA) (Majestic **107 p**
Light (USA)) [2001 7m³ 7g* 7d⁵ Oct 20]
    Which trainer has won three of the last five Two Thousand Guineas? Sir
Michael Stoute is the answer, of course. He is due a wait for another it could be
argued! Nevertheless, don't rule out the possibility of Comfy making it four
winners in the last six years for the yard in 2002, or at least putting up a bold show
at Newmarket. Interestingly, Comfy's career so far has followed a similar path to
that of King's Best, successful in the Guineas for the stable in 2000. Both colts
had one run in a maiden—in Comfy's case finishing third at Ascot in July—before
winning the Acomb Stakes at York in August. In a field of nine, Comfy was much
too good for the useful Asheer, in receipt of 3 lb, taking command as soon as Fallon
asked him to extend and merely being pushed out to win by two lengths. On the
strength of that performance Comfy started second favourite behind Rock of
Gibraltar in the Dewhurst Stakes in October at Newmarket, where he became short
of room on the rail as the race finally began in earnest and had to be switched wide
to make his effort, finishing only fifth of eight, beaten just under three lengths.
Comfy made no impression once in the clear, but time could show that the softer
ground than at York didn't suit him.

		Roberto	Hail To Reason
	Lear Fan (USA)	(b 1969)	Bramalea
	(b 1981)	Wac	Lt Stevens
Comfy (USA)		(b 1969)	Belthazar
(b.c. Jan 26, 1999)		Majestic Light	Majestic Prince
	Souplesse (USA)	(b 1973)	Irradiate
	(b 1990)	Nimble Feet	Danzig
		(b 1985)	Nimble Folly

    Comfy is bred to be a good horse. His dam Souplesse is out of Nimble Feet,
a half-sister to Flit, the dam of One Thousand Guineas winner Wince. Nimble Feet
is also the dam of Eltish, who won the Royal Lodge Stakes and finished second in
the Breeders' Cup Juvenile before being sixth in the Kentucky Derby. This is also
the family of a still more notable dirt performer in Skimming, whose dam Skimble
is closely related to Comfy's grandam. Comfy is the fourth foal of his dam and the
second winner following Cabrita Point (by Cox's Ridge), a mile winner in the

Paradime Acomb Stakes, York—Comfy looks a smart prospect in disposing of a useful field;
Asheer (noseband) is second with Toreador third

States. Souplesse gained her only success in a listed event in France over a mile and a quarter as a three-year-old, when she was also third in the Group 3 Prix de Psyche over the same trip. Comfy will be well suited by a step up to a mile and should stay a mile and a quarter; the average winning distance of his sire Lear Fan's three-year-old offspring is around nine furlongs. A strong, good sort, Comfy should train on into a smart performer at the very least. *Sir Michael Stoute*

COMMANCHE CUP (IRE) 8 b.g. Commanche Run 133 – Royal Cup (Politico – (USA) 124) [2001 f16.2g Jun 20] well held in Wolverhampton seller. *A. P. James*

COMMANCHE WIND (IRE) 6 b.g. Commanche Run 133 – Delko (Decent **49** Fellow 114) [2001 16f² Jul 9] first foal: dam unraced: second in claimer at Musselburgh. *E. W. Tuer*

COMMANDER 5 b.g. Puissance 110 – Tarkhana (IRE) (Dancing Brave (USA) 140) – [2001 65: 8s 7g Oct 6] fair maiden at best: well held both 5-y-o starts: tried tongue tied/visored: sent to Spain. *D. Morris*

COMMANDING 2 ch.c. (Apr 24) Pennekamp (USA) 130 – Lady Joyce (FR) (Galetto **80 p** (FR) 118) [2001 6m⁴ 6g* 7d⁵ Sep 26] 30,000Y: third foal: half-brother to 3-y-o Da Wolf: dam unraced half-sister to smart French/US middle-distance performers Lady Blessington and Lowell: fairly useful form: cosy winner of maiden at Folkestone in September: didn't get run of race in nursery at Chester final start: will stay 7f: probably capable of better. *Mrs A. J. Perrett*

COMMON CONSENT (IRE) 5 b.m. Common Grounds 118 – Santella Bell (Ballad **66** Rock 122) [2001 62: 8m⁴ 9f² 9f⁴ 9m³ 9f⁵ 9m 8m p10g³ p10g p10g Dec 22] smallish mare: fair handicapper: effective at 1m to 11.5f: acts on firm going and polytrack. *S. Woodman*

COMMON THOUGHT (IRE) 2 b.g. (May 15) Common Grounds 118 – Zuhal 67 **69 p** (Busted 134) [2001 6m 7m* Jul 13] IR 2,800F, IR 6,500Y: fourth living foal: half-brother to 3-y-o Grain Storm: dam Irish 1½m winner at 5 yrs: better effort in maidens (fair form) when winning at Lingfield in July by ½ length from Royal Eagle: subsequently gelded: will stay 1m: open to improvement. *P. W. Harris*

COMMON WORLD (USA) 2 ch.c. (Feb 3) Spinning World (USA) 130 – Spen- **91 p** derella (FR) (Common Grounds 118) [2001 6d⁵ 7d* Nov 6] 25,000 2-y-o: quite attractive colt: third foal: dam, lightly-raced French 1m winner, sister to useful French miler Raisonnable and half-sister to US Grade 1 1¼m winner Aube Indienne and 3-y-o Mare Nostrum: better effort in maidens (fairly useful form) when winning at Catterick comfortably by 1½ lengths from Olivia Rose despite still seeming green: will stay 1m: wore crossed noseband when slowly away on debut: should make a useful 3-y-o. *G. A. Butler*

COMMUNARD (IRE) 2 b.c. (Apr 28) Sri Pekan (USA) 117 – Broadway Rosie 101 **67** (Absalom 128) [2001 6m 7m⁵ 6m⁵ 6m* Sep 12] IR 34,000F, IR 50,000Y: seventh foal: half-brother to 3 winners, notably smart 6f winner Eastern Purple (by Petorius): dam Irish 5f to 7f winner: fair performer: won nursery at Goodwood in September by short head from unlucky Happy Guest: likely to prove best up to 7f: raced only on good to firm going: carried head awkwardly last 2 starts: sold 24,000 gns. *R. Hannon*

COMMUNICATE (IRE) 2 b.c. (Mar 15) Bigstone (IRE) 126 – Sada 74 (Mujtahid – (USA) 118) [2001 5m f6g Jun 8] sturdy colt: first foal: dam, sprint maiden, half-sister to useful 6f/7f performer Matila (dam of smart performer up to 9f Easaar): well beaten in claimer/seller. *T. D. Easterby*

COMO (USA) 3 b. or br.f. Cozzene (USA) – Merida (Warning 136) [2001 82p: 8.3s **95** 6m³ 6m* 6m* 6g³ 6g⁴ 5m³ 5d Oct 13] strong, good-topped filly: useful performer: won maiden at Southwell and minor event at Kempton in July: ran at least creditably in handicaps after, including when fourth to Torosay Spring at Kempton: was effective at 5f/6f: acted on good to firm and good to soft going: usually raced prominently: retired. *R. Charlton*

COMPANION 3 b.f. Most Welcome 131 – Benazir 91 (High Top 131) [2001 69: f8g³ **77** f7g⁵ f8g² e7g* f8g* f8g* 9s 8g 8m 8m² 9f 9m 7m 8m⁶ 8m p10g f8g p10g p10g⁶ p8g⁶ p8g **a87** Dec 28] tall, lengthy, good-topped filly: fairly useful on all-weather: claimed from W. Haggas before winning maiden at Lingfield and 2 handicaps at Southwell in March/April: below form final 5 starts: best up to 1m: acts on all-weather, firm and soft ground: has bolted to post/been led down: has been slowly away/taken good hold: races prominently. *B. A. Pearce*

COMPLETE CLASS (USA) 3 b.c. Dynaformer (USA) – Impertinent Lady (USA) – (Sham (USA)) [2001 10d Apr 17] $200,000Y: tall, good-topped colt: has plenty of scope: fifth foal: half-brother to several winners abroad, notably smart US performer up to 9f Cocky (by Valiant Nature): dam, winner in USA up to 7f (including at 2 yrs), half-sister to US Grade 2 7f winner She's Tops: well held in maiden at Newmarket: sent to USA. *H. R. A. Cecil*

COMPRADORE 6 b.m. Mujtahid (USA) 118 – Keswa 94 (Kings Lake (USA) 133) 72 § [2001 74: 7s 7m³ 7f⁵ 7g³ 8m 8g 7g² 7g³ 7d⁴ 7.1g⁵ 7.1g 6.1v 8s Oct 25] leggy, good-quartered mare: fair performer: effective at 6f (given a test) to easy 1m: acts on any going: tried blinkered: held up: often finds little/looks less than keen. *M. Blanshard*

COMPTON ADMIRAL 5 b.h. Suave Dancer (USA) 136 – Sumoto 101 (Mtoto 134) 105 [2001 10g³ May 30] smallish, sturdy horse: usually took the eye: had a quick, fluent action: very smart performer at 3 yrs, winner of Eclipse Stakes at Sandown: reported to have fractured a bone in his off-fore knee after final outing that year and suffered further set-back early in 2000: only useful form when 2½ lengths third to Dramatic Quest in minor event at Newbury (slowly away) only 5-y-o start: was best around 1¼m: acted on good to firm going: was held up: retired after suffering tendon injury in early-July: to stand at Hedgeholme Stud, nr Darlington, fee £2,000. *G. A. Butler*

COMPTON ARROW (IRE) 5 b.g. Petardia 113 – Impressive Lady 98 (Mr Fluoro- 78 carbon 126) [2001 79, a72: 7m³ 6m³ 7m⁵ 7d² 5s⁵ 6s 7d Oct 20] big, rangy gelding: has a quick action: fair handicapper: below form last 3 starts: effective at 6f to 1m: acts on soft going, good to firm and fibresand/equitrack: tried blinkered: sometimes tongue tied: sold 10,000 gns. *G. A. Butler*

COMPTON AVIATOR 5 ch.g. First Trump 118 – Rifada 103 (Ela-Mana-Mou 132) 76 [2001 87: 8m⁴ 16.2f 10.3m² 9d⁴ 10.1m 10.4g 10m 10s Sep 27] lengthy gelding: fair performer: effective at 1¼m, probably at 2m: acts on equitrack, good to firm and good to soft going: usually tongue tied: held up. *A. W. Carroll*

COMPTON BANKER (IRE) 4 br.g. Distinctly North (USA) 115 – Mary Hinge 99 100 (Dowsing (USA) 124) [2001 105p: 5s 6d 6g⁶ 5m 5m 5g Jul 14] small, strong, attractive gelding: useful performer: won 2 handicaps (including Portland at Doncaster) in 2000: generally disappointing at 4 yrs (highly tried on occasions): raced only at 5f/6f: acts on good to firm going: blinkered penultimate start: usually held up. *G. A. Butler*

COMPTON BOLTER (IRE) 4 b.c. Red Sunset 120 – Milk And Honey 102 (So 117 Blessed 130) [2001 112: e10g³ a8f 10m² 10m 12m⁴ 10m⁴ 12g* 10d 11f³ 12s⁶ p10g* Nov 24] smallish colt: has a quick action: smart performer: won listed events at Goodwood (rated stakes, by neck from Maniatis) in August and Lingfield (for second year running, edging left when beating Reef Diver by neck) in November: ran at least respectably otherwise when in frame, including 2 lengths second to Border Arrow in Brigadier Gerard Stakes at Sandown and third to Grandera in listed race at Newbury: stays 1½m: acts on dirt, equitrack and polytrack, has form on soft going, best turf efforts on good or firmer: blinkered (in USA) once as 3-y-o: has been tongue tied: held up. *G. A. Butler*

COMPTON CHICK (IRE) 3 b.f. Dolphin Street (FR) 125 – Cecina 100 (Welsh 55 Saint 126) [2001 48: e7g⁶ e7g 10s² 11.5f 9.9s Sep 25] modest maiden handicapper: stays 1¼m: acts on equitrack and soft going: usually tongue tied: said to have had breathing problem final start: sold 500 gns. *G. A. Butler*

COMPTON COMMANDER 3 ch.g. Barathea (IRE) 127 – Triode (USA) 105 99 (Sharpen Up 127) [2001 90: 10.3s² 10d 12.3f* 12f⁴ 11.9d 14g 13.9m 14g² 16d Nov 2] useful-looking gelding: useful handicapper: won at Chester in May: best effort when neck second to Riyadh at Newmarket penultimate start: should stay 2m: acts on any going: held up: very much on toes/found little final outing: has carried head awkwardly under pressure. *G. A. Butler*

COMPTON DICTATOR 2 b.c. (Apr 21) Shareef Dancer (USA) 135 – Princess Pati – p 124 (Top Ville 129) [2001 6d 6v p5g Nov 13] 55,000Y: leggy, useful-looking colt: closely related to 2 winners, notably smart middle-distance stayer Parthian Springs (by Sadler's Wells), and half-brother to several winners, including smart 9f/1¼m winner Pasternak (by Soviet Star): dam won Irish Oaks: in rear in maidens at Newmarket, Windsor and Lingfield: has carried head awkwardly: should do better at 1¼m+. *G. A. Butler*

COMPTON DRAGON (USA) 2 ch.c. (Feb 21) Woodman (USA) 126 – Vilikaia 87 P (USA) 125 (Nureyev (USA) 131) [2001 7d² p8g* Nov 28] IR 75,000Y: small colt: closely related to useful 7f (including at 2 yrs) and 1m (in UAE) winner Vilayet (by Machiavellian) and half-brother to 2 winners, including useful French/US performer up to 11f Legend of Russia (by Suave Dancer): dam, effective from 5f to 1m, sister to smart performer up to 9f Navratilovna: neck second of 3 to Studio Time in Newmarket Challenge Cup before winning maiden at Lingfield most impressively by 4 lengths from Land of Fantasy: likely to stay 1¼m: open to plenty more improvement, and potentially at least useful. *G. A. Butler*

COMPTON DYNAMO   2 b.c. (Mar 16) Wolfhound (USA) 126 – Asteroid Field **79**
(USA) 123 (Forli (ARG)) [2001 6d⁴ 7.1g³ Nov 7] 15,000F, IR 23,000Y: rather leggy colt: fourth foal: dam 7f (including Challenge Stakes) to 9f (US Grade 1) winner: fair form in maidens at Newmarket (wore crossed noseband) and Musselburgh (found little): will stay 1m. *G. A. Butler*

COMRADE CHINNERY (IRE)   8 ch.g. Jareer (USA) 115 – Phar Lapa 59 (Grundy   **–**
137) [2001 e13s 16g Jun 12] rather unfurnished gelding: of little account nowadays. *J. S. Moore*

COMTESSE NOIRE (CAN)   2 b.f. (Feb 3) Woodman (USA) 126 – Faux Pas (IRE) **67**
63 (Sadler's Wells (USA) 132) [2001 7m³ 6d³ 8m 6v⁶ Sep 28] $150,000Y: workmanlike filly: first foal: dam, Irish maiden who stayed 1½m, half-sister to smart performers Negligent (up to 1m), Ala Mahlik (up to 10.5f) and Ala Hounak (stayer): fair maiden: best effort on debut: should stay 1m. *I. A. Balding*

CONCINO (FR)   4 b.g. Zafonic (USA) 130 – Petronella (USA) (Nureyev (USA) 131)   **?**
[2001 –: 7.5f 7m 12f f16.2g 12.4m 15.8m³ 16.2s 12d Sep 25] leggy gelding: little form (probably flattered sixth start): tried visored. *Miss A. Stokell*

CONCLUDE (USA)   3 ch.c. Distant View (USA) 126 – Private Line (USA) 105 **107**
(Private Account (USA)) [2001 8g⁵ 8s² 10m* 10m⁵ 12g⁴ Jul 20] well-made, quite attractive colt: first foal: dam, 7f (at 2 yrs) to 8.5f (in USA) winner, half-sister to Prix de la Salamandre second Most Precious (dam of smart 1m to 1½m performer Matiara) from family of Sanglamore: useful form: won maiden at Ripon in May: edgy, best effort when 4 lengths fourth to Hill Country in minor event at Newmarket final start: stays 1½m: acts on soft and good to firm going: sold only 8,000 gns in October. *H. R. A. Cecil*

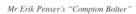

Mr Erik Penser's "Compton Bolter"

CONCUBINE (IRE) 2 b.f. (Apr 1) Danehill (USA) 126 – Bye Bold Aileen (IRE) **66** (Warning 136) [2001 5.6f 6m 5.2m⁴ 5g³ 5.1m p5g Nov 24] IR 70,000Y: close-coupled filly: has a quick action: first foal: dam, Irish maiden who seemed to stay 1¼m, half-sister to useful performers up to 1¼m Life At The Top and Gentilhomme: fair maiden: third in nursery at Beverley: should stay 6f: raced only on good going or firmer on turf, hampered on polytrack. *R. Guest*

CONEY KITTY (IRE) 3 ch.f. Lycius (USA) 124 – Auntie Maureen (IRE) 73 (Roi **103** Danzig (USA)) [2001 97: 8g 7m⁴ 8g 8.5f⁵ Oct 20] IR 12,000F, IR 13,000Y: big, good sort: second foal: half-sister to useful 2m winner Intrum Morshaan (by Darshaan): dam Irish 9f/1¼m winner from family of Halling: useful performer: won listed race at Cork at 2 yrs: ran very well when 1½ lengths fourth to Mozart in Jersey Stakes at Royal Ascot in June, then not discredited in Matron Stakes at the Curragh (eighth to Independence) and Grade 3 at Keeneland: stays 8.5f: acts on firm and good to soft going, below best on softer. *D. Hanley, Ireland*

CONGRATULATE 3 ch.g. Mark of Esteem (IRE) 137 – Kiss 88 (Habitat 134) [2001 **61** 9g⁵ 12m² 10v⁴ Oct 8] 20,000Y: half-brother to several winners, including smart Park Hill Stakes winner Casey and fairly useful 1994 2-y-o 7f winner who stayed 1¼m Alessia (both by Caerleon): dam sprinting half-sister to Park Hill winner Rejuvenate: modest form first 2 starts in maidens: stays 1½m: sent to UAE. *M. P. Tregoning*

CONISTON MILL (IRE) 4 b.f. Lake Coniston (IRE) 131 – Haiti Mill 68 (Free State **38** 125) [2001 69, a–: 6d 7m⁶ 7d⁴ Jul 18] poor maiden nowadays: stays 7f. *W. R. Muir*

CONNECT 4 b.g. Petong 126 – Natchez Trace 52 (Commanche Run 133) [2001 80, **88** a72: 6m 5.2m* 5m 5f⁴ 5g⁵ 5m⁵ 5g² 5m⁶ 5.2d* 6m f5g⁴ f5g⁵ Dec 8] strong, lengthy **a75** gelding: unimpressive mover: fairly useful handicapper on turf, fair on all-weather: won at Yarmouth in June and August: probably best at 5f: acts on good to soft going, fibresand and equitrack: tried visored/blinkered at 3 yrs: has hung. *M. H. Tompkins*

CONNOR (IRE) 2 ch.c. (Mar 2) Alhaarth (IRE) 126 – Ghayah (IRE) (Night Shift **87 p** (USA)) [2001 8g* 8f Sep 21] strong, rangy colt: has plenty of scope: has a quick action: first foal: dam, tailed off only start, out of half-sister to smart 7f/1m performer Hadeer: fairly useful form: won maiden at Kempton in September by neck from Charley Bates, quickening to lead 2f out: last and steadily to post, only seventh of 8 to Fight Your Corner in minor event at Newbury: will need to settle to stay beyond 1m: sort to do better as 3-y-o. *R. Hannon*

CONQUERING LOVE (IRE) 3 b.g. Pursuit of Love 124 – Susquehanna Days **65** (USA) 68 (Chief's Crown (USA)) [2001 –: 11.6g⁴ 10m⁵ 10.1m³ 10m² 10.9g² 11.9g* 12m² 12g⁵ 12m 11.9m⁴ 12g⁴ Sep 19] quite good-topped gelding: not a good walker: fair performer: won minor event at Brighton in July: stays 1½m: acts on good to firm going: has been mulish to post/flashed tail: consistent: sold 14,000 gns. *M. L. W. Bell*

CONQUESTADORA 3 b.f. Hernando (FR) 127 – Seren Quest 90 (Rainbow Quest **92 p** (USA) 134) [2001 10v³ 10g 14f* 13d* 14v* 13.9d 16g³ 16.5s* Nov 10] workmanlike filly: third foal: half-sister to 4-y-o Saddler's Quest and useful 1½m winner who stayed 2m Seren Hill (by Sabrehill), 1m winner at 2 yrs: dam 1¼m winner: fairly useful form: won maiden at Musselburgh and handicaps at Hamilton, Haydock and Doncaster (best effort, beat Allez Mousson 1¼ lengths) between July and November: will be suited by further than 2m: winner on firm ground, goes well on softer than good: progressive, and type to win a good prize at 4 yrs. *G. A. Butler*

CONSENSUS (IRE) 2 b.f. (Apr 29) Common Grounds 118 – Kilbride Lass (IRE) **91** (Lahib (USA) 129) [2001 6m⁴ 5m² 6d² 6m* 6m 6m* 6d³ 6d* Nov 6] IR 11,000Y: leggy filly: unimpressive mover: first foal: dam unraced out of half-sister to Arc winner Carroll House: fairly useful performer: won maiden at Ripon in August and nurseries at Ayr in September and Catterick in November: will stay 7f: yet to race on extremes of going: has edged left under pressure, and seems best held up: tough and consistent. *M. Brittain*

CONSIGNIA (IRE) 2 ch.f. (Feb 14) Definite Article 121 – Coppelia (IRE) (Mac's **67** Imp (USA) 116) [2001 6g 7m 6g 6d Oct 18] 9,000F, 16,000Y: lengthy, rather unfurnished filly: first foal: dam unraced half-sister to US Grade 2 1m winner Aberuschka out of half-sister to high-class sprinter Abergwaun: fair maiden: best effort penultimate start: likely to prove best up to 1m. *G. B. Balding*

CONSORT 8 b.g. Groom Dancer (USA) 128 – Darnelle 83 (Shirley Heights 130) **49 §** [2001 60§, a–§: 8m 8f⁴ 8d f8g Nov 26] good-topped gelding: poor handicapper: best at 1m/9f: acts on equitrack, best turf efforts on good going or firmer: has been tongue tied: best held up: unreliable. *Mrs J. R. Ramsden*

CONSPIRE (IRE) 3 b.f. Turtle Island (IRE) 123 – Mild Intrigue (USA) 91 (Sir Ivor **67**
135) [2001 81: e7g² e10g³ 11.1m² 10f³ 7g³ f9.4g³ 10f² 12g³ 10d Sep 21] leggy, quite
good-topped filly: has a quick, fluent action: fair maiden: will stay beyond 1½m: acts on
soft and good to firm going: blinkered final start: has been tongue tied. *G. A. Butler*

CONSTABLE 2 gr.g. (May 14) Efisio 120 – Tagiki (IRE) (Doyoun 124) [2001 6m⁵ **83 p**
6m* Sep 22] 45,000Y: fourth foal: half-brother to 4-y-o Peacock Alley and fairly useful
2000 2-y-o 6f winner Barathiki (by Barathea): dam, Italian 2-y-o 7f winner, granddaughter of high-class French sprinter Texanita: confirmed promise when beating
Rheinpark by 3 lengths in maiden at Catterick, sweeping through to lead final 1f: should
stay 7f: sold 32,000 gns in October, sent to USA: probably capable of better. *P. F. I. Cole*

CONSTITUTE (USA) 2 b.f. (Jan 27) Gone West (USA) – Appointed One (USA) **– p**
(Danzig (USA)) [2001 6g Oct 6] rather leggy filly: second foal: half-sister to 3-y-o
Matoaka: dam, minor 1m stakes winner in USA, sister to smart miler Emperor Jones and
closely related to top-class 1985 2-y-o Bakharoff: 12/1, never-dangerous thirteenth of 17
in maiden at Newmarket: should do better. *Sir Michael Stoute*

CONSULTANT 5 b.g. Man of May – Avenita Lady 57 (Free State 125) [2001 –, a66d: **–**
f6s Dec 15] good-bodied gelding: fair at best: well held only outing in 2001. *C. N. Kellett*

CONTACT DANCER (IRE) 2 b.c. (Mar 6) Sadler's Wells (USA) 132 – Rain **56 p**
Queen (Rainbow Quest (USA) 134) [2001 8d 8s 8.2s Oct 30] 240,000Y: well-made colt:
second foal: brother to Irish 17f winner Mutahamis: dam unraced half-sister to 3-y-o
Wareed out of smart French performer up to 10.5f Truly Special: modest form in maidens:
considerably handled last 2 starts: should be well suited by 1¼m+: type to do better in
handicaps. *J. L. Dunlop*

CONTACT (IRE) 4 br.g. Grand Lodge (USA) 125 – Pink Cashmere (IRE) (Polar **78**
Falcon (USA) 126) [2001 82+: 7d f5g f7s² Dec 15] fair handicapper, lightly raced: stays
7f: acts on good to soft ground and fibresand: twice blinkered at 2 yrs: has carried head
awkwardly. *M. Wigham*

CONTINENT 4 ch.g. Lake Coniston (IRE) 131 – Krisia (Kris 135) [2001 7d 6f³ 6f⁵ **111 p**
6m 6g 6m* 7s³ Sep 29] angular gelding: first foal: dam, French 1½m winner, out of very
smart winner up to 1m Interval: smart performer: trained by P. Bary in France in 2000,
winning minor event at Chantilly (sold 40,000 gns/gelded after final start): on upgrade at
4 yrs, twice having no luck in running, including in Stewards' Cup at Goodwood fifth
start, before winning Tote Ayr Gold Cup in September by neck from Brevity, quickening
smartly under confident ride: cruising long way when good third to Downland in Tote
Trifecta Stakes at Ascot following week: barely stays 7f when conditions are testing and

*Tote (Ayr) Gold Cup (Handicap)—David Nicholls trains the winner of the race for the second
year running and also completes the Ayr Silver and Gold Cup double as Continent beats
Brevity and Smokin Beau (both out of picture) with Antonio Canova (left) in fourth*

will prove as effective over 5f as 6f: acts on firm and soft ground: has run well when sweating: has been slowly away, and is waited with: very much type to win more good prizes at 5 yrs. *D. Nicholls*

CONTINUATION (IRE) 3 b.c. Sadler's Wells (USA) 132 – Sequel (IRE) (Law **86** Society (USA) 130) [2001 86p: 10d³ 12g² 10v³ 10m³ 12f a8.5f 8.9g³ Dec 27] quite attractive colt: fairly useful maiden: left J. Gosden after fifth outing: stays 1½m: acts on heavy going: visored last 2 starts in Europe (looked less than keen first time): tongue tied second to fifth outings: has worn crossed noseband. *S. Seemar, UAE*

CONTINUOUSLY (USA) 2 b.c. (Jan 25) Diesis 133 – Play On And On (USA) (Stop **95** The Music (USA)) [2001 7.1m² 7m* 7.1g⁶ Sep 1] half-brother to several winners, including 1998 2-y-o 7f/1m winner Joyeux Player (by St Jovite) and 7f winner (including at 2 yrs) Neverending (by Sabona): dam US 1m winner at 5 yrs: useful form: won maiden at Newmarket in July by 1¾ lengths from Prince Cyrano, pushed along throughout: only sixth to Redback in Solario Stakes at Sandown: will stay 1m. *H. R. A. Cecil*

CONTRABAND 3 b.g. Red Ransom (USA) – Shortfall 103 (Last Tycoon 131) [2001 **95** 67p: 8g² 8m⁵ 9m* 11.9d 12m* Jul 29] good-topped gelding: useful performer: won maiden at Musselburgh in June and handicap at Ascot in July, latter impressively by 5 lengths from Conquering Love, storming clear despite carrying head awkwardly: met minor setback afterwards: stays 1½m: yet to race on extremes of going: raced freely penultimate start. *W. J. Haggas*

CONTRARY MARY 6 b.m. Mujadil (USA) 119 – Love Street 62 (Mummy's Pet **81** 125) [2001 73, a66: 6m⁶ 6d³ 7m 6m³ 7m² 7g* 7.1f⁴ 6v* 7d² 7s² Nov 10] smallish, lightly-made mare: fairly useful performer: won claimer at Newmarket in August and handicap at Windsor (second run since leaving J. Akehurst) in October: effective at 6f/7f: acts on heavy going, good to firm and equitrack: has got upset in preliminaries: usually held up: sometimes looks difficult ride. *N. Hamilton*

CONUNDRUM (IRE) 3 ch.g. Dr Devious (IRE) 127 – Wasabi (IRE) (Polar Falcon **70** (USA) 126) [2001 8.2d³ 10v⁴ 10g⁵ Nov 5] 34,000F, IR 50,000Y: first foal: dam, unraced, out of useful mare to high-class American middle-distance stayer One On The Aisle: fair form first 2 starts in maidens: should stay 1½m. *P. W. Harris*

CONWY CASTLE 4 b.c. Sri Pekan (USA) 117 – Dumayla 78 (Shernazar 131) [2001 **81** 92: 11.9d 12m⁶ 16.1g⁵ 18.7m³ 14.8m Aug 24] leggy colt: fairly useful performer: probably stays 2¼m: acts on soft and firm going: on edge/pulled hard second start. *Mrs S. Lamyman*

COOKIE CRUMBLE 3 b.f. Never So Bold 135 – Well Tried (IRE) 43 (Thatching **58 d** 131) [2001 46: f6s* f8g⁵ f6g⁴ 7.1g⁴ 8.2g f7g⁶ 7.1m 7.1d 7s Oct 16] angular filly: unimpressive mover: modest performer: won maiden at Wolverhampton in January: below form after fourth start: stays 7f: acts on fibresand, best turf effort on good going. *R. Hollinshead*

COOL BATHWICK (IRE) 2 b.c. (Apr 7) Entrepreneur 123 – Tarafa 93 (Akarad **79 ?** (FR) 130) [2001 10d 10v⁵ Nov 27] 25,000F, IR 32,000Y: useful-looking colt: half-brother to several winners, including 1m (at 2 yrs) and 11f winner Tarajan and 9f winner Tarakana (both useful in Ireland, by Shahrastani): dam 1½m winner: well held in listed race at Newmarket and minor event at Saint-Cloud, though seemingly fair form when fifth to Pont d'Or in latter. *E. J. O'Neill*

COOL CHRON 2 b.f. (Feb 28) Polar Falcon (USA) 126 – Lough Graney (Sallust **46** 134) [2001 5m 6m 7m f7g³ 7.1s 8m Sep 20] 5,000Y: rather leggy, good-topped filly: half-sister to several winners, including fairly useful 1988 2-y-o 6f winner Safwah (by Ahonoora) and 7f winner (including at 2 yrs) The Multiyorker (by Digamist): dam, Irish 1½m winner, sister to 2000 Guineas winner Tap On Wood: poor maiden: stays 7f: best effort on fibresand. *N. Tinkler*

COOLERS QUEST 2 b.f. (May 2) Saddlers' Hall (IRE) 126 – Lucidity 67 (Vision **–** (USA)) [2001 7m⁵ Jun 27] 600F: third foal: dam 1m winner who stayed 1½m: green, very slowly away when last of 5 in maiden at Kempton. *W. G. M. Turner*

COOLING CASTLE (FR) 5 ch.g. Sanglamore (USA) 126 – Syphaly (USA) **–** (Lyphard (USA) 132) [2001 12.3s 10m Jun 22] fair 1¼m winner at 3 yrs: no show both 5-y-o starts. *Ronald Thompson*

COOLING OFF (IRE) 4 b.f. Brief Truce (USA) 126 – Lovers' Parlour 83 (Beldale **77** Flutter (USA) 130) [2001 79: f12g⁴ 12s² 12v² 12s 13.1m³ 14.4m⁵ 11.8m⁵ 14.4g Sep 8] good-topped filly: fair maiden: probably stays 1¾m: acts on heavy and good to firm ground. *J. R. Jenkins*

COOL INVESTMENT (IRE) 4 b.g. Prince of Birds (USA) 121 – Superb Invest- **84 d**
ment (IRE) (Hatim (USA) 121) [2001 98: 12s 10.4g 10.1m 14m⁵ 14v 12s² 14.1s⁵ Nov 5]
strong, rangy gelding: useful at 3 yrs: disappointing in 2001, leaving M. Johnston before
final start: effective at 1½m to 15f: seems to act on any going: blinkered (ran creditably)
once. *R. M. Stronge*

COOL PROSPECT 6 b.g. Mon Tresor 113 – I Ran Lovely (Persian Bold 123) [2001 **43**
65: f6s f6s f7s⁶ f6g f6g⁴ f5g f8.5g⁵ Mar 15] neat gelding: fluent mover: fair on turf at best:
poor form on all-weather at 6 yrs: best at 5f/6f: acts on firm going, good to soft and
fibresand: occasionally blinkered/visored: sometimes slowly away. *K. A. Ryan*

COOL SINGER 3 b.g. Sea Raven (IRE) 75 – Clean Singer 42 (Chief Singer 131) **55**
[2001 f8g f8g⁴ f8s⁶ f7g f7g Apr 14] second reported foal: dam poor maiden: modest
maiden: stays 1m: raced only on fibresand. *J. G. Given*

COOL SPICE 4 b.f. Karinga Bay 116 – Cool Run 87 (Deep Run 119) [2001 56: 11.9s* **79**
11.6g² 11.9d² 11.6g² 12.1m* 11.9m² 11.6m⁶ 11.6m 13.1d* 13.1m⁶ 12d⁵ Sep 3] fair handicapper: won at Brighton, Chepstow (apprentices) and Bath between May and August:
stays 13f: acts on soft and good to firm going: has raced freely/drifted left: consistent.
B. Palling

COOL STORM (IRE) 2 b.f. (Feb 1) Rainbow Quest (USA) 134 – Classic Park 115 **58 p**
(Robellino (USA) 127) [2001 8.2v Oct 4] 120,000Y: first foal: dam Irish 5f (at 2 yrs) to
1m (Irish 1000 Guineas) winner: 10/1, late headway under considerate handling when
ninth of 17 to Sheer Bliss in maiden at Nottingham: will stay at least 1¼m: sure to
improve. *P. W. Harris*

COOL TEMPER 5 b.g. Magic Ring (IRE) 115 – Ovideo 58 (Domynsky 110) [2001 **73**
81: f8.5g* f8.5g² e10g³ 8.5m 8m³ 8m 8m² f8g⁵ 7m 7.9m Sep 2] sturdy gelding: fairly **a82**
useful handicapper on all-weather, fair on turf: won at Wolverhampton in March: stays
easy 1¼m: acts on fibresand/equitrack and probably any turf going: has been tongue tied.
J. M. P. Eustace

COOL TUNE 2 b.g. (Feb 18) Piccolo 121 – Agony Aunt 81 (Formidable (USA) 125) **69 p**
[2001 6d 6d³ Oct 3] 16,000Y: first foal: dam, won at 1¼m, out of half-sister to Oaks
second Wind In Her Hair: odds on, better effort in maidens (fair form) when third to
Fangio's Quest at Newcastle, unable to sustain run final 1f: should stay at least 7f: likely
to improve. *J. R. Fanshawe*

COPCOURT ROYALE 3 b.f. Rock City 120 – Royal Meeting 44 (Dara Monarch **–**
128) [2001 56: f12g 10g 10m f12g f12g f16.2g f14g Dec 3] close-coupled filly: modest at
2 yrs: no form in 2001. *P. L. Clinton*

COPELAND 6 b.g. Generous (IRE) 139 – Whitehaven 116 (Top Ville 129) [2001 18.7f **98**
16.1f Jun 30] rather sparely-made gelding: useful performer: trained by H-A. Pantall in
France at 4 yrs, winning listed race at Lyon Parilly: better effort in 2001 when ninth at
Chester Cup in May: seems to stay easy 2¼m: raced mainly on good going or softer (acts
on heavy): usually blinkered/visored: gelded after final start: useful but none-too-resolute
hurdler. *M. C. Pipe*

COP MY GATOR (IRE) 2 b.g. (Apr 9) Danehill Dancer (IRE) 117 – Delta Blues **72**
(IRE) (Digamist (USA) 110) [2001 6m⁴ 5d⁵ 6m⁴ 7g* 7m⁶ 5s² Aug 18] IR 14,000F,
28,000Y: tall, rather leggy gelding: fourth foal: half-brother to winners up to 7.5f in Italy
by Distinctly North and College Chapel: dam ran once at 2 yrs in Ireland: fair performer:
won seller at Newmarket (idled, retained 24,500 gns) in July: good second in nursery at
Haydock, drifting right: effective at 5f to 7f: acts on soft and good to firm ground: gelded
and sold 2,500 gns. *N. A. Callaghan*

COPPERFIELDS LASS 2 b.f. (Mar 26) Millkom 124 – Salvezza (IRE) 97 (Super- **51 p**
power 113) [2001 6v⁶ Oct 8] 18,000Y: fourth foal: dam 2-y-o 6f winner and third in Nell
Gwyn: 33/1 and green, 14 lengths sixth of 20 to Overload in maiden at Windsor: will be
suited by 1m+: should do better. *Mrs Lydia Pearce*

COPPERMALT (USA) 3 b.g. Affirmed (USA) – Poppy Carew (IRE) 110 (Danehill **73**
(USA) 126) [2001 8s 8m⁴ 8.1m⁵ 7.2m Sep 22] first foal: dam 7f (at 2 yrs) to 1½m winner
who stayed 13.4f: fair maiden: may prove best around 7f: reluctant at stalls final start
(gelded after). *P. W. Harris*

COPPLESTONE (IRE) 5 b.g. Second Set (IRE) 127 – Queen of The Brush (Averof **68 §**
123) [2001 82: f8g 8.3d 8m⁵ 7d⁴ 8.1m 8d f8.5f f8g Dec 14] tall gelding: fair maiden: left **a– §**
P. Harris 2,500 gns after sixth outing: stays 9f: acts on firm going, good to soft and
fibresand: tried visored/tongue tied: not to be trusted. *J. R. Best*

COPY-CAT 3 b.f. Lion Cavern (USA) 117 – Imperial Jade 105 (Lochnager 132) [2001 – 60?: 5m May 26] modest form on debut: left impression something amiss 3 starts since. *W. R. Muir*

COPYFORCE GIRL 5 b.m. Elmaamul (USA) 125 – Sabaya (USA) 92 (Seattle **69** Dancer (USA) 119) [2001 70: 11.5f 10m 12m⁵ 14m³ 11.9s 12d p12g p16g Dec 4] angular **a57** mare: fair handicapper: effective at 1½m/1¾m: acts on firm and good to soft going: blinkered last 2 starts: usually tongue tied: usually claimer ridden: sold 2,800 gns. *Miss B. Sanders*

CORAL SHELLS 4 b.f. Formidable (USA) 125 – Elle Reef (Shareef Dancer (USA) – 135) [2001 –: e8g Jan 10] of little account nowadays. *R. M. Flower*

CORBLETS 4 b.f. Timeless Times (USA) 99 – Dear Glenda 66 (Gold Song 112) – [2001 65: 5v Apr 19] fair maiden at 3 yrs: well held only 4-y-o start. *J. J. Quinn*

CORK HARBOUR (FR) 5 ch.g. Grand Lodge (USA) 125 – Irish Sea 66 (Irish River **85** (FR) 131) [2001 76: 8s⁵ 10g 10m⁶ 10g 12m 7s² 7d² 7d² 10v p7g⁶ Dec 12] fairly useful handicapper: best at 7f/1m: has form on good to firm going/equitrack/polytrack, goes particularly well on softer than good: usually blinkered in 2001: hung badly right penultimate start: races prominently. *Mrs N. Smith*

CORNELIAN PRINCE 4 b.g. Sri Pekan (USA) 117 – Silent Girl 75 (Krayyan 117) – [2001 f8.5g f12g Dec 8] tall, lengthy gelding: fifth foal: half-brother to winners abroad by Law Society and Shalford: dam 1m (at 2 yrs) to 1½m winner: well held in maidens at Wolverhampton. *A. Senior*

CORNELIUS 4 b.g. Barathea (IRE) 127 – Rainbow Mountain 71 (Rainbow Quest **112** (USA) 134) [2001 107: 8d⁴ 8s⁵ 10.4g⁵ 8g* 9g⁴ 7.9d* 8s² Nov 3] tall, good-topped gelding: has an unimpressive, rather round action: smart performer: won minor event at Doncaster (by ½ length from Goggles) in July and handicap at York (beat dead-heaters Lots of Love and Sir Ninja 2½ lengths) in October: ran at least respectably otherwise, including when short-head second to Keltos in Prix Perth at Saint-Cloud final start: gelded afterwards: effective at 1m/1¼m: has form on good to firm going, raced mainly on good or softer: has been bandaged behind: tends to carry head high: reliable. *P. F. I. Cole*

CORRIDOR CREEPER (FR) 4 b.g. Polish Precedent (USA) 131 – Sonia Rose **92** (USA) (Superbity (USA)) [2001 90: 6m 5g* 5g 5g 5g Sep 15] useful-looking gelding: fairly useful handicapper: 14/1, won at Ascot in July by ½ length from Brave Burt: effective at 5f/6f: acts on firm and good to soft going: blinkered once at 3 yrs: tongue tied twice: has found little: sold 17,000 gns in November. *P. W. Harris*

CORSICAN SUNSET (USA) 3 b.f. Thunder Gulch (USA) 129 – Miss Evans **102** (USA) (Nijinsky (CAN) 138) [2001 10s 10.5s² 9.9d* 12.6m² 10g³ 12g³ 10g² 11.9m 12s⁴ 12s⁵ Nov 3] $67,000Y: good-topped filly: seventh foal: half-sister to several winners, notably smart French 1¼m/1½m performer Si Seductor (by Diesis), later winner in North America: dam, French 9f to 10.5f winner, half-sister to US Grade 3 6f to 7f winner Mamselle Bebette from very good family: useful performer: won maiden at Salisbury in May: ran well most starts after, including in Premio Mario Incisa at Milan (third to Honorifique) and listed races at Varese and Chantilly (fourth to Moon Queen) on sixth/ seventh/ninth starts: stays 1½m: acts on soft and good to firm going. *P. F. I. Cole*

CORTON (IRE) 2 b. or gr.g. (Apr 25) Definite Article 121 – Limpopo 49 (Green **88** Desert (USA) 127) [2001 7g⁵ 7m³ 8g⁴ 7m* 8m 8g³ Sep 13] IR 38,000F: strong gelding: brother to 3-y-o Smoothie and half-brother to several winners, notably 5-y-o Pipalong: dam maiden out of smart Irish 7f to 8.5f winner Grey Goddess: fairly useful performer: won maiden at Folkestone in August: very good third to Bollin Eric in nursery at Doncaster final start (gelded after): not sure to stay beyond 1m: raced only on good/good to firm going: hung markedly left/carried head high second start. *P. F. I. Cole*

CORUNDUM (USA) 2 b. or br.c. (Jan 30) Benny The Dip (USA) 127 – Santi Sana **76** 80 (Formidable (USA) 125) [2001 7.1s 7.5f² Jul 7] 62,000Y: good-bodied colt: fourth foal: half-brother to 1998 2-y-o 7f winner Minnesota (by Danehill): dam, 7f winner, sister to very smart 7f/1m performer Efisio: better effort (fair form) when 3½ lengths second of 6 to Receivedwiththanx in minor event at Beverley, flashing tail and never nearer: will stay 1¼m: sold 15,000 gns, joined J. Given. *M. H. Tompkins*

CORUNNA 4 b.g. Puissance 110 – Kind of Shy 61 (Kind of Hush 118) [2001 81: 5.1f **81** 6m 7f 7m² 7.6m* 7f⁴ 7m* 7m 8m 7.2g 7d Sep 13] good-bodied gelding: has a quick action: fairly useful performer: won minor events at Lingfield in June and Leicester in July: stays 7.6f: raced mainly on good ground or firmer: has idled in front: none too consistent. *A. Berry*

COSHOCTON (USA)   2 b.c. (Jan 22) Silver Hawk (USA) 123 – Tribulation (USA)   **103 p**
118 (Danzig (USA)) [2001 7m* 8d² Oct 13] strong, attractive colt: has scope: second
foal: dam Grade 1 1¼m winner in USA: useful form: won maiden at York in September
in quite good style by ¾ length from Simeon: some improvement when 5 lengths second
of 8 to Fight Your Corner in listed event at Ascot, not looking easiest of rides (possibly
still green) but keeping on well after being checked: should be suited by 1¼m/1½m:
capable of better. *M. A. Jarvis*

COSIMWORTHIT   5 b.m. Imp Society (USA) – Sasha Lea (Cawston's Clown 113) –
[2001 e12g 10m 6d 7f 9.7m 7d Jul 18] half-sister to 1½m winner Cedar Flag (by Jareer):
dam unraced: no form. *M. R. Ewer-Hoad*

COSMIC CASE   6 b.m. Casteddu 111 – La Fontainova (IRE) (Lafontaine (USA) 117   **66**
[2001 50: 12s 16v⁴ 14d 13d⁵ 13.1m² 13d² 12m* 12m* 12.1m* 12f 15f³ 12.4m² 12.1m³
14m² 15.9m 16.2m 14g³ 13d⁴ 14m³ 12.1m 16m Sep 30] angular mare: fair handicapper:
won at Pontefract, Musselburgh and Hamilton in May/June: effective at 1½m to easy 2m:
acts on any going: tried visored: held up: very tough. *J. S. Goldie*

COSMIC MILLENNIUM (IRE)   3 b.g. In The Wings 128 – Windmill Princess 55   **85**
(Gorytus (USA) 132) [2001 80: 8.3s 9m⁴ 6d 7.5f 7.6m Aug 22] quite attractive gelding:
fairly useful performer: not sure to stay beyond 9f: acts on good to firm going: free-going
sort: gelded after final outing. *R. Guest*

COSMIC RANGER   3 b.g. Magic Ring (IRE) 115 – Lismore 61 (Relkino 131) [2001   **44**
63: f7g 8g 10m 12m 16m 12m f12g⁵ Jul 20] leggy, useful-looking gelding: poor maiden
at 3 yrs: stays 1½m: acts on good to firm ground and fibresand: visored (slowly away/bit
reluctant early) sixth start. *N. P. Littmoden*

COSMIC SONG   4 b.f. Cosmonaut – Hotaria 68 (Sizzling Melody 117) [2001 58d: **43**
11s 9m* 10.1m⁵ 9.9f 8m 8m 8.5g 8m³ 8.9m 8f Sep 4] big filly: poor handicapper: won at
Redcar in May: effective at 1m/1¼m: acts on good to firm and good to soft going: has
given trouble in preliminaries (early to post nowadays): has carried head high: none too
consistent. *R. M. Whitaker*

COSMOCRAT   3 b.g. Cosmonaut – Bella Coola 50 (Northern State (USA) 91) [2001   **81**
79: 7f 10.2m⁶ 11.6m 8.1s* 8d 8.1v f9.4g Oct 23] fairly useful performer: won ladies
handicap at Chepstow in August: best efforts at 1m: goes well on soft ground: sold 8,000
gns, joined C. Cox. *M. Meade*

COST AUDITING   4 ch.f. Bluebird (USA) 125 – Elabella (Ela-Mana-Mou 132)   **–**
[2001 –: f16g f8.5s f5g e10g Feb 24] little form since 2 yrs: tried blinkered. *Andrew Reid*

COTEBROOK   2 ch.g. (Apr 17) First Trump 118 – Chantelys 52 (Ballacashtal   **64**
(CAN)) [2001 6d⁵ 7f⁶ 7d⁴ 7.5s 8.3s⁵ Aug 21] 3,000Y, resold 7,300Y, 12,000 2-y-o: strong
gelding: third foal: dam, 1¾m winner, half-sister to smart Irish 7f/1m performer Just
Three: modest maiden: fourth at Ayr: should stay at least 1m: gelded after final outing.
A. Bailey

COTE SOLEIL   4 ch.g. Inchinor 119 – Sunshine Coast 86 (Posse (USA) 130) [2001   **70**
84: 8s 7.1v 7m 9f* 9g⁵ 9d 10.1g⁴ 8m⁶ 8d⁴ Oct 15] smallish gelding: fair performer: won
minor event at Musselburgh in July: probably best at 1m/9f: acts on any going: tried
blinkered/visored: none too consistent. *M. L. W. Bell*

COTTAM LILLY   4 b.f. Sabrehill (USA) 120 – Karminski 70 (Pitskelly 122) [2001   **36**
–: 10v⁵ 10g 14.1m 12m 16.2f Jul 17] angular filly: poor maiden handicapper: stays 1½m:
acts on heavy going, probably on good to firm. *J. S. Wainwright*

COTTON HOUSE (IRE)   4 b.f. Mujadil (USA) 119 – Romanovna (Mummy's Pet   **107**
125) [2001 103: 6v 5v² 6d 5.1d⁵ 5f⁴ 6d⁴ 6m 5g 6m⁴ 6g⁵ 6d⁵ Aug 19] lengthy, useful-
looking filly: unimpressive mover: useful performer: several creditable efforts in 2001,
including when neck second to Dananeyev in listed race at Longchamp and fourth to
Cassandra Go in Temple Stakes at Sandown (fifth outing): stays 6f: acts on any going:
waited with. *M. R. Channon*

COTTON KID (IRE)   2 b.c. (Mar 5) Lake Coniston (IRE) 131 – La Suquet 72 (Puis-   **69**
sance 110) [2001 5.2m 5m⁴ 5m⁴ 7m 6d* 6d Oct 18] 27,000Y: rather leggy, unfurnished
colt: second living foal: half-brother to 5f to 7f (at 2 yrs) winner Castle Sempill (by
Presidium): dam 5f winner: fair performer: won nursery at Pontefract in October despite
wandering under pressure: stays 6f: yet to race on extremes of going: blinkered last 3
starts: possibly none too genuine: sold 12,000 gns, sent to Norway. *W. J. Haggas*

COTTONTAIL   3 b.g. Alzao (USA) 117 – Height of Passion (Shirley Heights 130)   **–**
[2001 –: 14.1m May 29] strong gelding: no form. *N. Tinkler*

COUAL CRYSTAL 2 b.f. (Apr 8) Cool Jazz 116 – Indian Crystal 66 (Petong 126) **54**
[2001 7g 7.1s⁶ 7.5g⁵ 7d 7g Oct 19] 2,100Y: small, lengthy, sparely-made filly: fourth foal:
half-sister to 1999 2-y-o 5f seller winner Gem of Wisdom (by Factual) and 3-y-o Eastern
Promise: dam 5f winner (including at 2 yrs): modest maiden: will prove best up to 1m:
usually visored. *J. R. Norton*

COUGHLAN'S GIFT 5 ch.m. Alnasr Alwasheek 117 – Superfrost 49 (Tickled Pink **62**
114) [2001 70: 10v⁶ 10v⁵ 10.9m 9.9m 9.9d p10g p10g⁵ p10g⁵ p10g⁴ Dec 28] smallish **a55 +**
mare: modest nowadays: stays 1¼m well: has form on good to firm ground and all-
weather, goes particularly well on soft/heavy: usually claimer ridden: has hung under
pressure. *J. C. Fox*

COUNSEL'S OPINION (IRE) 4 ch.g. Rudimentary (USA) 118 – Fairy Fortune 78 **88**
(Rainbow Quest (USA) 134) [2001 e12g* f12g* 12s⁴ 12m 10f 9g* 12d 10.1s³ 10v⁶ Nov
8] 22,000Y: big, useful-looking gelding: fifth foal: closely related to fairly useful 1998
2-y-o 6f winner Halloa (by Wolfhound) and half-brother to 2 winners, including Italian
winner up to 11f Quinolina (by Shareef Dancer): dam 7.6f winner out of useful close
relative to smart 1¼m colt Elegant Air: fairly useful performer: won maiden at Lingfield
in March, minor event at Southwell in April and handicap at Sandown in September:
effective at 9f to easy 1½m: acts on fibresand/equitrack and soft going, well beaten only
start on firm: tends to race freely. *S. P. C. Woods*

COUNT CALYPSO 3 ch.g. King's Signet (USA) 110 – Atlantic Air (Air Trooper 115) **65**
[2001 54, a67: f6s³ f6g* f6g* 6s 6m⁴ 6m 6g 7m Sep 11] sturdy, close-coupled gelding: **a82**
poor walker: fairly useful handicapper on all-weather, fair on turf: won at Wolverhampton in February and Southwell in March: better at 6f than 5f, and should stay 7f: acts on
fibresand and good to firm going: sometimes gives trouble at start. *D. J. Coakley*

COUNT DUBOIS 3 b.c. Zafonic (USA) 130 – Madame Dubois 121 (Legend of **104**
France (USA) 124) [2001 108: a8f³ Mar 1] strong, good-topped colt: useful performer:
won Gran Criterium at Milan at 2 yrs: respectable 8 lengths third to Street Cry in UAE
2000 Guineas at Nad Al Sheba only outing at 3 yrs: reportedly injured suspensory later in
March: unraced 1m: raced only on good going or softer on turf: had hung left and tended to
carry head awkwardly: visored/blinkered last 4 starts: reportedly retired to stud in South
Africa. *W. J. Haggas*

COUNTESS COLDUNELL 4 b.f. Bin Ajwaad (IRE) 119 – Beau's Delight (USA) **–**
(Lypheor 118) [2001 55?: f11g e16g Jan 27] little form: tried blinkered. *J. W. Payne*

COUNTESS PARKER 5 ch.m. First Trump 118 – Hoist (IRE) 75 (Bluebird (USA) **–**
125) [2001 –: 8.3g 6g 7d 9.2d Aug 15] useful-looking mare: disappointing maiden.
B. Mactaggart

COUNT FREDERICK 5 b.g. Anshan 119 – Minteen (Teenoso (USA) 135) [2001 –: **–**
f11g f8.5g 10.1m 10.9g Jul 6] of little account nowadays. *J. R. Jenkins*

COUNT ON THUNDER 4 ch.g. Thunder Gulch (USA) 129 – Count On A **35**
Change (USA) (Time For A Change (USA)) [2001 55d: f8.5g⁶ f8g⁶ 8v⁶ 11.1d May 6] big,
angular gelding: disappointing maiden: stays 1½m: acts on good to firm and good to soft
ground: visored once. *J. Hetherton*

COUNTRY BUMPKIN 5 ch.g. Village Star (FR) 131 – Malham Tarn (Riverman **–**
(USA) 131) [2001 –: f12g e10g f8.5g Nov 17] no form: left H. Haynes after penultimate
outing: blinkered once. *H. J. Manners*

COUNTRYWIDE GIRL (IRE) 2 ch.f. (Mar 21) Catrail (USA) 123 – Polish Saga **67**
59 (Polish Patriot (USA) 128) [2001 f5g 5m 6f⁵ 7g² 6g 6f² f6g 6g⁵ 6s* 5v* 5g Nov 7] IR **a–**
4,400F, IR 1,600Y: leggy, quite good-topped filly: second foal: half-sister to a winner in
Turkey by Persian Bold: dam, maiden best at 6f, half-sister to smart performer up to 11f
Tarawa: fair performer: won claimer (hung badly left) and seller at Lingfield in October:
needs good test at 5f, and stays 7f: best turf form on soft/heavy ground, no show on
fibresand. *A. Berry*

COUNTRYWIDE PRIDE (IRE) 3 ch.g. Eagle Eyed (USA) 111 – Lady's Dream **66 d**
85 (Mazilier (USA) 107) [2001 73: e10g⁶ e10s³ 10.9m⁴ 8m p10g Dec 29] fair sort: has a
round action: fair maiden: disappointing and clear signs of temperament in 2001: stays
1¼m: acts on fibresand/equitrack, good to firm and good to soft going: visored (took very
strong hold) second start. *K. R. Burke*

COUNTRYWIDE STAR (IRE) 3 ch.g. Common Grounds 118 – Silver Slipper 67 **70**
(Indian Ridge 123) [2001 f8f 6d 6.1v⁶ 6m⁶ 7.1g 7.1v* 7s 7v 8d p7g⁴ f6g p6g p7g Dec
12] sturdy gelding: has a round action: fourth foal: brother to fairly useful 1m winner

Commonwealth: dam, 2-y-o 7f seller winner, closely related to useful Irish performer up to 1¼m Irish Memory: fair performer: off over 3 months, won maiden at Haydock in September: stays 7f: acts on heavy going, good to firm and polytrack: visored (below form) last 2 starts. *K. R. Burke*

COUNT TIROL (IRE)   4 b.g. Tirol 127 – Bid High (IRE) (High Estate 127) [2001 –:   **46**
f9.4s³ f12g Mar 24] close-coupled gelding: poor maiden, lightly raced: stays 9.4f: acts on fibresand and good to firm going. *C. G. Cox*

COUNT TONY   7 ch.g. Keen 116 – Turtle Dove (Gyr (USA) 131) [2001 –: 14.1m⁵   **48**
16.2f⁴ Jul 7] sparely-made gelding: poor nowadays: probably stays 2m: acts on good to firm going and fibresand/equitrack: tried visored. *P. Bowen*

COURSE DOCTOR (IRE)   9 ch.g. Roselier (FR) – Faultless Girl (Crash Course   **67 d**
128) [2001 12g³ 12m³ 10.5d⁵ 16m⁵ 21m 16g Aug 13] big, strong gelding: one-time useful chaser/fair handicap hurdler: failed to confirm form of first 2 starts in maidens: should stay 2m. *A. Dickman*

COURTEOUS   6 b.h. Generous (IRE) 139 – Dayanata (Shirley Heights 130) [2001   **114**
11.6g⁶ 11.8d⁴ 12m² 14s³ 13.9g 14v⁶ Sep 28] tall, leggy horse: smart performer: won Grand Prix de Deauville at 4 yrs: not quite so good after a season off in 2001, best efforts when 2½ lengths second to Mubtaker in listed race at Newmarket and 2 lengths third to Generic in Prix Maurice de Nieuil at Maisons-Laffitte: stayed 1¾m: acted on soft and good to firm going: blinkered (ran poorly in Ebor) penultimate start: raced up with pace: to stand at Lismacue Stud, Co Tipperary, Ireland, fee €1,900, Oct 1st. *P. F. I. Cole*

COURTESY (USA)   2 b.f. (Apr 12) Diesis 133 – Muscadel (USA) (Nashwan (USA)   **76 p**
135) [2001 8d⁴ Sep 4] first foal: dam, French 1¼m/1½m winner, out of 1000 Guineas winner Musical Bliss: 13/2 and green, 6 lengths fourth of 7 to easy winner Fraulein in maiden at Yarmouth, best work at finish: will be suited by 1¼m+: sure to do better. *Sir Michael Stoute*

COURT EXPRESS   7 b.g. Then Again 126 – Moon Risk 62 (Risk Me (FR) 127)   **90**
[2001 84: 8g* 8.5m May 22] tall, angular gelding: fairly useful handicapper: won at Thirsk in May: broke down next start: was effective at 1m/1¼m: had run respectably on soft ground, but all wins on good or firmer: blinkered once in 1998: was held up: dead. *G. A. Swinbank*

COURTLEDGE   6 b.g. Unfuwain (USA) 131 – Tremellick 87 (Mummy's Pet 125)   **–**
[2001 –: f16.2g Dec 8] no form since 4 yrs. *M. J. Gingell*

COURT MUSIC (IRE)   2 b. or br.f. (Mar 21) Revoque (IRE) 122 – Lute And Lyre   **74**
(IRE) 96 (The Noble Player (USA) 126) [2001 6m 5f 6m⁴ 6m⁴ 6.1d* 6v⁵ Sep 28] 8,000Y: rather leggy, angular filly: fourth foal: half-sister to fairly useful 1999 2-y-o 7f winner who stayed 1¼m Travelling Lite (by Blues Traveller) and 1998 2-y-o 5f winner College Music (by College Chapel): dam Irish 5f (including at 2 yrs) winner: fair performer: clearly best effort when winning nursery at Nottingham in September: likely to stay 7f: acts on good to soft ground: tried blinkered. *T. D. Easterby*

COURT OF APPEAL   4 ch.g. Bering 136 – Hiawatha's Song (USA) (Chief's Crown   **81**
(USA)) [2001 87: 10s 10g 10v* 11.6g⁵ 12m² 10m³ 12g 10.3g 9.1m Sep 21] strong, lengthy gelding: fairly useful handicapper: stays 1½m: acts on heavy and good to firm going: has found little: sold 15,000 gns. *G. M. McCourt*

COURT ONE   3 b.g. Shareef Dancer (USA) 135 – Fairfields Cone (Celtic Cone 116)   **–**
[2001 –: 12f⁶ 11.6m 11.7g Jul 9] leggy gelding: shows knee action: no form. *R. J. Price*

COURT SHAREEF   6 b.g. Shareef Dancer (USA) 135 – Fairfields Cone (Celtic Cone   **92**
116) [2001 82: 12g³ 11.9m⁵ 11.6g 12m⁴ 14m*¹ 11.9d 16.2g⁵ 13.9g 13.9m 14m Sep 22] small gelding: fairly useful handicapper: won at Goodwood in June: effective at 1½m to 2m: acts on soft and good to firm going: sometimes finds little, and best coming late. *R. J. Price*

COVENT GARDEN   3 b.c. Sadler's Wells (USA) 132 – Temple Row (Aldross 134)   **94 +**
[2001 71p: 12m* 10g Sep 28] angular, useful-looking colt: has a fluent, round action: eighth foal: closely related to 1m winner Baalbek (by Barathea) and 13f winner Back Row (by In The Wings) and half-brother to 2 winners, including fairly useful 10.5f and 1½m winner Mount Row (by Alzao): dam unraced: coltish in preliminaries, won maiden at Doncaster in July by 13 lengths from Alunissage, leading at halfway: possibly unsuited by drop back in trip only start after: may stay beyond 1½m: sold 25,000 gns. *Sir Michael Stoute*

Ascot Stakes (Handicap), Royal Ascot—the race in which Kieren Fallon had a career-threatening fall the previous year; this time he galvanises Cover Up to beat First Ballot, Persian Waters (centre), Mana d'Argent (blaze) and Al Towd

COVER UP (IRE) 4 b.g. Machiavellian (USA) 123 – Sought Out (IRE) 119 (Rainbow **109** Quest (USA) 134) [2001 101: 18.7f⁴ 20m* 16.1f² 13.9g⁴ 18d⁶ 18d Oct 20] close-coupled, quite good-topped gelding: useful performer: better than ever in 2001, winning Ascot Stakes at Royal Ascot (by 1¼ lengths from First Ballot) despite flashing tail/wandering markedly: ran well in Northumberland Plate at Newcastle (neck second to Archduke Ferdinand), Ebor at York (fourth to Mediterranean) and Doncaster Cup (sixth to Alleluia) next 3 starts: early to post, ran respectably in Cesarewitch final one: stays 2½m: acts on firm and good to soft going, probably on heavy: tried visored: has raced lazily. *Sir Michael Stoute*

CO VIVANTE (IRE) 2 b.f. (Jan 29) Alzao (USA) 117 – Springtime (IRE) (Generous **67** (IRE) 139) [2001 6m 6m² 7m⁴ 6.5g 7s p7g Dec 29] leggy, close-coupled filly: first foal: dam unraced half-sister to smart May Hill Stakes/Fillies' Mile winner Tessla: fair maiden: below form after third start: should be suited by at least 1m. *R. Hannon*

COWBOYS AND ANGELS 4 b.g. Bin Ajwaad (IRE) 119 – Halimah 56 (Be My **76** Guest (USA) 126)) [2001 82: f7g 7s 7g 7g 7.1f² 8m⁵ 7v* p7g⁴ p7g² p7g³ p7g² p7g⁵ Dec 29] fair performer: won claimer at Doncaster (left W. Turner 6,000 gns) in October: best form around 7f: acts on any turf going, fibresand and polytrack: blinkered final start: usually races up with pace: consistent. *S. C. Williams*

COYOTE 3 b.f. Indian Ridge 123 – Caramba 114 (Belmez (USA) 131) [2001 51p: 7f² **91** 9m 8.3g⁴ 8d* 8g³ 8.1g⁵ Sep 1] leggy filly: fairly useful performer: won maiden at Ayr in August: ran at least respectably in listed events last 2 starts, third to Riberac at Ascot and fifth to Intrepidous at Sandown: best efforts around 1m (raced too freely over 9f): acts on firm and good to soft going: visored last 3 starts: races prominently. *Sir Michael Stoute*

COZETTE (IRE) 2 b.f. (Feb 6) Danehill Dancer (IRE) 117 – Great Splendour (Pharly **49** (FR) 130) [2001 5.7g 7g⁵ 8g⁴ Aug 24] IR 2,000Y resold IR 1,600Y: third foal: half-sister to a winner up to 7.5f in Germany by Forest Wind: dam, lightly-raced maiden, grand-daughter of very smart winner up to 1¼m Roussalka (herself half-sister to Oh So Sharp): poor maiden: fourth in claimer at Newcastle: will probably stay 1¼m. *E. J. O'Neill*

COZY MARIA (USA) 2 gr. or ro.f. (Mar 8) Cozzene (USA) – Mariamme (USA) 66 **95** (Verbatim (USA)) [2001 7g³ 7f³ 7d⁶ Oct 20] \$300,000Y: tall, rather unfurnished filly: has scope: third foal: half-sister to a winner in USA by Holy Bull: dam, won up to 1¼m in USA, half-sister to Breeders' Cup Turf winner Miss Alleged: useful maiden: easily best effort when third to Fraulein in minor event at Newbury on second start: possibly unsuited by softer ground in Rockfel Stakes at Newmarket final outing: should stay 1¼m: acts on firm going. *J. H. M. Gosden*

COZZIE 3 ch.f. Cosmonaut – Royal Deed (USA) 76 (Shadeed (USA) 135) [2001 57, **52** a60: e5g e6g* e5g⁵ e6s⁶ f5g f5f³ Mar 19] leggy filly: modest performer: won seller at Lingfield in January: stays easy 6f: acts on firm going, good to soft and fibresand/

224

equitrack: none too consistent: reportedly in foal to Dancing Spree, sold 3,000 gns in July, and sent to France. *J. G. Given*

CRACOW (IRE)   4 b.c. Polish Precedent (USA) 131 – Height of Secrecy (Shirley **99 §**
Heights 130) [2001 95: 10s 11.9m³ 12f² 12m 11.9d³ 14m 12g 10f 12d Oct 2] rather leggy, useful-looking colt: useful handicapper: ran creditably in 2001 only when placed, including third to Hannibal Lad in Old Newton Cup at Haydock fifth start: rather headstrong, but stays 1½m: yet to race on heavy going, acts on any other: tends to be on toes: often finds little: not to be trusted: sold 30,000 gns in October, 16,000 gns following month. *J. W. Hills*

CRAFTY   2 b.f. (Apr 1) Mistertopogigo (IRE) 118 – Tinkers Fairy (Myjinski (USA))   **–**
[2001 6f Jul 5] 1,000Y: smallish, short-backed filly: fifth foal: half-sister to 7-y-o College Princess: dam ran twice: tailed off in Haydock claimer. *J. R. Norton*

CRAIGARY   10 b.g. Dunbeath (USA) 127 – Velvet Pearl 52 (Record Token 128)   **24**
[2001 35: 13d 12m 13m 14f 13g⁶ 12.1s 11.1g Sep 2] bad handicapper: stays 13f: acts on soft going, probably on firm: effective blinkered/visored or not. *D. A. Nolan*

CRAIOVA (IRE)   2 b.c. (Feb 6) Turtle Island (IRE) 123 – Velvet Appeal (IRE) 101   **83 p**
(Petorius 117) [2001 6d⁴ Oct 18] 52,000F, 130,000Y: strong, deep-girthed colt: has a quick action: first foal: dam, Irish 7.7f winner, sister to smart performer up to 1m Sapieha and half-sister to smart French stayer Dajraan: 33/1, burly and green, promising fourth of 22 to Hiddendale in maiden at Newmarket, staying on well after slow start: will stay at least 1m: useful performer in the making, sure to win a race or 2. *B. W. Hills*

CRANDIUM   5 br.m. Presidium 124 – Crammond Brig (New Brig 120) [2001 f11g   **–**
Feb 2] eighth foal: half-sister to useful 2m/2½m jumper Easthorpe (by Sweet Monday): dam fair staying hurdler: well beaten in Southwell seller. *R. D. E. Woodhouse*

CRAZY LARRYS (USA)   3 ch.c. Mutakddim (USA) 112 – No Fear of Flying (USA)   **83**
(Super Concorde (USA) 128) [2001 95: 7g⁵ 8f⁶ 8f³ 8.5f 8f⁵ a8.5f Nov 15] useful winner at 2 yrs: left J. Noseda after below-par reappearance: probably best effort in US in claimer on penultimate start: stays 1m: raced only on good/good to firm going on turf. *P. Gallagher, USA*

CREAM CRACKERED   2 ch.f. (Feb 8) Dancing Spree (USA) – Badger Bay (IRE)   **–**
67 (Salt Dome (USA)) [2001 5m 5f Jun 13] second foal: dam unreliable maiden who stayed 1m: well held in claimer/seller: sent to Kuwait. *C. A. Dwyer*

CREAM TEASE   4 b.f. Pursuit of Love 124 – Contralto 100 (Busted 134) [2001 84:   **99 ?**
7g 7m⁵ 7.1d Jun 9] sturdy filly: fairly useful at 3 yrs: seemed to show useful form in face of stiff tasks first 2 starts at 4 yrs: stays 1m: acts on good to firm going, below form on softer than good: blinkered once at 3 yrs: has been edgy/on toes/early to post/hung right. *D. J. S. ffrench Davis*

CREDENZA MOMENT   3 b.c. Pyramus (USA) 78 – Mystoski 35 (Petoski 135)   **44**
[2001 46: 10s⁴ 11.6s 11.5m² 10f 11.6m 12f 11.9g² 10v⁶ Oct 29] sparely-made colt: poor maiden: left R. Hannon after seventh start: stays 1½m: acts on equitrack, heavy and good to firm going: blinkered (below form) twice. *M. Madgwick*

CREDIBILITY   3 ch.f. Komaite (USA) – Integrity 108 (Reform 132) [2001 65: f7g⁶   **48**
f9.4g e5s³ 5f 5.3g⁴ Aug 9] poor maiden: may prove best at 5f/6f: acts on equitrack and good to firm going. *M. Wigham*

CREDIBLE (USA)   2 ch.c. (Mar 6) Dixieland Band (USA) – Alleged Thoughts   **81**
(USA) (Alleged (USA) 138) [2001 7s 7d⁶ Nov 3] $230,000F, $250,000Y: small colt: second foal: dam unraced half-sister to Lancashire Oaks/Park Hill winner Niodini: better effort in maidens (fairly useful form) when close sixth of 27 to Prince Hector at Newmarket, fading only final 1f: bred to stay at least 1m: bandaged/wore crossed noseband both starts. *J. H. M. Gosden*

CREG WILLYS HILL (IRE)   2 b.c. (Apr 28) Distinctly North (USA) 115 – Need   **51**
You Badly 59 (Robellino (USA) 127) [2001 7g 6.1m 7f5g⁴ 5.7d f6g Nov 3] 2,800 2-y-o: first living foal: dam 5f winner out of half-sister to Lake Coniston: modest maiden: form only when fourth in seller at Wolverhampton: should stay 6f: acts on fibresand. *R. Ford*

CREPUSCULAIRE (FR)   4 ch.f. Hernando (FR) 127 – Guest Performer 117 (Be   **82**
My Guest (USA) 126) [2001 10v 9.9d⁴ 10s² 11.9s Oct 25] IR 16,000Y: workmanlike filly: half-sister to several winners, including smart German 6f/7f performer Global Player (by Tirol) and fairly useful 1½m to 2m winner Encore Une Fois (by Shirley Heights): dam 7f (Kiveton Park Stakes) winner: trained by J-C. Rouget in France at 3 yrs,

winning maiden, minor event and handicap in Provinces: fairly useful form in frame in handicaps in Britain: stays 1½m: acts on soft ground. *N. A. Callaghan*

CRESKELD (IRE) 2 b.c. (Apr 3) Sri Pekan (USA) 117 – Pizzazz 47 (Unfuwain (USA) 131) [2001 5v⁵ 5s² 6m 5m* 5m⁵ 7d 7s⁵ 7s Nov 10] IR 14,000Y: sparely-made colt: fourth foal: half-brother to French 6f (at 2 yrs) to 11f winner In The Trim (by Tirol): dam, French 5f winner, half-sister to Nell Gwyn winner Thrilling Day: fair performer: awarded maiden at Ripon in May: respectable efforts in nurseries last 2 starts: stays 7f: acts on soft and good to firm going. *J. L. Eyre* **72**

CRESSET 5 ch.g. Arazi (USA) 135 – Mixed Applause (USA) 101 (Nijinsky (CAN) 138) [2001 –, a69d: f12g⁵ f11s⁴ f11g f16.2g f16g f12g⁵ 16m 11.1d May 18] fair handicapper at best: has become disappointing: usually blinkered. *D. W. Chapman* **–**

CRESSEX KATIE 2 b.f. (Apr 12) Komaite (USA) – Kakisa 81 (Forlorn River 124) [2001 f6s p6g² Dec 28] 6,500Y: sister to 1997 2-y-o 5f winner Wait'N'See and half-sister to several winning sprinters, including fairly useful 5f performer Lake Mistassiu (by Tina's Pet): dam 5f/6f winner: much better effort in maidens in December when length second of 14 to Agincourt Warrior at Lingfield: slowly away both starts. *J. Cullinan* **63**

CREST WING (USA) 8 b.g. Storm Bird (CAN) 134 – Purify (USA) (Fappiano (USA)) [2001 16.2m May 26] tall gelding: no form. *Miss Z. C. Davison* **–**

CRETAN GIFT 10 ch.g. Cadeaux Genereux 131 – Caro's Niece (USA) 86 (Caro 133) [2001 112: f7g⁵ f6g³ 6v 6d 6g 6m⁴ 6f 6f⁴ 7m 5m 6d⁴ 6g Aug 21] lengthy gelding: smart on all-weather, useful on turf: some creditable efforts in 2001: races mainly over 6f/7f nowadays: acts on firm going, soft and fibresand: visored: has worn crossed/dropped noseband: tends to start slowly/get behind. *N. P. Littmoden* **100 a112**

CRICKETERS CLUB 3 b.g. Dancing Spree (USA) – Alacrity 62 (Alzao (USA) 117) [2001 52?: e8g⁶ e8g³ e10s⁵ 10.1g 6d⁵ f7g⁶ f8.5f p10g⁶ Dec 29] strong gelding: has a round action: modest maiden: stays 1m: acts on fibresand, equitrack and good to soft going: visored final start: has been reluctant at stalls. *R. Ingram* **52**

CRIMSON RIDGE 3 b.f. King's Signet (USA) 110 – Cloudy Reef 57 (Cragador 110) [2001 57: 6m⁵ 5g 5g 5m Sep 8] leggy, unfurnished filly: poor maiden handicapper: raced only at 5f/6f on good going or firmer. *R. Hollinshead* **47**

CRIMSON TIDE (IRE) 7 b.h. Sadler's Wells (USA) 132 – Sharata (IRE) (Darshaan 133) [2001 104: 7.9m⁴ 10.1m 8m Jun 20] tall, leggy horse: useful nowadays: ran creditably in 2001 only when fourth to Soviet Flash in handicap at York: effective at 1m to 1½m: acts on firm going, soft and equitrack: has raced freely/found little, and usually held up: sold 46,000 gns in December. *J. W. Hills* **105**

CRIPSEY BROOK 3 ch.g. Lycius (USA) 124 – Duwon (IRE) 55 (Polish Precedent (USA) 131) [2001 73: 8g⁵ 9m 8m⁴ 7m* 8.1f 8g Sep 28] tall gelding: fair handicapper: won maiden event at Brighton (final start for M. Wigham) in June: stays 1m: acts on good to firm and good to soft ground: sold 9,000 gns. *B. R. Millman* **72**

CRISTOFORO (IRE) 4 b.g. Perugino (USA) 84 – Red Barons Lady (IRE) (Electric 126) [2001 50p: f7g f7g f7g 6m Aug 18] showed promise in maidens at 2 yrs but well held in handicaps in 2001: stays 1m: raced mainly on fibresand: has started slowly. *B. J. Curley* **–**

CRISTOPHE 3 b.g. Kris 135 – Our Shirley 84 (Shirley Heights 130) [2001 12d f11g 12g 16m 15g f12g³ 16.2m 12g² 11.5g³ Aug 30] quite attractive gelding: half-brother to several winners, including fairly useful 5f (at 2 yrs) to 16.4f winner Pearl Venture (by Salse) and unguenine 6f (at 2 yrs) to 1m winner Soviet Express (by Siberian Express): dam 1¼m winner: modest maiden: should stay 1¾m: best efforts on good going: joined A. Crook. *S. P. C. Woods* **53**

CRITICAL STAGE (IRE) 2 b.g. (Apr 27) King's Theatre (IRE) 128 – Zandaka (FR) (Doyoun 124) [2001 6s⁶ 7d f8g Nov 19] IR 12,000Y: first foal: dam unraced half-sister to Poule d'Essai des Pouliches winner Zalaiyka: well held in maidens: gelded after final start. *John Berry* **–**

CROESO CROESO 3 b.f. Most Welcome 131 – Croeso-I-Cymru 96 (Welsh Captain 113) [2001 –: 5.1f 6m³ 5g³ 5.3g* 5g 6.1f 6s Sep 30] sturdy, deep-bodied filly: fair performer: won minor event at Brighton in August: raced only at 5f/6f: has started slowly: withdrawn after bursting through stall on intended debut. *J. L. Spearing* **67**

CROP CIRCLE 2 b.g. (Apr 9) Magic Ring (IRE) 115 – Surprise Surprise 91 (Robellino (USA) 127) [2001 5m 5.1g⁴ 5.7f Jul 26] 10,000Y: fifth foal: half-brother to 3 winners, including 3-y-o Factual Lad: dam 2-y-o 7f winner who stayed 1¼m: easily best **57**

effort in maidens (modest form) when fourth at Bath: should stay 6f: sold 1,600 gns. *I. A. Balding*

CROSBY DANCER 2 b.c. (Mar 23) Glory of Dancer 121 – Mary Macblain 49 (Damister (USA) 123) [2001 6m 7s 7s⁴ 8g Nov 5] leggy, angular colt: second foal: dam 1m winner: poor maiden: should stay 1¼m. *John A. Harris* **48**

CROSBY DONJOHN 4 ch.g. Magic Ring (IRE) 115 – Ovideo 58 (Domynsky 110) [2001 –: 9s 7m 6m 7m 8f⁴ 8g 10m² 8.3d* 9g⁶ 10g 8.3m³ 10v Oct 15] good-bodied gelding: has a round action: modest handicapper: won maiden event at Hamilton in August: stays 1¼m: acts on firm going, good to soft and fibresand: usually blinkered: none too consistent. *J. R. Weymes* **52**

CROSBY ROCKER 3 b.f. Rock Hopper 124 – Mary Macblain 49 (Damister (USA) 123) [2001 8d 10.4m Sep 2] first foal: dam 1m winner: well held in maidens. *John A. Harris* **–**

CROSSBREEZE (USA) 2 b.f. (Jan 28) Red Ransom (USA) – Crystal Crossing (IRE) 99 (Royal Academy (USA) 130) [2001 6g³ 6g 7m⁶ Sep 24] first foal: dam, 2-y-o 6f winner, sister to smart performer up to 8.5f Crystal Crossing: easily best effort in maidens (fairly useful form) when third of 5 to Distant Valley at Ascot: should stay 7f: sent to USA. *J. H. M. Gosden* **86**

CROSSWAYS 3 b.g. Mister Baileys 123 – Miami Dancer (USA) (Seattle Dancer (USA) 119) [2001 –: e10g³ 12m² 11.5f* 14.1g⁶ 12m* 12g³ 12.4g⁴ Aug 17] fair handicapper: won at Lingfield in June and Folkestone in July: should stay beyond 1½m: acts on firm ground. *C. F. Wall* **74**

CROWNFIELD 2 b.g. (Jan 21) Blushing Flame (USA) 109 – Chief Island 62 (Be My Chief (USA) 122) [2001 6m⁴ 6m 7f² Jul 4] tall, leggy gelding: second foal: half-brother to 3-y-o Celtic Island: dam once-raced daughter of useful 7f/8.5f winner Clare Island, herself half-sister to very smart 1½m performer Caliban: fair maiden: easily best effort on debut: should stay at least 1m: joined Mrs M. Reveley. *W. G. M. Turner* **67**

CROW WOOD 2 b.c. (Feb 12) Halling (USA) 133 – Play With Me (IRE) 73 (Alzao (USA) 117) [2001 6m⁵ 7m⁵ 7f7g* 8m 7.1s Sep 8] strong, close-coupled colt: half-brother to several winners, including useful sprinter Shawdon (by Inchinor) and 5-y-o Lincoln Dean: dam, 1¼m winner, half-sister to Oaks d'Italia winner Lady Bentley: fair on all-weather, modest on turf: won maiden at Wolverhampton in August: stiff tasks in nurseries last 2 starts: should stay 1m: acts on fibresand, soft and good to firm going: sold 22,000 gns. *Sir Mark Prescott* **63 a78**

CRUAGH EXPRESS (IRE) 5 b.g. Unblest 117 – Cry In The Dark (Godswalk (USA) 130) [2001 62: f8g e8g² 8s⁵ 8d 8.1m³ 6.9m² 7.1d 8.3g² 7g 7s⁴ 8m Sep 26] close-coupled gelding: modest performer: effective at 7f to 1¼m: acts on equitrack, soft ground and good to firm: effective blinkered or not: tongue tied last 2 starts: has looked none too keen. *G. L. Moore* **60**

CRUISE 4 ch.g. Prince Sabo 123 – Mistral's Dancer (Shareef Dancer (USA) 135) [2001 70?: e8g e8g e12g e10g 7m 7m 6f Jun 13] fair winner at 3 yrs: no show in 2001: tried blinkered. *R. M. Flower* **–**

CRUNCHY (IRE) 3 ch.g. Common Grounds 118 – Credit Crunch (IRE) 51 (Caerleon (USA) 132) [2001 7m 7f 6m⁴ 8.5d 9.7m⁶ 12m 10.1s 10s* f11g Dec 3] IR 24,000Y: third foal: brother to 1998 2-y-o 6f winner Golden Charm and fairly useful Italian 1999 2-y-o 6f/7f winner Zemira: dam lightly raced at 2 yrs in Ireland: modest handicapper: won at Brighton in October: should stay 1½m: acts on soft and good to firm going: tongue tied after third start. *J. A. R. Toller* **60**

CRUSADING TIMES 2 b.g. (Mar 2) Timeless Times (USA) 99 – Marie's Crusader (IRE) (Last Tycoon 131) [2001 5v f5g⁶ 5.1s⁶ Apr 16] 800Y, resold 1,000Y: small, sturdy gelding: third foal: dam unraced half-sister to smart 1m to 1½m performer Noble Patriarch: little form in maiden/sellers. *M. W. Easterby* **–**

CRUSTY LILY 5 gr.m. Whittingham (IRE) 104 – Miss Crusty 45 (Belfort (FR) 89) [2001 50, a–: 6f 5.3f⁵ 6.1f⁵ 6m 7m 5.5m³ 5.7g 6m³ 6m 6m⁶ Aug 30] smallish, lengthy mare: poor performer: effective at 5f to 7.5f: acts on firm and good to soft going. *N. P. Littmoden* **46 a–**

CRUZ SANTA 8 b.m. Lord Bud 121 – Linpac Mapleleaf 69 (Dominion 123) [2001 42: 13.8s Oct 20] lightly raced on Flat nowadays: modest hurdler. *Mrs M. Reveley* **–**

Lord Lloyd-Webber's "Crystal Music"

CRYFIELD 4 b.g. Efisio 120 – Ciboure 74 (Norwick (USA) 125) [2001 75: 7.6f 8m **73**
10m³ 10.5g⁴ 7g⁴ 9.1f⁴ f8g* 8m⁴ 7m* 7d⁵ 7.9m⁵ 7.2m⁵ 8g f8g 8s Nov 9] good-bodied
gelding: fair handicapper: won in large fields at Southwell (amateurs) in June and Ascot
(ladies) in July: has form at 1¼m, but gives impression best around 7f nowadays: acts on
any turf going and fibresand: often visored, effective without: has pulled hard. *N. Tinkler*

CRYSTAL CANYON 4 ch.f. Efisio 120 – Manor Adventure 75 (Smackover 107) **54**
[2001 –: f6g f6g 6g 5f⁴ 5m f5g f5g⁴ 5f³ 5.1m⁴ 5s⁴ 5g⁴ 5g f6g³ f6g f6g⁴ f6s Dec 15] robust
filly: modest maiden handicapper: raced only at 5f/6f: acts on firm going and fibresand:
sometimes slowly away: has carried head high: tends to race lazily. *B. Smart*

CRYSTAL CREEK (IRE) 5 b.g. River Falls 113 – Dazzling Maid (IRE) 64 (Tate **61**
Gallery (USA) 117) [2001 79: f7g 10f 8.3m⁵ 10f 10.5m² 10g⁴ 11.1s² 12d⁶ 9.2d 11.9s Oct
11] good-bodied gelding: modest handicapper nowadays: best at 1¼m/11f: acts on firm
and soft going. *D. Nicholls*

CRYSTAL FLITE (IRE) 4 b.f. Darshaan 133 – Crystal City (Kris 135) [2001 73d: **76**
11.8m* 12d 11.8m* 11.8g³ Jul 25] quite attractive filly: fair handicapper: won at Leices- **a–**
ter in June/July: stays 1½m: seems to act on any turf going, some promise on fibresand:
none too consistent: reportedly in foal to Singspiel. *W. R. Muir*

CRYSTAL GIRL 2 b.f. (Apr 11) Presidium 124 – Balgownie 43 (Prince Tenderfoot **–**
(USA) 126) [2001 7d f7g f8g Dec 10] leggy, unfurnished filly: eighth foal: dam 1¼m
winner at 6 yrs: well beaten in maiden/sellers. *M. Dods*

CRYSTAL LASS 5 b.m. Ardkinglass 114 – That's Rich (Hot Spark 126) [2001 46, **59**
a56: f7g f8f⁶ f7g f8g f8g f7g* f8g³ f7g* f8g³ f8g* f7g³ f7g⁶ 8s⁴ 9.9d f7g³ f8.5g f9.4g f9.4s **a77**
Dec 27] tall mare: fair on all-weather, modest on turf: won 2 apprentice handicaps and
claimer at Southwell in June/July: left J. Balding after twelfth start: stays 1m: acts on
fibresand, firm and soft going: effective blinkered, visored nowadays. *R. Brotherton*

228

CRYSTAL MUSIC (USA)   3 b.f. Nureyev (USA) 131 – Crystal Spray 75 (Beldale   **114**
Flutter (USA) 130) [2001 110p: 8g⁴ 8g² 8f² 10v⁶ 10f 9d⁴ Nov 25] tall, rangy filly: smart
performer: won all 3 starts at 2 yrs, notably Fillies' Mile at Ascot: good efforts first 3
outings in 2001, in 1000 Guineas at Newmarket (3 lengths fourth to Ameerat), Irish
equivalent at the Curragh (2 lengths second to Imagine) and Coronation Stakes at Royal
Ascot (1½ lengths second to Banks Hill): off 3½ months afterwards (reported in August
to have scoped unsatisfactorily) and just respectable efforts when seventh to impressive
Banks Hill in Breeders' Cup Filly & Mare Turf at Belmont (checked early in straight,
final appearance for J. Gosden) and Matriarch Stakes at Hollywood (6 lengths fourth to
Starine) on last 2 starts: should have stayed 1¼m: acted on firm and good to soft going,
possibly not on heavy: has been bandaged behind: tended to carry head awkwardly:
struck into on near-hind first two 3-y-o outings: retired, and visits Seeking The Gold.
N. D. Drysdale, USA

CRYSTAL SOLDIER   3 ch.f. Infantry 122 – Bottle Basher (Le Soleil 96) [2001 7m   **– §**
10f 10.2m Jun 1] 580 3-y-o: seventh foal: dam lightly raced in bumpers/over hurdles:
temperamental maiden: refused to race second outing. *D. Burchell*

CRYSTAL SPRINGS (IRE)   7 b.m. Kahyasi 130 – Aqua Lily (Kalaglow 132)   **74**
[2001 79: 20m 16s 16g* 16g 16s Nov 11] IR 15,000Y: first foal: dam, Irish 1¼m winner
who stayed 1½m, half-sister to William Hill Futurity winner Lanfranco: fair handicapper:
won at Tramore in August: well held otherwise in 2001, in Ascot Stakes on first start:
stays 2¼m: acts on soft and good to firm going. *Patrick Martin, Ireland*

CRYSTAL VALKYRIE (IRE)   2 b.f. (Feb 16) Danehill (USA) 126 – Crystal Cross   **79**
(USA) 88 (Roberto (USA) 131) [2001 6m⁶ 6.1d⁴ f6g* Nov 12] angular filly: fifth foal:
sister to 5-y-o Bright Hope, closely related to Irish 10.5f winner Blue Crystal (by Lure),
and half-sister to 6-y-o Al's Fella: dam, 11.6f to 1¾m winner, half-sister to very smart 6f/
7f performer Iktamal and smart French performer up to 12.5f First Magnitude: fair form:
some promise before landing odds in maiden at Southwell, making all: likely to stay 7f:
acts on fibresand. *B. W. Hills*

CUBA GOLD (USA)   2 b.f. (Feb 5) Red Ransom (USA) – Recoleta (USA) (Wild   **–**
Again (USA)) [2001 5d May 21] $55,000Y: first foal: dam, 1m winner in USA, out of
half-sister to US Grade 2 9f/1¼m winner Dynaformer: slowly away and well held in
maiden at Windsor. *J. L. Dunlop*

CUBISM (USA)   5 b.h. Miswaki (USA) 124 – Seattle Kat (USA) (Seattle Song (USA)   **101**
130) [2001 109: 6m⁵ 6m 6f³ 6g 7g 6m 7g³ 7m Sep 22] smallish, well-made horse: useful
performer: best efforts in 2001 when third in handicaps at Newbury (behind Kayo) and
Goodwood (behind Father Thames): stays 7f, at least when emphasis is on speed: raced
mainly on good going or firmer: tried visored: often tongue tied: usually held up: sold
23,000 gns. *J. W. Hills*

CUDDLES (FR)   2 b.f. (Jan 30) Anabaa (USA) 130 – Palomelle (FR) 112 (Moulin   **85**
103) [2001 7m⁶ 7g⁵ 8m⁶ 8s* 10s⁴ 7v⁴ p7g* Nov 13] leggy filly: second reported live
foal: half-sister to French 1m to 10.6f winner Girls Band (by Chimes Band): dam French
6f (at 2 yrs) to 1¼m (Prix de Psyche) winner: fairly useful performer: won nurseries at
Pontefract in September and Lingfield in November: seems best at 7f/1m: acts on heavy
going and polytrack: reliable. *C. E. Brittain*

CUIGIU (IRE)   4 b.g. Persian Bold 123 – Homosassa 82 (Burslem 123) [2001 58: 9.9f   **41**
8d 12m 8f⁶ 9.1d 10m 9.2d Aug 15] neat gelding: poor maiden nowadays: stays 1¼m: acts
on firm ground, soft and fibresand: tried blinkered/tongue tied: usually races prominently.
A. B. Mulholland

CULMINATE   4 ch.g. Afzal 83 – Straw Blade 66 (Final Straw 127) [2001 –: 12m   **38 ?**
11.5m 11.5m³ 16.4m 9.9m 11.6m 10v p10g Dec 12] poor maiden on balance. *J. E. Long*

CULTRA (IRE)   2 ch.c. (Feb 13) Spectrum (IRE) 126 – Ziggy Belle (USA) (Danzig   **66 p**
(USA)) [2001 6d 6v Nov 8] robust colt: fifth foal: half-brother to a 7f winner in UAE
by Persian Bold: dam, Irish 1¾m winner, closely related to Grand Criterium winner
Treizieme and half-sister to Gold Cup runner-up Eastern Mystic: better effort in maidens
(fair form) at Newmarket: ran as though still in need of race next time: will be suited by
1m+: should do better at 3 yrs. *R. Hannon*

CULZEAN (IRE)   5 b.g. Machiavellian (USA) 123 – Eileen Jenny (IRE) 112 (Kris   **96**
135) [2001 92: f8g² e10s 8v 10g 10m³ 10.1m⁴ 10.5g³ 10g³ 10g* 10m⁶ 10f p10g Dec 12]
leggy gelding: useful handicapper: won at Kempton in July by 3 lengths from Tarboush:
mostly respectable efforts otherwise: best at 1m/1¼m: acts on soft going, good to firm

and fibresand: blinkered twice at 4 yrs: sometimes fails to go through with effort. *R. Hannon*

CUMBRIAN CARLETON 2 b.g. (Mar 29) Polar Falcon (USA) 126 – Fly Dont **68** Run (USA) 59 (Lear Fan (USA) 130) [2001 5m³ 6m⁴ Jun 9] 6,500Y: leggy, useful-looking gelding: fourth foal: dam, maiden best at 1¼m, sister to smart 1¼m/1½m performer Run Don't Fly: better effort (fair form) when third in minor event at Newcastle: gelded after next outing: bred to stay 1m. *T. D. Easterby*

CUMBRIAN CRYSTAL 2 b.f. (Feb 25) Mind Games 121 – Crystal Sand (GER) **69 p** (Forzando 122) [2001 5m⁴ 5s³ Sep 7] 2,000F, 1,000Y resold 10,500Y: first foal: dam unraced: better effort (fair form) when third to Historic Treble in maiden at Haydock, again doing best work at finish: will stay at least 6f: capable of better. *T. D. Easterby*

CUMBRIAN HARMONY (IRE) 3 b.f. Distinctly North (USA) 115 – Sawaki 71 **73** (Song 132) [2001 64: 6g 6m 6m² 6g 6m* 7m 6m 6m 6g 7g⁴ 7.5m² 8m³ 7m* 7g² 7d Nov 6] workmanlike filly: fair performer: won handicaps at Thirsk in June and Catterick in September: probably stays easy 1m: acts on firm and soft going: has swished tail. *T. D. Easterby*

CUMBRIAN PRINCESS 4 gr.f. Mtoto 134 – Cumbrian Melody 83 (Petong 126) **60** [2001 49d: 8.2v 6g 6m³ 6.1d³ 6s² 6d⁴ 7g f7s⁴ f9.4s* Dec 27] leggy filly: modest handicapper: won at Wolverhampton in December: stays 9.4f: acts on fibresand, soft and good to firm going: has wandered. *M. Blanshard*

CUMWHITTON 2 b.f. (May 6) Jumbo Hirt (USA) 90§ – Dominance (Dominion **–** 123) [2001 6m 7.5m⁵ 8m⁶ Sep 8] leggy filly: eighth foal: sister to 1¾m/2m winner Onefourseven and half-sister to 6f (at 2 yrs) and 2m winner Can She Can Can (by Sulaafah): dam unraced daughter of Oaks/Irish Oaks winner Juliette Marny: little sign of ability in maidens/minor event. *P. C. Haslam*

CUPIDS CHARM 4 b.f. Cadeaux Genereux 131 – Chapka (IRE) 68 (Green Desert **76** (USA) 127) [2001 86: 6g 6m 7m 7m⁵ 7m 7g* Sep 5] small, angular filly: fair handicapper nowadays: won at Lingfield in September: stays 7f: acts on soft and good to firm going: none too consistent. *R. Guest*

CURATE (USA) 2 ch.c. (Apr 9) Unfuwain (USA) 131 – Carniola 104 (Rainbow **– p** Quest (USA) 134) [2001 7.2v⁶ 7d Nov 3] leggy, good-topped colt: second foal: half-brother to French 10.5f winner Kranjska (by Caerleon): dam, French 9f (at 2 yrs) to 1½m winner, sister to 3-y-o Exaltation out of half-sister to Arc winner Saumarez: signs of ability in maidens (reportedly had breathing problem final start): should do better. *M. P. Tregoning*

CURFEW 2 b.f. (Feb 18) Marju (IRE) 127 – Twilight Patrol 96 (Robellino (USA) 127) **77 +** [2001 7m* 7d⁶ Aug 26] 4,200Y, 21,000 2-y-o: second foal: dam 6f (at 2 yrs) to 1m winner: fair form: won maiden at Yarmouth in July in quite good style: pulled very hard when tailed-off last of 6 in Prestige Stakes at Goodwood: bred to stay at least 1m. *J. R. Fanshawe*

CURRENCY 4 b.g. Sri Pekan (USA) 117 – On Tiptoes 107 (Shareef Dancer (USA) **80** 135) [2001 –: 5v 6m 5m 6m* 6m* 6m* 6.1f* 6f² 6g²* 6f² Jul 5] fairly useful performer: one of most improved handicappers of 2001, winning at Redcar (amateurs), Pontefract, Goodwood (apprentices), Nottingham and Windsor between May and July: stays 6f: acts on firm going, well beaten on heavy. *J. M. Bradley*

CURTAIN TIME (IRE) 3 b.c. Sadler's Wells (USA) 132 – Alidiva 105 (Chief **104** Singer 131) [2001 10d* 12g⁶ 11m⁵ May 22] big, close-coupled colt: has plenty of scope: has a round action: seventh foal: closely related to French 9.5f winner Dear Girl and US 1m winner Anytime (both by Fairy King) and half-brother to 1000 Guineas winner Sleepytime and high-class 7f (at 2 yrs) to 9f winner Ali-Royal (both by Royal Academy) and very smart middle-distance horse Taipan (by Last Tycoon): dam, 6f to 1m winner, half-sister to high-class French middle-distance colt Croco Rouge: created very good impression when winning maiden at Newmarket in April by 2½ lengths from Rasid, despite hanging left: failed to take the eye when disappointing next time: looked ill at ease on track when 6¼ lengths fifth to Asian Heights in listed race at Goodwood final start: should stay 1½m: was well regarded. *H. R. A. Cecil*

CURTSEY 3 b.f. Mark of Esteem (IRE) 137 – Tabyan (USA) 68 (Topsider (USA)) **59** [2001 –: 6d 6g⁵ 5.3f 6m Jul 7] useful-looking filly: modest maiden: stays 6f: has worn crossed noseband: races freely: sold 5,000 gns. *R. Charlton*

CURULE (USA) 4 b. or br.c. Go For Gin (USA) 123 – Reservation (USA) (Crypto- **116** clearance (USA)) [2001 111: a8f³ a8f² a9f⁵ a8.5f a9f² Aug 11] smart performer: tongue tied, ran well when ¾-length second to Festival of Light in Godolphin Mile at Nad Al Sheba in March: below form in 3 allowance races in US after: effective at 1m/1¼m: raced only on dirt since debut: often comes from off pace. *Saeed bin Suroor*

CURZON RIDGE (IRE) 2 b.f. (Mar 4) Indian Ridge 123 – Curzon Street 70 (Night **69** Shift (USA)) [2001 5d² 7d⁶ 6d Nov 2] IR 54,000Y: first foal: dam, maiden who stayed 1½m (not one to trust implicitly), sister to high-class 1m to 1½m winner In The Groove: fair maiden: off 4 months after debut: should stay 1m. *E. Stanners*

CUSIN 5 ch.g. Arazi (USA) 135 – Fairy Tern 109 (Mill Reef (USA) 141) [2001 76: f7g **66** f8g 7m 10f⁵ 10m² 9.9m⁴ 8.5f 8m² 8g⁶ Aug 24] close-coupled, angular gelding: has a short action: fair nowadays: left D. Nicholls after second start: stays 1¼m: below form on heavy ground, acts on any other: blinkered once: tongue tied after second start: has been early to post: sometimes races too freely: often finds little. *M. E. Sowersby*

CUSTOMEYES 2 b.f. (Apr 25) Komaite (USA) – Mizog (Selkirk (USA) 129) [2001 **– §** 6m 6m 7m Aug 8] first foal: dam little sign of ability: no form, including in seller: withdrawn after unseating rider to post on intended debut: twice very slowly away. *B. A. Pearce*

CUSTOM MADE 2 ch.g. (Mar 30) Zafonic (USA) 130 – Asterita 103 (Rainbow **55** Quest (USA) 134) [2001 6s⁴ p8g p8g³ f7s Dec 18] second foal: half-brother to 2000 2-y-o 7f winner Gulchie (by Thunder Gulch): dam, 11.5f winner who stayed 2m, half-sister to smart 1¼m winner Rasm out of close relative to very smart miler Waajib: modest maiden: left G. Butler before running poorly final start (subsequently gelded): should stay 1¼m: acts on polytrack: carried head high third outing. *J. R. Best*

CUTE CAROLINE 5 ch.m. First Trump 118 – Hissma 84 (Midyan (USA) 124) **–** [2001 52, a–: f8g f7g⁶ f8s Jan 19] poor maiden at 4 yrs: no form in 2001: often visored/ blinkered. *A. Berry*

CUT RATE (USA) 3 ch.g. Diesis 133 – Itsamazing (USA) 85 (The Minstrel (CAN) **71** 135) [2001 –p: 10.2d³ 10m May 29] quite good-topped gelding: has scope: best effort in 3 maidens when 12¼ lengths third to Scarpe Rosse at Bath on reappearance: tongue tied next time: sold 8,500 gns in October, and gelded. *Mrs A. J. Perrett*

CYBER BABE (IRE) 4 b.f. Persian Bold 123 – Ervedya (IRE) (Doyoun 124) [2001 **51 d** 61: f8.5g 11.7d 11.9d 12g 12m⁶ 11.9m f12s Dec 27] modest performer: seems on the downgrade: stays 1½m: acts on fibresand, good to firm (probably on firm) and good to soft ground: often visored at 2 yrs: has found little. *A. G. Newcombe*

CYBER SANTA 3 b.g. Celtic Swing 138 – Qualitair Ridge (Indian Ridge 123) [2001 **59** 56: 10m 12.4g* 12g 12f p13g* Nov 13] big, useful-looking gelding: modest handicapper: won at Newcastle in July and Lingfield in November: little show otherwise: stays 13f: form only on good ground and polytrack: has been slowly away. *J. Hetherton*

CYBERTECHNOLOGY 7 b.g. Environment Friend 128 – Verchinina 99 (Star **49** Appeal 133) [2001 69: 8s 9.1m 9.9f 8g 9.1d⁶ 8.5g Aug 15] workmanlike gelding: carries condition: poor handicapper nowadays: probably best at 9f/1¼m nowadays: acts on firm and good to soft ground: blinkered/visored (no form) once each: held up: joined Miss V. Haigh. *M. Dods*

CYCLONE CONNIE 3 ch.f. Dr Devious (IRE) 127 – Cutpurse Moll 76 (Green **98** Desert (USA) 127) [2001 77: 5g⁵ Oct 4] smallish, sturdy filly: unimpressive mover: fair form both 2-y-o starts: useful form when fifth to Indian Prince in listed event at Newmarket only 3-y-o outing: refused to enter stall on intended reappearance in July. *C. A. Cyzer*

CYCLONIC STORM 2 b.f. (May 10) Catrail (USA) 123 – Wheeler's Wonder (IRE) **49** 43 (Sure Blade (USA) 130) [2001 6f 5m 7m⁶ 7.5g Sep 19] rather leggy filly: fourth foal: dam, 1½m and 2m winner, out of half-sister to Chief Singer: poor maiden: slowly away all outings. *R. A. Fahey*

CYMRU-AM-BYTH 4 ch.g. Primo Dominie 121 – Croeso-I-Cymru 96 (Welsh **–** Captain 113) [2001 6.9v 6g 10d 10f May 28] 9,500Y: first foal: dam 5f/6f winner: no form. *J. L. Spearing*

CYNARA 3 b.f. Imp Society (USA) – Reina 24 (Homeboy 114) [2001 65: 10g 8m⁵ **60** 10g³ 8.3d² 9m⁶ 8m⁶ 8.1s 12g 10.1v Oct 24] big, good-topped filly: modest performer: effective at 1m/1¼m: acts on good to firm and good to soft going: has idled. *G. M. Moore*

CYNOSURE 4 b.g. Runnett 125 – Polly Two (Reesh 117) [2001 f8s f11g f7g 7s 7m – 10m Jun 21] workmanlike gelding: no form. *J. R. Weymes*

CYPRESS AVENUE (IRE) 9 b.g. Law Society (USA) 130 – Flying Diva 100 – (Chief Singer 131) [2001 f16.2g⁵ 16m f16.2g f16g Jul 27] big, strong gelding: no longer of much account. *Mrs V. C. Ward*

CYRAZY 3 b.f. Cyrano de Bergerac 120 – Hazy Kay (IRE) 77 (Treasure Kay 114) – § [2001 56: 5d Apr 24] angular filly: modest maiden: blinkered, refused to race only 3-y-o start: may prove best at 5f: has hung right/carried head awkwardly. *J. G. Given*

CYRIAN (IRE) 7 b.g. Persian Bold 123 – Regina St Cyr (IRE) (Doulab (USA) 115) – [2001 18d Oct 20] tall, good-topped gelding: useful handicapper at 4 yrs for P. Cole, winning Northumberland Plate at Newcastle: suffered tendon problem and missed next 2 seasons: never dangerous in Cesarewitch only 7-y-o start. *M. C. Pipe*

CZARINA 3 b.f. Emperor Jones (USA) 119 – Topwinder (USA) (Topsider (USA)) – [2001 6d 8.1g 6m 6.1m Jun 18] 1,100F: angular filly: fourth living foal: half-sister to 3 winners, including 5f winner Piper's Clan (by Aragon) and 4-y-o Master George: dam ran twice in France: no form. *J. Gallagher*

CZARINA WALTZ 2 b.f. (Mar 10) Emperor Jones (USA) 119 – Ballerina Bay 75 **66 p** (Myjinski (USA)) [2001 7d 7d Nov 3] good-topped filly: has scope: third foal: half-sister to 6-y-o Wave of Optimism: dam 7f to 11.5f winner: fair form, not knocked about, in maidens at Leicester and Newmarket: will stay 1¼m: capable of better. *C. F. Wall*

CZAR WARS 6 b.g. Warrshan (USA) 117 – Dutch Czarina 45 (Prince Sabo 123) **72** [2001 59, a85: f6g⁶ f6g⁵ f6s* f6g³ f6g f6g* 6g f6g⁴ 6f* 6d 5d f6g Nov 19] sturdy gelding: **a89** fairly useful handicapper on all-weather, fair on turf: won at Southwell in January and April and Haydock in July: best at 6f/7f: acts on fibresand, firm and soft going: usually blinkered: has reportedly broken blood vessels. *J. Balding*

D

DAANA 2 b.f. (Feb 24) Green Desert (USA) 127 – Shining Water (USA) (Riverman **77** (USA) 131) [2001 6g 7v⁵ Oct 26] 50,000Y: small, strong filly: sixth foal: closely related to 4-y-o Bold Precedent and half-sister to useful French performers up to around 1½m Blue Water and Norton Sound (both by Bering): dam French 1¼m winner: better effort in maidens (fair form) when fifth of 12 to Proven at Doncaster: should stay 1m. *J. L. Dunlop*

D'ACCORD 4 ch.g. Beveled (USA) – National Time (USA) (Lord Avie (USA)) [2001 **74** 87: 6d 6m 6m 6g 6v⁶ 5v⁶ 6v f5g³ f5g p7g Dec 29] tall gelding: fairly useful handicapper **a87** on all-weather, fair on turf: left M. Kettle after fourth start: good third at Wolverhampton eighth outing: best at 5f/easy 6f: acts on fibresand/equitrack, heavy and good to firm going: visored (edged right) third start. *S. Kirk*

DADELAND (IRE) 2 b.f. (Mar 31) Desert King (IRE) 129 – Bubbling Heights (FR) **85** (Darshaan 133) [2001 6m² 7m⁵ 6m 8m³ 10v* 7.9s³ Oct 11] IR 35,000Y: leggy, quite attractive filly: fluent mover: second foal: dam, French 1¼m winner, out of half-sister to dam of Breeders' Cup Turf winner Kotashaan: fairly useful performer: won nursery at Nottingham in October easily: creditable third of 26 in similar event at York final start: will probably stay 1½m: best efforts ridden prominently on soft/heavy ground. *M. W. Easterby*

DAFFODIL GIRL 2 ch.f. (Mar 1) Vettori (IRE) 119 – Top Treat (USA) 101 (Topsider **64** (USA)) [2001 8.1g 7m 7d⁴ Nov 6] half-sister to several winners, including 5-y-o Oscietra and 1¼m/1½m winner Rehaab (by Mtoto): dam, 6f winner, probably stayed 1m: modest maiden: should stay at least 1m. *B. Palling*

DAFFS 3 b.f. Alhijaz 122 – Magnolia 52 (Petong 126) [2001 8d 7.1g⁵ 7.1s 10.2g Aug – 27] first foal: dam, ran twice, sister to useful sprinter Petula: little form. *P. J. Makin*

DAFNE 2 ch.f. (Feb 23) Nashwan (USA) 135 – El Opera (IRE) 100 (Sadler's Wells – p (USA) 132) [2001 8g 7.5g⁶ 7g Aug 23] strong filly: second foal: closely related to 3-y-o Rainshine: dam, 7f winner who stayed 1¼m well, closely related to smart sprinter Pharaoh's Delight: signs of ability in maidens: should do better in handicaps at 1¼m/1½m. *Sir Mark Prescott*

DAHLIDYA 6 b.m. Midyan (USA) 124 – Dahlawise (IRE) 76 (Caerleon (USA) 132) **50** [2001 –§, a72§: f6g* f6g² f6g⁴ f7s f6s f6g³ f6g² f6g³ f5g f6f³ f6g² f6g² f7g⁵ f6g 6g³ f6g 6f **a74**

232

6g f6s f6g Oct 1] angular mare: fair handicapper on all-weather, modest and lightly raced on turf: won at Southwell in January: best at 6f/7f: acts on fibresand, good to firm and good to soft going: tried blinkered: usually slowly away, often markedly so, and comes from well behind. *M. J. Polglase*

DAILY SPORT (USA)   2 b.c. (Mar 11) Forest Wildcat (USA) 120 – French Lake (USA) (Lac Ouimet (USA)) [2001 5m⁵ 6g³ 5.1f* 6m f5g⁴ Oct 9] $30,000Y, $77,000 2-y-o: big, good-topped colt: has scope: first foal: dam 7f/1m winner in USA: fairly useful performer: won minor event Bath in July: below-form favourite last 2 starts, blinkered on final one: will prove best at 5f/6f: acts on firm going: sold 25,000 gns. *B. J. Meehan*   **83**

DAILY TONIC   4 ch.c. Sanglamore (USA) 126 – Woodwardia (USA) 93 (El Gran Senor (USA) 136) [2001 63: f9.4f⁶ f14.8s* Dec 15] close-coupled colt: modest form: won seller at Wolverhampton in December: stays 14.8f: acts on fibresand: mulish at start and slowly away only outing at 3 yrs. *N. A. Twiston-Davies*   **53 +**

DAIMAJIN (IRE)   2 b.g. (Mar 14) Dr Devious (IRE) 127 – Arrow Field (USA) (Sunshine Forever (USA)) [2001 7s⁴ Sep 24] first foal: dam unraced: 33/1, 3½ lengths fourth of 10 to Lunar Sovereign in minor event at Leicester, hanging left but keeping on from rear: will stay at least 1m: should improve. *B. J. Meehan*   **74 p**

DAISY BUTTONS (IRE)   2 b.f. (Feb 21) Bluebird (USA) 125 – Centella (IRE) (Thatching 131) [2001 5m⁴ 6m⁵ 5m 5m⁵ 6g⁶ 6s 7g⁵ 8s⁶ Oct 22] IR 35,000Y: rather leggy, lengthy filly: half-sister to 5f seller winner Cameo (by Statoblest): dam, placed at 6f at 2 yrs in Ireland, granddaughter of Irish 1000 Guineas winner Lady Capulet: modest maiden: stays 7f, seemingly not testing 1m: acts on good to firm going: blinkered fourth to sixth starts (ran creditably first 2 occasions). *T. D. Easterby*   **57**

DAJAM VU   4 ch.f. Lyphento (USA) 108 – Dancing Diamond (IRE) 56 (Alzao (USA) 117) [2001 –: 17.2f 16f 18m Jul 7] no form. *J. S. King*   **–**

DAKHIRA   3 b.f. Emperor Jones (USA) 119 – Fakhira (IRE) 83 (Jareer (USA) 115) [2001 55p: 8m 7m⁴ 10m 7m 7m Aug 30] disappointing maiden: bred to prove best up to 1m: raced only on good/good to firm going. *D. R. C. Elsworth*   **65 d**

DAKISI ROYALE   4 ch.f. King's Signet (USA) 110 – Marcroft 91 (Crofthall 110) [2001 44: f8.5f³ Dec 5] small, sturdy filly: poor maiden: stays 8.5f: acts on fibresand, good to firm and good to soft going: tried visored: has worn near-side pricker. *P. D. Evans*   **48**

DAKOTA SIOUX (IRE)   4 ch.f. College Chapel 122 – Batilde (IRE) (Victory Piper (USA) 100) [2001 80: 6m 6m 8g* 8m² 10.5d 8s 7s* 8.2s⁶ Oct 30] unfurnished filly: fairly useful handicapper: won at Thirsk in June and Catterick in October: best at 7f/easy 1m: acts on good and good to firm going: effective blinkered/visored or not: often forces pace. *R. A. Fahey*   **81**

DALAL   2 b.f. (Mar 5) Cadeaux Genereux 131 – Proudfoot (IRE) (Shareef Dancer (USA) 135) [2001 7d Nov 3] 55,000Y: good-topped, angular filly: half-sister to several winners, including useful 1996 2-y-o 5f winner Head Over Heels (by Pursuit of Love) and 5-y-o Harlequin Dancer: dam, Irish 1¾m winner: 20/1, eleventh of 21 to Ballet Fame in maiden at Newmarket, not knocked about: will do better. *E. A. L. Dunlop*   **63 p**

DALAMPOUR (IRE)   4 b.c. Shernazar 131 – Dalara (IRE) 114 (Doyoun 124) [2001 115p: 12s³ 13.9g⁴ 10g 13.3f⁴ 10.3d Sep 14] lengthy, angular colt: smart performer: best efforts in 2001 at Newbury in John Porter (third to Lucido) and Geoffrey Freer (fourth to Mr Combustible) on first and fourth starts: at least as effective around 1½m as 2m: yet to race on heavy going, acts on any other: has worn crossed/dropped noseband: taken last and steadily to post in 2001 (mounted on track final start): refuses to settle, and best treated with caution: sold 100,000 gns. *Sir Michael Stoute*   **111 §**

DALBLAIR (IRE)   2 b.g. (May 19) Lake Coniston (IRE) 131 – Cartagena Lady (IRE) (Prince Rupert (FR) 121) [2001 6m⁴ 6m 6m Sep 2] IR 4,000F: rather leggy gelding: fluent mover: fifth foal: half-brother to 4-y-o Buying A Dream: dam unraced: modest form in maidens: gelded after final start: will stay 1m. *J. A. Glover*   **62**

DALBY OF YORK   5 ch.g. Polar Falcon (USA) 126 – Miller's Creek (USA) 62 (Star de Naskra (USA)) [2001 –: 16.2m May 12] strong gelding: no form in 2 starts since 1999: blinkered once. *M. E. Sowersby*   **–**

DALIAPOUR (IRE)   5 b.h. Sadler's Wells (USA) 132 – Dalara (IRE) 114 (Doyoun 124) [2001 122: 5d 10m⁵ 12g 10m⁶ 12g 12m⁶ Dec 16] small, quite attractive horse: good walker: has a short, fluent action: smart performer: successful 3 times in 2000, including Vodafone Coronation Cup at Epsom: well below best for I. Allan in Hong Kong first 4   **119**

starts in 2001: off 5 months and back with former stable, ran creditably when fourth past post behind Mutamam in Canadian International at Woodbine (demoted to seventh for causing interference on first turn) penultimate outing: only sixth when attempting repeat win in Hong Kong Vase at Sha Tin final start: best at 1½m: acts on soft and good to firm going, probably on firm: races up with pace. *Sir Michael Stoute*

DALYAN (IRE) 4 b.g. Turtle Island (IRE) 123 – Salette 110 (Sallust 134) [2001 55: 8m 16m⁴ f16g Jul 27] tall, workmanlike gelding: modest maiden handicapper: stays 2m: acts on good to firm going. *A. J. Lockwood*   **54**

DAMAGES 3 b.f. Contract Law (USA) 108 – Treasure Time (IRE) 65 (Treasure Kay 114) [2001 –: 8g 10.2s Aug 9] no form. *D. J. Wintle*   **–**

DAMALIS (IRE) 5 b.m. Mukaddamah (USA) 125 – Art Age (Artaius (USA) 129) [2001 103: 6v 5.1d⁶ 5.1f* 5g 6d³ 6.3g 5.1m³ 6.1m² 6g⁶ 6d 5.8s⁶ 6g² Oct 5] lengthy, sturdy mare: useful performer: won handicap at Chester (fourth course success) in May: several creditable efforts after, including in listed races at same track on seventh/eighth starts and handicap at Newmarket (second to Honesty Fair) on final one: best at 5f/6f: acts on firm and soft going: sometimes edgy/on toes: has run poorly when sweating: usually waited with (can make running). *E. J. Alston*   **106**

DAMASK ROSE (IRE) 3 ch.f. Dr Devious (IRE) 127 – Solac (FR) (Gay Lussac (ITY) 116) [2001 9.9d⁴ 14.1m* 12m⁶ 14g 13.9m 14m⁴ 14g³ 12s⁶ Nov 10] unfurnished filly: half-sister to several winners, notably very smart stayers Double Eclipse and Double Trigger (both by Ela-Mana-Mou): dam lightly-raced half-sister to Derby Italiano winner Sirlad: useful performer: won maiden at Redcar in June: mostly good efforts after, including sixth to Ranin in listed event, third to Riyadh in handicap (both at Newmarket), and sixth in November Handicap at Doncaster: stays 1¾m: acts on soft and good to firm going: reliable. *L. M. Cumani*   **100**

DAMASQUINER 4 b.f. Casteddu 111 – Hymn Book (IRE) 65 (Darshaan 133) [2001 56: e6g e7g³ e6s e7g⁴ 5m³ 6m 5f⁶ 6m Aug 18] smallish filly: modest performer: stays 1m: acts on equitrack and firm ground: none too consistent. *T. E. Powell*   **50**

DAME FONTEYN 4 b.f. Suave Dancer (USA) 136 – Her Honour 94 (Teenoso (USA) 135) [2001 66: e13g Mar 19] leggy filly: fair performer at 3 yrs: well held only 4-y-o start. *M. C. Pipe*   **–**

DAME SHARP 2 b.f. (Apr 12) Sabrehill (USA) 120 – Dame Helene (USA) (Sir Ivor 135) [2001 6d 7m⁵ 7.5m f6g f6s⁴ Dec 26] 2,000Y: fifth foal: half-sister to fairly useful 1998 2-y-o 7f winner Autocrat (by Polar Falcon): dam, no form, out of half-sister to high-class 7f to 9f performer Indian Lodge: modest maiden: should stay 1m: visored (slowly away, ran creditably) final start. *E. J. Alston*   **52**

DAMIEN'S LAW 4 b.g. Contract Law (USA) 108 – Cinderella Derek 61 (Hittite Glory 125) [2001 e12g f9.4g 7s Apr 12] no form. *A. D. Smith*   **–**

DANAKIL 6 b.g. Warning 136 – Danilova (USA) (Lyphard (USA) 132) [2001 75: f8.5s⁵ f8.5g 8.5s 8.3d 7m 7g 8f³ 9.7m⁵ 10.1g² 12g³ 11.9s⁴ p10g² p12g* p10g⁴ p12g* Dec 19] small gelding: unimpressive mover: fairly useful handicapper on all-weather, fair on turf: won at Lingfield in November (amateurs) and December: effective at 1m to 1½m: acts on fibresand/polytrack, firm and soft going: visored once at 5 yrs: reliable. *S. Dow*   **69 a81**

DANAKIM 4 b.g. Emarati (USA) 74 – Kangra Valley 56 (Indian Ridge 123) [2001 55: 7.1d⁶ 5d⁵ 5m 6m³ 5m² 5m³ 5.1f² 5m⁶ 5m⁶ 5f 5d 5g 6m* 5m⁵ 5g³ 6m⁵ 5m 6m 5f 5.3m⁴ 5d 7d 6d f6g Nov 27] lengthy, good-quartered gelding: fair performer: won maiden handicap at Ripon in July: best at 5f/6f: acts on firm and good to soft going, probably on heavy: tried blinkered: has been taken early to post: refused to enter stall final intended outing. *J. R. Weymes*   **65**

DANANEYEV (FR) 5 br.h. Goldneyev (USA) 114 – Danagroom (USA) (Groom Dancer (USA) 128) [2001 107: 7v³ 5v* 5.5v⁵ 5m* 5m* 5m 6d 5s Oct 7] tall horse: second foal: half-brother to useful French 6f (at 2 yrs) to 9f winner Frozen Groom (by Bering): dam French 2-y-o 7f winner: smart performer: in good form in first half of 2001, winning listed race at Longchamp in April, Prix de Saint-Georges at same track (by neck) in May and Prix du Gros-Chene at Chantilly (by ¾ length) in June, last 2 from Season's Greetings: below form after in King's Stand Stakes at Royal Ascot, Prix de Seine-Et-Oise at Maisons-Laffitte and Prix de l'Abbaye de Longchamp: best at 5f/6f: acts on heavy and good to firm going: races prominently: wore bandages and boots at Royal Ascot. *C. Laffon-Parias, France*   **114**

DANCEABOUT 4 b.f. Shareef Dancer (USA) 135 – Putupon 89 (Mummy's Pet 125) **110**
[2001 110: 8s⁴ 8g⁴ 9.9g⁶ 8g³ 8d 8g Oct 6] smallish, strong, attractive filly: reportedly
cracked pelvis in 1999: smart performer: won Sun Chariot Stakes at Newmarket at 3 yrs:
creditable efforts first 4 starts in 2001, including in Lockinge Stakes at Newbury (fourth
to Medicean), Falmouth Stakes at Newmarket (fourth to Proudwings) and Matron Stakes
at the Curragh (1¼ lengths third to Independence): was best at 1m/9f: acted on soft and
good to firm going: visored penultimate start: held up: reportedly retired. *G. Wragg*

DANCE ALIVE 3 b.c. Rainbow Quest (USA) 134 – Tashinsky (USA) (Nijinsky **69**
(CAN) 138) [2001 11s⁵ 10v May 19] half-brother to several winners, including useful 7f
(at 2 yrs)/1m winner Harry Wolton (by Distant Relative) and fairly useful 1¼m to 1¾m
winner Fanfare (by Deploy): dam, showed some ability in France, half-sister to very
smart miler Mukaddamah: fair form in maidens at Newbury: dead. *G. A. Butler*

DANCE ALL NIGHT 2 b.c. (Feb 19) Suave Dancer (USA) 136 – Lyndseylee 96 **54**
(Swing Easy (USA) 126) [2001 6d 6d 5s f5g Oct 9] tall, rather unfurnished colt: fourth
living foal: half-brother to 1998 2-y-o 6f winner Timelee and 5f winner (including at 2
yrs) Dande Flyer (both by Clantime): dam best at 5f: modest maiden: may prove best at
5f/6f: ran poorly on fibresand. *A. Berry*

DANCE DIRECTOR (IRE) 4 b.g. Sadler's Wells (USA) 132 – Memories (USA) **91**
(Hail The Pirates (USA) 126) [2001 91p: 14m May 24] fairly useful performer, lightly
raced: not discredited only 4-y-o start (gelded after): stays 1¾m: acts on soft and good to
firm going. *C. R. Egerton*

DANCEHALL DARCY 2 ch.f. (Mar 20) Bahamian Bounty 116 – Dancing Chimes **–**
(London Bells) (CAN) 109) [2001 5m Jun 27] half-sister to several winning sprinters,
including 11-y-o Palacegate Touch and 4-y-o Toleration: dam unraced: 16/1, in rear
throughout in maiden at Salisbury. *K. O. Cunningham-Brown*

DANCE IN THE DAY (IRE) 3 b.c. Caerleon (USA) 132 – One To One (Shirley **83**
Heights 130) [2001 –: 8.3g 10.9f² 11.9f² 11.5m* 13.1d³ 12m* 12m Sep 22] fairly useful
performer: won handicaps at Lingfield in July and Beverley in August: seems better
around 1½m/13f than shorter: acts on firm and good to soft ground: sold 20,000 gns.
E. A. L. Dunlop

DANCE LESSON 2 b.f. (Apr 25) In The Wings 128 – Be Discreet (Junius (USA) 124) **–**
[2001 8.2v 8.3v Oct 29] 23,000F: sturdy filly: half-sister to several winners, including
smart 7f/1m performer Gothenberg (by Polish Patriot) and useful 5f (at 2 yrs) to 1m
winner Omaha City (by Night Shift): dam won up to 7f in France: poor form in maidens.
S. Kirk

DANCE LITTLE LADY (IRE) 4 b.f. Common Grounds 118 – Kentucky Tears **–**
(USA) (Cougar (CHI)) [2001 57: 6m 5f 6g f11g Dec 3] angular filly: winning handi-
capper: well held in 2001, leaving M. Todhunter after penultimate start: tried blinkered.
M. Johnston

DANCE MASTER (IRE) 3 b.c. Nureyev (USA) 131 – Bay Queen 85 (Damister **72**
(USA) 123) [2001 8.3g 8m 8.2f 11m* 11.5m* 12.3f 10.9d⁶ 12.4m 11m Sep 26] 150,000Y:
rather sparely-made colt: unimpressive mover: third foal: closely related to 5-y-o Prairie
Wolf: dam 1¼m/1m1f winner: fair performer: won maiden at Redcar and handicap at
Lingfield in June: should be suited by at least 1½m: acts on good to firm going: sold 8,000
gns. *M. L. W. Bell*

DANCEMMA 4 ch.f. Emarati (USA) 74 – Hanglands (Bustino 136) [2001 64d: 10.5s **–**
f8.5g 6g f6s Dec 15] big, lengthy filly: disappointing maiden. *H. J. Collingridge*

DANCE ON THE TOP 3 ch.g. Caerleon (USA) 132 – Fern 100 (Shirley Heights **93 p**
130) [2001 83: 8g* 9m³ 12f⁶ Jun 21] close-coupled, good-topped gelding: poor mover:
fairly useful handicapper: won 28-runner race at Newmarket in May: creditable efforts
both starts after, sixth to Beekeeper in King George V Stakes at Royal Ascot final start
(jarred a knee): should prove better at 1¼m/1½m than shorter: acts on good to soft, well
below form on good to soft: type to do well at 4 yrs, providing all is well. *E. A. L. Dunlop*

DANCE THEATRE (IRE) 3 b.g. Sadler's Wells (USA) 132 – Noora Abu 113 **79 §**
(Ahonoora 122) [2001 12s² 10s⁴ 10m⁴ 10g⁵ 12m Sep 24] sixth foal: dam best up to 1¼m
in Ireland: fair maiden: left J. Bolger in Ireland 30,000 gns before final start: looked
reluctant (unseated rider to post) only start in Britain: stays 1½m: acts on soft going:
blinkered third/fourth outings. *J. R. Jenkins*

DANCING AL 6 br.g. Alnasr Alwasheek 117 – Lyne Dancer (Be My Native (USA) **43**
122) [2001 –: 14.1v³ 11.9s² 14.1s⁵ 11.9s Oct 3] poor maiden handicapper: stays 1¾m:
acts on good to firm and heavy going. *J. S. Moore*

Tote Exacta Stakes (Handicap), Ascot—a deserved win for Dancing Mystery, who holds on gamely from Guinea Hunter, Canterloupe (right), Sir Desmond (second right), Greenwood (far side) and Bali Royal

DANCING BAY 4 b.g. Suave Dancer (USA) 136 – Kabayil 75 (Dancing Brave (USA) 140) [2001 99: 12s 11.9m 13.9m 11.9m⁶ 14s⁶ 14v 13.1v* 12s Nov 10] close-coupled gelding: fairly useful handicapper: won at Ayr in October: ran poorly final start: stays 13f: best on going softer than good: has had tongue tied: usually held up (has gone in snatches/hung): joined N. Henderson. *Miss J. A. Camacho* — **93**

DANCING DERVISH 6 b.g. Shareef Dancer (USA) 135 – Taj Victory 68 (Final Straw 127) [2001 –: f16.2s f9.4g f12g⁵ f6g⁶ May 3] of no account nowadays. *D. Burchell* — **–**

DANCING DOLPHIN (IRE) 2 b.f. (Feb 7) Dolphin Street (FR) 125 – Dance Model (Unfuwain (USA) 131) [2001 6f 8d p7g Nov 20] 5,000Y: rangy, angular filly: first foal: dam, no form, half-sister to useful performer up to 7f Wantage Park: well beaten in maidens/claimer: trained on debut by M. Usher. *J. E. Long* — **–**

DANCING FREE 2 b.f. (May 1) Dancing Spree (USA) – Keep Quiet 54 (Reprimand 122) [2001 6g⁵ 7g⁵ 7.1f² 6g⁶ 7g⁵ f7g⁶ a6g² Dec 9] 2,400Y: smallish, quite good-topped filly: second living foal: half-sister to 4-y-o Villa Romana: dam, maiden who stayed 1m, from family of Tenby: poor maiden: raced only in sellers in Britain: left K. Burke before final start: should stay 1m: yet to race on ground softer than good. *J. H. Brown, Spain* — **46**

DANCING HILL 2 b.f. (Apr 24) Piccolo 121 – Ryewater Dream 72 (Touching Wood (USA) 127) [2001 5.1d 6m⁵ 5m⁶ 5.7f f5g⁵ 5d* 6.1s⁴ 7g f7g 5.3s⁶ Oct 3] 1,400Y: fifth foal: half-sister to fairly useful 9f winner Buzz (by Anshan) and 5-y-o It's Magic: dam 11.7f winner: modest on turf, poor on all-weather: left M. Blanshard after fourth start: won seller at Leicester in July: stays 6f: acts on soft ground, good to firm and fibresand. *W. G. M. Turner* — **55 a48**

DANCING JACK 8 ch.g. Clantime 101 – Sun Follower (Relkino 131) [2001 40, a50: e6g e5g e5g f5g e6g e5g 5.1m 5m 6m 6f 5m Jul 13] workmanlike gelding: poor performer: best at 5f/6f: acts on firm going, soft and equitrack: tried blinkered: refused to race third outing. *J. J. Bridger* — **– § a39 §**

DANCING KING (IRE) 5 b.g. Fairy King (USA) – Zariysha (IRE) (Darshaan 133) [2001 –: f14.8s 8.1d⁴ 8.1m 8d 8m 8m⁴ 8.1g Sep 13] modest form: stays 1m. *P. W. Hiatt* — **52**

DANCING KRIS 8 b.g. Kris 135 – Liska's Dance (USA) (Riverman (USA) 131) [2001 –: 10s 10d 10.5g³ 9m⁴ 8g 10d 10d 9g Oct 19] smallish, strong gelding: fractured splint bone in 1999: fair handicapper, on downgrade: stays 10.5f: acts on heavy and good to firm ground: blinkered once. *Ian Williams* — **75 d**

DANCING LILY 4 ch.f. Clantime 101 – Sun Follower (Relkino 131) [2001 45, a33: e10g⁴ e6g⁶ e7g³ e7g 6g 7m 6m 8f 7g 7.6g 9.9d Oct 3] poor maiden: barely stays easy 1¼m: acts on firm going, good to soft and equitrack: has hung right. *J. J. Bridger* — **– a39**

DANCING MARMY 3 b.f. Dancing Spree (USA) – Marmy 43 (Midyan (USA) 124) [2001 8s 6g 9f 10.2s 8.5g Aug 15] 1,700Y: smallish, workmanlike filly: first foal: dam, third in 6f seller at 2 yrs, out of half-sister to very smart miler Alhijaz: tailed off all starts: tried blinkered. *K. McAuliffe* — **–**

DANCING MARY 4 gr.f. Sri Pekan (USA) 117 – Fontenoy (USA) 63 (Lyphard's Wish (FR) 124) [2001 54, a47: f16g f12g² f12g² f12g 12g f14g Dec 14] leggy, — **– a45**

236

unfurnished filly: poor nowadays: left B. Smart after third start: stays 1¾m: acts on fibresand, firm and good to soft going: blinkered once. *J. S. Wainwright*

DANCING MILLY   3 ch.f. Dancing Spree (USA) – Maid Welcome 81 (Mummy's –
Pet 125) [2001 –: 6g 8.1m f6g Aug 10] little sign of ability: blinkered once. *P. J. Makin*

DANCING MYSTERY   7 b.g. Beveled (USA) – Batchworth Dancer 67 (Ballacashtal **112**
(CAN)) [2001 111+: f5g⁴ 5s⁵ 5m 5m⁵ 5f 5m 5m 5g 5g³ 5.1g 6m 5m 5s² 5d* 5d⁴ 5v² f5g²
Nov 21] close-coupled gelding: smart performer: won handicap at Ascot (beat Guinea
Hunter 1¼ lengths) in October: good second to Repertory (beaten 2½ lengths) in Prix du
Petit Couvert at Longchamp and to Juwwi (beaten a head) in handicap at Wolverhampton
last 2 starts: best at 5f: has form on firm ground/equitrack, best efforts on going softer
than good/fibresand: sometimes blinkered: takes strong hold and usually tracks pace: has
spoilt chance by rearing in stall. *E. A. Wheeler*

DANCING PENNEY (IRE)   3 b.f. General Monash (USA) 107 – Penultimate Cress **51 d**
(IRE) (My Generation 111) [2001 56: f7g⁴ f8g* f8.5s⁴ f8s² e7g e10s⁶ 7m⁶ 7s⁵ 10g⁶ 7f⁴ 6m
8m³ 8m 10f⁶ 7d 5.7g 7f⁶ f7g p7g Dec 12] angular filly: modest performer: won seller at
Southwell in January: left K. Ryan after fifth outing: stays 1m: acts on fibresand and firm
going, probably on soft: tried blinkered: has hung left/carried head awkwardly: on the
downgrade. *R. M. Flower*

DANCING PHANTOM   6 b.g. Darshaan 133 – Dancing Prize (IRE) 99 (Sadler's **105**
Wells (USA) 132) [2001 11.9g 13.1v² 12v Oct 27] quite attractive gelding: has a quick
action: useful handicapper: missed 2000 season: ran creditably in 2001 only when 2
lengths second to Dancing Bay at Ayr: stays 13f: acts on heavy going: sometimes edgy/
on toes in preliminaries: free-going sort, and usually races prominently: seems difficult to
train. *M. W. Easterby*

DANCING RIDGE (IRE)   4 b.g. Ridgewood Ben 113 – May We Dance (IRE) 57 **56**
(Dance of Life (USA)) [2001 –: 8s 7.1m 6m⁶ 5.1f⁶ f5g³ 5m f5g⁵ 5d³ f6g⁴ 6m f5g³ Aug
10] good-topped gelding: modest maiden handicapper: effective at 5f/6f: acts on fibresand, firm and good to soft ground: none too consistent. *A. Senior*

DANCING TILLY   3 b.f. Dancing Spree (USA) – L'Ancressaan 67 (Dalsaan 125) –
[2001 8d 11.9m 8.1d Jun 9] leggy filly: fifth foal: half-sister to 4-y-o Mr Cospector and
fairly useful 8.5f and 1¼m winner Komreyev Dancer (by Komaite): dam 2-y-o 6f winner:
well held in maidens (very slowly away on debut). *W. M. Brisbourne*

DANCING TSAR   3 b.c. Salse (USA) 128 – Lunda (IRE) 60 (Soviet Star (USA) 128 **76**
[2001 –P: e8g* f8g⁴ 11m 8.5f⁴ 7.1g 10g* 9.7g² 10.2g f9.4g⁵ f8g⁶ p10g Dec 28] small,
sparely-made colt: fair performer: won maiden at Lingfield in March and handicap at
Leicester in August: stays 1¼m: acts on fibresand and equitrack, best turf efforts on good
ground: left G. Butler before last 2 starts (below form). *J. M. Bradley*

DANCING WATER   2 gr.c. (Mar 10) Halling (USA) 133 – Gleaming Water 81 **86**
(Kalaglow 132) [2001 7f⁴ 8d Oct 19] leggy colt: has a quick action: seventh foal:
half-brother to 3 winners, including 1m to 10.4f winner Prince of Denial (by Soviet Star)
and middle-distance performer Faraway Waters (by Pharly), 6f winner at 2 yrs, both
useful: dam, 2-y-o 6f winner, sister to smart stayer Shining Water, herself dam of Tenby:
fairly useful form in maidens at Newbury (fourth of 18 to Al Mohallab) and Newmarket
(eighth of 20 to Rawyaan): will be suited by 1¼m/1½m. *R. F. Johnson Houghton*

DAN DE LION   2 b.c. (Mar 12) Danzig Connection (USA) – Fiorini 54 (Formidable –
(USA) 125) [2001 5f 7s 7d Oct 30] 2,200F, 5,200Y: good-bodied colt: sixth living foal:
closely related to 6f seller winner Light Breeze (by Hamas) and half-brother to 5f seller
winner Figlia (by Sizzling Melody): dam sprinter: no sign of ability in maidens/minor
event. *Jedd O'Keeffe*

DANDILUM   4 b.g. Dilum (USA) 115 – Renira 60 (Relkino 131) [2001 78: 7g 7s 7g 8f –
7.1f 6g 7.1d 7.1m 10m Aug 13] leggy, quite good-topped gelding: fair maiden at 3 yrs: no
form in 2001: sometimes blinkered. *J. M. Bradley*

DANDOONA   2 b.f. (Feb 20) Zafonic (USA) 130 – Speedybird (IRE) 71 (Danehill –
(USA) 126) [2001 5s 7d f6g Nov 12] leggy, good-topped filly: third foal: half-sister to
3-y-o A Bit Special: dam, 7f winner, out of half-sister to Mill Reef: little sign of ability in
minor event/maidens: looks wayward. *J. D. Czerpak*

Prince A. A. Faisal's "Dandoun"

DANDOUN   3 b.c. Halling (USA) 133 – Moneefa 73 (Darshaan 133) [2001 8d* 8m*   **114**
8m* 8m 10d⁵ Aug 15] useful-looking colt: has a moderate, quick action: second foal:
dam, 1¼m winner, half-sister to dam of 3-y-o Olden Times, out of smart sprinter Abha:
smart performer: won 28-runner newcomers event at Newmarket in April and minor
event at Doncaster and listed race at Kempton (by 1¾ lengths from Aldebaran, edging
left) in May: changed hands privately, then well held in St James's Palace Stakes at Royal
Ascot (edgy/took strong hold) next time: creditable fifth to Masterful in Prix Guillaume
d'Ornano at Deauville final start: best form at 1m: yet to race on extremes of going.
J. L. Dunlop

DANDY REGENT   7 b.g. Green Desert (USA) 127 – Tahilla 112 (Moorestyle 137)   **52**
[2001 60+, a–: 7m 8d 6d 8v⁴ 8s f8g Nov 19] angular gelding: modest performer: stays   **a–**
1m: acts on good to firm and heavy going: none too consistent. *John A. Harris*

DANE DANCING (IRE)   3 b.f. Danehill (USA) 126 – My Ballerina (USA) 94 (Sir   **62**
Ivor 135) [2001 68, a58: f7g⁴ f9.4s* e8g³ f8g⁴ f8.5g Feb 8] smallish, quite attractive filly:
modest performer: won maiden at Wolverhampton in January: stays 9.4f: acts on good to
soft ground and all-weather: blinkered nowadays. *A. Berry*

DANE FLYER (IRE)   3 b.c. Danehill (USA) 126 – Old Domesday Book 93 (High   **66**
Top 131) [2001 78: 6m 5m⁵ 6m³ 6m⁴ 5m⁵ 7m 5g 6g 7.1g 6.1f Sep 18] good-bodied colt:
good walker: has a quick action: fair maiden handicapper: stays 6f: acts on good to firm
going: tried tongue tied: sold 2,500 gns, sent to Sweden. *M. R. Channon*

DANEGOLD (IRE)   9 b.g. Danehill (USA) 126 – Cistus 123 (Sun Prince 128) [2001   **70**
60§: 17.2f⁵ 16.4m² 17.1m³ 18m* 16.2f³ 18m* 16.4m² 17.2m² 16m* 16.2m 16.4g⁴ Aug
17] compact gelding: fair handicapper: won at Chepstow then Newbury in July: effective

at 1¾m to 2¼m: acts on firm and soft going: usually visored early in career: usually gets behind: formerly unreliable. *R. T. Phillips*

DANEHURST 3 b.f. Danehill (USA) 126 – Miswaki Belle (USA) 73 (Miswaki **117** (USA) 124) [2001 108p: 5m 5g 5.1m* 5s 6d* 6s* Nov 10]

    Some individuals become inseparable in the public imagination . . . Gilbert and Sullivan, Nureyev and Fonteyn, Morecambe and Wise, Pinky and Perky, Ant and Dec. Racing's longest-running trainer-jockey combination of Sir Mark Prescott and George Duffield, now the senior jockey in the weighing room, comes into the same category. Their enduring partnership stretches back to April 1973, when the trainer was 'stuck for a jockey' for a two-year-old filly called So Valiant making her debut at Warwick. He says he turned to Duffield 'in desperation' and the filly won, initiating a twenty-nine-season unbroken alliance for trainer and jockey. Duffield rides work for Prescott at Newmarket twice a week but the pair don't socialise. 'As with most people who have been married a long time, words are often superfluous, but while I may have looked at other women, I have never looked at another jockey,' says the trainer, who lists fifty-five-year-old Duffield's main assets as his fitness, his strength, fearlessness and persistence ('he never gives up and is at his best on horses that need driving'), and his honesty and professionalism ('he is never late, never puts up overweight without telling me first and rings me straight after every race if I'm not at the course'). Prescott retains both Duffield, whose total of domestic winners is nearing 2,400, and Seb Sanders ('waiting patiently in the wings to take over'), and the pair have shared the six victories of the smart sprinting filly Danehurst, one of the stable's leading performers over the last two seasons.

    Duffield rode Danehurst to her most important success as a two-year-old in the Cornwallis Stakes at Newbury and was in the saddle when she defended her unbeaten record in the King's Stand Stakes over the same course on her reappearance at three. It had been decided over the winter that Danehurst would not run before Royal Ascot, but she managed only ninth of twenty-two behind Cassandra Go, tiring inside the final furlong after travelling smoothly with the leaders. Danehurst's next important target was the King George Stakes at Goodwood in July, but she missed the race with a pulled muscle, having warmed up with an impressive victory, ridden by Sanders, from Superstar Leo and Damalis in the Arthurs Dyke City Wall Stakes at Chester in mid-July. The Nunthorpe also went by without the sidelined Danehurst, who wasn't seen out again until running well below her best in the Prix de l'Abbaye in October. She was far from ideally drawn at Longchamp, which, in hindsight, probably had more bearing on her performance than the fact that she encountered soft ground for the first time. Underfoot conditions were similar for her two remaining races, both listed events which she won. The Travis Perkins Bentinck Stakes at Newmarket, a fortnight after the Abbaye, saw Danehurst stepped up to six furlongs for the first time and, with Duffield serving a suspension, Sanders was back on board. Probably in view of the

Arthurs Dyke City Wall Stakes, Chester—Danehurst quickens impressively to beat Superstar Leo (rail); Damalis (far left) stays on well for third with Eastern Purple (checked cap) coming next

extra furlong, riding tactics were modified slightly, and, after being restrained and moving strongly in the rear for a long way, Danehurst burst through inside the final furlong for a most impressive victory, Orientor and Bahamian Pirate filling the places in a particularly competitive event of its type. The Charles Sidney Mercedes Benz Wentworth Stakes, the final turf race of the season on November Handicap day at Doncaster, also attracted a strong field, half the runners having contested pattern races at some time during the season. Reunited with Duffield, Danehurst repeated the improved form she had shown in the Bentinck, edging ahead of the stand-side group entering the final furlong and holding on gamely from Eastern Purple, with Orientor, first home on the far side, in third.

Danehurst (b.f. 1998)	Danehill (USA) (b 1986)	Danzig (b 1977)	Northern Dancer Pas de Nom
		Razyana (b 1981)	His Majesty Spring Adieu
	Miswaki Belle (USA) (b 1992)	Miswaki (ch 1978)	Mr Prospector Hopespringseternal
		Belle Et Deluree (b 1985)	The Minstrel Sophisticated Girl

The smallish, barrel-shaped Danehurst is the second foal and only winner so far out of Miswaki Belle, who finished second over seven furlongs as a three-year-old on her only start. Miswaki Belle is closely related to Cherry Hinton winner and One Thousand Guineas third Dazzle, the pair being daughters of the Mr Prospector stallions Miswaki and Gone West respectively. Their dam Belle Et

Cheveley Park Stud's "Danehurst"

Deluree won at a mile as a two-year-old and over a mile and a quarter at three, and is herself closely related to Cheveley Park runner-up Dancing Tribute, the dam of Lowther winner Dance Sequence, who was beaten narrowly in the Cherry Hinton and finished sixth in the Guineas. Among the other winners bred by Dancing Tribute are the smart American two-year-olds Souvenir Copy and Gold Tribute, both of whom contested the Breeders' Cup Juvenile of their year. Danehurst's very successful sire Danehill has been represented by good winners over a range of distances, but Danehurst is unlikely to be tried over much further than six furlongs. She acts on fibresand, soft and good to firm going and seems suited by waiting tactics. Provided she trains on and keeps clear of injury, she should prove well capable of holding her own in pattern company as a four-year-old. If George Duffield is thinking of retirement, this filly could send him out in memorable style in the top sprints. *Sir Mark Prescott*

DANELOR (IRE) 3 b.c. Danehill (USA) 126 – Formulate 119 (Reform 132) [2001 **94** 8g⁶ 8m⁴ 7.1f* 8g³ Jul 21] IR 140,000Y: sturdy, good-bodied colt: half-brother to several winners, notably Oaks winner Shahtoush (by Alzao) and Oaks runner-up Game Plan (by Darshaan): dam top staying 2-y-o filly of 1978, ran only twice afterwards: fairly useful performer: won maiden at Haydock in July by 1¼ lengths from Masterful, making most: barely stays 1m: raced only on good going or firmer: has raced freely. *E. A. L. Dunlop*

DANEMERE (IRE) 2 b.f. (Apr 2) Danehill (USA) 126 – Kentmere (FR) (Galetto **79 p** (FR) 118) [2001 5f⁴ 6v* Oct 8] IR 60,000Y: tall, good-topped filly: third foal: half-sister to 13f winner Love Bitten (by Darshaan): dam, French 1m (at 2 yrs) and 11f winner, half-sister to Prix de Diane winner Lypharita: much better effort in maidens when winning at Windsor by 1¾ lengths from Ridley, leading final 1f: should stay 1m: likely to progress. *J. W. Hills*

DANESWOOD 2 b.g. (Mar 20) Be My Chief (USA) 122 – Floria Tosca § (Petong **60 §** 126) [2001 7m 7m 5.7f 7m² 7g⁴ 7s Oct 5] 4,800F, 8,000Y: fourth foal: half-brother to a 6f (including at 2 yrs) winner in Sweden by Rudimentary: dam, ran 3 times, one to avoid: modest maiden: second in claimer at Salisbury: stays 7f: acts on good to firm ground: blinkered/visored after debut: not to be trusted (appeared to drop himself out final start). *B. R. Millman*

DANGEROUS LIAISON 2 b.g. (Apr 12) Great Commotion (USA) 123 – Court- **75** isane (Persepolis (FR) 127) [2001 5.1v³ 5.3s³ 5.1s* 5.1f⁴ 5m 5g³ 6g 5m 5m* 5.1g* 5m² 5g 5.1m⁴ 5g f6g 5g² p6g Nov 28] 10,000Y: rather leggy, useful-looking gelding: half-brother to 3 winners, including 4-y-o Charming Lotte and an 11f winner in Germany by Caerleon: dam French 2-y-o 7f winner: fair performer: won maiden at Nottingham in April, claimer at Folkestone in July and seller at Bath (left B. Meehan) in August: best at 5f: acts on any turf going, some promise on fibresand/polytrack: usually blinkered/visored: races prominently. *C. A. Dwyer*

DANGEROUSLY GOOD 3 b.g. Shareef Dancer (USA) 135 – Ecologically Kind **70** (Alleged (USA) 138) [2001 7.9d⁴ 8g Dec 9] quite good-topped gelding: third foal: dam unraced: green, 10 lengths fourth of 6 to Carnival Dancer in maiden at York, never on terms after missing break: sold from D. Morris 1,500 gns and gelded, well held in minor event at Mijas 6 months later: will stay beyond 1m. *J. H. Brown, Spain*

DANGER OVER 4 b.c. Warning 136 – Danilova (USA) (Lyphard (USA) 132) [2001 **118** 116: 5m⁶ 6d² 6.5d⁵ 6g⁴ 6d Sep 18] smart performer: ran very well when head second to Sartorial, who received 4 lb, in Prix de Ris-Orangis at Deauville in August: bit disappointing otherwise in pattern races, though ran respectably when fourth to Do The Honours in Prix de Meautry at same course penultimate start: best at 6f/7f: acts on good to soft going, and disgraced once on good to firm: stays in training. *P. Bary, France*

DANIAVI (IRE) 3 ch.g. Kris 135 – Danishara (IRE) (Slew O' Gold (USA)) [2001 –p: **67 ?** 10s 11.7f⁴ 10s 14.1s p10g Dec 22] big, rather leggy gelding: has scope: maiden: seemed to show fair form second start: left Sir Michael Stoute and well beaten after, including in blinkers. *J. A. Glover*

DANIELLA RIDGE (IRE) 5 b.m. Indian Ridge 123 – Daniella Drive (USA) (Shelter **39** Half (USA)) [2001 63: e7g⁴ 10f⁶ 11.6g 12m 8m⁶ Jun 18] shallow-girthed mare: easy mover: poor maiden handicapper: barely stays 1¼m: acts on equitrack, firm and good to soft going: tried blinkered: has pulled hard/found little. *B. G. Powell*

DANIELLE'S LAD 5 b.g. Emarati (USA) 74 – Cactus Road (FR) (Iron Duke (FR) **92** 122) [2001 101, a–: 5.1v⁵ 5.2d 6.1v⁴ 6g 6m 6g³ 6m 5.1m 6.1m* 6g 5.2f⁵ 6g 7.1g³ 6g 6d **a–**

6d 7d⁴ p7g f6g f7g Dec 11] strong gelding: fairly useful nowadays: won minor event at Chepstow in July: stays 7f: acts on heavy and good to firm going, below form on fibresand/polytrack: usually blinkered in second half of 2001: tends to get on edge: has run poorly when sweating: jinked and unseated leaving stall penultimate start: often early to post: front runner. *B. Palling*

DANISH DECORUM (IRE)   2 ch.c. (Mar 21) Danehill Dancer (IRE) 117 –   **74**
Dignified Air (FR) 70 (Wolver Hollow 126) [2001 6m⁴ 7m* 8d Oct 19] IR 10,000F, 37,000Y: tall, leggy colt: has scope: half-brother to several winners, including useful Irish 7f winner (including at 2 yrs) Proud Titania (by Fairy King) and fairly useful Irish 6f winner who stayed 9.6f Luisa di Camerata (by Marju): dam 6f winner: fair form: won maiden at Salisbury in July: well beaten in nursery at Newmarket only subsequent outing: should stay 1m. *M. A. Jarvis*

DANITY FAIR   3 b.f. Cool Jazz 116 – Flute Royale 74 (Horage 124) [2001 38: f6g f6g   **33**
f6g f5g 5g 6g f6g⁵ Nov 16] poor maiden: probably stays 6f: form only on fibresand. *R. Bastiman*

D'ANJOU   4 b.g. Marju (IRE) 127 – Rose de Thai (USA) 99 (Lear Fan (USA) 130)   **116**
[2001 92: 8g 7g² 6.3g 6g* 6g² 7g* 7s⁶ Oct 7] fourth foal: half-brother to smart 7f (at 2 yrs)/1¼m winner Sandstone (by Green Desert) and smart Irish 1m and 1¼m winner Truth Or Dare (by Royal Academy): dam, French 1m winner (including at 2 yrs), granddaughter of Poule d'Essai des Pouliches winner Riverqueen: smart performer: much improved in 2001, winning handicaps at Fairyhouse in August and Leopardstown (very valuable Tote Exacta Handicap by ½ length from Montpelier Street, leading near line) in September: beaten head by Ishiguru in listed race at the Curragh in between: effective at 6f/7f: raced mainly on good ground or firmer (below form on soft final start): looks capable of winning listed/pattern races. *J. Oxx, Ireland*

DANKA   7 gr.g. Petong 126 – Angel Drummer 59 (Dance In Time (CAN)) [2001 –:   **–**
f12g e12g 14.1v 12m f14.8s⁵ Sep 6] seems of no account nowadays. *J. C. Fox*

DANNY BELL (IRE)   8 b.g. Be My Native (USA) 122 – Rhein Valley (IRE) (Kings   **–**
Lake (USA) 133) [2001 e12g Mar 31] bumper winner in 1998: tailed off in maiden. *J. G. M. O'Shea*

DANO-MAST   5 b.h. Unfuwain (USA) 131 – Camera Girl (Kalaglow 132) [2001 111:   **117**
9s* 12d* 12m⁵ 12g³ 12s³ Sep 9] closely related to a winner in Italy by Night Shift and half-brother to 2 winners, including useful 1m to 1¼m winner Captain Scott (by Polar Falcon): dam unraced: smart performer: better than ever in 2001, winning listed race at Klampenborg (by 12 lengths) in April and Prix Jean de Chaudenay at Saint-Cloud (by 2 lengths from Chiang Mai) in May: good third after to Valley Chapel in Scandinavian Open Championship at Klampenborg (beaten a length) and Stockholm Cup International at Taby (beaten 2 heads): stays 1½m: acts on soft and good to firm ground. *F. Poulsen, Denmark*

DANSEUSE D'ETOILE (FR)   2 gr.f. (Feb 13) Highest Honor (FR) 124 – Latifolia   **109 p**
73 (Dancing Brave (USA) 140) [2001 6g³ 8m* 8s² Oct 7] 1,000,000 francs Y: angular, quite attractive filly: second foal: half-sister to useful French 1998 2-y-o 9f winner Serse (by Persian Bold): dam twice-raced half-sister to smart French filly up to 1¼m Marble Maiden: won minor event at Longchamp in September: wearing crossed noseband, head second to Sulk in Prix Marcel Boussac on same course, leading final 1f but changing legs, hanging right and headed close home: likely to stay 1¼m: should make a smart 3-y-o. *R. Gibson, France*

DANTON (IRE)   3 ch.g. Cadeaux Genereux 131 – Royal Circle 95 (Sadler's Wells   **74**
(USA) 132) [2001 9d* 8.5m³ 11.9m 8g Oct 6] 12,000Y: very tall gelding, has scope: second foal: dam 1¼m winner who probably stayed 13.3f, out of Ribblesdale winner Queen Midas: fair form: won maiden at Newcastle in August: should stay beyond 9f: tended to hang second start. *M. Johnston*

DANZA MONTANA (USA)   3 ch.f. Diesis 133 – Valsora (IRE) (Tate Gallery (USA)   **–**
117) [2001 69: 8.3s⁶ 7.1m May 21] useful-looking filly: seemingly fair form on debut at 2 yrs: no form in 2001: sold 14,000 gns: sent to Australia. *L. M. Cumani*

DANZAS   7 b.g. Polish Precedent (USA) 131 – Dancing Rocks 118 (Green Dancer   **50**
(USA) 132) [2001 51, a41: 8f 7m 6m* 7.5f 5.7m 7d⁶ 7.1g 7.1m 8m 7m 8s Sep 30] lengthy   **a–**
gelding: modest on turf: won claimer at Folkestone in June: effective at 6f to 1m: acts on any turf going and fibresand/equitrack: blinkered: has had tongue tied: often slowly away: sold 400 gns. *J. M. Bradley*

DANZIGEUSE (IRE)   4 b.f. Zieten (USA) 118 – Baliana 75 (Midyan (USA) 124)   –
[2001 52: 7d 8m 8g 7m 5m Aug 18] seems of little account nowadays. *C. B. B. Booth*

DANZIG FLYER (IRE)   6 b.g. Roi Danzig (USA) – Fenland Express (IRE)   –
(Reasonable (FR) 119) [2001 –: 9.1m Sep 21] no form since 2 yrs. *M. Mullineaux*

DAPHNE ODORA   3 b.f. Elmaamul (USA) 125 – Heavenly Goddess (Soviet Star   **41**
(USA) 128) [2001 8.3m 10f³ 9.7m⁶ 10.9m 8g 8.3v⁵ f9.4f f8.5g⁵ Dec 11] second foal:
half-sister to 4-y-o Digital: dam unraced: poor maiden: probably stays 1¼m: acts on any
turf going, probably on fibresand. *B. G. Powell*

DAPHNE'S DOLL (IRE)   6 b.m. Polish Patriot (USA) 128 – Helietta 78 (Tyrnavos   **52**
129) [2001 54: e12s⁵ e8g e8g³ e7g 10g 8m⁵ 8m 7g 7g* 8.2m Sep 10] big mare: modest   **a44**
handicapper on turf, poor on all-weather: won at Lingfield in August: effective at 7f to
easy 1¼m: acts on good to firm going, heavy and equitrack (well held only run on
fibresand). *Dr J. R. J. Naylor*

DARA MAC   2 b.c. (Apr 24) Presidium 124 – Nishara (Nishapour (FR) 125) [2001 7f⁶   **39**
6m 8.5m Aug 26] 1,000Y: second foal: dam, of little account, half-sister to Irish 2000
Guineas winner Dara Monarch: poor maiden. *N. Bycroft*

DARAMSAN (IRE)   4 br.g. Doyoun 124 – Daralaka (IRE) (The Minstrel (CAN) 135)   **71 ?**
[2001 12.3m⁴ 8f Jun 30] IR 7,500 3-y-o: second foal: half-brother to useful French 1½m
winner Darghar (by Kahyasi): dam unraced dual bumper winner: fourth in slowly-run
maiden on Flat debut in June: broke down next time: dead. *Denys Smith*

DARANDALA (IRE)   3 b.f. Ashkalani (IRE) 128 – Daralinsha (USA) 116 (Empery   **105**
(USA) 128) [2001 10f* 10.2m⁵ 12m³ 11.9m 12s⁴ Nov 10] rather leggy, lengthy filly:
half-sister to several useful French winners up to 1½m, including Prix de Royallieu
runner-up Daraydala (by Royal Academy): dam, French 1m (at 2 yrs) to 1½m (Prix
Minerve) winner, half-sister to dam of very smart French performer up to 1½m Daryaba:
useful performer: won maiden at Pontefract in July: best effort in listed races after when
2¼ lengths third to Love Everlasting at Newbury in August: should be suited by 1¾m+:
has been equipped with rubber bit: sold 150,000 gns. *Sir Michael Stoute*

DARARA STAR (USA)   2 b.c. (Mar 19) Dariyoun (USA) 115 – Tuviah (USA)   **65**
(Eastern Echo (USA)) [2001 8m 7m 8d Oct 2] small, well-made colt: first foal: dam,
placed several times in USA, half-sister to smart performer up to 9f Duck Row: fair
maiden: should be suited by 1¼m+. *J. Noseda*

DARASIM (IRE)   3 b.g. Kahyasi 130 – Dararita (IRE) (Halo (USA)) [2001 10v³ 13d*   **108**
12g 14f* 13.4d⁴ 14.6d* 12.4v⁵ Sep 23] lengthy, quite good-topped gelding: third foal:
half-brother to 1½m and 13.4f winner Darariyna (by Shirley Heights): dam, French 12.5f
winner, half-sister to several smart performers at 1½m+, out of Prix Vermeille winner
Darara, herself half-sister to Darshaan: useful performer: won maiden at Wexford in May
and handicaps at Gowran in June (final start for J. Oxx) and Doncaster (held Ravenswood
by short head in Tote Exacta Mallard Stakes after poaching advantage under enterprising
ride) in September: well beaten at Dielsdorf final start: will stay 2m: probably acts on any
going: has been blinkered, including for last 2 wins. *M. Johnston*

DARCY DANCER   4 b.g. Be My Chief (USA) 122 – Little White Star (Mill Reef   –
(USA) 141) [2001 –: 15.4v Apr 24] disappointing maiden: tried blinkered.
D. J. S. Cosgrove

DARDANUS   3 ch.g. Komaite (USA) – Dance On A Cloud (USA) 76 (Capote (USA))   **81**
[2001 74: f12g* f12g³ 10.3s 12s* 11.6d 12m² 12g⁴ 12g⁵ 10g 10.1g 12m Sep 26]
good-topped gelding: fairly useful performer: won maiden at Southwell in January and
handicap at Pontefract in May: left E. Dunlop after eighth start: should stay beyond 1½m:
acts on fibresand, soft and good to firm going: tried visored: has carried head awkwardly:
none too consistent. *R. J. White*

DARE   6 b.g. Beveled (USA) – Run Amber Run (Run The Gantlet (USA)) [2001 70d: **70**
f12g* f9.4g 10s* f12f Dec 5] leggy gelding: fair performer: won minor event at Southwell
(had reportedly fractured a hock 5 months earlier) in October and handicap at Nottingham
in November: left P. D. Evans after: stays 1½m: acts on fibresand, heavy and good to firm
ground: usually blinkered/visored: tongue tied final start: has raced freely: tends to carry
head high. *R. Lee*

DARGO   7 b.g. Formidable (USA) 125 – Mountain Memory 109 (High Top 131) [2001   **48**
–: 16g³ Jun 12] lightly raced and poor on Flat nowadays: stays 2m: acts on fibresand and
heavy ground: races up with pace. *D. G. Bridgwater*

DARING DANCER 2 ch.f. (Apr 25) Bold Arrangement 127 – Glenrock Dancer (IRE) (Glenstal (USA) 118) [2001 6f 6m Aug 11] lengthy, angular filly: fourth foal: dam ran 3 times: no sign of ability in claimer/seller. *A. Berry* –

DARING GAMBLE 4 b.f. Barrys Gamble 102 – Rachel Sharp (Daring March 116) [2001 f6s⁵ f5g⁶ f5g Mar 8] first foal: dam ran twice: poor form in sellers at Wolverhampton. *R. A. Fahey* **42**

DARJINGLE 2 b.f. (Mar 4) Darshaan 133 – Delightful Chime (IRE) 79 (Alzao (USA) 117) [2001 7m 7.5m⁶ 7m Aug 11] third foal: dam, Irish 2-y-o 1m winner, sister to Cheveley Park/Moyglare Stud Stakes winner Capricciosa: poor maiden: will probably stay 1¼m. *T. D. Easterby* **45**

DARK BEFORE DAWN (USA) 4 ch.g. Sheikh Albadou 128 – Garza (Kris 135) [2001 f6g 6s 6m⁶ 6m 5s 6g⁴ 8.5g 9.1v 8v³ f7s Dec 18] 800 3-y-o: strong gelding: first foal: dam French 7f (at 2 yrs) and 1m (listed race) winner out of very smart French 7f to 1¼m winner Gabina: modest maiden: stays 1m: acts on heavy going and fibresand: blinkered 4 of last 5 starts: often wears tongue tie: has reared leaving stall. *A. Berry* **53 a43**

DARK DOLORES 3 b.f. Inchinor 119 – Pingin (Corvaro (USA) 124) [2001 –: 9.7m 7m² 6m Aug 30] poor maiden: stays 7f: acts on good to firm ground: has wandered. *C. Weedon* **43**

DARK FAIRY 3 br.f. Tragic Role (USA) – Sharp Fairy (Sharpo 132) [2001 7m⁴ 8g 8.2g⁴ 7m f8.5g⁶ 10s* Sep 24] 500Y: second live foal: half-sister to 7f winner Barnie Rubble (by Pharly): dam lightly-raced half-sister to top-class miler Desert Prince: modest performer: best effort when winning seller at Leicester (joined M. Pipe 21,000 gns) in September: stays 1¼m: acts on soft ground: won on hurdling debut in October. *P. W. D'Arcy* **64**

DARK FINISH (IRE) 3 b.f. Night Shift (USA) – Varnish 85 (Final Straw 127) [2001 60p: 7.6m⁵ 7m⁵ 6.1d Sep 21] 28,000 2-y-o: quite attractive filly: fifth foal: closely related to 4-y-o Queen of The May and half-sister to fairly useful 1996 2-y-o 5f winner Cherry Blossom (by Primo Dominie): dam 2-y-o 7f winner: modest maiden: should prove best at 5f/6f: acts on soft and good to firm going: sold 4,200 gns in December. *W. M. Brisbourne* **55**

DARK FLOWER (IRE) 2 b.f. (Apr 27) Sadler's Wells (USA) 132 – Marino Casino (USA) (Alleged (USA) 138) [2001 8m³ 7d⁴ 8v⁴ Oct 26] 120,000Y: well-made filly: second foal: dam once-raced half-sister to top-class miler Posse: best effort (fairly useful form) when third in maiden at Doncaster: should stay 1¼m: acts on good to firm ground: found little second outing. *B. W. Hills* **82**

DARK SHADOWS 6 b.g. Machiavellian (USA) 123 – Instant Desire (USA) 86 (Northern Dancer) [2001 62: 12.4d 12.3m 14.1g² 13.8s 12g Nov 7] big, good-topped gelding: has a high knee action: fair handicapper: stays 1¾m: acts on good to firm going. *W. Storey* **67**

DARK SOCIETY 3 b.g. Imp Society (USA) – No Candles Tonight 74 (Star Appeal 133) [2001 67: 10g 10g 10m 10.2f Sep 18] rather leggy, unfurnished gelding: fair maiden handicapper: stays 1¼m: acts on good to soft going: visored last 2 starts: has started slowly/hung. *P. W. Harris* **70**

DARK SORCERER 2 b.c. (Apr 13) So Factual (USA) 120 – Pipistrelle 62 (Shareef Dancer (USA) 135) [2001 5m³ 6f² 6m 6m* 6m⁶ 7.2m³ 6g 7s⁵ Oct 11] 5,000F, IR 30,000Y: strong, angular colt: carries condition: has a quick action: fifth foal: half-brother to ungenuine 1m to 11f winner Pip's Brave (by Be My Chief) and 2000 2-y-o 7.5f winner Sister Celestine (by Bishop of Cashel): dam 13f/1¾m winner who stayed 2¼m: fairly useful performer: second in listed race at Epsom: won in maiden at York in July: well below form last 2 starts: likely to stay 1m: acts on firm going: has gone freely to post/wandered under pressure: sold 60,000 gns, sent to USA. *A. P. Jarvis* **93**

DARK STORM 2 gr.g. (Apr 6) Terimon 124 – Norstock 52 (Norwick (USA) 125) [2001 6v p8g Nov 15] third foal: dam 2m winner, also winning jumper: well beaten in maidens. *J. White* –

DARK TROJAN (IRE) 5 b.h. Darshaan 133 – Trojan Miss 104 (Troy 137) [2001 97: 14d³ 20m 16s⁵ Oct 17] quite attractive horse: fairly useful maiden: stays 2m: acts on heavy ground: tends to wander. *P. Hughes, Ireland* **82**

DARK VICTOR (IRE) 5 b.g. Cadeaux Genereux 131 – Dimmer 108 (Kalaglow 132) [2001 62, a77: f8g 8.2s⁴ 8.3d f8g⁶ 9.2g 9.9s* 8d* 10g 8d⁶ 10d⁵ 13.8d² f12g⁶ f9.4g Dec 8] leggy, workmanlike gelding: fair handicapper: won at Beverley in September and Newcastle in October: effective at 1m/1¾m: acts on fibresand, seems best on going softer **73 a66**

than good on turf: sometimes blinkered/visored, latter for recent wins: usually patiently ridden: has his quirks. *D. Shaw*

DARWELL'S FOLLY (USA)   6 ch.g. Blushing John (USA) 120 – Hispanola (FR) – §
(Kris 135) [2001 49d: f9.4s f8g f11g² f12g 11.1g Sep 2] sturdy gelding: poor handicapper **a43** §
nowadays: left M. Johnston before final start: stays 11f: acts on soft going, good to firm
and fibresand: tried blinkered/visored/tongue tied: moody. *P. Monteith*

DARWIN (IRE)   3 b.c. Danehill (USA) 126 – Armorique (IRE) (Top Ville 129) [2001 **93**
99: 8g 7m* 7g⁵ 8m 10m 8m 10.4g 11g Dec 16] smallish, well-made, attractive colt:
unimpressive mover: fairly useful performer: easily landed odds in minor event at
Tipperary in May, but well held otherwise (finished lame once, out of depth several times,
acting as pacemaker in Britain fourth to seventh starts): sold from A. O'Brien in Ireland
9,000 gns before final outing: bred to be suited by further than 1m but tends to race freely:
acts on soft and good to firm ground. *G. Molteni, Italy*

DARWIN TOWER   3 gr.g. Bin Ajwaad (IRE) 119 – Floria Tosca § (Petong 126) [2001 **50**
56: 8s 8s 7.1g³ 7m 7f 7m 7d 6d Oct 12] sturdy gelding: poor mover: modest maiden:
should stay 1m: acts on heavy going: sometimes blinkered/visored: has hung badly left:
none too reliable. *B. W. Murray*

DARYABAD (IRE)   9 b.g. Thatching 131 – Dayanata (Shirley Heights 130) [2001 62, **72**
a69: 7g⁴ 8m² 7m⁶ 8d* 8.5g 7g Oct 6] big, strong gelding: fair handicapper: won at **a–**
Leicester in June: said to have injured eye next time: best at 7f/1m: acts on firm ground,
soft and fibresand/equitrack: usually blinkered: has started slowly/hung/carried head
awkwardly. *N. A. Graham*

DASHARAN (IRE)   8 b.g. Shahrastani (USA) 135 – Delsy (FR) (Abdos 134) [2001 –
17.1m Jun 11] workmanlike gelding: fairly useful handicapper for J. Oxx in Ireland in
1997: well beaten both Flat runs afterwards: dead. *Ian Williams*

DASH FOR GLORY   2 ch.c. (May 1) Bluegrass Prince (IRE) 110 – Rekindled Flame **59**
(IRE) (Kings Lake (USA) 133) [2001 6g 6v Oct 8] sixth foal: half-brother to 5-y-o
Goodenough Mover and 3-y-o Prince Pyramus: dam unraced: modest form in maidens:
should stay 1m. *M. Kettle*

DASH FOR GOLD   2 br.f. (Mar 18) Highest Honor (FR) 124 – Dashing Water 87 **62**
(Dashing Blade 117) [2001 7m 8d⁵ 8s⁵ Oct 25] third foal: half-sister to 1¼m winner Night
Diamond (by Night Shift): dam, 2-y-o 7f winner, half-sister to Nunthorpe winners
Lochsong and Lochangel: modest maiden: seemed not to cope with track at Brighton
final start: should stay 1¼m: sold 5,000 gns. *D. R. C. Elsworth*

DASHING BEAU (USA)   2 b.g. (Apr 14) Beau Genius (CAN) – Full O Cherries –
(USA) (Full Out (USA)) [2001 6s⁵ 6d 6m Sep 1] $11,000Y: leggy, close-coupled gelding:
half-brother to several winners in USA: dam, maiden in USA, half-sister to US Grade 1
1¼m winner Willow Hour: signs of only a little ability in maidens. *T. D. Barron*

DASHING BLUE   8 ch.g. Dashing Blade 117 – Blubella 86 (Balidar 133) [2001 100d: –
5g 5s 5g Sep 15] big, good-bodied gelding: formerly smart performer, very much on
downgrade: blinkered once. *I. A. Balding*

DASH OF MAGIC   3 b.f. Magic Ring (IRE) 115 – Praglia (IRE) 64 (Darshaan 133) **53**
[2001 –p: 7.1d³ 8.2d 7.5m² 10g Jun 16] leggy, quite good-topped filly: modest maiden:
should be suited by 1m+. *J. G. Given*

DASHOSKI (IRE)   4 b.f. Petoski 135 – Dashing March 62 (Daring March 116) [2001 –
8.1g 11.7f 10.2g Oct 1] second foal: dam, maiden who should have stayed beyond 6f,
half-sister to very smart hurdler Ra Nova: well held in maidens. *M. S. Saunders*

DATIN STAR   3 ch.f. Inchinor 119 – Halimah 56 (Be My Guest (USA) 126) [2001 48: **42**
f6g e6g⁵ f8g⁶ f5g³ f6g 5.3d 5.1m f6g⁶ Jun 15] poor maiden: effective at 5f to easy 7f: acts
on firm going and all-weather. *D. J. Coakley*

DAUNTED (IRE)   5 b.g. Priolo (USA) 127 – Dauntess (Formidable (USA) 125) **46**
[2001 –, a73: e10g* f9.4g⁴ e10g³ e12g⁴ e12g⁴ e10g⁴ 11.9s 11.6m³ f11g⁵ 12.6d f11g² **a61**
Dec 17] quite good-topped gelding: modest on all-weather, poor on turf: won claimer at
Lingfield in January: left G. L. Moore and off 5 months before running well final start:
barely stays 1½m: acts on fibresand, equitrack, good to firm and good to soft going:
usually wears blinkers: sometimes slowly away: carries head awkwardly. *R. Wilman*

DAVEYSFIRE   3 b.f. Gildoran 123 – Doubtfire 71 (Jalmood (USA) 126) [2001 –: 6m –
6m 6d Aug 15] good-bodied, workmanlike filly: little form. *A. R. Dicken*

DAVEY'S PANACEA (IRE) 4 ch.f. Paris House 123 – Pampoushka (Pampabird **48** 124) [2001 53: f5g f5g³ f5g⁵ Feb 15] poor maiden: stays 6f: acts on good to firm going and fibresand: blinkered: usually races prominently. *R. D. Wylie*

DAVIDE D'DONATELLO 4 b.c. Robellino (USA) 127 – Thimblerigger 62 (Sharpen **–** Up 127) [2001 –: e10g⁵ 12m 13d Jul 14] disappointing maiden: left J. W. Mullins after reappearance: tried blinkered/visored. *John J. R. Foley, Ireland*

DAVID WYNNE 3 b.c. Dolphin Street (FR) 125 – Statuette 57 (Statoblest 120) [2001 **40** –: e5g f5g⁵ e5g f5g 5m 5m 5m 7m 7.1d f8g f5g Dec 14] strong colt: poor maiden: stays 7f: acts on good to soft going and fibresand: blinkered once. *D. Shaw*

DA VINCI (IRE) 3 b.g. Inzar (USA) 112 – Tuft Hill 92 (Grundy 137) [2001 81: f6g **–** 5g 6s Sep 24] smallish, quite attractive gelding: fairly useful winner at 2 yrs: below form in 2001: best efforts at 5f: acts on soft going, possibly not on firm. *J. A. Osborne*

DAVIS ROCK 7 ch.m. Rock City 120 – Sunny Davis (USA) 71 (Alydar (USA)) [2001 **–** 56, a68: e10g³ f8g⁶ f8g⁶ f8g f8g Apr 27] modest performer: won handicap at Southwell **a64** in January: best form at 7f/1m: acts on any turf going and fibresand/equitrack: blinkered in 2001: none too consistent. *W. R. Muir*

DAWARI (IRE) 3 b.c. In The Wings 128 – Dawala (IRE) (Lashkari 128) [2001 94p: **99** 10s* 12.3f⁴ May 8] close-coupled, attractive colt: useful form: impressive winner of maiden at Windsor in April: favourite, didn't look at ease on sharp track/firmer going though creditable 5¾ lengths fourth to Mr Combustible in Chester Vase next time, soon off bridle: will be suited by further than 1½m: acts on soft going. *Sir Michael Stoute*

DAWN 4 b.f. Owington 123 – Realisatrice (USA) (Raja Baba (USA)) [2001 70: 5f Jun **–** 25] fair maiden at 3 yrs: well held only 4-y-o start. *J. S. Wainwright*

DAWN INVASION (IRE) 2 b.c. (Apr 18) Common Grounds 118 – Princess of **88 p** Zurich (IRE) (Law Society (USA) 130) [2001 7.1g² 8d* Oct 3] IR 210,000Y: sixth foal: half-brother to fairly useful 1999 2-y-o 5f/6f winner Princely Dream (by Night Shift) and a winner up to 1¼m in Italy by Thatching: dam, Irish 7f winner, half-sister to smart 6f/ 7f winner Prince Echo: fairly useful form: confirmed promise when winning maiden at Salisbury by 3 lengths from Araglin, quickening clear on seemingly disadvantaged stand side: likely to stay 1¼m: should make a useful 3-y-o. *Mrs A. J. Perrett*

DAWN'S SHARP SHOT (IRE) 2 b. or br.f. (Mar 2) Son of Sharp Shot (IRE) 105 – **68 p** Dawn Star 94 (High Line 125) [2001 8m⁵ Sep 11] half-sister to several winners, including Dawning Street (up to 9f, by Thatching) and 6-y-o Pairumani Star, both smart: dam 1¼m/ 11f winner: 25/1 and green, promising fifth of 13 to Aglow in maiden at Leicester, keeping on from off pace without being knocked about: will be suited by at least 1¼m: sure to improve. *J. L. Dunlop*

DAWN TRAVELLER (IRE) 4 b.f. Blues Traveller (IRE) 119 – All Alright **–** (Alzao (USA) 117) [2001 –: 8m Jun 20] sparely-made filly: little sign of ability. *H. J. Collingridge*

DA WOLF (IRE) 3 ch.g. Wolfhound (USA) 126 – Lady Joyce (FR) (Galetto (FR) **52** 118) [2001 –: 8s 6f 6m* 7f⁴ 7d 6m⁴ 7g 6m 8.2m Sep 10] strong gelding: modest handi-capper: won at Brighton in June: stays 7f: acts on firm going: usually blinkered in 2001: sold 1,500 gns. *W. R. Muir*

DAY-BOY 5 b.g. Prince Sabo 123 – Lady Day (FR) (Lightning (FR) 129) [2001 76: f8g **–** 8s 7.1m May 4] angular gelding: fair handicapper at best: no form in 2001. *Denys Smith*

DAYGLOW DANCER 3 b.g. Fraam 114 – Fading (Pharly (FR) 130) [2001 96: 8v* **95** 8s⁶ 8m³ 8m⁵ 7m 8f 7g⁵ 7.9d⁶ 8d Nov 3] rather sparely-made gelding: useful performer: won minor event at Doncaster in March: only some creditable efforts after, including when fifth to Free Rider in rated stakes at Newmarket in October: gelded after final start: stays 1m: acts on any going: usually races up with pace. *M. R. Channon*

DAYLILY (IRE) 4 ch.f. Pips Pride 117 – Leaping Water (Sure Blade (USA) 130) **52** [2001 62: 5d 8s f6g² 6m⁴ f7g f6g⁶ 5d f5g Jul 13] big, strong, long-backed filly: modest maiden handicapper: best form at 5f/6f: acts on fibresand and any turf going: has raced freely. *T. D. Easterby*

DAYS OF GRACE 6 gr.m. Wolfhound (USA) 126 – Inshirah (USA) 90 (Caro 133) **72** [2001 79, a75: e7g e5g⁶ f6g³ e6g³ e7g⁵ 6m 5m⁵ 5m⁵ 5s² 5g* f6s³ 5m⁵ 5.1d p7g f6g³ p6g Dec 19] lengthy mare: fair performer: won handicap at Sandown in September: effective at stiff 5f to easy 7f: acts on firm going, soft and fibresand/equitrack: usually races prominently: tough and reliable. *L. Montague Hall*

DAZZLING DAISY   4 b.f. Shareef Dancer (USA) 135 – Mariette 35 (Blushing   –
Scribe (USA) 107) [2001 44: e12s⁴ 10m 11.5g 11.9s 11.9s f8g f11s Dec 21] of little
account. *N. A. Graham*

DAZZLING QUINTET   5 ch.m. Superlative 118 – Miss Display 47 (Touch Paper   **48**
113) [2001 53: f5g f5g³ f5g³ f5g f5g 5.2m 5f² 5m 5f⁵ 5f Jul 25] sturdy mare: poor handicapper nowadays: probably best at 5f: acts on firm going, good to soft and fibresand:
usually visored: front runner: none too reliable. *C. Smith*

DAZZLING RIO (IRE)   2 b.g. (Feb 14) Ashkalani (IRE) 128 – Dazzling Fire (IRE)   **59**
78 (Bluebird (USA) 125) [2001 6m 6g⁴ 6d 6g⁴ 8s f7g⁵ Nov 16] 32,000Y: strong, sturdy
gelding: fifth foal: half-brother to 6f winner Mohawk (by Indian Ridge), later winner in
Scandinavia: dam 1½m winner: modest maiden: best efforts second to fourth starts: had
excuses final one: should stay at least 1m. *P. C. Haslam*

DEAL IN FACTS   2 ch.f. (Jan 2) So Factual (USA) 120 – Timely Raise (USA) (Raise   **61 d**
A Man (USA)) [2001 7m 7m⁶ 5.3m² 6.1s 7g 6g⁴ 5.3s f7g f6g f7g f6g Dec 17] tall, leggy
filly: half-sister to several winners, including 9f/1¼m winner Double Bluff (by Sharrood)
and 5f (at 2 yrs)/6f winner Poker Chip (by Bluebird), both useful: dam, miler in North
America, sister to smart middle-distance stayer Primitive Rising: modest maiden: below
form after third start: left R. Hannon after eighth one: likely to prove best at 5f/6f: acts on
good to firm going. *J. A. Pickering*

DEANO'S BEENO   9 b.g. Far North (CAN) 120 – Sans Dot 92 (Busted 134) [2001   **73**
18v³ Mar 23] angular gelding: only fair form when third in handicap at Doncaster only
Flat start since 1996: stays 2¼m: used to act on firm ground, probably best on good or
softer over hurdles nowadays (top-class front-running hurdler on his day). *M. C. Pipe*

DEAR BRIDIE (IRE)   2 ch.f. (Feb 18) Entrepreneur 123 – Shebasis (USA) (General   **66 p**
Holme (USA) 128) [2001 6m 6v⁴ Oct 26] IR 25,000Y: strong, angular filly: seventh
living foal: half-sister to several winners, including useful 1m/1¼m winner Sheba Spring
(by Brief Truce) and 6f winner Bank House (by Zafonic): dam unraced daughter of half-
sister to Alysheba: better effort in maidens (fair form) when fourth to Oases at Newbury,
keeping on under considerate handling: should stay 1m: will progress. *B. W. Hills*

DEAR DAUGHTER   3 ch.f. Polish Precedent (USA) 131 – Darayna (IRE) (Shernazar   **111**
131) [2001 79p: 8f* 8f² 8g⁵ 9.9g⁵ 10f⁴ Sep 22] lengthy filly: smart performer: won
maiden at Bath in June: ran very well when 1¼ lengths second to Independence in listed
rated stakes at Ascot second start: not discredited in Falmouth Stakes at Newmarket and
Nassau Stakes at Goodwood next 2 outings: should be at least as effective at 1¼m+ as
1m: acts on firm ground: sent to USA. *Sir Michael Stoute*

DEAREST DAISY   2 ch.f. (Apr 12) Forzando 122 – Sylhall (Sharpo 132) [2001 5m   **84**
6m³ 5m* 5m² 6m p6g Nov 28] 20,000Y: second foal: half-sister to 3-y-o Galy Bay: dam
unraced daughter of useful winner up to 1m No Cards: fairly useful performer: won
maiden at Musselburgh in August: likely to prove best at 5f/6f: raced only on good to firm
ground on turf (respectable effort on polytrack). *J. Noseda*

DEBBIE'S HOPE   5 ch.m. Be My Chief (USA) 122 – Appleton Heights (Shirley   **45 §**
Heights 130) [2001 10.9d 9.1d 8g⁴ 8m 8g 9.1v Oct 16] poor maiden nowadays: stays 1m:
acts on firm going: tongue tied last 4 starts: twice very slowly away: has flashed tail:
irresolute. *Mrs A. M. Naughton*

DEBBIES TREASURE (IRE)   2 b.g. (Apr 7) Idris (IRE) 118 – Treasure Ring (IRE)   –
(Treasure Kay 114) [2001 6g 6d f7g f8.5g f8g Nov 16] 3,000F, IR 6,500Y: third foal:
half-brother to a winner in Poland by Port Lucaya: dam ran once: no sign of ability,
including in sellers: left P. D. Evans after third start: visored final one. *Mrs N. Macauley*

DEBBIE'S WARNING   5 b.h. Warning 136 – Lomond Blossom 98 (Lomond (USA)   **84**
128) [2001 97: 7f³ 6d³ 6f 5m 6m 6m⁴ 6d Oct 12] big, useful-looking horse: poor mover:
has reportedly had soft palate operation: fairly useful nowadays: some creditable efforts
in 2001, heavily backed when equal-fourth to Tayif in Silver Cup (Handicap) at Ayr
(would have gone even closer had run started sooner) penultimate start: effective at 6f to
1m: acts on firm and good to soft going: has had tongue tied: has worn crossed noseband:
usually bandaged. *K. A. Ryan*

DEB'S SON   4 b.g. Minster Son 130 – Deb's Ball 70 (Glenstal (USA) 118) [2001 56:   –
14.1m 15.8g Aug 17] leggy, angular gelding: lightly-raced maiden. *D. Moffatt*

DECEITFUL   3 ch.g. Most Welcome 131 – Sure Care 62 (Caerleon (USA) 132) [2001   **91**
54: e10g e6g* f6g⁶ e7g* e6g⁵ f6g³ f6g 6.1f 6m 7.6m⁵ 7f* 5.2d⁴ 7f* 7m⁶ 6.1m 5d 5m
7.2m⁴ 7.1v⁴ 8s 7d 6g⁵ 7d* 7s* f6g p7g⁶ Dec 29] leggy, quite good-topped gelding:

fairly useful performer: much improved, and won handicaps at Lingfield in January and March, claimer at Brighton (final start for A. Reid) and handicaps at Catterick (2), Doncaster and Lingfield (beat Jelba a head) between August/December: best at 6f/7f: acts on any turf going/all-weather: has given trouble at stalls/been early to post: free-going sort: tough. *P. D. Evans*

DECEIVES THE EYE   3 b.g. Dancing Spree (USA) – Lycius Touch 50 (Lycius (USA) 124) [2001 –, a39: f7g f7g6 f8g Feb 16] small gelding: won seller at 2 yrs: no form in 2001: tried blinkered. *A. G. Newcombe*   –

DECEPTOR (USA)   2 b.c. (Apr 19) Machiavellian (USA) 123 – Satin Flower (USA) 115 (Shadeed (USA) 135) [2001 5f* 6m5 Jul 20] small, attractive colt: good walker: fifth living foal: closely related to smart 1998 2-y-o 6f (Middle Park Stakes) winner Lujain (by Seeking The Gold) and half-brother to 3-y-o Lilium: dam, won Jersey Stakes and second in US Grade 1 9f event, half-sister to US Grade 1 1¼m winner Martial Law: fairly useful form: won minor event at Doncaster in June: again favourite, raced freely when fifth to Kulachi in listed race at Newbury: will need to settle to stay beyond 6f. *D. R. Loder*   **89**

DECHTIRE (IRE)   2 b.f. (May 17) Thatching 131 – Derena (FR) (Crystal Palace (FR) 132) [2001 7g Sep 11] IR 15,000Y: fifth foal: sister to useful French 1m winner Dirca, later successful in USA, and half-sister to Irish 1¼m winner Kahrena (by Kahyasi) and a winner in France by Ballad Rock: dam unraced half-sister to very smart French middle-distance performer Deliorman: 25/1, well held in maiden at Lingfield, travelling well long way but running green once shaken up: should do better. *R. Hannon*   **– p**

DECIMA   2 b.f. (Mar 25) Puissance 110 – Kaleidophone 73 (Kalaglow 132) [2001 f5g2 f5g2 5s2 5.3s 5.1f4 6g3 6m* 5.1g3 5m f6g4 6m f5g2 f6g f6g4 f5g2 p6g Nov 28] 1,000 2-y-o: leggy, plain filly: seventh foal: half-sister to a winner abroad by Music Boy: dam, 1m winner, half-sister to useful Italian sprinter Plumbird: fair performer: won maiden at Windsor in June: left P. D. Evans after tenth start: second in Southwell nursery penultimate one: stays easy 6f: acts on fibresand, good to firm and soft going: often races up with pace. *Mrs N. Macauley*   **75**

DECOY   2 b.f. (May 11) Double Eclipse (IRE) 122 – Kilcoy (USA) (Secreto (USA) 128) [2001 10d6 8g5 Oct 19] lengthy, unfurnished filly: half-sister to several winners, including useful 1999 2-y-o 6f/7f winner Sheer Hamas (by Hamas) and 3-y-o Rose of America: dam unraced: signs of ability in maidens: likely to do better as 3-y-o. *M. Johnston*   **– p**

DEEKAZZ (IRE)   2 b.f. (May 23) Definite Article 121 – Lyric Junction (IRE) (Classic Secret (USA) 91) [2001 7f4 7f5 7g 8s Sep 27] IR 4,800Y, resold IR 15,000Y: lengthy, angular filly: third foal: sister to 3-y-o Flying Lyric: dam unraced from family of In Command, Lyric Fantasy and Royal Applause: modest maiden: well held in nursery final start: should stay 1m. *A. Berry*   **54**

DEEP BLUE   4 b.g. Lake Coniston (IRE) 131 – Billie Blue 63 (Ballad Rock 122) [2001 68+: f6s f6s 7g* 7.1s 7d 7g 7g 8.5g 7s 7d Oct 20] well-made gelding: fairly useful handicapper at best: won at Leicester in May: mainly well beaten after: stays 7f: acts on fibresand, soft and good to firm ground: tried visored: gelded after final start. *Dr J. D. Scargill*   **83 d**

DEEP DALE   5 b.g. Pharly (FR) 130 – L'Oraz (Ile de Bourbon (USA) 133) [2001 14g 12.6m 12f5 16.2f 16g Aug 13] robust gelding: third foal: dam lightly-raced daughter of German 1000 Guineas/Oaks winner Oraza: tailed off all starts (tongue tied last 2, hung badly left on penultimate). *Mrs S. Lamyman*   **–**

DEE PEE TEE CEE (IRE)   7 b.g. Tidaro (USA) – Silver Glimpse 108 (Petingo 135) [2001 –: 8m 11.9m 11.9s 8d4 10g Nov 5] tall gelding: has a round action: modest handicapper nowadays: stays 1½m: acts on soft and good to firm going. *M. W. Easterby*   **64**

DEEPER IN DEBT   3 ch.c. Piccolo 121 – Harold's Girl (FR) (Northfields (USA)) [2001 6g 6.1d6 f6g4 8.5s 8d f9.4g f9.4g3 f9.4g6 f8.5s Dec 26] 15,000F, 40,000Y: half-brother to several winners, including useful 7f/1m winner Jafn (by Sharpo): dam 2-y-o 6f winner in France, also successful over jumps: modest maiden: unlikely to stay much beyond 9.4f: acts on soft going, probably on fibresand: tried blinkered/tongue tied. *J. A. Osborne*   **55 a49**

DEEP RAVINE (USA)   3 ch.f. Gulch (USA) – Summertown (USA) 68 (Diesis 133) [2001 –: f12g3 f12g3 f11g f12g* Apr 17] $150,000Y: second foal: dam, ran 3 times (bred to stay beyond 7f), out of half-sister to El Gran Senor and Try My Best: modest performer: trained by A. O'Brien in Ireland only 2-y-o start: won on handicap debut at   **50**

Southwell in April: stays 1½m: raced only on fibresand in Britain: blinkered second start. *J. A. Osborne*

DEEP SPACE (IRE) 6 br.g. Green Desert (USA) 127 – Dream Season (USA) (Mr **106** Prospector (USA)) [2001 111: 6g 6g⁶ 5f³ 6m 7m⁴ 6g Aug 4] good-topped gelding: formerly smart, winner of Wokingham Handicap at Royal Ascot in 1999: only useful in 2001, below form after third to Bishops Court in listed rated stakes at Epsom in June: stayed easy 7f: seemed best on good going or firmer: visored third/fourth starts: occasionally taken early to post/reared stall: was usually held up, and best in strongly-run race: reportedly retired. *E. A. L. Dunlop*

DEFERLANT (FR) 4 ch.g. Bering 136 – Sail Storm (USA) 108 (Topsider (USA)) **80** [2001 16m⁵ Sep 12] first foal: dam, French 2-y-o 1m winner who probably stayed 1½m, out of half-sister to Allez France: fairly useful performer: had several trainers in France: first past post in claimers at 2 yrs at Maisons-Laffitte and at 3 yrs at Saint-Cloud (disqualified after failing dope test on first occasion, claimed from J. Bertran de Balanda for 183,000 francs after second): awarded claimer at Longchamp penultimate 3-y-o start: visored, far from discredited in handicap at Goodwood only 4-y-o outing: raced mainly up to 1½m on good ground or softer (acts on heavy): fairly useful but ungenuine hurdler. *M. C. Pipe*

DEFIANCE 6 b.g. Warning 136 – Princess Athena 119 (Ahonoora 122) [2001 –: 5m **51 §** 5.7g³ 5.1g⁴ 5.1g 5.5m² 6m⁵ 6g 5g Oct 6] tall gelding: modest nowadays: probably best at 5f/6f: best efforts on good/good to firm going: blinkered in 2001: unreliable. *A. P. James*

DEFINING 2 b.g. (Apr 27) Definite Article 121 – Gooseberry Pie 63 (Green Desert **72 p** (USA) 127) [2001 8d⁶ f8g³ Dec 10] 19,000F, 25,000Y: second foal: half-brother to 3-y-o Siena Star: dam, maiden who stayed 1m, half-sister to smart middle-distance stayer Rakaposhi King: better effort in maidens (fair form) when staying-on third at Southwell, still green: likely to prove best at 1¼m+: slowly away on debut: will do better still. *J. R. Fanshawe*

DEFINITE FLASH (IRE) 3 b.f. Definite Article 121 – Superflash (Superlative 118) **53** [2001 8m 8m⁶ 11.5g 11.9s⁶ Oct 3] IR 11,000Y: seventh foal: half-sister to 3 winners abroad: dam unraced: modest maiden: likely to prove better around 1½m than shorter. *G. C. Bravery*

DEFINITE GUEST (IRE) 3 gr.g. Definite Article 121 – Nicea (IRE) 90 (Dominion **82** 123) [2001 58: 8d 7f⁵ 7m³ 8m 7m* 7g 7g⁵ 6d⁵ 7m³ 7m² 7m³ 7d Sep 27] leggy gelding: fairly useful handicapper: won at Lingfield in July and Folkestone in September: seems best around 7f: acts on good to firm going: blinkered (very stiff task) once. *G. G. Margarson*

DEFINITELY SPECIAL (IRE) 3 b.f. Definite Article 121 – Legit (IRE) (Runnett **–** 125) [2001 10g Jul 8] IR 20,000Y: sixth foal: half-sister to 4-y-o Champion Lodge and 5-y-o Charles Spencelayh: dam, Irish maiden, half-sister to useful 1m to 1½m performer Ridgeway: 10/1, slowly away and always behind in Sandown maiden: sold 1,200 gns. *D. R. C. Elsworth*

DEFINITE RETURN (IRE) 3 ch.f. Definite Article 121 – Keen Note 69 (Sharpo **–** 132) [2001 39: 11.7m 7.1f Sep 18] no form in 2001. *B. Palling*

DEGREE OF POWER 3 b.f. Sure Blade (USA) 130 – One Degree 80 (Crooner 119) **–** [2001 –: 8.1g 10s 10s Oct 25] smallish, good-bodied filly: no form: left Miss D. McHale after reappearance. *Mrs L. Richards*

DE HAUTE LUTTE (USA) 5 b.m. Alleged (USA) 138 – Baranciaga (USA) (Bering **79** 136) [2001 16s 17.2f² 16.2f 11s² 16d⁴ 15.5m³ 12s* 12.5v³ Nov 20] lengthy mare: first foal: dam, French 1¼m and 10.5f winner, half-sister to smart French middle-distance colt Magistros: fair handicapper: trained by N. Gaselee first 3 starts only in 2001, second at Bath in May: rejoined former stable, ran well all subsequent starts, winning at Longchamp in October: effective at 1½m, stays 2¼m: acts on any ground: seems best in blinkers. *E. Danel, France*

DEIDAMIA (USA) 3 b.f. Dayjur (USA) 137 – Home Again (USA) (Forty Niner **–** (USA)) [2001 60: 8d 8m 7d Jul 18] unfurnished filly: modest maiden at 2 yrs: no form in 2001: visored final start. *P. W. Harris*

DELAWARE BAY 2 ch.g. (May 19) Karinga Bay 116 – Galacia (IRE) 52 (Gallic **67 d** League 119) [2001 5.1s² 5.1v² 5m f8.5g 8d 10d Nov 2] 2,800Y: leggy, plain gelding: first foal: dam, maiden who stayed 6f, also third over hurdles: fair maiden: ran poorly

after second start: bred to stay 1m: acts on heavy ground: has worn tongue strap.
W. G. M. Turner

DELAWARE TRAIL   2 b.g. (Mar 30) Catrail (USA) 123 – Dilwara (IRE) (Lashkari   –
128) [2001 7v Oct 26] 13,500Y: big, leggy gelding: third foal: half-brother to 3-y-o The
Bystander and 4-y-o Scottish Spice: dam French 10.5f winner: 50/1, burly and green,
showed nothing in Doncaster maiden. *J. S. Wainwright*

DELEGATE   8 ch.g. Polish Precedent (USA) 131 – Dangora (USA) 98 (Sovereign   **83**
Dancer (USA)) [2001 97: 6g 5m 6g 6m⁴ 6d⁴ 6m⁵ 5m⁴ 5g³ 5g⁶ 5g 6g 6g⁵ 5m* 5g 5d² 5m
6g 5v³ 5g* Nov 5] lengthy gelding: poor mover: fairly useful performer: won handicap at
Newmarket in August and minor event at Redcar in November: has form at 7f, probably
best at 5f nowadays: acts on any turf going and equitrack: sometimes slowly away/hangs:
usually held up. *N. A. Callaghan*

DELGADO   2 b.g. (Feb 3) Alhaarth (IRE) 126 – Nur (USA) 74 (Diesis 133) [2001   **83**
5.2d³ 5s² 6m³ 5m 5f⁴ 5g* 5g³ 5m 6g a8g Dec 16] 20,000F, 26,000Y: small, strong
gelding: fluent mover: half-brother to several winners, including temperamental 1997
2-y-o 5f winner who stayed 1m Kawafil (by Warning) and 1999 2-y-o 6f winner
Kamareyah (by Hamas), both fairly useful: dam, 2-y-o 5f/6f winner, sister to useful
sprinter Ra'a: fairly useful performer: gelded prior to winning minor event at Folkestone
in August: sold from B. Meehan 9,500 gns before final start: should stay 6f: acts on good
to firm and soft ground: ran poorly in blinkers/tongue strap. *J. H. Brown, Spain*

DELIUS (USA)   4 b. or br.c. A P Indy (USA) 131 – Hot Novel (USA) (Mari's Book   **112**
(USA)) [2001 11.6g⁴ 10m³ 12g³ 11.6m* 12g³ 10.9m³ Sep 22] big, rangy colt: smart
performer, lightly raced (missed 2000 season): won minor event at Windsor in August by
1½ lengths from Thari despite ducking right briefly: mostly creditable efforts otherwise,
notably when third in listed race at Newbury (beaten 4 lengths by Sakhee) and September
Stakes at Kempton (sweating and edgy, beaten 3½ lengths by Mutamam) on second/fifth
starts: stays 1½m: acts on good to firm going, won on soft only 2-y-o start: has shown
some temperament in preliminaries: no battler and a tricky ride: sold only 22,000 gns. *Sir
Michael Stoute*

DELLA FRANCESCA (USA)   2 b.c. (Mar 28) Danzig (USA) – La Affirmed (USA)   **110 p**
(Affirmed (USA)) [2001 6g³ 6g* 7g² Oct 5] strong, rangy colt: has scope: half-brother to
several winners, including US Grade 3 winners up to 9f Country Cat and Caress and
smart Irish 6f (including at 2 yrs)/7f winner Bernstein (all by Storm Cat): dam, US 1m
winner, closely related to Breeders' Cup Juvenile Fillies winner Outstandingly: smart
form: confirmed promise when landing odds in maiden at Leopardstown in September
by 2½ lengths from Fashion Guide: heavily-backed favourite, head second to Where
Or When in Somerville Tattersall Stakes at Newmarket, staying on strongly having
been soon off bridle: will stay 1m: capable of better still, and sure to win more races.
A. P. O'Brien, Ireland

DEL MAR SUNSET   2 b.g. (Mar 27) Unfuwain (USA) 131 – City of Angels (Wood-   **65**
man (USA) 126) [2001 8s p8g³ Nov 15] fourth foal: brother to 5-y-o Angels Venture and
half-brother to 4-y-o Charmer Venture: dam unraced close relative of useful middle-
distance performer Widyan: fair form in maidens at Yarmouth and Lingfield, in latter
around 5 lengths third of 11 to Azillion: subsequently gelded: will be suited by 1¼m+.
S. P. C. Woods

DELMO   6 ch.g. Democratic (USA) 101 – Charlotte Piaf (Morston (FR) 125) [2001   –
10m Aug 18] no form. *J. White*

DELPHYLLIA   3 b.f. Mind Games 121 – Euphyllia 70 (Superpower 113) [2001 43:   – §
5.3d 5.1m 6f 5f⁶ 5f 7g 10m Aug 29] temperamental maiden: blinkered/visored last 6
starts. *G. G. Margarson*

DELTA GEORGIA   5 ch.m. Tina's Pet 121 – Bacolet (Dominion 123) [2001 –: e10g⁶   –
Mar 19] lengthy, sparely-made mare: lightly-raced maiden. *A. Bailey*

DEMI BEAU   3 b.g. Dr Devious (IRE) 127 – Charming Life (NZ) (Sir Tristram 115)   **81**
[2001 10.4g⁴ 10m³ 12f³ 12g* Aug 15] tall, close-coupled gelding: fifth foal: half-brother
to several winners, notably very smart winners up to 1½m Kingfisher Mill (by Riverman)
and 4-y-o Wellbeing: dam, Australian 7f winner, sister to Zabeel and half-sister to Baryshnikov, both Australian Group 1 winners: fairly useful form: won maiden at Beverley
final start by 3½ lengths from Missouri (subsequently gelded): reportedly lost a shoe
penultimate outing: stays 1½m: has worn crossed noseband. *W. Jarvis*

DEMO BOYS (IRE)   5 b.g. Be My Guest (USA) 126 – Karine (Habitat 134) [2001   –
59: f12s Jan 9] modest performer at best: reportedly lame only 5-y-o start. *C. N. Allen*

DEMOCRACY (IRE)   5 ch.g. Common Grounds 118 – Inonder 31 (Belfort (FR) 89)   **57**
[2001 62d: 7d* 8f² 9m* 8m 9f⁵ 10.1m⁴ 9.9m⁶ 9.7m f8g⁴ f9.4g² p10g⁶ f9.4s³ Dec 27]
modest handicapper: won in large fields at Brighton (apprentice) in May and Goodwood
(amateurs) in June: stays easy 1¼m: acts on firm going, soft and fibresand: often visored/
blinkered earlier in career: held up. *P. G. Murphy*

DEMONSTRATE (USA)   3 ch.c. Storm Bird (CAN) 134 – Substance (USA) (Diesis   –
133) [2001 7m May 31] third foal: closely related to fairly useful 9f/1¼m (in Ireland)
winner Moratorium (by El Gran Senor): dam unraced half-sister to Ribblesdale Stakes
winner Ballinderry (dam of Sanglamore): evens favourite, gave impression something
amiss when tailed-off last in maiden at Goodwood. *J. H. M. Gosden*

DEMOPHILOS   3 b.c. Dr Devious (IRE) 127 – Graecia Magna (USA) 109 (Priv-   **119**
ate Account (USA)) [2001 85p: 11m 10m³ 10f 10g³ 12m² 11.9g³ 14.6g² Sep 15]
Following her breakthrough season as a trainer in 2000, when she had four
pattern wins (two of them Group 1) from Indian Lodge and top handicaps fell to
Bangalore, Give The Slip and Tillerman, Amanda Perrett went close to winning a
classic in 2001. Comfortably beaten by five lengths was, perhaps, not going close,
but the Perrett-trained Demophilos still finished in front of all except Milan
in a ten-runner field for the St Leger.

Demophilos went through his three-year-old season without a win, but
second in the St Leger and placings in lesser pattern events on his two previous
outings represented a massive triumph for a horse whose earlier inclinations on the
racecourse had sometimes seemed diametrically opposed to those of his riders and
tutors. The first phase of his career had seen one race offering a step forwards and
the next being two steps back. Winning a Newmarket maiden on his only start as a
two-year-old was promising, last of eleven in the Predominate Stakes at Goodwood
was not. That reappearance effort preceded two more outings in listed races, in
which a strong-finishing third of seven behind Potemkin at Newmarket suggested a
brighter future, but ninth of eleven at Ascot failed to realise. The most obvious
outward sign of what was amiss was a headstrong display at Goodwood. The
application of a net muzzle two starts later at Ascot, suggested that connections
were concerned about the horse's tractability. On his next two starts, Demophilos
was fitted with a crossed noseband and taken early to post, but on his two starts
after that, those procedures were dispensed with.

Unmuzzled, Demophilos showed smart form on all of his four starts after
Ascot. Third to Alphaeus and Askham in a £26,000 handicap at the Newmarket
July meeting, in which he carried top weight and raced off a BHB mark of 104, was
followed by praiseworthy efforts stepped up to a mile and a half when he came
second of eleven, beaten a neck, to Alexius in the Gordon Stakes at Goodwood,
followed by third of nine, beaten a length and three quarters, to Milan in the Great
Voltigeur at York. On his first start of the season, Demophilos seemed to have
forlorn hopes of ever staying an extended mile and three quarters, and he was not
initially given a St Leger entry. He was supplemented after the Voltigeur, which
also provided a blueprint for how he would be ridden in the St Leger, racing close
to the Ballydoyle pacemaker Saddler's Creek, who lasted for about a mile on both
occasions. Demophilos' turn up front was much more eye-catching at Doncaster,
Richard Quinn sending him for home and Demophilos passing the three-furlong
pole with a lead of about three lengths, with Milan still at the back of the leading
group in seventh. Demophilos had seen off his initial challengers, had made first
run on the rest and he wasn't flagging. Classic glory beckoned, but between two out
and one out the outlook changed. Demophilos maintained his advantage over his
other pursuers all the way to the line, but had no answer to Milan.

Demophilos stays an extended mile and three quarters and he acts on good
to firm and good to soft ground, having run poorly (at Ascot) on his only outing on
firm. He is a good-topped colt, a description which crops up regularly with the
offspring of his dam Graecia Magna. Big and strong are the other words most
commonly used, and Graecia Magna was herself a big, rangy, attractive filly when

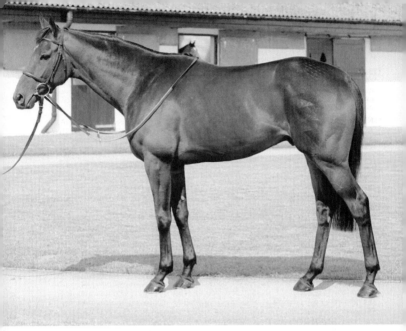

Mr Athos Christodoulou's "Demophilos"

		Ahonoora	Lorenzaccio
	Dr Devious (IRE)	(ch 1975)	Helen Nichols
	(ch 1989)	Rose of Jericho	Alleged
Demophilos		(b 1984)	Rose Red
(b.c. 1998)		Private Account	Damascus
	Graecia Magna (USA)	(b 1976)	Numbered Account
	(b 1982)	Dancing Peach	Nijinsky
		(b 1977)	Fleet Peach

she was in action as a three-year-old in 1985. Owned, like Demophilos, by Mr Christodoulou and trained by Mrs Perrett's father Guy Harwood, Graecia Magna was a useful two-year-old seven-furlong winner and won the Lancashire Oaks after coming second in the Ribblesdale. She cost 50,000 dollars as a yearling and is the best of three winners out of the unraced Dancing Peach, a daughter of the very smart 1973 American two-year-old Fleet Peach. Graecia Magna has passed on plenty of her ability as well as her looks. It is a close-run thing, in fact, as to whether Demophilos is the best of her offspring, as a high standard was set by her third foal, Thourios (by Green Desert). Given his chance in the 1992 Two Thousand Guineas and the Derby, in which he finished seventh of sixteen and tenth of eighteen respectively, Thourios won four races from seven furlongs to just short of a mile, one of them a listed event. He was also placed in four pattern events, notably when two and a half lengths third in the Dewhurst and when beaten a short head in the Prix de Meautry and a head in the Diomed Stakes. The first of Graecia Magna's seven winners was the useful Akamatis (by Kris), who is dam of the smart Irish six- and seven-furlong performer Theano. The latest is the 2001 two-year-old Bragadino (by Zilzal), who, trained by Sir Michael Stoute, won a Sandown maiden and was second in the Vintage Stakes at Goodwood. The winner of the Dewhurst and Derby which Thourios contested was Dr Devious, sire of Demophilos, who is from his first European crop. Others include the useful middle-distance performers Dr Greenfield and Shamdara, while Doc Holiday and Long Goodbye are useful two-year-olds from his second crop. Four crops in Japan produced Group 3 winners London Bridge and Takeichi Kento and a Group 1-placed performer in Olive Crown. *Mrs A. J. Perrett*

DEMOSTHENES (IRE) 2 b.g. (Mar 16) Lycius (USA) 124 – Fantasy Girl (IRE) 55 **66** (Marju (IRE) 127) [2001 6m 6.1f⁶ 6m⁶ Jul 13] first foal: dam, maiden who stayed 1½m, half-sister to useful performer up to 2¼m Height of Fantasy: easily best effort in maidens (fair form) when sixth at Nottingham: folded tamely next time: should stay at least 1m. *J. L. Dunlop*

DENARIUS SECUNDUS 4 ch.g. Barathea (IRE) 127 – Penny Drops 111 (Sharpo **–** 132) [2001 55?: 10g 11.6g 16.2m Jun 18] angular gelding: modest maiden for M. Tregoning at 3 yrs: well held in 2001: tried blinkered. *E. A. Wheeler*

DENBRAE (IRE) 9 b.g. Sure Blade (USA) 130 – Fencing (Viking (USA)) [2001 –: **55** f8.5s² f7g² f8.5g² f8g 7m f8g 6s⁵ Sep 30] lengthy gelding: modest handicapper: stays 8.5f: acts on firm ground, good to soft and fibresand/equitrack: often soon off bridle. *Mrs Lydia Pearce*

DENISE BEST (IRE) 3 ch.f. Goldmark (USA) 113 – Titchwell Lass 57 (Lead On **–** Time (USA) 123) [2001 ?: 8g 10.2m⁶ 10.3m⁵ 7m 8m⁵ 8m 8.3g 9m 8v⁵ 8v 8.2s Nov 5] little form at 3 yrs. *A. Berry*

DENISE MARGARET (IRE) 3 b.f. Flying Spur (AUS) – Rachel Pringle (IRE) **90** (Doulab (USA) 115) [2001 83: 8.3g² 10f* 12f 10m* 10.4m⁶ 9m⁶ 10.1m 10g Oct 5] IR 7,000F, IR 10,500Y: tall, workmanlike filly: sixth foal: half-sister to 2 winners, notably smart Irish 5f (at 2 yrs) to 7f winner Cobourg Lodge (by Unblest): dam third at 5f at 2 yrs in Ireland: fairly useful performer: trained by T. Regan in Ireland at 2 yrs: won maiden at Brighton in May and handicap at Sandown in July: stays 10.4f: acts on firm going: usually races up with pace. *J. Noseda*

DENMARK (IRE) 2 b.c. (Apr 8) Danehill (USA) 126 – Shamarra (FR) (Zayyani **81 p** 119) [2001 6v* f7g⁵ Nov 26] IR 100,000Y: tall, good sort: has scope: second foal: dam unraced half-sister to smart middle-distance performer Shantaroun: green, won 5-runner maiden at Newcastle in October by neck from Olivia Rose, travelling comfortably and forging ahead last 100 yds: quickly beaten once headed at Southwell next time: should stay at least 1m: likely to do better. *Sir Mark Prescott*

DENNIS BERGKAMP (IRE) 4 b.g. Night Shift (USA) – Indian Express 61 **–** (Indian Ridge 123) [2001 –: f5g f7g 12.3s 8m 10.3m⁵ 10f 6.1m 8.1d⁵ 8.1m 7g⁶ 8d 6.1d Sep 26] sturdy gelding: of little account nowadays. *W. Clay*

DENNIS EL MENACE 3 b.g. College Chapel 122 – Spanish Craft (IRE) 50 (Jareer **85** (USA) 115) [2001 78: 7d 8.1v³ 7.1g 8m 8m² 8.1f² 9m² 8.1m⁶ 7.6f² 8m³ 8g⁶ 8g² 9.2g* 8f² 8s 10v Nov 8] small, stocky gelding: fluent mover: fairly useful performer: won minor event at Hamilton in September: effective at 7.6f to 9f: seems best on good going or firmer on turf, some promise on fibresand: usually blinkered/visored nowadays: races up with pace. *W. R. Muir*

DENNIS OUR MENACE 3 b.g. Piccolo 121 – Free On Board 73 (Free State 125) **72** [2001 77: f9.4s³ e10g⁴ 10d 9s⁵ 9m 9s⁴ 8m² 8m² 8.2m 8g 8g Sep 28] sturdy gelding: fair maiden handicapper: probably stays 1¼m: acts on soft and good to firm going: has edged right. *S. Dow*

DENNIS'S BISMARCK 2 b.f. (Mar 24) Pyramus (USA) 78 – Lady Antoinette **–** (Pharly (FR) 130) [2001 6g⁵ 7m Sep 4] 3,000Y: seventh reported foal: dam unraced from family of Royal Lodge winner Reach and smart performer up to 1½m Papering: forced wide when well held in maidens at Brighton. *S. Dow*

DENON (USA) 3 b.c. Pleasant Colony (USA) – Aviance 112 (Northfields (USA)) **118** [2001 105p: 8v* 8m³ 9m³ 10d⁴ 9d* Nov 25] half-brother to several winners, including very smart miler Chimes of Freedom (by Private Account), smart performer up to 1½m Binkhaldoun (by Roberto) and to dam of top-class miler Spinning World: dam 6f/7f winner: smart performer: successful in Prix de Fontainebleau at Longchamp in April by 1½ lengths from Tarzan Cry: creditable efforts next 3 starts, 1¾ lengths fourth (promoted to third) behind subsequently disqualified Noverre in Poule d'Essai des Poulains on same course, very close third to Olden Times in Prix Jean Prat at Chantilly and fourth to Masterful in Prix Guillaume d'Ornano at Deauville (set more to do than principals): left J. Pease in France: won Hollywood Derby in November by a length from Sligo Bay: will prove fully effective at 1¼m: acts on heavy and good to firm going. *R. J. Frankel, USA*

DENSIM BLUE (IRE) 3 b.c. Lake Coniston (IRE) 131 – Surprise Visitor (IRE) (Be **69** My Guest (USA) 126) [2001 74: 7s 6g 6d⁶ 7f* 7m⁴ 7d 7m 7m⁵ 7d⁶ 7.6f⁶ 6f 6g f7g 7g⁵ 6s f7g Oct 23] smallish, good-topped colt: fair performer: won minor event at Lingfield in June: stays easy 7f: acts on firm and good to soft going: usually claimer ridden: races prominently: sold 1,400 gns. *N. E. Berry*

DEN'S-JOY 5 b.m. Archway (IRE) 115 – Bonvin (Taufan (USA) 119) [2001 71: 8.3g **85** 8.3d 9m⁴ 8m 9m 10m³ 8.3g* 8.3m* 8.3m* 8m* 9m 8s⁶ 8s Sep 30] close-coupled mare: fairly useful handicapper: won at Windsor (3) and Thirsk in August/September: best at 1m/9f: acts on good to firm and good to soft going, probably on soft (some promise on fibresand): visored fifth start: sometimes slowly away: usually held up: tough. *Miss D. A. McHale*

DEREK'S PRIDE (IRE) 3 b.f. General Monash (USA) 107 – Likeness 101 (Young **–** Generation 129) [2001 –: 8v 7s 6m 8f 9.9m 5g 6d Oct 9] little form: tried blinkered. *J. Parkes*

DERE LYN 3 b.g. Awesome 73 – Our Resolution (Caerleon (USA) 132) [2001 6.9v³ **61 ?** f9.4g 7f⁶ 9m 7d Jun 17] leggy, angular gelding: half-brother to 2 winners in Germany, including useful 6.5f to 7.5f winner See You Soon (by Distant Relative): dam no sign of ability: seemingly modest form on first and third starts. *D. Burchell*

DERICOU (IRE) 3 b.g. Sri Pekan (USA) 117 – Cartagena Lady (IRE) (Prince Rupert **54** (FR) 121) [2001 8g 7.5m⁵ 7.5f⁶ 10m 8g Oct 1] IR 24,000F, IR 60,000Y: leggy, quite good-topped gelding: fourth foal: half-brother to 4-y-o Buying A Dream: dam unraced: modest maiden: stays 1m: visored final start: sold 1,500 gns. *J. Noseda*

DERRYQUIN 6 b.g. Lion Cavern (USA) 117 – Top Berry 87 (High Top 131) [2001 **74** 78: 8g 7g 8m 7.6m⁶ 8g 6m⁶ 8m⁵ Aug 12] good-bodied gelding: fair performer: seems best around 1m: acts on firm and good to soft going: blinkered/visored nowadays: often sweating/edgy: races up with pace. *P. L. Gilligan*

DERWENT (USA) 2 b.c. (Mar 17) Distant View (USA) 126 – Nothing Sweeter **90 p** (USA) (Darby Creek Road (USA)) [2001 8d 8d³ Oct 19] $105,000Y: rangy, unfurnished colt: closely related to a winner in Japan by Kingmambo and half-brother to several winners, including useful Italian sprinter Secret Thing (by Secreto), also 7f winner in Britain: dam won up to 1¼m in USA, including minor stakes: better effort in maidens (fairly useful form) when 1¾ lengths third of 20 to Rawyaan at Newmarket, still green: not sure to stay much beyond 1m: joined J. Bethell: should progress and win a race or 2. *L. M. Cumani*

DESARU (USA) 5 br.g. Chief's Crown (USA) – Team Colors (USA) (Mr Prospector **70** (USA)) [2001 95?: 8v 7d 6m 8m 6d 10f⁵ 10.5m 9.2d 9.9m² 8m 12m⁴ 12.3m⁶ Sep 1] angular gelding: has a quick action: formerly useful, fair nowadays: probably stays 1½m: acts on firm going, probably on soft: visored once: has found little: none too consistent. *D. Nicholls*

DESERT AIR (JPN) 2 ch.c. (Apr 3) Desert King (IRE) 129 – Greek Air (IRE) 107 **71** (Ela-Mana-Mou 132) [2001 7g 7g² 7m⁴ Aug 27] 800,000 francs Y: close-coupled colt: has scope: third living foal: dam, French 1m listed winner, sister to very smart French performer up to 1¼m Grecian Urn (dam of smart performer up to 13f Dark Shell): fair maiden: second at Leicester: should stay 1¼m. *P. F. I. Cole*

DESERT ALCHEMY (IRE) 2 b.f. (Jan 29) Green Desert (USA) 127 – Waffle On **80 p** 89 (Chief Singer 131) [2001 7d⁴ Oct 15] 60,000Y: third foal: half-sister to useful French 9.5f winner La Frou Frou (by Night Shift), later successful in USA: dam, 2-y-o 6f winner, out of half-sister to high-class sprinter College Chapel: 16/1, 3 lengths fourth of 20 to Opening Ceremony in maiden at Leicester: will probably stay 1m: should improve. *Mrs A. J. Perrett*

DESERT CHARM 4 b.f. Desert Style (IRE) 121 – Autumn Fall (USA) (Sanglamore **–** (USA) 126) [2001 –: f12g Feb 27] leggy, unfurnished filly: no sign of ability: tried blinkered. *H. J. Manners*

DESERT CITY 2 b.g. (Mar 30) Darnay 117 – Oasis (Valiyar 129) [2001 5.2g³ 6m⁴ **73** 5.3m⁵ 7d⁴ 7g³ 8d³ Sep 27] 8,500Y: seventh foal: half-brother to 3 winners, including fairly useful 1999 2-y-o 6f/7f winner Water Hunter (by Mukaddamah) and 8-y-o White Settler: dam, winning hurdler, half-sister to smart 1991 2-y-o sprinter Magic Ring: fair maiden: good efforts in nurseries last 2 starts: will stay 1¼m: best efforts on good/good to soft ground. *R. Hannon*

DESERT DEER   3 ch.c. Cadeaux Genereux 131 – Tuxford Hideaway 102 (Cawston's   **106 p**
Clown 113) [2001 8v² 9.2m* 8m* 8.1g* Jul 8] 85,000Y: half-brother to several winners, notably smart 6f/7f performer Branston Abby (by Risk Me): dam sprinter: progressive form: won maiden at Hamilton and handicaps at Pontefract and Sandown (made all impressively by 3 lengths from Thihn) between May and July: should stay 1¼m: acts on good to firm ground: looked a smart performer in the making. *M. Johnston*

DESERT FIGHTER   10 b.g. Green Desert (USA) 127 – Jungle Rose 90 (Shirley   **48 +**
Heights 130) [2001 65: 12.4m⁵ 12.4g* 12.4d⁵ Aug 8] good-topped gelding: only poor form in 2001: won claimer at Newcastle in July: stays 1½m: acts on firm and soft ground: probably best held up. *Mrs M. Reveley*

DESERT FURY   4 b.g. Warning 136 – Number One Spot 71 (Reference Point 139)   **90**
[2001 85: 10g 8g² 8.1m² 7m³ 7m⁶ 7s* 8m⁵ 7.2m² 8g 8d Oct 19] small gelding: fairly useful performer: won minor event at Ayr in July: effective at 7f/1m: acts on soft and good to firm going. *B. Hanbury*

DESERT ISLAND DISC   4 b.f. Turtle Island (IRE) 123 – Distant Music (Darshaan   **45**
133) [2001 70, a–: 9.9d 8m 8m 8m 9.9d 8s 7d p12g p12g⁶ p10g p10g³ Dec 29] unfurnished filly: poor nowadays: probably stays easy 1½m: acts on heavy ground and polytrack. *J. J. Bridger*

DESERT KNIGHT   5 b.h. Green Desert (USA) 127 – Green Leaf (USA) 97 (Alydar   **–**
(USA)) [2001 104: 8s⁵ 6.1v⁶ 7m May 12] tall, good sort: useful performer at best: no form in 2001. *J. Noseda*

DESERT MUSIC   5 b.m. Ardkinglass 114 – Musical Princess 66 (Cavo Doro 124)   **41**
[2001 34: 12g⁵ 12m 16m⁵ 16f 12s Oct 20] small, sturdy mare: poor maiden handicapper: stays 2m: acts on good to firm going: none too consistent. *J. R. Weymes*

DESERT ROYAL (IRE)   2 ch.c. (Mar 8) Ali-Royal (IRE) 127 – Hajat 64 (Mujtahid   **72**
(USA) 118) [2001 5s⁵ 6f² 5f⁶ 6m 5m⁶ 7g³ 7m* 8d⁴ 10v⁶ 7d⁵ Oct 18] 15,000Y: leggy, close-coupled colt: first foal: dam, 5f winner, out of sister to sprinter Ra'a: fair performer: won claimer at Salisbury in August: stays 1m: acts on any going: consistent: sold 10,000 gns. *R. Hannon*

DESERT SPA (USA)   6 b.g. Sheikh Albadou 128 – Healing Waters (USA) (Temper-   **–**
ence Hill (USA)) [2001 –, a73: f12g* f12g f12s⁴ Dec 15] workmanlike gelding: has a   **a70**
round action: fair performer on all-weather: won claimer at Southwell in June: best at 1¼m/1½m: acts on fibresand: blinkered twice at 3 yrs. *P. J. Makin*

DESERT VALENTINE   6 b.g. Midyan (USA) 124 – Mo Ceri 63 (Kampala 120)   **61**
[2001 60: 10v 10.2f 12m 12.6d² 12.1m⁶ 12g⁵ 12g⁶ Sep 28] tall, lengthy gelding: has high knee action: modest handicapper: probably best at 1¼m/1½m: acts on heavy and good to firm going: has found little: tends to race freely. *L. G. Cottrell*

DESERT WARNING   2 b.c. (Mar 23) Mark of Esteem (IRE) 137 – Warning Belle   **98**
(Warning 136) [2001 7m* 7g⁴ 7d³ Oct 2] 300,000Y: close-coupled colt: first foal: dam unraced half-sister to high-class 1¼m performer Stagecraft from excellent family of Opera House and Kayf Tara: useful form: won maiden at Epsom in August: very good third (beaten under a length) to Sir George Turner in valuable sales race at Newmarket, leading until final 1f: will stay 1m. *D. R. Loder*

DESILU   4 b.f. Skyliner 117 – Munequita (Marching On 101) [2001 f7g Apr 10] lightly   **–**
raced and little form (tried tongue tied). *G. A. Swinbank*

DESIRE ME   3 b.f. Silca Blanka (IRE) 104 – Dazzle Me (Kalaglow 132) [2001 45: f7g   **39**
e7g⁶ 10s 8.2s 8m 7f 7f⁵ 7g 7m³ 10g f7g Oct 20] poor maiden: stays 7f: acts on firm going. *A. D. Smith*

DESRAYA (IRE)   4 b.g. Desert Style (IRE) 121 – Madaraya (USA) (Shahrastani   **80 d**
(USA) 135) [2001 84p: 5g 6m⁵ 6m⁶ 5m 6f 6m⁶ 6d 6m⁵ 7g 7m Sep 2] strong, lengthy gelding: fairly useful handicapper, on downgrade in 2001: best at 6f: yet to race on heavy ground, acts on any other: often blinkered/visored: has drifted left. *K. A. Ryan*

DESTINATION 4 ch.g. Deploy 131 – Veuve (Tirol 127) [2001 92, a77: 16v 16s 14.1g 13.3m f14g* p13g f16g Nov 19] tall, lengthy, angular gelding: fair performer on all-weather: won amateur handicap at Southwell in October despite tending to hang: left C. Cyzer afterwards: acts on fibresand/equitrack: tried visored: tends to carry head high. *B. A. Pearce* — a66

DESTINY BOUND 2 ch.c. (Apr 30) Bluegrass Prince (IRE) 110 – Eastbury Rose (Beveled (USA)) [2001 7s 6v p5g p7g Dec 12] sparely-made colt: first foal: dam once-raced daughter of Fred Darling winner Shapina: poor maiden. *E. A. Wheeler* —

DESTRUCTIVE (USA) 3 b. or br.c. Dehere (USA) 121 – Respectability (USA) (His Majesty (USA)) [2001 7.1m⁵ 8m 10m 8m⁶ 14.1m⁴ 14m² 14.1s 16v Oct 17] $20,000F, 40,000Y: rangy colt: has scope: third foal: half-brother to 5.5f to 8.5f winner in USA by Dixie Brass: dam, 7f/8.5f winner in USA, out of Prix Marcel Boussac winner Play It Safe: disappointing maiden: stays 1¾m: acts on good to firm going: sold 5,500 gns. *W. J. Haggas* — 61 d

DETACHING (IRE) 3 b.f. Thatching 131 – David's Star (Welsh Saint 126) [2001 45: f8g 9m Jun 6] no form at 3 yrs. *I. A. Balding* —

DETACHMENT (USA) 8 b.g. Night Shift (USA) – Mumble Peg (General Assembly (USA)) [2001 7s 12m⁶ Sep 24] disappointing maiden: tried blinkered/visored. *Miss Z. C. Davison* —

DETECTIVE 5 ch.g. Wolfhound (USA) 126 – Ivoronica 89 (Targowice (USA) 130) [2001 –: f6s⁴ e6g⁵ 6f May 28] strong gelding: poor maiden: best at 6f/7f: acts on firm going and fibresand/equitrack: blinkered last 4 starts. *Dr J. D. Scargill* — 47

DETENTION 2 b.c. (Mar 5) Reprimand 122 – June Fayre (Sagaro 133) [2001 6v 6s³ 6v⁴ Nov 8] 5,600Y: closely related to 1987 2-y-o 5f winner Very Special Lady (by Mummy's Game) and half-brother to several winners, including fairly useful 6f winner (including at 2 yrs) Feast of Romance (by Pursuit of Love): dam ran twice: fair form in maidens: in frame at Pontefract and Windsor: should prove best at 5f/6f. *W. J. Musson* — 70

DE TRAMUNTANA 4 b.f. Alzao (USA) 117 – Glamour Game 80 (Nashwan (USA) 135) [2001 79: 11.7d 14.4g Sep 8] workmanlike filly: temperamental maiden nowadays: virtually refused to race final start. *P. R. Hedger* — §

DEVISE (IRE) 2 b.g. (Jan 25) Hamas (IRE) 125§ – Soreze (IRE) 102 (Gallic League 119) [2001 5.2d⁴ 5g* 5m Jun 21] IR 34,000Y: smallish, close-coupled gelding: second foal: half-brother to smart 6f winner (including at 2 yrs) Strahan (by Catrail): dam Irish 5f winner: fairly useful form: won maiden at Warwick in May: ninth of 10 in Norfolk Stakes at Royal Ascot (subsequently gelded): may well prove best at 5f. *M. S. Saunders* — 80

DEVOLUTION (IRE) 3 b.g. Distinctly North (USA) 115 – Election Special 78 (Chief Singer 131) [2001 5m⁵ 6g² f8g³ 7m 7m 8g p8g* p8g* Dec 4] 13,000Y: third foal: half-brother to 5-y-o First Ballot and 4-y-o La Speziana: dam, 2-y-o 6f winner who probably stayed 1¼m, half-sister to dam of smart performers Grey Shot (stayer) and Night Shot (sprinter): fairly useful handicapper: much improved to win at Lingfield in November and December: stays 1m: acts on polytrack, probably on good to firm going: has been slowly away: refused to race fourth start. *J. M. P. Eustace* — 88

DEVON DREAM (IRE) 5 b.g. Paris House 123 – Share The Vision (Vision (USA)) [2001 6f 5g 8f 7m³ 7.1m³ 7.1g Sep 13] leggy gelding: poor nowadays: left M. Weeden before final start. *J. M. Bradley* — 48

DEVOTE 3 b.c. Pennekamp (USA) 130 – Radiant Bride (USA) (Blushing Groom (FR) 131) [2001 11g⁵ 13d 11.7d⁶ Aug 19] fourth foal: half-brother to fairly useful 1997 2-y-o 1m winner Giveaway (by Generous) and 9f winner Men of Wickenby (by Shirley Heights): dam, French 1m (at 2 yrs) to 1¼m winner, half-sister to US Grade 1 1¼m/1½m winner Vanlandingham and to dam of 4-y-o Distant Music: modest maiden: fifth in minor event at Le Touquet in June: sold from M. Zilber in France 5,500 gns after next outing: below form at Bath final start. *B. J. Llewellyn* — 64

DEXTROUS 4 gr.c. Machiavellian (USA) 123 – Heavenly Cause (USA) (Grey Dawn II 132) [2001 85: 9d 10s 9m⁶ 7m 8.5f⁶ 8g 12g 10.1f⁴ 10.9m 12d Oct 8] tall colt: modest maiden handicapper, on downgrade: stays 1¼m: acts on any going: tongue tied last 4 starts: sometimes races freely. *N. Tinkler* — 64 d

DHUHOOK (USA) 3 b.f. Dixieland Band (USA) – Basma (USA) 104 (Grey Dawn II 132) [2001 8m⁵ 9f* 8m² 10.3m² 9.9m⁵ 10g⁶ 8d Oct 19] tall, good-topped filly: good — 96

mover: fifth foal: half-sister to 1m winner Sadaka (by Kingmambo) and winner in USA by Dayjur: dam, 2-y-o 6f winner and third in Cheveley Park Stakes, sister to US Grade 3 8.5f winner Dawn Quixote: useful performer: won maiden at Lingfield in June: good second in handicaps at Newmarket and Doncaster (behind Sauterne) next 2 starts: stayed 1¼m: raced mainly on good ground or firmer: very slowly away on debut: usually raced prominently: visits Muhtarram. *B. Hanbury*

DIABLO DANCER (IRE)   5 b.g. Deploy 131 – Scharade 74 (Lombard (GER) 126)   –
[2001 72: 10s 10.9m 16m Sep 30] well-made gelding: useful handicapper at best: no form in 2001: dead. *A. C. Whillans*

DIABOLO (IRE)   3 b.g. Magic Ring (IRE) 115 – First Play 59 (Primo Dominie 121)   **51**
[2001 50: 6m 5m 7.1g² 6g 6g 6m 6m Jul 5] lengthy, dipped-backed gelding: had quick action: modest maiden handicapper: stayed 7f: blinkered after second start: had looked reluctant/difficult ride: was none too consistent: dead. *M. W. Easterby*

DIAGHILEV (IRE)   2 b.c. (May 5) Sadler's Wells (USA) 132 – Darara 129 (Top Ville   **102**
129) [2001 8d² 8d⁴ 8s⁵ Nov 3] 3,400,000Y: neat, attractive colt: brother to very smart French middle-distance performer Darazari (also Group 1 1¼m winner in Australia) and smart middle-distance stayer Rhagaas and half-brother to several winners, including smart performer up to 1½m Kilimanjaro (by Shirley Heights): dam, won Prix Vermeille, half-sister to Darshaan and to smart dam of Derby second Daliapour (by Sadler's Wells): useful form: in frame in maidens at Leopardstown (short-headed by Stage Call) in August and Newmarket (fourth of 20 to Rawyaan, taking strong hold and hanging off bridle) in October: never threatened but seemed to run well when fifth of 6 to Act One in Criterium International at Saint-Cloud: will be suited by 1¼m/1½m: wore crossed noseband, had 2 handlers and taken steadily to post at Newmarket: clearly capable of winning races. *A. P. O'Brien, Ireland*

DIAMILINA (FR)   3 gr.f. Linamix (FR) 127 – Diamonaka (FR) 105 (Akarad (FR)   **121**
130) [2001 12.5v² 12.5d* 12.5g* 12m* 10d* 12m² 12s Oct 7] good-topped filly: fourth foal: sister to 2 winners in France, notably smart 10.5f (Prix Cleopatre) winner Diamonixa, and half-sister to French 1999 2-y-o 1m winner Diamond Gift (by Cadeaux Genereux): dam, French 10.5f winner, half-sister to smart French middle-distance performer Diamond Mix (by Linamix): very smart performer: won minor events at Fontainebleau in May and Maisons-Laffitte in June, Prix de Malleret at Saint-Cloud (led close home to beat Volga short neck) in July and Prix de la Nonette at Deauville (beat Lady Lahar 1½ lengths) in August: very good short-neck second to Aquarelliste in Prix Vermeille at Longchamp penultimate start but well held in Prix de l'Arc de Triomphe there final outing: stays 12.5f: acts on good to firm and good to soft going. *A. Fabre, France*

Prix de Malleret, Saint-Cloud—
Diamilina (No.3) battles on well to lead close home from Volga (rail) and Shamdara

DIAMOND BEACH 8 b.g. Lugana Beach 116 – Cannon Boy (USA) (Canonero **41 §**
(USA)) [2001 12.6d⁴ 12g⁶ Aug 17] temperamental maiden: stays 1½m: acts on firm and
good to soft going. *B. J. Llewellyn*

DIAMOND CROWN (IRE) 10 ch.g. Kris 135 – State Treasure (USA) (Secretariat **36 §**
(USA)) [2001 36§: f14g 12.4g³ 15s² 16g Aug 13] leggy gelding: poor performer: stays
2m: acts on firm and soft going: visored once: unreliable. *Denys Smith*

DIAMOND DAGGER 2 ch.g. (May 26) Sabrehill (USA) 120 – Diamond Princess **–**
69 (Horage 124) [2001 f8g Dec 10] half-brother to several winners, including 4-y-o Girl's
Best Friend and fairly useful 1½m to 15f winner Princess Topaz (by Midyan): dam 1½m
winner: well held in seller at Southwell. *D. W. P. Arbuthnot*

DIAMOND DARREN (IRE) 2 ch.c. (Apr 4) Dolphin Street (FR) 125 – Deerussa **64**
(IRE) (Jareer (USA) 115) [2001 5.1s 5.1f f6g f6g⁶ 6f² 6d² 7m³ 6g² 6m Aug 27] IR
12,500Y: leggy, close-coupled colt: third foal: half-brother to fairly useful 2000 2-y-o 5f
winner Secret Index (by Nicolotte) and a winner in Italy by Archway: dam unraced:
modest maiden: effective at 6f/7f: acts on firm and good to soft going, some promise on
fibresand: usually visored/blinkered: difficult ride. *P. D. Evans*

DIAMOND DECORUM (IRE) 5 ch.g. Fayruz 116 – Astra Adastra (Mount Hagen **67**
(FR) 127) [2001 74, a–: f7g f7s⁶ e7g⁶ e7g f7s⁴ 7s 7m 7.1f* 6m² 6f⁶ 6m Aug 4] leggy,
workmanlike gelding: fluent mover: fair performer: left John Berry after fifth start: won
claimer at Musselburgh (left J. Hetherton £5,000) in June: best at 6f/easy 7f: acts on firm
and soft going: tried visored/tongue tied: races freely: has carried head awkwardly/hung
right. *Andrew Turnell*

DIAMOND DISCOVERY (USA) 3 b. or br.c. Weather Break 84 – Ali's Diamond **–**
(USA) (Caracolero (USA) 131) [2001 6g 10g f8g 8m 7g Oct 12] fourth foal: half-brother
to 3 winners in USA: dam lightly-raced winning sprinter in USA: no form: trained by
H. Candy on debut and I. Williams next 3 starts: has looked ungenuine. *Andrew Lee,
Ireland*

DIAMOND FALLS 2 b.f. (Apr 19) River Falls 113 – Compton Lady (USA) 100 **62**
(Sovereign Dancer (USA)) [2001 7m⁵ 8s⁶ Oct 25] leggy filly: seventh foal: half-sister to
a 1m/1¼m winner in Scandinavia by Slip Anchor: dam 7f (at 2 yrs) and 1½m winner:
modest form in maidens at Goodwood and Brighton 4 months apart: will probably stay
1¼m: sold 3,800 gns. *Mrs A. J. Perrett*

DIAMOND GEEZER (IRE) 5 br.g. Tenby 125 – Unaria (Prince Tenderfoot (USA) **74**
126) [2001 76, a84: f5g f6s 5.1d⁴ 5m 5m 5g² 5m² 5m 5g 5m 7m 5m 5v⁵ Sep 29] sturdy, **a78**
good-quartered gelding: fair handicapper: left R. Hannon after eighth start: effective at 5f
to easy 7f: acts on any turf going and fibresand/equitrack: blinkered once: usually races
prominently. *J. J. Quinn*

DIAMOND GREEN (ARG) 3 ch.c. Roy (USA) – Diamond Ring (ARG) (El Basco **62**
(USA)) [2001 8m 9.9d⁴ 10v Oct 8] first foal: dam Argentinian 1m winner: easily best
effort in maidens when 5¾ lengths fourth to Valley of Song at Goodwood. *B. R. Millman*

DIAMOND JAYNE (IRE) 3 ch.f. Royal Abjar (USA) 121 – Valiant Friend (USA) **–**
(Shahrastani (USA) 135) [2001 –: 8.2s 7m 10g Jun 12] big, plain filly: no form.
J. Hetherton

DIAMOND JOBE (IRE) 2 ch.g. (Apr 28) College Chapel 122 – Dazzling Maid **59**
(IRE) 64 (Tate Gallery (USA) 117) [2001 5g³ 5.3f⁵ 7g 6.1d Sep 21] IR 17,500Y: half-
brother to several winners, including 5-y-o Crystal Creek and 4-y-o Ravishing: dam
placed at 5f/6f at 2 yrs: modest maiden: well held last 2 starts (3 months apart): best
efforts at 5f: acts on firm ground. *A. Berry*

DIAMOND JOSHUA (IRE) 3 b.g. Mujadil (USA) 119 – Elminya (IRE) (Sure **53**
Blade (USA) 130) [2001 5.1s 6.1d 6m 7d 10m 12m 16.2g² 14.1s⁶ 15.8m Sep 22] IR
13,000Y: workmanlike gelding: fifth foal: brother to fair 7f (at 2 yrs) to 1½m winner
Soden and half-brother to fairly useful 1997 2-y-o 6f/7f winner Belle de Nuit (by
Statoblest): dam unraced half-sister to very smart 1¼m performer Ruby Tiger: modest
maiden handicapper: stays 2m: acts on good to firm ground: none too consistent. *John
Berry*

DIAMOND LOVER (IRE) 2 ch.c. (Feb 6) Alhaarth (IRE) 126 – Silent Love (USA) **88 p**
(Hansel (USA)) [2001 7.5g³ 8d* Oct 3] 25,000F: big, lengthy colt: has scope: first foal:
dam placed at 5f/6f in Germany at 2 yrs: better effort in maidens when beating Selective
by ¾ length in 13-runner event at Newcastle, pulling clear with runner-up final 2f: should
stay 1¼m: likely to make a useful 3-y-o. *N. A. Graham*

DIAMOND LYDIA (IRE)   3 gr.f. Petong 126 – Nagida 94 (Skyliner 117) [2001 5m⁶   –
5m 6m f8g Nov 26] IR 4,100F, IR 5,500Y: fourth foal: half-sister to 4-y-o Love You Too
and 1997 2-y-o 7f winner Chief Blade (both by Be My Chief): dam won Wokingham:
little form: left John Berry after third start. *P. D. Evans*

DIAMOND MAX (IRE)   3 b.c. Nicolotte 118 – Kawther (Tap On Wood 130) [2001   **109 ?**
78: f7g* f8.5g⁴ 7d³ 8g 7d² 8.1s* 8s 8s* 8s Nov 18] angular colt: useful performer: won
handicaps at Southwell in January and Chepstow in August and listed race at Longchamp
(seemingly much improved form to beat Texalina by neck) in October: not sure to stay
beyond 8.5f: acts on fibresand, best turf efforts on ground softer than good. *P. D. Evans*

DIAMOND MILL (IRE)   2 ch.f. (Apr 28) Desert King (IRE) 129 – Euromill (Shirley   **56**
Heights 130) [2001 5g⁵ 5m 7m⁴ Jun 27] smallish filly: ninth foal: half-sister to 3 winners,
including useful 6f (at 2 yrs) and 1m winner Tadwiga (by Fairy King): dam, Irish
middle-distance stayer, from family of Old Vic: modest maiden: should stay at least 1m.
R. Hannon

DIAMOND OLIVIA   4 b.f. Beveled (USA) – Queen of The Quorn 53 (Governor   –
General 116) [2001 70, a–: 8.2s 7d⁴ May 7] angular, workmanlike filly: fair performer at
best: no form in 2001: sent to Germany. *John Berry*

DIAMOND PROMISE (IRE)   4 b.f. Fayruz 116 – Cupid Miss (Anita's Prince 126)   –
[2001 57, a49: f5g p5g p6g p6g Dec 29] small filly: of little account nowadays. *R. Ingram*

DIAMOND RACHAEL (IRE)   4 b.f. Shalford (IRE) 124§ – Brown Foam (Horage   **63**
124) [2001 73, a75: f7g e7g⁵ e7g⁴ f6g⁴ f7g 7m 7m f7g f6g* f5g f7g⁶ f6g Dec 11] strong,   **a71**
plain filly: fair performer: left Mrs N. Macauley after seventh start, J. Hetherton after
eighth: won claimer at Southwell in November: effective at 6f to easy 1m: acts on good
to firm going, fibresand and equitrack: usually visored/blinkered: none too consistent.
P. S. McEntee

DIAMOND RING   2 b.f. (Jan 13) Magic Ring (IRE) 115 – Reticent Bride (IRE) 71   **73**
(Shy Groom (USA)) [2001 5m³ 5m* 5g² Jul 18] quite good-topped filly: fourth foal:
half-sister to fairly useful 6f winner Barnacla (by Bluebird) and a 6f winner in Italy by
Night Shift: dam, Irish 6f winner, sister to Lowther winner Miss Demure: fair form: won
maiden at Salisbury in June: short-headed by Celestien in minor event at Doncaster: will
prove best at 5f/6f. *J. L. Dunlop*

*Prix de Ranelagh, Longchamp—trainer David Evans' first runner in France, Diamond Max (No.6),
steps up on previous form to record a surprise win over Texalina and Special Discount*

DIAMOND ROAD (IRE)   4 b.g. Dolphin Street (FR) 125 – Tiffany's Case (IRE) 65   **67**
(Thatching 131) [2001 75: 9m 8m⁶ 9m⁵ 8m Sep 24] good-bodied gelding: fair maiden
handicapper: stays 1¼m: acts on good to firm going: has carried head high: free-going
sort. *C. A. Horgan*

DIAMOND SINEAD (IRE)   2 b.f. (Mar 5) Fayruz 116 – Pink Eyes (IRE) (Vision   **52**
(USA)) [2001 5v⁵ 5.1s² Apr 16] IR 900F, IR 2,500Y: plain, wiry filly: sister to Italian 5f
(at 2 yrs) to 7f winner Salomone: dam Belgian 1¼m/1½m winner: modest maiden:
second in seller at Nottingham: should stay 6f: withdrawn after proving reluctant at stalls
in May. *P. D. Evans*

DIAMOND ZOE   3 b.f. Whittingham (IRE) 104 – Sharp Gazelle 57 (Beveled (USA))   **40**
[2001 38: 5d f6g 6f 6g⁵ 6d 7d 6.1s Aug 6] quite attractive filly: unimpressive mover: poor
maiden handicapper: effective at 5f/6f: acts on good to soft ground: blinkered final start.
J. L. Eyre

DIANA PANAGAEA   2 ch.f. (Feb 3) Polar Falcon (USA) 126 – Pandrop (Sharrood   **75**
(USA) 124) [2001 6g* 6.5g Sep 28] workmanlike filly: first foal: dam once-raced
half-sister to Ribblesdale/Geoffrey Freer winner Phantom Gold: fair form: won maiden
at Lingfield in August by ½ length from Noble Nick: well held in valuable sales race at
Ascot (wore rope halter for stall entry): should stay at least 7f. *A. C. Stewart*

DIAPHANOUS   3 b.f. Beveled (USA) – Sharp Venita 84 (Sharp Edge 123) [2001 7s
6v 8.3v Nov 8] sturdy filly: sister to 5-y-o Absolute Fantasy and half-sister to several
winners, notably useful 7f/1m performer Sharpalto (by Noalto): dam sprinter: well beaten
in maidens (refused to enter stall on intended debut). *N. E. Berry*

DI CANIO   3 ch.g. Piccolo 121 – Conquista 87 (Aragon 118) [2001 –: f6g⁵ 7v f5g⁵ 6f⁵   **46**
Jun 5] modest maiden: should be suited by further than 6f: acts on firm ground and
fibresand: has been slowly away. *D. Nicholls*

DICK'N MICK   4 b.g. Secret Appeal – Gilboa 48 (Shirley Heights 130) [2001 6.9m⁵
8.1d 8m Jul 21] third foal: brother to fairly useful 1m/1¼m performer Pentagon Lad: dam
lightly-raced close relative of useful stayer Gondolier: well held in maidens/seller:
visored last 2 starts. *J. G. Smyth-Osbourne*

DICK THE TAXI   7 b.g. Karlinsky (USA) – Another Galaxy (IRE) (Anita's Prince   **64**
126) [2001 p12g³ p10g⁴ Nov 20] first foal: dam 2-y-o 6f winner in Ireland: smart bumper
performer in 1999/00: fairly useful 2m hurdler: better effort in maidens (modest form)
when third at Lingfield on Flat debut, slowly away. *R. J. Smith*

DICK WHITTINGHAM   2 ch.g. (Mar 30) Whittingham (IRE) 104 – Comme Une   **–**
Fleur (FR) (Sharpo 132) [2001 f6g 7.1d Jul 21] 2,500Y: second foal: dam French 1m
winner: well beaten in maidens. *D. Shaw*

DIDDYMU (IRE)   2 b.f. (Apr 6) Revoque (IRE) 122 – Family At War (USA) 71   **66**
(Explodent (USA)) [2001 7m 7.1m⁵ 8.2v Oct 4] IR 100,000Y: tall filly: has scope: sixth
foal: half-sister to 3 winners by Common Grounds, notably smart 5f (including at 2 yrs)
winner Flanders: dam 2-y-o 5f winner: fair maiden: best effort when fifth at Warwick:
should stay 1m. *M. R. Channon*

DIDNT TELL MY WIFE   2 ch.g. (Feb 17) Aragon 118 – Bee Dee Dancer (Balla-   **73**
cashtal (CAN)) [2001 6v 7d f6g² f6g f6g² p6g³ p7g* Dec 29] 3,500Y, 10,500 2-y-o: sixth
foal: half-brother to 6f winner Breakin Even (by Chilibang) and a 5f winner in Italy by
Superlative: dam well beaten only start: fair performer: won nursery at Lingfield comfortably by 1½ lengths from Steely Dan: stays easy 7f: acts on fibresand and polytrack, some
promise on turf. *S. C. Williams*

DID YOU MISS ME (IRE)   4 ch.f. Indian Ridge 123 – Upward Trend 112 (Salmon   **–**
Leap (USA) 131) [2001 59: 5d 8.3d 8m 6g Sep 2] modest maiden at 3 yrs: well held in
2001. *P. Monteith*

DIESAN (USA)   10 b.g. Diesis 133 – Bold Courtesan (USA) (Bold Bidder) [2001 8m   **–**
8m May 31] good-bodied gelding: useful at 3 yrs for J. Gosden: below form in Dubai
early in 1995 but ran well in Germany subsequently, winning handicaps at Gelsenkirchen
and Dortmund in 1996 for U. Ostmann: tailed off both 10-y-o starts. *S. Woodman*

DIETRICH (USA)   3 br.f. Storm Cat (USA) – Piquetnol (USA) 103 (Private Account   **115**
(USA)) [2001 96: 5d* 5m 5m* 5s Oct 7] leggy, good-topped filly: smart performer: won
4-runner Ballyogan Stakes at Leopardstown (by ¾ length from Final Exam) in June and
King George Stakes at Goodwood (by ¾ length from Afaan, squeezed for room early
but travelled strongly before leading final 1f) in July: below best in Prix de l'Abbaye at

King George Stakes, Goodwood—
Dietrich takes her second pattern race, beating the blinkered pair Afaan (rail) and Eastern Purple

Longchamp final start: easily best form at 5f: acts on soft and good to firm going: has worn crossed noseband. *A. P. O'Brien, Ireland*

DIFFERENTIAL (USA) 4 b. or br.c. Known Fact (USA) 135 – Talk About Home (USA) (Elocutionist (USA)) [2001 88: 6m⁴ 6g 6g 6g p7g p7g⁶ Dec 12] small, sturdy, quite attractive colt: fairly useful handicapper: good fourth to Brevity at Ascot in July: below form after (reportedly bled from nose next time): raced mainly over 5f/6f: raced only on good/good to firm going on turf: tried in net muzzle at 2 yrs: sometimes early to post: has raced freely. *B. Smart* **91 d**

DIG FOR GOLD 8 ch.g. Digamist (USA) 110 – Formidable Task 61 (Formidable (USA) 125) [2001 16m 16m⁵ 16.2f Jul 17] robust gelding: winning hurdler/poor maiden chaser: bad form on Flat: tried tongue tied. *R. D. E. Woodhouse* **26 +**

DIGGER (IRE) 2 ch.g. (Apr 10) Danzig Connection (USA) – Baliana 75 (Midyan (USA) 124) [2001 5.1g 6f 5.7g Oct 1] 10,500F, 19,000Y: big, workmanlike gelding: fourth foal: half-brother to 7f (at 2 yrs)/1m winner Bali Dance (by Rambo Dancer): dam unreliable sprinter: fair maiden: best effort when seventh at Bath on final start, late headway under hands and heels: likely to prove best at 7f/1m: tongue tied all starts. *G. B. Balding* **71**

DIGITAL 4 ch.g. Safawan 118 – Heavenly Goddess (Soviet Star (USA) 128) [2001 85: 8v² 10s 8g² 8m 8.5m 8m³ 7m* 8g 7s 9g Oct 6] workmanlike gelding: fairly useful handicapper: won 23-runner race at York in July by neck from Tornado Prince: effective at 7f/1m: acts on good to firm and heavy going: has carried head awkwardly: none too consistent. *M. R. Channon* **93**

DIGITAL IMAGE 4 b.c. Presidium 124 – Sally Tadpole 44 (Jester 119) [2001 –: e7g 8m⁶ 7d 7.8g Aug 15] useful-looking colt: has a quick action: fairly useful at 2 yrs: lightly raced and little form since: tried blinkered/tongue tied. *S. Donohoe, Ireland* **–**

DIGON DA 5 ch.g. Sparky Lad 89 – Fleur Power (IRE) 54 (The Noble Player (USA) 126) [2001 –: 8.3m f12g 8m 7m f6g f8g⁶ f9.4g⁶ f12g⁶ f14.8s Dec 15] fair maiden at 3 yrs: poor nowadays: tried visored: has looked wayward/headstrong. *R. Brotherton* **37**

DIHATJUM 4 b.g. Mujtahid (USA) 118 – Rosie Potts 83 (Shareef Dancer (USA) 135) [2001 69: 8s 7m 10f⁵ 8.1m² 10f 9g 8f 10m 9.7m² 12g⁵ 9.7d² 10m⁵ 12g Sep 15] rather leggy, workmanlike gelding: modest handicapper: probably stays 1½m: acts on firm and good to soft going: has worn visor/blinkers, including last 5 starts: often slowly away: held up. *R. M. Flower* **59**

DIL 6 b.g. Primo Dominie 121 – Swellegant 84 (Midyan (USA) 124) [2001 –, a95: f5g f5s* f5g f6g f5g 6m f6g f5g⁶ f5g⁵ f5g f6g* f6g⁴ f6s² Dec 21] lengthy, good-topped gelding: fair nowadays: won claimers at Wolverhampton (final start for Mrs N. Macauley) in January and December: best at 5f/easy 6f: acts on fibresand, lightly raced and little recent form on turf: sometimes visored: has worn net muzzle to post: sometimes starts slowly/looks difficult ride. *Andrew Reid* **–**
a73

261

DILEER (IRE)　2 b.c. (Mar 23) Barathea (IRE) 127 – Stay Sharpe (USA) (Sharpen Up　**86**
127) [2001 6f³ Jun 14] IR 37,000F, 80,000Y: half-brother to several winners, including
Manazil (1m/1¼m, by Generous), Jalaab (7f/1m, by Green Desert) and 4-y-o Takamaka
Bay, all useful: dam unraced half-sister to dam of Indian Skimmer: 14/1, 5 lengths third
of 20 to Waldenburg in maiden at Newbury, soon prominent and not knocked about once
held: bred to stay 1m: looked sure to improve. *M. R. Channon*

DILIZA　2 b.f. (Mar 17) Dilum (USA) 115 – Little White Lies 78 (Runnett 125) [2001　**45**
5.7f 6m 6.1m⁴ 6f⁵ 7g Sep 11] fifth foal: half-sister to 1m winner Singers Image (by Chief
Singer): dam, maiden who stayed 1m, half-sister to smart middle-distance filly So True,
herself dam of smart 1m/1¼m performer Bomb Alaska: poor maiden: likely to prove best
at 5f/6f. *G. B. Balding*

DILKUSHA (IRE)　6 b.g. Indian Ridge 123 – Crimson Glen 70 (Glenstal (USA) 118)　**74**
[2001 83: e7g e7s 6s 8d³ 8m 8f May 28] rather leggy gelding: has a quick action: fair
handicapper: stays 1m: acts on firm and good to soft going: tried blinkered: held up: has
looked less than genuine. *B. A. Pearce*

DILLY　3 br.f. Dilum (USA) 115 – Princess Rosananti (IRE) (Shareef Dancer (USA)　**70**
135) [2001 79: 7.1g 7.9g 8m 10m⁵ 9.7m⁴ p10g p10g p10g Dec 19] fair performer: stays　**a64**
9.7f: raced only on good/good to firm ground on turf (respectable effort on polytrack
penultimate outing): dropped away tamely last time. *P. R. Chamings*

DILSAA　4 ch.g. Night Shift (USA) – Llia 94 (Shirley Heights 130) [2001 76, a70:　**56**
f12s⁶ 5d 6m 7.5m⁶ 8d 8m 12f³ 14.1m* 14.1m Sep 6] strong, lengthy gelding: modest
handicapper: left P. Harris after reappearance: won at Nottingham in July, reportedly lame
final start: stays 1¾m: acts on soft going, firm and fibresand: tried blinkered: free-going
soft. *K. A. Ryan*

DILSHAAN　3 b.c. Darshaan 133 – Avila 76 (Ajdal (USA) 130) [2001 118p:　**119**
10.4m* 12f Jun 9]
　　Just a few days after Dilshaan and Time Away had underlined still further
Darshaan's influence as a stallion by winning the Dante Stakes and Musidora
Stakes respectively, the 1984 Prix du Jockey Club winner was found to have a
ruptured duodenum and had to be put down. Ironically, Darshaan's standing was
never higher than at the time of his death, something which the victory of his son
Olden Times in the Prix Jean Prat a couple of weeks later served to underline.
Though Darshaan had looked to have made a remarkable start to his career at
stud when Aliysa, from his first crop, passed the post first in the Oaks, her
disqualification meant that it was another year before he had his first Group 1
winner through Hellenic in the Yorkshire Oaks, and his rise to the top proved
gradual. In 1993 he was responsible for the US Horse of the Year Kotashaan and
three years later for Europe's top miler Mark of Esteem. Mark of Esteem himself is
already making his name at stud and is the sire of One Thousand Guineas winner
Ameerat. With Darshaan also having achieved fame as a broodmare sire, his
influence should continue to be far-reaching for many years to come. Let's not
forget, either, that he will be well represented on the racecourse for some time to
come, having already covered sixty-six of the eighty mares booked to him in his
final season by the time of his death.
　　Of those offspring who raced in the latest season, perhaps Dilshaan, who
stays in training, will be the one to enhance Darshaan's reputation further. He has
already made a notable contribution despite having been restricted to just four
races to date, his victory in the Group 2 Dante following on from that in the Group
1 Racing Post Trophy seven months earlier. His trainer, importantly, is second to
none when it comes to improving horses of Dilshaan's type. The form of the Racing
Post Trophy received a boost when runner-up Tamburlaine, whom Dilshaan beat by
two and a half lengths, finished runner-up to Dilshaan's stable-companion Golan in
the Two Thousand Guineas, the last-named immediately installed as favourite for
the Derby. Later in May Dilshaan, reportedly slow to come to hand in the spring,
was given his chance to enhance his Epsom claims when he lined up with five
others, all of them holding Derby entries, for the Convergent Communications
Dante at York, one of his opponents being none other than Olden Times. Paddock
inspection revealed Dilshaan, who was sent off favourite, lacking nothing in
fitness, but he didn't stride out to post on ground a good deal firmer than that which

Convergent Communications Dante Stakes, York—Dilshaan (right) gets the better of a sustained duel with Celtic Silence; Storming Home (left) and Aldwych come next

he had encountered at Doncaster. There was nothing in the way in which he came back to suggest that good to firm ground was a problem for him, though. Moving through to tackle pacesetter and second favourite Celtic Silence three furlongs out, Dilshaan showed just the right sort of attitude, getting the better of that horse in a sustained duel, gradually gaining the upper hand over the final furlong to win by half a length. Storming Home rallied to finish a close third, but Olden Times failed to do himself justice and beat only one home. Dilshaan reproduced the level of form shown in the Racing Post Trophy but did not give the impression at York that there was a lot better to come, at least not in the short term. Yet, by all accounts, Dilshaan's subsequent homework was impressive enough to suggest otherwise, and support for him grew until he was as short as 100/30 for the Derby on the morning of the race, just behind Galileo and Golan in the betting. He drifted to 5/1 on the day, failing to take the eye in the preliminaries, looking dull in his coat and scratching unimpressively to post. Dilshaan didn't shine in the race itself either, never really looking like mounting an effective challenge in the straight and finishing only seventh to Galileo, beaten around eight lengths. Dilshaan suffered a setback while being prepared for the Princess of Wales's Stakes at Newmarket in July and wasn't seen out again, an X-ray revealing a flake in one of his joints.

Dilshaan (b.c. 1998)	Darshaan (br 1981)	Shirley Heights (b 1975)	Mill Reef
			Hardiemma
		Delsy (br 1972)	Abdos
			Kelty
	Avila (b 1989)	Ajdal (b 1984)	Northern Dancer
			Native Partner
		Sweet Habit (b 1976)	Habitat
			Sweet Mimosa

We know plenty about Dilshaan's sire, but what about his dam Avila? She had a couple of runs at three, putting up easily her better effort when finishing third in a seven-furlong newcomers race at Newbury, and she produced four foals prior to Dilshaan. None has proved in the same league as him, though a close relation by Shirley Heights won over eight and a half furlongs in Austria, the modest Mama-San (by Doyoun) won at ten and a half furlongs and a colt by Lahib is a five-furlong winner in Greece. Avila's two-year-old colt by Halling, named Distinctive State, was in training with David Loder. A half-sister, among others, to the very smart mile-and-a-quarter performer Alleging and the Chester Vase winner Nomrood,

Avila is a daughter of the unraced Sweet Habit, herself a half-sister to the Irish Oaks second Fleur Royale. The next dam Sweet Mimosa, a sister to the top-class stayers Levmoss and Le Moss, won the 1970 Prix de Diane. Dilshaan certainly has plenty of stamina in his pedigree and is sure to prove fully effective at a mile and a half. A leggy, quite good-topped colt who acts on soft and good to firm going, he has hung and carried his head a shade awkwardly but is game. *Sir Michael Stoute*

DILYS 2 b.f. (Mar 1) Efisio 120 – Ramajana (USA) (Shadeed (USA) 135) [2001 5m³ 5.7g⁴ 6d 6v* Nov 8] 4,000F, 7,000Y: smallish, sturdy filly: second foal: dam 6f (at 2 yrs) and 1m winner in Germany: fairly useful form: won maiden at Windsor comfortably by 1½ lengths from The Last Cast, making all despite idling/flashing tail: will probably stay 7f: acts on heavy going. *W. S. Kittow* **84**

DIM BYD 2 ch.c. (Apr 7) So Factual (USA) 120 – Time Clash 67 (Timeless Times (USA) 99) [2001 6m Jul 30] second foal: dam 2-y-o 6f winner: 50/1, last in maiden at Windsor: broke out of stalls and withdrawn in August. *Mrs Merrita Jones* **–**

DIMPLE CHAD 2 b.c. (Apr 13) Sadler's Wells (USA) 132 – Fern 100 (Shirley Heights 130) [2001 7d Nov 3] good-topped colt: sixth foal: brother to fair 1½m winner Frangy and half-brother to 3 winners, including 1½y-o Dance On The Top: dam, 1½m winner, half-sister to Oaks second Shamshir: 20/1, tenth of 27 to Prince Hector in maiden at Newmarket, not knocked about once unable to quicken: will be suited by 1¼m+: sure to improve. *L. M. Cumani* **67 p**

DINAMI 3 b.g. Young Ern 120 – Born To Be 80 (Never So Bold 135) [2001 6g 7m 6m Jun 29] second reported foal: dam 5f winner: no form. *S. Dow* **–**

DINAR (USA) 6 b.h. Dixieland Band (USA) – Bold Jessie (Never So Bold 135) [2001 64: 8.2v f8g⁶ 8.5s 10d 12m⁵ 8.3g⁵ 10g² 9g⁴ 11.6m⁴ 11.5g⁴ 10m Sep 11] good-topped horse: fair handicapper: left R. Brotherton after fourth start: has won at 1½m, probably best at 1m/1¼m: acts on firm and soft going: races prominently. *B. J. Llewellyn* **65**

DINKY 4 ch.f. Floose 99 – Marinsky (USA) 63 (Diesis 133) [2001 –: f12g f11g Apr 10] small filly: little form. *M. J. Ryan* **–**

DINOFELIS 3 b.g. Rainbow Quest (USA) 134 – Revonda (IRE) (Sadler's Wells (USA) 132) [2001 62p: 10.2d 14.1m⁶ 14f⁶ 12.6d³ 12f⁴ 16g f11g 10.9v⁶ Oct 15] quite attractive gelding: modest maiden handicapper: left P. Harris after fifth start: seems to find 1½m on sharp side, and should stay 2m: acts on firm and good to soft ground: sold 2,500 gns. *K. A. Ryan* **57**

DION DEE 5 ch.m. Anshan 119 – Jade Mistress 51 (Damister (USA) 123) [2001 53: f16.2s⁶ f12s⁵ 14.1s 11.9s* 11.8m⁴ 12d³ Jun 17] tall mare: modest handicapper: won at Brighton in May: effective at 1¼m/1½m: acts on good to firm ground, soft and fibresand: often held up: has carried head awkwardly. *Dr J. R. J. Naylor* **54 a36**

DIRECT DEAL 5 b.g. Rainbow Quest (USA) 134 – Al Najah (USA) 96 (Topsider (USA)) [2001 72d: 10.9m 12.6d* Jul 21] rather leggy gelding: modest performer: made all in selling handicap at Warwick in July: stays 12.6f: acts on good to firm and good to soft going: blinkered once: often tongue tied. *G. M. McCourt* **63**

DIRECT DESCENDANT (IRE) 2 ch.g. (Mar 26) Be My Guest (USA) 126 – Prague Spring 66 (Salse (USA) 128) [2001 8g 8.2d 8d Oct 2] 10,000F, 28,000Y: good-topped gelding: has scope: good walker: second foal: dam, 1¼m winner, out of half-sister to Irish 2000 Guineas winner Wassl: fair maiden: seemingly best effort on debut: will stay 1¼m. *S. P. C. Woods* **65 ?**

DIRECT PLAY 2 b.c. (Apr 30) Muhtarram (USA) 125 – Direct Fortune (USA) (Java Gold (USA)) [2001 5.1d³ 6m* 6m⁵ 6d 6f* 7g⁵ 6.1m³ 7.1m³ 6d⁵ Oct 18] 3,500F: rather leggy colt: third foal: half-brother to a winner abroad by King's Signet: dam unraced: fairly useful performer: won maiden at Folkestone in June and nurseries at Kempton and Warwick in August: stays 7f: acts on firm and good to soft ground: consistent: sold 40,000 gns. *B. W. Hills* **83**

DISCERNING 3 b.f. Darshaan 133 – Tromond 94 (Lomond (USA) 128) [2001 10m⁵ 11.5g* 12m 12g³ 13.4d⁶ 16d⁶ Nov 2] tall, rather leggy filly: third foal: half-sister to very smart 1m (at 2 yrs) to 1½m winner Nowhere To Exit (by Exit To Nowhere) and useful 1m (including at 2 yrs) winner Embraced (by Pursuit of Love): dam, 9f winner who stayed 1½m, out of half-sister to Yorkshire Oaks winner and St Leger second Hellenic (by Darshaan): useful form: won maiden at Yarmouth in July: 9 lb out of handicap, best effort **96**

when sixth to Flossy in rated stakes at Chester penultimate start: should be suited by 2m+: yet to race on extremes of going: flashes tail. *J. R. Fanshawe*

DISCO VOLANTE   2 b.f. (Apr 4) Sadler's Wells (USA) 132 – Divine Danse (FR)   **79 p**
118 (Kris 135) [2001 7d⁵ Oct 15] rangy filly: sixth foal: closely related to 4-y-o Valentino and half-sister to 2 winners, including 7f (in France) and 9f (in USA) winner Djinn (by Mr Prospector): dam, French sprinter, half-sister to very smart 6f to 1m performer Pursuit of Love: 5/1, keeping-on fifth of 20 to Opening Ceremony in maiden at Leicester: will stay at least 1m: sure to improve. *J. H. M. Gosden*

DISGLAIR   3 b.f. River Falls 113 – Bold Dove (Never So Bold 135) [2001 –: 8m 8.1m   **–**
Jul 5] no form. *D. Burchell*

DISPOL CHIEFTAN   3 b.g. Clantime 101 – Ski Baby (Petoski 135) [2001 69: f5g   **54**
5.1s³ 6s 6m 7.5m 7.1f Jun 18] modest maiden: best at 5f: acts on heavy going: blinkered final start: tried tongue tied: usually races prominently: gelded. *Mrs A. Duffield*

DISPOL EVITA   2 ch.f. (Apr 30) Presidium 124 – She's A Breeze 35 (Crofthall 110)   **60**
[2001 5s 5d⁶ 6m³ 6f 7g* 7f* 7g⁴ 7m⁵ 7m⁴ 7m² f8.5g³ 8m p7g⁶ p8g* p7g³ f8.5s⁶ Dec 27] 1,200Y: rather leggy, close-coupled filly: fifth foal: half-sister to 1998 2-y-o 5f winner Dispol Clan (by Clantime): dam maiden: modest performer: won seller at Redcar in June, claimer at Brighton (left S. Kettlewell) in July and seller at Lingfield in November: barely stays 8.5f: acts on fibresand/polytrack and firm going: has been slowly away/edged left/ looked reluctant (refused to race fourth outing). *Andrew Reid*

DISPOL FOXTROT   3 ch.f. Alhijaz 122 – Foxtrot Pie 77 (Shernazar 131) [2001 49:   **53**
f9.4s f8g* e10s² f11g 10s⁴ 12s³ 9.9m⁶ 10f³ 10g 9.2s* 9.2g* 10.1m⁵ 10m 9.2g f8.5s Dec 26] close-coupled filly: bad mover: modest performer: won seller at Southwell in February and claimer and handicap at Hamilton in July: off nearly 4 months, ran badly final start (slowly away): probably best at 1m/1¼m: acts on fibresand, equitrack and soft going. *S. E. Kettlewell*

DISPOL JAZZ   4 ch.f. Alhijaz 122 – Foxtrot Pie 77 (Shernazar 131) [2001 58: f7g 7f   **–**
Sep 21] leggy filly: poor mover: fair at 2 yrs: little form since, leaving S. Kettlewell after reappearance. *D. Broad, Ireland*

DISPOL LAIRD   3 ch.g. Clantime 101 – She's A Breeze 35 (Crofthall 110) [2001 56:   **–**
5m⁶ 7m May 28] leggy, close-coupled gelding: disappointing maiden. *S. E. Kettlewell*

DISPOL ROCK (IRE)   5 b.g. Ballad Rock 122 – Havana Moon (Ela-Mana-Mou   **64**
132) [2001 58: 9m² 9.9f 12.4m 10.1m³ 10s² 12.3g² 11.9g² 10.1g 14.1m Sep 6] tall gelding: modest handicapper: stays 1½m: acts on firm and soft going: front runner: has hinted at temperament. *T. D. Barron*

DISTANT CHEERS (USA)   3 ch.f. Distant View (USA) 126 – With Cheer (CAN)   **55 ?**
(With Approval (CAN)) [2001 e8g³ 8.3s 8.1g⁶ 10m 8d 8m f8.5g f8.5g* f9.4g Oct 6] IR   **a77**
36,000Y: second foal: half-sister to winner in USA by Alydeed: dam unraced half-sister to minor North American stakes winners Canadian Silver (sprinter) and Cheery Knight (8.5f): fair performer: much improved form when making all in maiden handicap at Wolverhampton in September: stays 8.5f: acts on fibresand. *T. G. Mills*

DISTANT COUSIN   4 b.g. Distant Relative 128 – Tinaca (USA) (Manila (USA))   **60**
[2001 84: 13.9m 12m 12g 15g 15s 15.8d 12s³ 13.8d f14g² f14g⁴ p13g⁵ Dec 29] rather leggy gelding: modest nowadays: stays 1¾m: acts on all-weather, best turf form on soft going: visored (ran creditably) seventh/eighth starts. *M. A. Buckley*

DISTANT DAWN   3 b.f. Petong 126 – Turbo Rose 81 (Taufan (USA) 119) [2001 45:   **27 §**
e5g f7g⁴ f9.4g⁶ f8g Feb 12] bad maiden: stays 7f: acts on fibresand and any turf going: visored/blinkered: usually looks none too keen. *K. T. Ivory*

DISTANT DECREE (USA)   3 ch.f. Distant View (USA) 126 – Nobile Decretum   **–**
(USA) (Noble Decree (USA) 127) [2001 –: 8.1g 8.2d 9.9f 10m 8.1m Aug 1] smallish filly: no form: tried blinkered. *J. A. Osborne*

DISTANT DIVA   2 b.f. (Apr 14) Distant Relative 128 – Miss Poll Flinders (Swing   **86**
Easy (USA) 126) [2001 6.1m⁵ 5g² 5s* 6m⁴ 5g* 5g³ 5d Oct 13] good-topped filly: good walker: half-sister to several winners, including 1m (at 2 yrs)/1¼m winner Chilly Lad and fairly useful 1994 2-y-o 5f and 7f winner Duffertoes (both by High Kicker): dam tailed off only start at 2 yrs: fairly useful performer: won maiden at Beverley in August and nursery at Sandown in September: best effort when third in nursery at Newmarket: effective at 5f/6f: acts on soft and good to firm going. *N. A. Callaghan*

Goffs International Stakes, the Curragh—
Distant Music makes most and quickens readily to beat his two rivals Muakaad (right) and Bonnard

DISTANT MIST (USA) 2 ch.c. (Apr 4) Distant View (USA) 126 – Sage Mist (USA) **75**
(Capote (USA)) [2001 e5g* 5d⁵ 7d 7s p7g Dec 29] $30,000F, 82,000Y: third foal:
half-brother to a winner in USA by Virginia Rapids: dam won up to 1¼m in USA: fair
form: won maiden at Lingfield in March: ran creditably next start (6 months later): should
stay 7f. *J. Noseda*

DISTANT MUSIC (USA) 4 b.c. Distant View (USA) 126 – Musicanti (USA) **121**
(Nijinsky (CAN) 138) [2001 126: 9d⁴ 9g* 8m⁵ 10.4g⁵ 8d⁶ 10d⁶ Oct 20] tall, attractive
colt: very smart performer: leading 2-y-o of 1999: won 3-runner Goffs International
Stakes at the Curragh in July by 1½ lengths from Muakaad, making most: mainly only
respectable efforts after, including in Sussex Stakes at Goodwood (fifth to Noverre),
International Stakes at York (fifth to Sakhee) and Champion Stakes at Newmarket (sixth
to Nayef, kept on after being short of room): stayed 1¼m: acted on good to firm and
good to soft going: sometimes wore pads between feet and shoes, bandaged behind on
reappearance: had found little/hung under pressure: was usually held up: to stand at
Morristown Lattin Stud, Ireland, fee €9,500, Oct 1st. *B. W. Hills*

DISTANT PROSPECT (IRE) 4 b.g. Namaqualand (USA) – Ukraine's Affair (USA) **102**
(The Minstrel (CAN) 135) [2001 93: 18.7f 14m 16.1f⁵ 14m⁵ 18d* 16d⁴ Nov 2] unfurnished gelding: useful handicapper: 14/1, best effort when winning Tote Cesarewitch at
Newmarket (weaved through after travelling smoothly, got up close home to beat
stable-companion Palua by neck) in October: ran at least respectably otherwise, including
in Northumberland Plate at Newcastle third start: will stay beyond 2¼m: has form on firm
going, all wins on good or softer: held up: genuine. *I. A. Balding*

DISTANT SCENE (USA) 3 b.c. Distant View (USA) 126 – Dangora (USA) 98 **65**
(Sovereign Dancer (USA)) [2001 8m 7g² 7g⁵ 5.7m⁴ 7m⁵ Sep 22] tall, good sort: fifth
foal: closely related to fairly useful 1996 2-y-o 7f winner Corsini (by Machiavellian) and
half-brother to sprinters Danzari (at 2 yrs in France, by Arazi) and 8-y-o Delegate: dam,
2-y-o 6f winner, closely related to smart miler Zaizafon (dam of Zafonic): fair maiden:
stays 7f: raced only on good/good to firm going: has worn crossed noseband/raced freely/
carried head awkwardly: very slowly away first 2 starts: sold 5,000 gns. *B. W. Hills*

*Tote Cesarewitch (Handicap), Newmarket—a 1,2 for the Balding stable as Distant Prospect (far side)
snatches the verdict from Palua; next home are Give Notice, Establishment (No.31),
Guard Duty and the short-priced favourite Alleluia (rail)*

DISTANT SKY (USA)   4 ch.c. Distant View (USA) 126 – Nijinsky Star (USA)   **75**
(Nijinsky (CAN) 138) [2001 f11g 8.5s³ 10g³ 10m 12m 12g 13.9d 11.7d f12g⁵ Nov 17]   **a59 +**
30,000 3-y-o: lengthy, useful-looking colt: half-brother to several winners, including US
Grade 2 11f winner Revasser (by Riverman) and useful French 1m/1¼m winner Viviana
(by Nureyev): dam unraced half-sister to dam of Chief's Crown: fair maiden: below form
on turf after fourth start: stays 1¼m: acts on good to firm going: blinkered last 3 starts.
P. Mitchell

DISTANT STORM   8 ch.g. Pharly (FR) 130 – Candle In The Wind 90 (Thatching   **52 §**
131) [2001 52§: f16.2g 17.1s³ 21.6s⁴ 16.2m 18m 16.2mᵈ Jul 27] robust gelding: modest
handicapper: better at 2m/2¼m than shorter: acts on fibresand/equitrack, probably on any
turf going: blinkered/visored: tongue tied after reappearance: irresolute. *B. J. Llewellyn*

DISTANT VALLEY   2 b.f. (Mar 29) Distant Relative 128 – Down The Valley 73   **104**
(Kampala 120) [2001 6g* 7g* 7f² 7d* Oct 20] smallish, sturdy filly: half-sister to several
winners up to 1m, notably useful 6f (at 2 yrs) to 1m winner Mayaro Bay (by Robellino):
dam 2-y-o 5f winner who stayed 11f: useful performer: won maiden at Ascot in August,
minor event at Kempton in September and 10-runner Owen Brown Rockfel Stakes at
Newmarket (beat Lahinch by a head, rallying gamely) in October: should stay 1m: acts
on firm and good to soft ground: genuine: sent to USA. *R. Hannon*

*Owen Brown Rockfel Stakes, Newmarket—
Distant Valley (rail) battles back close home to edge out Lahinch, with Misterah (left) in third*

DISTINCTIVE DANCER (IRE) 3 b. or br.c. Distinctly North (USA) 115 – – Resiusa (ITY) (Niniski (USA) 125) [2001 f12g Dec 8] 10,000 2-y-o: half-brother to 3 winners, including 1996 2-y-o 5f/6f winner Rebec Girl (by Masterclass): dam Italian 7f (at 2 yrs) to 11f winner: last in maiden at Wolverhampton. *I. A. Wood*

DISTINCTIVE DREAM (IRE) 7 b.g. Distinctly North (USA) 115 – Green Side **68** (USA) 37 (Green Dancer (USA) 132) [2001 77d, a74d: f7g² f8.5s³ f7s f7s² f7g³ f7g f7g⁵ **a61** f7g³ f8g 8.3d⁶ 6m² 5d³ 7m* 5m³ 6m⁵ 5m⁵ 6m 6d* 6g² 6m Jul 1] strong, lengthy gelding: fair handicapper: won at Doncaster (apprentices) in May and Hamilton in June: effective at 5f (given bit of test) to 1m: acts on any turf going and fibresand/equitrack: often visored/blinkered, effective without: sometimes slowly away/looks less than keen. *A. Bailey*

DISTINCTLY EAST (IRE) 4 b.g. Distinctly North (USA) 115 – Raggy (Smoggy **45** 115) [2001 60: f7g f7s⁶ f8.5s⁴ f8.5s f8.5g f7f⁴ f8.5g⁵ f7g Jun 21] small, useful-looking gelding: fluent mover: poor performer: probably stays 1m: acts on soft going, good to firm and fibresand: tried visored/blinkered: has been slowly away. *Miss S. J. Wilton*

DISTINCTLY WELL (IRE) 4 b.g. Distinctly North (USA) 115 – Brandywell **58** (Skyliner 117) [2001 73: f9.4s f9.4g f8.5g f11g 8.2s 8f 8d 8m 10g³ 10m² 11.6m³ 9.9s Sep 25] angular gelding: modest handicapper nowadays: stays 11.6f: acts on firm going, soft and fibresand: tried visored/blinkered: often on toes/sweating. *B. A. McMahon*

DIVA LA VIDA (IRE) 2 ch.f. (Apr 8) Perugino (USA) 84 – First Nadia (Auction **44** Ring (USA) 123) [2001 5m 6m 5m 8.5m⁶ f7.5g 7g Oct 19] IR 5,500Y: tall filly: closely related to a 6f winner in Hong Kong by Fairy King and half-sister to several winners, including 3-y-o My Lucy Locket: dam lightly-raced maiden: poor maiden: stays 8.5f: raced only on good/good to firm going. *J. S. Wainwright*

DIVA'S ROBE (IRE) 3 b.f. Robellino (USA) 127 – High Note 82 (Shirley Heights **46** 130) [2001 58: 6d 8.1g 10g⁶ f12g Jul 2] small filly: poor maiden. *N. A. Graham*

DIVINE GRACE (IRE) 2 b.f. (Mar 2) Definite Article 121 – Grey Patience (IRE) – (Common Grounds 118) [2001 6m 7.6m Aug 22] IR 3,500Y: first foal: dam unraced half-sister to 4-y-o Cape Town: well beaten in maidens. *Mrs P. N. Dutfield*

DIVINE TASK (USA) 3 ch.c. Irish River (FR) 131 – Set In Motion (USA) (Mr **104** Prospector (USA)) [2001 8g 7g* 8g Oct 4] big, lengthy, attractive colt: first foal: dam, French 11f winner, half-sister to very smart 1m to 1½m performer Hatoof (by Irish River) out of half-sister to Mrs Penny: neck second to Rumpold in 1m private trial at Nad Al Sheba in April (then had named changed from Devine Task): well held in 2000 Guineas at Newmarket on British debut, then won maiden at Lingfield in September: useful form when 4 lengths seventh to Beckett in listed race at Newmarket final start: stays 1m. *Saeed bin Suroor*

DIVINE WIND 3 ch.f. Clantime 101 – Breezy Day 85 (Day Is Done 115) [2001 75§: **63 §** f7g⁵ 7.1g 6m² 6.1f⁴ f6g² 7f⁶ 6m⁴ f6g² 6m⁶ 5g³ a5.5f a7f 6g⁴ Dec 23] big, strong, lengthy **a68 §** filly: poor mover: fair performer: left B. McMahon after tenth outing: best at 5f/6f: acts on firm going, good to soft and fibresand: unreliable. *S. Seemar, UAE*

DIVORCE ACTION (IRE) 5 b.g. Common Grounds 118 – Overdue Reaction (Be **61 §** My Guest (USA) 126) [2001 70§: 10.3m 10v 10m³ 10.5g⁵ 9m Jul 1] modest handicapper: stays 11f: acts on good to firm and good to soft going: has been slowly away: usually held up: sometimes looks none too keen/edges left: not one to trust. *R. M. Stronge*

DIXIE DANCING 2 ch.f. (May 2) Greensmith 121 – Daylight Dreams 77 (Indian – Ridge 123) [2001 7d Oct 15] sturdy filly: first foal: dam, 2-y-o 5f winner who probably stayed 1m, from family of smart stayer Further Flight: 33/1, well held in maiden at Leicester. *C. A. Cyzer*

DIXIE ISLAND (USA) 4 b.g. Dixieland Band (USA) – Cranberry Island (USA) **79** (Private Account (USA)) [2001 f16.2g⁵ f9.4s⁶ e10g⁵ 8s⁴ 8d 10.3f³ 10g 10v May 18] $200,000Y: small gelding: type to carry condition: fourth foal: half-brother to a winner in USA by Conquistador Cielo: dam, maiden in USA, sister to US Grade 1 1¼m winner Corporate Report: trained in 2000 by Mme C. Head-Maarek in France, winning maiden at Cholet: fair form in Britain: left A. Murphy after third start: stays 1¼m: acts on firm going, soft and fibresand/equitrack: tried visored/blinkered. *B. J. Meehan*

DIXIE'S DARTS 3 b.g. Mistertopogigo (IRE) 118 – Maestrette 77 (Manado 130) **67** [2001 50: 6s⁵ 7.5m 6.1f⁵ 6d⁵ 6d⁴ 6g⁶ 7v⁵ p7g⁴ Dec 19] quite good-topped gelding: fair maiden: best efforts at 6f: acts on firm and soft going. *M. H. Tompkins*

DIZZY IN THE HEAD 2 b.g. (Mar 29) Mind Games 121 – Giddy 60 (Polar Falcon **79 d** (USA) 126) [2001 5s 5g* 5d² 5m 6g 5.2m³ 5s 6d 5g f6g 6v⁴ Oct 29] 14,500F, 30,000Y:

leggy gelding: second foal: closely related to fairly useful 2000 2-y-o 5f/6f winner Wally McArthur (by Puissance): dam, 1m winner, half-sister to smart 1m/1¼m performer Dance Turn: fair performer: won maiden at Windsor in May: not so good later in year, running badly ninth and tenth appearances: probably stays 6f: acts on heavy ground and good to firm: sometimes visored: sold 3,200 gns and gelded. *D. W. P. Arbuthnot*

DIZZY KNIGHT   4 b.f. Distant Relative 128 – Top Treat (USA) 101 (Topsider (USA))   – [2001 64: f5g f5g 6m Jun 11] rather angular filly: of little account nowadays. *B. Palling*

DIZZY TART (IRE)   2 b.f. (Feb 11) Definite Article 121 – Tizzy 79 (Formidable   **65** (USA) 125) [2001 5.2m⁵ 5m 7m³ 7g⁵ Aug 13] 6,000Y: half-sister to several winners, including useful 1989 2-y-o 5f winner La Galerie (by Glenstal) and 5f (including at 2 yrs) winner Penniless (by Common Grounds): dam 9f/1¼m winner: fair maiden: may prove best at 6f/7f. *Mrs P. N. Dutfield*

DJAIS (FR)   12 ch.g. Vacarme (USA) 121 – Dame de Carreau (FR) (Targowice (USA)   – § 130) [2001 –, a65: f16g e16g Jan 24] good-topped gelding: one-time smart performer: temperamental nowadays (usually visored). *J. R. Jenkins*

D J SUPREME (IRE)   2 b.c. (May 5) Blues Traveller (IRE) 119 – Musical Gem   **45** (USA) (The Minstrel (CAN) 135) [2001 5.3m 6m 7.1g 6v 8.2s p7g Nov 20] 2,500 2-y-o: sixth foal: half-brother to 1996 2-y-o 6f seller winner Hoh Surprise (by Mac's Imp): dam Irish 2-y-o 7f winner: poor maiden: left M. Quinn after second start: stays 7f: refused to settle only try in blinkers. *G. M. McCourt*

DOBERMAN (IRE)   6 br.g. Dilum (USA) 115 – Switch Blade (IRE) 60 (Robellino   **62** (USA) 127) [2001 52: f9.4g² f8.5s³ f12g⁵ 8g² 9f 8.2s² 8.1s³ 8m³ 8.3g⁴ 8.2m 8m 8s³ f8g²   **a71** f8.5s* Dec 26] rangy gelding: fair handicapper on all-weather, modest on turf: won at Wolverhampton in December: best at 1m/easy 1¼m: acts on fibresand/equitrack, firm and soft going: usually blinkered/visored: has worn tongue tie: usually races prominently: often ridden by inexperienced rider (not at Wolverhampton): sometimes looks none too resolute. *W. M. Brisbourne*

DOC HOLIDAY (IRE)   2 ch.c. (Mar 24) Dr Devious (IRE) 127 – Easter Heroine   **104** (IRE) 72 (Exactly Sharp (USA) 121) [2001 5s* 7m⁶ 6g⁴ 6g* 7.1g⁵ 6g³ 6v Oct 25] IR

Racegoers Club Owners Group's "Doc Holiday"

28,000Y: sturdy, close-coupled colt: second foal: dam, Irish maiden who stayed 1¼m, half-sister to useful sprinter Ocker: useful performer: won maiden at Salisbury in May and minor event at Haydock in August: best efforts when fourth of 5 to Meshaheer in July Stakes and third of 7 to Johannesburg in Middle Park Stakes, both at Newmarket: will need to settle to stay beyond 6f: acts on soft going (well beaten on heavy in Criterium de Maisons-Laffitte): races prominently: sold 135,000 gns, sent to USA. *B. J. Meehan*

DOCKLANDS LIMO   8 b.h. Most Welcome 131 – Bugle Sound 96 (Bustino 136)   – [2001 20m Jun 20] leggy horse: fairly useful handicapper for B. McMath in 1998: well held only Flat start since. *N. A. Twiston-Davies*

DOCK LEAF (USA)   2 ch.f. (Mar 5) Woodman (USA) 126 – Dokki (USA) (Northern   – Dancer) [2001 7m Jul 11] half-sister to several winners, notably Kentucky Derby and Belmont Stakes runner-up Aptitude (by A P Indy) and smart US 6.5f to 9f (Grade 1 event) winner Sleep Easy (by Seattle Slew): dam unraced half-sister to Belmont Stakes winner Coastal and US Grade 1 9f/1¼m winner Slew O'Gold: eighth of 11 in maiden at Kempton: joined R. Frankel in USA. *J. H. M. Gosden*

DOCTOR DENNIS (IRE)   4 b.g. Last Tycoon 131 – Noble Lustre (USA) 71   **73** (Lyphard's Wish (FR) 124) [2001 76, a82: 6.1v f6g 6.1d f6g* 6g 6f* 6d⁶ 6m 6m³ 6s³ 6v   **a78** f6g f7g p6g Dec 4] good-bodied gelding: fair performer: won handicap at Southwell in May and claimer at Lingfield (final start for B. Meehan) in June: left A. Reid after ninth start: effective at 6f/7f: acts on firm going, soft and fibresand: blinkered/visored after third start: none too consistent. *Mrs Lydia Pearce*

DOCTOR JOHN   4 ch.g. Handsome Sailor 125 – Bollin Sophie (Efisio 120) [2001   – 63: 14.1s 12.4d 11.8f 17.1m Jun 11] lengthy gelding: of little account nowadays. *Andrew Turnell*

DOCTOR NO NO (IRE)   3 b.g. Dr Devious (IRE) 127 – Silver Echo (Caerleon   **70** (USA) 132) [2001 10m⁵ 10s⁵ 10.2g² 10m⁵ 10.2g 10v 11g 7.5d Dec 29] IR 50,000Y: close-coupled, quite attractive gelding: seventh foal: half-brother to several winners, including smart French 1998 2-y-o 7f winner who stayed 9f Hello Soso (by Alzao) and useful Irish/US performer up to 1¼m Artema (by Common Grounds): dam unraced: fair maiden: sold 8,000 gns from J. Osborne after sixth outing: stays 1¼m: acts on soft and good to firm ground: blinkered (went with little enthusiasm) sixth start. *I. de Chirico, Italy*

DOCTOR SPIN (IRE)   5 b.h. Namaqualand (USA) – Madam Loving 99 (Vaigly   **108** Great 127) [2001 111: 6g 6m 5g 6m⁵ 6f⁴ 6m⁶ 7m 6m Aug 18] tall, leggy horse: usually looks well: useful performer: best efforts in 2001 when fifth to Nice One Clare in Wokingham Handicap at Royal Ascot (best of centre group), fourth to Volata in Chipchase Stakes at Newcastle and eleventh to Atavus in Tote International Handicap at Ascot (penultimate start): best at 6f/7f: acts on firm going, below form on soft: edgy sort, often sweats: has found little. *R. F. Johnson Houghton*

DODONA   3 b.f. Lahib (USA) 129 – Dukrame 76 (Top Ville 129) [2001 63§: 8.2s 11.6g   **64** 9m 11.5f⁵ 12.6f⁵ 8m⁴ 10g* 10g² 10.1s* 10.1g⁵ 11m 10s³ 11.6v⁵ Oct 29] modest handicapper: won at Brighton and Epsom (tended to hang left/carry head awkwardly) in August: best form at 1¼m: acts on soft going, probably on good to firm: has worn crossed noseband: free-going sort: attacked by dog before start on penultimate outing: has looked temperamental both in preliminaries/once racing. *T. D. McCarthy*

DOLFINESSE (IRE)   4 ch.f. Dolphin Street (FR) 125 – Gortadoo (USA) (Sharpen   **52** Up 127) [2001 51d: 9v² 8d* 7.1m³ f8g³ f8g 7.5f 8m f8g⁵ 7g* 9g 8.9m Sep 2] sparely-made filly: modest performer: won handicap at Musselburgh in April and seller at Leicester in August: effective at 7f to 9f: acts on fibresand, heavy and good to firm going: usually visored. *M. Brittain*

DOLLAR KING (IRE)   3 b.g. Ela-Mana-Mou 132 – Summerhill (Habitat 134)   **77 +** [2001 8d 8m⁵ 7.1f⁴ 7g⁶ 8.2g² 9m* 9d 8.1f 8g³ Sep 28] 65,000Y: lengthy, angular gelding: seventh foal: brother to 4-y-o Mana-Mou Bay and half-brother to 2 winners, including Irish 7f/1m winner Two Bandits (by Thatching): dam Irish 6f winner: fairly useful performer: won maiden at Redcar in August: ran very well in visor final start: gelded after: should prove best at 1m/9f: acts on firm ground. *J. Noseda*

DOLLAR LAW   5 ch.g. Selkirk (USA) 129 – Western Heights (Shirley Heights 130)   **66** [2001 8s⁵ 8f 8d f8g² 7.1g³ 7s 6v f8.5g 8.2s² Nov 5] leggy, short-backed gelding: fair handicapper: effective at 7f/1m: acts on soft ground (well held twice on fibresand): has been taken steadily/alone to post: has hung left: sometimes pulls too hard. *R. J. Price*

270

DOLLY DIMPLE   2 b.f. (Mar 22) Son Pardo 107 – Anne's Bank (IRE) 77 (Burslem   –
123) [2001 6m 6g 7f 7s Oct 5] fifth foal: dam Irish 7f (at 2 yrs)/1m winner who should
have stayed 1½m: poor maiden. *G. L. Moore*

DOLORES   2 b.f. (Feb 14) Danehill (USA) 126 – Agnus (IRE) (In The Wings 128)   **87 p**
[2001 8d² Oct 19] good-topped filly: second foal: dam, Belgian 7f (at 2 yrs) and 9f
winner, half-sister to smart performer up to 1m Wavy Run: 9/1 and backward, promising
length second of 20 to Rawyaan in maiden at Newmarket, taking strong hold just off pace
and run out of things only late on: not sure to stay beyond 1m: useful prospect, sure to win
races. *Mrs A. J. Perrett*

DOLPHIN DANCER   3 b.f. Dolphin Street (FR) 125 – Hot Lavender (CAN) 67   **45**
(Shadeed (USA) 135) [2001 7.1d 5m 6m 5m 6g Jun 19] 3,000Y: sturdy filly: third foal:
half-sister to 6f winner who stayed 1m Carinthia (by Tirol): dam, maiden, raced only at
5f: poor maiden: probably best at 5f: tongue tied on debut. *Miss J. F. Craze*

DOLPHINELLE (IRE)   5 b.g. Dolphin Street (FR) 125 – Mamie's Joy (Prince   **54 §**
Tenderfoot (USA) 126) [2001 70, a68d: e8g f8g e7g³ e7g e8g⁵ 8s 7m⁶ 8m⁵ 7g 6m 7m⁴ 7m   **a45 §**
7g⁶ 7.6g 7d p7g⁴ p7g p7g⁵ Dec 28] sturdy gelding: modest on turf, poor on all-weather:
probably best at 7f/1m: acts on firm going, soft, equitrack and polytrack (probably on
fibresand): tried visored, usually blinkered nowadays: inconsistent. *Jamie Poulton*

DOME   3 b.g. Be My Chief (USA) 122 – Round Tower 93 (High Top 131) [2001 8d   **60 d**
8.3g 8m 12.6f² 11.7g 14.1m 16g 12m Aug 13] big, good-topped gelding: half-brother to
several winners, including useful 1986 2-y-o 7f winner Roundlet (by Roberto) and fairly
useful 1½m winner Moat Garden (by Sportin' Life): dam, 1¼m winner, out of half-sister
to 1000 Guineas/Prix de Diane winner Highclere (grandam of Nashwan, Unfuwain and
Nayef): modest maiden at best: left R. Charlton 16,000 gns after fifth start: stays 12.6f:
tried visored: looked none too keen final outing. *S. Dow*

DOMINGUIN   2 b.c. (Feb 6) Distant Relative 128 – Derasara (IRE) (Dancing Dissident   –
(USA) 119) [2001 9v Nov 15] approx. 14,000Y in Italy: second foal: dam Italian 5f
(including at 2 yrs)/6f winner: seventh of 10 in maiden at Milan. *L. M. Cumani*

DOMINIC   2 b.c. (Apr 19) Primo Dominie 121 – Pleasant Memories 63 (Danehill   **69**
(USA) 126) [2001 6g⁴ 6d³ 6m 7g 8d a8g* Dec 16] 15,000F, 27,000Y: strong, lengthy colt:
third foal: dam, 1m winner, half-sister to Belmont Stakes runner-up My Memoirs: fair
performer: sold from G. Bravery 5,000 gns before final start: won minor event at Mijas in
December: stays 1m: acts on sand. *M. Alvarez, Spain*

DOMINICA   2 ch.f. (May 8) Alhaarth (IRE) 126 – Dominio (IRE) 99 (Dominion 123)   **105**
[2001 5g³ 6m³ 5m* 5d* Oct 13] sixth foal: half-sister to 6f winner East Winds (by Suave
Dancer), later useful sprinter in Sweden: dam, best at 5f, half-sister to Ya Malak and
from family of Cadeaux Genereux: useful performer: won maiden at Musselburgh in
September and 11-runner Cornwallis Stakes at Ascot (beat Berk The Jerk 1¾ lengths,
making virtually all) in October: will prove best at 5f/6f: yet to race on extremes of going:
flashes tail under pressure, but seems genuine. *M. P. Tregoning*

Willmott Dixon Cornwallis Stakes, Ascot—
Dominica puts up her best performance to beat Berk The Jerk (right) and Pachara

DOMINION PRINCE   3 b.c. First Trump 118 – Lammastide 93 (Martinmas 128)   –
[2001 66d: f8.5g e8g Feb 24] tall, rather leggy, good-topped colt: fair maiden: well held
both 3-y-o starts: bred to be best up to 1m. *R. Hannon*

DOMINIQUE   3 ch.f. Primo Dominie 121 – Tender Loving Care 105 (Final Straw   –
127) [2001 62: 6g 8.1m⁵ Jul 5] modest maiden at best: finished distressed final start.
R. Hannon

DOMQUISTA D'OR   4 b.g. Superpower 113 – Gild The Lily 83 (Ile de Bourbon   **57 d**
(USA) 133) [2001 –: f8.5s² f9.4s² f9.4g³ f9.4g⁴ 8.1m 10g 10.9g⁶ 7.1d 7.1s⁵ Aug 9] strong,
lengthy gelding: modest maiden, on downgrade: probably stays 11f: acts on soft ground
and fibresand: blinkered/visored last 3 starts. *G. A. Ham*

DON ALFRED (IRE)   3 b.g. Mark of Esteem (IRE) 137 – Jezyah (USA) 80 (Chief's   **68 §**
Crown (USA)) [2001 73: f9.4g² e8g⁴ 8f⁴ May 29] close-coupled gelding: fair maiden:
should stay 1¼m (below form in very testing ground when tried at 2 yrs): acts on
fibresand/equitrack, good to firm and good to soft going: effective blinkered or not: has
raced freely/found little: not one to trust implicitly: sent to Italy. *P. F. I. Cole*

DONATELLO PRIMO (IRE)   2 ch.c. (May 8) Entrepreneur 123 – Mystical River   **70**
(USA) (Riverman (USA) 131) [2001 5m⁴ 7m 5.7m⁴ 6m⁴ 6v⁵ Oct 29] 8,000F, 13,000
2-y-o: half-brother to several winners by El Gran Senor, including useful Irish 1m
(including at 2 yrs) winner Epic Tale: dam, ran twice in USA, half-sister to smart 1m
winner Maximilian: fair maiden: should stay 1m: acts on good to firm and heavy going:
joined L. Cumani. *G. L. Moore*

DONATUS (IRE)   5 b.g. Royal Academy (USA) 130 – La Dame du Lac (USA) (Round   **65**
Table) [2001 70: 13.9m 12m⁶ 12m³ 10.1d⁶ 12f⁵ 12m⁴ 12g p13g⁴ Dec 29] neat gelding:
fair maiden handicapper: probably stays 13f: acts on firm going, soft and equitrack/
polytrack: visored (ran creditably) final start: none too consistent. *S. Dow*

DON BOSCO (IRE)   5 ch.g. Grand Lodge (USA) 125 – Suyayeb (USA) (The   **60**
Minstrel (CAN) 135) [2001 71, a58: e8g⁵ 7g 8m⁴ 7m⁶ f8.5g⁴ 6.5d³ 7.5d³ Dec 29] strong   **a50**
gelding: easy mover: modest performer: sold 5,000 gns from E. Stanners after fifth start:
effective at 6.5f to easy 1¼m: acts on firm going, good to soft and fibresand/equitrack:
tried blinkered/visored/tongue tied. *E. Allegri, Italy*

DONE AND DUSTED (IRE)   5 ch.m. Up And At 'em 109 – Florentink (USA) (The   **53**
Minstrel (CAN) 135) [2001 75: f7s f6g⁴ f6g f6g⁶ f6g Mar 14] good-topped mare: modest
handicapper in 2001: best at 6f/7f: acts on good to firm going, good to soft and fibresand/
equitrack. *R. Brotherton*

DONEGAL SHORE (IRE)   2 b.c. (Apr 11) Mujadil (USA) 119 – Distant Shore   **98**
(IRE) 71 (Jareer (USA) 115) [2001 5g⁶ 6m 6v² 6d² Nov 2] IR 19,000F, 35,000Y: rather
leggy colt: second foal: dam, fourth at 7f in Ireland on only start, half-sister to smart
Irish 6f to 1m performer Nautical Pet: useful performer: won maiden at Folkestone in
September: good second in listed race at Doncaster and minor event at Newmarket
(beaten neck by Red Liaison) last 2 starts: will stay 7f: acts on heavy ground. *B. W. Hills*

DON FAYRUZ (IRE)   9 b.g. Fayruz 116 – Gobolino (Don 128) [2001 f11g 8.2s⁵ f8g   **62**
10f⁴ 8d⁴ 8f* 8.3g² Jul 9] good-topped gelding: modest nowadays: first win on Flat since
1994 in claiming handicap at Bath in June: effective at 1m/1¼m: acts on firm and soft
ground: has found little. *Mrs A. J. Bowlby*

DON FERNANDO   2 b.c. (Feb 2) Zilzal (USA) 137 – Teulada (USA) 61 (Riverman   **93 +**
(USA) 131) [2001 7.1g* 8f³ 8s Oct 22] 80,000Y: tall, good-topped colt: third foal: dam
lightly-raced half-sister to useful 1m winner Triode out of smart US Grade 2 8.5f winner
Triple Tipple: fairly useful form: won maiden at Sandown in September: very good
staying-on third to Fight Your Corner in minor event at Newbury later in month: not bred
to stay much beyond 1m: acts on firm ground, possibly not soft. *S. P. C. Woods*

DONNA'S DOUBLE   6 ch.g. Weldnaas (USA) 112 – Shadha 57 (Shirley Heights   **80**
130) [2001 76, a–: 8.3m⁶ 8.1m 8m² 10m* 7.9m 10m⁴ 9.2g 10.1f* 8m 8.9d 6v 7d Oct 30]   **a–**
rather leggy gelding: fairly useful handicapper: won at Ripon in June and Newcastle in
September: seems best at 1¼m nowadays: acts on firm going, soft and fibresand: usually
held up: has carried head awkwardly: none too consistent. *D. Eddy*

DONNINI (IRE)   4 ch.g. Kris 135 – La Luna (USA) (Lyphard (USA) 132) [2001 –:   –
12.6m Jun 18] big, strong gelding: well held in 2 maidens. *P. W. Harris*

DON QUIXOTE (IRE)   5 b.g. Waajib 121 – Maimiti (Goldhill 125) [2001 44+: e10g³   **54**
e8g⁴ e7g* e7g 7f 7f⁶ 8.5f Jul 5] close-coupled gelding: modest performer: won claimer at
Lingfield in January: best up to 7f: acts on firm going and fibresand/equitrack: tried
blinkered: tongue tied in 2001: sometimes slowly away. *Miss B. Sanders*

DON RUBINI 3 b.g. Emarati (USA) 74 – Emerald Ring 74 (Auction Ring (USA) 123) [2001 –: f6s⁶ Jan 23] no form. *B. Smart* –

DONTBESOBOLD (IRE) 4 b.g. River Falls 113 – Jarmar Moon (Unfuwain (USA) 131) [2001 64: f8g f7s Jan 23] leggy gelding: modest maiden at 3 yrs: no form in 2001: visored. *B. S. Rothwell* –

DON'T SIOUX ME (IRE) 3 b.c. Sadler's Wells (USA) 132 – Commanche Belle 74 (Shirley Heights 130) [2001 12f* 12g² 14.1m⁴ 12s Nov 10] brother to fairly useful Irish 1999 2-y-o 9f winner Commanche Saddle, closely related to 2 winners by Fairy King, notably smart 1993 2-y-o 7f and 1m (Fillies' Mile winner) Fairy Heights and half-brother to several winners, notably smart 7f (at 2 yrs) to 1½m winner Persian Brave (by Persian Heights): dam middle-distance maiden: won maiden at Newbury in July: useful form in minor events at Newmarket (neck second to Jalousie) and Salisbury (fourth to Hatha Anna) next 2 starts, well held in November Handicap at Doncaster final outing: barely stays 1¾m: acts on firm ground: free-going sort. *H. R. A. Cecil* **105**

DON'T TELL DAD 2 ch.c. (Apr 9) King's Signet (USA) 110 – Princess Tallulah 43 (Chief Singer 131) [2001 5.1v 5m 7m⁶ Jun 14] well-grown, leggy colt: third foal: brother to disqualified 2000 2-y-o 6f seller winner Princess Penny: dam maiden who stayed 1m: poor maiden: has worn tongue strap. *W. G. M. Turner* –

DONT WORRY BOUT ME (IRE) 4 b.g. Brief Truce (USA) 126 – Coggle 60 (Kind of Hush 118) [2001 64d: e10g⁵ e12g 10f* 10m 9.7d⁴ 10.2f Sep 18] modest performer: won handicap at Brighton in May: stays 1½m: acts on firm ground and fibresand/ equitrack: usually visored: needs to dominate: none too consistent. *T. G. Mills* **60**

DOODLE BUG 4 b.f. Missed Flight 123 – Kaiserlinde (GER) (Frontal 122) [2001 77, a–: f16g 14.1v Mar 28] fair maiden at 3 yrs: no form in 2001. *Jedd O'Keeffe* –

DORA CARRINGTON (IRE) 3 b.f. Sri Pekan (USA) 117 – Dorothea Brooke (IRE) 80 (Dancing Brave (USA) 140) [2001 106: 8g May 6] lengthy, good-quartered filly: useful performer at 2 yrs, winning Cherry Hinton Stakes at Newmarket: took strong hold when last in 1000 Guineas at Newmarket (reportedly lost near-hind shoe) only 3-y-o start: likely to prove best short of 1m: yet to race on extremes of going. *P. W. Harris* –

DORANS PRIDE (IRE) 12 ch.g. Orchestra 118 – Marians Pride (Pry) [2001 88: 14g⁶ 20m 22.2f³ 16d Oct 14] strong, workmanlike gelding: smart hurdler/high-class chaser: fairly useful and very lightly raced on Flat: not discredited both starts at Royal Ascot in June, eighth in Ascot Stakes then 6½ lengths third to Life Is Life in Queen Alexandra Stakes: stays 2¾m: acts on firm and soft ground. *Michael Hourigan, Ireland* **86**

DORCHESTER 4 b.g. Primo Dominie 121 – Penthouse Lady (Last Tycoon 131) [2001 88: 6m 5m 5g⁶ 5g 6g 5s 5g 5m 6g⁵ 5.2v 5s³ Nov 9] good-topped gelding: fairly useful handicapper, on downgrade: has form at 6f, but all successes at 5f: acts on firm going, soft and fibresand: blinkered once at 3 yrs: tends to edge right. *W. J. Musson* **85 d**

DOROTHEA SHARP (IRE) 4 b. or br.f. Foxhound (USA) 103 – Captain's Niece 84 (Vitiges (FR) 132) [2001 –: 7d⁴ f8g May 25] plain filly: bad maiden: stays 7f: acts on fibresand and good to firm going, probably on good to soft: visored twice in 2000. *Mrs A. Duffield* **28**

DO THE HONOURS (IRE) 3 br. or gr.f. Highest Honor (FR) 124 – Persian Secret (FR) 101 (Persian Heights 129) [2001 8s⁶ 5.5g³ 7d* 6g* 5g* 6g* 5s⁶ Oct 7] **121**

Despite the best efforts of Three Points, none of the major sprint prizes went the way of Godolphin in 2001, but it will be a surprise if they draw a blank in the next season. Not only will Three Points be doing duty again, but a more recent acquisition by the team promises to make her presence felt, too. This is Do The Honours, who has had two seasons' racing in France for Sheikh Mohammed and made remarkable progress in the latest one. The winner of a minor event at Angers on the second of three starts at two, Do The Honours developed into a very smart sprinter at three and won four races in succession during the summer.

Do The Honours' four-timer began in a seven-furlong handicap at Le Lion d'Angers, but it was over five and six furlongs at Deauville that she made a name for herself. Following another handicap success, she was stepped up to pattern-race company and won both the listed Prix du Cercle and the Group 3 Prix de Meautry Royal Barriere. Do The Honours won the former by two lengths from the sole British challenger Kyllachy and was even more impressive in accounting for the British-trained pair Invincible Spirit and Hot Tin Roof in the latter, for which she

*Prix de Meautry Royal Barriere, Deauville—a fine performance from Do The Honours,
who makes all for an easy success, beating Invincible Spirit (rail) and Hot Tin Roof (far side)*

started favourite. Perhaps Do The Honours had the run of the race to some extent in
the Meautry, allowed to dictate the pace, but there was a lot to like about the way
she quickly brushed aside her challengers when shaken up after two furlongs out
and stormed clear soon after. At the line, where she was being eased, Do The
Honours had three lengths to spare over Invincible Spirit, who had been produced
to hold every chance, with Hot Tin Roof a never-nearer third. This was up there
with the best sprinting performances by a three-year-old filly in the last five years,
but Do The Honours failed by a long way to reproduce it on her only subsequent
start, in the Prix de l'Abbaye. She did best of the three-year-olds at Longchamp but
still finished only sixth, possibly unsuited by the soft ground. Although Do The
Honours won her first race of the season on good to soft, she left that form a long
way behind at Deauville, where each of her races took place on good ground. She is
certainly well worth another chance to confirm herself a very smart sprinter.

		Kenmare	Kalamoun
Do The Honours (IRE)	Highest Honor (FR)	(gr 1975)	Belle of Ireland
(br. or gr.f. 1998)	(gr 1983)	High River	Riverman
		(b 1978)	Hairbrush
	Persian Secret (FR)	Persian Heights	Persian Bold
	(b 1993)	(ch 1985)	Ready And Willing
		Rahaam	Secreto
		(gr 1987)	Fager's Glory

There's another very smart sprinting filly in Do The Honours' immediate
family, her dam being a half-sister to Cassandra Go. Persian Secret is also a half-
sister to the Coventry Stakes winner and Irish 2000 Guineas runner-up Verglas,
who like Do The Honours is by the Prix d'Ispahan winner Highest Honor. Do The
Honours is the first foal of Persian Secret, a useful performer who was successful
over six furlongs at Ayr and Pontefract as a two-year-old, and in a listed event over
a mile in France for Do The Honours' trainer at three. Persian Secret's second foal
Seba (by Alzao), also owned by Sheikh Mohammed, won the seven-furlong
Chesham Stakes in June. Do The Honours is bred to stay a mile and was tried once
at the trip, but she has speed in abundance and it is at five and six that she will
continue to prove most effective. *H-A. Pantall, France*

DOTTIE DIGGER (IRE)   2 b.f. (May 11) Catrail (USA) 123 – Hint-Of-Romance   **57**
(IRE) 86 (Treasure Kay 114) [2001 7.2m 7.2v Oct 15] IR 5,500Y: heavy-topped filly:

second foal: dam won at 6f/7f in Ireland: better effort in maidens at Ayr (modest form) when seventh on debut. *I. Semple*

DOUBLE BAILEYS   5 b.g. Robellino (USA) 127 – Thimblerigger 62 (Sharpen Up 127) [2001 13.3m 18m 17.2m 14.1m 16.4g 16g Sep 5] tall gelding: little form in 2001: often visored/blinkered. *C. P. Morlock* —

DOUBLE BLADE   6 b.g. Kris 135 – Sesame 117 (Derrylin 115) [2001 72: 10m^2 10.3m^4 9f^2 10.3m 11m 8.9m 11d Oct 30] big, angular gelding: fair performer: below form after reappearance: effective at 9f to 2m: acts on firm and good to soft going: blinkered once: usually held up: carries head high and none too trustworthy. *Mrs M. Reveley* **72 d**

DOUBLE BREW   3 ch.g. Primo Dominie 121 – Boozy 111 (Absalom 128) [2001 83: 6m^3 5m^4 5g 5.1f 6g^4 6g 5g^6 f6g Nov 30] good-topped gelding: has scope: fairly useful maiden handicapper: left R. Hannon 9,000 gns before final outing: raced only at 5f/6f: acts on good to firm and good to soft going (last on all-weather debut): carries head high. *J. L. Eyre* **80**

DOUBLE CROSSED   3 b.f. Caerleon (USA) 132 – Quandary (USA) 104 (Blushing Groom (FR) 131) [2001 75p: 10v* 11.5g* 12s^6 Nov 10] big, rangy filly: has plenty of scope: useful form in 4 starts: made all in maiden at Sandown in April: first past post in 3-runner listed race at Lingfield following month, beating Silver Grey Lady by a neck, initially demoted, having hung across runner-up, but reinstated on appeal: off 6 months before below form in similar event at Doncaster final start: stayed 11.5f: stud. *H. R. A. Cecil* **102**

DOUBLE DESTINY   5 b.g. Anshan 119 – Double Gift 68 (Cragador 110) [2001 56: 7m^3 7m^3 7.6f 7m^3 7m 7g^6 7m^5 8.3g Aug 6] modest maiden handicapper: best around 7f: acts on good to firm ground: tried visored/blinkered. *K. T. Ivory* **56**

Mr K. Abdulla's "Double Crossed"

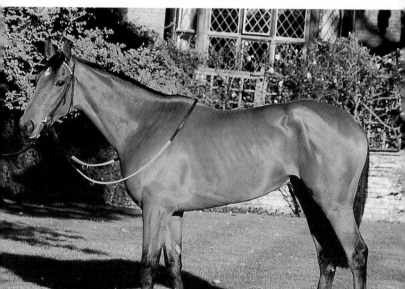

DOUBLE DIGIT 3 b.f. Timeless Times (USA) 99 – Kagram Queen 64 (Prince Ragusa – 96) [2001 –: 11m 8.2s 5g Aug 17] small, sturdy filly: no form. *D. W. Barker*

DOUBLE EM 2 b.g. (Mar 28) Balnibarbi 95 – Something Speedy (IRE) 53 (Sayf El **53** Arab (USA) 127) [2001 5v⁶ f5g 7g 7m 8g³ 8m 10v Oct 4] 2,800Y: workmanlike gelding: second foal: dam, 2-y-o 8.5f winner who stayed 1½m, half-sister to smart 1½m performer Murghem: modest maiden: well held in nurseries last 2 starts: should stay 1¼m: acts on heavy ground. *C. W. Fairhurst*

DOUBLE FANTASY 3 b.f. Mind Games 121 – Song's Best (Never So Bold 135) **71** [2001 83: f6g 6d 6s⁵ 6.1f 5.3f⁶ 6g 6m 5m 6m³ f7g Dec 1] leggy filly: fair performer: left D. Nicholls and off over 4 months after penultimate start: effective at 5f/easy 6f: probably acts on any going (off several months before both outings on fibresand): has been slowly away. *A. Bailey*

DOUBLE FARE 3 b.f. Mtoto 134 – Double Flutter 92 (Beldale Flutter (USA) 130) **69** [2001 8.2d⁵ 9m⁵ 10f³ 8m⁵ 8g⁵ 9.7m³ Aug 13] second foal: half-sister to 4-y-o It's Allowed: dam 7f to 1¼m winner: fair maiden: should be suited by 1¼m+: acts on good to firm going. *M. R. Channon*

DOUBLE FAULT (IRE) 4 br.f. Zieten (USA) 118 – Kashapour 81 (Nishapour (FR) – § 125) [2001 54d: f8g f16g Jan 12] angular filly: temperamental maiden: usually blinkered. *J. A. Gilbert*

DOUBLE GAMBLE 3 b.f. Ela-Mana-Mou 132 – Helen's Gamble (IRE) (Spectacular **76** Bid (USA)) [2001 12m⁴ 12.3m² 11.5g³ 11.5g⁶ 12m* 14.5g f12g Dec 1] 11,000 2-y-o: lengthy, unfurnished filly: fourth foal: half-sister to 3 winners abroad, including useful French 1m winner Chief Baron (by Wolfhound): dam, French 1¼m winner, half-sister to St Leger runner-up Air Marshall: fair performer: won maiden at Musselburgh in September: well held in listed race at Cologne (stiff task) and handicap at Wolverhampton after: should be suited by 1¾m+: raced only on good/good to firm ground on turf: tends to hang/carry head awkwardly, and temperament under suspicion. *M. Johnston*

DOUBLE HONOUR (FR) 3 gr.g. Highest Honor (FR) 124 – Silver Cobra **120** (USA) (Silver Hawk (USA) 123) [2001 80: 10d² 12m* 11.9d* 16.2m⁵ 16g² 18d 15.5v 14.6s* Nov 9]
        Double Honour began to make a name for himself in his own right in the latest season, having first hit the headlines as a two-year-old when becoming the thousandth winner on the Flat for Mark Johnston, Johnston reaching that milestone quicker than any other British-based trainer. Double Honour's record-breaking victory came in a Hamilton maiden, and he soon added to it on his return, picking up mile-and-a-half handicaps at Goodwood and Haydock. The best was still to come, when Double Honour was stepped up in trip again, and also in class. Fifth in the Queen's Vase at Royal Ascot on his first attempt at two miles, Double Honour then ran a cracking race in the Group 2 Goodwood Cup. One of only two three-year-olds in the twelve-runner field, Double Honour accounted for all bar Persian Punch, the pair having the race to themselves in the straight. Double Honour was sent on over three furlongs out, and stayed on most willingly, though the much more experienced Persian Punch rallied to regain the advantage shortly after and went on to beat him by a length and a half. It is possible that this hard race just took the edge off Double Honour for a while, as he failed to do himself justice on his next two starts, in the Doncaster Cup and Prix Royal-Oak. He was back on song at Doncaster in November, though, admittedly facing a straightforward task starting at 9/4-on in a minor event. But he could hardly have been more impressive, ridden with slightly more restraint than usual and simply toying with the opposition, storming well clear when given his head. All being well Double Honour will be more than ready for the much stiffer tests that await him on his return. His campaign will be geared around the Cup races, and no doubt Goodwood will be a particular target given that Johnston has won the race with Royal Rebel and three times with Double Trigger, the latter owned by Ron Huggins, who also runs the syndicate which has Double Honour.
        Double Honour, a 150,000-franc yearling, is the sixth foal of the French eleven-furlong and mile-and-a-half-mile winner Silver Cobra, herself a sister to the American Grade 1 nine-furlong winner Silver Ending. Four of Silver Cobra's previous offspring have won races, too. They include a couple of winners in France

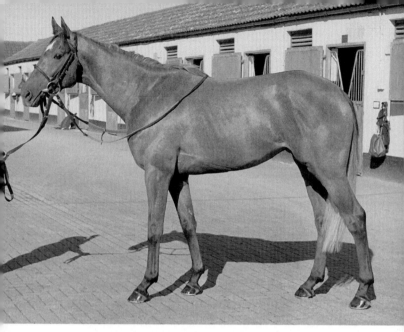

The 4th Middleham Partnership's "Double Honour"

		Kenmare	Kalamoun
Double Honour (FR) (gr.g. 1998)	Highest Honor (FR) (gr 1983)	(gr 1975)	Belle of Ireland
		High River	Riverman
		(b 1978)	Hairbrush
	Silver Cobra (USA) (b 1986)	Silver Hawk	Roberto
		(b 1979)	Gris Vitesse
		Copperhead	Hawaii
		(b or br 1979)	Basin

also sired by the French Guineas second and Prix d'Ispahan winner Highest Honor, notably the useful filly Silversword, who stayed a mile and a half. Double Honour, a leggy, close-coupled individual with a round action, was gelded after his final outing. He acts on soft and good to firm going. *M. Johnston*

DOUBLE KAY (IRE)   3 gr.g. Treasure Kay 114 – Heart To Heart (IRE) (Double   –
Schwartz 128) [2001 –: 6.1v 8.2f Jun 25] little form. *J. A. Glover*

DOUBLE M   4 ch.c. First Trump 118 – Girton Degree 41 (Balliol 125) [2001 57: e5g³   **59**
e6g² e6s e5g 6f 5g 5m⁴ 5m 5.1f⁶ 5m p5g³ p7g⁶ Dec 12] modest performer: stays easy
6f: acts on good to firm ground and all-weather: usually blinkered/visored: sometimes
slowly away. *Mrs L. Richards*

DOUBLE MARCH   8 b.g. Weldnaas (USA) 112 – Double Gift 68 (Cragador 110)   **55**
[2001 62: 6m⁴ 6.1f⁴ 6g⁶ 6m 7m 7.1g Sep 13] sturdy gelding: modest handicapper: stays
6f well: acts on any turf going and fibresand/equitrack: blinkered once: has been slowly
away. *H. Morrison*

DOUBLE OSCAR (IRE)   8 ch.g. Royal Academy (USA) 130 – Broadway Rosie   **69**
101 (Absalom 128) [2001 79, a88: f5g f5g⁶ f6g 5s 5m 5m⁶ 6m 5.1f 5m 5m⁴ 5g 6g² 5m²   **a88**
6g 5d 5g Sep 3] good-bodied gelding: fairly useful on all-weather, fair on turf: best at 5f/

277

6f: acts on firm going, soft and fibresand/equitrack: visored once, often blinkered nowadays: has had tongue tied: sometimes slowly away: usually held up. *D. Nicholls*

DOUBLE PING   3 gr.f. Petong 126 – Paircullis (Tower Walk 130) [2001 38: 9s 9.9m May 12] lengthy, leggy filly: no form in 2001. *M. W. Easterby*

DOUBLE PLAY (IRE)   2 b.c. (Mar 26) Mujadil (USA) 119 – Skinity (Rarity 129)   **89** [2001 5s² 5.3s* 5.2d² 5m* 6m Sep 12] 20,000Y: leggy, useful-looking colt: good walker: has a quick action: brother to fairly useful Irish 9f winner Tianyi and half-brother to 2 winners in Belgium: dam won 6 times in Belgium, including at 2 yrs: fairly useful performer: won maiden at Brighton in April and minor event at Redcar in August: should stay 6f: acts on soft and good to firm ground: sold 28,000 gns. *J. Noseda*

DOUBLE RANSOM   2 b.g. (Apr 15) Bahamian Bounty 116 – Secrets of Honour   **60** (Belmez (USA) 131) [2001 8g 8d⁵ f8.5s 7.9s 8d Nov 2] 8,000Y: good-topped gelding: has scope: third foal: half-brother to 3-y-o Another Secret: dam unraced half-sister to high-class sprinter Mr Brooks and to dam of Middle Park winner First Trump: modest maiden: easily best effort on second start: raced only around 1m: acts on good to soft ground, well held on fibresand. *C. A. Dwyer*

DOUBLE SPEY   2 b.g. (Apr 7) Atraf 116 – Yankee Special 60 (Bold Lad (IRE) 133)   **65** [2001 6g f7g 5g 6d³ Oct 8] 5,500Y, resold 5,500Y, 30,000 2-y-o: workmanlike gelding: half-brother to 6f (at 2 yrs) and 1m winner Langtonian (by Primo Dominie) and French winner up to 11f Soldiers Bay (by Robellino): dam sprint maiden: fair maiden: best effort when third in nursery at Pontefract, carrying head rather awkwardly: not sure to stay 7f. *P. C. Haslam*

DOUBLE SPICE   3 b.f. Saddlers' Hall (IRE) 126 – Island Lake 97 (Kalaglow 132)   **63** [2001 10v⁴ 12d³ f12g Dec 8] 5,200Y: sister to fair 1¾m to 17f winner Island Song and half-sister to several winners, including fairly useful 1m/1¼m winner Double Edged (by Sabrehill): dam 1½m winner: modest form in maidens: best effort when third at Catterick: should stay 2m+. *M. Johnston*

DOUBLE SPLENDOUR (IRE)   11 b.g. Double Schwartz 128 – Princess Pamela   **76** 70 (Dragonara Palace (USA) 115) [2001 78: f6f² f7g 6.1d⁵ 7m⁵ 6m² 6g 6g⁶ 6m* Aug 24] good-topped gelding: has been hobdayed: fair handicapper: won apprentice event at Newmarket in August: effective at 6f/7f: acts on firm going, soft and fibresand/equitrack: sometimes slowly away: held up. *P. S. Felgate*

DOUBLET   6 ch.g. Bustino 136 – Pas de Deux 80 (Nijinsky (CAN) 138) [2001 14s   **63** 18m⁵ 16m 15.4m⁶ 11.6g³ 14.1m Aug 16] leggy, rather angular gelding: modest maiden, lightly raced: stays 2¼m: acts on good to firm and good to soft ground. *B. R. Millman*

DOUBTLESS RISK   4 b.g. Risk Me (FR) 127 – Doubtfire 71 (Jalmood (USA) 126)   **–** [2001 –: 8.3m 8m 8f⁶ Jun 30] modest maiden at best: no form in 2001: tried blinkered. *A. R. Dicken*

DOVEBRACE   8 b.g. Dowsing (USA) 124 – Naufrage (Main Reef 126) [2001 61: 7.1f   **56** 7.6m 8g⁵ 7m² 8g 8d⁵ 8m 8f² 8.2m² 8f 7.5s Sep 25] leggy gelding: unimpressive mover: modest handicapper: effective at 7f to easy 9f: yet to race on heavy going, acts on any other turf and probably on equitrack: tried blinkered/visored: tends to be slowly away (has been markedly so). *A. Bailey*

DOVEDON SUPREME   3 b.f. Emperor Jones (USA) 119 – Secreto Bold (Never So   **–** Bold 135) [2001 –: 8.5m⁵ 10m Jul 12] leggy, short-backed filly: well held in maidens. *H. Akbary*

DOVE FROM ABOVE   8 b.g. Henbit (USA) 130 – Sally's Dove (Celtic Cone 116)   **–** [2001 14.1v Apr 3] first foal: dam winning hurdler: 100/1, well held in Nottingham minor event. *R. J. Price*

DOVE'S DOMINION   4 b.g. Primo Dominie 121 – Dame Helene (USA) (Sir Ivor   **–** 135) [2001 54: f12g e12g 8.1g 11.6m 15m Aug 1] of no account in 2001: dead. *A. J. Chamberlain*

DOWER HOUSE   6 ch.g. Groom Dancer (USA) 128 – Rose Noble (USA) 62   **96** (Vaguely Noble 140) [2001 10s 10.4g⁴ May 17] lengthy, rather leggy gelding: has a fluent, round action: useful performer, lightly raced: better effort in 2001 when fourth to Ferzao in handicap at York: best form at 8.5f to 1¼m: acts on firm going, probably soft: tongue tied both 6-y-o outings: takes good hold: joined A. Turnell. *M. W. Easterby*

DOWHATJEN   2 b.f. (Mar 22) Desert Style (IRE) 121 – Cupid Miss (Anita's Prince   **79** 126) [2001 5.7f⁴ 5.7m* 7m 6g 5g 7g* 7d³ 6d Oct 12] IR 8,000F, IR 24,000Y: lengthy filly: half-sister to several winners, including 3-y-o Montana Miss and ungenuine 11f winner Perecapa (by Archway): dam Irish 6f (at 2 yrs) and 1m winner: fair performer: won maiden at Bath in July and nursery at Epsom (made all) in September: may prove best at 6f/7f: acts on firm and good to soft going: usually races prominently. *M. R. Channon*

DOWNLAND (IRE)　5 b.g. Common Grounds 118 – Boldabsa 96 (Persian Bold 123)　**98 §** [2001 88: 7s 6s 6m 7m 8.1d³ 8f 8m 8.5m 7.1s 7s* 6g 7d 6v* f7g Dec 11] tall, good sort: useful handicapper: won at Ascot (40/1, beat I Cried For You by ½ length in Tote Trifecta Stakes) in September and Newcastle (beat CD Flyer by 5 lengths) in October: left T. D. Barron after penultimate start: effective at 6f to 1m: has won on good to firm going, goes very well on soft/heavy: blinkered last 3 starts at 4 yrs: has been taken early to post and mounted on track (withdrawn after unseating and running back to paddock intended penultimate start): inconsistent. *R. M. Beckett*

DOWNPOUR (USA)　3 b.g. Torrential (USA) 117 – Juliac (USA) (Accipiter (USA))　**76** [2001 –p: 13.1m⁴ f12g* 12.4g f11g* 10.9d² f12g² 11.9s³ Oct 11] useful handicapper on　**a96** all-weather, fair on turf: won at Southwell in June and July: good efforts after: effective at 11f/1½m: acts on fibresand, soft and good to firm going: has raced freely: sold 30,000 gns. *Sir Mark Prescott*

DOWN TO THE WOODS (USA)　3 ch.c. Woodman (USA) 126 – Riviera Wonder　**103** (USA) (Batonnier (USA)) [2001 109: 7d 6m 10.3m² 10f³ 10m⁵ 9.9g 10.5g³ 8m⁵ Aug 16] tall, leggy colt: good mover: useful performer: mostly creditable efforts at 3 yrs, including when placed in minor event at Doncaster, listed race at Ascot (1½ lengths third to Freefourinternet) and Rose of Lancaster Stakes at Haydock (9 lengths third to Nayef): stays 1¼m, at least when emphasis is on speed: acts on firm and soft going: blinkered (folded tamely) final start: tongue tied after reappearance: takes strong hold. *M. Johnston*

DOYLE (USA)　3 b.g. Odyle (USA) 116 – Miss Riverton (USA) (Fred Astaire (USA))　**52** [2001 8s f7g⁶ f8g⁶ 12.3v⁵ 9.9m 10.1g⁶ Aug 17] $11,000F: workmanlike gelding: fourth foal: half-brother to 3 winners, including useful 7.5f to 8.5f winner in Britain/UAE River Times (by Runaway Groom): dam won up to 1¼m in USA: modest maiden: stays 1¼m: acts on fibresand, best turf effort on good ground: sold 900 gns. *T. D. Easterby*

DRAGNET (IRE)　3 ch.f. Rainbow Quest (USA) 134 – River Dancer 118 (Irish River　**72** (FR) 131) [2001 72p: 9.9g* Sep 19] useful-looking filly: fair form: won maiden at Goodwood in September by head from Prickly Poppy, briefly swishing tail: will stay 1½m: never travelling well on heavy ground final start at 2 yrs. *Sir Michael Stoute*

DRAGON FLYER (IRE)　2 b.f. (Mar 11) Tagula (IRE) 116 – Noble Rocket (Rep-　**85 p** rimand 122) [2001 5m⁴ 5s* 5.2s* Oct 31] IR 2,000Y, 8,200 2-y-o: second foal: dam unraced sister to useful performer up to 8.5f in Britain/USA Royal Rebuke: left M. Quinn after debut: won maiden at Lingfield and nursery at Yarmouth (beat Effervescing by 1½ lengths) in October, quickening well each time: will prove best at 5f/6f: should make a useful 3-y-o. *G. M. McCourt*

Tote Trifecta Stakes (Handicap), Ascot—40/1-shot Downland returns to form, giving apprentice David Kinsella the most important of his twenty-four winners during the year; I Cried For You (far side) is second, with Continent next

DRAMA KING 9 b.g. Tragic Role (USA) – Consistent Queen 55 (Queen's Hussar **51** 124) [2001 17.1s* 21.6s Apr 23] sturdy gelding: modest handicapper: won at Pontefract (first Flat start for 3 yrs) in April by 11 lengths: stays 17f well: acts on fibresand and soft ground: often blinkered: none too consistent: won over hurdles in December. *B. J. Llewellyn*

DRAMA OF LIFE (USA) 2 ch.f. (Apr 1) Royal Academy (USA) 130 – Hot Princess **– p** 101 (Hot Spark 126) [2001 7s⁶ Oct 31] half-sister to several winners, including top-class 1m/1¼m winner Rodrigo de Triano (by El Gran Senor), also 6f/7f winner at 2 yrs, and 3-y-o Modigliani: dam, Irish 5f to 7f winner, later successful in USA: 8/1, backward and green, left behind final 2f when sixth of 10 in maiden at Yarmouth: sure to do better. *J. H. M. Gosden*

DRAMA PREMIERE 3 br.f. Emarati (USA) 74 – Dramatic Mood (Jalmood (USA) **75** 126) [2001 64: 7f 8.1g² 8.1d* 8.3g⁴ 8.1g⁵ 8g 8g Sep 28] good-topped filly: fair handicapper: won at Haydock (drifted left) in July: stays 1m: acts on good to soft ground. *I. A. Balding*

DRAMATIC QUEST 4 b.g. Zafonic (USA) 130 – Ultra Finesse (USA) 107 (Rahy **108** (USA) 115) [2001 101: 10g* 12d⁶ 12g² 12g³ Oct 5] rangy gelding: good mover: useful performer, lightly raced: won minor event at Newbury in May by short head from Man O'Mystery: much better effort in listed races after when creditable 6¼ lengths third to Mubtaker at Newmarket (carried head rather awkwardly): stays 1½m: acts on good to firm going: edgy penultimate start: sold 16,000 gns, joined Ian Williams. *M. Johnston*

DRAMATIC RING 2 b.c. (May 1) Magic Ring (IRE) 115 – Dramatic Mood (Jalmood **56** (USA) 126) [2001 6m⁶ 6g 5.7f 7m 6g 5.7g 6v Oct 8] 35,000Y: seventh foal: brother to useful 1997 2-y-o 6f/7f winner Merlin's Ring, later successful up to 9f in USA, and half-brother to 3 winners, including Irish 1½m winner Lifesforliving (by Aragon): dam unraced half-sister to useful Derby winner up to 2m Rada's Daughter: modest maiden: should stay 1m: acts on heavy ground: tried blinkered: sold 3,500 gns. *I. A. Balding*

DR BOOBY (IRE) 3 b.f. Bluebird (USA) 125 – Chellita (Habitat 134) [2001 10d 9m **–** 8m 14.1m Jul 24] 100,000Y: good-topped filly: half-sister to several winners, including May Hill Stakes and Fillies' Mile winner who stayed 1¼m Tessla (by Glint of Gold) and 13.4f winner Star Master (by Rainbow Quest): dam ran once at 2 yrs: well held in maidens/handicap. *N. A. Callaghan*

DR CHARLIE 3 ch.g. Dr Devious (IRE) 127 – Miss Toot 72 (Ardross 134) [2001 8d² **75** Apr 21] 210,000Y: well-made gelding: sixth living foal: half-brother to very smart 7f/ 1¼m winner Kool Kat Katie and smart 8.3f (at 2 yrs) and 1¼m winner who stays 1½m Kalypso Katie (both by Fairy King): dam 1¼m and 15f winner on only starts: well-supported 11/4-shot, encouraging ½-length second to Forest Leaf in maiden at Newbury, soon well there and keeping on: gelded afterwards: should stay at least 1¼m. *R. Charlton*

DR COMFORT (USA) 2 ch.g. (Mar 13) Spinning World (USA) 130 – Hot Thong **59** (BRZ) (Jarraar (USA) 78) [2001 8m⁴ Sep 26] first foal: dam, Brazilian Grade 3 7f winner and third in 1000 Guineas there, out of close relative to smart Ninotchka: well-held fourth of 6 to Mamool in maiden at Goodwood: sold 6,500 gns. *B. J. Meehan*

DR COOL 4 b.g. Ezzoud (IRE) 126 – Vayavaig 78 (Damister (USA) 123) [2001 60: **75** 11.9s² 11.6g* 12m⁴ 12d³ 11.6m 12g* 12g* 12g⁴ 11.9s Oct 11] quite good-topped gelding: fair handicapper: won at Windsor in June and Epsom and Goodwood (amateurs) in September: should stay beyond 1½m: acts on fibresand, good to firm and heavy going: tried visored/blinkered: tends to hang: held up. *J. Akehurst*

DREAM A DREAM 2 b.f. (Mar 28) Emperor Jones (USA) 119 – Thornbury (IRE) **–** (Tender King 123) [2001 7d 7s Oct 25] 5,000F: leggy filly: first foal: dam, ran once in Britain and later 13f winner in Norway, out of half-sister to smart winner up to 10.5f Church Parade: well beaten in maidens. *P. S. McEntee*

DREAM BIRD 3 b.f. Prince of Birds (USA) 121 – Baliana 75 (Midyan (USA) 124) **–** [2001 f7g 6.9v 7g⁶ 7.1g Jun 7] 6,500Y: angular, unfurnished filly: third foal: half-sister to 7f (at 2 yrs) and 1m winner Bali Dance (by Rambo Dancer): dam unreliable sprinter: well held in maidens/handicap. *N. A. Graham*

DREAM CARRIER (IRE) 13 b.g. Doulab (USA) 115 – Dream Trader (Auction **–** Ring (USA) 123) [2001 –: f8.5g e10g f7g 7m 8.1m 10d Aug 12] one-time fairly useful performer: no recent form: tried blinkered/visored. *R. E. Peacock*

DREAM EXPERIENCE 2 b. or br.f. (Mar 19) Reprimand 122 – Dependable (Form- **44** idable (USA) 125) [2001 5v⁴ f5g* e5g² 5.1s⁵ 7g Jun 12] 450Y: workmanlike filly: **a51**

seventh foal: half-sister to 6f (at 2 yrs) to 14.8f winner Certain Magic and 7f to 1¼m winner Elba Magic (both by Faustus): dam unraced: modest on all-weather, poor on turf: won seller at Wolverhampton in March: should stay at least 6f: acts on fibresand and equitrack, best turf run on heavy going: gave trouble at stalls final start. *J. S. Moore*

DREAMIE BATTLE   3 br.f. Makbul 104 – Highland Rossie 67 (Pablond 93) [2001 **52** 63: 6.1m 7f⁶ 8.1d⁵ 8m⁶ 7m⁵ 6f⁴ 8.1f⁶ 7m 7g f9.4g f8g f8.5f⁵ Dec 5] leggy, quite good-topped filly: modest maiden handicapper: probably stays easy 1m: unraced on heavy going, acts on any other turf (below form on fibresand). *R. Hollinshead*

DREAMING DIVA   2 ch.f. (Mar 28) Whittingham (IRE) 104 – Any Dream (IRE) 81 **71** (Shernazar 131) [2001 6d³ 7g* 7d* Aug 26] 600F, 1,000Y: strong, lengthy filly: third foal: dam, Irish 13f winner, half-sister to smart Irish 7f/1m performer Tarry Flynn: fair performer: trained on debut by R. Hannon: won seller at Newmarket and nursery at Goodwood, both in August: will stay 1m: sold 4,000 gns in December. *J. C. Fox*

DREAM MAGIC   3 b.g. Magic Ring (IRE) 115 – Pip's Dream 52 (Glint of Gold 128) **80** [2001 71: 8g 8.2f 8.1g 8m³ 10m 8.1s² 8m* 8g² 10g⁴ Oct 5] big, good-topped gelding: fairly useful handicapper: won at Goodwood in September: unlucky (stumbled twice closing stages) when short-headed by Beauchamp Pilot in 30-runner race at Ascot next time: may prove better at 1m than 1¼m: acts on firm and soft ground. *M. J. Ryan*

DREAM ON ME   5 b.m. Prince Sabo 123 – Helens Dreamgirl 95 (Caerleon (USA) **–** 132) [2001 34: e13g 11.9m⁴ 11.9f 11.5m 12m 11.7f Jul 26] of no account nowadays. *H. J. Manners*

DREAMS DESIRE   3 b.f. Mind Games 121 – Champenoise 64 (Forzando 122) [2001 **81 d** 90: 5s 5m 6m 6m⁵ 6m 6m 7g⁶ 5m 6m 6ds Dec 16] strong, good-topped filly: fairly useful performer: mostly disappointing at 3 yrs: sold from J. Glover 1,200 gns before final outing: stays 6f: acts on good to soft and good to firm going: blinkered penultimate start: has been slowly away. *Madeleine Smith, Sweden*

DREAM TIME   3 b.f. Rainbow Quest (USA) 134 – Grey Angel (Kenmare (FR) 125) **75** [2001 –: 11.9m³ 14m Aug 18] rangy filly: has scope: best effort in 3 maidens when 5 lengths third to Motto at Brighton: should stay 1¾m: visored both 3-y-o starts: sold 8,000 gns (in December). *Sir Michael Stoute*

DREAM WITH ME (FR)   4 b.g. Johann Quatz (FR) 120 – Midnight Ride (FR) (Fast **102** Topaze (USA) 128) [2001 12g⁶ 12s² 12s Nov 10] 320,000 francs Y: lengthy, quite attractive gelding: second foal: dam French maiden half-sister to Grand Criterium winners Lost World and Fijar Tango, latter also high-class up to 1½m: useful performer: won maiden and minor event at Compiegne and handicap at Deauville in 2000 then left J. Pease in France: very good efforts in handicaps last 2 starts at 4 yrs, 2 lengths second to Hannibal Lad in Betdaq Stakes at Ascot then eighth of 24 to Royal Cavalier in November Handicap at Doncaster (faded only final 1f): will be as effective back at 1¼m as 1½m: yet to race on ground firmer than good (acts on soft). *C. R. Egerton*

DRESS REHEARSAL   3 b.c. Machiavellian (USA) 123 – Dance To The Top 107 **91** (Sadler's Wells (USA) 132) [2001 61p: 10v 8.3m² 8f* 8g 7m 7f² Aug 29] tall, close-coupled, attractive colt: fairly useful performer: won maiden at Ripon in July: was effective at 7f/1m: acted on firm going: put down after reportedly being involved in accident with a car in September. *Sir Michael Stoute*

DRESS TO THRILL (IRE)   2 b.f. (Feb 19) Danehill (USA) 126 – Trusted Partner **104 p** (USA) 114 (Affirmed (USA)) [2001 7d⁵ 7m* 7g² Sep 2] half-sister to several winners, including useful Irish 1½m winner Blend of Pace and useful Irish 1½m/1¾m winner Archive Footage (both by Sadler's Wells): dam won Irish 1000 Guineas: won 4-runner listed race at the Curragh (by neck from Shah Jehan) in July: good ¾-length second of 17 to Quarter Moon in Moyglare Stud Stakes on same course, travelling well again and challenging 1f out: will stay 1m: should make a smart 3-y-o. *D. K. Weld, Ireland*

DR GORDON (IRE)   3 b.c. Definite Article 121 – Bristle 96 (Thatch (USA) 136) **72** [2001 –p: 9d 10s⁵ 11.5g 14.1m Jun 22] fair maiden on balance: flattered penultimate start: bred to be suited by 1¼m/1½m: sold 1,200 gns, sent to Holland. *C. E. Brittain*

DR GREENFIELD (IRE)   3 ch.c. Dr Devious (IRE) 127 – Memory Green (USA) **111** (Green Forest (USA) 134) [2001 84p: 10s* 10.3f* a12f Jun 9] useful-looking colt: smart performer: won minor event at Kempton in April and listed Philip Leverhulme Dee Stakes at Chester (beat Grandera by ½ length, always well placed and leading early in straight) in May: played up before start and slowly away when tailed-off last in Belmont Stakes (reportedly broke blood vessel) final start: should stay 1½m: acts on equitrack, firm and soft going: joined W. Mott in USA. *G. A. Butler*

DRIFT 7 b.g. Slip Anchor 136 – Norgabie 94 (Northfields (USA)) [2001 16v 15.4v² 57
16.2m f16.2s Dec 18] good-topped gelding: modest maiden handicapper: left **a–**
B. Llewellyn after penultimate start: stays 15.4f: acts on any turf going, no show on
fibresand: has worn blinkers/tongue strap. *J. M. Bradley*

DRINKIN TIME 2 ch.f. (Apr 9) Timeless Times (USA) 99 – Mashin Time 73 (Palm **68**
Track 122) [2001 5g⁵ 5s⁴ Sep 7] smallish filly: half-sister to 1m seller winner Tiffin Time
(by Lochnager): dam 6f to 1m winner: fair form in maidens at Pontefract and Haydock
(looked difficult ride): will stay 6f. *T. D. Easterby*

DRIPPING IN GOLD (IRE) 3 ch.f. Alhijaz 122 – Fanny's Choice (IRE) 90 (Fairy **–**
King (USA)) [2001 –: e5g⁶ Jan 6] sparely-made filly: bad maiden. *J. J. Bridger*

DROWNED IN BUBBLY 5 b.g. Tragic Role (USA) – Champenoise 64 (Forzando **–**
122) [2001 f16g Mar 26] workmanlike gelding: won over 15f in Jersey in 2000: no form
in Britain: tried blinkered/tongue tied. *J. G. Given*

DR STRANGELOVE (IRE) 3 ch.g. Dr Devious (IRE) 127 – Renzola (Dragonara **68 §**
Palace (USA) 115) [2001 7p: 10g⁵ 9f 10g³ 9g³ 10.1s Aug 31] close-coupled, quite
attractive gelding: fair maiden: should prove best short of 1¼m: visored (found nothing)
third start: one to treat with caution: sold 8,000 gns, gelded and joined A. Crook.
B. W. Hills

DRURIDGE BAY (IRE) 5 b.g. Turtle Island (IRE) 123 – Lady of Shalott 61 (Kings **– §**
Lake (USA) 133) [2001 –§: f7g f9.4g 8m 6m 7m⁶ 7f Aug 14] useful-looking gelding:
temperamental maiden: tried blinkered/visored. *D. G. Bridgwater*

DRYAD 6 ch.g. Risk Me (FR) 127 – Lizzy Cantle 52 (Homing 130) [2001 f6g⁵ f6g⁴ **58**
Mar 30] angular gelding: modest performer, lightly raced nowadays: stays 7f: acts on soft
going and fibresand: usually blinkered/visored: doesn't look an easy ride. *N. P. Littmoden*

DRYDEN HOUSE (IRE) 2 b.f. (Feb 14) Cadeaux Genereux 131 – For Example **70 p**
(USA) 66 (Northern Baby (CAN) 127) [2001 7m 6g⁴ Oct 19] IR 85,000Y: lengthy, quite
good-topped filly: third foal: half-sister to smart 1m (at 2 yrs) to 1¼m winner Forbearing
(by Bering): dam, third at 1¼m in Ireland, closely related to dam of Culture Vulture and
half-sister to dams of Zilzal and Polish Precedent: better effort in maidens (fair form)
when fourth to Wish at Redcar, keeping on under hands and heels: will probably stay 1m:
capable of better. *M. A. Jarvis*

DRY MARTINI 3 b.c. Darshaan 133 – Drei (USA) 67 (Lyphard (USA) 132) [2001 **73 ?**
10m⁵ 10m⁴ 8.1s³ 11.5g⁵ 9.9g⁶ Sep 19] 20,000Y: good-topped colt: third foal: half-brother
to 9.4f winner Trois (by Efisio) and 1¼m winner Triple Sharp (by Selkirk), both fairly
useful: dam once-raced daughter of smart 7f/1m winner Triple Tipple: maiden: seemingly
fair form at best: stays 11.5f: acts on good to firm going: very unruly in paddock on debut:
slowly away last 3 outings: possibly temperamental: sold 3,500 gns, sent to Holland.
J. W. Hills

DUBAIAN GIFT 2 b.c. (Apr 24) Bahamian Bounty 116 – Hot Lavender (CAN) 67 **66**
(Shadeed (USA) 135) [2001 6m⁴ 6f 5.7g⁶ Oct 1] 3,700F, 6,400Y: smallish colt: fourth
living foal: half-brother to 6f winner Carinthia (by Tirol): dam, maiden, raced only at 5f:
fair form in maidens: likely to prove best at 5f/easy 6f. *I. A. Balding*

DUBAI BELLE (USA) 2 b.f. (Apr 4) Mr Prospector (USA) – Flagbird (USA) 119 **79 p**
(Nureyev (USA) 131) [2001 8.1v² Sep 29] rather leggy filly: second foal: sister to 3-y-o
Marhoob: dam, 1m (including in France at 2 yrs) and 1¼m winner, half-sister to US
Grade 1 1m winner Prospector's Delite (herself dam of smart Irish 6f/7f winner Moon-
shee Mountain) and very smart US Grade 1 1¼m winner Runup The Colors: 4/1,
½-length second of 11 to Budoor in maiden at Haydock, leading 2f out and not given
unduly hard time once headed: joined H-A. Pantall in France: should improve.
D. R. Loder

DUBAI DESTINATION (USA) 2 b.c. (Feb 10) Kingmambo (USA) 125 – **119 p**
Mysterial (USA) (Alleged (USA) 138) [2001 6f² 7g* 7d* Sep 14]
   It seemed that hardly a week went by in the summer without David Loder
producing a two-year-old to win very easily on its racecourse debut. After the
disappointments with the Godolphin 'nursery' at Evry in France, Loder's return to
Newmarket yielded thirty individual juvenile winners of forty-two races to a ratio
of winners to runners approaching forty per cent. Eight of the stable's first nine
runners had already been successful (Steadfast And True's defeat at Yarmouth
being the only blot on the record) by the time the much vaunted Dubai Destination

made his own debut in a twenty-runner, six-furlong Newbury maiden in the middle of June. Dubai Destination's considerable home reputation had led to his name being altered earlier in the year from Copernican, a move comparable with that taken with Dubai Millennium, who had undergone a similar change after impressing on the Loder gallops in 1998 before his racecourse debut. Though presumably not forward enough to feature in the Loder team for Royal Ascot the following week, 2/1-on shot Dubai Destination was expected to dispose of his rivals at Newbury without too much difficulty. His short head defeat by the Gosden-trained Waldenburg, carrying owner Sheikh Mohammed's second colours, was, however, greeted with equanimity by Dubai Destination's trainer—'He went to the start shouting for his mother, and he's come back looking for her . . . when he grows up he'll be a different horse.'

Dubai Destination stayed on strongly at Newbury, finishing well clear of the rest of a promising bunch, and he duly got off the mark at 3/1-on next time when stepped up to seven furlongs in the traditionally-strong maiden that opens the Newmarket July meeting. Loder expressed himself 'more than satisfied' with Dubai Destination's three-and-a-half-length victory over newcomer Sohaib, though the winner had to be niggled along running into the Dip and needed a couple of smacks with the whip before asserting himself. This victory, incidentally, was followed later in the afternoon by that of Dubai Destination's long odds-on stable-companion Silent Honor in the Cherry Hinton, after which the season's record of the Loder juveniles stood at an amazing eighteen victories from twenty-four runs (all but two of the winners starting at odds on). Quotes for the Two Thousand Guineas ranged from 16/1 to 25/1 after Dubai Destination's Newmarket victory, but Hills and Ladbrokes had him as their 6/1 Guineas favourite after a tremendous display against Gimcrack winner Rock of Gibraltar in the Rothmans Royals Champagne Stakes at Doncaster in September. The race was billed as a test of strength between Loder and Aidan O'Brien, whose two-year-olds were enjoying a fantastic run in the big races. There seemed more market confidence behind O'Brien's 11/10 favourite Rock of Gibraltar than behind Dubai Destination, who eased from 2/1 to 3/1; the O'Brien second string Wiseman's Ferry, fourth to stable-companion Johannesburg in the Phoenix Stakes last time, and Sohaib, successful in an Ascot maiden since Newmarket, were next in the betting at 8/1. In receipt of 4 lb, Dubai Destination gave his main rival Rock of Gibraltar start and a beating, looking every inch a potential Guineas winner. With his pacemaker Ice And Fire disputing the lead at a good pace with the free-running Sohaib, Dubai Destination was dropped out last. Dettori seemed to set Dubai Destination plenty to do and the situation looked far from promising when Rock of Gibraltar struck the front two furlongs out and soon opened up a lead. Dubai Destination's response was breathtaking; he had no difficulty making up his ground when required to do so and produced a fine burst of speed to catch Rock of Gibraltar inside the final furlong and race away for a most decisive victory. Dettori was able to drop his hands before the post was reached and the winning margin of a length was far from

Rothmans Royals Champagne Stakes, Doncaster—Dubai Destination quickens in the style of a top-class performer in the making; Rock of Gibraltar (rail) is clear of Leo's Luckyman and Wiseman's Ferry (right)

a true reflection of Dubai Destination's superiority; it would have been at least doubled had Dubai Destination not been allowed to ease down.

The ability to make good opponents look much worse than they actually are is the hallmark of a top-notch performer. Dubai Destination made Rock of Gibraltar look pretty ordinary in the Champagne but, as he went on to show by winning the Grand Criterium and the Dewhurst on his next two starts, Rock of Gibraltar was far from ordinary. No-one could deny his right to be regarded as one of the season's best two-year-olds, yet Dubai Destination trounced him. The overall form of the Champagne Stakes looked very solid too. The first two finished clear, the useful Leo's Luckyman filling third, four lengths behind Rock of Gibraltar and half a length in front of fourth-placed Wiseman's Ferry with Sohaib a further three lengths away fifth. The stage looked set for Dubai Destination to tackle the Dewhurst next, but he suffered what connections described as 'a small setback . . . a ligament problem, not a bone problem.' He wasn't seen out again before being sent to Dubai for the winter to be prepared for the Godolphin classic challenge in 2002. Dettori said after the Champagne Stakes that Dubai Destination gave him the feel of a turf horse rather than a dirt horse, so it seems fairly certain that, provided all is well with him, his first major target will be the Two Thousand Guineas. His ante-post odds of

		Mr Prospector (b 1970)	Raise A Native
			Gold Digger
	Kingmambo (USA) (b 1990)	Miesque (b 1984)	Nureyev
Dubai Destination (USA) (b.c. Feb 10, 1999)			Pasadoble
		Alleged (b 1974)	Hoist The Flag
			Princess Pout
	Mysterial (USA) (b or br 1994)	Mysteries (b 1986)	Seattle Slew
			Phydilla

Sheikh Mohammed's "Dubai Destination"

around 9/2 for that race at the time of writing couldn't be described as a gift, but there is no doubting that, judged on the striking impression created by his victory at Doncaster, he fully deserves his place near the head of the market.

The rangy, quite attractive Dubai Destination, who cost 1,500,000 dollars as a yearling, has the physique of a colt who should train on, and he looks like developing into a good-looking three-year-old. There is no doubt that he will get the Guineas trip, and possibly further. His sire Kingmambo was a miler—he has already sired a winner of the Two Thousand Guineas in King's Best—but he has sired winners over significantly further, including the top-class colts El Condor Pasa and Lemon Drop Kid, both successful at up to a mile and a half, notably in the Japan Cup and in the Belmont Stakes respectively. Dubai Destination is the first foal of his dam, the twice-raced Mysterial, a daughter of Alleged, an influence for stamina, out of Mysteries, who finished a good third in the Musidora Stakes. Mysteries showed smart form at York but failed to win in a four-race career and was a keen, active type who gave the impression she might have proved ideally suited by distances short of a mile and a quarter. Mysteries has made her mark as a broodmare through the achievements of two Japanese-trained performers, the July Cup and Prix de l'Abbaye winner Agnes World (by Danzig) and Hishi Akebono (by Woodman), a very smart sprinter-miler; also among the offspring of Mysteries is the stakes-winning filly My Sea Castles (by Polish Navy), successful four times in the States. Dubai Destination's great grandam Phydilla was a high-class miler, winner of the Prix Quincey and fourth in the Prix du Moulin, but one of her half-brothers Observation Post was runner-up in the Irish Derby and the Coronation Cup. Dubai Destination, who has worn a crossed noseband and swished his tail under the whip at Newmarket, has yet to race under conditions softer than the good to soft going he encountered in the Champagne Stakes. Dubai Destination's excellent turn of foot looks sure to prove a potent weapon, and if he gets to Newmarket in May fully recovered from his autumn training setback he will take a good deal of beating in the Guineas, especially with the unbeaten Johannesburg thought likely to go for the Kentucky Derby instead. *D. R. Loder*

DUBAI EXCELLENCE   2 br.c. (Apr 2) Highest Honor (FR) 124 – Colorado Dancer   **89 p**
122 (Shareef Dancer (USA) 135) [2001 7.1g* Sep 13] half-brother to several winners, including outstanding 1m (including at 2 yrs) and 1¼m winner Dubai Millennium (by Seeking The Gold), useful French 1¼m winner Denver County (by Mr Prospector) and useful French 1½m winner Fort Morgan (by Pleasant Colony): dam, won 13.5f Prix de Pomone, daughter of outstanding broodmare Fall Aspen: 3/1-on, won 11-runner maiden at Chepstow by 3½ lengths from Noble Academy, challenging over 2f out and pulling away late on: will stay at least 1¼m: potentially at least useful. *D. R. Loder*

DUBAI MIDNIGHT (USA)   2 ch.c. (Feb 28) Saint Ballado (CAN) – Lituya Bay   **73 p**
(USA) (Empery (USA) 128) [2001 7f⁶ Aug 18] $430,000Y: strong, well-made colt: closely related to a winner in USA by Jolie's Halo and half-brother to several winners abroad, including smart winner up to 1½m in UAE Breathtaking View (by Country Pine), also 2.5-y-o winner in USA: dam minor 8.5f stakes winner in USA: 7/1 and backward, 4 lengths sixth of 17 to Flat Spin in maiden at Newbury, travelling strongly on heels of leaders good way and not given anything like a hard time: will stay at least 1m: sent to UAE: sure to do better. *J. H. M. Gosden*

DUBAI NURSE   7 ch.m. Handsome Sailor 125 – Lady Eccentric (IRE) (Magical   **42**
Wonder (USA) 125) [2001 –: 5d³ 5m⁵ 5m 5g⁴ 5f 6g 5g Aug 7] poor maiden: best at 5f: acts on firm and soft going: tried blinkered/visored: has started slowly/carried head awkwardly/found little. *A. R. Dicken*

DUBAI PRINCE (IRE)   2 b.g. (Apr 25) Anita's Prince 126 – Balqis (USA) 93   **70**
(Advocator) [2001 5m³ 6d⁴ 5g² 6g⁴ Aug 24] IR 12,000Y: half-brother to numerous winners, including useful 1m (at 2 yrs) to 1½m winner who stayed 1¾m Libk (by Kalaglow) and fairly useful 6f (including at 2 yrs) winner Marha (by Shaadi): dam 2-y-o 5f winner: fair maiden: stays 6f: yet to race on extremes of going. *D. Nicholls*

DUBAI SEVEN STARS   3 ch.f. Suave Dancer (USA) 136 – Her Honour 94 (Teenoso   **75**
(USA) 135) [2001 85: 10.3f⁴ 9.9s² 10.2m² 12m³ 14.1g⁶ 11.7d Oct 25] leggy, workman-like filly: fair maiden on Flat: stays 1½m: acts on firm and soft going: won on hurdling debut in December. *M. C. Pipe*

DUBAI STATUS (USA) 2 b.c. (Jan 31) Seeking The Gold (USA) – Possibly Perfect **89**
(USA) 122 (Northern Baby (CAN) 127) [2001 7m* 7m⁶ Sep 12] $700,000Y: strong,
attractive colt: second foal: closely related to US 8.5f (at 2 yrs) and 9f (Grade 3 event)
winner Promontory Gold (by Gone West): dam, champion turf mare in USA, multiple
Grade 1 winner at 9f/1¼m: fairly useful form: landed odds in maiden at Newmarket in
June by 1¼ lengths from Prince Domino: only sixth of 8 in minor event at Doncaster,
folding tamely: should stay 1m. *D. R. Loder*

DUBAI VISIT (USA) 3 b.f. Quiet American (USA) – Furajet (USA) 101 (The **101**
Minstrel (CAN) 135) [2001 a8f⁴ a9f³ 8s* 8v² Oct 30] rangy, angular filly: fifth foal:
half-sister to 4-y-o China Visit: dam, best at 5f, closely related to 2000 Guineas winner
King of Kings: useful performer: successful in maiden at Bay Meadows from 4 starts for
E. Harty in USA at 2 yrs: won minor event at Leicester in October: best efforts in 2001
when placed in UAE Oaks at Nad Al Sheba (third to Laoub) and listed race at
Maisons-Laffitte (made most, caught only close home when beaten length by First) final
start: stays 9f: acts on heavy going and dirt: blinkered at 2 yrs: has had tongue tied. *Saeed
bin Suroor*

DUBIANSTAR (USA) 3 b.f. Shadeed (USA) 135 – Dubian 120 (High Line 125) **–**
[2001 7d Apr 18] angular filly: sister to 3 winners, notably Cheveley Park and 1000
Guineas winner Sayyedati, and half-sister to 3 winners, including 5-y-o Golden Snake:
dam 7f (at 2 yrs) to 1½m winner who was placed in Oaks/Irish Oaks: 14/1 and backward
in coat/green, last of 28 in Newmarket maiden. *B. W. Hills*

DUCHAMP (USA) 4 b.g. Pine Bluff (USA) – Higher Learning (USA) (Fappiano **–**
(USA)) [2001 93: 20m Jun 20] tall, quite attractive gelding: shows knee action: fairly
useful handicapper at best: well beaten only 4-y-o start on Flat: should stay at least 1¾m:
yet to race on heavy going, acts on any other: visored once: possibly temperamental: fair
hurdler/chaser. *I. A. Balding*

DÚCHCOV 3 ch.f. Caerleon (USA) 132 – Amandine (IRE) (Darshaan 133) [2001 **101**
78p: 9.9m* 10f² Jun 14] tall, good-topped filly: won maiden at Beverley in May: useful
form when 1¾ lengths second of 6 to Nafisah in listed event at Newbury next time: should
stay 1½m: raced only on good to firm/firm going: sent to USA. *L. M. Cumani*

DUCK ROW (USA) 6 ch.g. Diesis 133 – Sunny Moment (USA) (Roberto (USA) **114**
131) [2001 110: 8.1m⁴ 8.5f⁵ 8g² 8m 8d* 8d⁵ 9g³ 9d⁵ Oct 19] sturdy, close-coupled
gelding: smart performer: won minor event at Bath in August by 2½ lengths from Blue
Mountain: best efforts when head second to Panis in Prix Messidor at Deauville in July
and 3½ lengths third to I Cried For You under top weight in Cambridgeshire Handicap at
Newmarket in October: stays 9f: acts on firm and good to soft going, below form on soft:
waited with: consistent. *J. A. R. Toller*

DUC'S DREAM 3 b.g. Bay Tern (USA) 86 – Kala's Image 55 (Kala Shikari 125) **73**
[2001 71: f9.4s⁴ 10.3s 8.1g⁵ 10m* 9.9m* 10m³ f12g³ 10.3v p12g p10g Dec 28] small
gelding: fair handicapper: won at Lingfield in May and Goodwood in June: below
form final 3 starts: stays 1½m: acts on fibresand, heavy and good to firm going: game.
D. Morris

DUDLEYS DELIGHT 2 b.f. (Feb 12) Makbul 104 – Steadfast Elite (IRE) 58 **82**
(Glenstal (USA) 118) [2001 5d* 5.1d* 5m 5f⁴ 5m⁴ 6v² Oct 26] 1,000F, 10,000Y: leggy,
close-coupled filly: second foal: sister to 2000 2-y-o 6f winner Ebullience: dam, 5f (at 2
yrs) to 11f winner, also successful over hurdles: fairly useful performer: won maiden at
Newmarket in April and minor event at Nottingham in May: finished tired when second
of 22 in sales race at Doncaster: will prove best at 5f/easy 6f: very best efforts on good
to soft ground: bolted to post and withdrawn third intended outing (early to post after):
reportedly broke blood vessel penultimate start: sold 14,000 gns. *A. Berry*

DUDS (IRE) 2 ch.g. (Apr 29) Definite Article 121 – Domino's Nurse 104 (Dom Racine **67 d**
(FR) 121) [2001 6m³ 8s 7.9d 7d Oct 18] 17,000Y: brother to 3-y-o Chemicalattraction
and half-brother to numerous winners, including fairly useful 5f (at 2 yrs) to 10.5f winner
Romios (by Common Grounds) and 13f winner Mujtahida (by Mujtahid): dam, Irish 7f
(at 2 yrs) and 1¼m winner, later successful in USA: fair form when third in maiden at
Catterick: no show after, blinkered in seller final start: should stay 1m: sold 3,800 gns.
P. F. I. Cole

DUEL ISLAND 6 b.g. Jupiter Island 126 – Duellist (Town Crier 119) [2001 f9.4s **–**
f16.2g Feb 22] smallish gelding: fair maiden at 3 yrs: well held on Flat since: tried
blinkered/tongue tied. *A. G. Hobbs*

DUELLO   10 b.g. Sure Blade (USA) 130 – Royal Loft 105 (Homing 130) [2001 58§: **76**
10.5g* 10m* 10.1m² 12.6d* 11.6g⁶ 12.3d⁵ 12g² f12g³ Nov 3] leggy gelding: has a round
action: fair performer: won amateur handicaps at Haydock and Warwick and minor event
at Brighton in June/July: effective at 1¼m (given good pace) to 1¾m (when conditions
aren't testing): acts on any turf going and fibresand: blinkered once at 3 yrs, visored
nowadays: usually held up: has hung and looked less than genuine. *M. C. Pipe*

DUE WEST   3 b.f. Inchinor 119 – Western Sal 75 (Salse (USA) 128) [2001 6s⁴ 7g 8m   **56**
May 30] 35,000Y: angular, good-bodied filly: second foal: half-sister to Italian 1999
2-y-o 7f winner Pemba (by First Trump): dam 1¼m/1½m winner who stayed 14.8f: best
effort when fourth to Fatwa in maiden at Pontefract: pulled hard next start, visored final
one: sold 3,400 gns. *Mrs J. R. Ramsden*

DUKE OF EARL (IRE)   2 ch.c. (Mar 26) Ali-Royal (IRE) 127 – Faye 79 (Monsanto   **85**
(FR) 121) [2001 5d 5g 6.9m³ 7g 7g 7d² 7g⁴ 8s* 8.3v* 8s Oct 22] IR 30,000F, IR 20,000Y:
useful-looking colt: half-brother to several winners by Sharp Victor, notably useful 1m/9f
winner Wray: dam, 2-y-o 6f winner, later successful in USA: fairly useful performer: won
maiden at Brighton in September and nursery at Windsor in October: will probably stay
1¼m: goes well on soft/heavy going. *S. Kirk*

DUKE OF MODENA   4 ch.g. Salse (USA) 128 – Palace Street (USA) 103 (Secreto   **109**
(USA) 128) [2001 107p: 7m⁶ 8.1m² 8m 7m 7m 7g 7.9m³ 7s 7.9d 8d Nov 3] sturdy
gelding: useful handicapper: best efforts when second to Calcutta at Sandown in May and
third to Tough Speed at York in August: effective at 7f/1m: acts on heavy and good to
firm going: has been bandaged all round: usually held up: genuine. *G. B. Balding*

DULCET SPEAR   2 b.c. (Apr 8) Vettori (IRE) 119 – Honeyspike (IRE) 79 (Chief's   **101**
Crown (USA)) [2001 7m* 7m* 7.1g Sep 1] 120,000Y: strong colt: fourth foal: half-
brother to 3-y-o Second Strike and fairly useful 2-y-o winners Unicamp (6f in 1998, by
Royal Academy) and Via Camp (7.5f in 1999, by Kris): dam, second at 1m in Ireland,
half-sister to smart 1¼m performer Casey Tibbs: useful performer: won maiden at
Southwell and minor event at Newbury (quickened well to beat Laissezalder by 3½
lengths) in July: ran poorly in Solario Stakes at Sandown: should stay 1m. *D. R. Loder*

DULCIFICATION   3 b.c. So Factual (USA) 120 – Dunloe (IRE) 54 (Shaadi (USA)   **68**
126) [2001 56: 6m² 5m² 5m⁴ 6m⁵ 8g 7m⁴ 8.1m³ 8.5s 7g Oct 19] fair maiden: stays 1m:
acts on good to firm going: blinkered final start: sold 3,600 gns. *J. R. Weymes*

DULZIE   4 b.f. Safawan 118 – Dulzura (Daring March 116) [2001 53: f9.4g⁶ f11g*   **40**
f12g* 11.9s 10d⁶ 11.8m³ 16.2m 11.8d 11.7m f12g f11g⁴ Nov 30] small filly: poor   **a49**
performer: won sellers at Southwell in March and April: stays 1½m: acts on fibresand
and firm going: none too consistent. *A. P. Jarvis*

DUMARAN (IRE)   3 b.g. Be My Chief (USA) 122 – Pine Needle 89 (Kris 135) [2001   **91**
–: 7.1g* 8.1s⁵ 9d* 9g 10.5v 7d⁶ Oct 13] rather leggy gelding: fairly useful performer: won
maiden at Chepstow in July and handicap at Goodwood in August: ran well final start:
stays 9f: acts on good to soft going (finished lame on good to firm). *I. A. Balding*

DUNBRODY RIVER (IRE)   4 b.f. River Falls 113 – Caria (Sure Blade (USA) 130)   **–**
[2001 52: f7g 10s Apr 28] second foal: dam unraced: poor maiden at 3 yrs: trained in
Ireland before well held both 4-y-o starts: stays 9.5f: acts on soft going: has had tongue
tied. *J. J. Quinn*

DUN DISTINCTLY (IRE)   4 b.g. Distinctly North (USA) 115 – Dunbally 57   **56**
(Dunphy 124) [2001 51: f12g⁴ f12g* f16.2g⁵ Nov 21] modest performer: won maiden
handicap at Southwell in January: should stay 1¾m: acts on fibresand, well beaten on
turf: visored once. *P. C. Haslam*

DUNDONALD   2 ch.g. (May 13) Magic Ring (IRE) 115 – Cal Norma's Lady (IRE) 87   **– p**
(Lyphard's Special (USA) 122) [2001 7.2v⁵ Oct 15] fourth foal: brother to 1997 2-y-o 6f
winner Magical, later Grade 3 1m winner in USA, and half-brother to Under Pressure (by
Keen) and 4-y-o Sabre Lady, both 2-y-o 5f winners: dam 2-y-o 6f/7f winner who stayed
1¼m: 25/1 and green, well-held fifth in maiden at Ayr, keeping on past beaten horses:
should do better. *K. A. Ryan*

DUNE   2 b.c. (Apr 4) Desert King (IRE) 129 – Flamands (IRE) 92 (Sadler's Wells   **66**
(USA) 132) [2001 7d 7s 7g⁶ Nov 26] IR 55,000Y: strong colt: second foal: dam, 1½m/
1¾m winner, sister to smart 1¼m performer Casey Tibbs out of Irish Oaks runner-up
Fleur Royale: fair form in maidens: easily best effort when seventh of 14 to Ballet Score
at Doncaster second start: gave trouble at stalls and slowly away at Southwell final one:
will be suited by at least 1¼m. *R. Charlton*

DUNEDIN RASCAL   4 b.g. Piccolo 121 – Thorner Lane 86 (Tina's Pet 121) [2001   **85 d**
88: f5g e5g* f6g e6g³ 5s⁶ 6s⁴ 5.1f² 6m 5g 5.1f 5m 5m 5m⁶ 5g 5.7m 5.1d f6g² p6g f5s⁶ p5g
Dec 22] smallish gelding: sixth foal: half-brother to several winning sprinters, including
useful Coffee 'n Cream (by Handsome Sailor): dam sprinter: fairly useful handicapper
at best: trained by T. Stack in Ireland until after reappearance: won at Lingfield in
March: only fair form most subsequent starts: raced only at 5f/6f: acts on any turf going
and fibresand/equitrack: tried blinkered at 3 yrs, and last 2 starts: usually held up.
E. A. Wheeler

DUNKELD CHAMP   4 br.g. Be My Chief (USA) 122 – Callipoli (USA) 81 (Green   –
Dancer (USA) 132) [2001 –: 9v 8v⁶ Apr 7] no form. *P. Monteith*

DUNKERRON   4 b.g. Pursuit of Love 124 – Top Berry 87 (High Top 131) [2001 10.3f³   **74**
11.5m⁴ 8d³ 8m 10s Oct 16] 4,000Y, 4,500 2-y-o: sturdy gelding: sixth foal: half-brother
to 3 winners, including 6-y-o Derryquin and 9.7f winner Star Entry (by In The Wings):
dam 1m winner: fair maiden: stays 1¼m: visored last 2 starts: sold 7,500 gns.
P. L. Gilligan

DUNKINEELY BOY (IRE)   3 b.c. Hamas (IRE) 125§ – Eimkar (Junius (USA) 124)   **70**
[2001 8d⁵ 10s⁶ 8s 8f² 8.3g 10g⁴ 9m³ 8.5d² 9.9m⁵ 10.1s⁶ 8s³ f9.4g Oct 23] IR 18,000Y:
tall, useful-looking colt: half-brother to untrustworthy 1997 2-y-o 6f seller winner Shannon (by Mujadil) and 1m winner Ladybower (by Pennine Walk): dam unraced half-sister
to high-class French miler Daring Display: fair maiden: barely stays 1¼m: acts on firm
and soft going: sold 12,000 gns. *R. Hannon*

DUNKIRK SPIRIT   3 b.g. Whittingham (IRE) 104 – Ruda (FR) (Free Round (USA))   –
[2001 58: 8.1g 8.3g f12g 8d Aug 8] big, strong gelding: maiden: well held in 2001. *Mrs
Lydia Pearce*

DUNN ALMU (IRE)   4 br.c. Hamas (IRE) 125§ – Art Age (Artaius (USA) 129) [2001   **56 ?**
–: 7g 9d⁵ 10g 9g a7g³ 8f 12g f9.4f Dec 5] IR 18,500Y: closely related to 9-y-o Artful
Dane and 1995 2-y-o 5f winner Happy Tycoon (by Polish Patriot) and half-brother to 2
winners, notably 5-y-o Damalis: dam unraced: modest maiden on balance: well beaten at
Wolverhampton final start: likely to prove best at short of 1¼m: sometimes blinkered.
Edward Butler, Ireland

DUNNES RIVER (USA)   3 b.f. Danzig (USA) – Elizabeth Bay (USA) 116 (Mr   **84**
Prospector (USA)) [2001 8m* Jun 8] second foal: sister to fairly useful 1998 2-y-o 7f
winner Jahaam: dam, French 1m (second in Coronation Stakes) and 9f performer who
later won in USA, out of US Grade 1 9f/1¼m winner Life At The Top: won maiden at
Goodwood by neck, getting up close home: visits Fantastic Light. *Saeed bin Suroor*

DUNSTON DURGAM (IRE)   7 b.g. Durgam (USA) – Blazing Sunset 55 (Blazing   –
Saddles (AUS)) [2001 f12s⁶ Jan 16] of little account. *R. Hollinshead*

DUPONT   2 b.c. (Apr 10) Zafonic (USA) 130 – June Moon (IRE) (Sadler's Wells   **96**
(USA) 132) [2001 6m² 6m* 7g* 7m 7d⁶ Oct 2] useful-looking colt: fifth foal: brother to 2
winners, including smart 7f (at 2 yrs)/1m winner Pacino, and half-brother to fairly useful
winner up to 1½m Winsome George (by Marju): dam unraced daughter of 1000 Guineas
runner-up and smart sprinter Kerrera: useful performer: won maiden at Doncaster in June
and minor event at Lingfield in August: set bit to do and not discredited in valuable sales
race at Newmarket final start: should stay 1m: acts on good to firm and good to soft
ground. *W. J. Haggas*

DURAID (IRE)   9 ch.g. Irish River (FR) 131 – Fateful Princess (USA) 95 (Vaguely   **89**
Noble 140) [2001 92: 8g 10m 8m 7.9m³ 8m⁵ 8m³ 7.9m³ 7d 8f⁵ 8.9d 7d⁴ Nov 6]
workmanlike gelding: has a round action: fairly useful handicapper: effective at 7f (given
a test) to 9f: acts on soft going, probably on firm, well beaten only start on fibresand:
visored once in 1998: tends to carry head high: held up. *Denys Smith*

DURANDANA (FR)   2 b.f. (Feb 9) Selkirk (USA) 129 – Damanka (IRE) (Slip Anchor   **58**
136) [2001 7g⁴ 8.2m⁴ Sep 10] rather leggy, lengthy filly: first foal: dam lightly-raced
half-sister to useful stayer Bondstone out of half-sister to Prix du Jockey Club winner
Darshaan: favourite, modest form when fourth in maidens at Thirsk and Nottingham:
should stay 1¼m: sent to France. *J. R. Fanshawe*

DURHAM   10 ch.g. Caerleon (USA) 132 – Sanctuary (Welsh Pageant 132) [2001 65:   **51 §**
17.1m 17.2g⁵ 18m 14.1m⁵ 14.1m 17.1g⁶ 14.1d f14.8s Sep 6] sparely-made gelding:
modest handicapper: stayed 17f: acted on equitrack, firm and soft going: was usually
blinkered/visored: tongue tied in 2001: was usually held up: was unreliable: dead.
J. Neville

DURKAR STAR (IRE)   3 b.g. Bin Ajwaad (IRE) 119 – Faith Alone 85 (Safawan   –
118) [2001 7g 5m 7.5m 5g Jul 25] IR 4,300F, IR 8,200Y, 5,000 2-y-o: neat gelding: first
foal: dam 5f to (at 2 yrs) 7f winner: well held in maidens. *M. C. Chapman*

DUSKY BLUE (IRE)   2 b.c. (Feb 25) Bluebird (USA) 125 – Massada 106 (Most   55
Welcome 131) [2001 5.2m⁶ 5g 5s Sep 7] 95,000Y: close-coupled colt: first foal: dam
German 2-y-o 7f/1m winner: modest maiden: will stay at least 6f. *Jonjo O'Neill*

DUSKY VIRGIN   4 b.f. Missed Flight 123 – Rosy Sunset (IRE) (Red Sunset 120)   62
[2001 62: 8f³ 7m⁵ Jun 22] modest handicapper: stays 8.5f: raced only on good going or
firmer: sold 8,000 gns (in December). *S. Woodman*

DUSKY WARBLER   2 br.g. (Jan 26) Ezzoud (IRE) 126 – Bronzewing 103 (Beldale   98 p
Flutter (USA) 130) [2001 7m* 10d² Nov 3] rangy gelding: half-brother to several
winners, including smart 7f (at 2 yrs) and 1¼m winner Merry Merlin (by Polar Falcon)
and fairly useful stayer Sun Grebe (by Arctic Tern): dam 6f and 1m winner: useful form:
awarded maiden at Newmarket in September after being short-headed by Moon Ballad,
carried left: 4 lengths second to Alexander Three D in listed event on same course, still
green but staying on well: will stay at least 1½m: will improve further and win more
races. *M. L. W. Bell*

DUST FLICKER   2 ch.f. (Mar 6) Suave Dancer (USA) 136 – Galaxie Dust (USA) 86   63 p
(Blushing Groom (FR) 131) [2001 7d Oct 15] strong, close-coupled filly: sister to smart
7f to 1½m winner Dust Dancer and half-sister to several winners, including very smart
middle-distance performer Zimzalabim (by Damister) and smart filly up to 1¼m Bulaxie
(by Bustino): dam 2-y-o 6f winner: 20/1, eighth of 20 to Opening Ceremony in maiden at
Leicester, late headway under considerate handling: should be suited by 1¼m/1½m: will
improve. *J. L. Dunlop*

DUST TO DUST (IRE)   2 ch.g. (Mar 23) College Chapel 122 – Poscimur (IRE)   63 d
(Prince Rupert (FR) 121) [2001 5s 5s⁶ f5g* 6m f5g f6g f6g f6g⁵ Dec 17] useful-looking
gelding: fourth foal: dam ran 3 times in Ireland: modest performer: won claimer at
Southwell in May: left W. Turner and off 4 months after next start: below form for new
stable: likely to prove best at 5f/6f: acts on fibresand and soft ground. *A. Crook*

DUSTY ANSWER   2 b.f. (Mar 13) Zafonic (USA) 130 – Dust Dancer 116 (Suave   84
Dancer (USA) 136) [2001 7m² 7f* Aug 1] 120,000Y: first foal: dam, 7f to 1½m winner
(including 1¼m Prix de la Nonette), half-sister to very smart performer up to 1½m
Zimzalabim: fairly useful form: confirmed promise when winning maiden at Kempton
by 4 lengths from Procession, making most: will stay 1m. *J. L. Dunlop*

DUSTY BANKES   2 ch.f. (Jan 30) Greensmith 121 – Heather Honey (Insan (USA)   59 d
119) [2001 f5g³ f5g² 5.1s³ f5g* 6f³ 5f* 6.1m² 5.1m 5m² 6g* 7m² 7m 7.1s⁶ f6g f8g p7g
Nov 20] 500Y: workmanlike filly: fourth foal: dam unraced: modest performer: won
sellers at Southwell in April and Musselburgh in June and claimer at Newcastle in July:
well below form last 5 starts: barely stays 7f: acts on firm going, soft and fibresand: has
drifted left under pressure: often makes running. *W. G. M. Turner*

DUSTY CARPET   3 ch.g. Pivotal 124 – Euridice (IRE) 66 (Woodman (USA) 126)   88
[2001 84: 7m³ 8m⁵ 7.6f² 10.3m³ 10m³ 10.3d² 10s² 11.8s Oct 15] sturdy, close-coupled
gelding: fairly useful performer: stays 1¼m: acts on soft ground, firm and fibresand: has
carried head awkwardly/edged left under pressure, but is consistent: sold 44,000 gns,
joined M. Weeden. *C. A. Dwyer*

DUSTY DEMOCRAT   3 b.g. Democratic (USA) 101 – Two Shots (Dom Racine   –
(FR) 121) [2001 40: f8.5s Jan 16] maiden: well held only 3-y-o start: tried visored.
W. G. M. Turner

DUSTY STAR   2 b.f. (Feb 26) Danzig Connection (USA) – Sindos 89 (Busted 134)   –
[2001 8.5m f8.5g Oct 20] half-sister to 1990 2-y-o 6f winner Hold Court and 2 winners in
Germany (all by The Noble Player): dam 7f and 1¼m winner: no sign of ability in
maiden/seller. *W. G. M. Turner*

DUSTY WUGG (IRE)   2 b.f. (Apr 25) General Monash (USA) 107 – Welsh Berry   70
(USA) (Sir Ivor 135) [2001 5m⁶ 5m⁴ 5m⁴ 6m⁴ 6d⁴ 7s² 7v Oct 27] IR 25,000Y: leggy filly:
has a quick action: half-sister to several winners, including unreliable 7.5f to 9f winner
Zahran (by Groom Dancer) and Irish 7.7f winner Hallucination (by Last Tycoon): dam,
ran twice in France, half-sister to Belmont Stakes winner Avatar and Prix du Jockey Club
winner Hours After: fair maiden: runner-up in nursery at Catterick: should stay 1m: acts
on good to firm and soft going: blinkered last 2 starts. *T. D. Easterby*

DUTCH DYANE 8 b.m. Midyan (USA) 124 – Double Dutch 100 (Nicholas Bill 125) [2001 47, a–: 16s f14g f16g 16.2m 16.4m⁴ Jul 12] poor maiden handicapper: stays 2m: acts on fibresand. *G. P. Enright* — **a43**

DUTCH NIGHTINGALE 7 b.m. Warrshan (USA) 117 – Double Dutch 100 (Nicholas Bill 125) [2001 e13g Feb 3] of little account nowadays. *G. P. Enright* —

DYNAMIC TIMES 2 ch.g. (Mar 21) Timeless Times (USA) 99 – Naufrage (Main Reef 126) [2001 5f 6g Jun 19] 2,000Y, resold 1,000Y: small gelding: half-brother to 8-y-o Dovebrace and 1¼m/1½m winner Kismetim (both by Dowsing): dam unraced: well beaten in claimer/seller. *M. W. Easterby* —

E

EACHY PEACHY (IRE) 2 ch.f. (Apr 28) Perugino (USA) 84 – Miss Big John (IRE) (Martin John) [2001 f5g 5m⁵ f5g³ f5g f7g 6g⁴ 8m⁴ 7.5g² 7d p7g⁶ Dec 29] IR 300F, 3,200 2-y-o: rather leggy filly: first foal: dam ran twice in Ireland: modest maiden: modest maiden: creditable efforts last 5 starts: stays 1m: acts on good to firm going, good to soft, fibresand and polytrack. *J. R. Best* — **55**

EAGER ANGEL (IRE) 3 b.f. Up And At 'em 109 – Seanee Squaw (Indian Ridge 123) [2001 6g 16m 5m 7.5f f6g⁴ 5g f6s Dec 15] small, good-quartered filly: poor maiden: left J. L. Eyre prior to final start: stays 6f: acts on fibresand and firm going: tried blinkered. *R. F. Marvin* — **38**

EAGLE PARK (IRE) 2 ch.g. (Apr 1) Eagle Eyed (USA) 111 – Avidal Park 68 (Horage 124) [2001 5m 7g 7.1f³ 7.5s⁴ 8m 8m⁴ 8.3m⁴ 8m⁴ Sep 30] 14,000Y: strong gelding: closely related to 1m winner (including in Hong Kong) Projectvision (by Roi Danzig) and half-brother to several winners, including 4-y-o Sarena Pride: dam 2-y-o 5f winner: fair maiden: creditable fourth in nursery at Musselburgh final start: will stay at least 1¼m: acts on firm and soft going. *J. L. Eyre* — **66**

EAGLERIDER (IRE) 3 b.g. Eagle Eyed (USA) 111 – What A Summer (USA) (What Luck (USA)) [2001 69p: 5f⁶ 8d 8.2s f6g Dec 10] workmanlike gelding: fair maiden at 2 yrs: little form in 2001: blinkered last 2 starts: dead. *J. G. Given* —

EAGLES FORTUNE (IRE) 3 ch.f. Eagle Eyed (USA) 111 – Black Orchid (IRE) (Persian Bold 123) [2001 f7g 5.1s 6g 5.3d⁵ 6m 6f f6g³ f6g Nov 26] IR 1,200F, IR 2,500Y: quite attractive filly: first foal: dam unraced out of half-sister to very smart sprinter Indian Ridge: poor maiden: stays 6f: acts on fibresand and good to soft going. *I. A. Wood* — **42**

EAGLES HIGH (IRE) 2 ch.g. (Feb 17) Eagle Eyed (USA) 111 – Bint Al Balad (IRE) 63 (Ahonoora 122) [2001 5.1f³ 5s 6f⁵ 6m⁴ 8d 7v³ p8g⁴ Dec 12] IR 7,800F, IR 30,000Y: sturdy gelding: third foal: dam twice-raced sister to Nell Gwyn winner A-To-Z: fair maiden: creditable efforts in nurseries last 3 starts: stays 1m: acts on polytrack and any turf going. *R. Hannon* — **71**

EAGLE'S LANDING 3 b.f. Eagle Eyed (USA) 111 – Anchorage (IRE) 86 (Slip Anchor 136) [2001 62: f8g² f8g³ f9.4g³ f11g* 11.6g a10.5g* a12g⁴ a10.5g³ a9g³ Dec 16] fair performer: won handicap at Southwell in March and, having been sold from N. Graham 8,800 gns after fifth outing, minor event at Mijas in August: stays 1½m: acts on sand/fibresand, well held only start on turf. *P. Haley, Spain* — **71**

EAGLET (IRE) 3 b.g. Eagle Eyed (USA) 111 – Justice System (USA) 57 (Criminal Type (USA)) [2001 62: f8f 8v⁶ 8.2s 5.1s 6d 5v Oct 24] small, sparely-made gelding: little form in 2001: tried blinkered. *A. Scott* —

EARLDOM 2 b.c. (Mar 18) Distant Relative 128 – Noble Story 61 (Last Tycoon 131) [2001 8.5g⁶ p8g⁵ f8g⁶ Dec 10] first foal: dam, ran twice, out of half-sister to dam of Derby winner Shaamit: modest form in maidens: should stay 1¼m. *P. F. I. Cole* — **62**

EARL OF DUNTON (IRE) 2 b.g. (Mar 28) Dr Devious (IRE) 127 – Jade Vine (IRE) (Alzao (USA) 117) [2001 5.3f⁶ 6m 7f Jul 25] 7,500Y: first foal: dam, ran once at 2 yrs in Ireland, out of useful Irish 2-y-o 5f/6f winner Grey Dream: well beaten in maidens: gelded after final start. *S. C. Williams* —

EARL SIGURD (IRE) 3 ch.g. High Kicker (USA) – My Kind 59 (Mon Tresor 113) [2001 10m⁵ 7.9d⁵ 8f⁴ 9.2g⁵ Sep 3] leggy gelding: first foal: dam 2-y-o 6f seller winner who stayed 1m: modest maiden: stays 9f: winning hurdler. *L. Lungo* — **64**

EARLY MORNING MIST (IRE)   3 b.f. Alzao (USA) 117 – Welsh Mist 102   **94 d**
(Damister (USA) 123) [2001 78: 7g³ 10.1m³ 10.4d³ 8f 8m 9m⁵ 10g³ 8d 10.3m⁶ 8f 8s²
p10g⁵ Nov 13] workmanlike filly: fairly useful performer: gradually regressed in 2001:
stays 1¼m: acts on soft going, good to firm and polytrack: blinkered seventh/eighth
starts: has looked irresolute. *M. Johnston*

EARLY WISH (USA)   3 ch.f. Rahy (USA) 115 – Heaven's Nook (USA) 96 (Great   **78**
Above (USA)) [2001 67: 7m⁶ 7m 10m 6m* 7g⁴ 6g⁶ Sep 2] good-quartered filly: fair
handicapper: won at Lingfield in July: best effort at 6f: acts on good to firm going,
some promise on good to soft and fibresand: blinkered last 3 starts: sold 28,000 gns in
December. *B. Hanbury*

EARTH SPIRIT   3 b.g. Ezzoud (IRE) 126 – Ideal Candidate 80 (Celestial Storm   **66**
(USA) 132) [2001 10s³ 12g f9.4g⁶ 11.8s⁶ 11.6v 14.1s Nov 5] third foal: half-brother to a
winner in Hungary by Second Set: dam 1¼m to 2m winner: fair form on debut in Windsor
maiden: below that level after: best effort at 1¼m: blinkered final start: dead. *C. A. Cyzer*

EASAAR   5 b.h. Machiavellian (USA) 123 – Matila (IRE) 98 (Persian Bold 123) [2001   **107**
117: 8s² 8.1m² May 25] good-bodied, attractive horse: has a quick action: smart performer at best, lightly raced: much better effort (useful form) in minor events in 2001
when second to Pulau Tioman at Kempton in May: stays 9f: acts on soft going, probably
on good to firm: sold only 10,500 gns in December. *M. P. Tregoning*

EASTBOROUGH (IRE)   2 b.g. (Apr 21) Woodborough (USA) 112 – Easter Girl   **70**
(Efisio 120) [2001 6m⁶ 7.1d* 7g⁵ 7m 6s⁵ f8.5g² 8.3v 6d f7g² p8g* Dec 12] 14,000Y: **a89**
close-coupled, quite good-topped gelding: first foal: dam unraced half-sister to smart 6f/
7f performer Bollin Knight: fairly useful on all-weather, fair on turf: won maiden at
Warwick in July and nursery at Lingfield in December: stays 8.5f: acts on fibresand,
polytrack and good to soft going. *A. P. Jarvis*

EAST CAPE   4 b.g. Bering 136 – Reine de Danse (USA) 78 (Nureyev (USA) 131)   **60 §**
[2001 82: 8s 10s f11g 8.5m 8.1m 10.5g 7m 8g 8.9m 9.1v² 10.1v² Oct 24] leggy, useful-
looking gelding: useful maiden in 2000, only modest at 4 yrs: acts on heavy and
good to firm going: tried visored: irresolute nowadays. *Don Enrico Incisa*

EASTER BONNET   3 ch.f. My Generation 111 – Flower Othe Forest (Indian   **–**
Forest (USA) 117) [2001 –: f12g⁵ Feb 20] small filly: well held in claimer/maiden.
N. M. Babbage

EASTERN BLUE (IRE)   2 ch.f. (Apr 11) Be My Guest (USA) 126 – Stifen (Burslem   **68**
123) [2001 5f⁴ 6m⁴ 5g 6.1g* 6g³ 6.1d³ 6g Oct 6] 7,000 2-y-o: sturdy filly: half-sister
to numerous winners, including 3-y-o Where's Jasper and 1m winner Reason Why (by
College Chapel): dam unraced: fair performer: won maiden at Nottingham in August:
good third in nurseries at Hamilton and Nottingham: should stay 1m: acts on good to soft
ground, probably on firm: has worn crossed noseband. *K. A. Ryan*

EASTERN BREEZE (IRE)   3 b.g. Sri Pekan (USA) 117 – Elegant Bloom (IRE) 84   **86**
(Be My Guest (USA) 126) [2001 73: 9s⁵ 10m⁴ 10g⁵ Jul 20] leggy gelding: fairly useful
maiden: stays 1¼m: acts on soft and good to firm going: edgy sort. *P. W. Harris*

EASTERN HOPE (IRE)   2 b.g. (Jan 18) Danehill Dancer (IRE) 117 – Hope And   **76**
Glory (USA) 87 (Well Decorated (USA)) [2001 6m⁵ 6m³ 7g³ 7m Jul 29] 14,500F,
19,000Y: tall, good-topped gelding: has plenty of scope: half-brother to several winners,
including 6f winner Never Think Twice (by Never So Bold) and fairly useful 1¼m winner
Saddlers' Hope (by Saddlers' Hall): dam, 6f winner, ran only at 2 yrs: fair maiden: third
at Ayr and Thirsk: will probably stay 1m. *K. A. Ryan*

EASTERN IMAGE (USA)   2 ch.c. (Apr 4) Gone West (USA) – My True Lady   **96 p**
(USA) (Seattle Slew (USA)) [2001 6m⁴ 7.1s⁴ 6s* 7d* Oct 30] well-made colt: fifth foal:
half-brother to a winner in USA by Half A Year: dam, US 8.5f minor stakes winner,
half-sister to useful 1996 2-y-o The West (by Gone West): useful form: won maiden at
Pontefract (by 8 lengths) in September and minor event at Redcar (beat Sholay by ½
length) in October, comfortably having led on bridle at halfway in latter: should stay
1m: acts on soft going: on toes at Redcar: should improve further and win more races.
J. L. Dunlop

EASTERN JEWEL   3 b.f. Anshan 119 – China's Pearl (Shirley Heights 130) [2001   **48 §**
–: 12v⁵ 11.6g 11.8f 14m 11.5m 10m³ 10m⁵ 10m² 10d 10s Oct 25] sparely-made filly:
poor maiden: seems to stay 11.6f: acts on good to firm ground: usually blinkered/visored:
has wandered/carried head awkwardly: finds little under pressure. *Mrs A. J. Perrett*

EASTERNKING 2 ch.f. (Mar 21) Sabrehill (USA) 120 – Kshessinskaya 99 (Hadeer – 118) [2001 7d 7.9d 8g Oct 19] 2,000Y: smallish, sturdy filly: third foal: half-sister to French 9.5f winner Noble Doble (by Shareef Dancer): dam 11.5f winner: well held in maidens. *J. S. Wainwright*

EASTERN PROJECT (IRE) 7 b.g. Project Manager 111 – Diandra (Shardari 134) – [2001 11.9g Aug 10] of little account on Flat nowadays. *A. Crook*

EASTERN PROMISE 3 gr.f. Factual (USA) 108 – Indian Crystal 66 (Petong 126) **62 d** [2001 61: 6m⁴ 7.1m 6m 8m⁶ 7.5f 10m⁵ 7g⁴ 9m 6f Sep 10] tall, quite good-topped filly: modest performer: below form after reappearance: should stay 7f: acts on firm and good to soft ground: tried visored: usually races prominently. *J. G. Given*

EASTERN PROPHETS 8 b.g. Emarati (USA) 74 – Four Love (Pas de Seul 133) **45** [2001 62: 6m 7.1m 5m 6m 6.1m 6g⁵ 7d f6s Dec 21] good-quartered gelding: poor nowadays: left M. Dods after penultimate outing: effective at 5f to 7f: acts on firm going, good to soft and fibresand/equitrack: usually blinkered/visored: sometimes on toes/ sweating. *Jedd O'Keeffe*

EASTERN PURPLE (IRE) 6 b.g. Petorius 117 – Broadway Rosie 101 (Absalom **116** 128) [2001 116: 5g 6m 6g⁴ 6m 5.1m⁴ 5m 5m³ 5.1g² 6f³ 5.6m⁵ 5.2f² 5s⁴ 6s² Nov 10] robust, strong-quartered gelding: usually takes the eye: smart performer: ran at least respectably most starts in 2001, including in King George Stakes at Goodwood (under length third to Dietrich, placed for second year running) seventh outing, and Portland Handicap at Doncaster (fifth to Smokin Beau) on tenth and Prix de l'Abbaye at Long-champ (fourth to Imperial Beauty) and listed race at Doncaster (½-length second to Danehurst) last 2: best at 5f/6f: acts on firm and soft going: tried visored, effective blinkered or not: game. *K. A. Ryan*

EASTERN RED 3 b.f. Contract Law (USA) 108 – Gagajulu 75 (Al Hareb (USA) 123) – [2001 48: f6g⁶ f7g f8g 10f⁵ 8.2f Jun 25] close-coupled, unfurnished filly: no form in 2001: tried blinkered. *Ronald Thompson*

EASTERN ROYAL 2 b.g. (Feb 2) Royal Applause 124 – Kentfield (Busted 134) **61** [2001 6m⁶ 7m Jul 29] 18,500Y: leggy gelding: half-brother to several winners, including useful 11f (in UAE) and 1¾m winner Saleel (by Salse) and 6-y-o Chief Cashier: dam once-raced half-sister to smart Irish sprinter Puissance: modest form in maiden at Doncaster and minor event at Ascot: will probably stay 1m. *K. A. Ryan*

EASTERN TRUMPETER 5 b.h. First Trump 118 – Oriental Air (IRE) 56 (Taufan **94** (USA) 119) [2001 87: f6g f5s* e5g* f5g 5m 5m³ 5g 5m³ 5m* 5d⁵ 5m 5f 5m² 5.2m⁴ 5.2f 5d Oct 13] compact horse: fairly useful handicapper: won at Wolverhampton in January, Lingfield in February and York in June: effective at 5f/easy 6f: acts on fibresand/ equitrack, firm and soft going: tough and game: sold 30,000 gns. *J. M. Bradley*

EASTERN VENTURE 4 b.g. Last Tycoon 131 – Imperial Jade 105 (Lochnager 132) **60** [2001 7m⁴ 6g 6m 6g 7m Jul 20] modest handicapper: gelded after final start: stays 6f: acts on good to firm going: tongue tied last 2 starts. *W. R. Muir*

EASTER OGIL (IRE) 6 ch.g. Pips Pride 117 – Piney Pass (Persian Bold 123) [2001 **69** 88d: f7g f7g⁶ f7g⁵ 7s 5.1d 7m 5.7m 7.1g⁴ 7.1m 7m p10g Nov 28] lengthy, good-topped **a59** gelding: unimpressive mover: fair performer nowadays: effective at 5.7f, probably at 1m: acts on any going except heavy: sometimes visored (only twice in 2001): often soon off bridle and tends to get behind: has edged left: often claimer ridden in 2001. *I. A. Balding*

EAST OF JAVA 3 b.g. Greensmith 121 – Krakatoa (Shirley Heights 130) [2001 73: **71** 6m⁴ 6g³ 5g 7m 6g Sep 5] workmanlike gelding: fair maiden: stays 6f: acts on good to firm and good to soft going. *P. J. Makin*

EASTWELL HALL 6 b.g. Saddlers' Hall (IRE) 126 – Kinchenjunga 67 (Darshaan **78** 133) [2001 92: 12s 14.1g 16.4m⁵ 20m Jun 20] tall, close-coupled gelding: fair handi-capper nowadays: stays 2½m: raced mainly on good going or softer: held up. *T. P. McGovern*

EASTWELL MANOR 3 b.g. Dancing Spree (USA) – Kinchenjunga 67 (Darshaan **54** 133) [2001 65: e10g⁶ 6.9v⁵ 7s 10m 10m 12m⁶ 6m Aug 22] modest maiden: probably stays 1½m: blinkered last 2 starts: sold 500 gns. *T. P. McGovern*

EASY DOLLAR 9 ch.g. Gabitat 119 – Burglars Girl 63 (Burglar 128) [2001 88: 7m **77** 6m 5g⁴ 5.7d 6g³ 7m² 6g³ Sep 15] tall, plain gelding: didn't impress in appearance: useful performer in his day, winner of 3 of his 63 races: reportedly sustained leg fracture final start and was put down: stayed 7f: acted on firm and good to soft going, probably on soft: was usually blinkered/visored: raced prominently. *B. Gubby*

EASY ENIGMA (IRE) 3 ch.c. Selkirk (USA) 129 – Moonlight Saunter (USA) 85 **54**
(Woodman (USA) 126) [2001 71: f8.5g³ 6m Aug 16] fair form both 2-y-o starts: below
that level in 2001: should stay 1m: sold 800 gns. *B. W. Hills*

EAU ROUGE 3 ch.f. Grand Lodge (USA) 125 – Tarsa 81 (Ballad Rock 122) [2001 **77**
63: 7.1d⁴ 6m⁴ 5m³ 5f* 5.1m² Jul 14] good-topped filly: fair performer: won maiden at
Musselburgh in June: effective at 5f/6f: acts on firm going, probably on good to soft.
M. A. Jarvis

EBINZAYD (IRE) 5 b.g. Tenby 125 – Sharakawa (IRE) (Darshaan 133) [2001 16.1m **–**
May 24] sturdy gelding: fluent mover: fairly useful performer for E. Dunlop in 1999: well
beaten only start since. *L. Lungo*

EBONY BOUND (USA) 3 b.c. Woodman (USA) 126 – Truly Bound (USA) (In **68 §**
Reality) [2001 8d 12m 10m⁵ 12m³ 14.1g⁶ 10d Sep 21] sturdy colt: brother to smart Irish
1996 2-y-o 7f winner Shell Ginger and half-brother to several winners, including useful
Irish 1m (at 2 yrs) to 1¾m winner Yeoman's Point (by Sadler's Wells): dam, US Grade 2
7f (at 2 yrs) and 8.5f winner, from very good family: fair maiden: stays 1½m: acts on
good to firm ground: has raced freely: carries head high, and probably none too genuine:
sold 4,000 gns. *M. L. W. Bell*

ECCLESIASTICAL 3 b.g. Bishop of Cashel 122 – Rachael Tennessee (USA) (Mat- **112**
sadoon (USA)) [2001 75p: 7g* 8.1m* 8m² 5m 7m² Dec 16] good-bodied gelding: smart
performer: won maiden at Leicester and Tote Credit Club Silver Bowl (Handicap) at
Haydock (by 2 lengths from Lord Protector) in May: excellent 1¾ lengths second to
Analyser in Britannia Stakes at Royal Ascot on third start: sold privately, left J. Fanshawe
and renamed Olympic Express: second in handicap at Sha Tin final outing: stays 1m: acts
on good to firm going. *I. W. Allan, Hong Kong*

ECHO RIVER (USA) 2 ch.f. (Feb 7) Irish River (FR) 131 – Monaassabaat (USA) **101**
105 (Zilzal (USA) 137) [2001 6g* 6g⁴ 7.1m* 8d² 7d⁵ Oct 20] close-coupled filly: third
foal: dam, 6f (at 2 yrs) to 1¼m winner, out of champion US filly and winner up to 1¼m
It's In The Air: useful performer: won minor event at Windsor in June and listed race at
Sandown (beat Sophorific by 1¼ lengths despite edging right) in July: good 2½ lengths
second to Half Glance in May Hill Stakes at Doncaster: only fifth in Rockfel Stakes at
Newmarket, folding tamely and flashing tail: likely to prove best at 7f/1m: yet to race on
extremes of going: has worn crossed noseband. *D. R. Loder*

EC LADY 2 ch.f. (Apr 24) Dilum (USA) 115 – Pooka 65 (Dominion 123) [2001 f5g⁴ **85**
f5g³ 6m* 6.1m 6m³ 7m⁴ 6g* 6m* 6.1g⁶ 6m⁴ 6g⁵ 6v⁴ Oct 26] 3,200Y: close-coupled filly:
sixth foal: half-sister to 4-y-o Chagall and a winner in Greece by Emarati: dam placed at
5f at 2 yrs: fairly useful performer: won seller at Goodwood in May and nurseries at
Leicester (seller) and Windsor in August: best efforts at 6f on good/good to firm going:
sometimes edgy/early to post: front runner: tough and consistent: sold 14,000 gns, sent to
USA. *J. L. Spearing*

ECSTASY 4 b.f. Pursuit of Love 124 – Gong 84 (Bustino 136) [2001 81: 10g³ 11.6g **73**
10.1m 9.9m 9.9m 10d⁴ Sep 21] unfurnished filly: fair performer: stays 1¼m: acts on good
to firm and good to soft going: has looked none too keen. *R. M. Beckett*

ECSTATIC 3 ch.f. Nashwan (USA) 135 – Divine Quest 81 (Kris 135) [2001 88: 7.6f⁴ **94**
9m 9s² 9f² 8g⁵ 8m² 8m³ 9f⁶ 7d Oct 13] leggy, useful-looking filly: fluent mover: fairly
useful performer: ran at least respectably most starts in 2001: stays 9f: acts on soft and
firm ground: sometimes races freely: tends to carry head high: sold 30,000 gns.
R. Hannon

EDDIE ROYALE (IRE) 3 b.g. Elbio 125 – Persian Royale 94 (Persian Bold 123) **–**
[2001 58: f7g⁵ 7d 7g 5m Sep 8] close-coupled gelding: little form at 3 yrs. *D. Nicholls*

EDDU 3 ch.g. Casteddu 111 – Cabra (Red Sunset 120) [2001 11.1s⁶ 10.9m² 10.5m 10.3f* **78**
12.3m 9.9m³ Jul 1] big, lengthy gelding: seventh foal: dam no form: fair performer: won
minor event at Chester in June: stays 1¼m (possibly not 1½m): acts on good to firm
ground: very edgy/gave trouble stalls final start. *W. M. Brisbourne*

EDDYS LAD 3 b.g. Lahib (USA) 129 – Glamour Model 78 (Last Tycoon 131) [2001 **65**
70: 7s² 7.1m f7g 7m 7g f8.5g⁴ 7s⁶ 7s⁴ 7s³ 7s f7s³ p7g² Dec 28] quite good-topped gelding: **a57**
fair maiden on turf, modest on all-weather: left R. Cowell after ninth start: probably stays
8.5f: acts on fibresand/polytrack, firm and soft going: tried visored: has had tongue tied:
has given trouble at stalls/wandered: has looked less than keen. *J. Balding*

EDEL'S JOY (IRE) 3 b.f. General Monash (USA) 107 – Belle-Cote 69 (Coquelin **–**
(USA) 121) [2001 10f 12g 11d Oct 30] fifth foal: half-sister to Irish 8.5f winner Rudi's

Pride (by Conquering Hero): dam, maiden who was best up to 7f, from family of high-class 1¼m/1½m performer Master Willie: no form. *J. Parkes*

EDIFICE (JPN) 5 ch.g. Carroll House 132 – Moon Tosho (JPN) (Steel Heart 128) [2001 74d: 10s 8s 8s 10f 8m⁴ 8m⁴ 10.1m 10.1m⁴ 9.9m 10.1g⁴ 11m² 14.1m⁴ 15.8m Sep 22] smallish, sturdy gelding: modest maiden handicapper: stays 1¾m: acts on good to firm ground: tried blinkered: has started slowly: sometimes looks none so keen. *B. Ellison* **50**

EDITOR IN CHIEF (USA) 2 b.c. (Jan 29) Kingmambo (USA) 125 – Cymbala (FR) (Assert 134) [2001 7.1m³ 8.1g* 10s² Oct 15] 140,000Y: strong, angular colt: first foal: dam won 5 times in France and USA, including Grade 3 9f event: won maiden at Chepstow (carried head awkwardly) in August: good second to Barathea Blazer in minor event at Leicester: should stay 1½m: acts on good to firm and soft going: races up with pace: should make a useful 3-y-o. *J. L. Dunlop* **86 p**

EDMO LIFT (IRE) 2 b.f. (Feb 12) Alhaarth (IRE) 126 – Pollyfidra (USA) (In Fijar (USA) 121) [2001 6m⁶ 5.1f² 6m⁶ 5f² 5m⁵ 5g⁶ 7.5s 5.1m 6m⁵ 5m⁶ 6d 7g Oct 19] IR 13,500Y: compact filly: fourth foal: half-sister to a winner in South Africa by Thatching: dam, French 1¼m to 13f winner, half-sister to smart French 1¼m/1½m performer Solid Illusion: fair maiden: below form after fifth appearance: should stay 7f: acts on firm going: blinkered (looked none too keen) sixth start: sold 800 gns. *T. D. Easterby* **66 d**

E DUBAI (USA) 3 b.c. Mr Prospector (USA) – Words of War (USA) (Lord At War (ARG)) [2001 a9f* a8.5f* a9s² a8.5s* a10f² a10s² Sep 23] $1,350,000Y: second foal: half-brother to smart 1m (in France) and 9f (US Grade 1) winner No Matter What (by Nureyev): dam US 5f (at 2 yrs) to 8.5f (minor stakes) winner: very smart performer: trained in US at 2 yrs by E. Harty: very impressive winner in 2001 of prestige race at Nad Al Sheba (by 9 lengths) in April, allowance race at Belmont in May and Grade 2 Dwyer Stakes on latter course in July: beat Windsor Castle by 5¾ lengths in last-named event, making all and ridden out: runner-up afterwards in Travers Stakes at Saratoga (ran very well when beaten 3½ lengths by Point Given, weakening last 100 yards) and Super Derby at Louisiana Downs (2/1-on, worn down and beaten ½ length by Outofthebox): will prove at least as effective back at 9f as at 1¼m: acts on a wet track. *Saeed bin Suroor* **122**

EFFERVESCE (IRE) 3 b.f. Sri Pekan (USA) 117 – Arctic Winter (CAN) (Briartic (CAN)) [2001 75: 7d 6d⁵ 5m² 5g 5g³ 5g³ 5g 6m 5g 6d Oct 12] strong filly: has scope: fair handicapper: effective at 5f/6f: acts on good to firm and good to soft going: has run well when sweating/edgy: has pulled hard: usually patiently ridden. *M. A. Buckley* **77**

EFFERVESCENT 4 b.f. Efisio 120 – Sharp Chief 71 (Chief Singer 131) [2001 77, a87: f6g* f6s² f6s² f6s* f7g⁴ 6m f6g⁵ 6d 7m³ 5.7m⁴ 7m⁵ 7d⁵ 7.5m 6v f7g³ p7g Nov 24] tall filly: fairly useful handicapper on all-weather, fair on turf: won at Southwell and Wolverhampton in January: effective at 6f/7f: acts on firm going, good to soft and fibresand: usually waited with. *A. G. Newcombe* **77 a89**

EFFERVESCING 2 ch.g. (Mar 1) Efisio 120 – Superspring (Superlative 118) [2001 f6g⁶ 6m² 5f³ 5m f6s⁵ 7d 6d 5.2s² f5g f6g Dec 14] 32,000Y: sturdy gelding: second foal: half-brother to 3-y-o Our Destiny: dam unraced sister to smart sprinter Superpower: fair maiden: left C. Egerton 12,000 gns after good second in nursery at Yarmouth eighth start: likely to prove best at 5f/easy 6f: acts on firm going, soft and fibresand. *Mrs A. Duffield* **70 a67**

EFFIE GRAY 2 b.f. (May 14) Sri Pekan (USA) 117 – Rose Bouquet 78 (General Assembly (USA)) [2001 7f⁶ 7m⁶ 7g Sep 14] eighth foal: half-sister to 8.5f winner Absalom's Lad (by Abalsom) and 10-y-o Rising Spray: dam, 2-y-o 6f winner, out of smart performer up to 1m Premier Rose: easily best effort in maidens (fair form) when sixth at Salisbury second start: should stay 1m. *P. W. Harris* **69**

EFHARISTO 12 b.g. Dominion 123 – Excellent Alibi (USA) (Exceller (USA) 129) [2001 8.3m 10m⁶ Jul 11] of little account nowadays. *J. White* **–**

EFIDIUM 3 b.g. Presidium 124 – Efipetite 54 (Efisio 120) [2001 66: f5s⁶ f6g f5g 6d 6m 5m 6g² 6g 6m 8m 8m 6m⁵ 6m* 6f 7g Oct 19] small gelding: modest performer: won minor event at Redcar in August: best at 5f/6f: acts on fibresand and good to firm going: blinkered last 3 starts. *N. Bycroft* **59**

EGYPT 3 b.g. Green Desert (USA) 127 – Just You Wait (Nonoalco (USA) 131) [2001 –p: f8g* 7m⁴ f7g* f8g² 8s² 8d² 7v² 8.2s⁴ Oct 30] big, good-topped gelding: has plenty of scope: fairly useful handicapper: won twice at Southwell in June: likely to stay 1¼m: acts on fibresand and heavy going, shaped well on good to firm: blinkered (raced freely, ran respectably) final start: gelded afterwards: sometimes wanders: sold 38,000 gns. *Sir Mark Prescott* **81**

EGYPTBAND (USA) 4 b.f. Dixieland Band (USA) – Egyptown (FR) 110 (Top Ville **117**
129) [2001 128: 10s² 12m* 12m³ 12s Oct 7] lengthy, attractive filly: had a quick action:
high-class performer at 3 yrs, winning Prix de Diane at Chantilly and second to Sinndar
in Prix de l'Arc de Triomphe at Longchamp: only smart form in 2001: won Grand Prix
de Chantilly in June by ¾ length from St Expedit, tending to idle: placed in Prix Ganay
at Longchamp (3 lengths second to Golden Snake) and Grand Prix de Saint-Cloud (found
to have strained off-fore fetlock when third behind Mirio): never threatened when
mid-division in Prix de l'Arc de Triomphe at Longchamp final outing: stayed 1½m
well: acted on good to firm going, probably on soft: has reportedly been retired.
Mme C. Head-Maarek, France

EHTEFAAL (USA) 10 b.g. Alysheba (USA) – Bolt From The Blue (USA) (Blue **50**
Times (USA)) [2001 16f² 18m 15m Aug 1] useful-looking gelding: modest nowadays,
lightly raced: stays 2¼m: acts on firm ground, probably on soft: tried visored/blinkered.
J. S. King

EIBH'N ABBIE 2 b.g. (May 9) Forzando 122 – Brookhead Lady 73 (Petong 126) **69 §**
[2001 5m⁵ 6m 5m² 6g 6d⁴ 6f 5d 5m f6g⁶ 5m³ 6d f6g² f6g⁴ f5g⁴ f6g⁵ p6g³ f5s² Dec 27]
14,000Y, 3,500 2-y-o: tall, close-coupled gelding: second foal: dam 5f/6f winner,
including at 2 yrs: fair maiden at best: usually ran in sellers in second half of year:
effective at 5f/6f: acts on fibresand, polytrack, good to firm and good to soft going:
usually visored/blinkered: unreliable. *P. D. Evans*

EIGHT (IRE) 5 ch.g. Thatching 131 – Up To You (Sallust 134) [2001 66: 9f⁶ 12.1m* **61**
14.1d³ 12g f14g 14.1g⁶ Oct 19] workmanlike gelding: modest handicapper: won amateur **a–**
event at Chepstow in July: stays 1¾m: acts on firm and good to soft going: usually
visored/blinkered in 2000. *C. G. Cox*

EIGHTY TWO (USA) 5 br.h. Theatrical 128 – Heaven Knows Why (USA) (Star de **85**
Naskra (USA)) [2001 90+: e12g³ 12d³ 12f⁵ 12g⁴ 10.3m* 10m⁵ 10g⁴ 10g 10.3g 10.4d Oct **a91**
12] big, lengthy, good-topped horse: fairly useful handicapper: won at Lingfield in March
and Chester in May: stays 1½m: acts on soft going, good to firm and fibresand/equitrack:
blinkered (well held) once in 2000: has found little: sold 11,000 gns. *S. P. C. Woods*

EIRAARDIA (IRE) 2 br.f. (Mar 4) Petardia 113 – Eiras Mood 57 (Jalmood (USA) **33**
126) [2001 5v⁶ f5g 7m f7g Jun 29] IR 3,200Y: fourth foal: sister to Italian winner up to
10.5f Marco Monaldi: dam, 1m/1¼m winner, out of close relation to high-class miler
Dara Monarch: poor form in maiden/sellers. *P. D. Evans*

EJAY 2 b.f. (Jan 17) Emperor Jones (USA) 119 – Lough Erne 83 (Never So Bold 135) **–**
[2001 p6g Dec 28] 600F, 2,000Y: first foal: dam, 6f winner, half-sister to useful sprinter
Power Lake: last of 14 in maiden at Lingfield, slowly away. *Julian Poulton*

EKRAAR (USA) 4 b.c. Red Ransom (USA) – Sacahuista (USA) (Raja Baba **125**
(USA)) [2001 126: a10f⁴ a10f 9.3m³ 12m⁴ 12g⁵ 12d* 12m² Dec 16]
Ekraar left it very late, but in coming within a whisker of lifting the Hong
Kong Vase in December he finally reproduced the high-class form he had shown on
his final outing as a three-year-old when trained by Marcus Tregoning. It had
required a drop in class on his outing prior to the Vase for Ekraar to open his account
for Godolphin, and as he had scrambled home on that occasion the chances of his
following up in a Group 1 contest hardly seemed bright. Yet, under an enterprising
ride from Dettori, Ekraar almost stole it, sent on before the turn and quickening so
well that he looked to have gone beyond recall early in the straight. He still held a
good lead entering the final furlong before his exertions began to tell and the
favourite Stay Gold came out of the pack to catch him in the last strides, the pair
finishing over six lengths clear of third-placed Indigenous. Somewhat surprisingly,
the ride given by Dettori, along with that by the same jockey aboard Sakhee in the
Breeders' Cup Classic, reportedly came in for criticism from co-owner Hamdan Al
Maktoum. Hong Kong was easily Ekraar's best performance since winning the
Select Stakes at Goodwood fifteen months beforehand, that victory his third in
succession, all gained over a mile and a quarter. Ekraar ended off at that distance in
the latest season, possibly not suited by the dirt on a couple of occasions at Nad Al
Sheba but then faring no better on his return to turf, finishing third in the Prix
d'Ispahan at Longchamp. Ekraar was then stepped up to a mile and a half, a distance
which on pedigree he wasn't certain to stay. Ekraar's first couple of attempts at the
trip cast doubts, but the manner in which he won the listed Amco Corporation Troy
Stakes at Doncaster in September left a very different impression, one which his

Amco Corporation Troy Stakes, Doncaster—
the visored Ekraar rallies in splendid fashion to beat Hill Country; Boreas is third

performance in Hong Kong confirmed. Ekraar set a sound pace on quite testing ground at Doncaster, was headed two out by Hill Country but rallied in splendid fashion to win by a head, despite being hit on the head by the whip of Hill Country's jockey.

	Ekraar (USA) (b.c. 1997)		
	Red Ransom (USA) (b 1987)	Roberto (b 1969)	Hail To Reason / Bramalea
		Arabia (b 1977)	Damascus / Christmas Wind
	Sacahuista (USA) (b 1984)	Raja Baba (b 1968)	Bold Ruler / Missy Baba
		Nalees Flying Flag (b 1975)	Hoist The Flag / Nalee

Ekraar's immediate pedigree is not that of a horse sure to get a mile and a quarter let alone a mile and a half. Most of his sire's runners seem best around a mile, while his dam did all her winning up to nine furlongs. Ekraar is the sixth foal of Sacahuista, who won the Grade 1 Oak Leaf Stakes at two and went on to do even better at three when she was champion three-year-old filly in the States after wins in the Grade 1 Breeders' Cup Distaff and Spinster Stakes. Three of Sacahuista's previous offspring are winners, including the stakes-placed Hussonet (by Mr Prospector). The well-made Ekraar, a good walker, acts on firm and soft going. He is usually fitted with a tongue strap nowadays, and often with either blinkers or a visor. *Saeed bin Suroor*

ELA ATHENA 5 gr.m. Ezzoud (IRE) 126 – Crodelle (IRE) (Formidable (USA) 125) **115** [2001 119: 11.6g² 12g² 12g² 11f³ Sep 8] tall, lengthy, quite good-topped mare: smart performer: successful in 2000 in Lancashire Oaks at Haydock: runner-up in 5 Group/ Grade 1s during career, including Gran Premio di Milano (beaten short head by Paolini after good battle) on second 5-y-o start: also ran creditably in 2001 in listed race at Windsor (½-length second to Water Jump), Sword Dancer Handicap at Saratoga and Man o'War Stakes at Belmont (placed for second year running, 2½ lengths third to With Anticipation): was effective at 1¼m/1½m: raced only on good going or firmer: had sweated up/been early to post: reportedly in season third outing at 5 yrs: was consistent but quirky, and reportedly best when not crowded: reportedly retired after suffering injury final start. *M. A. Jarvis*

ELA D'ARGENT (IRE) 2 b.f. (Feb 28) Ela-Mana-Mou 132 – Petite-D-Argent 91 **74 d** (Noalto 120) [2001 5s⁴ 5g⁴ 8g* 8g 8s 7s Nov 10] IR 10,000Y: angular, quite good-topped filly: second foal: sister to 4-y-o Mana d'Argent: dam 6f (at 2 yrs) and 7f winner: fair performer: won minor event at Newcastle in August: ran badly in nurseries after: should stay at least 1¼m: tongue tied final outing. *M. Johnston*

ELA-DARLIN-MOU 3 gr.f. Mtoto 134 – Ancestry (Persepolis (FR) 127) [2001 51: **–** 8m 6m 7m 8.2f Jun 25] sturdy filly: modest maiden at 2 yrs: well held in 2001: blinkered last 2 starts: sold 4,800 gns. *K. T. Ivory*

ELA JAY 2 b.f. (Feb 27) Double Eclipše (IRE) 122 – Papirusa (IRE) (Pennine Walk 120) [2001 5.7g Oct 1] third known foal: dam, won in Spain, out of half-sister to St Leger winner Snurge: 33/1 and very green, tailed off in maiden at Bath. *G. A. Butler* –

ELA MARATHONA (IRE) 2 b.c. (Feb 20) Doyoun 124 – Peace Melody (IRE) 69 (Classic Music (USA)) [2001 7s² 7.1g⁵ Nov 7] 21,000Y: first foal: dam, Irish maiden who stayed 1m, half-sister to National Stakes winner Manntari (by Doyoun): much better effort in maidens (fairly useful form) when ¾-length second to Miss Corniche at Yarmouth, staying on well: will probably stay 1¼m: slowly away final outing: joined J. Eustace. *L. M. Cumani* **84**

ELAYOON (USA) 2 b.f. (Jan 9) Danzig (USA) – Ajfan (USA) 112 (Woodman (USA) 126) [2001 6g² Oct 3] fourth foal: closely related to smart 5f/6f winner in Britain/UAE Mutamayyaz (by Nureyev) and half-sister to fairly useful 1997 2-y-o 7f winner Elsurur (by Storm Cat): dam, 7f (at 2 yrs)/1m winner who was third in 1000 Guineas, half-sister to smart performer up to 14.6f Minds Music: 15/8, 7 lengths second of 9 to Tikkun in maiden at Folkestone, racing up with pace: should stay 1m: will improve. *M. P. Tregoning* **76 p**

ELDER PRINCESS (IRE) 2 b.f. (May 31) Houmayoun (FR) 114 – Lanesra (IRE) (Taufan (USA) 119) [2001 7s 10d Nov 2] 2,800 2-y-o foal: sister to Italian 6f to 9f winner Super Papa, 7f winner at 2 yrs: dam ran once in Irish bumper: well held in maidens at Brighton. *T. P. McGovern* –

EL DOLOR (IRE) 4 br.g. Elbio 125 – Payne's Grey (Godswalk (USA) 130) [2001 f7g f5g* f6g³ 5m⁵ f5g³ 5m³ 5m f5g* 5d³ Jul 16] sturdy, good-bodied gelding: easy mover: fair performer: won maiden claimer in April and handicap in July, both at Southwell: effective at 5f/6f: acts on fibresand, good to firm and good to soft going: usually visored/blinkered in 2001: has carried head high. *R. A. Fahey* **64 a70**

ELECTRUM (IRE) 5 b.g. Up And At 'em 109 – Short Stay (Be My Guest (USA) 126) [2001 98: a8g² a9g* a8g a6g* 7m 6f⁵ a6g* a8g a8g² a8g* a8g³ Dec 9] half-brother to 3 winners, including 1997 2-y-o 5f/6f winner Ellenbrook (by Petorius): dam Irish middle-distance maiden: useful performer when trained by J. Hayden in Ireland, winning minor event at the Curragh at 3 yrs: successful at Mijas in 2001 in minor events in May (amateurs), June, September and November: soundly beaten in handicap at Epsom fifth start: has won at 9f, probably best at 6f to 1m: acts on soft ground and sand: has been blinkered/visored. *E. J. Creighton, Spain* **?**

ELEGANT ESCORT (USA) 4 b.g. Take Me Out (USA) – Get With It (USA) (King Pellinore (USA) 127) [2001 –: f8g f8g f9.4g Feb 20] fairly useful winner on all-weather at 2 yrs: no form since. *Mrs G. S. Rees* –

EL EMEL (USA) 4 b.g. Green Dancer (USA) 132 – Moivouloirtoi (USA) 106 (Bering 136) [2001 98: f8.5g⁵ f8.5g f9.4g Mar 15] useful performer at 3 yrs in Germany: little form in Britain: tried blinkered. *I. A. Balding* –

EL FUERTE 6 b.g. Perpendicular 119 – Sleekit 78 (Blakeney 126) [2001 f12s f12s f9.4g 14.1s 11.1d May 6] little form: tried visored/tongue tied. *W. Clay* –

EL GIZA (USA) 3 ch.g. Cozzene (USA) – Gazayil (USA) 80 (Irish River (FR) 131) [2001 –p: 12g⁵ 12.1g 14.1d Oct 3] big, lengthy, angular gelding: little sign of ability. *H. R. A. Cecil* –

EL GRAN HOMBRE (USA) 5 ch.g. El Gran Senor (USA) 136 – Conquistress (USA) (Conquistador Cielo (USA)) [2001 f12g 12.4g f8g⁶ 8g Aug 13] leggy, close-coupled gelding: has long, fluent stride: fairly useful performer for A. O'Brien in Ireland at 2/3 yrs: well held in 2001: stays 13f: raced only on good going or softer: has had tongue tied: has raced freely: reared badly leaving stalls on reappearance, very edgy/early to post final start. *D. Nicholls* –

ELGRIA (IRE) 3 b. or br.c. Distinctly North (USA) 115 – Perfect Swinger (Shernazar 131) [2001 75: 8m 7m³ 10m 8m⁶ 8.3g⁶ 8.5m* 9d 8g 7d p8g⁶ p8g p10g⁵ p12g Dec 19] sturdy colt: fair performer: won maiden at Epsom in August: left R. Hannon after tenth start: stays 8.5f: acts on polytrack, yet to race on extremes of going on turf. *S. Kirk* **76**

EL HAKMA 3 b.f. Shareef Dancer (USA) 135 – Clare Court 89 (Glint of Gold 128) [2001 9.7m⁴ 12.3d* 14.6m 14v⁴ Sep 28] 21,000Y: small filly: fifth foal: sister to smart Italian 9f/1¼m winner Snake Snap and half-sister to 4-y-o Chief of Justice: dam 1m (at 2 yrs) to 1¾m winner from family of Silver Patriarch: won 4-runner maiden at Chester in August: stiff tasks, fairly useful form in Park Hill Stakes at Doncaster (never-dangerous ninth to Ranin) and minor event at Haydock (fourth to Invermark) after: seemed to stay 1¾m: acted on heavy and good to firm ground: visits Fantastic Light. *C. E. Brittain* **94**

EL HAMRA (IRE)   3 gr.c. Royal Abjar (USA) 121 – Cherlinoa (FR) (Crystal Palace   **65**
(FR) 132) [2001 73: 7v⁶ 10d 8.2f 8.1f⁶ 8m³ 8.2m⁵ Jul 28] small, strong colt: fair
performer: best around 1m: acts on fibresand, heavy and good to firm going: seems
temperamental. *B. A. McMahon*

ELHEBA (IRE)   2 b. or br.g. (Mar 6) Elbio 125 – Fireheba (ITY) (Fire of Life (USA)   **52**
113) [2001 5.1s⁶ 5.1d 8m f8g³ 8.2s² 8.3v⁴ f8g⁴ p10g⁶ f8g³ Dec 10] big, leggy gelding: has   **a58**
scope: fifth foal: half-brother to 3 winners, including Irish 1½m/1¾m winner Pilgrim Star
(by Marju): dam, Italian 5f to 1m winner, from family of very smart performer up to 1½m
Filia Ardross: modest maiden: runner-up in seller at Nottingham: stays 1¼m: acts on soft
ground, fibresand and polytrack: visored (ran creditably) last 3 starts. *J. S. Moore*

ELIIPOP   3 b.g. First Trump 118 – Hasty Key (USA) (Key To The Mint (USA)) [2001   **68**
8m⁴ 7.5f³ 9m³ 10m² 9.9m Aug 15] 6,500F, 8,000Y: half-brother to several winners,
including useful winner up to 12.5f Cotteir Chief (by Chief Singer) and useful 1989 2-y-o
7f winner Cutting Note (by Diesis), later winner in USA: dam won up to 9f in USA: fair
maiden: stays 1¼m: raced only on ground firmer than good: has worn crossed noseband:
sold 6,000 gns. *J. R. Fanshawe*

ELJOHAR (IRE)   4 ch.c. Nashwan (USA) 135 – Mehthaaf (USA) 121 (Nureyev   **96**
(USA) 131) [2001 82: 10m² 10d² Jun 18] strong, stocky colt: useful maiden: runner-up at
Sandown in May and Windsor (7/4-on) in June: better at 1¼m than shorter: has worn
crossed noseband/tongue tie. *J. H. M. Gosden*

ELJUTAN (IRE)   3 b.g. Namaqualand (USA) – Camarat 69 (Ahonoora 122) [2001   **60**
8m 9f 8.1d 12d 12m⁴ 16g⁵ 16v Oct 17] IR 8,200F, 12,000Y: fourth living foal: half-
brother to 1996 2-y-o 6f winner Colombia (by Mujtahid) and winner abroad by Polish
Patriot: dam, 9f winner, half-sister to Park Hill winner Trampship and to dam of St Leger
second High And Low: modest maiden handicapper: may prove best around 1¾m: acts
on firm and good to soft going. *R. J. O'Sullivan*

EL KARIM (USA)   5 ch.h. Storm Cat (USA) – Gmaasha (IRE) (Kris 135) [2001 –:   **–**
9.9m 6m 6m 6m f7g Jun 21] disappointing maiden. *R. Ford*

ELLA CARISA   2 b.f. (Feb 3) Elmaamul (USA) 125 – Salty Girl (IRE) 70 (Scenic   **57**
128) [2001 7f 8.2d⁶ 7.9d 8d Oct 25] leggy filly: first foal: dam, disappointing maiden,
placed at 7f (at 2 yrs) and 1¼m: form in maidens only when sixth to Affray at Nottingham: should stay beyond 1m. *K. O. Cunningham-Brown*

ELLA FALLS (IRE)   6 ch.m. Dancing Dissident (USA) 119 – Over Swing (FR)   **55**
(Saint Cyrien (FR) 128) [2001 16f⁶ 16.4m* 15m⁶ 16m³ 16f² 16.2m Sep 17] leggy mare:
modest handicapper: first outings on Flat (winning pointer/hurdler) for almost 3 years
when winning at Musselburgh (apprentices) and Folkestone in July: stays 2m: acts on
firm going, good to soft and fibresand: tried blinkered. *Mrs H. Dalton*

ELLAMINE   7 b.m. Warrshan (USA) 117 – Anhaar (Ela-Mana-Mou 132) [2001 f12g   **36**
e13g³ e12g⁵ 16.2m² f14.8g⁴ Aug 10] poor performer: stays 2m: acts on all-weather and
good to firm ground: tried blinkered: won over hurdles in October, then joined M. Pipe
9,500 gns. *J. Neville*

ELLA PEE-ELLE   6 b.m. Elmaamul (USA) 125 – Alipampa (IRE) (Glenstal (USA)   **–**
118) [2001 –: 10m 10.2g Oct 1] behind in maidens. *R. J. Price*

ELLA-TINO   3 b.f. Reprimand 122 – Tino-Ella 73 (Bustino 136) [2001 65: 6s⁶ 6.1v   **–**
6m Jun 11] quite good-topped, close-coupled filly: had a round action: fair maiden at 2
yrs: well below form in 2001: visored once: dead. *J. A. Glover*

ELLENDUNE GIRL   3 b.f. Mistertopogigo (IRE) 118 – Perfidy (FR) (Persian Bold   **75**
123) [2001 60: 5.1d² 5.3d² 5m 6m 6.1m⁵ 6.1m 6m 5g 5.3m 6g⁴ 6.1d* 5.2v² 6d 6v⁵ f5g⁵
f6s Dec 15] quite good-topped filly: fair handicapper: won at Nottingham in September:
best at 5f/6f: acts on heavy and good to firm going, probably on fibresand: often slowly
away. *D. J. S. ffrench Davis*

ELLEN MOONEY   2 ch.f. (Apr 4) Efisio 120 – Budby 72 (Rock City 120) [2001 5v³   **78**
6.1g² 7.5m² 7.5s* 6d 7d² 7s* 7s Oct 20] 5,000Y: workmanlike filly: poor walker: second
foal: half-sister to a winner in Denmark by Most Welcome: dam 8.5f winner: fair
performer: won minor event at Beverley in August and nursery at Lingfield in October:
will stay 1m: acts on good to firm and soft ground: usually bandaged: slowly away last 3
starts, losing all chance final one (said to have been in season). *B. Smart*

ELLENS ACADEMY (IRE)   6 b.g. Royal Academy (USA) 130 – Lady Ellen 67   **111**
(Horage 124) [2001 86: 6v f6g* 6g⁵ 6m* 6m² 6f 5m² 6m³ 6m³ 6m 5s⁵ Sep 30] big,
useful-looking gelding: impresses in appearance: smart performer: won handicap at

ELN

Southwell in April and minor event at Doncaster in May: ran very well after when placed, including in Wokingham Handicap at Royal Ascot (neck second to Nice One Clare) on fifth start and handicap at Ascot in July on seventh: best at 5f (given stiff track)/6f: acts on fibresand and firm going, probably on soft: sometimes blinkered, not in 2001: sometimes slowly away: has wandered/looked faint-hearted in the past. *E. J. Alston*

ELLENS LAD (IRE) 7 b.g. Polish Patriot (USA) 128 – Lady Ellen 67 (Horage 124) **114**
[2001 116: 5.1v* 5f 5m 5g 5m 5m⁶ 5.1g⁵ 6m² 5.6m 5s 5g 5d Oct 18] sturdy, strong-quartered gelding: smart performer: won minor event at Nottingham in April: ran creditably only a few times after, including when second to Honesty Fair in handicap at York in September: well held last 4 starts: best at 5f/easy 6f: probably acts on any going: blinkered once at 4 yrs: usually held up, and has a good turn of foot. *W. J. Musson*

ELLE ROYAL (IRE) 2 br.f. (Mar 17) Ali-Royal (IRE) 127 – Silvretta (IRE) 73 **71**
(Tirol 127) [2001 7g 6v⁶ 8.3v³ Oct 29] IR 4,500F: first foal: dam 1½m winner: best effort in maidens (fair form) when keeping-on third to Ski For Me at Windsor: will stay at least 1¼m. *T. P. McGovern*

ELLIEBERRY (IRE) 3 ch.f. Lucky Guest 109 – Persian Flower (Persian Heights **–**
129) [2001 –: 7f⁶ 7m⁶ Aug 4] well held in maidens, tongue tied and pulling hard final start. *B. Ellison*

EL LUTE (GER) 7 b.h. Scenic 128 – Easily (Swing Easy (USA) 126) [2001 8s 8g* **115**
8g 8m Aug 28] smart performer: winner of 7 races prior to 2001, including handicap at Baden-Baden at 6 yrs: career-best effort when winning Emirates-Mile at same course in May by 2 lengths from Late Night Out: races mainly at 1m and on good ground or softer: has been blinkered, including last 3 starts. *D. Ilic, Germany*

ELLWAY HEIGHTS 4 b.g. Shirley Heights 130 – Amina 80 (Brigadier Gerard 144) **61**
[2001 61: 11.6g³ 11.9f³ 12d 12f f12g 10.9m³ Sep 17] modest maiden handicapper: should stay beyond 1½m: acts on firm ground: sold 5,000 gns. *I. A. Balding*

ELLWAY PRINCE 6 b.g. Prince Sabo 123 – Star Arrangement (Star Appeal 133) **54**
[2001 59, a78: e12g⁵ f9.4g⁶ e10g² e10g e10g e8g May 11] close-coupled gelding: modest performer: barely stays 1¼m: acts on good to firm going, good to soft and fibresand/equitrack: sometimes blinkered/visored: often races prominently. *Mrs N. Macauley*

ELLWAY QUEEN (USA) 4 b.f. Bahri (USA) 125 – Queen Linear (USA) (Polish **–**
Navy (USA)) [2001 71: 7.1f 10v Oct 4] quite attractive filly: fair winner at 3 yrs: well held both 4-y-o starts. *G. A. Butler*

EL MAXIMO (IRE) 3 b.g. First Trump 118 – Kentucky Starlet (USA) 69 (Cox's **68**
Ridge (USA)) [2001 76: 7.1g 8m 7f 7g* Sep 17] smallish, compact gelding: has a quick, fluent action: fair performer: well held in Britain first 3 starts in 2001, then won amateur event at Turin in September: stays 7f: acts on good to firm ground, below form on softer than good: blinkered/usually tongue tied nowadays: has been slowly away. *M. G. Quinlan*

ELMHURST BOY 5 b.h. Merdon Melody 98 – Young Whip (Bold Owl 101) [2001 **95**
91: e10g 8.1v* 10.4g 12f 10m 10g⁴ 9g⁵ 9g 10d 8d p8g⁶ Dec 28] good-topped horse: useful handicapper: won at Sandown in April by length from La Speziana: several credit-able efforts after: effective at 7f to 1¼m: acts on equitrack (probably on polytrack) and any turf going: effective in blinkers/visor (tried only once in 2001): usually gets behind: carries head high and sometimes fails to go through with effort. *S. Dow*

EL MISTI 2 b.f. (Mar 28) Elmaamul (USA) 125 – Sherrington 56 (Thatching 131) **49**
[2001 f5g 6m 6m⁵ f7g 6g 6d² f6g⁵ 5v³ 5.7d p7g⁴ Dec 29] third foal: dam lightly-raced maiden who stayed 1m: poor maiden: stays 7f: acts on heavy ground and polytrack, probably on fibresand: no easy ride. *M. D. I. Usher*

ELMONJED (USA) 3 b.c. Gulch (USA) – Aqaarid (USA) 116 (Nashwan (USA) **93**
135) [2001 85: 8v³ 10.5m² 12f 11.6g⁵ a8f³ a10f⁶ Nov 29] useful-looking colt: fairly useful performer: best effort when second to Lailani in handicap at Haydock in May: left J. Dunlop before penultimate outing: stays 10.5f: acts on heavy and good to firm going. *N. Robb, UAE*

ELMUTABAKI 5 b.g. Unfuwain (USA) 131 – Bawaeth (USA) 72 (Blushing Groom **–**
(FR) 131) [2001 111: 8m 10.3m 13.1m 10.4s Oct 11] tall, lengthy gelding: unimpressive mover: smart at 3/4 yrs: little form in 2001: blinkered (reportedly lame/bled from nose) when pulled up on reappearance. *D. Nicholls*

ELNAHAAR (USA) 3 b.c. Silver Hawk (USA) 123 – Futuh (USA) 95 (Diesis 133) **106**
[2001 97p: 9d³ Apr 19] lengthy, good-topped colt: useful form: won maiden and minor event in 2000: good 1¾ lengths third to Olden Times in listed race at Newmarket

299

only 3-y-o start: stayed 9f: reportedly put down after breaking leg in early-May. *E. A. L. Dunlop*

EL RAYMONDO 2 b.g. (Mar 22) Night Shift (USA) – Alaraby (IRE) 77 (Caerleon **49** (USA) 132) [2001 7.1g 8d p8g p7g Dec 29] 10,000F, 20,000Y: first foal: dam 1¾m winner: poor maiden: should stay 1¼m: acts on polytrack: tongue tied last 2 starts. *M. Blanshard*

ELREHAAN 3 b.f. Sadler's Wells (USA) 132 – Moss (USA) (Woodman (USA) 126) **96** [2001 91: 11.4f³ 12.6m* 12g Sep 28] smallish, rather sparely-made filly: useful performer: creditable ¾-length third to Rockerlong in listed event at Chester before winning 4-runner minor event at Warwick later in May by 2½ lengths from Corsican Sunset: on toes, well held in listed race at Ascot final start: stayed 1½m: acted on firm going, below form on soft: visits Bahri. *J. L. Dunlop*

ELSAAMRI (USA) 3 b. or br.c. Silver Hawk (USA) 123 – Muhbubh (USA) 108 **103** (Blushing Groom (FR) 131) [2001 85p: 11.8m⁵ 12f* 11.7m* 12m⁴ 10.4g 12m* 12d⁵ Oct 2] quite good-topped colt: useful performer: won maiden at Kempton and minor event at Bath in July and minor event at Kempton in September: also ran well in handicaps at Goodwood (Tote Gold Trophy, fourth to Ovambo) in August and Newmarket (fifth to High Pitched) in October: should prove at least as effective at 1¼m as 1½m: acts on firm going, probably on soft: has worn crossed noseband: has edged right/looked bit awkward under pressure. *M. P. Tregoning*

ELSIE PLUNKETT 3 b.f. Mind Games 121 – Snow Eagle (IRE) 57 (Polar Falcon **91** (USA) 126) [2001 92: 5s² 5.1d 6m 6d 6m⁵ 6m 6s 6g 6g⁵ 7d Oct 20] good-topped filly: fairly useful performer: best at 5f/easy 6f: probably acts on any going: tried blinkered: usually races prominently. *R. Hannon*

ELSUNDUS (USA) 3 b.c. Gone West (USA) – Aljawza (USA) 86 (Riverman (USA) **91** 131) [2001 8m* Aug 30] third foal: closely related to fairly useful 1998 2-y-o 6f winner Ishtihar (by Woodman), later 1m/8.5f winner in France/UAE: dam, Irish 2-y-o 6f winner, half-sister to Queen Mary and Cheveley Park winner Gay Gallanta and very smart Irish 1¼m performer Sportsworld from outstanding family: favourite, won maiden at Salisbury by 7 lengths from Claretelle, soon in clear lead and unchallenged: sold only 4,000 gns in December. *J. H. M. Gosden*

EL TALGO (IRE) 2 b.c. (May 2) Common Grounds 118 – Lovely Me (IRE) 70 **58** (Vision (USA)) [2001 5m f5g 5g 5g 5s 5g Sep 19] IR 20,000Y: leggy colt: third foal: half-brother to 3-y-o Red Millennium: dam maiden who stayed 7f: modest maiden: raced only at 5f: acts on soft going (showed little on fibresand): tongue tied last 4 starts. *N. Tinkler*

ELUCIDATE 2 ch.f. (Feb 4) Elmaamul (USA) 125 – Speed To Lead (IRE) 90 **60** (Darshaan 133) [2001 7m 5.2m⁴ 5.1d⁶ 6m 7m* 8m⁶ 6d 8d p7g* p8g Dec 12] tall, angular filly: first foal: dam, 2m winner who stayed 2¾m, out of half-sister to Poule d'Essai des Poulains winner Fast Topaze: modest performer: won nursery at Catterick in September and claimer at Lingfield in November: seems barely to stay 1m: acts on polytrack, yet to race on extremes of going on turf. *I. A. Wood*

EL UNO (IRE) 3 ch.g. Elmaamul (USA) 125 – Fawaakeh (USA) 84 (Lyphard (USA) **51** 132) [2001 51: 7.5m 7.5f 11m³ 10f⁴ 9.2s² 8.5d⁵ 8m 9.9g 10m Sep 1] strong, lengthy gelding: modest maiden: stays 11f: acts on fibresand and firm ground, probably on soft: blinkered on debut. *J. L. Eyre*

ELUSIVE TREASURE (IRE) 2 b.f. (Mar 27) Entrepreneur 123 – Hidden Crest **61** (USA) (Gold Crest (USA) 120) [2001 5m⁵ 6m⁵ 7.1f³ 6d⁵ 5.7g Aug 7] 18,000F, 17,500Y: good-topped filly: second foal: half-sister to a fairly useful Italian 2-y-o 7.5f winner by Fairy King: dam, winner around 1m in USA, half-sister to dam of Helissio: modest maiden: should stay 1m: visored (looked none too keen) final start: sold 3,700 gns. *R. M. Beckett*

ELVINGTON BOY 4 ch.g. Emarati (USA) 74 – Catherines Well 99 (Junius (USA) **84** 124) [2001 88: 5g 6m 5m² 5m 5m 5m 5f* 5g Aug 15] quite good-topped gelding: fairly useful handicapper: won at Musselburgh in July: seems best at 5f: acts on firm going, possibly not on soft: visored (well held) fourth and fifth starts: has had tongue tied: has got upset in stalls: usually races up with pace. *M. W. Easterby*

ELWOOD BLUES (IRE) 2 b.g. (Apr 28) Blues Traveller (IRE) 119 – Tolomena 61 **–** (Tolomeo 127) [2001 7g Oct 4] 18,000Y: angular gelding: fourth foal: half-brother to fairly useful 1994 2-y-o 7f/1m winner Menas Gold (by Heights of Gold): dam ungenuine maiden who stayed 2m: 50/1, always tailed off in maiden at Newmarket. *S. C. Williams*

EL ZITO (IRE)   4 b.g. Mukaddamah (USA) 125 – Samite (FR) (Tennyson (FR) 124)   –
[2001 88: f12g Mar 8] tall, angular gelding: fairly useful performer at best: tongue tied,
well held only 4-y-o start. *M. G. Quinlan*

EMALI   4 b.g. Emarati (USA) 74 – Princess Poquito (Hard Fought 125) [2001 68d, a–§:   – §
f8.5s e10g 9m 11.9f 8.1g Jul 6] temperamental maiden: tried visored. *J. S. Moore*

EMARATI'S IMAGE   3 b.g. Emarati (USA) 74 – Choir's Image 53 (Lochnager 132)   –
[2001 10.1m 9d³ 9m Aug 12] big, good-topped gelding: second foal: dam, lightly raced
on Flat, placed over hurdles: last in maidens. *W. S. Cunningham*

EMBER DAYS   2 gr.f. (Mar 15) Reprimand 122 – Evening Falls 82 (Beveled (USA))   67
[2001 7m 7s² f8.5g f8g⁵ Nov 19] 5,000Y: third foal: half-sister to 7f (at 2 yrs) to 11f (in
France) winner Chimney Dust (by Pelder): dam sprinter: best effort in maidens (fair
form) when second at Catterick: should stay 1m: acts on soft ground. *G. C. H. Chung*

EMERALD FIRE   2 b.f. (Mar 25) Pivotal 126 – Four-Legged Friend 101 (Aragon   73
118) [2001 5g⁵ 5.7m² 5m 6d* Oct 18] 10,500F, 15,000Y: small, leggy filly: seventh foal:
half-sister to 10-y-o Herr Trigger and 6-y-o Quite Happy: dam 2-y-o 5f winner: fair
performer: off 3 months, won 19-runner nursery at Newmarket by ½ length from Orlass:
likely to prove best at 5f/6f. *I. A. Balding*

EMERALD HUNTER (USA)   6 b. or br.g. Quest For Fame 127 – In Jubilation   –
(USA) (Isgala) [2001 f14g May 14] modest seller winner in 1999: tailed off
only 6-y-o start: tried blinkered. *K. O. Cunningham-Brown*

EMERALD IMP (IRE)   4 ch.f. Mac's Imp (USA) 116 – Lady Montekin (Montekin   –
125) [2001 –: 10m 7.6g 8m Sep 10] disappointing maiden. *M. S. Saunders*

EMERALD LAKE (USA)   3 b.c. Green Dancer (USA) 132 – Dame Avie (USA)   60
(Lord Gaylord) (USA) [2001 10s⁶ 10v 14g⁶ Jun 8] $70,000Y: tall, good sort: half-brother
to several winners in USA, notably Grade 3 9f winner and Grade 1 runner-up Primitive
Hall (by Dixieland Band): dam unraced out of half-sister to US champion 2-y-o Lord
Avie: modest form in maidens. *J. H. M. Gosden*

EMERALD MIST (IRE)   2 b.f. (May 1) Sacrament 118 – Jade's Gem (Sulaafah   –
(USA) 119) [2001 7m 7m 7g 8.3v 8.3v Nov 8] 34,000Y: smallish filly: first foal: dam,
lightly-raced maiden, out of sister to smart miler Just A Flutter and half-sister to smart
Italian performer up to 1½m Slicious: well held, including in sellers. *G. B. Balding*

EMERALD PALM   3 b.f. Green Desert (USA) 127 – Opus One 63 (Slip Anchor 136)   62
[2001 70p: e8g⁵ 8.3s³ 7m 9f Jun 13] leggy, close-coupled filly: modest maiden: not sure
to stay beyond 1m: acts on soft going, probably on heavy: free-going sort: looks none too
easy a ride (has found little): joined P. Hobbs. *J. Noseda*

EMERALD PEACE (IRE)   4 b.f. Green Desert (USA) 127 – Puck's Castle 92   103
(Shirley Heights 130) [2001 101: 5m⁴ 5m* 5m⁶ 6f⁵ Jun 30] sparely-made filly: useful
performer: won listed event at Kempton in May by neck from unlucky-in-running
Misraah: creditable efforts after, fifth to Volata in Chipchase Stakes at Newcastle: stays
6f: yet to race on soft/heavy going, acts on any other: has been bandaged near-hind:
ridden with more restraint than usual in 2001: reportedly in foal to Grand Lodge.
M. A. Jarvis

EMIGRATE   2 b.f. (Feb 8) Emarati (USA) 74 – Fly South (Polar Falcon (USA) 126)   64
[2001 f7g² f7g³ Dec 8] 3,800Y: first foal: dam unraced: modest form when placed in
maidens at Wolverhampton: likely to prove best up to 1m. *P. J. Makin*

EMILY DEE   2 b.f. (Mar 4) Classic Cliche (IRE) 128 – Alpi Dora (Valiyar 129) [2001   59
7.1d⁶ 7m⁴ 7m 6.1v⁵ Oct 22] 2,000YL, resold 1,200Y: quite good-topped filly: sixth foal:
half-sister to 4-y-o Windmill Lane and winners in Italy by Don't Forget Me and High
Estate: dam Italian 7.5f (at 2 yrs) and 8.5f winner: modest maiden: bred to be suited by
1¼m+: acts on good to firm and heavy ground. *J. M. Bradley*

EMINENTLY   2 b.g. (May 9) Deploy 131 – Lady Clementine 68 (He Loves Me 120)   63
[2001 7.6m 7m 7.1f⁵ 8.3v Oct 8] half-brother to several winners, including fairly useful
Much Sought After (by Adonijah), who probably stayed 2m, and 9f to 11.5f winner
Darling Clover (by Minster Son): dam 5f winner: modest maiden: should be suited by
1¼m+: acts on firm going, well held on heavy. *R. M. Beckett*

E MINOR (IRE)   2 b.f. (Mar 17) Blushing Flame (USA) 109 – Watch The Clock 93   54
(Mtoto 134) [2001 5.7g 6.1v 5d⁵ 7s Oct 25] IR 6,000Y: rather leggy filly: second foal:
dam 2-y-o 6f/7.5f winner who stayed 1¼m: modest maiden: should stay at least 1m.
G. A. Butler

EMISSARY 3 gr.g. Primo Dominie 121 – Misty Goddess (IRE) 63 (Godswalk (USA) **42** 130) [2001 59, a–: f11g⁶ 8m⁶ 9m 7m 8.2f Jun 25] sturdy gelding: modest maiden at 2 yrs: poor form in 2001, mostly over unsuitable trips: stays 6f: acts on firm and soft ground: blinkered (looked none too keen) final 2-y-o start: has hung left: usually races prominently. *N. P. Littmoden*

EMMA CLARE (IRE) 3 b.f. Namaqualand (USA) – Medicosma (USA) 80 (The **37** Minstrel (CAN) 135) [2001 52: f8g⁶ f9.4g⁴ f11g f9.4g 10.9f³ 10m 14.1s Aug 6] poor nowadays: stays 11f, at least with emphasis on speed: acts on firm ground and fibresand: sometimes blinkered: refused to enter stall once at 2 yrs. *J. A. Osborne*

EMMA-LYNE 5 b.m. Emarati (USA) 74 – Moreton's Martha (Derrylin 115) [2001 –: – f8g Apr 9] one-time fair performer: no show since 1999: tried visored. *G. Brown*

EMMAS HOPE 4 b.f. Emarati (USA) 74 – Ray of Hope 53 (Rainbow Quest (USA) – 134) [2001 –: f8g f12g 11.1d⁶ 11.9f 14.1g 10.3f 12.3m⁵ f14.8s Sep 6] little form: tried visored. *B. P. J. Baugh*

EMMA THOMAS 3 b.f. Puissance 110 – Clan Scotia 47 (Clantime 101) [2001 41: – f6g f5g f6g 5.1s 6g 5m 6f 6m 6m 5d 5g 6s 5m 5d Sep 25] of no account at 3 yrs. *A. Berry*

EMMERANNE 4 b.f. Warning 136 – Empress Matilda (IRE) (Sadler's Wells (USA) **65** 132) [2001 7.5f⁴ 8f⁴ 7.6m² 7m⁵ᵈ 8g 7g 8m⁴ Aug 22] 5,000 3-y-o: first foal: dam unraced daughter of very smart French/US performer up to 1¼m Reine Mathilde: fair maiden handicapper: stays 1m: raced only on good going or firmer: blinkered (ran poorly) penultimate start. *E. J. O'Neill*

EMMERVALE 2 b.f. (Mar 16) Emarati (USA) 74 – Raintree Venture (Good Times **63** (ITY)) [2001 5m⁴ 6m² 6g 5.1m⁴ 6s⁵ 6d Oct 19] angular, unfurnished filly: half-sister to a winner up to 1½m in Italy by Celestial Storm: dam, ran twice at 2 yrs, out of half-sister to dam of Oaks winner Polygamy: modest maiden: shapes as if will prove best at 5f/6f: acts on good to firm and soft going. *J. G. Portman*

EMMS (USA) 3 gr.c. Fastness (IRE) 127 – Carnation (FR) (Carwhite 127) [2001 101: **98** 8m 8m 8m Jul 22] tall, leggy, angular colt: has reportedly suffered from sore shins: useful handicapper: edgy and wearing stick-on shoes, respectable ninth to Analyser in Britannia Stakes at Royal Ascot on reappearance: disappointing both starts after: likely to be suited by 1¼m+: acts on good to firm and good to soft going: sold 5,500 gns. *P. F. I. Cole*

EMPEROR OF DREAMS 2 b.c. (Feb 18) Emperor Jones (USA) 119 – Girl of My **49** Dreams (IRE) 51 (Marju (IRE) 127) [2001 7m 6m 6m 8s 6s⁵ p6g Dec 28] 2,400Y: lengthy colt: first foal: dam 7f winner: poor maiden: seems not to stay testing 1m: forced pace last 3 starts. *R. Hannon*

EMPEROR'S CASTLE 2 b.g. (Mar 14) Emperor Jones (USA) 119 – Riyoom – (USA) 83 (Vaguely Noble 140) [2001 6m 7g 7g Aug 24] 9,000Y: fifth foal: closely related to fairly useful 1998 2-y-o 5f winner Shining Desert (by Green Desert) and half-brother to a winner up to 10.5f in France/Italy by Alzao: dam, Irish 2-y-o 1m winner, half-sister to US Grade 3 8.5f/9f winner Lt Lao: well held in sellers. *P. C. Haslam*

EMPERORS FOLLY 3 b.g. Emperor Jones (USA) 119 – Highest Bid (FR) (Highest – Honor (FR) 124) [2001 –: 7m 9f Jun 13] well held in maidens: sold to Kuwait. *C. A. Dwyer*

EMPEROR'S WELL 2 ch.g. (Apr 3) First Trump 118 – Catherines Well 99 (Junius **63** (USA) 124) [2001 5s⁵ 5m⁵ 5m³ 5m⁵ 5m 5m 5m Aug 26] 5,500Y: well-made gelding: sixth living foal: half-brother to 3 winners, including 4-y-o Elvington Boy and 7-y-o William's Well: dam sprinter: modest maiden: well held in nurseries last 2 starts: will prove best at 5f/6f: sometimes slowly away. *M. W. Easterby*

EMPORIO 3 b.g. Emperor Jones (USA) 119 – Lykoa (Shirley Heights 130) [2001 68: **66** 8s² 8d 10m⁴ 10d⁵ 9f⁶ Jul 9] big, leggy gelding: fair maiden handicapper: should stay 1½m: acts on soft and good to firm going: sold 10,500 gns, sent to Malaysia. *L. M. Cumani*

EMPRESS ALICE 4 b.f. Petoski 135 – Blue Empress (Blue Cashmere 129) [2001 –: – 7.1m 10m Sep 11] tailed off in maidens. *R. E. Peacock*

EMPRESS EMMILLINE 5 ch.m. My Generation 111 – Over The Mill (Milford – 119) [2001 8m 12.1d 10m 8m 12g f12g Nov 26] rather leggy, quite good-topped mare: second foal: dam unraced: seems of little account. *M. Mullineaux*

EMTEYAZ 3 b.c. Mark of Esteem (IRE) 137 – Najmat Alshemaal (IRE) 98 (Dancing **64** Brave (USA) 140) [2001 10.2f 11.5m⁶ 10m 12g 12m* 16.2s⁴ 14.1s 12g* 11g² Dec 23] second foal: dam 1¼m winner who stayed 14.6f: modest handicapper: won at Folkestone in August and, having left A. Stewart after seventh outing, Abu Dhabi in December: seems best around 1½m: acts on good to firm going: blinkered last 2 starts. *D. J. Selvaratnam, UAE*

ENCHANTED 2 b.f. (May 7) Magic Ring (IRE) 115 – Snugfit Annie 49 (Midyan **84** (USA) 124) [2001 6m⁵ 5m* 7m* 6m⁵ 6g⁴ Aug 4] quite good-topped filly: fourth reported foal: dam third in 6f seller at 2 yrs (only season to race): fairly useful performer: won maiden at Warwick in June and nursery at Salisbury in July: creditable efforts in nurseries last 2 starts: stays 7f: raced only on good/good to firm going. *N. A. Callaghan*

ENCHANTED OCEAN (USA) 2 b.f. (Apr 21) Royal Academy (USA) 130 – **76** Ocean Jewel (USA) (Alleged (USA) 138) [2001 7.2m⁴ 8v Oct 26] IR 20,000Y: big, leggy filly: half-sister to several winners, including useful German performer up to 2m Ocean Sea (by Bering) and 3-y-o Tjinouska: dam unraced: much better effort in maidens (fair form) when fourth to Legal Approach at Ayr: should be suited by at least 1m: possibly unsuited by heavy ground. *M. Johnston*

ENCHANTING (IRE) 3 b.f. Bistgone (IRE) 126 – Spire 75 (Shirley Heights 130) **–** [2001 –: 6.9v⁴ 7m 7s 10g May 30] quite attractive filly: reportedly had sore shins prior to only 2-y-o start: only a little sign of ability: blinkered (folded very tamely) final outing: sent to New Zealand. *B. J. Meehan*

ENCORE DU CRISTAL (USA) 4 b.f. Quiet American (USA) – Elegant Cham- **82** pagne (USA) (Alleged (USA) 138) [2001 –: 10d⁴ 9.9m* 9m 12m³ 10g Sep 8] rangy, angular filly: fairly useful performer: made all in maiden at Salisbury in June: barely stays 1½m: acts on good to firm going: free-going sort. *J. H. M. Gosden*

ENCORE MA FILLE 2 b.f. (May 8) Royal Applause 124 – Collide 102 (High Line **72** 125) [2001 6m 6.1g⁵ 5f* 5g⁵ 6m⁶ 6m Sep 21] 12,000F, 16,000Y: useful-looking filly: sixth foal: half-sister to Wolf Tooth and 3-y-o Collard, both 1m winners by Wolfhound: dam 1m winner: fair performer: won maiden at Ripon in July: creditable sixth in nursery at Doncaster: was effective at 5f/6f: raced only on good going or firmer: dead. *R. M. Whitaker*

ENCORE MY LOVE 2 b.f. (Feb 11) Royal Applause 124 – Lady Be Mine (USA) 76 **68** (Sir Ivor 135) [2001 6m² Jun 15] half-sister to several winners, including leading 1989 2-y-o (successful at 6f to 1m) Be My Chief and fairly useful 9f to 1¾m performer Chief Bee (both by Chief's Crown): dam, 1m winner, from family of Marwell and Marling: 11/1 and green, keeping-on 5 lengths second of 6 to stable-companion Massarra in maiden at Goodwood: should stay 7f. *J. L. Dunlop*

ENCOUNTER 5 br.g. Primo Dominie 121 – Dancing Spirit (IRE) 72 (Ahonoora 122) **68** [2001 59, a–: 7.1m 6m 7m⁵ 8m 7.5f⁶ 7.5m 7m* 7m² 7m 7d⁴ 7m⁴ 8g⁶ 7m* 7m 7g⁶ 7s* **a–** 10.4m 8.5g⁶ 7.2m 8g 6v 7d 7d 8s Nov 9] lengthy gelding: fair handicapper on turf: won at Newmarket (apprentices), Catterick and Epsom in the summer: effective at 6f to 7.5f: probably acts on any turf going: sometimes slowly away: usually held up. *J. Hetherton*

ENCYCLOPEDIA 3 b.f. So Factual (USA) 120 – Wakayi 87 (Persian Bold 123) **58** [2001 55: 6m³ 7m 6m 7g² Aug 24] close-coupled, quite good-topped filly: modest maiden: stays 7f: acts on good to firm ground: has been slowly away: sold 800 gns. *T. D. Easterby*

ENDLESS HALL 5 b.h. Saddlers' Hall (IRE) 126 – Endless Joy 90 (Law Society **121** (USA) 130) [2001 127: 12g⁴ 10f* 10m⁶ 10m 12m⁴ Sep 8]

Endless Hall's bumper pay day when winning the Singapore Airlines International Cup at Kranji in May was a timely financial boost for trainer Luca Cumani. The first prize of nigh on £690,000 was almost double the win prize money earned by Cumani's stable during the year in Britain when results showed—despite the presence among the ranks of the exciting classic prospect Gossamer—that the yard still has a long way to go to regain the prominence it enjoyed in the 'eighties and 'nineties, before the loss of the Aga Khan's patronage. In fact, but for the contributions of Endless Hall over the past couple of campaigns Cumani might have found himself in something of a pickle. The globetrotting Endless Hall has been by far the biggest earner for the stable with high-class wins as a four-year-old in the Group 1 Gran Premio di Milano and the Group 3 Sodexho Prestige Scottish Classic at Ayr preceding his valuable success as a five-year-old in Singapore.

The second running of the International Cup (which will be a new leg in the World Series in 2002) lived up to its name. Ten horses from eight different countries lined up, with Endless Hall the only British-trained representative. Among those opposing him were the previous year's second and third, the French-trained Jim And Tonic and the locally-trained Carry The Flag, as well as two other Europeans, Germany's Silvano, who had beaten Jim And Tonic in Hong Kong last time out, and France's With The Flow. The early pace was strong and Endless Hall was unable to adopt his customary front-running role, racing in second behind American challenger Lazy Lode. Approaching the three-furlong marker, Endless Hall was sent up to dispute the lead and, once in front, was kept up to his work, ridden out by regular jockey Jamie Spencer to hold off the challenge of Jim And Tonic; Endless Hall beat Jim And Tonic by three quarters of a length, with a short head back to the staying-on With The Flow. New Zealand's Hill of Grace was a further length and three quarters back in fourth, while Silvano came a never-nearer fifth, another half a length in arrears. As a matter of interest, the prize money on offer in the International Cup exceeded that for Europe's richest race the Derby, in which the latest winner Galileo earned £580,000, serving as a reminder that horseracing in the Far East is booming. At around the same time the Hong Kong Jockey Club announced significantly increased prize money at its International meeting in December, making the Group 1 Hong Kong Cup the fourth most valuable race in the world behind only the Dubai World Cup, the Japan Cup and the Breeders' Cup Classic. The growth of richly-endowed international races on the world stage has had the effect of pushing Europe's most important races further down the world rankings in terms of prize-money, something the leading European racing authorities could do with addressing.

European racegoers didn't see Endless Hall at his best as a five-year-old, his best run, apart from the International Cup, coming when fourth of sixteen in the Group 2 Dubai Sheema Classic at Nad Al Sheba in March on his reappearance; he finished four and a half lengths behind Stay Gold and Fantastic Light, leading until over a furlong out. Endless Hall remained in Dubai to be prepared for his foray to Singapore. After his return to Britain, Endless Hall was aimed at the Prince of Wales's Stakes at Royal Ascot, where he finished over seven and a half lengths

Singapore Airlines International Cup, Kranji—jockey Jamie Spencer celebrates victory aboard Endless Hall in the second running of this very valuable prize; they hold on from Jim And Tonic and With The Flow

Il Paralupo's "Endless Hall"

sixth of nine to Fantastic Light, paying a little for getting involved with a very strong pace; he then ran poorly in the Eclipse at Sandown in July, the first beaten and coming back tailed off. Worse was to come when Endless Hall couldn't take advantage of seemingly his easiest task of the year in the Group 2 Bosphorus Cup at Veliefendi in Turkey on his final outing, managing only fourth of six, seven and a half lengths behind the German winner King's Boy. In truth, he was never the same horse again in 2001 after his Kranji exertions.

		Sadler's Wells (b 1981)	Northern Dancer
	Saddlers' Hall (IRE) (b 1988)		Fairy Bridge
		Sunny Valley (b 1972)	Val de Loir
Endless Hall (b.h. 1996)			Sunland
		Law Society (br 1982)	Alleged
	Endless Joy (b 1987)		Bold Bikini
		La Joyeuse (b 1982)	Northern Dancer
			Rosa Mundi

Endless Hall's pedigree was covered extensively in *Racehorses of 2000*. There is little to add, other than to note that his fairly useful year-younger half-brother Fonic Joy (by Zafonic) was a winner over both a mile and a mile and a quarter in Italy in the latest season. A medium-sized, quite attractive horse with a quick action, Endless Hall is effective at a mile and a quarter to a mile and a half; though he has won on soft ground, all his best form is on firmer than good. He stays in training. *L. M. Cumani*

ENDLESS Q 2 ch.f. (May 21) Timeless Times (USA) 99 – Off Camera (Efisio 120) – [2001 5f Jul 9] 3,000Y: workmanlike filly: second foal: dam unraced sister to 7-y-o Jo Mell: 20/1, backward and green, tenth of 13 in maiden at Ripon, swishing tail. *T. D. Easterby*

END OF AN ERROR   2 b.f. (Apr 29) Charmer 123 – Needwood Poppy 29 (Rolfe **54** (USA) 77) [2001 6m f5g f7g[6] 7g[3] 8m* 7d 10s f8g f6g f8s[6] Dec 15] leggy filly: second **a—** foal: half-sister to 5-y-o Needwood Maestro: dam, maiden on Flat, winning staying hurdler: modest performer: won nursery at Leicester in September: left B. McMahon and below form after: should stay at least 1¼m: acts on good to firm ground, no form on fibresand. *M. C. Chapman*

ENDYMION (IRE)   4 ch.f. Paris House 123 – Vaguely Jade (Corvaro (USA) 124) **–** [2001 65: 6f 7f 7m 6m 6m Aug 22] sparely-made filly: fair maiden at 3 yrs: no form in 2001. *Mrs P. N. Dutfield*

ENGLISH HARBOUR   3 ch.f. Sabrehill (USA) 120 – Water Woo (USA) 102 (Tom **81** Rolfe) [2001 77: 10s* 10s[3] Apr 23] close-coupled, quite attractive filly: fairly useful performer: won maiden at Brighton in April: below form only start after: should stay 1½m: acts on heavy ground. *B. W. Hills*

ENGSTRUM (IRE)   3 ch.g. Grand Lodge (USA) 125 – Gentle Guest (IRE) (Be My **53** Guest (USA) 126) [2001 14g f11g[6] f12g[6] 16.2m[2] 16g[3] 16m* 16.2g 16v[6] Oct 4] 15,000Y: seventh foal: half-brother to 1m winner who stayed 1½m Freedom Chance (by Lahib): dam unraced: modest handicapper: won maiden event at Musselburgh in August: should prove best at 2m+: acts on good to firm ground: visored sixth/seventh starts: sold 8,000 gns. *H. Morrison*

ENIGMATIC SPIRIT (IRE)   2 b.f. (Jan 30) Petorius 117 – Bakema (IRE) 62 (King **–** of Clubs 124) [2001 6m 5m 7d 10s 8.2s 7d Nov 6] IR 2,000Y: sparely-made filly: first foal: dam Irish 1½m winner at 4 yrs: no form, including in seller: tried visored. *A. B. Mulholland*

ENJOY THE BUZZ   2 b.c. (Mar 22) Prince of Birds (USA) 121 – Abaklea (IRE) **57** (Doyoun 124) [2001 6m 6.1m 6s[5] 6v Oct 26] 2,500Y: small, sturdy colt: first foal: dam unraced out of half-sister to smart 1¾m winner Book At Bedtime: modest maiden: best effort on debut: should stay at least 1m. *E. J. Alston*

ENNOBLEMENT (IRE)   3 ch.c. Halling (USA) 133 – Royal Touch 121 (Tap On **107** Wood 130) [2001 10g* 10.3m[2] 10.3d 9.9m[3] Sep 26] leggy, useful-looking colt: fifth living foal: closely related to useful Irish 7f (at 2 yrs) and 1m winner Nobility (by Diesis) and half-brother to smart French 7f/1m winner Ethelinda (by Indian Ridge): dam, 7f to 9f (US Grade 2 event) winner, half-sister to very smart Irish 1½m/1¾m performer Foresee: useful performer: won maiden at Lingfield in May: good efforts after, including when beaten short head by Attache in minor event at Doncaster and 3 lengths when third to Mont Rocher in listed race at Goodwood: will stay at least 1½m: joined Godolphin. *M. P. Tregoning*

ENRICH (USA)   3 b.f. Dynaformer (USA) – Eternal Reve (USA) 116 (Diesis 133) **91** [2001 103p: a8f[5] 8.5m Jun 8] strong, compact filly: trained at 2 yrs by J. Oxx in Ireland, winning maiden at Cork and third in C. L. Weld Park Stakes at the Curragh: below that form in UAE 1000 Guineas at Nad Al Sheba and listed race at Epsom in 2001: stayed 7f: acted on soft going, also won on good to firm: visits Maria's Mon. *Saeed bin Suroor*

ENTAIL (USA)   4 b. or br.f. Riverman (USA) 131 – Estala (Be My Guest (USA) 126) **97** [2001 72: f8g 7.5m* 7.1s* 8m* 7m Jul 12] neat filly: improved into useful handicapper at 4 yrs: won at Beverley, Sandown and Newmarket (by ¾ length from Dhuhook) in June: below form final start: acted on soft and good to firm going: found little twice at 3 yrs: reportedly in foal to Kris. *W. Jarvis*

ENTHUSED (USA)   3 b.f. Seeking The Gold (USA) – Magic of Life (USA) 118 **107** (Seattle Slew (USA)) [2001 109: 8g[5] 8f 6m Jul 12] lengthy, quite attractive filly: useful performer: won Princess Margaret Stakes at Ascot and Lowther Stakes at York at 2 yrs: creditable efforts first 2 starts in 2001 in 1000 Guineas at Newmarket (4½ lengths fifth to Ameerat) and Coronation Stakes at Royal Ascot (6 lengths eighth to Banks Hill): always outpaced when last of 18 in July Cup at Newmarket final one: stayed 1m: acted on firm and good to soft going: has idled in front: reportedly retired, and sent to USA. *Sir Michael Stoute*

ENTITY   4 ch.g. Rudimentary (USA) 118 – Desert Ditty 67 (Green Desert (USA) 127) **86** [2001 77+: 9v 10.3m 8.5m 8.5m* 9.2d* 9.9m 9.2s Aug 21] big, lengthy gelding: fairly useful handicapper: made all at Beverley and Hamilton (tended to idle) in June: well held otherwise: stays 1¼m: acts on heavy and good to firm going: blinkered twice as 3-y-o: sometimes rears in stall/slowly away (took no part fifth 3-y-o start): effective ridden from front or held up: none too reliable. *T. D. Barron*

ENTRAP (USA) 2 b.f. (Mar 13) Phone Trick (USA) – Mystic Lure 70 (Green Desert **89** (USA) 127) [2001 6m* 6m⁴ 6m³ 7g Oct 6] $150,000Y: has scope: second foal: dam, maiden who stayed 7f, half-sister to top-class French/US 1m/9f winner Thrill Show: fairly useful performer: won maiden at Kempton (idled) in July: good efforts in Princess Margaret Stakes at Ascot (7½ lengths fourth to Leggy Lou) and listed event at Ayr (about 2 lengths third to Misterah): ran as though something amiss final outing: should stay 1m. *W. J. Haggas*

ENTROPY 5 b.m. Brief Truce (USA) 126 – Distant Isle (IRE) (Bluebird (USA) 125) **47** [2001 54, a46: f7g 7d⁵ 8f f7g Jun 21] close-coupled mare: fluent mover: poor handi- **a–** capper: best at 7f/1m: acts on equitrack (no show on fibresand), firm and good to soft going. *B. A. Pearce*

ENVIOUS 2 ch.g. (Jan 16) Hernando (FR) 127 – Prima Verde 81 (Leading Counsel **62** (USA) 122) [2001 8g 7s⁶ Oct 25] strong, lengthy gelding: has scope: first foal: dam 7.5f/ 1m winner: better effort in maidens (modest form) when sixth to Thrasher at Brighton: should stay 1¼m: sold 10,000 gns. *Sir Mark Prescott*

ENVIRONMENT AUDIT 2 ch.c. (May 19) Kris 135 – Bold And Beautiful 105 **78 p** (Bold Lad (IRE) 133) [2001 7d 6s³ Nov 10] 3,000Y: rather leggy colt: half-brother to several winners, including winner Bold Faith and smart French winner around 11f (third in 15f Prix de Lutece) Warbler (both by Warning): dam best at 1m: better effort in maidens (fair form) when 2¼ lengths third to Just James at Doncaster: should stay 1m: open to further improvement. *B. W. Hills*

EPICENTRE (USA) 2 b.c. (Mar 13) Kris S (USA) – Carya (USA) (Northern Dancer) **89 p** [2001 8g⁶ 8f⁵ Sep 21] quite attractive colt: fifth foal: closely related to very smart 7f (at 2 yrs) to 1¼m (including US Grade 1 turf events) winner Ryafan (by Lear Fan) and half-brother to 2 winners, including fairly useful 10.5f winner Stage Direction (by Theatrical): dam, ran 3 times in France, closely related to smart French middle-distance stayer Glorify from very good US family: stepped up on debut form when fifth to Fight Your Corner in minor event at Newbury, no extra from over 1f out after travelling better than most: bred to stay 1¼m: useful performer in the making, and should win a race or 2. *J. H. M. Gosden*

EPPING 3 b.f. Charnwood Forest (IRE) 125 – Dansara (Dancing Brave (USA) 140) **81** [2001 8d 8d³ f7g* Oct 20] lengthy filly: fourth foal: closely related to smart French performer up to 15.5f Self Defense and fairly useful French 9f winner Answer (both by Warning): dam unraced half-sister to Irish Oaks winner Princess Pati and high-class 1½m performer Seymour Hicks: progressed in maidens, winning at Wolverhampton by 11 lengths from Challenor: likely to stay 1¼m: sold 70,000 gns. *B. W. Hills*

EPITRE (FR) 4 b.c.Common Grounds 118 – Epistolienne (Law Society (USA) 130) **115** [2001 115: 12.5s³ 12.5g 12m⁶ 12v² 15.5v Oct 28] leggy, angular colt: smart performer: easily best effort in 2001 when ½-length second to Yavana's Pace in Prix du Conseil de Paris at Longchamp penultimate start, staying on well: disappointing in Prix Royal-Oak there week later: needs good test at 1½m and stays 15f: raced mainly on good ground or softer (acts on heavy): blinkered last 2 starts. *A. Fabre, France*

EQUERRY (USA) 3 b. or br.c. St Jovite (USA) 135 – Colour Chart (USA) 122 **119 p** (Mr Prospector (USA)) [2001 106p: 10d* Sep 23]

Equerry takes an unbeaten record into his four-year-old season, when he has the potential to develop into one of the leading lights among Godolphin's older horses. The winner of his three starts as a two-year-old in Sheikh Mohammed's colours when trained by Andre Fabre, Equerry's Derby hopes were all but dashed as early as March when it was reported that he had sustained an injury in training in Dubai and would be unlikely to be ready for Epsom. Even so, it was not until the five-day stage that Equerry was finally ruled out of the Derby. A wait for softer ground then meant that it was the autumn before Equerry finally made his reappearance. Originally that looked like being in a listed race at York in September, but the ground was deemed too firm and he was sent instead for the Group 3 Prix du Prince d'Orange at Longchamp, where he had signed off as a two-year-old in the Prix des Chenes just over twelve months earlier.

If Equerry had something to prove after a lengthy absence, so did a couple of his rivals. Maille Pistol was on trial for the Prix de l'Arc de Triomphe and attempting to re-establish his reputation after being beaten favourite in the Prix du Jockey Club, while Equerry's former stable-companion Sagacity, also well beaten

*Prix du Prince d'Orange, Longchamp—Equerry's only race of the year,
but he maintains his unbeaten record at the chief expense of subsequent Arc third Sagacity*

in the Jockey Club, had yet to fulfil the promise of his two-year-old campaign.
Maille Pistol set off in front in his usual style, opening up a clear lead with only
Equerry in hailing distance. As Maille Pistol gave way in the straight, Equerry took
over, soon establishing a lead of around four lengths over his weakening rival as the
rest tried to close. The only one to make any impression on Equerry was Sagacity,
who reduced his advantage to half a length at the line, without ever looking like
posing a serious threat. Poussin also passed Maille Pistol to take third, three lengths
behind the winner. Although Equerry was not seen out again (he was taken out of
the Champion Stakes on the day of the race), the placed horses enhanced the form
in no uncertain terms afterwards. Poussin continued his progress by giving weight
away all round when winning a listed race at Deauville, while Sagacity put up a
career-best effort, showing high-class form, to take third place in the Prix de l'Arc
de Triomphe.

Equerry will have come as a much-needed boost—of sorts—to the flagging
stud career of his sire St Jovite. An outstanding winner of the Irish Derby and
King George VI and Queen Elizabeth Diamond Stakes he may have been, but as a
twelve-furlong turf performer in Europe St Jovite has seemingly held little appeal
to breeders in America where he stands at stud. He covered only half a dozen mares
in 2001 at a fee of $5,000, just a fifth of the asking price for his services when he
started out in 1994. Equerry's dam Colour Chart has otherwise kept much more
fashionable company at stud, as befits a very smart mare who raced in top-level
company on both sides of the Atlantic over three seasons. The winner of her only
start at two over a mile at Longchamp, Colour Chart won the Prix de l'Opera and
Prix de la Nonette as a three-year-old (when also demoted from second in the Prix
de Diane) and the Prix du Muguet on her reappearance at four. That same season
she finished second attempting a repeat win in the Opera and also took the runner-
up spot in the Beverly D at Arlington. Kept in training at five, she made the frame
in three Grade 1 events at Santa Anita, coming nearest to winning one when second
to that year's Breeders' Cup Distaff winner Paseana in the Santa Maria Handicap.

Colour Chart's first two foals were by Danzig, Chirico being an ordinary
winner up to a mile and a quarter in Britain and the UAE, and later successful in
Saudi Arabia, and Kumait proving a useful performer over six and seven furlongs.
Her next two foals, both by Nureyev, managed just one run between them. Fifth
foal Equerry is already facing stiff competition from his two-year-old half-sister
Tempera (by A P Indy) for the honour of being his dam's best offspring; she took
the Breeders' Cup Juvenile Fillies for Godolphin's American two-year-old operation. Colour Chart also has a yearling filly by Kris S named Ostentation and
produced a colt foal to Theatrical in 2001. Equerry's immediate family is a very
good Canadian one. Grandam Rainbow Connection was the champion filly in
Canada at two and three, and, as well as Colour Chart and the smart Guy Harwood-
trained stayer Dance Spectrum, bred another Canadian champion Rainbows For
Life. Rainbow Connection was one of several good winners in Canada out of a

Godolphin's "Equerry"

maiden daughter of a mare named Auburn's Pride whom Dick Hern trained to win a maiden over five furlongs at Manchester as a two-year-old.

Equerry (USA) (b. or br.c. 1998)	St Jovite (USA) (b 1989)	Pleasant Colony (b 1978)	His Majesty Sun Colony
		Northern Sunset (ch 1977)	Northfields Moss Greine
	Colour Chart (USA) (b 1987)	Mr Prospector (b 1970)	Raise A Native Gold Digger
		Rainbow Connection (b 1978)	Halo Hangin Round

A big, good-topped colt with plenty of scope, Equerry is just the sort to improve further as a four-year-old, particularly as he has had very little racing. He will not be difficult to place either, never having won above Group 3 level. He should stay a mile and a half and has yet to race on extremes of ground, though it seems unlikely that he would be risked on firm going. *Saeed bin Suroor*

EREBUS (IRE)   4 b.g. Desert Style (IRE) 121 – Almost A Lady (IRE) 70 (Entitled 126) [2001 70?: 9m 7m 8f⁵ 8g 8s f8.5g³ 8v Oct 24] small, sturdy gelding: has a round action: modest maiden handicapper: stays 9f: acts on firm going and fibresand: visored after second start: has taken strong hold: sold 800 gns. *J. A. Glover*   **60**

ERIC LE BEAU (IRE)   2 ch.c. (Apr 3) Great Commotion (USA) 123 – Mirmande 66 (Kris 135) [2001 8d Oct 19] IR 13,500F, IR 34,000Y: third foal: dam maiden half-sister to smart 1¼m performer Dartrey: 50/1 and unimpressive to post, never-nearer seventh of 20 to Rawyaan in maiden at Newmarket: will probably stay 1¼m: sure to improve. *G. C. Bravery*   **81 p**

ERRACHT 3 gr.f. Emarati (USA) 74 – Port Na Blath (On Your Mark 125) [2001 76: **54 +** f5s f6g[4] f8g 6m* 6g* 6s[6] Sep 24] lengthy filly: modest performer: won sellers at Thirsk in June and Hamilton in July: effective at 5f/6f: acts on good to firm and heavy going, probably on fibresand: has made running: doesn't seem an easy ride. *P. C. Haslam*

ERRO CODIGO 6 b.g. Formidable (USA) 125 – Home Wrecker (DEN) (Affiliation **64 ?** Order (USA) 89) [2001 –: 6s[2] 5v 8s 6g May 10] strong, good-topped gelding: modest performer: below form after reappearance: best at 6f/7f: acts on fibresand, heavy and good to firm going: visored once at 3 yrs. *F. P. Murtagh*

ERTLON 11 b.g. Shareef Dancer (USA) 135 – Sharpina (Sharpen Up 127) [2001 58: **35** f8.5s e7g[4] e8g Feb 10] close-coupled gelding: poor performer: stays easy 1¼m: raced only on all-weather in 2001: blinkered once: has been tongue tied. *C. E. Brittain*

ERUPT 8 b.g. Beveled (USA) – Sparklingsovereign 53 (Sparkler 130) [2001 63§, **52 §** a46§: 7m 8m 7.5m 8d 8g[2] 8.9m[6] 8s 8v[6] 8d Oct 30] plain, leggy gelding: modest **a– §** performer: best at 7f/1m nowadays: acts on any turf going and fibresand: has won when visored, blinkered once: has been tongue tied: sometimes slowly away: has raced freely: held up: moody. *M. Brittain*

ESATTO 2 b.c. (Apr 25) Puissance 110 – Stoneydale 83 (Tickled Pink 114) [2001 f5g **67** 5.1f[2] 5g[4] 5m[4] 5f[5] f5g[3] 5m[4] 5d[5] 6s 5.1s 5g[5] f7g f5g Dec 11] 7,500Y, 9,200 2-y-o: big, quite **a60** good-topped colt: half-brother to several winners, including 5f/6f (at 2 yrs) winner Runs In The Family (by Distant Relative): dam sprinter: fair maiden on turf, modest on all-weather: left M. Polglase after seventh start: form only at 5f: acts on firm going, good to soft and fibresand: sometimes slowly away. *R. Hollinshead*

ESCALADE 4 b.g. Green Desert (USA) 127 – Sans Escale (USA) (Diesis 133) [2001 **78** –: 6m 8.3m[5] 8f[3] 8f[4] 8.3d[2] 8m 8.2m* 8.5g* 8s* 8.1v* 8.9d[4] 8.2s Oct 30] small, compact gelding: fair performer: won minor event at Leicester and handicaps at Nottingham, Beverley and Haydock (slowly away), all in September: will stay 1¼m: acts on any going. *W. M. Brisbourne*

ESCENICA (IRE) 2 b.f. (Apr 21) Charnwood Forest (IRE) 125 – Scenic Spirit (IRE) **76 p** (Scenic 128) [2001 7.6m[5] 7d[4] Oct 6] leggy, quite good-topped filly: second foal: half-sister to 3-y-o winner Achilles Spirit: dam unraced half-sister to Bob's Return: better effort in maidens (fair form) when keeping-on fourth to Atarama at Redcar: will probably stay 1¼m: should improve. *C. F. Wall*

ESCORT 5 b.g. Most Welcome 131 – Benazir 91 (High Top 131) [2001 14.1v 17.1s **–** Apr 10] strong, sturdy gelding: fairly useful handicapper at 3 yrs: well held both Flat outings since. *W. Clay*

ESENIN 2 b.c. (Feb 25) Danehill (USA) 126 – Boojum 101 (Mujtahid (USA) 118) **94** [2001 6g* 6m[5] 7g[6] Aug 30] 200,000Y: strong, lengthy colt: first foal: dam 2-y-o 6f/7f winner: created good impression and showed fairly useful form when winning minor event at Newmarket in July by 5 lengths from Gold Guest: only fifth to Mister Cosmi when favourite for Richmond Stakes at Goodwood next time: ran as if something amiss final start: should stay 7f. *N. A. Callaghan*

ESHER COMMON (IRE) 3 b.g. Common Grounds 118 – Alsahah (IRE) (Unfuwain **92** (USA) 131) [2001 94p: 8v[5] 8s[4] 7g 8.1m 7m 8m[4] Aug 30] tall, good-topped gelding: fairly useful performer: ran creditably most starts in 2001, including when fourth to Herodotus in listed race at Kempton on second one: stays 1m: acts on heavy and good to firm going: free-going sort: sold 10,500 gns. *T. G. Mills*

ESHRAAG 2 ch.c. (Apr 23) Lion Cavern (USA) 117 – Val d'Erica 119 (Ashmore (FR) **75** 125) [2001 7g 8g[2] 7g f8g* 8d Oct 19] 14,000F: big, strong colt: half-brother to numerous winners, including 3-y-o Astral Prince and Italian Group 3 1¼m winner Verardi (by Mill Reef): dam won Oaks d'Italia and second in Prix de Diane: fair performer: won minor event at Southwell in October: ran creditably in nursery at Newmarket final start: will stay 1¼m: acts on fibresand, yet to race on ground firmer than good: has worn crossed noseband. *P. W. D'Arcy*

ESLIGIER (IRE) 2 ch.f. (Mar 28) Sabrehill (USA) 120 – Norbella (Nordico (USA)) **87 +** [2001 f5g[2] 5.1g* 5g[2] 5m* 5d[5] Sep 13] good-topped filly: third foal: half-sister to useful 5f (at 2 yrs) to 1m winner Achilles Star (by Deploy): dam unraced: fairly useful performer: won maiden at Nottingham and minor event at Ripon in August: creditable effort when fifth to Astonished in all-aged listed event at Doncaster final start: will prove best at 5f: acts on good to firm and good to soft ground, shaped well on fibresand: races prominently. *B. A. McMahon*

Mr Hamdan Al Maktoum's "Esloob"

ESLOOB (USA) 2 b.f. (Jan 29) Diesis 133 – Roseate Tern 123 (Blakeney 126) [2001 **104 p**
7f* 8s³ Sep 29] smallish, sturdy filly: has fluent, slightly round action: sixth foal: half-
sister to useful 1¼m winner Siyadah (by Mr Prospector) and fairly useful 1997 2-y-o 7f
winner who stayed 1½m Fakhr (by Riverman): dam, won Yorkshire Oaks and placed
in Oaks/St Leger, half-sister to high-class performer up to 1¾m Ibn Bey: justified
favouritism in maiden at Newmarket in August by head from Snowfire: useful form when
3¾ lengths third to Gossamer in Fillies' Mile at Ascot, making most and keeping on
willingly: should be suited by 1¼m/1½m: capable of better. *M. P. Tregoning*

ESPADA (IRE) 5 b.g. Mukaddamah (USA) 125 – Folk Song (CAN) (The Minstrel **81**
(CAN) 135) [2001 99: 8v 8d 7m 7.1s³ 7s⁵ 8.1g Aug 11] strong, smallish gelding: fairly
useful handicapper: effective at 7f/1m: acts on any going: visored once: has raced freely/
hung left/found little. *J. A. Glover*

ESPANA 3 gr.f. Hernando (FR) 127 – Pamela Peach 81 (Habitat 134) [2001 67: f9.4s² **69**
f12g* 10.3s⁴ 10.2d⁵ 10.9m² 12f⁵ 12.3f⁴ Jun 30] leggy filly: has a round action: fair performer: won Wolverhampton maiden in February: stays 1½m: acts on fibresand, firm and
soft going: consistent: sold 15,000 gns in July, resold 18,000 gns in December. *B. W. Hills*

ESPERE D'OR 4 b.g. Golden Heights 82 – Drummer's Dream (IRE) 48 (Drumalis **–**
125) [2001 –: 7v Oct 27] of no account. *A. Streeter*

ESPRIT D'ARTISTE (IRE) 2 ch.c. (Apr 21) Selkirk (USA) 129 – Fracci (Raise A **65 p**
Cup (USA)) [2001 7d 8.2s 8.2s Nov 5] 45,000Y: tall colt: has scope: sixth foal: brother to
smart 7f/1m winner in Italy/France Field of Hope and half-brother to Italian 7f to 1¼m
winner Stage Set (by Old Vic): dam Italian 5f (at 2 yrs) to 7f winner, placed in Group 3
1m event: fair form in sales race/maidens: will probably stay 1¼m: looks type to do better
at 3 yrs. *C. E. Brittain*

311

ESSIE 4 b.f. Ezzoud (IRE) 126 – Safari Park 43 (Absalom 128) [2001 –: 14.1s Apr 16] – of no account. *Miss D. A. McHale*

ESTABELLA (IRE) 4 ch.f. Mujtahid (USA) 118 – Lady In Green (Shareef Dancer 52 (USA) 135) [2001 67: 16m 13.3f⁵ 12.1m 16.4g 10m 14.1s p13g⁵ f14.8g p16g Dec 4] modest performer: left R. Phillips after reappearance: stays easy 2m: acts on any turf going and fibresand/equitrack: blinkered/tried visored: races freely: has wandered/found little. *B. R. Johnson*

ESTABLISHED 4 gr.g. Not In Doubt (USA) 101 – Copper Trader 53 (Faustus (USA) 51 118) [2001 58: 16v 17.1s 16m⁶ 16.4m⁶ 16.2m⁴ 18m⁶ 16.4m³ 15.4m⁵ 16g 16.4g⁶ 16g² a– 16.2m⁶ 16d 15.8d⁴ 16s Oct 30] smallish, strong gelding: modest handicapper on turf: stays 2m: acts on firm and good to soft going (little form on fibresand/equitrack): tried blinkered: has been reluctant stalls: finished distressed thirteenth start. *J. R. Best*

ESTABLISHMENT 4 b.g. Muhtarram (USA) 125 – Uncharted Waters 68 (Celestial 85 Storm (USA) 132) [2001 74: 11.9f² 10g² 12g* 12m 13.3m³ 13.9m⁶ 16.2s² 18d⁴ 16.5s⁶ a76 p12g⁴ f16.2f⁵ Dec 5] smallish, workmanlike gelding: fairly useful handicapper on turf, fair on all-weather: won at Ascot in July: generally in good form otherwise, best effort when fourth to Distant Prospect in Cesarewitch at Newmarket (sweating, 66/1) eighth start: stays 2¼m: acts on equitrack, polytrack, firm and soft going: blinkered final 3-y-o start: has raced freely. *C. A. Cyzer*

ESTACADO (IRE) 5 b.m. Dolphin Street (FR) 125 – Raubritter (Levmoss 133) 44 § [2001 50§: e16g⁴ e16g Jan 27] smallish mare: poor maiden handicapper: will stay beyond 2m: acts on equitrack, soft and good to firm going: sometimes visored: ungenuine. *J. W. Mullins*

ESTEEMED MASTER (USA) 2 b.c. (Apr 5) Mark of Esteem (IRE) 137 – 87 Jasminola (FR) (Seattle Dancer (USA) 119) [2001 7.1m⁴ 7g³ 7m² 8m⁴ 10.2g² 10d* 8s² Nov 9] $20,000F, 28,000Y: close-coupled colt: second foal: dam, French 9.5f winner, out of half-sister to champion US filly Magic's: fairly useful performer: in frame all starts: won maiden at Brighton in November: 5 lengths second of 3 to Simeon in minor event at Doncaster final outing: stays 1¼m: yet to race on extremes of going: blinkered last 2 starts: lazy but consistent. *G. A. Butler*

ESTIHAN (USA) 3 b.f. Silver Hawk (USA) 123 – Dance Image (IRE) (Sadler's Wells 65 (USA) 132) [2001 68p: 11.9f⁴ 10.2m⁵ 11.9m 10m³ 14.1s⁴ 16.1d⁵ f12g⁴ 12d⁴ f12g Nov a57 23] fair maiden handicapper on turf, modest on all-weather: stays 1¾m: acts on soft going, good to firm and fibresand: sold 4,000 gns. *C. E. Brittain*

ESTOMAQUE 2 br.g. (Apr 12) Mark of Esteem (IRE) 137 – Allespagne (USA) – (Trempolino (USA) 135) [2001 8d Oct 19] close-coupled, quite good-topped gelding: second foal: half-brother to 3-y-o Larousse: dam useful French 1½m/1¾m winner: 33/1 and backward, always behind in maiden at Newmarket. *S. C. Williams*

ESTUARY (USA) 6 ch.g. Riverman (USA) 131 – Ocean Ballad 104 (Grundy 137) 56 [2001 56: e13g² f12s² f12g* f12g³ 8m² 8d 12.6d⁶ 10m Jul 27] big, workmanlike gelding: a64 modest performer: won maiden at Wolverhampton in February: stays 13f: acts on fibresand/equitrack and good to firm going: has had tongue tied: has found little. *Ms A. E. Embiricos*

ESYOUEFFCEE (IRE) 3 b.f. Alzao (USA) 117 – Familiar (USA) 96 (Diesis 133) 109 [2001 104: 10.1m³ 10.9m² 8g 10d* 10.5d⁴ 10.5v Nov 27] leggy, angular filly: useful performer: won listed race at Newmarket in October by ¾ length from Villa Carlotta, despite edging right: earlier placed in similar events at Newcastle (rated stakes, third to Moselle) and Ayr (4 lengths second to Albarahin): below form in France last 2 starts: stays 1¼m: acts on soft and good to firm going. *M. W. Easterby*

ETERNAL BLOOM 3 b.f. Reprimand 122 – Forever Roses 70 (Forzando 122) 45 [2001 f6g⁵ f6s³ Dec 15] 1,000F, 800Y: second foal: half-sister to useful 6f (at 2 yrs)/7f winner Free Rider (by Inchinor): dam, third at 5f only start, half-sister to smart sprinter Gallic League: poor form in fibresand maidens: may prove best at 5f/6f: carried head high second outing. *M. Brittain*

ETERNAL SPRING (IRE) 4 b.g. Persian Bold 123 – Emerald Waters (Kings Lake 107 (USA) 133) [2001 105: 12.3s² 13.9g³ 13.9m⁶ 18d Sep 13] close-coupled, quite good-topped gelding: useful performer, lightly raced: best effort in 2001 when 6 lengths third to Marienbard in Yorkshire Cup at York in May: gelded before tailed off in Doncaster Cup final start: stays 1¾m: acts on heavy going, probably on good to firm: has been taken steadily to post. *J. R. Fanshawe*

ETERNELLE   2 b.f. (Mar 17) Green Desert (USA) 127 – Eversince (USA) (Foolish   **– p**
Pleasure (USA)) [2001 7d Nov 3] lengthy filly: sister to useful sprinter Everset and
half-sister to fairly useful winner up to 1¼m Lady Lodger (by Be My Guest) and 7-y-o
Caitano: dam 1m winner at 2 yrs in France: 7/1-joint favourite but backward, well-held
seventeenth of 21 in Newmarket maiden: should do better. *Sir Michael Stoute*

ETISALAT (IRE)   6 b.h. Lahib (USA) 129 – Sweet Repose (High Top 131) [2001 64:   **56 d**
f9.4s⁴ f9.4g² e10g³ f8.5g e10g⁶ f8.5g 8m 10m 9.7m⁶ 9.2g 10g⁶ 8s Sep 30] quite good-
topped horse: modest handicapper, on downgrade: stays easy 1¼m: acts on fibresand/
equitrack and firm going: sometimes slowly away. *Mrs Lydia Pearce*

ETON (GER)   5 ch.g. Suave Dancer (USA) 136 – Ermione (Surumu (GER)) [2001   **74 d**
8g⁵ 11.9m 12m 11.9s Oct 11] half-brother to several winners, including smart German
performer at 7f/1m Erminus (by Highest Honor): dam winner in Germany and fourth in
Preis der Diana: useful in Germany for P. Rau in 1999: little form after first start in 2001:
stays 11f: tried blinkered. *D. Nicholls*

ETTRICK WATER   2 ch.c. (Feb 16) Selkirk (USA) 129 – Sadly Sober (IRE) 70 (Roi   **77**
Danzig (USA)) [2001 7f 7.1s³ 7s³ 8g² Nov 7] 65,000Y: strong colt: third foal: dam,
maiden who stayed 1¼m well, half-sister to smart winner up to 11f Overbury: fair
maiden: easily best efforts last 2 starts, runner-up at Musselburgh: should stay 1¼m.
L. M. Cumani

EUCALYPTUS (IRE)   4 ch.g. Mujtahid (USA) 118 – Imprecise 64 (Polish Precedent   **59**
(USA) 131) [2001 –: e7g⁵ 7s 7g 7m⁵ 6v p10g p10g² p10g⁵ Dec 22] big, lengthy gelding:
poor mover: modest maiden: barely stays 1¼m: acts on polytrack, soft and good to firm
going: visored last 2 starts: has been slowly away. *S. Dow*

EUROLINK ARTEMIS   4 b.f. Common Grounds 118 – Taiga 69 (Northfields (USA))   **75**
[2001 73: 8.1m 10.1m* 10f² 10m* 9.9f⁵ 10.5d 10.4d p10g Nov 15] useful-looking filly:
fair handicapper: won at Newcastle and Redcar in June: left M. Johnston 4,200 gns after
penultimate start: stays 1¼m: acts on soft and good to firm going. *Julian Poulton*

EUROLINK ROOSTER   3 b.g. Turtle Island (IRE) 123 – Eurolink Virago (Charmer   **80**
123) [2001 e7g⁴ 8d³ 7s⁵ 10d³ 9m*⁵ 9.2s⁶ 7.9m 8d f8g Oct 22] leggy, quite good-topped   **a69**
gelding: third foal: half-brother to 5f winner in Germany by Be My Chief: dam unraced
half-sister to smart 7f/1m performer Eurolink Thunder: fairly useful on turf, fair on
all-weather: left G. Butler after third start: won maiden at Redcar in August: may prove
best up to 1m: acts on good to soft going, winner on good to firm: has worn crossed
noseband: has been taken early/last to post and slowly away: tends to pull hard/find little:
sold 2,000 gns. *M. Johnston*

EUROLINK SUNDANCE   3 ch.f. Night Shift (USA) – Eurolink Mischief 84 (Be   **85**
My Chief (USA) 122) [2001 75: 7s 7m⁶ 6m 6g* 6g⁶ 6g 5s Nov 9] leggy, plain filly: fairly
useful handicapper: won at Newmarket in July: probably best at 5f/6f: raced mainly on
good/good to firm ground: usually races prominently. *J. L. Dunlop*

EUROLINK ZANTE (IRE)   5 b.g. Turtle Island (IRE) 123 – Lady Eurolink 55   **77**
(Kala Shikari 125) [2001 54+: 6g² 7m⁴ 8.1g⁴ 7.1s⁶ 7d Oct 30] fair maiden handicapper,
lightly raced: probably stays 1m: acts on soft and good to firm going. *T. D. McCarthy*

EUROPRIME GAMES   3 b.c. Mind Games 121 – Flower Princess (Slip Anchor   **51**
136) [2001 43p: 7d 7s 7m⁵ 6m 8.2m⁴ 11.5f Jul 25] good-topped colt: modest maiden: left
A. Berry after fourth start: stays 7f: acts on soft and good to firm going. *R. J. Smith*

EUROTWIST   12 b.g. Viking (USA) – Orange Bowl (General Assembly (USA))   **–**
[2001 e10g Apr 11] of little account nowadays. *Dr P. Pritchard*

EURO VENTURE   6 b.g. Prince Sabo 123 – Brave Advance (USA) 98 (Bold Laddie   **76**
(USA)) [2001 84: f5g⁵ f6f⁴ f6g⁶ f6g⁶ 6m 5f⁵ 7g 7m 6g 6f⁵ 7m 6d f6g³ f7g⁴ f6g⁴
f6g f6g² f6s* Dec 15] sturdy gelding: fair handicapper: won at Thirsk in August (left
D. Nicholls after thirteenth start) and Wolverhampton in December: has won at 7f,
probably best at 5f/6f: unraced on heavy going, acts on any other turf and fibresand.
Mrs H. L. Walton

EVENING CHASE (IRE)   3 b.g. Pursuit of Love 124 – Late Evening (USA)   **59**
(Riverman (USA) 131) [2001 6g 5.1f 5.1m f6g³ f7g* 6m 6g 8.5s 7g Oct 19] 40,000Y: **a62**
half-brother to several winners, including useful 7f (at 2 yrs) and 1m winner Joie de Soir
(by Caerleon) and fairly useful 7f winner Sleepless (by Night Shift): dam French maiden:
modest performer: won claimer at Southwell (final start for H. Morrison) in July:
effective at 6f/7f: acts on fibresand, probably on firm going: tongue tied (reportedly had
breathing problem) final start. *J. L. Eyre*

EVENING PRESS 2 b.f. (May 2) River Falls 113 – Shiny Kay 65 (Star Appeal 133) – [2001 6f 6g 7g Nov 5] 3,500 2-y-o: half-sister to several winners, including useful 1995 2-y-o 5f winner Home Shopping (by Superpower) and 6-y-o Kayo: dam 1½m winner: no encouragement in maidens. *T. J. Etherington*

EVENING SCENT 5 b.m. Ardkinglass 114 – Fresh Line 60 (High Line 125) [2001 – 66, a–: f16g Jan 5] fair handicapper at best: well held only 5-y-o start. *J. Hetherton*

EVENING SERENADE (IRE) 2 b.f. (Feb 14) Night Shift (USA) – Flying Diva 75 100 (Chief Singer 131) [2001 6m⁶ 7m² 7m* 7g⁶ 7.1m 7d Oct 2] well-made filly: seventh reported foal: closely related to 8-y-o White Plains and half-sister to French 1m winner Lovely (by Catrail) and useful 1998 2-y-o 5.5f (Prix Robert Papin)/6f winner Black Amber (by College Chapel): dam, 2-y-o 6f/7f winner, out of sister to 1000 Guineas and Champion Stakes winner Flying Water: fair performer: won maiden at Folkestone in July: form in nurseries after only on penultimate start: should stay 1m: acts on good to firm going, possibly best on soft. *M. L. W. Bell*

EVENTUALITY 5 b.m. Petoski 135 – Queen's Tickle 57 (Tickled Pink 114) [2001 58 + 77: 6f⁵ 6.9m 6m Jun 27] leggy, lengthy mare: modest in 2001: stays 7f: acts on firm going, soft and equitrack: has taken strong hold/edged left: probably best forcing pace. *R. F. Johnson Houghton*

EVERBOLD 4 b.f. Never So Bold 135 – Out of Hours (Lochnager 132) [2001 –: f9.4s – 6m Jun 27] no sign of ability: tried blinkered. *D. McCain*

EVEREST (IRE) 4 ch.g. Indian Ridge 123 – Reine d'Beaute 97 (Caerleon (USA) 78 132) [2001 96: 8v 7m 8m 7.9m 8m 10d⁶ 8d Oct 18] strong, deep-girthed gelding: fair handicapper nowadays: best at 1m/9f: acts on any going: has wandered: often races freely. *B. Ellison*

EVERLASTING LOVE 4 b.f. Pursuit of Love 124 – Now And Forever (IRE) (Kris 100 135) [2001 94+: 9g 10.4m³ 12g⁵ 10.1m⁶ 10f Sep 22] strong, well-made filly: useful performer: without a win since 2 yrs: best effort in 2001 when third to Moselle in listed race at York and fifth to Honorifique in Premio Mario Incisa at Milan: stays 1½m: acts on firm going, well below form on soft. *M. L. W. Bell*

EVERMOORE 3 b.f. Thatching 131 – Ganador 67 (Weldnaas (USA) 112) [2001 54d: – p7g Dec 19] modest form on second run at 2 yrs: little show since. *J. S. Moore*

EVER REVIE (IRE) 4 b.f. Hamas (IRE) 125§ – Lucy Limelight 98 (Hot Spark 126) – [2001 50, a–: 8.2s 8s May 2] leggy filly: modest 7f winner at 3 yrs: well held both 4-y-o starts: sometimes blinkered. *Miss S. J. Wilton*

EVERY RIGHT (IRE) 3 b.g. Common Grounds 118 – Incendio (Siberian Express – (USA) 125) [2001 –: f5f⁶ f7g f5g 5m 6g 6m f6g 6d 5f 6m Aug 4] no form: tried blinkered. *D. W. Chapman*

EVEZIO RUFO 9 b.g. Blakeney 126 – Empress Corina 74 (Free State 125) [2001 52, – § a68: f14g³ f11g⁴ f11s² f12s³ f16g⁴ f12g⁶ f16.2g⁴ f12g e16g f14g³ f12g⁵ f16g f12g f16g² **a63 §** f14g f16.2f³ f16.2s² Dec 18] neat gelding: modest handicapper: effective at 1½m to 2m: acts on fibresand/equitrack: blinkered/visored: has hung: no easy ride: not one to trust. *N. P. Littmoden*

EVIDENCE 3 ch.f. Machiavellian (USA) 123 – Beyond Doubt 87 (Belmez (USA) 65 131) [2001 9.9d 12f 12g⁵ Jul 18] first foal: dam, 1¼m/1½m winner, half-sister to very smart 1½m/1¾m winner Blueprint: fair form in maidens: will probably stay beyond 1½m: slowly away first 2 outings. *R. Charlton*

EVIYRN (IRE) 5 b.g. In The Wings 128 – Evrana (USA) (Nureyev (USA) 131) [2001 39 –: 12.6f⁶ 18m⁴ 16s Oct 30] poor maiden nowadays: stays 2¼m: acts on soft and good to firm ground: visored final start. *J. R. Jenkins*

EWAR BOLD 8 b.g. Bold Arrangement 127 – Monaneigue Lady (Julio Mariner 127) – [2001 14.1s Nov 5] disappointing maiden. *K. G. Wingrove*

EWAR VICTORIA (FR) 2 b.f. (Jan 27) Valanour (IRE) 125 – Ewar Empress (IRE) 59 d 57 (Persian Bold 123) [2001 5s 7m⁶ 7m 8g f8.5g 8d 8v p8g Nov 28] 50,000 francs Y: sparely-made filly: fourth foal: half-sister to 5-y-o Sharp Spice: dam, temperamental maiden, best at 7f at 2 yrs: modest maiden: best effort on second start: free-going sort, likely to prove best up to 1m. *K. O. Cunningham-Brown*

EXALTATION (IRE) 3 ch.c. Rainbow Quest (USA) 134 – Carnival Spirit 92 (Kris 112 135) [2001 8s* 10m² 10g* 12g⁵ 10s³ 10g³ Sep 8] rather leggy, lengthy colt: brother to useful French 9f (at 2 yrs) to 1½m winner Carniola and closely related to French winner up to 11.5f Robber's Dance (by Groom Dancer): dam, 1m winner, half-sister to Arc winner Saumarez: smart performer: won maiden in April and Gallinule Stakes in June, both at Leopardstown, latter by ¾ length from Jammaal: good efforts behind Galileo in Derrinstown Stud Derby Trial at Leopardstown (1½ lengths second) and Irish Derby at the Curragh (10½ lengths fifth) and behind Bach in Royal Whip Stakes on latter course (2 lengths third): below form final outing: stays 1½m: acts on soft and good to firm going: joined Godolphin. *J. Oxx, Ireland*

EXALTED (IRE)   8 b.g. High Estate 127 – Heavenward (USA) (Conquistador Cielo   **66** (USA)) [2001 66: 13d² 12.1m² 13.1m² 11.9d⁶ 13g* 13s³ 10.9m 12.1m Sep 24] good-topped gelding: has round action: fair handicapper: won ladies event at Hamilton in June: effective at 1½m/1¾m, possibly not 2m: acts on soft and good to firm ground. *T. A. K. Cuthbert*

EXCLUSIVE AIR (USA)   2 ch.c. (Apr 30) Affirmed (USA) – Lac Dessert (USA) 91   **65 p** (Lac Ouimet (USA)) [2001 7.2m⁵ 8d 7d⁶ f8g² Dec 3] $9,500Y: smallish, good-topped colt: second foal: dam 7f/7.5f winner at 2 yrs who later won in USA: fair maiden: best effort when staying-on second in nursery at Southwell: should stay 1¼m: acts on fibresand: should do better. *T. D. Barron*

EXEAT (USA)   5 b. or br.g. Dayjur (USA) 137 – By Your Leave (USA) (Private   **92 d** Account (USA)) [2001 107d: 8v 7g³ 8m* 7d 9.1m* 6d 8d Nov 3] good-topped gelding: unimpressive mover: formerly smart, on downgrade nowadays: won minor event at Goodwood (odds on) in May and claimer at Ayr (claimed from D. Nicholls £20,000) in September: needs further than 6f and stays 9f: acts on soft and good to firm going: sometimes visored earlier in career: sometimes races freely: possibly none too genuine. *J. S. Goldie*

EXECUTIVE CHOICE (IRE)   7 b.g. Don't Forget Me 127 – Shadia (USA) 53   **–** (Naskra (USA)) [2001 8.5s Aug 16] of little account nowadays. *B. Ellison*

EXECUTIVE NETWORK   3 b.g. Silca Blanka (IRE) 104 – Scene Stealer (Scenic   **55 ?** 128) [2001 11.9s f7g 10v⁴ f12g Nov 23] first foal: dam tailed off only start on Flat and pulled up over hurdles: form only in seller at Windsor penultimate start, tending to wander: ran in snatches final outing: stays 1¼m. *A. D. Smith*

EXELLENT ADVENTURE   3 ch.g. Gold Dust 84 – Freedom Weekend (USA)   **–** (Shahrastani (USA) 135) [2001 35: 10s 6g 8f 6m 8.1m Jul 5] tall, unfurnished gelding: little form. *D. Burchell*

EXHIBITION GIRL (IRE)   4 ch.f. Perugino (USA) 84 – Shy Jinks (Shy Groom   **37** (USA)) [2001 ?: 10d 10f 8m 12f⁵ f16g Jul 27] angular filly: poor maiden handicapper: stays 1½m: acts on firm going. *Andrew Turnell*

EXHIBIT (IRE)   3 b.c. Royal Academy (USA) 130 – Juno Madonna (IRE) (Sadler's   **69** Wells (USA) 132) [2001 10m 8.3m⁴ 8.3m 8.2m Sep 10] 90,000Y: good-bodied, quite attractive colt: second foal: dam unraced close relative of useful sprinters Title Roll and Northern Express: fair maiden: should be suited by further than 1m: raced only on good to firm going: sold 11,000 gns. *Sir Michael Stoute*

EXHIBITOR (USA)   2 b.f. (Feb 23) Royal Academy (USA) 130 – Akadya (FR)   **– p** (Akarad (FR) 130) [2001 7d Oct 15] $70,000Y: lengthy filly: sixth foal: half-sister to 3 winners, including useful French 1¼m/1½m winner Aka Lady (by Sanglamore): dam French 1¼m (at 2 yrs) and 12.5f (listed winner): 16/1, well held in maiden at Leicester: should do better. *J. R. Fanshawe*

EXILE   4 b.g. Emperor Jones (USA) 119 – Silver Venture (USA) (Silver Hawk (USA)   **83** 123) [2001 79: 13.3g 12m* 11.4g Jul 8] close-coupled gelding: fairly useful handicapper: made all at Kempton in June: stays 1½m: acts on firm going: blinkered twice at 2 yrs: possibly not easiest of rides. *R. T. Phillips*

EXJAYSIX   3 b.g. Chocolat de Meguro (USA) 98 – Secret Chant (Silly Prices 110)   **–** [2001 10d³ Jul 16] fourth reported foal: dam unraced: 50/1, distant third of 4 in maiden at Ayr. *M. A. Barnes*

EXOTIC FAN (USA)   3 b. or br.f. Lear Fan (USA) 130 – Green Moon (FR) (Shirley   **80** Heights 130) [2001 66: 7m 13.1f⁶ f8.5g* 10d* f12g* f8.5g* 9.9s⁵ 10.5v⁵ 10d p10g f12s⁵   **a97** Dec 21] useful on all-weather, fairly useful on turf: won handicaps at Wolverhampton (2) and Southwell and minor event at Lingfield in summer: has won at 1½m, probably best at 1m/1¼m: acts on fibresand and heavy going. *R. Guest*

EXPECTED BONUS (USA)   2 b. or br.c. (Mar 14) Kris S (USA) – Nidd (USA) 112   **96** (Known Fact (USA) 135) [2001 6g² 7g* 7d⁵ Oct 19] lengthy colt: poor walker: third foal: half-brother to 4-y-o Charango: dam, 5.5f and 7f winner (including Prix de la Porte Maillot), closely related to Breeders' Cup Classic winner Skywalker: useful form: won minor event at Kempton in September by short head from Right Approach despite carrying head awkwardly and edging left: hung right when only fifth of 6 to Century City in similar event at Newmarket, again making running: not certain to stay beyond 7f. *B. W. Hills*

EXPECTEDTOFLI (IRE)   3 b.f. Mujadil (USA) 119 – Zurarah (Siberian Express   **47** (USA) 125) [2001 6g 8m 6m 6d⁴ 7d p6g³ f7g⁵ p7g f7s Dec 18] IR 10,000Y: unfurnished filly: sister to a winner up to 7f in Italy and half-sister to 3 winners, including fairly useful 1995 2-y-o 6f winner Magarah (by Magical Strike): dam unraced half-sister to very smart 7f/1m performer Gabr: poor maiden: stays 7f: acts on fibresand/polytrack and on good to soft going: tongue tied after second outing. *C. N. Allen*

EXPLODE   4 b.g. Zafonic (USA) 130 – Didicoy (USA) 104 (Danzig (USA)) [2001   **–** 106p: 10g May 5] quite attractive gelding: useful at 3 yrs: well held only 4-y-o start:sold 6,000 gns, and gelded. *R. Charlton*

EXPLORING (IRE)   2 br.c. (Apr 20) Charnwood Forest (IRE) 125 – Caribbean Quest   **69** 90 (Rainbow Quest (USA) 134) [2001 7m⁵ 8g⁵ 8d Oct 3] IR 18,000Y: close-coupled, useful-looking colt: unimpressive mover: second foal: dam, 2-y-o 1m winner, from family of high-class sprinter/miler Golden Opinion: fair maiden: fifth twice at Kempton: not sure to stay much beyond 1m. *R. F. Johnson Houghton*

EXPLOSIVE   3 b.g. Saddlers' Hall (IRE) 126 – Pursuit of Glory 84 (Shirley Heights   **60 §** 130) [2001 –: e10g⁴ 14m 9.7m⁵ 12g f14.8s f11g Oct 1] leggy, sparely-made gelding: modest maiden: stays 1¼m: acts on equitrack, raced only on good/good to firm going on turf: blinkered (raced freely and unseated after saddle slipped) final start: seems temperamental (has hung/swerved badly), and one to treat with caution. *C. A. Cyzer*

EXPRESS TOUR (USA)   3 ch.c. Tour d'Or (USA) 108 – Express Fashion (USA)   **121** (Private Express (USA)) [2001 107p: a9f* a10f a7f⁶ a8f* 8f Oct 27]
   The newly-instituted UAE Derby, run on dirt and added to the Dubai World Cup programme at Nad Al Sheba in 2000, was quick to make its mark. Bachir, runner-up to the impressive China Visit in the first running, went on to win the French and Irish Two Thousand Guineas, sixth-placed Crimplene took the German and Irish One Thousand Guineas and ninth-placed Pacino won the German Two Thousand Guineas. The eighth Compton Bolter went on to finish a good fifth in the Two Thousand Guineas at Newmarket, a race bypassed by China Visit in favour of a tilt at the Kentucky Derby, in which he came sixth. The second running of the UAE Derby at Nad Al Sheba in March had a massive injection of prize-money, its first prize worth £836,571 (at prevailing exchange rates) dwarfing even those for the Kentucky Derby and the Derby at Epsom, the latter the most valuable race of the year in Europe. An increase in the distance of the UAE Derby is set to be the next change—from nine furlongs to the Kentucky Derby trip of a mile and a quarter.
   The Kentucky Derby was the initial target for the first two in the latest UAE Derby, the Godolphin-owned pair Express Tour and Street Cry, both of whom had gained experience of racing on dirt as two-year-olds in America. Express Tour had been purchased privately, for a sum reported to be in excess of a million dollars, after establishing himself as the best two-year-old in Florida by winning his last three races—all restricted to colts by Florida-based stallions—for Martin Wolfson. He was promoted to third favourite behind Point Given and Monarchos in ante-post betting on the Kentucky Derby after winning the UAE Derby by a short head from 6/4 favourite Street Cry. The pair had the finish to themselves—American-trained Lido Palace was six lengths back in third—and Express Tour deserved plenty of credit for battling back gamely to regain the lead close home after being headed inside the final furlong. Lido Palace had built up a very good record when trained in Chile and went on to further Grade 1 successes later in the year in the States in the Whitney Handicap and the Woodward Stakes. He would have been one of the leading home-trained contenders for the Breeders' Cup Classic if connections had elected to stump up the 800,000 dollars required to supplement him, but instead went for the Japan Cup Dirt at Tokyo, where he finished only eighth.

UAE Derby, Nad Al Sheba—the world's richest Derby goes to Express Tour (far side), who just gets the better of stable-companion Street Cry

Express Tour did make it to the Breeders' Cup at Belmont Park in October, coming tenth of twelve (three places behind Godolphin's first string Noverre) in the Breeders' Cup Mile on his first outing on turf. He had run three times in the meantime, recording his only other victory on his previous start in the Grade 2 Jerome Handicap over a mile at Belmont Park in September, racing with plenty of enthusiasm on his return after an absence of three and a half months, helping to set a strong pace from the start, and beating Illusioned by five and a half lengths. Express Tour's Kentucky Derby challenge—he started at 18/1 in a field of seventeen—ended in disappointment for his connections. He failed to repeat his UAE Derby form, managing only eighth after moving up smoothly on the far turn and seemingly having every chance as the field approached the home straight. Injury had ruled Street Cry out of the Kentucky Derby and Express Tour was also said to have missed work in the weeks leading up to the race after bruising his near-fore hoof. Connections were inclined, however, to put down Express Tour's failure to the fact that he had not stayed the trip, even though he seemed beaten before the distance became a factor. He was tried back at seven furlongs next time, finishing only sixth in a Grade 2 event at Belmont.

Express Tour (USA) (ch.c. 1998)	Tour d'Or (USA) (ch 1982)	Medaille d'Or (ch 1976)	Secretariat
			Fanfreluche
		Debby's Turn (b 1974)	Turn To Mars
			Gunnysdeb
	Express Fashion (USA) (b or br 1992)	Private Express (gr 1984)	Pass The Tab
			Sombranita
		Fashion Jet (b 1983)	Tri Jet
			Fashion Feature

Express Tour's sire Tour d'Or, who showed useful form at up to a mile as a two-year-old in Britain, was afterwards successful at up to nine furlongs in the States and was still racing as an eight-year-old, at which age he finished a close second over a mile and a quarter in the Grade 1 Gulfstream Park Handicap. Express Fashion, the dam of Express Tour, comes from a nondescript background and was raced only as a two-year-old, winning once in four starts. Express Tour is her second foal, following the minor winner Do Unto Others (by Unzipped). Express Tour lasted the nine furlongs of the UAE Derby well and should stay a mile and a quarter. He has raced with his tongue tied. *Saeed bin Suroor*

EXTRA GUEST 3 b.f. Fraam 114 – Gibaltarik (IRE) 68 (Jareer (USA) 115) [2001 **45** 79?: 7.1d 6m⁴ May 12] unfurnished filly: has knee action: fair maiden at 2 yrs: poor form in 2001: stays 7f: acts on any going: has edged right. *N. Tinkler*

EXTREMIST (USA) 2 b.c. (Apr 5) Dynaformer (USA) – Strumming (IRE) 75 **70** (Ballad Rock 122) [2001 7f 8.5g⁴ 10.2g⁶ Oct 1] $95,000Y: second foal: dam, 1m winner, from family of 4-y-o Best of The Bests: fair form in maidens: best effort when sixth to Stage By Stage at Bath: likely to stay at least 1½m. *R. Hannon*

EXUBERANT 3 ch.g. Exit To Nowhere (USA) 122 – Pitcroy 99 (Unfuwain (USA) **64 §** 131) [2001 10g 10d 9m⁵ 10m 8m Sep 26] 13,000Y: second foal: dam, 1¼m winner, half-sister to smart 7f/1m performer Ardkinglass: modest form in maidens first 2 starts only: stays 1¼m: acts on good to soft going: pulls hard: has carried head high: hung markedly left on debut: one to treat with some caution. *J. R. Fanshawe*

EYELETS ECHO 4 b.g. Inchinor 119 – Kinkajoo 53 (Precocious 126) [2001 73: 7m **62** 9m 10.1g 11.5f⁶ 11.9g⁵ 14.1d⁴ 14.1d 10g f14.8g f12g Nov 23] well-made gelding: modest **a48** handicapper on turf, poor on all-weather: stays 1¾m: acts on firm and soft going: sometimes visored/blinkered: has raced freely. *D. Morris*

EYE OF GOLD 3 b.f. Wolfhound (USA) 126 – Blade of Grass 78 (Kris 135) [2001 **?** 78p: 5m f6g⁴ Jun 29] promising effort only 2-y-o start: well below that form both runs in 2001: should be suited by at least 7f. *J. R. Fanshawe*

EYES DONT LIE (IRE) 3 b.g. Namaqualand (USA) – Avidal Park 68 (Horage 124) **51 d** [2001 53d: 9m² 8f 9.1m 8v⁶ 12g Nov 7] modest maiden at best: left I. Semple after third start: stays 9f: acts on good to firm ground: tried blinkered/visored/tongue tied. *D. A. Nolan*

EYES TO THE RIGHT (IRE) 2 ch.g. (Jan 16) Eagle Eyed (USA) 111 – Capable **62** Kate (IRE) (Alzao (USA) 117) [2001 5f 7g³ 6g 6g 7d* 8m 8m⁵ 7.6d⁵ f8g⁴ 8s f8g p7g⁵ f8.5g⁵ p7g Dec 12] 20,000Y: sturdy gelding: third living foal: half-brother to 6f winner Golden Biff (by Shalford): dam unraced: modest performer: won nursery at Newcastle in August: mostly creditable efforts, including in claimers, after (left Mrs J. Ramsden before eighth start): stays 1m: acts on good to soft ground, good to firm, fibresand and polytrack: tried visored: has started slowly/taken strong hold/wandered. *P. S. McEntee*

EYES WIDE OPEN 3 b.f. Fraam 114 – Dreamtime Quest (Blakeney 126) [2001 7.1v **–** 8.2v Oct 4] good-bodied filly: fourth foal: half-sister to fairly useful 7f (at 2 yrs) to 1¼m winner Interdream (by Interrex) and 1½m winner Courage Under Fire (by Risk Me): dam no form: well beaten in maidens at Haydock and Nottingham. *P. F. I. Cole*

EYES WIDE SHUT 4 b.g. Beveled (USA) – Dreamtime Quest (Blakeney 126) [2001 **–** 7m 10m 11.5g f11g Oct 1] 1,450Y: third foal: half-brother to fairly useful 7f (at 2 yrs) to 1¼m winner Interdream (by Interrex) and 1½m winner Courage Under Fire (by Risk Me): dam no form: tongue tied, well held in maidens/claimer. *D. W. P. Arbuthnot*

EZZ ELKHEIL 2 b.c. (May 10) Bering 136 – Numidie (FR) (Baillamont (USA) 124) **85 p** [2001 8m² Sep 24] 150,000Y: fifth foal: half-brother to 3 winners in France by Highest Honor, notably smart 1¼m (Prix Saint-Alary) winner Reve d'Oscar: dam French 10.5f (listed race) and 11.5f winner: 6/1, 1¼ lengths second of 11 to Mananan McLir in maiden at Kempton, staying on well despite tending to edge right: will be suited by 1¼m+: sure to improve. *J. W. Payne*

F

FABREZAN (FR) 2 b.g. (Apr 23) Nikos 124 – Fabulous Secret (FR) (Fabulous **–** Dancer (USA) 124) [2001 5.1s 7g 8d Oct 25] 40,000 francs Y: seventh foal: half-brother to 3 winners abroad, including French 1996 2-y-o 1m winner Bikain (by Exit To Nowhere): dam French 1¼m/1½m winner: well beaten in maidens. *Nick Williams*

FACE D FACTS 3 b.f. So Factual (USA) 120 – Water Well 96 (Sadler's Wells (USA) **76** 132) [2001 76: 6d 7s² 7m⁴ 7m⁵ 7g³ 7m 6d⁵ 7v Oct 26] quite good-topped filly: fair performer: below form last 3 starts: stays 7f: acts on soft and good to firm going: visored (found little) fourth start: has started slowly: sometimes hangs left: possibly none too hearty: sold 3,000 gns. *C. F. Wall*

FACE THE JUDGE (USA) 2 b.f. (May 9) Benny The Dip (USA) 127 – Lyrebird **59 d** (USA) (Storm Bird (CAN) 134) [2001 8f² 7.2m⁶ f8.5g⁶ 8v 8g p7g Dec 29] $18,000Y, 20,000 2-y-o: seventh foal: half-sister to 2 winners, including 1¼m winner Lady of Leisure (by Diesis): dam unraced sister to smart Cornwallis winner Mujadil and half-sister to high-class 1½m performer Fruits of Love: modest maiden: best efforts first 2 starts: should stay 1¼m: acts on firm going, below form on heavy/all-weather. *A. Berry*

FACE THE LIMELIGHT (IRE) 2 b.c. (Mar 6) Quest For Fame 127 – Miss Boni- **65** face 112 (Tap On Wood 130) [2001 6m 6m⁶ 7.1f⁴ 7m⁴ f7g⁴ 8f 7g⁵ 10v 8d² 7s* Nov 10] 21,000Y: leggy, quite good-topped colt: eighth foal: half-brother to a winner around 6f in USA by Chimes Band: dam won Ribblesdale Stakes: fair performer: made all in 21-runner nursery at Doncaster: should stay at least 1¼m: acts on any turf going and on fibresand: reliable. *J. G. Smyth-Osbourne*

FACILE TIGRE 6 gr.g. Efisio 120 – Dancing Diana 82 (Raga Navarro (ITY) 119) **– §** [2001 57§, a47§: f6g f6g f6s⁴ f6s 6s Sep 30] leggy, close-coupled gelding: poor handi- **a35 §** capper in 2001: was best at 5f/6f: acted on fibresand, equitrack, firm and soft going: was sometimes slowly away: was unreliable: dead. *R. Hollinshead*

FACT O' THE MATTER 2 b.g. (May 11) So Factual (USA) 120 – Edgeaway 70 **70** (Ajdal (USA) 130) [2001 6d³ 6.1m 6m³ 7g⁶ 6m⁵ 6.1d 7s² 7v⁴ Oct 26] fourth foal: half-brother to fairly useful 1m winner (including at 2 yrs) Hayes Way (by Lahib): dam, 7f winner, out of half-sister to high-class 1979 2-y-o Monteverdi: fair maiden: creditable efforts in nurseries last 2 starts: stays 7f: acts on heavy and good to firm going: tried blinkered. *M. Blanshard*

FACTUAL LAD 3 b.g. So Factual (USA) 120 – Surprise Surprise 91 (Robellino **88** (USA) 127) [2001 87: 8d⁴ 8.1m⁶ 7m⁴ 8m 8.2m³ 8g 8g 7d⁵ Sep 27] close-coupled, workmanlike gelding: poor mover: fairly useful handicapper: effective at 7f/1m: acts on good to firm and good to soft going, ran as if something amiss on firm: blinkered (hung right, fair effort) final start: usually races prominently. *B. R. Millman*

FADDAD (USA) 5 b.g. Irish River (FR) 131 – Miss Mistletoes (IRE) 89 (The Minstrel **–** (CAN) 135) [2001 10m 12m Jun 9] $220,000F: second foal: half-brother to a winner in USA by Kingmambo: dam, Irish 7f and 9f winner, out of half-sister to Le Moss and Levmoss: fairly useful performer at best: left K. Prendergast in 1999, and well beaten both Flat runs since: probably stays 1¼m: acts on heavy going, probably on good to firm: blinkered final 3-y-o start. *D. C. O'Brien*

FADHEL (USA) 5 b.g. Zilzal (USA) 137 – Nice Life (USA) (Sportin' Life (USA)) **–** [2001 12m 9.9f 16m Jun 27] fair maiden at best: left D. Weld in Ireland after third 3-y-o start, well held since: stays 9.5f: acts on good to firm going: tried blinkered at 3 yrs. *E. W. Tuer*

FAERIE REALM (IRE) 3 b.f. Fairy King (USA) – Marie Noelle (FR) 114 **83** (Brigadier Gerard 144) [2001 68p: 10s² 12g² Jul 18] leggy, rather unfurnished filly: fairly useful form in 3 maidens: runner-up at Sandown in June and Kempton (hung left) in July: stays 1½m: raced only on good going or softer: sold 35,000 gns in December. *Sir Michael Stoute*

FAHS (USA) 9 b. or br.g. Riverman (USA) 131 – Tanwi 101 (Vision (USA)) [2001 88: **–** f14g f12g 12m Jun 13] strong, good sort: fairly useful performer at best: well held in 2001. *N. Hamilton*

FAILED TO HIT 8 b.g. Warrshan (USA) 117 – Missed Again 84 (High Top 131) **–** [2001 –, a75: f12s* f12g⁴ f12g* f12g* e12g6 f14.8s³ f12g f12g⁴ f12g² p13g f14.8g² **a69** f14.8g Dec 1] lengthy gelding: fair performer on all-weather: multiple course winner at Wolverhampton, including in claimers (2) and amateur handicap in January/February: effective at 1½m/1¾m: acts on fibresand and equitrack: visored nowadays: best racing up with pace: runs the odd moody race. *N. P. Littmoden*

FAIR FINNISH (IRE) 7 b.g. Commanche Run 133 – Karelia (USA) 111 (Sir Ivor **–** 135) [2001 –: 12.3s 16.2m May 12] well held all 4 starts on Flat. *W. Clay*

FAIRGAME MAN 3 ch.g. Clantime 101 – Thalya (Crofthall 110) [2001 84: 6.1f 6m **91** 5.1m² 5.1f⁵ 5g⁵ 5s 5s 6g Nov 5] strong gelding: fairly useful handicapper: well beaten last 3 starts: best at 5f/6f: acts on firm going: slowly away from tape start penultimate outing. *A. Berry*

FAIRMEAD PRINCESS 3 b.f. Rudimentary (USA) 118 – Lessons Lass (IRE) 73 –
(Doyoun 124) [2001 8.1m 10v Oct 8] 1,000Y: first foal: dam, Irish maiden who stayed
2m, fairly useful winning hurdler: well held in 2 maidens. *C. F. Wall*

FAIR PRINCE 3 ch.g. Rakaposhi King 119 – Lady Llanfair 61 (Prince Tenderfoot –
(USA) 126) [2001 7s 8d f7g f12g Jun 21] smallish, sparely-made gelding: first foal: dam,
11.7f winner, also winning pointer/hunter chaser: well held in maidens/handicap: bred to
be suited by 1¼m+. *B. J. Meehan*

FAIR PRINCESS 3 b.f. Efisio 120 – Fair Attempt (IRE) (Try My Best (USA) 130) 76
[2001 83: 6g* 6s 6m 6m⁵ Aug 27] strong, lengthy filly: has a quick action: fair performer:
won maiden at Ripon in May: effective at 5f/6f: acts on good to firm ground, below best
on soft/heavy: blinkered (ran creditably) final outing: unseated rider in paddock and
withdrawn in September: sold 5,000 gns. *B. W. Hills*

FAIR PROMISE 2 b.g. (Apr 2) Rudimentary (USA) 118 – Birsay (Bustino 136) [2001 –
f8g f8s Dec 21] 11,000Y: second foal: half-brother to 3-y-o Yanus: dam unraced sister to
useful 1½m/1¾m winner Baffin Bay: well held in maidens at Southwell. *K. T. Ivory*

FAIR QUESTION (IRE) 3 b.c. Rainbow Quest (USA) 134 – Fair of The Furze 112 113
(Ela-Mana-Mou 132) [2001 94p: 10g² 11m 14.8g² 14g⁶ 14s* 15.5v Oct 28] unfurnished,
quite attractive colt: fluent mover: smart performer: runner-up in 2 listed events at
Newmarket, beaten neck by Rosi's Boy on reappearance and 4 lengths by Arrive on third
start: improved to win Deutsches St Leger at Dortmund in September by 10 lengths from
Stingray, making all: dropped right out after making most in Prix Royal-Oak at Longchamp final start: stays 1¾m: best effort on soft ground. *J. L. Dunlop*

FAIR STEP 3 ch.f. King's Signet (USA) 110 – Miss Hocroft (Dominion 123) [2001 55
44: 5.1m⁵ 5m 5d² 5f³ 5f² Jul 22] unfurnished filly: modest maiden: may prove ideally
suited by sharp 5f: yet to race on soft/heavy going, acts on any other: front runner.
G. A. Swinbank

Tessona Racing Limited's "Fair Question"

FAIR TIME (USA) 2 b.f. (Apr 1) Woodman (USA) 126 – Anakid (USA) (Danzig (USA)) [2001 8m 8d 8s Oct 31] $80,000Y: sturdy filly: first foal: dam unraced out of very smart Musidora Stakes winner and Oaks third Last Feather: easily best effort in maidens (fair form) when seventh at Newmarket on debut: said to have bled from nose final outing: should stay at least 1¼m. *E. A. L. Dunlop* **70**

FAIRTOTO 5 b.g. Mtoto 134 – Fairy Feet 78 (Sadler's Wells (USA) 132) [2001 55: 16.2m* 16.4m⁵ 15.8d² Oct 9] leggy, plain gelding: modest handicapper: won at Warwick in June: stays 2m well: acts on fibresand, soft and good to firm ground: tongue tied nowadays: pulled hard final start. *D. J. Wintle* **60**

FAIRY LOCH 2 b.f. (May 7) Sure Blade (USA) 130 – Tremloch (Tremblant 112) [2001 6f Jun 4] unfurnished filly: first foal: dam, ran once over hurdles, half-sister to useful 5f to 7f performer Loch Patrick: in rear in seller at Thirsk. *W. G. M. Turner* **–**

FAIRY MONARCH (IRE) 2 b.g. (Mar 25) Ali-Royal (IRE) 127 – Cookawara (IRE) (Fairy King (USA)) [2001 5.1s³ 5.3s⁴ 6m³ 6f⁵ 7f² 6m* 7m* 7g 6g 8g⁶ 7.6d³ 10s⁵ Oct 15] IR 21,000F, IR 40,000Y: neat gelding: third foal: half-brother to Irish 9f winner Kudrow (by Shalford) and a 7f winner abroad by Mukaddamah: dam Irish 2-y-o 6f winner (only season to race): fairly useful performer: won maiden at Epsom and nursery at Newmarket (hung badly left) in July: stays 7.6f: yet to race on heavy going, acts on any other: usually blinkered after fourth start: difficult ride: gelded after final outing. *B. J. Meehan* **83**

FAIRY PRINCE (IRE) 8 b.g. Fairy King (USA) – Danger Ahead (Mill Reef (USA) 141) [2001 67: 6.1d 6f 6m² 6m⁴ 6.1f 6m⁶ 5f⁶ 6m* 6g³ 6m³ 5m Aug 25] lengthy gelding: fair handicapper: won at Newmarket in July: raced only at 5f/6f nowadays: acts on firm going (probably on soft), well beaten only run on fibresand: effective visored/blinkered or not, hooded last 5 appearances: sometimes slowly away. *Mrs A. L. M. King* **68**

FAIRY STAR 3 b.f. Fairy King (USA) – Gold Rose (FR) (Noblequest (FR) 124) [2001 10m⁶ 8.1g³ 10.1g⁴ 10v² 8.3v* Nov 8] strong, long-backed filly: closely related to 1994 Grand Criterium winner Goldmark and French 1997 2-y-o 5.5f winner Gilded Leaf (both by Lyphard): dam, French 10.5f winner, half-sister to very smart 7f/1m performer Gabina and smart performer around 1¼m Galetto: fair performer: didn't need to repeat best form to land odds in maiden at Windsor final outing: effective at 1m/barely at testing 1¼m: seems to act on heavy going: has been bandaged behind. *D. R. C. Elsworth* **70**

FAITH AGAIN (IRE) 5 b.m. Namaqualand (USA) – Intricacy 65 (Formidable (USA) 125) [2001 –: f16.2s* f16g⁵ f16.2g⁵ Feb 6] neat mare: poor handicapper nowadays: won at Wolverhampton in January: stays 2m: acts on fibresand and good to firm going, probably on soft: tried blinkered at 3 yrs. *A. Streeter* **40**

FAITHFUL WARRIOR (USA) 3 ch.c. Diesis 133 – Dabaweyaa 118 (Shareef Dancer (USA) 135) [2001 74: 7.9g 8.1g* 8m 8d* 7.6d* 9g Oct 6] good-topped colt: improved into a useful handicapper: won at Sandown in June, Pontefract in August and Chester (beat James Stark comfortably by 2½ lengths) in September: sweating and last/steadily to post, respectable ninth to I Cried For You in Cambridgeshire at Newmarket final outing: may prove best at 7f/1m: best efforts on good/good to soft going: has worn crossed noseband: should progress further, and win a good prize. *B. W. Hills* **102 p**

FAIZA 2 b.f. (Jan 16) Efisio 120 – Nanouche (Dayjur (USA) 137) [2001 5m⁴ 5g⁵ Jul 8] smallish, sturdy filly: first foal: dam once-raced daughter of outstanding sprinter and 1000 Guineas third Habibti: fair form in maidens at Goodwood and Sandown: will stay 6f: flicked tail both starts. *R. Hannon* **68**

FAJARA BOY 2 b.g. (Jun 16) Cool Jazz 116 – Prudent Pet 65 (Distant Relative 128) [2001 5d f7g Nov 26] leggy, lengthy gelding: first foal: dam 7f (at 2 yrs) and 1m winner: soundly beaten in maiden at Redcar and seller at Southwell. *C. W. Fairhurst* **–**

FALCON GEORGIE 2 b.f. (Mar 28) Sri Pekan (USA) 117 – Georgia Stephens (USA) 64 (The Minstrel (CAN) 135) [2001 6g³ 6g 6.1d Sep 21] 14,000Y: neat filly: seventh foal: half-sister to fairly useful French 9f (at 2 yrs)/10.5f winner Sir Hamelin (by Hernando) and UAE 7f winner Heartbreak House (by Shavian): dam, maiden, out of US Grade 3 8.5f winner Ancient Fables: poor maiden. *N. Tinkler* **43**

FALCON GOA (IRE) 3 b.f. Sri Pekan (USA) 117 – Minden (IRE) (Bluebird (USA) 125) [2001 72: 5d 5g 6m 7m 6m⁵ 6g⁴ 6m* 5g* 6g 5d 5s Nov 9] leggy filly: fair handicapper: won at Doncaster and Newcastle in July: ran poorly last 3 starts: effective at 5f/6f: acts on fibresand, good to firm and good to soft going: visored 6 of last 7 starts. *N. Tinkler* **69**

FALCON HILL   2 b.c. (Apr 16) Polar Falcon (USA) 126 – Branston Jewel (IRE) 95   **102**
(Prince Sabo 123) [2001 5d⁵ 5m² 5m 5f* 6g³ 5.2m 6g³ 6g² 6m* 6g 6d⁶ 6v* 6.5d Dec 16]
20,000Y: quite good-topped colt: second foal: dam, 2-y-o 5f winner, half-sister to smart
6f/7f performer Branston Abby: useful performer: won maiden at Pontefract and nursery
at Ascot in July, nursery at Newmarket (drifted left) in August and listed race at Doncaster
(by 5 lengths from Donegal Shore) in October: well held in listed race at Pisa final start:
stays 6f: acts on any going: races prominently: tends to idle. *M. Johnston*

FALCONIDAE   4 ch.g. Polar Falcon (USA) 126 – Barbary Court (Grundy 137) [2001   **78 +**
89: 8.3m⁴ Jun 11] good-topped gelding: one-time fairly useful performer: stayed 1m:
acted on good to firm ground: dead. *P. J. Makin*

FALCON SPIRIT   5 b.g. Polar Falcon (USA) 126 – Amina 80 (Brigadier Gerard 144)   **–**
[2001 54: 11.1d 9m May 29] big, lengthy gelding: modest maiden at best: well beaten at
5 yrs: usually blinkered/visored:. *Mrs M. Reveley*

FALLACHAN (USA)   5 ch.g. Diesis 133 – Afaff (USA) (Nijinsky (CAN) 138) [2001   **78**
88d: f8g* f8g f8.5g* 8.3g 8.3d f8g f7g⁵ Aug 10] angular, good-topped gelding: fairly   **a84**
useful handicapper: won at Southwell in January and Wolverhampton in March: effective
at 7f/1m: acts on fibresand, good to firm and good to soft going (possibly not on soft/
heavy): has run poorly when sweating. *M. A. Jarvis*

FALLEN STAR   3 b.f. Brief Truce (USA) 126 – Rise And Fall (Mill Reef (USA) 141)   **108 p**
[2001 7d² 7m* 7d* 8s² Sep 29] 140,000Y: rangy filly: half-sister to several winners,
notably very smart miler Fly To The Stars (by Bluebird) and smart French 1¼m/1½m
performer Danseur Landais (by Damister): dam maiden daughter of smart sister to
Highclere: useful form: off 4 months after promising debut, reportedly with joint
problem: landed odds in maiden at Salisbury (hardly off bridle) in August and minor
event at Yarmouth in September: most unfortunate (rated 2-length winner) when head
second to Mowaadah in falsely-run listed rated stakes at Ascot on final start, pulling hard
in rear, still having a deal to do when switched over 1f out then finishing strongly:
free-going sort, likely to prove best at 7f/1m: acts on soft going: has proved difficult
(swished tail) preliminaries/stall: carries head awkwardly: potentially smart, and sure to
win more races if temperament holds. *J. L. Dunlop*

FALLS O'MONESS (IRE)   7 b.m. River Falls 113 – Sevens Are Wild 40 (Petorius   **48 §**
117) [2001 58§, a–§: 7d⁵ 8.3d 8m 8g³ 9m⁴ 8d³ 7.1m³ 7g 8m 7.2m 8d f7g f8g⁶ f8g Dec   **a43 §**
14] sparely-made mare: poor handicapper: best at 1m/1¼m: acts on firm and soft going,
probably on fibresand: tried blinkered/visored earlier in career: often slowly away:
headstrong and best held up: unreliable. *E. J. Alston*

FALSE PROMISE   3 b.g. Bluebird (USA) 125 – Funoon (IRE) 74 (Kris 135) [2001   **–**
–p: 10s Apr 16] strong, lengthy, good sort: has a fluent, round action: never dangerous in
3 maidens/handicap. *E. A. L. Dunlop*

FAMOUS (FR)   8 b.g. Tropular – Famous Horse (FR) (Labus (FR)) [2001 43§: e12g   **– §**
e16g⁵ e13g f12g⁵ e12g⁶ 11.9s 8s 8m 12m f11g Jul 2] temperamental handicapper: dead.
J. J. Bridger

FANAAR   4 ch.c. Unfuwain (USA) 131 – Catalonda (African Sky 124) [2001 108+: 9d³   **111**
8.1v⁶ 8m Jun 19] good-bodied colt: smart performer, lightly raced: good 2¾ lengths third
of 6 to Right Wing in Earl of Sefton Stakes at Newmarket in April: well held in Masai
Mile at Sandown and Queen Anne Stakes at Royal Ascot after: will stay 1¼m: raced
mainly on good going or softer: sent to USA. *J. Noseda*

FANDANGO DREAM (IRE)   5 ch.g. Magical Wonder (USA) 125 – Fandikos (IRE)   **44**
(Taufan (USA) 119) [2001 44: 12m 5m³ 12d* 12.1m 12f³ Aug 1] smallish, angular
gelding: poor handicapper: won at Epsom in July: effective at 1½m, probably at 2¼m:
acts on soft and firm going: tried blinkered/visored: usually held up. *M. D. I. Usher*

FANDANITA (IRE)   2 b.f. (Apr 18) Anita's Prince 126 – Fandangerina (USA) (Grey   **57**
Dawn II 132) [2001 5.3m³ 5g 6m² 5.1s⁴ 5m 6g⁶ Aug 20] IR 8,000Y: sister to useful 1999
2-y-o 6f winner Trinculo and half-sister to several winners, including useful 7f (at 2 yrs)
to 1½m winner Ocean Air (by Elegant Air): dam won up to 1m in USA: modest maiden:
will stay 7f: acts on good to firm ground. *N. P. Littmoden*

FANGIO'S QUEST   2 ch.c. (May 18) Piccolo 121 – Perioscope (Legend of France   **76 p**
(USA) 124) [2001 5g 6d* 6d⁴ Oct 30] smallish, strong colt: second living foal:
half-brother to 3 winners, including fairly useful 1995 2-y-o 7f winner Chuffed, later
winner up to 9f in Hong Kong, and French 6f (at 2 yrs) to 1¼m winner Pastavino (both by
Batshoof): dam placed at 6f in Scandinavia: fair form: won maiden at Newcastle in

October: creditable fourth in nursery at Redcar, travelling strongly long way: likely to prove best at 5f/6f: type to make his mark in handicaps. *T. D. Easterby*

FANNY BAY (IRE)   2 b.f. (Jan 29) Key of Luck (USA) 126 – Disregard That (IRE)   **76**
(Don't Forget Me 127) [2001 5.1d² 6s² May 19] IR 22,000Y: fourth foal: half-sister to 1997 2-y-o 5f/5.7f winner Eleventh Duke (by Imperial Frontier) and Irish 1998 2-y-o 1m winner Crosskeys Lass (by Petorius): dam unraced: fair form when second in maidens at Bath and Newbury: will need to settle to stay beyond 6f. *Mrs P. N. Dutfield*

FANTASTIC CHAMPION (IRE)   2 b.c. (Mar 21) Entrepreneur 123 – Reine   **–**
Mathilde (USA) 123 (Vaguely Noble 140) [2001 7m⁵ Jul 29] 180,000Y: half-brother to 3 winners, including 1¾m winner Swordking (by Kris) and French 8.5f winner Reine des Iles (by Nureyev): dam French 1m/1¼m and E P Taylor Stakes winner: 8/1, slowly away and never dangerous in maiden at Newmarket: sold 7,000 gns, joined P. D'Arcy. *Sir Michael Stoute*

FANTASTIC LIGHT (USA)   5 b.h. Rahy (USA) 115 – Jood (USA) 87 (Nijinsky   **134**
(CAN) 138) [2001 128: 12g² 10.5g* 10m* 12m² 10g* 12f* Oct 27]
When Fantastic Light passed the post first in the Breeders' Cup Turf at Belmont Park in October, he became the first horse in British racing history to pass the £4m mark in total prize-money. His twelve career victories, recorded in five different countries and on three continents, yielded £3,202,615 alone (at exchange rates prevailing at the time). The precise sum of £4,207,030 will be quoted in most record books for his total earnings, though exact figures are always open to question since they depend on the conversion rates used for overseas prize-money (annual statistics produced for the Jockey Club, for example, are based on arbitrary conversion rates that do not take account of currency movements over the year). Fantastic Light was trained in Dubai when earning £279,720 (at prevailing exchange rates) for finishing second, beaten a nose by the Japanese-trained Stay Gold, in the Dubai Sheema Classic on his reappearance in the latest season. But, even if that sum is discounted, Fantastic Light's total earnings still take him above those of the previous British record holder, Singspiel, who compiled a generally-quoted £3,671,039, also a record—before Fantastic Light came along—for a European-trained horse, which just about got him a place among the twenty leading career-earners in the world, a list dominated nowadays by Japanese and American horses.

Preoccupation with statistics of any kind has its hazards and prize-money earnings can never be a reliable guide to racing merit, principally because the level of prize-money rises over the years as the value of money falls (the vast majority of the world's top twenty earners raced in recent seasons). But Fantastic Light is not short of other claims to fame. His victories in the Irish Champion Stakes and at the Breeders' Cup, coupled with his second in the King George VI and Queen Elizabeth Stakes, enabled him to retain the Emirates World Series title, decided on points gained over twelve specified events. Fantastic Light had snatched the title the previous year with a victory in the final leg, the Hong Kong Cup, after which he had been led away in apparel bearing the monogram 'World Champion 2000'. As we pointed out in *Racehorses of 2000*, the eminently consistent Fantastic Light was nothing like the best horse in the world at the time. He was, however, better qualified by the end of the latest season, improving (as he did in each season he raced) and establishing himself as a nailing good performer at a mile and a quarter to a mile and a half. His record earned him the prestigious Horse of the Year title at the eleventh Cartier Racing Awards dinner, the most glittering occasion of its type in European racing. The Cartier awards, most of which are derived from an arbitrary points system for performances over the year, regularly come in for criticism in some quarters (including in these pages). The Cartier Horse of the Year in 2000 was the admirable three-year-old colt Giant's Causeway, but, like Fantastic Light, he was not a champion in the strictest sense—in that he did not prove himself superior to all his contemporaries. The dual Derby and Prix de l'Arc winner Sinndar was universally acknowledged as the year's top three-year-old (he won the Cartier award for top three-year-old colt, making Giant's Causeway's overall award—which also took account of a popular vote—look even more incongruous). Incontrovertibly the top horse in Europe in 2000 was Dubai Millennium, who was ignored at the Cartier awards (Kalanisi was Cartier's top older horse). Similarly, in the latest awards, there was no place for Sakhee, whose wide-margin victories in the International at York and in the Prix de l'Arc clearly established him as the best horse to race in Europe. We use the term 'in Europe' advisedly, aware that sporting performers and performances in many spheres are all too readily these days proclaimed 'the best in the world', often without those making the claim having the slightest idea of what the rest of the world is like.

One of the rewards from the World Series, inaugurated in 1999 when Daylami took the million-dollar championship bonus, has been its contribution towards achieving wider recognition for horseracing as a global sport. The organisers claim that each race in the latest series, staged in ten different countries and on four continents, was watched by a billion viewers round the world. The series may not be perfect—it is essentially a northern hemisphere middle-distance turf championship—but largely thanks to the support it has received from its founders the Maktoum family it has been beneficial. The World Series was framed around the existing structure of the world's top middle-distance races, themselves forming part of a much wider classification of all the major events in the leading racing countries. The greatest achievement of the seventh Earl of Carnarvon, who died in 2001, was the introduction of the pattern-race system which identified and classified the most important Flat races in Britain and became the prototype for the European pattern introduced in 1971 and adopted in similar form two years later by North America. Within a short time, the system had been adopted by almost every other racing country. Among other things, the Group-race and graded-race systems provide a structured guide—where none existed before—showing the relevant importance of prominent events around the world. But the limitation of such a system is that it is a guide only to a race's prestige, not to the level of performance by its winner. The quality of pattern races varies from one country to another, and from season to season, and 'quality control' has not been all it might have been over the years in some countries. The number of American graded races has grown significantly, from 276 in 1980, for example, to 473 in 2000; the total in Europe has

Tattersalls Gold Cup, the Curragh—Fantastic Light takes the measure of Golden Snake inside the final furlong; Kalanisi makes a satisfactory reappearance in third

Prince of Wales's Stakes, Royal Ascot—another triumph for the decision to upgrade this race to Group 1 as Fantastic Light puts up a top-class performance, settling matters with a fine change of pace; it turns out to be the final race for second-placed Kalanisi and fourth-placed Observatory; Hightori (right) stays on well for third

remained virtually constant, 315 in 1980 compared to the current number of 329, though even this disguises the fact that, within the European pattern, the increase is accounted for almost wholly by an increase in Group 1 races from 64 to 78. Pattern and graded designations of races, like racing championships and awards based on arbitrary points systems, are no substitute for ratings, the only clear and precise definition of quality. 'The ultimate accolade in the racing world', the sponsors' claim for the Cartier awards, would arguably be much more accurate if it was applied, say, to being the top-rated horse in the *Racehorses* annual or being recognised as the best by the International Classifications.

Fantastic Light is not the highest rated horse in *Racehorses of 2001*. That distinction belongs to his stable-companion Sakhee, whose six-length triumph in the Arc was an outstanding performance and equalled the record winning margin of Ribot and Sea Bird II in the race. None of Fantastic Light's form matched that or Sakhee's in the International either—so it is as well to keep a sense of proportion about Fantastic Light's achievements. His path never crossed that of Sakhee, but it seems evident from the decision to run Sakhee in preference to Fantastic Light in the Breeders' Cup Classic which horse Godolphin regarded as the better by the end of the season. Until Sakhee's somewhat belated return to the scene—he wasn't seen out until July—Fantastic Light was the standard-bearer for Godolphin in what seemed, at one time, likely to turn into something of a disappointing campaign by previous high standards. By the time Fantastic Light took the field for the Prince of Wales's Stakes at Royal Ascot—an event won in brilliant fashion the previous year by Dubai Millennium—Godolphin had chalked up only three Group 1 victories, the subsequently-expunged win by Noverre in the French Guineas and the narrow victories by the five-year-olds Mutafaweq and Fantastic Light in the Coronation Cup at Epsom and the Tattersalls Gold Cup at the Curragh respectively.

The Tattersalls Gold Cup at the end of May was the first outing of the year in Europe for Fantastic Light, and, after his stable-companion Give The Slip had set a strong pace, he got the better of a last-furlong duel with Prix Ganay winner Golden Snake to win by a neck. Give The Slip was again employed as a pacemaker for Fantastic Light at Royal Ascot, where the considerably-handled Tattersalls Gold Cup third Kalanisi started favourite to turn the tables, second favourite Fantastic Light and the Prix d'Ispahan winner and runner-up Observatory and Hightori being the only others shorter than 10/1 in the nine-runner line-up. Fantastic Light showed himself better than ever, making short work of his rivals and looking every inch a leading candidate for the King George VI and Queen Elizabeth Stakes, a race his stable had won four times in the previous six years. Fantastic Light quickened impressively at Royal Ascot once Dettori extricated him from something of a pocket in the straight and won by two and a half lengths and three quarters of a length from Kalanisi and Hightori, with Observatory fourth—top-class form independently confirmed by a very good timefigure, 1.16 fast (equivalent to a rating of 129), marginally the best of the British season by any horse. The Saeed bin Suroor-trained Swain and Daylami had both won the King George at the same age as Fantastic Light (Swain also won it as a six-year-old) and no three-year-old had won since Lammtarra, the Derby winner who began bin Suroor's run of success in Britain's most prestigious all-aged event in 1995. Sheikh Mohammed, the driving force behind the Godolphin operation, said after Fantastic Light's Prince of Wales's victory: 'We want to take on the best of the bests with him; we would love to have Galileo because what he did at Epsom was special.' At the time, the King George didn't figure in the plans announced for the Derby winner, but Sheikh Mohammed got his wish following a change of heart in the Ballydoyle camp after the unbeaten Galileo romped home in the Irish Derby at the end of June. There was also a change in Fantastic Light's intended programme at around the same time, connections deciding to bypass the Eclipse at Sandown 'just to give him a little more time'.

The King George VI and Queen Elizabeth Diamond Stakes became the most eagerly-anticipated race of the season—a clash of the generations, the three-year-olds represented not only by Galileo, but by such as the Prix du Jockey Club winner Anabaa Blue and the Derby Italiano winner Morshdi (who had come second to Galileo at the Curragh). Twelve lined up in a splendid renewal, though the race was billed in some quarters as little more than a 'lap of honour' for Galileo and in most others as effectively a match between Galileo (the 2/1-on favourite) and Fantastic Light, the bookmakers betting 18/1 (Anabaa Blue) and upwards bar the two. The race didn't disappoint, Galileo becoming the first since Generous in 1991 to land the Derby, Irish Derby and King George treble, but only after a tough battle with Fantastic Light, who was produced to have every chance approaching the final furlong; Fantastic Light appeared to edge into the lead for a stride or two before going down by two lengths to the hard-ridden Galileo after a pulsating race. Galileo's margin of victory would have been slightly less had Dettori not eased the faltering Fantastic Light, who lost absolutely no caste in defeat. Sheikh Mohammed crossed to the winner's circle to offer generous congratulations to Galileo's connections. 'We have no excuses; we were beaten by a better horse' seemed a fair summary at the time, the Sheikh hitting the nail on the head when adding 'Fantastic Light is a very good horse—but he is not Dubai Millennium.' The untimely death of Dubai Millennium, a victim of grass sickness at the end of April, was a big blow to the Sheikh's Dalham Hall breeding operation. He was the best to have raced for any member of the Maktoum family, the world's biggest owners, and one of the very best racehorses in our experience; he had reportedly covered around eighty mares in his first season at stud up to the time of his death.

Among the words of comfort offered to Sheikh Mohammed after the King George by Coolmore supremo John Magnier were 'It is just one day. There is always another day. As you know yourself, there is no finishing post.' There was indeed to be another day for Fantastic Light, and it came when he met Galileo again six weeks later at Leopardstown in Ireland's most prestigious all-aged prize the Irish Champion Stakes, or, to give it its full title in the latest season, the Ireland The Food Island Irish Champion Stakes. The strong pace set by Fantastic Light's pacemaker Give The Slip had resulted in a clutch of very good time performances in the King George—Galileo's 1.15 fast was the second best of the British season and the best by a three-year-old—and it had also ensured that the King George was a thorough test of stamina. In the end, however, Fantastic Light was effectively outstayed by Galileo at Ascot and there still remained a possibility that he was marginally better at around a mile and a quarter—the distance of the Prince of Wales's—than at a mile and a half, over which trip, incidentally, he had now been beaten seven times in a row.

The distance for the Irish Champion Stakes 'showdown'—a mile and a quarter—was not widely considered at the time to favour Fantastic Light, since Galileo himself was generally expected to prove every bit as effective dropped back in trip (his trainer was convinced he would prove even better at a mile and a quarter). Fantastic Light's connections, however, also pointed to a difference of

5 lb in the weights compared to Ascot, the official weight-for-age received by the three-year-olds coming down from 12 lb at the end of July to 7 lb by the second week in September. 'For me, the 5 lb is more significant than the distance,' said Fantastic Light's trainer. The average thoroughbred does not reach full maturity until the age of four and the weight-for-age scale, originated in the middle of the nineteenth century by Admiral Rous, compensates three-year-olds for their immaturity and allows them to compete against older rivals on fair terms. The Rous scale, which was purely empirical, remained more or less intact for over a century but has been revised at various times over the last thirty years in the light of practical experience as racing has changed, and usually after suggestions by trainers and handicappers. Even an apparently minor modification can, however, have a considerable bearing. The conditions set for the King George by the Ascot authority at the time of the epic clash between Derby winner Grundy and tip-top four-year-old Bustino in 1975 required older horses to concede 14 lb to three-year-olds. Grundy's winning distance was half a length and the recommended scale was amended by 1 lb in favour of the older horses the year after, to be followed by a further 1 lb in 1990. Had the same weight-for-age terms applied in 1975 as those now in existence, we might very well have been talking about Bustino's memorable victory over Grundy, rather than the other way round!

Galileo's victory in the King George was the twenty-sixth by a three-year-old in the fifty-one runnings of the race, a ratio which, in itself, demonstrates that the event has achieved the objective of its architect Sir John Crocker Bulteel to bring together the best of different generations in a true championship race. Some existing major events over other distances were also soon opened to older horses, new ones like the International at York were created, and it became possible for later-developing three-year-olds and for older horses to achieve the sort of profile and reputation which had, until the middle of the twentieth century, been almost the exclusive preserve of classic winners. The importance of races such as the King George and its French counterpart the Prix de l'Arc—raised in status by a huge increase in prize-money in 1949—has also obliged the leading three-year-olds to prove themselves against competition from outside their own age group. The desirability of having a weight-for-age scale at all, however, is still called into question by some, who point out that no other sport gives immature performers such an allowance against the best. For racing, however, there are clear benefits in intensifying top-level competition through events which capture the public imagination. The weight-for-age scale itself is bound to have its imperfections, some necessarily arising from the fact that all racehorses are given a common birthday of January 1st and treated for weight-for-age purposes, within their age group, as if they were the same age. Some such horses also inevitably and naturally mature faster than others, but such inadequacies should not be used as an argument

Ireland The Food Island Irish Champion Stakes, Leopardstown—a keenly anticipated renewal sees Fantastic Light reverse King George placings with Galileo in a rousing finish

Breeders' Cup Turf, Belmont—a sixth Group/Grade 1 victory for Fantastic Light, who is chased home by the strong-finishing Milan

against using a weight-for-age scale. Plenty of Derby winners down the years have owed their success not only to their intrinsic merit, but also, in some degree, to the fact that they were already, as three-year-olds, a good deal closer to full maturity than many of their contemporaries. According to our weight-for-age scale, a thoroughbred should, on average, be 13 lb better over a mile and a half by early June as a four-year-old than at the same time the previous year. Very few Derby winners in our long experience would have been capable of showing real improvement of around that magnitude from three to four, a fact not lost, we are sure, on many of those lucky enough to have had 'superstar' three-year-olds down the years. Keeping a champion three-year-old in training at four or five makes no sense from a commercial viewpoint anyway; connections have plenty to lose, risking a year's stud fees, not to mention the horse's reputation.

Talk of Fantastic Light's being 5 lb better off at the weights with Galileo at Leopardstown, compared to Ascot, seemingly had very little influence on the betting public, who sent off Galileo at 11/4-on. The Irish Champion, with its field of only seven, looked even more of a match on paper than the King George had looked. Fantastic Light started at 9/4, with 20/1-shot Bach, a stable-companion of Galileo, the only other runner to start at odds shorter than 50/1. Fantastic Light's pacemaker Give The Slip was fourth favourite at 50/1. Galileo's pacemaker Ice Dancer set off at a furious gallop and was soon six or seven lengths in front of Give The Slip, who in turn was three or four clear of Fantastic Light, in contrast to Ascot racing just ahead of Galileo. Richard Hills, diverted from Kempton to take the mount on Give The Slip, wisely made no attempt to match strides with Ice Dancer who was left to his own devices, his role effectively nullified. At around the three-furlong marker, as the runners began the turn for home, Give The Slip moved off the rail which gave Dettori the opening to make his move on Fantastic Light. Dashed through on the inside, Fantastic Light was in front just inside the two-furlong marker, hotly pressed by Galileo after he had come three-wide, on the outside of Give The Slip. To say that the race was won and lost by Give The Slip's manoeuvrings on the home turn, as some did, might have been an exaggeration, but discussion of the role of the two pacemakers and of the changed tactics with Fantastic Light were among the biggest post-race topics. Galileo never quite managed to get to the front as the pair battled head-to-head in the straight, Fantastic Light maintaining a fractional advantage as both he and Galileo responded valiantly to the urgings of their riders. The two came close together at one point as Fantastic Light drifted slightly away from the rail—Dettori was subsequently cautioned for his over-corrective use of the whip—but Fantastic Light answered every call and held on by a head in a rousing finish. Fantastic Light and Galileo were six lengths in front of third-placed Bach, with Give The Slip a further four away in fourth. The race had produced a climax to rival the two stirring battles between the previous year's Irish Champion winner Giant's Causeway and Kalanisi in the Eclipse and the International, and, with the score between Fantastic Light and Galileo now one-all, the racing public wanted to see a decider. This was pencilled in immediately after Leopardstown for the Breeders' Cup Classic at Belmont Park at the end of October, neither horse being an intended runner in the meantime (Giant's Causeway had contested the Queen Elizabeth II Stakes at Ascot between the Irish Champion and his close second in the Breeders' Cup Classic).

Frankie Dettori seemed in no doubt that Fantastic Light would beat Galileo again at Belmont Park. 'It will be like two heavyweight champions stepping into the ring again, but when you have knocked an opponent out once he is easier to knock down next time . . . That's why I would be more frightened of the American horses than Galileo.' However, Sakhee's runaway victory in the Prix de l'Arc four weeks after Leopardstown gave Godolphin another string to their bow and, in the week leading up to the Breeders' Cup, it was decided that Fantastic Light would revert to a mile and a half to tackle the Breeders' Cup Turf—'an easier race to win than the classic,' in the words of Godolphin's racing manager Simon Crisford. Godolphin enjoyed an outstanding Breeders' Cup meeting, sending out the first two in the Breeders' Cup Juvenile Fillies from its American stable run by Eoin Harty, and almost pulling off the Breeders' Cup Turf-Breeders' Cup Classic double. Before Sakhee had the Classic snatched from him close home by the previous year's winner Tiznow (with Galileo only sixth), Fantastic Light landed the Turf by three quarters of a length from Galileo's stable-companion Milan, the pair clear, with the Turf Classic winner, ex-Italian Timboroa, faring best of the home-trained runners in third. Fantastic Light didn't have the services of his own pacemaker in the Turf but still managed to break the course record for the sharp track in a time of 2m 24.36sec. He was always cruising before being sent clear early in the home straight, never looking in serious danger from the late thrust of Milan, despite again showing a tendency to drift off a true line, a trait which had first manifested itself as a three-year-old, when he also used to run in snatches. Fantastic Light was the only winning favourite on the Breeders' Cup card, none of those in the seven other events reaching the first three. Victories for Banks Hill (Breeders' Cup Filly & Mare Turf) and Johannesburg (Breeders' Cup Juvenile) added to a day to remember for European-trained challengers. There was speculation that Fantastic Light would round off his career in the Japan Cup, a race in which he had finished a close third the previous year, but the decision was taken to retire him after the Breeders' Cup. He begins his stallion career at Dalham Hall Stud, Newmarket, at a fee of £30,000 (October 1st, special live foal).

The strong, lengthy Fantastic Light, a fluent mover, ran in the colours of Maktoum Al Maktoum before being transferred to Godolphin as a four-year-old. Both his sire Rahy and his dam Jood also raced for Maktoum Al Maktoum, whose initial return on the two million dollars paid for the well-bred Jood as a yearling amounted to £1,215 for finishing third in maiden races at Goodwood and Sandown on her only two starts. The second of those efforts came over a mile and a quarter on her only start as a three-year-old, and she would probably have stayed a mile and a half. Jood is by triple crown winner Nijinsky, out of a champion Canadian mare Kamar, who won the Canadian Oaks over nine furlongs and is also the dam of numerous winners. Among those winners were another Canadian champion Key To The Moon, a triple US Grade 1 winner Gorgeous and a Kentucky Oaks winner

Godolphin's "Fantastic Light"

Fantastic Light (USA) (b.h. 1996)	Rahy (USA) (ch 1985)	Blushing Groom (ch 1974)	Red God
			Runaway Bride
		Glorious Song (b 1976)	Halo
			Ballade
	Jood (USA) (b 1989)	Nijinsky (b 1967)	Northern Dancer
			Flaming Page
		Kamar (b 1976)	Key To The Mint
			Square Angel

Seaside Attraction (herself the dam of numerous good winners), as well as, in Britain, the Princess Margaret Stakes winner Hiaam. Fantastic Light is far and away the best offspring of his dam, whose three other winners are the useful mile-and-a-quarter performer Westbound Road (by Gone West) and the Mr Prospector pair Madraar and Wanice, successful respectively in the United Arab Emirates and France. Fantastic Light's great grandam Square Angel also won the Canadian Oaks and, like Kamar, was named champion three-year-old filly of her year in Canada. Square Angel is the grandam of Swain, and Fantastic Light's sire Rahy also has a connection with one of the Maktoum family's other top-class international middle-distance performers, being a half-brother to Singspiel. Fantastic Light stayed well for a son of the miler Rahy, whose other major earner in Britain in the latest season was the Sussex Stakes winner Noverre. Fantastic Light was usually held up and was effective at a mile and a half, though he showed his very best form at a mile and a quarter. He acted on any going, except possibly heavy, and had his tongue tied as a five-year-old. Although he often sweated before his races, he was a tough and genuine racehorse and has plenty to offer as a stallion. He should do very well. *Saeed bin Suroor*

Betdaq Stakes (Handicap), Ascot—the fourth of five wins during the season for Fantasy Believer; Torosay Spring (white colours), Trace Clip (No.10), Polar Kingdom (left) and Rich Gift (rail) battle it out for the minor placings

FANTASY ADVENTURER 4 b.g. Magic Ring (IRE) 115 – Delicious 51 – (Dominion 123) [2001 54d: 6g f7g 6m f8.5g p6g Nov 15] tall, leggy gelding: no recent form: left J. Quinn after third start: tried visored. *J. Cullinan*

FANTASY BELIEVER 3 b.g. Sure Blade (USA) 130 – Delicious 51 (Dominion **103** 123) [2001 75: 6s 6s⁴ 6s⁵ 6m 5g 6m* 6m⁴ 6f² 5d 6d* 6g³ 6m* 6g⁵ 6m 6g* 6d 5v* Oct 27] sturdy gelding: useful handicapper: improved considerably, and won at Kempton in June, Lingfield in July, Ripon in August, Ascot (by ½ length from Torosay Spring) in September and Doncaster (beat Smart Predator by a neck) in October: effective at 5f/6f: acts on any going: left stall without jockey fourth outing: has worn near-side pricker and hung: effective held up or racing prominently: tough and game. *J. J. Quinn*

FANTASY CRUSADER 2 ch.c. (Mar 5) Beveled (USA) – Cranfield Charger **65 d** (Northern State (USA) 91) [2001 5f 7m* 7m 7d⁶ 5g 6m Sep 24] 1,500F, 5,000Y: third foal: brother to a winner in Greece: dam probably of little account: fair form when winning maiden at Lingfield in June, tending to wander: well held after: stays 7f: acts on good to firm going. *Mrs Lydia Pearce*

FANTASY FLIGHT 7 b.m. Forzando 122 – Ryewater Dream 72 (Touching Wood – (USA) 127) [2001 8m 7.5m Jun 8] no form. *N. Tinkler*

FANTASY PARK 4 b.g. Sanglamore (USA) 126 – Fantasy Flyer (USA) (Lear Fan **84 ?** (USA) 130) [2001 84+: 12m⁴ 15.9d 12g Sep 15] workmanlike gelding: fairly useful form at best, lightly raced: well held last 2 starts: stays 1½m: yet to race on extremes of going. *G. M. McCourt*

FANTASY RIDGE 3 ch.f. Indian Ridge 123 – Footlight Fantasy (USA) 68 (Nureyev **92** (USA) 131) [2001 91: 7m² 8f 6m 7m 8g 8m³ Aug 30] tall, unfurnished filly: good mover: reportedly hobdayed after final 2-y-o start: fairly useful performer: some creditable efforts in 2001, including third of 4 to easy winner Noon Gun in minor event at Salisbury (travelled best for most of way) final start: may well prove best at 7f: acts on firm going: sometimes races freely. *M. R. Channon*

FARAUDE 3 b.f. Farfelu 103 – Pennine Star (IRE) 68 (Pennine Walk 120) [2001 43: **55** f11g 8.2f³ 8.1m* 8g⁴ 8m² 10g³ 8m⁴ Aug 17] workmanlike filly: won seller at Chepstow (carried head awkwardly) in July: stays 1¼m: acts on firm and good to soft going: reared in stalls twice at 2 yrs. *W. R. Muir*

FARAWAY JOHN (IRE) 3 b.g. Farhaan 77 – Indiana Dancer (Hallgate 127) [2001 **59** –: f11g⁴ 10s² 11.6s* 11.6g⁶ 10s f14g p10g Dec 22] modest handicapper: won at Windsor in April: should stay further than 1½m: acts on soft going, fibresand and equitrack. *G. P. Enright*

FARAWAY LOOK (USA)   4 br.g. Distant View (USA) 126 – Summer Trip (USA) **90**
117 (L'Emigrant (USA) 129) [2001 96p: 10.5g² 10m 10m 8d Oct 19] good-bodied
gelding: fairly useful handicapper: no form after first start in 2001: stays 10.5f: acts on
fibresand, best turf effort on good going: has carried head high: joined P. Hobbs.
J. R. Fanshawe

FARFIELDS PRINCE   9 b.g. Weldnaas (USA) 112 – Coca (Levmoss 133) [2001 –
f12s Dec 27] probably of little account on Flat nowadays. *M. J. Wilkinson*

FARHA (USA)   3 b.f. Nureyev (USA) 131 – Arutua (USA) (Riverman (USA) 131) **85**
[2001 83p: 6g 7g⁶ 6m* Aug 15] fairly useful performer, lightly raced: won handicap at
Epsom in August: stayed 6f: acted on good to firm and good to soft going: visits Cadeaux
Genereux. *B. Hanbury*

FAR LANE (USA)   2 b.c. (Mar 11) Lear Fan (USA) 130 – Pattimech (USA) (Nureyev **70 p**
(USA) 131) [2001 6g Sep 15] IR 75,000Y: rangy colt: has scope: sixth foal: half-brother
to 1m winner Lamanka Lass (by Woodman), 3-y-o Riverina and a winner in USA by
Cox's Ridge: dam, won up to 7f in USA, sister to Grade 1 9f winner Annoconnor and
half-sister to Grand Prix de Paris and Melbourne Cup winner At Talaq: 14/1, green and
wearing crossed noseband, seventh of 10 to Inishowen in minor event at Doncaster,
taking fierce hold: will do better. *B. W. Hills*

FAR NOTE (USA)   3 ch.c. Distant View (USA) 126 – Descant (USA) (Nureyev **81**
(USA) 131) [2001 8d³ 7m³ 7g² 8.2d² 7s² Oct 15] sturdy, well-made colt: first foal: dam
unraced half-sister to 2000 Guineas winner Zafonic: fairly useful maiden: placed all 5
starts: stays 1m: pulled hard penultimate start: sold 50,000 gns. *B. W. Hills*

FAR PAVILIONS   2 b.c. (Feb 9) Halling (USA) 133 – Flambera (FR) (Akarad (FR) **91 p**
130) [2001 6m* 7.1s⁵ Aug 19] 23,000F, 25,000Y: quite good-topped colt: half-brother
to several winners, including very smart US performer up to 9f Jumron (by Sharpo) and
fairly useful 1¼m winner who stayed 13f Passionate Pursuit (by Pursuit of Love): dam
French 1¼m winner: very green, won maiden at Ascot in July by head from Nemo Fugat,
making most and rallying: ran in snatches and found little when only fifth in minor event
at Sandown: should be suited by 1m+: probably capable of better. *M. Johnston*

FARQAD (USA)   2 b.c. (Apr 1) Danzig (USA) – Futuh (USA) 95 (Diesis 133) [2001 **101 p**
6f* 6g⁴ Oct 4] robust, good-bodied colt: seventh foal: closely related to 2 winners by
Dayjur, including useful 1997 2-y-o 6f (Middle Park Stakes) winner Hayil, and half-
brother to 2 winners, including smart 6f (at 2 yrs) and 1¼m (in UAE) winner Tamhid (by
Gulch): dam 2-y-o 6f winner: 4/9, won 23-runner maiden at Newbury in September easily
by ½ length from Royal Quarters: useful form when 7 lengths fourth of 7 to Johannesburg
in Middle Park Stakes at Newmarket, no impression once shaken up: will probably stay
7f: probably capable of better, and should win more races. *D. R. Loder*

FARRIER'S GAMBLE   5 ch.m. Belmez (USA) 131 – Chrisanthy 81 (So Blessed –
130) [2001 –: 6m May 8] little form, including blinkered. *R. M. Flower*

FAR SOUTH TRADER   3 gr.g. Blushing Flame (USA) 109 – Podrida 48 (Persepolis –
(FR) 127) [2001 65: 11.9f⁵ May 25] lightly-raced maiden: reportedly finished lame on
reappearance. *R. J. O'Sullivan*

FAS   5 ch.g. Weldnaas (USA) 112 – Polly's Teahouse 68 (Shack (USA) 118) [2001 –: 7s –
7m May 28] lengthy gelding: no longer of much account. *J. D. Bethell*

FASHIONABLE MAN (USA)   2 ch.c. (Apr 3) Unbridled (USA) 128 – Too Chic **93 p**
(USA) (Blushing Groom (FR) 131) [2001 7.5m⁴ 7.1g³ 7m* 8m² Sep 21] $15,000Y: big,
leggy colt: good walker: has a rather splayed action: half-brother to several winners in
USA, notably Grade 1 winners Chic Shirine (8.5f) and Queena (7f to 8.5f), both by Mr
Prospector, latter dam of smart US 1m/9f performer Brahms: dam US Grade 1 1m
winner: won maiden at Newcastle in August: beaten head by Harnour in nursery at Ayr,
making most: will stay at least 1¼m: type to make a useful 3-y-o, and should win more
races. *M. Johnston*

FAST AND FURIOUS (IRE)   4 b.g. Brief Truce (USA) 126 – Zing Ping (IRE) 80 **82**
(Thatching 131) [2001 77: f9.4g⁴ 10s⁴ 10v⁴ 8.5m 9m⁶ 8.5g* 7d³ 8.5d⁴ 8g 9g 8m Sep 29]
second foal: brother to useful Irish 1998 2-y-o 6f winner Fear And Greed: dam Irish
maiden (best effort at 7f on 2-y-o debut): fairly useful performer: won maiden at
Wolverhampton in February and handicap at Killarney in July: stays 1¼m: acts on
fibresand, heavy and good to firm ground: usually tongue tied. *T. Stack, Ireland*

FAST AS LUCK   3 b.g. Pursuit of Love 124 – Dominio (IRE) 99 (Dominion 123)   –
[2001 f8.5g f8f 11s 9f⁵ 10.2f f11g 12g Aug 17] 20,000Y: workmanlike gelding: fifth foal:
half-brother to 6f winner East Winds (by Suave Dancer), later useful sprint winner in
Sweden: dam, best at 5f, half-sister to Ya Malak and from family of Cadeaux Genereux:
little form. *K. McAuliffe*

FAST CINDY (USA)   2 b.f. (Feb 28) Fastness (IRE) 127 – Forever Cindy (ARG)   65
(Forever Sparkle (USA)) [2001 6m 6m 6g 8d⁴ Nov 2] $20,000Y: tall, quite good-topped
filly: first foal: dam Argentinian Grade 1 1¼m winner: fair maiden: creditable fourth in
nursery at Brighton, finishing well after racing freely: likely to stay 1¼m: reportedly bled
from nose third start. *P. F. I. Cole*

FAST FOIL (IRE)   3 b.f. Lahib (USA) 129 – Fast Chick 93 (Henbit (USA) 130) [2001   70
72: 8v⁶ 7s* 8g⁶ 11m 8m⁵ 8f⁵ 10.2g f6g p8g p8g² Dec 28] sparely-made filly: fair
performer: won minor event at Brighton in May: left M. Channon after seventh start:
100/1, seemed to run very well in minor event at Lingfield final start: should stay at least
1¼m: acts on polytrack, heavy and good to firm going. *D. Burchell*

FAST FORTUNE   3 ch.f. Forzando 122 – High Cut 84 (Dashing Blade 117) [2001 –:   –
e10g⁴ e8g e10g e7g⁶ 8f f6g⁶ f9.4g 5.7m Jul 15] strong, close-coupled filly: little form.
M. Quinn

FAST FORWARD FRED   10 gr.g. Sharrood (USA) 124 – Sun Street 73 (Ile de   50
Bourbon (USA) 133) [2001 56: 15.4m⁴ Jul 30] big, lengthy gelding: shows knee action:
modest handicapper: stays 2¼m: acts on firm ground. *L. Montague Hall*

FASTINA (DEN)   3 b.f. Dunphy 124 – Farandole (DEN) (Gay Baron) [2001 65: 8.3s   77
9.9m³ 9.9m 10g* 10.1m 10.4s 10v² Oct 29] leggy filly: fair performer: won handicap at
Windsor in July: stays 1¼m: acts on firm going, probably on heavy: none too consistent.
R. Guest

FASTRACK TIME   4 ch.g. Clantime 101 – Bitch 53 (Risk Me (FR) 127) [2001 –: f8g   44
f6g⁴ e6s² e6g f5g f6g f6s Dec 15] angular gelding: poor maiden: stays 6f: acts on equitrack and good to firm going: tried visored. *S. Mellor*

FAST TRACK (IRE)   4 b.c. Doyoun 124 – Manntika 77 (Kalamoun 129) [2001 104:   70
8d 10g 8m² 7m⁴ 8m 10.2d Oct 25] lengthy colt: only fair nowadays: effective at 7f to
10.4f: acts on firm and good to soft ground. *G. M. McCourt*

FATEHALKHAIR (IRE)   9 ch.g. Kris 135 – Midway Lady (USA) 126 (Alleged   72
(USA) 138) [2001 70: f11g⁵ 12m³ 13.8d Nov 6] leggy, angular gelding: poor mover: fair   a45 +
handicapper on turf, poor on all-weather in 2001: stays 13f: acts on fibresand, firm and
good to soft going: visored once at 4 yrs: all wins on left-handed tracks: fairly useful
hurdler/chaser. *B. Ellison*

FATHER JUNINHO (IRE)   4 b.g. Distinctly North (USA) 115 – Shane's Girl (IRE)   100
(Marktingo) [2001 100: 12d 11.9m* 14m 12f⁴ 12m 12g Aug 3] strong, close-coupled
gelding: has a quick action: useful handicapper: won at York in May by 1¼ lengths from
Maniatis: creditable efforts next 3 starts, seventh to Takamaka Bay in Duke of Edinburgh
Stakes at Royal Ascot penultimate outing: stays 1½m: acts on firm and good to soft going,
though may not take much racing on former: visored once as 3-y-o: has been mulish in
preliminaries: moved poorly to post (well held) final start: held up. *A. P. Jarvis*

FATHER SEAMUS   3 b.g. Bin Ajwaad (IRE) 119 – Merry Rous 66 (Rousillon (USA)   43
133) [2001 –: 8s 6s 7s 7.6m 8m⁶ 8d⁶ 11.5m⁵ 11.9s 11.6v 8s Oct 25] leggy, workmanlike
gelding: poor maiden: stays 1m: acts on good to firm ground, probably on soft. *P. Butler*

FATHERS FOOTSTEPS   3 ch.g. Clantime 101 – Cousin Jenny (Midyan (USA)   35
124) [2001 –: 5m 5f⁵ 5f 5m 5.7m Sep 10] small gelding: poor maiden: best efforts at 5f on
ground firmer than good: tried blinkered. *C. Smith*

FATHER THAMES   3 b.c. Bishop of Cashel 122 – Mistress Thames 63 (Sharpo 132)   112
[2001 95p: 7g² 7.9m 7g* 8g⁴ 7d Oct 20] strong, lengthy colt: has plenty of scope: smart
performer, lightly raced: won handicap at Goodwood in September in impressive style
(travelled strongly/idled in front) by ½ length from Lapwing: creditable 2 lengths fourth
to Beckett in listed event at Newmarket penultimate start: below form in Challenge
Stakes at Newmarket final outing: may prove better at 7f than 1m: acts on soft and good
to firm going. *J. R. Fanshawe*

333

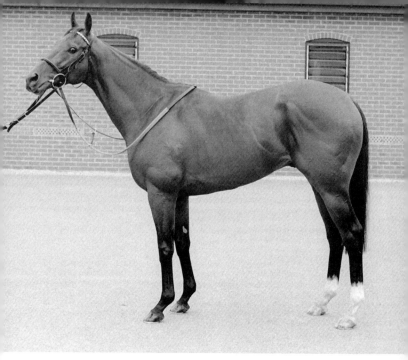

Mr Hamdan Al Maktoum's "Fath"

FATH (USA) 4 b.c. Danzig (USA) – Desirable 119 (Lord Gayle (USA) 124) [2001 **116**
108: 6d² 5g⁵ 5f⁵ 7.1d² 6m 7m* 7g* 8d 7d² Oct 20] smallish, good-topped colt: not the
best of movers: smart performer: won minor event at Chester in July and Theo Fennell
Lennox Stakes at Goodwood (beat Munir by ¾ length) in August: also ran well when
runner-up in Abernant Stakes at Newmarket, listed event at Haydock and Challenge
Stakes (beaten length by Munir) at Newmarket: effective at 5f to 7f, not at 1m: yet to race
on soft/heavy going, acts on any other: tried tongue tied at 3 yrs: sometimes bandaged/
wears crossed noseband/races freely: game and reliable. *M. P. Tregoning*

FATWA (IRE) 3 ch.f. Lahib (USA) 129 – Mayaasa (USA) 70 (Lyphard (USA) 132) **95**
[2001 6s* 7d² 7m⁶ May 12] rather leggy, unfurnished filly: fourth foal: sister to useful 6f
(at 2 yrs)/1m winner Hirasah and 6-y-o Zaha: dam, 1¼m winner, closely related to
high-class miler Maroof and to dam of Desert King: useful form: overcame slow start/
greenness to win maiden at Pontefract (beat Hata by 8 lengths) in April, and ran well
when ½-length second to Rolly Polly in Fred Darling Stakes at Newbury 11 days later:
only sixth to Palace Affair in listed race at Lingfield final start: stayed 7f: acted on soft
going: visits War Chant. *B. Hanbury*

FAUTE DE MIEUX 6 ch.g. Beveled (USA) – Supreme Rose 95 (Frimley Park 109) **74**
[2001 85: 5s 5m 5m⁵ 6m 5m p7g p7g⁶ Dec 28] useful-looking gelding: fair on turf, **a63**
modest on all-weather: trained until after fifth start by M. Kettle: effective at 5f/6f: acts
on any turf going and polytrack: blinkered once at 5 yrs: has had tongue tied. *S. Kirk*

FAVORISIO 4 br.g. Efisio 120 – Dixie Favor (USA) 82 (Dixieland Band (USA)) **73 §**
[2001 –, a80: f8g f11s⁵ f11g⁵ f12g⁴ 12g* 14.4m³ 14.1g f14g² f12s Dec 21] robust gelding:
fair performer: won minor event at Beverley in August: stays 1¾m: acts on fibresand and

good to firm going: visored last 5 outings: has been slowly away (seemed reluctant fourth start)/carried head awkwardly: not to be trusted. *Miss J. A. Camacho*

FAX TO SOOTY 2 b.g. (Mar 24) Factual (USA) 108 – Saltina (Bustino 136) [2001 6m⁶ 6m⁴ 6m⁶ 6m 6d 7m³ 7m³ 7g f7s⁵ p6g⁵ Dec 22] 2,600Y: lengthy gelding: eighth foal: half-brother to 1½m winner Mr Towser (by Faustus) and 1996 2-y-o 5f winner who stayed 1m Skyers Tryer (by Lugana Beach): dam little form: modest maiden: stays 7f: acts on good to firm going and fibresand: visored/blinkered and raced up with pace last 4 starts. *J. S. Moore* **58**

FAYDAH (USA) 2 b.f. (Feb 25) Bahri (USA) 125 – Lady Cutlass (USA) (Cutlass (USA)) [2001 7g 7d⁵ Nov 3] leggy, unfurnished filly: closely related to 2 winners by Riverman, notably high-class 1m/1¼m performer Lahib, and half-sister to several winners, including smart performer up to 1m Nwaamis (by Dayjur): much better effort (fair form) when fifth of 21 to Ballet Fame in maiden at Newmarket: refused to settle and carried head awkwardly on debut: should stay 1m: likely to do better. *J. L. Dunlop* **72 p**

FAYE ELLEN 2 ch.f. (Feb 7) Elmaamul (USA) 125 – Iradah (USA) 66 (Topsider (USA)) [2001 f5g³ 6m² 5.7f 6m⁴ 6d p7g Dec 12] 3,600Y: rather leggy filly: second living foal: dam, 5f winner, from very good family: modest maiden: finished lame final start: stays 7f: acts on fibresand/equitrack, good to firm and good to soft ground. *D. J. Coakley* **61**

FAYMIST (IRE) 2 ch.g. (Mar 23) Fayruz 116 – Grave Error (Northern Treat (USA)) [2001 5f⁴ 6d 5m⁵ 7m Sep 6] IR 8,000F, IR 15,000Y: good-bodied gelding: half-brother to several winners, including 6-y-o Muja's Magic and 6f (at 2 yrs) to 9.4f winner Miss Take (by Red Sunset): dam Irish 1½m winner: fair maiden: best effort on debut: should stay at least 6f: tongue tied last 2 starts. *J. L. Eyre* **66**

FAYR JAG (IRE) 2 b.c. (Mar 17) Fayruz 116 – Lominda (IRE) 80 (Lomond (USA) 128) [2001 5g² 5m* 6.1d² 6m 5s⁶ Oct 20] 8,000Y: compact, attractive colt: fourth foal: dam 2-y-o 6f winner: fair performer: off 3 months (had reportedly had blood disorder) before winning maiden at Thirsk in August: creditable efforts next 2 starts: effective at 5f/6f: acts on good to firm and good to soft going. *T. D. Easterby* **78**

FAZENDA 3 b.f. Piccolo 121 – Petra's Star 61 (Rock City 120) [2001 –: 10s Sep 24] well held in minor event/seller. *K. McAuliffe* **–**

FAZZANI (IRE) 3 b.f. Shareef Dancer (USA) 135 – Taj Victory 68 (Final Straw 127) [2001 80: 8v 10s 12m 8g 8m 8f 10m f12g Oct 20] small, useful-looking filly: fairly useful performer at 2 yrs: well held in handicaps in 2001: blinkered last 2 starts. *M. W. Easterby* **–**

FEARBY CROSS (IRE) 5 b.g. Unblest 117 – Two Magpies 43 (Doulab (USA) 115) [2001 88: 6s⁴ 6d 6m 6g 6g² 6m³ 5d* 5m 6g⁶ Oct 5] strong gelding: poor mover: fairly useful handicapper: won at Doncaster in September: best at 5f (given test)/6f: acts on soft and good to firm going: blinkered once at 3 yrs: has swished tail: usually held up. *W. J. Musson* **83**

FEAST OF ROMANCE 4 b.g. Pursuit of Love 124 – June Fayre (Sagaro 133) [2001 65, a78: f7s f6g² f6s⁴ f6g⁴ f6g* f6g* f7g⁶ f6g f5g⁵ 6m 5m f5g p6g f6g⁶ Dec 8] sturdy gelding: fairly useful performer: won handicap and minor event at Wolverhampton in March: below form after: best at 6f: acts on fibresand: tried blinkered. *N. P. Littmoden* **– a79**

FEATHERS FLYING (IRE) 2 b.f. (Apr 8) Royal Applause 124 – Dancing Feather 72 (Suave Dancer (USA) 136) [2001 7m* 7.1m² 7g⁴ 8d⁶ 7d 10d⁶ Nov 3] 3,500Y: angular filly: first foal: dam, 1m winner at 4 yrs who stayed 1½m, half-sister to 3-y-o Spring Oak and useful winner up to 11f Fragrant Hill (dam of very smart French middle-distance performer Fragrant Mix): fairly useful performer: won maiden at Lingfield in June: best effort when sixth to Half Glance in May Hill Stakes at Doncaster fourth start: seems not to stay 1¼m: unraced on extremes of going. *D. J. S. Cosgrove* **91**

FEATHERSTONE LANE 10 b.g. Siberian Express (USA) 125 – Try Gloria (Try My Best (USA) 130) [2001 –, a60§: f7g³ f7g⁴ f6g f6g 7m 6g Aug 17] workmanlike gelding: modest handicapper: below form after second start: stays 7f: acts on fibresand/equitrack: formerly visored: often gets behind, and sometimes doesn't go through with effort. *Miss L. C. Siddall* **– a54 §**

FEATHERTIME 5 b.m. Puissance 110 – Midnight Owl (FR) (Ardross 134) [2001 61: 10.3d⁴ 12d 10s³ 10g Nov 5] leggy, angular mare: modest handicapper: best up to 1¼m: best efforts on good to soft/soft going. *Mrs G. S. Rees* **58 a–**

FEBRUARY MOUNTAIN (IRE) 4 b.f. Symboli Heights (FR) – Mountain Sue (Lyphard's Special (USA) 122) [2001 65: f9.4g⁶ f12g⁴ f12g 12s 14.1s 14.1s Apr 23] second foal: dam, Irish maiden, stayed 1¾m: fair maiden at 3 yrs in Ireland: well held **–**

in Britain: stays 12.5f: raced mainly on good going or softer: blinkered final start. *B. A. McMahon*

FEET SO FAST 2 ch.g. (May 14) Pivotal 124 – Splice 114 (Sharpo 132) [2001 6v 6d* Nov 2] 8,000Y: lengthy gelding: fourth foal: half-brother to fairly useful 1998 2-y-o 5f winner Entwine (by Primo Dominie): dam sprinter: 66/1, stepped up markedly on debut form to win 20-runner maiden at Newmarket by ¾ length from Ridley, leading after 2f and needing only hand riding to hold on: may prove best at 5f/6f: should make a useful 3-y-o. *W. J. Musson*   **89 p**

FENWICKS PRIDE (IRE) 3 b.g. Imperial Frontier (USA) 112 – Stunt Girl (IRE) (Thatching 131) [2001 85: 6d 6d 5m 6m 6f⁵ 6m 6g 6d 5v⁴ 6v⁶ Nov 8] strong, lengthy gelding: fair handicapper: stays 6f: acts on any turf going: visored: has worn crossed noseband/hung under pressure: inconsistent. *B. S. Rothwell*   **78**

FERNY HILL (IRE) 7 b.g. Danehill (USA) 126 – Miss Allowed (USA) (Alleged (USA) 138) [2001 f11g² f12g f9.4g⁶ f12g⁴ f16.2g f12g* f11g² f11g⁴ 11.9m f14g⁴ 8.2s f14.8g f12g f11g Nov 30] lengthy gelding: formerly useful, modest nowadays: has reportedly had breathing problem/leg injury: left W. Muir after first start: won seller at Wolverhampton in March: mostly disappointing after: probably best around 1½m: acts on soft going, good to firm and fibresand: tongue tied final outing. *R. Brotherton*   **– a59**

FERZAO (IRE) 4 b.c. Alzao (USA) 117 – Fer de Lance (IRE) (Diesis 133) [2001 93, a99: 10.4g* 10g² 10g 10f 8m⁵ 8g 8g⁴ 10.4g Aug 22] strong colt: useful handicapper: won at York in May by 1¾ lengths from Jedi Knight: in-and-out form after, running well when close fourth to Persiano at Ascot penultimate start: tailed off final outing: best at 1m/ 1¼m: acts on equitrack, good to firm and good to soft going: has worn crossed noseband/ tongue strap: free-going sort, usually races up with pace: sold 17,000 gns, joined C. Mann. *Mrs A. J. Perrett*   **99**

FESTIVAL OF LIGHT (USA) 4 b.c. A P Indy (USA) 131 – Aurora (USA) (Danzig (USA)) [2001 a6f* a6.5f* a8f* Mar 24] $975,000Y: third foal: half-brother to 2 winners in USA by Kris S, notably high-class US Grade 1 1¼m winner Arch: dam, minor US stakes winner around 1m, sister to champion Japanese 2-y-o filly Yamanin Paradise out of champion US 2-y-o filly Althea: smart performer: unraced at 2 yrs, ran in USA at 3 yrs: much improved and won all 3 starts in 2001, maiden at Jebel Ali (by 7 lengths) in February, handicap (by 10 lengths) then Godolphin Mile (made all, beat Curule ¾ length), both at Nad Al Sheba in March: effective at 6f to 1m: raced only on dirt: blinkered last 2 starts in 2000, visored first in 2001: tongue tied last 2 outings. *Saeed bin Suroor*   **118**

Godolphin Mile, Nad Al Sheba—the much improved Festival of Light makes all; stable-companion Curule stays on to take second with Conflict (rail) third

FESTIVE AFFAIR 3 b.g. Mujadil (USA) 119 – Christmas Kiss 82 (Taufan (USA) **65**
119) [2001 –: e6g f6g³ f6g* 6.1v² f6g⁶ 5g 5.1g f6g⁵ 6.1v f6g⁴ f6g⁶ f7g⁶ Nov 23] fair
performer: won maiden at Southwell in February: best at 5f/6f: acts on fibresand and
heavy going. *B. Smart*

FEUER 3 br.c. Emperor Jones (USA) 119 – Strapless 84 (Bustino 136) [2001 a8g* **88**
a10g² 12m² 10f 10d⁵ a12g² a8s² Dec 9] 4,600Y, 10,000 2-y-o: good-topped colt: closely
related to useful 6f (at 2 yrs) and 7f winner Polish Admiral (by Roi Danzig), later
successful in USA, and half-brother to 3 winners, including fairly useful sprinter Faith
Alone (by Safawan), 7f winner at 2 yrs: dam 6f winner, including at 2 yrs: won minor
event at Taby in May: tongue tied, last of 11 in listed race at Ascot fourth start: second in
handicap and minor event at Taby last 2 starts: stays 1½m: acts on good to firm ground
and dirt: blinkered second outing. *B. Nilsson, Sweden*

FFAL FOREST 2 b.f. (Feb 17) Charnwood Forest (IRE) 125 – Manarah 76 (Marju **–**
(IRE) 127) [2001 6m 7g 8g Aug 24] 10,000Y: strong, close-coupled filly: first foal: dam,
Irish 1½m winner, half-sister to 4-y-o Muakaad: no form in maidens/minor event.
M. Dods

FFIFFIFFER (IRE) 3 b.c. Definite Article 121 – Merry Twinkle (Martinmas 128) **46**
[2001 –: 7g⁵ 7m⁶ 10.1g 8m 6m⁵ 6d³ a8g³ a8g Dec 9] tall, good-topped colt: poor maiden:
left A. Dickman after sixth start (visored, ran creditably): seems to stay 1m: acts on firm
and good to soft going, probably on sand. *P. Haley, Spain*

FFYNNON GOLD 4 b.f. Beveled (USA) – Sparklingsovereign 53 (Sparkler 130) **64**
[2001 53: 7m* 6.9m⁵ 6f² 6d 6g³ 6g* 6m⁵ 6m 6m² 5.7m 6.1d Sep 21] modest performer:
won claimer at Southwell in May and handicap at Windsor in July: has form at 1m, raced
mainly around 6f nowadays: acts on fibresand, firm and soft going: sometimes slowly
away: has found little. *J. G. Portman*

FIABA (USA) 3 b. or br.f. St Jovite (USA) 135 – Florie (FR) (Gay Mecene (USA) **–**
128) [2001 9m 10m May 26] half-sister to several winners, including smart filly up to
1½m Fanjica (by Law Society) and useful Italian performer up to 15f Almanor (by
Akarad): dam placed up to 1½m in France: no show in maidens at Milan (reportedly
finished lame) and Lingfield. *J. L. Dunlop*

FIAMMA ROYALE (IRE) 3 b.f. Fumo di Londra (IRE) 108 – Ariadne 79 (Bustino **68**
136) [2001 74: 6d 5g 6m⁵ 5m 5m⁵ 5.1g³ 5g 5g⁶ 5m 5g 7g f6g p7g³ p6g⁴ Dec 29] leggy, **a52 +**
quite good-topped filly: fair winner at 2 yrs: disappointing in 2001: best at 5f/sharp 6f:
acts on any going: has been on toes/pulled hard/hung. *Mrs P. N. Dutfield*

FICHE AND CHIPS 2 b.c. (Apr 9) Distant Relative 128 – Moorefield Girl (IRE) 57 **41**
(Gorytus (USA) 132) [2001 5v 7m f8.5g Sep 22] 6,000Y: tall colt: has scope: third foal:
dam Irish winner up to 2¼m on Flat, also successful over hurdles: poor form in maidens:
will stay at least 1m. *A. Dickman*

FIDDLER'S MOLL (IRE) 3 b.f. Dr Devious (IRE) 127 – Belle Bleue (Blazing **61**
Saddles (AUS)) [2001 62: 10d 10m f9.4g 10m 8d³ p10g Nov 28] modest maiden: should **a–**
be suited by 1¼m: best form on going softer than good: tried blinkered. *B. J. Meehan*

FIDDLESTICKS 3 b.f. Missed Flight 123 – Fiddling 82 (Music Boy 124) [2001 6s **55**
6.1d⁴ 6m 5m³ 6m³ 6m 5f 5m Sep 8] good-topped filly: fourth living foal: dam, 5f winner,
sister to useful sprinter Clantime: modest maiden handicapper: should stay 7f: acts on
firm and good to soft going. *Mrs J. R. Ramsden*

FIELD MASTER (IRE) 4 ch.g. Foxhound (USA) 103 – Bold Avril (IRE) (Persian **59**
Bold 123) [2001 70d: e10g e10g f9.4g² f9.4g⁵ e13g Mar 19] strong gelding: modest
performer: stays 10.5f: acts on fibresand, equitrack, good to firm and good to soft going
(well beaten on soft/heavy): sold 4,200 gns, then won over hurdles. *S. Dow*

FIELD OF VISION (IRE) 11 b.g. Vision (USA) – Bold Meadows 80 (Persian Bold **43**
123) [2001 55: 13d³ 11.1d⁵ 12.4m 13m³ 12m³ 12.4m² 12f⁵ 12g² 12.1s² 12.1g⁴ Sep 3] neat
gelding: has a quick action: poor performer nowadays: effective at 11f to 2m: acts on
fibresand, equitrack and any turf going: has worn blinkers, tried rarely nowadays: usually
held up. *Mrs A. Duffield*

FIELLA (IRE) 2 b.g. (Apr 22) Petorius 117 – Creggan Vale Lass (Simply Great (FR) **47**
122) [2001 5.1s 6g 5.7g Oct 1] IR 10,000F, 15,000Y: smallish gelding: fifth living foal:
brother to 4-y-o Keltech Gold and half-brother to a winner abroad: dam poor Irish
maiden: poor maiden. *B. R. Millman*

FIENNES (USA) 3 b. or br.g. Dayjur (USA) 137 – Artic Strech (USA) (Arctic Tern **65**
(USA) 126) [2001 53: e5g⁵ e7g⁵ f5g⁵ f5g* f6g⁴ f5g² f6g⁵ f6g 5.3d f5g f5g⁵ f6g² f6g⁴

f6g f6g f5g f6g* f5g⁴ f5g f6g² f5g² f6g³ Dec 17] small, sparely-made gelding: modest performer: sold 1,500 gns and left M. Bell after second start: won seller at Wolverhampton in March and claimer at Southwell in November: good efforts in handicaps last 3 starts: effective at 5f/6f: acts on good to firm going and fibresand: visored after reappearance: tried tongue tied: used to seem temperamental. *Mrs N. Macauley*

FIERY WATERS 5 b.g. Rudimentary (USA) 118 – Idle Waters 116 (Mill Reef (USA) 141) [2001 70: f14g⁶ f12g f14g² May 14] unfurnished gelding: modest handicapper: stays 1¾m: acts on fibresand: blinkered nowadays: tends to be slowly away. *D. W. P. Arbuthnot* **– a64**

FIESTA 3 ch.f. Most Welcome 131 – Taza (Persian Bold 123) [2001 7s 7.5f 8m⁴ 12g Aug 15] strong filly: third foal: half-sister to fairly useful 1999 2-y-o 7f winner who stays 2m Il Capitano (by Be My Chief): dam (no form) half-sister to very smart middle-distance performer Apache: no sign of ability in maidens. *C. W. Thornton* **–**

FIFE AND DRUM (USA) 4 b. or br.g. Rahy (USA) 115 – Fife (IRE) 95 (Lomond (USA) 128) [2001 58, a76: e10g 10g 10.1d 10m³ 10g* 10.1g⁵ 10.2f² Sep 18] smallish gelding: fair handicapper: won at Nottingham in August: better at 1¼m than 1½m: acts on equitrack (well held both runs on fibresand), best turf efforts on good going or firmer: tried blinkered. *J. Akehurst* **72**

FIFTEEN REDS 6 b.g. Jumbo Hirt (USA) 90§ – Dominance (Dominion 123) [2001 51§: f16g Jan 5] close-coupled gelding: temperamental maiden: often visored. *P. C. Haslam* **– §**

FIFTH EDITION 5 b.m. Rock Hopper 124 – Glossary (Reference Point 139) [2001 –: 12.3m 12.6f⁴ 18m 14.1m⁶ 16m⁴ 11.9s⁵ 11.9s⁶ Oct 25] poor maiden handicapper: probably stays 2¼m: acts on firm and soft going. *R. Guest* **40**

FIGAWIN 6 b.g. Rudimentary (USA) 118 – Dear Person (Rainbow Quest (USA) 134) [2001 f16g Feb 5] of little account nowadays. *Mrs H. L. Walton* **–**

FIGHT YOUR CORNER 2 b.c. (Apr 12) Muhtarram (USA) 125 – Dame Ashfield 90 (Grundy 137) [2001 6d* 6m³ 7m⁵ 8f* 8d* Oct 13] **114 p**
Fight Your Corner: it could be Mark Johnston's byword. Except that is for one thing: the Middleham-based trainer doesn't come across as a man who'd be satisfied with such a limited brief. In his regular Saturday column in the *Racing Post*, Johnston loads up his opinions and fires at will on a battery of topics. Targets identified in 2001 included: the future of ex-racehorses, media rights, the Levy Board, Saturday morning racing, racegoers' facilities at Newmarket, racecourse facilities in general, racecourse stabling, the state of the track at Newcastle, jockey bans, late abandonments, Tattersalls, sales catalogues, Ballydoyle, weight ranges in handicaps, rules H14 and H19, drunkenness on racecourses, starting stalls, racecourse rake-offs from sellers, the future of racing in general, the demise of greyhound racing, corruption in cricket and the photo the *Racing Post* had been using of M. J. as a mugshot. Johnston often adopted a 'shoot-to-kill' policy and his views, which sometimes left little room for him to discuss his horses, clearly weren't mellifluous to all, judging by the paper's own letters pages. Nevertheless, some topics did benefit from his front-line insight, something often missing from

Tom McGee Autumn Stakes, Ascot—the heavily backed Fight Your Corner justifies the support for a five-length success over Coshocton (right)

the columns of full-time racing journalists. Perhaps the horses will deserve more space in 2002.

    Johnston certainly hasn't let his writing commitments get in the way of training winners. Fight Your Corner's final success at Ascot in October brought up a domestic hundred for the stable for the eighth consecutive year, leaving the yard one short of Henry Cecil's record of nine successive seasonal hundreds achieved in the 'nineties. The latest landmark was reached in the listed Tom McGee Autumn Stakes. In a field of eight, Fight Your Corner beat the favourite Coshocton by five lengths, leading three furlongs out and responding generously under pressure as he drew clear. In winning the race, Fight Your Corner was following in the footsteps of Nayef the previous year, as he had been when successful in the Haynes, Hanson and Clark Stakes at Newbury in September, when he had beaten a promising field headed by Wing Commander by a length and a half. In hindsight, the opportunity to tackle a mile on his last two starts seemed to be the making of Fight Your Corner, though he had shown progressive form on his first three outings, winning a maiden over six furlongs at Newcastle in August on his debut before being beaten in minor events at Ripon and Doncaster.

Fight Your Corner (b.c. Apr 12, 1999)	Muhtarram (USA) (b 1989)	Alleged (b 1974)	Hoist The Flag
			Princess Pout
		Ballet de France (b 1981)	Northern Dancer
			Fabulous Native
	Dame Ashfield (b 1980)	Grundy (ch 1972)	Great Nephew
			Word From Lundy
		African Dancer (b 1973)	Nijinsky
			Miba

    Fight Your Corner's family is already quite well known to his trainer, who won a handful of races each with two of his dam Dame Ashfield's better previous foals, the handicappers Indigo Dawn (by Rainbow Quest) and Shirley Sue (by Shirley Heights); this pair were successful at up to two miles. Dame Ashfield was successful twice over a mile and a half and her dam, African Dancer, was successful in the Park Hill Stakes over the St Leger trip. African Dancer is also the dam of On Show, the dam of Coronation Stakes runner-up Inchmurrin, who went on to produce Inchinor, a smart performer over seven furlongs and a mile and now a successful sire; this is also the family of Sir George Turner, another promising colt in the yard. Fight Your Corner should be well suited by at least a mile and a quarter. His sire Muhtarram was probably best at that trip, winning the Prince of Wales's Stakes twice, but ran respectably on his only two outings at a mile and a half, including when fourth behind Dr Devious in the Derby. The tall, angular, useful-looking Fight Your Corner could well end up at Epsom himself, and on what he has done already over distances which will almost certainly prove inadequate at three, he looks likely to develop into a live contender—he is very much one to respect in the trials in the spring and 40/1 with the Tote, at the time of writing, could well look good Derby value come June. Fight Your Corner has yet to race on soft or heavy ground, but he has already shown he acts on any other. *M. Johnston*

FIG LEAF (FR)   2 b.f. (May 1) Distant Relative 128 – Shady Leaf (IRE) 56 (Glint of   **81** Gold 128) [2001 6g⁴ 7f² 7m Aug 30] tall, useful-looking filly: sixth foal: half-sister to fairly useful Irish 2m winner Academy House (by Sadler's Wells): dam, maiden who stayed 1½m, half-sister to Princess Royal Stakes winner Dancing Bloom and to dams of Spectrum and Millenary: fairly useful maiden: best effort when beaten neck by Shifty at Lingfield, staying on strongly after racing freely: should stay at least 1¼m. *R. F. Johnson Houghton*

FIGURA   3 b.f. Rudimentary (USA) 118 – Dream Baby (Master Willie 129) [2001 87:   **72** 8f 7m 11.6m 8g Sep 28] big, leggy filly: just fair form in handicaps in 2001, leaving K. McAuliffe after third start: best form at 7f: raced only on good ground or firmer. *C. G. Cox*

FIGUREHEAD   2 b.c. (Mar 7) Entrepreneur 123 – Noble Dane (IRE) 79 (Danehill   **77** (USA) 126) [2001 7.5m³ 7.5g³ 8.3g³ f8.5g² Sep 22] 300,000Y: good-bodied colt: first foal: dam, 1m winner at 2 yrs (stayed 1½m), sister to 9-y-o Amrak Ajeeb: fair maiden: placed at Beverley (2), Hamilton and Wolverhampton (visored): should stay 1¼m: acts on fibresand, and good to firm going. *Sir Michael Stoute*

FILIAL (IRE) 8 b.g. Danehill (USA) 126 – Sephira (Luthier 126) [2001 –: f11g f12g **43**
12.4m⁴ 14.1m 12.4d² 12.1s⁶ Aug 21] smallish gelding: poor performer: stays 13f: acts on
fibresand, equitrack, good to firm and heavy going: blinkered once. *Mrs A. Duffield*

FILLE D'ARGENT (IRE) 2 gr.f. (Apr 21) Desert Style (IRE) 121 – Talina (General **62**
Assembly (USA)) [2001 5f² 6m 5.1m⁴ 6g 8.3v 7g³ Oct 19] IR 15,500Y: strong, good sort:
fourth reported foal: half-sister to fairly useful 2m winner Talina's Law (by Law Society)
and 7f (at 2 yrs) and 9f winner Chateau Lina (by Paris House), both in Ireland: dam,
French 9f to 11f winner, half-sister to 2000 Guineas winner Zino: modest maiden: should
stay 1m: acts on firm going: visored (ran well) final start. *Mrs P. N. Dutfield*

FILLE DE BUCHERON (USA) 3 b.f. Woodman (USA) 126 – Special Secreto **76**
(USA) (Secreto (USA) 128) [2001 83p: 8.2f³ 7m² 8.5m³ f8g³ f8.5g⁴ f6s* Dec 15] strong, **a67**
angular filly: fair performer: left H. Cecil and off 5 months after third start: visored,
nowhere near best to win maiden at Southwell in December: stays 1m: acts on fibresand,
raced only on good to firm/firm ground on turf: carries head high. *S. R. Bowring*

FILLE DE DAUPHIN (IRE) 3 b.f. Dolphin Street (FR) 125 – Asturiana (Julio **–**
Mariner 127) [2001 –: f11g Feb 16] smallish filly: well held, including in seller.
N. Bycroft

FILLE DE JOIE (IRE) 3 b.f. Royal Academy (USA) 130 – Courtesane (USA) **67 d**
(Majestic Light (USA)) [2001 8m² 9m 7g² 8m⁶ 8d⁵ Oct 8] leggy filly: sixth foal:
half-sister to smart 10.4f to 14.6f winner Delilah (by Bluebird) and winners abroad by
Vigors and Assert: dam placed twice in USA: maiden: regressed after showing fair form
on debut: reportedly finished lame penultimate start: will stay 1¼m. *R. F. Johnson
Houghton*

FILLE GENEREUX 3 ch.f. Cadeaux Genereux 131 – Mohican Girl 112 (Dancing **46**
Brave (USA) 140) [2001 7g 8m³ 6.9m³ 8.5d³ 8.1m 8d f6g⁴ p7g Dec 28] lengthy,
unfurnished filly: third foal: half-sister to 7-y-o The Prince: dam, winner up to 11f,
half-sister to Yorkshire Oaks winners Sally Brown and Untold: poor maiden: stays 8.5f:
acts on fibresand, yet to race on extremes on turf. *R. M. H. Cowell*

FILUM TERMINALE (IRE) 2 b.c. (Apr 12) Mujadil (USA) 119 – Millie's Return **77**
(IRE) 71 (Ballad Rock 122) [2001 5s 5m² 5f⁴ 5m⁴ Jun 8] IR 16,000F, 30,000Y: rather
leggy, angular colt: third foal: half-brother to 4-y-o Paddywack: dam, Irish maiden who
stayed 1½m, out of sister to very smart stayer Assessor: fair maiden: bit below form after
second in minor event at Warwick: should stay at least 6f: acts on good to firm ground:
sold 4,000 gns, sent to France. *M. R. Channon*

FINAL DIVIDEND (IRE) 5 b.g. Second Set (IRE) 127 – Prime Interest (IRE) **62**
(Kings Lake (USA) 133) [2001 75: e12g* 10.3s e12g² 8s⁵ 9.9m 12.3m² 13.3f p12g³ p12g **a77**
Dec 19] close-coupled gelding: fair handicapper on all-weather, modest on turf: won
amateur event at Lingfield in January: probably best at 1¼m/1½m: acts on soft going,
firm and all-weather. *J. M. P. Eustace*

FINAL EXAM (IRE) 4 ch.g. College Chapel 122 – It Takes Two (IRE) (Alzao **113**
(USA) 117) [2001 109: 5s* 6s* 6g* 5d² 5g⁴ 5g⁴ 5s 5v⁶ Oct 28] IR 20,000F, IR 72,000Y:
robust gelding: second living foal: brother to French 1m winner El Bosco: dam, ran 3
times at 2 yrs in Ireland, half-sister to useful sprinter Wish List: smart performer: won
handicap at the Curragh, minor event at Cork and Weatherbys Ireland Greenlands Stakes
(by ½ length from One Won One) at the Curragh in April/May: in frame afterwards in
Ballyogan Stakes at Leopardstown, valuable listed race at the Curragh and Flying Five
(fourth to Ishiguru) at Leopardstown: effective at 5f to 7f: acts on soft going (not tried
on firmer than good since debut): blinkered: often races close to pace (slowly away at
Longchamp last 2 outings). *D. K. Weld, Ireland*

FINAL FAZE 2 ch.f. (Mar 23) Chaddleworth (IRE) 103 – Fine Fettle (Final Straw **– p**
127) [2001 7m Sep 22] lengthy filly: fifth reported foal: dam unraced: 50/1, faded when
eleventh of 18 in maiden at Newmarket: likely to do better. *J. G. Given*

FINAL LAP 5 b.g. Batshoof 122 – Lap of Honour 100 (Final Straw 127) [2001 62, a–: **–**
f16.2s 11.6g 15g Jul 6] angular gelding: one-time fair performer: well held in 2001, in
blinkers final start. *G. M. McCourt*

FINAL PURSUIT 3 b.f. Pursuit of Love 124 – Final Shot 91 (Dalsaan 125) [2001 91: **92 §**
7d 6s³ 6m 8m 7g⁵ 8m 7g Aug 3] tall filly: fairly useful performer: form in 2001 only when
third in minor event at Newbury in May and fifth in handicap at Newmarket in July: stays
7f: acts on soft going: has sweated/been slowly away/flashed tail: visored fourth start: not
one to trust. *D. Haydn Jones*

FINAL SETTLEMENT (IRE)   6 b.g. Soviet Lad (USA) – Tender Time (Tender   **71**
King 123) [2001 74: 16m 14.4m³ 14s⁴ 14.6f 14m⁵ 14.8m* 14g⁵ 14.8m⁵ 16g 16d⁶ Sep 27]
angular gelding: good mover: fair handicapper: won at Newmarket in July: was best at
1¾m/2m: acted on heavy and good to firm going: carried head awkwardly: was usually
held up: dead. *J. R. Jenkins*

FIND THE KING (IRE)   3 b.c. King's Theatre (IRE) 128 – Undiscovered (Tap On   **86**
Wood 130) [2001 46: 8d⁵ 9s 11m³ 12f* 12m⁴ 14m² 14g² 13.9m 14s Sep 8] sturdy, useful-
looking colt: has a round action: fairly useful handicapper: won at Newbury in June:
mostly creditable efforts after: stays 1¾m: acts on firm and good to soft going, probably
soft: sweating (well held) penultimate start: front runner: tough and genuine: joined
E. O'Grady in Ireland, successful on hurdling debut in December. *D. W. P. Arbuthnot*

FINE LOOKING WOMAN   3 ch.f. Imp Society (USA) – Pity's Pet 62 (Stanford   **–**
121§) [2001 f8g Nov 30] second reported foal: dam, maiden, best at 6f: 50/1, well beaten
in maiden at Southwell, slowly away. *D. J. Wintle*

FINISHED ARTICLE (IRE)   4 b.g. Indian Ridge 123 – Summer Fashion 84   **90**
(Moorestyle 137) [2001 82: 7s 8.3g⁵ 9m³ 8f² 8.5m⁶ 9d⁶ 9.9d* 9m² 8s 8d⁴ 8d Nov 3] small
gelding: fairly useful handicapper: won at Goodwood in August: good efforts after when
in frame: best at 1m/1¼m: acts on firm and good to soft going: gelded after final start.
D. R. C. Elsworth

FINMAR   3 b.g. Efisio 120 – Patiala (IRE) (Nashwan (USA) 135) [2001 70: 5d 6d⁵   **70 §**
8.3m³ 7m⁵ 7.1g² 7m⁴ 8.3m⁴ 8.3g² 10.9d 7s 8g⁵ Nov 7] strong gelding: fair maiden: should
stay beyond 1m: acts on good to firm and good to soft going. *Miss L. A. Perratt*

FINN MCCOOL (IRE)   3 b.g. Blues Traveller (IRE) 119 – Schonbein (IRE) 60   **58**
(Persian Heights 129) [2001 61: 10m f12g 10.1g* 10m 10f 10.1v⁴ Oct 24] workmanlike
gelding: modest handicapper: won at Newcastle in August: stayed 1¼m: probably acted
on any turf going and fibresand: dead. *R. A. Fahey*

FIORI   5 b.g. Anshan 119 – Fen Princess (IRE) 72 (Trojan Fen 118) [2001 89: f14g⁵ 16s   **87**
13.9m³ 16.1m⁶ 14g² 13.9m⁴ 15f⁴ 12.1m Sep 24] close-coupled gelding: has a round
action: fairly useful handicapper: effective at 10.4f (given test) to easy 2m: acts on any
turf going and fibresand: has been slowly away: tends to drift left (has worn near-side
pricker): usually races prominently: fairly useful winning hurdler. *P. C. Haslam*

FIREBREAK   2 b.c. (Mar 6) Charnwood Forest (IRE) 125 – Breakaway 98 (Song   **109**
132) [2001 5m* 5m* 6m² 6s* 6g⁴ 6f* Sep 21] 27,000Y: leggy, quite attractive colt:
half-brother to several winners, including 1997 2-y-o 5f winner who stayed 7f Stop By
(by Rudimentary) and 1m winner who stayed 1¼m Hippy (by Damister), both fairly
useful: dam 5f winner, including at 2 yrs: useful performer: won maiden at Goodwood in
May, minor event at Beverley in June, Prix de Cabourg at Deauville (held on gamely to

Dubai Duty Free Mill Reef Stakes, Newbury—
a second pattern-race success for the admirable Firebreak who finds plenty to ward off Irony

Kennet Valley Thoroughbreds I's "Firebreak"

beat Flying Dash a neck) in August and Dubai Duty Free Mill Reef Stakes at Newbury (by 1¼ lengths from Irony, travelling comfortably to lead 2f out and finding plenty) in September: also ran well when neck second of 20 to Landseer in Coventry Stakes at Royal Ascot and 4½ lengths fourth of 11 to Johannesburg in Prix Morny at Deauville: will stay 7f: acts on firm and soft going: reliable: sold 525,000 gns, joined Godolphin. *I. A. Balding*

FIRE DOME (IRE) 9 ch.g. Salt Dome (USA) – Penny Habit (Habitat 134) [2001 96+, a–: f7s 6v² 6d 6.1v* 6s⁶ 6g⁵ 6f⁶ 6m³ 6m 6f³ 6g* 6s² 6m 6d 6d 6v⁶ 7s Nov 10] rangy gelding: useful performer at best: won minor event at Warwick in April: mostly well below form in second half of season, including when winning claimer at Haydock in August: very best form at 6f on good going or softer: hung left/looked less than keen fifteenth outing: tried blinkered/visored: has had tongue tied: usually held up. *Andrew Reid*   **103 d a–**

FIRE IN ICE 2 b.f. (Apr 28) Missed Flight 123 – Boulabas (IRE) 66 (Nashamaa 113) [2001 5.1f 5f 7.1d 7.1s f6g f6g f6g f5f⁵ Dec 5] 1,200Y: leggy, close-coupled filly: fourth reported foal: dam 2-y-o 5f winner: poor maiden: barely stays 7f: acts on fibresand and good to soft going. *B. P. J. Baugh*   **38**

FIRE MOON (IRE) 2 b.g. (Feb 3) Royal Applause 124 – Welwyn 92 (Welsh Saint 126) [2001 5g⁶ 7f 6m⁴ 8m⁶ Sep 1] 57,000Y: smallish, well-made gelding: has a quick action: half-brother to 3 winners, including useful sprinter Welsh Mist (by Damister): dam, best at 6f, half-sister to smart sprinter Welshwyn: modest maiden: likely to prove best up to 7f: withdrawn after refusing to enter stall second intended start: sold 2,000 gns, and gelded. *M. R. Channon*   **60**

FIRESIDE LEGEND (IRE) 2 b.g. (May 24) College Chapel 122 – Miss Sandman 86 (Manacle 123) [2001 6m f6g* 7.1f⁵ 7g 6g f8.5g⁴ f8g³ 8.2s³ f8.5g² 8.3v Nov 8] IR

4,000F, IR 5,400Y: half-brother to several winners, including useful 7f (at 2 yrs) to 1¼m (in Italy) winner Arman's Sax (by Waajib): dam 2-y-o 5f winner: modest performer: won seller at Southwell in June: stays 8.5f: acts on fibresand and soft ground: sometimes runs in snatches/hangs under pressure. *W. G. M. Turner*

FIRESTONE (GER) 4 b.g. Dictator's Song (USA) – Fatinizza (IRE) (Niniski (USA) **79 ?**
125) [2001 9m⁵ 8.3m 8m Sep 24] tall, leggy gelding: first foal: dam German 6.5f winner, including at 2 yrs: seemingly fair form for E. Kurdu in Germany, winning maiden at Dusseldorf at 2 yrs and handicap at Hanover in 2000: fair form at best in 3 handicaps in Britain: probably stays 1¼m: acts on good to soft ground: tried blinkered earlier in career. *A. W. Carroll*

FIREWIRE 3 b.g. Blushing Flame (USA) 109 – Bay Risk (Risk Me (FR) 127) [2001 **74**
–: 10s 10m 10g* 10m² 10g⁴ Aug 8] smallish, workmanlike gelding: fair handicapper: won maiden event at Nottingham in June: good efforts after: should stay 1½m: acts on good to firm ground, well beaten on softer than good: has been heavily bandaged near-hind. *N. Hamilton*

FIREWORK 3 b.c. Primo Dominie 121 – Prancing 98 (Prince Sabo 123) [2001 85: 6d **78 §**
6m 6m 5f 6m³ 6g⁶ 6m³ 5f⁴ 7d³ 7s⁶ 6g⁴ 6v³ Oct 29] quite attractive colt: good walker: fair maiden: likely to prove best at 6f/easy 7f: acts on firm and soft going: blinkered/visored last 4 starts: sold 5,500 gns. *R. Guest*

FIROZI 2 b.f. (Mar 20) Forzando 122 – Lambast 70 (Relkino 131) [2001 5.7f 6m³ **61 §**
5.7m⁴ 7m 6s 7s 7v Oct 26] third living foal: half-sister to 5-y-o Angie Marinie: dam, maiden who stayed 1½m, sister to useful performer up to 1½m My Lamb and half-sister to useful sprinter Bay Bay: modest maiden: well below form last 2 starts: should stay 1m: acts on good to firm ground, probably on soft: blinkered last 3 outings: has played up in preliminaries: wanders under pressure: not one to trust. *C. G. Cox*

FIRST ALERT 2 ch.f. (Feb 28) Miswaki (USA) 124 – First Amendment (IRE) 78 **74**
(Caerleon (USA) 132) [2001 5s⁴ 6m³ 5m* 6.1m² 7.1m⁶ 7.1s* 7d Oct 2] sturdy filly: second foal: dam, 9f winner in USA (maiden in Britain who stayed 1½m), granddaughter of Musidora winner and Oaks third Last Feather: fair performer: landed odds in claimers at Beverley in July and Haydock in September: will stay 1m: acts on soft and good to firm going: sent to USA. *W. J. Haggas*

FIRST BACK (IRE) 4 b.g. Fourstars Allstar (USA) 122 – Par Un Nez (IRE) (Cyrano **52 d**
de Bergerac 120) [2001 56: 9m 9.9f⁶ 12.4m 9.9f 8g 10.1g⁵ 11m 9.1m Sep 21] lengthy, dipped-backed gelding: modest performer, on downgrade: seems to stay 1½m: acts on firm going, possibly on good to soft: tried visored/blinkered: none too reliable. *C. W. Fairhurst*

FIRST BALLOT (IRE) 5 b.g. Perugino (USA) 84 – Election Special 78 (Chief Singer **108**
131) [2001 92: 14.1g* 14m² 20m² 16.4m³ 14m* 16.2g² 13.9g Aug 22] tall, leggy, good-topped gelding: useful handicapper: made all at Salisbury in May and Goodwood (beat Moonjaz by a length) in July: mostly good placed efforts otherwise in 2001, including 1¼-length second to Cover Up in Ascot Stakes at Royal Ascot third start and length second to Moon Emperor in Shergar Cup (Stayers) at Ascot on penultimate outing: badly hampered in Ebor at York final outing: effective at 1¾m to 2½m: acts on firm and good to soft going: races prominently/leads: tough and consistent. *D. R. C. Elsworth*

FIRST BASE 2 ch.g. (Mar 1) First Trump 118 – Rose Music 86 (Luthier 126) [2001 5f **45**
6g 6m 8m Sep 20] 10,000F: quite good-topped gelding: half-brother to several winners, including 1¼m/11.5f winner Rose Alto (by Adonijah) and 7f to 1¼m performer Jal-musique (by Jalmood), both useful: dam 7f/1m winner: poor maiden: probably stays 1m: tried visored: sold 2,000 gns. *Mrs J. R. Ramsden*

FIRST CHARTER 2 b.c. (Mar 10) Polish Precedent (USA) 131 – By Charter 104 **94 p**
(Shirley Heights 130) [2001 8g 8d² Nov 2] 160,000F: seventh foal: closely related to 1995 2-y-o 7f winner Green Charter (by Green Desert) and half-brother to 3 winners, including fairly useful 1½m winner Careful Timing (by Caerleon): dam, 2-y-o 7f winner who seemed to stay 1½m, daughter of Time Charter: better effort at Newmarket (fairly useful form) when ½-length second of 5 to Ashdown Express in steadily-run minor event, staying on well after being caught flat-footed: will be suited by 1¼m/1½m: gave some trouble at stalls on debut: will improve further, and sure to win races. *Sir Michael Stoute*

FIRST DEGREE 3 br.f. Sabrehill (USA) 120 – Degree 81 (Warning 136) [2001 50: **–**
10s 12m Aug 3] modest maiden at 2 yrs: well held in handicaps nearly 4 months apart in 2001: should stay 1¼m: acts on heavy going. *S. C. Williams*

FIRST EAGLE   2 b.g. (Mar 19) Hector Protector (USA) 124 – Merlin's Fancy 62   –
(Caerleon (USA) 132) [2001 6f 7s 6v p6g³ p10g p7g⁴ Dec 29] 37,000Y: lengthy, rather   **a55**
unfurnished gelding: second foal: half-brother to 3-y-o Illusionist: dam, maiden who
probably stayed 1m, half-sister to top-class sprinter Cadeaux Genereux: modest maiden:
left M. Channon after fourth start: stays 1¼m: acts on polytrack, well beaten on turf.
S. Kirk

FIRST IMPRESSION   6 b.g. Saddlers' Hall (IRE) 126 – First Sapphire (Simply Great   **82**
(FR) 122) [2001 82: 10v³ 12s³ 13.3g³ 14.4m 13.1m² 11.6v* 11.7d Oct 25] workmanlike
gelding: fairly useful performer: won minor event at Windsor (despite hanging left) in
October: stays 13f: acts on heavy and good to firm going: edgy sort. *Mrs A. J. Perrett*

FIRST MAGNITUDE (IRE)   5 ch.h. Arazi (USA) 135 – Crystal Cup (USA) (Nijin-   **117**
sky (CAN) 138) [2001 117: 12d⁴ May 14] close-coupled horse: smart performer: won
Prix d'Hedouville at Longchamp and Prix Jean de Chaudenay at Saint-Cloud in 2000: off
11 months, creditable 3¾ lengths fourth to Dano-Mast in latter event only outing in 2001,
though never dangerous: stays 12.5f well: acts on heavy and good to firm ground: held
up: consistent. *A. Fabre, France*

FIRST MAITE   8 b.g. Komaite (USA) – Marina Plata (Julio Mariner 127) [2001 101,   **81**
a96: 7.1g⁶ 5m 6m² 6f 6d 6f⁶ 6m⁴ 6m 7d 5m⁶ 7m⁵ 5m 5v 8g² 9g³ 7d² 7d 8s* f8.5g² f8.5f³   **a88**
f8g* f9.4s Dec 26] tall, lengthy gelding: has a round action: fairly useful handicapper:
won at Doncaster (ladies) in November and Southwell in December: effective at 6f to 9f:
acts on good to firm going, soft and fibresand: often blinkered (has been visored), best
recent form when not: has been tongue tied/bandaged in front: sometimes hangs: usually
races prominently. *S. R. Bowring*

FIRST MEETING   3 b.f. Contract Law (USA) 108 – Sunday News'n'echo (USA) 78   –
(Trempolino (USA) 135) [2001 48: 6.1v 8m May 21] no form in 2001. *M. Dods*

FIRST OF MANY   2 b.f. (Jan 29) Darshaan 133 – Star Profile (IRE) 100 (Sadler's   **83 p**
Wells (USA) 132) [2001 7m⁵ Sep 6] first foal: dam, Irish 2-y-o 6f winner, closely related
to smart Irish sprinter Lady Alexander: weak 7/1-shot and green, 2 lengths fifth of 12 to
Sulk in maiden at Salisbury, staying on having been slowly away and soon off bridle: will
stay at least 1m: sure to do better. *Sir Michael Stoute*

FIRST ORDAINED   2 b.c. (Apr 17) Mujadil (USA) 119 – Ordinate (Nashwan   **76**
(USA) 135) [2001 5m⁶ 6m 6m³ 7m⁴ 7g² 7m³ 7g⁴ 8f² 7m² 8g 8m 8s⁵ 8g² f9.4g⁶ Nov 17]
IR 10,000F, 11,000Y: sturdy, lengthy colt: unimpressive mover: first foal: dam, French
9f winner, granddaughter of Prix Morny winner Madina: fair maiden: in frame 8 times,
including in sellers/nurseries: stays 1m: acts on firm going, possibly not on soft: usually
races prominently. *R. Hannon*

FIRST STEPS (IRE)   3 b.f. Brief Truce (USA) 126 – Wilsonic 78 (Damister (USA)   **68**
123) [2001 59: f8g f8g² f8s² f9.4g* f8.5g⁶ 10.3s 10g⁴ f9.4g² 11.6g⁴ 10m³ 10m* 9.7m⁴   **a74**
10m³ 10s⁴ f9.4g* f9.4g⁴ Oct 23] leggy filly: unimpressive mover: fair performer: won
maiden at Wolverhampton in February and handicaps at Newbury in August and Wolverhampton in October: stays 1¼m: acts on fibresand, soft and good to firm going: blinkered
last 9 starts: no easy ride, but is consistent: sold 10,000 gns, sent to Sweden. *B. Smart*

FIRST TOAST   3 ch.g. First Trump 118 – Toast (IRE) (Be My Guest (USA) 126)   –
[2001 8g 7m 7f Jun 5] 11,500Y: angular, workmanlike gelding: third living foal: dam,
lightly-raced Irish maiden, sister to smart French 7f to 1¼m winner What A Guest and
half-sister to very smart middle-distance performer Infantry: well held in maidens/
claimer. *Miss Gay Kelleway*

FIRST TO GO   2 ch.f. (Mar 19) First Trump 118 – Port Na Blath (On Your Mark 125)   **47**
[2001 6g 6d 7g 7d Oct 3] 1,600F, 9,000Y: strong filly: closely related to fairly useful 1991
2-y-o 6f winner Combination (by Primo Dominie), later winner abroad, and half-sister to
2 winners, including 3-y-o Erracht: dam, Irish 6f winner, from good family: poor maiden:
probably stays 7f. *M. Dods*

FIRST TRUTH   4 b.g. Rudimentary (USA) 118 – Pursuit of Truth (USA) 69 (Irish   –
River (FR) 131) [2001 94: 10s 8.9d 10g Nov 5] angular gelding: fairly useful handicapper
at 3 yrs: well held in 2001. *Mrs H. Dalton*

FIRST VENTURE   4 b.g. Formidable (USA) 125 – Diamond Wedding (USA) 65   **67**
(Diamond Shoal 130) [2001 73, a81: f6g³ f7g² f6g⁴ f7s f6g⁴ f6g e7g⁴ 7m² 7d³ 6f⁶ 5m⁴ 5m   **a80**
5m* 5m⁶ 5m 5.1g 6g 7s 5.3m³ p6g Dec 29] lengthy, useful-looking gelding: fairly useful
performer on all-weather, fair on turf: won handicap at Lingfield in June: best up to 7f:

acts on fibresand/equitrack, good to firm and good to soft going: often blinkered/visored: tries to dominate. *C. N. Allen*

FISHER ISLAND (IRE)   4 b. or br.f. Sri Pekan (USA) 117 – Liberty Song (IRE)   **49** (Last Tycoon 131) [2001 59: 8.2v 10v² 12m⁴ 11.8m² f12g³ 11.9f⁵ 9.9m³ 10m³ 9.9m² 14.1m⁶ 10f⁵ f12s² Dec 27] tall filly: poor handicapper nowadays: effective at 1¼m to 2m: acts on heavy going, good to firm and fibresand: often races prominently: said to have bled from nose final outing: consistent, but carries head awkwardly and doesn't always go through with effort. *R. Hollinshead*

FITTONIA (FR)   2 ch.f. (Jan 31) Ashkalani (IRE) 128 – Fly For Fame (Shaadi (USA)   **65 p** 126) [2001 7d⁵ Oct 6] workmanlike filly: first foal: dam, useful French 1¼m (at 2 yrs)/ 1½m winner, out of smart French performer around 1¼m Fly Me: 7 lengths fifth of 12 to Atarama in maiden at Redcar, slowly away: should improve. *J. D. Bethell*

FIVEEIGHTSARF   2 b.c. (Apr 27) Forzando 122 – Fair Eleanor (Saritamer (USA)   **40** 130) [2001 5m 7m 6g 6s Oct 5] 6,500Y, 9,000 2-y-o: sturdy, workmanlike colt: has been tubed: half-brother to several winners, including useful 2000 2-y-o 5f/6f winner Imperial Measure (by Inchinor) and 1¼m winner Nicolai (by Piccolo): dam maiden who stayed 1m: poor maiden. *B. R. Millman*

FIVE STARS   2 ch.f. (Feb 12) Bahamian Bounty 116 – Star Ridge (USA) (Storm Bird   **86 p** (CAN) 134) [2001 8.2s* Nov 5] half-sister to several winners, including smart 7f/1m winner On The Ridge (by Risk Me) and fairly useful 1m/1¼m winner Barrier Ridge (by Lycius): dam ran twice in France: 4/1, won maiden at Nottingham by 1½ lengths from Barman, initially green off bridle but wearing down runner-up near finish: not sure to stay beyond 1m: likely to make a useful 3-y-o. *H. R. A. Cecil*

FIZA (IRE)   2 b.g. (Feb 3) Revoque (IRE) 122 – Double Eight (IRE) 77 (Common   **–** Grounds 118) [2001 6d 6m 5d Oct 9] IR 62,000Y: quite attractive gelding: first foal: dam, 1½m winner, sister to 5-y-o Downland: signs of just a little ability in maidens: carried head awkwardly second start. *M. L. W. Bell*

FIZZY TREAT   3 b.f. Efisio 120 – Special Guest 67 (Be My Guest (USA) 126) [2001   **63** 8.1v² 7s 8.2s³ Oct 30] 40,000Y: lengthy filly: sister to useful 1997 2-y-o 5f/6f winner who later stayed 1m Hoh Chi Min and half-sister to several winners, including useful 7f winner Cragganmore (by Faustus): dam 2-y-o 7f winner who stayed 9f: easily best effort in maidens (modest form) when second at Haydock in September: likely to stay 1¼m. *R. Guest*

FLAG DAY (JPN)   2 b.c. (Apr 9) Sunday Silence (USA) – National Flag (JPN) (Dictus   **99 p** (FR) 126) [2001 7g* Jul 24] $748,000Y in Japan: fifth foal: brother to 1999 Japanese Group 3 2-y-o 1m winner Maruka Komachi and half-brother to 2 winners in Japan by Northern Taste: dam Japanese 1¼m winner: won 11-runner minor event at Chantilly by ¾ length from Bashful (pair 4 lengths clear), staying on strongly to lead near finish: will stay 1¼m: joined Godolphin: sure to improve. *A. Fabre, France*

FLAG FEN (USA)   10 b. or br.g. Riverman (USA) 131 – Damascus Flag (USA) (Dam-   **51** ascus (USA)) [2001 71: 10.3s³ 10v³ 11.5m⁶ 12m 10.1g⁶ Jul 3] rangy gelding: modest performer nowadays: stays 11.5f: acts on fibresand, firm and soft going: blinkered once: has tended to hang right: often apprentice ridden. *H. J. Collingridge*

FLAG OF DEMOCRACY (USA)   3 ch.c. Distant View (USA) 126 – Capital Hill   **72** (USA) (Temperence Hill (USA)) [2001 e8s* 8g f8g⁶ 8.1g² 8g 7s³ 7.5m 11g Dec 16] $135,000Y, resold 60,000Y: big, lengthy colt: seventh foal: closely related/half-brother to several minor winners in USA: dam unraced: fair performer: won maiden at Lingfield in February: sold 10,000 gns from J. Noseda after sixth outing: effective at 7f (at least given a test)/1m: acts on fibresand, equitrack and soft going: visored fourth to sixth starts (raced freely/hung markedly left on first occasion). *R. Feligioni, Italy*

FLAK JACKET   6 b.g. Magic Ring (IRE) 115 – Vaula 49 (Henbit (USA) 130) [2001   **80** 81: 5v 5s³ 7m 7f 6m² 5g⁴ 5d* 5g² 5m⁴ 6g* 6g 5d 5d 5s Oct 20] strong gelding: impresses in appearance: fairly useful handicapper: won at Haydock in July and Goodwood (for second successive year) in August: below form after: best at 5f/6f: acts on firm and soft going: blinkered once: often tongue tied: sometimes hangs right. *D. Nicholls*

FLAMBE   3 b.g. Whittingham (IRE) 104 – Uae Flame (IRE) (Polish Precedent (USA)   **71** 131) [2001 82: f6g⁵ f9.4s³ 6s 8d 8m* 8m* 8.1g 7m 8d f8g f8g Nov 12] good-topped gelding: fair handicapper: won at Newcastle in May and June: below form after: best at 7f/1m: acts on fibresand and good to firm going: usually races prominently: hung markedly fourth start. *P. C. Haslam*

FLAMEBIRD (IRE) 4 b.f. Mukaddamah (USA) 125 – Flamenco (USA) 116 (Dance –
Spell (USA)) [2001 –: e8g e10m⁶ 10.9g 6d 7m⁴ Aug 3] rangy filly: of little account
nowadays. *Mrs A. L. M. King*

FLAMENCA (USA) 2 b.f. (Feb 17) Diesis 133 – Highland Ceilidh (IRE) 100 (Scottish –
Reel 123) [2001 7.1v⁶ 10d Oct 8] sturdy filly: sixth living foal: sister to 3-y-o Carioca
Dream and half-sister to 1½m winner Nika Nesgoda (by Suave Dancer) and Penshiel
(by Mtoto), latter fairly useful: dam, 1m (at 2 yrs)/1¼m winner, from family of Halling
(by Diesis): only a little sign of ability in maidens, seeming in need of run each time: sold
7,000 gns. *Sir Mark Prescott*

FLAMING SPIRT 2 b.f. (Feb 8) Blushing Flame (USA) 109 – Fair Test 95 (Fair **74**
Season 120) [2001 6v⁵ f7g² f8g³ f8g* f8.5s³ Dec 27] half-sister to Irish 7f winner Bestbet-
eastwood (by Chief Singer) and 2 winners in Italy: dam 5f winner, including at 2 yrs: fair
performer: won maiden at Southwell in December: should stay 1¼m: acts on fibresand,
some promise on heavy going: has edged right/flicked tail. *J. S. Moore*

FLAMME DE LA VIE 3 b.g. Blushing Flame (USA) 109 – La Belle Vie 73 (Indian **54**
King (USA) 128) [2001 72: f11g² 10.9m 10g 16m⁵ Jul 5] rather sparely-made gelding:
modest maiden: form in 2001 only on reappearance: seems to stay 11f: acts on soft going
and fibresand: tongue tied final outing: sold 2,000 gns. *G. A. Butler*

FLAPDOODLE 3 b.f. Superpower 113 – My Concordia 58 (Belfort (FR) 89) [2001 **55**
55: f5g² f5s⁵ f5g f5g⁵ f5g³ e5g⁴ f5g 5g 5.3f⁵ f5g Dec 1] modest performer: likely to prove
best at 5f: acts on fibresand (below par on equitrack once), and probably on firm going:
sometimes wanders. *A. W. Carroll*

FLASHFEET 11 b.g. Rousillon (USA) 133 – Miellita 98 (King Emperor (USA)) –
[2001 51d, a–: 7m 8m 9.9d f8g p12g Nov 28] of little account nowadays. *P. D. Purdy*

FLASH OF LIGHT (IRE) 3 b.f. Brief Truce (USA) 126 – Dancing Light (Dancer's –
Image (USA)) [2001 52: 8m 10g 11.1m Jun 13] modest form on debut at 2 yrs: no show
since: tried visored/tongue tied. *P. D. Evans*

FLASHTALKIN' FLOOD 7 ch.g. Then Again 126 – Linguistic 95 (Porto Bello –
118) [2001 42, a–: f12s f8g⁵ e8g f8.5g⁶ e12g 10v Apr 3] of little account nowadays.
C. A. Dwyer

FLAT SPIN 2 b.c. (Feb 12) Spinning World (USA) 130 – Trois Graces (USA) (Alysheba **95**
(USA)) [2001 7f* 7m⁴ 7g Oct 5] rather leggy, useful-looking colt: easy mover: second
reported foal: dam, French 1m winner, half-sister to smart French sprinter/miler Crack
Regiment and Prix de l'Abbaye second La Grande Epoque: useful form: won maiden at
Newbury in August: good fourth to Hills of Gold in minor event at Doncaster: on toes,
ran no sort of race in Somerville Tattersall Stakes at Newmarket final start: likely to prove
best up to 1m: raced only on good going or firmer. *J. L. Dunlop*

FLAT STANLEY 2 b.c. (Feb 8) Celtic Swing 138 – Cool Grey 49 (Absalom 128) –
[2001 7.5g 7d 8g Oct 19] 3,200Y: workmanlike colt: first foal: dam in frame in 7f sellers
at 2 yrs: well beaten in maidens. *T. D. Easterby*

FLAXEN PRIDE (IRE) 6 ch.m. Pips Pride 117 – Fair Chance (Young Emperor 133) **39**
[2001 36: 11s 10m 10.1m⁵ 12.4m³ 9f⁵ 9.9m Aug 26] poor nowadays: may prove better at
1¼m than 1½m: acts on firm going: has been slowly away. *Mrs M. Reveley*

FLEDGE 2 b.f. (Feb 28) Botanic (USA) – Kitty Kitty Cancan 73 (Warrshan (USA) **52**
117) [2001 6d 6v Oct 26] useful-looking filly: second foal: dam maiden who should have
stayed 1½m+: never dangerous in maidens, better effort (modest form) at Newmarket on
debut: should stay at least 1m. *D. R. C. Elsworth*

FLEETING FANCY 4 b.f. Thatching 131 – Fleetwood Fancy (Taufan (USA) 119) –
[2001 59: e7g e7g f9.4g e7g⁵ e10g 10g 11.6m 11.9g Aug 9] modest maiden handicapper
in 2000: well held at 4 yrs: left S. Dow after fifth start: tried visored. *G. M. McCourt*

FLETCHER 7 b.g. Salse (USA) 128 – Ballet Classique (USA) 84 (Sadler's Wells **74**
(USA) 132) [2001 74: 11.9s³ 14.1g⁵ 12m* 14s³ 16.2f³ 13.3f* 12m⁶ 14m⁴
14.1m 14.1d 16d² 16v Oct 26] useful-looking gelding: easy mover: fair handicapper: won
ladies races for Mrs S. Bosley at Newmarket in June and Newbury in July: effective at
1½m to 2m: possibly unsuited by heavy going, acts on any other: visored once: usually
held up: sometimes looks none too keen. *H. Morrison*

FLIGHT OF DREAMS (IRE) 4 b.f. College Chapel 122 – Lady Portobello (Porto **55**
Bello 118) [2001 51+: f8g e8g² e8g² 8d 8f* 8m² 8m⁵ 9m⁵ 8d 8d Aug 8] modest handi-

capper: won at Brighton in May: stays 1m: acts on firm going and equitrack: blinkered once as 3-y-o. *M. Wigham*

FLIGHT OF EAGLES (IRE) 2 gr.c. (May 21) Paris House 123 – Wisdom To Know **74** (Bay Express 132) [2001 5.1f⁶ 5m³ 5.1m⁶ 5.2m Jul 21] 10,000Y: tall, leggy colt: half-brother to several winners, including smart 5f (at 2 yrs)/6f winner Selhurstpark Flyer (by Northiam) and 4-y-o Susie's Flyer: dam third at 6f: fair maiden: best effort when third at Lingfield: will prove best at bare 5f: wore tongue strap final start. *A. Berry*

FLIGHT OF FANCY 3 b.f. Sadler's Wells (USA) 132 – Phantom Gold 119 **114** (Machiavellian (USA) 123) [2001 97P: 10.4m⁴ 12m² Jun 8]
    What odds Flight of Fancy's breeding the Queen a Derby winner? Whatever they are, she looks the best addition to the band of Royal broodmares since Height of Fashion was sold out of the stud, only to go on to produce Nashwan for Sheikh Hamdan Al Maktoum, plus, of course, Unfuwain and Nayef. Among Flight of Fancy's obvious credentials are a fine physique, a high-class middle-distance pedigree and a second place in the Oaks, which could easily have been a first. Sadly, Lord Carnarvon, the Queen's racing manager for many years and the man largely held responsible for the decision to sell Height of Fashion, won't be around to see Flight of Fancy's progeny attempt to make amends; he died of a heart attack in September.
    Flight of Fancy's career drew a lot of column inches for a filly who had only four races. The coverage was understandable all the same. She left us in little doubt she was a genuine classic prospect as early as her second start when bursting to prominence in a Salisbury two-year-old maiden, winning easily by six lengths. Flight of Fancy was favourite for the Oaks by the time of her next start in the Musidora Stakes at York in May. Her running there was eye-catching in itself, but it earned still greater coverage after Lord Carnarvon publicly criticised her jockey Kieren Fallon, calling his ride 'awful'. Lord Carnarvon had backtracked somewhat by the Oaks itself, explaining that he hadn't been aware that Flight of Fancy had gone very freely to post at York. She had done likewise once under way in the

The Queen's "Flight of Fancy"

Musidora, but, with Fallon at pains to settle her, she was caught flat-footed as the pace quickened, showing her inexperience and unable to respond immediately before finishing best into fourth, about two lengths behind the winner Time Away. Flight of Fancy was ridden in closer touch at Epsom, where she started second favourite at 100/30 with Imagine at 3/1, but the race must have left connections with a still greater sense of what might have been. Admittedly, some of Flight of Fancy's problems were of her own making as she ran a little in snatches, again showing her inexperience, but she was just about to launch a challenge when checked noticeably by a weakening rival soon after the turn, thereafter never really balanced on the camber or able to get a clear run as Imagine went past wide. Switched entering the last furlong and rallying strongly, Flight of Fancy finished with plenty of running left in her, a head in front of Musidora second Relish The Thought this time, but a length and a quarter behind Imagine. She probably should have won.

Flight of Fancy (b.f. 1998)	Sadler's Wells (USA) (b 1981)	Northern Dancer (b 1961)	Nearctic
			Natalma
		Fairy Bridge (b 1975)	Bold Reason
			Special
	Phantom Gold (b 1992)	Machiavellian (b 1987)	Mr Prospector
			Coup de Folie
		Trying For Gold (b 1986)	Northern Baby
			Expansive

Flight of Fancy had no chance to make amends after Epsom. She was reportedly found to be lame on her off-hind once returning home, and, though she was said to be sound by the time of the Irish Oaks, she wasn't risked again. She was retired with form somewhat inferior to that of her dam Phantom Gold, who had the benefit of a much longer career and improved with age, winning the Ribblesdale and the St Simon Stakes at three and finishing on a high note by taking the Geoffrey Freer Stakes on her final start at four. Flight of Fancy, whose grandam Expansive also won the Ribblesdale, is the second foal of Phantom Gold, and there are produce by Green Desert and Daylami to come. Flight of Fancy had some of her dam's character, tending to carry her head awkwardly and not looking an altogether straightforward ride, though she did little to bring her generosity into question. She would have stayed beyond a mile and a half and raced only on good to firm ground after finishing second on good on her debut. She visits Danehill. *Sir Michael Stoute*

FLIGHT REFUND 4 ch.g. Missed Flight 123 – Settlement (USA) 75 (Irish River (FR) 131) [2001 –: f12g f12g⁴ f14.8s Dec 15] angular, workmanlike gelding: little sign of ability. *R. Hollinshead* –

FLIGHT SEQUENCE 5 b.m. Polar Falcon (USA) 126 – Doubles 85 (Damister (USA) 123) [2001 82: 10g* 10m³ Jun 11] fair performer, lightly raced: made all in minor event at Windsor in May: barely stays 1½m: best efforts on good going or firmer: twice visored at 4 yrs. *Lady Herries* 78

FLIGHT TO TUSCANY 3 b.f. Bonny Scot (IRE) 119 – Tuscan Butterfly (Beldale Flutter (USA) 130) [2001 f8g 10.2d 9.9s 14.1m 18m Jul 7] first reported foal: dam little sign of ability in bumpers/over hurdles: poor form in maidens/handicaps: should stay beyond 1¾m. *J. M. Bradley* 38

FLINT RIVER 3 b.c. Red Ransom (USA) – She's All Class (USA) (Rahy (USA) 115) [2001 84: 6m 6m⁶ 7m 7.1m 6m 6m⁴ 7g⁴ 7f 7d Oct 20] rather leggy, quite attractive colt: fairly useful handicapper: stays easy 7f: acts on firm going: tried blinkered: raced freely penultimate start: has run well when sweating: sold 22,000 gns. *R. F. Johnson Houghton* 83

FLIPSIDE (IRE) 3 b.g. Dolphin Street (FR) 125 – Trinity Hall 67 (Hallgate 127) [2001 –: e8s 8f 10.9f Jun 27] well beaten in varied company, including in seller. *J. W. Hills* –

FLIQUET BAY (IRE) 4 b.g. Namaqualand (USA) – Thatcherite (Final Straw 127) [2001 60§: 11.6g Jun 4] rather leggy gelding: temperamental maiden: often blinkered. *G. M. McCourt* – §

FLITE OF ARABY 4 b.g. Green Desert (USA) 127 – Allegedly Blue (USA) 106 (Alleged (USA) 138) [2001 65: f11g 12s 12m³ 12m⁶ 14.1m 11.5f 12s⁴ 13.8d f12g⁴ f11g f11g⁶ p13g Dec 29] leggy, close-coupled gelding: modest maiden handicapper: stays 55 a50

1½m: acts on firm going, soft and fibresand: tried visored: has played up in stall/taken good hold. *W. R. Muir*

FLOATING CHARGE   7 b.g. Sharpo 132 – Poyle Fizz (Damister (USA) 123) [2001   **84** 93: 8s 7.1g³ 8m 8g Aug 3] very tall gelding: fairly useful handicapper: best effort at 7 yrs when third in minor event at Warwick: best at 7f/1m: acts on any turf going and fibresand: blinkered/visored once apiece: has found little. *J. R. Fanshawe*

FLOATING EMBER   4 b.f. Rambo Dancer (CAN) 107 – Spark (IRE) 79 (Flash of   – Steel 120) [2001 42: f12g f14.8g 13.1m 11.1d 10.9f Jun 22] sparely-made filly: well held at 4 yrs, leaving J. L. Eyre after second start. *Miss L. A. Perratt*

FLOODGATE   4 b.g. Bin Ajwaad (IRE) 119 – Miss Haversham 81 (Salse (USA) 128)   – [2001 f9.4g May 19] first foal: dam maiden who stayed 1¼m: well beaten in maiden. *C. A. Cyzer*

FLOOT   3 b.c. Piccolo 121 – Midnight Owl (FR) (Ardross 134) [2001 73: 8.2v* 7.1g³   **76** 8.2f³ 10d 10.9d⁵ 9d 7.6g³ 8g 11m Dec 3] smallish, good-bodied colt: fair handicapper: justified favouritism at Nottingham in May: ran creditably afterwards only when third: sold 7,500 gns from J. Dunlop before final outing: stays 1m well: acts on any going: has raced freely. *G. Molteni, Italy*

FLORENTINE FLUTTER   2 b.c. (Feb 3) Machiavellian (USA) 123 – Party Doll   **72 p** 108 (Be My Guest (USA) 126) [2001 7g 6d Nov 2] 280,000Y: close-coupled, quite attractive colt: seventh foal: brother to French sprinters Titus Livius (smart) and Bahama Dream (useful), and half-brother to 3 winners, including fairly useful 1998 French 2-y-o 5.5f winner Party Zane (by Zafonic): dam French 5f (at 2 yrs) to 1m winner: mid-division in maidens at Newmarket, better effort (fair form) on debut: should do better. *J. H. M. Gosden*

FLORENZAR (IRE)   3 b.f. Inzar (USA) 112 – Nurse Tyra (USA) (Dr Blum (USA))   – [2001 8.3v Nov 8] 2,200 2-y-o: fifth foal: half-sister to 1999 2-y-o 5f and 7f winner Bescaby Blue (by Blues Traveller) and winners in Italy by Shalford and Petardia: dam unraced: 33/1, no encouragement in maiden at Windsor. *Miss S. West*

FLORHILL (IRE)   2 ch.c. (Mar 9) Danehill Dancer (IRE) 117 – Florissa (FR)   **90** (Persepolis (FR) 127) [2001 5g 5m⁴ 6f* 6.1m* 7.5f³ 7.5s* 8f⁴ 7g³ 8g⁴ 8g⁴ 8d⁵ Dec 9] IR 10,000F, 10,500Y, 5,000 2-y-o: workmanlike colt: half-brother to several winners, including fairly useful 1999 2-y-o 5f winner Tara's Girl and 5f (at 2 yrs) to 7f winner Santa Faye (both by Fayruz): dam Belgian 2-y-o 7f winner: fairly useful performer: won claimers at Brighton in June and Chepstow in July: sold from N. Littmoden 12,000 gns after fifth start and won minor event at San Sebastian later in July: good fifth, beaten about 1½ lengths by Maranilla, in listed event at Toulouse final start: stays 1m: acts on firm and soft ground. *F. Rodriguez, Spain*

FLORIAN   3 b.g. Young Ern 120 – Murmuring 69 (Kind of Hush 118) [2001 7m 7m   **56** 10.1f⁵ p6g⁴ p7g p7g⁶ Dec 28] third reported foal: dam 6f winner: modest maiden: should stay 1m: form only on polytrack: sometimes slowly away. *P. Mitchell*

FLORIDA (IRE)   3 b.f. Sri Pekan (USA) 117 – Florinda (CAN) (Vice Regent (CAN))   **44** [2001 –: f6s³ e6g f7g⁶ 10s⁶ f11g² 11.9f⁴ f12g 12f³ f12g⁶ 16.2s³ 16.2g 13.8m Sep 22] poor maiden handicapper: stays 2m: acts on firm going, soft and fibresand. *I. A. Wood*

FLORIE NIGHTINGALE   2 b.f. (Feb 17) Tragic Role (USA) – Florentynna Bay 61   **60** (Aragon 118) [2001 6m 5m⁴ 6f⁶ 7.1f² 7.1f² f7g⁶ 7g* 7m³ 7m Sep 22] smallish, leggy filly: half-sister to several winners, including smart 7f/1m performer Sunstreak (by Primo Dominie) and 8-y-o Albert The Bear: dam, 2-y-o 5f winner, half-sister to smart sprinter Superpower: modest performer: won selling at Thirsk in August: good third in nursery at Redcar: stays 7f: raced only on good ground or firmer on turf, below form on fibresand: usually races prominently. *K. A. Ryan*

FLOSSY   5 b.m. Efisio 120 – Sirene Bleu Marine (USA) (Secreto (USA) 128) [2001   **107** 107: 9g³ 10.4m⁵ 11.8d⁵ 11.9m 10d⁵ 12m⁴ 12g 12g 11.9m 13.4d* 14.6m 12g 12s⁵ 12d 10.5v 12s Nov 10] leggy, quite good-topped mare: useful performer: right back to best when winning listed rated stakes at Chester (beat Jalousie impressively by 4 lengths) in September: respectable efforts at best most other starts: was effective at 9f to 13f: acted on soft and good to firm going: had been bandaged near-fore: had taken strong hold/ wandered, and was best waited with: tough: reportedly retired to stud. *C. W. Thornton*

FLOUNCE   3 b. or gr.f. Unfuwain (USA) 131 – Flo Russell (USA) (Round Table)   **74** [2001 11m⁶ 12m² 12m² 11.5g⁴ 12m⁴ 11.8s Oct 15] closely related to smart Irish sprinter Flowing (by El Gran Senor) and useful Irish/US performer up to 1½m Crockadore (by

Nijinsky) and half-sister to several winners, including useful winner up to 1m Florazi (by Arazi): dam placed in USA: fair maiden: will be suited by 1¾m/2m: acts good to firm going, possibly not on soft: sold 37,000 gns. *Mrs A. J. Perrett*

FLOW BEAU   4 b.f. Mtoto 134 – Radiance (FR) 115 (Blakeney 126) [2001 49d: f12g   **33** f8f 8g 12f⁶ 16.2f 13.8g 16.2s⁶ f14.8g Sep 22] poor maiden: stays 1¾m: acts good to soft going and fibresand: often blinkered/visored: sometimes slowly away (has been markedly so)/races freely/looks less than keen. *J. O'Reilly*

FLOWING RIO   3 b.f. First Trump 118 – Deanta In Eirinn (Red Sunset 120) [2001   **–** 71: f7g f7g Mar 16] lengthy, rather unfurnished filly: fair performer on turf, modest on all-weather in 2000: well below form in sellers at 3 yrs. *P. C. Haslam*

FLOWLINE RIVER   3 b.f. Awesome 73 – Gymcrak Dancer 45 (Pennine Walk 120)   **–** [2001 –: 6s f9.4g⁶ 7s f7g 7m⁶ 5.7g Jun 16] no form. *D. Burchell*

FLOWNAWAY   2 b.c. (Mar 9) Polar Falcon (USA) 126 – No More Rosies 74 (Warpath   **80** 113) [2001 6m⁶ 7m⁴ 7g* 8m³ 7g Sep 15] 5,500F, 7,500Y: strong colt: has a quick action: half-brother to several winners, including 1¼m/1½m winner Eau de Cologne (by Persian Bold) and 1990 2-y-o 7f winner who stayed 15f Beachy Head (by Damister): dam 1¼m winner: fairly useful performer: won maiden at Thirsk in August: good third in valuable nursery at Newcastle: should stay 1¼m: took strong hold and hung left when well held final start. *W. Jarvis*

FLUENT   2 b.f. (May 7) Polar Falcon (USA) 126 – Lady Barrister (Law Society (USA)   **64 p** 130) [2001 7d 6v³ Nov 8] lengthy, good-bodied filly: sister to fairly useful 1997 2-y-o 6f winner Eloquent and half-sister to several winners, including fairly useful 1994 1m (in Italy) winner who stayed 1¾m Edipo Re (by Slip Anchor): dam unraced from family of Kings Lake and Salmon Leap: better effort in maidens (modest form) when third at Windsor: should stay at least 1m: should do better again. *M. L. W. Bell*

FLUR NA H ALBA   2 b.c. (Mar 25) Atraf 116 – Tyrian Belle 77 (Enchantment 115)   **88** [2001 6d⁶ 5f* 6m⁴ 5m Sep 20] strong colt: fifth foal: half-brother to 2 winners, including 1995 2-y-o 5f winner Purple Memories (by Don't Forget Me): dam sprinter: fairly useful performer: won maiden at Musselburgh in July: steadily to post, ran poorly in listed race at Ayr final start: will prove best at 5f/6f: acts on firm ground. *Miss L. A. Perratt*

FLY BACK   2 ch.g. (Feb 15) Fraam 114 – The Fernhill Flyer (IRE) 71 (Red Sunset   **–** 120) [2001 6s Sep 27] 800Y, resold 17,500Y: strong gelding: third foal: dam 2-y-o 5f/6f winner: last of 10 in maiden at Pontefract. *Mrs J. R. Ramsden*

FLY BOY FLY (USA)   3 b.g. Chief's Crown (USA) – Gillingham (USA) (Hatchet   **73** Man (USA)) [2001 68: f8g⁴ e10s⁶ f9.4g⁴ f9.4g³ 8.1f Jun 27] fair maiden: stays 9.4f: best turf efforts on good/good to soft going, and acts on fibresand: not an easy ride: sold 12,000 gns in July. *M. Johnston*

FLY GOLD AIR (USA)   2 ch.f. (Apr 3) Tactical Advantage (USA) – Festive Mood   **87** (USA) (Bering 136) [2001 5.1f³ 6g⁶ 5.1g² 6.1m³ 6m* 7g 6d³ Oct 18] $60,000Y, $92,000 2-y-o: useful-looking filly: third foal: half-sister to winners abroad by Saint Ballado (in USA) and Hazaam (in Italy): dam maiden half-sister to Racing Post Trophy winner Peter Davies: fairly useful performer: won 22-runner nursery at Doncaster in September: narrowly-beaten third in similar event at Newmarket final start, making most: stays 6f: acts on good to firm and good to soft going: free-going sort, possibly best allowed to stride along: sold 60,000 gns, sent to USA. *B. J. Meehan*

FLYING FAISAL (USA)   3 b.c. Alydeed (CAN) 120 – Peaceful Silence (USA)   **66** (Proper Reality (USA)) [2001 60: f6g⁶ f7g* f8g⁶ f7g⁶ e7g 7f 8.1f 10m 8.1g f8.5g 6.1m 6d² f6g⁶ f6g f7g f6g⁶ f6g⁵ f6g⁶ Dec 11] sturdy colt: fair handicapper: won at Wolverhampton in February: left J. Osborne after eighth start: best at 6f/7f: acts on good to soft going and fibresand: best form in blinkers: has had tongue tied: has very slowly away. *B. A. McMahon*

FLYING FLIP   7 b.m. Rolfe (USA) 77 – Needwood Sprite 58 (Joshua 129) [2001   **54** 16.2m 10.2f³ 13.8g³ 16m Aug 28] unfurnished mare: has a round action: modest handicapper nowadays: should prove best up to 1¾m: acts on firm and soft going: usually tongue tied. *R. Hollinshead*

FLYING FULMAR   2 ch.f. (Feb 5) Bahamian Bounty 116 – West Humble 93 (Pharly   **81** (FR) 130) [2001 6m² 5.1g* 6m* 6.1s³ 6m Aug 25] 42,000Y: leggy, quite good-topped filly: first foal: dam, 7f winner, half-sister to smart sprinter Leap For Joy out of half-sister to College Chapel: fairly useful performer: won maiden at Nottingham in June and nursery at Lingfield (drifted left) in July: should prove best at 5f/6f: acts on soft and good to firm going. *M. L. W. Bell*

FLYING GEM   2 ch.g. (Apr 6) Wing Park 104 – Manhattan Diamond 54 (Primo Dominie 121) [2001 5.1f⁴ 6d 6s⁵ 5f 6m 5.3s Oct 3] 3,000Y: leggy gelding: first foal: dam, maiden, effective at 6f to 8.5f: modest maiden: well below form last 3 starts (blinkered on first occasion). *A. Bailey*   **63 d**

FLYING LYRIC (IRE)   3 b.c. Definite Article 121 – Lyric Junction (IRE) (Classic Secret (USA) 91) [2001 85p: 10s² 12.3f⁵ 12v² 12f 14.8m 14s⁵ 16.2s⁵ 14g Oct 6] medium-sized colt: fairly useful performer: mostly creditable efforts at 3 yrs, including when 1¼ lengths second of 3 to Villa Carlotta in handicap at Newbury third outing: acts on any ground: probably stays 2m: joined A. King. *S. P. C. Woods*   **93**

FLYING MILLIE (IRE)   3 b.f. Flying Spur (AUS) – Sweet Pleasure 88 (Sweet Revenge 129) [2001 87: 6s⁵ 5f 6g* 6m³ 6g* 6g Sep 28] leggy, useful-looking filly: useful handicapper: won at Newmarket in July and Ascot (tended to idle when beating Ghazal by a head) in August: also ran well when close third to Idle Power at Yarmouth: last of 17 at Ascot final outing: effective at 5f/6f: acts on good to firm going. *R. M. Beckett*   **99**

FLYING PENNANT (IRE)   8 gr.g. Waajib 121 – Flying Beckee (IRE) 60 (Godswalk (USA) 130) [2001 51, a41: 8f 7.5f⁵ 7.1g 7.1m 8m⁵ Aug 29] strong gelding: has a quick action: poor handicapper: stays 1m: acts on any going: blinkered/visored: has given trouble at stalls: usually comes from off pace. *J. M. Bradley*   **44**

FLYING PETREL (USA)   3 b.f. Storm Bird (CAN) 134 – Olatha (USA) (Miswaki (USA) 124) [2001 58: 5d 6d 6m May 30] good-topped filly: modest maiden at 2 yrs: no form in 2001: sold 10,000 gns in July. *M. Johnston*   **–**

FLYING ROMANCE (IRE)   3 b.f. Flying Spur (AUS) – State Romance 67 (Free State 125) [2001 54: f6g 8.2v² 8.2s³ 8m f8g³ 8.3m 8f 10.3f⁴ 10m⁴ 12m* 10.9d³ f14.8g³ 11.7m⁵ 10m⁵ f12g⁵ f12g 12g f12s² Dec 26] angular filly: modest handicapper: left D. Barker after sixth start: won selling event at Beverley in July: stays 14.8f: acts on firm going, soft and fibresand: sometimes slowly away. *P. D. Evans*   **56**

FLYING RUN (IRE)   4 b.f. Lake Coniston (IRE) 131 – Kaskazi (Dancing Brave (USA) 140) [2001 40: 10m 8m³ 10f⁴ 8.5f⁵ 8.1m f8g 8d 8f 6m Aug 22] disappointing maiden: stays easy 1¼m: acts on firm going and fibresand: tried blinkered. *J. G. Portman*   **57 d**

FLYING SPIRIT (IRE)   2 b.c. (Mar 17) Flying Spur (AUS) – All Laughter (Vision (USA)) [2001 6m⁶ Jun 22] IR 3,800F, IR 4,000Y: fifth foal: half-brother to fairly useful Irish 9.5f winner Gabby Hayes (by Tirol): dam, placed at 7f/1m in Ireland at 2 yrs, half-sister to very smart Irish performer up to 1¾m Lord Duke: sixth of 11 in maiden at Newmarket: should stay 1m. *M. H. Tompkins*   **65**

FLYING TACKLE   3 ch.c. First Trump 118 – Frighten The Life (Kings Lake (USA) 133) [2001 –: 7m 8m 6g⁴ 6d³ 5g² 5g³ 5v² 6g* 7v Oct 26] strong, lengthy colt: fair performer: improved gradually, and won 23-runner maiden at Redcar in October: eased off once held in handicap at Doncaster final outing: best form at 5f/6f: acts on heavy going: visored last 6 starts: has wandered. *J. S. Wainwright*   **68**

FLYING TRAPEZE (USA)   3 ch.c. Trempolino (USA) 135 – Loen (USA) (Accipiter (USA)) [2001 –: 8s 7s 10g* 10.2f* 10.5m* 11f⁴ 10m⁶ 10g f9.4g Oct 9] strong, quite attractive colt: fair handicapper: won at Redcar, Bath and Haydock in June/July: ran creditably next 2 starts: will prove best up to 11f: acts on firm going. *J. Noseda*   **73**

FLYING TREATY (USA)   4 br.c. You And I (USA) 118 – Cherie's Hope (USA) (Flying Paster (USA)) [2001 71: f8g f8.5s² f9.4g² f9.4g² f8.5g* f12g² e12g* e12g 12.3g f12g³ f8g* f8g⁴ f7g² f8g f8g f12g⁶ p12g Dec 19] useful-looking colt: has reportedly been hobdayed: fairly useful performer: won handicap at Wolverhampton in February, minor event at Lingfield in March and handicap at Southwell in June: stays easy 1½m: acts on firm going (yet to race on softer than good), fibresand and equitrack: visored final start: usually races prominently: reportedly struck into eighth outing: tough. *Miss A. Stokell*   **–**
a85

FLYING TURK (IRE)   3 ch.g. Flying Spur (AUS) – Empress Wu 62 (High Line 125) [2001 74: 8s f8g 8.2g Jun 16] strong, compact gelding: fair maiden at 2 yrs: well below form in 2001. *J. A. Osborne*   **–**

FLY KICKER   4 ch.g. High Kicker (USA) – Double Birthday (Cavo Doro 124) [2001 –: f12g f8.5s⁴ f12g f11s Dec 21] poor form: may prove best up to 1m: raced only on fibresand: carried head awkwardly second outing. *E. J. Alston*   **38**

FLY MORE   4 ch.g. Lycius (USA) 124 – Double River (USA) (Irish River (FR) 131) **84**
[2001 79p: 5v 6m 6g⁴ 5m 6m³ 6m 5m 5.1g* 5m* 5m* 5.1g⁴ 5.7m 6v 5d² 5s⁶ Oct 20] very
big, strong, lengthy gelding: fairly useful handicapper: won at Bath (apprentice event),
Folkestone and Windsor in July: good second at York penultimate outing: effective at 5f/
6f: acts on good to firm and good to soft going, not on softer: hung left twelfth start.
J. M. Bradley

FLYOVER   4 b.f. Presidium 124 – Flash-By (Ilium 121) [2001 69: 11.9d 12d⁶ 12.1m   **43**
12f 10.9m⁵ Aug 27] fair handicapper in 2000: only poor form at 4 yrs: effective at 1¼m/
1½m: acts on soft and good to firm going, probably on firm: tried blinkered/visored:
sometimes slowly away: difficult ride. *B. R. Millman*

FLY WITH ME   3 b.g. Pharly (FR) 130 – Nelly Do Da 78 (Derring-Do 131) [2001   **101**
71p: e10g² e12g² 11m* 12m³ 12.3m³ 11.6m* 12m² 13.9m Aug 23] rangy gelding: useful
handicapper: progressed to win at Goodwood in May and Windsor in July: clearly best
effort when length second to Ovambo in Tote Gold Trophy at Goodwood in August:
gelded after final start (behind in Melrose Rated Stakes at York): stayed 1½m: acted on
equitrack and good to firm going: usually raced up with pace: dead. *T. G. Mills*

FOCUSED ATTRACTION (IRE)   3 b.g. Eagle Eyed (USA) 111 – Seattle Siren   **79**
(USA) 101 (Seattle Slew (USA)) [2001 71: f6s* e6g* 7v⁴ 6g 6m Jun 6] fairly useful   **a87**
handicapper on all-weather, fair on turf: won in good style at Wolverhampton in January
and Lingfield in February: below form last 2 starts: should prove best at 6f/7f: acts on
heavy going, good to firm and all-weather: sent to USA. *R. Hannon*

FOLAANN (IRE)   3 ch.c. Pennekamp (USA) 130 – Chaturanga (Night Shift (USA))   **74**
[2001 –p: 8g³ 10g 8f² 8.1d² f9.4g* a8f Dec 6] sturdy, good-bodied colt: type to carry condition: fair performer: won maiden at Wolverhampton (dismounted after line, reportedly
having gone lame for a few strides) in August: left M. Jarvis and off 4 months before final
outing: stays 9f: acts on good to soft going and fibresand. *D. J. Selvaratnam, UAE*

FOLEY MILLENNIUM (IRE)   3 ch.c. Tagula (IRE) 116 – Inshirah (USA) 90   **–**
(Caro 133) [2001 81: 6g 5.1m 7m 5.7f 5m Jun 29] tall, lengthy colt: fairly useful
performer at 2 yrs: well below form in 2001. *M. Quinn*

FOLIE DE GRANDEUR (USA)   2 ch.f. (Feb 16) Hennessy (USA) 122 – Shameem   **66**
(USA) 65 (Nureyev (USA) 131) [2001 6m 6m 6g³ 7g⁵ 7g Sep 11] $160,000F: fourth foal:
half-sister to 2 winners abroad, including a 7f winner in USA by Warning: dam thrice-
raced half-sister to US Grade 1 7f (at 2 yrs) and 9f winner Lucky Lucky Lucky: fair
maiden: best effort when third at Windsor: well held in nurseries last 2 starts: should stay
7f: hung markedly left second start: has worn tongue strap. *J. L. Dunlop*

FOLLOW A DREAM (USA)   3 b.f. Gone West (USA) – Dance A Dream 115   **90**
(Sadler's Wells (USA) 132) [2001 78p: 8f² 8.3m² 8.3g² Jul 23] smallish, attractive filly:
fairly useful maiden: good efforts at 3 yrs in handicaps at Newbury then twice at Windsor
(beaten head final occasion, wandering): bred to stay beyond 1m: acts on any going:
generosity under suspicion. *Sir Michael Stoute*

FOLLOW FLANDERS   2 b.f. (Mar 21) Pursuit of Love 124 – Pretty Poppy 67   **74 p**
(Song 132) [2001 p5g* Nov 13] 42,000Y: half-sister to several winners, including 3-y-o
Kyllachy, 5-y-o Borders and useful 5f performer Speed On (by Sharpo): dam 2-y-o 5f
winner who stayed 7.6f: 9/2, won maiden at Lingfield by ½ length from B Major, leading
late on having been slowly away: sure to improve. *H. Candy*

FOLLOW FREDDY   3 ch.g. Factual (USA) 108 – Forgiving (Jellaby 124) [2001 59:   **59**
8.5d 12g 12g⁶ Aug 15] leggy, lengthy gelding: modest maiden: should stay at least 1m:
raced only on good ground or softer. *M. Johnston*

FOLLOW LAMMTARRA (IRE)   4 ch.g. Lammtarra (USA) 134 – Felawnah   **91 d**
(USA) 111 (Mr Prospector (USA)) [2001 84: 12v⁴ 16s 16s⁴ 13.9m 17.1f 14m³ 15.9m⁵
17.2g 13.9d³ 16v² Oct 26] tall, useful-looking gelding: unimpressive mover: fairly useful
handicapper at best: below form after third outing: stays 2m: best form on going softer
than good (acts on heavy): visored seventh start: sold 32,000 gns. *M. R. Channon*

FOLLOW YOUR STAR   3 ch.g. Pursuit of Love 124 – Possessive Artiste 73 (Shareef   **70**
Dancer (USA) 135) [2001 77: 9s 10.2g³ Jul 9] sturdy gelding: fair maiden: stays 1¼m:
best efforts on good/firm going: visored (well below form) final 2-y-o start.
P. W. Harris

Victor Chandler Lupe Stakes, Goodwood—Foodbroker Fancy (breastgirth) finishes strongly to snatch it on the line from Arhaaff (third left) and Candice (left)

FOODBROKER FANCY (IRE) 3 ch.f. Halling (USA) 133 – Red Rita (IRE) 97§ **113** (Kefaah (USA) 124) [2001 83: 8s² 10.4m⁶ 9.9m* 12m 10.4g⁶ 8.1g⁶ 10f* 8g² Oct 6] smallish, sparely-made filly: smart performer: won listed races at Goodwood (by head from Arhaaff, leading post) in May and Newbury (by length from Candice) in September: best efforts when 11 lengths sixth to Sakhee in International Stakes at York fifth outing and when very good 1¼ lengths second to Independence in Sun Chariot Stakes at Newmarket final outing: equally effective at 1m/1¼m (well held in Oaks at Epsom at 1½m): unraced on heavy going, acts on any other: has been bandaged behind: held up. *D. R. C. Elsworth*

FOOLISH WHISPER 2 b.f. (Jun 4) Makbul 104 – Whisper Low (IRE) 63 (Shalford – (IRE) 124§) [2001 6s f5g Dec 3] unfurnished filly: first foal: dam, maiden, best at 5f: well beaten in maidens at Doncaster and Southwell. *R. Hollinshead*

FOOL ON THE HILL 4 b.g. Reprimand 122 – Stock Hill Lass 87 (Air Trooper 115) **78** [2001 76: 7m⁵ 7m 8m 8.3g 11.6g² 9.9d² 10.2d* 10v⁵ Nov 8] workmanlike gelding: fair handicapper: won at Bath in October: stays 11.6f: acts on heavy and good to firm going: visored last 5 starts. *L. G. Cottrell*

FOOLS RUSH IN (IRE) 2 b.c. (Jan 30) Entrepreneur 123 – Blinding (IRE) (High **87 p** Top 131) [2001 7f⁴ 7.1s² 7d⁵ Oct 2] 220,000F, 200,000Y: strong, attractive colt: fifth foal: half-brother to fairly useful 1998 2-y-o 5f winner High Priority (by Marju) and a winner in Denmark by Caerleon: dam twice-raced half-sister to smart 7f/1m performer Hadeer: fairly useful form: in frame in maidens at Newbury and Haydock prior to fifth of 16 to Sir George Turner in valuable sales race at Newmarket: should stay 1m: acts on firm and soft ground: useful prospect, and should win races. *T. G. Mills*

FOOTBALL CRAZY (IRE) 2 b.g. (Mar 29) Mujadil (USA) 119 – Schonbein (IRE) **84** 60 (Persian Heights 129) [2001 6m 6m 6m³ 7f 7m 7g² 7g⁶ 7s 7.9s* 8d Oct 19] 16,000Y: quite good-topped gelding: second foal: half-brother to 3-y-o Finn McCool: dam, lightly-raced Irish maiden, half-sister to smart sprinter Bradawn Breever: fairly useful performer: much improved to win 26-runner nursery at York in October, drifting left: ran poorly in similar event at Newmarket final start: gelded afterwards: better at 1m than shorter: acts on soft and good to firm going. *N. A. Callaghan*

FOOTPRINTS (IRE) 4 b.f. College Chapel 122 – Near Miracle (Be My Guest (USA) **73 d** 126) [2001 75: 6d 6m³ 6g 6m 7.6g 7m 6.1d 8s 7s Oct 16] sturdy, good-quartered filly: fair handicapper, on downgrade: stays 1m: acts on soft and good to firm going: tried blinkered/visored/tongue tied: has veered right/flashed tail/looked far from keen: sold 800 gns. *W. R. Muir*

FORCE FOUR (USA) 3 b.g. Gulch (USA) – Lantana Lady (CAN) (Vice Regent **66** (CAN)) [2001 10.1g⁵ 10m⁵ 12g 16v p12g⁴ f12g² Nov 26] $17,000Y, 22,000 2-y-o, resold 5,000 2-y-o: tall gelding: closely related to several winners, notably US Grade 3 7f winner Mineral Wells (by Mr Prospector) and half-brother to 2 winners, including useful 1m winner Chief Burundi (by Alleged): dam won up to 9f, including Canadian Grade 2 event: fair maiden: stayed 1½m: acted on fibresand and polytrack: dead. *D. Morris*

FORCE OF DESTINY 3 b.g. Polar Falcon (USA) 126 – Springs Welcome 86 (Blake- – ney 126) [2001 10m 12m Jun 24] workmanlike, angular gelding: sixth foal: half-brother to 3 winning stayers, including fairly useful Jonas Nightengale (by Deploy): dam 1¼m to 12.5f winner who stayed 2m: some promise in maiden at Sandown on debut: fatally injured next time. *C. A. Cyzer*

FOREIGN ACCENT 2 b.c. (Mar 25) Machiavellian (USA) 123 – Rappa Tap Tap (FR) **100 p**
111 (Tap On Wood 130) [2001 7v* Oct 26] 270,000Y: tall, good-topped colt: half-brother to several winners, including smart 1m winner Killer Instinct (by Zafonic), useful Irish 1m winner Oriane (by Nashwan) and useful 1998 2-y-o 7f winner Pick of The Pops (by High Top): dam, 6f and 1m winner, half-sister to Cezanne, Colorspin (also dam of Opera House and Kayf Tara) and Bella Colora (also dam of Stagecraft): 10/1, backward and green, impressive winner of 12-runner maiden at Doncaster by 5 lengths from Zaajel, ridden clear final 1f despite carrying head high: will stay at least 1m: probably a smart performer in the making. *J. H. M. Gosden*

FOREIGN AFFAIRS 3 ch.c. Hernando (FR) 127 – Entente Cordiale (USA) **117 p**
(Affirmed (USA)) [2001 94p: 10.1m² 9.9m* 9.9m* 10.4m* 13.9g² 12s Oct 7]
'Prescott, my office'. Presumably, the trainer, renowned for being a disciplinarian who doesn't suffer fools (or employ them), as much as for being a shrewd placer of his horses, felt obliged to give himself a tongue-in-cheek rollicking after the defeat of Foreign Affairs on his reappearance at Epsom. If Sir Mark knew the full extent of Foreign Affairs' ability at the time, he cannot have helped feeling more than a bit sheepish after seeing Foreign Affairs beaten off a BHB mark of 85 when well backed on his handicap debut. Here was a horse who was to finish the season running in the Arc. An explanation wasn't long in revealing itself, however. Lailani, who swept past Foreign Affairs late on conceding him 7 lb in the Vodafone Handicap on Oaks day, carried all before her in the following months. As it turned out, the Epsom race, which was run in a very fast timefigure incidentally, turned out to be a much more significant contest than it looked beforehand.

Like Lailani, Foreign Affairs progressed extremely well and never looked back after Epsom. He won his next three races, a minor event at Salisbury and a handicap at Goodwood in June and the valuable John Smith's Cup at York in July. Worth over £87,000 to the winner, the John Smith's Cup drew a typically competitive field, but Foreign Affairs still went off a hot favourite to beat eighteen rivals, backed down to 5/2 at the off. He made his task more difficult when failing to hold his place in the early hurly-burly, but showed a tremendous burst of speed when switched wide in the straight, so much so that the race was clearly all over as he led over a furlong out. Thereafter, he had just to be kept up to his work to beat the four-year-old Man O'Mystery by a length and three quarters, giving trainer and jockey

John Smith's Cup (Handicap), York—
Foreign Affairs justifies substantial support from Man O'Mystery and Golconda

their second success in the race in five years, following on from Pasternak in 1997. Foreign Affairs returned to York five weeks later for the Tote Ebor, being a confirmed runner only a few days before. His BHB handicap mark had risen a further 8 lb to 105 after the John Smith's Cup, but he was favourite again at 6/1. Foreign Affairs held his place more readily this time, and his rider was able to pick his moment before sending him on, gambling on his mount's stamina as he eased him to the front two furlongs out. Foreign Affairs ran on gamely, but he was cut down by his fellow three-year-old Mediterranean, who beat him by half a length in receipt of 4 lb. In the wake of this performance, connections considered supplementing Foreign Affairs for the St Leger, but opted instead to pay nearly £40,000 to supplement him for Longchamp. He was one of the outsiders on the pari-mutuel, but was by no means discredited, his rider trying to shadow Sakhee's every move before his mount was beaten quickly early in the straight, weakening into a well-held tenth of seventeen.

Foreign Affairs (ch.c. 1998)	Hernando (FR) (b 1990)	Niniski (b 1976)	Nijinsky
			Virginia Hills
		Whakilyric (b 1984)	Miswaki
			Lyrism
	Entente Cordiale (USA) (gr 1991)	Affirmed (ch 1975)	Exclusive Native
			Won't Tell You
		Likely Split (ro 1977)	Little Current
			Caterina

Foreign Affairs is from the second crop of the Prix du Jockey Club winner Hernando, who had another good year with his three-year-olds, after the success of Holding Court in 2000. Mr Combustible (Geoffrey Freer) and Asian Heights

The Speculators' "Foreign Affairs"

(Predominate Stakes) were other good winners in 2001 who will vie with Foreign Affairs as Hernando's best four-year-old in 2002. Hernando is also responsible for two other produce of the dam of Foreign Affairs, the once-raced Entente Cordiale, namely the two-year-old Affaire d'Amour and the four-year-old Bien Entendu. The latter was favourite for the Derby for a while after his debut success at Newmarket as a three-year-old, but he has been seen only once since because of a string of problems. Entente Cordiale is a half-sister to the smart middle-distance performer Pegnitz and further back this is the family of the very smart French sprinters Cricket Ball and Ancient Regime. It remains to be seen if Foreign Affairs, who was bred by one of his stable's principal owners Kirsten Rausing before being sold for 20,000 guineas as a yearling, has more speed than stamina. He may well prove better at ten furlongs and twelve furlongs than over the Ebor trip in the long run. Foreign Affairs is still inexperienced, the Arc having been only his sixth race on turf after two runs on the all-weather at Wolverhampton late on as a two-year-old, which yielded a second and an easy win. There should be more improvement in him. A quite good-topped colt, who had raced only on good ground or firmer prior to Longchamp, Foreign Affairs is a game and genuine sort and has been expertly handled so far. There are surely pattern races to be won with him. *Sir Mark Prescott*

FOREIGN EDITOR 5 ch.g. Magic Ring (IRE) 115 – True Precision 84 (Presidium 124) [2001 69, a92: f7s⁶ f6s⁵ f7g⁶ f7g⁶ f6g⁵ 7m 6m 7g 7g⁵ 7.1g f7g⁶ f7g⁶ f6g⁴ f8g³ Dec 14] workmanlike gelding: fairly useful handicapper: left K. Ryan after seventh start: stays 1m: acts on good to firm going, fibresand and equitrack: occasionally blinkered. *J. J. Quinn* — **62 a83**

FOREST BRIDE (USA) 4 ch.f. Woodman (USA) 126 – Lady In White 94 (Shareef Dancer (USA) 135) [2001 51: f12s f9.4g Feb 15] seems of little account nowadays. *J. A. Osborne* — **–**

FOREST DANCER (IRE) 3 b.c. Charnwood Forest (IRE) 125 – Forest Berries (IRE) (Thatching 131) [2001 90: 8d 8g³ 7.9g 7m⁴ 8.2f⁴ 8m 8f* 8m 7m⁵ 8s 8d Oct 18] tall, rather leggy colt: fairly useful handicapper: won at Newbury in July: creditable efforts otherwise only when in frame and when fifth: stays 1m: acts on firm going, good to soft and fibresand: tends to be slowly away: has carried head awkwardly: sold 12,500 gns. *R. Hannon* — **88**

FOREST DREAM 6 b.m. Warrshan (USA) 117 – Sirenivo (USA) 113 (Sir Ivor 135) [2001 51d: 16d⁶ 12f 16.4g 14.1d³ 16g Sep 5] modest handicapper at best nowadays: appeared to run well fourth outing (could be worth a rating of 57): stays 1¾m: acts on firm going, soft and fibresand: has had tongue tied. *L. A. Dace* — **?**

FOREST HEATH (IRE) 4 gr.g. Common Grounds 118 – Caroline Lady (JPN) (Caro 133) [2001 88: 10g 10m 10g⁵ 12m⁵ 10.5d³ 10d² 9.9d⁵ 8d p12g p12g Dec 19] quite good-topped gelding: not a good walker: has a short, round action: fairly useful handicapper: effective at 1¼m/easy 1½m: yet to race on heavy, acts on any other turf going and polytrack: sometimes visored (hung badly left once): has looked headstrong: possibly not one to trust implicitly. *H. J. Collingridge* — **88 a79**

FOREST LEAF (IRE) 3 b.g. Charnwood Forest (IRE) 125 – Besito 79 (Wassl 125) [2001 8d* 7.6m⁵ 8m⁶ 9g Sep 8] 18,000F, 27,000Y, 50,000 2-y-o: good-bodied gelding: fifth foal: half-brother to 3 winners, including 1m winner who stayed 1¼m Simlet (by Forzando) and 4-y-o Kinsman: dam 2m winner: fair form: won maiden at Newbury in April: not discredited, though unable to challenge, when fifth in minor event at Lingfield following month: sold from M. Jarvis 12,000 gns and well held after: should be as effective over 1¼m as 1m: sent to Macau. *Patrick Carey, Ireland* — **76**

FOREST LIGHT (IRE) 3 gr.f. Rainbow Quest (USA) 134 – Woodland Garden (Godswalk (USA) 130) [2001 –p: 10m 12f 12.6f* 11.9f 12m³ 14.1m Sep 6] rather leggy filly: fair handicapper: won maiden at Warwick in June: stays 1¾m: acts on firm going. *R. F. Johnson Houghton* — **69**

FOREST MOON 3 b.f. Charnwood Forest (IRE) 125 – Moon Watch 64 (Night Shift (USA)) [2001 53: e6g³ e7g⁵ e6g³ e6g⁶ 5m³ 6m⁴ 5g 6m 6g 6m 8m f8.5g f7g² f7s Dec 18] smallish, good-bodied filly: modest performer: stays 7f: acts on good to firm ground, equitrack and fibresand: sold 2,200 gns. *Andrew Reid* — **55**

FOREST PRIZE 2 b.f. (Apr 13) Charnwood Forest (IRE) 125 – Midnight's Reward 84 (Night Shift (USA)) [2001 6m⁵ 6m 6m* 6g* 7m 6m 7d 7d Oct 9] 13,500Y: leggy filly: half-sister to several winners, including 3-y-o Pasithea and French 9f winner Damaya (by — **77**

Formidable): dam 2-y-o 5f winner: fair performer: won maiden and minor event at Haydock in July/August: no better than mid-field in nurseries: should stay 7f. *T. D. Easterby*

FOREST QUEEN   4 b.f. Risk Me (FR) 127 – Grey Cree 64 (Creetown 123) [2001 –:   –
6m 8m 7f 8d 5m 6m 5m 5g 5g Sep 19] no form since 2 yrs. *J. S. Wainwright*

FOREST RIDGE   2 b. or br.g. (Mar 8) Charnwood Forest (IRE) 125 – Away To Me   – p
(Exit To Nowhere (USA) 122) [2001 8d Oct 25] 62,000Y: first foal: dam unraced: 10/1,
slowly away and not knocked about when well held in maiden at Bath: should do better.
Mrs A. J. Perrett

FOREST TUNE (IRE)   3 b.g. Charnwood Forest (IRE) 125 – Swift Chorus (Music   83 d
Boy 124) [2001 10s* 10s⁵ 8g 8.5f⁶ 8g 8g 8.1g 10.5v⁶ 8d⁴ 7v Oct 26] 33,000Y: well-made,
attractive gelding: fifth foal: half-brother to several winners, including 1999 2-y-o 5f
winner Welch's Dream (by Brief Truce) and 7f winner Miss Skye (by Common Grounds):
dam, Irish 2-y-o 6f winner, from very good middle-distance family: fairly useful performer at best: won maiden at Pontefract in April: creditable effort 2 outings after, but
mostly well below form subsequently, including in blinkers final one: gelded afterwards:
not sure to stay beyond 1¼m: acts on soft going: tongue tied seventh outing. *B. Hanbury*

FOREVER LOVED   2 ch.f. (Mar 3) Deploy 131 – Truly Madly Deeply (Most   72
Welcome 131) [2001 6m 7.1m 7g² 7m⁶ 8d Oct 19] heavy-topped filly: second foal: dam,
no form, half-sister to 3-y-o Superstar Leo: easily best effort (fair form) when ½-length
second of 17 to Sir George Turner in maiden at Leicester, rallying: well beaten in nursery
final start: should stay at least 1m. *D. Haydn Jones*

FOREVER MY LORD   3 b.g. Be My Chief (USA) 122 – In Love Again (IRE) 86   69 d
(Prince Rupert (FR) 121) [2001 75: 7s⁴ 7.9g 7m 7m⁶ 10g⁶ 10g⁶ 10m 8m Sep 12] good-
bodied gelding: fair performer at best, on the downgrade: usually races freely, and may
prove best around 7f: acts on soft and good to firm ground: tried blinkered/tongue tied.
R. F. Johnson Houghton

FOREVER TIMES   3 b.f. So Factual (USA) 120 – Simply Times (USA) 64 (Dodge   98
(USA)) [2001 74: f7g 6s 7.6f 7m* 7m² 7f* 7.1m⁶ 7g⁶ 7m² 7d² 7d 6g 6d* 6d⁴ Nov 2]
smallish, sparely-made filly: unimpressive mover: useful performer: won maiden at
Redcar in May, handicap at Chester in June and minor event (apprentices) at Catterick in
October: best effort when second to Mr Mahoose in handicap at Newmarket ninth outing:
effective at 6f/7f: probably acts on any turf going, well beaten only run on fibresand:
tough and consistent. *T. D. Easterby*

FOR EVVA SILCA   2 ch.f. (Apr 15) Piccolo 121 – Silca-Cisa 93 (Hallgate 127)   60
[2001 5.2s⁴ 6m 5m Jun 4] leggy, quite good-topped filly: half-sister to several winners,
notably 5-y-o Golden Silca: dam 5f winner, including at 2 yrs: modest maiden: may prove
best at 5f/6f: reportedly broke blood vessel final start. *M. R. Channon*

FORGE VALLEY LADY   2 ch.f. (Apr 9) Hamas (IRE) 125§ – Salul (Soviet Star   60
(USA) 128) [2001 5m⁴ 5g⁴ 6m³ 7g 7m 6d Oct 8] 2,000Y: workmanlike filly: third foal:
half-sister to 3-y-o Senator's Alibi and a winner in Sweden by Hernando: dam unraced
half-sister to 2 useful performers from very good US family: modest maiden: below form
in nurseries last 3 starts: should stay 7f. *J. L. Eyre*

FORGOTTEN INVITE   3 ch.f. Forzando 122 – Uninvited 73 (Be My Guest (USA)   –
126) [2001 9m 8d Aug 19] 500Y: fourth foal: dam, maiden on Flat, winning selling
hurdler: tailed off in maidens. *D. A. Nolan*

FORGOTTEN TIMES (USA)   7 ch.m. Nabeel Dancer (USA) 120 – Etoile d'Amore   75
(USA) 81 (The Minstrel (CAN) 135) [2001 80: 5m 5.3m 5m 5m⁵ 5m² 5m 5m 5g 5g⁶
5.3g⁶ 5.3m⁶ 5.7m 5g* 5m² Sep 26] small, good-quartered mare: fair handicapper: won at
Epsom in September: effective at 5f/easy 6f: acts on firm going, soft and equitrack:
blinkered once, usually visored: often claimer ridden: goes well on downhill tracks: sold
4,000 gns. *K. T. Ivory*

FOR HEAVENS SAKE   4 b.g. Rambo Dancer (CAN) 107 – Angel Fire (Nashwan   62 §
(USA) 135) [2001 67§: 8m 10.1m³ 12.6d 16.5m⁵ 10g⁶ 10d 8.5s Aug 16] compact gelding:
modest maiden handicapper: best at 1¼m: acts on firm going, soft and fibresand: tried
blinkered/visored: often looks ungenuine/finds little: sent to Spain. *B. S. Rothwell*

FORMAL PARTY   3 ch.f. Formidable (USA) 125 – Tea Colony (USA) (Pleasant   –
Colony (USA)) [2001 55: 8.2s 7m 6f 6.1m 6m 6m Aug 30] modest maiden at 2 yrs: well
held in 2001. *T. D. McCarthy*

FORMERIC   5 ch.g. Formidable (USA) 125 – Irish Limerick 89 (Try My Best (USA)   –
130) [2001 7m 7m 7m Jul 12] of little account. *Miss L. C. Siddall*

FORONLYMO 2 b.g. (Mar 20) Forzando 122 – Polish Descent (IRE) (Danehill   **70**
(USA) 126) [2001 5s² 6g² 6m⁶ 6m 6s⁴ f6g* 6d f6g⁶ p7g f6g² f6s* Dec 26] 8,500F,   **a82**
15,000Y: small gelding: second living foal: half-brother to a 1999 2-y-o 6f/7f winner in
Italy by Cyrano de Bergerac: dam unraced: fairly useful on all-weather, fair on turf: won
claimers at Wolverhampton in October and December: should stay 7f: acts on soft ground
and fibresand: visored last 6 starts. *K. R. Burke*

FORTHECHOP 4 b.g. Minshaanshu Amad (USA) 91§ – Cousin Jenny (Midyan   **–**
(USA) 124) [2001 42: f8g⁵ f9.4g f8.5s⁵ f8s f9.4g f12g f11g⁶ 17.1f f16.2g Jun 20] of little
account nowadays. *Mrs H. L. Walton*

FORT SUMTER (USA) 5 b.g. Sea Hero (USA) 124 – Gray And Red (USA) (Wolf   **–**
Power (SAF)) [2001 67: f12g³ f11g* f11g⁶ 11.6g 12s May 17] tall gelding: fair performer: **a67**
won handicap at Southwell in February: stays 1¾m, not 2m: acts on soft going, good to
firm and fibresand/equitrack: has run moodily when visored. *P. R. Hedger*

FORTUNE FOUND (IRE) 3 b.f. Fumo di Londra (IRE) 108 – Trillick (IRE) 71   **–**
(Treasure Kay 114) [2001 –: f7g Apr 27] strong filly: tongue tied when well held both
outings in maidens. *C. G. Cox*

FORTUNE ISLAND (IRE) 2 b.c. (Apr 2) Turtle Island (IRE) 123 – Blue Kestrel   **76 p**
(IRE) 70 (Bluebird (USA) 125) [2001 8d 8g⁴ 8s⁴ Nov 9] IR 24,000F, IR 180,000Y:
strong, lengthy colt: third foal: dam Irish 7f and 9f winner: fair form in maidens: fourth at
Redcar and Doncaster: will probably stay 1¼m: capable of better. *S. P. C. Woods*

FORTUNE POINT (IRE) 3 ch.g. Cadeaux Genereux 131 – Mountains of Mist   **66**
(IRE) 80 (Shirley Heights 130) [2001 89: 7g 7.1v² 6g³ Oct 19] strong, angular gelding:
fairly useful maiden at 2 yrs: only fair in 2001: should stay 1m: raced only on good going
or softer: visored final 2 starts: sold 18,000 gns. and gelded. *J. Noseda*

FORTUNE'S FOOL 2 b.c. (Mar 31) Zilzal (USA) 137 – Peryllys 67 (Warning 136)   **57 d**
[2001 6m³ 7m⁶ 7.1m 6d Oct 8] 4,000Y: leggy colt: third foal: half-brother to 4-y-o Honest
Warning and a winner in Belgium by Primo Dominie: dam, maiden who stayed 1m,
half-sister to smart sprinter Cragside: modest form on debut: showed little after: sold 600
gns. *B. Smart*

FORTY FORTE 5 b.g. Pursuit of Love 124 – Cominna (Dominion 123) [2001 78:   **78**
f8g² e10g⁶ f8.5g 9.2m f8g* f8g⁴ f8g² 10g³ f9.4g⁴ 8.2m 10.3d* 10v 11.7d f8g³ f8.5g*
f9.4g f9.4s⁴ Dec 26] fair handicapper: left T. D. Barron after third start: won at Southwell
(penultimate outing for K. Burke) in July, Chester (by 13 lengths, soon well clear under
excellent ride from 5-lb claimer G. Gibbons) in September and Wolverhampton in
November: best at 1m/1¼m: acts on heavy going, good to firm, fibresand and equitrack:
free-going front runner, needs to dominate. *Miss S. J. Wilton*

FORTY ON LINE 2 ch.f. (Mar 2) Pharly (FR) 130 – Charming Bride 56 (Charmer   **102 p**
123) [2001 6m⁴ 8f* 8f* Nov 23] second foal: dam 7f winner: fourth in maiden at Newmarket (only outing for S. Williams): won maiden at Santa Anita in October and Grade 3
Miesque Stakes at Hollywood (by a length from Riskaverse, making all) in November:
stays 1m: acts on firm going: useful, and may well improve again. *R. B. Hess jnr, USA*

FORUM FINALE (USA) 3 b.f. Silver Hawk (USA) 123 – Silk Masque (USA) 91   **73**
(Woodman (USA) 126) [2001 74: f9.4s² f8g² e10g e10g⁵ f12g² 11.6s 12.1m² 12.3m³
11.9f* 12m⁶ Aug 3] tall, quite good-topped filly: has scope: fair handicapper: ran well
last 4 starts, winning at Haydock in July: should stay beyond 1½m: acts on firm going,
soft and fibresand: tongue tied last 4 starts. *M. Johnston*

FORWOOD (IRE) 3 b.g. Charnwood Forest (IRE) 125 – Silver Hut (USA) 80 (Silver   **98**
Hawk (USA) 123) [2001 103: 8d⁶ 8m⁴ 7m Dec 16] rather leggy, useful-looking gelding:
useful performer: well held in Craven Stakes at Newmarket on reappearance: better
effort, though still below 2-y-o best, when fourth to Dandoun in minor event at Doncaster
in May: gelded, left M. Jarvis and off 7 months before final outing: stays 1m: yet to race
on extremes of going: usually held up. *P. Chapple-Hyam, Hong Kong*

FOR YOUR EYES ONLY 7 b.g. Pursuit of Love 124 – Rivers Rhapsody 104 (Dom-   **–**
inion 123) [2001 –: e10s f9.4g⁶ f6g Mar 10] one-time smart winner up to 1m: usually
blinkered. *C. E. Brittain*

FORZACURITY 2 ch.g. (Apr 10) Forzando 122 – Nice Lady 65 (Connaught 130)   **66**
[2001 6.1m⁶ 6g⁵ 7.1s² 7.5g* 8m² 8v³ Oct 16] 15,000Y: strong gelding: brother to 6f
winner Newlands Corner and half-brother to several winners, including 7f winner
Cinnamon Lady (by Emarati): dam second at 9.4f: fair performer: won selling nursery at
Beverley in September: good efforts in nurseries at Musselburgh and Ayr (visored) last 2
starts: stays 1m: acts on heavy and good to firm going: sold 7,000 gns. *R. M. Beckett*

FORZA FIGLIO 8 b.g. Warning 136 – Wish You Well 78 (Sadler's Wells (USA) 132) **72**
[2001 80: 10d³ 10m 10g³ 10g³ 10g* 10.2g⁶ 10g 10d 9.9d² 10.2d 10s³ Nov 5] strong, angular
gelding: fair handicapper nowadays: won at Windsor in July: stays 1½m: acts on soft and
good to firm going: tried blinkered. *M. Kettle*

FORZA GLORY 2 ch.f. (Feb 21) Forzando 122 – Glory Isle 60 (Hittite Glory 125) **57**
[2001 6g 6s 6v⁶ p8g Nov 15] 2,000Y: half-sister to several winners, including fairly
useful 7f (at 2 yrs) to 1¼m winner Rio Piedras (by Kala Shikari): dam 9f winner: easily
best effort in maidens (modest form) when sixth at Windsor: appeared to lose action final
outing: should stay 1m. *Miss B. Sanders*

FORZA VITALE 2 b.f. (Feb 26) Forzando 122 – Meeson Times 71 (Enchantment **–**
115) [2001 5d May 21] 11,000Y: second foal: half-sister to fairly useful 2000 2-y-o 5f
winner Mise En Scene (by Lugana Beach): dam 5f and (including at 2 yrs) 6f winner:
25/1, soundly beaten in maiden at Windsor. *G. B. Balding*

FOSTON FOX 4 b.f. Foxhound (USA) 103 – Enaam 65§ (Shirley Heights 130) [2001 **43 §**
45: 6m 7m 6d 6g 7d 7g³ 7m⁵ 8.1g Sep 13] small, sturdy filly: poor mover: poor maiden:
effective at 6f to 1m: acts on good to firm going, probably on heavy: often blinkered:
sometimes slowly away/looks reluctant: not one to trust. *C. B. B. Booth*

FOSTON SECOND (IRE) 4 ch.f. Lycius (USA) 124 – Gentle Guest (IRE) (Be My **–**
Guest (USA) 126) [2001 41: 11.6m 12.6f Jun 27] no longer of any account. *C. Weedon*

FOUETTE 3 b.f. Saddlers' Hall (IRE) 126 – Tight Spin (High Top 131) [2001 –: 10g **65**
10d 14.1m⁴ 16g⁵ 14.1s 11.6v⁶ Oct 29] sturdy, lengthy filly: fair maiden: should stay 2m
(beaten before stamina became issue when tried at trip): easily best efforts on good/good
to firm going: sold 2,100 gns. *N. A. Graham*

FOUNDRY LANE 10 b.g. Mtoto 134 – Eider 80 (Niniski (USA) 125) [2001 81: 14m **77**
16.2g³ 14m⁴ 16m⁴ 16m⁶ 16.1f² Sep 10] rangy gelding: fair handicapper nowadays:
should stay beyond 2m: acts on any going: not an easy ride, but is consistent. *Mrs
M. Reveley*

FOURDANED (IRE) 8 b.g. Danehill (USA) 126 – Pro Patria 86 (Petingo 135) [2001 **– §**
–§: 12g Aug 17] small gelding: temperamental maiden nowadays: tried blinkered.
Mrs L. C. Jewell

FOUR EAGLES (USA) 3 b.g. Lear Fan (USA) 130 – Bloomingly (ARG) (Candy **74**
Stripes (USA) 115) [2001 82p: 8s⁶ 8m³ 9.9m⁵ 8g⁵ 10m⁴ Jul 21] close-coupled gelding:
good mover: fair maiden: seems to stay 1¼m: acts on good to firm and good to soft
ground: blinkered penultimate outing. *D. R. C. Elsworth*

FOUR LEGS GOOD (IRE) 3 b.f. Be My Guest (USA) 126 – Karine (Habitat 134) **–**
[2001 58: 8m 7.5s 7s Oct 5] smallish, sturdy filly: modest maiden at 2 yrs: well held in
2001. *G. C. Bravery*

FOURLOCH (IRE) 3 b.f. Fourstars Allstar (USA) 122 – Loch Wee (IRE) (Colmore **45**
Row 111) [2001 10m⁴ 7.5f 7f⁵ 10.1m⁴ 8g f8g Dec 10] IR 900F, IR 1,200Y: small, sparely-
made filly: first foal: dam well held in bumper/over hurdles in Ireland: poor maiden:
pulled hard fourth outing. *N. G. Richards*

FOUR MEN (IRE) 4 b.g. Nicolotte 118 – Sound Pet (Runnett 125) [2001 41: f8.5s⁵ **–**
f9.4g f12g⁶ 10v 10s f12g 12.3s 10d 8.1m 7f 8m 7f⁶ 7.1g 8m 8.2f² 8f 7m 6m 7.1d 8g 8f 7s
8.1m 10d 8m 8d 8g 10.1d⁵ 7.2g 9.2g 8f 6m 7d 7g 8.2s Nov 5] of little account nowadays.
A. Berry

FOURSOME 2 b.f. (Feb 5) Makbul 104 – Ra Ra (Lord Gayle (USA) 124) [2001 5m³ **69**
6.1m⁵ 6.1v* 6d Oct 19] rather leggy filly: half-sister to several winners, including 1m and
11f winner Broctune Line (by Safawan) and two 6f winners by Efisio: dam unraced: fair
performer: easily best effort when winning maiden at Nottingham in September: well
held in sales race at Newmarket final start: will stay 7f: acts on heavy ground: sold 3,500
gns. *H. Candy*

FOURTH DIMENSION (IRE) 2 b.c. (Apr 27) Entrepreneur 123 – Isle of Spice **59 ?**
(USA) 74 (Diesis 133) [2001 8g⁴ 8m 8s Oct 16] 38,000Y: sturdy colt: second foal: closely
related to 3-y-o Zanzibar: dam, 9.7f winner, from good family: best effort in maidens
(modest form) when fourth at Kempton: should stay 1¼m. *A. C. Stewart*

FOURTH TIME LUCKY 5 b.g. Timeless Times (USA) 99 – Wych Willow (Hard **–**
Fought 125) [2001 31: f8.5s f6g 5.1v 6s 8.1m 7f 8m 7m Jun 23] of little account
nowadays. *B. W. Murray*

FOXCOTE 2 ch.c. (Jan 20) Lycius (USA) 124 – Birdlip (USA) (Sanglamore (USA) **84**
126) [2001 6g* 6m³ 5g³ 7d³ 7.1m Sep 17] sturdy colt: second foal: dam unraced half-
sister to high-class miler Distant View out of Prix Morny and Prix Robert Papin winner

Seven Springs: fairly useful performer: won maiden at Windsor in July: respectable efforts in nurseries last 2 starts: stays 7f: sold 8,000 gns, sent to Barbados. *B. W. Hills*

FOX COTTAGE (IRE)   3 ch.f. So Factual (USA) 120 – Ever So Artful (Never So – Bold 135) [2001 –: 8f 7.6g Aug 30] seemingly of little account. *D. W. P. Arbuthnot*

FOXES LAIR (IRE)   3 b.g. Muhtarram (USA) 125 – Forest Lair (Habitat 134) [2001   **56** 68: f7g⁴ 8d 8m 10g⁵ 7.1d 6g 10m 12d Oct 9] tall gelding: modest maiden handicapper: probably stays 1¼m (raced too freely at 1½m): acts on soft going (probably on good to firm) and fibresand: sometimes tongue tied. *M. Dods*

FOXY PRINCESS (IRE)   2 b.f. (Apr 8) College Chapel 122 – Love Dove (IRE)   **59** (Last Tycoon 131) [2001 5.2m 6m⁴ 6g f6g Oct 18] IR 16,000F, IR 30,000Y: fifth foal: dam, French 9.5f winner, out of close relative to very smart sprinter Nabeel Dancer: modest maiden: well held after fourth at Goodwood: not sure to stay beyond 6f: sold 800 gns. *R. Hannon*

FOXY ROCKETTE   2 ch.f. (Apr 13) Rock City 120 – Absolutley Foxed 45 (Absalom – 128) [2001 7g Aug 12] second foal: dam, maiden, out of half-sister to Oaks second Mabel: always behind in maiden at Leicester. *C. N. Kellett*

FOYS (FR)   2 b.g. (Feb 12) Danehill Dancer (IRE) 117 – Ack's Secret (USA) (Ack Ack   **74** (USA)) [2001 5.7f² Jul 26] 260,000 francs Y, 40,000 2-y-o: half-brother to several winners, including fairly useful 11.5f winner Ack's Again and 15f to 17.5f winner Hunting Ground (both by Dancing Brave): dam US Grade 1 9f/1¼m winner: short-head second of 11 to Piccolo Party in maiden at Bath: subsequently gelded. *R. Charlton*

FRAAMTASTIC   4 b.f. Fraam 114 – Fading (Pharly (FR) 130) [2001 e13g 10g 6m³   **48** 6g 7g 6s 8s p7g p7g Dec 28] fifth foal: sister to 3-y-o Dayglow Dancer: dam unraced: poor maiden: probably stays 7f: virtually no show on debut. *B. A. Pearce*

FRAGARIA GIRL   2 b.f. (Apr 21) Fraam 114 – Chaconia Girl (Bay Express 132) – [2001 6m 7.1m 10d Nov 2] eighth foal: half-sister to 7f/1m winner Digger Doyle (by Cragador): dam of little account: tailed off in maidens. *M. A. Allen*

FRAGRANT CLOUD   3 b.f. Zilzal (USA) 137 – Stardyn (Star Appeal 133) [2001 – 8m 7.1s 7m⁶ Aug 16] 19,000Y: seventh foal: half-sister to several winners, notably very smart 6f (at 2 yrs)/7f winner Young Ern (by Efisio): dam maiden who stayed 1½m: well held in maidens. *E. A. Wheeler*

FRAGRANT STORM (USA)   2 b.f. (Feb 10) Storm Bird (CAN) 134 – Subtle   **80** Fragrance (USA) (Crafty Prospector (USA)) [2001 5s⁴ 5m² 5.1f* 5m³ 5d 6.1g Aug 20] $30,000Y: smallish, rather leggy filly: first foal: dam winner up to 7f in USA at 2 yrs: fairly useful performer: won maiden at Nottingham in June, dictating pace: good third at York, best effort in nurseries after: should stay 6f: acts on firm going, not at best on softer than good. *M. Johnston*

FRAGRANT VIEW (USA)   2 ch.f. (Jan 30) Distant View (USA) 126 – Musicanti   **79 p** (USA) (Nijinsky (CAN) 138) [2001 7d² Oct 15] tall, useful-looking filly: has scope: second foal: sister to 4-y-o Distant Music: dam, French 14.5f winner, half-sister to top-class US middle-distance performer Vanlandingham: 3/1 and backward, neck second of 20 to Trojan Princess in maiden at Leicester, sweeping through to lead well over 1f out and headed only near line: should stay 1m: sure to improve and win a race. *B. W. Hills*

FRAMPANT   4 ch.f. Fraam 114 – Potent (IRE) (Posen (USA)) [2001 58: f6g 5.1v 5v – 5.1d 5m f6g Jul 20] of little account nowadays. *M. Quinn*

FRANCIS FLUTE   3 b.g. Polar Falcon (USA) 126 – Darshay (FR) 87 (Darshaan 133) – [2001 11.1d⁴ 10m⁶ f8.5g Dec 11] 20,000F, IR 60,000Y, 9,000 2-y-o: second foal: half-brother to useful winner up to 1¼m Deal Fair (by Grand Lodge): dam, fairly useful 2-y-o maiden, later won over 9f in Belgium at 4 yrs: little form: left B. MacTaggart and off over 6 months after second outing: likely to prove best short of 11f. *E. J. Alston*

FRANCKEN (ITY)   2 ro.g. (Apr 19) Petit Loup (USA) 123 – Filicaia 79 (Sallust 134) – [2001 6f 6.1d Sep 21] fourth foal: dam 5f/6f winner: last in maidens. *N. Tinkler*

FRANCPORT   5 b.g. Efisio 120 – Elkie Brooks 82 (Relkino 131) [2001 85: 6.1v³ 5v*   **80** 6d² 5m 6m 5m 6g⁶ 5m³ 6m 5v 5s⁴ f6g f6g⁶ p6g⁴ p7g Dec 12] big, lengthy gelding: fairly   **a67** useful handicapper on turf, fair on all-weather: won apprentice event at Ripon (edged right) in April: effective at 5f (given good test) to easy 7f: acts on fibresand/polytrack, heavy and good to firm going: tried blinkered: often slowly away. *K. A. Ryan*

FRANDANEIL   2 b.f. (Mar 20) Emarati (USA) 74 – Luminary (Kalaglow 132) [2001   **48** 5s⁴ 5m 6m 7g⁴ 6d⁴ f7g 7g Oct 19] 3,500F, IR 7,500Y: close-coupled filly: second foal:

dam unraced daughter of Cheveley Park and Coronation Stakes winner Jacinth: poor maiden: stays 7f. *J. J. Quinn*

FRANKIES DREAM (IRE) 2 b.c. (Mar 16) Grand Lodge (USA) 125 – Galyph (USA) 72 (Lyphard (USA) 132) [2001 7m⁴ 7m³ Sep 22] IR 80,000Y: sturdy colt: third foal: half-brother to Irish 7f winner Echo Canyon (by Lahib): dam, Irish 1¼m winner, from good family: fairly useful form in frame in maidens at Leicester and Newmarket, keeping on well when third of 18 to demoted Moon Ballad in latter: should stay 1¼m: well up to winning a race. *T. G. Mills* **92**

FRANKLIN-D 5 ch.g. Democratic (USA) 101 – English Mint 66 (Jalmood (USA) 126) [2001 –, a53: f7g⁵ f8.5g 7m f7g 7m⁵ 8g Aug 20] poor maiden nowadays: best up to sharp 7f: acts on firm going and fibresand/equitrack: visored twice. *J. R. Jenkins* **35**

FRANKLIN LAKES 6 ch.g. Sanglamore (USA) 126 – Eclipsing (IRE) 93 (Baillamont (USA) 124) [2001 44, a38: 5g 7m Aug 27] of little account nowadays. *M. R. Bosley* **–**

FRANK MOR (IRE) 2 ch.g. (May 3) Common Grounds 118 – Drowsy Maggie (Tumble Wind (USA)) [2001 f5g³ f5g 6m⁴ 6.3d 6.1g² 6m⁶ 7d² 7s Oct 20] IR 7,000Y: strong gelding: sixth foal: half-brother to 3 winners in Ireland, including 1992 2-y-o 6f winner State Of The Art (by Dominion Royale) and 7f winner Rachael's Delight (by Pips Pride): dam Irish maiden: fair maiden: second at Nottingham (nursery) and Newcastle: stays 7f: acts on good to firm and good to soft going. *K. A. Ryan* **75**

FRANK MURPHY 2 ch.g. (Feb 16) Dr Devious (IRE) 127 – Bacinella (USA) (El Gran Senor (USA) 136) [2001 5v f5g 6m 7.5f³ 7.5g Sep 19] 2,000Y: close-coupled gelding: first foal: dam unraced sister to useful 7f winner Mandarina from family of Derby runner-up City Honours: poor maiden: third in seller at Beverley: will stay at least 1m: acts on firm ground. *M. W. Easterby* **40**

FRANKSKIPS 2 b.g. (Feb 22) Bishop of Cashel 122 – Kevins Lady (Alzao (USA) 117) [2001 8d⁴ Oct 19] 1,600F: half-brother to a winner in Hungary by Slip Anchor: dam well beaten in bumper: 66/1, staying-on fourth of 20 to Music Club in maiden at Newmarket: showed a round action: should stay 1¼m: likely to improve. *B. R. Johnson* **87 p**

FRATERNITY 4 b.g. Grand Lodge (USA) 125 – Catawba 98 (Mill Reef (USA) 141) [2001 74: e12g* a10f a10f Dec 6] fair performer: won maiden at Lingfield in January: sold 16,000 gns from W. Jarvis following month, then well held after: stays 1½m: acts on good to soft going and equitrack. *C. Wroe, UAE* **66**

FRATERNIZE 3 ch.g. Spectrum (IRE) 126 – Proud Titania (IRE) 103 (Fairy King (USA)) [2001 8.2f² 10.5d² 9d² 9.7m⁵ Aug 27] first foal: dam Irish 7f winner (including at 2 yrs) who stayed 1m: runner-up in maidens at Nottingham, Haydock and Newcastle (again took strong hold, carried head awkwardly and unable/unwilling to go past): below form final outing: unlikely to stay beyond 10.5f: probably not one to trust: sold 8,500 gns in October, and gelded. *Sir Michael Stoute* **73**

FRAULEIN 2 b.f. (Mar 27) Acatenango (GER) 127 – Francfurter 89 (Legend of France (USA) 124) [2001 7g⁵ 8d* 7f* 8s⁵ Sep 29] big, good-bodied filly: third foal: half-sister to a German 6.5f (at 2 yrs) and 9f winner by Mtoto: dam, 1¼m winner, from good family: useful form: landed odds in maiden at Yarmouth and minor event at Newbury (by short head from Distant Valley) in September: 4¾ lengths fifth of 7 to Gossamer in Fillies' Mile at Ascot final start: will be suited by 1¼m/1½m: acts on firm and soft going: type to improve further. *E. A. L. Dunlop* **102 p**

FRAZER'S LAD 4 b.g. Whittingham (IRE) 104 – Loch Tain (Lochnager 132) [2001 52: 9.9m 8d⁶ 8m⁵ 8m 9.2d² 10.9d⁴ 8.1s f12g³ 8.3s Aug 21] angular, close-coupled gelding: modest maiden: seems to stay 1½m: acts on fibresand, soft going and good to firm: blinkered seventh start: sold 2,500 gns. *A. Bailey* **49 a55**

FRAZZLED 2 b.g. (Feb 8) Greensmith 121 – Time For Tea (IRE) 73 (Imperial Frontier (USA) 112) [2001 6m 6g⁴ 6s³ p7g² Dec 29] first foal: dam, maiden who stayed 1¼m, out of useful half-sister to Kalaglow: fair maiden: best effort when short-headed by Princess Petardia in nursery at Lingfield, slowly away: should stay 1m. *C. A. Cyzer* **79**

FREDDIE MERCURY (IRE) 2 ch.g. (Apr 17) Eagle Eyed (USA) 111 – So Far Away 48 (Robellino (USA) 127) [2001 5.1m⁵ 5.7f⁵ 5.1g² 5.1f 6s⁵ f5g f6g f5s Dec 27] IR 10,500F, IR 12,000Y: third living foal: dam, lightly-raced Irish maiden, out of useful 2-y-o 5f winner who stayed 1m Faraway Grey: modest performer: left D. Arbuthnot after fifth outing: stays 6f: acts on firm and soft ground, well held on fibresand: ungenuine. *J. Balding* **57 § a– §**

FREDDY FLINTSTONE   4 b.g. Bigstone (IRE) 126 – Daring Ditty (Daring March   **76 d**
116) [2001 90: 8v 8d 8m 7g 9f 9m 10g 8d 7m Aug 30] close-coupled gelding: good
walker: fairly useful maiden at 3 yrs: disappointing in 2001: should stay 1¼m: acts on
firm going, possibly not on softer than good: sometimes visored: has been slowly away.
R. Hannon

FREDERICK JAMES   7 b.g. Efisio 120 – Rare Roberta (USA) 118 (Roberto (USA)   **55**
131) [2001 55: e6g e6g⁴ f7g f7g 7.1g May 7] modest performer: stays 7.7f: acts on heavy
going, good to firm and fibresand/equitrack: blinkered. *H. E. Haynes*

FREDERICK LUIGI   2 b.g. (Feb 28) Bal Harbour 113 – Scented Message (Ivotino   **82**
(USA)) [2001 8.1g³ 8.2d 8d³ Oct 25] 1,000Y: fifth foal: dam unraced: clearly best effort
in maidens (fairly useful form) when staying-on third of 15 to Kaieteur at Bath, still
green: will be suited by 1¼m+. *H. Candy*

FRED'S DREAM   2 ch.f. (Apr 10) Cadeaux Genereux 131 – Vaguar (USA) (Vaguely   **67**
Noble 140) [2001 6d 7f 7g⁴ Nov 6] 2,500Y: fifth living foal: half-sister to French 1m winner
Un Melodie (by Caerleon) and 15.4f winner Ela Agapi Mou (by Storm Bird): dam French
1¼m winner out of half-sister to Lyphard and Nobiliary: better effort in maidens (fair
form) when slow-starting tenth at Newmarket: should stay 1m. *R. Guest*

FREE   6 ch.g. Gone West (USA) – Bemissed (USA) (Nijinsky (CAN) 138) [2001 67:   **66**
f16g² 16f⁵ 16.2f Jul 7] angular gelding: good mover: fair handicapper, lightly raced on
Flat since 4 yrs: stays 17f: acts on firm ground: has sweated/got on edge. *Mrs M. Reveley*

FREECOM NET (IRE)   3 b.g. Zieten (USA) 118 – Radiance (IRE) 54 (Thatching   **65**
131) [2001 49: f8s f7g* f8g³ 7m 7g 7.6g⁵ Sep 5] useful-looking gelding: fair performer:
won maiden at Wolverhampton in March: stays 1m: acts on fibresand, best turf effort on
good going. *A. P. Jarvis*

FREEDOM NOW (IRE)   3 b.g. Sadler's Wells (USA) 132 – Free At Last 115 (Shirley   **82**
Heights 130) [2001 72P: 12.3m² 12f⁶ 10g* 12g⁶ 10.3d⁵ Aug 31] compact gelding: fairly
useful performer: won maiden at Windsor in July: not discredited in handicap at Chester
final outing (subsequently gelded): will prove better at 1¼m than 1½m: acts on good to
firm and good to soft going. *L. M. Cumani*

FREEFOURINTERNET (USA)   3 b.c. Tabasco Cat (USA) 126 – Dixie Chimes   **106**
(USA) (Dixieland Band (USA)) [2001 90+: 8.2f* 10f* 10m⁶ Aug 25] small, compact
colt: good walker: has a quick action: useful performer: won maiden at Nottingham in
June and listed event at Ascot later in month by neck from Chianti, held up and leading
after 2f out: last in Winter Hill Stakes at Windsor only subsequent outing: stays 1¼m:
raced only on ground firmer than good. *B. J. Meehan*

FREE KEVIN   5 b.g. Midyan (USA) 124 – Island Desert (IRE) 55 (Green Desert   **34**
(USA) 127) [2001 –: 7m 10m 10m 10.2s⁶ 12g 10.9m⁶ 11.5g 9.9d Oct 3] poor maiden:
stays 11f: acts on good to firm going: blinkered last 3 starts. *Dr J. R. J. Naylor*

FREE OPTION (IRE)   6 ch.g. Indian Ridge 123 – Saneena 80 (Kris 135) [2001 101:   **–**
7m 8m Jul 21] strong, lengthy gelding: useful handicapper at best: well beaten both 6-y-o
outings. *B. Hanbury*

FREE RIDER   4 b.g. Inchinor 119 – Forever Roses 70 (Forzando 122) [2001 108: 6v⁶   **111**
7d³ 7.1s⁴ 7g 10g⁵ 8g³ 7g⁵ 7m⁴ 7d² 7g* 7.9d Oct 12] rangy, good-topped gelding: smart
performer: appeared to down tools third/fourth outings, and subsequently gelded: won
handicap at Newmarket in October by 1¼ lengths from Point of Dispute: otherwise ran
well only in handicap at Newmarket second start and Supreme Stakes at Goodwood on
ninth (2 lengths second of 4 to Late Night Out): best at 7f/1m: acts on heavy and good to
firm going: usually races prominently: none too reliable: sold 40,000 gns,
sent to USA. *I. A. Balding*

FREE WILL   4 ch.g. Indian Ridge 123 – Free Guest 125 (Be My Guest (USA) 126)   **79**
[2001 75: 12v 9d³ 10.1d² 8.3d³ 8f 8m 10.1f² 10f* 10g 10.4d Oct 12] well-made gelding:
fair performer: won maiden at Pontefract in September: stays 1¼m: acts on firm and good
to soft ground: found little third outing. *A. Scott*

FRENCH BRAMBLE (IRE)   3 ch.f. General Monash (USA) 107 – La Mazya (IRE)   **51 §**
(Mazaad 106) [2001 55, a47: 5.1v⁵ f6g 5m 6m⁶ 6m 5f⁵ 5m* 5g f5s Dec 27] leggy, quite   **a– §**
good-topped filly: modest handicapper: won at Doncaster in August: effective at 5f/6f:
acts on good to firm ground, poor form on fibresand at 2 yrs: usually blinkered/visored:
irresolute. *J. Balding*

FRENCH CONNECTION   6 b.g. Tirol 127 – Heaven-Liegh-Grey 90 (Grey Desire   **–**
115) [2001 54: 10v⁴ 12m 10.5s Aug 18] no form in 2001: blinkered final start. *B. D. Leavy*

FRENCH FANCY (IRE) 4 gr.f. Paris House 123 – Clipping 76 (Kris 135) [2001 43, **–**
a48: e8g⁵ f9.4s⁵ e8g e6g e8g* e7s⁵ f9.4g e7g⁵ e8g e8g⁴ e8g 7.6m Jun 26] leggy, plain **a42**
filly: poor performer: won seller at Lingfield in February: stays 1m: acts on any turf going
and fibresand/equitrack: tried visored/blinkered: sometimes slowly away. *B. A. Pearce*

FRENCH GUEST 2 ch.g. (Feb 12) Most Welcome 131 – Laleston 73 (Junius (USA) **–**
124) [2001 8d 7v Oct 26] smallish, strong, lengthy gelding: half-brother to several 5f
winners, including 1998 2-y-o winner Ewenny (by Warshaan): dam 5f winner: burly, well
held in maidens: gelded after final start. *M. A. Jarvis*

FRENCH LIEUTENANT 4 b.g. Cadeaux Genereux 131 – Madame Crecy (USA) **89**
(Al Nasr (FR) 126) [2001 93: 10g⁶ 9.9m* 10.3m⁴ Sep 12] angular, workmanlike gelding:
fairly useful performer, lightly raced: simple task to win maiden at Beverley in August:
creditable fourth to Celtic Island in minor event at Doncaster only subsequent start: stays
1¼m: acts on soft and good to firm going. *G. A. Butler*

FRENCH MANNEQUIN (IRE) 2 gr.f. (Mar 8) Key of Luck (USA) 126 – Paris **63**
Model (IRE) (Thatching 131) [2001 6g 6.1g 7g 6v* 7s⁶ Nov 10] 17,000Y: second foal:
dam, Irish 5f winner at 4 yrs, half-sister to smart performers Showbrook (5f/6f) and
Smarginato (1m/1¼m): modest performer: won nursery at Ayr in October by 3 lengths
from Night Shift Blue's: should stay 7f: raced only on good going or softer: visored last 2
starts. *R. M. Beckett*

FRENCHMANS BAY (FR) 3 br.c. Polar Falcon (USA) 126 – River Fantasy **118**
(USA) (Irish River (FR) 131) [2001 101p: 7d² 8g³ May 5]
        The 'best maiden in training' tag is one which will probably still be attached
to Frenchmans Bay when he finally returns to action, an injury apparently picked
up when he finished third in the Two Thousand Guineas having denied him
the opportunity to break his duck since. Frenchmans Bay, clearly well regarded,
showed useful form in Group 3 events on both his starts prior to the Guineas. He
looked green and shaped most encouragingly when third in the Horris Hill Stakes
at Newbury on his only start at two, and improved on that when runner-up in the
Greenham Stakes over the same course and distance on his reappearance. Frenchmans Bay's lack of experience was evident in the Greenham. Taking a strong hold
in a steadily-run race, he was caught flat-footed when the tempo increased but
stayed on best of those who chased home the two-and-a-half-length winner Munir.
The extra furlong plus a stronger gallop showed Frenchmans Bay to much better
advantage in the Guineas, for which he was sent off at 14/1. Patiently ridden once
again, Frenchmans Bay took a while to respond when initially asked for his finishing effort, changing his legs a few times. However, he began to stay on strongly
on meeting the rising ground and failed by only a neck to snatch second from the
Greenham fourth Tamburlaine, while also getting to within a length and a half of
the winner Golan. Unfortunately, Frenchmans Bay was found to have chipped a
bone in his near-fore knee and underwent a three-hour operation a few days later. A
report in August that Frenchmans Bay was back cantering suggested that he was
well on the way to making a complete recovery, and it is understood that all has
gone well since and he will be back in action in the next season. Frenchmans Bay
should soon make up for lost time when he does return, and it will be most
disappointing if he doesn't meet with far greater success than the last maiden placed
in the Two Thousand Guineas. Bellefella, a 100/1-shot when third to Doyoun in the
1988 running, was beaten at 9/4-on in a maiden on his next start and also failed to
come up to scratch when tried in blinkers in his following race. He didn't get off the
mark until sent to the States, winning a maiden at Belmont.

Frenchmans Bay (FR) (br.c. 1998)	Polar Falcon (USA) (b or br 1987)	Nureyev (b 1977)	Northern Dancer Special
		Marie d' Argonne (ch 1981)	Jefferson Mohair
	River Fantasy (USA) (ch 1991)	Irish River (ch 1976)	Riverman Irish Star
		Harbor Wine (br 1969)	Herbager Bourbon Mist

        Frenchmans Bay, a big, good-topped colt with scope, was sold for 42,000
guineas as a foal but fetched 7,000 guineas less as a yearling, surprising given that
he looks the part and is quite well bred. Though his dam River Fantasy showed no

worthwhile form, she is a half-sister to the Norfolk Stakes winner Romeo Romani and from a good family. Frenchman Bay's grandam Harbour Wine and great-grandam Bourbon Mist (who occupies the same place in Nuclear Debate's pedigree) both won in the States, and the latter's sister Ole Liz was not only one of the best two-year-old fillies of 1966 but also the dam of Kittiwake, one of the top fillies on turf in the early-'seventies and highly successful as a broodmare, too. Bourbon Mist herself is the grandam of Life's Magic, a champion filly in the States. Frenchmans Bay is the second foal of River Fantasy and a half-brother to the once-raced four-year-old Buttermans Bay (by Muhtarram). He may stay a bit beyond a mile, and to date has raced only on good and good to soft ground. *R. Charlton*

FRENCH MASTER (IRE)   4 b.g. Petardia 113 – Reasonably French (Reasonable **36 ?** (FR) 119) [2001 60d: f11g⁶ f12g⁶ 8m 10.9f 12.1m 10f 12g⁵ 16.2s 8.9m Sep 2] close-coupled gelding: poor performer at best nowadays: probably stays 11f: best turf form on good going or firmer, and acts on fibresand: sometimes visored/blinkered. *Jedd O'Keeffe*

FREUD (USA)   3 b.c. Storm Cat 78 – Mariah's Storm (USA) 116 (Rahy (USA) 115) **113** [2001 110: 6s² 8g* 8m³ 6m 6d⁶ 6g⁶ 6s 7s Oct 7] deep-girthed colt: smart performer: won maiden at the Curragh in May: very good 2½-length third to Harmonic Way in Cork And Orrery Stakes at Royal Ascot: failed to repeat that form (though better than bare result suggests when tenth to Mozart in July Cup at Newmarket next time): had form up to 1m, was probably best at 6f/7f: acted on good to firm and good to soft going: tried blinkered, better form without: had worn crossed noseband/tongue tie: idled markedly on reappearance, and had hung: to stand at Lakland North, Hudson, New York, fee $5,000. *A. P. O'Brien, Ireland*

FREYA ALEX   2 b.f. (Feb 6) Makbul 104 – Crissem (IRE) 70 (Thatching 131) [2001 **58** 5d 7d⁵ Nov 6] first foal: dam 2-y-o 5f winner who stayed 7f: better effort in maidens (modest form) when fifth at Catterick: showed knee action on debut. *R. Hollinshead*

FREYA'S DREAM (IRE)   2 b.f. (Mar 23) Danehill Dancer (IRE) 117 – Ruwy 77 **65** (Soviet Star (USA) 128) [2001 5s 6m⁶ 6f⁶ 5f⁵ 5s⁴ 7m Sep 22] IR 5,000F, 13,000Y: rather leggy, angular filly: second foal: dam 1m winner: fair maiden: likely to prove best at 5f/6f: acts on firm ground. *T. D. Easterby*

FRIAR TUCK   6 ch.g. Inchinor 119 – Jay Gee Ell 78 (Vaigly Great 127) [2001 88: **86** 6m² 5m⁶ 6m 6f 6m 6d⁵ 6m 6g 5m 6m 6v² 6v Oct 24] leggy, lengthy gelding: has reportedly had several wind operations: fairly useful handicapper nowadays: best at 5f/6f: acts on any going: none too consistent. *Miss L. A. Perratt*

FRIDAY'S TAKINGS   2 ch.c. (Mar 19) Beveled (USA) – Pretty Pollyanna (General **57 p** Assembly (USA)) [2001 5.7f f8s Dec 21] 21,000Y: fifth foal: half-brother to 3 winners, including 7f to 1¼m winner Polly Peculiar (by Squill) and useful 1m (including at 2 yrs) winner Peculiarity (by Perpendicular): dam unraced: modest form in maidens 6 months apart: should improve. *B. Smart*

FRIENDLY ALLIANCE   5 b.g. Shareef Dancer (USA) 135 – Snow Huntress 80 **57** (Shirley Heights 130) [2001 54: e13g⁶ e16g⁴ p16g³ f16.2s Dec 18] tall, workmanlike gelding: modest handicapper: off 11 months before third outing: stays 2m: acts on equitrack and polytrack, well held on fibresand. *R. M. Flower*

FRILLY FRONT   5 ch.m. Aragon 118 – So So 84 (Then Again 126) [2001 60, a82: **–** f5g e5g³ e5g f5g⁴ f5g⁶ Mar 15] compact mare: fair performer: effective at 5f/6f: acts **a74** on fibresand/equitrack: blinkered once: usually forces pace (can be slowly away): has wandered markedly: has given trouble at stalls/been withdrawn: none too reliable. *T. D. Barron*

FRINK (USA)   2 ch.f. (Mar 21) Royal Academy 130 – Crafty Buzz (USA) **–** (Crafty Prospector (USA)) [2001 8d Oct 19] rangy, unfurnished filly: second foal: dam minor stakes winner at 6f at 2 yrs in USA: 33/1, well beaten in maiden at Newmarket. *M. L. W. Bell*

FRISCO BAY   3 b.g. Efisio 120 – Kabayil 75 (Dancing Brave (USA) 140) [2001 –: 7m **–** Sep 22] sturdy gelding: second foal: half-brother to 4-y-o Dancing Bay: dam 1¼m winner and fairly useful hurdler: well held in 2 maidens over a year apart. *T. D. Easterby*

FRODO   2 b.c. (Feb 16) Magic Ring (IRE) 115 – Prompt (Old Vic 136) [2001 6s 5g 6d³ **77** 6f 6.1g* 6v³ 6d p8g p6g⁵ Dec 28] rather leggy, angular colt: second foal: half-brother to a winner in Greece by Efisio: dam once-raced half-sister to smart 1¼m winner Baron Ferdinand out of half-sister to Shirley Heights: fair performer: won nursery at Nottingham in August: sold 21,000 gns and left R. Charlton before penultimate start: should stay 1m: acts on heavy ground (probably on polytrack), well held on firm. *R. J. White*

FROGLET   2 b.f. (Apr 25) Shaamit (IRE) 127 – Frog 84 (Akarad (FR) 130) [2001 f6g   **58 p** 6v f6g Nov 19] second foal: half-sister to 3-y-o Sel: dam 1¼m/1½m winner: modest form, not knocked about, in maidens (twice slowly away): should do better at 1m+. *Sir Mark Prescott*

FROLICKING   6 b.m. Mujtahid (USA) 118 – Perfect Desire (USA) (Green Forest   – (USA) 134) [2001 f7g Jan 8] lightly-raced maiden nowadays: tried blinkered/visored. *B. S. Rothwell*

FROMSONG (IRE)   3 b.c. Fayruz 116 – Lindas Delight 54 (Batshoof 122) [2001   **105** 105p] 5.1s* 5m⁴ 6g Jun 2] tall, angular colt: useful performer: won minor event at Nottingham in April: better effort in listed races after when creditable 1¼ lengths fourth to Emerald Peace at Kempton (reportedly had troubled journey to course): speedy, and will prove best around 5f: acts on soft and good to firm going. *B. R. Millman*

FRONTIER FLIGHT (USA)   11 b.g. Flying Paster (USA) – Sly Charmer (USA)   – (Valdez (USA)) [2001 –: 8m⁴ Jul 1] no form on Flat after 1993: dead. *P. W. Hiatt*

FROSTY WELCOME (USA)   2 gr. or ro.f. (Apr 7) With Approval (CAN) – Light   **67 p** Ice (USA) (Arctic Tern (USA) 126) [2001 6s⁶ 6g⁵ Oct 19] $47,000Y: rather leggy, unfurnished filly: seventh foal: closely related to a winner in USA by Talkin Man and half-sister to winners in USA by Tejano and Seattle Song: dam, won up to 1¼m in USA, half-sister to US Grade 1 9f winner Al Mamoon: better effort in maidens (fair form) when fifth to Wish at Redcar, not knocked about: will stay 1m: should improve. *G. Wragg*

FROTTOLA   3 b.f. Muhtarram (USA) 125 – For My Love (Kahyasi 130) [2001 9m²   **59** 10g 8.1v⁵ 10v 8.2s⁴ Nov 5] tall, useful-looking filly: first foal: dam unraced half-sister to useful performers Be Fresh (sprinter) and How Long (up to 1m): fair form when second in maiden at Milan on debut: modest form at best in Britain afterwards, including in handicap final outing: best effort at 9f: acts on heavy and good to firm ground: returned to Italy. *L. M. Cumani*

FRUHLING FEUER (FR)   3 ch.f. Green Tune (USA) 125 – Reef Squaw (Darshaan   **80** 133) [2001 7d 8.2d* 9m⁴ 10.2g³ 10.5v⁵ 10d Nov 2] 200,000 francs F: leggy filly: first foal: dam, French 1¼m/11f winner, from family of very good French middle-distance performers Animatrice, Poliglote and Indian Danehill: fairly useful performer: won maiden at Nottingham in May: creditable efforts in handicaps next 2 starts only: stays 1¼m: acts on good to firm and good to soft going. *J. L. Dunlop*

FRUIT OF GLORY   2 b.f. (Mar 21) Glory of Dancer 121 – Fresh Fruit Daily 92   **91** (Reprimand 122) [2001 6g⁵ 6g² 6d² 7g* 7s² Sep 30] useful-looking filly: first foal: dam 9.7f to 1½m winner: fairly useful performer: won maiden at Epsom in September: excellent short-head second to Rapscallion in nursery at Ascot final start, prominent throughout: should stay 1¼m: raced only on good going or softer. *M. R. Channon*

FRUIT PUNCH (IRE)   3 b.f. Barathea (IRE) 127 – Friendly Finance (Auction Ring   **73** (USA) 123) [2001 64: 10s² 10g⁴ 11.9m⁶ 9m³ 9.9f² 9.9m⁴ 10g 10m 10m² 10.3d 10v³ 12d* Nov 18] sturdy filly: fair performer: won minor event at Saint-Brieuc in November by 3½ lengths: stays 1½m: acts on firm and soft going: blinkered in second half of year: has wandered under pressure: sold 52,000 gns. *T. D. Easterby*

FUDGE BROWNIE   5 b.g. Deploy 131 – Carte Blanche 67 (Cadeaux Genereux 131)   **60** [2001 8v³ 8d² 8.3d² 8m⁵ 8.5g Sep 19] workmanlike gelding: modest maiden: left D. Eddy and off 3½ months after fourth outing: should be suited by at least 1¼m: yet to race on firm going, probably acts on any other. *G. A. Swinbank*

FUEGIAN   6 ch.g. Arazi (USA) 135 – Well Beyond (IRE) 101 (Don't Forget Me 127)   – [2001 64d: e8g⁶ 7m 9m 7m 7d 10m Jul 30] rangy gelding: winning handicapper: no form in 2001: sometimes visored. *M. Madgwick*

FUERO REAL (FR)   6 b.g. Highest Honor (FR) 124 – Highest Pleasure (USA) (Fool-   – ish Pleasure (USA)) [2001 43: 10m 10d May 16] of no account nowadays. *R. J. Hodges*

FULL AHEAD (IRE)   4 b.g. Slip Anchor 136 – Foulard (IRE) (Sadler's Wells (USA)   **83** 132) [2001 91: f11g⁵ 16s Apr 21] smallish, robust gelding: fairly useful performer: tailed off final start: should stay 2m: acts on good going and fibresand. *A. King*

FULL EGALITE   5 gr.g. Ezzoud (IRE) 126 – Milva 56 (Jellaby 124) [2001 59: f12g³   **36** f12g⁶ f12g⁶ 15.4v 11.5m⁴ 12m 16.2m p12g Nov 28] smallish, sturdy gelding: poor   **a47** performer: reportedly lame when tailed off penultimate outing: stays easy 13f: acts on

soft and good to firm going, very best all-weather form on equitrack: usually blinkered/
visored. *B. R. Johnson*

FULL HOUSE (IRE)   2 br.c. (Feb 14) King's Theatre (IRE) 128 – Nirvavita (FR)   **84 p**
(Highest Honor (FR) 124) [2001 8.1s³ 8.3m* Sep 24] IR 15,000F, 37,000Y: second foal:
dam French 1m winner out of half-sister to very smart French 7f/1m performer Nikos:
fairly useful form: justified favouritism in maiden at Hamilton by 3 lengths from So
Royal, making all: will stay at least 1¼m: open to improvement. *P. F. I. Cole*

FULLOPEP   7 b.g. Dunbeath (USA) 127 – Suggia (Alzao (USA) 117) [2001 –: 14.1m²   **68**
14.8m 14.1g Oct 6] sturdy gelding: fair handicapper, lightly raced on Flat nowadays:
creditable second at Redcar in June: below form after: should stay beyond 2m: acts on
good to firm going. *Mrs M. Reveley*

FULL SPATE   6 ch.g. Unfuwain (USA) 131 – Double River (USA) (Irish River (FR)   **79**
131) [2001 76: 5v 6m⁴ 6m 6g³ 6d 6d 6m* 6m 6f 6g³ 7m 7m² 7m 7m* 7m⁵ 7.2m⁶ 7s Sep
30] leggy, quite good-topped gelding: fair performer: won handicap at Windsor (very
slowly away) in June and minor event at Folkestone in August: effective at 6f/7f: acts on
any going: sometimes slowly away: usually held up: none too consistent. *J. M. Bradley*

FULL STOP (IRE)   4 b.f. Zieten (USA) 118 – Scherzo Impromptu (Music Boy 124)   **45**
[2001 e5g Apr 11] IR 15,000F, IR 14,000Y: fourth foal: dam twice-raced half-sister to
smart sprinter Governor General: poor form in Lingfield maiden on debut. *B. J. Curley*

FULL TIME (IRE)   2 b.g. (Apr 18) Bigstone (IRE) 126 – Oiche Mhaith 74 (Night   **59**
Shift (USA)) [2001 5d f5g⁶ May 21] IR 7,800Y: fifth foal: half-brother to winners in
Italy by Catrail (5f) and Thatching (5f to 7.5f): dam Irish 6f winner: modest form at
Southwell on second start in maidens. *G. A. Swinbank*

FULLY INVESTED (USA)   3 b.f. Irish River (FR) 131 – Shirley Valentine 104   **99 +**
(Shirley Heights 130) [2001 85P: 10g 10v³ 8g⁶ 10d⁶ Oct 18] tall, slightly unfurnished
filly: useful performer: rather disappointing in listed events first 2 outings: off 5 months,
ran well when sixth in Sun Chariot Stakes at Newmarket (probably flattered
behind Independence) and listed race at Esyoueffcee): best effort at 1m (bred to stay at
least 1¼m): raced only on good going or softer: joined R. Frankel in USA. *H. R. A. Cecil*

FUNDAMENTAL   2 ch.g. (Apr 28) Rudimentary (USA) 118 – I'll Try 71 (Try My   **–**
Best (USA) 130) [2001 8.1s 8d 8g Oct 19] 13,000Y: strong gelding: closely related to
6-y-o John Ferneley and half-brother to several winners, including Irish middle-distance
stayer Steel Mirror (by Silver Hawk): dam 2-y-o 5f winner, later successful in USA: well
held in maidens. *T. P. Tate*

FUNFAIR WANE   2 b.g. (Mar 27) Unfuwain (USA) 131 – Ivory Bride 86 (Domynsky   **101**
110) [2001 6m² 6d* 7m* 6g⁵ 7m⁵ 5d Oct 13] lengthy, useful-looking gelding: has a long
stride: sixth foal: closely related to useful 5f (at 2 yrs) to 9f (in Italy) winner Cabcharge
Striker (by Rambo Dancer) and half-brother to 2 winners, including fairly useful 1m
winner Bride's Answer (by Anshan): dam 2-y-o 6f winner who stayed 1m: useful
performer: won maiden at York (by 7 lengths) in June and listed race at Newbury (by
head from Mamool) in August: below form in pattern races last 3 starts: shapes as though
will prove best up to 7f. *M. R. Channon*

FUNKSOULBOROUGH (IRE)   2 b.c. (Mar 3) Woodborough (USA) 112 – White   **79**
Paper (IRE) (Marignan (USA) 117) [2001 5f² 6g* 6m³ 7m⁵ 6.1g³ 7g 7d⁴ 6g Oct 6]
16,000F, 25,000Y: strong colt: first foal: dam unraced out of half-sister to high-class 1981
2-y-o 7f/1m performer Paradis Terrestre: fair performer: won maiden at Redcar in June:
creditable efforts when in frame in minor event/nurseries after: probably stays 7f: acts on
firm and good to soft ground: visored (pulled hard) sixth start: sold 24,000 gns. *W. Jarvis*

FUNNY GIRL (IRE)   4 b.f. Darshaan 133 – Just For Fun (FR) (Lead On Time (USA)   **68**
123) [2001 78: 8.1g³ 7.1m 7m⁶ Jun 22] compact filly: fair maiden: probably stays 1¼m:
acts on firm going. *W. R. Muir*

FUNNY VALENTINE (IRE)   3 ch.c. Cadeaux Genereux 131 – Aunt Hester (IRE)   **112**
68 (Caerleon (USA) 132) [2001 82: e6g² 5s⁴ 5.1m* 5m³ 5f² 5m Jul 7] lengthy, attractive
colt: won maiden at Lingfield in April and minor event at Bath in May: 100/1, improved
greatly (smart form) when 2¼ lengths third to Cassandra Go in King's Stand Stakes at
Royal Ascot: favourite, well below that form but unfortunate not to win handicap at Ascot
4 days later, switched then becoming unbalanced when ½-length second to Muja
Farewell: only eighth in listed event at Sandown final outing (subsequently found to have
sustained an injury): should prove at least as effective at 6f as 5f: acts on equitrack and
probably any turf going. *T. G. Mills*

FURNESS 4 b.g. Emarati (USA) 74 – Thelma (Blakeney 126) [2001 67: f16g³ a9g³ **62**
a10.5g⁶ a10.5g² a12g³ 11s³ 12d a12g Sep 15] leggy, workmanlike gelding: modest
performer: trained in Spain after first start: stays 2m: acts on fibresand/sand and good to
soft going, probably on good to firm: has rejoined A. Dickman. *P. Haley, Spain*

FURTHER OUTLOOK (USA) 7 gr.g. Zilzal (USA) 137 – Future Bright (USA) **110 d**
(Lyphard's Wish (FR) 124) [2001 109: 5s⁴ 6v⁴ 5.1v² 6d 5.2d⁵ 6g 6g 6m 6m 5.6m
7.2m 6d⁴ 6d Oct 13] big, strong gelding: carries condition: smart performer at best: on
downgrade after reappearance at Doncaster in 2001: untried on firm ground of late, acts
on any other: has been tongue tied/worn crossed noseband/bandaged in front: takes strong
hold, and usually races up with pace. *D. Nicholls*

FUSUL (USA) 5 ch.g. Miswaki (USA) 124 – Silent Turn (USA) (Silent Cal (USA)) **–**
[2001 –, a71: e12g⁶ e13s* e13g e12g⁶ Apr 2] tall, useful-looking gelding: fair performer: **a61**
won claimer at Lingfield in February: stays 13f, seemingly not 2m: acts on equitrack:
blinkered/tongue tied: races freely. *G. L. Moore*

FUTUNA (IRE) 3 b.f. Tagula (IRE) 116 – Pleasant Outlook (USA) 73 (El Gran Senor **–**
(USA) 136) [2001 7d Apr 20] 5,500F, 5,500Y: sturdy, close-coupled filly: third foal: dam,
Irish 7f winner, out of half-sister to high-class US 1980 2-y-o Cure The Blues: 33/1 and
backward, no promise in maiden at Newbury: sold 800 gns in July. *I. A. Balding*

FUTURE FLIGHT 3 b.f. Polar Falcon (USA) 126 – My Branch 111 (Distant Relative **78 +**
128) [2001 85p: 6.9v* 7.6m⁴ 7.1m 7.1v Sep 29] unfurnished filly: fair performer: easy
winner of maiden at Folkestone in April: ran respectably in minor event at Lingfield next
time: below form after in handicaps: likely to prove best at 6f/7f: acts on heavy and good
to firm ground. *B. W. Hills*

John Humphreys (Turf Accountants) Ltd's "Funny Valentine"

FUTURE PROSPECT (IRE) 7 b.g. Marju (IRE) 127 – Phazania (Tap On Wood **65** 130) [2001 70d, a–: 7.5f* 7.5m 8.5m⁶ 8.5g⁶ 8.9m³ 10.9m⁶ 9.9s² Sep 25] leggy gelding: **a–** has a round action: fair performer: won handicap at Beverley in June: stays 1¼m: acts on firm ground and good to soft: blinkered once: has drifted right/been slowly away. *M. A. Buckley*

F-ZERO 4 b.g. Bin Ajwaad (IRE) 119 – Saluti Tutti 77 (Trojan Fen 118) [2001 70: 10s **–** 10s Oct 22] lengthy gelding: one-time fair performer, lightly raced: well below form both 4-y-o outings. *C. F. Wall*

G

GABBY HAYES (IRE) 5 b.g. Tirol 127 – All Laughter (Vision (USA)) [2001 66: **–** f16.2g 13.1d Aug 19] third foal: dam placed at 7f/1m in Ireland at 2 yrs: fairly useful winner at 3 yrs: lightly raced and well held in handicaps on Flat since, leaving T. Walsh in Ireland prior to 2001: stays 1¼m: has won on good to firm ground, very best form on softer than good (acts on heavy): usually blinkered in Ireland. *B. G. Powell*

GABI (IRE) 3 ch.f. Gabitat 119 – Gabibti (IRE) 82 (Dara Monarch 128) [2001 –p: 8m **45** 8.3m 6f⁵ 7g⁶ Aug 10] poor maiden: stayed 6f: acted on firm going: dead. *B. Gubby*

GABLESEA 7 b.g. Beveled (USA) – Me Spede (Valiyar 129) [2001 61: f8.5g f9.4g 8s **47** 8.3m² 8f⁶ 10m 7.6m 10.5g 10.5s Aug 18] tall gelding: poor handicapper: stays 10.5f: acts on soft going, good to firm and fibresand: often visored, has been blinkered: has been slowly away: none too consistent. *B. P. J. Baugh*

GABOR 2 b.g. (Apr 28) Danzig Connection (USA) – Kiomi 65 (Niniski (USA) 125) **79** [2001 7g 8g³ 8.5m³ 8m² 10d Nov 2] tall gelding: fourth foal: dam maiden who would have stayed beyond 13.6f: fair maiden: best effort when second in nursery at Bath: gelded after final start: should stay at least 1¼m: acts on good to firm ground, well beaten on good to soft. *S. P. C. Woods*

GADGE 10 br.g. Nomination 125 – Queenstyle 58 (Moorestyle 137) [2001 43§: f7g f7g⁵ **40 §** Feb 1] sturdy, lengthy gelding: poor performer nowadays: stays 1m: acts on soft going and fibresand/equitrack: tried visored/blinkered, not since 1996: unreliable. *A. Bailey*

GAD YAKOUN 8 ch.g. Cadeaux Genereux 131 – Summer Impressions (USA) 70 **– §** (Lyphard (USA) 132) [2001 –: f5s f6g⁶ 5d 5g 5g Aug 6] lengthy gelding: temperamental handicapper: visored last 3 starts. *Mrs G. S. Rees*

GAELIC FORAY (IRE) 5 b.m. Unblest 117 – Rich Heiress (IRE) 49 (Last Tycoon **–** 131) [2001 40, a63: e7g³ e7g Jan 27] modest performer: seems best around 7f: best form **a63** on equitrack. *M. R. Ewer-Hoad*

GAELIC STORM 7 b.g. Shavian 125 – Shannon Princess (Connaught 130) [2001 **–** 118: 7m 7g 6v f8g Nov 19] small, sturdy gelding: smart performer at best, winner of 16 races: no form in 2001 (off 10 months before reappearance). *M. Johnston*

GAINFUL 2 ch.f. (Apr 16) Elmaamul (USA) 125 – Regain 86 (Relko 136) [2001 **61** 7.1m⁴ 7.1m 6.5g 8g Nov 5] leggy, narrow filly: lacks scope: half-sister to several winners, including 1986 2-y-o 7f winner Counter Attack (by Nishapour) and stayer White River (by Pharly): dam 1½m winner: modest form in maidens first 2 starts: well held after: bred to be suited by 1¼m/1½m. *B. Smart*

GALA AFFAIR 2 ch.f. (Apr 27) Zilzal 137 – Sally Slade 80 (Dowsing (USA) **50** 124) [2001 6g 6g⁶ Sep 11] second foal: dam 5f winner: better effort in maidens (modest form) when sixth at Lingfield: may prove best at 5f/6f. *C. A. Cyzer*

GALA GOLD 2 b.f. (Mar 19) Green Desert (USA) 127 – Melting Gold (USA) 108 **65 p** (Cadeaux Genereux 131) [2001 6g 7g⁵ Nov 5] lengthy filly: fourth foal: half-sister to French 9f winner Gold Venture (by Indian Ridge): dam, French 2-y-o 7f winner, out of half-sister to 2000 Guineas winner Shadeed: much better effort in maidens (fair form) when fifth to Sholay at Redcar, disputing lead until 1f out: likely to prove best up to 7f: should improve. *M. Johnston*

GALANT EYE (IRE) 2 ch.g. (Mar 8) Eagle Eyed (USA) 111 – Galandria 57 (Sharpo **46** 132) [2001 5m 6m 6.1m 7s Oct 5] IR 6,000F, 10,000Y: fifth reported foal: half-brother to 1m winner in Britain (and multiple winner in Belgium) Glossator (by Shardari): dam 9f/ 1¼m winner in France: poor maiden. *F. Jordan*

GALAPAGOS GIRL (IRE) 3 b.f. Turtle Island (IRE) 123 – Shabby Doll 69 (North- **80** fields (USA)) [2001 72: 8g³ 7.6f⁵ 8g f7g³ Sep 8] fairly useful performer, lightly raced:

stays 1m: raced only on good going or firmer on turf, acts on fibresand: has found little/flashed tail: sold only 800 gns in December. *B. W. Hills*

GALAPINO 8 b.g. Charmer 123 – Carousella 62 (Rousillon (USA) 133) [2001 55d: – §
15.4v⁴ 14s 16f⁶ 16.4m 17.2m 16.4g Aug 17] smallish gelding: temperamental handi-capper nowadays: has run well in blinkers. *Jamie Poulton*

GALAXY DRIVE (IRE) 2 b.f. (Feb 28) Perugino (USA) 84 – Madaraka (USA) 84 **47**
(Arctic Tern (USA) 126) [2001 5f 6m⁵ 5m⁴ f5g Oct 6] IR 1,600Y: small, sparely-made filly: second foal: dam Irish 1¼m winner and placed over hurdles: poor maiden. *A. Berry*

GALAXY FALLON 3 b.f. Dancing Spree (USA) – No Comebacks 70 (Last Tycoon –
131) [2001 7.5m 9m 12m⁶ 12.4g 12m Jul 31] 2,500Y: tall, quite good-topped filly: second foal: half-sister to 4-y-o New Options: dam, 1m to 1½m winner, out of half-sister to Irish 1000 Guineas winner Katies: well held in maidens/handicaps. *A. Berry*

GALAXY JEWEL 2 ch.f. (Apr 23) Bijou d'Inde 127 – Give Me A Day (Lucky **57**
Wednesday 124) [2001 5s f5g² f5g 6m 5f² f5g⁴ 5m* 5d⁴ 5m 5g⁵ f5g⁵ Oct 6] 800Y, resold 2,500Y: workmanlike filly: eighth foal: half-sister to 3 winners by Risk Me, including 8.5f to 9.4f winner Colins Choice: dam little form: modest performer: won maiden at Beverley in July: below form after next start: may prove best at 5f: acts on firm going, good to soft and fibresand: tried blinkered: races prominently: sold 1,500 gns, sent to Spain. *A. Berry*

GALAXY PASHA (IRE) 2 ch.g. (Feb 10) Hector Protector (USA) 124 – Blade of –
Grass 78 (Kris 135) [2001 6d Jul 18] 18,000Y: eighth foal: half-brother to useful sprinter Warning Star (by Warning), useful French 1m/1¼m winner Brindle (by Polar Falcon) and 1¼m/1½m winner Lawn Lothario (by Pursuit of Love): dam 7f winner: 14/1, soundly beaten in Lingfield maiden: subsequently gelded. *A. Berry*

GALAXY RETURNS 3 ch.g. Alhijaz 122 – Naulakha (Bustino 136) [2001 59: 7.1g **51**
6m 7m 8m⁴ 7.6f⁴ 7g 8.5m 7.5m 8m 6s Sep 24] workmanlike gelding: modest performer at best: barely stays 1m: acts on firm going: blinkered eighth start: sold 2,400 gns. *A. Berry*

GALAXY ROLE 2 b.g. (Mar 1) Tragic Role (USA) – Wasblest 59 (Statoblest 120) –
[2001 7s f6g 8s³ Nov 9] angular, workmanlike gelding: second foal: dam, 2-y-o 5f winner, later stayed 7f: well beaten in minor events/maiden. *A. Berry*

GALAXY SAM (USA) 2 ch.g. (Jan 18) Royal Academy (USA) 130 – Istiska (FR) **63**
(Irish River (FR) 131) [2001 5m 7.1g³ 8.2d⁵ 8.3v Nov 8] 35,000Y: tall, rather leggy gelding: half-brother to several winners, including fairly useful Irish 1m winner Fairy Water (by Warning) and 7f (fairly useful at 2 yrs) and 13f winner Noyan (by Northern Baby): dam, French maiden, from family of Enzeli, Ebadiyla and Edabiya: modest maiden: edged markedly left when third at Sandown: gelded after final start: should stay 1¼m. *A. Berry*

GALAXY TEE (IRE) 2 ch.f. (Apr 4) Goldmark (USA) 113 – Shepherd's Delight **56 d**
(Prince Sabo 123) [2001 6m 6m⁴ 5m f6g 7g 6d Oct 30] leggy, rather unfurnished filly: first reported foal: dam unraced: modest maiden: easily best effort when fourth at Catterick: should stay 7f: acts on good to firm going. *A. Berry*

GALAXY THUNDERBIRD 2 ch.g. (Feb 9) Bahamian Bounty 116 – Milva 56 **58**
(Jellaby 124) [2001 6m 6m³ 6.1d⁶ 5.1s⁵ Oct 30] 7,000F, 24,000Y: strong gelding: half-brother to numerous winners, including 6f winner (including at 2 yrs) Milagro (by King of Spain) and 1¾m winner Serious Time (by Good Times), both fairly useful: dam 6f winner: modest maiden: third at Lingfield: gelded after final start: likely to prove best at 5f/6f: acts on soft and good to firm ground. *A. Berry*

GALAXY TIMES 2 ch.f. (Mar 21) Presidium 124 – Oubeck 65 (Mummy's Game **55**
120) [2001 f5g f5g² 5m⁵ 5m² f5g² 5m Jul 11] 3,000Y: leggy filly: fourth foal: half-sister to 1998 2-y-o 5f seller winner Lune Lass (by Cyrano de Bergerac): dam 6f winner: modest maiden: will prove best at 5f/6f: raced only on fibresand and good to firm ground: often slowly away: sold 5,200 gns, sent to Kuwait. *A. Berry*

GALEY RIVER (USA) 2 ch.c. (Mar 29) Irish River (FR) 131 – Carefree Kate (USA) **70**
(Lyphard (USA) 132) [2001 6g³ 7s Oct 16] $5,000Y, 30,000 2-y-o: strong, close-coupled colt: third foal: brother to 3-y-o Tedstale: dam, US 9f winner at 4 yrs, half-sister to 6-y-o Arkadian Hero: much better effort in maidens (fair form) when third to Tikkun at Folkestone: bred to stay 1m. *J. J. Sheehan*

GALI 5 gr.g. Petong 126 – Wasimah 84 (Caerleon (USA) 132) [2001 44: 8f 8f⁵ 10m **40**
Aug 29] poor maiden handicapper: unlikely to stay beyond 1m: best effort on soft going: sometimes slowly away: visored once. *C. A. Horgan*

GALILEO (IRE) 3 b.c. Sadler's Wells (USA) 132 – Urban Sea (USA) 126 **134**
(Miswaki (USA) 124) [2001 107p: 10s* 10m* 12f* 12g* 12m* 10g² a10f⁶ Oct 27]

The traditional European notion of the ideal racehorse is slowly but surely being eroded. For most of the second half of the twentieth century, the popular idea of the consummate thoroughbred was the Derby winner, or the winner of the King George VI and Queen Elizabeth Stakes or the Prix de l'Arc de Triomphe—the top-class mile-and-a-half horse with speed. In the strictest sense, of course, there is no such animal as the ideal racehorse: there are simply horses, horses with different racing characters and different requirements. That's one of the reasons why the long-standing bias in the European racing programme towards middle-distance performers has often come in for criticism in these pages down the years. Middle-distance specialists in general still earn too great a share of racing's prestige and prize-money, though the sprinters, milers and even the stayers—in Britain at least—thankfully get a fairer crack of the whip than they used to. Far and away the biggest influence, however, in the steadily dwindling kudos attached to being a middle-distance champion has been the globalisation of the thoroughbred breeding business. North American racing has been contracted around a seven-furlong to a mile-and-a-quarter centre and potential stallions who make their name as racehorses exclusively or mostly at a mile and a half or further are nowhere near so attractive to American breeders as those who shine over shorter distances. The desire to breed for speed at the expense of stamina manifests itself in the stallion fees that are commanded. An exceptional group of top horses raced in the 2000 season in Europe, headed by the brilliant four-year-old Dubai Millennium who went to stud at a fee in the region of £100,000 to £120,000. He met the only defeat of his career in the Derby, the only time he was raced beyond a mile and a quarter. The 2000 Derby winner Sinndar, who also won the Irish Derby and the Arc, was retired at IR £30,000. The world order was also illustrated when the fees were set by Coolmore for the admirable pair Giant's Causeway and Montjeu. Montjeu was manifestly the better racehorse, showing himself a middle-distance champion of rare quality with wide-margin victories in 1999 in the French and Irish equivalents of the Derby, followed by victory in the Arc before an effortless win in 2000 over Fantastic Light in the King George. Giant's Causeway, never raced at around a mile and a half, recorded five successive Group 1 victories at a mile to an extended mile and a quarter and concluded his racing career with a narrow defeat in the Breeders' Cup Classic. Montjeu was retired to stud at IR 30,000 guineas, Giant's Causeway at IR 100,000 guineas, his fee going up from the IR 75,000 guineas announced before the Breeders' Cup.

Against this background, the latest season produced the extraordinary story of a top-class dual Derby and King George winner whose connections, judged by

Ballysax Stakes, Leopardstown—the race in which the previous year's Derby winner Sinndar met his only defeat; Galileo keeps his unbeaten record with a smooth victory over stable-companion Milan

Derrinstown Stud Derby Trial Stakes, Leopardstown—Galileo continues on 'the Sinndar route' to Epsom and confirms his position as second favourite in the ante-post Derby betting; Exaltation (rail) is second, ahead of El Bueno

some public pronouncements, seemed somewhat constrained by the colt's proven ability at a mile and a half and sought to create the impression that the horse ultimately would prove even better at shorter distances. Was this a calculated way of trying to boost potential stallion value, as some cynically whispered, or purely and simply an honest appraisal of the horse's racing character? It is a sign of the times that such a question has to be put. Galileo's strikingly impressive victory at Epsom over the Two Thousand Guineas winner Golan and the rest of a represent-ative field drew a string of superlatives, under examples of the headline-writers' art such as 'Galileo in orbit', 'Galileo powers to celestial status', 'Galileo the star turn'. The front-page headline in the *Racing Post* was the single word 'PERFECTION'. For trainer Aidan O'Brien, however, Galileo's Derby victory did not represent the pinnacle of achievement, or anything like it. 'This is a serious horse who is capable of producing the unbelievable; he has the speed of a sprinter and the strength of a miler, and this is something I have never seen before in a horse capable of winning a classic over a mile and a half,' said O'Brien. 'He is very explosive and very special.' Immediately after the Derby, O'Brien revealed an audacious plan—apparently hatched before the Derby but kept secret—to drop Galileo back to a mile and a quarter next time for the Eclipse at Sandown, then back to a mile for the Queen Elizabeth II Stakes at Ascot before attempting to avenge Giant's Cause-way's defeat in the Breeders' Cup Classic ('the dirt track won't bother him, he'd gallop on water').

For its boldness and its disregard for convention—if for no other reason—O'Brien's plans for Galileo came as a breath of fresh air. It also served to fuel the feeling, however, that in Galileo the Epsom crowd had been privileged to see an exceptional Derby winner—one for whom equine greatness beckoned, for all that, judged on substance rather than style, Galileo still had much to prove before joining the pantheon of racing's immortals. No sooner had the significance of O'Brien's plan begun to be appreciated, however, than an announcement came from Ballydoyle that, before embarking on a campaign over shorter distances,

Galileo would first attempt the Anglo-Irish Derby double, effectively ruling out the Eclipse and a first clash with older horses. Galileo's Irish Derby proved the proverbial 'steering job', but O'Brien was singing from the same hymn sheet again in the post-race interviews: 'I was never convinced he was a mile-and-a-half horse because he has always shown such speed. Horses with such a cruising pace are usually not. But he finds it easy to keep going.' O'Brien had said after Epsom that 'on the very first day he worked, Galileo was good enough to win any six-furlong maiden . . . that's how natural he is.' At the Curragh, O'Brien went further: 'Every bit of work suggested he would never be anything other than a champion.' The acting Irish Turf Club handicapper Geoffrey Gibbs joined the chorus, proclaiming that Galileo, one of the best Derby winners he felt he had seen, 'fulfils Sir Noel Murless's criterion for being a top-class racehorse—good enough to perform at the highest level from six furlongs to two miles.' Galileo's supposed versatility was not tested in his next race either when, after a late change of heart, connections rowed in once more with convention, sending Galileo to Ascot for the King George. After a pulsating race, in which Galileo had to work hard to get the better of the five-year-old Fantastic Light, O'Brien expressed himself as being 'relieved to have been wrong that a strongly-run mile and a half might be too far for Galileo.' It was still the intention, connections said, that, after taking in the Irish Champion Stakes, Galileo would be returned to Ascot for the Queen Elizabeth II Stakes over a mile before ending his career in the Breeders' Cup Classic. The papers had spent much of the summer trailing the proposed clash at Belmont Park with the champion American three-year-old Point Given, who had won two legs of the American triple crown. Victory over Point Given, it was claimed, would make Galileo 'the first hundred-million-dollar racehorse'.

O'Brien reported that in the discussions about sending Galileo for the King George he had been 'overruled'. 'I firmly believe Galileo is a better horse over a shorter trip and there will be less pressure for me in his last three races . . . he is a great horse and showed today how much courage he has.' If O'Brien had indeed been 'overruled', it was almost certainly by the head of the Coolmore breeding empire John Magnier, also controller of Ballydoyle stables, whose finest equine

Vodafone Derby Stakes, Epsom—Mr Combustible (rail) and Perfect Sunday dispute the lead round Tattenham Corner; Galileo is poised on their heels with Dilshaan and Putra Sandhurst on his inside

graduates nowadays go on to take up stud duties at Coolmore, or its associated studs in America and Australia. Coolmore's dominant position also enables it to acquire other good stallion prospects after their racecourse careers—Danehill and Grand Lodge, for example—as well as horses 'made' at other studs. Magnier's horses run in the name of his wife Sue and other partners, including Michael Tabor, now adopting the role of Robert Sangster, who played a major part in the rise of Coolmore in the 'seventies before cutting back his involvement in the late-'eighties. Magnier himself shuns the limelight and his public utterances are rare, but, under his guidance, the operation is run on strictly commercial lines, with the Coolmore stallions—some of them operating in two hemispheres—aggressively marketed to an international clientele. The Ballydoyle racing operation concentrates on blue-blooded two- and three-year-olds, many of them acquired at the world's premier yearling sales, with an eye to the future regarding potential stallions. Much of Ballydoyle's raw material comprises progeny of Coolmore-owned stallions or of other sires in which Coolmore has a vested interest, though Galileo himself was not purchased at auction, being bred in partnership by David Tsui, in whose colours Galileo's dam Urban Sea raced, and by Orpendale, an offshoot of Coolmore. An independent assessment, quoted in a series of articles on Coolmore by Tony Morris in the *Racing Post*, estimated that Coolmore's income from its Irish Flat stallions alone was over IR £46m in 2000, representing seventy per cent of the Irish market share and over forty-three per cent for Britain and Ireland combined (Darley Stud Management at just under ten per cent and Juddmonte at just under seven per cent being the next biggest in the combined category). The prize-money won by the Ballydoyle racehorses is peanuts compared to the earnings from the Coolmore stallions, a factor which undoubtedly influences the racing programmes selected for Ballydoyle's top horses, now reflected in the attention being given to the Breeders' Cup meeting.

Galileo's only appearance as a two-year-old had been when evens favourite for an end-of-season maiden over a mile on heavy going at Leopardstown. He won in sparkling style by fourteen lengths, earning quotes of between 16/1 and 20/1 in the winter ante-post betting on the Two Thousand Guineas and the Derby. Given his breeding and the fact that he was still running on strongly at the end of a testing mile, Galileo looked much more of a Derby prospect than a Guineas contender, and it came as no surprise when a middle-distance path was chosen for him in the spring. Galileo followed the route to Epsom taken the previous year by Sinndar, reappearing in the middle of April in the listed Ballysax Stakes over a mile and a quarter at Leopardstown and going one better than Sinndar, who met the only defeat of his career in the same race. Galileo was a smooth winner from stable-companion Milan, with Vinnie Roe third (second and third both future classic winners) and the bookmakers took no chances, promoting Galileo to the head of the Derby betting. With his position usurped in the interim by the Guineas winner Golan, Galileo maintained his own unbeaten record with another clear-cut victory in the Derrins-town Stud Derby Trial, again over a mile and a quarter at Leopardstown. Galileo won by a length and a half from another Derby entrant Exaltation, running on strongly at the finish and looking guaranteed to improve a fair bit over the Derby trip. The going was good to firm, vastly different to the testing conditions Galileo had encountered on his first two starts, and his notably fluent action and the ease with which he travelled through the race before beginning his challenge augured well for Epsom. The O'Brien horses in general tended to need the race at around this time and Galileo himself blew far more than the placed horses after the Derrinstown, suggesting there was a little more left to work on before the Derby.

Whilst Ballydoyle made a slow start to 2001—its Newmarket Guineas challenge, for example, making little impact—the stable's horses were thriving by Derby time. They dominated Guineas weekend at the Curragh, filling the first three places in the Irish Two Thousand and three of the first four in the Irish One Thousand. Two weeks later, Imagine won the Oaks—like the Derby sponsored by Vodafone—to set up an Epsom classic training double which had been achieved on only seven occasions in the previous century. The trials in Britain failed to unveil a Derby challenger to dislodge Golan (ridden by Eddery after stable jockey Fallon was suspended) and Galileo from the head of the Derby betting, the pair starting

*Vodafone Derby Stakes, Epsom—early in the home straight and Galileo is about to sweep past the leaders;
eventual second and third, Golan (No.5) and Tobougg (No.12), also challenge on the outside*

11/4 joint favourites on the day. The Lingfield Derby Trial winner Perfect Sunday
was next at 9/2, followed by the Dante Stakes winner Dilshaan at 5/1 and the
previous year's Dewhurst winner Tobougg, beaten favourite in the Two Thousand
Guineas last time, at 9/1. There was less discussion than usual before a modern-day
Derby about the supposed stamina—or rather lack of it—of some of the leading
contenders. Golan and Galileo both looked certain to stay on pedigree, as did
Dilshaan and Perfect Sunday, while one of Perfect Sunday's stable-companions,
the Chester Vase winner Mr Combustible, looked as stoutly bred as any of the
twelve runners in the smallest field since the same number tackled the race in
Nashwan's year.

Mr Combustible and Perfect Sunday shared the lead in the Derby for over a
mile, the pace steadying a little after the usual early scramble for positions. Galileo
moved smoothly just behind the leaders on the outside, tracked by Golan and
Tobougg, and was perfectly poised rounding Tattenham Corner. His rider Michael
Kinane followed to the letter his pre-race plan to 'let Galileo use himself, as he
should stay'. As soon as he was fully opened out in the straight, Galileo—
impressing with his extravagant stride—produced a devastating burst which took
him to the front with over two furlongs still to go. Storming clear, he was never in
the slightest danger afterwards and passed the post, his rider easing up, three and a
half lengths ahead of Golan for the most impressive Derby victory since Generous
recorded his five-length success in 1991 in similar style. Tobougg finished third,
a neck behind Golan, followed by three of the four Hills-trained runners, Mr
Combustible, the Dante third Storming Home and Perfect Sunday; Dilshaan came
seventh. Galileo's winning time was 2m 33.27sec, the second-fastest in the history
of the race (Lammtarra holds the record) and his time performance—he recorded a
timefigure of 0.99 fast—was a very good one in the circumstances, given the
relatively steady pace in the middle part of the race. The much discussed 'slow'
pace in the latest Derby, incidentally, was exaggerated in some quarters and any
suggestion that the 'real stayers' in the Derby field were compromised by the way
the race was run was mostly twaddle. The only Derby runner with any shred of an
excuse on the day was Storming Home, who might have finished a place closer but
for being hampered by Tobougg entering the final furlong.

Storming Home's 'traffic problems' were nothing compared to those encountered by many trying to make their way to Epsom on Derby Day. There were
long tailbacks on most of the approach roads, Golan's trainer Sir Michael Stoute
and Tobougg's rider Frankie Dettori being among the jockeys and trainers who
reportedly had to abandon their transport and walk the last part of the journey. The
publicity for 'Britain's biggest day out' exhorted the public to 'Be part of it', and
the Downs resonated as an estimated modern-day record of 150,000 flocked
to Epsom, some of the scenes resembling those black and white archive images.
Flat racing's greatest day also returned to BBC1 television for the first time in
twenty-two years, though the TV audience remained still substantially less than that

for the Grand National, far and away racing's biggest attraction with an audience in 2001 of ten million. An estimated three million watched the Derby live in Britain, just under a third of the terrestrial television audience watching at the time; this was compared to 2.4m who watched Channel 4's coverage the previous year (the figure of 3.9m claimed by Channel 4 and published in *Racehorses of 2000* appears to have been cumulative, incorporating figures for preview and recorded highlights programmes). Incidentally, two Derby institutions swapped mementoes before racing on Derby Day, Lester Piggott receiving his to celebrate the fiftieth anniversary of his first ride in the race and veteran BBC radio commentator Peter Bromley receiving his to mark his retirement. Four of Piggott's nine Derby winners were for the previous master of Ballydoyle Vincent O'Brien—father-in-law of John Magnier—who sent out six winners of the race in a most distinguished career. Galileo was Aidan O'Brien's first Epsom Derby winner, and O'Brien also emulated his namesake by becoming the champion trainer on the Flat in Britain in the latest season, the first overseas trainer to achieve the feat since 1977, when Vincent O'Brien took the title by winning eighteen races worth £439,124 (his string that year included Alleged and The Minstrel, the two best horses in Europe). Aidan O'Brien won twenty races in Britain in the latest season and his haul in first-three prize-money was £3,245,024, a record surpassing that set the previous year by Sir Michael Stoute. O'Brien enjoyed a phenomenally successful season—he was also champion trainer in Ireland for the fifth successive year—and won a record twenty-three Group 1 or Grade 1 races, including ten of the twenty-seven run in Britain. More about his achievements can be found in the essays on Black Minnaloushe and Johannesburg. The self-effacing O'Brien seemed unmoved by all the praise heaped on him during the latest season, describing his job with Ballydoyle's annual consignment of quality thoroughbreds simply as 'not to mess them up'. Vincent O'Brien's sixteen British classic winners included two Oaks winners, but he never achieved the Epsom classic double in the same year. Henry Cecil, who twice won the Derby and Oaks in the same year (1985 and 1999) and Dick Hern (1980) are the only other trainers to achieve that particular feat in the last forty years.

Galileo gave Michael Kinane his second Epsom Derby winner (following Commander In Chief), and his association with the Ballydoyle horses enabled him to ride seventeen Group 1 or Grade 1 winners during the year. Until the latest season, Kinane had never won the Irish Derby. Galileo was his eighteenth mount in his native Derby, which was sponsored by Budweiser, and he had an armchair ride. Galileo developed a tendency to sweat before his races, and he got particularly warm down at the start at the Curragh, a stalls handler using a handful of grass to wipe an excess of sweat from his neck. Once the race got under way, however,

Vodafone Derby Stakes, Epsom—
Galileo proves a class apart, recording the most impressive Derby victory for a decade;
Golan (light colours) stays on for second place ahead of Tobougg (left) and Mr Combustible (rail)

Kinane must never have had a moment's anxiety. Always close up travelling smoothly, Galileo stretched clear after being shaken up to lead two furlongs out and, eased slightly in the closing stages, won by four lengths and the same from the Derby Italiano winner Morshdi and the strong-finishing Golan. The front-running Pugin held on for fourth, ahead of Exaltation—winner of the Gallinule Stakes on his only outing since the Derrinstown Stud Derby Trial—and Mr Combustible. The 11/4-on Galileo, who virtually doubled the distances between himself and Golan and Mr Combustible compared to Epsom, was his trainer's second Irish Derby winner (following Desert King). He also provided Ballydoyle with its sixth European classic victory of the year, a tally which became seven when Milan won the St Leger. At first, it seemed that Galileo—like Sinndar after his Anglo-Irish Derby double—would bypass the King George VI and Queen Elizabeth Stakes. The main focus, it seemed, was now on the Breeders' Cup Classic at the end of October and the preferred route was the Irish Champion Stakes and the Queen Elizabeth II Stakes—'though he could well run somewhere before the Irish Champion.' That 'somewhere' did eventually turn out to be Ascot at the end of July for Britain's most prestigious all-aged middle-distance event. Galileo had proved himself to everyone's satisfaction the best three-year-old over a mile and a half, though those hailing him as one of the all-time greats were still being premature. Galileo's Irish Derby victory was achieved in a twelve-runner field in which half the runners started at 66/1 or longer, and his winning margin was not exceptional for the race these days, St Jovite, Balanchine, Zagreb, Dream Well, Montjeu and Sinndar all having won the race by further in the previous ten years. The twelve-length victory of St Jovite in 1992, the four-and-a-half length victory of Oaks winner Balanchine over Derby second and third King's Theatre and Colonel Collins in 1994, and Sinndar's nine-length win all represented better form than Galileo's—at least in our view—as did the three-length victory of Generous over Prix du Jockey Club winner Suave Dancer in the 1991 edition, the best performance in the race of modern times, judged strictly on form.

Victory in the King George VI and Queen Elizabeth Diamond Stakes took Galileo's reputation to new heights, though much of the Press coverage was a ludicrous over-reaction. On a sweltering afternoon and before a record crowd of 38,410, Ascot, it seemed to some, was to be the scene not of a contest but of a coronation; another victory for Galileo seemed a formality, whether in the runaway style of Generous (who won by a record seven lengths) or on a tight rein like Nijinsky and Montjeu. Sweating freely, Galileo started at 2/1-on, with 7/2-shot Fantastic Light—who had improved since being trounced in the race by Montjeu twelve months earlier—the only other runner to start at odds shorter than 18/1. The King George really caught the public imagination, helped by some attempts in the Press to promote it as a clash of two Titans, Fantastic Light having run out an

Budweiser Irish Derby, the Curragh—another striking performance as
Galileo provides jockey Michael Kinane with his first win in the race from eighteen attempts;
they are far too good for Derby Italiano winner Morshdi, Golan (right) and Pugin (rail)

King George VI and Queen Elizabeth Diamond Stakes, Ascot—
Galileo battles on splendidly and outstays Fantastic Light; Hightori (No.5) has to overcome
trouble in running before finishing third, ahead of Storming Home and Millenary (right)

impressive winner of the Prince of Wales's Stakes at the Royal meeting. The Titans finished first and second—Galileo winning a memorable race by two lengths in 2m 27.71 sec, the third fastest time in the event's history—but the bare result showed that the Titans weren't much bigger than their rivals. The racing media, however, predictably bathed Galileo in superlatives—'one of the true greats' seemed to be the majority view—conveniently glossing over the proximity at the finish of third- and fourth-placed Hightori and Storming Home. They were separated by a short head and were only three lengths adrift of Fantastic Light, restricting the view that could be taken of the form, added to which Hightori suffered serious interference in the straight and looked unlucky not to come second. Galileo had little in hand at the finish, the air of invincibility that had been constructed around him dispelled as the patiently-ridden Fantastic Light appeared to edge into the lead after being produced to challenge approaching the final furlong. With the result momentarily looking as if it could go either way, Galileo, ridden for stamina as at Epsom and the Curragh and taking over in front from early in the home straight, had to pull out all the stops. Kinane had secured the mount after a late injunction in the Dublin High Court against the Turf Club, over an appeal against a two-day ban for careless riding, and he excelled on Galileo at Ascot. Galileo responded splendidly to Kinane's strong handling in the final furlong and forged ahead again as Fantastic Light faltered near the finish. In a strongly-run race, in which both principals were accompanied by pacemakers, Galileo effectively outstayed Fantastic Light who was eased in the last few strides.

Although Galileo's performance at Ascot did not merit all the hyperbole it generated, it was nonetheless top-class, certainly above-average for the race in recent times. The field of twelve was the first double-figure line-up since 1994, when Kinane (who has now ridden four King George winners) was successful on King's Theatre. The latest edition attracted a thoroughly representative field, bringing the generations together with three Group 1 winners among the older horses (Golden Snake and Millenary, as well as Fantastic Light) and three from the current classic crop (Morshdi and Prix du Jockey Club winner Anabaa Blue joining Galileo). Galileo's timefigure of 1.15 fast, the second best recorded in Britain all year (just behind Fantastic Light's at Royal Ascot), provided independent confirmation of the value of the form. Galileo was the seventh horse to achieve the feat of winning the Derby at both Epsom and the Curragh and then go on to success in the King George. The others are Nijinsky, Grundy, The Minstrel, Troy, Shergar and Generous—not bad company to be in—while Mill Reef and Nashwan completed a similar treble, contesting the Eclipse instead of the Irish Derby between Epsom and Ascot. Some of those mentioned displayed a degree of versatility all too rarely seen in the modern thoroughbred, notably triple crown winner Nijinsky and Nashwan, the last horse to win the Two Thousand Guineas and the Derby.

Galileo's versatility was tested on his two remaining starts when he reverted to a mile and a quarter for the Irish Champion Stakes and the Breeders' Cup Classic, plans to tackle the Queen Elizabeth II Stakes being shelved after Galileo's narrow defeat at Leopardstown. The Irish Champion attracted tremendous publicity—the 'sequel' to Ascot's 'blockbuster'—and produced another memorable head-to-head between odds-on Galileo and Fantastic Light (the five other runners were sent off at odds ranging from 20/1 to 200/1). Fantastic Light's defeat in the King George was his seventh in a row at a mile and a half and he turned the tables over the shorter trip, inflicting the first defeat on Galileo in seven races. Both horses again had the services of pacemakers, but Galileo's was soon out on his own, virtually ignored. Fantastic Light kept tabs on his own pacemaker Give The Slip with Galileo tracking them. In a reversal of the King George tactics, Fantastic Light made the first move, striking for home as Give The Slip was eased off the rail on the final turn to allow him through. Galileo had to begin his own challenge three-wide, racing round the outside of Give The Slip, and was never quite able to get to the front as Fantastic Light maintained a fractional advantage in a drawn-out battle in the straight, both horses and both riders giving their all. The margin of victory was a head, though the result was not what the majority in a big crowd had been hoping for. 'We probably didn't shine tactically,' said O'Brien. 'I thought Give The Slip would go after Ice Dancer (Galileo's pacemaker) but he didn't and it was a difficult race for Michael to ride . . . maybe we should have had Galileo a bit handier.'

The summer dream of a Breeders' Cup meeting between Galileo and Point Given had been shattered at the end of August when Point Given returned with a career-ending injury to his near-fore after winning the Travers Stakes at Saratoga. The focus was now on a 'decider' between Galileo and Fantastic Light, both announced as likely runners next in the Breeders' Cup Classic, the Arc incidentally never being mentioned at any stage as a possible target for Galileo. Southwell's all-weather track staged a dress-rehearsal of sorts for the Ballydoyle Breeders' Cup contenders, as it had the previous year for Giant's Causeway, and a crowd estimated at five hundred saw Galileo, Mozart and Black Minnaloushe take part in three separate gallops, Galileo winning his by three lengths or so from his King George and Irish Champion pacemaker Ice Dancer ('We're happy with Galileo . . . he only came for the day out'). A late switch resulted in Arc winner Sakhee replacing Fantastic Light in the Breeders' Cup Classic. Fantastic Light ended his career in a blaze of glory by winning the Breeders' Cup Turf, instead while, in contrast, Galileo ended his in relative anonymity in the Classic, starting second favourite to Aptitude but managing only sixth of thirteen behind Tiznow on his first race on dirt and reportedly returning with swollen eyes and sore heels. Galileo will stand his first season at Coolmore in Ireland in 2002 at a fee of IR £50,000 with the October 1st concession.

The neat, attractive Galileo, who bears much more of a resemblance to his grandsire Northern Dancer than to his sire Sadler's Wells, is one of the finest movers anyone could wish to see, notably fluent with a tremendous stride (magnificently depicted in TV side-on shots of the field in the straight at Epsom). Galileo's Derby victory was the first for perennial champion sire Sadler's Wells, who had previously had five runners-up in the race. With Imagine leading home a one, two, three for Sadler's Wells in the Oaks—and providing him with his fourth winner of that classic—Galileo's victory made him the world's leading sire of Group 1/Grade 1 winners, Galileo being his forty-sixth such individual winner. Another landmark came with Milan's St Leger win, which gave Sadler's Wells a complete set of British and Irish classic winners. There is more on Sadler's Wells in the essay on Gossamer.

		Northern Dancer	Nearctic
	Sadler's Wells (USA)	(b 1961)	Natalma
	(b 1981)	Fairy Bridge	Bold Reason
Galileo (IRE)		(b 1975)	Special
(b.c. 1998)		Miswaki	Mr Prospector
	Urban Sea (USA)	(ch 1978)	Hopespringseternal
	(ch 1989)	Allegretta	Lombard
		(ch 1978)	Anatevka

Sadler's Wells earned the lion's share of the credit at the time for Galileo's Derby victory, but Galileo's pedigree is a notable illustration of success for that oldest of breeding adages—putting the best to the best and hoping for the best. Galileo's dam Urban Sea won the Prix de l'Arc de Triomphe and is a daughter of the splendid broodmare Allegretta, whose eight other winners include Two Thousand Guineas winner King's Best. Another of Allegretta's pattern-winning daughters

Allez Les Trois is also the dam of Prix du Jockey Club winner Anabaa Blue, while yet another of her daughters Anzille, who was placed four times in France, is the dam of the latest Deutschland-Preis winner Anzillero. Galileo's successes meant that three daughters of Allegretta were represented by Group 1 winners in the latest season; a fourth daughter, the listed winner Turbaine, also had a pattern winner in the US-bred Tertullian, who won the Prix de la Porte Maillot. The prospects of Allegretta's achieving lasting fame at stud looked remote when she passed through the ring at the December Sales for 24,000 guineas after her racing career in Britain, in which her achievements included wins at a mile and nine furlongs as a two-year-old and a second in the Lingfield Oaks Trial before her form went rapidly downhill. Galileo's dam Urban Sea, who cost 280,000 francs (approximately £28,000) as a yearling, raced for a relatively unfashionable dual-purpose stable which looked as if it might lose her when she was sent up to the Goffs Arc Sale in 1992 to dissolve a partnership also involving other horses. All were bought back by Mr Tsui, one of the partners, for three million francs (about £365,000). Urban Sea, a tough, sound, genuine filly, was a 37/1 outsider when successful in the following year's Arc; she was kept in training for a second tilt at the race but didn't make the line-up, retired through injury after a good spring campaign saw her win the Prix d'Harcourt and finish in the frame in the Prix Ganay and the Coronation Cup. Galileo is Urban Sea's third foal, and her third 'black type' performer following the Gallinule Stakes victor Urban Ocean (by Bering) and the listed winner Melikah (by Lammtarra), who finished third in the Oaks and second in the Irish Oaks. Urban Sea's fourth foal, Galileo's brother Black Sam Bellamy, contributed further to the family name when third in the Criterium de Saint-Cloud, and there is a yearling colt and filly foal, both also by Sadler's Wells. The filly foal made 1.1m guineas—to the

Mrs John Magnier & Mr M. Tabor's "Galileo"

bid of John Magnier who already had an interest in her—when sent up to the December Sales. The game and genuine Galileo acted on any going. He was equipped with a crossed noseband in his races and tended to sweat, though he did not get anything like so warm as usual before the Irish Champion, in which he showed himself nearly as good at a mile and a quarter as he was at his natural trip of a mile and a half. *A. P. O'Brien, Ireland*

GALLANT 4 b.c. Rainbow Quest (USA) 134 – Gay Gallanta (USA) 112 (Woodman (USA) 126) [2001 71: 8.3g⁶ 9m* 8m³ 10g² 8.5f³ 8g⁴ 9f⁶ Dec 26] smallish, useful-looking colt: unimpressive mover: fairly useful performer: won handicap at Goodwood in June: good efforts in similar events at Goodwood and Ascot (final start for M. Meade), then in frame in allowance races at Hollywood: stays 1¼m: acts on firm and soft going: slowly away on reappearance. *I. P. D. Jory, USA*   **89**

GALLANT BOY (IRE) 2 ch.c. (Apr 12) Grand Lodge (USA) 125 – Damerela (IRE) (Alzao (USA) 117) [2001 7f³ 7m² Sep 11] 57,000F, 140,000Y: rather leggy, quite good-topped colt: has scope: easy mover: third foal: half-brother to Irish 7f winner Crevelli (by Dolphin Street) and Irish 1½m to 2m winner Cincuenta (by Bob Back), both fairly useful: dam French maiden half-sister to dam of Daylami: shaped well in maidens at Newmarket (third to Savannah Bay) and Leicester (again caught flat-footed before staying on well, beaten ½ length by Indian Dreamer), well-backed favourite each time: will be well suited by 1¼m/1½m: useful prospect, sure to win races. *Sir Michael Stoute*   **84 p**

GALLA PLACIDIA (IRE) 3 b.f. Royal Abjar (USA) 121 – Merrie Moment (IRE) (Taufan (USA) 119) [2001 73: 7m 7.6m³ Jun 26] fair form in maidens at 2 yrs: only modest form in 2001: should stay 1¼m: raced only on good/good to firm going on turf, ran once on fibresand. *R. Ingram*   **54**

GALLEON BEACH 4 b.g. Shirley Heights 130 – Music In My Life (IRE) 59 (Law Society (USA) 130) [2001 85: 11.9g 16.4m⁵ 15.9d 16m⁶ 18f² 12g 18d Oct 20] sturdy, deep-girthed gelding: fairly useful performer nowadays: stays 2¼m: acts on firm and soft going: blinkered/tongue tied last 3 starts: unreliable. *J. W. Hills*   **92 §**

GALLEONS POINT 5 b.g. Sabrehill (USA) 120 – Rainbow Ring (Rainbow Quest (USA) 134) [2001 10m May 29] sparely-made gelding: fourth living foal: half-brother to winner up to 11f Raindeer Quest (by Hadeer): dam ran once: no sign of ability in bumpers/Flat maiden. *H. A. McWilliams*   **–**

GALLERY BREEZE 2 b.f. (Feb 6) Zamindar (USA) 116 – Wantage Park 104 (Pas de Seul 133) [2001 6.1m 5.1g⁴ 5s² 6m 5d⁴ f6g Oct 18] leggy, unfurnished filly: half-sister to several winners, including stayers Izza and Thornby Park (both by Unfuwain), latter fairly useful: dam stayed 7f: modest maiden: best effort when runner-up at Beverley: may prove best at 5f: acts on soft ground, probably on good to firm: blinkered last 4 starts: has hung left: tends to be slowly away. *T. D. Easterby*   **63**

GALLERY GOD (FR) 5 ch.g. In The Wings 128 – El Fabulous (FR) 111 (Fabulous Dancer (USA) 124) [2001 99: 12f* 12m³ 14m³ 14g⁴ 12s* 12d³ Nov 25] rangy gelding: has a quick action: smart performer: won handicap at Thirsk (for second year running) in June and listed race at Nantes (made all to beat Darakiyla 2 lengths) in November: good efforts in handicaps at Royal Ascot (third to Takamaka Bay in Duke of Edinburgh Stakes) and Goodwood then listed race at latter course (3½ lengths fourth to Shamaiel) in between: effective at 1½m/1¾m: acts on any going: often sweats/gets on edge/takes good hold: consistent. *G. Wragg*   **113**

GALLOWAY BOY (IRE) 4 ch.g. Mujtahid (USA) 118 – Supportive (IRE) (Nashamaa 113) [2001 100: 5s 6v 5s² 6g 5.1f 5m³ 6g 5g 6m 5m 5g³ 6m 5v 5d Oct 13] smallish, sturdy gelding: useful handicapper: creditable efforts only when placed at Epsom in April, York in May and Epsom in September: best at 5f: well held on heavy going, acts on any other: tried blinkered, visored final outing: usually tongue tied. *D. Nicholls*   **98**

GALY BAY 3 b.f. Bin Ajwaad (IRE) 119 – Sylhall (Sharpo 132) [2001 74: 8.1s² 8g 6g 9.1v* 8d Oct 30] leggy, unfurnished filly: modest performer: won seller at Ayr in October: stays 9f: raced only on good going or softer (acts on heavy): blinkered second/third starts: has been edgy/hung left. *A. Bailey*   **56**

GAME GURU 2 b.g. (Mar 20) First Trump 118 – Scarlett Holly 81 (Red Sunset 120) [2001 5s f5g⁴ f5g⁵ 5g⁵ 5s⁶ f6g³ 7s f6g⁶ f7g* f7g* Nov 30] 17,000Y: leggy, quite good-topped gelding: half-brother to several winners, including 4-y-o Scarlett Ribbon and 8.5f winner Little Scarlett (by Mazilier): dam 6f/7f winner: fairly useful on all-weather,   **61 a84**

modest on turf: won nurseries at Southwell in November: stays 7f: acts on fibresand, best turf effort on good going: blinkered fifth and last 2 starts. *T. D. Barron*

GAME LEADER (IRE)   2 b.f. (Jan 16) Mukadamah (USA) 125 – Fauna (IRE) 65   **72**
(Taufan (USA) 119) [2001 5.1d 5.1d² 5.7f² 5.7f* 5m 5.7m⁵ 6d Sep 14] 7,000Y: angular
filly: first foal: dam, maiden who stayed 1m, half-sister to useful 6f to 1m performer
Baaderah: fair performer: made all in maiden at Bath in June: ran poorly last 2 starts:
should stay 7f: acts on firm and good to soft ground. *D. Haydn Jones*

GAME N GIFTED   3 b.g. Mind Games 121 – Margaret's Gift 101 (Beveled (USA))   **79 d**
[2001 91: 5.1s⁴ 6s 7g 6g 6g 7.5m⁶ 11g Dec 16] fairly useful at 2 yrs: below form after
reappearance in 2001: sold 1,500 gns from B. Meehan after fifth outing: stays 6f: acts on
good to firm going: tried blinkered/tongue tied. *T. Minissale, Italy*

GAME PIE   3 ch.f. Selkirk (USA) 129 – Pigeon Hole (Green Desert (USA) 127) [2001   **–**
7m 7.1g Jul 20] first foal: dam lightly-raced half-sister to 1000 Guineas runner-up Niche:
twice-raced in maidens, hanging badly left on debut and reportedly breaking leg next
time: dead. *R. Hannon*

GAMES MISTRESS   2 b.f. (Feb 25) Mind Games 121 – Annaceramic 83 (Horage   **54 d**
124) [2001 5m⁵ f5g 5f 6g 6m Aug 11] 11,000Y: small, lightly-made filly: fourth foal: dam
best up to 7.5f: modest maiden: best effort on debut: should stay 6f. *T. D. Easterby*

GAME TIME   2 b.f. (May 7) Atraf 116 – Real Popcorn (IRE) 52 (Jareer (USA) 115)   **64**
[2001 5.1f 6g⁶ f7g³ f8.5g⁴ f8.5g⁴ f8.5g* f8g⁶ p8g* f8g p7g⁵ Dec 12] 14,000Y: third foal:
dam 1½m winner: modest performer: left A. Jarvis after third start: won selling nursery at
Wolverhampton and seller at Lingfield in November: stays 8.5f: acts on fibresand and
polytrack, some promise on turf: has raced freely/carried head high. *R. Brotherton*

GAME TUFTY   5 b.g. Sirgame – Melancolia 77 (Legend of France (USA) 124) [2001   **45 §**
52§, a54§: f12s⁵ f12g⁴ f11g* f11g 10f 12m 11.5m 11.6g f11g f14.8s f12s Dec 26]
workmanlike gelding: poor performer: won seller at Southwell in February: well beaten
last 6 starts: stays 1½m: acts on firm going, soft and fibresand: reportedly had breathing
problem second start: often looks less than keen. *P. Howling*

GAMITAS   3 b.f. Dolphin Street (FR) 125 – Driftholme 27 (Safawan 118) [2001 62:   **50**
f8s³ f11g³ 8d 8m 8m⁶ Aug 1] modest maiden handicapper: stays 11f: best form on   **a59**
fibresand: very reluctant to enter stall on reappearance: sold 5,000 gns. *A. P. Jarvis*

GAMUT (IRE)   2 b.c. (Mar 19) Spectrum (IRE) 126 – Greektown (Ela-Mana-Mou   **83 P**
132) [2001 7d² Nov 3] well-made colt: eighth living foal: closely related to smart 1¼m
and 13f winner Multicoloured (by Rainbow Quest) and half-brother to useful 7f (at 2
yrs) and 1¼m winner Athens Belle (by Groom Dancer): dam, French 1¼m/1½m winner,
half-sister to Prix du Cadran winner Sought Out: 10/1, shaped well when 1¼ lengths
second of 27 to Prince Hector in maiden at Newmarket, tracking pace and staying on well
having run bit green: will be suited by 1¼m/1½m: a useful prospect at least, and seems
sure to win races. *Sir Michael Stoute*

GANDON   4 ch.g. Hernando (FR) 127 – Severine (USA) 65 (Trempolino (USA) 135)   **63**
[2001 69: f12g* e13g f12g 10g 10.9m f8g⁴ 10g 12.1m⁴ f14.8g* 16.2m³ f14g Oct 1] IR
14,000Y: angular gelding: third foal: dam, 1½m winner, out of half-sister to Petoski:
modest performer: won maiden in March and apprentice handicap in August, both at
Wolverhampton: effective at 1½m to 2m: acts on firm going and fibresand: found little
penultimate start. *P. G. Murphy*

GANESHA   2 b.f. (Apr 12) Magic Ring (IRE) 115 – Breed Reference (Reference Point   **58 d**
139) [2001 6.1g³ 5f 6d 6.1m 6s 6.5g Sep 28] 900F, 2,500Y: good-bodied filly: fifth foal:
half-sister to fairly useful 6f/7f winner Jocasta (by Warning) and 10.5f seller winner
Home Force (by Chaddleworth): dam placed in France from 1¼m to 14.5f: modest
maiden: best effort on debut: should stay at least 7f. *J. G. Given*

GARDEN OF EDEN   3 b.f. Green Desert (USA) 127 – All The Time 59 (Dancing   **81**
Brave (USA) 140) [2001 –p: 10m² 10.2g f9.4g* Oct 23] tall, quite attractive filly: fairly
useful performer, lightly raced: won handicap at Wolverhampton in October: will
probably stay 1½m: acts on fibresand, best turf effort on good to firm going: sold 34,000
gns. *Sir Michael Stoute*

GARDEN SOCIETY (IRE)   4 ch.c. Caerleon (USA) 132 – Eurobird 118 (Ela-Mana-   **102**
Mou 132) [2001 98: 12s⁶ 13.4d³ 18d 16d Nov 2] small colt: useful performer, lightly
raced: best efforts when 9½ lengths sixth to Lucido in John Porter Stakes at Newbury in
April and 5¼ lengths third to Flossy in listed rated stakes at Chester in September: stays
13.4f: yet to race on heavy going, seems to act on any other. *J. A. R. Toller*

GARDOR (FR) 3 b.g. Kendor (FR) 122 – Garboesque (Priolo (USA) 127) [2001 63: **56**
10m 9f⁵ 7g 9.9g⁶ Aug 15] angular gelding: modest maiden: probably stays 1¼m: acts on
soft and good to firm going: edged left penultimate 2-y-o start. *J. G. FitzGerald*

GARDRUM (IRE) 3 ch.g. Lycius (USA) 124 – Kafayef (USA) 46 (Secreto (USA) **57 §**
128) [2001 –§: 7v 8v⁵ 9d 8.3m 6m* 7.1g⁶ 6g⁴ 6m 6f⁵ 7d⁶ 6d² 7g 7.1m 6v 8g Nov 7]
strong, close-coupled gelding: modest performer: won maiden at Newcastle in June:
best efforts at 6f: acts on firm and good to soft going: usually blinkered: refused to race
on debut: slowly away final outing: has hung left: one to treat with caution. *Miss
L. A. Perratt*

GARGOYLE GIRL 4 b.f. Be My Chief (USA) 122 – May Hills Legacy (IRE) 68 **–**
(Be My Guest (USA) 126) [2001 51: 10v 12g Nov 7] big, good-topped filly: modest
maiden at 3 yrs: behind both 4-y-o outings. *J. S. Goldie*

GARNOCK VALLEY 11 b.g. Dowsing (USA) 124 – Sunley Sinner 93 (Try My Best **60**
(USA) 130) [2001 68, a81: f6g f6s* f7g⁴ f7s⁵ f6g³ 5v⁴ 6s⁴ f6g⁶ f6g⁶ f6g f7g f7g⁵ f8g⁴ 8s **a67**
Jul 24] neat gelding: fair turf performer: won seller at Southwell in January: below form last 7
starts: stays 1m: best turf form on going softer than good, and acts on fibresand/equitrack:
has been blinkered/visored, not since 1999: sometimes slowly away, and often gets
behind. *A. Berry*

GARRISON (IRE) 3 b.f. College Chapel 122 – Milain (IRE) (Unfuwain (USA) 131) **55**
[2001 48: 6d² 6m 6m⁵ 6g 6g 5m 7m 5v Oct 15] unfurnished filly: modest maiden handicapper: seems best at 6f: acts on heavy and good to firm going: inconsistent. *Miss
L. A. Perratt*

GARW VALLEY 2 b.f. (May 9) Mtoto 134 – Morgannwg (IRE) 86 (Simply Great **62 p**
(FR) 122) [2001 7d Nov 3] rather leggy filly: fifth foal: sister to 4-y-o Welsh Dream and
half-sister to 6-y-o Black Army and 7f winner Penybont (by Unfuwain): dam 7f winner:
20/1, never-dangerous fourteenth of 21 in maiden at Newmarket: likely to prove suited
by at least 1¼m: should improve. *A. C. Stewart*

GASCON 5 b.g. Beveled (USA) – Lady Roxanne 65 (Cyrano de Bergerac 120) [2001 **70**
67: f6s 6.1v 6d² 6m* 6m² 6f⁶ 6m* 6m p7g⁶ p6g⁴ Dec 19] fair on turf, modest on all- **a52 +**
weather: won seller at Leicester in June and handicap at Salisbury in July: best at 6f: acts
on heavy ground, good to firm and polytrack: held up. *D. J. Coakley*

GAUDI PARC 3 ch.g. King's Signet (USA) 110 – Witch (Risk Me (FR) 127) [2001 **–**
10.4m 10f Sep 20] 500F, 750Y: big, strong, lengthy gelding: second foal: dam unraced:
tailed off in maidens at York and Pontefract. *J. Hetherton*

GAVRILOV (IRE) 2 b.c. (Apr 9) Danehill Dancer (IRE) 117 – Elminya (IRE) (Sure **73**
Blade (USA) 130) [2001 6f 6f 6m³ 7m⁶ 6.1d p5g³ p6g p6g Dec 28] IR 16,500F, IR
85,000Y: sixth foal: half-brother to 7f (at 2 yrs) to 1½m winner Soden (by Mujadil) and
fairly useful 1997 2-y-o 6f/7f winner Belle Nuit (by Statoblest): dam unraced half-sister
to very smart 1¼m performer Ruby Tiger: fair maiden: third at Epsom and Lingfield: will
probably stay 1m: acts on firm going and polytrack. *N. A. Callaghan*

GAY BREEZE 8 b.g. Dominion 123 – Judy's Dowry 80 (Dragonara Palace (USA) **72**
115) [2001 83d: f5g f6s⁶ f6g f5g 6.1v* 6m 6f f7g f6g 6g 6f⁴ 6m⁵ 5g 7m f6g 5v 6g² 6v² **a68**
Nov 8] compact gelding: fair handicapper: won at Nottingham (from flip start) in March:
effective at 5f to easy 7f: acts on any going: usually races prominently: none too consistent. *P. S. Felgate*

GAY CHALLENGER 3 b.g. Young Ern 120 – Ship of Gold 78 (Glint of Gold 128) **–**
[2001 48: e10g⁵ 10s⁶ 7d 7s 7d 6m 7m 6m⁶ 8m 8m 8m Jul 4] close-coupled gelding: has a
round action: little form in 2001: tried blinkered. *N. A. Callaghan*

GAYE LATINO 2 ch.f. (Apr 27) Wing Park 104 – Lombard Ships 73 (Orchestra 118) **–**
[2001 6g 6m Aug 13] first foal: dam 7f/1m winner: well held in seller/minor event.
P. S. McEntee

GAY HEROINE 3 b.f. Caerleon (USA) 132 – Gay Gallanta (USA) 112 (Woodman **105 d**
(USA) 126) [2001 77p: 11.4f² 12m⁶ 12f 10m² 12d 12.3d³ Aug 31] good-topped filly:
disappointing maiden: useful form when neck second to Rockerlong in listed race at
Chester in May and when 6¼ lengths sixth to Imagine in Oaks at Epsom in June: beaten
in maidens last 3 starts, twice at odds on: will probably be suited by 1¾m+: raced mainly
on going firmer than good: visored final start: often soon off bridle. *Sir Michael Stoute*

GAY LOVER 4 gr.f. Environment Friend 128 – Gay Ming 50 (Gay Meadow 52) [2001 **–**
–: 11.5g Sep 11] no form in maidens. *Dr J. R. J. Naylor*

GAZEILA 2 b.f. (Feb 24) Makbul 104 – Liberatrice (FR) (Assert 134) [2001 6g 8d 5v **43** p7g p8g³ p10g p7g Dec 12] second foal: dam maiden half-sister to smart French 1989 2-y-o 5.5f winner Zinarelle: poor maiden: third in seller at Lingfield: stays 1m: acts on polytrack. *J. J. Bridger*

GAZETTE IT TONIGHT 3 b.f. Merdon Melody 98 – Balidilemma 77 (Balidar **55 §** 133) [2001 f7g f9.4g⁵ 8.3m 8m⁴ 7m⁶ 7.1m 8.2f⁴ 7m* 7.5f 8m 8m² 7g³ 8m⁶ 8m⁶ 7s f7g³ f7g Nov 21] small, sparely-made filly: modest performer: won seller at Yarmouth in July: stays 1m: acts on firm going, soft and fibresand: has hung left: inconsistent. *A. Berry*

GDANSK (IRE) 4 b.g. Pips Pride 117 – Merry Twinkle (Martinmas 128) [2001 74: **86** 5v* 5g* 5m 5m 5m⁶ 5g 5m 6f⁵ 6s² 5g 6d 5g⁵ 5s² 5m 5v* 5d 5s⁶ 5v Oct 29] leggy, lengthy gelding: fairly useful performer: won minor event at Folkestone in April, and handicaps at Thirsk in May and Haydock in September: best at 5f/6f: has form on good to firm going, but ideally suited by soft/heavy: sometimes slowly away, and usually held up: has edged left/carried head high: none too reliable. *A. Berry*

GEE BEE BOY 7 ch.g. Beveled (USA) – Blue And White (Busted 134) [2001 48: 14.1f **–** Jun 11] strong gelding: winning handicapper: well beaten only 7-y-o start. *G. M. McCourt*

GEEGEE EMMARR 8 b.m. Rakaposhi King 119 – Fair Sara 65 (McIndoe 97) [2001 **–** –: f12g 6.1v 6s f8g⁶ 8.1m⁵ 7m 8m Jun 4] of little account. *A. Berry*

GEESPOT 2 b.f. (Apr 16) Pursuit of Love 124 – My Discovery (IRE) (Imperial **39** Frontier (USA) 112) [2001 6g 6.1m 5s⁵ 5.7d 5.1s Nov 5] 1,600Y: first foal: dam unraced: poor maiden: should stay 6f: acts on soft going. *D. J. S. ffrench Davis*

GEETEE EIGHTYFIVE 3 b.g. Magic Ring (IRE) 115 – Versaillesprincess (Legend **–** of France (USA) 124) [2001 –: 8.3v p6g Nov 15] well held in maidens. *J. J. Bridger*

GEM BIEN (USA) 3 b.c. Bien Bien (USA) 125 – Eastern Gem (USA) (Jade Hunter **82 §** (USA)) [2001 70: 8.3s² 8d³ 7.9g 8.1f 8m⁵ 8.2m* 8g 10m Aug 28] rather leggy, quite attractive colt: fairly useful handicapper: won at Nottingham in July: should stay at least 1¼m: acts on soft and good to firm ground: tongue tied final outing: not an easy ride, and none too genuine. *Andrew Turnell*

GEMIND 2 b.f. (Apr 14) Forzando 122 – Innocent Abroad (DEN) 53 (Viking (USA)) **–** [2001 f7g f7g f8s Dec 21] 900Y: third foal: dam, poor maiden, out of half-sister to Prix du Jockey Club winner Policeman: soon behind in maidens: very slowly away debut. *B. P. J. Baugh*

GEMTASTIC 3 b.f. Tagula (IRE) 116 – It's So Easy 63 (Shaadi (USA) 126) [2001 70: **62** f6g f6s e6g e6g⁴ f6g⁶ 5.3f 5.1m⁴ 6.1f³ 6f³ 5.7g⁴ 6.1m* 7f 6m* 5.1m 6g 5m Aug 4] small, **a57** sparely-made filly: modest handicapper: won at Warwick in June and Southwell in July: best form around 6f: acts on firm going, good to soft and all-weather: has flashed tail: usually races prominently. *P. D. Evans*

GENERAL 4 b.g. Cadeaux Genereux 131 – Bareilly (USA) (Lyphard (USA) 132) **69** [2001 10m 10d⁶ 10.1f⁴ 8s² Oct 3] 3,000 3-y-o: strong, heavy-bodied gelding: second living foal: dam unraced close relative of Prix de Diane second Baya out of sister to Triptych: fair maiden on Flat: effective at 1m/1¼m: acts on firm and soft going: edged left final outing: winning hurdler. *Mrs N. Smith*

GENERAL AMNESTY (IRE) 2 b.c. (Apr 11) General Monash (USA) 107 – **56** Beautyofthepeace (IRE) (Exactly Sharp (USA) 121) [2001 6m f6g⁵ f6g 6d 8s 8g f7g Nov 16] IR 9,500F, 12,000Y, 6,500 2-y-o: leggy, quite good-topped colt: fourth foal: half-brother to 5-y-o Windshift: dam unraced: modest maiden: best efforts second and fourth starts: should stay 7f: acts on good to soft going and fibresand. *D. Shaw*

GENERAL DOMINION 4 b.g. Governor General 116 – Innocent Princess (NZ) **–** (Full On Aces (AUS)) [2001 61: 7m f8g Nov 26] modest maiden at 3 yrs: reared at stalls and unseated on reappearance, then left F. Murtagh. *G. A. Swinbank*

GENERAL HAVEN 8 ch.g. Hadeer 118 – Verchinina 99 (Star Appeal 133) [2001 **34** 14.1m 12m 10m 10.1m 12.6d 10.1m 16.2s 17.1g 11.1g⁶ Sep 2] quite good-topped gelding: fairly useful in 1997: poor form in 2001 on first outings on Flat since: tried blinkered/visored. *J. S. Wainwright*

GENERAL HAWK (IRE) 3 b.g. Distinctly North (USA) 115 – Sabev (USA) (Saber **64** Thrust (CAN)) [2001 61: f7g 5d 6m 6f 6m⁵ 7g* 7m² 8m⁴ f7g⁴ 7g Oct 19] rather leggy, useful-looking gelding: modest handicapper: won at Newcastle in July: stays 1m: acts on good to firm going, probably on fibresand: has been slowly away (reared as stall opened fourth outing). *R. A. Fahey*

GENERAL JACKSON 4 ch.g. Cadeaux Genereux 131 – Moidart 90 (Electric 126) **63**
[2001 71: 10m 11.5f 17.2g⁴ 18m² 21m 16g² 16d Sep 21] big, good-topped gelding: modest maiden handicapper: suited by 2m+: acts on good to firm ground. *Jane Southcombe*

GENERAL JANE 3 ch.f. Be My Chief (USA) 122 – Brave Advance (USA) 98 (Bold –
Laddie (USA)) [2001 –: 7m 8.1m⁶ Jul 5] little sign of ability. *B. R. Millman*

GENERAL SMITH 2 b.c. (Apr 16) Greensmith 121 – Second Call 67 (Kind of Hush **60**
118) [2001 f6g f6g³ f7g Nov 17] second foal: dam 1m/1¼m winner, also winning hurdler/chaser: modest form in maidens: third at Wolverhampton: should stay at least 1m: raced only on fibresand. *J. M. Bradley*

GENERATE 5 b.m. Generous (IRE) 139 – Ivorine (USA) (Blushing Groom (FR) 131) –
[2001 66: f11g 13s f12g Apr 14] smallish, good-topped mare: fair performer at best: little show in 2001. *M. J. Polglase*

GENERIC (FR) 6 b.g. Hero's Honor (USA) – Tweed Girl (FR) (Windwurf (GER)) **121**
[2001 9v* 10v* 12.5v⁶ 10s⁴ 12s* 12g³ 15.5d* 15d* 14s* 15d* 15.5d³ 20v² 15.5v² Oct 28] fourth foal: half-brother to French winner at up to 9.5f Neyev Girl (by Goldneyev): dam French 1m to 1½m winner: very smart performer: off over 2 years before return in autumn 2000: in tremendous form in 2001, winning apprentice race at Compiegne, handicaps at Longchamp and Chantilly, listed races at Maisons-Laffitte and Chantilly (beat Pairumani Star a head), Prix Maurice de Nieuil at Maisons-Laffitte (beat Romantic Affair 1½ lengths) and Prix Kergorlay at Deauville (beat Samsaam short neck) between March and August: placed at Longchamp last 3 starts when third to Yavana's Pace in Prix Gladiateur, 6 lengths second to Germinis in Prix du Cadran and (best effort) 2½ lengths second to Vinnie Roe in Prix Royal-Oak: stays 2½m: acts on heavy ground: held up: tough and consistent. *J-P. Gallorini, France*

GENEROUS DIANA 5 ch.m. Generous (IRE) 139 – Lypharitissima (FR) (Lightning **90**
(FR) 129) [2001 84: 10.5v 10d 12d³ 12s Nov 10] fairly useful performer, quite lightly raced: best effort when close third to Bollin Nellie in handicap at Newmarket in November: stays 1½m: raced mainly on going softer than good (acts on heavy): wore tongue tie first 2 starts. *C. G. Cox*

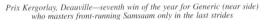

*Prix Kergorlay, Deauville—seventh win of the year for Generic (near side)
who masters front-running Samsaam only in the last strides*

GENEROUS WAYS 6 ch.g. Generous (IRE) 139 – Clara Bow (USA) (Coastal **67 §**
(USA)) [2001 74§, a71§: 13.1m 16.2f² 16m Jul 5] leggy, quite good-topped gelding: fair
handicapper: stays 2m: acts on firm going (possibly not on softer than good) and fibresand: blinkered once: sometimes slowly away: held up: reportedly finished distressed
final outing: weak finisher: sold 3,000 gns, joined R. Lee. *E. J. Alston*

GENIAL GENIE 5 b.g. Sizzling Melody 117 – Needwood Sprite 58 (Joshua 129) **78**
[2001 f7g³ f9.4g³ f7g⁶ f7g⁴ f8g f8.5g⁶ 8m 10g 7m³ 8f 6m² 6m* 6m⁴ 5g* 6m 7.1g* 7.5d²
7s³ 7d 7d² 7s⁴ f7g* f8g Dec 14] good-topped gelding: third foal: half-brother to 1¼m to
1¾m winner Flying Flip (by Rolfe): dam, 7f winner who stayed 1¾m, also successful
over hurdles: made into fair handicapper in first season: won at Thirsk and Pontefract in
August, Chepstow in September and Southwell in November: effective at stiff 5f to 1m:
acts on soft going, good to firm and fibresand: tongue tied: sometimes races freely:
reliable. *R. Hollinshead*

GENIE 3 ch.f. Cool Jazz 116 – Spice And Sugar 65 (Chilibang 120) [2001 8.3v⁶ p12g **–**
f8s Dec 21] first foal: dam 6f (at 2 yrs) and 1½m winner: well beaten in maidens/claimer.
J. S. Moore

GENIUS (IRE) 6 b.g. Lycius (USA) 124 – Once In My Life (IRE) 114 (Lomond (USA) **– §**
128) [2001 –, a54§: f12g Jan 6] big, good-bodied gelding: temperamental handicapper:
blinkered once at 2 yrs. *A. G. Juckes*

GENSCHER 5 b.g. Cadeaux Genereux 131 – Marienbad (FR) (Darshaan 133) [2001 **–**
–: 12.1m 13d 11.1g Sep 2] lengthy, workmanlike gelding: lightly raced and little form on
Flat since 1999: visored final outing. *R. Allan*

GENTLE MAGIC 3 b.f. Magic King (IRE) 115 – Gentle Stream 55 (Sandy Creek **–**
123) [2001 –: 9m 7m 7.1g Sep 13] leggy, unfurnished filly: little sign of ability. *H. Akbary*

GENTLEMAN VENTURE 5 b.g. Polar Falcon (USA) 126 – Our Shirley 84 **97**
(Shirley Heights 130) [2001 89: 10s* 10.1s³ 12f⁶ Jun 9] tall, quite attractive gelding:
useful handicapper: won Coral Eurobet Rosebery Stakes at Kempton in April, beating
Champagne Rider by 1¾ lengths, pair well clear, despite edging right: creditable efforts at
Epsom both starts after: best at 1¼m/1½m: acts on any going: free-going sort. *J. Akehurst*

GENUINE JOHN (IRE) 8 b.g. High Estate 127 – Fiscal Folly (USA) (Foolish **39**
Pleasure (USA)) [2001 39, a42: f11g* f11s⁴ f11g² f16g⁴ f16g⁵ 12d⁴ f11g f14g Dec 14] **a44**
sturdy gelding: poor handicapper: won at Southwell in January: effective at 11f to 2m:
acts on firm going, soft and fibresand: has run creditably in blinkers, not tried since 1999:
tongue tied: sometimes looks moody. *J. Parkes*

GEORGE ROMNEY (USA) 2 b.g. (May 22) Distant View (USA) 126 – Polish **78**
Socialite (USA) (Polish Navy (USA)) [2001 7.1v⁶ 7s³ p8g³ p8g³ Nov 28] $35,000Y,
70,000G 2-y-o: good-topped gelding: has scope: poor walker: fourth foal: half-brother to
1m (including at 2 yrs)/1¼m winner in USA by Seattle Song: dam unraced out of US
Grade 3 9f winner Social Business: fair maiden: third at Leicester and twice at Lingfield:
should stay 1¼m: acts on polytrack, raced only on soft/heavy going on turf: gelded after
final start. *P. F. I. Cole*

GEORGE STREET (IRE) 3 b.g. Danehill (USA) 126 – Sweet Justice (Law Society **62**
(USA) 130) [2001 8m 7.1f 8.3m 10m⁶ 12g² 16v Oct 17] 160,000Y: well-made gelding:
unimpressive mover: sixth foal: brother to useful Irish 7f to 1¼m winner Darina
and half-brother to 2 winners in Italy, including winner up to 11f by Bob Back: dam
French 9.5f winner: modest maiden: stays 1½m: raced mainly on good going or firmer:
blinkered/visored except third start (below form): sold 16,000 gns, gelded and joined
M. Pipe. *J. H. M. Gosden*

GEORGE STUBBS (USA) 3 b. or br.g. Affirmed (USA) – Mia Duchessa (USA) **82**
(Nijinsky (CAN) 138) [2001 52p: f7g³ f8g* 10g³ 10.2m* 9.9m⁴ 8d Oct 19] fairly useful
performer: won maiden at Southwell (wandered) in April and minor event at Bath in
May: off 3½ months before well held final outing: stays 1¼m: acts on good to firm going
and fibresand: makes running. *P. F. I. Cole*

GERI ROULETTE 3 b.f. Perpendicular 119 – Clashfern (Smackover 107) [2001 6m **47**
7.6m⁶ 10g⁴ 10m 10.9v⁶ f12g³ f11s² Dec 21] 800Y: second foal: dam unraced: poor
maiden: stays 11f: acts on fibresand: gave trouble at start on debut, flashed tail under
pressure final outing. *E. J. Alston*

Prix du Cadran - Casino Barriere de Cannes Croisette, Longchamp—
a fine training performance from Patrick Chevillard as Germinis defies a five-month absence
to outstay Generic (right) and the previous year's winner San Sebastian

GERMINIS (FR) 7 ch.g. Vaguely Pleasant (FR) 113 – Grey Valley (USA) (Vigors) **121**
[2001 107: 12.5s* 15.5v* 15v² 15.5s⁴ 20v* 15.5v³ Oct 28] fifth foal: brother to French
winners up to around 1¾m Greystar and Valley Pleasant and half-brother to 2 winners:
dam French 12.5f winner: very smart performer: better than ever at 7 yrs, winning listed
race at Cagnes-sur-Mer in February, minor event at Saint-Cloud in March and Prix
du Cadran - Casino Barriere de Cannes Croisette at Longchamp (off course 5 months,
beat Generic 6 lengths after leading 1m out) in October: creditable 2¾ lengths third to
Vinnie Roe in Prix Royal-Oak at Longchamp final start: has won at around 1½m but
ideally suited by 2m+: goes well on soft/heavy ground: won over hurdles in December.
P. Chevillard, France

GERONIMO 4 b.g. Efisio 120 – Apache Squaw 54 (Be My Guest (USA) 126) [2001 **67**
–, a64: e7g e10g e6g e8g² e8g f7g⁶ 6m* 6g² 6g⁴ 7s f6g f7s* p7g Dec 28] sparely-made
gelding: fair handicapper: won at Redcar in August and Wolverhampton in December:
effective at 6f to easy 1m: acts on good to firm going, fibresand and equitrack: blinkered
once. *M. Wigham*

GETATEM (IRE) 2 b.c. (Apr 5) Up And At 'em 109 – Fiaba 66 (Precocious 126) **66**
[2001 5m³ 5f² 5m⁵ 5m⁵ 5d⁵ 5m⁴ 5m² 6m 6v 6d 5g Nov 7] IR 3,600Y, 15,000 2-y-o: small,
compact colt: second foal: dam, 5f (at 2 yrs) to 1m winner, later won in Holland: fair
maiden: well below form last 4 starts: best at 5f: acts on firm ground. *Miss L. A. Perratt*

GET STUCK IN (IRE) 5 b.g. Up And At 'em 109 – Shoka (FR) 86 (Kaldoun (FR) **95**
122) [2001 92§: 5s² 5s⁴ 6g⁴ 5m 5m 5m² 6s⁵ 5d² 5m 6m 5s 5d Oct 13] leggy, quite
attractive gelding: useful handicapper: creditable efforts only when in frame: effective at
5f/6f: acts on any going: blinkered once: sometimes reluctant to post (has gone down
early)/slowly away: often leads: has carried head high/found little: remains none too
reliable. *Miss L. A. Perratt*

GEYSERVILLE 3 ch.g. Mujtahid (USA) 118 – Pennsylvania (USA) 83 (Northjet **–**
136) [2001 8m 8m 8.2s f8.5g f12g Nov 26] 19,000Y: angular gelding: sixth living foal:
half-brother to 3 winners, including fairly useful 7f (at 2 yrs)/1m winner East Liberty (by
Halo), later winner in USA, and a winner up to 1½m in Spain by Lahib: dam, maiden who
stayed 1¼m, daughter of high-class Mrs Penny: little form: left P. D'Arcy after second
start. *B. W. Duke*

GEZKAT 2 b.f. (Mar 3) Petong 126 – Petite Louie 45 (Chilibang 120) [2001 6g 6.1d **–**
7d⁶ Oct 19] close-coupled filly: has a round action: third foal: half-sister to 1½m winner
Crash Call Lady (by Batshoof): dam, maiden, daughter of half-sister to Environment
Friend: no promise in maidens/minor event. *S. C. Williams*

GHANNAM (USA) 2 b.c. (Mar 16) Langfuhr (CAN) 124 – Katerina Key (USA) (Key **95**
To The Mint (USA)) [2001 8f⁴ 6d² 6d³ Nov 2] $400,000Y: rather leggy, useful-looking
colt: good walker: closely related to 2 winners in USA, notably high-class Grade 1 9.5f/
11f winner Influent (by Ascot Knight) and half-brother to 3 winners: dam unraced out of
half-sister to high-class 5f to 1m performer (second in 1000 Guineas) Girl Friend: useful
maiden: best effort when ¾-length second of 22 to Hiddendale at Newmarket: third to
Feet So Fast there final start: likely to prove best at 7f/1m: acts on firm and good to soft
ground: well up to winning a race or 2. *M. P. Tregoning*

GHAYTH 3 b.c. Sadler's Wells (USA) 132 – Myself 110 (Nashwan (USA) 135) [2001 **90 d**
102: 7d 6m⁵ 7.5g 7.5g 10g Dec 13] small, stocky, attractive colt: has a quick, fluent
action: useful form at 2 yrs: disappointing in 2001, including in European Free Handicap

386

at Newmarket on reappearance: left Sir Michael Stoute after next outing, then off 4 months: stays 7f: acts on good to firm going. *K. P. McLaughlin, UAE*

GHAZAL (USA)   3 b.f. Gone West (USA) – Touch of Greatness (USA) (Hero's Honor (USA)) [2001 94p: 7d 6g² 6d* 6m Sep 22] sturdy, quite attractive filly: good mover: useful performer: off nearly 4 months after well held in Nell Gwyn Stakes at Newmarket on reappearance: improved form next 2 starts: head second to Flying Millie in quite valuable handicap at Ascot before winning minor event at Yarmouth in good style by 3 lengths from Hurricane Floyd: stayed 6f: acted on good to soft going, well below form in Ayr Gold Cup (Handicap) on good to firm: visits Danehill. *Sir Michael Stoute*   **103**

GHOST OF A CHANCE (IRE)   3 b.g. Indian Ridge 123 – Ma N'Ieme Biche (USA) (Key To The Kingdom (USA)) [2001 –: 7m⁴ 8f³ 7.5m 8m⁶ 7m⁵ 7s³ 7d⁴ 8v⁵ Nov 24] small, plain gelding: has a round action: poor maiden: sold 2,200 gns from M.Tompkins after fifth outing: unlikely to stay further than 1m: acts on firm and soft ground: tried blinkered. *F. Breuss, Germany*   **41**

GHUTAH   7 ch.g. Lycius (USA) 124 – Barada (USA) (Damascus (USA)) [2001 –: 16g⁶ Jun 12] little recent form on Flat: tried blinkered/visored. *G. A. Swinbank*   **–**

GIFTED FLAME   2 b.c. (May 14) Revoque (IRE) 122 – Little Lady Leah (USA) (Shareef Dancer (USA) 135) [2001 7f 7g 7.1m³ 8d 7v Oct 26] 6,500Y, 7,000 2-y-o: workmanlike colt: half-brother to 3-y-o Lucayan Chief and several winners abroad: dam unraced: fair maiden: form only when third at Warwick: should stay 1m: acts on good to firm ground. *P. G. Murphy*   **77**

GIFT FOUNTAIN   2 b.f. (Feb 11) Greensmith 121 – Bright Fountain (IRE) 47 (Cadeaux Genereux 131) [2001 8.1g³ Aug 27] first foal: dam poor maiden daughter of useful stayer High Fountain from very good middle-distance family: green, 3¾ lengths third of 11 in maiden at Chepstow: will be suited by 1¼m/1½m: should improve. *H. Candy*   **76 p**

GIFT OF GOLD   6 ch.g. Statoblest 120 – Ellebanna 69 (Tina's Pet 121) [2001 93, a72: 7d⁴ 8d 6g 7.2g² Aug 31] good-topped, close-coupled gelding: fairly useful handicapper: creditable efforts within 6 weeks only when in frame at Ayr: seems best around 7f nowadays: acts on good going, good to firm and fibresand/equitrack: tried blinkered, seems better when not. *A. Bailey*   **83 a–**

GIKO   7 b.g. Arazi (USA) 135 – Gayane 125 (Nureyev (USA) 131) [2001 57: 8.2s 8m 9f 10m³ 10m⁴ 12m⁴ 11.6m* 12.1s 13.1d³ 12g 12m Sep 26] leggy gelding: has a round action: modest handicapper: won at Windsor in July: stays 13f: acts on soft going, good to firm and fibresand: effective in blinkers, not used in 2001: tried in tongue tie. *Jane Southcombe*   **52**

GILDA (IRE)   3 b.f. Goldmark (USA) 113 – Pretty Precedent (Polish Precedent (USA) 131) [2001 79: e10g² e10g⁵ a8f⁶ Sep 30] fair performer: left R. Cowell after second outing, then off over 7 months: stays 1¼m: acts on equitrack. *J. M. Hilling, USA*   **75**

GILDED DANCER   3 b.g. Bishop of Cashel 122 – La Piaf (FR) (Fabulous Dancer (USA) 124) [2001 76: 8g² 8.1m³ May 26] small, good-bodied gelding: fairly useful maiden: ran very well in competitive large-field handicaps at Newmarket (head second to Dance On The Top) and Haydock (third to Ecclesiastical in Tote Credit Silver Bowl) only 3-y-o outings: gelded after: should prove best up to 1m: acts on good to firm ground. *W. R. Muir*   **89**

GILDEN MAGIC   3 b.g. Magic Ring (IRE) 115 – Have Form (Haveroid 122) [2001 7s 6.9v² 7m 8d 11.6m 10.2g f11g f12s Dec 27] 3,000Y, 15,000 2-y-o: close-coupled gelding: half-brother to useful sprinter (also won up to 1m) Shikari's Son (by Kala Shikari): dam maiden: modest maiden: disappointing after second outing: gelded and off over 4 months before penultimate start: should stay 1m: acts on heavy going. *M. Blanshard*   **62 d**

GILL'S DIAMOND (IRE)   3 ch.f. College Chapel 122 – Yafford (Warrshan (USA) 117) [2001 54: f6g⁴ 5m 5m 5g 6g f6g⁴ Oct 22] small, good-bodied filly: poor maiden in 2001: should prove best at 6f/7f: acts on soft going, good to firm and fibresand: tongue tied last 2 starts: reportedly broke blood vessel once at 2 yrs. *N. Tinkler*   **39**

GILL THE TILL (IRE)   2 ch.f. (May 19) Anshan 119 – Bilander 78 (High Line 125) [2001 7m 8.2m⁶ 8m f8.5g⁶ 5.7d 8.3v⁶ Nov 8] IR 6,000Y: workmanlike filly: half-sister to several winners, notably useful sprinter Humbert's Landing (by Cyrano de Bergerac): dam maiden who stayed 1½m: poor maiden: stays 1m: often slowly away. *M. R. Channon*   **43**

GILT TRIP (IRE)   3 b.g. Goldmark (USA) 113 – Opening Day (Day Is Done 115) [2001 –: f8g f9.4g* f11g⁵ f11g⁶ f12g f9.4g⁴ f12g 11.6m 15.8m⁶ Aug 7] poor performer: **– § a52 §**

won seller at Wolverhampton (sold from J. Osborne 2,500 gns) in February: sold from N. Littmoden 3,000 gns/off 4 months after fifth start: stays 9.4f: acts on fibresand, no form on turf: blinkered 7 starts before final one: ungenuine. *M. J. Polglase*

GINA (IRE)   3 b.f. Lahib (USA) 129 – Relankina (IRE) (Broken Hearted 124) [2001   –
49: f6g Jun 29] poor maiden: dead. *J. A. Glover*

GINANMIX (IRE)   3 gr.f. Linamix (FR) 127 – Mill Rainbow (FR) (Rainbow Quest   –
(USA) 134) [2001 6v Oct 29] first foal: dam, French 10.5f winner, out of half-sister to Prix Jacques le Marois winner Miss Satamixa (by Linamix): 25/1, well beaten in maiden at Windsor: bred to need 1¼m+. *S. Kirk*

GINGER ROGERS   7 ch.m. Gildoran 123 – Axe Valley 89 (Royben 125) [2001 f16g   –
May 21] probably of little account nowadays. *R. E. Peacock*

GINGKO   4 b.g. Pursuit of Love 124 – Arboretum (IRE) 83 (Green Desert (USA) 127)   **76**
[2001 74: f7g² f7g² f8.5g⁴ f7g 10g⁵ 10.3m* 10m 10.3m⁵ 10d 10v f8g* 10.2d p8g⁶ Nov 13] fair handicapper: won at Doncaster in May and Southwell in October: stays 1¼m: acts on good to firm going and fibresand. *J. G. Smyth-Osborne*

GINNER MORRIS   6 b.g. Emarati (USA) 74 – Just Run (IRE) 45 (Runnett 125)   **56**
[2001 51: f11g 9.1v 8v* f8g Dec 17] lengthy gelding: modest performer: won claiming   **a–**
handicap at Newcastle (for second successive year) in October: best at 1m/1¼m: acts on heavy ground: best form (including both wins) in blinkers: usually races prominently. *J. Hetherton*

GIN PALACE (IRE)   3 gr.c. King's Theatre (IRE) 128 – Ikala (Lashkari 128) [2001   **89**
73: 10s⁴ 10s* 11m⁶ 14g³ 13.9m 14g⁵ Oct 6] leggy, sparely-made colt: fairly useful performer: won maiden at Brighton in May: good efforts in handicaps when third to Big Moment at Goodwood in August and fifth to Riyadh at Newmarket in October: will stay 2m: acts on soft and good to firm going. *G. L. Moore*

GIRL FRIDAY   3 ch.f. Ajraas (USA) 88 – Miss Nonnie (High Kicker (USA)) [2001   **45**
–: 8.2g 7.5m⁶ 7s f6g² f7g Nov 12] first foal: dam no sign of ability in bumpers/over hurdles: poor maiden: short-headed at Southwell penultimate start: will probably stay 1m: acts on fibresand. *Mrs N. Macauley*

GIRL OF PLEASURE (IRE)   2 b.f. (Feb 14) Namaqualand (USA) – Shrewd Girl   **61**
(USA) 79 (Sagace (FR) 135) [2001 6m 7m³ 7m⁶ 7m 8g Sep 13] 8,500Y: good-topped filly: has scope: half-sister to several winners, including fairly useful Irish 7f to 9f winner Delirious Tantrum (by Taufan) and 3-y-o Rainbow River: dam, placed at 1m/1¼m, out of half-sister to Palace Music: modest maiden: third at Kempton: should stay at least 1m: raced only on good/good to firm going. *Mrs P. N. Dutfield*

GIRL'S BEST FRIEND   4 b.f. Nicolotte 118 – Diamond Princess 69 (Horage 124)   **77**
[2001 82: f7g⁶ 8.9d 9d p8g⁵ f9.4g* p8g⁶ f9.4g Nov 27] tall, lengthy filly: fair performer: won handicap at Wolverhampton in November: stays 9.4f: acts on soft going, fibresand and polytrack: blinkered (very slowly away) final 3-y-o outing: has been tongue tied. *D. W. P. Arbuthnot*

GIVE A LITTLE BACK (IRE)   3 b.g. College Chapel 122 – Daroura (USA) (Forli   –
(ARG)) [2001 f6s Dec 15] IR 5,000 3-y-o: sixth foal: half-brother to 3 winners in France, including 1¼m winner Darawar (by Shernazar) and 15f winner Daryapour (by Kahyasi): dam unraced from family of Doyoun: 12/1, always rear in maiden at Southwell: bred to be suited by 1m+. *B. J. Curley*

GIVE AN INCH (IRE)   6 b.m. Inchinor 119 – Top Heights (High Top 131) [2001 77:   –
16s 16.2m May 12] leggy, sparely-made mare: fair handicapper at best: well beaten both 6-y-o outings. *W. Storey*

GIVE BACK CALAIS (IRE)   3 b.g. Brief Truce (USA) 126 – Nichodoula 65   **98**
(Doulab (USA) 115) [2001 94: 6m* 5f 7.1m⁴ 7g 10m Aug 25] strong, compact gelding: useful performer: won maiden at Newbury in June: form in handicaps after only when good fourth to Lunar Leo at Sandown in July: stays 7f: raced only on good ground or firmer: blinkered (never going well) fourth outing: gelded after final start. *P. J. Makin*

GIVE ME A RING (IRE)   8 b.g. Be My Guest (USA) 126 – Annsfield Lady (Red   **80**
Sunset 120) [2001 f11g 12.1m* 12m* 12m* 12m 12f³ 12.4m Jun 28] useful-looking gelding: has a round action: useful in 1998: fairly useful on return in 2001, winning minor event at Hamilton and handicaps at Musselburgh and Doncaster, all in May: stays 1½m: acts on firm going and equitrack: below form in blinkers: usually races prominently: joined F. Murphy. *C. W. Thornton*

GIVEMETHEMOONLIGHT   2 ch.f. (Apr 16) Woodborough (USA) 112 –   **68 p**
Rockin' Rosie 59 (Song 132) [2001 6v⁶ 6v⁴ f6s² Dec 15] 6,800Y: sturdy filly: seventh
foal: half-sister to fairly useful 1999 2-y-o 6f winner Rule of Thumb (by Inchinor): dam
5f winner: fair form in maidens: second to B Major at Wolverhampton, leading 5f: likely
to prove best at 5f/6f: probably capable of better. *L. G. Cottrell*

GIVE NOTICE   4 b.g. Warning 136 – Princess Genista 108 (Ile de Bourbon (USA)   **105**
133) [2001 94: 12d² 14m⁴ 13.9m⁵ 16.1f 16.2g³ 14.8m* 14m³ 18d³ 16d* 15.5s³ Nov 23]
tall, sparely-made gelding: useful performer: had a good season, winning handicaps at
Newmarket in August (beat King Flyer by ¾ length) and November (beat L'Evangile ½
length in steadily-run listed rated stakes): also good third to Distant Prospect in
Cesarewitch at Newmarket (beaten 2 lengths) and to Crillon in listed race at Saint-Cloud
(beaten around ½ length) either side of second win: stays 2¼m: acts on firm and soft
going: has been rather on edge in preliminaries: has been bandaged in front: genuine and
consistent. *J. L. Dunlop*

GIVE THE SLIP   4 b.c. Slip Anchor 136 – Falafil (FR) (Fabulous Dancer (USA)   **121**
124) [2001 116: 12g* 12g⁵ 10.5g⁴ 10m⁵ 12m 10g⁴ 16d² Nov 6]
        European challengers for Australia's most prestigious race the Melbourne
Cup have sometimes had to put up with a hostile reception. Winning New Zealand
trainer Brian Jenkins, for example, used his acceptance speech in 1998 to have a
dig at the overseas visitors, advising them not to 'bring third-rate stayers to Melbourne'. There were four British-trained finishers in the first seven at Flemington
that year, Persian Punch faring best in third place, beaten a neck and half a length
by the New Zealanders Jezabeel and Champagne. Persian Punch was back in the
latest season for another crack at 'the race that stops a nation' and he was joined by
the Godolphin pair Marienbard and Give The Slip, with German-trained Caitano
making it a four-strong European challenge. All four were in good positions in the
big field turning for home and Give The Slip, in front from the start, nearly lived up
to his name, caught only in the dying strides by New Zealand-based Caulfield Cup
winner Ethereal after looking to have the race won when sent for home in earnest
early in the final straight and holding a clear lead with only a furlong or so to run.
Give The Slip went down by three quarters of a length—Godolphin's second
runner-up after Central Park in 1999—with Persian Punch holding off the rest,
Marienbard in seventh and the non-staying Caitano thirteenth. Remarkably, the
riders of Give The Slip and Persian Punch, Richard Hills and Richard Quinn, were
labelled 'cowboys' afterwards by sections of the Australian media, the latter
criticised for going too wide and the former for sticking to the inside rail when clear
in the home straight. 'Pommy jockey Richard Hills must have been asleep when the
first six races were being run . . . every other jockey knew that the best going was
out in the centre,' wrote *Sydney Daily Telegraph* columnist Ken Callander, who
wasn't the only critic to claim that Hills cost Give The Slip the race. Hills deserved
a better reception for a sterling effort that nearly gave Europe a Melbourne Cup
victory to add to the epic achievement in 1993 of Irish-trained Vintage Crop, the
only horse outside Australasia to win Australia's top race. It is very hard to believe
that sticking to the inner was such a significant disadvantage given that Give The
Slip beat the rest in a twenty-two runner field by six lengths or more, and to our eyes
Hills actually deserved a bouquet rather than a brickbat for demonstrating tactical
astuteness in dictating matters and quickening from the front. The criticisms
seemed partisan and smacked of sour grapes, though hopefully they won't prevent
European trainers and jockeys from showing similar enterprise in the future. Give
The Slip, incidentally, was said to have become 'buzzed up' after rearing over and
superficially grazing himself an hour before the race; he was also fractious in the
stalls and had to be taken out and eventually put in last.
        Most of Give The Slip's season was spent on pacemaking duties for
Fantastic Light in championship races in Europe, and he did a fine job in his allotted
role, usually running at least creditably into the bargain. Give The Slip was bought
privately as a three-year-old by Godolphin after winning Europe's richest handicap the Ebor at York—where he was never headed—for Amanda Perrett's stable.
Thereafter he made a smooth transition to pattern company, leading all the way in
the Dubai City of Gold at Nad Al Sheba to win by a length and a quarter from
Miletrian on his first outing for Godolphin at the end of February. After a creditable

fifth to Stay Gold in the Dubai Sheema Classic over the same course and distance the following month, Give The Slip looked well up to winning in pattern company in Britain in the summer until plans were changed. The saying 'If you're going to use a pacemaker, use a good one' certainly applies to the free-going Give The Slip, who showed himself a very smart middle-distance stayer in his own right, as well as a consistent one, in the latest season. He is probably most effective at a mile and a half to two miles, but it is worth noting that he was left in the Gold Cup at Royal Ascot until after the five-day stage and also recorded a particularly good effort when acting as pacemaker in the Tattersalls Gold Cup over an extended mile and a quarter at the Curragh in May, finishing fourth, just over four lengths behind Fantastic Light. Give The Slip, who has worn a crossed noseband, has yet to race on extremes of going.

Give The Slip (b.c. 1997)	Slip Anchor (b 1982)	Shirley Heights (b 1975)	Mill Reef
			Hardiemma
		Sayonara (b 1965)	Birkhahn
			Suleika
	Falafil (FR) (br 1986)	Fabulous Dancer (b 1976)	Northern Dancer
			Last of The Line
		Noble Tiara (b 1981)	Vaguely Noble
			Tayyara

The tall, leggy, close-coupled Give The Slip, who has a round action, is by the extremely well bred Derby winner Slip Anchor, who has been regrettably neglected by commercial breeders because of his stamina-biased pedigree. Best known as the sire of the outstanding filly User Friendly, Slip Anchor had another classic winner in the latest season in Derby Italiano victor Morshdi. Another son of Slip Anchor, the Gordon Stakes and Great Voltigeur winner Stowaway, is out of a half-sister to Give The Slip's dam Falafil, a winner at a mile and a quarter and eleven and a half furlongs in France. The grandam Noble Tiara showed smart form at a mile and a quarter and a mile and a half. Further details of the family can be found in the essay on Give The Slip in *Racehorses of 2000*. Falafil added to her list of winners when the three-year-old filly Josephine (by Emperor Jones) won claimers over fifteen furlongs at Chantilly and Maisons-Laffitte in the latest season. *Saeed bin Suroor*

GIVRE (IRE) 3 b.g. Houmayoun (FR) 114 – Interj (Salmon Leap (USA) 131) [2001 **51** 83: 8s 8g 8.5g 11.9s f11s Dec 21] IR 40,000Y: strong gelding: brother to smart Irish 9f winner Scottish Memories and half-brother to Irish 6.5f to 1¼m winner Dunrally Fort (by Toca Madera): dam unraced half-sister to smart 1m/1¼m performer Spindrift: fairly useful form on second 2-y-o outing: just modest since: left J. Mulhern in Ireland 8,000 gns after second 3-y-o start: should stay beyond 8.5f: raced only on good going or softer: very slowly away final outing. *R. A. Fahey*

GLADE RUNNER (USA) 2 br.f. (Feb 18) Woodman (USA) 126 – Maid of Camelot **63 p** 102 (Caerleon (USA) 132) [2001 6g⁴ Aug 6] first foal: dam, 1¼m winner, from family of smart performers up to 1m Inchmurrin and Inchinor: 6/4 favourite but green, 2 lengths fourth of 15 to Border Minstral in maiden at Windsor, briefly short of room: should stay at least 1m: should improve. *R. Charlton*

GLEAMING BLADE (USA) 3 ch.c. Diesis 133 – Gleam of Light (IRE) 81 (Dane- **98** hill (USA) 126) [2001 94: 7m⁵ 6g⁴ 8m⁴ 7m² 8g² 8d Oct 19] sturdy colt: useful performer: creditable second in minor events at Newmarket (¾ length behind Palatial) in September and Bath (2½ lengths behind Caughnawaga) in October: gave impression something amiss in handicap at Newmarket final outing: stays 1m: raced mainly on good going or firmer: often hangs left, markedly so final 2-y-o outing: headstrong and needs treating with caution: sold 52,000 gns. *Mrs A. J. Perrett*

GLEBE (USA) 2 b.c. (Apr 20) Meadowlake (USA) – Careful Approach (USA) **–** (Relaunch (USA)) [2001 7.9d 8s Oct 25] $50,000F, $85,000Y: leggy, unfurnished colt: fifth foal: half-brother to winners in USA by Geiger Counter and Cure The Blues: dam unraced: always behind in maidens: sold 3,200 gns. *M. R. Channon*

GLENBURN (IRE) 3 br.g. Dr Devious (IRE) 127 – Edwina (IRE) 63 (Caerleon **64** (USA) 132) [2001 8.3m 8.1m⁴ 8.1m⁴ 8d⁵ Aug 9] 60,000Y: good-bodied gelding: closely related to fairly useful 7f/1m winner Your The Lady (by Indian Ridge): dam maiden should have stayed further than 6f: modest form in maidens: worth a try beyond 1m: reluctant to enter stall/slowly away debut: sold 4,000 gns. *A. C. Stewart*

GLENDALE RIDGE (IRE)   6 b.g. Indian Ridge 123 – English Lily (Runnett 125)   –
[2001 63: f8g Feb 5] lengthy, workmanlike gelding: modest maiden at best: well beaten
only 6-y-o outing. *Jamie Poulton*

GLENDAMAH (IRE)   4 b.g. Mukaddamah (USA) 125 – Sea Glen (IRE) (Glenstal   **49**
(USA) 118) [2001 67d: 7.1m⁵ 7.1m 8m 10m 7g⁴ 8.5m 8.3s 8m Sep 8] good-bodied
gelding: poor performer: stays easy 7f: acts on any going: sometimes visored/blinkered.
J. R. Weymes

GLENHURICH (IRE)   4 b.f. Sri Pekan (USA) 117 – Forli's Treat (USA) (Forli   **52**
(ARG)) [2001 59: 8f 8.1g⁵ 8.3d 7m Sep 22] lengthy, unfurnished filly: modest maiden:
stays 1m: acts on firm ground: none too consistent. *J. S. Goldie*

GLENMORANGIE   2 gr. or br.g. (Feb 5) Danzig Connection (USA) – In The High-   **87**
lands (Petong 126) [2001 5s³ 6m* 5g* 7m 6m 6d Oct 18] IR 13,500Y: strong gelding: has
scope: second foal: dam, well beaten, half-sister to useful performer up to 1m In Like
Flynn: fairly useful performer: made all in maiden at Goodwood in May and minor event
at Windsor in June: well held after: should stay 7f: acts on soft and good to firm ground:
has given trouble in preliminaries/at start (withdrawn once): sold 20,000 gns. *R. Hannon*

GLEN PARKER (IRE)   8 ch.g. Bluebird (USA) 125 – Trina's Girl 78 (Nonoalco   –
(USA) 131) [2001 f8s Dec 21] sturdy, good-bodied gelding: one-time fairly useful
performer: very lightly raced nowadays: has been blinkered/visored. *R. F. Marvin*

GLENROCK   4 ch.g. Muhtarram (USA) 125 – Elkie Brooks 82 (Relkino 131) [2001   **90**
91: 6s³ 7.6f³ 6f 7.1g⁴ 7f 7.1f³ 7d² 7s⁴ 7m⁶ 6g⁶ 7d³ 6.1d* 6d 6v⁴ p7g⁴ f7g² Dec 11] quite
good-topped gelding: fairly useful performer: ended long losing sequence in minor event
at Chester in September: effective at 6f/7f: acts on any going and fibresand/polytrack: has
drifted right: usually races prominently. *A. Berry*

GLEN VALE WALK (IRE)   4 ch.g. Balla Cove 119 – Winter Harvest (Grundy 137)   **57**
[2001 51: 10f 10f³ 10.9g* 11.1s 10m⁴ 11.9g⁶ 10.1g 10f 12d 12g⁴ Nov 7] leggy gelding:
modest handicapper: won at Warwick in July: stays 1½m: acts on firm and good to soft
going: blinkered final outing: has wandered/found little: none too consistent. *Mrs
G. S. Rees*

GLITTER AND GLORY   2 b.g. (May 6) Classic Cliche (IRE) 128 – Veuve (Tirol   –
127) [2001 8s Oct 25] fourth foal: half-brother to 4-y-o Destination and a 1½m winner in
Sweden by Batshoof: dam unraced half-sister to smart miler Fizzed and useful sprinter
Premiere Cuvee: 33/1 and green, showed little in maiden at Brighton. *C. A. Cyzer*

GLOAMING   3 b.f. Celtic Swing 138 – Kandavu 87 (Safawan 118) [2001 7d 6g³   **67**
10.4m 7m 7m Jun 12] first foal: dam, 5f winner, raced only at 2 yrs: fair maiden: should
be suited by 1m+ (very stiff task at 10.4f): unraced on extremes of going. *J. Gallagher*

GLOBAL POWER (IRE)   2 ch.c. (Apr 10) Spinning World (USA) 130 – Petroleuse   **76**
104 (Habitat 134) [2001 7f⁶ 7.1g⁴ Sep 13] 1,400,000 francs Y: angular, useful-looking
colt: half-brother to several winners, including smart French/US middle-distance performer Parme (by Blushing Groom), US Grade 2 1½m winner Peinture Bleue (by
Alydar), now dam of Peintre Celebre, and useful Irish 1997 2-y-o 7f winner Chateau
Royal (by Personal Hope): dam, won up to 8.5f, half-sister to Pawneese: better effort in
maidens (fair form) when sixth at Newmarket: will stay 1m. *W. R. Muir*

GLOBAL PRINCESS (IRE)   2 b.f. (Feb 22) Dashing Blade 117 – Brandon Princess   **86**
(Waajib 121) [2001 5.7f³ 6m² 5.3m* 5m³ 5.2m 5m Sep 20] 3,500Y: rather leggy, quite
good-topped filly: first foal: dam unraced daughter of useful sprinter Bless The Match:
fairly useful performer: landed odds in maiden at Brighton in July, making all despite
seeming ill at ease on track: good third in nursery at Thirsk next time: below form in listed
events after: effective at 5f/6f: raced only on ground firmer than good. *I. A. Balding*

GLORIA DI MODENA   3 b.f. Glory of Dancer 121 – Star of Modena (IRE) (Waajib   **38**
121) [2001 10v 10d 8.5m⁴ 14.1m Jul 24] 7,500F: first foal: dam Italian 7f (at 2 yrs) to
1½m winner: poor form in maidens: visored (tailed off in handicap) final outing.
H. Akbary

GLORIOUS QUEST (IRE)   3 ch.c. Lake Coniston (IRE) 131 – Lassalia (Sallust   **70**
134) [2001 84p: 6g 6m² 7g⁶ 7g 7s⁴ f7g⁵ Oct 20] tall, quite good-topped colt: fair maiden:
stays 7f: acts on soft and good to firm going: sold 7,000 gns. *M. A. Jarvis*

GLORIOUS WELCOME   3 b.g. Past Glories 91 – Rest And Welcome 75 (Town   –
And Country 124) [2001 8d 12g 9.9m 8m Jul 22] second reported foal: dam poor maiden
on Flat (stayed 7.6f) and over hurdles: well held in maidens: blinkered/tongue tied final
outing. *Jane Southcombe*

GLORY DAYS (IRE)   3 ch.c. Lahib (USA) 129 – Gloire (Thatching 131) [2001 85:   **76**
6m 6m⁶ 6.1m⁶ 5.2f 8.1g 7f 7s p6g* Dec 19] good-topped colt: fairly useful winner only
run at 2 yrs: reportedly chipped a bone in a knee afterwards: fair form in 2001, winning
handicap at Lingfield in December: should prove best at 5f/6f: acts on soft going, good to
firm and polytrack: blinkered (below form) sixth/seventh starts. *R. Hannon*

GLORY OF LOVE   6 b.g. Belmez (USA) 131 – Princess Lieven (Royal Palace 131)   –
[2001 –: 21.6s Apr 23] disappointing maiden on Flat: tried visored. *Mrs A. M. Naughton*

GLORY QUEST (USA)   4 b.c. Quest For Fame 127 – Sonseri 95 (Prince Tenderfoot   **84**
(USA) 126) [2001 86: 8g 7.6d 10d⁶ f9.4g³ 10s⁵ 8s⁴ 10v f9.4g Nov 27] good-topped colt:
carries condition: fairly useful performer: creditable efforts only when in frame in handicap at Wolverhampton and minor event at Brighton: stays 1¼m: acts on firm going, soft
and fibresand: tried visored. *Miss Gay Kelleway*

GLOSSY EYED (IRE)   2 ch.g. (May 14) Eagle Eyed (USA) 111 – Hi-Gloss (IRE)   –
(Be My Guest (USA) 126) [2001 6m 7g 6m Sep 6] IR 2,000Y: first foal: dam unraced: no
sign of ability in sellers/maiden. *A. Berry*

GLOWING   6 b.m. Chilibang 120 – Juliet Bravo 61 (Glow (USA)) [2001 86: 5.1m²   **88**
6m 6m* 6m 6m 6g⁶ f6g⁵ p7g² f6g Dec 17] lengthy mare: fairly useful handicapper: won
at Goodwood in July by a head from Flak Jacket: broke leg at Southwell in December:
was effective at 5f to easy 7f: acted on firm going, good to soft and fibresand/polytrack:
occasionally wore tongue strap: was usually waited with: dead. *J. R. Fanshawe*

GLOWING LAKE (IRE)   2 b.f. (Feb 16) Lake Coniston (IRE) 131 – Glowing Lines   **54 §**
(IRE) 78 (Glow (USA)) [2001 5v 5v³ 5d⁴ f5g² f5g 6m 7.5m⁶ 6m 7g² 7.9m⁴ 8m³ 7.9s 7.9d
8s Oct 22] IR 6,500Y: smallish filly: second foal: dam, Irish 1¼m and 1¾m winner (also
won over hurdles), out of half-sister to Irish Derby winner Malacate: modest maiden:
runner-up in sellers: stays 1m: acts on good to firm and heavy going: often visored/
blinkered: tends to sweat: none too keen. *J. S. Wainwright*

GO AHEAD JO   2 b.f. (Apr 19) Classic Cliche (IRE) 128 – It's So Easy 63 (Shaadi   –
(USA) 126) [2001 6.1m 8.2v f8.5g Oct 9] quite good-topped filly: second foal: half-sister
to 3-y-o Gemtastic: dam 7f winner: no form in maidens. *A. P. James*

GOBLET OF FIRE (USA)   2 b.c. (Apr 23) Green Desert (USA) 127 – Laurentine   **85**
(USA) (Private Account (USA)) [2001 7d 8d⁴ Nov 2] 82,000Y: sturdy, attractive colt: has
scope: first foal: dam, French 1½m winner, half-sister to Oaks winner Love Divine: fairly
useful form when ninth of 16 to Sir George Turner in valuable sales race and fourth of 5 to
Ashdown Express in minor event (favourite and able to dictate pace), both at Newmarket:
should stay 1¼m. *B. J. Meehan*

GODMERSHAM PARK   9 b.g. Warrshan (USA) 117 – Brown Velvet 68 (Mansingh   –
(USA) 120) [2001 48, a56: f8g⁴ f8g f9.4g⁵ Feb 13] lengthy, good-topped gelding: poor   **a42**
performer: stays 9f: acts on fibresand: tried blinkered/visored: has given trouble stalls/
found little/hung. *P. S. Felgate*

GO FOR IT SWEETIE (IRE)   8 b.m. Brush Aside (USA) 125 – Arctic Mistress   –
(Quayside 124) [2001 –: f16g Jan 12] no sign of ability both Flat outings. *B. D. Leavy*

GO GABANA   2 b.g. (Mar 9) First Trump 118 – Have Form (Haveroid 122) [2001 5m⁶   **64 §**
6g 6g f7g 6g⁶ 6.1m 7s Oct 5] 3,000F, 8,000Y, 16,000 2-y-o: strong gelding: half-brother
to useful sprinter (also won up to 1m) Shikari's Son (by Kala Shikari): dam poor maiden
who stayed 7f: modest maiden: gelded after final start: stays 6f: blinkered last 3 starts
(best effort on first occasion): sometimes slowly away: ungenuine. *N. P. Littmoden*

GOGGLES (IRE)   3 b. or br.c. Eagle Eyed (USA) 111 – Rock On (IRE) (Ballad Rock   **109**
122) [2001 95p: 8d⁵ 7m⁵ 7m⁴ 7m 8g² 8g* Aug 4] strong, well-made colt: useful performer: mostly creditable efforts at 3 yrs, including when ½-length second to Cornelius
in minor event at Doncaster before winning listed race at Goodwood by ½ length from
Sonatina, responding generously: stays 1m: acts on good to firm going: joined J. Moore
in Hong Kong. *H. Candy*

GOG'S GIFT   3 b.g. So Factual (USA) 120 – Premium Gift 63 (Most Welcome 131)   –
[2001 42: 6m 6g Oct 19] strong gelding: poor maiden: well held at 3 yrs. *C. B. B. Booth*

GOING GLOBAL (IRE)   4 ch.g. Bob Back (USA) 124 – Ukraine Girl 121 (Targo-   **88**
wice (USA) 130) [2001 109: 10.1s 12d 10d Oct 13] smallish, angular gelding: useful
winner in 2000: well below form in handicaps in 2001 (off 5 months and gelded after
reappearance): stays 1½m: best efforts on soft/heavy going: tried visored/tongue tied: has
worn crossed noseband. *G. L. Moore*

GOLAN (IRE)   3 b.c. Spectrum (IRE) 126 – Highland Gift (IRE) 95 (Generous **125**
(IRE) 139) [2001 102P: 8g* 12f² 12g³ 12m* 12s⁴ 12f⁶ Nov 25]
      For four weeks in late-spring, the time it took from the Two Thousand
Guineas to the Derby, Golan could have been the next wonder of the age. He wasn't,
and, by the end of the season, there were seven other European three-year-olds
rated above him. In a late change of heart by his connections, Golan has been given
the opportunities presented by another season on the racecourse, but he will have to
go some to live up to the expectations that once attended him. But before this
particular springtime fancy is consigned to history as meaningless hype it is as well
to record that, in the run-up to the Derby, Coolmore, who already had Galileo to fly
their standard, thought enough of Golan to buy a controlling interest in him as well.
That fact is as telling an indication of Golan's once-exalted status as any entry in
the form-book.
      That said, no great study of the form-book, allied to one of the stud book, is
required before it becomes obvious why Golan was thought to have the world at his
feet—he had won the Two Thousand Guineas on just his second race and it
appeared on pedigree that he would do even better over middle distances. No
Guineas winner had gone on to take the Derby since Nashwan in 1989, and the last
before him was Nijinsky. Given the rarity nowadays even of horses that manage to
be placed in both races, the creature capable of winning both is becoming the stuff
of fable. But that has not stopped the continuing search for one. From eighteen
runners in the latest Two Thousand Guineas field, probably only five had any
realistic hope of staying the Derby distance—Tobougg, Nayef, Golan, Mayville
Thunder and Darwin, the last two reckoned, however, to have next to no hope of
winning the Guineas. The eighteen runners represented eighteen different sires,
with only one of those stallions—King's Theatre, responsible for King's Ironbridge, who is out of a dam who is a strong influence for speed—having shown his
form at a mile and a half. Breeders' almost slavish devotion to speed over stamina
nowadays is not virgin territory for racing and bloodstock writers. While the
Guineas line-up illustrates clearly enough that those waiting for the next Guineas
and Derby winner (let alone a triple crown winner) should not bother holding their
breath, the chance of just such a horse emerging had been the subject of much huff
and puff in the latest season even before the Guineas was run. Golan was not the
season's first 'wonder horse'. Nor would he be the last. On the morning of the
Craven Stakes, Nayef was generally quoted as 5/2 favourite for the Guineas, and
8/1 co-favourite (with Galileo) for the Derby; Golan was at 10/1 and 12/1 for the
Derby and 25/1 for classic glory at Newmarket. Nayef, Nashwan's half-brother, is
the colt of whom we wrote twelve months ago 'There is no better classic prospect'.
Defeat at 6/4-on behind King's Ironbridge and Red Carpet in the Craven very
effectively discounted any likelihood that he would be a Guineas winner (though he
was still sent off 10/1 fifth favourite for the race). Not that the trials had thrown up

Sagitta 2000 Guineas Stakes, Newmarket—Golan defies his inexperience, coming from last place
to beat Tamburlaine, Frenchmans Bay (left), Minardi (blaze), Red Carpet (rail) and Munir (striped cap)

many convincing alternatives. King's Ironbridge and Red Carpet had been separated by a head in a slowly-run race; the Greenham too had lacked any early pace, before Munir had comprehensively outsprinted Frenchmans Bay, Imperial Dancer, Racing Post Trophy runner-up Tamburlaine and Patsy's Double; and, in Dubai, Godolphin's private trial had been a muddling affair as well, in which Rumpold had just got home in front of Divine Task (who had not had a race under rules) and the Dewhurst winner Tobougg. Aidan O'Brien had kept his powder dry with the Middle Park winner Minardi, while an exceptionally wet spring had held up many British stables; Sir Michael Stoute's team had experienced some uninspiring results with its apparent trialists, but Golan and Tempest, the Dewhurst third, had not been among them.

As regards Golan, the most important thing to know was that one week earlier he had been backed down from 25/1 to 7/1 second favourite. Hardly anything else concrete was known about him because he had had only one race, a maiden at Chepstow the previous September. Starting at 5/4, he had beaten another well-bred colt, Clearing, trained by John Gosden, by a length and a quarter, with another nine lengths back to the third. Clearing had gone on to win the Horris Hill and the Free Handicap and was now being prepared for the Poule d'Essai des Poulains. This had to be useful form at least. The month of May was not over before the newspapers reported Golan to be working 'in his usual indolent fashion' and cautioned 'those less accustomed to his slothful ways', but his eye-catching market move prior to the Guineas hinted that these lacklustre tendencies on the gallops had not been entirely prevalent.

With this augury in the ante-post betting, it was hard enough to believe at the time that midweek rain had been required for stable-jockey Kieren Fallon to confirm his choice of Golan, rather than Tempest, and that there had then been a serious possibility that Golan's stall position on the complete outside of the field would prompt Fallon to change his mind. After the race, Fallon reflected: 'He had been lazy in his homework, but I knew as soon as I got on him in the paddock he was a different horse from the one I've been riding at home.' However highly Golan was rated beforehand, connections could hardly have conceived that he would win in the manner he did. With Red Carpet and Nayef setting the pace as the field bunched on the stand rail, Golan had been switched inside leaving the stalls, before having to be switched to the wide outside again not long afterwards. Of even more concern, he was right at the back and was off the bridle. The good news for Golan and Fallon three furlongs out, however, was that perhaps only Tamburlaine was travelling any better. At this stage for Golan there were at least a dozen horses for him to get past, but he had accomplished the task a furlong and a half later. This startling progress had not yet shaken off Tamburlaine, at his shoulder, but when Richard Hughes's mount was asked for his full effort it became immediately apparent that Golan had the greater momentum. The distance between them stretched to a length and a quarter at the line. Frenchmans Bay stayed on stoutly in their wake to finish a neck behind the runner-up, after which it was three lengths back to Minardi, who had met with some interference but not enough to affect the result; doubtful stayer Red Carpet hung on for fifth, scotching any suggestion that the early pace had been too strong and played into the hands of those who had come from the back. Nayef was eighth; Tobougg, the 4/1 favourite, ninth.

The best price for Golan for the Derby the next day was 5/2. Almost everything about his Guineas win suggested more improvement would be forthcoming, and his pedigree prompted the belief that it would probably come at a mile and a half. Lord Weinstock, Golan's owner, said later: 'I wasn't surprised by Golan's Two Thousand Guineas success, but it wasn't the plan. We couldn't find anywhere to work him. The ground wasn't decent and the best ground to work him on appeared to be on Newmarket racecourse. He suddenly showed he was coming to himself two or three weeks before the race and we thought we would take him there and see what happened.' For Sir Michael Stoute, Golan was a fifth Two Thousand Guineas winner, following Shadeed, Doyoun, Entrepreneur and King's Best. Since 1900 only Fred Darling has trained as many winners of the race as Stoute. John Scott holds the record with seven between 1842 and 1862.

Prix Niel - Casino Barriere d'Enghien-Les-Bains, Longchamp—
in a clash of two classic winners, Golan gets the better of Anabaa Blue

For Kieren Fallon Golan was a second Two Thousand Guineas victory in the space of twelve months for the Stoute stable following King's Best's win. Golan's could not have been any less sweet as the jockey was on the comeback trail, following the severe injury sustained to his shoulder in June 2000. Well below his best, as he himself later confessed, when he returned to race-riding in Britain at the end of March, Fallon stated at that time that 'the only way I won't be champion again this season is if I have another injury.' The Derby, however, would not be contributing towards any championship-winning total. Ten days before the race, and on the last day on which any riding bans would take in Derby Day, Fallon's performance in taking third place in a £3,136 handicap led the Ayr stewards to find him guilty of irresponsible riding of a minor nature. He was banned for three days. Under the rules, suspensions can be deferred for jockeys to ride on days that there are Group 1 events, but only if those suspensions are of one or two days.

It was not the last blow in the course of yet another turbulent season for Kieren Fallon, but the disappointment of losing the Derby ride did not turn out to be so great as it might have been. With Pat Eddery in the saddle, Golan was sent off 11/4 co-favourite with Galileo. Coolmore now had their stake in both horses, Golan's price a reported fifteen million dollars, with an extra five million if he should win the Derby, but if Coolmore had questioned whether Galileo could beat him at Epsom, they had their answer almost as soon as the runners turned into the straight. Golan came off the bit (one of the first to do so) as they started to race downhill to Tattenham Corner, though this did not rule him out remembering his performance in the Guineas, but Galileo's spectacular surge to the front two and a half furlongs out most certainly did. Golan could not match him; nothing in this field could. The two of them had raced on the outside almost from the off, with Golan tracking Galileo, but 'tracking' ceased to be the appropriate description as Golan almost immediately conceded four lengths on his rival, labouring into second place at the furlong pole by which stage Galileo was already being acclaimed the winner. The 'wonder horse' mantle had passed to new shoulders.

Golan clearly stayed a mile and a half at Epsom, but he had not improved significantly for it, hanging left under a right-handed drive. The firm ground, the course's eccentricities and perhaps Golan's own inexperience seemed at the time as if they might have been contributory factors, but Golan did not show any markedly better form in four races afterwards. The Irish Derby at the Curragh was his worst race of the season. Starting 4/1 second favourite behind 11/4-on Galileo, Golan was showing such a lack of zest entering the straight over three furlongs out that he looked set to end up out with the washing. For him eventually to emerge in third place seemed miraculous, Fallon later conceding that his mount had shown little interest while being forced to race wide and had only run on when switched inside. On this occasion, Galileo beat Golan eight lengths, easing down, with Italian Derby winner Morshdi four lengths in front of Golan as well.

After the Curragh, Golan was put aside until the autumn, when with Galileo about to be tested at a mile and a quarter there might be some good opportunities. The Prix Niel - Casino Barriere d'Enghien-Les-Bains, or the Niel as we will henceforth refer to it, provided a winning return to action at Longchamp in September, Golan leading a furlong and a half out and appearing to idle in front before holding Prix du Jockey Club winner Anabaa Blue by three quarters of a length. The previous five Arc winners had all contested the Niel, but with the contestants for the 2001 Arc far from clear, Golan's ante-post quote with the major bookmakers was as short as 3/1 and as long as 10/1. In a wider historical context, it is clear that Golan did not possess Arc-winning form; indeed his form falls well short of what is usually required to win the race. The 2001 Two Thousand Guineas turned out to be a modest renewal, as evinced on a pretty regular basis by runner-up Tamburlaine and fourth-placed Minardi (third-placed Frenchmans Bay having been sidelined though injury). This was already becoming apparent after the Irish Guineas. That hardly counted, at the time, against Golan's prospects in the top mile-and-a-half events, in which he faced a radically different test. Always close up in the Arc, Golan came off the final turn in fifth place and responded in good enough style to move into a clear second a furlong and a half out. He was then left well behind by the previous year's Derby runner-up Sakhee. It looked, as at Epsom, as though Golan was the second-best horse in the race, but on this occasion he also lost out close home to Aquarelliste and Sagacity. That was on soft ground. On firm in the Japan Cup at Tokyo seven weeks later, Golan was unable to take up so prominent a position early on and could not muster the pace to mount a challenge, beaten almost five lengths and finishing sixth of fifteen to Jungle Pocket. Lord Weinstock, who will retain part-ownership of Golan at stud, had already expressed his hope that the horse would race on as a four-year-old, and, after it was initially determined that Golan would take up stallion duties in 2002, the change of plan was announced in December.

A visual impression of Golan's Arc performance—if not the form—suggests he might well be tried at a mile and a quarter in 2002. Golan does seem to find a mile and a half stretching him, in soft ground at least, though other factors could come into play if he is to improve as a four-year-old. Physical improvement is a possible candidate, as Golan—a rather leggy, close-coupled attractive colt—often struck our racecourse reporters as being on the weak side in his three-year-old season. There is not much difference between his form on firm and soft going.

When Golan returns to action, it seems highly unlikely that it will be with Kieren Fallon. At the end of October, following plenty of racecourse rumour, the news came that he had lost his job at Freemason Lodge. Jamie Spencer and Johnny Murtagh, currently holding retainers with Luca Cumani and John Oxx respectively, were mentioned as desirable replacements in the media, but Sir Michael Stoute stated: 'My stable will not be retaining a jockey for the 2002 season. Not all of my owners wish to use Kieren Fallon, but his association with the stable will continue with those that do. Kieren assures me that he is keen to do so.' At this stage, though, it was still expected that Fallon would ride Golan in Japan. Eleven days later Fallon won the Prix Fille de l'Air at Toulouse on the Stoute-trained Goncharova, but a largely unexplained sequence of events followed, in which the jockey was fined 2,000 francs for weighing out one kilogram heavy before the race, without having declared in advance that he would do so, and was suspended for four days for having weighed 2.1 kilograms heavier still when coming back in. 'Kieren Fallon did not contest either decision,' reported a stewards' spokesman. 'His only worry was whether he would be able to ride Golan in the Japan Cup.' The ban did not cover the day of the Japan Cup, but two days later it was announced that Golan would be ridden by Johnny Murtagh. The news of Fallon's lost retainer with Stoute had come close to eclipsing the massive achievement of his returning to be champion jockey, after an injury that required a six-and-a-half-hour operation and left a scar that stretches from his elbow to the top of his shoulder. The 2000 champion Kevin Darley put up a sterling defence of his title, but when the Jockeys' Association 2001 championship race came to an end on November Handicap day Fallon had 166 winners, Darley 158.

		Rainbow Quest (b 1981)	Blushing Groom
	Spectrum (IRE) (b 1992)		I Will Follow
		River Dancer (b 1983)	Irish River
Golan (IRE) (b.c. 1998)			Dancing Shadow
		Generous (ch 1988)	Caerleon
	Highland Gift (IRE) (b 1993)		Doff The Derby
		Scots Lass (b 1982)	Shirley Heights
			Edinburgh

Golan is a triumph for Lord Weinstock's Ballymacoll Stud, which bred him, as well as his sire and his dam. Sire Spectrum and broodmare Highland Gift are both descended from mares that were present at the stud when it was owned by Dorothy Paget. The results of her Flat-breeding enterprises were generally disappointing, but Weinstock and his father-in-law Sir Michael Sobell, who bought the stud following Miss Paget's death in 1960, have certainly had their moments. Spectrum's relatives are the better known, his grandam Dancing Shadow for instance being a half-sister to Sun Princess and Saddlers' Hall. There is no shortage of pattern winners on Highland Gift's side of the pedigree either, including her half-brother Bonny Scot, who took the Great Voltigeur Stakes and Gordon Stakes, and Sought Out, the Prix du Cadran, Prix Kergorlay and Prix de Lutece winner who is a half-sister to Golan's grandam Scots Lass. Although it was widely assumed that Golan would stay a mile and a half, neither his sire nor dam showed their form at the trip, both returning with injuries on their sole attempts. Spectrum's came in the Derby, in which, following his victory in the Irish Two Thousand Guineas, he started 5/1 second favourite but finished thirteenth of fifteen. Absent until the autumn, he returned to win the Champion Stakes but his four-year-old season was

Lord Weinstock's "Golan"

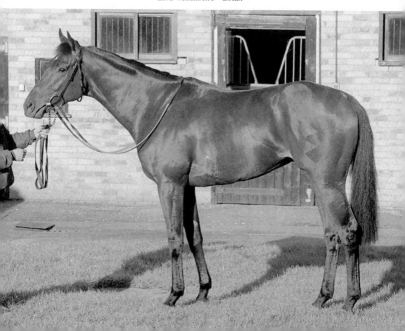

spoiled by recurrences of his Derby injury. Highland Gift made her debut at a mile and a half, in a Newmarket maiden in April as a three-year-old, but jarred her knees and was off the course until the autumn, when she looked useful in two races at a mile and a quarter, hacking up in a Newbury maiden. Golan is from Spectrum's first crop and is Highland Gift's first foal. He is way out in front of the rest among Spectrum's three-year-olds, although Chronos (another product of Ballymacoll, incidentally) had useful middle-distance form in France; one of Spectrum's brightest hopes, Hemingway, the winner of both his starts as a two-year-old, including the listed Acomb Stakes at York, never ran in 2001 following a series of injuries, and was sent to Australia. Spectrum's second crop has a number of useful or fairly useful performers, notably Prism and the Irish-trained duo Rum Charger and Marionnaud. Highland Gift's second foal is Mount Street (by Pennekamp), who was second in a Salisbury maiden in August but did not run again. She is followed by the colts Highland Games (by Singspiel) and Gift Voucher (by Cadeaux Genereux) and, not too surprisingly, Highland Gift was covered by Spectrum again in 2001.

Once bitten, twice shy, is not an approach to which the media tends to pay much attention in its quest for the next unbeaten equine 'superstar'. In the latest season, Nayef, Golan and Galileo all had the tag at one stage, only to lose it. In a short-term context, Golan's season must consequently have been viewed as somewhat disappointing. In a much broader historical perspective, all three horses deserve to be celebrated for what they achieved rather than damned for what they didn't. Golan, with another season in which to improve his record, is already a rare commodity on two fronts, increasingly rare as a horse that was capable of showing his form at Group 1 level over both a mile and a mile and a half, and, for all that Lammtarra had pulled off a similar feat six years earlier, exceedingly rare as one that was capable of winning a classic on just his second outing. *Sir Michael Stoute*

GOLCONDA (IRE) 5 br.m. Lahib (USA) 129 – David's Star (Welsh Saint 126) **92** [2001 92: 10g⁶ 10m⁴ 10.4m³ 10.2m⁶ Jul 27] workmanlike mare: fairly useful performer: creditable efforts last 3 starts, in listed events at Kempton and Chepstow and in John Smith's Cup (Handicap) at York (2¾ lengths third to Foreign Affairs having been short of room) in between: best around 1¼m: acts on firm going, soft and fibresand/equitrack: visored once: usually held up. *Lady Herries*

GOLD ACADEMY (IRE) 5 b.g. Royal Academy (USA) 130 – Soha (USA) 58 **102** (Dancing Brave (USA) 140) [2001 112: 10.3f³ 9.9m⁵ 10g⁴ 10f 10.1m² 9.9m 10.4g⁶ 8g Sep 15] big, close-coupled, good sort: usually takes the eye: generally disappointing since 1999: just useful form at 5 yrs, runner-up to Chianti in minor event at Epsom in July: barely stays 1½m: acts on firm and good to soft going: sent to Singapore. *R. Hannon*

GOLD ACE (USA) 2 ch.c. (Mar 13) Gulch (USA) – Najecam (USA) (Trempolino **70** (USA) 135) [2001 6d² 6m 7d Sep 26] $155,000Y: first foal: dam, 6f (at 2 yrs) to 8.5f winner in USA, placed in Grade 2 events when second in maiden at Haydock: well held in similar events after: sold 3,600 gns. *J. Noseda*

GOLD BLADE 12 ch.g. Rousillon (USA) 133 – Sharp Girl (FR) 114 (Sharpman) **36** [2001 51: f12g f12g³ f12g 12m 11.5m⁶ 13g⁵ 10g 9.9m Jul 31] big gelding: poor handi- **a45** capper: stayed 13f: acted on any turf going and fibresand/equitrack: was sometimes blinkered earlier in career: was usually held up: dead. *Mrs Lydia Pearce*

GOLDBROOK 3 b.g. Alderbrook 120 – Miss Marigold (Norwick (USA) 125) [2001 **–** 10.2d 10.2f 10g 10.2f Jun 27] first foal: dam, no form on Flat, unreliable winning hurdler/ chaser: well held in maidens/handicap. *R. J. Hodges*

GOLDEN APPLES (IRE) 3 b.f. Pivotal 124 – Loon (FR) (Kaldoun (FR) 122) [2001 **115** 9v² 9.5d* 9.5m⁴ 10d³ 9f* 10g² 9f* 9d³ Nov 25] 19,000Y: half-sister to several winners, including French/US winner up to 1¼m La Piaf (by Fabulous Dancer), second in Grade 3 8.5f event: dam French 1m (at 2 yrs) to 1½m winner: smart performer: won maiden at Gowran in May and creditable 2¼ lengths third to Rebelline in Pretty Polly Stakes at the Curragh following month, final start for D. Hanley in Ireland: improved form in USA, winning Del Mar Oaks (by length from Affluent) in August and Grade 2 handicap at Santa Anita in November: set plenty to do when 3 lengths third to Starine in Matriarch Stakes at Hollywood final outing: stays 1¼m: probably acts on any going: held up of late. *B. D. A. Cecil, USA*

GOLDEN BOOT 2 ch.g. (Apr 15) Unfuwain (USA) 131 – Sports Delight (Star **81** Appeal 133) [2001 7g⁴ 7m⁵ 8.1s* 8m 7.9s 8.3v⁶ Nov 8] strong gelding: fifth living foal: dam unraced half-sister to dam of Irish 2000 Guineas winner Turtle Island: fairly useful performer: won maiden at Haydock in September: left R. Beckett after fifth start: creditable sixth in nursery at Windsor: will stay 1¼m: acts on heavy going. *A. Bailey*

GOLDEN BOUNTY 2 b.c. (Feb 20) Bahamian Bounty 116 – Cumbrian Melody 83 **92** (Petong 126) [2001 6m⁴ 6m³ 6g³ 5f* 5d⁵ Oct 13] 29,000F, 65,000Y: good-bodied colt: half-brother to several winners, including 4-y-o Cumbrian Princess and 7f winner Titanium Honda (by Doulab): dam 2-y-o 5f/6f winner: fairly useful performer: won maiden at Pontefract (swished tail repeatedly in paddock) in September: creditable fifth to Dominica in Cornwallis Stakes at Ascot: best efforts at 5f: acts on firm and good to soft going. *R. Hannon*

GOLDEN BRIEF (IRE) 3 ch.g. Brief Truce (USA) 126 – Tiffany's Case (IRE) 65 **57** (Thatching 131) [2001 64: f7g f7g⁵ 7.1g 7m 7.1f⁴ 9m⁴ 8.2m³ 8f f8g p7g* p7g⁵ p7g⁴ p8g⁵ **a64** Dec 22] strong gelding: modest performer: won handicap at Lingfield in November: best form at 7f: acts on firm going, polytrack and equitrack: visored last 5 starts: usually tongued tied: sometimes slowly away. *K. R. Burke*

GOLDEN CHANCE (IRE) 4 b.g. Unfuwain (USA) 131 – Golden Digger (USA) 66 **74 §** (Mr Prospector (USA)) [2001 82: 8g 8.5m 8m 11.9d³ 12.3m* 12.4m 9.9m² 11.9g 12m² 10.9m⁵ 13.9d Oct 13] strong, sturdy gelding: fair handicapper: won ladies event at Ripon in June: stays 1½m: acts on firm and good to soft going: has sweated/flashed tail/found little: inconsistent. *M. W. Easterby*

GOLDEN CHIMES (USA) 6 ch.g. Woodman (USA) 126 – Russian Ballet (USA) **64** (Nijinsky (CAN) 138) [2001 64: 17.1f⁶ 14m² 14.1m Jun 23] close-coupled gelding: modest handicapper: effective at 1¾m to 2¼m: acts on soft and good to firm going: tried blinkered/tongue tied: has reportedly had breathing problem. *E. W. Tuer*

GOLDEN DRAGON 3 ch.g. Piccolo 121 – Aunt Judy (Great Nephew 126) [2001 **98** 7d⁶ 7m² 6m* 7.6f* 8m 7f² 7d⁵ 7g Oct 5] 28,000Y: strong, useful-looking gelding: ninth foal: half-brother to 3 winners, including fairly useful 1988 2-y-o 7f winner who stayed 1m Island Mead (by Pharly): dam, well beaten, out of Oaks winner Juliette Marny: useful performer: won maiden at Southwell in May and minor event at Chester in June: best effort when neck second to A Touch of Frost in handicap at Newbury sixth outing, just failing: didn't have things go his way last 2 starts: stays 7.6f: acts on firm going: has taken good hold, and held up: sent to USA. *M. A. Jarvis*

GOLDEN DRAGONFLY (IRE) 3 ch.g. Eagle Eyed (USA) 111 – Shanna (BEL) **49 d** (River Smile (USA)) [2001 51: f7g f8g² f7s f8s⁶ f7g⁴ 8m⁶ 10m⁴ 11m⁴ 12m⁵ 10m⁴ Sep 1] sturdy gelding: poor maiden: should prove best at 1m/1¼m: acts on good to firm going and fibresand: has had tongue tied: has wandered. *D. Nicholls*

GOLDEN FACT (USA) 7 b.g. Known Fact (USA) 135 – Cosmic Sea Queen (USA) **90 d** (Determined Cosmic (USA)) [2001 103: 8s 8m⁴ 9d 12g 8.5d 8.5d 8d 8s 8s f9.4s⁶ Dec 15] angular, close-coupled gelding: fairly useful handicapper, on downgrade: well held at Wolverhampton final start: best at 1m/9f: acts on heavy and good to firm ground: blinkered twice. *Michael McElhone, Ireland*

GOLDEN FORTUNA 3 b.f. Turtle Island (IRE) 123 – Shady Bank (USA) 62 **66** (Alleged (USA) 138) [2001 67: f8g³ 8.3m⁴ 9m Jul 11] fair form in maidens: ran poorly in handicap final outing: should stay 1¼m: raced only on good to firm going/fibresand. *J. W. Hills*

GOLDEN HIND (USA) 3 ch.f. Seeking The Gold (USA) – Min Elreeh (USA) 68 **82** (Danzig (USA)) [2001 77+: f7g² f7g⁵ f8.5g³ Feb 8] sturdy, compact filly: first foal: dam once-raced daughter of Yorkshire Oaks winner Roseate Tern, herself half-sister to high-class middle-distance performer Ibn Bey out of half-sister to Teleprompter: fairly useful performer: creditable efforts when placed in handicaps at Wolverhampton: stays 8.5f: has run only on fibresand except for debut (on turf): has been slowly away: sold 52,000 gns in December. *Sir Mark Prescott*

GOLDEN LEGEND (IRE) 4 b.g. Last Tycoon 131 – Adjalisa (IRE) 65 (Darshaan **69** 133) [2001 65: f9.4g 6d 7m 6m² 8m³ 7.5m 6m⁴ f7g 6.1f 9f* 8.1g² 8m Jul 15] useful- **a–** looking gelding: fair handicapper: won amateur event at Kempton in July: claimed out of A. Coogan's stable £5,000 2 days later: stays 9f: acts on firm and good to soft going: tried tongue tied. *R. J. Price*

GOLDEN LOCKET 4 ch.f. Beveled (USA) – Rekindled Flame (IRE) (Kings Lake **73 d** (USA) 133) [2001 70: 7g⁵ 7m⁵ 7.1f⁶ f7g 8d f8.5g⁶ f6g Nov 3] tall, workmanlike filly: fair maiden handicapper: below form after second start: stays 7f: acts on good to firm and good to soft going and fibresand: has raced freely: joined A. Jarvis. *M. Kettle*

GOLDEN NEEDLE (IRE)   3 b.f. Prince of Birds (USA) 121 – Royal Thimble (IRE) **43** 83 (Prince Rupert (FR) 121) [2001 56: f7g³ Jan 4] poor maiden: ran in seller only 3-y-o outing: looked likely to be suited by 1m+. *Noel T. Chance*

GOLDEN OSCAR   4 ch.g. Primo Dominie 121 – Noble Destiny 89 (Dancing Brave **34** (USA) 140) [2001 60?: 8.2v 7.5f 8f 7.1f⁴ 7m Aug 28] strong, lengthy gelding: poor maiden: raced only at 7f to 1m. *Andrew Turnell*

GOLDEN ROD   4 ch.g. Rainbows For Life (CAN) – Noble Form (Double Form 130) **53** [2001 64: f11g* e12g f11g⁸ 10g 11.8f* 10.9m 14.1m³ 12d⁴ 12g⁴ f12g* f12g² f12g⁴ Nov **a64** 17] close-coupled, angular gelding: modest handicapper: won at Southwell in March, Leicester (apprentices) in May and Wolverhampton in September: stays 1¾m: acts on any turf going and fibresand: has bled from nose: races prominently: has found little: quirky. *P. W. Harris*

GOLDEN SHELL   2 ch.f. (May 7) Hatim (USA) 121 – Sonnenelle 71 (Sonnen Gold **–** 121) [2001 5m Sep 30] first known foal: dam 5f winner: 100/1, well beaten in maiden at Musselburgh. *A. C. Whillans*

GOLDEN SILCA   5 ch.m. Inchinor 119 – Silca-Cisa 93 (Hallgate 127) [2001 115: **115** 8.9g² 8.9g⁴ 8m 8g² 8m Aug 1] lengthy, sparely-made mare: smart performer: creditable efforts in 2001 when ½-length second to Mahfooth in prestige race then 3 lengths fourth to Jim And Tonic in Dubai Duty Free, both at Nad Al Sheba in March, and when 1¼ lengths second to Royal Dragon in Berlin Brandenburg-Trophy at Hoppegarten in July: well beaten otherwise in Queen Anne Stakes at Royal Ascot and Sussex Stakes at Goodwood: best at 1m/9f: acts on soft and good to firm going: has won when edgy: usually held up: stays in training. *M. R. Channon*

GOLDEN SNAKE (USA)   5 b.h. Danzig (USA) – Dubian 120 (High Line 125) **127** [2001 121: 10s* 10.5g² 12m⁶ Jul 28]

    Two years after he was first due to take up stallion duties at the National Stud, Golden Snake is finally in residence there, a knee injury possibly sustained in the King George VI and Queen Elizabeth Diamond Stakes having brought his racing career to an end. Apparently breeders showed little interest in Golden Snake when he was first offered to them at a fee of £6,500, hence his return to the racecourse; but, given his subsequent achievements, being snubbed has turned out a blessing in disguise. Golden Snake had shown himself to be very smart in two seasons' racing for Barry Hills's stable before being purchased by the National Stud, gaining one of his three victories in the Prix Jean Prat, but he developed into a high-class performer after being brought back into training with John Dunlop and gained three more Group 1 wins. He will surely be a lot more popular with breeders this time around, even though his fee has been raised to £8,000.

    Apart from in the King George, Golden Snake never raced in Britain for Dunlop. In the 2000 season he won in Germany (the Preis von Europa) and Italy (the Gran Premio del Jockey Club) and also travelled to Japan after starting off in Ireland and France. The last two countries were as far as he got in the latest season. Making his reappearance in the Prix Ganay at Longchamp in April, with his stable

Prix Ganay, Longchamp—a fourth career Group 1 win for Golden Snake, who makes all and is never in danger; Egyptband (right) is second, ahead of With The Flow (blinkers) and Little Rock

in top form and the ground in his favour, Golden Snake proceeded to show himself better than ever in winning the nine-runner event by three lengths from the previous season's Arc second Egyptband, making all. Next stop for Golden Snake was the Tattersalls Gold Cup at the Curragh, a race in which he had finished fourth twelve months earlier. A career-best performance saw Golden Snake go very close to winning his fifth pattern contest. The betting suggested the race lay between Fantastic Light and Kalanisi, yet Golden Snake not only managed to split the pair but also failed only by a neck to hold off the first-named after being sent to the front over two furlongs out. Golden Snake finished a long way behind Fantastic Light in the King George, and being found to have a chipped bone in the near-fore knee a week or so later could be one reason why he failed to give his running. Another is that the ground at Ascot was unsuitable for him. On the five occasions Golden Snake encountered ground firmer than good he ran well below his best. He acted very well on soft going, and indeed all of his pattern wins were gained on such a surface.

		Danzig (USA) (b 1977)	Northern Dancer (b 1961)	Nearctic
				Natalma
Golden Snake (USA) (b.h. 1996)			Pas de Nom (b or br 1968)	Admiral's Voyage
				Petitioner
		Dubian (b 1982)	High Line (ch 1966)	High Hat
				Time Call
			Melodina (br 1968)	Tudor Melody
				Rose of Medina

The essay on Golden Snake at the end of his four-year-old season mentioned that he would have a fair amount to recommend him when the time came for him to take up stallion duties, and his performances on his first two starts in his final campaign only strengthened his position. A rangy, attractive individual, he

The National Stud's "Golden Snake"

certainly looks the part, and he also has a pedigree to match his ability, being by Danzig out of the very smart Dubian. A winner over seven furlongs on her only start at two, Dubian went on to show smart form at up to a mile and a half, winning three more races including the Royal Whip and Premio Lydia Tesio as a four-year-old. She was also placed in the Musidora Stakes, Oaks and Irish Oaks and finished fourth in the Phoenix Champion Stakes. Her dam Melodina, whose other winning produce include triple champion hurdler See You Then, and grandam Rose of Medina were racehorses with a similarly high level of ability who also stayed a mile and a half well. Dubian has produced numerous winners, the pick of them after Golden Snake being Sayyedati (by Shadeed) and Race Leader (by Gone West). The former won the 1993 One Thousand Guineas, while the latter was a smart winner over a mile in 2000. Golden Snake, a thoroughly genuine performer who was effective at a mile and a quarter and a mile and a half, has already done plenty on the racecourse to help revive the fortunes of the National Stud. Let's hope he continues in the same vein in his new career. *J. L. Dunlop*

GOLDEN SONATA (USA) 2 b.f. (Feb 16) Mr Prospector (USA) – Elissa Beet- –
hoven (Royal Academy (USA) 130) [2001 6m Jul 12] tall, leggy filly: second foal: dam, French maiden, out of half-sister to dam of high-class 1m/1¼m performer Palace Music: very green, ninth of 11 in maiden at Newmarket. *J. Noseda*

GOLDEN SPARROW 3 ch.f. Elmaamul (USA) 125 – Moon Spin 83 (Night Shift **102**
(USA)) [2001 93p: 10d* 10f a8.5f⁶ a10s³ 8d Nov 4] smallish, workmanlike filly: useful form when winning handicap at Newmarket in April by 2 lengths from Double Honour (left J. Dunlop after): below form in North America, changing trainers twice more: will stay 1½m+: acts on soft going. *R. Attfield, Canada*

GOLDEN SPECTRUM (IRE) 2 ch.c. (May 8) Spectrum (IRE) 126 – Plessaya **94**
(USA) (Nureyev (USA) 131) [2001 7g² 7f² Aug 18] 10,500F, 28,000Y: leggy, quite good-topped colt: seventh foal: brother to 3-y-o Smart Dancer and half-brother to 2 winners abroad by Highest Honor, including useful German/UAE 7f to 1½m performer Paris Sport: dam lightly-raced half-sister to high-class French middle-distance performer Persepolis: fairly useful form when runner-up in maidens at Goodwood and Newbury (kept on well, beaten neck by Flat Spin) in August: will stay at least 1m. *R. Hannon*

GOLDEN SYMBOL 4 ch.f. Wolfhound (USA) 126 – Nuriva (USA) 100 (Woodman **54 d**
(USA) 126) [2001 –: f6g⁵ e7g⁴ 7m⁶ 8.1m 10.1m 8d 8m 6d 7.1m⁵ 8f f7g Nov 23] modest maiden, on downgrade: left N. Littmoden after second start and T. Keddy after eighth: should prove best up to 7f: acts on heavy going, good to firm and equitrack: tried blinkered: sometimes slowly away: sold 12,500 gns. *J. G. Given*

GOLDEN WELLS (IRE) 3 b.g. Sadler's Wells (USA) 132 – Golden Bloom (Main **115**
Reef 126) [2001 9d* 10s* 12.3f³ 12f 11.9d⁵ 12m⁶ 10d* 10s⁶ 12s³ Nov 10] 44,000Y: close-coupled, good-topped gelding: seventh foal: closely related to 4-y-o Stratton, and half-brother to 2 winners, including smart US Grade 2 1½m winner Golden Pond (by Don't Forget Me), earlier 6f (at 2 yrs) to 1m winner in Britain: dam unraced: smart performer: won maiden at Musselburgh (by 11 lengths) and minor event at Newbury in April, and handicap at Ascot (by neck from Nadour Al Bahr) in October: best effort when close third to Royal Cavalier in November Stakes (Handicap) at Doncaster (blinkered, slowly away, wandered and looked hard ride) final outing: gelded after: will stay 1¾m: has form on firm going, possibly best on softer than good. *M. Johnston*

GOLDEN WHISPER (IRE) 3 b.f. Priolo (USA) 127 – Gold Wind (IRE) 79 (Marju –
(IRE) 127) [2001 55, a–: f8g 9.9m 8f⁵ 8.2f⁶ 8.2m 7d 7s Oct 5] leggy, sparely-made filly: modest maiden at 2 yrs: little form in 2001. *P. Howling*

GOLDEN WIND 5 ch.m. Blaze O'Gold (USA) 86 – Cool Wind 64 (Windjammer –
(USA)) [2001 f9.4s f9.4g f6g 8.1g⁵ 5.7m 8.1m May 26] fifth foal: dam won at 5f/6f (including at 2 yrs) to 11f: little form. *C. J. Price*

GOLDEVA 2 gr.f. (May 9) Makbul 104 – Gold Belt (IRE) 61 (Bellypha 130) [2001 **85 +**
5.1f* 5m² 6f² 6g² 6.1d⁵ 5d 5d² Sep 25] leggy filly: has a quick action: half-sister to 3 winners, including 4-y-o Royal Cavalier and 5-y-o Nathan's Boy: dam 1m winner: fairly useful performer: won maiden at Chester in May: second in 4 minor events after: seemed to run well in all-aged listed event at Doncaster penultimate start: will prove best at 5f/6f: acts on firm and good to soft ground. *R. Hollinshead*

GOLD FERVOUR (IRE) 2 b.g. (Mar 15) Mon Tresor 113 – Fervent Fan (IRE) 65 **50**
(Soviet Lad (USA)) [2001 6d 6m⁵ 7g⁵ 7.1s³ 7.5g⁴ f5g Oct 6] 4,500F: quite good-topped

gelding: first foal: dam 2-y-o 6f winner: modest maiden: stays 7.5f: acts on soft and good to firm going. *W. M. Brisbourne*

GOLD GUEST   2 ch.c. (Feb 8) Vettori (IRE) 119 – Cassilis (IRE) (Persian Bold 123)   **91**
[2001 5d⁶ 5.3s* 6m⁶ 5m 6g² 6m² 7m⁵ 7g 7d³ Aug 19] 16,500F, 44,000Y: tall colt: first foal: dam unraced half-sister to smart German miler Sinyar and to dam of smart performer up to 9f Ventiquattrofogli: fairly useful performer: won maiden at Brighton in May: placed in minor events and listed race (respectable third of 4 to Red Briar at Deauville) after: should stay 1m: acts on soft and good to firm ground: joined G. Margarson. *M. R. Channon*

GOLDIE   3 b.f. Celtic Swing 138 – Hotel California (IRE) 58 (Last Tycoon 131) [2001   **80**
73: 8g 7.1g⁵ 9f⁶ 8.3m⁴ 7.1m* 7g⁴ 7.1g p8g² p8g Dec 22] leggy, sparely-made filly: fairly useful handicapper: won at Warwick in August: stays 1m: acts on firm going, good to soft and polytrack: tends to race freely. *D. J. Coakley*

GOLD KRIEK   4 b.g. High Kicker (USA) – Ship of Gold 78 (Glint of Gold 128) [2001   –
43: 10s 12m Jun 26] probably of little account. *M. E. Sowersby*

GOLDON FRIENDSHIP (IRE)   2 b.f. (Apr 6) College Chapel 122 – Claire's   **51**
Thatch (Thatch (USA) 136) [2001 5s 5m⁵ 6.1g 5m 6m Sep 22] 1,200Y: angular filly: half-sister to several winners abroad, including The Imps (by Mac's Imp), also 5f seller winner in Britain at 2 yrs: dam Irish 1½m winner: modest maiden: likely to prove best at 5f/6f. *J. R. Weymes*

GOLD POINT (IRE)   2 b.g. (Mar 20) Goldmark (USA) 113 – Flashing Raven (IRE)   **82**
(Maelstrom Lake 118) [2001 6d² 7g* Jul 28] 5,000F, 9,500Y: quite good-topped gelding: fourth foal: brother to 3-y-o Regatta Point and half-brother to fairly useful 7f (at 2 yrs) to 1½m winner Perfect Moment (by Mujadil): dam unraced: fairly useful form: 7 lengths second to Funfair Wane in maiden at York (coltish and green): gelded before justifying favouritism in similar event at Newcastle: bred to stay 1¼m. *A. P. Jarvis*

GOLD RIDER (IRE)   4 b.g. Common Grounds 118 – Baydon Belle (USA) 64 (Al   –
Nasr (FR) 126) [2001 –: f12g 10.1g 10d 14.1s Oct 31] little form: left Mrs L. Pearce after reappearance: tried blinkered/tongue tied. *Mrs C. A. Dunnett*

GOLD STANDARD (IRE)   3 ch.g. Goldmark (USA) 113 – Miss Audimar (USA)   **86**
(Mr Leader (USA)) [2001 75p: 10g 10.2m⁶ 11.4g 11.6m 11.7g³ 14.1m³ 14.1m* 12m² 16f² 14g Oct 6] rather unfurnished gelding: fluent mover: fairly useful handicapper: won at Salisbury in August: good second on same course and at Newbury (best effort, 3 lengths behind Hirapour) next 2 starts: ran as if something amiss final outing (reportedly banged head when being saddled): better at 2m than shorter: acts on firm going: has raced freely: genuine. *D. R. C. Elsworth*

GOLD STATUETTE (IRE)   3 ch.g. Caerleon (USA) 132 – Nawara 75 (Welsh   **91**
Pageant 132) [2001 73: 8g³ 10.9m* 12m 12m² 12g⁴ Aug 27] lengthy, useful-looking gelding: fairly useful handicapper: won at Warwick in May: best efforts at Epsom last 2 starts when ½-length second to Serengeti Bride then (didn't get much room in amateur event) 1¾ lengths fourth to Rutland Chantry: will probably stay 1¾m: yet to race on extremes of going: sold 24,000 gns, gelded and joined T. McGovern. *J. W. Hills*

GOLDTHROAT (IRE)   2 b.f. (Mar 24) Zafonic (USA) 130 – Winger 70 (In The   **77**
Wings 128) [2001 7g 7m* 8f 8d Sep 27] IR 100,000Y: close-coupled filly: second foal: half-sister to fairly useful Irish 2000 2-y-o 5f winner Warrior Wings (by Indian Ridge): dam, Irish 9f winner, half-sister to 1m winner Killer Instinct (by Zafonic), out of smart half-sister to Irish Oaks winner Colorspin (dam of Opera House and Kayf Tara) and Bella Colora (dam of Stagecraft): fair performer: won maiden at Redcar in August: well held in nurseries after, looking reluctant final start: should stay 1m. *J. L. Dunlop*

GOMPAS PAL   3 b.g. Petong 126 – Impala Lass 81 (Kampala 120) [2001 50: 8.1v⁵   **50**
7m³ 9m 8m³ 8.2f 7g³ 7d 7m Sep 4] strong gelding: modest maiden: stays 1m: acts on good to firm going and equitrack: usually visored: none too consistent: sold 1,300 gns. *K. R. Burke*

GONCHAROVA (USA)   3 b.f. Gone West (USA) – Pure Grain 121 (Polish Precedent   **112**
(USA) 131) [2001 82: 7d 10.5d* 11.9m 10d³ 10.5d* Nov 11] smallish, well-made filly: smart performer: won handicap at Haydock in August and Prix Fille de l'Air at Toulouse in November, never far away and leading just inside final 1f to beat Side of Paradise 1½ lengths in latter: close third to Esyoueffcee in listed race at Newmarket penultimate start, racing freely then staying on well after meeting trouble: should stay 1½m: acts on heavy going, well held on good to firm. *Sir Michael Stoute*

Weatherbys Super Sprint, Newbury—Good Girl proves herself a bargain buy as a yearling;
Online Investor (breastgirth) is second, ahead of Lady Links

GONE'N'DUNNETT (IRE) 2 b.c. (Apr 27) Petardia 113 – Skerries Bell 71 (Taufan **58 d**
(USA) 119) [2001 5f 6m 6m⁵ 5.6f⁶ 6m⁵ f8g 7s Oct 5] 9,000Y: strong colt: second living
foal: half-brother to a winner in Greece by Blues Traveller: dam, Belgian 7f to 9f winner,
half-sister to smart sprinter Indian Rocket: modest maiden: clearly best effort on third
start: stays 6f: acts on good to firm ground: tried blinkered/visored. *Mrs C. A. Dunnett*

GONE TOO FAR 3 b.g. Reprimand 122 – Blue Nile (IRE) 70 (Bluebird (USA) 125) **62**
[2001 65: 8d 8m⁶ 10.1m 8m³ 8m⁴ 8.5f⁶ 10.9d⁴ 12.4g³ 16f³ Sep 4] rather unfurnished
gelding: modest handicapper: probably stays 2m: acts on firm ground. *M. Dods*

GOODBYE GOLDSTONE 5 b.g. Mtoto 134 – Shareehan (Dancing Brave (USA) **–**
140) [2001 74d, a–: 10s Apr 23] sparely-made gelding: fair handicapper at best: well held
only 5-y-o outing. *Miss J. A. Camacho*

GOODENOUGH MOVER 5 ch.g. Beveled (USA) – Rekindled Flame (IRE) **80**
(Kings Lake (USA) 133) [2001 88: 7s³ 6g 8m⁴ 8m² 7d³ 8.1m² 7m 7.6g 8m 10.2d Oct 25]
rangy gelding: fairly useful handicapper: below form last 4 starts: has won at 1m, may
prove best at 6f/7f: acts on soft and good to firm going: slowly away penultimate outing,
otherwise often makes running. *J. S. King*

GOOD FRIDAY (IRE) 4 b.f. Tenby 125 – Sign of Peace (IRE) 78 (Posen (USA)) **–**
[2001 66: 16.2m May 26] lengthy filly: maiden handicapper: well held only 4-y-o outing.
Mrs P. N. Dutfield

GOOD GIRL (IRE) 2 b.f. (Mar 4) College Chapel 122 – Indian Honey (Indian King **100**
(USA) 128) [2001 f5g² 5g* 5m* 5m⁵ 5.2m* 6m⁴ 5g⁶ 6m² 6d³ Oct 2] IR 9,000Y: workmanlike filly: half-sister to several winners, including Irish 6f and 1m winner Honeys-
choice (by Distinctly North) and 1m to 1½m winner Jack The Lad (by Shalford): dam
unraced: useful performer: won maiden at Ripon in May, listed event at Beverley (by
neck from Roundtree) in June and Weatherbys Super Sprint at Newbury (beat Online
Investor by length) in July: good efforts in listed event at Ayr and Cheveley Park Stakes
at Newmarket (bandaged off-hind, 9 lengths third to Queen's Logic) last 2 starts: stays 6f:
unraced on extremes of going (some promise on fibresand): excitable in preliminaries
fourth and seventh outings (in season when below form on second occasion): has been
early to post: consistent. *T. D. Easterby*

GOODGOLLYMISSMOLLY 3 b.f. Factual (USA) 108 – Chardonnay Girl (Hubbly **–**
Bubbly (USA)) [2001 40: 9.9m 6.9m 10m 7g Aug 10] big, plain filly: little form.
M. A. Allen

GOODIE TWOSUES 3 b.f. Fraam 114 – Aliuska (IRE) 70 (Fijar Tango (FR) 127) **91 ?**
[2001 90: 7m 8.5m⁶ 8f⁴ 7m 7s 8g 7d Oct 20] workmanlike filly: has a round action: fairly
useful performer: clearly best efforts in 2001 in listed races at Epsom and Goodwood on
second/fourth starts: stays 8.5f, at least when conditions aren't testing: acts on soft and
good to firm going: best treated with caution. *R. Hannon*

GOOD STANDING (USA) 3 b.f. Distant View (USA) 126 – Storm Dove (USA) **91**
108 (Storm Bird (CAN) 134) [2001 88p: 7d 8m³ 8m⁴ 9d⁵ 7m⁴ 8d Nov 3] rather leggy
filly: fairly useful handicapper: best efforts at 3 yrs when in frame at Ayr, Ripon and
Salisbury: stays 1m: won on soft going on debut, unraced on extremes since: sold 16,000
gns. *B. W. Hills*

GOOD TIMING 3 bl.g. Timeless Times (USA) 99 – Fort Vally 58 (Belfort (FR) 89) **61**
[2001 58: f7g⁴ 8m⁶ 8.1g³ 10m⁵ 8m⁶ 7g² 7.1d 7.1f² 8.5s⁴ Sep 25] lengthy, sparely-made
gelding: modest maiden handicapper: should prove best at 7f/1m: acts on any turf going
and fibresand: free-going sort: has edged left. *J. J. Quinn*

404

GOODWOOD PROMISE 2 b.c. (Mar 24) Primo Dominie 121 – Noble Destiny 89 **55**
(Dancing Brave (USA) 140) [2001 6m 6f 7s Oct 16] 10,000F, 20,000Y: neat colt: brother
to useful 5f winner (including at 2 yrs) Noble One and half-brother to several winners,
including fairly useful 1¼m winner Maiden Castle (by Darshaan): dam, 2-y-o 7f winner,
disappointing at 3 yrs: modest form in maidens: sold 5,000 gns. *J. L. Dunlop*

GOOGOOSH (IRE) 2 b.f. (Feb 10) Danehill (USA) 126 – Literary 79 (Woodman **77**
(USA) 126) [2001 6g³ 7g³ 6.1m² 7.5m² 8s⁵ Sep 27] 60,000F, 1,300,000 francs Y: lengthy
filly: first foal: dam, 1m winner, out of half-sister to Middle Park winner Lycius: fair
maiden: blinkered, second at Nottingham and Beverley: stays 1m: acts on soft and good
to firm ground: has raced freely/hung left. *E. A. L. Dunlop*

GORDONS FRIEND 3 ch.g. Clantime 101 – Auntie Fay (IRE) (Fayruz 116) [2001 **50**
41: 8m 8m 7.1g* 6g³ 6m⁵ 7d² 8d³ 7.1m Aug 23] smallish gelding: modest handicapper:
won at Haydock in June: effective at 6f to 1m: acts on good to firm and good to soft going:
visored (raced freely) on reappearance. *B. S. Rothwell*

GORETSKI (IRE) 8 b.g. Polish Patriot (USA) 128 – Celestial Path 101 (Godswalk **74**
(USA) 130) [2001 70: f6g f6g f6s² f5g² f5g f5g³ f5g² f5g⁴ f6g² 5m 5m 5g⁴ 5.1f⁵ 5f³ 5m
5d 6g 5g² 5s* 5m⁶ 5f 6f⁶ 5s 5.2v* 5s² p5g² f5g³ Dec 14] tall gelding: unimpressive
mover: fair handicapper: won at Hamilton in August, Newbury in October and Wolverhampton in December: has won at 6f, best form at 5f: acts on any turf going, fibresand
and polytrack: effective blinkered or not: races prominently: tough. *N. Tinkler*

GORMIRE 8 ro.m. Superlative 118 – Lady of The Lodge 60 (Absalom 128) [2001 6m **– §**
8g 8f 5g Aug 6] temperamental nowadays. *B. W. Murray*

GORSE 6 b.h. Sharpo 132 – Pervenche (Latest Model 115) [2001 116: 6d 6m* 6s* **116**
6m Jul 12] big, strong, lengthy horse: smart performer: successful 8 times during career,
including 5 pattern races: won Benazet-Rennen at Baden-Baden (by 1½ lengths from
Barrow Creek) in May and Holsten-Trophy at Hamburg (for second time, also second in
2000, by 2½ lengths from Irish Man) in July: raced alone down centre and never
threatened in July Cup at Newmarket final outing: raced only around 6f: acted on soft and
good to firm going: raced prominently: was genuine and consistent: to stand at East
Burrow Farm, Devon, fee £2,500, Oct 1st. *H. Candy*

GOSHIN'S LAD (USA) 2 b.c. (Mar 7) Nicholas (USA) 111 – Maratha (USA) **67 p**
(Devil's Bag (USA)) [2001 7.9d 7d⁶ p5g⁶ p6g* Dec 22] $42,000F: fifth foal: closely
related to a winner in USA by Danzig Connection and half-brother to 2 winners abroad:
dam, French 6f and (at 2 yrs) 1m winner, out of champion US turf filly De La Rose: fair
performer: tongue tied, best effort to win seller at Lingfield in December in good style:
stays 6f: acts on polytrack: should progress. *G. A. Butler*

GOSSAMER 2 b.f. (Feb 20) Sadler's Wells (USA) 132 – Brocade 121 (Habitat **114 p**
134) [2001 6m* 7d* 8s* Sep 29]

　　　Another Group 1 juvenile pattern winner for Sadler's Wells? Yes, but Gossamer is one with a difference, since, unlike Ballingarry, High Chaparral, Quarter
Moon and Sholokhov, she won over six furlongs and is no certainty to be suited by
middle distances. That sets her apart from the vast majority of her sire's progeny,
because nearly all runners with Sadler's Wells in the pedigree can be expected to
have stamina in excess of speed. Among three-year-olds and upwards, the offspring
of Sadler's Wells from fourteen crops have gained just one success over sprint
distances compared with getting on for five hundred at a mile and a quarter or more.
The same goes for the sire's juveniles, with fewer than thirty victories at five or six
furlongs and almost one hundred and fifty at seven furlongs or more. Gossamer
may be untypical in one respect, but in having abundant ability—unbeaten in three
starts, culminating in the Meon Valley Stud Fillies' Mile at Ascot—she is very
much her sire's daughter and clearly has a bright future. She did not have to show
top form to win on her debut over six furlongs in an eleven-runner maiden race at
Newmarket in July. Starting at 12/1, Gossamer came to challenge Karamah
entering the Dip and knuckled down well to win readily by a length. An impressive
performance, but much better followed in the Touchdown In Malaysia Prestige
Stakes at Goodwood the following month, Gossamer moving effortlessly to the
front two furlongs from home and quickening clear in a matter of strides to
defeat previous winners Protectorate and Kootenay by seven lengths and a length
and three quarters. Gossamer was immediately installed as favourite for the One
Thousand Guineas at 8/1, and few could envisage her losing the Fillies' Mile, in

Meon Valley Stud Fillies' Mile, Ascot—Gossamer, a sister to Barathea, takes her second pattern race; Maryinsky (No.5) stays on strongly for the runner-up spot, in front of Esloob (striped cap), Half Glance (centre), Fraulein (spots) and Moon Safari

which she started at odds on to beat six rivals headed by May Hill Stakes winner Half Glance, once-raced Aidan O'Brien contender Maryinsky, the improving Fraulein, winner of her last two races, and Esloob, successful in a Newmarket maiden. In what proved a tactical race, with the tempo not increasing significantly until the home turn, Gossamer was short of room early in the straight and had to manoeuvre her way into a challenging position. Once clear, she responded willingly to assert approaching the final furlong and soon put distance between herself and the rest, beating Maryinsky emphatically by two and a half lengths with Esloob third. At that stage Gossamer definitely looked the one to beat in the Guineas but Queen's Logic's scintillating display in the Cheveley Park Stakes changed the picture, leaving Gossamer with quite a bit to find on form to beat that filly. Still, she is a good-looking filly, strongly made, and with an equable temperament and fine turn of foot, so she will be difficult to keep out of the winner's enclosure for long as a three-year-old, regardless of how she fares at Newmarket.

		Sadler's Wells (USA) (b 1981)	Northern Dancer (b 1961)	Nearctic
				Natalma
Gossamer			Fairy Bridge (b 1975)	Bold Reason
(b.f. Feb 20, 1999)				Special
		Brocade (b 1981)	Habitat (b 1966)	Sir Gaylord
				Little Hut
			Canton Silk (gr 1970)	Runnymede
				Clouded Lamp

The prize-money Gossamer has already won, £145,577, has gone towards a good cause, because her owner-breeder Gerald Leigh raced her and all his other runners during the season in the interests of the charity CancerBACUP. Leigh, who has cancer, has shown exceptional judgement and enjoyed phenomenal success as a breeder, with a succession of top-notchers led by Bosra Sham, Barathea, Markofdistinction and the latest Criterium International winner Act One produced from a smallish broodmare band at his Cayton Park then Eydon Hall Studs. One of the foundation mares for his operation, the five-furlong specialist Canton Silk, is grandam of Gossamer via her daughter Brocade, a very smart filly who won at a mile but was best at seven furlongs, over which trip she landed the Prix de la Foret as a three-year-old and the Challenge Stakes at four. She was the best of Canton Silk's eight winners—the others include the dam of very smart sprinter Desert Style. Brocade has been even better than her dam as a broodmare, getting six other winners. They are headed by Gossamer's brother Barathea, who landed the Irish Two Thousand Guineas, the Queen Anne Stakes and the Breeders' Cup Mile; smart French mile- to mile-and-a-quarter performer Zabar (by Dancing Brave), successful in four Group 3 races; and Free At Last (by Shirley Heights), a Grade 3 winner in the States and dam of Coretta, a multiple Grade 2 scorer there. In the last two years at the Newmarket December Sales Brocade's daughters Brocatelle (by

Gerald W. Leigh - CancerBACUP's "Gossamer"

Green Desert) and Zibilene (by Rainbow Quest) have fetched 1,700,000 guineas, a European record for a broodmare, and 1,500,000 guineas respectively. Gossamer's value can only be guessed at. The family is essentially a speedy one, and although Brocade has had winners by Shirley Heights and Generous, plus Zibilene, who were effective at a mile and a half, her best runners generally have not possessed great stamina. Barathea was never raced beyond a mile, a very rare occurrence for a horse by Sadler's Wells. While Gossamer is relaxed enough to suggest she will stay a mile and a quarter, a mile and a half will surely be a different matter. Barathea was also untypical of his sire's offspring in being fully effective on firm going; Gossamer's debut was on good to firm but the Fillies' Mile was on soft. *L. M. Cumani*

GOT ALOT ON (USA)   3 b. or br.g. Charnwood Forest (IRE) 125 – Fleety Belle   –
(GER) (Assert 134) [2001 57: 10s f8g Apr 28] leggy, quite attractive gelding: modest
form at 2 yrs: no show in handicaps in 2001. *Mrs J. R. Ramsden*

GO THUNDER (IRE)   7 b.g. Nordico (USA) – Moving Off (Henbit (USA) 130)   **35**
[2001 47: 8.3m 6m 9.2d⁶ 9.2g⁶ 8f 8.3d⁴ 9.2g⁵ 8f 7s⁶ 9.2d 8.3s⁴ 9.2g 8f 9.1v Oct 16] poor
performer nowadays: effective at 1m/9f, had form at 1¾m earlier in career: acts on soft
and good to firm going: tongue tied: tends to carry head awkwardly. *D. A. Nolan*

GOT TO BE CASH   2 ch.f. (Apr 26) Lake Coniston (IRE) 131 – Rasayel (USA) 79§   **66**
(Bering 136) [2001 5.1s⁴ 5.1f 5m 6d⁴ 7g 6s² f6s⁶ Sep 6] 4,500Y: strong, lengthy filly: first
foal: dam 1¼m to 1¾m winner who became unreliable: fair maiden: second at Haydock:
should stay 7f: acts on soft ground, some promise on fibresand. *B. A. McMahon*

GOT TO GO   3 b.f. Shareef Dancer (USA) 135 – Ghost Tree (IRE) 88 (Caerleon   **92**
(USA) 132) [2001 99: 10g⁵ 9.9m 8g² 7d⁶ 8d⁴ 8g 7v p10g Nov 13] useful-looking filly:
fairly useful performer: hasn't won since debut: best efforts in listed races at Newmarket

on reappearance, Ascot (6 lengths second to Riberac) third start and Doncaster next outing: flattered when eighth in Sun Chariot Stakes at Newmarket sixth start: stays 1¼m: acts on good to soft going, possibly not on soft/heavy: tongue tied last 3 starts: sold 55,000 gns in December. *B. W. Hills*

GO WITH THE WIND   8 b.g. Unfuwain (USA) 131 – Cominna (Dominion 123)   **41 §** [2001 51§: 11.1d 13m² 12m⁴ 16f Jul 2] lengthy gelding: unimpressive mover: poor performer: reportedly finished lame final outing: stays 2m: acts on firm and good to soft going: visored/blinkered once in 1996: irresolute tail swisher. *R. A. Fahey*

GRACEFUL EMPEROR   3 b.g. Emperor Jones (USA) 119 – Juvenka (Shirley   **–** Heights 130) [2001 –: 10.3v f12g⁵ 11.1d⁵ 12.3m Jun 10] leggy gelding: little form. *D. Eddy*

GRACIA   2 gr.f. (Jan 29) Linamix (FR) 127 – Francia 59 (Legend of France (USA)   **–** 124) [2001 8.2s Nov 5] third foal: half-sister to 4-y-o Suave Performer: dam 7f (at 2 yrs) and 1½m winner: very green, behind in maiden at Nottingham. *S. C. Williams*

GRACILIS (IRE)   4 b.g. Caerleon (USA) 132 – Grace Note (FR) 99 (Top Ville 129)   **93** [2001 59: 14.1s² f16g² 17.1m¹ 18m* 16.4m* 21m² Aug 1] heavy-topped gelding: fairly useful performer: progressed in handicaps at 4 yrs, winning at Southwell in May, twice at Pontefract in June and Sandown (beat King Flyer by length) in July: good 2½ lengths second to Hugs Dancer at Goodwood final outing: best at 2m+: acts on soft going, good to firm and fibresand: sometimes flashes tail/edges left. *G. A. Swinbank*

GRACIOUS AIR (USA)   3 b.f. Bahri (USA) 125 – Simply Bell (USA) (Simply   **49** Majestic (USA)) [2001 –p: 7f 7.5m⁵ 8g 12m⁴ 14.4d 9.9m 9m⁵ 10m⁶ 12d³ 12g Nov 7] tall, leggy, good-topped filly: poor maiden handicapper: stays 1½m: acts on good to firm going: ran as if something amiss third outing. *J. R. Weymes*

GRACIOUS KING   3 ro.c. King's Signet (USA) 110 – Gracious Gretclo 54 (Common   **48** Grounds 118) [2001 7s 5.1m³ 7m 6.1f 5.1f Jul 26] first foal: dam, maiden who stayed 6f, sister to smart 6f/7f performer Rich Ground: poor form in maidens/handicap/claimer: best effort second start. *R. J. Hodges*

GRADY   2 ch.c. (May 13) Bluegrass Prince (IRE) 110 – Lady Sabina 61 (Bairn (USA)   **67** 126) [2001 5.7g⁶ Oct 1] 4,000Y: first foal: dam 1¼m winner out of useful sprinter Calibina: never-nearer sixth of 16 to Rosie's Posy in maiden at Bath: should stay 7f. *Miss Jacqueline S. Doyle*

GRAFT   2 b.c. (Apr 19) Entrepreneur 123 – Mariakova (USA) 84 (The Minstrel (CAN)   **81 p** 135) [2001 7g 7m³ p8g* Nov 15] 68,000F, 95,000Y: quite good-topped colt: half-brother to 5f (at 2 yrs) to 1m winner Well Beyond (by Don't Forget Me) and 1¼m winner Krispin (by Kris), both useful, and 1½m winner Society Ball (by Law Society): dam, placed at 6f and 1m only starts, sister to dam of Zafonic: fairly useful form in maidens: won at Lingfield by 1¼ lengths from Quite A Night, leading near finish: likely to stay 1¼m: should progress. *B. W. Hills*

GRAIG PARK   3 b.g. Mind Games 121 – Flicker Toa Flame (USA) 85 (Empery   **–** (USA) 128) [2001 –: 7m May 28] no form, including in seller. *A. Berry*

GRAIN OF GOLD   2 b.f. (Feb 4) Mr Prospector (USA) – Pure Grain 121 (Polish   **57 p** Precedent (USA) 131) [2001 7m Aug 30] second foal: closely related to 3-y-o Goncharova: dam 7f (Prestige Stakes at 2 yrs) to 1½m (Irish/Yorkshire Oaks) winner: 16/1, never-dangerous tenth of 16 to Brown Eyes in maiden at Salisbury: sure to improve. *Sir Michael Stoute*

GRAIN STORM (IRE)   3 b.f. Marju (IRE) 127 – Zuhal 67 (Busted 134) [2001 62:   **50** 9.9m 8m⁶ 8m 8.2f* 9.2s⁵ 8m 7g Aug 8] lightly-made filly: modest performer: won selling handicap at Nottingham in June: stays 1m: acts on firm going: very slowly away final outing: has been early to post: headstrong. *P. C. Haslam*

GRALMANO (IRE)   6 b.g. Scenic 128 – Llangollen (IRE) 87 (Caerleon (USA) 132)   **89** [2001 91, a96: f8.5g³ f8.5g 12.3s⁵ 8g⁵ 10.4g 10m 10.5g⁵ 10m 10m⁶ 10m 12m 10.3g 10g   **a96** Oct 6] strong gelding: unimpressive mover: useful handicapper on all-weather, fairly useful on turf nowadays: below form after sixth start at 6 yrs: best at 9f/1¼m: acts on firm going (probably on soft): has been visored/blinkered, only once in 2001: edgy sort: usually races prominently: has looked none too keen: fairly useful winner over hurdles. *K. A. Ryan*

GRAMPAS (USA)   4 b. or br.c. El Gran Senor (USA) 136 – Let There Be Light (USA)   **111** (Sunny's Halo (CAN)) [2001 97+: 10f* Jun 23] rather leggy, quite attractive colt: smart form: 20/1, improved effort only 4-y-o outing when winning handicap at Ascot by

½ length from Nadour Al Bahr, quickening well from behind: stays 1¼m: acts on firm going, yet to race on softer than good: swished tail continuously/found little third 3-y-o start, rider seemed reluctant to use whip final one: held up: sent to USA. *J. H. M. Gosden*

GRAMPIAN 2 b.c. (Feb 15) Selkirk (USA) 129 – Gryada 93 (Shirley Heights 130) **89** [2001 7g⁴ 7g* 7m Sep 12] 200,000Y: rather leggy, useful-looking colt: second foal: half-brother to 3-y-o Guaranda: dam, 2-y-o 7f/1m winner, closely related to useful stayer Gondolier: fairly useful form: won maiden at Newmarket in August despite idling and hanging left: seventh of 8 in minor event at Doncaster (on toes, had 2 handlers) final start: should stay at least 1m: joined J. Given. *L. M. Cumani*

GRAN CLICQUOT 6 gr.m. Gran Alba (USA) 107 – Tina's Beauty 41 (Tina's Pet **52** 121) [2001 8f* 7.6g Sep 5] 700Y: fourth living foal: dam maiden: pulled up in a bumper in 1999: modest form: 100/1, successful Flat debut in seller at Brighton in August: stays 1m: acts on firm ground. *G. P. Enright*

GRAND AUNT DEE (IRE) 2 b.f. (Mar 28) Distant Relative 128 – Willow Dale **64 p** (IRE) 89 (Danehill (USA) 126) [2001 6g Oct 6] 5,000F, IR 18,000Y: first foal: dam 5f/6f winner, including at 2 yrs: 50/1, never-dangerous tenth of 17 in maiden at Newmarket: will probably improve. *D. R. C. Elsworth*

GRAND BAHAMIAN (USA) 4 gr.g. Distant View (USA) 126 – Flora Scent (USA) **–** (Fluorescent Light (USA)) [2001 77: 8g 7m 6.1v Oct 4] well-made gelding: fair performer at 3 yrs: no form in 2001: tried blinkered. *Miss J. Feilden*

GRAND BANKES 2 b.g. (Apr 7) Mistertopogigo (IRE) 118 – Mayday Kitty 38 **–** (Interrex (CAN)) [2001 5f Jun 13] second foal: dam maiden who stayed 1½m: always behind in Lingfield seller. *W. G. M. Turner*

GRAND CRU 10 ch.g. Kabour 80 – Hydrangea 73 (Warpath 113) [2001 51§, a56§: **– §** f16g f14g 14.1v Mar 28] angular gelding: temperamental handicapper nowadays: visored/blinkered. *J. Cullinan*

GRANDE DAME (IRE) 2 b.f. (Jan 30) Grand Lodge (USA) 125 – Royal Hostess **57 p** (IRE) (Be My Guest (USA) 126) [2001 7m 7m Sep 24] 27,000F: second foal: dam, ran twice in France, half-sister to Prix du Cadran winner Sought Out and to grandam of 3-y-o Golan: green, modest form in maidens: slowly away both starts: should be suited by 1¼m/1½m: likely to do better. *I. A. Balding*

GRANDERA (IRE) 3 ch.c. Grand Lodge (USA) 125 – Bordighera (USA) **124** (Alysheba (USA)) [2001 106p: 10.3f² 12m³ 10m² 10.4g² 11f* Sep 22]

The acquisition of Grandera by Godolphin in October from James Fanshawe's yard for an undisclosed sum seemed to pass almost unnoticed at the time, yet in terms of form Grandera is one of the best horses recruited for the stable in recent years. Only seven such recruits over the last five years have been rated Grandera's equal or higher by Timeform: Daylami in 1998, Derby winner High-Rise and Xaar in 1999, Arc winner Sagamix and Bertolini in 2000, and Sakhee and Ekraar in 2001. Their fortunes in the Godolphin colours proved mixed to say the least. While Daylami and Sakhee went on to record top-class performances in the best middle-distance races in Europe and North America, the five others mustered only a couple of victories in listed events between them (courtesy of High-Rise and Ekraar). It remains to be seen how Grandera will fare for his new owners. In spite of showing very smart form, he has yet to win in pattern company, though he was involved in a close finish in both the Prix du Jockey Club at Chantilly and the Coral Eclipse Stakes at Sandown, leaving the impression on the first occasion that had things fallen his way he might even have won. He was also second in the Juddmonte International at York. Grandera has progressed well so far, which bodes well for his career as a four-year-old when an international campaign seems likely to be mapped out for him. With that in mind, he couldn't be in better hands, as the globe-trotting achievements of the likes of Fantastic Light and Kutub in the latest season testify.

Grandera reappeared in the Dee Stakes at Chester in May and, in finishing half a length second to Dr Greenfield, he repeated his similarly useful two-year-old form, which included a close second to King Charlemagne in the Somerville Tattersall Stakes at Newmarket. Though Grandera did well, he still looked to have a bit to find to make a serious impression in his second race of the season, the Prix

Dubai Arc Trial, Newbury—very smart performances from the first two as Grandera gets the better of Mubtaker; Compton Bolter (noseband), Miletrian (left) and Chancellor complete the field

du Jockey Club over three weeks later. But Grandera ran a cracker to come third of fourteen behind Anabaa Blue, running on really well once he saw daylight in the final furlong after enjoying anything but a smooth passage, being short of room against the rail for much of the straight. Grandera was beaten a diminishing half a length by Anabaa Blue with Chichicastenango splitting the pair. Okawango was close behind in fourth with subsequent St Leger winner Milan fifth. On Grandera's next outing, in the eight-runner Eclipse Stakes, it was more a case of the line not coming soon enough for him. The two pacemakers Darwin and Broche, acting respectively for the Ballydoyle and Godolphin camps, set a furious gallop and Grandera, who edged into a narrow lead under pressure, after mastering Bach entering the final furlong, was just unable to hold the late surge of Medicean, who swept past to win by half a length with Bach a neck away in third, just ahead of Tobougg. Grandera had no excuses when beaten seven lengths by Sakhee in the International in August but nevertheless ran well, keeping on from mid-division and managing to turn the tables on Medicean, who finished a length behind Grandera in third, with Black Minnaloushe fourth. Grandera gained a deserved win when dropped into listed company on his final outing in the Dubai Arc Trial at Newbury, beating Mubtaker comfortably by a length and a half in a fairly steadily-run affair.

			Chief's Crown	Danzig
	Grand Lodge (USA)		(b 1982)	Six Crowns
	(ch 1991)		La Papagena	Habitat
Grandera (IRE)			(br 1983)	Magic Flute
(ch.c. 1998)			Alysheba	Alydar
	Bordighera (USA)		(b 1984)	Bel Sheba
	(ch 1992)		Blue Tip	Tip Moss
			(b 1982)	As Blue

Grandera's sire Grand Lodge is best known as the sire of dual Derby and Prix de l'Arc de Triomphe winner Sinndar and was also represented by the champion two-year-old filly Queen's Logic in the latest season. But many of Grand Lodge's best offspring—in his admittedly short time at stud—have gone on to make their mark as four-year-olds, among them the high-class Indian Lodge, Island House and Sandmason. Grandera's dam Bordighera was a useful winner in France over a mile and three furlongs as a three-year-old. She is a daughter of Blue Tip, a smart performer in France who won the Prix Penelope over ten and a half furlongs

Lael Stable & Mrs V. Shelton's "Grandera"

and was also third in the Prix de l'Opera. Grandera has a couple of half-sisters in France, the year-older Fifty Five (by Lake Coniston), who has won at a mile and a quarter, and the year-younger Tropezina (by Entrepreneur), who has yet to race. Grandera, a good-topped individual and a fluent mover, usually takes the eye in the paddock. He seems best at a mile and a quarter to a mile and a half, and has raced mainly on going firmer than good, though he does act on good to soft (he was well held on his only outing on soft, in the Racing Post Trophy on his final outing at two). It should be pointed out, however, that Grandera appeared not fully at ease on firm going at Chester and Newbury in the latest season, though it is just possible there could be a bit more to that than meets the eye. While with Fanshawe, Grandera was reported on the trainer's website as being 'a bit of a character' at home, something the horse hinted at on the racecourse too, when carrying his head awkwardly at Chester and when tending to hang left at Newbury. Grandera fetched IR 46,000 guineas as a foal but, interestingly, only IR 30,000 guineas as a yearling, a disparity possibly accounted for by the fact that he reportedly appeared a little lame in the sale-ring. Whatever the reason, he is certainly worth a good deal more now. *J. R. Fanshawe*

GRAND ESTATE 6 b.g. Prince Sabo 123 – Ultimate Dream 74 (Kafu 120) [2001 62, a50: 6m 5f⁴ 6g⁵ 6g 6m⁶ 5g² 6f Sep 10] strong gelding: modest handicapper: effective at 5f/6f: yet to race on heavy ground, acts on any other turf going and on fibresand: possibly best blinkered nowadays: none too genuine. *D. W. Chapman* **62 a–**

GRAND FROMAGE (IRE) 3 ch.g. Grand Lodge (USA) 125 – My First Paige (IRE) 53 (Runnett 125) [2001 10.2d⁶ 10v 10g 12m⁵ 14.1m² 14.1g⁴ 16g* 15.9d Sep 26] IR 16,000Y, 17,500 2-y-o: quite good-topped gelding: third foal: half-brother to 1998 2-y-o **75**

411

5f winner Sweet As A Nut (by Pips Pride) and 1½m winner Second Paige (by Nicolotte): dam, 6f winner who ran only at 2 yrs, from family of top-class miler To-Agori-Mou: fair handicapper: won at Kempton in September: better around 2m than shorter: acts on good to firm ground. *H. Candy*

GRAND HARBOUR (IRE) 2 b.c. (Apr 24) Grand Lodge (USA) 125 – Port Isaac **71** (USA) 64 (Seattle Song (USA) 130) [2001 8g³ 8d Oct 3] IR 60,000Y: fifth foal: half-brother to 4-y-o Howard's Lad and a winner in Italy (both by Reprimand): dam lightly-raced maiden from very good US family: much better effort in maidens (fair form) when third of 6 at Goodwood: should stay 1¼m. *R. Hannon*

GRAND ILLUSION (IRE) 2 b.c. (Apr 18) Mukaddamah (USA) 125 – Saint **50** Cynthia (Welsh Saint 126) [2001 5m 5g⁴ 6g⁶ Sep 3] 2,500F, 4,000Y: half-brother to several winners, including untrustworthy Irish 1½m winner Tittle Tattle (by Soviet Lad) and 6f (at 2 yrs)/7f winner who was later successful abroad Saint Caligula (by Petorius), both fairly useful: dam, Irish 1¾m winner who also won over hurdles, half-sister to dam of July Cup winner Compton Place: modest maiden: should stay 1m: slowly away first 2 starts: carried head awkwardly final one. *P. Mitchell*

GRANDMA GRIFFITHS 3 b.f. Eagle Eyed (USA) 111 – Buck Comtess (USA) **–** (Spend A Buck (USA)) [2001 –: 10s 16m May 30] angular filly: of little account. *Mrs L. Stubbs*

GRANDMA LILY (IRE) 3 b.f. Bigstone (IRE) 126 – Mrs Fisher (IRE) 94 (Salmon **88** Leap (USA) 131) [2001 f8g 10m⁵ f6g* f7g* f9.4g² Aug 18] big, lengthy filly: has scope: fifth foal: half-sister to fairly useful 1m (and at 2 yrs) 8.5f winner Pedro (by Brief Truce): dam 7f winner (including at 2 yrs): fairly useful form: progressed well to win maiden and minor event at Wolverhampton in July/August: further improvement when second to Inver Gold in handicap there final outing (carried head slightly awkwardly): stays 9.4f: acts on fibresand: sold 10,500 gns. *Sir Mark Prescott*

GRAND VIEW 5 ch.g. Grand Lodge (USA) 125 – Hemline 77 (Sharpo 132) [2001 **62** 67: f6g³ e6g f6g 5m* 6m⁵ 5m² 5m 6m 6.1m* 5f* 6m 6g 5g 5g f6g p5g⁴ f6g⁵ f6s Dec 15] **a49** modest performer: won seller at Musselburgh in May, then claimed from D. Nicholls after sixth start, and won seller at Nottingham and claimer at Musselburgh in July: best at 5f/6f: acts on soft going, good to firm and all-weather: blinkered first 3 starts in 2001 (finished lame second outing). *H. A. McWilliams*

GRANGE CLARE (IRE) 2 b. or br.f. (Feb 22) Bijou d'Inde 127 – Scarlet Slipper **72** (Gay Mecene (USA) 128) [2001 f5g* 6f³ Jun 3] IR 10,500Y, 9,000 2-y-o: workmanlike filly: half-sister to several winners, including 7f winner Shimmering Scarlet (by Glint of Gold) and useful French miler Sao (by Dolphin Street): dam, French 1m winner, out of smart French performer up to 1m Silk Slipper: fair form: overcame greenness to win maiden at Southwell in May: improved when third of 5 to Barzah in minor event at Pontefract following month: should stay 7f. *P. D. Evans*

GRANGE PRINCE (IRE) 2 b.g. (Feb 23) Mujadil (USA) 119 – Cashel Princess **60 ?** (IRE) 91 (Fayruz 116) [2001 6g 5.3s p6g p5g Nov 24] IR 20,000Y, 4,000 2-y-o: second foal: dam Irish 9f/1¼m winner: beaten some way in sellers/maiden (left P. D. Evans after second start), though seemingly modest form in tongue tie final start. *Mrs L. C. Jewell*

GRANITE CITY 4 ro.g. Clantime 101 – Alhargah (Be My Guest (USA) 126) [2001 **48** 58: 8d 7.1m 8m 7.1f⁵ 8f 8f 9f* 10g⁶ 8f⁵ 8.3m 6v³ 8d³ 8g³ Nov 7] leggy gelding: poor mover: poor handicapper: won amateur event at Musselburgh in August: needs good test at 6f, barely stays 1¼m: acts on any turf going: consistent. *J. S. Goldie*

GRANNY'S PET 7 ch.g. Selkirk (USA) 129 – Patsy Western 81 (Precocious 126) **110** [2001 111: 7g⁴ 7f⁴ 7m³ 7.3m⁴ 7g⁵ 7g* 7m² 7s⁴ 7v⁶ Oct 27] angular, close-coupled gelding: has a quick action: smart performer: won handicap at Goodwood in August, bursting through to beat Softly Tread by a neck: some creditable efforts otherwise at 7 yrs, including when ¾-length fourth to Kayo in handicap at York (made frame for fourth year running) on eighth start: best at 7f: acts on soft and good to firm going: usually waited with: tried blinkered earlier in career. *P. F. I. Cole*

GRANTLEY 4 b.g. Deploy 131 – Matisse 65 (Shareef Dancer (USA) 135) [2001 50, **46** a62: f8g⁶ f8g⁴ f9.4g 9v⁴ 8d³ 8g* 10g⁴ 9.3m³ 8d² 8g* 8s* Dec 2] modest performer on **a57** all-weather, poor on turf: left J. Bethell after fifth start: successful at Frankfurt in maiden in June and handicaps in November and December: stays 1¼m: acts on fibresand and heavy going: visored/blinkered nowadays. *H. Hesse, Germany*

GRASSLANDIK 5 b.g. Ardkinglass 114 – Sophisticated Baby 39 (Bairn (USA) **–**
126) [2001 57: f7g f8.5s f8s⁶ 7g 5g f6g² f6g f5g f6s⁴ Dec 21] poor performer: left **a49**
A. Newcombe after third start: probably stays 1m: acts on good to firm going, good to
soft and fibresand/equitrack: blinkered twice at 4 yrs: none too consistent. *Miss A. Stokell*

GREAT AS GOLD (IRE) 2 b.g. (Apr 28) Goldmark (USA) 113 – Great Land (USA) **56**
(Friend's Choice (USA)) [2001 5m⁵ f6g f7g⁵ 6g⁶ 6m 8g³ 7.9m³ 6g 7m 10v 7.9s f8.5g⁵ f8g **a49**
f8g⁵ Dec 10] 3,000Y, 5,000 2-y-o: unfurnished gelding: half-brother to several winners,
including fairly useful 7f to 1½m winner Able Choice (by Taufan) and 3-y-o Sean's
Honor: dam winner up to 9f in USA: modest maiden: should stay 1¼m: acts on good
to firm going and fibresand: effective blinkered or not: has looked difficult ride.
Miss V. Haigh

GREATDREAM (IRE) 2 ch.c. (Apr 26) Hamas (IRE) 125§ – Simply A Dream **64**
(IRE) (Simply Great (FR) 122) [2001 f6g⁴ f6g⁵ p8g Nov 15] third foal: dam placed at
1¼m in France: modest form in maidens: probably stays 1m. *E. J. O'Neill*

GREATER GLORY (IRE) 2 br.c. (Mar 11) Mtoto 134 – Folgore (USA) 83 (Irish **70 p**
River (FR) 131) [2001 9s³ Nov 24] first foal: dam, 7f winner at 2 yrs, half-sister to smart
middle-distance filly Fanjica: dead-heated for third in minor event at Milan: bred to stay
1½m: likely to do better. *J. L. Dunlop*

GREAT HOPPER 6 b.m. Rock Hopper 124 – Spun Gold 106 (Thatch (USA) 136) **–**
[2001 –: f8s f12g⁴ 13.1m 12m 12f⁶ Sep 4] of little account. *F. Watson*

GREAT NEWS 6 b.g. Elmaamul (USA) 125 – Amina 80 (Brigadier Gerard 144) [2001 **89**
93: 8.1d⁶ 6f 7m 8m* 7s 7d f8g Nov 12] tall, angular gelding: fairly useful handicapper: **a–**
won Tote Ayrshire Handicap at Ayr (for second year running, by ¾ length from Marnor)
in September: left W. Haggas 21,000 gns before final start: best at 7f/1m: acts on soft and
good to firm going: edged right for win, but game. *N. Tinkler*

GREAT ORATION (IRE) 12 b. or br.g. Simply Great (FR) 122 – Spun Gold 106 **49**
(Thatch (USA) 136) [2001 16m 17.1g 16m⁴ 16.1f Sep 10] angular gelding: has round
action: one-time fair handicapper, only poor nowadays: best at 2m+: acts on any turf
going and fibresand: sometimes visored much earlier in career: usually held up. *F. Watson*

GREAT VIEW (IRE) 2 b.g. (Apr 2) Great Commotion (USA) 123 – Tara View (IRE) **90**
(Wassl 125) [2001 5d⁶ 6m² 6.1m* 6.1s² 7g⁴ 7d 7m Sep 26] 10,500F, IR 23,000Y: lengthy
gelding: fourth foal: half-brother to 1998 2-y-o 5f winner Wind In Winnipeg (by
Midhish): dam, unraced, out of half-sister to 2000 Guineas winner Roland Gardens: fairly
useful performer: won maiden at Chepstow in July: good efforts in nursery and listed race
(fourth to Comfy at York) next 2 starts: gelded after final one: stays 7f: acts on soft and
good to firm going. *B. J. Meehan*

GRECIAN HALO (USA) 3 b.f. Southern Halo (USA) – Modern Grecian (USA) **59**
(Mr Leader (USA)) [2001 51: e8g* e10g⁴ 8f f9.4g Jun 20] modest performer: won
handicap at Lingfield in January: stays 1¼m: acts on equitrack: sold 25,000 gns in July,
resold 16,000 gns in December. *M. L. W. Bell*

GREEK DREAM (USA) 3 ch.f. Distant View (USA) 126 – Wandesta 121 (Nash- **75**
wan (USA) 135) [2001 79: 8f³ 7f² 7m* 7f Aug 29] quite attractive filly: fair form: easily
landed odds in maiden at Thirsk in August: ran as if something amiss when tailed off in
handicap at Catterick next time: stayed 7f: acted on firm going: stud. *B. W. Hills*

GREENAWAY BAY (USA) 7 ch.g. Green Dancer (USA) 132 – Raise 'n Dance **80**
(USA) (Raise A Native) [2001 84: f8.5g 8v⁶ 8g 8.1d 8f 10.5g 7.9m 8g 9g² 8.2s* 10v⁴ **a78**
f8.5g⁶ f8g⁴ f8s² f8.5s⁴ Dec 27] quite good-topped gelding: fairly useful handicapper: won
at Nottingham in October: effective at 1m/1¼m: has form on firm going/fibresand, very
best efforts on soft/heavy: usually waited with. *K. R. Burke*

GREEN BOPPER (USA) 8 b.g. Green Dancer (USA) 132 – Wayage (USA) (Mr **68**
Prospector (USA)) [2001 65, a76: f12g 12f* 12.4m 10.5d 10.1d 12.3d* 10.5s⁶ 12g⁶ Nov
7] close-coupled gelding: fair handicapper: won at Musselburgh in June and Chester
(amateur event) in August: effective at 1¼m/1½m: acts on firm going, soft and fibresand:
visored once at 3 yrs: front runner: none too consistent. *J. L. Eyre*

GREENBOROUGH (IRE) 3 b.g. Dr Devious (IRE) 127 – Port Isaac (USA) 64 **–**
(Seattle Song (USA) 130) [2001 67: 9m 8.3d f12g Jul 20] tall gelding: fair maiden at 2
yrs: well held in handicaps in 2001 (gelded after final start): sold 3,000 gns. *P. F. I. Cole*

GREEN CARD (USA) 7 b.h. Green Dancer (USA) 132 – Dunkellin (USA) (Irish **86**
River (FR) 131) [2001 90: 16m May 26] quite attractive horse: fairly useful performer:

not disgraced only 7-y-o outing on Flat: raced mainly at up to 1½m: acts on good to firm and good to soft going, probably on firm: tried blinkered/visored, better without: often held up: winning hurdler. *S. P. C. Woods*

GREEN CASKET (IRE)   4 b.g. Green Desert (USA) 127 – Grecian Urn 123   **79**
(Ela-Mana-Mou 132) [2001 68: f7g f8s⁴ f9.4g 9.9f 9.9m* 9.9m* 10m² 9.9s 10m 10m 12g³ Oct 4] fair performer: won handicaps at Beverley in June and July: stays 1½m: acts on soft going, good to firm and fibresand: tried tongue tied: has carried head awkwardly: has reportedly had breathing problems: usually races up with pace: none too consistent. *J. A. Glover*

GREEN CRYSTAL   2 b.f. (May 13) Green Dancer (USA) 132 – Dunkellin (USA)   **57**
(Irish River (FR) 131) [2001 7g⁶ 7m 7f Aug 24] close-coupled filly: sister to 7-y-o Green Card, closely related to a sprint winner in USA by Seattle Dancer and half-sister to 3 winners, including 8-y-o Irish Sea: dam sprint winner in USA: modest form, though well held, in maidens at Folkestone and Newmarket (2): will stay at least 1m. *S. P. C. Woods*

GREEN EYED LADY   2 b.f. (Feb 1) Greensmith 121 – Dark Eyed Lady (IRE) 82   **78**
(Exhibitioner 111) [2001 e5g³ e5g* f5g² 5f* a5.5f⁴ a6.5f* a6f⁵ Oct 21] third living foal: half-sister to 3-y-o Oh So Dusty: dam 5f/6f winner, including at 2 yrs: fair performer: won claimers at Lingfield in April and Leicester (final start for B. Meehan) in May and non-graded stakes at Fairplex (by 6 lengths) in September: stays 6.5f: acts on firm ground, equitrack, fibresand and dirt. *P. G. Aguirre, USA*

GREEN GINGER   5 ch.g. Ardkinglass 114 – Bella Maggio (Rakaposhi King 119)   **56**
[2001 70d: f7g 10m 10g 8m³ 8.2m⁵ Sep 10] modest performer nowadays: seems to stay 1m: acts on good to firm going: tried visored. *A. Streeter*

GREEN GREEN GRASS   3 b.f. Green Desert (USA) 127 – Hulm (IRE) 79 (Mujtahid   –
(USA) 118) [2001 56: 6g 5m f6g 6g 7.5m⁶ 7m p6g p6g Dec 19] smallish, sturdy filly: modest form in maidens at 2 yrs: little form in 2001, including visored: looked hard ride final outing. *N. P. Littmoden*

GREENHILLS   2 br.c. (Feb 7) Greensmith 121 – Free As A Bird 62 (Robellino (USA)   **87**
127) [2001 6m² 6m* 5.2m 5s 6m³ 6m² 6g⁴ 7d 6g 6d Oct 19] 16,000Y: neat colt: first foal: dam, maiden who stayed 7f, half-sister to useful 7f/1m performers Cragganmore and Hoh Chi Min: fairly useful performer: won maiden at Lingfield in July: in frame in nursery and 2 minor events after: stays 6f: acts on good to firm going, well held on softer than good: sold 40,000 gns, sent to USA. *M. Blanshard*

GREENHOPE (IRE)   3 b.g. Definite Article 121 – Unbidden Melody (USA)   **85**
(Chieftain II) [2001 74p: f8f² f8g 11m⁴ 12m² 12f² 12m³ 11f* 10.1m⁴ Aug 16] big, useful-looking gelding: fairly useful handicapper: won at Redcar in July: stays 1½m: acts on firm going (possibly on soft) and fibresand: usually races prominently: consistent: joined N. Henderson, and won first 3 races over hurdles. *J. A. Osborne*

GREEN IDEAL   3 b.c. Mark of Esteem (IRE) 137 – Emerald (USA) (El Gran Senor   **95**
(USA) 136) [2001 10m* 11.6m⁵ Aug 25] seventh living foal: half-brother to 3 winners, including fairly useful 11.5f winner Pendant and 1993 2-y-o 7f winner Tufa (both by Warning): dam unraced close relation of Danehill: won 4-runner maiden at Sandown in July by ½ length from Gay Heroine: useful form when 10 lengths fifth of 7 to Delius in minor event at Windsor: will be at least as effective back at 1¼m as at 11.6f: slowly away debut: held up both starts: sold 58,000 gns, joined N. Henderson and fairly useful form when making successful hurdling debut in December. *Mrs A. J. Perrett*

GREENLEES   3 b.f. Greensmith 121 – Scawsby Lees 62 (Stanford 121§) [2001 –:   –
12s⁶ f9.4g 7s May 17] well beaten, including in sellers. *W. G. M. Turner*

GREEN MAGICAL (IRE)   5 ch.m. Magical Strike (USA) 114 – Green Legend   **35 +**
(IRE) (Montekin 125) [2001 –: f12g f11g f14g⁶ f16.2g³ Jun 20] poor maiden: left B. Curley after second start: seems to stay 2m: acts on firm going, soft and fibresand: tried blinkered: joined T. Hogan in Ireland. *J. Cullinan*

GREEN MISSILE   6 b.g. Green Ruby (USA) 104 – Amber Missile VII (Damsire   –
Unregistered) [2001 22.2f Jun 22] workmanlike gelding: tailed off in Queen Alexandra Stakes at Royal Ascot only Flat outing. *G. B. Balding*

GREEN PURSUIT   5 b.g. Green Desert (USA) 127 – Vayavaig 78 (Damister (USA)   **57**
123) [2001 58, a48: 7m⁵ 8m f8g² f8g⁴ 8f⁴ 8.1g Sep 13] modest performer nowadays: left J. Osborne after fifth outing: stays 1m: acts on good to firm going, good to soft and fibresand: tried blinkered. *J. G. M. O'Shea*

GREEN RANSOM (USA) 3 b.c. Red Ransom (USA) – Arjunand (USA) (Diesis –
133) [2001 8d Apr 18] $525,000Y: rather leggy, unfurnished colt: third foal: half-brother
to useful US 1m/8.5f winner Boyum (by Valiant Nature): dam unraced sister to useful
1m/9f performer Badawi: 16/1 and looking very green, never on terms in newcomers race
at Newmarket: sent to USA. *H. R. A. Cecil*

GREENSLADES 2 ch.c. (Mar 30) Perugino (USA) 84 – Woodfield Rose 41 (Scottish **82 p**
Reel 123) [2001 8d⁶ Oct 19] 13,000F, 18,000Y: workmanlike colt: first foal: dam, Irish
1¾m winner, half-sister to dam of 8-y-o Persian Punch: well-backed 8/1-shot but
backward, sixth of 20 to Rawyaan in maiden at Newmarket, no extra only late on: sure to
improve. *P. J. Makin*

GREEN TAMBOURINE 3 b.f. Green Desert (USA) 127 – Maid For The Hills 101 **84**
(Indian Ridge 123) [2001 82+: 7m 6m Sep 24] well-made, attractive filly: has a free,
round action: fairly useful performer, lightly raced: better effort at 3 yrs (off over 4
months after reappearance) when tenth of 13 in handicap at Kempton: needs to settle
better to stay further than 6f: raced only on good/good to firm going. *R. Charlton*

GREENWOOD 3 ch.c. Emarati (USA) 74 – Charnwood Queen 61 (Cadeaux Genereux **93**
131) [2001 92: 6m 6m 6m² 5g 6d 5d⁵ f5g Nov 21] strong, lengthy colt: fairly useful
handicapper: creditable efforts at 3 yrs when second at Yarmouth (beaten neck by Idle
Power) and fifth at Ascot (beaten 3 lengths by Dancing Mystery): effective at 5f/6f: acts
on good to firm and good to soft going: blinkered last 3 starts: has pulled hard.
J. M. P. Eustace

GREMLIN ONE 4 ch.g. Democratic (USA) 101 – Calcutta Queen 51 (Night Shift –
(USA)) [2001 –: 5m 7m 6m 7.1f⁶ 8f 8m Aug 28] of little account. *W. Storey*

GRENADIER (IRE) 4 b.g. Sadler's Wells (USA) 132 – Sandhurst Goddess 103 **74 d**
(Sandhurst Prince 128) [2001 80: 7g 8m³ 9f⁴ 9.9m 10.1m⁵ 8m⁵ 8d³ 8m 7.9m 8m Sep
12] smallish, strong gelding: fair maiden handicapper, on downgrade: stays easy 1¼m:
probably acts on any turf going: tried blinkered: sold 13,000 gns. *W. R. Muir*

GREYCOAT 3 ch.g. Lion Cavern (USA) 117 – It's Academic 73 (Royal Academy –
(USA) 130) [2001 45: 6d 8m⁵ 7m 8.1m⁵ 7g Aug 12] little form in 2001: left Mrs
J. Ramsden 1,000 gns after reappearance. *Jean-Rene Auvray*

GREY COSSACK 4 gr.g. Kasakov – Royal Rebeka (Grey Desire 115) [2001 71: 7g **75**
6m 5m⁴ 6d 5f 6m⁵ 6g⁴ 6d* 6g 5g 6g³ 5v 5d 6d² Oct 12] leggy, workmanlike gelding: fair
handicapper: won at Ayr in July: will prove best at 5f/6f: acts on good to firm and good to
soft going: tried visored: has been slowly away. *M. Brittain*

GREY EMINENCE (FR) 4 gr.c. Indian Ridge 123 – Rahaam (USA) 91 (Secreto **98**
(USA) 128) [2001 106: 6d 7m May 12] big, good-topped colt: useful performer: not
disgraced both 4-y-o starts: likely to prove best at 6f: acts on heavy and good to firm
going: has carried head awkwardly/been edgy/had 2 handlers. *R. Hannon*

GREY EXPECTATIONS 6 gr.g. Terimon 124 – Flammable (IRE) (Prince Rupert –
(FR) 121) [2001 10f f11g Jun 15] lengthy gelding: no form on Flat: blinkered second
outing. *A. Crook*

GREYFIELD (IRE) 5 b.g. Persian Bold 123 – Noble Dust (USA) (Dust Commander **70**
(USA)) [2001 78: 10f 10d⁴ 12g 10m Sep 11] leggy gelding: fair handicapper: best at
1¼m/1½m: acts on firm and soft going: usually held up. *K. Bishop*

GREY FLYER 4 gr.g. Factual (USA) 108 – Faraway Grey 99 (Absalom 128) [2001 **50**
62: e6g⁵ e5g⁵ e6g 5m 7m 5g 5m 5m 5g Aug 17] leggy, angular gelding: modest
performer: form only on second start in 2001: left Mrs L. Stubbs 3,400 gns after third: has
hung/been early to post/been reluctant to race. *L. R. James*

GREY IMPERIAL (IRE) 3 gr.g. Imperial Frontier (USA) 112 – Petrel 62 (Petong **57**
126) [2001 55: 8.5m⁴ Aug 16] modest form in 3 maidens: pulled hard only 3-y-o outing.
P. W. Harris

GREY PEARL 2 gr.f. (Jan 21) Ali-Royal (IRE) 127 – River's Rising (FR) 88 **67**
(Mendez (FR) 128) [2001 7d 6s⁴ Nov 10] 10,000Y: sturdy filly: half-sister to fairly useful
1996 2-y-o 7f winner Mudflap (by Slip Anchor) and several winners abroad: dam 1m
winner: better effort in maidens (fair form) when 5¼ lengths fourth to Just James at
Doncaster: should stay at least 7f. *Miss Gay Kelleway*

GREY SON 2 gr.g. (Apr 16) Son Pardo 107 – Faraway Grey 99 (Absalom 128) [2001 –
5s f5g 7m 5m⁵ Jul 7] 7,000Y: good-topped gelding: half-brother to 4-y-o Grey Flyer,

fairly useful 5f/6f winner Royal Dream (by Ardkinglass) and 1m winner Mrs Dawson (by Sharrood): dam 2-y-o 5f winner who stayed 1m: little form: sent to Kuwait. *Mrs L. Stubbs*

GRIZEDALE (IRE) 2 ch.g. (Jan 29) Lake Coniston (IRE) 131 – Zabeta (Diesis 133) **89**
[2001 6d² 6m³ 6m* 6g 7v³ Oct 27] 15,000F, 37,000Y: strong gelding: fifth foal: half-brother to 3 winners, including 1999 2-y-o 7f winner Lady of Honour (by Bigstone) and 5f (at 2 yrs) and 7f winner Turtle's Rising (by Turtle Island): dam, French 1m winner, out of half-sister to Prix de Diane winner Harbour: fairly useful performer: landed odds in maiden at Newmarket in July: creditable efforts in Two-Year-Old Trophy at Redcar (wore crossed noseband) and nursery at Doncaster (raced very freely early on, third to Allenby) last 2 starts: gelded afterwards: stays 7f: acts on good to firm and heavy going: carries head high. *E. A. L. Dunlop*

GRIZEL 2 b.f. (Jan 31) Lion Cavern (USA) 117 – Polska (USA) 103 (Danzig (USA)) **72**
[2001 5d 6m 5m³ 5m 6f⁵ 6m f6g* 5d⁵ 5g 5.1f 6s f6g* p6g⁶ f5g* Dec 11] 45,000Y: **a93**
workmanlike filly: has a quick action: second foal: dam, 2-y-o 6f winner, closely related to useful 5f performer Millstream: fairly useful on all-weather, fair on turf: won nursery at Southwell in July and claimer/nursery at Wolverhampton in October/December: will prove best at 5f/6f: acts on fibresand/polytrack, firm and good to soft ground: blinkered after sixth start: usually races up with pace: sometimes looks none too keen. *B. J. Meehan*

GROESFAEN LAD 4 b.g. Casteddu 111 – Curious Feeling (Nishapour (FR) 125) **63 d**
[2001 70§: f9.4g f8.5g² f8.5g³ e8g⁵ f8g 7.1m 8.1m 10f⁴ 10f f16.2g⁴ f11g⁶ f16.2g 11.7f⁵ Jul 26] workmanlike gelding: modest performer, on downgrade: stays 9.4f: acts on firm going (possibly not on softer than good), and on fibresand: sometimes blinkered/visored. *P. S. McEntee*

GROOMS GOLD (IRE) 9 ch.g. Groom Dancer (USA) 128 – Gortynia (FR) (My **26 §**
Swallow 134) [2001 26§, a40§: e13g f16.2g³ Feb 8] lengthy gelding: bad performer: stays 2m: acts on firm going, good to soft and fibresand/equitrack: often blinkered/visored: can't be trusted. *J. Pearce*

GROOVEJET 2 b.g. (Apr 28) Emperor Jones (USA) 119 – Sir Hollow (USA) (Sir **–**
Ivor 135) [2001 7s⁶ Oct 16] tall, rather unfurnished gelding: sixth living foal: brother to 4-y-o Moon Emperor and half-brother to 2 winners abroad, including French 1¼m to 11.5f winner Knight of Honor (by Highest Honor): dam French 1m winner: very green, well beaten in minor event at Leicester. *J. R. Jenkins*

GROUNDSFORDIVORCE (IRE) 3 ch.g. Common Grounds 118 – Nikki's Groom **72 d**
(Shy Groom (USA)) [2001 f8g f9.4g² f8.5g³ f9.4g⁵ f7g 8.2v⁵ 10s 6v f8.5g p10g Dec 22] IR 3,800F, IR 8,500Y: sixth foal: brother to fairly useful 6f winner Compatibility, and half-brother to 7f/1m winner Pinheiros Dream (by Grand Lodge) and a German 1½m winner by Ballad Rock: dam fourth at 1¼m in Ireland: fair form in maidens at Wolverhampton second/third starts: well held after: should prove as effective at 1m as 9.4f: acts on fibresand. *M. Blanshard*

GROUNDSWELL (IRE) 5 b.g. Common Grounds 118 – Fuchsia Belle (Vision **64**
(USA)) [2001 14.4m⁴ f14.8g³ 14.1g⁵ Oct 6] fair performer at 3 yrs, winning handicap at Gowran and claimers at Killarney/Down Royal: modest nowadays: left M. Grassick in Ireland before reappearance: should stay 2m: acts on soft going, good to firm and fibresand. *C. W. Thornton*

GROVE DANCER 3 b.f. Reprimand 122 – Brisighella (IRE) (Al Hareb (USA) 123) **61**
[2001 61: 8m² 10.1m³ 8m 10g 8m⁴ f9.4f Dec 5] smallish, workmanlike filly: modest handicapper: stays 1m (seemingly not 1¼m): acts on good to firm and good to soft going: tried blinkered/visored: has been reluctant at stalls. *B. G. Powell*

GRUB STREET 5 b.h. Barathea (IRE) 127 – Broadmara (IRE) 91 (Thatching 131) **40**
[2001 59: f8g f8g 8.5m f8.5g f11g⁶ Dec 3] big, lengthy horse: poor performer nowadays. *M. Brittain*

GRUFF 2 ch.g. (Apr 1) Presidium 124 – Kagram Queen 64 (Prince Ragusa 96) [2001 **67**
6f⁶ 5f³ 5.1s³ 5g 5m² 6m⁶ 6m 5d⁴ 6d f5s Dec 21] sturdy gelding: third foal: dam (at 2 yrs) to 11f winner: fair maiden: likely to prove best at 5f/6f: acts on firm and soft ground. *D. W. Barker*

GRUINART (IRE) 4 br.g. Elbio 125 – Doppio Filo (Vision (USA)) [2001 77: 8s 10f **61 d**
8m 10f 11.6m* 11.6m 12m⁶ 12g Oct 4] leggy gelding: has a quick, fluent action: modest performer, on downgrade: won seller at Windsor in July: stays 11.6f: unraced on heavy going, seems to act on any other: sent to Italy. *H. Morrison*

GRYFFINDOR   3 b.c. Marju (IRE) 127 – Hard Task 82 (Formidable (USA) 125)   **106**
[2001 86: 8s* 8s² 10v³ 11m 10d⁴ 12f 8d⁵ 9f* Sep 22] strong, sturdy colt: carries plenty of
condition: useful performer: won maiden at Doncaster in March and minor event at
Newbury (dictated pace, beat Alunite by neck) in September: best efforts when neck
second to Herodotus in listed race at Kempton, 5¾ lengths third of 5 to Chancellor in
Classic Trial at Sandown in April and 6 lengths fourth to Zollner in Grosser Muller
Brot-Preis at Munich in June: effective at 1m to 11f: acts on any going: blinkered 3 of last
4 outings. *B. J. Meehan*

GUARANDA   3 b.f. Acatenango (GER) 127 – Gryada 93 (Shirley Heights 130) [2001   **97**
83p: 10g* 11s 12.3f* 12m 9.9m³ 10.1m 10g Oct 5] rangy filly: useful performer: won
maiden at Lingfield in May and handicap at Chester (beat Bylaw by 1¾ lengths) in June:
ran well after only on next 2 starts in listed races at Newmarket and Salisbury (4 lengths
third to Premier Prize): should stay beyond 1½m: acts on firm going. *W. Jarvis*

GUARD DUTY   4 b.g. Deploy 131 – Hymne d'Amour (USA) 58 (Dixieland Band   **85**
(USA)) [2001 87§: 16s* 18.7f 20m⁶ 16.4m⁴ 18d⁵ Oct 20] small gelding: fairly useful
handicapper: 9/2f, won Queen's Prize at Kempton in April by neck from You're Special:
creditable efforts all starts after, including fifth to Distant Prospect in Cesarewitch at
Newmarket (heavily backed) final outing: stays 2½m: acts on firm and soft going:
blinkered third 3-y-o start: tongue tied: has looked none too genuine, but did nothing
wrong in 2001. *M. C. Pipe*

GUARDED SECRET   4 ch.g. Mystiko (USA) 124 – Fen Dance (IRE) 82 (Trojan   **79**
Fen 118) [2001 82: 10s⁶ 10g⁵ 11.6g 10s² p10g p12g⁶ Dec 19] workmanlike gelding: fair   **a74**
handicapper: stays easy 1½m: acts on polytrack, soft and good to firm going, probably on
fibresand: races freely. *P. J. Makin*

GUARDIA   3 ch.f. Grand Lodge (USA) 125 – Gisarne (USA) 104 (Diesis 133) [2001   **–**
77p: 10s⁶ 11m May 22] lengthy filly: fair maiden at 2 yrs: well held in 2001, reportedly
lame after final outing: sold 6,000 gns in July: sent to Bahrain. *J. L. Dunlop*

GUDLAGE (USA)   5 b.g. Gulch (USA) – Triple Kiss 106 (Shareef Dancer (USA)   **88 §**
135) [2001 –: 8g³ 10m 10m⁶ 10.4m Jul 14] strong, lengthy gelding: fairly useful
handicapper nowadays: easily best effort at 5 yrs when third at Thirsk in May: stays 1¼m:
acts on good to firm and good to soft going: blinkered (swerved and almost unseated from
stall) final outing: sometimes tongue tied: should be treated with caution. *M. W. Easterby*

GUEST ENVOY (IRE)   6 b.m. Paris House 123 – Peace Mission (Dunbeath (USA)   **53**
127) [2001 59: f7g⁶ f6g f7g⁵ f7g* f7g² f7g⁶ f7g f7g³ f8g⁵ 7.6m 7m³ 7d² 8g 7g Aug   **a58**
15] sparely-made mare: modest handicapper: won at Wolverhampton in March: stays
easy 8.5f: acts on any turf going and fibresand: tried visored/tongue tied earlier in career:
has taken good hold/looked none too keen: held up: none too consistent. *C. N. Allen*

GUEST LINE (FR)   2 ch.g. (Feb 20) Ashkalani (IRE) 128 – Double Line (FR) (What   **63**
A Guest 119) [2001 5.2g⁶ 6f⁶ Jul 4] 26,000F, 420,000 francs Y: sixth foal: half-brother to
2 winners, notably useful performer up to 15f Royal Line (by Saint Estephe), 9f winner in
France at 2 yrs: dam, third at 1½m in France at 4 yrs, half-sister to dam of Poule d'Essai
des Pouliches winner Pearl Bracelet: modest form in maiden at Newbury and minor event
at Kempton (looked ill at ease on firm ground): should stay at least 1m. *B. J. Meehan*

GUILDED FLYER   2 b.c. (Mar 23) Emarati (USA) 74 – Mo Ceri 63 (Kampala 120)   **43**
[2001 6m 7m 6f Sep 21] 17,000Y: big, lengthy colt: half-brother to several winners,
including 7f to 11f winner Mazilla (by Mazilier) and 6-y-o Desert Valentine: dam 1½m
winner: poor form in maidens. *W. S. Kittow*

GUILD'S DELIGHT (IRE)   2 b.g. (Apr 3) College Chapel 122 – Tamburello (IRE)   **70**
(Roi Danzig (USA)) [2001 5.1g⁶ 6.1m³ 6.1g 7.1g 7.1f³ 7v⁶ Oct 26] 5,000F, 8,500Y:
workmanlike gelding: first foal: dam, 2-y-o sprint maiden, half-sister to useful performer
up to 9.4f Reported: fair maiden: third twice at Chepstow: stays easy 7f: acts on firm
going, possibly not heavy: has hung right. *W. S. Kittow*

GUILSBOROUGH   6 br.g. Northern Score (USA) – Super Sisters (AUS) (Call   **76**
Report (USA)) [2001 ?, a89: f8g⁴ f7s f7g⁵ f8g² 8.1g⁵ 8.1m* 8.2f 8d² 8g* 8d 8m* 8.2m²   **a95**
f8g² f9.4g* f9.4s⁴ f9.4s² Dec 26] close-coupled, workmanlike gelding: useful handicapper on all-weather, fair on turf: won at Warwick (amateurs) in May, Bath (2) in August
and (having left J. Smyth-Osbourne after twelfth start) Wolverhampton in December:
stays easy 9.4f: acts on good to firm going, good to soft and fibresand: visored once: idles
in front, and best with waiting tactics. *D. Haydn Jones*

Vodafone Stewards' Cup (Handicap), Goodwood—the most important success of Guinea Hunter's career; Halmahera (No.24) repeats his 1999 placing ahead of the visored Undeterred and Perfect Peach (No.18)

GUINEA HUNTER (IRE)   5 b.g. Pips Pride 117 – Preponderance (IRE) 85 (Cyrano de Bergerac 120) [2001 107: 6.1v² 6g 5m³ 6m 5m 6g* 5.6m³ 6m 5s⁶ 5d² 6d⁴ Oct 19] big, lengthy, good sort: usually takes the eye: smart performer: 33/1, won Vodafone Stewards' Cup at Goodwood in August by neck from Halmahera, running on strongly, despite edging right (survived lengthy enquiry): good efforts most starts after, including in Portland Handicap at Doncaster (close third to Smokin Beau), quite valuable handicap at Ascot (1¼ lengths second to Dancing Mystery) and listed event at Newmarket (short of room when 3¼ lengths fourth to Danehurst): raced only at 5f/6f: acts on soft and good to firm going: effective blinkered or not: has edged right: usually waited with: consistent: sold 53,000 gns, sent to Singapore. *T. D. Easterby*   **114**

GULF SHAADI   9 b.g. Shaadi (USA) 126 – Ela Meem (USA) (Kris 135) [2001 75§: f12g e12g² e12g⁶ 10.3s⁵ f11g² f11g² f12g² f11g³ 10.1d⁵ 10m⁶ f9.4s f11g³ f11g f12s Dec 27] lengthy gelding: has a quick action: fair performer, on downgrade: stays easy 1½m: acts on fibresand, equitrack and any turf going: visored once: has had tongue tied: usually early to post/sometimes starts slowly: held up: unreliable. *A. G. Newcombe*   **73 d**

GULZAAR   2 b.f. (Mar 3) Kris 135 – Kilma (USA) 97 (Silver Hawk (USA) 123) [2001 8d⁶ Oct 25] first foal: dam won around 1½m: poor form in maidens: bred to be suited by 1¼m/1½m. *M. P. Tregoning*   **49**

GUMLAYLOY   2 ch.c. (Apr 21) Indian Ridge 123 – Candide (USA) 74 (Miswaki (USA) 124) [2001 6d 6m 6f 6m Sep 21] IR 55,000Y: leggy, quite good-topped colt: second foal: dam, Irish 7f winner, from family of Hector Protector and Bosra Sham: no sign of ability in maidens/nursery. *Miss L. A. Perratt*   **–**

GUMPTION   3 b.g. Muhtarram (USA) 125 – Dancing Spirit (IRE) 72 (Ahonoora 122) [2001 71p: 8s⁵ 10m⁵ 14g 11.9s⁴ 14v² 14.1g⁴ 16.5s Nov 10] good-topped gelding: fairly useful maiden: best efforts when in frame in handicaps at Haydock in September and Redcar in October: should stay 2m: raced mainly on good going or softer (acts on heavy). *J. L. Dunlop*   **85**

GUN HILL (IRE)   4 b.g. Ridgewood Ben 113 – Lils Fairy (Fairy King (USA)) [2001 f7g f6g f8g f5g 6s 6m Jun 4] 1,000F, IR 5,000Y: third foal: half-brother to ungenuine 5f winner Tinker's Surprise (by Cyrano de Bergerac): dam unraced: no form. *M. C. Chapman*   **–**

GUNNA B NUTS   3 ch.g. Gunner B 126 – Absolutely Nuts 73 (Absalom 128) [2001 8f May 28] third foal: dam 5f/6f winner: 66/1, tailed off in maiden at Leicester. *B. P. J. Baugh*   **–**

GUNS BLAZING   2 b.c. (Apr 10) Puissance 110 – Queen of Aragon 76 (Aragon 118) [2001 5.1d* 5m⁴ 5m³ 5d² 6m Aug 13] 4,800Y: leggy colt: half-brother to 7f winner Midyan Queen and a 1m winner in Spain (both by Midyan): dam 5f winner: fairly useful performer: won maiden at Bath in May: in frame in minor events after: may well prove best at 5f. *B. A. McMahon*   **81**

Prix La Rochette Royal Thalasso Barriere, Longchamp—
Guys And Dolls steps up in class, winning cleverly from Bernebeau

GURU 3 b.g. Slip Anchor 136 – Ower (IRE) 71 (Lomond (USA) 128) [2001 –: 12g³ **81 ?**
10.2m 11.7g⁵ 11.7g f9.4s 11.6v³ 16v Oct 17] unfurnished gelding: fairly useful: form
only when third in maiden at Salisbury in May and minor event at Windsor in October:
stays 1½m: acts on heavy going: has found little: sold 13,000 gns, joined S. Dow and won
over hurdles in December. *I. A. Balding*

GUYS AND DOLLS 2 ch.c. (May 1) Efisio 120 – Dime Bag 87 (High Line 125) [2001 **113**
6g* 6m² 7m* 8s³ Nov 3] 25,000F, 58,000Y: leggy, quite good-topped colt: fourth foal:
half-brother to 4-y-o Pawn Broker, useful 2000 2-y-o 7f winner Blushing Bride (by
Distant Relative) and fairly useful Irish 7f winner Blushing Melody (by Never So Bold):
dam 1½m to 2m winner: smart performer: won maiden at Newmarket in August and Prix
La Rochette Royal Thalasso Barriere at Longchamp (by ¾ length from Bernebeau) in
September: best effort when staying-on 1¼ lengths third of 6 to Act One in Criterium
International at Saint-Cloud: should stay 1¼m: acts on soft and good to firm ground:
capable of winning more races. *P. F. I. Cole*

GWENER DDA 3 b.g. Mistertopogigo (IRE) 118 – Good Holidays 60 (Good Times **–**
(ITY)) [2001 7.1m 5.7m Sep 10] third foal: dam maiden who stayed 7f: well held in
maidens. *J. M. Bradley*

GWENLLIAN LYN 3 b. or br.f. Awesome 73 – Regency Brighton (Royal Palace **–**
131) [2001 f8g 12v⁶ 12g f11g May 25] half-sister to 7f seller winner Royal Resort (by
King of Spain) and 1m winner Return To Brighton (by Then Again): dam showed little:
well beaten in maidens/minor event: has been slowly away/shown clear signs of
temperament. *D. Burchell*

GYPSY (IRE) 5 b.g. Distinctly North (USA) 115 – Winscarlet North (Garland Knight **71**
92) [2001 76: f8g f12g f9.4g³ f9.4g⁶ 8.5s³ 8s⁶ 10g May 14] leggy, sparely-made gelding: **a58**
fair performer on turf, modest on all-weather: effective at 8.5f and 1¼m, barely at 1½m:
acts on good to firm going, soft and fibresand: blinkered once: has looked none too keen:
sold 2,000 gns. *P. R. Chamings*

H

HAAFEL (USA) 4 ch.g. Diesis 133 – Dish Dash 118 (Bustino 136) [2001 –: 10v⁵ **64**
14.1s* Oct 31] modest form: unraced at 2 yrs, and off 16 months after debut: easily best
effort when winning claimer at Yarmouth (hanging left): will probably stay 2m: won over
hurdles in November. *G. L. Moore*

HAALIM 3 b. or br.c. Lahib (USA) 129 – Cancan Madame (USA) (Mr Prospector **64 d**
(USA)) [2001 10s 7f⁵ 12m 8.3m 7.6g f12g Sep 22] half-brother to 3 winners, notably
high-class French 1¼m/1½m performer Dancehall (by Assert): dam 9f winner in USA:
modest form in maidens first 2 starts: sold from K. Prendergast in Ireland 7,500 gns after
third outing: well held in Britain (said to have had a breathing problem final outing): best
effort at 7f on firm ground. *C. P. Morlock*

HAASIL (IRE) 3 b.c. Machiavellian (USA) 123 – Mahasin (USA) 90 (Danzig (USA)) **88**
[2001 73p: 8s² 8v* 8m 8g 8g 8d Oct 18] big, strong colt: has scope: good walker: fairly
useful performer: easily landed odds in Ripon maiden in April: best efforts when seventh
in 30-runner handicaps at Redcar and Newmarket last 2 starts: likely to stay 1¼m: raced
mainly on good going or softer (acts on heavy): sent to UAE. *J. L. Dunlop*

The Mail On Sunday Mile Final (Handicap), Ascot—
Hail The Chief returns to form to beat Norfolk Reed, Lady Bear, College Rock and Thihn

HADAANI 3 b.f. Mtoto 134 – Trude (GER) (Windwurf (GER)) [2001 8f⁵ 8.2f⁵ 9m⁴ **54** 12m⁴ 12m⁶ Aug 16] 7,000Y: half-sister to numerous winners, including 5-y-o Westender and German winner up to 15f Trudeau (by Belmez), both useful: dam German 6f (at 2 yrs) and 1m (listed race) winner: modest maiden: should stay 1¾m: sold 4,000 gns in October, joined P. Murphy. *W. J. Haggas*

HADDICE (USA) 2 b.c. (Jan 28) Dixieland Band (USA) – Bevel (USA) (Mr Prospector (USA)) [2001 8d Oct 2] fifth foal: half-brother to 1m winner Bevier (by Nashwan): dam French 1m winner, out of half-sister to Ajdal, Formidable and the dam of Arazi: 33/1, backward and green, eleventh of 21 to Hathaal in maiden at Newmarket, considerably handled when weakening: should improve. *C. E. Brittain* **70 p**

HADEQA 5 ch.g. Hadeer 118 – Heavenly Queen (Scottish Reel 123) [2001 –: f12g **–** f12g Feb 13] small gelding: good mover: fair winner as 3-y-o: no form since: usually visored/blinkered. *F. Jordan*

HADLEIGH (IRE) 5 b.h. Perugino (USA) 84 – Risacca (ITY) (Sir Gaylord) [2001 **66** 66: e8g⁶ e8g* e10g⁵ e8g 7.6f⁵ 8f³ 9g 8.2g³ 8.3m⁴ 8m³ 8m⁴ 8.5g p10g⁴ p8g⁴ Dec 22] leggy horse: fair handicapper: won at Lingfield in January: stays 1¼m: acts on firm going, soft and polytrack/equitrack: sometimes slowly away: usually held up: wears visor: none too resolute, but largely consistent. *H. J. Collingridge*

HAGLEY PARK 2 b.f. (Mar 21) Petong 126 – Gi La High 68 (Rich Charlie 117) **56** [2001 f5g* 5g⁶ 5.1f⁶ 5m f5g³ f5g* f6g⁶ f5g⁵ f5g⁶ f5s³ Dec 15] 3,200Y: smallish, **a62** workmanlike filly: first foal: dam 5f winner, including at 2 yrs: modest performer: won maiden at Southwell in April and seller at Wolverhampton in September: won minor event at Southwell on seventh start: ran well in Southwell nursery final one: best at 5f: acts on fibresand and firm going: usually races prominently. *G. M. McCourt*

HAIL SHEEVA 4 ch.f. Democratic (USA) 101 – Sun Storm (Sunyboy 110) [2001 –: **44** 10.2s³ 10d Sep 21] poor maiden: stays 1¼m: acts on soft ground. *Miss K. M. George*

HAIL THE CHIEF 4 b.c. Be My Chief (USA) 122 – Jade Pet 90 (Petong 126) [2001 **87** 78, a116: f8.5s* f8.5g² e10g² e10g 8v 8.3g 8m⁴ 8g 9d 9g 8.5g 8s* 9g Oct 6] rather **a109** sparely-made colt: good mover: useful on all-weather, fairly useful on turf: won minor event at Wolverhampton in January and 31-runner Mail On Sunday Mile Final (Handicap) at Ascot (by 1½ lengths from Norfolk Reed, wandering) on first start: very good second in minor event also at Wolverhampton on second start: best at 1m to 9.4f: acts on soft going, good to firm and fibresand/equitrack: races prominently: sent to USA. *R. Hannon*

HAILWOOD (USA) 2 b.c. (Mar 7) Twining (USA) 120 – Beat (USA) (Nijinsky **76** (CAN) 138) [2001 6d⁴ 7f* 7d⁵ Aug 31] $35,000F, IR 42,000Y: rather finely-made colt: seventh foal: half-brother to 3 winners, including 1¼m/11f winner in Britain/UAE Merry

Festival (by Private Account): dam, 1m/9f winner in USA, half-sister to US Grade 1 1m winner Too Chic, herself dam of champion US older mare Queena: fair form: clearly best effort when winning maiden at Redcar in July: well held in nursery at Chester final start, taking fierce hold and not handling bends: will have to settle better to stay 1m: has twice reared leaving stall. *T. D. Easterby*

HAIRY NIGHT (IRE)   2 b.f. (Feb 25) Night Shift (USA) – Snowcap (IRE) (Snow   **73** Chief (USA)) [2001 5s² 5m² 6m² 6m⁵ 6m² 7m² 6.1m² 7m² 7m⁴ 6m 6.5g 7d 6g⁴ 6v 7v Oct 26] 20,000Y: small filly: first foal: dam lightly-raced daughter of Breeders' Cup Sprint winner Very Subtle: fair maiden: runner-up 7 times: stays 7f: acts on good to firm and soft going, possibly not heavy: usually races prominently. *M. R. Channon*

HAITHEM (IRE)   4 b.g. Mtoto 134 – Wukk (IRE) (Glow (USA)) [2001 67: f8g f8g   **56 §** 8s f8.5g 7m⁴ 7.5f 8d f9.4g Nov 3] close-coupled gelding: modest handicapper nowadays: stays 8.5f on all-weather, best form up to 7f on turf: acts on good to firm going and fibresand: held up: temperamental. *D. Shaw*

HAIYFOONA   2 b.f. (Apr 1) Zafonic (USA) 130 – Itqan (IRE) 92 (Sadler's Wells   **–** (USA) 132) [2001 8.2s Nov 5] sixth foal: half-sister to 3 winners, including smart 1996 2-y-o 6f and 1m winner Hello (by Lycius), later 8.5f winner in USA, and fairly useful 1m winner Crown Lodge (by Grand Lodge): dam 1½m and 15f winner: 25/1, slowly away and always behind in maiden at Nottingham. *J. D. Czerpak*

HAJEER (IRE)   3 b.g. Darshaan 133 – Simouna (Ela-Mana-Mou 132) [2001 12m⁵   **–** 11.5g⁶ 12d p12g f11g Dec 17] 90,000Y: lengthy, angular gelding: fourth foal: half-brother to 3 winners in Ireland, including useful 1998 2-y-o 7f/1m winner Athlumney Lady (by Lycius): dam unraced daughter of half-sister to Seymour Hicks and Princess Pati: little form: left A. Stewart 2,800 gns after second start. *P. W. Hiatt*

HAKEEM (IRE)   6 ch.g. Kefaah (USA) 124 – Masarrah 91 (Formidable (USA) 125)   **61 d** [2001 68, a–: 7g⁵ 8m 7.9m 7.6m 6g 8s Sep 24] sturdy, lengthy gelding: modest handi-   **a–** capper, on downgrade: probably best at 7f/1m: acts on firm and soft going: often races prominently. *M. Brittain*

HAKEYMA (USA)   3 ch.f. Gone West (USA) – United Kingdom (USA) 93 (Danzig   **80** (USA)) [2001 7d⁴ 8s* 10v⁴ 10f⁴ Jun 3] tall, leggy, angular filly: third foal: dam, 1m (in France) and 1¼m winner, closely related to smart 1¼m winner La Confederation out of Oaks winner Unite: fairly useful form: unraced at 2 yrs because reportedly didn't have best of joints: won 3-runner minor event at Kempton (by 5 lengths) in May: not discredited when fourth of 5 to Santa Isobel in listed event at Newbury next time: seemed to stay 1¼m: acted on heavy ground, tailed off (reportedly lame) on firm final outing: visits Gilded Time. *M. R. Channon*

HALAWAN (IRE)   3 b.c. Muhtarram (USA) 125 – Haladiya (IRE) (Darshaan 133)   **96 +** [2001 94p: 9g* 11.9g 9f⁵ Sep 22] sturdy, lengthy colt: easily landed odds in 4-runner maiden at Sandown in August: well held in Great Voltigeur at York next time: good effort when 2½ lengths fifth of 7 to Gryffindor in minor event at Newbury final outing: should stay further than 9f: sold 50,000 gns, sent to Singapore. *Sir Michael Stoute*

HALAWELLFIN HALA   2 ch.c. (Mar 17) Kris 135 – Tegwen (USA) 79 (Nijinsky   **90 p** (CAN) 138) [2001 7.9d² 8s⁶ Nov 3] tall, rangy colt: has plenty of scope: third living foal: closely related to 1¾m winner Tegyra (by Trempolino) and half-brother to Fillies' Mile winner/Ribblesdale second Teggiano (by Mujtahid): dam 11.5f winner: green, staying-on 1½ lengths second of 14 to Him of Distinction in maiden at York: seemed to show similar form when 12¾ lengths last of 6 to Act One in Criterium International at Saint-Cloud, leading until under 2f out: should stay 1½m: missed break both starts, very much so on debut: should do better. *C. E. Brittain*

HALCYON DAZE   3 ch.f. Halling (USA) 133 – Ardisia (USA) 87 (Affirmed (USA))   **82** [2001 79: 8.1v⁴ 11.5m* 12m 11.9s 11.6v² 12d⁶ Nov 2] unfurnished filly: has a short action: fairly useful performer: won maiden at Yarmouth in July: creditable efforts last 2 starts in minor event at Windsor and handicap at Newmarket: stays 1½m: acts on heavy and good to firm going. *L. M. Cumani*

HALCYON MAGIC   3 b.g. Magic Ring (IRE) 115 – Consistent Queen 55 (Queen's   **67 d** Hussar 124) [2001 65: 6d⁶ f7g 6m 6g⁵ 6m 6g 6g³ 7s 6d p6g Dec 19] sturdy gelding: fair   **a42** maiden handicapper: generally below form after reappearance in 2001: should stay 7f: acts on firm and good to soft going, seemingly not on softer: tends to hang, and looks a tricky ride. *Pat Mitchell*

Rothmans Royals May Hill Stakes, Doncaster—
Half Glance provides trainer Henry Cecil with his twelfth success in the race in twenty-four years;
she wins convincingly from Echo River (left) and Shadow Dancing (right)

HALF GLANCE 2 b.f. (Mar 15) Danehill (USA) 126 – Fleeting Glimpse 109 (Rainbow Quest (USA) 134) [2001 7g* 8d* 8s⁴ Sep 29] strong, lengthy filly: has scope: easy mover: first foal: dam, French 1¼m winner and second in Prix Saint-Alary on only starts, sister to 6-y-o Ulundi and half-sister to 1000 Guineas winner Wince: won maiden at Newmarket (by 3½ lengths from Snowfire) in August and Rothmans Royals May Hill Stakes at Doncaster (by 2½ lengths from Echo River) in September, in latter stretching clear final 1f despite still seeming green: rather edgy, seemed to run creditably when about 4 lengths fourth to Gossamer in Fillies' Mile at Ascot, though gave impression possibly not at home on going: should stay 1¼m: likely to make a smart 3-y-o. *H. R. A. Cecil* **104 p**

HALF MOON BAY 4 b.g. Cyrano de Bergerac 120 – Tarnside Rosal 68 (Mummy's Game 120) [2001 –: f5g 5s f5g 5f⁶ 5d 5f 5g Aug 19] tall, rather unfurnished gelding: has a quick action: fairly useful winner at 2 yrs: disappointing since: raced only at 5f: best efforts on going firmer than good: headstrong. *T. D. Barron* **–**

HALF TIDE 7 ch.g. Nashwan (USA) 135 – Double River (USA) (Irish River (FR) 131) [2001 51: e16g² e12g⁴ 15.4v f14g May 14] modest handicapper: stays 2m: acts on soft going (pulled up on heavy penultimate start) and fibresand/equitrack: looked less than keen final outing. *P. Mitchell* **a55**

HAL HOO YAROOM 8 b.g. Belmez (USA) 131 – Princess Nawaal (USA) 86 (Seattle Slew (USA)) [2001 62: 14.1d Aug 26] angular gelding: winning handicapper, very lightly-raced nowadays. *J. R. Jenkins* **–**

HALLAND 3 ch.c. Halling (USA) 133 – Northshiel 85 (Northfields (USA)) [2001 87p: 7.1m 8m² 10f* 9g² Oct 6] quite attractive colt: useful and progressive form in handicaps: won 4-runner race at Newbury in August by 2½ lengths from Muthaaber: best effort when 2 lengths second to I Cried For You in Cambridgeshire at Newmarket (wore rope halter) final outing, one of last to be asked for effort but staying on strongly and nearest finish: will stay 1½m: acts on any going: refused to enter stall once at 2 yrs: unseated/got loose during preliminaries on reappearance: carries head high: quirky, but has the makings of a smart 4-y-o, likely to win a good prize. *G. Wragg* **108 p**

HALLAND PARK LAD (IRE) 2 ch.c. (Feb 2) Danehill Dancer (IRE) 117 – Lassalia (Sallust 134) [2001 6m 7m 7.6m⁶ 7m³ 6s f8.5g* 8d* 8.3v p8g Nov 20] 9,500F, 8,500Y: half-brother to numerous winners, including smart 1¼m performer Free Flyer (by Bluebird), 7f winner at 2 yrs, and Irish 1½m winner Snowy Lane (by Commanche Run): dam placed from 6f to 9.5f in Ireland: fair performer: won maiden at Wolverhampton in October and nursery at Brighton in November: stays 8.5f: acts on fibresand, good to firm and good to soft ground. *S. Kirk* **77**

HALLAND PARK LASS (IRE) 2 ch.f. (Mar 12) Spectrum (IRE) 126 – Palacegate Episode (IRE) 111 (Drumalis 125) [2001 5s 5g Sep 3] second foal: half-sister to a 6f winner in Sweden by Danehill: dam 5f (including at 2 yrs) winner: last in maidens: has pulled hard/carried head high. *S. Kirk* **–**

422

Mr K. Abdulla's "Half Glance"

HALLIVIEN (IRE)   3 ch.f. Halling (USA) 133 – Blasted Heath 105 (Thatching 131)   –
[2001 10.2d 9.9m 7m 7m 10g Aug 20] 27,000F: leggy, angular filly: seventh foal: half-
sister to 3 winners, including fairly useful 1¼m and 11f winner Hamlet (by Danehill):
dam, Irish 5f (at 2 yrs) and 1m winner, half-sister to Middle Park winner Balla Cove:
little form: visored penultimate start: has started slowly/raced freely. *W. G. M. Turner*

HALMAHERA (IRE)   6 b.g. Petardia 113 – Champagne Girl 67 (Robellino (USA)   **96**
127) [2001 109: 5.2d⁶ 6s² 6g 5g 6m 7f 6m³ 6g² 6g 6m⁶ 6m 6d³ 5d Oct 13] rather leggy,
good-topped gelding: has a round action: useful performer: not the force of old in
2001, but several creditable efforts, including when placed in handicaps at Ascot and
Goodwood (neck second to Guinea Hunter in Stewards' Cup, edged out only close home)
seventh/eighth starts: best at 6f/stiff 5f: acts on any turf going: visored last 2 starts:
sometimes slowly away: well suited by strong pace: tends to carry head awkwardly: sold
40,000 gns. *I. A. Balding*

HAMADEENAH   3 ch.f. Alhijaz 122 – Mahbob Dancer (FR) (Groom Dancer (USA)   **90 d**
128) [2001 78: 7m 6m⁶ 6d 7.5f⁶ 6m⁴ 7g Oct 6] unfurnished filly: fairly useful performer
at best: good efforts in valuable handicaps at York and Newmarket first 2 starts: well
below form after: stays 7f: acts on good to firm going, possibly not on good to soft: has
raced freely/carried head high/found little): reared at stalls penultimate start. *K. A. Ryan*

HAMASKING (IRE)   3 b.f. Hamas (IRE) 125§ – Sialia (IRE) (Bluebird (USA) 125)   –
[2001 53: 8.2s 8.1v 6.1v⁵ 7m May 30] lengthy filly: seller winner at 2 yrs: well held in
2001. *T. D. Easterby*

HAMATARA (IRE)   3 ch.g. Tagula (IRE) 116 – Arctic Poppy (USA) 67 (Arctic Tern   **78**
(USA) 126) [2001 68: e6g f6s² f6g f7g* 6s Sep 24] quite good-topped gelding: fair
performer: won handicap at Wolverhampton in February: well beaten when next seen

423

out: stays 7f: acts on fibresand, heavy and good to firm going: tongue tied: sold 8,000 gns in October. *I. A. Balding*

HAMBLEDEN   4 b.g. Vettori (IRE) 119 – Dalu (IRE) 72 (Dancing Brave (USA) 140) [2001 92: 12s² 14m* 13.9m⁶ 11.9d⁵ 12m³ 12g⁵ 13.9m² 16f⁵ Sep 21] tall gelding: useful handicapper: won at Sandown in May: creditable efforts otherwise, notably when head second to King Flyer at York on penultimate start: stays at least 1¾m: acts on soft going, good to firm and fibresand: hung left final outing: has taken good hold: held up: consistent. *M. A. Jarvis*   **103**

HAMBLETON HIGHLITE (IRE)   3 ch.g. Paris House 123 – Sempreverde (USA) (Lear Fan (USA) 130) [2001 76d: f5s f5f⁵ f7g 6m 6m f6g f9.4g³ 8.5f 10m Sep 1] plain, unfurnished gelding: fair winner at 2 yrs: on downgrade in 2001: seems to stay 9.4f: acts on firm and good to soft going, probably on fibresand: tried blinkered/visored. *K. A. Ryan*   **50 d**

HAMEEDA   2 b.f. (Mar 2) Hector Protector (USA) 124 – Habibti 136 (Habitat 134) [2001 6m⁵ 7g³ 7m 6s² Oct 3] strong filly: has a quick action: half-sister to Irish 1994 2-y-o 5f winner Desert Lily (by Green Desert) and to dam of Derby Italiano winner Morshdi: dam outstanding sprinter: fairly useful maiden: best effort when second in nursery at Brighton: should stay at least 7f. *R. Hannon*   **81**

HAMISH G   4 ch.g. Sure Blade (USA) 130 – Horton Line 89 (High Line 125) [2001 –: p7g⁴ Dec 28] quite good-topped gelding: lightly-raced maiden: first form when fourth at Lingfield on only outing of 2001: should be suited by 1m+: acts on polytrack. *John Berry*   **56**

HAMLYN (IRE)   4 gr.g. Lure (USA) 131 – Passamaquoddy (USA) (Drone (USA)) [2001 75: e7g² 7g⁴ 8m 7.1s 8.5m⁵ Aug 15] attractive, good-bodied gelding: fair maiden: below current best last 3 starts: stays 1m: acts on good to firm going, good to soft and equitrack: tried blinkered: tends to carry head high: sold 3,200 gns. *D. R. C. Elsworth*   **72**

HAMMER AND SICKLE (IRE)   4 b.g. Soviet Lad (USA) – Preponderance (IRE) 85 (Cyrano de Bergerac 120) [2001 86: 5s 6m 5m 8m 7m⁵ 6f³ 6g 5.1m³ 5m 6g Aug 17] good-topped gelding: fair handicapper nowadays: best at 5f/6f (pulled very hard at 7f): acts on firm and good to soft going: blinkered last 5 outings, tongue tied penultimate one: usually races prominently: none too consistent: sold 2,000 gns. *M. Johnston*   **67**

HAMMER AND TONGS (IRE)   5 ch.g. Hamas (IRE) 125§ – Bag Lady 86 (Be My Guest (USA) 126) [2001 f9.4g Jan 25] modest performer at 3 yrs and in 2000 when winning 3 times for M. Hofer in Germany: tailed off only 5-y-o outing: usually blinkered in second half of 2000. *Miss V. Haigh*   **–**

HAMMOCK (IRE)   3 b. or br.g. Hamas (IRE) 125§ – Sure Victory (IRE) 75 (Stalker 121) [2001 47§: 7m 16m⁶ May 30] temperamental maiden: tried blinkered/visored. *P. S. McEntee*   **– §**

HAMPTON LUCY (IRE)   2 b.f. (Feb 1) Anabaa (USA) 130 – Riveryev (USA) (Irish River (FR) 131) [2001 5g Aug 19] 30,000F, 65,000Y: strong, lengthy filly: half-sister to several winners, including 1m (at 2 yrs) to 1½m winner Okabango (by Unfuwain) and 1996 2-y-o 5.5f and 7f (Prix du Calvados) winner Shigeru Summit (by Be My Chief), both useful in France: dam French maiden: 33/1 and backward, well held in maiden at Pontefract, not knocked about once tiring: swished tail in paddock: should do better. *M. A. Buckley*   **– p**

HAMUNAPTRA   2 ch.c. (Feb 7) Alhijaz 122 – Princess Dancer (Alzao (USA) 117) [2001 5f 7g 7g 6d 7d Oct 18] 1,300Y: stocky colt: seventh foal: half-brother to fairly useful 7f (at 2 yrs) and 9f winner who probably stayed 1½m Northern Sun (by Charmer): dam ran once at 2 yrs: little form in maidens/sellers: tried blinkered. *P. L. Gilligan*   **–**

HANDA ISLAND (USA)   2 b.c. (Mar 26) Pleasant Colony (USA) – Remote (USA) (Seattle Slew (USA)) [2001 8m⁵ 8d⁵ Oct 19] $210,000Y: big, strong, close-coupled colt: has a quick action: second foal: dam, ran twice in USA, half-sister to smart performers Hibernian Gold (1¼m) and Irish Shoal (5f/6f): fairly useful form when fifth in maidens at Doncaster (behind Wahchi) and Newmarket (behind Music Club): should stay 1¼m: probably capable of better. *H. R. A. Cecil*   **85 p**

HAND CHIME   4 ch.g. Clantime 101 – Warning Bell 88 (Bustino 136) [2001 95p: 7g 7m³ 7m 7f² 7m² 7g³ 6s* 7s 6d Oct 13] angular, unfurnished gelding: useful performer: creditable efforts in handicaps when placed at Lingfield, Ayr and at Newmarket (twice, 3 lengths second to Atavus in Bunbury Cup first occasion) before winning 22-runner minor event at Haydock in September: well held last 2 starts: has won at 1m, but best form at 6f/7f: yet to race on heavy going, acts on any other turf and on fibresand. *W. J. Haggas*   **97**

HANDFUL (IRE)   2 b.g. (Feb 10) Woodborough (USA) 112 – Volkova 60 (Green Desert (USA) 127) [2001 5f³ Jun 5] IR 11,500F, 17,000Y, 23,000 2-y-o: third foal: dam,   **76**

maiden who should have stayed beyond 1m, granddaughter of Irish 1000 Guineas/ St Leger winner Pidget: fair form when keeping-on third in maiden at Lingfield. *W. J. Haggas*

HANDSOME BADSHA (IRE) 3 b.c. Petardia 113 – Cape Shirley (Head For Heights 125) [2001 57: f7g Jan 6] modest maiden at 2 yrs: well held only 3-y-o outing: tried tongue tied. *J. A. Osborne*   –

HANGOVER SQUARE (IRE) 7 ch.h. Jareer (USA) 115 – Dancing Line (High Line 125) [2001 108: a8g* a8.7g 9.8m³ 9m* 10g 7m 10g⁶ Aug 31] leggy, close-coupled horse: useful performer: successful in 2001 in minor event at Taby in April and listed race at Klampenborg in June: mostly creditable efforts otherwise, though well beaten in Tote International Handicap at Ascot penultimate start (sweating and very edgy): has won up to 1½m, at least as good at 1m: acts on good to firm ground and dirt. *Lennart Reuterskiold, Sweden*   **105**

HANNAH PARK (IRE) 5 b.m. Lycius (USA) 124 – Wassl This Then (IRE) 74 (Wassl 125) [2001 16v 12d⁵ 9.2d⁴ 12m⁵ 13.1m⁶ 13m⁶ 14f³ 14f⁵ 13d⁶ Aug 15] workmanlike mare: won 3 times when trained by M. Hofer in Germany in 2000: modest form on return to Britain: stays 1¾m: acts on firm and soft going: has been blinkered (including when successful)/visored: has looked none too keen. *P. Monteith*   **58**

HANNAVEE 2 br.g. (Mar 8) Hamas (IRE) 125§ – Secret Rapture (USA) (Woodman (USA) 126) [2001 8.2s Oct 30] 7,800Y: second foal: dam unraced close relative of useful 1¼m performer Obsessive from very good US family: green, slowly away and always behind in maiden at Nottingham. *S. C. Williams*   –

HANNIBAL LAD 5 ch.g. Rock City 120 – Appealing 49 (Star Appeal 133) [2001 90: f9.4s³ e12g³ e12g* e12g² e10s e12g³ 12m⁴ 12m* 11.9d* 11.9m⁴ 12g⁶ 12g⁶ 13.9g 12g 12g 12s* Sep 30] leggy gelding: useful handicapper: had fine season, and won at Lingfield in January, Goodwood in June, Haydock (Tote Old Newton Cup, beat Steel Band by 1½ lengths) in July and Ascot (Betdaq Stakes, best effort to beat Dream With Me by 2 lengths) in September: stays 1½m: acts on any turf going and fibresand/equitrack: sometimes slowly away: usually held up: tough, game and reliable. *W. M. Brisbourne*   **100**

HANNON (FR) 2 br.c. (Feb 27) Exit To Nowhere (USA) 122 – Delphania (FR) (Fabulous Dancer (USA) 124) [2001 8d⁵ Oct 3] 140,000 francs Y: third foal: dam, French 10.5f winner, half-sister to useful French middle-distance stayer Dona Bella: 12/1, weakened only final 1f when fifth of 17 to Dawn Invasion in maiden at Salisbury: sure to improve. *R. Hannon*   **61 p**

HANS ANDERSON (USA) 3 b.c. Deputy Minister (CAN) – Sister Dot (USA) (Secretariat (USA)) [2001 86P: 10m* 10f⁴ Jun 26] useful form: successful at Cork in maiden only 2-y-o outing and in 4-runner minor event (comfortably landed odds) in June: best effort but looked ill at ease on very firm ground when 7 lengths fourth of 5 to Chichicastenango in Grand Prix de Paris at Longchamp (reluctant at stalls) later in month: stays 1¼m: sent to Saudi Arabia. *A. P. O'Brien, Ireland*   **107**

HANWORTH (IRE) 2 b.f. (Mar 18) Prince of Birds (USA) 121 – Regal Fanfare (IRE) 94 (Taufan (USA) 119) [2001 f5g⁶ 7g 7m 6m⁴ 5m Aug 25] tall, leggy filly: second foal: dam 2-y-o 6f winner out of half-sister to 1999 Cherry Hinton winner Torgau: ungenuine maiden: sold 800 gns, sent to Sweden. *M. H. Tompkins*   – §

Betdaq Stakes (Handicap), Ascot—Hannibal Lad puts up a career-best effort; Dream With Me, Thundering Surf, Saltrio (No.8) and Harlequin follow him home

HAPPY ARE THEY 2 b.f. (May 12) Makbul 104 – Safe Bid 44 (Sure Blade (USA) – 130) [2001 6m 8d Oct 3] fourth living foal: half-sister to unreliable winner around 1m Heathyards Jake (by Nomination): dam ran 3 times at 2 yrs: no sign of ability in maidens. *R. M. Flower*

HAPPY CHANGE (GER) 7 ch.g. Surumu (GER) – Happy Gini (USA) (Ginistrelli – (USA) 117) [2001 113: e10g 10m⁵ 12g Jul 20] strong, angular gelding: smart performer in 2000: no form at 7 yrs. *M. Johnston*

HAPPY CLAPPER 2 b.f. (Jun 5) Royal Applause 124 – Coir 'a' Ghaill 38 (Jalmood 70 (USA) 126) [2001 6f 6g⁶ 8.3v Oct 29] angular filly: seventh foal: half-sister to a winner in Italy by Piccolo: dam maiden who stayed 15f: best effort in maidens (fair form) when sixth to Scarlet Ribbons at Newmarket: hampered and not knocked about final start: should stay 1m. *J. G. Portman*

HAPPY DAYS 6 b.g. Primitive Rising (USA) 113 – Miami Dolphin 85 (Derrylin 115) – [2001 42: 13d 14.1m Sep 6] winning handicapper: well beaten both 6-y-o outings: blinkered once. *D. Moffatt*

HAPPY DIAMOND (USA) 4 b.c. Diesis 133 – Urus (USA) (Kris S (USA)) [2001 116 116: 10g* 8.9g Mar 24] sturdy colt: smart performer: won handicap at Nad Al Sheba in February by ¾ length from Inchlonaig: well beaten in Dubai Duty Free there only subsequent start: stays 1¼m: acts on firm and good to soft going. *Saeed bin Suroor*

HAPPY GO LUCKY 7 ch.m. Teamster 114 – Meritsu (IRE) 54 (Lyphard's Special – (USA) 122) [2001 65: 11.7d 13.1m⁵ 12d 12.1s Aug 9] sparely-made mare: fair handicapper at best: well beaten at 7 yrs. *M. J. Weeden*

HAPPY GUEST (IRE) 2 b.g. (Feb 9) Be My Guest (USA) 126 – Happy Lucy (IRE) 82 (Alzao (USA) 117) [2001 5g⁵ 5g² 6g⁴ 6g² 7.6m 6m² 6g Oct 6] IR 45,000Y: useful-looking gelding: first foal: dam unraced sister to smart 7f to 1¼m performer Aldbourne: fairly useful maiden: short-headed by Communard in nursery at Goodwood sixth start: gelded after final one: should stay 7f: raced only on good/good to firm going: wears tongue tie: very slowly away final outing: has carried head awkwardly. *E. Stanners*

HAPPY UNION 2 b.g. (Apr 16) First Trump 118 – Heights of Love 51 (Persian 67 Heights 129) [2001 6.1f 5.6f² 6d⁶ 6d 6m⁶ 6v⁴ 6v Oct 15] 13,000Y: close-coupled gelding: second foal: dam, headstrong maiden, best effort at 5f at 2 yrs: fair maiden: best effort when runner-up at Doncaster: gelded after final outing: will stay 7f: acts on any ground. *K. R. Burke*

HARBOUR BELL 2 b.c. (Mar 16) Bal Harbour 113 – Bellara 65 (Thowra (FR)) 59 [2001 7.1d 7m⁴ 7.1m Aug 27] 7,000Y: first foal: dam 1¾m winner: modest maiden: should be suited by 1¼m+. *B. R. Millman*

HARBOUR HOUSE 2 b.g. (Apr 2) Distant Relative 128 – Double Flutter 92 80 p (Beldale Flutter (USA) 130) [2001 7d 7.1g* Nov 7] leggy gelding: third foal: half-brother to 4-y-o It's Allowed: dam 7f to 1¼m winner: better effort in maidens when winning at Musselburgh by head from Red Forest: should stay 1m: open to improvement. *M. R. Channon*

HARBOUR ISLAND 9 b.g. Rainbow Quest (USA) 134 – Quay Line 117 (High Line – 125) [2001 17.2f May 22] rather leggy gelding: fairly useful handicapper in 1996: tailed off only Flat outing since: blinkered/visored: fair but ungenuine hurdler nowadays. *B. J. Llewellyn*

HARCELANTE (FR) 4 b.f. Balleroy (USA) 115 – Hekabe (GER) (Surumu (GER)) – [2001 67: 8.5s 10g 11.6m f7g f6g f9.4f Dec 5] successful in 3 claimers in France at 3 yrs: no show in Britain: blinkered once. *P. W. Hiatt*

HARD DAYS NIGHT (IRE) 4 b.g. Mujtahid (USA) 118 – Oiche Mhaith 74 (Night 53 § Shift (USA)) [2001 53: 14.1v 11.9m⁶ 17.2f³ 14.1m⁶ 16.4m⁴ 17.2g 12.6f² 11.9f⁶ 12d 14.1m 16.4g⁵ 16g 15.9d Sep 26] neat gelding: has a quick action: poor maiden handicapper: stays 17f: acts on firm ground: tried blinkered/visored: has raced freely/hung badly/found little: not one to trust. *M. Blanshard*

HARD LINES (USA) 5 b.g. Silver Hawk (USA) 123 – Arctic Eclipse (USA) (North- 57 ern Dancer) [2001 67: f8g 8m⁶ 10f* 9.9m⁵ 10.1g* f11g f14g Nov 26] rangy gelding: modest performer, lightly raced: trained by M. Hammond first start: won sellers at Ripon in July and Newcastle in August: stays 1¼m well: acts on any turf going. *A. Crook*

HARD TO CATCH (IRE) 3 b.g. Namaqualand (USA) – Brook's Dilemma 80 74 (Known Fact (USA) 135) [2001 75: f6g e7g⁴ e7g³ e7g² e6g² 7s 6m* 6m* 6m⁵ 6d⁶ 5m **a70** 6m⁶ p6g⁵ Dec 4] close-coupled gelding: fair performer: won minor event at Brighton and handicap at Goodwood in June: effective at 6f/7f: acts on firm going and all-weather: probably best in blinkers: usually races prominently. *K. T. Ivory*

HARD TO KNOW (IRE)   3 b.c. Common Grounds 118 – Lady Fern (Old Vic 136)   –
[2001 67?: f8.5g Dec 11] small, well-made colt: fair maiden in 2000: well held only 3-y-o start. *D. J. S. Cosgrove*

HARD TO LAY (IRE)   3 br.f. Dolphin Street (FR) 125 – Yavarro 44 (Raga Navarro   60
(ITY) 119) [2001 55: f8g 7m³ 8f² 7.5m Jun 8] smallish, workmanlike filly: modest maiden: stays 1m: acts on good to soft ground, probably on firm. *D. J. S. Cosgrove*

HAREWOOD END   3 b.g. Bin Ajwaad (IRE) 119 – Tasseled (USA) (Tate Gallery   86 d
(USA) 117) [2001 8d f8g* 10.2f³ 10.1m³ 8m 10g 8.1g⁶ 10g 10.3v⁶ f8g Nov 19] sturdy gelding: fifth foal: half-brother to several winners, notably smart performer up to 1¾m in Britain and USA Deploy Venture (by Deploy): dam, ran 3 times in USA, closely related to dam of smart 2-y-o Rock of Gibraltar out of half-sister to Riverman: fairly useful performer: won maiden at Southwell in April: looked sure to follow up for long way in handicap at Bath next time, but idled markedly: disappointing after fourth outing, leaving S. Woods 12,000 gns before final start: should prove best at 1m/1¼m: blinkered penultimate outing. *A. Crook*

HARIK   7 ch.g. Persian Bold 123 – Yaqut (USA) 77 (Northern Dancer) [2001 –, a87:   53
e12g f16.2s⁶ e16s* f16.2g⁴ e13g² 16.2m 15g⁶ f16.2f* Dec 5] rather leggy gelding: fairly   a85
useful handicapper on all-weather nowadays, modest on turf: won at Lingfield in February and Wolverhampton (visored) in December: probably best around 2m: acts on good to firm going and fibresand/equitrack: reportedly had breathing problem second start, mostly tongue tied after. *G. L. Moore*

HARLEQUIN   3 b.c. Halling (USA) 133 – Russian Grace (IRE) (Soviet Star (USA)   97
128) [2001 71: 9s 10.2m² 11.7g⁴ 12.3m* 12s⁵ 12d Oct 18] quite attractive colt: good walker: useful performer: won minor event at Bath then handicap at Ripon in June: off 3 months (reportedly pulled muscle) before creditable fifth to Hannibal Lad in £40,000 handicap at Ascot and seventh to Mesmeric in handicap at Newmarket: should stay further than 1½m: acts on soft and good to firm going: tended to run in snatches penultimate start: sold 60,000 gns. *Sir Michael Stoute*

HARLEQUIN DANCER   5 b.g. Distant Relative 128 – Proudfoot (IRE) (Shareef   54
Dancer (USA) 135) [2001 –: 9.9m 7m³ 10.1m 8.1s 10m Aug 29] strong, good-topped gelding: fairly useful performer in 1999: modest form at best since: best around 1m: acts on good to firm going, possibly not softer than good: has been visored: has hung. *N. A. Callaghan*

HARLESTONE BAY   2 b.g. (Mar 7) Shaamit (IRE) 127 – Harlestone Lake 78 (Ribo-   –
boy (USA) 124) [2001 7s Nov 9] smallish, sturdy gelding: brother to 3-y-o Harlestone Grey and half-brother to 2 winners, including fairly useful 1½m to 2½m winner Harlestone Brook (by Jalmood): dam out-and-out stayer: 20/1 and burly, well held in maiden at Doncaster. *J. L. Dunlop*

HARLESTONE GREY   3 gr.g. Shaamit (IRE) 127 – Harlestone Lake 78 (Riboboy   101 p
(USA) 124) [2001 12m 11.7f* 12g⁶ 14g⁴ 13.9m³ 14.6d Sep 14] tall, lengthy gelding: ninth foal: half-brother to 2 winners, including fairly useful 1½m to 2½m winner Harle-stone Brook (by Jalmood): dam out-and-out stayer: useful form: won maiden at Bath in June: best efforts when 1¼ lengths fourth to Big Moment in handicap at Goodwood then ½-length third to Artillery in Melrose Rated Stakes at York (edged right when challenging but run out of it only close home) in August: bred to be well suited by 2m+: acts on firm ground: lightly raced, and should make a smart stayer at 4 yrs. *J. L. Dunlop*

HARMONIC (USA)   4 b.f. Shadeed (USA) 135 – Running Melody 86 (Rheingold   73
137) [2001 80: 8.3g⁴ 8m 8.1m 6m⁵ 6m 8m 8m⁴ 8d⁴ 10.2d Oct 25] quite attractive filly: fair maiden handicapper: stays 8.5f: acts on soft and good to firm going: has been slowly away/edged right: sold 11,000 gns. *D. R. C. Elsworth*

HARMONIC WAY   6 ch.h. Lion Cavern (USA) 117 – Pineapple 77 (Superlative   121
118) [2001 117: 6g⁴ 6m 6g* 6m* 6m 5m 6s Sep 29]
Harmonic Way's style of running is idiosyncratic, so idiosyncratic that he has produced some worthwhile pictures for the BBC's 'jockey cam'. Harmonic Way's trademark is to come from last to first in big fields of sprinters, and he is good enough to do it. Of course, it simply isn't possible to pull off this sort of trick at every time of asking, or anything like it. Nonetheless, after a frustrating period which lasted nearly two years after his successful two-year-old debut, with strategy

Cork And Orrery Stakes, Royal Ascot—Harmonic Way gets the better of favourite Three Points to win at the meeting for the second successive year; Freud is third with Tillerman fourth

and tactics undergoing some experimentation and fine-tuning, this Beckhampton stalwart has emerged as a big-race winner in each of the last three seasons. Luckily for the BBC, he has been successful at their showpiece meetings of Glorious Goodwood and Royal Ascot.

Often, the 'jockey cam', the attachment of a camera to a jockey's helmet, results in the BBC's Flat-racing viewers receiving some fine views of grass, thin air, mud on the lens and a pair of large wiggling ears. Sometimes—and this really is a cardinal sin—these startling insights are transmitted not just in replays but during the race itself. What viewers need most is an overall view of what is happening in the race, the best view of what is unfolding on the way to a result, indicating what has happened to the horses they have wagered their money on, and not, if they're lucky, whether or not Kieren Fallon or Frankie Dettori needs to clean his breeches. If the intention was to show us something of what it is like to be a jockey, the 'jockey cam' has succeeded in giving some extra appreciation of the problems jockeys face during a race, given that it is apparently possible to see very little of what is happening from a hemmed-in position towards the back of a big field.

The steady hands controlling Harmonic Way for most of the last three years have been those of Richard Hughes. On his fifth ride on the horse, in 1999, Harmonic Way broke a losing run of sixteen races in the Stewards' Cup at Goodwood, and the following June the pair won the Wokingham Handicap at Royal Ascot. In the latest season Harmonic Way was back at the Royal meeting in the Group 2 Cork And Orrery Stakes (which is to be promoted to Group 1 from 2002 and to be run as the Golden Jubilee Stakes with prize-money doubled). Hughes was there as well, but this time endeavouring to pull off a similarly audacious stroke on board Tillerman, for whose owner he had a retainer, leaving Steve Drowne to test his nerve on Harmonic Way. Drowne and Harmonic Way had warmed up in impressive style with a victory at the first attempt together in the sixteen-runner listed Tote Scoop6 Leisure Stakes at Windsor at the start of the month, when Harmonic Way was brought to catch stable-mate Tamarisk on the line without the winning jockey resorting to his whip. The stage was set for an eventful encounter in the Cork And Orrery because both Harmonic Way and Tillerman had a good chance, and were sent off as two of the five 10/1 co-third favourites, behind Three Points and Primo Valentino. The two market leaders, together with Modigliani, were about to leave no possible excuses for those held up on grounds of lack of pace. With a total field of twenty-one, however, there was bound to be trouble in running and Hughes met plenty of it on Tillerman, eventually running on into fourth, while Drowne had shown him the way home on Harmonic Way, enjoying uninterrupted progress towards the stand rail, hitting the front sooner than intended in fact, just inside the final furlong before going on to beat Three Points by a length.

In 2000 it was said that Harmonic Way would eventually stand at his owner's stud in Greece. He has somewhat exceeded expectations since then of course, but a trip to Greece could still be the favoured option if he fails to add to his winning record and attract interest from larger stud operations. For now though, he races on, with retirement beckoning only, according to his trainer, 'when he is not earning money and not giving pleasure'. A Group 1 win might provoke British and Irish stud masters into taking more of an interest, but Harmonic Way was no better than fourth in two outings at such level in 2000 and three—the July Cup, Nunthorpe and Haydock Sprint Cup—in 2001. The ground was against him at Haydock and again when he finished his season with tenth of fifteen in the Diadem Stakes at Ascot.

Mrs Chandris is listed as Harmonic Way's breeder, as well as his owner, having bought the broodmare Pineapple for 28,000 guineas when she was carrying him at the Newmarket December Sales in 1994 and sold her again, when she was in foal to Night Shift, for 24,000 guineas at the same venue twelve months later. Pineapple was exported to India, and that Night Shift colt is consequently only her third reported foal, her second by Night Shift, following Passiflora who was a fair six-furlong winner as a two-year-old. Pineapple's liaisons with Night Shift were predictable given that her dam Pine Ridge had combined with the stallion in 1986 to produce In The Groove, winner of seven races, including the Irish One Thousand Guineas, the International Stakes, the Champion Stakes and the Coronation Cup. Pine Ridge was still being represented in the latest season, by her two-year-old son Barry Island. Pine Ridge has so far foaled eight winners and Pineapple was one of them, capable of fair form as a three-year-old when she won a three-runner maiden at Beverley over a mile and a half. Pine Ridge was herself a fair mile-and-a-half winner. Harmonic Way's sire, Gone West's brother Lion Cavern, has stood in Kentucky for the last two seasons, at 10,000 dollars in 2000 and 15,000 in 2001, and, typically, has had his most noteworthy results in Europe since being exported, with Crimplene in 2000 and now with Harmonic Way.

Harmonic Way (ch.h. 1995)	Lion Cavern (USA) (ch 1989)	Mr Prospector (b 1970)	Raise A Native
			Gold Digger
		Secrettame (ch 1978)	Secretariat
			Tamerett
	Pineapple (ch 1988)	Superlative (ch 1981)	Nebbiolo
			Clariden
		Pine Ridge (b 1980)	High Top
			Wounded Knee

An angular horse, Harmonic Way has improved his rating in every season on the racecourse. Capable of useful form over seven furlongs back in 1998, he has since been raced almost exclusively over six. He has useful form on soft ground, but is best on good or firmer. He was tried in a tongue strap in 1999 and a net muzzle has also been used. Now, however, it looks as if the key to him is getting the run of the race in view of the tactics used on him. As we have said, that does not happen too often and consequently, although he is a tough performer, one would struggle to call Harmonic Way consistent. Or perhaps not. When Harmonic Way has found himself in a field of twenty or more runners in the last three seasons, except for two occasions (in the autumn of 1999) when the ground was too soft for him, he has won. With twenty-nine rivals despatched in the 1999 Stewards' Cup, twenty-eight in the 2000 Wokingham and twenty in the 2001 Cork & Orrery, perhaps Harmonic Way confirms the saying 'the bigger the field the bigger the certainty'! *R. Charlton*

HARMONY HALL   7 ch.g. Music Boy 124 – Fleeting Affair 98 (Hotfoot 126) [2001   **65** 74: 8m⁵ 8f⁶ 7.5f 8f 8.3g 8.3g* 7.9m³ 8g² 8.5m⁵ 8g⁴ 8.3m² 7.5d³ Sep 25] big, lengthy gelding: fair handicapper: won at Windsor in July: creditable efforts next 5 starts: has form at 1½m, races mainly around 1m nowadays: acts on firm and good to soft going: visored once: usually waited with. *J. M. Bradley*

HARMONY ROW   3 ch.c. Barathea (IRE) 127 – Little Change 70 (Grundy 137)   **?** [2001 90p: 8v⁴ a10.5g* a12g² Dec 16] strong, useful-looking colt: fairly useful maiden winner in 2 starts at 2 yrs: shaped as if retaining ability/needing race in minor event at Ayr on reappearance: sold from E. Dunlop 15,000 gns, won minor event at Mijas in December: stays 1½m. *J. H. Brown, Spain*

HARNOUR   2 ch.c. (Feb 5) Desert King (IRE) 129 – Irish Light (USA) 91 (Irish River   **92** (FR) 131) [2001 5m³ 7m² 7m⁵ 7.5m² 8.3s³ 8.3g* 8m* 8s 10d⁵ Nov 3] 90,000Y: compact colt: first foal: dam, 1m winner, out of half-sister to smart US 6f/7f performer Gold Land:

429

fairly useful performer: won maiden at Hamilton and nursery at Ayr in September: creditable fifth to Alexander Three D in listed race at Newmarket final start: stays 1¼m: acts on soft and good to firm going: races up with pace. *M. R. Channon*

HARRYANA 4 b.f. Efisio 120 – Allyana (IRE) 83 (Thatching 131) [2001 –: e5g f9.4g Feb 3] small, strong filly: fair performer at 2 yrs: soundly beaten since: one to treat with some caution. *M. Johnston* –

HARRY BENNETT 3 b.g. Mind Games 121 – Edraianthus 78 (Windjammer (USA)) [2001 f7g⁴ 7.1d 8m 7m 8.3d⁶ 7.1f⁶ 9.9g Aug 15] 12,000F, 16,500Y: ninth foal: half-brother to useful 1m (in France at 2 yrs)/9f (in USA) winner Esquive (by Safawan) and fairly useful 1993 2-y-o 6f winner Close To Reality (by Dreams To Reality), later winner in USA: dam maiden who was best at 6f: modest maiden: probably stays 1m: sold 800 gns. *R. A. Fahey* **53**

HARRY HORSE 3 b.g. Cosmonaut – Bonny Melody 58 (Sizzling Melody 117) [2001 f6g 6m 7m 6m 5g 10d Oct 15] second foal: dam 5f and 7f winner: poor form, including in seller. *R. J. Hodges* **41**

HARRY JAKE 2 b.c. (Mar 25) Royal Applause 124 – Flora Wood (IRE) 77 (Bob Back (USA) 124) [2001 7m³ 6.1g* 7s⁶ Nov 6] 14,000F, 18,000Y, 35,000 2-y-o: fourth foal: dam, Irish winner around 1m, out of sister to sprinters Hot Spark (high class) and Bitty Girl (very smart): odds on, confirmed promise when bolting up in maiden at Nottingham in August by 4 lengths from Zelensky: left H. Cecil, below-form last of 6 in listed race at Maisons-Laffitte: may prove best at 6f/7f. *J.-P. Gallorini, France* **98**

HARRY JUNIOR 3 b.g. River Falls 113 – Badger Bay (IRE) 67 (Salt Dome (USA)) [2001 47§: f6g f8g 7.6f 8m 7.1d 5f 7m 8.5m 6s 8f 5d 5g Nov 5] temperamental maiden: trained first 2 starts by C. Dwyer: tried blinkered/visored/tongue tied. *B. W. Murray* – §

HARRY M 3 ch.g. River Falls 113 – Sylvan Rime (Weldnaas (USA) 112) [2001 f7g f7s Feb 9] first reported foal: dam of no account: last in 2 Southwell sellers, including in blinkers. *J. A. Glover* –

HARRY THE BEAVER (IRE) 2 b.g. (Mar 8) Bigstone (IRE) 126 – Moon River (FR) (Groom Dancer (USA) 128) [2001 7m 7g 7.9m Sep 5] IR 11,500Y: first foal: dam, third at 2m in France, half-sister to useful French performers up to 13f Blue Water and Norton Sound: poor maiden: should stay at least 1¼m: twice slowly away. *M. H. Tompkins* **41**

HARVARD (USA) 3 b. or br.g. Zafonic (USA) 130 – Bright Generation (IRE) 111 – (Rainbow Quest (USA) 134) [2001 7d Apr 19] fourth foal: closely related to US 1m winner Sunburst (by Gone West) and half-brother to fairly useful 1999 2-y-o 6f winner Barakula (by Barathea): dam 6f (at 2 yrs) to 1½m (Oaks d'Italia) winner: 20/1 and backward, never a threat in maiden at Newmarket: sold 1,000 gns in October. *L. M. Cumani*

HARVEY LEADER 6 b.g. Prince Sabo 123 – Mrs Leader (USA) (Mr Leader (USA)) [2001 75+: f8g* f8.5s f7g⁴ f8g g8g⁶ f8g 8g 6m f8g⁶ f8.5g⁵ Nov 17] fairly useful handicapper: won at Southwell in January: probably best around 1m: acts on fibresand: sometimes carries head high: usually races up with pace: unreliable. *Miss J. Feilden* – § **a80** §

HARVEY'S FUTURE 7 b.g. Never So Bold 135 – Orba Gold (USA) 67 (Gold Crest (USA) 120) [2001 61: e7g e7g³ f8g⁵ 7g Aug 11] rather sparely-made gelding: modest performer: stays 7f (raced freely at 1m): acts on soft going, good to firm and fibresand/equitrack: tried blinkered: has refused to enter stall. *P. L. Gilligan* **53**

HASIKIYA (IRE) 3 b.f. Green Desert (USA) 127 – Hasainiya (IRE) 109 (Top Ville 129) [2001 8.3g Aug 6] second foal: dam Irish 1¼m winner: 8¾ lengths seventh in maiden at Windsor on debut, slowly away: sold 18,000 gns in December. *Sir Michael Stoute* **52**

HASTA LA VISTA 11 b.g. Superlative 118 – Falcon Berry (FR) (Bustino 136) [2001 54, a–: 14d³ 13d⁶ 12m² 13m 12.1d* f16g³ 12.1s³ 15.8m 12g³ f16.2s Dec 18] compact gelding: has a round action: poor handicapper: won at Hamilton in July: effective at 1½m to 2m: acts on any turf going and fibresand: has been blinkered, visored nowadays: usually makes running. *M. W. Easterby* **49 a46**

HASTY PRINCE 3 ch.g. Halling (USA) 133 – Sister Sophie (USA) (Effervescing (USA)) [2001 78: 8.2f⁴ 10.3f* 10g 12m⁵ 10.5s⁴ 10f⁶ Sep 22] tall, quite attractive gelding: has a round action: useful performer: won maiden at Doncaster in June: best effort when fifth to Ovambo in Tote Gold Trophy at Goodwood in August: not discredited last 2 starts in competitive handicaps at Haydock and Newbury: gelded afterwards: stays 1½m: acts on firm and soft going: spoils chance with slow start. *B. Hanbury* **97**

HATA (IRE) 3 ch.f. Hamas (IRE) 125§ – Enaya 99 (Caerleon (USA) 132) [2001 69: **94** 6s² 6.1v* 6g² 6s⁴ 5v 7d Oct 13] rangy filly: fairly useful performer: won maiden at Warwick in April by 6 lengths, despite flashing tail and drifting right: easily best effort when second in handicap at Salisbury following month: stayed 6f: raced mainly on good ground or softer: slowly away penultimate outing: possibly of suspect temperament: visits Nashwan. *N. A. Graham*

HATALAN 2 ch.f. (Feb 25) Mark of Esteem (IRE) 137 – Elbaaha 97 (Arazi (USA) **74** 135) [2001 7m 7g² p8g⁶ f6g⁴ Dec 1] first foal: dam, 11.5f winner who stayed 14.6f, out of smart performer around 1¼m Gesedeh, herself half-sister to Ardross and to smart 1½m performer Larrocha: best effort in maidens (fair form) when second at Redcar: found little last 2 starts: will need to settle to stay beyond 7f. *M. R. Channon*

HATHAAL (IRE) 2 b.c. (May 21) Alzao (USA) 117 – Ballet Shoes (IRE) 75 (Ela- **95 p** Mana-Mou 132) [2001 8g² 8d* Oct 2] 230,000Y: good-topped colt: has short, unimpressive action: fifth foal: half-brother to 3 winners, including 4-y-o Petrushka and 3-y-o Colorado Falls: dam, 5f winner, half-sister to Spectrum: 9/2, confirmed promise when beating Sting Like A Bee a head in 21-runner maiden at Newmarket, never far away and holding on gamely: will stay 1¼m: already useful, and capable of better still. *Sir Michael Stoute*

HATHA ANNA (IRE) 4 b.c. Sadler's Wells (USA) 132 – Moon Cactus 118 (Kris **115** 135) [2001 106: 12m² 12m⁴ 10.5d* 14.1m* 12g² 12.5g* Nov 10] quite attractive colt: has a round action: smart performer, lightly raced: won maiden at Haydock in July, minor event at Salisbury (beat Alunissage comfortably by neck) in September and Group 2 Queen Elizabeth Stakes at Flemington (beat Ascana by head) in November: at least respectable efforts otherwise: unlucky neck second to Ulundi in minor event at Goodwood and 2 lengths fourth to Takamaka Bay in Duke of Edinburgh Stakes (Handicap) at Royal Ascot first 2 starts, and 5 lengths second to Mubtaker in listed event at Newmarket (visored) penultimate: stays 1¾m: acts on firm and good to soft ground: has been bandaged behind. *Saeed bin Suroor*

HATTER'S LAD (IRE) 2 b.c. (Apr 16) Alzao (USA) 117 – Shamsana (USA) **86 p** (Nijinsky (CAN) 138) [2001 7.5g⁴ f8.5g* Oct 9] IR 22,000F, 24,000 2-y-o: strong colt: half-brother to French 7f listed winner Shamaniya (by Doyoun) and French 10.5f and 1½m winner Shamawna (by Darshaan): dam unraced half-sister to Prix Vermeille winner Sharaya: well-backed favourite, better effort in maidens (fairly useful form) when beating High Diva by 4 lengths at Wolverhampton, drawing clear soon after halfway and eased: will stay 1¼m: has worn crossed noseband: capable of better. *J. A. Osborne*

HATTINGTON 3 b.g. Polish Precedent (USA) 131 – Ruffle (FR) (High Line 125) **–** [2001 11.9s⁵ 11.7d 10g Nov 5] 50,000F, 27,000Y: seventh foal: half-brother to 3 winners in France, including useful 1m and (at 2 yrs) 9f winner Go Between (by Highest Honor) and 11f winner Determined (by Darshaan): dam, won 1¼m Prix Gontaut-Biron, out of sister to Mtoto: little form in maidens: gelded after final start. *M. R. Channon*

HAULAGE MAN 3 ch.g. Komaite (USA) – Texita 65 (Young Generation 129) [2001 **63 +** 55: 8m⁵ 7g 6f* 7.2m Sep 22] modest handicapper: won at Newcastle in September: stays 7f, at least ridden with plenty of restraint: raced mainly on good going or firmer: slowly away final outing: has edged left. *D. Eddy*

HAUNT THE ZOO 6 b.m. Komaite (USA) – Merryhill Maid (IRE) 71 (M Double M **–** (USA))³ [2001 43, a69: f6g⁵ f7g⁵ f8s* f8g f6g f8g f7g⁴ f7g f7g f8g³ f8g* f8.5g³ f9.4s* **a66** f9.4g⁵ f8g f8g p10g Dec 28] tall mare: fair performer: won handicap in January and claimer in July, both at Southwell, and handicap at Wolverhampton in September: stays 9f: acts on fibresand/equitrack: held up. *John A. Harris*

HAVANA (IRE) 5 b.m. Dolphin Street (FR) 125 – Royaltess (Royal And Regal **54 d** (USA)) [2001 71d: 9.9m 16m 16.2f² 16.2f 16g 16.2m 17.1d Oct 8] close-coupled mare: maiden handicapper: on the downgrade and just modest form at best in 2001: stays 2m: probably acts on any turf going: tried blinkered: tongue tied: has been slowly away: sometimes makes running. *R. Ford*

HAVOC 2 b.c. (May 15) Hurricane Sky (AUS) – Padelia (Thatching 131) [2001 7s 8s² **80 p** Oct 31] well-made colt: half-brother to several winners, including useful miler Polar Boy (by Northern Baby) and fairly useful stayer Shining High (by Shirley Heights): dam unraced: better effort in maidens (fairly useful form) when 1¾ lengths second to Jawwala at Yarmouth, staying on again after being short of room: will probably stay 1¼m: should improve. *E. A. L. Dunlop*

HAWAYIL (USA) 2 b.f. (Apr 25) Halling (USA) 133 – Avice Caro (USA) 85 (Caro **61**
133) [2001 6.1m⁴ 7g⁵ 8.2v Oct 4] leggy filly: fourth foal: closely related to useful French
1m winner who stayed 1¼m Actoris (by Diesis) and half-sister to fairly useful but
ungenuine 1¼m winner Anschluss (by Alzao): dam, 1¼m winner, half-sister to smart
milers Sensation and Superiority out of Breeders' Cup Juvenile Fillies winner Outstandingly: modest maiden: best effort on second start: will stay 1¼m. *C. E. Brittain*

HAWK 3 b.c. A P Jet (USA) – Miss Enjoleur (USA) (L'Enjoleur (CAN)) [2001 82: 5f³ **90 §**
5f² 6g⁵ 5m³ 5.7m* 5g Oct 4] big, strong, good-bodied colt: fairly useful form: won
maiden at Bath in September: speedy, and will prove best around 5f: acts on firm ground:
tongue tied/carried head awkwardly final 2-y-o outing: has worn crossed noseband: has
found little: unreliable: sold 10,000 gns. *R. Hannon*

HAWKES RUN 3 b.g. Hernando (FR) 127 – Wise Speculation (USA) (Mr Prospector **79**
(USA)) [2001 73: 9s² 12s² 10.9m³ 14.1d⁴ Jun 17] tall, angular, unfurnished gelding: fair
maiden handicapper: stays 1½m: acts on fibresand, good to firm and soft ground: tends
to carry head awkwardly: joined C. Mann and showed fairly useful form over hurdles.
B. J. Meehan

HAWKEYE (IRE) 3 b.c. Danehill (USA) 126 – Tea House 107 (Sassafras (FR) **122**
135) [2001 89p: 8s⁴ 8d* 8m* 8s* 8d³ 8s³ 10d⁴ 10m⁴ Dec 16]
We have no idea how much Gary Tanaka paid for Hawkeye, sold in a private
deal out of Aidan O'Brien's stable after finishing fourth in the Champion Stakes at
Newmarket; but there's little doubt the amount will have far exceeded the colt's
original purchase price. Not that Hawkeye came cheaply when sent up to the
December Sales as a foal, a bid of 450,000 guineas being required to secure a colt
who had plenty to recommend him on pedigree. However, by the time of his latest
sale, Hawkeye's performances on the racecourse made him look something of a
bargain even at that price. Mr Tanaka has already seen a return on his outlay,
Hawkeye earning over £85,000 when finishing fourth in the Hong Kong Cup, and

Desmond Stakes, the Curragh—Hawkeye improves again to beat Pebble Island (right) and Maumee

there should be much more to come in the next season. The relatively lightly-raced Hawkeye may be capable of improving on the very smart form he has shown already and looks sure to continue to do well in pattern races over a mile and a mile and a quarter.

Hawkeye was one of the more obscure members of the very powerful O'Brien string in the first half of the season, but it didn't take him long to start making a name for himself in the second. After getting off the mark in a maiden at the Curragh in June, he followed up in a minor event there and completed a course hat-trick in the Group 3 Desmond Stakes, beating his stable-companion Pebble Island in good style by a length. Hawkeye failed to add to those victories but did go on to show even better form in making the frame in four subsequent races, each of them a Group 1 contest. Kept to a mile, he finished third in both the Prix du Moulin de Longchamp and the Queen Elizabeth II Stakes at Ascot, beaten four and a half lengths by Slickly in the former and three lengths by Summoner in the latter. On each occasion Hawkeye ran a bit better than the bare form suggested, being set plenty to do given the way the races were run. If Hawkeye's next performance, behind Nayef in the Champion Stakes, beaten five lengths, failed conclusively to prove that he was just as effective at a mile and a quarter, that in the Hong Kong Cup left no room for doubt. Handily placed from the start, Hawkeye came under pressure on the home turn and stuck to his task so well that he finished within a length of the first two, Agnes Digital and Tobougg.

	Danehill (USA)	Danzig	Northern Dancer
	(b 1986)	(b 1977)	Pas de Nom
Hawkeye (IRE)		Razyana	His Majesty
(b.c. 1998)		(b 1981)	Spring Adieu
	Tea House	Sassafras	Sheshoon
	(ch 1980)	(b 1967)	Ruta
		House Tie	Be Friendly
		(b 1975)	Mesopotamia

By the time Hawkeye appeared in the sale-ring in 1998 all but one of the nine live foals previously produced by his dam Tea House were winners, including Hawkeye's full sister Danish, who also raced up to a mile and a quarter and was of similar ability. She too was sold at the December Sales, though not until the end of her two-year-old season, when she fetched 18,000 guineas. At that stage Danish had only one win to her name, in a maiden at Leopardstown, but she left her previous form well behind at three, first of all racing in France where she gained one of her two wins in a listed event, and then in North America where she won the Grade 1 Queen Elizabeth II Challenge Cup. Hawkeye is also closely related to a couple of useful performers, including Teishebaini (by Hamas) who won at up to a mile in Italy; and one of his half-brothers is the very smart hurdler and high-class chaser Sybillin (by Henbit). There's another notable jumper in the family, too, the 1995 Champion Hurdle winner Alderbrook, who was also very smart on the Flat. Like Hawkeye, Alderbrook is a grandson of House Tie, a winning daughter of the Chesham Stakes winner Mesopotamia. Hawkeye's dam Tea House, a useful performer up to a mile in Ireland, was one of several winners produced by House Tie, the pick of them Academic, who showed smart form both in France and the States. Hawkeye, a tall, angular, quite good-topped colt, has shown himself effective on ground ranging from soft to good to firm. *M. A. Jarvis*

HAWKLEY 2 ch.c. (Feb 1) Arctic Tern (USA) 126 – Last Ambition (IRE) 29 **54**
(Cadeaux Genereux 131) [2001 7g 5m 6g 5.1f Sep 18] IR 2,000F, IR 8,000Y, 26,000 2-y-o: lengthy, rather unfurnished colt: first foal: dam, maiden, seemed best at 5f/6f: modest maiden: should stay 7f. *N. P. Littmoden*

HAWKWIND (USA) 2 ro.c. (Feb 7) El Prado (IRE) 119 – Pleasantly Quick (USA) **71**
(Roanoke (USA)) [2001 8d 8s Oct 31] $160,000Y: lengthy colt: fluent mover: first foal: dam, 2-y-o sprint winner in USA, half-sister to US Grade 3 8.5f winner Forcing Bid, also placed in Grade 1 events at 9f/1¼m: mid-field in maidens at Newmarket (green and burly, better effort) and Yarmouth. *J. H. M. Gosden*

HAWK WING (USA)   2 b.c. (Mar 15) Woodman (USA) 126 – La Lorgnette   **116 p**
(CAN) (Val de L'Orne (FR) 133) [2001 7m* 6g² 7g* 7m* Sep 16]

    For a while in October, the ante-post favourite for the Two Thousand
Guineas wasn't the unbeaten Johannesburg, even though he had already proved
himself comfortably the top juvenile colt in Europe with three smooth Group 1
victories. Nor was it Rock of Gibraltar, successful in the Grand Criterium and
Dewhurst Stakes, nor even Landseer or Tendulkar, both beaten narrowly in the
Dewhurst. No, the market leader, at around 5/1, vying with Godolphin's Dubai
Destination, was their stable-companion Hawk Wing, whose position at the top
of the list testified to the remarkable strength in depth of Aidan O'Brien's
two-year-olds (he was responsible for half of the twenty-two rated 110 and more by
Timeform), and owed as much to the trainer's oft-stated high opinion of the colt as
to the form-book. That's not to say Hawk Wing is an ordinary performer on
form—far from it, as his record stands at three wins from four starts culminating in
the Group 1 Aga Khan Studs National Stakes at the Curragh—and as he looks more
likely to improve than some of his stable mates he is certainly an exciting prospect.
Hawk Wing lined up for the National Stakes as winner of a maiden race at
Tipperary in May by a short head and of the King of Kings EBF Futurity Stakes at
the Curragh in August. In the latter race, upgraded to Group 2, Hawk Wing quickened splendidly after being held up and beat his stable-companion Sholokhov
easily by three lengths. In between, dropped back to six furlongs in the Railway
Stakes, also at the Curragh, he had gone down by two lengths to Rock of Gibraltar
after racing freely. The National Stakes drew a field of seven, three of them trained
by O'Brien—his other contenders were Sholokhov again and Monarchoftheglen.
Naheef and Funfair Wane came from Britain, the former, winner of the Vintage
Stakes at Goodwood, representing David Loder and going off second favourite.
Hawk Wing was odds on and gained another easy success, responding impressively
two furlongs out after being held up at the rear and having only to be pushed clear
to score by two and a half lengths from Naheef with Sholokhov third. Winners
of the National Stakes have a pretty good recent record, including Desert King,

*Aga Khan Studs National Stakes, the Curragh—Hawk Wing puts himself at the forefront
of the Guineas betting with an impressive success over Naheef and Sholokhov*

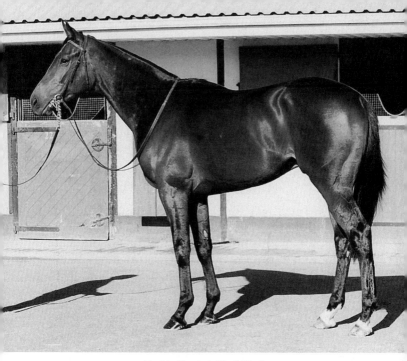

Mrs John Magnier's "Hawk Wing"

King of Kings and Sinndar, and O'Brien's comments about Hawk Wing were also encouraging. He said: 'He's a wonderful-looking colt with great presence, and looks more like a four-year-old than a two-year-old. The sky's the limit—he has a lot of class and a huge stride, and a lot of speed, but there is plenty of stamina in his pedigree, so he'll have no shortage of options next year.'

Hawk Wing (USA) (b.c. Mar 15, 1999)	Woodman (USA) (ch 1983)	Mr Prospector (b 1970)	Raise A Native / Gold Digger
		Playmate (ch 1975)	Buckpasser / Intriguing
	La Lorgnette (CAN) (b 1982)	Val de L'Orne (b 1972)	Val de Loir / Aglae
		The Temptress (b 1973)	Nijinsky / La Sevillana

Hawk Wing will be better suited by a mile and a mile and a quarter, though there's no cast-iron guarantee that he will prove fully effective at a mile and a half. His sire Woodman, rather like Danehill, gets winners over all sorts of distances and the dam La Lorgnette was the best of her age in Canada as a three-year-old, beating the colts in the Queen's Plate over a mile and a quarter after landing the Canadian Oaks. She is continuing the excellent stud record of fillies who have won the latter race. They are headed by Flaming Page, dam of Nijinsky, and South Ocean, dam of Storm Bird and of Canadian Oaks winner Northernette, herself dam of a Grade 1 winner. Backing up that pair are Square Angel and Classy 'n Smart. The former is grandam of Swain and dam of another Canadian Oaks winner, Kamar, who in turn

435

is dam of Grade 1 winners Gorgeous and Seaside Attraction and grandam of Fantastic Light. Classy 'n Smart is dam of a Grade 1 winner and of Dance Smartly, who earned an Eclipse Award with a tally including the Breeders' Cup Distaff and Canadian Oaks and has foaled the last two winners of the Queen's Plate in Scatter The Gold and Dancethruthedawn. Six of La Lorgnette's other foals have hit the target, notably the Canadian stakes performer Alexandrina (by Conquistador Cielo), dam of Canadian International winner Thornfield. The grandam The Temptress, successful as a juvenile, did not produce any other stakes winners. Hawk Wing has been through the sale-ring twice, for 225,000 dollars as a foal and 300,000 dollars as a yearling at Saratoga. He was not bought by any of the Coolmore connection at the latter sale but they seem to have a bargain—however they got hold of him. His return to action is awaited with interest. *A. P. O'Brien, Ireland*

HAYDN BOWEN 2 ch.c. (May 6) Most Welcome 131 – Hi-Li (High Top 131) [2001 8d f8g Dec 10] 1,000Y: seventh foal: dam unraced half-sister to useful miler Pfalz from very good family of Central Park: no form in maidens at Salisbury (pulled up) and Southwell. *R. M. Flower*

HAYLEY'S AFFAIR (IRE) 3 b.f. Night Shift (USA) – Sea Mistress (Habitat 134) 51 [2001 70p: 7s 6.9v 7.1m 8s⁶ 8d Oct 25] leggy, unfurnished filly: modest form only 2-y-o start: below form in 2001: races freely, and should prove as effective at 6f as 7f: acts on soft going: tongue tied last 3 starts: sold 4,200 gns. *P. W. Harris*

HAYMAKER (IRE) 5 b.g. Thatching 131 – Susie Sunshine (IRE) 81 (Waajib 121) 70 [2001 8d 8.2s³ 7.1v f6g⁶ f7g² f7g² f8g³ 9.1d⁴ 10.5g⁵ 10.5s f9.4s⁴ 9g Oct 19] quite good- a76 topped gelding: fair handicapper: left B. Rothwell after sixth start and G. Swinbank for 1,700 gns after penultimate: stays 1¼m, at least when conditions aren't testing: acts on heavy going, good to firm and fibresand: sometimes slowly away. *R. Craggs*

HAYSTACKS (IRE) 5 b.g. Contract Law (USA) 108 – Florissa (FR) (Persepolis (FR) 62 127) [2001 57: 16v 12.1m⁶ 15s³ 14.4d³ 16.1f* Sep 10] strong, close-coupled gelding: modest handicapper: won at Newcastle in September: should stay beyond 2m: acts on any going: usually visored before 2001: has pulled hard/looked none too keen/hung markedly left. *D. Moffatt*

HAZIMAH (USA) 2 b.f. (Mar 20) Gone West (USA) – Elrafa Ah (USA) 105 (Storm 74 Cat (USA)) [2001 7g³ 8d⁴ Oct 3] fourth foal: closely related to 3-y-o Raajiya and half-sister to Dewhurst Stakes winner Mujahid (by Danzig): dam 5f (at 2 yrs)/6f winner who stayed 1m: fair form in maidens at Folkestone and Newcastle 6 weeks apart: not sure to stay beyond 1m. *M. P. Tregoning*

HAZIRAAN (IRE) 4 b.g. Primo Dominie 121 – Hazaradjat (IRE) 82 (Darshaan 133) 46 [2001 49: e7g f6g f6g⁴ f6g f7g⁵ 7.1m⁶ 8.2f f7g Jun 15] poor maiden: may prove best around 6f: acts on fibresand: has been slowly away/wandered. *R. A. Fahey*

HAZY MORN 2 gr.f. (Feb 25) Cyrano de Bergerac 120 – Hazy Kay (IRE) 77 51 (Treasure Kay 114) [2001 5s 5g 5.7f 5m⁴ 5m 5.1g⁴ 5m⁶ 5g⁶ 6.1m 5.1f f6g Oct 9] 6,000Y: close-coupled filly: fifth foal: half-sister to 1998 2-y-o 5f winner Clara Blue (by Alhijaz): dam, disappointing maiden who should have stayed beyond 7f, out of sister to Middle Park winner Steel Heart: modest maiden: should stay 6f: acts on good to firm ground: tried blinkered. *N. J. Hawke*

HEADFORT ROSE (IRE) 4 b.f. Desert Style (IRE) 121 – Tamarsiya (USA) (Shah- 63 rastani (USA) 135) [2001 76: 8s 9m 8g 7f 8m 7.8f² 7g 9g 8m f8.5g f8.5g Oct 20] third foal: half-sister to winners abroad by Namaqualand and Roi Danzig: fair handicapper at best: won at Bellewstown in 2000: modest form at 4 yrs: left M. Cunningham in Ireland after eighth start: no show in Britain: stays 8.5f: acts on firm going: usually blinkered, including for win. *M. Meade*

HEAD IN THE CLOUDS (IRE) 3 b.f. Rainbow Quest (USA) 134 – Ballerina 114 (IRE) 88 (Dancing Brave (USA) 140) [2001 94p: 10g⁴ 12f⁶ 11.9m* 13.5s² 11.9g 12d* 12d² Nov 2] leggy, light-framed filly: smart performer: easily landed odds in maiden at York in July, and impressive winner of Princess Royal Willmott Dixon Stakes at Ascot in October, latter by 5 lengths from Love Everlasting: creditable efforts most other starts, notably when ½-length second to Abitara in Prix de Pomone at Deauville fourth outing and 1¼ lengths second to High Pitched in St Simon Stakes at Newmarket final start: only below-par effort when last in Yorkshire Oaks fifth outing: should stay 1¾m: best efforts on good to soft/soft going: has been early to post: has pulled hard under restraint, and best making running. *J. L. Dunlop*

HEADLAND (USA) 3 b. or br.c. Distant View (USA) 126 – Fijar Echo (USA) (In **89**
Fijar (USA) 121) [2001 71: f5g² 6.1v² 6g 6m² 5m f6g* 5.5d f7g* 7.1v f8g⁶ p7g⁴ Dec 29]
well-made colt: fairly useful performer: won maiden in July and handicap in September,
both at Wolverhampton: creditable efforts otherwise when in frame: stays 7f: acts on
heavy going, good to firm, fibresand and polytrack: front runner. *J. M. P. Eustace*

HEAD SCRATCHER 3 ch.g. Alhijaz 122 – Sabrata (IRE) (Zino 127) [2001 55: f7g* **53**
f9.4s f8.5g⁵ Jan 25] modest performer: won seller at Southwell in January: should stay
1m: acts on firm going and fibresand. *A. Bailey*

HEALEY (IRE) 3 ch.g. Dr Devious (IRE) 127 – Bean Siamsa (Solinus 130) [2001 **–**
88?: 7.5d 7.6f 8.1m 10f³ 10.4d 10g Oct 6] lengthy, quite good-topped gelding: fairly
useful 6f winner at 2 yrs: no form in 2001: tried tongue tied. *J. D. Bethell*

HEATHER MIX 3 gr.f. Linamix (FR) 127 – Craigmill 85 (Slip Anchor 136) [2001 **84**
10.5s* 11.6g⁴ 10.5v Sep 28] second foal: dam, 2-y-o 7f winner, half-sister to Park Hill
winner Coigach and smart performer up to 1¾m Applecross (dam of Craigsteel and
Invermark): fairly useful form when overcoming inexperience to win 5-runner maiden at
Haydock in May: very disappointing after in minor event and (off nearly 4 months,
looked most reluctant) handicap: should stay at least 1½m. *J. L. Dunlop*

HEATHER VALLEY 5 ch.m. Clantime 101 – Sannavally (Sagaro 133) [2001 47: 7g **–**
5m 6s f5s Dec 15] maiden handicapper: no form at 5 yrs. *J. Akehurst*

HEATHMAN (IRE) 5 b.g. Common Grounds 118 – Dul Dul (USA) (Shadeed (USA) **–**
135) [2001 7m 11.7f 7.1s Aug 9] well beaten, including in seller. *R. J. Baker*

Mr L. Neil Jones's "Head In The Clouds"

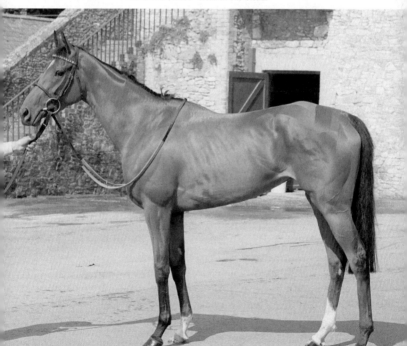

DGH Partnership's "Heavenly Whisper"

HEATHYARDSBLESSING (IRE) 4 b.g. Unblest 117 – Noble Nadia (Thatching **74**
131) [2001 –: 5.1g 5m 5d³ 6d Oct 13] quite good-topped gelding: useful winner at 2 yrs,
just fair nowadays: should prove best at 5f/easy 6f: yet to race on soft/heavy going, acts
on any other: has carried head awkwardly. *R. Hollinshead*

HEATHYARDS FRIEND 2 b.g. (Mar 29) Forest Wind (USA) 111 – Heathyards **–**
Lady (USA) 76 (Mining (USA)) [2001 7.1m 10d Oct 8] leggy, unfurnished gelding: first
foal: dam 6f to 8.5f winner: little sign of ability in maidens. *R. Hollinshead*

HEATHYARDS GUEST (IRE) 3 ch.g. Be My Guest (USA) 126 – Noble Nadia **60**
(Thatching 131) [2001 71: f9.4s² 10s 10.3f⁵ 10m 8.2f³ 9m⁴ 10g 10.3d 12d 10.9v Oct 15]
leggy, unfurnished gelding: modest maiden: probably stays 1½m: acts on firm and good
to soft going: visored last 2 starts: sold 5,000 gns. *R. Hollinshead*

HEATHYARDS LAD (IRE) 4 b.g. Petardia 113 – Maiden's Dance 65 (Hotfoot **–**
126) [2001 63: 8.3g 8g 6g Aug 31] leggy gelding: winning handicapper: well held at 4
yrs: visored/blinkered last 2 starts. *M. Wigham*

HEATHYARDS MATE 4 b.g. Timeless Times (USA) 99 – Quenlyn (Welsh Pageant **–**
132) [2001 46, a65: f11g f11g Dec 17] sturdy, close-coupled gelding: fair on all-weather
at 3 yrs: well held in 2001. *R. Hollinshead*

HEATHYARDS SIGNET 3 b.g. King's Signet (USA) 110 – Heathyards Gem 64 **61 ?**
(Governor General 116) [2001 –: 6.1d⁵ 6m 6.1f* 6m 6m⁵ f6g³ 7.1d 5g f5s 5.1d f6s
Dec 21] workmanlike gelding: modest performer: seemingly best effort when winning
claimer at Chester in June: stays 6f: acts on firm ground and fibresand: slowly away final
outing: has hung right. *D. McCain*

438

HEATHYARDS SWING 3 b.c. Celtic Swing 138 – Butsova 93 (Formidable (USA) **79**
125) [2001 8s 7g² 10.5m² 8.1d⁶ 10m* 10.3m 10.5d 11.9s 11.8s f9.4g Oct 23] 4,000Y,
11,000 2-y-o: rather leggy, quite good-topped colt: half-brother to 2 winners by Bustino,
including fairly useful 11f winner who stayed 2m Bustinetta: dam, 6f winner, half-sister
to Terimon: fair performer: won maiden at Ripon in June: mainly well held after: stays
10.5f: acts on good to firm and good to soft going: has flashed tail: probably not an easy
ride. *R. Hollinshead*

HEAVEN FORBID 3 b.g. Beveled (USA) – Fayre Holly (IRE) 57 (Fayruz 116) **54**
[2001 6m⁵ f6g 5g 5g f5g 5.2v Oct 26] 1,500Y: first foal: dam maiden who may have
proved best as a sprinter: modest form in Lingfield maiden on debut: well held after:
raced only at 5f/6f: slowly away on debut. *J. G. Portman*

HEAVENLY WHISPER (IRE) 3 b.f. Halling (USA) 133 – Rock The Boat 52 (Slip **105**
Anchor 136) [2001 87: 8s* 10.4m³ 10d⁶ 8g² 8s 8g Oct 6] useful-looking filly: has a short,
round action: useful performer: won listed race at Kempton in April by ½ length from
Mauri Moon: good efforts in pattern company next 3 starts, notably when 2 lengths third
to Time Away in Musidora Stakes at York and 2 lengths second to Proudwings in
Falmouth Stakes at Newmarket: poor efforts last 2 starts: stays 10.4f: yet to race on firm
ground, acts on any other: races prominently: genuine. *M. L. W. Bell*

HEFIN 4 ch.g. Red Rainbow 105 – Summer Impressions (USA) 70 (Lyphard (USA) **56**
132) [2001 51: 10.1v 10g³ p13g* Dec 29] modest performer, lightly raced: won handicap at Lingfield in December: stays 13f: acts on good to firm ground and polytrack.
S. C. Williams

HEIR TO BE 2 b.c. (Feb 12) Elmaamul (USA) 125 – Princess Genista 108 (Ile de **– p**
Bourbon (USA) 133) [2001 7s 8s Nov 9] angular colt: half-brother to useful performers
Tsarnista and Sovinista (both best up to 1m, by Soviet Star), Tomos (up to 1½m, by Sure
Blade) and 4-y-o Give Notice: dam, 1m (including at 2 yrs) winner, stayed 15f: some
promise in maidens at Leicester and Doncaster: should do better. *J. L. Dunlop*

HEJAZIAH (USA) 3 b.f. Gone West (USA) – Top Trestle (USA) (Nijinsky (CAN) **76**
138) [2001 89: 8s⁶ Apr 14] leggy, useful-looking filly: fairly useful listed winner in Italy
at 2 yrs: below that form in similar race at Kempton only 3-y-o outing: should stay 1m:
acts on firm and soft going: sent to USA. *P. F. I. Cole*

HELALI MANOR 3 b.f. Muhtarram (USA) 125 – Royal Mazi 58 (Kings Lake **–**
(USA) 133) [2001 –: 6g 5m 8.1m 8m 7f 10m 11.9d f8g 9.9m 6s 8d 6m⁶ 5d 7d 5g 10.3s
Nov 9] of little account. *G. P. Kelly*

HELEN ALBADOU (USA) 4 b.f. Sheikh Albadou 128 – Sister Troy (USA) (Far **69**
North (CAN) 120) [2001 64: f6g⁴ 7f f5g⁵ f6g Jul 20] fair performer, lightly raced: stays
6f: acts on heavy going and fibresand: sent to USA. *K. R. Burke*

HELEN BRADLEY (IRE) 2 ch.f. (Apr 25) Indian Ridge 123 – Touraya (Tap On **85**
Wood 130) [2001 6.1d* 7g Oct 6] 19,000Y, 64,000 2-y-o: rather leggy, angular filly: ninth
foal: sister to useful 7f winner Modern British (later 1m/9f winner in Hong Kong where
known as Good Record), and half-sister to 2 winners by Dominion, including Irish 1000
Guineas third Tarwiya, 5f and 7f winner at 2 yrs: dam French 1m winner: won maiden at
Nottingham in September by ½ length from Al Maali: similar form when eleventh of 12
in listed event at Newmarket: likely to prove best up to 1m. *N. P. Littmoden*

HELICAL GIRL 3 b.f. Presidium 124 – Oubeck 65 (Mummy's Game 120) [2001 **40**
7m⁴ 8.1s f7g⁴ f8.5g⁵ f8.5g³ f8.5s Dec 26] 3,200Y: third foal: half-sister to 1998 2-y-o 5f
seller winner Lune Lass (by Cyrano de Bergerac): dam 6f winner: poor maiden: stays
8.5f: acts on fibresand: blinkered/visored all starts. *R. M. H. Cowell*

HELLOFABUNDLE 3 b.g. Phountzi (USA) 104 – Helleborus (King of Spain 121) **–**
[2001 –: 11.5m 8.2f 8.5d 10s 10d Oct 15] of little account. *T. D. McCarthy*

HELLO HOLLY 4 b.f. Lake Coniston (IRE) 131 – Amandine (IRE) (Darshaan 133) **59**
[2001 50: 10f 10g 10.1g² 10.1g² 11.5m² 10m⁴ 12g³ 12m⁵ 9.9m³ 13.1m* 16d Sep 27] big,
lengthy filly: modest handicapper: won at Bath in September: stays 13f: acts on good to
firm going: unseated/bolted before fifth outing: races prominently. *Mrs A. L. M. King*

HELLOIMUSTBEGOING (USA) 2 b.f. (Apr 4) Red Ransom (USA) – Arsaan **76 p**
(USA) 106 (Nureyev (USA) 131) [2001 7g² Aug 17] seventh living foal: half-sister to 3
winners, including fairly useful 1¼m winner Allgrit (by Shadeed): dam, 7f (at 2 yrs)/1m
winner, half-sister to US Grade 1 winners Menifee (9f) and Desert Wine (up to 1¼m)
and to dam of Fasliyev: 6/1, 2½ lengths second of 10 to Bright And Clear in maiden at
Newmarket, always close up: should improve. *E. A. L. Dunlop*

HELLO SCHATZI 5 b.g. Ardkinglass 114 – Hotaria 68 (Sizzling Melody 117) [2001 –
f9.4g May 19] half-brother to 4-y-o Cosmic Song: dam 6f winner, including at 2 yrs: well
held in maiden at Wolverhampton. *Miss A. Stokell*

HELLO SWEETY 3 b.f. Shaamit (IRE) 127 – Madam Brady (USA) (Lomond (USA) **78**
128) [2001 49: 10m* 10m⁵ Jul 21] fair performer, lightly raced: won maiden at Kempton
in June: stays 1¼m: took good hold (well held) final outing. *G. C. Bravery*

HELLO VEGAS 4 b.g. First Trump 118 – Meet Again (Lomond (USA) 128) [2001 –
60: f7g f12g f11g 10s 11.8s 14.1s Oct 31] strong, good-topped gelding: well beaten at 4
yrs: tried visored. *Mrs Lydia Pearce*

HELVETIUS 5 b.g. In The Wings 128 – Hejraan (USA) 73 (Alydar (USA)) [2001 –: **70**
f14g 11.9m⁴ 12s⁶ 13.3g May 30] tall, leggy gelding: fair handicapper nowadays: stays
1½m: acts on firm and soft going: blinkered once. *P. C. Ritchens*

HENRI LEBASQUE (IRE) 2 b.c. (Apr 5) Sri Pekan (USA) 117 – Almost A Lady **109 p**
(IRE) 70 (Entitled 126) [2001 6m⁶ 7m³ 8g* Sep 19] 30,000Y: leggy, quite good-topped
colt: fourth foal: half-brother to 3-y-o Thanks Max: dam, second at 1m at 2 yrs in Ireland,
half-sister to very smart 1¼m performer Insatiable: won minor event (green) in June and
6-runner listed race (by ¾ length from Sparkling Water, leading late on) in September,
both at Goodwood: wrong in coat and blanketed for stall entry, 1¾ lengths third to Hills
of Gold in minor race at Doncaster: should stay 1¼m: joined Godolphin: smart performer
in the making, sure to win more races. *P. F. I. Cole*

HENRY HALL (IRE) 5 b.h. Common Grounds 118 – Sovereign Grace (IRE) 101 **101**
(Standaan (FR) 118) [2001 100: 5m⁵ 5m⁴ 5g² 5f 5m 5g⁴ 5m 5g 5g⁵ 5m* 5d Oct 18] leggy
horse: has a round action: useful handicapper: won at Newmarket (beat Mungo Park 2
lengths) in September: creditable efforts otherwise only at Windsor on third start and
Ascot on sixth: best at 5f: acts on firm and soft going: visored once: usually waited with:
none too consistent. *N. Tinkler*

HENRY HARBER (IRE) 3 b.g. Dilum (USA) 115 – Marguerite Bay (IRE) 73 (Dar- –
shaan 133) [2001 f8g 9m⁶ 8.3m 7g Sep 11] 4,500Y: second foal: dam 7f winner: no sign
of ability. *T. E. Powell*

HENRY ISLAND (IRE) 8 ch.g. Sharp Victor (USA) 114 – Monterana 99 (Sallust **72 §**
134) [2001 –§: f16g⁶ f12g* f12g² 16m 11.8g⁴ 11.9g 14.4g 12g* 16.5s⁴ Nov 10] **a80 §**
workmanlike gelding: good mover: fairly useful on turf nowadays, fair on all-weather:
won minor event at Southwell in February and handicap at Musselburgh in November:
effective at 1½m, probably at 2¼m: acts on soft going, good to firm and fibresand: tends
to sweat: has looked reluctant: untrustworthy. *Mrs A. J. Bowlby*

HENRY PEARSON (USA) 3 ch.c. Distant View (USA) 126 – Lady Ellen (USA) **59**
(Explosive Bid (USA)) [2001 68: 7d 6s 8.1m 10.3f 10f 10d⁶ 10.5g⁴ 10.5s 11.9s Sep 7]
strong, lengthy colt: modest maiden handicapper: stays 1¼m: acts on soft ground: visored
seventh/latest outings, running creditably first time. *T. H. Caldwell*

HENRY'S HERO 2 b.c. (Mar 18) Pyramus (USA) 78 – Casbatina 71 (Castle Keep **65**
121) [2001 5m 6m⁵ 5.3s* f5s² f5s⁴ Dec 21] second reported foal: dam 2-y-o 6f seller
winner: fair performer: left G. Brown prior to landing gamble in seller at Brighton in
October: good second in nursery at Southwell despite hanging right: likely to prove best
at 5f/easy 6f: acts on fibresand and soft ground. *C. A. Dwyer*

HENRY TUN 3 b.g. Chaddleworth (IRE) 103 – B Grade 59 (Lucky Wednesday 124) **54**
[2001 51: f6g³ f6g⁶ f5g* 5g⁵ 5m⁶ f5g f5g f6g² 6.1s⁵ 5f⁵ f5s f5g⁶ 5d f5g⁵ Dec 1] tall, quite **a57**
good-topped gelding: modest handicapper: won at Southwell in April: stays sharp 6f: acts
on firm going (possibly on soft) and fibresand: tried visored: tongue tied: slowly away
final outing: usually races prominently. *Miss J. F. Craze*

HERACLES 5 b.g. Unfuwain (USA) 131 – La Masse (High Top 131) [2001 78: 11.9m –
May 8] fair performer at 4 yrs: well held only 5-y-o start. *B. G. Powell*

HERBIE'S MOVE 3 b.g. Contract Law (USA) 108 – Megan's Move 66 (Move Off –
112) [2001 12d Nov 6] half-brother to 1½m and 2m winner Here Comes Herbie (by
Golden Lahab): dam 9.4f and hurdles winner: 100/1, tailed off in maiden at Catterick.
W. Storey

HERE COMES TOM 3 b.g. Puissance 110 – Young Holly (Risk Me (FR) 127) –
[2001 7s 6v Oct 29] first foal: dam unraced: well beaten in maidens at Leicester and
Windsor. *Jamie Poulton*

HERETIC 3 b.g. Bishop of Cashel 122 – Barford Lady 93 (Stanford 121§) [2001 90p: **96**
8s* 8g 7m Jun 22] good-bodied gelding: has a short, round action: fourth foal: closely

related to 7-y-o Warningford: dam 7f/1m winner: useful performer, lightly raced: won minor event at Kempton (merely pushed out to beat Foodbroker Fancy by 2½ lengths) in April: last in 2000 Guineas at Newmarket next time, then creditable seventh in handicap there final start: likely to prove best up to 1m: acts on soft and good to firm going. *J. R. Fanshawe*

HERMIT'S HIDEAWAY   4 b.g. Rock City 120 – Adriya 94 (Vayrann 133) [2001   **49**
51: e7g 5m 5g 6v f12g⁴ f11g² f9.4s⁵ Dec 15] useful-looking gelding: poor maiden: stays
easy 1½m: acts on fibresand and firm going: has sweated/wandered. *T. D. Barron*

HERNANDITA   3 b.f. Hernando (FR) 127 – Dara Dee 87 (Dara Monarch 128) [2001   **83**
72: 8.2v³ 10s* 10g 10v 11.7d² Oct 25] leggy, rather unfurnished filly: fairly useful
performer: won minor event at Nottingham in April: best effort when second in handicap
at Bath final outing: stays 11.7f: acts on heavy and good to firm going: sold 13,000 gns,
joined M. Pipe and winner on hurdling debut in December. *J. L. Dunlop*

HERODOTUS   3 b.g. Zafonic (USA) 130 – Thalestria (FR) 91 (Mill Reef (USA) 141)   **104**
[2001 8s* 10v⁵ 11m 12f 10g⁵ 9f⁴ 12s 7s Oct 11] big, good sort: has plenty of scope:
usually takes the eye: half-brother to several winners, including winner up to 11f in
Britain/France Soldier's Leap (by Warning) and 9.7f to 13f winner Amazon Express (by
Siberian Express): dam 7f (at 2 yrs) and 11f (in France) winner: useful performer: won
listed race at Kempton in April in good style by neck from Gryffindor: creditable 2
lengths fourth behind that colt in minor event at Newbury in September: ran poorly last 2
starts (gelded afterwards): should be suited by 1¼m/1½m: acts on firm and soft going:
blinkered/tongue tied final outing. *C. E. Brittain*

HEROS FATAL (FR)   7 ch.g. Hero's Honor (USA) – Femme Fatale (FR) (Garde   **103**
Royale 120) [2001 96: 16.1f³ 16.2g⁴ 18d Oct 20] smallish, deep-bodied gelding: useful
handicapper, lightly raced on Flat: good efforts at 7 yrs when 2¼ lengths third to Archduke Ferdinand in Northumberland Plate at Newcastle (not best of runs) in June then
unlucky fourth at Ascot (short of room much of straight, but for which may well have
won when 2 lengths behind Moon Emperor) in August: below form bidding for repeat
win in Cesarewitch final outing: stays 2½m: probably acts on any going: effective in
blinkers at 4 yrs in France. *M. C. Pipe*

HERO'S SON (FR)   5 ch.g. Hero's Honor (USA) – Happy Waki (USA) (Miswaki   **–**
(USA) 124) [2001 18.7f May 9] big, lengthy gelding: useful performer at best: trained by
J-M. Capitte at 3 yrs, winning minor event at Saint-Cloud and amateur race at Lyon
Parilly: last in Chester Cup on only Flat outing since: stays 11f: acts on soft going: tried
blinkered. *Jonjo O'Neill*

HER OWN WAY (USA)   4 b.f. Danzig (USA) – Formidable Lady (USA) (Silver   **76**
Hawk (USA) 123) [2001 87: 8.1g 12g Sep 28] big, lengthy, heavy-bodied filly: has a
fluent, round action: fair maiden at 4 yrs, lightly raced: should prove best up to 1m:
blinkered final outing: sent to USA. *J. H. M. Gosden*

HERRING GREEN   4 b.g. Greensmith 121 – Jane Herring (Nishapour (FR) 125)   **–**
[2001 –: 7f 7f Jun 5] leggy gelding: no sign of ability. *E. A. Wheeler*

HERR TRIGGER   10 gr.g. Sharrood (USA) 124 – Four-Legged Friend 101 (Aragon   **–**
118) [2001 47: 12m 10.1g Jul 3] leggy gelding: fairly useful at best: lightly raced
nowadays. *Dr J. D. Scargill*

HE'S A RASCAL (IRE)   3 b.g. Fumo di Londra (IRE) 108 – Lovely Ali (IRE) 69   **–**
(Dunbeath (USA) 127) [2001 8m 11.7d⁵ 12.1g⁶ f12g 14.1d 11.8s 10v Oct 29] IR 7,200F:
third foal: dam Irish 1m/9f winner at 5 yrs: little form: tried blinkered/visored.
H. Morrison

HESPERUS (IRE)   2 ch.g. (May 19) Catrail (USA) 123 – Sweet Pleasure 88 (Sweet   **– p**
Revenge 129) [2001 6g 5f 5.7g Oct 1] well-made gelding: half-brother to several
winners, including 3-y-o Flying Millie and fairly useful 1½m/1¾m winner Haddaaj (by
Ela-Mana-Mou): dam 2-y-o 6f winner: signs of ability in maidens: raced very freely on
debut: slowly away next time: looks type to do better. *R. M. Beckett*

HETRA HAWK   5 ch.g. Be My Guest (USA) 126 – Silver Ore (FR) 94 (Silver Hawk   **–**
(USA) 123) [2001 –: 12g f14g Dec 14] quite good-topped gelding: little form.
W. J. Musson

HETRA REEF   3 b.g. First Trump 118 – Cuban Reef 54 (Dowsing (USA) 124) [2001   **–**
–: 8.2s f8g 8.2f 10m Sep 1] smallish, plain gelding: of little account. *W. J. Musson*

HEVER GOLF GLORY   7 b.g. Efisio 120 – Zaius 94 (Artaius (USA) 129) [2001   **– §**
39§, a63d: f11g⁵ f8g⁶ f11g³ f11g Dec 3] smallish gelding: poor handicapper: probably   **a40 §**

stays 1½m: acts on firm ground, good to soft and fibresand/equitrack: tried blinkered/visored: inconsistent. *C. N. Kellett*

HE WHO DARES (IRE) 3 b.g. Distinctly North (USA) 115 – Sea Clover (IRE) 77 (Ela-Mana-Mou 132) [2001 7v⁴ 7s 8.2v² Oct 4] IR 10,500Y: rather leggy, quite good-topped gelding: fourth foal: half-brother to 5f winner Knockemback Nellie (by Forzando): dam 2-y-o 7f winner: fair form in maidens: best efforts when in frame at Doncaster in March and Nottingham in October: gelded after final start: not bred to stay beyond 1m: raced only on soft/heavy going. *I. A. Balding* **69**

HIBAAT 5 ch.g. Zafonic (USA) 130 – Realisatrice (USA) (Raja Baba (USA)) [2001 –: f16g Jan 1] disappointing maiden. *M. C. Chapman* **–**

HIBERNATE (IRE) 7 ch.g. Lahib (USA) 129 – Ministra (USA) (Deputy Minister (CAN)) [2001 77: 12.1m² 11.9d* 12.4m 8.5f⁴ 15.9m 12m* 12g³ 10.4m⁴ 10.4s⁴ 12s⁶ p12g f11g Dec 17] big, lengthy gelding: fair performer: won Queen Mother's Cup (ladies handicap) at York in June and claimer at Musselburgh in August: below form last 4 starts: effective at 1¼m/1½m: acts on firm going, good to soft and equitrack/polytrack: tried visored: usually front runner. *K. R. Burke* **70 a–**

HI BUDDY 4 br.g. High Kicker (USA) – Star Thyme (Point North 73) [2001 10v 13.8s Oct 20] modest maiden at 2 yrs: well held in 2001 on first outings since: tried blinkered/visored. *J. Mackie* **–**

HICKLETON DREAM 4 b.f. Rambo Dancer (CAN) 107 – Elegant Approach 48 (Prince Ragusa 96) [2001 –: 10m 12.4g⁶ 12f 14.1m² 14.1m³ 15.8m Sep 22] sparely-made filly: poor maiden: left A. Mulholland after reappearance: stays 1¾m: acts on good to firm going. *G. A. Swinbank* **45**

Queen Mother's Cup (Ladies) Handicap, York—Hibernate is given a well-judged ride by Claire Stretton; Miss Fara is second and Golden Chance third

HIDDENDALE (IRE) 2 br.f. (Apr 4) Indian Ridge 123 – That'll Be The Day (IRE) **90 p**
68 (Thatching 131) [2001 6m⁴ 6.5g³ 6d* Oct 18] 180,000Y: good-bodied filly: fourth
foal: half-sister to 5-y-o Majestic Bay and Italian winner (including listed race) up to 7.5f
That's The Way (by Hamas): dam, 2-y-o 5f winner in Britain who later won up to 7f in
Italy, half-sister to performers up to 1¼m Candy Glen (very smart) and Ashley Park
(smart): on toes/edgy, third of 28 to Madame Boulangere in sales race at Ascot: justified
favouritism in 22-runner maiden at Newmarket by ¾ length from Ghannam, jinking left
leaving stall but travelling strongly and quickening clear 2f out: should stay 7f: likely to
make a useful 3-y-o. *B. J. Meehan*

HIDDEN ENEMY 5 b.g. Meqdaam (USA) – Orchard Bay 47 (Formidable (USA) –
125) [2001 –: 8.2s f16.2g f11g Dec 3] sturdy gelding: little form. *R. Hollinshead*

HIDDEN FORT 4 ch.g. Mujtahid (USA) 118 – Temple Fortune (USA) 74 (Ziggy's **71**
Boy (USA)) [2001 –: 7m 5g f5g f6s Dec 21] robust gelding: fairly useful winner at 2 yrs,
lightly raced since: fair form in 2001: left Mrs A. Perrett 2,000 gns after second start:
stays 7f: best efforts on good to firm/firm ground: races freely. *D. W. Chapman*

HIDDEN LAKE (IRE) 3 b.g. Lake Coniston (IRE) 131 – Valmarana (USA) 51 –
(Danzig Connection (USA)) [2001 –: f8g f11g⁴ f12g 11.5f 12.6f 16.2m⁶ 16.2m Jul 23]
little form. *Mrs A. J. Bowlby*

HIDDEN MEANING 3 ch.f. Cadeaux Genereux 131 – Cubby Hole (Town And **58**
Country 124) [2001 66: 6g⁶ 7.1m May 28] sturdy, lengthy filly: modest maiden, lightly
raced: well held on handicap debut final outing: likely to prove best up to 1m. *R. Hannon*

HIDDEN PEACE (USA) 3 ch.g. Gilded Time (USA) – Sanctuary (Welsh Pageant –
132) [2001 6d Apr 17] big, angular gelding: half-brother to several winners, including
high-class sprinter Sheikh Albadou (by Green Desert) and useful 1¾m/2m winner
Captain Jack (by Salse): dam unraced half-sister to Gold Cup winner Little Wolf: 12/1,
green and coltish, slowly away and never dangerous in maiden at Newmarket: gelded
after: seemed sure to improve: sold 3,500 gns in July, resold 1,200 gns in October. *Sir Michael Stoute*

HIDEAWAY HEROINE (IRE) 2 ch.f. (Mar 8) Hernando (FR) 127 – Dulcinea 73 **76**
(Selkirk (USA) 129) [2001 7f 7g³ 7.9d³ 8d³ Oct 25] 40,000Y: first foal: dam, 7f/1m
winner, half-sister to smart French performer up to 1¼m Amato out of smart winner up to
10.5f Ahohoney: fair maiden: favourite and tongue tied, third to Indian Solitaire at Bath
final start, making running and rallying: should stay at least 1¼m: acts on firm and good
to soft ground. *J. W. Hills*

HI-FALUTIN 5 b.m. Lugana Beach 116 – Hitravelscene (Mansingh (USA) 120) –
[2001 –: 10.3f 10f 8f Jul 22] seems of no account. *W. M. Brisbourne*

HIGH AND MIGHTY 6 b.g. Shirley Heights 130 – Air Distingue (USA) 120 (Sir **88**
Ivor 135) [2001 12d 16s 18.7f² 16m⁴ 20m Jun 20] sturdy, angular gelding: good mover:
useful handicapper in 1999: fairly useful nowadays: ¾-length second to Rainbow High in
Chester Cup in May then fourth at Kempton later in month: favourite, ran poorly in Ascot
Stakes final start: stays 2½m well: acts on firm and soft going: usually visored: seems
difficult to train. *G. Barnett*

HIGH BARN 4 b.f. Shirley Heights 130 – Mountain Lodge 120 (Blakeney 126) [2001 –
72p: 14v 13.9d Oct 13] rather leggy, lengthy filly: fair form in maidens at 3 yrs: well
beaten both starts in 2001: should be well suited by 1¾m+. *J. R. Fanshawe*

HIGH BEAUTY 4 br.f. High Kicker (USA) – Tendresse (IRE) 60 (Tender King 123) –
[2001 40: f16.2g Feb 8] probably of little account nowadays. *M. J. Ryan*

HIGH BLADE 3 b.f. Kris 135 – High Atlas 65 (Shirley Heights 130) [2001 10.4g³ **60**
10g³ 12d 9g Oct 9] medium-sized, quite good-topped filly: first foal: dam, ran once (twice
withdrawn after giving trouble at stalls), out of half-sister to high-class performer up to
1½m Sanglamore: modest maiden: sold from R. Charlton 4,000 gns after second start:
stays 1½m: blinkered (well beaten in claimer) final outing: very green/moved poorly to
post on debut. *Michael Cunningham, Ireland*

HIGHBURY LEGEND 6 ch.g. Mazilier (USA) 107 – Jans Contessa 68 (Rabdan –
129) [2001 e8g f12s⁵ Jan 16] winning handicapper in 1998: tailed off in 2001 on first Flat
outings since: visored twice at 2 yrs. *G. Brown*

HIGHCAL 4 gr.g. King's Signet (USA) 110 – Guarded Expression 51 (Siberian –
Express (USA) 125) [2001 56: 12m 12m 12.1d 12.3g 15.8m Sep 22] good-bodied
gelding: modest handicapper at best: well held in 2001: blinkered final outing. *Ronald Thompson*

Racing Post Trophy, Doncaster—High Chaparral (right) continues Aidan O'Brien's domination of the two-year-old colts' Group 1s; odds-on favourite and stable-companion Castle Gandolfo is caught near the finish; Redback, Mount Joy (left) and O'Brien's other runner Camp David follow them home

HIGH CHAPARRAL (IRE)   2 b.c. (Mar 1) Sadler's Wells (USA) 132 – Kasora   **115 p**
(IRE) (Darshaan 133) [2001 7.5g^2 7s* 8v* Oct 27]

'Sorry to disturb you, but I'm thinking your horse will beat the other one.' That, at least, is how one eaves-dropping correspondent reported the opening line of a phone call from champion trainer Aidan O'Brien to Kevin Darley three hours before the Racing Post Trophy at Doncaster in October. 'He was very green when he won last time at Tipperary. He has a lot of potential and if you can wait until the last furlong I think he'll go past Castle Gandolfo in this ground,' continued O'Brien, as related by Brough Scott in the *Sunday Telegraph*. Having whittled down his forty original entries to ten at the five-day stage and three at the final declarations, O'Brien, in America for the same day's Breeders' Cup meeting, had still given himself plenty to think about.

Darley's horse was High Chaparral. Unraced until the end of September, he had run in two maiden races over seven furlongs, when a short-head second to Hot Trotter at 15/8-on at Punchestown and a two-and-a-half-length winner when 3/1-on at Tipperary one week later. O'Brien had two other maiden winners in the Racing Post field, with Castle Gandolfo starting the 13/8-on favourite: in addition to his maiden success, Castle Gandolfo had taken the Group 3 Beresford Stakes at the Curragh, in which Camp David, the third Ballydoyle runner (a 20/1-shot) at Doncaster, was seven lengths back in second. The trio were all ridden by English jockeys, Darley joined by George Duffield on the favourite and Steve Drowne on Camp David. Castle Gandolfo had been odds on since the lists opened, with his smart form in the Beresford Stakes the most positive sign, though Duffield's booking was also reckoned to have significance as he had partnered Aristotle to victory for Ballydoyle in the same race two years earlier. Aristotle himself, however, had been the longest-priced of three O'Brien runners in the opening show on his Racing Post day, before going on to give his evidence in what is now a compelling case, that assumptions about the relative merits of those making up an Aidan O'Brien raiding party should not be made too readily. The trainer has doubtless always been aware of that. One indication that someone else also had an inkling came as High Chaparral was priced up at 33/1 with one bookmaker for the latest Racing Post at the five-day stage, at 20/1 after the final declarations, at a top price of 9/1 on the morning of the race and finally went off at 9/2.

No mention has so far been made of the British challenge for the British season's final Group 1 and little is required—the British trainers did not want to play. Richard Hannon saddled Redback (12/1) and James Given had Mr Sandancer (66/1), both exposed as useful at best after nine and five starts respectively. Godolphin put up a challenger in Mount Joy, having his first run for them and his second overall following his second in a Doncaster maiden at the start of August when trained by Barry Hills. He was sent off at 6/1 in a contest switched from the round course, but his contribution to the race was spoiled in the first two furlongs when he fought for his head. Over the last two furlongs, the prize was clearly on its way to Ballydoyle. Castle Gandolfo made smooth headway on the outside to challenge, and even with High Chaparral following him through, he was soon being acclaimed the winner. Darley's ride on High Chaparral had been far from easy, with High Chaparral running in snatches, and it did not get any easier, as the colt carried his head high and hung in to his left behind Castle Gandolfo. But eventually High Chaparral began to make up ground and hit the front in the last fifty yards to win going away by three quarters of a length. Redback was a further five lengths back in third.

High Chaparral (IRE) (b.c. Mar 1, 1999)	Sadler's Wells (USA) (b 1981)	Northern Dancer (b 1961)	Nearctic
			Natalma
		Fairy Bridge (b 1975)	Bold Reason
			Special
	Kasora (IRE) (b 1993)	Darshaan (br 1981)	Shirley Heights
			Delsy
		Kozana (br 1982)	Kris
			Koblenza

Sons and daughters of Sadler's Wells from Ballydoyle are not exactly a rarity and three yearling colts by Sadler's Wells were bought by Ballydoyle's agent Demi O'Byrne at the 2000 sales, all at the Houghton. The 3,400,000-guinea colt out of Darara is now called Diaghilev and was fifth of six in the Criterium de Saint-Cloud, and the 2,000,000-guinea son of La Papagena is Sorcerous, who won

Mr M. Tabor & Mrs John Magnier's "High Chaparral"

a Leopardstown maiden. High Chaparral cost 270,000 guineas, exactly the same sum that his dam Kasora had fetched at the Newmarket sale-ring, also unraced, but as a three-year-old at the December Sales rather than as a yearling. Kasora was trained by John Oxx and came from the Aga Khan Studs, as good a guarantee as any that she is well related. Half-sisters Kotama and Khanata both won listed One Thousand Guineas Trials at Leopardstown and a half-brother, Khoraz, was third in the National Stakes, but the star of the show is their dam Kozana, three times a winner over a mile and once over a mile and a quarter, twice in pattern events, before she was second to Rousillon in the Prix du Moulin, hampered but beaten only a length and a half, and third next time out behind Sagace and Rainbow Quest in the Arc, beaten by a neck and two lengths. Kozana's dam Koblenza won the 1969 Poule d'Essai des Pouliches and also produced the 1983 Prix du Cadran winner Karkour. Kasora's only foal before High Chaparral is the year-older Oriental Ben (by Ridgewood Ben), a fairly useful miler in Ireland who, however, got off the mark only in September of the latest season, at the tenth attempt. High Chaparral will stay a good deal further and is a candidate for one of the European Derbys. Which one, is very hard to say at this stage. Much may depend on whether connections think High Chaparral's round action will be able to cope with good ground or firmer—he clearly goes very well on heavy—and the gradients of Epsom, but there is also the question of his status among the massed ranks of plausible classic candidates housed at Ballydoyle. It may well be some time before that question is finally answered. High Chaparral has the scope to train on, but whether he does so also depends on his temperament. Greenness can sometimes eventually turn into a worse character trait, but the conclusion immediately after his Racing Post Trophy was that High Chaparral still seemed far from the finished article, a colt who was taking a while to get the hang of racing. He eventually got the hang of things in that race; if it also proves true of his career, then there is a great deal to look forward to. *A. P. O'Brien, Ireland*

HIGH DIVA　2 b.f. (Mar 15) Piccolo 121 – Gifted (Shareef Dancer (USA) 135) [2001 **65** 7m³ 7m³ f8.5g² Oct 9] 10,000Y: third foal: half-sister to a winner in Poland by Tirol: dam, of little account, half-sister to smart stayers Sergeyevich and Princess Sobieska: fair maiden: second to Hatter's Lad at Wolverhampton: should stay 1¼m. *J. W. Hills*

HIGHDOWN (IRE)　2 b.c. (Apr 2) Selkirk (USA) 129 – Rispoto 58 (Mtoto 134) **100** [2001 5.2m² 6m 6m* 7m⁴ 7m⁶ 7d 7s* 6v⁵ Oct 25] 34,000Y: leggy, useful-looking colt: fourth foal: half-brother to Irish 1999 2-y-o 1m winner Mitsubishi Trium (by Formidable) and Irish 9f winner Sweet Surrender (by Pennekamp): dam, 1½m winner, half-sister to smart performer up to 1¾m Jahafil: useful performer: won maiden at Goodwood in July and minor event at York (sweating, beat Jelani ¾ length) in October: respectable fifth to Captain Rio in Criterium de Maisons-Laffitte: will probably stay 1m: acts on soft and good to firm going. *M. R. Channon*

HIGH DRAMA　4 b.g. In The Wings 128 – Maestrale (Top Ville 129) [2001 63?: 10g **50** f12g 14.1g⁴ 16m³ 18m⁶ 16.2m⁶ 15m³ 16.2s 16m 16.2m* 15.8m* 17.2g 15.8d Oct 9] leggy gelding: modest handicapper: won at Warwick (apprentices) and Catterick in September: seems best at 1¾m/2m: acts on good to firm going: blinkered once: held up: sold 15,000 gns. *W. R. Muir*

HIGHER CIRCLE (USA)　2 ch.f. (Jan 24) Diesis 133 – Captive Island 116 (North- **82** fields (USA)) [2001 7m⁵ 7.5g⁵ 7d² Oct 6] angular filly: closely related to Derby Italiano/US Grade 1 1¾m winner Single Empire (by Kris) and half-sister to several winners, notably smart performer up to 2m Court of Honour (by Law Society): dam French 6f and 1m winner, including at 2 yrs: best effort in maidens (fairly useful form) when 1¼ lengths second to Atarama at Redcar, well there until inside final 1f: should stay 1¼m: joined N. O'Callaghan in USA. *J. H. M. Gosden*

HIGH ESTEEM　5 b.g. Common Grounds 118 – Whittle Woods Girl 80 (Emarati **62** (USA) 74) [2001 57, a65: f6s⁶ f6g f8s f7g³ f7g⁵ 6g 5g* 5s 5g⁴ 5v 5d* f6g* Dec 10] big gelding: modest performer: won handicaps at Ripon (seller) and Southwell and claimer at Catterick in second half of year: effective at 5f to 7f: acts on any turf going and fibresand: has hung left: none too consistent. *M. A. Buckley*

HIGHEST (IRE)　2 b.c. (Apr 28) Selkirk (USA) 129 – Pearl Kite (USA) 106§ (Silver **98 p** Hawk (USA) 123) [2001 8d² Oct 19] 125,000Y: strong, useful-looking colt: fourth foal: half-brother to 4-y-o Shamaiel and Irish 6.5f winner Pearl Barley (by Polish Precedent):

dam, 2-y-o 1m winner who stayed 1¾m, not one to trust: 12/1, burly and green, shaped very well when head second of 20 to Music Club (pair 4 lengths clear) in maiden at Newmarket, off bridle in mid-field some way out before finishing strongly: will be suited by 1¼m/1½m: had 2 handlers in paddock, and moved unimpressively to post: sure to win a similar event before going on to better things. *Sir Michael Stoute*

HIGHFIELD FIZZ   9 b.m. Efisio 120 – Jendor 82 (Condorcet (FR)) [2001 52, a–: 16s 13.1m⁶ 16.1m 14.1m⁵ 17.1m⁵ 14.1m 16f* 16.2f 16f 15s⁶ 14.1m 17.5m 17.1d Oct 8] good-topped mare: has a round action: poor handicapper: won at Musselburgh in June: stays 2¼m: acts on any turf going: tried visored: has reportedly had breathing problems: tends to carry head high. *C. W. Fairhurst*   **41** **a–**

HIGH FINALE   2 b.f. (Apr 21) Sure Blade (USA) 130 – High Velocity 53 (Frimley Park 109) [2001 5d 5m² 5m² 5m² 5.1m* 5m⁵ 5.2m 5m⁵ 5f Sep 4] leggy, workmanlike filly: sister to fairly useful 1997 2-y-o 5f winner Banningham Blade and half-sister to 3 winners, including 5f (at 2 yrs) to 1¼m winner Anokato (by Tina's Pet): dam 5f performer: fairly useful performer: made all in maiden at Chester in July: below form last 3 starts: likely to prove best at 5f: tried visored. *K. T. Ivory*   **85**

HIGH HOYLAND   5 b.g. High Estate 127 – Waffling 68 (Lomond (USA) 128) [2001 8f Jul 9] fair maiden in 1999: reportedly finished lame only outing since: blinkered once. *Jedd O'Keeffe*   **–**

HIGHLAND FLIGHT   3 gr.f. Missed Flight 123 – In The Highlands (Petong 126) [2001 57: 5.2m 5m p5g⁵ p6g⁶ Dec 19] smallish filly: poor maiden handicapper: best form at 5f: acts on polytrack and good to firm going. *Bob Jones*   **49**

HIGHLAND GAIT   2 ch.f. (Mar 12) Most Welcome 131 – Miller's Gait 74§ (Mill Reef (USA) 141) [2001 6g 6m 6.1m⁵ Jul 14] half-sister to 3 winners, including 9-y-o Welton Arsenal and smart stayer Bold Gait (by Persian Bold): dam, ungenuine middle-distance maiden, half-sister to high-class stayer/hurdler Royal Gait: modest form in maidens: should be suited by at least 1¼m. *T. D. Easterby*   **59**

HIGHLAND GOLD (IRE)   4 ch.g. Indian Ridge 123 – Anjuli (Northfields (USA)) [2001 57: 9v 8d⁶ 11.1d* 8.3m 12f² 13d² 12.4m 14f² 13s² 10.5d⁶ 11.1d⁴ 11.1d⁵ 14m⁶ 12.1g⁵ 17.5m⁶ Sep 21] big gelding: fair performer: won maiden at Hamilton in May: best up to easy 1¾m: acts on any going: held up: none too consistent. *Miss L. A. Perratt*   **65**

HIGHLAND REEL   4 ch.g. Selkirk (USA) 129 – Taj Victory 68 (Final Straw 127) [2001 98p: 8v² 10s 8s 8m 8.5m³ 7m 8g 8g⁶ Aug 11] leggy, unfurnished gelding: useful handicapper: good 2 lengths second to Nimello in Lincoln at Doncaster in March: in-and-out form after, not discredited when close third at Epsom fifth outing and sixth at Ascot (met trouble) on final one: best around 1m: acts on heavy and good to firm going: races freely: has wandered: saddle reportedly slipped fourth outing. *D. R. C. Elsworth*   **106**

HIGHLAND SHOT   3 b.f. Selkirk (USA) 129 – Optaria 83 (Song 132) [2001 7m⁶ 8.1v⁴ Sep 28] quite good-topped filly: fifth foal: half-sister to 3 winners, notably smart performers Grey Shot (up to 2m, by Sharrood) and Night Shot (sprinter, by Night Shift): dam sprinter: better effort in maidens 3½ months apart (modest form) at Haydock final outing. *I. A. Balding*   **57**

HIGHLAND WARRIOR   2 b.c. (Feb 18) Makbul 104 – Highland Rowena 59 (Royben 125) [2001 6m⁴ 5d 5m 6g Aug 21] 19,000F, 38,000Y: big, leggy colt: sixth foal: brother to 6f winner Kilbrannan Sound and 6-y-o Lord Kintyre, and half-brother to 2 winning sprinters, including useful Crofters Ceilidh (by Scottish Reel): dam sprinter: fair maiden: well beaten in nursery at York final start: likely to prove best at 5f/6f. *J. S. Goldie*   **71**

HIGHLAND WELCOME   5 b.g. Most Welcome 131 – Highland Hannah (IRE) (Persian Heights 129) [2001 f11g⁴ f12g⁵ Jan 8] first foal: dam, unraced, out of useful sprinter who became untrustworthy Hana Marie: poor form in maidens at Southwell when belatedly tried on Flat: stays 1½m: looked none too keen final outing. *W. Jarvis*   **48**

HIGHLY FANCIED   5 b.m. High Kicker (USA) – Angie's Darling (Milford 119) [2001 –: 7s 12f Aug 1] fair maiden at 2 yrs: little form since: tried tongue tied. *A. C. Whillans*   **–**

HIGHLY PLEASED (USA)   6 b.g. Hansel (USA) – Bint Alfalla (USA) (Nureyev (USA) 131) [2001 54+: 8.3m f8.5g² f9.4g Nov 21] quite good-topped gelding: poor maiden, lightly raced nowadays: left J. Fox after reappearance: stays 8.5f: acts on firm ground and fibresand: reportedly bled from nose final start. *P. Burgoyne*   **46**

HIGHLY SOCIABLE   4 b.f. Puissance 110 – Come To Tea (IRE) (Be My Guest   –
(USA) 126) [2001 –: 6.1f f6g⁶ Jul 20] maiden: no form since 2 yrs. *B. A. McMahon*

HIGH PADDY   2 b.g. (Mar 19) Master Willie 129 – Ivy Edith (Blakeney 126) [2001   –
8.1g Sep 13] second foal: dam fairly useful 2m hurdler: tailed off in maiden at Chepstow.
R. Ingram

HIGH PASTURE (USA)   3 b. or br.f. El Gran Senor (USA) 136 – Summer Retreat   62
(USA) 78 (Gone West (USA)) [2001 60: 8m 8g⁵ 10m Jul 20] unfurnished filly: modest
maiden, lightly raced: stays 1m: best efforts on good/good to soft going: sold 25,000 gns
in December. *R. Charlton*

HIGH PITCHED   3 ch.c. Indian Ridge 123 – Place de L'Opera 98 (Sadler's Wells   116 p
(USA) 132) [2001 12m² 12m³ 11.9g* 12g* 12d* 12d* Nov 2]
      As in 1998, the Group 3 St Simon Stakes was transferred to the following
week's Newmarket fixture after Newbury's final scheduled meeting of the season
had to be abandoned because the course was waterlogged. Five of the eight
declared to run at Newbury turned out at Newmarket—Little Rock the only notable
absentee—which left Mubtaker, Head In The Clouds and High Pitched as the chief
contenders. The first two had run out five-length winners of their previous starts,
Mubtaker in a listed event over the course and distance and Head In The Clouds in
the Group 3 Princess Royal Stakes at Ascot. High Pitched, on the other hand, was
taking a marked step up in class, though he was improving rapidly and the smart
form he had shown when winning a handicap on his previous start, also over a mile
and a half at Newmarket, suggested strongly that he was more than capable of
making an impact at this level. That victory had been his third in succession,
following on from those in a maiden at Haydock and a handicap at Doncaster, and
High Pitched had justified strong support in good style by two lengths from Celtic
Mission, making smooth progress to lead inside the final furlong and running on
strongly. The strong pace at which both the handicaps were run suited High Pitched
ideally, as he is a tricky ride, best produced late. Fortunately for High Pitched, Head
In The Clouds ensured that the Levy Board St Simon Stakes was a truly-run contest
too. The closing stages concerned only this pair, the odds-on Mubtaker having
folded tamely when asked for his effort. High Pitched's tendency to hang left under
pressure was even more pronounced this time and he ended up against the stand
rail, but he still managed to collar Head In The Clouds near the finish to win by a
length and a quarter. Once again High Pitched was going on strongly at the finish,
and there's no doubt that he will stay at least a mile and three quarters. That's the
distance of the Yorkshire Cup, a race which looks an obvious starting point for his
four-year-old campaign. The chances are that High Pitched will stay even further,
and he could also prove a major contender for good races at two miles. High Pitched
still has further improvement to make to reach the standard set by the leading
stayers, but he should continue on the upgrade for some time yet and eventually
bridge that gap. Unraced at two years, High Pitched has had only six outings and is
still relatively inexperienced. With more runs under his belt, it is also possible his
wayward tendencies may be ironed out.

		Ahonoora	Lorenzaccio
	Indian Ridge	(ch 1975)	Helen Nicholls
	(ch 1985)	Hillbrow	Swing Easy
High Pitched		(ch 1975)	Golden City
(ch.c. 1998)		Sadler's Wells	Northern Dancer
	Place de L'Opera	(b 1981)	Fairy Bridge
	(b 1993)	Madame Dubois	Legend of France
		(ch 1987)	Shadywood

     High Pitched, a 38,000-guinea yearling, is from a family which has proved
highly successful for Warren Place over many years, first of all for Sir Noel Murless
and since then for Henry Cecil. All three mares on the bottom line of the pedigree
won races for Cecil, High Pitched's grandam Madame Dubois (also dam of the
2000 Gran Criterium winner Count Dubois) the pick of this trio. Her five victories
as a three-year-old included those in the Park Hill Stakes and Prix de Royallieu.
Madame Dubois' daughter Place de L'Opera fractured a sesamoid and, like High
Pitched who is her first foal, was not raced at two. She quickly developed into a

useful performer at a mile and a half at three, though, winning a maiden at Thirsk and a minor event at Leicester; and she might have shown even better form given the opportunity to race over further. The good-bodied High Pitched has yet to race on extremes of going, and gained his wins on good and good to soft ground. *H. R. A. Cecil*

HIGH POINT (IRE) 3 b.c. Ela-Mana-Mou 132 – Top Lady (IRE) 83 (Shirley Heights 130) [2001 p10g Dec 29] 11,000 3-y-o: second foal: dam, 1½m and 1¾m winner, half-sister to high-class middle-distance performer Emmson (by Ela-Mana-Mou): 33/1, soon behind in maiden at Lingfield on debut. *G. P. Enright* —

HIGH POLICY (IRE) 5 ch.g. Machiavellian (USA) 123 – Road To The Top 84 (Shirley Heights 130) [2001 65: f16.2s⁴ 16v⁵ 14.1s 14m⁴ 14g 14.1m 16m⁶ 16d* 17.1d² 18s 13.8d³ f16g* f16g* f14g* f14.8g³ Dec 11] well-made gelding: fairly useful handicapper on all-weather, modest on turf: won at Nottingham in September and Southwell (3) in November: effective at 1¾m to 17f: acts on heavy going and fibresand: tried visored, not in 2001: held up: has started slowly/flashed tail. *R. Hollinshead* **61 a84**

HIGH PROSPECT (IRE) 3 b.g. Lycius (USA) 124 – Pay The Bank 81 (High Top 131) [2001 10d 10s 10g 9.7d⁶ 9.9s 9.9d 11.8s⁵ Oct 16] 22,000Y: tall, rather leggy, quite good-topped gelding: sixth foal: half-brother to several winners, including smart 5f (at 2 yrs) to 7f winner My Branch (by Distant Relative) and 4-y-o Banco Suivi: dam 2-y-o 1m winner who stayed 1¼m: modest maiden: should stay beyond 1¼m: had breathing problem on third start: sold 8,000 gns. *N. A. Graham* **56**

HIGH ROCK HENRY (IRE) 2 ch.c. (Feb 1) Pennekamp (USA) 130 – Belsay 68 (Belmez (USA) 131) [2001 6g⁵ 6g 6m⁴ 6.1d Sep 21] 29,000F, 42,000Y: first foal: dam, ran twice in Ireland, closely related to smart performer up to 1m Crystal Gazing and half-sister to useful performer up to 1¼m Wainwright: fair maiden: fourth at Brighton: will probably stay 1m: sold 7,000 gns. *J. Noseda* **65**

HIGH SHOW 3 ch.g. Superlative 118 – Just Like You (Sandhurst Prince 128) [2001 8.3g 11.7m Sep 10] first reported foal: dam ran twice: well beaten in maidens. *N. M. Babbage* —

HIGH SIERRA (IRE) 2 b.c. (Feb 20) Danehill (USA) 126 – Direct Lady (IRE) (Fools Holme (USA)) [2001 8m* 8s⁵ Sep 29] small, compact colt: fourth foal: half-brother to fairly useful 1998 Irish 2-y-o 7f winner Aeraiocht (by Tenby): dam, Irish 11f/1½m winner (also successful over hurdles), half-sister to good Irish 2-y-o winners Cois Na Tine and Eva Luna: useful maiden: justified favouritism in maiden at Tralee in August by 4 lengths from Kasparov: 11/2 and wearing crossed noseband, 5½ lengths fifth of 9 to stable-mate Mutinyonthebounty in Royal Lodge Stakes at Ascot, under pressure before straight: should be suited by 1¼m/1½m: open to further improvement. *A. P. O'Brien, Ireland* **100 p**

HIGH SOCIETY LADY (IRE) 3 ch.f. General Monash (USA) 107 – Bardia 42 (Jalmood (USA) 126) [2001 37: f8g f8g f11g 8.2s 7m 8m 6g Jun 19] plain, good-topped filly: of little account nowadays. *N. Bycroft* —

HIGH SPOT 3 b.f. Shirley Heights 130 – Rash Gift 78 (Cadeaux Genereux 131) [2001 67: 10.2m³ 12m 11.8d⁴ 12m Aug 30] strong, good-bodied filly: fair maiden: disappointing after eye-catching reappearance: should stay 1½m: acts on good to firm going: blinkered (raced freely/found little/wandered) penultimate start, visored final one: has run in snatches: sold 6,000 gns in December. *R. Charlton* **73**

HIGHSTREET FLIGHT (IRE) 2 br.g. (Apr 28) Darnay 117 – La Calera (Corvaro (USA) 124) [2001 f8g f7g Dec 14] IR 5,500F, IR 7,800Y: half-brother to fairly useful 1990 2-y-o 6f/7f winner Spice Trader (by Burslem) and 3 winners abroad: dam Irish 1¼m winner: last in maidens. *J. Nicol* —

HIGH SUN 5 b.g. High Estate 127 – Clyde Goddess (IRE) 92 (Scottish Reel 123) [2001 54: 8d³ 8d 8.3d² 8.3m* 8m² 9f⁵ 9.2d⁵ 8f³ 9.2g² 7.1f² 9f⁴ 9.2g⁴ 8f 8.3m⁶ 8g Nov 7] heavy-topped gelding: modest handicapper: won at Hamilton in May: effective at 7f to 1¼m: acts on firm and good to soft going: tried blinkered: sometimes slowly away. *P. Monteith* **54**

HIGH TEMPO 3 b.g. Piccolo 121 – Reem Fever (IRE) 79 (Fairy King (USA)) [2001 –: 8.1v 8m 7m 10f 10m f11g Nov 30] workmanlike gelding: no form: has been blinkered/tongue tied. *K. R. Burke* —

HIGH TENSION (USA) 6 b.h. Sadler's Wells (USA) 132 – Very Confidential –
(USA) (Fappiano (USA)) [2001 12m⁵ 16d Nov 2] tall horse: fairly useful winner at 3 yrs:
showed little only 2 outings since. *Miss Z. C. Davison*

HIGHTORI (FR) 4 b.c. Vettori (IRE) 119 – High Mecene (FR) (Highest Honor **129**
(FR) 124) [2001 119: a10f* a10f³ 9.3m² 10m³ 12m³ 12m* 12s Oct 7]
    Good enough to run in the top championship races, but not good enough
to win them might seem a fair summary of Hightori judged strictly on his racing
record. But there is a little more to it than that. He came agonisingly close to
winning the Group 1 Prix d'Ispahan at Longchamp in May, having his head in front
a stride before and a stride after the line, and was unlucky not to finish second to
Galileo—some thought he might have won—when suffering serious interference
early in the straight in the King George VI and Queen Elizabeth Stakes. Hightori's
effort at Ascot was the best of his career; he finished third beaten two lengths
and a length by Galileo and Fantastic Light in a strong renewal of Britain's most
prestigious all-aged race, keeping on after being badly hampered by Fantastic
Light's weakening pacemaker Give The Slip. The King George was only Hightori's
second race over a mile and a half—he had come a good fifth to Sinndar in the
Arc the previous year—and his regular jockey Gerald Mosse gave him a patient
ride. He did, though, come in for criticism for trying to make his run against the far
rail. The owner Gary Tanaka's associate Andy Smith, who was responsible for the
purchase of Hightori just before his tilt at the Arc as a three-year-old, said after the
King George: 'He should have come down the outside. The horse got completely
blocked and the jockey almost fell off. When he got through he was full of running.'
Hightori still finished closer to Fantastic Light than he had in their encounter in
the Prince of Wales's Stakes over a mile and a quarter at Royal Ascot, where the
staying-on Hightori went down by two and a half lengths and three quarters of a
length to the winner and Kalanisi. Hightori had Observatory—to whom he had lost
by a short head in the Prix d'Ispahan—a length and a quarter behind him in fourth.
Mosse also set Hightori a fair bit to do at Royal Ascot, eliciting from the horse's
trainer the view that 'he was too far out of his ground, this wasn't the last handicap
of the afternoon.'
    On the face of it at least, reverting to a mile and a half in the King George
seemed to suit Hightori and he was generally ante-post second favourite with
bookmakers for the Prix de l'Arc de Triomphe when he took the field for one of
the main trials, the Prix Foy, over the Arc course and distance in mid-September.
Hightori hadn't run since the King George, missing an intended outing in the
Grosser Preis von Baden, for which he had been supplemented, when found to
have a dental problem (necessitating the removal of two teeth). There was some
speculation that Mosse might lose the ride on Hightori, but he was in the saddle

Prix Foy - Gray d'Albion Barriere, Longchamp—Hightori pulls out no more than required;
Idaho Quest (No.3) battles on for second place, ahead of Slew The Red (No.1) and Little Rock

again in the Prix Foy in which he kept the odds-on Hightori close up throughout. Mosse rode confidently but Hightori was anything but impressive, racing lazily once in front and pulling out no more than was required to hold off Idaho Quest and Slew The Red by half a length and three quarters of a length. With the Arc shaping up into a far better race than had appeared likely at one stage, Hightori started only fifth favourite on the day, behind Sakhee, Aquarelliste, Milan (coupled with his pacemaker) and Golan. He was beaten by all four, managing only seventh, a place behind the Prix Foy fourth Little Rock and beaten ten lengths by the runaway winner Sakhee. Mosse couldn't be blamed this time, Hightori never travelling with his usual fluency through the race—on and off the bit before keeping on steadily in the straight—and clearly running below his best. Hightori was successful in very testing conditions as a two-year-old, winning the Prix Thomas Bryon, so it could well be that there is an explanation other than the going being unsuitable for his performance. It is interesting to note that he wore blinkers when winning the Maktoum Challenge (Round III) at Nad Al Sheba in March on his reappearance by half a length from Broche, and an eyecover when beaten three lengths and half a length by Captain Steve and To The Victory in the Dubai World Cup on the same course later in the month. Perhaps he needs his mind to be kept on the job in hand.

			Machiavellian	Mr Prospector
		Vettori (IRE)	(b 1987)	Coup de Folie
		(b 1992)	Air Distingue	Sir Ivor
Hightori (FR)			(b 1980)	Euryanthe
(b.c. 1997)			Highest Honor	Kenmare
		High Mecene (FR)	(gr 1983)	High River
		(b 1990)	Belle Mecene	Gay Mecene
			(b 1982)	Djaka Belle

Hightori, a tall individual, was not guaranteed on pedigree to prove fully effective over as far as a mile and a half. His sire Vettori was a miler, winner of the Poule d'Essai des Poulains and third in the St James's Palace Stakes, though he wasn't discredited when sixth in the Derby. Hightori's dam High Mecene never saw a racecourse but is closely related to the very smart French miler Kendor (who is by High Mecene's grandsire Kenmare out of the unraced Belle Mecene). Hightori is the second foal out of High Mecene, whose first Loi d'Homme (by Homme de Loi) has been successful at up to a mile and a quarter in the French Provinces. The consistent Hightori was sold after the Arc and is to continue his career in Saudi Arabia, where, on his first appearance, he finished in mid-division in the Crown Prince's Cup over an extended two miles on dirt at Riyadh in November. *P. H. Demercastel, France*

HIGH YIELDER (IRE)   3 b. or br.g. Namaqualand (USA) – Cadisa 82 (Top Ville   –
129) [2001 10d 10m 14m 11.5g 14.1s Oct 31] IR 3,600F, 8,000Y: eighth foal: half-brother to 3 winners, including fairly useful Irish 1¾m winner Caliandak (by Darshaan) and Irish 1¼m winner Calounia (by Pharly): dam 11f winner: looks of little account. *Pat Mitchell*

HI HO SILCA   2 b.f. (Feb 17) Atraf 116 – You Make Me Real (USA) [Give Me   **56**
Strength (USA)] [2001 6m⁶ 6g² Aug 20] 37,000F, 52,000Y: sixth foal: half-sister to 4-y-o Natural and 3 winners in Ireland, including useful 1998 2-y-o 5f/6f winner Camargo (by Brief Truce), later successful in USA, and 9f and 1¾m winner Real Guest (by Be My Guest): dam minor winner in USA: modest form in maidens at Hamilton and Brighton (4 lengths second to Zamyatina): should stay 7f. *M. R. Channon*

HILL COUNTRY (IRE)   3 b.c. Danehill (USA) 126 – Rose of Jericho (USA)   **115**
(Alleged (USA) 138) [2001 109p: 11m 12g* 12m 11.9g⁶ 12d² Sep 14] well-made colt: smart performer: game winner of minor event at Newmarket in July by head from Nooshman: best effort when head second to Ekraar in listed race at Doncaster final start, never quite able to shake off winner and touched off close home: well held otherwise at 3 yrs, including in Gordon Stakes at Goodwood and Great Voltigeur Stakes at York: stays 1½m: best on good going or softer (acts on heavy ground): unimpressive to post first 2 starts at 3 yrs: sold privately. *J. H. M. Gosden*

HILLESLEY HENRY   6 gr.g. Zambrano – Diddy Girl 42 (Comedy Star (USA) 121)   –
[2001 8m Jun 4] no show in bumpers or claimer on Flat debut. *Dr P. Pritchard*

HILL FARM DANCER   10 ch.m. Gunner B 126 – Loadplan Lass 63 (Nicholas Bill   **42**
125) [2001 42, a51: f12g* f12g⁴ f12g⁵ f14g⁶ f12g f12g⁴ Mar 24] sparely-made mare:
fluent mover: poor handicapper: won amateur race at Wolverhampton in February:
effective at 1½m to 2m: acts on firm going, soft and fibresand: held up: often slowly
away: has wandered/refused to race: often claimer ridden. *W. M. Brisbourne*

HILL MAGIC   6 br.g. Magic Ring (IRE) 115 – Stock Hill Lass 87 (Air Trooper 115)   **75**
[2001 83: 7s 6g 6m³ Aug 16] close-coupled, useful-looking gelding: fair handicapper:
best at 6f/7f: acts on firm and good to soft going: none too consistent. *L. G. Cottrell*

HILLS OF GOLD   2 b.c. (Mar 21) Danehill (USA) 126 – Valley of Gold (FR) 117   **103 p**
(Shirley Heights 130) [2001 7m* Sep 12] big, lengthy colt: has scope: has a fluent, quick
action: second foal: dam, 1¼m/11f (Oaks d'Italia) winner, granddaughter of US Grade 1
8.5f/1¼m winner White Star Line: 20/1, created good impression when winning 8-runner
minor event at Doncaster by 1¾ lengths from Mr Sandancer, quickening to lead over 1f
out and keeping on well despite looking green: will stay at least 1m: smart performer in
the making, sure to win more races. *B. W. Hills*

HILLTOP WARNING   4 b.g. Reprimand 122 – Just Irene 50 (Sagaro 133) [2001 84:   **101**
e6g⁶ 7m* 7m* 7m⁵ 7m* 7g³ 7g⁴ Sep 19] smallish gelding: useful handicapper: had a
good season, winning at Goodwood in May, Yarmouth in June and Epsom (beat Whale
Beach by 1¾ lengths despite carrying head awkwardly) in August: creditable efforts at
Goodwood last 2 starts: best around 7f: easily best form on good/good to firm ground:
blinkered once at 3 yrs: tends to edge left: held up: reliable. *S. P. C. Woods*

HILL WELCOME   3 ch.f. Most Welcome 131 – Tarvie 101 (Swing Easy (USA) 126)   **50**
[2001 52: e7g f7s⁵ f11g e10g Feb 24] small, workmanlike filly: modest maiden: stays 7f:
acts on firm going, good to soft and fibresand: tongue tied on reappearance: sold 3,000
gns in March. *B. W. Hills*

HILTON HEAD   3 b.f. Primo Dominie 121 – Low Hill (Rousillon (USA) 133) [2001   **76**
66p: 8m⁶ 6m 6d 6f⁴ 6d² 5m 5s Sep 8] sturdy filly: fair performer: ran mostly creditably in
handicaps/minor events: best effort at 6f, should prove equally as effective at 5f: acts on
firm and good to soft going. *T. D. Easterby*

HILTON PARK (IRE)   2 b.f. (Mar 27) Dolphin Street (FR) 125 – Test Case 90   **34**
(Busted 134) [2001 f5g f5g⁵ f6g⁶ 7g f9.4g Dec 8] IR 4,000Y, 2,000 2-y-o: leggy filly:
seventh living foal: half-sister to 1½m winner Mock Trial (by Old Vic) and 5-y-o Red
Cafe: dam 1m winner: poor maiden: should stay 6f: tried visored. *P. D. Evans*

HIM OF DISTINCTION   2 br.c. (Apr 19) Rainbow Quest (USA) 134 – Air of   **93 p**
Distinction (IRE) 99 (Distinctly North (USA) 115) [2001 7g⁵ 7.9d* Oct 13] smallish colt:
second foal: closely related to 3-y-o Man of Distinction: dam Irish 6f winner, including
Anglesey Stakes at 2 yrs: fairly useful form: still not fully wound up, justified favouritism
in maiden at York by 1½ lengths from Halawellfin Hala, never far away: will stay 1¼m:
capable of better. *J. L. Dunlop*

HI MUJTAHID (IRE)   7 ch.g. Mujtahid (USA) 118 – High Tern 93 (High Line 125)   **– §**
[2001 37§, a52§: f9.4s e8g f8.5s 8f 9.9d f8g f8.5g f6g p7̄g Dec 19] lengthy, good-
quartered gelding: temperamental handicapper nowadays: tried blinkered. *J. M. Bradley*

HINCHLEY WOOD (IRE)   2 b.g. (Feb 22) Fayruz 116 – Audriano (IRE) (Cyrano   **–**
de Bergerac 120) [2001 f8.5s 7.9d Oct 12] IR 9,600F, 10,000Y: second foal: dam ran once
in Ireland: well beaten in maidens. *K. McAuliffe*

HINDI   5 b.g. Indian Ridge 123 – Tootsiepop (USA) (Robellino (USA) 127) [2001 74:   **–**
f11g Jan 12] workmanlike gelding: fair maiden handicapper at best: well beaten only
5-y-o outing: tried blinkered. *N. A. Graham*

HI NICKY   5 ch.m. High Kicker (USA) – Sharp Top 62 (Sharpo 132) [2001 48: 8v f12g   **–**
f14g f14g f8s Dec 21] of little account nowadays. *M. J. Polglase*

HINT OF MAGIC   4 b.g. Magic Ring (IRE) 115 – Thames Glow 69 (Kalaglow 132)   **71 d**
[2001 79d: e10g⁶ e8g* 8s³ 7m 8m 8.1m 8m 8s Sep 24] tall, leggy gelding: fair handicapper: won at Lingfield in March: ran poorly last 5 starts: stays 1¼m: acts on soft going
and equitrack: blinkered penultimate start: tongue tied twice in 2000: carries head
awkwardly. *J. G. Portman*

HIRAETH   3 b.f. Petong 126 – Floppie (FR) (Law Society (USA) 130) [2001 76: 7s   **58**
6f⁴ f7g 6v Nov 8] good-topped filly: fair form at 2 yrs: well below that level in 2001,
including when making all in maiden at Catterick in August: stays 6f: probably acts on
any turf going. *B. Palling*

HIRAPOUR (IRE) 5 b.g. Kahyasi 130 – Himaya (IRE) (Mouktar 129) [2001 101: **107**
12m* 12m 13.4d[5] 16f* 18d Oct 20] strong, workmanlike gelding: has a round action:
useful performer: won minor event at Newmarket (by 1½ lengths from Carly's Quest) in
June and handicap at Newbury (comfortably by 3 lengths from Gold Standard) in
September: shaped better than result suggests when eighth of 31 to Distant Prospect in
Cesarewitch at Newmarket final outing, becoming poorly placed as principals kicked
then staying on when switched: stays 2¼m: acts on firm and soft going: blinkered (below
form) twice at 4 yrs: effective racing prominently or held up. *Mrs A. J. Perrett*

HI RED 2 ch.f. (Feb 5) Atraf 116 – Red River Rose (IRE) 51 (Red Sunset 120) [2001 **75 d**
5d[2] 5.1d[4] 6m 6m 7m[4] 7m[5] 7m[5] 7m* 8g[2] 8m[6] 8s f8g p8g Dec 12] 13,000Y: sparely-made
filly: second foal: dam 2-y-o 6f winner who stayed 1m: fair performer: won claimer at
Salisbury in August: below form after next start: stays 1m: acts on good to firm and good
to soft going: blinkered 5 of last 6 starts: possibly temperamental. *J. G. Portman*

HIRVINE (FR) 3 ch.g. Snurge 130 – Guadanella (FR) (Guadanini (FR) 125) [2001 **–**
12v[6] Apr 7] 75,000 francs Y: half-brother to 3 winners in France, including 10.5f to 1½m
winner Harebelle (by Hero's Honor): dam French 1¼m to 13f winner: 33/1, ran as if
needing race when well held in Musselburgh maiden. *T. P. Tate*

HISTORIC TREBLE 2 b.c. (May 9) Lycius (USA) 124 – Alfaaselah (GER) 97 **81 +**
(Dancing Brave (USA) 140) [2001 6m[4] 6f[4] 6s[2] 6m[2] 5s* 5g 6v[2] Oct 17] rather leggy colt:
second foal: half-brother to French 11f/1½m winner Benhabeebi (by Bin Ajwaad),
ungenuine in Britain: dam, 7f (at 2 yrs) to 9.5f (in Germany) winner, from family of
Urban Sea and Galileo: fairly useful performer: won maiden at Haydock in September:
good efforts in nursery and minor event (possibly improved when second to Lady Links
at Lingfield) after: should stay 7f: acts on any going. *B. Hanbury*

HIT THE TRAIL (IRE) 3 b.f. Treasure Kay 114 – Shoot The Dealer (IRE) 74 **–**
(Common Grounds 118) [2001 54: 5.1s 6s May 2] medium-sized, workmanlike filly:
modest form in maiden only 2-y-o start: no encouragement both starts at 3 yrs. *J. L. Eyre*

HOAX (IRE) 2 b.c. (Apr 3) Robellino (USA) 127 – Hocus 88 (High Top 131) [2001 **93**
5.1m[4] 6m* 6f[4] 7.1f* 7m[4] 7m[4] 7g 8g[2] 7g[2] 7s Sep 30] IR 22,000Y: half-brother to several
winners, including 5f (at 2 yrs in Ireland) to 1m (in Hong Kong) winner Jamieson (by Be
My Chief) and 8.5f and 9.4f winner High Noon (by Shirley Heights): dam 7f winner:
fairly useful performer: won maiden at Southwell in May and minor event at Warwick in
June: good second in nurseries at Doncaster and Epsom: stays 1m: acts on firm going, ran
poorly on soft: blinkered (well beaten) seventh start: sold 52,000 gns, joined D. Vienna in
USA. *R. F. Johnson Houghton*

HO CHOI 2 b.c. (Feb 13) Pivotal 124 – Witch of Fife (USA) 91 (Lear Fan (USA) 130) **102**
[2001 6f[6] 6g[2] 6m[4] Sep 12] 20,000Y: good-topped colt: has scope: first living foal: dam,
2-y-o 6f/7f winner, half-sister to 6-y-o Hudood: won maiden at Ayr in June: useful form
when 3 lengths second of 9 to Rock of Gibraltar in Gimcrack Stakes at York: respectable
fourth of 22 to Acclamation in valuable sales race at Doncaster: should be suited by 7f/
1m: raced only on good going or firmer. *Miss L. A. Perratt*

HOH EXPRESS 9 b.g. Waajib 121 – Tissue Paper 95 (Touch Paper 113) [2001 20m **–**
Jun 20] rangy gelding: fairly useful handicapper on Flat in 1998: well held in Ascot
Stakes at Royal Ascot on only Flat outing since: usually held up. *P. R. Webber*

HOH GEM 5 b.g. Be My Chief (USA) 122 – Jennies' Gem 95 (Sayf El Arab (USA) **–**
127) [2001 53, a58: f8g f9.4g[3] f8s[6] f8g Mar 13] big, lengthy gelding: modest handi- **a49**
capper: sold out of B. R. Millman's stable 6,000 gns after second start, left N. Tinkler
after third: stayed 9.4f: acted on heavy going and on fibresand: often got well behind:
dead. *Don Enrico Incisa*

HOH INVADER (IRE) 9 b.g. Accordion – Newgate Fairy (Flair Path 122) [2001 **78**
10.1d[4] 12.4m[3] 10g[2] 16m[2] 16.1f[6] f14g f16g Nov 12] tall gelding: fairly useful hurdler/ **a–**
chaser: fair maiden on Flat: may prove best at 1¼m/1½m: acts on good to firm going:
often races prominently: has found little/been blinkered over jumps. *Mrs A. Duffield*

HOH NO 5 b.g. Efisio 120 – Primetta (Precocious 126) [2001 10g 10m 10m 10m **58**
10.1g[3] 10.2g[3] 12g 17.2g Oct 1] tall gelding: fairly useful performer at 3 yrs: only modest
form at 5 yrs: sold from M. Bell 6,000 gns after sixth start: best form around 1¼m: acts on
firm going. *R. M. Stronge*

HOH'S BACK 2 b.c. (Feb 26) Royal Applause 124 – Paris Joelle (IRE) (Fairy King **83**
(USA)) [2001 8.2m 8.2d 7s[2] f8.5g* p7g[5] Nov 13] 8,500F, 10,500Y, resold 13,500Y:
well-made colt: second living foal: dam ran once at 2 yrs: fairly useful performer: won

maiden at Wolverhampton in November by ¾ length from No Question, making most: stays 8.5f: acts on fibresand/polytrack and soft ground. *S. Kirk*

HOLBECK (IRE)   3 b.f. Efisio 120 – Autumn Fall (USA) (Sanglamore (USA) 126)   – [2001 –: 5f 8m 8s Oct 16] small, sturdy filly: no form: left M. Johnston after second start. *R. Wilman*

HOLDING COURT   4 b.c. Hernando (FR) 127 – Indian Love Song 68 (Be My Guest   **120** (USA) 126) [2001 125: 12g³ 12g³ 12.5g* 12s Oct 7] tall, good sort: shows plenty of knee action: won Prix du Jockey Club at Chantilly at 3 yrs: not discredited in 2001 when third in Jockey Club Stakes at Newmarket (5 lengths behind Millenary) and Princess of Wales's Stakes on same course (beaten 2¼ lengths by Mutamam) prior to winning Grand Prix de Deauville Lucien Barriere in August by 2½ lengths from Marienbard, allowed clear early lead and never looking in danger: well beaten in Prix de l'Arc de Triomphe at Longchamp next time: should stay beyond 12.5f: acts on heavy going: blinkered last 3 starts in Europe: best making running: sold to race in Saudi Arabia, where renamed Wakaad, and finished unplaced in 2m Crown Prince's Cup there in November. *M. A. Jarvis*

HO LENG (IRE)   6 ch.g. Statoblest 120 – Indigo Blue (IRE) 56 (Bluebird (USA) 125)   **97 §** [2001 112: 6m 5f 6m 6f 7m 6g 6m 6g 6m⁴ 5.6m 6m Sep 22] leggy, lengthy gelding: useful handicapper: best effort at 6 yrs when twelfth of 30 to Nice One Clare in Wokingham at Royal Ascot third start and length fourth to Honesty Fair at York on ninth: effective at 5.6f, barely at 1m: acts on firm going, below form on softer than good: very slowly away when last on final 2 starts, said to have bled from nose on second occasion: unreliable. *Miss L. A. Perratt*

HOLLYBELL   2 b.f. (Mar 8) Beveled (USA) – Fayre Holly (IRE) 57 (Fayruz 116)   **68** [2001 5.1d⁵ 5f 5.7g³ 6.1g⁵ 5.1m* 6s f5s Dec 21] second foal: dam maiden who may have proved best at 5f/6f: fair performer: won maiden at Bath in September, dictating: likely to prove best at 5f/easy 6f: acts on good to firm and good to soft ground, some promise on fibresand. *J. Gallagher*

HOLLYBUSH (IRE)   2 b.f. (Mar 4) Ali-Royal (IRE) 127 – Another Baileys 60   **55** (Deploy 131) [2001 6d⁵ 7d⁶ 6d⁵ 8m 8v⁴ Oct 16] 7,000Y: fourth foal: half-sister to 3-y-o Kaluga, 4-y-o Ridgewood Bay and 5-y-o Irish Cream: dam, 7f winner, ran once at 2 yrs: modest maiden: raced only at Ayr: respectable efforts in nurseries last 2 starts: stays 1m: acts on good to firm and heavy ground. *J. S. Goldie*

HOLLY GAMES   2 b.f. (Feb 12) Mind Games 121 – Young Holly (Risk Me (FR) 127)   – [2001 5f⁵ 5m 5.1m Aug 24] second foal: dam unraced: well beaten in maidens: reportedly sprained off-fore final start. *M. R. Bosley*

HOLLY ROSE   2 b.f. (Jan 26) Charnwood Forest (IRE) 125 – Divina Luna 96   **46** (Dowsing (USA) 124) [2001 6m⁶ 6m 6g Sep 11] first foal: dam, 7f/1m winner, from good family: poor form in maidens: twice slowly away. *Pat Mitchell*

HOLY ISLAND   4 b.f. Deploy 131 – Bells 63 (Sadler's Wells (USA) 132) [2001 66+:   **81** 9.9s 12.4m 10g* 10.1m* 11.8g² 10m³ 10.4d⁴ 12d Nov 2] smallish, strong, dipped-backed filly: fairly useful handicapper: won at Brighton and Yarmouth in July: good efforts at Nottingham (minor event) and York sixth/seventh starts: best from at 1¼m: acts on soft and good to firm going: has shown reluctance at stalls/carried head awkwardly: best held up. *L. M. Cumani*

HOLY ORDERS (IRE)   4 b.c. Unblest 117 – Shadowglow (Shaadi (USA) 126) [2001   **99** 96: 12g* 12m 12d Aug 31] IR 11,000Y: smallish colt: first foal: dam, ran once in Ireland, half-sister to useful performers Alpenglow (up to 1m) and Attitre (up to 1½m): useful handicapper: won at the Curragh in May: good eighth to Takamaka Bay in Duke of Edinburgh Stakes at Royal Ascot next time: well below form final start: stays 1½m: acts on heavy and good to firm going: useful hurdler. *W. P. Mullins, Ireland*

HOME BY SOCKS (IRE)   2 ch.f. (Mar 4) Desert King (IRE) 129 – Propitious (IRE)   **56** 101 (Doyoun 124) [2001 5v 5m f6g 6.1g 7.5m 7.5s⁴ 7.9m 8m 8s⁶ 10v 10d 10s⁶ f8g Nov   **a–** 19] 10,000Y: leggy, close-coupled filly: third foal: dam Irish 1m winner: modest maiden: probably stays 1¼m: acts on soft and good to firm going, well beaten both runs on fibresand: edgy type. *M. C. Chapman*

HOME COMING   3 br.g. Primo Dominie 121 – Carolside 108 (Music Maestro 119)   – [2001 f8g⁶ 8g 8m 6m 6m Aug 3] lengthy, angular gelding: brother to fairly useful 1995 2-y-o 5f winner Oh Whataknight and half-brother to several winners, including useful 1m to 9f winner Eton Lad (by Never So Bold): dam 2-y-o 5f winner who didn't progress: little form: very slowly away on debut. *S. P. C. Woods*

454

HOMELIFE (IRE) 3 b.g. Persian Bold 123 – Share The Vision (Vision (USA)) [2001 **92**
67: f12g* 10.3s f12g* 12.3f⁶ 12f 14.1g⁵ 16d² 16.1g* 16.2s 16v⁵ 16.5s p12g⁴ f16.2f² Dec
5] tall, useful-looking gelding: fairly useful handicapper: won at Wolverhampton/
Southwell in March and Newmarket in August: best effort final outing: will stay
beyond 2m: acts on soft going and fibresand/polytrack: has worn net muzzle to post.
P. W. D'Arcy

HOMELY SORT (IRE) 2 b.f. (Apr 27) Petardia 113 – Safe Home 94 (Home Guard **–**
(USA) 129) [2001 f5g 6m 5.1f 6m f5g f6g 5.1s 6d f5g Nov 16] leggy filly: half-sister to
1m (in Ireland)/1¼m winner who stayed 17.5f Home Counties (by Ela-Mana-Mou) and
winners in Italy by Shardari and Blues Traveller: dam Irish 5f winner, best at 2 yrs: little
form, including in seller: tried blinkered: looks a difficult ride. *M. J. Polglase*

HOMESPUN 2 b.f. (Apr 14) Reprimand 122 – Home Truth 98 (Known Fact (USA) **75**
135) [2001 6m³ 6g² 7.1m Sep 17] rather leggy filly: half-sister to several winners,
including very smart 7f performer Susu (by Machiavellian) and 7-y-o Cadeaux Cher:
dam 7f/1m winner: fair maiden: seemed not to handle track when second at Goodwood:
should stay 7f. *B. W. Hills*

HONEST BORDERER 6 b.g. Selkirk (USA) 129 – Tell No Lies 96 (High Line 125) **86**
[2001 87: 7m⁴ 8m³ 7.6m 8g 8m 10m⁶ 8m Sep 24] very tall gelding: fairly useful
handicapper: effective at 7f to 1¼m: acts on firm and soft going: tried blinkered: found to
be suffering from fibrillating heart fourth outing: none too consistent: joined T. Easterby.
J. L. Dunlop

HONEST OBSESSION (IRE) 3 b.c. Sadler's Wells (USA) 132 – Valley of Gold **–**
(FR) 117 (Shirley Heights 130) [2001 –: 7d 8m Jun 2] strong, good-topped colt: well held
in 3 maidens: sold 3,800 gns in October. *B. W. Hills*

HONEST VILLAIN (USA) 4 b.g. St Jovite (USA) 135 – Villandry (USA) 113 **–**
(Lyphard's Wish (FR) 124) [2001 –: 14.1m Jul 27] leggy, unfurnished gelding: modest
maiden as 2-y-o: well beaten both outings since. *I. A. Balding*

HONEST WARNING 4 b.g. Mtoto 134 – Peryllys 67 (Warning 136) [2001 68: 6.9m **76**
7.5m* 7m 7m 7m 7g⁶ 7.6g p7g⁶ p7g p8g⁵ p10g p10g Dec 22] rather sparely-made **a65**
gelding: fair handicapper: won at Beverley in June: left B. Smart after fourth outing:
effective at 7f/1m: acts on firm going and polytrack: races freely: very slowly away final
outing. *J. R. Best*

HONESTY FAIR 4 b.f. Reprimand 122 – Truthful Image 90 (Reesh 117) [2001 102p: **110**
6g 5m 5g 6m 5g* 6g⁵ 6g³ 6g³ 6m* 7d⁵ 6m 6g* 6d 6.5f Dec 31] sparely-made filly:
unimpressive mover: smart performer: won handicaps at Newmarket in July, York in
September and Newmarket (beat Damalis by a length) in October: also ran creditably in

*Peterhouse Group Rated Stakes (Handicap), York—Honesty Fair battles on strongly
to get up well inside the final furlong, beating half-brothers Ellens Lad and Ellens Academy*

Ayr Gold Cup (twelfth of 28 to Continent) eleventh outing: left J. Glover before final start: effective at 5f/6f: acts on good to firm and good to soft going: reluctant to post twice in 2001 (has been mounted on course): has been bandaged/run well when sweating: usually held up: tough and reliable. *Kathy Walsh, USA*

HONEY FOR MONEY (IRE)   2 b.f. (May 7) Alzao (USA) 117 – Classical Flair **61 p**
(USA) (Riverman (USA) 131) [2001 6m³ 7g⁶ 6.1v⁶ Oct 4] 62,000 2-y-o: small, leggy filly: half-sister to several winners, including fairly useful Irish 1999 2-y-o 7f winner River Sounds (by Shalford), later winner in USA, and useful Irish/US performer up to 1¾m Orange Sunset (by Roanoke): dam ran twice in USA at 2 yrs: modest form in maidens, not knocked about: should be suited by 1¼m/1½m: capable of better. *J. R. Fanshawe*

HONEYMOONER (IRE)   2 ch.f. (Mar 31) Pursuit of Love 124 – Bathe In Light **47**
(USA) 72 (Sunshine Forever (USA)) [2001 5d 6m 7m⁵ 7m 7m⁵ Aug 15] 5,000Y: first foal: dam, 1½m/1¾m winner, out of sister to King Edward VII Stakes winner Open Day: poor maiden: should stay at least 1¼m. *J. G. Portman*

HONEYPOINT   2 b.f. (Mar 18) Robellino (USA) 127 – Short And Sharp 88 (Sharpen **53**
Up 127) [2001 6g⁸ 7g 7m Jul 24] dipped-backed filly: half-sister to several winners, including useful performer up to 1m Golden Fortune (by Forzando), 6f/7f winner at 2 yrs: dam, placed at 6f/7f, ran only at 2 yrs: modest form when overcoming greenness to win seller at Yarmouth in July, leading final 50 yds: well held in similar events after: should stay 1m: reluctant at stalls first 2 outings. *D. Morris*

HONEY'S GIFT   2 b.f. (Feb 5) Terimon 124 – Honeycroft (Crofter (USA) 124) [2001 **56**
5v² 5.1v⁴ f6g⁶ 7m⁵ 7d⁴ f7g 7d³ 8s 8d Nov 2] eighth foal: dam ran once on Flat/winning hurdler: modest maiden: below form in nurseries last 2 starts: should stay 1m: acts on heavy going. *G. G. Margarson*

HONOR ROUGE (IRE)   2 ch.f. (Apr 11) Highest Honor (FR) 124 – Ayers Rock **73**
(IRE) 95 (In The Wings 128) [2001 7f 7g³ 8f* 7.9s Oct 11] IR 20,000F, IR 25,000Y: good-topped filly: first foal: dam, Irish 1¼m/1½m winner, granddaughter of Cherry Hinton (herself dam of Dante winner Red Glow): fair form: won maiden at Musselburgh in September: well beaten in nursery final start: should be suited by 1¼m+: acts on firm ground, possibly not on soft. *P. W. Harris*

HONOR'S LAD   2 ch.c. (Jan 30) Sabrehill (USA) 120 – Ackcontent (USA) (Key To **–**
Content (USA) 120) [2001 6g Aug 8] 7,000Y: half-brother to several winners, including winners up to 7f Eager To Please (by Keen) and No Sympathy (by Ron's Victory), both successful at 2 yrs: dam ran once in USA: 50/1, looked difficult ride when well beaten in maiden at Leicester. *C. N. Kellett*

HONOURABLE CHIEF   4 b.g. Be My Chief (USA) 122 – Magic Orb 81 (Primo **–**
Dominie 121) [2001 f8.5g p6g p7g Dec 28] little form. *G. Prodromou*

HO PANG YAU   3 b. or gr.g. Pivotal 124 – La Cabrilla 89 (Carwhite 127) [2001 63: **63**
7.1d⁵ 7m⁶ 8m 8.3m⁶ 8.3d⁴ 7f 6s⁶ 6d⁵ 6m³ 6d⁵ 6f³ 6g³ 5m⁶ 5m 5v Oct 15] close-coupled gelding: modest maiden: has form at 1m, but seems best at 6f: acts on firm and good to soft going: blinkered (below form) once. *Miss L. A. Perratt*

HOPEFUL HENRY   5 ch.g. Cadeaux Genereux 131 – Fernlea (USA) (Sir Ivor 135) **54**
[2001 46: e6g* e6g² e7g⁵ f6g 6m⁵ Aug 22] modest handicapper: won amateur event at Lingfield in January: stays 6f: acts on good to firm going and equitrack: has been slowly away. *G. L. Moore*

HOPE JO'ANNA (USA)   3 ch.f. Chimes Bundle (USA) 117 – Banker's Bundles **–**
(USA) (Majestic Light (USA)) [2001 8.2d 8d 10g Nov 5] $37,000F, $210,000Y: lengthy, well-made filly: third foal: half-sister to winner in North America by Leo Castelli: dam winner up to 1m in North America: well held in maidens. *N. A. Graham*

HORMUZ (IRE)   5 b.g. Hamas (IRE) 125§ – Balqis (USA) 93 (Advocator) [2001 66: **67**
8f 9m⁵ 8m² 9m⁴ 7.9m² 10.1d 8m³ 8m⁴ 8.5s* 8m 9m* 10f Sep 20] big, well-made gelding: fair handicapper: claimed from J. M. Bradley after third start: won at Beverley (amateurs) in August and Ripon in September: effective at 1m/easy 1¼m: acts on firm going, soft and equitrack: usually front runner: consistent. *D. Nicholls*

HORNBY BOY   3 b.g. Dolphin Street (FR) 125 – Miss Walsh (Distant Relative 128) **–**
[2001 –: f7s f7g⁵ f6g f6g 8m⁶ 7.5f 12m 8.1d 9m Aug 23] seems of little account. *J. Hetherton*

HOROSCOPE (IRE)   2 b.g. (Mar 10) Eagle Eyed (USA) 111 – Council Rock 74 **88**
(General Assembly (USA)) [2001 5f⁴ 5.1f* 6m² 6g² 6m⁵ Dec 16] half-brother to several

456

winners, notably 3-y-o Superstar Leo and 5-y-o Royal Artist: dam, maiden best at 1¼m, daughter of Nassau winner Dancing Rocks: fairly useful performer: won maiden at Nottingham in June: runner-up in nurseries next 2 starts: left W. Haggas before fifth at Sha Tin final one: not sure to stay much beyond 6f: raced only on good going or firmer. *P. F. Yiu, Hong Kong*

HORSECALLEDCHARLIE   3 ch.g. Charmer 123 – Ordima (Sylvan Express 117)   – [2001 7m 7m 6f Jun 13] second foal: dam no sign of ability: well beaten in maidens/ claimer. *J. Akehurst*

HORTON DANCER   4 b.g. Rambo Dancer (CAN) 107 – Horton Lady 46 (Midyan   **45** (USA) 124) [2001 49: f12g⁴ f12g f11g 12f³ 12g 16.2s 9.9m* 8.9m 10f⁶ f14g⁴ Dec 14] close-coupled gelding: poor handicapper: left J. Parkes after third start: won apprentice maiden event at Beverley in August: effective at 1¼m to 1¾m: acts on firm going and fibresand: tried visored/tongue tied: races prominently. *D. W. Barker*

HO SEC (IRE)   3 ch.g. Goldmark (USA) 113 – Londubh (Tumble Wind (USA)) [2001   – f7g a6.8g⁶ Dec 1] IR 5,500Y: third foal: dam unraced: tailed off in seller at Southwell for J. Eustace on debut: 6½ lengths sixth in minor event at Taby 11 months later. *A. Borger, Sweden*

HOSSRUM (IRE)   3 b.c. Definite Article 121 – Petite Maxine 70 (Sharpo 132) [2001   – 71: 8f May 28] rangy colt: fair maiden at 2 yrs: tongue tied, said to have had breathing problem when tailed off only 3-y-o outing: sold 2,000 gns in July, sent to Kuwait. *E. A. L. Dunlop*

HOTCALLIE LEGEND   2 b.c. (Apr 14) Faustus (USA) 118 – Alice Holt (Free State   **57** 125) [2001 6.9m 6.9m 7.6m Aug 22] fourth reported thoroughbred foal: dam, lightly-raced maiden, half-sister to smart sprinter Tickled Pink: modest maiden: likely to prove best up to 1m. *Mrs A. J. Perrett*

HOTELGENIE DOT COM   3 gr.f. Selkirk (USA) 129 – Birch Creek (Carwhite   – 127) [2001 107+: 9d 8.1g 7d Sep 13] rather leggy, close-coupled, useful-looking filly: has a quick action: useful winner at 2 yrs, when also placed in Moyglare Stud Stakes at the Curragh and Fillies' Mile at Ascot: well below form in 2001: visored final outing. *M. R. Channon*

HOTELIERS' DREAM   3 b.f. Reprimand 122 – Pride of Britain (CAN) 67 (Linkage   – (USA)) [2001 8f⁶ 10g 8.1g 8.3v Nov 8] second foal: dam 1½m and 2m winner: well held in maidens. *W. S. Kittow*

HOT JAVA (USA)   2 b.f. (Apr 19) Twining (USA) 120 – Coffee Ice 92 (Primo Dominie   – 121) [2001 5v 5m a6g a6g Dec 9] 10,000Y: fourth foal: sister to a 6f winner in USA: dam, 2-y-o 5f winner, later sprint winner in USA: little sign of ability: left T. Easterby after second start. *P. Haley, Spain*

HOT JAZZ   2 ch.f. (May 10) Midyan (USA) 124 – Fascinating Rhythm 85 (Slip Anchor   **75** 136) [2001 7m⁵ 7.1g⁴ f7g⁴ Nov 27] first foal: dam, 2-y-o 1m winner who disappointed both 3-y-o starts, from family of Opera House and Kayf Tara: fair form first 2 starts in maidens: will stay at least 1m. *J. R. Fanshawe*

HOT PANTS   3 ch.f. Rudimentary (USA) 118 – True Precision 84 (Presidium 124)   **63** [2001 63: e5g* f5s e5s 5.3d⁴ 5.3f⁴ 6m 6m⁶ 5m 5.3g² 5g⁵ 5g⁴ 6g⁶ 5g p5g⁴ Dec 22] sturdy, close-coupled filly: modest performer: won maiden at Lingfield in January: mainly creditable efforts after: best at 5f: acts on firm going, good to soft, equitrack and poly- track: has carried head awkwardly/edged left: tried blinkered. *K. T. Ivory*

HOT POTATO   5 b.h. Roman Warrior 132 – My Song of Songs (Norwich (USA) 125)   – [2001 43: f8.5s f12g 9.2d May 6] poor maiden at 4 yrs: no form in 2001: tried visored. *J. S. Wainwright*

HOT PRODUXION (USA)   2 ch.g. (Apr 8) Tabasco Cat (USA) 126 – Princess   **86** Harriet (USA) (Mt Livermore (USA)) [2001 7g 7m⁵ 8m³ 10d² Oct 8] $100,000Y: strong, useful-looking gelding: has scope: has a quick, fluent action: second foal: dam, maiden in USA, half-sister to US Grade 3 9.5f winner Autobot: fairly useful maiden: best effort when second to Kayseri at Pontefract, disputing lead much of way: gelded after: stays 1¼m. *Mrs A. J. Perrett*

HOT TIN ROOF (IRE)   5 b.m. Thatching 131 – No Reservations (IRE) 87 (Com-   **109** manche Run 133) [2001 112: 6.1v³ 6m 6g³ 6d² 6g* 6.5d 6g³ 6s 7d 6s⁵ Nov 10] angular, good-topped mare: unimpressive mover: useful performer: won minor event at Newmarket in July: creditable efforts otherwise in listed races at Windsor (1¾ lengths third to Harmonic Way) and Haydock (1¼ lengths second to Summerhill Parkes) third/ fourth outings, and in Prix de Meautry at Deauville (4½ lengths third to Do The Honours) and Diadem Stakes at Ascot (2¾ lengths seventh to Nice One Clare) on seventh/eighth: best at 6f/7f: has form on good to firm going, best efforts on good or softer: usually held up: game: sold 230,000 gns. *T. D. Easterby*

HOT TROTTER   2 b.c. Halling (USA) 133 – Born To Glamour (Ajdal (USA) 130)   **92** [2001 7d 7s² 7s³ 7.5g* 8g⁵ Nov 24] fifth foal: half-brother to 3 winners, including 5-y-o Sailing Shoes and fairly useful Irish 1¼m winner (later 1m to 1½m winner in Sweden) Tarbaan (by Nashwan): dam Irish 2-y-o 6f winner: fairly useful performer: won maiden at Punchestown in September by short head from High Chaparral: sold from K. Prendergast in Ireland 50,000 gns in October: respectable fifth in Grade 3 at Hollywood: stays 7.5f. *J. H. M. Gosden*

HOUSE DOCTOR   2 ch.g. (Apr 14) Rudimentary (USA) 118 – Persian Air (Persian   **54** Bold 123) [2001 6.1f 6.9m Jul 12] 11,000F, IR 26,000Y: brother to useful Irish 2-y-o 7f winner Setmatt and half-brother to 3 winners, including unreliable 1997 2-y-o 5f winner who stayed 7f Persian Fortune (by Forzando): dam well beaten: modest form in maidens: gelded after final start: should stay at least 1m. *K. McAuliffe*

HOUSE OF DREAMS   9 b.g. Darshaan 133 – Helens Dreamgirl 95 (Caerleon (USA)   **48** 132) [2001 58, a44: 14.1m 15s 13.8g² 12g Aug 17] small gelding: has stringhalt: **a–** very slow mover: poor performer: stays 2m: acts on firm and soft going: held up. *Mrs M. Reveley*

HOUSEPARTY (IRE)   3 b. or br.g. Grand Lodge (USA) 125 – Special Display   **93** (Welsh Pageant 132) [2001 62p: 8g² 8.1m² 10.5d* 10.4g Aug 22] good-bodied gelding: fairly useful performer: won maiden at Haydock (made virtually all to beat Hyderabad by head) in August: not discredited on handicap debut at York next time: stays 1¼m: raced mainly on good going or softer: sold 42,000 gns in October, joined J. Old and gelded. *Sir Michael Stoute*

HOUSTON PARK (IRE)   2 ch.c. (Mar 26) Persian Bold 123 – Harina (Pentotal)   **92** [2001 7g⁵ 7f 6m 6g 9s* 8s* 9s² Nov 24] approx. 11,800Y in Italy: half-brother to 3 winners in Italy, including 1m/1¼m winners Houston Sky (by Mukaddamah) and Houston Street (by Astronef): dam Italian 9f to 1½m winner: fairly useful performer: ran in Britain second to fourth starts: much improved to win minor events at Milan in October/November: creditable second in similar event there: will stay 1¼m: acts on soft ground. *L. M. Cumani*

HOUT BAY   4 ch.g. Komaite (USA) – Maiden Pool 85 (Sharpen Up 127) [2001 60:   **72** f5g³ e5g² f7s³ f5g⁶ 5f² 6m² 5.3f* 6f 5g 6m⁶ 6m 5f* 5.3m⁵ f6g Sep 22] big, lengthy gelding: fair performer: won handicaps at Brighton in July and Catterick in August: best form at 5f: acts on firm going, good to soft and fibresand/equitrack: consistent. *S. E. Kettlewell*

HOWARDS DREAM (IRE)   3 b.g. King's Theatre (IRE) 128 – Keiko 76 (Generous   **–** (IRE) 139) [2001 –p: 10.9m⁵ 12.1d⁵ 14.1m 13.1f⁵ 13s 14f⁵ 16m Aug 22] compact gelding: little form: tongue tied penultimate start: headstrong. *I. Semple*

HOWARDS HEROINE (IRE)   2 ch.f. (Mar 5) Danehill Dancer (IRE) 117 –   **61 §** Romangoddess (IRE) (Rhoman Rule (USA)) [2001 5v 6m⁵ 7.1f³ 7d³ 7m 6f⁶ 7.5g³ 7d⁶   **a52 §** 8g⁵ f7g f7s² Dec 18] IR 4,000Y: good-topped filly: sixth foal: half-sister to fairly useful 1999 2-y-o 7f winner Clonmany (by Petardia), 6-y-o Petara and 5-y-o Kuwait Thunder: dam Irish 2-y-o 7f winner: modest maiden: best efforts around 7f: acts on fibresand and good to soft going: visored penultimate start: often slowly away: probably ungenuine. *I. Semple*

HOWARDS HERO (IRE)   2 gr.g. (Apr 28) Paris House 123 – Gold Braisim (IRE)   **59** 77 (Jareer (USA) 115) [2001 5m⁴ 5m⁶ 5m⁴ 6g⁶ 5g⁴ Sep 2] IR 11,000Y: fifth foal: half-brother to 6-y-o Madame Jones and 5-y-o Thorntoun Gold: dam Irish 6f winner: modest maiden: should stay 6f: looks difficult ride. *I. Semple*

HOWARD'S LAD (IRE)   4 b.g. Reprimand 122 – Port Isaac (USA) 64 (Seattle Song   **52 §** (USA) 130) [2001 62§: 9v 7.1m 7m² 8.3m*⁶ 7.1f⁴ 8f 9.2g 8f² 9.2g 6f⁵ 6v f6g Dec 8] rangy   **a45 §** gelding: modest performer: effective at 6f to 1m: acts on firm and soft going, probably on fibresand: sometimes slowly away: usually blinkered/visored: ungenuine. *I. Semple*

HOW DO I KNOW   3 gr.f. Petong 126 – Glenfield Portion 86 (Mummy's Pet 125)   **91** [2001 78: 6d* 6g⁴ 7m 6g³ 7d Oct 20] leggy filly: fairly useful handicapper: won 30-runner race at Newmarket in May: off 5 months then best effort on same course

penultimate start: ran poorly final outing: stays 6f: yet to race on extremes of going.
G. A. Butler

HOWE TIMELY 4 b.g. Timeless Times (USA) 99 – Adder Howe (Amboise 113) –
[2001 6m 5f 10.5d 7m 8f f12g Nov 26] seems of little account. *N. Bycroft*

HUB HUB 3 b.c. Polish Precedent (USA) 131 – Ghassanah 73 (Pas de Seul 133) [2001 **69 d**
8.3g 6.9m⁴ 8m 7.1s³ 8.1s 8g 8d 8.2s p7g⁵ Dec 28] half-brother to several winners,
including 5f/6f winner Alzianah (by Alzao) and 7-y-o Return of Amin, both useful: dam
7f winner: fair maiden, on downgrade: stays 7f: visored last 3 starts: has been slowly
away. *R. Hannon*

HUDOOD (USA) 6 ch.g. Gone West (USA) – Fife (IRE) 95 (Lomond (USA) 128) **93**
[2001 99: 10s 10g⁵ 12m³ 10g Jun 15] good-topped gelding: poor mover: fairly useful
performer nowadays: best effort at 6 yrs when fifth in handicap at Newmarket in May:
stays easy 1½m: acts on good to firm going, good to soft and dirt: has been visored (best
form when not)/tongue tied: returned to UAE. *C. E. Brittain*

HUFFLEPUFF (IRE) 2 b.f. (Mar 15) Desert King (IRE) 129 – Circle of Chalk (FR) **81**
74 (Kris 135) [2001 6m² 6m* 6d² 7.1m⁶ Jul 26] third foal: half-sister to 5-y-o Avebury:
dam, French 1¼m winner, sister to useful French 1½m winner From Beyond and
half-sister to 3-y-o Enthused out of Coronation Stakes winner Magic of Life: fairly useful
performer: won maiden at Pontefract in June: best effort when short-headed by Sandy
Lady in minor event at Haydock in July, making most: will need to settle to stay 7f.
J. L. Dunlop

HUGH THE MAN (IRE) 2 b.c. (Apr 20) Hamas (IRE) 125§ – Run To Jenny 105 **64 ?**
(Runnett 125) [2001 7v 6s f7g Nov 27] IR 8,200Y, 15,000 2-y-o: close-coupled, good-
topped colt: third foal: half-brother to winners abroad by Jovial and Last Tycoon: dam,
Irish 2-y-o 5f winner, later best at 1m/won in USA: seemed to show modest form at
Doncaster on first of 3 starts in maidens. *N. P. Littmoden*

HUGS DANCER (FR) 4 b.g. Cadeaux Genereux 131 – Embracing 91 (Reference **83**
Point 139) [2001 71: 8.5m 8m⁴ 12.4m* 12.4m³ 14f* 15.9m³ 16f² 21m* 13.9m 15.9d 18d
Oct 20] workmanlike gelding: fairly useful performer: won minor event at Newcastle in
June and handicaps at Musselburgh in July and Goodwood (beat Gracilis by 2½ lengths)
in August: stays 21f: best form on good ground or firmer: usually visored, tried blinkered:
tends to race lazily/idle in front: consistent. *J. G. Given*

HUGWITY 9 ch.g. Cadeaux Genereux 131 – Nuit d'Ete (USA) 90 (Super Concorde **69**
(USA) 128) [2001 78, a88: e10g e12g f12g² e12g³ f14g⁵ f11g⁴ e10g* e10g* f8g* e8g⁶ **a79**
10m 10f 8m³ 8g² 8.2g⁴ 8.5m⁴ 8m² 8d⁵ 7.6g Sep 11] big, good-topped gelding: fair handicapper nowadays: successful at Lingfield (2) and Southwell in March/April: effective at
1m to easy 1½m: acts on firm going, good to soft and fibresand/equitrack: tends to race
up with pace. *G. C. Bravery*

HUME'S LAW 3 b.c. Puissance 110 – Will Be Bold 79 (Bold Lad (IRE) 133) [2001 –
71: e6g f7g 6m 5m 6g 7.1f 5f 5f 5f f7g 7g⁵ 6g 8.5m⁶ 7.5m 7.2g 6s 5m 8f 6m⁴ 5d 7d 7g 6d⁶
6d 8v 5g f6g f6s Dec 21] sparely-made colt: has a round action: little form in 2001: tried
blinkered, often tongue tied: possibly none too genuine. *A. Berry*

HUNTING GROUND 13 b.g. Dancing Brave (USA) 140 – Ack's Secret (USA) –
(Ack Ack (USA)) [2001 16m May 4] probably of little account nowadays. *M. Mullineaux*

HUNTING LION (IRE) 4 b.c. Piccolo 121 – Jalopy 71 (Jalmood (USA) 126) [2001 **115**
112: 6d 6g⁷ May 6] leggy colt: had a quick action: smart performer: won valuable
handicap at Newmarket and third in Jersey Stakes at Royal Ascot at 3 yrs: good ¾-length
second to Munjiz in handicap at Newmarket in May: stayed 7f: acted on firm going,
below form on good to soft: to stand at Hedgeholme Stud, nr Darlington, fee £2,000 nfnf.
M. R. Channon

HUREYA (USA) 3 b.f. Woodman (USA) 126 – Istiqlal (USA) (Diesis 133) [2001 73: **82**
7g² 8m* 7d³ 8m⁶ Jul 4] fairly useful handicapper: made all at Yarmouth in May: ran
creditably next time: effective at 7f/1m: acted on good to firm and good to soft going: had
raced freely/wandered markedly/carried head awkwardly: visits Alhaarth. *J. L. Dunlop*

HURLINGHAM STAR (IRE) 3 b.g. Distinctly North (USA) 115 – Charrua 55 –
(Sharpo 132) [2001 50: e5g⁴ e5g⁴ e6g⁶ f6g e6s⁵ f8.5g⁶ f7g e7g 7v f6g Nov 16] poor
performer: left M. Quinn after fifth start and P. D. Evans after eighth: stays 6f: acts on
fibresand/equitrack: sometimes visored. *W. M. Brisbourne*

459

Lucayan Stud's "Hurricane Floyd"

HURRICANE COAST   2 b.g. (Apr 27) Hurricane Sky (AUS) – Tread Carefully 51   **70** (Sharpo 132) [2001 7.5m 7g 6f³ 7d³ 7.9s Oct 11] tall gelding: has scope: fourth foal: dam, maiden who stayed 1m, half-sister to high-class stayer and Champion Hurdle winner Royal Gait: fair maiden: third at Newcastle and Chester: should stay 1m: acts on firm and good to soft going: has carried head awkwardly. *T. D. Easterby*

HURRICANE DAN   2 b.g. (Apr 2) Emarati (USA) 74 – Bellateena 57 (Nomination   **69** § 125) [2001 5s f5g² f5g⁵ 6g 5g⁴ 7d 6m⁴ 6g³ 6g 5m³ 5f⁴ 6m 6d f6g Oct 20] 7,500F: strong gelding: first foal: dam 1m/1¼m winner: fair maiden: well below form last 3 starts: stays easy 6f: acts on fibresand and firm going: blinkered last 8 starts: sometimes sweating/edgy: untrustworthy: sold 3,800 gns, sent to Spain. *M. W. Easterby*

HURRICANE FLOYD (IRE)   3 ch.c. Pennekamp (USA) 130 – Mood Swings   **110** (IRE) 77 (Shirley Heights 130) [2001 101: 7m² 7m⁶ 7m⁶ 6g⁵ 6d² Aug 26] strong, quite attractive colt: has a quick action: smart performer: best efforts when 2 lengths second to Malhub in listed event at Newmarket in June and 1½ lengths sixth of 28 to Atavus in Tote International Handicap at Ascot third outing: not discredited in valuable minor event at Ascot penultimate start, badly hampered when over 5 lengths fifth to Orientor (would probably have finished second otherwise): will prove best at 6f/7f: acts on good to firm ground: visored (missed break and below form) final outing: tends to grind teeth in paddock: finished lame final 2-y-o start: joined D. Nicholls. *J. Noseda*

HUTCH   3 b.g. Rock Hopper 124 – Polly's Teahouse 68 (Shack (USA) 118) [2001   **63** 12.3m⁵ 8f⁵ 10f⁵ 12d Oct 8] plain, lengthy gelding: half-brother to 3 winners by Weldnaas, including 8-y-o Polly Golightly and unreliable 4-y-o Tea For Texas: dam sprint maiden:

modest form: should prove better at 1¼m than shorter: slowly away second outing. *J. D. Bethell*

HUTCHIES LADY   9 b.m. Efisio 120 – Keep Mum 63 (Mummy's Pet 125) [2001 44:   **44**
9v³ 9.2d 11.1d⁴ 8m⁶ 11.9g⁵ 10.5g 16g² 9.2m* 13d⁴ 10.9f 13g³ 9.2m⁶ 11.1s⁵ 9.2d 10.9d²
7s 12f 9.1d⁵ 11.9g 8m 8.3s⁵ 7.2g 11.1g⁴ 9.1m 6m Sep 24] small, sparely-made mare: poor
performer: won handicap at Hamilton in June: has form from 9f to 2m: acts on heavy and
good to firm going: sometimes blinkered/visored: has looked less than keen/started
slowly: tends to get behind: tough. *J. S. Goldie*

HWISPRIAN   3 b.f. Definite Article 121 – No Islands (Lomond (USA) 128) [2001 68:   **80**
10g⁵ 10d² 9.9m Jun 27] fairly useful maiden: ran as if something amiss final outing: may
prove best around 1¼m: acts on good to soft ground. *M. Blanshard*

HYDE HALL   3 b.f. Barathea (IRE) 127 – Catawba 98 (Mill Reef (USA) 141) [2001   **90**
–p: 10m² 10g* 10.5d⁴ 10.1g Aug 27] compact, quite attractive filly: unimpressive mover:
ninth foal: closely related to fairly useful 1¼m to 1½m winner Licorne (by Sadler's
Wells) and half-sister to several winners, including Yorkshire Oaks winner Catchascatchcan (by Pursuit of Love): dam, 1¼m winner, out of Ribblesdale Stakes winner
Catalpa: fairly useful form: won maiden at Pontefract in July: best effort when fourth to
Goncharova in handicap at Haydock next time: will stay 1½m: yet to race on extremes of
going: possibly unsuited by track at Epsom final outing. *H. R. A. Cecil*

HYDE PARK (IRE)   7 b.g. Alzao (USA) 117 – Park Elect (Ahonoora 122) [2001 56:   **60**
f8g 8d⁵ 7.1m³ 7.1m⁵ 8f 8g⁶ 7g* 7.5m⁶ Aug 25] robust gelding: modest handicapper:
won at Catterick in August: effective at 7f, barely at 9f: suited by good ground or firmer
on turf, and acts on fibresand/equitrack: blinkered once: usually races prominently.
D. Nicholls

HYDERABAD   3 ch.c. Deploy 131 – Ajuga (USA) 102 (The Minstrel (CAN) 135)   **95**
[2001 –p: 12d² 12.3f 12m³ 12f 10.5d² 11.7d* 14m 14g Oct 6] strong, stocky colt: has a
round action: useful performer: won maiden at Bath in August: creditable efforts otherwise when placed in small-field maidens at Newmarket (twice) and Haydock: unlikely to
stay beyond 1½m: has form on good to firm going, best efforts on good to soft: sold
55,000 gns, joined M. Morris in Ireland and impressive winner over hurdles in December.
B. W. Hills

HYPERACTIVE (IRE)   5 b.g. Perugino (USA) 84 – Hyannis (FR) (Esprit du Nord   **52**
(USA) 126) [2001 73: f7g 8m 7m 7m 8m⁵ 8f⁵ 8f 7d⁶ 8v Oct 24] rather dipped-backed
gelding: modest performer nowadays: stays easy 1m: acts on firm and good to soft going:
tried blinkered. *B. Ellison*

HYPERSONIC   4 b.g. Marju (IRE) 127 – Hi-Li (High Top 131) [2001 –: 10m 10.2d   **–**
Oct 25] fair maiden at 2 yrs: no form since. *C. L. Popham*

HYPOTHESIS (IRE)   4 b.g. Sadler's Wells (USA) 132 – Surmise (USA) 75 (Alleged   **–**
(USA) 138) [2001 12v 12g 16f Sep 4] no show on Flat. *A. Bailey*

I

IAMATMEWHITZEND   4 ch.f. Whittingham (IRE) 104 – The Fernhill Flyer (IRE)   **–**
71 (Red Sunset 120) [2001 –: f8g Feb 26] tailed off both outings. *A. Berry*

IBIS ROUGE (IRE)   2 ch.f. (Feb 19) Forzando 122 – Aquiletta 67 (Bairn (USA) 126)   **–**
[2001 6f 7g Oct 19] small filly: second foal: half-sister to 4-y-o Tick Tock: dam, maiden,
effective at 6f/7f: no sign of ability in maiden/claimer: dead. *C. B. B. Booth*

I CAN'T REMEMBER   7 br. or gr.g. Petong 126 – Glenfield Portion 86 (Mummy's   **48**
Pet 125) [2001 60d: 10s³ 8s⁵ 12m 10f⁶ 12m 14.1g³ Jun 16] small, compact gelding: poor
performer: stays 1¾m: acts on firm going, soft and fibresand/equitrack: tried visored/
blinkered/tongue tied: none too consistent. *S. R. Bowring*

ICARESSA   3 b.f. Anabaa (USA) 130 – Dance Quest (FR) 117 (Green Dancer (USA)   **–**
132) [2001 7d Apr 18] angular filly: half-sister to several winners, including very smart
6f to 1m performer Pursuit of Love (by Groom Dancer) and smart French sprinter Divine
Danse (by Kris): dam, French 5f/6f winner (including at 2 yrs), half-sister to Prix de la
Salamandre winner Noblequest: 14/1 and backward in coat, mid-division in 28-runner
maiden at Newmarket. *H. R. A. Cecil*

461

Tote Scoop6 Cambridgeshire (Handicap), Newmarket—run in a downpour,
I Cried For You provides James Given with his biggest win in three years of training;
the progressive Halland is second ahead of (from right to left) Duck Row, Smirk and Thihn

ICE 5 b.g. Polar Falcon (USA) 126 – Sarabah (IRE) 83 (Ela-Mana-Mou 132) [2001 **97 §**
100§: 8.5m⁶ 8.9m 7.9m* 10m⁴ 8g 7.9m 8.9m⁴ 7.9d Oct 12] deep-bodied gelding: useful
performer: won handicap at York (5 wins on course) in July: claimed from M. Johnston
£16,000 after seventh start: stayed 1¼m: acted on any going: visored: was best forcing
pace: carried head high/tended to wander: unreliable: winning hurdler, fell fatally in
December. *S. E. Kettlewell*

ICEALION 3 b.g. Lion Cavern (USA) 117 – Icecapped 91 (Caerleon (USA) 132) **–**
[2001 –: f7s Dec 15] angular, workmanlike gelding: well held in maidens. *M. W. Easterby*

ICE AND FIRE 2 b.g. (Mar 12) Cadeaux Genereux 131 – Tanz (IRE) 79 (Sadler's **72 p**
Wells (USA) 132) [2001 7m³ 7d Sep 14] quite good-topped gelding: half-brother to
several winners, including useful 7f winner (stayed 11.4f) Tanzilla (by Warning) and
7-y-o Tarxien: dam, 1½m winner, sister to smart middle-distance stayer Spring and
closely related to Pentire: fair form when third of 7 to Continuously in maiden at Newmarket: acted as pacemaker for Dubai Destination in Champagne Stakes at Doncaster,
finishing tailed off: gelded after: should stay 1¼m: capable of better. *D. R. Loder*

ICE CRYSTAL 4 b.g. Slip Anchor 136 – Crystal Fountain (Great Nephew 126) [2001 **–**
74: 16v Oct 17] fair maiden at 3 yrs: well beaten only Flat outing at 4 yrs. *S. Woodman*

ICE DANCER (IRE) 3 b.c. Sadler's Wells (USA) 132 – Tappiano (USA) (Fappiano **112**
(USA)) [2001 10v² 12m* 11g² 12g 12m 10g⁵ 10s* Oct 29] good-topped colt: fifth
reported living foal: half-brother to 3 minor winners in USA: dam, US 2-y-o Grade 1 6f
to 9f winner, from family of Known Fact and Gone West: smart performer: won maiden
in May and listed race (gamely by head from Taraza) in October, both at Leopardstown:
pacemaker for Galileo in Irish Derby, King George VI and Queen Elizabeth Diamond
Stakes and Irish Champion Stakes: stays 1½m: acts on heavy and good to firm going.
A. P. O'Brien, Ireland

ICE MAIDEN 3 b.f. Polar Falcon (USA) 126 – Affair of State (IRE) 99 (Tate Gallery **61**
(USA) 117) [2001 76: 8m 8m² 8m 7g⁵ 6.5d⁶ Dec 22] small filly: has a short, quick action:
fair winner at 2 yrs: only modest form at best in 2001: sold from M. Channon 1,200
gns before final outing: probably stays 1m: acts on good to firm and good to soft going:
reportedly finished lame final 2-y-o start. *P. Migheli, Italy*

ICENI QUEEN 3 b.f. Formidable (USA) 125 – Queen Warrior 74 (Daring March **–**
116) [2001 9.2m⁵ 10.1m⁶ 7.1f 8d 10.9v Oct 15] 1,600Y: third living foal: half-sister to
fairly useful 1m winner Malleus (by Hamas): dam 1m winner who stayed 1¼m: well
beaten in maidens/claimers: twice slowly away. *W. McKeown*

ICE PACK 5 gr.m. Mukaddamah (USA) 125 – Mrs Gray 61 (Red Sunset 120) [2001 **33**
37: 14.1m 16g⁵ 12m⁶ 16.2f 12.4m⁵ 15.8m⁴ 16g 16m Aug 22] leggy mare: poor maiden:
stays 17f: acts on any turf going and fibresand: visored recently. *Don Enrico Incisa*

ICE PRINCE 3 b.c. Polar Falcon (USA) 126 – The Jotter 99 (Night Shift (USA)) **78 +**
[2001 64: f8.5g² f8.5g² f8.5g* 8f 8.5f⁶ 8f⁴ 8f⁶ 6.5f³ 9f⁵ a8.5s 8f² a6.5f⁵ Dec 29] smallish,
sturdy colt: type to carry condition: fair form: runner-up in handicaps at Wolverhampton
prior to winning maiden on same course in March by 3 lengths (left J. Osborne after):
placed in US afterwards in claimers at Santa Anita in October and Hollywood in
December: stays 8.5f: acts on firm going and fibresand/dirt. *J. Cassidy, USA*

ICHIBAN   4 gr.g. Kasakov – First Slice 51 (Primo Dominie 121) [2001 e7g⁵ Feb 21]   –
second foal: dam second at 5f at 2 yrs: tailed off only start. *J. J. Bridger*

I CRIED FOR YOU (IRE)   6 b.g. Statoblest 120 – Fall of The Hammer (IRE)   **104**
(Auction Ring (USA) 123) [2001 95, a–: 7d 8s⁴ 7.1g⁶ 7m⁵ 8m⁴ 7g² 7.1s 7s² 9g* 8d⁵   **a–**
Nov 3] angular gelding: useful handicapper: better than ever when winning Tote Scoop6
Cambridgeshire at Newmarket in October by 2 lengths from Halland, always travelling
smoothly: also ran well when ½-length second to Downland in Tote Trifecta Stakes at
Ascot on previous outing and 4 lengths fifth to Soller Bay at Newmarket final one:
effective at 7f to 9f: probably acts on any turf going: tried visored/blinkered earlier in
career: usually tracks pace: sometimes idles: tough and consistent. *J. G. Given*

ICY   2 b.f. (Apr 14) Mind Games 121 – Snow Eagle (IRE) 57 (Polar Falcon (USA) 126)   **44**
[2001 6m⁵ 6m 5m 7.5g Sep 19] 2,000F, 12,000Y: small, leggy filly: sister to 3-y-o
Elsie Plunkett: dam, maiden who stayed 8.5f, ran only at 2 yrs: poor maiden: best efforts
first 2 starts. *M. W. Easterby*

IDAHO QUEST   4 br.c. Rainbow Quest (USA) 134 – Javandra (USA) (Lyphard   **118**
(USA) 132) [2001 10.5v 10v 12s⁸ 12v³ 12g² 12.5s⁶ 12.5g³ 12m² 12s Oct 7] good-topped
colt: second foal: dam, placed at 1¼m in France, sister to Dancing Brave and Jolypha:
smart performer: sold from M. Zilber 13,000 gns after final start at 3 yrs: won minor
event at Bordeaux in April: improved efforts on seventh/eighth starts in Grand Prix de
Deauville (4½ lengths third to Holding Court) and Prix Foy at Longchamp (½-length
second to Hightori, battling on): well held in Prix de l'Arc de Triomphe at Longchamp
final outing: stays 12.5f: acts on heavy and good to firm going: held up. *H.-A. Pantall,
France*

IDLE POWER (IRE)   3 b. or br.g. Common Grounds 118 – Idle Fancy 79 (Mujtahid   **95 +**
(USA) 118) [2001 91: 6d 6g⁵ 6m* 6g⁵ 6g³ 6m 6d Oct 13] rather leggy, close-coupled
gelding: useful handicapper: won at Yarmouth in July: best effort when close third to
Smokin Beau at Goodwood following month: stays 6f: acts on good to firm and good to
soft going. *P. W. Harris*

I DO   2 ch.f. (Jan 18) Selkirk (USA) 129 – Acquiesce (Generous (IRE) 139) [2001 7f⁴   **81 p**
7m 7.5m 7.1g* 6.9d* 7m⁵ Sep 6] strong filly: first foal: dam unraced half-sister to smart
2000 2-y-o 6f winner Endless Summer out of sister to Dewhurst dead-heater Scenic:
fairly useful performer: won nurseries at Sandown (made all) and Folkestone (easily)
within 3 days in September: respectable effort (third run in a week) final start: will stay at
least 1m: acts on good to soft going, probably on good to firm: should make a useful
3-y-o. *Sir Mark Prescott*

IF BY CHANCE   3 ch.c. Risk Me (FR) 127 – Out of Harmony 79 (Song 132) [2001   **63**
56: e6g* e6g⁴ e6g³ f6g³ 5g 5d⁶ 6m⁶ 5m² 5m³ 5m 5m 5g 5g f6g f6g³ f7s Dec 15] strong,   **a68**
close-coupled maiden: fair performer: made virtually all when winning at Lingfield in January: left
D. Arbuthnot 2,500 gns after thirteenth start: stays 6f: acts on heavy going, good to firm,
fibresand and equitrack: visored eleventh outing. *M. A. Buckley*

IFFAH (IRE)   3 ch.f. Halling (USA) 133 – Taroob (IRE) 72 (Roberto (USA) 131)   **86**
[2001 71p: 10s² 11.9f* 12f⁴ 11.9f² 14m⁴ 14m⁴ Aug 11] lengthy, angular filly: fairly useful
performer: landed odds in maiden at Brighton in May: good efforts in handicaps next 3
starts: stayed 1¾m: acted on firm and soft going: had hung left/carried head
awkwardly: tricky ride: visits Sahm. *J. L. Dunlop*

IFTITAH (USA)   5 ch.h. Gone West (USA) – Mur Taasha (USA) 108 (Riverman   –
(USA) 131) [2001 101, a110: 6m⁶ 6g 5g Jul 14] strong, robust horse: type to carry plenty
of condition: smart on dirt, useful at best on turf: well below form at 5 yrs: stays 1m: acts
on good to firm ground and dirt: visored and tongue tied final outing: has been bandaged
behind. *J. H. M. Gosden*

IGNITE (IRE)   4 b.g. Bluebird (USA) 125 – Save Me The Waltz 86 (Kings Lake   –
(USA) 133) [2001 68: 14.1s Nov 5] strong, well-made gelding: good mover: fair maiden
at best: well beaten only 4-y-o outing: blinkered twice at 2 yrs. *R. T. Phillips*

I GOT RHYTHM   3 gr.f. Lycius (USA) 124 – Eurythmic 58 (Pharly (FR) 130) [2001   **50 +**
47: f11g³ 10s³ 9.2s³ 12.4g⁵ 12m³ 15.8m* 14.1m² 13.8m⁴ 16.1d⁴ Oct 3] leggy filly: has a
round action: modest performer: won seller at Catterick in August: appeared to run very
well final outing: stays 2m: acts on soft going, good to firm and fibresand: won over
hurdles in November. *Mrs M. Reveley*

IGUASSU FALLS   3 b.f. Machiavellian (USA) 123 – Ivrea 109 (Sadler's Wells   **59 d**
(USA) 132) [2001 11v³ 12s⁵ 12.5d 12v 10m 14.1g 10.1v Oct 24] lengthy, workmanlike

ex-French filly: fourth foal: sister to French 1¼m/11.5f winner Colchica, closely related to fairly useful 1994 2-y-o 7f winner who stayed 1¼m Hedera (by Woodman) and half-sister to 1¾m winner Itatinga (by Riverman): dam, 2-y-o 7f winner who was second in Ribblesdale Stakes, half-sister to Italian Oaks winner Ivyanna: third in newcomers event at Durtal in March: generally well held after, leaving H. Pantall in France 30,000 gns before penultimate start. *J. Parkes*

IHTIMAAM (FR) 9 b.g. Polish Precedent (USA) 131 – Haebeh (USA) 88 (Alydar (USA)) [2001 –§: e16g Jan 6] temperamental handicapper. *H. E. Haynes* – §

IKBAL 3 ch.c. Indian Ridge 123 – Amaniy (USA) 96 (Dayjur (USA) 137) [2001 –p: 8d 8d² 8.5m⁴ 7.1s f6s⁵ f8.5s Dec 26] lengthy colt: modest maiden: left M. Tregoning 5,600 gns after reappearance: sometimes races freely, and will prove best up to 8.5f. *E. J. Alston* 64

IKENGA (IRE) 2 ch.f. (Apr 25) Spectrum (IRE) 126 – Thistle Hill (IRE) 58 (Danehill (USA) 126) [2001 8.2m³ 7.5g* 7d* 7d Oct 20] IR 16,000Y, 9,000 2-y-o: small, good-bodied filly: poor mover: second foal: dam, Irish 1¼m winner, out of half-sister to Ardross: fairly useful performer: won maiden at Beverley in September and nursery at Catterick (made most, flashed tail) in October easily: behind in Rockfel Stakes at Newmarket final start: should stay 1¼m. *M. L. W. Bell* 88

IKIS ZEB T BOB 4 b.g. Rock Hopper 124 – Ikis Girl 83 (Silver Hawk (USA) 123) [2001 11.5m 10m Sep 11] second foal: dam maiden who stayed 1¼m: well held in maidens on Flat. *S. Gollings* –

IKTINAS 2 b.c. (Mar 31) Unfuwain (USA) 131 – Midway Lady (USA) 126 (Alleged (USA) 138) [2001 6g³ 7f⁴ Aug 24] half-brother to several winners, including smart 6f winner (including at 2 yrs) Haafiz and useful 7f/1m winner who stayed 1¼m Umniyate (both by Green Desert): dam won 1000 Guineas and Oaks: fairly useful form in maidens at Newmarket: sweating and unimpressive to post when fourth to Savannah Bay: should stay 1¼m. *B. Hanbury* 82

IL CAVALIERE 6 b.g. Mtoto 134 – Kalmia (Miller's Mate 116) [2001 75p: 14g⁵ 16.4m 15.9m 16m⁴ 14.4d⁶ 14.4m² 14.1m² 16m 14.1g* 16g² Nov 7] good-topped gelding: fairly useful handicapper: won at Redcar in October: stays 2m: acts on firm going, probably on good to soft: consistent. *Mrs M. Reveley* 81

IL DESTINO 6 b.g. Casteddu 111 – At First Sight (He Loves Me 120) [2001 64, a–: f12g⁶ 8.1g⁶ 8.1m 10m 10m Jun 26] lengthy gelding: modest handicapper: probably best around 1¼m: acts on good to firm going, good to soft and equitrack: blinkered (raced freely) once/visored final outing: broke blood vessel on reappearance. *J. G. M. O'Shea* 52

ILE MICHEL 4 b.g. Machiavellian (USA) 123 – Circe's Isle (Be My Guest (USA) 126) [2001 80: 7m 7m⁵ 8f* 7m 7m⁴ 7g 7.1g³ 7s 8d Oct 18] good-topped gelding: fairly useful performer: won minor event at Ayr in June: mostly creditable efforts in handicaps otherwise: effective at 7f/1m: raced mainly on good going or firmer: has hung left/carried head high. *Lady Herries* 87

IL FALCO (FR) 7 ch.g. Polar Falcon (USA) 126 – Scimitarlia (USA) 84 (Diesis 133) [2001 16.4m Jun 7] modest maiden in 1997: tailed off only outing on Flat since. *R. Curtis* –

ILLEGAL IMMIGRANT (CZE) 2 br.g. (Mar 5) Thatching 131 – Silindhra (GER) (Windwurf (GER)) [2001 f8g 8.2s f6g Dec 17] first known foal: dam ran 3 times in Germany: no form in sellers. *Miss J. F. Craze* –

ILLEGAL (IRE) 2 b.c. (Feb 22) Eagle Eyed (USA) 111 – Lady Bodmin (IRE) (Law Society (USA) 130) [2001 5m 6m³ 7.1m* 7m 7.5s⁶ 6g Aug 25] IR 9,500F, IR 23,000Y: workmanlike colt: fifth reported foal: half-brother to a 1m and 1½m winner in Italy by Dancing Dissident: dam unraced: fair performer: won maiden at Warwick in July, despite carrying head awkwardly and edging right: should stay at least 1m: acts on good to firm going, probably on soft. *N. P. Littmoden* 66

ILLUMINATE 8 b.g. Marju (IRE) 127 – Light Bee (USA) 86 (Majestic Light (USA)) [2001 e12g Jan 13] lightly raced and well beaten since 5 yrs. *D. C. O'Brien* –

ILLUMINATION 3 b.f. Saddlers' Hall (IRE) 126 – Warning Light (High Top 131) [2001 10s³ 10g* 11.9m⁶ 10.5s⁶ 10d Oct 18] good-topped filly: has scope: sixth foal: sister to 7f (at 2 yrs)/1m winner Qui Vivra Verra and half-sister to 6f (at 2 yrs) to 1m winner Twilight Patrol (by Robellino) and 1m winner Polar Challenge (by Polar Falcon), all fairly useful: dam unraced from family of Nashwan and Unfuwain: useful performer: impressive winner of maiden at Windsor in August: good 3½ lengths sixth to Inchiri in listed race at York next time, but ran no sort of race after: stays 1½m: best effort on good to firm going: visored final outing: tail flasher, and not an easy ride. *J. R. Fanshawe* 101

ILLUSIONIST 3 b.g. Mujtahid (USA) 118 – Merlin's Fancy 62 (Caerleon (USA) **63** 132) [2001 66: e7g² e7g* f6g⁴ f6g* 8d 7f 6m² 7f⁶ 7d² 7.6f 7f 7.1g 7s Oct 5] quite attractive **a70** gelding: fair performer: won maiden at Lingfield in February: left E. Dunlop after eighth start, poor efforts last 4: probably best around 7f: acts on equitrack, good to soft and good to firm going: visored last 7 outings: has looked hard ride/less than keen. *Mrs N. Macauley*

ILLUSIVE (IRE) 4 b.g. Night Shift (USA) – Mirage 60 (Red Sunset 120) [2001 77, **68** a84: f5g e7g² f6g⁵ f6g* f5g² e5g² f6g³ 6g 5m 5m³ 5g f7g p6g² Dec 29] fairly useful **a93** handicapper on all-weather, fair on turf: in excellent form early in 2001, winning at Wolverhampton in March and running well next 3 starts: respectable efforts at best after: best at 5f/6f: acts on firm going, fibresand and equitrack: usually blinkered: has been slowly away/carried head awkwardly/seemed not to go through with effort: difficult ride. *M. Wigham*

ILLUSTRIOUS DUKE 3 b.c. Dancing Spree (USA) – Killick 69 (Slip Anchor 136) **–** [2001 61: f8.5g* f8g* f8s* f8.5g⁵ 7.6f 8m 7g f9.4g p8g f8.5g f8.5g⁴ f8s⁴ Dec 15] **a76** workmanlike colt: fair performer on all-weather: won maiden at Wolverhampton in January and handicaps at Southwell (2) in February: stays 8.5f: acts on fibresand: races prominently. *M. Mullineaux*

ILTON 2 ch.g. (Mar 14) Dr Devious (IRE) 127 – Madame Crecy (USA) (Al Nasr (FR) **52** 126) [2001 7g 7.2m Sep 20] 20,000Y: strong gelding: fifth foal: closely related to French 1m winner Which Hand (by Indian Ridge), later winner in USA, and half-brother to 3-y-o Jools and 4-y-o French Lieutenant: dam, third at 1m in France, half-sister to high-class sprinter/miler Polar Falcon: modest form when tenth of 12 in maidens at Newcastle and Ayr: should stay at least 1m. *J. D. Bethell*

I'M A BIRD (IRE) 2 b.f. (Mar 27) Prince of Birds (USA) 121 – E Sharp (USA) 49 **44** (Diesis 133) [2001 6m⁵ 6f 7m⁶ 6m 6f Jul 5] IR 3,800Y: small filly: second foal: half-sister to Italian 5f (including at 2 yrs) and 6.5f winner by Bishop of Cashel: dam, second at 7f, granddaughter of US Grade 1 9f winner Chain Bracelet: poor maiden: best effort on debut: tried visored. *G. A. Swinbank*

IMAGINATIVE 4 b.g. Last Tycoon 131 – Imaginary (IRE) 94 (Dancing Brave **–** (USA) 140) [2001 15.9d Sep 1] third foal: half-brother to 6-y-o Rainbow High: dam, 1¼m winner, half-sister to Lowther Stakes winner Kingscote: fairly useful form at best: won maiden at Le Croise Laroche at 2 yrs and handicap at Longchamp at 3 yrs (sold from M. Zilber 20,000 gns after final start): blinkered, well held only 4-y-o Flat outing: stays 11f: acts on good to soft going, yet to race on firmer than good: winning hurdler. *W. Jenks*

IMAGINE (IRE) 3 b.f. Sadler's Wells (USA) 132 – Doff The Derby (USA) **119** (Master Derby (USA)) [2001 108: 7s² 7g³ 8g* 12m* Jun 8]
On pedigree, no great stretch of the imagination was required to picture this filly as a classic winner, though the form of her first eight starts threw a different light on it. A Sadler's Wells half-sister to Generous, Imagine wasn't so good as her half-brother as a two-year-old and she wasn't so good as him at three, the latter certainly too much to ask, but she emulated Generous in stepping up markedly on her juvenile form and she succeeded where he had failed in winning a classic at a mile before going on to glory at Epsom.
The broodmare Doff The Derby had had eight other attempts since Generous to come up with something of the same ilk. A 1989 Sadler's Wells colt died as a foal and a 1990 Lomond colt never saw the racecourse. A lack of European classic success for her next three foals, Osumi Tycoon (by Last Tycoon), Matikane-benizakura (by Royal Academy) and Shinko Hermes (by Sadler's Wells), cannot really be held against them because, as the names hint, they were in Japan, the first two having been sold for 440,000 guineas and 538,348 guineas respectively, the latter being a private sale—at the time a European record for a foal; the first two were winners, the former doing easily the better as he took two Group races and total prize money worth £1,759,634. Doff The Derby's 1994, 1996 and 1997 foals all remained to be trained in Ireland though, where the first of them, 240,000-guinea Strawberry Roan (by Sadler's Wells), had three stabs at classic glory, finishing second in the One Thousand Guineas, eighth in the Derby and fourth in the Oaks; 360,000-guinea foal Genghis Khan (by Sadler's Wells) beat only one home in his two classics and has not gone to Asia, nor embarked on any empire-building, winning two races in Ireland where he performed at plating-class level in 2001;

Entenmann's Irish 1000 Guineas, the Curragh—Imagine puts up an improved effort to beat Crystal Music, Toroca and Sequoyah (light colours), Aidan O'Brien saddling three of the first four home

2,500,000-guinea foal Padua's Pride (by Caerleon), Generous's full brother and the highest-priced foal ever, was in training with Dermot Weld but never ran in Europe, taking a 42,000-dollar race in the United States during the latest season.

In October 1998, Tote bookmakers laid their first bet on the 2000 classics, £10 each-way at 150/1 about Padua's Pride for the Derby. It was not an inspired wager. In May of the latest season, punters fought shy of Imagine when she lined up in the Entenmann's Irish One Thousand Guineas at the Curragh. Four stable mates were also in the line-up, two of them 100/1-shots but the other two both ahead of Imagine in the betting, the Newmarket Guineas third Toroca at 11/2, with Michael Kinane on board, and the Moyglare Stud Stakes winner Sequoyah at 14/1 ridden by Jamie Spencer. Imagine was a 16/1 chance, with Newmarket fourth Crystal Music (9/2), listed winner Cool Clarity (6/1), Leopardstown Trial winner Rebelline (8/1), Newmarket flop Karasta (8/1), Tetrarch Stakes second Scarlet Velvet (10/1), Gladness winner Softly Tread (11/1) and listed winner Speirbhean (12/1) all also preferred to Imagine in a sixteen-runner line-up. Imagine had useful form, lots of it. Eight previous starts made her the most experienced horse in the field—none of the others had had more than five—and she had won two of them, a maiden at Gowran and the C. L. Weld Park Stakes at the Curragh the previous September. In between those two starts, she had been four and a half lengths fourth of nine to Crystal Music in the Fillies' Mile at Ascot. Her last three outings had seen her placed over seven furlongs in the Rockfel Stakes at Newmarket and the listed races won by Rebelline and Cool Clarity. As Aidan O'Brien observed after the Guineas, most of his horses had needed a run. Imagine had needed two, and a much improved performance was in the offing from the two-furlong marker. British challengers Crystal Music and Karasta were about to emerge at the front but Toroca and Imagine were after them, Imagine grabbing the lead from Crystal Music just inside the final furlong and extending her advantage all the way to the line. Ridden by the Ballydoyle number two Seamus Heffernan, Imagine won by two lengths. Toroca was a further two lengths back in third, with Sequoyah arriving late to get fourth from Rebelline and a tame Karasta to give Aidan O'Brien three of the first four finishers, a disappointment no doubt after the previous afternoon's Two Thousand one, two, three.

Ten years earlier, Generous finished only fourth in his Guineas at Newmarket. Six years after that, Strawberry Roan met trouble in running in the Irish One Thousand and finished strongly to go down by a length to her lesser-fancied stable-mate Classic Park in Aidan O'Brien's first classic victory. On their next outings, Generous was transformed by a mile and a half, Strawberry Roan failed to find any improvement. One could not be sure therefore that Imagine would be suited by the Oaks distance, but she looked certain to stay beyond a mile, she was bred to get a mile and a half, and there were no lesser-fancied stable companions for her to contend with in the Vodafone Oaks at Epsom. In a fourteen-runner line-up, only one horse was seriously backed against her. The Queen's Flight of Fancy had been winter favourite for the race and, unlike Imagine, clearly needed a mile and a half on the evidence of her fourth in the Musidora Stakes at York. Imagine was sent off at 3/1, Flight of Fancy at 100/30. The rest, who started at 9/1 and longer, included Italian Oaks winner Zanzibar, Musidora second Relish The Thought, the

Pretty Polly Stakes first and second Mot Juste and Tarfshi, Gay Heroine, who had been second in the Cheshire Oaks, and Silver Patriarch's sister Silver Grey Lady, a close second in the Lingfield Oaks Trial.

Half of the Oaks field appeared to lose their chances on the descent to Tattenham Corner. The early pace was not particularly strong and the run downhill sorted them out instead, with a group of six—outsiders Santa Isobel and Mameha, followed by Relish The Thought, Tarfshi, Flight of Fancy and Mot Juste—entering the straight clear of the remainder. Imagine was the only one to bridge the gap. Uneasy on the descent, she then had five lengths to make up just to get into contention, but the crucial point of the race came approaching the three-furlong marker where Flight of Fancy, in close attendance on the leaders, was impeded for half a dozen strides and lost her momentum, while Imagine was closing fast and uninterrupted on the outer. Only Relish The Thought and Mot Juste remained to be caught and Imagine passed them just inside the final furlong, Flight of Fancy staying on after having to be switched to get second close home with the final distance between them a length and a quarter. Without the interference, Flight of Fancy probably would have won, though, to view it another way, Imagine had the pace to overcome her travails and Flight of Fancy didn't. A rematch would have been fascinating, but three months later neither filly had run again and both were in retirement. Flight of Fancy returned lame from Epsom. Imagine suffered a stone bruise at the start of July, when being prepared for the Irish Oaks, and put on so much weight while recovering from the setback that connections decided that to bring her back would be an unequal struggle.

The Oaks result prompted an updating of several dusty records. Most strikingly, Imagine from Flight of Fancy and Relish The Thought represented a one, two, three for stallion Sadler's Wells (who achieved the same feat in 1999 in the Irish Derby). This was not an unprecedented feat in the British classics, as Rubens, Sultan and Hermit had done the same in the One Thousand Guineas, as had Waxy and Irish Birdcatcher in the Oaks, Sir Peter Teazle and Stockwell in the Derby and Comus (who sired the first four) in the St Leger, but those results had been celebrated in, respectively, 1822, 1836, 1882, 1813, 1852, 1803, 1866 and 1818. Stockwell could also be said to have achieved the feat in the Two Thousand Guineas of 1862, siring the first two and one of the dead-heaters for third place. The day after Imagine's Oaks, one could still read in the newspapers of Sadler's Wells's supposed inability to sire a Derby winner, somewhat incongruously one might think

Vodafone Oaks, Epsom—Imagine does well to come from a poor position and collar eventual third Relish The Thought (right); Flight of Fancy (noseband) has a troubled run before rallying strongly for second place, the first three all sired by Sadler's Wells; Mot Juste and Sunstone come next

seeing as Imagine's win had put him within striking distance of the most wins by any sire in the Oaks, a fourth success (after Salsabil, Intrepidity and Moonshell) taking him level with Hyperion and one behind St Simon. A first Derby win for Sadler's Wells duly arrived thanks to Galileo. This made him the first sire to complete the double in the same year since Blushing Groom in 1989—with Nashwan and, eventually, Snow Bride—hot on the heels of Solario in 1937. Twenty broodmares had two individual British classic winners in the twentieth century, the most recent of them being Glass Slipper, the dam of Light Cavalry and Fairy Footsteps. Two more broodmares had two classic winners in the period spanning the nineteenth and twentieth centuries. Doff The Derby's double success with Generous and Imagine is the first for a dam with Derby and Oaks winners since the same broodmare, Doris, produced Sunstar (1911 Two Thousand Guineas and Derby) and Princess Dorrie (1914 One Thousand Guineas and Oaks). Set Free (with Juliette Marny, Julio Mariner and Scintillate in the 'seventies) is the only dam born in nearly a hundred and forty years to have had three British classic winners.

		Northern Dancer	Nearctic
	Sadler's Wells (USA)	(b 1961)	Natalma
	(b 1981)	Fairy Bridge	Bold Reason
Imagine (IRE)		(b 1975)	Special
(b.f. 1998)		Master Derby	Dust Commander
	Doff The Derby (USA)	(ch 1972)	Madam Jerry
	(b 1981)	Margarethen	Tulyar
		(b 1962)	Russ-Marie

Sadly, Doff The Derby now has no chance of joining Scintillate, following the death as a foal of her 1999 colt by Entrepreneur and her own death later that year because of laminitis. Most of her foals have already been mentioned in this essay, but there were also two before Generous, the US listed-placed winner Windy Triple K (by Jaklin Klugman) and Irish Group 3 and US Grade 3 winner Wedding

Mrs John Magnier & Mrs David Nagle's "Imagine"

Bouquet (by Kings Lake). That takes their dam's overall record to nine winners from ten runners. Doff The Derby never raced herself, reportedly because her tail was broken in an accident. She was first covered as a two-year-old. Her sale to the Barronstown Stud early as a four-year-old, for 82,000 dollars, was probably not unconnected with news that Doff The Derby's half-sister Trillion (herself winner of the Ganay and second in the Arc) had a useful three-year-old with David O'Brien called Triptych. Doff The Derby is more distantly related to King Charlemagne and Meshaheer, brothers who were pattern winners in the latest season. This fine year for the family in general, and for Imagine in particular, provides a timely advertisement for Generous, who will be returning to stallion duties in Britain in 2002, at the Plantation Stud for a fee of £8,000 (October 1st). He was sold to Japan in 1995 after four British covering seasons which produced nothing approaching his own standard—his first Group 1 winner came via the German filly Catella in 2000—but which did yield three-year-olds of almost guaranteed stamina and a high median rating. A much more poignant reminder of Generous and his glory days came in July when his owner Prince Fahd Salman died of a heart attack, aged just forty-six. Generous was easily his best horse, but there were other Group 1 successes with Bint Pasha, Knight's Baroness, Ibn Bey, Zoman, Time Star and Ramruma.

It is a shame that Imagine never got the chance to build an extensive record, like relatives such as Generous, Trillion or Triptych, but her two classic wins in the space of thirteen days made her the first to achieve that particular double since Valoris in 1966. On her best form Imagine would have gone close, at the very least, in races like the Irish Oaks and Yorkshire Oaks, though it has to be said that, overall, the latest season's middle-distance fillies were an uninspiring collection. Gaining classic wins at a mile and at a mile and a half, though, set Imagine apart, with her Irish Guineas form marginally the better. Those classic wins, both with waiting tactics employed, came on good and good to firm ground, but she also won on soft as a two-year-old. A strong, stocky, close-coupled filly, Imagine had a relaxed disposition and was a game and genuine filly. *A. P. O'Brien, Ireland*

IMARI   4 b.f. Rock City 120 – Misty Goddess (IRE) 63 (Godswalk (USA) 130) [2001 68: 13.1m⁴ 14.1m 10.2f 8g⁶ 9.9m 8d³ 10.2f Sep 18] fair winner at 3 yrs: modest form at best in 2001: probably stays 13f: acts on good to firm going, good to soft and fibresand. *R. G. Frost*   **61**

IMBACKAGAIN (IRE)   6 b.g. Mujadil (USA) 119 – Ballinclogher (IRE) (Creative Plan (USA)) [2001 52, a48: f7s f7g f7s³ f7g⁶ f7g f6g* f6g f6g f7g Apr 10] strong, close-coupled gelding: modest performer: won seller at Southwell in February: effective at 6f to 9f: acts on fibresand: visored last 7 starts: has had tongue tied: has been slowly away: tricky ride: unreliable. *N. P. Littmoden*   **– §**
a52 §

IMBIBING (IRE)   2 ch.c. (Apr 28) Halling (USA) 133 – Polar Fizz (Polar Falcon (USA) 126) [2001 7f 8d Oct 19] IR 20,000F, IR 40,000Y: leggy, useful-looking colt: third foal: half-brother to fairly useful 1999 2-y-o 5f winner Saffizz (by Safawan): dam, unraced half-sister to smart 1m/1¼m performer Port Lucaya, out of half-sister to Diminuendo: better effort in maidens (fairly useful form) when eighth of 20 to Music Club at Newmarket on second start: should stay 1¼m: should improve. *R. F. Johnson Houghton*   **83 p**

I'M LULU   3 b.f. Piccolo 121 – Everdene (Bustino 136) [2001 53: e7g³ a8s² 5.8g a6.8g a8g a10g a6s Dec 23] poor maiden: sold from Mrs A. Perrett 1,000 gns after reappearance (blinkered) and trained next 4 starts by O. Stenstrom: best effort at 7f on soft going. *Y. Durant, Norway*   **?**

IMMACULATE CHARLIE (IRE)   3 ch.f. Rich Charlie 117 – Miners Society (Miner's Lamp 114) [2001 37: 11.1d 8m Jun 1] no form at 3 yrs: visored final outing. *L. Lungo*   **–**

IMOYA (IRE)   2 b.f. (Apr 25) Desert King (IRE) 129 – Urgent Liaison (IRE) (High Estate 127) [2001 6m 7m⁴ 7m⁴ 8v² Oct 26] second foal: dam unraced half-sister to very smart performer up to 1¼m Great Dane from family of Croco Rouge and Sleepytime: fairly useful maiden: beaten ½ length by Teresa Balbi at Doncaster final start: should be suited by 1¼m/1½m: acts on heavy and good to firm going. *B. J. Meehan*   **84**

IMPALDI (IRE)   6 b.m. Imp Society (USA) – Jaldi (IRE) 75 (Nordico (USA)) [2001 49, a–: 6s 5m⁴ 6m 5m³ 7.1f 6m 5g Aug 6] angular mare: poor maiden: raced mainly at 5f/ 6f: acts on firm and good to soft going: blinkered once: has hung. *B. Ellison*   **46**
a–

IMPAVIDO (IRE)   2 b.c. (May 25) Sadler's Wells (USA) 132 – Tis Juliet (USA)   **65 p**
(Alydar (USA)) [2001 8m 8d⁵ Oct 3] IR 35,000Y: big, strong, angular colt: half-brother
to winners abroad by Wild Again and Dayjur: dam, US Grade 1 9f winner, out of
champion US sprinter My Juliet: better effort in maidens (fair form) when never-nearer
fifth to Diamond Lover at Newcastle: should stay 1¼m: should progress. *M. Johnston*

IMPELLER (IRE)   2 ch.g. (May 14) Polish Precedent (USA) 131 – Almaaseh (IRE)   **86**
63 (Dancing Brave (USA) 140) [2001 6m⁴ 7m* 8m³ 8d Oct 19] 21,000Y: tall gelding:
sixth foal: half-brother to 3 winners, including smart 5f performer Almaty (by Dancing
Dissident) and useful 1¼m and (in France) 11f winner Salee (by Caerleon): dam
twice-raced daughter of Irish 1000 Guineas winner Al Bahathri: fairly useful form: won
maiden at Salisbury in August: good third in nursery at Bath: likely to prove best at 7f/
1m: has raced freely/carried head awkwardly, and gelded after final start. *W. R. Muir*

IMPERIAL BEAUTY (USA)   5 b.m. Imperial Ballet (IRE) 110 – Multimara   **118**
(USA) (Arctic Tern (USA) 126) [2001 111: 5m⁴ 5m⁴ 5m 6d³ 5s* Oct 7]
      For most of the year the 950,000 guineas spent on Imperial Beauty at the
2000 Newmarket December Sales received a scant return on the track, around
£14,000 from four starts. After leaving Peter Makin's stable and joining John
Hammond's, she finished in the frame in the Prix Saint-Georges at Longchamp,
Prix du Gros-Chene at Chantilly and Prix de Seine-et-Oise at Maisons-Laffitte
(third to Deep Sleep) but was well beaten in the King's Stand Stakes at Royal Ascot,
and on the balance of her form, looked the best part of a stone worse than she had
been in her prime. On the face of it, she looked set to be retired to the paddocks
boasting creditable performances in top company—principally seconds in the 1998
Cheveley Park Stakes and 1999 Prix de l'Abbaye de Longchamp—but with a win
tally consisting of just a minor event and two listed races. All that changed on her
final appearance, when she went one better in the Abbaye on Arc day with a gutsy
success in the biggest field to have contested France's premier sprint. The number
of runners, nineteen, reflected the altered conditions referred to in the essay on
Nuclear Debate in *Racehorses of 2000*, which at last allowed geldings to run. Eight
did so, including Nuclear Debate, but for all the bold remarks afterwards from one
of the Channel 4 pundits about the race having 'the best field lined up for a very
long time' the Abbaye, even though highly competitive, did not take a great deal
of winning by its usual standards. There was no Mozart, King Charlemagne nor
Cassandra Go, only one Group 1 winner from the latest season in Nuclear Debate
and one from the year before, Pipalong, plus seven Group 3 winners and one in
Group 2. The draw seemed to have a marked effect, with low numbers dominating
and the four highest drawn occupying the last four places. Imperial Beauty, drawn
one, was always prominent under Yutaka Take, improved to lead a furlong out and
held on well by half a length from Bahamian Pirate (drawn five) with Pipalong
(drawn three) two and a half lengths away third. This was only the second time
since 1978 that a home-trained runner had won the race, and the twelfth time that a
filly or mare had won it in the same period, but Imperial Beauty's performance has
been rated as no better than smart—she has the lowest rating ever in *Racehorses* for
an Abbaye winner, behind Agnes World, Carmine Lake and Silver Fling on 120 and
L'Epinay on 121. The fact that three of the five just mentioned have won in the last

Prix de l'Abbaye de Longchamp - Majestic Barriere, Longchamp—
a record-sized field, due in no small part to geldings being eligible for the first time;
the mare Imperial Beauty improves on her second placing in 1999, with Bahamian Pirate runner-up
ahead of Pipalong and the blinkered Eastern Purple

five years reflects an undoubted decline in the quality of the race, thanks in part to the drawing power of the Breeders' Cup, but also to a general decline in the sprinting department in Europe and perhaps a lack of returns—the latest Abbaye was worth £47,215 to the winner, the same as the Prix du Cadran but some way behind all the other Group 1 races on Arc day, and a huge amount behind the £403,000 on offer for the Hong Kong Sprint. Whatever the cause, it looks far from promising, since the average rating of Abbaye winners in the last decade is 124, compared to 127 in the previous period and 131 and 128 in the preceding two. However, both the Abbaye and the Cadran will have their prize-money increased by fifty per cent in 2002.

An oddity of the Abbaye concerns the winner's time. The official figure of 1m 0.3sec is more than a second slower than our hand-timed 58.88sec, allowing 0.3 seconds added to the hand time to compensate for the slightly delayed reaction, both consistent and unavoidable, when the stalls open. Nor was this the only occasion at the Arc meeting that the official times were suspect. The difference compared to our hand times was 0.70 seconds or higher in four other races, the Prix de Royallieu, Prix Dollar, Prix de l'Opera and Prix Marcel Boussac, and in four races at the September meetings including the Prix Vermeille. The most extreme

Imperial Beauty (USA) (b.m. 1996)	Imperial Ballet (IRE) (b 1989)	Sadler's Wells (b 1981)	Northern Dancer Fairy Bridge
		Amaranda (b 1975)	Bold Lad Favoletta
	Multimara (USA) (b 1990)	Arctic Tern (ch 1973)	Sea Bird II Bubbling Beauty
		Evening Air (br 1982)	J O Tobin Nellie Forbes

Mrs John Magnier's "Imperial Beauty"

examples in recent years came in the 1997 Poule d'Essai des Poulains and Poule d'Essai des Pouliches, where the official times were 0.85 seconds slower and 2.05 seconds faster than our hand times—the latter equates to around ten lengths. It doesn't require a master of mathematics to work out that something is drastically wrong with some of the clocking at Longchamp, with a ridiculous degree of inconsistency. Until action is taken to improve the situation anyone setting store by the official times is likely to make serious miscalculations.

Imperial Beauty is the best runner by far for both her sire and dam, which made her auction price the previous year seem all the more remarkable. Imperial Beauty is also a granddaughter of Sadler's Wells, which rather reduces the options for her Coolmore owners when it comes to mating her (she is thought to be visiting Danehill), given the strong links several of the stud's best sires have with him. Imperial Beauty's dam Multimara, who was placed twice in the States, has had three other winners including the three-year-old sprint handicapper King's Ballet, also by Imperial Ballet. Her yearling colt by the same sire was bought by Mark Johnston for 30,000 dollars at the Keeneland September Sale. The unraced second dam Evening Air produced May Hill Stakes winner Midnight Air, dam of a good filly in Midnight Line, who finished third in the Oaks as well as winning the Grade 2 Long Island Handicap. Imperial Beauty, a smallish, lengthy mare and a good mover, was effective at five and six furlongs and acted on any going. *J. E. Hammond, France*

IMPERIAL DANCER 3 b.c. Primo Dominie 121 – Gorgeous Dancer (IRE) (Nordico (USA)) [2001 103: 7d³ 8g 8m 6g 7g⁴ 8v* 7v⁴ 8d³ 8s⁵ Nov 18] smallish, angular colt: useful performer: won minor event at Ayr (beat Caughnawaga by 1¼ lengths) in October: best effort when 3 lengths third to Munir in Greenham Stakes at Newbury in April: not discredited otherwise in handicap at Ascot on fourth outing or listed event at Newmarket (third to Riberac) at Rome (fifth to Giovane Imperatore) last 2 starts: will prove best at 7f/1m: acts on any going: tended to carry head high for win: none too consistent. *M. R. Channon*   **105**

IMPERIAL JEWEL (FR) 3 b.f. Deploy 131 – Imperial Prospect (USA) (Imperial Falcon (CAN)) [2001 8.3g 8.1m⁵ 8.3g³ 8.1g⁵ 10g 8.1m 8m 8d Oct 15] lengthy filly: first foal: dam, ran once on Flat and in bumper, from very good US family: fair maiden: should stay 1¼m: yet to race on extremes of going: has looked temperamental, including in blinkers sixth start. *J. J. Sheehan*   **66**

IMPERIAL RACER (IRE) 2 b.g. (Mar 18) Blues Traveller (IRE) 119 – Reasonably French (Reasonable (FR) 119) [2001 7.2g 8g 8m f7g Oct 22] IR 14,000Y: lengthy, rather unfurnished gelding: brother to US 8.5f minor stakes winner Aswhatilldois, fairly useful 7f winner in Britain at 2 yrs, and half-brother to 3 winners, including 4-y-o French Master: dam Irish 2-y-o 7f winner: little form in maidens/sellers. *M. R. Channon*   **–**

IMPERIAL THEATRE (IRE) 2 b.c. (Feb 4) Sadler's Wells (USA) 132 – Aunt Pearl (USA) (Seattle Slew (USA)) [2001 7v³ Oct 26] big, lengthy colt: has plenty of scope: fifth foal: closely related to useful performer up to 1m Kalidasa, 7f winner at 2 yrs, and fairly useful 1997 2-y-o 6f/7f winner Social Charter (both by Nureyev), latter later US Grade 3 9.5f winner: dam, won up to 7f at 4 yrs in USA, from family of Stravinsky and Dowsing: 10/1, burly and green, 3 lengths third of 12 to Proven in maiden at Doncaster, staying on late after missing break: will stay at least 1m: very much on toes and attended by 2 handlers: probably a smart performer in the making, sure to win races. *J. H. M. Gosden*   **90 P**

IMPERO 3 b.g. Emperor Jones (USA) 119 – Fight Right (FR) (Crystal Glitters (USA) 127) [2001 –: 11.5m 10m 11.7g⁶ Aug 7] modest maiden handicapper: stays 1¼m: tongue tied (tailed off) final outing: sold 800 gns. *Miss B. Sanders*   **50**

IMPISH JUDE 3 b.f. Imp Society (USA) – Miss Nanna 56§ (Vayrann 133) [2001 8.2d 7.1m⁴ 8.2f⁶ 7d⁶ 8.2m 8.1s Sep 7] 500Y: leggy filly: sixth foal: half-sister to 1994 2-y-o 5f winner who stayed 1¼m and became ungenuine Cumbrian Minstrel (by Efisio) and 7f/1m winner Sis Garden (by Damister): dam temperamental maiden who stayed 6f: modest maiden: stays 1m: acts on firm and good to soft going. *J. Mackie*   **59**

IMPISH LAD 3 b.g. Imp Society (USA) – Madonna Da Rossi 53 (Mtoto 134) [2001 56: f7g f8g² f8s* f8g f8g⁶ f7g² f7g² f7g⁶ f7g³ f7g⁵ f7g⁵ 8.1v⁶ f11g⁴ 8.2v 9.9m 7m 8.2s⁶ 7g 10m 10.2g 10s 11.8s Oct 16] small, sturdy gelding: modest performer: won claimer at Southwell (final start for B. Rothwell) in January: mostly below form after: effective at   **–**   **a60**

7f/easy 1m: acts on firm going and fibresand: often blinkered/visored: sold 2,600 gns. *M. J. Polglase*

IMPRESSIVE WAY (IRE)   5 b.h. Archway (IRE) 115 – Way Ahead 81 (Sovereign   **64**
Path 125) [2001 10d 7m⁶ 10d 8s⁶ f9.4s Dec 15] half-brother to 1m/9f winner Quietly
Impressive (by Taufan): dam Irish 1m winner: form (modest) only when sixth in handicap
at Thurles fourth start: well beaten at Wolverhampton final outing: stays 1m: acts on soft
ground. *Michael McElhone, Ireland*

IMPREVUE (IRE)   7 ch.m. Priolo (USA) 127 – Las Bela 75 (Welsh Pageant 132)   **58**
[2001 66: e12g² e12s² e12g* e10g² e12g⁵ e12g* e10g 12.3m⁵ 10m 10s⁶ p10g Dec 19]   **a68**
lengthy mare: fair performer: won claimer at Lingfield (then left R. O'Sullivan) in March
and handicap there in April: left A. Reid after ninth start: has form at 2m, but seems
best at 1¼m/1½m: acts on firm ground, soft and equitrack: usually blinkered: sometimes
slowly away/wanders: usually held up. *R. J. O'Sullivan*

IMPREZA   3 b.f. Mistertopogigo (IRE) 118 – Little Redwing 37 (Be My Chief (USA)   **–**
122) [2001 –: 12m f12g 12g Aug 7] compact filly: no form: tried visored. *Miss A. Stokell*

IMPULSIVE AIR (IRE)   9 b.g. Try My Best (USA) 130 – Tracy's Sundown (Red   **54 §**
Sunset 120) [2001 51§: f11g⁵ f8.5g⁵ 9v⁶ 8m 9m⁴ 8m 9f 10.9f⁵ 9.9f* 10g 10.9d⁶ 10m*
11m⁵ 10.4m 10.1f 10.9m 9.9s Sep 25] strong gelding: unimpressive mover: modest
handicapper: won at Beverley and Nottingham (dead-heated) in July: effective at 1m to
11f: acts on firm going, good to soft and fibresand: tried visored early in career: untrustworthy. *J. R. Weymes*

I'M SOPHIE (IRE)   4 ch.f. Shalford (IRE) 124§ – Caisson 67 (Shaadi (USA) 126)   **64**
[2001 53: f6g⁵ f8.5s³ f5g 5v⁵ 5.1d 6m* 5d 6.1v Oct 4] lengthy filly: modest performer:
won maiden handicap at Brighton in May: off nearly 5 months after and well below form
last 2 starts: should prove best at 5f/6f: acts on heavy going, good to firm and fibresand:
often races prominently. *D. Burchell*

I'M THE GUV'NOR (IRE)   2 b.c. (Apr 21) College Chapel 122 – Star of Aran   **–**
(Artaius (USA) 129) [2001 8.3v p8g Nov 24] 6,000Y: half-brother to several winners,
including fairly useful Irish winner around 7f Grianan Realta (by Elbio) and Irish 1997
2-y-o 1m winner Precise Direction (by Distinctly North), later winner in USA: dam
lightly-raced maiden: well held in sellers: blinkered final start. *J. Akehurst*

IMTIHAN (IRE)   2 ch.c. (Apr 8) Unfuwain (USA) 131 – Azyaa 101 (Kris 135) [2001   **– p**
8d 8d Oct 19] good-topped colt: has a quick action: brother to 8-y-o Yarob, closely related
to 2 winners, including 4-y-o Samsaam, and half-brother to 3 winners, including useful
7f/1m performer Ihtiraz (by Soviet Star): dam 7.5f winner from good middle-distance
family: never dangerous in maidens at Newmarket: will probably do better. *B. W. Hills*

IMTIYAZ (USA)   2 ro.c. (Mar 14) Woodman (USA) 126 – Shadayid (USA) 122   **96**
(Shadeed (USA) 135) [2001 7.1s* 7m³ 7s⁵ Oct 7] leggy colt: sixth foal: closely related to
7f winner (including in USA) Shawaf (by Mr Prospector), and half-brother to 3 winners,
including 1m/1¼m performer Bint Shadayid (by Nashwan) and 3-y-o Alshadiyah, all
useful: dam, won Prix Marcel Boussac and 1000 Guineas, from very good family: useful
form: won maiden at Sandown in June by 6 lengths from Sparkling Water: disappointing
after in listed race at Newmarket (odds on) and Grand Criterium at Longchamp (visored,
last of 5), finding little: should stay 1m. *D. R. Loder*

IN A TWINKLING (IRE)   4 b.f. Brief Truce (USA) 126 – Glim (USA) (Damascus   **–**
(USA)) [2001 65: 8d 10f 8m Jun 4] leggy, angular filly: fair maiden at best: little show in
2001. *M. Blanshard*

INCANTATION   2 b.f. (Apr 8) Magic Ring (IRE) 115 – Songsheet 74 (Dominion 123)   **–**
[2001 7m 6g 8s Sep 30] 5,600Y: first foal: dam best at 5f: well beaten in maidens/seller.
Dr J. D. Scargill

INCA WARRIOR (USA)   3 ch.c. Diesis 133 – Urus (USA) (Kris S (USA)) [2001   **79**
8m³ 8m³ 10f² 10m⁴ Jul 27] close-coupled, quite attractive colt: second foal: brother to
Happy Diamond: dam won up to 1¼m in USA, including minor stakes: fair maiden: stays
1¼m: carried head awkwardly final outing: sold 1,800 gns in October. *J. W. Hills*

INCHALONG   6 b.m. Inchinor 119 – Reshift 94 (Night Shift (USA)) [2001 –: 7.1m 6g   **–**
7m May 30] small mare: unimpressive mover: fair handicapper in 1999: well held since:
visored. *M. Brittain*

INCH BY INCH   2 b.f. (Mar 6) Inchinor 119 – Maid Welcome 81 (Mummy's Pet 125)   **52**
[2001 7g 7d p10g Dec 4] second foal: dam 5f to 1m winner: modest form in maidens:
seems barely to stay 1¼m. *P. J. Makin*

INCHCAPE   3 b.g. Indian Ridge 123 – Inchmurrin 114 (Lomond (USA) 128) [2001   **102**
85p: 6d* 7g³ May 6] good-topped gelding: useful form: won maiden at Newmarket in
April by 1¾ lengths from Indian Prince: ran well when 3¼ lengths third to Jentzen in
minor event there only subsequent start: gelded after: will probably stay 1m: raced only
on good going or softer. *R. Charlton*

INCHCOONAN   3 b.f. Emperor Jones (USA) 119 – Miss Ivory Coast (USA) (Sir Ivor   **64**
135) [2001 7s 6g 7.5m 8m⁶ 8m* 10.9m f7g f8g³ f8g* f8g⁴ Dec 14] 15,000F: strong filly:
fifth foal: half-sister to 7-y-o Abajany: dam French 9f winner: modest performer: won
handicaps at Musselburgh (hung badly left) in August and Southwell in December: stays
1m: acts on fibresand and good to firm ground. *K. R. Burke*

INCHDURA   3 ch.g. Inchinor 119 – Sunshine Coast 86 (Posse (USA) 130) [2001 53p: **92**
8g 8s 7m² 7m* 7.1m 7.6g* 7.6g² 8f* 8d Nov 3] quite attractive gelding: fairly useful
handicapper: won at Salisbury in June, Lingfield in August and Newbury (beat Dennis El
Menace by neck) in September: stays 1m: best on going firmer than good: has won with
tongue tied: sometimes edgy (unseated in paddock on reappearance): gelded after final
start. *R. Charlton*

INCH HIGH   3 ch.g. Inchinor 119 – Harrken Heights (IRE) (Belmez (USA) 131)   **–**
[2001 7.1f 10.5d Jul 15] first foal: dam no form: tailed off in maidens. *J. S. Goldie*

INCHING CLOSER   4 b.g. Inchinor 119 – Maiyaasah 75 (Kris 135) [2001 88: 12d   **93**
12s⁶ 12g² 12v² 14m 13.3m* 16.1f Jun 30] sturdy gelding: fairly useful handicapper: won
at Newbury in June by short head from Arabian Moon: also ran well previously when
second at Newmarket and Newbury: stays extended 13f: acts on any going: sold 50,000
gns, joined F. Murphy and winner over hurdles. *N. A. Callaghan*

INCHINNAN   4 b.f. Inchinor 119 – Westering 54 (Auction Ring (USA) 123) [2001 74:   **78**
10v 8.5s⁶ 10m⁵ 9m³ 9f³ 10.1d² 10.5g 10.5s* 12g Sep 28] small filly: fair handicapper:
won amateur contest at Haydock in September: stays 10.5f: has form on firm going,
seems at very best on soft/heavy. *C. Weedon*

INCHIRI   3 b.f. Sadler's Wells (USA) 132 – Inchyre 102 (Shirley Heights 130) [2001   **108**
95p: 12v³ 10s* 11.4f⁴ 10f⁶ 10.2m³ 11.9m* 12m 12d⁵ 10.5v⁵ 10.5v Nov 27] small, rather
leggy filly: useful performer: won maiden at Ripon in April and listed race at York in
August, in latter doing well to beat Panna a neck after getting clear run only just inside
final 1f: not discredited when 8½ lengths eighth to Aquarelliste in Prix Vermeille at
Longchamp next time: below form after: will stay 1¾m: very best form on good to
firm ground, has won on soft: sometimes slowly away (markedly so eighth outing).
G. A. Butler

INCH PERFECT   6 b.g. Inchinor 119 – Scarlet Veil 75 (Tyrnavos 129) [2001 92, a87:   **95**
8.9m² 11.9d 8m 10m⁵ 11.9g⁵ 13.9m 12g 12d⁶ Oct 2] tall, good-topped gelding: useful
handicapper: ran well when neck second to Pension Fund at York in June: ran respectably
at best after: stays 1¾m: yet to race on heavy going, acts on any other turf and on
fibresand: tongue tied once: has idled, and usually held up: tough. *R. A. Fahey*

INCLINE (IRE)   2 b.g. (Mar 22) Danehill (USA) 126 – Shalwar Kameez (IRE)   **–**
(Sadler's Wells (USA) 132) [2001 5m May 11] IR 90,000Y: first foal: dam, unraced sister
to useful Irish performer up to 1¾m Family Tradition, from outstanding family of
Rainbow Quest, Warning and Commander In Chief: 10/1 and very green, last of 12 in
maiden at Lingfield: subsequently gelded. *T. G. Mills*

*Peugeot Sun Chariot Stakes, Newmarket—another major prize goes to an Ed Dunlop-trained filly
as Independence gains a decisive success from Foodbroker Fancy and Riberac*

INDABA (IRE) 3 ch.f. Indian Ridge 123 – Sedulous 107 (Tap On Wood 130) [2001 **98**
6s² 6g² 6g² 6g* 7d* 6g³ 7d² 7v* 6v³ Nov 14] IR 75,000Y: useful-looking filly: half-sister
to several winners, including useful 1m winner So Sedulous (by The Minstrel), herself
dam of smart German middle-distance colt Subiaco: dam, Irish 2-y-o 5f to 1m winner,
later successful in USA: useful performer: won maiden at Newmarket in August and
minor events at Yarmouth (hung right) in September and Doncaster (beat Watching by
1½ lengths in race started by tape) in October: creditable third to Chercheuse in listed
race at Maisons-Laffitte final start: effective at 6f/7f: raced only on ground softer than
good (acts on heavy): has been early to post/slowly away: has been bandaged in front/
worn crossed noseband: sold 110,000 gns in December. *J. Noseda*

INDEFINITE STAY 3 b.g. Beveled (USA) – Wassl's Sister (Troy 137) [2001 53: 8s **–**
10g 9.7d f9.4s Sep 6] tall gelding: modest maiden at 2 yrs: no form in 2001. *W. R. Muir*

INDELIBLE 2 br.f. (Feb 27) Polar Falcon (USA) 126 – Ink Pot (USA) 73 (Green **63**
Dancer (USA) 132) [2001 6m⁴ f6g³ 6m³ 7.5s 7g² Oct 19] small, good-bodied filly: has a
round action: second foal: half-sister to fairly useful 2000 2-y-o 6f/7f winner Quink (by
Selkirk), later 1m winner in Hong Kong: dam maiden who would have stayed at least
1¼m: modest maiden: runner-up in claimer at Redcar: stays 7f: acts on good to firm
ground and fibresand, ran as if something amiss on soft: sold 5,000 gns. *W. J. Haggas*

INDEPENDENCE 3 b.f. Selkirk (USA) 129 – Yukon Hope (USA) 75 (Forty Niner **116**
(USA)) [2001 80p: 7m² 7.1m⁴ 7.1g* 8f* 7m³ 8g* 8g* Oct 6] tall, useful-looking filly:
smart performer: progressed well at 3 yrs, winning minor event at Sandown and listed
rated stakes at Ascot, both in June, Trusted Partner Matron Stakes at the Curragh (beat
Toroca a length) in September and Peugeot Sun Chariot Stakes at Newmarket (by 1¼
lengths from Foodbroker Fancy) in October: effective at 7f/1m: acts on firm going:
sometimes edgy: has worn crossed noseband/gone early to post: races freely and usually
held up, but just as effective making running: genuine and reliable. *E. A. L. Dunlop*

Cliveden Stud's "Independence"

INDEPENDENCE HALL (IRE)   4 b.c. Sadler's Wells (USA) 132 – Fruition 89   –
(Rheingold 137) [2001 86: 14s⁶ 14d 16g 12s 13d p16g p13g Dec 29] IR 40,000Y: brother
to top-class Breeders' Cup Turf winner Northern Spur, closely related to high-class stayer
Kneller (by Lomond) and useful 1¼m/11f winner Oenothera (by Night Shift), and
half-brother to 2 winners, including smart stayer Great Marquess (by Touching Wood):
dam maiden half-sister to dam of Salsabil: unraced at 2 yrs, then fairly useful at 3 yrs
(winner over 1½m): no form in 2001 (sold from T. Stack in Ireland 3,500 gns after fifth
start), at Lingfield last 2 outings: stays 1½m: form only on good/good to soft going.
J. E. Long

INDEPENDENT DANCER   4 b.g. Shareef Dancer (USA) 135 – Ecologically Kind   –
(Alleged (USA) 138) [2001 f12s Dec 26] 4,000Y, 3,500 2-y-o: second foal: dam unraced:
tailed off in seller. *Mrs A. Duffield*

IN DEPTH (USA)   3 b.f. Defensive Play (USA) 118 – Popularity (USA) 58 (Blushing   **58**
Groom (FR) 131) [2001 f12g² f11s Dec 21] 15,000 3-y-o: fourth foal: half-sister to 1¾m
winner Devilish Charm (by Devil's Bag) and French 10.5f winner Attention Seeker (by
Exbourne): dam, ran twice, half-sister to US Grade 1 1¼m/1½m winner Vanlandingham
and to dam of 4-y-o Distant Music: much better effort in maidens (modest form) when 2
lengths second to easy winner Speed of Light at Wolverhampton: slowly away later in
month. *Mrs H. Dalton*

INDIANA JONES (IRE)   4 b.g. Emperor Jones (USA) 119 – Broadway Rosie 101   –
(Absalom 128) [2001 –: f9.4g f7g Apr 10] good-topped gelding: no sign of ability.
D. W. Chapman

INDIANA SPRINGS (IRE)   4 b.g. Foxhound (USA) 103 – Moss Agate (Alias   **46 §**
Smith (USA)) [2001 48§, a34§: f11g f12g⁵ f16g⁴ f16.2g* f16.2g Feb 22] good-topped
gelding: poor performer: won selling handicap at Wolverhampton in February: stays 2m:
acts on good to firm going, good to soft and fibresand: tried visored/blinkered (including
last 4 starts): has wandered/carried head high. *J. G. Given*

INDIAN BAZAAR (IRE)   5 ch.g. Indian Ridge 123 – Bazaar Promise 58 (Native   **67**
Bazaar 122) [2001 52: 5d 5m* 5.2m* 5.7g⁴ 5m* 5m 5f³ 5m⁴ 5g 5g³ 5m³ 5m 5.7m⁵
5.1g* 5m⁴ 6.1v Oct 4] big, good-topped gelding: fair handicapper: won at Goodwood/
Yarmouth in May, Lingfield in June and Chepstow in September: best at 5f: acts on soft
and good to firm going: usually races up with pace. *J. M. Bradley*

INDIAN BEAT   4 ch.g. Indian Ridge 123 – Rappa Tap Tap (FR) 111 (Tap On Wood   **68**
130) [2001 8m 10m* 9m² 10.3f⁴ 10g⁵ 9g 8m Aug 25] 130,000Y, 4,000 3-y-o: leggy,
useful-looking gelding: half-brother to several winners, including smart miler Killer
Instinct (by Zafonic) and fairly useful 1¼m winner Tap On Air (by Caerleon): dam, 6f (at
2 yrs) and 1m winner, half-sister to Colorspin (dam of Opera House and Kayf Tara) and
Bella Colora (dam of Stagecraft): fair maiden: unlikely to stay beyond 1¼m: raced only
on good going or firmer: visored (well beaten) last 2 starts: sold 5,200 gns. *Mrs L. Stubbs*

INDIAN BLAZE   7 ch.g. Indian Ridge 123 – Odile (Green Dancer (USA) 132) [2001   **76**
89d, a–: 8m 8m 7.6f 6m² 8f* 8m 8m³ 6v Nov 8] workmanlike gelding: fair handicapper:
won at Kempton in August: effective at 6f to 1m: acts on any turf going and fibresand:
blinkered once: takes good hold: often hangs right. *D. R. C. Elsworth*

INDIAN BRAVE   7 b.g. Indian Ridge 123 – Supreme Kingdom 85 (Take A Reef 127)   **46**
[2001 –: f8g f9.4g f12g 7m⁶ 7f³ 8m Jun 20] lengthy gelding: poor maiden: left Jamie
Poulton after third start: stays 7f: acts on firm and soft ground: tried blinkered: has carried
head awkwardly/hung. *P. Howling*

INDIAN CREEK   3 br.c. Indian Ridge 123 – Blue Water (USA) 104 (Bering 136)   **117**
[2001 8.3g⁴ 8m* 9.9m* 10g⁵ 9.9g³ 10g* 10d³ 10d⁴ Nov 2] 46,000Y: tall, rather leggy,
useful-looking colt: first foal: dam French 1m to 1½m (listed race) winner: smart
performer: won maiden in June and handicap (went in snatches) in July, both at
Goodwood, and minor event at Ascot (beat Tissifer by neck) in September: excellent 4¾
lengths third to Nayef in Dubai Champion Stakes at Newmarket penultimate start, but
only fourth of 5 behind Lagudin in listed race there final outing: better around 1¼m than
shorter: acts on good to firm and good to soft going: found little fourth start: often slowly
away: quirky, and no easy ride. *D. R. C. Elsworth*

INDIAN DANCE   5 ch.g. Indian Ridge 123 – Petronella (USA) (Nureyev (USA) 131)   –
[2001 56, a78: f7g f7g⁶ f9.4s⁵ f8.5s f7g f8g 8.1g May 7] big, lengthy gelding: fair   **a70**
performer: form only on all-weather at 5 yrs: stays 9.4f: acts on fibresand: has had tongue
tied: reportedly broke blood vessel 3 times in 2001, including final start. *P. D. Evans*

INDIAN DREAMER (IRE)   2 b. or br.c. (Feb 10) Indian Ridge 123 – Truly A   **88**
Dream (IRE) 116 (Darshaan 133) [2001 7m* 7d Oct 2] 400,000Y: smallish, good-bodied
colt: third foal: half-brother to French 2000 2-y-o 1m winner Truly Yours (by Barathea):
dam, won at 1m (at 2 yrs) to 1½m in France and Canada, half-sister to 3-y-o Wareed and
dam of Prix Saint-Alary winner Cerulean Sky: won maiden at Leicester in September by
½ length from Gallant Boy: similar form when seventh of 16 to Sir George Turner in
valuable sales race at Newmarket (wore crossed noseband, unimpressive to post): will
stay at 1m. *D. R. Loder*

INDIAN DRIVE (IRE)   4 b.g. Indian Ridge 123 – Daniella Drive (USA) (Shelter   **–**
Half (USA)) [2001 64: 5g 7.5g 6g 12.5d f5g Dec 14] sturdy gelding: disappointing
maiden: left L. Browne in Ireland after penultimate start. *E. J. Alston*

INDIAN FILE   3 ch.c. Indian Ridge 123 – Shining Water 111 (Kalaglow 132) [2001   **98**
–p: 7d² 10.2f* 10.1m 10.3m² 11.9d* 12g* 14.8m Aug 24] sturdy, good-bodied colt:
useful performer: won maiden at Bath in May and handicaps at Haydock (got up late to
beat Celtic Mission by neck) and Newmarket (set steady pace when beating Mesmeric ½
length) in August: found to be distressed after final outing: was better at 1½m than 1¼m:
acted on firm and good to soft going: was game: dead. *B. W. Hills*

INDIAN GIFT   2 ch.f. (Jan 26) Cadeaux Genereux 131 – Vanishing Trick (USA) 80   **58**
(Gone West (USA)) [2001 7g 8.2v 7s Oct 31] strong filly: first foal: dam, 2-y-o 7f winner
who stayed 1¼m, from family of Nureyev and Sadler's Wells: modest form in maidens:
should stay 1¼m. *E. A. L. Dunlop*

INDIAN GIVER   3 ch.f. Cadeaux Genereux 131 – About Face (Midyan (USA) 124)   **81**
[2001 57: 8d² 7m* 8.1v² 7g Nov 3] fairly useful performer, lightly raced: won maiden at
Salisbury in June: well held on handicap debut at Newmarket over 4 months later: should
prove best at 7f/1m: yet to race on extremes of going. *R. Hannon*

INDIAN JUSTICE   2 b.g. (Apr 25) Bijou d'Inde 127 – Legal Sound 85 (Legal Eagle   **–**
126) [2001 7m⁴ Aug 25] 1,500Y, resold 2,000Y: half-brother to 3 winners, including
useful 1989 2-y-o sprinter Brisas (by Vaigly Great): dam 6f winner: 14/1, tailed-off last
of 4 in minor event at Redcar. *R. A. Fahey*

INDIAN MUSIC   4 b.g. Indian Ridge 123 – Dagny Juel (USA) 75 (Danzig (USA))   **77**
[2001 71: f5g³ f6g² f6f* 5v⁵ 5d* 6m f6g³ 5m⁵ 5.1f⁶ 5m 6m⁶ f5g 5d 5m 5m 6.1v f5g* f6g⁴
f5g⁴ f6g Dec 17] sturdy, lengthy gelding: fair performer: won handicaps at Southwell in
March and Musselburgh in April, and claimer at Southwell in November: will prove best
at 5f/6f: acts on heavy going (probably on firm) and fibresand: sometimes blinkered (at
least as effective when not): sometimes slowly away: tends to carry head high. *A. Berry*

INDIAN PLUME   5 b.g. Efisio 120 – Boo Hoo 68 (Mummy's Pet 125) [2001 87: 8s   **96**
7.1g 7m³ 8m* 8g³ 8m² 8.1v² 7g Oct 5] smallish, sturdy gelding: useful handicapper: won
at Yarmouth in July: easily best efforts when second at Ripon and Haydock: effective at
7f to 8.5f: acts on good to firm and heavy going: front runner: game. *T. G. Mills*

INDIAN PRINCE (IRE)   3 ch.g. Indian Ridge 123 – Lingering Melody (IRE) 59   **112**
(Nordico (USA)) [2001 e6g² 6d² 6.1v⁴ 5m³ 5f 6d² 5.1f* 5g³ 5.2f² 5g 5.6m 6m⁵ 5g* 6d

JRA Nakayama Rous Stakes, Newmarket—Indian Prince (right) shows appreciable improvement
to defeat Smokin Beau; The Trader takes third place

Oct 19] IR 34,000F, IR 50,000Y: sturdy gelding: second foal: half-brother to fairly useful 7f winner (including at 2 yrs) Rainbow Melody (by Rainbows For Life): dam, Irish maiden who stayed 1m, half-sister to very smart miler Alflora from family of Ardross: much improved with racing and developed into smart performer, winning handicap at Bath in July and listed event at Newmarket in October: 33/1, best effort when beating Smokin Beau by neck in latter race: respectable tenth to Danehurst in similar contest on same course final start: will prove best at 5f: acts on firm and good to soft going: sometimes starts slowly: reliable. *B. J. Meehan*

INDIAN SHORES   2 b.f. (Apr 22) Forzando 122 – Cottonwood 80 (Teenoso (USA)   **66** 135) [2001 5.1f 5m⁵ 6g³ 5f⁴ 5f⁵ f5g 6d Oct 19] 3,000Y: neat filly: sixth foal: half-sister to 3-y-o White Star Lady, 4-y-o Lady Jeannie and a winner abroad by Primo Dominie: dam, 1¼m winner, half-sister to smart Italian sprinter Arranvanna: fair maiden: will prove best at 5f/6f: raced mainly on good going or firmer on turf, ran poorly on fibresand: races prominently. *E. J. Alston*

INDIAN SILK (IRE)   3 b.f. Dolphin Street (FR) 125 – Scammony (IRE) (Persian   **74** Bold 123) [2001 f7g⁴ f7g⁴ 6.1v* 7s* 8.1g f7g⁴ 8.1m³ 10.2g f8g 8d Nov 2] 16,000F: second foal: dam once-raced sister to dam of top-class sprinter Lake Coniston: fair performer: won seller at Southwell in February and handicaps at Nottingham in March and Newbury in May: well held last 3 starts: stays 1m: acts on heavy going, good to firm and fibresand: tongue tied. *J. A. Osborne*

INDIAN SOLITAIRE (IRE)   2 b.c. (Mar 26) Bigstone (IRE) 126 – Terrama Sioux   **91 p** (Relkino 131) [2001 7m² 7.1f³ 8d* Oct 25] 30,000Y: half-brother to several winners, including 1½m winner Dakota Brave (by Exactly Sharp): dam unraced: placed in maidens at Folkestone and Chepstow before winning similar event at Bath by 1½ lengths from Celtic Style, leading well inside final 1f: will be suited by 1¼m/1½m: should make a useful 3-y-o. *Mrs A. J. Perrett*

INDIAN SPARK   7 ch.g. Indian Ridge 123 – Annes Gift (Ballymoss 136) [2001 109:   **112** 6v 5.2d 6s 6g 5m 6m⁴ 5m* 7m 5.1g³ 5g² 6m 5s 6v Oct 26] close-coupled gelding: poor mover (reportedly fractured off-fore joint earlier in career): smart performer: won Northern Rock Gosforth Park Cup (Handicap) at Newcastle (cosily by ¾ length from Get Stuck In) in June: ran well otherwise only when in frame in Wokingham Stakes (3¼ lengths fourth to Nice One Clare), well-contested minor at Nottingham (over ½-length third to Astonished) and Miller Flying Five at Leopardstown (head second to Ishiguro): best at 5f/6f: acts on any going: usually takes a few runs to hit form. *J. S. Goldie*

INDIAN SUN   4 ch.g. Indian Ridge 123 – Star Tulip 99 (Night Shift (USA)) [2001 79:   **67 d** f8g* f8.5g f9.4g f8.5g⁶ 7s⁶ 8m f8g 10f² 12.1m f11g* f11g⁴ 11.5m⁶ 10.3m f8g 11.5g 16.2m⁵ f12g⁵ 15.9d f11g⁵ 11.8s* f14g 14.1s f12g⁴ f12g f11g* f12g⁴ f11g⁵ f11g f12s Dec 26] angular gelding: fair performer at best: won claimer (only outing for Mrs L. Jewell) in February and seller in June, both at Southwell, claimer at Leicester in October and seller at Southwell in November: probably stays 2m: acts on any turf going and fibresand: tried blinkered/visored: tongue tied: sometimes slowly away. *P. D. Evans*

INDIAN SUNSET   8 ch.g. Indian Ridge 123 – Alanood 85 (Northfields (USA)) [2001   **32** f14g f14g⁴ 17.1m⁶ 12.3m 16f⁵ 15m⁵ Aug 1] compact, good-bodied gelding: poor maiden: **a42** stays 2m: acts on firm going and fibresand. *J. A. Osborne*

INDIAN SWINGER (IRE)   5 ch.h. Up And At 'em 109 – Seanee Squaw (Indian   **–** Ridge 123) [2001 –, a60d: f8g² f8.5s⁴ Jan 11] modest performer: stays 8.5f: acts on   **a51** fibresand/equitrack: sometimes slowly away: none too reliable: sold only 620 gns in April. *P. Howling*

INDIAN WARRIOR   5 b.g. Be My Chief (USA) 122 – Wanton 106 (Kris 135) [2001   **56** 52, a59: f6g⁴ f6g 6f 6m⁵ 6m* 7s³ f7g⁵ f6g² p7g Dec 28] small, quite attractive gelding: modest performer nowadays: won selling handicap at Lingfield in August: best form at 6f/7f: acts on firm going, soft and fibresand: tried visored/blinkered: has been steadily/ last to post: sometimes starts slowly/races freely. *W. J. Musson*

INDIGO BAY (IRE)   5 b.g. Royal Academy (USA) 130 – Cape Heights (Shirley   **38 §** Heights 130) [2001 50§, a71d: e16g f11g f11g⁶ 10s 12.3s 10d 8.1m 16m 16m 13m⁴ 12f⁴ 12m⁶ 12g 12m 11.1g 12d² 11d f12g Nov 3] leggy gelding: poor performer: best form around 1½m: acts on firm going and fibresand/equitrack: usually blinkered/visored: tried tongue tied: usually front runner: unreliable. *R. Bastiman*

IN DISGUISE   2 ch.g. (Jan 23) Nashwan (USA) 135 – Conspiracy 98 (Rudimentary   **78** (USA) 118) [2001 7m⁶ 7g² 8m 8d Oct 19] strong, lengthy gelding: has a fluent, round action: first foal: dam, 2-y-o 5f winner, closely related to high-class sprinter Gayane out of very smart filly up to 1¼m Roussalka, herself half-sister to Oh So Sharp: fair maiden: second of 19 to Grampian at Newmarket: disappointing both starts after, including in nursery on same course (then gelded): should stay at least 1m. *J. L. Dunlop*

INDIUM 7 b.g. Groom Dancer (USA) 128 – Gold Bracelet § (Golden Fleece (USA) **74** 133) [2001 85: 7.1m⁴ 8m* 8.1m² 10.1d³ 8.5s p10g Dec 12] tall, leggy gelding: fair performer: won claimer at Yarmouth in July: effective at 1m/1¼m: acts on any going: has run well sweating: has worn crossed noseband: held up. *D. E. Cantillon*

INDUCEMENT 5 ch.g. Sabrehill (USA) 120 – Verchinina 99 (Star Appeal 133) [2001 **86** 91: 12d 10d Oct 2] tall, good-topped gelding: has a fluent, round action: fairly useful handicapper: better effort on Flat at 5 yrs (off 6 months in between) at Newmarket second outing: best efforts around 1¼m: acts on good to firm and good to soft going: has been equipped with rope halter. *Mrs A. J. Perrett*

INDY ROSE (USA) 2 b.f. (Mar 12) A P Indy (USA) 131 – Chelsey Flower (USA) **94 §** 116 (His Majesty (USA)) [2001 7g* 7.1m⁵ 7g⁵ 7g 7d Oct 20] $950,000Y: second foal: dam US Grade 1 1¼m winner: fairly useful performer: won maiden at Yarmouth in July: creditable tenth of 17 in Moyglare Stud Stakes at the Curragh on fourth start: most disappointing otherwise, visored when last of 10 in Rockfel Stakes at Newmarket: bred to stay at least 1m: usually races prominently: has flashed tail/seemed to take no interest when headed: joined H-A. Pantall in France. *D. R. Loder*

INEXPENSIVE 5 b.m. Puissance 110 – Sojourn 87 (Be My Guest (USA) 126) [2001 **–** 72+: f8.5g 8.5s 8d 8f 9m 8m 8.3g 8.3g Jul 9] fair winner at 3 yrs: little form in 2001: tried blinkered/tongue tied. *M. Kettle*

INFAMOUS (USA) 8 ch.g. Diesis 133 – Name And Fame (USA) (Arts And **–** Letters (USA)) [2001 f16.2g 17.2f May 22] angular gelding: one-time fairly useful performer: well beaten both 8-y-o outings, first since 1999: tried blinkered/tongue tied. *B. J. Llewellyn*

Mr Frank Brady's "Indian Spark"

INFINITE RISK 2 gr.c. (Mar 11) Vettori (IRE) 119 – Dolly Bevan 53 (Another Realm **61 ?**
118) [2001 6m 7m 8m⁵ Sep 24] 23,000F, 76,000Y: eighth foal: half-brother to 3 winners,
including fairly useful 6f (at 2 yrs) to 1m winner Pengamon and useful 6f (including at 2
yrs) winner Oggi, both by Efisio: dam, 2-y-o 6f winner who stayed 1m, half-sister to
smart sprinter Pips Pride: seemingly best effort in maidens (modest form) when fifth in
steadily-run race at Kempton: appears to stay 1m. *R. Hannon*

INFINITE SPIRIT (USA) 2 ch.f. (Mar 19) Maria's Mon (USA) 121 – Eternal Reve **94**
(USA) 116 (Diesis 133) [2001 6m* 7g⁴ 8s² Oct 22] quite attractive filly: fluent mover:
third foal: half-sister to 3-y-o Enrich: dam, French 6f (at 2 yrs) to 1m winner, half-sister
to US Grade 1 9f winner Eternity Star out of half-sister to Miswaki: fairly useful form:
landed odds in maiden at Redcar in May: better form when in frame in listed events at
Newmarket and Pontefract (didn't take eye beforehand, 9 lengths second of 12 to Bandari) in October: not sure to stay further than 1m: acts on soft and good to firm ground.
D. R. Loder

IN FOR THE CRAIC (IRE) 2 b.c. (Apr 30) Our Emblem (USA) – Lucky State **–**
(USA) (State Dinner (USA)) [2001 8.2m f9.4g Nov 17] IR 16,000Y: seventh foal: closely
related to 3 winners, including 1m winner Gold Lance (by Seeking The Gold) and
half-brother to a Brazilian Grade 3 winner by Thunder Gulch: dam, French 1m winner,
half-sister to 1000 Guineas winner Ravinella: slowly away and signs of just a little ability
in maidens. *S. Kirk*

INFOTEC (IRE) 4 b. or br.g. Shalford (IRE) 124§ – Tomona (Linacre 133) [2001 79: **72**
f6s f6f 7.1v² 7g 8.3d 8m 5s 6v Oct 16] strong, close-coupled gelding: fair handicapper: **a–**
should stay 1m: raced mainly on going softer than good (acts on heavy): sold 1,000 gns.
H. Akbary

INFRA RED 2 ch.c. (Apr 7) Most Welcome 131 – Flying Wind 51 (Forzando 122) **–**
[2001 6m Jul 6] 2,100Y: small, compact colt: fourth foal: half-brother to 7f winner My
Emily (by King's Signet) and 4-y-o Master Luke: dam, poor maiden (stayed 1m), half-
sister to smart 1m to 1½m performer Karinga Bay: 25/1 and very green, always tailed off
in maiden at Haydock. *C. Grant*

INGLEMOTTE MISS 3 ch.f. Hatim (USA) 121 – Phantom Singer 58 (Relkino 131) **–**
[2001 –: 6.1v 8m May 30] no sign of ability. *Miss J. F. Craze*

INGLENOOK (IRE) 4 b.c. Cadeaux Genereux 131 – Spring 112 (Sadler's Wells **112**
(USA) 132) [2001 112: 8g⁴ 10.5g⁴ 10.3d⁶ 9.3v³ Sep 23] lengthy, quite attractive colt:
reportedly suffers from knee problems: smart performer: creditable efforts at 4 yrs when
fourth to Bach in listed race at the Curragh in July and when length third to Denaro in
Group 2 event at Cologne (made most) in September: below form both outings in Britain
in between, in Rose of Lancaster Stakes at Haydock and minor event at Doncaster:
effective at 1m to 10.5f: acts on heavy and good to firm going: has been bandaged in
front: usually held up: has found little. *J. L. Dunlop*

INGLETONIAN 12 b.g. Doc Marten 104 – Dreamy Desire 50 (Palm Track 122) **–**
[2001 16m May 4] fair hurdler: well held on belated Flat debut. *B. Mactaggart*

INGLIS DREVER 2 b.c. (Mar 18) In The Wings 128 – Cormorant Creek 73 (Gorytus **65 p**
(USA) 132) [2001 6s⁴ 6s⁶ 6v Oct 26] 130,000Y: good-bodied colt: has scope: fourth foal:
half-brother to fairly useful 6f (at 2 yrs) to 1m winner Far Removed (by Distant Relative)
and 17f winner Spartan Royale (by Shareef Dancer): dam, 10.4f winner, half-sister to
Champion Stakes winner Cormorant Wood, herself dam of Rock Hopper: shaped very
well first 2 starts in maidens: ran no sort of race final one: will be suited by at least 1m:
type to do well in handicaps. *Sir Mark Prescott*

IN GOOD FAITH 9 b.g. Beveled (USA) – Dulcidene 71 (Behistoun 131) [2001 –: **–**
10f Jun 3] of little account nowadays. *R. E. Barr*

IN GOOD TIME 2 b.g. (Feb 25) Classic Cliche (IRE) 128 – Primum Tempus 49 **–**
(Primo Dominie 121) [2001 8.3g⁶ 7d Sep 26] fourth foal: half-brother to three 2-y-o 5f
winners, including 3-y-o Time N Time Again and Rythm N Time (also won at 3 yrs), both
by Timeless Times: dam sprint maiden: well held in maidens. *E. J. Alston*

INIGO JONES (IRE) 5 b.g. Alzao (USA) 117 – Kindjal 84 (Kris 135) [2001 103: **100**
12d 12g⁴ 10m 12v Oct 27] rather leggy, angular gelding: useful handicapper: easily best
effort at 5 yrs (after 4 months off) when fourth to Thundering Surf at Ascot in August:
effective at 1½m to 2m: acts on firm and soft going: has been bandaged in front: sometimes edgy at stalls: has tended to hang/find little: headstrong: not one to trust implicitly:
sold 16,000 gns, joined G. Brown. *P. W. Harris*

INISHOWEN (IRE) 2 b.c. (Mar 9) Alhaarth (IRE) 126 – Naaman (IRE) 61 (Marju **89 p**
(IRE) 127) [2001 6g* 7s⁴ Sep 30] 27,000F, 30,000Y: compact colt: has a quick action:
first foal: dam, ran 3 times, out of half-sister to very smart miler Shaikiya: fairly useful
form when beating Addeyll by a neck in minor event at Doncaster in September,
hampered twice and weaving through to lead near line: possibly unsuited by soft going in
similar contest at Ascot: bred to stay 1m. *B. W. Hills*

INITIATIVE 5 ch.g. Arazi (USA) 135 – Dance Quest (FR) 117 (Green Dancer (USA) **–**
132) [2001 –: f6g f7g 8m f8g 8f 11d f8s Dec 21] smallish, leggy gelding: fairly useful
winner at 3 yrs: little form since, leaving B. Murray after fifth start: twice blinkered.
J. Hetherton

INJAAZ 3 ch.f. Sheikh Albadou 128 – Ferber's Follies (USA) (Saratoga Six (USA)) **99**
[2001 84: 7d* 7m 7m⁴ 8f⁵ 8g³ 7m Aug 2] leggy, sparely-made filly: has a fluent, round
action: useful performer: won 27-runner handicap at Newmarket in April, despite hanging right: best effort in listed races on last 4 starts when 4 lengths fifth to Independence in
rated stakes at Ascot: stays 1m: acts on firm and good to soft going: carries head
awkwardly. *J. L. Dunlop*

INJUN 2 ch.c. (Feb 11) Efisio 120 – Lassoo 87 (Caerleon (USA) 132) [2001 7g Nov 5] **–**
half-brother to 8-y-o Mustang and 1½m winner Sioux (by Kris): dam maiden half-sister
to very smart middle-distance performer Apache: 100/1, always behind in maiden at
Redcar. *C. W. Thornton*

INKWELL 7 b.g. Relief Pitcher 120 – Fragrant Hackette 32 (Simply Great (FR) 122) **– §**
[2001 –§, a42§: 10m 11.9f 11.6m 8m Jun 18] smallish, robust gelding: temperamental
handicapper: tried visored/blinkered. *M. R. Ewer-Hoad*

IN LUCK 3 b.f. In The Wings 128 – Lucca (Sure Blade (USA) 130) [2001 9.7m⁴ 9m³ **72**
Jun 22] 42,000Y: third foal: half-sister to a winner in Japan by Keen: dam, behind in
bumper, sister to smart 1m to 1½m performer Needle Gun, and half-sister to smart/very
smart performers up to 1½m Cloud Castle (by In The Wings) and Luso: better effort in
maidens (fair form) on debut: should be suited by 1½m. *B. Smart*

INNES 5 b.m. Inchinor 119 – Trachelium 65 (Formidable (USA) 125) [2001 –: f16g Jan **–**
29] lightly-raced maiden on Flat. *Miss S. E. Hall*

INNKEEPER 4 b.g. Night Shift (USA) – Riyoom (USA) 83 (Vaguely Noble 140) **62 d**
[2001 71: e8g² f8g e8g⁵ e10g⁶ e6g³ e7g Mar 19] smallish, good-topped gelding: disappointing maiden: stays 1m: acts on firm going, good to soft and equitrack: blinkered: has
looked none too keen. *G. L. Moore*

INNOCENT (IRE) 3 b.g. Lure (USA) 131 – Miss Declared (USA) (Alleged (USA) **41**
138) [2001 6m 5g 6g p5g⁶ Nov 20] IR 140,000Y: tall, good-topped gelding: second foal:
dam unraced: poor maiden: form only in handicap final outing: bred to stay at least 7f.
J. A. Osborne

IN 'N' OUT 2 ch.g. (Apr 30) Dancing Spree (USA) – Aquarula 88 (Dominion 123) **83 d**
[2001 5v* 5s* 5d 5.1f 5g f6g f8.5g⁴ Nov 27] 4,000Y: leggy gelding: half-brother to 3
winners, including 6f winner Aquatic Queen (by Rudimentary) and 1½m winner To Be
Fair (by Adonijah): dam 2-y-o 5f/6f winner: fairly useful performer: won maiden seller at
Doncaster in March and minor event at Musselburgh in April: well below form after,
trained by D. Nicholls fourth start only (then off course 6 months): likely to prove best
short of 1m: acts on heavy ground: tried visored: very upset in stall third start. *P. D. Evans*

INNOVATOR (IRE) 2 b.c. (Feb 8) Entrepreneur 123 – Midnight Angel (Machia- **65**
vellian (USA) 123) [2001 6f 7m⁵ 7m 7g 8.3v Oct 8] 30,000Y: first foal: dam unraced
daughter of useful sprinter Night At Sea: fair maiden: well held in nurseries last 2 starts,
visored (slowly away and wandered) on first occasion: stays 7f: acts on good to firm
ground: sold 3,500 gns. *R. Hannon*

INQUISITIVE 2 b.f. (Mar 20) Nashwan (USA) 135 – Ingenuity 68 (Clever Trick **67**
(USA)) [2001 6m³ 7m⁴ 5.7g⁶ 6.5g Sep 28] 10,000Y: close-coupled filly: fourth foal:
half-sister to fairly useful 1999 2-y-o 5f winner Inventive (by Sheikh Albadou): dam, 6f
winner, bred to stay at least 1m: fair maiden: creditable ninth of 28 in valuable sales race
at Ascot, racing on unfavoured stand side: should stay 1m: sold 10,000 gns. *R. Hannon*

INSENOR (USA) 4 ch.f. El Gran Senor (USA) 136 – Informatrice (USA) 95 (Trempo- **–**
lino (USA) 135) [2001 91: 10.4m 10m 8f 11g⁶ 8.3g 10.1m⁶ Aug 15] angular filly: second
foal: dam, lightly-raced 2-y-o 7f winner, bred to be best at 1¼m+: useful performer at
best: trained at 2 and 3 yrs by J. Oxx in Ireland, winning maiden at Roscommon and fifth

in listed race at Leopardstown in 2000: well held in Britain in 2001: stays 1½m: acts on firm ground: blinkered final start. *E. J. O'Neill*

INSHEEN (IRE) 3 b.g. Inzar (USA) 112 – Moonshine Lady (Ballad Rock 122) [2001 49: e10g⁶ e8g⁶ e12g⁴ Feb 3] poor maiden at 2 yrs: little form in 2001. *J. S. Moore*

INSIGNIS (IRE) 2 b.f. (Mar 21) Inzar (USA) 112 – Negria (IRE) (Al Hareb (USA) **44** 123) [2001 6m 7.1f⁵ 6f⁵ 7g⁶ 5.3s Oct 3] 3,500Y: sparely-made filly: second foal: half-sister to 3-y-o Church Mice: dam, German 2-y-o 6f winner, half-sister to useful 1996 2-y-o sprinter Miss Stamper: poor maiden: well held in sellers last 2 starts: stays 7f. *Mrs P. N. Dutfield*

IN SPACE (USA) 2 ch.c. (Jan 26) Sky Classic (CAN) – Thrilling Day 112 (Groom **95** Dancer (USA) 128) [2001 5d⁵ 5s⁵ 6m* 6g⁵ 7m² 7m³ 8g⁵ Sep 19] 100,000Y: close-coupled colt: fluent mover: first foal: dam, 6f (at 2 yrs) to 8.5f (US Grade 3) winner, also won Nell Gwyn Stakes: useful performer: won maiden at Yarmouth in July: creditable placed efforts in minor event at Thirsk and listed race at Newbury (third of 4 to Funfair Wane): stays 7f, probably not 1m: acts on good to firm ground, well below form on soft. *S. P. C. Woods*

INSPECTOR BLUE 3 ch.g. Royal Academy (USA) 130 – Blue Siren 113 (Bluebird **63 ?** (USA) 125) [2001 –p: 8m 7g 8m 8.1f 8m Sep 26] leggy, quite good-topped gelding: seemingly modest form: best efforts at 1m on good to firm ground. *D. R. C. Elsworth*

INSPECTOR GENERAL (IRE) 3 b.g. Dilum (USA) 115 – New Generation 91 **96** (Young Generation 129) [2001 90: 8s 5.1s 6g 7m 8.1m 7.1g* 7.1m⁵ 8g⁷g 7d Oct 20] good-topped gelding: unimpressive mover: useful performer: won minor event at Haydock in June: ran well in handicaps after only when good fifth at Sandown: seems best around 7f: acts on soft and good to firm ground. *P. F. I. Cole*

IN SPIRIT (IRE) 3 b.g. Distinctly North (USA) 115 – June Goddess (Junius (USA) **74** 124) [2001 75: f7g* 8.3s 9s⁴ 10m² 9m 8.1f* 10m 8m 8g f9.4g⁶ Oct 23] fair performer: won maiden at Southwell in January and handicap at Warwick in June: well held last 3 starts: stays 1¼m, at least when conditions aren't testing: acts on firm going and fibresand: tried blinkered. *D. J. S. Cosgrove*

INTANGIBLE (USA) 2 ch.f. (Mar 13) Diesis 133 – Flamboyance (USA) 94 (Zilzal **72 p** (USA) 137) [2001 8m 8s* Oct 25] first foal: dam, 7f and (in USA) 8.5f winner, out of half-sister to US Grade 1 9f winner Reluctant Guest: better effort in maidens when winning at Brighton by ½ length from Shove Ha'Penny, carried wide early but leading final 1f: will probably stay 1¼m: should improve further. *H. R. A. Cecil*

INTEGRATE (USA) 3 b. or br.g. You And I (USA) 118 – September Kaper (USA) **62** (Peterhof (USA) 116) [2001 10m 8f³ 7g 8d⁴ 8.5m⁵ 10m Sep 6] $77,000F, 60,000Y: smallish, good-bodied gelding: poor mover: fifth foal: half-brother to useful Irish 1m (at 2 yrs) and 9f winner Cambodian (by Roanoke) and winner in USA by Mi Cielo: dam, won up to 1m in USA, out of half-sister to US Grade 1 2-y-o 6f winner Stub: modest maiden: probably stays 8.5f: acts on good to firm and good to soft going: sold 2,500 gns. *M. H. Tompkins*

INTERNAL AFFAIR (USA) 6 b.g. Nicholas (USA) 111 – Gdynia (USA) (Sir Ivor **–** 135) [2001 –, a73: e12g Mar 28] sturdy gelding: fair performer in 2000: well held only 6-y-o outing: sent to USA. *D. L. Williams*

INTERNATIONALGUEST (IRE) 2 b.c. (Mar 27) Petardia 113 – Banco Solo **73** (Distant Relative 128) [2001 5s 6m 6.9m⁵ 7m⁴ 6.9d² 8d⁶ 7s³ Oct 20] 24,000Y: close-coupled colt: first foal: dam unraced sister to smart 7f/1m performer My Branch: fair maiden: creditable efforts in nurseries last 3 outings: likely to prove best at 7f/1m: acts on soft and good to firm going: blinkered last 5 starts. *G. G. Margarson*

INTERSKY CHAMPAGNE 2 b.g. (Apr 23) Emperor Jones (USA) 119 – Cham- **77 §** pagne Grandy 84 (Vaigly Great 127) [2001 5s⁶ 5m* 5m² 5.1m 5m Aug 1] 4,800Y: leggy, close-coupled gelding: third foal: half-brother to 1999 2-y-o 5f winner Ninety Degrees (by Piccolo): dam 5f to 7f winner: fair performer: clearly best effort when winning maiden at Newcastle in June: raced only at 5f: acts on good to firm ground: tends to give trouble in preliminaries/find little: probably ungenuine: sent to Macau. *A. Berry*

INTHAAR 4 b.g. Nashwan (USA) 135 – Twafeaj (USA) 110 (Topsider (USA)) [2001 **–** f9.4g² f8s f9.4g⁴ f11g f8g⁶ 10d f8g² f7g³ f7g 8.1g f12g* f16g f12g f9.4g p12g f11g⁵ Dec **a58** 17] 14,000 2-y-o: third foal: dam, best around 6f, won Moyglare Stud Stakes: modest performer: claimed from G. M. Moore £5,000 after ninth start: won seller at Southwell in July: stays 1½m: acts on fibresand: blinkered/visored last 10 starts. *R. Brotherton*

IN THE ARENA (USA)　4 ch.g. Cadeaux Genereux 131 – Tajfah (USA) (Shadeed　–
(USA) 135) [2001 76: 7.1d f6g 5m 8m 7.5s Sep 25] big, strong gelding: fair winner in
2000: showed nothing at 4 yrs. *D. Shaw*

IN THE FRAME (IRE)　2 b.g. (Mar 21) Definite Article 121 – Victorian Flower　**69**
(Tate Gallery (USA) 117) [2001 6m 6f 7f⁶ 7g Sep 15] IR 20,000Y: quite good-topped
gelding: fifth foal: half-brother to 2 winners abroad, including a 8.5f and 11.5f winner in
Italy by Common Grounds: dam, ran twice, closely related to useful 1¼m performer
Splendid Career: fair maiden: best effort when sixth at Newbury: should stay 1m: has
carried head awkwardly. *R. Hannon*

IN THE GREEN　2 b.g. (Jan 20) Greensmith 121 – Carn Maire 83 (Northern Prospect　**72**
(USA)) [2001 5m³ 5f³ 5.1m³ 5d 6g⁶ 5f* 5g Oct 4] good-topped gelding: has a short
action: half-brother to several winners, including fairly useful 1999 2-y-o 5f winner
Passion Flower (by Forzando) and 6f winner Maple Burl (by Dominion): dam 2-y-o 5f
winner: fair performer: third in claimer/maidens prior to winning nursery at Musselburgh
in September: should stay 6f: acts on firm ground, below form on good to soft: sold
15,000 gns. *R. A. Fahey*

IN THE STARS (IRE)　3 ch.g. Definite Article 121 – Astronomer Lady (IRE)　**60**
(Montekin 125) [2001 10d⁴ 10g 11.7d Oct 25] IR 8,500Y: third foal: half-brother to a
2-y-o 6f winner abroad by Unblest: dam unraced: best effort in maidens (modest form) on
second start: gelded after final outing. *Mrs A. J. Perrett*

IN THE STOCKS　7 b.m. Reprimand 122 – Stock Hill Lass 87 (Air Trooper 115)　**49**
[2001 55: 10d 11.6g 10.9m⁵ 11.5m 12.6d⁵ 10.9m* 11.8s² Oct 16] small mare: poor
performer: won seller at Warwick in August: barely stays 1½m: acts on soft and good to
firm going: usually held up: game. *L. G. Cottrell*

INTOTHEDRINK　3 b.f. River Falls 113 – Miss Alkie 58 (Noalcoholic (FR) 128)　–
[2001 10s f7g f9.4g May 3] 4,200Y: seventh foal: half-sister to 7f/1m winner Corona
Gold (by Chilibang) and a winner in Italy by Alhijaz: dam won 6f seller: well held in
maidens/seller. *J. A. Osborne*

INTREPIDOUS　3 b.f. Polar Falcon (USA) 126 – Silver Braid (USA) 101 (Miswaki　**100**
(USA) 124) [2001 7.1g⁵ 8m² 8.3g* 10m 8.1g* 8g Oct 6] lengthy, quite good-topped filly:
fifth foal: half-sister to 8-y-o Kass Alhawa and 4-y-o Beading: dam, 2-y-o 7f winner, later
suited by 1m: useful performer: won maiden at Windsor in July and listed race at
Sandown (best effort when beating Sayedah ½ length) in September: behind in Sun
Chariot Stakes at Newmarket final outing: stays 1m: raced only on good/good to firm
going: reportedly suffered overreach after slipping on fourth outing: front runner: sent to
Saudi Arabia. *B. J. Meehan*

INTRICATE WEB (IRE)　5 b.g. Warning 136 – In Anticipation (IRE) 93 (Sadler's　**91**
Wells (USA) 132) [2001 77, a81: f7s* f7s² f7g* f7g* 7g* 7m² 7f 7f² 7m 8m⁶ 7.6m 7.2g*　**a99**
7s 7d⁵ 7d⁵ Nov 3] sturdy, angular gelding: useful handicapper on all-weather, fairly useful
on turf: better than ever at 5 yrs, winning at Wolverhampton in January, Southwell in
February and March, Thirsk in May and Ayr (minor event) in August: has form at 1m,
very best efforts at 7f: well beaten on heavy going, acts on any other turf and fibresand:
tried blinkered/visored, not in 2001: sometimes slowly away. *E. J. Alston*

INVADER　5 b.h. Danehill (USA) 126 – Donya 74 (Mill Reef (USA) 141) [2001 86,　**87 §**
a94: f6s e7g f8.5g* e10g⁴ 8s 8f 9f³ 10f 10m⁵ 8m⁴ 8d f8g p7g⁴ f8.5f f9.4s Dec 26] big,　**a96 §**
strong horse: carries condition: useful on all-weather, fairly useful on turf: won valuable
handicap at Wolverhampton in March: good fourth to Sergeant York in listed event at

*Ed Weetman Haulage And Storage Lincoln Trial Stakes (Handicap), Wolverhampton—the most valuable
handicap of the all-weather season goes to Invader; Wahj is a good second, in front of The Prince*

Lingfield next time: best at 1m/easy 1¼m: acts on firm going and all-weather: seems effective blinkered or not, sometimes visored: moody. *C. E. Brittain*

INVER GOLD   4 ch.c. Arazi (USA) 135 – Mary Martin (Be My Guest (USA) 126)   **74**
[2001 83: f9.4s⁵ e12g 10m⁴ 11.9d 10g⁵ 12.3m 12d f9.4g* 10.4m² 9.9d⁵ p12g f9.4g⁶ f9.4s⁶
Dec 26] fair handicapper: won at Wolverhampton in August: best at 8.5f to 1¼m: acts on
good to firm going, good to soft, fibresand and equitrack: often takes while to warm to
task. *A. G. Newcombe*

INVERMARK   7 b.g. Machiavellian (USA) 123 – Applecross 117 (Glint of Gold 128)   **114**
[2001 14v* 16d² Oct 20] tall, workmanlike gelding: smart performer: second in Gold Cup
at Royal Ascot in 1999: off 2 years (reportedly due to suspensory trouble) before winning
minor event at Haydock in September by neck from Murghem: creditable ½-length
second to Capal Garmon in Jockey Club Cup at Newmarket final start: stays 2½m: acts
on heavy and good to firm going: seems best held up: flashes tail under pressure, but
game enough. *J. R. Fanshawe*

INVESTMENT FORCE (IRE)   3 b.g. Imperial Frontier (USA) 112 – Superb   **69**
Investment (IRE) (Hatim (USA) 121) [2001 68: f8g⁴ f7g 6m⁶ 7m² 6d⁶ 6m³ 6g⁴ 6m² Aug
3] small, strong gelding: fair maiden handicapper: effective at 6f/7f: yet to race on
extremes of going on turf, below form on fibresand/equitrack: blinkered/visored last 6
starts. *M. Johnston*

INVESTOR (IRE)   2 b.c. (Mar 11) Marju (IRE) 127 – Shine On Me (Machiavellian   **72 +**
(USA) 123) [2001 6s 7m² 7d³ 7m* 7d⁵ 7.1m 7s Oct 20] 210,000 francs F, 400,000 francs
Y: strong colt: good mover: first foal: dam useful French 7f (at 2 yrs)/1m winner: fair
performer: made all in maiden at Chester in August: below form in nurseries after: stays
7f: acts on good to firm ground, possibly not on softer than good: visored (looked none
too keen) final start: has raced freely: sold 14,000 gns. *P. F. I. Cole*

INVESTOR RELATIONS (IRE)   3 b.g. Goldmark (USA) 113 – Debach Delight   **52**
97 (Great Nephew 126) [2001 62: 10s⁵ 10.2d 8.1g May 7] modest maiden: should stay
beyond 1¼m: acts on soft and good to firm going: has raced freely: hung badly right on
reappearance: blinkered final outing: sold 4,200 gns. *B. J. Meehan*

INVICTRESS (DEN)   6 b.m. Prince Mab (FR) 124 – Joe's Lake (DEN) (Kings Lake   **–**
(USA) 133) [2001 16.2f Jun 23] Danish-bred mare: fairly useful in Denmark in 1998
when trained by S. Jensen, winning 4 times: well held on return. *P. J. Hobbs*

INVINCIBLE   3 b.f. Slip Anchor 136 – Blessed Honour 77 (Ahonoora 122) [2001   **76**
64p: 11.1m* 11.7g³ Jun 16] second foal: half-sister to 1999 2-y-o 6f/7f winner Icicle (by
Polar Falcon) who stayed 8.5f: dam, 2-y-o 7f winner on only start, half-sister to smart
middle-distance stayer Sacrament: fair performer: landed odds in maiden at Hamilton in
May: creditable third in minor event at Bath only subsequent start, racing shade freely:
should stay beyond 1½m: acts on good to firm going, showed promise on soft only 2-y-o
outing. *J. R. Fanshawe*

INVINCIBLE SPIRIT (IRE)   4 b.c. Green Desert (USA) 127 – Rafha 123 (Kris 135)   **115**
[2001 106: 7g⁴ 6m* 6m 6m* 6g² 6m* Sep 15] strong, well-made colt: has a powerful,
round action: smart performer: won minor event at Goodwood (by ¾ length from Kier
Park) in May, listed race at Newbury (beat Mugharreb 1½ lengths) in July and Aon
MacDonagh Boland Stakes at the Curragh (by short head from Toroca, leading on line) in
September: also ran well when 3 lengths second to Do The Honours in Prix de Meautry at
Deauville penultimate start: best at 6f: acts on good to firm going: usually held up, and
has good turn of foot. *J. L. Dunlop*

INVIRAMENTAL   5 b.g. Pursuit of Love 124 – Corn Futures 78 (Nomination 125)   **45**
[2001 53: e10g e8g³ e8g Apr 3] good-topped gelding: poor maiden: stays 1m: acts on
fibresand/equitrack: usually blinkered/visored: sold 3,800 gns. *Mrs L. C. Jewell*

INVISIBLE FORCE (IRE)   4 b.g. Imperial Frontier (USA) 112 – Virginia Cottage   **–**
45 (Lomond (USA) 128) [2001 51: 10s 10s Apr 28] lengthy gelding: modest handicapper
at best: well beaten both 4-y-o outings: blinkered/visored. *B. S. Rothwell*

INVITADO (IRE)   2 ch.g. (Mar 25) Be My Guest (USA) 126 – Lady Dulcinea (ARG)   **–**
(General (FR)) [2001 7.9m 8d 8g 8g Nov 5] IR 15,000Y: leggy, unfurnished gelding:
brother to 5-y-o It's Our Secret and half-brother to 3 winners in Italy: dam won in Peru
and USA: no form in maidens/nursery. *J. G. FitzGerald*

INVITATION   3 b.g. Bin Ajwaad (IRE) 119 – On Request (IRE) 53 (Be My Guest   **84**
(USA) 126) [2001 60p: 10g* 10g 12m⁵ 11.9s⁶ 10g³ 10d Nov 2] quite attractive gelding:
fairly useful performer: won maiden at Windsor in May: best effort in handicaps after

when third at Newmarket, despite wandering: may prove best short of 1½m: raced mainly on good going or softer: ran poorly (raced freely) final outing: carried head awkwardly last 2 starts. *K. O. Cunningham-Brown*

IN XANADU (IRE) 2 b.c. (Apr 2) Persian Bold 123 – Dromoland (Cadeaux Genereux 131) [2001 6f 7s 7d Nov 3] IR 10,000F, 25,000Y: small colt: first foal: dam unraced daughter of smart sprinter Al Sylah: fair form in maidens: caught the eye when never-nearer ninth of 27 to Prince Hector at Newmarket final start: should stay 1m: type to do well in handicaps. *J. L. Dunlop* **72 p**

INZACURE (IRE) 3 b.g. Inzar (USA) 112 – Whittingham Girl 58 (Primo Dominie 121) [2001 87p: 6d 6m 6s 7m 7d Jun 17] small gelding: fairly useful winner at 2 yrs: disappointing in 2001. *R. M. Beckett* **–**

INZARMOOD (IRE) 3 b.f. Inzar (USA) 112 – Pepilin (Coquelin (USA) 121) [2001 –: 8m 6.1m 8m f9.4g2 9.9m 9.1v f11g Nov 30] neat filly: poor maiden: form only at 9.4f on fibresand: usually visored. *K. R. Burke* **– a42**

IONIAN SPRING (IRE) 6 b.g. Ela-Mana-Mou 132 – Well Head (IRE) (Sadler's Wells (USA) 132) [2001 77, a94: f7s e10g4 e10s4 f12g2 f12g* f12f5 10g 17.2f 10.2g* 10.3g6 10.4d* Oct 12] fairly useful handicapper: won at Southwell in March, Chepstow in August (first start since leaving C. Egerton) and York (idled when beating McGillycuddy Reeks by length) in October: stays easy 1½m: acts on good to firm going, good to soft and fibresand/equitrack: has edged left. *C. G. Cox* **89**

IPANEMA BEACH 4 ch.f. Lion Cavern (USA) 117 – Girl From Ipanema 106 (Salse (USA) 128) [2001 67: 8.3g 7g f7g f8.5g* f8g* f8g f8.5s Dec 26] leggy, lengthy, angular filly: fair performer nowadays: form at 4 yrs only when winning seller at Wolverhampton and handicap at Southwell in December: stays 8.5f: acts on fibresand, raced only on good going or softer on turf. *Andrew Reid* **65**

I PROMISE YOU 4 b.g. Shareef Dancer (USA) 135 – Abuzz 101 (Absalom 128) [2001 75: e6g 8g 8.1m 7.5m 7m 8g 8f4 10g 7m 8.2s5 f7g2 f9.4g p7g3 f8.5s4 Dec 26] small, sturdy gelding: modest performer: stays 1m: acts on firm going and all-weather: sometimes blinkered. *C. E. Brittain* **64 a61**

IRELAND'S EYE (IRE) 6 b.g. Shareef Dancer (USA) 135 – So Romantic (IRE) 97 (Teenoso (USA) 135) [2001 59d: 14.1v4 16.2m6 17.1m Jun 11] small gelding: poor maiden handicapper: stays 17f: acts on heavy and good to firm going: tried visored in 2000: sometimes hangs: winning hurdler. *J. R. Norton* **43**

Ruinart Champagne Stakes (Hackwood), Newbury—the second of three wins during the year for the smart Invincible Spirit; Mugharreb (right) finishes second with Bouncing Bowdler third

IRIDESCENT 3 b.f. Spectrum (IRE) 126 – Ingenuity 68 (Clever Trick (USA)) [2001 – 46: 11.5m 7.1g Jun 7] poor form only outing at 2 yrs: well held in 2001: refused to enter stalls on 3 occasions and has been banned from racing from stalls. *W. M. Brisbourne*

IRIE RASTA (IRE) 2 ch.c. (Mar 15) Desert King (IRE) 129 – Seeds of Doubt (IRE) **62** (Night Shift (USA)) [2001 7f 7m⁶ 8.1s⁵ Aug 19] 28,000Y: first foal: dam unraced close relative to useful Irish middle-distance stayer Blazing Spectacle and half-sister to smart Irish winner up to 1½m Token Gesture: modest maiden: should be suited by 1¼m+. *S. Kirk*

IRINA (IRE) 5 b.m. Polar Falcon (USA) 126 – Bird of Love 82 (Ela-Mana-Mou 132) – [2001 91: 7.1s⁵ 5m 10m 6m Jun 9] fifth living foal: dam maiden half-sister to smart middle-distance stayer Water Boatman: fairly useful winner for P. Martin in Ireland at 3/4 yrs: no form in Britain: stays 1m: acts on soft going: sometimes slowly away. *E. J. O'Neill*

IRISH BLESSING (USA) 4 b.g. Ghazi (USA) – Win For Leah (USA) (His Majesty – (USA)) [2001 75: 14v Sep 29] fair performer: won amateur maiden at Sligo in 2000: sold from D. Weld in Ireland 9,000 gns after final 3-y-o start: well held on return to Flat: stays 1¾m: acts on soft and good to firm going: blinkered last 5 starts at 3 yrs. *F. Jordan*

IRISH CREAM (IRE) 5 b.m. Petong 126 – Another Baileys 60 (Deploy 131) [2001 **a50** 35, a56: f16.2g⁴ f12g³ f12g⁵ f12g⁴ f12g* 14.1v f16.2g⁴ f12s Dec 26] small, workmanlike mare: modest handicapper: won at Wolverhampton in March: effective at 1½m to 2m: acts on heavy going and fibresand: usually visored/blinkered: tongue tied last 2 starts. *J. L. Spearing*

IRISH DISTINCTION (IRE) 3 b.g. Distinctly North (USA) 115 – Shane's Girl **73 d** (IRE) (Marktingo) [2001 65: 8d 6g 11m² 11.5m⁵ 10.1m⁶ 10g 11.9g 10.2g f12g Oct 22] good-bodied gelding: fair maiden: below form after third start: left A. Jarvis after penultimate outing: should stay 1½m: acts on good to firm going: has flashed tail. *Simon Earle*

IRISH PADDY (IRE) 2 b.g. (Apr 23) Idris (IRE) 118 – Ceili Queen (IRE) 77 – (Shareef Dancer (USA) 135) [2001 8.1s 7.1m Sep 21] IR 4,200F, IR 5,000Y: angular gelding: first foal: dam, Irish 1¼m winner, also winning hurdler/chaser: blinkered, tailed off in maidens. *K. McAuliffe*

IRISH SEA (USA) 8 b.g. Zilzal (USA) 137 – Dunkellin (USA) (Irish River (FR) 131) **48** [2001 17.1s 15.4v* 18m 17.2m 16.2m Jul 27] leggy, close-coupled gelding: poor performer nowadays, gaining belated first win on Flat in handicap at Folkestone in April: stays 2¼m: acts on heavy going: tried blinkered. *B. J. Llewellyn*

IRISH STREAM (USA) 3 ch.c. Irish River (FR) 131 – Euphonic (USA) 113 (The **78** Minstrel (CAN) 135) [2001 78: 6d 7m 6m⁴ 6m² Jun 23] big, strong, good sort: fair maiden: blinkered, beaten short head on final outing (caught close home, rider seemingly not wanting to use whip): free-going sort, and should prove best around 6f: acts on soft and good to firm going: missed break/carried head awkwardly on reappearance, saddle slipped next time. *R. Charlton*

IRISH VALE 2 ch.c. (Mar 27) Wolfhound (USA) 126 – Valencia 79 (Kenmare (FR) **95** 125) [2001 5.1m⁶ 5d³ 5.1g* 5m 6m² 6m 5.5d⁶ 5m* 7v Oct 26] small, strong colt: first foal: dam, second at 1m at 2 yrs on only start, half-sister to very smart performers Wandesta (up to 13.5f in Britain/USA) and De Quest (up to 12.5f in France): useful performer: won minor event at Bath (subsequently left R. Charlton 32,000 gns) in June and listed race at Ayr (beat Master Robbie by short head, battling on splendidly) in September: will prove best at 5f/6f: acts on good to firm and good to soft ground: races up with pace: sold 43,000 gns, sent to USA. *M. Meade*

IRIS' TEMPEST (USA) 2 b.f. (Feb 12) Trempolino (USA) 135 – Ivory Dance – (CAN) (Sir Ivor 135) [2001 7m Sep 24] $32,000F, IR 110,000Y: fifth foal: sister to a winner in North America and half-sister to a winner there by Leo Castelli: dam won 5 races and second in 9f Canadian Oaks: 10/1, last of 12 in maiden at Kempton. *Sir Michael Stoute*

IRON DRAGON (IRE) 3 b.g. Royal Academy (USA) 130 – Kerry Project (IRE) 79 – (Project Manager 111) [2001 64: 6.1v 6m Jul 21] quite attractive gelding: modest maiden at 2 yrs: well held in 2001 (gelded after final outing): twice slowly away, very much so final start at 2 yrs: wears tongue strap. *J. Noseda*

IRON MASK (USA) 3 b.c. Danzig (USA) – Raise A Beauty (USA) (Alydar (USA)) **117** [2001 112: 7v 6f* a6f⁶ a6f Sep 29] small, strong colt: smart performer: successful in Prix d'Arenberg at Chantilly at 2 yrs: returned to best when winning very valuable Singapore Airlines KrisFlyer Sprint at Kranji in May, beating Trillion Win by ½ length: off nearly 3 months, well held in Grade 2 at Saratoga (final start for Mme C. Head-Maarek) and non-graded event at The Meadowlands: best at 5f/6f: acts on firm going, has won on good to soft: usually races prominently. *T. A. Pletcher, USA*

IRON MOUNTAIN (IRE) 6 b.g. Scenic 128 – Merlannah (IRE) (Shy Groom (USA)) [2001 86: 8s 10g² 10d² 10.1m⁵ 8g 8m 8m 8d⁵ 8.5s² 10.3g³ 10d p12g⁴ p10g⁵ Dec 28] good-topped gelding: fairly useful handicapper: creditable efforts when in frame, leaving N. Callaghan before penultimate start: effective at 1m (given a test) to easy 1½m: acts on polytrack, firm and soft going: blinkered once at 2 yrs: has wandered: usually held up. *Mrs L. C. Jewell* **86**

IRONY (IRE) 2 gr.c. (Apr 22) Mujadil (USA) 119 – Cidaris (IRE) (Persian Bold 123) [2001 5m* 5m* 5m² 5g⁶ 5g⁵ 6f² 5d⁶ Oct 13] IR 9,000F, 8,500Y, 35,000 2-y-o: good-topped colt: first foal: dam, ran once at 2 yrs in Ireland, out of sister to 2000 Guineas winner Mystiko: useful performer: won maiden at Haydock in May and Windsor Castle Stakes at Royal Ascot (made all to beat Steaming Home by neck) in June: best efforts when runner-up in Molecomb Stakes at Goodwood (beaten ½ length by Whitbarrow) and Mill Reef Stakes at Newbury (beaten 1¼ lengths by Firebreak): effective at 5f/6f: acts on firm going, below form on good to soft: shade edgy when running poorly fourth start: often early to post: races up with pace. *J. A. Osborne* **102**

IROQUOIS CHIEF (USA) 2 b.c. (Feb 14) Known Fact (USA) 135 – Celtic Shade (Lomond (USA) 128) [2001 6d⁶ 7d 5f⁴ Sep 20] $32,000Y: good-topped colt: third foal: half-brother to French 1m winner Famous Celt (by Quest For Fame): dam, third at 1m/ 10.5f in France, half-sister to very smart performer up to 1½m Urgent Request and smart stayer Sanmartino: easily best effort in maidens (fair form) when fourth to Golden Bounty at Pontefract, not given hard time after tracking leaders: should stay at least 6f: probably capable of better. *M. L. W. Bell* **66 p**

IRREVOCABLE (IRE) 2 b.f. (Apr 10) Revoque (IRE) 122 – Nellie's Away (IRE) 72 (Magical Strike (USA) 114) [2001 7d 8.3v Oct 29] quite good-topped filly: third foal: dam, third at 1½m in Ireland, half-sister to 2000 Guineas winner Tap On Wood: well held in maidens. *N. A. Graham* **–**

IRSAL 7 ch.g. Nashwan (USA) 135 – Amwag (USA) 106 (El Gran Senor (USA) 136) [2001 –§, a37§: f12g f11g⁶ f11g f8g Mar 21] temperamental handicapper nowadays: usually blinkered. *D. W. Chapman* **– §**

Windsor Castle Stakes, Royal Ascot—Irony provides former jump jockey Jamie Osborne with one of his twenty-nine training successes during the year; filling the frame are Steaming Home (No.23), Leggy Lou (near side) and Simianna

IRVINGTON (IRE) 3 br.c. Lahib (USA) 129 – Snoozy Time 65 (Cavo Doro 124) **81**
[2001 7m 8m⁴ 8g 7.1m⁵ 9m* 10.2g⁵ 8f 8g⁵ 7s p7g p10g³ p10g² Dec 28] 15,500F, IR
48,000Y: rangy colt: half-brother to numerous winners, including useful 1999 2-y-o 5f/6f
(Cherry Hinton) winner Torgau (by Zieten) and fairly useful 1½m to 2m winner Fujiyama
Crest (by Roi Danzig): dam, 2-y-o 5f winner, half-sister to smart performer up to 7f Grey
Desire: fairly useful performer: won maiden at Newbury in August: several creditable
efforts in handicaps after: likely to prove best up to 1¼m: acts on polytrack and good to
firm ground: races prominently. *R. Hannon*

ISABELLA D'ESTE (IRE) 3 ch.f. Irish River (FR) 131 – Vienna Charm (IRE) 67 **65**
(Sadler's Wells (USA) 132) [2001 8g⁶ 10m⁶ 10m⁴ 10m 12f⁴ Sep 4] 36,000Y: second foal:
dam Canadian 7f winner: fair maiden, lightly raced: should stay 1½m: raced only on good
going or firmer. *P. W. Harris*

ISADORA 4 b.f. Sadler's Wells (USA) 132 – Ahead 113 (Shirley Heights 130) [2001 **106**
91p: 11.6g² 11.9m 14.6m⁴ 12g² 12d⁴ 12s² Nov 3] big, lengthy filly: useful performer:
improved at 4 yrs and made frame most starts, notably in autumn in Park Hill Stakes at
Doncaster (2¾ lengths fourth to Ranin, keeping on strongly from poor position) and
listed races at Ascot (no match for Lilium) and at Milan (1¼ lengths second to Villa
Carlotta) on 3 of last 4 outings: stays 1¾m: acts on soft and good to firm ground: sent to
USA. *L. M. Cumani*

ISCHIA 2 ch.f. (Mar 13) Lion Cavern (USA) 117 – Royal Passion 78 (Ahonoora 122) **64**
[2001 7m⁶ 7.5m³ 7.1s⁴ 7d Sep 26] fifth living foal: half-sister to 3 winners, including
3-y-o Attache and 8-y-o Tadeo: dam 1¼m winner: modest maiden: easily best effort when
third at Beverley: should stay at least 1m: acts on good to firm going. *M. Johnston*

ISHAAM 3 ch.f. Selkirk (USA) 129 – Elaine's Honor (USA) (Chief's Crown (USA)) **76**
[2001 –p: 8m⁴ 9.7m³ 10d 8.1m* Aug 1] good-bodied filly: fair performer: won minor
event at Warwick in August: probably stayed 9.7f: acted on good to firm going: hung
penultimate start: visits Muhtarram. *Sir Michael Stoute*

ISHIGURU (USA) 3 b.c. Danzig (USA) – Strategic Maneuver (USA) (Crypto- **112 +**
clearance (USA)) [2001 114p: 5m² 5m 5g² 6m 6g* 5g* 5s Oct 7] strong colt: smart
performer: won listed race at the Curragh in August by a head from D'Anjou (just held on
in blanket finish) and Miller Flying Five at Leopardstown in September by head from
Indian Spark (idled a little): not discredited in King's Stand Stakes at Royal Ascot, listed
event at the Curragh (head second to Repertory, just failing) and July Cup second to
fourth outings: raced only at 5f/6f: acts on good to firm and good to soft going: wears
crossed noseband. *A. P. O'Brien, Ireland*

ISKAN (GER) 6 b.g. Perceive Arrogance (USA) – Ifakara (GER) (Athenagoras **–**
(GER)) [2001 8.3d May 6] successful 3 times at 3/4 yrs when trained by N. Sauer in
Germany, including handicap at Cologne in March 1999: well beaten only Flat outing at
6 yrs. *Jonjo O'Neill*

ISLAND DESTINY 2 ch.f. (Feb 20) Kris 135 – Balnaha 67 (Lomond (USA) 128) **79**
[2001 6g³ 6d Nov 2] 220,000F: strong filly: has a round action: fifth foal: sister to smart
1m (Coronation Stakes) winner Balisada, 7f winner at 2 yrs, and half-sister to 1½m
winner Talk To Mojo (by Deploy): dam, 1m winner, sister to Inchmurrin (dam of Inchinor) and closely related to Guest Artiste, both smart milers: shaped well when third of 19
to Ringmoor Down in maiden at Kempton, staying on well after slow start: only eleventh
of 20 in similar event at Newmarket: bred to stay 1m: took very strong hold to post both
times, and may need to settle better to fulfil potential. *G. Wragg*

ISLAND FLIGHT 2 b.f. (Mar 18) Missed Flight 123 – Island Mead 86 (Pharly (FR) **57 ?**
130) [2001 5d 6m 7g 7g⁵ 8s f8.5g f8g Nov 16] 500Y, resold 1,400Y: smallish, unfurnished
filly: half-sister to several winners, including 2-y-o winners Island Prince (6f in 1996, by
Prince Sabo) and Jobber's Fiddle (7f in 1994, by Sizzling Melody): dam 2-y-o 7f winner:
easily best effort (modest form) when fifth in maiden at Thirsk: well held in seller/claimer
last 2 starts: should stay 1m: sometimes slowly away. *C. W. Thornton*

ISLAND HOUSE (IRE) 5 ch.h. Grand Lodge (USA) 125 – Fortitude (IRE) (Last **118**
Tycoon 131) [2001 117: 12g 10v* 10.3f² 10g³ 10d³ 10d⁶ 12g⁴ Oct 5] tall, quite good-
topped horse: smart performer: won Heathorns Bookmakers Gordon Richards Stakes at
Sandown in April by ½ length from Border Arrow: eased prematurely and beaten short
head by Adilabad in 4-runner listed race at Chester next time: creditable efforts after
when in frame in La Coupe at Longchamp (2¼ lengths third to Slew The Red), Scottish
Classic at Ayr (3¾ lengths third to Carnival Dancer) and listed event at Newmarket
(6¾ lengths fourth to Mubtaker): effective at 1¼m/1½m: acts on any going: reliable.
G. Wragg

ISLAND LIGHT   3 b.g. Inchinor 119 – Miss Prism 60 (Niniski (USA) 125) [2001   **85 p**
8.1m 8d² 8.2s* Oct 30] 5,000F, 10,000Y: well-made gelding: first foal: dam maiden who
stayed 2m: fairly useful form: won maiden at Nottingham in October by 2 lengths from
Anadonis, coming with a sustained run: will be suited by 1¼m+: lightly raced and should
improve further. *A. C. Stewart*

ISLAND MINT (USA)   2 b.f. (Jan 28) Hennessy (USA) 122 – Mintecy (USA) (Key   **80 ?**
To The Mint (USA)) [2001 6m 6m⁶ 6m⁵ 7g Sep 15] useful-looking filly: half-sister to 3
winners, including US Grade 2 1¼m winner Prophet's Warning (by Storm Bird) and Irish
1½m winner Innovative Step (by Summer Squall): dam won in USA, including 6.5f
minor stakes at 2 yrs: seemingly fairly useful form when sixth of 7 in listed race at
Newbury: fair at best in maidens/nursery otherwise: should stay 7f. *B. J. Meehan*

ISLAND OF PARADISE   2 b.f. (Mar 6) Turtle Island (IRE) 123 – Mighty Squaw 58   **61**
(Indian Ridge 123) [2001 5.7f 5m⁵ 7m⁵ 7.1g Sep 1] first foal: dam, maiden who stayed
1½m, half-sister to smart performer up to 8.5f in USA Mighty Forum: modest maiden:
will stay at least 1m. *B. R. Millman*

ISLAND PRINCESS (IRE)   4 b.f. Turtle Island (IRE) 123 – Classic Dilemma   **–**
(Sandhurst Prince 128) [2001 76d: f16g 10v f12g Sep 8] good-bodied filly: fair maiden at
best: well beaten at 4 yrs, leaving E. Wheeler after reappearance and S. Williams after
second start: tried blinkered. *K. O. Cunningham-Brown*

ISLAND QUEEN (IRE)   3 b.f. Turtle Island (IRE) 123 – Holy Devotion (Commanche   **76**
Run 133) [2001 69: 8.3g³ 8m³ 9m 9m 10m* Jul 29] fair performer: won claimer at
Newmarket in July, hanging left when asserting (unseated rider in preliminaries): stays
1¼m: yet to race on heavy ground, acts on any other: very slowly away/far from keen
third outing: probably temperamental. *R. Hannon*

ISLAND SANDS (IRE)   5 b. or br.h. Turtle Island (IRE) 123 – Tiavanita (USA) (J O   **115**
Tobin (USA) 130) [2001 109+: 8v² 8.1v³ 8.1m* 8m Jun 19] strong, lengthy horse: had
only 9 races: very smart performer at best, successful in 2000 Guineas at Newmarket in
1999: reportedly had foot problem after only subsequent start that year: left Saeed bin
Suroor after only 4-y-o outing: visored and wearing crossed noseband, best effort in 2001
when length third of 7 to Nicobar in Masai Mile at Sandown in April: won minor event at
Haydock in June: gave impression something amiss in Queen Anne Stakes at Royal
Ascot final outing: raced mainly around 1m: best effort on good to firm going, though had
form on any: has been retired. *D. R. Loder*

Heathorns Bookmakers Gordon Richards Stakes, Sandown—
Island House gains his first pattern-race success as he holds on gamely from Border Arrow (right);
Pawn Broker (white blaze) and Island Sound contest third place

ISLAND SOUND 4 b.g. Turtle Island (IRE) 123 – Ballet 61 (Sharrood (USA) 124) **109**
[2001 116: 10s⁴ 10v⁴ 12g³ 12.5s 10.3d 12g Oct 5] lengthy, angular gelding: has round
action: useful performer: not discredited when fourth of 5 to Island House in Gordon
Richards Stakes at Sandown on second start and 2¼ lengths third to Hill Country in minor
event at Newmarket on third: below form otherwise: stays 1½m: possibly best on good
going or softer: visored (tailed off) penultimate start: usually makes running: far from
reliable: fair form over hurdles. *D. R. C. Elsworth*

ISLAND STREAM (IRE) 2 b.g. (Apr 4) Turtle Island (IRE) 123 – Tilbrook (IRE) **54**
78 (Don't Forget Me 127) [2001 7.1s 7.5g⁶ 6d Oct 3] IR 8,800Y: big gelding: second foal:
half-brother to 2000 German 2-y-o 7f winner Directa Irlandia (by Mujadil): dam, 1m
winner, half-sister to smart Irish winner up to 7f Bufalino: modest maiden: bred to stay
1m: edgy type: refused to enter stall fourth intended outing. *J. L. Eyre*

ISLAND WARRIOR (IRE) 6 b.g. Warcraft (USA) – Only Flower § (Warpath 113) **–**
[2001 11.9s⁵ Aug 18] fair form at best in bumpers for G. Stewart in Ireland before
sold 9,500 gns Doncaster May Sales: tailed off in minor event on belated Flat debut.
B. P. J. Baugh

ISLE OF CEBU 3 b.f. Aragon 118 – Salala 83 (Connaught 130) [2001 10.1g f14.8s **–**
Sep 6] seventh foal: half-sister to several winners, including 5-y-o Mindanao and 7f
winner My Nominee (by Nomination): dam 7f winner: no encouragement in seller/
claimer. *Miss J. A. Camacho*

ISLINGTON (IRE) 2 b.f. (Feb 12) Sadler's Wells (USA) 132 – Hellenic 125 (Dar- **100 p**
shaan 133) [2001 7g⁶ 7g³ Oct 6] quite good-topped filly: sixth foal: sister to very smart
1¼m performer Greek Dance and smart stayer Election Day and half-sister to useful 7f/
1m winner Desert Beauty (by Green Desert): dam won Yorkshire Oaks and second in St
Leger: much better effort (useful form) when narrowly-beaten third of 12 to Protectress
in listed event at Newmarket, staying on well: will be suited by 1¼m+: smart prospect,
sure to win races. *Sir Michael Stoute*

ISTHEREANYGOODINU (IRE) 4 ch.f. Forest Wind (USA) 111 – Solar Flash **–**
(IRE) 40 (Shy Groom (USA)) [2001 f11g Mar 13] first foal: dam Irish 1m winner: behind
in seller: dead. *P. Howling*

ISTIHSAAN (IRE) 3 b.g. Barathea (IRE) 127 – Ghazwat (USA) (Riverman (USA) **67**
131) [2001 67: 8v⁵ 8m 9.9m 7d* 7.1d 8g⁵ 9g 8.1s 8d 7g a12g Dec 16] sturdy, quite
attractive gelding: fair handicapper: won at Ayr in July: sold from R. Fahey 2,500 gns
before final start: effective at 7f/1m: form only on good going or softer: usually visored:
very slowly away penultimate outing. *J. H. Brown, Spain*

I SWEAR 2 b.c. (Jan 30) Barathea (IRE) 127 – Karlafsha (Top Ville 129) [2001 7m⁴ **83 p**
Jul 13] 875,000Y: good-topped colt: has scope: seventh foal: half-brother to
3 winners in France, including winner up to 13.5f Kelemar (by Doyoun) and useful
winner up to 11f Karliyka (by Last Tycoon), latter dam of 3-y-o Karasta: dam French 7f/
1m (listed race) winner: 5/2 favourite but backward, keeping-on length fourth of 11 to
Martin House in maiden at York: will stay 1¼m: should do better, all being well.
J. L. Dunlop

IS WONDERFUL (USA) 3 ch.c. Diesis 133 – Falling In Love (IRE) 48 (Sadler's **87**
Wells (USA) 132) [2001 –: 10s² 10v 11.7g² 14.1g* 14g 13.9m⁵ 14s 17.2g³ Oct 1] strong
colt: poor mover: fairly useful performer: won maiden at Yarmouth in June: better form
in handicaps on 3 of last 4 outings: may prove best up to 2m: probably acts on soft and
good to firm going: tongue tied: has worn crossed noseband. *Mrs A. J. Perrett*

ITALIAN AFFAIR 3 ch.f. Fumo di Londra (IRE) 108 – Sergentti (IRE) 76 (Common **50**
Grounds 118) [2001 54, a47: e6g e6s² 5m⁴ 5m 5f⁴ 5f f5g Aug 10] leggy, unfurnished filly:
modest performer: effective at 5f/6f: acts on firm going and all-weather: usually races up
with pace. *A. Bailey*

ITALIAN COUNSEL (IRE) 4 b.g. Leading Counsel (USA) 122 – Mullaghroe **–**
(Tarboosh (USA)) [2001 –: f6s⁵ f11g f12g 7f 9v Oct 31] no form: left R. Hollinshead after
third start and back with former yard. *A. J. Martin, Ireland*

ITALIAN MIST (FR) 2 b.g. (Feb 26) Forzando 122 – Digamist Girl (IRE) (Digamist **73**
(USA) 110) [2001 5m 5.2m³ p5g² Nov 13] 13,000Y, resold 21,000Y: second foal:
half-brother to 3-y-o Chispa: dam winning sprinter in Belgium: fair maiden: carried head
awkwardly when second at Lingfield: should stay 6f: raced only on good to firm going
and polytrack. *B. J. Meehan*

ITALIAN SYMPHONY (IRE) 7 b.g. Royal Academy (USA) 130 – Terracotta Hut **–**
99 (Habitat 134) [2001 64, a93: 6m Jun 11] close-coupled gelding: fairly useful on

all-weather, modest on turf at best: well held only 7-y-o outing: has been blinkered, usually visored. *J. J. Quinn*

ITCANBEDONE AGAIN (IRE) 2 b.c. (Apr 16) Sri Pekan (USA) 117 – Maradata **68** (IRE) 68 (Shardari 134) [2001 6g⁴ 7m³ 7m³ 6d⁵ 7d⁴ 6d 10v⁴ Oct 4] 30,000Y: tall, good-topped colt: has scope: unimpressive mover: second foal: dam, 1¼m and (in France) 11f winner, half-sister to smart performer up to 2m Maridpour: fair maiden: should stay 1½m: acts on good to firm and heavy going: consistent. *R. Hollinshead*

I T CONSULTANT 3 b.g. Rock City 120 – Game Germaine (Mummy's Game 120) **68** [2001 75p: f6f⁶ f6g 6g⁸ 6d f6g⁵ f6g f6g Nov 3] fair handicapper: won ladies handicap at **a64** Thirsk in June: likely to prove best at 5f/6f: yet to race on extremes of going on turf, and acts on fibresand: slowly away final outing: subsequently gelded. *A. G. Newcombe*

ITHRAIR (IRE) 2 ch.c. (Feb 27) Machiavellian (USA) 123 – Saleemah (USA) 96 **78** (Storm Bird (CAN) 134) [2001 7m³ 7f⁴ 7m 6d⁶ Oct 18] leggy, rather unfurnished colt: second foal: brother to 3-y-o Medraar: dam won around 1m: fair maiden: third at Newmarket: shaped quite well in nursery there final start: should stay 1m: sent to UAE. *J. L. Dunlop*

I TINA 5 b.m. Lycius (USA) 124 – Tintomara (IRE) (Niniski (USA) 125) [2001 66: **62** e10g* e12g e10g² 10g 10m⁵ 10.2g* 10m 10.2f³ f11g p10g p10g p13g Dec 29] modest performer: won maiden at Lingfield in January (left M. Tregoning after next start) and handicap at Chepstow in August: best form around 1¼m: acts on firm going, soft and equitrack: tried visored: has pulled hard/carried head high: best with waiting tactics. *J. G. Portman*

IT IS AS IT IS 2 b.g. (Apr 29) Aragon 118 – Hatimena (Hatim (USA) 121) [2001 5g **–** 7g Oct 19] small gelding: first foal: dam well beaten in 3 starts: well held in maiden/ claimer. *J. S. Wainwright*

IT'SAFACT 2 ch.f. (Apr 3) So Factual (USA) 120 – Axed Again (Then Again 126) **62** [2001 f5g⁵ 5.1g* 6d* 6f³ 6g⁶ f5s Dec 15] 1,000Y: angular filly: third foal: dam, no sign of ability, sister to Stewards' Cup winner For The Present: modest performer: won seller at Bath and nursery at Ayr in July: likely to prove best at 5f/6f: acts on firm and good to soft ground. *P. D. Evans*

IT'S ALLOWED 4 b.f. Piccolo 121 – Double Flutter 92 (Beldale Flutter (USA) 130) **–** [2001 73: 7.5m 7m 7.5m 7m Sep 22] fair handicapper at best: dead. *T. D. Barron*

ITSANOTHERGIRL 5 b.m. Reprimand 122 – Tasmim 63 (Be My Guest (USA) **69** 126) [2001 77: f8.5g f8g f8g 8.2v 12d 8s 8.3d 7m 10.5s* 8.5g 10v* 10s⁴ f12s Dec 15] **a–** leggy mare: fair handicapper: won at Haydock (landed gamble after 8 unplaced runs) in August and Ayr in October: stays at 1m (given a test) to 1¼m: has form on good to firm going, goes very well on soft/heavy (well held on all-weather): blinkered last 5 outings: usually held up: has hung left. *M. W. Easterby*

IT'S A SECRET 3 b.f. Polish Precedent (USA) 131 – Secret Obsession (USA) 89 **95** (Secretariat (USA)) [2001 7m⁵ 8m* 8m 9m* 9f 10m² 10.1m² 8g³ 10d Oct 18] strong, lengthy filly: sister to fairly useful 1¼m winner Secret's Out and half-sister to several winners, including 1995 2-y-o 6f winner Obsessive (by Seeking The Gold), later useful at 1¼m, and useful winner around 1m (including at 2 yrs) Secret Agent (by Machiavellian): dam, 1¼m winner, half-sister to smart 1½m performer Beyton: useful performer: won maiden at Newmarket and handicap at Newcastle in June: also ran well when second in handicap at Ascot and listed rated stakes at Newcastle (to Moselle): may prove best around 1¼m: acts on good to firm going. *W. J. Haggas*

ITS ECCO BOY 3 ch.g. Clantime 101 – Laena 72 (Roman Warrior 132) [2001 68p: **78** 8m⁴ 7m 8m⁵ 6d⁴ 7f⁴ 7g³ 7d 7s Nov 10] tall, useful-looking gelding: good walker: fair maiden handicapper: likely to prove best at 6f/7f: acts on good to firm and good to soft going. *K. R. Burke*

ITSFORNOWT (IRE) 2 b.f. (Mar 8) Royal Abjar (USA) 121 – Ewar Snowflake **43** (Snow Chief (USA)) [2001 6g 6f 5m⁵ 5m⁶ 5m⁶ Aug 23] 500Y: unfurnished filly: first foal: no form, out of Norfolk Stakes winner Petillante: poor maiden: likely to prove best at 5f. *D. W. Barker*

ITSGOTTABDUN (IRE) 4 b.g. Foxhound (USA) 103 – Lady Ingrid (Taufan (USA) **–** 119) [2001 56: f6g e8g Jan 10] modest performer at 3 yrs: well held both 4-y-o outings: usually visored/blinkered. *Andrew Reid*

IT'S MAGIC 5 b.g. Magic Ring (IRE) 115 – Ryewater Dream 72 (Touching Wood **64 +** (USA) 127) [2001 78d: 7g³ 8m⁴ 8m⁴ Jun 2] leggy, shallow-girthed gelding: modest handicapper: effective at 7f to easy 1¼m: acts on firm ground and equitrack: usually blinkered. *B. Hanbury*

IT'S OUR SECRET (IRE) 5 ch.g. Be My Guest (USA) 126 – Lady Dulcinea **76** (ARG) (General (FR)) [2001 72: 8s* 8d 8m* 8.3d² 9.1d 8d⁴ 8m² 8m⁶ 8.3g 8m 8g² Nov 7] lengthy, sturdy gelding: fair handicapper: won at Brighton in May and Ayr in June: best at 1m/1¼m: acts on fibresand/equitrack, soft and good to firm going: tried visored, not since 1999: reportedly bled from nose final 4-y-o outing. *M. H. Tompkins*

IT'S SMEE AGAIN 3 ch.f. Mizoram (USA) 105 – Mountain Dew (Pharly (FR) 130) **–** [2001 59: e10g 6s 6m 5m 6.1f 6m Aug 4] tall, useful-looking filly: modest performer at 2 yrs: no form in 2001. *Ronald Thompson*

IT'S THE LIMIT (USA) 2 b.c. (Mar 29) Boundary (USA) 117 – Beside (USA) **– p** (Sportin' Life (USA)) [2001 8d Oct 2] $80,000Y: tall, rather leggy colt: has scope: sixth foal: half-brother to fairly useful 1½m winner Marsul (by Cozzene) and winners in USA by Lord At War and Sunny's Halo: dam unraced: 14/1 and very green, sixteenth of 21 in maiden at Newmarket, missing break and always behind: likely to do better. *Mrs A. J. Perrett*

ITS YOUR BID 3 b.f. Dilum (USA) 115 – By Arrangement (IRE) 60 (Bold Arrange- **58** ment 127) [2001 –: 8.3s 10s 10m 11.5m⁴ 12m³ 16.4g⁵ 16g⁴ Sep 5] first foal: dam 1m to 16.5f winner: modest handicapper: 25/1, 12 lb out of weights and carrying overweight, improved to win at Epsom in August: ran creditably final outing: stays 2m: acts on good to firm going, well beaten on soft/heavy. *S. Woodman*

IT WAS MEANT TO BE 2 b.f. (Mar 22) Distant Relative 128 – Belle Vue 78 (Petong **62** 126) [2001 5d 6m² 6m* 7m 7m* 7.5s 8g² 8m² 7d f6g* f8g² f6g* p7g* Dec 12] 1,000Y: **a69** rather dipped-backed filly: first foal: dam, 6f winner from 2 starts at 2 yrs, out of half-sister to Forzando, very smart sprinter at 2 yrs and later Grade 1 1m winner in USA: fair on all-weather, modest on turf: won maiden at Lingfield in July, claimer at Thirsk (left K. Ivory) in August, nursery at Southwell and claimer at Wolverhampton in November and claimer at Lingfield in December: barely stays 1m: acts on good to firm going, good to soft and fibresand/polytrack: tends to wander/carry head awkwardly: consistent. *P. C. Haslam*

IVAN'S BABY (IRE) 2 b. or br.f. (Feb 11) Distinctly North (USA) 115 – Alexander **61 d** Goddess (IRE) (Alzao (USA) 117) [2001 5g² 5.7f 5f⁵ 6m⁴ 7m 5m⁶ f5g p6g p7g p10g p6g Dec 22] IR 11,500Y: first foal: dam unraced from family of very smart US 1m/1¼m performer Victory Speech: disappointing maiden: left R. Hannon after fourth start: tried blinkered/visored: sometimes hangs left: irresolute. *B. A. Pearce*

IVORSAGOODUN 2 b.f. (Apr 12) Piccolo 121 – Malibasta 83 (Auction Ring (USA) **61** 123) [2001 5.7f 6m⁶ 5.7f⁶ 7.1g 7.1m Sep 17] 13,000Y: sixth foal: sister to fairly useful 2000 2-y-o 5.7f winner Sibla and half-sister to 6f (at 2 yrs) and 7f winner Lamorna (by Shavian) and 1¼m (including at 2 yrs) and 11f winner Mystagogue (by Mystiko): dam 6f (at 2 yrs) and 1m winner: modest maiden: stays 7f: raced only on good going or firmer: blinkered (edgy, ran creditably) final start. *Mrs P. N. Dutfield*

IVOR'S FLUTTER 12 b.g. Beldale Flutter (USA) 130 – Rich Line (High Line 125) **–** [2001 16m 14g⁶ 16g 16d Sep 27] workmanlike gelding: one-time fairly useful winner: lightly raced on Flat in recent years: stayed 2¼m: acted on heavy and good to firm going: usually came from off pace: useful hurdler at best: was one to treat with caution: reportedly retired. *D. R. C. Elsworth*

IVORY BAY 2 b.g. (May 18) Piccolo 121 – Fantasy Racing (IRE) 86 (Tirol 127) [2001 **78 d** 6m² 6m 5m² 5d 5m 6g 5.7g 5g Nov 7] 15,500 2-y-o: rather leggy gelding: has a quick action: third foal: half-brother to a winner in Greece by Inchinor: dam 5f (including at 2 yrs) to 7f winner: fair maiden: well beaten after third start, leaving I. Balding before final one: likely to prove best at 5f/6f: acts on good to firm going: blinkered (found nothing) sixth start: gelded after final one. *J. Hetherton*

IVORY DAWN 7 b.m. Batshoof 122 – Cradle of Love (USA) 87 (Roberto (USA) **70** 131) [2001 85: 6s 6m 7m 6d 6m 6m⁵ Jul 13] leggy, workmanlike mare: fair handicapper: respectable efforts at best at 7 yrs: probably stays easy 7f: possibly unsuited by heavy going, acts on any other turf: below form in visor (including penultimate start): usually held up. *K. T. Ivory*

IVORY'S JOY 6 b.m. Tina's Pet 121 – Jacqui Joy 63 (Music Boy 124) [2001 109: **107 d** 5.2d 5.1d² 5g 5g 5f² 5g⁶ 5.1m 5m 5.1g 5g 5m² 5d 5.2f⁵ 5s 5d⁵ 5v Oct 27] leggy mare: useful performer: mostly below form after second to Bishops Court in valuable rated stakes at Epsom fifth outing: stays easy 6f: probably acts on any turf going and on fibresand: has won in blinkers, tried only once since 2 yrs: usually bandaged: usually waited with. *K. T. Ivory*

I WALKED BY NIGHT   2 ch.c. (Mar 20) Primo Dominie 121 – Malwiya (USA) – (Shahrastani (USA) 135) [2001 7d Nov 3] 28,000Y: good-bodied colt: fifth foal: half-brother to 4-y-o Malarkey and winners abroad by Polish Patriot and Be My Chief: dam unraced daughter of very smart French filly up to 10.5f Masmouda: 20/1 and backward, no show in maiden at Newmarket: sold 5,000 gns. *H. R. A. Cecil*

I WANT YOU NOW (IRE)   3 ch.f. Nicolotte 118 – Christle Mill (Pas de Seul 133) – [2001 f8.5f p10g Dec 29] IR 8,000Y: seventh foal: half-sister to fairly useful 1997 2-y-o 6f winner Conectis (by River Falls), later minor 6.5f stakes winner in USA, and winner in Italy by Mac's Imp: dam ran twice in Ireland at 2 yrs: well held in maidens at Wolverhampton (slowly away) and Lingfield. *D. J. S. Cosgrove*

I WISH   3 ch.f. Beveled (USA) – Ballystate 71 (Ballacashtal (CAN)) [2001 8.3s⁶ 9.9d   **58 ?** p10g Dec 29] second foal: sister to 4-y-o Bless: dam, maiden on Flat, fair hurdler (stayed 2¾m): best effort in maidens (apparently modest form) on debut: raced freely next time, off over 7 months before final outing: should stay at least 1¼m. *M. Madgwick*

IZMAIL (IRE)   2 b.g. (Feb 20) Bluebird (USA) 125 – My-Lorraine (IRE) 77 (Mac's   **94** Imp (USA) 116) [2001 5g⁵ 5m* 5m 6g⁴ 5d⁴ 5g² 6g⁴ 5m Sep 20] IR 150,000Y: useful-looking gelding: first foal: dam, Irish 5f and 6.5f winner, half-sister to smart Irish sprinter Catch The Blues (by Bluebird): fairly useful performer: won maiden at Newcastle in April: in frame in listed races at York (beaten ¾ length by Pepperoni) and Kempton sixth/seventh starts: will prove best at 5f/easy 6f: yet to race on extremes of going: has been slowly away: tends to race freely. *E. A. L. Dunlop*

IZWAH (USA)   2 b.f. (Mar 5) Bahri (USA) 125 – Firdous (Nashwan (USA) 135) [2001   **97** 5f* 6m³ Jun 30] useful-looking filly: third foal: dam, unraced sister/half-sister to 3 smart performers, out of 1000 Guineas, Oaks and Irish Derby winner Salsabil: useful form: landed odds in maiden at Sandown in May: beaten 2 necks when staying-on third of 5 to Massarra in listed event at Newmarket: should stay 1m: wore crossed noseband both starts. *D. R. Loder*

IZZET MUZZY (FR)   3 ch.g. Piccolo 121 – Texanne (BEL) 66§ (Efisio 120) [2001   **68** 52, a67: f6g² f6g² f6g f7g² f6g f6g⁴ f8.5g f6s⁶ f6g* 5v⁴ 6g f6g* f6g⁴ 6v f6g Nov 19] good-   **a92** bodied gelding: unimpressive mover: fairly useful handicapper on all-weather, fair on turf: left C. Kellett after sixth start: much improved when winning at Wolverhampton in September and Southwell (best effort, hung across to stand rail) in October: effective at testing 5f to easy 7f: acts on any turf going and fibresand: effective visored or not: races prominently. *R. Wilman*

J

JABAAR (USA)   3 gr.c. Silver Hawk (USA) 123 – Sierra Madre (FR) 119 (Baillamont   **85 p** (USA) 124) [2001 10m⁵ 8d* Oct 8] strong, lengthy colt: third foal: half-brother to high-class 7f/1m winner Aljabr (by Storm Cat) and useful French 1999 2-y-o 6f winner Makaarem (by Danzig): dam won Prix Marcel Boussac and Prix Vermeille: better effort in maidens over 2 months apart (fairly useful form) to beat Island Light by 3 lengths at Pontefract (wore crossed noseband), still appearing green (edged right) but soon well in control in straight: capable of better still. *E. A. L. Dunlop*

JABULANI (IRE)   2 b.c. (Apr 21) Marju (IRE) 127 – Houwara (IRE) (Darshaan 133)   **79 p** [2001 7g⁵ Oct 4] IR 12,500Y: half-brother to 11f seller winner Milltown Classic (by Classic Secret): dam unraced: 25/1, fifth of 21 to Millennium Dragon in maiden at Newmarket, staying on well after taking strong hold both to post and early in race: sure to improve. *W. Jarvis*

JACANA (USA)   3 ch.f. Woodman (USA) 126 – Storm Teal (USA) (Storm Bird   **65 +** (CAN) 134) [2001 74: 6m⁴ 6m Jul 27] rather leggy filly: first living foal: dam unraced sister to smart Coventry Stakes winner and Dewhurst second Stonehatch and half-sister to US Grade 1 1¼m winner Danger's Hour: fair form in 2 maidens at 2 yrs: below that level in maidens in 2001, both times looking ill at ease on ground: should stay 1m: unimpressive to post final 2-y-o start: has reportedly had breathing problem (tongue tied at 3 yrs): sold 13,500 gns in December. *J. H. M. Gosden*

JACK CARTER (IRE)   2 ch.c. (Feb 23) Desert King (IRE) 129 – Miss Garuda 94   **69**
(Persian Bold 123) [2001 7f Aug 18] 26,000F, 80,000Y: robust colt: seventh foal: half-
brother to 3 winners, including fairly useful 7f winner Bali Batik (by Barathea) and 1993
2-y-o 8.5f winner Pampered Guest (by Be My Guest): dam 2-y-o 7f winner: fair form
when ninth of 17 in maiden at Newbury: dead. *M. L. W. Bell*

JACK DAWSON (IRE)   4 b.g. Persian Bold 123 – Dream of Jenny 73 (Caerleon   **80**
(USA) 132) [2001 82: 10g 10m⁴ 12m 15f* 14f³ 15.9m* 21m 13.9m 13.3f⁶ 16m* Sep 30]
neat gelding: fairly useful handicapper: won at Ayr in June, Chester in July and Musselburgh in September: best at 1¾m/2m: acts on firm and soft going: usually held up:
reliable. *John Berry*

JACKERIN (IRE)   6 b.g. Don't Forget Me 127 – Meanz Beanz (High Top 131) [2001   **59 §**
52§: f5g f5g⁵ e6g* e6g² e5g⁴ e5g² 6m⁴ 5m* 5m⁶ 5m Jun 8] strong gelding: modest   **a62 §**
performer: won seller at Lingfield in March and handicap at Hamilton in May: was best
at 5f/easy 6f: acted on any turf going and fibresand/equitrack: was usually visored/
blinkered: raced up with pace: often hung/finished weakly: dead. *Miss J. F. Craze*

JACK FLUSH (IRE)   7 b.g. Broken Hearted 124 – Clubhouse Turn (IRE) (King of   **–**
Clubs 124) [2001 10s Apr 10] leggy gelding: one-time rated 1m handicapper: well held
only Flat outing since 1999: tried blinkered/visored. *M. E. Sowersby*

JACKIE'S BABY   5 b.g. Then Again 126 – Guarded Expression 51 (Siberian Express   **–**
(USA) 125) [2001 90: 5.1f 5.1m May 21] big, good-topped gelding: fairly useful
handicapper at best: well beaten both 5-y-o outings: sometimes wanders. *W. G. M. Turner*

JACKS BIRTHDAY (IRE)   3 b.g. Mukaddamah (USA) 125 – High Concept (IRE)   **56**
(Thatching 131) [2001 –: f6g 8.3g 10.9g⁵ 11.5g Aug 10] modest maiden handicapper:
may prove best around 1¼m: blinkered second and final starts. *R. J. O'Sullivan*

JACKSMILES   2 b.g. (May 10) Puissance 110 – Cassiar 84 (Connaught 130) [2001 5s   **–**
6m f5g 7d 7.6m 6g Sep 5] 1,000Y: brother to fairly useful 5f/6f winner Ultra Beet and
half-brother to several winners, including fairly useful 5f/6f performer Persistent Bell
(by Belfort): dam 11.5f winner: no sign of ability in maidens/sellers: tried blinkered.
J. J. Bridger

JACK THE TRACK (IRE)   2 b.g. (Feb 6) Barathea (IRE) 127 – Babushka (IRE)   **88**
(Dance of Life (USA)) [2001 8m* 8s Oct 22] 47,000Y: good-topped gelding: fourth foal:
half-brother to 4-y-o Julius and 1997 2-y-o 5f winner Dancing Icon (by Mujtahid), later
successful abroad: dam Irish 2-y-o 1m winner out of half-sister to high-class miler Then
Again: fairly useful form: won maiden at Kempton in September by 1½ lengths from
Lewis Island: only seventh in listed event at Pontefract: will stay 1¼m. *J. Noseda*

JACK TO A KING   6 b.g. Nawwar 76 – Rudda Flash (General David) [2001 –, a64:   **–**
f5g² f5g⁴ f5g² f7g⁵ f5g f5g⁵ f5g f5g 5m⁶ f5g⁶ 5g f12g³ f12g f14g Dec 3] modest   **a60**
handicapper: well below form after sixth start: raced mainly over 5f, seems to stay easy
1½m: acts on fibresand/equitrack, little form on turf: usually blinkered/visored: has worn
tongue tie. *M. J. Polglase*

JACMAR (IRE)   6 br.g. High Estate 127 – Inseyab 65 (Persian Bold 123) [2001 56:   **36**
5v 7.1m 6m 5d 5m 6m 6d⁵ 6g⁴ 5f 6g⁶ 7.1f⁶ 7d 6d⁶ 5s 5g⁵ Sep 3] smallish, good-bodied
gelding: poor handicapper: stays 7f: below form on heavy going, acts on any other turf:
sometimes slowly away. *Miss L. A. Perratt*

JADEERON   2 b.g. (Feb 22) Green Desert (USA) 127 – Rain And Shine (FR) 78   **59**
(Rainbow Quest (USA) 134) [2001 6m 7m 6g Aug 15] useful-looking gelding: first foal:
dam, Irish 1½m winner who stayed 2m, closely related to smart 1m/1¼m performer
Kabool and granddaughter of Fall Aspen: modest maiden: blinkered and tongue tied,
tailed off final start: should stay at least 1m. *B. Hanbury*

JADE'S PROMISE   2 b.g. (Apr 12) Definite Article 121 – Zacinta (USA) (Hawkster   **60**
(USA)) [2001 7m 6.1g⁶ 7.1g Sep 2] 3,000Y, 30,000 2-y-o: first foal: dam ran once in
Italy: modest maiden: should stay 1m. *J. R. Best*

JADE TIGER   5 ch.g. Lion Cavern (USA) 117 – Precious Jade 72 (Northfields (USA))   **52 §**
[2001 –§, a58§: f12g f8.5g 8s 8.1g 8.1m⁴ 11.6g f9.4g⁴ 10.9m 8.1g³ Sep 13] smallish
gelding: modest performer: stays 9.4f: acts on good to firm going, good to soft and
fibresand: irresolute. *F. Jordan*

JADE WARRIOR   2 b.g. (Jan 24) Sabrehill (USA) 120 – Jade Pet 90 (Petong 126)   **70**
[2001 7.1s⁶ 7.9m 7s⁶ Nov 9] 5,200F, 9,000Y: big, lengthy gelding: third foal: half-brother
to 4-y-o Hail The Chief and 5-y-o Just Wiz: dam, 5f winner, half-sister to dam of smart

sprinter Sampower Star: easily best effort in maidens (fair form) at Doncaster final outing: gelded after: not sure to stay 1m. *P. Howling*

JAHANGIR 2 b.c. (Mar 31) Zamindar (USA) 116 – Imperial Jade 105 (Lochnager 132) [2001 5m^6 5.2m Jul 21] 32,000Y: close-coupled, useful-looking colt: half-brother to several winners, notably smart sprinter Averti (by Warning): dam sprinting sister to smart sprinter Reesh: clear signs of ability in maiden at Sandown and valuable sales race at Newbury, fair form in latter. *W. R. Muir* **73**

JAHASH 3 ch.g. Hernando (FR) 127 – Jalsun (Jalmood (USA) 126) [2001 –: 12m 12.1d^3 15m 16m^2 16.2g* 15.8m^4 Sep 22] modest handicapper: won at Chepstow in August: will stay beyond 2m: acts on good to soft ground: blinkered last 3 starts: has looked reluctant (early reminders after slow start at Chepstow). *Sir Mark Prescott* **55**

JAILHOUSE ROCKET 4 gr.g. Petong 126 – Selvi (Mummy's Pet 125) [2001 –: f6g f8g 6f 5g 9m 8.3g 9f 8.1s^2 8.5g 10s Oct 25] poor handicapper: left C. Dwyer after second start: stays 1m: acts on soft and good to firm going. *Miss B. Sanders* **47**

JALINDI (IRE) 4 ch.f. Indian Ridge 123 – Jaljuli 107 (Jalmood (USA) 126) [2001 84: 12d 10g 7.1m^2 7m 7g^4 7m^4 7m 7.1m^5 Aug 1] sixth foal: half-sister to 1m/1¼m performer Jubilee Scholar (by Royal Academy) and a winner in Japan by Persian Bold: dam, 5f/6f winner at 2 yrs, half-sister to Kooyonga: fair performer: trained in 2000 by J. Oxx in Ireland, winning maiden at Dundalk: creditable efforts at 4 yrs when in frame in handicaps: probably best at 7f/1m: acts on firm and good to soft ground: tongue tied: usually blinkered/visored in 2001: carries head awkwardly: probably ungenuine. *E. J. O'Neill* **77 §**

JALONS STAR (IRE) 3 b.g. Eagle Eyed (USA) 111 – Regina St Cyr (IRE) (Doulab (USA) 115) [2001 46: e10s^4 e10g f12g^6 10.3s^5 10s* 11.6s^2 12s^5 11.6g May 14] tall gelding: fair handicapper: won at Nottingham in April: should stay 1½m: best efforts on soft going: makes running. *M. Quinn* **67 a–**

JALOUSIE (IRE) 3 b.f. Barathea (IRE) 127 – Duende 75 (High Top 131) [2001 68p: f11g* 11.8g^4 f12g* 12f 11.8g* 12g* 13.4d^2 14.6m^3 12g^3 12d^6 Oct 13] well-made filly:

Mr Dennis Yardy's "Jalousie"

useful performer: won maiden at Southwell in April, handicaps at Southwell in June and Leicester in July and minor event at Newmarket (by neck from Don't Sioux Me) in August: good placed efforts in listed rated stakes at Chester (4 lengths second to Flossy) and Park Hill Stakes at Doncaster (staying-on 2¾ lengths third to Ranin) next 2 starts only: stays 1¾m: acts on good to soft going (probably on firm) and fibresand: races prominently: tough and genuine. *S. P. C. Woods*

JAMAICAN FLIGHT (USA) 8 b.h. Sunshine Forever (USA) – Kalamona (USA) **60 d**
(Hawaii) [2001 78d: f11s⁴ f16g⁴ f12g 18v⁴ 17.1s 16.2n 12d⁵ 16d f16.2g⁴ Nov 21] leggy horse: modest handicapper in 2001, continued on downgrade: probably suited by 2m+ nowdays: acts on any turf going and fibresand: tried visored: has given trouble start: front runner. *Mrs S. Lamyman*

JAMES DEE (IRE) 5 b.g. Shalford (IRE) 124§ – Glendale Joy (IRE) (Glenstal **65**
(USA) 118) [2001 69, a87: f7f² 6s⁵ 6m⁵ 7f Jul 5] fair handicapper: effective at 6f/7f: acts on firm going, good to soft and fibresand/equitrack: has swerved left at start/not found much: sold 4,200 gns in September. *A. P. Jarvis*

JAMES STARK (IRE) 4 b.g. Up And At 'em 109 – June Maid 56 (Junius (USA) **92**
124) [2001 95: 6m 6m 6m 5g 5.5d⁴ 6m³ 6g 6m 5.2d⁵ 7.6d² 7d⁶ 6m 6g 7d 7d 5v f6g* 7s f6g* f6g³ f5g* Dec 8] leggy gelding: has a quick, fluent action: fairly useful performer: won minor event then 2 handicaps at Wolverhampton in November and December: effective at 5f to 7.5f: acts on any turf going and fibresand/equitrack: best blinkered/visored: sometimes slowly away, but usually races prominently: tends to wander, and probably best with strong handling: none too consistent. *N. P. Littmoden*

JAMESTOWN 4 b.g. Merdon Melody 98 – Thabeh 57 (Shareef Dancer (USA) 135) **74**
[2001 71, a81: f9.4g⁴ f8.5g f8g³ f7g 7.1d* 7.6f 8.5s⁴ 7.9m 7.5s 7s⁴ f7g⁴ f8.5g f7g⁶ Dec 8] **a76**
workmanlike, close-coupled gelding: fair performer: won minor event at Musselburgh in April: races mainly at 7f/1m: acts on firm going, soft and fibresand: visored final outing: none too consistent. *C. Smith*

JAMIE ANN 4 b.f. Son Pardo 107 – Taine Sands (Record Run 127) [2001 8.3v Nov 8] **–**
seems of little account. *Miss S. West*

JAMIE MY BOY (IRE) 3 b.g. Common Grounds 118 – House of Fame (USA) **–**
(Trempolino (USA) 135) [2001 59: 7d 8.1g f11g f7g Jul 13] leggy gelding: modest maiden at 2 yrs: well held in 2001: blinkered final outing. *T. Keddy*

JAMMAAL 4 b.c. Robellino (USA) 127 – Navajo Love Song (IRE) 43 (Dancing **115**
Brave (USA) 140) [2001 121: 10s* 10g² 10m³ 10s² 10s* 10s³ Oct 29] strong, close-coupled colt: carries condition: smart performer: landed odds in 4-runner minor event at Cork in April and listed race at the Curragh (held on gamely by short head from Chamela Bay) in October: good efforts otherwise when ¾-length second to Exaltation in Gallinule Stakes at Leopardstown and when beaten ½ length by Bach in Royal Whip Stakes at the Curragh then third to Ice Dancer in listed event at Leopardstown final outing: effective at 1¼m to 1½m: seems suited by good ground or softer (acts on heavy), well below form in Singapore Derby on good to firm third start: blinkered nowadays. *D. K. Weld, Ireland*

JAMMIE DODGER 5 b.g. Ardkinglass 114 – Ling Lane (Slip Anchor 136) [2001 **–**
43: f12g f8.5s⁶ f9.4s⁶ f8.5g f6g e10g f7g f9.4g f6g e12g e8g f12g Apr 14] seems of no account nowadays. *D. Burchell*

JAN BRUEGHEL (USA) 2 ch.g. (Feb 9) Phone Trick (USA) – Sunk (USA) (Polish **82 p**
Navy (USA)) [2001 5.2m⁶ 6d⁵ Oct 18] $45,000F, 70,000Y: good-bodied gelding: second foal: dam, winner around 1m in USA, half-sister to Rockfel Stakes winner At Risk: off 3 months, much better effort in maidens (fairly useful form) when fifth of 22 to Hiddendale at Newmarket: should stay 7f: likely to progress. *P. F. I. Cole*

JANEFER JOHN (IRE) 4 ch.f. Magical Wonder (USA) 125 – John's Vision (IRE) **–**
(Vision (USA)) [2001 85: 5m 6g 7g Jul 17] fairly useful maiden in Ireland in 2000: showed nothing in handicaps at 4 yrs. *D. J. S. Cosgrove*

JANGLYNYVE 7 ch.m. Sharpo 132 – Wollow Maid 73 (Wollow 132) [2001 8m 12m **–**
6m 8.1m⁵ 7m 10.1d⁶ 10g⁵ Aug 20] leggy mare: modest performer at 3 yrs: little form since: has bled from nose. *C. A. Dwyer*

Mr Hamdan Al Maktoum's "Jammaal"

JANICELAND (IRE) 4 b.f. Foxhound (USA) 103 – Rebecca's Girl (IRE) (Nashamaa **75 d** 113) [2001 71: e7g³ e7g² e8g e7g³ e7s⁵ e8g³ 6f⁶ 7m⁶ 7m* 7m 7g³ 7g 7m f7g f7g f6g f8g Dec 10] strong, close-coupled filly: fair handicapper: made virtually all at Brighton in July: no form last 5 starts (left M. Wigham after thirteenth): stays easy 1m: raced only on good going or firmer on turf, better form on equitrack than fibresand: tried visored: has been bandaged behind. *S. E. Kettlewell*

JANOUEIX (IRE) 2 b.c. (Apr 28) Desert King (IRE) 129 – Miniver (IRE) (Mujtahid **59 p** (USA) 118) [2001 7m 6v p10g⁵ Dec 4] 28,000Y: first foal: dam, ran once in Ireland at 2 yrs, half-sister to high-class performer up to 1½m Legal Case and useful performer up to 1¾m La Sky (dam of Oaks winner Love Divine): best effort in maidens (modest form) when not-knocked-about fifth at Lingfield: will stay at least 1½m: should do better. *G. A. Butler*

JAPAN (IRE) 3 ch.f. Caerleon (USA) 132 – Culture Vulture (USA) 118 (Timeless **59** Moment (USA)) [2001 f6g⁵ f6g² f7g* 7s⁶ 7s 7.1m 6g⁵ 6g 6.1m Sep 10] strong, **a69** workmanlike filly: poor mover: third foal: dam, won Prix Marcel Boussac and Poule d'Essai des Pouliches, out of half-sister to dams of Zilzal and Polish Precedent: fair performer on all-weather, modest on turf: easily best effort when winning maiden at Southwell in March: finds 6f a minimum, and should stay 1m: acts on fibresand, best turf effort on good ground: blinkered (soundly beaten) final outing: sold 80,000 gns in December. *P. F. I. Cole*

JARDINES LOOKOUT (IRE) 4 b.g. Fourstars Allstar (USA) 122 – Foolish Flight **119** (IRE) 57 (Fools Holme (USA)) [2001 112: 13.9g⁵ 16.4m 20f³ 16g 15.9g² 18d⁵ Sep 13]

497

Mr Ambrose Turnbull's "Jardines Lookout"

leggy, sparely-made gelding: shows knee action: smart performer: best efforts when 5 lengths third to Royal Rebel in Gold Cup at Royal Ascot in June and head second to Persian Punch in Lonsdale Stakes at York in August: ran respectably at best otherwise in Yorkshire Cup at York, Bonusprint Stakes (Henry II) at Sandown, Goodwood Cup and Doncaster Cup: stays 2½m: acts on firm and soft going: tends to hang under pressure. *A. P. Jarvis*

JARN　4 b.c. Green Desert (USA) 127 – Alkariyh (USA) 79 (Alydar (USA)) [2001 103: **111** 6g 7.9m 6m* 6f⁶ 5m⁴ 6m⁴ 6d⁵ 6m Sep 5] strong, attractive colt: usually takes the eye: fluent mover: smart performer: won minor event at Yarmouth in June by short head from Palanzo: best effort when length fourth to Antonio Canova in Great St Wilfrid Stakes (Handicap) at Ripon on sixth outing: ran badly on second and final starts: should prove as effective at 7f as 6f: acts on firm going, well held on soft: usually tongue tied: blinkered last 6 starts: held up: sold 21,000 gns in October, sent to France. *B. Hanbury*

JARV (IRE)　3 b.f. Inzar (USA) 112 – Conditional Sale (IRE) (Petorius 117) [2001 61: **60** 8.2s 8.3g 8.3g⁶ 8.5d⁶ 6m 8m* 8.5g³ 7s⁵ 8d 8.2s Nov 5] modest handicapper: won at Brighton in September: may prove best at 1m/9f: acts on soft and good to firm going: blinkered of late. *J. Akehurst*

JASKINI　5 b.g. Lion Cavern (USA) 117 – Sharka 97 (Shareef Dancer (USA) 135) **–** [2001 –: f9.4s Jan 18] formerly useful in France: tailed off at Wolverhampton only 5-y-o outing. *W. M. Brisbourne*

JASMICK (IRE)　3 ch.f. Definite Article 121 – Glass Minnow (IRE) 59 (Alzao (USA) **88** 117) [2001 40: 8.3d³ 8m⁴ 10d³ 9.9m⁴ 10.3m 12m* 11.9m² 13.3f⁵ 14g⁴ 12d Nov 2] smallish filly: fairly useful handicapper: progressive form at 3 yrs, winning at Salisbury in August: good efforts next 3 starts at York, Newbury and Newmarket: effective at 1½m/1¾m: acts on firm and good to soft going: consistent. *H. Morrison*

JASMINE BREEZE 2 b.f. (Apr 29) Saddlers' Hall (IRE) 126 – Regal Peace 94 (Known Fact (USA) 135) [2001 7m Sep 22] lengthy, rather unfurnished filly: fifth foal: half-sister to useful 2000 2-y-o 6f winner Earl Grey (by Twining) and 3 winners in USA: dam, Irish sprinter, later successful in USA: 33/1, never-dangerous eighth of 18 to demoted Moon Ballad in maiden at Newmarket: should improve. *W. Jarvis* **61 p**

JATO DANCER (IRE) 6 b.m. Mukaddamah (USA) 125 – Que Tranquila 65 (Dominion 123) [2001 34: f12s⁴ f12g³ f7s f11g f12s⁵ f12g⁴ f12g⁴ f11g⁵ f7f f11g f8g⁵ f11g⁴ f11g³ 11.9m⁶ 11.8d 12g 10.9m Aug 27] poor performer: stays 1½m: acts on firm going, good to soft and fibresand/equitrack: tried blinkered: often claimer ridden. *R. Hollinshead* **36**

JAVELIN 5 ch.g. Generous (IRE) 139 – Moss (Alzao (USA) 117) [2001 58d: e10g Mar 31] disappointing maiden: blinkered once. *Ian Williams* **–**

JAWAH (IRE) 7 br.g. In The Wings 128 – Saving Mercy 101 (Lord Gayle (USA) 124) [2001 §§: 14.1m 14.1f⁵ 16.2f 16.2s Aug 16] lengthy, sparely-made gelding: fairly useful handicapper at best, but irresolute and best avoided: tried in blinkers/visor. *J. R. Jenkins* **§§**

JAWHARI 7 b.g. Lahib (USA) 129 – Lady of The Land 75 (Wollow 132) [2001 73: f5g* f6g³ f5g⁵ 5.3m² 5.3m* 6s f6g³ p5g² Dec 22] small, sturdy gelding: has a quick action: fair performer: won seller at Wolverhampton in February and minor event at Brighton in September: races mainly over 5f/6f nowadays: acts on good to firm going (probably on soft), fibresand and polytrack: blinkered once: has found little: none too consistent. *T. G. Mills* **70**

JAWHIRJI 4 b.g. Owington 123 – Dream Baby (Master Willie 129) [2001 7m 7g Aug 12] 170,000Y, 4,500 3-y-o: third foal: half-brother to fairly useful 1998 2-y-o 6f winner Dreaming and 1997 2-y-o 7f winner Only In Dreams (both by Polar Falcon): dam, ran once, out of half-sister to high-class French 1¼m/1½m performer Apple Tree: well held on Flat in maiden and seller. *Mrs Lydia Pearce* **–**

JAWRJIK (IRE) 3 b.g. Blues Traveller (IRE) 119 – Eva Fay (IRE) (Fayruz 116) [2001 –: 12g⁶ Aug 15] useful-looking gelding: well held in maidens. *B. S. Rothwell* **–**

JAWWALA (USA) 2 b.f. (Mar 28) Green Dancer (USA) 132 – Fetch N Carry (USA) (Alleged (USA) 138) [2001 8s* Oct 31] $25,000F, $100,000Y: half-sister to several minor winners in USA: dam, US maiden, half-sister to dam of smart 1m/1¼m performer Light of Morn: 25/1, beat Havoc by 1¾ lengths in maiden at Yarmouth, dropped out and switched wide before leading over 2f out: will stay at least 1¼m: sure to improve. *J. W. Payne* **84 p**

JAYANJAY 2 b.g. (Feb 23) Piccolo 121 – Morica 88 (Moorestyle 137) [2001 5.2m 5m⁴ 5m⁴ 5s* 5g² 6m⁶ Sep 12] half-brother to 3 winners, including 1992 2-y-o 5f winner Carnbrea Snip (by Robellino) and 6f/7f winner Espla (by Sure Blade): dam, 2-y-o 6f winner who stayed 1¼m, half-sister to smart 7f/1m performer Aragon: fair performer: won nursery at Sandown in August: unlucky head second in similar event there next time: will prove best at 5f/6f: acts on soft and good to firm going: sometimes slowly away. *B. R. Johnson* **78**

JAYANNPEE 10 ch.g. Doulab (USA) 115 – Amina 80 (Brigadier Gerard 144) [2001 5g 6g 5.1g 5.7m 5m 6m 5d 6m 5m Sep 26] good-topped gelding: useful performer in his prime: stayed 6f: acted on firm and good to soft ground: tongue tied in 2001: was sometimes early to post/slowly away: usually came from off pace: dead. *I. A. Balding* **60**

JAYCAT (IRE) 3 ch.f. Catrail (USA) 123 – Improviste (CAN) (The Minstrel (CAN) 135) [2001 –: 6v³ 8.2s² 8.1g 7s⁵ 9m f8.5g 9.9s 6d Oct 9] unfurnished filly: modest maiden: well below form last 4 outings: should stay beyond 1m: acts on heavy going: looked none too genuine in blinkers sixth start: has started slowly: sold 450 gns. *G. A. Butler* **56**

JAZAN (IRE) 2 b.f. (Jan 31) Danehill (USA) 126 – Babita 107 (Habitat 134) [2001 8.1g² 7d Oct 6] good-bodied filly: eighth foal: half-sister to 3 winners, including useful 7f (at 2 yrs) to 11f (in USA) winner Babinda (by Old Vic) and 4-y-o 8f winner Amjad: dam best at 6f at 2 yrs: seemed to show fairly useful form when 1¼ lengths second of 3 to Sundari in minor event at Sandown: second favourite, only seventh of 12 in maiden at Redcar. *C. E. Brittain* **94 ?**

JAZMEER 2 ch.f. (Jan 28) Sabrehill (USA) 120 – Saabga (USA) 83 (Woodman (USA) 126) [2001 6m⁶ 7m* Jun 29] lengthy filly: has scope: first foal: dam, second at 7f at 2 yrs on only start, half-sister to smart middle-distance performers Close Conflict and **83**

499

Newton's Law out of unraced sister to Secreto: much better effort in maidens (fairly useful form) when winning maiden at Goodwood by 1¼ lengths from Thrasher: should stay 1¼m. *M. P. Tregoning*

JAZZAAM 2 ch.f. (Mar 29) Fraam 114 – Aldwick Colonnade 62 (Kind of Hush 118) – [2001 6v Nov 8] third foal: half-sister to 6f to 2m winner Coastguards Hero (by Chilibang): dam 1m winner/winning hurdler: green, twelfth in maiden at Windsor. *M. D. I. Usher*

JAZZY MILLENNIUM 4 ch.g. Lion Cavern (USA) 117 – Woodcrest 82 (Niniski 65 (USA) 125) [2001 65: 7g 6f 6.1f 9f 7g 7m* 7g² 6m* 7.1g⁴ 6s* Sep 30] quite attractive gelding: won seller at Brighton in July, and handicaps at Lingfield in August and Brighton in September: effective at 6f/7f: acts on firm and soft going: blinkered last 6 starts: best making running. *B. R. Millman*

JEBA TO 2 b.f. (Mar 9) Petong 126 – Sunley Stars (Sallust 134) [2001 6f Jun 4] – 4,000Y, 4,200 2-y-o: workmanlike filly: eighth foal: half-sister to fairly useful 1m (in UAE)/9.4f winner Don Sebastian (by Indian Ridge) and 1995 2-y-o 5f winner All She Surveys (by Mazilier): dam, poor maiden, out of sister to high-class sprinter Runnett: very green, well beaten in seller at Thirsk. *M. W. Easterby*

JEDEYDD 4 b.g. Shareef Dancer (USA) 135 – Bilad (USA) (Riverman (USA) 131) 95 [2001 64p: 8m² 7m* 7m⁶ 7.1f² 6m² 7m 8g 7d 5v Oct 29] lengthy gelding: useful performer: won maiden at Yarmouth in May: good efforts in handicaps next 3 starts: below form after: effective at 6f/7f: acts on firm ground, probably not on softer than good: slowly away final outing: usually races up with pace. *B. Hanbury*

JEDI KNIGHT 7 b.g. Emarati (USA) 74 – Hannie Caulder (Workboy 123) [2001 94: 93 10s 10.4g² 8.1m⁶ 10.1m⁴ 8.9m⁶ 10.4m Jul 14] tall, good-topped gelding: fairly useful handicapper: creditable efforts when in frame at York in May and Epsom in June: best at 1m/1¼m nowadays: acts on firm ground, probably on heavy: blinkered once: has high head carriage: has been bandaged: often races up with pace. *M. W. Easterby*

JEFFREY ANOTHERRED 7 b.g. Emarati (USA) 74 – First Pleasure 73 (Dominion 72 123) [2001 72, a–: 7.1v³ 7g² 7g³ 7m⁵ 7m 7d 7.2m 7d f8.5g Nov 17] small gelding: fair a– handicapper: on a lengthy losing run: stays 7.6f: acts on heavy going, probably on good to firm: tried visored, not in 2001: usually held up. *M. Dods*

JELANI (IRE) 2 b.c. (Feb 21) Darshaan 133 – No Rehearsal (FR) (Baillamont (USA) 98 p 124) [2001 7.1s* 7.2m² 7s² Oct 11] 70,000Y: quite good-topped colt: sixth foal: half-brother to fairly useful French winner around 5f/6f Lever To Heaven (by Bluebird): dam French 8.5f and 1¼m winner out of half-sister to Miesque: useful form: won maiden at Haydock in September: runner-up in minor events at Ayr and York after, beaten ¾ length by Highdown in latter: should be suited by 1m/1¼m: probably capable of better. *Andrew Turnell*

JELBA 3 b.f. Pursuit of Love 124 – Gold Bracelet § (Golden Fleece (USA) 133) [2001 87 80: 7d 7.6f⁵ 10g 7m⁶ 7m 6g² 6m² 6.1m² f6g² 6g* 7d⁴ 8.5g⁴ 7g f6g⁴ 6d⁶ p7g³ p7g² p7g* f7g p7g² p7g* Dec 29] tall, quite good-topped filly: fairly useful performer: won maiden at Newmarket in July and handicaps at Lingfield in November and December: effective at 6f/7f: acts on firm ground, good to soft, fibresand and polytrack: blinkered twice, usually visored: often slowly away: has found little/looked none too keen. *N. P. Littmoden*

JELLYBEEN (IRE) 5 ch.m. Petardia 113 – Lux Aeterna (Sandhurst Prince 128) – § [2001 –§: f9.4g f12g³ f16g⁶ e12g 13.8g 12g Aug 15] workmanlike mare: temperamental handicapper nowadays: tried blinkered/visored. *Miss A. Stokell*

JENKO (IRE) 4 b.g. College Chapel 122 – Flicker of Hope (IRE) 53 (Baillamont – (USA) 124) [2001 –: f8g e7g f8g⁶ f8.5g Mar 15] of little account nowadays. *Miss J. Feilden*

JENNASH 3 b.f. Sabrehill (USA) 120 – Kayartis 57 (Kaytu 112) [2001 –: f11g 8.1v – Apr 25] rather leggy, plain filly: little sign of ability in maidens/handicap. *C. A. Dwyer*

JENNIFER JENKINS 3 b.f. Komaite (USA) – Joemlujen (Forzando 122) [2001 –: – 6f 10s Oct 3] well held in maidens/handicap. *P. D. Evans*

JENTZEN (USA) 3 b.c. Miswaki (USA) 124 – Bold Jessie (Never So Bold 135) 108 [2001 85p: 7d⁴ 7g* 7g³ 7m* 7m 6g³ 6g 7s⁴ Aug 31] big, strong, good-bodied colt: useful performer: won minor event at Newmarket (beat Caughnawaga 1¾ lengths) in May and listed race at Epsom (beat Amicable ½ length) in June: good efforts otherwise when fourth in minor event at Newmarket, 1¾ lengths third to Lunasalt in Prix du Palais-Royal at Longchamp and 4 lengths third to Orientor in Shergar Cup Sprint at Ascot: effective at 6f/7f: acts on good to firm going: sent to USA. *R. Hannon*

JEPAJE 4 b.g. Rambo Dancer (CAN) 107 – Hi-Hunsley 82 (Swing Easy (USA) 126) [2001 55, a46: f7g³ f7s³ f6s e7g² e7g* e7g 7.1m 7d 8f 8f Jul 9] modest handicapper: won at Lingfield in March: no form after: stays 7f, possibly not 8.5f: acts on heavy going, good to firm and fibresand/equitrack: tried blinkered: has twice unseated rider after finishing line: none too consistent, and sometimes looks none too keen. *A. Bailey* **52 d**

JERPAHNI 2 b.f. (Apr 27) Distant Relative 128 – Oublier L'Ennui (FR) 79 (Bellman (FR) 123) [2001 5s⁴ 6m 6g 7g Sep 11] 26,000Y: tall, leggy filly: sixth foal: sister to 6-y-o Shudder and half-sister to 4-y-o Arctic High: dam, probably stayed 1½m on Flat, winning hurdler/chaser: modest maiden: best effort on debut: reportedly threw rider 3 times in preliminaries before third start: looked none too keen (carried head awkwardly) final one: should stay 7f: one to treat with caution: sold 1,200 gns. *G. Wragg* **58 §**

JERVAULX FLICKA 2 b.f. (Feb 25) Magic Ring (IRE) 115 – Tirolina (IRE) (Thatching 131) [2001 6m⁶ Jul 27] lengthy filly: second foal: dam, unraced half-sister to useful Irish sprinter Sharp Point, out of half-sister to 2000 Guineas winner Tirol: 20/1, last in maiden at Thirsk. *C. W. Fairhurst* **–**

JESSICA'S DREAM (IRE) 3 b.f. Desert Style (IRE) 121 – Ziffany 68 (Taufan (USA) 119) [2001 6m⁵ 7.1g⁶ 6m* 6f* 6d² 6g³ 5g* 5g* 5.6m 6m 5s* 5s* Oct 21] IR 2,200F: smallish, workmanlike filly: second foal: dam, 7f seller winner, ran only at 2 yrs: thrived on racing and developed into smart performer: won maiden at Newcastle, handicaps at Ripon, York, Sandown (by ½ length from Smokin Beau) and Ascot (beat Dancing Mystery comfortably by 1½ lengths) and Premio Omenoni at Milan (led inside final 1f to beat Herve Leger ½ length) between June and October: has won at 6f, but will prove best at 5f: acts on firm and soft going: has edged right: a credit to connections. *J. G. Given* **114**

JESSIE 2 ch.f. (Mar 23) Pivotal 124 – Bold Gem 68 (Never So Bold 135) [2001 6m⁶ 7s* 7g⁴ 7f 8s Sep 27] lengthy filly: third foal: dam, 5f winner, half-sister to smart pair Just A Flutter (miler) and Slicious (up to 1½m): fair performer: won maiden at Epsom in August: ran creditably next 2 starts: stays 7f: acts on soft going, probably on firm: sold 7,000 gns. *B. J. Meehan* **77**

JESSINCA 5 b.m. Minshaanshu Amad (USA) 91§ – Noble Soul 67 (Sayf El Arab (USA) 127) [2001 52, a57: f9.4s² f8g⁵ f8g² f7g² f8f² f7g³ e8g⁵ 8m 7f⁵ 8.3g 8g 6m f9.4s f8g Nov 26] leggy mare: modest handicapper on all-weather, poor on turf: effective at 7f/1m: acts on good to firm going, soft and fibresand: tried visored. *A. P. Jones* **42 a59**

JESS REBEC'S PET (IRE) 4 b.f. Petorius 117 – Jess Rebec 63 (Kala Shikari 125) [2001 –: f9.4s f12g f9.4g Feb 20] of little account. *P. D. Evans* **–**

Riggs Bank Rated Stakes (Handicap), Ascot—one of six wins during the year for Jessica's Dream, who comes from some way back to beat Dancing Mystery and Smart Predator

JE'THAME (IRE) 3 ch.f. Definite Article 121 – Victorian Flower (Tate Gallery (USA) 117) [2001 61: 10g 8.3g 8d 7f Jun 30] rather leggy, workmanlike filly: modest maiden at 2 yrs: little show in 2001: sometimes blinkered. *P. L. Gilligan* —

JETSTREAM FLYER 3 b.f. Distant Relative 128 – Persian Air (Persian Bold 123) [2001 –: 7s³ f8g 7d 10.1m⁶ 8d 7m 7m Sep 4] poor maiden: little form after reappearance in 2001: stays 7f: best effort on soft going: blinkered last 2 starts. *J. M. P. Eustace* **43 d**

JETTA (IRE) 2 b.g. (Mar 28) Tagula (IRE) 116 – Freedom's Flame (IRE) 48 (Caerleon (USA) 132) [2001 5m⁴ 5m 5m⁶ Sep 30] IR 8,000F: good-topped gelding: second foal: dam ran twice in Ireland (third at 12.5f at 6 yrs): modest maiden: should have stayed at least 6f: dead. *A. Berry* **50**

JEVINGTON GREY 2 gr.c. (Jan 16) Bal Harbour 113 – Bercheba (Bellypha 130) [2001 7m Jun 24] 1,500Y: closely related to 2 winners, including 1½m winner Shirl (by Shirley Heights), and half-brother to a winner abroad by Midyan: dam lightly raced in France: tailed off in maiden at Lingfield. *R. M. Flower* —

JEWEL OF INDIA 2 ch.c. (Feb 25) Bijou d'Inde 127 – Low Hill (Rousillon (USA) 133) [2001 5.7f³ 7g⁴ Aug 17] IR 17,000F, 21,000Y: half-brother to several winners, including 3-y-o Hilton Head and 6-y-o Aix En Provence: dam Italian 2-y-o 5f winner: fair form in frame in maidens at Bath and Newcastle, well-backed favourite when fourth to Miss Opulence in latter: will probably stay 1m. *Sir Mark Prescott* **73**

JEZADIL (IRE) 3 b.f. Mujadil (USA) 119 – Tender Time (Tender King 123) [2001 54+, a66: f9.4g⁶ f12g⁵ f9.4g³ f11g 10.2d⁴ 11.6g 16m⁵ 10m⁶ 11.9f* 11.5m² 11.5m⁴ 11.5m 11.9m 16.4g⁶ f12g* 10f 10s² f12g f12g⁶ p13g f11g Dec 3] sparely-made filly: modest handicapper: won at Brighton in June and Wolverhampton (selling event, left P. McEntee 7,000 gns) in September: stays 1½m: acts on firm going, soft and fibresand: blinkered (well below form) once: none too consistent. *Mrs L. Stubbs* **52 a63**

JEZEBEL 4 b.f. Owington 123 – Just Ice 90 (Polar Falcon (USA) 126) [2001 104: 5g 6f 6g³ Aug 4] well-made, attractive filly: useful performer at 3 yrs: well held in 2001: stays 6f: probably acts on any going: sold 105,000 gns in December. *C. F. Wall* **94 ?**

JIBEREEN 9 b.g. Lugana Beach 116 – Fashion Lover 70 (Shiny Tenth 120) [2001 54, a75d: f8g³ Jan 1] big, strong gelding: modest performer: third in seller only 9-y-o outing: stays 1½m: acts on soft going, good to firm and fibresand: tried blinkered. *J. Pearce* **— a49**

JIM AND TONIC (FR) 7 ch.g. Double Bed (FR) 121 – Jimka (FR) (Jim French (USA)) [2001 124: 8.9g* 10m² 10f² 10d* 8s² 10m⁵ Dec 16] **124**

The race of the night on a very impressive Dubai World Cup programme at Nad Al Sheba in March was the Dubai Duty Free on turf, which produced a cracking climax involving Jim And Tonic from France, Fairy King Prawn from Hong Kong and Sunline from New Zealand. The last two had fought out a photo finish to the Hong Kong Mile at Sha Tin the previous December, on the same day that Jim And Tonic had finished a good third to Fantastic Light in the Hong Kong Cup. Far East form was borne out in a truly international race for the Dubai Duty Free, which also attracted runners from the United States, Japan, Britain, Germany, Italy and Saudi Arabia, as well as from the host country, the United Arab Emirates. Front-running Sunline was not allowed to have matters all her own way, harried by Slickly until managing to shake him off after the home turn, and she deserves plenty of credit for keeping on so well in the home straight. The patiently-ridden Jim And Tonic, suited by the strong pace, quickened to take over from Sunline inside the final furlong, only to be challenged by Fairy King Prawn, coming from even further back. Fairy King Prawn led briefly but Jim And Tonic would not be denied and rallied in the gamest fashion to win by a neck and half a length from Fairy King Prawn and Sunline in a pulsating finish: British-trained Golden Silca and Arkadian Hero came fourth and fifth, with Slickly sixth in a field of fifteen, the form of the principals suggesting they would not have been far away in the World Cup itself, assuming they could have repeated their form on the dirt surface.

The Dubai Duty Free, worth £836,571 to the winner, was not the first mammoth prize won by Jim And Tonic, who has become a regular on the international circuit. He earned £465,863 when winning the Hong Kong Cup in 1999. Sha Tin, in fact, has been a happy hunting ground for Jim And Tonic, who has also won two other big events there, the Queen Elizabeth II Cup, worth £249,437 to the winner, in 1999 and the Hong Kong International Bowl, worth £292,248, in 1998. In seven

Dubai Duty Free, Nad Al Sheba—a truly international race with French-trained Jim And Tonic (centre) gaining his fourth victory outside Europe; he beats Hong Kong's Fairy King Prawn, the New Zealand mare Sunline (rail) and Golden Silca from Britain

outings at Sha Tin, Jim And Tonic has finished out of the first three only once, when a respectable fifth in the latest Hong Kong Cup in December to Agnes Digital. Jim And Tonic also contested his third Queen Elizabeth II Cup in April, finishing runner-up for the second successive year, beaten a length and three quarters by German-trained Silvano. The very valuable Singapore Airlines International Cup at Kranji, moved from March to the middle of May in the latest season, looks like providing an attractive stopping-off point for globe-trotters who have been to Dubai in March and, perhaps, Hong Kong in April. It took place three weeks after the Queen Elizabeth II Cup in the latest season and both Silvano, third earlier in the Dubai Sheema Classic, and Jim And Tonic were in the line-up. Jim And Tonic reversed Hong Kong form with Silvano, who managed only fifth, but he couldn't improve on his second in the inaugural running in 2000, going down by three quarters of a length to British-trained Endless Hall, who had finished a place behind Silvano in the Sheema Classic on his most recent outing. Jim And Tonic was off the course for four months after the International Cup but returned as good as ever to win La Coupe de Maisons-Laffitte, conceding weight all round, in the middle of September. He should almost certainly have won his next race too, the Prix du Rond-Point at Longchamp on Arc weekend when his rider set him too much to do in the home straight, the strong-finishing Jim And Tonic still a length adrift of the enterprisingly-ridden China Visit at the post.

		Be My Guest	Northern Dancer
	Double Bed (FR)	(ch 1974)	What A Treat
	(b 1983)	Claire's Slipper	Welsh Saint
Jim And Tonic (FR)		(b 1974)	Semislipper
(ch.g. 1994)		Jim French	Graustark
	Jimka (FR)	(br 1968)	Dinner Partner
	(b 1978)	Kastueuse	Kashmir II
		(b or br 1970)	Vertueuse

The medium-sized, good-topped Jim And Tonic is by some way the most celebrated winner sired by the very smart middle-distance performer Double Bed, who was trained by Jim And Tonic's trainer. Jim And Tonic's dam Jinka also raced for the Doumen stable, winning seven races at up to ten and a half furlongs in a long career. Her racing programme included over seventy races on the Flat and a few more over hurdles, but it did not affect her stud potential. She has bred nine winners so far on the Flat or over jumps, or—in the notable case of Jim And Tonic's even more prolific older brother Jimble—both. The tremendously tough, game and consistent Jim And Tonic is effective at a mile to a mile and a quarter and acts on any going. He has a fine turn of foot and is usually held up. Jim And Tonic, who has been bandaged in front, was said by his trainer after the latest Hong Kong Cup to have 'had a niggling problem with one fetlock'. Provided the injury clears up, Jim And Tonic is set to begin his 2002 campaign with another tilt at the Dubai Duty Free. *F. Doumen, France*

JIMGAREEN (IRE) 4 b. or br.f. Lahib (USA) 129 – Sharp Circle (IRE) 83 (Sure – Blade (USA) 130) [2001 59d: 10s 8d 14.1v May 1] disappointing maiden: tried blinkered. *M. Johnston*

JIMJONPADDAL (IRE) 2 b.c. (Apr 21) Key of Luck (USA) 126 – Rich Heiress **76** (IRE) 49 (Last Tycoon 131) [2001 7g⁵ 8.5s⁴ 8g 8m² 8g⁴ 7s p7g p6g⁵ Dec 28] fourth foal: **a62** half-brother to 7f winner Gaelic Foray (by Unblest): dam maiden who stayed 1m: fair maiden on turf, modest on all-weather: in frame in nurseries at Listowel and Gowran: left D. Gillespie, Ireland, after next start: stays 1m: acts on soft going, good to firm and polytrack: blinkered 3 of last 4 starts. *J. M. Bradley*

JIMMY FLOYD (IRE) 2 b.g. (Mar 21) Dolphin Street (FR) 125 – Queen Sigi (IRE) – (Fairy King (USA)) [2001 8g 8.2d Sep 21] IR 8,000F, 11,000Y: well-made gelding: first foal: dam, ran once at 2 yrs, out of half-sister to smart performer up to 2m Harbour Dues: no form in maidens. *I. A. Balding*

JIMMY SWIFT (IRE) 6 b.g. Petardia 113 – Grade A Star (IRE) (Alzao (USA) 117) – [2001 35: 11.9f May 23] of little account nowadays. *P. R. Hedger*

JIMORANNI 2 b.f. (May 19) Rock City 120 – Cornflower Blue (Tyrnavos 129) [2001 – 6m May 29] 1,000Y: leggy filly: fifth reported foal: half-sister to fairly useful 7.5f to 8.5f winner Blooming Amazing (by Mazilier): dam, ran twice, half-sister to dam of smart 6f/ 7f performer Branston Abby: well beaten in maiden at Redcar. *J. R. Norton*

JINGLE ROSE (FR) 4 b.g. Missolonghi (USA) – Quelle Etoile V (FR) (Mitsoupam – (FR)) [2001 11.7f⁴ 12.5s⁵ Oct 27] brother to French 10.5f winner Christina III: dam unraced: contested non-thoroughbred events in France in 2000 for T. Chenu, winning 1¼m maiden: fourth in seller on return to Flat in 2001: sold 5,000 gns from P. Hobbs after reappearance. *T. Trapenard, France*

JINGLING GEORGIE 2 b.f. (Feb 15) Ali-Royal (IRE) 127 – Golden Daring (IRE) **51** (Night Shift (USA)) [2001 f5g f7g 7.1d⁵ 8d f8.5g Nov 3] 9,200Y: first foal: dam, Italian 2-y-o 6f winner, out of sister to very smart sprinter Ballad Rock: modest maiden: easily best effort on third start: will need to settle to stay 1m. *B. Palling*

J M W TURNER 2 b.c. (Apr 29) Forzando 122 – Noor El Houdah (IRE) 61 (Fayruz **80** 116) [2001 5m⁶ 6g⁵ 6g³ 6g* 6m 6g 7g⁴ 6.1d⁵ 6m* 6g p7g⁶ p6g* f6g* Dec 1] 16,000Y, **a95** 40,000 2-y-o: sturdy colt: third foal: dam, 5f to 7f winner (including at 2 yrs), half-sister to useful 1998 2-y-o 6f/7f winner Smittenby: useful on all-weather, fairly useful on turf: won minor event in June and nursery in September, both at Hamilton, and nurseries (easily) at Lingfield in November and Wolverhampton in December: best form at 6f: acts on fibresand, polytrack and good to firm going: blinkered/visored 5 of last 6 starts: races freely, and best waited with. *N. P. Littmoden*

JOCKO GLASSES 4 ch.g. Inchinor 119 – Corinthia (USA) (Empery (USA) 128) – [2001 92p: 12g May 6] lengthy gelding: fairly useful winner at 3 yrs: well held only Flat outing in 2001: fair hurdler. *N. J. Henderson*

JODEEKA 4 ch.f. Fraam 114 – Gold And Blue (IRE) (Bluebird (USA) 125) [2001 77: **97** 6m 5m* 6d 5m* 5m 5.5d² 5g² 6m 5.6m Sep 12] strong, close-coupled filly: made into useful handicapper: won at Ripon in June and Hamilton in July: very good efforts when runner-up at Warwick and Haydock, but mostly well held otherwise (reportedly lame final outing): likely to prove best around 5f: yet to race on extremes of going. *J. A. Glover*

JOEL ASH 6 b.g. Crofthall 110 – Lady Carol 42 (Lord Gayle (USA) 124) [2001 6m – 6m 5m f5g Jun 20] of little account nowadays. *D. Shaw*

JOELY GREEN 4 b.g. Binary Star (USA) – Comedy Lady 46 (Comedy Star (USA) **62** 121) [2001 65: f12g⁵ f11g f9.4g³ f11g⁴ 11.9m⁵ 11.5m³ 12m⁴ 11.9f⁶ f12s⁵ Dec 27] tall, **a59** workmanlike gelding: modest handicapper: barely stays 1½m: acts on fibresand and equitrack, raced only on ground firmer than good on turf: blinkered/visored: sometimes looks less than easy ride. *N. P. Littmoden*

JOE TAYLOR (CAN) 3 b.g. Known Fact (USA) 135 – Shore Mist (USA) (Coastal (USA)) [2001 –: 7m 7.5m⁴ 8.1g 7d 8.1d 8.5f 10m 9.9m 10.9m Aug 27] smallish gelding: left D. Arbuthnot after reappearance: modest form only on next outing. *C. N. Kellett* **53 d**

JOEY-HO 4 b.g. Kasakov – Little Wilma 41 (Zalazl (USA) 120) [2001 e8s e7g 6g 5.1m May 21] first foal: dam second in 8.5f seller: well held in maidens/minor event. *J. J. Bridger* **–**

JOEY THE JOLLY 5 b.g. Belfort (FR) 89 – Divine Penny 65 (Divine Gift 127) [2001 5d Sep 25] probably of little account. *John A. Harris* **–**

JOEY THE SCHNOZE 3 ch.g. Zilzal (USA) 137 – Linda's Design (Persian Bold 123) [2001 5m 7m Sep 22] 7,000F, 10,000Y: sixth reported foal: half-brother to fairly useful 6f (at 2 yrs) to 1¼m winner Busy Banana (by Insan), later winner in USA, and to a winner in Sweden: dam maiden half-sister to very smart pair Prominent and Dominion: last in maidens at Beverley and Catterick (tongue tied). *S. J. Magnier* **–**

JOEY TRIBBIANI (IRE) 4 b.g. Foxhound (USA) 103 – Mardi Gras Belle (USA) 65§ (Masked Dancer (USA)) [2001 –: f8g e8g⁵ Jan 17] tall gelding: poor maiden in 2001. *C. N. Allen* **41**

JOHANNESBURG (USA) 2 b.c. (Feb 23) Hennessy (USA) 122 – Myth (USA) (Ogygian (USA)) [2001 6m* 5m* 6.3g* 6d* 6g* 6g* a8.5f* Oct 27] **127**
Predictability doesn't necessarily equate with monotony, although those trainers—a minority—who have been prepared to take on the all-conquering teams of juveniles trained by Aidan O'Brien over the last three years may care to disagree. After providing hard acts to follow in 1999, with sixty-five races won, including fourteen pattern races and five Group 1s, and again in 2000, with fifty races won, nine pattern races and four Group 1s, the trainer compiled a record in the latest season that looks unassailable. Fifty-five two-year-olds raced for the O'Brien stable, landing sixty-two races, including nine of the ten European Group 1 events open to colts, the Group 1 Moyglare Stud Stakes for fillies, the Grade 1 Breeders' Cup Juvenile, three Group 2s and six Group 3s. Without the stable's runners the best colts' races for this age group would have been pretty sorry affairs, since O'Brien saddled twenty-six of the seventy-nine contestants in the Group 1s, gaining clean sweeps of the places in the Dewhurst Stakes and Criterium de Saint-Cloud and a one, two in the Racing Post Trophy. The O'Brien fillies didn't make

Norfolk Stakes, Royal Ascot—Johannesburg comes on the outside to beat Waterside (white blaze), Lord Merlin (centre) and Kulachi (rail)

Independent Waterford Wedgwood Phoenix Stakes, Leopardstown—a fourth consecutive success in the race for Aidan O'Brien as Johannesburg produces a tremendous turn of foot; Miss Beabea (spots on cap) is second and Agnetha (on Miss Beabea's right) third

anything like such a mark, but besides Quarter Moon they gained four places in Group I company, which was a failure only by comparison with the colts. Given the quality of the latest yearling intake at Ballydoyle, 2002 looks a fair bet to offer more of the same. This may create a problem, since systematic dominance has the potential to become self-perpetuating if other trainers increasingly hold up their hands and take the easy route by not bothering to take on O'Brien's runners. This may well benefit Coolmore, and O'Brien for that matter, but it surely will not benefit racing as a whole. That's in the future, though, and a possibility, not a certainty. What's there in black and white is that the star of the O'Brien two-year-old show was undoubtedly Johannesburg, who went through the season unbeaten in seven races including the Independent Waterford Wedgwood Phoenix Stakes, the Prix Morny Casinos Barriere, the Middle Park Stakes and the Bessemer Trust Breeders' Cup Juvenile, success in which confirmed him the outstanding colt of his age in the northern hemisphere. Not bad for a 200,000-dollar yearling, about whom owner Michael Tabor said this to the *Racing Post* at Royal Ascot: 'This is obviously a decent horse and he is up there, but is not the best (in the yard). There is a nice Group race in him, one would have thought, but I haven't discussed it with Aidan yet.'

It would have been fascinating to have been a fly on the wall at those discussions, because within two months of Tabor's remarks Johannesburg was favourite for the Two Thousand Guineas. The colt's journey to the top was a smooth one, starting with a facile victory at 3/1-on in a six-furlong maiden at Fairyhouse at the end of May followed by the race at Royal Ascot his owner was alluding to, the Norfolk Stakes, which saw Johannesburg stepping down in trip and running green in what amounted to his first competitive race before beating Waterside by a length and a quarter. Another Group 3 came Johannesburg's way in the Anglesey Stakes at the Curragh in July, when he gave weight all round and readily beat his stable-companion Wiseman's Ferry by four lengths. It was now time for his line to be cast in deeper waters. Not that the Phoenix Stakes at Leopardstown in August usually has a field worthy of its Group 1 status—seventeen of the twenty-three winners since the race was elevated from Group 2 in 1979 have failed to register another Group 1 success and only Turtle Island has landed one after the age of two. Not an inspiring record, and the opposition to Johannesburg, who went off the 5/2-on favourite, was pretty flimsy. He crushed them, quickly putting daylight between himself and the rest once asked to accelerate entering the final furlong and scoring impressively by five lengths from Miss Beabea, winner of an auction event on the same course, and Agnetha, who had scored in listed company. The best the ten beaten horses could manage during the rest of the year was one listed victory, which says all that needs to be said about them as Group 1 contenders. Still, Johannesburg could do no more than beat them easily, in the process gaining his trainer a fourth successive win in the race. O'Brien has some way to go before matching Paddy Prendergast's record of seven wins in a row but the way things are going, few would bet against his increasing his tally. O'Brien had also won two of the three previous runnings of the Prix Morny at Deauville, for which Johannesburg lined up against a much better field. Meshaheer had won the July Stakes, Whitbarrow the Molecomb Stakes, Zipping the Prix Robert Papin, Firebreak the Prix de Cabourg and Berk The Jerk a listed event. None of them could cope with Johannesburg, who quickened well to lead a furlong out and beat Zipping by a length and a half despite losing his near-fore shoe and pulling off a small part of his hoof. Previously 6/1 favourite for the Guineas, Johannesburg was cut to 3/1 with one firm on the strength of this display. The injury did not impede his training programme and he had little difficulty adding the Middle Park Stakes at Newmarket in October to his tally, despite being rather on edge beforehand—as usual, he was attended by two handlers. He started at 100/30-on with only Zipping and the very promising Newbury maiden-race winner Farqad, trained by David Loder, at shorter than 20/1 among his six opponents. Johannesburg was soon cruising behind the strong gallop set by his pacemaker Line Rider and, showing his customary turn of foot from the Dip, accounted for Zipping again, this time by three lengths, with a similar margin back to Doc Holiday in third place. A fast timefigure provided confirmation of Johannesburg's ability and of his speed over six furlongs under sharpish conditions.

By this stage Johannesburg had been joined at the head of the market for the Guineas by both Dubai Destination and Hawk Wing. Hawk Wing's form was some way inferior but he was seen as a better bet to be suited by a mile. There was a choice for Johannesburg's final race: the Dewhurst Stakes or the Breeders' Cup Juvenile. Besides proving that he stayed beyond six furlongs, winning the Dewhurst would do little for his reputation or tell us anything new about him. A tilt at the Breeders' Cup Juvenile would prove his stamina and have the added advantage, when it came to advertising him as a stallion, of confirming him the best of his age in the northern hemisphere—provided he were to win it. Advertising potential often

Prix Morny Casinos Barriere, Deauville—Johannesburg gives Aidan O'Brien
and Michael Kinane their third success in the race in the last four years;
he quickens readily to account for Zipping, Meshaheer (rail) and Firebreak (No.5)

Middle Park Stakes, Newmarket—the same 1,2 as Johannesburg extends his advantage over Zipping; Doc Holiday (left) and Farqad battle it out for third

seems a consideration with the top Ballydoyle horses bound for Coolmore and, as there were more than adequate deputies for the Dewhurst in Rock of Gibraltar and Landseer, Johannesburg was sent to Belmont Park. He was not in the Ballydoyle group that visited Southwell for a spin on the fibresand and, as with Giant's Causeway the previous year, O'Brien did not work him on the track in America either, leaving his first experience of dirt until the day. Facing eleven opponents including virtually all the best American juveniles, four of whom were unbeaten, Johannesburg started third favourite at a shade over 7/1. Odds-on Officer had gained five straight victories, the latest in the Grade 1 Champagne Stakes over the course by nearly four lengths in a canter from another Breeders' Cup contender, Grade 2 winner Jump Start. Grade 1 Hopeful Stakes winner Came Home had won three from three while Grade 2 scorers Publication and Siphonic had each won both their starts. Johannesburg did not break so fast as Officer, who was soon close behind pacesetter Came Home at a sound though not breakneck gallop. Mick Kinane pretty quickly had Johannesburg taking closer order and the colt showed his turn of foot to pass half the field in the twinkling of an eye and move into fifth on the rail. Entering the home straight Johannesburg, evidently at home on the surface and going best of all, was switched for a run with a furlong to go and quickened really well without coming under undue pressure to beat Repent by a length and a quarter with Siphonic the same distance away third and Officer only fifth.

Officer suffered two more defeats, the first of which came only a week after the Breeders' Cup, but Siphonic won the Grade 1 Hollywood Futurity (with Officer third) in December and both Repent and Breeders' Cup Juvenile eighth Saarland won Grade 2s, so even if the opposition wasn't outstanding the form was pretty solid. Johannesburg's margin of victory didn't come close to matching Arazi's five lengths at Churchill Downs a decade earlier, but Johannesburg was primarily ridden to win the race, not to score by as far as possible, and the result was still a tremendous feather in the cap for both the winner and his trainer. It impressed the bookmakers too, who put Johannesburg back as favourite for the Two Thousand Guineas at 2/1 with a run, short enough odds even allowing for his superiority over the other European two-year-olds. British firms also made him favourite for the Kentucky Derby, one at the laughable odds of 3/1.

Johannesburg's connections, especially Michael Tabor, who has owned a Kentucky Derby winner before in Thunder Gulch, understandably expressed an interest in the American classic, but connections said no decision would be taken until the spring. The prospect of returning to America must be tempting, but delaying a decision until then leaves it very late for what the Americans would consider to be a full preparation. For some time there have been arguments in Europe about the Derby and Prix du Jockey Club coming too soon for three-year-olds, but there is simply no comparison as regards the demands made on American three-year-olds going for the Triple Crown, involving three very tough races, of which the Kentucky Derby is the first leg, in the space of just five weeks.

Nowadays it is an exception to see any of the principals in the Kentucky Derby enjoying an uninterrupted campaign subsequently. In the last six years, more than half the twenty-four colts in the first four places at Churchill Downs were not raced after August due to leg injury or, in one instance, 'depression'. Of the winners, Grindstone broke down, Silver Charm was off the track for six months after the Belmont Stakes, Real Quiet wasn't seen out after the Belmont, Charismatic fractured his near-fore in the Belmont, Fusaichi Pegasus injured a foot in the Preakness Stakes but came back, and Monarchos fractured a knee in July. In the same period, four others who had won Grade 1 races in the run-up to the Kentucky Derby had to be retired before the Belmont due to injury and Point Given, winner of the latest Preakness and Belmont Stakes, injured his near-fore suspensory in August and was packed off to stud. Criticism of some of the foreign raiders for the Kentucky Derby, in particular China Visit's challenge in 2000, has centred around the lack of race-hardened experience gained in the months beforehand. However, it can hardly be said that Johannesburg is short of experience and, considering the aforementioned injuries sustained by others in the pursuit of classic glory, there would seem to be a good case for flying in the face of convention if the Kentucky Derby is eventually chosen as an objective. Other things such as Johannesburg's ability to see out the mile and a quarter, and his physical development over the winter are likely to be more important factors come May 4th. Arazi enjoyed a similarly highly successful campaign as a two-year-old in 1991, winning the last seven of his eight races, including the Prix Morny, Prix de la Salamandre and Grand Criterium, as well as the Breeders' Cup Juvenile, but he wasn't the same force the following year. Plenty of good two-year-olds fail to make the requisite progress to maintain their dominance even early on into their three-year-old careers.

The decision for Johannesburg's connections will be a tough one. Let's consider his stamina, since he is not certain to get a mile and a quarter. His sire Hennessy raced only at two, when successful in four of his nine starts, including the Hopeful Stakes over seven furlongs, and beaten a neck by Unbridled's Song in the Breeders' Cup Juvenile. Hennessy has retired after injuring his near-fore fetlock and has covered massive books of mares at Ashford Stud, Coolmore's American arm, with over a hundred foals in each of his first two crops. He covered in Japan in the latest season but will be back at Ashford in 2002 at a fee of 45,000 dollars, increased from the 20,000 dollars announced for him after the Breeders' Cup. Johannesburg comes from Hennessy's second crop and is his best winner, though

Bessemer Trust Breeders' Cup Juvenile, Belmont—Johannesburg takes well to the dirt and maintains his unbeaten record, quickening really well to beat Repent (left) and Siphonic (right); odds-on favourite Officer (blinkered, behind Siphonic) is only fifth

he is also responsible for Grade 2 scorers Keats and Distilled. Hennessy is unlikely to be a prime influence for stamina and Johannesburg's dam, sprint winner Myth, comes from a fast and precocious family. She is a half-sister to another Ashford stallion, Tale of The Cat (by Hennessy's sire Storm Cat), who was smart at up to nine furlongs but best at seven, and to Minardi, winner for O'Brien of the Phoenix Stakes and Middle Park Stakes in 2000 but not notably successful at three. The grandam Yarn was a useful sprinter.

Johannesburg is the first live foal out of Myth, who was sold for 350,000 dollars at the Keeneland November Sale in 1997 and for 250,000 dollars at the same venue in 1999; her new owners, Barronstown Stud, exercised a breeding right to Storm Cat and the resultant filly foal must be worth a small fortune. Given his family, it was no surprise that the Coolmore team was interested in Johannesburg when he appeared at the Keeneland September Sale as a yearling, having fetched 240,000 dollars as a foal. That they were able to buy him for 200,000 dollars must go down as one of the biggest bargains they've obtained during a mammoth spending spree over the last few years. Since 1997 Coolmore and its associates have purchased more than fifty foals, yearlings and two-year-olds each costing at least a million dollars, or its equivalent in Europe. The forty-one of racing age have yielded six Group/Grade 1 winners, none of whom could fairly be called outstanding—Saffron Walden (Irish Two Thousand Guineas), High Yield (Hopeful Stakes, Fountain of Youth Stakes and Blue Grass Stakes), Beckett (National Stakes), Minardi, Yonaguska (Hopeful Stakes) and King Charlemagne (Prix Maurice de Gheest). Notable failures have included Norway, who cost three million dollars and

Mr M. Tabor & Mrs John Magnier's "Johannesburg"

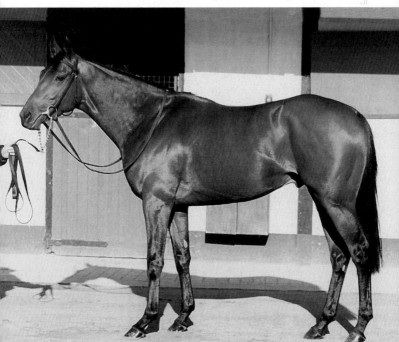

didn't win in six starts before retiring to stud, and Gala Performance, who cost two million dollars, and never even reached the racetrack. The latest collection of two-year-olds was headed by Tasmanian Tiger, a 6.8 million-dollar yearling who finished a modest third in a maiden race at the Curragh on his debut; Diaghilev, a 3.4 million guineas buy who has yet to win in three starts; Shah Jehan, a 4.4 million-dollar yearling who looks fully exposed as no better than useful; and Sophisticat, a 3.4 million-dollar filly who has been placed in four pattern events, including a second in the Cheveley Park Stakes, but has yet to get her head in front in one. On the brighter side, Sorcerous (two million guineas) and Century City (two million punts) looked distinctly promising in winning a maiden at Leopardstown and the Houghton Stakes at Newmarket respectively. Moreover, proving that it pays to spread the net wide, there were several good and relatively cheap buys besides Johannesburg, notably Tendulkar at 200,000 dollars, High Chaparral at 270,000 guineas and Mutinyonthebounty at 100,000 guineas as a foal.

		Storm Cat	Storm Bird
Johannesburg (USA) (b.c. Feb 23, 1999)	Hennessy (USA) (ch 1993)	(b or br 1983)	Terlingua
		Island Kitty	Hawaii
		(ch 1976)	T C Kitten
	Myth (USA) (b 1993)	Ogygian	Damascus
		(b 1983)	Gonfalon
		Yarn	Mr Prospector
		(b or br 1987)	Narrate

Johannesburg is a well-made colt, who has yet to race on extremes of going and has worn a crossed noseband. Given his breeding and style of racing, our money would be on his turning out to be best at up to a mile, and a colt who could be a formidable opponent in the Guineas. Even if Johannesburg fails there, or in the Kentucky Derby, there will still be the option of trying to turn him into the next champion sprinter for the O'Brien stable—with his natural speed he would be a much more obvious candidate for such honours than were Stravinsky or Mozart at the same stage. Whatever else he does, Johannesburg has already guaranteed himself a place at stud and has a record of which to be proud, which also applies to his connections over the way he was campaigned. *A. P. O'Brien, Ireland*

JOHANNIAN   3 b.c. Hernando (FR) 127 – Photo Call 73 (Chief Singer 131) [2001   **108**
10.3f³ 10.5m* 16.2m 12g⁵ 11.9s³ 12d⁵ 10d⁵ 12v Oct 27] quite good-topped colt: unimpressive mover: fourth foal: dam, 9f (at 2 yrs) and 11f winner, granddaughter of 1000 Guineas second Photo Flash: useful performer: won maiden at Haydock in May: easily best efforts when 2¼ lengths third of 5 to Yavana's Pace in minor event at Haydock fifth outing and when 2½ lengths fifth to Golden Wells in handicap at Ascot (able to dictate pace) penultimate start: stays 1½m: best efforts on good to soft/soft going: has been bandaged off-hind. *M. A. Jarvis*

JOHAYRO   8 ch.g. Clantime 101 – Arroganza 62 (Crofthall 110) [2001 67: 5d 5m 6d   **60**
5d⁶ 7.1m⁶ 7m⁶ 5m 6m 5m 6m* 5m⁴ 6g 6m 5f³ 5d 6m 5m² 6g 5m Sep 20] close-coupled gelding: has a quick action: modest handicapper nowadays: second race in 24 hrs when winning amateur event at Hamilton in June: effective at 5f to sharp 7f: acts on firm and good to soft going, below form on soft/heavy: occasionally blinkered/visored: usually races up with pace. *J. S. Goldie*

JOHN FERNELEY   6 b.g. Polar Falcon (USA) 126 – I'll Try 71 (Try My Best (USA)   **95**
130) [2001 110: 6v 7f 8f Sep 5] tall, sparely-made gelding: has a long stride: smart performer in 2000: below form in 2001 (left Mrs J. Ramsden 35,000 gns after second start): seems best at 7f/1m: acts on heavy going, good to firm and fibresand: tried blinkered: races freely, and best waited with. *N. D. Drysdale, USA*

JOHN FOLEY (IRE)   3 b.g. Petardia 113 – Fast Bay (Bay Express 132) [2001 54§:   **49 §**
8.3g³ 8m 7.1d f8.5g⁵ f12g f16.2g⁶ Dec 8] big gelding: poor maiden: left W. M. Brisbourne after third start: seems to stay 2m: acts on firm going, fibresand and equitrack: tried blinkered/visored: wayward and probably ungenuine. *J. W. Unett*

JOHN HUNTER (IRE)   4 b.g. Unfuwain (USA) 131 – Aigue 96 (High Top 131)   **94**
[2001 7s² 10g⁶ 10m* 8.9m 11.9m 12g 10f 10d 10.4d Oct 12] 180,000Y, 6,000 3-y-o: strong, rangy gelding: fifth foal: brother to useful 7f (at 2 yrs) and 1¼m winner Mezzo-giorno (also third in Oaks) and half-brother to fairly useful winner around 1¼m Rainbow Top (by Rainbow Quest): dam, 1m winner, sister to smart middle-distance performer

Torchon: fairly useful performer: won maiden at Redcar in May: creditable efforts in handicaps next 2 starts only: will probably prove better over 1¼m than 1½m: acts on good to firm ground: free-going sort: tongue tied final start: sold 20,000 gns, joined M. Pipe and gelded. *B. W. Hills*

JOHNNY NO NAME (IRE)   4 b.g. Fairy King (USA) – Zariysha (IRE) (Darshaan 133) [2001 f9.4g f6g 6s f5g f7g May 14] IR 120,000Y, 10,500 2-y-o: sturdy gelding: second foal: dam unraced sister to Greenham winner/King Edward VII second Zayyani: no form, including in sellers: tried in visor/blinkers. *K. R. Burke*   –

JOHNNY OSCAR   4 b.g. Belmez (USA) 131 – Short Rations (Lorenzaccio 130) [2001 74: 12d 14m² 14s⁵ 16.2f⁶ 16m³ 14.8m* 14.8m⁶ Aug 24] tall, leggy, unfurnished gelding: fairly useful form: won handicap at Newmarket in July: ran well most other starts, notably in handicap at Newmarket (in poor position 2f out but finished strongly) final outing: will prove well suited by return to 2m+: acts on firm and soft going: from late-maturing family, and looks capable of better still if all is well. *J. R. Fanshawe*   **91 p**

JOHNNY REB   3 b.g. Danehill (USA) 126 – Dixie Eyes Blazing (USA) 56 (Gone West (USA)) [2001 73: 8m 7m⁶ 8m* 8m 8g⁶ 8f³ 7m 8m f7g f8.5g Dec 8] strong gelding: fair handicapper: made all in apprentice race at Salisbury in June: sold from R. Hannon 12,500 gns after eighth start, gelded after final one: will prove best up to 1m: acts on firm going, probably on fibresand: tongue tied last 3 starts in 2000: best when able to dominate. *J. G. Given*   **69 d**

JOHNNY STACCATO   7 b.g. Statoblest 120 – Frasquita (Song 132) [2001 39§, a–§: 5.3s 11.9f⁴ 14.1g⁵ 10.1g 10g² 8g* 10m⁵ 8g⁴ 10m f9.4s Sep 6] leggy gelding: modest handicapper: won ladies event at Newmarket in July: effective at 1m/1¼m: probably acts on any going: tried visored before 2001: unreliable. *C. Drew*   **53 §**
a– §

JOHN O'GROATS (IRE)   3 b.g. Distinctly North (USA) 115 – Bannons Dream (IRE) (Thatching 131) [2001 –: 5.1s* 6s* 6m² 6d 5m 6m 5d 5s Oct 22] tall, close-coupled, good-topped gelding: fairly useful performer: won maiden at Nottingham in April and handicap at Haydock in May: better at 6f than 5f: acts on soft and good to firm going: has worn crossed noseband. *M. Dods*   **81**

JOHNSON'S POINT   3 ch.f. Sabrehill (USA) 120 – Watership (USA) (Foolish Pleasure (USA)) [2001 81: 10.3s 9v 8v 10s 9.9m 12m 12.3m⁶ 9.9f* 12g⁶ 10.1m² 12m³ 12g² 9.9m⁴ 13.9d Oct 13] fair handicapper nowadays: won at Beverley in July: may prove best at 1¼m/1½m: acts on firm and good to soft going: blinkered 3 starts before final one. *M. W. Easterby*   **65**

JOHN STEED (IRE)   4 b.g. Thatching 131 – Trinity Hall 67 (Hallgate 127) [2001 48: 11.9g⁴ 11.7m Aug 24] smallish gelding: maiden: little form in 2001. *C. Weedon*   –

JOHNSTON'S DIAMOND (IRE)   3 b.g. Tagula (IRE) 116 – Toshair Flyer 88 (Ballad Rock 122) [2001 51: f7g⁵ 5f 6m² Jul 4] sparely-made gelding: modest maiden, lightly raced: stays 7f: acts on firm ground and fibresand. *E. J. Alston*   **63**

JOIN THE PARADE   5 b.m. Elmaamul (USA) 125 – Summer Pageant 81 (Chief's Crown (USA)) [2001 65d: 11.5m 10.1g 10.1g 10m 14.1d 12g Oct 4] leggy, plain mare: poor handicapper nowadays: best form at 1¼m: acts on firm going, possibly not on softer than good. *P. Howling*   **46**

JOINT INSTRUCTION (IRE)   3 b.g. Forzando 122 – Edge of Darkness 62 (Vaigly Great 127) [2001 73: f6g f6g³ f6g³ f7g² 7v f7g 5v 6.1v 5g f7g f6g f6g⁶ f6g Dec 10] smallish, sturdy gelding: fair performer at best: below form after third start, including in sellers: best form around 6f: acts on any turf going and fibresand: tried visored: has raced freely/found little/flashed tail. *D. Nicholls*   **70 d**

JOKESMITH (IRE)   3 b.g. Mujadil (USA) 119 – Grinning (IRE) (Bellypha 130) [2001 8s* 9.9m² 10m⁴ 10.4g 10.5s 10g* Oct 5] 30,000F, 40,000Y: leggy, lengthy gelding: fourth live foal: half-brother to fairly useful Irish 7f/8.5f winner Smiling Brave (by Indian Ridge) and winner abroad (up to 13f) by Old Vic: dam unraced: useful performer: won maiden at Newbury in May and handicap at Newmarket in October: best effort when coming from last to beat Canada by ½ length) in October: stays 1¼m: acts on soft and good to firm ground: reportedly had breathing problem when tailed off penultimate start. *B. J. Meehan*   **102**

JOLLANDS   3 b.g. Ezzoud (IRE) 126 – Rainbow Fleet 66 (Nomination 125) [2001 64: f6g 8s* 10s² 10s 10d 10.2m 11.6g⁶ 8.3m 9.9m Jun 27] quite good-topped gelding: fair performer: won minor event at Brighton in April: disappointing after third outing: stays   **74 d**

1¼m: acts on soft and good to firm ground: visored last 2 starts (gelded after final one).
D. Marks

JOLLY SHARP (USA) 4 ch.c. Diesis 133 – Milly Ha Ha 106 (Dancing Brave (USA) **93**
140) [2001 96: 12g 14m 12m Jun 19] good-topped, attractive colt: fairly useful handicapper, lightly raced: ran poorly final start in 2001: probably stays 1¾m: yet to race on
firm going, on any other: has worn crossed noseband. *H. R. A. Cecil*

JO MELL 8 b.g. Efisio 120 – Militia Girl (Rarity 129) [2001 101: 7d 8g⁶ 7.9m 8.1d **92 d**
8.9m 7m Jul 14] strong, lengthy gelding: has a round action: smart performer at best, on
downgrade: stays 8.5f: acts on any going: often takes good hold/leads. *T. D. Easterby*

JONA HOLLEY 8 b.g. Sharpo 132 – Spurned (USA) 91 (Robellino (USA) 127) **–**
[2001 50: 10.1v Oct 24] big gelding: modest performer at best: well beaten only 8-y-o
outing: usually visored/blinkered nowadays. *A. Streeter*

JONALTON (IRE) 2 b.c. (Feb 15) Perugino (USA) 84 – Vago Pequeno (IRE) (Posen **44**
(USA)) [2001 6.1f 8g 8.2m 10d Oct 8] 5,000F, IR 5,000Y, 7,200 2-y-o: first foal: dam
unraced half-sister to smart Irish performer up to 1¼m Alianna: poor maiden. *Mrs P. Sly*

JONES'FOLLY (IRE) 2 b.g. (May 13) Anita's Prince 126 – Dame's Folly (IRE) **49**
(Kings Lake (USA) 133) [2001 7.1d⁶ 8.1g⁵ f7g 5.7d Oct 25] IR 1,000Y: third foal: dam
unraced half-sister to useful but ungenuine Irish performer up to 2m Try For Ever: poor
maiden: gelded after final start: likely to prove best up to 7f. *B. Palling*

JONESY 3 b.g. Emperor Jones (USA) 119 – Don't Jump (IRE) 71 (Entitled 126) [2001 **–**
8f 8.3m Jun 25] 4,500F, 4,000Y, 1,300 2-y-o: second foal: dam 1m winner who stayed
1¼m: tailed-off last in maidens. *J. Gallagher*

JONI WIKABE (IRE) 2 b.g. (May 5) Nicolotte 118 – Shoot To Kill 64 (Posse (USA) **–**
130) [2001 f5g 5m f6g Aug 18] 8,200 2-y-o: sixth foal: half-brother to 1997 2-y-o 5f
winner Diamond Steve (by Rambo Dancer), later winner abroad, and a 1m winner in Italy
by Most Welcome: dam maiden who stayed 1m: no sign of ability in maidens/sales race.
R. M. H. Cowell

JONJO 3 b.g. Charnwood Forest (IRE) 125 – Katy-Q (IRE) 58 (Taufan (USA) 119) **–**
[2001 8.1d 10.5d⁴ 10.9m Aug 27] good-bodied gelding: first foal: dam 2-y-o 5f winner:
well held in maidens/seller. *J. G. Given*

JONLOZ 4 ch.g. Presidium 124 – Stratford Lady 48 (Touching Wood (USA) 127) **44**
[2001 55: 12m 12m 14.1m 9.4f⁴ 12.3m 12m 12.3g⁴ᵈ 12m⁶ 11.8s Oct 16] sparely-made
gelding: poor handicapper nowadays: stays 1½m: acts on firm going and good to soft: has
been edgy/sweating: highly-strung, and a difficult ride. *A. B. Mulholland*

JONNY EBENEEZER 2 b.g. (Apr 21) Hurricane Sky (AUS) – Leap of Faith (IRE) **84**
65 (Northiam (USA)) [2001 6f 7s³ 7d 6d* p7g Nov 13] quite good-topped gelding: fourth
foal: dam 2-y-o 5f/6f winner who stayed 1¼m: fairly useful performer: won maiden at
Brighton in November, disputing lead throughout: well held in nursery final outing: stays
7f: acts on soft going. *I. A. Wood*

JOOLS 3 b.c. Cadeaux Genereux 131 – Madame Crecy (USA) (Al Nasr (FR) 126) **72**
[2001 f7g⁴ f7s* f8.5g e10g⁶ 7f 8m* 8m* 8m⁴ 8.1g⁵ 7.6m⁴ 8g Sep 28] 46,000Y: rather
leggy colt: fourth foal: brother to 4-y-o French Lieutenant and half-brother to French 1m
winner Which Hand (by Indian Ridge), later winner in USA: dam, third at 1m in France,
half-sister to Polar Falcon: fair performer: won maiden at Wolverhampton in January and
2 claimers at Newmarket (left W. Haggas after first of them) in June: stays 1m: acts on
good to firm going and fibresand: visored (not discredited in 30-runner handicap at
Ascot) final outing. *Mrs N. Macauley*

JORDAN'S RIDGE (IRE) 5 br. or b.g. Indian Ridge 123 – Sadie Jordan (USA) **58**
(Hail The Pirates (USA) 126) [2001 58: 16v³ 14d² 13d May 6] modest maiden handicapper, quite lightly raced on Flat: stays 17f: acts on any turf going: blinkered once at 3
yrs, visored last 2 starts. *P. Monteith*

JORROCKS (USA) 7 b.g. Rubiano (USA) – Perla Fina (USA) (Gallant Man) [2001 **?**
74, a83: f8g* f9.4s² f7s* f8.5g* a10f a8f* a8.5f⁴ a8.5f⁶ a8f* a8f⁵ 6.5f⁴ a7.5f³ a8.5f⁵ Nov **a108**
23] sturdy gelding: has a short, round action: useful performer: revitalised on all-weather
early in 2001, and successful in 2 handicaps at Southwell and minor event at Wolverhampton, last-named by 5 lengths from Hail The Chief: left M. Easterby: won non-graded
handicap at Bay Meadows in April and optional claimer at Del Mar in August: effective
at 6.5f to 9.4f: acts on soft going, fibresand and dirt: blinkered once at 4 yrs and on final 2
starts in 2001: has hung left: tends to carry head awkwardly. *R. B. Hess jnr, USA*

JOSEPH WILLIAM (IRE)   2 b.c. (Mar 23) College Chapel 122 – Murroe Star   –
(Glenstal (USA) 118) [2001 7.1f 7d f6g 6d Oct 30] IR 2,600Y, resold 3,000Y: lengthy
colt: sixth foal: half-brother to 1½m to 2m winner In Behind (by Entitled) and a winner up
to 9f in Italy by Foxhound: dam unraced: only a little sign of ability in maidens/nursery.
C. N. Kellett

JOVIAL LAD (IRE)   5 b.g. Soviet Lad (USA) – Vital Spirit 65 (Tachypous 128)   –
[2001 –: f8.5s Dec 26] no form: trained by G. Lyons in Ireland at 3/4 yrs: tried blinkered.
W. Jenks

JOYCE'S CHOICE   2 b.g. (Apr 23) Mind Games 121 – Madrina 70 (Waajib 121)   72
[2001 5f⁵ 5g* 6.1d³ 6d 5s⁴ 6d Nov 6] 21,000Y: leggy, unfurnished gelding: second
foal: half-brother to 3-y-o Laurel Dawn: dam, 6f winner, out of half-sister to very smart
sprinter Bolshoi: fair performer: won maiden at Thirsk in August: ran creditably last 2
starts: gelded after final one: seems to stay 6f: acts on firm and soft going. *A. Berry*

JOYFUL ILLUSION   2 br. or b.f. (Mar 19) Robellino (USA) 127 – Sharp Falcon   –
(IRE) 76 (Shaadi (USA) 126) [2001 6m 5g 7m f8g p10g f9.4g⁶ f7s Dec 18] 4,000 2-y-o:
small, good-topped filly: has a markedly round action: first living foal: dam, 1¼m/12.5f
winner, half-sister to smart performer up to 10.5f Ahohoney: little form in maidens/
sellers. *M. D. I. Usher*

JOYFULL DREAM (FR)   3 ch.f. Midyan (USA) 124 – Villa Maria Pia (FR)   43 d
(Alwasmi (USA) 115) [2001 e5g² e7g f5f 6.1v f5g f9.4g 6.1s 6s f6g f6s Dec 21] 60,000
francs Y: second foal: half-sister to French 9f and 12.8f winner Cigare (by Saumarez):
dam ran once in France: fair form at 2 yrs, winning claimer at Chantilly (final run for
R. Collet): form in Britain only on reappearance (final start for A. Spanu in France) in
January: stays 6f: acts on good to soft going and equitrack: usually blinkered/visored.
Mrs N. Macauley

JOY OF NORWAY   3 b.g. Halling (USA) 133 – Triple Joy 104 (Most Welcome 131)   68
[2001 e7g⁴ e7g⁴ f8.5g² 8m 7s 7.5d* Dec 29] 110,000Y: third foal: half-brother to smart 6f
(at 2 yrs) and 1m winner Triple Dash (by Nashwan): dam, 6f/7f winner, half-sister to
smart middle-distance performer Talented and to dam of 4-y-o Three Points: fair
performer: sold from Sir Mark Prescott 2,000 gns prior to winning amateur event at Pisa
in December: stays 8.5f: acts on fibresand, probably on equitrack: raced freely/wandered
third outing: blinkered/tongue tied (needed early reminders) fifth start. *F. Castellini, Italy*

J R STEVENSON (USA)   5 ch.g. Lyphard (USA) 132 – While It Lasts (USA) 78   99
(Foolish Pleasure (USA)) [2001 99d: 8s* 7d⁵ 8s 8.5m⁶ 8m⁶ 8g 10.4g 8g Sep 15] strong,
close-coupled gelding: has a quick action: useful handicapper: won at Brighton in
April: not discredited at Epsom fourth outing and at Royal Ascot (sixth of 30 to Surprise
Encounter in Hunt Cup) on fifth: effective at 1m/1¼m: acts on soft and good to firm
going: tried visored. *P. R. Webber*

J'UBIO   2 b.f. (Jan 15) Bijou d'Inde 127 – Eternal Triangle (USA) 76 (Barachois   43
(CAN)) [2001 7m 6d 7m p10g p7g Dec 29] 1,800F, 2,500Y: fifth living foal: half-sister to
fairly useful 1997 2-y-o 5f winner Mister Bankes, later winner abroad, and German 2000
2-y-o 7f winner Gianni (both by Risk Me): dam 2-y-o 5f/6f winner who stayed 1m: poor
maiden: stays 7f: acts on polytrack. *B. A. Pearce*

JUDGE DAVIDSON   2 b.c. (Mar 9) Royal Applause 124 – Without Warning (IRE)   90 p
(Warning 136) [2001 6g³ 6.1m² 7d* Nov 6] 22,000Y: good-bodied colt: second foal: dam
once-raced half-sister to useful performers Berillon (up to 1½m) and Opera Buff (up to
1¾m): placed in maidens prior to winning one at Catterick comfortably by 1¼ lengths
from Scurra despite hanging badly right: will stay at least 1m: should make a useful
handicapper. *J. R. Fanshawe*

JUDIAM   4 b.f. Primo Dominie 121 – Hoist (IRE) 75 (Bluebird (USA) 125) [2001 68:   59
5.2v⁴ 5s p5g⁵ f5g f5g Dec 14] tall, leggy filly: modest handicapper nowadays: best at 5f:
acts on heavy ground and all-weather. *C. A. Dwyer*

JUDICIOUS (IRE)   4 b.g. Fairy King (USA) – Kama Tashoof 72 (Mtoto 134) [2001   92
92p: 8v 7f* 8f³ 7m Jul 12] big, good-topped gelding: fairly useful performer: won minor
event at Thirsk in June: better effort in handicaps after when third at Newbury: should
prove best at 7f/1m: acts on any ground: may benefit from exaggerated waiting tactics:
sold 11,000 gns in October, joined C. Mann and gelded. *G. Wragg*

JUFISCEA   2 b.g. (Mar 2) Efisio 120 – Jucea 77 (Bluebird (USA) 125) [2001 6m² 6m   59
6m Sep 12] first foal: dam 5f and 5.7f winner: modest form at Lingfield (very slowly

away) and Brighton first 2 starts in maidens: gave impression something amiss final start: will probably stay 7f. *M. R. Channon*

JULIET TURNER (IRE)   2 b.f. (Apr 5) General Monash (USA) 107 – Solway Lass – (IRE) (Anita's Prince 126) [2001 f6g 5.2g Jun 25] IR 2,300Y: first foal: dam little sign of ability at 2 yrs: well held in sellers. *J. S. Moore*

JULIUS (IRE)   4 b.f. Persian Bold 123 – Babushka (IRE) (Dance of Life (USA))   **96** [2001 95: 9.7m² 12f⁵ 10f Jun 23] angular filly: useful performer: creditable efforts in 2001 when second in minor event at Folkestone, narrowly-beaten third in handicap at Epsom (demoted to fifth) and seventh in handicap at Ascot final outing: effective at 9.7f to 1½m: acts on firm and good to soft going: has tended to wander: usually races handily: reported in July to have split a pastern. *M. Johnston*

JUMAIREYAH   3 b.f. Fairy King (USA) – Donya 74 (Mill Reef (USA) 141) [2001   **91** 81p: 8m⁵ 10.5d² 10.5d 10.5s² 10.3g* 12s 10v Nov 8] lengthy, quite attractive filly: fairly useful handicapper: won at Doncaster in September: ran well most other starts, particularly when twice second at Haydock and when seventh at Ascot penultimate outing: barely stayed 1½m: acted on soft going: sometimes took strong hold/raced freely: visits Mark of Esteem. *L. M. Cumani*

JUMBO JADE   5 ch.m. Jumbo Hirt (USA) 90§ – Miss Mac (Smackover 107) [2001   – 9d 10.1d 9.9m 17.1m Jun 11] lengthy mare: first foal: dam of little account: well held on Flat in maidens/handicap. *E. J. Alston*

JUMBO JET   4 b.g. Emarati (USA) 74 – Mithi Al Gamar (USA) 68 (Blushing Groom   – (FR) 131) [2001 71: 7g 6d May 21] quite good-topped gelding: fair maiden at 3 yrs: no form in 2001: tried tongue tied. *B. R. Millman*

JUMBO'S FLYER   4 ch.g. Jumbo Hirt (USA) 90§ – Fragrant Princess (Germont)   – [2001 67, a52: f12g Jan 8] close-coupled, sturdy gelding: fair handicapper at 3 yrs: well beaten only 4-y-o outing. *J. L. Eyre*

JUMEIRAH DREAM (USA)   2 ch.c. (Feb 19) Diesis 133 – Golden Vale (USA)   **76** (Slew O' Gold (USA)) [2001 6f 7m² 7.1s Sep 8] $70,000Y: first foal: dam 1m/9f winner in USA and placed in minor stakes: fair maiden: best effort when second to Tholjanah at Kempton: pulled too hard final start: bred to stay at least 1m. *E. A. L. Dunlop*

JUMEIRAH SONG (USA)   2 b.c. (Mar 18) Sultry Song (USA) – Sunnytime Lady   – (USA) (Majestic Light (USA)) [2001 8.2d 10.2g Oct 1] $62,000F, $60,000Y: good-bodied colt: fifth foal: half-brother to 3 winners in USA, including 1999 2-y-o 6f minor stakes winner Heavenly Sunshine (by West By West): dam placed in USA: signs of just a little ability in maidens: sold 5,500 gns. *M. R. Channon*

JUMP (USA)   4 b.g. Trempolino (USA) 135 – Professional Dance (USA) (Nijinsky   – (CAN) 138) [2001 59d: f14g f8g 10g 11.6g Jul 23] of little account nowadays. *A. W. Carroll*

JUNGLE LION   3 ch.g. Lion Cavern (USA) 117 – Star Ridge (USA) (Storm Bird   **83** (CAN) 134) [2001 94p: 10.3m⁴ 8d Aug 19] lengthy, quite good-topped gelding: fairly useful winner of only 2-y-o outing (tongue tied): well below that form in minor events both starts at 3 yrs: should stay at least 1m: sold 1,200 gns in October, and gelded. *H. R. A. Cecil*

JUNGLE POCKET (JPN)   3 b.c. Tony Bin 134 – Dance Charmer (USA) (Nureyev   **131** (USA) 131) [2001 9f* 10f³ 12d* 10f³ 15f⁴ 12f* Nov 25] third living foal: brother to a winner in Japan: dam unraced daughter of US Grade 2 2-y-o 1m winner Skillful Joy from family of Breeders' Cup Sprint winner Precisionist: top-class performer: won 2 of his 3 starts at 2 yrs: successful at Tokyo in 2001 in Group 3 event in February, Tokyo Yushun (Japanese Derby, by 1½ lengths from Dantsu Flame) in May and 15-runner Japan Cup (led final strides to beat previous year's winner T M Opera O a neck) in November: stays at least 1½m (beaten 2½ lengths in 15f Japanese St Leger penultimate start): acts on firm and good to soft ground: may be campaigned in Europe during 2002. *S. Watanabe, Japan*

JUNIKAY (IRE)   7 b.g. Treasure Kay 114 – Junijo (Junius (USA) 124) [2001 79: 10s   **83** 10g⁴ 10m* 10.1m 10f⁵ 10g⁶ 10g³ 9d⁵ 10g 10g* 10.3g 10f 10.4d 11.7d⁶ Oct 25] work-manlike gelding: fairly useful handicapper: won at Southwell in May and Kempton in September: best form at 9f to 11.5f: acts on soft and good to firm going: tried blinkered early in career: usually held up. *R. Ingram*

JUNIOR BRIEF (IRE)   3 b.g. Case Law 113 – Sharpnkeen 74 (Keen 116) [2001 41:   – f11g⁵ f8g f7g 6m f9.4g 11.6g 11.6m Jul 16] of no account in 2001. *K. McAuliffe*

JUNIPER (USA) 3 b.c. Danzig (USA) – Montage (USA) (Alydar (USA)) [2001 100:   **105**
6g³ 6m 5m⁶ Jul 7] well-made, good sort: useful performer, lightly raced: good 2 lengths
third to Final Exam in Greenlands Stakes at the Curragh in May: not discredited when 3½
lengths sixth to Misraah in listed event at Sandown (slowly away) on final outing: well
held in Cork And Orrery Stakes at Royal Ascot in between: will stay beyond 6f: unraced
on extremes of going: slowly away final outing. *A. P. O'Brien, Ireland*

JUNKANOO 5 ch.g. Generous (IRE) 139 – Lupescu 102 (Dixieland Band (USA))   **66 p**
[2001 12v⁴ 10f 8.2v 14.1g 16s* Oct 30] strong, good-topped gelding: first foal: dam 9f/
1¼m winner in Britain/USA who stayed 1½m: fair form on Flat: improved effort to win
handicap at Nottingham in October: should stay beyond 2m: acts on soft ground: usually
slowly away: useful bumper winner and winner on hurdling debut in December: promising, and should win more handicaps on Flat. *Mrs M. Reveley*

JUNO BEACH 5 ch.m. Jupiter Island 126 – Kovalevskia 71 (Ardross 134) [2001 69:   **72**
14.1m* 14.4m 16.2f 14.8m⁵ Jul 29] fair performer, lightly raced: won handicap at
Yarmouth in May: will probably stay beyond 1¾m: acts on good to firm going. *D. Morris*

JUPITERS PRINCESS 3 b.f. Jupiter Island 126 – Capricious Lass (Corvaro (USA)   **54**
124) [2001 7d 6d 7m⁶ 9f 11.5m⁶ 12m 10m Jul 23] close-coupled filly: first reported foal:
dam ran once in Ireland: modest maiden at best: should stay 1½m: form only on going
firmer than good: reluctant stalls on debut. *C. E. Brittain*

JUST A CARAT (IRE) 2 b.f. (Mar 28) Distinctly North (USA) 115 – Justice System   **65**
(USA) 57 (Criminal Type (USA)) [2001 5.7f⁶ 5.3m* 6m⁵ 7g 6g 7s p6g* f6g⁶ Nov 21] IR
9,000Y: leggy filly: third foal: dam, Irish maiden, half-sister to 6-y-o Lear Spear: fair
performer: won maiden at Brighton in June and seller at Lingfield in November: stays 6f:
acts on good to firm going and polytrack: tongue tied fourth/fifth starts: looks no easy
ride. *R. Hannon*

JUSTAFANCY 3 b.g. Green Desert (USA) 127 – Justsayno (USA) (Dr Blum (USA))   **67**
[2001 f7g 7s⁴ 6s⁶ 6m³ 7f⁵ 10.9d Jul 21] 54,000Y: leggy, close-coupled gelding: seventh
foal: half-brother to several winners, including fairly useful 1997 2-y-o 7f winner Casino
King (by Fairy King), later winner in USA, and 12.5f winner Tintara (by Caerleon): dam
5f winner and placed in Grade 1 events in USA at 2 yrs: fair maiden: well held in
handicaps last 2 starts: likely to prove best at up to 1m (pulled hard final outing and
subsequently gelded): blinkered fourth start. *E. A. L. Dunlop*

JUSTALORD 3 b.g. King's Signet (USA) 110 – Just Lady 72 (Emarati (USA) 74)   **72 d**
[2001 68, a73: e5g* f6s e5s² e5g⁶ 5m 5.3d 5m 5m 5.1g 5.5m 5m 5m 6s Sep 24] lengthy
gelding: fair handicapper at best: won at Lingfield in January: below form last 8 starts:
best at 5f: acts on firm going, good and soft and fibresand/equitrack: has carried head
high: seems best racing from front, but can spoil chance by starting slowly: ungenuine.
T. Keddy

JUST ARTHUR 3 b.g. Aragon 118 – Spark Out (Sparkler 130) [2001 7.1f 10d 11.9g⁵   **–**
Aug 11] leggy gelding: half-brother to 3 winners, including 6-y-o Shamwari Song: dam
probably of little account: tailed off in maidens. *B. P. J. Baugh*

JUST EMERALD 2 ch.f. (Apr 15) Emarati (USA) 74 – Bichette 66 (Lidhame 109)   **65**
[2001 7d 7s³ 6v⁵ Nov 8] good-topped filly: half-sister to 4-y-o Soller Bay: dam 7f winner,
including at 2 yrs: fair form in maidens: raced freely when third at Brighton: will probably
stay 1m: raced on going softer than good. *G. L. Moore*

JUST ERN 2 ch.g. (Mar 16) Young Ern 120 – Just Run (IRE) 45 (Runnett 125) [2001   **61**
5f⁶ 6m³ 6m⁶ 8m 8m Sep 30] 17,000F, 11,000Y: compact gelding: fifth foal: half-brother
to 3 winners by Emarati, including Just Lady (5f at 2 yrs) and 6-y-o Ginner Morris: dam
ran twice: modest maiden: seemed to lose action final start: probably stays 1m: raced on
going firmer than good: has looked tricky ride. *P. C. Haslam*

JUST FOR YOU JANE (IRE) 5 b.m. Petardia 113 – Steffi 67 (Precocious 126)   **–**
[2001 42: 6m Jun 29] of little account nowadays. *T. J. Naughton*

JUST GOOD FRIENDS (IRE) 4 b.g. Shalford (IRE) 124§ – Sinfonietta (Foolish   **–**
Pleasure (USA)) [2001 –: 13s 12.1s Aug 21] sturdy gelding: little form: tried blinkered/
tongue tied. *Denys Smith*

JUSTINIA 3 b.f. Inchinor 119 – Just Julia (Natroun (FR) 128) [2001 53: 7d 11m⁵ 10.9v   **–**
12d Nov 6] leggy, unfurnished filly: modest maiden at 2 yrs: well beaten in 2001, leaving
E. O'Neill after second start: stays 7f: acts on firm going: very slowly away on reappearance: visored last 2 starts: has given trouble at stalls. *Miss S. E. Hall*

JUST JAMES   2 b.c. (Mar 30) Spectrum (IRE) 126 – Fairy Flight (IRE) 86 (Fairy King **84 p**
(USA)) [2001 7v⁶ 6s* Nov 10] 20,000F, 80,000Y: strong, compact colt: first foal: dam,
Irish 2-y-o 6f winner, sister to useful sprinter King of The East: confirmed promise and
showed fairly useful form when winning maiden at Doncaster by 1½ lengths from
Colonel Cotton, travelling strongly in touch and ridden out to assert final 1f: bred to stay
at least 1m: open to improvement. *J. Noseda*

JUST JAZZ   2 b.g. (Jan 10) Alhijaz 122 – Jersey Belle 53 (Distant Relative 128) [2001 **–**
5g 6m Aug 27] sturdy gelding: second foal: dam 6f winner: well beaten in maiden/seller.
J. Balding

JUST MAGICAL   4 b.f. Emperor Jones (USA) 119 – Magnetic Point (USA) 60 **63 p**
(Bering 136) [2001 7s* p8g Dec 22] 12,000F, 8,500Y, 800 3-y-o: fourth foal: half-sister
to a 2-y-o winner abroad by Most Welcome: dam, maiden who stayed 1¼m, half-sister to
US 2-y-o Grade 1 2-y-o 6.5f winner Great Navigator: ran in bumpers prior to winning
maiden at Wolverhampton on Flat debut (25/1, beat Best Bond by 2½ lengths): stiff
task in minor event at Lingfield later in December: stays 1m: should do better yet.
A. B. Coogan

JUST MICHAEL   2 b.c. (Apr 4) Bluegrass Prince (IRE) 110 – Plucky Pet 50 (Petong **61**
126) [2001 5m 6m⁴ 5f 6d⁵ 7.1f⁵ 7d 7d 6v 7d⁶ f6g⁶ f5s Dec 27] 4,800F, 5,800Y: small,
well-made colt: good walker: third foal: dam, poor maiden, half-sister to 3-y-o Pomfret
Lad: modest maiden: seems best at 5f/6f: acts on heavy going and good to firm, some
promise on fibresand: blinkered last 4 starts. *A. Berry*

JUST MIDAS   3 b.g. Merdon Melody 98 – Thabeh 57 (Shareef Dancer (USA) 135) **58 §**
[2001 60: 8.2v 8m 8.1g⁵ 8f 8.1m f8.5g⁶ 10.9v Oct 15] angular gelding: modest maiden
handicapper: form at 3 yrs only when fifth: may prove best around 7f: edgy sort: none too
genuine. *K. R. Burke*

JUST MISSED   3 b.f. Inchinor 119 – Lucky Round 82 (Auction Ring (USA) 123) **–**
[2001 58: 10m 9.9s Sep 25] rather leggy filly: modest maiden at 2 yrs: no form in 2001:
stayed 1¼m: acted on soft going, probably on good to firm: dead. *M. W. Easterby*

JUST MO (IRE)   2 ch.f. (Jan 23) Common Grounds 118 – Nomadic Dancer (IRE) 52 **–**
(Nabeel Dancer (USA) 120) [2001 f5g 5.1f 6s f5g Nov 17] IR 13,000Y: second foal:
maiden who stayed 6f, half-sister to useful French performer up to 9f Touching Love: no
form, including in seller. *K. R. Burke*

JUST MURPHY (IRE)   3 b.g. Namaqualand (USA) – Bui-Doi (IRE) 58 (Dance of **88**
Life (USA)) [2001 62: 6g⁵ 8m* 8m³ 10m* 10m⁶ 11f³ 10.5d⁵ 9.2s* 10.5s³ 10s⁴ Sep 27]
leggy gelding: fairly useful handicapper: progressed well at 3 yrs, winning at Thirsk in
May, Pontefract in June and Hamilton in August: good third at Haydock penultimate
start: stays 11f: acts on firm and soft going: tends to carry head awkwardly: consistent:
sold 32,000 gns, joined N. Henderson. *G. A. Swinbank*

JUST NICK   7 b.g. Nicholas (USA) 111 – Just Never Know (USA) (Riverman (USA) **92 +**
131) [2001 79: 8g 8.1m* 8m² 8m 8.1s 9g³ 9m 8s⁶ 8d* Oct 18] smallish, good-topped
gelding: fairly useful handicapper: won at Sandown in May and Newmarket (best effort
when beating Sabo Rose 1¼ lengths in 30-runner event) in October: good efforts also
when placed at Kempton and Sandown: effective at 1m/9f: acts on heavy and good to
firm going: usually held up: very slowly away seventh and final starts. *W. R. Muir*

JUST SERENADE   2 ch.f. (Apr 2) Factual (USA) 108 – Thimbalina 63 (Salmon Leap **66**
(USA) 131) [2001 6m⁵ 6g 6g⁵ 5g⁵ 5.1m³ 6s 5.2s⁶ Oct 31] fifth foal: half-sister to 1½m
and 16.5f winner Saint Albert (by Keen): dam, 1¼m/1½m winner, from family of
Halling: fair maiden: good efforts in nurseries fourth/fifth starts: should stay 7f: acts on
good to firm ground, below form on soft. *M. J. Ryan*

JUSTSILV   2 ch.f. (Feb 11) Democratic (USA) 101 – Smocking 39 (Night Shift (USA)) **–**
[2001 f6g f7g Jun 29] second foal: dam maiden who stayed 1½m: well beaten in sellers.
Miss K. M. George

JUST THE JOB TOO (IRE)   4 b. or br.g. Prince of Birds (USA) 121 – Bold **–**
Encounter (IRE) 69 (Persian Bold 123) [2001 57: f8g f8s³ f12g* f12g⁵ f11g f11g f14.8g **a59**
12.1g Sep 3] good-topped gelding: modest performer: won selling handicap at Wolverhampton in January: stays easy 1½m: acts on fibresand/equitrack, little form on turf.
P. C. Haslam

JUST THE TRICK (USA)   2 b. or br.f. (Feb 27) Phone Trick (USA) – Tammi's Pal **48**
(USA) (Lear Fan (USA) 130) [2001 5s⁶ 5.1m⁶ 5.1g⁶ 5.1m⁶ f6g f6g p5g⁶ f7g f5s f5s⁴ Dec
27] $42,000F, 34,000Y: third foal: closely related to a 6f winner in USA by Clever Trick

and half-sister to a 2-y-o winner there by Manila: dam winner up to 1m in USA, including minor stakes: poor maiden: will prove best at 5f/6f: acts on good to firm ground and firesand: blinkered last 3 starts. *W. R. Muir*

JUST WIZ 5 b.g. Efisio 120 – Jade Pet 90 (Petong 126) [2001 50, a76: 10g 10f f9.4g* p12g f9.4g⁵ f9.4g² f12g⁴ f9.4s* f9.4s⁵ Dec 26] small gelding: fairly useful on all-weather, poor on turf: won handicaps at Wolverhampton in October and December: best form at 9f/1¼m: acts on fibresand and equitrack: usually blinkered/visored earlier in career: tough. *N. P. Littmoden* **45 a84**

JUST WOODY (IRE) 3 br.g. Charnwood Forest (IRE) 125 – Zalamera 45 (Rambo Dancer (CAN) 107) [2001 71?: 7.1d 7m 8m⁵ 7.1f 8.3d* 8.3m 9.2g 9m³ 9.2g 8.3m 8d 8g f7g Nov 16] modest performer: won minor event at Hamilton in June: likely to prove best around 1m: acts on good to firm and soft going: inconsistent. *A. Berry* **63 §**

JUTHJOOR (IRE) 3 b.g. Marju (IRE) 127 – Deyaajeer (USA) 64 (Dayjur (USA) 137) [2001 12g Aug 7] 800 3-y-o: second foal: dam once-raced half-sister to Nashwan, Nayef and Unfuwain: behind in claimer at Catterick. *J. O'Reilly* **–**

JUWWI 7 ch.g. Mujtahid (USA) 118 – Nouvelle Star (AUS) (Luskin Star (AUS)) [2001 101, a94: f5g⁵ f6s f5s⁶ f6s es5g³ f6g⁶ f5g⁵ 5g 5m⁶ 6m* 6m² 6g 6m 6g⁴ 6m 6m 6.1m⁴ 6m* 6m 6g 6g 6m 6g 6g 5m 6m 5v 6d⁶ 6d 6g f5g* f6g³ f5s* Dec 15] robust gelding: useful handicapper: won at Southwell in January, Thirsk in May, York in July, Wolverhampton in November and Southwell (by length from Prime Recreation) in December: best at 5f/easy 6f: acts on any turf going and fibresand/equitrack: has reportedly bled: usually claimer ridden: quirky and starts slowly, often getting long way behind: very tough. *J. M. Bradley* **97 a101**

JUYUSH (USA) 9 b.g. Silver Hawk (USA) 123 – Silken Doll (USA) (Chieftain II) [2001 16s 16m⁶ 14g 16f* 16m² 16.2m² 16m 16.2s 18d Oct 20] big, strong gelding: fairly useful performer: won claimer at Nottingham in June: creditable efforts in handicaps after only when second at Newbury and Ascot: stays 2m: acts on firm and soft ground: often races prominently. *R. M. Stronge* **83**

K

KADISKAR (IRE) 3 b.c. Ashkalani (IRE) 128 – Kadissya (USA) 107 (Blushing Groom (FR) 131) [2001 12m⁵ 11.7d⁴ Oct 25] half-brother to several winners, notably Derby winner Kahyasi (by Ile de Bourbon), smart 11.5f/15f winner Kadaka (by Sadler's Wells) and smart 1¼m/1½m winner Kaliana (by Slip Anchor): dam, French 1¼m listed winner, half-sister to grandam of St Leger winner Milan: fair form in maidens at Kempton and Bath: should stay 1¾m: sold 62,000 gns. *Sir Michael Stoute* **79**

KAFEZAH (FR) 3 br.f. Pennekamp (USA) 130 – Yakin (USA) 86 (Nureyev (USA) 131) [2001 85: 7d⁵ 7f³ 6g⁵ 8f* 7g⁴ 9m* 8g⁶ 9d⁶ 8g⁶ Oct 5] lengthy filly: fairly useful performer: won maiden at Brighton in July and handicap at Goodwood (beat Omniheat by neck) in August: stayed 9f: acted on firm and good to soft going: blinkered sixth/seventh starts, taking strong hold second occasion: sometimes edgy: visits Nashwan. *B. Hanbury* **93**

KAFIL (USA) 7 b. or br.g. Housebuster (USA) – Alchaasibiyeh (USA) 85 (Seattle Slew (USA)) [2001 44, a53: 7d p7g Dec 28] seems of little account nowadays. *J. J. Bridger* **–**

KAGOSHIMA (IRE) 6 b.g. Shirley Heights 130 – Kashteh (IRE) 79 (Green Desert (USA) 127) [2001 63: 16.2m 16.1m⁴ 17.1f* 18m Jun 24] deep-bodied gelding: fair handicapper: won at Pontefract in June: ran badly final start: stays 2¼m: has form on good to soft going, but goes very well on firm/good to firm: visored nowadays: has drifted left: held up. *J. R. Norton* **73**

KAHTAN 6 b.h. Nashwan (USA) 135 – Harmless Albatross 115 (Pas de Seul 133) [2001 112: 22.2f² Jun 22] good-topped horse: good walker/easy mover: smart performer at best: very lightly raced on Flat nowadays: 4 lengths second to Life Is Life in Queen Alexandra Stakes at Royal Ascot only Flat outing at 6 yrs: stays 18.7f: yet to race on heavy going, acts on any other turf: front runner/races prominently: winner over hurdles in October. *N. J. Henderson* **89 +**

KAHZIMA (USA) 2 b. or br.f. (Mar 16) Gulch (USA) – Gharayib (USA) (Nureyev (USA) 131) [2001 5m⁵ 6m³ 5f* 5m⁴ Jul 14] smallish filly: first foal: dam 1m winner in **79**

USA: fair performer: won maiden at Kempton in July: creditable fourth in nursery at York: should stay 6f: raced only on going firmer than good: has given trouble at start. *E. A. L. Dunlop*

KAIAPOI 4 ch.c. Elmaamul (USA) 125 – Salanka (IRE) 68 (Persian Heights 129) **85** [2001 87: 10v 12.3f* 12m⁵ 11.9d 12g² 12m³ 10.3g 15.9d Sep 26] leggy, rather plain colt: fairly useful handicapper: won at Chester in May: was best at 1¼m/1½m: won on soft going at 2 yrs, but best form on good or firmer: tended to hang: unseated leaving stall third start at 3 yrs: was sometimes slowly away: dead. *R. Hollinshead*

KAIETEUR (USA) 2 b.c. (Mar 25) Marlin (USA) 124 – Strong Embrace (USA) **93 p** (Regal Embrace (CAN)) [2001 7f² 8d* Oct 25] big, strong, well-made colt: has plenty of scope: fourth foal: half-brother to a winner in USA by Red Ransom: dam won 11 races in USA, including 6f minor stakes at 2 yrs: shaped well when second to Al Mohallab in maiden at Newbury: won similar event at Bath following month easily by ¾ length from Statim despite edging left: will probably stay 1¼m: acts on firm and good to soft ground: useful prospect, should win more races. *B. J. Meehan*

KAILAN SCAMP 8 gr.m. Palm Track 122 – Noble Scamp (Scallywag 127) [2001 –: **–** 9f 9.9m⁵ Aug 26] of little account. *J. Parkes*

KAI ONE 3 b.c. Puissance 110 – Kind of Shy 61 (Kind of Hush 118) [2001 81: 7.1g* **86** 8m 7g 8.1g Sep 2] tall, leggy colt: fairly useful performer: won maiden at Haydock in June: well beaten in handicaps after: may prove best around 7f: raced mainly on good going or firmer: sold 18,000 gns. *R. Hannon*

KALABELL PRINCE 2 br.c. (May 22) Bluegrass Prince (IRE) 110 – Shikabell **46** (Kala Shikari 125) [2001 5.2g 6f 6.1m⁶ 7g⁶ 7m⁶ 7m 8m 5.7d p8g Nov 24] leggy colt: fourth foal: dam, maiden who stayed 1¾m, winning hurdler: poor maiden: stays 7f: acts on good to firm and good to soft ground: tried blinkered. *J. C. Fox*

KALAHARI FERRARI 5 ch.g. Clantime 101 – Royal Agnes 71 (Royal Palace 131) **–** [2001 –: 9.9d Oct 3] lightly raced on Flat nowadays: tried visored. *A. G. Hobbs*

KALANISI (IRE) 5 b.h. Doyoun 124 – Kalamba (IRE) (Green Dancer (USA) **129** 132) [2001 132: 10.5g³ 10m² Jun 20]
The enforced early retirement of Kalanisi provided a reminder of how fortunes can fluctuate in horse racing. Success as a four-year-old, when his victories included the Champion Stakes and the Breeders' Cup Turf, contributed to an outstanding 'millennium season' for his owner-breeder the Aga Khan, who also had that year's top three-year-old Sinndar. With Sinndar at stud, Kalanisi began the latest season as the Aga Khan's principal flag-bearer but, after coming second of nine to Fantastic Light in the Prince of Wales's Stakes at Royal Ascot, he was found to have sustained a hairline fracture to his near-fore shin. With Kalanisi out of action, the Aga Khan's chances of retaining his title as leading owner in Britain were dealt a mortal blow; in the end, he didn't make the top ten in Britain and his horses had a poor year generally, when compared to the exceptional achievements in both 1999 and 2000.

Kalanisi's contribution to his owner-breeder's racecourse winnings in 1999 consisted of spring victories in a maiden at Folkestone on his debut, a minor event at Newmarket and a listed race at Kempton before a training setback kept him off the course for the rest of the campaign. Switched from Cumani's stable at the end of the year, Kalanisi made his mark in pattern company by winning the Queen Anne Stakes at Royal Ascot on his second start as a four-year-old; as well as those memorable end-of-season victories in the Champion Stakes at Newmarket and the Breeders' Cup Turf at Churchill Downs, Kalanisi had added to his reputation in the summer when just coming off worse in thrilling battles with Giant's Causeway in the Eclipse Stakes at Sandown and the Juddmonte International at York. Kalanisi looked all set to figure in more top contests as a five-year-old after his pleasing reappearance in the Tattersalls Gold Cup at the Curragh in May against race-fit rivals; Kalanisi wasn't given too hard a time of it once it was clear he wouldn't be able to trouble the principals Fantastic Light and Golden Snake, and he finished just over three lengths third of six. Reopposing the winner at Royal Ascot, Kalanisi ran closer to his best, despite scratching his way to post and never travelling particularly fluently. After improving under pressure in the straight he kept on gamely once headed in the final furlong, this time beaten by two and a half lengths.

Kalanisi (IRE) (b.h. 1996)	Doyoun (br 1985)	Mill Reef (b 1968)	Never Bend
			Milan Mill
		Dumka (br 1971)	Kashmir II
			Faizebad
	Kalamba (IRE) (b 1991)	Green Dancer (b 1972)	Nijinsky
			Green Valley
		Kareena (b 1979)	Riverman
			Kermiya

Plans were up in the air at first after the discovery of Kalanisi's injury, but once a firm diagnosis was made that it would be difficult to get him back for an autumn campaign he was retired; the announcement was made at the end of July and he will begin his career as a stallion in 2002 at the Gilltown Stud in County Kildare at a fee of €15,000 (Oct 1st), alongside another son of Doyoun, Daylami. The good-topped Kalanisi, who had a quick action, is the first foal of the lightly-raced Kalamba, who was third at nine furlongs and a mile and a quarter. Kalamba is out of the genuine and smart miler Kareena. Kalanisi's year-younger half-sister Kalimanta (by Lake Coniston) was unplaced for John Oxx in two listed races in Ireland late on as a three-year-old. Kalamba's three-year-old filly Kalambara (by Bluebird) won a minor event over an extended nine furlongs at Chateauroux for Alain de Royer-Dupre in the latest season, while her two-year-old gelding Kalambari (by Kahyasi) was with Kalanisi's trainer. Kalanisi showed very smart form at a mile and stayed a mile and a half. He was successful on firm going in the Breeders' Cup Turf, though he showed his very best form on good or softer. The most genuine and consistent Kalanisi was usually waited with to make best use of his turn of foot; his third in the Tattersalls Gold Cup was the only occasion in which he finished out of the first two. *Sir Michael Stoute*

KALARRAM   4 ch.f. Muhtarram (USA) 125 – Kalandariya 78 (Kris 135) [2001 5g Jul 30] well beaten both outings. *C. B. B. Booth*   –

KALA SUNRISE   8 ch.h. Kalaglow 132 – Belle of The Dawn (Bellypha 130) [2001 81: 8.9d Oct 13] tall, workmanlike horse: fairly useful performer at best: pulled up (reportedly lame) only 8-y-o outing. *C. Smith*   –

KALINGALINGA   4 b.g. Zafonic (USA) 130 – Bell Toll 87 (High Line 125) [2001 f6g⁶ f9.4g⁵ f11g 10g 5.2m 8.5d* 8.5g 8d 8.2s Nov 5] 750,000 francs Y, 5,000 3-y-o: fifth foal: half-brother to 3 winners, including 10-y-o Prince Babar and 1m (at 2 yrs) to 11.5f (in France) winner Warning Order (by Warrshan), both useful: dam, 2-y-o 7f/1m winner, sister to dam of very smart Prix Jean Prat winner Suances: modest performer: won handicap at Galway comfortably in August: well held in Britain all other starts: best effort at 8.5f: acts on good to soft ground: blinkered fifth start. *B. J. Curley*   60 +

KALOUSHKA (IRE)   3 b.f. Inzar (USA) 112 – Petova (IRE) (Petorius 117) [2001 f7g⁵ f6g⁵ f9.4g f11g⁴ Mar 30] second foal: dam, poor maiden, from family of smart sprinter Governor General: no form, including in seller. *R. Brotherton*   –

KALUANA COURT   5 b.m. Batshoof 122 – Fairfields Cone (Celtic Cone 116) [2001 –: 12m 12m⁵ 15g² 17.2m* 15m* 17.1g* 16d 16d Sep 27] modest handicapper: won at Bath in July and Warwick and Pontefract in August: should stay beyond 17f: acts on good to firm ground, probably not softer than good: genuine. *R. J. Price*   63

KALUGA (IRE)   3 ch.f. Tagula (IRE) 116 – Another Baileys 60 (Deploy 131) [2001 47: f11g 12s¹⁴ f12g 14.1d May 11] strong, angular, lengthy filly: poor performer: won seller at Pontefract in April: leaves firm impression 1½m: will prove a minimum: acts on soft going: visored last 2 starts: sold 4,600 gns in June. *I. A. Balding*   47

KAMAKAZI KNIGHT (IRE)   2 b.g. (May 9) Night Shift (USA) – Kaskazi (Dancing Brave (USA) 140) [2001 7m 6g 8m Sep 24] 10,000Y: sixth foal: half-brother to 5-y-o Trinity: dam, Irish 9f/1¼m winner, out of smart French middle-distance filly Fly With Me: no form in maidens. *R. M. Flower*   –

KAMA SUTRA   3 b.c. Pursuit of Love 124 – Note Book 94 (Mummy's Pet 125) [2001 93p: 7g 6g² p6g² f7g² f7s⁴ Dec 15] well-made, attractive colt: fair maiden: stays 7f: acts on good to soft going and fibresand/polytrack: blinkered last 2 starts: irresolute. *W. Jarvis*   67 §

KAMA'S WHEEL   2 ch.f. (Feb 11) Magic Ring (IRE) 115 – Tea And Scandals (USA)   **51**
(Key To The Kingdom (USA)) [2001 f5g f5g⁵ 6g³ 5d⁴ 6m³ 7g⁴ 6g⁴ 6d 6.5g f6g⁴ Oct 9]
1,000Y: workmanlike filly: closely related to French 1m winner The Dude (by Owington)
and half-sister to high-class sprinter Ron's Victory (by General Holme): dam French 6f
winner: modest maiden: in frame 6 times, including 4 sellers: stays 7f: acts on fibresand,
unraced on extremes of going on turf: edgy sort: often slowly away. *John A. Harris*

KAMEYNN (IRE)   3 b.c. Green Desert (USA) 127 – Continuous (IRE) 89 (Darshaan   **81 §**
133) [2001 7d⁴ 7f³ 8.3m³ 7m⁴ 7g² 7g* 8.5m* 8.1g 7.5g⁶ Nov 29] IR 170,000Y: smallish,
quite attractive colt: good walker: third foal: half-brother to 7f winner in Hong Kong by
Persian Bold: dam, Irish 2-y-o 7f winner, half-sister to Italian Derby winner In A Tiff and
very smart miler Pennine Walk: fairly useful performer: won maiden at Ascot (hung left)
and minor event at Beverley in August: mostly creditable efforts in maidens/handicaps
most other starts except penultimate one when looked far from keen (left M. Tregoning
afterwards): not sure to stay beyond 8.5f: acts on firm and good to soft going: races up
with pace: consistent, but not one to trust. *D. J. Selvaratnam, UAE*

KANDYMAL (IRE)   3 ch.f. Prince of Birds (USA) 121 – Gentle Papoose (Comman-   **49**
che Run 133) [2001 52: 8m 7.5m² 8m 8f 7s³ 8m³ 8.3s³ 10m² 8.1f⁵ 9.1v⁶ Oct 16] angular,
sparely-made filly: poor maiden: stays 1¼m: acts on soft and good to firm going: well
held in visor (forced too strong a gallop) fourth start: front runner: has looked less than
keen. *R. A. Fahey*

KANGARILLA ROAD   2 b.g. (Feb 5) Magic Ring (IRE) 115 – Kangra Valley 56   **56**
(Indian Ridge 123) [2001 5s 6s⁶ f6g⁵ Nov 12] rather leggy gelding: third foal: half-
brother to 3-y-o Beverley Macca and 4-y-o Danakim: dam 2-y-o 5f winner: modest form
in minor event/maidens. *Mrs J. R. Ramsden*

KANZINA   2 b.f. (Mar 27) Machiavellian (USA) 123 – Kanz (USA) 115 (The Minstrel   **72**
(CAN) 135) [2001 7d 7d Nov 3] smallish filly: has a quick action: closely related to 5-y-o
Kanz Wood and half-sister to several winners, including useful 10.5f to 2m winner Kansk
(by Top Ville): dam, 1m (including at 2 yrs) winner, second in Yorkshire Oaks: better
effort in maidens (fair form) when seventh of 21 to Maid To Perfection at Newmarket on
second start, no extra final 2f: should be suited by 1¼m/1½m. *R. Hannon*

KANZ WOOD (USA)   5 ch.g. Woodman (USA) 126 – Kanz (USA) 115 (The   **69**
Minstrel (CAN) 135) [2001 75: f8g f6g² 6m 7m 7.1g 6g⁵ f7g² 8s 8m² 8.2s⁶ f6g³ f7g Dec   **a76**
3] strong gelding: fair performer: left W. Muir after seventh start: effective at 6f to 1m:
acts on good to firm going, good to soft and fibresand: has carried head high: has
reportedly had wind operation: none too consistent. *A. W. Carroll*

KAPAROLO (USA)   2 ch.c. (Mar 11) El Prado (IRE) 119 – Parliament House (USA)   **73 p**
(General Assembly (USA)) [2001 8s³ Oct 16] $42,000F, IR 45,000Y: strong colt: sixth
foal: half-brother to 3 winners, including useful 1998 2-y-o 7f/1m winner who stayed
1¾m Mixstarthetrixster (by Alleged): dam, sprint winner in USA at 4 yrs, half-sister to
Prix du Cadran winner Molesnes from very good family: 12/1, 5 lengths third of 15 to
Master In Law in maiden at Leicester, staying on late: should be suited by 1¼m+: should
do better. *Mrs A. J. Perrett*

KARAKUM   2 b.c. (Jan 30) Mtoto 134 – Magongo 103 (Be My Chief (USA) 122)   **75**
[2001 7m⁶ 7f⁴ Jul 25] close-coupled colt: first foal: dam, 5f (at 2 yrs) and 9f (in UAE)
winner, half-sister to Irish 1000 Guineas winner Classic Park: better effort in maidens
(fair form) when fourth to Shifty at Lingfield: should stay at least 1¼m. *M. A. Jarvis*

KARAMAH   2 b.f. (Mar 15) Unfuwain (USA) 131 – Azdihaar (USA) 81 (Mr   **78 p**
Prospector (USA)) [2001 6m² Jul 12] well-made filly: third foal: half-sister to useful
French 1999 2-y-o 6.5f winner Sand Pigeon (by Lammtarra): dam, 7f winner, half-sister
to 1000 Guineas winner Shadayid and 4-y-o Fath: 13/2, length second of 11 to Gossamer
in maiden at Newmarket, clear of remainder: should do better, all being well. *J. L. Dunlop*

KARAMEG (IRE)   5 b.m. Danehill (USA) 126 – House of Queens (IRE) (King of   **88**
Clubs 124) [2001 90: 7s 7g² 6g⁶ 7m⁵ 7g⁴ 7d² Aug 26] useful-looking mare: fairly useful
handicapper: best effort at 5 yrs when ¾-length second to Madame Jones at Yarmouth
final outing: best around 7f: acts on soft and good to firm going: sold 12,500 gns.
P. W. Harris

KARASTA (IRE)   3 b.f. Lake Coniston (IRE) 131 – Karliyka (IRE) (Last Tycoon 131)   **106**
[2001 107p: 8g 8f 7m Jun 20] very big, useful-looking filly: easy mover: useful
performer: won May Hill Stakes at Doncaster and finished second in Prix Marcel Boussac
at Longchamp in 2000: failed to progress at 3 yrs, best effort when 5¾ lengths sixth to
Imagine in Irish 1000 Guineas at the Curragh in May: well held in 1000 Guineas at

Newmarket (9/2f) and Jersey Stakes at Royal Ascot otherwise: stayed 1m well: raced only on good/good to firm going: stud. *Sir Michael Stoute*

KAREEB (FR)   4 b.g. Green Desert (USA) 127 – Braari (USA) 97 (Gulch (USA))   **87**
[2001 86: 7.6f 8m⁴ 8.5m⁴ 8.3m⁶ 8.1g 8m⁵ 6m⁴ 7g² 7.6g⁵ 7f² Sep 21] smallish, robust gelding: fairly useful handicapper: mostly at least creditable efforts at 4 yrs, notably when ¾-length second to Stratton at Newbury final outing: effective at 6f to 8.5f: acts on firm and soft going: tried blinkered at 3 yrs: has hung/looked faint-hearted: sold 20,000 gns. *W. R. Muir*

KARINDEE   3 ch.f. Karinga Bay 116 – Jaydeebee (Buckley 117) [2001 –: e6g e8g 10g   –
10g Aug 20] no form. *M. Madgwick*

KARIN'S LAD (IRE)   4 b.g. Up And At 'em 109 – Sharp Goodbye (Sharpo 132)   –
[2001 –: f11g 17.1s Apr 10] no sign of ability. *G. M. Moore*

KARITSA   3 b.f. Rudimentary (USA) 118 – Desert Ditty 67 (Green Desert (USA) 127)   **56**
[2001 67: 5.1v 6s 5g 5.3d⁶ 5.3f 6f³ 5m⁵ 6.1m 5g 6m f5g 5.2v p7g Dec 19] lengthy filly: fair winner at 2 yrs: just modest form in 2001, leaving M. Channon after penultimate start: effective at 5f/6f: acts on any going. *G. L. Moore*

KARMAFAIR (IRE)   5 b.m. Always Fair (USA) 121 – Karmisymixa (FR) (Linamix (FR) 127) [2001 12v 12.3s 16m⁶ May 4] first foal: dam unraced sister to useful Kalimisik and half-sister to smart Karmiska, both 1¼m performers in France: little form on Flat. *C. B. B. Booth*

KARMINSKEY PARK   2 b.f. (Mar 28) Sabrehill (USA) 120 – Housefull 81 (Habitat   **64**
134) [2001 5m 5g³ Aug 13] 12,500Y: heavy-bodied filly: seventh foal: half-sister to 1992 2-y-o 5f winner Greenlet (by Green Desert) and French 9f winner Dolforwyn (by Caerleon): dam, 1m winner, out of 1000 Guineas winner Full Dress II: much better effort in maidens (modest form) when third at Thirsk: should stay 6f. *T. J. Etherington*

KAROWNA   5 ch.m. Karinga Bay 116 – Misowni (Niniski (USA) 125) [2001 70:   –
12.3f 15.9m 13.9d Oct 13] rather leggy, useful-looking mare: little form on Flat in 2001: left S. Brookshaw after second start. *Ian Williams*

KARPASIANA (USA)   3 ch.f. Woodman (USA) 126 – Redwood Falls (IRE) 107   **79**
(Dancing Brave (USA) 140) [2001 54p: e8g⁵ 6s e10m* f11g* 10g⁴ f12g* 14g 9.9m* Aug 26] sturdy filly: fair handicapper: progressed steadily in 2001, winning at Lingfield and Southwell (apprentices, hung left/took long time to find stride) within 4 days in May, Wolverhampton in June and Beverley in August: effective at 1¼m/1½m: acts on good to firm going and fibresand/equitrack: has raced freely/idled: sold 62,000 gns in December. *M. A. Jarvis*

KARSAVINA (IRE)   3 b.f. Sadler's Wells (USA) 132 – Dumfries Pleasure (USA)   **114**
(Pleasant Colony (USA)) [2001 98: 10s² 11g* 10d⁴ 12g³ 11.9g⁴ 12m⁵ Sep 16] $650,000F, 450,000Y: leggy, good-topped filly: half-sister to 3 winners, notably smart US Grade 1 8.5f/1¼m winner Urbane (by Citidancer): dam ran once in USA: smart performer: won minor event at Naas in June: best efforts when 1¼ lengths third to Lailani in Irish Oaks at the Curragh in July and when 4¾ lengths fifth to Aquarelliste in Prix Vermeille at Longchamp final start, staying on both times: respectable fourth to Super Tassa in Yorkshire Oaks at York in between: will stay beyond 1½m: acts on good to firm ground: has worn crossed noseband: sent to USA. *A. P. O'Brien, Ireland*

KASAMBA   2 b.f. (Mar 15) Salse (USA) 128 – Kabayil 75 (Dancing Brave (USA)   **78**
140) [2001 6g⁶ 6m⁵ 7g* 7d 8s Oct 22] quite good-topped filly: has a quick action: third foal: half-sister to 4-y-o Dancing Bay: dam 1¼m winner and fairly useful hurdler: fair performer: shade edgy when winning maiden at Newmarket in July: well held last 2 starts: should stay at least 1m. *C. G. Cox*

KASHMOR (USA)   2 b.c. (Feb 26) Nashwan (USA) 135 – Millstream (USA) 107   **78 P**
(Dayjur (USA) 137) [2001 8s* Sep 27] useful-looking colt: second foal: half-brother to 3-y-o Baaridd: dam, 5f winner (including Cornwallis Stakes) who stayed 6f, from very good family: 9/4 on, beat Systematic by 5 lengths in 4-runner maiden at Pontefract, leading over 3f out: should stay 1¼m: sure to do considerably better. *D. R. Loder*

KASHRA (IRE)   4 b.f. Dancing Dissident (USA) 119 – Tudor Loom (Sallust 134)   **81**
[2001 95: 6f 6g⁶ 6g 6g Aug 21] close-coupled filly: fairly useful performer at best nowadays: form in handicaps at 4 yrs on second outing: stays 7f: acts on firm and good to soft going: often races freely: wore tongue tie/slowly away final outing. *M. Johnston*

KASS ALHAWA 8 b.g. Shirley Heights 130 – Silver Braid (USA) 101 (Miswaki **56** (USA) 124) [2001 77, a65: 7.1m 8m 7.5f 8m 8g 8f 8.5m⁴ 7m³ 7g 7.5d⁵ f11g² 12s⁵ 8v⁵ **a50** f7s⁵ f9.4s Dec 27] good-topped gelding: modest performer: effective at 7f to 11f: acts on firm going, soft, fibresand and equitrack: sometimes blinkered: best held up: none too consistent. *D. W. Chapman*

KASTANEA 3 ch.f. Tharqaam (IRE) – Adana (FR) (Green Dancer (USA) 132) [2001 **–** –: f9.4s f8g f11g f11g 11.8m 10m 8.2v Oct 4] of little account. *Mrs N. Macauley*

KASTINA 2 b.f. (May 22) Lancastrian 126 – Kit 34 (Green Ruby (USA) 104) [2001 **–** p8g Nov 28] first live foal: dam, poor sprint maiden at 2 yrs, failed to complete in points: 100/1, slowly away and always behind in maiden at Lingfield. *M. J. Gingell*

KATALI 4 ch.f. Clantime 101 – Portvally (Import 127) [2001 7.1m⁶ 5f 7v Oct 27] **–** 5,000Y: sister to fairly useful sprinter No Monkey Nuts and half-sister to 1989 2-y-o 6f seller winner Stop High (by Crofthall): dam unraced: well held in maidens/claimer. *A. Bailey*

KATATONIC (IRE) 8 b.g. Waajib 121 – Miss Kate (FR) (Nonoalco (USA) 131) [2001 **–** f12g⁴ Feb 20] seems of little account nowadays. *A. G. Juckes*

KATES SON (IRE) 4 ch.g. Fayruz 116 – Kates Choice (IRE) 86 (Taufan (USA) 119) **61** [2001 62: 7.1f 7g² 8f f8.5g⁵ f8g p10g⁴ Dec 22] strong, lengthy gelding: first foal: dam **a55** Irish 8.5f winner: modest maiden handicapper: trained by S. Treacy in Ireland at 3 yrs: best effort in Britain when second at Kempton: effective at 7f to 1¼m: acts on firm ground and polytrack, well held on fibresand. *Noel T. Chance*

KATHAKALI (IRE) 4 b.c. Dancing Dissident (USA) 119 – Shes A Dancer (IRE) **63** (Alzao (USA) 117) [2001 63, a89: f9.4s e10g 10d 10m² 10g 9.9m 9.7d 10.9m 8m³ 8s* **a76** 10s p8g⁴ p8g⁴ Dec 22] angular colt: fair performer on all-weather, modest on turf: won seller at Brighton in September: effective at 1m to easy 1¼m: acts on soft going, good to firm and all-weather: tried visored at 2 yrs: none too consistent. *S. Dow*

KATHANN 3 ch.f. Presidium 124 – Travel Mystery 99 (Godswalk (USA) 130) [2001 **–** 43: 14.1d 14.1g Jun 16] big, lengthy filly: poor maiden at 2 yrs: tailed off in 2001. *J. A. Glover*

KATHIES PET 6 b.m. Tina's Pet 121 – Unveiled 76 (Sayf El Arab (USA) 127) [2001 **34** e8g e8g f8.5g⁴ f7g Apr 27] rather leggy mare: poor handicapper nowadays: stays easy 1m: acts on fibresand. *R. J. Hodges*

KATHINKA 2 b.f. (Mar 17) Bin Ajwaad (IRE) 119 – Promissory (Caerleon (USA) **69 ?** 132) [2001 7d 8.3v⁶ 8d Nov 3] leggy, quite good-topped filly: second foal: dam, maiden, out of sister to smart 5f/6f winner Jester: fair form at best in maidens then listed event: should stay beyond 1m. *C. E. Brittain*

KATHOLOGY (IRE) 4 b.g. College Chapel 122 – Wicken Wonder (IRE) 71 (Distant **96 d** Relative 128) [2001 102: f5g 5.2d 6g³ 7m 6g 7.1g² 6m 6g 7.6d 6g 5d Oct 3] smallish, sturdy gelding: useful performer: on downgrade at 4 yrs after being placed in handicap at Newmarket and minor event at Haydock: effective at 5f/6f, almost certainly at 7f: acts on soft and good to firm going: usually races prominently. *M. Johnston*

KATHYS JACK 3 b.g. Silca Blanka (IRE) 104 – Kathy Fair (IRE) 46 (Nicholas Bill **–** 125) [2001 8.1m 6v Oct 29] close-coupled gelding: first foal: dam, maiden who stayed 1¼m and was temperamental over hurdles, half-sister to smart stayer Silence In Court: well beaten in maidens. *A. D. Smith*

KATIE KOMAITE 8 b.m. Komaite (USA) – City To City 55 (Windjammer (USA)) **44** [2001 44: 12.4d⁵ 10m 10.9f 10.5s⁵ 12.1s⁴ 11.1g* 9.9d Oct 3] angular mare: poor handicapper: won apprentice event at Hamilton in September: stays 12.5f: acts on soft and good to firm going: usually blinkered/visored earlier in career: has been difficult at stalls: tends to start slowly: often races freely/finishes weakly. *Mrs G. S. Rees*

KATIES CHIMES (IRE) 4 b.f. African Chimes 100 – The Monks Sister (IRE) **–** (Tony Nobles (USA)) [2001 6m 8.3m 10.1m⁴ 10g p7g Dec 28] first known foal: dam unraced: little sign of ability. *R. Ingram*

KATIES DOLPHIN (IRE) 3 ch.f. Dolphin Street (FR) 125 – Kuwah (IRE) 77 (Be **49** My Guest (USA) 126) [2001 56: 8.1d 6m 7.1f Sep 4] leggy, close-coupled filly: poor maiden at 3 yrs: best form at 5f/6f: acts on good to firm ground (possibly not on softer than good): blinkered/visored 4 of last 5 starts. *J. L. Eyre*

KATIES GENIE 3 b.f. Syrtos 106 – Reine de La Chasse (FR) (Ti King (FR) 121) **–** [2001 7f 8m 8f³ 8.3m 8.5f Jul 17] first foal: dam French 10.5f and 15f winner: no show in

maidens/handicap: reportedly broke loose on way to post on debut when slowly away.
B. N. Doran

KATIES TIGHT JEANS   7 b.m. Green Adventure (USA) 119 – Haraka Sasa (Town   –
And Country 124) [2001 7.1m 10d 6m 5.7m f9.4s p7g Dec 28] first foal: dam well beaten
over hurdles: well beaten in maidens/handicap. *R. E. Peacock*

KATIE'S VALENTINE   4 b.f. Balnibarbi 95 – Ring Side (IRE) (Alzao (USA) 117)   **54 d**
[2001 57, a–: 5g 6s⁴ 7.1f 6d 7g 9.2g 6m Sep 24] lengthy filly: modest maiden, very   **a–**
much on downgrade: should stay 7f: acts on soft going: tried visored/tongue tied.
T. A. K. Cuthbert

KATIYPOUR (IRE)   4 ch.g. Be My Guest (USA) 126 – Katiyfa (Auction Ring   **73**
(USA) 123) [2001 75: p8g⁶ Dec 22] quite attractive gelding: fair maiden: ran creditably
in handicap at Lingfield only Flat outing in 2001: stays 1¼m: acts on good to firm ground
and polytrack. *P. R. Webber*

KAT SLATER (IRE)   2 b.f. (Apr 8) Eagle Eyed (USA) 111 – Taniokey (Grundy 137)   –
[2001 5m 7.1f f6g Jul 13] 10,000Y: half-sister to several winners, including 3-y-o Bram
Stoker and fairly useful 1¼m/1½m winner Wafir (by Scenic): dam Irish 1m winner: no
form in claimer/maidens: refused to enter stall intended debut. *G. A. Swinbank*

KATTEGAT   5 b.g. Slip Anchor 136 – Kirsten 77 (Kris 135) [2001 86: 16s 13.3m   –
14.8m⁶ Jul 21] tall, unfurnished gelding: one-time useful performer: very lightly raced on
Flat nowadays. *J. A. B. Old*

KATY NOWAITEE   5 b.m. Komaite (USA) – Cold Blow 67 (Posse (USA) 130)   **107**
[2001 112p: 9d⁶ 9g² 9.9m² Oct 6] smart performer at best: won Cambridgeshire in
2000: only useful form in 2001 (reportedly suffered from back and muscle problems),
including when sixth in Earl of Sefton Stakes at Newmarket in April, and second in listed
events at Newmarket (behind Cayman Sunset) in May and Salisbury (behind Premier
Prize) in August: has won at 1¼m, but may prove best at 1m/9f: yet to race on extremes
of going: free-going sort: sold 40,000 gns. *P. W. Harris*

KATY O'HARA   2 b.f. (Apr 26) Komaite (USA) – Amy Leigh (IRE) 78 (Imperial   **66**
Frontier (USA) 112) [2001 6m 6m 6s 6v f6g* f5s* Dec 21] 3,000Y, 8,200 2-y-o: good-
bodied filly: first foal: dam 5f (including at 2 yrs)/6f winner: fair performer: improved to
win nurseries at Southwell in December: stays 6f: acts on fibresand, some promise on
turf. *Miss S. E. Hall*

KAURI (USA)   3 b.f. Woodman (USA) 126 – No Ordinary Storm (USA) (Storm Bird   –
(CAN) 134) [2001 54: e12g² f11g³ f11g* f12g³ 9.9m 10.1m 12f Jul 9] sparely-made filly: **a63**
modest performer: won handicap at Southwell in April: races freely, and may prove best
up to 1f: acts on fibresand/equitrack. *M. Johnston*

KAWANBAIK   2 ch.f. (Jan 19) Inchinor 119 – Sky Music 85 (Absalom 128) [2001 6d⁵   **49**
6g⁵ 6d p6g Dec 19] 15,000Y: leggy, quite good-topped filly: third foal: half-sister to 4-y-o
Polar Haze: dam, 6f/7f winner, half-sister to useful sprinter Lago di Varano: poor maiden:
tried blinkered. *K. McAuliffe*

KAYO   6 b.g. Superpower 113 – Shiny Kay 65 (Star Appeal 133) [2001 105, a78: 6f*   **105**
f8g⁶ 7g⁵ 6m 8m* 7m² 7s* 7d Oct 20] tall, leggy gelding: useful performer: won handicap   **a–**
at Newbury (beat Marsad by length) in July, claimer at Ripon in August and handicap at
York (beat Needwood Blade by short head) in October: pulled up reportedly lame final
outing: was effective at 6f to 1m: acted on any going: was tried blinkered: sometimes
sweated/got on toes/swished tail in preliminaries: usually raced prominently: carried
head awkwardly: was none too consistent: dead. *M. Johnston*

KAYSERI (IRE)   2 b.c. (Mar 16) Alzao (USA) 117 – Ms Calera (USA) (Diesis 133)   **90 p**
[2001 7f 8.5g² 10d* Oct 8] IR 105,000Y: stocky colt: second foal: dam, maiden in USA,
half-sister to Irish St Leger winner Authaal: progressive form in maidens: won at
Pontefract in October by 2½ lengths from Hot Produxion, asserting inside final 2f: will
stay at least 1½m: useful prospect, and should win more races. *M. A. Jarvis*

KAZANA   3 b.f. Salse (USA) 128 – Sea Ballad (USA) (Bering 136) [2001 76: e8g*   **63**
9.9g 10f 11.8m⁴ 7g 8s⁶ p12g Nov 28] strong, angular filly: modest performer: won
maiden at Lingfield in March: well held after, leaving S. Woods 10,000 gns and off over
2 months after fourth start: should be suited by 1¼m/1½m: acts on good to soft ground
and equitrack. *G. L. Moore*

KAZEEM   3 b.f. Darshaan 133 – Kanz (USA) 115 (The Minstrel (CAN) 135) [2001   –
73p: 10s Apr 20] strong, good sort: fair maiden in 2 starts in 2000: well held only 3-y-o
outing: should stay at least 1½m. *B. W. Hills*

KAZZIA (GER) 2 b.f. (Apr 12) Zinaad 114 – Khoruna (GER) (Lagunas) [2001 7s* **105 p** 8d* Oct 14] third foal: half-sister to German 1m (at 2 yrs)/9f winner Kalimas (by Lomitas) and German 7.5f/1m winner Kimbajar (by Royal Abjar): dam German 7f (at 2 yrs) and 11f winner: won maiden at Hoppegarten in September and Premio Dormello at Milan in October, useful form in latter to beat Kootenay by 2¼ lengths, leading near finish: will stay 1¼m: joined Godolphin: should progress. *A. Wohler, Germany*

KEBREYA (USA) 2 ch.c. (Jan 30) Affirmed (USA) – Minifah (USA) 69 (Nureyev **66** (USA) 131) [2001 8.1s⁶ 8.2s⁵ Nov 5] half-brother to several winners, including useful 1m (at 2 yrs) and 1¼m (in UAE) winner Ethmaar (by Silver Hawk) and useful 1m winner Bintalshaati (by Kris): dam, maiden who stayed 1½m, half-sister to Kentucky Derby winner Winning Colors: better effort in maidens (fair form) when fifth to Five Stars at Nottingham: will stay 1¼m. *J. L. Dunlop*

KEEN HANDS 5 ch.g. Keen 116 – Broken Vow (IRE) (Local Suitor (USA) 128) – [2001 66, a88: f6g⁵ f7g f7s* f8g f8.5g⁶ f8g⁴ f8.5g f7g³ f6g² f7g² f6g 6.1d f6g 8d f8g f6g **a83** f6g f8g f7s* Dec 15] compact gelding: fairly useful handicapper on all-weather: won at Wolverhampton in January and December: effective at 6f to easy 1m: acts on fibresand, no recent form on turf: usually visored, but effective without: tends to drift left: none too consistent. *Mrs N. Macauley*

KEEP DREAMING 3 b.f. Mistertopogigo (IRE) 118 – Ominous 91 (Dominion 123) – [2001 –: e7g f11g⁵ f8g Feb 19] strong, lengthy filly: little form. *M. Johnston*

KEEPERS HILL (IRE) 2 b.f. (May 9) Danehill (USA) 126 – Asnieres (USA) **95** (Spend A Buck (USA)) [2001 5g² 5g² 5m 5g² Jul 22] unfurnished filly: third foal: half-sister to a 7f winner in Hong Kong by Rahy: dam, 9f winner in France at 4 yrs, half-sister to Breeders' Cup Classic winner Arcangues and to dams of Cape Verdi and 3-y-o Aquarelliste: useful maiden: made much of running when seventh of 20 to Queen's Logic in Queen Mary Stakes at Royal Ascot: runner-up at the Curragh (twice, beaten ¾ length by Mahsusie in listed event on second occasion) and Tipperary (odds on): should stay 6f. *M. Halford, Ireland*

KEEP IKIS 7 ch.m. Anshan 119 – Santee Sioux (Dancing Brave (USA) 140) [2001 66: **66** 16m 16.1m³ 17.1f⁴ 18m⁶ 16.2f³ 21m Aug 1] leggy, short-backed mare: fair handicapper: needs at least 2m: acts on firm and good to soft going: patiently ridden. *Mrs M. Reveley*

KEEP TAPPING (IRE) 4 b.g. Mac's Imp (USA) 116 – Mystery Bid (Auction Ring **62** (USA) 123) [2001 76: f6s³ f6g⁵ f7g f5g 6m 6m 5m 5m 6m⁵ Jun 29] useful-looking gelding: has a quick action: modest performer: probably best at 6f: acts on soft going, good to firm and fibresand: often visored/blinkered: often slowly away nowadays: sold 1,000 gns in October. *N. P. Littmoden*

KEEP THE PEACE (IRE) 3 br.g. Petardia 113 – Eiras Mood 57 (Jalmood (USA) **66** 126) [2001 60: 6.1d⁵ 8.3g 8d² 10m Jul 7] tall gelding: has a quick action: fair maiden handicapper, lightly raced: shapes as if will stay 1¼m: yet to race on extremes of going: visored last 2 starts: sold 1,100 gns in September. *I. A. Balding*

KEEP THE SILVER 2 gr.c. (Jan 20) Petong 126 – Marjorie's Memory (IRE) 76 **79** (Fairy King (USA)) [2001 5s 5.1f 5s 6m² 5m* 5d³ 6m⁵ f6g² Oct 22] 16,000Y: quite **a85** attractive colt: third foal: brother to 4-y-o Mind The Silver and 3-y-o Pay The Silver: dam 5f winner, including at 2 yrs: fairly useful on all-weather, fair on turf: won nursery at York in July: good efforts after when placed in similar events at Goodwood and Southwell: effective at 5f/6f: acts on fibresand, good to firm and good to soft going: races prominently: game: sold 30,000 gns, joined D. Vienna in USA. *A. P. Jarvis*

KEE RING 5 ch.g. Keen 116 – Rose And The Ring (Welsh Pageant 132) [2001 54: e6g **46** f6g⁵ f5g e6g² 6f⁵ 6f⁴ 5.3f⁴ 5m Jul 12] leggy gelding: poor maiden: best at 5f/6f: acts on firm going (probably on good to soft) and equitrack: usually blinkered nowadays: tends to hang and carry head awkwardly. *P. R. Chamings*

KEETCHY (IRE) 2 b.c. (Apr 19) Darshaan 133 – Ezana (Ela-Mana-Mou 132) [2001 **76 p** 8g⁶ 8m 10.2g³ Oct 1] 190,000Y: rather leggy, unfurnished colt: brother to smart Irish 7f (at 2 yrs) to 1½m winner Ebaziya (dam of 3 Group 1 winners, including Gold Cup winner Enzeli) and half-brother to 2 winners, including fairly useful 1½m winner Erzadjan (by Kahyasi): dam French 11.5f winner: fair form in maidens: not given hard time once headed when third to Stage By Stage at Bath: will be suited by 1½m+: raced only on good/good to firm going: type to do well in handicaps. *J. L. Dunlop*

KELBURNE (USA) 4 b.g. Red Ransom (USA) – Golden Klair 115 (Damister (USA) **90** 123) [2001 56?: 8.3d 8m* 8.3m* 9.1f⁶ 9.2m* 10.5d 8m* 8m* 7.9m 9.2g² 8m 8g⁵ 8d Oct

19] big, lengthy gelding: has a quick action: fairly useful performer: much improved in 2001, winning handicap at Newcastle and minor event at Hamilton in June and handicaps at Hamilton, Ascot and Goodwood in July: seems best at 1m/9f: acts on good to firm ground, not disgraced on good to soft: sometimes flashes tail. *I. Semple*

KELSEY ROSE 2 b.f. (Mar 26) Most Welcome 131 – Duxyana (IRE) (Cyrano de **93** Bergerac 120) [2001 f5g² 5.3s² 5.1s⁵ f5g* 5g* 5.1f⁵ 5f⁵ 5m⁴ 5m 5.1m² 5m⁶ 5.2m* 6m³ 6.1d³ 6m⁵ 7s⁶ Sep 30] 1,100Y: leggy filly: fifth foal: half-sister to fairly useful 6f winner Vista Alegre (by Petong): dam unraced half-sister to dam of smart sprinter Indian Rocket: fairly useful performer: won maiden at Southwell in April and minor events at Thirsk in May and Yarmouth in July: creditable 2 lengths third to Resplendent Cee in listed contest at Ripon on thirteenth start: best at 5f/6f: acts on fibresand, soft and firm going: sometimes edgy: tends to hang right: tough and consistent. *P. D. Evans*

KELTECH GOLD (IRE) 4 b.g. Petorius 117 – Creggan Vale Lass (Simply Great **67** (FR) 122) [2001 83: 8f 8m 8m 7d 7s 8.2s³ p10g f8g Dec 17] heavy-topped gelding: fair **a–** handicapper: stays 1m: acts on soft and good to firm going: tried blinkered: has been early to post: front runner. *B. Palling*

KELTIC FLUTE 2 b.g. (May 12) Piccolo 121 – Nanny Doon (Dominion 123) [2001 **53** 8d 8m⁶ f8g f8g⁶ f8g Dec 10] 4,800Y: fourth foal: half-brother to winner around 9f Lord Harley (by Formidable) and a winner abroad by Alflora: dam well beaten both starts: modest form at best, including in seller: tried blinkered. *D. Morris*

KELTOS (FR) 3 gr.c. Kendor (FR) 122 – Loxandra 76 (Last Tycoon 131) [2001 8v* **116** 8v* 8m⁵ 8g* 8m⁶ 8s* Nov 3] close-coupled, useful-looking colt: third foal: half-brother to useful French 7f/1m winner Iridanos (by Sabrehill): dam, 1m winner, half-sister to several useful winners, including 3-y-o Halland: smart performer: won minor events at Saint-Cloud in March and Longchamp (by 10 lengths) in April, listed race at Chantilly in May and Prix Perth at Saint-Cloud (led on line to beat Cornelius short head) in November: best effort when 2¼ lengths sixth of 11 to Black Minnaloushe in St James's Palace Stakes at Royal Ascot penultimate start: stays 1m: acts on heavy and good to firm ground: usually races prominently. *C. Laffon-Parias, France*

KENNET 6 b.g. Kylian (USA) – Marwell Mitzi 50 (Interrex (CAN)) [2001 77, a68: **73** f12g³ f16s⁵ f14g⁵ f11g 10g 11.9m 13.3g⁴ 13.3m³ 13.3f Jul 5] leggy, plain gelding: fair **a59** handicapper on turf, modest on all-weather: probably best at 1½m/1¾m: acts on soft going, good to firm and fibresand/equitrack: tried blinkered/visored. *P. D. Cundell*

KENNYTHORPE BOPPY (IRE) 3 ch.g. Aragon 118 – Spark (Flash of **54** Steel 120) [2001 54: 8m 12m 11.1m³ 12f 12g 11.9s Oct 11] tall, leggy gelding: modest maiden: stays 1½m: acts on good to firm going: visored final outing. *J. S. Wainwright*

KEN'S DREAM 2 b.c. (Apr 13) Bin Ajwaad (IRE) 119 – Shoag (USA) (Affirmed **69** (USA)) [2001 8s⁵ 8s Nov 9] 9,000Y: half-brother to several winners, including fairly useful 7f performer in Britain/UAE Showgi (by Topsider): dam once-raced close relative of US Grade 1 1¼m winner Sisterhood: better effort in maidens (fair form) when fifth at Yarmouth: wore crossed noseband (took strong hold) next time. *Ms A. E. Embiricos*

KENT 6 b.g. Kylian (USA) – Precious Caroline (IRE) 60 (The Noble Player (USA) **50** 126) [2001 –, a56: f16g* f16.2s² f16g* f16g* f16g² f16g³ 17.2f⁶ 13.3g f16g f14g* **a72** f14.8g⁴ Dec 11] very big gelding: fair performer on all-weather, modest on turf: has gained all 6 wins at Southwell, including 3 handicaps and a minor event in 2001, 2 of them for amateur riders: best at 1¾m/2m: acts on fibresand and firm ground: often blinkered/visored: has hung/run in snatches/found little/carried head high. *P. D. Cundell*

KENTUCKY BOUND (IRE) 3 b.g. Charnwood Forest (IRE) 125 – Blown-Over **–** 41 (Ron's Victory (USA) 129) [2001 60: 6g 6m 7m 6m 5m Sep 8] rather leggy gelding: modest maiden at 2 yrs: little form in 2001: blinkered last 2 starts. *J. W. Payne*

KENTUCKY BULLET (USA) 5 b.g. Housebuster (USA) – Exactly So (Caro 133) **46 §** [2001 60: f9.4s² f11s² f12g⁶ 11.9s 10f⁵ 12m² 10g⁶ f9.4g⁵ 11m f12g⁶ f12g⁵ f12s³ Dec 27] **a64 §** leggy, angular gelding: modest handicapper on all-weather, poor on turf: stays 1½m: acts on firm going, good to soft and fibresand: often blinkered/tongue tied in 1999, tried once in 2001: irresolute. *A. G. Newcombe*

KEPLER (USA) 2 ch.c. (Jan 24) Spinning World (USA) 130 – Perfect Arc (USA) 120 **94 P** (Brown Arc (USA)) [2001 6v* Nov 8] first foal: dam won 10 of her 13 starts in USA, notably Grade 1 9f event: 8/1 from 4/1, impressive winner of maiden at Windsor by 3 lengths from Ridley, green early, soon pushed along well off pace but storming home for only one backhander to get well on top near finish, despite edging left: will be well suited by 7f/1m: smart prospect, sure to win more races. *P. F. I. Cole*

KERALA (IRE) 2 b.f. (May 12) Mujadil (USA) 119 – Kalisz (IRE) (Polish Precedent —
(USA) 131) [2001 6g Oct 19] 5,200 2-y-o: small filly: dam ran once: 200/1, tailed off in
maiden at Redcar. *Don Enrico Incisa*

KEROUNI (IRE) 3 ch.c. Rainbow Quest (USA) 134 – Kerita 111 (Formidable (USA) —
125) [2001 10m May 29] lengthy, angular colt: seventh foal: half-brother to 3 useful
winners in Ireland, including 1993 2-y-o 5f/6f winner Keraka and 7f/1m winner Keriyoun
(both by Storm Bird): dam 7f winner, including in Supreme Stakes: weak 12/1, tailed off
in maiden at Sandown: sold 1,800 gns in July, sent to Kuwait. *Sir Michael Stoute*

KESTLE IMP (IRE) 3 b.f. Imp Society (USA) – Dark Truffle 69 (Deploy 131) [2001 —
54?: e10g f9.4s⁵ Jan 20] little form since debut: visored last 2 starts. *R. M. H. Cowell*

KESTLE SKY (IRE) 2 b.f. (May 21) Woodborough (USA) 112 – Dark Truffle 69 —
(Deploy 131) [2001 6m 7g 5.3s f7g Oct 22] second foal: dam, third at 1m, out of
half-sister to very smart performer up to 11f Running Stag: no sign of ability in maidens/
sellers. *M. R. Ewer-Hoad*

KESTRAL 5 ch.g. Ardkinglass 114 – Shiny Kay 65 (Star Appeal 133) [2001 64, a46:   **72 +**
f8g* f8g⁴ f8g⁵ f8s 9m* 8.5m² 8m* 8.5f⁴ 8g* 7g 8.2g 9m³ 8m Sep 22] leggy, angular   **a52**
gelding: fair handicapper on turf, modest on all-weather: won at Southwell (apprentices)
in January, Redcar in May, Thirsk in June and Doncaster (did very well given way race
was run) in July: didn't have things go his way when below form 3 of last 4 starts: best at
1m/1¼m: acts on firm going and fibresand: tried tongue tied at 4 yrs. *T. J. Etherington*

KEW 2 b.g. (Jan 26) Royal Applause 124 – Cutleaf 81 (Kris 135) [2001 6m 7m⁵ 7g³ 7g   **50**
8d p8g p7g Dec 12] IR 46,000F, IR 100,000Y: fifth foal: half-brother to 3 winners,
including 1999 2-y-o 1m winner High Cheviot (by Shirley Heights) and 7f (at 2 yrs) and
1½m winner Goodwood Lass (by Alzao): dam, 10.5f winner, half-sister to Ribblesdale
winner Strigida and to dam of Yorkshire Oaks winner Catchascatchcan: modest maiden:
left Sir Mark Prescott after third in maiden at Catterick: probably stays 1m: acts on
polytrack: often visored/blinkered: gelded after final outing. *J. J. Bridger*

KEWARRA 7 b.g. Distant Relative 128 – Shalati (FR) (High Line 125) [2001 67: f12g —
14.1m 10.9m Sep 17] one-time useful handicapper: well held at 7 yrs: tried blinkered/
visored. *A. Streeter*

KEW GREEN (USA) 3 b. or br.g. Brocco (USA) 124 – Jump With Joy (USA) (Link-   **78 p**
age (USA)) [2001 7g 7.1g² 10d* Jul 19] $90,000Y: rangy gelding: has scope: seventh
foal: half-brother to several winners, including smart Japanese sprinter Washington Color
(by Black Tie Affair): dam winning US sprinter: fair form: won maiden at Leicester in
July by neck from Annabelle, chased along in rear early on and just getting on top close
home: gelded after: stays 1¼m: looks capable of better still. *W. J. Haggas*

KEY TO THE CITY (IRE) 7 b.g. Shalford (IRE) 124§ – Green Wings (General —
Assembly (USA)) [2001 f7g f11g Jun 15] fair winner at 5 yrs: well held on first Flat
outings since: sometimes blinkered. *D. G. Bridgwater*

KEY VIRTUE (USA) 2 ch.f. (Apr 10) Atticus (USA) 121 – Questionablevirtue   **72**
(USA) (Key To The Mint (USA)) [2001 7m³ 7d Oct 15] $130,000Y: rather leggy filly:
seventh foal: closely related to very smart 7f/1m (including Sussex Stakes) winner
Among Men (by Zilzal) and half-sister to a winner in USA by Lost Code: dam unraced
half-sister to 1990 US Grade 1 2-y-o 6.5f winner Deposit Ticket: favourite, much better
effort in maidens (fair form) when third to Red Rioja at Kempton: will probably prove
best up to 1m. *Mrs A. J. Perrett*

KEZ 5 b.g. Polar Falcon (USA) 126 – Briggsmaid 70 (Elegant Air 119) [2001 57§:   **77**
11.9m³ 10f* 11.5f* 10m* 10.1g* 10g 10.1m* 12m⁵ 10d 10g³ 10m 10.2d⁶ Oct 25] lengthy
gelding: has a quick action: fair handicapper: won at Brighton in May, Lingfield in June
and Yarmouth (ladies event) and Epsom in July: effective at 1¼m/1½m: acts on firm
going, probably on good to soft: visored once: held up. *P. R. Webber*

KHALED (IRE) 6 b.g. Petorius 117 – Felin Special (Lyphard's Special (USA) 122)   **44**
[2001 72: 8g 6g 6g 9.7d⁶ 8f f12g f16.2s⁵ Dec 18] tall gelding: poor performer nowadays:
seems to stay 2m: acts on good to firm going and fibresand: has had tongue tied: bled on
5-y-o reappearance: has hung right. *T. Keddy*

KHALIK (IRE) 7 br.g. Lear Fan (USA) 130 – Silver Dollar 106 (Shirley Heights 130)   **71**
[2001 71: 5g⁵ f5g 5.1d 6v Nov 8] smallish, sturdy gelding: unimpressive mover: fair
handicapper: creditable effort in 2001 only on first outing: probably best at 5f (given a
test)/6f nowadays: acts on any turf going: effective blinkered or not: wears tongue tie.
Miss Gay Kelleway

KHAYSAR (IRE) 3 b.g. Pennekamp (USA) 130 – Khaytada (IRE) 111 (Doyoun 124) – [2001 78: 8m⁶ 8g 10v 14.1s⁶ Nov 5] small gelding: second foal: dam, Irish 6f (at 2 yrs) to 1m winner and third in Irish 1000 Guineas, out of useful sprinter Khaydara: fair maiden in 2000: left J. Oxx in Ireland after second 3-y-o start: well held both starts in Britain (gelded after final one): bred to stay 1m. *R. Curtis*

KHAYYAM (USA) 3 b.g. Affirmed (USA) – True Celebrity (USA) (Lyphard (USA) 82 132) [2001 70p: 7m 8m² 10g⁶ 8m* 8.1g³ 8g⁵ 7m⁴ 8d f8g⁶ Nov 12] well-made gelding: fairly useful performer: won claimer at Newbury in August: effective at 7f/1m: acts on good to firm ground, some promise on fibresand final start (subsequently gelded): usually leads/races prominently. *P. F. I. Cole*

KHAZAYIN (USA) 3 b.f. Bahri (USA) 125 – Thawakib (IRE) 108 (Sadler's Wells 74 (USA) 132) [2001 8d 10m² 10m² Sep 11] fourth foal: sister to 4-y-o Sakhee, closely related to smart 7f (at 2 yrs) and 1¼m winner Nasheed (by Riverman) and half-sister to useful 1997 2-y-o 7f winner Alharir (by Zafonic): dam, 7f (at 2 yrs) and 1½m (Ribblesdale Stakes) winner, half-sister to top-class middle-distance performer Celestial Storm: fair form in maidens: second at Kempton and Leicester: stayed 1¼m: carried head awkwardly final outing: visits Seeking The Gold. *J. L. Dunlop*

KHITAAM (IRE) 3 b.c. Charnwood Forest (IRE) 125 – Queen's Ransom (IRE) 70 90 (Last Tycoon 131) [2001 89: 7s⁴ 7g 7.1m² 8.1d* 8m Jul 29] big, good-topped colt: has scope: fairly useful performer: best effort to make all in maiden at Warwick in July, despite hanging right: shaped as though something amiss final start: stays 1m: acts on good to firm and good to soft going: refused to settle third outing: sent to UAE. *B. Hanbury*

KHUCHN (IRE) 5 b.h. Unfuwain (USA) 131 – Stay Sharpe (USA) (Sharpen Up 127) – [2001 58: f11g⁶ 10s 12m⁶ 9.9f 9.9m Jul 23] strong, good-topped horse: little form in 2001: has worn tongue strap. *M. Brittain*

KHULAN (USA) 3 b.f. Bahri (USA) 125 – Jawlaat (USA) 91 (Dayjur (USA) 137) 99 [2001 103p: 7d⁴ 6g 6m³ Jun 29] tall, imposing filly: useful performer: failed to fully confirm 2-y-o promise: best effort in 2001 when length third to Autumnal in minor event at Newmarket final outing: free-going sort, probably didn't stay 7f: acted on good to firm and good to soft going: visits Machiavellian. *J. L. Dunlop*

KI CHI SAGA (USA) 9 ch.g. Miswaki (USA) 124 – Cedilla (USA) 111 (Caro 133) – § [2001 –§, a32§: e10g 11.9s May 3] stocky gelding: temperamental handicapper nowadays: usually visored/blinkered/tongue tied. *Jean-Rene Auvray*

KIDOLOGY (IRE) 5 b.g. Petardia 113 – Loveville (USA) (Assert 134) [2001 –: 9m – May 29] seems of little account. *W. Storey*

KID'Z'PLAY (IRE) 5 b.g. Rudimentary (USA) 118 – Saka Saka (Camden Town 81 125) [2001 66: 10.3s* 9v* 10s 12d* 12m 11.9m 16m 12.1m 9.2d³ 12.4m 13s 9.2s Aug 21] fairly useful handicapper: won at Doncaster (ladies) in March and Musselburgh (twice, allowed to dictate both times) in April: creditable effort after only when third: best at 9f (given test) to 1½m: acts on any going: has been early to post: looked most temperamental once as 4-y-o: often leads. *J. S. Goldie*

KIERCHEM (IRE) 10 b.g. Mazaad 106 – Smashing Gale (Lord Gayle (USA) 124) 45 [2001 45: 8m 10f⁴ 10f⁴ 10.1m² 8f Jul 22] useful-looking gelding: poor handicapper nowadays: stays 1½m: acts on any turf ground and fibresand: blinkered once. *C. Grant*

KIER PARK (IRE) 4 b.c. Foxhound (USA) 103 – Merlannah (IRE) (Shy Groom 114 (USA)) [2001 111: 5.1v 5g 6m² 5m 6.5d³ 5m 6s⁶ 5s Oct 7] tall, quite good-topped colt: smart performer: reportedly split pastern after only 3-y-o outing: ran well when ¾-length second to Invincible Spirit in minor event at Goodwood in May, and (best efforts) when 2¼ lengths third to King Charlemagne in Prix Maurice de Gheest at Deauville and 3¾ lengths fifth to Mozart in Nunthorpe Stakes at York, both in August: well below form otherwise, including in King's Stand Stakes at Royal Ascot fourth outing, and Sprint Cup at Haydock (raced too freely) and Prix de l'Abbaye at Longchamp (poorly drawn) last 2 starts: effective at 5f to 6.5f: acts on soft and good to firm going. *M. A. Jarvis*

KIGEMA (IRE) 4 ch.f. Case Law 113 – Grace de Bois (Tap On Wood 130) [2001 54: – e7g e8g f8g Feb 12] small filly: modest performer at 3 yrs: no form in 2001. *C. N. Allen*

KILBARCHAN 3 ch.f. Selkirk (USA) 129 – Haitienne (FR) (Green Dancer (USA) 40 132) [2001 64?: 8v⁵ 5d 8.3m 8m 9.9f⁶ 7d 6m⁶ 6d 7.5m Aug 26] stocky filly: poor maiden: should be suited by 7f+: acts on good to firm going. *Miss L. A. Perratt*

KILCREGGAN 7 b.g. Landyap (USA) 112 – Lehmans Lot (Oats 126) [2001 54: 16f⁴ **52**
16m Aug 12] rangy gelding: modest handicapper: stays 2m: acts on firm ground and
fibresand: has worn crossed noseband: held up: sold 3,500 gns. *Mrs M. Reveley*

KILDARE CHILLER (IRE) 7 b.g. Shahrastani (USA) 135 – Ballycuirke (Taufan **59**
(USA) 119) [2001 –: f11g⁴ 11.9s⁶ May 3] fair handicapper in Ireland in 2001: only
modest nowadays on Flat: stays 11f: acts on heavy going and fibresand. *P. R. Hedger*

KILDRUMMY 3 br.g. Timeless Times (USA) 99 – Rynavey 67 (Rousillon (USA) **64**
133) [2001 9d⁶ 8.2s³ 7g⁴ 7m³ 10.1m² 9.1m² 8.3m³ 9f 8.3d⁶ 7.1f⁴ 9.2m⁵ Sep 24] sparely-
made gelding: fourth foal: half-brother to 1998 2-y-o 6f winner Dipple (later useful
winner up to 9f in Norway, by Komaite) and 1999 2-y-o 6f winner Zestril (by Zilzal):
dam, middle-distance maiden, half-sister to smart winner up to 13f Applecross (dam of
Craigsteel and Invermark): modest maiden: effective at 7f to 1¼m: acts on soft and good
to firm going: tried visored/blinkered (ran poorly in latter): consistent: sold 5,500 gns,
sent to Denmark. *Denys Smith*

KILKENNY CASTLE (IRE) 5 b.g. Grand Lodge (USA) 125 – Shahaamh (IRE) 85 **88**
(Reference Point 139) [2001 8m 8m 9g 7g³ 8d 8d Nov 3] 21,000Y: big gelding: third foal:
half-brother to Italian 7f winner Coco Passion (by Polish Precedent): dam, 1¼m winner
who stayed 1¾m, closely related to useful stayer Haitham: useful 7.5f winner (blinkered)
for C. O'Brien in Ireland in 1999: unraced in 2000: easily best effort in handicaps in
Britain (fairly useful form) when third of 28 to Stratton at Newmarket in October: stays
9f: yet to race on extremes of going. *S. Dow*

KILLARNEY 3 gr.f. Pursuit of Love 124 – Laune (AUS) 68 (Kenmare (FR) 125) **65**
[2001 –: 7m 8.2f⁵ 8g 9.7m 10.1m³ 10g 10m⁴ 10.1g Sep 14] lengthy, deep-girthed filly:
fair maiden handicapper: stays 1¼m: acts on good to firm ground: blinkered (raced freely
and ran poorly) final outing: has hung left: sold 3,800 gns. *R. Hannon*

HRH Sultan Ahmad Shah's "Kier Park"

KILLARNEY JAZZ 6 b.g. Alhijaz 122 – Killarney Belle (USA) (Irish Castle (USA)) –
[2001 –, a64: e6g⁵ e7g² e7g⁶ e6g⁴ f7g² f6g³ f7g⁴ f6g⁴ f7g⁴ f8g Jul 27] angular **a57**
gelding: modest performer: effective at 7f to 9f: acts on fibresand/equitrack: tried
visored/blinkered, including final outing (ran badly): has had tongue tied: has hung right:
consistent. *G. C. H. Chung*

KILMEENA LAD 5 b.g. Minshaanshu Amad (USA) 91§ – Kilmeena Glen (Beveled **73 +**
(USA)) [2001 64, a89: f6s e7s⁶ 6m⁶ 6f* 7g* Jul 18] good-quartered gelding: fair handicapper: reportedly finished distressed second start then left E. Wheeler: won at Kempton
twice in July, comfortably on second occasion: effective at 6f to easy 1m: acts on any turf
going, much better form on equitrack than fibresand: tried blinkered: tends to edge left:
has run well sweating: has reared leaving stall. *J. C. Fox*

KILMEENA STAR 3 b.c. So Factual (USA) 120 – Kilmeena Glen (Beveled (USA)) **51**
[2001 47p: 6g 6f⁶ 6m 6.1f⁵ 5m 5m⁴ 6d f8.5g p6g Dec 19] modest maiden: left E. Wheeler **a–**
after sixth start: effective at 5f/6f: acts on firm going, well held on all-weather: races
prominently. *J. C. Fox*

KILMENY (IRE) 3 b.f. Royal Abjar (USA) 121 – Mouchez Le Nez (IRE) 41 (Cyrano **74**
de Bergerac 120) [2001 f8.5g⁴ f8f* 8m² 8.1g* 9.2s 7.9m 7.1f⁵ 8g f8g* 7d Nov 3] 2,500Y: **a87**
robust filly: second foal: half-sister to winner in Belgium by Case Law: dam, lightly-
raced maiden, from family of Cheveley Park winners Pass The Peace and Embassy: fairly
useful on all-weather, fair on turf: won maiden at Southwell in March and handicaps at
Haydock in August and Southwell (apprentice race) in October: should prove at least as
effective at 7f as 1m: acts on good to firm going and fibresand. *H. Morrison*

KILMORY 2 b.f. (Apr 24) Puissance 110 – Lizzy Cantle 52 (Homing 130) [2001 6d –
6g Jul 3] fifth reported foal: half-sister to 6-y-o Dryad: dam 7f winner: last in maiden/
seller. *G. G. Margarson*

KIMOE WARRIOR 3 ch.g. Royal Abjar (USA) 121 – Thewaari (USA) 68 (Eskimo **43**
(USA)) [2001 47: 8.1v³ 11.1d 10.3f f8g f6g⁶ 7.6m 7.1v⁵ f8.5g Dec 11] tall, close-coupled
gelding: poor maiden: stays 1m: acts on heavy ground and fibresand. *M. Mullineaux*

KINAN (USA) 5 b.g. Dixieland Band (USA) – Alsharta (USA) (Mr Prospector **70**
(USA)) [2001 92: 7s 8g 8g 8.1d 8f 8s⁵ 7.5s³ f7g³ p6g⁶ Dec 19] quite attractive gelding:
fair handicapper nowadays: probably stays 1m: best form on good going or softer/fibre-
sand (eye-catching effort on polytrack final start): possibly no easy ride. *T. D. Barron*

KIND EMPEROR 4 br.g. Emperor Jones (USA) 119 – Kind Lady 56 (Kind of Hush **60 §**
118) [2001 72d: 6v 8m* 8m 8.3g 7m² Jul 24] leggy, sparely-made gelding: modest
performer: made all in handicap at Yarmouth in May: stays 1m: acts on firm and soft
going: refused to race in visor tenth 3-y-o outing: hung markedly right third start:
unreliable. *P. L. Gilligan*

KIND OF LOVING 2 ch.f. (Apr 24) Diesis 133 – Gentilesse 81 (Generous (IRE) **63 p**
139) [2001 7d Nov 3] smallish filly: first foal: dam, won at 1¼m only start, daughter of
smart winner around 1m in France As You Desire Me: 16/1, twelfth of 21 to Maid To
Perfection in Newmarket maiden, held up and not given unduly hard time: should
improve. *J. L. Dunlop*

KINDRED FALLS 4 b.f. Bin Ajwaad (IRE) 119 – Rising River (Warning 136) [2001 –
12g 11.8s 8.3v Nov 8] 3,000F: first foal: dam no sign of ability: well beaten in claimers/
maiden. *P. R. Hedger*

KING CAREW (IRE) 3 b.c. Fairy King (USA) – Kareena 110 (Riverman (USA) 131) **88**
[2001 90: 12f 12f 8f* 10.1m⁵ 9.9g 10f³ 8f 8d 8d Nov 3] rather leggy colt: unimpressive
mover: fairly useful performer: won maiden at Newcastle in June: in-and-out form
otherwise, and flattered in Derby at Epsom on reappearance: probably stays 1½m:
probably acts on any going: tried visored: has carried head awkwardly: may not have
ideal temperament. *M. R. Channon*

KING CHARLEMAGNE (USA) 3 b.c. Nureyev (USA) 131 – Race The Wild **120**
Wind (USA) 121 (Sunny's Halo (CAN)) [2001 108p: 7g* 7g* 6.5d* Aug 12]
       Thursday April 16th 1987 marked the end of an era in the world of thor-
oughbred breeding when Northern Dancer, the most successful commercial stallion
and the most influential, was retired from stud duties. Less than three weeks later, it
seemed that the industry might also lose one of his foremost sons when Nureyev
broke his off-hind hock in a paddock accident. An operation to insert four screws in
his leg—after which he had to be supported by a sling—was given only a ten per

cent chance of saving his life. Failure threatened to be a grievous blow but Nureyev lived for another fourteen years. Covering in each of them, he became beyond doubt an outstanding stallion. Not that there was much room for doubt, even in 1987. In his crops conceived before the accident, his best included Al Sylah, Theatrical, Vilikaia, Lead On Time, Sonic Lady, Gayane, Miesque, Soviet Star, Stately Don, Alwuhush, Great Commotion, Zilzal and Polar Falcon; those that came afterwards include Wolfhound, Mehthaaf, Spinning World, Peintre Celebre, Reams of Verse, Skimming, Stravinsky, Fasliyev, Crystal Music and King Charlemagne. Nureyev's first crop, the only one conceived in France, included an amazing seven pattern winners from just twenty-four foals. One indication of the unremitting quality of his offspring is contained in the latest *Timeform Stallion Statistical Review*, which shows that over the last four seasons of British racing only one sire, Danzig, has produced runners with a higher median rating. As a sire of winners of European pattern races, Nureyev, whose crops exceeded fifty on just three occasions, stands second only to Sadler's Wells, whose foals each year are usually now into three figures. The end of the Nureyev era came on October 29th 2001 in the aftermath of an operation on his off-fore hoof. 'It was cancer in his foot,' reflected John T. L. Jones junior, owner of the Walmac International stud in Kentucky. 'We tried to take it out a month ago and it just didn't work. We didn't put him down—he just laid down in his stall.'

It is equally straightforward to remember the details of Nureyev's racing career, aided, of course, by there being so little of it. Transferred from Peter Walwyn's stable as an unraced two-year-old, he had three runs for Francois Boutin, seizing the attention with six-length triumphs in both the Prix Thomas Bryon and the Prix Djebel. His third start was the Two Thousand Guineas, in which he became the first winner of the race to be disqualified, one of only six horses to be demoted from first place in any British classic, and the first to suffer such a fate since 1918; a most impressive last-to-first run from the 13/8 favourite saw him beat Known Fact by a neck but, under a most ill-judged ride from Philippe Paquet, Nureyev had nearly brought down third-placed Posse in the process. A virus ruled him out of the Derby and he was not seen again. Nureyev raced in the colours of Stavros Niarchos, who outbid Robert Sangster to get him at the Keeneland July Sale for 1,300,000 dollars, at that time the second highest price ever for a yearling at auction. A fine pedigree had outweighed his lack of size (Timeform later described him as a smallish, lengthy, good-quartered colt). One year after Nureyev's Guineas, that pedigree was about to get better still when his half-sister Fairy Bridge gave birth to another Northern Dancer colt, Sadler's Wells, and one year on from that Nureyev was standing his first Kentucky season after his syndication for upwards of fourteen million dollars. From the moment he stepped into the public eye, he was a success story, and remained one from start to finish.

If the stallion masters had, greedily, wished for anything more from Nureyev, it would have been better fertility. His ninety-one mares in 1997, for instance,

Prix Maurice de Gheest, Deauville—a fifth consecutive win for King Charlemagne (left), who has a neck to spare over Three Points; Kier Park is third with Mount Abu (right) fourth

produced only twenty-nine live foals. One of those successful liaisons was with Race The Wild Wind, and victory in the Prix Maurice de Gheest at Deauville in August saw her son King Charlemagne become Nureyev's twenty-ninth individual Group/Grade 1 winner. Sold for 1,500,000 dollars as a foal, King Charlemagne raced for the Coolmore team of Magnier and Tabor. His racing career was twice as long as that of Nureyev, but still too short, as he left the field with a record of steady improvement and the possibility of potential still untapped. King Charlemagne's debut brought only second place when 5/4-on in the Convivial Maiden at the York Ebor meeting, but he never tasted defeat after that. In September as a two-year-old he won a maiden at Leopardstown comfortably at 7/1-on and won the Somerville Tattersall Stakes gamely, in a tight finish with Grandera and Patsy's Double at Newmarket. An abscess had reportedly kept him out of the Prix de la Salamandre in between those two races and he again had to wait for his Group 1 chance as a three-year-old. Slow to come to hand and absent from the classics, he reappeared in mid-June to win the five-runner Ballycorus Stakes at Leopardstown in clear-cut fashion by a length and a half from One Won One. His battling qualities were called upon again, however, a month later when King Charlemagne took his third Group 3 on the trot in denying Mull of Kintyre and Just Special by a neck and a head in the six-runner Emirates Airline Minstrel Stakes at the Curragh. Brought to challenge inside the final furlong for both of those wins as a three-year-old, King Charlemagne repeated the trick in better company for the Maurice de Gheest. Sent off at 5/4-on and anchored at the back of the nine-runner field by Jamie Spencer, he was clearly going best two furlongs out but still had to make up about four lengths on the trail-blazing Three Points; edging left into the whip, he managed it under ten strides from home to win by a neck, with Kier Park third and Mount Abu fourth.

		Northern Dancer	Nearctic
	Nureyev (USA)	(b 1961)	Natalma
	(b 1977)	Special	Forli
King Charlemagne (USA)		(b 1969)	Thong
(b.c. 1998)		Sunny's Halo	Halo
	Race The Wild Wind (USA)	(ch 1980)	Mostly Sunny
	(b or br 1989)	Redpath	Indian Chief
		(b 1974)	Lady Marguery

The remainder of King Charlemagne's season was rather like that of Nureyev's after the Guineas, but without quite the same suspense. He was a surprise absentee from the Haydock Park Sprint before a challenge for the Breeders' Cup Sprint or Mile was mooted, but 'a little injury' forced him to miss the Ballydoyle team practice at Southwell and his retirement was announced in October. King Charlemagne was going the right way prior to that premature exit, but, as things stand, his form cannot be described as high class. He gave the impression on a couple of occasions that he would stay a mile, but, a coincidence perhaps, his best form was when dropped to six and a half furlongs, and he showed no lack of speed on that occasion. An angular, quite good-topped colt, King Charlemagne never raced on firm or soft going. Details of the dam's side of his pedigree can be found in the essay on his two-year-old brother, the July Stakes winner Meshaheer. Nureyev is gone but King Charlemagne begins his stallion career at Coolmore at a fee of IR £8,000, October 1st, no foal no fee. *A. P. O'Brien, Ireland*

KINGCHIP BOY 12 b.g. Petong 126 – Silk St James (Pas de Seul 133) [2001 –, a53d: f8g⁶ f8g⁴ f8g⁵ f8g f8s f7g 7s 10d 6f May 25] compact gelding: poor nowadays: stays 9.7f: acts on fibresand/equitrack: effective blinkered/visored or not: often forces pace. *M. J. Ryan*   **a37**

KING CREOLE 2 b.c. (Feb 4) Slip Anchor 136 – Myrrh (Salse (USA) 128) [2001 8.2d 8d Oct 19] 7,500F, 62,000Y: strong, well-made colt: has a quick action: third foal: half-brother to Rudy Spice (by Rudimentary), 7f winner in Italy: dam lightly-raced half-sister to Celeric and Sesame: fair form in mid-division in maidens at Nottingham and Newmarket, never dangerous or knocked about: likely to be suited by 1½m+: almost certainly capable of better. *J. Noseda*   **70 p**

KING DAVID 2 b.c. (Mar 19) Distant Relative 128 – Fleur Rouge 71 (Pharly (FR) 130) [2001 f6g⁵ Nov 12] 31,000Y: brother to fairly useful 6f winner Always On My Mind   **58 p**

and half-brother to several winners, including 3-y-o Red Carpet and 5-y-o Red Lion: dam 2-y-o 6f winner: 10/1, fifth of 8 to Crystal Valkyrie in maiden at Southwell, slowly into stride and not knocked about: should do better. *J. A. Osborne*

KING EIDER   2 b. or br.g. (Jan 29) Mtoto 134 – Hen Harrier 94 (Polar Falcon (USA) **68 p** 126) [2001 7g 8s 8s⁵ Nov 9] smallish, good-topped gelding: first foal: dam, 7f (at 2 yrs) to 1¼m winner, granddaughter of Oaks winner Circus Plume: fair form in maidens: will be suited by 1¼m/1½m: capable of better. *J. L. Dunlop*

KINGFISHER EVE (IRE)   3 b.f. Hamas (IRE) 125§ – Houwara (IRE) (Darshaan   – 133) [2001 –: 8d Aug 19] well held in maidens a year apart. *C. Grant*

KINGFISHERS BONNET   5 b.m. Hamas (IRE) 125§ – Mainmast 63 (Bustino 136)   **40** [2001 58: 9.7v⁵ 11.7d 11.9s 11.1d 10f 10s Sep 30] rather leggy mare: poor handicapper: barely stays 1½m: best on good going or softer nowadays. *J. M. Bradley*

KING FLYER (IRE)   5 b.g. Ezzoud (IRE) 126 – Al Guswa 98 (Shernazar 131) [2001   **90** 79, a–: 12g 14m³ 14.4m³ 20m 16.4m² 14.8m² 16.1g² 14.8m² 13.9m* 14.6d 18f⁴ Sep 20]   **a–** leggy, workmanlike gelding: fairly useful handicapper: gained deserved success at York in September by head from Hambleden: previously good second firstly at Sandown then 3 times at Newmarket: stays 2¼m: possibly needs good going or firmer on turf, and acts on equitrack: blinkered once: tongue tied: held up: reliable. *Miss J. Feilden*

KING FOR A DAY   5 b.g. Machiavellian (USA) 123 – Dizzy Heights (USA) (Danzig   **36** (USA)) [2001 49: 14.1m 14.1m 16m⁵ 12g Aug 23] poor handicapper: below form in 2001: stays 2m, at least with emphasis on speed: acts on heavy and good to firm ground: blinkered twice at 3 yrs, often visored nowadays: none too reliable. *Bob Jones*

KING HARSON   2 b.g. (Mar 22) Greensmith 121 – Safari Park 43 (Absalom 128)   **80 +** [2001 5f* 5d³ 5f³ 5.2m 5m⁶ 6m 5g 6v* Oct 26] 3,900Y: close-coupled, good-bodied gelding: third foal: dam maiden on Flat and poor winning hurdler: fairly useful performer: won maiden at Pontefract in June and 22-runner sales race at Doncaster (raced alone when beating Dudleys Delight by 1¾ lengths) in October: should stay 7f: acts on any ground: visored fourth/fifth starts, blinkered at Doncaster: gelded after final one. *J. D. Bethell*

KING NICHOLAS (USA)   2 b.c. (Apr 24) Nicholas (USA) 111 – Lifetime Honour   **– p** (USA) (Kingmambo (USA) 125) [2001 6d 6s Nov 10] $6,500F, 25,000Y: good-topped colt: first foal: dam unraced half-sister to US Grade 2 9f winner Composer out of useful Irish performer up to 1m Honoria: signs of ability in maidens at Newmarket and Doncaster: capable of better. *M. A. Jarvis*

KING OF ADOC   2 ch.c. (Apr 2) Dr Devious (IRE) 127 – Urchin (IRE) (Fairy King   **49** (USA)) [2001 6v 8d p10g p7g⁵ Dec 29] 29,000F: first foal: dam unraced half-sister to several winners, including smart sprinter Lugana Beach, out of half-sister to Mtoto: poor maiden: blinkered last 2 starts. *S. Kirk*

KING OF HAPPINESS (USA)   2 ch.c. (Apr 11) Spinning World (USA) 130 –   **105 p** Mystery Rays (USA) 122 (Nijinsky (CAN) 138) [2001 7m* Aug 4] 220,000Y: rather leggy, good-topped colt: half-brother to several winners abroad, including useful French 1995 2-y-o 1m winner Metaphor (by Woodman) and French 11f winner Estery des Bois (by Bering): dam, 1m (at 2 yrs) to 1½m (Prix Minerve) winner, closely related to smart 6f to 1m performer Robin des Pins: 7/2 and better for race, won 7-runner maiden at Doncaster by 1¼ lengths from Mount Joy, asserting from over 1f out: will be suited by 1m/1¼m: swished tail repeatedly in paddock: should go on to better things, all being well. *Sir Michael Stoute*

KING OF MOMMUR (IRE)   6 b.g. Fairy King (USA) – Monoglow (Kalaglow   **50** 132) [2001 59: 11.9f³ 13.1m⁴ Sep 10] lengthy, angular gelding: modest maiden, lightly raced on Flat nowadays: stays 2m: acts on good to firm going: sometimes blinkered, not in 2001: has worn tongue strap. *B. G. Powell*

KING OF PERU   8 br.g. Inca Chief (USA) – Julie's Star (IRE) 45 (Thatching 131)   **68** [2001 79, a89: f5g f5g* f6g⁶ f5g 5v 6s 5v 5m 5m³ 5m² 5.2m² 5m f5g³ f6g 5f³ Jul 25] tall,   **a77** leggy gelding: has a quick action: fair performer: won claimer at Southwell in January: effective at 5f to 7f: acts on hard going, soft and fibresand: effective blinkered/visored or not: often a weak finisher. *D. Nicholls*

KING OF TARA (IRE)   3 b.c. Fairy King (USA) – La Bella Fontana (Lafontaine   **116** (USA) 117) [2001 8v* 7v* 8m* 9m² 10g* 12m⁶ 9.8d³ a10.5g Nov 24] good-topped colt: seventh foal: brother to 2 winners, notably very smart miler Revoque, Prix de la Sala-mandre and Grand Criterium winner at 2 yrs: dam once-raced half-sister to useful 5f/

7f winner Abuzz: smart performer: won maiden at the Curragh in April, minor event at Tipperary and listed race at Leopardstown (beat Tarry Flynn a short head) in May, and Prix Eugene Adam at Deauville (by 1½ lengths from Stardan) in also: also ran well when head second of 5 to Olden Times in Prix Jean Prat at Chantilly on fourth start, final one for A. O'Brien: best effort in autumn when creditable staying-on 4 lengths third of 5 to Albarahin in Prix Dollar at Longchamp (blinkered) penultimate start: stays 1¼m: yet to race on firm ground, probably acts on any other turf (soundly beaten in Japan Cup Dirt final outing). *F. Doumen, France*

KING OF THE TWEED (IRE) 2 b.g. (Feb 26) Robellino (USA) 127 – River **66**
Tweed 61 (Selkirk (USA) 129) [2001 5m 5g6 6f Sep 21] 13,000F, IR 15,000Y, 18,500 2-y-o: first foal: dam, maiden who stayed 1m, half-sister to smart French/US performer up to 1½m Bon Point: fair maiden: clearly best effort when sixth at Folkestone: should stay 1m: has been edgy/worn crossed noseband. *J. J. Sheehan*

KING OF TRUMPS 2 ch.c. (Mar 8) First Trump 118 – Sea of Stone (USA) 71 **60**
(Sanglamore (USA) 126) [2001 7m 7f6 7d6 7s Oct 25] 11,000F, 9,000 2-y-o: second foal: dam lightly-raced maiden who stayed 1¾m: modest maiden: clearly best effort on second start: should stay 1m: acts on firm going: sold 2,000 gns. *T. G. Mills*

KING O' THE MANA (IRE) 4 b.c. Turtle Island (IRE) 123 – Olivia Jane (IRE) –
(Ela-Mana-Mou 132) [2001 112: 10m5 12g4 Sep 8] sturdy, quite attractive colt: not a good mover: smart performer at 3 yrs: off 10 months before well held in Group 3 events at 4 yrs (bandaged, reportedly finished lame final outing): stays 15f: acts on soft and good to firm going. *R. Hannon*

KING PRIAM (IRE) 6 b.g. Priolo (USA) 127 – Barinia (Corvaro (USA) 124) [2001 **95 d**
100: f8.5g 8v3 10s3 10g 7.9m 8m5 8.1d 10m f12g* 8f 8.5f3 10g 10m 8.3g 10g 10d2 10.3d 10g* 8.9d 8d 10.2d2 10g2 f8g4 p10g f9.4g3 f12g3 f12g4 f12s3 Dec 21] sturdy gelding: poor mover: useful performer at best: placed in Lincoln Handicap at Doncaster (6 lengths third to Nimello) in March for second consecutive year: below that form after, including when winning claimer at Southwell in June and handicap at Redcar in October: effective at 1m to 1½m: acts on fibresand and probably any turf going: blinkered: has had tongue tied: usually held up: bled from nose sixteenth start: sometimes takes little interest early on, and not one to trust. *M. J. Polglase*

KINGSADE (IRE) 3 b.f. King's Theatre (IRE) 128 – Haiti Mill 68 (Free State 125) **66**
[2001 8.3s3 10d 11.7f5 11.7g2 12.1s Aug 21] 8,000Y: eighth foal: half-sister to 7f winner Level Up (by Beveled) and 6f (at 2 yrs)/7f winner Nigel's Lucky Girl (by Belfort): dam, maiden miler, out of sister to Petong: fair maiden: ran as though something might have been amiss final outing: likely to prove better around 1½m than shorter: acts on soft going. *B. Smart*

KING'S BALLET (USA) 3 b.c. Imperial Ballet (IRE) 110 – Multimara (USA) **94**
(Arctic Tern (USA) 126) [2001 84p: 5f 6g 5g 5.1d* 5d Oct 13] strong, lengthy colt: fairly useful handicapper: won at Chester (started slowly) in September by 2½ lengths from Xsynna: poor efforts otherwise: likely to prove best at 5f/6f: acts on soft going: has hung/wandered when successful: inconsistent: sold 6,000 gns. *P. J. Makin*

KING'S CHAMBERS 5 ch.g. Sabrehill (USA) 120 – Flower Girl 108 (Pharly (FR) **37**
130) [2001 40: 10s 12.3m4 16m 16.2s2 12m Sep 22] poor maiden handicapper: stays 2m: acts on heavy ground, seemingly on good to firm: used to wear blinkers: tongue tied nowadays: races prominently. *J. Parkes*

KINGSCLERE 4 b.g. Fairy King (USA) – Spurned (USA) 91 (Robellino (USA) 127) **84 §**
[2001 108§: 8s 10g 8.9m 10f 8m6 7.2g5 8f 7.6g* Nov 16] tall, attractive gelding: good walker: has a quick action: useful performer at best: has become disappointing: left I. Balding before winning minor event at Marseille-Vivaux in November: effective at 7.6f, probably stays 1½m: acts on any going: races freely: usually wears fulmar bridle/Australian noseband: tongue tied first 3 starts, blinkered last 2 in Britain: unreliable. *J. Rossi, France*

KING'S CREST 3 b.g. Deploy 131 – Classic Beauty (IRE) 65 (Fairy King (USA)) **83**
[2001 70: 10v5 12s3 13.3g 10.1g3 10g* 12g2 12f* 12g 14.1g Oct 6] medium-sized gelding: fairly useful handicapper: won at Brighton, Folkestone and Catterick, all in August: well beaten last 2 starts, reportedly pulling muscle in back on penultimate one: stays 1½m: acts on firm and good to soft going, below form on fibresand: usually held up: game. *S. C. Williams*

KINGSCROSS 3 ch.g. King's Signet (USA) 110 – Calamanco 71 (Clantime 101) **76 p**
[2001 63p: 6.1d 5g 5d 5g* 5d Oct 12] strong, good-bodied gelding: fair performer: won

at Newmarket in October: will prove best at 5f/6f: raced only on good going or softer: slowly away second outing: lightly raced, and should do better still. *M. Blanshard*

KINGSDON (IRE) 4 b.g. Brief Truce (USA) 126 – Richly Deserved (IRE) (Kings **74** Lake (USA) 133) [2001 98: 8v 10.1s 10.3f 10m 7m⁶ 10.1m² 8m 8d³ 8.9d 7s⁶ Oct 20] sturdy, useful-looking gelding: only fair handicapper nowadays: probably best at 1m to 10.5f: seems to act on any going: visored final 3-y-o start/last 2 at 4 yrs: usually tongue tied in 2000: has found little. *D. Nicholls*

KINGSDOWN TRIX (IRE) 7 b.g. Contract Law (USA) 108 – Three of Trumps **–** (Tyrnavos 129) [2001 f12g f16.2g f16g 18m Jul 5] seems of little account nowadays. *R. J. Smith*

KING'S ENVOY (USA) 2 b.g. (Apr 30) Royal Academy (USA) 130 – Island of **73 p** Silver (USA) 107 (Forty Niner (USA)) [2001 7m⁵ 7g 7.1g⁶ Sep 2] tall gelding: third foal: half-brother to fairly useful UAE 1m to 1½m winner Borneo Boy (by Danzig): dam winner up to 1¼m in Britain/UAE/USA: fair form in maidens, shaping better than result each time: should stay 1m: type to do better in handicaps at 3 yrs. *E. A. L. Dunlop*

KING'S IRONBRIDGE (IRE) 3 b.c. King's Theatre (IRE) 128 – Dream Chaser **114** 92 (Record Token 128) [2001 103p: 8d* 8g 7g⁶ 8m⁴ Aug 16] tall, good sort: easy mover: smart performer: won Macau Jockey Club Craven Stakes at Newmarket in April by head from Red Carpet: well below form in 2000 Guineas at Newmarket (then left R. Hannon), Lennox Stakes at Goodwood and listed event at Salisbury afterwards, on all 3 occasions finding little after racing freely up with pace: rather headstrong, and unlikely to stay beyond 1m: acts on good to firm and good to soft ground. *B. J. Meehan*

KING'S MILL (IRE) 4 b.c. Doyoun 124 – Adarika (Kings Lake (USA) 133) [2001 **96** 106: 10s 10g⁵ 12m 12m⁶ 13.9g Aug 22] rangy colt: poor walker, but good mover: useful performer: not at best at 4 yrs, though some respectable efforts, including when ninth in Ebor at York final outing: probably stays 1¾m: acts on firm and good to soft going: usually patiently ridden: sold 23,000 gns in October. *N. A. Graham*

KINGS OF EUROPE (IRE) 3 b.g. Rainbow Quest (USA) 134 – Bemissed (USA) **82 §** (Nijinsky (CAN) 138) [2001 79: 11.9f³ 14g² 14.1m⁴ 12.4m* 14g⁴ 14.1g⁵ 16.2m³ 16v Oct 4] angular, quite good-topped gelding: good mover: fairly useful performer: won maiden at Newcastle in July: stays 2m: acts on good to firm going, possibly not on heavy: blinkered/visored 4 starts before final one: carries head high, and ungenuine: sold 10,000 gns. *B. W. Hills*

KING SOLOMON (FR) 2 gr.c. (Mar 29) Simon du Desert (FR) 116 – All Square **99** (FR) (Holst (USA) 119) [2001 7d³ 7.9d² 8s* 8s* Nov 23] 160,000 francs Y: good-topped colt: second foal: dam, French 2-y-o 7f and (demoted) 1m winner: useful performer: placed in minor event at Salisbury and maiden at York: won 4-runner minor event at Maisons-Laffitte and listed race at Saint-Cloud (by 1½ lengths from Begueule) in November, making much of running both times: should stay 1¼m. *P. F. I. Cole*

KING SPINNER (IRE) 4 b.g. Mujadil (USA) 119 – Money Spinner (USA) 61 **75 §** (Teenoso (USA) 135) [2001 83: 10s 10g 9.9m 10g 12g³ 11.9g 12g f14g* f16g⁶ f14g⁵ Dec 17] lengthy gelding: poor walker/mover: fair handicapper: won at Southwell in October: stays 1¾m: acts on fibresand, raced mainly on good/good to soft going on turf: visored last 3 starts: difficult ride: inconsistent. *A. P. Jarvis*

KING'S REGARDS (IRE) 3 b.c. Machiavellian (USA) 123 – Hagwah (USA) 109 **76** (Dancing Brave (USA) 140) [2001 8d 10m⁵ 10.1f² 11.6m⁴ 10m⁴ 9.7g⁴ Aug 23] first foal: dam, winner at 1m to 1½m, half-sister to smart miler Sarafan: fair maiden handicapper: probably stays 11.6f: raced on good going or firmer after debut: visored last 2 starts, tongue tied final one: races freely: sold 14,000 gns in October, sent to Holland. *Sir Michael Stoute*

KING'S SECRET (USA) 3 ch.c. Kingmambo (USA) 125 – Mystery Rays (USA) **72 §** 122 (Nijinsky (CAN) 138) [2001 100p: 10.1g³ 9g⁴ Sep 2] useful maiden at 2 yrs: off 11 months, gave temperamental displays when favourite both outings at 3 yrs: should stay 1¼m: carries head high/finds little: sent to UAE. *Sir Michael Stoute*

KINGS SIGNAL (USA) 3 b.c. Red Ransom (USA) – Star of Albion 61 (Ajdal **76** (USA) 130) [2001 60: 10.1v 7.1m⁴ 7f³ 7m² 7d² 8f⁶ 7m⁴ 8.2m* 9f⁶ 8d 8m 8.1f Sep 18] good-topped colt: fair performer: mostly good efforts before first win in minor event at Nottingham in July: below form after: stays 1m: acts on firm and good to soft going: usually held up. *M. R. Channon*

KING'S THOUGHT 2 b.c. (May 28) King's Theatre (IRE) 128 – Lora's Guest 99 **76 P**
(Be My Guest (USA) 126) [2001 7s⁴ Oct 16] 110,000Y: good-topped colt: has scope:
closely related to smart miler Centre Stalls (by In The Wings) and half-brother to 4-y-o
Catchy Word and fairly useful 1¾m winner Nawahil (by Shirley Heights): dam, 7f
winner, sister to 1000 Guineas winner On The House: 16/1, coltish and lethargic, length
fourth of 19 to Allenby in maiden at Leicester, quickly recovering from slowish start
to race mid-field and keeping on strongly despite wandering: wore crossed noseband:
will stay at least 1m: type to improve considerably, and looks sure to win races.
E. A. L. Dunlop

KINGSTON BILL 4 b.g. Then Again 126 – Tricata (Electric 126) [2001 f11g 7m **53**
8m⁶ 11.6m³ Jun 11] lengthy, good-topped gelding: fair winner at 2 yrs: only modest form
in 2001, though would have won claimer at Windsor on final outing with clear run (later
said to have bled from nose): seems to stay 11.6f: acts on heavy ground, probably on good
to firm. *W. G. M. Turner*

KINGSTON BLUE 2 b.c. (Apr 16) Bluegrass Prince (IRE) 110 – Miss Pokey (Uncle **45**
Pokey 116) [2001 7m 8g 10.2g 8.2s Oct 30] fourth living foal: dam winning stayer on Flat
and over hurdles: poor maiden. *W. G. M. Turner*

KINGSTON GAME 2 b.c. (Apr 21) Mind Games 121 – Valmaranda (USA) (Sir Ivor **55**
135) [2001 5m 5g 6f f6g⁶ 8.2s f7g⁶ f7s⁶ Dec 18] 2,800Y: workmanlike colt: has scope:
fourth reported living foal: dam, Irish 1½m winner at 4 yrs, also successful over hurdles:
modest maiden: probably stays 7f: tried blinkered: has been mulish at stalls/slowly away:
none too consistent. *A. Berry*

KINGSTON WISH (IRE) 2 b.c. (Jan 20) Mujadil (USA) 119 – Well Wisher (USA) **69**
(Sanglamore (USA) 126) [2001 5d³ 5m 6d Jun 20] 7,500Y: leggy colt: second foal: dam
unraced from family of Known Fact, Gone West and Lion Cavern: fair maiden: best effort
when third at Newcastle: should stay 6f: sold 1,800 gns in November. *A. Berry*

KINGS TO OPEN 4 b.g. First Trump 118 – Shadiyama 58 (Nishapour (FR) 125) **53**
[2001 59: e12g f9.4g⁶ f12g⁵ 8g f9.4g² f11s¹⁴ f9.4s² Dec 27] angular, workmanlike gelding:
modest maiden: probably best at 1m/9.4f: acts on good to firm going and fibresand: tried
blinkered/tongue tied. *P. W. Hiatt*

KING'S TRAVEL (FR) 5 gr.g. Balleroy (USA) 115 – Travel Free (Be My Guest **–**
(USA) 126) [2001 10.3f⁴ May 10] tall, rather leggy gelding: useful performer in France
at 3 yrs, winning 1m newcomers event at Saint-Cloud and runner-up in 3 listed events:
sold out of J. Bernard's stable 580,000 francs after final start in 1999: unraced in 2000,
and last of 4 to Adilabad in listed race at Chester only 5-y-o Flat outing: should stay
beyond 1m: raced mainly on good ground or softer. *G. M. McCourt*

KING'S WELCOME 3 b.c. Most Welcome 131 – Reine de Thebes (FR) 67 (Darshaan **97**
133) [2001 90: 10s² 10d⁶ 10.4m² 11.9d² Jun 9] rather leggy, quite good-topped colt:
useful performer, lightly raced: good efforts in handicaps at Newmarket, York and
Haydock (1¾ lengths second to Double Honour) last 3 starts: stays 1½m: acts on heavy
and good to firm going: reliable. *C. W. Fairhurst*

KING TUT 5 ch.g. Anshan 119 – Fahrenheit 69 (Mount Hagen (FR) 127) [2001 53,
a44: 8.2v 8s May 2] big, leggy, plain gelding: modest maiden at best: well held both starts
in 2001. *J. G. Given*

KINNINO 7 b.g. Polish Precedent (USA) 131 – On Tiptoes 107 (Shareef Dancer **53**
(USA) 135) [2001 50: f8.5g⁵ e10g³ e10g* e10g³ 10.9m* 10g⁴ p10g p10g⁶ Dec 29] sturdy
gelding: modest performer: won seller at Lingfield in March and apprentice handicap at
Warwick in June: stays 11f: acts on firm going, soft and all-weather: effective blinkered
or not. *G. L. Moore*

KINSMAN (IRE) 4 b.g. Distant Relative 128 – Besito 79 (Wassl 125) [2001 72, a90+: **79**
e7g⁴ e7g⁵ e8g* e10s f8.5g⁵ 7m 7m⁶ 8.5m 8m 6m p10g p7g⁶ p7g p8g p8g Dec 28] leggy, **a92**
useful-looking gelding: fairly useful handicapper on all-weather, fair on turf: won at
Lingfield in February: effective at 7f to easy 1¼m: acts on firm going, soft and all-
weather: sometimes blinkered/visored: tried tongue tied: broke blood vessel fifth start,
said to have had breathing problem final one: has started slowly/carried head high/hung
badly right: held up. *Andrew Reid*

KIPPAX BLUES (IRE) 3 b.c. Grand Lodge (USA) 125 – Bird In Blue (IRE) 57 **–**
(Bluebird (USA) 125) [2001 9d 10.5m 7g Jun 19] 18,000Y, 17,000 2-y-o: leggy colt:
second foal: dam, maiden, sister to smart 7f/1m performer Bluegrass Prince: well beaten
in maidens: tongue tied. *J. L. Eyre*

KIRAT 3 b.g. Darshaan 133 – Kafsa (IRE) (Vayrann 133) [2001 10m May 29] 51,000Y: –
tall, leggy gelding: fourth foal: half-brother to Irish 1½m winner Count Us In (by Persian
Bold): dam, Irish 2-y-o 1m winner, half-sister to Yorkshire Oaks winner Key Change (by
Darshaan) from family of Kahyasi: 20/1 and fit but very green, slowly away and well
held in maiden at Sandown (unseated and galloped loose before start): sold 3,000 gns.
R. Charlton

KIRIKOU 3 b.g. Mtoto 134 – Nevis 61 (Connaught 130) [2001 10.2f⁶ 10g 10d⁵ 10.9f* **69 d**
10g 10.3d 12d Oct 9] small gelding: fifth foal: half-brother to 3 winners, including 1999
2-y-o 5f winner Aunt Doris (by Distant Relative) and 6f (at 2 yrs) and 1m winner
Naivasha (by Petong): dam twice-raced half-sister to very smart sprinter Paris House: fair
performer: didn't have to repeat form of his first 3 starts to win seller at Warwick (final
start for F. J. Houghton) in June: well beaten in handicaps after: should be suited by at
least 1½m: acts on firm and good to soft going. *D. J. Wintle*

KIRISNIPPA 6 b.g. Beveled (USA) – Kiri Te (Liboi (USA) 76) [2001 61: f11g f12g* –
e12g f12g⁴ f14g 14.1m f11g p12g f14.8g* Dec 11] tall gelding: fair handicapper: won at **a69**
Wolverhampton in January (final start for Derrick Morris) and (having left R. Curtis after
sixth outing) December: stays 15f: acts on fibresand, well held only turf outing in 2001:
tried blinkered/visored: sometimes slowly away. *A. P. Jones*

KIRKBY'S TREASURE 3 b.g. Mind Games 121 – Gem of Gold 52 (Jellaby 124) **75**
[2001 55: 5d⁴ 6g 6d⁴ 6m 6m⁴ 7f⁴ 7.1f⁶ 6s² 5g⁴ 6m 5m 5m² 6f² 6m² 5g² 7m² 6d* f6g Nov
3] tall, leggy gelding: has a round action: fair performer: won maiden at Catterick (started
slowly/hung markedly left) in October: effective at 5f to 7f: well beaten on heavy going,
acts on any other turf, and seemingly on fibresand: largely consistent. *A. Berry*

KIROV 2 b.f. (Mar 21) Darshaan 133 – Dance To The Top 107 (Sadler's Wells (USA) **72 p**
132) [2001 8m Sep 22] leggy, quite good-topped filly: fourth foal: half-sister to 3-y-o
Dress Rehearsal, fairly useful 1¼m winner Audition (by Machiavellian) and useful
French 1m to 10.5f winner Cheshire (by Warning): dam, 2-y-o 7f winner (second in
Fillies' Mile) who stayed 10.4f, from good family: 20/1 and backward, never dangerous
and not unduly knocked about when eighth of 12 to Revealing in maiden at Newmarket:
will be suited by 1¼m/1½m: sure to improve. *Sir Michael Stoute*

KIROVSKI (IRE) 4 b.g. Common Grounds 118 – Nordic Doll (IRE) 71 (Royal **91**
Academy (USA) 130) [2001 97: 8v 8m 8m 8m 9g 10f² 9g 8d⁶ Nov 3] tall, quite attractive
gelding: fairly useful handicapper: some creditable efforts in 2001: effective at 1m/1¼m:
acts on firm and soft going: usually races prominently. *P. W. Harris*

KIRTLE 2 b.f. (Jan 16) Hector Protector (USA) 124 – Kyle Rhea 104 (In The Wings **81 p**
128) [2001 7m⁶ 7d³ Oct 6] rather leggy filly: first foal: dam, 1¼m/11.4f winner, half-
sister to smart performer up to 1¾m Applecross, herself dam of 7-y-o Invermark and very
smart winner up to 1¾m Craigsteel: better effort in maidens (fairly useful form) when
third to Atarama at Redcar, keeping on well without being given hard time: should stay at
least 1¼m: capable of better. *J. R. Fanshawe*

KIRUNA 3 b.f. Northern Park (USA) 107 – Kiliniski 119 (Niniski (USA) 125) [2001 **68**
58: 12d 10g⁵ 12g 13d⁴ f16g⁴ Nov 12] half-sister to 1½m winner Kilshanny (by Groom **a71**
Dancer) and winner in Belgium by Green Desert: dam, 1½m winner, out of half-sister to
Nureyev and dam of Sadler's Wells: fair maiden: should stay 1¾m: acts on good to soft
ground (ran at Southwell final outing) fibresand: blinkered final 2-y-o start: none too
consistent: joined R. Guest. *J. S. Bolger, Ireland*

KISMET 3 b.f. Tirol 127 – Belamcanda (Belmez (USA) 131) [2001 7g⁶ 8f⁶ 8d Oct 8] –
1,200Y: first foal: dam unraced out of useful 6f (at 2 yrs) winner who stayed 1½m
Neenah, herself half-sister to Irish Oaks winner Swiftfoot: well held in maidens. *Don
Enrico Incisa*

KISS CURL 3 ch.f. Beveled (USA) – Laquette (Bairn (USA) 126) [2001 –: 8d 7m 10g –
11.9m Aug 29] of little account. *M. Madgwick*

KISSED BY MOONLITE 5 gr.m. Petong 126 – Rose Bouquet 78 (General –
Assembly (USA)) [2001 –: f6g f7g 14.1g Jun 16] no form in 2001. *R. Hollinshead*

KISSING TIME 4 b.f. Lugana Beach 116 – Princess Athena 119 (Ahonoora 122) **67 d**
[2001 75: 5m⁵ 5m⁵ 5f 8.3g 8.3m⁵ 8.2s 5m³ 5.3m² 5.1g 5m⁶ f5g p7g f5g Nov 30] tall filly:
fair performer, on downgrade: left P. Cole 17,000 gns after eleventh start: best at 5f/6f:
acts on good to firm and good to soft going: tried blinkered/visored. *M. R. Channon*

KITCHENER (USA) 3 br.g. Lord At War (ARG) – Visiting Bee (USA) (Drone **65**
(USA)) [2001 11.9g³ 11.5g 12m 16v f16g f14g Nov 26] $52,000Y: lengthy, rather

sparely-made gelding: fifth foal: brother to 3 winners up to 9f in USA: dam 8.5f winner in USA: fair maiden: stays 1½m: acts on good to firm going and fibresand: has run in snatches. *P. W. Harris*

KITE MARK 3 ch.f. Mark of Esteem (IRE) 137 – Shadywood 96 (Habitat 134) [2001 **58** 9.9s⁶ May 17] half-sister to several winners, including very smart 9f to 14.6f (Park Hill Stakes) winner Madame Dubois (by Legend of France) and fairly useful 1991 2-y-o 6f winner Sun And Shade (by Ajdal): dam 1¼m winner from good family: 7/2, modest form in maiden at Salisbury on only outing: sold 55,000 gns in December. *H. R. A. Cecil*

KITTY BANKES 3 b.f. Forzando 122 – St Kitts 43 (Tragic Role (USA)) [2001 –: **—** 11m f9.4g Aug 18] no sign of ability in 3 starts, including in sellers. *W. G. M. Turner*

KITTYLEE 2 b.f. (May 29) Bal Harbour 113 – Courtesy Call (Northfields (USA)) **—** [2001 5.1s f8s Dec 21] half-sister to several winners, including 1¼m winner Royal Passion (by Ahonoora), herself dam of 8-y-o Tadeo and 3-y-o Attache: dam, maiden, should have stayed 1½m: always behind in maidens. *R. M. Whitaker*

KIVOTOS (USA) 3 gr.g. Trempolino (USA) 135 – Authorized Staff (USA) **—** (Relaunch (USA)) [2001 63: 8.2v⁶ 10s 8m May 19] leggy, close-coupled gelding: modest maiden at 2 yrs: little form in 2001. *Mrs J. R. Ramsden*

KNAVE'S ASH (USA) 10 ch.g. Miswaki (USA) 124 – Quiet Rendezvous (USA) **—** (Nureyev (USA) 131) [2001 49: 8.3m Jun 14] probably of little account nowadays. *M. Todhunter*

KNAVESMIRE DREAM 2 b.g. (Mar 5) Mujadil (USA) 119 – Dreams Are Free **56** (IRE) 71 (Caerleon (USA) 132) [2001 5m 7.1f⁶ 7d⁴ 7d 7g 8m⁶ 7g f8.5g Nov 3] 16,000Y: fifth foal: half-brother to 3 winners, including 4-y-o Bogus Dreams and 5-y-o Live To Tell: dam 1¼m winner: modest maiden: barely stayed 1m: acted on good to soft and firm going: blinkered last 3 starts: dead. *M. Johnston*

KNAVESMIRE OMEN 2 b.g. (Apr 24) Robellino (USA) 127 – Signs 91 (Risk Me **73** (FR) 127) [2001 6g⁶ 7f⁵ 7g² 7.6m³ 7.2g³ 7g 6d 7d³ f8g⁵ Nov 16] 20,000Y: sturdy gelding: third foal: half-brother to a 7.5f winner in Germany by Alzao: dam 2-y-o 5f winner who stayed 7f: fair maiden: placed in various races, including seller: should stay 1m: acts on firm and good to soft ground: blinkered (looked none too enthusiastic) sixth start: gelded after final one. *M. Johnston*

KNIGHT CROSSING (IRE) 3 b.g. Doyoun 124 – Princess Sarara (USA) (Trem- **57** polino (USA) 135) [2001 50: f7g 9m 10.1m 8m³ 7m Sep 22] close-coupled gelding: modest maiden: stays 1¼m: acts on soft and good to firm going. *Mrs A. Duffield*

KNIGHTED 5 b.g. Bigstone (IRE) 126 – Missed Again 84 (High Top 131) [2001 18v* **77** 16v 16s⁵ 16m 16.5s Nov 10] leggy gelding: has a markedly round action: fair handicapper on Flat, lightly raced: won at Doncaster in March: creditable effort after only when fifth: stays 2¼m well: best efforts on ground softer than good, and acts well on heavy. *T. D. Easterby*

KNIGHT OF SILVER 4 gr.g. Presidium 124 – Misty Rocket 75 (Roan Rocket 128) **—** [2001 e10g Mar 31] modest maiden in 1999: no show only Flat outing since. *S. Mellor*

KNIGHT'S EMPEROR (IRE) 4 b.g. Grand Lodge (USA) 125 – So Kind 90 (Kind **65** of Hush 118) [2001 70: 7g 8d² 8m² 7.5m⁶ 8.3g 8.2g 9.9m Aug 15] rangy, good sort: fair maiden handicapper: stays 1m: acts on good to soft and good to firm going: blinkered once: winning novice hurdler. *J. L. Spearing*

KNOCKDOO (IRE) 8 ch.g. Be My Native (USA) 122 – Ashken (Artaius (USA) **55** 129) [2001 49: 17.1s² 21.6s² Apr 23] modest handicapper: sold from F. Flood in Ireland 20,000 gns after final 7-y-o start: second at Pontefract both outings at 8 yrs, in visor on second occasion: stays 2¾m: raced mainly on good going or softer, and acts on heavy. *Jonjo O'Neill*

KNOCKEMBACK NELLIE 5 b.m. Forzando 122 – Sea Clover (IRE) 77 (Ela- **65** Mana-Mou 132) [2001 70d: 5v 5m⁵ 5g³ 5.3f* 5m 5m² 5m 5f⁵ 5g² 5.3g⁵ 5m Sep 26] smallish mare: fair handicapper: won at Brighton in June: effective at 5f/6f: acts on firm going, soft and equitrack: blinkered: has had tongue tied: often leads: sold 1,700 gns in October. *P. W. Harris*

KNOCKHOLT 5 b.g. Be My Chief (USA) 122 – Saffron Crocus 83 (Shareef Dancer **96** (USA) 135) [2001 102: 16g 14m 16.2g⁴ 14m² 13.3m Jul 21] rather unfurnished, useful-looking gelding: fluent mover: useful handicapper: creditable efforts second to fourth starts only: stays 2m: acts on firm going, well beaten only start on ground softer than good: visored second and last 2 starts: often makes running: none too consistent. *S. P. C. Woods*

KNOCK (IRE) 3 b.c. Mujadil (USA) 119 – Beechwood (USA) (Blushing Groom (FR) 131) [2001 78: e6g⁵ 7s³ 6.1f 6g 7m* 7g 7f⁴ 8.5m⁶ 7d Aug 26] compact colt: fair performer: won minor event at Goodwood in June: good fourth in handicap at Kempton on seventh start: probably best around 7f: acts on soft going, good to firm and all-weather: has run creditably when sweating/edgy: inconsistent: sold 10,000 gns in October. *R. Hannon* — **77 §**

KNOCKTOPHER ABBEY 4 ch.g. Pursuit of Love 124 – Kukri (Kris 135) [2001 83: 8.1m 7.6f² 7.6m³ 8f⁶ 8m 8m² 8.1g⁶ 7.6g⁶ 8s p10g* p12g Dec 19] angular, plain gelding: fairly useful handicapper: won at Lingfield in December: stays easy 1½m: acts on polytrack, firm and good to soft ground: none too consistent. *B. R. Millman* — **82**

KNOTTY ASH GIRL (IRE) 2 ch.f. (Feb 15) Ashkalani (IRE) 128 – Camisha (IRE) 82 (Shernazar 131) [2001 6d⁴ 6.1g³ 7.1s³ 10v² Oct 4] IR 19,000F, 4,800 2-y-o: leggy, close-coupled filly: half-sister to Irish winners around 1½m Tacobarry (by Northern Baby) and Berkeley Bay (by Fit To Fight): dam Irish 11f/1½m winner: fair maiden: second in nursery at Nottingham: will stay at least 1½m: acts on heavy going. *B. A. McMahon* — **76**

KNOTTY HILL 9 b.g. Green Ruby (USA) 104 – Esilam 62 (Frimley Park 109) [2001 –: f8g f7g f6g 6g 8.3s 6m⁶ Aug 25] tall, workmanlike gelding: little form in 2001. *R. Craggs* — **–**

KNOWN MANEUVER (USA) 3 b.g. Known Fact (USA) 135 – Northern Maneuver 73 (USA) (Al Nasr (FR) 126) [2001 f6g* 6m 12m⁵ 8.9m 11m³ Sep 26] $65,000F, IR 70,000Y: smallish gelding: sixth foal: half-brother to 2 sprint winners in USA by Phone Trick: dam, sprint winner in USA, half-sister to US Grade 1 2-y-o 1m winner Proud Lou (dam of smart French miler Houseproud): fair performer: won maiden at Southwell in June: creditable effort only in handicaps third and final outings: gelded after: stays 1½m: acts on fibresand, raced only on good to firm ground on turf. *P. F. I. Cole*

KOINCIDENTAL (IRE) 4 b.f. Mtoto 134 – Floris (Master Willie 129) [2001 53: 14d Apr 12] modest maiden at best: well held only 4-y-o Flat outing. *C. Grant* — **–**

KOKOPELLI STAR 2 b.f. (Mar 12) Hernando (FR) 127 – Celebrity 101 (Troy 137) [2001 8d Oct 25] half-sister to 3 winners, including 9.7f to 2m winner Stompin (by Alzao): dam 1¼m winner: always behind in maiden at Bath. *B. Smart* — **–**

KOLLEGIO (IRE) 2 b.g. (Feb 25) College Chapel 122 – Steal 'em 66 (Efisio 120) [2001 6g 5m 5.1m 7s Oct 5] IR 6,500F, 7,000Y: first foal: dam, fair winner, half-sister to smart sprinter Perryston View: little form in maidens/nursery. *P. W. Harris* — **–**

KOMALUNA 3 ch.g. Komaite (USA) – Sugar Token 66 (Record Token 128) [2001 –: f5g⁴ f6g⁶ 7.1g 6m³ f6s Dec 15] lengthy gelding: poor maiden: may prove best around 6f: acts on fibresand and good to firm ground: reportedly suffered breathing problem third 2-y-o start, tongue tied next one. *D. Shaw* — **41**

KOMASEPH 9 b.g. Komaite (USA) – Starkist 81 (So Blessed 130) [2001 –§, a40§: f8g f6s⁴ f6s f6g⁶ f7g f6f Mar 19] workmanlike gelding: poor performer: best at 6f/7f: acts on good to firm going and fibresand: tried blinkered/visored: sometimes tongue tied: inconsistent. *R. F. Marvin* — **– §** / **a35 §**

KOMEDERA 2 b.g. (Mar 28) Danzig Connection (USA) – Musica 82 (Primo Dominie 56 121) [2001 6g² 5d⁶ 5m⁶ 5f Sep 20] 8,500Y: second foal: half-brother to 4-y-o Coco de Mer: dam 5f winner, including at 2 yrs: modest maiden: best effort when second at Newcastle: may prove best at 5f/6f. *A. Berry* — **56**

KOMENA 3 b.f. Komaite (USA) – Mena 58 (Blakeney 126) [2001 84: 7m 7d 7d Nov 3] tall, lengthy filly: fairly useful winner at 2 yrs: well held in 2001: has been edgy/reluctant stalls/raced too freely: temperament under suspicion. *J. W. Payne* — **–**

KOMPLIMENT 3 ch.g. Komaite (USA) – Eladale (IRE) (Ela-Mana-Mou 132) [2001 71 79: 6f 6m 5.1m Jul 5] big, lengthy, workmanlike gelding: fair performer: may prove best at 5f/6f: acts on good to firm going. *Mrs H. Dalton* — **71**

KONICA 2 b.f. (May 23) Desert King (IRE) 129 – Haboobti (Habitat 134) [2001 6.1m⁶ 57 5s 6.1v⁶ Oct 4] 16,000Y: good-bodied filly: eighth foal: half-sister to 3 winners, including 1996 2-y-o 6f/7f winner Boojum (by Mujtahid) and 7f/1m winner Abeyr (by Unfuwain), both useful: dam lightly-raced daughter of sister to high-class miler Noalcoholic: best effort in maidens (modest form) when sixth to Foursome at Nottingham on final start: should stay 1m. *P. S. Felgate*

KONKER 6 ch.g. Selkirk (USA) 129 – Helens Dreamgirl 95 (Caerleon (USA) 132) **76**
[2001 66: 10v³ 12d* 10.1v* 10d⁴ Oct 30] unfurnished gelding: fair handicapper on Flat, lightly raced: won at Pontefract (apprentice race after 6-month break) and Newcastle (after slow start) in October: stays 1½m: acts on heavy going, probably on good to firm: usually held up. *Mrs M. Reveley*

KOOL (IRE) 2 b.c. (Feb 5) Danehill Dancer (IRE) 117 – New Rochelle (IRE) 65 **87**
(Lafontaine (USA) 117) [2001 5.2d⁶ 5.1g² 5m² 5m² 5g* 6d² 6g Oct 6] IR 11,000F, 72,000Y: well-made colt: third foal: half-brother to 4-y-o Tower of Song: dam, Irish 1¾m winner at 5 yrs, sister to smart 1½m to 2m performer Shambo: fairly useful performer: won maiden at Pontefract in August: good ½-length second of 22 to Advance Party in sales race at Doncaster penultimate start: free-going sort, not sure to stay 7f. *P. F. I. Cole*

KOORI 3 b.f. Komaite (USA) – Unadorned (Never So Bold 135) [2001 –: e6g Jan 13] **–**
always behind both starts in maidens. *B. A. Pearce*

KOOTENAY (IRE) 2 ch.f. (Mar 10) Selkirk (USA) 129 – Llia 94 (Shirley Heights **100**
130) [2001 7m⁴ 7g* 7d³ 7.5s* 8d² Oct 14] rather unfurnished filly: third foal: half-sister to 4-y-o Dilsaa: dam, 2-y-o 7f winner who stayed 1½m, out of smart performer up to 9f Llyn Gwynant: useful performer: won maiden at Goodwood in August and listed race at Milan (by 5 lengths from Torrigiana) in September: placed in Prestige Stakes at Goodwood (below form behind Gossamer) and Premio Dormello at Milan (2¼ lengths second to Kazzia): will stay at least 1¼m: acts on soft ground: front runner. *J. L. Dunlop*

KOSEVO (IRE) 7 b.g. Shareef Dancer (USA) 135 – Kallista (Zeddaan 130) [2001 49, **–**
a56: f6g e6g² e5g f6s f5g f6g f5g f5g⁶ f5g 7m 5m 6m 5s 6m Aug 25] good-topped **a51 d**
gelding: modest handicapper: below form after second start, leaving D. Shaw after twelfth outing: stays 7f: acts on firm going, soft and fibresand/equitrack: wears visor/ blinkers. *J. Balding*

KOSMIC LADY 4 b.f. Cosmonaut – Ktolo 80 (Tolomeo 127) [2001 55, a49: f8g 7s* **55**
8.1g² 10g 10v 8.1m² 7s 7d f8g Nov 19] strong, lengthy filly: poor walker: modest **a–**
performer: won seller at Brighton in April: stays 1m: acts on soft and good to firm going: tried blinkered/tongue tied: has been edgy/carried head high. *P. W. Hiatt*

KOTORI (IRE) 2 gr.g. (Mar 22) Charnwood Forest (IRE) 125 – La Kermesse (USA) **–**
58 (Storm Bird (CAN) 134) [2001 5s 5.1s 5.7g Oct 1] 12,000F, IR 16,500Y: fifth reported foal: half-brother to French 10.5f winner Kermor (by Suave Dancer) and French 11f/1½m winner La Kempa (by Saumarez): dam 7f winner: little form in maidens. *M. S. Saunders*

KOURNAKOVA (IRE) 2 b.f. (Mar 16) Sadler's Wells (USA) 132 – Bermuda Classic **102 p**
98 (Double Form 130) [2001 7m 8s³ 8s* Oct 17] strong filly: half-sister to 3 winners, including very smart French miler Shake The Yoke (by Caerleon) and very smart sprinter Tropical (by Green Desert): dam, Irish 2-y-o 5f/6f winner, half-sister to dam of 4-y-o Kutub: useful form when 3¼ lengths third to Sulk in Prix Marcel Boussac at Longchamp, staying on strongly: landed odds in 18-runner maiden at Navan by 4½ lengths from Ciara's Delight: likely to stay 1¼m: capable of better. *A. P. O'Brien, Ireland*

KRATO (USA) 5 b.h. Theatrical 128 – Claxton's Slew (USA) 100 (Seattle Slew **?**
(USA)) [2001 6s 5m 5m 8m 8m⁶ 7.9m⁶ 9.9s 8m Aug 27] sturdy horse: sixth foal: brother to 2 winners, notably smart Irish performer up to 1¾m Humbel, and half-brother to 2 winners, notably Breeders' Cup Distaff winner Escena (by Strawberry Road): dam Irish 7f to 9f winner: fairly useful performer at best: won 3 times from 12 starts in USA for W. Mott, including allowance races at Gulfstream and Belmont in 2000: mostly well beaten in Britain, pulling hard in blinkers final outing: probably best around 1m: acts on firm going: sold 2,000 gns. *T. D. Easterby*

KRISKOVA (USA) 2 b.c. (Apr 3) Kris S (USA) – Tereshkova (USA) 113 (Mr Pros- **102 p**
pector (USA)) [2001 7.1m* 8g³ Sep 19] useful-looking colt: second foal: half-brother to French 1½m winner Russian Range (by St Jovite): dam, 6f (at 2 yrs in France) to 1m (in UAE) winner, sister to Middle Park winner and 2000 Guineas runner-up Lycius: long odds on, won 4-runner minor event at Sandown in July by ½ length from Titchfield: useful form when 2¼ lengths third of 6 to Henri Lebasque in listed event at Goodwood, quickening to lead over 2f out but no extra final 1f: may prove best at 7f/1m: should improve further and win more races. *D. R. Loder*

KRISTENSEN 2 ch.g. (Feb 12) Kris (USA) – Papaha (FR) 103 (Green Desert **71**
(USA) 127) [2001 6g³ 5m³ 5g 6m³ 7g 7m⁵ Sep 22] 47,000Y: good-bodied gelding: has scope: first foal: dam, 8.5f winner, out of half-sister to Old Vic: fair maiden: shaped well

under patient rides more often than not: should prove best at 7f/1m: raced only on good/ good to firm ground: edgy third/fourth starts. *Mrs J. R. Ramsden*

KRISTINEAU 3 ch.f. Cadeaux Genereux 131 – Kantikoy (Alzao (USA) 117) [2001 **57** –p: 7v[5] 8.2s[2] 8.1v 8.2g 10m 9.9s Sep 25] lengthy, good-topped filly: modest maiden handicapper: ran poorly last 4 starts, off over 2 months before final one: should prove suited by 1¼m/1½m: raced mainly on soft/heavy going: sold 5,500 gns. *C. F. Wall*

KROISOS (IRE) 3 b.g. Kris 135 – Lydia Maria 70 (Dancing Brave (USA) 140) [2001 **50** 11.8m 12m 12f[5] 16.2m f12g[2] 14.1s f14g Dec 14] fifth foal: half-brother to 3 winners, including useful 6f (at 2 yrs) and 10.4f winner Premier Bay (by Primo Dominie) and 7f (at 2 yrs) and 1¾m winner Taufan Boy (by Taufan): dam maiden who stayed 1¼m: form (modest) only when short-headed in maiden handicap at Wolverhampton: left *P. Harris* and off over 3 months before final start: stays 1½m: acts on fibresand. *R. Curtis*

KRUGERRAND (USA) 2 ch.c. (Mar 15) Gulch (USA) – Nasers Pride (USA) (Al **94** Nasr (FR) 126) [2001 6m[3] 6d[2] 7.1m* Sep 17] $190,000Y: deep girthed, attractive colt: has scope: fifth living foal: closely related to winner in USA by Woodman and half-brother to 8.5f winner there by Rahy: dam, US 2-y-o 1m (including minor stakes) winner, second in Grade 1 1m event: fairly useful form: short-priced favourite all starts: best effort when head second to Asheer in maiden at Lingfield: tongue tied, travelled strongly long way but only scrambled home in similar event at Warwick: likely to prove best up to 7f. *M. L. W. Bell*

KRYSTAL MAX (IRE) 8 b.g. Classic Music (USA) – Lake Isle (IRE) (Caerleon **72** (USA) 132) [2001 –, a79: e6g[6] e5g[2] e6g[3] f5s e5g[4] e7s[3] e6g* e5g[6] e6g f6g 5.3m[6] 6m **a79** 6m 5.1g[2] 5.7m[3] 7g[6] 5g 6g 5.7d p7g p7g Dec 28] smallish, good-topped gelding: fair handicapper: won at Lingfield in February: effective at 5f to easy 7f: acts on fibresand/ equitrack, firm and good to soft ground: blinkered once at 2 yrs. *P. S. McEntee*

KULACHI (IRE) 2 b.c. (Feb 24) Royal Applause 124 – Silly View (IRE) 75 (Scenic **96** 128) [2001 6m* 5m[4] 6m* 6g 6f Sep 21] 26,000F, 110,000Y: tall, rather leggy colt: has a fluent, round action: second foal: half-brother to a 6f (at 2 yrs) to 11.5f winner in Scand-inavia by Mujtahid: dam, Irish 9f winner at 4 yrs, half-sister to dam of Racing Post Trophy winner Seattle Rhyme: useful performer: won maiden at Goodwood in June and listed race at Newbury (by neck from Approval) in July: below form in Gimcrack Stakes at York and Mill Reef Stakes at Newbury (hung left) last 2 starts: bred to stay 7f: raced only on good going or firmer. *M. R. Channon*

KUMAKAWA 3 ch.g. Dancing Spree (USA) – Maria Cappuccini 70 (Siberian Express **– §** (USA) 125) [2001 86: e8g[3] f7g[2] f9.4g[4] 10.3s 10d 8m 7.1g 8f f7g[2] f8g f8g f8.5g[5] f7g f8g **a86 d** f8g f7g f12f Dec 5] tall gelding: fairly useful performer at best: well below form in second half of year: stays easy 9.4f: acts on soft going, good to firm and fibresand: tried visored/blinkered: has looked difficult ride/been edgy and reluctant at stalls: not one to trust implicitly. *M. J. Polglase*

KUMON EILEEN 5 ch.m. Anshan 119 – Katie Eileen (USA) 49 (Bering 136) [2001 **–** –: e13g Feb 7] no form: tried visored. *J. R. Jenkins*

KUNDALILA 3 b.f. River Falls 113 – Kalou 71 (K-Battery 108) [2001 53: 8m 8.3m **–** 8f 8.3d[5] 7s Jul 24] modest maiden at 2 yrs: well held in 2001. *A. C. Whillans*

KUNDOOZ 2 b.c. (Feb 9) Sabrehill (USA) 120 – Reem Albaraari 81 (Sadler's Wells **97** (USA) 132) [2001 7m[5] 7g[4] 7.6d[2] Sep 26] sturdy, well-made colt: sixth foal: half-brother to 3-y-o Morshdi: dam, maiden who stayed 9f, out of top-class sprinter Habibti: useful form: won minor event at Doncaster in July: in frame in similar 5-runner races at New-market and Chester (neck second to Lascombes, leading 2f out until near line): should stay 1m. *M. A. Jarvis*

KUROFUNE (USA) 3 gr.c. French Deputy (USA) 118 – Blue Avenue (USA) (Classic **118** Go Go (USA)) [2001 10f* 8f* 12d[5] 10f[3] a8g* a10.5g* Nov 24] $70,000Y, $430,000 **a130** 2-y-o: third foal: closely related to a winner in USA by Silver Deputy: dam, 1m minor stakes winner in USA, half-sister to US Grade 1 8.5f/9f winner Brought To Mind: top-class performer: won twice at 2 yrs: successful in 2001 in Group 3 at Hanshin in March, NHK Mile Cup at Tokyo (by ½ length from Grass Eiko O) in June, another Group 3 at Tokyo (by 9 lengths from Eagle Cafe) in October and 16-runner Japan Cup Dirt (by 7 lengths from previous year's winner Wing Arrow) in November: stayed 10.5f (fifth in Japanese Derby at 1½m): acted on firm ground, clearly went well on dirt: looked capable of making his mark in top company outside Japan, but reportedly suffered tendon injury and to stand at Shadai Stallion Station, fee 5m yen. *K. Matsuda, Japan*

KUSTER 5 b.h. Indian Ridge 123 – Ustka 60 (Lomond (USA) 128) [2001 92: a10f⁵ **95**
a12f⁶ 8.5m 10f⁶ 12g⁴ 9.9m* 13.9g 9g Oct 6] good-bodied horse: unimpressive mover:
useful handicapper: won Bet Direct Summer Stakes at Goodwood in July by 1¼ lengths
from Parisien Star: no luck in running in Cambridgeshire at Newmarket final start:
best at 1¼m/1½m: acts on firm and soft going: blinkered last 3 starts: sent to UAE.
L. M. Cumani

KUSTOM KIT KEVIN 5 b.g. Local Suitor (USA) 128 – Sweet Revival 41 (Claude **–**
Monet (USA) 128) [2001 48, a62: 7m 8f Jul 22] tall gelding: modest performer at 4 yrs:
well beaten both 5-y-o outings: blinkered once: has had tongue tied. *S. R. Bowring*

KUT O ISLAND (USA) 3 br.g. Woodman (USA) 126 – Cherry Jubilee (USA) **59**
(Coastal (USA)) [2001 –p: f8f⁵ Mar 19] modest form only 3-y-o outing (slowly away):
tongue tied last 2 starts: gelded and sold 2,200 gns in November. *G. A. Butler*

KUTUB (IRE) 4 b.c. In The Wings 128 – Minnie Habit (Habitat 134) [2001 116: **123**
12g⁴ 12g 10m² 10s* 12v* 12s* 11g* Nov 10]
Not many races can have had a greater bearing on so many big events
worldwide during the rest of the season, or, in hindsight, drawn a field with quite so
much strength in depth, as the Dubai Sheema Classic at Nad Al Sheba in March.
Behind the subsequent Hong Kong Vase winner Stay Gold came runner-up Fan-
tastic Light, who went on to win three Group 1 races in Europe and the Breeders'
Cup Turf; third-placed Silvano took the Queen Elizabeth II Cup in Hong Kong
and the Arlington Million; fourth-placed Endless Hall won the Singapore Airlines
International Cup next time out; and fifth came future Melbourne Cup runner-up
Give The Slip. Eighth-placed Mutafaweq won the Coronation Cup on his return to
Britain, while Island House (ninth) also made a successful return to Britain in the
Gordon Richards Stakes. Back in twelfth came the 40/1 outsider of the sixteen-
runner field Kutub, whose record hardly paled in comparison by the end of the year,
by which time he had won three Group 1 events in Europe and a very valuable event
in the Far East, netting more than half a million pounds in win prize money in the
process.
Kutub's achievements were overshadowed by his top-class stable-
companions Sakhee and Fantastic Light, but even fourth-best (Ekraar is also rated
above him) among the older middle-distance performers in the Godolphin stable
equates to being more than a match for most of the best performers that Germany
and Italy have to offer. Kutub met nothing like the strength of opposition he faced
in Dubai in his remaining races. That said, he was beaten into second by the very
smart German colt Paolini on his next outing in the Premio Presidente della
Repubblica at Rome, going down by a length and a half, but he then turned the
tables on him under much softer conditions in the Grosser Dallmayr-Preis (Bay-
erisches Zuchtrennen) at Munich in August. Paolini was only third this time,
and in a field that otherwise consisted of German three-year-olds, it was Deutsches
Derby also-ran Krombacher who fared best of Kutub's rivals, although beaten
comprehensively by four lengths.
A heavy 'home defeat' in Munich had also occurred on the football field by
the time Kutub returned to Germany in September for the Deutsche Post Euro
Express Preis von Europa at Cologne. His rivals this time included not only the
German Derby winner Boreal, but the Russian and Polish Derby winners
respectively, Bor and Kombinacja. Kutub's biggest rival came from closer to home,
however, in the form of the previous year's runner-up Yavana's Pace, but after
leading two furlongs out Kutub ran on well for a comfortable win, the margin of
victory officially four lengths again. Kutub's task had been made much easier by
the heavy fall taken by Boreal as the field bunched on the first turn. Boreal escaped
with concussion and a lost tooth, and while jockey John Reid was also able to walk
away relatively unscathed, the fall prompted Reid to call a halt to his long and
distinguished career in the saddle. Reid, who was awarded the MBE in 1997, won
four British classics, notably the 1992 Derby on Dr Devious, during a particularly
successful partnership with the Peter Chapple-Hyam stable. He also won the King
George VI and Queen Elizabeth Diamond Stakes on Ile de Bourbon in 1978 and
Swain in 1997, and the Prix de l'Arc de Triomphe on Tony Bin in 1988.

Kutub's two wins in Germany had seen him put up the best performances of his career to date, but the field of seven that contested the Gran Premio del Jockey Club at Milan in October was a weak one and he did not need to be anywhere near his best to make all and land the odds by two and a half lengths from one of four German horses in the line-up, Monos. Two of the others, Noroit (third at Cologne) and Passimo, looked to be his main rivals beforehand but both ran poorly. Kutub's final outing of the year came in the very valuable New Zealand Bloodstock Singapore Gold Cup at Kranji in November, a handicap worth more than £250,000 to the winner. Kutub carried joint-top weight in the sixteen-runner field, but seeing that he carried the same weight as the other European runner, With The Flow, whose recent efforts were about a stone below Kutub's best form, he looked well treated. Ridden more patiently than at Milan, Kutub landed the odds by three lengths from one of the local runners, Saddle Up, with the leading Singapore performer Bocelli, who had contested the Queen Elizabeth II Stakes at Ascot, in third. Kutub has yet to race in Britain, though he is reportedly to be campaigned here for at least some of 2002. As a three-year-old he held a prominent position in betting on the Derby after winning the Prix Noailles impressively, but ended up contesting the Prix du Jockey Club instead, finishing fourth behind Holding Court, one of several creditable efforts that season for Freddie Head.

Kutub went through the sale-ring twice, fetching 130,000 guineas as a foal at Newmarket and then 220,000 guineas at the Houghton Sales, making him easily the most expensive In The Wings yearling of 1998. His dam Minnie Habit had produced two winners by then, Child Prodigy (by Ballad Rock), who won over six furlongs at two and over a mile in the States at three, and the Irish mile-and-three-quarter winner Blue Bit (by Bluebird), who has also won over hurdles. Kutub has a close relative by Sadler's Wells in the two-year-old filly On The Nile, who has made a promising start for Aidan O'Brien, winning a nine-furlong listed race at Leopardstown. Their dam got off the mark as a four-year-old in a Tipperary maiden over nine furlongs. Her half-sister Bermuda Classic was a useful sprinter/miler in Ireland whose two wins came in Group 3 company as a two-year-old in the Railway Stakes and the Curragh Stakes. She has already bred two fillies of a very similar standard to Kutub: Irish sprinter Tropical and the French-trained Coronation Stakes

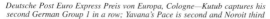

Deutsche Post Euro Express Preis von Europa, Cologne—Kutub captures his second German Group 1 in a row; Yavana's Pace is second and Noroit third

Godolphin's "Kutub"

winner Shake The Yoke. Like her half-sister, Bermuda Classic was also represented by a useful Aidan O'Brien-trained daughter of Sadler's Wells in the latest season, Kournakova, who was third in the Prix Marcel Boussac. Grandam Minnie Tudor won over six furlongs (at two) and a mile in Ireland, and was out of a lightly-raced half-sister to the Lingfield Oaks Trial winner Javata and the Fred Darling winner Rotisserie.

Kutub (IRE) (b.c. 1997)	In The Wings (b 1986)	Sadler's Wells (b 1981)	Northern Dancer / Fairy Bridge
		High Hawk (b 1980)	Shirley Heights / Sunbittern
	Minnie Habit (b or br 1987)	Habitat (b 1966)	Sir Gaylord / Little Hut
		Minnie Tudor (b 1976)	Tudor Melody / Tiny Toque

Kutub is a compact, attractive colt. He stays a mile and a half, and while the pick of his form is on good ground or softer (he acts on heavy), he has run several sound races on good to firm. Indeed, Kutub has shown a consistent level of form throughout his career, finishing out of the frame for the only time in that ultra-competitive Dubai Sheema Classic, though there was no disgrace in that. Kutub has tended to race lazily and was tried in blinkers in the Prix du Jockey Club as a three-year-old. He was visored for all his starts in the latest season, except for his reappearance when fourth to Give The Slip at Nad Al Sheba in the Group 3 Dubai City of Gold. *Saeed bin Suroor*

544

KUUIPO 4 b.f. Puissance 110 – Yankee Special 60 (Bold Lad (IRE) 133) [2001 48: f11g f9.4s⁴ f8g f9.4g 10s⁵ 8s² 9s² 10m 8.2f 8m Jun 22] quite good-topped filly: poor maiden handicapper: effective at 1m to 1¼m: acts on soft and good to firm going: visored once: often tongue tied. *B. S. Rothwell* **48 a35**

KUWAIT DAWN (IRE) 5 b.m. Pips Pride 117 – Red Note (Rusticaro (FR) 124) [2001 75: f7g⁶ f7g⁴ f8g 10v 8f 8g Jun 19] big, lengthy mare: poor mover: fair performer, on downgrade: stays 1m: acts on good to firm going, good to soft and fibresand: tried visored: often sweating/edgy: sold 5,000 gns in September. *D. Nicholls* **71 d**

KUWAIT FLAVOUR (IRE) 5 b.g. Bluebird (USA) 125 – Plume Magique (Kenmare (FR) 125) [2001 67: f9.4g 10.9m 7m f8g p6g Dec 19] small, stocky gelding: fair maiden at 4 yrs: well held in 2001: visored final start. *G. Prodromou* **–**

KUWAIT MILLENNIUM 4 b.g. Salse (USA) 128 – Lypharitissima (FR) (Lightning (FR) 129) [2001 69: 20m Jun 20] fair maiden at 3 yrs: soundly beaten in Ascot Stakes at Royal Ascot only 4-y-o Flat outing. *M. C. Pipe* **–**

KUWAIT ROSE 5 b.g. Inchinor 119 – Black Ivor (USA) (Sir Ivor 135) [2001 72: 7.1m 9f³ 8f² 8m 7.5m⁵ 9.2g* Sep 2] smallish, sturdy gelding: fair performer: won seller at Hamilton in September: stays 9f: acts on firm going, good to soft and fibresand: blinkered (ran creditably) penultimate start: withdrawn after refusing to enter stalls final intended Flat outing Sep 21. *K. A. Ryan* **69**

KUWAIT SAND 5 b.g. Lugana Beach 116 – Soon To Be 84 (Hot Spark 126) [2001 f9.4g f7s Dec 15] of little account nowadays. *G. A. Ham* **–**

KUWAIT THUNDER (IRE) 5 ch.g. Mac's Imp (USA) 116 – Romangoddess (IRE) (Rhoman Rule (USA)) [2001 43§: f11g f11g³ 9m⁵ 8m² f8g⁵ 10g 8f³ 7m* 8f³ Sep 4] rather leggy, quite good-topped gelding: poor mover: poor handicapper: first win (at thirty-eighth attempt) in apprentice event at Thirsk in August: effective at 7f to easy 1½m: acts on firm going, good to soft and fibresand: often visored up to first outing at 5 yrs: weak finisher, and not to be trusted. *J. L. Eyre* **49 §**

KUWAIT TROOPER (USA) 4 b. or br.c. Cozzene (USA) – Super Fan (USA) (Lear Fan (USA) 130) [2001 111: 11.6g³ 20f 14s 13.3f³ Aug 18] leggy, close-coupled colt: smart performer: below form in listed event at Windsor, Gold Cup at Royal Ascot and Prix Maurice de Nieuil at Maisons-Laffitte before (with blinkers reapplied) creditable 6 lengths third of 5 to Mr Combustible in Geoffrey Freer Stakes at Newbury: should stay 2m: acts on firm going, possibly not on soft: also blinkered last 2 outings at 3 yrs: tongue tied once as 4-y-o: sent to Kuwait. *G. A. Butler* **112**

KUZI 2 br.f. (Apr 6) Bin Ajwaad (IRE) 119 – Petonellajill 73 (Petong 126) [2001 5.1s 5.1f 6m May 29] 800Y: leggy, unfurnished filly: third foal: half-sister to 3-y-o Piquet: dam 7f winner: well held in maidens. *M. Mullineaux* **–**

KWAHERI 3 b.f. Efisio 120 – Fleeting Affair 98 (Hotfoot 126) [2001 61: 11.6d 14.1d⁵ 11.6m 12m Aug 13] smallish, sturdy filly: modest maiden at 2 yrs: little show in handicaps in 2001. *Mrs P. N. Dutfield* **–**

KWIKPOINT 7 ch.g. Never So Bold 135 – Try The Duchess 99 (Try My Best (USA) 130) [2001 8m 7.1m Aug 22] of little account nowadays. *R. F. Fisher* **–**

KYDA (USA) 3 b.f. Gulch (USA) – Trampoli (USA) 115 (Trempolino (USA) 135) [2001 10m² 10m⁴ 10.5d³ 8d² 8s³ 8.3v² Nov 8] third foal: half-sister to fairly useful 10.5f winner who stays 2m First Officer (by Lear Fan): dam, 1¼m to 1½m winner in France/USA, half-sister to very smart middle-distance performers Luth Dancer and Roi Normand: fair maiden: stays 1¼m: acts on good to firm and good to soft going: carried head high third start. *H. R. A. Cecil* **75**

KYLKENNY 6 b.g. Kylian (USA) – Fashion Flow (Balidar 133) [2001 52: f12g* f12g* f12g f11g³ 10.3s f11g² 11.6g 12m 10m² 10f* 10d* 10.4d p12g Nov 20] angular, workmanlike gelding: fair handicapper: had a good season, winning at Southwell in January and February, Pontefract in September and Newmarket in October: effective at 1¼m/easy 1½m: acts on firm going, good to soft and fibresand: has won for amateur/apprentice. *H. Morrison* **66**

KYLLACHY 3 b.c. Pivotal 124 – Pretty Poppy 67 (Song 132) [2001 91p: 5s* 5g² 5.1g⁴ 5s⁴ Sep 30] strong, well-made colt: smart performer: progressed again at 3 yrs, winning handicap at Sandown (impressively by 5 lengths) in April: in frame after in listed contest at Deauville (2 lengths second to Do The Honours), well-contested minor event at **111**

Nottingham (1½ lengths fourth to Astonished) and handicap at Ascot (4¼ lengths fourth to Jessica's Dream): will prove best at 5f/easy 6f: yet to race on firm going, seems to act on any other: held up. *H. Candy*

KYLMAX   2 b.g. (Apr 15) Classic Cliche (IRE) 128 – Dame Lorraine 56 (Damister –
(USA) 123) [2001 7.2m 8g Oct 19] 2,800Y: third living foal: dam maiden who stayed 1m:
well held in maidens. *H. A. McWilliams*

L

LABASHEEDA (IRE)   3 ch.f. Lahib (USA) 129 – Hebat (Kris 135) [2001 10m²   **75**
11.9m⁴ 10m f9.4g Oct 23] IR 23,000Y: first foal: dam unraced out of half-sister to US
Grade 1 winner (including Belmont Stakes) Creme Fraiche: fair form in maiden at
Kempton on debut: well beaten after (very upset stalls second start, raced freely): has
been slowly away. *J. Cullinan*

LA BIRBA (IRE)   4 b.f. Prince of Birds (USA) 121 – Ariadne 79 (Bustino 136) [2001 –
–: f9.4s f11s 11.9s 14.1m May 29] little form: tried blinkered. *D. Morris*

LABRETT   4 b.g. Tragic Role (USA) – Play The Game 70 (Mummy's Game 120)   **93**
[2001 81: e6g* 6s² 7m* 7m³ 6g⁵ 6g³ 7m 6m⁵ 7m 6g 6g 7g 6g 6d 7d Oct 20] workmanlike
gelding: fairly useful handicapper: won at Lingfield in April and May (ladies race): ran
creditably most other starts: effective at 6f/7f: acts on equitrack, soft and good to firm
going: usually blinkered earlier in career (once in 2001): has swished tail in preliminaries:
sometimes slowly away: usually set plenty to do. *B. J. Meehan*

LADY ABAI   4 b.f. Bin Ajwaad (IRE) 119 – Charmed I'm Sure (Nicholas Bill 125) –
[2001 –: 11.9s May 3] no form. *J. Cullinan*

LADY ALRUNA (IRE)   2 ch.f. (Feb 10) Alhaarth (IRE) 126 – In Tranquility (IRE)   **76 p**
(Shalford (IRE) 124§) [2001 6m⁵ 5.1m³ 5.7g³ Oct 1] 15,000Y: first foal: dam unraced
half-sister to smart 6f (including Prix Morny at 2 yrs)/7f winner Tagula from family of
dual Breeders' Cup Mile winner Da Hoss: progressive form in maidens: third to Royal
Quarters at Bath final start, finishing well without being knocked about after having to
race very wide: will stay 7f: should make a fairly useful 3-y-o. *P. J. Makin*

LADY ANASTASIA (IRE)   4 b.f. Unblest 117 – Cry In The Dark (Godswalk (USA) –
130) [2001 –: 9.2g⁶ 7m 10v 10s f11g Dec 3] fourth foal: sister to 5-y-o Cruagh Express
and half-sister to fairly useful Irish 6.5f to 1m winner Classic Express (by Classic Music):
dam Irish 1m winner: only a little sign of ability (trained by Miss I. Oakes in Ireland only
3-y-o start): blinkered final outing. *P. L. Gilligan*

LADY ANGOLA (USA)   3 ch.f. Lord At War (ARG) – Benguela (USA) 76 (Little   **83**
Current (USA)) [2001 77: 10.2d 10m² 9.7g f12g* p10g p12g Nov 24] lengthy filly: fairly
useful handicapper: won at Wolverhampton in October: stays 1½m: acts on fibresand and
polytrack, best turf form on going firmer than good: none too consistent. *J. L. Dunlop*

LADY ANSELL   2 b.f. (Apr 10) Puissance 110 – Rare Indigo 80 (Timeless Times   **73**
(USA) 99) [2001 f5g* 5.1f 5.1f² Jun 1] 3,000Y: tall, unfurnished filly: first foal: dam
2-y-o 5f winner: fair form: landed odds in maiden at Southwell in April: best effort when
second to Bella Chica in minor event at Nottingham (edgy), leading 4f: will prove best at
5f. *A. Berry*

LADY ARNICA   2 b.f. (Feb 17) Ezzoud (IRE) 126 – Brand (Shareef Dancer (USA) –
135) [2001 7d Nov 3] lengthy, angular filly: fifth foal: half-sister to fairly useful 6f to 1m
winner Double Brandy (by Elmaamul): dam, unraced half-sister to useful performer up to
1½m Clever Cliche, from family of Unfuwain, Nashwan and Nayef: 16/1, always behind
in Newmarket maiden. *I. A. Balding*

LADY BASE   3 b.f. Blushing Flame (USA) 109 – Lady Marguerrite (Blakeney 126) –
[2001 12.6m Jun 18] lengthy, angular filly: third foal: dam, ran twice, from family of St
Leger/Gold Cup winner Classic Cliche and Prix Vermeille/Yorkshire Oaks winner My
Emma: 100/1, well held in Warwick maiden. *W. S. Kittow*

LADY BATHWICK (IRE)   2 ch.f. (Apr 9) General Monash (USA) 107 – Forget   **58**
Paris (IRE) (Broken Hearted 124) [2001 5d² 6g² 7.1m 8m f7g Sep 22] IR 5,000Y: first
foal: dam no form: modest maiden: second in sellers at Leicester and Lingfield: should
stay 1m: sold 3,500 gns. *B. R. Millman*

LADY BEAR (IRE)   3 b.f. Grand Lodge (USA) 125 – Boristova (IRE) 79 (Royal   **87 §**
Academy (USA) 130) [2001 86: 8v* 10s⁴ 10.4m 10.1m 7.1f⁴ 7m 8m 9.2s⁵ 8.3g 8m 8s³
8.9d⁶ 8s⁴ f8g⁴ f8g* f8.5g³ f8.5f⁴ Dec 5] useful-looking filly: fairly useful handicapper:
won at Ripon in April and Southwell in November: seems best at 1m/1¼m: acts on any
turf going and fibresand: effective visored or not: has been very slowly away/edged left:
moody. *R. A. Fahey*

LADY BIRGITTA   3 b.f. Emperor Jones (USA) 119 – Badiane (USA) (Green Forest   **91**
(USA) 134) [2001 9g* 8d⁶ 8g* 7g² 9v p7g⁵ f9.4s² p8g³ Dec 28] ex-French filly: third
foal: dam, French maiden, half-sister to very smart French performer up to 13.5f (dual
winner of Prix de Pomone) Bright Moon: fairly useful performer: won maiden at
Salon-de-Provence in May and minor event at Deauville in July for J-C. Rouget: ran
creditably last 2 starts: should stay 1¼m: acts on fibresand and polytrack, well beaten on
heavy ground. *R. Guest*

LADY BLUE   5 b.m. Puissance 110 – Blueit (FR) 101 (Bold Lad (IRE) 133) [2001 5g   **–**
f6g f6s Dec 15] sturdy mare: half-sister to several winners, mostly sprinters, including
useful Blues Indigo (by Music Boy) and fairly useful Indigo (by Primo Dominie), latter
dam of smart sprinters Astonished and Bishops Court: dam 2-y-o 5f winner: well held in
maidens. *P. T. Dalton*

LADY BOXER   5 b.m. Komaite (USA) – Lady Broker 54 (Petorius 117) [2001 91: 6s³   **88 +**
7.6f 6m 7.6d 6s⁵ 6m 6.1d 6g 6d³ 6v³ 7d 6s f8g Nov 19] close-coupled mare: fairly useful
performer: appeared to run particularly well tenth start: effective at 6f to 7.6f: revels in
the mud: has been early to post: sometimes slowly away: usually comes from off pace:
none too consistent. *M. Mullineaux*

LADY BREANNE (IRE)   5 b.m. Woods of Windsor (USA) – Tootsie Roll (Comedy   **48**
Star (USA) 121) [2001 47: e8g² f9.4s³ e7g* f8.5g³ e8g² e8g⁴ e8g* 8m 9.7m³ 9m 8f 10m⁶   **a57**
Aug 22] modest handicapper: won at Lingfield in January (maiden event) and April:
effective at 7f to 9.7f: acts on fibresand/equitrack, firm and good to soft going: blinkered
nowadays: tends to get behind/look none too keen: sold 620 gns. *G. L. Moore*

LADYCHATTERLY   2 ch.f. (Feb 22) Botanic (USA) – Gay Sarah (Last Fandango   **74**
125) [2001 5m³ 6g² f6g* p7g Nov 13] 3,600Y, 8,000 2-y-o: unfurnished filly: seventh
foal: half-sister to winners in Belgium by Dominion Royale and Imperial Frontier: dam
winner in Belgium: fair performer: got up near finish to beat Lloyd a neck in maiden at
Wolverhampton in October: ran creditably in nursery next time: stays 7f: acts on
fibresand and polytrack. *J. W. Hills*

LADY COLDUNELL   5 b.m. Deploy 131 – Beau's Delight (USA) (Lypheor 118)   **67**
[2001 61, a67: f14g⁵ f16s² e16s² e13g* 16.1m² 14g 14s⁶ 16.1g 16.2f 16m⁵ 16.2m⁶ Jul 27]
workmanlike mare: fair handicapper: won at Lingfield in April: stays 17f: acts on
fibresand/equitrack, soft and good to firm going: sometimes blinkered/visored: tends to
race lazily. *H. J. Collingridge*

LADYCROMBY (IRE)   3 ch.f. Lycius (USA) 124 – Havinia (Habitat 134) [2001 8d   **–**
10g 7m f12g Aug 18] 10,000Y: leggy, workmanlike filly: fourth foal: half-sister to 2
winners abroad, notably smart performer up to 1¼m in France/USA Lord Cromby (by
Risen Star): dam French 1m winner: no sign of ability. *E. J. O'Neill*

LADY CYRANO   4 b.f. Cyrano de Bergerac 120 – Hazy Kay (IRE) 77 (Treasure Kay   **–**
114) [2001 46, a38: f6g Feb 16] poor maiden at 3 yrs: well beaten only 4-y-o start: tried
visored/blinkered. *Mrs N. Macauley*

LADY DANCER   3 b.f. Aragon 118 – Hi-Hunsley 82 (Swing Easy (USA) 126) [2001   **–**
6s 6m May 25] leggy, sparely-made filly: half-sister to several winners, including 8-y-o
Myttons Mistake: dam sprinter: last in maidens at Pontefract. *A. Smith*

LADY DE BATHE   2 b.f. (Mar 15) Robellino (USA) 127 – Langtry Lady 91 (Pas de   **70**
Seul 133) [2001 7s⁵ 7.5g Sep 19] leggy filly: sixth foal: half-sister to 3 winners,
including 1996 2-y-o 6f winner Sharp Return (by Sharpo), later useful sprinter in
Scandinavia, and 5-y-o Nowell House: dam 6f to 9f winner: much better effort in maidens
(fair) when never-nearer fifth of 6 at Epsom: should stay at least 1m. *I. A. Balding*

LADY DEVIKA   2 b.f. (Apr 26) Sri Pekan (USA) 117 – The Frog Lady (IRE) 52 (Al   **54 p**
Hareb (USA) 123) [2001 7f Sep 22] 36,000Y: quite good-topped filly: third foal:
half-sister to useful 2000 2-y-o 6f winner Piccolo Player (by Piccolo) and 1999 2-y-o 7f
seller winner The Frog Queen (by Bin Ajwaad): dam, maiden, best at 1¼m/1½m: 33/1
and burly, faded when tenth of 18 to Al Mohallab in maiden at Newbury: should do better.
R. Hannon

LADY DOMINATRIX (IRE)   2 b.f. (Feb 11) Danehill Dancer (IRE) 117 – Spout   **89**
House (IRE) 55 (Flash of Steel 120) [2001 5m* 5.2s² 5m 6m 5.2m 7g² 8d Sep 13] IR
1,400F, IR 2,000Y: tall, leggy filly: third foal: half-sister to an Italian 7.5f (at 2 yrs) to 11f
winner by Mukaddamah: dam maiden who stayed 1½m: fairly useful performer: won
minor event at Doncaster in May: clearly best efforts when second in similar event at
Newbury and listed race at Newmarket (beaten 5 lengths by Muklah): should stay 1m:
acts on soft and good to firm ground: edgy final start. *Mrs P. N. Dutfield*

LADY EBERSPACHER (IRE)   3 b.f. Royal Abjar (USA) 121 – Samriah (IRE)   –
(Wassl 125) [2001 68: 8.3s 6m 6f 6m 5v Oct 15] fair maiden at 2 yrs: no form in 2001.
Mrs P. N. Dutfield

LADY EL EE   2 b.f. (Feb 26) Komaite (USA) – Mountain Harvest (FR) 64§ (Shirley   **51**
Heights 130) [2001 6m 5m 7.2v Oct 15] 14,000Y: sixth foal: half-sister to 3-y-o Takaroa
and winners in Italy by Sabrehill and Cyrano de Bergerac: dam ungenuine maiden who
seemed to stay 1¾m: best effort in maidens (modest form) when eighth of 20 at Ayr on
debut: should stay 7f. *Miss L. A. Perratt*

LADY FEARLESS   4 b.f. Cosmonaut – Lady Broker 54 (Petorius 117) [2001 –: f7g   –
6s May 2] unfurnished filly: little form. *M. Mullineaux*

LADY HIGH HAVENS (IRE)   2 b.f. (Feb 18) Bluebird (USA) 125 – Blanche   **102**
Dubois (Nashwan (USA) 135) [2001 6g⁴ 6m² 6f* 6g² 7m* 7d² 8d Sep 13] 50,000Y:
close-coupled, workmanlike filly: first foal: dam unraced half-sister to useful 2000
2-y-o 6f to 1m (Gran Criterium) winner Count Dubois out of Park Hill winner Madame
Dubois: useful performer: won minor events at Ascot in June and July: short-headed by
Silent Honor in Cherry Hinton Stakes at Newmarket in between: 1½ lengths second to Ya
Hajar in Prix du Calvados at Deauville penultimate start: reportedly returned with abscess
on off-fore final start: should stay 1m: acts on firm and good to soft ground: races
prominently. *P. W. D'Arcy*

LADY HOPPER   2 ch.f. (Mar 20) Muhtarram (USA) 125 – Lady Sheriff 90 (Taufan   –
(USA) 119) [2001 6f Jun 4] small filly: first foal: dam, 5f winner, including at 2 yrs: 50/1,
tailed off throughout in seller at Thirsk. *M. W. Easterby*

LADY INCH   3 b.f. Inchinor 119 – Head Turner 61 (My Dad Tom (USA) 109) [2001   –
–: f8g f9.4g f11g Mar 30] little form. *B. Smart*

LADY INGABELLE (IRE)   3 b.f. Catrail (USA) 123 – Lady Anna Livia (Ahonoora   **71 ?**
122) [2001 f9.4s 10v⁵ 9.9s⁴ 9.7m 11.6g 8.3g Jul 9] IR 16,000F, 4,500Y: heavy-topped
filly: half-sister to several winners, including fairly useful 1990 2-y-o 7f winner Plan of
Action (by Krayyan) and Irish 9f winner Karoi (by Kafu): dam winner in Holland:
apparently fair form at best: best efforts around 1¼m: visored final start: sold 4,500 gns.
T. G. Mills

LADY IN THE NIGHT (IRE)   3 ch.f. Royal Academy (USA) 130 – Pig Tail 98   **47**
(Habitat 134) [2001 50: 7m 7m³ 7s Oct 5] poor maiden: bred to stay 1m: acts on good to
soft going: has pulled hard. *J. A. R. Toller*

LADY IRENE (IRE)   5 br.m. Tirol 127 – Felsen (IRE) 54 (Ballad Rock 122) [2001 –:   –
11.9f May 23] of little account nowadays. *T. J. Naughton*

LADY JEANNIE   4 b.f. Emarati (USA) 74 – Cottonwood 80 (Teenoso (USA) 135)   **64**
[2001 45: e7g 8.5s⁶ 7m 6m⁴ 6m⁶ 8.3g* 8.3g 7.6g² 8m p7g Nov 15] modest performer: **a54**
won handicap at Windsor in July: stays 1m: acts on good to firm going, probably on
equitrack/polytrack: often forces pace. *M. J. Haynes*

LADY JONES   4 b.f. Emperor Jones (USA) 119 – So Beguiling (USA) 49 (Woodman   **65**
(USA) 126) [2001 68: 10f 10g 9.9s⁵ 14.1d* 10.1v 12d p16g⁵ Dec 4] fair handicapper:
won at Salisbury in October: stays 1¾m: has form on firm going, best efforts on good
to soft/soft: blinkered final start: often comes from off pace: none too consistent.
P. L. Gilligan

LADY KINVARRAH (IRE)   3 b.f. Brief Truce (USA) 126 – Al Corniche (IRE) 62   **79**
(Bluebird (USA) 125) [2001 72p: 8.1g 9m* 10m⁶ 9d³ 10.2g⁴ 11m 10.3v Oct 26] fair
handicapper: won at Kempton in July: stays 1¼m: acts on good to firm and good to soft
going: tends to race freely: has been slowly away. *P. J. Makin*

LADY LAHAR   3 b.f. Fraam 114 – Brigadiers Bird (IRE) (Mujadil (USA) 119) [2001   **106 +**
102: a8f⁴ 8.3g* 8g³ 8g⁴ 10d² 8.9m⁵ 10d Oct 18] angular filly: has a round action: useful
performer: off 4 months (reportedly injured) after reappearance at Nad Al Sheba: landed
odds in minor event at Hamilton in June: in frame in Falmouth Stakes at Newmarket (2½

Barry Walters Catering's "Lady Lahar"

lengths third to Proudwings), listed race at Goodwood (fourth to Goggles) and Prix de la Nonette at Deauville (1½ lengths second to Diamilina) next 3 starts: stays 1¼m: acts on heavy going, has won on good to firm but gave impression not entirely at ease on it penultimate start: returned to UAE. *M. R. Channon*

LADY LAP DANCER   3 b.f. Shareef Dancer (USA) 135 – Jelabna (Jalmood (USA)   **42 +**
126) [2001 8m³ 9m⁵ 11m² Jul 28] 2,200Y, 500 2-y-o: small filly: second foal: dam once-raced half-sister to useful 6f to 1m performer Baaderah: modest maiden: will be suited by 1½m+. *Mrs M. Reveley*

LADY LAUREATE   3 b.f. Sir Harry Lewis (USA) 127 – Cyrillic 88 (Rock City 120)   **79**
[2001 54: f11g 10.2d 11.6g⁵ 14.1m² 11.5f² 11.5m* 11.5m* 11.9g³ 12m 12g² 11.9m* 12g 17.2g* 14.1g 16g Nov 7] small, sparely-made filly: fair handicapper: progressed well, and won at Lingfield (2), Brighton and Bath between June/October: stays 17f: acts on firm and soft going: has turn of foot. *G. C. Bravery*

LADY LAUREN   5 b.m. Cyrano de Bergerac 120 – Wandering Stranger 69 (Petong   **–**
126) [2001 7s 5m Jun 6] seems of little account nowadays. *J. O'Reilly*

LADY LENOR   3 b.f. Presidium 124 – Sparkling Roberta 55 (Kind of Hush 118)   **58**
[2001 62: 6s 6m 5.1g⁵ 6m 5f 5d 5v⁵ Oct 15] modest performer: bred to stay 1m, but raced only at 5f/6f: acts on good to soft ground (probably on heavy) and fibresand: has started slowly/drifted left/carried head awkwardly. *Mrs G. S. Rees*

LADY LINDSAY (IRE)   2 ch.f. (Feb 5) Danehill Dancer (IRE) 117 – Jungle Jezebel   **82 p**
107 (Thatching 131) [2001 6g* 5.7m* Aug 24] IR 10,000F, 12,000Y: eighth foal: half-sister to 3 winners, including fairly useful 1¼m winner Bluebell Wood (by Bluebird) and 1997 2-y-o 7f winner Jungle Story (by Alzao): dam 2-y-o 7f winner: fairly useful form: won maiden at Windsor in July and minor event at Bath (beat Waterside by a length, quickening to lead final 1f) in August: should stay 7f: capable of better. *R. Guest*

LADY LINKS 2 b.f. (Feb 22) Bahamian Bounty 116 – Sparky's Song 63 (Electric **95** 126) [2001 5m² 5.2m³ 6g⁴ 6.5g⁶ 6g⁴ 6v* 6v* Nov 9] 12,000F, 22,000Y: angular filly: second foal: dam, 1¼m/1½m winner, half-sister to very smart sprinter Bold Edge: useful performer: third in Super Sprint at Newbury and fourth (on fifth start) in Two-Year-Old Trophy at Redcar: won minor event at Lingfield in October and listed race at Saint-Cloud (made all, beat Skyrock by 2½ lengths) in November: likely to stay 7f: acts on heavy and good to firm ground. *R. Hannon*

LADY-LOVE 4 b.f. Pursuit of Love 124 – Lady Day (FR) (Lightning (FR) 129) [2001 **62 d** 65: 7.1m 8f 6m 8.3m 8m 5f 6g 6m 5s 5m 8f Sep 4] quite attractive filly: modest handicapper, on downgrade: stays 7f: yet to race on heavy going, acts on any other: tried blinkered/visored: races freely: sold 2,100 gns. *Denys Smith*

LADY MILETRIAN (IRE) 3 b.f. Barathea (IRE) 127 – Local Custom (IRE) (Be **103** My Native (USA) 122) [2001 72: 8v* 8s⁴ 7d⁴ 7m³ 9g⁵ 8.5m² 8f 8g 7m Aug 2] tall, lengthy filly: useful performer: won maiden at Musselburgh in April: best efforts fourth to seventh starts, in listed races at Lingfield, Baden-Baden and Epsom (½-length second to Sheppard's Watch) and Coronation Stakes at Royal Ascot (shade flattered when 6¼ lengths ninth to Banks Hill): should be suited by 1¼m+: acts on any going: sold 150,000 gns. *M. R. Channon*

LADY NETBETSPORTS (IRE) 2 b.f. (Apr 16) In The Wings 128 – Auntie Mau- **76** reen (IRE) 73 (Roi Danzig (USA)) [2001 6f² 7m 8m² 8.2v⁴ 8v³ Oct 16] IR 52,000Y: leggy filly: third foal: half-sister to Irish 2000 2-y-o 6f winner Coney Kitty (by Lycius) and 2m winner Intrum Morshaan (by Darshaan), both useful: dam Irish 9f/1¼m winner from family of Halling: fair maiden: will be suited by 1¼m/1½m: seems to act on any ground. *B. S. Rothwell*

LADY OF GDANSK (IRE) 2 ch.f. (Mar 26) Danehill Dancer (IRE) 117 – Rebecca's **–** Girl (IRE) (Nashamaa 113) [2001 6s Nov 10] IR 5,000F, 7,700Y: big, lengthy filly: half-sister to several winners, including 4-y-o Janiceland and 5-y-o Waterford Spirit: dam unraced: 33/1, burly and green, showed little after slow start in maiden at Doncaster. *H. J. Collingridge*

LADY OF KILDARE (IRE) 3 b.f. Mujadil (USA) 119 – Dancing Sunset (IRE) **100 ?** 111 (Red Sunset 120) [2001 93: 7g⁵ 6g⁵ 6d⁶ 7m⁵ 6g Aug 25] well-made filly: useful performer: won maiden at Tipperary and listed race at the Curragh at 2 yrs: ran well when 4½ lengths fifth to Cool Clarity in listed event at the Curragh on reappearance: just respectable efforts in Prix de Ris-Orangis at Deauville and listed race at Goodwood third/ fourth starts: effective at 6f/7f: acts on good to firm and good to soft going: blinkered (well held) final start: has been slowly away. *T. J. Taaffe, Ireland*

LADY OF TA'PINU 2 ch.f. (May 5) Greensmith 121 – Pitcairn Princess (Capricorn **– §** Line 111) [2001 5.1g⁵ 6.5g f6g f9.4g Nov 17] 700Y: third foal: half-sister to a winner up to 10.5f in Italy by Tragic Role: dam tailed off in maidens at 2 yrs: no sign of ability: has looked reluctant/refused to enter stall. *C. N. Kellett*

LADY OF THE BRAES 2 b.f. (Feb 12) Mind Games 121 – Mary From Dunlow 49 **–** (Nicholas Bill 125) [2001 5s 5d⁶ 5f 5m 5g Sep 2] sixth foal: half-sister to 7-y-o Smokey From Caplaw and a winner in Scandinavia by Clantime: dam 2-y-o 5f winner: no form in maidens/minor event: reportedly bled from nose final start. *H. A. McWilliams*

LADY OF THE INN (IRE) 2 ch.f. (Feb 22) Hamas (IRE) 125§ – Faakirah (Dragon- **55** ara Palace (USA) 115) [2001 p7g⁶ Dec 22] IR 10,000F, 7,500Y: closely related to fairly useful Irish 1996 2-y-o 5f winner Klinsman (by Danehill), later winner in USA, and half-sister to numerous winners, including 11.5f winner Henrietta Holmes (by Persian Bold): dam twice-raced sister to Cherry Hinton winner Crime of Passion: modest form when sixth in minor event at Lingfield, making most. *B. J. Meehan*

LADY OF WINDSOR (IRE) 4 ch.f. Woods of Windsor (USA) – North Lady **– §** (Northfields (USA)) [2001 73§: f7s 7.1d 8m 7m 8.3m⁴ 7m 8g f8.5g⁵ Dec 1] sturdy, lengthy filly: fair performer at 3 yrs: little form in 2001: visored/blinkered. *I. Semple*

LADY PAHIA (IRE) 3 ch.f. Pivotal 124 – Appledorn 99 (Doulab (USA) 115) [2001 **81** 77: 7d 7m³ 7.1m 7m* 7m* 8.1d² 7f⁵ 7g 8g 7d Oct 13] tall, leggy filly: fairly useful handicapper: won at Kempton and Goodwood in June: stays 1m: acts on good to firm and good to soft going: sometimes hangs left. *A. P. Jarvis*

LADY PEKAN 2 b.f. (Feb 14) Sri Pekan (USA) 117 – Cloudberry 88 (Night Shift **87** (USA)) [2001 5d f5g⁴ 5m² 6m⁶ 5.1g² 5m³ 5m⁴ 5m* 5g² 5g* 5.2m 6m Sep 12] 30,000Y: smallish, strong filly: first foal: dam, 2-y-o 5f winner (only season to race), out of sister to

550

smart sprinter Argentum: fairly useful performer: left P. McEntee after fourth start: won nurseries at Kempton in July and Sandown (idled markedly) in August: seems best at 5f: reliable. *J. Balding*

LADY RATH (IRE)   3 b.f. Standiford (USA) – Jalopy 71 (Jalmood (USA) 126) [2001 – e6g 7s 7m 5.1f May 22] leggy, unfurnished filly: half-sister to several winners, including 13f winner Classy Chief (by Be My Chief) and 4-y-o Hunting Lion: dam, 5f winner, half-sister to smart sprinter Point of Light: no sign of ability. *L. A. Dace*

LADY ROCK   3 b.f. Mistertopogigo (IRE) 118 – Bollin Victoria 51 (Jalmood (USA)   **65** 126) [2001 63: 5m 6m 5m 6m* 6.1s⁶ 6m 6f 7m⁴ f6g³ f6g⁴ Nov 3] lengthy, workmanlike filly: fair handicapper: won at Southwell in July: effective at 5f to easy 7f: acts on firm going and fibresand: usually races prominently. *R. Bastiman*

LADY SANDROVITCH (IRE)   4 b.f. Desert Style (IRE) 121 – Mauras Pride (IRE)   **36** (Cadeaux Genereux 131) [2001 37: f7s⁴ f6s Jan 30] poor maiden: seems to stay 7f: acts on fibresand: blinkered final start. *R. A. Fahey*

LADY SANTANA (IRE)   4 b.f. Doyoun 124 – Santana Lady (IRE) 72 (Blakeney 126) [2001 61: f9.4g Feb 22] modest maiden at 3 yrs: well held only outing in 2001. *Mrs Merrita Jones*

LADY SAPPHIRE   2 b.f. (May 8) Dancing Spree (USA) – Lady Broker 54 (Petorius   **35** 117) [2001 5.1f 5m 5.1f 7.1s 6m f6g 6s Nov 10] leggy, workmanlike filly: fourth foal: half-sister to 5-y-o Lady Boxer: dam 7f winner: poor maiden: sweating/edgy/wandered markedly final start. *M. Mullineaux*

LADY SHARP SHOT (IRE)   3 b.f. Son of Sharp Shot (IRE) 105 – Ski For Gold 76   – (Shirley Heights 130) [2001 71p: f11g⁴ 13.1m Sep 10] lengthy, useful-looking filly: fair form on debut: well held in 3 outings since: should be suited by 1¼m/1½m. *J. L. Dunlop*

LADY SOPHIA   2 ch.f. (Mar 8) Atraf 116 – Miss Lear (Lear Fan (USA) 130) [2001   **42** 5g 5m⁵ 6f⁶ 7m³ f7g 6g 6g 8m Sep 11] leggy, unfurnished filly: first foal: dam unraced: poor maiden: left W. Turner after third start: stays 7f: raced only on good going or firmer on turf: tried visored. *Andrew Reid*

LADY'S SECRET (IRE)   2 b.f. (Mar 28) Alzao (USA) 117 – Kaaba (Darshaan 133)   **88 p** [2001 f⁴ 7g Oct 6] IR 68,000Y: useful-looking filly: first foal: dam unraced close relation to smart 1½m performer Konigsberg: fairly useful form when fourth in minor event at Newbury and eighth in listed race at Newmarket: should be well suited by 1¼m/1½m: probably capable of better, and looks sure to win a race or 2. *B. W. Hills*

LADY STRATAGEM   2 gr.f. (Mar 14) Mark of Esteem (IRE) 137 – Grey Angel   **61** (Kenmare (FR) 125) [2001 7m 6d⁶ 7m 7d Nov 3] 19,000Y: sturdy filly: has a round action: fourth foal: half-sister to 4-y-o Welcome Shade: dam won 8 races in South Africa at 7f/1m, including Grade 3 event: modest maiden: should stay 1m. *R. Hannon*

LADY TILLY   4 b.f. Puissance 110 – Lady of Itatiba (BEL) (King of Macedon 126)   – [2001 40: 8.3g⁵ 9.2d 7s Jul 24] workmanlike filly: poor maiden at 3 yrs: no form in 2001: blinkered once. *A. C. Whillans*

LADY TWO K (IRE)   4 b.f. Grand Lodge (USA) 125 – Princess Pavlova (IRE)   **85** (Sadler's Wells (USA) 132) [2001 85p: 11.7d² 12.3g² 10.5v 11.9s 12v Oct 27] sturdy, lengthy filly: fairly useful performer: should stay beyond 1½m: acts on soft ground, possibly not on heavy. *J. Mackie*

LADY WARD (IRE)   3 b.f. Mujadil (USA) 119 – Sans Ceriph (IRE) 75 (Thatching   **64** 131) [2001 59: 8m⁴ 7f 8m* 8.2s* 10.1g³ 8.1s 7m f8g Dec 10] leggy filly: modest   **a–** performer: won claimers at Leicester and Nottingham in August: well below form after: seems best around 1m: acts on soft and good to firm ground: often carries head high/hangs. *M. H. Tompkins*

LADYWELL BLAISE (IRE)   4 b.f. Turtle Island (IRE) 123 – Duly Elected (Persian   **52 §** Bold 123) [2001 63: e7s e6g e7g e8g 8s⁶ 6v 8.3g 7.6m 6d⁴ 5m 7f² 7m⁴ 7m³ 7m⁵ 8.3g 7d 9.7m³ 7g 7g 7d 7g 6g Sep 15] modest performer: effective at 6f/7f: acts on fibresand/equitrack, firm and good to soft going: blinkered once: has been very slowly away. *J. J. Bridger*

LAFAYETTE (IRE)   3 b.c. General Monash (USA) 107 – Bezee (Belmez (USA) 131)   **90** [2001 57: 7m 10m* 11.4g² 12m⁴ 9.9g* 10g 10s* 10g Oct 5] sturdy, good-bodied colt: fairly useful handicapper: won at Sandown in May, Beverley in August and Pontefract in September: should stay 1½m: acts on soft and good to firm going: sold 35,000 gns. *A. C. Stewart*

LAFFAH (USA)   6 b.g. Silver Hawk (USA) 123 – Sakiyah (USA) (Secretariat (USA))   **72**
[2001 74: 16s 14m 20m 16.2f⁴ 18m 21m Aug 1] heavy-topped gelding: fair handicapper:
stays 2½m: acts on firm going: visored once, blinkered final start: tongue tied: has
seemed lazy, but runs on gamely. *G. L. Moore*

L'AFFAIRE MONIQUE   2 b.f. (Feb 12) Machiavellian (USA) 123 – Much Too   **73 p**
Risky 87 (Bustino 136) [2001 7g Oct 4] sister to smart 1m to 13.5f winner Whitewater
Affair and half-sister to several winners, including 5-y-o Little Rock: dam 2-y-o 7f/1m
winner: 16/1, shaped quite well when seventh of 21 to Millennium Dragon in maiden at
Newmarket, keeping on having been soon niggled along off pace: likely to be suited by
1¼m/1½m: sure to improve. *Sir Michael Stoute*

LAGGAN MINSTREL (IRE)   3 b.c. Mark of Esteem (IRE) 137 – Next Episode   **84**
(USA) (Nijinsky (CAN) 138) [2001 66: f7s³ 8d* 8.1g⁵ 8.3g² 8.2m² 7.6f* 7g Aug 4] fairly
useful handicapper: won at Salisbury in May and Lingfield in July: stays 1m: acts on
fibresand/equitrack, firm and good to soft going: carries head high. *R. Hannon*

LAGO   3 b.g. Maelstrom Lake 118 – Jugendliebe (IRE) (Persian Bold 123) [2001 –: f8g   **52**
5.1s 10m⁴ 12.1m² 10g 14.1s⁴ 14.1m⁵ Aug 25] robust gelding: modest maiden: probably
stays 1¾m: acts on good to firm ground, probably on soft. *M. W. Easterby*

LAGO DI COMO   4 b.c. Piccolo 121 – Farmer's Pet 90 (Sharrood (USA) 124) [2001   **62**
65: 8.5s 11.6g 11.7f 11.9g⁵ 10m* 10m* f9.4s² 8.5g p10g Dec 22] sturdy colt: has a round   **a56**
action: modest performer: won seller at Lingfield and amateur handicap at Brighton in
August: best at 9f/1¼m: acts on firm going and fibresand/equitrack: tried blinkered/
visored: front runner. *T. J. Naughton*

LAGO DI LEVICO   4 ch.g. Pelder (IRE) 125 – Langton Herring (Nearly A Hand   **42**
115) [2001 57d: e6g⁴ e7g³ f8.5g⁵ e10g 10m 7.1g Aug 27] poor performer: stays 1m:
acts on equitrack: tried visored/tongue tied: has started slowly/wandered markedly.
H. S. Howe

LAGO DI VARANO   9 b.g. Clantime 101 – On The Record 72 (Record Token 128)   **88**
[2001 95: 6s* 6g 6g 6g 6g 6g⁶ 5g 6.1d 5d² 6d⁴ 5s 6g Nov 5] strong gelding: fairly useful
performer: won minor event at Windsor in April: best at 5f/6f: acts on any going: visored/
blinkered: normally races up with pace. *R. M. Whitaker*

LAGUDIN (IRE)   3 b.c. Eagle Eyed (USA) 111 – Liaison (USA) (Blushing Groom   **112**
(FR) 131) [2001 98p: 8g³ 8g⁴ 7g³ 10.4g² 10.3d* 9d³ 10d* Nov 2] good-topped, quite
attractive colt: smart performer: won minor event at Doncaster (by 1¼ lengths from
Aldebaran) in September and listed race at Newmarket (by short head from Chianti) in
November: best form around 1¼m: acts on soft going, yet to race on firmer than good:
has worn crossed noseband: tends to flash tail: has gone freely, and best waited with:
consistent. *L. M. Cumani*

*Joy UK Conditions Guaranteed Sweepstakes, Doncaster—a smart performance from Lagudin,
who gains the upper hand from Aldebaran inside the last furlong*

LAGUNA BAY (IRE) 7 b.m. Arcane (USA) – Meg Daughter (IRE) (Doulab (USA) —
115) [2001 –: f16g Feb 16] close-coupled mare: modest handicapper in 1999: well held in
3 starts since. *G. M. McCourt*

LAGUNA SECA 2 b.f. (Feb 23) General Monash (USA) 107 – Cavatina 72 (Chief **63 p**
Singer 131) [2001 5d³ p5g⁶ Nov 24] lengthy, angular filly: second foal: dam 6f/7.5f
winner: modest form in maidens at Redcar (swerved left leaving stall) and Lingfield (still
green and not at all knocked about): should do better. *R. Guest*

LAHAAY 4 ch.g. Lahib (USA) 129 – Jasarah (IRE) 70 (Green Desert (USA) 127) **74**
[2001 74: e10g e10g⁴ 10m 10.1m⁶ 8f⁵ 9.7m* 10.2d f9.4g p10g p10g Dec 22] quite **a66**
good-topped gelding: fair performer, better on turf than all-weather: won handicap at
Folkestone in August: stays 1¼m: twice well beaten on heavy ground, acts on any other
turf going and on equitrack/polytrack: none too consistent. *J. Akehurst*

LAHBERHORN (USA) 2 ch.c. (Jan 26) Affirmed (USA) – Skiable (IRE) (Niniski **71 p**
(USA) 125) [2001 7f Aug 18] strong colt: third foal: half-brother to fairly useful French
1½m winner Grail (by Quest For Fame): dam, French/US winner up to 9f, half-sister to
dam of Dansili and 3-y-o Banks Hill: 7/1 and backward, eighth of 17 to Flat Spin in
maiden at Newbury, travelling well up with pace and not unduly knocked about when
fading: should do better. *B. W. Hills*

LAHINCH (IRE) 2 b.f. (Feb 20) Danehill Dancer (IRE) 117 – Dublah (USA) (Private **104**
Account (USA)) [2001 7s 6g⁴ 5m* 6d⁴ 5s* 7d² Oct 20] IR 200,000Y: strong, deep-girthed
filly: has plenty of scope: half-sister to several winners, including useful 5f (at 2 yrs) and
8.5f (in USA) winner Perugino Bay (by Perugino) and 6-y-o Bandbox: dam unraced:
useful performer: won maiden at the Curragh in September and listed race at Tipperary
(beat Church Cross by 4 lengths) in October: set pace when respectable 9¾ lengths fourth
to Queen's Logic in Cheveley Park Stakes at Newmarket in between: wearing crossed
noseband, head second to Distant Valley in Rockfel Stakes at Newmarket: stays 7f: acts
on soft and good to firm ground. *A. P. O'Brien, Ireland*

LAHOOQ 2 b.c. (Mar 21) Indian Ridge 123 – Woodsia 97 (Woodman (USA) 126) **96 p**
[2001 8g* 8s Sep 29] well-made, attractive colt: has a fluent, slightly round action: first
foal: dam, Irish 1m/1¼m winner, half-sister to useful 5f performer Millstream: useful
form: justified strong support in 12-runner maiden at Kempton (beat Hathaal by neck) in
September, set fair bit to do in slowly-run race but quickening well: co-favourite and in
fine shape, never a threat and eased once held in Royal Lodge Stakes at Ascot: not sure to
stay much beyond 1m: worth another chance to show himself a smart colt. *D. R. Loder*

LAILANI 3 b.f. Unfuwain (USA) 131 – Lailati (USA) 66 (Mr Prospector (USA)) **122**
[2001 75p: 8.3s* 10g* 10.5m* 10.1m* 12g* 10g* 10f Oct 27]
 The best horses to run in handicaps each year are invariably capable of
making their presence felt in pattern company. In the latest season Alleluia
(Doncaster Cup), Atavus (Hungerford Stakes), Harmonic Way (Cork And Orrery
Stakes), High Pitched (St Simon Stakes), Independence (Matron Stakes and Sun
Chariot Stakes) and Nice One Clare (Diadem Stakes) all won a Group 2 or 3 race,
but even this sextet were outshone by Lailani. She started 2001 winning a maiden
race and ran off a mark of 80 in her first handicap (a slightly higher mark than both

*Kildangan Stud Irish Oaks, the Curragh—Lailani (No.4) makes a seamless transition
from handicaps to classic success, edging out Mot Juste to give trainer Ed Dunlop a 1,2;
Karsavina, Sequoyah (both partially hidden), Lime Gardens and Time Away are next*

Alleluia and Atavus did on their first runs of the year in handicaps); she finished it as one of the top three middle-distance fillies in Europe, behind only Banks Hill and Aquarelliste, with wins in Group 1 races in Ireland and Britain and a Grade 1 in the States on the scoresheet. Her name is a perfect one to quote when anybody trots out that silly standard insult about a runner being 'only a handicapper'.

Lailani's rate of improvement seemed to take her connections by surprise, since she wasn't mentioned in a stable tour of her trainer's in the *Racing Post* in April and wasn't entered in the classics, having to be supplemented for the Kildangan Stud Irish Oaks in July at a cost of IR £28,000. The expense seemed justified given that by the end of June she had picked up four races, starting with that maiden, at Windsor in April, her third start in such company after making no show when not knocked about at Doncaster and Newmarket at the backend as a two-year-old. Lailani trotted up by ten lengths from modest opposition at Windsor then justified favouritism in handicaps at Newmarket and Haydock in May and Epsom in June, on the last-named course beating Foreign Affairs with something in hand by a length and a quarter in the Vodafone Handicap. Lailani's timefigure at Epsom was an eye-opener and, although she clearly needed to improve to extend her winning run in the Irish Oaks at the Curragh, she looked just the type to continue on the upgrade. Another point in her favour was that the Irish Oaks could not be regarded as vintage by any means in the absence of Imagine. In a field of twelve Lailani started second favourite behind Oaks third Relish The Thought, ahead of Prix de Diane third Time Away, Pretty Polly Stakes winner Rebelline and Mot Juste, also trained by Ed Dunlop and fourth in the Oaks. In a cracking finish dominated by the two stable companions, Lailani improved over a furlong out after being held up and quickened well to catch Mot Juste in the last fifty yards to score by a neck, with Karsavina, who had been only fourth in the Pretty Polly Stakes, a length away third. This was the third Group 1 success for Dunlop, whose father John has compiled a formidable record as a trainer over the last thirty years— Dunlop junior's earlier winners were Iktamal in the Haydock Park Sprint Cup and Ta Rib in the Poule d'Essai des Pouliches, both in 1996. As well as Lailani and Mot Juste, Sun Chariot Stakes winner Independence, Surprise Encounter, who took the Royal Hunt Cup, and Park Hill winner Ranin were all a great credit to Dunlop, who is adept at placing his horses, knows the handicap system well—as one would expect of a Dunlop—and travels far and wide with his runners, having won races at twenty-six different British courses during the latest season. That is a record from which some other trainers could draw a useful lesson. In passing, it should also be mentioned that Dunlop twice fell foul of the Jockey Club's H2 guideline relating to schooling in public, being fined £1,000 on the first occasion and £2,000 on the second; the latter was quashed on appeal.

Having made her mark once in Group 1 company, Lailani stayed at the top for the remainder of her campaign, starting with the Vodafone Nassau Stakes at Goodwood in August. Although dropping back in distance, Lailani was the clear pick on form and went off 5/4 favourite against six opponents, only one of whom, Time Away, had landed a pattern race during the season. After tracking the pace behind the enterprisingly-ridden Snowflake, Lailani gradually responded to pressure to wear down the leader in the final furlong and draw away to win by a length and a half. Initially, the intention was to run Lailani next in the Prix Vermeille followed by the Prix de l'Arc de Triomphe, but her owner reportedly wished her to remain racing against her own sex and to have her covered in Kentucky as a four-year-old. This made an autumn campaign in the States a logical course, with two obvious Grade 1 events to go for—the Flower Bowl Invitational and the Breeders' Cup Filly & Mare Turf, both over a mile and a quarter at Belmont Park. In the interim, in mid-August, Lailani met with a setback when getting loose and falling over, sustaining cuts on her off-side. This necessitated some patching up and, combined with problems in quarantine when the filly was unable to eat her normal food, it seemed that she had a lot on her plate in the Flower Bowl at the end of September against England's Legend, a near-eight-length winner of the Grade 1 Beverly D Stakes last time, and Starine, recent wide-margin winner of a Grade 2. England's Legend set a good pace with Lailani close up. Once asked for her effort, the latter always looked like getting there, battling past the leader to win by three quarters of a length with Starine the same distance away third. This was pretty clearly Lailani's best performance of the year and she looked to have good prospects at the Breeders' Cup a month later. Unfortunately, she was drawn wide, which can be regarded as unhelpful, and, after a long season, failed to run anywhere near her best in eighth, becoming warm and edgy at the stalls and never posing a threat. England's Legend and Starine both finished behind her, which could be taken to indicate that the Flower Bowl had taken something out of all of them.

Lailani is the third Irish Oaks winner sired by Unfuwain, following Bolas and Petrushka. Unfuwain died in January 2002 from a sudden illness, his stud career, from lesser opportunities, more than matching that of his illustrious

Maktoum Al Maktoum's "Lailani"

half-brother Nashwan. There had been some cause for concern over a recurring problem on the left side of Unfuwain's jaw, with cancerous growths appearing in 1992, 1993, 1997 and in the autumn, but his death was reportedly connected to a neurological condition. Unfuwain's books of mares improved in the wake of his success at stud, with more black-type performers visiting him, so his record may well get even better. Only one of his six Group 1 winners is out of a mare who earned any black type, and Lailani is among the majority since her dam Lailati was only fair at best, finishing third in two maiden races at around a mile and a quarter.

Lailani (b.f. 1998)	Unfuwain (USA) (b 1985)	Northern Dancer (b 1961)	Nearctic
			Natalma
		Height of Fashion (b 1979)	Bustino
			Highclere
	Lailati (USA) (ch 1990)	Mr Prospector (b 1970)	Raise A Native
			Gold Digger
		Carduel (b 1978)	Buckpasser
			Minstrelete

The next two dams on the bottom line of Lailani's pedigree, Carduel and Minstrelete, weren't up to much on the track either, winning a race apiece, but Lailati is a half-sister to two good performers, Always Fair and Faithful Son. The former won the Coventry Stakes and Prix Quincey and the latter the Prince of Wales's Stakes as well as running second in the Eclipse Stakes and Juddmonte International. Lailati's sister Golden Digger is dam of the useful juvenile Naheef. Lailati herself has foaled three other winners, geldings by Rock Hopper and Green Desert and the French colt Copper Carnival (by Petit Loup), successful in a listed race over a mile and a half in the Provinces. She foaled a filly by Green Desert named Laikipia in 2000. Lailani, an angular, quite attractive filly who acted on soft and good to firm going, has been retired and visits Fantastic Light's sire Rahy. Although she carried her head a bit high and flashed her tail on occasions early in the season she lacked nothing in courage and, until her below-form effort at the Breeders' Cup, was a model of consistency. She was well handled by Frankie Dettori in Europe, after her maiden win, and by Jerry Bailey in the States. *E. A. L. Dunlop*

LAI SEE (IRE)   3 b.g. Tagula (IRE) 116 – Sevens Are Wild 40 (Petorius 117) [2001 73: f6s e5s 8d f5g 6m 8d p7g Dec 19] quite attractive gelding: fair maiden at 2 yrs: well held in 2001: visored once as 2-y-o. *A. P. Jarvis*   –

LAISSEZALLER (USA)   2 gr. or ro.c. (Mar 26) End Sweep (USA) – Laissez Faire (USA) (Talinum (USA)) [2001 7f* 7m² 8d³ Nov 2] $77,000Y: close-coupled, useful-looking colt: second foal: dam 8.5f winner in USA: won maiden at Newbury in July: useful form when placed in minor events there and at Newmarket (after 3½ months off, length third of 5 to Ashdown Express): not sure to stay much beyond 1m: acts on firm and good to soft ground: unseated rider and got loose before second outing, upset in stall and withdrawn next intended one. *Mrs A. J. Perrett*   95

LAJADHAL (FR)   12 gr.g. Bellypha 130 – Rose d'Amour (USA) (Lines of Power (USA)) [2001 –: 14.1m 18m Jul 7] of little account on Flat. *P. D. Purdy*   –

LAKATOI   2 b.f. (Mar 18) Saddlers' Hall (IRE) 126 – Bireme 127 (Grundy 137) [2001 7d 7d Nov 3] good-bodied filly: half-sister to several winners, including fairly useful 1¼m winner Flagship and useful 1992 2-y-o 7f winner Yawl (both by Rainbow Quest): dam won Oaks: signs of a little ability in maidens at Leicester and Newmarket: likely to do better at 1¼m+. *B. W. Hills*   – p

LAKE DORSET (IRE)   3 b.c. Night Shift (USA) – Lara's Dream (Dominion 123) [2001 9m² 8s 7g 7g 10g⁴ 10m 10m⁶ 8.5m 8.5d 6d Nov 23] first foal: dam, Italian 1m winner, closely related to smart Italian middle-distance performer Lara's Idea: modest maiden: left L. Cumani after fifth start: showed little at Rome for new stable (fell ninth outing): stays 1¼m: acts on good to firm ground. *L. Camici, Italy*   62

LAKE EYRE (IRE)   2 b.f. (Mar 15) Bluebird (USA) 125 – Pooh Wee 71 (Music Boy 124) [2001 6g 6g 7d⁵ Sep 26] IR 17,000F, IR 32,000Y: seventh foal: half-sister to fairly useful 1997 2-y-o 5f winner Pacifica (by Robellino) and a winner in Hungary by Tragic Role: dam, 6f (at 2 yrs) and 1m winner, half-sister to smart miler Nicolotte: modest form in maidens: not best of runs at Chester on final start: will probably stay 1m. *D. Shaw*   57

LAKE KINNERET (IRE)　3 b.f. Danehill (USA) 126 – Dancing Shadow 117　**70**
(Dancer's Image (USA)) [2001 69p: 10g 8.3m² 8d* 8d⁵ 8.1g Sep 2] lengthy, good sort:
fair performer: landed odds in maiden at Pontefract in August: should stay at least 1¼m:
acts on good to firm and good to soft ground: flicked tail/tended to edge left second start.
Sir Michael Stoute

LAKELAND PADDY (IRE)　4 b.g. Lake Coniston (IRE) 131 – Inshad 81 (Indian　**–**
King (USA) 128) [2001 78: 6g 8.3d 6d p7g Nov 15] rather unfurnished gelding: fair
handicapper at 3 yrs: well held in 2001. *M. Blanshard*

LAKE SUNBEAM　5 b.g. Nashwan (USA) 135 – Moon Drop 103 (Dominion 123)　**61**
[2001 73: 8.5m³ 8m² 8.9m 8s² Sep 30] rangy, angular gelding: very good mover: has
reportedly had wind operation: modest nowadays: stays 1¼m: acts on firm and good to
soft going (probably not on soft). *W. R. Muir*

LAKE VERDI (IRE)　2 ch.c. (Mar 2) Lake Coniston (IRE) 131 – Shore Lark (USA)　**88**
(Storm Bird (CAN) 134) [2001 5g* 5d⁴ 6f* 6m 6g⁴ 7m⁴ 6m 7g 6d Oct 19]　IR 5,700F,
12,500Y: quite good-topped colt: first foal: dam unraced half-sister to smart performers
Tipsy Creek (5f/6f) and Wathik (1m/9f, in UAE): fairly useful performer: won maiden at
Newmarket in May and minor event at Newbury in June: creditable efforts, including in
nurseries, after: stays 7f: acts on firm and good to soft going: tongue tied first 4 starts:
consistent. *B. Hanbury*

LA KOCA (FR)　3 b.f. Thatching 131 – Green Maid (USA) (Green Dancer (USA)　**44**
132) [2001 8.2d 8g 7g⁶ 6g p10g Dec 29] 100,000 francs Y: second foal: half-sister to
French 11f/12.5f winner Gold Point (by Arctic Tern): dam French 7.5f and 9f winner:
poor maiden: best effort at 7f. *H. J. Collingridge*

LAKOTA BRAVE　7 ch.g. Anshan 119 – Pushkinia (FR) 95 (Pharly (FR) 130) [2001　**–**
64+, a79?: e7g e8g⁵ 7m p8g⁴ p7g* p7g² Dec 29] lightly-raced gelding: fairly useful　**a87**
performer: won claimer at Lingfield in December: very good effort when short-headed
in handicap there final outing: effective at 7f/easy 1m: acts on equitrack and polytrack,
well held only outing on turf in 2001: often tongue tied: has started slowly/raced freely.
C. N. Allen

LA MARTINA　2 b.f. (Apr 22) Atraf 116 – Dance Steppe (Rambo Dancer (CAN) 107)　**100**
[2001 7g* 7.1m³ 8f* 8f⁴ Nov 23] 1,000F, 4,800Y: second foal: dam no form: useful
performer: won maiden at Milan in June and non-graded stakes at Santa Anita (having
left M. Quinlan, by 2½ lengths) in October: in frame in listed race at Sandown (1½
lengths third to Echo River) and Grade 3 at Hollywood (fourth to Forty On Line): better
at 1m than 7f: acts on firm going. *Jenine Sahadi, USA*

LAMBADORA　3 ch.f. Suave Dancer (USA) 136 – Lust (Pursuit of Love 124) [2001　**55**
–: 8m 14.1m³ 14.1m⁵ 16m² 16.2m⁶ 14.1s 16m Aug 22] tall, good-topped filly: modest
maiden handicapper: will stay beyond 2m: acts on good to firm going. *Miss
J. A. Camacho*

LAMBAY ISLAND (IRE)　3 b.g. Turtle Island (IRE) 123 – Ullapool (Dominion　**66**
123) [2001 –: f7g 10s 14d 12g⁴ 13d Oct 24] IR 10,000Y: brother to fairly useful Irish 9f/
1¼m winner Cotopaxi and half-brother to several winners, including fairly useful winner
up to 1½m Mad Militant (by Vision): dam unraced: fair maiden: left N. Chance after
reappearance: stays 1½m: yet to race on ground firmer than good. *Sean Gannon, Ireland*

LAMBROOK　3 b.f. (Mar 15) Emarati (USA) 74 – Shalverton (IRE) (Shalford (IRE)　**54**
124§) [2001 f5g6 f5g 5.1g² 5.7f 5m p6g⁶ Dec 22] 12,000Y: first foal: dam, ran 3 times,　**a45**
half-sister to smart 1995 2-y-o 6f (including Mill Reef Stakes) winner Kahir Almaydan:
modest maiden on turf, poor on all-weather: second at Bath: stays easy 6f: acts on
polytrack, best turf effort on good going. *W. R. Muir*

LAMMOSKI (IRE)　4 ch.g. Hamas (IRE) 125§ – Penny In My Shoe (USA) (Sir Ivor　**–**
135) [2001 42: f6g f5g 6m 5.2m 5m 12m⁵ 11.6m 8.5s 8.9m Sep 2] of little account
nowadays. *M. C. Chapman*

LA MONDOTTE (IRE)　3 b.f. Alzao (USA) 117 – Saucy Maid (IRE) 69 (Sure Blade　**60 §**
(USA) 130) [2001 57p: f11g³ f11g⁴ 14.1d 11m⁴ 10.1g 12d f12g⁵ f12g² f11g f14.8g f12g³　**a66 §**
f12s Dec 27] fair maiden: should stay 1¾m: acts on fibresand, probably on soft going: has
looked difficult ride. *J. A. Osborne*

L'AMOUR (USA)　3 ch.f. Gone West (USA) – Midnight Air (USA) 111 (Green　**81**
Dancer (USA) 132) [2001 8d 8.1g* 9.9m May 23] sturdy filly: has a round action: third
living foal: half-sister to smart 7f (at 2 yrs) to 1½m (in USA) winner Midnight Line (by
Kris S) and 8.5f winner Midnight Watch (by Capote): dam won May Hill Stakes and first

past post in Fillies' Mile: fairly useful form: won maiden at Warwick in May by 3½ lengths from Santa Isobel: disappointing in listed race at Goodwood next time: stayed 1m: retired. *H. R. A. Cecil*

LAMZIG 2 b.g. (Mar 15) Danzig Connection (USA) – Lamsonetti 68 (Never So Bold – 135) [2001 8d Oct 19] fourth foal: dam, 7f winner, half-sister to 4-y-o Orientor: 50/1, soundly beaten in maiden at Newmarket. *Mrs Lydia Pearce*

LANCE FEATHER (IRE) 3 b.c. Petardia 113 – Fantasticus (IRE) 78 (Lycius – (USA) 124) [2001 47: 10g 10.9d Aug 3] leggy, useful-looking colt: poor maiden at 2 yrs: well held in 2001. *J. L. Eyre*

LANCER (USA) 9 ch.g. Diesis 133 – Last Bird (USA) (Sea Bird II 145) [2001 67§, **61 §** a–§: 12s³ 11.9s⁴ 11.9s⁵ 14.1m² 12m⁶ 15g⁴ 14.1m 12g* 11.5g⁶ 12d* 11.8s 11.9s* Oct 25] **a– §** workmanlike gelding: modest performer: won sellers at Folkestone and Beverley and apprentice handicap at Brighton between August and October: effective at 1½m to 15f: acts on any turf going and fibresand/equitrack: blinkered twice, usually visored: tends to start slowly/look none too keen: held up: not one to trust implicitly. *Mrs Lydia Pearce*

L'ANCRESS PRINCESS 4 b.f. Rock City 120 – Premier Princess 45 (Hard Fought – 125) [2001 –: 12m⁶ Jul 11] smallish filly: of no account. *Mrs A. M. Naughton*

LAND GIRL 3 b.f. General Monash (USA) 107 – Charming Madam (General Holme – (USA) 128) [2001 –: 9.2g Sep 2] well held in claimer and seller. *Miss S. E. Hall*

LANDICAN LAD 4 b.g. Petong 126 – Dancing Daughter 79 (Dance In Time (CAN)) – [2001 57d: f6s Jan 30] little form. *A. C. Whillans*

LANDINGS 2 ch.f. (May 7) Deploy 131 – Sandblaster 55 (Most Welcome 131) [2001 **54** 6.9m 7.1f* 8m 8m Sep 30] first foal: dam 1m winner at 4 yrs: modest performer: won seller at Musselburgh in July despite hanging right (then left W. Turner): should stay 1¼m: raced only on going firmer than good. *Miss L. A. Perratt*

LANDING SLOT (USA) 6 b.g. Personal Hope (USA) 118 – Durability (USA) – (Affirmed (USA)) [2001 f11g Jan 8] useful performer in Ireland in 1999: well held only Flat start since: best form at 9f/1¼m: acts on soft and good to firm ground: blinkered twice in 1999. *E. W. Tuer*

LAND OF FANTASY 2 ch.c. (Apr 12) Hernando (FR) 127 – Height of Folly 81 **74** (Shirley Heights 130) [2001 8g p8g² Nov 28] 21,000Y: quite good-topped colt: half-brother to several winners, including 5-y-o Sarangani: dam stayer: much better effort in maidens (ran for S. Dow on debut when burly) when staying-on 4 lengths second of 12 to Compton Dragon at Lingfield: will be suited by 1¼m+. *K. T. Ivory*

LANDSEER 2 b.c. (Feb 28) Danehill (USA) 126 – Sabria (USA) (Miswaki **115** (USA) 124) [2001 5s⁴ 7d* 6m* 7d² 7d² 8s² Nov 3]

The first out and one of the last back—that was Landseer, who got the campaign of Aidan O'Brien's powerful team of juveniles under way at Leopardstown on April 16th and ended his season at Saint-Cloud on November 3rd, with only the Criterium de Saint-Cloud to come. Landseer had six races in all, and, although he didn't win above Group 3 level, he did himself great credit by finishing second in two Group 1s, almost winning the Dewhurst Stakes thanks to a skilful piece of jockeyship. In contrast, Landseer's debut distinctly failed to go according to plan as he was beaten into fourth in a blanket finish to a maiden at odds on. Upped in distance, to seven furlongs in a similar race at Gowran a month later, he made no mistake, showing a turn of foot to land the odds readily this time. But he was still only a 20/1-shot for the Coventry Stakes over a furlong shorter at Royal Ascot, twice the odds of his stable-companion Rock of Gibraltar and even further behind the favourite Meshaheer. In a record-equalling field of twenty runners, a good proportion of leading trainers were represented. Due to bunching on the stand side there was no shortage of hard-luck stories after Landseer triumphed by a neck from Firebreak, with Meshaheer the same distance away third and Redback fourth. Landseer showed signs of greenness, improving on the outside over two furlongs out, quickening in good style to lead at the distance but then drifting markedly left under a right-handed drive before going back the other way into the whip close home. Landseer's rider, Jamie Spencer, received a six-day ban for careless riding and misuse of the whip.

On the day most were convinced that Meshaheer, who had a terrible run, should have gained a clear-cut victory, while Rock of Gibraltar in sixth also had

Coventry Stakes, Royal Ascot—a record-equalling field for the race of twenty runners;
Landseer takes the honours, ahead of Firebreak (far side),
the unlucky Meshaheer (near side) and Redback

nothing like a clear passage. In the event, Landseer proved a better two-year-old than Meshaheer and not far behind Rock of Gibraltar. He missed the important summer races, in which Johannesburg and Rock of Gibraltar dominated for the stable, and returned in the Tattersalls Houghton Sales Stakes at Newmarket in October, a race in which O'Brien can virtually be guaranteed to have a significant contender given the amount of money on offer and the number of eligible yearlings purchased by the Coolmore team each year. The stable had won the race with Mozart the year before and was unlucky not to land it again as Landseer enjoyed anything but a smooth passage, finding trouble several times when trying to improve, then bumping another runner when switched left over a furlong out; despite never being really balanced, he stayed on strongly to be beaten a head by Sir George Turner. If Landseer didn't enjoy the rub of the green that day, fortune almost compensated him in spades in the Dewhurst Stakes on the same course later in the month. While two of his stable companions, odds-on Rock of Gibraltar and Tendulkar, got into trouble Landseer enjoyed an uninterrupted passage on the outside. Spencer, who consistently shows tactical awareness, appreciated what was happening to the rest of the field and rousted Landseer into the lead over a furlong out, snatching an advantage which Rock of Gibraltar had to fight hard to eliminate before scoring by a short head, with Tendulkar a head away third. A creditable display by Landseer was followed by another in the Criterium International at Saint-Cloud, in which he improved to challenge over a furlong out but never looked like overtaking the half-length winner Act One. The mile trip that day posed no problems for Landseer, and he should stay a mile and a quarter. While it is hard to envisage him as a classic prospect to vie with the best of his stable companions, he is game and consistent and likely to give a good account of himself whatever the company, whether or not he proves up to winning a Group 1 race.

Landseer is a well-made, attractive colt (his portrait was taken late in the year) who acts on soft and good to firm going. He cost 115,000 guineas as a foal and 260,000 guineas as a yearling at the Houghton Sales and comes from a family without any exceptional performers close up. His dam never ran and has produced two other winners, the fillies Ghita (by Zilzal), successful over a mile and at nine furlongs in France, and Sabreon (by Caerleon), awarded a mile-and-a-quarter maiden at Chepstow. She had an Unfuwain colt in 2000 (now named Ikhtyar, and with John Gosden) who fetched 65,000 guineas as a foal then 380,000 guineas as a

Mr M. Tabor & Mrs John Magnier's "Landseer"

	Danehill (USA) (b 1986)	Danzig (b 1977)	Northern Dancer Pas de Nom
Landseer (b.c. Feb 28, 1999)		Razyana (b 1981)	His Majesty Spring Adieu
	Sabria (USA) (b 1991)	Miswaki (ch 1978)	Mr Prospector Hopespringseternal
		Flood (b or br 1983)	Riverman Hail Maggie

yearling to a bid from Shadwell Estates—perhaps buying siblings of yearlings purchased by the Coolmore team is a profit-making venture worth trying by pinhookers. The grandam Flood produced four winners, the pick of them Grand Criterium and Cumberland Lodge Stakes third King Sound. Things improve with the third dam Hail Maggie. She was a half-sister to top-notch racemare Trillion, dam of Triptych, and to Doff The Derby, dam of Generous and Imagine, and foaled a good runner herself in Sabona, winner of the Grade 1 Californian Stakes. *A. P. O'Brien, Ireland*

LANE COVE (IRE) 2 b.f. (Apr 26) Turtle Island (IRE) 123 – Shining Creek (CAN) **54**
(Bering 136) [2001 5.7g 6d p6g Dec 28] IR 9,500Y: first foal: dam, Italian winner around 7f (including at 2 yrs), half-sister to dam of smart French performer up to 15f Russian Hope: modest form in maidens: likely to be suited by 1m+. *P. J. Makin*

LANESBOROUGH (USA) 3 ch.c. Irish River (FR) 131 – Hot Option (USA) **–**
(Explodent (USA)) [2001 87p: 7m 8m 9.2s Aug 21] medium-sized, useful-looking colt: fairly useful winner at 2 yrs: well held in 2001: blinkered second outing: sent to USA. *G. A. Butler*

LANOSO (IRE) 3 b.g. Charnwood Forest (IRE) 125 – Silver Spark (USA) (Silver **–**
Hawk (USA) 123) [2001 –: 8m 8.3g 12.6f Jun 27] no form. *C. R. Egerton*

LA NOTTE 3 b.f. Factual (USA) 108 – Miss Mirror 77 (Magic Mirror 105) [2001 88: **84**
7g 8.1m⁵ 7m Sep 22] lengthy, good-topped filly: fairly useful performer: off 4 months
before final start: not sure to stay beyond 1m: acts on firm and soft ground. *W. Jarvis*

LANTIC BAY 4 b.f. Afzal 83 – Silent Dancer 76 (Quiet Fling (USA) 124) [2001 35: **–**
11.7f⁶ 10.2s Aug 9] little form in sellers. *J. C. Tuck*

LANZERAC 4 b.g. Lycius (USA) 124 – Watership (USA) (Foolish Pleasure (USA)) **81 ?**
[2001 12m⁵ 12g⁵ 12d⁵ Nov 6] 5,000 3-y-o: tall, angular, close-coupled gelding: half-
brother to several winners, including 1¼m winner Blue (by Bluebird) and winner up to
2¼m Captain's Guest (by Be My Guest), both useful: dam maiden half-sister to North
American Grade 1 13f winner Great Neck: seemed to show fairly useful form when 5
lengths fifth to Turn of A Century in maiden at Newmarket second start: well held
otherwise: will stay beyond 1½m: hung left on debut: won over hurdles in December.
John A. Harris

LANZLO (FR) 4 b. or br.g. Le Balafre (FR) 116 – L'Eternite (FR) (Cariellor (FR) **–**
125) [2001 71: 12g Aug 27] lightly-raced maiden. *P. J. Hobbs*

LAPADAR (IRE) 2 b. or br.f. (Mar 27) Woodborough (USA) 112 – Indescent Blue 63 **52**
(Bluebird (USA) 125) [2001 7g f7g³ 7.1d⁴ f7g f8g² 8s f8.5g³ f8g* f7g* Nov 26] 3,200Y: **a80**
leggy, lengthy filly: second foal: dam, maiden, raced mainly at 1m: fairly useful on all-
weather, modest on turf: won maiden and minor event at Southwell in November: likely
to prove best at 7f/1m: acts on fibresand, best turf effort on good to soft going: tough.
J. R. Weymes

LA PAOLA (IRE) 5 ch.m. Common Grounds 118 – Lotte Lenta (Gorytus (USA) 132) **–**
[2001 f6g f8.5g 7m 6f⁶ 5m 7m 7g Aug 11] leggy mare: fair winner in 1999: little form
since, leaving Jamie Poulton after second start in 2001: blinkered once. *P. Howling*

LA PASSIONE (USA) 3 ch.f. Gulch (USA) – Larking (USA) 86 (Green Forest **80**
(USA) 134) [2001 83p: 8d 9m² 8m 8.1v* 8s⁵ Oct 25] strong, angular filly: fairly useful
performer: won maiden at Haydock in September: stays 9f: acts on good to firm and
heavy ground. *H. R. A. Cecil*

LA PAZ 2 b.f. (Mar 22) Nashwan (USA) 135 – Las Flores (IRE) 102 (Sadler's Wells **70 p**
(USA) 132) [2001 8v⁵ Oct 26] strong, lengthy filly: third foal: half-sister to useful 1¼m
winner Jalisco (by Machiavellian) and 3-y-o Spanish Spur: dam, 1¼m winner and
third in Oaks d'Italia, half-sister to 4-y-o Bach: 20/1, never-dangerous fifth of 11 to
Teresa Balbi in maiden at Doncaster: should be suited by 1¼m/1½m: type to do better.
J. H. M. Gosden

LA PERLA 2 gr.f. (Apr 1) Royal Applause 124 – Lammastide 93 (Martinmas 128) **69 §**
[2001 5g⁴ 5.3f² f6g³ f7g² 7d⁵ 6g⁴ 7g² 7m 8m 8.2v⁶ 7.9s 7d³ f7g⁶ f6g⁶ f8g f8g f6g* Dec
17] 25,000Y: leggy filly: half-sister to several winners up to 1m, including 8-y-o Amber
Fort: dam 2-y-o 5f winner: fair performer: left W. Haggas after seventh start: rather
disappointing prior to winning seller at Southwell: effective at 6f to easy 1m: acts on
firm ground, good to soft and fibresand: blinkered twice, including when successful:
ungenuine. *M. C. Chapman*

LAPWING (IRE) 3 b.c. Tagula (IRE) 116 – Wasaif (IRE) 79 (Lomond (USA) 128) **101**
[2001 82: 7g⁴ 7m² 8m* 8m 7.1m 7g⁴ 8m² 8g³ 7g² 7s³ 7d Oct 20] strong, attractive colt:
poor mover: useful handicapper: won at Newmarket in June: mainly creditable efforts
otherwise, notably when ½-length third to Kayo at York penultimate start: better form
at 7f than 1m: acts on firm and soft going: waited with: sold 42,000 gns, sent to UAE.
B. W. Hills

LARA FALANA 3 b.f. Tagula (IRE) 116 – Victoria Mill 59 (Free State 125) [2001 –p: **60**
7m 7m 8d² 8f* 10m* 9.7d⁴ 8.1f² Sep 18] smallish, good-topped filly: modest handicapper: won at Brighton and Ripon in August: stays 1¼m: acts on firm and good to soft
going: has worn tongue tie: has started slowly. *J. A. Osborne*

LARA RUBY (IRE) 2 b.f. (Apr 11) Sri Pekan (USA) 117 – Atisayin (USA) (Al Nasr **40**
(FR) 126) [2001 5d 5m 7m 6g 8g Aug 24] 4,200F: smallish, good-topped filly: fourth
foal: dam, poor maiden, half-sister to dam of Derby winner Benny The Dip: poor maiden:
stays 7f: acts on good to firm ground: tried blinkered. *P. L. Gilligan*

LARA'S DELIGHT 6 b.m. Then Again 126 – Sarah Dream (IRE) (Strong Gale 116) **–**
[2001 –: 7m 9.7m 10.2s 10m Aug 18] little form. *M. J. Weeden*

LA REINE ROXANNE 2 b.f. (Apr 14) Cyrano de Bergerac 120 – Sylvandra 81 **40**
(Mazilier (USA) 107) [2001 5m⁵ 6m 5d 6s Oct 22] 2,000Y: small, strong filly: second
foal: dam, 2-y-o 6f winner, later stayed 1m: poor maiden: reportedly finished lame final
start. *L. R. James*

LARKWOOD SIENNA (IRE)   2 ch.f. (Apr 14) Woodborough (USA) 112 – Luisa   **?**
di Camerata (IRE) 81 (Marju (IRE) 127) [2001 5.2g⁶ 6g a6g² Nov 6] 2,800Y: first foal:
dam Irish 6f winner who stayed 9.4f: well held in sellers first 2 starts (visored on second
occasion), then left C. Dwyer: second in maiden at Taby: stays 6f: acts on dirt. *Patrick
Wahl, Sweden*

LAROUSSE   3 ch.f. Unfuwain (USA) 131 – Allespagne (USA) (Trempolino (USA)   **70**
135) [2001 57: 6d 10g⁵ 12m* 12.3f³ 12g* 14.1s³ Sep 4] big, lengthy filly: fair performer:
won handicaps at Beverley in June and Newmarket in August: will stay 2m: acts on any
going. *S. C. Williams*

LASCOMBES   2 b.g. (Mar 6) Bluebird (USA) 125 – Arinaga (Warning 136) [2001   **96**
6m⁴ 6m 7.1g* 7g 7.1s⁴ 7.6d* 8d⁵ 7v Oct 26] 43,000F, 110,000Y: sturdy, close-coupled
gelding: first foal: dam, Norwegian 2-y-o 1m winner, out of smart French winner up to
11f Brillante (herself half-sister to top-class French miler Bellypha): useful performer:
won maiden at Haydock in August and minor event at Chester (beat Kundooz a neck
under exaggerated waiting tactics in steadily-run race) in September: may prove best
around 7f: acts on soft and good to firm going: visored (ran poorly) final start, and
subsequently gelded: has been slowly away/run in snatches. *J. Noseda*

LASER CRYSTAL (IRE)   2 b.f. (Mar 24) King's Theatre (IRE) 128 – Solar Crystal   **67 p**
(IRE) 110 (Alzao (USA) 117) [2001 7g⁶ Aug 4] second foal: half-sister to 3-y-o Lunar
Crystal: dam, 2-y-o 6f and 1m (May Hill) winner who should have stayed 1½m,
half-sister to 3 smart winners, including 3-y-o Crystal Music: 9/1 and green, shaped well
when sixth of 9 to Half Glance in maiden at Newmarket, getting hang of things late on:
should do better, all being well. *D. R. C. Elsworth*

LASHING NIGHT (IRE)   4 b.f. Shalford (IRE) 124§ – Lashing (USA) 98 (Storm   **–**
Bird (CAN) 134) [2001 66: 10s 11m 13m p10g Dec 22] seventh foal: half-sister to 7f to
1¼m winner Straw Thatch (by Thatching): dam 6f (at 2 yrs) to 1m winner: fair maiden at
3 yrs: little form in 2001, leaving C. Collins in Ireland before final start (at Lingfield):
best form up to 1¼m on soft ground: blinkered last 2 outings. *P. D. Evans*

LA SPEZIANA (IRE)   4 b.f. Perugino (USA) 84 – Election Special 78 (Chief Singer   **90 d**
131) [2001 86+: v1.2v² 8s 7.1m⁶ 8f 8s 7d Oct 20] useful-looking filly: fairly useful
handicapper: well below form after second at Sandown in April: stays 1m: has won on
good to firm going, very best efforts on heavy: has been slowly away: sold 9,500 gns.
D. R. C. Elsworth

LAS RAMBLAS (IRE)   4 b.g. Thatching 131 – Raise A Warning 57 (Warning 136)   **74**
[2001 86: f6g² e5g f6g⁴ 7.1v 6.1d² 6m May 26] compact gelding: poor mover: fair
performer: best around 6f: acts on fibresand, firm and good to soft going: visored
nowadays, has been blinkered: none too consistent: sold only 500 gns. *Andrew Reid*

LAST EXHIBIT   3 b.f. Royal Academy (USA) 130 – Noirmant (Dominion 123) [2001   **67**
6v⁶ p6g* p6g² Dec 19] seventh foal: half-sister to several winning sprinters, including
4-y-o Rozel: dam unraced half-sister to very smart middle-distance stayer Braashee: fair
form: won maiden at Lingfield in November: good neck second in handicap there
following month: may prove best at 6f/7f: acts on polytrack: slowly away all starts.
R. Guest

LAST GESTURE   2 b.g. (Mar 20) Jester 119 – Suile Mor 65 (Satin Wood 117) [2001   **56**
6.1m 7m* 7g² 7g 7g p7g Dec 29] 2,000Y: first foal: dam, 2-y-o 7f winner who stayed 11f,
possibly temperamental: modest performer: won seller at Brighton in August: well held
in nurseries last 3 starts: left B. R. Millman and gelded before final one: stays 7f: acts on
good to firm going: races prominently: has looked wayward. *Jean-Rene Auvray*

LAST IMPRESSION   3 b.f. Imp Society (USA) – Figment 75 (Posse (USA) 130)   **–**
[2001 69: 5d 6d 6m May 12] fair at 2 yrs: well held in 2001. *J. S. Goldie*

LASTMAN (USA)   6 b. or br.g. Fabulous Dancer (USA) 124 – Rivala (USA) (River-   **– §**
man (USA) 131) [2001 65§: 12.6d Jul 6] tall, leggy gelding: temperamental maiden
nowadays. *Jonjo O'Neill*

LAST MASTER   2 b.c. (Apr 17) Master Willie 129 – Oatfield 69 (Great Nephew 126)   **– p**
[2001 8d Oct 3] brother to fairly useful 6f winner High Sevens and 5f winner Oatey,
closely related to useful miler Barley Bill (by Nicholas Bill) and 2m winner High Plains
(by High Line), and half-brother to several winners, including smart performers up to
11.5f and 2m respectively Munwar and Hateel (both by Kalaglow): dam ran 3 times: 25/1
and green, in rear throughout in maiden at Salisbury: likely to do better. *H. Candy*

LASTOFTHECASH   5 b.g. Ballacashtal (CAN) – Blue Empress (Blue Cashmere   –
129) [2001 –: 7.1s 5.1m[6] Aug 24] no form. *Dr P. Pritchard*

LAST OF THE MICE   3 b.g. Deploy 131 – Top Mouse (High Top 131) [2001 53:   **69**
8.3g f9.4g[5] 10m[5] 11.4g 11.6m* 12m Jul 12] strong, good-bodied gelding: fair performer:
won handicap at Windsor in June: better at 11.6f than shorter: acts on good to firm
ground: blinkered last 2 starts: has found little. *J. A. Osborne*

LAST SYMPHONY   4 b.g. Last Tycoon 131 – Dancing Heights (IRE) 80 (High   **71 d**
Estate 127) [2001 73+: e8g 7m[6] 8.5m 9g 10g 8.3m 8.5m 7m Aug 27] leggy, unfurnished
gelding: fair performer, on downgrade: probably stays 9f: acts on soft ground, probably
on good to firm: visored last 2 starts: has started slowly/looked difficult ride: sold 2,000
gns. *P. Mitchell*

LA SYLPHIDE   4 ch.f. Rudimentary (USA) 118 – Primitive Gift 38 (Primitive Rising   **?**
(USA) 113) [2001 46: f7g[7] f8g* f7g* 6.1d f7g Nov 3] workmanlike filly: shows knee   **a71**
action: fair performer on all-weather: won 3 handicaps at Southwell between April/June:
best at 7f/1m: acts on fibresand, well beaten on turf in 2001. *Mrs A. Duffield*

LA TANIA   2 b.f. (Mar 30) Polish Precedent (USA) 131 – Highsplasher (USA) (Buck-   **56**
splasher (USA)) [2001 7m 8d[5] Sep 4] sixth reported foal: half-sister to fairly useful 1¼m
winner Sunny Isle (by Cadeaux Genereux) and 1993 2-y-o 7f winner Dulford Lad (by In
Fijar), later useful winner in Scandinavia up to 1¾m: dam won 6 races in USA: modest
form in maidens at Kempton and Yarmouth. *C. F. Wall*

LATE ARRIVAL   4 b.g. Emperor Jones (USA) 119 – Try Vickers (USA) 72 (Fuzz-   **52**
buster (USA)) [2001 63: 8g 8m 9.9f 12.1d[5] 9f[2] 9.9m[6] Aug 25] tall, sparely-made gelding:
modest maiden handicapper: stays 1¼m: acts on firm going: tried blinkered/visored.
A. Crook

LATE NIGHT OUT   6 b.g. Lahib (USA) 129 – Chain Dance 88 (Shareef Dancer   **116**
(USA) 135) [2001 112: 7.1s* 8g[2] 7.1d[3] 8m* 8m[2] 8g[3] 8d[3] 7d* 7d[4] Oct 20] compact
gelding: has had knee problems: smart performer: better than ever in 2001, winning listed
events at Haydock in May and Goodwood (by 1¼ lengths from Proceed With Care) in
July and Charlton Hunt Supreme Stakes at Goodwood (by 2 lengths from Free Rider) in
September, all in small fields: ran creditably otherwise, including in Celebration Mile at
Goodwood (under 2 lengths third to No Excuse Needed) and Park Stakes at Doncaster (3
lengths third to Tough Speed) on sixth/seventh starts: effective at 7f/1m: acts on soft and
good to firm going: game and consistent. *W. Jarvis*

Mr J. M. Greetham's "Late Night Out"

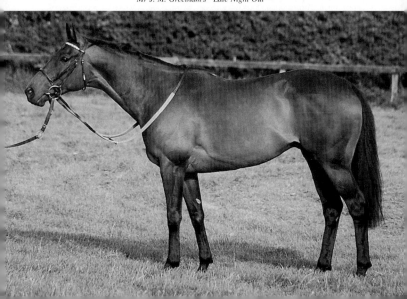

LATENSAANI   3 b.g. Shaamit (IRE) 127 – Intoxication 73 (Great Nephew 126) [2001   **49**
–: 6.9v 12m⁴ 16.2m³ 15.8g 11.9m³ Sep 4] poor maiden: stays 2m: acts on good to firm
ground. *W. J. Haggas*

LATE SUMMER (USA)   3 b.f. Gone West (USA) – Sun And Shade 93 (Ajdal (USA)   **71**
130) [2001 64P: 10m⁴ 10m⁴ 8m⁶ 10m 8.3m⁴ 8g Oct 6] smallish, good-topped filly:
unimpressive mover: fair maiden: not sure to stay much beyond 1¼m: acts on good to
firm going, showed promise on heavy: races prominently. *H. R. A. Cecil*

LATIN BAY   6 b.g. Superlative 118 – Hugging 78 (Beveled (USA)) [2001 –, a53:   **38**
13.3f⁶ 13.1d 9.9d f12f Dec 5] small, leggy gelding: poor performer: stays 13f: acts on
firm going and equitrack: has been tongue tied. *A. E. Jones*

LATIN LYNX (USA)   2 b. or br.f. (Feb 24) Forest Wildcat (USA) 120 – Senita Lane   **96**
(CAN) (Ascot Knight (CAN) 130) [2001 5m* 5m⁴ 5d⁴ Aug 21] $240,000Y: small, sturdy
filly: first foal: dam US 2-y-o winner around 6f, including minor stakes: landed odds
easily in maiden at Leicester in June: fourth in Queen Mary Stakes at Royal Ascot (beaten
1½ lengths by Queen's Logic, useful form) and listed race at Deauville (below best,
having made running): should stay 6f: has worn crossed noseband. *D. R. Loder*

LATINO BAY (IRE)   4 ch.g. Perugino (USA) 84 – Slightly Latin (Ahonoora 122)   **38**
[2001 54: f7s f7s⁵ a7g 14f 12.3f⁴ 16.6g Aug 15] poor performer: left N. Littmoden after
second start: stays 1½m: acts on fibresand/equitrack and firm ground: tried blinkered: has
looked none too keen. *Cathal McCarthy, Ireland*

LA TRAVIATA   3 b.f. Spectrum (IRE) 126 – Opera Lover (IRE) 97 (Sadler's Wells   **59**
(USA) 132) [2001 –P: 10s* 10s Oct 30] big, good-topped filly: has plenty of scope:
modest form: best effort when winning handicap at Brighton (flashed tail) in October:
stays 1¼m: raced only on soft/heavy going: sold 10,000 gns. *Sir Mark Prescott*

LATTERLY (USA)   6 b.g. Cryptoclearance (USA) – Latest Scandal (USA) (Two   **25**
Davids (USA)) [2001 f14.8g f12g⁶ f16.2g Feb 22] disappointing maiden: trained by
K. Prendergast in Ireland in 1999: stays 1¼m: acts on good to firm and good to soft going:
tried blinkered. *F. Jordan*

LAUGHING GIRL (USA)   3 ch.f. Woodman (USA) 126 – Milly Ha Ha 106   **85**
(Dancing Brave (USA) 140) [2001 10m³ 12m³ 10m* 11.9m⁴ Oct 11] third foal: half-sister
to 4-y-o Jolly Sharp: dam, 1¼m winner who stayed 1¾m, half-sister to 3-y-o Bosham
Mill out of smart middle-distance performer Mill On The Floss: fairly useful performer:
won maiden at Leicester in September: good fourth to Zilarator in minor event at York
final start: should stay 1¾m. *H. R. A. Cecil*

LAUND VIEW LEONA   3 ch.f. Piccolo 121 – Punta Leona (IRE) (Shernazar 131)   **– §**
[2001 –: f7g⁵ f7g⁶ f8g f7g⁶ 8.1v 8g 7g 8.1m 8m 7m 6m 7.5m 6s 6.1d 7d 7v 8.2s Nov 5]
little form. *R. Bastiman*

LAURA BETH   2 b.f. (Jan 20) Danehill Dancer (IRE) 117 – Cantata (IRE) (Saddlers'   **65**
Hall (IRE) 126) [2001 6g⁴ 6m⁴ 6m⁵ 5d Aug 2] 4,000F, 9,500Y: lengthy, good-bodied
filly: first foal: dam ran twice in France: fair maiden: best effort on debut: should prove
best at 5f/6f. *A. Dickman*

LAUREL DAWN   3 gr.g. Paris House 123 – Madrina 70 (Waajib 121) [2001 81: e5g*   **84 d**
5.1f 5m⁴ 5m 5f 5f⁴ 5m 5.1f 6g 5m 5d 5g⁶ 5s Oct 20] leggy, plain gelding: fairly useful   **a90**
handicapper: won at Lingfield in April: below form last 7 starts: best at 5f: acts on firm
going and fibresand/equitrack: usually races prominently. *A. Berry*

LAURIE SHEARER   5 b. or br.m. Show-A-Leg 107 – Grand Teton 64 (Bustino 136)   **–**
[2001 –: f12g Jan 8] tailed off in fibresand maidens. *R. C. Spicer*

LAURIESTON FLO (IRE)   3 b.f. Nicolotte 118 – Brown Foam (Horage 124) [2001   **51**
49: e8g³ 10s 12s⁴ f9.4g³ May 3] lengthy, heavy-bodied filly: fifth foal: half-sister to
4-y-o Diamond Rachael and 1m winner Pass The Rest (both by Shalford): dam ran twice:
modest maiden at best: stays 1m: tried blinkered: sold 2,000 gns. *B. J. Meehan*

LAUTREC   5 b.g. Shareef Dancer (USA) 135 – Pride of Paris (Troy 137) [2001 –:   **–**
f11g f12g⁶ f12g Mar 22] lightly-raced maiden nowadays: tried blinkered/visored.
R. M. Stronge

LAVYS DREAM   2 b.f. (Mar 31) Lugana Beach 116 – Gaelic Air 65 (Ballad Rock   **52 d**
122) [2001 f5g² 5.7m 5m f6s f6g f5g Nov 23] 2,000Y: fifth foal: half-sister to fairly useful
Irish 1m/9f winner Quite Chuffed (by Emarati): dam lightly-raced maiden: only form
(modest) when second in seller at Wolverhampton: should stay 6f: hung markedly left
leaving stall final outing. *M. J. Polglase*

LAW BREAKER (IRE)   3 ch.g. Case Law 113 – Revelette (Runnett 125) [2001 62,   **72**
a70: f6g³ f5s² f6s³ f5g² f5g* e5g³ 5g 5d³ 5g 6m 6g f5g⁶ f5g Dec 8] fair performer: won   **a78**

handicap at Southwell in March: best at 5f: acts on soft going, good to firm, fibresand and equitrack: visored (very slowly away) ninth start. *J. Cullinan*

LAW COMMISSION 11 ch.g. Ela-Mana-Mou 132 – Adjala 89 (Northfields (USA)) **69**
[2001 72: 5.7m 6g 7g⁴ 7.1m⁴ 8g 7m 8m 7m⁶ 7.1g* 7s f8g⁵ p7g p7g f8.5g Dec 8] small, **a62**
sturdy gelding: fair handicapper on turf, modest on all-weather: won at Chepstow in
September: effective at 6f to easy 1m: acts on fibresand and polytrack, best recent form
on good going or firmer: sometimes starts slowly/hangs under pressure: held up. *S. Kirk*

LAWFUL CONTRACT (IRE) 6 br.g. Contract Law (USA) 108 – Lucciola (FR) **–**
(Auction Ring (USA) 123) [2001 10.9m Aug 27] no form. *Graeme Roe*

LAYAN 4 b.f. Puissance 110 – Most Uppitty 69 (Absalom 128) [2001 64, a58: f6g⁶ f6g **55**
f5g² 6m² 6m⁴ 6m 5g³ f5g⁶ 6m⁴ f5g Dec 14] leggy filly: modest maiden on turf, poor on **a44**
all-weather: stays 6f: unraced on heavy going, acts on any other turf and on fibresand.
J. Balding

LAY DOWN SALLY (IRE) 3 ch.f. General Monash (USA) 107 – Sally Fay (IRE) **54**
66 (Fayruz 116) [2001 53: 6g 5m 6m⁴ 5m³ 5g 5.7m⁶ f6g f6g p6g³ Dec 19] modest maiden:
probably stays 7f: acts on soft ground, good to firm, fibresand and polytrack: tried
blinkered. *J. White*

LA YOLAM 3 ch.f. Unfuwain (USA) 131 – Massorah (FR) 108 (Habitat 134) [2001 **85**
7m⁶ 8g³ 10.1g* 10.1m⁵ 10m⁵ Sep 21] 45,000Y: good-bodied filly: sister to fairly useful
1999 2-y-o 7f winner Miss Orah, closely related to several winners, including fairly
useful 6f winner Massiba (by Shareef Dancer), and half-sister to winner abroad: dam
French sprinter: fairly useful performer: easily won Yarmouth maiden in August: better
effort after when fifth to Moselle in listed rated stakes at Newcastle next time: stays 1¼m:
raced only on good/good to firm going: swished tail repeatedly in paddock final start:
free-going sort: sold 30,000 gns. *B. Hanbury*

LAZZAZ 3 b.g. Muhtarram (USA) 125 – Astern (USA) 67 (Polish Navy (USA)) [2001 **55**
72: 10s 10s 11.6m 11m⁵ 10g³ 9.9s 10d² f9.4s³ Dec 27] modest maiden: left Miss H. Irving
after fourth start: unlikely to stay further than 1¼m: acts on fibresand, soft and good to
firm ground. *P. W. Hiatt*

LEADERSHIP 2 b.c. (Feb 24) Selkirk (USA) 129 – Louella (USA) (El Gran Senor **84 p**
(USA) 136) [2001 7m² 7.1g* 7.9s Oct 11] 42,000F, IR 350,000Y: well-made, attractive
colt: first foal: dam, French maiden, sister to useful 1¼m performer Himself: fairly useful
form: won maiden at Sandown in September by 1½ lengths from Olimolimoo: favourite,
well held in nursery at York (poorly positioned when race began in earnest) final start:
should stay at least 1m: probably capable of better. *Sir Michael Stoute*

LEANADIS ROSE 3 b.f. Namaqualand (USA) – Fiorini 54 (Formidable (USA) 125) **–**
[2001 –: 11.1s f7g f12g⁶ Nov 26] seems of little account. *Miss A. Stokell*

LEAPING CHARLIE 5 b.g. Puissance 110 – Impala Lass 81 (Kampala 120) [2001 **66**
61: f5g f6g 5v⁵ 5m* 5m⁴ 5m 5m 5f* 5d 5m 6f 5d Nov 6] leggy, angular gelding: fair
handicapper: won in large fields at Ayr in May and Beverley in July: effective at 5f/6f:
acts on fibresand and any turf going: blinkered once. *Mrs A. Duffield*

LEARNED LAD (FR) 3 ch.c. Royal Academy (USA) 130 – Blushing Storm (USA) **74**
102 (Blushing Groom (FR) 131) [2001 77p: 12m⁵ 11.7f⁶ 11.9m⁵ 11.7m⁵ 12m 8s Oct 3]
big, rather leggy colt: has plenty of scope: fair maiden: found little penultimate outing:
stays 1½m: acts on good to firm and good to soft going: sold 5,500 gns. *D. R. C. Elsworth*

LEAR SPEAR (USA) 6 b.h. Lear Fan (USA) 130 – Golden Gorse (USA) (His **116**
Majesty (USA)) [2001 120: 12m³ Jun 30] tall, workmanlike horse: usually impressed
in appearance: had a long, round action: very smart performer at best: won 6 races,
including Cambridgeshire at Newmarket in 1998 and Prince of Wales's Stakes at Royal
Ascot and Select Stakes at Goodwood in 1999: reportedly had shoulder injury after
second 5-y-o start: left D. Elsworth prior to respectable 3¼ lengths third to Mubtaker in
Fred Archer Stakes at Newmarket only outing in 2001: very best form at 1¼m: acted on
dirt, best turf form on good going or firmer: was usually held up: genuine: to stand at
Rathbarry Stud, Co Cork, Ireland, fee €2,500. *H. R. A. Cecil*

LEASE 3 ch.g. Lycius (USA) 124 – Risanda (Kris 135) [2001 10m* 12f⁵ 10.1g⁶ Sep **90**
14] fourth foal: half-brother to fairly useful 10.5f winner Andalish (by Polish Precedent):
dam unraced half-sister to Cheveley Park Stakes winner Prophecy out of Lancashire Oaks
winner Andaleeb: fairly useful performer: won maiden at Lingfield in June: similar form
in minor events after, last of 5 to Rajam at Newbury and sixth to Blue Sugar at Epsom
(slowly away/raced freely/found little): stays 1½m: sold 13,000 gns. *Mrs A. J. Perrett*

LEATHERBACK (IRE)   3 b.g. Turtle Island (IRE) 123 – Phyllode (Pharly (FR)   **85**
130) [2001 77p: 10d 10d 12g⁵ 12g 10.4d⁵ 10.3v* 11.6v³ Oct 29] strong, useful-looking
gelding: fairly useful handicapper: suspended for 40 days (trainer fined, jockey banned)
under non-triers' rule second start: won at Doncaster in October: best effort at 1¼m:
goes well on soft/heavy going: visored when refusing to enter stall on intended debut.
N. A. Callaghan

LE CAVALIER (USA)   4 b.g. Mister Baileys 123 – Secret Deed (USA) (Shadeed   **26**
(USA) 135) [2001 –, a63: f11g f12g f12s⁶ e13g⁴ e13g³ f12g³ e16s³ f16.2g³ f12g⁵ f14g   **a48**
e13g⁵ 9s 11.1d 10.3f f9.4g³ 10g f14.8s f12g² Sep 8] poor maiden: left C. Allen after
eleventh start: stays 2m: acts on good to firm going and fibresand/equitrack: tried
blinkered/visored/tongue tied: often races prominently. *A. Bailey*

LEDGENDRY LINE   8 b.g. Mtoto 134 – Eider 80 (Niniski (USA) 125) [2001 61:   **–**
14.1g 18s⁴ Oct 22] good-topped gelding: useful jumper: little form on Flat in 2001: stays
17f: acts on good to firm and heavy going: usually held up, and has found little.
Mrs M. Reveley

LEEN   4 b.f. Distant Relative 128 – St James's Antigua (IRE) 79 (Law Society (USA)   **49**
130) [2001 53d: 5.1v 7d* 9.2m⁶ f8g⁶ 7m 7.1f⁵ 6.1f 7m Jul 12] small filly: has a quick
action: poor performer: made all in claimer at Newcastle in May: probably stays 1m: acts
on firm and soft going: visored once. *M. J. Polglase*

LE FANTASME   3 b.g. Fairy King – La Splendide (FR) (Slip Anchor 136)   **72**
[2001 –: 8d 8s 7d⁴ 10g 7.1g⁶ 8g⁴ 8s⁴ 8d* 10d⁵ Nov 2] strong, good-bodied gelding: fair
handicapper: won at Bath in October: stays 1m: acts on soft going, yet to race on firmer
than good: tends to race freely: gelded after final start. *S. Dow*

LE FOLLIE (CHI)   4 ch.f. Hussonet (USA) – Whisper Loud (CHI) (Worldwatch   **–**
(USA)) [2001 –: 8.3m Aug 13] well held in maidens. *B. W. Hills*

LEGAL APPROACH   2 b.c. (Apr 9) Zafonic (USA) 130 – Legaya 94 (Shirley Heights   **100 p**
130) [2001 7.2m* 7s* Sep 30] useful-looking, slightly unfurnished colt: first foal: dam,
Irish 1½m winner, daughter of Oaks winner Jet Ski Lady: won maiden at Ayr (by neck
from Night Passion) and minor event at Ascot (by neck from Yasey, rallying gamely),
both in September: will stay 1¼m: useful already, and capable of better still. *M. Johnston*

LEGAL COUP   3 gr.f. Contract Law (USA) 108 – What A Coup (Malicious) [2001   **–**
9.7m 11.5g 11.9s Sep 30] 500Y, 1,200 2-y-o: ninth reported foal: dam winning hurdler/
chaser: tailed off in maidens. *B. A. Pearce*

LEGAL LUNCH (USA)   6 b.g. Alleged (USA) 138 – Dinner Surprise (USA)   **78**
(Lyphard (USA) 132) [2001 75§: 18v² 13.3m 16g 16d³ 17.2g⁶ Oct 1] well-made gelding:
useful hurdler: fair handicapper on Flat: stays 2¼m: acts on any turf going and equitrack:
effective visored/blinkered or not: has hung right/found little. *R. M. Stronge*

LEGAL NATIVE (IRE)   5 br.m. Be My Native (USA) 122 – Tullahought (Jaazeiro   **–**
(USA) 127) [2001 10.2g Oct 1] sister to winning hurdler: dam winning hurdler: 33/1,
well held in maiden at Bath. *R. J. Price*

LEGAL SET (IRE)   5 gr.g. Second Set (IRE) 127 – Tiffany's Case (IRE) 65 (Thatch-   **80**
ing 131) [2001 81: 9.1f 7m⁵ 7d* 8.1m⁴ 7g² 7f² 6g* f6g 6d³ 7v³ p7g³ f6g⁶ f6g p7g* p6g*
Dec 29] rather leggy, close-coupled gelding: fairly useful performer: won claimer at
Lingfield in July, handicap at Ayr in August and 2 claimers at Lingfield in December: best
form at 6f/7f: acts on good to firm going, heavy and polytrack, well held on fibresand:
tried visored/tongue tied: reportedly had breathing problem twelfth start: races freely,
often making running. *K. R. Burke*

Princess Margaret Stakes, Ascot—
Leggy Lou benefits from the step up in trip to record a five-length success over Pastel

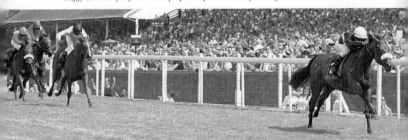

LEGAL VENTURE (IRE)   5 ch.g. Case Law 113 – We Two (Glenstal (USA) 118)   –
[2001 44, a55: 5m Aug 27] small, sturdy gelding: modest at 4 yrs: well held only outing
in 2001: usually blinkered/visored. *Julian Poulton*

LEGENDAIRE (USA)   4 gr.g. Fly Till Dawn (USA) – Iolani 59 (Alzao (USA) 117)   –
[2001 59, a65: p7g Dec 28] fair maiden in 2000: off 17 months, folded tamely only outing
at 4 yrs. *K. T. Ivory*

LEGENDARY LOVER (IRE)   7 b.g. Fairy King (USA) – Broken Romance (IRE)   **69**
(Ela-Mana-Mou 132) [2001 57: 11.6g* 11.8g⁶ 16g p13g Dec 29] strong, rangy gelding: **a–**
poor mover: fair performer: won minor event at Windsor in May: well held after: best at
1¼m/1½m: acts on soft and good to firm going: visored once: probably not one to trust
implicitly. *J. R. Jenkins*

LEGGIT (IRE)   3 b.f. Night Shift (USA) – Scales of Justice 85 (Final Straw 127)   **60 §**
[2001 61: e8g f7g f8g 8s 8.1v 8.1g 6m⁴ 11.6g³ 7m 10m 8.3g⁴ 9.7m⁵ 10g² 10m³ 10g²
10.1g⁵ 10g 10s Sep 30] modest maiden: stays 1¼m: acts on firm ground and fibresand:
visored (below form) once: tried tongue tied: tends to hang under pressure: unreliable.
Andrew Reid

LEGGY LADY   5 b.m. Sir Harry Lewis (USA) 127 – Lady Minstrel (Tudor Music   **46**
131) [2001 54, a–: f16g f16.2g² f16.2g* f16g⁴ 15.4v⁶ Apr 24] tall, angular mare: poor
performer: won handicap at Wolverhampton in February: stays 2m: acts on firm ground
and fibresand/equitrack. *B. J. Llewellyn*

LEGGY LOU (IRE)   2 b.f. (Feb 19) Mujadil (USA) 119 – Alzeam (IRE) 61 (Alzao   **108**
(USA) 117) [2001 5f⁵ 5m³ 5m* 6m* 6m Aug 23] IR 50,000Y: strong, lengthy, good-

Lucayan Stud's "Leggy Lou"

topped filly: fourth foal: sister to fairly useful 1999 2-y-o 6f winner Dashing Duke and half-sister to a 5.5f winner in Italy by Case Law: dam, lightly-raced maiden, from family of Salsabil and Marju: useful performer: won maiden at Windsor and Princess Margaret Stakes at Ascot (by 5 lengths from Pastel, clearly best effort) in July: 100/30, never travelling with fluency when last of 8 in Lowther Stakes at York: should stay 7f: raced only on ground firmer than good: has been blanketed for stall entry: sold 500,000 gns in December: joined G. Butler. *J. Noseda*

LEGS BE FRENDLY (IRE)   6 b.g. Fayruz 116 – Thalssa (Rusticaro (FR) 124)   – § [2001 71: f6g f7g f6s Jan 22] angular gelding: fair performer at 5 yrs: little form in 2001: often blinkered, tried visored: virtually refused to race final outing. *D. Nicholls*

LEILA   6 b.m. Aragon 118 – Carpe Diem 82 (Good Times (ITY)) [2001 –: 11.9s 17.2f   – May 22] little form: dead. *Miss E. C. Lavelle*

LEMARATE (USA)   4 b.g. Gulch (USA) – Sayyedati 122 (Shadeed (USA) 135)   63 [2001 58: 7s⁶ 8m 8.5m⁶ 10m 10.9g 10g 9.7m f8.5g 10.1v Oct 24] quite attractive gelding: modest maiden handicapper: left C. Brittain after seventh start, gelded after final one: stays 8.5f: acts on good to firm going: tried blinkered. *D. W. Chapman*

LE MERIDIEN (IRE)   3 ch.f. Magical Wonder (USA) 125 – Dutch Queen (Ahonoora   61 122) [2001 60: 5.1s 6g⁴ 6m³ 6m 5f⁴ 6m⁶ 5g⁶ 6m 5m* Aug 25] robust filly: modest performer: tongue tied, made all in maiden at Beverley in August: effective at 5f/6f: acts on firm ground, probably on soft: tried visored. *J. S. Wainwright*

LEMON BRIDGE (IRE)   6 b.g. Shalford (IRE) 124§ – Sharply (Sharpman) [2001   77 75: 12d 12g 13.9m* 14m⁶ 14.4m 16.2f 14.6f* 15.9m 12g⁴ Aug 3] well-made gelding: fair handicapper: won at York in May and Doncaster in June: stays 1¾m: acts on any going: often slowly away (looked reluctant leaving stalls sixth start). *C. N. Allen*

LEMURIA (IRE)   2 b.f. (Apr 10) Idris (IRE) 118 – Tiempo 50 (King of Spain 121)   45 [2001 5.3s 5m⁴ 5f⁴ 5f f5g Oct 6] sixth foal: half-sister to fairly useful 1997 2-y-o 1m winner Ten Bob (by Bob Back): dam, sprint maiden, half-sister to smart sprinter Grey Desire: poor maiden: trained first 3 starts by M. Tompkins: sent to Denmark. *Miss J. F. Craze*

LENANGO (GER)   8 b.g. Acatenango (GER) 127 – Lekana (GER) (Ile de Bourbon   – (USA) 133) [2001 f12s Feb 9] useful in Germany at 3 yrs, winning ladies race at Mannheim: no show only start on Flat in 2001. *R. G. Frost*

LENGAI (USA)   2 br.c. (Feb 2) Dixieland Band (USA) – La Pepite (USA) (Mr   85 Prospector (USA)) [2001 7m⁴ 7m² 7.2m⁵ Sep 20] $60,000Y: close-coupled, quite good-topped colt: half-brother to several winners, including useful 1m/1¼m winner Asly (by Riverman) and a winner in USA up to 1m by Slew O'Gold: dam, maiden in USA, out of champion US filly Fanfreluche: fairly useful maiden: 5 lengths second to impressive Trilogy at Salisbury: again favourite when only fourth to Legal Approach at Ayr: should stay at least 1m. *E. A. L. Dunlop*

LENNEL   3 b.g. Presidium 124 – Ladykirk 78 (Slip Anchor 136) [2001 68: 8v² 8v*   75 10s⁴ 8m* 10.9m⁴ 8m 8g 8g Oct 6] leggy, close-coupled gelding: fair performer: won maiden in April and minor event in May, both at Musselburgh: effective at 1m/1¼m: seems to act on any going: sold 16,000 gns. *Denys Smith*

LENNY THE LION   4 b.g. Bin Ajwaad (IRE) 119 – Patriotic 43 (Hotfoot 126) [2001   – § 57: 11.1d May 18] temperamental maiden handicapper: blinkered twice at 3 yrs. *Mrs M. Reveley*

LEONICA   2 b.f. (Mar 26) Lion Cavern (USA) 117 – South Shore 102 (Caerleon   92 (USA) 132) [2001 6m³ 6m² 6g² Aug 12] quite attractive filly: half-sister to 3 winners, including useful 7f/1m winner South Rock (by Rock City) and 15f winner Stonecutter (by Warning): dam, 1¼m/1½m winner, half-sister to very smart 7f/1m performer Soviet Line: refused to enter stalls on intended debut: fairly useful form when runner-up in 5-runner maidens at Ascot, beaten 1¾ lengths by Ya Hajar and ¾ length by Distant Valley: should stay 1m. *M. L. W. Bell*

LEONORA TRUCE (IRE)   2 b.f. (Apr 1) Brief Truce (USA) 126 – Eleonora   53 d'Arborea 78 (Prince Sabo 123) [2001 f5g⁴ f5g³ 5f 6.1m³ f6g⁶ 6s 6v p6g⁶ f6g p7g⁶ p6g Dec 22] 5,500Y: first foal: dam 2-y-o 6f winner (only season to race): modest maiden: barely stays 7f: acts on fibresand, polytrack and good to firm ground: often visored. *K. McAuliffe*

LEOPHIN DANCER (USA)   3 b.g. Green Dancer (USA) 132 – Happy Gal (FR)   70 (Habitat 134) [2001 8d⁴ 9m² 10f² 12d⁶ f12g f9.4s Dec 18] 12,000Y: tall, leggy, un-furnished gelding: brother to very smart French winner up to 15f Tarator and half-brother to several winners, including fairly useful Irish 1¼m/1½m winner Halcyon (by Diesis): dam French 9.5f winner: fair maiden: left M. Johnston after fifth start: stays 1½m: acts on firm and good to soft ground, well held on fibresand. *P. W. Hiatt*

LEOPOLD 2 b.c. (Jan 29) Lion Cavern (USA) 117 – Warning Star 104 (Warning 136) **46** [2001 6g 7d 6s Oct 5] 22,000Y: second foal: half-brother to Italian 7f (at 2 yrs) and 1m winner Sele Alt (by Zafonic): dam 5f (including at 2 yrs)/6f winner: poor maiden: should stay 7f: sold 800 gns. *M. L. W. Bell*

LEO'S LUCKYMAN (USA) 2 b. or br.c. (Feb 15) Woodman (USA) 126 – Leo's **103 p** Lucky Lady (USA) (Seattle Slew (USA)) [2001 7f* 7m³ 7g⁶ 7d³ Sep 14] $50,000Y: big, strong, attractive colt: has scope: fifth living foal: brother to a winner in Japan and half-brother to a 6f winner in USA by Deputy Minister: dam, winner in USA up to 6f (including at 2 yrs), daughter of 1000 Guineas second Konafa and from family of Awaasif, Hector Protector and Bosra Sham (last 2 by Woodman): useful form: impressive 8-length winner of maiden at Ayr in June: third behind Naheef in Vintage Stakes at Goodwood (seemed rather ill at ease on bends, beaten 2½ lengths at evens) and Dubai Destination in Champagne Stakes at Doncaster (beaten 5 lengths): last in Futurity Stakes at the Curragh in between: should stay 1m: acts on firm and good to soft ground: raced up with pace first 3 starts: looks type to train on into a smart colt. *M. Johnston*

LEOZIAN 3 b.g. Lion Cavern (USA) 117 – Alzianah 102 (Alzao (USA) 117) [2001 **89** 76: 6d 6m 5d⁴ 5.3m* 5m⁴ 5m 5.1m* 5g 6m 5g 5g 5g 5g Oct 4] strong, stocky gelding: fairly useful handicapper: won at Brighton in June and Chepstow in July: well held last 2 starts: best at 5f: acts on equitrack, firm and soft going: has been edgy/on toes/had 2 handlers/been taken down early: joined R. White. *E. A. L. Dunlop*

LERMONTOV (USA) 4 b. or br.g. Alleged (USA) 138 – Prospect Dalia (USA) (Mr **93** Prospector (USA)) [2001 96: 8.5f 12m 10.3f 10.4m 8g 14m 8.3m² 9g² 10.1g⁵ 8g⁵ 10d⁴ 10.1s⁶ 12s p12g Nov 24] lengthy, sparely-made gelding: fairly useful performer: left D. Nicholls after sixth outing: below form last 3 starts, possibly something amiss final one: effective at 1m/1¼m: acts on soft and good to firm going, probably on firm: sometimes takes strong hold (has worn crossed noseband). *W. R. Muir*

LE RUBAN BLEU (IRE) 2 ch.c. (Mar 17) Bluebird (USA) 125 – Minervitta – (Warrshan (USA) 117) [2001 7m 8.2s Oct 30] 280,000 francs Y: second foal: dam useful French 1¼m/1½m winner: signs of a little ability at Nottingham on second of 2 starts in maidens, forcing pace. *H. J. Collingridge*

LE SAUVAGE (IRE) 6 b.g. Tirol 127 – Cistus 123 (Sun Prince 128) [2001 –: f16g – Jan 5] probably of little account nowadays. *D. W. Barker*

LESMACADAM (IRE) 10 b.m. Digamist (USA) 110 – Fiodoir (Weavers' Hall 122) – [2001 –: f6g f7g f9.4g 11.1d 8m 14m 8.3g⁶ 12.1m 12f 16f Jul 22] of no account. *D. A. Nolan*

LETHALS LADY 3 b.f. Rudimentary (USA) 118 – Madiyla 73 (Darshaan 133) **113** [2001 8v³ 9v⁶ 8d* 8m³ 8m² 8f⁴ 8s⁴ 8d 8d 7s 9d² Nov 25] 5,000Y: leggy, quite attractive filly: fourth foal: half-sister to French 1998 2-y-o 1m winner Miracle (by Ezzoud): dam, 1½m winner, half-sister to smart 1993 Irish 2-y-o Manntari: smart performer: much improved in 2001, winning listed race at Toulouse in May: good efforts after in Poule d'Essai des Pouliches at Longchamp (very close third to Rose Gypsy), Prix de Sandringham at Chantilly (1½ lengths second to Banks Hill), Coronation Stakes at Royal Ascot (2½ lengths fourth to Banks Hill) on sixth start and Matriarch Stakes at Hollywood (2½ lengths second to Starine): stays 9f: acts on firm and soft going: tough. *R. Collet, France*

LET ME GO (GER) 3 ch.g. Java Gold (USA) – Leventina (GER) (Kris 135) [2001 – 11.1s f11g 11.5m⁵ 14.1m 12f f12g Jul 13] 19,000Y: smallish gelding: second foal: dam unraced half-sister to German Derby winner Luigi: disappointing maiden: tried blinkered. *S. P. C. Woods*

LET RIP 7 b.g. Nalchik (USA) – Delbounty (Bounteous 125) [2001 f14.8s Jan 18] well – held in maiden. *W. M. Brisbourne*

LETS REFLECT 4 b.f. Mtoto 134 – Lets Fall In Love (USA) (Northern Baby (CAN) – 127) [2001 64: 10g⁶ 7m May 28] modest maiden at best: well beaten in 2001. *L. R. James*

L'EVANGILE 3 b.f. Danehill (USA) 126 – Dubai Lady 78 (Kris 135) [2001 7g 10m³ **105** 12.1g² 12g⁴ 11.7d² 16d² Nov 2] 65,000Y: workmanlike filly: has powerful, round action: eighth foal: sister to smart 1m (at 2 yrs) and 1¼m winner who stayed 1½m Ela-Aristokrati: dam, middle-distance maiden, half-sister to smart performer up to 9f Bluegrass Prince: useful maiden: easily best effort when ½-length second to Give Notice in listed rated stakes at Newmarket final start: will stay beyond 2m: yet to race on extremes of going. *J. W. Hills*

LEVEL HEADED 6 b.m. Beveled (USA) – Snowline (Bay Express 132) [2001 68, a51: f9.4s* f11s⁵ f9.4g³ e10g f9.4g³ e10g³ 8.2f 9f 10m⁵ 9.7m* 8.5f 9.7m³ 10m⁵ Jul 13] **65 a55** strong mare: fair handicapper on turf, modest on all-weather: won at Wolverhampton in January and Folkestone in June: was effective at 9f/1¼m: acted on fibresand/equitrack and any turf going: was blinkered twice at 4 yrs: front runner: reportedly in foal to Bien Bien. *P. W. Hiatt*

LEVENDI (IRE) 4 ch.g. Mukaddamah (USA) 125 – Christle Mill (Pas de Seul 133) **–** [2001 –: 8s 5m 8.2f Jun 1] rather leggy gelding: no form. *J. S. Wainwright*

LEWIS ISLAND (IRE) 2 b.c. (Feb 27) Turtle Island (IRE) 123 – Phyllode (Pharly **85** (FR) 130) [2001 7.1s³ 8.1s² 8m² Sep 24] IR 38,000Y, IR 60,000Y: third foal: brother to 3-y-o Leatherback and half-brother to 5-y-o College Dean: dam, maiden who stayed 1½m, half-sister to Ribblesdale winner Strigida and to dam of Yorkshire Oaks winner Catchascatchcan: fairly useful form in maidens: best effort when beaten 1¼ lengths by Jack The Track at Kempton final start: will stay at least 1¼m: acts on soft and good to firm ground. *T. G. Mills*

L FOR LEISURE 2 ch.g. (Mar 28) Cosmonaut – York Street (USA) (Diamond Shoal **–** 130) [2001 8.5m 10.2g 8d Oct 25] sixth reported live foal: dam little form on Flat at 2 yrs/ over hurdles: well beaten in maidens. *W. G. M. Turner*

LIBERTY BOUND 3 b.f. Primo Dominie 121 – Tshusick 81 (Dancing Brave (USA) **62** 140) [2001 58: f6g² 5.1v³ f6g⁴ f6g 6m² 5m⁵ 5s⁶ 5g⁵ f5g* Oct 18] workmanlike filly: fair **a69** handicapper on all-weather, modest on turf: won at Southwell in October: raced only at 5f/6f: acts on fibresand, good to firm and heavy going: visored once. *D. Shaw*

LIBERTY ROYAL 2 b.c. (Mar 21) Ali-Royal (IRE) 127 – Hope Chest 70 (Kris 135) **83 p** [2001 p8g* Nov 28] 10,000F, 20,000Y: first foal: dam, lightly-raced maiden, would have proved best up to 1½m: joint favourite, won 12-runner maiden at Lingfield shade comfortably by 1½ lengths from Climate, green and having to wait for run before leading final 1f: should stay 1¼m: sure to improve. *P. J. Makin*

LICENCE TO THRILL 4 ch.f. Wolfhound (USA) 126 – Crime of Passion 115 **70** (Dragonara Palace (USA) 115) [2001 83: 5m 5.2m 5.7f³ 5m³ 5.1g⁵ Aug 7] fair performer: best at bare 5f: acts on fibresand/equitrack and good to firm ground: has gone left leaving stalls/looked far from keen. *D. W. P. Arbuthnot*

LIEUDAY 2 b.g. (Apr 22) Atraf 116 – Figment 75 (Posse (USA) 130) [2001 6m² 6s⁴ **68** Oct 22] 10,500Y: rather leggy gelding: sixth foal: half-brother to 3-y-o Last Impression and 4-y-o Annijaz: dam, somewhat temperamental 5f/6f winner, half-sister to smart sprinter Prince Reymo: fair form in frame in maidens at Ripon and Pontefract: likely to prove best short of 1m. *J. L. Eyre*

Queen Alexandra Stakes, Royal Ascot—an easy win for Life Is Life, who breaks the course record; Kahtan takes second place ahead of the twelve-year-old Dorans Pride

LIFE IS BEAUTIFUL (IRE) 2 b.f. (Mar 27) Septieme Ciel (USA) 123 – Palombella **65**
(FR) (Groom Dancer (USA) 128) [2001 5d⁶ 5m⁴ 6.1m⁶ 6m 8s 7d⁴ Oct 18] 300,000 francs
Y: good-bodied filly: sixth foal: half-sister to 3 winners in France by Highest Honor,
including smart 1m/9f winner Orso and fairly useful 1½m winner who stayed 15f Highest
Land: dam, French 11f to 13f winner, half-sister to dam of Lit de Justice, Colonel Collins
and Commander Collins: fair maiden: fourth of 30 in seller at Newmarket final start: stays
7f (raced too freely at 1m): acts on good to firm and good to soft ground: withdrawn once
after unseating rider/running loose (has been early to post). *M. L. W. Bell*

LIFE IS LIFE (FR) 5 b.m. Mansonnien (FR) 122 – La Vie Immobile (USA) (Alleged **114**
(USA) 138) [2001 112: 16.4m⁴ 22.2f* 16g 18d⁴ Sep 13] tall, angular mare: smart per-
former: good 1¼ lengths fourth to Solo Mio in Bonusprint Stakes (Henry II) at Sandown
in May, then justified favouritism in Queen Alexandra Stakes at Royal Ascot (beat
Kahtan 4 lengths) in June: better subsequent effort when respectable fourth in Doncaster
Cup: stays 2¾m: acts on any going: free-going sort: usually held up. *M. A. Jarvis*

LIFE MATCH (FR) 3 b.c. Polish Precedent (USA) 131 – Life Watch (USA) **85 +**
(Highland Park 66) [2001 11d⁴ 14.6g 10m 13s* Oct 17] 1,400,000 francs Y: big, lengthy
attractive colt: third foal: dam twice-raced sister to Poule d'Essai des Pouliches second
Duckling Park: fairly useful form: won maiden at Navan in October: very stiff task in St
Leger at Doncaster second start: stays 13f: acts on soft ground: has worn crossed
noseband: sold 30,000 gns. *A. P. O'Brien, Ireland*

LIFFORD LADY 3 b.f. Syrtos 106 – Sally Maxwell (Roscoe Blake 120) [2001 –: **58 d**
8.2s* 8.2v⁶ 7m⁶ 10g⁵ 10m 10d 8.1m⁵ 10.2g 8m 10v f8.5g Dec 1] close-coupled filly:
modest performer: below form after easily winning handicap at Nottingham in April: best
effort at 1m: acts on soft ground: has started slowly/raced freely: flashes tail: ungenuine.
B. N. Doran

Mr & Mrs Raymond Anderson Green's "Life Is Life"

LIGHT BRIGADE 2 b.g. (Mar 4) Kris 135 – Mafatin (IRE) 74 (Sadler's Wells **59** (USA) 132) [2001 7.1m 7m 6.1g⁵ Aug 20] 5,000Y: fourth foal: half-brother to a winner in Poland by Bahri: dam, 1¼m winner, half-sister to 1000 Guineas winner Fairy Footsteps and St Leger winner Light Cavalry: modest form in maidens: best effort when fifth at Nottingham: likely to be suited by at least 1m. *J. M. P. Eustace*

LIGHT DUTIES 3 gr.c. Dancing Spree (USA) – Goody Four Shoes 56 (Blazing **–** Saddles (AUS)) [2001 8m Aug 29] first foal: dam 5f (including at 2 yrs) and 6f winner: 20/1, slowly away when well held in Brighton claimer. *A. G. Newcombe*

LIGHT EVIDENCE 3 ch.f. Factual (USA) 108 – Blazing Sunset 55 (Blazing **49** Saddles (AUS)) [2001 64: f6s⁴ f7g⁶ f9.4g f6g Feb 19] poor performer in 2001: stays easy 7f: acts on fibresand. *R. Hollinshead*

LIGHTNING BLAZE 5 ch.m. Cosmonaut – Royal Deed (USA) 76 (Shadeed (USA) **45** 135) [2001 6m 5.3f 5m⁴ f6g 5m 6g⁴ 5g 5.1g 6d Aug 26] small, sturdy mare: poor form nowadays: barely stays 6f: acts on firm ground: often races prominently. *P. S. McEntee*

LIGHTNING RIDGE 3 b.f. Lightning Dealer 103 – Amazing News 47 (Mazilier **–** (USA) 107) [2001 10g 11.6m 8.1m 10v Oct 29] first foal: dam sprint maiden: no sign of ability. *D. R. C. Elsworth*

LIGHTNING STAR (USA) 6 b.g. El Gran Senor (USA) 136 – Cuz's Star (USA) **–** (Galaxy Libra 104) [2001 72: 20m 12m⁶ 11.6g Aug 6] fair handicapper at 5 yrs: no form in 2001: blinkered last 4 starts. *T. P. McGovern*

LIGHT OF DAWN (USA) 3 b. or br.c. Dynaformer (USA) – Dixie Morn (USA) **56** (Dixieland Band (USA)) [2001 8s May 7] $40,000Y: second foal: half-sister to a 1m winner in USA by Chief Honcho: dam unraced half-sister to smart winner up to 1½m in Britain and USA Fool's Prayer: 25/1, signs of ability when mid-division in maiden at Kempton, making some late headway. *P. W. Harris*

LIGHT OF FASHION 3 b.f. Common Grounds 118 – May Light 62 (Midyan (USA) **–** 124) [2001 39: 8.2s f7g Apr 30] smallish, workmanlike filly: poor maiden at 2 yrs: well held in 2001. *B. Smart*

LIGHT PROGRAMME 7 b.g. El Gran Senor (USA) 136 – Nashmeel (USA) 121 **56** (Blushing Groom (FR) 131) [2001 –: f11g 10f⁶ 12.6d² 9.9m⁵ 12g³ 16.2m⁴ f14g Oct 1] sturdy gelding: modest nowadays: stays 12.6f: acts on good to firm and good to soft going: has had tongue tied: tends to hang right. *A. L. Forbes*

LIGHT SCENT (USA) 2 ch.c. (Apr 19) Silver Hawk (USA) 123 – Music Lane **93 p** (USA) (Miswaki (USA) 124) [2001 7m⁵ 8.1s² Aug 19] $300,000Y: strong, close-coupled colt: third foal: dam, sprint winner in USA, half-sister to several smart performers by Silver Hawk, including US Grade 1 winner up to 1½m Hawkster and French middle-distance performer Silver Lane: better effort in maidens (fairly useful form) when clear 4 lengths second to impressive Shadow Dancing at Sandown, not unduly punished once clearly held: will be suited by 1¼m/1½m: should improve and win races. *Sir Michael Stoute*

LIGHT THE ROCKET (IRE) 5 ch.g. Pips Pride 117 – Coolrain Lady (IRE) 74 **–** (Common Grounds 118) [2001 89: 6s 6g 6m 5g 6m 6g 6g 6v Oct 8] leggy, rather lightly-made gelding: smart in 1999 for R. Hannon: deteriorated markedly: was tried blinkered: dead. *W. J. Musson*

LIGNE GAGNANTE (IRE) 5 b.g. Turtle Island (IRE) 123 – Lightino (Bustino **88 +** 136) [2001 100: 11.9g Aug 21] useful-looking gelding: useful handicapper: not entirely discredited only 5-y-o start: has form at 1¾m, probably best around 1½m: acts on firm and soft going. *M. Johnston*

LIHOU ISLAND 2 b.f. (Apr 16) Beveled (USA) – Foreign Mistress (Darshaan 133) **89** [2001 5d³ 5m⁵ 5.7m³ 6g* 6g⁴ 6m 6d 7d⁵ 7v² Oct 26] 7,000Y: leggy, sparely-made filly: sixth foal: sister to 6f winner Nicholas Mistress, closely related to a 7f winner in Italy by Sharpo and half-sister to 1997 2-y-o 8.5f winner Pink Ticket (by Emarati): dam maiden in Italy: fairly useful performer: won nursery at Newmarket in August: very good second in similar event at Newbury: should stay 1m: acts on heavy going. *N. P. Littmoden*

LIKELY LADY (IRE) 2 b.f. (Jan 6) Revoque (IRE) 122 – Harmer (IRE) 72 (Alzao **51** (USA) 117) [2001 6m 5.1g⁶ 5.2m⁴ 8g p5g p6g⁵ p6g⁶ Dec 28] quite attractive filly: sixth living foal: half-sister to fairly useful 1995 2-y-o 5f winner Amaretto Bay (by Common Grounds), later sprint winner abroad, and a 1m winner in Germany by Silver Kite: dam maiden who stayed 7f: modest maiden: stays 6f: acts on good to firm going and polytrack. *N. P. Littmoden*

LILIUM 3 b.f. Nashwan (USA) 135 – Satin Flower (USA) 115 (Shadeed (USA) 135) **111**
[2001 95p: 9.9m6 10.1f4 12g* 12d3 Oct 13] leggy, angular filly: smart performer: on toes
after 3-month break, best effort when winning listed race at Ascot in September by 5
lengths from Isadora, soon clear straight, though not for first time flashing tail: just
respectable third to Head In The Clouds in Princess Royal Stakes at same track final start:
stayed 1½m: acted on firm going, probably on good to soft: sometimes ran in snatches:
visits Seeking The Gold. *Sir Michael Stoute*

LILLEMAN 3 b.g. Distant Relative 128 – Lillemor (Connaught 130) [2001 80, a70: **70**
e5g* 5s 5s 5m 5f 5s 5s 5s Sep 8] strong, compact gelding: has quick action: fair performer: won
3-runner maiden at Lingfield in March: no form last 4 starts: not sure to stay beyond 6f:
acts on heavy going: blinkered (ran well) final 2-y-o start: has worn tongue strap/crossed
noseband/been early to post: carries head awkwardly: sold 1,800 gns, sent to Italy.
G. A. Butler

LILLIAN VIOLET 2 b.f. (Mar 25) Beveled (USA) – Grey Twig 68 (Godswalk –
(USA) 130) [2001 5d f6g 6m Jun 12] 1,000Y: half-sister to several winners, including
fairly useful 1986 2-y-o 6f winner Grey Wolf Tiger (by Rolfe): dam, maiden, ran only at
5f at 2 yrs: little form in maidens/seller. *J. S. Moore*

LILLIES BORDELLO (IRE) 2 b.f. (Jan 29) Danehill Dancer (IRE) 117 – Lunulae **81**
(Tumble Wind (USA)) [2001 5m3 5d2 6m2 5.2m 5m* 6g3 5.1m 5m5 Sep 20] IR 9,000F,
IR 7,800Y: lengthy, quite good-topped filly: seventh foal: half-sister to 3 winners, including Irish 1997 2-y-o 7f winner Super Sonic Sonia (by Tirol) and 7f to 1¼m winner Lunar
Mission (by Waajib), both fairly useful: dam, Irish 2-y-o 7f winner, also successful over
hurdles: fairly useful performer: won maiden at Musselburgh in August: good fifth in
listed event at Ayr: effective at 5f/6f: unraced on extremes of going: reliable. *K. A. Ryan*

LILLI'S LAD 3 ch.g. Selkirk (USA) 129 – Langtry Lady 91 (Pas de Seul 133) [2001 –
9.9m 12g Jul 18] 52,000F, IR 55,000Y: fifth foal: closely related to 1996 2-y-o 6f winner
Sharp Return (by Sharpo), later useful sprinter in Scandinavia, and half-brother to 2
winners, including 5-y-o Nowell House: dam 6f to 9f winner: last in maidens at Salisbury
and Kempton. *P. W. Harris*

LIL'S JESSY (IRE) 3 b.f. Kris 135 – Lobmille (Mill Reef (USA) 141) [2001 91: 7d* **101**
8m 8f 8g 7d Sep 13] well-made filly: useful performer: won Shadwell Stud Nell Gwyn
Stakes at Newmarket (beat Zaheemah ¾ length) in April, quickening in good style:
seemed to run at least creditably in face of stiff tasks in Poule d'Essai des Pouliches at
Longchamp, Coronation Stakes at Royal Ascot (under 10 lengths twelfth to Banks Hill)
and Falmouth Stakes at Newmarket next 3 starts: probably stays 1m: yet to race on soft/
heavy going, acts on any other: has been bandaged behind. *J. Noseda*

LILY OF THE GUILD (IRE) 2 ch.f. (May 4) Lycius (USA) 124 – Secreto Bold **53 §**
(Never So Bold 135) [2001 5f 6.1g 5.1m 6s Sep 24] 3,000F, 5,800Y: close-coupled filly:
second foal: dam French 2-y-o 6f/7f winner: modest maiden: form only on third start:
should stay 6f: has swished tail/hung markedly/pulled hard: unreliable. *W. S. Kittow*

LIMBO LAD 2 b.g. (Apr 24) Millkom 124 – Bumble Boogie (IRE) (Bluebird (USA) **58**
125) [2001 6f 8g6 7m f7g3 Nov 30] 3,200F, 7,500 2-y-o: first foal: dam unraced from
family of 8-y-o Persian Punch: modest maiden: third in nursery at Southwell, best effort:
bred to stay at least 1m. *P. C. Haslam*

LIMBURG (IRE) 3 b. or br.g. Hamas (IRE) 125§ – Tambora 75 (Darshaan 133) –
[2001 –: f8g5 7m f8g 8.1m f8.5g f9.4s Dec 18] little form: left W. Muir after fourth outing:
tried visored. *P. D. Evans*

LIME GARDENS 3 b.f. Sadler's Wells (USA) 132 – Hatton Gardens 96 (Auction **113**
Ring (USA) 123) [2001 99: 10f2 12f 12g5 12.5g* 12m Sep 16] 200,000Y: heavy-topped
filly: closely related to several winners, including useful 7f (at 2 yrs) to 10.4f winner
Ludgate (by Lyphard) and champion South African filly Kundalini (by El Gran Senor):
dam, Irish 6f to 1m winner, half-sister to high-class 1m/1¼m filly Kooyonga: smart
performer: ran well when short-head equal second to Adonesque in listed race at Cork
and when 2¼ lengths fifth to Lailani in Irish Oaks at the Curragh prior to winning Prix
Minerve at Deauville in August by length from Moon Queen: below best in Ribblesdale
Stakes at Royal Ascot and Prix Vermeille at Longchamp on other starts: stays 12.5f:
probably acts on any going: has carried head awkwardly. *M. J. Grassick, Ireland*

LINCOLN DANCER (IRE) 4 b.c. Turtle Island (IRE) 123 – Double Grange (IRE) **107**
(Double Schwartz 128) [2001 119: 7.1d4 6m 6d2 6s 8g 7v3 6s Nov 10] compact, sturdy,
attractive colt: poor mover: smart winner at 3 yrs: subsequently twice reportedly underwent surgery, firstly for chipped fetlock then for severe colic: useful form at best in 2001,

including when fourth to Mount Abu in listed race at Haydock and second to Welcome Friend in minor event at Yarmouth: probably best at 6f/7f: goes well on ground softer than good: has worn stick-on shoes. *M. A. Jarvis*

LINCOLN DEAN 5 b.g. Mtoto 134 – Play With Me (IRE) 73 (Alzao (USA) 117) [2001 52, a–: 8d⁵ 8d 8.3d* 8.3m 8.3d 8m² 9f 9.2m 10.1m 11.1d³ 10d 10.1g⁴ 9.2g 10.1f 8.3m 9.1v Oct 16] small, sturdy gelding: modest handicapper: won NH jockeys race at Hamilton in May: probably stays 11f: acts on firm going, good to soft and equitrack: has been early to post: often races prominently: has found little: unreliable: sold 1,000 gns, joined F. Murtagh. *J. S. Goldie* **52 §** **a– §**

LINDINIS (USA) 3 b.c. Distant View (USA) 126 – Annual Dance (USA) (Nostalgia (USA)) [2001 8.2v 8.2s⁵ 10g Nov 5] $68,000F, 140,000Y: second foal: dam won 9 races in USA, including 7f minor stakes: modest form in maidens: probably stays 1¼m. *S. Kirk* **53**

LINEA-G 7 ch.m. Keen 116 – Horton Line 89 (High Line 125) [2001 73: f16.2s³ f12g² f16g³ 13s⁴ 13.1m* 14m* 13.1m* 14.1f³ 12f⁴ 12g 14.4d Aug 8] strong mare: fair performer: won handicap and minor event at Ayr and minor event at Musselburgh in May/June: best form around 1¾m: acts on fibresand, firm and good to soft going: often held up. *Mrs M. Reveley* **63** **a69**

LINENS GIRL 5 br.m. Thowra (FR) – Stocktina 42 (Tina's Pet 121) [2001 e8g 8f May 23] no form. *B. G. Powell* **–**

LINE RIDER (USA) 2 b.c. (Apr 6) Danzig (USA) – Freewheel (USA) 88 (Arctic Tern (USA) 126) [2001 5m⁴ 5d² 6m* 6.3g 7m³ 6d 6g 6g⁶ Oct 4] $650,000Y: fourth foal: half-brother to a winner in USA by Gulch: dam, 6f/7f winner in Britain (including at 2 yrs), later Grade 3 1½m winner in USA: useful performer: won maiden at Leopardstown in July: good 3 lengths third of 4 to Dress To Thrill in listed race at the Curragh: set strong pace for long way in Group 1 events won by stable-companion Johannesburg last 3 starts: stays 7f: sent to USA. *A. P. O'Brien, Ireland* **97**

LINGO (IRE) 2 b.g. (Mar 24) Poliglote 121 – Sea Ring (FR) (Bering 136) [2001 6d³ 6g 6m Sep 6] 300,000 francs Y: strong gelding: third foal: closely related to 5-y-o Torrealta: dam, French 8.5f/10.5f winner, from family of smart French performer up to 10.5f Goldamix: modest form in maidens: third at Newcastle: likely to be suited by at least 1¼m: should do better in handicaps. *Mrs J. R. Ramsden* **53 p**

LINUS 3 b.g. Bin Ajwaad (IRE) 119 – Land Line (High Line 125) [2001 10g 11.8m⁶ 12.6m 12.1g³ 14.1s⁵ Aug 6] 8,500Y, 16,500 2-y-o: sturdy, quite attractive gelding: unimpressive mover: fifth living foal: half-brother to 1½m/1¾m winner Dalwhinnie (by Persian Bold) and 7f winner Michellisa (by Indian Ridge): dam unraced sister to Park Hill winner Quay Line: fair maiden: stays 1¾m: acts on soft and good to firm going. *S. Kirk* **65**

LIONARDO 5 b.h. Lion Cavern (USA) 117 – Pravolo (Fools Holme (USA)) [2001 ?: 8v 8v² 8d* 7g⁶ 8.3d 8g* 8f³ 8g⁴ 8d 8g* 10d 8g³ 7.5g Dec 27] fair performer: won minor events at Compiegne in May (amateurs) and Ostend in July and handicap at Deauville in August: not discredited in handicap at Windsor fifth start: left P. Smith in Belgium before penultimate outing: stays 1¼m: acts on any going. *A. Smith, UAE* **78**

LIONEL ANDROS 3 b.g. Lion Cavern (USA) 117 – Guyum (Rousillon (USA) 133) [2001 50: 7s 5v⁶ 5.1m² 5.7g 6m 5.1g 5.1f⁴ 6m Aug 18] modest maiden: seems best at 5f: goes well on going firmer than good: blinkered (slowly away) once. *R. J. Hodges* **50**

LION OF JUDAH 4 b.c. Caerleon (USA) 132 – Lyndonville (IRE) (Top Ville 129) [2001 –: 12v 8.5s 7.1g 10d 8.1m⁶ 11.9g Jun 7] of little account nowadays. *R. Brotherton* **–**

LION'S DOMANE 4 b.g. Lion Cavern (USA) 117 – Vilany 87 (Never So Bold 135) [2001 58: f8g f8g 8.3d 7m* 8m⁶ 8f⁴ 7.1f³ 6g⁶ 7.6m* 7.1f* 7g⁴ 7d 7g⁴ 7.1m* 7m 8g f8.5g f7s⁵ Dec 18] strong, workmanlike gelding: fair on turf, modest on all-weather: left P. Haslam after second outing: won seller at Thirsk, apprentice handicaps at Chester/Musselburgh and minor event at Musselburgh between May and August: seems best around 7f: acts on firm going and fibresand: tried visored (raced too freely): occasionally wayward at 2 yrs (has been equipped with net muzzle): often forces pace: none too consistent. *I. Semple* **67** **a54**

LION SONG 3 b.g. Savahra Sound 111 – Lucky Candy 61 (Lucky Wednesday 124) [2001 –: e5g 8.2v⁶ Mar 28] leggy gelding: little form in maidens (left N. Littmoden after reappearance): tried blinkered. *M. J. Polglase* **–**

LIPICA (IRE) 3 b.f. Night Shift (USA) – Top Knot (High Top 131) [2001 99p: 8s 10.2m Jul 27] big, strong, lengthy filly: useful form at 2 yrs: disappointing in listed races at Kempton (took strong hold, later said to have swallowed tongue) and Chepstow (tongue tied) over 3 months apart in 2001: stays 7f: acts on heavy going. *K. R. Burke*

LIPSTICK 2 b.f. (Mar 13) Zamindar (USA) 116 – Final Shot 91 (Dalsaan 125) [2001 **99 p** 5.2m⁵ 5.1m* 6g* 6.5g² Sep 28] 95,000Y: rather angular filly: half-sister to several winners, including 5f (at 2 yrs)/6f winner Double Action (by Reprimand) and 6f (including at 2 yrs) winner Sir Nicholas (by Cadeaux Genereux), both smart: dam won Ayr Gold Cup: won maiden at Bath in August and listed event at Kempton (beat Twilight Blues by ½ length) in September: good length second of 28 to Madame Boulangere in valuable sales contest at Ascot, staying on strongly having been dropped right out: will stay 7f: raced only on good/good to firm going: smart filly in the making, and should win more races. *M. R. Channon*

LIQUIDAMBAR 2 ch.f. (May 24) Atraf 116 – Precious Ballerina 66 (Ballachashtal **49** (CAN)) [2001 7d 7s⁴ 7d Nov 6] 2,500Y: leggy, close-coupled filly: fifth living foal: dam 1m maiden at 6 yrs: poor maiden. *J. R. Norton*

LIQUORICE 3 b.f. Robellino (USA) 127 – Missed Blessing 115 (So Blessed 130) **–** [2001 7g⁵ Aug 12] 63,000 2-y-o: half-sister to several winners, notably smart 6f/7f performer Unblest (by Alzao): dam 6f/1m winner: 4/1, looked green when fifth of 6 in maiden at Ascot on debut. *W. J. Haggas*

LISA-B (IRE) 4 b.f. Case Law 113 – Nishiki (USA) (Brogan (USA) 110) [2001 41, **–** a46: f16.2g Dec 8] leggy, sparely-made filly: poor performer at 3 yrs: off 1½ years before only outing in 2001: usually blinkered/visored. *D. L. Williams*

LISA'S LOONEY 2 b.f. (Apr 12) Bahamian Bounty 116 – Starfida (Soviet Star **44 §** (USA) 128) [2001 5.1g 5s 6g 6.1m 7d f7g p6g f6g f5f Dec 5] strong, close-coupled filly: second foal: dam once-raced half-sister to dam of very smart sprinter Pivotal: poor maiden: visored last 3 starts: probably temperamental. *Mrs C. A. Dunnett*

LISHTAR (IRE) 2 b.g. (Feb 27) Mtoto 134 – Lilissa (IRE) (Doyoun 124) [2001 8s³ **79 p** Nov 9] quite attractive gelding: third foal: closely related to useful 9f winner Livadiya (by Shernazar) and half-brother to useful 1¼m/1½m winner Lidakiya (by Kahyasi): dam, French 9f/10.5f winner, half-sister to smart French filly up to 13.5f Linnga: 7/1 but green, 6½ lengths third of 17 to Zone in maiden at Doncaster, keeping on encouragingly: gelded after: will stay at least 1¼m: sure to improve. *Sir Michael Stoute*

LISIANSKI (IRE) 3 b.g. Fairy King – Tough Lady 91 (Bay Express 132) **82** [2001 8.3g 8m 7f 6g 6m³ 5g* 5g* 5m* 5d 6g Sep 28] 105,000Y: quite good-topped gelding: has scope: closely related to 3 winners, including useful Irish sprinters Title Roll (stayed 7f, by Tate Gallery) and Northern Express (by Northern Guest), and half-brother to winner abroad by Pas de Seul: dam 2-y-o 6f winner: fairly useful handicapper: won at Folkestone, Goodwood and Salisbury in August/September: speedy, and best at 5f: acts on good to firm ground: visored fifth to ninth starts: has been slowly away. *I. A. Balding*

LISSOME (USA) 2 b.f. (Apr 2) Lear Fan (USA) 130 – Miss Otis (USA) (One For All **–** (USA)) [2001 6g Aug 6] third foal: dam US Grade 3 8.5f winner at 5 yrs: 20/1, well beaten in maiden at Windsor. *I. A. Balding*

LITANY 2 b.f. (Apr 21) Colonel Collins (USA) 122 – Hymn Book (IRE) 65 (Darshaan **– §** 133) [2001 6.9m 7.1m 7m 6g Aug 10] third living foal: half-sister to 4-y-o Damasquiner: dam maiden who should have stayed 15f: soundly beaten in maidens/sellers: tried visored: temperamental. *J. G. Smyth-Osbourne*

LITERARY SOCIETY (USA) 8 ch.h. Runaway Groom (CAN) – Dancing Gull **91** (USA) (Northern Dancer) [2001 92: 6g⁵ 6m 5m 6m 6g Oct 5] small, sturdy horse: has a quick action: fairly useful handicapper: effective at 5f/6f: best efforts on good ground or firmer: usually comes from off pace. *J. A. R. Toller*

LITHGOW FLASH (IRE) 3 b.f. Mark of Esteem (IRE) 137 – Innocence 73 **79** (Unfuwain (USA) 131) [2001 10m⁶ 10m⁶ 11.9m³ 11.7g⁵ 11.7m² f12g³ Oct 20] 160,000Y: second foal: half-sister to fairly useful 6f winner Najeyba (by Indian Ridge): dam, maiden who stayed 1½m, half-sister to Melbourne Cup winner Jeune and King Edward VII Stakes winner Beneficial: fair maiden: should stay 1¾m: acts on fibresand, raced only on good/good to firm going on turf. *J. H. M. Gosden*

LITTLE ACORN 7 b.g. Unfuwain (USA) 131 – Plaything 69 (High Top 131) [2001 **–** –: 14v Sep 29] fairly useful handicapper in 1998: well held both starts since: tried blinkered. *D. Moffatt*

LITTLE AMIN 5 b.g. Unfuwain (USA) 131 – Ghassanah 73 (Pas de Seul 133) [2001 **92** 82: 7g* 8m* 8.5m* 9m² 10.4m⁵ 8g³ 7.9m Aug 23] smallish, well-made gelding: has marked knee action: fairly useful handicapper: won at Goodwood in May and Epsom (by neck from Thihn in valuable contest) in June: mostly creditable efforts after, including when third to Riberac in William Hill Mile at Goodwood: has won at 1½m, probably ideally suited by 1m/1¼m: acts on good to firm and good to soft going. *K. R. Burke*

LITTLE BLUEBELL 2 ch.f. (May 9) Greensmith 121 – Bluebell Copse (Formidable   – (USA) 125) [2001 5.3s 5v 5.7d Oct 25] fifth foal: sister to 1997 2-y-o 5f seller winner Sage, later 5f/6f winner in Sweden, and half-sister to a winner in Italy by Faustus: dam, winner in Jersey, half-sister to very smart middle-distance stayer Sapience: last in sellers. *W. G. M. Turner*

LITTLE BRAVE 6 b.g. Kahyasi 130 – Littlemisstrouble (USA) (My Gallant (USA))   – [2001 65, a–: f16.2s⁵ f16.2g² f16g f16g Nov 19] lengthy gelding: fair handicapper: below   **a78** form after 9-month break last 2 starts: stays 2¼m: acts on fibresand/equitrack, firm and soft going: not a straightforward ride. *J. M. P. Eustace*

LITTLE CALLIAN 3 ch.f. Charmer 123 – Eucharis 41 (Tickled Pink 114) [2001 66:   **61 d** e5g² e5s⁵ e5g² 5.1s³ 5.1d 5g 5m 5m 5m Sep 26] strong, good-bodied filly: modest maiden: on downgrade: seems best at sharp 5f: acts on equitrack, soft and good to firm going: tried visored: usually races prominently. *T. M. Jones*

LITTLE CHAPEL (IRE) 5 b.m. College Chapel 122 – Istaraka (IRE) (Darshaan   – 133) [2001 52d: 12.1m 10.5s Aug 18] quite good-topped mare: disappointing maiden. *G. H. Yardley*

LITTLE CINNAMON 5 ch.h. Timeless Times (USA) 99 – Belltina 41 (Belfort (FR)   – 89) [2001 5f 5m 5f Sep 10] probably of little account nowadays. *J. Balding*

LITTLE DAISY 3 ch.f. Factual (USA) 108 – Twice In Bundoran (IRE) 70 (Bold   – Arrangement 127) [2001 7s Oct 15] strong filly: second foal: dam 5f winner, including at 2 yrs: 66/1, well beaten in maiden at Leicester. *A. B. Mulholland*

LITTLE DOCKER (IRE) 4 b.g. Vettori (IRE) 119 – Fair Maid of Kent (USA) 68   – (Diesis 133) [2001 71: 15.9d 10g Oct 6] big, workmanlike gelding: fair maiden at 3 yrs: well held both 4-y-o starts: won over hurdles in December. *T. D. Easterby*

LITTLE EDWARD 3 gr.g. King's Signet (USA) 110 – Cedar Lady (Telsmoss 91)   **76** [2001 6m² 5g* Aug 8] eighth foal: half-brother to 5-y-o Addition: dam, of little account, sister to smart 5f to 7f performer Hard To Figure: confirmed debut promise when winning maiden at Sandown by 2 lengths from Mishka, racing freely and leading 2f out: will prove best at 5f/6f: refused to enter stall and withdrawn Sep 10. *B. G. Powell*

LITTLE EMMA 3 b.f. Safawan 118 – Little Vixen (Aragon 118) [2001 6m 6m 8m   – 8m Jul 21] 620Y: second foal: dam unraced: well held in maidens/seller. *C. W. Fairhurst*

LITTLE FOX (IRE) 6 br.m. Persian Bold 123 – Dance Land (IRE) (Nordance   **55** (USA)) [2001 11.6g 8f⁶ 9f³ 10m² 14.1m⁶ 10m⁴ 10m² 8g² 11.9s p10g⁴ p10g⁴ p10g³ p10g²   **a62** p13g³ Dec 29] modest handicapper: won maiden at Lingfield in November: ran well in handicaps there after: effective at 1m to 13f: acts on equitrack/polytrack and firm going: has been slowly away: refused to enter stall fifth intended outing: consistent. *J. J. Bridger*

LITTLE JOHN 5 b.g. Warrshan (USA) 117 – Silver Venture (USA) (Silver Hawk   **63 §** (USA) 123) [2001 66: 12s 9v 13s⁶ 12d⁶ 9.2d⁵ 8.3m 12.1m⁵ 11.1d² 13.1m³ 12.4m² 12.1m⁴ 14m⁴ 14f² 13g² 16f² 12f² 12g³ 13g³ 14f³ 16m² 12m² 14g² 16m³ Aug 22] big, lengthy gelding: modest maiden handicapper: stays 2m: acts on any going: occasionally blinkered/visored: has run creditably when sweating profusely: usually finds little. *Miss L. A. Perratt*

LITTLE KENNY 8 b.m. Warning 136 – Tarvie 101 (Swing Easy (USA) 126) [2001   – f16.2g Feb 6] probably of little account nowadays. *R. J. Price*

LITTLE LES 5 b.g. Jumbo Hirt (USA) 90§ – Hand On Heart (IRE) 62 (Taufan (USA)   – 119) [2001 31: 7.1f 6m 9f⁵ Aug 1] of little account nowadays. *J. L. Eyre*

LITTLE NOBBY 2 b.g. (Apr 30) Makbul 104 – Simply Style (Bairn (USA) 126)   **55** [2001 6m⁵ 6d 6d f6g 7.1s³ f6g⁶ f6s Dec 26] 2,700 2-y-o: leggy gelding: seventh foal: half-brother to 3 winners, including fairly useful 1997 2-y-o 5f winner Lady Moll (by King's Signet), later sprint winner in USA, and unreliable 1m winner Loch Style (by Lochnager): dam unraced: modest maiden: stays 7f: acts on fibresand, good to firm and soft going. *R. Hollinshead*

LITTLE OAK (IRE) 3 b.f. Tagula (IRE) 116 – Blue Goose (Belmez (USA) 131)   – [2001 8d⁵ 7g 6f Aug 29] IR 1,000Y: first foal: dam ran 3 times in France: never dangerous in maidens. *G. A. Swinbank*

LITTLE PEARL (IRE) 3 b.f. Bigstone (IRE) 126 – Congress Lady 93 (General **55**
Assembly (USA)) [2001 f7g⁵ f8g⁵ f8g f8g 10s⁴ f12g⁴ 16m 12f* 12f* 12g Aug 4] IR
15,000Y: quite good-topped filly: half-sister to several winners, including useful Scandinavian performer up to 8.5f Senador (by Alzao) and fairly useful 1m/1¼m winner Ganga
(by Generous): dam French 8.5f winner: modest performer: won handicaps at Pontefract
(seller) and Musselburgh in July: stays 1½m: acts on soft ground, firm and fibresand: sold
2,200 gns. *T. D. Easterby*

LITTLE PIPPIN 5 ch.m. Rudimentary (USA) 118 – Accuracy 83 (Gunner B 126) **85**
[2001 90: 12s⁴ 14.1g⁴ 12d³ 12g 14v Sep 29] rather unfurnished mare: has a round action:
fairly useful handicapper: stays 1¾m: raced mainly on good going or softer: has worn
tongue strap: edgy sort. *G. B. Balding*

LITTLE PIXIE (USA) 3 ch.f. Woodman (USA) 126 – Tryarra (IRE) 99 (Persian **48 §**
Heights 129) [2001 –: 10s⁶ 10.1d 8m 8m 7.1g* 7m 7d 7.1d 7.1m⁵ 8.1f Sep 18] smallish,
good-topped filly: poor handicapper: won at Haydock in June: should stay beyond 7f:
acts on good to firm going: sold 8,000 gns in December. *N. Tinkler*

LITTLE ROBS' GIRL 2 ch.f. (Mar 19) Cosmonaut – David James' Girl 65 (Faustus **54**
(USA) 118) [2001 5s⁶ 5m Sep 30] smallish, angular filly: first foal: dam 5f (at 2 yrs) to
1m winner: better effort in maidens (modest form) when sixth at Haydock: should stay 6f.
A. Bailey

LITTLE ROCK 5 b.h. Warning 136 – Much Too Risky 87 (Bustino 136) [2001 118: **121**
10s⁴ 12g² 12g 12m⁴ 12s⁶ 10d³ Nov 18] smallish, lengthy, angular horse: very smart
performer: ran well in 2001 when 1½ lengths second to Mutamam in Princess of Wales's
Stakes at Newmarket (won race at 4 yrs) in July and 9½ lengths sixth to Sakhee in Prix de
l'Arc de Triomphe at Longchamp in October: stays 1½m well, seemingly not 1¾m: yet to
race on firm going, acts on any other: sometimes wanders: joined F. Doumen in France.
Sir Michael Stoute

LITTLE TASK 3 b.g. Environment Friend 128 – Lucky Thing (Green Desert (USA) **–**
127) [2001 67: 10g 10m 12.4m⁶ 12.4g 8m 7.5m 8.9m Sep 2] smallish, close-coupled
gelding: fair at 2 yrs: little form in 2001, leaving H. McWilliams after fifth start: tried
blinkered (including when successful). *J. S. Wainwright*

LITTLE TOBIAS (IRE) 2 ch.g. (Apr 12) Millkom 124 – Barbara Frietchie (IRE) **68**
(Try My Best (USA) 130) [2001 5m 6m⁵ 6f⁵ 6d Oct 8] smallish, good-topped gelding:
first foal: dam, Italian 6f and 1m winner, closely related to useful performer up to 1½m
Roses In The Snow from family of Tenby: fair maiden: best effort at Newcastle on
penultimate start: should stay 1m. *Andrew Turnell*

LITTLETON BOREAS (USA) 2 b. or br.c. (Feb 4) Foxhound (USA) 103 – Susita **52**
Song (USA) (Seattle Song (USA) 130) [2001 6d 7.6m f6g⁶ Nov 12] $11,000Y, 23,000
2-y-o: leggy colt: second foal: dam unraced: best effort in maidens (modest form) when
sixth at Southwell. *R. J. White*

LITTLETON TZAR (IRE) 2 b.c. (Mar 25) Inzar (USA) 112 – Solo Symphony **74**
(IRE) 67 (Fayruz 116) [2001 6m 6g⁴ 6g 5.1f⁵ 6s³ f6g⁴ 6d⁵ Nov 2] 7,600Y, 30,000 2-y-o:
small colt: first foal: dam, sprint maiden, out of half-sister to useful sprinter Whittingham:
fair maiden: ran well in nurseries fourth to sixth starts: should stay 7f: acts on fibresand,
firm and soft going. *R. J. White*

LITTLETON ZEUS (IRE) 2 ch.g. (Apr 13) Woodborough (USA) 112 – La Fan- **45**
dango (IRE) 51 (Taufan (USA) 119) [2001 6g 6.1m 7s p8g p8g⁶ f9.4g⁵ Dec 8] 17,000Y:
second foal: dam maiden who stayed 1m: poor maiden: probably stays 9.4f: acts on soft
and good to firm going, polytrack and fibresand: visored final start: has looked
headstrong. *R. J. White*

LITTLE TUMBLER (IRE) 6 b.m. Cyrano de Bergerac 120 – Glass Minnow (IRE) **62**
59 (Alzao (USA) 117) [2001 53: 10f 9m 10m² 9f² 8g⁴ 10m 10m* 8.5g⁵ Sep 14] neat mare:
modest handicapper: won at Brighton in September: probably best at 9f/1¼m: goes well
on going firmer than good: sometimes slowly away. *S. Woodman*

LITTLE WOODSTOCK (IRE) 2 ch.g. (Apr 22) Woodborough (USA) 112 – Penul- **65**
timate Cress (IRE) (My Generation 111) [2001 5.3s 5.3m⁴ 5.3m² 6m f7g³ Sep 22] IR
4,200Y: strong gelding: third foal: half-brother to 3-y-o Dancing Penney: dam unraced:
fair maiden: ran in seller final start: stays 7f: acts on good to firm ground: blinkered last 3
starts. *D. J. S. Cosgrove*

LITUUS (USA) 8 gr. or ro.g. El Gran Senor (USA) 136 – Liturgism (USA) (Native **–**
Charger) [2001 a10f a10f⁵ 8f a7f 8g 12m Aug 27] good-topped gelding: has a round

action: won maiden at Nad Al Sheba in 1997: left S. Seemar in Dubai before well held
last 2 starts: stays 1m: acts on dirt and good to firm ground: sometimes visored/blinkered.
Miss Gay Kelleway

LITZINSKY 3 b.g. Muhtarram (USA) 125 – Boulevard Girl 80 (Nicholas Bill 125) **81**
[2001 59: 10s² 11s⁴ 13.9m⁵ 14.1m 11.9d⁵ 13.1d⁴ 16.2s* 15m⁴ 14v 18d 16.5s³ Nov 10]
rather leggy, lengthy gelding: fairly useful handicapper: made all at Haydock in August:
ran well final start: stays 2m well: has form on good to firm going, goes well on soft.
C. B. B. Booth

LIVE DANGER (USA) 2 b.c. (Mar 9) Affirmed (USA) – Personal Colors (USA) **54 p**
(Danzig (USA)) [2001 7.1g⁶ Sep 2] $62,000F, $160,000Y: second foal: half-brother to a
winner in US by Miner's Mark: dam, unraced, out of sister to Breeders' Cup Distaff
winner Personal Ensign: 6/1 and green, slowly away and not knocked about when sixth
of 10 to Don Fernando in maiden at Sandown: should stay 1¼m: sent to UAE: likely to
improve. *M. R. Channon*

LIVE IN LOVER (IRE) 3 b.g. Up And At 'em 109 – Inesse (Simply Great (FR) **–**
122) [2001 –: f7g f7g 10m Sep 1] quite good-topped gelding: little form. *P. C. Haslam*

LIVELY FELIX 4 b.g. Presidium 124 – Full of Life 85 (Wolverlife 115) [2001 53: **–**
e7g Feb 10] modest maiden at 3 yrs: well held only 4-y-o start. *S. Mellor*

LIVELY LADY 5 b.m. Beveled (USA) – In The Papers 87 (Aragon 118) [2001 94: 6s⁶ **84**
5.1d f5g 6g 5.2d⁶ 5v 5d 5v Oct 29] sturdy mare: poor mover: fair handicapper nowadays: **a–**
effective at 5f/6f: acts on good to firm and heavy going, probably on fibresand: usually
visored/blinkered: usually held up: tends to wander. *J. R. Jenkins*

LIVE THE DREAM 3 b.f. Exit To Nowhere (USA) 122 – Inveraven 53 (Alias Smith **57**
(USA)) [2001 48: f8g f8g⁵ f11g 10m 9.9m 16f⁴ 13.8m* Sep 22] angular filly: modest
performer: won seller at Catterick (joined M. Pipe 8,500 gns) in September: better at
1¾m/2m than shorter: acts on firm going: fairly useful hurdler. *J. Hetherton*

LIVE TO TELL 5 ch.m. Primo Dominie 121 – Dreams Are Free (IRE) 71 (Caerleon **–**
(USA) 132) [2001 5.1m⁶ 5g 6v 5.1d Oct 25] fair performer at 3 yrs: little form on return
in 2001. *W. G. M. Turner*

LIVIUS (IRE) 7 b.g. Alzao (USA) 117 – Marie de Beaujeu (FR) 108 (Kenmare (FR) **89**
125) [2001 92: 12d 12g⁴ 12f 12m⁶ 11.9d⁴ 12g⁴ 14.6d 12.1m 12g Oct 4] big gelding:
fairly useful handicapper: stays 1½m: acts on firm and good to soft going, probably on
soft: blinkered once: often sweats: usually held up. *C. A. Dwyer*

LIZZEY LETTI 3 ch.f. Grand Lodge (USA) 125 – Crystal Ring (IRE) 83 (Kris 135) **99**
[2001 64p: 10m³ 10m 10f⁵ 10s* Oct 20] strong, lengthy filly: useful performer: best effort
when making all in listed race at Gelsenkirchen (beat Homita ½ length) in October:
reportedly lame third outing: may stay 1½m: acts on equitrack, firm and soft
ground: joined P. Schiergen in Germany. *G. Wragg*

LLOYD 2 b.g. (Apr 11) Glory of Dancer 121 – Broughtons Bird (IRE) (Exhibitioner **77 §**
111) [2001 5s 6g 7g⁶ 8g f7g⁶ f6g² f6g f6g⁴ Oct 23] strong gelding: third foal: half-brother
to a winner in Greece by Contract Law: dam no sign of ability: fair maiden: second at
Wolverhampton in October, easily best effort: stays 6f: acts on fibresand: tongue tied last
4 starts: difficult ride: unreliable. *J. O'Reilly*

LOBLITE LEADER (IRE) 4 b.g. Tirol 127 – Cyrano Beauty (IRE) (Cyrano de **54**
Bergerac 120) [2001 –: 9.2d 11.1d* 10.9f 9.2m⁴ 11.1s³ 14.4d* 14m* 14v Sep 29] good-
topped gelding: modest handicapper: won at Hamilton (seller, final start for D. Eddy) in
May and Newcastle and Musselburgh (amateurs) in August: stays 14.4f: acts on soft and
good to firm going. *G. A. Swinbank*

LOBUCHE (IRE) 6 b.g. Petardia 113 – Lhotse (IRE) 67 (Shernazar 131) [2001 –§: **– §**
f7g Mar 13] temperamental handicapper: tried blinkered/tongue tied. *M. C. Chapman*

LOCH AILORT 5 b.m. Be My Chief (USA) 122 – Lochbelle 70 (Robellino (USA) **44**
127) [2001 46: 11g³ f8g⁵ f9.4s⁵ f9.4g f8s² f11g⁵ f8g Mar 16] poor maiden handicapper:
stays 11f: raced only on fibresand since debut: visored: often starts slowly: sold 2,000
gns. *Miss V. Haigh*

LOCHARIA 2 b.f. (Apr 19) Wolfhound (USA) 126 – Lochbelle 70 (Robellino (USA) **91**
127) [2001 5m³ 5g 5m* 5d⁴ Oct 13] 16,000Y: third foal: dam, 1¼m winner who stayed
1½m, half-sister to Nunthorpe winners Lochsong and Lochangel: fairly useful performer:
won maiden at Musselburgh in September by 5 lengths: beaten same margin when
good fourth to Dominica in Cornwallis Stakes at Ascot, keeping on: should stay 6f.
Mrs L. Stubbs

LOCH INCH 4 ch.g. Inchinor 119 – Carrie Kool 69 (Prince Sabo 123) [2001 –: 6m 6g **63** 6g f6g[6] 6.1v 5d 5.2v Oct 26] smallish gelding: modest handicapper: stays 7f: acts on good to firm going, good to soft and fibresand: visored once, often blinkered. *K. McAuliffe*

LOCH LAIRD 6 b.g. Beveled (USA) – Daisy Loch (Lochnager 132) [2001 83d: 7m[5] **69** 7s[3] 6m[5] 6m 6m 7m 6g 7.6g[5] 5m Sep 26] lengthy gelding: fair handicapper: best at 6f/ 7f: acts on firm and soft ground: tried visored/blinkered: has carried head awkwardly. *M. Madgwick*

LOCH MAREE 2 b.f. (Feb 22) Primo Dominie 121 – Aurora Bay (IRE) (Night Shift **65 d** (USA)) [2001 5s[6] 6g[3] 6m 6d 6d Oct 30] 5,200Y: angular, quite good-topped filly: first foal: dam, no form, out of useful half-sister to high-class 1¼m performer Shady Heights: easily best effort (fair form) when third in maiden at Thirsk: stays 6f. *M. W. Easterby*

LOCHRIDGE 2 ch.f. (Mar 27) Indian Ridge 123 – Lochsong 129 (Song 132) [2001 **87 p** 7m[3] 7m[2] Sep 24] third foal: dam best at 5f (won Prix de l'Abbaye twice and Nunthorpe): better effort in maidens (fairly useful form) when 2 lengths second of 12 to Purple Haze at Kempton: will stay 1m: should improve and win a race or 2. *I. A. Balding*

LOCHSPRITE 3 ch.f. So Factual (USA) 120 – Lochspring (IRE) (Precocious 126) **58** [2001 75: 6g[6] 5.1f[2] 5g[3] f7g Oct 1] modest maiden: will prove best at 5f/6f: acts on firm and good to soft ground: has found little: sold 1,000 gns. *I. A. Balding*

LOCK INN 2 b.g. (Jan 31) Dolphin Street (FR) 125 – Highest Bid (FR) (Highest **–** Honor (FR) 124) [2001 8d p10g Dec 4] 7,500F, 10,000Y: second foal: dam French 7.5f (at 2 yrs) to 1¼m winner: well beaten in maidens. *Miss D. A. McHale*

LOCKSTOCK (IRE) 3 b.g. Inchinor 119 – Risalah (Marju (IRE) 127) [2001 f7g 8d[4] **67** 10.2d 7m 8d[3] 8m 8.5d f9.4g[2] f8g* f9.4g Dec 8] second foal: half-brother to 4-y-o Atlantic Ace: dam ran once: fair performer: won maiden at Southwell (edged left) in November: stays 9.4f: acts on good to soft ground and fibresand. *M. S. Saunders*

LOCOMBE HILL (IRE) 5 b.g. Barathea (IRE) 127 – Roberts Pride 62 (Roberto **64** (USA) 131) [2001 83: 8d 7g 10g[6] 8.3g[5] 8.3m[6] 10g 9.9d Oct 3] very big, rather dipped-backed gelding: one-time useful performer, just modest nowadays: stays 1½m: acts on good to firm and heavy going: often takes good hold: none too consistent: sold 8,500 gns. *M. Blanshard*

LOCOMOTIVE 2 b.g. (Feb 18) Bin Ajwaad (IRE) 119 – Saluti Tutti 77 (Trojan Fen **65 p** 118) [2001 7d 8d[4] Oct 3] eighth foal: brother to 4-y-o F-Zero and half-brother to 5f (at 2 yrs) to 1m winner Mazeeka (by Glow): dam sprint maiden: fair form, not knocked about, in maidens: fourth of 17 to Dawn Invasion at Salisbury: should do better. *C. F. Wall*

LODESTONE (IRE) 3 b.c. Distant Relative 128 – Magnetic Point (USA) 60 (Bering **–** 136) [2001 8v 7m 6.9m[6] Jun 29] 1,000Y: fifth foal: half-brother to a 2-y-o winner abroad by Most Welcome and 4-y-o Just Magical: dam, maiden who stayed 1¼m, half-sister to US Grade 1 2-y-o 6.5f winner Great Navigator: no form in maidens and a claimer. *J. M. Bradley*

LOGO'S DREAM 2 b.c. (Feb 7) Mind Games 121 – Yukosan 69 (Absalom 128) **53** [2001 5.1v[3] 5m f6g Jul 13] 1,200F, 4,500Y, resold 4,000Y: fifth living foal: half-brother to 3 winners by Risk Me, including fairly useful 1998 2-y-o 5f winner Little Movie Star and 15f winner The Great Flood: dam, 5f (at 2 yrs) and 6f winner, half-sister to very smart German performer up to 1½m Kornado: modest maiden: well held on fibresand. *B. A. McMahon*

LOKOMOTIV 5 b.g. Salse (USA) 128 – Rainbow's End 83 (My Swallow 134) [2001 **– §** 57§, a–§: 11.5m 9.9f 12m 12f 12.6d 11.9g Aug 9] quite attractive gelding: temperamental handicapper nowadays: tried visored, usually blinkered. *J. M. Bradley*

LONDOLOZI LAD (IRE) 2 b.g. (Apr 24) Ali-Royal (IRE) 127 – Ashdown (Pharly **38** (FR) 130) [2001 6m 6m f8.5s Sep 6] 2,500F, 8,000Y: eighth foal: half-brother to 5f (at 2 yrs)/6f winner Standown (by Reprimand) and a 2-y-o 1m winner in Italy by Alhijaz: dam lightly-raced: poor form in sellers/maiden. *P. C. Haslam*

LONDONER (USA) 3 ch.g. Sky Classic (CAN) – Love And Affection (USA) (Exclu- **104** sive Era (USA)) [2001 98: 10.4g[3] 12f 10.1m[3] Jul 12] tall, rather unfurnished gelding: has scope: useful performer: at least creditable efforts in 2001 on first 2 starts, 1½ lengths third to Musha Merr in listed race at York and 7¼ lengths seventh to Storming Home in King Edward VII Stakes at Royal Ascot: barely stays 1½m: yet to race on soft/heavy going, acts on any other: made running in 2001: sold 100,000 gns, joined M. Pipe and gelded. *H. R. A. Cecil*

LONDON EYE 3 b.f. Distinctly North (USA) 115 – Clonavon Girl (IRE) 44 (Be My   **52 ?**
Guest (USA) 126) [2001 59, a53: e7g³ e8g² e8g e7g² e8g 6f 6m 7m 6m 6g Sep 15] modest   **a52**
performer: stays 1m: acts on firm going, good to soft and equitrack: usually blinkered:
none too reliable. *K. T. Ivory*

LONDON FOLLIES (IRE) 2 b.g. (Mar 3) Danehill Dancer (IRE) 117 – Savona   **70**
(IRE) 70 (Cyrano de Bergerac 120) [2001 7m 6m⁴ 6m* 6.1s* 6g 6g 6d⁴ 7s⁶ Oct 25] tall,
leggy, unfurnished gelding: has scope: first foal: dam maiden who should have stayed 7f:
fair performer: won seller at Brighton in July and nursery at Chepstow (carried head high)
in August: should stay easy 7f: acts on soft and good to firm going: sold 13,000 gns, sent
to USA. *N. A. Callaghan*

LONDON LIGHTS 7 b.g. Slip Anchor 136 – Pageantry 83 (Welsh Pageant 132)   **–**
[2001 f12g f12g f14.8s Jan 18] useful-looking gelding: disappointing maiden, lightly
raced: trained by L. Woods in Ireland in 1999. *D. J. Wintle*

LONE CHIEF (USA) 2 b.g. (Mar 10) Cozzene (USA) – Alcando 113 (Alzao (USA)   **89**
117) [2001 6m* 5f² 7m³ 8m Aug 27] $5,000Y: neat colt: fifth living foal: half-brother to
3 winners, including useful 2000 2-y-o 6f winner Bring Plenty (by Southern Halo) and
smart 7f (including at 2 yrs) winner/1000 Guineas fourth Capistrano Day (by Diesis):
dam 5f (at 2 yrs) to 1¼m winner (including US Grade 1 9f event at 5 yrs): fairly useful
performer: won maiden at Ripon in June: dictated pace when good third of 5 in minor
event at Thirsk: stays 7f: raced only on going firmer than good: has run well when
sweating/edgy. *T. D. Barron*

LONE PIPER 6 b.g. Warning 136 – Shamisen 86 (Diesis 133) [2001 80§, a103§: 6v   **71**
7.1d 8s 5g 5m 5m 6g 5f² 5m² 5g* 5g⁵ 6m 6m 5m³ 5m⁵ f6s 5g² 5m 5m* 5s 5s Nov 9]
small, close-coupled gelding: poor mover: fair handicapper nowadays: won at Doncaster
(apprentices) in July and Goodwood in September: below form after: successful at 7f,
raced mainly at 5f/6f nowadays: acts on fibresand, firm and soft going: tried visored/
tongue tied: held up. *Jedd O'Keeffe*

LONER 3 b.g. Magic Ring (IRE) 115 – Jolis Absent 57 (Primo Dominie 121) [2001 77:   **–**
7.9g 9.7g 10.4m 12g Sep 15] strong gelding: fair winner at 2 yrs: well beaten in 2001.
M. Wigham

LONGCHAMP DU LAC 3 b.g. Lake Coniston (IRE) 131 – Kaprisky (IRE) (Red   **39**
Sunset 120) [2001 –: 6.1v 6m 7.1g 9.2g Jun 27] good-bodied gelding: poor maiden: tried
blinkered. *A. Berry*

LONG GOODBYE (IRE) 2 ch.c. (Mar 26) Dr Devious (IRE) 127 – Lady Nessa   **99 p**
(USA) (Al Nasr (FR) 126) [2001 8g* 9d* Oct 14] IR 65,000Y: fourth foal: half-brother to
smart French 1¼m/1½m winner Pretty (by Darshaan): dam Irish maiden half-sister to US
Grade 1 9.5f winner Dancers Countess: won maiden in September and listed event
(awarded race, having been beaten head by Nordhal) in October, both at Milan: should be
suited by 1¼m/1½m: open to improvement. *P. F. I. Cole*

LONG TALL SALLY (IRE) 2 b.f. (Apr 30) Danehill Dancer (IRE) 117 – Miss   **69**
Galwegian (Sandford Lad 133) [2001 5.7m⁶ 5.7g⁴ 5.1m³ 6g⁴ 6s Sep 24] IR 2,000F,
15,000 2-y-o: lengthy, unfurnished filly: half-sister to several winners, including 13f
winner Western Rainbow (by Rainbows For Life) and 1992 2-y-o 6f winner A Bridge Too
Far (by The Noble Player), later winner abroad: dam third at 6f at 2 yrs in Ireland: fair
maiden: third at Bath: effective at 5f/6f: acts on good to firm ground, well beaten on soft.
D. W. P. Arbuthnot

LONG WEEKEND (IRE) 3 b.c. Flying Spur (AUS) – Friday Night (USA) (Trem-   **45**
polino (USA) 135) [2001 55: f7g⁶ f9.4s 7.1g f8g f8.5s Dec 26] sturdy, angular colt:
modest maiden at 2 yrs: poor form in 2001: should stay at least 1m: acts on good to firm
ground: tried blinkered/visored. *D. Shaw*

LOOK AND LEARN (FR) 6 ch.g. Rock Hopper 124 – Lailati (USA) 66 (Mr Pros-   **–**
pector (USA)) [2001 f6g f9.4g Mar 10] half-brother to 3-y-o Lailani: fairly useful winner
in France in 1998 (sold 1,800 gns): tongue tied, no show in minor events both starts since.
R. F. Marvin

LOOK AWAY NOW 2 ch.c. (Apr 28) Timeless Times (USA) 99 – Petite Elite 47   **66 +**
(Anfield 117) [2001 f5g⁵ 6m² 6m Jun 25] 3,000F, 10,000Y, 17,000 2-y-o: eighth foal:
brother to 2 winning sprinters, including 4-y-o Christopherssister, and half-brother to 3
winners, including fairly useful 7f winner (including at 2 yrs) who stayed 8.5f Efferves-
cence (by Efisio): dam maiden who stayed 7f: fair maiden: best effort when beaten ½
length by Terfel in minor event at Yarmouth: will probably stay 7f. *W. A. O'Gorman*

LOOK FIRST (IRE) 3 b.c. Namaqualand (USA) – Be Prepared (IRE) (Be My Guest **71**
(USA) 126) [2001 70: e10g⁵ f8g* f8g* f12g 10.3s f12g⁶ 8.3m 8f* 10.2f² Jun 27] leggy
colt: fair performer: won handicaps at Southwell in January/February and claimer at
Leicester in May: stays 1¼m: acts on fibresand, soft and firm going: visored last 2 starts:
tends to be soon off bridle. *A. P. Jarvis*

LOOK HERE NOW 4 gr.g. Ardkinglass 114 – Where's Carol 67 (Anfield 117) [2001 **71**
79: 6v 6m 6d 6f 7d 7m Jul 28] workmanlike gelding: fair performer: ran respectably at
best in 2001: better form at 6f than 7f: acts on soft going: has looked none too keen.
B. A. McMahon

LOOKING FOR LOVE (IRE) 3 b.f. Tagula (IRE) 116 – Mousseux (IRE) (Jareer **81**
(USA) 115) [2001 81: 9s⁴ 9.9g⁴ 10g³ 9m⁴ 8m 8.3m³ 8.3g⁶ 8g 7d* 7.1g 7d⁶ 7g Oct 6]
leggy filly: fairly useful performer: won minor event at Goodwood in August: effective
at 7f to 1¼m: acts on soft and good to firm ground: often races prominently: reliable.
J. G. Portman

LOOP THE LOUP 5 b.g. Petit Loup (USA) 123 – Mithi Al Gamar (USA) 68 **91**
(Blushing Groom (FR) 131) [2001 99: 13.9m⁶ 16.1f 13.9g 14.6d⁶ 13.9d Oct 13] smallish,
workmanlike gelding: fairly useful handicapper: should be suited by 2m+: acts on firm
and soft going: blinkered third (raced freely)/fourth outings: usually held up. *Mrs
M. Reveley*

LOOSE CHIPPINS (IRE) 3 b.f. Bigstone (IRE) 126 – Fortune Teller (Troy 137) **–**
[2001 –: e5g 8.1g f8g May 14] tall, rangy filly: little form. *G. L. Moore*

LORD ADVOCATE 13 br.g. Law Society (USA) 130 – Kereolle (Riverman (USA) **–**
131) [2001 –: 13d 12.1m 13d³ 13g⁴ 12.1m 13g 10d⁵ 13d 7.2g 11.1g 10.9m⁵ 16m⁶ Sep 30]
of little account nowadays. *D. A. Nolan*

LORD ALASKA (IRE) 4 b.g. Sir Harry Lewis (USA) 127 – Anchorage (IRE) 86 **93**
(Slip Anchor 136) [2001 87p: 16m* May 12] workmanlike gelding: fairly useful handi-
capper: successful on 4 of last 5 starts, including at Thirsk (by 1¼ lengths from Mental
Pressure) in May: suffered a slight tendon strain and not seen out again: better at 1¾m/2m
than shorter: acts on good to firm going, yet to race on extremes: sometimes slowly away.
J. A. R. Toller

LORD ASHMORE 2 ch. or gr.g. (Apr 29) Greensmith 121 – Flair Lady 55 (Chili- **58**
bang 120) [2001 5.7f 5m³ 5.1g² 6m⁶ 5.1g 5m² 5.1f 5v 5.7d Oct 25] 900Y: second foal:
brother to 3-y-o Montev Lady: dam 6f (at 2 yrs) and 1m winner: modest maiden: below
form in nursery/sellers last 3 outings: may prove best at 5f: acts on good to firm ground:
tried visored. *W. G. M. Turner*

LORD BANKES 4 b.g. Presidium 124 – Marfen (Lochnager 132) [2001 f5g Oct 18] **–**
probably of little account nowadays. *W. G. M. Turner*

LORD CHAMBERLAIN 8 b.g. Be My Chief (USA) 122 – Metaphysique (FR) **–**
(Law Society (USA) 130) [2001 11.8s 12d⁵ 8.3v⁶ f12g Nov 17] 36,000Y, 2,100 2-y-o:
dam, French 1¼m winner, out of sister to Try My Best and El Gran Senor: little form.
J. M. Bradley

LORD CONYERS (IRE) 2 b.f. (May 7) Inzar (USA) 112 – Primelta 55 (Primo **51**
Dominie 121) [2001 6m 8.2m 7.5g⁴ f7g f6g³ f7g⁶ f7g f6g⁴ Dec 17] 2,000 2-y-o resold
3,400 2-y-o: leggy filly: first foal: dam, 7f winner, half-sister to 5-y-o Lots of Magic:
modest maiden: third in seller at Southwell: stays 7.5f: acts on fibresand. *Miss V. Haigh*

LORD DUNDEE (IRE) 3 ch.c. Polish Precedent (USA) 131 – Easy To Copy (USA) **87**
108 (Affirmed (USA)) [2001 11.8m³ Jun 4] 60,000Y: closely related to fairly useful Irish
1996 2-y-o 6f winner Desert Ease (by Green Desert) and half-brother to several winners,
notably smart Irish 7f to 1¼m performer Two-Twenty-Two (by Fairy King): dam, Irish
1m (at 2 yrs) to 1½m winner, sister to Irish 1000 Guineas winner Trusted Partner: 20/1
and visored, 2¾ lengths third to Artillery in maiden at Leicester, smooth headway early in
straight and keeping on well without being knocked about: stays in training. *H. R. A. Cecil*

LORD EUROLINK (IRE) 7 b.g. Danehill (USA) 126 – Lady Eurolink 55 (Kala **87**
Shikari 125) [2001 74: 7m⁶ 8m 10f* 10.1m 10d³ 9.9s* 10.5s 12.1m⁵ 12g 10.4d³ Oct 12]
strong, lengthy gelding: fairly useful handicapper: won at Newbury (amateurs) in June
and Beverley in August: stays 1½m: acts on fibresand, firm and soft going: usually
visored in 2000: has worn tongue tie. *M. H. Tompkins*

LORD FERNANDO 2 ch.g. (Feb 27) Forzando 122 – Lady Lacey 66 (Kampala 120) **65**
[2001 5g 5s 5m 7.1d³ 7m 7g 7s² 6d 8d Nov 2] 16,000Y: sturdy, workmanlike gelding:

second foal: dam 7f to 1¼m winner: fair maiden: second in nursery at Lingfield: not sure to stay 1m: acts on soft going: none too consistent. *G. B. Balding*

LORD GG (IRE)   2 b.g. (Mar 26) Fayruz 116 – Cnoc Ban (IRE) (On Your Mark 125)   **50 d**
[2001 6m 6m 6.1m f6g f8.5s 5.7g Oct 1] 5,000 2-y-o: second reported foal: half-brother to a winner up to 8.5f in Germany by Silver Kite: dam second at 7f in Ireland at 2 yrs: disappointing maiden: visored last 3 starts. *J. S. Moore*

LORD GIZZMO   4 ch.g. Democratic (USA) 101 – Figrant (USA) (L'Emigrant (USA)   **57**
129) [2001 58: f9.4s⁴ f11g² f12g* f12g⁴ f11g e13g⁶ p13g Nov 13] modest performer: won handicap at Wolverhampton in February: left R. Beckett and off 7 months before well held final start: stays 1½m: acts on fibresand. *R. M. Stronge*

LORD INVINCIBLE   3 b.g. Dancing Spree (USA) – Lady Broker 54 (Petorius 117)   **45**
[2001 f6g⁵ 5g⁶ 8.2g 7.1m Aug 23] third foal: half-brother to 5-y-o Lady Boxer: dam 7f winner: poor maiden: likely to prove best up to 7f: gelded after final start. *M. Mullineaux*

LORD JIM (IRE)   9 b.g. Kahyasi 130 – Sarah Georgina 79 (Persian Bold 123) [2001   **96 +**
–: 12f* 20m Jun 20] good-bodied gelding: useful performer, lightly raced nowadays: 25/1, won Vodafone Handicap at Epsom in June by neck from Cracow, coming from well back: never dangerous in Ascot Stakes only start after: effective at 1½m, probably at 2¾m: acts on soft and firm going, probably on fibresand: usually visored earlier in career: joined R. Hodges. *G. A. Butler*

LORD JOSHUA (IRE)   3 b.c. King's Theatre (IRE) 128 – Lady Joshua (IRE) 88   **92**
(Royal Academy (USA) 130) [2001 52p: 8s 7s⁵ 10g⁴ 11.6d² 14.4m* 12m 13.3m² 13.9m 14s 16.2s 11.7d* Oct 25] angular, unfurnished colt: fairly useful performer: won minor event at Kempton in June and handicap at Bath (drifted left) in October: shaped better than bare form on several other occasions: effective at 11.6f to 1¾m: acts on good to soft and good to firm going, probably on soft: sold 130,000 gns, joined N. Henderson. *G. A. Butler*

LORD KINTYRE   6 b.g. Makbul 104 – Highland Rowena 59 (Royben 125) [2001   **113**
109: 5.2d 5g 5f 5m⁴ 5m³ 5.1g 5d 5d⁶ 5s 5d 5v³ Oct 27] good-topped gelding: smart performer: best efforts when 1¾ lengths fourth to Misraah in listed race at Sandown and 2½ lengths third to Smokin Beau in valuable handicap at Ascot in July: raced only at 5f/ 6f: acts on any going: has started slowly: none too consistent. *B. R. Millman*

LORD LAMB   9 gr.g. Dunbeath (USA) 127 – Caroline Lamb 74 (Hotfoot 126) [2001   **–**
98: 16.2g⁵ Jun 7] tall, good-topped gelding: useful performer at best, very lightly raced on Flat nowadays: stays 2m: acts on heavy and good to firm going: no easy ride: useful hurdler/fairly useful chaser. *Mrs M. Reveley*

LORD LIAM (USA)   3 b.g. Foxhound (USA) 103 – Crackling Sike 77 (Salse (USA)   **58 d**
128) [2001 69, a–: 6d 7s 8f⁴ 8.5m 7d 6d 7m 10m f8g f11g f11s Dec 21] modest maiden: **a–**
soundly beaten after fourth start: stays 1m: acts on firm and soft ground, below form on fibresand: tongue tied first 8 starts at 3 yrs: has started slowly/gone sharply right leaving stalls/raced freely. *T. Keddy*

LORD MELBOURNE (IRE)   2 b.c. (Feb 10) Lycius (USA) 124 – Adana (IRE)   **52**
(Classic Music (USA)) [2001 6g f6g⁵ f6s⁵ Dec 15] IR 13,000F, IR 29,000Y: first foal: dam 5f (including at 2 yrs) to 7f winner in Italy: modest form in maidens: took good hold on debut: should stay 1m: has carried head awkwardly. *J. A. Osborne*

LORD MERLIN (IRE)   2 b.g. (Mar 5) Turtle Island (IRE) 123 – My-O-My (IRE)   **96**
105 (Waajib 121) [2001 5s* 5m³ 6g³ 5d Oct 13] IR 40,000Y: strong gelding: fourth foal: half-brother to a 2-y-o winner in South Africa by Royal Academy: dam, Irish 5f winner, out of half-sister to useful Irish 5f to 7f performer Title Roll: useful form: won maiden at Pontefract in May: third in Norfolk Stakes at Royal Ascot (1¼ lengths behind Johannesburg) and valuable sales race at the Curragh: will prove best at 5f/6f: acts on soft and good to firm ground: has given plenty of trouble at stalls (withdrawn 3 times): needs treating with some caution. *D. Nicholls*

LORDOFENCHANTMENT (IRE)   4 ch.g. Soviet Lad (USA) – Sauvignon (IRE)   **63**
63 (Alzao (USA) 117) [2001 62: f6g 6g 7m² 6m 7.5m² 7m* 7.5m⁶ 7m⁵ 7m 7.5s* Sep 25] strong gelding: modest handicapper: won at Southwell in July and Beverley (drifted right/ carried head awkwardly) in September: stays 7.5f: acts on good to firm and heavy ground: sometimes visored before 2001. *Don Enrico Incisa*

LORD OF LOVE   6 b.g. Noble Patriarch 115 – Gymcrak Lovebird 84 (Taufan (USA)   **–**
119) [2001 17.1d Oct 8] leggy gelding: has a round action: modest maiden: well held only Flat outing since 1998. *D. Burchell*

LORD OF METHLEY 2 gr.c. (Apr 23) Zilzal (USA) 137 – Paradise Waters 73 **70** (Celestial Storm (USA) 132) [2001 6m 7.1g⁵ 7g⁴ 7.1s⁵ 7s Nov 10] 25,000 2-y-o: leggy, quite good-topped colt: second foal: dam, 7f (at 2 yrs) to 13f winner, from family of Grand Criterium and Dante winner Tenby: fair maiden: fourth at Thirsk: likely to stay at least 1¼m: acts on soft going. *R. M. Whitaker*

LORD OF THE EAST 2 b.g. (Feb 21) Emarati (USA) 74 – Fairy Free (Rousillon **67** (USA) 133) [2001 6f⁶ 6m 5g 5m² 5s⁵ 6.1m⁵ 5.1m² Sep 10] 15,000Y: lengthy, rather unfurnished gelding: fourth foal: dam, maiden who stayed 1¼m in Ireland, half-sister to smart miler Protection: fair maiden: second in claimer at Folkestone and nursery at Nottingham: effective at 5f/6f: acts on firm and soft ground: tongue tied last 4 starts: has looked wayward. *B. R. Millman*

LORD OMNI (USA) 4 ch.g. El Prado (IRE) 119 – Muskoka Ice (USA) (It's Freezing **73** (USA) 122) [2001 75: f7s f6s³ f6g* f7g 6d 6f 7m Jul 28] big, useful-looking gelding: fair **a78** handicapper: won at Southwell in February: raced only around 6f/7f: acts on fibresand and firm ground, probably on good to soft: tongue tied once. *T. D. Barron*

LORD PACAL (IRE) 4 b.g. Indian Ridge 123 – Please Believe Me 93 (Try My Best **93** (USA) 130) [2001 97: 7d 6g 6g 7m⁴ 7f⁴ 6m 6g² 6g⁵ 7d 7g Oct 5] leggy gelding: fairly useful handicapper: creditable efforts in 2001 when in frame, runner-up to Antonio Canova at Newmarket in August: probably best at 6f/7f: acts on firm and good to soft going: blinkered sixth start: usually races prominently: sold 30,000 gns, joined D. Vienna in USA. *N. A. Callaghan*

LORD PIERCE 3 b.g. Tragic Role (USA) – Mirkan Honey 83 (Ballymore 123) [2001 **94** 11.1s⁵ 10v* p12g² p12g f12s Dec 21] 7,000F, IR 15,000Y: good-bodied gelding: half-brother to several winners, including 5f/6f winner Lee Artiste (by Tate Gallery) and 6f/7f winner (later stayed 1¼m) Fleet Hill (by Warrshan), both useful: dam Irish 2m winner: fairly useful form: off 6 months after debut: won maiden at Ayr in October by 12 lengths: at least creditable efforts in minor event/handicap at Lingfield next 2 starts: should stay 1¾m+: acts on polytrack and heavy going, well beaten on fibresand. *M. Johnston*

LORD PROTECTOR (USA) 3 b.g. Nicolotte 118 – Scared (Royal Academy (USA) **95** 130) [2001 83: f7g* 7m³ 8.1m² 8m⁶ 8g² 7f Aug 18] lengthy gelding: useful performer: won maiden at Southwell in April: good efforts in valuable handicaps next 4 starts, including runner-up at Haydock (behind Ecclesiastical) and Newmarket (behind Putra Pekan): stays 1m: acts on fibresand and good to firm ground: waited with. *D. W. P. Arbuthnot*

LORD STRADBROKE (USA) 2 b.g. (Feb 24) Lear Fan (USA) 130 – Encorenous **72 p** (USA) (Diesis 133) [2001 8d 8.2s⁵ Oct 30] strong, lengthy gelding: second foal: dam unraced half-sister to very smart German 7f/1m performer Royal Abjar: much better effort in maidens (fair form) when fifth to Balakheri at Nottingham, keeping on under considerate handling: will stay 1¼m: should improve. *M. A. Jarvis*

LORENZINO (IRE) 4 ch.g. Thunder Gulch (USA) 129 – Russian Ballet (USA) **–** (Nijinsky (CAN) 138) [2001 78: 10s 10.5s Sep 7] sixth foal: half-brother to several winners by Woodman, notably very smart 1¼m to 1¾m winner/Irish Derby second Dr Johnson: dam twice-raced close relative of Try My Best and El Gran Senor: fair maiden at best: trained by C. O'Brien in Ireland at 3 yrs: winning hurdler for current trainer, but well held both starts on Flat in 2001: should stay 1¼m: acts on good to soft ground. *Jonjo O'Neill*

LORI'S DANCER 2 ch.f. (May 12) Zilzal (USA) 137 – Brush Away (Ahonoora 122) **63** [2001 7f f7g⁶ Oct 23] 15,000Y: close-coupled, useful-looking filly: closely related to useful 1997 2-y-o 6f winner (stayed 1m) Bintang (by Soviet Star) and half-sister to several winners, including fairly useful 1998 2-y-o 7.5f winner Glanwydden (by Grand Lodge): dam unraced: modest form at Newmarket on first of 2 starts in maidens: should stay 1m: sent to USA. *W. Jarvis*

LOST AT SEA (IRE) 3 b.g. Exit To Nowhere (USA) 122 – Night At Sea 107 (Night **77** Shift (USA)) [2001 86: 7g 7m⁶ 8m 6m 7.5f⁵ 8m Aug 27] strong, good-bodied gelding: fairly useful at 2 yrs: largely disappointing in 2001 (gelded after final start): stays 7f: raced only on good ground or firmer: tongue tied: headstrong. *K. R. Burke*

LOST IN HOOK (IRE) 4 b.f. Dancing Dissident (USA) 119 – Rathbawn Realm **?** (Doulab (USA) 115) [2001 83d: a6g* a6g⁶ a8g 7m 5m 7m 8g 7g 7m f8.5g Oct 20] strong, good-quartered filly: trained by M. Lambert in Spain first 3 starts in 2001, winning minor event at Mijas in February: no form back in Britain: stays 6f: acts on sand: has been blinkered/tongue tied. *P. S. McEntee*

LOST SPIRIT 5 b.g. Strolling Along (USA) – Shoag (USA) (Affirmed (USA)) [2001 **63** 47, a60: e10g e13g* e12g² f12s⁴ f12g* e12g e12g* e12g* e12g* f12g f12f e12g e12g **a71** 12m² 12m 12g⁶ 12g 12m⁶ f12g f12g f12s Dec 27] strong gelding: fair handicapper: successful at Lingfield (4 times) and Southwell (amateurs) in January/February: stays 13f: acts on soft going, good to firm and fibresand/equitrack: blinkered twice at 2 yrs: front runner (sometimes drops away tamely). *P. W. Hiatt*

LOTS OF LOVE (USA) 3 b.g. Woodman (USA) 126 – Accountable Lady (USA) **102** (The Minstrel (CAN) 135) [2001 88: 7.6d⁹ 10.5d⁶ 7.9m 7.1s* 7.1v* 7.9d² 8d 8d f9.4s Dec 26] lengthy gelding: unimpressive mover: useful performer: won minor event at Lingfield in July and handicaps at Haydock (second one by neck from Millennium Force) in September: creditable second to Cornelius in handicap at York in October, but well held last 3 starts: probably best at 7f/1m: raced mainly on going softer than good: has been slowly away/edged left: tends to carry head awkwardly: usually takes a while to warm to his task. *M. Johnston*

LOTS OF MAGIC 5 b.h. Magic Ring (IRE) 115 – Pounelta 91 (Tachypous 128) **95** [2001 107: 7g 7g 7f³ 7.1d 6m 7.9m⁵ 7g 6g⁵ 7m Sep 22] tall, quite good-topped horse: fluent mover: has had wind operation: very smart 3-y-o, just useful nowadays: some creditable efforts in 2001: probably stays easy 1m: acts on firm going, probably not on softer than good: had had tongue tied: has found little. *R. Hannon*

LOTUS EATER 2 gr.f. (Feb 27) Linamix (FR) 127 – La Adrada (Arazi (USA) 135) **–** [2001 6d Nov 2] 35,000F: leggy, quite good-topped filly: first foal: dam, placed around 11f in France, out of smart Spanish middle-distance filly Teresa: 50/1, last of 20 in maiden at Newmarket. *S. C. Williams*

LOUD AND PROUD 2 b.g. (Apr 11) Polish Precedent (USA) 131 – Echo Cove (Slip **42** Anchor 136) [2001 7.9m 8d 8.2s Oct 30] 10,000Y: sparely-made gelding: sixth foal: half-brother to 2 winners abroad and to 2000 2-y-o 7f winner Persian Cat (by Persian Bold): dam French 11f winner: poor maiden. *R. A. Fahey*

L'OUEST (USA) 4 br.c. Gone West (USA) – La Carene (FR) 111 (Kenmare (FR) 125) **56** [2001 63: 7s⁶ 8.3g Aug 6] modest maiden: stays 1m: acts on soft ground: refused to enter stall second intended start. *G. Wragg*

LOUGH BOW (IRE) 3 b.g. Nicolotte 118 – Gale Force Seven (Strong Gale 116) **–** [2001 –: 8.5m 10m 10m Sep 6] quite good-topped gelding: little form in 2001. *M. W. Easterby*

LOUGHLORIEN (IRE) 2 b.g. (Mar 8) Lake Coniston (IRE) 131 – Fey Lady (IRE) **69 §** (Fairy King (USA)) [2001 f5g 5m 5m⁴ 5m² 5.1m⁵ 6d⁶ 5m 6g 6v Sep 28] 6,500F, IR 28,000Y: close-coupled, good-topped gelding: first foal: dam unraced half-sister to smart Irish/US performer up to 1½m Baba Karam: fair maiden: second at Redcar: below form in nurseries after: should stay 6f: acts on good to firm ground: blinkered/visored 5 times: often slowly away: probably ungenuine. *K. A. Ryan*

LOUIS GEORGIO 2 b.c. (Mar 21) Royal Applause 124 – Swellegant 84 (Midyan **61** (USA) 124) [2001 5f⁶ 5s Oct 5] 36,000F, 80,000Y: smallish colt: fifth foal: half-brother to 6-y-o Dil and 3-y-o Racina: dam, 2-y-o 5f winner, half-sister to very smart sprinter Prince Sabo: considerate introduction (modest form) when sixth to Golden Bounty in maiden at Pontefract: got worked up in stall when well held only other start. *J. Noseda*

LOUP CERVIER (IRE) 4 b.g. Wolfhound (USA) 126 – Luth d'Or (FR) (Noir Et Or **–** 125) [2001 50: e8g e7g 10f 8m 10f 7m 11.9g 16.4g Aug 17] quite good-topped gelding: modest maiden at best: little form in 2001: tried visored/tongue tied. *S. Dow*

LOU'S WISH 4 b.g. Thatching 131 – Shamaka 53 (Kris 135) [2001 –, a66: f16g f11g⁶ **41** f11g³ f9.4g f8.5g f12g⁵ f11g f11g⁵ f12g f8g 8.1g 10.4s f11g⁴ f12s f11g Dec 17] leggy **a49** gelding: poor nowadays: stays easy 1½m: acts on good to firm going, good to soft and fibresand: often blinkered: has started slowly/hung right/found little. *M. J. Polglase*

LOUVOLITE (IRE) 2 b.f. (Apr 3) Fayruz 116 – Non Dimenticar Me (IRE) 63 (Don't **81** Forget Me 127) [2001 5m 5m³ 5m* 5m⁵ Jun 6] 17,000Y: strong, well-made filly: third foal: sister to useful 1999 2-y-o 5f/6f winner Master Fay and half-sister to 3-y-o Zarin: dam 5f winner who stayed 7f: fairly useful performer: made all in minor event at Redcar in May: edgy, helped force strong pace when fifth in listed event at Beverley: raced only at 5f on good to firm ground: hung left second start. *J. A. Glover*

LOVE DIAMONDS (IRE) 5 b.g. Royal Academy (USA) 130 – Baby Diamonds **–** (Habitat 134) [2001 49, a76: f8g⁴ f9.4s⁴ f9.4s³ f8g 10g Jul 17] modest performer: left **a58**

N. Littmoden after third start: probably best around 1¼m: acts on fibresand/equitrack: tried blinkered/visored: has wandered/flashed tail/found nil. *R. Dickin*

LOVE EVERLASTING 3 b.f. Pursuit of Love 124 – In Perpetuity 90 (Great **112** Nephew 126) [2001 91p: 10g⁶ 8.1m 8f³ 10.1f⁵ 11.9m* 12m² 12m* 11.9m³ 12s⁴ 12d² 12d⁵ Nov 2] tall, lengthy filly: smart performer: won handicap at York in July and listed race at Newbury (by 1¼ lengths from Nafisah) in August: ran at least respectably most other starts, including in listed races at Newmarket (1¾ lengths second to Ranin) and York (close third to Inchiri) and Princess Royal Stakes at Ascot (5 lengths second to Head In The Clouds) on sixth, eighth and tenth starts: ran poorly final outing: better around 1½m than shorter, and should stay at least 1¾m: yet to race on heavy going, acts on any other: tends to race lazily: tough. *M. Johnston*

LOVE IN THE MIST 2 gr.f. (Jan 17) Pursuit of Love 124 – Misty Goddess (IRE) 63 **67** (Godswalk (USA) 130) [2001 5s⁶ f8.5g 7d⁶ 8g⁶ f8.5g³ f7g⁵ f9.4g* Dec 8] workmanlike filly: fourth foal: half-sister to 4-y-o Imari: dam 7f (at 2 yrs) to 11f winner: fair performer: joint favourite, won seller at Wolverhampton: stays 9.4f: acts on good to soft going and fibresand: has been early to post. *N. P. Littmoden*

LOVE (IRE) 3 b.g. Royal Academy (USA) 130 – Kentmere (FR) (Galetto (FR) 118) **66 d** [2001 61: 9.2m 9f³ 8g 8.5m 7g f8.5g 8f 5v Oct 15] rather leggy, lengthy gelding: fair maiden handicapper: no form after second start: stays 9f: raced mainly on good going or firmer: tried blinkered: has had tongue tied. *M. Johnston*

LOVE KISS (IRE) 6 b.g. Brief Truce (USA) 126 – Pendulina 102 (Prince Tenderfoot **–** (USA) 126) [2001 60: 7m 8m 10.1m 10m 9m 8f 10.1f Sep 10] tall gelding: modest handicapper at 5 yrs: well held in 2001: tried tongue tied. *W. Storey*

LOVELEAVES 2 b.f. (Feb 18) Polar Falcon (USA) 126 – Rash (Pursuit of Love 124) **84 p** [2001 6v² Oct 26] 15,000F: strong, rangy filly: first foal: dam unraced half-sister to useful 2-y-o sprinters Maid For Walking and Maid For The Hills: 10/1, shaped well when 1½ lengths second of 17 to Oases in maiden at Newbury, going on well at finish: sure to do better. *M. A. Jarvis*

LOVELY SPARK (BEL) 4 gr.f. Abbey's Grey – Spark Haven (Hot Spark 126) **?** [2001 6g³ 5g 7f 6g* 6g* 6g* 6f 5d² 5g* 5.5d³ 6s p7g Dec 12] Belgian-bred filly: won minor event and 3 handicaps at Ostend between July and September: well held in seller at Lingfield on British debut: best at 5f/6f: acts on heavy ground and dirt. *Mrs V. Elsen, Belgium*

LOVE REGARDLESS (USA) 2 b. or br.c. (Feb 10) Storm Bird (CAN) 134 – **98 P** Circus Toons (USA) (Wild Again (USA)) [2001 6f* Sep 10]

No one has trained more winners on the Flat in Britain than Mark Johnston over the past eight seasons, but the victory of Mister Baileys at the start of this period in the 1994 Two Thousand Guineas remains the stable's only British classic success. The near-thousand winners saddled by the Middleham trainer in the meantime have come with thoughtful placing, and Johnston hasn't been one to run horses in classics just for the sake of it. Far from it, in fact. Mister Baileys, who went on to finish fourth at Epsom, has been his only Derby runner to date, for example, and he has yet to have a runner in the Oaks. The stable will almost certainly mount a more concerted classic challenge in 2002, at least for the colts' races. Bandari, Fight Your Corner, Leo's Luckyman, Legal Approach and Sir George Turner are among what their trainer described in October as his best bunch of two-year-olds since the days of Lend A Hand. Those named are no mean bunch either, yet reportedly considered better than all of them is the lesser-known Love Regardless, who is scheduled to reappear in the Two Thousand Guineas. Mister Baileys was making his reappearance when winning the Guineas, as were Johnston's only other runners in the race so far, Bijou d'Inde and Lend A Hand, when they were placed at Newmarket. All were vastly more experienced than Love Regardless will be come May, however, each having had at least five races at two. Love Regardless had only one race as a juvenile, winning a six-furlong maiden at Newcastle in September. In a field of sixteen runners, he was overshadowed in the betting that day by David Loder's newcomer Access Denied, who started odds on, but Love Regardless made his own odds of 4/1 look very generous, soon close up and quickly asserting from two furlongs out to beat the favourite going away by five lengths, with a similar margin back to the third horse. It was an impressive

Racecourse Video Services Maiden Stakes, Newcastle—Love Regardless creates a good impression on his debut, beating the odds-on Access Denied by five lengths

start, and the form was boosted by the subsequent successes of Access Denied, who won a similar event at Pontefract easily by six lengths, and of fourth-placed Red Rioja, who won twice, including the Group 3 C. L. Weld Park Stakes at the Curragh.

		Northern Dancer (b 1961)	Nearctic Natalma
Storm Bird (CAN) (b 1978)		South Ocean (b 1967)	New Providence Shining Sun
Love Regardless (USA) (b. or br.c. Feb 10, 1999)		Wild Again (b 1980)	Icecapade Bushel-N-Peck
Circus Toons (USA) (b 1992)		Circus Poster (b 1982)	Crimson Satan Show Notice

Love Regardless was reasonably expensive compared to Johnston's other two-year-olds. He sold as a foal for 135,000 dollars and made IR 60,000 guineas when re-sold as a yearling. He is from the final crop of Storm Bird and the first foal out of Circus Toons, a minor stakes winner in the States over six furlongs and eight and a half furlongs. Storm Bird has not had much recently to rival the best of his produce, which include Indian Skimmer, Balanchine and Bluebird. Love Regardless has a long, long way to go to rival them, but he looks a colt of great potential, however he fares in the Guineas. He should stay a mile, if not much further. *M. Johnston*

LOVE'S DESIGN (IRE) 4 b. or br.g. Pursuit of Love 124 – Cephista 61 (Shirley Heights 130) [2001 74: f7g⁴ f9.4s⁶ f8g e8g* f7g³ e8g* e8g* e7g* 8g 7m⁴ 9m 8f⁴ 8m 8g* 7m 7.6m 7m 7.9m p7g p8g* Dec 28] fairly useful performer, better on all-weather than turf: won seller and 3 handicaps at Lingfield and handicap at Brighton between January/July, and minor event at Lingfield in December: best at 7f/1m: acts on firm going, good to soft, and all-weather: usually visored: probably best with exaggerated waiting tactics. *Miss J. Feilden* **83 a91**

LOVE SONG 3 b.f. Kris 135 – Heart's Harmony (Blushing Groom (FR) 131) [2001 7d 7g 10m⁴ 10m³ 9m⁶ 9.9m⁵ 10s* 10v Oct 8] rather sparely-made, useful-looking filly: **75**

fifth foal: half-sister to 1¼m winners National Anthem (smart, by Royal Academy) and Lullaby (by Unfuwain): dam, second at 1m from 2 starts in France, closely related to useful 1¼m and 1¾m winner Proposing: fair performer: won minor event at Pontefract in September: stays 1¼m: acts on soft and good to firm going. *Sir Michael Stoute*

LOVES TO DARE (IRE) 2 b.f. (Mar 12) Desert King (IRE) 129 – Loves To Dance (FR) (Sadler's Wells (USA) 132) [2001 5v 7f 7d f7g Oct 22] 170,000 francs F: sturdy, close-coupled filly: third foal: half-sister to 1999 French 2-y-o 8.5f winner Midiana (by Midyan): dam rarc twice in France: no form, including in sellers: trained on debut by R. Collet in France: blinkered final start. *B. J. Meehan* –

LOVE THEE FOREVER 2 ch.f. (Apr 24) Millkom 124 – Exceptional Beauty 94 (Sallust 134) [2001 6g Aug 8] 2,200Y, 18,000 2-y-o: half-sister to 2-y-o 5f winners Good Fetch (in 1993) and Winterbound (in 1994), both by Siberian Express: dam 1½m winner: 25/1, well held in maiden at Leicester. *N. P. Littmoden* –

LOVE THING 3 b.f. Phountzi (USA) 104 – Devils Dirge 68 (Song 132) [2001 68: 6g² 7m 5.1m⁶ 6m⁶ 6g⁴ 6m² 6g² 6f⁵ 6v Oct 24] lengthy, rather unfurnished filly: unimpressive mover: fair handicapper: seems best at 6f: acts on firm and good to soft going: usually visored/blinkered: edgy sort: has wandered. *R. A. Fahey* **68**

LOVE TUNE 3 b.f. Alhijaz 122 – Heights of Love 51 (Persian Heights 129) [2001 61: 5.1v⁶ 5d⁴ 5v⁵ 5m 5f 5g 5g Aug 24] small, unfurnished filly: modest maiden handicapper: well below form after second outing: effective at 5f/6f: acts on fibresand, good to firm and good to soft going: visored final start. *K. R. Burke* **61 d**

LOVE YOU TOO 4 ch.f. Be My Chief (USA) 122 – Nagida 94 (Skyliner 117) [2001 84d: 6m 6f 6m³ 6m⁴ 6m* 6g² 6g 6g³ 7m* 7m 7d Aug 26] big, close-coupled filly: fairly useful handicapper: won at Salisbury in June and July: effective at 6f/7f: acts on good to firm going: visored after second outing: has worn crossed noseband/been taken early to post: started slowly/hung left/looked lazy. *K. T. Ivory* **82**

LOWESWATER (USA) 2 b.c. (Mar 23) Nureyev (USA) 131 – River Empress (USA) (Riverman (USA) 131) [2001 6m² 6m* 7m⁵ Aug 1] $525,000F, 330,000Y: strong, close-coupled colt: fourth foal: dam, ran 3 times in USA, from family of high-class US Grade 1 winner around 9f Jewel Princess: useful form: won maiden at Doncaster in July by ¾ length from Serieux, getting up well inside final 1f: 2¾ lengths fifth to Naheef in Vintage Stakes at Goodwood, never nearer: should stay 1m: has had 2 handlers and been on toes. *J. H. M. Gosden* **102**

LOW ON FUNDS (USA) 4 b.g. Eagle Eyed (USA) 111 – Miss Sanmar (USA) (Recitation (USA) 126) [2001 –: e8g 8m 7m 7d f8g⁶ 9.9m⁴ 10.1d 10m⁵ 10g⁴ Aug 20] quite attractive gelding: poor maiden: left T. Mills after reappearance: stays 1¼m: tried blinkered/visored/tongue tied: has edged left. *I. A. Wood* **36**

LOWRY (USA) 3 b. or br.g. Gulch (USA) – Aviara (USA) (Cox's Ridge (USA)) [2001 10.2d 10.2f 9.9m⁶ Jun 28] fourth foal: closely related to 1999 2-y-o 8.3f winner Kingdom of Gold (by Gone West): dam, French 9f winner, out of close relative to Ajdal from family of Arazi: well held in maidens. *J. S. King* –

LOXLEY 2 b.g. (Jan 1) Ezzoud (IRE) 126 – Shewillifshewants (IRE) (Alzao (USA) 117) [2001 7m⁵ 7g 7.2g Aug 31] smallish, sturdy gelding: first foal: dam unraced half-sister to smart performer up to 12.5f Fairy Queen: only a little sign of ability in maidens. *M. A. Buckley* –

LOYAL TYCOON (IRE) 3 br.g. Royal Abjar (USA) 121 – Rosy Lydgate 53 (Last Tycoon 131) [2001 81: 7d 7g 7.9g 6m⁵ 7.1g³ 6m* 6g 5.7d 7g 6g 6g Oct 5] robust, close-coupled gelding: fairly useful handicapper: won at Lingfield in June: ran respectably most other starts: stays 7f: acts on soft and good to firm going: sweating (below form) third outing: gelded after final start: sold 16,000 gns in October, joined D. Nicholls. *S. Dow* **85**

LUBOHENRIK (IRE) 4 b.f. Perugino (USA) 84 – Febian John (FR) (Shafaraz (FR) 124) [2001 –: 5d 5g 6m 5f Jul 9] small, unfurnished filly: no form: tried visored. *P. Monteith* –

LUCAYAN CHIEF (IRE) 3 b.c. With Approval (CAN) – Little Lady Leah (USA) (Shareef Dancer (USA) 135) [2001 97: 9d⁴ 10.5g⁶ 10m⁶ 12f 14.8g⁶ 14g 14m⁶ Sep 22] smallish, quite attractive colt: has a quick, fluent action: useful performer: generally quite highly tried in 2001, though not entirely discredited on occasions, including when 4¼ lengths fourth to Olden Times in listed race at Newmarket in April: seems to stay 15f: acts on any going: visored final start: sold 20,000 gns, joined D. Vienna in USA. *S. P. C. Woods* **101**

LUCAYAN LEGACY (IRE)   2 b.c. (Feb 11) Persian Bold 123 – Catherinofaragon   **81** (USA) (Chief's Crown (USA)) [2001 7m² 7g* 7d* 8m 10s 10s] 12,000F, IR 130,000Y: useful-looking colt: second foal: half-brother to 3-y-o Catstreet: dam unraced half-sister to US Grade 3 8.5f/1¼m winner Gold Alert: fairly useful performer: landed odds in small-field minor events at Newcastle in July and Yarmouth (beat Stage By Stage a neck) in August: well below form last 2 starts: should stay 1m: acts on good to firm and good to soft ground. *S. P. C. Woods*

LUCAYAN MONARCH   3 ch.g. Cadeaux Genereux 131 – Flight Soundly (IRE) 78   **71** (Caerleon (USA) 132) [2001 e8s⁴ f9.4g* 10s⁵ 8m 10s f12g f9.4s f8s³ Dec 21] 16,000Y: lengthy, unfurnished gelding: second foal: half-brother to 1999 2-y-o 5f winner Jaybird (by Common Grounds): dam 2-y-o 6f winner out of Queen Mary winner Night of Wind: fair performer: trainer fined/jockey suspended/horse banned for 30 days under schooling in public rule on debut: won maiden at Wolverhampton in March: mainly disappointing after, leaving J. Noseda after fourth start and D. Nicholls 3,000 gns after fifth one: unlikely to stay much beyond 9.4f: acts on fibresand. *R. Wilman*

LUCEFER (IRE)   3 b.g. Lycius (USA) 124 – Maharani (USA) (Red Ransom (USA))   **75 ?** [2001 83: 7.1f* 7.2m 7.1v 10s f7g Nov 3] leggy, close-coupled gelding: fair form at best in 2001: won maiden at Musselburgh in September: well held last 3 starts: should stay 1m: acts on firm and soft ground: blinkered/tongue tied penultimate start: has carried head high. *G. C. H. Chung*

LUCID DREAMS (IRE)   2 b.g. (Mar 9) Sri Pekan (USA) 117 – Scenaria (IRE)   **–** (Scenic 128) [2001 7s 8s f9.4g Nov 17] 15,000F, 14,500Y: rather leggy, good-topped gelding: first foal: dam unraced half-sister to 3-y-o Mujado: well held in maidens. *M. L. W. Bell*

LUCIDO (IRE)   5 b.h. Royal Academy (USA) 130 – Lady Ambassador (General   **116** Assembly (USA)) [2001 112: 12v* 12s* 12f⁶ 12g⁶ Jul 10] strong, rangy horse: reportedly had stress fracture of pelvis as 3-y-o: smart performer, lightly raced: at least as good as ever early in 2001, winning minor event at Doncaster and John Porter Stakes at Newbury (impressively by 3½ lengths from Salford Express) in March/April: respectable sixth to Sandmason in Hardwicke Stakes at Royal Ascot penultimate start, but well below form in Princess of Wales's Stakes at Newmarket final one: stays 1½m: winner on good to firm ground, very best efforts on good or softer (acts on heavy): usually waited with: sent to Germany, joined P. Lautner. *J. L. Dunlop*

LUCILLE (IRE)   3 b.f. Sadler's Wells (USA) 132 – Lady Ambassador (General   **79** Assembly (USA)) [2001 59p: 10m 12g³ 12.4g⁵ 14v⁵ 10.5v² 10v Dec 2] strong, useful-looking filly: fair maiden: left J. Dunlop after fourth start: barely stays 1¾m: acts on heavy going. *P. Lautner, Germany*

LUCK AND DOUGH   2 b.g. (May 25) Forzando 122 – Lucky Song 91 (Lucky   **–** Wednesday 124) [2001 7g 6m 7.1f Jul 25] 8,000Y: half-brother to 3 winners, including 1991 2-y-o 6f/7f winner X My Heart (by Aragon): dam 5f and 7f winner: well held in maidens/seller. *M. W. Easterby*

LUCKY ARCHER   8 b.g. North Briton 67 – Preobrajenska 93 (Double Form 130)   **67** [2001 –: e8g⁴ 8.1m 8m* 8d 9m 8.1m* 8g 8.9m⁵ 8m Sep 6] smallish, well-made gelding: fair performer: won claimers at Leicester in June and Sandown in July: stays 8.5f: acts on hard and good to soft going: blinkered once at 3 yrs: often races up with pace. *Ian Williams*

LUCKY BEA   8 b.g. Lochnager 132 – Knocksharry 58 (Palm Track 122) [2001 35: f8g   **–** Jan 1] of little account nowadays. *K. A. Ryan*

LUCKY BOY   3 b.g. Magic Ring (IRE) 115 – Etourdie (USA) (Arctic Tern (USA)   **–** 126) [2001 10m Jul 11] 4,500Y: seventh foal: half-brother to 3 winners, including 4-y-o Stoney Garnett and a winner up to 1½m in France by Glint of Gold: dam unraced: 12/1, virtually refused to race when tailed off in seller at Lingfield. *W. G. M. Turner*

LUCKY BREAK (IRE)   3 ch.c. Brief Truce (USA) 126 – Paradise Forum 78 (Prince   **69** Sabo 123) [2001 60: 7.1m⁶ 8.1g³ 10m 7.6f⁵ 9.9m⁶ Aug 15] small colt: fair maiden: barely stays 1¼m: raced only on good going or firmer. *C. A. Horgan*

LUCKY CHRYSTAL (IRE)   3 b.g. Lucky Guest 109 – Chrysilia (USA) (Tilt Up   **62** (USA)) [2001 58: f7g⁵ 5.1s⁵ 7m 7m³ 8.5d* 8.5m a10.5g a8g Dec 9] rather leggy, close-coupled gelding: modest handicapper: won maiden event at Epsom in July: sold from E. Dunlop 6,000 gns after seventh start: stays 8.5f: acts on good to firm and good to soft going. *P. Haley, Spain*

LUCKY COVE 5 gr.g. Lugana Beach 116 – Port Na Blath (On Your Mark 125) [2001 58?: 5v f5g 5m f5g⁶ 5f 6g 5g f6s⁴ Dec 15] seemingly poor maiden: best at 5f: acts on good to firm going, heavy and fibresand: sometimes blinkered. *N. Tinkler*   **45 ?**

LUCKY FOR GEORGE 3 b.c. Theatrical Charmer 114 – Jeedamaya 57 (Taufan (USA) 119) [2001 12g 11.8s Oct 16] 8,200Y: sparely-made colt: sixth foal: half-brother to 1m/1¼m winner in France by Sizzling Melody: dam maiden who stayed 1m: well held in claimers. *Ms A. E. Embiricos*   **–**

LUCKY GITANO (IRE) 5 br. or b.g. Lucky Guest 109 – April Wind 91 (Windjammer (USA)) [2001 95p: 8v 8.1v 8g⁶ May 18] leggy, quite attractive gelding: useful handicapper at 3 yrs: well below form in 2001: was best at 7f/1m: acted on firm and soft going: tended to take good hold (usually held up): retired. *J. L. Dunlop*   **–**

LUCKY HEATHER (IRE) 4 b.f. Soviet Lad (USA) – Idrak 68 (Young Generation 129) [2001 11.6g 10.2s* 11.7m Aug 24] poor performer, lightly raced: won seller at Chepstow in August: stays 1¼m well: acts on soft going. *R. J. Baker*   **47**

LUCKY HETTIE 3 b.f. Alzao (USA) 117 – Halo's Charm (USA) (Halo (USA)) [2001 45p: 6.1v 8.3m⁴ 9.9f⁵ f8.5g² 7m⁵ 7g Aug 10] angular, quite attractive filly: modest maiden handicapper: should stay 1¼m: acts on good to firm ground and fibresand: blinkered (looked temperamental) final start: has been slowly away: sold 2,200 gns. *C. R. Egerton*   **55**

LUCKY JACASA 2 b.f. (Mar 4) Whittingham (IRE) 104 – Lucky Dip 68 (Tirol 127) [2001 5s⁴ May 17] 6,000Y: first foal: dam 5f winner: modest form when fourth of 17 to Doc Holiday in maiden at Salisbury, edging right. *Mrs P. N. Dutfield*   **62**

LUCKY JUDGE 4 b.g. Saddlers' Hall (IRE) 126 – Lady Lydia 66 (Ela-Mana-Mou 132) [2001 69: 13d* 16.1m⁵ 14m³ 16f² 16f⁵ 13d⁵ 16g³ 16m⁵ Sep 30] close-coupled gelding: fair handicapper: won at Hamilton in May: effective at 13f to 2m: acts on any going: visored (raced too freely) final start: has carried head high: won over hurdles in December. *G. A. Swinbank*   **78**

LUCKY LILLY (IRE) 3 b.f. Definite Article 121 – Nordic Doll (IRE) 71 (Royal Academy (USA) 130) [2001 7s 11.7d p12g Nov 13] rather leggy filly: second foal: half-sister to 4-y-o Kirovski: dam 7f winner who stayed 1m: well held in maidens. *P. J. Hobbs*   **–**

LUCKY MAN 2 b.c. (Feb 21) Robellino (USA) 127 – Vannozza 58 (Kris 135) [2001 6.1m³ 6m⁶ 7m 6d Sep 14] 17,000Y: leggy, plain colt: fifth living foal: half-brother to 5f (in Ireland)/6f winner Steval (by Efisio): dam, ran twice, out of high-class 5f to 1m performer Vilikaia: fair maiden: eighth of 22 in sales race at Doncaster final start: stays 7f. *G. C. Bravery*   **74**

LUCKY PRINCESS 2 b.f. (Jun 2) Bijou d'Inde 127 – Thinkluckybelucky (Maystreak 118) [2001 5g 6g⁴ 6m 6.1v Oct 4] smallish, sturdy filly: sixth reported foal: half-sister to 2 winners, notably useful but unreliable 6f to 1m winner Hornbeam (by Rich Charlie): dam sprint maiden: no form in maidens/minor events: tried visored. *J. D. Czerpak*   **–**

LUCKY RAINBOW (USA) 3 b.f. Rainbow Quest (USA) 134 – Tinaca (USA) (Manila (USA)) [2001 10v² 11.9m⁴ 10v* Oct 8] tall, leggy, light-bodied filly: fourth foal: half-sister to 4-y-o Distant Cousin: dam, ran twice in France, half-sister to very smart French middle-distance performer Panoramic and to dam of Giant's Causeway: fair form: off over 4 months before winning maiden at Windsor in October by 8 lengths from   **75**

Rainworth Lady: should be suited by 1½m+: acts on heavy going, possibly on good to firm: sold 30,000 gns. *J. L. Dunlop*

LUCKY ROMANCE 2 b.f. (May 2) Key of Luck (USA) 126 – In Love Again (IRE) **68 p** 86 (Prince Rupert (FR) 121) [2001 f6g⁴ Nov 19] 23,000Y: third foal: closely related to 3-y-o Forever My Lord: dam, 2-y-o 5f winner, half-sister to high-class sprinter Hallgate: 10/1, under a length fourth of 11 to Bond Jovi in maiden at Southwell, soon recovering from slow start but tiring late on: should improve. *R. F. Johnson Houghton*

LUCKY'S SON (IRE) 4 gr.g. Lucky Guest 109 – April Wind 91 (Windjammer **50** (USA)) [2001 50, a–: f7g 5.2m 5m⁶ 6.1f Jun 25] good-topped gelding: modest performer: **a–** stays 6f: raced mainly on good going or firmer: has had tongue tied: has pulled hard/ flashed tail: sold 2,500 gns. *P. Howling*

LUCKY STAR 4 b.f. Emarati (USA) 74 – Child Star (FR) 58 (Bellypha 130) [2001 **46** 60: f7g 7.1g 6f⁴ 7m⁵ 7f 6m 12.1m Jul 27] leggy filly: poor handicapper: left D. Marks **a?** after sixth start: effective at 6f to 8.5f: acts on fibresand/equitrack and firm going: visored once. *Mrs Merrita Jones*

LUCY TUFTY 10 b.m. Vin St Benet 109 – Manor Farm Toots 70 (Royalty 130) [2001 **–** –: f12g Jan 26] of little account. *G. Prodromou*

LUDERE (IRE) 6 ch.g. Desse Zenny (USA) – White Jasmin 53 (Jalmood (USA) 126) **–** [2001 45: f16.2g Feb 8] good-bodied gelding: well held only Flat outing in 2001: blinkered once: won over hurdles in December. *B. J. Llewellyn*

LUDYNOSA (USA) 2 b.f. (Apr 23) Cadeaux Genereux 131 – Boubskaia (Niniski **74 p** (USA) 125) [2001 7d⁴ Nov 3] 2,100,000 francs Y: quite good-topped filly: closely related to several winners abroad, including smart French miler Daneskaya (by Danehill) and useful French 1m winner Beriskaio (by Bering): dam French 1m winner: 14/1 and backward, 2 lengths fourth of 21 to Ballet Fame in maiden at Newmarket, slowly away but leading penultimate 1f: sure to improve. *L. M. Cumani*

LUGANA MIST 2 gr.f. (Apr 12) Lugana Beach 116 – Swallow Bay 54 (Penmarric **–** (USA) 111) [2001 6m 6d 7m 5v p6g f6g Nov 21] 1,200 2-y-o: half-sister to several winners, including 3-y-o Chaweng Beach: dam, 2-y-o 6f winner, barely stayed 1¼m: no form, including in sellers. *J. C. Fox*

LULUWA (IRE) 2 b. or br.f. (Feb 26) Zafonic (USA) 130 – Affection Affirmed **83 p** (USA) (Affirmed (USA)) [2001 8d⁵ Oct 19] strong, lengthy filly: has scope: half-sister to several winners, including smart but untrustworthy 6.5f to 8.5f winner in Britain/USA River Deep (by Riverman) and useful performer up to 1½m in Britain/USA Dreamer (by Zilzal): dam, US 1m/9f winner, half-sister to dam of Zoman: 10/1 and green, shaped well when fifth of 20 to Rawyaan in maiden at Newmarket, fading only final 1f having travelled well just off pace: sure to improve. *H. R. A. Cecil*

LUMIERE D'ESPOIR (FR) 3 br.f. Saumarez 132 – Light of Hope (USA) 101 **81** (Lyphard (USA) 132) [2001 –p: 10s⁶ 10.2d* 14.6m* 12f Jun 21] rather leggy, quite good-topped filly: fairly useful performer: won handicaps at Bath and Doncaster (very easily) in May: stays and very stiff task, behind in Ribblesdale Stakes at Royal Ascot (slowly away) final start: will stay 2m: sold 15,000 gns in October. *S. Dow*

LUMIERE DU SOLEIL 3 b.f. Tragic Role (USA) – Pounelta 91 (Tachypous 128) **55** [2001 60: 6g 8.3m⁶ 8m 14.1m f8g⁵ 8.5f 8.1d³ f8g³ Dec 17] tall filly: modest maiden: stays 1m: acts on fibresand, good to firm and good to soft going: tried blinkered/visored/tongue tied. *K. A. Ryan*

LUMING (USA) 3 b.f. Miesque's Son (USA) 117 – Lucky State (USA) (State Dinner **60** (USA)) [2001 8.2g⁵ 9m² 9.7m⁴ Aug 27] $15,000Y, resold 15,500Y: sixth foal: closely related to 3 winners, including 1m winner Gold Lance (by Seeking The Gold), and half-sister to a Brazilian Grade 3 winner by Thunder Gulch: dam, French 1m winner, half-sister to 1000 Guineas winner Ravinella: modest form in maidens: stays 9.7f. *R. Guest*

LUNACY (IRE) 2 b.f. (Mar 22) Alzao (USA) 117 – Lunar Ridge (Indian Ridge 123) **69** [2001 7.1m² 8f Oct 19] 18,000Y: quite attractive filly: first foal: dam unraced half-sister to US Grade 3 6.5f winner Wrekin Pilot: neck second of 9 to Carrozzina in maiden at Warwick for G. Bravery: well held in non-graded stakes at Santa Anita month later: should stay 1m. *M. G. Harte, USA*

LUNAJAZ 4 ch.g. Alhijaz 122 – Lunagraphe (USA) (Time For A Change (USA)) **–** [2001 –: 7f 8m 11.5m Jun 30] no form: tried visored. *T. M. Jones*

LUR

LUNALUX 4 b.f. Emarati (USA) 74 – Ragged Moon 72 (Raga Navarro (ITY) 119) **43** [2001 55: 5d 5v 5m 5.1m 6d 6m⁴ 6.1m⁵ 5m 5m 5d 7g Oct 6] unfurnished filly: poor maiden: best at 5f/easy 6f: acts on firm going, good to soft and fibresand: sometimes visored/blinkered: usually races up with pace. *C. Smith*

LUNA MOTH (USA) 2 b.f. (Jan 4) Silver Hawk (USA) 123 – Night And Dreams **78 p** (USA) (Fappiano (USA)) [2001 7f 7m⁶ 8.2s³ Nov 5] strong, well-made filly: third foal: half-sister to 2 winners abroad, including smart French 6f winner Deep Sleep (by Rahy): dam, US 6f winner, half-sister to champion USA sprinter Housebuster: fair form in maidens: not knocked about when never-nearer third to Five Stars at Nottingham final start: stays 1m: likely to do better in handicaps. *E. A. L. Dunlop*

LUNA NOVA 3 b.g. Aragon 118 – Lucidity 67 (Vision) [2001 7s 6.1d 7m 10m **–** 12m 8.3d Aug 15] second foal: dam 1m winner who stayed 1½m: little form: tried blinkered. *C. W. Thornton*

LUNAR CRYSTAL (IRE) 3 b.g. Shirley Heights 130 – Solar Crystal (IRE) 110 **90** (Alzao (USA) 117) [2001 104: 8s⁵ 10.3f⁶ 8m⁴ 8m 10m⁵ Jul 29] quite attractive, good-topped gelding: good mover: useful at 2 yrs: just fairly useful in 2001, best effort when 10 lengths fourth to Dandoun in listed event at Kempton in May: should stay 1½m: acts on heavy going, probably on good to firm: has been slowly away: sold 18,000 gns, joined M. Pipe and gelded. *D. R. C. Elsworth*

LUNAR LEO 3 b.g. Muhtarram (USA) 125 – Moon Mistress 82 (Storm Cat (USA)) **98** [2001 86: 6m 7.1m* 7g³ 7.9m 8g⁴ p7g² Nov 24] useful handicapper: won at Sandown in July: very good second to Point of Dispute at Lingfield final start: should prove best at 6f/7f: yet to race on extremes of going, acts on good to firm and polytrack: usually tongue tied: often early to post. *S. C. Williams*

LUNAR LORD 5 b.g. Elmaamul (USA) 125 – Cache (Bustino 136) [2001 46: 14.1v³ **64** 14.1s* 14m³ 12m³ 17.1d Oct 8] close-coupled gelding: modest performer: won handicap at Nottingham in April: stays 1¾m: acts on heavy going, probably on good to firm. *D. Burchell*

LUNAR SOVEREIGN (USA) 2 b. or br.c. (Feb 28) Cobra King (USA) 122 – **95 p** January Moon (USA) (Apalachee (USA) 137) [2001 7s* 7d² Oct 19] $140,000Y: lengthy, attractive colt: second foal: dam, winning sprinter in USA, half-sister to useful Irish sprinter Flawless Image, herself dam of smart miler Darnay: useful form: landed odds in minor event at Leicester in September: wearing crossed noseband, 3 lengths second to Century City in similar event at Newmarket, travelling strongly much of way but no impression late on and eased: will stay 1m: capable of better. *D. R. Loder*

LUNA WAIN 4 b.g. Unfuwain (USA) 131 – Lunafairy (FR) 110 (Always Fair (USA) **–** 121) [2001 6.9v 10g 9.9m Jun 28] second foal: half-brother to a winner in USA by Generous: dam, French 6f (at 2 yrs) to 1m winner, half-sister to very smart French/US middle-distance performer Luazur out of half-sister to Linamix: well beaten in maidens. *G. L. Moore*

LUNCH DATE 2 b.f. (Jan 28) Robellino (USA) 127 – Darkness At Noon (USA) **–** (Night Shift (USA)) [2001 f5g⁴ f5g f6g⁵ May 21] 1,500Y: third foal: half-sister to 1999 2-y-o 5f seller winner Dimming of The Day (by Muhtarram) and a winner in Greece by Rudimentary: dam unraced: visored, no form in sellers. *K. McAuliffe*

LUNCH PARTY 9 b.g. Beveled (USA) – Crystal Sprite 74 (Crystal Glitters (USA) **56** 127) [2001 68: 6m 7m⁵ 6g 7m 8g 7g 8f² 7.5d⁴ f7g Nov 21] good-bodied gelding: not a good walker: modest handicapper: effective at 6f to 1m: acts on firm and soft going, probably on fibresand: tongue tied last 3 starts: has been early to post/slowly away: reportedly finished lame once in 2000: usually races prominently. *R. A. Fahey*

LUNEVISION (FR) 3 b.f. Solid Illusion (USA) 117 – Lumiere Celeste (FR) (Always **–** Fair (USA) 121) [2001 67: 7d 6.1d⁶ 6m⁶ 8m 6m Jul 23] smallish, sturdy filly: fair maiden at 2 yrs: well held in 2001: tongue tied final outing. *H. J. Collingridge*

LUPINE (IRE) 2 b. or br.f. (May 4) Lake Coniston (IRE) 131 – Prosaic Star (IRE) 81 **82** (Common Grounds 118) [2001 5d⁴ 5d* 6m⁴ Jun 30] lengthy, rather unfurnished filly: third foal: half-sister to useful 1999 2-y-o 5f winner Barringer (by Nicolotte), later 6f winner in Sweden: dam Irish 2-y-o 1m winner: fairly useful form: won maiden at Haydock in June: about 3 lengths fourth of 5 to Massarra in listed race at Newmarket final start: may prove best at 5f/6f. *M. R. Channon*

LURDI (IRE) 3 b.c. Lure (USA) 131 – Headrest (Habitat 134) [2001 7g³ 7m 8.1d 8m⁴ **79** 10m* 12m 11.9s³ Sep 7] IR 50,000Y, 36,000 2-y-o: good-bodied colt: sixth foal: closely

591

related to useful Irish 7f (including at 2 yrs) and 1¼m winner Polaire (by Polish Patriot) and half-brother to 11f winner in Hong Kong by Kalaglow: dam lightly-raced sister to Princess Royal winner One Way Street, herself dam of good performers Grape Tree Road, Red Route and Windsor Castle: fair handicapper: dead-heated at Nottingham in July: stays 1½m: acts on soft and good to firm going: visored (ran respectably) fourth start. *J. R. Fanshawe*

LURINA (IRE) 3 b.f. Lure (USA) 131 – Alligatrix (USA) 111 (Alleged (USA) 138) **111** [2001 80p: 7g* 8m³ 8f Jun 22] stocky, lengthy filly: good mover: won maiden at Newmarket (on toes, swished tail and attended by 2 handlers in preliminaries) in May: smart form when 1½ lengths third to Banks Hill in Prix de Sandringham at Chantilly (reluctant to post) following month: sweating freely, last in Coronation Stakes at Royal Ascot final start: stays 1m: acts on good to firm going, showed promise (on debut) on soft. *J. H. M. Gosden*

LUSHS LAD 3 b.c. Wolfhound (USA) 126 – Helsinki (Machiavellian (USA) 123) **55** [2001 –: e5g⁶ e7g³ e7g⁵ e7g* 7.1g 8d⁵ 7m 8m 8.3g Jul 9] IR 7,500Y: first foal: dam, **a62** useful French 1¼m winner, sister to 3-y-o Street Cry out of Irish Oaks winner Helen Street: modest performer: trained in Ireland only 2-y-o start: won 4-runner maiden at Lingfield in March: stays 7f: acts on equitrack. *G. L. Moore*

LUSONG (IRE) 4 ch.c. Fayruz 116 – Mildred Anne (IRE) (Thatching 131) [2001 61: **55** e8g⁶ e7g⁴ 7m Jun 12] modest maiden: barely stays easy 7f: acts on equitrack (shaped well first of 2 outings on fibresand) and good to firm going: blinkered second start: sold 500 gns. *R. Hannon*

LUTINE BELL 6 b.g. Fairy King (USA) – Bell Toll 87 (High Line 125) [2001 –: 7m – 8m May 25] leggy gelding: little form on the Flat: dead. *H. J. Collingridge*

LUXOR 4 ch.g. Grand Lodge (USA) 125 – Escrime (USA) 92 (Sharpen Up 127) [2001 **58** 85: e12g 10.1s 10g 7.6m⁴ 10d 8g 8g 9.7d 8m Sep 12] rangy gelding: fluent mover: fairly useful at 3 yrs: just modest at best in 2001: stays 1½m: acts on firm going: visored last 4 starts: has worn tongue tie: headstrong: sold 4,500 gns. *P. Mitchell*

LYCHEEL 3 ch.g. Lycius (USA) 124 – Talon d'Aiguille (USA) (Big Spruce (USA)) **52** [2001 63: f8g f8g⁴ 8m⁵ 8.2s 10.2g 9.7d 8m 8f Sep 20] modest maiden: stays 1m: acts **a59** on fibresand and good to firm going: blinkered final start: sometimes slowly away. *W. R. Muir*

LYCIAN (IRE) 6 b.g. Lycius (USA) 124 – Perfect Time (IRE) (Dance of Life (USA)) **63** [2001 71+: 10g 10.3f⁶ 9m 10m³ p10g⁶ p10g² p10g Dec 28] tall, angular gelding: fair **a71** handicapper: effective at 1m/1¼m: acts on all-weather and firm going, probably on good to soft. *J. A. R. Toller*

LYCIAT SPARKLE (IRE) 3 b.g. Lycius (USA) 124 – Benguiat (FR) (Exceller **36** (USA) 129) [2001 –: 8f⁵ 12m 8.1d 10.9m⁴ 13.8m⁶ 10.9v Oct 15] angular, close-coupled gelding: poor maiden: stays 1¾m: acts on good to firm going: has looked headstrong. *Mrs G. S. Rees*

LYDIA'S LOOK (IRE) 4 b.f. Distant View (USA) 126 – Mrs Croesus (USA) (Key **65** To The Mint (USA)) [2001 52: 5m⁴ 5m f5g⁴ 5g* 5f⁴ 6m* 6m 5g² 6f f6g f6g Nov 26] **a53** close-coupled filly: fair handicapper on turf, modest on all-weather: won at Hamilton in June and Thirsk in July: effective at 5f/6f: acts on fibresand and firm going. *T. J. Etherington*

LYGETON LAD 3 b.g. Shaamit (IRE) 127 – Smartie Lee 66 (Dominion 123) [2001 **56** f9.4g⁶ 8.2m f9.4g⁴ 7m f7g f8.5g* f7g Nov 23] 1,000Y: fourth foal: half-brother to 5-y-o Santandre and 4-y-o Super Dominion: dam, 7f (at 2 yrs) to 1½m winner who stayed 2m, also winning hurdler: modest performer: won maiden at Wolverhampton in November: stays 8.5f: acts on fibresand and good to firm ground: tongue tied last 5 starts. *Miss Gay Kelleway*

LYNTON LAD 9 b.g. Superpower 113 – House Maid 95 (Habitat 134) [2001 65, a57: – f9.4g² f8.5s⁴ f9.4s⁵ f6g f9.4g Feb 13] good-topped gelding: modest performer: left **a57** P. McEntee before final start (when reportedly lost action): stayed 9.4f: acted on soft going, good to firm and fibresand: often blinkered/visored: unreliable: dead. *M. J. Gingell*

LYRICAL 3 b.f. Shirley Heights 130 – La Sky (IRE) 107 (Law Society (USA) 130) **65** [2001 10v 10g⁴ 12.3d² 12.1g⁴ Sep 13] well-made filly: fifth foal: half-sister to several winners, notably Oaks winner Love Divine (by Diesis): dam, 1¼m winner (probably stayed 1¾m), closely related to Champion Stakes winner Legal Case: fair maiden: jinked and unseated rider having seemed to panic when tape was released (flip start) on debut: likely to stay 1¾m+: raced only on good going or softer. *H. R. A. Cecil*

LYRICAL LAD   2 b.g. (Feb 21) Primo Dominie 121 – Lyrical Bid (USA) 77 (Lyphard   **64 ?**
(USA) 132) [2001 7m 8m⁴ 8s Oct 16] 14,500F, 22,000Y: smallish gelding: first foal: dam,
2-y-o 7.5f winner on only start, half-sister to useful winner up to 2m On Call: modest
maiden: possibly flattered when fourth at Kempton: may prove best up to 1m.
P. W. Harris

LYRICAL WAY   2 b.g. (Feb 9) Vettori (IRE) 119 – Fortunate (Reference Point 139)   **59**
[2001 7.1m 7.1f⁶ 8d Oct 3] 10,000Y: fourth foal: half-brother to winners in Greece by
Selkirk and Hernando: dam unraced half-sister to useful 6f/7f winner Royal Loft: modest
maiden: form only when sixth at Chepstow: gelded after final start: will probably stay
1m. *P. R. Chamings*

LYRIC MAESTRO   2 b.g. (Mar 5) Merdon Melody 98 – Dubitable 59 (Formidable   **77**
(USA) 125) [2001 6d 7m 8g³ Sep 7] 8,000Y: good-bodied gelding: fourth reported foal:
dam, maiden who stayed 1½m, out of very smart performer up to 1¼m Duboff: easily
best effort in maidens (fair form) when third to Connor at Kempton (subsequently
gelded): not sure to stay beyond 1m. *S. Dow*

LYRINGO   7 b.m. Rustingo 94 – Lyricist (Averof 123) [2001 f14g Jun 8] well held in   **–**
claimer: winning hurdler. *P. D. Evans*

LYSANDER'S QUEST (IRE)   3 br.g. King's Theatre (IRE) 128 – Haramayda (FR)   **–**
(Doyoun 124) [2001 87?: 10d 9.9m 12m 11m Sep 26] tall gelding: seemed to show fairly
useful form at 2 yrs: well held in 2001. *L. Montague Hall*

M

MA BELLE BLEUE   2 b.f. (Feb 18) Bluegrass Prince (IRE) 110 – My Bonus 79   **66 d**
(Cyrano de Bergerac 120) [2001 5d⁵ 5.6f 5m⁴ 7m 6.1g 7g 6m⁶ 6m 6v 7d 7f7g⁴ f5g Dec 17]
12,500Y: small filly: second foal: closely related to fairly useful 2000 2-y-o 5f winner My
Lovely (by Dolphin Street): dam 5f (including at 2 yrs) winner: disappointing maiden:
left T. Easterby after eighth start: tried blinkered: has hung under pressure. *Miss A. Stokell*

MABRUM (IRE)   2 b.c. (May 27) Alhaarth (IRE) 126 – Absaar (USA) 76 (Alleged   **– p**
(USA) 138) [2001 7g⁶ Aug 12] fourth living foal: half-brother to 3 winners, including
5-y-o Munjiz and 3-y-o Mobtaker: dam, 11f winner, half-sister to Grand Prix de Paris and
Melbourne Cup winner At Talaq: 10/1, caught the eye when well-beaten sixth of 16 in
maiden at Leicester, short of room in rear and not at all knocked about: should do fair bit
better. *J. L. Dunlop*

MACADAMIA (IRE)   2 b.f. (Feb 1) Classic Cliche (IRE) 128 – Cashew 80 (Sharrood   **82 p**
(USA) 124) [2001 7.1f⁴ 8g* Oct 19] strong, lengthy filly: third foal: half-sister to useful
1998 2-y-o 5f/6f winner Pistachio (by Unblest), later winner in Scandanavia, and 3-y-o
Prime Version: dam 1m winner: confirmed promise when winning 19-runner maiden at
Redcar comfortably by 1¾ lengths from Nirvana: will stay at least 1¼m: useful prospect.
J. R. Fanshawe

MACAROON (IRE)   3 ch.f. Tagula (IRE) 116 – Almond Flower (IRE) (Alzao (USA)   **105 ?**
117) [2001 6s³ 7f7g* 8g² 7.1m³ 7m³ 7m* 6g³ 7g 7f⁴ 7m* 6g 7d⁷ Oct 16] IR 12,000Y: big,
lengthy filly: closely related to winner abroad by Taufan and half-sister to 2 winners
abroad, including German 1m winner Almujta (by Mujtahid): dam, Irish 5f winner, ran
only at 2 yrs: useful performer: won maiden at Southwell in April, handicaps at Lingfield in June and Salisbury in September, and listed race at Maisons-Laffitte (dictated,
seemingly improved effort to beat Inventing Paradise by length) in October: best at 6f/
7f: acts on firm going, good to soft and fibresand: races up with pace: sold 72,000 gns.
M. L. W. Bell

MACAW (IRE)   2 b.c. (Jan 27) Bluebird (USA) 125 – No Quest (IRE) (Rainbow   **88**
Quest (USA) 134) [2001 6m⁴ 7d² 7.2v² Oct 15] IR 160,000Y: good-topped colt: second
foal: half-brother to French 9f/1¼m winner Nakos (by Turtle Island): dam, French
maiden, half-sister to very smart French performer up to 1¼m No Pass No Sale: fairly
useful form: second to Angelus Sunset in minor event at Salisbury and to Night Passion
(beaten a head) in maiden at Ayr: will stay 1m: sold 42,000 gns. *J. H. M. Gosden*

MAC BE LUCKY   4 b.g. Magic Ring (IRE) 115 – Take Heart 84 (Electric 126) [2001   **67**
74: 7.1g 8m 7.9m 7d 7.5d 8d Oct 3] strong, lengthy gelding: fair maiden handicapper:
stays 1m: yet to race on firm ground, acts on any other: has raced freely. *T. D. Barron*

MACDUNE (FR) 3 b.g. Machiavellian (USA) 123 – Sandhill (IRE) 96 (Danehill **67** (USA) 126) [2001 71: 8s 7.1m 7s 6d[4] f6g Nov 21] small, lightly-made gelding: fair maiden, lightly raced: free-going sort, and may prove best at 6f: increasingly warm/short to post second start, gelded after final one. *E. A. L. Dunlop*

MACEO (GER) 7 ch.g. Acatenango (GER) 127 – Metropolitan Star (USA) 84 **79** (Lyphard (USA) 132) [2001 10.5g 10.1m[3] 13.1d* 13.8g* 12g[4] 13.1v[4] 13.8d[5] Nov 6] good-topped gelding: brother to winner in Germany and half-brother to winners there by Surumu and Law Society: dam, 1m winner, out of high-class sprinter/miler Sanedtki: smart performer at best in Germany, winning listed races at Hamburg and Hoppegarten and third in Deutsches St Leger at Dortmund at 3 yrs: won minor events at Munich and Vienna for P. Schiergen in 1999: only fair nowadays: won minor event at Ayr in July and handicap at Catterick in August: stays 1¾m: acts on soft and good to firm ground. *Mrs M. Reveley*

MACONACHIE 2 b.g. (Apr 14) Bahamian Bounty 116 – Madurai 71 (Chilibang 120) **69** [2001 6s 6v[4] 5.1s[3] Oct 30] useful-looking gelding: third foal: half-brother to fairly useful 1999 2-y-o 6f winner Maestersinger (by Piccolo) and a 1m and 11f winner abroad by First Trump: dam 6f winner: fair maiden: third to Acorazado at Nottingham, forcing pace: may prove best at 5f/6f: raced only on soft/heavy ground. *J. L. Dunlop*

MAC'S DREAM (USA) 6 b.g. Mister Frisky (USA) – Annie's Dream (USA) (Droll **–** Role (USA)) [2001 –: 6s 6s 8.1m[3] 8m 10g 8.1m 10.2s 7.1g 7m p10g Nov 20] little form nowadays: tongue tied. *A. W. Carroll*

MAC'S JEWEL 2 ch.c. (Apr 30) Bijou d'Inde 127 – Elabellou (IRE) 41 (Ela-Mana- **67** Mou 132) [2001 p10g[4] f7g[2] p7g Dec 22] 8,000F, 13,000Y: first foal: dam, maiden, should have stayed beyond 1¼m: fair form at best in maidens at Lingfield (2) and Southwell: stays 1¼m: tended to edge left final outing. *W. A. O'Gorman*

MACS MIESQUE (USA) 3 b.c. Miesque's Son (USA) 117 – Santella (USA) (Coastal **58** (USA)) [2001 7d 8g May 6] 10,000Y: sturdy colt: closely related to a winner in USA by Afleet and half-brother to several winners, including fairly useful 1m winner who stayed 11f Highland Legend (by Storm Bird): dam unraced half-sister to dam of Miesque: better effort in maidens at Newmarket when tenth on second start (on toes). *W. A. O'Gorman*

MACTIRE 2 b.c. (Mar 10) Celtic Swing 138 – High Desire (IRE) 59 (High Estate 127) **64** [2001 6s 6f 7m 7m 7.1m[3] 7d 7s Oct 5] leggy colt: first foal: dam maiden who stayed 1½m: modest maiden: seemingly best efforts on first and fifth starts: should stay 1m: acts on good to firm and soft ground. *J. C. Fox*

MADAME BOULANGERE 2 b.f. (Mar 27) Royal Applause 124 – Jazz 76 (Shar- **91** rood (USA) 124) [2001 5g[2] 6m* 6g[3] 7d[5] 6d[3] 6.5g* Sep 28] 29,000Y: leggy, useful-looking filly: fourth living foal: dam, maiden who stayed 1¼m, half-sister to smart US Grade 2 9f winner Sign of Hope: fairly useful performer: won minor event at York in May and valuable 28-runner sales race at Ascot (improved form, beat Lipstick by a length, making virtually all) in September: should stay 7f: unraced on extremes of going: usually races prominently. *R. Hannon*

Watership Down Stud Sales Race, Ascot—an improved effort by Madame Boulangere, who makes virtually all to beat the fast-finishing Lipstick, with Hiddendale (No.2) third

MADAME BUTTERFLY   3 b.f. Reprimand 122 – Mill d'Art (Artaius (USA) 129)   –
[2001 51: e7g⁶ e10s 8m Jun 11] lightly-made filly: little form at 3 yrs: blinkered last 4
starts. *D. J. S. Cosgrove*

MADAME JONES (IRE)   6 ch.m. Lycius (USA) 124 – Gold Braisim (IRE) 77   **72**
(Jareer (USA) 115) [2001 51, a48: f12g⁴ f9.4s⁴ f9.4g⁶ f8g* f9.4g* f9.4g* f7g³ f7g*   **a79**
f8.5g³ f8.5g² f8f⁵ f8g* f8.5g f9.4g⁴ e8g⁶ e8g f8g f8.5g f8g* 8f² 8.1m³ 8m⁴ 8m⁵ f8g
8m 8f⁶ 7.1f⁴ 7.6m⁵ 8m f8g² 8f² 8.2g* 8g³ 7g⁴ f8.5g* 7d* 8.3g 8d² 8m⁴ 8.2m* 7m³
10.3d⁶ 8.1v⁴ f7g² f8.5g² f8g⁵ 8.2s f8.5g⁵ 8g³ f8g p8g⁴ p8g f8.5g³ f7g* f7g* f8g⁴ f7g
f8g f8s³ p8g⁶ f8.5s Dec 27]
   The year's most notable record-breakers included the mare Madame
Jones, who became the first horse in well over a century to win ten handicaps in a
season on the Flat when successful at Nottingham in September. She gained her
earlier wins at Southwell (four), Wolverhampton (three), Nottingham and Yarmouth. Another handicap victory at Wolverhampton in December apparently made
Madame Jones only the third in British racing history to record such eleven such
victories in a calendar year (following Misty Morn in 1858 and Honesty in 1869).
A further victory at Wolverhampton—in a non-handicap—took Madame Jones's
total for the year to twelve, one short of the post-war record number of wins by a
filly or mare in a single year, set by the two-year-old Nagwa in 1975. The
introduction of artificial surfaces and of a twelve-month season has changed Flat

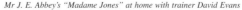

Mr J. E. Abbey's "Madame Jones" at home with trainer David Evans

racing since Nagwa's day. Her thirteen victories came from twenty starts, the last ten crammed into the final two months of the season, which finished at the beginning of November. Madame Jones ran twelve times after the end of the latest turf season, a figure that would have been thirteen but for severe frost causing the abandonment of Wolverhampton's fixture on New Year's Eve. Five of Madame Jones's victories—the first of them off a BHB mark of only 32—were recorded in the first part of the year, before the turf season got under way.

Resting on its laurels is rarely an option for any horse trained by Abergavenny trainer David Evans, whose previous jobs have included car park attendant, supermarket shelf-stacker, self-employed window cleaner and jockey. Even by the standards of an Evans-trained handicapper, Madame Jones was raced particularly hard. After being claimed for 5,000 guineas out of a seller at Wolverhampton in early-January on her first outing of the year (for Andrew Murphy), Madame Jones ran another sixty times (thought also to be a record but virtually impossible to verify). The previous post-1900 record of nine handicap wins was shared by the geldings Chaplins Club (1985, 1988), Glencroft (1988), Star Rage (1994), Vindaloo (1995), Sihafi and Soaked (both 1998) and Nineacres (2000), all from yards noted for campaigning suitable horses vigorously. Toughness and durability alone do not explain their achievements though, nor do they explain those of Madame Jones, who positively thrived on hard work and improved by around two stones over the year (she actually ran her last few races off BHB marks in the 70s). Madame Jones's victories in 2001 were achieved at distances ranging from seven to nearly nine and a half furlongs, nine of them on fibresand and three victories on turf on going ranging from good to firm to good to soft. The tall Madame Jones, who often takes a good hold in her races, has been tried blinkered but was visored on most of her starts in 2001. By the sprinter-miler Lycius out of the Irish six-furlong winner Gold Braisim, Madame Jones is reportedly to be covered by Diktat in 2002. *P. D. Evans*

MADAM ELSA (IRE)   3 b.f. Lycius (USA) 124 – Extra Time 66 (Shadeed (USA) **65**
135) [2001 f7g 7s 7g⁶ 8m⁴ 10d 10m 10.9d³ 10g f12g* Oct 18] 3,500Y: angular filly: third
foal: dam, maiden who stayed 1¾m, out of Ribblesdale Stakes winner Expansive: fair
handicapper: won at Southwell in October: will stay 1¾m: acts on good to firm going,
good to soft and fibresand: visored (raced bit freely) penultimate start: sold 4,000 gns.
R. M. Beckett

MADAME MAXI   7 ch.m. Ron's Victory (USA) 129 – New Pastures (Formidable **61**
(USA) 125) [2001 8g² 8d⁵ 8m⁶ 7.1g* 7f 8d 7d Nov 3] angular mare: shows knee action: **a–**
modest handicapper: won at Sandown in September: effective at 7f/1m: acts on firm and
good to soft going: tried blinkered in 1999: often makes running. *H. S. Howe*

MADAME MAXINE (USA)   2 b. or br.f. (Mar 23) Dayjur (USA) 137 – Political **69**
Parody (USA) (Doonesbury (USA)) [2001 6v f6g* f7s⁴ p6g* Dec 28] IR 90,000Y: half-
sister to smart French 1m winner Panis (by Miswaki), 6f/9f winner at 2 yrs, and to US
stakes-winning sprinter Political Whit (by Lines of Power): dam winning sprinter in US:
fair performer: won maiden at Southwell in November and nursery at Lingfield in
December: raced too freely in between: likely to prove best at 5f/6f: acts on fibresand and
polytrack, soundly beaten only run on turf. *B. J. Meehan*

MADAME ROUX   3 b.f. Rudimentary (USA) 118 – Foreign Mistress (Darshaan **65**
133) [2001 54: 7g⁵ 6.1d³ Sep 21] fair maiden: stays 7f: acts on good to soft going: has
wandered under pressure. *G. Wragg*

MADAM JENKOV   2 ch. or ro.f. (Mar 10) Baryshnikov (AUS) – Joemlujen (Forzando **–**
122) [2001 7g 6g f7g f8g Oct 18] second foal: dam unraced: no form in maidens/sellers.
P. D. Evans

MADAM SHOOLAY   7 b.m. Tragic Role (USA) – Lady Alone 59 (Mr Fluorocarbon **–**
126) [2001 6m Jun 29] angular mare: third foal: half-sister to 11f winner Dancing-Alone
(by Adbass): dam sprinter: 100/1, tailed off in minor event at Newmarket. *D. Mullarkey*

MAD CAREW (USA)   2 ch.g. (Mar 20) Rahy (USA) 115 – Poppy Carew (IRE) 110 **70**
(Danehill (USA) 126) [2001 7f 8g⁴ 8m⁵ 8.3v Oct 8] sturdy gelding: second foal: dam 7f
(at 2 yrs) to 1½m winner: fair maiden: well beaten in nursery final start (subsequently
gelded): should stay 1¼m: acts on good to firm going. *P. W. Harris*

MADDORA (IRE)   2 b.f. (Apr 30) Mark of Esteem (IRE) 137 – Almuhtarama (IRE)   **63**
84 (Rainbow Quest (USA) 134) [2001 7.5m⁴ 8d⁶ Oct 3] sixth foal: half-sister to useful 6f
(at 2 yrs) to 1m (in UAE) winner Man Howa (by Lycius): dam 1¼m winner: encouraging
fourth (modest form) to Plymsole in maiden at Beverley: raced too freely only subsequent
start. *M. P. Tregoning*

MADELINE BASSETT (IRE)   3 b.f. Kahyasi 130 – Impressive Lady 98 (Mr Fluoro-   **85 +**
carbon 126) [2001 66p: 8.3d 7f⁶ 10m⁴ 10m 12d* 12m² 11.8s² 12d p10g* p10g⁵ Nov 24]   **a95**
smallish filly: fluent mover: useful on all-weather, fairly useful on turf: won minor event
at Folkestone in September and handicap at Lingfield (readily) in November: ran well
when 2¾ lengths fifth to Compton Bolter in listed race at Lingfield final start: effective at
1¼m/1½m: acts on soft going, good to firm and polytrack: waited with. *G. A. Butler*

MAD GENIUS   2 b.g. (Feb 16) Makbul 104 – Rinca (Unfuwain (USA) 131) [2001 f6g   **–**
f8.5g Nov 27] second foal: dam twice-raced half-sister to smart 1989 2-y-o 6f to 7.5f
winner Call To Arms: tailed-off last in maiden/claimer at Wolverhampton. *T. H. Caldwell*

MAD HABIT   3 b.g. Minshaanshu Amad (USA) 91§ – Shady Habitat (Sharpo 132)   **–**
[2001 –: 11.6m Jul 16] little form. *W. R. Muir*

MADIBA   2 b.c. (Feb 19) Emperor Jones (USA) 119 – Priluki 65 (Lycius (USA) 124)   **69 p**
[2001 7s⁴ Oct 31] 5,000Y: first foal: dam, won at 13.6f, out of sister to 1000 Guineas/
Oaks winner Midway Lady: 33/1, 8 lengths fourth of 10 to Miss Corniche in maiden at
Yarmouth, staying on having been last 2f out: will stay 1¼m: should improve. *R. Guest*

MADIES PRIDE (IRE)   3 b.f. Fayruz 116 – June Lady (Junius (USA) 124) [2001 48:   **52**
5.1v 6s 5m* 5f f5s 5s Sep 27] rather leggy filly: modest handicapper: won at Beverley in
June: probably best at 5f: acts on good to firm going: has looked wayward. *J. J. Quinn*

MAD MICK (IRE)   6 b.g. Homo Sapien 121 – Yougotit (Orange Reef 90) [2001 11.9m   **§§**
f11g Jun 15] last in claimer (very reluctant to race) and seller (looked most wayward in
blinkers): dead. *K. McAuliffe*

MADONNA FAN (IRE)   3 b.g. Lear Fan (USA) 130 – Madonna Sprite (Saint Cyrien   **69**
(FR) 128) [2001 8m 7g 10g⁵ 10.2g⁵ 12g Sep 19] 1,000,000 francs Y: fifth living foal:
half-brother to 3 winners in France, including useful performer up to 12.5f Reve Parisien
(by Trempolino): dam, French 2-y-o 7f winner, half-sister to Gran Criterium winner
Will Dancer: fair maiden: best efforts at 1¼m: has started slowly: sold 6,500 gns.
L. M. Cumani

MADRASEE   3 b.f. Beveled (USA) – Pendona 72 (Blue Cashmere 129) [2001 72: e6g   **70**
e7g³ e6g⁴ e7g³ 5.1d 6d⁵ 5.3f 6m⁴ 5f 6m 6s⁴ 6d* p7g p5g* Dec 22] fair handicapper: left
M. Blanshard after tenth start: won at Brighton in November and Lingfield in December:
has form at easy 7f, probably best at 5f/6f: acts on firm going, soft, equitrack and
polytrack: usually races prominently: none too consistent. *L. Montague Hall*

MAGDALEON   3 b.f. Lion Cavern (USA) 117 – Magdala (IRE) (Sadler's Wells   **51**
(USA) 132) [2001 –: 7m 6m⁵ 7m⁶ 6m 6.1f f8g f7g f8.5g³ f8g⁶ Dec 17] leggy, lengthy
filly: modest maiden: left R. Charlton after sixth start: barely stays 8.5f: acts on fibresand
and good to firm going: races freely. *R. Ford*

MAGELTA   4 b.g. Magic Ring (IRE) 115 – Pounelta 91 (Tachypous 128) [2001 79,   **73**
a86p: 7m 6.9m⁶ 8m⁵ 9f 7d 7f³ 6g 7m³ Sep 4] big, useful-looking gelding: fair performer:
stays 1m: acts on good to firm going, good to soft and fibresand/equitrack: tried tongue
tied: has edged left. *R. Hannon*

MAGENTA (IRE)   2 b. or br.f. (Jan 20) Spectrum (IRE) 126 – Bird In My Hand (IRE)   **–**
57 (Bluebird (USA) 125) [2001 7g⁵ Jul 3] IR 34,000Y: first living foal: dam thrice-raced
half-sister to very smart stayer Yawa: very green, well-held fifth of 6 in maiden at
Yarmouth: sold 800 gns, sent to Sweden. *M. L. W. Bell*

MAGGIE FLYNN   3 b.f. Imp Society (USA) – Lonely Street 93 (Frimley Park 109)   **–**
[2001 –: f7g⁶ Mar 14] well held in maidens at Wolverhampton. *A. P. Jarvis*

MAGHAS (IRE)   7 ch.g. Lahib (USA) 129 – Rawaabe (USA) 87 (Nureyev (USA)   **47**
131) [2001 57: 5m⁵ 5g⁶ 5m 5m f5g Dec 14] modest handicapper at best: won at Down
Royal in 1999: poor form in 2001: best at 5f: acts on heavy ground, well held on fibresand
final start: blinkered. *G. Stack, Ireland*

MAGIC AIR   3 b.f. Magic Ring (IRE) 115 – Exhibit Air (IRE) 77 (Exhibitioner 111)   **37**
[2001 –: e8g e10g⁵ 8.2s 7m⁴ 7s 7.5m³ 8m 7d 6f⁶ 7m Aug 8] sturdy filly: poor performer:
stays 7.5f: acts on firm going: tried blinkered. *J. S. Moore*

MAGICAL BAILIWICK (IRE) 5 ch.g. Magical Wonder (USA) 125 – Alpine –
Dance (USA) 62§ (Apalachee (USA) 137) [2001 66: 8.2s Nov 5] fair performer at 4 yrs:
below form only 5-y-o Flat outing: blinkered. *R. J. Baker*

MAGICAL DAY 2 ch.f. (May 22) Halling (USA) 133 – Ahla 90 (Unfuwain (USA) 52
131) [2001 6m 7m⁵ 7.5g Sep 19] rather leggy filly: second foal: dam 1½m winner:
modest maiden: should be suited by 1¼m/1½m. *Mrs J. R. Ramsden*

MAGICAL FLUTE 3 ch.f. Piccolo 121 – Stride Home 78 (Absalom 128) [2001 72,
a75: 7v Mar 24] strong filly: fair performer in 2000: well held only 3-y-o start.
M. R. Channon

MAGICAL FOOL 2 b.g. (Apr 1) Magic Ring (IRE) 115 – Vera's First (IRE) 69 –
(Exodal (USA)) [2001 6m 5m 7.5g Sep 19] 4,500Y, 10,000 2-y-o: compact, workmanlike
gelding: second foal: dam 2-y-o 7f seller winner: well beaten in maidens. *N. Wilson*

MAGICAL KNIGHT 3 b.g. Sir Harry Lewis (USA) 127 – Formal Affair 78 (Rousil- 68
lon (USA) 133) [2001 8m 8.1d⁶ 10m⁴ Sep 11] second foal: dam 7f (at 2 yrs) to 1¼m
winner who was also successful over hurdles: fair maiden: best effort on third start: will
be suited by 1½m. *R. T. Phillips*

MAGICAL MYTH 2 b.f. (Apr 30) Robellino (USA) 127 – Sinking (Midyan (USA) 50 p
124) [2001 5f Jul 17] 17,000Y: sturdy, good-quartered filly: has scope: fifth foal:
half-sister to 5f (at 2 yrs)/6f winner Molly Brown (by Rudimentary) and Italian 7f/1m
performer Stato King (by Statoblest), both useful: dam unraced: backward, seventh of 15
in maiden at Beverley, not given hard time: should do better. *D. Nicholls*

MAGICAL NATURE (IRE) 2 ch.f. (May 5) Petardia 113 – Sweet Nature (IRE) 71 58
(Classic Secret (USA) 91) [2001 5g 6g⁵ Sep 11] 16,000 2-y-o resold 6,400 2-y-o: second
foal: half-sister to 1998 2-y-o 5.7f winner Ivans Bride (by Inzar), later winner in Holland:
dam, 2-y-o 6f winner, half-sister to useful 1994 2-y-o sprinter Princely Hush: much better
effort in maidens (modest form) when fifth of 14 at Lingfield, never nearer under
inexperienced claimer: should stay 7f: sent to USA. *N. P. Littmoden*

MAGICAL POWER (IRE) 2 ch.c. (Mar 29) Magic Ring (IRE) 115 – Try Vickers 71
(USA) 72 (Fuzzbuster (USA)) [2001 6.1g 7.9d f7g² f8.5g⁵ f8g² f8g⁵ f7s⁵ Dec 18]
12,000Y: half-brother to several winners, including sprinter Nordico Princess (by Nordico) and 1½m winner Hurgill Dancer (by Rambo Dancer): dam, maiden, stayed 1¼m:
fair maiden: second at Wolverhampton and Southwell: stays 8.5f: acts on fibresand:
blinkered/visored last 3 starts: difficult ride. *W. R. Muir*

MAGICAL RIVER 4 ch.f. Lahib (USA) 129 – Awtaar (USA) 67 (Lyphard (USA) 47
132) [2001 –: f8g 7.1d 6m* 6m 7g⁶ 6m 7d Aug 26] poor handicapper: won maiden
event at Brighton in July: stays 7f: acts on firm going: has started slowly/raced freely.
J. M. Bradley

MAGICAL SHADOWS 2 b.g. (Mar 28) Whittingham (IRE) 104 – She Knew The 43
Rules (IRE) 45 (Jamesmead 86) [2001 f5g⁶ f5g⁵ 5g⁵ 5.1f 6d Jun 17] angular gelding:
second foal: dam 2m seller winner: poor maiden. *D. Burchell*

MAGIC ARROW (USA) 5 b.g. Defensive Play (USA) 118 – Magic Blue (USA) –
(Cure The Blues (USA)) [2001 f14g⁴ 14m⁶ 18m 16.2f Jul 7] seems of little account
nowadays. *I. Emmerson*

MAGIC BABE 4 b.f. Magic Ring (IRE) 115 – Head Turner 61 (My Dad Tom (USA) –
109) [2001 64d: e7g⁵ e8g 7m 6.9m 7f 9.7m⁶ 10s Sep 30] leggy filly: one-time modest 7f
winner: well held in 2001: tried blinkered. *Jamie Poulton*

MAGIC BENGIE 2 b.g. (May 10) Magic Ring (IRE) 115 – Zinzi (Song 132) [2001 56
7f 6v 6d Nov 2] 10,000Y: good-topped gelding: has scope: brother to 1998 Irish 2-y-o 1m
winner River Gorge and half-brother to several winners, including smart sprinter Sarcita
(by Primo Dominie) and useful 1999 2-y-o 5f (including Flying Childers Stakes) winner
Mrs P (by First Trump): dam Irish 5f winner: modest form at best in maidens: not sure to
stay 7f. *Mrs L. Stubbs*

MAGIC BOX 3 b.g. Magic Ring (IRE) 115 – Princess Poquito (Hard Fought 125) 75 d
[2001 74: 9.9g⁶ 10.4m 8m 8f 7m 8m 8.2s³ 8.9m Sep 2] strong, good-bodied gelding: fair
performer: generally disappointing in 2001: acts on firm and good to soft going,
possibly on soft: tried visored: races freely. *A. P. Jarvis*

MAGIC CHARM 3 b.f. Magic Ring (IRE) 115 – Loch Clair (IRE) 53 (Lomond 44
(USA) 128) [2001 44: e7g 7s² 8.5f³ 8.1m 10g 10m 10.1g⁶ 10s f9.4g⁴ f12f⁶ p10g⁵ Dec

29] angular filly: poor maiden handicapper: stays 1¼m, at least when emphasis is on speed: acts on firm going, fibresand and polytrack: has started slowly. *N. P. Littmoden*

MAGIC EAGLE   4 b.g. Magic Ring (IRE) 115 – Shadow Bird 70 (Martinmas 128) **56** [2001 62+: f7g* f7s 7m⁴ 5.7m f7g f6g² 7d⁴ p8g p6g* p7g Dec 19] quite good-topped **a76** gelding: fair on all-weather, modest on turf: won handicap at Southwell in January and minor event at Lingfield in December: best form at 6f: acts on fibresand/polytrack, soft and good to firm going: possibly needs to dominate. *G. L. Moore*

MAGIC FEATHERS   3 b.g. Anabaa (USA) 130 – Plume Magique (Kenmare (FR) **50** 125) [2001 e8g 9.9m 10.4m 13.8m³ Sep 22] fifth foal: half-brother to UAE 1¼m winner Moreeb (by Unfuwain): dam French 1m winner: modest maiden: trained by E. Dunlop on debut: unlikely to stay beyond 1¾m. *M. E. Sowersby*

MAGIC FLUTE   5 ch.m. Magic Ring (IRE) 115 – Megan's Flight 74 (Welsh Pageant **71** 132) [2001 70: 8d³ 8f⁴ 8m* 8m Sep 12] good-bodied mare: fair handicapper: won at Bath in July: said to have bled from nose final start: best at 1m: acts on good to firm and good to soft going: has been tongue tied. *R. J. Baker*

MAGIC GEM (IRE)   3 gr.g. Petong 126 – Fairy Magic (IRE) (Fairy King (USA)) **42** [2001 50?: e5g² e6g e5g⁴ e5s 5.3g⁶ 6m 7.1g Sep 13] poor maiden: should stay 6f: acts on equitrack, raced only on good going or firmer on turf: tried blinkered/tongue tied: inconsistent. *J. A. Osborne*

MAGIC HANNE   2 ch.f. (Feb 20) Magic Ring (IRE) 115 – Sunfleet 59 (Red Sunset **–** 120) [2001 7v⁴ f8s Dec 21] 15,000Y, 20,000Y: rather leggy filly: half-sister to several winners, including 1997 2-y-o sprinter Pool Music (later 8.5f winner in USA) and 7f/1m winner Russian Music (both useful, by Forzando): dam 1¼m maiden: well held in maidens at Newcastle and Southwell. *S. E. Kettlewell*

MAGIC HARP (IRE)   3 b.f. Common Grounds 118 – Princess of Zurich (IRE) (Law **–** Society (USA) 130) [2001 –p: 7m May 11] only a little sign of ability in maidens. *M. A. Jarvis*

MAGIC LODGE   2 b.c. (Feb 12) Grand Lodge (USA) 125 – Samsung Spirit 79 **67** (Statoblest 120) [2001 7m⁶ 7g 6m⁶ 6.9d Sep 3] 32,000Y: sturdy colt: first foal: dam, 6f winner (including at 2 yrs), half-sister to dam of smart 6f/7f performer Indian Rocket: fair form in maidens second/third starts: ran poorly in nursery final one: stays 7f: sold 6,200 gns. *M. R. Channon*

MAGIC MAID   2 b.f. (May 2) Presidium 124 – Mrs Magic (Magic Mirror 105) [2001 **–** 5.7g 7m 5.1m Sep 10] 3,200Y: fifth foal: sister to German 7f winner Tricky Dick: dam unraced: well held in maidens. *H. S. Howe*

MAGIC MILL (IRE)   8 b.g. Simply Great (FR) 122 – Rosy O'Leary (Majetta 115) **58** [2001 70d: 7s³ 7d³ 7m³ 8f⁵ 6g⁵ 8s² 7d² 6d 9.2g 9.1m 9.1v⁵ Oct 16] sparely-made gelding: modest performer: best at 7f/1m: acts on equitrack and any turf going: tried visored: has been slowly away: often races prominently. *J. S. Goldie*

MAGIC MUSIC (IRE)   2 b.f. (Mar 13) Magic Ring (IRE) 115 – Chiming Melody 71 **67** (Cure The Blues (USA)) [2001 6g⁶ 7f 6g³ 6m 7v³ Oct 24] 18,500 2-y-o: tall, plain filly: half-sister to several winners, including 1999 2-y-o 5f winner Alustar (by Emarati) and fairly useful 8.5f to 1½m winner Ocean Park (by Dominion): dam 1m winner: fair maiden: third at Kempton (sales race) and Newcastle: not sure to stay beyond 7f: probably acts on any going. *A. Bailey*

MAGIC OF LOVE   4 b.f. Magic Ring (IRE) 115 – Mistitled (USA) 54 (Miswaki **99** (USA) 124) [2001 99: 6g⁵ 6g 5f⁶ 6m² 5.7m³ 6g⁴ 6m⁵ 5.6m 7m⁶ 6g⁶ Oct 5] leggy, workmanlike filly: useful performer: generally respectable efforts at least in 2001, including when ¾-length second to Autumnal in minor event at Newmarket in June: best at 5f/6f: acts on firm and good to soft going: has been bandaged behind/run well when sweating: held up: sold 48,000 gns. *M. L. W. Bell*

MAGIC RAINBOW   6 b.g. Magic Ring (IRE) 115 – Blues Indigo 103 (Music Boy **85** 124) [2001 93: 6g 6m⁵ 5m 5.1m* 5m Sep 22] leggy gelding: poor mover: fairly useful performer: won minor event at Bath in August: effective at 5f to easy 7f: seems unsuited by soft/heavy going, acts on any other turf and fibresand/equitrack: sometimes starts slowly. *M. L. W. Bell*

MAGIC'S BEAUTY   2 b.f. (May 18) Magic Ring (IRE) 115 – Tocco Jewel 44 (Reesh **61** 117) [2001 6g 6g 5.1m⁵ 6s Oct 3] first foal: dam 1m winner: modest maiden: stays 6f: acts on good to firm ground, well held on soft. *M. J. Ryan*

MAGIC SONGBIRD 2 b.f. (May 8) Magic Ring (IRE) 115 – Winsong Melody **50** (Music Maestro 119) [2001 6g 5m 6g Sep 5] half-sister to numerous winners, including useful 5f winner El Yasaf (by Sayf El Arab), fairly useful 1997 2-y-o 6f winner Tobler-song (by Tirol) and 7-y-o Swinging The Blues: dam sprint maiden: modest form at best in maiden/sellers: stays 6f. *C. A. Dwyer*

MAGIC SOUND 3 ch.g. Savahra Sound 111 – Ace Girl 58 (Stanford 121§) [2001 f7g **52** 5g⁶ 5m 5f³ 6g f6g Nov 16] 1,200Y: fourth reported foal: brother to 1998 2-y-o 5f winner Sound's Ace: dam 1m winner: modest maiden: stays 6f: visored (needed early reminders) final start. *Mrs A. Duffield*

MAGIC TO DO (IRE) 3 b.g. Spectrum (IRE) 126 – Smouldering (IRE) (Caerleon – (USA) 132) [2001 60p: 11.7d Oct 25] better effort in maidens when ninth at Doncaster only 2-y-o start: has been gelded. *R. F. Johnson Houghton*

MAGIC TRICK 2 b.c. (Jan 11) Magic Ring (IRE) 115 – Les Amis 70 (Alzao (USA) **91** 117) [2001 5s³ 5d* 5.1f³ 6m⁴ 6g³ 7g 6m 6m⁶ 6g p7g⁴ Nov 13] 6,000F, 22,000Y: big, well-made colt: fifth foal: half-brother to a 1m/9f winner in Italy by Never So Bold: dam 6f (at 2 yrs) and 1m winner: fairly useful performer: won maiden at Newmarket in April: mostly creditable efforts after, especially in Lingfield nursery final start: should stay 1m: acts on firm going, good to soft and polytrack: sometimes sweating/on toes. *B. W. Hills*

MAGIC WATERS 3 b.g. Ezzoud (IRE) 126 – Paradise Waters 73 (Celestial Storm **67** (USA) 132) [2001 65: 8v⁴ 10s² 11.1m³ 10m 12.3f⁶ 16.2f 10m³ 14.1m⁴ 10m⁴ Sep 6] strong, useful-looking gelding: fair maiden handicapper: effective at 1¼m, probably at 1¾m: seems to act on any going: blinkered (below form) fourth start: fair hurdler. *T. D. Easterby*

MAGIQUE ETOILE (IRE) 5 b.m. Magical Wonder (USA) 125 – Shes A Dancer – (IRE) (Alzao (USA) 117) [2001 64, a57: 7m 6m 10m 10g Sep 11] good-bodied mare: modest maiden handicapper at 4 yrs: no form in 2001: tried blinkered/visored. *Dr J. R. J. Naylor*

MAGNANIMOUS 3 ch.g. Presidium 124 – Mayor 86 (Laxton 105) [2001 50: 5.1s – 5m 6m 6g Jun 12] workmanlike gelding: little form in 2001: often visored. *N. Tinkler*

MAGNUSSON 3 b.c. Primo Dominie 121 – Nunsharpa 87 (Sharpo 132) [2001 83: **79 +** 6.9m³ 8.3g² 8.2d* Sep 21] tall, rather leggy, quite attractive colt: fair performer: won maiden at Nottingham in September by 1½ lengths from Far Note, making most: not sure to stay much beyond 1m: yet to race on extremes of going: free-going sort: sold 25,000 gns. *J. H. M. Gosden*

MAGS CRYSTAL DREAM 4 b.g. Holly Buoy 60 – Keep Mum 63 (Mummy's Pet – 125) [2001 16f 10d³ Jul 16] sixth foal: half-brother to 3 winners, including 1m winner who stayed 1¾m Seconds Away (by Hard Fought): dam, sprint maiden, best at 2 yrs: tailed off in claimer and maiden. *J. S. Goldie*

MAGZAA (IRE) 3 gr.c. Marju (IRE) 127 – Labibeh (USA) 109 (Lyphard (USA) 132) **84 d** [2001 69p: 10g² 9.9m² 12m² 12s 12d 12d 7d 13d⁶ Aug 11] big, strong colt: fairly useful maiden: left J. Dunlop 23,000 gns after third start: well below form after: stays 1½m: acts on good to firm going: tried blinkered. *Luke Comer, Ireland*

MAHALA 4 b.f. Lugana Beach 116 – Little Nutmeg 38 (Gabitat 119) [2001 –: f6g Jan – 4] no form. *J. Balding*

MAHFOOTH (USA) 4 ch.c. Diesis 133 – I Certainly Am (USA) (Affirmed (USA)) **117** [2001 109: 8g² 8.9g* 8.9g 7g⁶ 8g* 8g Jul 8] sturdy, lengthy colt: smart performer: won prestige race at Nad Al Sheba (by ½ length from Golden Silca) in March and Prix du Chemin de Fer du Nord at Chantilly (by neck from Up And Away) in June: below form otherwise: stays 9f: acts on good to firm going and dirt: has been bandaged behind: has left Godolphin. *Saeed bin Suroor*

MAHLSTICK (IRE) 3 b.g. Tagula (IRE) 116 – Guv's Joy (IRE) 72 (Thatching 131) **43** [2001 –: e8g 6m⁵ 6f 9f 7v p7g p7g⁶ Dec 28] small, sturdy gelding: poor maiden: seems to stay 9f: acts on firm ground and polytrack: tried visored. *W. P. Arbuthnot*

MAHSUSIE (IRE) 2 gr.f. (Apr 14) Mukaddamah (USA) 125 – La Susiane (Persepolis **97** (FR) 127) [2001 5s³ 6m* 5g* 6m⁵ 7s⁵ 7g 6m Sep 12] 6,500Y: big, good-topped filly: third foal: dam, won 1½m bumper, half-sister to useful 1¼m winner Gisarne: useful performer: won maiden at Leopardstown (hung left) and listed race at the Curragh (by ¾ length from Keepers Hill) in May: ran creditably when fifth in Coventry Stakes at Royal Ascot on fourth start and seventh in Moyglare Stud Stakes at the Curragh on sixth one: bred to stay

1m: acts on good to firm ground, below form on soft: often forces pace. *Francis Ennis, Ireland*

MAIDEN VOYAGE 3 b.f. Slip Anchor 136 – Elaine Tully (IRE) 80 (Persian Bold **47** 123) [2001 10.4m⁵ 10m⁶ 8.1v Sep 28] lengthy, good-bodied filly: second foal: dam, 1m to 1¾m winner, also fairly useful staying hurdler: poor form in maidens: bred to be suited by at least 1½m. *Mrs J. R. Ramsden*

MAID FOR FREEDOM (USA) 3 gr.f. Trempolino (USA) 135 – Spectacular Native **64** (USA) (Spectacular Bid (USA)) [2001 –p: 7d 7f⁵ May 9] leggy, unfurnished filly: best effort in 3 maidens when ninth of 28 to Victoria Cross at Newmarket on reappearance, hampered leaving stalls: should stay at least 1m. *G. A. Butler*

MAID FOR ROMANCE 3 ch.f. Pursuit of Love 124 – High Savannah 77 (Rousillon **71** (USA) 133) [2001 10m³ Jul 25] 100,000F: fifth foal: half-sister to 3 winners, including smart 5f (at 2 yrs) to 1¼m winner who stayed 1½m Lady In Waiting (by Kylian) and 5-y-o Smart Savannah: dam maiden who stayed 1½m: 8/1, 5½ lengths third of 4 to Green Ideal in maiden at Sandown, close up over 2f out then running green, only outing. *D. R. C. Elsworth*

MAID FOR RUNNING 2 b.f. (Apr 4) Namaqualand (USA) – Scarlet Lake 60 (Rep- **80** rimand 122) [2001 5m² 5d* 7g 6.5g⁵ 6g Oct 6] 8,000F, 40,000G: close-coupled filly: second foal: half-sister to 3-y-o Polar Kingdom: dam lightly-raced half-sister to useful sprinters Maid For The Hills and Maid For Walking and to dam of smart 1¼m filly Lady In Waiting: fairly useful performer: won maiden at Hamilton in August, idling: good fifth of 28 to Madame Boulangere in valuable sales race at Ascot: probably stays 7f: unraced on extremes of going. *G. A. Butler*

MAID OF ARC (USA) 3 b.f. Patton (USA) 110 – Holy Speed (CAN) (Afleet (CAN)) **41** [2001 58: 7d 6f 7m 8g 6m Aug 27] quite attractive filly: poor performer: should stay 1m: acts on firm ground: often tongue tied: has raced too slowly away. *Lady Herries*

MAID TO LOVE (IRE) 4 ch.f. Petardia 113 – Lomond Heights (IRE) (Lomond **45** (USA) 128) [2001 62: f8s⁶ f8g f8g f7g f8f⁴ f11g e8g e10g² f12g³ e10m⁴ f12g³ May 19] poor maiden: left T. D. Barron after sixth outing: stays 1½m: acts on fibresand/equitrack, best turf efforts on good going: blinkered/visored last 7 starts: has had tongue tied: has looked difficult ride/less than keen: sold 2,900 gns, joined M. Pipe. *I. A. Wood*

MAID TO PERFECTION 2 b.f. (Mar 31) Sadler's Wells (USA) 132 – Maid For **84 p** The Hills 101 (Indian Ridge 123) [2001 7g⁵ 7d* Nov 3] leggy, finely-made filly: second foal: half-sister to 3-y-o Green Tambourine: dam, 2-y-o 6f winner, half-sister to dam of smart 1¼m filly Lady In Waiting: considerately handled on debut (on toes), and 2 months later fairly useful form to win 21-runner maiden at Newmarket by 1¾ lengths from Silken Brief, leading over 1f out: will stay at least 1m: should make a useful 3-y-o. *J. L. Dunlop*

MAILLE PISTOL (FR) 3 ch.c. Pistolet Bleu (IRE) 133 – Bric Mamaille (FR) **117** (Bricassar (USA) 119) [2001 10.5v* 10.5v* 12d* 12m 10d⁴ 12v Oct 21] 165,000 francs Y: first foal: dam French 10.5f/hurdles winner: smart performer: won minor event at Saint-Cloud at 2 yrs and progressed well on return, winning listed race there in March, Prix Greffulhe (by 6 lengths from Nolt) in April and Prix Hocquart (gradually opened up clear lead and beat Sagacity by 8 lengths) in May, last 2 at Longchamp: disappointing afterwards in Prix du Jockey Club at Chantilly (favourite, only eighth to Anabaa Blue), and in Prix du Prince d'Orange (fourth to Equerry) and Prix du Conseil de Paris (reportedly choked when last of 11), both at Longchamp in autumn: stays 1½m: seems suited by ground softer than good (acts on heavy going): has given trouble at stalls: front runner. *J.-C. Rouget, France*

MAIMANA (IRE) 2 b. or br.f. (Feb 23) Desert King (IRE) 129 – Staff Approved 94 **79** (Teenoso (USA) 135) [2001 7g 8d³ 8.2v² Oct 4] IR 230,000Y: good-topped filly: fifth living foal: half-sister to smart 7f (including at 2 yrs) to 1¼m winner Polar Prince (by Distinctly North) and useful 7f (at 2 yrs) and 1m winner Housekeeper (by Common Grounds), later winner in USA: dam 2-y-o 1m winner: progressive in maidens, fair form when short-headed by Sheer Bliss at Nottingham (led briefly final 1f): should stay 1¼m. *M. A. Jarvis*

MAINE LOBSTER (USA) 3 ch.f. Woodman (USA) 126 – Capades (USA) (Over- **71** skate (CAN)) [2001 70: 8.3s⁵ 10g⁵ 10m⁵ Jun 1] angular, workmanlike filly: fair maiden: stays 1¼m: acts on soft and good to firm going: has raced freely: sold 15,000 gns in December. *J. L. Dunlop*

MAIRI'S WEDDING 2 b.f. (Jan 17) Atraf 116 – Crofters Ceilidh 101 (Scottish Reel **59** 123) [2001 5m⁶ 5m⁶ 5f⁴ 5m⁵ 6.1g 5f⁶ 6m 7d⁶ Oct 9] 15,500Y: rather unfurnished filly:

first foal: dam, 5f winner (including at 2 yrs), half-sister to 6-y-o Lord Kintyre: modest maiden: should stay 7f: acts on firm and good to soft ground: consistent. *J. S. Goldie*

MAI TAI (IRE) 6 b.m. Scenic 128 – Oystons Propweekly 74 (Swing Easy (USA) 126) **46** [2001 47, a61: f7g f8g f11s f8s 9v f8g² f8g⁶ 7s² 7d f8g* f7g* f7g³ 8m Jun 24] good-bodied **a64** mare: modest on all-weather, poor on turf: won seller and handicap at Southwell in May/June: effective at 7f/1m: acts on soft going, good to firm and fibresand/equitrack: blinkered once, often visored. *D. W. Barker*

MAJESTIC BAY (IRE) 5 b.g. Unfuwain (USA) 131 – That'll Be The Day (IRE) 68 **93** (Thatching 131) [2001 90: 12s⁶ 13.9m 13.3m* 13.3m⁶ 14s³ 14v Sep 29] sturdy gelding: fairly useful handicapper: won at Newbury in July: good third to Caqui d'Or at Haydock penultimate start: effective at 13f to 2m: acts on heavy and good to firm ground: blinkered once as 4-y-o: often leads: has shown temperament: sold 32,000 gns, joined J. Old. *P. W. Harris*

MAJESTIC QUEST (IRE) 3 b.g. Piccolo 121 – Teanarco (IRE) 94 (Kafu 120) **55** [2001 72d: 7f 6m 7m f6g 7.1g³ 7.1m 6m 6g Sep 5] fair at 2 yrs: just modest form at best **a–** in 2001: stays 7f. *J. Neville*

MAJESTIC WIND (IRE) 4 ch.g. College Chapel 122 – Columbian Sand (IRE) **–** (Salmon Leap (USA) 131) [2001 54: f6g³ f7g⁶ f9.4s f6g f12g Feb 27] IR 10,500F, IR 15,000Y: third foal: half-brother to 7-y-o Arc: dam unraced: modest maiden at 3 yrs (sold from T. Stack in Ireland 3,500 gns after final start): little form in 2001: seems to stay 9f: acts on soft going: tried blinkered/tongue tied. *M. G. Quinlan*

MAJHOOL 2 b.g. (Apr 29) Mark of Esteem (IRE) 137 – Be Peace (USA) (Septieme **71 d** Ciel (USA) 123) [2001 6m² 6g 6f 7s Oct 5] IR 4,400Y, 19,000 2-y-o: tall, useful-looking gelding: has scope: second foal: half-brother to a winner in Greece by Lion Cavern: dam German 1m (at 2 yrs) and 1¼m winner: disappointing after fair form when second in maiden at Newmarket: needs to settle to stay beyond 6f: has worn crossed noseband. *G. L. Moore*

MA JOLIE 3 ch.f. Shalford (IRE) 124§ – Scalford Brook (Handsome Sailor 125) **78** [2001 78: 7d 7s⁴ 7f⁴ 7g 8m* 7.6g 7.1v 6d Oct 12] workmanlike filly: fair handicapper: won at Doncaster in August: effective at 7f/1m: acts on good to firm and heavy going: none too consistent. *H. Akbary*

MAJOR ATTRACTION 6 gr.g. Major Jacko 78 – My Friend Melody (Sizzling **64** Melody 117) [2001 49: 12s 13.1m⁵ 12m² 10.5g 12.1m 10.9f* 12m² 12m² 12.3m³ 12d 12.3m⁴ 12g⁵ 12.3d⁶ 12.1g Sep 3] sturdy gelding: modest handicapper: won at Ayr in June: probably stays 13f: acts on fibresand and firm going: tried blinkered/visored: has been early to post: sometimes slowly away: held up: none too consistent. *W. M. Brisbourne*

MAJOR DRIVE (IRE) 3 b.c. Sadler's Wells (USA) 132 – Puck's Castle 92 (Shirley **84** Heights 130) [2001 8d 10.2d 10.5m⁶ 9.9m² 9.9d Sep 27] IR 170,000Y: medium-sized, quite attractive colt: second foal: half-brother to 4-y-o Emerald Peace: dam, 1m winner who ran only at 2 yrs (bred to be suited by 1¼m/1½m), half-sister to Cheveley Park winner Embassy out of winner of same race Pass The Peace: fairly useful maiden: best effort when 2 lengths second to Foreign Affairs in handicap at Goodwood in June: reportedly lost action on bend at same track final start: will stay 1½m: acts on good to firm going: has worn crossed noseband: sold 13,000 gns. *J. H. M. Gosden*

MAJOR LAUGH 2 ch.c. (Feb 18) Colonel Collins (USA) 122 – Joytime (John de **92** Coombe 122) [2001 5.1d³ 5.7f⁴ 6m 6m² f7g* 7d³ 7g* 7m⁵ 6m⁵ 6m 6d* p7g³ Nov 13] 2,500F: useful-looking colt: half-brother to 7f winner Jolto (by Noalto) and 1½m/1¾m winner All The Joys (by Adbass): dam ran once: fairly useful performer: won maiden at Southwell in July, nursery at Newmarket in August and 30-runner sales race at Newmarket (led close home to beat Protectorate by ¾ length) in October: good third to Cuddles in nursery at Lingfield final start: effective at 6f/7f: acts on firm ground, good to soft and fibresand/polytrack: races prominently: consistent. *B. W. Hills*

MAJOR REVIEW (IRE) 3 b.f. Definite Article 121 – Fresh Look (IRE) 64 (Alzao **53** (USA) 117) [2001 –: 10m 8m⁴ 10m 10.1m⁵ 11.6m 16.2g 10d Oct 15] smallish filly: modest maiden: stays 11.6f: acts on good to firm going: blinkered final start: has been slowly away: sent to Spain. *M. L. W. Bell*

MAKARIM (IRE) 5 ch.g. Generous (IRE) 139 – Emmaline (USA) (Affirmed (USA)) **89 §** [2001 –, a91: f16g* f16.2s³ f16.2g³ f12f² 11.9d 14.1m² 14.4m² 12m* 12d⁴ 12.3m⁴ 14.4g² **a92 §** 13.3f³ f12g³ Oct 6] tall gelding: fairly useful handicapper: won at Southwell in January and Kempton in July: effective at 1½m to 2m: acts on fibresand/equitrack and firm ground: blinkered once: has hung badly right: usually held up: consistent, but no battler. *M. R. Bosley*

MAKASSEB 4 ch.g. Kris 135 – Shefoog 90 (Kefaah (USA) 124) [2001 79: f16g⁴ e16g* a7.5f Dec 6] strong, angular gelding: fair handicapper: won amateur event at Lingfield in January: left M. Channon and off 11 months after: stays easy 2m: acts on heavy, good to firm going and fibresand/equitrack. *D. J. Selvaratnam, UAE* **77**

MAKBOOLA (IRE) 3 b.f. Mujtahid (USA) 118 – Haddeyah (USA) 68 (Dayjur (USA) 137) [2001 83: 8d⁶ 9s 9m 8g³ 8f Jul 5] lengthy, rather unfurnished filly: good walker: fairly useful handicapper: stays 1m: acts on good to firm ground, probably on soft: tends to carry head awkwardly: possibly none too genuine. *J. L. Dunlop* **85**

MAKELOVELAST (IRE) 3 b.f. Darshaan 133 – Touch And Love (IRE) (Green Desert (USA) 127) [2001 8d 10m 12.6m³ 10.2m⁴ 12m⁴ Jul 11] smallish, sturdy filly: sixth foal: sister to French 9.5f winner Antique Pearl and half-sister to French 7f winner Tinged With Love (by Kris): dam, useful French sprinter, out of half-sister to top-class miler Sure Blade: fair maiden: likely to stay beyond 1½m: acts on good to firm ground. *B. W. Hills* **74**

MAKE MY HAY 2 b.g. (May 1) Bluegrass Prince (IRE) 110 – Shashi (IRE) 79 (Shaadi (USA) 126) [2001 7s Oct 16] leggy, sparely-made gelding: first foal: dam 5f (at 2 yrs) to 7f winner: 50/1, very slowly away when eleventh of 19 in maiden at Leicester. *M. Kettle* **–**

MAKE THE CALL 4 b.f. Syrtos 106 – Dawn Call (Rymer 121) [2001 12.6m Jun 18] rather sparely-made filly: first foal: dam well beaten over hurdles: 66/1, well behind in maiden at Warwick. *B. N. Doran* **–**

MAKING WAVES (IRE) 2 b.f. (Apr 13) Danehill (USA) 126 – Wavey 93 (Kris 135) [2001 7d Oct 6] rather leggy, unfurnished filly: second foal: dam, 7.5f (at 2 yrs) and 1¼m (French listed race) winner, sister to useful French 1¼m/1½m performer Rebuff: 10/1, weakened final 2f when tenth of 12 in maiden at Redcar: should improve. *J. H. M. Gosden* **– p**

MAKNAAS 5 ch.h. Wolfhound (USA) 126 – White-Wash 94 (Final Straw 127) [2001 –, a84: 16m 16m² 16.2g³ 16.4g f14.8s³ 16.2m Sep 17] smallish, lengthy horse: modest performer in 2001: stays 2m: acts on fibresand/equitrack, soft and good to firm going: tried blinkered at 3 yrs: tends to race lazily, and best forcing pace: sent to Portugal. *P. S. McEntee* **57**

MAKTAVISH 2 b.c. (Feb 12) Makbul 104 – La Belle Vie 73 (Indian King (USA) 128) [2001 5.1s* 5g² 5f² 5m 5d* 6g Oct 6] close-coupled colt: fifth foal: half-brother to fairly useful 5f winner Paradise Lane (by Alnasr Alwasheek): dam 6f/7f winner: useful performer: won maiden at Nottingham (by 8 lengths) in April and minor event at Beverley (beat Goldeva by 2½ lengths) in September: ¾-length second to Shiny in listed race at Sandown third start: likely to prove best at 5f: acts on firm and good to firm ground. *B. R. Millman* **97**

MALAAH (IRE) 5 gr.g. Pips Pride 117 – Lingdale Lass 60 (Petong 126) [2001 50: e8g* e8g² e7g² e8g⁵ e7g² e7g⁵ 6v e8g 7m⁴ 8.5m 7g 6m⁶ 7.6g p7g p8g Dec 22] good-topped gelding: fair on all-weather, modest on turf: won maiden at Lingfield in January: best at 7f/1m: acts on firm going and equitrack: blinkered earlier in career: none too consistent. *Julian Poulton* **54 a72**

MALADERIE (IRE) 7 b.g. Thatching 131 – Native Melody (Tudor Music 131) [2001 65d: 7.1m 6m⁶ 6f 5d⁵ 6m⁴ 6g⁴ 6f² 5d 6g 6f⁶ 6s³ f8g p7g Dec 28] close-coupled gelding: modest nowadays: best at 5f/6f: acts on firm and soft going: usually visored, blinkered once: has had tongue tied. *M. Dods* **50 a42**

MALARKEY 4 b.g. Mukaddamah (USA) 125 – Malwiya (USA) (Shahrastani (USA) 135) [2001 72: f9.4g* e10g³ f8g 9.9m⁴ 11.8f⁶ 14.4m⁵ 17.2g² 16.2f 17.2m³ 14.1m⁴ 14.1m 16g⁶ 17.2g⁴ 18d Oct 20] tall, rather angular gelding: has a high knee action: fair performer: won maiden at Wolverhampton in February: probably needs at least 1¾m nowadays: acts on soft going, good to firm and fibresand/equitrack: blinkered eleventh start: has found little: consistent: sold 26,000 gns, joined P. Hedger. *J. A. Osborne* **78**

MALCHIK 5 ch.g. Absalom 128 – Very Good (Noalto 120) [2001 –, a63: f8.5s² f9.4g f8.5g³ f9.4g* f8.5g* f9.4g f12g 11.6m 8g 11.6g f9.4g⁶ f9.4s⁶ p12g f8.5g⁴ p7g f8.5s² Dec 26] leggy gelding: modest performer: won 2 sellers at Wolverhampton in February: effective at 8.5f to easy 1½m: acts on fibresand and equitrack, little form on turf since 1998: blinkered once at 2 yrs: has drifted right: best forcing pace. *P. Howling* **a61**

Mr Hamdan Al Maktoum's "Malhub"

MALHUB (USA) 3 b. or br.c. Kingmambo (USA) 125 – Arjuzah (IRE) 110 (Ahonoora **115**
122) [2001 94p: 7m* 8m 8g⁵ 7d Oct 20] quite attractive colt: fluent mover: smart
performer, lightly raced: won listed race at Newmarket in June by 2 lengths from
Hurricane Floyd: respectable 3 lengths fifth to Beckett in similar event at Newmarket
(after 4-month break, having reportedly undergone wind operation): below form in St
James's Palace Stakes at Royal Ascot and Challenge Stakes at Newmarket otherwise:
stays 1m: acts on good to firm going: has worn crossed noseband: tongue tied in 2001.
J. H. M. Gosden

MALLARD (IRE) 3 b.g. Tagula (IRE) 116 – Frill (Henbit (USA) 130) [2001 10d **49**
8.2d⁶ 8d Oct 8] 22,000Y: workmanlike gelding: eighth foal: closely related to fairly
useful 1½m to 2m winner Sudest (by Taufan) and half-brother to 3 winners, including
fairly useful 11f winner Shakieyl (by Grand Lodge): dam Irish 1½m winner: best effort in
maidens when sixth at Nottingham (after 5-month break): reportedly lost action final
start: should stay 1¼m. *N. A. Graham*

MALLIA 8 b.g. Statoblest 120 – Pronetta (USA) (Mr Prospector (USA)) [2001 76: f6g **54 §**
f6g³ f6s* f6g⁵ f6g³ f6g³ f6g² f6g* 6.1v⁵ f6g 6m 6d 6.1f 6m² 6m 6g 6g 6g⁴ f6s⁴ f6g⁶ f6g **a65 §**
f6g* f6g⁴ f6g f6g Dec 11] lengthy, dipped-backed gelding: fair on all-weather, modest on
turf: won seller in January and handicaps in March and November, all at Wolverhampton:
best at 6f: acts on any turf going and fibresand/equitrack: usually blinkered, occasionally
visored: has started slowly/edged right: held up: sometimes finds little. *T. D. Barron*

MALMAND (USA) 2 ch.c. (Mar 16) Distant View (USA) 126 – Bidski (USA) **60 p**
(Explosive Bid (USA)) [2001 6.1d⁴ 8s Oct 25] $25,000Y resold 47,000Y: quite attractive
colt: fourth foal: half-brother to winners in US by My Memoirs and Halissee: dam

604

winning sprinter in USA: modest form in maidens at Nottingham and Brighton, not at all knocked about when eighth of 13 in latter: capable of better. *M. A. Jarvis*

MALUMLA (IRE)   2 b.f. (Apr 14) Marju (IRE) 127 – Pearl Shell (USA) (Bering 136)   –
[2001 8s Nov 9] IR 5,000Y: good-topped filly: second foal: half-sister to fairly useful 7f winner Pearly Gates (by Night Shift): dam, French 1½m winner, out of top-class French middle-distance performer Paulista: 33/1, green and swished tail in preliminaries, well held in maiden at Doncaster. *J. Nicol*

MAMBOESQUE (USA)   3 b.g. Miesque's Son (USA) 117 – Brawl (USA) (Fit To   **60 ?**
Fight (USA)) [2001 f7g 8v 7s 8m f12g 8.3d⁵ 9.9m 10d* Oct 15] $7,500Y: good-topped gelding: sixth foal: half-brother to 2 winners in USA, including sprinter by Irish River: dam 7f to 8.5f winner in USA: modest performer: 20/1, apparently much improved form when winning seller at Leicester in October: stays 1¼m: acts on good to soft ground: blinkered last 3 starts. *T. D. Barron*

MAMCAZMA   3 gr.c. Terimon 124 – Merryhill Maid (IRE) 71 (M Double M (USA))   **74**
[2001 80: 8m f12g⁵ f11g² 12m² 14.1s² Sep 4] strong, lengthy colt: fair performer: left A. Smith after third start: stays 1¾m: acts on fibresand, soft and good to firm going: has carried head awkwardly. *D. Morris*

MAMEHA   3 b.f. Rainbow Quest (USA) 134 – Musetta (IRE) 107 (Cadeaux Genereux   **94**
131) [2001 91: 8g 9.9m⁵ 12m 10m³ Jun 26] close-coupled filly: easy mover: fairly useful maiden: creditable efforts (in face of stiff tasks) in 1000 Guineas at Newmarket (eleventh to Ameerat), listed race at Goodwood (fifth to Foodbroker Fancy) and Oaks at Epsom (ninth to Imagine) first 3 starts: stays 1½m: yet to race on extremes of going: free-going sort. *C. E. Brittain*

MAMEYUKI   2 ch.f. (Mar 6) Zafonic (USA) 130 – Musetta (IRE) 107 (Cadeaux   **81**
Genereux 131) [2001 6m 6m* Jul 16] second foal: dam 7f (at 2 yrs) and 1¼m winner who was fourth in Oaks: still green, much better effort (fairly useful form) when winning 5-runner minor event at Windsor by ¾ length from Bright Edge, racing freely before quickening to assert final 1f: will stay at least 7f. *C. E. Brittain*

MAMMA'S BOY   6 b.g. Rock City 120 – Henpot (IRE) 68 (Alzao (USA) 117) [2001   **60**
58: 8d 8d⁴ 7.1m* 7.1m* 7m³ 9f⁶ 7m 8f 8g 7.1f³ 7m 8m 8f Sep 4] sturdy gelding: modest handicapper: successful 6 times at Musselburgh, including twice in May: probably stays 9f: acts on any turf going: blinkered once at 4 yrs: usually held up. *A. Berry*

MAMMAS F-C (IRE)   5 ch.m. Case Law 113 – Wasaif (IRE) 79 (Lomond (USA)   **71**
128) [2001 44: f6g 6.1v 5.7m 5m* 5.7f 5f⁵ 5f³ 6f* 6m³ 5f* 6m⁴ 5.1g* 5m⁴ 6m⁵ 5.7m⁶   **a–**
5.1g⁶ 6f Sep 20] good-bodied mare: fair handicapper: won at Lingfield (twice), Pontefract and Bath between May and August: effective at 5f to easy 7f: acts on hard going, soft and fibresand/equitrack: usually held up: has found little: consistent. *J. M. Bradley*

MAMOOL (IRE)   2 b.c. (Mar 19) In The Wings 128 – Genovefa (USA) 107 (Wood-   **101**
man (USA) 126) [2001 7g² 7m² 8m* 8s⁴ Oct 21] rangy colt: third foal: half-brother to useful French 1999 2-y-o 1m winner Ejlaal (by Caerleon) and French 13f winner Genova (by Darshaan): dam, won 1½m Prix de Royaumont, closely related to smart French 1m/1¼m winner Grafin: useful performer: beaten narrowly in minor event at Newmarket and listed race at Newbury (head second of 4 to Funfair Wane) first 2 starts: landed odds easily in maiden at Goodwood in September, making all: creditable 3¼ lengths fourth to Sholokhov in Gran Criterium at Milan: will stay at least 1¼m: acts on soft and good to firm ground: has worn crossed noseband. *D. R. Loder*

MAMORE GAP (IRE)   3 b.c. General Monash (USA) 107 – Ravensdale Rose (IRE)   **89**
(Henbit (USA) 130) [2001 89: 7d 8g 8f³ 8.1d* 8g¹* 8g⁴ 9d² 8g⁶ 8d Oct 18] smallish, useful-looking colt: fairly useful performer: won minor event at Warwick in July: generally respectable efforts at least otherwise: stays 9f: acts on equitrack, firm and good to soft ground: sold 16,000 gns. *R. Hannon*

MAMOUNIA (IRE)   2 b.f. (Apr 26) Green Desert (USA) 127 – Maroussie (FR) 115   **81**
(Saumarez 132) [2001 6s³ 6d² 6d² Nov 2] rather leggy filly: first foal: dam French 1¼m (including Prix Fille de l'Air) winner: fairly useful maiden: runner-up at York (behind Pic Up Sticks) and Brighton (set bit to do when beaten neck by Jonny Ebeneezer): should stay 1m. *B. W. Hills*

MAMZUG (IRE)   4 b.g. Hamas (IRE) 125§ – Bellissi (IRE) 77 (Bluebird (USA) 125)   **85 d**
[2001 85: 8s 10.3f⁵ 8.5m² 8.3g 9.1f 10.3m 7m 7g f6g Sep 22] strong, sturdy gelding: fairly useful handicapper: ran badly last 4 starts: stays 1¼m: acts on firm going: tried blinkered/tongue tied: races prominently: sold 800 gns. *B. Hanbury*

MANA D'ARGENT (IRE)   4 b.g. Ela-Mana-Mou 132 – Petite-D-Argent 91 (Noalto   **96**
120) [2001 95: f14g³ 18.7f⁵ 13.9m 12f 20m⁴ 16.1f 11.9m² 12m² 14m⁵ 12g² 13.9g 12g
13.1m⁴ 12s⁶ 13.1v⁵ 12v² 12s Nov 10] small, quite attractive gelding: good walker:
unimpressive mover: useful handicapper: generally respectable efforts at least in 2001,
including when fourth to Cover Up in Ascot Stakes and runner-up at York, Ascot (twice)
and Doncaster: effective at 1½m to 2½m: acts on any turf going and fibresand: often
blinkered/visored: sometimes wanders: tough. *M. Johnston*

MANA-MOU BAY (IRE)   4 b.g. Ela-Mana-Mou 132 – Summerhill (Habitat 134)   **99**
[2001 100: 8s⁴ 8.3g⁵ 8m 9.7m⁴ 8m 8.3m* 8g³ p10g Nov 24] good-topped gelding: useful
performer: made all in handicap at Windsor (beat Lermontov by 1¾ lengths) in August:
left R. Hannon 26,000 gns before final start: stays 9.7f: acts on good to firm going,
probably on good to soft: visored last 3 starts: has worn crossed noseband: often front
runner: none too consistent. *D. Nicholls*

MANANAN MCLIR (USA)   2 b.c. (Jan 28) Royal Academy (USA) 130 – St   **88**
Lucinda (CAN) 71 (St Jovite (USA) 135) [2001 6m 6g² 6m² 7f⁴ 7g 8m* 7d Oct 13]
$180,000F: good-topped colt: has scope: first foal: dam 6f (at 2 yrs) and 9f (in USA)
winner: fairly useful performer: won maiden at Kempton in September: stays 1m: acts on
firm ground, well held on good to soft: visored last 2 starts: usually races prominently:
sold 60,000 gns, sent to USA. *J. H. M. Gosden*

MANA POOLS (IRE)   2 b.f. (Mar 13) Brief Truce (USA) 126 – Pipers Pool (IRE) 94   **53**
(Mtoto 134) [2001 5.1f 6m 5f 7.1d 6s 8.2s⁴ 8g⁴ f8g³ f8g Dec 3] 2,500Y: good-topped
filly: fourth foal: half-sister to Irish 6f winner Pipewell (by Lake Coniston) and useful
French/US 1m/9f winner Miss Chryss (by Indian Ridge): dam, maiden who stayed 1¼m,
closely related to smart middle-distance stayer Pipsted: modest maiden: will stay 1¼m:
yet to race on heavy going, acts on any other turf and fibresand: blinkered/visored after
fourth start: possibly none too genuine. *J. A. Glover*

MANDELSON (USA)   2 ch.c. (Apr 5) Spinning World (USA) 130 – Draconienne   **52**
(USA) (Trempolino (USA) 135) [2001 7g 6s⁶ 6m f6s 7g 7s⁴ Oct 5] $125,000Y: third foal:
half-brother to 1999 2-y-o 8.5f winner in USA by Woodman: dam, French 2-y-o 6f and
1m (listed race) winner, from very good family: modest maiden: barely stays 7f: acts on
soft ground: blinkered (ran creditably) final start: sold 9,000 gns. *Sir Mark Prescott*

MANDERINA   2 b.f. (Mar 2) Mind Games 121 – Millaine 69 (Formidable (USA) 125)   **–**
[2001 6g⁵ 6m 5f Sep 20] 12,000Y: leggy filly: closely related to 8-y-o River Tern and
half-sister to several winners, including useful sprinter Amber Mill (by Doulab): dam
maiden who stayed 1¼m: last in minor event/maidens. *A. Berry*

MANDOOB   4 b.g. Zafonic (USA) 130 – Thaidah (CAN) 105 (Vice Regent (CAN))   **71**
[2001 79: 12m 9f 10g 7m* 8m 10v* 10.2d⁵ p13g Dec 29] big, close-coupled gelding: fair
performer: won seller at Brighton in September and handicap at Nottingham in October:
stays 1¼m: acts on any ground: has given trouble at stalls/been slowly away/hung under
pressure. *B. R. Johnson*

MANDOWN   2 b.c. (Apr 21) Danehill Dancer (IRE) 117 – Golden Decoy 73 (Decoy   **58**
Boy 129) [2001 5d 7.9d 6v Oct 26] 2,000Y: seventh reported foal: half-brother to 1993
2-y-o 5f/6f winner Dangerous Shadow (by Absalom) and 5f (at 2 yrs)/6f winner For Real
(by Tina's Pet): dam 7f winner: modest maiden: probably stays 1m. *K. McAuliffe*

MANDY'S COLLECTION   2 ch.f. (Mar 28) Forzando 122 – Instinction (Never So   **52**
Bold 135) [2001 6m f6g f5g³ Nov 16] 1,700Y: fourth foal: half-sister to 6-y-o Nickles:
dam unraced out of smart 5f performer Princess Athena: modest maiden: third at Southwell: will prove best at 5f/6f. *A. G. Newcombe*

MAN FROM HAVANA (USA)   2 b.g. (May 29) Green Dancer (USA) 132 – Charmie   **75**
Carmie (USA) (Lyphard (USA) 132) [2001 7.1s⁴ 7f³ 7.5m⁴ 8.1s Sep 8] brother to 1998
2-y-o 6f winner Sundae Girl and half-brother to several winners, including South
American Grade 1 winner Faaz (by Fappiano) and fairly useful 6f/7f winner (including at
2 yrs) Himmah (by Habitat): dam, placed in USA, from excellent family: fair maiden:
shied at whip on debut: hung badly left at Beverley third start: should stay 1m: acts on
firm and soft ground. *P. F. I. Cole*

MANGUS (IRE)   7 b.g. Mac's Imp (USA) 116 – Holly Bird (Runnett 125) [2001 53§,   **49 §**
a81d: f5s f5g³ f5g³ e5g² 5.3s⁴ 5m f5g⁵ 5m⁶ f5g f5s⁴ 5m f5g³ p5g Nov 20] workmanlike   **a66 §**
gelding: fair on all-weather, poor on turf: raced mainly at 5f: acts on firm going, soft
and fibresand/equitrack: sometimes starts slowly: not an easy ride: untrustworthy.
K. O. Cunningham-Brown

MANIATIS   4 b.c. Slip Anchor 136 – Tamassos 67 (Dance In Time (CAN)) [2001 99p: **103**
12d 11.9m² 12m 13.9m² 12g² 13.9g Aug 22] tall, good sort: usually looks well: useful
handicapper: ran well in 2001 when runner-up, including in listed rated stakes at York
(beaten 2½ lengths by Akbar) and Goodwood (neck behind Compton Bolter) on fourth/
fifth starts: badly hampered in Ebor final start: effective at 1½m/1¾m: acts on soft and
good to firm going: has been taken steadily to post/blanketed for stall entry: tends to race
freely up with pace. *P. F. I. Cole*

MANICANI (IRE)   3 ch.g. Tagula (IRE) 116 – Pluvia (USA) (Raise A Native) [2001 **74 +**
59: 8.2v⁵ 7s² Apr 16] tall, useful-looking gelding: has scope: short to post, clearly best
effort in 3 maidens when 7 lengths second to Zarin at Kempton: reportedly had some leg
trouble subsequently and was blistered (also gelded): should stay 1m. *I. A. Balding*

MANIKATO (USA)   7 b.g. Clever Trick (USA) – Pasampsi (USA) (Crow (FR) 134) **40**
[2001 47: 10f⁴ 10.1g⁴ Jul 3] close-coupled gelding: poor handicapper: stays 1½m: acts on
firm going, good to soft and fibresand/equitrack: sometimes visored earlier in career: has
worn crossed noseband. *R. Curtis*

MANILENO   7 ch.g. K-Battery 108 – Andalucia 57 (Rheingold 137) [2001 f14g f12g   **–**
f12g⁶ f14g f14g⁵ Jun 8] seems of little account nowadays. *Miss S. J. Wilton*

MAN OF DISTINCTION   3 b.c. Spectrum (IRE) 126 – Air of Distinction (IRE) 99 **72**
(Distinctly North (USA) 115) [2001 79: 6s³ 9s May 7] rather leggy, useful-looking colt:
fair performer, lightly raced: reportedly lost action and lame second outing: should stay
7f: acts on firm going, probably on good to soft: has been slowly away. *D. R. C. Elsworth*

MAN O'MYSTERY (USA)   4 b.g. Diesis 133 – Eurostorm (USA) 104 (Storm Bird **115**
(CAN) 134) [2001 112: 10s 10g⁴ 10g² 10.4m² 10g³ Aug 10] sturdy, lengthy gelding:
unimpressive mover: smart performer: best effort when 1¾ lengths second to Foreign

Ecurie Pharos' "Man O'Mystery"

Affairs in John Smith's Cup (Handicap) at York penultimate start: ran respectably at best otherwise: stays 10.4f: acts on good to firm going, probably on soft: held up: gelded after final start. *J. Noseda*

MANON LYN   3 b.f. Awesome 73 – Sea Challenger (Seaepic (USA) 100) [2001 8.1m   –
5.7m 7.1g 7.1g 8.1f Sep 18] first foal: dam winning pointer: little form. *D. Burchell*

MANORBIER   5 ch.g. Shalford (IRE) 124§ – La Pirouette (USA) 73 (Kennedy Road   **95 +**
(CAN)) [2001 111?: f5g f6g⁵ 6v⁵ 6d 6s 6g 6f⁵ Jun 3] strong, close-coupled gelding: poor
mover: smart in 2000: only useful form in 2001: best at 5f/6f: acts on firm going, soft and
fibresand: held up. *K. A. Ryan*

MANOR FROM HEAVEN   3 ch.f. Most Welcome 131 – Manor Adventure 75   –
(Smackover 107) [2001 8.1g 8.1m 6v⁶ f8.5f Dec 5] 6,000Y: leggy filly: third foal: dam,
5f winner, half-sister to useful sprinter Bunty Boo: little form. *R. Hannon*

MANOR LAKE   3 b.f. Puissance 110 – Harifa (Local Suitor (USA) 128) [2001 61:   **59**
5.1s 6.1v 6m³ 5.1f⁵ 7f 6.1m⁶ 6d⁶ 5f Jul 25] angular filly: modest maiden: best efforts at
5f/6f: acts on firm and good to soft going: blinkered final start. *R. F. Johnson Houghton*

MANORSON (IRE)   2 ch.c. (Apr 23) Desert King (IRE) 129 – Familiar (USA) 96   **83 p**
(Diesis 133) [2001 p8g⁵ p10g² Dec 4] IR 21,000Y, 82,000 2-y-o: half-brother to several
winners, including 3-y-o Esyoueffcee: dam, 1m winner, half-sister to 1m/1¼m winner
and Oaks second All At Sea: better effort in maidens at Lingfield when 5 lengths second
to Playapart, finishing strongly without being at all knocked about: will stay 1½m: sure to
improve and win races. *D. W. P. Arbuthnot*

MAN THE GATE   2 b.c. (Apr 2) Elmaamul (USA) 125 – Girl At The Gate 53 (Formid-   **61**
able (USA) 125) [2001 f7g⁴ f8g⁶ 7s Oct 25] third foal: dam 2-y-o 7f winner: modest
maiden: should stay 1m. *P. W. Harris*

MANTILLA   4 b.f. Son Pardo 107 – Well Tried (IRE) 43 (Thatching 131) [2001 69§:   **43 §**
f8.5s⁵ f9.4s⁵ f9.4g⁵ 7m⁵ 7.5m³ 8m 10.5g 9.9m 10f Sep 20] poor maiden nowadays:
stays 9.4f: acts on fibresand, firm and soft going: has been slowly away: ungenuine.
R. Hollinshead

MANTLES PRIDE   6 b.g. Petong 126 – State Romance 67 (Free State 125) [2001 90:   **78**
7.1d⁴ 7.1v 7.6f 8f³ 7.5f* 7m 7m⁴ 7d² 8m³ 7.5m 7m* 7m* 7d 8s p7g Dec 29] useful-
looking gelding: fluent mover: fair performer: won handicap at Beverley (dead-heated)
in June and minor event at Redcar and claimer at Newmarket (29 ran) in September:
left J. Glover 6,200 gns before penultimate start: best around 7f/1m: acts on any turf
going: usually wears visor/blinkers: sometimes slowly away: reportedly broke blood
vessel second outing: tends to carry head awkwardly: probably best with strong handling.
M. Dods

MANUKA TOO (IRE)   3 ch.f. First Trump 118 – Kukri (Kris 135) [2001 55: 8f 9m³   **68**
10g² 10.9g³ 11.5f³ 14.1d* 16.4g² Aug 23] smallish filly: fair handicapper: won ladies
race at Yarmouth in August: stays 2m: acts on firm and good to soft going: has been
awkward leaving stall. *C. F. Wall*

MANZONI   5 b.g. Warrshan (USA) 117 – Arc Empress Jane (IRE) (Rainbow Quest   **68**
(USA) 134) [2001 51: 10f² 14f* 14.1m* 12m⁴ 14m* 15.9d* 14.1m 15.9d⁶ 17.1d Oct
8] small gelding: fair handicapper: won at Musselburgh (twice), Redcar and Chester
between June and September: stays 2m: acts on firm going, good to soft and fibresand:
effective blinkered, visored once: ridden by claimer S. Hitchcott in 2001: usually races
prominently. *M. W. Easterby*

MAP BOY   3 b.g. Chaddleworth (IRE) 103 – Chaconia Girl (Bay Express 132) [2001   –
–: 9g Sep 2] last in maidens at Lingfield and Sandown. *Jamie Poulton*

MAPLE HOUSE   2 ch.f. (Mar 23) Emperor Fountain 112 – Strathrusdale (Blazing   **54**
Saddles (AUS)) [2001 5m 6m 6f² f6g⁴ 7d⁶ 7.1m⁵ 6d Oct 12] smallish, sparely-made filly:
fourth reported living foal: dam showed signs of ability in bumpers: modest maiden:
second in seller at Thirsk: stays 7f: acts on firm and good to soft going. *M. W. Easterby*

MARAAMI   2 b.f. (Jan 31) Selkirk (USA) 129 – Tansy 75 (Shareef Dancer (USA) 135)   **83**
[2001 6g³ 6g⁶ Oct 19] small filly: fourth foal: half-sister to French 1m winner Tanasie and
useful 1¼m winner Trahern (both by Cadeaux Genereux): dam, 2-y-o 6f winner who
stayed 1¼m, ungenuine close relative of Most Welcome: fairly useful form when third
to Scarlet Ribbons in maiden at Newmarket: looked difficult ride (wandered/carried
head awkwardly) when only sixth in similar event at Redcar: should stay 1m: joined
H-A. Pantall in France. *D. R. Loder*

MARABAR   3 b.f. Sri Pekan (USA) 117 – Erbaya (IRE) (El Gran Senor (USA) 136)   **81**
[2001 75: 6m* 6.1m³ Sep 10] progressive and fairly useful form in 4 starts: won maiden
at Lingfield in August, making virtually all: third to Uhoomagoo in handicap at Nottingham final outing: stays 6f: acts on good to firm going: lightly raced. *P. J. Makin*

MARAGUN (GER)   5 b.g. General Assembly (USA) – Marcelia (GER) (Priamos   –
(GER) 123) [2001 12s May 17] winner of 4 races in Germany for N. Sauer, including
handicap at Mulheim at 4 yrs: well held in Britain only 5-y-o Flat start: stays 11f: acts on
heavy and good to firm ground: useful hurdler. *M. C. Pipe*

MARAKABEI   3 ch.f. Hernando (FR) 127 – Kirsten 77 (Kris 135) [2001 10.5d⁶ 8.3g   –
12m⁵ 10.1v Oct 24] IR 8,000Y: fifth foal: half-sister to 2 winners, including 5-y-o
Kattegat: dam, 1½m winner, half-sister to Petoski: well held in maidens/handicap: should
be suited by 1½m+. *R. Guest*

MARAKASH (IRE)   2 b.c. (Feb 4) Ashkalani (IRE) 128 – Marilaya (IRE) 96   **77 p**
(Shernazar 131) [2001 8.2s⁴ Nov 5] first foal: dam, 9f and 10.5f winner, out of half-sister
to smart French middle-distance performers Modaiyn and Malakim: 7/1 and green, not
unduly punished when around 4 lengths fourth to Star Cross in maiden at Nottingham:
will stay 1¼m: should improve. *Sir Michael Stoute*

MARANI   3 ch.f. Ashkalani (IRE) 128 – Aquamarine 89 (Shardari 134) [2001 73p: **106**
9m* 12f³ 11.9d Jul 7] tall, leggy filly: won maiden at Goodwood in May: useful form
when 2 lengths third to Sahara Slew in Ribblesdale Stakes at Royal Ascot next start: tailed
off (reportedly lost action) in Lancashire Oaks at Haydock final one: stays 1½m: acts on
firm going: stays in training. *J. H. M. Gosden*

MARANILLA (IRE)   2 b.c. (Apr 11) Desert King (IRE) 129 – Queen Moranbon   **94**
(USA) 65 (Bering 136) [2001 7m⁵ 7.1m⁶ 7s² 8s⁴ 8d* Dec 9] leggy, workmanlike colt:
second foal: dam placed up to 10.5f in Ireland/France: fairly useful performer: ran in
maidens in Britain first 3 starts: fourth in listed event at Saint-Cloud before winning
similar race at Toulouse by head from Lost Bay: will stay 1¼m: acts on soft ground.
E. J. O'Neill

MARCASSIN   7 b.g. Unfuwain (USA) 131 – Coir 'a' Ghaill 38 (Jalmood (USA) 126)   –
[2001 f12g Jan 8] well held in maiden. *Bob Jones*

MARCHING ORDERS (IRE)   5 b.g. Nashwan (USA) 135 – Minstrels Folly (USA)   –
(The Minstrel (CAN) 135) [2001 –: 10.5s Sep 7] of little account nowadays. *R. Ford*

MARCOSA   2 b.f. (Feb 25) Cosmonaut – Maria Cappuccini 70 (Siberian Express (USA)   **54**
125) [2001 f6g⁶ f6g 6.1m⁴ Aug 1] 2,600 2-y-o: sixth foal: half-sister to 3 winners, including 3-y-o Kumakawa and 7f winner Agent (by Anshan): dam, 5f winner who stayed 7f,
half-sister to smart performer up to 7f Marina Park: modest maiden: will probably stay
7f. *J. G. Given*

MARCOVINA (IRE)   3 ch.g. Erins Isle 121 – Irish Call (USA) (Irish River (FR) 131)   –
[2001 –: 12v⁵ 12g 13.8g Aug 7] sixth foal: half-brother to Irish 1¼m winner River Run
(by Nordico): dam Italian 5f/6f winner: little form: left J. Bolger, Ireland, before final
start: blinkered once. *M. Todhunter*

MARCUS AURELIUS (IRE)   2 b.c. (Apr 30) Alzao (USA) 117 – Kaguyahime   **85 p**
(Distant Relative 128) [2001 5g² 5g* 5s² Oct 20] 27,000Y: strong colt: has a quick action:
third foal: dam, French 9f winner, half-sister to high-class 1m/1¼m performer Bijou
d'Inde: fairly useful form: made all in maiden at Beverley in September: best effort when
5 lengths second to Welsh Emperor in minor event at Catterick final start, chasing winner
throughout: likely to prove best at 5f/6f: type to do better still. *T. D. Barron*

MARCUS MAXIMUS (USA)   6 ch.g. Woodman (USA) 126 – Star Pastures 124   –
(Northfields (USA)) [2001 82: 12d 10g 13.9m 10g⁶ 12m⁵ 10f Jun 14] rather leggy
gelding: has a round action: one-time very smart performer: little form in 2001: carries
head high. *N. A. Callaghan*

MARECHAL GEORGE   2 b. or br.c. (Apr 22) Deerhound (USA) 64 – Lady of   **75**
Limerick (IRE) (Thatching 131) [2001 6m⁶ 6d 5m⁵ 5m³ 5f* 5f⁵ 5.1m 5.1f³ 6m⁴ 5g Oct 4]
9,000F, 19,000Y: small, strong colt: second foal: dam, ran once in USA, out of close
relation to smart French 9f performer L'Irresponsable: fair performer: won maiden at
Catterick in August: creditable efforts in nurseries last 3 starts: will prove best at 5f/6f:
acts on firm ground: sold 10,000 gns, sent to USA. *A. Berry*

MARENGO   7 b.g. Never So Bold 135 – Born To Dance 76 (Dancing Brave (USA)   **57**
140) [2001 68: f6g³ f7g² f6g f6s f6g³ f6g* f7s² f6g⁵ f5g⁴ f6g 6s⁵ f6g⁶ 7m⁵ 6m⁵ f6g f6g⁵   **a61**
5m 5g f7g² f6g 5.5m* 5g⁶ 6d 6g⁴ 7.1g³ f5g² 6g f6g f7g f6g⁵ f6s³ Dec 21] small

gelding: modest performer: won seller at Southwell in February and apprentice claimer at Warwick in August: stays 7f: acts on fibresand, firm and soft going: tried visored: has been free to post/seemed reluctant/started slowly: held up. *M. J. Polglase*

MARE NOSTRUM 3 b.f. Caerleon (USA) 132 – Salvora (USA) (Spectacular Bid (USA)) [2001 9.3s* 10m² 10.5m⁵ 12m³ 12.5d⁶ Oct 6] strong, angular filly: half-sister to several winners, including smart US Grade 1 1¼m winner Aube Indienne (by Bluebird) and useful French miler Raisonnable (by Common Grounds): dam French 1¼m winner: smart performer: won minor event at Longchamp at 2 yrs and Prix Vanteaux there in April by ¾ length from Snataka: head second of 7 to Nadia in Prix Saint-Alary on same course following month, then staying-on fifth to Aquarelliste in Prix de Diane at Chantilly: best effort when 2¾ lengths third to Aquarelliste in Prix Vermeille at Longchamp penultimate start: best at 1½m: has won on soft ground, best form on good to firm. *P. Bary, France* **117**

MARE OF WETWANG 3 ch.f. River Falls 113 – Kudos Blue (Elmaamul (USA) 125) [2001 44: f8g⁴ f8g f11g⁴ 12s² 9.9m⁵ 14.1m 11.6m⁵ 10m* Sep 1] workmanlike filly: poor performer: won apprentice selling handicap at Ripon (seemed to idle) in September: probably stays 1¾m: acts on fibresand, soft and good to firm ground. *J. D. Bethell* **42**

MARGARET'S DANCER 6 b.g. Rambo Dancer (CAN) 107 – Cateryne (Ballymoss 136) [2001 55: 8s 7m 8m 8m 8f Jul 22] sturdy gelding: winning handicapper: no form in 2001: often blinkered at 2 yrs: usually tongue tied. *J. L. Eyre* **–**

MARGOT 3 b.f. Sadler's Wells (USA) 132 – Glatisant 104 (Rainbow Quest (USA) 134) [2001 10.2g 11.7d Oct 25] second foal: half-sister to fairly useful 1998 2-y-o 6f winner Frappe (by Inchinor): dam, 2-y-o 6f and 7f (Prestige Stakes) winner who became one not to trust implicitly, out of Nassau Stakes winner Dancing Rocks: well beaten in maidens at Bath: blinkered final start. *J. H. M. Gosden* **–**

MARHOOB (USA) 3 b. or br.c. Mr Prospector (USA) – Flagbird (USA) 119 (Nureyev (USA) 131) [2001 a8f* a9f 10.1g* 9.9m² 9d⁶ Oct 19] good-bodied, attractive colt: first foal: dam, 1m (including in France at 2 yrs) and 1¼m (including Italian Group 1) winner, half-sister to very smart US Grade 1 1¼m winner Runup The Colors and to Grade 1-winning dam of smart Irish 1999 2-y-o 6f/7f winner Monashee Mountain: smart form: won maiden at Nad Al Sheba in February and 4-runner minor event at Epsom (by 9 lengths from Bogus Dreams) in August: creditable neck second to Mont Rocher in listed race at Goodwood penultimate start: disappointing (steadily to post) final one: stays 1¼m: acts on good to firm going and dirt: wears tongue strap: made running all 3 starts in Britain. *Saeed bin Suroor* **111**

MARIANA 6 ch.m. Anshan 119 – Maria Cappuccini 70 (Siberian Express (USA) 125) [2001 31, a35: f11g f12g Jan 15] probably of little account nowadays. *T. T. Clement* **–**

MARIE DE COURT 2 b.f. (Mar 5) Muhtarram (USA) 125 – Marie de Sologne (Lashkari 128) [2001 7.1m 7.1f 6s Oct 5] 4,400Y: fourth foal: half-sister to 8.5f winner Two To Tango (by Anshan) and useful French 1¼m/1½m winner Minervitta (by Warrshan): dam unraced: little sign of ability in maidens/claimer. *M. G. Quinlan* **–**

MARIENBARD (IRE) 4 b.c. Caerleon (USA) 132 – Marienbad (FR) (Darshaan 133) [2001 115: 13.9g* 20f⁵ 12.5g² 14m³ 16d Nov 6] big, good-topped colt: smart performer: won Merewood Homes Yorkshire Cup in May by length from Samsaam (pair clear), tending to idle: ran well after when 2½ lengths second to Holding Court in Grand Prix de Deauville and 4½ lengths third to Vinnie Roe in Irish St Leger at the Curragh: respectable seventh in Melbourne Cup at Flemington final start: best at 1¾m to 2m (not disgraced, though weakened noticeably final 2f in Gold Cup over 2½m): acts on any going: visored/blinkered in 2001. *Saeed bin Suroor* **119**

MARIGLIANO (USA) 8 b.g. Riverman (USA) 131 – Mount Holyoke 93 (Golden Fleece (USA) 133) [2001 –: 10d May 11] tall gelding: fair performer at best: well held both Flat outings since 1999: fairly useful handicap hurdler/chaser. *K. A. Morgan* **–**

MARIINSKY 2 gr.c. (May 21) Royal Applause 124 – Mainly Dry (The Brianstan 128) [2001 5.1s⁴ 5m* 5g⁴ Sep 15] rather unfurnished, useful-looking colt: half-brother to numerous winning sprinters, notably very smart 5f performer Bolshoi (by Royal Academy): dam unraced: useful form: won maiden at Lingfield in August: 4 lengths fourth of 13 to Saddad in Flying Childers at Doncaster: likely to prove best at 5f/easy 6f: should do better still at 3 yrs. *B. J. Meehan* **100 p**

MARIKA 3 b.f. Marju (IRE) 127 – Nordica 99 (Northfields (USA)) [2001 –: 11.4f⁵ 8.1d* 8m³ Jul 12] tall filly: has scope: has marked knee action: won maiden at Haydock in June: much improved (useful form) when 1¾ lengths third to Smirk in handicap at **102**

Newmarket final start: effective at 1m to 11.4f: acts on firm and good to soft going.
B. W. Hills

MARINKA 3 b.f. Pivotal 124 – Roxy Hart (High Top 131) [2001 f8.5g⁵ f9.4g Nov 27] —
8,200Y: half-sister to several winners, including fairly useful 6f (at 2 yrs) and 1m winner
Don't Presume (by Pharly) and 1½m to 2m winner Chahaya Timor (by Slip Anchor): dam
unraced: achieved little in maidens at Wolverhampton. *D. Haydn Jones*

MARINO STREET 8 b.m. Totem (USA) 118 – Demerger 61 (Dominion 123) [2001 **54**
67, a46+: f5g⁶ f6g⁵ 6m 6d 5f⁶ Jun 27] small, leggy mare: modest handicapper on turf, **a42**
poor on all-weather: best at 5f/6f: acts on any turf going and fibresand/equitrack:
often blinkered/visored before 1999. *B. A. McMahon*

MARINO TINO (IRE) 2 ch.f. (Apr 24) Fayruz 116 – Zestino (Shack (USA) 118) —
[2001 6m f6g f6g Dec 17] 5,200Y, 5,000 2-y-o: half-sister to 3 winners, including 11f
winner who stayed 1¾m Briggs Lad (by Be My Native): dam unraced half-sister to Oaks
winner Ginevra: well held in maidens/seller: trained by C. Weedon on debut: blinkered
final start. *Miss V. Haigh*

MARINO WOOD (IRE) 2 ch.f. (Apr 12) Woodpas (USA) 85 – Forgren (IRE) **47**
(Thatching 131) [2001 5f³ 5.2m⁴ 5f³ 6d 5d 5m⁵ 5.1g³ 5m Aug 23] 3,000 2-y-o: first foal:
dam unraced: poor maiden: likely to prove best at 5f: acts on firm going, below form on
good to soft. *J. S. Moore*

MARION HASTE (IRE) 2 ch.f. (May 15) Ali-Royal (IRE) 127 – Coryana 104 **69 d**
(Sassafras (FR) 135) [2001 5.1v* 6f³ 5m⁶ 5m⁵ 6d 6v 5g 6v Oct 15] 20,000F, IR 20,000Y:
strong filly: half-sister to numerous winners, notably very smart miler Waajib (by Try My
Best) and useful French/US performer up to 13f Cote d'Azur (by Arazi): dam Irish 6f (at
2 yrs) and 1¼m winner: fair performer: won minor event at Nottingham in May: last or
pulled up last 4 starts: stays 6f: acts on any ground. *A. Berry*

MARISKA 2 b.f. (Apr 2) Magic Ring (IRE) 115 – Prima Silk 82 (Primo Dominie 121) **65**
[2001 6g⁵ 7f⁴ 6g 6s⁶ 5v⁶ Oct 17] useful-looking filly: second foal: dam 5f to 7f winner:
fair maiden: favourite in Lingfield seller final start: stays 7f: acts on firm going.
N. A. Callaghan

MARITSA (IRE) 3 b.f. Danehill (USA) 126 – Marwell 133 (Habitat 134) [2001 6m³ **59 +**
Jun 29] half-sister to numerous winners, notably very smart performers up to 1m Marling
(by Lomond) and Caerwent (by Caerleon): dam, champion sprinter who was also fourth
in 1000 Guineas: weak 7/2-shot and blinkered, 4 lengths third to Jessica's Dream in
maiden at Newcastle, soon ridden along: stud. *Sir Mark Prescott*

MARITUN LAD 4 b.g. Presidium 124 – Girl Next Door 58 (Local Suitor (USA) 128) —
[2001 54, a68: f5g f5g 5m f5g Jun 15] good-topped gelding: fair handicapper in 2000: no
form at 4 yrs: visored/blinkered nowadays. *D. Shaw*

MARJEUNE 4 b.f. Marju (IRE) 127 – Ann Veronica (IRE) (Sadler's Wells (USA) **70 d**
132) [2001 70: f16g² 12s 14.1v f16g⁴ 16.2m⁶ 16.5m 12.1s f14g⁶ Oct 1] lengthy filly: fair
handicapper: well below form last 3 starts: stays 2m: acts on soft going, good to firm and
fibresand: blinkered penultimate start. *J. G. Smyth-Osbourne*

*Merewood Homes Yorkshire Cup, York—Marienbard, in a first-time visor,
has more to spare than the margin suggests over Samsaan; Eternal Spring, Dalampour,
Jardines Lookout (right) and Royal Rebel (behind Dalampour) come next*

MARJURITA (IRE) 2 b.f. (Feb 2) Marju (IRE) 127 – Unfuwaanah 74 (Unfuwain **81** (USA) 131) [2001 6m⁶ 6m³ 5m 5f 6g⁵ 5.1g³ 6g* 6v Oct 26] 13,000Y: leggy, lengthy filly: second foal: half-sister to 4-y-o Arizona Lady: dam 7f winner: fairly useful performer: won nursery at Hamilton in September: should stay 7f: acts on firm ground, had excuse when well held on heavy: sweating (well below form) fourth start. *N. P. Littmoden*

MARKET AVENUE 2 b.f. (Apr 7) Factual (USA) 108 – The Lady Vanishes (Robin **62** Des Pins (USA) 119) [2001 5m 6m⁴ 5f³ 7d² 7g 6d 6v Oct 26] 2,800Y: leggy, quite good-topped filly: has a quick action: first foal: dam unraced: modest maiden: second in nursery at Chester: stays 7f: acts on firm and good to soft going. *R. A. Fahey*

MARKING TIME (IRE) 3 b.g. Goldmark (USA) 113 – Tamarsiya (USA) (Shahras- **57** tani (USA) 135) [2001 –: e10g 9.2m⁴ 11.5m³ 14.1g* 16f 13.8m² Sep 22] smallish gelding: modest performer: won selling handicap at Nottingham in June: should stay 2m: acts on good to firm going (returned jarred up on firm penultimate start). *K. R. Burke*

MARK IT 2 b.g. (Feb 22) Botanic (USA) – Everdene (Bustino 136) [2001 8d⁵ Oct **– p** 25] fifth foal: half-brother to 5f (at 2 yrs)/5.7f winner Hever Golf Express (by Primo Dominie): dam, French 1¼m winner, half-sister to useful sprinter Great Deeds: 25/1, well-held fifth to stable-companion Indian Solitaire in maiden at Bath, late headway after starting slowly: should improve. *Mrs A. J. Perrett*

MARK OF PROPHET (IRE) 6 b.g. Scenic 128 – Sure Flyer (IRE) (Sure Blade **62** (USA) 130) [2001 75: 12g⁵ Jun 19] tall, close-coupled gelding: very lightly-raced handi-capper nowadays, modest form only 6-y-o start: stays 1¾m: acts on good to firm ground. *E. Stanners*

MARK OF RESPECT 2 b.f. (Mar 2) Mark of Esteem (IRE) 137 – Bassmaat (USA) **–** 81 (Cadeaux Genereux 131) [2001 7m 7g 7m Aug 15] 15,000Y, 20,000Y: useful-looking filly: third foal: half-sister to fairly useful Irish 2000 2-y-o 1m winner El-Libaab (by Unfuwain): dam, 7f winner, out of smart French performer up to 1½m Mangayah: no form, including in seller: sold 500 gns. *B. J. Meehan*

MARK ONE 3 b.g. Mark of Esteem (IRE) 137 – One Wild Oat 63 (Shareef Dancer **85** (USA) 135) [2001 79: f12g⁴ 9m⁴ 11.7f³ 10.2g* 10m 9g⁴ 12d* 12m⁶ 14s 12v³ 12s Nov 11] fairly useful performer: won 3-runner maiden at Bath (subsequently sold from B. Hills 16,500 gns) in July and handicap at Tramore in August: stays 1½m: acts on heavy ground, probably on firm: free-going sort. *J. G. Burns, Ireland*

MARKOVA'S DANCE 2 ch.f. (Jan 18) Mark of Esteem (IRE) 137 – Tanouma **64** (USA) 114 (Miswaki (USA) 124) [2001 6.1m³ 7.1s⁵ 7d Oct 2] 125,000Y: small, leggy filly: half-sister to several winners, including smart middle-distance stayers Azzilfi (by Ardross) and Khamaseen (by Slip Anchor) and useful 1995 2-y-o 6f/7f winner Tamnia (by Green Desert): dam 6f (at 2 yrs)/7f winner: modest maiden: third at Nottingham: will need to settle better to stay 1m. *J. G. Smyth-Osbourne*

MARKUSHA 3 b.g. Alhijaz 122 – Shafir (IRE) 68 (Shaadi (USA) 126) [2001 68: **70** 6m 7m² 8f 8g 8m³ 10m³ 10g⁵ 10.9m 8d f8.5g² 7v³ Oct 26] leggy gelding: fair maiden handicapper: effective at 7f to 1¼m: acts on soft going (probably on heavy), good to firm and fibresand: sold 10,000 gns. *Mrs J. R. Ramsden*

MARLO 2 b.c. (Apr 20) Hector Protector (USA) 124 – Tender Moment (IRE) 78 **95** (Caerleon (USA) 132) [2001 6v³ f6g* 6v* 6d³ Nov 6] half-brother to several winners, including fairly useful 1m winner Spring Fever (by Indian Ridge) and 5-y-o Summer Bounty: dam 7f winner: useful form: won maiden at Southwell and nursery at Windsor (beat Sir Northerndancer by 6 lengths) in October: bit below form final start: should stay 1m. *B. W. Hills*

MARMADUKE (IRE) 5 ch.g. Perugino (USA) 84 – Sympathy 77 (Precocious 126) **63** [2001 61: f11g* f11g⁵ e12g⁵ 11.6g* 12g⁵ p10g³ Dec 28] tall gelding: modest handi- **a57** capper: won at Southwell in February and Windsor (amateurs) in August: stays 1¾m: probably acts on any turf going/all-weather: races freely: tried visored. *M. Pitman*

MARNIE 4 ch.f. First Trump 118 – Miss Aboyne 64 (Lochnager 132) [2001 65: e7g² **68** e7g³ e7s² e8g* 7d³ 7m 7d p8g p8g p8g Dec 22] sturdy, lengthy filly: fair handicapper: **a75** won at Lingfield in February: stays 1m: acts on firm going, good to soft and equitrack (probably on polytrack). *J. Akehurst*

MARNOR (USA) 5 ch.h. Diesis 133 – Love's Reward (Nonoalco (USA) 131) [2001 **79** 6.1v 6g 5m 5m 5.5d 10.3g 8m² 8.1v 10g⁶ 8d Oct 18] big, strong, lengthy horse: has markedly round action: missed 2000 season, and only fair handicapper nowadays:

612

probably best at 1m/1¼m: acts on firm and good to soft going: blinkered (pulled very hard) final start: sold 8,500 gns. *M. W. Easterby*

MAROMITO (IRE)   4 b.g. Up And At 'em 109 – Amtico (Bairn (USA) 126) [2001 71:   **79**
f6g f5g² 5m* 5m² f5g⁴ 5.1f⁵ 5m² 5g⁴ 5g⁴ Sep 15] well-made gelding: fair handicapper: **a66 +**
won at Musselburgh in May: best at bare 5f: acts on firm going, good to soft and fibre-sand: sometimes sweats/on edge/early to post: has hung left: front runner. *R. Bastiman*

MARON   4 b.g. Puissance 110 – Will Be Bold 79 (Bold Lad (IRE) 133) [2001 60, a48:   **–**
e6g f6g⁴ f5g² f6g⁶ f5g f5g* f5g² e6g* e5g⁶ e5g⁵ f6g² 6.1d 5d 5m f6g f6g⁵ 5.5m f5s f6g f6s   **a67 d**
Dec 26] rather leggy gelding: fair performer: won handicaps at Wolverhampton in February and Lingfield in March: on downgrade after eighth start, and sold 800 gns after penultimate: stays 6f: acts on fibresand/equitrack. *A. Berry*

MARQUISE   2 gr.f. (Mar 17) Petong 126 – Jewel (IRE) 64 (Cyrano de Bergerac 120)   **–**
[2001 6m 5.1m 6.1m Sep 17] 10,000Y: rather leggy filly: first foal: dam, lightly-raced maiden, half-sister to smart 1996 2-y-o 5f/6.5f winner Deadly Dudley: well held in maidens. *R. Hannon*

MARRAKECH (IRE)   4 ch.f. Barathea (IRE) 127 – Nashkara (Shirley Heights 130)   **103**
[2001 86: 10.5d⁴ 12m* 11.9m⁵ 12s Nov 10] tall, rather leggy filly: useful performer, lightly raced: won handicap at Ascot in July by 1¼ lengths from Mana d'Argent: better effort after more creditable 2½ lengths fifth to Inchiri in listed race at York: seems better at 1½m than shorter: acts on good to firm and good to soft going. *P. W. Harris*

MARREL   4 b.g. Shareef Dancer (USA) 135 – Upper Caen (High Top 131) [2001 58:   **60**
11.6s 11.5f⁴ 14.1g f12g³ f12g³ 16.2m* 16m⁴ 16.4g 12f⁴ Aug 29] strong, workmanlike gelding: modest handicapper: won at Beverley in July: stays 2m: acts on fibresand and firm going: blinkered last 2 starts. *B. Hanbury*

MARRIFORTH   2 ch.f. (Apr 9) Wolfhound (USA) 126 – Ghassanah 73 (Pas de Seul   **51**
133) [2001 5s⁶ 6m⁶ 6m 6g 7.5g⁶ 6.5g Sep 28] 7,500Y: smallish, sparely-made filly: closely related to 6-y-o Sand Hawk and 7f winner Willisa (by Polar Falcon), and half-sister to several winners, including useful 5f/6f winner Alzianah (by Alzao) and 7-y-o Return of Amin: dam 7f winner: modest maiden: should stay 7f: twice blinkered. *J. D. Bethell*

MARSAD (IRE)   7 ch.g. Fayruz 116 – Broad Haven (IRE) (Be My Guest (USA) 126)   **99**
[2001 96: 6v 7s² 6g* 6m² 6m 6f² 6g 6g⁵ 6m⁶ 6d⁵ 6v⁵ 6v⁶ Nov 14] lengthy, good-topped gelding: useful handicapper: won 29-runner event at Newmarket in May: mostly credit-able efforts otherwise, including when runner-up at Goodwood (beaten 1¼ lengths by Seven No Trumps) and Newbury (length behind Kayo) on fourth/sixth starts and when sixth to Chercheuse in listed race at Maisons-Laffitte final outing: effective at 6f/7f: acts on any going: has run creditably when sweating: consistent. *J. Akehurst*

MARSHAL BOND   3 b.g. Celtic Swing 138 – Arminda (Blakeney 126) [2001 65:   **75**
f8f⁴ 8v* 10s* 10d⁴ 10s 10.3f⁵ 11.4g 10.2f⁵ 10m 10.2g⁴ 9.9m³ 12g 10d³ f11g f12g Nov   **a62**
17] workmanlike gelding: fluent mover: fair handicapper: won at Musselburgh (maiden event) in March and Brighton in April: stays 1¼m: seems to act on any turf going (below best on fibresand): blinkered final start: usually races prominently. *B. Smart*

MARSHALL NEIGH (USA)   2 ch.c. (Apr 24) French Deputy (USA) 118 – Jamie   **–**
de Vil (USA) (Digression (USA) 116) [2001 f7g f8g Oct 18] 15,000 2-y-o: first foal: dam, maiden in USA, half-sister to dam of smart sprinter Pharaoh's Delight: well held in sellers: tongue tied on debut: sold 500 gns. *P. F. I. Cole*

MARSHALL ROOSTER   2 gr.g. (May 26) Greensmith 121 – Petinata (Petong 126)   **69 p**
[2001 5d² Oct 30] 2,400Y: close-coupled, good-topped gelding: fourth foal: half-brother to 7f winner Starlight (by King's Signet) and a winner in Sweden by Beveled: dam twice-raced half-sister to useful sprinter Peatswood Shooter: 10/1 and burly, 4 lengths second of 8 to Aldora in maiden at Redcar: will stay at least 6f: should do better. *T. D. Barron*

MARSHALLSPARK (IRE)   2 b.g. (Apr 1) Fayruz 116 – Lindas Delight 54 (Batshoof   **75**
122) [2001 6m 6d² f6g⁴ Oct 18] IR 13,500F, 14,000Y: sturdy, lengthy gelding: third foal: brother to 3-y-o Fromsong: dam 6f seller winner at 2 yrs (only season to race): fair maiden: best effort when second to Fangio's Quest at Newcastle: may well prove best at 5f/6f. *R. A. Fahey*

MARSHMAN (IRE)   2 ch.g. (Feb 2) College Chapel 122 – Gold Fly (IRE) (Be My   **81**
Guest (USA) 126) [2001 5s³ 5m* 5m² 6f³ 5g³ 6m⁶ 6m 6g⁶ 6d* 6d⁵ Nov 6] 8,000F, IR 8,000Y: good-topped gelding: first foal: dam unraced out of half-sister to very smart miler Shaikiya: fairly useful performer: won maiden at Hamilton in May and nursery at York in

October: likely to stay 7f: yet to race on heavy going, seems to act on any other: gelded after final start: reliable. *M. H. Tompkins*

MARTELLO   5 b.g. Polish Precedent (USA) 131 – Round Tower 93 (High Top 131)   **69 §**
[2001 64: f8g² e8g³ f8g⁵ f8.5g⁶ Mar 22] strong, rangy gelding: fair maiden: effective at 1m to 1½m: acts on fibresand, good to firm and heavy going: tried visored, blinkered last 2 runs: irresolute. *R. Charlton*

MARTHA DALY   2 b.f. (Feb 18) Royal Applause 124 – Primulette 82 (Mummy's Pet   **67 d**
125) [2001 5d⁴ 5.1d⁶ 5m* 5m* 5m⁵ 5m 6m 6.1d f6g⁶ f6g f5g Nov 23] 15,000Y: small, workmanlike filly: half-sister to numerous winners, including fairly useful 1996 2-y-o 6f winner Makhbar (by Rudimentary) and 7f (at 2 yrs) and 1½m winner Boogy Woogy (by Rock Hopper): dam 5f (at 2 yrs) and 1m winner: fair performer: won sellers at Beverley (left M. Channon) in May and Musselburgh in June: generally below form after: should stay 6f: acts on good to firm and good to soft going: tried visored. *R. M. Whitaker*

MARTHA P PERKINS (IRE)   3 b.f. Fayruz 116 – Cake Contract (IRE) (Contract   **– §**
Law (USA) 108) [2001 51: 8g 8m f6g Oct 22] modest maiden at 2 yrs: no form in 2001 (virtually refused to race on reappearance, left J. Osborne after next start). *T. J. Naughton*

MARTHA REILLY (IRE)   5 ch.m. Rainbows For Life (CAN) – Debach Delight 97   **–**
(Great Nephew 126) [2001 51: 16v 17.1s 21.6s⁵ Apr 23] smallish, sparely-made mare: modest handicapper at 4 yrs: well held in 2001: tried blinkered. *Mrs Barbara Waring*

MARTIAL EAGLE (IRE)   5 b.g. Sadler's Wells (USA) 132 – Twine (Thatching   **–**
131) [2001 –: f12s f16g f16s f16.2g Feb 22] of little account nowadays. *N. Tinkler*

MARTINEZ (IRE)   5 b.g. Tirol 127 – Elka (USA) (Val de L'Orne (FR) 133) [2001 –:   **–**
f16g May 21] angular, good-bodied gelding: little form. *C. W. Thornton*

MARTIN HOUSE (IRE)   2 b.c. (Apr 27) Mujadil (USA) 119 – Dolcezza (FR)   **89**
(Lichine (USA) 117) [2001 7m* 7g⁴ 7s⁴ Oct 11] 35,000Y: tall, leggy colt: sixth foal: half-brother to 3 winners abroad, including German 9.5f/1¼m winner C'Est Fantastique (by Hernando): dam unraced close relation of smart French performer up to 10.5f Caprarola: fairly useful form: 33/1-winner of maiden at York in July: best effort when around 4 lengths fourth to Steenberg in minor event at Ascot second start: sweating, ran respectably behind Highdown in similar event at York: will stay 1m. *J. D. Bethell*

MARTIN'S PEARL (IRE)   4 gr.g. Petong 126 – Mainly Dry (The Brianstan 128)   **56**
[2001 –: 7m 7.5m⁶ 8d 6g 8d Aug 8] lengthy gelding: modest maiden: best efforts around 7f: acts on good to firm ground: blinkered penultimate start. *W. R. Muir*

MARTIN'S SUNSET   3 ch.g. Royal Academy (USA) 130 – Mainly Sunset (Red   **80 §**
Sunset 120) [2001 71: 9m 8m 8.1g 8g² 8.1s 10.2g 8f⁴ 8s 10d⁶ 10v p12g Nov 24] sparely-made gelding: fairly useful maiden handicapper: best efforts at 1m: acts on firm and soft ground: often blinkered/visored: usually soon off bridle: has found little: gelded after final start: unreliable. *W. R. Muir*

MARTON MERE   5 ch.g. Cadeaux Genereux 131 – Hyatti 74 (Habitat 134) [2001   **54**
57: 9.9m 8m 7.5m 7.5f 8m⁶ 7.5f² 10g⁶ Jul 10] angular gelding: modest performer: stays 1¼m: acts on firm going. *A. J. Lockwood*

MARVEL   4 b.f. Rudimentary (USA) 118 – Maravilla 73 (Mandrake Major 122) [2001   **?**
63: f8g 8.2s 7d⁶ a10.5g² a6g⁴ a8g* a8g a8g a9g Dec 16] smallish, workmanlike filly: modest performer in 2000: left Don Enrico Incisa after second start and N. Tinkler after third: won minor event at Mijas in September: little form otherwise: stays 10.5f: acts on heavy going, good to firm and sand: has been early to post. *M. Lambert, Spain*

MARWEH   6 b.g. Prince Sabo 123 – Born To Dance 76 (Dancing Brave (USA) 140)   **101**
[2001 110: 6m⁴ 5.6m 7g 6d Oct 13] strong, compact gelding: smart performer when trained in 2000 by J. Hammond in France, winning handicap at Deauville and minor event and listed race at Maisons-Laffitte: best effort in 2001 when respectable 5 lengths fourth to Vision of Night in minor event at Doncaster (trainer fined, jockey suspended, horse banned for 30 days under schooling in public rule) in August: not knocked about in handicaps after: stays 6.5f: acts on heavy going, probably on good to firm. *Mrs J. R. Ramsden*

MARY DOLL (IRE)   2 b.f. (Feb 2) Distinctly North (USA) 115 – Robin Red Breast   **54 d**
74 (Red Alert 127) [2001 f5g⁶ 5m² 5m⁴ 5m⁴ 5d⁵ 5m⁶ f5g⁶ 5.1s f5g f5f f7g Dec 10] 6,000Y: half-sister to three 5f winners, including Pious Bird (by Tender King) and Rosey Nosey (at 2 yrs in 1994, by Cyrano de Bergerac): dam 2-y-o 5f winner (only season to race): modest maiden: on downgrade after third start: left P. Haslam after sixth: raced mainly at 5f: acts on good to firm ground: sometimes starts slowly. *D. W. Chapman*

MARY HANNAH   8 b.m. Lugana Beach 116 – Bloomsbury Girl 63 (Weepers Boy –
124) [2001 5g Oct 6] very lightly-raced handicapper nowadays. *J. Balding*

MARYINSKY (IRE)   2 b.f. (Apr 10) Sadler's Wells (USA) 132 – Blush With   **107 p**
Pride (USA) (Blushing Groom (FR) 131) [2001 7m² 8s² 7d* Oct 11]
As stable-companion Imagine demonstrated so vividly in 2001, compre-
hensive defeat in the Fillies' Mile at Ascot need not destroy a filly's classic
prospects. It indicates that improvement is required, and Maryinsky, runner-up in
the latest Fillies' Mile, is a good bet to make improvement. Queen's Logic and
Gossamer ended the season in advance of the other fillies, but Maryinsky is a
leading candidate to bridge the gap, if any filly can.
There's no denying that Maryinsky was beaten comprehensively in the
Fillies' Mile. In fact, the two and a half lengths between her and Gossamer at the
post somewhat underestimated Gossamer's superiority. But Maryinsky's performance was encouraging for an attractive filly contesting a Group 1 only a fortnight
after her racecourse debut. Despite the recent spate of successes by her stable
companions, not much seemed to be expected of Maryinsky, who drifted from 10/1
to 12/1 in a line-up dominated by Gossamer, fresh from her seven-length romp in
the Prestige Stakes. The lack of each-way opportunities in a seven-runner field
will not have encouraged those looking for value outside the 5/4-on favourite, but
Maryinsky turned out to be the clear second best. Held up, she still had only one
behind her approaching the final furlong, after being switched from the inner
entering the straight and forced wider still when Gossamer was manoeuvred into
the open. Maryinsky was unable to match the favourite's turn of foot at around the
furlong marker, but stayed on well thereafter and was a length and a quarter clear of
the rest at the end of a race that was not truly run. She had similarly found her stride
only in the closing stages when going down by a neck at 10/1 (with two stable mates
at shorter odds) in an IR £12,795 event at the Curragh on her debut. Maryinsky
justified 7/4-on favouritism comfortably in a fourteen-runner maiden at Gowran
twelve days after Ascot. Both of her Irish races were over seven furlongs, but
Maryinsky will stay at least a mile and a quarter.

		Northern Dancer	Nearctic
	Sadler's Wells (USA)	(b 1961)	Natalma
	(b 1981)	Fairy Bridge	Bold Reason
Maryinsky (IRE)		(b 1975)	Special
(b.f. Apr 10, 1999)		Blushing Groom	Red God
	Blush With Pride (USA)	(ch 1974)	Runaway Bride
	(ch 1979)	Best In Show	Traffic Judge
		(ch 1965)	Stolen Hour

Maryinsky's immediate family has seen action mostly at around a mile.
Three of the dam Blush With Pride's first six foals were unraced and the other three
(one colt by Nijinsky, two by Devil's Bag) were minor winners in the United States.
Her seventh foal was the smart Andre Fabre-trained filly Smolensk (by Danzig),
winner of the Prix d'Astarte and Prix de Sandringham, runner-up to Ridgewood
Pearl in the Coronation Stakes and two and a half lengths fifth in the Moulin. Ninth
foal Fire Thunder (by Dayjur) was a useful winner in Dubai and the tenth, Better
Than Honour (by Deputy Minister), was a smart two-year-old in the United States,
successful in the Grade 2 Demoiselle Stakes and placed in two Grade 1s. A second
visit to Deputy Minister resulted in Turnberry Isle, the 2000 Beresford Stakes
winner and Royal Lodge runner-up for Aidan O'Brien. Turnberry Isle shaped as if
he would stay a mile and a quarter but achieved nothing in his three-year-old
campaign for D. Wayne Lukas. Maryinsky is followed by another filly by Sadler's
Wells. They are related to countless pattern-class performers, as Blush With Pride
is a half-sister to Gielgud, Malinowski, Monroe (the dam of Xaar), Minnie Hauk
(ancestress of Aviance, Chief Contender, Chimes of Freedom and Spinning World)
and to Sex Appeal (the dam of Try My Best and El Gran Senor). Blush With Pride
was no mug herself, winner of two Grade 1 races—the Santa Susana Stakes (now
run as the Santa Anita Oaks) and the Kentucky Oaks—as a three-year-old and of
two other graded races, including the Golden Harvest Handicap over ten and a
half furlongs, the furthest trip she ever attempted. Maryinsky is a good-topped,

attractive filly who looked in great shape at Ascot but showed an unimpressive, quick action on the way to post. She should add to her family's fine record in 2002. *A. P. O'Brien, Ireland*

MARY JANE 6 b.m. Tina's Pet 121 – Fair Attempt (IRE) (Try My Best (USA) 130) **67** [2001 52, a–: 5v 5m³ 5m² 5f⁶ 5g² 5m⁴ 5f² f5g f5g 5g* 5m² 5f³ f5s 5m⁴ 5s³ 5d⁴ 5d 5v⁵ Oct **a60** 24] smallish, sturdy mare: fair handicapper: won at Thirsk (apprentices) in August: has won at 6f, best at 5f: acts on any turf going and fibresand/equitrack: blinkered once at 3 yrs: has wandered: tough. *N. Tinkler*

MARZELLE (FR) 3 b.f. Sillery (USA) 122 – Marzipan (IRE) 74 (Green Desert **76** (USA) 127) [2001 10v⁴ 10f² 10m⁵ 11.6m⁵ 10m⁵ 10g² 11.9m⁶ 10.1g² 10s Sep 30] 150,000 francs Y: tall, workmanlike filly: second foal: dam, maiden who should have stayed beyond 1¼m, half-sister to smart 7f to 9f performer Anshan: fair maiden: probably stays 1½m: acts on firm going: tends to wander. *S. Dow*

MASHHOOR (USA) 3 b.c. Thunder Gulch (USA) 129 – Memorive (USA) 81 **52** (Riverman (USA) 131) [2001 10s 11.5g⁴ 12.1g Sep 13] fourth living foal: half-brother to 2 winners abroad, including a winner in Italy up to 1¼m by Alzao: dam, 1m winner, sister to very smart French/US winner up to 13.5f River Memories from family of Sakhee: modest form in maidens: bred to be suited by 1¼m/1½m: sold 3,600 gns. *C. E. Brittain*

MASILIA (IRE) 4 b.f. Kahyasi 130 – Masmouda 123 (Dalsaan 125) [2001 16m* **109** 12.3f* 12g* 12d² 14.6m² 12d² 12.5v⁶ Nov 19] angular filly: useful performer: missed 2000 season: progressed well in 2001, winning maiden at Clonmel and handicaps at Down Royal (dead-heated in Ulster Harp Lager Derby) and the Curragh between May/ July: good second in listed race at Leopardstown (head behind Sadlers Wings), Park Hill

H.H. Aga Khan's "Masilia"

Stakes at Doncaster (boxed in as race began in earnest, beaten 2 lengths by Ranin) and listed race at the Curragh (beaten ½ length by Diamond Trim): stays 1¾m: acts on firm and good to soft going. *J. Oxx, Ireland*

MASQUE TONNERRE (USA) 3 b.c. Thunder Gulch (USA) 129 – Veiled Lady **61** (USA) (Professor Blue (USA)) [2001 63: f11g 12m⁴ 12m 10.9g Jul 6] deep-bodied gelding: modest maiden handicapper: stays 1½m: acts on good to firm ground: sold 500 gns. *M. A. Jarvis*

MASSARRA 2 b.f. (Apr 9) Danehill (USA) 126 – Rafha 123 (Kris 135) [2001 6m² **99** 6m* 6m* 5.5g² 6m 6d⁶ Oct 2] lengthy, rather angular filly: closely related to 4-y-o Invincible Spirit and half-sister to several winners, notably smart 7.6f (at 2 yrs) to 1¾m winner Sadian (by Shirley Heights): dam 6f (at 2 yrs) to 11.5f winner (including 10.5f Prix de Diane): useful performer: made all in maiden at Goodwood and listed race at Newmarket (beat Pastel by a neck) in June: good neck second of 5 to Zipping in Prix Robert Papin at Maisons-Laffitte in July: raced too freely in good company last 2 starts: will prove best at 5f/6f: acts on good to firm going: has been edgy in preliminaries: wore crossed noseband final start. *J. L. Dunlop*

MASSENET (IRE) 6 b.g. Caerleon (USA) 132 – Massawippi (Be My Native (USA) – 122) [2001 10v Apr 3] maiden: well held only start since 1998. *D. J. Wintle*

MASSEY 5 br.g. Machiavellian (USA) 123 – Massaraat (USA) (Nureyev (USA) 131) – [2001 55, a70: f9.4s* f11g⁴ 11s 9m f8.5g⁴ f8g² f9.4g f9.4g⁴ f8s* Dec 15] fair performer: **a78** won apprentice handicap at Wolverhampton in January and minor event at Southwell in December: effective at 1m to 1½m: acts on fibresand, little form on turf: sometimes visored in 2000: front runner. *T. D. Barron*

MASTER BEVELED 11 b.g. Beveled (USA) – Miss Anniversary §§ (Tachypous **55** 128) [2001 63: 15.9m 10g⁵ 11.6g Aug 6] lengthy gelding: fairly useful performer at best, successful 11 times: modest form in last 2 seasons: stayed 1½m: acted on any turf going and fibresand/equitrack: was often blinkered/visored, but was at least as effective when not: reportedly retired. *P. D. Evans*

MASTER BLUE 3 b.g. Mind Games 121 – Sandicroft Jewel (Grey Desire 115) [2001 **46** 7g⁶ 6m 6m⁵ 6.1s 6f Sep 10] 1,200Y: leggy gelding: first foal: dam unraced: poor maiden: seems to stay 7f. *J. R. Norton*

MASTER COOPER (IRE) 7 b.g. Kahyasi 130 – Arabian Princess (Taufan (USA) **82** 119) [2001 80: 10g* 11.9m 12v May 19] leggy gelding: fairly useful handicapper: left D. Hanley in Ireland 13,000 gns after final 6-y-o start: won 30-runner event at Newmarket in May: stays 1½m: acts on good to soft and good to firm ground: often blinkered in Ireland. *D. R. C. Elsworth*

MASTER ELLIS (IRE) 2 b.g. (May 1) Turtle Island (IRE) 123 – Take No Chances – (IRE) 94 (Thatching 131) [2001 7m 8.1s 8.3g⁵ Sep 3] second foal: dam Irish 5f (at 2 yrs) to 9f winner: only a little sign of ability in maidens: has raced freely. *P. D. Evans*

MASTER FELLOW 3 ch.g. First Trump 118 – Take Charge (Last Tycoon 131) [2001 **47** 63: 8m 10g 8m 10.9m 15.8d f11g⁵ f9.4g Dec 11] sparely-made gelding: disappointing maiden: tried blinkered. *J. G. Given*

MASTERFUL (USA) 3 b.c. Danzig (USA) – Moonlight Serenade (FR) (Dictus **119** (FR) 126) [2001 74: 6m² 7f² 7.1f² 8g* 10m* 9.9g² 10d* Aug 15]
Once he got his head in front Masterful's career took off, and in the space of just over a month he went from fairly useful maiden to pattern-race winner. Masterful's first win, which ended a run of seconds, was gained over a mile at Ascot in July, but it was a further step up in trip, to a mile and a quarter, that helped bring out the best in him. Returned to Ascot for a minor event, he was again impressive, making all, quickening clear off the home turn and eased considerably inside the last furlong, but for which he would have beaten Serge Lifar by at least six lengths instead of a length and three quarters. Five days later Masterful ran a cracking race to finish three lengths second to Askham, who was receiving 9 lb, in an extremely competitive three-year-old handicap at Goodwood (Indian Creek was third), a performance which earned him his place in the Group 2 Prix Guillaume d'Ornano at Deauville. Masterful was one of four British challengers in the nine-runner field at Deauville, with Chancellor, Dandoun and Potemkin the others, and he was sent off second favourite behind Denon, in the frame in the Poule d'Essai des Poulains and the Prix Jean Prat on his two previous starts. Front-running tactics were

Prix Guillaume d'Ornano, Deauville—Masterful takes the step up from handicap to Group 2 company in his stride, making all to beat Chancellor (No.4) and Sagacity

re-employed on Masterful after he had been ridden with some restraint at Goodwood and he was able to dictate matters. Shaken up turning for home, Masterful quickened well and never really looked like being caught, winning by a length from Chancellor, who just got the better of Sagacity for second. The first three home had occupied those positions virtually throughout in a race in which those held up, including fourth-placed Denon, were at a disadvantage. Masterful wasn't seen out again and is a likeable sort who may have more improvement in him. He should continue to do well in 2002, when he will be racing for Godolphin.

			Northern Dancer	Nearctic
	Danzig (USA)		(b 1961)	Natalma
	(b 1977)		Pas de Nom	Admiral's Voyage
Masterful (USA)			(b or br 1968)	Petitioner
(b.c. 1998)			Dictus	Sanctus
	Moonlight Serenade (FR)		(ch 1967)	Doronic
	(ch 1979)		Tres Snobe	Snob
			(b 1967)	Trezene

Masterful, a 250,000-dollar yearling, is his dam's fourteenth foal and ninth winner. The best of Moonlight Serenade's previous produce were Corviglia (by Cresta Rider) and River Rhythm (by Riverman). The former, closely related to Masterful, was useful as a two-year-old in France, winning the Criterium de Maisons-Laffitte over seven furlongs, while the latter won eleven races in France and the States, and also finished second in the Grade 1 San Luis Rey Stakes. Moonlight Serenade herself won over a mile and a half in France, while the next dam Tres Snobe was successful a couple of times there. Masterful, said by his trainer to have been a 'scrawny yearling', has clearly made considerable physical progress since and is now a good-bodied individual. He acts on good to firm and good to soft going. *J. H. M. Gosden*

MASTER GATEMAKER 3 b.g. Tragic Role (USA) – Girl At The Gate 53 (Formid- – able (USA) 125) [2001 63: 8.2v 10g 10m 9m f8g Jul 2] modest form both 2-y-o starts: little form in 2001: tried visored. *P. W. Harris*

MASTER GEORGE   4 b.g. Mtoto 134 – Topwinder (USA) (Topsider (USA)) [2001   –
89: 16.4m 13.3m 14m 13.3m Aug 17] quite good-topped gelding: fairly useful performer
at 3 yrs: little form in 2001: tried visored. *I. A. Balding*

MASTER HENRY (GER)   7 b.g. Mille Balles (FR) 124 – Maribelle (GER) (Wind-   –
wurf (GER)) [2001 73: e8g Apr 2] formerly useful in Germany: well held only 7-y-o start
on Flat: winning hurdler/chaser. *Ian Williams*

MASTER IN LAW (IRE)   2 ch.c. (Apr 24) Polish Precedent (USA) 131 – Clara Bow   85
(USA) (Coastal (USA)) [2001 7.1m² 8s* 10v Nov 13] 28,000Y: leggy colt: half-brother
to several winners, including fairly useful Irish 1991 2-y-o 7f to 1¼m winner Fawaayid
(by Vaguely Noble) and 6-y-o Generous Ways: dam US 6f to 8.5f winner: confirmed
promise when winning maiden at Leicester in October by 3 lengths from Araglin: tailed
off in Criterium de Saint-Cloud: should stay at least 1¼m. *G. C. Bravery*

MASTER LUKE   4 b.g. Contract Law (USA) 108 – Flying Wind 51 (Forzando 122)   54
[2001 64, a71: 6v⁵ 6s 7m f7g 6m⁴ 5g³ 6s 7s p7g p6g Dec 19] modest performer: effective   a59
at stiff 5f to easy 7f: acts on all-weather, soft and good to firm going: usually blinkered.
G. L. Moore

MASTER MCGRATH (IRE)   3 b.c. Common Grounds 118 – Darabaka (IRE)   75 p
(Doyoun 124) [2001 10s⁴ 10.5d⁴ 11.5m 14.1s* Sep 4] 10,000F, 50,000Y: fourth foal:
half-brother to 3 winners, notably smart 1½m to 2¼m winner Far Cry (by Pharly), also
runner-up in Gold Cup: dam unraced half-sister to dam of Prix de Diane winner Daryaba:
fair form: visored, best effort when winning handicap at Yarmouth in September by 2½
lengths from Mamcazma, tending to idle (swished tail once): better at 1¾m than shorter,
and will stay 2m+: acts on soft ground: lightly raced, and should make quite a useful
4-y-o. *J. Noseda*

MASTERMIND (IRE)   4 ch.g. Dolphin Street (FR) 125 – Glenarff (USA) (Irish River   112
(FR) 131) [2001 108: 8v⁴ 8d* 7.9m 8m 8g³ Jul 1] strong gelding: good walker: fluent
mover, though has a splayed action: smart performer: fourth in Lincoln at Doncaster then
won Bet Direct Spring Cup (Handicap) at Newbury in April by 1¼ lengths from Pulau
Tioman: at least respectable efforts after, third to Bach in listed contest at the Curragh
final start: effective at 1m (given test)/1¼m: acts on any turf going: best held up: sold
380,000 gns, sent to Saudi Arabia. *Mrs J. R. Ramsden*

MASTERPIECE (USA)   4 b. or br.g. Nureyev (USA) 131 – Lovely Gemstone   61
(USA) (Alydar (USA)) [2001 83: f8g f8g 8v 9v 8s 11s 7.1m a8.5f a8.5s a8s* Dec 15]
rather leggy gelding: modest performer in 2001: left K. Burke after seventh start, and off
5½ months: won claimer at Philadelphia Park in December: should stay 1¼m: acts on
heavy and good to firm going, and on dirt: tried visored/tongue tied, blinkered last 4
starts. *R. Allen, USA*

MASTER ROBBIE   2 b.g. (Apr 14) Piccolo 121 – Victoria's Secret (IRE) 70 (Law   95
Society (USA) 130) [2001 5g³ 6m² 6g* 6.1d⁵ 5m² 5d Oct 13] close-coupled colt: third
foal: brother to Italian 7f (at 2 yrs)/1m winner: dam 1½m winner at 4 yrs: useful
performer: won maiden at Goodwood in August: clearly best effort when short-headed
by Irish Vale in listed race at Ayr fifth start: will prove best at 5f/6f: acts on good to firm
going, well beaten on good to soft: gelded after final outing. *M. R. Channon*

MASTER SODEN (USA)   4 b.g. Pembroke (USA) 113 – Lady Member (FR) (Saint   80 +
Estephe (FR) 123) [2001 64: f11g⁴ f8.5g* f8g 7s 7m* 7m* 6d 8m² 7m* 7d 7m⁴ 7m³ 7.5g
6.5d² 7.5d⁶ Dec 29] sturdy gelding: fairly useful performer: won handicaps at Wolverhampton and Yarmouth, seller at Redcar and claimer at Salisbury between February and
July: sold from T. Mills 10,000 gns after twelfth start: best form at 7f: acts on fibresand,
good to soft and good to firm ground: has raced freely/hung left, and may prove best with
strong handling: front runner. *I. de Chirico, Italy*

MASTER SUN (IRE)   2 b.g. (Mar 20) Grand Lodge (USA) 125 – Mersada (IRE) 65   55
(Heraldiste (USA) 121) [2001 7d 7s p10g Dec 4] IR 19,000F, IR 25,000Y: smallish
gelding: fourth foal: half-brother to Irish 7f to 9f winner One For The Money (by Doubletour): dam lightly-raced Irish maiden: modest form in maidens: gelded after final start:
seems to stay 1¼m. *R. Charlton*

MASTER TRUMP   3 b.g. First Trump 118 – Anhaar (Ela-Mana-Mou 132) [2001   –
10.9m⁶ 14g f9.4g Aug 10] 6,800F, 11,000Y, 37,000 2-y-o: sixth foal: brother to Irish
1¾m/2m winner Midnight Coup and half-brother to 7-y-o Ellamine: dam bad maiden:
well held in maidens. *Jonjo O'Neill*

MASTER T (USA) 2 b.g. (Mar 6) Trempolino (USA) 135 – Our Little C (USA) **67**
(Marquetry (USA) 121) [2001 7g⁶ 7.6m⁴ 7.9m⁵ 8s Sep 30] $9,000Y, 5,000 2-y-o: sparely-
made gelding: first foal: dam unraced half-sister to US Grade 3 9f winner Vigorous Lady:
fair form first 2 starts in maidens: wandered/found little after: should stay 1m: acts on
good to firm ground: needs treating with some caution. *G. L. Moore*

MATERIAL WITNESS (IRE) 4 b.g. Barathea (IRE) 127 – Dial Dream (Gay **86 §**
Mecene (USA) 128) [2001 93§: 8d 8s 8.1g⁵ 7.2g³ 8.3g² 10.3g 8.1v 8.9d p8g f9.4g p8g² **a74 §**
Dec 22] strong gelding: fairly useful performer on turf, fair on all-weather: stays 1m: acts
on soft going and polytrack: tried blinkered/visored: carries head high, and not one to
trust. *W. R. Muir*

MATHMAGICIAN 2 ch.g. (Apr 7) Hector Protector (USA) 124 – Inherent Magic **43**
(IRE) 95 (Magical Wonder (USA) 125) [2001 5g f5g f6g⁴ f7g⁶ 7g 7.1s f7g Oct 22] strong
gelding: third foal: dam 5f winner, including at 2 yrs: poor maiden: stays 6f: form only on
fibresand: sold 800 gns. *W. R. Muir*

MATINS (IRE) 2 ch.f. (Feb 22) College Chapel 122 – Krayyalei (IRE) 94 (Krayyan **50**
117) [2001 f6g⁶ 7s Oct 25] IR 50,000Y: third foal: half-sister to 4-y-o Romanyeli: dam
Irish 6f/6.5f winner: better effort in maidens (modest form) when sixth at Southwell:
slowly away both starts: sold 3,000 gns. *W. J. Haggas*

MATLOCK (IRE) 3 b.c. Barathea (IRE) 127 – Palio Flyer (Slip Anchor 136) [2001 **83**
86: 8s³ 7.6f 10.5m 8m 6.5f 8f⁵ 8f* Oct 31] good-topped colt: fairly useful performer: left
P. Cole after fourth start: won claimer at Santa Anita in October: best form at 7f/1m: acts
on soft and firm going, some promise only start on fibresand: free-going sort, usually
races prominently. *M. Chew, USA*

MATOAKA (USA) 3 b.f. A P Indy (USA) 131 – Appointed One (USA) (Danzig **92**
(USA)) [2001 90p: 9.9d² 8.5m 6.9m* 7g³ 7g Aug 3] rangy, quite attractive filly: fairly
useful performer: won maiden at Folkestone in June by 12 lengths: better effort in
handicaps after when third at Newmarket: at least as effective at 7f as 1m: yet to race on
extremes of going: has been taken steadily to post: sometimes races freely. *Sir Michael
Stoute*

MATRON (IRE) 3 b.f. Dr Devious (IRE) 127 – Matrona (USA) (Woodman (USA) **–**
126) [2001 83p: 7s⁶ Oct 15] quite attractive filly: fairly useful form in 2 maidens in 2000:
slowly away and well below that level only 3-y-o start: should stay 1m: raced only on
soft/heavy ground. *L. M. Cumani*

MATTAN 5 b.g. Chaddleworth (IRE) 103 – Gilded Omen (Faustus (USA) 118) [2001 **–**
14.1v 21.6s Apr 23] seems of no account on Flat nowadays. *B. J. Llewellyn*

MATTY TUN 2 b.g. (Apr 12) Lugana Beach 116 – B Grade 59 (Lucky Wednesday **63**
124) [2001 f5g⁴ f5g⁶ 6m Aug 18] 7,500Y: sixth foal: half-brother to 6-y-o Tom Tun and
3-y-o Henry Tun: dam 6f winner: modest maiden: will prove best at 5f/6f: wandered
second start: found little final one. *Miss J. F. Craze*

M'AULD SEGOISHA (IRE) 3 gr.f. Dolphin Street (FR) 125 – September Tide **70**
(IRE) 58 (Thatching 131) [2001 79p: 7.5m² f8g⁴ 7.1d² 7g 7.5d 7g Oct 19] strong filly:
fair maiden: stays 7.5f: yet to race on extremes of going on turf, some promise only run
on fibresand: tried tongue tied. *J. G. FitzGerald*

MAUNBY ROLLER (IRE) 2 b.g. (Mar 25) Flying Spur (AUS) – Brown Foam **65**
(Horage 124) [2001 6s⁶ 5d⁶ f6g⁶ f8g³ Dec 3] 9,500Y: strong gelding: sixth foal: half-
brother to 4-y-o Diamond Rachael and fairly useful 1m winner Pass The Rest (by
Shalford): dam ran twice: fair maiden: carried head high when third in nursery at
Southwell: stays 1m: acts on fibresand. *P. C. Haslam*

MAUNSELL'S ROAD (IRE) 2 b.g. (Apr 18) Desert Style (IRE) 121 – Zara's **74**
Birthday (IRE) 71 (Waajib 121) [2001 7g 8.1g² 7.1f² 7.9d 7v Oct 26] IR 8,000F, 22,000Y:
strong gelding: third foal: half-brother to 4-y-o Blair and Irish 1½m winner Pigeon Top
(by Paris House): dam Irish maiden who stayed 1½m: fair maiden: form only when
second twice at Chepstow: gelded after final outing: should stay 1¼m: acts on firm going.
S. Kirk

MAURANGI 10 b.g. Warning 136 – Spin Dry (High Top 131) [2001 10s Apr 28] of no **–**
account nowadays. *B. W. Murray*

MAURI MOON 3 b.f. Green Desert (USA) 127 – Dazzling Heights 99 (Shirley **104**
Heights 130) [2001 90p: 8s² 7m 10f⁴ 7m* 7g 8g Oct 6] angular, quite attractive filly:
useful performer: won listed race at Goodwood (made all to beat Sheppard's Watch by
neck) in August: ran well otherwise only when ½-length second to Heavenly Whisper in

similar event at Kempton: best efforts at 7f/1m: acts on soft and good to firm going: sometimes finds little: has worn rope halter/given trouble in preliminaries (has had 2 handlers in paddock and been accompanied by expert in stall entry). *G. Wragg*

MA VIE   4 b.f. Salse (USA) 128 – One Life (USA) (L'Emigrant (USA) 129) [2001 69: 10.1g* Aug 15] sturdy filly: has a quick action: fair performer: made all in minor event at Yarmouth only 4-y-o start: best around 1¼m: acts on good to firm and good to soft going, probably on soft: visored last 3 outings at 3 yrs: reportedly in foal to Cadeaux Genereux. *J. R. Fanshawe*   **65**

MAWDSLEY   4 b.f. Piccolo 121 – Legendary Dancer 90 (Shareef Dancer (USA) 135) [2001 –: 8m 7m 10.1m 8m 12.3g 10.1g 9.9m 8m Sep 8] of little account. *A. B. Mulholland*   **–**

MAWHOOB (USA)   3 gr.g. Dayjur (USA) 137 – Asl (USA) 114 (Caro 133) [2001 76: 8.2f² 8.5m⁵ Aug 25] good-bodied gelding: has a round action: fair maiden: left J. Dunlop 9,000 gns after reappearance (edged left), took strong hold next time: not sure to stay beyond 1m: acts on firm going, showed promise (on debut) on good to soft. *Mrs N. Macauley*   **79**

MAWINGO (IRE)   8 b.g. Taufan (USA) 119 – Tappen Zee (Sandhurst Prince 128) [2001 69: e10g² f11g³ 10.1g p10g Nov 28] leggy gelding: fair handicapper: hardly stays 11f: acts on any turf going and fibresand/equitrack: blinkered twice: has won for apprentice: held up. *G. Wragg*   **67**

MAWJUD   8 b.h. Mujtahid (USA) 118 – Elfaslah (IRE) 107 (Green Desert (USA) 127) [2001 7.9m 6s f12g Oct 23] fairly useful handicapper in Dubai at 4/5 yrs: well held in Britain. *A. W. Carroll*   **–**

MAX BEE JAY   3 b.g. Imp Society (USA) – Dulzura (Daring March 116) [2001 –: f7g 6d 6f 7g Aug 8] no form. *A. P. Jarvis*   **–**

MAX (FR)   6 gr.g. L'Emigrant (USA) 129 – Miss Mendez (FR) (Bellypha 130) [2001 42: e10g f12g⁵ f12g⁶ e12g 7s 7.6m 11.6m 8.5f Jul 5] of little account nowadays. *J. J. Bridger*   **–**

MAX'S MICRO (IRE)   2 b.g. (Mar 25) Inzar (USA) 112 – Guess Who 76 (Be My Guest (USA) 126) [2001 f7g⁴ f9.4g f8g⁶ Dec 10] 5,000Y: half-brother to fairly useful 1¼m/1½m winner Hazard A Guess (by Digamist) and several winners abroad: dam disqualified 10.4f winner: modest form in sellers: should stay beyond 1m: visored final start. *P. D. Evans*   **50**

MAY BALL   4 b.f. Cadeaux Genereux 131 – Minute Waltz (Sadler's Wells (USA) 132) [2001 104: 7.1s³ 7m 7g* 7d⁵ 8s³ Nov 3] big, strong filly: useful performer: won minor event at Redcar (after 5-month break) in October: fifth to Toffee Nosed in listed event at Ascot (reportedly lost a shoe and finished lame, having looked winner 2f out) next start, then good effort when around 1½ lengths third to Keltos in Prix Perth at Saint-Cloud: probably best at 7f/1m: acts on soft going, probably on heavy: races prominently. *J. H. M. Gosden*   **104**

MAYBE BABY (IRE)   2 b.g. (Mar 26) Lake Coniston (IRE) 131 – Nadedge (IRE) 78 (Petorius 117) [2001 6g 6g 5f Sep 20] IR 500Y, 10,000 2-y-o: leggy, sparely-made gelding: second foal: dam Irish maiden who stayed 1m: modest maiden: best effort in sales race at Kempton on second start. *J. L. Eyre*   **53**

MAYBE SHADES   2 b.f. (Mar 30) Thornberry (USA) 110 – My Moody Girl (IRE) (Alzao (USA) 117) [2001 6m 6v Oct 8] fifth foal: dam no form: well held in maidens. *G. F. H. Charles-Jones*   **–**

MAYCOCKS BAY   3 b.f. Muhtarram (USA) 125 – Beacon (High Top 131) [2001 67p: 7g³ 7.1f⁵ 8m³ 10m² 9.9m³ 10m³ 10m⁵ 12d⁴ f12g 10s² Nov 5] strong, compact filly: fairly useful maiden: stays 1½m: acts on soft and good to firm ground, below form only start on all-weather: has worn crossed noseband: usually takes good hold/held up: consistent. *J. A. Glover*   **81**

MAY I SAY (IRE)   5 b.m. Night Shift (USA) – Monoglow (Kalaglow 132) [2001 f9.4g 9v 10s 10s f8g f14.8s Dec 15] close-coupled mare: trained by M. Hofer in Germany at 4 yrs, winning maiden at Bremen and handicap at Cologne: no show back in Britain in 2001, leaving Mrs A. Duffield after third start: stays 11.4f: probably acts on any going: tried blinkered/visored/tongue tied. *R. Brotherton*   **–**

MAY KING MAYHEM   8 ch.g. Great Commotion (USA) 123 – Queen Ranavalona (Sure Blade (USA) 130) [2001 58: 9.9m 12m³ 11.5f² Jun 5] close-coupled gelding: has a   **58**

round action: modest handicapper: effective at 11.5f to 15f: acts on firm going, soft and fibresand: usually blinkered/visored. *Mrs A. L. M. King*

MAYLANE 7 b.g. Mtoto 134 – Possessive Dancer 118 (Shareef Dancer (USA) 135) – §
[2001 112§: 11.8d 12m Jun 30] smallish, leggy gelding: smart performer at up to 2½m at best: virtually refused to race on reappearance and took little interest only start after: blinkered twice at 5 yrs: temperamental. *A. C. Stewart*

MAY PRINCESS 3 ch.f. Prince Sabo 123 – Mim 39 (Midyan (USA) 124) [2001 56: **61 d**
7m⁵ 8m 7.6f³ 8m 7m 7g f7g p6g Dec 19] quite good-topped filly: disappointing maiden handicapper: should stay 1m: raced mainly on good going or firmer on turf: has carried head high. *D. Morris*

MAY QUEEN MEGAN 8 gr.m. Petorius 117 – Siva (FR) (Bellypha 130) [2001 43: **50**
f8g f9.4g* f9.4g⁵ f9.4g 8.2f* 9f⁵ 9f 8d* 8g 8g 10m Aug 29] leggy mare: modest handi- **a43**
capper: won at Wolverhampton (amateur event) in January, Nottingham (apprentice race after 3½-month break) in June and Pontefract in July: effective at 1m/1¼m: acts on fibresand, firm and soft going: blinkered once at 3 yrs: held up. *Mrs A. L. M. King*

MAYREAU LEGEND (IRE) 2 b.g. (Mar 23) Distinctly North (USA) 115 – Crystal **62**
River (Jester 119) [2001 6m⁵ 6d⁴ 6m 7.1g 8m 7d 6d² Oct 30] IR 5,000F, IR 11,000Y: sturdy gelding: third reported foal: dam lightly-raced bumper performer: modest maiden: good second in nursery at Redcar (subsequently gelded): should stay 7f: acts on good to soft going. *M. H. Tompkins*

MAYSBOYO 3 b.g. Makbul 104 – Maysimp (IRE) (Mac's Imp (USA) 116) [2001 –: –
f8g 8f 8.1g 10m 7.6f f9.4g 8.1d Aug 9] of no account. *B. P. J. Baugh*

MAYTIME 3 ch.f. Pivotal 124 – May Hinton 82 (Main Reef 126) [2001 55: 6m 5m **51**
6.1m 8m² 7.1d 8s⁵ 8g 7s⁵ Oct 5] unfurnished filly: modest maiden: stays 1m: yet to race on heavy going, probably acts on any other: blinkered (looked none too keen) second start: has raced freely: often races prominently. *H. Morrison*

MAYVILLE THUNDER 3 ch.c. Zilzal (USA) 137 – Mountain Lodge 120 (Blakeney **109**
126) [2001 84p: e10g* 8g May 5] rangy colt: has scope: unimpressive mover: has had just 4 outings, but has shown useful form: won handicap at Lingfield in March: excellent effort when 5½ lengths seventh to Golan in 2000 Guineas at Newmarket next time (later reported to have been jarred up): should stay beyond 1¼m: has form on soft going, good to firm and equitrack: stays in training. *G. A. Butler*

MAZURY (USA) 2 b.c. (Feb 24) Langfuhr (CAN) 124 – Assurgent (USA) (Damascus **68 p**
(USA)) [2001 6d 7d³ Oct 30] $40,000Y: unfurnished colt: half-brother to numerous winners abroad, notably US minor stakes winners Lady Ack (6f, by Ack Ack) and Touch of Love (7f/1m, by Alydar): dam, US 2-y-o 7f winner, half-sister to Grade 1 winners Tiffany Lass (up to 9f) and Valdez (1¼m): better effort (fair form) when third to Eastern Image in minor event at Redcar, shaping as if still in need of race: should stay 1m: will improve further. *M. Johnston*

MBELE 4 b.g. Mtoto 134 – Majestic Image 86 (Niniski (USA) 125) [2001 105: 16.4m⁵ **116**
20f⁶ 14s⁶ 16g Aug 2] close-coupled, useful-looking gelding: smart performer: best effort when 2¾ lengths fifth to Solo Mio in Bonusprint Stakes (Henry II) at Sandown, tending to hang and short of room (said to have lost a shoe): edgy, respectable sixth to Royal Rebel in Gold Cup at Royal Ascot next start: well below form in Prix Maurice de Nieuil at Maisons-Laffitte (didn't handle one of bends) and Goodwood Cup (stirred up in blinkers) last 2: gelded after: should stay beyond 2m: acts on heavy and good to firm going: gave trouble stalls first 2 starts in 2000: not an easy ride. *W. R. Muir*

MCBAIN (USA) 2 br.c. (Mar 27) Lear Fan (USA) 130 – River City Moon (USA) **80**
(Riverman (USA) 131) [2001 5m 6m⁴ 6m² 7m⁶ 7m 8d² 8g* 8.3v* Nov 8] $52,000Y, resold IR 35,000Y: leggy colt: first foal: dam, US 2-y-o 1m winner, out of half-sister to very smart sprinter Dowsing and US Grade 1 9.5f winner Fire The Groom (dam of Stravinsky): fairly useful performer: won nurseries at Redcar and Windsor (by 1¼ lengths from Birdie) in November: will stay 1¼m: yet to race on firm going, acts on any other. *R. F. Johnson Houghton*

MCGILLYCUDDY REEKS (IRE) 10 b.m. Kefaah (USA) 124 – Kilvarnet 78 **79**
(Furry Glen 121) [2001 77: 11s⁶ 11.9m⁴ 10m⁵ 10m⁴ 12g* 10.3f² 12.3m² 10.3m⁵ 11.9g 11.9m 10s⁵ 10.4d² 12v⁴ 10.3s² Nov 9] small mare: fair handicapper: won at Thirsk in June: best at 1¼m/1½m: acts on fibresand and any turf going: has worn tongue strap: takes good hold: often held up: tough. *Don Enrico Incisa*

MCQUILLAN   4 b.g. Maledetto (IRE) 103 – Macs Maharanee 85 (Indian King (USA)   **43**
128) [2001 –: f6g⁶ f7g f6g³ f7g Jun 8] poor maiden: stays 6f: acts on fibresand.
P. S. Felgate

MEA CULPA (IRE)   3 b.f. Blues Traveller (IRE) 119 – Tolomena 61 (Tolomeo 127)   **–**
[2001 46: 7s May 3] leggy filly: no form since debut at 2 yrs. *T. D. Easterby*

MEASURE UP   2 ch.c. (Mar 7) Inchinor 119 – Victoria Blue (Old Vic 136) [2001   **74**
6.1m 6m⁴ 7m⁵ Sep 5] 7,000F, 15,000Y: second foal: dam unraced: fair form at Epsom and
York on last 2 starts in maidens: should stay 1m. *R. Hannon*

MEDELAI   5 b.m. Marju (IRE) 127 – No Islands (Lomond (USA) 128) [2001 52: f16g   **–**
f16.2g f16.2g 16f 16.4m⁶ 16.2s f14.8s⁶ Dec 15] little form in 2001. *A. G. Juckes*

MEDIA BUYER (USA)   3 b. or br.g. Green Dancer (USA) 132 – California Rush   **61**
(USA) (Forty Niner (USA)) [2001 65d: f7g³ f6g⁴ f8.5g⁵ f8.5g Mar 10] small, sturdy
gelding: modest maiden: stays 7f: acts on fibresand and good to soft ground: often
blinkered at 2 yrs: none too consistent. *R. J. Price*

MEDIA PUZZLE (USA)   4 ch.c. Theatrical 128 – Market Slide (USA) 94 (Gulch   **116**
(USA)) [2001 116: 14g* 14g² May 23] big, strong, lengthy colt: fluent mover: smart
performer: made all in 4-runner minor event at the Curragh (beat Ancelin by 1½ lengths)
in May: creditable 1½ lengths second to enterprisingly-ridden Rostropovich in listed race
at Leopardstown only start after: effective at 1½m to 14.6f: acts on firm going, has won
on soft: blinkered last 3 starts in 2000. *D. K. Weld, Ireland*

MEDICEAN   4 ch.c. Machiavellian (USA) 123 – Mystic Goddess (USA) 94   **128**
(Storm Bird (CAN) 134) [2001 121: 8s* 8m* 10m* 10.4g³ Aug 21]
     The Ballydoyle and Godolphin stables took fifteen of Britain's twenty-
seven Group 1 events between them—winning ten and five respectively—in the
latest season, with Sir Michael Stoute's Freemason Lodge and Beech Hurst complex the only other yard to get on the scoresheet more than once. Golan's Two
Thousand Guineas win and the victories of Medicean (who, like Golan, was trained
at Beech Hurst) in the Juddmonte Lockinge Stakes at Newbury and in the Coral
Eurobet Eclipse Stakes at Sandown helped Stoute to divide Aidan O'Brien and
Saeed bin Suroor in the trainers' table—with first-three prize-money earnings of
£1,967,583—though a seventh British trainers' title was out of reach long before
the end of the season. Medicean provided another fine advertisement for his
trainer's skill with older horses, something that will be tested again in the next
season after the late decision to keep Golan in training as a four-year-old. Medicean
improved between three and four, as did such Stoute stars as Opera House, Rock
Hopper, Singspiel, Pilsudski and Kalanisi before him. Opera House and Pilsudski
went on to provide Stoute with Eclipse victories in the 'nineties as five-year-olds
—as did another late-developer Ezzoud—and Medicean went one better in the race
than three other four-year-old Stoute runners-up Stagecraft, Opera House and
Kalanisi, the last-named beaten in a nip-and-tuck finish with Giant's Causeway
in 2000.

Juddmonte Lockinge Stakes, Newbury—a successful reappearance for Medicean;
Warningford (right) and Swallow Flight (centre) fill the places

Medicean, unraced at two, quickly progressed from minor events to pattern company as a three-year-old, crossing swords himself with Giant's Causeway when third to him in both the St James's Palace Stakes at Royal Ascot and the Sussex Stakes at Goodwood. Medicean went on to record his first pattern victory in the Celebration Mile at Goodwood in August before his progress temporarily came to an end when only fourth on his final start behind the Celebration Mile runner-up Observatory and Giant's Causeway in the Queen Elizabeth II Stakes at Ascot. Observatory and Medicean both had the Juddmonte Lockinge Stakes pencilled in for their reappearance in May. Observatory was a late defector to the Prix d'Ispahan on the same weekend because of the prevailing soft going at Newbury, but Medicean still had to work very hard for a narrow victory over Warningford and Swallow Flight. With no established front-runner in the line-up, the early pace in the Lockinge was muddling and it was past halfway before the race began in earnest, the waited-with Medicean running on strongly to lead near the line, winning by a neck and the same. Medicean had to defy a Group 1 penalty on his next outing in the Queen Anne Stakes at Royal Ascot, a race that was almost a re-run—the retired Giant's Causeway apart—of the previous year's St James's Palace Stakes, with runner-up Valentino and fourth-placed Shibboleth (heavily-backed favourite for the Queen Anne) also in the line-up. Medicean shrugged off the weight concession to his rivals, enjoying a clear passage against the stand rail and coming through to win by a length from Swallow Flight, who would have run the winner very close but for finding trouble in running. Arkadian Hero was a further neck away third, with Valentino, another who met trouble, fourth and Shibboleth only eighth.

Apart from Medicean, the older generation was not strongly represented in the Coral Eurobet Eclipse at Sandown in July. The Derby third Tobougg started favourite at 9/4, ahead of Irish Two Thousand Guineas and St James's Palace winner Black Minnaloushe at 5/2, with Medicean third favourite at 7/2. The Eclipse was Medicean's second race at around a mile and a quarter, following a poor effort from a wide draw when hot favourite off a favourable-looking handicap mark in the John Smith's Cup at York as a three-year-old. Medicean's stamina was tested to the full at Sandown, where both Tobougg and Black Minnaloushe were provided with pacemakers. The field was soon strung out with Medicean settled towards the rear, but ahead of Tobougg and Black Minnaloushe. Medicean closed early in the straight, making his move first, and stayed on really well under a very strong ride from Kieren Fallon to edge ahead close home in a blanket finish. Less than a length covered the first five, Medicean winning by half a length from the Prix du Jockey Club third Grandera, with four-year-old Bach a neck away third and the strong-finishing Tobougg and Black Minnaloushe a head and the same further behind. The Eclipse produced an exciting finish but the race itself was not a vintage renewal, the occasion also dampened by the arrival of forecast bad weather and by coming up against a very strong sporting programme on the day, including morning TV coverage of a vital Lions rugby union match, the prospect of British glory at Wimbledon and a gripping Test match. If Eclipse day lacked its usual atmosphere, the Sandown executive did not have far to look for valid reasons.

Victory in the Eclipse marked the high point of Medicean's career. Whether there was ever any serious possibility of his staying in training as a five-year-old was never revealed, though he looked just the tough and genuine type to continue to do well, his ability to show his form on any going and his effectiveness at a mile and at a mile and a quarter giving his connections plenty of options. Medicean's trainer said after the Eclipse: 'This horse can dig deep. It was not a difficult decision to persevere with him as a four-year-old as he is very sound and has the most laid-back temperament you can imagine. You take him to the races and he goes to sleep.' Medicean's almost unbroken progress up to the Eclipse suggested he might have had even more to offer, but he was seen out only once afterwards, when a bit below his best in third behind Sakhee and Grandera in the Juddmonte International at York in August. Medicean had missed the Sussex Stakes at Goodwood after a minor setback and was also absent from the acceptors for his intended autumn target the Dubai Champion Stakes after bruising a foreleg in training. He has been retired to the Cheveley Park Stud, Newmarket, and will stand at £15,000.

The strong, good-bodied Medicean, a fluent mover, really let down as a four-year-old and very much took the eye before all his races; he looked in tremendous shape when our photographer visited Beech Hurst to take posed portraits in August. Medicean's pedigree, as well as his racing record, should appeal to commercial breeders. His sire, the versatile Mr Prospector stallion Machiavellian and his dam Mystic Goddess, winner of the Sweet Solera Stakes and placed in races like the Queen Mary and the Cherry Hinton, both matured early. Machiavellian, the top two-year-old of his year in France, went on to finish second in the Two Thousand Guineas but only just got a mile, over which trip Mystic Goddess also showed fairly useful form as a three-year-old, despite not training on so well as expected. Medicean is the third foal produced by Mystic Goddess, and her first winner. She now has a second, Medicean's fairly useful, year-younger half-sister Moon Goddess (by Rainbow Quest), successful in a maiden at Yarmouth in the latest season. Medicean's grandam Rose Goddess is out of Cocarde, who won

Coral Eurobet Eclipse Stakes, Sandown—with just over a length covering the first five, Medicean is in front where it matters; Grandera (cross belts) is second, Bach (rail) third, with Tobougg (right) and Black Minnaloushe well clear of the rest

Cheveley Park Stud's "Medicean"

		Mr Prospector (b 1970)	Raise A Native
Medicean (ch.c. 1997)	Machiavellian (USA) (b 1987)		Gold Digger
		Coup de Folie (b 1982)	Halo
			Raise The Standard
	Mystic Goddess (USA) (ch 1990)	Storm Bird (b 1978)	Northern Dancer
			South Ocean
		Rose Goddess (b 1979)	Sassafras
			Cocarde

at a mile and a quarter and was a half-sister to the top-class racehorse and successful stallion Caro. Rose Goddess herself did not see a racecourse but produced several winners, including Solario Stakes victor Sanam, who was at his best as a two-year-old, improving with time and distance and ending his campaign with victories over a mile in pattern races in Ireland and Italy (the latter the Gran Criterium). *Sir Michael Stoute*

MEDITERRANEAN 3 b.c. Sadler's Wells (USA) 132 – Pato 90 (High Top 131) **114** [2001 91P: 16.2m 14d² 14g⁶ 13.9g* 14.6g Sep 15] stocky colt: smart performer: runner-up to Chimes At Midnight in Curragh Cup prior to best effort (16/1) when winning Tote Ebor (Handicap) at York in August by ½ length from Foreign Affairs, quickening in good style: 7/1, broke down badly 5f out in St Leger at Doncaster final start: stayed 1¾m: acted on good to soft going, successful on heavy only 2-y-o start: wore crossed noseband: reportedly retired. *A. P. O'Brien, Ireland*

MEDKHAN (IRE) 4 ch.g. Lahib (USA) 129 – Safayn (USA) 82 (Lyphard (USA) **–** 132) [2001 74?: 12.6m⁶ 10.3f⁵ 10g 12.3d 8g f12g Nov 23] disappointing maiden: left

D. Weld in Ireland 7,500 gns after final 3-y-o start: stays 1¼m: acts on any ground: tried blinkered. *F. Jordan*

MEDRAAR 3 b.c. Machiavellian (USA) 123 – Saleemah (USA) 96 (Storm Bird (CAN) 134) [2001 –p: 8v* 8d² 8.1g⁴ 8m² 8.1m⁴ Jul 13] leggy, useful-looking colt: fairly useful performer: won maiden at Ripon in April: at least creditable efforts in handicaps after: stays 1m: unraced on firm going, probably acts on any other turf: gives impression may be worth a try in blinkers/visor: found less than seemed likely last 2 starts: sent to UAE. *J. L. Dunlop* **82**

MEGA (IRE) 5 b.m. Petardia 113 – Gobolino (Don 128) [2001 39: 10.3f 14.1m 11.8g Aug 8] of little account nowadays. *M. H. Tompkins* **–**

MEHMAAS 5 b.g. Distant Relative 128 – Guest List 85 (Be My Guest (USA) 126) [2001 69§: 8.3d 7m 8m⁴ 8.2f³ 7m³ 7m 8f² 7.5m⁴ 7m* 7m 7.1m³ 8m³ 7m 7m³ 8.5g³ 7.5s² 8g 7s 7d⁶ 8g⁶ f8.5g Nov 17] smallish, sturdy gelding: fair performer: won amateur minor event at Redcar in July: effective at 7f/1m: acts on firm going, soft and fibresand: visored at 5 yrs, has been blinkered: front runner. *R. E. Barr* **72**

MEIYING 3 br.f. Cyrano de Bergerac 120 – Hong Kong Girl 94 (Petong 126) [2001 6m⁶ 5m 6m 5.7m 7.1f Sep 18] fifth reported foal: half-sister to 6-y-o Bound To Please and 6f winner Jersey Belle (by Distant Relative): dam best at 5f: no form: reluctant to race first 2 outings (early to post/unruly at start second one): one to leave alone. *M. Kettle* **– §**

MELANZANA 4 b.f. Alzao (USA) 117 – Melody Park 104 (Music Boy 124) [2001 89: f7g 6g* 6m 6d 6f⁴ 6m 6g⁵ 6g² 6g³ 6g Sep 8] rather leggy filly: fairly useful handicapper: won at Leicester in May: creditable efforts after when in frame: best at 5f/6f: acts on firm and good to soft going: often races freely: sold 6,500 gns, sent to Saudi Arabia. *E. A. L. Dunlop* **85**

MELLEDGAN (IRE) 4 b.f. Catrail (USA) 123 – Dark Hyacinth (IRE) 65 (Darshaan 133) [2001 49: 6v 6m f7g³ 8m 7.1f* 7m 8g 7g 8m³ 10.9m* 10.4s f12g Oct 22] angular filly: modest performer: won claimers at Musselburgh in June and Warwick (claimer, final start for R. Guest) in September: stays 11f: acts on fibresand and firm going: winner over hurdles in November. *Miss S. J. Wilton* **56**

MELLOW PARK (IRE) 2 b.f. (Jan 28) In The Wings 128 – Park Special (Relkino 131) [2001 7d⁵ Nov 3] sister to very smart 6f (at 2 yrs) to 1½m winner who stayed 2m Central Park and half-sister to 3 winners, notably useful 6f (including Lowther Stakes) and 1¼m winner Velvet Moon (by Shaadi): dam Irish 1¼m winner: 15/2, fifth of 21 to Maid To Perfection in Newmarket maiden, keeping on without being given hard time: should stay at least 1¼m: sure to do better. *J. Noseda* **73 p**

MELODIAN 6 b.h. Grey Desire 115 – Mere Melody 88 (Dunphy 124) [2001 79: 8v* 8d 8g 8.9m⁵ 8.1g 8.1s 8s 7d 10s Nov 5] leggy horse: fairly useful handicapper: won Randombet.com Spring Mile at Doncaster in March by 10 lengths from Digital: mostly well below that form after: probably best at 7f/1m: has won on firm ground, best efforts on softer than good (well beaten only try on fibresand): blinkered: often races up with pace. *M. Brittain* **91 d**

Tote Ebor (Handicap), York—a smart renewal as Mediterranean foils the favourite Foreign Affairs, with the unlucky Brother Joe third and Cover Up fourth

MELODY LADY   5 ch.m. Dilum (USA) 115 – Ansellady 67 (Absalom 128) [2001   –
53, a–: 12.3m 16f Jul 2] probably of little account nowadays. *K. A. Ryan*

MELOMANIA (USA)   9 b.g. Shadeed (USA) 135 – Medley of Song (USA) (Secre-   – §
tariat (USA)) [2001 –§: e8g f12g e10g 8m Jun 2] temperamental handicapper: tried
blinkered/visored/tongue tied. *T. T. Clement*

MELS BABY (IRE)   8 br.g. Contract Law (USA) 108 – Launch The Raft (Home Guard   38
(USA) 129) [2001 –: 10s 12m⁶ 9f 10g 10.1g 10g Aug 31] tall, light-bodied gelding:
one-time fair handicapper: poor and lightly raced nowadays: effective at 1m/1¼m: acts
on firm going, soft and fibresand: tried blinkered/visored. *J. L. Eyre*

MELSTAIR   6 b.g. Terimon 124 – Kevins Lady (Alzao (USA) 117) [2001 12v Apr 7]   –
no show in maiden. *A. R. Dicken*

MEMAMEDA   5 b.m. Cigar 68 – Mamzooj (IRE) (Shareef Dancer (USA) 135) [2001   31
–: f12g f12s 7m 8g 8f⁵ 14.1m 8.3d Aug 15] poor maiden: should stay 1¼m: acts on firm
ground. *K. A. Ryan*

MEMPHIS DANCER   6 b.m. Shareef Dancer (USA) 135 – Wollow Maid 73   –
(Wollow 132) [2001 21.6s Apr 23] big, strong, lengthy mare: fair maiden at best: well
held both starts since 1998. *M. W. Easterby*

MEMSAHIB   3 b.f. Alzao (USA) 117 – Indian Queen 115 (Electric 126) [2001 –:   –
12.1g 12m Sep 24] well held in maidens. *D. R. C. Elsworth*

MENAGGIO (USA)   3 b.g. Danehill (USA) 126 – Mayenne (USA) (Nureyev (USA)   82 +
131) [2001 8m* 8d⁶ 8d Oct 18] 750,000 francs Y: first foal: dam unraced close relation of
Carnegie out of Detroit (both won Prix de l’Arc de Triomphe): fairly useful from when
winning maiden at Newmarket (having reportedly been held up by sore shins) in August:
well held both starts after (taken quietly to post/left impression something amiss on
penultimate): should be suited by further than 1m: has been gelded. *P. W. Harris*

MEN OF WICKENBY   7 b.g. Shirley Heights 130 – Radiant Bride (USA) (Blushing   –
Groom (FR) 131) [2001 –: f11g Jun 15] of little account nowadays. *G. A. Swinbank*

MENTAL PRESSURE   8 ch.g. Polar Falcon (USA) 126 – Hysterical 68 (High Top   74
131) [2001 66: 16m² 14.1m* 16.2f⁵ 16f* 16m³ 13.9m⁵ 16m² 14.1g 16g⁵ Nov 7] rangy
gelding: fair handicapper: won at Redcar in May and July: stays 2m: yet to race on soft/
heavy going, acts on any other: usually held up: most consistent. *Mrs M. Reveley*

MERANTI   8 b.g. Puissance 110 – Sorrowful (Moorestyle 137) [2001 –: 6m 6m⁶ 6g   43
5.7m 7d³ 7.1d⁶ 6f⁵ 5g Aug 6] leggy gelding: poor performer: seems to stay 7f: acts on
firm and good to soft ground: blinkered final start. *J. M. Bradley*

MERCEDE (IRE)   4 b.f. Perugino (USA) 84 – Miss Busybody (IRE) (Phardante (FR)   ?
123) [2001 –: 10v 8v 8.8g² 8.5s⁴ 10g 8.5g 8g* 8g⁶ 8.5d 10d f8g Nov 19] leggy filly: won
handicap at Mulheim in July (left B. Hellier in Germany before well beaten in Britain last
2 starts): joined N. Wilson. *J. Balding*

MERCERNARY (IRE)   2 b.g. (Apr 24) General Monash (USA) 107 – Battle Rage   –
(IRE) (Shernazar 131) [2001 5v f5g 6g f5g Dec 17] IR 6,000Y: smallish gelding: second
foal: dam Irish maiden on Flat/over hurdles: well held in maidens/seller. *A. Berry*

MERCHANT PRINCE   5 b.g. Flying Tyke 90 – Bellinote (FR) 71 (Noir Et Or 125)   –
[2001 –: 7m 8m 10.1g⁵ 5g Sep 19] of little account nowadays. *A. Smith*

MERCHANT PRINCESS   2 ch.f. (Feb 4) Dashing Blade 117 – Running Tycoon   –
(IRE) 62 (Last Tycoon 131) [2001 6d⁵ Oct 3] half-sister to 2-y-o 6f winners Dillionaire
(in 1998, by Dilum) and Tycando (in 1999, by Forzando), both later successful abroad:
dam, ran only at 2 yrs, best effort at 7f: 25/1, well-beaten last of 5 in minor event at
Salisbury: sold 900 gns. *I. A. Balding*

MERCURY RISING (IRE)   3 b.c. Sadler’s Wells (USA) 132 – Silwana (FR)   89
(Nashwan (USA) 135) [2001 8d⁴ 10.1d³ 12m 11.6v² p12g Nov 13] tall, unfurnished colt:
first foal: dam, useful French 2-y-o 1m winner who stayed 1¼m, granddaughter of Arc
winner Gold River: fairly useful maiden: injured near-fore second start and off over 4
months: best effort when second in handicap at Windsor: should have stayed 1¾m: acted
on heavy going: dead. *J. W. Hills*

MERDIFF   2 b.c. (Apr 28) Machiavellian (USA) 123 – Balwa (USA) 101 (Danzig   –
(USA)) [2001 8s Oct 31] seventh foal: half-brother to 1½m winner Laazim Afouz (by
Mtoto): dam 5f (at 2 yrs) and 7f winner from very good family: 8/1 from 7/2, well beaten
in maiden at Yarmouth, reluctant stall, edging left leaving it and virtually pulled up
closing stages: bred to do better. *M. A. Jarvis*

MERELY A MONARCH 2 b.g. (Feb 16) Reprimand 122 – Ruby Princess (IRE) 70 **69**
(Mac's Imp (USA) 116) [2001 6m 6g* 6.1d f6g* f7g⁴ Nov 16] first foal: dam ran once:
fair performer: won seller at Lingfield in September and nursery at Southwell in October:
stays 7f: acts on fibresand, unraced on extremes of going on turf: hung left first 3 starts.
I. A. Wood

MERIDEN MIST 3 b.f. Distinctly North (USA) 115 – Bring On The Choir 87 (Chief **74**
Singer 131) [2001 75: 7d⁶ 8g⁶ 8m² 8g⁵ 8.5g³ 8g 10v 10.2d Oct 25] sparely-made filly: fair
handicapper: stays 8.5f: acts on firm and soft ground: usually held up: sold 8,000 gns.
P. W. Harris

MERLIN'S MISTRESS 3 b.f. Magic Ring (IRE) 115 – Jubilata (USA) 65 (The **–**
Minstrel (CAN) 135) [2001 11m 15.8m Aug 7] second foal: dam, 11f seller winner, also
won seller over hurdles: well beaten in sellers. *W. G. M. Turner*

MER LOCK 3 b.f. Piccolo 121 – Sojourn 87 (Be My Guest (USA) 126) [2001 –: 6m **–**
Aug 22] behind in 2 maidens at Lingfield. *T. J. Naughton*

MERLY NOTTY 5 ch.m. Inchinor 119 – Rambadale 68 (Vaigly Great 127) [2001 38: **–**
f12g 12.4m 10m 12f 12.4g 16f Sep 4] of little account nowadays. *W. Storey*

MER MADE 3 b.f. Prince Sabo 123 – Blue Zulu (IRE) 94 (Don't Forget Me 127) **–**
[2001 40: 6m 5f 7m 8m⁶ Aug 29] little form at 3 yrs: blinkered second appearance: veered
markedly right leaving stall third outing. *T. J. Naughton*

MERRYVALE MAN 4 b.g. Rudimentary (USA) 118 – Salu 65 (Ardross 134) [2001 **70**
73: 13.1m f12g 13d⁶ 11.1s* 11.6g 12.1s⁵ 10.5s³ 10.9m f14g⁴ 10.1v* 13.8d⁴ f12g Nov 23] **a–**
leggy gelding: fair handicapper: won at Hamilton (amateurs) in July and Newcastle in
October: effective at 1¼m (given a test) to 1¾m: acts on fibresand, heavy and good to
firm going: blinkered once: races up with pace: sometimes finds little. *J. M. Jefferson*

MERSEY MIRAGE 4 b.g. King's Signet (USA) 110 – Kirriemuir 51 (Lochnager **77**
132) [2001 94: 7d 6g 6m 7g 6m 6d 6g⁴ 6m² 7g⁵ 6m⁵ 7m⁵ 6v Oct 8] neat gelding: fair
nowadays: effective at 6f/7f: acts on firm and good to soft going: visored twice: sold
4,200 gns, and gelded. *R. Hannon*

MERSEY SOUND (IRE) 3 b.c. Ela-Mana-Mou 132 – Coral Sound (IRE) 67 (Glow **96**
(USA)) [2001 93p: 10.4g⁴ 10m⁴ 12f p10g⁵ p10g³ Dec 29] rather leggy, quite attractive
colt: useful maiden, lightly raced: best effort when seventh to Beekeeper in King George
V Handicap at Royal Ascot third start: ran at Lingfield last 2 starts, off nearly 6 months
before penultimate and very disappointing at odds on final one: stays 1½m well: raced
only on good ground or firmer on turf. *D. R. C. Elsworth*

MESHAHEER (USA) 2 b.c. (Mar 18) Nureyev (USA) 131 – Race The Wild **113**
Wind (USA) 121 (Sunny's Halo (CAN)) [2001 6m* 6m³ 6g* 6g³ Aug 26]
If he never rode another winner there, Frankie Dettori's name would forever
be celebrated at Ascot after his 'Magnificent Seven' in 1996. But he will never have
another day at the course like that again and sometimes, inevitably, days at Ascot
will go badly. The Ascot Festival in September 2001, for instance, was an obvious
disappointment for the jockey, first when withdrawals reduced him to four rides
on the card and then when none of them managed a win, one of them, Noverre,
suffering the ignominy of being beaten by his pacemaker. Before racing, he was
also unveiled, for posterity, in a rather curious-looking pose in a statue to com-
memorate the 'Magnificent Seven', a statue that depicts him in the early, crouched
stages of a flying dismount. Three months earlier, on the Tuesday of Royal Ascot,
those punters who used permutations of Dettori's six mounts for multiple bets, or
even just for singles, may also have felt somewhat uncomfortable. Last of ten in the
Queen Anne Stakes got things off to an inauspicious start and five subsequent
reverses included those on Noverre, caught near the post in the St James's Palace,
on Hatha Anna, who ran on strongly from the rear for fourth place in the Duke of
Edinburgh, and on When In Rome, who went down by a neck in the Queen's Vase.
And then there was Meshaheer. 2/1 favourite for the Coventry Stakes, for a change
the final race on the card, the 'getting-out' stakes, Meshaheer was the subject of
some £60,000 in recorded on-course bets alone. Getting behind from stall one in a
field of twenty made things difficult for a start, and Dettori was forced to switch
him round virtually the entire field before being forced to cut back inside again
late on. Meshaheer eventually finished strongly for third, beaten two necks behind

TNT July Stakes, Newmarket—Meshaheer requires only hand riding
to maintain his advantage over Scottish River, with Prince Dayjur and Doc Holiday (right) next home

Landseer and Firebreak. To cut a long and tortuous story short, Meshaheer should have won. He should have won decisively.

Happily, normal service for Dettori was resumed as soon as the following day, when he rode a treble on Fantastic Light in the Prince of Wales's Stakes, Surprise Encounter in the Royal Hunt Cup and Seba in the Chesham. There were wins too for Meshaheer either side of the Coventry Stakes. At 100/30-on, he took a strong hold before beating eight others easily in a maiden at Doncaster near the end of May, and at 3/1-on he won the TNT July Stakes at Newmarket. There were only five runners at Newmarket and he came through to lead over a furlong out and beat Scottish River by a length and a quarter, clearly the best horse in the race without being particularly impressive. That Meshaheer still had some way to go to figure among the top juveniles was evident when he finished three lengths third of eleven to Johannesburg in the Prix Morny at Deauville, held up in rear, unable to keep up when tracking the winner through but keeping on well nonetheless. 'The plan was always for him to have just four runs and he will not run again this season,' reported trainer David Loder in September.

		Northern Dancer	Nearctic
	Nureyev (USA)	(b 1961)	Natalma
	(b 1977)	Special	Forli
Meshaheer (USA)		(b 1969)	Thong
(b.c. Mar 18, 1999)		Sunny's Halo	Halo
	Race The Wild Wind (USA)	(ch 1980)	Mostly Sunny
	(b or br 1989)	Redpath	Indian Chief
		(b 1974)	Lady Marguery

Meshaheer, who is quite an attractive colt, was rather unfurnished as a two-year-old, but he doesn't have the physical scope to suggest he'll improve greatly from two to three. He races freely (he wore a crossed noseband after Royal Ascot) but his effort at Deauville indicated that he will stay seven furlongs. A look at the three-year-old career of his brother King Charlemagne, however, hints that he may not get the Guineas trip. We thought King Charlemagne should have stayed a mile, but his trainer never gave him the chance to prove it, and he showed his best form at six and a half furlongs. Their sire Nureyev needs no introduction and his magnificent career is detailed in the essay on King Charlemagne. The dam Race The Wild Wind won five races in the United States, including two Grade 2 events and the Grade 1 eight-and-a-half-furlong Santa Maria Handicap. Her three previous foals—Chasethewildwind (by Forty Niner), Chasetheragingwind (by Dayjur) and Chasethewinterwind (by Rahy)—were winners who did not have much in common as racehorses with their dam beyond their names. Meshaheer cost 425,000 dollars as a foal and 525,000 as a yearling. For all Nureyev's fertility problems, he clicked again with Race The Wild Wind in 1999, which resulted in a colt who was bought by Meshaheer's owner for 70,000 dollars as a foal. Race The Wild Wind herself changed hands for 700,000 when in foal with King Charlemagne, having already made 21,000 as a foal, 22,000 as a yearling and 59,000 in March as a two-year-old. Her dam Redpath and grandam Lady Marguery both won a minor race. The former had a poor producing record, but Lady Marguery's eight winners from nine foals included the 1981 Kentucky Derby third Partez and she herself was a half-sister to Margarethen, ancestress of Trillion, Triptych, Generous and Imagine. *D. R. Loder*

MESMERIC (IRE)   3 b.c. Sadler's Wells (USA) 132 – Mesmerize (Mill Reef (USA)   **111**
141) [2001 8g² 10g⁴ 10g⁶ 12.6m⁴ 10g³ 12g² 12.1g* 13.3f* 12d 12d* 12s² Nov 10]
good-topped colt: brother to smart performer up to 1½m Tanaasa, closely related to 2
winners, including smart 6f (at 2 yrs) to 1¼m winner Just Happy (by Night Shift), and
half-brother to several winners, including smart 1990 2-y-o 6f (Gimcrack Stakes) winner
Mujtahid (by Woodman): dam unraced: smart performer: won maiden at Chepstow and
handicaps at Newbury and Newmarket (beat Scorned by length) in September/October:
good head second to Royal Cavalier in November Handicap at Doncaster final start: stays
13f: yet to race on heavy going, acts on any other: visored fifth to ninth starts: sometimes
carries head awkwardly: unseated on way to post fourth outing. *E. A. L. Dunlop*

MESMERIC LADY   2 ch.f. (Apr 29) Zilzal (USA) 137 – Blue Brocade 91 (Reform   **62 d**
132) [2001 5m⁶ 6d 6m 7.1g f6g f7g Oct 22] 10,000Y: half-sister to 3 winners, including
very smart 1¾m/2m winner Orchestra Stall (by Old Vic): dam 10.6f winner: modest
maiden: well beaten last 3 starts: should stay 1m: sold 1,000 gns. *R. Hannon*

METALICO   2 b.f. (Apr 9) Piccolo 121 – Pewter Lass 56 (Dowsing (USA) 124) [2001   **59**
6.1m f8.5g⁵ f7g⁶ Oct 23] 1,400Y: close-coupled filly: third foal: sister to 4-y-o Tinsel
Whistle: dam maiden half-sister to useful 1991 2-y-o 6f winner Misterioso: modest
maiden: best effort on second start: likely to prove best up to 1m: acts on fibresand.
M. Blanshard

METEORITE (IRE)   5 b.g. Bigstone (IRE) 126 – Winning Appeal (FR) 62 (Law   **63**
Society (USA) 130) [2001 14.1m⁴ 14.1m Jul 24] leggy gelding: modest maiden: very
lightly raced nowadays: stays 2m: acts on firm and good to soft going, seemingly not on
soft. *J. M. P. Eustace*

METEOR STRIKE (USA)   7 ch.g. Lomond (USA) 128 – Meteoric 102 (High Line   **– §**
125) [2001 54§: 10g 11.9g 12d Sep 25] big, lengthy gelding: temperamental handicapper:
tried blinkered/tongue tied. *D. Burchell*

METICULOUS   3 gr.g. Eagle Eyed (USA) 111 – Careful (IRE) 59 (Distinctly North   **–**
(USA) 115) [2001 8.2f 8.3m Jun 25] 26,000F, 5,000Y: leggy, quite good-topped gelding:
first foal: dam, maiden best at 6f at 2 yrs, should have stayed further: well held in
maidens at Nottingham (moved poorly to post) and Windsor (failed to handle first bend).
R. F. Johnson Houghton

MEXICAN (USA)   2 b.c. (Mar 19) Pine Bluff (USA) – Cuando Quiere (USA)   **78**
(Affirmed (USA)) [2001 7m⁴ 7d³ 7m Sep 22] $180,000Y: well-grown, close-coupled
colt: sixth foal: half-brother to 3 winners in USA, notably Grade 3 9f winner Cuando
Puede (by Lord At War): dam maiden in USA: fair form when in frame at Ascot and
Yarmouth on first 2 starts in maidens: should stay 1¼m. *C. E. Brittain*

M FOR MAGIC   2 ch.g. (Feb 9) First Trump 118 – Celestine 62 (Skyliner 117) [2001   **72**
5.1f⁶ 6m⁵ 6g⁵ 6.1m⁵ 6v³ 6s Nov 10] 7,000F, 18,000Y: useful-looking gelding: third
living foal: half-brother to 6-y-o Prix Star and 5-y-o Ringside Jack: dam 5f (at 2 yrs) to 7f
winner: fair maiden: third at Windsor: should stay 7f: acts on good to firm and heavy
going: tried blinkered: reportedly lost action third start. *J. L. Spearing*

MIA   4 b.f. Contract Law (USA) 108 – Sianiski (Niniski (USA) 125) [2001 f8.5s f7s⁶   **–**
e7g Jan 27] 7,000Y: third foal: half-sister to 1998 2-y-o 7f winner Sweet Compliance (by
Safawan) and useful 7f (at 2 yrs) to 11f winner Sick As A Parrot (by Casteddu): dam
lightly raced: well held in maidens. *T. D. Barron*

MIA'S REFORM   2 b.g. (Apr 19) Lugana Beach 116 – Lady Caroline Lamb (IRE) 68   **53**
(Contract Law (USA) 108) [2001 5d⁶ 5m 5m 5m 5f⁵ f5g² f5g⁶ 5m⁵ 5g f5g f5s f5s Dec 27]
5,000Y: first foal: dam 5f winner (including at 2 yrs): modest maiden: second in seller at
Southwell: will prove best at bare 5f: acts on fibresand and good to firm ground: tried
blinkered. *H. A. McWilliams*

MI CASTANO (IRE)   2 ch.g. (Mar 22) Fayruz 116 – Tadasna (IRE) (Thatching 131)   **57**
[2001 6g 5.1d⁴ 6m 6.1d f8.5g Oct 9] IR 8,000Y, 13,000 2-y-o, resold 5,200 2-y-o:
useful-looking gelding: first foal: dam unraced half-sister to smart performer up to 1½m
Ela-Aristokrati: modest maiden: well held last 3 starts (gelded after final one): should
stay 7f. *N. P. Littmoden*

MICE DESIGN (IRE)   4 b.g. Presidium 124 – Diplomatist 69 (Dominion 123) [2001   **52**
55: f16g* f16g⁶ f16s 11.6m f14.8s⁵ Sep 6] modest performer: won handicap at Southwell
in January: stays 2m: acts on fibresand, firm and good to soft going. *N. P. Littmoden*

MICE IDEAS (IRE)   5 ch.g. Fayruz 116 – Tender Encounter (Prince Tenderfoot   **38**
(USA) 126) [2001 53, a58: f11s* f12g f11g³ f11g⁵ f11g⁶ 11.5m f11g 9.9m 10m⁶ f12g³   **a60 d**
f11g⁶ f8.5g Dec 1] tall, angular gelding: modest handicapper on all-weather, none on turf:
won at Southwell in January: on downgrade after, leaving N. Littmoden after penultimate
start: stays 1½m: acts on good to firm going, good to soft and fibresand: has taken fierce
hold: sometimes looks none too keen: usually held up. *O. O'Neill*

MICE WORLD (IRE)   4 b.g. River Falls 113 – Naglaa (USA) (State Dinner (USA))   **–**
[2001 f16g e13g⁵ f16g Feb 16] lengthy, workmanlike gelding: little form. *N. P. Littmoden*

MICHAEL MAHER   2 b.c. (May 3) Indian Ridge 123 – Well Proud (IRE) (Sadler's   **– p**
Wells (USA) 132) [2001 7d Nov 3] tall, quite good-topped colt: third foal: dam unraced
half-sister to middle-distance fillies Ghaiya (smart) and Fiesta Gal (high class in USA):
16/1, not knocked about at any stage when well held in 27-runner maiden at Newmarket:
should do better. *M. A. Jarvis*

MICHAELS DREAM (IRE)   2 b.g. (Feb 15) Spectrum (IRE) 126 – Stormswept   **68 d**
(USA) 74 (Storm Bird (CAN) 134) [2001 6m 6m⁵ f6g⁵ 7f³ 7d 7m 8m⁵ 10v 8s Oct 22]
smallish, good-looking gelding: fifth foal: half-brother to 1m winners Amico (by Efisio)
and 4-y-o Stormswell: dam, 2-y-o 5f winner, closely related to Colonel Collins, Lit de
Justice and Commander Collins: fair maiden: below form after third at Redcar: stays 7f:
acts on firm going and fibresand, possibly not on softer than good: tried visored/
blinkered: often races freely. *R. A. Fahey*

MICHAELS GIRL   2 ch.f. (Apr 24) Bluebird (USA) 125 – Bonnie Lassie 74 (Efisio   **66 d**
120) [2001 5s f5g² f5g* 6m⁴ 5.1f⁵ 5m 5g 6d f5g f5s f5s Dec 21] 3,700F, 7,500Y: strong
filly: first foal: dam 2-y-o 1m winner: fair performer: won maiden at Wolverhampton
in May: well held last 5 starts: stays 6f: acts on good to firm going and fibresand.
M. C. Chapman

MICKLEY (IRE)   4 b.g. Ezzoud (IRE) 126 – Dawsha (IRE) 75 (Slip Anchor 136)   **80 d**
[2001 89: e10g f16.2g⁵ 14m 14s 9.9m 11.4g 11.6m 12g f12g³ f12g f14g³ f12g³ f14g⁵
f14g⁵ p13g³ Dec 29] tall, short-backed gelding: fairly useful handicapper at best: on
downgrade in 2001, leaving M. Hammond after second start: barely stays 2m: acts on
firm going, good to soft, fibresand and polytrack: often visored/blinkered: carries head
awkwardly. *P. R. Hedger*

MICKLOW MAGIC   3 b.f. Farfelu 103 – Scotto's Regret (Celtic Cone 116) [2001   **75**
67: 8m* 8m³ 10m 8g⁴ 8g 7f³ 6f Sep 20] strong, workmanlike filly: fair performer: won
maiden at Thirsk in May: stays 1m: acts on firm going, well held on heavy. *C. Grant*

MIDDLETHORPE   4 b.g. Noble Patriarch 115 – Prime Property (IRE) 60 (Tirol 127)   **71**
[2001 71: 12.4d 11.9m 12d* 14s 10.3d⁵ 11.9s⁶ Oct 16] rather sparely-made gelding:
poor mover: fair handicapper: won at Pontefract in August: best at 1¼m/1½m: acts on
soft going, well beaten on firmer than good/fibresand: usually blinkered nowadays:
unseated after exiting paddock on reappearance: tends to wander. *M. W. Easterby*

MIDDLETON GREY   3 gr.g. Ashkalani (IRE) 128 – Petula 103 (Petong 126) [2001   **70**
6m⁵ 6g 6m⁶ 6.1m⁴ 7m f8g* f8g* f8g² p7g⁴ p8g Dec 28] IR 48,000Y: leggy gelding: third   **a91**
foal: half-brother to 5f (at 2 yrs)/6f winner Night Life (by Night Shift) and 6f winner
Etienne Lady (by Imperial Frontier): dam 2-y-o 5f/6f winner: fairly useful on all-weather,
fair on turf: won minor event and handicap at Southwell in October/November: stays
1m: acts on good to firm going and fibresand/polytrack: visored final 2 starts: genuine.
D. W. P. Arbuthnot

MIDHISH TWO (IRE)   5 b.g. Midhish 109 – Tudor Loom (Sallust 134) [2001 69d: **–**
f5g 5m 6m⁵ 5m f7g 6s Nov 10] leggy gelding: has a quick action: fairly useful handicapper in 1999: disappointing since, leaving B. Ellison 520 gns before final start: tried
blinkered/visored/tongue tied. *P. Mitchell*

MIDNIGHT ARROW   3 b.f. Robellino (USA) 127 – Princess Oberon (IRE) 91   **–**
(Fairy King (USA)) [2001 81: 8.3s 7s a6g⁵ a8g a6g a9g Dec 16] leggy, useful-looking

filly: easy mover: fairly useful winner in 2000: well below form in 2001, leaving I. Balding 8,000 gns after second start: blinkered once. *P. Haley, Spain*

MIDNIGHT CAFE (IRE)   2 b. or br.f. (Feb 27) Sri Pekan (USA) 117 – Midnight   **49**
Heights 104 (Persian Heights 129) [2001 6m 6.9m 7f Jul 25] 52,000Y: first foal: dam, 1m to (in Italy) 1½m winner, half-sister to smart performer up to 1¼m Galitzin: poor form in maidens: should be suited by at least 1m. *J. L. Dunlop*

MIDNIGHT COUP   5 br.g. First Trump 118 – Anhaar (Ela-Mana-Mou 132) [2001   –
16.2m 16d Sep 27] fair winning handicapper for G. Hourigan in Ireland in 1999: well held both starts since: stays 17f: acts on firm and good to soft going. *B. G. Powell*

MIDNIGHT CREEK   3 b.g. Tragic Role (USA) – Greek Night Out (IRE) 54   **76**
(Ela-Mana-Mou 132) [2001 67: 11.6g 14m⁴ 16.2m⁴ 12g* 12d³ 11m 11.9s⁴ Oct 25] leggy gelding: fair handicapper: won maiden event at Goodwood in August: best efforts at 1½m: acts on soft and good to firm going. *Mrs A. J. Perrett*

MIDNIGHT ESCAPE   8 b.g. Aragon 118 – Executive Lady 59 (Night Shift (USA))   –
[2001 86: 6m May 26] close-coupled gelding: fairly useful at 7 yrs: well held only 8-y-o start. *C. F. Wall*

MIDNIGHT PARKES   2 b. or br.c. (Apr 11) Polar Falcon (USA) 126 – Summerhill   **63 p**
Spruce 70 (Windjammer (USA)) [2001 6s⁵ 6d Oct 18] half-brother to several winning sprinters, including useful 5f performers My Melody Parkes (by Teenoso) and Lucky Parkes (by Full Extent) and 3-y-o Summerhill Parkes: dam 6f winner: better effort in maidens (modest form) when fifth at Pontefract: hampered leaving stall next time: should do better. *M. A. Jarvis*

MIDNIGHT VENTURE   3 b.g. Night Shift (USA) – Front Line Romance 89 (Caer-   **75**
leon (USA) 132) [2001 75: 6g 6g 6g 6g⁴ 6g 7d* Sep 27] lengthy, rather dipped-backed gelding: fair handicapper: made all at Goodwood in September: stays 7f: acts on soft going, probably on good to firm. *Mrs L. Stubbs*

MIDNIGHT WATCH (USA)   7 b.g. Capote (USA) – Midnight Air (USA) 111   –
(Green Dancer (USA) 132) [2001 –, a52: f9.4s f8g f8g p7g Dec 19] leggy gelding: modest handicapper at 6 yrs: well held in 2001, leaving I. Wood after penultimate start: tried blinkered/tongue tied. *M. A. Allen*

MIDSHIPMAN   3 b.c. Executive Man 119 – Midler (Comedy Star (USA) 121) [2001   **80**
84: 6d 7g 8m 6g f6g⁶ 7s² f8g² f9.4g* f12g* f9.4s* Dec 26] good-topped colt: useful on   **a109**
all-weather, fairly useful on turf: left Mrs D. Haine 8,000 gns after third start: won handicap in November then minor event and handicap in December, all at Wolverhampton: most impressive for final success, beating Guilsborough 3 lengths without needing to be hard ridden: won at 1½m, best effort at 9.4f: acts on fibresand and soft ground, possibly not on good to firm: races prominently. *P. W. D'Arcy*

MIDY'S RISK (FR)   4 gr.g. Take Risks (FR) 116 – Martine Midy (FR) (Lashkari 128)   **83**
[2001 e10g² 10g² 10d³ 12g Jul 14] tall, sparely-made gelding: half-brother to winners in France by Baby Turk and Phantom Breeze: dam French 11f winner: fairly useful maiden: ran twice for A. Hosselet in France at 3 yrs: stays 1¼m: acts on soft going and equitrack. *Mrs N. Smith*

MI FAVORITA   3 b.f. Piccolo 121 – Mistook (USA) (Phone Trick (USA)) [2001 –: 7d   **39**
6s 5.3f 7.1g f6g² f6g 6m 5m 6f⁶ 6m 6d⁴ f6g² f7g⁵ f8g⁵ f6s⁴ Dec 15] small, quite attractive   **a44**
filly: poor maiden: left B. Meehan after sixth start: stays 1m: acts on firm going, good to soft and fibresand: tried blinkered/visored. *Don Enrico Incisa*

MIGHTY MAGIC   6 b.m. Magic Ring (IRE) 115 – Mighty Flash 81 (Rolfe (USA)   –
77) [2001 –: e12g Jan 13] angular mare: very lightly-raced maiden nowadays: tried blinkered/visored. *Mrs P. N. Dutfield*

MIGHTY MAX   3 b.g. Well Beloved 86 – Jokers High (USA) (Vaguely Noble 140)   –
[2001 11.7d Aug 19] half-brother to 1995 2-y-o 5f seller winner Swiss Valley Lady (by Tout Ensemble) and 7f winner Blue Room (by Gorytus): dam unraced: 66/1, tailed off in Bath maiden. *G. A. Ham*

MIGHTY PIP (IRE)   5 b.g. Pips Pride 117 – Hard To Stop 77 (Hard Fought 125)   **68 d**
[2001 68: 13d 10m* 12m⁶ 8d 9f f11g p12g p10g Nov 28] fair handicapper: won at Clonmel in May: below form after, leaving P. Roche in Ireland after fifth start: stays 1¼m: acts on heavy and good to firm ground: tried blinkered: has had tongue tied. *M. R. Bosley*

MIGWAR   8 b.g. Unfuwain (USA) 131 – Pick of The Pops 109 (High Top 131) [2001   – §
–§, a58§: f14g May 25] deep-girthed gelding: one-time useful performer: sometimes
blinkered/visored: tried tongue tied: temperamental. *R. Craggs*

MIKE'S DOUBLE (IRE)   7 br.g. Cyrano de Bergerac 120 – Glass Minnow (IRE) 59   – §
(Alzao (USA) 117) [2001 –§, a49d: f7g⁶ f7g f7s⁵ f9.4g Feb 13] sturdy gelding:
temperamental handicapper: tried blinkered, usually visored. *Mrs N. Macauley*

MILADY LILLIE (IRE)   5 b.m. Distinctly North (USA) 115 – Millingdale Lillie   –
119 (Tumble Wind (USA)) [2001 58: f7g⁴ e8g Jan 13] winning handicapper, lightly raced
nowadays: blinkered once. *K. T. Ivory*

MILAN   3 b.c. Sadler's Wells (USA) 132 – Kithanga (IRE) 117 (Darshaan 133)   **129**
[2001 100p: 10s² 10.5m³ 12m⁵ 12f⁴ 11.9g* 14.6g* 12s⁵ 12f² Oct 27]

The quality of the St Leger in recent years has usually failed to match the
spectacle, but the oldest classic had a very good winner in 2001. Timeform's rating
for Milan's performance on Town Moor was 126+, average at best for most editions
of the race in the second half of the twentieth century but significantly ahead of
most renewals in the 'nineties, when only the St Legers won by Snurge (130) in
1990 and Mutafaweq (129) in 1999 produced higher figures. Milan won with some
ease and, as his second in the Breeders' Cup Turf demonstrated clearly enough, is
capable of better than the bare form of his St Leger victory. His winning margin of
five lengths has been bettered only twice in the St Leger in the last thirty-five years,
by the Charles St George-owned pair Bruni and Michelozzo, winners by ten lengths
and eight respectively in 1975 and 1989, the latter when the race was transferred to
Ayr. No other St Leger winner in that time has triumphed with the same authority as
Milan. His position among St Leger winners may do less than full justice to Milan
with a modern-day readership, and perhaps it would mean more to say instead that
only Galileo was rated his superior among European middle-distance three-year-
olds in the latest season.

For most of the season, it would have seemed ridiculous to suggest that
there was just 5 lb between Galileo and Milan. The previous October, Milan had
also apparently been thought the inferior of another stable companion by Sadler's
Wells called Leopard Spot, who started 2/1 favourite (with Michael Kinane on
board) to Milan's 9/1 in a maiden at the Curragh. Milan beat him by three and a half
lengths (Leopard Spot, by the way, ended 2001 a gelding and still a maiden, and is
now with Jonjo O'Neill). On the one and only time that Milan and Galileo crossed
swords on the racecourse, Galileo started at 3/1-on and Milan at 7/1. In this race,
the listed Ballysax Stakes over a mile and a quarter at Leopardstown in April, the
betting proved an accurate guide as Galileo came out the better by three and a half
lengths at level weights; with Vinnie Roe a length behind Milan, it turned out to be
a remarkably good renewal.

To have lost out in this manner to Galileo was no disgrace, but, much more
worryingly for Milan's status, over his next three outings he was also pushed down
in the European league tables by Chichicastenango, Anabaa Blue, Grandera,

Great Voltigeur Stakes, York—Milan shows improved form,
quickening well to account for favourite Storming Home and Demophilos

Rothmans Royals St Leger Stakes, Doncaster—favourite this time, Milan storms clear at the end of a well-run race to give Aidan O'Brien his seventh European classic success of the year; the supplemented Demophilos is second, with Mr Combustible just holding on for third from When In Rome

Okawango, Storming Home, Snowstorm and Theatre Script, all of these colts beating Milan at level weights, Chichastenango and Anabaa Blue doing so twice. Milan ran only in Group/Grade 1 or Group 2 events after the Ballysax, and his first such venture was promising as he finished strongest of all in a muddling race for the Prix Lupin over ten and a half furlongs at Longchamp, going down by a neck and a head to Chichastenango and Anabaa Blue, looking to have an obvious chance of turning the tables in the Prix du Jockey Club at Chantilly three weeks later given a stiffer test of stamina. However, when Milan tried and failed to come from last to first, again in the Jockey Club, held up last of fourteen, this too proved beyond him. Milan gave Anabaa Blue and Chichastenango a start of five or six lengths early in the straight and, after being checked as well, was not disgraced in finishing fifth, two lengths behind the winner. Kinane stated later in the season that Milan had been unlucky and should have won. That Grandera ended up coming from a similar position but finished a length and a half in front of him, and that a 40/1-chance called Foundation Spirit made up an almost identical amount of ground to Milan, shows clearly, however, that Milan was not the same calibre of horse he became in the autumn. Nineteen days after the French Derby, Milan was sent off 13/8 favourite in the King Edward VII Stakes at Royal Ascot, but could only struggle into fourth, this time ridden from mid-division and meeting no trouble, three lengths behind the winner Storming Home. This display, looking somewhat one paced on the firm ground, would serve to highlight Milan's subsequent transformation all the more clearly.

Milan would not have started favourite, or anything like it, in the St Leger on his performance at Royal Ascot, but his prospects looked a good deal brighter following the Great Voltigeur Stakes at York. Seven of the nine runners held St Leger entries and Milan was the winner, and in striking style too. One plausible explanation for his repeated staying-on-too-late efforts previously over a mile and a half was that he needed a stiffer test of stamina, probably a longer trip. He did not get either at York but still did most of his work on the bridle; also flying in the face of previous evidence, he then surged past leaders Demophilos and Xtra approaching the two-furlong marker, the favourite Storming Home producing his challenge much too late. Milan beat him by a length and a half.

In a ten-runner field for the St Leger, only two from the Voltigeur field took on Milan again, one of those his own pacemaker Saddler's Creek. Demophilos was in the field again, while Storming Home's trainer fielded the Derby fourth and Geoffrey Freer winner Mr Combustible. Aidan O'Brien had a useful second string in the Ebor winner Mediterranean, a half-brother to the 1995 St Leger winner Classic Cliche. A further significant Irish challenger was John Oxx's Pugin, the Irish Derby fourth since touched off in a listed race by Vinnie Roe, the latter providing a late boost to Pugin's prospects by landing the Irish St Leger twenty minutes before the Doncaster version. Godolphin had the seemingly late-developing Alunissage, whose claims seemed to rely more on pedigree (by Rainbow Quest out of Moonshell) than performance. And Beyond and When In

Rome had been first and second in the Queen's Vase. Milan shared favouritism with Mr Combustible in the morning lists, just in front of the Gordon Stakes winner Alexius who, however, had sustained a tendon injury the day before and did not make the line-up. One feature of the latest St Leger, relatively unusual for a modern-day running, was the absence of stamina doubts over nearly all of the participants and Saddler's Creek ensured a good test before weakening to leave Demophilos in front on the final turn. Milan was travelling supremely well and Kinane was riding him with supreme confidence, even switching his mount in behind horses again after finding trouble early in the straight—the reason for the tactics, as he later explained, to avoid a headwind. When finally produced two furlongs out Milan had five lengths to make up on Demophilos; he closed the gap before the furlong marker and put the same distance again between himself and the tiring Demophilos before the line, the runner-up clear of third-placed Mr Combustible and fourth-placed When In Rome.

Milan's St Leger victory showed that he is a markedly better horse than Demophilos and the others at Doncaster, although some, including Mr Combustible, did not run to their best. Though Milan possesses stamina aplenty, he went on to prove himself capable of performing at least as well over a sharp mile and a half. That opportunity did not arrive in a soft-ground Arc de Triomphe on his next start, when he was a bit below his St Leger form, catching the eye however in the closing stages; losing his early position and, as in the French Derby, finding himself on the rail with more than a dozen horses to pass, Milan was still labouring out of the first ten when switched to the outside early in the straight before staying on stoutly in the final furlong to finish fifth of seventeen, eight lengths behind the winner Sakhee but only two behind runner-up Aquarelliste. Circumstances would not have had to be very different for Milan to have finished second. The Arc, incidentally, had

Mr M. Tabor & Mrs John Magnier's "Milan"

provided another striking illustration of the lengths and expense the Ballydoyle team are prepared to go to to get things just right for their runners. Four days before the race, their Shoal Creek, frequently used as a pacemaker, still had an Arc entry but appeared instead on the Southwell all-weather as a work companion to Breeders' Cup Classic hopeful Black Minnaloushe. Milan still had his pacemaker at Longchamp, however, in the shape of Sadler's Creek who was supplemented into the race at a cost of 400,000 francs. At Belmont Park twenty days after the Arc, the option of providing a pacemaker for Milan in the Breeders' Cup Turf was, even for the Ballydoyle team, not viable, and he had no need of one anyway as the American front-runners, aided by the prevailing firm ground, set up a course record. In markedly different conditions to those for the Arc—the winning time was over eleven seconds quicker than at Longchamp—Milan showed his career-best form to run Fantastic Light to three quarters of a length, the pair finishing nearly six lengths ahead of the rest. Held up as usual, Milan was driven along to make his ground on the wide outside around the final turn; fourth entering the straight, he had four lengths to make up on Fantastic Light, who was about to be sent clear, and kept on well, closing noticeably in the final furlong. It was a particularly commendable effort given the relative test of speed the conditions provided on the sharp track.

A rather leggy, useful-looking colt, Milan is effective at a mile and half and stays an extended mile and three quarters well. He acts on soft and good to firm going and, given the way he is ridden, is best with a strong pace. Like so many of his stable companions, he wears a crossed noseband. Milan was bred by Luca Cumani's Fittocks Stud, which, when added to his own St Leger win as a trainer with Commanche Run, reportedly makes Cumani the first person to taste success in both roles since William l'Anson in 1864. Milan's dam, Kithanga, was bred, owned and trained by Cumani. One of his eight winners of the Galtres Stakes in the 'nineties, Kithanga followed up with an easy six-length triumph in the St Simon Stakes but had a disappointing campaign as a four-year-old. Her dam Kalata ran once in France, to no effect, before being sent to the sales as a three-year-old. Cumani's buying her, for 38,000 guineas, might have had something to do with his having recently sent out a two-year-old maiden winner called Kahyasi, a son of Kalata's half-sister Kadissya. As usual with the Aga Khan's studs, good horses abound in the family; one is the 1996 Yorkshire Oaks winner Key Change, a daughter of another half-sister to Kalata. Kithanga, however, is her dam's only winner. Kalata was even mated with her own relation Kahyasi, the dual Derby winner, in 1992 and 1993, but the resulting foals both died before they reached racing age and Cumani sold her in 1995 for 60,000 guineas. Milan is Kithanga's second foal, following the poor maiden Single Currency (by Barathea). Kithanga's 1999 foal is Katmandu, a brother to Milan who is in training with Cumani but did not race in 2001. Kithanga aborted to Peintre Celebre in 1999, had a colt by Machiavellian in 2001 and was barren to her 2001 covering by Sadler's Wells. Milan entered his current ownership for 650,000 guineas at the 1999 Houghton Sales.

Milan (b.c. 1998)	Sadler's Wells (USA) (b 1981)	Northern Dancer (b 1981)	Nearctic
			Natalma
		Fairy Bridge (b 1975)	Bold Reason
			Special
	Kithanga (IRE) (b 1990)	Darshaan (br 1981)	Shirley Heights
			Delsy
		Kalata (b 1984)	Assert
			Kalkeen

Before leaving the subject of Milan's pedigree, his sire and dam's sire are worth further comment. Sadler's Wells and his accomplishments have become the stuff of legend, while Darshaan scarcely needs an introduction either, but the pair's record in conjunction has also become a striking success story. Over the last five seasons on the Flat in Britain and Ireland there have been thirteen runners sired by Sadler's Wells out of Darshaan mares. One of those has been listed-placed, one Group 1-placed, one a listed winner, one a Group 2 winner and no fewer than five—Greek Dance, Ebadiyla, Milan, Quarter Moon and High Chaparral—have been Group 1 winners. It is an extraordinary statistic, and Milan, who stays in training, is fully expected to add further honours to all those connected with him in 2002. *A. P. O'Brien, Ireland*

MILES   3 ch.f. Selkirk (USA) 129 – Tricorne 92 (Green Desert (USA) 127) [2001 8.1d   –
8.2d Sep 21] 50,000Y: quite good-topped filly: third foal: dam 2-y-o 6f winner out of half-sister to Old Vic: pulled hard when well held in maidens at Haydock and Nottingham 3 months apart. *M. A. Jarvis*

MILETRIAN (IRE)   4 b.f. Marju (IRE) 127 – Warg (Dancing Brave (USA) 140) [2001   **113**
113: 12g² 12g 13.9g 16.4m 16g 14.6m⁶ 11f⁴ 12g Sep 28] strong, lengthy, workmanlike filly: smart performer: won Ribblesdale Stakes at Royal Ascot and Park Hill Stakes at Doncaster at 3 yrs: good 1¼ lengths second to Give The Slip in Dubai City of Gold at Nad Al Sheba in February: largely disappointing after, though showed useful form on occasions: stays 1¾m: acts on any going: stood still when stall opened once at 3 yrs: sold 700,000 gns in December. *M. R. Channon*

MILIANA (IRE)   4 b.f. Polar Falcon (USA) 126 – Mirana (IRE) (Ela-Mana-Mou 132)   **108**
[2001 10g* 8.5m⁴ 8d 8s 10m³ 10.5d² 10.5v* Oct 29] leggy, lengthy filly: fourth foal: half-sister to useful 1¼m winner Mirjan (by Tenby) and fairly useful 1½m winner Mirarima (by Shernazar): dam useful Irish 1½m winner from good family: useful performer: won minor event at Longchamp in May and Prix de Flore at Saint-Cloud (by head from Kentucky Rose) in October: creditable efforts when in frame in listed races, including when 1¾ lengths fourth to Sheppard's Watch at Epsom second start despite looking all at sea on track: stirrup broke third outing: stays 10.5f: acts on heavy and good to firm going. *A. de Royer Dupre, France*

MILL AFRIQUE   5 b.m. Mtoto 134 – Milinetta (Milford 119) [2001 39: 14.1m² 16.2s   **39**
Aug 16] rather leggy mare: poor maiden: should stay 2m: acts on firm going: blinkered once at 3 yrs. *Mrs M. Reveley*

MILL DOT KOM   2 ch.g. (Apr 25) Millkom 124 – Bear To Dance 46 (Rambo Dancer   **46 §**
(CAN) 107) [2001 f5g³ f5g f6g³ f6g⁵ 7m⁵ 5.2g⁵ Jun 25] 3,000F, 1,500Y, resold 500Y: **a51 §**
second foal: dam poor maiden out of half-sister to smart miler Nicolotte: modest maiden on all-weather, poor on turf: stays 7f: acts on fibresand and good to firm going: tried visored: probably ungenuine: gelded after final start. *W. G. M. Turner*

MILLENARY   4 b.c. Rainbow Quest (USA) 134 – Ballerina (IRE) 88 (Dancing   **124**
Brave (USA) 140) [2001 122: 12g* 12m³ 12m⁵ 13.3f² 14m² Sep 15]
    Hopes were entertained that the 2000 St Leger winner Millenary would prove good enough to compete successfully at the highest level over a mile and a half in the latest season, but he didn't manage to live up to those expectations. That's not to say his four-year-old season was a let down. Far from it. Millenary improved a little on his three-year-old form, won a Group 2 event on the first of his five starts and ran below form only when failing to act on the course at Epsom. If he is to win a Group 1 race at a mile and a half, however, he will probably have to follow in the footsteps of stable-companion Golden Snake and travel abroad. Either that or the Coronation Cup will have to be run on a more conventional course. Millenary started a short-priced favourite for the latest running of the Coronation Cup which the 1997 St Leger winner, Silver Patriarch, also trained by John Dunlop, had gone on to win the following year. This time around it fell to the 1999 Leger winner Mutafaweq with Millenary only third, beaten four lengths. Millenary, had not looked entirely at ease at Goodwood when winning the previous year's Gordon Stakes and he found the even more undulating track at Epsom very much against him, hanging left from the moment the pace quickened in the straight.
    A repeat of the form Millenary had shown when winning the Sagitta Jockey Club Stakes at Newmarket on his reappearance would have been enough to ensure victory in the Coronation Cup. Millenary and the Prix du Jockey Club winner Holding Court conceded weight all round at Newmarket, the St Leger second Air Marshall receiving 2 lb and the four remaining runners, including the favourite Wellbeing, 5 lb. In a race run at a sound pace, Millenary went with considerable zest and could be named the probable winner some way out. Moving easily into the lead two furlongs out, he galloped on strongly when pushed along and won by two lengths from the favourite's stable-companion Sandmason. Wellbeing, who finished only fourth, went on to finish a short-head second to Mutafaweq at Epsom, where he met Millenary at level weights. The King George VI and Queen Elizabeth

Sagitta Jockey Club Stakes, Newmarket—Millenary gains the fourth pattern-race success of his career, beating Sandmason, with Holding Court and Wellbeing chasing them home

Diamond Stakes at Ascot was the race chosen for Millenary's third outing of the season, and it provided him with much his stiffest task to date. In finishing fifth to Galileo, beaten six lengths, Millenary ran every bit as well as could be expected and the result merely served to underline his limitations. Millenary also acquitted himself well when stepped back up in trip for his last two starts, but found a three-year-old just too good for him on each occasion. Mr Combustible, receiving 6 lb more than weight for age, beat Millenary by two and a half lengths in the Geoffrey Freer Stakes at Newbury; and Vinnie Roe beat him by two lengths in the Irish St Leger at the Curragh, Pat Eddery easing his mount slightly when held by the winners in both races.

Millenary (b.c. 1997)	Rainbow Quest (USA) (b 1981)	Blushing Groom (ch 1974)	Red God
			Runaway Bride
		I Will Follow (b 1975)	Herbager
			Where You Lead
	Ballerina (IRE) (b 1991)	Dancing Brave (b 1983)	Lyphard
			Navajo Princess
		Dancing Shadow (b 1977)	Dancer's Image
			Sunny Valley

Millenary's pedigree was dealt with fully in *Racehorses of 2000*. Suffice to say here that he is the second foal of Ballerina, who gained her sole success in two seasons' racing in a seven-furlong maiden on her only start at two. Her third foal Head In The Clouds, a full sister to Millenary and also his stable companion, developed into a smart performer in the latest season and won the Princess Royal Stakes. A two-year-old half-sister to the pair, also with Dunlop and named Angel of The Gwaun (by Sadler's Wells) has yet to race. Millenary, a leggy, attractive colt, is a good walker and a fluent mover in his faster paces. He has won on soft going, but has done more of his racing on good or firmer and acts on firm. *J. L. Dunlop*

MILLENIUM MOONBEAM (USA)   4 ch.c. Phone Trick (USA) – Shywing (USA)   **85**
(Wing Out (USA)) [2001 101: 7g 7f⁵ 6m 6.1m⁵ 6m 6g 7d⁵ 7s 8d Oct 18] rangy colt: fairly useful handicapper nowadays: left M. Pitman after sixth outing: stays 1m: acts on good to firm and good to soft ground: has had tongue tied: very awkward leaving stall final start. *G. G. Margarson*

MILLENNIA STAR (USA)   3 b.f. Hennessy (USA) 122 – Woodyoubelieveit (USA)   **45**
(Woodman (USA) 126) [2001 f8.5g³ p10g⁵ Nov 20] first foal: dam, US 2-y-o minor stakes winner up to 7f, out of US Grade 3 9f winner Tricky Fingers: poor form in maidens at Wolverhampton and Lingfield: sold 8,000 gns. *J. H. M. Gosden*

MILLENNIUM BUG   5 b.m. Rock Hopper 124 – So Precise (FR) (Balidar 133)   **47**
[2001 –: 11.9s 11.7d³ 11.9s³ 11.5f³ 12d² 11.6g⁵ 11.9m Jul 23] poor maiden: stays 1½m: acts on firm and good to soft ground. *M. Madgwick*

MILLENNIUM CADEAUX (IRE)   3 ch.g. Cadeaux Genereux 131 – Quest of Fire   **73**
(FR) (Rainbow Quest (USA) 134) [2001 75p: 10.5m 9m⁶ 11.5g³ 12.4m² 14.4g⁶ 16v 11m Dec 3] leggy gelding: unimpressive mover: fair maiden: sold from E. Dunlop 5,000 gns before final start: stays 1¾m: acts on good to firm ground, probably on good to soft. *G. Macchi, Italy*

MILLENNIUM DAWN (IRE)   3 b. or br.f. Cadeaux Genereux 131 – Rasaael   **–**
(Warning 136) [2001 8m Aug 25] second foal: dam unraced sister to smart performer up to 9f Mudeer from family of Kayf Tara and Opera House: 16/1, well held in Newmarket maiden: sold 3,000 gns in December. *B. Hanbury*

MILLENNIUM DRAGON   2 b.c. (Jan 29) Mark of Esteem (IRE) 137 – Feather   **97 p**
Bride (IRE) (Groom Dancer (USA) 128) [2001 7d² 7g* 7v⁵ Oct 26] 25,000Y: well-made, quite attractive colt: third foal: closely related to 1¼m winner Bless The Bride (by Darshaan) and half-brother to a winner in Greece by Bluebird: dam, French 10.5f winner, from family of Breeders' Cup Turf winner Kotashaan: won 21-runner maiden at Newmarket in October by 1¼ lengths from Mingora, making most: favourite, best forgiven disappointing effort under very testing conditions in Horris Hill Stakes at Newbury: will stay at least 1m: should make a smart 3-y-o. *M. A. Jarvis*

MILLENNIUM FORCE   3 b.g. Bin Ajwaad (IRE) 119 – Jumairah Sun (IRE) 98   **90**
(Scenic 128) [2001 8s⁶ 8m⁶ 10g 10s⁴ 9.9m⁴ 8m² 8.2m⁴ 8d³ 9g³ 7m* 7.1v² 7d 8.2s³ Oct 30] tall, lengthy, rather unfurnished gelding: has scope: second foal: half-brother to 1999 2-y-o 6f winner Joonayh (by Warning): dam 1¼m winner who stayed 1½m: fairly useful performer: won maiden at Catterick in September: best efforts at 7f/1m: yet to race on firm going, acts on any other: visored (ran well) fifth start: has edged left: held up: gelded after final outing: consistent. *M. R. Channon*

MILLENNIUM HALL   2 b.c. (Feb 25) Saddlers' Hall (IRE) 126 – Millazure (USA)   **75**
71 (Dayjur (USA) 137) [2001 8g 7.1m 8s³ Oct 31] leggy colt: has a quick action: second foal: dam, ran 4 times (should have stayed beyond 7f), daughter of top-class miler Milligram: easily best effort in maidens (fair form) when third to Jawwala at Yarmouth: likely to be suited by 1¼m+: acts on soft ground. *L. M. Cumani*

MILLENNIUM KING   2 b.g. (Feb 22) Piccolo 121 – Zabelina (USA) 57 (Diesis   **85**
133) [2001 6g* 6m⁵ 6m Sep 2] 36,000Y: fourth foal: half-brother to 9f to 11f winner Zorba (by Shareef Dancer) and a 9.5f winner in France by Soviet Star: dam, maiden who stayed 1m, half-sister to US Grade 1 1¼m winner Dance Teacher: fairly useful form: green, won maiden at Newmarket in July by neck from Treetops Hotel: met trouble next time: heavily-backed favourite, lost all chance by rearing as stall opened in nursery at York: will probably stay 7f. *W. Jarvis*

MILLENNIUM KNIGHT   3 ch.g. Kris 135 – High Stepping (IRE) (Taufan (USA)   **75 d**
119) [2001 14.1m³ 14.1g⁵ 11.5m f14g 16v Oct 17] second foal: half-brother to 4-y-o Bint Habibi: dam unraced: disappointing maiden: stays 1¾m: sold 2,500 gns. *B. Hanbury*

MILLENNIUM LADY (USA)   3 ch.f. Woodman (USA) 126 – Salina Cookie (USA)   **54**
(Seattle Dancer (USA) 119) [2001 70: 12f⁴ f8.5g f8.5g f12g Sep 22] quite attractive filly:

fair form in maidens at 2 yrs: well below that level in 2001: should stay at least 1m: sold 3,000 gns in December. *B. W. Hills*

MILLENNIUM MAGIC 3 b.f. Magic Ring (IRE) 115 – Country Spirit (Sayf El **72** Arab (USA) 127) [2001 78: f8.5s⁵ e10g e8g* a6f⁴ a8f⁵ Nov 18] small, good-bodied filly: fair performer: won claimer at Lingfield in February, final start for J. Portman: stays 1m: acts on firm ground and equitrack: edgy sort. *J. M. Hilling, USA*

MILLFIELDS DREAMS 2 b.c. (Apr 2) Dreams End 93 – Millfields Lady 75 (Sayf **–** El Arab (USA) 127) [2001 6f Jun 14] first foal: dam 6f (at 2 yrs, seller) and 1m winner: 100/1, tailed off in maiden at Newbury. *R. Brotherton*

MILLIEMETER 2 ch.f. (Apr 26) Millkom 124 – Whirling Words 75 (Sparkler 130) **–** [2001 f9.4g Dec 8] half-sister to fairly useful 1996 2-y-o 5f winner Chili Concerto (by Chilibang): dam 1m winner: 8/1, well held in seller at Wolverhampton. *P. J. Makin*

MILLIKEN PARK (IRE) 3 ch.f. Fumo di Londra (IRE) 108 – Miss Ironwood **57 d** (Junius (USA) 124) [2001 65: 5m⁵ 5m⁴ 6m 6m 6g Sep 2] workmanlike filly: fair at 2 yrs: modest at best in 2001: raced only at 5f/6f: acts on firm and soft going: has given trouble in preliminaries/been led to post. *Miss L. A. Perratt*

MILLION PERCENT 2 b.c. (Feb 8) Ashkalani (IRE) 128 – Royal Jade 82 (Last **96** Tycoon 131) [2001 5v³ 6m* 6m 6.3g⁴ 6g* 6m² 6g⁶ 6g p7g³ Dec 22] 37,000Y: small, strong colt: second foal: half-brother to 3-y-o Xaloc Bay: dam, 7f winner, half-sister to smart 5f/6f performer Averti: useful performer: won small-field minor events at Yarmouth in May and Ripon (beat Tough Love 5 lengths) in August: good second to Resplendent Cee in listed race at Ripon: shaped well long way final start: best around 6f: acts on good to firm ground. *K. R. Burke*

MILLIONS 4 b.g. Bering 136 – Miznah (IRE) 102 (Sadler's Wells (USA) 132) [2001 **49 §** 68§: f8g f8.5s f12g f7g 10.3s 8s³ 8s 11.1d 12m May 21] strong gelding: poor maiden: left D. Nicholls after second start: effective at 1m (given a test) to 11.6f: acts on soft and good to firm ground: tried blinkered: has been slowly away/virtually refused to race: most untrustworthy. *K. A. Ryan*

MILLKOM ELEGANCE 2 b.f. (Apr 8) Millkom 124 – Premier Princess 45 (Hard **52** Fought 125) [2001 7.5m⁵ 7g 7m Aug 11] 3,000Y: leggy, quite good-topped filly: fourth foal: half-sister to 9.4f winner Rosie Jaques (by Doyoun): dam winning stayer on Flat/over hurdles: modest maiden: best effort on debut: will stay at least 1¼m. *K. A. Ryan*

MILL LORD (IRE) 8 b.g. Aristocracy 111 – Millflower (Millfontaine 114) [2001 **–** 11.6m Jun 11] well held in claimer only Flat start. *C. J. Drewe*

MILLSEC 4 b.f. Petong 126 – Harmony Park 55 (Music Boy 124) [2001 –: 6.1v 6s 5m **–** 8g 5g 7d 6g 7v 10.3s Nov 9] no form in 2001: tried blinkered. *R. Bastiman*

MILLYS FILLY 3 b.f. Polish Precedent (USA) 131 – Lemon's Mill (USA) 80 **–** (Roberto (USA) 131) [2001 12m 12d⁶ Nov 6] first foal: dam, 1½m winner, also useful hurdler/fairly useful chaser up to 3¼m: little sign of ability in maidens at Kempton (in mid-field when hampered and unseated before halfway) and Catterick (reportedly returned lame). *R. Charlton*

MILLY'S LASS 3 b.f. Mind Games 121 – Millie's Lady (IRE) (Common Grounds **–** 118) [2001 79: 5v 5s Nov 9] sparely-made filly: fair performer at 2 yrs: well held both 3-y-o starts: effective at 5f/6f: acts on any going: has started slowly. *M. R. Channon*

MINARDI (USA) 3 br.c. Boundary (USA) 1†7 – Yarn (USA) (Mr Prospector (USA)) **116** [2001 119p: 8g⁴ 8g³ 8m 6.5d⁶ 6s Sep 8] rather leggy, quite attractive colt: fine mover, with a fluent, round action: smart performer: won Phoenix Stakes at Leopardstown and Middle Park Stakes at Newmarket in 2000: in frame first 2 starts at 3 yrs, in 2000 Guineas at Newmarket (4½ lengths fourth to Golan, staying on after being slightly short of room) and Irish equivalent at the Curragh (best effort in 2001, 2¾ lengths third to Black Minnaloushe): below form after in St James's Palace Stakes at Royal Ascot, Prix Maurice de Gheest at Deauville and Sprint Cup at Haydock (poorly drawn): stayed 1m: acted on good to firm and good to soft going: to stand at Walmac International, Kentucky, fee $12,500, Sept 1st. *A. P. O'Brien, Ireland*

MINASHKI (IRE) 2 b.c. (Jan 11) Ashkalani (IRE) 128 – Blushing Minstrel (IRE) 85 **95** (Nicholas (USA) 111) [2001 5g⁴ 5m* 6.3d² 6d 5s* 6g² 5g Sep 15] IR 21,000F, IR 14,000Y: well-made colt: first foal: dam Irish 2-y-o 6f winner: useful performer: won maiden in May and minor event (beat Colourfast by 5 lengths) in August, both at Tipperary: creditable 1½ lengths second to Steaming Home in listed race at the Curragh penultimate start: well beaten in Flying Childers Stakes at Doncaster final one: should stay 7f: acts on soft and good to firm going. *H. Rogers, Ireland*

MINDAHRA   3 b.f. Mind Games 121 – Indiahra 76 (Indian Ridge 123) [2001 –: 7f 5f   –
5g f6g Oct 22] angular, plain filly: no form: tried visored. *M. Mullineaux*

MINDANAO   5 b.m. Most Welcome 131 – Salala 83 (Connaught 130) [2001 92: 12.3s⁶   **79**
10m 11.9d 12m* 10.5d 12g* 11.9s* 14.1g³ Oct 19] leggy mare: fair performer: won
claimers at Beverley and Catterick and apprentice handicap at York between June and
October: effective at 1½m/1¾m: acts on any going: held up: sold 23,000 gns, joined
F. Murtagh. *Miss J. A. Camacho*

MINDEROO   3 b.g. Efisio 120 – Mindomica 63 (Dominion 123) [2001 6d 6g 5.1f   **61**
5g⁴ 7g f8.5g⁵ 7s Oct 15] quite good-topped gelding: third living foal: dam, 7f winner
(including at 2 yrs), half-sister to Fred Darling winner/Oaks fourth Sueboog, herself dam
of 4-y-o Best of The Bests: modest maiden: should stay 1m: acts on good to soft ground
(ran as if something amiss on firm): gelded after final start. *B. W. Hills*

MIND OVER MATTER   3 b.g. Muhtarram (USA) 125 – Veuve (Tirol 127) [2001 –:   **36**
10s⁶ f11g 14.1d 11.5m 10m 12d³ Aug 15] angular gelding: has a round action: poor
maiden: left C. Cyzer 3,000 gns after fifth start: stays 1½m: acts on soft ground.
Patrick J. Flynn, Ireland

MIND SONG   3 b.f. Barathea (IRE) 127 – Discomatic (USA) (Roberto (USA) 131)   **53 +**
[2001 10.2g³ 11.7d Oct 25] seventh living foal: half-sister to 3 winners, including smart
1¾m winner Tuning (by Rainbow Quest): dam, French 9f winner, half-sister to smart
1987 2-y-o 6f performer Digamist: better effort in maidens at Bath in October when 14
lengths third to Najah: retired. *H. R. A. Cecil*

MIND THE SILVER   4 gr.g. Petong 126 – Marjorie's Memory (IRE) 76 (Fairy King   **– §**
(USA)) [2001 63§, a–§: f8g f8g f8s 7m 8m 8m 8d 8m 7.1g 8.1s 8.3m 6m⁶ 7m Aug 30]
temperamental handicapper: tried visored/blinkered. *J. M. Bradley*

MINE FOREVER   2 br.g. (Mar 13) Royal Academy (USA) 130 – Overseas Romance   **49**
(USA) (Assert 134) [2001 5m 5m⁶ 7.5f⁴ 7.1f⁴ 7m 7g 8g⁵ 6g 7g Oct 19] 4,000 2-y-o:
tall, sparely-made gelding: seventh foal: half-brother to fairly useful Irish 7f/1m winner
Foreign Love (by Gulch): dam unraced half-sister to Irish 1000 Guineas winner Trusted
Partner: poor maiden: seems beat at 7f/1m: raced on good going or firmer: looked
wayward (reminders at halfway/hung badly right) sixth start. *A. Berry*

MINE HOST   2 b.c. (Apr 2) Elmaamul (USA) 125 – Divina Mia 66 (Dowsing (USA)   **92**
124) [2001 6m* 7m⁴ 6g Aug 25] 5,500F, IR 25,000Y: good-topped colt: has scope: third
foal: half-brother to 3-y-o So Divine: dam, 2-y-o 6f winner who stayed 11f, out of useful
half-sister to Shirley Heights: fairly useful form: won maiden at Yarmouth in May: stayed
on well when 2¾ lengths fourth to Seba in Chesham Stakes at Royal Ascot: towards rear
throughout in 29-runner sales race at the Curragh: should stay at least 1m. *M. L. W. Bell*

MINE (IRE)   3 b.c. Primo Dominie 121 – Ellebanna 69 (Tina's Pet 121) [2001 71:   **82**
7.1g³ 6m⁴ 8m* 8.2m² 8g* Aug 13] tall, useful-looking colt: fairly useful performer: won
handicaps at Doncaster in July and Thirsk (hung right briefly) in August: stays 1m: raced
only on good/good to firm ground. *J. D. Bethell*

MINGLING   4 b.g. Wolfhound (USA) 126 – On The Tide 72 (Slip Anchor 136) [2001   **85**
82: 12m² 12m⁶ 9f⁵ 10.1g⁴ 10.1m* 10g* 10g 11.8d² 12.3m³ 10.1f³ 12m Sep 22] good-
topped gelding: fairly useful performer: won minor event at Newcastle in June and
handicap at Sandown in July: best at 1¼m/1½m: yet to race on soft/heavy going, acts on
any other: visored final 3-y-o start: has been sweating/edgy: has raced freely/found little:
sold 20,000 gns, joined C. Mann. *M. H. Tompkins*

MINGORA (USA)   2 b.f. (Feb 26) Mtoto 134 – Silk Braid (USA) 105 (Danzig (USA))   **89 p**
[2001 7g² Oct 4] small filly: sixth foal: sister to fairly useful 1996 2-y-o 7f winner Velour
and half-sister to 2 winners, notably smart 7f winner Beraysim (by Lion Cavern): dam, 9f
and 1½m winner, half-sister to Belmont/Preakness winner Risen Star: 14/1, shaped well
when 1¼ lengths second of 21 to Millennium Dragon in maiden at Newmarket, soon
handy and keeping on: bred to be suited by 1¼m/1½m: sure to improve. *D. R. Loder*

MINIHAHA   3 ch.f. First Trump 118 – Indian Lament 52§ (Indian Ridge 123) [2001   **71**
65p: 7m² 8m⁵ 8.2g³ 9.7m* 10m 10s 10.2d⁴ Oct 25] workmanlike filly: second foal: sister
to fairly useful 1999 2-y-o 6f winner Follow Suit: dam, one to avoid, out of sister to very
smart sprinter Prince Sabo: fair performer: won maiden at Folkestone in August: barely
stays 1¼m: acts on firm and good to soft going: races prominently: sold 11,000 gns.
Mrs A. J. Perrett

MINI LODGE (IRE) 5 ch.g. Grand Lodge (USA) 125 – Mirea (USA) 104 (The – Minstrel (CAN) 135) [2001 81: 10d 10.4d 12s Nov 10] tall, close-coupled gelding: fairly useful handicapper at 4 yrs: well held in 2001: sometimes visored. *J. G. FitzGerald*

MINISTRY OF MAGIC (USA) 3 ch.f. Pine Bluff (USA) – Record Setter (USA) **61** (Damascus (USA)) [2001 10s 8s 6v² p6g f7s² f8.5s* Dec 26] $100,000Y, $285,000 2-y-o: useful-looking filly: fifth foal: closely related to winner in USA by Polish Navy: dam, won up to 9f in USA, half-sister to US Grade 2 1½m winner Euphrosyne: modest maiden: stays 8.5f: acts on heavy ground and fibresand: blinkered last 2 starts. *B. J. Meehan*

MINIVET 6 b.g. Midyan (USA) 124 – Bronzewing 103 (Beldale Flutter (USA) 130) **80** [2001 11.9m 12m 11.9d 10m⁵ 10.5d⁵ 12g Aug 3] workmanlike gelding: fairly useful handicapper: stays 1½m, not 1¾m: acts on soft and good to firm going: blinkered (raced too freely) fourth start: often held up. *T. D. Easterby*

MIN MIRRI 3 b.f. Selkirk (USA) 129 – Sulitelma (USA) 63 (The Minstrel (CAN) **85** 135) [2001 77: 10.2f⁵ 7m⁵ 7m⁴ 7m² 7g 7f 8m³ 7m 7.2g⁴ 7d⁶ Sep 4] leggy, close-coupled filly: fairly useful performer: has won at 1m, best efforts at 7f: goes well on good to firm going: sold 6,000 gns, sent to Israel. *M. R. Channon*

MINNIE BLOO MIN (IRE) 2 b.f. (Mar 1) Blues Traveller (IRE) 119 – White **49** Jasmin 53 (Jalmood (USA) 126) [2001 5m² 6g² 5.2g² f5g* f6g³ 7m 6g f6s⁴ 7s⁶ 5v f6g⁶ Dec 17] 500 2-y-o: good-bodied filly: seventh reported foal: half-sister to 1996 2-y-o 7f winner who stayed 1¼m The Deejay (by Desse Zenny) and 6-y-o Ludere: dam 2m winner: poor performer: won seller at Southwell in July: stays 7f: acts on fibresand and good to firm going: consistent. *Miss V. Haigh*

MINSKIP MERLIN 2 b.g. (Apr 17) Sea Raven (IRE) 75 – Minskip Miss 41 (Lucky **72** Wednesday 124) [2001 6m⁶ 5g⁶ 6g² 6m² Sep 22] leggy, good-topped gelding: fourth foal: dam maiden (possibly best at 7f): fair maiden: runner-up at Thirsk (carried head awkwardly) and Catterick: will prove best at 5f/6f: gelded after final start. *T. D. Barron*

MINT APPROVAL (USA) 2 gr. or ro.g. (Mar 24) With Approval (CAN) – Mint – Bell (USA) (Key To The Mint (USA)) [2001 5s 5s 5f Jul 4] third foal: dam, maiden in USA, sister to US 2-y-o 1m minor stakes winner Mintecy: well beaten in maidens: gave trouble at start final outing. *B. J. Meehan*

MINT CAKE 2 b.f. (Mar 3) Namaqualand (USA) – Caroline Connors (Fairy King **42 d** (USA)) [2001 6m 6m⁴ 6f 6g 8g 8m Sep 20] IR 1,500F, IR 2,200Y: close-coupled filly: fourth foal: sister to 3-y-o Wattno Eljohn: dam, winner in Sweden from 6f to 1m, half-sister to useful sprinter El Yasaf: poor maiden: below form after second start. *N. Tinkler*

MINT JULEP (IRE) 3 br.g. Piccolo 121 – Kingdom Princess 69 (Forzando 122) – [2001 8v 8f⁶ 8m 7f 7g 8.1f f9.4g Oct 9] 17,500F, 47,000Y: strong gelding: first foal: dam 7f/1m winner: little form in maidens/handicaps: sent to Denmark. *K. R. Burke*

MINT LEAF (IRE) 4 b.f. Sri Pekan (USA) 117 – Suaad (IRE) 88 (Fools Holme – (USA)) [2001 –: 10m 10.2f Jun 1] of little account nowadays. *Julian Poulton*

MINT ROYALE (IRE) 3 ch.f. Cadeaux Generous 131 – Clarentia 111 (Ballad Rock **44** 122) [2001 –: 6v⁵ 6s 6s 5m 6m Jul 21] neat filly: poor maiden: should stay 6f. *T. D. Easterby*

MINUSCOLO 3 b.f. Piccolo 121 – Wrangbrook (Shirley Heights 130) [2001 66: 5d – 6m 7m 8s p7g f8g Dec 10] fair maiden at 2 yrs: little form in 2001. *J. A. Osborne*

MINUS FOUR (IRE) 3 b.c. Standiford (USA) – Minibar 33 (Dominion 123) [2001 **46** –: 10s⁵ f11g Oct 1] sparely-made colt: poor maiden: not sure to stay beyond 1¼m. *L. A. Dace*

MI ODDS 5 b.g. Sure Blade (USA) 130 – Vado Via 56 (Ardross 134) [2001 48+, a75: **62** f11g³ f11g* f12g² f12g⁴ f11g* e10s³ e10g f9.4g² f12f⁴ 12m⁵ 10f⁴ 10.1g 7m Jul 7] **a87** fairly useful performer on all-weather, modest on turf: won handicaps at Southwell in January and February: effective at 9.4f to 1½m: acts on fibresand/equitrack and good to firm going: usually waited with and races with enthusiasm. *Mrs N. Macauley*

MIRACLE ISLAND 6 b.g. Jupiter Island 126 – Running Game 81 (Run The Gantlet **63** (USA)) [2001 –: f8g⁶ f9.4g 16m 10.9f 11.9g² 10g⁶ 11.6m⁶ 12g Aug 27] tall gelding: fair **a72** on all-weather, modest on turf: effective at 1¼m/1½m: acts on fibresand, soft and firm going: visored once: sometimes tongue tied. *K. R. Burke*

MIRAFIORI (IRE) 2 br.f. (May 4) Inzar (USA) 112 – Monaco Lady 83 (Manado **47** 130) [2001 f5g 7f 7g* 8m 8m f8.5g Nov 3] 4,500 2-y-o: sparely-made filly: half-sister to several winners, including 9f/1¼m winner Twice The Groom (by Digamist) and winner around 1m Missy-S (by Sarab): dam second at 1m: poor performer: won seller at Folkestone in August: probably stays 1m: raced only on good going or firmer on turf, below form on fibresand. *G. C. H. Chung*

MIRIO (FR) 4 ch.c. Priolo (USA) 127 – Mira Monte (Baillamont (USA) 124) **124** [2001 10v* 10.5v* 10.5g³ 12m* Jul 1]

Saint-Cloud's big race was officially titled the Grand Prix de Saint-Cloud-Prix du Centenaire to mark the track's centenary but the field it attracted did not really rise to the occasion. In any case, the winners of the two most recent editions, Montjeu and El Condor Pasa, would have been tough acts to follow. The previous year's Arc runner-up Egyptband started the hot favourite on the back of a recent win in the Grand Prix de Chantilly, with Lingfield Derby Trial winner Perfect Sunday considered her main rival. The rest looked an odd assortment. Neither of the other four-year-old fillies, Acceleration and Beyond The Waves, looked good enough, and neither did the other three-year-old colts, Nolt and Roman Saddle. Denmark's representative Dano-Mast was worthy of a bit more respect on his course-and-distance win in the Prix Jean de Chaudenay in May, but Italy's Super Tassa had yet to show the sort of form that was to win her the Yorkshire Oaks later in the summer.

And then there was Mirio, who had never contested a pattern race of any sort in his life, let alone a Group 1. Mirio might have been venturing into unknown territory so far as the class of the race was concerned, but he was on familiar ground at Saint-Cloud, where he had contested eight of his thirteen previous starts. Four of those runs at Saint-Cloud had produced victories, and he had also won on his reappearance at Longchamp. Only once had he been tried outside minor company, catching the eye with a fast-finishing third to the John Dunlop-trained Inglenook in a listed race at Saint-Cloud the previous autumn. Mirio's best effort prior to the Grand Prix had come at the same track in May in a race which left two very contrasting impressions. On the one hand it was hard not to be impressed by the way he barely came off the bridle in hacking up by eight lengths, giving weight away all round to some useful rivals. Few races, however, can have been won so easily with the winner looking so unenthusiastic, Mirio drawing clear carrying his head awkwardly and flashing his tail vigorously.

It usually pays to race handily at Saint-Cloud, where the straight is only a couple of furlongs long. Nonetheless, Mirio was anchored in last place in the Grand Prix, his rider relating afterwards that, realistically, he had been riding to obtain third or fourth place at best. Turning for home, it soon became clear that Mirio would be playing a bigger part in the finish. As Egyptband delivered her challenge to the front-running Perfect Sunday, Mirio found a perfect run on the rail to lead over a furlong out, running on strongly but again flashing his tail. Perfect Sunday held the below-form Egyptband (later found to have sustained an injury) by a neck, a length and a half behind the winner, the first three finishing clear of the remainder. Regrettably, Mirio had neither the opportunity to confirm his improvement nor to make more of a name for himself. He was being prepared for the Prix de l'Arc de Triomphe when it was announced in September that he had tendonitis in both forelegs and would miss the rest of the season.

Grand Prix de Saint-Cloud—Mirio proves a relevation on his debut in pattern company;
Perfect Sunday (rail) keeps favourite Egyptband out of the runner-up's spot

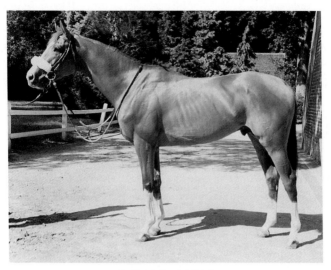

Mr E. Soderberg's "Mirio"

Mirio (FR) (ch.c. 1997)	Priolo (USA) (b 1987)	Sovereign Dancer (b 1975)	Northern Dancer
			Bold Princess
		Primevere (br 1982)	Irish River
			Spring Is Sprung
	Mira Monte (b 1989)	Baillamont (b 1982)	Blushing Groom
			Lodeve
		Mirea (ch 1979)	The Minstrel
			Mlle Vitesse

Mirio, a fourth foal and the third to race, was bought for 520,000 francs as a yearling at Deauville. His dam's first two foals also showed above average form for the de Choubersky stable. Montemiro (by Kris) proved a useful miler in France before moving to the USA, where he won the Grade 3 Inglewood Handicap at Hollywood over eight and a half furlongs. Mira Monte's second foal Mountjoy (by Bering) had more stamina, showing smart form at a mile and a half, including when sixth to Dream Well in the Prix du Jockey Club. The late Francois Boutin figures large in Mirio's history, as he trained not only his sire and dam, but three of his grandparents. Mira Monte won her only outing as a two-year-old over a mile at Deauville by four lengths, securing her a short comment in *Racehorses of 1991*, but she failed to add to that success at three. It was a similar story for grandam Mirea, she too gaining her only win as a two-year-old, over seven furlongs at Maisons-Laffitte. Mirea was out of an unraced half-sister to the Prix Morny winner Filiberto, the Kentucky Oaks winner White Star Line, and to the dam of another Boutin inmate, the top-class middle-distance filly Northern Trick. A flashy chestnut, Mirio stays a mile and a half well. The Grand Prix de Saint-Cloud was his first race on ground firmer than good, and most of his other starts, and all his previous wins, had come on soft or heavy ground. Mirio may not look the most enthusiastic in the closing stages of a race, but his record of never having finished out of the frame shows him in a better light. Good older middle-distance horses are thin on the ground in France these days and it is to be hoped Mirio is able to return as a five-year-old. *J-M. de Choubersky, France*

MISALLIANCE 6 ch.m. Elmaamul (USA) 125 – Cabaret Artiste (Shareef Dancer –
(USA) 135) [2001 –, a46: f12g 17.1s Apr 10] smallish mare: of little account nowadays.
M. E. Sowersby

MISBEHAVIOUR 2 b.g. (May 10) Tragic Role (USA) – Exotic Forest 66 (Dominion **70**
123) [2001 6g 6g³ 6g³ 5.1m 6d Oct 19] leggy, unfurnished gelding: fourth foal: half-
brother to 3-y-o Threezedzz and 4-y-o Zoena: dam 1m winner: fair maiden: best efforts
when third at Folkestone and Lingfield: should stay 7f. *J. G. Portman*

MISCHIEF 5 ch.g. Generous (IRE) 139 – Knight's Baroness 116 (Rainbow Quest **45 §**
(USA) 134) [2001 51d, a46§: e16g e13g f14.8s⁶ e16g⁶ 16g⁶ 15.4m² 14.1d 10m² 14.1s
f14g⁵ f14g³ Dec 3] compact gelding: poor performer: left M. Quinn after fifth start:
effective at 1¼m to easy 2m: acts on fibresand/equitrack and any turf going: sometimes
blinkered/visored: has looked reluctant to race: unreliable. *K. Bell*

MISCHIEVIOUS (IRE) 2 ch.f. (Mar 27) Dr Devious (IRE) 127 – Last Affaire (IRE) –
(Roi Danzig (USA)) [2001 6m 7m 7g Aug 10] IR 6,000Y: smallish, good-topped filly:
second foal: half-sister to Hong Kong 1m winner Best News (by Turtle Island): dam
unraced half-sister to US Grade 1 winners Mourjane and Anka Germania: no sign of
ability in maidens/seller: sold 400 gns. *H. J. Collingridge*

MISCK (IRE) 2 ch.f. (Apr 20) Desert King (IRE) 129 – Sedra 116 (Nebbiolo 125) **– p**
[2001 7d 7d Nov 3] smallish, sturdy filly: half-sister to several winners, including smart
1¼m to 2m winner Samraan (by Green Dancer) and useful 6f (at 2 yrs) to 1m winner Star
Talent (by Local Talent): dam 6f (at 2 yrs) to 1¼m winner: signs of a little ability in
maidens at Leicester and Newmarket: likely to do better. *J. L. Dunlop*

MISCONDUCT 7 gr.m. Risk Me (FR) 127 – Grey Cree 64 (Creetown 123) [2001 58: **49**
11.7d⁵ 14.1m Aug 16] lengthy mare: poor handicapper: stays 1¾m: acts on good to firm
going, soft and fibresand/equitrack: winning hurdler. *J. G. Portman*

MISDEMEANOR 3 b.f. Presidium 124 – Fair Madame 88 (Monseigneur (USA) 127) –
[2001 –: 10s Apr 23] leggy, angular filly: little form: sent to Norway. *J. S. Wainwright*

MISHEAD 3 ch.c. Unfuwain (USA) 131 – Green Jannat (USA) (Alydar (USA)) [2001 –
10d 10g 5m 7m 12d f7g f8g f11g Nov 30] strong, good-topped colt: second foal: half-
brother to winner in Germany by Green Desert: dam, lightly-raced maiden, half-sister to
very smart 1m to 1½mile performer Faithful Son and to dam of Lailani: little form,
including in sellers: trained on debut by Sir Michael Stoute. *M. C. Chapman*

MISHKA 3 b.g. Mistertopogigo (IRE) 118 – Walsham Witch 61 (Music Maestro 119) **81 §**
[2001 71: e6g² 5s³ 6g 5m³ 5f 5m⁴ 6m⁵ 5g² 5s⁴ 5g³ 5.7m⁵ 5g 5g 5d³ 5v f6g⁵ f5g p6g² p7g³ **a71 §**
Dec 28] strong, close-coupled gelding: fairly useful maiden on turf, fair on all-weather:
probably stays easy 7f: acts on heavy going, good to firm and all-weather: often blinkered
(raced freely/tended to wander first occasion)/visored nowadays: carries head awkwardly: unreliable. *Julian Poulton*

MISRAAH (IRE) 4 ch.g. Lure (USA) 131 – Dwell (USA) 96 (Habitat 134) [2001 **120 +**
109: 6d⁵ 6m 5m² 6m⁵ 5m* 6m³ 7m⁴ 7.3f⁵ Aug 18] close-coupled, useful-looking gelding:
improved into very smart performer at 4 yrs: won listed event at Sandown (squeezed
halfway, stormed home to beat Aleganza ½ length) in July: good efforts in July Cup at
Newmarket (4½ lengths third to Mozart) and Tote International Handicap at Ascot (close
fourth to Atavus, fared best of those drawn high) next 2 starts: effective at 5f to 7f: acts on
good to firm and good to soft going: nervy sort, has sweated up: sometimes mulish in
preliminaries (has been very reluctant to go to post/mounted on track/blanketed for stall
entry): has gone freely: usually waited with. *Sir Michael Stoute*

MISS ALL ALONE 6 ch.m. Crofthall 110 – Uninvited 73 (Be My Guest (USA) 126) –
[2001 –: 14.1v May 1] probably of little account nowadays. *J. A. Glover*

MISS AMAZER 2 b.f. (Apr 26) Shaamit (IRE) 127 – Kiss On Time (Lead On Time **63 d**
(USA) 123) [2001 f5g f5g 5v⁶ 5.7f³ 5.7f 6d 6.1s⁵ 6.1m⁶ 7m Aug 30] 900F, 800Y: second
foal: sister to a winner in Spain: dam, French maiden, probably stayed 9f: modest maiden:
third at Bath, easily best effort: stays 6f: acts on firm going. *J. M. Bradley*

MISS AMBER NECTAR 4 b.f. Theatrical Charmer 114 – Avenmore Star 47 –
(Comedy Star (USA) 121) [2001 –: e12g Jan 3] no form. *E. A. Wheeler*

MISS BANANAS 6 b.m. Risk Me (FR) 127 – Astrid Gilberto 75 (Runnett 125) [2001 –
49, a44: e6g f5g* f6s⁴ f5g⁶ f5g⁶ f5g Mar 21] workmanlike mare: poor handicapper: won **a48**
at Southwell in January: best at 5f/6f: acts on fibresand/equitrack, soft and good to firm
going: often tongue tied: none too consistent. *C. N. Kellett*

MISS BEADY (IRE) 3 b.f. Eagle Eyed (USA) 111 – Regal Fanfare (IRE) 94 (Taufan (USA) 119) [2001 54§: 7s 6g⁶ 6m 6m⁵ 7g⁴ 8m⁶ 6g Aug 31] tall, sparely-made filly: poor mover: modest maiden: stays 6f: acts on firm and good to soft ground: tried blinkered: has flashed tail/found little: not one to trust. *Don Enrico Incisa* **52 §**

MISS BEETEE (IRE) 3 b.f. Brief Truce (USA) 126 – Majestic Amber (USA) (Majestic Light (USA)) [2001 60: 6g 5d 6f 7m f6g f8.5g 8.5d Jul 19] smallish, sturdy filly: modest maiden at 2 yrs: little form in 2001. *J. J. Bridger* **–**

MISS BRIEF (IRE) 3 b.f. Brief Truce (USA) 126 – Preponderance (IRE) 85 (Cyrano de Bergerac 120) [2001 72d: e5g⁶ e5g⁵ e5g 5f 8.2m⁵ 6f 7g Aug 8] small filly: fair maiden on turf, modest on all-weather: below best in 2001: best efforts at sharp 5f: acts on firm ground and equitrack: tried visored: sometimes tongue tied: probably not one to trust implicitly. *P. D. Evans* **53 d**

MISS C 2 b.f. (Mar 18) Tachyon Park 87 – Fallal (IRE) 47 (Fayruz 116) [2001 5m³ 5f* 5.1f⁴ 5.1m f5g³ f5g⁶ f6g f5g f5s Dec 21] smallish filly: second foal: dam maiden who stayed 7f: fair on turf, modest on all-weather: won claimer at Beverley in June: in frame in minor events after: will prove best at 5f/easy 6f: acts on fibresand and firm going. *R. Hollinshead* **69 a62**

MISS CASH 4 b.f. Rock Hopper 124 – Miss Cashtal (IRE) (Ballacashtal (CAN)) [2001 43: 9.9m³ 9m Sep 6] workmanlike filly: poor maiden at best: should be suited by 1½m+. *M. E. Sowersby* **35**

MISS CONCEPT (IRE) 2 b.f. (May 18) Frimaire – Hard Sweet (Hard Fought 125) [2001 7.1g Sep 13] half-sister to 3 winners, including useful Irish 7f (at 2 yrs) to 1¼m winner Sweet Nasha (by Nashamaa): dam unraced: 66/1, tailed off in maiden at Chepstow. *F. Jordan* **–**

MISS CORNICHE 2 b.f. (Jan 24) Hernando (FR) 127 – Miss Beaulieu 106 (Northfields (USA)) [2001 7m² 7s* Oct 31] sister to useful 1m winner Miss Riviera Golf, closely related to 2 winners by Niniski, including fairly useful 1¼m and 12.5f winner Riviera Magic, and half-sister to several winners, including useful performer up to 1m Miss Riviera (by Kris): dam 6f (at 2 yrs) and 1¼m winner: 5/4 on, confirmed promise when winning maiden at Yarmouth comfortably by ¾ length from Ela Marathona, racing freely early but quickening well: will stay at least 1m: should make a useful 3-y-o. *G. Wragg* **81 p**

MISS CROISETTE 2 ch.f. (Mar 24) Hernando (FR) 127 – Miss Riviera 103 (Kris 135) [2001 6m 6d Nov 2] strong filly: first foal: dam, 2-y-o 6f winner (later best at 7f/ 1m), half-sister to useful 1m winner Miss Riviera Golf (by Hernando): modest form in maidens at Goodwood and Newmarket 3 months apart, never-nearer eighth of 20 to Feet So Fast on second occasion: will stay 1m: capable of better. *G. Wragg* **60 p**

*Porcelanosa Sprint Stakes, Sandown—an improved performance by Misraah,
who storms past almost the entire field to beat Alegranza (left), with Astonished (No.1) third
and Lord Kintyre (partially hidden) fourth*

MIS

MISS DAMASK 3 b.f. Barathea (IRE) 127 – Startino 111 (Bustino 136) [2001 f8g² **70 +** 8.3g 7s⁵ f8.5g² p10g p10g³ f9.4s* Dec 18] 30,000Y: rangy filly: half-sister to several winners, including 1¼m winner Stoney Valley (by Caerleon) and 4-y-o Second Affair, both fairly useful: dam, 1m and 1½m winner, also third in Park Hill Stakes: fair performer: won maiden at Wolverhampton in December: may prove best up to 1¼m: acts on fibresand and polytrack. *J. A. Osborne*

MISS DAMINA 3 b.f. Primo Dominie 121 – So Beguiling (USA) 49 (Woodman **46** (USA) 126) [2001 52: 8m⁶ 8.2g⁶ 7m 8f 7m 10g³ 10m 13.8m f12g f8.5g⁶ f14.8g f9.4f Dec **a32** 5] smallish, sturdy filly: poor maiden handicapper: left P. Gilligan after eighth start: stays 1¼m: acts on firm going and fibresand, unraced on soft/heavy: tried blinkered/visored. *J. D. Czerpak*

MISS DEVIOUS (IRE) 3 ch.f. Dr Devious (IRE) 127 – Lothlorien (USA) 80 **50** (Woodman (USA) 126) [2001 –: e8g f11g⁴ f12g² f12g⁴ f12g³ 14.1d 16m³ 12f 16g² 15.8g⁴ **a47** 16.2g 13.1m³ 11.9s³ f12g⁵ Nov 26] good-topped filly: modest maiden handicapper: left R. Guest 6,200 gns after eighth start: stays 2m: acts on fibresand, soft and good to firm going: races freely. *Miss J. Feilden*

MISS DORDOGNE 4 b. or br.f. Brief Truce (USA) 126 – Miss Bergerac (Bold Lad **77** (IRE) 133) [2001 81: 8s⁴ 8.1v⁶ Apr 27] lengthy filly: fair performer: stays 1m: acts on soft going: has raced freely/swished tail/carried head high: sold only 1,200 gns (in December). *G. Wragg*

MISSED THE BOAT (IRE) 11 b.g. Cyrano de Bergerac 120 – Lady Portobello **–** (Porto Bello 118) [2001 –: f12g f16.2g Jun 20] of little account on Flat nowadays. *G. A. Ham*

MISS EQUINOX 3 b.f. Presidium 124 – Miss Nelski 84 (Most Secret 119) [2001 54: **48** 6m 7.5m 7.1m⁶ 5f* 5f³ 5m 6.1s³ 5g⁶ 6g 6f 6s 6d Oct 8] tall filly: has a round action: poor handicapper: dead-heated in selling event at Musselburgh in July: effective at 5f/6f: acts on firm and soft going: has drifted right: sent to Spain. *N. Tinkler*

MISS FARA (FR) 6 ch.m. Galetto (FR) 118 – Faracha (FR) (Kenmare (FR) 125) **90** [2001 64: 11.9d² 13.3f² 12m² 13.1m* 14.4g* 13.3f⁴ Sep 22] leggy, angular mare: fairly useful handicapper: won at Bath in August and Kempton in September: stays 1¾m: acts on firm and good to soft going: tough and reliable. *M. C. Pipe*

MISS FIT (IRE) 5 b.m. Hamas (IRE) 125§ – Soucaro (Rusticaro (FR) 124) [2001 **64** 78d: 5d⁵ 5m² 5f 6m 5m³ 5d⁶ 5g 6m 5g² 6f f5g⁵ f5g Nov 30] unfurnished mare: modest **a56** handicapper: best at 5f/6f: acts on fibresand, firm and soft going: visored once: often tongue tied: has been mounted on track/early to post: not an easy ride. *Mrs G. S. Rees*

MISS FLIRTATIOUS 4 b.f. Piccolo 121 – By Candlelight (IRE) 84 (Roi Danzig **75** (USA)) [2001 42: f7g⁴ f6g* e7g f6g* f6g* 6d* 6.1f² f6g* f5g* f6g* 5.1m* 6m f6g f6g f5s Dec 18] tall, useful-looking filly: fair performer: much improved, and won 7 of 8 starts between April and July, namely seller at Southwell and handicaps at Wolverhampton, Leicester, Southwell (3) and Chepstow: well held last 4 outings: effective at 5f/6f: acts on good to soft going, firm and fibresand: tried visored, blinkered nowadays: front runner: game. *D. Haydn Jones*

MISS GEORGE 3 b.f. Pivotal 124 – Brightside (IRE) 99 (Last Tycoon 131) [2001 7d **84** 7m⁴ 7m⁴ 6m² 5f⁴ 5f* 5g Aug 4] 2,600F, 4,600Y: big, workmanlike filly: second foal: dam 2-y-o 1m winner who stayed 1½m: fairly useful performer: won maiden at Beverley in July: effective at 5f/6f: acts on firm ground: has hung left. *K. T. Ivory*

MISS GIGI 2 br.f. (Feb 8) Deploy 131 – Sunley Sinner 93 (Try My Best (USA) 130) **78** [2001 7m³ 7.6m² 8.1g³ 8s⁴ 7.9d Oct 12] quite attractive filly: half-sister to several winners, including 11-y-o Garnock Valley and fairly useful 7f (at 2 yrs) and 1m winner Sunley Seeker (by Elmaamul): dam 2-y-o 7f winner: fair maiden: close fourth in Pontefract nursery: should stay 1¼m: acts on soft and good to firm ground. *M. R. Channon*

MISS GLORY BE 3 b.f. Glory of Dancer 121 – Miss Blondie (USA) (Stop The **42** Music (USA)) [2001 6d 5m 5.1f f8.5g³ 7m 6m f8.5g* f8.5s Dec 26] first foal: dam **a56** unraced: modest performer: best effort when winning maiden at Wolverhampton in December: stays 8.5f: acts on fibresand: has carried head awkwardly. *Miss Gay Kelleway*

MISS HIT 6 b.m. Efisio 120 – Jennies' Gem 95 (Sayf El Arab (USA) 127) [2001 77, **–** a82: f6g 6m 6m Jun 27] sturdy mare: fairly useful handicapper on all-weather, fair on turf at best: only signs of retaining ability in 2001 (trainer fined/jockey suspended/horse banned for 40 days under non-triers' rule on reappearance). *G. A. Butler*

648

MISSILE TOE (IRE) 8 b.g. Exactly Sharp (USA) 121 – Debach Dust 64 (Indian **63**
King (USA) 128) [2001 57, a–: 10g* 8m 10f³ 10.1m 10g 10m³ 10g² 10.4m⁶ Sep 5] **a–**
good-topped gelding: poor walker: modest handicapper: won at Windsor in May: stays
1¼m: acts on firm and good to soft going: tried blinkered/visored (not since 1996): often
slowly away: pulls hard. *D. Morris*

MISS INDIGO 3 b.f. Indian Ridge 123 – Monaiya (Shareef Dancer (USA) 135) [2001 **62**
8g⁴ 8m⁶ 10.2g⁴ 8d Oct 25] IR 90,000Y: lengthy, unfurnished filly: sixth foal: half-sister
to several winners, notably useful 7f (at 2 yrs) and 1¼m winner who stayed 1½m Musetta
(by Cadeaux Genereux): dam French winner around 1m: modest maiden: best effort at
1m: pulled too hard second start. *J. H. M. Gosden*

MISS INFORM 3 b.f. So Factual (USA) 120 – As Sharp As 64 (Handsome Sailor **51**
125) [2001 49: 5v² 5g 5m⁶ f5g⁴ 5g 6.1f⁴ 5m 6v⁵ Oct 29] modest maiden handicapper: **a56**
raced only at 5f/6f: acts on fibresand and any turf going: usually races prominently.
K. O. Cunningham-Brown

MISSING 2 b.f. (Mar 23) Singspiel (IRE) 133 – Misbelief 107 (Shirley Heights 130) **55 p**
[2001 7.5g⁵ 7m⁶ Aug 27] 77,000Y: workmanlike filly: second foal: half-sister to a 7.5f
winner in Italy by Polar Falcon: dam 1¼m to 1¾m winner: modest form in maidens at
Beverley (took strong hold) and Newcastle: should do better at 1¼m/1½m. *T. D. Easterby*

MISSING DRINK (IRE) 3 ch.g. Idris (IRE) 118 – Miss Tuko (Good Times (ITY)) **–**
[2001 49: 10.2f Jun 27] workmanlike gelding: poor maiden in 2000: last only 3-y-o
outing: stays 7f: raced only on good ground or firmer on turf, no form on fibresand: tried
tongue tied: has been slowly away/wandered. *P. D. Evans*

MISSION HILLS 6 b.m. Faustus (USA) 118 – Hot Case 92 (Upper Case (USA)) **44**
[2001 63: e10g e10g e10m³ 10f⁶ 11.9g Aug 9] half-sister to 7f and 1m winner Aitch
N'Bee (by Northfields): dam best at 7f: modest performer for P. Flynn in Ireland in 2000:
poor form in 2001, reportedly lame final start: should stay 1½m: acts on soft going, good
to firm, sand and equitrack: sometimes slowly away. *B. G. Powell*

MISSION TO MARS 2 b.g. (Mar 23) Muhtarram (USA) 125 – Ideal Candidate 80 **–**
(Celestial Storm (USA) 132) [2001 7s 8.2s f9.4g Nov 17] fourth foal: half-brother to
winner in Hungary by Second Set: dam 1¼m to 2m winner: only a little sign of ability in
maidens. *C. A. Cyzer*

MISS JINGLES 2 b.f. (Apr 21) Muhtarram (USA) 125 – Flamingo Times 60 (Good **57**
Times (ITY)) [2001 7g 7m⁴ 7g 7g 7.1m* 7g 7d⁶ Oct 19] leggy filly: fourth foal: half-
sister to French 1½m winner Kaigani (by Pharly): dam 1½m winner: modest performer:
left S. Williams after second start: won nursery at Musselburgh in August: sweating,
soundly beaten in similar event at Newmarket final outing: should stay at least 1m: yet to
race on extremes of going. *J. A. Gilbert*

MISS LIPPY 4 b.f. Emperor Jones (USA) 119 – Anatroccolo 47 (Ile de Bourbon **–**
(USA) 133) [2001 6m Jun 24] 3,800 2-y-o: third foal: dam 7f (including at 2 yrs) and 1m
winner: 12/1, well beaten in maiden at Lingfield. *P. J. Hobbs*

MISS LORILAW (FR) 4 b.f. Homme de Loi (IRE) 120 – Miss Lorika (FR) (Bikala **104**
134) [2001 104: 12m⁵ 11g⁵ 11.9d⁴ 13.5s 15.9g 10f³ 10g⁵ Sep 28] rather leggy, angular
filly: useful performer: best efforts in 2001 on first 2 starts, fifth to Ulundi in minor event
at Goodwood (beaten 8 lengths) and to Abitara in Deutscher Herold-Preis at Hamburg
(beaten 5 lengths): best at 1¼m/1½m: acts on firm going, probably on good to soft: sold
46,000 gns in December. *J. W. Hills*

MISS MANETTE 4 br.f. Dilum (USA) 115 – Lucy Manette 53 (Final Straw 127) **–**
[2001 –: 6.9m 9.7m 8f Sep 4] little form: left R. Curtis after second start. *P. Monteith*

MISS MARPLE 4 b.f. Puissance 110 – Juliet Bravo 61 (Glow (USA)) [2001 63: f6g **54**
6m 5.1f 5f³ 5.7g 6m Jun 27] modest maiden handicapper: best efforts at 5f/6f: raced only
on good going or firmer on turf, well beaten both starts on fibresand. *J. M. Bradley*

MISS MOORE (IRE) 2 b.f. (Apr 6) Tagula (IRE) 116 – Thatcherite (Final Straw **–**
127) [2001 5g 6.1d 6v 7d Oct 18] IR 10,000Y: sparely-made filly: closely related to 1¼m/
11f winner Bajan (by Taufan) and half-sister to 3 winners, including useful 5f (at 2 yrs)
and 1¼m winner Unconditional Love (by Polish Patriot): dam unraced half-sister to very
smart 6f to 1m performer Kampala: well beaten: visored in seller final start. *I. A. Balding*

MISS MOSELLE (IRE) 3 b.f. Zieten (USA) 118 – Topseys Tipple (IRE) 76 (Hatim **79**
(USA) 121) [2001 73: 9m⁵ 10m 11.6g⁶ 10m⁶ 10m² 10.1m* 10.1s² 10.2g 10s² 10s Oct 22]

strong filly: fair performer: won handicap at Epsom in August: stays 1¼m: acts on soft and good to firm ground: visored after third start: held up: sold 15,000 gns. *P. W. Harris*

MISS MOUGINS 3 b. or br.f. Polar Falcon (USA) 126 – Miss Bergerac (Bold Lad **61**
(IRE) 133) [2001 7g 7m May 23] rangy, rather unfurnished filly: seventh foal: half-sister to several winners, including useful 7f winner Allez Cyrano (by Alzao) and 6-y-o Noble Cyrano: dam unraced sister to Cyrano de Bergerac: better effort in maidens when eye-catching eighth to Lurina at Newmarket on debut: likely to stay 1m. *G. Wragg*

MISS NINOTCHKA (IRE) 4 b.f. Petardia 113 – Sin Sceal Eile (IRE) (Pitskelly **–**
122) [2001 –: 9.9m 5m⁶ 5m Jun 11] good-topped filly: no form. *N. Wilson*

MISS OPULENCE (IRE) 2 b.f. (Mar 17) Kylian (USA) – Oriental Splendour 85 **74**
(Runnett 125) [2001 7m³ᵈ 7g* 7.1g² 8g 7g 7d Oct 2] good-topped filly: seventh foal: half-sister to 3 winners, including fairly useful Irish 7f (at 2 yrs) to 1½m winner Really Chuffed (by Shavian) and 5f/6f winner Sizzling (by Sizzling Melody): dam best at 7f: fair performer: won maiden at Newcastle in August: easily best effort in nurseries after when second at Sandown: should stay 1m. *Miss V. Haigh*

MISSOURI 3 b.f. Charnwood Forest (IRE) 125 – Medway (IRE) 60 (Shernazar 131) **84**
[2001 69: 10m² 12m⁴ 10g 12g² 10m³ 11.5g² 15m* 16g Nov 7] big, rather unfurnished filly: fairly useful performer: won handicap at Ayr in September: better at 15f than shorter: raced only on good/good to firm going. *M. H. Tompkins*

MISS PEACHES 3 b.f. Emperor Jones (USA) 119 – Dear Person (Rainbow Quest **54**
(USA) 134) [2001 7d 8g⁶ 6v⁴ Oct 29] 3,200Y: quite good-topped filly: half-sister to 1997 2-y-o 6f seller winner Figawin (by Rudimentary): dam twice-raced half-sister to Galtres Stakes winner Startino: modest form in maidens: stays 1m: gave trouble at stalls on debut. *G. G. Margarson*

MISS PHANTINE (IRE) 3 ch.f. Be My Guest (USA) 126 – Rosananti 107 (Blushing **–**
Groom (FR) 131) [2001 –: 10g 10m 12m Sep 24] well held in maidens. *R. Hollinshead*

MISS PINKERTON 2 b.f. (Mar 28) Danehill (USA) 126 – Rebecca Sharp 122 **81 p**
(Machiavellian (USA) 123) [2001 5m 6.1d* Sep 21] first foal: dam, 7f/1m (Coronation Stakes) winner, from family of 1000 Guineas winner On The House: 9/1, improved markedly when winning maiden at Nottingham by ¾ length from Zandicular, leading late on: should stay 7f: capable of better. *G. Wragg*

MISS PITZ 3 b.f. Cadeaux Genereux 131 – Catch The Sun (Kalaglow 132) [2001 58: **75**
9m 10.1m* 10.1m³ 11.9s⁵ 10m³ 10s⁴ 10v⁵ Oct 15] leggy filly: fair performer: won handicap at Newcastle in July: probably better at 1¼m than 1½m: acts on soft and good to firm going: looked tricky ride sixth start. *E. A. L. Dunlop*

MISS POLLY 3 b.f. Democratic (USA) 101 – My Pretty Niece (Great Nephew 126) **–**
[2001 –: 11.6g 11.5f 8.5d 9.7m 10.1g Sep 14] little form. *J. R. Best*

MISS PROGRESSIVE (IRE) 3 b.f. Common Grounds 118 – Kaweah Maid **48**
(General Assembly (USA)) [2001 52: f8g f8g 8.2s 6.1v² 6d 6.1f 7.1m Jun 17] small filly: poor performer: best at 6f/7f: acts on heavy going and fibresand: inconsistent. *N. Tinkler*

MISS SADIE (IRE) 2 b.f. (Apr 24) Distinctly North (USA) 115 – Raggy (Smoggy **49**
115) [2001 5d 5f⁴ 5f⁴ f5g Jul 2] IR 1,250F, 2,600Y: angular filly: seventh living foal: sister to 4-y-o Distinctly East and half-sister to a winner in Holland by Shalford: dam French 9f winner: poor maiden: should stay 6f: acts on firm ground, well beaten (favourite for seller) on fibresand. *J. J. Quinn*

MISS SAMANTHA 3 b.f. Emarati (USA) 74 – Puella Bona 60 (Handsome Sailor **–**
125) [2001 7d f6g 9g Sep 2] second foal: half-sister to 11f winner Bobona (by Interrex): dam, maiden, should have stayed 1m: well held in maidens. *M. D. I. Usher*

MISS SKICAP 4 b.f. Welsh Captain 113 – Miss Nelski 84 (Most Secret 119) [2001 –: **–**
f7s f9.4s f7g 7.1g 7f 10f 10.5g Jun 8] fair winner at 2 yrs: little form since, leaving Miss S. Wilton after third 4-y-o start: tried blinkered. *W. Clay*

MISS SUTTON 3 b.f. Formidable (USA) 125 – Saysana 63 (Sayf El Arab (USA) 127) **a50**
[2001 40: f8s⁵ f8g² f8g³ f7g* f7g⁴ f7g 8d f7g³ 8m Jul 27] lengthy filly: modest performer: won seller at Southwell in February: effective at 7f/1m: acts on fibresand: visored after third start: usually races up with pace: sold 2,000 gns. *T. G. Mills*

MISS T 2 b.f. (Jan 19) Sabrehill (USA) 120 – Pourville (USA) (Manila (USA)) [2001 **– p**
8s Nov 9] 1,400F: big, useful-looking filly: has scope: first foal: dam, second at 1½m in

France, daughter of top-class Prix Vermeille winner Paulista: 33/1, very green when well held in maiden at Doncaster: looks type to do better. *J. R. Fanshawe*

MISS TANGO 4 b.f. Batshoof 122 – Spring Flyer (IRE) 66 (Waajib 121) [2001 12.3f **61** 11.8f[2] 12m 11.9f[4] Jul 4] modest maiden, lightly raced: stays 1½m: acts on firm ground: visored once: sometimes slowly away: fair hurdler. *M. C. Pipe*

MISS TEAK (USA) 3 b.f. Woodman 126 – Miss Profile (IRE) (Sadler's Wells **95 d** (USA) 132) [2001 83p: 8v[2] 9.9m[4] 10m 10m[5] 8.1s[2] 8.1g[6] 6.1d[5] 6d Oct 12] tall filly: has a round action: maiden: useful effort when 2½ lengths fourth to Foodbroker Fancy in listed race at Goodwood in May, but well below that level otherwise: stays 1¼m: acts on soft and good to firm going: blinkered sixth start, tongue tied fourth: sometimes slowly away (has gone right from stalls): carries head awkwardly/finds little: ungenuine: sold 7,000 gns, sent to Germany. *G. A. Butler*

MISS TEXAS 2 ch.f. (Feb 26) Master Willie 129 – Houston (GER) (Surumu (GER)) – [2001 8v Oct 26] heavy-topped filly: first known foal: dam, 6f to 1¼m winner in Germany: well beaten in maiden at Doncaster: dead. *D. Morris*

MISS TOPOGINO 3 b.f. Mistertopogigo (IRE) 118 – Bitch 53 (Risk Me (FR) 127) – [2001 –: 9.9m 6d[6] 6g Oct 19] strong filly: little form. *J. Parkes*

MISS TRESS (IRE) 3 b.f. Salse (USA) 128 – Circulate (High Top 131) [2001 67: – 8.1m 8m Jul 27] close-coupled, quite attractive filly: fair maiden in 2000: well held both 3-y-o starts. *W. Harris*

MISS ULUWATU (IRE) 2 b.f. (Apr 19) Night Shift (USA) – Miss Kinabalu 50 **64** (Shirley Heights 130) [2001 6m 7.1m[6] 7.9m[2] 7g[5] 7d Oct 2] 10,500F, 9,000Y, 5,200 2-y-o: third foal: closely related to Irish 9f and 1½m winner Miskilette (by Nicolotte) and half-sister to 3-y-o Spinetail Rufous: dam maiden who stayed 1m: modest maiden: second at York: best effort in Epsom nursery next time: barely stays 1m. *E. J. O'Neill*

MISS VALENTINE 2 b.f. (Feb 14) Cosmonaut – Miss Mariner (Rock Hopper 124) – [2001 7g Aug 12] first foal: dam unraced: always behind in maiden at Leicester. *J. F. Coupland*

MISS WORLD (IRE) 4 b.f. Mujadil (USA) 119 – Great Land (USA) (Friend's – § Choice (USA)) [2001 –, a65d: f12g[3] f12g[4] e16g f9.4g f9.4g[5] f12g[2] f11g f12g 10.1m 10f **a41** § 11.5m f12g 9.7m[5] 12g 10g[6] f9.4g[5] 6d Aug 26] leggy, angular filly: poor performer: stays 1½m: acts on fibresand/equitrack: sometimes blinkered/visored/tongue tied: unreliable. *P. S. McEntee*

MISTANOORA 2 b.g. (Apr 12) Topanoora 118 – Mistinguett (IRE) 77 (Doyoun 124) **67 ?** [2001 8.1g[4] 7.1f 8d Oct 3] first foal: dam, 2-y-o 1m winner and later very smart staying hurdler, out of close relative to dam of Sinndar: seemingly best effort in maidens when fourth of 5 at Chepstow: should be suited by 1½m+. *M. R. Channon*

MISTERAH 2 b.f. (Apr 11) Alhaarth (IRE) 126 – Jasarah (IRE) 70 (Green Desert **103** (USA) 127) [2001 6m* 6m[2] 6m* 7d[3] Oct 20] sturdy, quite attractive filly: fifth foal: half-sister to 5-y-o Muqtarb and 4-y-o Lahaay: dam, second at 7f, from good middle-distance family: useful form: won maiden at Newbury in August and listed event at Ayr (beat Good Girl by a head, seeming to idle) in September: under a length third to Distant Valley in Rockfel Stakes at Newmarket, staying on well once switched under 2f out and possibly shade unlucky: will stay 1m. *M. P. Tregoning*

MISTER BENJI 2 b.g. (Mar 20) Catrail (USA) 123 – Katy-Q (IRE) 58 (Taufan **88** (USA) 119) [2001 5d* 6m* 6m 6m 6g[5] 6g Oct 6] quite good-topped gelding: second foal: dam 2-y-o 5f winner: fairly useful performer: won maiden at Musselburgh in April and minor event at Pontefract in May: best effort when fifth to Inishowen in minor event at Doncaster: should stay 7f: unraced on extremes of going: reportedly finished lame third start: short to post next time: gelded after final outing. *J. G. Given*

MISTER BUCKET (IRE) 3 ch.g. Superlative 118 – Rose Bouquet 78 (General **49** Assembly (USA)) [2001 53: 10s 10.2g[3] 9.9m 12m f14.8s Sep 6] poor maiden: probably stays 1¼m. *P. W. Harris*

MISTER CLINTON (IRE) 4 ch.g. Lion Cavern (USA) 117 – Thewaari (USA) 68 **74** (Eskimo (USA) 68) [2001 68: 8s 7f[6] 7m[5] 7.5f[4] 6.1f* 6f[5] 6g 7g 6g 6g[2] 6g[2] 7.6g* 7.6g 7s[5] Sep 30] tall, lengthy gelding: fair performer: won handicap at Nottingham in June and minor event at Lingfield in September: effective at 6f to 7.6f: acts on firm going, probably not on softer than good: has been slowly away: held up. *K. T. Ivory*

651

*Gerrard Richmond Stakes, Goodwood—Mister Cosmi passes the packed stands with great gusto,
ahead of Prince Dayjur and Anna Walhaan (partially hidden)*

MISTER COSMI 2 b.c. (Apr 12) Royal Applause 124 – Degree 81 (Warning 136) **107**
[2001 5m* 6m² 6m⁴ 6m* 6g 6f⁵ 8s³ Oct 21] 18,000Y: leggy, quite good-topped colt:
fluent mover: second foal: dam 1m winner at 4 yrs: useful performer: won maiden at
Hamilton in June and Gerrard Richmond Stakes at Goodwood (by length from Prince
Dayjur) in July: respectable efforts in Mill Reef Stakes at Newbury and Gran Criterium at
Milan (3 lengths third to Sholokhov) last 2 starts: probably stays 1m: acts on firm and
soft going: reportedly sustained cuts to a fetlock while being loaded on to horsebox after
Richmond Stakes, and said to have reopened wound next time. *M. Johnston*

MISTER DOC 3 ch.g. Most Welcome 131 – Red Poppy (IRE) 58 (Coquelin (USA) **61 ?**
121) [2001 –: 11.1d⁵ 10.9m³ 12m 14.1m 10g 10.9f Jun 22] maiden: seemingly best effort
(modest form) on second outing: stays 11f: sometimes slowly away. *D. W. Barker*

MISTER FALCON (FR) 4 b.g. Passing Sale (FR) 125 – Falcon Crest (FR) (Cadoudal **–**
(FR) 124) [2001 14.1v Mar 28] fair performer at best: won claimer at Maisons-Laffitte
for B. Secly (subsequently bought 126,700 francs) in 2000: well held only 4-y-o start on
Flat (flashed tail): stays 13f: raced only on good going or softer: won over hurdles in June/
July (one to treat with caution). *M. C. Pipe*

MISTER HAVANA 4 br.g. Pelder (IRE) 125 – Cee Beat § (Bairn (USA) 126) [2001 **–**
–: f11g 11.6g 8m 11.6g 16v Oct 17] little form. *E. A. Wheeler*

MISTER JOHN 2 b.g. (Mar 17) Unfuwain (USA) 131 – Natural Key 74 (Safawan **–**
118) [2001 7m f8.5g f9.4g p7g Dec 29] first foal: dam 5f/6f winner, including at 2 yrs: no
form, including in seller: blinkered final start. *M. Wigham*

MISTER MAL (IRE) 5 b.g. Scenic 128 – Fashion Parade (Mount Hagen (FR) 127) **92**
[2001 85, a75: 6v⁴ f7g 6s* 6m² 6m 6f 6g² 6m Jun 23] big, strong, lengthy gelding: fairly **a–**
useful handicapper: won at Brighton in May: ran well otherwise when runner-up, beaten
length by Sartorial at York penultimate start: best at 6f/7f: acts on soft and good to firm
ground (below form on firm in 2001): often unruly at stalls (sometimes slowly away):
free-going sort who usually races prominently. *D. Nicholls*

MISTER MCGOLDRICK 4 b.g. Sabrehill (USA) 120 – Anchor Inn 48 (Be My **66**
Guest (USA) 126) [2001 75?: f12g⁶ 10s f12g² f14g Dec 14] fair handicapper, lightly
raced: form in 2001 only when second at Southwell: stays 1½m: acts on heavy ground
and fibresand. *J. G. Given*

MISTER MOUSSAC 2 b.g. (May 3) Kasakov – Salu 65 (Ardross 134) [2001 7.2m **–**
6v⁴ Oct 24] tall, unfurnished gelding: fourth foal: closely related to 5-y-o Clarinch

Claymore and half-brother to 4-y-o Merryvale Man: dam, 11f to 2m winner, out of half-sister to Middle Park winner Creag-An-Sgor: signs of a little ability in maidens at Ayr and Newcastle. *J. M. Jefferson*

MISTER PQ   5 ch.g. Ardkinglass 114 – Well Off (Welsh Pageant 132) [2001 –: 18m   –
16.4m 15m Aug 1] winning handicapper: little form since 1999, including blinkered.
J. G. Smyth-Osbourne

MISTER PUTT (USA)   3 b. or br.g. Mister Baileys 123 – Theresita (GER) (Surumu   **69**
(GER)) [2001 f8g⁶ 8d⁶ f11g 11.6g 11.8f³ 14m³ 14.1g 18m Jul 7] 23,000Y: big, strong
gelding: half-brother to several winners abroad, including French 1¼m and 13f winner
Tamana (by Northern Baby): dam, German 1¼m winner, sister to German Derby winner
Temporal: fair maiden handicapper: barely stays 2¼m: acts on firm ground: has looked
none too keen. *J. A. Osborne*

MISTER RAMBO   6 b.g. Rambo Dancer (CAN) 107 – Ozra 63 (Red Alert 127)   **77 d**
[2001 87: 8v 8s⁵ 7g⁴ 7.6f* 8m 7m⁴ 7f 7d⁶ 7m² 8m 7m 7m 7.2m³ 7g 7s⁵ Oct 20] strong,
lengthy gelding: fair handicapper: won at Chester in May: on downgrade after sixth start:
stays 1m: acts on firm and soft going: tried blinkered: often races up with pace: has started
slowly/carried head awkwardly: sometimes finds little. *D. Nicholls*

MISTER SANDERS   3 ch.g. Cosmonaut – Arroganza 62 (Crofthall 110) [2001 55:   **48**
8g 6m 6m 7.5f 7m 8.5f 11m³ 9m 7m³ 8f⁴ 7.1g 6d 6d⁶ Nov 2] leggy gelding: poor maiden:
effective at 6f, barely at 11f: acts on firm and good to soft ground: has worn visor,
including last 5 starts: has started slowly/raced freely: carries head awkwardly/wanders.
R. M. Whitaker

Miss Elisabetta Tulliani's "Mister Cosmi"

MISTER WATERLINE (IRE) 2 b.c. (Mar 26) Mujadil (USA) 119 – Cree's Figurine **65** 63 (Creetown 123) [2001 5s e5g² f5g³ 5.1f⁴ 5.1m 6m 5.1m⁴ Jul 14] 11,000Y: leggy, **a74** angular colt: half-brother to several winners, notably useful 5f (including at 2 yrs)/6f winner Royale Figurine (by Dominion Royale): dam 2-y-o 5f winner: fair maiden: second at Lingfield: should stay 6f: acts on firm ground, equitrack and fibresand: tongue tied last 2 starts. *P. D. Evans*

MISTER WEBB 4 b.g. Whittingham (IRE) 104 – Ruda (FR) (Free Round (USA)) **41** [2001 66: f14g 13.1m 16d 14.1d Oct 3] fair maiden at 3 yrs: poor form in 2001, leaving B. Smart after first start: stays 13f, seemingly not 2m: acts on good to firm going: has taken strong hold. *Dr J. R. J. Naylor*

MISTER WESTSOUND 9 b.g. Cyrano de Bergerac 120 – Captivate 79 (Mansingh **38 §** (USA) 120) [2001 61d: 7.1m 7d 6m 7.1f 5d⁶ 6g Jul 18] workmanlike gelding: poor handicapper nowadays: stays 7f: acts on any going: tried visored, usually blinkered: tends to start slowly/get behind/hang: not one to trust. *Miss L. A. Perratt*

MIST 'N RAIN 2 b.f. (Mar 5) Ezzoud (IRE) 126 – Uncharted Waters 68 (Celestial **66 p** Storm (USA) 132) [2001 7g⁶ Sep 8] tall, lengthy, unfurnished filly: has scope: third foal: half-sister to 4-y-o Establishment: dam 1¼m/1½m winner: 33/1, never-dangerous sixth of 10 to Distant Valley in minor event at Kempton: should be suited by 1¼m+: probably capable of better. *C. A. Cyzer*

MIST OF TIME (IRE) 2 b.f. (Feb 23) Danehill (USA) 126 – Lothlorien (USA) 80 **72 p** (Woodman (USA) 126) [2001 7g⁴ Aug 17] second foal: dam, 1m winner who stayed 1½m, sister to smart 1¼m/1½m performer Monsajem out of close relative to Sadler's Wells: 10/1, 4 lengths fourth of 10 to Bright And Clear in maiden at Newmarket, unable to sustain effort: should improve. *J. H. M. Gosden*

MISTRAL SKY 2 b.c. (Mar 7) Hurricane Sky (AUS) – Dusk In Daytona 64 (Beveled **–** (USA)) [2001 6m 6v Oct 26] 13,000Y: first foal: dam 7f winner (later won in Jersey): well held in minor event/maiden. *R. Hannon*

MISTRESS MOUSE 2 br.f. (Mar 31) Mistertopogigo (IRE) 118 – Perfidy (FR) **–** (Persian Bold 123) [2001 e5g⁶ e5g⁵ 6m⁶ 6d 6v Oct 26] 500Y: fourth foal: sister to 3-y-o Ellendune Girl and half-sister to a 6f/7f winner abroad by Lead On Time: dam no form: little form, including in sellers. *T. M. Jones*

MISTRESS OFTHEHALL 3 b.f. Son Pardo 107 – Covent Garden Girl 67 (Sizzling **–** Melody 117) [2001 8v 8.3s 10s May 3] second foal: half-sister to a 5f winner in Belgium by Noble Patriarch: dam 5f winner: well held in maidens. *P. D. Evans*

MISTY BOY 4 br.g. Polar Falcon (USA) 126 – Misty Silks 81 (Scottish Reel 123) [2001 **53** 48: f7g 6m 5.2m⁵ f7g 6m* 6.1f⁴ 6m⁴ 6d Jul 19] lengthy gelding: modest handicapper: won at Yarmouth in June: fell final start: best efforts at 6f: acts on firm going, probably on heavy and fibresand: usually blinkered nowadays. *M. J. Ryan*

MISTY DANCER 2 g.r.g. (Mar 16) Vettori (IRE) 119 – Light Fantastic 66 (Deploy **75** 131) [2001 7.1g³ 8g² Sep 19] 12,000Y: third foal: dam, second from 2 starts at 1m, out of half-sister to smart middle-distance performer Icona: fair form in maidens at Sandown and Goodwood (beaten 3 lengths by Simeon) in September: will stay 1¼m. *G. L. Moore*

MISTY EYED (IRE) 3 gr.f. Paris House 123 – Bold As Love (Lomond (USA) 128) **112** [2001 105: 5f 5m² 6d³ 5m⁶ 5d³ 5.2f³ Sep 22] smallish, strong, useful-looking filly: smart performer: best efforts when fast-finishing 1¼ lengths second to Cassandra Go in King's Stand Stakes at Royal Ascot, length third to Sartorial in Prix de Ris-Orangis at Deauville and 4¼ lengths sixth to Mozart in Nunthorpe Stakes at York: also third in listed races at Doncaster (shade unlucky behind Astonished) and Newbury (to The Trader) last 2 starts: effective at 5f/6f: yet to race on soft/heavy going, acts on any other: genuine and consistent. *Mrs P. N. Dutfield*

MISTY MAGIC 4 b.f. Distinctly North (USA) 115 – Meadmore Magic 68 (Mansingh **–** (USA) 120) [2001 59, a–: 8m 7f 6g 7m⁶ 6m 6m 7g 6g⁶ Aug 27] neat filly: modest maiden at 3 yrs: little form in 2001: often blinkered. *K. T. Ivory*

MISTY MAN (USA) 3 ch.g. El Gran Senor (USA) 136 – Miasma (USA) 92 (Lear **56 +** Fan (USA) 130) [2001 8.3v² Nov 8] $60,000Y, resold IR 125,000Y, 1,500 3-y-o: first foal: dam, 6f (at 2 yrs) and 9f (in USA) winner, out of half-sister to high-class US Grade 1 8.5f/9f winner Hidden Lake: 33/1 and tongue tied, 4 lengths second to Fairy Star in maiden at Windsor, staying on after slow start. *Miss J. Feilden*

MITAWA (IRE)   2 b.f. (Apr 14) Alhaarth (IRE) 126 – Susquehanna Days (USA) 68   **73 +**
(Chief's Crown (USA)) [2001 5g⁶ 7d* 7g 7d Oct 2] strong filly: fifth foal: closely related
to fairly useful 1999 2-y-o useful 6f winner Tioga (by Unfuwain) and half-sister to 3
winners, including 5-y-o Balladonia and useful 6f (including at 2 yrs) winner Clef of
Silver (by Indian Ridge): dam, 1m winner, half-sister to dam of Silver Patriarch: fair
performer: won maiden at Ayr in July: well held in nurseries after (raced freely in lead on
first occasion): should stay 1m. *B. W. Hills*

MITCHAM (IRE)   5 br.g. Hamas (IRE) 125§ – Arab Scimetar (IRE) (Sure Blade   **99**
(USA) 130) [2001 100: 5.2d 5m 5m² 5g 6m 5m 5g 5m 6g⁶ 6m 6g 6g³ Sep 19] strong
gelding: usually impresses in appearance: won King's Stand Stakes at Royal Ascot in
1999: only useful handicapper nowadays: several creditable efforts in 2001, including
when placed at Haydock (head second to Coastal Bluff) and Goodwood (third to Baby
Barry): best at 5f/6f: acts on good to firm going, probably on soft: blinkered final 4-y-o
outing: usually held up: has found little: none too consistent. *T. G. Mills*

MITCHELLS MAYHEM   4 b.f. Mistertopogigo (IRE) 118 – Mayday Kitty 38 (Inter-   **–**
rex (CAN)) [2001 –: f5g Mar 8] no form. *Mrs N. Macauley*

MITHRAIC (IRE)   9 b.g. Kefaah (USA) 124 – Persian's Glory (Prince Tenderfoot   **38**
(USA) 126) [2001 38: 12.4d³ 10.1g Aug 17] big, lengthy gelding: has been tubed: poor
nowadays: stays 1½m: acts on firm and soft going: tried blinkered. *W. S. Cunningham*

MITREBEENJANE   2 b.f. (Apr 2) Beveled (USA) – Jane Herring (Nishapour (FR)   **–**
125) [2001 7m 6v Oct 26] fourth foal: dam lightly-raced half-sister to useful but
temperamental 5f/6f performer Sylvan Breeze: well beaten in maidens. *D. J. S. ffrench
Davis*

MITSUKI   2 b.f. (Apr 22) Puissance 110 – Surrealist (ITY) (Night Shift (USA)) [2001   **86**
5.1f 5m 6f* 6m² 6g⁴ 5m 5m* 6g 5f³ 5m⁴ Sep 20] 3,000Y: big, leggy, useful-looking filly:
second foal: dam unraced half-sister to smart Italian 5f to 1m winner Arranvanna: fairly
useful performer: won seller at Thirsk in June and (after being claimed from A. Berry
next start) nursery there in August: clearly best effort when 1¼ lengths fourth to Irish Vale
in listed event at Ayr final start: effective at 5f/6f: raced only on good ground or firmer.
J. D. Bethell

MIXED MARRIAGE (IRE)   3 ch.c. Indian Ridge 123 – Marie de Flandre (FR) 109   **65**
(Crystal Palace (FR) 132) [2001 8d 8.3g 10g⁶ 12g 16.2s 13.1m Sep 10] 33,000F, IR
65,000Y: quite attractive colt: half-brother to several winners, including 7-y-o Solo Mio
and fairly useful 1¼m winner Count of Flanders (by Green Desert): dam, French 1¼m
winner, half-sister to Prix Morny winner Sakura Reiko: fair maiden: probably stays 1¼m:
sold 5,000 gns. *J. W. Hills*

MIZHAR (USA)   5 b. or br.g. Dayjur (USA) 137 – Futuh (USA) 95 (Diesis 133) [2001   **88**
83: f5g⁴ f6s f6g f7s f5g* f6g⁴ f5g⁵ 5s 5g 6m⁶ 6m⁴ 6f⁶ f5g* 6f³ 6g 5s f6g f5g f5g f5s
Dec 15] sturdy gelding: fairly useful handicapper: won for 7-lb claimer Dawn Watson at
Wolverhampton in February (first start after leaving D. Nicholls) and June: off 4 months
before well held last 6 starts: best at 5f/6f: acts on fibresand, firm and good to soft going:
usually blinkered/visored. *D. Shaw*

MIZILLABLACK (IRE)   2 b.f. (Mar 12) Eagle Eyed (USA) 111 – Sketch Pad 78   **93**
(Warning 136) [2001 5s³ 5g* 5f⁴ 5m 5g⁴ 5.2m⁵ 5m 5.2m³ 6g³ Oct 6] IR 2,800F, IR
17,500Y: strong filly: first foal: dam third at 5f at 2 yrs (only season to race): fairly useful
performer: won minor event at Salisbury in May: third in listed race at Newbury (2½
lengths behind Swiss Lake) and Two-Year-Old Trophy at Redcar (beaten 2 lengths by
Captain Rio) on last 2 starts: effective at 5f/6f: acts on firm going. *Mrs P. N. Dutfield*

MIZZEN MAST (USA)   3 gr.c. Cozzene (USA) – Kinema (USA) (Graustark) [2001   **117**
106p: 9v⁴ 9.3g* 10f² 10d 9f 8f* a7f* Dec 26] tall, good sort: smart performer: impressive
winner of Prix de Guiche at Longchamp in May by 6 lengths from Kadence, then ran
well when 1½ lengths second to Chichicastenango in Grand Prix de Paris there following
month, opening up clear lead both times: left Mme C. Head-Maarek in France after fourth
outing: successful in non-graded stakes at Hollywood in November and Malibu Stakes
at Santa Anita in December, latter by 2½ lengths from Giant Gentleman: effective at 7f
to 1¼m: acts on firm going and dirt, probably unsuited by ground softer than good.
R. J. Frankel, USA

MOBAADER (USA)   3 b.c. Danzig (USA) – Retrospective (USA) (Easy Goer (USA))   **84**
[2001 8.2f* 7d² Oct 3] $400,000Y: strong, medium-sized, quite attractive colt: second
foal: brother to 4-y-o Mull of Kintyre: dam, winner up to 9f in USA, half-sister to US

Grade 1 9f/1¼m winner Broad Brush: won maiden at Nottingham in June: creditable second in minor event at Newcastle when next seen out: unlikely to stay beyond 1m: joined J. Sadler in UAE. *Saeed bin Suroor*

MOBIL-ONE DOT COM   3 b.g. Magic Ring (IRE) 115 – Not So Generous (IRE) 68 **49** (Fayruz 116) [2001 9.2d 9.2m³ 10.1m³ May 24] 8,200F, 4,800Y, 2,000 3-y-o: tall gelding: second living foal: dam 5f winner, including at 2 yrs: poor maiden on balance: probably flattered final start: stays 1¼m. *J. S. Goldie*

MOBO-BACO   4 ch.g. Bandmaster (USA) 97 – Darakah 78 (Doulab (USA) 115)   **55** [2001 58: f7g⁵ 6m 5.7f⁴ 6m 6m 8m* 10.2f⁴ f12g Nov 17] good-bodied gelding: modest performer: won selling handicap at Bath in September: stays 1¼m: acts on firesand and probably any turf going. *R. J. Hodges*

MOBTAKER (IRE)   3 b.c. Marju (IRE) 127 – Absaar (USA) 76 (Alleged (USA) 138)   **77** [2001 70p: 8d² 8d* 8f 8d Oct 8] well-made, quite attractive colt: fair performer, lightly raced: won maiden at Pontefract in August: stiff tasks in handicaps after: not sure to stay beyond 1m: yet to race on soft/heavy going, probably acts on any other: sent to UAE. *B. W. Hills*

MODEL QUEEN (USA)   3 ch.f. Kingmambo (USA) 125 – Model Bride (USA)   **76** (Blushing Groom (FR) 131) [2001 66p: 7d 7.5f* 10.3m³ 10d⁴ 8m⁴ Aug 16] good-topped filly: fair performer: won maiden at Beverley in June: stays 1¼m: acts on good to firm ground (gave impression not entirely at ease on firm), seemingly on good to soft: sold 92,000 gns in December. *B. W. Hills*

MODEM (IRE)   4 b.g. Midhish 109 – Holy Water (Monseigneur (USA) 127) [2001   **53** 57: f6g 7m 7.1d⁴ 7m 8d 8g* 7s⁶ f8g f8.5s⁶ Dec 26] modest handicapper on turf, poor   **a41** on all-weather: won selling event at Thirsk in August: stays 1m: acts on soft going and fibresand: tried blinkered, visored after second start: none too consistent. *D. Shaw*

MODESTY   3 b.f. Bin Ajwaad (IRE) 119 – Penny Dip 86 (Cadeaux Genereux 131)   **52 d** [2001 –: 6.1d⁴ 5.1f 5.1d f6g f8.5s Dec 26] smallish filly: disappointing maiden: form only on reappearance: probably stays 6f: blinkered penultimate start. *B. N. Doran*

MODIGLIANI (USA)   3 b.c. Danzig (USA) – Hot Princess 101 (Hot Spark 126) [2001   **106** 98: 7g* 8m 6m Jun 21] close-coupled colt: useful performer: won Desert King European Breeders Fund Tetrarch Stakes at the Curragh in May by head from Scarlet Velvet, making virtually all: creditable efforts after in Poule d'Essai des Poulains at Longchamp (ninth to Noverre) and 6 days later and in Cork And Orrery Stakes at Royal Ascot (seventh to Harmonic Way): effective at 6f to 1m: acts on soft and good to firm going: effective blinkered or not: has hung right and looked difficult ride: sent to USA. *A. P. O'Brien, Ireland*

MODRIK (USA)   3 ch.c. Dixieland Band (USA) – Seattle Summer (USA) (Seattle   **100** Slew (USA)) [2001 96: 8d³ 8g⁴ 10f² 10g⁵ 10.5d³ Aug 9] useful-looking colt: fluent mover: useful performer: good efforts in 2001 after reappearance, including in handicaps at Newmarket (fifth to Alphaeus) and Haydock (blinkered, third to Goncharova) last 2 starts: effective at 1m to 10.5f: yet to race on heavy going, acts on any other: sent to UAE. *N. A. Graham*

MODUS OPERANDI (USA)   5 b.g. Known Fact (USA) 135 – Proud Lou (USA)   **57** (Proud Clarion) [2001 73, a81d: e12g⁵ f12s* f11g⁵ f12g³ 11.6m 12m⁵ Aug 26] strong,   **a64** close-coupled gelding: modest handicapper: won at Southwell in January: stays 1½m: acts on firm going, good to soft and fibresand/equitrack: often slowly away: sometimes races freely/finds little/carries head awkwardly: none too consistent. *T. Keddy*

MOJAVE FLOWER (IRE)   2 b.f. (Feb 28) Desert Style (IRE) 121 – Torrmana   **57 d** (IRE) (Ela-Mana-Mou 132) [2001 e5g 6m⁴ 6m 6m 6g 6g 8.3v⁵ p8g⁴ Nov 24] 1,500Y: first foal: dam unraced: modest maiden: best effort second start: likely to prove best at 5f/6f: blinkered 3 of last 4 outings: has looked a difficult ride. *M. J. Haynes*

MOJO   5 gr.g. Mtoto 134 – Pepper Star (IRE) (Salt Dome (USA)) [2001 10m f6g 10.5d   **–** 6g Aug 10] angular gelding: third foal: brother to 1¼m winner Gunboat Diplomacy: dam unraced half-sister to Kribensis: no form. *Miss L. C. Siddall*

MOJO MAN   2 b.c. (Feb 15) Millkom 124 – Prima Sinfonia 64 (Fairy King (USA))   **70** [2001 7.1g⁵ 8.1s⁴ 7.1v 8s⁵ Oct 16] 35,000Y: sturdy colt: third living foal: half-brother to a winner in Japan by Tragic Role: dam twice-raced half-sister to 3 useful performers, including Italian stayer London Bank: fair maiden: best efforts second and final starts: should be suited by 1¼m+: raced only on good going or softer. *R. Hannon*

MOLAAF 2 b.f. (May 5) Shareef Dancer (USA) 135 – Amber Fizz (USA) (Effervescing **75** (USA)) [2001 6g⁵ 5m⁶ 7m³ 6m 6m Aug 28] small, lengthy filly: sister to unreliable 1¼m/ 1½m winner Ambidextrous, closely related to 7f winner Wasaif (by Lomond) and half-sister to 3 winners, including smart 5f/6f winner Cool Jazz (by Lead On Time): dam ran once: fair maiden: well beaten in Princess Margaret Stakes at Ascot and nursery at Ripon last 2 starts: should stay at least 1m: has run well when sweating. *C. E. Brittan*

MOLAKEM 3 b.c. Darshaan 133 – Calpella 81 (Ajdal (USA) 130) [2001 10.2f 12g⁴ **54** 9.9d 11.8s Oct 15] third living foal: half-brother to useful 1m (at 2 yrs) and 1¼m winner Naskhi (by Nashwan): dam, 1m winner, out of smart Irish 1m and 1¼m winner Calandra (herself half-sister to Oaks winner Intrepidity): reportedly suffered injury to pedal bone at 2 yrs: modest maiden: best effort at 1¼m: sold 4,000 gns. *C. E. Brittain*

MOLLY MALONE 4 gr.f. Formidable (USA) 125 – Pharland (FR) (Bellypha 130) **60** [2001 –: 5.7m⁵ 6m³ 6d 6m⁴ 8m⁵ 8m 7g⁵ Aug 10] leggy, workmanlike filly: modest maiden handicapper: barely stays 1m: acts on good to firm going, possibly not on softer than good: blinkered final start: has started slowly/drifted right. *J. C. Tuck*

MOLLY'S SECRET 3 b.f. Minshaanshu Amad (USA) 91§ – Secret Miss 55 **61** (Beveled (USA)) [2001 f7g⁶ 8m⁵ 7m⁵ 8.1m 8.5m* 10.1s 8.1f f9.4g³ f9.4g² p10g² Dec 19] first foal: dam 5f winner: modest performer: won handicap at Epsom in August: ran well last 2 starts: stays 1¼m: acts on fibresand, polytrack and good to firm ground. *C. G. Cox*

MOLOKO (USA) 2 b. or br.f. (Apr 9) Boundary (USA) 117 – Future Starlet (USA) **54** (Theatrical 128) [2001 7f 6v 6v Nov 8] $60,000Y: fourth foal: half-sister to a winner in USA by Rubiano: dam, won up to 9f in USA and third in Grade 3 9f event, half-sister to US Grade 3 6f/7f winner Spring Beauty: modest form on first start in maidens (tongue tied after). *J. W. Hills*

MOLOMO 4 b.f. Barathea (IRE) 127 – Nishan (Nashwan (USA) 135) [2001 103: 10g³ **104** 12m* 10g⁵ 10d² 10m⁵ 12d 10m⁴ 9.5g² 10d⁵ Oct 18] angular filly: first foal: dam French maiden: useful performer: won maiden at Roscommon in May: mostly creditable efforts at best otherwise, including when runner-up in Pretty Polly Stakes at the Curragh (beaten 2 lengths by Rebelline) and listed event at Gowran (neck behind Julie Jalouse), and fifth to Esyoueffcee in listed race at Newmarket final outing: stays 1½m: yet to race on extremes of ground: tends to carry head awkwardly: has pulled hard. *N. Meade, Ireland*

MOMENT 2 ch.f. (Jan 30) Nashwan (USA) 135 – Well Away (IRE) (Sadler's Wells **59 p** (USA) 132) [2001 7d Oct 15] smallish, sturdy filly: fifth foal: half-sister to 2000 2-y-o 6f (Richmond Stakes) winner Endless Summer (by Zafonic): dam, French 2-y-o 1m winner, sister to Dewhurst dead-heater Scenic from excellent family: 6/1, eleventh of 20 to Opening Ceremony in maiden at Leicester: should do better. *J. H. M. Gosden*

MOMENTOUS JONES 4 b.g. Emperor Jones (USA) 119 – Ivory Moment (USA) **50** (Sir Ivor 135) [2001 50: 10.2f 14.1d 16v⁴ Oct 17] leggy gelding: modest maiden handicapper, lightly raced: stays 2m: acts on heavy going. *M. Madgwick*

MOMENTS IN TIME 3 b.f. Emperor Jones (USA) 119 – Dame Helene (USA) (Sir – Ivor 135) [2001 56d: 10s 11.6s 11.8f f12g⁶ 11d Oct 30] leggy filly: unimpressive mover: modest maiden at 2 yrs: well held in 2001: blinkered last 2 starts. *M. J. Ryan*

MOMENTUM (USA) 3 b.c. Nureyev (USA) 131 – Imprudent Love (USA) (Foolish **115** Pleasure (USA)) [2001 8m³ 8f² 9m* 10g 8m* 8m² 8.9m* 8f² a9f² Dec 9] lengthy, quite attractive colt: half-brother to several winners, including useful 6f (at 2 yrs) and 1¼m winner Indiscreet (by St Jovite): dam won up to 1½m in USA: smart performer: won maiden at Goodwood in June, handicap at Newmarket (beat Halland by head) in July and listed race at York (beat Summoner by neck) in September: also good ¾-length second to Umistim in listed event at Salisbury sixth outing: left J. Hills: won Grade 3 event at Hollywood in December: stays 9f: raced only on good ground or firmer on turf, acts on dirt: tongue tied all starts in Britain. *C. Dollase, USA*

MONACLE 7 b.g. Saddlers' Hall (IRE) 126 – Endless Joy 90 (Law Society (USA) **36** 130) [2001 48: f16g⁵ e16g⁵ e13g⁴ 14.1v Mar 28] big gelding: blind on his off-side: poor handicapper: stays 2m: acts on fibresand/equitrack and firm ground: tried blinkered: has been slowly away/looked ungenuine. *John Berry*

MONALINGA (IRE) 3 ch.g. General Monash (USA) 107 – Malinga (USA) (Alwasmi (USA) 115) [2001 7v f8g 8d 6d 6m Jun 4] IR 4,000F, 10,500Y: close-coupled gelding: first foal: dam unraced: little form: tried blinkered. *M. Brittain*

MONARCHOFTHEGLEN (USA)   2 b.c. (Feb 22) A P Indy (USA) 131 – Milliardaire (USA) (Alydar (USA)) [2001 6g* 7m³ 7g⁴ 7m⁴ Sep 16] $1,500,000Y: rather leggy, attractive colt: closely related to 2 winners in USA by Seattle Slew, notably smart Grade 1 winner up to 9f Lakeway, and half-brother to a winner in USA by Dayjur: dam, US sprinter, won both starts, sister to Saratoga Six and half-sister to Dunbeath: useful performer: landed odds in maiden at the Curragh in May: 2 lengths third to Seba in Chesham Stakes at Royal Ascot: fourth to Hawk Wing in Futurity Stakes (beaten 5¾ lengths) and National Stakes (blinkered, beaten 8 lengths) at the Curragh: should stay 1m: sent to USA. *A. P. O'Brien, Ireland*   **101**

MONASH FREEWAY (IRE)   3 ch.c. General Monash (USA) 107 – Pennine Pearl (IRE) (Pennine Walk 120) [2001 –: 11.6s 12g 8m 11.5f 10g⁴ 16.2g Aug 27] poor maiden handicapper: probably stays 2m: tried blinkered. *Miss Jacqueline S. Doyle*   **40**

MONASH LADY (IRE)   3 ch.f. General Monash (USA) 107 – Don't Be That Way (IRE) (Dance of Life (USA)) [2001 49: e10g* e10g* e10g* e10g⁶ f12g 10s⁶ 10.2d 11.6g⁴ 11.6d⁶ 10g 10g³ 12m⁶ 8s p10g⁵ p10g Dec 19] workmanlike filly: fair performer, better on all-weather than turf: won claimer, handicap and minor event at Lingfield in January: stays 11.6f: acts on firm going, good to soft and equitrack/polytrack: very slowly away final start. *J. S. Moore*   **65 a76**

MONASH PRINCE (IRE)   2 b.c. (Feb 25) General Monash (USA) 107 – Elinor Dashwood (IRE) 61 (Fools Holme (USA)) [2001 6s 6s 6d⁶ 6d³ f5g p6g⁴ Dec 28] IR 6,000F, IR 7,000Y: first foal: dam, Irish maiden best at 1m at 2 yrs, half-sister to useful Irish performer up to 1½m Identify: fair maiden on turf, modest on all-weather: left C. Collins, Ireland, before penultimate start: stays 6f: acts on good to soft going and polytrack. *R. M. Beckett*   **77 a63**

MONDURU   4 b.g. Lion Cavern (USA) 117 – Bint Albadou (IRE) 91 (Green Desert (USA) 127) [2001 70d: 8.1m 10g 8d 10.1g² 10.5s 10g⁴ 9.9s⁶ f11g⁵ 10s³ Oct 25] good-topped gelding: modest maiden handicapper: stays 1¼m: acts on heavy going, probably on good to firm: sold 6,500 gns. *W. R. Muir*   **53**

MONICA GELLER   3 b.f. Komaite (USA) – Rion River (IRE) (Taufan (USA) 119) [2001 70, a60: f8.5s e8g² f8g e10g 9s³ 9s* 9m 8s 8.9d 8s 10v p8g p10g Dec 19] leggy filly: fairly useful handicapper on turf, modest on all-weather: below form after winning at Kempton in May: stays 9f: acts on all-weather, soft and good to firm going: often slowly away. *C. N. Allen*   **86 a59 +**

MONKSFORD   2 b.g. (Mar 12) Minster Son 130 – Mortify (Prince Sabo 123) [2001 5m² 6d² 6d³ 5f⁴ 6f 6m Sep 24] leggy gelding: first foal: dam unraced: fair maiden: runner-up at Newcastle and Hamilton: stays 6f: took strong hold/found little third start: reportedly hit head on stall fifth one. *Denys Smith*   **73**

MONKSTON POINT (IRE)   5 b.g. Fayruz 116 – Doon Belle (Ardoon 124) [2001 108: 5s 5.2d* 6s* 6g⁴ 6s³ 6s 6d⁶ 5v³ 6s⁴ Nov 10] sturdy, good sort: smart performer: better than ever in 2001, winning handicap at Newbury (for second successive year) in April and minor event at Haydock (by 2 lengths from Halmahera) in May: generally respectable efforts at least after, including when third in Sprint Cup at Haydock (3¾ lengths behind Nuclear Debate) and Prix du Petit Couvert at Longchamp: effective at 5f/6f: has form on good to firm ground, goes very well on softer than good: usually visored: has been bandaged: has been early to post (mulish to post sixth outing). *D. W. P. Arbuthnot*   **114**

Tote Ten To Follow Rated Stakes (Handicap), Newbury—Monkston Point lands the race for the second successive year; Blue Velvet is second ahead of Repertory (spotted cap) and Munjiz (striped cap)

MONNAVANNA (IRE) 3 ch.f. Machiavellian (USA) 123 – Mezzogiorno 108 **109** (Unfuwain (USA) 131) [2001 7d³ 7f* 8m² 8f 7d* 8s 6d* 6d² 5g Oct 4] angular filly: good walker: first foal: dam, 7f (at 2 yrs) and 1¼m winner, third in Oaks: useful performer: won maiden at Chester in May and listed races at Deauville (beat Stunning impressively by 5 lengths) in July and Pontefract (beat Perfect Peach by head) in August: good neck second to Deep Sleep in Prix de Seine-et-Oise at Maisons-Laffitte penultimate start: effective at 6f to 1m (soon outpaced over 5f final outing): yet to race on heavy going, acts on any other: reliable: sent to USA. *G. Wragg*

MONO LADY (IRE) 8 b.m. Polish Patriot (USA) 128 – Phylella (Persian Bold 123) **81 §** [2001 76: f12g³ e12s 11.9m* 12m 12d 12g⁵ Jul 18] leggy mare: fairly useful handicapper: won at Brighton in May: probably best around 1½m: acts on good to firm going, good to soft and fibresand/equitrack: blinkered/visored: virtually refused to race last 2 starts: ungenuine. *D. Haydn Jones*

MONOLITH 3 b.c. Bigstone (IRE) 126 – Ancara 109 (Dancing Brave (USA) 140) **83** [2001 9.9m⁴ 10g³ 11.5m⁶ 10v* Oct 8] second foal: half-brother to fairly useful 1¼m winner Anamore (by Sanglamore): dam, French 1¼m and 1½m winner, from very good middle-distance family: fairly useful performer: won maiden at Windsor in October by 1¾ lengths, making most: should stay 1½m: sold 25,000 gns. *Mrs A. J. Perrett*

MON PETITE (IRE) 2 ch.f. (Mar 20) General Monash (USA) 107 – Wide Outside **57** (IRE) 50 (Don't Forget Me 127) [2001 5v f5g 5m 6g* 6g 7m* 7m³ 7d⁵ 7.5s Aug 16] IR 5,000F, IR 12,000Y: small filly: third foal: half-sister to 1999 2-y-o 1m seller winner Timaru (by Shalford): dam maiden sister to smart US Grade 3 9f winner Eastern Memories: modest performer: won sellers at Thirsk in June and Yarmouth in July: stays 7f: acts on good to firm and good to soft going: visored last 6 starts. *J. A. Glover*

MON PREFERE (FR) 6 ch.g. Pistolet Bleu (IRE) 133 – Salve (Sallust 134) [2001 **71** 76: e10g⁵ f9.4g* f12g² e10g* e12g³ e10g⁶ 10s f9.4g p8g p10g Nov 28] fair performer: won claimer at Wolverhampton (left I. Wood £8,000) in February and minor event at Lingfield in March: stays 1½m: acts on heavy going and fibresand/equitrack: blinkered last 2 starts. *R. Brotherton*

MONSAL DALE (IRE) 2 ch.c. (Feb 28) Desert King (IRE) 129 – Zanella (IRE) 87 **65** (Nordico (USA)) [2001 6m⁶ 6m Jun 22] IR 45,000F, IR 85,000Y: strong gelding: second foal: half-brother to unreliable Irish 6.5f winner Paws (by Brief Truce): dam, Irish 2-y-o 7.7f winner who stayed 1¼m, sister to useful Irish performer at 1m/1¼m Malvernico and half-sister to smart stayer Biennale: better effort in Newmarket maidens (fair form) when slow-starting sixth to Class Leader: should stay at least 1m. *J. A. R. Toller*

MON SECRET (IRE) 3 b.c. General Monash (USA) 107 – Ron's Secret 92 (Efisio **65** 120) [2001 74: 6g⁶ 6m 7g⁴ 7g 7.1m⁴ 7g 6d Oct 3] sparely-made colt: fair performer: stays 7f: acts on good to soft ground: has hung right. *J. L. Eyre*

MONSIEUR LE BLANC (IRE) 3 b.g. Alzao (USA) 117 – Dedara (Head For **83 §** Heights 125) [2001 78: 10d 11.8g² 11m 13.3m⁴ 14.1m⁵ 12.5s⁶ 11.8d⁵ Aug 12] quite good-topped gelding: fairly useful maiden: stays 13.3f: acts on good to firm going: blinkered (ran well despite taking strong hold and tending to wander) final 2-y-o start, visored last 5: unreliable: sold 11,000 gns, sent to Spain. *I. A. Balding*

MONTAGU BREEZER (IRE) 3 b.g. Paris House 123 – Forever 'n' Ever (Jasmine **–** Star 113) [2001 6g 6m 5m Jun 29] fourth reported foal: dam Irish maiden: no form. *Jamie Poulton*

MONTANA LADY (IRE) 4 ch.f. Be My Guest (USA) 126 – Invisible Halo (USA) **–** 75 (Halo (USA)) [2001 83: 7s 7m 7f Jun 23] fifth foal: half-sister to 3 winners in Italy: dam 2-y-o 6f winner: fairly useful winner in Ireland in 2000 (trained by J. Bolger/ P. Martin): little form in 2001: stays 1m: acts on good to firm and good to soft ground: has been blinkered/tongue tied. *E. J. O'Neill*

MONTANA MISS 3 b.f. Earl of Barking (IRE) 119 – Cupid Miss (Anita's **80** Prince 126) [2001 78: 8.3s f8g² 7m² 8.2f 8.1f 7.6f³ 8.1s 7.6m f7g 6s Sep 24] rather angular, good-quartered filly: fairly useful performer: effective at 7f/easy 1m: acts on firm going, soft and fibresand: blinkered (sweating/raced too freely) final start: usually front runner: none too consistent. *B. Palling*

MONTANA MOON (IRE) 2 b.g. (Mar 21) Ajraas (USA) 88 – Batilde (IRE) **64** (Victory Piper (USA) 100) [2001 5m 6m² 7d⁶ 7d f6g f7g² f8s Dec 15] IR 7,000Y: small **a57**

gelding: second foal: half-brother to 4-y-o Dakota Sioux: dam placed in Italy: modest maiden: second at Ayr (hung badly left) and Southwell (seller): probably stays 7f: acts on good to firm going and fibresand: tried visored. *R. A. Fahey*

MONTAUROUX (IRE)   2 b.g. (Apr 6) Eagle Eyed (USA) 111 – Lyrical Vision (IRE)   – (Vision (USA)) [2001 6d Oct 18] IR 5,000F, IR 4,500Y: fourth foal: half-brother to 2 winners abroad, including Italian 6.5f (at 2 yrs) and 1m winner Lyrical Song (by Waajib): dam unraced: 66/1, green and very burly, tailed off in Newmarket maiden. *T. M. Jones*

MONTE CARLO (IRE)   4 b.g. Rainbows For Life (CAN) – Roberts Pride 62   – (Roberto (USA) 131) [2001 102: 12g 10g⁶ 13.3m⁵ 21m 16.2s Sep 29] big, close-coupled gelding: has a quick action: useful at 2/3 yrs for R. Hannon: well held in handicaps in 2001. *L. Montague Hall*

MONTECASSINO ABBEY (IRE)   2 b.g. (Mar 26) Danehill (USA) 126 – Battle   **77** Mountain (IRE) (Dancing Brave (USA) 140) [2001 5m⁴ 6g² 6.1d³ Sep 21] 55,000Y: sturdy gelding: second foal: dam, ran twice in France, half-sister to high-class French 7f to 1¼m performer Bigstone: fair form in maidens: placed at Folkestone and Nottingham: gelded after: should stay 7f. *P. W. Harris*

MONTECASTILLO (IRE)   4 b.g. Fairy King (USA) – Arcade (Rousillon (USA)   **113 ?** 133) [2001 85: 7s⁵ 8s² 8m³ 8g² 8d 8m 8g³ 9g⁶ 8m³ 7s⁴ 7g⁴ 7s⁸ Oct 7] quite attractive gelding: seemingly improved performer in 2001, winning minor event (by 10 lengths) in August and Coolmore Stud Home of Champions Concorde Stakes (by 1½ lengths from Toroca, appearing to put up easily best effort) in October, both at Tipperary: respectable tenth to Surprise Encounter in Hunt Cup at Royal Ascot on sixth outing: stays 1m: acts on firm and soft going: tongue tied at 3 yrs: blinkered/visored fourth to seventh outings: sold 120,000 gns, sent to USA. *Charles O'Brien, Ireland*

MONTECRISTO   8 br.g. Warning 136 – Sutosky 78 (Great Nephew 126) [2001 91:   **95** 16s⁵ 12m* 11.9d⁵ 16m³ a16g² 16m⁴ 13.1v³ 16g⁶ Nov 7] leggy, sparely-made gelding: useful handicapper: dead-heated at Southwell in May: generally in good form after: effective at 1½m to 2m: acts on good to firm going, heavy and fibresand/equitrack/dirt: held up: has won twice for a lady rider: genuine. *R. Guest*

MONTE MAYOR GOLF (IRE)   3 b.f. Case Law 113 – Nishiki (USA) (Brogan   **80** (USA) 110) [2001 64, a79: f8.5g³ f8.5g² Feb 8] fairly useful performer: will stay beyond 8.5f: acts on good to soft going and fibresand/equitrack: usually races prominently: tends to flash tail. *D. Haydn Jones*

MONTE MAYOR LADY (IRE)   2 b.f. (Mar 8) Brief Truce (USA) 126 – Busker   – (Bustino 136) [2001 6g 6.1m f8.5g Oct 20] IR 5,000F, 5,200Y: half-sister to several winners, including 7f winner Yellow Ribbon (by Hamas): dam twice-raced half-sister to smart stayer Arden: no form: blinkered in seller final start. *D. Haydn Jones*

MONTESSORI MIO (FR)   2 b.g. (Feb 22) Robellino (USA) 127 – Child's Play   **63** (USA) (Sharpen Up 127) [2001 7s⁵ 8g⁴ f6g³ Nov 12] 75,000Y: good-topped gelding: has scope: fourth foal: brother to 5-y-o Sharp Play and half-brother to 4-y-o Pax: dam, French 10.5f winner, out of half-sister to Precocious and Jupiter Island: modest form in maidens: in frame at Musselburgh and Southwell: gelded after: should stay 1¼m. *M. Johnston*

MONTEV LADY   3 ch.f. Greensmith 121 – Flair Lady 55 (Chilibang 120) [2001 59:   **53** 5.7f 5m³ 5f 5.1f 5.7g⁶ 5g 5.3m⁶ 6.1f 6s f7g⁵ 7d Nov 2] modest performer: below form last 4 starts: effective at 5f/easy 6f: acts on good to firm ground, probably on soft: visored once: tends to wander. *W. G. M. Turner*

MONTOYA (IRE)   2 b.g. (Apr 24) Kylian (USA) – Saborinie 56 (Prince Sabo 123)   **74 ?** [2001 6m⁵ 7f⁵ 6g f8g⁴ Oct 1] 9,000 2-y-o: close-coupled gelding: second foal: dam lightly-raced Irish maiden: easily best effort (fair form, possibly flattered) when fifth in maiden at Newbury second start: should stay 1m: gelded after final outing. *P. D. Cundell*

MONTRAVE   12 ch.g. Netherkelly 112 – Streakella 79 (Firestreak 125) [2001 13.1v⁶   – Oct 16] very lightly-raced maiden on Flat nowadays. *Miss Lucinda V. Russell*

MONT ROCHER (FR)   6 gr.g. Caerleon (USA) 132 – Cuixmala (FR) (Highest   **113** Honor (FR) 124) [2001 113: 8v² 10.6d⁶ 12g* 12m³ 9.9m* 12v 12d* Dec 9] first foal: dam unraced half-sister to Montjeu: smart performer: won minor event at La Teste in May and listed races at Goodwood (beat Marhoob by a neck) in September and Toulouse (by short head from Jomana, repeating win in race in 1999) in December: also good third to

Egyptband in Grand Prix de Chantilly fourth start: effective at 1¼m to 15.5f: acts on soft and good to firm going: has had tongue tied: sometimes blinkered earlier in career. *J. E. Hammond, France*

MONTS MEMORY 2 ch.g. (Apr 5) Fraam 114 – Miss Derby (USA) (Master Derby (USA)) [2001 6m⁵ f6g² 7g³ 6m⁴ 7.5s 7.1s⁴ 8m 7g f7g² Oct 22] 500Y, resold 7,000Y: leggy gelding: half-brother to several winners, including 1998 2-y-o 1m winner Oo Ee Be (by Whittingham) and 5f (including at 2 yrs) winner Miss Siham (by Green Forest): dam won up to 9f in USA: modest maiden: runner-up in sellers at Southwell: will stay 1m: acts on good to firm going, soft and fibresand: blinkered sixth and final appearances: sold 1,400 gns, sent to Denmark. *K. A. Ryan* **56**

MONTURANI (IRE) 2 b.f. (Mar 9) Indian Ridge 123 – Mezzogiorno 108 (Unfuwain (USA) 131) [2001 7d³ Nov 3] big, good-topped filly: has scope: second foal: half-sister to 3-y-o Monnavanna: dam, 7f (at 2 yrs) and 1¼m winner, third in Oaks: 12/1, promising 3 lengths third of 21 to Maid To Perfection in maiden at Newmarket, soon bustled along but staying on strongly once starting to get hang of things: will stay at least 1m: sure to win a maiden before going on to better things. *G. Wragg* **77 P**

MOO-AZ (USA) 4 b.g. Red Ransom (USA) – Fappies Cosy Miss (USA) (Fappiano (USA)) [2001 90: 10.4s 7s p8g p7g p7g Dec 12] quite good-topped, workmanlike gelding: only modest form at best in 2001: stays 1m: acts on good to firm ground: tried visored. *C. A. Dwyer* **59**

MOOCHA CHA MAN 5 b.g. Sizzling Melody 117 – Nilu (IRE) 58 (Ballad Rock 122) [2001 60+, a67: f7g⁵ f6s f6g⁵ f6g⁶ f6g⁴ Mar 15] lengthy gelding: modest performer: probably best at 5f/6f: acts on fibresand, good to firm and heavy going: usually blinkered, has been visored: sold 1,900 gns, sent to Sweden. *B. A. McMahon* **56**

MOOJAZ 3 b.f. Lahib (USA) 129 – Numuthej (USA) 50 (Nureyev (USA) 131) [2001 8.3m³ 8.3m* 7.6g 8d Oct 8] medium-sized filly: third foal: half-sister to 1¼m winner Big Wheel (by Mujtahid) and winner in Greece by Zafonic: dam once-raced sister to smart French winner up to 7.5f Robin des Pins and closely related to very smart French winner up to 1½m Mystery Rays: fair performer: won maiden at Windsor in August: below form in handicaps after: stayed 1m: visits Sahm. *A. C. Stewart* **74**

MOONA'S MAGIC (IRE) 2 b.f. (Mar 27) Inzar (USA) 112 – Moona (USA) 73 (Lear Fan (USA) 130) [2001 6m 6g⁶ 7m 6.1d Sep 21] IR 16,000Y, 15,000 2-y-o: leggy filly: sister to 3-y-o Rare Old Times and half-sister to several winners abroad: dam 7f winner: modest maiden: probably stays 7f. *R. Hannon* **58**

MOON AT NIGHT 6 gr.g. Pursuit of Love 124 – La Nureyeva (USA) 83 (Nureyev (USA) 131) [2001 76: 8d 8g⁶ 8.3g³ 8m 7.1g 8m Sep 26] leggy gelding: modest handicapper: stays 1m: acts on firm and good to soft going: visored (tailed off) final start: front runner. *W. S. Kittow* **60**

MOON BALLAD (IRE) 2 ch.c. (Mar 4) Singspiel (IRE) 133 – Velvet Moon (IRE) 108 (Shaadi (USA) 126) [2001 7m² Sep 22] 350,000Y: strong, lengthy colt: third living foal: half-brother to useful 1m winner Velvet Lady (by Nashwan): dam, 6f (at 2 yrs, including Lower Stakes) and 1¼m winner, half-sister to very smart 1¼m to 2m performer Central Park: 5/4 favourite, demoted after beating Dusky Warbler a short head in 18-runner maiden at Newmarket, soon recovering from sluggish start to travel strongly just off pace, leading over 1f out and keeping on well despite edging left: should stay 1¼m: smart performer in the making, sure to win races as a 3-y-o. *D. R. Loder* **98 p**

MOONCELL 2 b.g. (Apr 7) Exit To Nowhere (USA) 122 – Lady Liska (USA) (Diesis 133) [2001 7m f8g 8g Oct 19] 13,000Y: fourth foal: half-brother to fairly useful 1¼m winner Ikatania (by Highest Honor): dam, French 7.5f winner, half-sister to dam of Breeders' Cup Sprint winner Cardmania: well held in maidens/minor event. *M. W. Easterby* **–**

MOON COLONY 8 b.g. Top Ville 129 – Honeymooning (USA) (Blushing Groom (FR) 131) [2001 –: 16.2m 15g³ 14.1m² 12m 13.8g⁶ Aug 7] quite attractive gelding: one-time fairly useful handicapper: modest nowadays: stays 15f: acts on soft and good to firm ground: tried blinkered/tongue tied. *A. L. Forbes* **55**

MOON EMPEROR 4 b.g. Emperor Jones (USA) 119 – Sir Hollow (USA) (Sir Ivor 135) [2001 93: e12g* e12g e10g⁶ 10s⁵ 12g⁵ 12m⁶ 13.9m² 16.1g⁴ 16.2g* 13.9g⁶ 14.6d⁴ 16d⁶ Oct 20] tall, close-coupled gelding: useful handicapper: better than ever in 2001, winning at Lingfield in January and Ascot (by length from First Ballot) in August: good **108**

Millennium And Copthorne Shergar Cup Stayers (Rated Stakes Handicap), Ascot—
Moon Emperor gains his most important success; also in the frame (from left to right) were
First Ballot, Give Notice and Heros Fatal; the Shergar Cup format underwent another overhaul,
the focus switching from teams of owners to jockeys;
Rest of the World beat Great Britain and Ireland by 125 points to 115

efforts after when sixth to Mediterranean in Ebor at York and close fourth to Darasim in Mallard Stakes at Doncaster: stiff task when sixth of 7 in Jockey Club Cup at Newmarket final start: stays 2m: acts on equitrack, good to firm and good to soft going (has won on soft): held up. *J. R. Jenkins*

MOON GODDESS   3 ch.f. Rainbow Quest (USA) 134 – Mystic Goddess (USA) 94 **98** (Storm Bird (CAN) 134) [2001 8m² 8g* 9m³ 10.3g⁵ 10d Oct 18] leggy filly: fourth foal: half-sister to 4-y-o Medicean: dam, 2-y-o 6f/7f winner (stayed 1m), half-sister to smart 2-y-o 6f to 1m (Gran Criterium) winner Sanam: useful form: won maiden at Yarmouth in June: good efforts after, 5½ lengths seventh to Esyoueffcee in listed race at Newmarket (never dangerous) final start: stays 1¼m: yet to race on extremes of going: free to post/hung right on debut: has been taken last/steadily to post. *Sir Michael Stoute*

MOONJAZ   4 ch.c. Nashwan (USA) 135 – Harayir (USA) 119 (Gulch (USA)) [2001 **104** 88p: 10m³ 12g* 14m² Jul 31] good-topped colt: useful performer, lightly raced: won maiden at Pontefract in July: good length second to First Ballot in handicap at Goodwood next time: will probably stay 2m: acts on good to firm going, showed promise on soft: sold 36,000 gns. *M. P. Tregoning*

MOONLIGHT DANCER   3 b.g. Polar Falcon (USA) 126 – Guanhumara (Caerleon **73** (USA) 132) [2001 68§: f7g e7g e8g⁵ e7g⁶ 8m 8.3g* 8f* 9f² 9f* p8g p10g Dec 12] lengthy, **a61 +** quite attractive gelding: fair on turf, modest on all-weather: won handicaps at Windsor and Musselburgh and minor event at Redcar in June/July: stays 1¼m: acts on firm going, good to soft and all-weather: withdrawn after breaking out of stall/bolting intended sixth start at 2 yrs: has looked none too keen. *K. R. Burke*

MOONLIGHTING   4 b.f. Lugana Beach 116 – White Flash 39 (Sure Blade (USA) **–** 130) [2001 9.9m p7g Dec 19] 800 4-y-o: second foal: dam, maiden who should have stayed beyond 1m, out of smart 7f winner Princess Matilda: well held in claimers nearly 5 months apart (left D. Elsworth 2,000 gns after debut). *B. R. Johnson*

MOONLIGHT INVADER (IRE)   7 br.g. Darshaan 133 – Mashmoon (USA) 80   –
(Habitat 134) [2001 21.6s Apr 23] little form after 2 yrs: dead. *J. G. Portman*

MOONLIGHT MONTY   5 ch.g. Elmaamul (USA) 125 – Lovers Light (Grundy   –
137) [2001 58: 12s Mar 22] lengthy gelding: modest maiden at 4 yrs: well held only 5-y-o
start on Flat: won over hurdles in May. *B. Ellison*

MOONLIGHT SONG (IRE)   4 b.f. Mujadil (USA) 119 – Model Show (IRE) 82   **57**
(Dominion 123) [2001 68, a73: f7g* f8g² e7g⁴ f7g f7g f7g f7g² f7g 6g 7g 7d⁵ 8d⁴ 8m⁵ 7m   **a71 d**
7s³ 8g⁴ f7g f7g f7s³ p7g Dec 28] fair at best on all-weather, modest on turf: won claimer
at Southwell in January: left W. Jarvis after third start, and below best last 5: effective at
7f/easy 1m: acts on fibresand/equitrack, soft and good to firm going. *John A. Harris*

MOON MASTER   3 b.c. Primo Dominie 121 – Sickle Moon (Shirley Heights 130)   **43**
[2001 65: f6g⁶ f7g 10m⁴ Aug 29] poor maiden: probably stays 1¼m: tongue tied (slowly
away) penultimate start: has carried head awkwardly. *J. A. Osborne*

MOON PARADE (ARG)   5 br.h. Parade Marshal (ARG) – Moon Fitz (ARG)   **92**
(Fitzcarraldo (ARG)) [2001 8v a6g³ a8.7g⁶ a10g⁶ 9.8m 8g² a8.8g² 7m 8.8d² a8g Sep 9]
ex-Argentinian horse: won twice in native country in 1999, including Group 2 event: best
effort in Europe in 2001 (fairly useful form) when sixth in listed race at Jagersro in May:
heavily bandaged all round and wore crossed noseband, well held in Tote International
Handicap at Ascot eighth start: effective at 1m to 1½m: acts on dirt: blinkered fourth start.
Diego Lowther, Sweden

MOONRAKING   8 gr.g. Rusticaro (FR) 124 – Lunaire (Try My Best (USA) 130)   **– §**
[2001 –§, a46§: f12s⁶ f11s³ 10f 10f f11g Oct 1] leggy, close-coupled gelding: poor   **a39 §**
performer nowadays: left Miss S. Wilton after second start: stays 1½m: acts on fibresand:
blinkered/visored: moody. *W. Clay*

MOON ROYALE   3 ch.f. Royal Abjar (USA) 121 – Ragged Moon 72 (Raga Navarro   **53**
(ITY) 119) [2001 51: 10s 8m 8m* 8f 8m 9f 8m* 7.1m³ 8m 8g Nov 7] close-coupled filly:
modest performer: won sellers at Pontefract in June and Thirsk (handicap) in July: should
stay 1¼m: acts on good to firm going: none too consistent. *Denys Smith*

MOON SAFARI (USA)   2 b.f. (Feb 16) Mr Prospector (USA) – Video (USA)   **101**
(Nijinsky (CAN) 138) [2001 6g⁵ 8.5s³ 7s* 7g 8s⁶ Sep 29] big, lengthy filly: ninth foal:
sister to 2 winners in USA, notably Grade 1 1m/9f winner Scan, and closely related to
2 winners there by Forty Niner: dam, 8.5f winner in USA, sister to Caerleon: useful
performer: won maiden at Tipperary in August: 50/1, best effort when 5 lengths sixth of 7
to Gossamer in Fillies' Mile at Ascot, fading: stays 1m: acts on soft going. *A. P. O'Brien,
Ireland*

MOON SOLITAIRE (IRE)   4 b.c. Night Shift (USA) – Gay Fantastic (Ela-   **110**
Mana-Mou 132) [2001 103: 10s³ 10g* 12m³ 12f³ 12m 12g⁴ 10.4g Aug 22] strong colt:
smart handicapper: favourite, won at Newmarket in May by head from Shamaiel: in
frame most other starts, including when very good close fourth (promoted a place) to
Lord Jim in Vodafone Handicap at Epsom fourth start: effective at 1¼m/1½m: acts on any
going: tried visored, including last 2 starts: has had tongue tied: sometimes wanders/finds
little: sent to USA. *E. A. L. Dunlop*

MOORLANDS AGAIN   6 b.g. Then Again 126 – Sandford Springs (USA) 67   **59 d**
(Robellino (USA) 127) [2001 75+: 8m 10d 9.9m⁴ 10.2g⁶ 9.9s 8g 11.9s 10s⁵ Oct 22] big
gelding: maiden handicapper, on downgrade in 2001: stays 1¼m: acts on soft and good to
firm going: blinkered final start. *J. M. Bradley*

MOORTOP LADY   2 b.f. (Mar 23) Mtoto 134 – Octavia Girl 104 (Octavo (USA)   **44**
115) [2001 f5g 5s f5g 10d p8g⁴ Nov 24] IR 7,200Y: smallish, close-coupled filly: sister to
useful winner around 1½m Toto Caelo and half-sister to several winners, including 7f/1m
winner Festival Mood (by Jalmood) and 1m (at 2 yrs) and 15f winner Lofty Lady (by
Head For Heights), both fairly useful: dam, 2-y-o 6f winner, later stayed 1m: poor
maiden: should stay at least 1¼m: acts on polytrack: has had tongue tied. *J. L. Eyre*

MOOSE MALLOY   4 ch.g. Formidable (USA) 125 – Jolimo 92 (Fortissimo 111)   –
[2001 –: 16m⁶ Jul 30] big, workmanlike gelding: no form. *M. J. Ryan*

MOOTAFAYILL (USA)   3 b.c. Danzig (USA) – Ruznama (USA) 105 (Forty Niner   **80**
(USA)) [2001 95: 7m² 8m³ Jul 12] good-topped, imposing colt: has quick action: fairly
useful maiden: ran just respectably both 3-y-o starts (didn't seem to apply himself fully

under pressure final one): probably stays 1m: yet to race on extremes of going: hung right final start in 2000: sent to UAE. *B. W. Hills*

MOPPY MAY (IRE) 2 b.f. (Apr 28) Alhaarth (IRE) 126 – Lacinia 107 (Groom – Dancer (USA) 128) [2001 7m 7g⁵ Sep 14] 42,000Y: second foal: dam Irish 6f (at 2 yrs) and 11f winner: signs of just a little ability in maidens. *T. G. Mills*

MOQUI MARBLE (GER) 5 b.g. Petit Loup (USA) 123 – Margo's New Hope – (USA) (Cannonade (USA)) [2001 6d 8.5m Aug 15] won 3 of his 4 starts in Germany at 3 yrs and handicap at Dusseldorf in 2000 when with P. Rau: well held in Britain both 5-y-o starts: stays 8.5f: acts on heavy ground. *John Berry*

MORAHIB 3 ch.c. Nashwan (USA) 135 – Irish Valley (USA) (Irish River (FR) 131) – [2001 10.1s⁵ Aug 31] ninth foal: closely related to high-class 7f (Dewhurst Stakes) to 9.8f (Prix Dollar) winner who stayed 1½m Alhaarth (by Unfuwain) and half-brother to 3 winners, including useful French 1990 2-y-o 7f (Prix du Calvados) winner Green Pola (by Nijinsky): dam maiden half-sister to Green Dancer: favourite, weakened quickly 3f out when remote fifth in maiden at Epsom in August: joined M. Tregoning. *Saeed bin Suroor*

MORE MODERN (USA) 3 ch.c. Mt Livermore (USA) – A La Mode (USA) 77 **93** (Known Fact (USA) 135) [2001 7₇p: 7s³ 7m* 8.1m 7.1m² 7f* 7f* 7d 7g⁶ Sep 19] close-coupled, quite attractive colt: has a quick action: fairly useful performer: won maiden and minor event, both at Lingfield, and handicap at Kempton (made all to beat Mr Mahoose by length, despite flashing tail) between May and August: stays 7f: best form on good going or firmer: blinkered last 4 starts: joined R. Frankel in USA. *R. Charlton*

MOREOVER (IRE) 3 b.f. Caerleon (USA) 132 – Overcall (Bustino 136) [2001 58p: **69** 12m² 11.8g³ f12g⁵ 12f³ f14.8g² 13.8s² Oct 20] strong, good-bodied filly: fair maiden: stays 15f: acts on soft going, good to firm and fibresand: blinkered (pulled hard) fourth start: has flashed tail: sold 33,000 gns, joined M. Easterby. *Sir Mark Prescott*

MORE SIRENS (IRE) 3 ch.f. Night Shift (USA) – Lower The Tone (IRE) 74 (Phone **78** Trick (USA)) [2001 8m 7.5m³ 10m⁴ 8.2f* 8m² 8f Jul 1] 42,000Y: tall, good-topped filly: first foal: dam, Irish 1m winner, half-sister to 6-y-o Pantar: fair performer: trained at 2 yrs by R. Gibson in France: won handicap at Nottingham in June: stays 1m: acts on soft and firm ground: sold 20,000 gns. *Mrs J. R. Ramsden*

MORE SPECIFIC 2 ch.c. (Apr 24) Definite Article 121 – Blue Lamp (USA) 68 **71** (Shadeed (USA) 135) [2001 7m³ 7.1d² 6g⁶ 8m⁴ 7.9s⁴ 7s f8g* f8g* Dec 3] 20,000Y: **a85** smallish colt: first foal: dam maiden who stayed 1¼m: fairly useful on all-weather, fair on turf: visored, won maiden in November and nursery (carried head awkwardly) in December, both at Southwell: will stay 1¼m: acts on soft going, good to firm and fibresand. *A. P. Jarvis*

MORGAN LE FAY 6 b.m. Magic Ring (IRE) 115 – Melody Park 104 (Music Boy – 124) [2001 61: f6g² f6g³ f6g⁶ f8s⁵ f6s³ f7g 6g 6g 6f f7g⁵ f7g³ f6g⁶ f6g⁶ Dec 10] leggy **a60** mare: modest handicapper: effective at 6f/7f: acts on firm ground, good to soft and fibresand: visored final start: has been slowly away. *Don Enrico Incisa*

MORGANS ORCHARD (IRE) 5 ch.g. Forest Wind (USA) 111 – Regina St Cyr **66** (IRE) (Doulab (USA) 115) [2001 73, a76: f12f³ f14g² 13.3g⁶ 12m⁵ 12.4m⁴ 15.9m⁶ 12f* **a76** 12g f14g Oct 22] workmanlike gelding: fair handicapper: made all in apprentice event at Kempton in August: effective at 1½m, and should stay easy 2m: acts on fibresand and probably any turf going: tends to wander/idle in front. *A. G. Newcombe*

MORLESS 2 b.f. (Mar 21) Morpeth § – Bush Radio (Hot Grove 128) [2001 f9.4g Dec – 8] 3,600Y: third reported foal: dam poor novice hurdler/chaser: 20/1, well beaten in seller at Wolverhampton. *B. R. Millman*

MORNING SKY (IRE) 2 b.f. (Apr 21) Machiavellian (USA) 123 – Dizzy Heights **79 p** (USA) (Danzig (USA)) [2001 6m 7g 6d* Aug 26] leggy, quite good-topped filly: second foal: sister to 5-y-o King For A Day: dam, French 9f and 11f winner, half-sister to US Grade 1 9f/1¼m winner Life At The Top: progressive in maidens, fair form when beating Fruit of Glory by 1¼ lengths at Goodwood, hampered stall and leading close home: should stay at least 1m: capable of better. *E. A. L. Dunlop*

MORNINGS MINION 4 b.g. Polar Falcon (USA) 126 – Fair Dominion 107 **89** (Dominion 123) [2001 90: 8d⁶ 10g 10v 8.3m 8m² 8g* 8d* 8g⁵ 8s 7.9d⁵ Oct 12] big, lengthy gelding: fairly useful handicapper: made all at Newmarket and Leicester in August: stays 1m: acts on firm and soft going: visored (below form) once: has wandered: sold 30,000 gns, joined D. Vienna in USA. *R. Charlton*

MORNING SUNSET   2 b.f. (Mar 16) Zafonic (USA) 130 – Eclipsing (IRE) 93   –
(Baillamont (USA) 124) [2001 6.1m Jul 27] fifth foal: half-sister to useful performer up
to 1½m Vagabond Chanteuse (by Sanglamore), 7f winner at 2 yrs, and fairly useful 1998
2-y-o 6f winner Esteraad (by Cadeaux Genereux): dam 1m winner: favourite, seventh of
15 in maiden at Chepstow: dead. *P. W. Harris*

MORNIN RESERVES   2 b.g. (May 3) Atraf 116 – Pusey Street Girl 87 (Gildoran   55
123) [2001 5.1g³ 6m Jul 11] 12,000Y: first foal: dam 7f winner: modest form in maidens
at Bath (favourite) and Lingfield: may prove best at 5f/6f: sold 2,900 gns in November
and gelded. *M. R. Channon*

MOROCCO (IRE)   12 b.g. Cyrano de Bergerac 120 – Lightning Laser 68 (Monseig-   –
neur (USA) 127) [2001 52: 7.5f 8f 8.2s Aug 6] probably of little account nowadays.
J. A. Osborne

MOROUJ (USA)   2 br.f. (Jan 22) Gone West (USA) – Chicarica (USA) 112 (The   84
Minstrel (CAN) 135) [2001 6m⁴ 5m² 6m⁵ 5d* Oct 9] sturdy, angular filly: has a short,
quick action: fourth living foal: closely related to fairly useful 1997 2-y-o 6f winner Court
Lane (by Machiavellian), later 1m winner in France: dam, 6f performer (won Cherry
Hinton Stakes), out of sister to very smart 2-y-o performer up to 7f Romeo Romani: fairly
useful performer: visored, landed odds in maiden at Catterick by 5 lengths from Twice
Upon A Time, making all (drifted right): free-going sort, likely to prove best at 5f/6f: has
worn crossed noseband. *D. R. Loder*

MORRIS DANCING (USA)   2 b.g. (Feb 3) Rahy (USA) 115 – Summer Dance 86   75
(Sadler's Wells (USA) 132) [2001 7s⁵ 8s⁴ f8s Dec 21] first foal: dam, 1m winner,
daughter of smart 1m winner Hyabella, herself half-sister to high-class 1¼m performer
Stagecraft from family of Opera House and Kayf Tara: fair form at Leicester and
Yarmouth first 2 starts in maidens, then left Sir Michael Stoute: gelded after final outing:
should stay 1¼m. *B. P. J. Baugh*

MORRO CASTLE (USA)   3 b. or br.c. Kris S (USA) – Fuerza (USA) (Distinctive   83
Pro (USA)) [2001 10m⁴ 11.5m³ 12g 9g* 10f Sep 22] $95,000Y: big, good-topped colt:
fourth foal: brother to 6f winner in USA and half-brother to 2 winners, notably very smart
Irish 6f (at 2 yrs) to 9.5f winner Pro Trader (by Lyphard), later winner in North America:
dam US Grade 3 6f winner at 2 yrs who later won up to 7f: fairly useful performer: made
all in maiden at Sandown in September: ran respectably in handicap final start: stays
1¼m: raced only on good going or firmer. *C. E. Brittain*

MORSHDI   3 b.c. Slip Anchor 136 – Reem Albaraari 81 (Sadler's Wells (USA)   123
132) [2001 94: 10g³ 12f* 12g² 12m 12d* Sep 2]
Who'd have thought it? The Derby Italiano, generally regarded as a viable
alternative for horses trained in Britain, France, Germany and Ireland who fall short
of the standard required to win the equivalent events at Epsom, Chantilly, Hamburg
and the Curragh, was the fourth most valuable race to take place in Europe in the
latest season, behind only the Derby itself, the Prix de l'Arc de Triomphe and the
King George VI and Queen Elizabeth Diamond Stakes. A doubling of the prize
money, with around £400,000 on offer to the winner, cannot, however, be said to
have resulted in a significantly better contest in terms of quality. But at least the
latest running, at Rome at the end of May, was a slightly above-average one with an
international flavour. Maybe maintaining the current level of money on offer will
produce an even stronger challenge from outside Italy in future, which will make
the task of keeping the prize at home even more difficult than it is already. No
Italian-trained horse has won the Derby Italiano since Tisserand edged out the
following year's Arc winner Carroll House back in 1988.
Carroll House's trainer Michael Jarvis, who went one better in the following
year's race with Prorutori, was responsible for one of the six challengers from
outside Italy in the latest edition. The Jarvis representative Morshdi was one of
the least experienced members of a field which also included Godolphin's Atlantis
Prince, Irish challengers King's County and Vinnie Roe, and the German pair
Iberus and Limerick Boy. Morshdi was having only his fifth race, having won a
maiden at Haydock from three starts as a two-year-old before leaving that form well
behind when a close third to Rosi's Boy in the mile-and-a-quarter listed Newmarket
Stakes at Newmarket on his return. The step up to a mile and a half in the Derby
Italiano showed Morshdi in an even better light. He raced nothing like so freely as
at Newmarket, was travelling well in seventh turning into the straight, where the

Derby Italiano - Yoga, Rome—Morshdi is ridden right out to win one of Europe's richest races; Falbrav is second and Iberus (black cap) third, whilst Vinnie Roe (stars) gains fourth after encountering trouble in running

field began to fan out across the course, and found plenty under pressure to take command over a furlong out. Morshdi kept on strongly after hitting the front, and, with the Italian-trained Falbrav putting in some good work to take second, ran out the winner by two and three quarter lengths. The enterprise shown by Morshdi's connections had paid off handsomely, and they continued to adopt an attacking policy. On his next two starts, Morshdi took on Derby winner Galileo in the Irish Derby and the King George VI and Queen Elizabeth Stakes. Supplemented at a cost of IR £90,000 for the former, Morshdi showed further improvement in finishing four lengths second to Galileo, staying on without ever threatening the winner. He failed to do himself justice at Ascot, finishing only eighth, beaten over fifteen lengths after moving up to the leaders four furlongs out. Nothing came to light to explain Morshdi's disappointing run, but he put it well behind him when returned to action in September in the UAE Grosser Preis von Baden. This was the least valuable of the four Group 1s contested by Morshdi, but it still had more than £320,000 on offer to the winner. The race, which had been won by Jarvis in 1988 with Carroll House, might have lacked Germany's top older horse Silvano, being campaigned in North America, but it did contain its two best three-year-olds, Boreal and Sabiango. Morshdi, however, needed only to reproduce his Irish Derby form to take care of that pair and the nine others, all but one of which were home-based runners. Making his move on the outside turning for home, Morshdi

UAE Grosser Preis von Baden, Baden-Baden—Morshdi plunders more valuable foreign prize-money, seeing off Germany's top three-year-olds Boreal and Sabiango (black sleeves); Paolini (hooped sleeves) is fourth

ran on strongly to lead inside the final furlong and win by a length and a quarter from Boreal, who in turn finished a length and a half ahead of third-placed Sabiango. This victory took Morshdi to the top of the Emirates World Series rankings, though his reign was a brief one. Later in September it was announced that Morshdi had injured a near-fore tendon while being prepared for the Arc and would be out for the rest of the season; and that was followed by the news that he had been retired to stud in Germany at the Gestut Friedrichsruh at a fee of €4,000, the injury more serious than first thought.

		Slip Anchor (b 1982)	Shirley Heights (b 1975)	Mill Reef Hardiemma
Morshdi (b.c. 1998)			Sayonara (b 1965)	Birkhahn Suleika
	Reem Albaraari (b 1988)	Sadler's Wells (b 1981)	Northern Dancer Fairy Bridge
		Habibti (br 1980)	Habitat Klairessa

Morshdi, a good-topped colt with a long, round action, was bred by his owner and comes from a good family. He is the fifth foal of Reem Albaraari, a filly who showed promise as a two-year-old but failed to train on. That 510,000-guinea yearling Reem Albaraari, a daughter of Sadler's Wells and the brilliant sprinter Habibti, did not manage to win a race must have been a bitter disappointment to her connections, but she has more than made up for that now. Morshdi, her first winning produce, was quickly followed by her second in Kundooz (by Sabrehill), a useful two-year-old also trained by Jarvis. Conversely, Habibti was a great deal

Sheikh Ahmed Al Maktoum's "Morshdi"

more successful on the racecourse than she's been at stud, having produced only one minor winner to date. There is a lot more stamina than speed in Morshdi's make-up, and he would probably have stayed a mile and three quarters (he was made favourite for the St Leger after the Irish Derby, but connections ruled him out of the race after success at Baden-Baden). He seemed not to be beholden to the state of the ground, having won on soft at two and on firm and good to soft in Italy and Germany respectively. *M. A. Jarvis*

MORSHID (USA) 3 b.g. Gulch (USA) – Possessive Dancer 118 (Shareef Dancer (USA) 135) [2001 77: 10.3s 12.3v² 14.6m⁴ 10.9m⁶ 10.3f⁴ 12.3m a8f⁶ Dec 13] leggy, lengthy gelding: fair performer: left M. Channon and off nearly 6 months before final outing: stays 1½m: acts on heavy going, possibly on firm: tried visored: has raced freely/carried head awkwardly. *D. J. Selvaratnam, UAE* — **77**

MORTON (IRE) 2 b.g. (Apr 12) Lake Coniston (IRE) 131 – Tannerrun (IRE) 65 (Runnett 125) [2001 5.6f Jul 1] IR 5,500Y, 4,500 2-y-o: workmanlike gelding: third foal: half-brother to 4-y-o Africa: dam, 2-y-o 5f winner, half-sister to useful performer up to 7f Nashcash: 50/1, tailed off in Doncaster maiden. *R. F. Marvin* — **–**

MOSAAHIM (IRE) 3 b.c. Nashwan (USA) 135 – Azdihaar (USA) 81 (Mr Prospector (USA)) [2001 83: 8d Apr 21] rangy, angular colt: has scope: best effort in 3 maidens on debut (edgy/tended to wander next time): should stay at least 1m: sent to Germany. *J. L. Dunlop* — **–**

MOSAYTER (USA) 3 b.c. Storm Cat (USA) – Bashayer (USA) 103 (Mr Prospector (USA)) [2001 80p: 10.4g⁶ 8f³ 8m* 8g* 9m Sep 12] strong, rangy colt: useful performer: won maiden and minor event (by 1¼ lengths from Turku) at Thirsk in August: not discredited in handicap final start: barely stays 9f: acts on firm going: sent to USA. *M. P. Tregoning* — **95**

MOSCA 3 ch.f. Most Welcome 131 – Moidart 90 (Electric 126) [2001 65p: 10m⁶ 14.1m⁴ 14.1m* Jul 27] rather leggy, quite good-topped filly: fairly useful performer: best effort when winning handicap at Salisbury in July by neck: better at 1¾m than shorter: lost all chance when rearing as stalls opened on reappearance. *J. R. Fanshawe* — **83**

MOSELLE 4 b.f. Mtoto 134 – Miquette (FR) (Fabulous Dancer (USA) 124) [2001 101: 9g⁴ 10.4m* 10.5g 12m 11.9d⁵ 12g 10.1m* 10m Sep 16] rather leggy filly: useful performer: won listed races at York (by 2 lengths from Valentine Band) in May and Newcastle (rated stakes by ¾ length from It's A Secret) in August: well held in Blandford Stakes at the Curragh final outing: best around 1¼m: acts on firm and good to soft going: edgy type: has pulled hard: sold 180,000 gns in December. *W. J. Haggas* — **108**

MOSSPAT 2 b.g. (Apr 17) Reprimand 122 – Queen And Country (Town And Country 124) [2001 5s³ 5s 6m⁵ 7g⁵ 7m Jun 23] 2,500F: sturdy gelding: half-brother to several winners, including 2000 2-y-o 5f winner Nine To Five (by Imp Society): dam twice-raced half-sister to Ayr Gold Cup winner Polly's Brother: poor maiden: seems barely to stay 7f: visored (well beaten) final start: temperament under suspicion. *W. G. M. Turner* — **44**

MOSTABSHIR (IRE) 3 b.g. Unfuwain (USA) 131 – Istibshar (USA) 78 (Mr Prospector (USA)) [2001 –p: 10.5m³ 11m³ 11.6m³ 12m⁴ 12.3m⁴ 12m* 14g Oct 6] big, strong, lengthy gelding: has scope: has round action: fairly useful performer: made all in maiden at Kempton in September: stays 1½m: acts on good to firm going: tongue tied after second start: sent to UAE. *J. H. M. Gosden* — **85**

MOSTARSIL (USA) 3 ch.g. Kingmambo (USA) 125 – Naazeq 80 (Nashwan (USA) 135) [2001 10m⁶ 12m* 10.3m⁶ 10g² 12.3m⁵ Aug 18] medium-sized, useful-looking gelding: first foal: dam, 10.5f winner, sister to smart performer up to 2½m Shaya: fairly useful performer: won maiden at Pontefract in June: best effort when second in handicap at Newmarket: left impression something amiss final start (subsequently gelded): effective at 1¼m/1½m: raced only on good/good to firm ground: sold 6,500 gns. *A. C. Stewart* — **89**

MOST-SAUCY 5 br.m. Most Welcome 131 – So Saucy 59 (Teenoso (USA) 135) [2001 82: e8g* f8.5s² e8g⁴ e8g² f8.5g f8.5g 8.3g 7m⁴ 8.5f² 10.5d f8g f8g⁴ 7.6m 7.9m 6f⁶ 8s² f7g* 8d⁵ 7s⁶ 8s p7g² p8g³ f8.5f p8g Dec 22] lengthy mare: fairly useful handicapper on all-weather, fair on turf: won at Lingfield in January and Southwell in October: best at 7f/1m: acts on firm going, soft and all-weather. *I. A. Wood* — **66 a86**

MOST STYLISH 4 ch.f. Most Welcome 131 – Corman-Style 52 (Ahonoora 122) [2001 69: 12.4d* 11.1g⁵ 14.1g Oct 6] leggy, useful-looking filly: modest performer: won apprentice seller at Newcastle in August: stays 1¾m: acts on soft going, good to firm and fibresand: sold 900 gns. *L. Lungo* — **58**

MOTEN SWING 2 b.c. (Apr 28) Kris 135 – Lady Bankes (IRE) 69 (Alzao (USA) **75**
117) [2001 5.1f⁴ 6f 6m* 7.1g⁴ Sep 1] 21,000F, 200,000 francs Y: sturdy, good-bodied
colt: second foal: dam, 1¼m winner, half-sister to smart performer up to 9f in Britain and
USA Circle of Gold: fair performer: won maiden at Salisbury in July: ran creditably in
nursery at Sandown final start: should stay 1m. *R. Hannon*

MOTHER CORRIGAN (IRE) 5 gr.m. Paris House 123 – Missed Opportunity (IRE) –
(Exhibitioner 111) [2001 64d: f8g 6m 5f 6m Aug 11] lengthy, angular mare: modest
handicapper at 4 yrs: little form in 2001: visored/blinkered. *M. Brittain*

MOTHER MOLLY (USA) 4 b. or br.f. Irish River (FR) 131 – Charming Molly – §
(USA) 86 (Diesis 133) [2001 63: 8.3g 7m 10g Aug 11] temperamental maiden.
P. S. McEntee

MOTH HIL (USA) 2 b.c. (Feb 17) Danzig (USA) – Siyadah (USA) 106 (Mr –
Prospector (USA)) [2001 8.2s Oct 30] first foal: dam, 1¼m winner, daughter of Yorkshire
Oaks winner Roseate Tern (also third in Oaks and St Leger), herself half-sister to
high-class middle-distance performer Ibn Bey: 10/1, folded tamely when last in maiden
at Nottingham. *J. L. Dunlop*

MOT JUSTE 3 b.f. Mtoto 134 – Bunting 102 (Shaadi (USA) 126) [2001 87p: 10g* **115**
12m⁴ 12g² 11.9g 12m⁴ 10v² 10f Oct 27] rangy, quite attractive filly: has scope: smart
performer: won listed race at Newmarket in May: at least creditable efforts when in frame
in Oaks at Epsom (4½ lengths fourth to Imagine, tending to wander), Irish Oaks at the
Curragh (beaten neck by Lailani) and Prix Vermeille (4¾ lengths fourth to Aquarelliste)
and Prix de l'Opera (1½ lengths second to Terre A Terre) at Longchamp: well below form
in Yorkshire Oaks at York and Breeders' Cup Filly & Mare Turf at Belmont otherwise:

Mohammed Al Nabouda's "Mot Juste"

stays 1½m: acts on heavy and good to firm going, possibly not on firm: races prominently: joined Godolphin. *E. A. L. Dunlop*

MOTTO (FR) 3 b.f. Mtoto 134 – Coigach 110 (Niniski (USA) 125) [2001 –P: 10m⁴ **95** 10m² 11.9m* 14.6m 12g 12d 10.3s⁴ Nov 9] rather unfurnished filly: useful performer: won maiden at Brighton in August: best efforts when seventh to Ranin in steadily-run Park Hill Stakes at Doncaster (slightly flattered) and handicap at Newmarket on fourth and sixth starts: stays 1¾m: acts on good to firm and good to soft ground. *H. R. A. Cecil*

MOUNT ABU (IRE) 4 b.c. Foxhound (USA) 103 – Twany Angel (Double Form **123** 130) [2001 112: 7g³ 7.1d* 6m⁶ 6.5d⁴ 6s² 6s⁶ 7s* 8m Dec 16]

Just a week after winning a Group 1 event at Longchamp with Sulk, John Gosden repeated the feat with Mount Abu in the Prix de la Foret. Whereas the former had been supplemented at a late stage for the Prix Marcel Boussac, Mount Abu's victory was a triumph for long-term planning. 'This was his target all year,' said Gosden after the colt had put up a career-best performance in a race dominated by British-trained runners. One of those, China Visit, started a short-priced favourite on the strength of his victory in the Prix du Rond-Point over the same course eight days earlier; and Warningford was also sent off at much shorter odds than Mount Abu, who had run with credit at the top level earlier in the season without quite proving good enough. Mount Abu was a different proposition on this occasion, however. As usual over the seven-furlong course at Longchamp it paid to race handily, and Mount Abu had the front-running China Visit in his sights from the off. Quickening to lead two furlongs out, Mount Abu ran on well to draw two lengths clear of China Visit, who just held Warningford for second, with Nicobar completing a clean sweep for the British.

This was Mount Abu's second win of the season and his sixth all told. Successful only once at two, in a maiden at Newbury, Mount Abu won listed events at Ascot and Lingfield as well as the Group 3 Supreme Stakes at Goodwood at three; and he opened his account at four in another listed event, the bet365.com John of Gaunt Stakes at Haydock in June. Sent off favourite in this ten-runner event, Mount Abu, conceding weight all round, made smooth headway over two furlongs out, was driven to lead entering the final furlong and held on by a short head from Fath. In between Haydock and Longchamp, Mount Abu confirmed that he is almost as effective at six furlongs as over seven, his best efforts at the former trip coming in the July Cup at Newmarket and the Sprint Cup at Haydock. Mount Abu finished sixth of eighteen behind Mozart in the former, keeping on without ever seriously threatening, and second of twelve to Nuclear Debate in the latter. Mount Abu came through to make his challenge over a furlong out at Haydock, but couldn't match the speed of Nuclear Debate and was beaten three lengths. Whether or not Mount Abu will be able to show his form at a mile is another matter. It has to be open to doubt; he beat just one home on his only attempt at that distance, in the fourteen-runner Hong Kong Mile at Sha Tin in December. However, Mount Abu was in trouble that day before stamina became an issue, so drawing firm conclusions from that one performance would be unwise.

Prix de la Foret, Longchamp—a very smart performance from Mount Abu, who beats China Visit, with Warningford (hooped cap) finishing well in third

Gary Seidler & Andy J. Smith's "Mount Abu"

		Foxhound (USA) (b 1991)	Danzig (b 1977)	Northern Dancer Pas de Nom
Mount Abu (IRE) (b.c. 1997)			Lassie Dear (b 1974)	Buckpasser Gay Missile
		Twany Angel (ch 1981)	Double Form (b 1975)	Habitat Fanghorn
			Athy Angel (ch 1976)	Three Dons Frozen Blonde

Mount Abu, along with smart sprinter Kier Park, is from the first crop of the extremely well-bred Foxhound, a useful performer up to seven furlongs who will be standing at stud in Britain in 2002 following spells in Ireland and the States. The dam Twany Angel, who raced in France, didn't manage to win, but the grandam and great grandam each won three races, Athy Angel and Frozen Blonde also finishing second in a Group 3 event in Ireland and the Princess Royal Stakes respectively. Twany Angel has certainly proved her worth at stud, though, and Mount Abu, her eighth foal, is her seventh winner. The pick of the remainder are Mount Abu's close relative Melleray (by Danehill), a useful two-year-old five-furlong winner in Ireland in 1996, who later won in the USA, and his half-sister Chiquita Linda (by Mujadil), whose five wins included one in a six-furlong listed event in Italy. Mount Abu, an IR 16,500-guinea foal who fetched 60,000 guineas as a yearling, is a rather leggy, quite attractive colt and usually takes the eye. He showed in the July Cup that he acts on good to firm going, but all his wins have been gained on good to soft or soft. *J. H. M. Gosden*

MOUNT ELBRUS 3 b.f. Barathea (IRE) 127 – El Jazirah (Kris 135) [2001 8d³ 10m* **106**
p10g³ 10.5v* Nov 27] 160,000Y: first foal: dam unraced sister to Prix de Diane winner
Rafha and half-sister to 4-y-o Chiang Mai: useful form: won maiden at Leicester (by 7
lengths) in September and listed race at Saint-Cloud (visored) in November, latter by
length from Shamdara, rallying after headed over 1f out: should stay 1½m: winner on
good to firm going, goes well on heavy ground: reportedly to join H-A. Pantall in France.
J. H. M. Gosden

MOUNT JOY 2 br.c. (Jan 31) Mtoto 134 – Nightitude 93 (Night Shift (USA)) [2001 **102 p**
7m² 8v⁴ Oct 27] 7,500F, 45,000Y: sturdy, lengthy colt: fourth foal: half-brother to fairly
useful Italian 7.5f/1m winner (including at 2 yrs) Golden Cavern (by Lion Cavern): dam,
2-y-o 5f winner, became one to treat with caution: promising 1¼ lengths second to King
of Happiness in maiden at Doncaster when trained by B. Hills, then sold privately: 6/1,
similarly useful form when 8¾ lengths fourth of 6 to High Chaparral in Racing Post
Trophy at Doncaster, pulling very hard early on and tiring over 1f out, shaping better than
result: will need to settle to stay beyond 1m: capable of better, and sure to win races.
Saeed bin Suroor

MOUNT PARK (IRE) 4 b.f. Colonel Collins (USA) 122 – Make Hay (Nomination **46 §**
125) [2001 50, a41: f6g 5s⁴ 5m 5f 5m⁶ 6.1f f5g 5f 5g Aug 7] strong filly: poor
handicapper: stays 6f: acts on soft going, good to firm and fibresand: usually blinkered:
has been slowly away/swerved violently under starter's stalls: unreliable. *D. W. Chapman*

MOUNTRATH ROCK 4 b.f. Rock Hopper 124 – Point of Law (Law Society (USA) **45 §**
130) [2001 52§: a8g⁶ a9g⁶ a10.5g 8m⁶ 8s p12g⁴ p10g Dec 28] small filly: poor performer:
raced at Mijas for E. Creighton first 3 starts: stays easy 1¼m: acts on polytrack, firm and
good to soft going: usually visored/blinkered/tongue tied: has been reluctant to race: not
one to trust. *Miss B. Sanders*

MOUNT ROYALE (IRE) 3 ch.g. Wolfhound (USA) 126 – Mahabba (USA) 74 **60**
(Elocutionist (USA)) [2001 –: 8d⁶ 8m 7.1g⁶ f6g³ 6m 6m³ f7g* 7s² 6.1s 7.1m² 7g² 6.1f
Sep 18] close-coupled gelding: has knee action: modest performer: won claimer at
Southwell in July: stays 7f: acts on fibresand, soft and good to firm going: sometimes
tongue tied: races prominently. *N. Tinkler*

MOUNT STREET (IRE) 2 b.f. (Mar 6) Pennekamp (USA) 130 – Highland Gift **82 P**
(IRE) 95 (Generous (IRE) 139) [2001 7m² Aug 30] second foal: half-sister to 3-y-o
Golan: dam, 1¼m winner, half-sister to smart middle-distance stayer Bonny Scot and
smart 1¼m/1½m winner Mary Stuart: 7/4 favourite, shaped well when 1½ lengths second
of 16 to Brown Eyes in maiden at Salisbury, running green just off the pace and not
unduly knocked about: will stay 1¼m: sure to improve considerably and win races. *Sir
Michael Stoute*

MOUSEHOLE 9 b.g. Statoblest 120 – Alo Ez 100 (Alzao (USA) 117) [2001 78: 5v **79**
5g 5.1f³ 5.2m 5.1f* 5m² 5m⁴ 5g 5m² 5g 5m⁴ 5m 5g 5.1d Oct 25] strong gelding: fair
handicapper: won at Nottingham in June: races mainly at 5f nowadays: best on good
ground or firmer: successful in blinkers, not tried since 1996: comes from behind, and
often soon off bridle. *R. Guest*

MOUTON (IRE) 5 b.m. Dolphin Street (FR) 125 – The Queen of Soul 75 (Chief **–**
Singer 131) [2001 35: e6g e7g e6g⁵ e7g⁶ e6g Mar 7] unfurnished mare: little form in
2001. *J. J. Bridger*

MOUWADH (USA) 3 b. or br.f. Nureyev (USA) 131 – Min Alhawa (USA) 108 **64**
(Riverman (USA) 131) [2001 8.3g⁴ 8.2d Sep 21] first foal: dam, 7f (at 2 yrs) and 1¼m
winner, half-sister to 1000 Guineas winner Harayir: better effort in maidens when 2¾
lengths fourth to Silver Bracelet at Windsor: visits Green Desert. *M. P. Tregoning*

MOVIE KING (IRE) 2 ch.c. (Mar 26) Catrail (USA) 123 – Marilyn (IRE) 72 (Kings **67**
Lake (USA) 133) [2001 5m³ 6m 7f f7g⁴ f8s⁶ Dec 21] IR 4,000F, IR 8,500Y: fourth foal:
dam, Irish 12.5f/13f winner (also won over hurdles), out of smart sprinter Welshwyn: fair
maiden: best efforts on debut and (visored) penultimate outing: should stay 1m: acts on
fibresand, raced only on going firmer than good on turf. *A. P. Jarvis*

MOVING EXPERIENCE (IRE) 4 b.f. Nicolotte 118 – Sound Performance (IRE) **72**
63 (Ahonoora 122) [2001 61: 8m* 9m² 9m³ 8.3g⁵ 8m* 8d p8g⁶ p10g Dec 19] fair
handicapper: won at Brighton in June and Goodwood (after 2-month break, claimer) in
September: stays 9f, possibly not 1¼m: acts on soft going, good to firm and probably on
polytrack: goes well fresh. *D. W. P. Arbuthnot*

MOWAADAH (IRE)   3 b.f. Alzao (USA) 117 – Mahrah (USA) 89 (Vaguely Noble   **93**
140) [2001 8m² 8m² 8d* 8g* 8s* 8d Nov 3] leggy, angular filly: seventh foal: half-sister
to smart 1m to 1¼m winner Fahim (by Green Desert) and useful Irish 1½m and 1¾m
winner Hadeb (by Unfuwain): dam, 1m winner, half-sister to smart Irish 1½m winner
Andros Bay: fairly useful performer: won maiden at Pontefract and handicaps at
Kempton and Ascot (beat Fallen Star by head in listed rated stakes) in August/September:
ran respectably in 30-runner handicap at Newmarket final start: raced only at 1m: acted
on soft going, probably on good to firm: had good turn of foot: visits Swain. *A. C. Stewart*

MOWBRAY (USA)   6 b. or br.g. Opening Verse (USA) 126 – Peppy Raja (USA)   **89**
(Raja Baba (USA)) [2001 102: 16s⁶ 14m May 24] tall gelding: good mover: useful at 5
yrs: well below form both starts in 2001: best around 1¾m nowadays: acts on any ground:
tried blinkered/visored: has gone in snatches/looked none too keen: has worn near-side
pricker. *G. L. Moore*

MOWELGA   7 ch.g. Most Welcome 131 – Galactic Miss 78 (Damister (USA) 123)   **–**
[2001 109: 12g Oct 5] short-backed gelding: useful performer at best, lightly raced:
bandaged behind, tailed off in listed event at Newmarket only 7-y-o start. *Lady Herries*

MOYNE PLEASURE (IRE)   3 b.c. Exit To Nowhere (USA) 122 – Ilanga (IRE) 92   **69**
(Common Grounds 118) [2001 82: f7g³ f7g⁵ f8.5g* f9.4g* e10g 8d 9.9g 8m 10.3f³ 8m   **a87**
8g⁶ 9f 8.3g Aug 6] small, sparely-made colt: fairly useful on all-weather, fair on turf: won
handicap and minor event at Wolverhampton in February/March: not sure to stay much
beyond 1¼m: acts on fibresand and firm ground. *J. A. Osborne*

MOYNOE PRINCESS (IRE)   7 b.m. Distinctly North (USA) 115 – First String   **–**
(FR) (What A Guest 119) [2001 –: f14g f11g e16g Jan 24] poor maiden handicapper:
trained in 2000 by D. Hassett in Ireland: no form in 2001: stays 1½m: acts on firm and
good to soft going: visored final start. *P. D. Evans*

MOZART (IRE)   3 b.c. Danehill (USA) 126 – Victoria Cross (USA) (Spectacular   **131**
Bid (USA)) [2001 111p: 8s³ 7g³ 8g² 7m* 6m* 5m* a6f Oct 27]
     The composer was different but the outcome was the same. Two years after
Stravinsky was brought back in distance, after failing to find his metier over seven
furlongs, and developed into one of the best sprinters of the 'nineties, Mozart, also
trained by Aidan O'Brien, followed suit. After starting out over a mile, Mozart
proceeded to outclass the opposition in Europe's two most strongly-contested races
for sprinters, the Darley July Cup and Victor Chandler Nunthorpe Stakes. Yet for
all the similarities between Stravinsky and Mozart there was one crucial difference
between them. Much more so than Stravinsky, never guaranteed to be fully
effective beyond sprint distances, Mozart initially fooled a number of observers
about his stamina, ourselves included. On the evidence of his two-year-old
campaign, consisting of three races over seven furlongs including success in the

Jersey Stakes, Royal Ascot—after helping to cut out a furious pace,
Mozart just holds on in this seven-furlong event from Aldebaran, with Ratio (noseband) third;
next are Coney Kitty and Pan Jammer (left)

Tattersalls Houghton Sales Stakes and fourth in the Dewhurst, and his pedigree, *Racehorses* concluded: 'He will be well suited by further than seven furlongs.' Not that O'Brien, a master of his art, was any more accurate in his assessment. Even after the season had started, on April 13th to be precise, the trainer was quoted as saying: 'If we have a runner in the Kentucky Derby this year he could be the one.' A month later Mozart was left in the Dante Stakes at the five-day stage, but by this time a change in plan was in the offing. Mozart had run twice, below form each time. Starting at 4/1-on for the Leopardstown 2000 Guineas Trial, he made the running but faded, finishing third of five to Dr Brendler and looking as though possibly in need of the outing. Odds on again and ridden more patiently in the Tetrarch Stakes at the Curragh, Mozart was beaten into third in a photo-finish behind his stable-companion Modigliani. Given these performances, it was no surprise to see Mozart's starting at 20/1 for the Irish Two Thousand Guineas back at the Curragh at the end of May. He proved a revelation, setting off in front, leading for much of the way and being clear two furlongs out, but then having nothing in reserve when his stable-mate Black Minnaloushe collared him well inside the final furlong. Mozart was beaten two lengths. Mozart was clearly capable of smart form at the trip, but the speed he showed, plus the fact that the winner gave O'Brien a top alternative candidate for races at around a mile, made the decision to campaign Mozart over shorter distances a relatively easy one.

Stamina in the thoroughbred is dependent on various factors, including heredity, temperament and conformation, but an important element is how the horse's muscles are arranged. There is a mix between 'fast-twitch' and 'slow-twitch' muscles in all thoroughbreds and the division, it is thought, crucially affects the distance over which a runner is effective. Fast-twitch muscles, which use glycogen, not oxygen, are able to expand and contract quickly, providing rapid movement for short periods of time. If dominant, they make for a sprinter. A preponderance of slow-twitch muscles, which use oxygen for power and have a slower expansion and contraction time, enables a horse to receive energy at a steadier pace and to stay further. Unfortunately, even allowing for differences in appearance or temperament, there is no easy way for a trainer to ascertain precisely how the muscles of any of his horses are arranged. Once the racecourse has given a clear indication, though, skilful training can change the balance and enhance one type of muscle at the expense of the other. In other words, a sprinter doesn't have to be born, he can be made, providing the ability and muscle make-up are there in the first place. The drawback is that the effects of introducing a new training regime are not immediate. Presumably O'Brien started working Mozart much faster than previously after the Irish Guineas, but he did not try the colt over the minimum trip in the King's Stand Stakes at Royal Ascot. Instead, he ran him over the intermediate trip of seven furlongs in the Jersey Stakes. Backed as if defeat was out of the question, Mozart set a scorching pace, seeing off those who tried to live with him but leaving himself vulnerable to late challengers, one of whom, Aldebaran, got to within a neck at the line, where Mozart looked out on his feet.

The form of the Jersey Stakes was not so good as that of the Irish Guineas, but, given O'Brien's expertise, the signs were there that by the time of the colt's next intended start, the July Cup, he would be even sharper and faster—O'Brien said at Ascot: 'I've never seen a horse with his pace. Speed is his thing.' So it proved in astonishing fashion at Newmarket, where eighteen runners faced the starter. Besides Mozart, they included horses who had, on their last start, won Group 2 races (Cassandra Go, Harmonic Way), Group 3 races (Gorse, Shibboleth, Volata) and listed events (Mount Abu, Misraah), so there was no shortage of in-form contenders. Mozart, who very nearly got away from his rider on the way to post, proved ideally drawn on the stand side—the low-drawn runners who raced towards the far side were seriously disadvantaged—and, away like lightning, he soon left the others trailing when asked to quicken approaching the two-furlong pole, storming clear to defeat Cassandra Go by three and a half lengths with Misraah third. A breathtaking display, comfortably the best by a sprinter all year, and in the second-fastest time in the race's history. After this, it looked as though only ill-luck could prevent Mozart's adding the five-furlong Victor Chandler Nunthorpe Stakes to his tally at York the following month. His nine opponents, six of whom started at 20/1 or longer, were not so good a bunch as at Newmarket—the second favourite, Nuclear Debate, seemed to be struggling to recapture the form which had won him the race the previous year. After just missing the break, Mozart was niggled along to find his stride, improved to lead two furlongs out and responded well when given a couple of reminders in the final furlong to run out a comfortable two-length winner from Nuclear Debate. Michael Kinane finished the race with his saddle having slipped a long way back after Mozart left the stalls awkwardly, which cannot have helped the colt's cause and paid tribute to the jockey's balance—this only four years after Kevin Darley's heroics riding without reins on Coastal Bluff in the same race. With the saddle in the right place Mozart would surely have won more cosily, but to claim, as his owner did, that the margin might have been ten lengths is fanciful in the extreme.

The Breeders' Cup Sprint was immediately named as Mozart's next and final target before retirement to Coolmore, and his preparation included a work-out at Southwell. The extent to which the Breeders' Cup Sprint poses particular problems for European runners has been noted before. Regardless of which track it is run on, the Europeans face, usually for the first time, the combination of a large field going round a turn at a ferocious end-to-end gallop on an unfamiliar surface with kickback. At Belmont Park, Mozart was attempting to become the first overseas challenger to finish in the frame since Sheikh Albadou won the Sprint in 1991. In coming home eleventh of fourteen behind Squirtle Squirt at a shade over 11/1, Mozart fared worse than Stravinsky, who ran sixth, but much the same as Green Desert, Lochsong and Royal Applause, who all finished out with the washing. As at York, Mozart was a shade slowly away, which virtually put paid to any chance of success, and, according to his jockey, he couldn't handle the kickback either. An unfortunate end to a career which had blossomed fruitfully and shown the genuine Mozart to be well up to scratch as the season's champion sprinter.

Victor Chandler Nunthorpe Stakes, York—a further drop in trip
and Mozart is still good enough to see off his rivals, despite a slipping saddle; Nuclear Debate is second,
ahead of Bishops Court (noseband), Repertory (partially hidden) and Kier Park (far side)

Mr M. Tabor & Mrs John Magnier's "Mozart"

		Danzig (b 1977)	Northern Dancer
	Danehill (USA) (b 1986)		Pas de Nom
Mozart (IRE) (b.c. 1998)		Razyana (b 1981)	His Majesty
			Spring Adieu
	Victoria Cross (USA) (b 1983)	Spectacular Bid (gr 1976)	Bold Bidder
			Spectacular
		Glowing Tribute (b 1973)	Graustark
			Admiring

Even though he will be standing alongside his sire Danehill, at a fee of IR £30,000 (October 1st), Coolmore should have no difficulty filling Mozart. He passes muster in appearance (a wrong portrait appeared in *Racehorses of 2000*), being a well-made colt, and there can be no complaints about his breeding—his sale price of 340,000 guineas as a yearling looks a tremendous bargain now. Danehill enjoyed an exceptional year with three other Group 1 winners to his tally, Aquarelliste, Banks Hill and Rock of Gibraltar. Mozart's dam the unraced Victoria Cross is a half-sister to the Kentucky Derby winner Sea Hero and has bred three other winners. Victoria Cross's 1999 foal, also by Danehill, died during the year without reaching the racecourse, but she has another colt, by Polish Precedent, coming along and she was returned to Danehill in the latest season. The Polish Precedent colt, named Highest Honour, and in training with Ian Balding in 2002, fetched only 30,000 guineas at the Houghton Sales in October. Mozart, who occasionally had his tongue tied and wore a crossed noseband, showed smart form at seven furlongs and a mile but was clearly best at shorter distances. Effective on good to firm and good to soft going, he has every chance of siring progeny effective over a mile or more. *A. P. O'Brien, Ireland*

MR BLUE SKY (IRE) 2 b.c. (Jan 23) Blues Traveller (IRE) 119 – Faypool (IRE) **72** (Fayruz 116) [2001 5m⁶ 6m³ 5.7g⁵ 6v⁵ f7g* p8g² p8g Dec 12] 6,000Y: useful-looking **a82** colt: first foal: dam, maiden in Switzerland, half-sister to smart sprinter Croft Pool: fairly useful on all-weather, fair on turf: won maiden at Wolverhampton in October: ran well in nursery at Lingfield next time: stays 1m: acts on heavy ground, fibresand and polytrack. *G. C. H. Chung*

MR BOUNTIFUL (IRE) 3 b.g. Mukaddamah (USA) 125 – Nawadder 73 (Kris 135) **58** [2001 55: 6.1v 5m 5m² 6m 7g 6m 5f 5m² 5s⁶ f5g f6g p6g⁴ p7g* Dec 28] angular gelding: has a fluent, rather exaggerated action: modest performer: left Mrs J. Ramsden 4,200 gns before penultimate start: won maiden at Lingfield in December: stays easy 7f: acts on polytrack, soft and good to firm going. *M. Dods*

MR BUSBY 8 b.g. La Grange Music 111 – Top-Anna (IRE) 71 (Ela-Mana-Mou 132) **–** [2001 f12g⁵ Feb 13] modest hurdler/novice chaser: well held in maiden at Wolverhampton (slowly away/soon off bridle). *J. L. Harris*

MR CARRIGANN (IRE) 8 b.g. Commanche Run 133 – Madam's Well (Pitpan) **–** [2001 7.1m 12f Jul 1] fair bumper winner/novice hurdler for D. Hassett in Ireland in 1999/00: well held in maidens on Flat. *M. Tate*

MR CHESTNUT TREE 2 b.g. (Apr 8) Forzando 122 – Sure Flyer (IRE) (Sure **56** Blade (USA) 130) [2001 5.1d 5.7f 6m³ 7m⁶ 7m 7g³ 8m² 7.5g f7g Oct 22] 17,000Y: half-brother to several winners, including useful Irish 2000 2-y-o 5f winner Sure Mark (by Goldmark) and 6-y-o Mark of Prophet: dam Irish maiden half-sister to dam of 4-y-o Jardines Lookout: modest maiden: placed in seller/nurseries: stays 1m: acts on good to firm ground: visored (ran poorly) fifth start: sold 4,000 gns. *M. R. Channon*

MR COMBUSTIBLE (IRE) 3 b.c. Hernando (FR) 127 – Warg (Dancing Brave **121** (USA) 140) [2001 88p: 10.3v² 12.3f* 12f⁴ 12g⁶ 13.3f* 14.6g³ Sep 15]

The St Leger tends to be an after-thought or a consolation prize for so many modern-day trainers and owners, and enthusiasm for the race is equally hard to drum up among the ante-post odds-makers. So when a leading trainer names the race as a target for one of his horses in early-May, more than four months before the event, it is worthy of notice, even though it might persuade some simply to put a line through that horse's name as a Derby contender. There might seem something perverse therefore in reporting that Mr Combustible ran a fine race when 20/1 in the Derby, while his performance when 3/1 second favourite in the St Leger came as something of a let-down. In the one race he seemed tailor-made for, Mr Combustible failed to ignite.

There is no suggestion in these opening remarks that Mr Combustible is a better horse than the St Leger winner Milan, but on form, as viewed on the day of the race and from an end-of-season perspective, Mr Combustible was clearly the second-best horse to line up for the race. He had the form to beat the runner-up Demophilos and should have finished further ahead of fourth-placed When In Rome than three quarters of a length. Mr Combustible was also good enough to have won or gone very close in several renewals of the classic in the last decade. Enough, however, of what should have happened. What did happen was that as soon as Mr Combustible was let down three and a half furlongs out, he began to hang under pressure, with his tongue lolling out. It was only in the last half furlong that he got the better of 50/1-shot When In Rome.

Mr Combustible had already twice come up against Ballydoyle's top colt Galileo, when second best was more than he was capable of. Fourth in the Derby and sixth in the Irish Derby, Mr Combustible was some way removed from the top as a mile-and-a-half horse, though his five and a half lengths fourth of twelve at Epsom was an improved showing and a game one too as he disputed the lead until Galileo went past, followed afterwards by Golan and Tobougg. Mr Combustible was clearly below form at the Curragh, weakening in the final two furlongs after tracking the leader, but either side of his two Derbys he won two pattern events. The Victor Chandler Chester Vase put him in line for Epsom as he made the running and kept on gamely to deny Snowstorm, who looked to be travelling the better for a

Stan James Geoffrey Freer Stakes, Newbury—Mr Combustible quickens well to collar Millenary, with Pat Eddery accepting things on the runner-up

long way, by three quarters of a length. Mr Combustible was one of two Barry Hills-trained maidens in a seven-runner field and started at 12/1, further confirmation that Hills's runners at the Chester May meeting are always worth a second look. The St Leger plan got back on track in fine style with a victory by two and a half lengths over the previous season's St Leger winner Millenary in the Stan James Geoffrey Freer Stakes over an extended thirteen furlongs at Newbury. Millenary had to concede Mr Combustible 6 lb more than weight for age, but Mr Combustible, waited with this time, was a smooth winner.

Mr Combustible is a half-brother to Miletrian (by Marju), who won the Park Hill Stakes—the 'fillies St Leger'—and the Ribblesdale. Add this smart pair to Marksman (by Marju), a useful two-year-old six-furlong winner on his only start, and Parkside (by Common Grounds), a fairly useful mile winner in his day, and it is clear that Warg has a very good record as a broodmare, though she died in January 2000 and her 1999 foal died young. Warg, who failed to make the racecourse, was covered as a three-year-old and sold for IR 26,000 guineas that November. Her dam Um Lardaff has a solid stud record—the useful two-year-old Mr Sandancer is the best of her four winners—after managing to retrieve only about £5,000 of a 260,000-guinea yearling price through winning two middle-distance races, at Granville-St-Pair-sur-Mer and Rochefort-sur-Loire. That yearling price is easily explained, as Um Lardaff is a sister to Shirley Heights. Their half-sister Bempton produced pattern winners Gull Nook (by Mill Reef), Mr Pintips and Banket, and Gull Nook is also the dam of Pentire. Mr Combustible, an IR £30,000 yearling, is by the 1993 Prix du Jockey Club winner Hernando, who has made such a good start at stud, beginning with last year's Prix du Jockey Club winner Holding Court. Autumn Rhythm failed to live up to early-season expectations, but Foreign Affairs and Asian Heights, as well as Mr Combustible, helped to keep Hernando in the spotlight. Despite this, Hernando's fee for 2002 has been reduced by £500 to £7,500.

Mr R. A. N. Bonnycastle's "Mr Combustible"

		Niniski (b 1976)	Nijinsky
			Virginia Hills
	Hernando (FR) (b 1990)	Whakilyric (b 1984)	Miswaki
Mr Combustible (IRE) (b.c. 1998)			Lyrism
		Dancing Brave (b 1983)	Lyphard
	Warg (b 1991)		Navajo Princess
		Um Lardaff (b 1986)	Mill Reef
			Hardiemma

A strong, rangy, attractive colt, Mr Combustible certainly has a future as a four-year-old if looks are anything to go by. Capable of smart form at a mile and a half, Mr Combustible showed in the Geoffrey Freer that he should be suited by at least a mile and three quarters. After showing promise on ground softer than good on his first three outings, his three best efforts were all on firm going. Apparently, and as the media took pleasure in pointing out on a regular basis, Mr Combustible is supposedly named after his allegedly sometimes irascible trainer. *B. W. Hills*

MR COSPECTOR   4 b.g. Cosmonaut – L'Ancressaan 67 (Dalsaan 125) [2001 72:   **69** 10v² 8s 10.5g 14m⁶ Jul 6] tall, close-coupled gelding: fair performer: stays 10.5f: best form on soft/heavy going. *T. H. Caldwell*

MR DINOS (IRE)   2 b.c. (Feb 19) Desert King (IRE) 129 – Spear Dance (Gay   **89 p** Fandango (USA) 132) [2001 7m² Jul 27] IR 40,000Y, 42,000 2-y-o: good-topped colt: closely related to smart Irish 7f (at 2 yrs) to 1¼m winner who stayed 1¾m Risk Material (by Danehill) and half-brother to several winners, including 6f winner Lambada Girl (by

679

Petorius): dam, Irish 7f/1m winner, sister to Jersey Stakes winner Rasa Penang: 14/1, fairly useful form when neck second of 6 to Sohaib in maiden at Ascot, keeping on after running green: should do better if all is well. *P. F. I. Cole*

MR ED (IRE)   3 ch.g. In The Wings 128 – Center Moriches (IRE) 74 (Magical Wonder   **69**
(USA) 125) [2001 –: 9f⁶ 9.9m⁵ 11.6m² 14m 9.9m* 11m Sep 26] fair handicapper: won at Salisbury (tended to edge right) in August: should stay 1½m: acts on good to firm going. *D. R. C. Elsworth*

MR FITZER   2 b.g. (Mar 7) Robellino (USA) 127 – Tiszta Sharok 81 (Song 132)   **–**
[2001 5.7f 5f 7g 5m f8g f7g Dec 10] 10,000 2-y-o: big gelding: half-brother to several winners, including 1993 2-y-o 6f winner Peter Rowley (by Absalom) and Irish 9f/1¼m winner Petofi (by Petong), both fairly useful: dam 2-y-o 5f winner (only season to race): only a little sign of ability in maidens/nursery. *M. C. Chapman*

MR FORTYWINKS (IRE)   7 ch.g. Fools Holme (USA) – Dream On 54 (Absalom   **73**
128) [2001 70: 16s* 16m 16m 15f⁵ 13g² 16g 15.9d 14.1g 13.9d⁴ 16g Nov 7] sparely-made gelding: fair handicapper: won at Ripon in April: effective at 13f to 2m: has form on firm going, probably at very best on good or softer, and acts on fibresand and equitrack: tried tongue tied: tends to sweat: usually races up with pace. *J. L. Eyre*

MR GEORGE SMITH   4 b.g. Prince Sabo 123 – Nellie's Gamble 66 (Mummy's   **–**
Game 120) [2001 64: e7g f8s e7s⁶ e7g Mar 19] modest handicapper: little form in 2001: blinkered final start. *G. L. Moore*

MR GISBY (USA)   3 b. or br.g. Chief's Crown (USA) – Double Lock 104 (Home   **63**
Guard (USA) 129) [2001 10g⁴ 9m⁵ 9.9g⁵ 12g Oct 4] $40,000Y: lengthy gelding: half-brother to several winners, including top-class miler Sure Blade (by Kris) and 1¼m to 13f winner Ringlet (by Secreto): dam 1¼m winner: modest maiden: stays 1¼m. *D. R. C. Elsworth*

MR LEAR (USA)   2 b.g. (Feb 25) Lear Fan (USA) 130 – Majestic Mae (USA) (Crow   **49**
(FR) 134) [2001 5m⁶ 5f 5m Jul 30] $20,000Y: sturdy gelding: brother to 3 winners in USA, including 1994 2-y-o 6f minor stakes winner Hamlets Ghost, and half-brother to 3 winners in USA: dam winning sprinter in USA: poor maiden: best effort on debut: gelded after final start. *T. D. Barron*

MR MAHOOSE (USA)   3 b.g. Rakeen (USA) 99 – Golden Hen (USA) (Native   **105 p**
Prospector (USA) 90) [2001 71p: f8g⁵ 6m* 7.1d* 7f² 7m* 7s⁶ Sep 29] tall, quite good-topped gelding: useful form: won maiden at Newcastle in June, minor event at Haydock in July and handicap at Newmarket (quickened well despite edging left when beating Forever Times by ¾ length) in August: respectable sixth to Downland, set good deal to do, in Tote Trifecta Handicap at Ascot final start: should prove best at 6f/7f: acts on firm and good to soft ground: should make a smart performer, and win a good prize. *W. J. Haggas*

MR MICKY (IRE)   3 b.g. Rudimentary (USA) 118 – Top Berry 87 (High Top 131)   **54**
[2001 10s 12m⁶ 10.5m 12d Oct 9] 11,000F, 4,800Y: big, workmanlike gelding: has a round action: seventh foal: half-brother to 3 winners, including 6-y-o Derryquin: dam 1m winner: modest maiden: probably stays 1½m. *T. D. Easterby*

MR MIDAZ   2 ch.g. (Feb 19) Danzig Connection (USA) – Marmy 43 (Midyan (USA)   **67**
124) [2001 5f⁴ 5g³ 7g 6m 7m² 6d Oct 18] 2,600F: good-bodied gelding: second foal: dam, third in 6f seller at 2 yrs, out of half-sister to very smart miler Alhijaz: fair maiden: 50/1, best effort when beaten neck in nursery at Redcar: gelded after final start: will probably stay 1m: acts on firm ground: often races prominently. *Jedd O'Keeffe*

MR MONROE   2 b.c. (Apr 28) Mistertopogigo (IRE) 118 – Highland Heights (IRE)   **43**
(Lomond (USA) 128) [2001 8d⁵ f6g f6g f6g Dec 17] 500Y: smallish, quite good-topped colt: second foal: dam bad maiden hurdler: poor maiden. *C. Smith*

MR OBOE   3 b.g. Charnwood Forest (IRE) 125 – Miss Clarinet (Pharly (FR) 130)   **–**
[2001 11.1d⁶ 8.1v⁶ 10v Oct 16] 23,000F, 20,000Y: lengthy gelding: second living foal: dam once-raced half-sister to very smart sprinter Piccolo: poor maiden. *Andrew Turnell*

MR PERRY (IRE)   5 br.g. Perugino (USA) 84 – Elegant Tune (USA) 51 (Alysheba   **–**
(USA)) [2001 60d: e8g f6g Apr 17] one-time fair handicapper: very much on down-grade on Flat: sometimes blinkered/visored: winner of selling hurdle in October. *M. D. Hammond*

MR PERTEMPS   3 b.g. Primo Dominie 121 – Amber Mill 96 (Doulab (USA) 115)   **58**
[2001 53p: 5g 7s² Oct 5] tall, lengthy gelding: modest maiden handicapper: stays 7f: best efforts on soft going. *S. C. Williams*

MR PIANO MAN (IRE)   3 gr.g. Paris House 123 – Winter March (Ballad Rock 122)   –
[2001 63: 6m 5m May 26] close-coupled gelding: modest maiden at 2 yrs: well beaten
both starts in 2001. *J. L. Eyre*

MR PITZ   2 ch.c. (Apr 28) Hector Protector (USA) 124 – Moogie 103 (Young   **86**
Generation 129) [2001 7f⁴ 7d² 7m² 7g* Aug 27] 30,000Y: ninth foal: half-brother to 3
winners, including 4-y-o Pup's Pride and fairly useful 1996 2-y-o 7f winner Catwalk (by
Shirley Heights): dam, 2-y-o 6f winner, later best at 9f: fairly useful form: runner-up
twice before winning 3-runner maiden at Epsom by 1½ lengths from Sir Northerndancer,
making most: settled better with each run, and should stay 1m: acts on good to firm and
good to soft ground. *E. A. L. Dunlop*

MR RICCIOLO (IRE)   2 b.g. (May 6) Highest Honor (FR) 124 – Just Rainbow (FR)   –
(Rainbow Quest (USA) 134) [2001 8m Sep 24] IR 15,000F, IR 25,000Y: third foal:
brother to French 9f/1¼m winner Just Wood: dam unraced half-sister to useful French
middle-distance performer Justful (by Highest Honor): tailed off in maiden at Kempton,
looking wayward. *B. J. Curley*

MR SANDANCER   2 b.c. (Feb 20) Zafonic (USA) 130 – Um Lardaff (Mill Reef   **102**
(USA) 141) [2001 6f* 7m⁴ 7.1g 7m² 8d⁶ 8v⁶ Oct 27] 21,000F, 62,000Y, 30,000 2-y-o:
strong, attractive colt: good walker: eighth foal: brother to useful 1997 2-y-o 7f winner
Fantasy Island, later winner in UAE, and half-brother to 2 winners, including fairly useful
7f (at 2 yrs) and 1¼m winner Expensive Taste (by Cadeaux Genereux): dam, French 11f/
1½m winner, grandam of 3-y-o Mr Combustible and sister to Shirley Heights: useful
performer: won maiden at Newcastle in June: clearly best efforts when 2½ lengths fourth
to Naheef in Vintage Stakes at Goodwood and 1¾ lengths second to Hills of Gold in
minor event at Doncaster: should stay at least 1m: acts on good to firm going, possibly
not softer than good. *J. G. Given*

MRS ANNA   2 b.f. (Mar 11) Charnwood Forest (IRE) 125 – Jezyah (USA) 80 (Chief's   **60**
Crown (USA)) [2001 5s⁴ 6m³ 6m⁵ 7.5m³ 6m Sep 2] 10,000Y: rangy filly: second foal:
dam 2-y-o 7f winner out of half-sister to Derby third Star of Gdansk: modest maiden:
stays 7.5f: acts on soft and good to firm ground: has raced freely. *T. D. Easterby*

MRS CUBE   2 ch.f. (May 13) Missed Flight 123 – Norska 67 (Northfields (USA))   **41**
[2001 5.7f 5m 6.1m 6g Aug 6] 1,700Y: well-grown filly: half-sister to several winners,
including 1¾m winner Eponine (by Sharpo): dam maiden who stayed 1¼m: poor maiden.
J. M. Bradley

MRS JOHNSON (IRE)   3 b.f. Brief Truce (USA) 126 – Zara Whetei (IRE) (Lomond   –
(USA) 128) [2001 8m 10s f7g f8g f9.4f Dec 5] 3,800Y, 3,500 2-y-o: first foal: dam winner
in Italy at 7f (at 2 yrs) to 1¼m: little form, including in sellers. *J. A. Osborne*

MRS KANNING   2 ch.f. (Mar 8) Distant View (USA) 126 – Red Hot Dancer (USA)   **61**
(Seattle Dancer (USA) 119) [2001 5m 8d 8v Oct 26] 14,500Y, 7,000 2-y-o: small,
good-bodied filly: third foal: half-sister to a winner in USA by Technology: dam, placed
in USA, half-sister to useful stayer Zero Watt and to dam of Poule d'Essai des Pouliches
winner Ta Rib: form in maidens (modest) only when twelfth of 20 at Newmarket on
second start. *M. H. Tompkins*

MRS NASH   3 b.f. Night Shift (USA) – Nashkara (Shirley Heights 130) [2001 8m 9m²   **66**
10v Oct 8] 21,000F, 125,000Y: eighth foal: closely related to 2 winners abroad and
half-sister to 4-y-o Marrakech and a winner abroad by Kahyasi: dam Irish 1½m winner
from family of Shergar: fair maiden: second at Newbury, best effort: raced freely final
start: should stay 1¼m. *R. Charlton*

MR SPEAKER (IRE)   8 ch.g. Statoblest 120 – Casting Vote (USA) 54 (Monteverdi   **58**
129) [2001 –: 10g 7.6m 8.1s⁶ 8g³ 8d* Sep 4] close-coupled, workmanlike gelding:
modest handicapper: made all at Yarmouth (apprentices) in September: seems best at 1m/
9f: acts on firm and soft going: none too consistent. *C. F. Wall*

MRS PICKLES   6 gr.m. Northern Park (USA) 107 – Able Mabel 77 (Absalom 128)   –
[2001 f14g Dec 14] probably of little account nowadays. *M. D. I. Usher*

MR SPLIFFY (IRE)   2 b.g. (Apr 18) Fayruz 116 – Johns Conquerer (IRE) 74 (Con-   **65**
quering Hero (USA) 116) [2001 5g 6m 5m 7g 5d 5d f5g⁴ f5g f5g⁵ f5g³ Dec 17] IR 3,800F,
IR 5,000Y, 3,500 2-y-o: heavy-topped gelding: second foal: dam Irish 2-y-o 6f winner:
fair maiden: best effort when third at Southwell: will prove best at 5f: acts on fibresand,
probably on good to soft going: has bolted to post: difficult ride. *M. C. Chapman*

MRS PLUM   2 b.f. (Mar 16) Emarati (USA) 74 – Aubade (Henbit (USA) 130) [2001   **72**
f6g³ 7g⁶ f6g⁴ f5g⁶ Dec 3] 2,600F: seventh foal: half-sister to winners abroad by Sharpo

and Reprimand: dam, French 12.5f winner, sister to smart French middle-distance colt Ordinance: fair maiden: third at Southwell (hung left), best effort: needs to settle to stay beyond 6f. *D. Morris*

MRS POOTERS (IRE) 2 b.f. (Apr 4) Petardia 113 – Mrs Hooters (Glint of Gold **66** 128) [2001 7m 6v³ f6g⁶ Nov 19] IR 10,000Y: sixth foal: sister to Italian 7.5f winner (including at 2 yrs) In Creek Ata and half-sister to winners in Italy by Broken Hearted and Superpower: dam, Irish maiden, stayed 1½m: easily best effort in maidens (fair form) when 8 lengths third to Kepler at Windsor: should stay 1m: has carried head awkwardly: edged left final outing. *D. W. P. Arbuthnot*

MR SQUIGGLE (IRE) 3 b.g. Persian Bold 123 – Soul Fire (IRE) (Exactly Sharp **51** (USA) 121) [2001 49: 7.5m 8m 8.5f 11m* 12g 10m Sep 1] leggy, workmanlike gelding: modest performer: won maiden seller at Redcar in July: little other form: stays 11f: acts on good to firm going. *A. Dickman*

MRS TIGGYWINKLE 3 b.f. Magic Ring (IRE) 115 – Upper Sister (Upper Case **47 §** (USA)) [2001 54§: f6g³ f6g f6g f8g 5f³ 6m 6g 5f⁵ 6d² 5v Oct 15] sparely-made filly: poor maiden: left N. Littmoden after second outing, J. M. Bradley after fourth: effective at 5f to 8.5f: acts on firm going, good to soft and fibresand: sometimes blinkered at 2 yrs: ungenuine. *Miss L. A. Perratt*

MR STYLISH 5 b.g. Mazilier (USA) 107 – Moore Stylish 65 (Moorestyle 137) [2001 **83** 86: f5g 6m⁶ 5.1m 6g⁶ 5m 6m² 6m 6s⁶ 7m 6m⁴ 5.7d 5.7m⁴ 5.1g 5m 6g 6v³ 5s³ f6g* f6g Nov 3] lengthy gelding: fairly useful handicapper: won at Wolverhampton in October: best at 5f/6f: acts on fibresand and any turf going: tried blinkered (reportedly bled from nose), usually visored: tongue tied: carries head awkwardly. *J. S. Moore*

MR TOAD (IRE) 2 b.c. (Feb 6) Marju (IRE) 127 – Zany (Junius (USA) 124) [2001 5f **99** 6m³ 6m* 6g 5g² 6m⁵ 6s* 6g³ 6g⁶ 7m³ 6g⁵ Oct 4] 20,000Y: good-topped colt: good mover: half-brother to several winners, including useful Irish 1997 2-y-o 7f/8.5f winner Magical Minty (by Magical Wonder), later 9f winner in Hong Kong: dam Irish 9.5f/1¼m winner at 4 yrs: useful performer: won maiden at Kempton in June and nursery at Epsom in August: good 2 lengths third to Lipstick in listed event at Kempton in September: not at best last 3 starts (stiff task in Middle Park final one): headstrong, and may prove best at 5f/6f: acts on soft and good to firm ground: has worn crossed noseband: tongue tied last 7 starts: carries head awkwardly: has found little. *J. A. Osborne*

MR TOP FLIGHT (IRE) 2 b.g. (Mar 2) Night Shift (USA) – Native Rhythm (IRE) **55** 71 (Lycius (USA) 124) [2001 7d 6s f6g Nov 12] 16,000F, IR 20,000Y: first foal: dam, maiden who stayed 7f, out of half-sister to Prix Marcel Boussac winner Play It Safe and Washington International winner Providential: modest form in maidens: not knocked about final start: should stay 1m. *Mrs G. S. Rees*

MR WENSLEYDALE 2 b.g. (Mar 28) Alzao (USA) 117 – Third Watch 114 (Slip **61** Anchor 136) [2001 7g 7.1g 8.5g⁵ 8.3v 8d⁶ Nov 2] 20,000Y: close-coupled, good-topped gelding: half-brother to a several winners, including 3-y-o Watchkeeper and useful 1½m winner Rainwatch (by Rainbow Quest): dam, won Ribblesdale Stakes, from very good family: modest maiden: has raced freely, but should stay 1¼m: slowly away 3 times: has carried head awkwardly: gelded after final start. *G. L. Moore*

MR WHIZZ 4 ch.g. Manhal – Panienka (POL) 70 (Dom Racine (FR) 121) [2001 6v* **69** f8.5g⁶ f8s⁵ Dec 15] third reported foal: half-brother to 6f/7f winner Itch and 7-y-o Whizz Kid (both by Puissance): dam stayer on Flat, also won over hurdles: 33/1, fair form to make winning debut in maiden at Windsor in October by length from Vincentia: well held on all-weather both subsequent outings. *M. R. Bosley*

MSHINDA 3 b.f. Mtoto 134 – Nibabu (FR) 101§ (Nishapour (FR) 125) [2001 7m⁴ **61** 5.7m² f6g⁵ Oct 22] 10,000Y: half-sister to several winners, notably smart 7f/1m performer Nijo (by Top Ville): dam, maiden, best at 7f/1m: modest maiden: second at Bath: free-going sort, may prove best short of 1m: sold 4,500 gns. *P. J. Makin*

MUAKAAD 4 b.c. Muhtarram (USA) 125 – Forest Lair (Habitat 134) [2001 113: 10g* **118** 10.5g⁶ 9g² 10m* 10d⁶ 10g* Sep 8] good-bodied colt: smart performer: won listed race at the Curragh in May, Meld Stakes there (by 1½ lengths from Bonnard) in July and listed race at Leopardstown in September: ran well when 1½ lengths second to Distant Music in International Stakes at the Curragh on third outing: well-held sixth in Arlington Million penultimate one: stayed 1¼m: acted on soft and good to firm going: was usually tongue tied: twice blinkered: suffered fatal injury on gallops in November. *D. K. Weld, Ireland*

MUBAAH 2 ch.c. (Apr 13) Cadeaux Genereux 131 – Numuthej (USA) 50 (Nureyev **64 p** (USA) 131) [2001 6v⁵ 6d⁴ Nov 2] fourth foal: half-brother to 1¼m winner Big Wheel (by

Mujtahid), 3-y-o Moojaz and a winner in Greece by Zafonic: dam once-raced sister to smart French winner up to 7.5f Robin des Pins and closely related to very smart French winner up to 1½m Mystery Plays: modest form in maidens at Windsor and Brighton, forced wide and again not knocked about when fourth to Jonny Ebeneezer in latter: will stay 1m: capable of better. *A. C. Stewart*

MUBKERA (IRE) 2 ch.f. (May 5) Nashwan (USA) 135 – Na-Ayim (IRE) 68 (Shirley **86 p** Heights 130) [2001 8.1g* Aug 27] fifth foal: sister to 7.5f winner Hishmah and half-sister to fairly useful 1¼m winner Tajawuz (by Kris) and 3-y-o Wa-Naam: dam, 2-y-o 6f winner, out of half-sister to Oaks second/excellent broodmare Slightly Dangerous: 5/1, looked useful prospect when winning maiden at Chepstow by 1¾ lengths from Alexander Three D, travelling strongly just off pace and leading over 1f out: should stay at least 1¼m: sure to improve. *E. A. L. Dunlop*

MUBTAKER (USA) 4 ch.c. Silver Hawk (USA) 123 – Gazayil (USA) 80 (Irish **123** River (FR) 131) [2001 103p: 10s³ 10g² 9.9m* 11.8d² 12m* 11f² 12g* 12d³ Nov 2]
  Mubtaker's racing career began in earnest in the latest season. Once-raced at two, for David Loder in France, and seen out only twice at three, when he won a maiden at Newbury, he made eight appearances in 2001 and was successful on three of them, developing into a very smart performer. Indeed, such was the progress made by Mubtaker that he ended the season rated not far behind his more vaunted stable companion the Champion Stakes winner Nayef, whom he will be accompanying to Dubai to be prepared for the 2002 World Cup meeting.
  Mubtaker has been entered for the Dubai Sheema Classic, run over a mile and a half on turf. He seemed not to stay when first tried at that trip on his final

Mr Hamdan Al Maktoum's "Mubtaker"

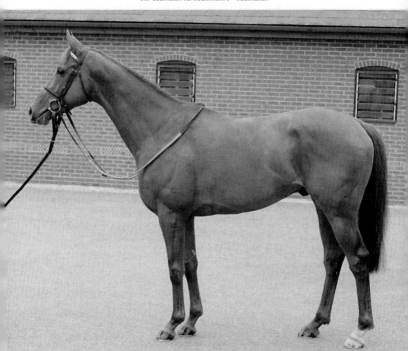

outing at three, and began his four-year-old campaign racing over a mile and a quarter, winning the listed Badger Brewery Festival Stakes at Goodwood in May on his third start by a head from Nooshman. It was, however, the step back up to a mile and a half which seemed to bring out the best in Mubtaker, who was successful in two more listed events, both of them at Newmarket. In June, Mubtaker won the seven-runner Ladbrokes Fred Archer Stakes by two and a half lengths from Courteous, who received 3 lb, then in October he gave an impressive performance in accounting for eight rivals in the Fishpools Furnishings Godolphin Stakes. Mubtaker was still travelling easily when coming through to lead over two furlongs out in the latter, and he forged clear when shaken up, value for still more than the five lengths which separated him from his nearest pursuer, Hatha Anna, at the line. Mubtaker also acquitted himself well when second in listed races immediately prior to his last two wins, going down by a short head to subsequent Hardwicke runner-up Zindabad, who received 3 lb, at Leicester and by a length and a half to Grandera at Newbury. Mubtaker was probably past his best for the season when beaten at odds on for the St Simon Stakes back at Newmarket on his final start, though at least he maintained his record of never having finished out of the first three.

			Roberto		Hail To Reason
	Silver Hawk (USA)		(b 1969)		Bramalea
	(b 1979)		Gris Vitesse		Amerigo
Mubtaker (USA)			(gr 1966)		Matchiche II
(ch.c. 1997)			Irish River		Riverman
	Gazayil (USA)		(ch 1976)		Irish Star
	(ch 1985)		Close Comfort		Far North
			(b 1979)		Caterina

Mubtaker is the fifth foal of Gazayil, who won a seven-furlong maiden at Chepstow for Henry Cecil on her only start at two but failed to make the frame in a couple of outings at three. She was later successful in Australia, where three of her earlier foals won races. Another, Crystal Downs (by Alleged), showed useful form over seven furlongs and a mile for Aidan O'Brien, including when runner-up in the Prix Marcel Boussac and fourth in the 1999 Irish One Thousand Guineas. Gazayil, a half-sister to the smart mile-and-a-quarter-winner Husyan, is a daughter of an unraced half-sister to Ancient Regime, the leading French two-year-old filly of 1980. Mubtaker's third dam Caterina, a half-sister to the high-class middle-distance colt Scottish Rifle, won the Nunthorpe Stakes and is also the third dam of Foreign Affairs. The lengthy Mubtaker, an unimpressive mover who acts on any going, may still be capable of a bit more improvement and is certainly well up to winning pattern races below the highest level. *M. P. Tregoning*

MUCHANA YETU 4 b.f. Mtoto 134 – Bobbie Dee 93 (Blakeney 126) [2001 64d: 6m⁴ 8.1m Jul 13] close-coupled filly: disappointing maiden: has worn tongue strap/ blinkers. *Mrs P. N. Dutfield* —

MUCHEA 7 ch.h. Shalford (IRE) 124§ – Bargouzine 67 (Hotfoot 126) [2001 106: 8d 8s³ 7.9m³ 8.1m⁵ 8m³ 7m 8g⁵ 7.9m 8g⁴ 7s 7s 6v⁶ 8.2s² Nov 5] good-topped horse: useful performer: creditable efforts when in frame in handicaps (including 2 lengths third to Surprise Encounter in Royal Hunt Cup at Royal Ascot fifth outing) and minor event: stays 1m: acts on heavy and good to firm going: sometimes visored at 6 yrs: sometimes sweats: has been bandaged: usually held up. *M. R. Channon* **105**

MUCHO GUSTO 3 b.g. Casteddu 111 – Heather Honey (Insan (USA) 119) [2001 –: f6g 7g 8d 7.5m 10m⁴ f7g f8g Nov 26] poor maiden: form only when fourth at Leicester: stays 1¼m: tongue tied both outings before final one. *R. F. Marvin* **46**

MUCH TOO MUCH (IRE) 3 b.f. Mujadil (USA) 119 – Spoilt Again 91 (Mummy's Pet 125) [2001 6g 6f f6g³ f6g f8.5g Sep 22] 1,500Y: half-sister to several winners, including fairly useful 7f to 9f winner High Spirits (by Great Commotion) and 1¼m and 1¾m winner Teen Jay (by Teenoso): dam, 9f/1¼m winner, daughter of Park Hill winner Reload: modest maiden: should stay beyond 6f: acts on fibresand: sold 900 gns. *K. McAuliffe* **52**

MUDDY WATER 5 b.m. Salse (USA) 128 – Rainbow Fleet 66 (Nomination 125) [2001 63d, a55d: e8g² f8.5g⁵ 8m³ 8.1g⁴ 8.1m⁵ f8g* 8m³ 7.1g⁶ 8f 8s³ f8.5g⁶ f8g* f8g² f8g f8g⁶ Dec 17] modest performer: left D. Marks after second start: won claimer in July and **51**
a63

seller (final start for I. Wood) in November, both at Southwell: stays 1m: acts on soft going, good to firm and fibresand/equitrack: occasionally tongue tied: held up. *R. Wilman*

MUDLARK   9 b.g. Salse (USA) 128 – Mortal Sin (USA) 65 (Green Forest (USA) 134)   –
[2001 f16g Jan 12] probably of little account nowadays. *J. Norton*

MUFFIN MAN   4 b.c. Timeless Times (USA) 99 – Allesca 69 (Alleging (USA) 120)   **45**
[2001 52: 7g 6f 7m 8f⁶ 8f³ 9f 10.2g⁵ 8.1m 10m 10g Aug 3] workmanlike colt: poor maiden handicapper: barely stays 1¼m: acts on firm and good to soft going: sometimes slowly away: none too consistent. *M. D. I. Usher*

MUFFIT (IRE)   2 b.f. (Apr 18) Alhaarth (IRE) 126 – Calash (Indian King (USA) 128)   **63**
[2001 6.1g 6m 7m 6g* 7.1m² 7g⁶ 6.9d⁴ 7m 7m³ 7s⁵ 6d² 7d 8v² 7d f8.5g³ f8g f7g⁵ f7s Dec   **a56**
18] IR 20,000Y: smallish, sturdy filly: half-sister to several winners, including Irish 8.5f winner Hill Style (by Desert Style) and 1996 2-y-o 7f winner Briska (by River Falls): dam ran twice at 2 yrs: modest performer: won seller at Lingfield in August: left M. Channon after fifteenth outing: stays 8.5f: acts on good to firm going, heavy and fibresand: flicked tail/found little penultimate start. *P. Howling*

MUFREH (USA)   3 b.c. Dayjur (USA) 137 – Mathkurh (USA) 97 (Riverman (USA)   **65 +**
131) [2001 6.1m³ 7v⁵ f8.5g⁴ f7g² Nov 23] sixth foal: brother to useful 1997 2-y-o 5f/6f (Cherry Hinton) winner Asfurah, closely related to fairly useful 5f (at 2 yrs)/6f winner Alumisiyah (by Danzig) and half-brother to 2 winners, including smart US 6f/7f performer Istintaj (by Nureyev): dam 5f (at 2 yrs)/6f winner: modest maiden: trained by N. Graham on first start: best effort in handicap at Southwell on final one (hung left): may prove best at 7f: twice slowly away. *A. G. Newcombe*

MUGHARREB (USA)   3 b.c. Gone West (USA) – Marling (IRE) 124 (Lomond   **117**
(USA) 128) [2001 94P: 8g* 8g⁶ 8.1m³ 6m² 6g 6f* 6d Oct 19] strong colt: very good mover: smart performer: won maiden in May and listed event (held up, best effort to beat

Mr Hamdan Al Maktoum's "Mugharreb"

Welcome Friend by 1¾ lengths in 5-runner contest) in August, both at Newmarket: well held final start: better form at 6f than 1m: acts on firm going. *B. Hanbury*

MUHAREB (USA)   2 ch.c. (Apr 20) Thunder Gulch (USA) 129 – Queen of Spirit   **76**
(USA) (Deputy Minister (CAN)) [2001 7s 8.2s⁴ Nov 5] $72,000Y: third foal: half-brother
to winners in US by Miner's Mark and Hennessy: dam, US maiden, half-sister to US
Grade 1 9f/1¼m winner Tactile out of Grade 1 winner Only Queens: better effort (fair
form) when fourth to Five Stars in maiden at Nottingham: should stay 1¼m. *C. E. Brittain*

MUHTAFEL   7 b.g. Nashwan (USA) 135 – The Perfect Life (IRE) 106 (Try My   –
Best (USA) 130) [2001 9m 11.6g Jul 9] big gelding: formerly useful handicapper:
showed little in 2001 (reportedly lame second start): occasionally visored/tongue tied.
J. R. Jenkins

MUJAALED (IRE)   4 b.g. Elmaamul (USA) 125 – Balaabel (USA) 83 (Sadler's   –
Wells (USA) 132) [2001 –: f8g 7m 7m May 28] of little account. *D. W. Chapman*

MUJADILLY   3 b.f. Mujadil (USA) 119 – Casbah Girl 79 (Native Bazaar 122) [2001   –
6v⁶ 7f⁶ 8s⁶ 6d f6g Dec 10] 3,500Y: workmanlike filly: half-sister to several winners,
including useful 5f (including at 2 yrs) winner Sabre Rattler (by Beveled): dam 6f/7f
winner: well held, including in handicaps. *W. M. Brisbourne*

MUJADO (IRE)   3 b.f. Mujadil (USA) 119 – Unaria (Prince Tenderfoot (USA) 126)   **95**
[2001 86: 6m 5f 6g* 6m⁵ 6g Aug 11] leggy, workmanlike filly: useful performer: won
minor event at Yarmouth in June: creditable fifth to Palace Affair in listed race at York
next time: should stay 7f: acts on good to firm going, probably on good to soft: tongue
tied last 4 starts: joined C. Clement in USA. *W. J. Haggas*

MUJA FAREWELL   3 ch.f. Mujtahid (USA) 118 – Highland Rhapsody (IRE) 78 (Kris   **94**
135) [2001 89p: 6d⁵ 5f* 5g 5g Aug 22] strong, lengthy filly: fairly useful handicapper:
best effort when winning 20-runner event at Ascot in June by ½ length from Funny
Valentine, making all: probably best at 5f: acts on firm and good to soft going: sometimes
on toes/early to post. *T. D. Barron*

MUJAGEM (IRE)   5 br.m. Mujadil (USA) 119 – Lili Bengam (Welsh Saint 126)   –
[2001 49+, a58: 5g⁶ f5s 6v Oct 16] tall mare: modest handicapper at 4 yrs: no form in
2001 (broke blood vessel second start): often blinkered. *M. W. Easterby*

MUJALIA (IRE)   3 b.g. Mujtahid (USA) 118 – Danalia (IRE) 78 (Danehill (USA)   – §
126) [2001 –: e10g² f9.4s⁵ e10s* e10g³ 10s 7m 10d 10v Oct 29] modest performer: won   **a62 §**
claimer at Lingfield in February: left S. Dow after sixth start: stays easy 1¼m: acts on
equitrack, no form on turf: showed considerable temperament last 2 outings. *Jamie
Poulton*

MUJALINA (IRE)   3 b.c. Mujadil (USA) 119 – Talina's Law (IRE) 83 (Law Society   –
(USA) 130) [2001 85?: 11v⁵ 13s⁶ 12.5g Jun 5] leggy colt: won maiden at Southwell at 2
yrs: well held on Flat in 2001, leaving E. O'Neill after reappearance (very stiff task in
Prix Noailles at Longchamp): should stay 1¼m: acts on fibresand, firm and soft going:
blinkered (ran poorly) seventh 2-y-o outing: winner over hurdles for G. Macaire in France
and for M. Pipe. *E. Lellouche, France*

MUJASINA (IRE)   2 b.c. (Mar 4) Mujadil (USA) 119 – Camassina (IRE) 62 (Taufan   **70**
(USA) 119) [2001 5m⁴ 5m* 5f⁴ 6f⁴ 7d 7.1m 8v f7g Nov 30] IR 10,500F, IR 15,000Y:
rather leggy, workmanlike colt: first foal: dam, Irish maiden, stayed 9f: fair performer:
won maiden at Musselburgh in May: ran poorly in nurseries 3 of last 4 starts: stays easy
7f: acts on firm going: sometimes tongue tied: has hung/been slowly away. *J. L. Eyre*

MUJA'S MAGIC (IRE)   6 b.m. Mujadil (USA) 119 – Grave Error (Northern Treat   **a58 d**
(USA)) [2001 57, a70: f6g f7s³ f7g f8s⁴ f8g⁴ f7g f7g⁶ f7g f7g⁵ f8g Apr 9] leggy,
workmanlike mare: modest handicapper, on downgrade: stays easy 1m: acts on firm
going, good to soft and fibresand/equitrack: blinkered/visored: sometimes slowly away/
looks hard ride: sold 800 gns. *Mrs N. Macauley*

MUJKARI (IRE)   5 ch.g. Mujtahid (USA) 118 – Hot Curry (USA) (Sharpen Up 127)   **54 d**
[2001 44§: f9.4s e10g* e12g e13s² 11.8f³ 12m³ 12m⁵ 10m 12m⁴ 12m⁶ 12.3g⁵ 13.8g
10.2g² Aug 27] lengthy gelding: modest handicapper: won at Lingfield in January: below
best after sixth start: stays easy 13f: acts on firm going, good to soft and fibresand/
equitrack: visored/blinkered: none too keen. *J. M. Bradley*

MUKLAH (IRE)   3 b.f. Singspiel (IRE) 133 – Maraatib (IRE) 93 (Green   **101**
Desert (USA) 127) [2001 7f² 7m* 7g* Aug 11] smallish, quite attractive filly: half-sister
to several winners, including useful 5f/6f winner (including at 2 yrs) Khasayl and fairly
useful 6f (at 2 yrs) to 1¼m winner Mazeed (both by Lycius): dam 5f (including at 2 yrs)/

6f winner: won maiden at Kempton in July and listed race at Newmarket (beat Lady Dominatrix by 5 lengths) in August, making all on first occasion and most on second: will stay at least 1m: raced on good going or firmer: useful. *B. W. Hills*

MULABEE (USA) 2 br.c. (Jan 5) Gulch (USA) – Shir Dar (FR) (Lead On Time (USA) 123) [2001 7m⁶ 7m² 7.5g⁴ 7g* Aug 30] $120,000Y: useful-looking colt: second foal: dam, winner up to 1m in France, later US Grade 2 8.5f winner: fairly useful form: twice shaped encouragingly prior to winning nursery at Lingfield by head from Football Crazy, leading 1f out: should stay 1m: open to improvement. *E. A. L. Dunlop* **84 p**

MULDOON (IRE) 2 b.c. (Apr 24) Fumo di Londra (IRE) 108 – Caroline's Mark (On Your Mark 125) [2001 5s⁴ 5g f5g⁴ f5g³ 5.1s⁶ f6s 5.3s 5v 5.7d⁶ f6g³ f5s Dec 27] IR 3,000F, 2,000Y: half-brother to several winners, including fairly useful Irish 1¼m winner Bothsidesnow (by Exhibitioner) and 6f winner One To Go (by Petorius): dam Irish 2-y-o 5f winner: modest maiden: should stay 7f: acts on fibresand, raced only on good ground or softer on turf: wandered markedly eighth outing. *B. Palling* **53**

MULLAGHMORE (IRE) 5 b.g. Petardia 113 – Comfrey Glen 63 (Glenstal (USA) 118) [2001 61, a79: e10g 10f⁵ 11.6g⁴ 10m³ 8.3g⁶ 10g 14.1d Oct 3] strong gelding: modest performer: effective at 1m, probably at 1¾m: acts on firm going (probably on good to soft) and equitrack: sometimes blinkered/visored, hooded penultimate outing: tongue tied early in career: usually slowly away: unreliable. *M. Kettle* **60 §**
a– §

MULLING IT OVER (IRE) 3 b.f. Blues Traveller (IRE) 119 – Wonderment 72 (Mummy's Pet 125) [2001 56d: 6m⁶ May 28] leggy filly: modest maiden: well held only outing in 2001. *T. D. Easterby* **–**

MULL OF KINTYRE (USA) 4 b.c. Danzig (USA) – Retrospective (USA) (Easy Goer (USA)) [2001 8m⁶ 7g² 7g³ 6s⁴ 7s⁶ Oct 14] sturdy, good-topped colt: smart performer: won Gimcrack Stakes at York at 2 yrs: missed 2000 with injured pedal bone: in frame in Minstrel Stakes at the Curragh (neck second to King Charlemagne), Lennox Stakes at Goodwood (1¼ lengths third to Fath) and Sprint Cup at Haydock (4 lengths fourth to Nuclear Debate): only sixth in Prix de la Foret at Longchamp final start: effective at 6f to 8.5f: acted on dirt, soft and good to firm going: usually raced up with pace: to stand at Coolmore Stud, Ireland, fee IR £5,000 Oct 1st, nfnf. *A. P. O'Brien, Ireland* **114**

MULSANNE 3 b.c. Clantime 101 – Prim Lass 65 (Reprimand 122) [2001 –: 7.1m 6.1m 7.1g Jul 20] seems of little account. *P. A. Pritchard* **–**

MULTIPLOY 2 b.f. (Apr 8) Deploy 131 – Multi-Sofft 30 (Northern State (USA) 91) [2001 5.7f 6m⁶ 7m 7.6m Aug 22] 6,500Y: smallish, sturdy filly: fourth foal: half-sister to 4-y-o Bold State and a winner in Turkey by Magic Ring: dam, maiden who probably stayed 1¾m, out of Cheshire/Lancashire Oaks winner One Over Parr: modest maiden: should be suited by 1m+. *I. A. Wood* **56**

MUMBLING (IRE) 3 ch.g. Dr Devious (IRE) 127 – Valley Lights (IRE) (Dance of Life (USA)) [2001 –: 10d 10s³ 12.1m* 10.9m⁹ 14.1d³ 12f 11.9m⁴ 13.1m³ 11.9s⁵ 10.3v Oct 26] strong, useful-looking gelding: fairly useful handicapper: won at Pontefract, Hamilton and Ayr in May: good third twice after: stays 1¾m: acts on soft and good to firm going (possibly not on heavy): blinkered (well held) fifth start: sold 20,000 gns. *M. H. Tompkins* **89**

MUNADIL 3 ch.c. Nashwan (USA) 135 – Bintalshaati 95 (Kris 135) [2001 87: 11m⁵ 10m² 10.1m* 10s⁶ 8d Oct 18] angular, good-topped colt: fluent mover: fairly useful performer: won 4-runner maiden at Epsom in August: ran poorly in handicaps after: should stay 1½m: acts on good to firm and good to soft going: tongue tied second and third starts: sold 17,000 gns. *M. P. Tregoning* **86**

MUNCHIE 2 ch.f. (Apr 9) Bluegrass Prince (IRE) 110 – Hoyland Common (IRE) (Common Grounds 118) [2001 7g 5m 5m 6m Aug 11] 4,000Y: first foal: dam, no form, half-sister to useful sprinter Barrys Gamble: poor maiden. *N. Tinkler* **36**

MUNDO RARO 6 b.g. Zafonic (USA) 130 – Star Spectacle (Spectacular Bid (USA)) [2001 10s f8g f8g 7.5m 8.5g⁵ 9.9s 8v Oct 24] robust gelding: modest handicapper: stays 8.5f: acts on good to firm going, good to soft and probably fibresand. *J. G. FitzGerald* **54**

MUNGO PARK 7 b.g. Selkirk (USA) 129 – River Dove (USA) 86 (Riverman (USA) 131) [2001 87§: 5s⁵ 5.1m³ 5.1f⁴ 5g³ 5d² 5m² 5m⁶ 6s 5g 5g⁶ 5m² 5d 5s 6g Nov 5] big gelding: impresses in appearance: has a round action: fairly useful handicapper: effective at 5f/6f: acts on any going: sometimes visored/blinkered earlier in career: sometimes unruly stalls: irresolute tail flasher, best held up as long as possible. *M. Dods* **85 §**

Victor Chandler Challenge Stakes, Newmarket—with Darryll Holland in the saddle for the first time,
Munir produces a career-best performance; Fath (striped cap) makes it a 1,2
for owner Hamdan Al Maktoum; Warningford (hooped cap) and Late Night Out (armlets) come next

MUNIR   3 ch.c. Indian Ridge 123 – Al Bahathri (USA) 123 (Blushing Groom (FR) 131)   **118**
[2001 92p: 7d* 8g⁶ 7m 7g² 8g⁴ 7d⁴ 7d* Oct 20] strong colt: smart performer: won Lane's
End Greenham Stakes at Newbury (by 2½ lengths from Frenchmans Bay) in April and
Victor Chandler Challenge Stakes at Newmarket (beat Fath by a length) in October: best
effort in pattern races in between when creditable ¾-length second to Fath in Lennox
Stakes at Goodwood (wandered and carried head bit awkwardly): was effective at 7f,
barely at 1m: acted on heavy going: refused to settle in blinkers penultimate appearance:
to stand at Station d'Etalons, France, fee €8,300. *B. W. Hills*

Mr Hamdan Al Maktoum's "Munjiz"

MUNJIZ (IRE)   5 b. or br.h. Marju (IRE) 127 – Absaar (USA) 76 (Alleged (USA) **113**
138) [2001 103?: 6v³ 5.2d⁴ 6g* 6m⁶ 6m 5.7m* 6d³ 6f⁴ 6s 6d⁵ Oct 19] good-topped horse:
smart performer: won handicap at Newmarket (by ¾ length from Hunting Lion) in May
and minor event at Bath in July: creditable efforts after, including when length third to
Bahamian Pirate in Phoenix Sprint Stakes at Leopardstown and fifth to Danehurst in
listed race at Newmarket final outing: seems best around 6f: probably acts on any going:
sold 70,000 gns, joined D. Vienna in USA. *B. W. Hills*

MUNQITH (USA)   2 b.c. (Feb 14) Bahri (USA) 125 – Indihash (USA) 81 (Gulch **82 p**
(USA)) [2001 7d⁴ Nov 3] good-topped colt: first foal: dam, 2-y-o 7f winner, out of smart
6f/7f winner Linda's Magic: 25/1 and backward, 1½ lengths fourth of 27 to Prince Hector
in maiden at Newmarket, staying on without being unduly knocked about: will stay at
least 1m: sure to improve. *E. A. L. Dunlop*

MUQTARB (IRE)   5 ch.g. Cadeaux Genereux 131 – Jasarah (IRE) 70 (Green   **–**
Desert (USA) 127) [2001 78: 6m 6m 6d 6f 5g 8v Oct 24] strong gelding: useful winner
at 2 yrs: injured cannon bone after and little form in 2001: sometimes tongue tied.
W. J. Musson

MURDINGA   2 br.g. (Feb 19) Emperor Jones (USA) 119 – Tintinara (Selkirk (USA) **65**
129) [2001 7s p8g² p8g Nov 28] tall, rather unfurnished gelding: second reported foal:
dam unraced: fair maiden: 5 lengths second to Azillion at Lingfield: will need to settle to
stay beyond 1m. *Lady Herries*

MURGHEM (IRE)   6 b.h. Common Grounds 118 – Fabulous Pet (Somethingfab- **108**
ulous (USA)) [2001 117: 12g 12s⁵ 16g 14v² 12d⁵ Oct 14] rangy horse: smart performer at
5 yrs: only useful at best in 2001: neck second to Invermark in minor event at Haydock in
September: stays 1¾m: acts on any ground: blinkered once at 4 yrs: usually races up with
pace. *M. Johnston*

Mr A. Al-Rostamani's "Murghem"

MURJANA (IRE) 3 b.f. Pleasant Colony (USA) – Golden Reef (USA) (Mr Prospector **80** (USA)) [2001 8.2d 8.2f² 10m² 10g² 10g³ 8.5m² 10m* 12m Sep 22] $500,000Y: big, heavy-topped filly: fluent mover: seventh foal: sister to 2 winners around 1m in USA and closely related to minor stakes winner there by Cherokee Colony: dam US Grade 2 2-y-o 6f winner and placed in Grade 1 7f event: fairly useful performer: placed most starts in maidens prior to winning one at Ripon in September: stayed 1¼m, probably not 1½m: acted on firm ground: often forced pace: visits Alhaarth. *B. W. Hills*

MURRENDI (IRE) 3 b.g. Ashkalani (IRE) 128 – Formaestre (IRE) 56 (Formidable **68** (USA) 125) [2001 82: 9s 10g⁶ 9.9m⁶ 9s 10m² 10.2g⁵ 10m⁶ 11.7g⁴ 10.1g* 9m 10m 10.9v Oct 15] workmanlike gelding: fair performer: made all in claimer at Yarmouth in August: below form after: stays easy 1¼m: acts on good to firm and good to soft going, below form on soft/heavy: tends to race freely: sold 10,000 gns. *M. R. Channon*

MURRON WALLACE 7 gr.m. Reprimand 122 – Fair Eleanor (Saritamer (USA) – 130) [2001 33: f12s Jan 9] probably of little account nowadays. *D. Haydn Jones*

MURZIM 2 b.g. (Feb 19) Salse (USA) 128 – Guilty Secret (IRE) 109 (Kris 135) [2001 **59 ?** 10.2g 7.9d 8d Oct 25] fifth foal: half-brother to useful 1m/9f winner Mawsoof (by Alzao) and 3-y-o Abyssinian Wolf: dam, 1½m winner and second in Park Hill Stakes, half-sister to dam of Derby second City Honours: seemingly modest form in maidens at Bath (2) and York: should be suited by 1½m+: unruly in preliminaries and withdrawn on intended debut: gelded after final start. *G. A. Butler*

MUSHA MERR (IRE) 3 b.c. Sadler's Wells (USA) 132 – Valdara (Darshaan 133) **109** [2001 98p: 10.4g* 12m 12f⁶ Jun 22] rangy, good sort: useful performer: won listed race at York in May by a neck from Potemkin, carrying head awkwardly: twelfth in Prix du Jockey Club at Chantilly (visored, below form) and sixth in King Edward VII Stakes at Royal Ascot (ran creditably, beaten 4¼ lengths by Storming Home) afterwards: stays 1½m: raced only on good going or firmer: joined K. McLaughlin in UAE. *Saeed bin Suroor*

MUSH (IRE) 4 b.g. Thatching 131 – Petite Jameel (IRE) (Ahonoora 122) [2001 80: **75** 8.3g 9m⁵ 8m² 8m³ 8m³ 8m⁵ 7m f8g p8g f7g Dec 1] quite good-topped gelding: fair **a–** handicapper: ran as if something amiss seventh start and well beaten last 3: seems best at 1m/9f: acts on firm going: carries head awkwardly: has pulled hard: gelded after final outing. *N. P. Littmoden*

MUSICAL FLUTE 2 b.f. (Mar 31) Piccolo 121 – Stride Home 78 (Absalom 128) **68 d** [2001 5.7f⁴ 5.1g⁴ 6.9m⁵ 6.1m⁵ 7g⁵ 6d Sep 4] fifth foal: sister to 3-y-o Magical Flute and half-sister to 4-y-o Pedro Pete: dam 5f (at 2 yrs) to 1¼m winner: fair maiden: well below form, including in seller, last 3 starts: should stay 7f: acts on firm ground. *M. R. Channon*

MUSICAL HEATH (IRE) 4 b.g. Common Grounds 118 – Song of The Glens **87** (Horage 124) [2001 83: 8g 8m 8.5m* 7.6g³ 8m 8d Oct 18] fairly useful handicapper: won at Epsom in July: good third at Lingfield, easily best effort after: should prove best at 7f/ 1m: acts on good to firm going: tongue tied at 3 yrs: races prominently. *P. W. Harris*

MUSICAL MAYHEM (IRE) 8 b.g. Shernazar 131 – Minstrels Folly (USA) (The – Minstrel (CAN) 135) [2001 11.8d Jul 19] one-time fairly useful 1½m and 2m winner in Ireland: well beaten in claimer only start in 2001: tried blinkered: won claiming hurdle in August. *D. J. Wintle*

MUSIC CLUB (USA) 2 b.f. (Feb 27) Dixieland Band (USA) – Long View (USA) **93 p** (Damascus (USA)) [2001 8d* Oct 19] big, useful-looking filly: has a fluent, round action: half-sister to 3 winners in USA, including 2000 2-y-o 8.5f minor stakes winner Overview (by Kingmambo): dam, US 9f minor stakes winner, half-sister to smart 1m/1¼m winner Flagbird and US Grade 1 winners Prospector's Delite (1m/8.5f) and Runup The Colors (1¼m): 12/1, beat Highest by a head (pair 4 lengths clear) in 20-runner maiden at Newmarket, niggled along before leading well over 1f out then idling: will be suited by 1¼m/1½m: sure to win more races. *J. H. M. Gosden*

MUSIC MAID (IRE) 3 b.f. Inzar (USA) 112 – Richardstown Lass (IRE) (Muscatite **69** 122) [2001 74: 7m 7.1m⁵ 7.6f⁶ 8m⁶ 8m³ 7d⁵ 7m 8g Sep 28] angular filly: fair handicapper: stays easy 1m: acts on firm going, probably on soft: has swished tail/wandered under pressure. *H. S. Howe*

MUSTANG 8 ch.g. Thatching 131 – Lassoo 87 (Caerleon (USA) 132) [2001 50§: f8g⁶ **– §** f8.5s f9.4g Jan 25] strong, lengthy gelding: temperamental handicapper nowadays: blinkered/visored. *J. Pearce*

MUST BE MAGIC   4 b.g. Magic Ring (IRE) 115 – Sequin Lady (Star Appeal 133)   **66**
[2001 70: e12g⁴ e10g² 8.5s 10d 9m 9m* 10.1g⁵ 8.5m² 10.1d 8s² Sep 24] smallish, good-topped gelding: fair performer: won handicap at Kempton in June: probably best at 1m/1¼m: acts on equitrack, soft and good to firm going: sometimes visored, not at Kempton. *H. J. Collingridge*

MUTABARI (USA)   7 ch.g. Seeking The Gold (USA) – Cagey Exuberance (USA)   **–**
(Exuberant (USA)) [2001 44, a65: f7g⁶ f7g Mar 27] rangy gelding: fluent mover: modest   **a51**
handicapper: barely stays 1¼m: acts on fibresand, equitrack and any turf going: effective visored or not: sold 2,000 gns. *R. Hollinshead*

MUTABASSIR (IRE)   7 ch.g. Soviet Star (USA) 128 – Anghaam (USA) 80 (Diesis   **70**
133) [2001 71: 8m 7f 8m* 7f* 8g⁴ 7m⁴ 7m 7.6g p7g⁵ p8g² Dec 22] fair performer: won seller in June and handicap in July, both at Brighton: stays easy 1m: acts on all-weather, very best turf efforts on good going or firmer. *G. L. Moore*

MUTADARRA (IRE)   8 ch.g. Mujtahid (USA) 118 – Silver Echo (Caerleon (USA)   **52 §**
132) [2001 69§: 9m³ 9m 11.6m Jul 30] tall, angular gelding: modest handicapper: effective at 9f to 1½m: yet to race on heavy going, acts on any other turf: tried blinkered early in career: held up and tends to hang: unreliable: sold 4,200 gns. *G. M. McCourt*

MU-TADIL   9 gr.g. Be My Chief (USA) 122 – Inveraven 53 (Alias Smith (USA))   **29 §**
[2001 36§: f16.2g⁵ f16.2g⁴ 21.6s 17.2f 17.2g 16f 15g 16.2m 15m⁴ 16.2s⁴ f14.8s Sep 6] sturdy gelding: bad maiden handicapper: reportedly lame final start: stays 2¼m: acts on firm and soft going, probably on fibresand: tried blinkered: usually slowly away: ungenuine. *J. Gallagher*

MUTAFAWEQ (USA)   5 b.h. Silver Hawk (USA) 123 – The Caretaker 113   **120**
(Caerleon (USA) 132) [2001 122: 12g 12m* 12f³ 12d 11f 12g⁶ Sep 29]
The now-retired Mutafaweq won four Group/Grade 1 races in his career but seems likely to be remembered longest by British racegoers for his parlous plight after a hard-fought victory in the 1999 St Leger. Racecourse and television audiences watched in amazement as he entered the winner's enclosure lashing out in an apparent frenzy. He seemed close to collapse when eventually led away and had to be treated with a sedative, an anti-inflammatory drug and painkillers, in addition to ten litres of a glucose saline solution fed intravenously. Mutafaweq's St Leger form—winning by two lengths from the Oaks, Irish Oaks and Yorkshire Oaks winner Ramruma—exceeded anything he had shown at up to that time. He failed to reproduce his Doncaster form as a four- and five-year-old but showed that he had suffered no long-lasting ill-effects by adding the WGZ Bank-Deutschland Preis and the Canadian International to his record as a four-year-old.

Only three of Mutafaweq's twelve outings in his last two seasons were in Britain, but he advertised his battling qualities once again when holding the sustained challenge of Wellbeing by a short head in the Vodafone Coronation Cup

Vodafone Coronation Cup, Epsom—in a race featuring three classic winners,
Mutafaweq (right) is given a shrewd front-running ride by Frankie Dettori
and just has the edge over Wellbeing; Millenary, Ekraar (rail) and Petrushka come next

in June. The Coronation Cup has tended to be overshadowed by the Derby and Oaks since the Epsom meeting became condensed into two days in the mid-'nineties, but the latest renewal attracted three classic winners, Mutafaweq and the St Leger and Irish Oaks winners from the previous year, Millenary and Petrushka. Mutafaweq started 11/2 fourth favourite in a field of six, behind the 6/4 favourite Millenary and 7/2-shots Petrushka and Wellbeing, and benefited from an astute ride by Frankie Dettori. With none of his rivals keen to go on, Dettori set only a steady pace on Mutafaweq until sending him into a clear lead rounding Tattenham Corner. Wellbeing was the only one to make a race of it with Mutafaweq, who responded most gamely to Dettori's urgings to get the better of a duel over the last two furlongs. There was a gap of four lengths back to third-placed Millenary, who failed to act on the undulating course. Mutafaweq went on to contest the Hardwicke Stakes at Royal Ascot, his Group 1 penalty meaning he had to concede weight all round in the race for the second year running. Seventh of nine in 2000 was improved to a creditable third of seven in 2001, beaten a head and two and a half lengths by Sandmason and Zindabad, both of whom received 5 lb from Mutafaweq. The rest of Mutafaweq's campaign was a sorry disappointment: he had three more outings, all Group/Grade 1s, and finished last each time in the Credit Suisse Private Banking Pokal at Cologne in August and in the Man o' War and the Turf Classic, both at Belmont Park in September.

		Roberto	Hail To Reason
	Silver Hawk (USA)	(b 1969)	Bramalea
	(b 1979)	Gris Vitesse	Amerigo
Mutafaweq (USA)		(gr 1966)	Matchiche II
(b.h. 1996)		Caerleon	Nijinsky
	The Caretaker	(b 1980)	Foreseer
	(b 1987)	Go Feather Go	Go Marching
		(b 1972)	Feather Bed

The sturdy, attractive Mutafaweq is by Derby third Silver Hawk, one of the leading middle-distance sires in Britain despite a limited number of runners (Mubtaker and Albarahin also represented him with distinction in the latest season). Mutafaweq's dam The Caretaker was a smart racemare, successful in listed events at seven furlongs and a mile in Ireland as a three-year-old after winning the Cartier Million as a juvenile. The Caretaker was then raced for three seasons in the States, being third in a Grade 3 event on turf, before being retired to the paddocks and producing Mutafaweq as her first foal. He is her only winner so far. Both Mutafaweq's grandam, the five-furlong juvenile winner Go Feather Go, and great grandam, Feather Bed, bred numerous winners; Go Feather Go's other winners included the nine-furlong Grade 3 turf winner Go Honey Go and the useful sprinter Feather's Lad. On pedigree, therefore, it was no surprise that Mutafaweq should prove effective returned to distances short of the St Leger trip. He acted on firm going and ran well below form on the two occasions he encountered softer than good. Sometimes bandaged, he tended to swish his tail in the preliminaries and drifted left under pressure on his last two starts as a three-year-old. He was set to start as a stallion at Wood Farm Stud, Shropshire, at a fee of £2,500 in 2002, but the deal fell through and he has been sent to Japan. *Saeed bin Suroor*

MUTAHADETH 7 ch.g. Rudimentary (USA) 118 – Music In My Life (IRE) 59 (Law — Society (USA) 130) [2001 –, a66: f8g f8g f9.4g f9.4g f11g 7.1d 8g⁵ 8m 8.5s Aug 16] angular gelding: fair handicapper in 2000: generally well held in 2001: usually blinkered/visored. *D. Shaw*

MUTAKARRIM 4 ch.c. Mujtahid (USA) 118 – Alyakkh (IRE) 78 (Sadler's Wells **112** (USA) 132) [2001 102: 10s² 12m⁵ 12g³ 12g² 13.9g 12m* Sep 11] good-topped colt: third foal: brother to fairly useful Irish 1m winner Hawas and half-brother to fairly useful Irish 1½m winner Bashashah (by Kris) and 3-y-o Nafisah: dam, 1m winner, out of Irish 1000 Guineas winner Al Bahathri: smart performer: placed in minor event at Cork and handicaps at the Curragh prior to winning listed race at Galway in September by head from Affianced: fifth in Duke of Edinburgh Stakes at Royal Ascot and mid-division in Ebor at York other 2 appearances: stays 1½m, possibly not 1¾m: acts on heavy and good to firm going: usually blinkered: sold 135,000 gns. *D. K. Weld, Ireland*

MUTAMAM   6 b.h. Darshaan 133 – Petal Girl 96 (Caerleon (USA) 132) [2001 **122**
123: 12g* 12m 12g* 12g* 12f Oct 27]

Mutamam was a sick horse in the spring and he ended the year with an uncomfortable-sounding malady, but in between those two indignities he was his usual honest self on the racecourse and built on an impressive career record that has now won him a place at the National Stud. Mutamam won eleven of his twenty-one starts, including five Group 3s, a Group 2 and Grade 1, with battling qualities his hallmark. 2001 told us nothing new about him, but saw him maintain an impressive ratio of wins and register his most prestigious triumph.

That was a long way off when Mutamam was hit by a serious stomach infection in May. He had already missed a trip to Dubai for the Sheema Classic, when 'moving poorly' at the end of January, and had the Coronation Cup and Royal Ascot ruled out as well when, as his trainer explained, he was struck down by 'a colic viral infection and overnight lost all his condition.' When he finally did reappear though, in the Princess of Wales's Pearl And Coutts Stakes at the Newmarket July meeting, it was the same old Mutamam, his ability and enthusiasm undiminished. Sent off at 11/2 in a wide-open renewal with nine runners, he won in clear-cut fashion by a length and a half after being sent on well over two furlongs out; Little Rock, Holding Court and Zindabad were unable to reel him in.

Now the task for connections was to find Mutamam a good Group or Grade 1 opportunity. He had had four previous attempts, in the Racing Post Trophy (third) as a two-year-old, the Derby (thirteenth) and Champion Stakes (fourth) as a three-year-old and the Breeders' Cup Turf (close fourth to Kalanisi) as a five-year-old. Another such target presented itself soon after Mutamam's Newmarket victory, probably too soon. The King George came eighteen days later and Mutamam may not have got over his exertions. Either way, he was well beaten, briefly disputing the lead coming off the final turn. Odds of 20/1 accurately indicated though that Mutamam was a most unlikely winner in this company, even at his best. Reportedly very stiff the following day, he was put away for an autumn campaign. That got under way against just three opponents in a poor renewal of the Milcars September Stakes at Kempton, a race Mutamam had won twelve months earlier and had little difficulty winning again, at 6/4-on dictating a steady pace before galloping on strongly to beat Perfect Sunday by a length and a half. The race proved an excellent warm-up for the £393,013 Canadian International at Woodbine just over three weeks later. The Canadian International was the sixth round of the Emirates World Series and attracted three runners from the United States, four from Canada, Slew The Red from France, Paolini from Germany and Mutamam, Zindabad and Daliapour from Britain. Favourite was Strut The Stage, who had a good record in Canada and had been touched off in the Secretariat Stakes in August. Mutamam was ridden by Richard Hills, bidding to follow up his Queen Elizabeth II Stakes success the previous day, and was sent off second favourite at 425/100. Nearly all the field had a chance entering the straight but Mutamam was a hard horse to pass once he had his head in front. Paolini resorted to trying to take a bite out of Mutamam or his jockey just before they passed the post, but Mutamam won by half a length, with Zindabad third and Daliapour fourth, both of them subsequently

Princess of Wales's Pearl And Coutts Stakes, Newmarket—Mutamam returns from a serious viral infection in the spring to beat Little Rock; Holding Court (blinkers) and Zindabad complete the frame

demoted for causing interference. Although the Canadian International was easily Mutamam's biggest win, it might not have been his best form. Exactly which race was his best effort is hard to pin down, as he ran at or very near his best on a regular basis. By our reckoning he ran to a rating of between 114 and 123 on at least ten of his twenty-one outings. Sadly, but no great slight on his overall record, Mutamam's final outing was not among those ten, being a very tame effort in last of eleven in the Breeders' Cup Turf.

	Darshaan (br 1981)	Shirley Heights (b 1975)	Mill Reef / Hardiemma
Mutamam (b.h. 1995)		Delsy (br 1972)	Abdos / Kelty
	Petal Girl (ch 1989)	Caerleon (b 1980)	Nijinsky / Foreseer
		Amazer (b 1967)	Mincio / Alzara

A smallish, quite attractive horse and a good mover, Mutamam will stand at a fee of £6,000 on October 1st terms. He was going to be sold to the National Stud for syndication, but that deal was cancelled when he failed the vet, returning from the Breeders' Cup with klebsiella, an infection of the genitalia. It is thought that he will still be able to cover in 2002, though in the ownership of Sheikh Hamdan's Shadwell Estates, who paid 185,000 guineas for him at the 1996 Houghton Yearling Sales. This is the fourth essay devoted to Mutamam in *Racehorses* and it is only necessary to recap on the striking aspects of his pedigree. He is out of a half-sister to Mtoto, his dam's next foal being Pretty Girl (by Polish Precedent), trained in Norway by Wido Neuroth, for whom she was runner-up to Mozart in the 2000 Houghton Sales Stakes and winner of the 2001 Norsk One Thousand Guineas. A further update is that the dam's 2001 two-year-old is the 180,000-guinea colt Lafi (by Indian Ridge). Mutamam was best at a mile and a half and acted on firm and

Mr Hamdan Al Maktoum's "Mutamam"

good to soft going; he never ran on soft. Not noted for a turn of foot, he either made the running or was ridden close to the pace, and proved both genuine and durable. *A. C. Stewart*

MUTAMARKIZ (IRE) 4 b.c. Rainbow Quest (USA) 134 – Pharaoh's Delight 112 **77** (Fairy King (USA)) [2001 7s* 8s⁵ 10m May 26] 375,000Y: good-topped colt: fourth foal: half-brother to useful Irish 1998 2-y-o 6f winner Pharmacist (by Machiavellian) and a winner in Japan by Caerleon: dam sprinter, won Phoenix Stakes at 2 yrs: fair form when winning maiden at Kempton in April: beaten long way in minor race/handicap on same course following month: should have stayed at least 1m: to stand at Tall Trees Stud, Longburton, Sherborne, Dorset, fee £1,250. *M. P. Tregoning*

MUTARAFAA (USA) 2 b.c. (Jan 26) Red Ransom (USA) – Mashaarif (USA) (Mr **76** Prospector (USA)) [2001 6m² 6m 7d⁵ 7g⁶ 8d Oct 19] strong, rangy colt: half-brother to several winners, including fairly useful 1998 2-y-o 6f winner Itlak (by A P Indy) and 9-y-o Tajar: dam unraced half-sister to smart miler Magic of Life (dam of 3-y-o Enthused): fair maiden: second at Goodwood: should stay 1m: sold 15,000 gns. *J. H. M. Gosden*

MUTARASED (USA) 3 b. or br.g. Storm Cat (USA) – Sajjaya (USA) 97 (Blushing **88** Groom (FR) 131) [2001 91: 7m 7m⁴ 8g Aug 12] small, stocky gelding: fairly useful handicapper: sold from J. Dunlop 25,000 gns prior to poor effort final start: should stay 1m: acts on soft and good to firm ground, though has looked ill at ease on latter. *R. J. White*

MUTARED (IRE) 3 b.c. Marju (IRE) 127 – Shahaada (USA) 57 (Private Account **78 +** (USA)) [2001 7.5s 7m 6g⁶ 11.7d 8s² f8g* p8g³ Dec 4] 70,000F: third foal: half-brother to Italian 1997 2-y-o 7f/1m winner Melissanthe (by Elmaamul) and 6f winner in Japan by Barathea: dam, maiden who stayed 1¼m, out of smart 6f/7f performer Linda's Magic: fairly useful performer: trained by J. Hammond in France only 2-y-o outing: won handicap at Southwell in November: may prove as effective at 7f as 1m: acts on soft going, fibresand and polytrack: raced freely (steady pace) final outing. *M. Wigham*

MUTASAWWAR 7 ch.g. Clantime 101 – Keen Melody (USA) 60 (Sharpen Up 127) **65** [2001 55, a71: e5g⁵ e6g e5g⁶ 5.3s 5v³ 5m² 5d² 5m² 5.3m² 5m⁴ 5m 5f* 5d 5g³ 5m⁶ 5g³ 5m⁶ 5m f6s⁵ Dec 26] lengthy gelding: fair handicapper: won at Beverley in July: effective at 5f/easy 6f: acts on all-weather and any turf going: sometimes blinkered early in career: tough and consistent. *J. M. Bradley*

MUTAWAQED (IRE) 3 ch.g. Zafonic (USA) 130 – Waqood (USA) 75 (Riverman **82 p** (USA) 131) [2001 –: 6.9v 8s f7g* f6g² f8.5g⁴ f8g* p7g* Dec 28] heavy-bodied gelding: fairly useful form: sold from M. Tregoning 3,500 gns after second start and off 5½ months: won handicaps at Southwell (2) and Lingfield (final start, comfortably) in November and December: effective at 6f to 1m: acts on fibresand/polytrack, no form on turf: tongue tied and blinkered/visored last 5 starts: progressive. *D. W. P. Arbuthnot*

MUTED GIFT 3 ch.f. King's Signet (USA) 110 – Ballet On Ice (FR) 46 (Fijar Tango **–** (FR) 127) [2001 –: 5v⁴ 6.1v 7m⁵ 7s 6f⁶ May 25] little form. *W. G. M. Turner*

MUTHAABER 3 br.c. Machiavellian (USA) 123 – Raheefa (USA) 75 (Riverman **102** (USA) 131) [2001 89p: 7.1m* 7.1g 8m³ 8m⁴ 9.9g⁵ 10f² 6g⁶ a8f³ Dec 6] close-coupled, useful-looking colt: useful performer: won maiden at Haydock in May: good efforts in handicaps after when third at Royal Ascot (2 lengths behind Analyser in Britannia Stakes) and second at Newbury (beaten 2½ lengths by Halland, final outing for J. Gosden): stays easy 1¼m: unraced on heavy going, acts on any other turf, ran respectably on dirt: often wears crossed noseband/early to post. *K. P. McLaughlin, UAE*

MUTINY 3 ch.g. Selkirk (USA) 129 – Indian Love Song 68 (Be My Guest (USA) 126) **–** [2001 10.5m 11.8m 14.1m Jun 22] half-brother to several winners, notably 4-y-o Holding Court and smart winner up to 7f Tomba (by Efisio): dam maiden who stayed 1½m: only a little sign of ability in maidens. *M. Johnston*

MUTINYONTHEBOUNTY 2 b.c. (Apr 26) Sadler's Wells (USA) 132 – Threat- **112** ening 95 (Warning 136) [2001 7m³ 8g* 8s* 8s⁴ Nov 3]
    Unusually, Mutinyonthebounty has had a different jockey in each of his four races to date and his stable's number-one rider Michael Kinane has not been among them. Kinane didn't even enter the equation involving riding plans for Mutinyonthebounty until the colt's third outing. When Mutinyonthebounty fin-ished third in a maiden at Tipperary on his debut, Kinane was involved in trying to overturn a careless-riding ban which started that day; and when he won a similar

*Hackney Empire Royal Lodge Stakes, Ascot—Mutinyonthebounty quickens nicely
in the testing conditions to beat Tholjanah (No.9), with Parasol third*

event at Gowran next time Kinane was at York riding Mozart in the Nunthorpe. On
those occasions Mutinyonthebounty was partnered by the claimers Paul Scallan
and Colm O'Donoghue respectively. The Gowran success was achieved in no more
than workmanlike style and represented just fairly useful form, so it was hardly a
surprise that Mutinyonthebounty was passed over by Kinane in favour of High
Sierra, the four-length winner of a maiden on his only start, when the pair did duty
for the O'Brien yard in the Hackney Empire Royal Lodge Stakes at Ascot at the end
of September. The other runners included another once-raced maiden winner in
Lahooq, as well as Bragadino and Tholjanah, runners-up in the Vintage Stakes and
Solario Stakes respectively, and this trio shared favouritism at 4/1. High Sierra
started at 11/2 with Mutinyonthebounty, the mount of Jamie Spencer, at 16/1.
Muntinyonthebounty, a strong, good-topped colt and a good walker, took the eye in
the paddock but not on the way to post, his action short and unimpressive. There
was plenty to like about the manner in which he made the return journey, though.
On ground much more testing than he had encountered on his first two starts, the
patiently-ridden Mutinyonthebounty quickened on the inside to lead entering the
final furlong and win with a little to spare by a length and a half from Tholjanah,
High Sierra back in fifth. Mutinyonthebounty ran respectably without being able to
improve on this smart form when faced with similar conditions in the Criterium
International at Saint-Cloud, where he was partnered by Johnny Murtagh. Kinane
made the correct decision this time, choosing Landseer, who finished second to Act
One, Mutinyonthebounty taking fourth, two and three quarter lengths behind the
winner. Held up last of the six runners, Mutinyonthebounty was never really able to
get on terms, as at Ascot carrying his head awkwardly. He shaped as though in need
of a stiffer test of stamina, and his pedigree also suggests that he'll prove well suited
by further than a mile. A mile and a half should pose no problems at three, when
he'll be in the care of Beau Greely in the States.

Mutinyonthebounty (b.c. Apr 26, 1999)	Sadler's Wells (USA) (b 1981)	Northern Dancer (b 1961)	Nearctic
			Natalma
		Fairy Bridge (b 1975)	Bold Reason
			Special
	Threatening (br 1991)	Warning (b 1985)	Known Fact
			Slightly Dangerous
		Pato (b 1982)	High Top
			Patosky

Although Mutinyonthebounty's dam Threatening failed to win over further
than seven furlongs, she did show her form over nine and there is plenty of stamina,
as well as quality, on her side of the pedigree. She is a half-sister to the St Leger and
Gold Cup winner Classic Cliche, the Prix Vermeille and Yorkshire Oaks winner My
Emma and the latest Ebor winner Mediterranean, the last-named, like Mutinyonthebounty, a son of Sadler's Wells. Their dam Pato, a sister to the very smart
sprinter Crews Hill, was fairly useful and stayed a mile and a quarter. Threatening

gained both her wins at two but showed even better form at three, including when finishing second in the Masaka Stakes and twelfth in the One Thousand Guineas. Mutinyonthebounty is Threatening's fourth foal and second winner, her second foal, a colt by Kris named Seasons Glory, having been successful over six furlongs in Hong Kong in the latest season. It is too early to say that Mutinyonthebounty needs soft going, but he does act well on it and, given his action, there has to be some doubt about his proving so effective back on ground firmer than good. *A. P. O'Brien, Ireland*

MUWAKLEH 3 b.f. Machiavellian (USA) 123 – Elfaslah (IRE) 107 (Green **115** Desert (USA) 127) [2001 a8f* a8f* 8g^2 May 6]

For the second year running, Godolphin drew a blank in the British classics. Godolphin's run of classic victories in the 'nineties was widely seen as vindicating the experiment undertaken by Sheikh Mohammed to see how horses reacted to spending the winter in a warmer climate, though the true effects—if any—on Godolphin's potential classic horses have always been difficult to judge. That said, if ever horses wintered in Dubai were going to enjoy an advantage in the early part of the British season, it was going to be in the latest one. Trainers in most parts of Britain found conditions very difficult in a cold and record-breakingly wet spring, while Godolphin's team enjoyed an unhindered preparation in the Dubai sun before being flown to Britain at the beginning of Guineas week. The first runner for Godolphin was Mahfooth in the Leicestershire Stakes, transferred to Newmarket because Leicester was waterlogged, but he managed only sixth of eleven. The next day, the favourite Tobougg, Rumpold and Divine Task finished ninth, fourteenth and sixteenth respectively for Godolphin in the Two Thousand Guineas.

Rumpold had won one of the two private trials staged at Nad Al Sheba in April for Godolphin's three-year-old colts, with Divine Task and Tobougg close behind in second and third. On the same day, Tempting Fate ran out a clear-cut winner of the fillies' trial but was immediately announced as an intended runner in the Poule d'Essai des Pouliches. Godolphin's principal hope for the Sagitta One Thousand Guineas, in a year when they believed they were 'a little bit light on quality fillies', was Muwakleh, who had been unraced at two. Muwakleh did not take part in the fillies' trial, having won the Moonshell Mile (with Tempting Fate third) in February and the inaugural running of the UAE 1000 Guineas in March, both prestige races at Nad Al Sheba, with Zahwah second each time. Muwakleh's performances, particularly her five-and-a-half-length victory in the UAE Guineas, set the standard for the British classic fillies to aim at in their trials. Assuming she translated her dirt form to turf, Muwakleh looked sure to play a major part at Newmarket and she started fourth favourite on the day at 13/2 (drifting from 5/1) in a field which looked a pretty good one at the time. With Express Tour adding to Godolphin's woes by failing to reproduce the form of his UAE Derby victory in the Kentucky version, Muwakleh brought some relief the following day with a fine second place at Newmarket (though Godolphin had to wait until the final day of the York May meeting for its first European winners of the year). Sent straight to the front and setting a good gallop in the Guineas, Muwakleh kept on strongly under firm riding but wasn't quite able to hold off Ameerat, who caught her well inside the final furlong and beat her by a neck, with Irish-trained Toroca a length and three quarters further back in third. Unfortunately, Muwakleh returned lame and was later found to have sustained a fractured knee. She was immediately retired and starts her career as a broodmare with a visit to Diesis in 2002.

Muwakleh (b.f. 1998)	Machiavellian (USA) (b or br 1987)	Mr Prospector (b 1970)	Raise A Native
			Gold Digger
		Coup de Folie (b 1982)	Halo
			Raise The Standard
	Elfaslah (IRE) (b 1988)	Green Desert (b 1983)	Danzig
			Foreign Courier
		Fair of The Furze (b 1982)	Ela-Mana-Mou
			Autocratic

Muwakleh is the sixth foal of her dam, the listed mile-and-a-quarter-winner Elfaslah, whose third foal was Almutawakel, a full brother to Muwakleh. While

Muwakleh's run in the Guineas was her first on turf, Almutawakel had the distinction of winning the Dubai World Cup on his first outing on an artificial surface. Even on the best of his turf form (winning the Prix Jean Prat and coming second in the Grand Prix de Paris), Almutawakel looked to face a stiff task in the Dubai World Cup but he beat off a strong American challenge, becoming the first winner of the race for Godolphin. Almutawakel's older half-brothers Mawjud (by Mujtahid) and Fayik (by Arazi) also did better when switched from turf to dirt, Mawjud showing fairly useful form in Dubai and Fayik winning four races in a row on the all-weather in Britain before finishing third in the inaugural Winter Derby at Lingfield. Another of Muwakleh's half-sisters Inaaq (by Lammtarra) was a useful performer (raced only on turf), successful at a mile and a quarter and fully effective at a mile and a half. Muwakleh's pedigree on the distaff side is basically a middle-distance one—her dam is a half-sister to Italian Derby winner and King George/Arc runner-up White Muzzle—and Muwakleh herself shaped as though she would have stayed beyond a mile.—*Saeed bin Suroor*

MUYASSIR (IRE) 6 b.h. Brief Truce (USA) 126 – Twine (Thatching 131) [2001 91: 8m 8m* 8.3m⁶ 9g 8d p10g p10g Dec 4] compact, deep-bodied horse: fairly useful handicapper: won at Kempton in July: below form otherwise: sold from P. Makin 10,000 gns before penultimate outing: effective at 1m/easy 1¼m: acts on firm going and equitrack: held up. *Miss B. Sanders*   **88 a74**

MY AMERICAN BEAUTY 3 ch.f. Wolfhound (USA) 126 – Hooray Lady 92 (Ahonoora 122) [2001 69: 6g 5m 5m* 5f* 6f⁴ 5.1m* 5g* 5g³ 6m Sep 21] big, lengthy filly: fairly useful performer: won minor event at Pontefract in June and handicaps at Ayr later in June, Nottingham in July and Beverley in August: has won at 6f, probably best at 5f: acts on firm going, possibly not soft: edgy sort. *T. D. Easterby*   **87 +**

MY BAYARD 2 ch.c. (Apr 21) Efisio 120 – Bay Bay 101 (Bay Express 132) [2001 6m f8.5g⁵ Sep 22] 42,000Y: half-brother to several winners, including useful 5f/6f winner Boast (by Most Welcome) and 7-y-o Butrinto: dam 7.6f winner: well held in maidens. *P. F. I. Cole*   **–**

MY BOLD BOYO 6 b.g. Never So Bold 135 – My Rosie (Forzando 122) [2001 57d: 12.1m 8.1s⁴ 10.2g⁵ Aug 27] sturdy, close-coupled gelding: poor handicapper: barely stays 1½m: acts on equitrack and firm going, probably on soft: sometimes blinkered before 2001. *K. Bishop*   **37**

MYBOTYE 8 br.g. Rambo Dancer (CAN) 107 – Sigh 75 (Highland Melody 112) [2001 64: 7.1m⁴ f7g 7m⁴ 7m⁶ 7m 7.5d Sep 25] sturdy gelding: modest handicapper: best around 7f: well beaten on heavy going, probably acts on any other turf and on fibresand: tried blinkered earlier in career: tongue tied: sometimes hangs. *A. B. Mulholland*   **56 a–**

MY BROTHER 7 b.g. Lugana Beach 116 – Lucky Love 65 (Mummy's Pet 125) [2001 45: 6m² 6g⁵ 7m⁶ 5g⁶ 6m Sep 26] modest handicapper: best at 5f/6f: acts on good to firm going: visored once as 5-y-o: sometimes starts slowly. *Dr J. R. J. Naylor*   **54**

MY DANCER (IRE) 2 b.f. (Apr 15) Alhaarth (IRE) 126 – Dance Land (IRE) (Nordance (USA)) [2001 5.1f² 5f 5m 5.1g* 5m³ 6g Aug 3] 9,000F, 24,000Y: strong, lengthy filly: fifth foal: half-sister to Irish 1½m winner Dariole (by Priolo) and 6-y-o Little Fox: dam unraced half-sister to smart 2-y-o sprinter Easy Landing from family of smart performers Lord of Men (up to 12.5f) and Her Ladyship (up to 10.5f): fair performer: won maiden at Bath in July: good third in nursery at Kempton next time, flashing tail: should stay 6f: raced only on good ground or firmer. *R. Hannon*   **79**

MY DILEMMA 5 b.m. Pursuit of Love 124 – Butosky 71 (Busted 134) [2001 –: 11.8g Aug 8] of little account. *J. A. Gilbert*   **–**

MY DING A LING 2 b.f. (Apr 18) Librate 91 – Dawn Bell 55 (Belfort (FR) 89) [2001 5v⁵ f5g Apr 30] fourth reported foal: dam 6f winner: well beaten in maiden/seller. *J. M. Bradley*   **–**

MY FRIEND JACK 3 b.g. Petong 126 – Spring Collection (Tina's Pet 121) [2001 56, a49: e6g⁴ e6g³ e6s⁴ 6m 5m 5.3m Aug 29] poor maiden: stays easy 6f: acts on heavy going, good to firm and equitrack. *J. Akehurst*   **43**

MYHAT 3 ch.f. Factual (USA) 108 – Rose Elegance 83 (Bairn (USA) 126) [2001 71: 8d 7f 7m 7m 6g 6.1s Aug 6] modest handicapper: probably stays 7f: acts on firm and good to soft going: blinkered once at 2 yrs. *K. T. Ivory*   **–**

MY LADY 4 b.f. Derrylin 115 – Brianstan Rose (The Brianstan 128) [2001 10.5d[5] 8d – Aug 19] unfurnished filly: well held in 3 maidens: dead. *B. P. J. Baugh*

MY LAST BEAN (IRE) 4 gr.g. Soviet Lad (USA) – Meanz Beanz (High Top 131) **73** [2001 76: f12g[3] f12g f11g[3] 14.1g f12g[3] f11s[3] Dec 21] fair maiden: well below form last 3 starts (off 6 months before final one): stays 1½m: acts on fibresand, raced only on good going and softer on turf. *B. Smart*

MY LEGAL EAGLE (IRE) 7 b.g. Law Society (USA) 130 – Majestic Nurse 80 **55** (On Your Mark 125) [2001 66d, a51d: f12g[6] 14.1v[2] 17.1g[4] 16.2m[2] 15.9d[2] 17.2g[2] 17.1d **a43** 16s[5] f16.2s Dec 18] smallish gelding: modest handicapper on turf, poor on all-weather: stays 17f: acts on good to firm going, heavy and fibresand: occasionally blinkered before 2001: usually held up. *R. J. Price*

MY LINE 4 b.g. Perpendicular 119 – My Desire 88 (Grey Desire 115) [2001 –: 15.8g[2] **58 p** 16d[6] 15.8d* Oct 9] lengthy gelding: modest form: won handicap at Catterick in October, held up and quickening well despite edging left: will stay beyond 2m: acts on good to soft going: banned for 30 days under non-triers rule after hurdling debut in November: progressive on Flat, and looks one to follow in handicaps in 2002. *Mrs M. Reveley*

MY LUCY LOCKET (IRE) 3 b.f. Mujadil (USA) 119 – First Nadia (Auction Ring **88** (USA) 123) [2001 87: 7.1m[5] 7m[4] 8.3m* 7f[2] 8m* 8f 8s[4] 7d 8d Nov 3] rather leggy, angular filly: unimpressive mover: fairly useful handicapper: won at Windsor in July and Salisbury in August: good fourth (dictated pace, possibly slightly flattered) in listed rated stakes at Ascot in September: stays 1m: probably acts on any going: used to hang left under pressure. *R. Hannon*

MY MAN FRIDAY 5 b.g. Lugana Beach 116 – My Ruby Ring 72 (Blushing Scribe **45** (USA) 107) [2001 39: f8.5s e10g[5] e7g[2] e8g 5m 6s 6v[5] Oct 29] unfurnished gelding: poor maiden handicapper: effective at 6f/7f: unraced on firm going, acts on any other turf and on equitrack: has carried head high/flashed tail. *Dr J. R. J. Naylor*

MY MATE HENRY 2 ch.g. (Feb 16) Pursuit of Love 124 – Gopi 64 (Marju (IRE) 127) – [2001 5m Jul 26] first foal: dam, maiden who stayed 7f, out of sister to smart performer up to 1¼m Visto Si Stampi: soundly beaten in maiden at Sandown. *M. Madgwick*

MY ONLY SUNSHINE 2 b.g. (Feb 15) First Trump 118 – Fiveofive (IRE) 61 (Fairy **76** King (USA)) [2001 5g[4] 5g[6] 7m[2] 7m* 6d Oct 19] fourth foal: half-brother to 1½m winner Sweet Angeline (by Deploy): dam 5f (at 2 yrs) and 1m winner: fair performer: made all in maiden at Folkestone in September: creditable eighth of 30 in sales race at Newmarket: should stay at least 1m: yet to race on extremes of going. *G. G. Margarson*

MY PETAL 5 gr.m. Petong 126 – Najariya (Northfields (USA)) [2001 –: 5.7m 5s Sep – 24] tall mare: fairly useful 5f/6f winner at 2 yrs: lightly raced since: tried blinkered. *J. M. Bradley*

MY PLACE 3 b.f. Environment Friend 128 – Verchinina 99 (Star Appeal 133) [2001 – 75, a59: e8g[4] f8g p7g[3] Nov 20] fair maiden at 2 yrs: showed little in 2001, leaving B. Hills after second start. *Mrs L. Richards*

MY PLEDGE 6 b.g. Waajib 121 – Pollys Glow (IRE) 91 (Glow (USA)) [2001 **64** 64: 11.6m[2] 11.5g p13g Dec 29] modest handicapper: best at 1¼m/1½m: acts on good to firm and good to soft going: tongue tied earlier in career: sometimes slowly away/races freely: held up. *C. A. Horgan*

MY POPPET 6 b.m. Midyan (USA) 124 – Pretty Poppy 67 (Song 132) [2001 6g f5g – 6m Jun 29] of little account. *N. J. Hawke*

MY RAGGEDY MAN 2 b.c. (Apr 7) Forzando 122 – Ragged Moon 72 (Raga Navarro **81** (ITY) 119) [2001 5.7f[4] 7m[5] 7d 7s* 8s[2] p8g* p8g[5] Dec 12] 6,500Y, resold 18,000Y: brother to 2 winners, notably useful 1991 2-y-o 6f winner who stayed 8.5f Misterioso, later winner in USA, and half-brother to several winners, including fairly useful 1992 2-y-o 7f winner Benevolent (by Robellino): dam 1m seller winner: fairly useful performer: won nurseries at Lingfield in October and November: likely to prove best at 7f/1m: acts on soft going, good to firm and polytrack: visored last 2 starts: tends to wander under pressure. *R. Hannon*

MY RETREAT (USA) 4 b.c. Hermitage (USA) – My Jessica Ann (USA) (Native **88** Rythm) [2001 90: f8g 8d f7g[4] 7v f9.4f* f9.4s[3] f8.5s* Dec 27] sturdy colt: fairly useful performer: left B. Hills 3,000 gns before winning claimer and handicap at Wolverhampton in December: stays 9.4f: acts on heavy going and fibresand: blinkered (below form) once at 3 yrs. *I. Semple*

MY SHARP GREY 2 gr.f. (Jan 25) Tragic Role (USA) – Sharp Anne 74§ (Belfort **54**
(FR) 89) [2001 6g³ 6m⁶ 5.7m 6m⁶ Aug 13] 4,200Y: eighth foal: half-sister to 3 winners,
including fairly useful 1997 2-y-o 5f winner Its All Relative (by Distant Relative) and
4-y-o Valentines Vision: dam unreliable 5f/6f performer: modest maiden: best effort
when third in minor event at Windsor: should stay 7f. *K. O. Cunningham-Brown*

MYSTERI DANCER 3 b.g. Rudimentary (USA) 118 – Mystery Ship 105 (Decoy **83**
Boy 129) [2001 77: 8s 7s 6m 6m⁶ 6.1m³ 7g³ 7f³ 7.6m* 7.6g⁴ 8s⁶ p10g Dec 4] fairly useful
handicapper: won at Lingfield in August: respectable efforts most other starts: seems best
around 7f: unraced on heavy going, acts on any other turf and probably on fibresand.
R. J. O'Sullivan

MYSTERIOUS FORCE 2 b.f. (Mar 6) Forzando 122 – Mystique (Mystiko (USA) **60**
124) [2001 6m 6.9m³ 7m³ 7.1m 7m Sep 6] first foal: dam unraced half-sister to smart
performer up to 1m in Britain/UAE Bahamian Bandit: modest maiden: third at Folkestone and Catterick (left J. Dunlop in between): ran poorly in nurseries last 2 outings
(reluctant to post final one): stays 7f. *D. W. Barker*

MYSTERIUM 7 gr.g. Mystiko (USA) 124 – Way To Go 69 (Troy 137) [2001 65: f9.4s **62**
f12g f12g⁵ f12g³ f12g f12f² f9.4g⁵ f12s² f12s p13g⁶ Dec 29] tall, leggy gelding: modest
handicapper: stays easy 13f: acts on firm going, fibresand and equitrack, probably on
polytrack: tried visored: usually held up: has hung left. *N. P. Littmoden*

MYSTIC FOREST 2 b.g. (Jan 28) Charnwood Forest (IRE) 125 – Mystic Beauty **75**
(IRE) (Alzao (USA) 117) [2001 6m 6g⁵ 6m⁶ 7.1g³ 7g⁶ 8d* 8d Oct 19] 9,200F, 14,500Y:
first foal: dam unraced out of half-sister to high-class performer Bluebird: fair performer:
won nursery at Goodwood in September: should stay 1¼m: yet to race on extremes of
going: gelded after final start. *B. J. Meehan*

MYSTIC MAN (FR) 3 b.g. Cadeaux Genereux 131 – Shawanni 105 (Shareef Dancer **74**
(USA) 135) [2001 8m 7.9d³ 8.3m⁵ 8.3g⁵ 8.3m⁴ 7g 8s* Oct 3] strong, angular gelding:
first foal: dam, 7f winner at 2 yrs, out of Rockfel Stakes winner and 1000 Guineas third
Negligent: fair performer: tongue tied, won maiden at Brighton in October comfortably:
free-going sort, but stays 1m: acts on soft and good to firm going: hung left fourth start:
sold 9,500 gns, then gelded. *E. A. L. Dunlop*

MYSTIC VENTURE (IRE) 2 b.g. (May 9) Woodborough (USA) 112 – Paganina **62**
(FR) (Galetto (FR) 118) [2001 5.1f⁵ 5s³ 6m² 5m* 6m² 6g 7.5g⁵ 7g⁴ Oct 19] IR 6,200F,
IR 5,000Y, 5,200 2-y-o: smallish, quite good-topped gelding: third foal: dam unraced
half-sister to smart French 7f performer Philippi: modest performer: won seller at
Musselburgh in August: stays 7.5f: acts on firm and soft going: has worn crossed nose-
band: has been slowly away: consistent. *K. A. Ryan*

MYSTIC WITCH 2 b.f. (Apr 25) Mistertopogigo (IRE) 118 – Walsham Witch 61 **49**
(Music Maestro 119) [2001 5g 5m⁵ 6.1m⁶ 6s 6v f5g f7g Dec 14] 2,200Y: smallish filly:
fourth foal: half-sister to 7f winner who probably stayed 1½m Bunnies Own (by Flockton's Own) and 1999 2-y-o 5f winner Chiko (by Afif): dam 2-y-o 6f winner who probably
stayed 2m: poor maiden: stays 6f: acts on good to firm ground, well held on fibresand.
E. J. Alston

MY TESS 5 br.m. Lugana Beach 116 – Barachois Princess (USA) 62 (Barachois (CAN)) **72**
[2001 74, a89: f7s⁴ f6s f7g³ f7g 8.1v 8g 7v 7s³ f8g³ f8.5g² f7g* Dec 11] big, strong, **a90**
lengthy mare: fairly useful handicapper on all-weather, fair on turf: won at Wolverhampton in December: best at 7f to easy 8.5f: acts on fibresand, soft and good to firm
going: front runner: sometimes wanders. *B. A. McMahon*

MYTHIC 2 ch.f. (Feb 23) Zafonic (USA) 130 – Fetlar (Pharly (FR) 130) [2001 7d⁶ **70 p**
Nov 3] lengthy filly: half-sister to several winners, including 1994 2-y-o 6f/7f winner
who stayed 1¼m Be Mindful (by Warning) and 1m winner Incredulous (by Indian
Ridge), both useful: dam unraced half-sister to Jersey Stakes winner Ardkinglass: 16/1,
sixth of 21 to Ballet Fame in maiden at Newmarket, soon prominent after sluggish start
and not knocked about once held: sure to do better. *J. R. Fanshawe*

MYTHICAL KING (IRE) 4 b.g. Fairy King (USA) – Whatcombe (USA) 88 (Alleg- **88**
ed (USA) 138) [2001 87: 10g 10m⁵ 10.3f* 9m⁶ 10f³ 10.3m⁵ 11.8g² 12.3m³ 12g 10.1f 8m
10g² 10s Oct 16] quite attractive, deep-girthed gelding: fairly useful handicapper: won at
Chester in June: creditable efforts when placed after: seems best at 1¼m/1½m: acts on
firm and good to soft going: has wandered: seems best when able to lead: gelded after
final start. *B. Palling*

MY TRIVET (IRE)   10 b.g. Thatching 131 – Blue Scholar 60 (Blue Cashmere 129) –
[2001 62: 5.2m 5m Jun 15] modest handicapper: trained at 9 yrs by J. Gorman in Ireland:
well beaten both starts in 2001: stayed 6f: acted on heavy ground, good to firm and sand:
was effective blinkered or not: was tried tongue tied: dead. *M. H. Tompkins*

MYTTON'S AGAIN   4 b.g. Rambo Dancer (CAN) 107 – Sigh 75 (Highland Melody   **76**
112) [2001 77, a65: f8g* f8.5s² f8s² f8.5g⁴ f8.5g⁴ e8g* 8d 8.3m 8d 7m* 8m³ 8.1d 8.3d⁵
8m⁴ 8m³ 7f³ 8m 6g² 7m³ 7d⁶ f7g 7m 8m⁴ 7g 7s 7d 8g 7s⁶ p8g f8.5g² Nov 17] sparely-
made gelding: fair handicapper: won at Southwell in January, Lingfield in March and Ayr
in May: effective at 6f to easy 8.5f: acts on firm going, soft, fibresand and equitrack:
effective blinkered or not: usually held up: none too consistent. *A. Bailey*

MYTTONS MISTAKE   8 b.g. Rambo Dancer (CAN) 107 – Hi-Hunsley 82 (Swing   **62**
Easy (USA) 126) [2001 62, a–: 7m* 7g⁵ 8.1s 8m p7g p10g⁵ Dec 29] leggy, workmanlike   **a44**
gelding: modest handicapper on turf, poor on all-weather: easily best effort in 2001 when
winning at Kempton in July: effective at 7f/1m: acts on firm going, good to soft (possibly
not softer) and all-weather: tried blinkered. *R. J. Baker*

MYTTON'S MOMENT (IRE)   5 b.g. Waajib 121 – Late Swallow (My Swallow   – §
134) [2001 54§: 14.1s Apr 16] temperamental handicapper: usually blinkered. *A. Bailey*

MY VERY OWN (IRE)   3 ch.g. Persian Bold 123 – Cossack Princess (IRE) 72   **82**
(Lomond (USA) 128) [2001 70, a74: f9.4s 10.3m⁴ 12g² 11.9g 11.9m 14g 10s Nov 5]
lengthy gelding: fairly useful handicapper: second at Newmarket, comfortably best effort
in 2001: stays 1½m: acts on fibresand, equitrack and good to firm going: tends to go in
snatches: joined K. Bailey. *N. P. Littmoden*

N

NACHO VENTURE (FR)   2 b.f. (Apr 25) Rainbow Quest (USA) 134 – Pearl   **88**
Venture 92 (Salse (USA) 128) [2001 7f 8d² f8.5g³ 8.2v³ 10d⁴ Nov 3] well-made filly:
second foal: dam 5f (at 2 yrs) to 2m winner: fairly useful maiden: best effort when
never-dangerous 6¾ lengths fourth to Alexander Three D in listed event at Newmarket:
will be suited by 1½m+: acts on heavy going: should win a race. *S. P. C. Woods*

NADIA   3 ch.f. Nashwan (USA) 135 – Nazoo (IRE) 99 (Nijinsky (CAN) 138) [2001   **116**
10.5v² 10m* 10.5m² 12m 10v⁴ Oct 7] tall, attractive filly: sixth foal: half-sister to 2

Prix Saint-Alary, Longchamp—Nadia rallies to hold the renewed challenge of Mare Nostrum

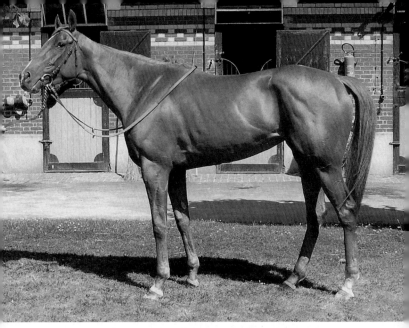

Maktoum Al Maktoum's "Nadia"

winners abroad, including French 9.5f winner Hedonic (by Gone West): dam, 2-y-o 6f/7f winner who probably stayed 1m, from very good family: smart performer: won minor event at Maisons-Laffitte at 2 yrs and Prix Saint-Alary at Longchamp in May by head from Mare Nostrum, rallying after headed briefly 1½f out: ran well when 1½ lengths second to Aquarelliste in Prix de Diane at Chantilly following month: bit below that form at Longchamp last 2 starts, in Prix Vermeille and Prix de l'Opera (fourth to Terre A Terre, taking strong hold): will prove best at around 1¼m: acts on heavy and good to firm going: races prominently: tail flasher. *C. Laffon-Parias, France*

NADOUR AL BAHR (IRE)   6 b.g. Be My Guest (USA) 126 – Nona (GER) (Cortez (GER)) [2001 97§: 12s 10.1s⁶ 10g 10g⁴ 10f² 10m* 12g³ 10m⁵ 10f⁵ 9g 10d² Oct 13] tall, close-coupled gelding: unimpressive mover: useful handicapper: won at Ascot in July by 2½ lengths from Bogus Dream: creditable efforts after, notably when neck second to Golden Wells on same course final start: better form at 1¼m than 1½m: acts on equitrack and any turf going: tailed off in blinkers (looked reluctant) final 2000 start: sometimes slowly away/races freely/wanders, and is held up. *T. G. Mills*   **102**

NAFISAH (IRE)   3 ch.f. Lahib (USA) 129 – Alyakkh (IRE) 78 (Sadler's Wells (USA) 132) [2001 94: 8d* 10v² 10f* 12f² 12m² 11.9g⁶ 12g⁵ Sep 28] tall filly: made into useful performer: won handicap in April and listed event (by 1¾ lengths from Duchcov) in June, both at Newbury: good second in Ribblesdale Stakes at Royal Ascot (beaten head by Sahara Slew) and listed race at Newbury (beaten 1¼ lengths by Love Everlasting), best efforts after: stayed 1½m: acted on firm and soft going: raced prominently: visits Kingmambo. *B. Hanbury*   **109**

NAFITH   5 ch.g. Elmaamul (USA) 125 – Wanisa (USA) (Topsider (USA)) [2001 53, a57: f9.4s f11g 16m* 16g 14m Aug 22] poor performer: won amateur claimer at Musselburgh in May for E. James after first start: possibly went amiss final start: stays 2m: acts on good to firm going, heavy and fibresand: tried blinkered/tongue tied: often gets behind. *L. R. James*   **37**

702

Ballymacoll Stud Stakes, Newbury—
Nafisah gallops on resolutely to beat the Luca Cumani-trained pair Duchcov (centre) and Rizerie

NAHEEF (IRE) 2 b.c. (Feb 15) Marju (IRE) 127 – Golden Digger (USA) 66 (Mr **109**
Prospector (USA)) [2001 7d* 7m* 7m² Sep 16] unfurnished colt: second foal: half-
brother to 4-y-o Golden Chance: dam, maiden who failed to progress from only start at 2
yrs, sister to dam of 3-y-o Lailani and half-sister to very smart performers Always Fair (at
7f/1m) and Faithful Son (up to 1½m): useful form: won maiden at Epsom (landed odds
by 5 lengths) in July and Champagne Lanson Vintage Stakes at Goodwood (by 2 lengths
from Bragadino, leading 1f out and staying on strongly) in August: creditable 2½ lengths
second to Hawk Wing in National Stakes at the Curragh: will stay at least 1m. *D. R. Loder*

NAJAH (IRE) 3 b.f. Nashwan (USA) 135 – Mehthaaf (USA) 121 (Nureyev (USA) **110**
131) [2001 8m² 12m 12f 10.2g* 10g* Oct 28] big, strong filly: third foal: sister to fairly
useful 1½m winner Raaqi: dam, 6f (at 2 yrs) to 1m (Irish 1000 Guineas) winner, closely
related to July Cup winner Elnadim and granddaughter of outstanding broodmare Fall
Aspen: smart performer: successful in October in maiden at Bath (simple task, by 9
lengths) and Premio Lydia Tesio-Darley at Rome (by 4 lengths from Cincischiando): had
earlier finished good ½-length second to Speirbhean in listed race at Leopardstown, but
was well held in Oaks at Epsom and Ribblesdale Stakes at Royal Ascot: stayed 1¼m:
raced only on good going or firmer: visits Danehill. *Saeed bin Suroor*

NAJDA (IRE) 3 b.f. Halling (USA) 133 – Danishkada 119 (Thatch (USA) 136) [2001 –
10g 9.7m Aug 27] closely related to smart French performer up to 6.5f Danakal (by
Diesis) and half-sister to a winner in USA by Lyphard: dam won Grand Criterium: well
held in maidens: sold 13,000 gns in December. *H. R. A. Cecil*

Champagne Lanson Vintage Stakes, Goodwood—Naheef stays on really strongly to beat (from right to
left) Bragadino, Leo's Luckyman, Mr Sandancer, Loweswater (partially hidden) and Highdown

NAJ-DE 3 ch.g. Zafonic (USA) 130 – River Jig (USA) 98 (Irish River (FR) 131) [2001 **68** 77p: 7s 7.1m² 7m 7g 8.3m⁵ 8m 10v Oct 8] close-coupled gelding: fair maiden: stays 1m: acts on good to firm going: blinkered (respectable effort) penultimate start: sold 11,000 gns. *P. F. I. Cole*

NAKED OAT 6 b.g. Imp Society (USA) – Bajina (Dancing Brave (USA) 140) [2001 **53 §** 53: f9.4s* f9.4s³ f9.4s f9.4g f9.4g* f9.4g f11g³ f11g* 10g 11.6g⁶ 10.9m³ 12m³ 9.9m **a81 §** 10m 10g⁴ 9.7d f12g⁵ p13g⁶ f12g⁵ f12g⁵ Dec 8] smallish, strong gelding: fairly useful on all-weather, modest on turf: won apprentice handicap at Wolverhampton in January, claimer there in March and handicap at Southwell in April: stays 11f: acts on firm, good to soft going (not soft/heavy), fibresand and equitrack: blinkered once: unreliable. *B. Smart*

NAKWA (IRE) 3 b.g. Namaqualand (USA) – Cajo (IRE) (Tirol 127) [2001 –: 8s⁵ f8g **70** 8d* 8m³ 10m 8g⁶ 8d 10d Oct 30] tall gelding: fair handicapper: won at Newcastle in May: stays 1m: acts on good to firm and good to soft ground: often makes running. *E. J. Alston*

NAMLLAMS 3 b.c. Magic Ring (IRE) 115 – White Flash 39 (Sure Blade (USA) 130) **60 d** [2001 65: 5m 6g 6m 8m 8f 10m⁴ 12.4g 10m 10m a8g Nov 25] strong colt: disappointing maiden handicapper: left A. Dickman before final start: stays 6f: raced only on good ground or firmer: visored sixth (ran respectably) and seventh starts. *P. Haley, Spain*

NANCY'S BOY 3 b.g. Perpendicular 119 – Derry's Delight (Mufrij) [2001 –: 10.5m – 7.5f Jul 17] smallish gelding: little sign of ability, including in claimer: dead. *J. Hetherton*

NANDOO 2 b.f. (Mar 24) Forzando 122 – Ascend (IRE) (Glint of Gold 128) [2001 6m **60** 7m⁵ 7m⁶ 7.1g⁵ Sep 1] 10,000Y: third living foal: half-sister to 1¼m/1½m winner Elms Schoolgirl (by Emarati): dam unraced: modest maiden: should stay 1m. *P. W. Harris*

NANETTE 3 b.f. Hernando (FR) 127 – No Restraint 84 (Habitat 134) [2001 7.1s³ **60** 9.7m³ 9.9d Sep 27] half-sister to several winners, including useful Spanish performer up to 15f Alexandrovich (by Mtoto) and Irish 1½m winner Zetonic (by Zafonic), also 11f winner in France: dam, 1m/1¼m winner, from very good family: modest form when third in maidens: should prove better around 1¼m than shorter. *S. C. Williams*

NAPA VALLEY 2 ch.f. (Feb 23) Most Welcome 131 – Eccolina 65 (Formidable – (USA) 125) [2001 7m 7f f7g Aug 18] fifth foal: dam, maiden who seemed to stay 1¼m, sister to very smart sprinter Chilibang: well held in maidens. *M. Blanshard*

NAPIER STAR 8 b.m. Inca Chief (USA) – America Star (Norwick (USA) 125) [2001 – 38, a47: f7g 6s f7g 7s May 3] of little account nowadays. *A. B. Mulholland*

NASEEM REEF (IRE) 2 b.c. (Apr 3) College Chapel 122 – Bay Supreme (Martin- – mas 128) [2001 6m Sep 22] IR 4,200Y, resold 6,500Y: half-brother to several winners, including UAE 5f/6f winner Shantarskie (by Mujadil) and 6f (at 2 yrs) and 7f winner Pesidanamich (by Mummy's Treasure): dam unraced: 10/1, tailed off in maiden at Catterick: sold 500 gns. *A. Berry*

NASHAAB (USA) 4 b.g. Zafonic (USA) 130 – Tajannub (USA) 104 (Dixieland Band **94** (USA)) [2001 70: f8g* 6v 8s⁶ 10s 8.1m⁵ 8f* 9f 8.5m⁵ 8.9m³ 8f* 8.1g 8m 7.6m* 8.1s 7d² 8s 7.9d Oct 12] small, quite attractive gelding: fairly useful handicapper: won at South-well in January, Leicester in May, Doncaster (originally demoted but reinstated on appeal) in July and Chester in August: good second at Doncaster, only form after: effective at 7.5f to 9f: acts on fibresand, firm and good to soft going: visored final start: often slowly away: held up: none too consistent: sent to UAE. *P. D. Evans*

NASHIRA 3 ch.f. Prince Sabo 123 – Aldevonie 75 (Green Desert (USA) 127) [2001 – 78: 8.5g 8g Sep 28] fair 5f winner at 2 yrs: well beaten in handicaps in 2001. *C. R. Egerton*

NASH ME (IRE) 3 b.c. Nashwan (USA) 135 – Queen's View (FR) 103 (Lomond **88** (USA) 128) [2001 10.4m* 12d Sep 14] big, lengthy, good sort: has scope: fourth foal: brother to useful French 1999 2-y-o 1m winner (stays 1¼m) Dubai Two Thousand and half-brother to fairly useful UAE 7f and 8.5f winner Canyonlands (by Gulch): dam, 6f (at 2 yrs)/7f winner, out of half-sister to Irish Oaks winner Give Thanks (grandam of 1000 Guineas winner Harayir): impressive winner of maiden at York in September by 12 lengths from Quizzical, making all: well-beaten last in listed race won by Ekraar at Doncaster 12 days later: should stay 1½m: joined J. Wickham in UAE. *D. R. Loder*

NASMATT 3 b.f. Danehill (USA) 126 – Society Lady (USA) 75 (Mr Prospector **96** (USA)) [2001 89: 6m⁴ 6d 6g⁵ 5.7m² 6g⁵ Aug 4] lengthy, angular filly: useful performer: in frame in handicap at Newmarket (good fourth) and minor event at Bath: looked far from keen when running badly final start: free-going sort, raced mostly around 6f: unraced on firm going, acted on any other turf: visits Gilded Time. *M. R. Channon*

NASSAU NIGHT   2 b.g. (Apr 14) Bahamian Bounty 116 – Leave At Dawn (Slip **– p**
Anchor 136) [2001 7m Aug 8] 3,500F, IR 8,400Y, 15,500 2-y-o: fourth foal: half-brother
to a 1m winner in Sweden by Bin Ajwaad: dam unraced out of half-sister to smart miler
Trojan Fen: 33/1, green when eighth of 11 in maiden at Brighton: should do better.
R. M. H. Cowell

NASTY NICK   2 gr.g. (Mar 4) Petong 126 – Silver Spell 54 (Aragon 118) [2001 6m **–**
Jul 29] 9,000Y, 5,200 2-y-o: second foal: brother to 3-y-o Warden Warren: dam, 2-y-o 5f
winner (only season to race), sister to smart sprinter Argentum: 16/1, tailed off in maiden
at Newmarket. *M. Wigham*

NATALIE JAY   5 b.m. Ballacashtal (CAN) – Falls of Lora 107 (Scottish Rifle 127) **81**
[2001 88: 10m 8m⁵ 9m 9m 8g⁵ 8m⁵ 7m* 7.9m 7m Sep 6] angular mare: fairly useful
handicapper: won at Salisbury (apprentices) in August: acts on equitrack and
probably any turf going: held up: none too consistent. *M. R. Channon*

NATHAN'S BOY   5 gr.g. Tragic Role (USA) – Gold Belt (IRE) 61 (Bellypha 130) **66 §**
[2001 –: f12s⁶ f11g⁵ 10s⁵ 8.5m³ 10m 10.3f⁴ 9.9f³ 9.9m⁵ 12f 10.5s⁶ 12.3d Aug 31] leggy **a– §**
gelding: fair handicapper: trained first 8 starts by R. Hollinshead: probably best at 1¼m/
1½m: acts on any turf going: often gets behind: visored final start: not to be trusted.
A. Streeter

NATIAIN   2 ch.g. (Apr 6) Danzig Connection (USA) – Fen Princess (IRE) 72 (Trojan **–**
Fen 118) [2001 6s 8.2s Nov 5] 10,000Y: big, strong gelding: fifth foal: half-brother to 3
winners, including 5-y-o Fiori and 1996 2-y-o 7f winner Ben's Ridge (by Indian Ridge),
later useful winner around 1m in USA: dam 15f winner at 4 yrs: well held in maidens.
P. C. Haslam

NATIONAL DANCE   4 b.g. Deploy 131 – Fairy Flax (IRE) 97 (Dancing Brave **61**
(USA) 140) [2001 82: 10v 12m 12f⁶ 10.1m 9.9s⁶ 11m 12.1g Sep 3] small, strong gelding:
modest handicapper: probably stays 1½m: acts on good to firm going, soft and fibresand,
probably on equitrack: ran as if amiss final start: sold 800 gns. *Mrs J. R. Ramsden*

NATIONAL PARK   2 gr.g. (Feb 15) Common Grounds 118 – Success Story 60 **94**
(Sharrood (USA) 124) [2001 5g² 6s 6m* 6s² 7d⁸* 7d⁴ 8g³ Nov 24] tall, quite good-topped
gelding: fourth foal: half-brother to useful 1¼m/1½m winner Film Script (by Unfuwain)
and 1m/1¼m winner Champagne (by Efisio): dam, 1¼m winner, out of smart 1¼m
performer Starlet: fairly useful performer: won maiden at Lingfield (by 7 lengths) in
August and nursery (given excellent ride from front to beat Ellen Mooney
easily by 2 lengths) in September: left R. Hannon after next start: creditable third to
Mountain Rage in Grade 3 event at Hollywood: stays 1m: acts on soft and good to firm
going: raced prominently in Britain. *R. B. Hess jnr, USA*

NATION (USA)   3 b.c. Miesque's Son (USA) 117 – Erica's Fault (USA) (Muttering **90**
(USA)) [2001 81: 10g⁴ 12m 9m² 10.1s* 10.5v³ 11.9s⁶ Oct 11] strong colt: fairly useful
performer: won maiden at Epsom in August, making most: ran creditably after: stays
1½m: unraced on firm going, acts on any other turf: sold 86,000 gns. *Sir Michael Stoute*

NATIVE FORCE (IRE)   3 b.f. Indian Ridge 123 – La Pellegrina (IRE) 73 (Be My **82**
Guest (USA) 126) [2001 67p: 8m⁵ 8.1s* Aug 19] workmanlike filly: fairly useful
performer: won maiden at Sandown in August: may prove best around 1m: tends to carry
head high: sold 8,000 gns in December. *J. H. M. Gosden*

NATIVE TITLE   3 b.g. Pivotal 124 – Bermuda Lily 78 (Dunbeath (USA) 127) [2001 **87**
80: 8d² 8s² 7g² 7f* 6g⁶ 6m 7g 7d 7s Oct 31] big, close-coupled gelding: fairly useful
performer: won maiden at Newbury in June: creditable effort in handicaps after only on
next start: should prove as effective at 5f/6f as 7f: acts on firm and soft going: ran as if
something amiss sixth outing, gelded after final one. *M. Blanshard*

NATMSKY (IRE)   2 b.g. (Apr 28) Shadeed (USA) 135 – Cockney Lass 117 (Camden **48**
Town 125) [2001 6g 8.5m 7m 8s f8.5g f6g³ f7g² f6g² Dec 14] IR 4,000Y: quite **a71**
good-topped gelding: half-brother to several winners, including useful Irish 1m winner
Vinka (by Strawberry Road), later winner in USA, and Irish 7f to 9f winner Rockny (by
Theatrical): dam, best at 1¼m, won Tattersalls Rogers Gold Cup: fair maiden on all-
weather, poor on turf: second at Wolverhampton and Southwell (nursery): best efforts at
6f/easy 7f: acts on fibresand, best turf run on good to firm going: often makes running.
K. A. Ryan

NATSMAGIRL (IRE)   4 b.f. Blues Traveller (IRE) 119 – Top The Rest (Top Ville **45 §**
129) [2001 49, a–: 5s 9m³ 8g 8m 10f 12.4g 9.2d⁶ 9.9m⁶ 10.1f f11g f8g² Dec 10] small,

sparely-made filly: poor handicapper: stays 1¼m: acts on firm going and fibresand: visored twice in 1999: unreliable. *R. E. Barr*

NATURAL DANCER 2 b.f. (Apr 22) Shareef Dancer (USA) 135 – Naturally Fresh – 91 (Thatching 131) [2001 8d Oct 19] workmanlike filly: half-sister to 3 winners abroad, including German winner up to 10.5f Never To Louse (by Petoski): dam 2-y-o 5f winner: 66/1 and backward, well held in maiden at Newmarket. *C. N. Allen*

NATURAL (IRE) 4 b.g. Bigstone (IRE) 126 – You Make Me Real (USA) (Give Me 67 Strength (USA)) [2001 65: 7m 10f 9.2m³ 11.1d* 11.8g 14.1d 12s Oct 20] strong, rangy gelding: fair handicapper: won at Hamilton in July: mostly well below form otherwise: stays 11f: acts on good to firm and good to soft going: visored final start: possibly none too genuine: sold 8,200 gns. *John Berry*

NATURE (IRE) 2 b.f. (Feb 10) Bluebird (USA) 125 – Nawaji (USA) 45 (Trempolino 49 (USA) 135) [2001 5.2m 6m⁵ 7f⁶ 6.9d f6g⁶ Oct 9] IR 30,000Y: second foal: dam, maiden who stayed 13f, sister to smart 9f to 1½m performer Triarius: poor maiden: should stay at least 1m: tongue tied final start: sold 1,200 gns. *R. Hannon*

NAUGHTY KNIGHT 3 ch.g. King's Signet (USA) 110 – Maid of Mischief (Be My 56 Chief (USA) 122) [2001 58: 7f²g* f7g² f8s³ f7g³ f6g⁵ 8.1m⁶ 8d⁶ 7.5m³ 8m f7g⁶ f8g f11g Dec 3] modest performer: won seller at Southwell in January: creditable efforts after when placed, leaving A. Berry before sixth start: barely stays 7.5f: acts on soft ground, good to firm and fibresand: usually blinkered/visored: sometimes races freely. *P. W. D'Arcy*

NAUGHTY NELL 2 b.f. (Feb 17) Danehill Dancer (IRE) 117 – Hana Marie 101§ 69 p (Formidable (USA) 125) [2001 7m Sep 24] half-sister to winner up to 10.5f in Italy by Turtle Island: dam, 2-y-o sprint winner, became unreliable: favourite, shaped better than position suggests when seventh of 12 to Purple Haze in maiden at Kempton, up with pace until wandering and weakening final 2f: should improve. *J. Noseda*

NAUTICAL LIGHT 4 b.f. Slip Anchor 136 – Lighted Glitter (FR) (Crystal Glitters – (USA) 127) [2001 –: 8.3d 9.7m 9.9m f8.5g 8.3g 10m 10.9m 11.9s 10s Oct 25] disappointing maiden. *D. W. P. Arbuthnot*

NAUTICAL STAR 6 b.g. Slip Anchor 136 – Comic Talent 105 (Pharly (FR) 130) 51 [2001 –: 12s 14m 16f⁴ 12.1g⁵ 12f 12g³ f14.8s⁴ Sep 6] good-topped gelding: formerly useful, modest nowadays: stays 2m: acts on firm and soft going: tried visored. *J. W. Hills*

NAUTICAL WARNING 6 b.g. Warning 136 – Night At Sea 107 (Night Shift (USA)) – [2001 –, a86: e7g e8g⁶ f8.5g⁶ 7.6f 5.3m 5g p7g⁵ p7g⁴ p8g* p7g p8g* Dec 22] sturdy a81 gelding: fairly useful handicapper: trained first 4 starts by B. Johnson: won twice at Lingfield (all 8 wins there) in December: possibly better at 1m than 7f nowadays: acts on all-weather, little form on turf nowadays: sometimes visored, blinkered last 3 starts: usually tongue tied: has swished tail. *Jamie Poulton*

NAVARRE SAMSON (FR) 6 b. or br.g. Ganges (USA) 119 – L'Eternite (FR) 52 + (Cariellor (FR) 125) [2001 63: 16.2m²* 16.4g Aug 17] leggy, close-coupled gelding: modest performer: won claimer easily at Chepstow in July: ran no sort of race next time: stays 2m: acts on soft and good to firm going: tongue tied last 3 starts. *P. J. Hobbs*

NAVIASKY (IRE) 6 b. or br.g. Scenic 128 – Black Molly (IRE) (High Top 131) 80 [2001 86: 6m 8.3g 7m 8m⁶ 7.5m 8m 9d 8.5g² 7g 9g 8m* 7.9m² 7.6g 8m³ 8s 7d 8d Oct 18] big, strong gelding: fairly useful performer: won claimer at Brighton in August: form in handicaps after only when placed: best at 7f/1m, probably on good going or firmer: sometimes slowly away: best held up. *D. Nicholls*

NAWADER (USA) 5 b. or br.h. Silver Hawk (USA) 123 – Music Lane (USA) 46 (Miswaki 124) [2001 6m⁴ 6g 5m 7m 10g⁵ 8d⁶ 9.9s f14g Oct 1] $675,000Y, 1,500 5-y-o: good-topped horse: first foal: dam, sprint winner in USA, half-sister to US Grade 1 winner up to 1½m Hawkster, smart French middle-distance filly Silver Lane and smart French 1991 2-y-o Silver Kite (all by Silver Hawk): poor maiden handicapper: seems to stay 1¼m. *M. C. Chapman*

NAYEF (USA) 3 b.c. Gulch (USA) – Height of Fashion (FR) 124 (Bustino 136) 129 [2001 123p: 8d³ 8g 12m³ 10.5g* 9.9m* 12s* 10d* Oct 20]
Unlike the Delphic Oracle, the *Racing Post*'s banner headline on Tuesday July 31st—'Return of the fallen hero'—was both concise and explicit. The supposed fallen hero was Nayef, having his first outing since the Two Thousand Guineas twelve weeks earlier. Within another twelve weeks the headlines had

changed to 'Tregoning star proves his true worth' and 'Nayef win a delight for owner', which summed up a topsy-turvy year for Nayef and paid a tremendous compliment to his trainer, whose skill and patience in bringing the colt back from the brink of ignominy to the status of 'horse most likely to in 2002' were a model for any in his profession. Make no mistake, Nayef is a marvellous prospect as a four-year-old, though with Sakhee still in training it may not be that easy keeping the two apart. As a reminder, if one is needed, Nayef's crushing victory in the listed Autumn Stakes over a mile on heavy going at Ascot on the second of his two successful starts as a two-year-old marked him down as the leader of his generation, at least potentially. Backed up by his pedigree and exceptional looks, it also marked him down as the best classic prospect in Europe but, for various reasons, that wasn't quite how it turned out. When Nayef lined up for the Craven Stakes at Newmarket in April, he headed the market for the Two Thousand Guineas as short as 9/4 and was joint-favourite with Galileo for the Derby at 8/1. In a muddling race, despite the presence of a pacemaker, Nayef was never travelling that well, had to be nudged along before halfway and came home a one-paced third behind King's Ironbridge. A performance undoubtedly below expectations but not exactly a disaster, since horses have won the Guineas after failing in the Craven—King's Best in 2000, for instance—and, as noted in *Racehorses of 2000*, Tregoning's stable invariably takes time to hit peak form, having notched just three wins in sixty-one starts from March to the end of May in its first three years. Equally, Nayef's performance revealed none of the pace and sharpness required in a Guineas winner, and, having been deserted by regular rider Richard Hills for Munir, he started at 10/1 under Willie Supple on the big day and was swept aside in the final furlong after being ridden close to the pace, finishing around six lengths eighth to Golan. Within a month Tregoning had decided to bypass the Derby:'He's a big, tall horse who did a lot of growing in January and February, and I think he needs to fill out a bit. He'll certainly be a bit stronger later in the year; I just feel his strength has gone for the time being.'

The time spent away from the track, and not resuming full work until the end of June, evidently did Nayef a power of good and he looked in great shape for the Gordon Stakes at Goodwood. He didn't win, but in finishing under two lengths third, not unduly knocked about, behind Alexius he proved that he stayed a mile and half and gave a strong indication that his campaign might well get back on track. The confidence boosting continued in three Group 3 races, the Petros Rose of Lancaster Stakes at Haydock, the Select Stakes at Goodwood, in both of which Nayef made most of the running, and the Royal Court Theatre Cumberland Lodge Stakes at Ascot. He was particularly impressive at Goodwood in hammering Askham, who is no slouch, by six lengths; at Ascot, in pretty testing conditions, Nayef accounted for the Norwegian raider Sagittarius by a length and a quarter. With three relatively straightfoward races under his belt, the time was clearly approaching for Nayef to have another crack at Group 1 company. After Haydock, the St Leger had been dismissed on the grounds that a hard race over a trip possibly beyond his capabilities might harm his prospects as a four-year-old, and after

Dubai Champion Stakes, Newmarket—
Nayef dispels any niggling doubts about his true ability with a first Group 1 success,
running on really strongly to gain the upper hand over Tobougg (rail), with Indian Creek third

Goodwood the Prix de l'Arc de Triomphe was ruled out once it was decided Sakhee would be running there. That left the Dubai Champion Stakes and Nayef was one of twelve to line up for the race on Champions Day at Newmarket.

Giving a race meeting the title Champions Day is, in a sense, acting as a hostage to fortune since the presumption must be that more than one race on the card will settle a championship every year. The Newmarket event was created in 1997 by concentrating all the quality of the three-day fixture into one, switching the Challenge Stakes from Thursday and the Dewhurst Stakes and Rockfel Stakes (since elevated to Group 2) from the Friday to the Saturday to be staged alongside the Champion. Since then there have been some excellent performances by such as Xaar, Distant Music, Pilsudski and Kalanisi in the two races with genuine aspirations to producing a championship display, but no more than there used to be. Besides the newly-revamped Arc day at Longchamp, which now boasts six Group 1 races and therefore holds more realistic claims to be a day for champions, especially as the races cover a full range of ages and distances, the greatest headache for the Newmarket executive is the proliferation of valuable alternative prizes across the world right through to December. These mean that Champions Day does not bring down the curtain on top-quality racing for the year, and poses a potential problem with possible Newmarket runners being sidetracked. However, the only international option for juveniles is the Breeders' Cup, and, until Johannesburg, none of Europe's best had gone to the States since Arazi in 1991, so the Dewhurst Stakes is really under no serious threat.

As regards the latest Champions Day, run only a week before the Breeders' Cup, Johannesburg might have been a loss to the Dewhurst, but Aidan O'Brien fielded a pretty fair set of deputies, and while Sakhee and/or Fantastic Light would undoubtedly have gone for the Champion Stakes had the Breeders' Cup not existed the same cannot be said with any certainty about Galileo, Banks Hill or Lailani. The claim that the horses who play a leading part in the Champion Stakes invariably go on to the Breeders' Cup Turf or Classic simply doesn't hold water. In the seventeen runnings of the American event from 1984 to 2000, twenty-two Champion Stakes runners, including seven winners and nine placed horses, went on to the States, with Pebbles and Kalanisi completing a notable double. But ten winners and twenty-five placed horses didn't try their luck, which puts matters in perspective and raises questions about the somewhat heated reaction of the Newmarket executive to the news that the Breeders' Cup will also be held only a week after Champions Day in the next three years. To claim that the British event will inevitably be badly affected is, anyway, merely blowing in the wind, given that Breeders' Cup Ltd is under no obligation to bother about the consequences of its actions on the pattern of racing in Europe. Breeders' Cup day is perceived as the most important day's racing anywhere in the world but the various world racing authorities have no jurisdiction over the timing of it. Like it or not—and Newmarket clearly doesn't—Champions Day will never truly be able to live up to its grandiose title in any meaningful way in its current form, though it will continue to provide a first-class card with strong competition and a good number of high-class runners, which should be enough to satisfy anyone.

In the event, with Medicean and Kalanisi added to the list of absentees through retirement, and Equerry withdrawn on the day, the latest Champion Stakes was not representative of the best ten-furlong horses around. Even so, Nayef faced four Group 2 winners from the current season—his stable-companion Albarahin, Distant Music, No Excuse Needed and Rebelline—together with Group 3 winners Carnival Dancer, who had been trained specifically for the race since winning the Scottish Classic in July, Chancellor and Hawkeye, plus two Group 1 scorers from 2000 in Beckett and Tobougg. Nayef started favourite and justified the confidence in good fashion. Tracking the leaders, he briefly looked like becoming boxed in two furlongs out but produced a good turn of foot to catch Tobougg, who had got first run, seventy-five yards out and stayed on strongly to get the better of the argument by three quarters of a length. Indian Creek at 66/1 ran the race of his life to be four lengths away third, which cast some doubt on the form, though this was still a high-class performance by the winner, and the prolonged applause Tregoning received when his trophy was handed over was richly deserved. The applause for owner Hamdan Al Maktoum was similarly appropriate, since, without his patience and readiness to listen to his trainer, Nayef's season might well have come to nought. The victory was Tregoning's first in a Group 1 event and one of a personal-best total of fifty-three gained in Britain during the year, forty-one of which came after July 1st. Tregoning's ratio of winners to runners of almost one in four—behind only David Loder and Saeed bin Suroor among the leading hundred British-based trainers—proves how well he places his horses, and if he can ever manage to get the ball rolling a bit earlier in the season he could make an even bigger name for himself.

		Gulch (USA) (b 1984)	Mr Prospector (b 1970)	Raise A Native
Nayef (USA) (b.c. 1998)				Gold Digger
			Jameela (b or br 1976)	Rambunctious
				Asbury Mary
		Height of Fashion (FR) (b 1979)	Bustino (b 1971)	Busted
				Ship Yard
			Highclere (b 1971)	Queen's Hussar
				Highlight

The good news for Tregoning is that, unlike Ekraar in the latest season, Nayef will stay with him as a four-year-old rather than joining Godolphin, but not before the colt has wintered in Dubai. Reportedly Nayef's first intended start is the Dubai World Cup, with Tregoning preparing him, and, while Sakhee is obviously the Maktoum family's prime hope for that race, Nayef should be a magnificent back-up. His first reported target in Europe is the Coronation Cup and, wherever he goes after that, he will be a very tough nut to crack over either a mile and a quarter or a mile and a half. If we had to put our money on which trip will suit Nayef

Mr Hamdan Al Maktoum's "Nayef"

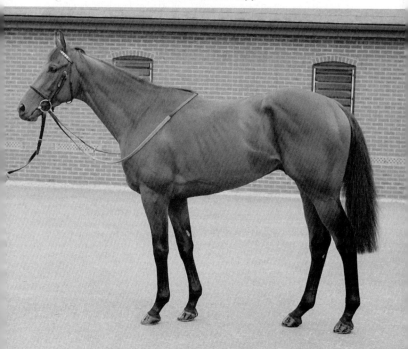

better, we'd say a mile and a half. On breeding that would be no surprise because, as pointed out in detail in *Racehorses of 2000*, Height of Fashion's progeny, including six stakes winners, have tended to take after her rather than their respective sires in terms of stamina. All of her eight winning foals have stayed at least a mile and a quarter, among them three by Mr Prospector, one by Blushing Groom, one by Danzig and one by Gulch, none of whom was a middle-distance performer. In this respect Height of Fashion was the complete opposite of the celebrated broodmare Mrs Moss, who seemed to act as a non-interfering receptacle for stamina in her offspring. Apart from Dayjur, Nayef's sire Gulch is the least successful stallion Height of Fashion visited, and the sprinter-miler had no significant runners in Europe besides Nayef during the season. The family has had another good winner recently in Blueprint, a son of Height of Fashion's half-sister Highbrow. After landing the Jockey Club Stakes in 2000 Blueprint was sold to be trained in the States and added the Grade 2 San Luis Rey Stakes and Sunset Handicap to his tally. One thing you can be sure of—there will be no more imposing four-year-old in training than Nayef, a rangy individual who always impresses in appearance. A resolute galloper, he is also a good mover with a long stride and he acts on heavy and good to firm ground. His four-year-old campaign is one to look forward to with relish. *M. P. Tregoning*

NAYYEL 2 b.c. (Jan 29) Zafonic (USA) 130 – The Perfect Life (IRE) 106 (Try My **94 p** Best (USA) 130) [2001 7f² 7.1m* Jul 25] fifth foal: half-brother to useful 1995 2-y-o 6f winner Najiya, 7-y-o Muhtafel and smart 7f (at 2 yrs) to 1½m (Gordon Stakes) winner Rabah (all by Nashwan): dam, French 5f (at 2 yrs) and 7f winner, sister to Last Tycoon: confirmed promise when landing odds in 4-runner maiden at Sandown by 2 lengths from Savannah Bay, dictating steady pace and needing only to be shaken up: will probably stay 1m: useful prospect at least, provided all is well. *J. L. Dunlop*

NAZARETH (IRE) 2 b.c. (Mar 11) Woodborough (USA) 112 – Tinos Island (IRE) **80** (Alzao (USA) 117) [2001 7.1m³ 7g⁶ 7m² 7.1m² Sep 17] IR 8,000Y: small, strong colt: first foal: dam thrice-raced granddaughter of top-class French middle-distance performer Northern Trick: fairly useful maiden: best effort in nursery at Warwick final start: will stay at least 1m: raced only on good/good to firm going: sold 18,000 gns. *R. Guest*

NDOLA 2 b.g. (May 14) Emperor Jones (USA) 119 – Lykoa (Shirley Heights 130) **–** [2001 8.2d 8d 8.2s Oct 30] 3,200F, 8,500Y: rather leggy, quite good-topped gelding: eighth foal: brother to French 1m/11f winner Roilyko and half-brother to 3 winners abroad: dam, French 1½m winner, sister to Prix de Pomone winner Light The Lights: well beaten in maidens. *B. J. Curley*

NEARLY A FOOL 3 b.g. Komaite (USA) – Greenway Lady (Prince Daniel (USA)) **94** [2001 90: 6d 5.1f⁴ 6m 6d 5f 5f 5.1m 5.1f⁶ 5g Aug 4] close-coupled gelding: fairly useful handicapper: fourth at Chester in May, best effort: effective at 5f/6f: acts on any turf ground: has been edgy. *B. A. McMahon*

NEAR MISS (USA) 3 b.f. Capote (USA) – Devon Diva (The Minstrel (CAN) **–** 135) [2001 11.5g⁵ Jul 3] half-sister to numerous winners, notably very smart 7f (at 2 yrs) to 1¼m (US Grade 1 event) winner Tinners Way (by Secretariat) and smart 5f to 6.5f performer (including in USA) Western Approach (by Gone West): dam, 9f winner in USA at 4 yrs, out of Cheveley Park winner Devon Ditty: showed little in maiden at Yarmouth: sold 160,000 gns in December. *H. R. A. Cecil*

NEEDWOOD BLADE 3 ch.c. Pivotal 124 – Finlaggan 83 (Be My Chief (USA) 122) **111** [2001 47: f6g 6v* 6s* 6.1f² 7m* 8m 7m⁴ 7m⁵ 6g 7m³ 6m 7s⁵ 7s² Oct 11] strong, compact colt: usually takes the eye: improved dramatically for new stable, and made into smart performer: won maiden at Doncaster in March and handicaps at Ripon in April and York (by neck from Lapwing) in May: mostly good efforts after, including when in frame in Bunbury Cup at Newmarket and listed race (¾-length third to Priors Lodge) and handicap at York (short-head second to Kayo): stays 7f, possibly not quite 1m: acts on any turf going: tough and genuine: a credit to his stable. *B. A. McMahon*

NEEDWOOD BRAVE 3 b.g. Lion Cavern (USA) 117 – Woodcrest 82 (Niniski **–** (USA) 125) [2001 63: 9.9m 10.1m 10m 8d 12m f14g Dec 14] rangy gelding: modest maiden at 2 yrs: well held in 2001: tried blinkered. *J. G. FitzGerald*

NEEDWOOD MAESTRO 5 b.g. Sizzling Melody 117 – Needwood Poppy 29 (Rolfe **–** (USA) 77) [2001 51: 11.9g 12g Oct 4] small gelding: modest performer at 4 yrs: tongue tied, reportedly finished lame final start in 2001: stayed 1¾m: acted on firm and soft going: visored: dead. *J. Mackie*

NEEDWOOD MISSILE 5 b.g. Sizzling Melody 117 – Sea Dart 55 (Air Trooper 115) [2001 12.1d May 18] half-brother to 7f winner Needwood Sprite (by Joshua) and 2m winner Needwood Muppet (by Rolfe): dam 11f seller winner: well beaten in maiden at Hamilton. *J. L. Spearing*

NEEDWOOD MYSTIC 6 b.m. Rolfe (USA) 77 – Enchanting Kate (Enchantment 115) [2001 55: 11.9s* 11.9s² 11.9d* 12m 11.9m* 10s Sep 30] smallish, workmanlike mare: fair handicapper: won at Brighton in April (ladies), May and August: stays 1½m: acts on firm and soft going (well held only outings on heavy and fibresand): usually leads. *Mrs A. J. Perrett* — **70**

NEEDWOOD SPIRIT 6 b.g. Rolfe (USA) 77 – Needwood Nymph 45 (Bold Owl 101) [2001 64: f16.2g 13g⁶ 16g³ 17.1g³ 16m 17.5m 17.1d³ 18s² Oct 22] smallish gelding: modest handicapper: stays 2¼m: best form on good ground or softer: visored once: winning hurdler. *Mrs A. M. Naughton* — **60**

NEEDWOOD TRICKSTER (IRE) 4 gr.g. Fayruz 116 – Istaraka (IRE) (Darshaan 133) [2001 66: f5g f6s⁴ f5s⁴ f5g f6g³ f7g⁴ f6g² f5g f6g⁵ 6f 7.1f f6s⁵ p6g Dec 29] close-coupled gelding: modest handicapper: barely stays easy 7f: acts on fibresand, equitrack and probably any turf going: tried tongue tied. *R. Brotherton* — **a56**

NEEDWOOD TRIDENT 4 b.f. Minshaanshu Amad (USA) 91§ – Needwood Nymph 45 (Bold Owl 101) [2001 49: f14.8g⁵ f16.2g f16.2g Feb 22] small filly: disappointing maiden. *J. Pearce* — **–**

NEEDWOOD TROOPER 4 br.g. Puissance 110 – Blueit (FR) 101 (Bold Lad (IRE) 133) [2001 60: e6g 6f 5f f5g 5d 5d 5m Sep 8] of little account nowadays. *J. Balding* — **–**

NEEDWOOD TRUFFLE (IRE) 4 ch.f. Brief Truce (USA) 126 – Green Wings (General Assembly (USA)) [2001 –: f6g f9.4s Jan 18] fair 5f winner at 2 yrs: has shown little since. *J. Hetherton* — **–**

NEGLIGEE 2 gr.f. (Feb 14) Night Shift (USA) – Vax Star 96 (Petong 126) [2001 6m⁶ 6m* 6.1d* 6m 6d Oct 13] 55,000Y: small, sturdy filly: first foal: dam, 2-y-o 5f winner, became one to treat with caution: fairly useful performer: won maiden at Salisbury (hung badly left) and minor event at Chester (beat White Rabbit comfortably by head) in August: well below best in listed events last 2 starts: not sure to stay beyond 6f: usually makes running. *B. W. Hills* — **94**

NELLIE MELBA 2 b.f. (Apr 15) Hurricane Sky (AUS) – Persuasion 79 (Batshoof 122) [2001 6g⁴ 7.1m⁴ 7d⁵ p8g⁵ f8g⁴ Nov 30] leggy filly: second foal: half-sister to 3-y-o So Tempting: dam 1¼m/1½m winner: should stay 1¼m: acts on good to firm going, good to soft, fibresand and polytrack. *D. J. Coakley* — **68**

NELSONS FLAGSHIP 3 b.g. Petong 126 – Marie's Crusader (IRE) (Last Tycoon 131) [2001 44: 10s 10m May 26] small, strong gelding: poor maiden: well beaten in handicaps in 2001. *J. Akehurst* — **–**

NEMO FUGAT (IRE) 2 b.c. (Feb 21) Danehill Dancer (IRE) 117 – Do The Right Thing 71 (Busted 134) [2001 6m² 6g⁴ 6g* 6d³ Oct 3] IR 12,000F, 34,000Y: useful-looking colt: second foal: dam, 1½m winner, half-sister to 3-y-o Bram Stoker: fairly useful performer: in frame in maidens at Ascot and York before winning similar event at Lingfield in September: creditable 4 lengths third to Prism in minor event at Salisbury: should stay 7f: unraced on extremes of going. *R. Hannon* — **91**

NEPTUNE 5 b.g. Dolphin Street (FR) 125 – Seal Indigo (IRE) 93 (Glenstal (USA) 118) [2001 41: 12m 12.6f⁴ 14.1m f14.8g Dec 1] leggy gelding: poor maiden handicapper: stays 15f: acts on fibresand, firm going and good to soft: has given trouble at stalls. *J. C. Fox* — **32**

NEPTUNE'S GIFT 2 b.f. (Apr 28) Lugana Beach 116 – Not So Generous (IRE) 68 (Fayruz 116) [2001 5m² 5f⁵ 5f 5m³ 5g⁶ 5g 5d 6v 5g³ f5fg* f5f² f5g⁴ f5s f5s⁵ Dec 27] 2,800Y: close-coupled filly: third living foal: dam 5f winner, including at 2 yrs: modest performer: won maiden at Southwell in November: left A. Berry after twelfth start: should prove best at 5f: acts on good to firm ground and fibresand: has edged left/wandered. *Andrew Reid* — **60**

NERONIAN (IRE) 7 ch.g. Mujtahid (USA) 118 – Nimieza (USA) 70 (Nijinsky (CAN) 138) [2001 40§: f9.4g f8.5s⁵ e12g 7s 7.6m 7d 10.1m 8m 12m Jun 10] tall, lengthy — **– §**

gelding: temperamental handicapper nowadays: trained first 2 starts by Miss D. McHale: tried blinkered/visored. *J. A. Gilbert*

NETHERHALL   5 ch.g. Rudimentary (USA) 118 – Legal Precedent (Star Appeal   **43** 133) [2001 –: f16.2s⁴ f16.2s⁶ f16g Feb 16] poor handicapper: stays 2m: raced mostly on fibresand. *R. D. Wylie*

NETTLES   3 br.g. Cyrano de Bergerac 120 – Sylvandra 81 (Mazilier (USA) 107) [2001   **– §** 55§, a–§: f7g Jan 26] temperamental maiden: sometimes blinkered. *Denys Smith*

NETTLETON KNIGHT   3 b.g. Beveled (USA) – Mybella Ann (Anfield 117) [2001   **–** 9m 8.2f 8.1d 7m Aug 8] fourth foal: dam little sign of ability: no form, including in handicap: somewhat headstrong. *J. M. Bradley*

NEVER CAN TELL   5 ch.g. Emarati (USA) 74 – Farmer's Pet 90 (Sharrood (USA)   **–** 124) [2001 f8.5g Mar 15] disappointing maiden: visored once. *B. P. J. Baugh*

NEVER DISS MISS   4 b.f. Owington 123 – Pennine Pink (IRE) 72 (Pennine Walk   **76** 120) [2001 80: 12s 12s 10g³ 10m⁴ 10g Jul 8] small, sturdy filly: fair handicapper: stays 11.6f: acts on heavy and good to firm ground: none too consistent. *N. A. Graham*

NEVER END   3 b.f. Alzao (USA) 117 – Eternal (Kris 135) [2001 74p: 8s 10.2m Jul 5]   **–** compact filly: fair 7f winner at 2 yrs: well beaten in listed race and handicap in 2001. *B. W. Hills*

NEVER ENDING STORY   3 b.f. Deploy 131 – Bold Gem 68 (Never So Bold 135)   **–** [2001 7f 7.1m 8.1d 12.3m 16.2s 12.3d Aug 31] 3,000Y: lengthy filly: second foal: dam, 5f winner who probably stayed 7f, half-sister to smart performers Just A Flutter (miler) and Slicious (up to 1½m): well held in maidens/handicaps. *E. J. Alston*

NEVER FEAR   3 b.f. Mistertopogigo (IRE) 118 – Never Say So 48 (Prince Sabo 123)   **–** [2001 –: f6g f6g f5g f5g 12s Apr 23] of no account. *Mrs S. Lamyman*

NEVER PROMISE (FR)   3 b.f. Cadeaux Genereux 131 – Yazeanhaa (USA) 68   **66** (Zilzal (USA) 137) [2001 72: f9.4g⁵ 10m⁴ 8m 10.2f³ 10.2g* 9.7m² 10g⁵ 10.1g Sep 14] smallish filly: fair handicapper: won at Chepstow in July: stays 1¼m: acts on good to firm ground: visored on reappearance, blinkered after: has raced freely/found little: sold 4,500 gns in December. *B. W. Hills*

NEW CALADONIA (USA)   2 ch.c. (Mar 8) Trempolino (USA) 135 – Tea Cozzy   **63** (USA) (Irish River (FR) 131) [2001 7m 6.9m⁶ 7f⁶ Jul 25] $10,000F, 30,000Y: first foal: dam unraced half-sister to US Grade 2 9f winner Mugatea: modest form in maidens: should be suited by 1¼m/1½m: sold 19,000 gns. *I. A. Balding*

NEW DEVELOPMENT   5 b.g. Sizzling Melody 117 – Silver's Girl 58 (Sweet   **–** Monday 122) [2001 11.7f Jul 26] fifth foal: half-brother to 1m winner Hamilton Silk (by K-Battery): dam 1¼m winner: well beaten in seller at Bath. *T. Wall*

NEW HORIZON (IRE)   3 b.g. General Monash (USA) 107 – Gulf Craft (IRE)   **53 §** (Peterius 117) [2001 f7g⁵ f8g⁵ 8d 6m 7g² 7g Aug 12] 17,000Y: good-bodied, lengthy gelding: fifth living foal: half-brother to 1997 2-y-o 5f seller winner Flash d'Or (by Shalford): dam unraced half-sister to smart sprinter Ginny Binny: modest maiden: barely stays 1m: acts on fibresand, best turf run on good going: blinkered last 3 starts: looks far from keen. *J. A. Osborne*

NEW OPTIONS   4 b.g. Formidable (USA) 125 – No Comebacks 70 (Last Tycoon   **99** 131) [2001 a6g⁴ 4.5g² 5.8m⁶ 6g 5.1m⁵ a6g⁴ 5.8g³ 5.8s Sep 9] 10,500Y, 3,000 2-y-o: first   **a104** foal: dam, 1m to 1½m winner, out of half-sister to Irish 1000 Guineas winner Katies: useful performer: had tremendous season in 2000, winning 8 races in Scandinavia: best effort in 2001 when 2 lengths fourth to Waquaas in listed race at Jagersro sixth start: not at all discredited (didn't get run of race) when fifth of 11 to Danehurst in similar event at Chester time before: stays 6f: acts on good to firm ground and dirt: usually blinkered. *Rune Haugen, Norway*

NEWPARK LADY (IRE)   4 b.f. Foxhound (USA) 103 – Toledana (IRE) (Sure Blade   **101** (USA) 130) [2001 94: 5s⁴ 6m⁶ 5g² 6f 6.3g 5g* 6g* 6d⁶ 5g⁶ 5m 5s Oct 6] good-topped filly: first foal: dam ran once: useful performer: won handicap at the Curragh (Ladbroke Rockingham) then minor event at Leopardstown (by length from Kalamunda) in July: just respectable efforts after, in listed race at Pontefract on first occasion: best at 5f/6f: acts on soft and good to firm going: blinkered (ran poorly) fifth start. *K. F. O'Brien, Ireland*

NEW PROSPECTIVE   3 b.c. Cadeaux Genereux 131 – Amazing Bay 100 (Mazilier   **?** (USA) 107) [2001 9m⁵ a8g⁵ a8g³ a10.5g² a8g⁵ a10g⁶ Nov 25] 23,000 2-y-o: first foal:

dam, 2-y-o 5f/6f winner, from family of Nunthorpe winners Lochsong and Lochangel: tongue tied, last of 5 in maiden at Musselburgh for D. Nicholls on debut: placed in minor event and handicap for new stable at Mijas: stays 10.5f: acts on sand. *J. H. Brown, Spain*

NEWRYMAN 6 ch.g. Statoblest 120 – With Love (Be My Guest (USA) 126) [2001 –: — 6s 8.1m 10f 7f 8m 10d⁵ 10m 7m 10m⁵ 10.1m 10.3f⁴ 6m 12.4m 6m 10.5d 8g 6m 8m 8d 9.9m 8.9m 6s 10.3m 8f 6m 14v 11.9s Oct 11] probably of little account. *G. P. Kelly*

NEWSCASTER 5 b.g. Bluebird (USA) 125 – Sharp Girl (FR) 114 (Sharpman) [2001 — –: e10g Jan 13] close-coupled gelding: fair 9f winner at 3 yrs: lightly raced and well beaten since. *T. E. Powell*

NEWSIMPLEJOY 3 b.f. Marju (IRE) 127 – Hesperia (Slip Anchor 136) [2001 7m — 7m 8g Jun 25] first foal: dam, useful 11f/1½m winner in France and Italy, out of half-sister to champion US filly Go For Wand: well held in maidens. *M. L. W. Bell*

NEW WONDER 3 b.f. Presidium 124 – Miss Tri Colour 37 (Shavian 125) [2001 53: — f6s e5g⁶ f5g Nov 30] modest maiden at 2 yrs: well beaten in 2001. *J. G. Given*

NEXT CHAPTER (IRE) 3 b. or br.f. Cois Na Tine (IRE) 101 – Book Choice (North **55** Summit) [2001 –: f8s f9.4g 12.1m⁵ 11.9d³ 16m* 14.1m³ 16.2g Aug 27] modest perform- **a–** er: won claimer at Yarmouth in May: stays easy 2m: acts on good to firm and good to soft going (well beaten both runs on fibresand): sold 1,200 gns. *A. P. Jarvis*

NEXT FLIGHT (IRE) 2 b.c. (Feb 22) Woodborough (USA) 112 – Sans Ceriph **76** (IRE) 75 (Thatching 131) [2001 7g⁵ 8g³ 8d⁶ Aug 26] IR 22,000Y: good-bodied colt: third living foal: half-brother to 3-y-o Lady Ward and a 5f (at 2 yrs) to 8.5f winner in Italy by Lahib: dam Irish 7f winner: fair maiden: third at Newmarket: stays 1m. *A. P. Jarvis*

NIAGARA (IRE) 4 b.g. Rainbows For Life (CAN) – Highbrook (USA) 88 (Alpha- **79** batim (USA) 126) [2001 73: 7m 9.2d² 9.1f* 10g* 10.3m⁴ 11.6m⁴ 11m³ 9.2g* 9m 10s⁴ Oct 16] stocky gelding: fair performer: won handicap at Ayr in June, minor event at Windsor in July and handicap at Hamilton in September: effective at 9f to 11.6f: acts on firm and good to soft going: usually races prominently. *M. H. Tompkins*

NIAMH (IRE) 2 br.f. (Feb 20) Atraf 116 – Island Girl (IRE) 58 (Elbio 125) [2001 5.1s — 7m f7g Jul 27] IR 1,000F, 4,000Y: small, workmanlike filly: first foal: dam 2-y-o 6f seller winner: no sign of ability in maiden/sellers. *D. Shaw*

NICANDER (USA) 3 b.c. Rahy (USA) 115 – Night Secret 86 (Nijinsky (CAN) 138) **61** [2001 64p: 11.1s 10s 11.6d 10m⁶ 12m³ 16d a9f a10f Nov 29] quite attractive colt: modest maiden: left M. Tregoning before penultimate outing: stays 1½m: acts on good to firm going: blinkered/visored fourth to seventh starts. *K. P. McLaughlin, UAE*

NICE BALANCE (USA) 6 b.g. Shadeed (USA) 135 – Fellwaati (USA) (Alydar — (USA)) [2001 49d: f8g f11g f9.4g⁵ f8g⁵ f8s f8g f8g⁴ f8g 8g f8g⁶ f8g f11g⁶ f8s⁴ Dec 21] **a39 +** big gelding: poor performer: stays 11f: acts on fibresand: tried blinkered: sometimes slowly away: tends to hang right. *M. C. Chapman*

NICE ONE CLARE (IRE) 5 b.m. Mukaddamah (USA) 125 – Sarah-Clare 67 **117** (Reach 122) [2001 105: 6g³ 6m* 7m⁴ 7m² 6d⁴ 7d* 6s* 7d⁵ 5m⁶ Dec 16]

    If great minds think alike then the country need look no further for some of its top brains than the leading bookmakers. The high street odds-setters seem to have a remarkable knack of coming up with similar prices, even on races which, at the same time, punters are being told are among the calendar's most difficult puzzles. If these races are such brain-teasers how come the bookies seem to agree so often on which horses should lead the market, and on what odds they should be? Take the Wokingham at Royal Ascot, for example. Of the four firms quoted when the opening prices were published on May 31st, Ladbrokes and Surrey had the same seven horses at the top of their betting, both companies agreeing that Capricho should be favourite at 14/1 and that the six others were all 16/1 shots, these seven plucked from 122 entries. Hills, basing their market round the same seven horses, had Seven No Trumps favourite at 12/1, Nice One Clare at 14/1, and had four of the five others, including Capricho, also as 16/1 shots. Only Coral were in any way out on a limb, offering 25/1 Capricho, odds pretty rapidly slashed the same morning incidentally. Ante-post prices weren't much more varied on the Royal Hunt Cup judged by the odds published by the leading bookmakers on the same day. It begs a question. As familiar high street names in the wider world outside racing have their price-setting brought under closer scrutiny, how far off is the day when bookmakers come under regulatory examination?

Nice One Clare attracted a good deal of support for the Wokingham, as she did in most of her races in 2001, during which Ladbrokes reportedly described her as their worst 'losing horse' of the season. She started at 7/1 favourite in a field of thirty at Royal Ascot, having finished fifth in the race the previous year, when she had also run well in defeat in two other valuable handicaps without having much luck in running. Things went smoothly at last in the Wokingham. Held up as usual, Nice One Clare got a good split as she made ground typically strongly to challenge in the stand-side group, and she had to be driven out only because she idled after quickening ahead inside the last furlong, holding Ellens Academy by a neck as the pair drew clear. Nice One Clare came off worse in a photo for the even more valuable Tote International Handicap when returned to Ascot two starts later, going down by a short head to Atavus, conceding the winner 13 lb. That was it so far as handicaps were concerned. After a rare below-par effort when only fourth in a fillies listed event at Pontefract in August (one of only two occasions during the year when she wasn't partnered by Johnny Murtagh), Nice One Clare showed her true colours again to take a similar contest, the betabet Sceptre Stakes over seven furlongs at Doncaster's St Leger fixture, where she beat Softly Tread by half a length. Better still was to come in the Group 2 Betdaq Diadem Stakes at Ascot's Festival of Racing. Nice One Clare started at 6/1 in a field of fifteen, second favourite behind Mount Abu, the recent second in the Stanley Leisure Sprint Cup at Haydock. Several others from Haydock took their chance too in a highly-competitive renewal of the Diadem, but Nice One Clare took things in her stride, swooping through, after Orientor had briefly taken command, and then holding him and the unlucky Bahamian Pirate by a neck and a short head with Pipalong also close up in fourth, Mount Abu only sixth. Nice One Clare had two runs after the

Wokingham Stakes (Handicap), Royal Ascot—the first three home come from stalls 4, 3 and 2 respectively; Nice One Clare is driven out to beat Ellens Academy, with Seven No Trumps (No.22) and Indian Spark (No.8) filling the frame; fifth home is Doctor Spin (No.5), who fares best of those in the centre of the course

Betdaq Diadem Stakes, Ascot—
Nice One Clare is produced with a typically late run to snatch the spoils from Orientor (spots);
Bahamian Pirate (No.5) is an unlucky third, with Pipalong (right) a very close fourth

Diadem. She finished a creditable joint-fifth of fourteen behind Munir in the
Challenge Stakes at Newmarket, beaten little more than a length and a half, despite
not getting the clearest of runs, then was sent to Sha Tin for the Hong Kong Sprint,
her first attempt at five furlongs, in which she ran respectably to finish sixth behind
the Australian-trained Falvelon, finishing well and beaten only about a length and
a half.

Nice One Clare (IRE) (b.m. 1996)	Mukaddamah (USA) (b 1988)	Storm Bird (b 1978)	Northern Dancer / South Ocean
		Tash (b or br 1977)	Never Bend / Natashka
	Sarah-Clare (b 1988)	Reach (b 1982)	Kris / Gift Wrapped
		Northern Dynasty (b 1975)	Breeders Dream / Broken Half

Nice One Clare defied all reasonable expectation on pedigree. Her sire
Mukaddamah has generally been disappointing at stud, though he was also boosted
in the latest season by the Dubai Duty Free Stakes (Fred Darling) winner Rolly
Polly. Nice One Clare's dam Sarah-Clare was only a fair handicapper, though she
won six races at a mile to a mile and a quarter, and, like Nice One Clare, was better
than ever as a five-year-old. Nice One Clare has reportedly been retired, and will be
covered by Grand Lodge. In three seasons she raced almost exclusively over six
and seven furlongs and proved equally effective at both distances, though speed
was definitely her main asset and she would almost certainly have proved fully
effective over five furlongs given more opportunities. Nice One Clare was
generally well suited by a sound gallop, as she was invariably held up for a late run,
and she did go too freely in a race run at a muddling pace once in 2001. A sturdy
mare, untried on heavy ground but proven on any other, she was game and reliable,
and very much enhanced the latest season in terms of excitement. She was a credit
to her connections. *J. W. Payne*

NICHOL FIFTY 7 b.g. Old Vic 136 – Jawaher (IRE) 60 (Dancing Brave (USA) 140) **60**
[2001 77: f16.2s⁵ f12g⁶ 12.1m³ 14.1m 16g⁴ 12g 12.1s 10.9m⁴ 15.8m² 12d 18s f14g Dec
14] workmanlike gelding: modest handicapper: effective at 1½m to 17f: acts on soft and
good to firm going, probably on fibresand: tried blinkered/visored. *D. Nicholls*

NICIARA (IRE) 4 b.g. Soviet Lad (USA) – Verusa (IRE) (Petorius 117) [2001 54: **–**
f11s Jan 22] lengthy gelding: maiden handicapper: well held only run in 2001: stays 2m:
acts on fibresand, good to soft and good to firm ground: often visored/blinkered: sometimes slowly away/carries head awkwardly. *M. C. Chapman*

NICKLES 6 b.g. Lugana Beach 116 – Instinction (Never So Bold 135) [2001 58+: f5g **44**
f5g f5g⁴ f5g Mar 13] poor performer: best at bare 5f: yet to race on heavy going, acts on
any other turf and fibresand: reportedly had breathing problem final start. *S. R. Bowring*

NICKLETTE 2 b.f. (Mar 16) Nicolotte 118 – Cayla (Tumble Wind (USA)) [2001 8d **67**
p7g⁴ Dec 22] tall, good-topped filly: half-sister to several winners, including sprinters
Touch of White (by Song) and Factuelle (by Known Fact): dam showed signs of ability:
much better effort (fair form) when fourth to Stratus in minor event at Lingfield: bred to
prove best up to 1m. *C. N. Allen*

NICOBAR 4 b.c. Indian Ridge 123 – Duchess of Alba 75 (Belmez (USA) 131) [2001 **117**
112: 8s³ 8.1v* 8m* 8.5f⁶ 8g⁶ 7s⁴ Oct 14] quite attractive colt: smart performer: won
Masai Mile at Sandown (led close home to beat Swallow Flight by ¾ length) in April and
Premio Emilio Turati at Milan (by length from Caluki) in May: respectable 4 lengths
fourth to Mount Abu in Prix de la Foret at Longchamp final start: best at 7f/1m: acts on
heavy and good to firm going: sometimes sweats: tried tongue tied as 3-y-o: races freely
(withdrawn after going too freely to post fifth intended outing): goes well on turning
track: sent to USA. *I. A. Balding*

NICOLAI 4 b.g. Piccolo 121 – Fair Eleanor (Saritamer (USA) 130) [2001 66p: e10g **64**
10.1m* 9m⁴ 10.9m 9.9m Jul 23] robust gelding: modest handicapper: won at Yarmouth
in May: below form otherwise: stays 1¼m: acts on good to firm going, possibly not on
softer than good. *M. L. W. Bell*

NICOLE'S DANCER 4 b.f. Rambo Dancer (CAN) 107 – Emma Woodford 62 **–**
(Master Willie 129) [2001 –: f7g Jan 15] seems of little account. *N. Hamilton*

NICOL (IRE) 3 b.f. Nicolotte 118 – Frensham Manor (Le Johnstan 123) [2001 –: f11g **–**
Feb 23] well held in sales race (at 2 yrs) and claimer (reportedly lame). *K. McAuliffe*

Exors of the late Mr Robert Hitchins' "Nicobar"

NIEVE LADY 2 b.f. (Mar 22) Komaite (USA) – Nikoola Eve 69 (Roscoe Blake 120) **71** [2001 6d 5.2m⁵ 6g 5d² 5g 5g⁴ 6d Oct 12] leggy filly: sixth living foal: half-sister to 1¼m winner Vin St Koola (by Vin St Benet): dam, 1½m and 2m winner, also successful over hurdles: fair maiden: in frame at Hamilton and Newmarket (nursery): should stay 6f: yet to race on extremes of going. *D. Shaw*

NIFTY ALICE 3 ch.f. First Trump 118 – Nifty Fifty (IRE) 97 (Runnett 125) [2001 80: **69 d** 5.1v 5.1f 5m⁶ 5f 5g 5g 5v 6g Nov 5] leggy, lengthy filly: fair handicapper: trained by A. Berry first 5 starts: below form after: best at 5f: acts on firm and good to soft going: has started slowly: usually races prominently: tends to wander. *E. J. Alston*

NIFTY DAN 2 b.g. (Apr 26) Suave Dancer (USA) 136 – Nifty Fifty (IRE) 97 (Runnett **45** 125) [2001 5d 6m⁶ 6d Jul 16] 10,000Y: good-bodied gelding: fifth foal: half-brother to 3-y-o Nifty Alice, 4-y-o Nifty Major and 7-y-o Nifty Norman: dam 2-y-o 5f winner: poor maiden. *A. Berry*

NIFTY MAJOR 4 b.g. Be My Chief (USA) 122 – Nifty Fifty (IRE) 97 (Runnett 125) **74 d** [2001 82§: 5d⁶ 5g⁵ 5m 5f⁴ 6d 5f 5m 5d 5.1g 5g 5g 5m⁵ 5d 6v 5v p5g* Nov 20] tall, workmanlike gelding: fair handicapper: on downgrade in 2001, though won at Lingfield in November: best at 5f: acts on soft going, firm and polytrack: visored last 2 starts: has twice refused to race: often races prominently: tends to hang right/carry head high: unreliable. *A. Berry*

NIFTY NORMAN 7 b.g. Rock City 120 – Nifty Fifty (IRE) 97 (Runnett 125) [2001 **–** 72, a83: a6g⁶ a6g⁴ 6s 5v 6g 6d f5g f5g f6g Dec 8] leggy, angular gelding: one-time fairly useful 5f/6f winner: no form in 2001, trained first 2 starts by P. Haley in Spain: often blinkered earlier in career, visored final outing. *D. Nicholls*

NIGEL'S LAD (IRE) 9 b.g. Dominion Royale 112 – Back To Earth (FR) (Vayrann **75** 133) [2001 16s⁶ 16m⁴ 16m² 17.1f Jun 3] sturdy gelding: fair handicapper: stays 2¼m: acts on good to firm ground, soft and fibresand/equitrack: visored (went in snatches but ran creditably) penultimate start: useful jumper. *P. C. Haslam*

NIGHT AURORA 2 ch.c. (Feb 17) Pennekamp (USA) 130 – India Atlanta (Ahonoora **96** 122) [2001 7.1s⁵ 7m² 7g²* 7.2m⁴ Sep 21] 180,000Y: rather leggy colt: half-brother to several winners, notably smart performer up to 9f Ventiquattrofogli (by Persian Bold), 6f to 1m winner at 2 yrs: dam unraced half-sister to smart German miler Sinyar: useful performer: landed odds in maiden at Leicester in August by 8 lengths: creditable 2 lengths fourth of 6 to Al Moughazel in minor event at Ayr: will probably stay 1m: races up with pace. *E. A. L. Dunlop*

NIGHT CAP (IRE) 2 ch.g. (Feb 28) Night Shift (USA) – Classic Design (Busted **55** 134) [2001 6v f6g 5.1s p6g p6g² Dec 28] 52,000Y: ninth foal: brother to very smart 5f performer Eveningperfomancc and half-brother to 1m winner Well Drawn (by Dowsing): dam unraced half-sister to 2000 Guineas winner Tirol: modest maiden: best effort when second in nursery at Lingfield: likely to prove best at 5f/6f: acts on polytrack: slowly away/reluctant stall first 2 starts. *Sir Mark Prescott*

NIGHT CITY 10 b.g. Kris 135 – Night Secret 86 (Nijinsky (CAN) 138) [2001 65§, **– §** a72§: f9.4s e12g e8g⁵ f12g e10g* e10g⁶ 10s 16m⁵ f11g² 11.7f f11g Oct 1] sturdy gelding: **a45 §** poor performer: won seller at Lingfield in March: left K. Burke after second in claimer at Southwell in May: effective at 1¼m to 1¾m, possibly not 2m: acts on any turf going and fibresand/equitrack: blinkered/visored once each: often goes clear early on then hangs right/downs tools: unreliable. *A. G. Juckes*

NIGHT DRIVER (IRE) 2 b.g. (Feb 5) Night Shift (USA) – Highshaan (Pistolet **76** Bleu (IRE) 133) [2001 7.1s 7m⁵ 6m² 7s p8g⁵ p10g³ Dec 4] 400,000 francs Y: big, strong gelding: first foal: dam fairly useful French 9f (at 2 yrs) and 10.5f winner: fair maiden: placed at Newmarket and Lingfield: barely stays 1¼m: acts on good to firm going and polytrack. *B. W. Hills*

NIGHT FALL (IRE) 3 ch.f. Night Shift (USA) – Tumble (Mtoto 134) [2001 73, **68 d** a60: 7.1g 10m⁴ 11.9f² 11.5m³ 12m⁶ 11.9m⁵ 14.1m 11.9m⁶ 11.9m Sep 4] smallish, strong, **a–** close-coupled filly: has a quick action: fair handicapper: below form after fourth start: stays 1½m: acts on firm ground and equitrack: sometimes tongue tied: sold 8,200 gns in December. *M. Blanshard*

NIGHT FLIGHT 7 gr.g. Night Shift (USA) – Ancestry (Persepolis (FR) 127) [2001 **92** 98: f6g 5s 5s 6g 5m 5m⁴ 6g⁵ 5m 5m⁴ 5g⁶ 5g⁶ 6m⁵ 6g² 6m 5.6m 6m Sep 21] good-bodied gelding: fairly useful handicapper: runner-up at York in August: had taken time to find form, and also well below best last 2 starts: best at 5f/easy 6f: acts on soft going, good to firm and fibresand. *R. A. Fahey*

NIGHT HAVEN   3 gr.f. Night Shift (USA) – Noble Haven 74 (Indian King (USA)   **99**
128) [2001 83: 6g* 6f* 6m 6g³ 6m² 7m 6g Aug 12] good-bodied filly: useful performer:
won handicap at Salisbury then minor event at Leicester in May: good placed efforts after
in minor event at Yarmouth and listed contest at York (strong-finishing 2½ lengths second
to Palace Affair): stays 6f: acts on firm and good to soft going: has been early to post/
slowly away. *M. L. W. Bell*

NIGHT MARKET   3 ch.c. Inchinor 119 – Night Transaction 59 (Tina's Pet 121)   **64**
[2001 8.5m² 9m² 8d 9.2g⁶ f8g² Nov 30] 16,000Y: strong colt: fifth foal: half-brother to
4-y-o Prime Recreation and fairly useful 6f winner Silca Key Silca (by Polar Falcon):
dam 1m winner: modest maiden: stays 9f: acts on good to firm going and fibresand.
B. Smart

NIGHT OF GLASS   8 b.g. Mazilier (USA) 107 – Donna Elvira 80 (Chief Singer 131)   **–**
[2001 84: 8m 7d 7.5d 9g Oct 19] small gelding: formerly useful 7f/8.5f winner: no form
in 2001: sometimes blinkered/visored/bandaged. *Miss J. F. Craze*

NIGHT OF NIGHTS   3 b. or br.f. Never So Bold 135 – Shamasiya (FR) (Vayrann   **48**
133) [2001 –: 7.1d 6m² 6g 6m 7.1f 7.1f⁵ Sep 4] leggy filly: poor maiden: stays 7f: acts on
firm going. *M. Dods*

NIGHT OMEN (IRE)   4 ch.g. Night Shift (USA) – Propitious (IRE) 101 (Doyoun   **46**
124) [2001 –: 8s 7m f5g 8m 6m² 7m² 7g 8m 6f Sep 10] heavy-topped gelding: poor
maiden: stays 7f: acts on good to firm ground: sometimes tongue tied: none too
consistent. *S. C. Williams*

NIGHT ON THE TOWN   3 b.g. Dancing Spree (USA) – Ling Lane (Slip Anchor   **69**
136) [2001 71p: f8g* 9s 10.2d⁶ 10m 11.6m² Jun 25] quite good-topped gelding: fair
performer: won maiden at Southwell in January: stays 11.6f: acts on good to firm ground,
good to soft and fibresand: refused to race second outing: sold 17,000 gns, sent to
Malaysia. *B. Smart*

NIGHT PASSION   2 b.c. (Apr 4) Night Shift (USA) – Nedaarah 83 (Reference Point   **88**
139) [2001 8d⁴ 7.2m² 7.2v* Oct 15] 28,000Y: sturdy colt: first living foal: dam, won in
Britain at 1¼m and in France at 9.5f/11f (and over jumps), from family of July Cup
winner Agnes World: fairly useful form: won maiden at Ayr by head from Macaw, getting
up well inside final 1f: should be suited by at least 1m: acts on good to firm and heavy
ground: has hung left: joined D. Vienna in USA. *K. R. Burke*

NIGHT RHAPSODY (IRE)   4 ch.f. Mujtahid (USA) 118 – Double On (IRE) 110   **80**
(Doubletour (USA)) [2001 81: 10g³ 8.1m 8g 8g Aug 11] IR 40,000Y: rather leggy,
lengthy filly: first foal: dam, Irish 1m to 1½m winner, from family of Nocturnal Spree
and Moonax: fairly useful handicapper: trained at 3 yrs by J. Bolger in Ireland: well
below form after first start in 2001: stays 1¼m: acts on soft going, well held on firmer:
often blinkered/visored. *K. R. Burke*

NIGHT RUNNER   2 b.c. (Mar 23) Polar Falcon (USA) 126 – Christmas Kiss 82   **65**
(Taufan (USA) 119) [2001 5s⁵ 5m⁵ 6g 7g⁴ 8m 7.1s 6m Sep 21] 15,000Y: lengthy, angular
colt: second foal: half-brother to 3-y-o Festive Affair: dam 5f/6f winner: fair maiden:
stays 7f: acts on good to firm going, probably on soft: raced too freely in blinkers final
outing. *T. D. Easterby*

NIGHT SHIFT BLUE'S (IRE)   2 b.c. (Apr 17) Night Shift (USA) – Tommelise   **75**
(USA) (Dayjur (USA) 137) [2001 5m³ 5g² 5d 6v² 6d⁵ f8g 8fg Dec 3] 9,000 2-y-o: strong,
close-coupled colt: first foal: dam, French 6f winner, closely related to US Grade 2 1½m
winner Ampulla: fair maiden: second at Hamilton and Ayr (nursery): stays 6f: acts on
good to firm and heavy going (well beaten on fibresand). *M. Johnston*

NIGHT SHIFTER (IRE)   4 b.f. Night Shift (USA) – Atsuko (IRE) (Mtoto 134)   **–**
[2001 –: 6.1v May 1] seems of little account nowadays. *Jamie Poulton*

NIGHT SIGHT (USA)   4 b.g. Eagle Eyed (USA) 111 – El Hamo (USA) (Search For   **64 §**
Gold (USA)) [2001 87: f8g f6g⁵ f7s f11g³ f12g⁴ f11g* f12f* 12v⁵ 10.1s 10.3m 12m⁶ 8g   **a94 §**
14.8m 12g 10m³ 12m 10v 10.4d 9g f8g f7g⁶ f8g f12s Dec 21] smallish, stocky gelding:
fluent mover: fairly useful handicapper on all-weather, fair on turf: won at Southwell in
February and March: mostly out of form after: probably best at 1¼m/1½m: acts on
fibresand and any turf going: blinkered once: has carried head bit high/been slowly away:
races freely. *M. C. Chapman*

NIGHTWATCHMAN (IRE)   2 b.c. (Jan 19) Hector Protector (USA) 124 – Nightlark (IRE) 85 (Night Shift (USA)) [2001 7.1g 8d 7d Nov 3] IR 60,000F, IR 75,000Y: first foal: dam, 1½m winner, half-sister to smart 9f to 11f performer Overbury from family of Vintage Crop: modest form in maidens: should be suited by 1¼m/1½m. *W. R. Muir*   **53**

NIGRASINE   7 b.h. Mon Tresor 113 – Early Gales (Precocious 126) [2001 104: 5s 6g 7m 7f⁶ 8f² 8f 6g* 6m 7d⁵ 6g 6m 8f* 8s 8g⁵ 7d f8g p8g Dec 4] close-coupled horse: fluent mover: fairly useful performer nowadays: won handicap in July and minor event in September, both at Pontefract: effective at stiff 6f to 1m: acts on any turf going: usually visored/blinkered: normally races up with pace: has wandered. *J. L. Eyre*   **88**

NIKITA'S STAR (IRE)   8 ch.g. Soviet Lad (USA) – Sally Chase 101 (Sallust 134) [2001 –: f16g⁶ f16g⁵ f16.2g² 12.4d f14g³ f16g f14g f16.2g² 16.2f f16g⁵ 16g Aug 13] sturdy gelding: unimpressive mover: poor handicapper: stays 2m: acts on fibresand, little recent form on turf: occasionally visored/blinkered: none too consistent. *M. Brittain*   **– a46**

NIKITIN   2 b.g. (Apr 10) Emarati (USA) 74 – Choral Sundown 81 (Night Shift (USA)) [2001 6g⁵ 6g⁴ 6g 8d 8d p8g² p8g Dec 12] 10,000Y: rather sparely-made gelding: half-brother to several winners, including 3-y-o Snowstorm and 1m to 1½m winner Celestial Welcome (by Most Welcome): dam effective from 1m to 1½m: fair maiden on turf, modest on all-weather: second in seller at Lingfield: stays 1m: acts on polytrack, raced only on good/good to soft going on turf: visored/blinkered last 3 starts. *R. M. Beckett*   **72 a55**

NIMBLE TRAVELLER (IRE)   2 b.f. (Feb 23) Blues Traveller (IRE) 119 – Be Nimble (Wattlefield 117) [2001 6m 5d 5s Oct 20] 3,500Y: unfurnished filly: seventh foal: half-sister to 3 winners, including 5f (including at 2 yrs) and 6f winner Trentesimo (by Imperial Frontier): dam, Irish 7f winner, half-sister to smart sprinter Carol's Treasure: little form in maidens/minor event. *K. R. Burke*   **–**

NIMELLO (USA)   5 b.g. Kingmambo (USA) 125 – Zakota (IRE) (Polish Precedent (USA) 131) [2001 94: f8.5g* 8v* 8s* 7.9g 7g 8.2s³ Nov 5] smallish, well-made gelding: smart performer: won handicaps at Wolverhampton then Doncaster (Randombet.com Lincoln, by 2 lengths from Highland Reel) in March and Kempton (Doubleprint Stakes, by 1¼ lengths from Bold King) in May, favourite in last 2 named: well below form last 3 starts (off 3 months between each one): seems best around 1m: has won on firm ground, goes particularly well on soft/heavy and fibresand: blinkered twice in 2000 and on final start. *P. F. I. Cole*   **111**

Randombet.com Lincoln (Handicap), Doncaster—Nimello becomes trainer Paul Cole's third winner of the race in five years as he quickens clear of Highland Reel, with King Priam (blinkers) placed for the second year in succession and Mastermind (striped sleeves) fourth

NINEACRES 10 b.g. Sayf El Arab (USA) 127 – Mayor 86 (Laxton 105) [2001 98, **88**
a95: f5g 5s 5.1f 5m 5m 5g⁶ 5m 5d³ 5m 5.1m² 5d⁶ 5.2m⁵ 6m⁶ 5.7d 5.2d 6m⁵ 6g 6m 5d⁶
5s⁵ f5g f6g f5s Dec 15] angular, workmanlike gelding: fairly useful handicapper: several
creditable efforts but failed to win in 2001 (successful 9 times in 2000): best at 5f/6f:
unraced on heavy, acts on any other turf going and fibresand/equitrack: tried visored,
blinkered nowadays: has given trouble at stalls: tough. *J. M. Bradley*

NINETEENNINETYNINE 4 b.g. Warning 136 – Flower Girl 108 (Pharly (FR) 130) **–**
[2001 –: f12g Jan 8] disappointing maiden: sometimes visored. *Mrs N. Macauley*

NINNOLO (IRE) 4 b.g. Perugino (USA) 84 – Primo Stampari 78 (Primo Dominie **69 +**
121) [2001 73: 8.1m⁶ May 29] fair maiden handicapper: sixth at Sandown, only run in
2001: stays 1½m, probably not 1¾m: acts on good to firm going and good to soft: usually
tongue tied at 3 yrs. *C. N. Allen*

NIRVANA 2 b.f. (Apr 25) Marju (IRE) 127 – Charming Life (NZ) (Sir Tristram 115) **78 p**
[2001 7f⁶ 8g² Oct 19] unfurnished filly: half-sister to several winners, notably very smart
1½m performers Kingfisher Mill (by Riverman) and 4-y-o Wellbeing: dam, Australian 7f
winner, sister to Zabeel and half-sister to Baryshnikov, both Australian Group 1 winners:
fair form in minor event at Newbury and maiden at Redcar, second of 19 to Macadamia
in latter: will stay 1¼m: capable of better. *J. L. Dunlop*

NISA TIME 3 ch.f. Timeless Times (USA) 99 – Stork Hill (Crofthall 110) [2001 5.1s **–**
6.1v 9.9m May 12] third foal: dam unraced: seems of little account. *N. Tinkler*

NISR 4 b.g. Grand Lodge (USA) 125 – Tharwa (IRE) 63 (Last Tycoon 131) [2001 81: **87**
7m³ 7m* 7f⁵ 7d⁶ Oct 20] lengthy gelding: fairly useful handicapper: won at Folkestone in
July: ran well both starts after: should stay 1m: acts on firm and good to soft going,
possibly not soft. *J. W. Payne*

NITE-OWL FIZZ 3 b.g. Efisio 120 – Nite-Owl Dancer 75 (Robellino (USA) 127) **67**
[2001 8.2s 7.5m f7g⁴ f8.5g* f8g* f7s⁶ Dec 18] second foal: half-brother to 4-y-o Nite-
Owl Mate: dam 5f winner: fair performer: won maiden at Wolverhampton and handicap
at Southwell in December: stays 8.5f: acts on fibresand: slowly away first 2 outings.
J. O'Reilly

NITE-OWL LADY (IRE) 2 b.f. (Apr 24) Elbio 125 – Persian Royale 94 (Persian **40**
Bold 123) [2001 5f⁶ 7.5f 6m⁶ 5m f6g Oct 20] IR 1,200Y, 2,800 2-y-o: small filly: half-
sister to 3 winners, including French 1½m winner Priola Royale (by Priolo) and Irish 7f/
1m winner Elizabeth's Pet (by Vision), both fairly useful: dam won Irish Cambridgeshire:
poor maiden. *J. O'Reilly*

NITE-OWL MATE 4 b.g. Komaite (USA) – Nite-Owl Dancer 75 (Robellino (USA) **–**
127) [2001 49§, a74§: f7g Mar 16] smallish, angular gelding: one-time fair 6f winner: has
lost his way: tried blinkered: often tongue tied. *J. O'Reilly*

NIVERNAIS 2 b.g. (Mar 19) Forzando 122 – Funny Wave 65 (Lugana Beach 116) **76 p**
[2001 5m⁶ 5m* 5.1f² Sep 18] 2,000Y: first foal: dam ran once: won maiden at Folkestone
in August: short-headed in nursery at Chepstow: will stay 6f: should make a fairly useful
handicapper. *H. Candy*

NIYABAH (IRE) 3 ch.f. Nashwan (USA) 135 – Gharam (USA) 108 (Green Dancer **85**
(USA) 132) [2001 62p: 8d² 10g* Nov 5] fairly useful form: won maiden at Redcar in
November by 4 lengths: stayed 1¼m: raced only on good going or softer: visits Mut-
amam. *A. C. Stewart*

NO ARGUMENT 2 b.g. (Apr 26) Young Ern 120 – As Sharp As 64 (Handsome Sailor **58**
125) [2001 7m 6d⁶ 6g⁴ 7g³ 7g² 6.1m⁴ Aug 27] 5,200F, 9,500Y: fourth foal: half-brother
to 1998 2-y-o 6f winner Bodfari Street (by Dolphin Street), later useful in Scandinavia:
dam, 7f winner, out of half-sister to dam of very smart 1¼m/1½m performer Glory of
Dancer: modest maiden: placed in nurseries: will probably stay 1m: yet to race on
extremes of going: sold 5,000 gns, and gelded. *N. A. Callaghan*

NOBELIST 6 b.g. Bering 136 – Noble Peregrine (Lomond (USA) 128) [2001 105: **96**
7.9m 10m⁶ 11.5m* 10m⁶ Jul 29] lengthy, angular gelding: useful performer: easily landed
odds in seller at Lingfield (bought in 20,000 gns) in June: best effort in handicaps second
start: probably best around 1¼m: acts on firm and good to soft going: visored last 7
outings: returned to UAE. *C. E. Brittain*

NOBILISSIME 2 b.f. (Feb 6) Halling (USA) 133 – Keswa 94 (Kings Lake (USA) **73 p**
133) [2001 6m⁶ 6.5g Sep 28] seventh foal: closely related to Italian winner up to 13.5f
Keswama (by Elmaamul) and half-sister to 3 winners, including 6-y-o Compradore: dam
1m (at 2 yrs) and 1½m winner from family of Sakhee and Celestial Storm: fair form: won

maiden at Newmarket in August: very edgy and poorly drawn when tenth of 28 in valuable sales race at Ascot: bred to stay at least 1m: probably capable of better. *W. Jarvis*

NOBLE ACADEMY (USA)   2 ch. or ro.c. (Mar 20) Royal Academy (USA) 130 –   **79** Aristocratique 71 (Cadeaux Genereux 131) [2001 6.1g 7.1g² 7f⁶ 6g 6s p5g* p6g Dec 19] 16,000F, 25,000Y: leggy, rather unfurnished colt: first foal: dam, Irish sprint maiden, half-sister to useful 6f/7f winner Royal Loft: fair performer: won maiden at Lingfield in November: shapes as though will prove best at 5f: acts on polytrack, best turf run on good going. *R. Hannon*

NOBLE ARC   3 b.c. Noble Patriarch 115 – Time For Joy 42 (Good Times (ITY)) [2001   – –: f6g Feb 19] stocky colt: last in 2 maidens. *B. S. Rothwell*

NOBLE CALLING (FR)   4 b.c. Caller I D (USA) – Specificity (USA) 103 (Alleged   **65** (USA) 138) [2001 67, a75: 8m⁶ 10m 10m⁶ 9m* 9g 10m⁴ 11.6g⁴ 8d⁴ 8m⁵ Sep 6] angular   **a–** colt: fair handicapper: won at Goodwood in July: mostly ran creditably after: effective at testing 1m to easy 1½m: acts on good to firm going, good to soft and equitrack: usually visored nowadays. *R. J. Hodges*

NOBLE CYRANO   6 ch.g. Generous (IRE) 139 – Miss Bergerac (Bold Lad (IRE)   **53 §** 133) [2001 74d: 9v⁵ 8d 9.1m 11.8f 12.4m* 12.3g⁶ 14.4d² 14m 14.1m 16d f14g Oct 22] tall, angular gelding: modest performer: won claimer at Newcastle in June: effective at 1½m/1¾m, seemingly not 2m: acts on good to firm going, heavy and fibresand: usually races up with pace: unreliable. *Jedd O'Keeffe*

NOBLE INVESTMENT   7 b.g. Shirley Heights 130 – Noble Destiny 89 (Dancing   – Brave (USA) 140) [2001 51: f8.5g Feb 17] heavy-topped gelding: winning handicapper: well held only outing in 2001: tried blinkered. *B. J. Llewellyn*

NOBLE LOCKS (IRE)   3 ch.g. Night Shift (USA) – Imperial Graf (USA) (Blushing   **65** John (USA) 120) [2001 59: f7g² f6g⁵ f6g 7v⁵ 6g³ 7.1g 7d 7g 7.1m f6g 7g 8d Oct 30] fair maiden: below form in second half of 2001: effective at 6f/7f: acts on fibresand and heavy ground: tried tongue tied/blinkered. *K. A. Ryan*

NOBLE NICK   2 b. or br.g. (Apr 20) Primo Dominie 121 – Pericardia 60 (Petong 126)   **78 §** [2001 5m⁴ 5f³ 7m⁴ 6m² 5d 6g² f6s³ 6g³ 6d Oct 18] 25,000F, 60,000Y: leggy, useful-looking gelding: fourth foal: closely related to 4-y-o Card Games and half-brother to a winner in Italy by Deploy: dam lightly-raced half-sister to smart 6f/7f performer Prince Ferdinand: fair maiden: left M. Channon after fifth start: in frame 7 times, including in nurseries: stays 6f: acts on firm going and fibresand: looks none too keen (gelded after final start): one to treat with caution. *S. P. C. Woods*

NOBLE PASAO (IRE)   4 b.g. Alzao (USA) 117 – Belle Passe (Be My Guest (USA)   **78** 126) [2001 74: 8f 9.9m³ 10.1m⁶ 8m* 10g² 11.9m⁵ 13.1m 11.9s Oct 11] close-coupled gelding: has a round action: fair performer: won handicap at Thirsk (apprentices) in July: effective at 1m to easy 1½m: acts on firm going, good to soft and fibresand: blinkered once. *Andrew Turnell*

NOBLE PURSUIT   4 b.g. Pursuit of Love 124 – Noble Peregrine (Lomond (USA)   **89** 128) [2001 93: 8s 8.1v 7m 8m 8m 7.6m* 8m⁵ 8.3m⁵ 7g⁴ 7d³ 8s 8d 7d Nov 3] workmanlike gelding: fairly useful handicapper: won at Lingfield in June: several creditable efforts after: effective at 7f/1m: possibly unsuited by soft/heavy going, acts on any other turf: sometimes races freely. *T. G. Mills*

NOBLE VIEW (USA)   2 ch.f. (Apr 26) Distant View (USA) 126 – Proud Lou (USA)   **68** (Proud Clarion) [2001 5.2m⁴ 6s⁴ Jul 24] half-sister to several winners, notably smart 5.5f (at 2 yrs) to 1m (Poule d'Essai des Pouliches) winner Houseproud (by Riverman) and useful French 7f/1m winner Proud Fact (by Known Fact): dam US Grade 1 2-y-o 1m winner: favourite, fair form when fourth in maidens at Newbury and Ayr: should stay 7f. *B. W. Hills*

NO DISS GRACE   3 b.g. Cigar 68 – Llanelly (FR) 51 (Kenmare (FR) 125) [2001 44:   – f7g 8m May 30] seems of little account now. *P. C. Haslam*

NOD'S NEPHEW   4 b.g. Efisio 120 – Nordan Raider 81 (Domynsky 110) [2001 69,   **64** a57: f7g 7.1m⁵ 7.5m 7.5f 6g 6g² 7g³ 7.5m 7.5s⁴ 6v f7g⁴ f6g Dec 8] lengthy gelding: modest performer: sold from Miss J. Camacho 7,000 gns after penultimate start: effective at 6f to 7.5f: acts on heavy and good to firm going, probably on fibresand: usually races prominently: none too consistent. *D. E. Cantillon*

NOELS GANADOR (USA)   2 b.c. (Feb 9) Our Emblem (USA) – Carolita (USA)   **72** (Caro 133) [2001 a5.5g⁵ 7m³ f6g³ a8g² a6g* a8g⁶ Dec 16] $10,000Y, 17,000 2-y-o: half-brother to several winners in USA: dam winning sprinter in USA: fair performer:

third in maiden at Brighton and sales race at Wolverhampton: won maiden at Mijas in December: stays 1m: acts on sand/fibresand. *E. J. Creighton, Spain*

NO EXCUSE NEEDED 3 ch.c. Machiavellian (USA) 123 – Nawaiet (USA) **121** (Zilzal (USA) 137) [2001 109+: 8m⁵ 8m² 8g* 10d Oct 20]

    Should they be needed there are a couple of perfectly plausible excuses for this very smart miler trailing home last of twelve in the Champion Stakes at Newmarket on his final start. One, he doesn't stay a mile and a quarter, and two, he is unsuited by ground softer than good. No Excuse Needed's performance in the race suggested that the going is the more likely explanation as he was beaten before stamina became an issue. One of the first off the bridle, No Excuse Needed began to lose his place fully two furlongs from home and was eased when clearly held. Connections will probably give him another chance at the trip, but whether they will run him again when the ground is on the soft side is another matter. No Excuse Needed had missed his intended previous engagement, in the Queen Elizabeth II Stakes, when the going turned soft, and he would also have been taken out of the Champion if conditions had become any worse.

    Apart from when finishing a below-par fifth on soft ground in the Royal Lodge Stakes at Ascot on his final start at two—he'd won a maiden at Sandown and the Champagne Lanson Vintage Stakes at Goodwood on his previous two outings —No Excuse Needed had raced only on good and good to firm ground until Newmarket. He had been due to make his seasonal reappearance on dirt, in the UAE Derby, but a setback, 'a bit of filling round his tendons', ruled him out three days beforehand. He didn't return to action until June, in the St James's Palace Stakes at Royal Ascot. Looking in very good shape, he ran even better than his fifth-of-eleven position behind Black Minnaloushe suggests, having a far from clear run. Just beaten to a gap by the winner a furlong out and forced to check, No Excuse Needed wasn't punished unduly once his chance had gone but was still beaten only a couple of lengths by the winner. No Excuse Needed enjoyed a clear passage and turned the tables on Black Minnaloushe on his next start, in the Champagne Lanson Sussex Stakes at Goodwood, the pair finishing second and third respectively behind the St James's Palace Stakes runner-up Noverre. It looked as though No Excuse Needed might win when he swept through to lead approaching the final furlong, but Noverre finished to even greater effect to beat him by two lengths. With no Noverre or Black Minnaloushe in the field, No Excuse Needed was sent off at odds on when returned to Goodwood just over three weeks later for the Celebration Mile, the Two Thousand Guineas second Tamburlaine the pick of his five rivals. No Excuse Needed, waited with in the early stages of the race, had to be pushed along vigorously as Nicobar increased the pace at halfway, but he gradually warmed to his task, took command over a furlong out and forged

Celebration Mile, Goodwood—No Excuse Needed responds to Kieren Fallon's urgings; Tamburlaine (rail), Late Night Out and Munir (right) are next home

clear to win by a length and a half from Tamburlaine. Twelve months earlier another son of Machiavellian, No Excuse Needed's stable-companion Medicean, had won the same race after also being placed in the Sussex Stakes. Medicean went on to do even better at four, winning the Lockinge, Queen Anne and Eclipse, and, while it might be too much to expect No Excuse Needed to emulate that colt's achievements, there's every reason to think he can train on well from three to four. A rangy, quite attractive individual, he has had just seven races to date and is with a trainer who is second to none when it comes to improving horses of this type.

No Excuse Needed (ch.c. 1998)	Machiavellian (USA) (b or br 1987)	Mr Prospector (b 1970)	Raise A Native
			Gold Digger
		Coup de Folie (b 1982)	Halo
			Raise The Standard
	Nawaiet (USA) (ch 1991)	Zilzal (ch 1986)	Nureyev
			French Charmer
		Greenland Park (ch 1976)	Red God
			Centre Piece

There has to be a doubt about whether No Excuse Needed can prove, as Medicean did, as effective over a mile and a quarter as he is at a mile. There's more speed than stamina on the dam's side of his pedigree, that's for sure. The dam Nawaiet gained her only success in five outings in a six-furlong event at Maisons-Laffitte as a three-year-old and is a daughter of the very smart sprinter Greenland Park. The latter was sold in 1981 for a then-European record broodmare price of 730,000 guineas carrying her first foal, a filly by Kris. Named Fitnah, she went on to prove every bit as good as her dam, though requiring much longer distances to show her worth, all of her wins coming at around a mile and a quarter, while she also showed her form at a mile and a half with second place in the Prix Vermeille. Greenland Park has produced nothing so good as Fitnah, though Emerald Park, a full sister to Nawaiet, is a useful winner at up to a mile in France. No Excuse Needed is himself the third foal of Nawaiet, and so far the only one to have raced. Nawaiet also has a two-year-old by Selkirk and a yearling full sister to No Excuse Needed. No Excuse Needed, who has a quick action, is likely to make into an even more imposing looking colt as a four-year-old, and it is to be hoped racegoers are able to have a longer time to view him in the preliminaries than those at Goodwood on Sussex Stakes day did. He was brought very late into the paddock on that occasion, something not uncommon for the stable's big-race runners. Not only does this short change the paying public but it's unfair on the other runners who are brought in on time; at Goodwood, several had been paraded for a good ten minutes on what was a particularly humid afternoon, before No Excuse Needed appeared. Sadly, no excuse was sought by the stewards for this state of affairs. *Sir Michael Stoute*

NO ILLUSIONS 2 b.c. (Mar 7) Bluegrass Prince (IRE) 110 – Dancing Years (USA) 56 (Fred Astaire (USA)) [2001 5.3s 6m⁶ 6g 7f 7m⁶ 6m 7g Aug 23] 3,500Y: sparely-made colt: third reported foal: dam German 1¼m winner: modest maiden: stays 7f: acts on firm and soft ground: visored last 3 starts. *R. Ingram* **53**

NOIRIE 7 br.g. Warning 136 – Callipoli (USA) 81 (Green Dancer (USA) 132) [2001 45§: f12s f11g 12.4d May 7] sparely-made gelding: temperamental handicapper: tried blinkered/visored. *M. Brittain* **– §**

NO JOKE 3 b. or br.f. Bin Ajwaad (IRE) 119 – Round Midnight 64 (Star Appeal 133) [2001 6s 8.3d 7m 10m⁶ 10.1g 8v Oct 24] rather leggy filly: half-sister to several winners, including 7f to 1¼m winner Midnight Jazz (by Shardari): dam, maiden, ran only at 5f/6f at 2 yrs: little form: has been slowly away/looked wayward. *C. F. Wall* **–**

NO LANGUAGE PLEASE (IRE) 7 ch.g. Arapahos (FR) 117 – Strong Language 58 (Formidable (USA) 125) [2001 55: 10.3s 11.9s⁶ 11.9m³ 12m 16.4m³ 14.1d⁶ Aug 8] strong, lengthy gelding: poor performer: effective at 1½m to 2m: acts on firm ground. *R. Curtis* **46**

NO MERCY 5 ch.g. Faustus (USA) 118 – Nashville Blues (IRE) 94 (Try My Best 54 (USA) 130) [2001 75§: 8s 10g 13.3g 10m f8g² 10g⁴ 10m³ 11.5f 9.9d 9.7d p7g f7g* f8g* a74 p7g Dec 28] big, lengthy gelding: fair performer on all-weather, modest on turf: won handicap in November and minor event in December, both at Southwell, making most each time: stays easy 1¼m: acts on any turf going, fibresand and equitrack: visored last 3 starts, tried blinkered/tongue tied earlier in career: sometimes races freely. *B. A. Pearce*

NOMINATOR LAD   7 b.g. Nomination 125 – Ankara's Princess (USA) 81 (Ankara (USA) 106) [2001 80, a74: f8g f8g 10m Aug 1] sturdy gelding: poor mover: formerly fairly useful winner: no form in 2001, reportedly lame final start: often blinkered at 6 yrs. *B. A. McMahon*

NOMORE MR NICEGUY   7 b.h. Rambo Dancer (CAN) 107 – Lariston Gale 81   **74** (Pas de Seul 133) [2001 81, a85: 7.6f 7.1m³ 7f⁴ 8.1d⁴ 8m⁵ 8g⁵ 7.9m⁶ 7.5m² 7.6m⁴ 8.1s⁶ 7m⁴ 7g f6g p7g Nov 28] big horse: one-time useful performer: only fair at 7 yrs: left E. Alston 8,000 gns after penultimate outing: stayed easy 8.5f: acted on any turf going/fibresand and equitrack: ran poorly in blinkers: was sometimes slowly away/looked less than keen: dead. *D. Nicholls*

NO NAME CITY (IRE)   3 ch.c. Royal Abjar (USA) 121 – Broadway Gal (USA)   **61** (Foolish Pleasure (USA)) [2001 55: f8.5g⁵ e8g³ 8d 8d⁶ Oct 25] modest maiden: stays 8.5f: acts on fibresand and equitrack. *J. W. Hills*

NO NELLIE NO   7 ch.m. Formidable (USA) 125 – Now In Session (USA) (Diesis   **–** 133) [2001 11.6m f11g 10m Jul 11] seems of no account. *M. A. Allen*

NON VINTAGE (IRE)   10 ch.g. Shy Groom (USA) – Great Alexandra (Runnett 125)   **–** [2001 –: 14.1g Jun 16] of little account on Flat nowadays. *M. C. Chapman*

NOON GUN   3 ch.c. Ashkalani (IRE) 128 – Lady Kris (IRE) (Kris 135) [2001 80p: **109** f7g* 7d 8m 8m* 8m* Aug 30] rather leggy colt: useful performer: won maiden at Southwell in March, then handicap and minor event (clearly best effort when beating Ecstatic 5 lengths in 4-runner race) at Salisbury in July/August: behind in competitive handicaps other 2 starts: stays 1m: acts on fibresand and good to firm going: held up: sent to Hong Kong, where renamed Sunseen. *W. R. Muir*

NOOSHMAN (USA)   4 ch.g. Woodman (USA) 126 – Knoosh (USA) 113 (Storm   **110** Bird (CAN) 134) [2001 117: a9f³ a10f5 9.9m² 10m² 12g² 10.3d³ Sep 14] rangy, good-topped gelding: smart performer: ran in UAE first 2 starts: runner-up in listed events at Goodwood (beaten head by Mubtaker) and Kempton (to Blue Gold) and minor event at Newmarket (beaten head by Hill Country) after: barely stays 1½m: acts on heavy and good to firm going: usually held up. *Saeed bin Suroor*

NO QUESTION   2 b.f. (Mar 12) Salse (USA) 128 – Opalette 75 (Sharrood (USA)   **77** 124) [2001 7g⁵ 8m⁴ f8.5g² f8.5g² f8g⁴ Nov 19] 11,000Y: first foal: dam 1¼m winner: fair maiden: twice runner-up when favourite at Wolverhampton: will stay at least 1¼m: acts on fibresand and good to firm going. *B. W. Hills*

NORCROFT LADY   3 b.f. Mujtahid (USA) 118 – Polytess (IRE) (Polish Patriot   **–** (USA) 128) [2001 85: 8g 9m 7g 7g 7m⁶ Aug 27] big, useful-looking filly: fairly useful 6f winner at 2 yrs: showed little in 2001. *N. A. Callaghan*

NORDIC HERO (IRE)   8 b.g. Nordico (USA) – Postscript (Final Straw 127) [2001   **–** f12g f11g f12g May 19] probably of little account now. *J. Balding*

NORDIC SABRE   3 b.f. Sabrehill (USA) 120 – Nordico Princess 71 (Nordico (USA))   **–** [2001 76: 5.1f 6m 5m 5m 6g Aug 15] leggy filly: fair 5f winner at 2 yrs: well held in handicaps in 2001: blinkered final start. *Mrs L. Stubbs*

NORFOLK REED (IRE)   4 b.g. Thatching 131 – Sawaki 71 (Song 132) [2001 88:   **92** 8s⁶ 7.1m* 7m⁵ 8.3g* 8f⁴ 8m⁴ 8.5m⁴ 8m 8m 8s² 8d Oct 19] leggy, close-coupled gelding: fairly useful performer: won minor event at Warwick in May and handicap at Windsor in June: good second of 31 to Hail The Chief in handicap at Ascot in September: effective at 7f to easy 8.5f: acts on soft and good to firm going: sometimes blinkered/visored earlier in year: none too consistent: sold 24,000 gns, sent to USA. *R. Hannon*

NORMAN CONQUEST (USA)   7 ch.g. Miswaki (USA) 124 – Grand Luxe (CAN)   **–** (Sir Ivor 135) [2001 12.1s 16f Sep 4] heavy-bodied gelding: winning chaser, disappointing maiden on Flat: tried visored. *A. Crook*

NOROIT (GER)   3 b.c. Monsun (GER) 124 – Noble Princesse (GER) (Windwurf   **116** (GER)) [2001 10s* 10g⁵ 10d⁴ 12s³ 12.1g* 12v³ 12s⁶ Oct 21] fourth foal: half-brother to 3 winners in Germany, notably smart middle-distance stayer Noel (by Acatenango): dam German 1¼m winner: smart performer: won maiden at Munich in April and improved effort when winning EuropaChampionat-Grosser Preis der Frankfurter Sparkasse at Frankfurt in August by 3½ lengths from Street Poker: much the better of last 2 starts in

Group 1 company when 4½ lengths third to Kutub in Preis von Europa at Cologne: will stay beyond 1½m: acts on heavy ground. *W. Figge, Germany*

NORTH ARDAR 11 b.g. Ardar 87 – Langwaite (Seaepic (USA) 100) [2001 46: f12s⁴ f11g⁶ f16.2g Feb 22] probably of little account nowadays. *R. Brotherton* —

NORTH BY NORTH (IRE) 3 b.g. Distinctly North (USA) 115 – Winscarlet North (Garland Knight 92) [2001 –: 6d 8.3m⁴ 8m⁵ f7g² 7d⁶ 7d 7m⁴ 7g⁵ Sep 3] leggy gelding: modest maiden: effective at 7f/1m: acts on fibresand, good to firm and good to soft going: sent to Spain. *M. H. Tompkins* **54 a57**

NORTH CIDER ROSE (IRE) 2 ch.f. (Mar 28) Goldmark (USA) 113 – Scotia Rose (Tap On Wood 130) [2001 5.7f 7.1m 7m 8.2s Oct 30] IR 5,400Y: has a round action: half-sister to several winners, including 14.6f to 2¼m winner Amiarge (by Reference Point) and fairly useful 1997 2-y-o 1m winner Herminius (by Ballad Rock): dam Irish 1½m winner: no form in maidens/seller: left M. Quinn after third start. *G. M. McCourt* —

NORTHERN DANZIG 2 b.f. (Jan 14) Danzig Connection (USA) – Kristiana (Kris 135) [2001 f5g Apr 10] 4,700Y: first foal: dam unraced half-sister to 4-y-o Rozel: well held in Southwell maiden. *E. J. Alston* —

NORTHERN DESERT (IRE) 2 b.c. (Mar 29) Desert Style (IRE) 121 – Rosie's Guest (IRE) (Be My Guest (USA) 126) [2001 6g² 6s² Oct 5] IR 9,500F, 35,000Y: second foal: half-brother to a 7f (at 2 yrs)/7.5f winner in Italy by Case Law: dam Irish maiden: green, fair form when second in maidens at Lingfield: beaten 4 lengths by Zandicular on second occasion: will stay 1m: capable of better. *G. Wragg* **76 p**

NORTHERN ECHO 4 b.g. Pursuit of Love 124 – Stop Press (USA) 93 (Sharpen Up 127) [2001 56: 12.4d 14m⁴ 17.1m 13.1f³ 10.9g Jul 6] strong gelding: poor maiden handicapper: stays easy 13f: acts on firm and soft going: visored final start, sometimes blinkered at 3 yrs. *M. Dods* **46**

NORTHERN EXPOSURE 2 ch.f. (Mar 22) Polar Falcon (USA) 126 – Lucky Round 82 (Auction Ring (USA) 123) [2001 6.1d Sep 21] strong filly: eighth foal: half-sister to 1¼m winner Missfortuna (by Priolo) and French 11f winner Harmonie du Soir (by Top Ville): dam, 1¼m winner, sister to very smart 7f/1m performer Lucky Ring: 50/1 and burly, well held in maiden at Nottingham. *John Berry* —

NORTHERN FLEET 8 b.g. Slip Anchor 136 – Kamkova (USA) 62 (Northern Dancer) [2001 66: 11.8f 11.6g⁵ 20m Jun 20] quite good-topped gelding: modest handicapper: best at 1¾m+: acts on good to firm going: blinkered once at 4 yrs. *Mark Campion* **62**

NORTHERN GAMES 2 b.c. (Feb 7) Mind Games 121 – Northern Sal 59 (Aragon 118) [2001 6d 6g⁵ 7d⁶ 7.1f⁶ Sep 18] leggy, useful-looking colt: first foal: dam 2-y-o 5f winner: fair maiden: stays 7f: acts on firm and good to soft ground: soon off bridle last 2 starts. *A. Berry* **67**

NORTHERN GOLD 3 b.g. Goldmark (USA) 113 – Scottish Royal (IRE) (Night Shift (USA)) [2001 f9.4g⁴ May 3] 13,000F, 5,600Y: first foal: dam unraced out of half-sister to Dancing Brave and Jolypha: well backed, won seller at Wolverhampton in May by 4 lengths, edging left, only outing. *J. G. Given* **59**

NORTHERN MOTTO 8 b.g. Mtoto 134 – Soulful (FR) (Zino 127) [2001 55: 15.8m Sep 22] leggy gelding: modest handicapper at 7 yrs: well held only outing in 2001: sometimes visored/blinkered. *J. S. Goldie* —

NORTHERN NYMPH 2 b.g. (Apr 14) Makbul 104 – Needwood Sprite 58 (Joshua 129) [2001 6g⁶ 7d f7g⁵ f8.5s* Dec 27] 1,200Y: good-topped gelding: fourth foal: half-brother to 5-y-o Genial Genie and 7-y-o Flying Flip: dam, 7f winner who stayed 1¾m, also successful over hurdles: fairly useful performer: shaped encouragingly in maidens prior to winning nursery at Wolverhampton: likely to stay 1¼m. *R. Hollinshead* **80**

NORTHERN RAIDER (IRE) 3 b.g. College Chapel 122 – Pepper And Salt (IRE) (Double Schwartz 128) [2001 11.1d³ 10d² 12g 16.2m 10s Sep 24] IR 8,800F, IR 7,200Y: good-topped gelding: first foal: dam unraced: poor maiden: blinkered final 2 starts: joined N. Wilson, successful in selling hurdle in December. *Andrew Turnell* **46**

NORTHERN SVENGALI (IRE) 5 b.g. Distinctly North (USA) 115 – Trilby's Dream (IRE) (Mansooj 118) [2001 77: 5v⁶ 5d 5g 6m 5m 5m 5m* 5m 5.1f³ 5m* 5f⁵ 5m 5m 5g 5g 5g 5m 5g⁴ 5.1g 5s f5g f6g³ f6g³ 5d⁶ f6g³ f6g Nov 27] small, sturdy gelding: fair handicapper: won at Newcastle (apprentice event) then Hamilton in June: effective at 5f to easy 7f: acts on any turf going, fibresand and equitrack: sometimes blinkered/slowly away: unreliable. *T. D. Barron* **68 § a62 §**

NORTHERN TARA (IRE) 2 b.f. (Apr 10) Fayruz 116 – Mitsubishi Style (Try My **84**
Best (USA) 130) [2001 5s² 5.1f³ 5m 5m* 5d² 6g⁶ 5m³ 5m 5s Oct 20] IR 6,000F, 26,000Y:
stocky filly: half-sister to 3 winners, including fairly useful Irish 1992 2-y-o 5f winner
Preponderance (by Cyrano de Bergerac): dam third at 1m in Ireland: fairly useful
performer: won maiden at Ripon in July: creditable efforts in nurseries/minor event next
3 starts: possibly something amiss final start: will prove best at 5f/6f: acts on firm and
good to soft going: sold 12,000 gns. *J. J. Quinn*

NORTHERN TIMES (USA) 4 ch.g. Cahill Road (USA) – Northern Nation (USA) **49**
(Northrop (USA)) [2001 58: f8.5s⁶ f14.8s³ f14.8g⁴ f12g³ f11g² e10g* f8g f11g f11g⁵ f11g
p10g Dec 29] compact gelding: poor performer: won seller at Lingfield in April: well
held after: effective at 1¼m to easy 15f: acts on fibresand, equitrack and good to soft
going: usually blinkered/visored. *R. Brotherton*

NORTHERN UNION (CAN) 10 b.g. Alwasmi (USA) 115 – Loving Cup (USA) **–**
(Big Spruce (USA)) [2001 22.2f Jun 22] very lightly raced on Flat nowadays: winning
hurdler. *A. Parker*

NORTHFIELDS DANCER (IRE) 3 ch.c. Dr Devious (IRE) 127 – Heartland 72 **93**
(Northfields (USA)) [2001 93: 8s 10.1s⁵ 7.6m 8m 8m 8g² 8g* 7g 8d 10s Oct 17] strong,
compact colt: fairly useful handicapper: left R. Hannon after fifth start: below form after
winning at Tralee in August: stays 1m: acts on soft and good to firm ground: blinkered
last 5 starts: none too consistent. *K. F. O'Brien, Ireland*

NORTHGATE (IRE) 5 b.g. Thatching 131 – Tender Time (Tender King 123) [2001 **52 §**
55§: 8m⁵ 8f 7.5f³ 7.5m 7m 8f³ 7m 7d³ 7m⁵ 8.9m 8.3m Sep 24] leggy gelding: modest
handicapper: was best at 7f/1m: acted on firm and soft going: was usually blinkered:
unreliable: dead. *M. Brittain*

NORTH (IRE) 3 br.g. Mukaddamah (USA) 125 – Flamenco (USA) 116 (Dance Spell **60**
(USA)) [2001 f11g 8v⁵ Apr 19] 21,000Y: half-brother to several winners, including fairly
useful 7f/1m winner Set Pattern (by Affirmed) and useful 1¼m/1½m winner Darrery (by
Darshaan): dam, 2-y-o 6f/7f winner, should have stayed beyond 1m: modest form on
second of 2 starts in maidens: sold 500 gns. *Miss J. A. Camacho*

NORTH OF KALA (IRE) 8 b.g. Distinctly North (USA) 115 – Hi Kala (Kampala **52**
120) [2001 51: 12m* 13.3f³ 12f Aug 1] modest handicapper: dead-heated in apprentice
event at Salisbury in June: ran well next time: stays 13f: acts on firm going and equitrack:
tried blinkered. *G. L. Moore*

NORTH POINT (IRE) 3 b.g. Definite Article 121 – Friendly Song 48 (Song 132) **79**
[2001 67: f8g⁴ 9.2m² 10m* 9.9m Jun 15] smallish, useful-looking gelding: fair performer: won handicap at Leicester in June: reportedly lame next time: stays 1¼m: acts on good
to firm ground. *A. P. Jarvis*

NORTHSIDE LODGE (IRE) 3 b.g. Grand Lodge (USA) 125 – Alongside 58 (Slip **71**
Anchor 136) [2001 10s 10s⁶ 10.3f⁶ 12m 12g 10m* 10.1g 10g f12g⁶ p10g* p10g* Dec 12]
IR 28,000Y: good-topped gelding: third foal: half-brother to fairly useful winner around
1½m Common Cause (by Polish Patriot): dam, Irish 9f winner, half-sister to smart
French/US 1m/1¼m winner Kirkwall: fair handicapper: won at Redcar in September and
Lingfield in November and December: probably best around 1¼m: acts on soft going,
good to firm and polytrack: blinkered fifth to seventh starts: best form ridden up with
pace. *P. W. Harris*

NORTON (IRE) 4 ch.g. Barathea (IRE) 127 – Primrose Valley 99 (Mill Reef (USA) **98**
141) [2001 86: 10m 10.5d 8m⁶ 8.1g* 7.1s⁵ 7f⁴ 7s⁴ 8d⁶ 8d Nov 3] useful-looking gelding:
useful handicapper: won at Haydock in August: creditable efforts after, particularly when
fourth in valuable event at Ascot (ridden less prominently than usual) seventh start:
effective at 7f/1m: acts on firm and soft going: gelded after final outing. *T. G. Mills*

NORWAY (USA) 3 ch.c. Storm Cat (USA) – Weekend Surprise (USA) (Secretariat **88**
(USA)) [2001 73p: 7s 8m² 8g⁵ 12f 10d Jun 30] $3,000,000Y: heavy-topped colt: closely
related to 2 winners, notably Preakness winner/Kentucky Derby second Summer Squall
(by Storm Bird), and half-brother to several winners, notably Belmont Stakes/Breeders'
Cup Classic winner A P Indy (by Seattle Slew): dam US Grade 3 6f and 8.5f winner at 2
yrs, later placed in Grade 1 events up to 1¼m: fairly useful maiden: second at Navan in
May: well behind in King George V Handicap at Royal Ascot penultimate start: stayed
1m: acted on good to firm going: to stand at Double L Farm, nr Bosque, New Mexico,
USA, fee $3,500, live foal. *A. P. O'Brien, Ireland*

NORWOOD ORIGO 2 ch.c. (Feb 18) Elmaamul (USA) 125 – Miller's Creek (USA) **68**
62 (Star de Naskra (USA)) [2001 6m 6.9m² Jun 29] 27,000Y: half-brother to several
winners, including useful 1993 2-y-o 6f winner Fast Eddy (by Sharpo), later 7f winner in
Germany, and useful 6f (at 2 yrs) to 1¼m winner Stone Mill (by Caerleon): dam maiden
miler: much better effort in maidens (fair form) when second to Bishop's Wood at
Folkestone: will stay 1m. *M. L. W. Bell*

NO SAM NO 3 b.f. Reprimand 122 – Samjamalifran (Blakeney 126) [2001 47: f7g⁶ **49 §**
6.1d f8.5g 8.2m⁴ 8d² 10.1g⁶ 10g 10m Sep 1] leggy filly: poor maiden: stays 1m: acts on
good to soft going: sometimes slowly away/seemingly reluctant. *J. A. Osborne*

NOSE THE TRADE 3 b.g. Cyrano de Bergerac 120 – Iolite 85 (Forzando 122) [2001 **107**
76: f7g⁴ f8.5g* f8.5g* f8.5g* e10g⁵ 9m⁵ 8m 7.1m 7d* 8d f8.5f² f9.4s Dec 26] strong,
sturdy gelding: useful handicapper: greatly improved in 2001, winning at Wolverhampton in January and February (twice), and Newmarket (27-runner event, by ¾ length
from Cork Harbour) in October: very good 4 lengths second to Celtic Thatcher at
Wolverhampton penultimate start: best at 7f/8.5f: acts on fibresand and good to soft
going, probably on good to firm: blinkered (very slowly away/pulled too hard) eighth
outing: usually held up. *J. A. Osborne*

NOSEY NATIVE 8 b.g. Cyrano de Bergerac 120 – Native Flair 87 (Be My Native **44 +**
(USA) 122) [2001 54, a–: f12g f16g 14.1v 10f 12.3m 13.3f 14.1d⁴ 14.1d⁶ Aug 26] leggy **a–**
gelding: poor handicapper: stays 2m: acts on any turf going: tried visored early in career:
tends to get behind. *Mrs Lydia Pearce*

NO SURRENDER 3 ch.f. Brief Truce (USA) 126 – Furry Dance (USA) (Nureyev **– §**
(USA) 131) [2001 36: e7g⁵ f7s f6g f6g⁵ f5g 5m 5d 6m f5g 5f Jul 22] maiden handicapper:
little form in 2001: usually blinkered: ungenuine. *D. W. Chapman*

NOSY BE 3 b.g. Cyrano de Bergerac 120 – Blossomville (Petong 126) [2001 73: f6g⁴ **67 d**
7f 7g f6s p7g Dec 28] fair maiden: well below form after second start: stays easy 7f: acts
on firm ground and fibresand: visored final outing: has been slowly away/hung under
pressure. *P. J. Makin*

NOTATION (IRE) 7 b.g. Arazi (USA) 135 – Grace Note (FR) 99 (Top Ville 129) **35 §**
[2001 35§: f14g f16g f12g f16.2g⁶ f16g f8g⁵ f11g f12g⁶ 16m² f11g⁴ 11.1d 11.9f 12m
13m 16f 12.1d 16.2s⁵ 12.1s Aug 21] quite good-topped gelding: poor performer: stays
2m: acts on fibresand, soft and good to firm going: usually blinkered: often gets behind:
unreliable. *D. W. Chapman*

NOTECARD 3 b.c. Zafonic (USA) 130 – Lead Note (USA) 62 (Nijinsky (CAN) 138) **82**
[2001 8m* 8d⁶ 10.3m Sep 12] rangy colt: third living foal: dam, 2-y-o 1m winner on only
start, half-sister to Rainbow Quest and from family of Commander In Chief and Warning:
fairly useful form: won maiden at Doncaster in July: seemed to run creditably in minor
event at Bath next time: should stay 1¼m: sold 30,000 gns, sent to USA. *B. W. Hills*

NOT FADE AWAY 3 b.g. Ezzoud (IRE) 126 – Green Flower (USA) 56 (Fappiano **–**
(USA)) [2001 –: 10v 11.8s Oct 16] strong gelding: well held in maidens/claimer.
R. M. Beckett

NOTHING DAUNTED 4 ch.c. Selkirk (USA) 129 – Khubza 86 (Green Desert **103**
(USA) 127) [2001 99: 7d² 7m 8m 7g 7d Oct 20] quite attractive colt: fluent mover:
useful handicapper, lightly raced: disappointing after good second at Newmarket in
April: stays 1m: acts on soft and good to firm going: visored final start: sold only 6,000
gns. *E. A. L. Dunlop*

NOTIONAL (IRE) 5 b.m. Lucky Guest 109 – Sportin' Notion (USA) (Sportin' Life **–**
(USA)) [2001 8d 11.7d Oct 25] disappointing maiden handicapper: tried blinkered/
tongue tied. *J. L. Spearing*

NOT JUST A DREAM 3 b.f. Mujadil (USA) 119 – Red Cloud (IRE) 61 (Taufan **54**
(USA) 119) [2001 56: 6g⁴ 7.5m⁶ 7m 6m 6m 6m Aug 22] leggy, sparely-made filly:
modest maiden: stays 6f: acts on firm and good to soft ground: sold 1,500 gns. *A. Berry*

NOT PROVEN 2 br.c. (Feb 7) Mark of Esteem (IRE) 137 – Free City (USA) (Danzig **70**
(USA)) [2001 7.5g 8d 8.2s⁴ Oct 30] 500,000 francs Y: useful-looking colt: fifth foal:
half-brother to a winner up to 1½m in Belgium by Suave Dancer: dam, French 1m winner,
out of half-sister to US Grade 1 winner up to 1¼m Chief's Crown: easily best effort in
maidens (fair form) when never-nearer fourth to Balakheri at Nottingham: will stay 1¼m.
J. G. FitzGerald

NOUF 5 b.m. Efisio 120 – Miss Witch 59 (High Line 125) [2001 81: 8.3d 7m 8.1d* 8g⁵ **83**
8m* 9.2g³ 10m Sep 21] good-topped mare: unimpressive mover: fairly useful handi-

capper: won at Haydock in June and Redcar in August: best at 1m/1¼m: acts on heavy and good to firm going. *K. A. Ryan*

NOUKARI (IRE)   8 b.g. Darshaan 133 – Noufiyla 68 (Top Ville 129) [2001 85: f12g⁴ e12g e13g⁴ f12g f11g 16m³ 12.3f⁵ 13.9m 12m³ 13.1m⁵ Jun 1] workmanlike gelding: fair handicapper: stays 1¾m, not 2m: possibly unsuited by heavy going, acts on any other turf, fibresand and equitrack: visored (tended to race freely) 4 starts prior to final one: sometimes slowly away. *P. D. Evans*   **69**

NOVAK   2 b.c. (Jan 22) Revoque (IRE) 122 – Most Uppitty 69 (Absalom 128) [2001 8m 7g 6d Oct 18] strong, useful-looking colt: third foal: dam 5f (at 2 yrs)/6f winner: well held in maidens: sold 3,000 gns, sent to Germany. *B. J. Meehan*   **–**

NOVA ZEMBLA   2 b.f. (Mar 29) Young Ern 120 – Candarela 41 (Damister (USA) 123) [2001 f5g Mar 30] third foal: dam, maiden, half-sister to useful 1¼m performer Game Ploy: 16/1, last in maiden at Southwell. *W. G. M. Turner*   **–**

NOVERRE (USA)   3 b.c. Rahy (USA) 115 – Danseur Fabuleux (USA) 106 (Northern Dancer) [2001 113: a8f² 8m*ᵈⁱˢ 8m² 8m* 8d³ 8s² 8f Oct 27]   **125**

The magnificent campaign enjoyed by Godolphin's four-year-olds and upwards, who notched fourteen Group/Grade 1 contests internationally, was in stark contrast to the relative lack of success with the three-year-olds, who contributed only one victory at the highest level—Noverre's in the Sussex Stakes. This shortfall in an age group which in the last few years has truly come up with the goods only twice—in 1998 with such as Cape Verdi and Nedawi and 1999 when the standard-bearers included Dubai Millennium, Aljabr and Island Sands—must be a cause for concern for the Dubai operation. In the latest season it certainly helps explain why the Coolmore/Ballydoyle team outpointed Godolphin in the Group 1 tally, since the former's classic horses notched twelve races in that category. The performances of the Godolphin three-year-olds were not boosted in the slightest by the purchases made at the end of 2000, since Atlantis Prince, Bad As I Wanna Be, Celtic Silence, Rumpold, Tempting Fate and West Order—some of which had valid reasons for their disappointing campaigns—won just one race and gained just one pattern placing between them. Tobougg, transferred from Mick Channon's stable, also failed to score but did at least finish third in the Derby and second in the Champion Stakes and the Hong Kong Cup. As regards winning, it was left to Noverre, in the team from the outset with David Loder in France. Right well he flew the flag too, showing himself the best specialist miler of his age in Europe.

Noverre's two-year-old form was smart and consistent, highlighted by victories in the July Stakes and Doncaster's Champagne Stakes and second place in the Dewhurst. After wintering in Dubai, he had three starts before the Sussex Stakes, losing out by two lengths to Street Cry in the UAE 2000 Guineas on the dirt at Nad Al Sheba before being first past the post in the Poule d'Essai des Poulains at Longchamp in May, when he held the strong-finishing Vahorimix by a head after squeezing through. That race, rather than the Two Thousand Guineas, in which Tobougg, Rumpold and Divine Task represented Godolphin, had been Noverre's designated target from early-March. But the seeming success of the Longchamp plan came to nought when in July the colt tested positive to the cortico steroid methylprednisolone, a drug commonly used to treat arthritic problems to which Noverre apparently is prone. Noverre was disqualified at a hearing in July, making him only the third classic winner to suffer this fate after testing positive, as did Dancer's Image in the 1968 Kentucky Derby and Aliysa in the 1989 Oaks; Saeed bin Suroor received the maximum fine of 100,000 francs. Godolphin did not dispute the findings but their explanation of what had happened made it plain how fraught using banned race-day substances in training can be, and how little the racegoing public knows about the medications runners may have been treated with in the run-up to races. Racing manager Simon Crisford reported that the same cycle for methylprednisolone had been used both previously and subsequently, and there had been no traces of the drug in Noverre's system on any other occasion, including after his next start following the Poulains, the St James's Palace Stakes at Royal Ascot, in which he went down by a neck to Black Minnaloushe after nosing ahead a furlong out and drifting right. Godolphin had followed veterinary advice about when to stop giving the drug in time for it to leave Noverre's system, but all the evidence suggests that hard-and-fast rules about how long it takes to metabolise drugs even in one horse, let alone the whole thoroughbred population, are not completely reliable. The so-called 'clearance rate' can be affected by any number of factors, including exercise, diet, sweating and the amount drunk, and one leading vet said the withdrawal time for methylprednisolone after injection can vary from between five to forty-two days. That leaves a big margin for error, and, to all intents and purposes, expertise in creating a raft of medications to deal with specific problems or weaknesses in thoroughbreds appears not to be matched by a similar level of precision in exhaustive clinical tests to ascertain every consequence of applying a drug. The only absolutely safe route—the route which automatically precludes all chance of disqualification—is to avoid administering medication in training that is banned on race days. Since this would almost certainly hinder some runners' fitness and speed of recovery from injury, there seems little possibility of owners and trainers conforming to it, Noverre being a particularly noteworthy example. Doubtless most owners and trainers will still carry on as before.

Noverre started third favourite for the Sussex Stakes, sponsored for the last time by Lanson Champagne. Quite why the Goodwood executive should have such trouble getting and keeping sponsors for the track's biggest race is a mystery. The Sussex is run in midsummer, receives abundant publicity and is invariably won by a good horse but, despite this, after Swettenham Stud ceased its six-year support in 1989 there were nine unsponsored years before Lanson took up the baton in 1999. The latest edition attracted nine other runners, headed by Black Minnaloushe, who started favourite at 3/1. The third and fifth from the St James's Palace Stakes, Olden Times and No Excuse Needed, were also there along with One Thousand Guineas winner Ameerat and the champion two-year-old of 1999, Distant Music, who had landed a Group 2 race in Ireland last time. Noverre put up a smashing display, the best of his career so far. Ridden patiently, he started to make a forward move over two furlongs out and produced a cracking turn of foot to lead and go clear in the final furlong, drifting left a little but still accounting for No Excuse Needed emphatically by two lengths, with Black Minnaloushe a length and a half back in third. It was difficult to believe after this performance that Noverre would go through the rest of the season without a win, but that's exactly what happened. He did not have the run of the race when just over a length fourth to subsequently-disqualified Proudwings in the Prix Jacques le Marois at Deauville, suffering a serious bump, and in the Queen Elizabeth II Stakes at Ascot his jockey allowed pacemaker Summoner too much rope before going down by a length and a half. Noverre was favourite both times, and was so again on his final outing in the

Champagne Lanson Sussex Stakes, Goodwood—
Noverre produces a fine turn of foot to go clear of No Excuse Needed;
Black Minnaloushe (partially hidden), Olden Times (light epaulets) and Distant Music (right) are next

Godolphin's "Noverre"

Breeders' Cup Mile at Belmont Park, where reportedly Noverre had something go amiss behind when five lengths seventh of twelve behind Val Royal.

Noverre (USA) (b.c. 1998)	Rahy (USA) (ch 1985)	Blushing Groom (ch 1974)	Red God
			Runaway Bride
		Glorious Song (b 1976)	Halo
			Ballade
	Danseur Fabuleux (USA) (b 1982)	Northern Dancer (b 1961)	Nearctic
			Natalma
		Fabuleux Jane (ch 1974)	Le Fabuleux
			Native Partner

There is nothing to add to the details of Noverre's breeding given in *Racehorses of 2000*. A rather angular, good-quartered colt, with a fluent, quick action, who acts on dirt, good to firm going and probably on soft, Noverre wears a crossed noseband and had his tongue tied on his last three starts in Britain. Providing all is well, Noverre stays in training and, as a tough, game and consistent performer, looks the type to do well at up to a mile and a quarter, a trip he hasn't yet attempted but should stay—he has been entered in the Dubai World Cup. The Lockinge Stakes looks a perfect race in which to start a British campaign. *Saeed bin Suroor*

NOWELL HOUSE 5 ch.g. Polar Falcon (USA) 126 – Langtry Lady 91 (Pas de Seul **95** 133) [2001 85: f11g 13s² 12d* 12s⁵ 11.9m 13.9m 14v⁶ 12d³ 12v³ 12s Nov 10] smallish, lengthy gelding: useful handicapper: won at Newmarket in April: creditable third on same course and at Doncaster after: stays 1½m, possibly not 1¾m: seems best on good ground or softer: visored (well below form) final outing: usually held up: has pulled hard/ carried head awkwardly/wandered. *M. W. Easterby*

NOW IS THE HOUR   5 ch.g. Timeless Times (USA) 99 – Macs Maharanee 85   –
(Indian King (USA) 128) [2001 35+, a51: f6g⁵ f7g f7g f7g f6g Jul 2] small gelding: poor   **a44**
performer: stays 7f: acts on fibresand and good to firm ground: tried blinkered at 4 yrs:
sometimes looks ungenuine. *P. S. Felgate*

NOW LOOK HERE   5 b.g. Reprimand 122 – Where's Carol 67 (Anfield 117) [2001   **111**
110: 6v* 6d 5g³ 6m 7m 6g 7d 6v² Oct 26] leggy gelding: unimpressive mover: smart
performer: won listed race at Doncaster in March by 3½ lengths from Fire Dome: placed
after in Palace House Stakes at Newmarket (2¾ lengths third to Rushcutter Bay) and
handicap at Newbury (¾-length second to Seven No Trumps): probably best at 5f/6f:
has form on any turf going, though wins on soft/heavy: blinkered (raced freely) once.
B. A. McMahon

NOWT BUT TROUBLE (IRE)   3 ch.g. Midhish 109 – Shinadeosee (IRE)   –
(Adonijah 126) [2001 56: f6g f6g 6.1f 6m 5f Jul 2] good-topped gelding: disappointing
maiden: blinkered second start. *D. Nicholls*

NOWT FLASH (IRE)   4 ch.g. Petardia 113 – Mantlepiece (IRE) (Common Grounds   **36**
118) [2001 67d: f8g 8m 6g 8f 7d 7g Aug 12] compact gelding: poor performer: stays 1m:
acts on firm going, good to soft and fibresand: tried blinkered at 2 yrs, visored
penultimate start: has looked less than keen. *B. S. Rothwell*

NUCLEAR DEBATE (USA)   6 b.g. Geiger Counter (USA) – I'm An Issue (USA)   **126**
(Cox's Ridge (USA)) [2001 127: a6f² a6f⁴ 5f³ 5m 5m² 6s* 5s 5.5f⁵ 5m Dec 16]
        It took 180,000 guineas to buy six-year-old sprinter Nuclear Debate at the
Autumn Horses In Training Sales at Newmarket in October and it is interesting to
speculate what might have been required to get him twelve months earlier and six
weeks later. 'I suppose he was very expensive for an old gelding!' his new trainer,
the California-based Darrell Vienna, was reported to have joked after Nuclear
Debate had taken his turn in the sale-ring. There is little doubt that a year-younger
Nuclear Debate, fresh from triumphs in the Prix du Gros-Chene, the King's Stand
Stakes and the Nunthorpe, would have fetched a good deal more than 180,000
guineas, for although Nuclear Debate proved just as good, judged strictly on form,
in 2001, he had one more season under his belt and also ended his six-year-old
campaign with just the one win and with something of a question mark over his
reliability. Vienna squeezed in two more races with him at the end of the year, but
these resulted only in fifth of ten in the Grade 3 Hollywood Turf Express Handicap
at Hollywood Park, albeit beaten less than two lengths, and an unplaced effort in
the Hong Kong Sprint at Sha Tin.
        The Hong Kong Sprint has never been a happy hunting ground for Nuclear
Debate, and he has finished ninth in the last three runnings of the race. There was
disappointment for him in Europe too in the latest season. In 2000 he had been the
leading contender for champion sprint honours throughout the summer and right up
until Namid's late show in the Prix de l'Abbaye, a race for which Nuclear Debate,
as a gelding, was not eligible. That iniquitous feature of the French programme
book was scrapped, not before time, for 2001, but Nuclear Debate, who was sent
off the 2/1 favourite, could not make the most of his belated opportunity and finished only eighth of nineteen. Stall eleven in a race dominated by the low numbers did
not help, but excuses of some degree were also called for after the Dubai Golden
Shaheen at Nad Al Sheba in March and the King's Stand Stakes at Royal Ascot, in
both of which Nuclear Debate also headed, or jointly headed, the betting.
        On the other hand, there are the four races in 2001 in which Nuclear Debate
ran to his best or near to it. A short-head defeat by Active Bo Bo, from Macau, in a
six-furlong prestige event on his first start at Nad Al Sheba in March was highly
creditable, particularly as Nuclear Debate saw more daylight than is ideal for him.
It promised better than fourth place (beaten seven lengths by the very speedy
US-trained Caller One) in the Golden Shaheen. Nuclear Debate's suitability for
being covered up for a late run invites trouble in running, even if the necessary
cover can be found, and things did not go well for him on his reappearance in
Europe when a close third to Cassandra Go in the Temple Stakes at Sandown;
Yutaka Take, having his first and only ride on Nuclear Debate, seemingly showed
his inexperience of the track in switching him off the favoured far rail and right over
to the centre of the course. Allow for Nuclear Debate's Group 1 penalty as well—he

Stanley Leisure Sprint Cup, Haydock—Nuclear Debate proves himself at least as effective over six furlongs as at the minimum trip with a victory from Mount Abu, Monkston Point (visored) and Mull of Kintyre (third right); the previous year's winner Pipalong (right) is well below form in seventh

was giving Cassandra Go 10 lb—and Nuclear Debate unquestionably ran well that day.

Back in Group 1 events for his last three starts in Europe, Nuclear Debate had no problem getting a run in the Nunthorpe Stakes at York, where he simply came up against a better horse. Mozart was a markedly better sprinter than any of those that Nuclear Debate crossed swords with during 2000 and Nuclear Debate never looked likely to catch him, beaten two lengths in second. There was nothing of Mozart's quality in the Stanley Leisure Sprint Cup at Haydock but it was still a decent renewal, with a twelve-runner field including the previous year's winner Pipalong and a quartet—Three Points, Kier Park, Mount Abu and Minardi—who had finished second, third, fourth and sixth in the Prix Maurice de Gheest. If the race looked competitive beforehand, it certainly didn't turn out that way as Nuclear Debate swept through from the rear. Six furlongs on soft ground presented a rare challenge for him—he had not faced such a combination since his three-year-old reappearance, and he had not been raced at all over six during 2000—but there was no questioning his superiority once the field fanned out across the track a furlong and a half out to give Gerald Mosse and Nuclear Debate all the room they required. Clear through the final furlong, Nuclear Debate won by three lengths, with Mount Abu, Monkston Point and Mull of Kintyre taking the minor honours. It was trainer John Hammond's third success in the race, following those of Polar Falcon in 1991 and Cherokee Rose in 1995. A disagreement among the owners about who should train Nuclear Debate in 2002 led to his sale after the Abbaye. Jack and Lynda Ramsden, the biggest shareholders in the six-strong partnership that owned him, wanted Nuclear Debate transferred back to their care—they had trained him back in 1998—and a decision was taken to decide the issue in the sales ring. None of Nuclear Debate's existing owners, however, was willing to match the final bid on behalf of Darrell Vienna. 'He has lots of opportunities at Hollywood Park and Santa Anita,' said Vienna. 'We also have the added dimension that he can run on dirt.'

Nuclear Debate (USA) (b.g. 1995)	Geiger Counter (USA) (b 1982)	Mr Prospector (b 1970)	Raise A Native
			Gold Digger
		Thong (b 1964)	Nantallah
			Rough Shod
	I'm An Issue (USA) (b 1990)	Cox's Ridge (b 1974)	Best Turn
			Our Martha
		Answers N' Issues (b 1981)	Jacinto
			Bourbon Mist

A big, strong gelding, Nuclear Debate is effective at five and six furlongs and on firm going, on heavy and on dirt. He is usually covered up for a late run, tactics which are not always easy to execute and may help to explain his apparent inconsistency in 2001. Nuclear Debate's American pedigree was described thoroughly in last year's Annual. An update is that his two-year-old half-brother Seems So Easy (by Palmister) has now run in Britain, though whether he will prove capable of updating the family's record with another winner remains to be seen after his last of eleven in a maiden at Catterick. *D. Vienna, USA*

732

NUCLEON COUNT (IRE) 5 b.g. Nucleon (USA) 94 – Clare's Hope (IRE) (Erin's   –
Hope 117) [2001 f11g 8m⁶ 7.1m 10g 6g Jul 10] IR 3,300 3-y-o: angular gelding: second
foal: dam unraced: little form. *J. G. Given*

NUGGET (IRE) 3 b.g. Goldmark (USA) 113 – Folly Vision (IRE) 58 (Vision (USA))   46
[2001 68: e8g 8.1g 10m 8.3g f12g⁶ p10g Nov 28] strong, sturdy gelding: poor maiden
handicapper: seems to stay 1¼m: acts on fibresand, probably on polytrack. *P. Mitchell*

NUMERATE 3 b.f. Bishop of Cashel 122 – Half A Dozen (USA) 57 (Saratoga Six   69 d
(USA)) [2001 62: 7d⁴ f7g 8.3m⁶ 10d³ 10v³ f9.4g⁵ f8g⁶ f11g Nov 30] compact filly: fair
performer: below best after reappearance, leaving M. Bell after third start: probably stays
1¼m: acts on heavy going and fibresand: blinkered penultimate outing. *M. Wigham*

NUTMEG (IRE) 4 ch.f. Lake Coniston (IRE) 131 – Overdue Reaction (Be My Guest   49
(USA) 126) [2001 55d: f8g 7.5m⁶ 7m⁴ 6m⁴ 6g 6f Sep 10] poor maiden: barely stays 1m: a–
acts on firm and good to soft going: blinkered once. *M. H. Tompkins*

NU TO ME 2 b.f. (Feb 27) So Factual (USA) 120 – Mubadara (IRE) 80 (Lahib (USA)   52
129) [2001 6m⁶ 7.1f⁴ 6d 7d 7.1m 6f Sep 10] 1,200Y: small, close-coupled filly: first foal:
dam Irish 2-y-o 6f winner out of half-sister to high-class miler Montekin: modest maiden:
well held last 3 starts: barely stays 7f: acts on firm ground. *J. R. Weymes*

NUTWOOD 3 br.c. Charnwood Forest (IRE) 125 – Ma Pavlova (USA) 102 (Irish   66
River (FR) 131) [2001 8m⁴ 11.5g 9.9d Sep 27] 8,200Y: half-brother to several winners,
including useful Irish 9f and 1½m winner L'Opera (by Old Vic): dam French 2-y-o 6.5f
winner: fair maiden: should stay beyond 1m: sold 15,500 gns. *R. Charlton*

NYSAEAN (IRE) 2 b.c. (Jan 22) Sadler's Wells (USA) 132 – Irish Arms (FR) (Irish   83 p
River (FR) 131) [2001 7d³ Nov 3] 6,000,000 francs Y: good-topped colt: closely related
to useful French stayer Lady Slave (by In The Wings), and half-brother to several
winners, including useful French 6f (at 2 yrs) to 1¼m winner Irish Steel (by Shining
Steel): dam French 12.5f winner: 10/1, 1¼ lengths third of 27 to Prince Hector in maiden
at Newmarket, soon to fore and sticking on well: will stay at least 1¼m: sure to improve
and win a race or 2. *R. Hannon*

NZAME (IRE) 3 b.c. Darshaan 133 – Dawnsio (IRE) 102 (Tate Gallery (USA) 117)   82
[2001 70: 8.2v² 9m 11.4g* 14.1m⁴ 12.3f⁴ 10.1m³ 12.4m³ 11.8s³ 11.6v⁴ Oct 29] close-
coupled colt: fairly useful handicapper: won at Sandown in June: mostly creditable
efforts after: probably stays 1¾m: acts on any turf going: visored last 4 starts: has carried
head awkwardly/hung right: sold 13,000 gns. *J. L. Dunlop*

O

OAKLEY JOY 3 ch.f. Beveled (USA) – Lillicara (FR) (Caracolero (USA) 131) [2001   –
–: e7g f8.5f Dec 5] well held in 4 maidens. *R. Hannon*

OAKLEY RAMBO 2 br.c. (May 19) Muhtarram (USA) 125 – Westminster Waltz   81
(Dance In Time (CAN)) [2001 7m⁶ 6m² 7.1s² 7.1f* 7d Oct 3] half-brother to several
winners, including 3-y-o Star Seventeen and 5-y-o Calldat Seventeen: dam, ran twice, out
of half-sister to top-class 1¼m/1½m performer Busted: fairly useful performer: landed
odds in maiden at Chepstow in September: should be suited by 1¼m/1½m: acts on soft
and firm going. *R. Hannon*

OAKWELL ACE 5 b.m. Clantime 101 – Fardella (ITY) (Molvedo 137) [2001 48: f7f   57
f7g f7g 6m* 6m² 6d⁴ 6f⁵ 5g 6m⁵ 6d² 6f⁴ 6f Sep 10] modest performer: won claimer at
Doncaster in May: races mainly over 6f nowadays: acts on soft and firm going, below
form on fibresand: tried visored: has been slowly away/carried head awkwardly.
J. Balding

OARE KITE 6 b.m. Batshoof 122 – Portvasco 90 (Sharpo 132) [2001 56, a48: f8s f6g³   57
f6g⁶ f6g² f7g f6g 6g⁴ f6g³ 7m⁴ 6d 6.1f f6g 6m⁴ 5f² 5g 6m³ 7d⁶ 5s* Sep 24] close-coupled   a46
mare: modest handicapper on turf, poor on all-weather: won at Leicester (fourth course
success) in September: effective at 5f to easy 1m: acts on firm going, soft and fibresand:
usually wears visor/blinkers: has carried head awkwardly/wandered/found little.
P. S. Felgate

OARE PINTAIL 4 b.f. Distant Relative 128 – Oare Sparrow 75 (Night Shift (USA))   –
[2001 64: f5g 5m Jul 13] smallish, sturdy filly: modest maiden at 3 yrs: well below form
both starts in 2001 (tongue tied first one). *R. M. Beckett*

OASES   2 ch.g. (Apr 5) Zilzal (USA) 137 – Markievicz (IRE) 73 (Doyoun 124) [2001   **92 p**
6v* Oct 26] 8,000Y: rather leggy, quite good-topped gelding: fourth foal: half-brother to
6-y-o Paarl Rock: dam Irish 6.5f winner: 20/1, won 17-runner maiden at Newbury by 1½
lengths from Loveleaves, tracking pace until leading over 1f out: will stay 1m: should
make a useful 3-y-o. *B. J. Meehan*

O B COMFORT   3 b.g. College Chapel 122 – Crystal Magic 92 (Mazilier (USA) 107)   **67**
[2001 5.1s⁶ 7g 6m 6m* 6f⁴ 6g 6g 7d 6g 6m f6g Oct 20] 17,500F, 11,000Y: good-topped
gelding: first foal: dam 2-y-o 5f winner out of sister to high-class sprinter Petong: fair
performer: won maiden at Newcastle in June: should prove best at 5f/6f: acts on firm
ground: has looked no easy ride: sold only 800 gns. *Mrs J. R. Ramsden*

OBEE GOOD   3 b.g. Zambrano – Tout de Val 41 (Tout Ensemble) [2001 10.9f 10m   **–**
11.6m 12g Aug 17] first foal: dam 1½m seller winner: seems of little account.
W. G. M. Turner

OBSERVATORY (USA)   4 ch.c. Distant View (USA) 126 – Stellaria (USA) 98   **127**
(Roberto (USA) 131) [2001 131: 9.3m* 10m⁴ Jun 20]
    John Gosden might have been forgiven for casting a rueful eye towards the
heavens after the enforced retirement of Observatory in July. Observatory's injury
was the third blow in fairly quick succession for the team at Manton, following the
injuries to Observatory's half-brother Terrestrial, who fractured a cannon bone in
May during his preparation for the Prix du Jockey Club, and the Poule d'Essai des
Poulains second Clearing, who had to be put down after shattering a hind pastern
on the gallops in June. Observatory's racing career ended when he was found to
have sustained a hairline fracture of the pelvis after returning from Royal Ascot,
where he had finished fourth to Fantastic Light in the Prince of Wales's Stakes.
Most trainers—whatever the size of their string—would suffer after losing three of
their best performers and Gosden certainly did; his stable finished outside the top
ten in the trainers' championship for the first time since 1991 and recorded its
lowest prize-money total since 1995.
    Probably no inmate of Manton carried higher hopes at the start of the season
than the four-year-old Observatory, who had done nothing but progress at three,
capping a fine season with a top-class performance to win the Queen Elizabeth II
Stakes at Ascot from Giant's Causeway. Observatory had looked the sort to make a
formidable opponent in the top weight-for-age races at around a mile in the latest
season, though, as it turned out, both his outings came at further. Observatory was
due to reappear in the Lockinge—the first European Group 1 of the year over a mile
—in May, but he was switched to the nine-furlong Prix d'Ispahan at Longchamp on
the same weekend after the ground at Newbury came up 'too gluey', according to
his trainer. Racing beyond a mile for the first time, Observatory started 11/10
favourite and ran out a short-head winner of the five-runner d'Ispahan, racing in
second in a truly-run contest until leading over a furlong out and holding on

Prix d'Ispahan, Longchamp—
Observatory (rail) just beats Hightori to gain his sixth career victory; pacesetting Ekraar is third

determinedly to beat Hightori, who was in front a stride before and a stride after the post. Observatory was stepped up further in trip at Royal Ascot, where, in spite of sweating and being on edge beforehand and going very freely to post, he ran at least as well as in the d'Ispahan, though the form was some way short of his very best. First impressions were that he did not see out the trip quite so well as those ahead of him—he held every chance a couple of furlongs from home—but any such reading of the race has to be tempered by the fact that Observatory was found to be lame afterwards. For the record, Observatory finished four and a half lengths behind the winner Fantastic Light, beaten also by Kalanisi and Hightori, the latter a length and a quarter ahead at the line.

		Mr Prospector (b 1970)	Raise A Native
Observatory (USA) (ch.c. 1997)	Distant View (USA) (ch 1991)		Gold Digger
		Seven Springs (ch 1982)	Irish River
			La Trinite
	Stellaria (USA) (ch 1986)	Roberto (b 1969)	Hail To Reason
			Bramalea
		Victoria Star (ch 1972)	Northern Dancer
			Solometeor

Observatory's pedigree was covered fully in *Racehorses of 2000*, though it is worth repeating the salient points. Observatory remains the best of the progeny of the high-class miler Distant View, who is also the sire of the leading juvenile of 1999 Distant Music, who showed very smart form in the latest season, winning over nine furlongs. Observatory is the fifth winner out of Stellaria, a fairly useful performer whose three wins in Britain included a listed contest at Newbury over six furlongs at two before later winning in the States. One of Observatory's half-sisters the Irish River maiden winner (at nearly six furlongs) En Garde, in foal to Giant's Causeway, fetched 550,000 guineas at the Newmarket December Sales in the latest season, more than twelve times the amount she had made at the end of her two-year-old days. Stellaria is a granddaughter of Canadian Oaks winner Solometeor. Observatory's year-younger half-brother Terrestrial (by Theatrical) ran three times, achieving smart form and winning a minor event at Newmarket in the spring before his untimely setback. Stellaria slipped a foal to Quest For Fame in 1999, but had a filly by him in 2000, and foaled a brother to Observatory in 2001. She was due to visit Distant View again in 2001. The genuine and reliable Observatory was unraced on extremes of going but acted on good to firm and good to soft going; he showed in the d'Ispahan that he stayed nine furlongs, though his very best form was at a mile. He was usually held up.

It goes almost without saying that the curtailing of Observatory's racing career was among the season's biggest disappointments but he is a strong, well-made, attractive colt with a good pedigree and he should make an impact as a stallion. He has been retired to the Banstead Manor Stud, Newmarket, and will stand at a fee of £12,500, live foal. *J. H. M. Gosden*

OCCAM (IRE) 7 ch.g. Sharp Victor (USA) 114 – Monterana 99 (Sallust 134) [2001 6g 8.3s 10g⁴ 9.1m 11.9s* 15.8d 10.1v f14g⁴ f12g⁶ f11g Dec 3] leggy gelding: fluent mover: poor handicapper: won at Brighton (amateur maiden) in October: should stay 1¾m: acts on fibresand, good to firm and soft going. *A. Bailey* **48 a41**

OCEAN AVENUE (IRE) 2 b.c. (May 17) Dolphin Street (FR) 125 – Trinity Hall 67 (Hallgate 127) [2001 8g⁶ 8s Oct 25] IR 5,800Y: third foal: dam, 6f winner, half-sister to smart 5f/6f performer Emma Peel: signs of a little ability in maidens: raced freely second start. *C. A. Horgan* **–**

OCEAN DRIVE (IRE) 5 b. or br.g. Dolphin Street (FR) 125 – Blonde Goddess (IRE) (Godswalk (USA) 130) [2001 57§: 10.3s 8.3d⁴ 9.1m 13d⁴ May 18] robust gelding: poor handicapper: stays 1½m: acts on firm and soft going: held up: has hung: no battler. *Miss L. A. Perratt* **48 §**

OCEAN ESTATES 3 ch.f. Inchinor 119 – Colleen Liath (Another Realm 118) [2001 –: f9.4g e8g a10.5g Dec 2] no form: left K. Ivory before final start. *P. Haley, Spain* **–**

OCEAN LINE (IRE) 6 b.g. Kefaah (USA) 124 – Tropic Sea (IRE) (Sure Blade (USA) 130) [2001 55, a58: f12g Mar 15] leggy, angular gelding: modest performer at 5 yrs: well beaten only Flat start in 2001: fair winning hurdler. *Jonjo O'Neill* **–**

OCEAN LOVE (IRE) 3 b.f. Dolphin Street (FR) 125 – Scuba Diver (Kings Lake **45**
(USA) 133) [2001 61: 11.6s 10g 12m 8g³ 8.3d Aug 15] workmanlike filly: poor maiden:
should stay 1¼m: acts on good to firm ground: blinkered third start. *M. L. W. Bell*

OCEAN RAIN (IRE) 4 ch.g. Lake Coniston (IRE) 131 – Alicedale (USA) (Trempo- **62**
lino (USA) 135) [2001 75: 8g 8m 8f 7.1f⁶ 10g 10.5g⁶ 10g 8m⁵ Sep 10] smallish, sturdy
gelding: modest handicapper: barely stays 10.5f: acts on soft ground, probably on firm:
often visored/blinkered: lazy sort: sold only 500 gns. *C. G. Cox*

OCEAN ROAD 3 ch.g. Inchinor 119 – Executive Lady 59 (Night Shift (USA)) [2001 **–**
65: 7.1g 10d Jun 18] smallish, sturdy gelding: fair maiden at 2 yrs: well held in 2001.
Mrs A. J. Perrett

OCEAN SONG 4 b.f. Savahra Sound 111 – Marina Plata (Julio Mariner 127) [2001 **53 d**
61: f8g f11g⁴ 11s 10m 12m 8g f11g f12g f16g⁵ f16.2g⁶ f14g³ Dec 14] rangy filly: modest
maiden handicapper: below form after second start: stays 1½m, probably not 2m: acts on
good to soft going and fibresand: occasionally blinkered. *S. R. Bowring*

OCEAN SOUND (IRE) 2 b.c. (Apr 3) Mujadil (USA) 119 – Ossana (USA) (Tejano **94**
(USA)) [2001 5g 6m³ 6m* 6g² 6m 7g³ 6g 7.6d⁴ Sep 26] 14,000F, IR 50,000Y: well-made
colt: has a quick, fluent action: first foal: dam, 2-y-o 5f winner in Germany and winning
jumper in France, from family of French Group 1 winners Gabina, Galetto and Goldmark: fairly useful performer: won minor event at Ayr in May: good placed efforts in
minor events at Doncaster and Ascot (2¾ lengths third to Steenberg) after: stays 7f: acts
on good to firm ground, possibly not good to soft: tried blinkered: sold 50,000 gns.
B. W. Hills

OCEAN TIDE 4 b.g. Deploy 131 – Dancing Tide (Pharly (FR) 130) [2001 75: 7.1m **82**
12.4m³ 13m* 13d* 12m* 14.6f⁴ 14m 16m⁵ 11.9g⁶ Aug 21] angular gelding: fairly useful
handicapper: won at Hamilton (twice) and Newmarket in June: respectable efforts at best
after next start: probably stays 14.6f: seems to act on any turf going: usually visored in
2001: no easy ride: sold 10,000 gns. *J. G. Given*

OCTANE (USA) 5 b.g. Cryptoclearance (USA) – Something True (USA) 119 (Sir **71**
Ivor 135) [2001 80: 12f 12.4m 10.5m³ Jul 6] good-bodied gelding: fluent mover: fair
handicapper: best at 1¼m/1½m on good going or firmer: tried blinkered: tongue tied
in 1999: usually held up: has refused to enter stalls, and twice failed stall tests.
W. M. Brisbourne

OCTAVIUS CAESAR (USA) 4 ch.c. Affirmed (USA) – Secret Imperatrice (USA) **96**
(Secretariat (USA)) [2001 95p: 12m² 12g 12.3m* 11.9g 12g 12d Oct 18] close-coupled
colt: useful handicapper: won at Chester in August by 6 lengths, given good ride from
front: ran poorly after: should stay beyond 1½m: acts on firm ground: tongue tied 3 of last
4 outings: sold only 6,000 gns. *P. F. I. Cole*

OCTENNIAL 2 gr.c. (Feb 9) Octagonal (NZ) – Laune (AUS) 68 (Kenmare (FR) 125) **76**
[2001 6v 6v f6g* Dec 1] 26,000Y: leggy, unfurnished colt: third foal: half-brother to
fairly useful 1999 2-y-o 5f winner Launfal (by Rudimentary): dam, 2-y-o 5f winner,
became unenthusiastic: fair form in maidens: won 6-runner event at Wolverhampton by
1¾ lengths from Victor Valentine: not sure to stay beyond 6f: hung left penultimate start:
tends to carry head high. *R. Hannon*

ODDSANENDS 5 b.g. Alhijaz 122 – Jans Contessa 68 (Rabdan 129) [2001 53, a67: **–**
6v Apr 24] small gelding: fair performer at 4 yrs: well beaten only run in 2001: tried
blinkered. *B. R. Johnson*

ODYN DANCER 4 b.f. Minshaanshu Amad (USA) 91§ – Themeda 69 (Sure Blade **–**
(USA) 130) [2001 –, a49: f16g³ f11g f12g⁵ f16.2g⁵ Feb 8] poor handicapper: stays 2m: **a39**
acts on fibresand/equitrack: visored penultimate start. *M. D. I. Usher*

OFFA'S DYKE (IRE) 2 b.c. (Feb 27) Emperor Jones (USA) 119 – Fakhira (IRE) 83 **76**
(Jareer (USA) 115) [2001 7g⁴ 7f 7g⁴ 7g⁴ 8g⁶ f8.5g⁵ 7.1m⁵ 7v² Oct 27] 10,000F, IR **a93**
26,000Y: strong, useful-looking colt: third foal: brother to 4-y-o Akhira: dam, Irish
2-y-o 5f winner, half-sister to smart 6f/7f performer Danehill Dancer: fairly useful on
all-weather, fair on turf: won nursery in August and minor event in September, both at
Wolverhampton: wandered when good second in nursery at Doncaster: stays 8.5f: acts on
fibresand, good to firm and heavy going: didn't handle track at Epsom second start: races
up with pace: sold 30,000 gns. *S. P. C. Woods*

OFF HIRE 5 b.g. Clantime 101 – Lady Pennington 51 (Blue Cashmere 129) [2001 62: **65**
f5g⁵ f5g⁵ f5g* f5g* f5g⁵ f5g³ 5v² 5v² 5.1d³ 5m⁵ 5m f5g⁴ 5f 5g³ f5s f6s⁶ Dec 26] leggy, **a69**

angular gelding: fair handicapper: won twice at Wolverhampton in February: mostly creditable efforts after: probably best at 5f: acts on any turf going and fibresand: visored: races prominently. *C. Smith*

OFFICIAL FLAME (USA) 2 ch.c. (Jan 8) Deputy Minister (CAN) – Fire The **98** Groom (USA) 115 (Blushing Groom (FR) 131) [2001 6g* 6f 6g Oct 4] $1,600,000Y: quite attractive colt: fourth living foal: half-brother to top-class sprinter Stravinsky (by Nureyev): dam, winner up to 1m in Britain and 9.5f Grade 1 winner in USA, half-sister to high-class sprinter Dowsing: useful form when winning maiden at York in August by ¾ length from Expected Bonus: disappointing in Mill Reef Stakes at Newbury (favourite) and Middle Park Stakes at Newmarket (raced freely in visor) after: raced only at 6f on good going or firmer: has worn crossed noseband. *D. R. Loder*

OH JAMILA 3 b.f. Ezzoud (IRE) 126 – True Bird (IRE) 63 (In The Wings 128) [2001 **–** –: 11.5m 10.9f⁶ 11.6m 11.9g Aug 9] seems of little account. *W. R. Muir*

OH NO NOT HIM 5 b.g. Reprimand 122 – Lucky Mill 50 (Midyan (USA) 124) **50 §** [2001 –: 7m⁶ 8.3m 8f 10.3f 8.1g 8m* 8f 12f 8.5g³ 10.9m 10g 8.3m Sep 24] rather sparely-made gelding: modest performer: won seller at Ripon in July: stays 1m: acts on good to firm going: tried blinkered: often reluctant/refuses to race. *W. M. Brisbourne*

OH SO DUSTY 3 b.f. Piccolo 121 – Dark Eyed Lady (IRE) 82 (Exhibitioner 111) **71** [2001 80: f6g e5g⁴ f6g⁵ 6d f6g f8g Oct 22] smallish, sturdy filly: fair performer: probably best at 5f: acts on equitrack and good to firm ground: blinkered twice at 2 yrs: sold 1,500 gns. *J. Hetherton*

O I BANDI 2 ch.c. (Apr 11) Spectrum (IRE) 126 – Nottash (IRE) 74 (Royal Academy **–** (USA) 130) [2001 6m 6g Aug 15] third foal: half-brother to a winner in Norway by Bluebird: dam, 7f winner, half-sister to top-class sprinter Lake Coniston: well held in maidens at Yarmouth: dead. *J. R. Fanshawe*

OKAWANGO (USA) 3 b.c. Kingmambo (USA) 125 – Krissante (USA) (Kris 135) **115** [2001 115p: 8v³ 8m⁴ 12m⁴ 10f⁵ Jun 26] smart performer: unbeaten in 3 races at 2 yrs, notably Grand Criterium at Longchamp: creditable efforts in 2001 only when 2¾ lengths fifth (later promoted to fourth) to Noverre in Poule d'Essai des Poulains on same course and when 1¼ lengths fourth to Anabaa Blue in Prix du Jockey Club at Chantilly: stays 1½m: acts on good to firm and good to soft ground, well beaten on firm in Grand Prix de Paris at Longchamp final outing. *Mme C. Head-Maarek, France*

OK TWIGGY 4 b.f. Kylian (USA) – B B Glen 52 (Hadeer 118) [2001 –: 10v Oct 8] **–** probably of little account. *J. Akehurst*

OLD BLUE EYES 2 b.c. (Mar 3) Whittingham (IRE) 104 – Special One 66 (Aragon **100** 118) [2001 5m⁴ 5m⁵ 5.2m² 5g* 6m² 6g² Oct 6] 12,000Y: well-made colt: third living foal: brother to useful 5f winner (including Molecomb Stakes at 2 yrs) Inya Lake: dam, 2-y-o 5f winner, better at 6f: useful performer: won maiden at Sandown in July and minor event at Newcastle in August: good second in valuable 22-runner sales race at Doncaster (beaten 2½ lengths by Acclamation) and 25-runner Two-Year-Old Trophy at Redcar (beaten 1¼ lengths by Captain Rio) last 2 starts: will prove best at 5f/6f: raced only on good/good to firm ground: often races prominently. *P. W. Harris*

OLD CALIFORNIA (IRE) 2 b.c. (May 9) Sadler's Wells (USA) 132 – Turban 80 **89 p** (Glint of Gold 128) [2001 7f 8d 8d³ Oct 19] rangy colt: easy mover: eighth foal: brother to Irish 13f winner Paris In The Fall, closely related to 3 winners, including useful 1m/ 8.5f winner Barboukh and 1m and 1½f winner Lovely Lyca (both by Night Shift), and half-brother to 2 winners by Green Desert: dam, 1¼m winner, half-sister to Old Vic (by Sadler's Wells): 50/1, clearly best effort (fairly useful form) in maidens when staying-on 4 lengths third of 20 to Music Club at Newmarket: will stay at least 1½m: should improve and win a race or 2. *J. L. Dunlop*

OLDEN TIMES 3 b.c. Darshaan 133 – Garah 107 (Ajdal (USA) 130) [2001 87p: **121** 9d* 10.4m⁵ 9m* 8m³ 8m⁴ 8d⁴ Sep 9]

By a Prix du Jockey Club winner out of a useful five- and six-furlong performer, Olden Times fell somewhere between the two in respect of his distance requirements. A defeat in the Dante Stakes, in which he seemed to hang left in the closing stages, put paid to any idea that his Derby entry was worth taking up, and he was returned to shorter trips with highly satisfactory results, winning the Prix Jean Prat and finishing in the frame in three other Group 1 contests.

Prix Jean Prat, Chantilly—Olden Times ends the unbeaten record of King of Tara (rail); Denon is third

Olden Times had shaped well when fourth in a maiden on his only start as a two-year-old and got off the mark at the first time of asking on his return, though it was by only a short head from 50/1-shot Sunny Glenn that he managed to justify good support in the listed Feilden Stakes at Newmarket. His margin of victory in the Prix Jean Prat was also very narrow. There were only four opponents for Olden Times, the sole British challenger in a no more than average renewal of this event, which, like the Feilden Stakes, is restricted to three-year-olds and run over nine furlongs. They included the Aidan O'Brien-trained King of Tara, unbeaten in three starts, and two smart French colts in Amiwain and Denon, who on their previous outings had been fourth past the post in the Prix Lupin and Poule d'Essai des Poulains respectively. Amiwain set a sound pace until a furlong and a half out, where King of Tara took over, but the latter was collared by Olden Times shortly after. Olden Times had to work very hard to hang on to his advantage as King of Tara stuck to his task, only a head separating the pair at the line, with just a short head back to Denon, who finished strongly to take third. All three of Olden Times's remaining races were over a mile, and he ran at least creditably in each of them. Indeed, a very close third behind Black Minnaloushe and Noverre in the St James's Palace Stakes at Royal Ascot, briefly looking like he might prevail, represents Olden Times's best form to date. That pair again finished ahead of Olden Times next time, in the Sussex Stakes at Goodwood, Olden Times beaten a little over four lengths in fourth behind Noverre. On his final start Olden Times dead-heated for fourth with Warningford in the Prix du Moulin de Longchamp, the pair finishing five lengths behind the winner Slickly.

Olden Times has run just seven times and has scope for further improvement—he's a big, good-topped, attractive colt who takes the eye. His dam, Garah, was unraced at two when reportedly splitting a pastern, and then won the first three of her seven starts in her three-year-old season. Though successful only once the following year, she was rated slightly higher, and had several good placed efforts to her name, including in the Duke of York Stakes, Temple Stakes and Hopeful Stakes. Garah was a speedy filly, as she was bred to be. By Ajdal, she is a daughter of the smart Abha, who, like Garah, was trained by Henry Cecil. Abha, raced exclusively at five and six furlongs and only at three years, winning four races and also finishing an excellent fourth in the King's Stand Stakes. Olden Times is Garah's

Prince A. A. Faisal's "Olden Times"

Olden Times (b.c. 1998)	Darshaan (br 1981)	Shirley Heights (b 1975)	Mill Reef
			Hardiemma
		Delsy (br 1972)	Abdos
			Kelty
	Garah (b 1989)	Ajdal (b 1984)	Northern Dancer
			Native Partner
		Abha (b 1982)	Thatching
			Hardware

third foal and third winner following Idma (by Midyan), a fair maiden in Britain who later won over six furlongs in the States, and the modest handicapper All Good Things (by Marju), who stays a mile and a half. Olden Times, a good walker, acts on good to firm and good to soft going. He was withdrawn from the Prix Jacques le Marois at Deauville in August because the ground was considered to be too soft for him. It is also worth noting that Olden Times's trainer was reported as saying that the undulating course at Goodwood possibly hadn't been ideal for the colt. *J. L. Dunlop*

OLDENWAY 2 b.c. (May 24) Most Welcome 131 – Sickle Moon (Shirley Heights 130) [2001 6m 5m³ 6m⁵ 6m 8v⁵ Oct 16] 15,500 2-y-o: sixth foal: half-brother to German 1m winner Misty Moon (by Polar Falcon): dam unraced: modest maiden: below form in nurseries last 2 starts: should stay 1m. *R. A. Fahey* **62**

OLDE OAK 7 ch.g. Precocious 126 – Quisissanno 76 (Be My Guest (USA) 126) [2001 f8.5s 7m 10m 10f 10.1m 7m 10.5d 8f 8.5g Aug 15] big gelding: brother to 3 winners, **–**

OLD

notably useful Euro Festival (up to 7f), and half-brother to several winners: dam 1½m winner: little form: left J. Wainwright before final start: tongue tied. *B. Ellison*

OLD FEATHERS (IRE) 4 b.g. Hernando (FR) 127 – Undiscovered (Tap On Wood 130) [2001 61: f16g* f16g⁴ 21.6s 16.2m a12g* 14v² a12g* a12g³ Dec 2] leggy, quite attractive gelding: fair performer: won handicap at Southwell in March: sold from J. FitzGerald 15,000 gns after fourth start: won minor events at Mijas in August and September and ran very well when length second to Persian Ruler in Gran Premio de San Sebastian in between: effective at 1½m, should stay further than 2m: acts on good to firm going, heavy and sand/fibresand: visored final start in Britain. *P. Haley, Spain* **? a65**

OLD HUSH WING (IRE) 8 b.g. Tirol 127 – Saneena 80 (Kris 135) [2001 52d: f16g 13d f14g Dec 17] seems of little account nowadays. *Mrs S. J. Smith* **–**

OLD OPIUM 2 b.f. (Mar 31) Dilum (USA) 115 – Ancient Secret (Warrshan (USA) 117) [2001 6.1v⁴ f6g⁴ f8.5g* 8g⁶ 8.3v³ 7s² f8g Dec 3] good-topped filly: third foal: sister to 1999 2-y-o 6f (including in USA) winner Secret Spice and half-sister to 3-y-o Artifact: dam unraced half-sister to smart stayer Primitive Rising: fair performer: left S. Kirk after winning seller at Wolverhampton in October: placed in nurseries at Windsor and Doncaster: should stay 1¼m: acts on fibresand and heavy ground. *P. S. McEntee* **70**

OLD RED (IRE) 11 ch.g. Ela-Mana-Mou 132 – Sea Port (Averof 123) [2001 14.4d 14.4m⁶ 17.5m⁵ Sep 21] poor handicapper: best at 2m+: acts on any turf going and fibresand: won over hurdles in October. *Mrs M. Reveley* **45**

OLD ROUVEL (USA) 10 b.g. Riverman (USA) 131 – Marie de Russy (FR) (Sassafras (FR) 135) [2001 16s Apr 21] tall gelding: one-time useful winner on Flat: tried visored: fairly useful hurdler. *A. King* **–**

OLENKA 3 gr.f. Grand Lodge (USA) 125 – Sarouel (IRE) (Kendor (FR) 122) [2001 74: 6d 10s f6g f7g f7g⁶ Dec 3] sturdy, lengthy filly: fair 6f winner only start at 2 yrs: well held in 2001: reared badly stall penultimate start: one to treat with caution. *Mrs J. R. Ramsden* **– §**

OLIMOLIMOO (IRE) 2 gr.g. (May 19) Ali-Royal (IRE) 127 – Classy 59 (Kalaglow 132) [2001 6m⁴ 7.1g² 7d Oct 13] IR 8,000Y: fourth foal: half-brother to an Italian 2-y-o 5f winner by Distant Relative: dam, maiden who was placed up to 1½m, from family of Oath: fairly useful maiden: 1½ lengths second to Leadership at Sandown: should stay at least 1m. *M. J. Haynes* **81**

OLIRANAR 5 gr.g. Gran Alba (USA) 107 – April Rain (Lepanto (GER)) [2001 36: e8g 7g f6g f8g Nov 19] of little account. *J. R. Best* **–**

OLIVERS TRAIL 3 ch.g. Catrail (USA) 123 – Carmenoura (IRE) (Carmelite House (USA) 118) [2001 –: 7g 10.1g Aug 17] little form. *A. Smith* **–**

OLIVIA GRACE 3 ch.f. Pivotal 124 – Sheila's Secret (IRE) 97 (Bluebird (USA) 125) [2001 e5g* 6m⁶ 5.1d* f6g² f6g* Dec 3] 29,000Y: second foal: half-sister to 4-y-o Our Fred (5f winner): dam 5f winner, including at 2 yrs: useful performer: won maiden at Lingfield in April and handicaps (readily) at Bath in October and Southwell (beat Travel Tardia by 2½ lengths) in December: will prove best at 5f/6f: acts on good to soft going, equitrack and fibresand: probably has further improvement in her. *T. G. Mills* **103 p**

OLIVIA ROSE (IRE) 2 b.f. (Apr 25) Mujadil (USA) 119 – Santana Lady (IRE) 72 (Blakeney 126) [2001 7d 6d⁴ 6v² 7d² f7g⁶ f7g* f7s³ Dec 18] 13,000Y: third foal: half-sister to 3-y-o Port Moresby: dam 1m to 1¼m winner who stayed 2m: fair performer: won nursery at Southwell in December: should stay at least 1m: acts on heavy going and fibresand: sometimes slowly away. *M. Johnston* **74**

OLIVO (IRE) 7 ch.g. Priolo (USA) 127 – Honourable Sheba (USA) (Roberto (USA) 131) [2001 11.9m 13.3g 12m 18m⁴ 16.4m⁴ 17.2m⁶ 15.4m³ Jul 30] strong, close-coupled gelding: poor handicapper: stays 2¼m: possibly needs good going or firmer: has gone in snatches. *C. A. Horgan* **45**

OLOROSO 4 b.g. Piccolo 121 – Saunders Lass 68 (Hillandale 125) [2001 –: f8.5s³ f9.4g 11.9s 8.2f⁵ 7m f11g³ Jul 2] poor maiden: seems to stay 11f: best efforts on fibresand. *J. Neville* **43**

OLYMPIC PRIDE (IRE) 3 b.f. Up And At 'em 109 – So Far Away 48 (Robellino (USA) 127) [2001 –: f7g Apr 27] no form in 3 maidens. *C. N. Allen* **–**

OLY'S GILL (IRE) 3 b.f. Eagle Eyed (USA) 111 – Jealous One (USA) (Raise A Native) [2001 34: e5g⁵ e6g² f7g⁴ f7g f5g f6g⁶ f6g 5.1v 5d 5.1s 6.1v⁵ 6s 7.1g 5m 6f⁵ 7m 8m 7m 7.1g Jun 8] disappointing maiden. *A. Berry* **–**

740

OLY'S WHIT   3 ch.g. Whittingham (IRE) 104 – Nellie O'Dowd (USA) (Diesis 133)   **60**
[2001 35: 10s⁵ 12.1m³ May 12] modest maiden: easily best effort at 1½m: acts on good to
firm ground: tried visored at 2 yrs. *Jonjo O'Neill*

OMEY STRAND (IRE)   2 b.g. (Apr 1) Desert Style (IRE) 121 – Ex-Imager (Exhibi-   **71**
tioner 111) [2001 6m⁴ 6d 7m⁴ 8m f8g2 p7g³ Nov 20] IR 28,000Y: strong gelding: eighth   **a56**
foal: brother to fairly useful Italian 5f to 7f winner Modern Style and half-brother to
winners abroad by Gallic League and Dancing Dissident: dam unraced: fair maiden on
turf, modest on all-weather: stays 1m: acts on fibresand, best turn run on good to firm
going: blinkered last 2 starts: has run in snatches. *B. J. Meehan*

OMNI COSMO TOUCH (USA)   5 b.g. Trempolino (USA) 135 – Wooden Pudden   **§§**
(USA) (Top Ville 129) [2001 83: 11.7d Oct 25] fairly useful in Ireland for L. Browne in
1999/2000: winner over hurdles (also refused to race) prior to refusing to race only outing
in 2001. *O. Sherwood*

OMNIHEAT   4 b.f. Ezzoud (IRE) 126 – Lady Bequick 81 (Sharpen Up 127) [2001 80,   **84**
a66: 8d 8.3g 8d⁶ 8f 8m⁵ 8m⁶ 9f⁴ 9m² 9g² 9m² 10m 9m² 10m² 9m 10.5v 8d³ 10d* 10g*   **a–**
Nov 5] small filly: fairly useful performer: won minor event in October and handicap
(in good style) in November, both at Redcar: best at 1m/1¼m: acts on any turf going,
fair form on fibresand in 2000: occasionally blinkered/visored: held up: consistent.
M. J. Ryan

OMNISCIENT (IRE)   2 br.f. (Jan 26) Distinctly North (USA) 115 – Mystic Shadow   **77**
(IRE) 80 (Mtoto 134) [2001 5.7f 5.1f³ 6m 6.1g 10v 7g²* 7v⁵ Oct 26] IR 3,400Y: quite
good-topped filly: second foal: half-sister to a 6f/7f winner in Italy by Up And At 'em:
dam Irish 2-y-o 6f winner: fair performer: best effort when winning claimer at Redcar in
October by 7 lengths, leading halfway: stays 7f: sometimes puts head in air/wanders.
Mrs P. N. Dutfield

ONCE MORE FOR LUCK (IRE)   10 b.g. Petorius 117 – Mrs Lucky (Royal Match   **56**
117) [2001 71: 12.4m⁶ 11.9g³ 10m⁵ 12m* 11.9m² 12.1d² 12m³ 12g⁴ 14.1m³ 12m 12d³
12s 11d⁵ Oct 30] sturdy gelding: modest performer: won claimer at Beverley in June:
stays 1¾m: acts on any turf going and fibresand: sometimes slowly away: held up.
Mrs M. Reveley

ONCE REMOVED   3 b.f. Distant Relative 128 – Hakone (IRE) 78 (Alzao (USA)   **41 d**
117) [2001 65: e6g e7g e7g⁴ e5g³ e6s³ f5g e6g⁵ f6g Mar 21] smallish filly: disappointing
maiden in 2001: stays easy 7f: acts on firm going, good to soft and equitrack: blinkered
final start. *C. N. Allen*

ON COO LAY (IRE)   2 b.f. (Mar 4) Definite Article 121 – Glass Minnow (IRE) 59   **51 §**
(Alzao (USA) 117) [2001 6d⁴ f7g 6m⁵ 7g⁴ 6m⁴ 8m³ f8.5g⁶ f8g f8.5g 8.2s⁶ 8g 8.3v³ p8g⁵   **a39 §**
f8g p7g Dec 12] small, angular filly: fifth foal: sister to 3-y-o Jasmick and half-sister to
6-y-o Little Tumbler and 7-y-o Mike's Double: dam maiden who stayed 9f: modest
maiden on turf, poor on all-weather: should stay 1¼m: acts on good to firm, heavy going
and polytrack: tried visored: has shown signs of temperament: inconsistent. *P. D. Evans*

ONE BELOVED   3 b.f. Piccolo 121 – Eternal Flame 73 (Primo Dominie 121) [2001   **–**
48: f5g 6m Jun 4] poor maiden at 2 yrs: well held in sellers in 2001. *A. G. Juckes*

ONE DINAR (FR)   6 b.h. Generous (IRE) 139 – Lypharitissima (FR) (Lightning (FR)   **70**
129) [2001 70, a85: 9v⁴ 8s⁵ 8s* 9.1m² 8.3d 8d f8g f8g f9.4g f9.4f³ f8s⁴ Dec 21] big   **a74**
horse: has a markedly round action: fair handicapper: won ladies race at Ripon in April:
effective at 1m/9f: acts on any turf going and fibresand: visored once. *D. Nicholls*

ONE FOR ME   3 br.f. Tragic Role (USA) – Chantallee's Pride (Mansooj 118) [2001   **62**
7g 9.9g 10v 8d f9.4g² f8.5g² f9.4s³ Dec 18] 1,300Y: fourth foal: sister to 1¼m and 11.4f
winner Tragic Dancer: dam unraced: modest maiden: will stay 1¼m: acts on fibresand,
showed promise on good to soft going. *Jean-Rene Auvray*

ONE FOR US   2 ch.c. (Mar 23) Superlative 118 – One For Jeannie 68 (Clantime 101)   **87 ?**
[2001 5m⁶ 5s² 5s³ 5g²* 6g 6v⁶ Oct 26] 1,200Y: second foal: dam 5f/6f winner: fairly useful
performer: won maiden at Hoppegarten in July: ran well when third to Flying Dash in
national listed race at Hamburg time before but below form last 2 starts, in sales race at
Doncaster final one: best form at 5f: acts on soft ground. *B. Hellier, Germany*

ONE LIFE TO LIVE (IRE)   8 gr.g. Classic Music (USA) – Fine Flame (Le Prince   **–**
98) [2001 33: f12s Feb 9] of little account nowadays. *D. W. Barker*

ONE MIND   3 b.c. Mind Games 121 – Cafe Solo 51 (Nomination 125) [2001 –p: 6m   **49**
7.1s⁵ 6g 7s Oct 5] good-topped colt: poor maiden: better form at 6f than 7f: looked hard
ride final start. *R. Hannon*

ONE QUICK LION   5 b.g. Lion Cavern (USA) 117 – One Quick Bid (USA) (Com-   **46**
memorate (USA)) [2001 63d: f8.5s⁶ f12s f7s³ e8g Feb 10] poor maiden: trained on first
start by R. Armstrong: stays 1m: acts on fibresand. *J. Pearce*

ONES ENOUGH   5 b.g. Reprimand 122 – Sea Fairy 64 (Wollow 132) [2001 55: 6m   **–**
7d Jul 18] close-coupled gelding: has only one eye: modest performer at 4 yrs: well
beaten in claimers in 2001: has worn eyecover/blinkers/been tongue tied. *T. P. McGovern*

ONE TO GO (IRE)   6 b.g. Petorius 117 – Caroline's Mark (On Your Mark 125) [2001   **–**
f8g f7g Feb 22] winning handicapper: has lost his form: tried blinkered. *Mrs A. J. Bowlby*

ONE WON ONE (USA)   7 b.g. Naevus (USA) – Havards Bay (Halpern Bay (USA))   **113**
[2001 115: 7f* a8f 6g² 8d* 7g² 8g⁵ 7g⁵ 6d² 6g³ 8m* 7g⁵ 7s⁵ 6d⁵ 7s³ Nov 11] good-topped,
attractive gelding: smart performer: won listed races at Abu Dhabi in January, Leopardstown (by ½ length from Bach) in June and Tralee (readily) in August: second in
Greenlands Stakes at the Curragh and in Ballycorus Stakes and Phoenix Sprint Stakes
(beaten short head by Bahamian Pirate) at Leopardstown: effective at 5f (given test) to
1m: acts on any turf going, well beaten only start on dirt: blinkered once at 5 yrs: has
sweated: held up: very tough, genuine and consistent. *Ms Joanna Morgan, Ireland*

ON GUARD   3 b.g. Sabrehill (USA) 120 – With Care 78 (Warning 136) [2001 75p: 7d   **75**
8m f7g f6g f9.4g² f9.4g⁴ f8g f11g³ f11g* f12s³ f9.4s* Dec 27] fair handicapper: left
W. Jarvis after second start: won at Southwell and Wolverhampton (despite carrying head
awkwardly and drifting right) in December: stays 1½m: acts on fibresand and good to
soft going: effective visored or not. *Mrs N. Macauley*

ONLINE INVESTOR   2 b.c. (Mar 23) Puissance 110 – Anytime Baby 56 (Bairn   **95**
(USA) 126) [2001 5.1d⁴ 5.7f* 5m 5.2m² Jul 21] 5,000Y: leggy, close-coupled colt:
second foal: half-brother to 3-y-o Acorn Catcher: dam 5f winner: useful performer: won
maiden at Bath in May despite tending to wander: best effort when length second of 25 to
Good Girl in Weatherbys Super Sprint at Newbury: will prove best around 5f: acts on
firm going, showed promise on good to soft: unseated and bolted at Royal Ascot before
third start. *C. G. Cox*

ONLY FOR GOLD   6 b.g. Presidium 124 – Calvanne Miss 48 (Martinmas 128) [2001   **89**
64, a58: f7s² f7g* f7g⁵ 7.1v* 8.1d 7g² 7m* 7.6m² 7d* 7.6m³ 8.1s⁵ 7.6d⁶ 7.1s² 6m³ 7d 7d   **a57**
Oct 30] rangy gelding: fairly useful on turf, modest on all-weather: won handicaps at
Wolverhampton in February and Warwick in April, minor event at Southwell in July and
handicap at Ayr later in July: effective at 6f, barely at 1m: acts on heavy going, good to
firm and fibresand: visored once at 4 yrs: usually races handily: tough. *A. Berry*

ONLY FOR SUE   2 ch.g. (Apr 6) Pivotal 124 – Barbary Court (Grundy 137) [2001 7s⁵   **62 p**
Sep 24] 12,500Y: eighth foal: closely related to 4-y-o Falconidae and half-brother to 2
winners, including fairly useful miler Mazcobar (by Mazilier): dam poor maiden: 100/1,
fifth of 10 to Lunar Sovereign in minor event at Leicester, fading after being bumped:
should improve. *W. S. Kittow*

ONLY ONE LEGEND (IRE)   3 b.g. Eagle Eyed (USA) 111 – Afifah 66 (Nashwan   **81**
(USA) 135) [2001 80: 6d⁵ 7g 6m 6m³ 5.1m 6g² 5g 6g 5g 6m⁶ 5v 6d 7d Oct 30] lengthy
gelding: fairly useful handicapper: ran badly last 3 starts: best at 5f/6f: acts on firm and
good to soft ground. *T. D. Easterby*

ONLY PENANG (IRE)   2 b.f. (Apr 8) Perugino (USA) 84 – Unalaska (IRE) 65 (High   **77**
Estate 127) [2001 6m 7m* 8f⁵ 8g 8d² Sep 27] IR 14,000Y: leggy, rather unfurnished filly:
third foal: dam, ran twice in Ireland, half-sister to useful 1989 2-y-o 6f performer Makbul:
fair performer: won maiden at Newbury in July: edged right when second in nursery at
Goodwood: stays 1m: acts on firm and good to soft going. *B. R. Millman*

ONLYTIME WILL TELL   3 ch.g. Efisio 120 – Prejudice 83 (Young Generation 129)   **86**
[2001 70: 8s³ 8.2v⁴ 7m* 7s* 8m 7.5f² 8g⁶ 9.1m 6d* f6g³ 7v* Oct 26] lengthy, useful-   **a73**
looking gelding: fairly useful on turf, fair on all-weather: won claimers at Brighton
then Salisbury (left C. Dwyer) in May and similar race at Pontefract then handicap at
Doncaster in October: best at 6f/7f: acts on fibresand, goes well on ground softer than
good on turf (though has won on good to firm): sometimes slowly away/wanders.
D. Nicholls

ONLY WHEN PROVOKED (IRE)   3 b.g. General Monash (USA) 107 – Lyzia   –
(IRE) 77 (Lycius (USA) 124) [2001 –: f12g f12g 14.1g Jun 16] seems of little account.
A. Streeter

ONLY WORDS (USA)   4 ch.g. Shuailaan (USA) 122 – Conversation Piece (USA)   **41**
(Seeking The Gold (USA)) [2001 51: 9s 9.9m 12m f7g 7.5f 10f 8f 8m 9.9m² 9.9m⁴ 9m
10.4s 13.8s⁴ 12d⁶ Nov 6] sturdy gelding: poor maiden handicapper: stays 1¼m: acts on
good to firm going: tried tongue tied at 3 yrs. *A. J. Lockwood*

ON MY HONOUR   3 b.f. Pyramus (USA) 78 – Princess Matilda 110 (Habitat 134)   –
[2001 –: 8d 6g 6f 6.1m 6m 7.1d 8.1s 7m⁵ 5.7m Sep 10] little form: blinkered last 2 starts.
J. C. Fox

ON PORPOISE   5 b.g. Dolphin Street (FR) 125 – Floppie (FR) (Law Society (USA)   –
130) [2001 50: 8g 10m Jul 27] lengthy gelding: modest handicapper at 4 yrs: well below
form both starts in 2001. *P. W. D'Arcy*

ON SHADE   4 ch.f. Polar Falcon (USA) 126 – Vagrant Maid (USA) 85 (Honest   –
Pleasure (USA)) [2001 44: 11s 10m 8m Jun 22] disappointing maiden. *N. Tinkler*

ON STAGE (USA) — see Stage By Stage (USA)

ON THE FAIRWAY (IRE)   2 b.f. (Feb 5) Danehill Dancer (IRE) 117 – Asta Madera   **54 p**
(IRE) 67 (Toca Madera 111) [2001 7m⁴ 6m 6f Sep 10] IR 1,700Y, 16,000 2-y-o: tall filly:
second foal: best effort in maidens (modest form) when seventh
of 16 at Newcastle final start, travelling well long way: type to do better in handicaps.
T. D. Easterby

ON THE LINE   3 ch.f. Alhijaz 122 – Join The Clan 95 (Clantime 101) [2001 –: f8g   –
Jan 26] no show in 3 maidens at Southwell: visored only run in 2001. *Mrs N. Macauley*

ON THE NILE (IRE)   2 b.f. (Mar 1) Sadler's Wells (USA) 132 – Minnie Habit (Habi-   **103 p**
tat 134) [2001 7m 7s 8s³ 8d⁶ 9s* Nov 11] closely related to 4-y-o Kutub and half-sister to
2 winners: dam, Irish 9f winner, half-sister to dam of Tropical and Shake The Yoke:
useful performer: plenty of improvement to win 10-runner listed race at Leopardstown by
2 lengths from Wrong Key, leading over 1f out and running on well: will be suited by
1¼m/1½m: acts on soft ground: capable of better still. *A. P. O'Brien, Ireland*

ON THE TAKE (IRE)   4 b.g. Kahyasi 130 – Malmada (USA) (Fappiano (USA))   –
[2001 f9.4g f12g f12g Mar 8] IR 7,000 3-y-o: second foal: dam unraced daughter of very
smart French 9f to 10.5f winner Masmouda: last in maidens: blinkered final start.
B. J. Curley

ON THE TRAIL   4 ch.g. Catrail (USA) 123 – From The Rooftops (IRE) (Thatching   **58**
131) [2001 43: f7s* f7s* e7g² 5f 5m 6g f6g 6m 5m f5s⁶ f5g f6g f7g⁵ f7s⁴ f6s* Dec 21] fair   **a65**
on all-weather, modest on turf: won sellers at Wolverhampton (2, left S. Dow after second
of them) in January and Southwell in December: stays easy 7f: acts on good to
ground, good to firm, fibresand and equitrack: sometimes tongue tied: often takes strong
hold up with pace. *T. D. Barron*

ONYX KNIGHT   2 b.g. (Apr 21) Awesome 73 – Lady of The Realm (Prince Daniel   –
(USA)) [2001 f6s p6g Dec 28] second foal: dam ran 3 times: slowly away and well beaten
in maidens at Wolverhampton and Lingfield. *J. Neville*

OOMPH   3 b.f. Shareef Dancer (USA) 135 – Seductress 94 (Known Fact (USA) 135)   **79**
[2001 83: 7m³ 7m 7g*⁷ 7d³ 8g f7g³ Nov 16] fair performer: landed odds in maiden at
Newcastle in July: creditable efforts after: may prove best at 7f/1m: acts on soft and good
to firm ground, probably on fibresand. *W. Jarvis*

OPAL'S HELMSMAN (USA)   2 b.c. (Mar 3) Helmsman (USA) 121 – Opal's   –
Notebook (USA) (Notebook (USA)) [2001 5.1d 6g 6v Oct 8] $37,000Y, 30,000 2-y-o:
second foal: dam unraced: well held in maidens. *R. M. Beckett*

OPEN ARMS   5 ch.g. Most Welcome 131 – Amber Fizz (USA) (Effervescing (USA))   **62**
[2001 70: 8m 10m 10g 10.9m 9.9s Sep 25] strong gelding: modest handicapper: stays
1¼m: acts on good to firm and good to soft going: ran badly in blinkers final start.
Mrs A. L. M. King

OPEN GROUND (IRE)   4 ch.g. Common Grounds 118 – Poplina (USA) (Roberto   **58**
(USA) 131) [2001 66, a–: e13g* 14.1g 16s Oct 30] lengthy gelding: modest handicapper:
won at Lingfield in March: off 7 months then well held both starts after: stays 2m: acts on
heavy going and equitrack. *Ian Williams*

OPENING CEREMONY (USA)   2 br.f. (Jan 28) Quest For Fame 127 – Gleam of   **87 p**
Light (IRE) 81 (Danehill (USA) 126) [2001 7d* Oct 15] second foal: half-sister to 3-y-o

Gleaming Blade: dam, 7.5f winner, out of half-sister to 2000 Guineas winner Don't Forget Me: 8/1, won 20-runner maiden at Leicester by short head from Sunray Superstar, responding well to lead near finish: should stay 1¼m: should make a useful 3-y-o. *Mrs A. J. Perrett*

OPEN WARFARE (IRE) 3 b. or br.f. General Monash (USA) 107 – Pipe Opener 58 **60 §** (Prince Sabo 123) [2001 79: f7g 6g² 5g 6g³ 5g 5f 5s f7g Nov 23] small, strong filly: has a **a– §** round action: modest performer: refused to race on reappearance (only start for D. Eddy): stays 6f: acts on heavy and good to firm going: untrustworthy. *G. A. Swinbank*

OPERATION ENVY 3 b.g. Makbul 104 – Safe Bid 44 (Sure Blade (USA) 130) [2001 **–** 58d: e10g Jan 10] disappointing maiden. *R. M. Flower*

OPIUM 2 b.f. (Apr 25) Polish Precedent (USA) 131 – Brecon Beacons (IRE) 71 (Shirley **–** Heights 130) [2001 7d Oct 15] compact filly: fifth foal: half-sister to a winner in Poland by Wolfhound: dam, maiden best at 2 yrs (should have stayed at least 1¼m), half-sister to smart French middle-distance performer Ordinance: 25/1, always towards rear in maiden at Leicester. *R. Hannon*

OPPORTUNE (GER) 6 br.g. Shirley Heights 130 – On The Tiles (Thatch (USA) **60** 136) [2001 39: 13d³ 12.1m* 15g* 14.1m³ 13g* 14.8m³ 13.1d² 13.1m³ 16.2m* 16m³ 16.2s 12d⁴ Oct 8] deep-bodied gelding: modest handicapper: won at Hamilton (2, first apprentice event) and Warwick (2) in summer: effective at 1½m to easy 2m: acts on soft and good to firm going: consistent. *W. M. Brisbourne*

OPTIMAITE 4 b.g. Komaite (USA) – Leprechaun Lady 57 (Royal Blend 117) [2001 **98 §** 108d: 12s 9.7m* 10.3f⁶ 10m² 12g 12f⁴ 12g 10.1g⁴ 12m² 9g Oct 6] tall, workmanlike gelding: easy mover: useful performer: won minor event at Folkestone in June: mostly disappointing after next 2 starts: stays 1½m, seemingly not 2m: acts on firm and good to soft going: visored (reluctant to race) seventh start: tongue tied: usually slowly away: has hung right/found little: ungenuine. *B. R. Millman*

OPTIMAX 4 ch.g. Rudimentary (USA) 118 – Zipperti Do 70 (Precocious 126) [2001 **–** 7m 7f f8g 8s Oct 3] half-brother to 5f to 7f winner Nobalino (by Sharpo) and 1¼m winner Wonderful Day (by Niniski): dam 1m winner: well beaten in maidens/claimers (first 3 starts for M. Quinlan). *P. D. Evans*

ORAKE PRINCE 2 b.g. (Apr 25) Bluegrass Prince (IRE) 110 – Kiri Te (Liboi (USA) **51** 76) [2001 7s 8d Oct 25] fourth foal: half-brother to 7f/1m winner Kanawa (by Beveled) and 6-y-o Kirisnippa: dam unraced: modest form in maidens at Brighton and Bath (slowly away, subsequently gelded): should stay 1¼m. *J. G. Portman*

ORANGE PLACE (IRE) 10 ch.g. Nordance (USA) – Little Red Hut (Habitat 134) **–** [2001 12s Mar 22] of little account nowadays. *B. J. Llewellyn*

ORANGERIE (IRE) 3 b.g. Darshaan 133 – Fleur d'Oranger 110 (Northfields **86** (USA)) [2001 65: 14.1m³ 16g* 14.1s² 13d³ 16m² 15m⁵ 16v³ Oct 4] tall, close-coupled gelding: fairly useful handicapper: won at Nottingham in August: ran creditably when placed 4 times after: stays 2m: acts on heavy and good to firm going: sold 41,000 gns, joined P. Hobbs. *Sir Mark Prescott*

ORANGETREE COUNTY (IRE) 3 b.f. Dolphin Street (FR) 125 – Empress Kim **39** (Formidable (USA) 125) [2001 –: 7g⁵ 5m 7.6f 10m 5g⁴ 5g 8d Nov 2] poor maiden. *C. A. Dwyer*

ORANGE TREE LAD 3 b.g. Tragic Role (USA) – Adorable Cherub (USA) 58 (Halo **64** (USA)) [2001 70: 6m 6m⁴ 6m² Jul 5] well-grown gelding: modest maiden handicapper: should stay 7f: acts on soft and good to firm ground. *M. L. W. Bell*

ORANGINO 3 b.c. Primo Dominie 121 – Sweet Jaffa 73§ (Never So Bold 135) [2001 **46 +** –: 6s 6m 7.1g 5m³ 6m 6d Jul 19] unfurnished colt: unimpressive mover: poor maiden handicapper: seems best at 5f/6f: acts on soft and good to firm going: blinkered last 3 starts. *C. W. Thornton*

ORCHESTRA STALL 9 b.g. Old Vic 136 – Blue Brocade 91 (Reform 132) [2001 **–** 119: 16g May 5] good-topped gelding: had a splayed, round action: formerly very smart, though had leg problems and was lightly raced: won 8 races, including Sagaro Stakes at Ascot in 1997 and 2000: tailed off long way out in same event at Newmarket only run in 2001: seemed best at 1¾m/2m: acted on soft and good to firm going: wore bandages: retired. *J. L. Dunlop*

ORDER 5 b.g. Deploy 131 – Gong 84 (Bustino 136) [2001 12g² 12.1d* 14g* 16.1g **90** Jul 11] strong, long-backed gelding: second foal: half-brother to 4-y-o Ecstasy (6.7f, at 2 yrs, and 1¼m winner): dam, 1¼m winner, half-sister to smart middle-distance stayer Waterfield: useful in bumpers: fairly useful performer: won maiden at Hamilton in May and handicap at Haydock in June: ran poorly final start: stays 1¾m: yet to race on ground firmer than good. *R. M. Beckett*

OREANA (FR)   3 b.f. Anabaa (USA) 130 – Lavinia Fontana (IRE) 116 (Sharpo 132)   **81** [2001 97p: 5s 6m 6s Sep 7] sturdy filly: useful 6f winner at 2 yrs: form in 2001 only on reappearance: stud. *J. L. Dunlop*

ORIENTAL EMPRESS   2 b.f. (Mar 24) Emperor Fountain 112 – Beijing (USA) 89   **–** (Northjet 136) [2001 7d 8g f9.4g Nov 17] 2,000Y: small, angular filly: half-sister to several winners, including useful 1¼m (at 2 yrs) and 1¾m winner Blaaziing Joe (by Alzao) and fairly useful but unreliable 1¼m/1½m winner Danjing (by Danehill): dam, won from 1½m to 2m, half-sister to very smart stayer Protection Racket: no show in maidens. *C. W. Thornton*

ORIENTAL MIST (IRE)   3 gr.g. Balla Cove 119 – Donna Katrina (Kings Lake   **73 d** (USA) 133) [2001 69: 8v 8.3m 7.1m 8g³ 8.1s⁴ 15m³ 10.5v 12d 10.9v⁴ Oct 15] leggy gelding: fair performer: best efforts of 2001 when third in handicaps at Ayr: seems to stay 15f: acts on heavy and good to firm going. *Miss L. A. Perratt*

ORIENTAL MOON (IRE)   2 ch.f. (Mar 4) Spectrum (IRE) 126 – La Grande   **70** Cascade (USA) (Beaudelaire (USA) 125) [2001 6f f7g 7g⁵ 7.5m 7g² 7d 8v Oct 16] 50,000 francs Y: leggy filly: fourth foal: dam French 2-y-o 1m winner: fair maiden: second of 20 in nursery at Doncaster: well held in similar events after: will probably stay 1m: form only on good going. *G. C. H. Chung*

ORIENTOR   3 b.c. Inchinor 119 – Orient 106 (Bay Express 132) [2001 86: 6v² 7s*   **118** 7m⁴ 6m³ 6m³ 6d* 6m 7m 6g* 7m⁵ 6s⁵ 6s² 6d² 6s³ Nov 10] close-coupled colt: made into smart performer: had an excellent season, winning maiden at Redcar in May, William Hill Trophy (Handicap) at York (stormed home to catch Armagnac on post) in June and

William Hill Trophy (Handicap), York—Orientor and Armagnac (far side) are well clear,
Kieren Fallon extracting maximum effort from the former to lead close home;
the race was the principal event on the 31st Timeform Charity Day,
which yielded record proceeds of £229,864

Mr S. Bruce's "Orientor"

valuable conditions event at Ascot (showed fine turn of foot to beat Pan Jammer 4 lengths) in August: ran well after when second to Nice One Clare in Diadem Stakes at Ascot (beaten a neck) and to Danehurst in listed event at Newmarket (beaten 1½ lengths): best form at 6f: has form on good to firm going, but seems ideally suited by good or softer: best with waiting tactics in well-run race: tough and reliable. *J. S. Goldie*

ORINOCO'S FLIGHT (IRE) 3 ch.g. Spectrum (IRE) 126 – Silk Route (USA) 55 **56** (Shahrastani (USA) 135) [2001 8.2s⁴ 10g Nov 5] 5,000F, IR 6,000Y, 12,000 2-y-o: third foal: dam once-raced half-sister to smart French filly up to 1m Fairy Path: modest form in maidens at Nottingham then Redcar. *J. G. Given*

ORINOCOVSKY (IRE) 2 ch.c. (Mar 31) Grand Lodge (USA) 125 – Brillantina **78 p** (FR) (Crystal Glitters (USA) 127) [2001 8m³ Sep 24] IR 29,000F, 45,000Y: fourth foal: half-brother to winners by Law Society (2) and Dashing Blade: dam German 7.7f winner at 4 yrs: favourite, 3½ lengths third of 10 to Jack The Track in maiden at Kempton, always prominent after veering left leaving stall: should improve. *P. F. I. Cole*

ORIOLE 8 b.g. Mazilier (USA) 107 – Odilese 82 (Mummy's Pet 125) [2001 57, a–: 8f **49** 7m 7m 8s 7m 8m⁶ 8g 7d Oct 30] leggy gelding: poor handicapper: stays 1m: acts on any turf going and fibresand: tried blinkered/visored: said to have bled from nose final outing. *Don Enrico Incisa*

ORLANDO SUNRISE (IRE) 4 ch.f. Dolphin Street (FR) 125 – Miss Belgravia **58** (USA) (Smarten (USA)) [2001 62: 10f 11.8m 12.6f 10.2f⁵ 10.2g⁴ 10m Sep 11] workman-like filly: modest maiden handicapper: stays 1½m: acts on firm and good to soft going: blinkered (ran creditably) penultimate start. *Ian Williams*

ORLASS (IRE) 2 br.f. (Apr 13) Hamas (IRE) 125§ – Rockbourne 57 (Midyan (USA) **89**
124) [2001 f5g² f5g² 6f* 6g⁶ 6v* 5g 6d² 6v³ 6.5d⁶ Dec 16] IR 4,000F: leggy filly: fifth
foal: half-sister to fairly useful Irish 5f (at 2 yrs) and 6f winner Fiddler's Rock (by Ballad
Rock) and a 7f/1m winner in Italy by Cyrano de Bergerac: dam 6f winner who stayed 1m:
fairly useful performer: won claimer at Haydock in July and nursery there in September:
best effort when 2½ lengths third to Lady Links in listed race at Saint-Cloud: should stay
7f: acts on fibresand and any turf going: races prominently. *M. G. Quinlan*

ORLEANS (IRE) 6 b.g. Scenic 128 – Guest House (What A Guest 119) [2001 f12g **–**
16v Apr 3] of little account. *G. A. Ham*

ORMELIE (IRE) 6 gr.g. Jade Hunter (USA) – Trolley Song (USA) (Caro 133) [2001 **–**
101: 12d Apr 18] leggy, lightly-made gelding: unimpressive mover: useful handicapper
at 5 yrs: well behind only run in 2001: blinkered once. *C. A. Dwyer*

OR ROYAL (FR) 10 ro.g. Kendor (FR) 122 – Pomme Royale (FR) (Shergar 140) **73**
[2001 f12g⁵ 14.1s³ 18.7f f16g 16.2m 12m 18m 11.9g f14.8s* f14.8g⁴ 15.8d f14g² f16g³ **a67**
f16.2g* Nov 21] workmanlike gelding: ran 3 times on Flat at 3 yrs for A. Fabre, winning
minor event at Evry: high-class chaser/useful hurdler since (most unreliable of late): fair
at best on Flat in 2001: won claimer in September and handicap in November, both at
Wolverhampton: stays 2m: acts on soft going and fibresand: blinkered/visored first 7
starts. *R. Lee*

ORTHODOX 2 gr.c. (Mar 7) Baryshnikov (AUS) – Sancta 106 (So Blessed 130) [2001 **73**
7.1g 10.2g⁴ Oct 1] 15,000Y: half-brother to several winners, including smart 7f (at 2 yrs)
and 1¼m winner Carmelite House (by Diesis) and useful stayer Saint Keyne (by Sadler's
Wells): dam 1m/1¼m winner: much better effort in maidens (fair form) when fourth to
Stage By Stage at Bath: will stay 1½m. *G. L. Moore*

OSCAR PEPPER (USA) 4 b.g. Brunswick (USA) 119 – Princess Baja (USA) (Con- **73**
quistador Cielo (USA)) [2001 67, a97: f7s⁵ f6g⁴ f7g* f7g² 7m 7m² 7.5m³ 7f 7.1f 7m 7m **a103**
f6g⁶ Dec 3] close-coupled, useful-looking gelding: useful on all-weather, fair on turf:
won minor event at Wolverhampton in March: creditable efforts in handicaps after only
when placed, including when beaten short head by Intricate Web at Southwell next time:
stays 7.5f: acts on fibresand, firm and good to soft ground: tried blinkered earlier in
career: usually held up, and best in strongly-run race. *T. D. Barron*

OSCIETRA 5 b.m. Robellino (USA) 127 – Top Treat (USA) 101 (Topsider (USA)) **37**
[2001 56: 10m 12m 9m 10.5s 9.1v³ 11d² Oct 30] good-topped mare: poor performer:
effective at 9f to 11f: probably best on going softer than good: tried visored at 4 yrs: none
too reliable. *W. M. Brisbourne*

OSHIPONGA 3 ch.f. Barat[hea (IRE) 127 – Ingozi 91 (Warning 136) [2001 f7g 7d 7m **72**
9m* 9.9f³ 10m Aug 5] angular, close-coupled filly: third foal: half-sister to 5-y-o Tissifer
and a winner in Hong Kong by Cadeaux Genereux: dam, 7f/1m winner, half-sister to
smart 6f/7f colt Inchinor, out of smart sprint winner up to 1m Inchmurrin: fair handicapper: won
at Redcar in June: stays 1¼m: acts on firm going: blinkered (wandered and found little)
final appearance: sold 38,000 gns in December. *R. Charlton*

OSTARA (IRE) 4 b.g. Petorius 117 – Onde de Choc (USA) (L'Enjoleur (CAN)) [2001 **61 d**
71: f8g 8s 8f 7g 10.5m 8m⁴ 8.1g 8m⁴ 7.1g⁵ Sep 13] tall gelding: modest performer, on
downgrade: left K. Ryan before final start: should stay 1¼m: acts on soft and good to firm
going: tried blinkered: edgy sort, has gone freely/hung. *R. C. Spicer*

OTHER CLUB 7 ch.g. Kris 135 – Tura (Northfields (USA)) [2001 f11g* f11g³ Apr **53**
28] lengthy, good-bodied gelding: modest handicapper: won at Southwell in March:
stayed 11f: acted on fibresand: raced prominently: dead. *J. G. Portman*

OTHER ROUTES 2 ch.c. (May 4) Efisio 120 – Rainbow Fleet 66 (Nomination 125) **47**
[2001 6m 6s 7s Oct 25] 11,000Y: fifth foal: half-brother to 3-y-o Muddy Waters, 3-y-o
Jollands and a winner in Hong Kong by Polar Falcon: dam 5f (at 2 yrs) and 6f winner:
poor maiden: may prove best at 5f/6f. *G. L. Moore*

OTIME (IRE) 4 b.g. Mujadil (USA) 119 – Kick The Habit 94 (Habitat 134) [2001 68, **49**
a76: f8g e6g⁴ e6g⁵ e7g e8g⁶ 7f⁵ 7m 8d Aug 8] lengthy, quite good-topped gelding: modest **a57**
performer: below form after second start: stays easy 1m: acts on firm going, fibresand
and equitrack: sometimes blinkered/visored: tongue tied: sold 380 gns. *Andrew Reid*

OUEST BANQUE (USA) 2 b.f. (Mar 11) Red Ransom (USA) – Mrs West (USA) 86 **80**
(Gone West (USA)) [2001 6g² 6m³ 7m² 7g³ 8m³ Sep 1] useful-looking filly: fifth

foal: closely related to fairly useful 1998 2-y-o 7f winner Meneer (by Silver Hawk) and half-sister to fairly useful 1999 2-y-o 1m winner Western Summer (by Summer Squall): dam, 2-y-o 6f/7.5f winner, later placed in USA: fairly useful maiden: favourite, third in nurseries last 2 starts: stays 1m: has hung right: sent to USA. *J. L. Dunlop*

OULTON BROAD 5 b.g. Midyan (USA) 124 – Lady Quachita (USA) (Sovereign – Dancer (USA)) [2001 16.4m Jul 12] lightly-raced maiden: well beaten only Flat run since 1999: tried visored. *M. R. Ewer-Hoad*

OUNDLE SCOUNDREL (FR) 2 b.c. (Mar 29) Spinning World (USA) 130 – Tidal **66 ?** Treasure (USA) (Crafty Prospector (USA)) [2001 7v 7d Nov 3] quite good-topped colt: third foal: half-brother to useful French 5.5f to 1m winner Igman (by Mt Livermore): dam unraced close relative of dam of high-class French 1m/1¼m performer Green Tune and smart French sprinter Pas de Reponse: mid-field in maidens at Doncaster (on toes, took strong hold) and Newmarket (led until past halfway), seemingly fair form in former. *M. Johnston*

OUR ALBERT (IRE) 8 b.g. Durgam (USA) – Power Girl 77 (Tyrant (USA)) [2001 – 5f 5g Sep 19] of little account. *J. Balding*

OUR CHELSEA BLUE (USA) 3 ch.f. Distant View (USA) 126 – Eastern Con- **79** nection (USA) (Danzig Connection (USA)) [2001 6d 5m⁴ 5m³ 5m 5g² 5m² Aug 18] $52,000F, 31,000Y: first foal: dam US 8.5f/9f winner: fairly useful maiden: second at Goodwood (handicap, easily best effort) then Ripon in August: likely to prove best at 5f/6f: tongue tied last 3 starts. *T. G. Mills*

OUR COLONEL 3 b.c. Darshaan 133 – Dance By Night 84 (Northfields (USA)) **66** [2001 10.3v⁶ f11g³ f11g⁶ 14.1d³ 14m Jun 15] 250,000Y: half-brother to several winners, including very smart French 7f (Prix de la Foret)/1m (Poule d'Essai des Pouliches) winner Danseuse du Soir (by Thatching) and smart 1¼m/1½m performer Don Corleone (by Caerleon), 7f winner at 2 yrs: dam 2-y-o 7f winner: fair maiden: ran poorly final start: stays 1¾m: acts on fibresand and good to soft going. *G. A. Butler*

OUR DESTINY 3 b.g. Mujadil (USA) 119 – Superspring (Superlative 118) [2001 75: **65** f7g f6g 8m 6m⁴ 6g⁵ 7d⁵ 6m 7g 5m⁵ 5g 6m³ 6g 6f 6s³ 7s 7g⁴ f8g⁴ f9.4g⁴ f11g* f11g Dec 3] big, lengthy gelding: fair performer: won seller at Southwell in November: stays 11f: acts on fibresand, firm and soft going: often visored. *M. A. Buckley*

OUR EMILY (IRE) 3 b.f. Charnwood Forest (IRE) 125 – Lacinia 107 (Groom Dancer – (USA) 128) [2001 61: 11.5m 14.1s 13.8m Sep 22] disappointing maiden: trained first 2 starts by K. Burke: blinkered in seller final one. *T. Keddy*

OUR FIRST LADY 4 b.f. Alzao (USA) 117 – Eclipsing (IRE) 93 (Baillamont (USA) **73** 124) [2001 71: 7m 7m² 8m p7g p8g Dec 4] fair maiden handicapper: stays 7f: acts on **a63** good to firm going, probably on polytrack: tongue tied once at 3 yrs. *D. W. P. Arbuthnot*

OUR FRED 4 ch.g. Prince Sabo 123 – Sheila's Secret (IRE) 97 (Bluebird (USA) 125) **85** [2001 88: f5s² f5g³ 5m 5.2m 5.1f 5m⁴ 5m² 5g² 5m 5.1m³ 5m 5g 5.1d³ f5s Dec 15] lengthy **a89** gelding: fairly useful performer: best at 5f: acts on soft going, good to firm and fibresand: usually blinkered: usually front runner. *T. G. Mills*

OUR GLENARD 2 b.c. (Feb 14) Royal Applause 124 – Loucoum (FR) 93 (Iron Duke **72** (FR) 122) [2001 5.1d⁵ 5m⁵ 5g 6d Oct 18] 35,000Y: neat colt: half-brother to several winners, including 3-y-o Brilliantrio, fairly useful 1m winner Iktasab (by Cadeaux Genereux) and 5-y-o Rigadoon: dam, third in 5f Prix d'Arenberg at 2 yrs, later won 7 races in USA, mostly around 1m: fair maiden: should stay at least 7f: twice slowly away. *B. W. Hills*

OUR INDULGENCE (IRE) 3 ch.g. Prince of Birds (USA) 121 – Megan's Dream **38** (IRE) 56 (Fayruz 116) [2001 45: 8.2v 6m⁴ 6g f6g 6m⁶ 8m⁵ 8.1d 10.1g⁶ Aug 17] strong gelding: poor maiden: seems to stay 1¼m: acts on good to firm going. *T. D. Easterby*

OUR KRISSIE 3 b.f. Kris 135 – Shehana (USA) 86 (The Minstrel (CAN) 135) [2001 **65** 10g⁶ 12.4m⁶ 12g³ 12.4m⁴ 10m 12m 10.5v Sep 29] 52,000F: plain, leggy filly: half-sister to several winners, including useful 1995 2-y-o 6f winner who later won in USA React (by Reprimand) and 1½m winner Legion of Honour (by Ahonoora): dam 2-y-o 9f winner who seemed to stay 1½m: fair maiden handicapper: below form after fourth start: likely to stay beyond 1½m: acts on good to firm going: blinkered fifth and sixth appearances. *M. Johnston*

OUR LAD 3 ch.g. Phountzi (USA) 104 – Lady Kalliste (Another Realm 118) [2001   –
10m 10d 7d Jul 18] third foal: brother to 1¼m/11.5f winner Lady Jo: dam no form: no
form in maidens/claimer. *S. Dow*

OUR MONOGRAM 5 b.g. Deploy 131 – Darling Splodge (Elegant Air 119) [2001   57
59: 18m 14.1m³ 16m* Aug 28] big gelding: modest handicapper: won at Ripon in
August: best at 2m+: acts on firm and good to soft going, possibly not soft. *A. C. Stewart*

OUR ROSY 3 ch.f. First Trump 118 – Cadeau Elegant 64 (Cadeaux Genereux 131)   –
[2001 6m⁶ 6g Aug 11] first foal: dam lightly-raced sprint maiden: little form.
G. G. Margarson

OUR SHELLBY (IRE) 3 b. or br.f. Petardia 113 – Davenport Goddess (IRE)   –
(Classic Secret (USA) 91) [2001 –: f11g⁶ 14.1d⁶ 14f 12f Jul 2] probably of little account.
J. L. Eyre

OUR WEDDINGPRESENT (USA) 2 ch.g. (May 4) Known Fact (USA) 135 – All   49
A Lark (General Assembly (USA)) [2001 6v 7.9d 6d Nov 2] $23,000F, $13,000Y, 28,000
2-y-o: leggy, workmanlike gelding: half-brother to several winners, including useful
1¼m winner Pier Damiani (by Shareef Dancer): dam, Irish 1m/9f winner, half-sister to
dam of Irish 2000 Guineas winner Flash of Steel: poor maiden: gelded after final start:
should stay at least 1m. *M. C. Pipe*

OUT FOR A STROLL 2 b.g. (Mar 27) Zamindar (USA) 116 – The Jotter 99 (Night   67
Shift (USA)) [2001 5.3s 5f 5m⁵ 5.1f Sep 18] 22,000F, 66,000Y: sturdy, deep-girthed
gelding: has scope: third foal: half-brother to useful 1999 2-y-o 6f winner Final Row (by
Indian Ridge), later winner in USA, and 3-y-o Ice Prince: dam, 2-y-o 5f/6.5f winner,
granddaughter of Irish 1000 Guineas winner Front Row: fair maiden: best effort when
fifth at Ripon: slowly away and not given hard time final start: should stay 6f: retained
24,000 gns. *S. C. Williams*

OUTLAW 2 b.c. (May 10) Danehill (USA) 126 – Sabaah Elfull 75 (Kris 135) [2001 7g   – p
7d Sep 1] 60,000F, 140,000Y: sturdy, lengthy colt: good walker: second foal: dam, 5f
winner who stayed 7.5f, closely related to smart French sprinter Pole Position, from
family of Pushy and Jupiter Island: signs of a little ability, not knocked about, in maidens
at Leicester and Chester: type to do better. *Sir Michael Stoute*

OUT OF DANGER (IRE) 2 b.f. (Mar 23) Darnay 117 – Achtung Lady (IRE) 53   –
(Warning 136) [2001 5f⁴ 5m⁶ 7.1f⁶ 8g Aug 24] third foal: dam, ran 3 times in Ireland at 2
yrs, out of half-sister to disqualified Oaks winner Aliysa: no form in sellers/claimer: often
slowly away. *A. Berry*

OUT OF RETIREMENT 3 b.g. Beveled (USA) – Incatinka 63 (Inca Chief (USA))   –
[2001 7f 8.3v Nov 8] 11,500F, 18,000Y: first foal: dam lightly-raced maiden: well held in
maidens 5 months apart: dead. *G. C. H. Chung*

OUT OF SEASON (IRE) 2 ch.f. (Jun 8) Brief Truce (USA) 126 – Red Partridge   58
(Solinus 130) [2001 5.1d 5.1m⁴ 6g² Sep 5] 1,500Y: half-sister to several winners,
including smart Irish/Italian 9f to 1½m winner Firing Line (by Slip Anchor) and 1m
winner Bird of Prey (by Last Tycoon): dam Irish 2-y-o 1m winner: modest maiden:
second in seller at Lingfield: will probably stay 1m. *W. G. M. Turner*

OUT OF SIGHT (IRE) 7 ch.g. Salse (USA) 128 – Starr Danias (USA) (Sensitive   –
Prince (USA)) [2001 65, a82: f8g f7g 10m 10.5g 10.5s f9.4s Sep 6] one-time fairly useful
7f/1m winner: showed little in handicaps in 2001: dead. *B. A. McMahon*

OUT OF THIS WORLD 2 ch.f. (May 6) Beveled (USA) – Martian Melody 62   59 p
(Enchantment 115) [2001 f6g* Nov 23] winter to 5f/6f winner Random and half-sister to
5f/6f winner Mister Raider (by Ballacashtal): dam best at 6f: 8/1, won 14-runner seller at
Southwell comfortably by ¾ length from Woodboro Minstrel, slowly away and short of
room penultimate 1f: should improve. *S. Kirk*

OUTRAGEOUSE 3 b.g. Be My Chief (USA) 122 – Pink Brief (IRE) 71 (Ela-Mana-   –
Mou 132) [2001 53: f8g 10m 7f 7m 10.4m 13.1m 16v Oct 4] disappointing maiden.
Andrew Reid

OUTSTANDING TALENT 4 gr.f. Environment Friend 128 – Chaleureuse (Final   48
Straw 127) [2001 44: f9.4s⁴ f7g⁵ f9.4g⁴ f9.4g² f8f f9.4g* e8g f8.5g 11.8m⁶ f12g⁴ 12.1m⁴   a55
10.2f⁶ f12g⁵ Sep 8] tall filly: modest handicapper: won at Wolverhampton in March:
barely stays 1½m: acts on fibresand, firm and good to soft going. *A. W. Carroll*

Tote Gold Trophy Stakes (Handicap), Goodwood—Ovambo produces another improved performance, staying on very strongly to beat Fly With Me (rail), Tomasino and Elsaamri (right)

OVAMBO (IRE) 3 b.g. Namaqualand (USA) – Razana (IRE) 71 (Kahyasi 130) [2001 **108** 77: 10s 10d* 12m* 12m* 13.9m² Aug 23] sturdy gelding: useful handicapper: won at Windsor in June, Salisbury in July and Goodwood (Tote Gold Trophy, by length from Fly With Me) in August: good neck second to Artillery in Melrose Rated Stakes at York final start: stays 1¾m: acts on good to firm going, some promise on soft: usually held up. *P. J. Makin*

OVERLOAD (USA) 2 b.f. (Jan 25) Forest Wildcat (USA) 120 – Magical Avie (USA) **85** (Lord Avie (USA)) [2001 7m³ 6v* 8v Oct 23] $132,000Y: fourth foal: dam won up to 9f in USA and second in Grade 3 1m event: fairly useful form: justified favouritism in maiden at Windsor in October by 3½ lengths from Woodland Spirit: stiff task, always behind in Prix des Reservoirs at Deauville: may prove best up to 7f: acts on good to firm and heavy ground. *C. R. Egerton*

OVERSMAN 8 b.g. Keen 116 – Jamaican Punch (IRE) (Shareef Dancer (USA) 135) **– §** [2001 49§: f12g⁶ 17.2m Jul 15] one-time fairly useful 1½m winner: has lost his form and enthusiasm: sometimes blinkered. *B. J. Llewellyn*

OVERSPECT 3 b.c. Spectrum (IRE) 126 – Portelet 91 (Night Shift (USA)) [2001 **89** 100: 8d⁴ 10.1g⁴ 12g Sep 15] close-coupled colt: fairly useful performer: fourth in minor events at Bath and Epsom: may prove best around 1m: acts on good to firm going and good to soft, possibly not soft. *P. F. I. Cole*

OZAWA (IRE) 4 gr.g. Brief Truce (USA) 126 – Classy 59 (Kalaglow 132) [2001 40: **–** e8g e8g⁶ 9s⁵ f11g 10m f8g 9.9m 8f Sep 20] tall gelding: little form in 2001: trained first 6 starts by J. Payne: tried tongue tied: sent to Denmark. *M. E. Sowersby*

P

PAARL ROCK 6 ch.h. Common Grounds 118 – Markievicz (IRE) 73 (Doyoun 124) **55** [2001 63: f16.2s* f16.2g⁴ f16.2g⁵ 12.3s Apr 28] quite good-topped horse: modest handicapper: won at Wolverhampton in January: stays 2m: acts on fibresand, good to firm and good to soft ground: usually blinkered/visored: front runner. *G. Barnett*

PACHARA 2 b.c. (Apr 9) Mind Games 121 – Miss Mercy (IRE) 62 (Law Society **98** (USA) 130) [2001 5d³ 5.1f² 5m* 6g³ 6m³ 6m 6d² 5d³ 6v⁴ Oct 27] 25,000Y: well-made colt: has scope: third foal: half-brother to 3-y-o That's Jazz: dam, 2-y-o 6f winner, out of sister to smart 7f/1m performer Arjuzah: useful performer: won minor event at Warwick in May: good 4¼ lengths third to Dominica in Cornwallis Stakes at Ascot penultimate start: stays 6f: acts on firm and good to soft ground, well below form on heavy: tough and consistent. *M. L. W. Bell*

PACHINCO 3 ch.c. Bluebird (USA) 125 – Lady Philippa (IRE) 77 (Taufan (USA) –
119) [2001 –: 11.9s Sep 30] has shown nothing in 2 maidens. *P. Mitchell*

PACIFIC ALLIANCE (IRE) 5 b.g. Fayruz 116 – La Gravotte (FR) (Habitat 134) **66 d**
[2001 83: 8v f8g 8.1m 7.9m 8.3g 8.1g⁶ 7g 8m 8.2m 9.9s 12d⁵ 11.9s Oct 11] fairly useful
handicapper at 4 yrs: on downgrade at most 1m: acts on good to firm and
and good to soft going: sometimes blinkered. *J. G. Given*

PACIFIC PLACE (IRE) 4 gr.g. College Chapel 122 – Kaitlin (IRE) (Salmon Leap **48**
(USA) 131) [2001 60: 5m 5m 6m 6g 5f⁶ 5m⁵ 6m 5d⁶ 6g 5s⁵ 5m 5g⁶ 6f 6m⁵ 7d 6v Oct 16]
good-bodied gelding: poor maiden handicapper: effective at 5f/6f: acts on firm and soft
going: visored (ran poorly) once: has found little: sent to Denmark. *J. S. Goldie*

PACIFIC SHORE (USA) 3 b.f. Gone West (USA) – Youm Jadeed (IRE) 105 **74**
(Sadler's Wells (USA) 132) [2001 8f⁴ 8f³ 10m⁴ 9.2m⁶ Sep 24] quite attractive filly: has a
short action: third foal: closely related to winner in Spain by Machiavellian and half-sister
to 1½m winner Youhadyourwarning (by Warning): dam, French 1¼m/1½m performer,
sister to dam of Derby runner-up City Honours: fair maiden: well below form last 2 starts:
should stay beyond 1m: sold 42,000 gns. *Sir Michael Stoute*

PACIFYC (IRE) 6 b.g. Brief Truce (USA) 126 – Ocean Blue (IRE) 70 (Bluebird –
(USA) 125) [2001 f11g 11.8d 14.1m 17.1g f14g Dec 3] won in Germany in 2000: little
form on Flat in Britain in 2001: stays 1½m: acts on heavy ground and sand: tried visored/
tongue tied last 2 starts: winning selling hurdler. *John A. Harris*

PADDY MCGOON (USA) 6 ch.g. Irish River (FR) 131 – Flame McGoon (USA) –
(Staff Writer (USA)) [2001 52: f12g Jan 15] disappointing maiden: tried blinkered.
S. E. H. Sherwood

PADDY MUL 4 ch.c. Democratic (USA) 101 – My Pretty Niece (Great Nephew 126) **38**
[2001 40: 10m³ 10f Sep 20] sparely-made colt: poor maiden: seems to stay 1¾m: acts on
firm and soft going: visored once in 2000: tongue tied. *W. Storey*

PADDY'S RICE 10 ch.g. Hadeer 118 – Requiem (Song 132) [2001 –§: 7m 8m Jun 2] – §
one-time fair 6f to 1m winner: temperamental nowadays. *A. P. Jones*

PADDYWACK (IRE) 4 b.g. Bigstone (IRE) 126 – Millie's Return (IRE) 71 (Ballad –
Rock 122) [2001 62, a79: f6s f6s³ f6g⁶ f6g f6g Dec 10] small gelding: fair handicapper: **a71 d**
off over 9 months before well held last 2 starts: best at 5f/6f: acts on good to firm going,
good to soft, fibresand and equitrack: blinkered: front runner. *D. W. Chapman*

PAGAN PRINCE 4 br.g. Primo Dominie 121 – Mory Kante (USA) (Icecapade **69**
(USA)) [2001 65: 8s⁴ 8m 8d⁵ 10g⁴ 10g⁵ 9d³ 8.1g* 8m⁶ 9g⁴ Oct 19] leggy gelding: fair
handicapper: won at Sandown (apprentices) in August: gelded after final start: effective
at stiff 1m to 1¼m: acts on soft and good to firm going: consistent. *J. A. R. Toller*

PAGAN PRINCESS 3 b.f. Mujtahid (USA) 118 – Dalu (IRE) 72 (Dancing Brave **54**
(USA) 140) [2001 10m 10m 7.1f 8.2s⁴ 8s⁶ Sep 24] 48,000Y: second foal: half-sister to
4-y-o Hambleden: dam, 1m winner, half-sister to useful Cornwallis Stakes winner
Mubhij (by Mujtahid): modest maiden: may prove best around 1m. *J. A. R. Toller*

PAGEANT 4 br.f. Inchinor 119 – Positive Attitude 82 (Red Sunset 120) [2001 82d, **52**
a62: f8g² f8s f8g f8g³ f9.4g f8g⁵ 8v e10g f7g 7m 8m² 8m² 8f⁶ f8g⁶ 7d 8m² 7.1g⁵ 8f² 7s⁴ **a60 d**
7d f8g⁴ f8g³ Dec 10] rather leggy, useful-looking filly: modest performer at best in 2001:
left Mrs L. Pearce after fourteenth start: stays 8.5f: acts on fibresand, equitrack and
probably any turf going. *J. M. Bradley*

PAGEBOY 12 b.g. Tina's Pet 121 – Edwins' Princess 75 (Owen Dudley 121) [2001 –
42: f7g Jan 4] one-time fairly useful 5f/6f winner: very lightly raced nowadays: sometimes blinkered/visored. *P. C. Haslam*

PAGE NOUVELLE (FR) 3 b.f. Spectrum (IRE) 126 – Page Bleue (Sadler's Wells –
(USA) 132) [2001 80: 12.6m⁴ 9.7m⁵ 14.6m Sep 12] strong, lengthy filly: fairly useful
performer at 2 yrs: little form in 2001: out of depth in Park Hill Stakes at Doncaster final
start: stays 1½m: sold 35,000 gns in December. *B. W. Hills*

PAID UP 3 b.g. Mind Games 121 – Indian Summer 78 (Young Generation 129) [2001 **53**
58: 7v 8d 8s 5m² 5f⁶ 5f 5m 6m 5m 5v⁴ f6s Dec 15] small, sparely-made gelding: modest
maiden handicapper: best at bare 5f: probably acts on any going: blinkered last 2 starts:
usually front runner: none too consistent. *M. W. Easterby*

PAINTED ROOM (USA)   3 ch.c. Woodman (USA) 126 – All At Sea (USA) 124   **93**
(Riverman (USA) 131) [2001 96p: 8d⁵ 8g³ 10.5m⁴ May 26] angular, useful-looking colt:
fairly useful maiden: fifth in Craven Stakes at Newmarket before in frame on same course
and at Haydock (below form, found little): should stay 1¼m: sold 45,000 gns.
H. R. A. Cecil

PAIRING (IRE)   3 ch.g. Rudimentary (USA) 118 – Splicing 82 (Sharpo 132) [2001   **80**
80: 6d p8g f8.5s³ Dec 27] smallish, lengthy gelding: fairly useful performer: off a year
before reappearance: ran well in handicap at Wolverhampton final start: stays 8.5f: acts
on fibresand, best turf run on good ground. *H. Morrison*

PAIRUMANI STAR (IRE)   6 ch.h. Caerleon (USA) 132 – Dawn Star 94 (High Line   **110**
125) [2001 110: 13.4f² 14f⁴ 15d² 16g Aug 2] lengthy horse: smart performer: in frame in
Ormonde Stakes at Chester (10 lengths second to St Expedit), Premio Carlo d'Alessio at
Rome and listed race at Chantilly (beaten head by Generic) in 2001, best effort in last-
named: last in Goodwood Cup final start: unraced on heavy going, acted on any other turf:
blinkered twice at 3 yrs: usually raced prominently: sometimes
ran in snatches, and needed strong handling: to stand at Islanmore Stud, Co. Limerick,
Ireland. *J. L. Dunlop*

PAIYDA   3 b.f. Danehill (USA) 126 – Meadow Pipit (CAN) 113 (Meadowlake (USA))   **–**
[2001 91p: 7.1g⁶ 10g Sep 28] rangy filly: fairly useful winner only start at 2 yrs: well
beaten in minor events in 2001: needs to settle to stay beyond 7f: sold 11,000 gns in
December. *E. A. L. Dunlop*

PALACE AFFAIR   3 ch.f. Pursuit of Love 124 – Palace Street (USA) 103 (Secreto   **112**
(USA) 128) [2001 99: 7d² 7m* 7m⁵ 7m 6m* 7m 6d Aug 19] quite good-topped filly:
smart performer: neck second to Clearing in Free Handicap at Newmarket on reappearance: won listed races at Lingfield (by neck from Pearly Gates) in May and York (by 2½
lengths from Night Haven) in July: well below form in similar events last 2 starts: best at
6f/7f: acts on good to firm and good to soft going: blinkered at 2 yrs: edgy when running
poorly in Jersey Stakes at Royal Ascot fourth outing: tends to carry head awkwardly.
G. B. Balding

PALACEGATE TOUCH   11 gr.g. Petong 126 – Dancing Chimes (London Bells   **59**
(CAN) 109) [2001 56, a71: f6s² e7g⁴ f6g² f6g² f6g⁵ f7g* e6g² f6g* f5g⁴ f7g* f6g⁵ 6m³   **a68**
f7g² 7m² 6m f7g 6m f7g⁴ 6g f7g⁵ 5d p7g f7g* f6g⁵ f6s Dec 21] tall, good-topped gelding:
fair on all-weather, modest on turf: won seller/claimer at Wolverhampton in February/
March and sellers at Southwell in April and December (dead-heated): probably best at
6f/7f: acts on fibresand, equitrack, firm and soft going, probably on polytrack: often
blinkered/visored before 2001: tends to hang left/race with head high: claimer ridden:
very tough, and has won 33 of his 183 career starts. *A. Berry*

PALACE LAKE   2 b.f. (Apr 27) Whittingham (IRE) 104 – Oh Whataknight 85 (Primo   **53**
Dominie 121) [2001 5v f5g⁴ f5g⁴ 5.3m⁵ May 8] 6,000Y: quite good-topped filly: first
foal: dam 2-y-o 5f winner who didn't train on: modest maiden: should have stayed 6f:
acted on fibresand and good to firm going: dead. *N. P. Littmoden*

PALAIS (IRE)   6 b.g. Darshaan 133 – Dance Festival 101 (Nureyev (USA) 131) [2001   **–**
–: f11g f16g f11g f11g Mar 26] seems of little account. *J. L. Harris*

PALAMEDES   2 b.c. (Jan 25) Sadler's Wells (USA) 132 – Kristal Bridge 75 (Kris   **78 p**
135) [2001 7g Oct 4] first foal: dam, maiden who was best around 1¼m, out of Nassau
Stakes and Yorkshire Oaks winner Connaught Bridge: 20/1, eighth of 21 to Millennium
Dragon in maiden at Newmarket, late headway without being knocked about: will be
suited by 1¼m/1½m: sure to improve. *P. W. Harris*

PALANZO (IRE)   3 b.g. Green Desert (USA) 127 – Karpacka (IRE) 99 (Rousillon   **108**
(USA) 133) [2001 101: 7d⁵ 8m⁵ 6m² 6m* 6m² 6m² 6g 6g⁴ 6d⁶ 6v⁴ Oct 26] lengthy
gelding: useful performer: won £32,500 handicap at Newmarket in June by head and a
neck from Type One and Orientor: creditable efforts when in frame in handicaps and
minor events otherwise, beaten short head by Jarn at Yarmouth on fifth start: effective
at 6f, probably at 7f: acts on good to firm and heavy going: blinkered (ran poorly)
penultimate start: slowly away last 2 starts, usually front runner previously. *P. W. Harris*

PALATIAL   3 b.f. Green Desert (USA) 127 – White Palace 80 (Shirley Heights 130)   **101**
[2001 93: 7d 8m² 8f 8g⁵ 7m* 8g⁶ 6d Oct 19] deep-girthed filly: useful performer: won

minor event at Newmarket in September by ¾ length from Gleaming Blade: good 3¼ lengths sixth to Beckett next start, much better effort in listed races on same course after: effective at 7f/1m: acts on good to firm and good to soft going: patiently ridden: genuine. *J. R. Fanshawe*

PALATIAL POISE   3 b.f. Rock Hopper 124 – Kamaress 85 (Kampala 120) [2001   – 10.5d 9m⁶ 8d⁶ 9.9m 10m Sep 1] 600F, 1,600Y: angular filly: fifth foal: dam 5f (at 2 yrs) and 9f winner: seems of little account. *N. Bycroft*

PALAWAN   5 br.g. Polar Falcon (USA) 126 – Krameria 72 (Kris 135) [2001 82: f6g f5g   **77** 5m 5.1f⁵ 5m⁴ 5.7g⁵ 6m³ 5.1m 5m⁴ p6g⁶ p5g⁶ Dec 22] lengthy gelding: fair handicapper: effective at 5f to easy 7f: acts on fibresand, polytrack, firm and soft going: tried visored: often apprentice ridden: consistent. *I. A. Balding*

PALISANDRA (USA)   3 b.f. Chief's Crown (USA) – Placer Queen (Habitat 134)   – [2001 7d 7g 8.3m f12g Jul 20] sturdy filly: half-sister to several winners, including 7-y-o Beyond Calculation and 1m winner Agnes Flemming (by Al Nasr): dam ran 3 times in Britain before winning up to 1¼m in Canada: well held in maidens/handicap. *P. W. Harris*

PALLIUM (IRE)   13 b.g. Try My Best (USA) 130 – Jungle Gardenia (Nonoalco   – (USA) 131) [2001 –: 5d 5f 6g 7s 5f⁶ 7m 7.2g 6m Sep 24] no longer of any account. *D. A. Nolan*

PALOMO (IRE)   2 b. or br.g. (Feb 9) Petardia 113 – Miss Barcelona (IRE) 53 (Mac's   – Imp (USA) 116) [2001 p7g Dec 22] 15,000Y, 14,000 2-y-o: first foal: dam, maiden who probably stayed 1½m, half-sister to Rockfel winner Name of Love and useful performer up to 1¼m Annapurna: 25/1, always outpaced in minor event at Lingfield. *R. M. Beckett*

PALUA   4 b.g. Sri Pekan (USA) 117 – Reticent Bride (IRE) 71 (Shy Groom (USA))   **91 §** [2001 88§: 16s³ 14s 12g 16.2s⁶ 18d² Oct 20] tall, useful-looking gelding: fairly useful maiden handicapper: ridden by 7-lb claimer, very good neck second to stable-companion Distant Prospect in Cesarewitch at Newmarket final start: stays 2¼m: acts on firm and soft going: occasionally blinkered: tends to wander/carry head high: probably ungenuine. *I. A. Balding*

PALVIC LADY   5 b.m. Cotation – Palvic Grey (Kampala 120) [2001 49§: f5g⁶ f6s²   **45 d** f5g f6g f6g f5g 5.2m 5m f6g 5f 7m f5g 5m Jul 31] tall mare: poor performer: on down-grade in 2001, leaving C. Smith after sixth start: stays 6f: acts on soft going and fibresand: usually blinkered/visored: has been slowly away/looked difficult ride. *L. R. James*

PAMELA ANSHAN   4 b.f. Anshan 119 – Have Form (Haveroid 122) [2001 43: f7g   – f9.4g Mar 14] of little account nowadays. *J. Cullinan*

PANAMINT (USA)   3 br.f. Silver Hawk (USA) 123 – Kamsi (USA) (Afleet (CAN))   – [2001 10m 10m 10g Jul 23] second foal: dam, French 9f winner, half-sister to US Grade 1 1¼m winner Vaudeville: little form in maidens. *J. R. Fanshawe*

PANCAKEHILL   2 ch.f. (Mar 7) Sabrehill (USA) 120 – Sawlah (Known Fact (USA)   **63** 135) [2001 6g 7.1m⁶ 7d⁶ Sep 26] quite good-topped filly: half-sister to a winner abroad by Cadeaux Genereux: dam, Irish 2-y-o 5f winner, half-sister to high-class sprinter Sheikh Albadou: modest maiden: will probably stay 1m: swished tail (before and during race) second start. *G. A. Butler*

PANDJOJOE (IRE)   5 b.g. Archway (IRE) 115 – Vital Princess (Prince Sabo 123)   **69** [2001 62: f7g f6g 6s* 7d⁵ 7.6m 6g 6g 6v Oct 16] sturdy gelding: fair handicapper: off 6 months, won at Hamilton in July: well below form last 2 starts: best at 5f/6f: acts on any turf going and fibresand: blinkered once at 4 yrs. *R. A. Fahey*

PANGO   2 ch.g. (May 8) Bluegrass Prince (IRE) 110 – Riverine (Risk Me (FR) 127)   **77** [2001 6m⁶ 7f³ 7s Oct 16] rather unfurnished gelding: fluent mover: second foal: dam, ran twice, out of half-sister to Yorkshire Oaks winner Hellenic, herself dam of very smart 1¼m performer Greek Dance: easily best effort in maidens (fair form) when third to Shifty at Lingfield: hung right final start (gelded after): should stay 1¼m: acts on firm going. *H. Morrison*

PAN JAMMER   3 b.g. Piccolo 121 – Ingerence (FR) (Akarad (FR) 130) [2001 99: 7d   **111** 6g⁴ 6m 7m³ 7m⁵ 6f³ 6m⁵ 6g² Aug 11] strong, smallish gelding: type to carry plenty of condition: smart performer: good efforts in listed race at Epsom (third to Jentzen), Jersey Stakes at Royal Ascot (1¾ lengths fifth to Mozart), Chipchase Stakes at Newcastle (¾-length third to Volata) and valuable conditions event at Ascot (4 lengths second to Orientor): effective at 6f/7f: acts on firm going, has won on good to soft: tends to get behind (sometimes slowly away): sent to Hong Kong. *M. R. Channon*

PANJANDRUM 3 b.g. Polar Falcon (USA) 126 – Rengaine (FR) (Music Boy 124) [2001 f5g e5g f5g* 5g f5g* 6m⁶ 6.1f² 5m 5.1g f6g⁴ f6g⁶ f5g⁶ f5s* Dec 27] 16,000Y: lengthy, sparely-made gelding: seventh living foal: half-brother to 3 winners, notably smart 5f (at 2 yrs) to 1m (Prix Chloe) winner Holly Golightly (by Robellino): dam French 8.5f and 11f winner: fair on all-weather, modest on turf: won claimer at Southwell in April, seller at Wolverhampton (then left P. Cole) in May and claimer at latter track in December: will prove best at 5f/sharp 6f: acts on fibresand and firm going: effective visored or not: none too consistent. *P. D. Evans* **54 + a69**

PANNA 3 b.f. Polish Precedent (USA) 131 – Gull Nook 120 (Mill Reef (USA) 141) [2001 83p: 8g 8.3g² 10m* 11.9m² Aug 23] quite attractive filly: useful performer, lightly raced: won handicap at Ascot in July by 6 lengths: further marked improvement when neck second to Inchiri in listed race at York in August, leading over 1f out but caught near line: better at 1½m than shorter: acts on good to firm going. *G. Wragg* **106**

PANOORAS LORD (IRE) 7 b.g. Topanoora 118 – Ladyship 76 (Windjammer (USA)) [2001 –: 10s⁵ 12.3s 10f 10f 10m 16m 8m 9.9m² 9.2g 12m 11.9s Oct 11] stocky gelding: seemingly poor maiden: appears to stay 1¼m. *J. S. Wainwright* **41 ?**

PANTAR (IRE) 6 b.g. Shirley Heights 130 – Spring Daffodil 97 (Pharly (FR) 130) [2001 104: f8.5g 8v 8.1v³ 8s 8m³ 10m² 10g* 10m⁴ 10.4m 9.9m⁶ 7.9m 9m³ 9g⁶ Oct 6] rangy gelding: useful handicapper: won at Sandown in June: several other creditable efforts, including second in Zetland Gold Cup at Redcar and fourth to Ulundi in Tote Exacta Stakes at Sandown and in Cambridgeshire at Newmarket (short of room, finished strongly) final start: seems best around 9f/1¼m: acts on fibresand and any turf going: sometimes blinkered, only on reappearance in 2001: usually held up: consistent: sent to USA. *I. A. Balding* **103**

PANTS 2 b.f. (Mar 14) Pivotal 124 – Queenbird 90 (Warning 136) [2001 6g⁴ 6g³ 6.1g³ 6.1d⁴ 6m 6m 8s⁶ Sep 30] 1,800Y: sparely-made filly: third foal: half-sister to 3-y-o Temper Tantrum: dam, 2-y-o 5f to 7f winner, not one to trust implicitly: fair maiden: well below form last 3 starts: likely to prove best at 6f/7f: acts on good to soft ground: has hung/been slowly away. *Andrew Reid* **78 d**

PAOLINI (GER) 4 ch.c. Lando (GER) 128 – Prairie Darling (Stanford 121§) [2001 116: 10m* 12g* 10s³ 12d⁴ 12g² 12f Nov 25] very smart performer: won 2 Group 1s in 2001, Premio Presidente della Repubblica at Rome (by 1½ lengths from Kutub) in May and Gran Premio di Milano (by short head from Ela Athena) following month: creditable 3½ lengths fourth to Morshdi in Grosser Preis von Baden before very good ½-length second to Mutamam in Canadian International at Woodbine, though attempted to bite winner close home: always behind in Japan Cup at Tokyo final start: stays 1½m: acts on good to firm going, not at best on soft. *A. Wohler, Germany* **121**

PAPAGENA (USA) 4 b. or br.f. Robellino (USA) 127 – Morning Crown (USA) (Chief's Crown (USA)) [2001 53: f12g f12g f11g⁶ Feb 2] small filly: has a round action: modest maiden at 3 yrs: well held in 2001: usually blinkered: sent to USA. *C. W. Thornton* **–**

PAPA MIO 2 br.f. (Mar 11) Ventiquattrofogli (IRE) 118 – Judys Girl (IRE) (Simply Great (FR) 122) [2001 5v 5d⁶ f5g³ 6m³ 7g 8m Sep 11] 2,200Y: angular filly: sixth foal: half-sister to 1996 2-y-o 7f winner who stayed 1½m Grate Times (by Timeless Times): dam of little account: poor maiden: stays 6f: acts on good to firm ground and fibresand: sent to Holland. *M. W. Easterby* **47**

PAPER CHASE (FR) 2 ch.f. (Mar 9) Machiavellian (USA) 123 – Papering (IRE) 114 (Shaadi (USA) 126) [2001 7g² 7g Aug 2] close-coupled, rather sparely-made filly: first foal: dam 7f (at 2 yrs) to 11f winner who was second in Yorkshire Oaks: better effort in maidens (fair form) when short-headed by Kasamba at Newmarket, drifting left: wearing crossed noseband, well-held favourite at Goodwood: should stay at least 1m: joined H-A. Pantall in France. *D. R. Loder* **78**

PAPERWEIGHT 5 b.m. In The Wings 128 – Crystal Reay 59 (Sovereign Dancer (USA)) [2001 64, a74: e10g² f9.4s⁶ f9.4s⁴ f9.4g⁴ f9.4g² f11g 9.7v 11.6g f12g² **a70** **–**

Jun 8] fair handicapper: stays 1½m: acts on fibresand/equitrack, well held only turf start in 2001: tried blinkered/visored earlier in career: sometimes runs lazily. *Miss K. M. George*

PAPINGO 3 b.f. Charnwood Forest (IRE) 125 – Maracuja (USA) (Riverman (USA) – 131) [2001 8f Jul 9] 8,000F: tall filly: sixth foal: half-sister to 3 winners, including useful German performer up to 1¾m Massada (by Most Welcome) and 7-y-o Chakra: dam, French 2-y-o 1m winner, from very good family of Wolfhound and A P Indy: well behind in maiden at Ripon. *K. R. Burke*

PAPI SPECIAL (IRE) 4 b.g. Tragic Role (USA) – Practical 95 (Ballymore 123) 50 [2001 62: 16v² 14d⁶ 13d 13.1m³ 13d⁵ 14m³ 16m⁶ 14f⁶ 18m 16f Jul 9] close-coupled, good-bodied gelding: poor mover: modest handicapper: stays 2m: acts on any turf going: usually visored/blinkered. *I. Semple*

PARACHUTE 2 ch.g. (Feb 12) Hector Protector (USA) 124 – Shortfall 103 (Last 62 p Tycoon 131) [2001 7d 7s⁶ 6v 6d Oct 30] 100,000Y: big, strong, lengthy gelding: has scope: second foal: half-brother to 3-y-o Contraband: dam, 1¼m/1½m performer who later won in USA, daughter of St Simon Stakes winner Upend from family of Royal Gait: modest form in maidens/nursery: type to do fair bit better at 1¼m/1½m as 3-y-o. *Sir Mark Prescott*

PARADE (IRE) 3 ch.g. Lycius (USA) 124 – Cheviot Amble (IRE) 105 (Pennine Walk 69 120) [2001 f7s² f7g³ Feb 15] IR 24,000F, IR 62,000Y: fourth foal: half-brother to smart 1m/1¼m winner Amalia (by Danehill): dam Irish 6f to 1¼m winner: placed in maidens at Wolverhampton, slightly better effort (fair form) on debut: should be suited by at least 1m: sold 5,400 gns. *W. J. Haggas*

PARADISE BLUE (IRE) 3 gr.f. Bluebird (USA) 125 – Safka (USA) 104 (Irish 63 River (FR) 131) [2001 7d 6g⁴ 6g⁵ 7g 7g 6.1d Sep 21] 63,000Y: half-sister to several winners, including smart 6f (at 2 yrs) and 1m winner Speedfit Too (by Scenic), also winner in UAE, and useful Irish 1994 2-y-o 7f winner Sannkaya (by Soviet Star): dam, 2-y-o 5f winner, half-sister to smart performer up to 1m Safawan: modest maiden: stays 7f: raced only on good/good to soft going: sold 7,800 gns in December. *R. Hannon*

PARADISE GARDEN (USA) 4 b.g. Septieme Ciel (USA) 123 – Water Course 44 + (USA) (Irish River (FR) 131) [2001 91d: 12d 11.4g 10.9d* 9g 16s 14.1s Nov 5] tall gelding: fluent mover: formerly useful: poor form when winning seller at Ayr (left M. Johnston) in July: stays 11f: acts on good to soft going, lightly raced on firmer than good. *P. L. Clinton*

PARADISE YANGSHUO 4 b.f. Whittingham (IRE) 104 – Poly Static (IRE) 43 ? (Statoblest 120) [2001 49: a6g* a6g² a6g³ a6g⁴ a8g a8g⁶ a6g⁵ a6g³ a6g* a6g³ a6g³ a6g⁴ f6g f8g Dec 17] angular filly: won handicap in January and minor event in July, both at Mijas: left P. Haley in Spain and off 4 months before well held at Southwell final 2 starts: best at 5f/6f: acts on soft and firm going, and on sand. *D. Nicholls*

PARADISO PARADIS (IRE) 3 b.f. Tagula (IRE) 116 – Shanamara (IRE) 77 – (Shernazar 131) [2001 8.3g 7g⁶ Aug 20] 12,000Y: second foal: dam Irish 2m winner: well held in maidens: hung left on debut. *J. A. Osborne*

PARA GLIDER (FR) 3 br.c. Jeune Homme (USA) 120 – Idee Folle (FR) (Crystal 87 Palace (FR) 132) [2001 80p: f9.4g³ e8s² 8.3s³ f8g* 8.1g⁴ 8f 10v² 10.3v⁴ Oct 26] leggy, rather unfurnished colt: fairly useful handicapper: won at Southwell in April: good second at Windsor, best effort after: stays 1¼m: acts on fibresand, equitrack and heavy going (well below form on firm): sent to UAE. *G. C. Bravery*

PARAGON OF VIRTUE 4 ch.g. Cadeaux Genereux 131 – Madame Dubois 121 84 (Legend of France (USA) 124) [2001 88: 8d p10g Dec 4] lengthy, quite attractive gelding: good walker: fairly useful maiden: ran creditably in handicap at Lingfield final start: stays 1¼m: acts on polytrack, soft and good to firm ground. *P. Mitchell*

PARASOL (IRE) 2 br.c. (Mar 17) Halling (USA) 133 – Bunting 102 (Shaadi (USA) 107 126) [2001 6g* 7m² 8d⁴ 8s³ 7d⁶ Oct 20] big, rangy colt: has scope: usually takes the eye: easy mover: third foal: half-brother to 3-y-o Mot Juste and 4-y-o Sudra: dam, 1m (at 2 yrs)/1¼m winner, third in Italian Oaks: useful performer: first past post in maiden at Haydock in June and listed race at Deauville (made all, disqualified and placed fourth for causing interference) in August: good efforts when 2½ lengths third to Mutinyon-

Mohammed Al Nabouda's "Parasol"

thebounty in Royal Lodge Stakes at Ascot and 3 lengths sixth to Rock of Gibraltar in Dewhurst Stakes at Newmarket: should stay 1¼m: acts on soft and good to firm going: tends to hang under pressure: joined Godolphin. *M. R. Channon*

PARDISHAR (IRE) 3 b.c. Kahyasi 130 – Parapa (IRE) (Akarad (FR) 130) [2001 **105** 10g* 9g³ 11.9s⁴ Aug 18] fourth foal: half-brother to useful French/US 1m/1¼m winner Porbandar (by Shahrastani): dam French 1m winner: useful performer: won maiden at Sandown in July: staying-on 3½ lengths third to Slickly there next time, better effort in 5-runner minor events after (soon off bridle and edged left final start): should stay 1½m: sold 40,000 gns. *Sir Michael Stoute*

PARIS FLASH (IRE) 2 gr.f. (Apr 5) Paris House 123 – Flash Donna (USA) 70 (Well **46** Decorated (USA)) [2001 7.1v 7g Oct 19] IR 4,600Y: leggy filly: half-sister to 3 winners, including fairly useful 5f (at 2 yrs) to 9f winner Second Chance (by Digamist), later winner in Canada: dam maiden best at 7f: better effort (poor form) when seventh of 21 in claimer at Redcar second start: should stay 1m. *A. B. Mulholland*

PARISIAN EIRE (IRE) 2 gr.g. (Apr 27) Paris House 123 – La Fille de Feu (Never **–** So Bold 135) [2001 5m 6g Aug 30] third foal: dam unraced: no form in maidens. *M. R. Channon*

PARISIAN ELEGANCE 2 b.f. (Feb 19) Zilzal (USA) 137 – Tshusick 81 (Dancing **90** Brave (USA) 140) [2001 5s⁴ f5g* 5m* 5m 6m³ 6m³ 6m⁶ 5.5d 6f Sep 21] sturdy, good-quartered filly: third foal: half-sister to 4-y-o Tribal Prince and 3-y-o Liberty Bound: dam, 7f winner, out of useful sprinter Infanta Real: fairly useful performer: won maiden at Southwell in April and minor event at Thirsk in May: ran creditably when third in listed race at Newbury and Princess Margaret Stakes at Ascot (6¾ lengths behind

Leggy Lou) and when close seventh of 8 in Prix d'Arenberg at Chantilly on eighth start: stays 6f: acts on soft going, good to firm and fibresand. *R. M. H. Cowell*

PARISIAN LADY (IRE)   6 b.m. Paris House 123 – Mia Gigi (Hard Fought 125)   **45** [2001 53, a58: 11.8f 12m⁴ 12.1m 10g Jul 17] tall, rather shallow-girthed mare: poor handicapper: stays easy 1½m: acts on fibresand, equitrack and firm going, possibly not on soft: tried blinkered earlier in career: tends to get behind. *A. G. Newcombe*

PARISIENNE HILL   5 b.m. Lapierre 119 – Snarry Hill 34 (Vitiges (FR) 132) [2001   **–** –: 12v 14.1v 10s 8.1m 10f 8m 10.3f³ 12.4m 10.5d 9f 8m 8d 9.9m⁶ 8.9m 8f 7g Oct 6] probably of little account nowadays. *B. W. Murray*

PARISIEN STAR (IRE)   5 ch.g. Paris House 123 – Auction Maid (IRE) (Auction   **94** Ring (USA) 123) [2001 97: 7d 8m⁵ 10.1m² 8m 10.4m 9.9m² 8g 8.1s⁴ 10.1d⁴ 9m⁵ 10v Nov 8] leggy gelding: poor mover: fairly useful handicapper: second at Epsom and Goodwood in summer: effective at 1m/easy 1¼m: ran poorly on heavy going final start, acts on any other turf: usually held up: tough and consistent. *N. Hamilton*

PARIS KNIGHT (IRE)   3 b.g. Paris House 123 – Bykova (Petoski 135) [2001 f6g⁵   **–** 6m f6g⁶ 7s 6m 7g 7.5m 10v Oct 29] IR 1,900F, IR 1,500Y: third foal: closely related to winner abroad by Petardia: dam unraced: little form: trained prior to final start by A. Berry: stays 6f: sometimes slowly away. *B. J. Llewellyn*

PARK CITY   2 b.c. (Jan 22) Slip Anchor 136 – Cryptal (Persian Bold 123) [2001 7m   **–** f8s Dec 21] 8,000F: poor mover: third foal: dam unraced: well held in maidens at York and Southwell (slowly away). *P. Howling*

PARKER   4 b.g. Magic Ring (IRE) 115 – Miss Loving 89 (Northfields (USA)) [2001   **86** 78: e8g* f7s⁵ e8g³ f7g⁵ e8g² 8.1m 7f* 7m² 7.6m 7.1g 7.6g Sep 11] neat gelding: fluent   **a81** mover: fairly useful performer: won maiden at Lingfield in January and handicap at Chester in June: well below form in handicaps last 3 starts: stays easy 1m: acts on fibresand, equitrack, firm and good to soft going. *B. Palling*

PARKSIDE (IRE)   5 b.g. Common Grounds 118 – Warg (Dancing Brave (USA) 140)   **–** [2001 79d: 10g May 4] one-time fairly useful performer: has lost his form. *W. R. Muir*

PARKSIDE PROPHECY   3 ch.g. Aragon 118 – Fairgroundprincess 46 (Kalaglow   **–** 132) [2001 53: f8g 8.2f 7m⁶ 8m Jul 21] well held in sellers in 2001. *M. R. Channon*

PARKSIDE PROSPECT   4 b.f. Piccolo 121 – Banner (USA) 75 (Known Fact   **–** (USA) 135) [2001 49: e6g e7g⁵ e6g Feb 7] one-time fair 5f/6f winner: has lost her form: tried blinkered. *E. A. Wheeler*

PARKSIDE PURSUIT   3 b.g. Pursuit of Love 124 – Ivory Bride 86 (Domynsky 110)   **75** [2001 67: 7v 6g 5.7g* 5.7f* 6d³ 5m³ 6d 5.1f* 5m 5m⁵ 5s 6s f6g f5g Nov 17] lengthy,   **a–** dipped-backed gelding: fair performer: won seller and minor event in June and claimer (left M. Channon) in July, all at Bath: best at 5f/6f: acts on firm ground, possibly not on soft (below form both runs on fibresand). *J. M. Bradley*

PARNDON BELLE   2 ch.f. (Feb 3) Clan of Roses – Joara (FR) (Radetzky 123) [2001   **–** 5m 7g Aug 24] third reported foal: dam, lightly raced on Flat/winning hurdler, sister to useful but ungenuine stayer Petrizzo: no sign of ability in claimer/seller. *J. S. Wainwright*

PARSIFAL   2 b.c. (Mar 23) Sadler's Wells (USA) 132 – Moss (USA) (Woodman   **85** (USA) 126) [2001 8d 8s Oct 31] 170,000F, IR 160,000Y: rangy colt: has scope: has a quick action: brother to 3-y-o Elrehaan and half-brother to 4-y-o Rousing Thunder: dam once-raced half-sister to high-class sprinter Committed from very good family: fairly useful form when seventh of 20 to Music Club in maiden at Newmarket, late headway after slow start: disappointing joint favourite in similar event at Yarmouth: will be suited by 1¼m/1½m. *L. M. Cumani*

PARTING SHOT   3 b.g. Young Ern 120 – Tribal Lady 80 (Absalom 128) [2001 64:   **71** 8v² 7g 7.5m* 8m⁴ 7m² 6f 7m⁶ 7f⁴ 7m² 7.2m 8g Oct 6] quite good-topped gelding: fair performer: won maiden at Beverley in May: creditable efforts in handicaps/minor event after until last 2 starts: best at 7f/1m: acts on any turf going: usually races prominently. *T. D. Easterby*

PARTNER (IRE)   3 b.g. Turtle Island (IRE) 123 – Sorara (Aragon 118) [2001 8.1m   **–** 8.2v f7g 10v Oct 29] 7,200F, 12,000Y: first foal: dam once-raced half-sister to dam of very smart miler Revoque: well held in maidens/seller: dead. *C. E. Brittain*

PARTY CHARMER   3 b.f. Charmer 123 – Party Game 70 (Red Alert 127) [2001 83:   **–** 6g 8g 5d 7s Nov 10] tall, good-topped filly: has a round action: fairly useful 5f winner at

2 yrs: reportedly injured in spring, and well beaten in 4 starts in 2001 (pulled up lame final one). *C. E. Brittain*

PARTY PLOY 3 b.g. Deploy 131 – Party Treat (IRE) 69 (Millfontaine 114) [2001 62: **74** 8.3s 11.6g* 11.6d³ 12.3m⁴ 12.3f⁵ 12g 12d³ f12g² 14.1s³ p12g² f12s Dec 15] small gelding: poor mover: fair performer: won handicap at Windsor in May: creditable efforts after when in frame: barely stays 1¾m when conditions are testing: acts on soft going, good to firm and fibresand/polytrack: reportedly broke blood vessel sixth start. *K. R. Burke*

PARTYTIME (IRE) 2 ch.f. (Feb 26) Tagula (IRE) 116 – Camarat 69 (Ahonoora 122) **91** [2001 5g² 5.2s³ 5f* 5d⁴ 5m 5.2m 6g² 5d Oct 13] IR 25,000Y: rather sparely-made filly: fifth living foal: half-sister to 1996 2-y-o 6f winner Colombia (by Mujtahid) and a winner in Austria by Polish Patriot: dam, 9f winner, half-sister to Park Hill winner Trampship: fairly useful performer: made all in maiden at Leicester in May and minor event at Salisbury in June: best effort when length second of 29 to Bella Chica in valuable sales race at the Curragh (reportedly returned with a gash on off-hind hoof): ran poorly final start: should stay 7f: acts on firm and good to soft ground: sold 30,000 gns. *R. Hannon*

PARVENUE (FR) 3 b.f. Ezzoud (IRE) 126 – Patria (USA) 76 (Mr Prospector (USA)) – [2001 79: 8.1v⁵ Apr 25] small filly: fair 6f winner at 2 yrs: well beaten in minor event at Warwick only start in 2001: sold 4,000 gns in December. *E. A. L. Dunlop*

PASADA LLAMADA 2 b.g. (Feb 9) College Chapel 122 – First Play 59 (Primo – Dominie 121) [2001 5g³ 6m 5m Sep 30] 7,000F, 8,000Y: workmanlike gelding: fourth foal: half-brother to a winner in Greece by Emarati: dam 6f winner out of sister to high-class French sprinter Kind Music: no form in minor event/maidens: looked difficult ride final start. *S. E. Kettlewell*

PAS DE PROBLEME (IRE) 5 ch.g. Ela-Mana-Mou 132 – Torriglia (USA) (Nijinsky **61** (CAN) 138) [2001 71: 10s⁶ 10g 10d⁴ 10m³ 9.9d⁶ f11g 11d Oct 30] lengthy gelding: modest handicapper: effective at 1¼m/easy 1½m: acts on good to firm and heavy going: tends to swish tail in preliminaries/get on toes: usually races prominently: sold 700 gns. *J. G. Portman*

PAS DE SURPRISE 3 b.g. Dancing Spree (USA) – Supreme Rose 95 (Frimley Park **68** 109) [2001 –: 10.2d⁵ 10g 8.3g⁵ 8.1g 8m⁶ 8.5d 8m 7.6m f11g⁶ Oct 1] fair maiden: well below form last 5 starts: may prove best around 1m: acts on good to soft ground: blinkered penultimate start. *J. G. Portman*

PASITHEA (IRE) 3 b.f. Celtic Swing 138 – Midnight's Reward 84 (Night Shift **90** (USA)) [2001 82: 8v⁴ 8d 7s³ 8m³ 8m⁴ 8s⁴ 9.9s² 11.9s* 12g 10.5v⁴ 11.9s 12s Nov 10] leggy, useful-looking filly: has a quick action: fairly useful handicapper: won at Haydock in September: several other creditable efforts: better at 1¼m/1½m than shorter: has form on good to firm going, very best efforts on soft/heavy: reliable. *T. D. Easterby*

PASO DOBLE 3 b.g. Dancing Spree (USA) – Delta Tempo (IRE) (Bluebird (USA) **77** 125) [2001 79: 9s 7.1m 7f³ 8.1f³ Jun 27] fair maiden handicapper: stays 1m: acts on firm going: usually races prominently. *B. R. Millman*

PASSERINE 3 b.f. Distant Relative 128 – Oare Sparrow 75 (Night Shift (USA)) [2001 **57 d** 5v⁶ 6g³ 6m⁴ 5f 5f⁶ f6g 6d f6g f7g Nov 12] smallish, good-topped filly: second foal: dam 6f/7f winner: modest maiden at best: little form after third start: stays 6f: acts on good to firm going: blinkered last 2 outings. *J. R. Weymes*

PASSIMO (GER) 4 ch.c. Lomitas 129 – Partida (GER) (Acatenango (GER) 127) **116** [2001 12g 11g⁴ 11g³ 12d⁴ 12d⁵ 12s Oct 21] approx. 24,000Y in Germany: second foal: half-brother to German 1999 2-y-o 7f winner Parla (by Lagunas): dam, German 2-y-o 7f winner, half-sister to Preis der Diana winner Padang: smart performer: trained by W. Figge at 3 yrs, winning maiden and handicap at Munich, national listed race at Baden-Baden and handicap at Cologne: progressed again in 2001, best efforts when 2½ lengths fourth to Sabiango in Credit Suisse Private Banking Pokal at Cologne and 5½ lengths fifth to Morshdi in Grosser Preis von Baden fourth/fifth outings: tailed off in Gran Premio del Jockey Club at Milan final start: stays 1½m: acts on heavy ground. *G. Kussatz, Germany*

PASSING GLANCE 2 b.c. (Mar 11) Polar Falcon (USA) 126 – Spurned (USA) 91 **94 p** (Robellino (USA) 127) [2001 6m⁵ 7m* 7m³ Jul 21] tall, unfurnished colt: half-brother to several winners, notably smart 7f/1m (at 2 yrs) winner Hidden Meadow (by Selkirk) and 6-y-o Scorned: dam 2-y-o 7f winner who stayed 1¼m: fairly useful form: won maiden at Salisbury in June by 2 lengths from Harnour, allowed to stride on after failing to settle first 2f: respectable 5¼ lengths third of 5 to Dulcet Spear in minor event at Newbury: will need to settle to stay 1m: type to make a better 3-y-o. *I. A. Balding*

PASSION FOR LIFE   8 br.g. Charmer 123 – Party Game 70 (Red Alert 127) [2001 95: 6m 6m 6g 5g 6g³ 6g 6d* 6v 6d⁶ 7s Oct 31] good-topped gelding: unimpressive mover: fairly useful handicapper: made all at Salisbury in October: seems best at 6f on good going or softer nowadays: tried blinkered earlier in career: needs to dominate (has downed tools): unreliable. *J. Akehurst*   **86 §**

PASTEL   2 ch.f. (Apr 11) Lion Cavern (USA) 117 – Dancing Spirit (IRE) 72 (Ahonoora 122) [2001 5g² 5d² 5m* 5m⁶ 6m² 6m² 5.2m² 6m⁵ 6.5g Sep 28] close-coupled filly: has a quick action: fifth foal: half-sister to 3 winners, including 1m winner Hazy Heights (by Shirley Heights) and fairly useful 6f (including at 2 yrs) and 1m (in Spain) winner Beware (by Warning): dam, 6f winner, sister to smart filly up to 1¼m Feminine Wiles: useful performer: made all in maiden at Goodwood (blinkered) in May: runner-up in listed races at Newmarket and Newbury and Princess Margaret Stakes at Ascot (beaten 5 lengths by Leggy Lou) fifth to seventh starts: lacklustre efforts last 2 outings: effective at 5f/6f: yet to race on extremes of going: races prominently. *B. J. Meehan*   **95**

PASTICHE   7 b.m. Kylian (USA) – Titian Beauty (Auction Ring (USA) 123) [2001 15.4m 11.5g 10m Sep 4] one-time modest 1m winner: produced a foal in 1999: no form in 3 handicaps in 2001. *Mrs L. C. Jewell*   **–**

PASTICHIO MEDLEY   2 b.c. (Mar 24) Celtic Swing 138 – Blue Nile (IRE) 70 (Bluebird (USA) 125) [2001 6m 7.5f⁵ 7g Aug 13] 23,000Y: lengthy colt: has scope: third foal: half-brother to 3-y-o Gone Too Far: dam, 1¼m winner, half-sister to smart 1¼m performer Revelation: only a little sign of ability in minor event/maidens: blinkered final start: dead. *T. D. Easterby*   **–**

PATAVELLIAN (IRE)   3 b.g. Machiavellian (USA) 123 – Alessia 91 (Caerleon (USA) 132) [2001 10g 10.5d³ 9g² 8g 8g 7d Nov 3] tall, sparely-made gelding: first foal: dam, 2-y-o 7f winner who stayed 1¼m, sister to Park Hill winner Casey: fair maiden: free-going sort, should prove at least as effective at 7f as 1m/9f: raced only on good/good to soft going. *W. R. Muir*   **71**

PATH OF HONOUR (IRE)   2 b.f. (Jan 31) Marju (IRE) 127 – Zorilla (Belmez (USA) 131) [2001 8.1v 7d f6g Oct 18] IR 18,000Y: first foal: dam, French 2-y-o 1m winner, out of half-sister to dam of very smart 1¼m performer Sabrehill: well held in maidens. *M. Johnston*   **–**

PATIENTES VIRTIS   2 ch.f. (Mar 18) Lion Cavern (USA) 117 – Alzianah 102 (Alzao (USA) 117) [2001 5s Oct 5] 14,000Y: third foal: sister to 3-y-o Leozian and half-sister to 4-y-o Waffles of Amin: dam 5f/6f winner, including at 2 yrs: 14/1 and green, well held in maiden at Lingfield. *Miss Gay Kelleway*   **–**

PATRICIAN FOX (IRE)   3 b.f. Nicolotte 118 – Peace Mission (Dunbeath (USA) 127) [2001 55, a50: 5.1v* f5g 6s⁴ 6d 5f* 5g⁵ 5.1m 6d 5g 5g 5s 6.1d Sep 21] rather unfurnished filly: unimpressive mover: fair handicapper: won at Nottingham in April and Beverley in June: lost form later on: stays 6f: acts on any turf going, probably on fibresand: visored final start. *J. J. Quinn*   **67 §** **a– §**

PATRICIA PHILOMENA (IRE)   3 br.f. Prince of Birds (USA) 121 – Jeewan 82 (Touching Wood (USA) 127) [2001 7.5m³ 7g³ 7g² 7f⁵ 7.5m Aug 26] 1,100Y: leggy, close-coupled filly: fifth reported foal: half-sister to 7f to 1¼m winner Harry Browne (by Al Hareb) and 6f winner Bello Gallico (by Gallic League): dam 1½m winner: modest maiden: ran poorly in claimer final start: raced only around 7f on good going or firmer. *T. D. Barron*   **59**

PATRINGTON BOY   8 b.g. Sayf El Arab (USA) 127 – Gunnard 62 (Gunner B 126) [2001 7.1m Aug 27] probably of no account. *G. T. Gaines*   **–**

PATRITA PARK   7 br.m. Flying Tyke 90 – Bellinote (FR) 71 (Noir Et Or 125) [2001 44: 10g Jul 10] small mare: poor handicapper: stays easy 1¾m: acts on good to firm ground, good to soft and fibresand: usually held up. *A. Smith*   **45**

PATRIVALOR (USA)   3 b.c. Diesis 133 – False Image (USA) 79 (Danzig (USA)) [2001 7d 8g 8.3g 8f³ 9.9s f9.4g Nov 21] $100,000Y: sturdy colt: sixth living foal: closely related to winner in Italy by Trempolino and half-brother to 2 winners abroad, including French winner up to 1¼m (ungenuine in Britain) Antarctictern (by Arctic Tern): dam winner up to 7f in USA at 4 yrs: modest maiden: form only when third in handicap at Musselburgh: left L. Cumani before final start: should stay 1¼m: acts on firm going. *M. Dods*   **57**

PATSY CULSYTH 6 b.m. Tragic Role (USA) – Regal Salute 68 (Dara Monarch 128) **52** [2001 50: f6g f7g⁶ 6.1v⁴ 5s³ 7m² 6m 7.5f³ 6g* 7d³ 8m² 6f⁵ 6v Oct 16] useful-looking **a–** mare: modest performer: won seller at Newcastle in July: effective at testing 5f to easy 1m: acts on any turf going, well held on fibresand: usually visored. *Don Enrico Incisa*

PATSY'S DOUBLE 3 b.g. Emarati (USA) 74 – Jungle Rose 90 (Shirley Heights 130) **112** [2001 106: 7d⁵ 8g 7m 7.3m³ 6g* 6f⁵ 7.3f² 6g 6v Oct 26] tall, leggy, useful-looking gelding: unimpressive mover: smart performer: won handicap at Leicester in August by ½ length from Rasoum: creditable efforts otherwise only when beaten ¾ length in minor event at Newbury (third to Umistim) and listed race at Newbury (second behind Welcome Friend): effective at 6f/7f (twelfth in 2000 Guineas at 1m): acts on firm and good to soft going: tends to sweat: races prominently: gelded after final outing. *M. Blanshard*

PATSY STONE 5 b.m. Jester 119 – Third Dam (Slip Anchor 136) [2001 77, a–: 7.1v **70** 7g⁵ 8.1m 8.5m 8.3d⁶ 8f Jun 27] leggy, sparely-made mare: poor mover: fair handicapper: **a–** stays 1m: acts on soft and good to firm going: sometimes slowly away: held up. *M. Kettle*

PAT THE BUILDER (IRE) 3 b.g. Common Grounds 118 – Demoiselle (Midyan **51** (USA) 124) [2001 56: e5g* e5g f5g⁴ f5g⁶ e7g 5f Jul 2] modest performer: made all in seller at Lingfield in January: below form after: stays easy 6f: acts on fibresand, equitrack and firm going: visored (poor effort) final 2-y-o start: sold 800 gns. *K. R. Burke*

PAULA'S PRIDE 3 ch.f. Pivotal 124 – Sharp Top 62 (Sharpo 132) [2001 71: 9.9m³ **74 d** 10d³ 10m 8.1s⁶ 8f² 10g⁵ 9.7g⁶ 7.6g⁶ 8s Oct 3] strong filly: fair performer: well below form last 3 starts: stays 1¼m: acts on firm and soft going: blinkered (ran poorly) fourth start: sometimes finds little. *J. R. Best*

PAWN BROKER 4 ch.c. Selkirk (USA) 129 – Dime Bag 87 (High Line 125) [2001 **116 §** 116: 10s² 10v³ 9.9m³ 10m³ Jun 27] tall, leggy, angular colt: smart performer: good head second to Border Arrow in listed race at Kempton in April: third after in Gordon Richards Stakes at Sandown (beaten 5½ lengths by Island House) and races at Goodwood (to Mubtaker) and Kempton (to Blue Gold): effective at 1¼m/1½m: acts on any going: tends to find little: blinkered last 2 starts: not one to trust implicitly. *J. L. Dunlop*

PAWN IN LIFE (IRE) 3 b.g. Midhish 109 – Lady-Mumtaz (Martin John) [2001 52: **67 +** f6g* f6g f6g⁴ p6g⁶ Dec 19] lengthy gelding: fair handicapper, lightly raced: won at Southwell in February (off course nearly 8 months after) and Lingfield in December: stays 6f: acts on fibresand and polytrack. *T. D. Barron*

PAX 4 ch.g. Brief Truce (USA) 126 – Child's Play (USA) (Sharpen Up 127) [2001 85: **–** 6g 7m 8.3g 8m 9g⁵ 8m 7m 8d Oct 15] tall gelding: one-time fairly useful 6f winner: showed little in 2001 (blinkered once). *J. W. Payne*

PAYS D'AMOUR (IRE) 4 b.c. Pursuit of Love 124 – Lady of The Land 75 (Wollow **94** 132) [2001 96: 7s⁶ 6s² 6g 7m³ 6m⁴ 6g 6g 7d 6m 6g³ 7s p7g Nov 24] strong colt: unimpressive mover: fairly useful handicapper: best effort in 2001 when third in Bunbury Cup at Newmarket on fourth start: best at 6f/7f: acts on firm and soft going: usually leads: none too consistent. *R. Hannon*

PAY THE SILVER 3 gr.g. Petong 126 – Marjorie's Memory (IRE) 76 (Fairy King **80** (USA)) [2001 70: f8.5g⁶ 9m² 9m² 8.1g 9.2m 10.1s⁵ 10.1g* 11m p10g f9.4g p10g³ p12g **a75** Dec 19] close-coupled, good-bodied gelding: fairly useful handicapper on turf, fair on all-weather: won at Epsom in September: stays easy 1¼m: acts on soft and good to firm ground and polytrack: sometimes races too freely. *A. P. Jarvis*

PAY TIME 2 ch.f. (Feb 22) Timeless Times (USA) 99 – Payvashooz 78 (Ballacashtal **58** (CAN)) [2001 f5g² f5g⁴ Dec 3] 500Y: sixth foal: dam 5f (at 2 yrs) to 7f winner who stayed 1m: modest form in maidens at Southwell: should stay 6f: slowly away on debut. *M. Brittain*

PAY TO PLAY 3 br.g. Puissance 110 – Times of Times (IRE) 78 (Distinctly North **–** (USA) 115) [2001 e5g Feb 7] first foal: dam won at 6f (including at 2 yrs): well held in seller at Lingfield. *Andrew Reid*

PEACE BAND (IRE) 3 b.c. Desert Style (IRE) 121 – Anita's Love (IRE) 53 (Anita's **60** Prince 126) [2001 72: f6g⁵ 5f⁴ 6g 5g⁶ 6.1m Sep 10] smallish, sturdy colt: modest maiden: will prove best at 5f/6f: acts on firm and good to soft ground: blinkered (well below form) penultimate start: sold 1,500 gns. *M. H. Tompkins*

PEACEFUL PARADISE 3 b.f. Turtle Island (IRE) 123 – Megdale (IRE) 74 (Waajib **98** 121) [2001 98: 8g 8m⁵ 8f⁶ 7.9m 8.1g³ 8v⁴ 8v³ Oct 15] lengthy filly: has a round action: useful performer: mostly creditable efforts, including tenth in 1000 Guineas at Newmarket on reappearance and third in listed race at Sandown (beaten 1¾ lengths by

Intrepidous despite not getting run of things) on fifth start: likely to stay 1¼m: acts on firm ground, possibly not on heavy: tongue tied 2 of last 3 starts: sold 62,000 gns in December. *J. W. Hills*

PEACEFUL SARAH   6 b.m. Sharpo 132 – Red Gloves 83 (Red God 128§) [2001 8g   **82** 7m 9g 8s* 9g² 8d* 10s* 8s 8s² p8g 10.5v Dec 1] leggy, angular mare: fairly useful mare: trained in 1999 by R. Ingram (in Britain) then S. Donohoe: better than ever (fairly useful) on return in the autumn, winning handicaps at the Curragh (2, both apprentices), Navan and Thurles: well held at Lingfield (all-weather debut) and Saint-Cloud (stiff task in listed race) last 2 starts: stays 1¼m: has won on good to firm going, goes well on softer than good: usually apprentice ridden in Ireland. *P. Mooney, Ireland*

PEACE WITHIN (IRE)   3 b.f. Brief Truce (USA) 126 – More Candy 98 (Ballad   **68** Rock 122) [2001 e6g⁶ f7g³ 7m⁵ 5g³ 7m Sep 29] IR 18,500F, IR 55,000Y: half-sister to several winners, notably smart 5f/6f performer Sunset Reigns (by Taufan): dam Irish 6f winner: fair maiden: trained first 2 starts by J. Noseda: best effort at 5f. *Edward Lynam, Ireland*

PEACOCK ALLEY (IRE)   4 gr.f. Salse (USA) 128 – Tagiki (IRE) (Doyoun 124)   **96** [2001 98: 7.9m 8m 8m 7m Jul 12] strong, smallish filly: good walker: useful handicapper: well below form after first start in 2001: stays 1m: acts on heavy and good to firm going. *W. J. Haggas*

PEACOCK THEATRE   3 b.g. Red Rainbow 105 – Fine Art (IRE) (Tate Gallery   **–** (USA) 117) [2001 8.2f 7.1g Jul 20] 800Y: first foal: dam unraced: no show in 2 maidens: won selling hurdle for A. Streeter in September. *J. M. Bradley*

Mr Raymond Tooth's "Pawn Broker"

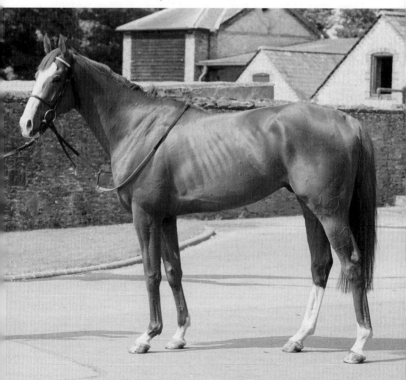

PEAK PRACTICE 3 b.f. Saddlers' Hall (IRE) 126 – High Habit 79 (Slip Anchor –
136) [2001 f11g⁶ 10g May 14] fifth foal: half-sister to 5-y-o Alegria and a 1¼m to 13f
winner in Scandinavia by Robellino: dam, second at 11.5f, half-sister to smart sprinter
Blue Siren: well held in 2 maidens: pulled very hard second time. *J. M. P. Eustace*

PEARLY BROOKS 3 b.f. Efisio 120 – Elkie Brooks 82 (Relkino 131) [2001 64: e5g⁴ **77**
5.1f 6m⁶ 6g* 6g Sep 2] sturdy filly: fair handicapper, lightly raced: won at Yarmouth in
August: may prove best at 5f/6f: best effort on good ground, showed promise on soft.
T. J. Naughton

PEARLY GATES (IRE) 3 b.f. Night Shift (USA) – Pearl Shell (USA) (Bering 136) **104**
[2001 7d* 7m² 7m 7m⁵ 7m⁴ 6g⁴ 7d 7s Nov 3] IR 110,000Y: neat filly: first foal: dam
French 1½m winner out of top-class French middle-distance filly Paulista: useful
performer: won maiden at Newbury in April: mostly good efforts after, including when in
frame in listed races at Lingfield (neck second to Palace Affair) and York (fourth to Priors
Lodge) and handicap at Newmarket and when 4¼ lengths seventh to Munir in Challenge
Stakes at Newmarket penultimate start: stays 7f: acts on good to firm and good to soft
going, well held in Premio Chiusura at Milan on soft: sold 48,000 gns. *B. W. Hills*

PEARTREE HOUSE (IRE) 7 b.g. Simply Majestic (USA) – Fashion Front (Habitat **94**
134) [2001 100, a–: 8v 7d 8g 8.5m 8.5m 8m 7.1f 7.9m* 7d⁴ 7m 7g 7.9m⁶ 8.3g 8g 8m⁶ 7s
Sep 29] rangy gelding: fairly useful handicapper: won at York in July: probably best at 7f/
1m: acts on firm and soft ground: has awkward head carriage: often races prominently/
freely: tried visored: none too consistent: sold 13,000 gns, joined Mrs M. Reveley.
D. Nicholls

PEASE BLOSSOM (IRE) 2 b.f. (Apr 30) Revoque (IRE) 122 – Saneena 80 (Kris **63**
135) [2001 6g 7m 7g⁴ 6.5g Sep 28] 11,000Y: tall, useful-looking filly: half-sister to
several winners, including 6-y-o Free Option and 8-y-o Old Hush Wing: dam 1½m
winner: modest maiden: fourth at Epsom: stiff task final start: should stay at least 1m.
C. A. Dwyer

PEDRO JACK (IRE) 4 b.g. Mujadil (USA) 119 – Festival of Light (High Top 131) **76**
[2001 87: 6g 6m⁶ 6m 6d 6m 6f³ 6m⁴ 5.7g² 6g f6g* f6g² p7g f6g⁶ f6s* Dec 26] tall gelding: **a85**
fairly useful on all-weather, fair on turf: won handicaps at Wolverhampton in October and
December (amateurs): best around 6f: acts on fibresand/polytrack, best on good ground
or firmer on turf: tried blinkered/visored: usually races prominently. *B. J. Meehan*

PEDRO PETE 4 ch.g. Fraam 114 – Stride Home 78 (Absalom 128) [2001 84: 10.3f **85**
11.6g* 12m³ Jun 27] close-coupled gelding: fairly useful handicapper: won at Windsor in
June: barely stayed 1½m: acted on soft and good to firm ground: dead. *N. J. Henderson*

PEGGYS ROSE (IRE) 4 b.f. Shalford (IRE) 124§ – Afrique Noir (IRE) (Gallic –
League 119) [2001 65d: f6g Mar 15] one-time fair 6f winner: has lost her form: tried
blinkered. *P. D. Evans*

PEGGY'S SONG 3 b.f. Mind Games 121 – Miss Whittingham (IRE) 68 (Fayruz 116) –
[2001 33: e5g⁶ e5g f5g 5.1m 5.3m 5.7m Sep 10] of little account in 2001. *D. L. Williams*

PEKANESE (IRE) 4 b.g. Sri Pekan (USA) 117 – Tootle (Main Reef 126) [2001 74: **?**
12.1m 10.2s⁴ 10m Aug 18] strong gelding: fluent mover: fair maiden at 3 yrs (reportedly
fractured shinbone before final start): little form in 2001, though fourth in seller: probably
stays 1¼m: acts on heavy going: blinkered last 2 starts: tends to carry head awkwardly.
R. T. Phillips

PEKAN HEIGHTS (USA) 5 b.g. Green Dancer (USA) 132 – Battle Drum (USA) –
(Alydar (USA)) [2001 65: 10f May 25] fair performer in 2000: well beaten only run at 5
yrs: usually visored/blinkered. *P. D. Evans*

PEKAN KU (USA) 2 b.g. (Feb 25) Kingmambo (USA) 125 – Star of Albion 61 –
(Ajdal (USA) 130) [2001 7g Jul 10] 120,000Y: good-topped gelding: sixth living foal:
half-brother to 1m winner Kings Signal (by Red Ransom): dam, 2-y-o 7f winner, closely
related to US Grade 1 9f/1¼m winner Sabin and half-sister to Musidora Stakes winner
Fatah Flare: 33/1, burly and bandaged behind, well held in maiden at Newmarket.
M. A. Jarvis

PEKANOORA (IRE) 3 b.g. Sri Pekan (USA) 117 – Shanoora (IRE) 53 (Don't –
Forget Me 127) [2001 –: 10s 8d f8g Nov 26] no form: blinkered final start. *W. R. Harris*

PEKAY 8 b.g. Puissance 110 – K-Sera 95 (Lord Gayle (USA) 124) [2001 61: 10.5s **58**
9.9s⁴ 12d³ 11.9s³ Oct 25] leggy gelding: modest handicapper: stays 1½m: acts on heavy
and good to firm ground: sometimes blinkered earlier in career: usually held up. *B. Smart*

PELAGIA (IRE)   3 b.f. Lycius (USA) 124 – Sahara Breeze 85 (Ela-Mana-Mou 132)   –
[2001 77: 7d 8d 7m 7g 8.3v f9.4g Nov 17] good-topped filly: disappointing maiden.
R. Hannon

PELLI   3 b.f. Saddlers' Hall (IRE) 126 – Pellinora (USA) (King Pellinore (USA) 127)   **37**
[2001 33: e10g³ e10g f8g³ f9.4g 7m 8g⁵ 10.1g p10g Dec 29] workmanlike filly: has a
round action: poor maiden: stays 1¼m: acts on good to firm ground, fibresand and equitrack. *P. Howling*

PENALTA   5 ch.g. Cosmonaut – Targuette (Targowice (USA) 130) [2001 57: f16g⁵   **53**
f16.2g² e16g⁴ f16g² 14.1s 16.2m May 12] modest handicapper: pulled up penultimate
start: stays 2m: acts on heavy going and fibresand: visored 3 of last 4 starts: tongue tied
final one: has hung: usually races prominently. *M. Wigham*

PENDULUM   3 ro.f. Pursuit of Love 124 – Brilliant Timing (USA) (The Minstrel   **82**
(CAN) 135) [2001 65p: 7f* 7.6m² 7g Sep 14] big, rangy filly: fairly useful performer:
won maiden at Thirsk in July: good second at Lingfield (hung right), much better effort
in handicaps after: likely to prove best up to 1m: raced only on good going or firmer.
W. J. Haggas

PENG (IRE)   4 ch.g. Case Law 113 – Real Bold (Never So Bold 135) [2001 –: f7g f7g   –
e6g e7g⁴ f7g 7m May 28] good-topped gelding: little form: tried visored/tongue tied.
R. Bastiman

PENGUIN BAY   5 b.g. Rock Hopper 124 – Corn Lily 78 (Aragon 118) [2001 12.3m⁵   **73 d**
14.1m⁵ 12f³ 9f³ 12.3g 14.4m⁵ 16d Sep 21] second foal: dam, effective at 1½m/1¾m, also
won over hurdles: fair maiden at best: well held last 3 starts: should stay beyond 1¾m:
acts on firm going. *Mrs M. Reveley*

PENNECHIP   2 ch.f. (Mar 14) Pennekamp (USA) 130 – Poker Chip 106 (Bluebird   **65**
(USA) 125) [2001 6m 5m⁶ 6.1m⁴ 6f 6m 6s Oct 3] useful-looking filly: third foal:
half-sister to 1999 2-y-o 5f winner Poker Polka (by Salse): dam 5f (including Flying
Childers Stakes)/6f winner: fair maiden: fourth at Nottingham: well held in nurseries
after: should stay 7f: sold 6,000 gns, sent to Holland. *R. Hannon*

PENNE DANCER (IRE)   2 gr.c. (Feb 27) Pennekamp (USA) 130 – Talama (FR)   **77**
(Shakapour 125) [2001 6m⁴ 6m⁴ 7f* 7m⁴ 7g Sep 15] 34,000Y: fifth foal: half-brother to
fairly useful UAE 1m to 1½m winner Taku (by Kahyasi) and a winner up to 1¾m in
Scandinavia by Second Set: dam French 1½m winner: fair performer: won maiden at
Lingfield in July: respectable efforts after: likely to be suited by 1¼m/1½m: raced on
good going or firmer: sold 25,000 gns. *R. Hannon*

PENNELESS DANCER   2 b.g. (Mar 15) Pennekamp (USA) 130 – Villella (Sadler's   **69**
Wells (USA) 132) [2001 5.3s⁶ 5.2g⁴ 6m⁶ 7m³ 6m⁵ 6d⁶ 7m f8.5g⁴ 8.3v 7s Oct 25] sixth
foal: closely related to French 10.5f/11.5f winner Periwinkle (by Bering): dam unraced
daughter of smart performer up to 1½m Ghaiya, herself sister to US Grade 1 9f/1¼m
winner Fiesta Gal: fair maiden: stays 8.5f: acts on fibresand, good to firm and good to soft
going: tends to edge left: consistent: gelded after final start. *M. Blanshard*

PENNINE LASS (IRE)   6 b.m. Archway (IRE) 115 – Pennine Girl (IRE) (Pennine   –
Walk 120) [2001 e13s Feb 14] first foal: dam, Irish staying maiden, half-sister to
high-class miler Sandhurst Prince: last in claimer at Lingfield. *L. A. Dace*

PENNY FARTHING   3 b.f. Mind Games 121 – Souveniers (Relko 136) [2001 65: 8d   **63**
7m⁵ 7m 8m 10g 13.1d⁵ 11.9m² 9.9s Sep 25] modest maiden handicapper: stays 13f: acts
on good to firm and good to soft going: visored last 2 starts: quirky sort (often slowly
away), but is consistent: sold 11,000 gns. *H. Candy*

PENNY HA'PENNY   2 b.f. (May 2) Bishop of Cashel 122 – Madam Millie 99   **51**
(Milford 119) [2001 6d⁶ 6d Oct 12] rather leggy filly: half-sister to 3-y-o Celtic Mill and
to 1½m winners Millie's Dream (by Petoski) and My Millie (by Midyan): dam sprinter:
better effort in maidens (modest form) when sixth at Newcastle: should stay at least 7f.
D. W. Barker

PENNY PICTURES (IRE)   2 b.c. (Feb 17) Theatrical 128 – Copper Creek 78 (Habi-   **83**
tat 134) [2001 6m⁴ 6f³ 7m* 7m⁶ 8g Sep 13] 85,000Y: close-coupled, quite good-topped
colt: half-brother to several winners, notably 5f/6f performer Tipsy Creek (by Dayjur)
and 6f (at 2 yrs) to 9f (in UAE) winner Wathik (by Ogygian), both smart: dam, 6f winner,
from good family: fairly useful performer: won maiden at Catterick in August, rallying:
below form in nurseries after: should stay 1m: raced only on good going or firmer.
M. Johnston

Cadogan Silver Salver Handicap, York—
Pension Fund holds on well from Inch Perfect to gain his third success on the course; Nashaab is third

PENNYS FROM HEAVEN   7 gr.g. Generous (IRE) 139 – Heavenly Cause (USA)   **58**
(Grey Dawn II 132) [2001 61: f16g f16g² f16.2s⁶ f12s² f12g f16g⁶ 12s⁶ 16v⁵ 12m⁴ 12.3g*
13d⁶ 12m² 16m 13m 16f 9.9m 12m³ 16g f14g f14g Nov 16] tall gelding: modest
handicapper: won at Ripon in May: ran badly last 3 starts: best at 1½m to easy 2m: acts
on any turf going and fibresand: tried blinkered at 3 yrs: has pulled hard/hung fire: not
one to trust implicitly: sold 4,200 gns. *D. Nicholls*

PENNYS PRIDE (IRE)   6 b.m. Pips Pride 117 – Mursuma (Rarity 129) [2001 76:   **66**
12s 8s³ 9.2m² 10m³ 12.4m² 8g 11.9f⁴ 12g³ 10m* 9.9m 10m* 10g Nov 5] tall mare: fair
handicapper: won at Redcar in August and Ayr in September: seems best at 1m/1¼m: acts
on soft and firm going: visored (ran poorly) once: sometimes races freely: found little
final start: usually held up. *Mrs M. Reveley*

PENSION FUND   7 b.g. Emperor Fountain 112 – Navarino Bay 102 (Averof 123)   **85**
[2001 87: f8.5s⁴ f12g⁶ f9.4g² f7g³ 8v 9v 10.3f* 8.9m* 10.4m 10m² 10f 8.9d 8.2s Oct 30]   **a77**
tall gelding: fairly useful handicapper on turf, fair on all-weather: won at Chester in May
and York in June: effective at 7f to 1¼m: acts on any other turf
and fibresand: blinkered once in 1997: not an easy ride. *M. W. Easterby*

PENTECOST   2 ch.g. (Mar 5) Tagula (IRE) 116 – Boughtbyphone 62 (Warning 136)   **90**
[2001 5f² 5m 6m³ 5f² 5.1f² 6m* 6m² 6g 6d Oct 19] 6,500F, 5,000Y: sturdy, close-coupled
gelding: first foal: dam, Irish maiden who stayed 1½m, out of half-sister to smart French
middle-distance stayer Whitehaven: fairly useful performer: won maiden at Epsom in
August: good efforts when second in nursery at Newmarket and seventh in Two-Year-Old
Trophy at Redcar next 2 starts: effective at 5f/6f: acts on firm ground, well held (visored)
on good to soft: sometimes slowly away: gelded after final start. *I. A. Balding*

PENTLAND (JPN)   3 br.g. Pentire 132 – Lay Claim (USA) (Mr Prospector (USA))   **84**
[2001 66: 10d 9.9m* 11f² 12.3m³ 10.4d Oct 12] smallish, good-bodied gelding: fairly
useful performer: won minor event at Salisbury in June: creditable efforts in handicaps
after when placed: stays 1½m: acts on firm going: reportedly had breathing problem on
reappearance (subsequently gelded): sold 13,500 gns, joined J. L. Eyre. *G. Wragg*

PENWELL HILL (USA)   2 b.g. (Feb 17) Distant View (USA) 126 – Avie's Jill   **58 ?**
(USA) (Lord Avie (USA)) [2001 7.1m⁴ 7.2m⁶ 6v Oct 8] $22,000Y: quite good-topped
gelding: second foal: dam winner in USA around 6f: apparently modest form in minor
events first 2 starts: gelded after final one. *T. D. Barron*

PEPPERCORN (GER)   4 b.c. Big Shuffle (USA) 122 – Pasca (GER) (Lagunas)   **115**
[2001 115: 8s 8v² 8g⁶ 8.8g² 8g² 8m⁴ 8m⁴ 8s³ 8.5v* 8.5v* Oct 28] smart performer: best
efforts when winning Grosser Preis von Dusseldorf (for second year running, by 3 lengths
from Up And Away) and Grosser Preis der Landeshauptstadt Dusseldorf (by 1¼ lengths

from Limerick Boy), both in October: ran at least creditably in frame in several listed/pattern races earlier in year, including when ½-length second to Banyumanik in Grosser Preis der Dortmunder Wirtschaft at Dortmund fourth start: stays 8.8f: acts on good to firm and heavy ground: blinkered once at 3 yrs. *U. Ostmann, Germany*

PEPPERDINE (IRE) 5 b.g. Indian Ridge 123 – Rahwah 73 (Northern Baby (CAN) **63** 127) [2001 102: 5s 6s 7m 7f 6d 6f² 7m 7s 7.5d Dec 29] strong, lengthy, good sort: formerly useful, modest at best in 2001: sold from D. Nicholls only 900 gns before final start (pulled up previous one): stays 7f: acts on firm and good to soft going: tried blinkered/visored earlier in career: has reportedly had breathing problems (twice tongue tied). *E. Castelli, Italy*

PEPPERONI (IRE) 2 b.g. (Apr 12) Nicolotte 118 – Enchantica 67 (Timeless Times **96** (USA) 99) [2001 5g⁴ f6g⁴ 5m* 5.1f² 5.2m⁶ 6g⁶ 6m* 5g* Aug 22] 15,000Y: lengthy gelding: second foal: dam, 5f maiden, out of half-sister to top-class sprinter Lochnager: useful performer: won maiden at Redcar in June and minor event at Ripon and listed event at York (beat Izmail ¾ length) in August: effective at 5f/6f: acts on fibresand, raced only on good going or firmer on turf: races prominently: game. *T. D. Easterby*

PEPPER RIDGE 2 b.f. (May 14) Bishop of Cashel 122 – Chief Celebrity (USA) 85 **56** (Chief's Crown (USA)) [2001 7.1v⁴ 7d Oct 15] 1,000Y: good-topped filly: seventh foal: half-sister to fairly useful 1m winner who stayed 2½m Go Britannia (by Machiavellian): dam, 1½m winner, half-sister to Grand Prix de Paris and Melbourne Cup winner At Talaq: better effort in maidens (modest form) when fourth to Albanova at Haydock: bred to stay at least 1m. *B. A. McMahon*

PEPPER ROAD 2 ch.g. (Apr 3) Elmaamul (USA) 125 – Floral Spark 69 (Forzando **58** 122) [2001 5m 5g⁴ 5.1s⁵ 5m⁶ 5g³ 6m Sep 24] 600F, 7,800Y: fourth foal: half-brother to 4-y-o Willemgeo and 3-y-o Sunridge Rose: dam 5f winner: modest maiden: third in nursery at Hamilton: probably stays 6f: acts on good to firm going: sometimes slowly away/wanders. *R. Bastiman*

PEPPIATT 7 ch.g. Efisio 120 – Fleur du Val (Valiyar 129) [2001 69: f7g 8s 6m 7.5f² 7f **59** 6d⁶ 7d⁴ 7m 6g⁵ 6g 6d 6v⁶ 7d Oct 30] robust gelding: modest handicapper: effective at 6f to 7.5f: acts on any turf going, well beaten both runs on fibresand: tried blinkered: sometimes slowly away: none too consistent. *N. Bycroft*

PEQUENO MUNDO (IRE) 4 b. or br.g. Marju (IRE) 127 – Maryinsky (USA) **–** (Northern Dancer) [2001 8.2f f11g p10g f8.5s Dec 26] half-brother to several winners, notably high-class 1¼m/1½m performer Legal Case (by Alleged) and useful performer up to 1¾m La Sky (by Law Society), latter dam of Oaks winner Love Divine: dam winner up to 9f in USA: well held on Flat in maidens/claimer. *A. B. Coogan*

PERCHANCER (IRE) 5 ch.g. Perugino (USA) 84 – Irish Hope (Nishapour (FR) **72 §** 125) [2001 66§, a70§: f8g⁴ f9.4g⁶ f11g* 10s³ 9.9m² f11g 10.1m³ 10f* 10.5g² f8.5g 9m **a67 §** f12g f11g⁴ Nov 12] strong gelding: fair handicapper: won apprentice events at Southwell in April and Pontefract in June: stays easy 11f: acts on fibresand, equitrack, firm and soft ground: tried visored/blinkered earlier in career: usually held up: has carried head high/found little: sometimes very slowly away: winner over hurdles in November. *P. C. Haslam*

PERCHANCE TO WIN 4 b.f. Pelder (IRE) 125 – French Plait (Thatching 131) **67** [2001 8m 7.1g³ 7.1s² 8m 10d 8d Oct 15] closely related to 7f winner French Ginger (by Most Welcome) and half-sister to 3 winners, including 7f/1m winner Rural Lad (by Town And Country): dam seemingly of little account: fair maiden: well held last 3 starts: should stay at least 1m: acts on soft ground. *P. J. Makin*

PERCHINO 4 b.g. Wolfhound (USA) 126 – Last Request 92 (Dancer's Image (USA)) **–** [2001 –: f12g⁵ f12g Jun 29] no sign of ability in maidens/claimer. *Miss J. Feilden*

PEREGIAN (IRE) 3 b.g. Eagle Eyed (USA) 111 – Mo Pheata (Petorius 117) [2001 **?** 88: p7g⁶ Nov 28] stocky gelding: type to carry condition: fairly useful performer for M. Johnston at 2 yrs: apparently not discredited only 3-y-o start: stays 1m: acts on firm and good to soft going, below form on soft: has hung. *Jamie Poulton*

PERESTROIKA (IRE) 3 ch.g. Ashkalani (IRE) 128 – Licentious 45 (Reprimand **81** 122) [2001 –p: 10s⁴ f9.4g 12f⁴ 14.1g* 14.1m* 15.9m Jul 14] leggy gelding: fairly useful performer: won handicaps at Yarmouth in June and July: well beaten final start: gelded after: better at 1¾m than shorter: acts on firm going, well beaten only outing on fibresand. *E. A. L. Dunlop*

PERFACTO 2 b.g. (May 1) Factual (USA) 108 – Hala 57 (Persian Bold 123) [2001 6s 7d Oct 18] unfurnished gelding: seventh foal: dam, maiden, should have stayed further than 7f: no sign of ability in claimer/seller. *J. S. Moore* —

PERFECT FUN 2 b.f. (Feb 8) Marju (IRE) 127 – Most Charming (FR) (Darshaan 133) [2001 6m* Jun 21] leggy, useful-looking filly: first foal: dam, French 2-y-o 1m winner, granddaughter of Cheveley Park/1000 Guineas winner Ma Biche: 9/2, fairly useful form when winning 12-runner maiden at Ripon by 1½ lengths from Mananan McLir, making most: should stay 1m. *B. W. Hills* **87**

PERFECT LOVER (IRE) 3 ch.g. Pursuit of Love 124 – Elabella (Ela-Mana-Mou 132) [2001 –: p6g Dec 19] heavy-topped gelding: little form in maidens/minor event. *D. J. S. ffrench Davis* —

PERFECTLY HONEST 3 b.f. Charnwood Forest (IRE) 125 – Carina Clare (Slip Anchor 136) [2001 –: 8m 9m⁴ 9.7m 8d Oct 25] good-topped filly: modest maiden: should stay beyond 9f. *B. Smart* **51**

PERFECT PEACH 6 b.m. Lycius (USA) 124 – Perfect Timing 107 (Comedy Star (USA) 121) [2001 91?: 5.1d 5m 6d⁶ 6m 6f 6m⁶ 6g⁴ 6d² 5.6m 6m 5s 6d Oct 19] quite good-topped mare: useful performer, but on a long losing run: largely creditable efforts in 2001, including when in frame in Stewards' Cup at Goodwood (fourth to Guinea Hunter) and listed race at Pontefract (beaten head by Monnavanna): best at 5f/6f: acts on firm and good to soft going: blinkered once as 4-y-o: usually slowly away. *C. W. Fairhurst* **100**

PERFECT PIROUETTE (JPN) 3 b.f. Warning 136 – Prancing Ballerina (USA) (Nijinsky (CAN) 138) [2001 72p: 10m 10m³ 10v⁵ 10d Nov 2] fair maiden: not sure to stay beyond 1¼m: acts on good to firm going, possibly not on heavy. *M. L. W. Bell* **72**

PERFECT STORM 2 b.c. (May 8) Vettori (IRE) 119 – Gorgeous Dancer (IRE) (Nordico (USA)) [2001 6f³ 6f⁴ 6f* 6g³ Jul 14] 32,000Y: lengthy colt: has scope: fourth living foal: half-brother to 3-y-o Imperial Dancer and useful 1m to 10.4f winner Lafite (by Robellino): dam, Irish 1m winner who stayed 1¾m, out of half-sister to Irish Oaks winner Give Thanks (grandam of 1000 Guineas winner Harayir): fairly useful form: won minor event at Kempton in July: creditable never-nearer third in nursery at Ascot: will stay at least 1m. *M. Blanshard* **85**

PERFECT SUNDAY (USA) 3 b. or br.c. Quest For Fame 127 – Sunday Bazaar (USA) (Nureyev (USA) 131) [2001 96: 12d* 11.5g* 12f⁶ 12m² 12m 12g² Sep 8] sturdy colt: very smart performer: won maiden at Newmarket in April and Arena Racing Derby Trial Stakes at Lingfield (made all, beat Putra Sandhurst by 2½ lengths) in May: good efforts when 6¼ lengths sixth to Galileo in Derby at Epsom and when 1½ lengths second in Grand Prix de Saint-Cloud (to Mirio) and in September Stakes at Kempton (short of room early in straight behind Mutamam): rare poor effort in Gordon Stakes at Goodwood penultimate start: should stay beyond 1½m: acts on firm and good to soft ground: usually races prominently. *B. W. Hills* **120**

PERFECT VENUE (IRE) 8 b.g. Danehill (USA) 126 – Welsh Fantasy 104 (Welsh Pageant 132) [2001 11.8d⁴ Jul 19] useful winner in 1997 in Ireland for C. O'Brien: poor form only start since: will stay beyond 1½m: acts on soft going: sold 4,500 gns. *N. J. Henderson* **48**

PERFIDIOUS (USA) 3 b.g. Lear Fan (USA) 130 – Perfolia (USA) 104 (Nodouble (USA)) [2001 71: f9.4s⁶ e10g² 10.2m⁴ 10.3m⁵ 11m⁵ 10.9m Sep 20] sturdy gelding: fair handicapper: stays 1¼m: acts on fibresand, equitrack and good to firm going: often soon off bridle, and has found little (gelded after final start): sold 10,000 gns. *Sir Mark Prescott* **70 a79**

PERIGEUX (IRE) 5 b.g. Perugino (USA) 84 – Rock On (IRE) (Ballad Rock 122) [2001 65, a72: f5g⁴ e6g² e5g* e5g e5g² f5g e5g e5g* 5.3s 5v 5s⁵ 5.1d 5m 5.1f 5m f5s Dec 27] small, good-bodied gelding: fair on all-weather, modest on turf: won handicap in January and claimer (then left K. Ivory) in April, both at Lingfield: well held last 5 starts, off 7 months and leaving A. Reid before final one: best at 5f/easy 6f: acts on fibresand, equitrack, good to firm and probably on soft going: often blinkered, has been visored: sometimes unruly stalls: often races prominently. *J. M. Bradley* **58 a78**

PERLE D'AZUR 2 b.f. (Feb 11) Mind Games 121 – Pearls (Mon Tresor 113) [2001 5m² 5d 6m⁴ 7g² 7m³ 6g* 6g* 6m² Aug 13] 15,000Y: leggy filly: second foal: closely related to 3-y-o Wilson Blyth: dam unraced half-sister to Oaks third Pearl Angel: fairly useful performer: won maiden at Pontefract in July and nursery at Goodwood in August, leading late on both times: good second in nursery at Windsor final start, edging right: best form at 6f: unraced on extremes of going: reliable. *A. Berry* **91**

PERLE DE SAGESSE 4 b.f. Namaqualand (USA) – Pearl of Dubai (USA) (Red –
Ransom (USA)) [2001 61, a51: e7g⁶ e7g⁷ 7g 7g 6m f6s 7m p7g⁶ p10g Dec 29] leggy filly: **a47**
poor performer: raced mainly at 6f/7f: acts on firm going and polytrack: often early to
post: somewhat temperamental. *Julian Poulton*

PERLINA (IRE) 2 ch.f. (Apr 21) Woodborough (USA) 112 – Kingdom Pearl 57 **50**
(Statoblest 120) [2001 5.1m 6.1v f6g Oct 6] IR 27,000Y: plain, leggy filly: first foal: dam,
1½m winner, half-sister to 7f/1m winner Russian Music and 1997 2-y-o 5f winner Pool
Music, both useful: modest maiden: best effort on debut: should stay 7f: sold 1,200 gns.
B. W. Hills

PERPETUITY 3 ch.g. Timeless Times (USA) 99 – Boadicea's Chariot (Commanche **65**
Run 133) [2001 6s³ 7m 7.5m⁴ 7.1g 7.1d⁴ 8s Jul 24] 15,000Y: lengthy, quite good-topped
gelding: third foal: brother to 4-y-o Agrippina (useful 7f winner at 2 yrs): dam, Irish 1½m
winner, later winner over hurdles: fair maiden: best efforts at 6f/7f on good to soft/soft
ground: has hung under pressure: looked unwilling in blinkers final start. *A. Bailey*

PERPETUO 4 b.f. Mtoto 134 – Persian Fountain (IRE) 67 (Persian Heights 129) **81**
[2001 70: 12m 12.1m⁵ 18m 13s⁴ 12m* 12.3g⁴ 11.9m⁴ 12.1m³ 13.9d² 16g Nov 7] sparsely-
made filly: poor mover: fairly useful handicapper: won at Beverley in July: good placed
efforts at Hamilton and York after: stays 1¾m: acts on soft and good to firm going:
usually comes from off pace (wandered in front fourth start). *R. A. Fahey*

PERSIAN BANDIT (IRE) 3 b.g. Idris (IRE) 118 – Ce Soir (Northern Baby (CAN) **?**
127) [2001 69: e8g⁵ f9.4s a6g³ a10.5g⁴ a6g² a10.5g³ a8g³ a6g a10.5g⁴ a8g⁵ a8g³ a6g a9g
a10.5g⁵ a6g* a6g² a6g* a8g a10g a6g a9g Dec 16] fair performer at best: left M. Quinn
after second start (looked none too cooperative on reappearance): won handicaps at Mijas
in July and August: best at 6f: acts on soft and good to firm ground and on sand: tried
blinkered. *E. J. Creighton, Spain*

Mr K. Abdulla's "Perfect Sunday"

PERSIAN DOLLAR (IRE) 2 b.g. (Jan 25) Persian Bold 123 – Dollar Magic (Fairy King (USA)) [2001 7m 6d f6g Aug 18] 3,000 2-y-o: fourth foal: half-brother to 2 winners abroad by Lycius: dam, twice-raced half-sister to Ebor winner Deposki: well held in maidens/sales race. *E. J. O'Neill*   **–**

PERSIAN FACT 2 b.g. (Apr 30) Greensmith 121 – Forest Song 60 (Forzando 122) [2001 f6g⁵ f6g f6g³ f6g⁵ f6g⁵ p6g p7g Dec 29] 600F, 2,200Y: fourth foal: half-brother to German 2000 2-y-o 5.5f winner Lady Ambition (by Emarati) and 4-y-o Come On Murgy (by Taufan): dam, maiden, should have stayed 1m: modest maiden: third at Southwell: likely to prove best at 5f/6f: raced only on fibresand/polytrack. *K. R. Burke*   **61**

PERSIAN FAYRE 9 b.g. Persian Heights 129 – Dominion Fayre 49 (Dominion 123) [2001 70, a–: 7m⁴ 7m 8.3m² 8f* 9.2d 7d 9.2g² 8m⁵ 9.1m 8s Nov 9] sturdy gelding: fair performer: won selling handicap at Ayr in June: probably best at 7f/1m: acts on any turf going, well beaten on fibresand: probably needs to dominate: none too consistent. *A. Berry*   **68 a–**

PERSIAN FLIGHT 3 ch.f. Catrail (USA) 123 – Persian Victory (IRE) (Persian Bold 123) [2001 8m Aug 30] fifth living foal: half-sister to Italian 2-y-o 7f winner by Selkirk: dam unraced: looked wayward when last in maiden at Salisbury. *Miss E. C. Lavelle*   **–**

PERSIAN KING (IRE) 4 ch.g. Persian Bold 123 – Queen's Share (Main Reef 126) [2001 90: f11g 12s Apr 25] IR 30,000F, IR 25,000Y: fourth living foal: half-brother to fairly useful 1994 2-y-o 6f winner Masruf (by Taufan): dam Irish sprinter: fairly useful winner for D. Gillespie in Ireland at 3 yrs (sold 47,000 gns after final start): well beaten in 2 handicaps in 2001: tried tongue tied. *J. A. B. Old*   **–**

PERSIAN LIGHTNING (IRE) 2 b.g. (Feb 11) Sri Pekan (USA) 117 – Persian Fantasy 94 (Persian Bold 123) [2001 6m³ 7g⁵ 8g⁶ 7g⁵ 7s Nov 10] strong, angular gelding: fourth foal: half-brother to useful 1¾m/2m winner Height of Fantasy (by Shirley Heights): dam 1½m winner who stayed 2m: fair form when third in maiden at New-   **73 p**

market: shaped better than result all starts after, never placed to challenge in nursery at Doncaster final one (subsequently gelded): should be suited by 1¼m/1½m: very much type to make his mark in handicaps as 3-y-o. *J. L. Dunlop*

PERSIANO   6 ch.g. Efisio 120 – Persiandale (Persian Bold 123) [2001 108: 7d 8s 8m² 8g⁶ 8g 8g* 7.1g³ 7m³ 9g Oct 6] big, lengthy gelding: unimpressive mover: useful performer: won handicap at Ascot in August by ½ length from Smart Ridge: best at 7f/ 1m: probably unsuited by soft/heavy going, acts on any other: visored once as 4-y-o. *J. R. Fanshawe*   **107**

PERSIAN PEARL   2 b.f. (Feb 2) Hurricane Sky (AUS) – Persian Fountain (IRE) 67 (Persian Heights 129) [2001 6d 6.1g² 5m* Aug 28] 1,000Y: third foal: half-sister to 4-y-o Perpetuo: dam, 2-y-o 7.5f winner who stayed 1¼m, out of sister to Middle Park winner Steel Heart: fair form: justified favouritism in maiden at Ripon by 2 lengths from Betty's Pride, giving trouble at start and edging right under pressure: bred to stay at least 7f. *B. A. McMahon*   **73**

PERSIAN PRIDE (IRE)   3 ch.g. Barathea (IRE) 127 – Glenarff (USA) (Irish River (FR) 131) [2001 82: 10.5d* 12m 11.9g 10g 12d 10v Nov 8] strong, compact gelding: useful performer at best: won maiden at Haydock in July: ran well when seventh in Tote Gold Trophy Handicap at Goodwood next start: lost form after: stays 1½m: acts on good to firm and good to soft ground: gelded after final outing. *P. W. Harris*   **96 d**

PERSIAN PUNCH (IRE)   8 ch.g. Persian Heights 129 – Rum Cay (USA) 75 (Our Native (USA)) [2001 122: 16g⁴ 16.4m³ 20f² 16g* 15.9g* 14m⁴ 16d³ Nov 6]   **124**

    'Persian Punch will not give in'. It seems as if the commentators have had cause to utter those words countless times. This horse is massive in stature and in heart. There is no secrecy about the conditions he needs to show his best and what is required to beat him, but those that do beat him generally know they have been in a battle. A thorough stayer and a relentless galloper, Persian Punch needs a good pace to bring those strengths into play and to try to run the finish out of his opponents. Which more often than not means that he has to set the pace himself. In most instances, when a front runner is passed it is usually a clear sign that it is beaten, but being headed is not the end of the matter with Persian Punch, not by a long chalk. A rallying Persian Punch has become a familiar and favourite sight on British racecourses, a status that has been hard-fought and hard-won in the course of six seasons' endeavour, and he has also impressed racegoers in Ireland, France and Australia. Persian Punch's battling spirit is not extraordinary in itself, but his continued ability and willingness to show it after all these years surely is. 'Persian Punch has always been trained with the long-term in mind, and now we are reaping the benefits,' said trainer David Elsworth. That was back in 1998 and it was more true than ever in 2001.

    One blot on Persian Punch's record over the years has been his perform-ances in the Gold Cup at Royal Ascot. This was a matter put right in the latest season, with his fifth appearance in the race, the fault with the previous four being not so much that he had not won, but that he had never come close to winning. There was nothing about the race that might explain his performances. He had run well at the track before, when placed in the Queen's Vase as a three-year-old and the Sagaro Stakes in 2000, and the extreme distance should have suited him, yet he managed only twelfth in 1997, sixth in 1998, twelfth in 1999 and sixth in 2000, markedly below form on all four occasions. As we reported in *Racehorses of 2000*, his trainer's New Year's resolution was 'to finally get Persian Punch to the Ascot Gold Cup in the right condition to win the race.' His route there in 2001 was an encouraging run in the Sagaro Stakes at Newmarket and a good one, beaten just over a length in third to Solo Mio, in the Henry II Stakes at Sandown. Persian Punch was, nonetheless, a weak 10/1-chance in a twelve-runner field for the Gold Cup, but he finally did himself justice. A three-length advantage seven furlongs out quickly stretched to six, but Royal Rebel and Marienbard closed to within a length entering the straight and approaching two furlongs out there were three in line. With Marienbard soon cracking, Royal Rebel edged into the lead just inside the two-furlong pole, going about half a length up. Persian Punch's fightback thereafter was an awesome spectacle and, after looking held inside the final furlong, he rallied markedly in the last fifty yards, the post coming just in time for Royal Rebel.

The Gold Cup experience did nothing for the winner, judged by his performances on his next four outings, but Persian Punch's appetite for the fight was undiminished. The JPMorgan Private Bank Goodwood Cup and the Weatherbys Insurance Lonsdale Stakes at York both featured nearly all of the leading stayers, and, in a competitive year for the division, there were plenty of them, but Persian Punch was the only one who kept on giving his running and that was good enough to give him victory in both events. Pattern-race win number eight came in a memorable set-to with the three-year-old Double Honour at Goodwood. As at Royal Ascot, the vast majority of the field never threatened a challenge to Persian Punch, but the one that did materialise got him into a protracted battle. Double Honour was a length up approaching the three-furlong marker. Afterwards, Jeff Smith, Persian Punch's owner, observed: 'If it had been a furlong out, I would have been worried. But this horse loves an argument,' and at Goodwood Persian Punch eventually had the better of that argument by a length and a half. At York under three weeks later, Smith was given cause for concern, even under his own criteria. This time the threat came from the Gold Cup third Jardines Lookout, to whom Persian Punch was conceding 5 lb, and it came late, after Persian Punch, not this time having to make the running, had been sent clear early in the straight. It was a close call over the last half furlong, though Persian Punch always had his nose just in front.

With victories at Goodwood and York, Persian Punch was showing the best form of his career and the best by any horse in the latest season over two miles or more. Two defeats followed, however, though Persian Punch's reputation did not suffer. First, dropped back to a mile and three quarters in the Irish St Leger, it was no great surprise that he was outpaced in the closing stages by Vinnie Roe, Millenary and Marienbard. He was also tightened up after the others had gone past, something that has happened before. Persian Punch's being taken up the centre of the track in his Goodwood Cup victory was reportedly because connections had been worried about just such an eventuality. In the Melbourne Cup at Flemington in November, such riding tactics were criticised by the locals after Persian Punch had been pushed up on the outside to take a prominent position. What brooked no criticism was the manner in which Persian Punch, carrying top weight, stuck to his guns up the straight to finish third, behind Ethereal and Give The Slip, the same position he filled on a previous trip 'down under' three years earlier. The criticism of his jockey, Richard Quinn, also on board at Royal Ascot, Goodwood and York, betrayed some unfamiliarity with the racing character of Persian Punch. Unless, of

*Weatherbys Insurance Lonsdale Stakes, York—another game display by Persian Punch,
who rallies as Jardines Lookout (left) threatens; Qaatef (striped cap) is third,
with the John Dunlop-trained pair San Sebastian (checks) and Romantic Affair fourth and fifth*

course, the early pace is too fast, Persian Punch's relentless stride and implacable courage are assets best suited to having him racing prominently or making the running.

Persian Punch (IRE) (ch.g. 1993)	Persian Heights (ch 1985)	Persian Bold (br 1975)	Bold Lad
			Relkarunner
		Ready And Willing (b 1971)	Reliance II
			No Saint
	Rum Cay (USA) (ch 1985)	Our Native (b 1970)	Exclusive Native
			Our Jackie
		Oraston (ch 1978)	Morston
			Orange Cap

The details of Persian Punch's pedigree have been described several times in these pages. He is a half-brother to the 1993 Solario Stakes winner Island Magic (by Indian Ridge). Their dam Rum Cay won over an extended fourteen furlongs, as well as a bumper at Towcester, and is a stamina influence, as also indicated in the latest season by the three-year-old Red Bartsia (by Barathea), who won a mile-and-a-half maiden at Tralee. Rum Cay's 2001 two-year-old Wadmaan (an 800,000 guinea yearling by Singspiel) has not seen the racecourse yet for Godolphin, and she foaled a Rainbow Quest filly in 2000. Persian Punch is from the final crop of Persian Heights. He is suited by further than a mile and three quarters nowadays and stays two and a half miles. He acts on any going. Many a jumps trainer would have cast an envious eye over Persian Punch, a big, strong gelding who impresses in appearance and has a powerful, round action. Not unconnected to his physique perhaps, he has something more in common with jumping stock in having revealed his best form at the age of eight, an advanced age to do so for a Flat horse. There is another connection to be stressed though. For durability and immense gameness, think also of Desert Orchid and Floyd. Their long and celebrated careers, and now that of Persian Punch, are all powerful tributes to their trainer, the same man, David Elsworth. *D. R. C. Elsworth*

PERSIAN SPIRIT   3 b.f. Persian Bold 123 – Big Story 50 (Cadeaux Genereux 131)   –
[2001 54: 9.7m 7m⁶ 8m Sep 10] modest maiden at 2 yrs: little form in 2001. *R. Hannon*

PERSIAN WATERS (IRE)   5 b.g. Persian Bold 123 – Emerald Waters (Kings Lake   **80**
(USA) 133) [2001 76: 16m* 20m³ Jun 20] lengthy, quite good-topped gelding: fairly useful handicapper, lightly raced: won at Ripon in May: good third to Cover Up in Ascot Stakes at Royal Ascot following month: stays 2½m: acts on soft and good to firm going. *J. R. Fanshawe*

PERSPICACIOUS 2 b.f. (Feb 13) Prince Daniel (USA) – Perspicacity (Petorius 117) –
[2001 7.5m 7m f7g Oct 1] first reported foal: dam, showed little on Flat, modest winning
hurdler: no encouragement in maidens/seller. *G. M. Moore*

PERSUADE 3 ch.g. Lure (USA) 131 – Shapely (USA) 81 (Alleged (USA) 138) [2001 **83 §**
76: e10g⁴ f9.4g² e10g* f8.5g³ e10g⁵ f9.4g³ e10g⁵ 8v³ 8d 7.6f² 9m 8.1m 8.2f⁵ 6m³ 7.1g
6m⁴ 7f² 6d 7m⁶ 7f⁴ pDec 28] leggy, attractive gelding: fairly useful performer: won
handicap at Lingfield in February: left M. Quinn and off 5 months before final outing:
effective at 6f to easy 1¼m: acts on all-weather and any turf going: tried tongue tied: has
raced freely/hung left/found little: not one to trust. *R. J. White*

PERTEMPS BOYCOTT (IRE) 3 b.g. Indian Ridge 123 – Coupe d'Hebe 87 (Ile de –
Bourbon (USA) 133) [2001 –: 7.1g 6m 8.3s Aug 21] of little account. *W. J. Haggas*

PERTEMPS FC 4 b.g. Prince Sabo 123 – Top Mouse (High Top 131) [2001 57: f5g³ **57**
f6g 5m 5m³ 5m 5m⁴ 5f 5d² 5f* 5m 5d² 6m 5m 5m 5.1d⁵ 5d⁶ 5v Oct 24] lengthy gelding:
modest handicapper: won at Musselburgh in July: effective at 5f/easy 6f: acts on firm
going, good to soft (possibly not heavy) and fibresand: blinkered once: tried tongue tied:
sometimes edgy/spoils chance with slow start: sold 1,800 gns. *T. D. Easterby*

PERTEMPS GILL 3 b.f. Silca Blanka (IRE) 104 – Royal Celerity (USA) (Riverman **39**
(USA) 131) [2001 30: 5.3d 5.3f³ 6.1m⁴ 6m 6.1m⁵ 6m 6m⁵ Aug 8] close-coupled,
sparely-made filly: poor maiden handicapper: stays 7f: acts on firm and good to soft
ground: consistent. *A. D. Smith*

PERTEMPS JACK 3 br.g. Silca Blanka (IRE) 104 – Stella Royale (Astronef 116) –
[2001 –: 9m 8m Jul 4] seems of little account. *A. D. Smith*

PERTEMPS JARDINE (IRE) 3 b. or br.g. General Monash (USA) 107 – Indescent **51**
Blue 63 (Bluebird (USA) 125) [2001 60: f6g f6g f5g f6g 7d 8d 5g 6g 6v Oct 16]
angular gelding: modest maiden handicapper: stays 7f: acts on good to soft ground: has
been slowly away/flashed tail: visored (ran respectably) then blinkered last 2 starts.
R. A. Fahey

PERTEMPS MISSION 7 b.g. Safawan 118 – Heresheis 69 (Free State 125) [2001 –
f16g 16.2m 16.2m Jun 18] no longer of any account. *Mrs Lydia Pearce*

PERTEMPS THATCHER 3 b. or br.f. Petong 126 – Nadema (Artaius (USA) 129) **58**
[2001 69: 7v 6s 6m 8s⁴ Nov 7] unfurnished filly: modest maiden in 2001: left S. Williams
before final start: stays 1m: acts on soft going. *Michael Hourigan, Ireland*

PERU GENIE (IRE) 4 b.g. Perugino (USA) 84 – High Concept (IRE) (Thatching **71**
131) [2001 55d: 6.5v³ 8m 5m 6m 6m⁴ 6.5g⁵ 7.8f⁴ 6v 5g³ 6.5s⁵ 6m* 5s³ 6d* f6s Dec 15]
good-topped gelding: fair handicapper: won at Cork in September and Leopardstown in
October: not discredited at Wolverhampton final start: stays 6f: acts on good to firm and
good to soft ground, probably on fibresand: blinkered last 4 starts: has worn tongue strap.
Michael McElhone, Ireland

PERUVIAN CHIEF (IRE) 4 b.g. Foxhound (USA) 103 – John's Ballad (IRE) **94**
(Ballad Rock 122) [2001 98: f5g⁵ f6s⁶ 7d 6m³ 6m³ 6m 6m⁵ 6m 6f 5g³ 5g³ 5g⁴ 6g² 6g 6m
5v 6g² 5d 6g Nov 5] good-topped gelding: fairly useful handicapper: several creditable
efforts in 2001, including second at Goodwood and Newmarket: best at 5f/6f: acts on
fibresand, equitrack, firm and soft going: has edged left: effective blinkered/visored or
not: tough and consistent. *N. P. Littmoden*

PERUVIAN JADE 4 gr.f. Petong 126 – Rion River (IRE) (Taufan (USA) 119) –
[2001 72: f6g f6g Feb 3] leggy filly: formerly fair 6f winner: well beaten in 2001.
N. P. Littmoden

PERUVIAN WAVE (USA) 3 b. or br.g. Alydeed (CAN) 120 – Polish Devil (USA) **58**
(Devil's Bag (USA)) [2001 8s 9d 8.2v⁵ 7m⁶ 6g³ 6f 5v f5g⁵ f5g³ f5g⁵ f6s⁴ Dec 21]
$30,000Y, resold 15,000Y, 50,000 2-y-o: sturdy gelding: fifth foal: brother to a 2-y-o
winner in Japan and half-brother to 6f winner Deviletta (by Trempolino): dam unraced
daughter of Prix de l'Abbaye winner Polonia: modest maiden handicapper: effective at
5f/6f: acts on fibresand, best turf run on good going: has high head carriage, and has hung
left/folded tamely. *Mrs J. R. Ramsden*

PERZIAN CLOUD 3 b.g. Ezzoud (IRE) 126 – Persian Smoke 45 (Persian Bold 123) –
[2001 5.1s Apr 16] unfurnished gelding: first foal: dam 1¾m winner: well beaten in
maiden at Nottingham. *John Berry*

PETALITE 3 gr.f. Petong 126 – Veuve Hoornaert (IRE) 88 (Standaan (FR) 118) [2001 **53**
48: 6.9v⁴ 7m f5g² 5f 6m⁶ 6m⁵ f6g Dec 10] modest maiden handicapper: should prove best **a63**
at 5f/6f: acts on fibresand and good to firm going. *M. A. Jarvis*

PETARA (IRE)   6 ch.g. Petardia 113 – Romangoddess (IRE) (Rhoman Rule (USA))   –
[2001 40: 10f 8m 10f Jul 9] of little account nowadays. *J. S. Wainwright*

PETARGA   6 b.m. Petong 126 – One Half Silver (CAN) (Plugged Nickle (USA))   87
[2001 81: 5.1m 5.2m⁴ 5.7g* 5m 6m⁶ 6g⁴ 5.7d 6f Sep 20] close-coupled mare: fairly useful
handicapper: won at Bath in June: effective at 5f/6f: acts on firm and good to soft going:
sometimes slowly away: held up: none too consistent: sold 5,200 gns. *J. A. R. Toller*

PETER PERFECT   7 gr.g. Chilibang 120 – Misdevious (USA) (Alleged (USA) 138)   –
[2001 –: f8g f11g Feb 2] of little account. *Mrs S. Lamyman*

PETER'S IMP (IRE)   6 b.g. Imp Society (USA) – Catherine Clare 58 (Sallust 134)   65 d
[2001 83, a60: 7.6f 8.1m 7m 7f⁵ 7.5m 7.6m 8g 7.5m 7m 7.6m 8.1g⁴ 7g 7.5s 8d Oct 30]   a–
good-bodied gelding: fair handicapper: mostly disappointing in 2001: stays 1m: acts on
firm and soft going: occasionally blinkered/visored. *A. Berry*

PETER THE GREAT (IRE)   2 b.c. (Mar 23) Hector Protector (USA) 124 – Perfect   78
Alibi (Law Society (USA) 130) [2001 6m 8m² p8g⁴ Nov 15] 25,000Y: half-brother to
several winners, including 9-y-o Acquittal and fairly useful 6f (including at 2 yrs) winner
Likely Story (by Night Shift): dam unraced half-sister to Prix du Cadran winner Chief
Contender and Phoenix Stakes winner Aviance (dam of Chimes of Freedom): best effort
in maidens (fair form) when 6 lengths second of 6 to Mamool at Goodwood: will stay
1¼m. *R. M. Beckett*

PET EXPRESS FLYER (IRE)   5 b.g. Mukaddamah (USA) 125 – Take The Option   –
(USA) (Bold Bidder) [2001 f8g Jan 1] close-coupled gelding: fairly useful 6f/7f winner
at 2 yrs: favourite, pulled up in seller only run since 1999. *P. C. Haslam*

PETITE DANSEUSE   7 b.m. Aragon 118 – Let Her Dance (USA) (Sovereign Dancer   –
(USA)) [2001 42, a55: f6g f7g May 25] small mare: modest handicapper in 2000: well
held in 2001: blinkered/visored once. *D. W. Chapman*

PETITE FUTEE   2 b.f. (Apr 25) Efisio 120 – Q Factor 90 (Tragic Role (USA)) [2001   60
7.1m⁵ 6.1m⁵ 5.7g⁵ 6.9d³ 7.1m⁴ 7s⁵ 7s⁵ Nov 10] small filly: first foal: dam 6f (at 2 yrs) to
1m winner: modest maiden: should stay 1m: acts on soft and good to firm going: has
flashed tail: often soon off bridle. *D. Haydn Jones*

PETIT MARQUIS (FR)   4 b.g. Lost World (IRE) 119 – Ephemeride (USA) (Al Nasr   98
(FR) 126) [2001 91: 7m³ 7.1f* 8m 8.1g⁴ 8s 8g* 8f³ Dec 31] good-bodied gelding: useful
performer: won handicap at Haydock in July and minor event at Newmarket in October:
sold from J. Fanshawe 30,000 gns: third in optional claimer at Santa Anita final outing:
stays 1m: acts on fibresand and any turf going. *M. Chew, USA*

PETONGSKI   3 b.g. Petong 126 – Madam Petoski 61 (Petoski 135) [2001 79: 6m 6d   79
5f 6m 5g⁴ 6g 5g 5m 6f⁶ 5d 6s⁵ 6.1v* 6v* 6v Oct 24] good-bodied gelding: fair performer:
won minor event at Nottingham then handicap at Ayr in October: effective at 5f/6f: acts
on heavy and good to firm going: visored/blinkered (below form) once each: has taken
strong hold/hung right/flashed tail: none too consistent. *D. W. Barker*

PETRAIL (IRE)   3 b.f. Catrail (USA) 123 – Smart Pet 77 (Petong 126) [2001 59p: –
6m⁶ Jul 14] smallish, sturdy filly: modest maiden at 2 yrs: well held only run in 2001:
raced only at 5f/6f. *W. R. Muir*

PETRA NOVA   5 ch.m. First Trump 118 – Spinner 59 (Blue Cashmere 129) [2001 –:   –
f6s⁵ Jan 22] of little account. *R. M. Whitaker*

PETREAN   2 gr.f. (Jan 19) Petong 126 – Star 83 (Most Welcome 131)   42
f6g Oct 23] 15,000Y: dam 5f winner who ran only at 2 yrs: poor form, not knocked about,
in maidens. *M. A. Jarvis*

PETRIE   4 ch.g. Fraam 114 – Canadian Capers 70 (Ballachtal (CAN)) [2001 54d: –
5.1m 10g f7g 5.7f 8.1m Jul 13] of little account now. *A. J. Chamberlain*

PETROV   3 b.c. Cadeaux Genereux 131 – Anna Petrovna (FR) 90 (Wassl 125) [2001   82
63: 11.6s⁶ 10g* 11m⁵ 10m² 12f³ 12m³ 12m⁵ Jul 29] big, good-topped colt: fairly useful
handicapper: won easily at Leicester in May: ran creditably after: stays 1½m: acts on firm
going: blinkered/visored fourth to sixth starts: looks none too resolute: sold 24,000 gns.
E. A. L. Dunlop

PETRULA   2 ch.g. (Feb 17) Tagula (IRE) 116 – Bouffant (High Top 131) [2001 6g 6f   79
7m² 6s* 6d 6d² Nov 6] good-bodied gelding: has a round action: eighth foal:
closely related to 2 winners by Taufan, including fairly useful 1¼m winner Sahil, and
half-brother to 3 winners by Polish Patriot, including fairly useful 1¼m/1½m winner
High Tatra: dam Irish middle-distance maiden: fair performer: won maiden at Haydock

in August despite veering right leaving stall and edging left final 1f: good second in nursery at Catterick final start (subsequently gelded): should stay 7f: acts on soft going. *A. Berry*

PETRUSHKA (IRE) 4 ch.f. Unfuwain (USA) 131 – Ballet Shoes (IRE) 75 (Ela- **102** Mana-Mou 132) [2001 126: 12m⁵ Jun 8] strong, rangy filly: good walker: fluent mover: high-class performer at 3 yrs, successful in Irish Oaks at the Curragh, Yorkshire Oaks at York and Prix de l'Opera at Longchamp, and also in frame in 1000 Guineas and Oaks: reportedly sustained small chip on off-hind fetlock while being prepared for Dubai World Cup in March: 10 lengths fifth of 6 to Mutafaweq in Coronation Cup at Epsom only run in 2001 (later found to have strained tendon in off-fore and retired later in June): was best at 1¼m/1½m: acted on good to firm and good to soft going: was held up: bought privately by Darley Stud after Epsom, reportedly for more than $5m: visits Machiavellian. *Sir Michael Stoute*

PETRUS (IRE) 5 b.g. Perugino (USA) 84 – Love With Honey (USA) (Full Pocket **82** (USA)) [2001 72: e7g² 7m* 8d⁴ 7m 7.6f* 7.6m⁵ 7m³ 8m 7.6g 7f⁵ 10d p8g³ p8g p8g* Dec 22] smallish, compact gelding: fairly useful handicapper: won at Brighton in May and Lingfield in June and December: best at 7f/1m: acts fibresand and polytrack, best on good going or firmer on turf: tongue tied earlier in career: has worn net muzzle/been taken early to post. *C. E. Brittain*

PETUNTSE 7 b.g. Phountzi (USA) 104 – Alipampa (IRE) (Glenstal (USA) 118) **59** [2001 11s³ 12m⁶ 10.9f³ 10.1m* 8f 10.5g* 10.5s³ 10g 10.1v³ Oct 24] tall gelding: usually impresses in appearance: modest handicapper: won at Newcastle in July and Haydock in August: best around 1¼m: acts on soft and good to firm ground: waited with: genuine: won twice over hurdles in November. *Mrs M. Reveley*

PEYTO PRINCESS 3 b. or br.f. Bold Arrangement 127 – Bo' Babbity 75 (Strong **79** Gale 116) [2001 70: 5.1s⁵ 5m² 5m⁵ 6m² 6m⁶ 6m* 5g 6.1m 6m 6g Nov 5] strong, lengthy filly: fair performer: won minor event at Pontefract in June: creditable effort in handicaps after only on next start: will prove best at 5f/6f: acts on firm and good to soft ground: sometimes wanders. *C. W. Fairhurst*

PFENNIG 2 b.c. (Feb 6) Petong 126 – Petriece 64 (Mummy's Pet 125) [2001 7m⁶ 7.9d **68** Oct 12] 45,000Y: good-topped colt: seventh foal: brother to 1993 2-y-o 5f winner Smart Pet and 6-y-o Solly's Pal and half-brother to useful sprinter Amazing Bay (by Mazilier): dam, 7f winner, half-sister to dam of Lochsong and Lochangel: fair form in maidens at Newmarket and York (visored): bred to be best short of 1m: joined J. Wickham in UAE. *D. R. Loder*

PHARAOH HATSHEPSUT (IRE) 3 b.f. Definite Article 121 – Maid of Mourne **64 d** (Fairy King (USA)) [2001 57: 6g* 7m 6g 5f 8.1d⁴ 7d 6m 6g⁶ 8.1s 6g 6v 7v Oct 26] good-topped filly: modest performer: won minor event at Thirsk in May: generally well held after: left J. Goldie after ninth start: stays 6f, seemingly not testing 1m: acts on heavy going. *R. A. Fahey*

PHARLY REEF 9 b.g. Pharly (FR) 130 – Hay Reef 72 (Mill Reef (USA) 141) [2001 **–** 10d 10.2g 12m Sep 24] of little account. *D. Burchell*

PHARMACY'S PET (IRE) 3 b.f. Petardia 113 – Pharmacy 80 (Mtoto 134) [2001 **–** –: 6m & 10m 6m 5.1g 5f 7g⁶ 5.7m p10g Nov 20] small filly: little form. *H. S. Howe*

PHAROAH'S GOLD (IRE) 3 b.g. Namaqualand (USA) – Queen Nefertiti (IRE) **88 d** 61 (Fairy King (USA)) [2001 70: 6s² 8m⁶ 6m 6d⁵ f6s⁵ Dec 21] smallish gelding: fairly useful performer: below form after, in claimer and seller final 2 starts (left W. Jarvis in between): probably stays 1m: acts on soft ground: visored last time. *D. Shaw*

PHAZED 2 b.f. (Feb 6) Zamindar (USA) 116 – Ypha (USA) (Lyphard (USA) 132) **67** [2001 7f³ Aug 1] fourth foal: half-sister to French 1½m winner Seasonal (by Generous): dam, French winner around 1¼m, half-sister to very smart French/US middle-distance performer Louis Le Grand: fair form when third in maiden at Kempton, hanging right late on: dead. *B. W. Hills*

PHECKLESS 2 ch.g. (Apr 20) Be My Guest (USA) 126 – Phlirty (Pharly (FR) 130) **43** [2001 6v f5g⁵ Dec 17] third foal: half-brother to 5f (at 2 yrs) to 1½m winner Pheisty (by Faustus): dam tailed off both starts: finished lame on debut: poor form when fifth in maiden at Southwell. *R. F. Johnson Houghton*

PHILAGAIN 4 b.f. Ardkinglass 114 – Andalucia 57 (Rheingold 137) [2001 46: 9v 8d **–** 7m 7m 8m 6m 7.1f 8f 6g 7.1f Jul 25] of little account now. *Miss L. A. Perratt*

PHILATELIC LADY (IRE)   5 ch.m. Pips Pride 117 – Gold Stamp (Golden Act   –
(USA)) [2001 85: 10.1s Apr 25] fairly useful handicapper at best: well held only outing
in 2001. *M. J. Haynes*

PHILBOY   2 b.g. (Apr 21) Young Ern 120 – Just Lady 72 (Emarati (USA) 74) [2001 5s   **62**
5s 5m⁵ 5m⁵ f5g⁶ 5m³ 5f 5m⁵ 5d² 5d⁴ 5g Nov 7] 11,000Y: angular gelding: second foal:
half-brother to 3-y-o Justalord: dam 2-y-o 5f winner: modest maiden: second at Catterick:
raced only at 5f: acts on good to firm and soft ground: blinkered (well below form on
fibresand) fifth start: tongue tied last 6. *C. W. Fairhurst*

PHILGIRL   2 ch.f. (Feb 25) Bijou d'Inde 127 – Ballagarrow Girl 66 (North Stoke 130)   **60**
[2001 5d⁶ 5d³ 6m⁴ 6m³ 7f 7.11f⁵ 6d² 6g 6m⁶ 6m⁶ 7d⁵ 6v⁶ 6d Oct 30] 3,200Y, resold
9,000Y: leggy filly: half-sister to several winners, including 1990 2-y-o 5f winner Northern Nation (by Nomination): dam, maiden, best at 1¼m: modest maiden: second at
Hamilton: probably stays 7f: acts on good to firm and heavy going. *C. W. Fairhurst*

PHILIPPI   3 b.g. Alzao (USA) 117 – Lighted Glitter (FR) (Crystal Glitters (USA) 127)   **?**
[2001 58: 8m 10.1m a7g⁴ a8g a8g⁴ a8g⁶ a10.5g* a8g² a8g² a9g Dec 16] compact
gelding: no form in handicaps for Mrs J. Ramsden first 2 starts in 2001, then sold 4,200
gns: won handicap at Mijas in September: stays 10.5f: acts on sand: has been blinkered.
M. Calcines, Spain

PHOEBE BUFFAY (IRE)   4 b.f. Petardia 113 – Art Duo 86 (Artaius (USA) 129)   **74**
[2001 67: f8g⁴ f9.4g⁴ f8f* f7g² e8g* e10m⁵ p10g Dec 19] close-coupled filly: fair
performer: won apprentice handicap at Southwell in March and minor event at Lingfield in April: seems better at 7f/1m than 1¼m: acts on good to firm going, fibresand and
equitrack: blinkered once: races prominently. *C. N. Allen*

PHOEBE ROBINSON (IRE)   3 b.f. Alzao (USA) 117 – Savelli (IRE) (Vision   **78**
(USA)) [2001 71: 8m³ 8f 8f 8.5f² 8.5f* Nov 10] fair performer: left G. Bravery after
reappearance: won maiden at Golden Gate Fields in November: stays 8.5f: acts on any
going. *D. Vienna, USA*

PHOTO FLASH (IRE)   2 ch.f. (Feb 15) Bahamian Bounty 116 – Zoom Lens (IRE)   **69**
65 (Caerleon (USA) 132) [2001 7m 7f⁴ 7f² 8s Sep 27] leggy, unfurnished filly: fourth
living foal: closely related to fairly useful 1997 2-y-o 1m winner Close Up (by Cadeaux
Genereux) and half-sister to 2 winners, notably 2000 Royal Lodge Stakes winner Atlantis
Prince (by Tagula): dam in frame up to 1½m: easily best effort (fair form) when ½-length
second to Princess Petardia in maiden at Brighton: well beaten in nursery next time:
should stay at least 1m: acts on firm ground. *J. L. Dunlop*

PHOTOGRAPHER (USA)   3 b. or br.g. Mountain Cat (USA) – Clickety Click   **90 ?**
(USA) (Sovereign Dancer (USA)) [2001 8m⁵ 8f⁵ 8.5m* 10f³ 10d Oct 13] $23,000F, IR
115,000Y: close-coupled gelding: fourth foal: brother to 2 winners in USA: dam, won up
to 9f in USA, including minor stakes: fairly useful performer: left Sir Michael Stoute after
winning maiden at Beverley in June by 7 lengths: appeared to run creditably when third
of 4 in handicap at Newbury next time: probably stays 1¼m: raced only on ground firmer
than good prior to final start (pulled too hard). *Mrs N. Smith*

PHURTIVE   3 b.g. Factual (USA) 108 – Phlirty (Pharly (FR) 130) [2001 –: 8.2s 10.2d   –
7m 7m Jun 12] smallish, workmanlike gelding: little form. *R. F. Johnson Houghton*

PHYSICAL FORCE   3 b.g. Casteddu 111 – Kaiserlinde (GER) (Frontal 122) [2001   **63**
–: 11.6s 10.2d 11.6g⁶ 14.1m 11.5f³ 12g² 10.1s³ 12d² 12d⁵ 11.9s⁵ p13g² f14.8g³ p13g² Dec
29] leggy gelding: modest maiden handicapper: stays 14.8f: acts on fibresand/polytrack,
firm and soft going: tried blinkered: has carried head awkwardly/flashed tail. *J. R. Best*

PHYSICAL GRAFFITI (USA)   4 b.g. Mister Baileys 123 – Gleaming Water (USA)   **58 +**
(Pago Pago) [2001 78: f12s⁴ Jan 22] $28,000F, 50,000Y: half-brother to numerous
winners abroad, notably US Grade 3 6.5f winner Middlefork Rapids (by Wild Again):
dam unraced: fair form in maidens first 2 starts at 3 yrs for C. O'Brien in Ireland: modest
form in similar event at Southwell only run at 4 yrs: should stay 1¾m: acts on fibresand,
raced only on soft/good to soft going on turf. *J. A. B. Old*

PIANO POWER   3 b.c. Cool Jazz 116 – Panayr (Faraway Times (USA) 123) [2001 –:   **53**
5f⁴ 6m 5g⁵ Jul 18] modest form, lightly raced: will prove best at 5f: hung right final start.
Miss L. A. Perratt

PICCADILLY   6 ch.m. Belmez (USA) 131 – Polly's Pear (USA) (Sassafras (FR) 135)   –
[2001 43: 14f Jun 18] lengthy mare: winning handicapper: well beaten only run in 2001:
tried blinkered. *Miss Kate Milligan*

PICCALILLI   4 ch.f. Piccolo 121 – Hat Hill (Roan Rocket 128) [2001 –: 10m 10d   –
11.5m 11.6m 12g Aug 17] of little account. *S. Woodman*

PICCLED   3 b.g. Piccolo 121 – Creme de Menthe (IRE) (Green Desert (USA) 127)   **67**
[2001 67: 7v 6m 5.1d 5.1d f5g² Dec 14] close-coupled gelding: fair handicapper: easily
best effort at 3 yrs on final start: best at 5f: acts on fibresand and good to soft going: twice
slowly away. *E. J. Alston*

PICCOLEZZA   2 b.f. (May 5) Piccolo 121 – Sound Check 62 (Formidable (USA)   **75 p**
125) [2001 f6g² f5g* Dec 3] 5,200Y: second foal: dam 7f (at 2 yrs)/1m winner: confirmed
promise when winning maiden at Southwell by head from Brilliant Basil: stays 6f: should
progress. *D. E. Cantillon*

PICCOLITIA   3 ch.f. Piccolo 121 – Miss Laetitia (IRE) (Entitled 126) [2001 –: 6s⁵   **51**
6.1v 6d 7.1g 6m 8.5f² 8m³ 8f⁴ 7g Sep 3] lengthy, workmanlike filly: modest maiden
handicapper: stays 8.5f: acts on firm ground: sometimes races freely. *N. A. Graham*

PICCOLITO   2 b.c. (Jun 13) Piccolo 121 – Feather Glen (Glenstal (USA) 118) [2001   –
6m 6g Aug 25] good-topped colt: half-brother to winners abroad by Grand Lodge and
Tirol: dam ran twice in Ireland: no show in maidens: reportedly struck into second start.
T. J. Naughton

PICCOLO CATIVO   6 b.m. Komaite (USA) – Malcesine (IRE) 46 (Auction Ring   **61**
(USA) 123) [2001 53, a–: 8s⁴ 8.3d⁶ 8.2f f7g f7g 7.1d² 6d* 6g³ 6v* Oct 16] smallish mare: **a–**
modest handicapper: won at Hamilton in August and Ayr in October: probably needs bit
of test at 6f nowadays and barely stays 1m: acts on good to firm going, heavy and
fibresand: has flashed tail/drifted left: has gone well fresh: usually ridden by 7-lb claimer
Angela Hartley. *Mrs G. S. Rees*

PICCOLO LADY   2 b.f. (Mar 13) Piccolo 121 – Tonic Chord 49 (La Grange Music   **63**
111) [2001 7g³ 6m 8s Sep 30] 3,600Y: workmanlike filly: second foal: dam, maiden who
raced only at 2 yrs, out of half-sister to useful sprinter Clantime: easily best effort in
maidens (modest form) when third at Leicester: not sure to stay 1m. *Mrs Lydia Pearce*

PICCOLO PARTY   2 b.c. (Apr 11) Piccolo 121 – Silankka 70 (Slip Anchor 136)   **74 d**
[2001 6m³ 5.7f* 7m⁵ 6m 6m 6m f8g³ 7d 5.7d⁴ Oct 25] useful-looking, unfurnished colt:
first foal: dam, 1½m/13f winner, out of half-sister to Ibn Bey and Roseate Tern: fair
performer: mostly below form after winning maiden at Bath in July: ran in seller there
final start: stays 1m: acts on fibresand, good to soft and firm ground: sold 6,500 gns.
M. R. Channon

PICKENS (USA)   9 b.g. Theatrical 128 – Alchi (USA) 112 (Alleged (USA) 138)   –
[2001 –, a59: f16g³ f16g* f11s² f16g² f12s² f16g* f14g² f16g⁶ f16g⁶ f12g* f16g³ May 21]   **a62**
stocky gelding: modest performer: won handicap and 2 claimers at Southwell between
January and April: effective at 11f to 2m: acts on fibresand (unraced on turf since 1997):
tried blinkered earlier in career: has had tongue tied: genuine and consistent. *Don Enrico
Incisa*

PICKETT POINT   3 b.g. Magic Ring (IRE) 115 – Bay Runner (Bay Express 132)   –
[2001 –: 9m 6m 7.6f 10.1s 8.3v f9.4f Dec 5] no form: twice very slowly away.
J. J. Bridger

PICKWICK AYR   2 b.g. (Feb 21) Bijou d'Inde 127 – Ayr Classic (Local Suitor (USA)   **58**
128) [2001 7.2g⁵ 6m 7.2v Oct 15] 22,000Y: angular gelding: fifth foal: half-brother to
1992 2-y-o 5f winner Able Ayr (by Formidable), 5-y-o Class Wan and 1995 2-y-o 1m
winner People Direct (by Ron's Pet), later winner at 7f to 8.5f: dam 2-y-o 5f/6f winner:
modest maiden: not sure to stay 1m: acts on good to firm ground, well held on heavy.
J. S. Goldie

PICO   3 ch.f. Piccolo 121 – Chatterberry 67 (Aragon 118) [2001 71p: 6m³ May 28] big,   **62**
strong, useful-looking filly: reportedly sustained a chip after final 2-y-o start: modest
form in 3 maidens: likely to prove best at 5f/6f: needs to learn to settle. *C. E. Brittain*

PICOBELLA (IRE)   3 b.f. Piccolo 121 – Chelsea Classic (IRE) 53 (Classic Music   –
(USA)) [2001 7s f7g p10g Nov 20] 4,000Y: sturdy filly: second foal: dam twice raced:
well beaten in maidens. *R. J. White*

PICTURE MEE   3 b.f. Aragon 118 – Heemee 81 (On Your Mark 125) [2001 41: f8g⁴   **55 d**
f9.4s* f11g⁶ f11g⁵ 8.2v* 8.2v⁴ 8.2s* 8.1v f8g f8g Dec 14] quite attractive filly: modest
performer: won sellers at Wolverhampton in January and Nottingham in March, and
handicap on latter course in April: soundly beaten last 3 starts (off 6 months before final
one): effective at testing 1m/easy 9f: acts on fibresand, heavy and good to firm ground.
B. S. Rothwell

PICTURE PALACE 3 ch.g. Salse (USA) 128 – Moviegoer 104 (Pharly (FR) 130) **59**
[2001 –: 11.5f 12f² 16.2m⁵ 12f² 16f* Sep 4] lengthy gelding: modest handicapper: won at
Musselburgh in September (pulled hard, tended to wander): stays easy 2m: acts on firm
ground: blinkered in 2001. *Sir Mark Prescott*

PIC UP STICKS 2 gr.c. (Apr 28) Piccolo 121 – Between The Sticks 83 (Pharly (FR) **89**
130) [2001 5g² 6m 6f³ 5m² 6d⁴ 6v³ Oct 27] 16,500Y: unfurnished colt: fourth foal:
half-brother to 1999 2-y-o 5f winner Magic Grand (by Magic Ring) and an Italian sprint
winner by Forzando: dam 2-y-o 5f winner: fairly useful performer: won maiden at York
in October by 1¼ lengths from Mamounia: below-form third in listed race at Doncaster
final start: stays 6f: acts on firm and good to soft ground. *M. R. Channon*

PIE HIGH 2 ch.f. (Apr 5) Salse (USA) 128 – Humble Pie 92 (Known Fact (USA) 135) **74**
[2001 8m 7d 6s f7g* f7s² p7g⁵ Dec 29] 7,500Y, 21,000 2-y-o: half-sister to several
winners, including smart sprinter Leap For Joy (by Sharpo) and 5-y-o Rimatara: dam,
2-y-o 6f winner, half-sister to very smart 6f/7f performer College Chapel: fair performer:
won maiden at Wolverhampton in December: good second in nursery there: will stay 1m:
acts on fibresand (probably on polytrack) and good to soft going. *N. P. Littmoden*

PIERDETE (IRE) 3 br.g. Lahib (USA) 129 – Distinct Element (IRE) (Doyoun 124) **44**
[2001 f7g f8g f8g⁶ f8g⁵ 10s f11g May 21] IR 9,200F, 15,000Y: second foal: dam unraced
half-sister to useful 6f/7f performer Selking: poor maiden: stays 1m: acts on fibresand:
blinkered last 3 starts. *T. D. Easterby*

PIERPOINT (IRE) 6 ch.g. Archway (IRE) 115 – Lavinia (Habitat 134) [2001 70: f6g **66**
f6g⁴ f7g f6g² f6f³ f6g f6g⁵ f5g³ f6g 6.1d³ f6g 5m⁵ 5m³ 5m² 6f f5g Aug 10] smallish
gelding: poor mover: fair performer: left D. Nicholls after third start: best at 5f/6f:
acts on firm going, soft and fibresand: effective visored/blinkered or not: usually races
prominently: joined J. M. Bradley. *D. Shaw*

PIES AR US 4 b.g. Perpendicular 119 – Jendor 82 (Condorcet (FR)) [2001 –: f11g **39**
f11g f8.5g 14.1v 10s 9s 11.1d³ 9m 13m 12m Jun 26] poor maiden: stays 11f: acts on good
to soft going: visored last 4 starts. *C. W. Fairhurst*

PIETA (IRE) 4 b.f. Perugino (USA) 84 – Auction Maid (IRE) (Auction Ring (USA) **52**
123) [2001 52?: f5g f6g* f6g³ f6g f6g⁴ 6g f6g f7g⁵ f5g Jun 8] small, workmanlike filly:
modest performer: won seller at Wolverhampton in March: seems to stay 7f: acts on
fibresand, little form on turf: usually forces pace. *K. McAuliffe*

PIETER BRUEGHEL (USA) 2 b.c. (Feb 9) Citidancer (USA) – Smart Tally (USA) **101**
(Smarten (USA)) [2001 6m⁴ 5.2g* 5m 5g⁴ 6.1d* 6g⁶ 7v⁶ Oct 26] $27,000F, 62,000Y: neat
colt: first foal: dam 1m winner in USA: useful performer: won maiden at Newbury in
May and minor event at Chester (by 10 lengths from Fayr Jag) in September: fourth in
listed race at York in between: creditable sixth of 25 to Captain Rio in Two-Year-Old
Trophy at Redcar penultimate start: well held in Horris Hill Stakes at Newbury final one:
should stay 7f: acts on good to firm and good to soft ground. *P. F. I. Cole*

PIETRO BEMBO (IRE) 7 b.g. Midyan (USA) 124 – Cut No Ice 97 (Great Nephew –
126) [2001 14.1m Jul 27] workmanlike gelding: fair handicapper at 3 yrs: well beaten
only Flat run since: tried blinkered. *J. Akehurst*

PIETRO SIENA (USA) 3 b. or br.c. Gone West (USA) – Via Borghese (USA) 116 **82 p**
(Seattle Dancer (USA) 119) [2001 73p: 6d³ 7s* Oct 15] useful-looking colt: fairly useful
form in just 3 maidens: good third at Newmarket on reappearance, then off 6 months prior
to winning at Leicester in October by 2½ lengths from Far Note, taking time to respond to
pressure but well on top at finish: will stay 1m: raced only on going softer than good:
should do better still. *E. A. L. Dunlop*

PIGEON 6 b.m. Castedijo 111 – Wigeon 80 (Divine Gift 127) [2001 5d 5d⁴ 6g 6g 5d 6d **57**
Oct 9] smallish, sturdy mare: modest handicapper: form in 2001 only on second start
(said to have had breathing problem final outing): stays 6f: acts on soft and good to firm
going. *D. W. Barker*

PIKESTAFF (USA) 3 ch.g. Diesis 133 – Navarene (USA) (Known Fact (USA) 135) **63**
[2001 6v 6g 6m 8.5s 8d Oct 8] sturdy gelding: second foal: half-brother to useful French
1m winner Serene View (by Distant View): dam, French maiden, half-sister to US 2-y-o
Grade 1 1m winner Contredance: maiden: left Mme C. Head-Maarek after second start:
modest form at best in 3 handicaps in Britain: stays 7f. *T. D. Barron*

PILGRIM GOOSE (IRE) 3 ch.g. Rainbows For Life (CAN) – Across The Ring **48 §**
(IRE) (Auction Ring (USA) 123) [2001 53§: 11.5m⁴ 10f⁶ 10.9f⁵ f12g⁴ 11.6m³ 12m² 15.8g **a45 §**

12m[4] 12.1g f11g f11g Nov 30] poor maiden: stays 1½m: acts on fibresand, raced mainly on good going or firmer on turf: blinkered last 6 starts: irresolute. *M. H. Tompkins*

PILGRIM PRINCESS (IRE) 3 b.f. Flying Spur (AUS) – Hasaid Lady (IRE) 69 **49** (Shaadi (USA) 126) [2001 35: f5g f6g 5d f7g[2] 7.1g 8m 7d 6d* 7g[6] 7.1d[5] f7g f6g[2] f6g[6] f6s **a52** Dec 15] rather angular, good-quartered filly: modest handicapper: won at Hamilton in July: should prove as effective over 5f as 6f/7f: acts on fibresand and good to soft going: tried blinkered: none too reliable. *E. J. Alston*

PILLAGER 4 b.g. Reprimand 122 – Emerald Ring 74 (Auction Ring (USA) 123) **–** [2001 62: f16g f16g f8g Apr 14] big, good-topped gelding: modest maiden in 2000: well held at 4 yrs, running as if something amiss final start. *Mrs A. J. Bowlby*

PILOT'S HARBOUR 5 b.g. Distant Relative 128 – Lillemor (Connaught 130) **– §** [2001 –§: 14f Jun 18] temperamental handicapper on Flat nowadays: tried blinkered. *F. P. Murtagh*

PINA COLADA 2 ch.f. (May 21) Sabrehill (USA) 120 – Drei (USA) 67 (Lyphard **77** (USA) 132) [2001 5.3s[2] 5.3f* 7m Jun 20] 2,000Y: small filly: fourth foal: half-sister to 9.4f winner Trois (by Efisio) and 1¼m winner Triple Sharp (by Selkirk), both fairly useful: dam once-raced daughter of smart 7f/1m winner Triple Tipple: fair form: won maiden at Brighton in May: ninth of 11 in Chesham Stakes at Royal Ascot: should stay 1m: acts on firm and soft ground: edged left first 2 starts: sent to USA. *R. Hannon*

PINBALL WIZARD (IRE) 2 b.g. (Apr 10) College Chapel 122 – Miss Bagatelle **–** 70 (Mummy's Pet 125) [2001 5.1s 5s 6m 7.1s 5d 6s Oct 22] 8,000Y: strong gelding: half-brother to French 1997 2-y-o 7f winner Baghamas (by Hamas) and a 7f/1m winner in Hong Kong by Nabeel Dancer: dam, Irish 6f winner, half-sister to Gold Cup winner Arcadian Heights: only a little sign of ability in maidens/claimer: usually blinkered. *J. D. Bethell*

PINCHANINCH 4 ch.g. Inchinor 119 – Wollow Maid 73 (Wollow 132) [2001 72: **72** 12.1s[3] 11.6m[2] 13.1m[5] 12g 14.1d f16g Nov 12] small, lengthy gelding: fair handicapper: **a–** well held last 3 starts (gave trouble stalls and ran thoroughly moody race final one): stays 1½m: acts on any turf going: blinkered twice in 2000. *J. G. Portman*

PINCHBECK 2 b.c. (Jan 27) Petong 126 – Veuve Hoornaert (IRE) 88 (Standaan (FR) **61 p** 118) [2001 6d 6d Nov 2] 15,000Y: strong, good sort: second foal: dam, 2-y-o 5.7f winner, from speedy family: burly and green, never on terms in maidens at Newmarket, not at all knocked about second start: type to do fair bit better. *M. A. Jarvis*

PINCHINCHA (FR) 7 b.g. Priolo (USA) 127 – Western Heights (Shirley Heights **95** 130) [2001 88: 8g[4] 10m[5] 10g[4] 10m 10.4m 10.3m[2] 10g[2] 10.3g[2] 10d[2] 10.4d 10.1s* Oct 31] workmanlike gelding: useful performer: in frame in 6 of 10 starts in handicaps prior to winning minor event at Yarmouth in October by ½ length from Tikram: best at 9f/1¼m: acts on fibresand, equitrack, heavy and good to firm going: tried visored, not in 2001: usually held up: tough and consistent. *D. Morris*

PINJARRA 2 b.f. (Apr 7) Petong 126 – Hoh Dancer 66 (Indian Ridge 123) [2001 6g **– p** Oct 6] 13,000Y: well-made filly: first foal: dam, disappointing maiden, half-sister to useful 1987 2-y-o 5f winner Infanta Real: 25/1 and backward, never-dangerous fourteenth of 17 in maiden at Newmarket: showed a quick action: should do better. *J. A. R. Toller*

PINK CHAMPAGNE 3 ch.f. Cosmonaut – Riviere Rouge (Forzando 122) [2001 –: **–** 5.7m 5.1f f5g 5m Sep 26] little form. *S. G. Knight*

PINNACLE DOLPHIN 2 b.g. (Mar 10) Dolphin Street (FR) 125 – Shifting Time 70 **–** (Night Shift (USA)) [2001 7.1f f8.5s 7.5g Sep 19] 600F, IR 5,500Y: sparely-made gelding: first foal: dam, 6f winner at 4 yrs, half-sister to useful sprinter Poker Chip: little sign of ability in maidens. *J. L. Eyre*

PINOT NOIR 3 b.g. Saddlers' Hall (IRE) 126 – Go For Red (IRE) (Thatching 131) **80** [2001 10m 12m[6] 12f[2] 12m[6] 11.5g[5] 12m[4] Sep 26] rather leggy, useful-looking gelding: third foal: brother to useful 1m (at 2 yrs) to 1½m winner Primary Colours: dam unraced: fairly useful maiden: may prove best at 1¼m/1½m: acts on firm going: flashed tail penultimate start. *H. Morrison*

PIOUS 2 b.f. (Apr 6) Bishop of Cashel 122 – La Cabrilla 89 (Carwhite 127) [2001 6.1v[3] **74 p** f6g* Nov 3] compact filly: half-sister to several winners, including 7f/8.5f winner Mister Rm (by Dominion) and French 1½m to 15f winner and high-class hurdler Teaatral (by Saddlers' Hall): dam, 2-y-o 5f/6f winner who stayed 1m, half-sister to smart sprinter Ya Malak: 5/4-on, confirmed promise when winning maiden at Wolverhampton by 5 lengths from Didnt Tell My Wife: bred to stay 1m: should progress. *J. R. Fanshawe*

PIPADASH (IRE)   4 b.f. Pips Pride 117 – Petite Maxine 70 (Sharpo 132) [2001 92d: **89 +**
6v f7g 5v³ 5s 6g⁴ 6m 6f² 6m⁴ 6f 6g 6d⁴ 6g* 5s* 5d⁶ 5m² 5v³ 6d* 6v³ 6g* Nov 5] big, leggy
filly: good walker: fairly useful performer: won handicaps at Hamilton and Haydock in
September, minor event at York in October and handicap at Redcar (beat Gay Breeze by
1¾ lengths) in November: effective at 5f/6f: acts on any going: tried blinkered, not since
early-2000. *T. D. Easterby*

PIPALONG (IRE)   5 b.m. Pips Pride 117 – Limpopo 49 (Green Desert (USA)   **121**
127) [2001 117: a6f 5g 6m* 6m 6m 5m 6s 6s⁴ 5s³ Oct 7]
       Twelve months after missing her first engagement at the December Sales,
Pipalong fulfilled her second one and fetched 600,000 guineas, reportedly for a stud
in Ireland. The sale finally brought the curtain down on a racing career spanning
four seasons, during which Pipalong established herself as one of the best and
certainly most popular sprinters of recent years. In terms of ability, Pipalong fell
short of the standard set by others of her sex in the sprinting category, such as
Marwell, Habibti and Lochsong, but her attitude was second to none. Well-
documented back problems failed to dampen her enthusiasm for racing and she was
better than ever at the age of five, fully justifying the decision to keep her in training
for another season.
       Pipalong kicked off her final season by becoming her trainer's first runner
outside Europe when contesting the Group 3 Dubai Golden Shaheen at Nad Al
Sheba. On what turned out to be Pipalong's only experience of an artificial surface,
she made little impact, and it transpired that she had lost a shoe during the race.
Back on turf it didn't take Pipalong long to show her worth. All the sharper for a run
at Newmarket, she defied a Group 1 penalty in the Group 3 Duke of York Victor
Chandler Stakes at York in May, a race in which the first six home were covered by
little more than a length. Pipalong travelled well on the heels of the leaders and
probably held a narrow advantage for most of the final furlong, having a neck to
spare over Tedburrow at the line. A loss of form followed this hard-fought victory,
and Pipalong was well held in top company, including the July Cup, the Nunthorpe
and the Haydock Sprint in all three of which she'd been placed in 2000, recording
her career highlight when successful at Haydock. Pipalong was very much back on
song at the end of September, when she finished fourth behind Nice One Clare in
the Diadem Stakes at Ascot. Conceding weight to all but one of her fourteen rivals,
Pipalong rallied with typical courage close home to take fourth place, only around
half a length behind the winner. The return to five furlongs wasn't in Pipalong's
favour when she made her final appearance, in the Prix de l'Abbaye de Longchamp,
and, in finishing third in the race for the second successive year, on this occasion
behind Imperial Beauty and Bahamian Pirate, she was far from discredited. Third-
place prize-money brought Pipalong's career-earnings to over £420,000, not bad
for a 7,000-guinea yearling. Her ten victories all told also included those in
Redcar's Two-Year-Old Trophy, the Great St Wilfrid Handicap as a three-year-old
and the Palace House Stakes as well as Haydock's Sprint Cup in her four-year-old

*Duke of York Victor Chandler Stakes, York—Pipalong (No.1), giving weight all round, beats Tedburrow,
Astonished (noseband), Bertolini (partially obscured by winner) and Vision of Night (right)*

season; the Haydock race provided her trainer Tim Easterby with his first Group 1 success on the Flat. Pipalong will be very much missed at Habton Grange.

Pipalong (IRE) (b.m. 1996)	Pips Pride (ch 1990)	Efisio (b 1982)	Formidable
			Eldoret
		Elkie Brookes (b 1981)	Relkino
			Cresset
	Limpopo (gr 1989)	Green Desert (b 1983)	Danzig
			Foreign Courier
		Grey Goddess (gr 1983)	Godswalk
			Thiella

Pipalong, a neat mare, takes after her dam Limpopo where size is concerned, but in terms of ability there's a vast difference between them. Limpopo was very much lacking in that department, managing only to be placed in a couple of maidens, at Southwell and Hamilton, from five starts as a juvenile. She has certainly shown her worth at stud, though, producing two winners to Common Grounds, notably the useful 1999 two-year-old Out of Africa, and two to Definite Article since. The latter pair are the three-year-old Smoothie, a fair performer who stays a mile and a quarter, and the fairly useful two-year-old seven-furlong winner Corton. The next dam Grey Goddess, who has foaled only three ordinary winners on the Flat and one over jumps, was a smart performer in Ireland and won five races at seven furlongs and a mile, including the Matron Stakes and Gladness Stakes. Apart from when tried, to no avail, over seven furlongs at two and once at a mile at three, Pipalong did all of her racing at five and six furlongs, and six suited her ideally. She was partnered for the most part early in her career by Lindsay Charnock and nearly always by Kevin Darley in her last two seasons. She acted on any going. *T. D. Easterby*

PIPED ABOARD (IRE) 6 b.g. Pips Pride 117 – Last Gunboat 50 (Dominion 123) [2001 79d: f9.4g f12g⁴ f8.5g f9.4g² f8g f12g² e10g³ f16g f12g⁵ 10m⁴ 10d⁴ 11.9f² May 23] good-bodied gelding: poor walker: modest performer: left T. D. Barron after sixth start: needs further than 1m and stays 1½m (probably not 2m): acts on soft going, firm and fibresand: sometimes blinkered/visored: has run in snatches/carried head high. *R. Brotherton*   **57**

PIPE DREAM 5 b.g. King's Signet (USA) 110 – Rather Warm 103 (Tribal Chief 125) [2001 48, a52: 10f p7g p7g Dec 19] of little account nowadays. *Jean-Rene Auvray*   **–**

PIPE MUSIC (IRE) 6 b.g. Mujadil (USA) 119 – Sunset Cafe (IRE) 68 (Red Sunset 120) [2001 48, a66: f16g f14.8s* f14.8g 16.2s f14.8g⁶ f16.2g f14.8s⁵ Dec 15] compact gelding: only poor form in 2001, winning seller at Wolverhampton in January: stays 2m: acts on good to firm ground, good to soft, fibresand and equitrack: effective blinkered/visored or not: tried tongue tied. *P. C. Haslam*   **48**

PIPER DREAM 3 b.g. Contract Law (USA) 108 – Good Fetch 66 (Siberian Express (USA) 125) [2001 f7g 7m f11g⁵ f11g 8.2f⁵ f11g f8s⁶ Dec 21] 2,500Y: leggy gelding: second foal: dam, 2-y-o 5f winner, also successful over hurdles: poor maiden: seems to stay 11f: acts on firm going and fibresand: has carried head awkwardly, and been reluctant to race/slowly away: blinkered. *J. Balding*   **39**

PIPIJI (IRE) 6 gr.m. Pips Pride 117 – Blue Alicia (Wolver Hollow 126) [2001 33: f6g⁶ f8g 7.1m Aug 1] of little account nowadays. *M. Wellings*   **–**

PIPPAS PRIDE (IRE) 6 ch.g. Pips Pride 117 – Al Shany 92 (Burslem 123) [2001 44, a71: f6s⁴ f7s⁶ f6g f7g f7g³ 6m f7g f6g 7m May 30] strong gelding: modest performer: left P. McEntee after fifth start: stays 1m: acts on good to firm going, good to soft, fibresand and equitrack: has worn tongue strap. *R. Hollinshead*   **– a51**

PIPS MAGIC (IRE) 5 b.g. Pips Pride 117 – Kentucky Starlet (USA) 69 (Cox's Ridge (USA)) [2001 88: 6v 5s 6m⁴ 6m³ 5m 6m 5m 6d 6m³ 6f⁶ 6m* 6m³ 6m⁶ 6g* 6m 6m 6m Sep 21] good-bodied gelding: fairly useful performer: won minor event at Doncaster in July and handicap at Ripon in August: better form at 6f than 5f nowadays: acts on firm and soft going: refused to enter stall once in 2000. *J. S. Goldie*   **86**

PIPSSALIO (SPA) 4 b.c. Pips Pride 117 – Tesalia (SPA) (Finissimo (SPA)) [2001 84+: 10s 10.1s 10g 10g 10g 9.9m³ 10g 10m 12g 9.9d³ f12g² Nov 17] workmanlike colt: fair handicapper: stays 1½m: acts on fibresand, best turf form on soft/heavy going: sometimes blinkered. *Jamie Poulton*   **74**

PIPS SONG (IRE)   6 ch.g. Pips Pride 117 – Friendly Song 48 (Song 132) [2001 86:   **80**
f6g⁵ f6g f6g⁶ f6g 6s 7.1g 7m 6d⁴ 6v p6g p7g⁴ Dec 19] lengthy gelding: poor mover:
fairly useful handicapper: effective at 6f/7f: acts on any turf going and fibresand: tried
blinkered: has been awkward leaving stall: none too consistent. *Dr J. D. Scargill*

PIPS WAY (IRE)   4 ch.f. Pips Pride 117 – Algonquin Park (High Line 125) [2001 83:   **73**
10v 8s 8g 10m⁵ 7.9m 10.3d 10.5v⁶ Sep 29] rangy filly: fluent mover: fair handicapper in
2001, form only on fourth start: stays 1¼m: best efforts on good going or softer (acts on
heavy): visored once: usually held up: has pulled hard: refused to enter stall once at 3 yrs:
reportedly in foal to Mind Games. *K. R. Burke*

PIQUET   3 br.f. Mind Games 121 – Petonellajill 73 (Petong 126) [2001 66, a55: e6g⁶   **75**
6m 7s 6f* 7m⁶ 6.1m 6m³ 7m⁵ 7m⁴ 6m* 7.1f 6s 6d⁶ 5.2v f6g p7g³ Dec 19] unfurnished   **a54**
filly: fair handicapper on turf, modest on all-weather: won at Lingfield in June and
Brighton in August: effective at 6f (both wins)/7f: acts on equitrack, polytrack and any
turf going: has started slowly/edged left. *R. Hannon*

PIRANDELLO (IRE)   3 ch.g. Shalford (IRE) 124§ – Scenic Villa (Top Ville 129)   **73**
[2001 11.5g⁴ 12m 10v² 11.7d Oct 25] half-brother to 1m/1½m winner Globe Runner
(by Adbass): dam poor maiden: fair maiden: stays 11.5f: acts on heavy going. *Miss
K. B. Boutflower*

PIRRO (IRE)   6 ch.g. Persian Bold 123 – Kindness Itself (IRE) 89 (Ahonoora 122)   **82**
[2001 10m 10f 11.4g⁴ 12g⁴⁸ 12m⁵ 12d² 12m⁶ 10g Sep 8] strong gelding: first foal: dam
Irish 7f winner: fairly useful handicapper: trained by J. Oxx in Ireland at 3/4 yrs: won at
Doncaster in July: stays 1½m: acts on soft and good to firm ground: withdrawn once after
breaking out of stall: usually front runner: sold only 2,700 gns. *M. H. Tompkins*

PIVOTABLE   3 ch.f. Pivotal 124 – Lady Dowery (USA) (Manila (USA)) [2001 63:   **57 +**
f6g* 6d f6g* 6.1f 6m 7f⁵ 8m 6g f6g f6g f7g² f7s³ p7g Dec 28] lengthy filly: fair performer   **a75**
on all-weather, modest on turf: won maiden and handicap at Wolverhampton in February/
May: left M. Bell after next start: stays easy 7f: acts on soft ground (probably on firm)
and fibresand: visored (pulled too hard) once. *K. R. Burke*

PIVOT D'AMOUR   2 ch.f. (Apr 10) Pivotal 124 – Miss Loving 89 (Northfields   **56**
(USA)) [2001 6g 5s³ 6m 5.1f Sep 18] 6,800F, IR 25,000Y: leggy, plain filly: half-sister to
several winners, including fairly useful sprinter Love Returned (by Taufan) and 4-y-o
Parker: dam 2-y-o 5f and 7f winner: modest maiden: not sure to stay beyond 6f: reluctant
stalls on debut, slowly away final start. *J. J. Quinn*

PLACATE   3 b.f. Rainbow Quest (USA) 134 – Princess Borghese (USA) 82 (Nijinsky   **75**
(CAN) 138) [2001 12f⁴ 10m³ 12g Aug 11] close-coupled, quite good-topped filly: fourth
foal: dam, 10.5f winner, from very good family of Sanglamore: fair form in frame in
maidens at Newbury and Ascot: well held in similar event at Newmarket (edgy/swished
tail beforehand) final start: should prove better at 1½m than 1¼m: sold 6,000 gns in
December. *J. H. M. Gosden*

PLAIN CHANT   4 b.g. Doyoun 124 – Sing Softly 112 (Luthier 126) [2001 –: 12.6f⁶   **48**
14.1m⁵ 16d³ Jul 18] poor maiden handicapper: should be suited by 2m+: acts on firm
ground. *P. W. Harris*

PLATEAU   2 b.c. (Jan 19) Zamindar (USA) 116 – Painted Desert 89 (Green Desert   **94**
(USA) 127) [2001 6d* 6m³ Aug 13] third foal: dam, 2-y-o 5.7f winner, out of sister to
Lowther winner Kingscote: won maiden at Ayr in July: fairly useful form when ½-length
third to Resplendent Cee in minor event at Windsor, travelling strongly before drifting
left: not sure to stay beyond 6f. *B. W. Hills*

PLATINUM DUKE   2 br.g. (Mar 28) Reprimand 122 – Princess Alaska (Northern   **81**
State (USA) 91) [2001 6m² 6m² 7f⁵ 7.1m* 7.5m² 7g⁶ 8m⁶ Aug 27] 4,200F, IR 18,000Y:
tall, close-coupled gelding: third living foal: half-brother to 3-y-o Prince Shaamaal: dam
unraced half-sister to smart 1m winner Royal Philosopher: fairly useful performer: won
maiden at Musselburgh in July: sixth in valuable nursery at Newcastle final start: stays
1m: raced only on good going or firmer. *K. A. Ryan*

PLATONIC   2 b.f. (Feb 6) Zafonic (USA) 130 – Puce 112 (Darshaan 133) [2001 7f⁴   **79**
8m⁶ Sep 22] leggy, light-bodied filly: first foal: dam 1¼m/1½m winner who stayed 14.6f
well: fair form in maidens at Newmarket: should stay 1¼m. *L. M. Cumani*

PLAYAPART (USA)   2 b.c. (Mar 19) Theatrical 128 – Spotlight Dance (USA)   **107 p**
(Miswaki (USA) 124) [2001 7f³ 7d² p10g* Dec 4] $270,000Y: rather leggy, angular colt:
has a long, round action: third living foal: half-brother to a winner in USA by Holy Bull:
dam unraced half-sister to US Grade 1 winners Sewickley (7f) and Shared Interest (8.5f):

useful form: placed in maiden at Newbury and minor event at Ascot (best effort, short-headed by Rapscallion) prior to landing odds in maiden at Lingfield easily by 5 lengths from Manorson: stays 1¼m: open to improvement, and sure to win more races. *G. A. Butler*

PLAYBACK (IRE)   2 b.c. (Feb 1) Revoque (IRE) 122 – Sound Tap (IRE) (Warning   **81**
136) [2001 7g 7m⁵ 8m⁴ 10d³ 10d² Nov 2] IR 23,000F, IR 30,000Y: leggy, good-topped colt: first foal: dam French 6f to 1m winner: fairly useful maiden: second to Esteemed Master at Brighton: likely to stay 1½m: acts on good to firm and good to soft ground. *R. Hannon*

PLAYFUL CHARLIE   6 b.g. Librate 91 – Hayley's Lass (Royal Boxer 112) [2001 –:   **–**
f8.5s Jan 9] no form in 2 maidens at Wolverhampton. *J. M. Bradley*

PLAYFUL SPIRIT   2 b.f. (Jan 27) Mind Games 121 – Kalimat 74 (Be My Guest   **88**
(USA) 126) [2001 6m⁶ 6m* 7m⁶ 6m Aug 13] 15,000Y: leggy, useful-looking filly: first foal: dam, 1m winner, half-sister to US Grade 1 1m/9f winner In Excess: fairly useful form: won maiden at Goodwood in June and minor event at Salisbury in July: something possibly amiss last 2 starts, carrying head awkwardly on first occasion: should stay 7f. *P. W. Harris*

PLAY GAMES (USA)   13 ch.g. Nijinsky (CAN) 138 – Playful Queen (USA)   **–**
(Majestic Prince (USA)) [2001 f14g Oct 1] fair 2m handicap chaser, lightly raced on Flat nowadays. *R. Lee*

PLAYGIRL (IRE)   3 b.f. Caerleon (USA) 132 – Stage Struck (IRE) 83 (Sadler's   **77**
Wells (USA) 132) [2001 10g² 10g² 8.1g⁴ Sep 1] second foal: sister to useful 1¼m winner who stayed 1½m Drama Class: dam, 1½m winner, sister to high-class performer up to 1¼m Prince of Dance, out of Oaks/St Leger winner Sun Princess: runner-up in maidens at Windsor first 2 starts: apparently something amiss (dismounted after line) final outing: will stay beyond 1¼m. *Sir Michael Stoute*

PLAYMAKER   8 b.g. Primo Dominie 121 – Salacious (Sallust 134) [2001 –:   **–**
10s Apr 28] of little account on Flat nowadays. *F. P. Murtagh*

PLAY MISTY (IRE)   2 b.f. (Mar 16) Dr Devious (IRE) 127 – Mystic Step (IRE) 90   **56**
(Fairy King (USA)) [2001 f5g⁶ 6.1g⁴ 5m⁶ 5m³ 6g 5.3s² 7s p6g f6g⁴ p6g⁴ Dec 19] 3,000 2-y-o: leggy, unfurnished filly: first foal: dam third at 7f and 9f in Ireland: modest maiden: second in seller at Brighton: stays 6f: acts on fibresand/polytrack, good to firm and soft ground: blinkered first 3 starts. *John Berry*

PLAY TIME   3 b.f. Unfuwain (USA) 131 – Break Point (Reference Point 139) [2001   **84**
76p: 10d⁶ 10g² 10m* 12m⁶ Jun 27] tall, leggy, useful-looking filly: fairly useful form, lightly raced: ½-length second to Lailani in handicap at Newmarket prior to winning maiden there in June by ¾ length from Hyde Hall, quickening well once gap appeared: something possibly amiss final start: bred to be suited by 1½m+: acts on good to firm ground: may prove best on galloping tracks. *D. R. C. Elsworth*

PLAZZOTTA (IRE)   4 b.g. Sri Pekan (USA) 117 – Porte Des Iles (IRE) 76 (Kris 135)   **–**
[2001 –: f8g f6s⁶ f11g f12g f11g 6m f12g 7g f7g Dec 3] good-topped gelding: no form. *M. C. Chapman*

PLEADING   8 b.g. Never So Bold 135 – Ask Mama 83 (Mummy's Pet 125) [2001 65,   **61**
a71: f6f⁵ f7g 7.1d³ 7d³ 7m⁵ 7.1g 7g³ 7m 8d 8s f6g⁶ f7g Dec 3] smallish, good-topped gelding: modest performer: needs good test at 6f, and stays 1m: acts on any turf going and fibresand: usually visored nowadays, has been blinkered: sometimes slowly away: usually held up: none too consistent. *M. A. Buckley*

PLEASANT MOUNT   5 b.g. First Trump 118 – Alo Ez 100 (Alzao (USA) 117)   **–**
[2001 70, a74: 16v 16m⁵ 15.8m Sep 22] good-bodied gelding: fair handicapper at 4 yrs: well below that level in 2001. *G. M. Moore*

PLEASURE   6 ch.m. Most Welcome 131 – Peak Squaw (USA) 75 (Icecapade (USA))   **56 §**
[2001 55: f6g³ f5g⁶ 6.1v f6g f5g⁵ f6g⁴ f6g f5g⁵ 6g f5g f7g f6s Dec 21] unfurnished mare: modest handicapper: left A. Smith before penultimate start: reportedly finished lame final outing: stays 7f: acts on heavy going and fibresand: sometimes blinkered and hooded: has looked none too keen: inconsistent. *P. R. Wood*

PLEASURE DOME   3 b.f. Most Welcome 131 – Hickleton Lady (IRE) 64 (Kala   **72**
Shikari 125) [2001 77: f7g² f7g⁴ 6m⁵ 6g 6g⁶ 6g 5.3m 8s* 8d* 10s p8g* p8g⁵ p8g³ Dec 4] lengthy filly: fair performer: won minor events at Brighton and Leicester in October and handicap at Lingfield in November: should prove as effective at 7f as 1m: acts on

fibresand, polytrack, soft and good to firm going: blinkered (raced freely) sixth start: has wandered. *J. M. P. Eustace*

PLEASURE TIME 8 ch.g. Clantime 101 – First Experience 58 (Le Johnstan 123) **66** [2001 73: 5g 5m 5d 5g 5.1g 5m² 5f⁶ f5g³ f5g* f5g Dec 14] leggy, good-topped gelding: fair 5f handicapper: won at Southwell in November: acts on fibresand, best turf form on good going or firmer: has worn blinkers, visored nowadays: front runner. *C. Smith*

PLEINMONT POINT (IRE) 3 b.g. Tagula (IRE) 116 – Cree's Figurine 63 (Cree- **67** town 123) [2001 64: 7v² 6s 6m 6.1f Sep 18] big, workmanlike gelding: fair maiden handicapper: below form after reappearance (reportedly returned lame final start): stays 7f: acts on heavy ground: tongue tied third start. *P. D. Evans*

PLOUGH BOY 3 br.g. Komaite (USA) – Plough Hill (North Briton 67) [2001 f7s **56** e7g⁶ f7g⁶ 7m² 6.1m 7m 8d* 10g² 10s⁴ Sep 24] third foal: brother to 4-y-o Robin Hood: dam unraced: modest performer: won selling handicap at Yarmouth in August: best around 1m: acts on good to firm and good to soft going: winner of both outings in juvenile hurdles in November. *D. E. Cantillon*

PLUM BEAUTIFUL 3 b.f. Wolfhound (USA) 126 – Miss Haversham 81 (Salse **56** (USA) 128) [2001 8.3s 8m⁴ 7d 8m⁴ 7m⁶ 8m p7g f9.4f⁵ Dec 5] second foal: dam maiden who stayed 1¼m: modest maiden at best: seems to stay 9.4f: acts on fibresand, best efforts on turf on good to firm going. *C. A. Cyzer*

PLURALIST (IRE) 5 b.g. Mujadil (USA) 119 – Encore Une Fois (IRE) 84 (Shirley **–** Heights 130) [2001 77: f16.2g⁶ f11g 15.4v 15g 16.2m p13g Dec 29] small, lengthy gelding: fair performer at 4 yrs: well held in 2001: tried tongue tied. *Miss K. M. George*

PLYMSOLE (USA) 2 ch.f. (Mar 15) Diesis 133 – Pump (Forli (ARG)) [2001 **79 p** 7g⁴ 7.5m* Aug 25] sister to very smart miler Dockside and half-sister to several winners, including useful middle-distance performer Classic Sport (by Nijinsky): dam unraced from excellent family: favourite, confirmed promise when winning maiden at Beverley by ¾ length from Googoosh, leading 2f out: will stay at least 1m: should progress. *J. L. Dunlop*

POCKET STYLE (IRE) 2 b.f. (Mar 21) Desert Style (IRE) 121 – Practical 95 **64** (Ballymore 123) [2001 6f⁴ 5m³ 6d 7g⁵ 8.1s 7d 8s Oct 22] IR 4,000F, IR 10,000Y: smallish, workmanlike filly: half-sister to several winners, including fairly useful 6f winner Be Practical (by Tragic Role) and 4-y-o Papi Special: dam Irish 9f/1¼m winner: modest maiden: should stay 1m: acts on good to firm going: has worn crossed noseband: has hung under pressure. *C. Grant*

POINT GIVEN (USA) 3 ch.c. Thunder Gulch (USA) 129 – Turko's Turn (USA) **134** (Turkoman (USA)) [2001 116p: a8.5f* a9f* a10f⁵ a9.5f* a12f* a9f* a10f* Aug 25] second foal: half-brother to a winner in USA by Dehere: dam, US 5f (at 2 yrs) to 1m winner, also won 5.5f minor stakes at 2 yrs: top-class performer: won 6 of his 7 races at 3 yrs, Grade 2 San Felipe Stakes at Santa Anita, Santa Anita Derby (by 5½ lengths), Preak- ness Stakes at Pimlico (by 2¼ lengths from A P Valentine), Belmont Stakes, Haskell Invitational Handicap at Monmouth (made hard work of it) and Travers Stakes at Saratoga: best efforts in Belmont Stakes, in which he put up a magnificent performance, leading 4f out and winning by 12¼ lengths from A P Valentine, and Travers Stakes, in which he beat E Dubai by 3½ lengths: favourite, weakened tamely in straight when only fifth to Monarchos in Kentucky Derby at Churchill Downs on third outing: very best effort at 1½m: won only outing in wet fast conditions: wore blinkers: very fractious before being loaded penultimate appearance, less so final start: tended to hang left: retired in late-August after reportedly straining tendon in near-fore: to stand at Three Chimneys Farm, Kentucky, fee $125,000 live foal. *R. Baffert, USA*

POINT OF DISPUTE 6 b.g. Cyrano de Bergerac 120 – Opuntia (Rousillon (USA) **101** 133) [2001 97: 6m 6g⁴ 7f³ 7g² f8g⁶ p7g³ p7g Dec 29] tall, useful-looking gelding: useful handicapper: won at Lingfield in November by ½ length from Lunar Leo: best at 6f/7f: acts on fibresand, polytrack, firm and good to soft going: visored nowadays: has tended to sweat/get on edge: has been early to post: often held up: tends to carry head awkwardly/ wander/find little on occasions. *P. J. Makin*

POKER SCHOOL (IRE) 7 b.g. Night Shift (USA) – Mosaique Bleue (Shirley **–** Heights 130) [2001 f12g⁴ f16g f12g⁵ f12g³ f12g³ e13g⁵ f14g f14g⁴ f11g Dec 17] smallish, **a58** sturdy gelding: modest performer: effective at 1½m to 2m: acts on fibresand and equi- track: tried blinkered/visored: has worn tongue strap. *M. R. Bosley*

POLAR BEAUTY (IRE)   4 b.f. Distinctly North (USA) 115 – How Gorgeous   **56** (Frimley Park 109) [2001 6s 7.1m⁶ 5.1f³ 5f⁴ f5g Jul 13] IR 6,400F, 4,000Y: fourth foal: sister to Irish 1996 2-y-o 8.5f winner Mount Rushmore and half-sister to a winner in Germany by Nashamaa: dam ran twice: modest form in maidens and a handicap: should stay 6f: reportedly broke blood vessel final start. *B. A. McMahon*

POLAR BEN   2 b.g. (Mar 5) Polar Falcon (USA) 126 – Woodbeck 90 (Terimon 124)   **86 p** [2001 7.1m* Aug 27] 12,500Y, 24,000 2-y-o: first foal: dam, 7f winner, out of half-sister to Prix de Diane winner Madam Gay: won 12-runner maiden at Warwick, seeming green and missing break but leading over 1f out and beating River Reine by ¾ length: gelded after: will stay 1m: could well be a useful performer in the making. *J. R. Fanshawe*

POLAR DANCE (USA)   3 gr. or ro.c. Nureyev (USA) 131 – Arctic Swing (USA)   **–** (Swing Till Dawn (USA)) [2001 7f 8.1d 8.3m Aug 13] eighth foal: brother to winner in Japan and half-brother to several winners, including a Grade 2-placed winner in USA by Capote: dam sprint winner in USA: behind in maidens. *J. W. Hills*

POLAR HAZE   4 ch.g. Polar Falcon (USA) 126 – Sky Music 85 (Absalom 128) [2001   **52** 66: 6g 6m 5g 5m⁵ f5g* 5v f5g⁴ Dec 14] lengthy, good-quartered gelding: modest   **a60** handicapper: won at Southwell (edged left) in October: best at 5f/6f: acts on fibresand, firm and good to soft ground: visored last 4 starts. *Miss S. E. Hall*

POLAR IMPACT   2 br.c. (May 14) Polar Falcon (USA) 126 – Boozy 111 (Absalom   **76 +** 128) [2001 5m⁵ 5f⁵ 5g² 6.1m³ 5s² 6d⁶ Oct 12] 8,500Y: strong, short-backed colt: seventh foal: half-brother to 5f (including at 2 yrs) winner Gwespyr (by Sharpo): dam best at 5f: fair maiden: seemed to run very well when second at Lingfield penultimate start: will prove best at 5f/easy 6f: acts on good to firm and soft going, ran as if something amiss on firm. *A. Berry*

POLAR KINGDOM   3 b.g. Pivotal 124 – Scarlet Lake 60 (Reprimand 122) [2001   **101** 6d⁴ 6g* 6s* 6d³ 6g⁵ 7g⁵ 7.1s 6g⁴ 6d² Oct 13] 24,000F, 70,000Y: rangy gelding: usually looks well: first foal: dam lightly-raced half-sister to useful performers up to 7f Maid For The Hills and Maid For Walking and to dam of smart 1¼m performer Lady In Waiting: useful and generally progressive form, winning maiden at Salisbury and handicap at Newbury in May: very good ¾-length second to Abbajabba in handicap at York final start: effective at 6f (given bit of a test)/7f: acts on good going or softer: visored (slowly away and below form) seventh outing: sold 80,000 gns. *J. Noseda*

POLAR LADY   4 ch.f. Polar Falcon (USA) 126 – Soluce 98 (Junius (USA) 124) [2001   **66** 69: f8g f7g⁶ f8s² f8g f7s* f8g⁶ f8g³ f7g⁵ May 14] strong, lengthy filly: fair performer: won seller at Southwell in February: effective at 7f/1m: acts on soft going, good to firm and fibresand: visored once at 3 yrs: has played up in stall/found little: sold 3,000 gns. *D. Morris*

POLAR MIST   6 b.g. Polar Falcon (USA) 126 – Post Mistress (IRE) 79 (Cyrano de   **60** Bergerac 120) [2001 63, a59: f5g⁶ f5g* f5g⁴ f5g² f5g f5g⁴ 5.1d⁵ 5m 5.2v p5g Nov 20]   **a65** quite good-topped gelding: fair handicapper: won at Wolverhampton in February: best at 5f/6f: acts on soft going, good to firm and fibresand: visored/blinkered/tongue tied: sometimes slowly away: usually races prominently. *M. Wigham*

POLAR RED   4 ch.g. Polar Falcon (USA) 126 – Sharp Top 62 (Sharpo 132) [2001   **106** 110: 13.9g 12g⁵ Oct 5] good-topped gelding: has a round action: only useful form in 2001: stiff tasks in Ebor at York (eighth to Mediterranean) and listed race at Newmarket (beaten 7 lengths behind Mubtaker), fading on both occasions: very best form around 1¼m: acts on heavy and good to firm going: blinkered first 3 starts at 2 yrs: has had to be mounted in saddling box/worn rope halter (refused to go to post once at 3 yrs). *M. C. Pipe*

POLAR ROCK   3 ch.f. Polar Falcon (USA) 126 – South Rock 102 (Rock City 120)   **66** [2001 55: 6.1v³ 7.1g⁶ 9.1m⁵ 8.2g³ 7.6m⁶ 7g 8s Oct 3] lengthy, rather unfurnished filly: fair maiden: well below form final 3 starts: stays 1m: acts on heavy going: hung penultimate start, ran as if something amiss final outing: not one to trust implicitly: sold 1,500 gns. *M. L. W. Bell*

POLAR STAR   4 b.g. Polar Falcon (USA) 126 – Glowing With Pride 114 (Ile de   **65** Bourbon (USA) 133) [2001 80?: e12g⁴ 12.3f May 10] big, quite good-topped gelding: fair maiden: stayed 1½m: acted on soft going and equitrack: headstrong: broke leg over hurdles in October: dead. *M. C. Pipe*

POLAR TRYST   2 ch.f. (Apr 24) Polar Falcon (USA) 126 – Lovers Tryst 91 (Castle   **65** Keep 121) [2001 8s 10d⁵ Nov 2] leggy, lengthy, unfurnished filly: sixth reported foal: dam 1¼m winner: still green, better effort in maidens (modest form) when fifth to

Esteemed Master at Brighton: will probably stay 1½m: very slowly away on debut. *Lady Herries*

POLE STAR 3 b. or br.g. Polar Falcon (USA) 126 – Ellie Ardensky 100 (Slip Anchor **103** 136) [2001 97p: 8f* 9s³ 10g⁴ 12g 12d⁴ Oct 2] tall, good-topped gelding: useful performer: won maiden at Leicester in May: mostly creditable efforts in handicaps after, 5¼ lengths fourth to High Pitched at Newmarket final outing, running in snatches (subsequently gelded): stays 1½m: yet to race on heavy going, probably acts on any other. *J. R. Fanshawe*

POLICASTRO 3 b.c. Anabaa (USA) 130 – Belle Arrivee 87 (Bustino 136) [2001 56p: **66** 8.3m 8m 10g 10.1g 10v⁶ f12g⁶ Oct 22] fair maiden: should stay 1¾m: acts on fibresand and heavy ground: tongue tied last 2 starts: sold 10,000 gns. *J. W. Hills*

POLI KNIGHT 4 b.f. Polish Precedent (USA) 131 – River Spey 96 (Mill Reef (USA) **50** 141) [2001 77d: e12g⁴ Jan 3] leggy filly: fair performer at best: modest form only outing in 2001: stays 1¼m: acts on good to firm going: tried tongue tied. *J. W. Hills*

POLISH BARON (IRE) 4 b.g. Barathea (IRE) 127 – Polish Mission (Polish Pre- **73** cedent (USA) 131) [2001 69: 11.9g* 12m⁵ 11.9m³ 11.7m* Aug 24] IR 25,000Y: useful-looking gelding: first foal: dam unraced half-sister to very smart 6f to 1m performer Interval from very good family: fair performer: trained by N. Meade in Ireland in 2000: won claimer at Haydock in June and seller at Bath (sold 6,200 gns) in August: stays 1½m: acts on soft and good to firm going: has been bandaged in front: joined J. White, and fair winner over hurdles. *P. J. Hobbs*

POLISH CORRIDOR 2 b.g. (Feb 10) Danzig Connection (USA) – Possibility 59 **63** (Robellino (USA) 127) [2001 5.2g 6f⁴ 7g Aug 17] 20,000Y: tall gelding: has scope: third foal: half-brother to a winner in Switzerland by Dancing Spree: dam 7f winner: modest maiden: should stay 7f. *M. Dods*

POLISHED UP 4 b.f. Polish Precedent (USA) 131 – Smarten Up 119 (Sharpen Up **51** 127) [2001 51: 9.9m⁶ 8m 6m Jun 22] quite attractive filly: modest maiden at 3 yrs: little form in 2001: visored penultimate start. *R. M. Beckett*

POLISH FALCON (IRE) 5 b.g. Polish Patriot (USA) 128 – Marie de Fresnaye – (USA) (Dom Racine (FR) 121) [2001 9.7v 11.9s 12m 10.1d 11.9s Oct 3] modest maiden at 3 yrs: well held in handicaps in 2001: blinkered final start. *Mrs N. Smith*

POLISH FLAME 3 b.g. Blushing Flame (USA) 109 – Lady Emm (Emarati (USA) **71** 74) [2001 75p: 9m⁴ 8d⁶ 16.1d² Oct 3] fair maiden, lightly raced: creditable second in handicap at Newcastle final start: stays 2m: acts on heavy going: promising juvenile hurdler, winner in November/December. *Mrs M. Reveley*

POLISH OFF 3 b.g. Polish Precedent (USA) 131 – Lovely Lyca 76 (Night Shift (USA)) **87** [2001 88: 8s³ 10.4m⁶ 10.1m 8.1d² 8.1d* 9m⁴ 8f³ 8g 8s Nov 9] strong gelding: fairly useful performer: made all in maiden at Warwick in July: sold from B. Hills and gelded after penultimate start: stays 10.4f: acts on firm and good to soft going. *R. M. Beckett*

POLISH PADDY (IRE) 3 b.g. Priolo 127 – Polish Widow 74 (Polish **65** Precedent (USA) 131) [2001 71: 8d 8f⁶ 8m³ 10.2g 7.1d² 7m 8m⁶ 7.1g f9.4g⁵ Oct 9] small gelding: fair handicapper: effective at 7f (given test) to 9.4f: acts on fibresand, soft and good to firm going, probably on firm: blinkered after reappearance: none too consistent. *R. Hannon*

POLLY FLINDERS 3 b.f. Polar Falcon (USA) 126 – So True 116 (So Blessed 130) **65** [2001 7d 8.3d 7.1v⁴ 8d 10s⁴ Oct 30] rangy filly: has scope: sister to smart miler Bomb Alaska and half-sister to 1m winner Phonetic (by Shavian) and 1m/9f winner Keep Your Word (by Castle Keep): dam, 5f (at 2 yrs) and 1m winner, best at 1½m: fair maiden: will stay 1½m: raced only on going softer than good: still seemed green final start. *G. B. Balding*

POLLY GOLIGHTLY 8 ch.m. Weldnaas (USA) 112 – Polly's Teahouse 68 (Shack **67** (USA) 118) [2001 77: 5m 5.1f 5m 5.1m Jul 5] smallish mare: fair handicapper: best at 5f: untried on heavy going, acts on any other: blinkered: has swished tail and tends to edge left: best racing up with pace. *M. Blanshard*

POLWHELE 3 ch.g. Mujtahid (USA) 118 – Safayn (USA) 82 (Lyphard (USA) 132) **41** [2001 46: f6g f7s⁶ f8g 7m 7m f7g² Jul 13] poor maiden: stays 7f: best efforts on fibresand: often visored: tongue tied last 5 starts: sent to Spain. *R. M. H. Cowell*

POLY AMANSHAA (IRE) 9 b. or br.g. Nashamaa 113 – Mombones (Lord Gayle (USA) 124) [2001 f16g Mar 21] of little account on Flat nowadays. *W. Jarvis* –

POLYPHONIC 3 b.f. Binary Star (USA) – Plainsong 71 (Ballad Rock 122) [2001 –: 6f 5m 8.2m 6m 5g Aug 17] smallish, workmanlike filly: little form: left A. Mulholland after second start: visored final outing: tail swisher. *B. S. Rothwell* –

POMFRET LAD 3 b.g. Cyrano de Bergerac 120 – Lucky Flinders 77 (Free State 125) [2001 107p: 6m³ 6g Jun 2] tall, good-topped gelding: useful performer: looking to have done well physically, creditable length third to Invincible Spirit in minor event at Goodwood: disappointing next time, and gelded after: races freely, and will prove at least as effective at 5f as 6f: yet to race on extremes of ground: had looked a smart prospect. *P. J. Makin* 107

POMME D'OR 3 b.f. Celtic Swing 138 – Glitter (FR) 70 (Reliance II 137) [2001 10m 12.6m 12g f14.8g⁶ Sep 22] unfurnished, angular filly: half-sister to several winners, notably top-class French 1½m performer Village Star (by Moulin) and smart French 1¼m/1½m performer For Valour (by Trempolino): dam 1¼m winner: no sign of ability. *K. O. Cunningham-Brown* –

POMME SWINGER (FR) 3 b.f. Celtic Swing 138 – Tarte Aux Pommes (USA) (Local Talent (USA) 122) [2001 8.2d 8s⁵ 8.3v p7g f11g Dec 1] 180,000 francs Y: leggy, sparely-made filly: first foal: dam winner in France (stayed 10.5f) before showing nothing in Britain: little form: sent to France. *K. O. Cunningham-Brown* –

POMPEII (IRE) 4 b.g. Salse (USA) 128 – Before Dawn (USA) (Raise A Cup (USA)) [2001 85: 16m 8.5s 12m 12m⁵ 10.4s⁵ 14.1g Oct 19] rangy gelding: fairly useful performer at 3 yrs: on downgrade in 2001, leaving R. Phillips after first start: stays 1½m: acts on good to firm and heavy going: ridden prominently. *N. Wilson* 69 d

POPOCATEPETL (FR) 2 br.f. (Feb 13) Nashwan (USA) 135 – Dimakya (USA) 83 (Dayjur (USA) 137) [2001 7d Nov 3] 70,000Y: leggy, quite good-topped filly: second foal: half-sister to 1999 2-y-o 6f winner Tereed Elhawa (by Cadeaux Genereux): dam, French 7.5f winner who probably stayed 1¼m, daughter of smart French/US performer around 1¼m Reloy: 20/1, tenth of 21 to Maid For Perfection in Newmarket maiden: should stay 1¼m: should do better. *B. W. Hills* 66 p

POPPAEA (IRE) 3 b.f. Definite Article 121 – Classic Ring (IRE) 50 (Auction Ring (USA) 123) [2001 51: 8.3s⁵ 8.1g⁶ 7s 7f 6m 8d⁵ 8d f7g⁶ Dec 1] rather leggy filly: modest maiden: stays 1m: acts on soft going, probably on fibresand: sold 800 gns. *R. Hannon* 59

POP SHOP 4 b.c. Owington 123 – Diamond Park (IRE) 91 (Alzao (USA) 117) [2001 69: 6f 5g Aug 6] strong, good-topped colt: fair handicapper at best: well held in 2001: tried blinkered: has worn tongue tie. *J. W. Payne* –

POP THE CORK 4 ch.g. Clantime 101 – Hyde Princess 75 (Touch Paper 113) [2001 62, a–: 5g 5m 5m 5m 5m³ 5m* 5m⁶ 5f 5g 5g⁵ 5m* 5m* 5.3m³ 5.1g³ Sep 13] strong-quartered gelding: fair handicapper: won at Beverley in June and Musselburgh (on successive days) in August, twice in apprentice events: raced mainly at 5f: acts on firm and good to soft going: reportedly broke blood vessel final 3-y-o outing: races prominently. *R. M. Whitaker* 75 a–

PORAK (IRE) 4 ch.g. Perugino (USA) 84 – Gayla Orchestra (Lord Gayle (USA) 124) [2001 60: e7g e8s³ e10g e10g⁵ 9.7v* 11.9m² 10g⁴ 10f 10m 10g⁶ 9g 12g⁵ 12g² 10s* Oct 16] big gelding: fair handicapper: won at Folkestone in April and Leicester (idled) in October: best at 1¼m/1½m: acts on equitrack and heavy going, probably on good to firm. *G. L. Moore* 78 a69

PORTACASA 2 b.f. (Jan 18) Robellino (USA) 127 – Autumn Affair 100 (Lugana Beach 116) [2001 6m⁴ 7g Aug 13] 4,000Y, resold 3,200Y: leggy filly: second foal: dam 2-y-o 6f winner who stayed 1m: poor form in maidens: should stay 1m. *R. A. Fahey* 49

PORT LOUIS (IRE) 3 b.g. Fairy King (USA) – Search For Spring (IRE) (Rainbow Quest (USA) 134) [2001 f8.5f Dec 5] 8,500Y: fifth foal: half-brother to fairly useful French 1¼m winner who stayed 1½m Siamoise (by Caerleon): dam, Irish maiden, half-sister to Prix Saint-Alary winner Grise Mine and US Grade 1 1¼m winner Kostroma: 12/1, soon pushed along when last in maiden at Wolverhampton. *C. A. Cyzer* –

PORT MORESBY (IRE) 3 b.g. Tagula (IRE) 116 – Santana Lady (IRE) 72 (Blakeney 126) [2001 74, a67: 10d 7.9g 9m³ 9f* 10.1m 10m* 10g* 10d* 10.4g 9g 12d p10g² p12g⁵ p10g⁶ Dec 28] compact, good-bodied gelding: useful handicapper on turf, fairly 96 a86

useful on all-weather: won at Lingfield, Newmarket (2) and Pontefract (beat Rutland Chantry by 3 lengths) in summer, twice in amateur events: should stay easy 1½m: acts on firm going, soft and all-weather: tried blinkered, better form when not: has worn tongue tie. *N. A. Callaghan*

PORT NATAL (IRE)   3 b.g. Selkirk (USA) 129 – Play Around (IRE) 105 (Niniski   **83 ?** (USA) 125) [2001 11g 10.5m⁴ 10d⁵ 12s f16g f12g Nov 26] 500,000 francs Y: ex-French gelding: second foal: dam French 1¼m and 1½m winner: fairly useful maiden in France, lightly raced: best effort in 2001 when fifth in minor event at Deauville in July: left R. Collet and off 4 months, well held at Southwell last 2 outings: ran as if something amiss final outing: stays 1¼m: acts on good to soft going: blinkered last 5 starts. *B. J. Meehan*

PORT OF CALL (IRE)   6 ch.g. Arazi (USA) 135 – Port Helene 107 (Troy 137)   **–** [2001 50: f6g 9.9m⁶ f14.8s Sep 6] big, lengthy, deep-girthed gelding: modest maiden at 5 yrs: no form in 2001. *R. F. Marvin*

PORTRACK JUNCTION (IRE)   4 b.g. Common Grounds 118 – Boldabsa 96   **–** (Persian Bold 123) [2001 39: 10m 10m 10.1m 12.4m 9f 10d⁶ 16m 8f Sep 20] of little account nowadays. *A. B. Mulholland*

PORT ST CHARLES (IRE)   4 b. or br.g. Night Shift (USA) – Safe Haven (Blakeney   **74** 126) [2001 81: 6.1v 5v² 6s³ 6m⁵ 7g³ 7g³ 6g* 7g⁵ 6d Oct 12] tall gelding: fair performer: jockey suspended, trainer fined and horse banned for 40 days under non-triers rule following third start: won minor event at Folkestone in August: effective 6f/7f: acts on heavy and good to firm going: free-going sort, usually held up: found little/wandered penultimate start: sold 8,500 gns. *N. A. Callaghan*

POSITIVE (IRE)   2 ch.g. (Mar 20) Fayruz 116 – Interj (Salmon Leap (USA) 131)   **82** [2001 5.2m f6g² 6m² f6g 7f² f7g⁵ 8.1s⁵ 7m* 7s 7v Oct 26] IR 24,000F, IR 40,000Y: strong gelding: half-brother to 3 winners, notably smart Irish 9f winner Scottish Memories (by Houmayoun): dam unraced half-sister to smart performer up to 1¼m Spindrift: fairly useful performer: made all in minor event at Goodwood in September: may prove best at 7f/1m: acts on good to firm ground, well below form on soft/heavy: blinkered last 3 starts: has found little: sold 20,000 gns, sent to USA. *B. J. Meehan*

POSITIVE PROFILE (IRE)   3 b.g. Definite Article 121 – Leyete Gulf (IRE) (Slip   **68** Anchor 136) [2001 11.1s 12g 8m⁶ 10d 10g 14.1s f8.5g 10s* 10s p10g⁶ f12s* f14g* f12s²   **a80** Dec 21] 27,000Y: workmanlike gelding: fifth foal: half-brother to 3 winners, including 1995 2-y-o 6f winner Ocean Grove (by Fairy King) and Irish 1m winner Absoluta (by Royal Academy), both fairly useful: dam unraced half-sister to smart 1¼m performer Missionary Ridge: fairly useful handicapper on all-weather, fair on turf: won at Ponte-fract (first outing after leaving N. Graham) in October and at Wolverhampton and Southwell (by 10 lengths) in December: stays 1¾m: acts on soft ground and fibresand: has flicked tail under pressure/been slowly away: tends to carry head high. *P. C. Haslam*

POST BOX (USA)   3 b.c. Quest For Fame 127 – Crowning Ambition (USA) 65   **89** (Chief's Crown (USA)) [2001 78: 10s² 12.3f⁴ 14.1d* 14g 13.9m 14s 15.9d⁴ 14g⁶ Oct 6] close-coupled, useful-looking colt: has a round action: fairly useful handicapper: won at Salisbury in June: probably stays 2m: yet to race on heavy going, acts on any other: consistent: sold 15,000 gns. *R. Charlton*

POTEMKIN (IRE)   3 ch.c. Ashkalani (IRE) 128 – Ploy 87 (Posse (USA) 130) [2001   **112** 8d² 8s* 10.4g² 10m* 10g³ 10d Aug 15] IR 30,000Y: big, strong, good sort: half-brother to several winners, including smart Italian miler Poliuto (by Last Tycoon) and useful Irish 9f and 1¼m winner High King (by Fairy King): dam maiden half-sister to Sun Princess and Saddlers' Hall: smart performer: won maiden at Kempton in May and listed race at Newmarket by neck from Aldwych, dictating pace and rallying) in June: also ran well when 1½ lengths third of 5 to King of Tara in Prix Eugene Adam at Deauville (made much of running) penultimate start: disappointing in Prix Guillaume d'Ornano at same course final outing: stays 10.4f: acts on soft and good to firm ground: genuine. *R. Hannon*

POT OF GOLD (FR)   3 gr.g. Kendor (FR) 122 – Golden Rainbow (FR) (Rainbow   **61** Quest (USA) 134) [2001 61: f8g⁴ f8g Dec 14] modest maiden, lightly raced: off 11 months before well held second start: should be suited by 1¼m+. *J. G. FitzGerald*

POTSDAM   3 ch.c. Rainbow Quest (USA) 134 – Danilova (USA) (Lyphard (USA)   **63** 132) [2001 11.7d 9g⁵ Sep 2] fourth foal: half-brother to 4-y-o Danger Over and 6-y-o Danakil: dam unraced half-sister to high-class 9f to 1½m performer Sanglamore: better effort in maidens when fifth at Sandown (tongue tied), again slowly away and weakening: bred to stay further than 9f, but has raced freely both starts: sold 2,500 gns. *J. H. M. Gosden*

POTTED SHRIMP (USA) 2 ch.c. (May 2) Prized (USA) – Mint Callee (USA) (Key **48** To The Mint (USA)) [2001 6d f6g 8.1s 8m Sep 20] $1,400Y, resold $9,000Y, 15,000 2-y-o: smallish, good-bodied colt: second foal: dam ran once in USA: poor maiden: best effort second start. *A. Berry*

POUNCE (IRE) 3 ch.f. Grand Lodge (USA) 125 – Mary Ellen Best (IRE) 64 **59** (Danehill (USA) 126) [2001 60: 7.6m 7.6g³ 9.9s⁶ f9.4g⁵ Nov 17] modest maiden: stays 1¼m: acts on soft and good to firm going. *J. A. Osborne*

POUR NOUS 3 gr.g. Petong 126 – Pour Moi 73 (Bay Express 132) [2001 –: 6d 8m 6m – 7s Jul 24] leggy gelding: little form: visored final outing. *J. J. Quinn*

POUSSIN (IRE) 3 b.c. Alzao (USA) 117 – Paix Blanche (FR) (Fabulous Dancer **115** (USA) 124) [2001 10.5m² 10g* 12g³ 10d³ 10v* Oct 23] second living foal: half-brother to useful French 1½m/12.5f (Prix Minerve) winner Prairie Runner (by Arazi): dam French 9f winner (including at 2 yrs) who stayed 10.5f: smart performer: trained by A. Fabre only outing at 2 yrs: won minor event at Chantilly in July and listed race at Deauville (led inside final 1f to beat Luna Sacra ¾ length) in October: ran well when 3 lengths third to Equerry in Prix du Prince d'Orange at Longchamp penultimate start: stays 1¼m: acts on heavy ground. *E. Lellouche, France*

POWDER RIVER 7 b.g. Alzao (USA) 117 – Nest 65 (Sharpo 132) [2001 60: f12g – f12s Dec 27] fair handicapper at 5 yrs: very lightly raced since. *A. G. Newcombe*

POWER AND DEMAND 4 b.g. Formidable (USA) 125 – Mazurkanova 63 (Song – 132) [2001 –, a49: f5g f5g⁵ f5g⁵ Feb 20] poor maiden handicapper: barely stays 6f: acts **a40** on fibresand and equitrack, has shown little on turf: usually blinkered. *D. Shaw*

POWER GAME 8 b.g. Puissance 110 – Play The Game 70 (Mummy's Game 120) – [2001 –: 6m 8m 8m 8m 9.2g 8f 6m 12.1d 8f 7s 10d 8m 7.2g 6m Sep 24] of little account nowadays. *D. A. Nolan*

POYLE JENNY 2 b.f. (May 12) Piccolo 121 – Poyle Amber 55 (Sharrood (USA) – 124) [2001 5m Aug 22] fifth foal: sister to 4-y-o Railroader and half-sister to 6f (at 2 yrs) to 1½m winner Wilton (by Sharpo): dam, sprint maiden, half-sister to smart sprinter Poyle George: 66/1, last in maiden at Lingfield. *K. T. Ivory*

POYLE MAGIC 2 b.g. (Mar 5) Magic Ring (IRE) 115 – Poyle Fizz (Damister (USA) **86** 123) [2001 5d³ 5m* 6m 5.1f* 5.2m⁶ Jul 30] 13,000Y: fourth foal: closely related to useful 1999 2-y-o 5f/6f (including Lowther Stakes) winner Jemima (by Owington) and half-brother to 2 winners, including 7-y-o Floating Charge: dam unraced: fairly useful performer: won maiden at Ayr (jinked left leaving stall) in May and minor event at Chester (beat Pepperoni short head) in June: may prove best at 5f: acts on firm going: lost all chance when rearing as stall opened final start: usually forces pace. *W. G. M. Turner*

POYLE PICKLE 3 b.f. Piccolo 121 – Hithermoor Lass 75 (Red Alert 127) [2001 –: – 6g 5g Sep 19] little sign of ability. *M. S. Saunders*

PRACTICAL MAGIC 2 ch.f. (Apr 3) Polar Falcon (USA) 126 – Beneficiary 69 – (Jalmood (USA) 126) [2001 5m 7m Sep 8] 3,000F, 4,000Y: fourth foal: half-sister to a winner in Austria by Lahib: dam, 6f and (including at 2 yrs) 7f winner, half-sister to very smart 7f/1m performer Decorated Hero: well held in maidens. *J. D. Bethell*

PRAETORIAN FORCE 2 b.g. (Jan 15) Atraf 116 – Zaima (IRE) 92 (Green Desert – (USA) 127) [2001 6m 7m 6.1d Sep 21] 10,500F, 27,000Y: first foal: dam, 7f winner at 2 yrs, out of half-sister to very smart miler Alhijaz: no form in minor event/maidens: tried visored/blinkered. *K. McAuliffe*

PRAGUE 3 b.g. Cyrano de Bergerac 120 – Basenite (Mansingh (USA) 120) [2001 9g⁶ – 12m Sep 24] 2,000F, 3,600Y, resold 7,700Y: fifth foal: half-brother to winner in Italy by Statoblest: dam poor sister to high-class sprinter Petong: well beaten in maidens. *N. Hamilton*

PRAGUE EXPRESS 2 ch.g. (Mar 31) Shaddad (USA) 75 – Express Girl 75 (Sylvan **42** Express 117) [2001 5d⁴ 6m 6g Jun 19] strong gelding: first foal: dam 5f winner at 2 yrs: poor form when fourth in maiden at Hamilton: well held in minor event/seller. *D. Moffatt*

PRAIRIE FALCON (IRE) 7 b.g. Alzao (USA) 117 – Sea Harrier (Grundy 137) **90** [2001 90: 18v 18.7f³ 14m 13.9m* 16.1f 16.1g⁶ 16.2m 13.3m 13.9m³ 14s 13.1m* 13.9d 16g⁴ Nov 7] attractive gelding: good mover: fairly useful handicapper: won at York in

June and Ayr in September: effective at 13f to 2¼m: acts on firm and soft going. *B. W. Hills*

PRAIRIE WOLF   5 ch.g. Wolfhound (USA) 126 – Bay Queen 85 (Damister (USA)   **100** 123) [2001 96: 10g 9.7m³ 10m² 9.9m³ 9m* 10.1g³ Sep 14] big, strong gelding: useful performer: won at Goodwood in September by ½ length from Finished Article: stays 1¼m: acts on firm going, good to soft and fibresand: has run well when sweating/edgy: consistent. *M. L. W. Bell*

PRAYERS FOR RAIN (IRE)   2 b.f. (Mar 18) Darshaan 133 – Whispered Melody   **85** 68 (Primo Dominie 121) [2001 6m⁴ 7m* 7d 8d Nov 3] IR 130,000F, IR 300,000Y: first foal: dam, 1m winner, half-sister to smart 9f/1¼m winner Supreme Sound and useful stayer Top Cees out of Lancashire Oaks winner Sing Softly: fairly useful performer: won maiden at Kempton in June, making most: well held in Prix du Calvados at Deauville and listed race at Newmarket (something possibly amiss) after: bred to stay 1¼m. *M. A. Jarvis*

PRECEDENT (USA)   2 b. or br.c. (May 15) El Prado (IRE) 119 – Sheikh Fortysix   **69** (USA) (Sheikh Albadou 128) [2001 7d 8.2d⁴ 10d⁵ Oct 8] $70,000F, IR 115,000Y: strong colt: first foal: dam, 1m/8.5f winner in USA, out of half-sister to very smart US Grade 1 1m winner Buckhar: backward, fair form in maidens: best effort when fourth to Affray at Nottingham: should stay 1¼m: sold 28,000 gns. *Sir Michael Stoute*

PRECIOUS   3 b.f. Danehill (USA) 126 – National Treasure 72 (Shirley Heights 130)   **65** [2001 7g⁴ 10v Oct 16] good-topped filly: first foal: dam lightly-raced sister to smart filly up to 1½m Free At Last and half-sister to high-class miler Barathea and 2-y-o Gossamer: 20/1, green and burly, encouraging fourth to Lurina in Newmarket maiden on debut, despite hanging right in Dip: ran as if something amiss over 5 months later: should be suited by 1¼m+. *W. J. Haggas*

PRECISO (IRE)   3 b.g. Definite Article 121 – Symphony (IRE) (Cyrano de Bergerac   **79** 120) [2001 72: 12f³ 14m 14.4g 12g Oct 4] quite attractive gelding: has a quick action: fair maiden: stays 1½m: acts on firm and soft ground: visored last 2 starts: sold 4,500 gns. *Mrs A. J. Perrett*

PREEN   2 b.f. (Feb 20) Lion Cavern (USA) 117 – Made of Pearl (USA) 107 (Nureyev   **72 p** (USA) 131) [2001 8g³ Oct 19] leggy filly: half-sister to several winners, including useful 1997 2-y-o 7f winner Flawless (by Warning) and 1½m winner Cultured (by Saint Cyrien): dam French 7f/1m winner: 16/1, 4¼ lengths third of 19 to Macadamia in maiden at Redcar, keeping on well, not knocked about: sure to improve. *J. R. Fanshawe*

PREFERRED (IRE)   3 b.g. Distant Relative 128 – Fruhlingserwachen (USA) (Irish   **78** River (FR) 131) [2001 88: 8d 7.6f 8m³ 9.9m³ 9.9m³ Jun 27] sturdy gelding: fair performer: stays 1¼m: acts on firm ground: visored (ran creditably but found little) final start: gelded after. *R. Hannon*

PREMIER ACCOUNT   3 b.g. Mark of Esteem (IRE) 137 – Gemaasheh (Habitat   **61** 134) [2001 8v⁴ 7g⁴ f9.4g⁴ 9.1m⁶ 10m 10m 8g 8.5s³ 8g Oct 6] 10,000F, IR 50,000Y: useful-looking gelding: poor mover: eighth foal: half-brother to fairly useful Irish 1m/9f winner Dance Academy and 6-y-o Reachforyourpocket (both by Royal Academy): dam unraced half-sister to smart 1¼m performer Dartrey: modest maiden handicapper: stays 9.4f: acts on heavy going and fibresand. *R. A. Fahey*

PREMIER AMBITIONS   3 b.g. Bin Ajwaad (IRE) 119 – Good Thinking (USA)   **60** (Raja Baba (USA)) [2001 –p: 10g 12.4m⁵ 10s⁵ 8d² 8s⁶ Nov 9] modest maiden handicapper: stays 1¼m (raced freely at 1½m): acts on soft going. *W. J. Haggas*

PREMIER BARON   6 b.g. Primo Dominie 121 – Anna Karietta 82 (Precocious 126)   **91** [2001 91, a–: 5.1v⁴ 7d 6g 7m⁵ 7m⁶ 7m 7.1s 7m* 7f³ 5g 6m⁵ 6g⁴ 7g⁶ 6m 7d 7g 7d⁴ 7d   **a–** 7s* Oct 31] smallish gelding: fairly useful handicapper: won at Newmarket in June and Yarmouth (beat Midshipman by 3½ lengths) in October: mainly creditable efforts otherwise: probably best at 6f/7f: acts on fibresand, firm and soft going: tried blinkered in 2000. *P. S. McEntee*

PREMIER BOY (IRE)   3 b.g. Blues Traveller (IRE) 119 – Little Min (Nebbiolo 125)   **–** [2001 43: 10m 8.5s Sep 25] leggy, angular gelding: poor maiden at 2 yrs: well held in 2001: visored at 2 yrs. *B. S. Rothwell*

PREMIERE FOULEE (FR)   6 ch.m. Sillery (USA) 122 – Dee (Caerleon (USA)   **44** 132) [2001 37: f16g⁴ f16.2s f12g³ f16.2g 15.4v 16.2m² 11.8m⁵ 14.1g² 16f 16.4m⁵ 16.2m   **a–** Sep 17] sturdy mare: poor handicapper: stays 2m: acts on soft and good to firm going: tried visored/blinkered. *F. Jordan*

PREMIERE VALENTINO   4 b.g. Tragic Role (USA) – Mirkan Honey 83 (Bally- –
more 123) [2001 –: 12m 12.6f 11.9f⁵ Jul 4] little form: tried blinkered/visored.
D. W. P. Arbuthnot

PREMIER GUEST   3 br.c. Primo Dominie 121 – Song of Hope 103 (Chief Singer –
131) [2001 7g⁵ 7.1m 7m 7d 6m Jul 23] 25,000F, 76,000Y: half-brother to several winners,
including fairly useful 5f (at 2 yrs)/7f winner Song of Skye (by Warning) and 7f/1m
winner Kingdom Princess (by Forzando): dam 2-y-o 5f winner: well held in maidens/
handicaps: blinkered last 2 starts: sent to Sweden. *G. G. Margarson*

PREMIER PRIZE   4 ch.f. Selkirk (USA) 129 – Spot Prize (USA) 108 (Seattle   **105**
Dancer (USA) 119) [2001 90: 12m 9g⁵ 9.9m* 10m³ 9.9m³ 8g⁵ 7d⁶ Oct 13] big, strong,
lengthy filly: useful performer: reportedly had bone chips removed from hind legs early
in 2001: won listed event at Salisbury (by 2 lengths from Katy Nowaitee) in August: ran
creditably after when 2¾ lengths third to Adilabad in Winter Hill Stakes at Windsor, last
of 3 to Nayef in Select Stakes at Goodwood and 5-length fifth to Independence in Sun
Chariot Stakes at Newmarket: needs further than 7f and stays 1¼m: acts on good to firm
going. *D. R. C. Elsworth*

PREMIUM PRINCESS   6 b.m. Distant Relative 128 – Solemn Occasion (USA)   **77 d**
(Secreto (USA) 128) [2001 78, a–: 5s 5s² 5m 6f 6m 5g 5g 6g Sep 2] good-bodied mare: **a–**
fair handicapper: good second at Redcar in May: well below form after: stays 6f: acts on
any going: usually held up: sold 5,000 gns. *J. J. Quinn*

PRESENTATION (IRE)   4 b.f. Mujadil (USA) 119 – Beechwood (USA) (Blushing   **82**
Groom (FR) 131) [2001 98: 6g 6g 6m⁶ 6m 6g 7f 6g Oct 5] smallish, lengthy filly:
unimpressive mover: fairly useful form at best in 2001: stays 6f: acts on heavy and good
to firm going: sometimes sweating and edgy: usually soon under pressure: sold 42,000
gns. *R. Hannon*

PRESENT CHANCE   7 ch.g. Cadeaux Genereux 131 – Chance All (FR) 88 (Glenstal   –
(USA) 118) [2001 68, a53: 7fg f6s⁵ f5g⁵ f6s Feb 9] strong, good-bodied gelding: poor   **a42**
handicapper nowadays: effective at 5f to 7f: acts on firm ground, soft and fibresand:
sometimes blinkered: has worn tongue strap: sometimes wanders. *D. Shaw*

PRESENT 'N CORRECT   8 ch.g. Cadeaux Genereux 131 – Emerald Eagle 78   **48**
(Sandy Creek 123) [2001 5m 5.3g³ 5.3m* 6s f6s Dec 26] workmanlike gelding: poor
handicapper nowadays: won at Brighton in August: effective at 5f to easy 7f: acts on any
turf going, fibresand and equitrack. *J. M. Bradley*

PRESSIONAGE   2 b.f. (Jan 28) Puissance 110 – My Girl 39 (Mon Tresor 113) [2001   **47**
5.7f 5d³ 6m³ 7m⁴ 7m 7d 5.7d Oct 25] 1,000Y: first foal: dam sprint maiden: poor maiden:
probably stays 7f: acts on good to firm and good to soft ground. *H. S. Howe*

PRESUMING   3 b.f. Mtoto 134 – D'Azy 91 (Persian Bold 123) [2001 53p: 8.3g⁶ Jul   **67**
9] better effort in maidens (8 months apart) when sixth at Windsor in July: bred to stay at
least 1¼m: sold 14,000 gns in December. *J. H. M. Gosden*

PRETENDING   4 b.g. Primo Dominie 121 – Red Salute (Soviet Star (USA) 128)   –
[2001 55: f8g 8s 7m 8m 8f Jun 22] leggy gelding: disappointing maiden. *J. D. Bethell*

PRETIOSA (IRE)   3 ch.f. Royal Abjar (USA) 121 – Thatcherite (Final Straw 127)   **47**
[2001 9m⁴ 9.7m⁶ 10.4m³ 8g 10s Oct 3] 6,500Y: half-sister to several winners, including
useful 5f (at 2 yrs) and 1¼m winner Unconditional Love (by Polish Patriot) and 1¼m/
11f winner Bajan (by Taufan): dam unraced half-sister to very smart 6f to 1m performer
Kampala: poor form in maidens/handicap: stays 10.4f: acts on good to firm going (ran in
snatches on soft). *N. P. Littmoden*

PRETRAIL (IRE)   4 b.g. Catrail (USA) 123 – Pretty Lady 98 (High Top 131) [2001   **95**
81: f8g e8g³ f8.5s* e10g f8g⁴ p10g* Dec 28] strong, deep-bodied gelding: has a round
action: useful performer: won handicaps at Wolverhampton in January and (having
reportedly finished lame next time, then gelded and off 10 months) Lingfield in December, in apprentice event on latter course: stays 1¼m: acts on good to soft going, fibresand
and polytrack. *P. W. D'Arcy*

PRETTY CLEAR (USA)   2 b.f. (Apr 23) Mr Prospector (USA) – Seven Springs   **89**
(USA) 114 (Irish River (FR) 131) [2001 6m² 7m² 6g² Oct 6] smallish, leggy filly: sister
to high-class miler Distant View, closely related to 3-y-o Seven Sing and half-sister to 3
winners abroad: dam won Prix Robert Papin and Prix Morny and later stayed 1m: fairly
useful form when runner-up in maidens at Newbury, Salisbury and Newmarket, free early

on when beaten 2½ lengths by Scarlet Ribbons on last-named course: will need to settle better to stay 1m. *H. R. A. Cecil*

PRETTY INDULGENT 4 b.g. Mistertopogigo (IRE) 118 – American Beauty 74 **49** (Mill Reef (USA) 141) [2001 f9.4g⁵ f9.4g³ f8g 8m⁶ Jul 21] poor maiden: barely stays 9.4f: acts on fibresand. *B. Smart*

PRETTY OBVIOUS 5 ch.m. Pursuit of Love 124 – Settlement (USA) 75 (Irish River **–** (FR) 131) [2001 –: 16v 17.1s Apr 10] fair performer in 1999: well held on Flat since: tried blinkered. *Mrs M. Reveley*

PRICELESS SECOND 4 b.g. Lugana Beach 116 – Early Gales (Precocious 126) **–** [2001 57: f8g⁵ f11g Jan 12] close-coupled, sparely-made gelding: modest performer at 3 yrs: well held in 2001: tried blinkered/visored: sent to Denmark. *J. A. Glover*

PRICKLY PEAR (USA) 3 b. or br.f. Polar Falcon (USA) 126 – Tootsiepop (USA) **–** (Robellino (USA) 127) [2001 f6g Feb 19] seventh foal: half-sister to smart German 1997 2-y-o 5f to 1m winner El Maimoun (by Royal Academy): dam, won in USA, half-sister to Gimcrack winner Splendent: weak 9/1-shot, well held in Southwell maiden, soon poorly placed after slow start. *Sir Mark Prescott*

PRICKLY POPPY 3 b.f. Lear Fan (USA) 130 – Prickwillow (USA) 75 (Nureyev **72** (USA) 131) [2001 58p: 8.1g⁵ 9.9g² 10v⁵ Oct 8] first foal: dam, 1¼m winner, daughter of smart performer around 1¼m Braiswick from very good family: fair form in maidens: probably better at 1¼m than shorter: sold 6,000 gns in December. *M. P. Tregoning*

PRIDDY FAIR 8 b.m. North Briton 67 – Rainbow Ring (Rainbow Quest (USA) 134) **–** [2001 37: 12f 13g⁴ Jul 20] lightly-raced maiden. *B. Mactaggart*

PRIDE IN ME 3 ch.f. Indian Ridge 123 – Easy Option (IRE) 115 (Prince Sabo 123) **77** [2001 74p: e7g³ 6m* 6m² 5g Aug 4] leggy, lengthy filly: fair performer: won maiden at Thirsk in May: better form in handicaps after: effective at 5f/6f: acts on soft and good to firm going: sold 85,000 gns in December. *E. A. L. Dunlop*

PRIDE OF BRIXTON 8 b.g. Dominion 123 – Caviar Blini 80 (What A Guest 119) **–** [2001 54, a81: f5g³ f5g⁶ f6g⁴ f6g⁶ f5g² f5g⁴ f5g f5s⁵ f5s⁵ Dec 27] lengthy gelding: **a76** fair performer: effective at 5f/easy 6f: acts on fibresand: visored once: front runner. *Andrew Reid*

PRIDE OF DUBAI (USA) 2 b.g. (Feb 11) Seeking The Gold (USA) – Bint Baladee **– p** 101 (Nashwan (USA) 135) [2001 7v⁵ Oct 26] compact, attractive gelding: first foal; dam, 1m/1¼m winner, out of half-sister to top-class French/US 1m/9f performer Thrill Show: weak 3/1-shot and backward, well-held fifth of 12 to Foreign Accent in maiden at Doncaster, not knocked about once beaten: gelded after: should do better. *D. R. Loder*

PRIDE OF INDIA (IRE) 4 b.g. Ezzoud (IRE) 126 – Indian Queen 115 (Electric **89** 126) [2001 66: 14.1v* 16v* 16s 17.1f² 20m 21m⁶ Aug 1] big, good-topped gelding: fairly useful handicapper: won at Nottingham in March and April: was suited by 1¾m+: acted on any ground: was visored last 2 starts: dead. *J. L. Dunlop*

PRIDE OF PERU (IRE) 4 b.f. Perugino (USA) 84 – Nation's Game 51 (Mummy's **42** Game 120) [2001 44: f7s⁴ f6g² 5m⁴ 6g f6g f7g⁶ Nov 23] tall, unfurnished filly: modest **a52** maiden: barely stays 1m: acts on fibresand, firm and good to soft ground: often races prominently. *M. Brittain*

PRIDE OF THE PARK (FR) 2 b.g. (Apr 26) Marju (IRE) 127 – Taj Victory 68 (Final Straw 127) [2001 6f 7.5g 8.5g Nov 3] 16,000Y: angular gelding: sixth foal: half-brother to 3 winners, including 4-y-o Highland Reel and 3-y-o Fazzani: dam, 1¼m to 13f winner, half-sister to Gold Cup winner Indian Queen: well held in claimer/maidens. *P. C. Haslam*

PRIDEWAY (IRE) 5 b.m. Pips Pride 117 – Up The Gates (Captain James 123) [2001 **57 d** 64§, a76§: 8f³ 9.2d⁶ 8m f8g 8.1g 8f f8.5g 9.1v⁴ 8v 7v⁶ 7d Nov 2] leggy, sparely-made mare: modest performer, on downgrade: races mainly at 7f/1m: acts on any turf going and fibresand: tried blinkered: tongue tied: sometimes slowly away. *W. M. Brisbourne*

PRIMAROSA 2 ch.f. (Mar 26) Atraf 116 – Prim Lass 65 (Reprimand 122) [2001 5v **52** f5g f5g* f5g 6v 8g Nov 5] 2,800Y: leggy filly: second foal: dam, maiden, may have proved best at 5f/6f and hinted at temperament: modest performer: won seller at Southwell in April: seemed to run creditably penultimate start: stays 6f: acts on heavy going and fibresand: inconsistent. *John A. Harris*

NGK Spark Plugs Abernant Stakes, Newmarket—in a much larger field than usual Primo Valentino makes all to beat Fath (black cap) and Superior Premium (centre, predominantly white colours)

PRIMA STELLA   2 br. or gr.f. (Mar 15) Primo Dominie 121 – Raffelina (USA)   **67**
(Carson City (USA)) [2001 5.1s 5f⁶ 5m⁶ 5m* 5m⁴ 5.1m 6.1d 6s² 5.1s Nov 5] 11,000Y:
leggy filly: first foal: dam unraced: fair performer: won seller at Leicester in July: good
second of 21 in nursery on same course: effective at 5f/6f: acts on soft and good to firm
going: sometimes races freely. *B. R. Millman*

PRIMA VENTURE   3 b.f. Pursuit of Love 124 – Prima Cominna 86 (Unfuwain   **46**
(USA) 131) [2001 56: 6s 7.1d 8m f8g f7g³ f6g 7s Jul 24] smallish, good-bodied filly: poor
maiden: stays 7f: acts on soft ground and fibresand: blinkered final start. *M. Dods*

PRIMEFLIGHT (IRE)   2 b.f. (Apr 4) Primo Dominie 121 – Auction Hall 59   **–**
(Saddlers' Hall (IRE) 126) [2001 6s Sep 27] 5,000 2-y-o: first foal: dam, maiden who
stayed 1¼m, half-sister to useful sprinter Bid For Blue (by Primo Dominie): 16/1, last in
maiden at Pontefract: sent to Sweden. *B. A. McMahon*

PRIME MUSIC   4 ch.g. Primo Dominie 121 – Rose Music 86 (Luthier 126) [2001 f7s
e7g e6s f7g f6g f7g 8f 8m Jun 22] of little account. *Mrs H. L. Walton*

PRIME OFFER   5 b.g. Primo Dominie 121 – Single Bid 68 (Auction Ring (USA)   **71**
123) [2001 70: 7m² 7.6f⁶ 6m 7m⁶ 8.1g 7m⁴ 8m p7g² p7g² Dec 28] useful-looking gelding:
fair handicapper: should stay easy 1m: acts on polytrack and firm going: usually races
prominently. *D. Morris*

PRIME RECREATION   4 b.g. Primo Dominie 121 – Night Transaction 59 (Tina's   **84**
Pet 121) [2001 68: f5g⁴ f5g² f5g* f6g f5g² 5g³ f5g 5d 5.5d³ 5m 5v⁶ 5d* 5g 5s⁵ f5s² Dec
15] strong, rangy gelding: fairly useful handicapper: won at Southwell in March and York
in October: best at 5f: acts on fibresand and heavy ground: has been slowly away/found
little: speedy. *P. S. Felgate*

PRIME TRUMP   3 b.g. First Trump 118 – Maristax 74 (Reprimand 122) [2001 73: 8g   **78**
8m⁵ 11.4g⁵ 11.5m² 12m² 11.9s Sep 7] angular gelding: fair maiden handicapper: stays
1½m: acts on good to firm going, possibly not on soft: has carried head high/wandered:
races prominently. *P. W. Harris*

PRIMEVAL   7 b.g. Primo Dominie 121 – Class Adorns (Sadler's Wells (USA) 132)   **48**
[2001 –: f12g 11.9s⁴ May 3] one-time fair performer: lightly-raced and only poor
nowadays: stays 1½m: acts on fibresand, equitrack and soft ground: tried visored/tongue
tied. *J. C. Fox*

PRIME VERSION   3 b.g. Primo Dominie 121 – Cashew 80 (Sharrood (USA) 124)   **–**
[2001 93p: 7d⁶ 8m 6g 8f 10m⁶ 7m Sep 22] lengthy gelding: fairly useful winner of 6f
maiden at Newbury only 2-y-o start: lost way badly at 3 yrs. *P. F. I. Cole*

PRIMO CARIAD (IRE)   2 b.f. (Feb 23) Primo Dominie 121 – Croeso Cynnes 70   **–**
(Most Welcome 131) [2001 5m 7f Jul 25] small, workmanlike filly: first foal: dam 5f and
(including at 2 yrs) 6f winner: last in maidens. *R. Brotherton*

PRIMO DANCER   2 b.c. (Apr 29) Primo Dominie 121 – Whittle Woods Girl 80   **–**
(Emarati (USA) 74) [2001 6m 7m⁵ 7.1g⁶ 7g Aug 24] 15,000Y: lengthy colt: fourth foal:
half-brother to 5-y-o High Esteem: dam, 6f winner, sister to useful 6f/7f performer
Emerging Market and half-sister to smart sprinter Atraf: well held in maidens/seller: tried
blinkered. *C. W. Fairhurst*

PRIMO DAWN   2 b.c. (Apr 15) Primo Dominie 121 – Sara Sprint (Formidable (USA)   **69**
125) [2001 6d 7d f7g² Nov 17] 5,200F, IR 8,400Y, 16,000 2-y-o: big, lengthy colt: fifth

foal: brother to fairly useful 6f/7f winner The Downtown Fox (became unreliable) and half-brother to 2 winners: dam, Italian 7f winner, half-sister to very smart miler Radetzky: easily best effort in maidens (fair form) when 5 lengths second to Red Forest at Wolverhampton: likely to stay 1m: acts on fibresand. *N. P. Littmoden*

PRIMO DORIA   2 ch.f. (Jan 16) Primo Dominie 121 – Il Doria (IRE) 66 (Mac's Imp   – (USA) 116) [2001 6g⁴ Aug 25] good-bodied filly: first foal: dam, sprint maiden, half-sister to smart 5f performer Palacegate Episode: 10/1 and bandaged behind, never-dangerous fourth of 6 in maiden at Goodwood. *J. H. M. Gosden*

PRIMO VALENTINO (IRE)   4 b.c. Primo Dominie 121 – Dorothea Brooke (IRE)   **116** 80 (Dancing Brave (USA) 140) [2001 115: 6d* 6m 6m Jul 12] quite good-topped colt: had a quick, fluent action: smart performer: won Middle Park Stakes at Newmarket at 2 yrs: as good as ever when making all in 23-runner listed Abernant Stakes on same course in April, beating Fath readily by 1¼ lengths: forced to miss next intended engagement with inflamed throat: well beaten subsequently in Cork And Orrery Stakes at Royal Ascot and July Cup at Newmarket: best form at 6f, but should have been just as effective at 5f: acted on soft and early to post: twice ran poorly abroad in 2000: to stand at Bearstone Stud, Shropshire, fee £3,500, Oct 1st. *P. W. Harris*

PRIMO VENTURE   3 b.f. Primo Dominie 121 – Jade Venture 67 (Never So Bold 135)   – [2001 –: f7g⁵ f9.4s f8g 8.2f 7m 8m 10.1g Aug 15] probably of little account. *P. Howling*

PRIMROSE AND ROSE   2 b.f. (Apr 22) Primo Dominie 121 – Cointosser (IRE) 66   **72** (Nordico (USA)) [2001 f5g* 5s² 5m³ 6g⁶ 6m 6d f6g⁵ p6g f5f⁴ p6g p6g² Dec 22] 10,000Y: **a59** plain, sparely-made filly: first foal: dam, 7f/1m winner, also won over hurdles: fair on turf, modest on all-weather: won maiden at Southwell in April: left J. Eustace after sixth start: second in seller at Lingfield final one: will prove best at 5f/easy 6f: acts on soft going, good to firm, fibresand and polytrack. *J. J. Bridger*

PRINCE ALBERT   3 ch.g. Rock City 120 – Russell Creek 80 (Sandy Creek 123)   **51** [2001 –: 7d f8g 7m⁵ 8m⁵ 10m 7s⁴ Oct 5] leggy, lengthy gelding: modest maiden handicapper: should prove at least as effective at 1m as 7f: acts on soft and good to firm ground. *J. R. Jenkins*

PRINCE ALEX (IRE)   7 b.g. Night Shift (USA) – Finalist 78 (Star Appeal 133)   **98 +** [2001 109: 10.4m Jul 14] big, sturdy gelding: has a quick action: useful handicapper, lightly raced: bit backward on first run for 10 months when not disgraced in John Smith's Cup at York only outing in 2001, short of room straight: possibly better at 1¼m than 1½m: acts on good to firm going: tongue tied: ridden for turn of foot. *Mrs A. J. Perrett*

PRINCE AMONG MEN   4 b.g. Robellino (USA) 127 – Forelino (USA) 62§ (Trem-   **64** polino (USA) 135) [2001 83: 12g 14m⁵ 13g⁵ 11.9g⁴ 12g 12g³ 13.8s⁶ Oct 20] sparely-made gelding: modest maiden: stays 1¾m: acts on soft and good to firm going: tried blinkered. *M. Todhunter*

PRINCE ATRAF   2 b.c. (Mar 8) Atraf 116 – Forest Fantasy 61 (Rambo Dancer   **88** (CAN) 107) [2001 5.1v* 6f³ 7.1m³ 7g⁵ 7s 7d⁶ Oct 13] 14,000F, 30,000Y: useful-looking colt: first foal: dam, 1m/9f winner, closely related to US Grade 3 6.5f winner Imperial Star: fairly useful performer: won maiden at Nottingham in April: best effort when fifth to Steenberg in minor event at Ascot: should stay 1m: acts on any going: blinkered final start. *B. R. Millman*

PRINCE BABAR   10 b.g. Fairy King (USA) – Bell Toll 87 (High Line 125) [2001 90:   **72 +** 8v⁵ Mar 23] sparely-made gelding: has a round action: fairly useful handicapper in 2000: not seen out again in 2001 after shaping well in March: effective at 7f/1m, probably not quite 1¼m: acts on any going: sometimes bandaged: visored once: tends to drift left. *R. A. Fahey*

PRINCE CASPIAN   4 ch.g. Mystiko (USA) 124 – Real Princess 78 (Aragon 118)   **63** [2001 88: 7.1s f6g* p7g Dec 28] leggy, angular gelding: modest form in 2001: won seller at Wolverhampton in December: may prove best at 6f/7f: acts on firm going, soft and fibresand. *Miss E. C. Lavelle*

PRINCE CYRANO   2 b.g. (Mar 1) Cyrano de Bergerac 120 – Odilese 82 (Mummy's   **100** Pet 125) [2001 7m 7m² 6g* 6m⁴ 6g* 5.5d² 6f⁴ 5s Oct 7] 10,500Y, 30,000 2-y-o: quite good-topped gelding: eighth foal: half-brother to 8-y-o Oriole and 5f (including at 2 yrs) winner Tutu Sixtysix (by Petong): dam 6f winner: useful performer: won maiden at Folkestone in August and 23-runner sales race at Kempton (by 5 lengths from Lady-chatterly) in September: good equal-second (beaten short neck) to Dobby Road in Prix d'Arenberg at Chantilly and fourth to Firebreak in Mill Reef Stakes at Newbury next 2 starts: midfield in Prix de l'Abbaye at Longchamp final start: likely to prove best at 5f/6f:

acts on firm and good to soft going: blinkered (very slowly away/looked wayward) on debut: takes strong hold (has been early to post): bandaged near hind/wore severe noseband last 3 starts in Britain: sold 120,000 gns, joined W. Musson. *S. C. Williams*

PRINCE DAYJUR (USA) 2 b. or br.c. (Mar 16) Dayjur (USA) 137 – Distinct **104** Beauty (USA) (Phone Trick (USA)) [2001 5m² 6m* 6g³ 6m² 6g Aug 22] $20,000F, IR 55,000Y: close-coupled, quite attractive colt: second foal: dam, 8.5f winner in USA, out of half-sister to high-class miler Last Fandango: useful performer: made all in minor event at Salisbury in July, beating Prism by 6 lengths: good efforts in July Stakes at Newmarket (2½ lengths third to Meshaheer) and Richmond Stakes at Goodwood (strong-finishing length second to Mister Cosmi) next 2 starts: ran poorly in Gimcrack Stakes at York final outing: should stay 7f: raced on good/good to firm going: sold 150,000 gns. *R. Hannon*

PRINCE DIMITRI 2 ch.g. (May 25) Desert King (IRE) 129 – Pinta (IRE) (Ahonoora **64** 122) [2001 7g 8m³ 7m Sep 22] close-coupled gelding: fourth foal: closely related to 3-y-o Stiletto and half-brother to fairly useful 1999 2-y-o 6f winner Teodora (by Fairy King): dam 2-y-o 5f (in Ireland) and 7.5f (Italian listed race) winner, also 7f winner in Italy at 3 yrs, out of half-sister to high-class 9f/1¼m filly Timarida: best effort in maidens (modest form) when third at Thirsk, making most: something possibly amiss final start: not sure to stay much beyond 1m. *S. P. C. Woods*

PRINCE DOMINO 2 b.c. (Apr 9) Primo Dominie 121 – Danzig Harbour (USA) **86** (Private Account (USA)) [2001 7m² 7f* 7g² 7g 6g 7s³ 7s⁴ Oct 16] 16,500F, 24,000Y: leggy, useful-looking colt: seventh foal: brother to two 5f winners, including fairly useful 1997 2-y-o Lord Lieutenant, and half-brother to 2 winners, including 1994 2-y-o 6f winner Puppet Master (by Prince Sabo): dam Irish 7f winner: fairly useful performer: won maiden at Epsom in July: good placed efforts in minor races at Ascot and Leicester after: may prove best at 6f/7f: acts on firm and soft going: races prominently. *R. Hannon*

PRINCE DU SOLEIL (FR) 5 b.g. Cardoun (FR) 122 – Revelry (FR) (Blakeney **69** 126) [2001 70: 8.2v² 8.2s 8m 8m 8.3d⁴ 8.3g 7g³ 8d p8g Dec 22] quite attractive gelding: fair handicapper: probably best around 1m: acts on heavy and good to firm going: below form in visor sixth start: tongue tied final outing. *J. R. Jenkins*

PRINCE GRIGORI (IRE) 3 ch.g. Prince of Birds (USA) 121 – Zinovia (USA) 80 **–** (Ziggy's Boy (USA)) [2001 51: 6m 7d 6d 6d 8.1d⁶ 8.1s⁴ 7m f8.5g f8.5s Dec 26] heavy-bodied gelding: modest maiden at 2 yrs: little form in 2001: usually blinkered/tongue tied. *E. J. Alston*

PRINCE HECTOR 2 ch.c. (Jan 30) Hector Protector (USA) 124 – Ceanothus (IRE) **86 p** 61 (Bluebird (USA) 125) [2001 7s⁴ 7d* Nov 3] strong, close-coupled colt: first foal: dam, maiden who stayed 1½m, half-sister to 3-y-o Golden Wells and 4-y-o Stratton: 6/1 joint favourite, won 27-runner maiden at Newmarket by 1¼ lengths from Gamut, leading over 1f out: will probably stay 1¼m: very slowly away on debut: useful performer in the making. *Mrs A. J. Perrett*

PRINCE JACK 3 b.g. Puissance 110 – Sabo Song 67 (Prince Sabo 123) [2001 –: 6m **–** 5f Jul 7] smallish, lengthy gelding: tailed off in maidens. *H. A. McWilliams*

PRINCELY VENTURE (IRE) 2 ch.c. (Apr 2) Entrepreneur 123 – Sun Princess **82 P** 130 (English Prince 129) [2001 7d⁵ Nov 3] strong, lengthy colt: has scope: closely related to several winners by Sadler's Wells, notably high-class 7f (at 2 yrs) and 1¼m winner Prince of Dance, and half-brother to 3 winners, including 7-y-o Royal Castle: dam won Oaks and St Leger: 33/1, 1¾ lengths fifth of 27 to Prince Hector in maiden at Newmarket, staying on having been niggled along just behind leaders at halfway: should stay at least 1¼m: sure to do good deal better and win races. *Sir Michael Stoute*

PRINCE MILLENNIUM 3 b.c. First Trump 118 – Petit Point (IRE) 78 (Petorius **52** 117) [2001 74: 9s 9m 7m 8m⁶ 7m² 8d⁴ 8f 10s³ 10d⁶ 10s Oct 25] neat colt: modest maiden: probably stays 1¼m: acts on soft and good to firm ground, probably on equitrack: usually blinkered/visored in 2001: has carried head high: sold 4,800 gns. *R. Hannon*

PRINCE MINATA (IRE) 6 b.g. Machiavellian (USA) 123 – Aminata 98 (Glenstal **67** (USA) 118) [2001 –: f8.5g* e10g 8s 10s 8.5s 8f⁵ 8.2f³ 9m 8d 8f* 8.3g 8g⁴ 8m² 8.2g 8f 8m **a75** f9.4s Dec 26] sturdy gelding: fair performer: trained in 2000 by Lindsay Woods in Ireland: won maiden at Wolverhampton in March and handicap at Musselburgh in July: well held last 4 starts: barely stays easy 8.5f: acts on fibresand, firm and soft going: has reportedly broken blood vessels. *P. W. Hiatt*

PRINCE NICHOLAS   6 ch.g. Midyan (USA) 124 – Its My Turn 80 (Palm Track   –
122) [2001 63: 12d Oct 8] sparely-made gelding: modest handicapper at 5 yrs: well held
only outing in 2001. *K. W. Hogg, Isle of Man*

PRINCE NICO (IRE)   4 b.g. Nicolotte 118 – Chummy's Friend (IRE) 47 (Be My   **51 +**
Guest (USA) 126) [2001 67+: e5g* e6g⁵ f5g³ e5g⁵ f5g* 5m 5.2m⁶ May 29] fair on all-   **a77**
weather, modest on turf: won handicaps at Lingfield in January and Wolverhampton in
May: best at 5f/6f: acts on fibresand, equitrack and good to firm going: has been slowly
away: usually races close to pace: joined T. Pinfield in USA. *R. Guest*

PRINCE OF BLUES (IRE)   3 b.c. Prince of Birds (USA) 121 – Reshift 94 (Night   **88 §**
Shift (USA)) [2001 87: 7d 5.1f⁶ 6.1f 5m² 6f 5f 5f 5.1f 5.1m 5g 5.2m 5g5 5g 5g² 5.1d   **a79 §**
5d⁴ 5g 5g⁴ f5g³ f5g f5g³ f5s⁴ f5s Dec 18] good-topped, useful-looking colt: fairly useful
handicapper: effective at 5f/6f: acts on fibresand, firm and good to soft going: often
blinkered in second half of year: has got upset in stall and started slowly: none too
genuine. *N. P. Littmoden*

PRINCE OF MY HEART   8 ch.h. Prince Daniel (USA) – Blue Room 70 (Gorytus   **81 d**
(USA) 132) [2001 85: 10g 9g 10v p12g f12g Dec 8] tall horse: fairly useful handicapper,
lightly raced nowadays: no form in 2001 after leaving H. Cecil after first start: stays 1½m:
raced mainly on good ground or softer on turf nowadays: visored once at 5 yrs. *J. Neville*

PRINCE OF MYSTERY (IRE)   4 b. or br.g. Shalford (IRE) 124§ – Mary Kate
Danagher (Petoski 135) [2001 53: f12g Jan 26] sturdy gelding: modest maiden at 3 yrs:
well held only outing in 2001: blinkered once. *A. B. Coogan*

PRINCE OMID (USA)   4 b.g. Shuailaan (USA) 122 – Matilda The Hun (USA)
(Young Bob (USA)) [2001 71: f14g p10g Dec 12] fair maiden at 3 yrs: well held in 2001:
visored once. *Mrs Merrita Jones*

PRINCE PROSPECT   5 b.g. Lycius (USA) 124 – Princess Dechtra (IRE) 65   **61**
(Bellypha 130) [2001 85§: e6g³ 5m 6d 6m f7g³ p7g f7g³ f8.5g* f8g⁵ f8g⁴ f8.5s* p10g   **a72**
Dec 28] sturdy gelding: unimpressive mover: fair handicapper on all-weather, modest on
turf: won twice at Wolverhampton in December, both times edging left: stays 8.5f: acts
on firm going, good to soft and fibresand: visored once at 2 yrs: often soon off bridle:
none too consistent. *Mrs L. Stubbs*

PRINCE PYRAMUS   3 b.g. Pyramus (USA) 78 – Rekindled Flame (IRE) (Kings   **83 d**
Lake (USA) 133) [2001 84: 6.1f⁵ 6f⁶ 6m 6d⁵ 6g 6m 5d 6d 7g 7d Oct 30] well-made
gelding: usually takes the eye: fairly useful performer at best: on the downgrade: should
stay 7f: acts on any turf going: blinkered (raced too freely) sixth start. *C. Grant*

PRINCE SHAAMAAL   3 b.g. Shaamit (IRE) 127 – Princess Alaska (Northern State   **75 §**
(USA) 91) [2001 79p: 10s⁵ 9s 8.1g p12g⁵ f12g Dec 8] tall, leggy gelding: fair winning
form only run at 2 yrs: disappointing in 2001, looking none too keen last 3 starts (gelded
after final one): should stay 1¼m: acts on polytrack, raced mainly on soft ground on turf:
pulled hard second outing: one to treat with caution. *K. Bell*

PRINCE SLAYER   5 b.g. Batshoof 122 – Top Sovereign (High Top 131) [2001 86:   **74**
10.1s⁴ 10g 10g May 14] well-made gelding: fair form in 2001 only on first start: best at
1m/1¼m: acts on good to firm and soft going (possibly not on heavy): blinkered final
4-y-o start: tends to carry head high: has drifted right. *T. P. McGovern*

PRINCE'S PASSION   2 b.f. (Jan 13) Brief Truce (USA) 126 – Green Bonnet (IRE)   **80**
(Green Desert (USA) 127) [2001 5.1d³ 5.1f⁵ 6m⁴ 5.7f* 6g² 6m⁴ 6g⁵ 6m 6.5g Sep 28]
7,500Y: small, good-bodied filly: first foal: dam, French maiden, half-sister to useful
French performer around 1¼m All Glory: fairly useful performer: won maiden at Bath in
June: creditable efforts in nurseries/minor event next 3 starts: should stay 7f: acts on firm
going. *D. J. Coakley*

PRINCESS ALMORA   3 b.f. Pivotal 124 – Drama School 72 (Young Generation   **88**
129) [2001 6g* 6m 6m⁵ 6g² 7.1m² 6m* 7g² 7m 6g 6m* 6d⁵ Oct 13] 16,000Y: rather
unfurnished filly: half-sister to several winners, including 5-y-o Rada's Daughter and
fairly useful Irish 1m winner Annie Laurie (by Aragon): dam maiden who stayed 1m:
fairly useful performer: won maiden at Windsor in June and handicaps on same course in
July and Kempton in September: effective at 6f/7f: yet to race on extremes of going: held
up. *I. A. Wood*

PRINCESS CHLOE   3 br.f. Primo Dominie 121 – Louise Moillon 79 (Mansingh   **74**
(USA) 120) [2001 72p: 6g 6m 6g⁴ 6d* 6g 6v Oct 8] lengthy, rather unfurnished filly: fair

performer: won minor event at Pontefract in August, wandering in front: not sure to stay much beyond 6f: acts on good to soft ground: blinkered last 4 starts: sold 5,000 gns. *M. A. Jarvis*

PRINCESS CLAUDIA (IRE)   3 b.f. Kahyasi 130 – Shamarra (FR) (Zayyani 119)   **58**
[2001 57: 12v³ 14.6m³ 16m⁵ 16.2m⁴ 11m⁵ 16.2g 15.8m Sep 22] small, compact filly: fluent mover: modest maiden handicapper: left T. Easterby after fifth start: below form subsequently: stays 2m: acts on good to firm going, probably heavy: blinkered final outing. *Mrs H. Dalton*

PRINCESS ELECTRA (IRE)   2 b.f. (Feb 10) Lake Coniston (IRE) 131 – Elect   **66**
(USA) 113 (Vaguely Noble 140) [2001 5m⁶ 5m 5f³ 5.6f* 5m⁶ 6.1m⁵ 6m 6m 6m⁵ 7d² 7v⁶ 7s Nov 10] well-grown filly: half-sister to several winners, including US Grade 3 8.5f winner Aquaba (by Damascus) and Irish 2m winner Electorate (by Caerleon): dam, 1¼m/1½m winner, from very good family: fair performer: won maiden at Doncaster in July: mostly creditable efforts in nurseries after: will stay 1m: acts on any going: sometimes wanders. *K. A. Ryan*

PRINCESS EMERALD   3 b.f. Mtoto 134 – Diamond Princess 69 (Horage 124)   –
[2001 –: 10g 12f 16.2m Jul 23] unfurnished filly: no form in 5 runs. *D. W. P. Arbuthnot*

PRINCESS EMILY (IRE)   3 b.f. Dolphin Street (FR) 125 – Partita (Polish   **49**
Precedent (USA) 131) [2001 68: 10d 9.9m 8m² 9m 8m 7.5f⁵ 8m 7.5m⁴ 8.9m Sep 2] small filly: fair performer at 2 yrs: only poor in 2001: best at 7f/1m: acts on soft and good to firm ground: visored (reared as stalls opened) seventh outing: has raced freely. *B. S. Rothwell*

PRINCESS GRACE   2 b.f. (Feb 23) Inchinor 119 – Hardiprincess (Keen 116) [2001   –
6v 6g 5.1s Oct 30] leggy, angular filly: second foal: half-sister to 3-y-o Anne-Sophie: dam well beaten both starts: only a slight sign of ability in maidens. *M. L. W. Bell*

PRINCESS LILLI   2 b.f. (Jan 28) Vettori (IRE) 119 – Move Darling (Rock City 120)   –
[2001 7.9d 8s 8s Nov 9] leggy, unfurnished filly: second foal: half-sister to Italian 2000 2-y-o 6f winner Sabrehill Star (by Sabrehill): dam ran twice: well held in maidens. *P. S. McEntee*

PRINCESS MILETRIAN (IRE)   2 b.f. (Feb 19) Danehill (USA) 126 – Place of   **80**
Honour (Be My Guest (USA) 126) [2001 6m³ 6m Aug 17] 78,000F, IR 110,000Y: useful-looking filly: half-sister to several winners, notably smart German miler Sinyar (by Machiavellian): dam Irish 1¼m winner out of Coronation Stakes winner Sutton Place: green, fair form when third to Tashawak in maiden at Goodwood: disappointing favourite in similar event at Newbury: should stay 1m: sold 46,000 gns in December. *M. R. Channon*

PRINCESS OF GARDA   3 b.f. Komaite (USA) – Malcesine (IRE) 46 (Auction Ring   **79 d**
(USA) 123) [2001 76: 6s³ 6m 5f⁶ 6d 5.1m⁶ 5m 5g 5.1d⁶ 5s 5.1d 5d⁵ Oct 12] good-topped filly: fair handicapper: generally on downgrade after reappearance: best at 5f/6f: has form on good to firm going, best efforts on good or softer: veered sharply left leaving stall and unseated on debut: has carried head awkwardly/wandered/pulled hard: visored/blinkered once each in 2001. *Mrs G. S. Rees*

PRINCESS OF PERSIA (IRE)   2 ch.f. (Jan 22) Persian Bold 123 – Kazimiera   **52 +**
(IRE) 77 (Polish Patriot (USA) 128) [2001 7g 5.1m Sep 10] IR 18,000Y: neat filly: first foal: dam, placed up to 1m, half-sister to useful 1994 2-y-o 5f/6f winner Fallow: modest form in maidens at Goodwood (needed race) and Bath (unsuited by drop in trip): should stay 1m. *M. R. Channon*

PRINCESS PETARDIA (IRE)   2 b. or br.f. (Mar 17) Petardia 113 – Coolrain Lady   **76**
(IRE) 74 (Common Grounds 118) [2001 5d³ 5d⁴ 6m⁵ 5.2m 6m² 7f* 8g p7g⁵ p7g* Dec 29] IR 10,000F, 23,000Y: leggy filly: has a quick, fluent action: fourth foal: half-sister to useful 2000 2-y-o 1m winner La Vita E Bella (by Definite Article) and 5-y-o Light The Rocket: dam placed at 1m/1¼m in Ireland: fair performer: won maiden at Brighton in August and nursery at Lingfield in December: stays 7f: acts on firm going, good to soft and polytrack. *R. Hannon*

PRINCESS RIA (IRE)   4 b.f. Petong 126 – Walking Saint 73 (Godswalk (USA) 130)   **29**
[2001 –: f12g f11g³ f9.4g⁶ 9v 9.2g⁵ 8.1g Jul 6] leggy, sparely-made filly: poor performer   **a47**
nowadays: left A. Bailey after fourth start: should stay easy 1½m: acts on fibresand. *N. P. Littmoden*

PRINCESS ROYALE (IRE)   2 b.f. (Jan 30) Royal Applause 124 – On The Bank   **61**
(IRE) (In The Wings 128) [2001 6m⁶ 6m⁶ 7g³ Aug 27] IR 52,000Y: third foal: dam

unraced half-sister to dam of Grand Prix de Paris winner Limpid: modest maiden: should stay 1m. *G. A. Butler*

PRINCESS SLANE   4 ch.f. Prince Daniel (USA) – Singing Slane (Cree Song 99)   –
[2001 8d Aug 19] third foal: dam unraced: 100/1, tailed off in maiden at Pontefract. *C. Grant*

PRINCESS SOFIE   2 b.f. (Feb 19) Efisio 120 – Dust 61 (Green Desert (USA) 127)   **84**
[2001 5m² 5m² 5f* 5d* 5f² 6g 5.2m⁴ 5.2m 6m Aug 27] 12,500Y: smallish, well-made filly: first foal: dam, 1m winner, out of smart sprinter Storm Warning: fairly useful performer: won maiden at Pontefract and minor event at Windsor in June: in frame in minor event at Doncaster and Weatherbys Super Sprint at Newbury (fourth of 25 to Good Girl) after: well held last 2 starts, blinkered final one: should stay 6f: acts on firm and good to soft ground. *T. D. Easterby*

PRINCESS TITANIA (IRE)   3 b.f. Fairy King (USA) – Chiquelina (FR) (Le   **96**
Glorieux 127) [2001 65: 7s 10m² 9.9f⁴ 10m² 12.3f⁵ 10m* 10.5s* 12g 10g⁴ Sep 28] leggy, angular filly: useful performer: made all in minor event at Newmarket (beat Alowmdah 7 lengths) in July and handicap at Haydock (beat Jumaireyah 2½ lengths) in September: stays 10.5f: acts on firm and soft going. *N. A. Callaghan*

PRINCES STREET   3 b.g. Sri Pekan (USA) 117 – Abbey Strand (USA) 78 (Shadeed   **66**
(USA) 135) [2001 72: e7g² e5g⁴ 7s³ 7f³ 8.3g 8m 8f⁶ 6m² 6g² 6f* 6.1f 5m³ 5g⁴ 6d Nov 2] fair performer: left R. Hannon after fourth start: won handicap at Newcastle in September: probably best at 5f/6f: acts on any turf going and equitrack: tongue tied for new stable: sometimes reluctant at start/slowly away: free-going sort: has found little. *G. G. Margarson*

PRINCES THEATRE   3 b.g. Prince Sabo 123 – Frisson (Slip Anchor 136) [2001   **74**
78p: 8g³ 8m 8.5m² 10g 8.1m² 10f 8d Oct 8] good-topped gelding: fair maiden: well held in handicaps final 2 starts: best at 7f/1m: acts on good to firm going: has been bandaged/ tongue tied. *I. A. Balding*

PRINCETOWN   2 b.g. (Feb 24) Cotation – The Prussian Queen (Dilum (USA) 115)   –
[2001 6g 7s Oct 11] strong, plain gelding: first foal: dam tailed off only start: 100/1, well beaten in minor events. *C. Smith*

PRINCE TULUM (USA)   2 ch.c. (Mar 27) Bien Bien (USA) 125 – Eastsider (USA)   **74**
(Diesis 133) [2001 6m³ 6m⁶ 6m³ 7g² 6.9d 7m⁵ 6g 7d Oct 20] IR 22,000Y: tall colt: second foal: half-brother to a 5.5f and 7f winner in USA by Exbourne: dam ran twice in USA: fair maiden: out of depth final start: stays 7f: yet to race on extremes of going. *N. P. Littmoden*

PRINCIPAL BOY (IRE)   8 br.g. Cyrano de Bergerac 120 – Shenley Lass (Prince   **35**
Tenderfoot (USA) 126) [2001 40: f8g⁵ f8g f11g³ f7g⁴ f7f 9v Mar 29] compact gelding: has a round action: poor performer: stays 9f: acts on any turf going and fibresand: tried blinkered/visored: sometimes slowly away: often takes good hold. *G. M. Moore*

PRINGIPESSA'S WAY   3 b.f. Machiavellian (USA) 123 – Miss Fancy That (USA)   **72**
99 (The Minstrel (CAN) 135) [2001 9m⁶ 8.1g² 9.9g⁴ Sep 19] 8,000Y, 28,000 2-y-o: half-sister to 3 fairly useful winners, including 7f/1m winner Super Monarch (by Cadeaux Genereux) and 1¾m winner Fancy Heights (by Shirley Heights): dam, 2-y-o 7f winner, closely related to top-class French 1m/9f winner Thrill Show: best effort in maidens when second at Sandown, really finding stride in final 1f: disappointing later in month, racing freely and swishing tail: should stay 1¼m. *P. R. Chamings*

PRINISHA   4 gr.f. Prince Sabo 123 – Nisha (Nishapour (FR) 125) [2001 63: 8.1g f7g   –
Jun 21] tall, lengthy filly: modest maiden at 3 yrs: well beaten in 2001: sent to Saudi Arabia. *Mrs L. Richards*

PRINS WILLEM (IRE)   2 b.g. (Feb 23) Alzao (USA) 117 – American Garden   **69 p**
(USA) (Alleged (USA) 138) [2001 6g 6.1g⁴ 6s Oct 5] IR 26,000F, IR 32,000Y: seventh foal: half-brother to Italian 1m winner Gran Patriot (by Polish Patriot): dam unraced: easily best effort in maidens (fair form) when fourth to Harry Jake at Nottingham: poorly drawn final start (subsequently gelded): bred to be suited by 1¼m/1½m: capable of better. *J. R. Fanshawe*

PRINTSMITH (IRE)   4 br.f. Petardia 113 – Black And Blaze (Taufan (USA) 119)   **56**
[2001 65: 7m 7m 6d⁶ 7.1f 7m Aug 12] leggy, unfurnished filly: modest handicapper: well held in 2001 bar third start: stays 7f: acts on good to soft and good to firm going: sold 4,800 gns. *J. R. Norton*

Lady Tennant's "Priors Lodge"

PRIORS LODGE (IRE)   3 br.c. Grand Lodge (USA) 125 – Addaya (IRE) (Persian **115**
Bold 123) [2001 94p: 8m³ 7.3m⁵ 7g* 7m* 7.3f 8g² Oct 4] rather unfurnished, useful-
looking colt: smart performer, much improved at 3 yrs: won minor event at Goodwood
and listed race at York (beat Toroca ½ length) in August: very good ¾-length second to
Beckett (who rec 4 lb) in listed event at Newmarket final start: will prove best at 7f/1m:
acts on good to firm going, probably on soft: game. *R. Hannon*

PRISA (USA)   2 b.f. (Apr 11) Danehill (USA) 126 – Cantonese (USA) 76 (Easy Goer **56**
(USA)) [2001 5m 6m³ f6g Jun 20] $135,000F: first foal: dam, 2-y-o 7f winner, out of US
Grade 2 8.5f winner Queen of Song: modest maiden: gave impression something amiss
final start: should stay at least 7f: slowly away first 2 outings. *J. Noseda*

PRISM   2 b.g. (Apr 11) Spectrum (IRE) 126 – Seal Indigo (IRE) 93 (Glenstal (USA) **108**
118) [2001 6d* 6m² 7g⁴ 6g* 6g 6d* 6d* Oct 13] 14,000Y: useful-looking, slightly
unfurnished gelding: unimpressive mover: sixth foal: half-brother to 1999 2-y-o 6f
winner who stayed 8.5f Bhutan Prince (by Robellino) and 3-y-o Cielito Lindo: dam, best
at 1½m, out of half-sister to Irish Oaks winner Give Thanks: useful performer: won
maiden at Leicester (awarded race) in June, nursery at York in August and minor event at
Salisbury and listed race at York (best effort, beat Carinae by 1½ lengths despite drifting
left) in October: stays 6f: yet to race on extremes of going. *M. P. Tregoning*

PRIVATE KELLY (IRE)   2 b.g. (Apr 30) General Monash (USA) 107 – Flying **67 §**
Tribute (USA) (Fighting Fit (USA)) [2001 5d 5f 5f* 5m 5m⁵ 5m 5d Aug 2] IR 4,000F, IR
19,000Y: useful-looking gelding: eighth foal: half-brother to Irish 1994 2-y-o 5f winner
CKR Sport (by Nordico): dam lightly-raced maiden: fair performer: won seller at
Lingfield in June: left K. Ivory and ran creditably only once after: raced only at 5f:

acted on firm going: blinkered 3 times: often made running: difficult ride: ungenuine: dead. *J. R. Best*

PRIVATE SEAL 6 b.g. King's Signet (USA) 110 – Slender 79 (Aragon 118) [2001 47§: e8g* f9.4g 10m f8.5g 8m 8m 11.5m² 10m² 11.6g⁴ 11.6m⁵ 10m 10.9m 9.7d p10g Dec 29] workmanlike gelding: modest performer: won seller at Lingfield in January: stays 11.5f: acts on equitrack, polytrack and firm going: tried blinkered, wore eyeshields first 2 starts in 2001: usually tongue tied: has carried head awkwardly/flashed tail: one to treat with caution. *Julian Poulton* **49 §** **a54 §**

PRIVILEGE (USA) 2 b.c. (Mar 17) Foxhound (USA) 103 – Pretty Miswaki (USA) (Miswaki (USA) 124) [2001 6.1m 8g⁴ a8f Dec 20] $27,000Y, resold 150,000Y: third foal: dam ran once in USA: visored, best effort in maidens (fair form) when fourth of 6 to Simeon at Goodwood: left J. Gosden and off 3 months before final outing: seems to stay 1m. *N. Robb, UAE* **68**

PRIX STAR 6 ch.g. Superpower 113 – Celestine 62 (Skyliner 117) [2001 65, a–: 6.1v² f5g 6g³ 6m 6m⁴ 6m 6m⁵ 6g* 6m² 6m 6g⁶ 6g* 6g* 6g⁴ 6m 6v⁵ 7d Nov 6] angular gelding: fair handicapper: won at Hamilton, Newcastle and Newmarket in the summer: has form at 7f, but seems best at 6f: acts on fibresand, equitrack and any turf going: best form visored nowadays. *C. W. Fairhurst* **78** **a–**

PRIYA 3 b.f. Primo Dominie 121 – Promissory (Caerleon (USA) 132) [2001 73: 7d⁵ 7g⁶ 7m³ 6m 6.1d 5g Oct 4] rather leggy, useful-looking filly: poor mover: fairly useful maiden: fifth to Rolly Polly in Fred Darling Stakes at Newbury in April: well below that form after: stays 7f: acts on good to firm and good to soft ground. *C. E. Brittain* **86 d**

PRIZE DANCER (FR) 3 ch.g. Suave Dancer (USA) 136 – Spot Prize (USA) 108 (Seattle Dancer (USA) 119) [2001 73: 10m³ 12f 9.9m⁶ 14.1m* 14m⁶ 13.9m 14.4g³ 17.2g⁵ Oct 1] useful-looking gelding: fairly useful performer: won maiden at Salisbury in July: stays 17f: acts on firm going: free-going sort: consistent. *D. R. C. Elsworth* **81**

PRIZEMAN (USA) 3 b.g. Prized (USA) – Shuttle (USA) (Conquistador Cielo (USA)) [2001 103p: a9f 12.3f⁵ 11m⁶ 16.2m 14.8g Jul 11] strong, lengthy gelding: useful performer: creditable efforts when sixth to Asian Heights in listed race at Goodwood and ninth to And Beyond in Queen's Vase at Royal Ascot (travelled sweetly long way) next time: barely stays 2m: acts on firm and soft going: hung markedly left final start: gelded, and joined N. Henderson. *R. Hannon* **105**

PRIZE WINNER 3 b.c. Mtoto 134 – Rose Show (Belmez (USA) 131) [2001 10.3v* 10s³ 12g² 11.5g 12m 10.4m 10m³ 10.4g Aug 22] small colt: first foal: dam unraced: useful performer: won maiden at Doncaster in March: mostly good efforts after, including ¾-length second to Terrestrial in minor event at Newmarket and 3½ lengths third to Nadour Al Bahr in handicap at Ascot: well held final start: effective at 1¼m/1½m: yet to race on firm going, acts on any other. *J. Noseda* **108**

PROCEDURE (USA) 5 b. or br.g. Strolling Along (USA) – Bold Courtesan (USA) (Bold Bidder) [2001 10s³ 12s 12v 10d Oct 13] big, useful-looking gelding: fairly useful form in 2001 only on first start: best up to 1½m: acts on good to firm and heavy ground: tends to carry head high. *J. A. B. Old* **85**

PROCEED WITH CARE 3 b.g. Danehill (USA) 126 – Ultra Finesse (USA) 107 (Rahy (USA) 115) [2001 101: 7d* 7m 8m² 7m 8g⁶ 7g Aug 25] good sort: useful performer: won minor event at Newmarket in April: good 1¼ lengths second of 4 to Late Night Out in listed event at Goodwood in July: below form last 3 starts: stays 1m: acts on good to firm and good to soft ground, well beaten on soft/heavy: blinkered final outing: sold 16,000 gns, sent to USA. *M. Johnston* **106**

PROCESSION 2 b.f. (Mar 23) Zafonic (USA) 130 – Applaud (USA) 105 (Rahy (USA) 115) [2001 7f² 7m⁴ Aug 11] second foal: dam 2-y-o 5f/6f (Cherry Hinton) winner: fair form in maidens at Kempton (runner-up to Dusty Answer) and Redcar (favourite, took strong hold): will need to settle to stay 1m. *Sir Michael Stoute* **71**

PROFILE 3 b.g. Spectrum (IRE) 126 – Famosa (Dancing Brave (USA) 140) [2001 7f 8.3m⁶ 8.1d³ 10.2g³ 10m⁴ 12g⁵ 8s Sep 24] rather leggy gelding: fifth foal: half-brother to several winners, including useful miler Brave Kris (by Kris) and 11f to 1½m winner Caerosa (by Caerleon): dam, French 1½m winner, half-sister to Lowther winner Kingscote: fair maiden: below form and looked tricky ride last 3 starts: should stay 1½m: visored fifth/sixth starts: sold 4,000 gns, sent to Holland. *M. L. W. Bell* **67**

PROFITEER (IRE) 2 b.g. (Feb 22) Entrepreneur 123 – Champagne Girl 67 (Robellino (USA) 127) [2001 6d⁵ 6f⁶ Sep 21] 160,000Y: smallish, sturdy gelding: fourth foal: **98 ?**

half-brother to 3 winning sprinters, including 6-y-o Halmahera and 3-y-o Speedy Gee: dam, 2-y-o 5f winner, half-sister to useful sprinter Deep Finesse: favourite (started slowly) in Pontefract maiden on debut: blinkered, seemingly useful form when under 3 lengths sixth of 10 to Firebreak in Mill Reef Stakes at Newbury, making pace 4f: gelded after: not sure to stay much beyond 6f. *D. R. Loder*

PROLETARIAT 3 gr.g. Petong 126 – Primulette 82 (Mummy's Pet 125) [2001 78: 6g^4 6.1d* 8.2f* 8m 8m Jul 22] close-coupled gelding: fairly useful performer: won maiden (blinkered) and handicap at Nottingham in May/June, carrying head rather high in latter: well below form after: stays 1m, at least with emphasis on speed: acts on firm and good to soft going: went in snatches fourth start: sold 11,500 gns. *H. Candy* **90**

PROMISCUOUS 3 ch.g. Pursuit of Love 124 – Sparkly Girl (USA) (Danehill (USA) 126) [2001 f8.5g^6 f8f^6 Mar 19] 5,000Y: second foal: half-brother to 4-y-o Spark of Life: dam Irish 1m to 1½m winner: well held in maidens at Wolverhampton and Southwell. *P. F. I. Cole* **–**

PROMISED (IRE) 3 b.f. Petardia 113 – Where's The Money 87 (Lochnager 132) [2001 90: 6v 5.1f 6s 6m^5 Jun 2] short-backed, leggy filly: fairly useful performer: ran well in 2001 only when fifth to Palanzo in handicap at Newmarket final start: should stay 7f: acts on good to firm and good to soft going: visored (stiffish task) once: sweating/edgy (below form) once at 2 yrs. *J. A. Glover* **89**

PROMISING (FR) 3 ch.f. Ashkalani (IRE) 128 – Sea Thunder 83 (Salse (USA) 128) [2001 8.2d 7s f7g f8g^6 f6s^6 Dec 15] 1,100,000 francs Y, 2,200 2-y-o: first foal: dam 6f winner: well held in maidens. *M. C. Chapman* **–**

PROMOTE 5 gr.g. Linamix (FR) 127 – Rive (USA) (Riverman (USA) 131) [2001 8.2s Nov 5] second foal: half-brother to 6-y-o Brevity: dam French 2-y-o 1¼m winner: fairly useful form both starts in France in 1998: off 3½ years and tongue tied, well held only outings at 5 yrs: will stay at least 1¼m. *Ms A. E. Embiricos* **–**

PROMPT PAYMENT (IRE) 3 b. or br.f. In The Wings 128 – Lady Lucre (IRE) 73 (Last Tycoon 131) [2001 10g^3 11.5g* 10g^5 10.1s^4 Oct 31] IR 20,000Y: tall filly: first foal: dam, ran once, from family of 3-y-o Golan: fairly useful performer: won maiden at Lingfield in September: creditable efforts after: bred to stay beyond 11.5f but isn't short of speed: swished tail continuously in paddock penultimate start. *J. R. Fanshawe* **87**

PROPER SQUIRE (USA) 4 b.g. Bien Bien (USA) 125 – La Cumbre (Sadler's Wells (USA) 132) [2001 75: 15.4v^3 16.2m f16.2g* f16.2g^3 16.2m^4 14.8m 16g 16d* 16v Oct 26] strong, well-made gelding: fair performer: won seller at Wolverhampton in June and NH jockeys handicap at Goodwood in September: will stay beyond 2m: acts on fibresand, good to firm and heavy going: blinkered last 5 outings: joined C. Mann, and fair form when successful over hurdles in December. *B. J. Meehan* **75**

PROPERTY ZONE 3 b.g. Cool Jazz 116 – Prime Property (IRE) 60 (Tirol 127) [2001 –: 8.5f 12m^4 16g 12f^6 f8.5s^3 Dec 26] smallish, workmanlike gelding: poor maiden handicapper: stays 1½m: acts on firm ground and fibresand. *M. W. Easterby* **43**

PROSERPINA 3 b.f. Most Welcome 131 – Hever Golf Lady 62 (Dominion 123) [2001 8f 10m 12.3m^6 Aug 27] quite attractive filly: first foal: dam 1¼m and 2m winner, half-sister to smart French middle-distance performer Lady Tamara: well held in maidens. *K. R. Burke* **–**

PROSERPINE 2 b.f. (Apr 16) Robellino (USA) 127 – Hymne d'Amour (USA) 58 (Dixieland Band (USA)) [2001 6g^5 7m^2 8d^2 8v* Oct 16] fifth foal: half-sister to smart performer up to 1¾m in Britain/USA Chelsea Barracks, 1m winner at 2 yrs, and 4-y-o Guard Duty (both by Deploy): dam, lightly raced on Flat and winning hurdler, out of half-sister to Alzao: useful form: short-headed by Sulk and then Shanty in maidens at Salisbury second and third starts, drifting left on second occasion: landed odds in similar event at Ayr in just workmanlike style: will be suited by 1¼m/1½m: should progress. *M. P. Tregoning* **95 p**

PROSPECTORS CORAL 2 b.f. (Apr 17) Primo Dominie 121 – St Louis Lady 71 (Absalom 128) [2001 5m 5m 6g f5g Oct 6] 2,500Y: third foal: dam 7f winner: well held in maidens/sellers: reared as stall opened and unseated rider final start: twice failed stall test later in year. *Mrs Lydia Pearce* **–**

PROSPECTOR'S COVE 8 b.g. Dowsing (USA) 124 – Pearl Cove 63 (Town And Country 124) [2001 77, a68: f8s f7g f8.5g^5 f11g 7f 8m 10f^3 10m^3 10.1g 10g 16f^5 8g 10.1d^5 8m^5 9.7d^5 8.2m 8s f11g 11.8s^6 10s 7d Nov 2] workmanlike gelding: modest performer, on downgrade: stays 1¼m: acts on fibresand, equitrack and on any turf going: **64 d a52 d**

has run poorly when visored: often slowly away: tends to wander: usually held up: banned from racing from stalls. *Mrs Lydia Pearce*

PROTAGONIST   3 b. or br.g. In The Wings 128 – Fatah Flare (USA) 121 (Alydar   71
(USA)) [2001 11.1s⁴ 10.2d⁴ 13.9m⁶ May 15] 42,000Y: leggy gelding: half-brother to several winners, including useful 6f (at 2 yrs) and 7f winner Flavian (by Catrail) and fairly useful 1¼m winner who stayed 1½m Refugio (by Reference Point): dam 6f (at 2 yrs) and 10.5f (Musidora Stakes) winner: fair form in maidens first 2 starts: stiff task when well-held last of 6 in minor event at York final outing: sold 12,000 gns, and gelded. *M. R. Channon*

PROTECTORATE   2 ch.f. (Apr 8) Hector Protector (USA) 124 – Possessive Lady   91
62 (Dara Monarch 128) [2001 5.1s* 7d² 6.5g 6d² 8d Nov 3] leggy filly: fifth foal: half-sister to 1½m winner Basher Jack (by Suave Dancer) and useful French 1¼m winner Morini (by Unfuwain): dam, 1m winner, half-sister to Irish Oaks winner Possessive Dancer: fairly useful performer: won maiden at Nottingham in August: best effort when 7 lengths second of 6 to Gossamer in Prestige Stakes at Goodwood next time: ¾-length second of 30 to Major Laugh in sales race at Newmarket (veered right when in front over 1f out) penultimate start: should stay 1m: raced only on good ground or softer. *I. A. Wood*

PROTECTRESS   2 ch.f. (Mar 23) Hector Protector (USA) 124 – Quota 102 (Rainbow   103 p
Quest (USA) 134) [2001 7g* Oct 6] rather leggy, useful-looking filly: second foal: dam, lightly-raced 1¼m winner, sister to Racing Post Trophy winner and St Leger second Armiger: 11/4 favourite, highly promising debut when beating Snowfire a head in listed race at Newmarket, slowly away, good headway to lead over 1f out and holding on gamely: bred to stay at least 1¼m: smart prospect, and should win races in pattern company. *H. R. A. Cecil*

Mr K. Adbulla's "Protectress"

PROTOCOL (IRE) 7 b.g. Taufan (USA) 119 – Ukraine's Affair (USA) (The **50**
Minstrel (CAN) 135) [2001 52: f16g⁴ f16s⁶ 10s⁴ 14.1v² 12.4d⁶ 11.8f 12m 10f 16.5m 12g⁴ **a32**
17.1g 16m 10.5s⁵ 18f⁵ 18s 14.1s Nov 5] rather leggy gelding: modest handicapper on
turf, poor on all-weather: effective at stiff 1¼m to 17f: acts on heavy going, good to firm,
fibresand and equitrack: visored once in 1999: tongue tied. *Mrs S. Lamyman*

PROUD BOAST 3 b.f. Komaite (USA) – Red Rosein 97 (Red Sunset 120) [2001 92: **93**
5.1f² 5m 6f 6d Jun 16] rather leggy, angular filly: fairly useful handicapper: below form
after reappearance: best at 5f: acts on firm and good to soft ground: usually held up.
Mrs G. S. Rees

PROUD CAVALIER 5 b.g. Pharly (FR) 130 – Midnight Flit 89 (Bold Lad (IRE) 133) **–**
[2001 33, a36: 10f⁵ 10g 11.7f³ 11.6g 10.1d Aug 8] little form in 2001. *K. Bell*

PROUD CHIEF 4 ch.g. Be My Chief (USA) 122 – Fleur de Foret (USA) 61§ (Green **66 §**
Forest (USA) 134) [2001 80d: f7g f7g 8s 7m 6m 5m 6m* 6f Jul 25] small, strong gelding:
fair handicapper nowadays: won at Epsom in July: stays 7f: acts on good to soft and good
to firm going: tried visored: unreliable. *A. P. Jarvis*

PROUD MONK 8 gr.g. Aragon 118 – Silent Sister 78 (Kind of Hush 118) [2001 f11g **39**
11.9g⁶ 10.5g 10m⁵ 11.8d Jul 19] strong, lengthy gelding: poor performer: probably stays
1½m: acts on soft and good to firm going: tried blinkered/visored/tongue tied. *K. Bell*

PROUD NATIVE (IRE) 7 b.g. Imp Society (USA) – Karamana (Habitat 134) [2001 **108**
114: 5.2d 5m³ 5f⁵ 5s* 5g³ 5g⁵ 5m 5m 5m⁴ 5d Sep 25] sturdy gelding: poor walker/mover:
useful performer: won minor event at Sandown in June: ran creditably earlier in season
when length third to Dananeyev in Prix de Saint-Georges at Longchamp and when fifth
to Bishops Court in listed rated stakes at Epsom: well held on 3 of last 4 starts: barely
stays 6f: acts on firm and soft going (possibly not at best on heavy): well held only try
in blinkers: edgy sort: often early to post: sometimes bandaged in front: waited with.
D. Nicholls

PROUD PROTECTOR (IRE) 2 ch.g. (May 3) Hector Protector (USA) 124 – **62**
Hooray Lady 92 (Ahonoora 122) [2001 6f 8.1s 6.1d⁵ Sep 21] seventh foal: half-brother to
3 winners, including fairly useful 5f to 7.5f winner Carlton (by Thatching) and useful 5f
(at 2 yrs) to 6.5f (including US Grade 3 events) winner Desert Lady (by Danehill): dam
winner around 1m and seemed to stay 1½m: modest form on first start in maidens (gelded
after final one). *T. D. Easterby*

PROUD REFLECTION 3 b.c. Petong 126 – Fleur de Foret (USA) 61§ (Green **–**
Forest (USA) 134) [2001 68: 6m 5g 8s Sep 24] maiden: fair form only run at 2 yrs: well
held in 2001, leaving A. Jarvis after second start: dead. *J. G. Portman*

PROUD WESTERN (USA) 3 b.c. Gone West (USA) – Proud Lou (USA) (Proud **73**
Clarion) [2001 8m 8m⁴ 8.2s⁵ f8g² f8.5g³ Dec 11] ex-French colt: half-brother to several
winners, notably smart 5.5f (at 2 yrs) to 1m (Poule d'Essai des Pouliches) winner Houseproud (by Riverman): dam US 2-y-o Grade 1 1m winner: fair maiden: in frame all starts
at 2 yrs: left A. Fabre 48,000 gns after second start in 2001: stays 1m: acts on fibresand
and soft ground. *B. Ellison*

PROUDWINGS (GER) 5 b.m. Dashing Blade 117 – Peraja (FR) (Kaiseradler) **118**
[2001 108: 8s³ 8v* 8g 8g* 8d*ᵈⁱˢ 8s 8f* 8m Dec 16]
    Proudwings' connections had at least three reasons to look back on her final
season with plenty of pride; there was an impressive win in France, an historic
victory in Britain and a valuable success in Japan. But there were disappointments
too, the greatest one when losing a Group 1 prize in the stewards' room. Few who
saw Proudwings' final-furlong swerve to her left in the Prix Jacques le Marois at
Deauville would have backed her to keep the race; even her own connections were
resigned to losing first place. But when the Deauville stewards disqualified her and
placed her last, rather than demoting her to third or fourth place, Proudwings'
owner, Dr Rolf Wilhelms, saw fit to appeal.
    At the end of a steadily-run race in the Jacques le Marois, the nine-runner
field was virtually line abreast entering the final furlong, spearheaded by Proudwings, who had begun to take a narrow advantage. But, under the whip, she went
quite sharply left into the path of Noverre forcing him in turn to bump Banks Hill,
Christophe Soumillon's switching of his stick to his left hand on Proudwings
coming too late to undo the damage. Proudwings passed the post first with half a
length to spare over Vahorimix, who had avoided all the trouble. The two main

sufferers, Banks Hill and Noverre, were third and fourth, just over a length behind the winner. Crucially though, another party was involved in the interference, Amonita who passed the post in eighth place. She had been tracking Noverre and Banks Hill and looking for room between the two of them when the gap closed. Proudwings' owner's appeal was based on the view that Amonita had *already* been hampered in an earlier incident and that Proudwings had not directly interfered with Amonita. However, the French stewards upheld the view that Amonita's chances of picking up some prize-money (which extended to fifth place) had been compromised by Proudwings coming off a true line, and the local stewards therefore had no option but to place Proudwings behind her in last.

Soumillon, riding Proudwings for the first time, was dealt a four-day ban. His view that Proudwings 'was frightened by something' was not received with much sympathy by her owner. 'We asked Monsieur Soumillon not to use his whip. But he did and she didn't like it. Whether he didn't listen, or didn't understand, I don't know.' After the decision to disqualify Proudwings was upheld, Dr Wilhelms issued a statement which read: 'The decision of the stewards was not justified. It is considered by expert insiders to be the exaggerated influence on France-Galop, and French racing in general, of the major sponsors and owners involved. In contrast to Italy and England, small owners from abroad can be expected to be treated neither in a friendly nor a fair manner.' The main beneficiary of Proudwings' disqualification, Vahorimix, was owned by France-Galop president Jean-Luc Lagardere.

Proudwings' other ventures abroad had much happier results for the most part. She ran only once in her native Germany all season, finishing third in a well-contested listed race at Cologne on her reappearance. Her first success came in the Prix du Muguet at Saint-Cloud in May, when she struck up a successful partnership with Japanese jockey Yutaka Take, newly based in France. They took the Muguet in really good style, bursting through a gap over a furlong out and quickening clear to beat Dionello four lengths. Take was unavailable for Proudwings' next start, also in France, in the Prix du Chemin de Fer du Nord at Chantilly, and she beat only two home in a blanket finish after being poorly placed when the pace quickened.

With Take back on board the following month for the Falmouth Stakes at Newmarket, Proudwings was ridden more prominently in another rather muddling affair. Always in control after quickening to lead over a furlong out, Proudwings beat Heavenly Whisper by two lengths. Her win broke new ground for German breeding, as Proudwings became the first German-bred winner of a British pattern race. She was also the first German-trained winner of such an event since the 1975 Eclipse winner Star Appeal. Proudwings was now the winner of two Group 2 events and an attempt to win a Group 1 was the logical next step. Take had to miss the ride in the Jacques le Marois with a broken wrist but was fit again for Proudwings' rematch with Vahorimix and Noverre in the Queen Elizabeth II Stakes at Ascot. She started third favourite behind that pair but, in a race where all the market leaders were guilty of giving Godolphin's pacemaker Summoner too much rope, Proudwings was in rear throughout and beat only one home. It transpired that there

Falmouth Stakes, Newmarket—Yutaka Take partners German mare Proudwings to success over Heavenly Whisper and Lady Lahar (No.7)

*Capital Stakes, Tokyo—Proudwings, winning in a fifth different country,
takes one of the sixteen races open to foreign competition on the Flat in Japan in 2001*

was more to her poor showing than met the eye, as she was found to be suffering
from 'nettle fever', seemingly an allergy to something in the hay.

Germany's most valuable international success had come in the 1995 Japan
Cup at Tokyo with Lando. One of his sons, Paolini, represented Germany without
success in the latest running, but on the same card Proudwings gained her tenth and
final career win in the Capital Stakes. Open to foreign-trained horses for the first
time, the Capital Stakes does not have pattern or graded status, yet was worth the
equivalent of around £140,000 to the winner, a very similar prize to the one
Proudwings had lost at Deauville. Take's presence in the saddle, rather than Proudwings' European form, no doubt contributed most to her starting the 11/10
favourite and she came home the half-length winner from some smart Japanese
milers headed by Daiwa Rouge. Proudwings had probably had enough for the
season when finishing only ninth in the Hong Kong Mile at Sha Tin in December.

		Elegant Air (b 1981)	Shirley Heights
Proudwings (GER) (b.m. 1996)	Dashing Blade (b 1987)		Elegant Tern
		Sharp Castan (ch 1977)	Sharpen Up
			Sultry One
	Peraja (FR) (b 1977)	Kaiseradler (b 1957)	Nebelwerfer
			Kaiserwurde
		Perette (b 1970)	High Hat
			Perine

Hyperion is a name that recurs in the further reaches of Proudwings'
extended pedigree. He is the grandsire of her grandam Perette and the sire of her
fourth dam La Perie, and is also a distant ancestor of her sire Dashing Blade. Those
connections are too remote to have much significance for Proudwings but Hyperion
has been a strong influence on Dr Wilhelms' breeding and racing operation. He
explained that all five of his broodmares are inbred to the 1933 Derby winner and
he has taken the name 'Hyperion Breeding' as his *nom de course*. Proudwings is
much the best recent member of the family, which has French origins. Her dam

has been a reliable producer of winners however, with five in Germany prior to Proudwings, as well as Proudwings' four-year-old full brother Proudfox, a seven-furlong winner. Like Proudwings, her dam Peraja raced until she was five, winning five races up to eleven furlongs in Germany. Peraja was one of several winners out of the French two-year-old seven-furlong winner Perette. Great grandam Perine was a once-raced half-sister to Prix de Diane winner Belle Sicambre out of a half-sister to the 1955 Derby winner Phil Drake. Proudwings was sold for an undisclosed sum after her final start to Teruya Yoshida in Japan, where she will be covered by Sunday Silence. Dr Wilhelms retains an option on the first filly foal she produces as part of the deal.

A mix of success and misfortune was a feature of Proudwings' career as a whole, not just of her final season. She must have been a contender for the title of most improved horse in training in Germany as a four-year-old, when she completed a four-timer in handicaps before winning a listed race and the Group 3 Premio Sergio Cumani, both at Milan. But her earlier career had evidently been much less straightforward. She was unraced at two and managed only four starts (and a win in maiden company) as a three-year-old. A legacy of some of her problems at around this time was that she reportedly had pins in a cannon bone. A rather leggy, good-topped mare, Proudwings was best at around a mile and acted on any ground. She was usually held up in touch and had a good turn of foot. She showed a tendency to sweat and get on edge before both her races in Britain, though that did not affect her performance, at least not at Newmarket. Although there have been plenty of better horses trained in Germany in recent seasons, few have done more than Proudwings to promote her country's racing and breeding inter-nationally. *R. Suerland, Germany*

PROVENDER (IRE) 2 b.c. (Apr 29) Ashkalani (IRE) 128 – Quiche 83 (Formidable **75** (USA) 125) [2001 7f⁵ 6.1m² 6m Sep 20] IR 25,000Y: good-topped colt: half-brother to several winners, including smart 6f performer Lionhearted (by Catrail) and useful 5f to 7f performer (in Ireland and France) Symboli Kildare (by Kaldoun): dam 6f winner: best effort in maidens (fair form) when second to Chateau Nicol at Warwick: will need to settle to stay 7f. *Sir Mark Prescott*

PROVEN (USA) 2 br.c. (Feb 17) Benny The Dip (USA) 127 – Night Fax (USA) **96 p** (Known Fact (USA) 135) [2001 7v* Oct 26] 150,000Y: strong, angular colt: second foal: half-brother to a 2-y-o winner in US by Thunder Gulch: dam US Grade 2 1¼m winner: 14/1 and backward, useful form when winning 12-runner maiden at Doncaster by ½ length from Sting Like A Bee despite drifting left under pressure: should stay at least 1¼m: wore crossed noseband: sure to improve. *J. H. M. Gosden*

PSALMIST 4 ch.f. Mystiko (USA) 124 – Son Et Lumiere (Rainbow Quest (USA) 134) **–** [2001 59: 8.1g 13.3g May 30] modest maiden at best: well held in 2001. *Noel T. Chance*

PSYCHIC (IRE) 2 b.f. (Mar 7) Alhaarth (IRE) 126 – Mood Swings (IRE) 77 (Shirley **60 P** Heights 130) [2001 7g⁶ Sep 11] IR 75,000Y: second foal: half-sister to 3-y-o Hurricane Floyd: dam 2-y-o 6f winner: 20/1, sixth of 17 to Snowfire in maiden at Lingfield, moving smoothly into contention 2f out and not at all knocked about once fading: likely to do good deal better, and should win races. *M. L. W. Bell*

PTAH (IRE) 4 b.g. Petardia 113 – Davenport Goddess (IRE) (Classic Secret (USA) **50** 91) [2001 58§, a49§: f16g f16.2s 16v* 17.1s⁶ 13d 16.2m 15.8m⁵ 15.8d 16s Oct 30] small gelding: modest handicapper: won at Musselburgh in March: stays 2m: acts on fibresand, equitrack, heavy and good to firm going: has given trouble in preliminaries: blinkered second start, usually tongue tied of late: none too consistent. *J. L. Eyre*

PTARMIGAN RIDGE 5 b.h. Sea Raven (IRE) 75 – Panayr (Faraway Times (USA) **94 §** 123) [2001 86: 5m⁵ 5d⁴ 5d⁴ 5g* 6m 5s 5v 5d 5s* 5v Oct 27] quite good-topped horse: reportedly had foot problems in 1999: fairly useful handicapper: won at Haydock in August and Catterick (beat Regal Song by 3½ lengths) in October: best at 5f: acts on good to firm and soft going (possibly not on heavy). *Miss L. A. Perratt*

PUDDLE DUCK 2 b.g. (Feb 14) First Trump 118 – Aunt Jemima (Busted 134) [2001 **–** 6m 7.9m Sep 5] 9,000Y: sturdy, lengthy gelding: eighth foal: half-brother to 3 winners, notably useful 6f (at 2 yrs) to 1½m winner Azhar (by Night Shift): dam unraced half-sister to 4-y-o Compton Bolter: behind in maidens, looking difficult ride: refused to enter stall in between. *T. D. Easterby*

Lady Clague's "Pugin"

PUFFIN   3 b.f. Pennekamp (USA) 130 – Spring 112 (Sadler's Wells (USA) 132) [2001   **81**
77p: 9s* 10s⁵ 8m⁶ 8g⁶ 8g 8d Oct 8] smallish filly: had a short action: fairly useful
handicapper: won at Kempton in April: stayed 9f: acted on soft going: stud. *J. L. Dunlop*

PUGIN (IRE)   3 b.c. Darshaan 133 – Gothic Dream (IRE) 113 (Nashwan (USA) 135)   **115**
[2001 10s* 12g² 10g* 12g⁴ 14g² 14.6g⁵ Sep 15] strong colt: has stringhalt: third foal:
half-brother to Irish 2m winner Gothic Theme (by Zafonic): dam, Irish 2-y-o 7f winner
and third in Irish Oaks, daughter of Irish St Leger winner Dark Lomond: smart performer:
won maiden at Navan in April and listed race at the Curragh (made virtually all to beat
March King ¾ length) in May: ran well next 2 starts, 8½ lengths fourth to Galileo in
Irish Derby at the Curragh and head second to Vinnie Roe in listed race on same course:
below-par fifth to Milan in St Leger at Doncaster final start: stays 1¾m: yet to race on
ground firmer than good. *J. Oxx, Ireland*

PULAU PINANG (IRE)   5 ch.m. Dolphin Street (FR) 125 – Inner Pearl (Gulf Pearl   **97**
117) [2001 84: f12g⁵ f12f 10m* 9.9m* 11.8m 9g 10m² 12.1m* 12d p10g* p12g* p10g*
Dec 4] leggy mare: useful handicapper: won at Sandown in May, Beverley in June,
Hamilton in September and Lingfield in November (twice) and December: best at 1¼m
to 13f: goes well on polytrack, best turf efforts on good to firm going (though has form on
good to soft): usually tongue tied: has raced freely: suffered from fibrillating heart fifth
start: waited with: reliable. *G. A. Butler*

PULAU TIOMAN   5 b.h. Robellino (USA) 127 – Ella Mon Amour 65 (Ela-Mana-   **112**
Mou 132) [2001 112d: 8v⁵ 8d² 8s* 8.5f* 8g 10m⁴ Aug 25] compact horse: smart
performer: as good as ever in 2001, runner-up to Mastermind in Spring Cup at Newbury before winning minor event at Kempton (beat Easaar by 1¾ lengths) in May and
Vodafone Diomed Stakes at Epsom (led near finish to beat Cauvery by a head) in June:

Vodafone Diomed Stakes, Epsom—Pulau Tioman (second left) is produced with a typically late effort to catch Cauvery (No.8), with Soviet Flash (No.6) third

only fair fourth to Adilabad in Winter Hill Stakes at Windsor final outing: reportedly split a pastern shortly after: very best form at 7f/8.5f: acts on any going: held up: remains in training. *M. A. Jarvis*

PULSAAR 2 br.c. (Apr 2) Hamas (IRE) 125§ – Sure Victory (IRE) 75 (Stalker 121) **62 §** [2001 6m 6.1m⁴ 5.1g³ 6g 5m² 5g⁵ 5.3s p6g² f5g⁶ p6g Dec 22] 5,000 2-y-o: sixth living foal: half-brother to a 1m/1¼m winner in Germany by Midyan: dam 6f to 1m winner: modest maiden: runner-up in sellers: likely to prove best at 5f/easy 6f: acts on good to firm going and polytrack: blinkered (raced too freely) fourth outing: usually races prominently: not to be trusted. *R. M. Beckett*

PULSE 3 b.c. Salse (USA) 128 – French Gift 99 (Cadeaux Genereux 131) [2001 50p: **64** 8m 8.1m 7.6g 6.1f⁵ f6g³ f6g p7g Nov 20] modest maiden: best at 6f: acts on fibresand, raced only on good going or firmer on turf. *R. Hannon*

PUNCTUALITY 3 b.f. Chaddleworth (IRE) 103 – Never Late 56 (Never So Bold **–** 135) [2001 –: 8.2v Mar 28] last all 3 starts, including in seller. *M. R. Ewer-Hoad*

PUNISHMENT 10 b.h. Midyan (USA) 124 – In The Shade 89 (Bustino 136) [2001 **76 §** 83§, a87§: f9.4s e12g³ e12g⁴ e10g⁴ f12g* e13g³ 10f² 9.9m⁴ 10d² 12m 10g³ 10v³ 10v p10g f9.4g⁴ Nov 27] workmanlike horse: won minor event at Wolverhampton in March: effective at 1¼m to easy 13f: acts on any turf going, fibresand and equitrack: visored once in 1999: tongue tied: unreliable. *K. O. Cunningham-Brown*

PUPPET KING 2 b.g. (Mar 25) Mistertopogigo (IRE) 118 – Bold Gift 61 (Persian **56** Bold 123) [2001 6f 7.1m 6g 7m Aug 3] 8,000Y: half-brother to several winners, including useful 9f winner Poddington (by Crofthall): dam 2-y-o maiden who stayed 7f: modest maiden: will probably stay 1m: sold 1,200 gns. *I. A. Balding*

PUPPET PLAY (IRE) 6 ch.m. Broken Hearted 124 – Fantoccini (Taufan (USA) **72** 119) [2001 71, a65: f6g* f6g* f7g² 6g 6m 6f³ 7m⁶ 7m³ 7m 6m Sep 6] workmanlike mare: **a82** fairly useful handicapper on all-weather, fair on turf: won at Wolverhampton and Southwell in February: has won at 1m, but best at 6f/7f: acts on firm going (below best on softer than good) and fibresand: tried blinkered: has idled/found little, and best held up. *E. J. Alston*

PUP'S PRIDE 4 b.g. Efisio 120 – Moogie 103 (Young Generation 129) [2001 53, a65: **46** f6g f6s* e7g f7g³ f7g⁴ f7g³ f7g⁶ 6m f6g² f6g³ f7g⁴ t6g⁶ f8g³ f12g f9.4g² f9.4g⁴ f8g³ f8.5s² **a64** Dec 26] modest handicapper on all-weather, poor on turf: won at Wolverhampton in January: effective at 6f to 9.4f: acts on fibresand and good to firm going: often visored/blinkered: often slowly away/gets behind: has found little/carried head high: consistent. *R. A. Fahey*

PURE BRIEF (IRE)   4 b.g. Brief Truce (USA) 126 – Epure (Bellypha 130) [2001 46:   –
f12g Nov 23] poor maiden at 3 yrs: well held only 4-y-o outing. *A. Streeter*

PURE COINCIDENCE   6 b.g. Lugana Beach 116 – Esilam 62 (Frimley Park 109)   **87 d**
[2001 81, a84: f5g 5s* 5s 5s 6d 5d⁵ 5s p5g* Dec 4] rather leggy gelding: has a short
action: fairly useful performer: on downgrade after winning handicap at Doncaster in
March, though won seller at Lingfield in December: reportedly lame fifth start, off 5½
months after: probably best at 5f: acts on firm ground, soft, fibresand and polytrack:
effective visored/blinkered or not: usually early to post: races prominently. *K. R. Burke*

PURE ELEGANCIA   5 b.m. Lugana Beach 116 – Esilam 62 (Frimley Park 109)   **72**
[2001 75: 5m³ 5m 5m 5m 5g 5m 5.2m 5.3g⁴ 5m 5g 5m f5g⁴ 5.2v p5g* p6g² Dec 19] rather
leggy, workmanlike mare: fair handicapper: left K. Ivory after winning at Lingfield in
November: barely stays sharp 6f: acts on firm going, fibresand and polytrack: very slowly
away fourth outing: tried visored/blinkered: none too consistent. *G. A. Butler*

PURE MIRACLE   2 b.f. (Feb 8) Royal Applause 124 – Deerlet 64 (Darshaan 133)   –
[2001 5.1g Aug 3] second foal: dam maiden who should have been suited by further than
1½m: 20/1, well held in maiden at Nottingham. *I. A. Balding*

PURE MISCHIEF (IRE)   2 b.g. (Apr 17) Alhaarth (IRE) 126 – Bellissi (IRE) 77   **92**
(Bluebird (USA) 125) [2001 7f 7.2v⁴ 8.2s² Oct 30] IR 40,000F, IR 42,000Y: third foal:
half-brother to 4-y-o Mamzuc: dam, Irish 7f/1m winner, sister to smart Irish 7f winner
Wild Bluebell and half-sister to Moyglare Stud Stakes winner Priory Belle: best effort in
maidens (fairly useful form) when clear second to Balakheri at Nottingham, not unduly
punished when held: gelded after: should stay 1¼m: moved poorly to post and raced too
freely on debut. *E. A. L. Dunlop*

PUREPLEASURESEEKER (IRE)   2 ch.f. (Mar 9) Grand Lodge (USA) 125 –
Bianca Cappello (IRE) (Glenstal (USA) 118) [2001 6m 7g 7m Sep 24] 50,000Y: second
foal: half-sister to useful 2000 2-y-o 6f/6.5f (Prix Eclipse) winner Potaro (by Catrail),
later successful up to 1¼m in USA: dam, no form, half-sister to smart Irish 7f to 1¼m
performer Idris: only a little sign of ability in maidens. *P. F. I. Cole*

PURPLE FLAME (IRE)   5 b.m. Thatching 131 – Polistatic 53 (Free State 125) [2001   **42**
–: 11.6m⁵ 12.6f 11.5m 9.9d⁶ 10s Oct 25] workmanlike mare: poor maiden handicapper:
stays 1½m: acts on good to firm going, probably not on soft: tongue tied final start.
C. A. Horgan

PURPLE FLING   10 ch.g. Music Boy 124 – Divine Fling (Imperial Fling (USA) 116)   –
[2001 –, a66: f6g Feb 16] strong gelding: fair performer in 2000: well held only start in
2001. *Andrew Reid*

PURPLE HAZE (IRE)   2 b.f. (Feb 23) Spectrum (IRE) 126 – Isticanna (USA) 96   **92 p**
(Far North (CAN) 120) [2001 7m* 7g⁵ Oct 6] half-sister to several winners, notably 3-y-o
Chancellor: dam 2-y-o 5f/6f winner: fairly useful form: won maiden at Kempton in
September by 2 lengths from Lochridge: edgy (reared over in paddock), some improvement when fifth to Protectress in listed event at Newmarket 2 weeks later, again racing
freely: should stay 1m: needs to learn to settle, but probably capable of further
improvement. *G. A. Butler*

PURSUIT OF DREAMS   4 ch.g. Pursuit of Love 124 – Follow The Stars 86 (Sparkler   **58**
130) [2001 68: 10d⁶ f8.5g³ 11.6g 10m⁵ f9.4g Oct 6] fair handicapper on all-weather,   **a68**
modest on turf: stays 9.4f: acts on fibresand, good to soft and good to firm ground: sold
3,000 gns. *P. W. Harris*

PUSEY SANCE   3 br.g. Puissance 110 – Pusey Street 96 (Native Bazaar 122) [2001   –
8m 10m 8.1m 12s Oct 20] plain gelding: half-brother to several winners, including 7f
winner Pusey Street Girl (by Gildoran) and 1m/1¼m winner Windrush Lady (by Risk
Me): dam sprinter: well beaten in maidens/claimer. *M. R. Bosley*

PUTRA PEKAN   3 b.c. Grand Lodge (USA) 125 – Mazarine Blue 65 (Bellypha 130)   **105**
[2001 92: 7d⁵ 7g⁴ 8m 8g* 7g 7.9m⁴ 9g 8d³ Nov 3] good-topped colt: good walker: useful
handicapper: won at Newmarket (beat Lord Protector 2½ lengths) in July: creditable
efforts after when fourth to Tough Speed at York in August and third to Soller Bay at
Newmarket final outing: best around 1m: acts on good to firm and good to soft going:
often blinkered: free-going sort. *M. A. Jarvis*

PUTRA SANDHURST (IRE)   3 b.c. Royal Academy (USA) 130 – Kharimata   **115**
(IRE) (Kahyasi 130) [2001 85p: 11.5g² 12f 10m² 12m* 14g² Aug 25] big, lengthy, good
sort: has plenty of scope: smart performer: won maiden at Newmarket in July: good

efforts when 2½ lengths second to Perfect Sunday in Derby Trial at Lingfield on reappearance, 9 lengths eighth to Galileo in Derby at Epsom (thoroughly coltish in preliminaries) and ¾-length second to Shamaiel in listed race at Goodwood final start: will stay 2m: acts on firm going (showed promise on soft only run at 2 yrs). *M. A. Jarvis*

PUZZLE 3 b.g. First Trump 118 – Eldoret 100 (High Top 131) [2001 –: 10g 13.8d Nov 6] strong, lengthy gelding: good walker: little form: tried tongue tied: gelded after final outing. *Lady Herries* –

PUZZLEMENT 7 gr.g. Mystiko (USA) 124 – Abuzz 101 (Absalom 128) [2001 79: e12g² e10g² e12g 12m Jun 22] big, good-bodied gelding: fair handicapper: effective at 1¼m/easy 1½m: acts on fibresand, equitrack good to firm and soft going. *C. E. Brittain* 77

PYRAM BAY 3 b.f. Pyramus (USA) 78 – Navarino Bay 102 (Averof 123) [2001 f8g Nov 30] sister to 1999 2-y-o 6f seller winner Olivias Choice and half-sister to several winners, including 7-y-o Pension Fund: dam 2-y-o 5f winner who stayed 1½m: 33/1, well beaten in maiden at Southwell. *C. A. Dwyer* –

PYRRHIC 2 b.c. (Feb 13) Salse (USA) 128 – Bint Lariaaf (USA) (Diesis 133) [2001 6s⁶ Sep 27] second living foal: dam French 1m (including at 2 yrs) winner: 6/4-favourite, sixth of 10 to Eastern Image in maiden at Pontefract, not given hard time when beaten: joined M. Johnston: capable of better. *D. R. Loder* 61 p

PYTHAGORAS 4 ch.g. Kris 135 – Tricorne 92 (Green Desert (USA) 127) [2001 73: 10s 10g 13.3g 7.6m 10m Jul 13] strong gelding: disappointing maiden: blinkered final start. *W. R. Muir* –

Q

QAATEF (IRE) 3 b.c. Darshaan 133 – Solo de Lune (IRE) (Law Society (USA) 130) [2001 10m* 11.6m³ 11.9d³ 15.9g³ 15s⁵ Oct 6] 400,000Y: strong, attractive colt: fourth foal: brother to smart 1m (including at 2 yrs) and 1¼m (Prix Saint-Alary) winner who stayed 1½m Cerulean Sky, and half-brother to 2 winners in France: dam, French 11f winner, half-sister to smart French middle-distance filly Truly A Dream (by Darshaan) and 3-y-o Wareed: smart form: won maiden at Sandown in May: much better form next 3 starts, notably when 3¼ lengths third to Persian Punch in Lonsdale Stakes at York in August: well beaten (pulled hard early on) in Prix Hubert de Chaudenay at Longchamp final start: stays 2m: acts on good to firm ground: visored last 2 appearances. *Sir Michael Stoute* 115

QANDIL (USA) 5 ch.g. Riverman (USA) 131 – Confirmed Affair (USA) (Affirmed (USA)) [2001 41: e6g e7g* f7g e6g⁶ e7g³ f7g Apr 10] poor handicapper: won maiden event at Lingfield in January: stays 7f: better form on equitrack than fibresand, well held twice on turf: blinkered once at 4 yrs, visored last 5 starts. *Miss J. Feilden* 46

QUALITAIR SURVIVOR 6 gr.g. Terimon 124 – Comtec Princess 73 (Gulf Pearl 117) [2001 40: 10.5g 9f 8f 8f 11.8d Jul 19] maiden: no form in 2001: tried visored. *J. Hetherton* –

QUALITAIR WINGS 2 b.g. (May 12) Colonel Collins (USA) 122 – Semperflorens (Don 128) [2001 7s 8s 7d³ Nov 6] 2,500F: quite good-topped gelding: half-brother to 1¼m winner Sweet Revival (by Claude Monet) and a winner in Italy by Deploy: dam ran 3 times at 2 yrs: fair maiden: not clear run when third to Judge Davidson at Catterick: should stay 1m: raced only on going softer than good. *J. Hetherton* 67

QUALITY SLEEP (IRE) 2 b.f. (Mar 11) Mukaddamah (USA) 125 – Blue Bell Lady 75 (Dunphy 124) [2001 5.3s 5f⁵ 6d⁵ 5.1g⁵ 6m³ 6g Aug 8] 5,500Y: sixth foal: half-sister to 1996 2-y-o 5f seller winner Taome (by Roi Danzig): dam 6f seller winner: poor maiden: third in seller at Brighton: should stay 7f: probably ungenuine. *S. Dow* 43 §

QUANTICA (IRE) 2 b.g. (Feb 13) Sri Pekan (USA) 117 – Touche-A-Tout (IRE) (Royal Academy (USA) 130) [2001 f7g⁶ 7m 7g 6d* 5.1s* Nov 5] IR 10,000Y, 17,500 2-y-o: workmanlike gelding: second foal: dam, unraced daughter of Prix Saint-Alary winner Tootens, herself half-sister to 1000 Guineas winner Nocturnal Spree: fair performer: tongue tied, much improved to win nurseries at Redcar in October and Nottingham (beat Aahgowangowan comfortably by 1¾ lengths) in November: effective at 5f/6f: acts on soft ground: has been early to post. *N. Tinkler* 77

QUANTUM LADY   3 b.f. Mujadil (USA) 119 – Folly Finnesse 80 (Joligeneration   **76**
111) [2001 79: 7d 5s 6g 7m f7g 6m² 6g⁶ 6.1d⁶ 7s 6v⁴ f6g f5g p6g Dec 19] sparely-made,   **a57**
angular filly: fair handicapper on turf, modest on all-weather: left B. R. Millman before
well beaten last 3 starts: best around 6f: acts on fibresand, heavy and good to firm going:
usually races prominently. *I. A. Wood*

QUANTUM LEAP   4 b.g. Efisio 120 – Prejudice 83 (Young Generation 129) [2001   **80**
7m⁴ 7m⁵ 6m* 8g⁶ 8m 7g⁶ 7g⁴ 8d 7d Nov 3] 36,000Y: quite good-topped gelding: brother
to several winners, including fairly useful 7f/1m winner Al Moulouki (later successful up
to 1½m in Italy), and half-brother to fairly useful 6f to 1m performer Hob Green (by
Move Off): dam, maiden miler, half-sister to smart 7f/1m performer Casteddu (by Efisio):
fairly useful performer: won maiden at Lingfield in June: mostly creditable efforts in
handicaps after: best form at 7f/1m: acts on good to firm and good to soft going. *S. Dow*

QUARTER MASTERS (IRE)   2 b.c. (Apr 12) Mujadil (USA) 119 – Kentucky   **–**
Wildcat 64 (Be My Guest (USA) 126) [2001 6m 7g 8d 7g Oct 19] 17,000Y, resold IR
23,000Y: workmanlike colt: brother to 2 winners, including 15f winner Pawsible, and
half-brother to 3 winners: dam staying maiden: little sign of ability in maidens/claimer.
J. L. Eyre

QUARTER MOON (IRE)   2 b.f. (Jan 31) Sadler's Wells (USA) 132 – Jude 53   **106 p**
(Darshaan 133) [2001 7s² 7g* Sep 2]
For the second successive year the Moyglare Stud Stakes was won by an
Aidan O'Brien-trained daughter of Sadler's Wells, Quarter Moon following in the
footsteps of Sequoyah in this Group 1 contest for two-year-old fillies run over
seven furlongs at the Curragh in September. Whereas Sequoyah was making her
fourth appearance when she contested the race, Quarter Moon, one of four in the
seventeen-runner field trained by O'Brien, was having only her second outing.
Such had been the promise shown by Quarter Moon on her debut, when a head
second to Saranac Lake in the ten-runner Group 3 Debutante Stakes over the same
course and distance, that she was sent off favourite for the Moyglare. She started at
7/2, with one of her stable-companions Sophisticat, runner-up in both the Queen
Mary and Lowther Stakes, at 4/1. Next in the betting came the Chesham Stakes
winner Seba, one of the three British-trained runners in the race. Another O'Brien
runner Ardara set the pace, with Quarter Moon, who pulled hard early on, dropped
out in rear, the winner not making her move until over two furlongs out, where
Sophisticat took up the running. Quarter Moon, one of half a dozen still in with a

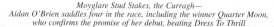

Moyglare Stud Stakes, the Curragh—
Aidan O'Brien saddles four in the race, including the winner Quarter Moon,
who confirms the promise of her debut, beating Dress To Thrill

chance going into the final furlong, continued to run on strongly under pressure, collared Sophisticat near the finish and passed the post with three quarters of a length to spare over Dress To Thrill, a filly owned by the race's sponsors, who came through to split the pair. It was just an average renewal of the Moyglare and Quarter Moon showed no more than useful form in winning it, but she should prove smart over longer distances at three. Quarter Moon could develop into a strong contender for the One Thousand Guineas, but distances of a mile and a quarter and upwards will see her to best advantage and, at this stage, she looks more of an Oaks filly. Quarter Moon will surely go on to prove more successful than Sequoyah, whose win in the Moyglare proved to be her last, though she did finish fourth in both the Irish One Thousand Guineas and the Irish Oaks.

	Sadler's Wells (USA) (b 1981)	Northern Dancer (b 1961)	Nearctic Natalma
Quarter Moon (IRE) (b.f. Jan 31, 1999)		Fairy Bridge (b 1975)	Bold Reason Special
	Jude (b 1994)	Darshaan (br 1981)	Shirley Heights Delsy
		Alruccaba (gr 1983)	Crystal Palace Allara

Quarter Moon is the first foal of Jude, a modest maiden who failed to finish in the first three on her four starts. Jude might have had little to recommend her on form when she came up for sale at the end of her three-year-old season, but her pedigree ensured that it took a bid of 92,000 guineas to secure her. By Darshaan out

Mrs Richard Henry's "Quarter Moon"

of the fairly useful two-year-old six-furlong winner Alruccaba, Jude is a sister to the useful Irish mile-and-a-half winner Alouette, third in the 1992 Moyglare Stud Stakes, and to Arrikala, a smart winner at up to a mile and three quarters and an unlucky third in the Irish Oaks; and she is a half-sister to several winners, notably the Nassau Stakes and Sun Chariot Stakes winner Last Second. Jude's pedigree was made to look even better in the two years following her sale, with Alouette's daughter Alborada, her first foal, winning the Champion Stakes in both 1998 and 1999; and it received a further boost in the latest season when another of Jude's half-sisters Alleluia won six races at up to two and a quarter miles, notably the Doncaster Cup. Quarter Moon's third dam is Allara, a half-sister to the dams of Aliysa and Nishapour, and a winner at seven furlongs in the French Provinces. *A. P. O'Brien, Ireland*

QUATREDIL (IRE) 3 b.f. Mujadil (USA) 119 – Quatre Femme 76 (Petorius 117) **67 d** [2001 65: e7g⁸ f8.5g⁶ e7g⁵ e7g⁴ 7.1g 6d² 7m 6m* 6m⁶ 7g³ 6g 7m 6s f7g² p7g p7g f8.5s Dec 26] leggy filly: fair handicapper: won at Lingfield in January and Leicester in July: well below form last 7 starts, leaving R. Hannon before last 3: effective at 6f/easy 7f: acts on good to firm ground, good to soft, fibresand and equitrack. *J. S. Moore*

QUAZAR (IRE) 3 b.c. Inzar (USA) 112 – Evictress (IRE) 70 (Sharp Victor (USA) **68** 114) [2001 61: 8d⁴ 8.3m² 8.1g⁴ 8.5d 10.4m Sep 5] smallish, strong colt: has a round action: fair maiden handicapper: best around 1m: acts on good to firm going, probably on heavy: visored (well held) final start: won first 4 starts over hurdles. *Jonjo O'Neill*

QUEBECK 3 b.g. Rainbow Quest (USA) 134 – Purbeck (IRE) (Polish Precedent **78** (USA) 131) [2001 12f² 12g⁴ 12.3m³ 11.8s Oct 15] 80,000Y: rather leggy gelding: second foal: dam unraced sister to top-class 1¼m/1½m performer Pilsudski: fair maiden: should stay beyond 1½m: acts on firm ground, below par on soft final start: sold 10,000 gns, and gelded. *H. R. A. Cecil*

QUECHA (IRE) 3 b.f. Indian Ridge 123 – Spain Lane (USA) 115 (Seeking The Gold **45** (USA)) [2001 7g⁴ 8.2s 17g⁴ 7m Nov 23] second foal: half-sister to 1m winner (in France at 2 yrs/UAE) Levantine (by Sadler's Wells): dam, French 5f (won Prix du Gros-Chene) and 6f performer, closely related to US Grade 1 9f/1¼m winner Marquetry: useful form when second at Maisons-Laffitte on only start at 2 yrs (trained by D. Loder): off 10 months then poor form in maidens (trained by Saeed bin Suroor on reappearance) in 2001: headstrong. *E. A. L. Dunlop*

QUEDEX 5 b.h. Deploy 131 – Alwal (Pharly (FR) 130) [2001 92, a67: 10s⁴ 18.7f May **83** 9] neat horse: has a round action: fairly useful handicapper: respectable efforts only starts **a–** in 2001, not getting run of race in Chester Cup: probably stays 2¼m: acts on soft and good to firm going. *E. L. James*

QUEENBORO CASTLE (FR) 2 b.f. (Jan 21) Night Shift (USA) – Magic Motion (USA) (Green Dancer (USA) 132) [2001 7d Oct 15] 100,000 francs Y: first foal: dam third both starts at 1¼m in France: 33/1, last of 20 in maiden at Leicester: sold 600 gns. *B. J. Meehan*

QUEENIE 3 b.f. Indian Ridge 123 – Bint Zamayem (IRE) 95 (Rainbow Quest (USA) **82** 134) [2001 81p: 7d³ 7.9d² 7.6m* 8.1d² 8g 7d Nov 6] useful-looking filly: fairly useful performer: won maiden at Chester in July (didn't seem comfortable round bends): ran as if something amiss final outing: stays 1m: yet to race on extremes of going: sometimes carries head high: sold 37,000 gns. *B. W. Hills*

QUEEN OF FASHION (IRE) 5 b.m. Barathea (IRE) 127 – Valuewise (IRE) 70 **54 d** (Ahonoora 122) [2001 62: 12d 12.6f⁵ 16.4m 11.6g 12f⁶ 11.5g 16g Sep 5] tall, rather angular mare: modest maiden handicapper at best: below form after second start: stays 12.6f: acts on firm ground: pulled hard in visor once. *J. J. Sheehan*

QUEEN OF THE MAY (IRE) 4 b.f. Nicolotte 118 – Varnish 85 (Final Straw 127) **–** [2001 80, a61: f6g⁴ f5g f5g Feb 1] small filly: only modest handicapper in 2001 (blink- **a58** ered): stays 6f: acts on firm going, soft and fibresand/equitrack: usually waited with. *D. Shaw*

QUEENS BENCH (IRE) 4 ch.f. Wolfhound (USA) 126 – Zafaaf 105 (Kris 135) **63** [2001 86d: 5v 6g 7m 8g⁴ 9m³ 9.2g f8.5g 9f.4g* f8.5g⁴ p10g Dec 22] lengthy filly: modest maiden: won at Wolverhampton in November: stays 9.4f: acts on fibresand, firm and good to soft ground (well held on softer): has had tongue tied: sometimes races freely: has run well sweating: none too consistent. *P. C. Haslam*

QUEENSBERRY 2 b.c. (May 5) Up And At 'em 109 – Princess Poquito (Hard —
Fought 125) [2001 6m 7.2m Sep 20] 5,000F, 24,000Y: heavy-topped colt: seventh foal:
half-brother to several winners, including 3-y-o Magic Box and 1m winner Eurobox
Boy (by Savahra Sound): dam unraced half-sister to smart 1¼m to 1¾m filly Senorita
Poquito: well held in maidens. *A. P. Jarvis*

QUEEN'S COLLEGE (IRE) 3 b.f. College Chapel 122 – Fairy Lore (IRE) 89 **46**
(Fairy King (USA)) [2001 57: f6g 7m 6.1m 6m 6m² 6g f6g Nov 27] sparely-made filly:
poor maiden handicapper: should stay 7f: acts on good to firm ground: visored final
outing. *M. L. W. Bell*

QUEEN'S LOGIC (IRE) 2 ch.f. (Feb 21) Grand Lodge (USA) 125 – Lagrion **125**
(USA) 68 (Diesis 133) [2001 5.2s* 5m* 6m* 6d* Oct 2]
Unbeaten Johannesburg's splendid campaign, capped by a striking 'away
victory' on dirt in the Breeders' Cup Juvenile, deservedly clinched for him the title
of Europe's champion two-year-old. But, on form, it was still a close thing between
him and the unbeaten filly Queen's Logic. No filly has topped the Timeform
juvenile ratings since Jacinth back in 1972. Jacinth also topped the Free Handicap
that year and the only filly to equal that achievement in the interim was Ravinella,
joint top in the International Classifications of 1987 with Warning (Timeform's
clear top-rated that year). Jacinth and Ravinella both ended their first season
unbeaten and cemented their positions as the outstanding two-year-old filly of their
year with impressive victories in the Cheveley Park Stakes at Newmarket. Jacinth
turned the race into a procession, running out a five-length winner from a strong
field, and Ravinella blinded her rivals for speed, unleashing a tremendous run after
being waited with and winning with her ears pricked by a length and a half. Both
started at 5/4-on for the following year's One Thousand Guineas. Jacinth ran below
her best on Guineas day and was beaten by 11/1-shot Mysterious (who landed the
Oaks next time). Jacinth went a fair way to restoring her lofty reputation with
victories in the Coronation Stakes, the Falmouth Stakes and the Goodwood Mile
and a second to the tip-top colt Thatch in the Sussex Stakes. Ravinella came from
behind in trademark style to become the shortest-priced winner of the One
Thousand Guineas since Hula Dancer in the 'sixties (Shadayid and Bosra Sham
have been odds-on winners of the race since Ravinella), and she went on to add the
Poule d'Essai des Pouliches before suffering a shock defeat in the Coronation
Stakes. Her last two races came in North America, where she was successful at
Laurel Park before finishing among the also-rans behind the previous year's One
Thousand Guineas winner Miesque in the Breeders' Cup Mile, on the way to
fetching 1,400,000 guineas, then a European record for a three-year-old filly, at that
year's December Sales. Whilst not rated so highly as Jacinth as a two-year-old,

Peugeot Lowther Stakes, York—Queen's Logic and Sophisticat repeat their Queen Mary placings;
Silent Honor (No.1) takes third, ahead of Good Girl

Queen's Logic won the Shadwell Stud Cheveley Park by seven lengths and could hardly have been more impressive. Generally available at 3/1 in the winter ante-post lists, she is a worthy favourite for the One Thousand Guineas and, at this stage, looks very much the one to be on at Newmarket on May 5th.

Though pattern-race form as a two-year-old is not nowadays widely regarded as being so important as it once was for a colt with genuine classic potential, the same does not seem to apply to Guineas fillies. The Cheveley Park was won by nine subsequent One Thousand Guineas winners in the second half of the twentieth century and was a classic guide second to none in Jacinth's and Ravinella's time. No Cheveley Park winner has gone on to Guineas success since Sayyedati in 1993 but One Thousand Guineas winners have still tended to emerge from pattern races. Of the last seven One Thousand Guineas winners, Harayir and Cape Verdi were beaten in the Cheveley Park Stakes, but both won the Lowther Stakes, whilst Bosra Sham (Fillies' Mile) and Lahan (Rockfel Stakes) also won pattern events as juveniles. Sleepytime was unlucky not to do likewise when third in the Fillies' Mile, and Ameerat was second in the May Hill Stakes. The latest Cheveley Park was weakened by five eleventh-hour withdrawals after overnight and morning rain, which left a field of eight, only two of which, Queen's Logic and French challenger Ziria, had won a pattern event. In the absence of Silent Honor, who would have been her closest market rival, Queen's Logic was sent off the 11/10-on favourite, with the Aidan O'Brien-trained Sophisticat, runner-up to Queen's Logic in the Queen Mary and the Lowther, second favourite at 11/4, ahead of another Irish challenger 7/1-shot Steaming Home, a winner of her last two races but making a sizeable jump in class. Good Girl, fifth in the Queen Mary and fourth in the Lowther, came next at 12/1, with the four others at odds between 16/1 and 33/1.

There is always a tendency to react to a wide-margin victory with the question 'But what did it beat?' Runaway winners, it is true, sometimes turn out to be overrated but, as with another oft-used generalisation—that in a bunched finish 'they can't all be good'—it is wisest to come to a considered view after weighing the evidence. A degree of scepticism about Queen's Logic's Cheveley Park form is

Shadwell Stud Cheveley Park Stakes, Newmarket—Queen's Logic puts up the best performance by a two-year-old filly in fifteen years as she delivers a much bigger beating to Sophisticat; Good Girl (partially hidden by runner-up) again makes the frame, ahead of Lahinch (rail)

evidenced by the fact that she is challenged in the Guineas betting by the Fillies' Mile winner Gossamer—actually joint-favourite with Hills as we write—but there is little doubt that Queen's Logic comfortably bettered the form shown three days earlier at Ascot by Gossamer, whom, it should be said, ought to make the greater progress over the winter, though she has plenty to find. Sophisticat and Good Girl proved to be Queen's Logic's main opposition at Newmarket but none saw the way she went after she made smooth progress to lead two furlongs out. Queen's Logic stretched right away, still extending her advantage as the post was reached; Sophisticat—beaten around a length into third in the Moyglare Stud Stakes on her only start since the Lowther—confirmed her superiority over Good Girl, who was two lengths away third, followed home by the O'Brien second string Lahinch and the creditable Moyglare sixth Sweet Deimos.

Judged simply on Sophisticat (fifth afterwards in the Breeders' Cup Juvenile Fillies) and Good Girl—over which pair Queen's Logic extended her superiority every time they met—and on Lahinch's good second in the Rockfel later in the month, the form of the Cheveley Park looks cast-iron. But there are other reasons to support our assessment of Queen's Logic's run as the best recorded by a two-year-old filly in Europe for fifteen years—since that of the subsequently-disqualified Forest Flower in the Cheveley Park of 1986. The form of the latest Cheveley Park, which was, incidentally, run on ground less testing than the officially-returned soft, was independently confirmed by the winner's timefigure— 1.05 fast—which was, by some way, the fastest recorded in Britain by any two-year-old in the latest season, and the fastest by a two-year-old filly since Timeform timefigures were reintroduced in 1975 using the computer program now employed. A Timeform computer timefigure is a representation in figures of the *time value* of a performance. Simply knowing that a race is run 'below standard time', for example, means very little unless weather conditions, such as the wind strength and direction, and the going are properly taken into account. Actual times recorded on different courses are not comparable because of different track conformations, and getting to the real value of a time performance involves quantifying many seemingly imponderable factors and compensating for their effects. It is a complex procedure, requiring the collation of vast amounts of data—part of the reason manually calculated Timeform timefigures were discontinued after the early-'sixties and hence the necessity for computers to enable them to be resurrected. At Timeform, once the data has been analysed, the timefigure is expressed in decimal notation in seconds (per five furlongs) faster or slower than a certain standard. Through simple mental arithmetic, this figure can be expressed in pounds to put it on a comparable scale to Timeform ratings (Queen's Logic's timefigure translates to a timerating of 126). A timefigure is, of course, an expression of a *single performance only* but only a good horse is capable of producing a very fast timefigure. That said, two-year-olds who have recorded outstanding timefigures have not always gone on to make quite the same impression as three-year-olds. The three best figures among the two-year-olds of the 'nineties, for example, were Celtic Swing's absolutely outstanding 1.51 fast in the 1994 Racing Post Trophy, Xaar's 1.19 fast in the 1997 Dewhurst and Armiger's 1.00 fast in the 1992 Racing Post Trophy, all classic-standard timefigures. These examples may lend support to the observation that when expectations run so highly they seldom seem to end up being fulfilled. Logic, however, dictates that the prospects of any new two-year-old champion should be judged on the evidence provided by the animal itself and by its performances, not on the subsequent records of earlier title-holders.

Though Queen's Logic showed plenty of pace as a two-year-old, winning the Queen Mary at Royal Ascot under conditions which placed the emphasis firmly on speed, she finished the Lowther and the Cheveley Park—both over six furlongs—in the manner of a filly who would have been suited by seven furlongs by the end of her two year old season, and she should certainly prove effective over a mile at three. Queen's Logic was the first to complete the Queen Mary/Lowther/ Cheveley Park treble since Dead Certain in 1989, and she improved with every race. Royal Ascot was already said to have been on the agenda before Queen's Logic made a promising start by beating previous winner Lady Dominatrix a shade comfortably by three quarters of a length (the pair ten lengths clear) in a minor event on heavy going at Newbury in mid-May. Queen's Logic took the eye as one of the better sorts, with scope for physical development, before the Queen Mary. She started third favourite at 13/2 in a field of twenty behind the Loder-trained hotpot Latin Lynx, a tiddler by comparison to the lengthy, attractive Queen's Logic. Making good headway towards the stand side of the main group over a furlong out, Queen's Logic ran on strongly to lead well inside the final furlong and won by half a length from Sophisticat, with Roundtree, Latin Lynx and Good Girl close behind. Given her physique and her pedigree—which we will come to shortly—this was a most encouraging performance from Queen's Logic, who looked very much the type to progress.

Given a two-month break 'to allow her to mature', Queen's Logic wasn't seen out again until the Peugeot Lowther Stakes at the York August meeting, where the powerful Loder stable again provided the favourite, this time in the shape of the highly regarded Silent Honor, winner of the Cherry Hinton at Newmarket in July. The Lowther attracted a strong field, which also included the runaway Princess Margaret winner Leggy Lou, the Prix Robert Papin runner-up Massarra, Carinae from the Stoute stable, and Sophisticat and Good Girl. Queen's Logic, a generous 7/1-shot, readily maintained her unbeaten record, tracking the leaders before quickening well to hit the front inside the final furlong. She beat Sophisticat by a length and a quarter, conceding the runner-up 3 lb into the bargain, with Silent Honor the same distance away third, and a further three back to Good Girl; Leggy Lou finished last and was subsequently found to be lame. As at Ascot—and subsequently at Newmarket—Queen's Logic impressed as having more physical scope than almost any of her opponents, particularly encouraging with her three-year-old career in mind. The Lowther was also run in a fast time, Queen's Logic recording a timefigure of 0.38 fast, not far below her Timeform rating after the race of 112. Queen's Logic's trainer Mick Channon completed the Queen Mary/ Lowther double in 1998 with the ill-fated Bint Allayl, and he was asked after the Lowther to compare the two. 'Bint Allayl was a monster from day one, Queen's Logic has just kept on improving,' he said. 'She settles so well and, for a filly, is so level-headed with a brilliant attitude.' Queen's Logic's jockey Steve Drowne, who retained the ride for the rest of the season after taking over from the suspended Craig Williams at Royal Ascot, added: 'She is almost not happy in third or fourth gear, but when she hits fifth she stretches out and is away. There might even be a sixth gear lurking somewhere.'

			Chief's Crown	Danzig
		Grand Lodge (USA)	(b 1982)	Six Crowns
Queen's Logic (IRE)		(ch 1991)	La Papagena	Habitat
(ch.f. Feb 21, 1999)			(br 1983)	Magic Flute
			Diesis	Sharpen Up
		Lagrion (USA)	(ch 1980)	Doubly Sure
		(ch 1989)	Wrap It Up	Mount Hagen
			(ch 1979)	Doc Nan

Queen's Logic passed through the sale-ring twice before being sent into training. She made IR 19,000 guineas as a foal and a million francs (approximately £95,000) as a two-year-old. Her somewhat bargain-basement pedigree wouldn't have attracted prospective purchasers. Queen's Logic is from the fourth European crop of her globe-trotting sire Grand Lodge whose first four crops were produced at fees of no more than IR 10,000 guineas (he first stood at IR 9,000 guineas). Grand Lodge was a consistent racehorse in top company at up to a mile and a quarter, gaining his biggest wins in the Dewhurst and the St James's Palace Stakes and finishing runner-up in the Two Thousand Guineas. His career at stud received an enormous boost with the emergence from his second crop of dual Derby and Prix de l'Arc de Triomphe winner Sinndar, after which his fee was raised to IR 35,000 guineas. Grandera, placed three times in Group 1 company at a mile and a quarter to a mile and a half in the latest season, is the best from Grand Lodge's third crop while Queen's Logic was the only pattern-race winner among his latest two-year-old crop, which numbered ninety. Given that the best performer from Grand Lodge's first crop was the late-developing miler Indian Lodge, who didn't score at pattern level until the age of four, it is difficult to detect any clear pattern among

Mr Jaber Abdullah's "Queen's Logic"

Grand Lodge's best performers. One discernible trend, however, is illustrated by the significant difference between the median rating of Grand Lodge's British-raced colts and geldings (80) and his fillies (60); Queen's Logic is the only filly among his northern hemisphere progeny rated at 100 or higher. The dam of Queen's Logic, the Diesis mare Lagrion, was a sister to Middle Park runner-up Pure Genius but never won a race. Lagrion was not raced at two and did all her racing over middle distances. She produced two minor winners before Queen's Logic, the mile-and-a-quarter winner Tulsa (by Priolo) and a nine-furlong to mile-and-a-half winner in Italy, Carlo Bank (by Lahib). Lagrion's yearling filly by Titus Livius was bought by Shadwell Estates for IR £380,000 at Goffs the week after Queen's Logic's win in the Cheveley Park. There is a colt foal by General Monash. Queen's Logic's family on the distaff side is fairly undistinguished, though her grandam Wrap It Up, who never won a race, is a half-sister to the Lingfield Oaks Trial winner Gift Wrapped, the dam of Royal Lodge winner Reach and of Oaks d'Italia runner-up and Lancashire Oaks third Wrapping, herself the dam of Yorkshire Oaks and Prix Vermeille runner-up Papering. As we have said, Queen's Logic should certainly get the Guineas trip and, on pedigree, should stay further. She acts on soft and good to firm going. The best juveniles owned by the Maktoum family or their associates—Queen's Logic's owner is reportedly a close friend of Sheikh Maktoum —usually end up joining the Godolphin team, as did the Channon-trained pair Gimcrack winner Josr Algarhoud and Dewhurst winner Tobougg, for example. Queen's Logic, however, remains at West Ilsley for a three-year-old campaign that could well feature further prestigious successes. *M. R. Channon*

817

QUEENS MUSICIAN 3 b.g. Piccolo 121 – Queens Welcome 60 (Northfields **52** (USA)) [2001 72: 7v 6g 6m 5m 7m 10m⁵ Aug 11] short-backed gelding: modest maiden: left Mrs J. Ramsden before final start: probably stays 1¼m: acts on firm going: blinkered (no show) third start: has found little. *G. A. Swinbank*

QUEEN'S PAGEANT 7 ch.m. Risk Me (FR) 127 – Mistral's Dancer (Shareef **77** Dancer (USA) 135) [2001 77: 10g⁶ 11.6g⁴ 10g² 10m² 11.6g* 10g 10s⁶ 11.7d Oct 25] big mare: fair handicapper: won at Windsor in July: stays easy 11.6f: acts on heavy going, good to firm and fibresand: blinkered once: held up: refused to enter stall on 3 occasions in 2001, and has been banned from racing from stalls. *J. L. Spearing*

QUEEN'S SONG 3 ch.f. King's Signet (USA) 110 – Darakah 78 (Doulab (USA) 115) **40** [2001 48: 5v 6d⁵ 5.1m 5.7g 8.1m² 7m⁴ 7m 6m Aug 27] poor maiden handicapper: best at 6f/7f: acts on good to firm and good to soft going. *R. J. Hodges*

QUEENS STROLLER (IRE) 10 b.m. Pennine Walk 120 – Mount Isa (Miami **–** Springs 121) [2001 –: f9.4g⁵ f9.4s f9.4s² f9.4g 7m 11.7m⁶ 11.7f 10d 11.6m⁶ Aug 25] poor **a34 ?** performer at best nowadays: stays 1¼m: acts on fibresand/equitrack: tried blinkered/ visored. *R. E. Peacock*

QUEST FOR GLORY (IRE) 2 b.c. (Feb 24) Fayruz 116 – Moyhora (IRE) (Nasha- **87** maa 113) [2001 f5g⁴ 5m³ 6f* 6f 6g² 6d 6g 5g* 6m f5g* Oct 9] 10,000Y: close-coupled colt: third foal: half-brother to 7f winner Detroit City (by Distinctly North): dam unraced: fairly useful performer: won minor events at Brighton in May, Hamilton in September and Wolverhampton (beat Decima a length) in October: effective at 5f/6f: acts on firm ground and fibresand: races prominently: sold 27,000 gns. *G. C. Bravery*

QUEST ON AIR 2 b.g. (May 12) Star Quest 79 – Stormy Heights 62 (Golden Heights **–** 82) [2001 7d Nov 3] fourth foal: closely related to 4-y-o Stormy Rainbow: dam, sprint winner, held up, including at 2 yrs: 33/1, well held in 27-runner maiden at Newmarket. *J. R. Jenkins*

QUIBBLE 4 ch.g. Lammtarra (USA) 134 – Bloudan (USA) (Damascus (USA)) [2001 **55** 10.5d 12.4m⁴ 8d⁵ 13.1m Sep 10] sixth living foal: half-brother to 3 winners, including very smart 1m to 1½m winner in France and USA Radevore (by Generous): dam unraced half-sister to Al Bahathri: fairly useful maiden at 3 yrs for A. Fabre in France: modest form at best in Britain: stays 12.5f: acts on good to firm and good to soft ground: tried blinkered. *A. Bailey*

QUICKNAP (USA) 2 ch.c. (May 30) Hennessy (USA) 122 – Time Knap (USA) **65** (Timeless Native (USA)) [2001 5.1f³ 6m⁵ 6s⁵ Oct 5] $28,000F, 22,000 2-y-o: third foal: half-brother to a 6f and 1m winner in USA by Gourami: dam, sprint winner in USA, half-sister to very smart German/US performer up to 1½m Que Belle from very good family: fair maiden: will stay 7f: wandered second start: sent to UAE. *H. Candy*

QUICK TO PLEASE (USA) 3 b.f. Danzig (USA) – Razyana (USA) 87 (His Majesty **101** (USA)) [2001 93P: 8m³ 10f 8.5f³ Nov 10] good-topped, attractive filly: good walker: most impressive winner of maiden at Doncaster only run at 2 yrs: reportedly pulled muscles in her back early in 2001: useful form when 1¾ lengths third to Sheppard's Watch in listed race at Goodwood in May: short of room in similar event at Ascot following month (final start for H. Cecil), then off 4½ months: held in third in allowance race at Hollywood on US debut: not sure to stay beyond 1m. *R. J. Frankel, USA*

QUIDS INN 4 br.g. Timeless Times (USA) 99 – Waltz On Air 86 (Doc Marten 104) **–** [2001 54, a47: e8g e7g e7g e8g³ e8g⁵ Feb 21] leggy gelding: poor maiden: stays 1m: acts **a43** on good to firm ground and equitrack: blinkered once. *M. Quinn*

QUIET READING (USA) 4 b.g. Northern Flagship (USA) 96 – Forlis Key (USA) **–** (Forli (ARG)) [2001 61, a66: f12s³ f12g² f12g⁴ f12g⁵ f11g 9.9m f12g p16g Dec 4] big, **a63** lengthy gelding: modest maiden: effective at 1½m/1¾m: acts on heavy going, fibresand and equitrack: has looked less than keen. *M. R. Bosley*

QUIET TRAVELLER (IRE) 3 b.g. Blues Traveller (IRE) 119 – Quietly Impressive **76** (IRE) 66 (Taufan (USA) 119) [2001 39: 8v 8.3m* 8m⁴ 10.1m⁴ 8.1g² 9m² 8m² 9f* 10m* 9g³ 8g² 8g⁵ 8d³ 10.3v⁵ 8g⁶ Nov 7] tall, quite good-topped gelding: fair handicapper: won at Hamilton in May and Musselburgh and Redcar in July: effective at 1m to easy 1¼m: acts on firm and good to soft going: blinkered once: usually held up: reliable. *Miss L. A. Perratt*

QUIET VENTURE 7 b.g. Rainbow Quest (USA) 134 – Jameelaty (USA) 96 (Nureyev **–** (USA) 131) [2001 66, a76: f7g⁵ f6g f7g Nov 3] big, lengthy gelding: fair performer: form **a71** in 2001 only on first start in 2001, leaving B. Hills after second: stays 7f: acts on fibresand

and firm going: often visored, blinkered final outing: usually wears tongue tie: races prominently. *J. A. Glover*

QUINTA LAD 3 b.g. Alhijaz 122 – Jersey Belle 53 (Distant Relative 128) [2001 67: 8.2v⁶ 7g⁵ 7v f8g f8g Dec 14] quite good-topped gelding: modest maiden: stays 7f: raced only on good going or softer and fibresand: has worn tongue strap. *J. Balding* — **58 a–**

QUITE A NIGHT 2 b.c. (May 13) Night Shift (USA) – Ellebanna 69 (Tina's Pet 121) [2001 7d p8g² p8g⁴ Nov 28] 35,000Y: half-brother to several winners, including useful 7f winner King Midas (by Bluebird), later winner in UAE, and 3-y-o Mine: dam, 5f (including at 2 yrs) winner, half-sister to very smart sprinter Bolshoi: tongue tied, fair form in frame in maidens at Lingfield: likely to prove best at 7f/1m: acts on polytrack. *J. W. Hills* — **75**

QUITE FRANKLY 3 b.g. Environment Friend 128 – Four-Legged Friend 101 (Aragon 118) [2001 8d 8g 8f 12g 8d Nov 2] leggy, close-coupled gelding: sixth foal: half-brother to fairly useful 1m (including at 2 yrs) and 1¼m winner Herr Trigger (by Sharrood) and 6-y-o Quite Happy: dam 2-y-o 5f winner: no sign of ability. *Dr J. D. Scargill* — **–**

QUITE HAPPY (IRE) 6 b.m. Statoblest 120 – Four-Legged Friend 101 (Aragon 118) [2001 69: 5g 5m 6f Jul 4] sturdy mare: fair performer at 5 yrs: little form in 2001: tried visored/blinkered. *W. J. Musson* — **–**

QUITE REMARKABLE 2 b.g. (Mar 10) Danzig Connection (USA) – Kathy Fair (IRE) 46 (Nicholas Bill 125) [2001 5.1s³ 5.3s⁵ 5m* f5g 5m⁴ Jul 30] workmanlike gelding: second foal: dam, maiden who stayed 1¼m on Flat and was temperamental over hurdles, half-sister to smart stayer Silence In Court: fair performer: made all in claimer at Thirsk in May: folded tamely next time, carried head high final start: will prove best at 5f: acts on soft and good to firm ground: not to be trusted. *W. G. M. Turner* — **73 §**

QUITTE LA FRANCE 3 b.f. Saddlers' Hall (IRE) 126 – Tafila 101 (Adonijah 126) [2001 86p: 8v⁴ 8v 8d 8m 12f 11.9d³ 11.9d⁴ Aug 9] strong filly: poor mover: fairly useful performer: left Mrs J. Ramsden after fourth start: will probably stay 1¾m: acts on soft going: blinkered (unseated after 2f) fourth appearance: has flashed tail: failed to impress with finishing effort final start. *J. G. Given* — **80**

QUI WARRANTO (IRE) 3 ch.g. Spectrum (IRE) 126 – Braneakins (Sallust 134) [2001 67: 8g 9.9m 9.9m 10m Aug 11] rangy, slightly unfurnished gelding: fair maiden at 2 yrs: no form in 2001, reportedly finishing lame second start. *J. G. FitzGerald* — **–**

QUIZZICAL 3 ch.g. Indian Ridge 123 – Mount Row 94 (Alzao (USA) 117) [2001 8g 10.4m² 12m 10s Oct 22] well-made gelding: first foal: dam, 11f/1½m winner, out of half-sister to smart sprinter Colmore Row: reported to have sustained a stress fracture on debut in May: modest form in maiden at York 4 months later: ran as if something amiss final 2 starts: sold 2,500 gns. *A. C. Stewart* — **60**

R

RAAHYEH (USA) 3 ch.f. Rahy (USA) 115 – Queen's Gallery (USA) 98 (Forty Niner (USA)) [2001 62: e5g³ f6g 5.1v Apr 3] small, sparely-made filly: poor maiden: effective at 5f/6f: acted on fibresand: looked none too keen penultimate start: visits Josr Algarhoud. *M. R. Channon* — **49**

RAAJIYA (USA) 3 ch.f. Gulch (USA) – Elrafa Ah (USA) 105 (Storm Cat (USA)) [2001 7m* 8g Aug 12] third foal: half-sister to Dewhurst Stakes winner who stayed 1¼m Mujahid (by Danzig): dam 5f (at 2 yrs) and 6f winner who stayed 1m: won 7f maiden at Goodwood in May by 1¼ lengths from Royal Millennium, racing freely in share of lead and carrying head high: well held in listed race at Ascot when next seen out: visits Red Ransom. *M. P. Tregoning* — **83**

RA-BOOB (IRE) 2 b.f. (Mar 17) Alhaarth (IRE) 126 – Harmless Albatross 115 (Pas de Seul 133) [2001 7g 8.2v Oct 4] rather leggy filly: half-sister to several winners (most at least useful), including smart 11f/1½m winner Ghataas (by Sadler's Wells), 6-y-o Kahtan and very smart performer up to 1½m Volochine (by Soviet Star): dam French miler: better effort in maidens (modest form) when eleventh of 17 at Nottingham second start: should be suited by 1¼m/1½m: capable of better. *J. L. Dunlop* — **55 p**

RABWAH (USA) 2 ch.f. (Feb 6) Gone West (USA) – Mamlakah (IRE) 104 **66 p**
(Unfuwain (USA) 131) [2001 6g⁶ Aug 15] second foal: closely related to fairly useful
Irish 7f/1m winner Al Mamaaliq (by Gulch): dam 2-y-o 7f/1m (May Hill Stakes) winner:
6/4 favourite, 6 lengths sixth of 13 to Tahitian Storm in maiden at Yarmouth: should
improve. *Sir Michael Stoute*

RACHEL GREEN (IRE) 3 b.f. Case Law 113 – Alzeam (IRE) 61 (Alzao (USA) **–**
117) [2001 46: e5g f5g f5g f6g 6d⁵ Oct 9] angular filly: little form in 2001. *C. N. Allen*

RACINA 3 ch.f. Bluebird (USA) 125 – Swellegant 84 (Midyan (USA) 124) [2001 93: **103**
5g 6m⁴ 6d 5m⁶ 6d Aug 26] sturdy, lengthy filly: has a quick, fluent action: useful
performer: best effort when 3 lengths fourth to Volata in listed rated stakes at Haydock
second start: likely to prove best at 5f/6f: acts on good to firm going (well held on softer
than good). *W. J. Haggas*

RACING BAILEY'S 2 b.c. (Feb 12) Zamindar (USA) 116 – Sioux City (Simply **96**
Great (FR) 122) [2001 5d⁵ 5v⁴ 6s* 7g 6s* 6g 6m⁵ 6g² 6d Oct 19] 11,500Y: close-coupled,
good-topped colt: fourth foal: half-brother to 1m/1¼m winner Northern Accord (by
Akarad) and French winner up to 1½m Dorsoduro (by Highest Honor): dam useful
French 1¼m/1½m winner: useful performer: won maiden at Ayr in July and minor event
at Hamilton in August: beaten head in 21-runner nursery at Newmarket penultimate start:
should stay at least 1m: acts on soft and good to firm going. *M. Johnston*

RACINGFORMCLUB BOY 2 ch.c. (Apr 12) Blushing Flame (USA) 109 – Sonoco **53**
61 (Song 132) [2001 5d 5g 5m f6g 8d 7m⁴ f8.5g⁶ 7d Oct 18] 1,200Y: useful-looking colt:
fourth foal: dam sprint maiden: modest maiden: probably stays 1m: acts on good to firm
ground, good to soft and fibresand: visored (tailed off) seventh start. *P. S. McEntee*

RACINGFORYOU LASS 3 b.f. Moujeeb (USA) 70 – Kentucky Mole VII (Damsire **–**
Unregistered) [2001 –: f12g 16.5m Jul 12] non-thoroughbred filly: no sign of ability on
Flat. *A. Streeter*

RACKET (IRE) 2 b.f. (Mar 3) Great Commotion (USA) 123 – Susie Sunshine (IRE) **–**
81 (Waajib 121) [2001 5d 5.3m 5g 5m Aug 25] IR 5,000Y: fourth foal: half-sister to 3-y-o
Shoeshine Boy and 5-y-o Haymaker: dam Irish 2-y-o 9f winner who stayed 1½m: no
form in maidens/seller: tried blinkered. *D. J. S. Cosgrove*

RADANPOUR (IRE) 9 b.g. Kahyasi 130 – Rajpoura 118 (Kashmir II 125) [2001 **56**
16g* 16f³ 16f* 14.1m* 14m⁵ Aug 22] fair maiden for W. Mullins in Ireland in 1996:
modest performer nowadays: successful in claimers at Redcar (2) and Musselburgh in
summer: stays 2m: acts on firm and good to soft going: blinkered nowadays: held up:
reportedly finished lame over hurdles later in August: sold 1,400 gns in October.
Mrs M. Reveley

RADA'S DAUGHTER 5 br.m. Robellino (USA) 127 – Drama School 72 (Young **107 d**
Generation 129) [2001 107: 10g³ 13.3v⁴ 11.6g⁵ 12f 11.9d 11m⁵ 13.4d 14.1m⁵ Sep 6] big,
good-bodied mare: useful performer at best: seemed to run well when 6½ lengths fourth
of 5 to Water Jump in slowly-run listed event at Newbury second start: well below form
otherwise: probably best at 1½m to 2m: acts on heavy and good to firm going: usually
held up: has run lazily and probably needs strong handling. *I. A. Balding*

RADIANT SKY (IRE) 3 ch.f. Spectrum (IRE) 126 – Shakey (IRE) (Caerleon (USA) **62**
132) [2001 8d 9.9d⁶ 9.7m 10.2f 7g f9.4s⁶ Dec 15] 12,500F, 24,000Y: second foal: dam
unraced half-sister to useful Irish 1990 2-y-o 7f winner Rinka Das from family of very
smart middle-distance stayer Seismic Wave: modest maiden: ran as if something amiss
fourth/fifth starts (blinkered second occasion) then off 4 months: likely to stay 1½m:
sometimes slowly away. *L. G. Cottrell*

RADICAL JACK 4 b.g. Presidium 124 – Luckifosome 45 (Smackover 107) [2001 –: **–**
9v 8f 8.3m Jun 13] of little account. *Denys Smith*

RAED 8 b.g. Nashwan (USA) 135 – Awayed (USA) 108 (Sir Ivor 135) [2001 56§: f8g **43 §**
9.1d 12m⁴ f12g f11g Dec 3] sturdy gelding: poor performer: effective at 1m to 1½m: acts
on fibresand, firm and soft going: inconsistent. *Mrs A. M. Naughton*

RAFFERTY (IRE) 2 ch.c. (Mar 29) Lion Cavern (USA) 117 – Badawi (USA) 103 **80**
(Diesis 133) [2001 6m³ 7f³ 7m 8g Sep 13] angular colt: fifth foal: half-brother to 3
winners, including useful 1m winner Badagara (by Warning): dam 1m/9f winner: fairly
useful maiden: out of depth in Vintage Stakes at Goodwood third start: well beaten in
nursery final one: should stay 1m. *C. E. Brittain*

RAFIYA 3 b.f. Halling (USA) 133 – Nemesia 111 (Mill Reef (USA) 141) [2001 8s² **89**
10v⁵ 9f² 10f³ 12.3m* 14.6m⁵ 12g⁶ 12d 16d Nov 2] 45,000Y: tall, rather unfurnished filly:

seventh foal: half-sister to French 9f winner Tikosia (by Mystiko) and winners in Germany by Niniski and Terimon: dam, 1¼m and 13.5f winner, closely related to smart 1¼m performer Elegant Air: fairly useful performer on balance: won maiden at Ripon in August: far from discredited in Park Hill Stakes at Doncaster (though probably flattered a bit when fifth to Ranin) and listed race at Ascot (sixth to Lilium) next 2 starts: well held last 2 outings: stayed 1¾m: probably acted on any going: had run well when sweating: visits Daylami. *C. E. Brittain*

RAFTERS MUSIC (IRE) 6 b.g. Thatching 131 – Princess Dixieland (USA) (Dixieland Band (USA)) [2001 61, a73: f7s f6g³ f6g⁴ f6s* 6v* 6s 6g⁵ 5.7m⁶ 6g⁵ 6d* 6f* 6f² 6g 6m³ 6g 5.7d² 6g⁶ 6g 6d f6g² f6g⁵ f7g⁶ Dec 11] good-bodied gelding: fairly useful handicapper: won at Southwell in February, Folkestone (apprentices) in April and Windsor/Doncaster in June: effective at 6f/7f: acts on equitrack/fibresand and any turf going: tried blinkered/tongue tied earlier in career: tends to hang: often held up. *B. W. Hills* **85**

RAGAMUFFIN 3 ch.g. Prince Sabo 123 – Valldemosa 81 (Music Boy 124) [2001 80p: 5.1f 5m 5m² 6d 6m 5m⁵ 6m 5g 6g 6m 6.1d⁶ 5s⁴ 6g⁴ Nov 5] sturdy gelding: fairly useful handicapper: best at 5f/easy 6f: acts on good to firm and good to soft ground: held up. *T. D. Easterby* **90**

RAGASAH 3 b.f. Glory of Dancer 121 – Slight Risk 72 (Risk Me (FR) 127) [2001 f6g⁶ 10m f9.4g⁵ f9.4g f11s* f12s Dec 27] first foal: dam 1¼m/1½m winner: modest performer: won maiden at Southwell in December: should stay at least 1½m: has looked difficult ride. *Miss Gay Kelleway* **55**

RAGDALE HALL (USA) 4 b.g. Bien Bien (USA) 125 – Gift of Dance (USA) (Trempolino (USA) 135) [2001 87: f11g⁶ 10m² 10f 10.1m³ 10m³ 9g 8m 11.7d Oct 25] big, well-made gelding: fairly useful handicapper: below form last 3 starts: best at 1¼m/1½m: acts on good to firm ground, possibly not good to soft: tried blinkered, has run well visored: has been blanketed for stall entry: sold 23,000 gns. *J. H. M. Gosden* **84**

RAHEIBB (IRE) 3 ch.c. Lion Cavern (USA) 117 – Abeyr 106 (Unfuwain (USA) 131) [2001 –: e7g² 8.3s 7.1g* 7.1m* 8m 7.1m³ 7.1m* 7f³ a6f³ Dec 21] smallish, stocky colt: not the best of movers: useful handicapper: won at Warwick and Sandown in May and Sandown again in July: good efforts last 2 starts when third at Newbury (didn't get run of race when beaten 1½ lengths by A Touch of Frost, final outing for A. Stewart) and Jebel Ali (beaten ½ length by Rayyaan): races freely, and better at 6f/7f than 1m: acts on equitrack/dirt and firm going (well beaten on softer than good). *D. J. Selvaratnam, UAE* **100**

RAHJEL SULTAN 3 b.c. Puissance 110 – Dalby Dancer 71 (Bustiki) [2001 8.3m⁵ 8.3m Aug 13] 21,000Y: fifth living foal: brother to 1997 2-y-o 5f winner Rejected and half-brother to 2 winners, including smart 7.5f to 1¼m winner Yabint El Sultan (by Safawan): dam won up to 2m: better effort in Windsor maidens on debut. *B. A. McMahon* **57**

RAHLEX (IRE) 3 ch.g. Rahy (USA) 115 – Lady Express (IRE) (Soviet Star (USA) 128) [2001 f6g f6g⁵ 6m 8.1d 5g⁴ f9.4g f7s⁶ Dec 6] 45,000Y: lengthy, sparely-made gelding: third foal: dam, 7f winner in France, half-sister to smart Irish performer up to 1¼m Dazzling Park and Japanese Group 1-winning sprinter Shinko Forest out of very smart Irish performer up to 1½m Park Express: modest maiden: left P. Cole/off nearly 4 months after fifth start, gelded after final one: may prove best around 6f. *Ronald Thompson* **55**

RAHWAAN (IRE) 2 b.c. (Mar 14) Darshaan 133 – Fawaakeh (USA) 84 (Lyphard (USA) 132) [2001 8.2d³ 8s⁴ Oct 25] good-topped colt: fourth foal: half-brother to smart 1m/1¼m (in UAE) winner Elghani (by Lahib): dam, 2-y-o 6f winner, closely related to high-class miler Maroof and to dam of Irish 2000 Guineas and Irish Derby winner Desert King: fair form when third to Affray in maiden at Nottingham: favourite when only fourth for similar race at Brighton: will be suited by 1¼m/1½m: should do better. *J. L. Dunlop* **78 p**

RAILROADER 4 ch.g. Piccolo 121 – Poyle Amber 55 (Sharrood (USA) 124) [2001 86: 6m 5m³ 6f⁶ 6m a7f⁶ a7f* a7f Dec 29] sturdy gelding: has a quick action: fairly useful performer: left G. Balding after fourth start: won allowance race at Laurel in December: stays 7f: acts on firm and soft going, and on dirt. *James L. Lawrence II, USA* **80**

RAINBOW CHASE (IRE) 3 b.g. Rainbow Quest (USA) 134 – Fayrooz (USA) 74 (Gulch (USA)) [2001 11s² 12g 14g⁵ 14.1g⁴ 11.6v Oct 29] tall, leggy, light-bodied gelding: third foal: half-brother to 1½m winner Beryl (by Bering): dam 2-y-o 7f winner out of half-sister to El Gran Senor and Try My Best: fairly useful maiden: easily best effort on debut, leaving J. Dunlop and off 4 months prior to final start: stays 11f: acts on soft going: blinkered penultimate outing. *S. J. Magnier* **82 d**

Tote Chester Cup (Handicap)—Rainbow High produces a notable weight-carrying performance to win the race for the second time, beating the visored High And Mighty, Prairie Falcon (behind runner-up) and Cover Up (third left)

RAINBOW D'BEAUTE   2 ch.f. (Apr 18) Rainbow Quest (USA) 134 – Reine   **– p**
d'Beaute 97 (Caerleon (USA) 132) [2001 7d 8s Oct 16] close-coupled filly: half-sister to several winners, most of them useful, including Irish 1m winner Reina Blanca (by Darshaan) and German winner up to 11f Silver Sign (by Shirley Heights): dam, 1m/9f winner, half-sister to smart but untrustworthy performer up to 1¼m Intimate Guest: signs of ability in valuable sales race at Newmarket (hampered early) and maiden at Leicester: should do better at 1¼m+. *M. A. Jarvis*

RAINBOW HIGH   6 b.h. Rainbow Quest (USA) 134 – Imaginary (IRE) 94 (Dancing   **117**
Brave (USA) 140) [2001 117: 12s 18.7f* 16.4m 20f 16g³ 15.9g⁶ 18d² 16d Oct 20] quite attractive horse: smart performer: won Tote Chester Cup (for second time) in May by ¾ length from High And Mighty under 9-13, quickening well in steadily-run race: in-and-out form after, good efforts when placed in Goodwood Cup (4½ lengths third to Persian Punch) in August and Doncaster Cup (¾-length second to Alleluia), rallied having been hampered by winner and switched) in September: stays 2¼m: unraced on heavy going, acts on any other: usually goes freely (pulled hard when well beaten third and final outings), and is waited with (sometimes finds little), though won from front earlier in career: none too reliable: stays in training. *B. W. Hills*

RAINBOW HILL   4 b.g. Rainbow Quest (USA) 134 – Hill Hopper (IRE) 106   **56**
(Danehill (USA) 126) [2001 89: 6s 7g 8.5m 6m 8m 7g⁶ 8m³ 10.5m 8s 7m 6m 9g 9.2g³ 8m 8f⁴ Sep 20] angular gelding: modest performer: stays 9f: acts on good to firm going: tried visored: sometimes takes good hold: none too consistent. *J. J. Quinn*

RAINBOW PRINCESS (IRE)   3 b.f. Spectrum (IRE) 126 – Richly Deserved (IRE)   **–**
(Kings Lake (USA) 133) [2001 –: f8.5g⁶ f8g 7d f7g 10m May 26] well held in maidens/handicap. *P. W. D'Arcy*

RAINBOW RAIN (USA)   7 b.g. Capote (USA) – Grana (USA) (Miswaki (USA)   **60**
124) [2001 67: e7g⁵ e7g⁶ e10g⁶ f9.4g² f8.5g⁴ 9m 10m 9m 10.1m² 9g Jul 18] well-made gelding: has a long stride: modest handicapper: best form at 9f/1¼m nowadays: acts on firm ground, good to soft and fibresand/equitrack: edgy sort: has been tongue tied. *S. Dow*

RAINBOW RAVER (IRE)   5 ch.m. Rainbows For Life (CAN) – Foolish Passion   – §
(USA) (Secretariat (USA)) [2001 –§: 16m 12.4m 12.1m 16f⁶ 12.4g Jul 18] sturdy mare:
little recent form: tried visored/tongue tied: ungenuine. *J. L. Eyre*

RAINBOW RIVER (IRE)   3 ch.g. Rainbows For Life (CAN) – Shrewd Girl (USA)   72
79 (Sagace (FR) 135) [2001 60: f8g⁵ f8g⁵ f8g⁴ f8f³ f12g⁴ f11g* f12g⁴ 10s³ 9.9m³ 7.9g   **a75**
12m³ 10m 12f³ 11.6m⁶ 13.9m 12f Aug 29] close-coupled gelding: shows plenty of knee
action: fair performer: left P. Haslam after second start: won maiden at Southwell in
April: best at 1¼m/1½m: acts on fibresand, soft and firm ground: sometimes visored/
blinkered: sometimes races freely/hangs right. *M. C. Chapman*

RAINBOW SPIRIT (IRE)   4 b.g. Rainbows For Life (CAN) – Merrie Moment   71
(IRE) (Taufan (USA)) 119) [2001 73: f16g* f16g 14.4m² 20m 16m³ 16m Aug 12] big,
lengthy gelding: fair handicapper: won at Southwell in February: probably stays 2½m:
yet to race on heavy going, acts on any other turf and fibresand/equitrack: tried visored:
sold 15,000 gns. *A. P. Jarvis*

RAINBOW VIEW (IRE)   5 b.g. Rainbows For Life (CAN) – L'Anno d'Oro (Habitat   49
134) [2001 –: 9m 6.1f⁶ 6f⁶ 6g 8f Jul 22] good-bodied gelding: poor mover: poor
performer: effective at 6f to 8.5f: acts on firm going. *W. M. Brisbourne*

RAINING   3 b.f. Mukaddamah (USA) 125 – Piney River 63 (Pharly (FR) 130) [2001   57
5.1f⁵ 5m⁴ 5m² Jul 11] 15,000Y: seventh foal: half-sister to fairly useful 1996 2-y-o 5f
winner Eye Shadow (by Mujtahid) and 1m winner Gushing (by Formidable): dam,
maiden suited by 7f, half-sister to smart sprinter Monaassib: modest form in maidens:
swerved right leaving stalls penultimate start: sold 1,200 gns. *R. Charlton*

Mr K. Abdulla's "Rainbow High"

RAIN OR SHINE (IRE) 3 ch.g. Rainbow Quest (USA) 134 – Fitnah 125 (Kris 135) –
[2001 f8f e8g⁶ 8v⁶ 11.8f May 29] good-topped gelding: seventh living foal: half-brother
to several winners, including useful French 1997 2-y-o 6.5f winner who stayed 1¾m
Fantastic Quest (by Sadler's Wells): dam won Prix Saint-Alary and second in Prix de
Diane and Prix Vermeille: little sign of ability in maidens/handicap: tongue tied: has been
slowly away: sold 1,500 gns in July, sent to Kuwait. *E. A. L. Dunlop*

RAINSHINE 3 br.f. Rainbow Quest (USA) 134 – El Opera (IRE) 100 (Sadler's Wells **87**
(USA) 132) [2001 8m⁶ 10m² 10.2m* 12m³ 12m⁶ 10.1m Aug 27] leggy, quite good-
topped filly: first foal: dam, 7f winner who stayed 1¼m well, closely related to smart
sprinter Pharaoh's Delight: fairly useful performer: won maiden at Chepstow in July:
creditable effort after only in handicap at Ascot next start: should stay beyond 1½m: raced
only on good to firm going: sold 50,000 gns in December. *Sir Mark Prescott*

RAINSTORM 6 b.g. Rainbow Quest (USA) 134 – Katsina (USA) 98 (Cox's Ridge **56**
(USA)) [2001 46, a53: f11g f9.4g⁵ f8.5s* f8.5g⁶ f7g⁶ f8g 9f³ 9g 9.9m* 8.2s 11m⁶ 9.7d²
f9.4s⁵ 10.9m² 10d Oct 2] stocky gelding: modest handicapper: won at Wolverhampton
(amateurs) in January and Beverley (ladies) in July: stays easy 11f: acts on fibresand/
equitrack and firm going, probably on soft: tried visored: none too consistent.
W. M. Brisbourne

RAINWORTH LADY 4 b.f. Governor General 116 – Monongelia 98 (Welsh Pageant **50**
132) [2001 43: 12g 10.2f 8.2s⁶ 10.5g 8.3m 7g 10.2g 10v² 10.1v f8.5g p12g⁶ Nov 13]
angular filly: modest maiden: stays 1½m: acts on heavy going, good to firm and polytrack: tried blinkered/tongue tied. *P. W. Hiatt*

RAINY RIVER (IRE) 3 b.f. Irish River (FR) 131 – Forest Storm (USA) (Woodman –
(USA) 126) [2001 65: f6g⁶ 7s 8d Jun 17] fair maiden at 2 yrs: well held in 2001: sold
3,000 gns. *B. W. Hills*

RAISA'S GOLD (IRE) 3 b.f. Goldmark (USA) 113 – Princess Raisa (Indian King **43**
(USA) 128) [2001 –: f7s⁶ f8g 11.1m⁴ 10m 16m Jun 27] leggy filly: poor maiden: stays
11f: acts on good to firm going. *B. S. Rothwell*

RAISE A MELODY (IRE) 2 ch.f. (Feb 1) Hector Protector (USA) 124 – Dumayla –
78 (Shernazar 131) [2001 8d Oct 3] sixth foal: half-sister to 4-y-o Conwy Castle and
French 1½m and 17f winner Dunaysir (by Kahyasi): dam, third at 1m/1¼m (only
starts), half-sister to Doyoun: 33/1, stumbled and unseated early in maiden at Salisbury.
E. Stanners

RAISE A PRINCE (FR) 8 b.g. Machiavellian (USA) 123 – Enfant d'Amour (USA) **75**
(Lyphard (USA) 132) [2001 95: f14g 16s 14.1s⁴ f14g² f14g f14g6 Dec 17] rather leggy
gelding: unimpressive mover: only fair handicapper nowadays: stays 2m: acts on
equitrack/fibresand, best turf form on good ground or softer: visored (won) once at 4 yrs:
tongue tied: usually held up. *S. P. C. Woods*

RAISED THE BAR (USA) 2 ch.f. (Feb 24) Royal Academy (USA) 130 – Barari **71**
(USA) (Blushing Groom (FR) 131) [2001 5m² 5g² 5.6f⁴ 7d Oct 2] leggy, angular filly:
half-sister to several winners, including 6f to 1¼m (US Grade 1 event) winner White
Heart (by Green Desert) and 7.5f (at 2 yrs) to 1½m winner Kind Regards (by Unfuwain),
both smart: dam unraced half-sister to very smart French/US performer up to 10.5f
Colour Chart, herself dam of 3-y-o Equerry and Breeders' Cup Juvenile Fillies winner
Tempera: fair maiden: first past post (hung right and demoted) at Ripon on debut: ran
creditably in nursery at Newmarket final start: should stay 1m: acts on good to firm and
good to soft going. *M. Johnston*

RAISON GARDE (IRE) 2 b.f. (Feb 15) Ashkalani (IRE) 128 – Didjala (USA) (Irish **86**
River (FR) 131) [2001 7m⁶ 7.5g* 8s⁶ Oct 22] lengthy filly: third living foal: half-sister to
French 1m to 1½m winner Kings Widow (by Generous): dam won in France at 1¼m:
fairly useful form: won maiden at Beverley in September: creditable staying-on sixth to
Bandari in listed event at Pontefract final start: acts on soft ground: has been heavily bandaged in front. *J. G. FitzGerald*

RAJAB 2 br.c. (Apr 8) Selkirk (USA) 129 – Putout 69 (Dowsing (USA) 124) [2001 6g⁶ **94 p**
6m* 7v Oct 26] 42,000Y: tall, quite good-topped colt: has scope: fifth foal: closely related
to 6-y-o Bedevilled and half-brother to useful German 1999 2-y-o 5f/6f winner Palanca

(by Inchinor): dam, 5f winner, half-sister to 4-y-o Danceabout and smart French sprinter Pole Position: won maiden at Goodwood in September by 2 lengths from Zargus: 11/2, dropped away from halfway under gruelling conditions in Horris Hill Stakes at Newbury final start: should stay 7f: likely to make a useful 3-y-o. *M. Johnston*

RAJAH EMAN (IRE) 3 b.g. Sri Pekan (USA) 117 – Jungle Book (IRE) (Ballad **82** Rock 122) [2001 10d f11g² f9.4g* 11.9d⁶ Jun 9] 9,500F, IR 21,000Y: lengthy, rather sparely-made gelding: unimpressive mover: third foal: half-brother to a 6f winner in Italy by Thatching: dam unraced half-sister to useful 1997 2-y-o 6f/1m winner Silent Tribute: fairly useful form: won maiden at Wolverhampton in May: tailed off final start: stays 11f: acts on fibresand. *S. P. C. Woods*

RAJAM 3 b.g. Sadler's Wells (USA) 132 – Rafif (USA) 68 (Riverman (USA) 131) **102** [2001 10g² 12m* 12f* 12g² 14m Sep 22] fourth foal: closely related to useful performer up to 1¾m Kadir (by Unfuwain): dam, 1¼m winner, out of close relative to Ribblesdale Stakes winner Thawakib (by Sadler's Wells and herself dam of Sakhee): useful performer: trained both starts at 2 yrs by D. Loder in France: dictated steady pace when winning maiden at Kempton in June and minor event at Newbury (beat Celtic Island ½ length) in August: good 1½ lengths second to Thundering Surf in handicap at Kempton penultimate start: reportedly suffered from breathing problem when tailed-off last final outing (subsequently gelded): stays 1½m: acts on firm and soft going: blinkered (pulled hard/wandered) final start at 2 yrs: carried head awkwardly/edged left on reappearance. *A. C. Stewart*

RAKEEB (USA) 6 ch.g. Irish River (FR) 131 – Ice House 89 (Northfields (USA)) **– §** [2001 73§: f12s 12s 16g 16m Aug 28] big, strong gelding: one-time fair handicapper: well held in 2001 (broke a blood vessel final start): sometimes blinkered: tends to hang: unreliable. *M. W. Easterby*

RAKE HEY 7 gr.g. Petong 126 – Dancing Daughter 79 (Dance In Time (CAN)) [2001 **48** 51: f16.2s f14.8s² e13g² f12g² Feb 15] poor maiden: stays 14.8f: acts on fibresand/ equitrack, good to firm and soft going: sometimes blinkered/visored/tongue tied. *D. G. Bridgwater*

RALLENTANDO 2 b.f. (May 16) Piccolo 121 – Wrangbrook (Shirley Heights 130) **–** [2001 f5g 5g 7g 8m Sep 20] 4,200Y: good-bodied filly: sister to 4-y-o Wintzig and half-sister to 2 winners, including useful 1990 2-y-o 6f/7f winner Punch N'Run (by Forzando), later winner in Italy: dam third at 1½m: no form in maidens/sellers. *G. M. Moore*

RAMBAGH 3 b.f. Polish Precedent (USA) 131 – My Preference (Reference Point **69** 139) [2001 68: 10s⁶ 12s⁴ 10m⁴ 8.2g³ 8m² 8m³ 9.9m f8.5g 8s⁵ Oct 3] unfurnished filly: fair maiden handicapper: stays 1¼m: acts on soft and good to firm going: blinkered/ visored last 7 starts: stumbled and unseated rider at start on penultimate outing: has wandered/flashed tail/found little. *J. L. Dunlop*

RAMBLING BEAR 8 ch.h. Sharrood (USA) 124 – Supreme Rose 95 (Frimley Park **–** 109) [2001 112: 5g 6g 5.7m⁵ Jul 15] leggy, good-topped horse: smart performer at best: won 7 races, including King George Stakes at Goodwood in 1996 and Palace House Stakes at Newmarket in 1999: well below best in 2001: barely stayed 6f: acted on firm and good to soft going, possibly not on soft/heavy: blinkered once: was often taken alone to post: free-going sort, and was best patiently ridden in strongly-run race: to stand at Hedgeholme Stud, Darlington, Co. Durham, fee £1,200 (concessions for winners). *M. Blanshard*

RAMBLIN' MAN (IRE) 3 b.g. Blues Traveller (IRE) 119 – Saborinie 56 (Prince **54** Sabo 123) [2001 55: f7g f7g³ f8.5g⁴ 8.2s⁵ 8.1g⁴ 10g² 9m⁴ 10g³ 10.2f¹ 10m 11.6m² 11.6m 12m 11.7m² 10m³ 10s³ f14.8g⁴ Dec 1] neat gelding: modest maiden: stays 11.6f: acts on fibresand, soft and good to firm going: gelded after final outing. *M. Blanshard*

RAMBO NINE 4 b.g. Rambo Dancer (CAN) 107 – Asmarina 50 (Ascendant 96) **–** [2001 –: f6s f5g f7g f11g f8g f7g 7s May 3] of little account. *S. R. Bowring*

RAMBO WALTZER 9 b.g. Rambo Dancer (CAN) 107 – Vindictive Lady (USA) **71 d** (Foolish Pleasure (USA)) [2001 62, a81: f9.4g* f9.4s* f9.4s⁵ f9.4g f12g³ f11g³ f12g³ 8.1g⁴ 10.2f 10f 8m f8g 12g 10.9m f9.4f f11g f12s³ Dec 26] smallish, sturdy gelding: prone to lameness: fair performer: won 2 claimers at Wolverhampton in January: well below form in second half of year: seems to stay 1½m: acts on heavy going, good to firm and fibresand: visored once: good mount for inexperienced rider. *Miss S. J. Wilton*

RAMPANT (IRE) 3 b.g. Pursuit of Love 124 – Flourishing (IRE) 85 (Trojan Fen 118) **89**
[2001 77p: 8v² 8.3g* 8.1m 9s⁵ 10.3g 10.5v⁴ 11.8s* 12v 12s Nov 10] tall, useful-looking
gelding: fairly useful performer: won maiden at Windsor in May and handicap at
Leicester in October: well beaten last 2 outings, gelded after final one: stays 11.8f: acts
on heavy ground: tongue tied last 4 starts. *R. M. Beckett*

RAMPART 4 b.g. Kris 135 – Balliasta (USA) (Lyphard (USA) 132) [2001 –: 7m 8.2f **50**
9.9m 8.3d⁴ 9.9m f8.5g f6g⁵ f7g f6s² p7g Dec 28] strong, workmanlike gelding: modest
maiden: stays 1m: acts on fibresand: tried blinkered: has raced freely: sometimes slowly
away. *D. Shaw*

RAMZAIN 3 b.c. Alzao (USA) 117 – Romoosh 69 (Formidable (USA) 125) [2001 **74**
f7g² f8g* 8g May 6] first reported foal: dam, 1¼m winner, half-sister to smart 6f/7f
performer Unblest (by Alzao): won maiden at Southwell in April (wandered): only
mid-field in handicap at Newmarket final start: will stay 1¼m, probably 1½m.
P. W. D'Arcy

RANDOM KINDNESS 8 b.g. Alzao (USA) 117 – Lady Tippins (USA) 83 (Star de **–**
Naskra (USA)) [2001 –, a84d: 11.5f 14.4m⁶ 14.1m Jul 27] sturdy, angular gelding:
one-time fairly useful performer: well held in 2001. *R. Ingram*

RANDOM QUEST 3 b.g. Rainbow Quest (USA) 134 – Anne Bonny 105 (Ajdal **94**
(USA) 130) [2001 86p: 12s² 12m⁵ May 31] leggy, useful-looking gelding: fairly useful
performer, lightly raced: good second of 3 in minor event at Salisbury in May, dictating
pace: well held in handicap at Goodwood only subsequent run: gelded after: should stay
1¾m+: acts on soft ground. *P. F. I. Cole*

RANDOM TASK (IRE) 4 b.c. Tirol 127 – Minami (IRE) (Caerleon (USA) 132) **–**
[2001 83: f6g f6g 7m 6d Jun 18] good-topped colt: fairly useful handicapper at 3 yrs: well
held in 2001: has won in blinkers, tried visored. *D. Shaw*

RANEEN NASHWAN 5 b.g. Nashwan (USA) 135 – Raneen Alwatar 80 (Sadler's **–**
Wells (USA) 132) [2001 80: 16.5s Nov 10] lengthy, angular gelding: fairly useful winner
at 2 yrs: very lightly raced since. *M. R. Channon*

RANGE TRADER (NZ) 7 gr.g. Truly Vain (AUS) – Respectful (NZ) (Standaan **–**
(FR) 118) [2001 8.1m⁴ 10.3f² 6m⁶ 6g 8.1g Aug 10] tall gelding: winner of 3 of his 12
races in New Zealand, including over 1m in 2000: little form on Flat in 2001: stays 1m:
acts on firm going. *E. J. Alston*

RANIN 3 b.f. Unfuwain (USA) 131 – Nafhaat (USA) 91 (Roberto (USA) 131) [2001 **112**
81: 8.3g² 10m* 10m* 10f 11.9d² 12m* 13.5s⁵ 11.9m⁴ 14.6m* 12.5d² 12d Oct 13] good-
topped filly: made into a smart performer: won maiden at Lingfield in May, handicap at
Newbury in June, listed race at Newmarket (by 1¾ lengths from Love Everlasting) in
July and Rothmans Royals Park Hill Stakes at Doncaster (by 2 lengths from Masilia) in
September: good nose second to Moon Queen in Prix de Royallieu at Longchamp
penultimate start (drifted right): probably hadn't recovered when well held week later:
stayed 1¾m: well held on firm going, probably acted on any other: game and genuine:
visits Seeking The Gold. *E. A. L. Dunlop*

RANVILLE 3 ch.g. Deploy 131 – Kibitka (FR) (Baby Turk 120) [2001 –: 10d 10g **102 p**
14.1m² 14.1s* 14g* 15.9d⁴ 16.1d⁴ 16v* 16.5s Nov 10] heavy-bodied gelding: poor
mover: made into a useful handicapper: won at Nottingham and Haydock in August,
Chester in September then Newcastle and Newbury (easily beat Follow Lammtarra by 5
lengths) in October: probably over top for season when beaten favourite at Doncaster
final start: will stay 2¼m: acts on heavy and good to firm going: races prominently: most
genuine: type to win a good prize at 4 yrs. *M. A. Jarvis*

Rothmans Royals Park Hill Stakes, Doncaster—
Ranin gains her first pattern-race success, beating Masilia (white breastgirth), Jalousie and Isadora

RAPADASH (IRE) 2 ch.c. (Jan 30) Boundary (USA) 117 – Imelda (USA) (Manila **81**
(USA)) [2001 5g⁴ f6g³ f6g* 7m³ Jul 6] IR 80,000Y: first foal: dam once-raced half-sister
to very smart French miler Shaanxi: fairly useful performer: won maiden at Southwell in
June: looked difficult ride when creditable third in nursery at Salisbury final start: stays
7f: acts on fibresand, raced only on good/good to firm going on turf: blinkered last 3
starts: sent to USA. *B. J. Meehan*

RAPHAEL (IRE) 2 b.f. (Apr 14) Perugino (USA) 84 – Danny's Miracle (Superlative **75**
118) [2001 5s³ 5d⁵ 5f² 6g⁴ 7m² 7g² 7g* 8m* 7d Oct 2] IR 6,000Y: leggy, quite good-
topped filly: half-sister to several winners, including fairly useful Irish 1m/9f winner Per
Amore (by General Monash): dam unraced: fair performer: made all in maiden at Thirsk
in August and nursery at Ripon in September: stays 1m: acts on firm and soft ground.
T. D. Easterby

RAPID LINER 8 b.g. Skyliner 117 – Stellaris (Star Appeal 133) [2001 36?: f16g **–**
f12g⁶ f14g Dec 3] of little account nowadays. *J. Gallagher*

RAPPAREE (USA) 3 b.f. Red Ransom (USA) – Pixie Erin 110 (Golden Fleece **78**
(USA) 133) [2001 8g⁵ 9m³ 10.4g* 10.3m⁵ 10.1m 10.3m 11.7d Oct 25] $40,000Y: sturdy
filly: has a quick action: seventh foal: half-sister to several winners, including fairly
useful 1999 2-y-o 7f winner Strasbourg (by Dehere) and useful 6f winner (including at 2
yrs) Bint Albaadiya (by Woodman): dam, 7f to 1¼m winner, half-sister to very smart filly
up to 1¼m Star Pastures: fair performer: won maiden at York in June: should stay 1½m.
J. W. Hills

Vodafone Horris Hill Stakes, Newbury—in barely raceable conditions Rapscallion produces another game display; Samhari (left) makes the winner pull out all the stops, with Advance Party third

RAPSCALLION (GER) 2 b.c. (Feb 16) Robellino (USA) 127 – Rosy Outlook (USA) **107**
79 (Trempolino (USA) 135) [2001 5m⁵ 6g³ 6g* 7s* 7d* 7v* Oct 26] leggy, unfurnished colt: first foal: dam, 6f winner, out of half-sister to very smart French performers Squill (up to 1¼m) and Baiser Vole (up to 1m): useful performer: won maiden at Lingfield in August, nursery at Ascot in September and minor event at Ascot (sweating, rallied to beat Playapart by short head) and Vodafone Horris Hill Stakes at Newbury in October: game effort to beat Samhari a neck at Newbury, all runners out on their feet at finish: will stay 1m: raced only on good going or softer after debut (acts on heavy): edged left last 2 starts. *J. M. P. Eustace*

RAPT (IRE) 3 b.g. Septieme Ciel (USA) 123 – Dream Play (USA) (Blushing Groom **70** (FR) 131) [2001 56: f6g* f7g² 7d 6m³ 6g³ 7m 7g f7g⁵ p8g Dec 22] leggy, useful-looking **a78** gelding: fair performer: won maiden at Southwell in March: sold from W. Jarvis 12,000 gns before penultimate start: may prove best up to 7f: acts on fibresand and good to firm going. *P. W. D'Arcy*

RAPTOR (IRE) 3 ch.g. Eagle Eyed (USA) 111 – Ahakista (IRE) (Persian Bold 123) **43 ?**
[2001 –: 14m⁶ 11.1m⁵ 12f 12g⁶ 15.8g Aug 17] strong, lengthy gelding: poor maiden: stays 11f, probably not 1¾m: visored (well held) last 2 starts. *S. E. Kettlewell*

RA RA RASPUTIN 6 b.g. Petong 126 – Ra Ra Girl 77 (Shack (USA) 118) [2001 –§, **– §** a55d: f7g f7s f8.5s f7s⁶ f9.4s f11g 10f 11.8d⁶ Aug 12] strong gelding: temperamental performer nowadays: sometimes blinkered/visored. *B. P. J. Baugh*

RARE GENIUS (USA) 5 ch.g. Beau Genius (CAN) – Aunt Nola (USA) (Olden **70** Times) [2001 71: 16.2m⁵ 14g⁴ Jun 8] tall gelding: fair maiden handicapper: stays 2m: acts on soft and good to firm ground. *Ian Williams*

RARE OLD TIMES (IRE) 3 b.f. Inzar (USA) 112 – Moona (USA) 73 (Lear Fan **64 d** (USA) 130) [2001 72: 5g⁶ 5d 6m⁶ 6m 5m⁵ 5g 5v 6v 5.2v Oct 26] leggy, good-topped filly: modest performer: well below form last 4 outings: stays 6f: acts on good to firm going, probably on good to soft: blinkered 4 of last 5 starts. *Mrs P. N. Dutfield*

RARE QUALITY 3 b.f. Chaddleworth (IRE) 103 – Pink Mex (Tickled Pink 114) **– p** [2001 8.3v Nov 8] seventh foal: half-sister to several winners, including useful 1995 2-y-o 6f to 1m winner Believe Me (by Beveled) and fairly useful 1m to 1¼m winner Tragic Hero (by Tragic Role): dam little form: 7/1, clear signs of ability when well-held twelfth of 15 in maiden at Windsor, eased right up after travelling comfortably until 2f out: almost certainly capable of better. *P. J. Makin*

RARE TALENT 7 b.g. Mtoto 134 – Bold As Love (Lomond (USA) 128) [2001 71: **69 d** 12.3f⁴ 12m 10.3f⁵ 11.9d 12f 9.9f 9.9m³ 12g Aug 17] good-bodied gelding: unimpressive mover: fair performer, on downgrade: stays 1½m: best form on good going or firmer: visored once: usually held up. *S. Gollings*

RASHBAG 2 b.c. (Mar 2) Reprimand 122 – Pleasuring 68 (Good Times (ITY)) [2001 **108**
6f* 7g* 8d² 8.3d* 9v* Oct 21] 5,000F, 220,000 francs Y: fourth foal: brother to 3-y-o
Suggestive and 5-y-o Swynford Pleasure: dam, sprint maiden, from very good family:
useful performer: won 2 minor events at La Teste in July, listed race at Craon (by short
neck from Guana) in September and 5-runner Prix de Conde at Longchamp (made all, ran
on well to beat Caesarion 1½ lengths) in October: also ran well when length third to
disqualified Parasol in listed race at Deauville (promoted to second): likely to stay 1¼m:
probably acts on any ground. *J-C. Rouget, France*

RASHIK 7 ch.h. Cadeaux Genereux 131 – Ghzaalh (USA) 87 (Northern Dancer) [2001 **59**
–: f8.5g³ f8g⁵ f12g² f11g f12g⁴ f11g* 12.3m⁶ f11g⁵ f14g Nov 16] useful-looking horse:
covered a handful of mares in 1999 and 2000: modest form on return, winning claimer at
Southwell in May: stays 1½m: acts on fibresand. *A. Streeter*

RASID (USA) 3 b.g. Bahri (USA) 125 – Makadir (USA) (Woodman (USA) 126) **88 p**
[2001 10d² Apr 17] rangy gelding: third foal: half-brother to a 7f/1m winner in USA by
Holy Bull: dam, 1m/9f winner in USA, third in Grade 3 8.5f event at 2 yrs: 16/1 and
green, shaped very well when 2½ lengths second to Curtain Time in maiden at Newmarket, held up some way off steady pace and staying on strongly without being unduly
knocked about: gelded after: not sure to stay beyond 1¼m: looked open to good deal of
improvement, and should win races when all is well again. *E. A. L. Dunlop*

RASMALAI 4 b.f. Sadler's Wells (USA) 132 – Raymouna (IRE) (High Top 131) –
[2001 71: 8.5s 8s May 3] quite good-topped filly: fair maiden at 3 yrs: well held in 2001:
sold 60,000 gns in December. *R. Hannon*

RASOUM (USA) 3 gr.c. Miswaki (USA) 124 – Bel Ray (USA) (Restivo (USA)) **113**
[2001 114: 7d⁶ 6m⁴ 6m 6d 6g² 7m 5g Oct 4] close-coupled colt: smart performer: best
effort at 3 yrs when strong-finishing ½-length second to Patsy's Double in handicap at
Leicester in August: well held in listed races after: best at 6f: probably best on good going
or softer (acts well on heavy): blinkered (ran poorly) third start: has been bandaged in
front: has hung left/pulled hard: sent to USA. *E. A. L. Dunlop*

RASSENDYLL 3 b.c. Rudimentary (USA) 118 – La Lutine 95 (My Swallow 134) **46**
[2001 49: 8.2g⁶ 7.1s⁴ 6g f7g 7.1v Sep 28] leggy colt: poor maiden: probably stays 1m.
A. Bailey

RATEEBA (IRE) 3 b.f. Green Desert (USA) 127 – Wathbat Mtoto 88 (Mtoto 134) –
[2001 –: 7g May 18] strong filly: good walker: well held in 3 maidens: visits Lujain.
A. C. Stewart

RATHKENNY (IRE) 3 b.c. Standiford (USA) – Shine (Sharrood (USA) 124) [2001 **96**
96: 10.1s⁴ 10.3f 8m⁶ 10f* 12f 10d⁶ Jul 16] small, sturdy colt: useful performer: won
minor event at Pontefract in June by ½ length from Modrik, best effort in 2001: should be
suited by 1½m+: acts on any ground. *J. G. Given*

RATIFIED 4 b.g. Not In Doubt (USA) 101 – Festival of Magic (USA) 73 (Clever Trick **44**
(USA)) [2001 62: 12s f11g 10s f12g f11g 14.1m f16g Jul 27] good-bodied gelding: poor
form in 2001: should stay 1¾m: acts on heavy going. *M. C. Chapman*

RATIO 3 ch.c. Pivotal 124 – Owdbetts (IRE) 69 (High Estate 127) [2001 6g* 7m² 7m³ **106**
8.1m⁴ 8s² 7m⁶ Aug 23] 14,500F, 34,000Y: angular, quite good-topped colt: first foal: dam
7f (including at 2 yrs) and 1¼m winner: useful performer: won maiden at Salisbury in
May: best efforts after when placed in Jersey Stakes at Royal Ascot (length third to
Mozart, having gone unimpressively to post) and listed race at Deauville (length second
to Domedriver): appeared not to be putting it all in when below form in listed race at York
final outing: stays 1m: acts on soft and good to firm going. *I. A. Balding*

RATTLE 8 b.g. Mazilier (USA) 107 – Snake Song 94 (Mansingh (USA) 120) [2001 –: –
8m 13m Jun 14] small gelding: no form since 1996. *D. A. Nolan*

RAVENGLASS (USA) 2 b.c. (Mar 23) Miswaki (USA) 124 – Urus (USA) (Kris S **72**
(USA)) [2001 6s⁵ May 19] $250,000Y: third foal: half-brother to 4-y-o Happy Diamond:
dam won up to 1¼m in USA, including minor stakes: fair form when fifth in maiden at
Newbury. *J. H. M. Gosden*

RAVENSWOOD (IRE) 4 b.c. Warning 136 – Green Lucia 116 (Green Dancer **101**
(USA) 132) [2001 94: 16.1f⁴ 13.9g⁵ 14.6d² 18d Oct 20] leggy colt: useful handicapper:
good efforts in 2001 when fourth in Northumberland Plate at Newcastle, fifth in Ebor at
York, and short-head second to Darasim in Mallard Stakes at Doncaster (forced to check
on a couple of occasions): travelled easily for a long way in Cesarewitch at Newmarket

final outing: stays 2m when conditions aren't testing, will probably prove as effective at 1½m: acts on firm and good to soft going: tongue tied: waited with: reliable. *M. C. Pipe*

RAVE ON (ITY)   2 b.f. (Apr 13) Barathea (IRE) 127 – Kalliopina (FR) (Arctic Tern   **73**
(USA) 126) [2001 6m 5.1m² 6m Aug 1] 300,000 francs Y: rather leggy filly: fifth foal:
half-sister to 3 winners abroad, including useful Italian performer up to 1¼m Lady Bi
(by Alzao): dam, Italian 8.5f/9f winner, half-sister to smart French 7f to 1¼m performer
Goofalik: easily best effort (fair form) when short-head second of 6 to Bonny Ruan in
minor event at Chepstow, staying on: bred to stay at least 1m. *R. Hannon*

RAVISHING (IRE)   4 b.f. Bigstone (IRE) 126 – Dazzling Maid (IRE) 64 (Tate   **83**
Gallery (USA) 117) [2001 82d: 6m³ 6m⁵ 6f² 6m* 6m 6g⁶ 6m 6m³ 5g² 5m² 6g⁵ Sep 19]
angular filly: fairly useful performer: won handicap at Yarmouth in July (despite edging
right): ran well last 3 starts: effective at stiff 5f to 7f: acts on firm and good to soft going,
possibly not on soft/heavy: often blinkered. *W. J. Haggas*

RAW SILK   3 b.g. Rudimentary (USA) 118 – Misty Silks 81 (Scottish Reel 123) [2001   **40**
–: 8s 8.1v⁴ 10g 8m 10.1v Oct 24] good-topped gelding: poor maiden: probably stays 1m:
acts on heavy going, probably on good to firm: blinkered final start. *M. J. Ryan*

RAWYAAN   2 b.c. (Feb 25) Machiavellian (USA) 123 – Raheefa (USA) 75 (Riverman   **94 p**
(USA) 131) [2001 7f⁵ 8d* Oct 19] close-coupled, quite attractive colt: has a round action:
second foal: brother to 3-y-o Muthaaber: dam, 1¼m winner, granddaughter of US
champion older mare Cascapedia (Grade 1 9f winner): 10/1, improved to win 20-runner
maiden at Newmarket by length from Dolores, taking very strong hold to post but leading
2f out and holding on bravely: will need to settle better to stay beyond 1m: has worn
crossed noseband: useful performer in the making. *J. H. M. Gosden*

RAYANA (FR)   3 b.f. Midyan (USA) 124 – High Kash (FR) (Highest Honor (FR) 124)   **39**
[2001 8s f7g⁴ Nov 23] lengthy, plain filly: first foal: dam, third over 9f at 2 yrs in France,
sister to smart French/US 1¼m performer Admise: left J. Piednoel in France after only
start at 2 yrs: poor form in maidens in Britain: should stay beyond 1m. *Ms A. E. Embiricos*

RAYBAAN (IRE)   2 b.g. (Jan 31) Flying Spur (AUS) – Genetta (Green Desert (USA)   **79**
127) [2001 6m³ 6d² 7.5s² 8d* 8g Sep 13] IR 12,500Y: good-bodied gelding: third foal:
dam, French maiden, out of half-sister to top-class performer up to 1½m Kalaglow: fair
performer: made all in maiden at Yarmouth in August: well beaten in nursery final start:
should stay 1¼m: acts on soft and good to firm going. *M. H. Tompkins*

RAYHAN   2 b.f. (Jan 16) Unfuwain (USA) 131 – Karawan 82 (Kris 135) [2001 7.1m³   **69**
6.1v⁴ Oct 4] small, rather angular filly: first foal: dam, 7f winner, sister to Prix de la
Salamandre winner Common Grounds and half-sister to smart French/US performer up
to 1¼m Angel In My Heart: better effort in maidens (fair form) when third of Carrozzina
at Warwick, pulling hard but staying on: hung left next time: will need to settle better to
stay 1m. *J. H. M. Gosden*

RAYIK   6 br.g. Marju (IRE) 127 – Matila (IRE) 98 (Persian Bold 123) [2001 61, a86:   **54 §**
e12g² e13g³ e12g e12g e12g² e16g⁶ e12g 11.9s 10f⁴ 11.9m* 12m 12m³ 12.6d⁵ 11.5f   **a66 §**
11.6m* 12g f12g p13g³ p12g³ p13g⁴ Dec 29] sparely-made gelding: fair on all-weather,
modest on turf: won ladies claimer at Brighton in June and handicap at Windsor in
August: stays 13f: acts on all-weather and good to firm going (well below form on soft):
tried visored in 1999: has been tongue tied: sometimes pulls hard: unreliable. *G. L. Moore*

RAYWARE BOY (IRE)   5 b.h. Scenic 128 – Amata (USA) (Nodouble (USA)) [2001   **49 §**
44, a55: f9.4s³ f12g⁵ f12g³ f12g f11g f12f⁴ f12s⁵ Dec 27] leggy, short-backed horse:
poor handicapper: stays 1½m: acts on fibresand/equitrack, probably on firm going: tried
visored, usually blinkered nowadays: tends to get behind and look none too keen.
D. Shaw

RAZKALLA (USA)   3 b.g. Caerleon (USA) 132 – Larrocha (IRE) 116 (Sadler's   **73 p**
Wells (USA) 132) [2001 9m* Sep 6] well-made gelding: first foal: dam, 1¼m/1½m
winner, half-sister to Ardross: 5/1-on, won maiden at Redcar by 1½ lengths from Leophin
Dancer, pushed along quite firmly and looking better the further he went: gelded after:
will be suited by at least 1½m: will improve. *D. R. Loder*

RAZZLE (IRE)   2 b.f. (Mar 26) Green Desert (USA) 127 – Organza 105 (High Top   **– p**
131) [2001 7d Oct 15] sturdy, lengthy filly: seventh reported foal: sister to very smart
Irish 6f/7f performer Desert Style and closely related to Irish 1½m winner Dansk
(by Danehill): dam, 1¼m winner, half-sister to very smart dam of Baratbea and 2-y-o
Gossamer: 20/1 and backward, never-dangerous eleventh of 20 to Trojan Princess in
maiden at Leicester: should do better. *J. L. Dunlop*

REACHFORYOURPOCKET (IRE) 6 b.g. Royal Academy (USA) 130 – Gema- **52 d**
asheh (Habitat 134) [2001 55, a73: e12g⁴ e10g e10g e10g⁵ e8g³ e8g³ e8g³ e10g 6m 7m³ **a68 d**
7f⁵ 7m 8g³ 10m 10m f8.5g f9.4s f12g p10g p10g⁶ Dec 28] fair handicapper at best on
all-weather, modest on turf: well held last 7 starts: best at 1m/1¼m: acts on firm going
and equitrack: tried blinkered/visored, not in 2001: has had tongue tied: has hung right.
M. D. I. Usher

READY TO ROCK (IRE) 5 b.g. Up And At 'em 109 – Rocklands Rosie (Muscatite **61**
122) [2001 57: f5g⁵ f6s f5g² f5g⁶ f5g* f5g² f5g⁵ f5g⁶ f5g⁵ e5g³ e5g³ f5g 5.1d 5m⁴ 5d 5.2m **a67**
p5g f5g p5g f5s Dec 27] fair handicapper: won at Wolverhampton in February: well held
last 4 starts: best at 5f: acts on fibresand/equitrack, soft and good to firm going: usually
blinkered: races prominently. *J. S. Moore*

REAL AMBITION (IRE) 2 b.g. (Apr 24) Fayruz 116 – Mauradell (IRE) (Mujadil **77**
(USA) 119) [2001 6g⁶ 6d 6.1m² f6g³ f6g² f6g⁵ Oct 22] IR 11,000F, 17,000Y: sturdy
gelding: third foal: half-brother to a 5f (including at 2 yrs) and 7f winner in Italy by
Shardari: dam unraced from family of very smart French 1¼m/1½m performer Diamond
Mix: fair maiden: second at Warwick and Southwell: may prove best at 5f/6f: acts on
good to firm ground and fibresand: blinkered last 4 starts: has wandered: sold 5,000 gns.
B. J. Meehan

REAL DELIGHT (IRE) 2 b.f. (Apr 30) Nicolotte 118 – Jumbo Delight (IRE) (Don't **82**
Forget Me 127) [2001 6g² 5m 5m* 5g* 6g 5g 5s³ 5s⁴ Oct 17] IR 700F: lengthy filly:
second foal: half-sister to Irish 1m winner Clare Rose (by Shalford): dam lightly raced on
Flat/over hurdles in Ireland: fairly useful performer: eleventh of 20 in Queen Mary Stakes
at Royal Ascot second start: won maiden at Bellewstown and minor event at the Curragh
in July: good fourth in nursery at Navan: likely to prove best at 5f: acts on soft and good
to firm going. *Patrick Carey, Ireland*

REAP 3 b.g. Emperor Jones (USA) 119 – Corn Futures 78 (Nomination 125) [2001 59: **54**
8s⁴ f9.4g 8d Oct 15] rather leggy, good-topped gelding: modest maiden: stays 1m: acts on
fibresand and equitrack, probably on soft ground: tried visored: has wandered. *Mrs Lydia
Pearce*

REAR GUARD ACTION 5 b.g. Almoojid 69 – Belle Deirdrie (Mandamus 120) **–**
[2001 12m Sep 24] rangy gelding: no form. *P. Butler*

REAR WINDOW 7 b.g. Night Shift (USA) – Last Clear Chance (USA) (Alleged **50**
(USA) 138) [2001 11.6g 14.1m³ 15.8d f14g 14.1s² 12g² Nov 7] compact gelding: modest
handicapper: effective at 1½m to easy 2m: acts on good to firm going, heavy and fibresand: tried visored/blinkered/tongue tied earlier in career. *M. J. Ryan*

REASONING 3 ch.f. Selkirk (USA) 129 – Attribute 69 (Warning 136) [2001 9.9d **65**
10m 9.7m⁶ 8g 7g 8m² f9.4g³ f8g⁴ f8.5g⁶ f9.4s² Dec 18] IR 60,000Y: first foal: dam,
maiden daughter of half-sister to Xaar, from family of El Gran Senor: fair maiden handicapper: left M. Bell 7,500 gns after seventh start: stays 1¼m: acts on good to firm, good
to soft ground and fibresand. *B. S. Rothwell*

REASON (IRE) 3 b.c. Sadler's Wells (USA) 132 – Marseillaise (Artaius (USA) 129) **102**
[2001 12g⁴ 14g* 16.2m Jun 19] 315,000F, 1,200,000Y: close-coupled, quite attractive
colt: eighth foal: closely related to 2 winners in France, including useful 6f to 9f (Prix
Daphnis) winner Regal Archive (by Fairy King) and half-brother to several winners: dam
unraced half-sister to Irish 2000 Guineas winner Northern Treasure and to dam of
Yorkshire Oaks winner Only Royale: useful form: won maiden at Haydock in June by
5 lengths: better form when twelfth in Queen's Vase at Royal Ascot final start, tending
to go in snatches: stays 2m: raced only on good ground or firmer: visored on debut.
H. R. A. Cecil

REBELLE 2 b. or br.g. (Mar 19) Reprimand 122 – Blushing Belle 74 (Local Suitor **–**
(USA) 128) [2001 7m 7m f6g Oct 6] 4,000 2-y-o: third foal: dam 10.6f seller winner at 2
yrs, also won over hurdles: well held in maidens. *K. Bell*

REBELLINE (IRE) 3 b.f. Robellino (USA) 127 – Fleeting Rainbow 65 (Rainbow **112**
Quest (USA) 134) [2001 106p: 7s* 8g⁵ 10d* 12g 10v³ 10d Oct 20] 28,000F, IR 68,000Y:
quite attractive filly: fifth foal: sister to smart Irish 5f (at 2 yrs) to 11f winner Quws:
dam, should have stayed 1½m, from good family: smart performer: won listed race at
Leopardstown (by 5½ lengths from Imagine) in April and Hunston Financial Pretty Polly
Stakes at the Curragh (beat Molomo 2 lengths) in June: good 3½ lengths third to Terre À
Terre in Prix de l'Opera at Longchamp penultimate start: below form in Dubai Champion
Stakes at Newmarket final outing: effective at 1¼m (seemed not to stay 1½m in Irish

Oaks): acts on heavy going, yet to race on ground firmer than good. *K. Prendergast, Ireland*

REBORN (IRE) 3 b.f. Idris (IRE) 118 – Tantum Ergo 106 (Tanfirion 110) [2001 7g **48** 10g 7g 7g 7m 8d³ 8g Nov 7] IR 20,000Y: leggy filly: fourth living foal: half-sister to Irish 6f winner (stays 1½m) Sacrementum (by Night Shift): dam Irish 2-y-o 6f/7f (C. L. Weld Park Stakes) winner: poor maiden: left T. Keddy after fifth start: should stay beyond 1m. *E. J. O'Neill*

RECEIVED WISDOM (USA) 3 b.c. Gone West (USA) – Sleep Easy (USA) 116 **54 +** (Seattle Slew (USA)) [2001 8g⁶ f8.5f² Dec 5] 10,500 3-y-o: first foal: dam, US Grade 1 9f winner, closely related to high-class Grade 1 1¼m winner Aptitude: probably flattered when sixth of 8 in minor event at Milan in October, then (modest form) 5 lengths second in maiden at Wolverhampton: likely to be suited by 7f. *Edward Butler, Ireland*

RECEIVEDWITHTHANX (IRE) 2 b.c. (Apr 16) Celtic Swing 138 – Sabrata **86** (IRE) (Zino 127) [2001 5s 7g* 7.5f* 7m 6m Sep 12] 19,000Y: rather leggy, close-coupled colt: third foal: half-brother to 3-y-o Head Scratcher: dam French 2-y-o 4.5f winner: fairly useful performer: won maiden at Thirsk in June and minor event at Beverley (made all, beat Corundum by 3½ lengths) in July: well held in Vintage Stakes at Goodwood and sales race at Doncaster last 2 starts: will probably stay 1¼m: acts on firm ground. *A. Dickman*

RECIPROCAL (IRE) 3 gr.f. Night Shift (USA) – African Light 65§ (Kalaglow 132) **88** [2001 65: 9.9d⁵ 10m³ 10m 9m* 9f* 8m³ 9m 8m⁶ 10g 8.5g⁶ Sep 15] tall filly: has scope: fairly useful handicapper: won at Kempton in June and July: below form last 4 starts (visored, said to have had a breathing problem final one): stays 1¼m: acts on soft and firm going: front runner. *D. R. C. Elsworth*

RECOLETA 4 b.f. Ezzoud (IRE) 126 – Hug Me 96 (Shareef Dancer (USA) 135) **–** [2001 –: f16g Apr 9] no form: tried blinkered/visored. *Miss H. M. Irving*

REDBACK 2 ch.c. (Apr 7) Mark of Esteem (IRE) 137 – Patsy Western 81 (Precocious **107 +** 126) [2001 5d² 5g² 5g* 6m⁴ 6g⁴ 7m* 7m 7.1g* 7g⁴ 8v³ Oct 27] 40,000Y: close-coupled colt: half-brother to several winners, including 7-y-o Granny's Pet and fairly useful 1¾m winner Way Out Yonder (by Shirley Heights): dam twice-raced 6f winner: useful performer: won minor event at Windsor in May, listed race at Newmarket in July and Ford Solario Stakes at Sandown (had run of race in beating Tholjanah by 4 lengths, could be rated much higher on bare form) in September: fourth in Coventry Stakes at Royal Ascot, Railway Stakes at the Curragh and Somerville Tattersall Stakes at Newmarket, and 5¾ lengths third (ridden with more restraint than usual) to High Chaparral in Racing Post Trophy at Doncaster: stays 1m: acts on good to firm and heavy going: often makes running: consistent. *R. Hannon*

RED BRIAR (IRE) 2 b.c. (Mar 30) Desert King (IRE) 129 – Rose Society (Caerleon **100** (USA) 132) [2001 5.1f³ 5d* 6d* 7d* 8g Nov 24] IR 40,000Y: quite attractive colt: fifth foal: half-brother to 3 winners, including 1m/1¼m winner Silverani (by High Estate), later winner in USA: dam Irish maiden who stayed 1½m: useful performer: won maiden at Hamilton in June, 4-runner minor event at Doncaster in July and 4-runner listed race at Deauville (made all, beat Sky Quest by short head) in August: reportedly sold privately out of M. Bell's stable: well held in Grade 3 at Hollywood final outing: should stay 1m: acts on good to soft going. *Jenine Sahadi, USA*

RED CAFE (IRE) 5 ch.m. Perugino (USA) 84 – Test Case 90 (Busted 134) [2001 **61** 65: f11g⁴ f11g³ f12g⁵ f12g Feb 13] leggy mare: modest performer: left P. D. Evans after penultimate start: stays 1½m: acts on heavy, good to firm going and fibresand: tried blinkered/visored: sometimes looks none too keen/hangs left: usually held up. *P. Howling*

RED CANYON (IRE) 4 b.g. Zieten (USA) 118 – Bayazida (Bustino 136) [2001 68: **–** 14.1d Aug 8] fair handicapper in 2000: well held only run of 2001. *B. I. Case*

RED CARNATION (IRE) 3 b.f. Polar Falcon (USA) 126 – Red Bouquet (Refer- **103** ence Point 139) [2001 82: 7m⁵ 6.9m⁵ 8g* 8.1g² 10.5v* 12s⁴ 10.5v⁴ Dec 1] quite attractive filly: useful performer: won handicaps at Newmarket in August and Haydock in September: fourth after in November Handicap at Doncaster (¾ length behind Royal Cavalier) and listed race at Saint-Cloud (best effort, beaten 1¾ lengths by Bedford Forrest): stays 1½m: acts on heavy ground: has been slowly away. *M. A. Jarvis*

RED CARPET 3 ch.c. Pivotal 124 – Fleur Rouge 71 (Pharly (FR) 130) [2001 112: 8d² **113** 8g⁵ May 5] tall, close-coupled colt: has scope: good mover: smart performer: good efforts at Newmarket both starts in 2001, runner-up to King's Ironbridge (took very strong hold, beaten a head) in Craven Stakes prior to 4½ lengths fifth to Golan in 2000 Guineas, leading until over 1f out in latter: reportedly suffered from lameness after: will prove at least as effective back at 6f/7f as 1m: acts on firm and good to soft ground. *M. L. W. Bell*

RED CHARGER (IRE)   5 ch.g. Up And At 'em 109 – Smashing Pet (Mummy's Pet 125) [2001 53: 6v 5v⁶ Oct 24] tall, leggy gelding: modest handicapper: best at 5f/6f: acts on any going: blinkered once: has been slowly away. *D. Nicholls*   **56 +**

RED CHERRY   4 ch.f. Never So Bold 135 – Romany Home (Gabitat 119) [2001 8v 9d 11.1d 8m 6g 9.1m 12m 9.1v Oct 16] strong, lengthy filly: half-sister to 5f winner Ballantrae Boy (by Safawan) and winner in Greece by Local Suitor: dam unraced: well held, including in seller. *J. S. Goldie*   **–**

RED CHINA   2 ch.c. (Apr 19) Inchinor 119 – Little Tramp (Trempolino (USA) 135) [2001 6m 6g 6d³ 5m⁵ 5g³ 5.1g⁵ 5.7g f6g 5.2s³ p5g³ Nov 13] 22,000Y: first foal: dam unraced daughter of smart 6f (at 2 yrs) and 1m winner Chipaya: fair maiden: likely to prove best at 5f/6f: acts on polytrack, good to firm and soft ground, below form on fibresand. *M. Blanshard*   **69**

Ford Solario Stakes, Sandown—Redback strides away from several useful performers, including Tholjanah (striped cap), Asheer (noseband), Where Or When and Doc Holiday (rail)

RED CONQUEST 3 ch.f. Lycius (USA) 124 – Crimson Conquest (USA) 85 (Diesis **55 d**
133) [2001 10s 10g 10m 10m 8f 7m² 8m 8d 8g f9.4g Nov 21] close-coupled, good-topped
filly: sixth foal: sister to 8.5f winner Crimson Glory, closely related to very smart 6f (at 2
yrs) to 1¼m winner Crimplene (by Lion Cavern) and half-sister to 2 winners up to 1m:
dam 2-y-o 6f winner who stayed 1¼m: modest maiden: well held last 3 starts: probably
stayed 1¼m: acted on good to firm ground: blinkered/visored last 6 starts: sometimes
raced freely: visits Agnes World. *C. E. Brittain*

RED CRYSTAL 3 b.f. Presidium 124 – Crystallography (Primitive Rising (USA) –
113) [2001 –: f8g Jan 12] leggy, plain filly: no form in 3 maidens. *J. Norton*

RED DELIRIUM 5 b.g. Robellino (USA) 127 – Made of Pearl (USA) 107 (Nureyev –
(USA) 131) [2001 72: f7g² f7s³ f6s⁶ f7g f8g³ f8g² 8.1g 8.1m 11.6g 7.1g f8.5g f8g f8.5g **a71**
f7g⁴ f8.5g f7g* p7g f8s³ f8.5s⁶ Dec 26] small, sturdy, close-coupled gelding: fair
performer: dead-heated in seller at Southwell in December: effective at 7f/1m: acts on
firm going, good to soft and fibresand: effective blinkered/visored or not: has worn
tongue strap: bled from nose ninth start. *R. Brotherton*

REDDENING 3 b.f. Blushing Flame (USA) 109 – Music In My Life (IRE) 59 (Law **82**
Society (USA) 130) [2001 10g 16m* 14.8m⁴ Jul 29] 8,000F: fifth foal: half-sister to
several winners, including useful 1999 2-y-o 1m winner (stays 1¼m) Galleon Beach (by
Shirley Heights) and fairly useful 1997 2-y-o 6f winner Premium Pursuit (by Pursuit
of Love): dam, maiden who stayed 1m, out of half-sister to 4-y-o Bach: fairly useful form:
won maiden at Southwell in July by 5 lengths: creditable fourth in handicap at
Newmarket only subsequent run: will prove best up to 2m. *J. R. Fanshawe*

RED DIAMOND 2 b.g. (Feb 18) Mind Games 121 – Sandicroft Jewel (Grey Desire **61**
115) [2001 5g 6s³ 7d⁵ Nov 6] 2,600Y: leggy gelding: second foal: dam unraced: modest
maiden: third at Pontefract: stays 7f. *A. Berry*

RED EAGLE (IRE) 2 b.f. (Feb 7) Eagle Eyed (USA) 111 – Dawn's Folly (IRE) 47 **61**
(Bluebird (USA) 125) [2001 5d* 5g⁵ f5g³ 5m⁶ f5g⁴ f5g* 5d⁶ f5g³ 5g³ f5g² f5g⁴ f5f⁶
Dec 5] 3,800Y: smallish, leggy filly: first foal: dam Irish maiden (probably stayed 7f)
out of half-sister to high-class miler Be My Guest: modest performer: won maiden at
Musselburgh in April and seller at Southwell in July: will prove best at 5f: acts on good to
soft ground and fibresand: often forces pace. *A. Berry*

RED FANFARE 3 ch.f. First Trump 118 – Corman-Style 52 (Ahonoora (122) [2001 –
61, a45: f8.5s f8s f6g f12g f11g 7m f6g 6d Jun 17] small filly: modest maiden at 2 yrs:
little form in 2001, leaving N. Tinkler after second start. *S. R. Bowring*

RED FLYER (IRE) 2 br.g. (Feb 28) Catrail (USA) 123 – Marostica (ITY) (Stone **67**
124) [2001 7s⁶ 7d⁴ f6g f7g⁵ Dec 10] sturdy gelding: half-brother to several winners in
Italy up to 1½m: dam Italian 7.5f to 8.5f winner: fair maiden: best effort when fourth in
minor event at Redcar: will probably stay 1m: slowly away first 3 starts. *P. C. Haslam*

RED FOREST (IRE) 2 b.c. (Feb 8) Charnwood Forest (IRE) 125 – High Atlas 65 **80**
(Shirley Heights 130) [2001 6s³ f6g² 7.1g² f7g* Nov 17] 10,000Y: second foal: dam,
ran once (twice withdrawn after giving trouble at stalls), out of half-sister to high-class
performer up to 1½m Sanglamore: fairly useful performer: won maiden at Wolverhampton by 5 lengths from Primo Dawn: has pulled hard, but should stay 1m: acts on
fibresand. *B. W. Hills*

RED HALO 2 b.c. (Jan 16) Be My Guest (USA) 126 – Pray (IRE) (Priolo (USA) 127) **75 p**
[2001 7m³ 8m⁵ Sep 6] IR 100,000Y: first foal: dam unraced half-sister to smart performer
up to 9f in Britain/USA Anshan: fair form when third in maiden at Kempton and last in
minor event at Salisbury: should stay 1¼m: probably capable of better. *R. Hannon*

REDHILL 4 b.f. Tragic Role (USA) – Indivisible 56 (Remainder Man 126§) [2001 –: –
f12g f14.8g Feb 3] rather leggy, unfurnished filly: little form. *R. Hollinshead*

REDISHAM 2 ch.f. (Feb 8) Hector Protector (USA) 124 – Barsham 94 (Be My Guest **73**
(USA) 126) [2001 7d² 8d p8g³ p10g² p8g³ f8s* Dec 21] 26,000Y: useful-looking filly:
half-sister to several winners, including useful 1996 2-y-o 6f to 1m winner Falkenham
(by Polar Falcon), later 9f winner in USA, and fairly useful 1¼m winner Jameel Asmar
(by Rock City): dam 1¼m winner: fair performer: claimed from W. Haggas £10,000 after
second in Newmarket seller on debut: won maiden at Southwell: should stay 1½m: acts
on polytrack, fibresand and good to soft ground. *J. R. Best*

RED LIASON (IRE) 2 ch.f. (Mar 30) Selkirk (USA) 129 – Red Affair (IRE) 95 **95 p**
(Generous (IRE) 139) [2001 6m³ 6.1m³ 6.1m* 7s² 6d* Nov 2] big, useful-looking filly:
has plenty of scope: first foal: dam, Irish 1¼m winner, half-sister to 8-y-o Brilliant Red

out of sister to Rainbow Quest: useful form: won maiden at Nottingham in July and minor event at Newmarket (ridden more prominently than previously, beat Donegal Shore by a neck) in November: effective at 6f/7f: acts on soft and good to firm going: capable of better. *J. L. Dunlop*

RED LION   5 ch.g. Lion Cavern (USA) 117 – Fleur Rouge 71 (Pharly (FR) 130) [2001   **69** 87d: 6m 7m 7g 6m Sep 6] useful-looking gelding: fair handicapper: left J. Payne after third start: stays 7f: unproven on firm going, acts on any other: blinkered twice: usually held up. *S. Gollings*

RED LION (FR)   4 ch.g. Lion Cavern (USA) 117 – Mahogany River (Irish River (FR)   **73** 131) [2001 74: 12.3m 16m⁴ 16.1g⁴ Aug 10] big, rather angular gelding: fair maiden handicapper: probably stays 2m: acts on good to firm and good to soft going: has pulled hard. *B. J. Meehan*

RED MAGIC (FR)   3 b. or br.c. Grand Lodge (USA) 125 – Ma Priere (FR) (Highest   **?** Honor (FR) 124) [2001 97: 7m 11f 10f 8.5f³ Nov 21] big, strong, close-coupled colt: useful form at 2 yrs: well beaten in Jersey Stakes at Royal Ascot, then left R. Hannon: best effort in 3 starts for new stable when third in claimer at Aqueduct final outing: probably stays 8.5f. *C. Clement, USA*

RED MAIL (USA)   3 b.g. Red Ransom (USA) – Seattle Byline (USA) (Slew City   **43** Slew (USA)) [2001 f11g³ 16m² 12m 16m 16.4g Aug 23] $54,000Y: first foal: dam 6f to 8.5f winner in USA: poor maiden: left M. Bell after second start: well held in handicaps last 2 starts. *T. D. McCarthy*

RED MILLENNIUM (IRE)   3 b.f. Tagula (IRE) 116 – Lovely Me (IRE) 70 (Vision   **102** (USA)) [2001 99: 5.1s⁶ 5.1d* 5f 5f 5g 5.1m⁵ 5m⁵ 5g⁴ 5.2f Sep 22] quite attractive, good-quartered filly: useful performer: made all in listed event at Bath (beat Ivory's Joy by ¾ length) in May: seemed to run well when 2¼ lengths fifth to Dietrich in King George Stakes at Goodwood and when close fourth to Jessica's Dream in handicap at York seventh/eighth starts: raced only at 5f: acts on firm and soft going: races prominently. *A. Berry*

RED MITTENS   4 ch.f. Wolfhound (USA) 126 – Red Gloves 83 (Red God 128§)   **–** [2001 43: 7m 7m 10f 8m 6g 8f 9m³ 8m 9.9m 7d 6g f8.5g⁶ Nov 17] of little account nowadays. *R. E. Barr*

RED N' SOCKS (USA)   4 ch.c. Devil's Bag (USA) – Racing Blue (Reference Point   **101** 139) [2001 98: 7d 7.6m* 8m 8f² 8m 7.6d² 7f 8g² 7g 8d a7.5g⁴ Dec 9] big, useful-looking colt: useful performer: won minor event at Lingfield in May: ran well after when second, beaten 1¼ lengths by Calcutta in handicap at Doncaster eighth start: left J. Dunlop before final outing: best at 7f/1m on good going or firmer: waited with, and sometimes races freely. *P. Lautner, Germany*

RED OCARINA   3 ch.f. Piccolo 121 – Morica 88 (Moorestyle 137) [2001 –: 6s 8m   **–** Jul 27] leggy, sparely-made filly: no form, including in sellers. *R. N. Bevis*

RED OPAL (IRE)   2 b.f. (Mar 18) Flying Spur (AUS) – Tamaya (IRE) (Darshaan   **81** 133) [2001 5f³ 5m 6m² 7m³ 6m 5.7g⁵ 6g Oct 6] IR 13,500F, 500,000 francs Y: rather leggy, good-topped filly: fifth foal: half-sister to useful 11f winner Tamitas (by Lomitas) and 6f/7f winner Tamarez (by Saumarez), both in Germany: dam French maiden: fairly useful maiden: creditable eighth of 25 in Two-Year-Old Trophy at Redcar final start: free-going sort, likely to prove best up to 7f: raced only on good going or firmer. *R. Hannon*

RED OSCAR   2 b.c. (Apr 6) Atraf 116 – Late Matinee 84 (Red Sunset 120) [2001 6g   **64 §** 6m 7m² 7m⁴ f7g 7g 7s³ 7d 8s 8.2s⁵ 8.3v Nov 8] 3,800Y: lengthy colt: seventh foal: half-brother to 5-y-o Stitch In Time: dam 2-y-o 6f winner: modest maiden: below form last 4 starts, looking ungenuine in blinkers on final one: stays 7f: acts on soft and good to firm going: sold 900 gns. *S. Kirk*

REDOUBLE   5 b.g. First Trump 118 – Sunflower Seed 70 (Mummy's Pet 125) [2001   **65** 67, a–: f12g⁵ 11.9s⁴ 12m* 14.1m⁶ 12.6d⁴ 12m³ 12.1m³ 12.3d⁴ 12g 12g Sep 28] good-   **a–** topped gelding: fair handicapper: dead-heated in amateur event at Salisbury in June: stays 1¾m: yet to race on heavy going, acts on any other turf. *B. R. Millman*

REDOUBTABLE (USA)   10 b.h. Grey Dawn II 132 – Seattle Rockette (USA)   **66 §** (Seattle Slew (USA)) [2001 85, a88: e6g* e7g f7s e7g f6g f6g* f6g* e8g² f7g f6g 6m 7m   **a78 §** 8.3d² 6g 6m 7d* 7m 6g 7m f8g p6g f7g Dec 8] small, sturdy horse: fair performer: won minor events at Lingfield, Wolverhampton and Southwell between January/March, and handicap at Newcastle in August: effective at 6f to easy 1m: acts on any turf going and fibresand/equitrack: no show in blinkers: unreliable. *D. W. Chapman*

RED RAMONA 6 b.g. Rudimentary (USA) 118 – Apply 87 (Kings Lake (USA) 133) **86 §**
[2001 –§: 14g⁴ 14.8m³ 14s 16.2s³ 16.5s Nov 10] lengthy, quite attractive gelding: fairly useful handicapper: probably best at 1¾m/2m nowadays: yet to race on heavy going, acts on any other: blinkered (raced freely) final start: withdrawn from Cesarewitch after proving most reluctant to post: has looked less than keen, and not one to rely on. *J. Akehurst*

RED REVOLUTION (USA) 4 ch.g. Explosive Red (CAN) 119 – Braided Way **–**
(USA) (Mining (USA)) [2001 80: 5m 5m Jun 17] strong, lengthy gelding: fairly useful in 2000: well beaten in 2001 (tongue tied first start). *B. Mactaggart*

RED RIOJA (IRE) 2 b.f. (Mar 1) King's Theatre (IRE) 128 – Foreign Relation (IRE) **98**
57 (Distant Relative 128) [2001 6f⁴ 7m* 7s* 7d⁴ Oct 20] second foal: dam, maiden, out of half-sister to dam of very smart 7f/1m performer Brocade, herself dam of Barathea and 2-y-o Gossamer: useful form: won maiden at Kempton in September and C. L. Weld Park Stakes at the Curragh (beat Lady Digby by ¾ length) in October: creditable fourth to Distant Valley, beaten about 4 lengths, in Rockfel Stakes at Newmarket final start, though never travelling well: will stay at least 1m: acts on soft and good to firm going. *E. J. O'Neill*

RED RIVER REBEL 3 b.g. Inchinor 119 – Bidweaya (USA) 45 (Lear Fan (USA) **74**
130) [2001 56: 8m 10.1m⁵ 10g³ f12g⁵ 10m 10g 12.4g* 12.4m* 12g* 14.1g³ 14.1g⁵ Oct 19] tall, leggy gelding: fair handicapper: won at Newcastle (2) and Beverley in August/ September: barely stays 1¾m: acts on good to firm and good to soft going (no show only start on fibresand). *J. R. Norton*

RED ROONEY 2 b.g. (Mar 26) Astronef 116 – Mica Male (ITY) (Law Society (USA) **55 d**
130) [2001 5d⁶ 6g 6m⁴ 7d 6g 6s Oct 5] 1,600Y: strong gelding: second foal: half-brother to a winner in Italy by Dancing Dissident: modest form on debut: well held after, including in seller. *P. Butler*

RED ROSES (IRE) 5 b.m. Mukaddamah (USA) 125 – Roses Red (IRE) 64 (Exhibi- **–**
tioner 111) [2001 30: f11g f11g 11.9g Jun 7] of little account nowadays. *Don Enrico Incisa*

RED ROSIE (USA) 3 b.f. Red Ransom (USA) – Do's Gent (CAN) (Vice Regent **81**
(CAN)) [2001 66p: 10.2m* 9.9m³ 12m Jul 29] medium-sized, workmanlike filly: fairly useful performer: won maiden at Bath in June: stays 1¼m: acts on good to firm ground: sometimes makes running. *Mrs A. J. Perrett*

RED ROULETTE (IRE) 2 ch.f. (Jan 24) Tagula (IRE) 116 – Mini Project (IRE) 94 **44**
(Project Manager 111) [2001 5s⁴ 6g 6m³ 8m f7g Oct 22] 4,200Y: close-coupled filly: poor mover: second foal: dam lightly-raced 1994 Irish 2-y-o 6f winner who stayed 11f: poor maiden: ran as if something amiss last 2 starts: should stay 1m. *A. Berry*

RED RYDING HOOD 3 ch.f. Wolfhound (USA) 126 – Downeaster Alexa (USA) **83**
(Red Ryder (USA)) [2001 79: f5g* e5g⁴ f6g³ 6g⁵ 6s 5.3m 5m* 5f⁵ 5m⁶ 6f 6g 5m² 5g⁶ 5g 5g⁶ 5m⁵ 6.1m⁵ Sep 10] big, lengthy filly: fairly useful performer: won maiden at South-well in March and handicap at Folkestone in June: best at 5f: acts on fibresand, equitrack, good to firm and good to soft going: tried visored/blinkered: sometimes sweating and edgy. *C. A. Dwyer*

RED SATIN (IRE) 2 b.c. (Feb 26) Mujadil (USA) 119 – Satinette 109 (Shirley Heights **–**
130) [2001 7.1v 6d 6v Oct 26] IR 16,000Y: strong, lengthy colt: half-brother to several winners, including 1988 2-y-o 1m winner (later placed in USA) Code Satin (by Secreto): dam 7f/1m winner at 2 yrs: well held in maidens. *B. A. McMahon*

RED SEPTEMBER 4 b.g. Presidium 124 – Tangalooma 56 (Hotfoot 126) [2001 –: **44**
12.4d³ 16m⁴ 15.8g Aug 17] tall, leggy gelding: poor maiden handicapper: stays 2m: acts on good to soft and good to firm ground: tried blinkered. *G. M. Moore*

RED STORM 2 ch.f. (May 21) Dancing Spree (USA) – Dam Certain (IRE) 61 **60**
(Damister (USA) 123) [2001 6m 5f 6v 6v⁵ 6d Nov 2] third living foal: half-sister to a winner in Italy by Chaddleworth: dam, 7f to 9f winner, from family of Shaamit: modest maiden: below form last 2 starts: should stay 7f. *R. Ingram*

RED SUN 4 b.g. Foxhound (USA) 103 – Superetta 65 (Superlative 118) [2001 f11g² **–**
f14g* f14g³ f16g 15.9d Sep 26] modest handicapper: won at Southwell in May: should **a60**
stay 2m: acts on fibresand. *A. Streeter*

RED SUNRISE   2 gr.f. (Apr 14) Beveled (USA) – Sun In The Morning 61 (Petardia **43**
113) [2001 f5g² f5g⁴ e5g⁴ 5.1s⁴ 5m May 12] 2,000Y: leggy filly: second foal: dam 2-y-o
5f winner: poor maiden. *A. Berry*

REDSWAN   6 ch.g. Risk Me (FR) 127 – Bocas Rose 106 (Jalmood (USA) 126) [2001 **72 §**
74§: 7s 8.3d 7m³ 6g 8d³ 8m Sep 26] big, workmanlike gelding: fair handicapper: best at
7f/1m: acts on firm going, good to soft and fibresand: sometimes blinkered/tongue tied
(not in 2001): held up: often races freely/finds little: bled from nose several occasions in
2001: unreliable. *A. W. Carroll*

RED SYMPHONY   5 b.m. Merdon Melody 98 – Woodland Steps 86 (Bold Owl 101)   **– §**
[2001 53§: f5g f6s⁶ Jan 22] modest performer at 4 yrs, though unreliable: well beaten in
2001: usually visored/blinkered. *M. J. Polglase*

RED TAPE   2 ch.g. (May 4) Danzig Connection (USA) – Jolizal 52 (Good Times   **–**
(ITY)) [2001 5g Sep 19] good-bodied gelding: fourth foal: half-brother to 5-y-o The
Last Word: dam 1m winner: 20/1 and burly, slowly away and well behind in maiden at
Beverley: sold 2,000 gns. *R. Hollinshead*

RED THATCH   4 ch.g. Pelder (IRE) 125 – Straw Castle (Final Straw 127) [2001 –: f12s **41**
f8g⁶ 6.9v⁶ 6d⁴ 7m⁵ 6.9m⁴ 7f⁶ 8.1m 5.7g 5m⁴ Aug 13] poor maiden: left M. Muggeridge
after first start: stayed 7f: acted on firm and good to soft going: tried tongue tied: dead.
A. P. Jones

RED TO VIOLET   2 b.f. (Mar 3) Spectrum (IRE) 126 – Khalsheva 55 (Shirley **77 p**
Heights 130) [2001 7s 6.1v⁵ 6s* Oct 22] 10,000Y: good-topped filly: has scope: second
foal: half-sister to fairly useful Irish 1m winner Moyeala (by Royal Academy): dam
lightly-raced maiden who should have been suited by test of stamina: best effort (fair
form) when winning maiden at Pontefract by 2½ lengths from Tomillie, asserting from
over 1f out despite flashing tail: will stay 1m: should do better. *J. A. Glover*

RED TOWER   6 b.g. Damister (USA) 123 – Tower of Ivory (IRE) (Cyrano de   **–**
Bergerac 120) [2001 7m Sep 4] of little account nowadays. *L. Wells*

REDUIT   3 ch.c. Lion Cavern (USA) 117 – Soolaimon (IRE) 71 (Shareef Dancer **106**
(USA) 135) [2001 106p: 10g⁶ 11m⁴ 9f 8f⁴ 9f² 10f* 9f² 9f⁴ Dec 16] tall, unfurnished colt:
useful performer: creditable staying-on 5 lengths fourth to Asian Heights in listed race at
Goodwood in May, final outing for G. Butler: won allowance race at Belmont in October:
stays 11f: acts on soft and good to firm going. *T. J. Skiffington, USA*

RED VELVET   3 ch.f. So Factual (USA) 120 – Amber Fizz (USA) (Effervescing   **–**
(USA)) [2001 7d Apr 20] 5,200Y: strong filly: half-sister to several winners, including
smart sprinter Cool Jazz (by Lead On Time) and unreliable 1¼m/1½m winner Ambidextrous (by Shareef Dancer): dam ran once: 25/1, backward and bandaged in front, last of
18 in Newbury maiden. *K. T. Ivory*

RED WHITE AND BLUE   4 b.f. Zafonic (USA) 130 – Malham Tarn (Riverman   **–**
(USA) 131) [2001 –: e7g Jan 13] no sign of ability. *K. O. Cunningham-Brown*

RED WINE   2 b.g. (Apr 23) Hamas (IRE) 125§ – Red Bouquet (Reference Point 139) **75 p**
[2001 f6g⁴ f8g² Nov 30] 17,000Y: second foal: half-brother to 3-y-o Red Carnation: dam,
1½m/13f winner in Germany, half-sister to smart filly up to 1m Red Camellia from family
of Ibn Bey and Roseate Tern: better effort in maidens (fair form) when second to More
Specific at Southwell, making most: likely to prove best up to 1m: capable of further
improvement. *J. A. Osborne*

RED WOOD   3 b.g. Kris 135 – Pearl Venture 92 (Salse (USA) 128) [2001 8.3m 7g   **–**
10.4m Sep 2] first foal: dam 5f (at 2 yrs) to 2m winner: well held in maidens/seller.
A. W. Carroll

REEDS RAINS   3 b.f. Mind Games 121 – Me Spede (Valiyar 129) [2001 72: 7v 6m   **–**
7.1g 7m 9.9f 10m⁶ 8d Aug 8] lightly-made filly: fair at 2 yrs: little form in 2001: blinkered
last 4 starts. *T. D. Easterby*

REEF DIVER   3 b.c. Pursuit of Love 124 – Triple Reef (Mill Reef (USA) 141) [2001 **109**
8g* 8m³ 8g 9f³ 9g p10g² p10g* Dec 12] useful-looking colt: impresses in appearance:
half-brother to several winners, including smart 1¼m/1½m performer Talented (by
Bustino), useful 6f/7f winner Triple Joy (by Most Welcome) and useful stayer Trifolio
(by Touching Wood): dam unraced from very good family: useful performer: won maiden
at Newmarket in May and minor event at Lingfield in December: good placed in listed
races at Kempton (2 lengths third to Dandoun) on second start and Lingfield (neck second
to Compton Bolter) on sixth: stays 1¼m: acts on polytrack, raced only on good ground or
firmer on turf: joined B. Cecil in USA. *Mrs A. J. Perrett*

REEFS SIS   2 ch.f. (May 16) Muhtarram (USA) 125 – Horseshoe Reef 88 (Mill Reef   **91**
(USA) 141) [2001 5.1f⁵ 5m 6m* 6g⁵ 7m² 8.1g³ 6m² 8s 6d³ Nov 2] 3,000 2-y-o: smallish,
quite attractive filly: half-sister to several winners, including 8-y-o Warning Reef and 1m
winner who probably stayed 1¾m Pumice (by Salse): dam, 1¼m winner, half-sister to
dam of Derby/Irish Derby second City Honours: fairly useful performer: won maiden at
Hamilton in June: good efforts after when placed, finishing well when third to Red Liason
in minor event at Newmarket final start: effective at 6f to 1m: acts on good to firm and
good to soft ground. *E. J. Alston*

REEL BUDDY (USA)   3 ch.c. Mr Greeley (USA) 122 – Rosebud 80 (Indian Ridge   **113**
123) [2001 97: 7d³ 7g* 7m* 7m³ 7m 7m² 7g⁵ 7.3f⁶ 7.3f⁶ Sep 21] tall, strong, close-
coupled colt: smart performer: won handicaps at Newmarket and Goodwood (beat
Baccura by 1¼ lengths) in May: placed in listed event and Criterion Stakes (strong-
finishing 1¼ lengths second to Shibboleth), both at Newmarket in June, would have gone
close with better run when fifth to Fath in Lennox Stakes at Goodwood seventh start, and
not suited by run of race last 2 starts: stays 7f: acts on good to firm and good to soft going:
has turn of foot and waited with: rather headstrong and best in well-run race. *R. Hannon*

REFA'AH (IRE)   2 b.f. (Jan 26) Lahib (USA) 129 – Shurooq (USA) 94 (Affirmed   **79**
(USA)) [2001 6.1m 7g⁴ Oct 4] rather unfurnished filly: sister to 1m winner Ghaazi and
half-sister to several winners, including useful 1¼m (including in UAE) winner who
stayed 1½m Ijlal (by Unfuwain) and fairly useful sprinter Maraatib (by Green Desert):
dam 2-y-o 6f/7f winner who stayed 1½m: much better effort in maidens (fair form)
when fourth to Millennium Dragon at Newmarket, never far away: should stay 1m.
E. A. L. Dunlop

REFERENDUM (IRE)   7 b.g. Common Grounds 118 – Final Decision (Tap On   **74 d**
Wood 130) [2001 81: e5g⁶ f6g 5s 5v 5v⁴ 6g² 5d* 5m 5m 6m 5f 5m 6m 6g* 7g 5m 6g³
6d 5g 5m 5s Sep 27] good-topped gelding: has a fluent, round action: fair handicapper:
won at Hamilton in May (apprentices) and July (amateurs): mostly below form after: best
at 5f/6f: acts on firm going, good to soft and equitrack: tried blinkered earlier in career:
sometimes on toes/slowly away: inconsistent. *D. Nicholls*

REFLEX BLUE   4 b.g. Ezzoud (IRE) 126 – Briggsmaid 70 (Elegant Air 119) [2001   **76**
83: 12g 12v 14.4m* 16.2f 14m⁴ 14m⁶ 13.1m⁴ p12g Nov 28] lengthy, angular gelding: fair
handicapper: won at Kempton in June: probably best at 1½m/1¾m: acts on firm and good
to soft going, well held only outing on polytrack: sometimes blinkered: none too reliable.
J. W. Hills

REFRACT   3 b.g. Spectrum (IRE) 126 – Sofala 103 (Home Guard (USA) 129) [2001   **–**
67p: p6g f6s Dec 15] angular gelding: fair form in maiden, only 2-y-o outing: off over a
year before well held in similar events in 2001. *D. E. Cantillon*

REGAL AIR (IRE)   3 b.f. Distinctly North (USA) 115 – Dignified Air (FR) 70   **60 §**
(Wolver Hollow 126) [2001 68, a56: f6g f5g 7m 5m 5.1g 5g 6.1s² 6g 5.3m 6.1f 7s f6g⁴ 6d   **a– §**
Nov 2] neat filly: modest maiden handicapper: below form last 6 starts: best at 5f/6f: acts
on good to firm going, soft and fibresand: blinkered/visored nowadays: has been slowly
away: carries head awkwardly: unreliable. *B. I. Case*

REGAL ALI (IRE)   2 ch.g. (May 22) Ali-Royal (IRE) 127 – Depeche (FR) (Kings   **–**
Lake (USA) 133) [2001 5s 5m 7.5f⁶ 6m Sep 6] IR 7,000F, IR 9,000Y: smallish, close-
coupled gelding: sixth foal: half-brother to 3 winners abroad, including fairly useful 9.5f
(in UAE)/1¼m winner Sharh (by Elmaamul): dam, French maiden, from family of
Daylami: well beaten in maidens/sellers: blinkered final start. *J. S. Wainwright*

REGAL APPLAUSE   2 b.f. (Mar 5) Royal Applause 124 – Panchellita (USA) 78   **–**
(Pancho Villa (USA)) [2001 7g 6g 6v Nov 8] leggy, rather unfurnished filly: third foal:
half-sister to 4-y-o Colne Valley Amy: dam 6f (at 2 yrs)/7f winner: well held in maidens.
G. L. Moore

REGAL DARCEY (IRE)   3 b.f. Darshaan 133 – Royal Ballet (IRE) (Sadler's Wells   **–**
(USA) 132) [2001 10s 12f Jul 5] fourth foal: sister to smart 1½m winner Talaash and
half-sister to 6-y-o Battle Warning: dam twice-raced sister to high-class winner up to
1½m King's Theatre and half-sister to high-class 1988 2-y-o High Estate: little form in
maidens at Sandown and Newbury. *H. Candy*

REGAL GALLERY (IRE)   3 b.f. Royal Academy (USA) 130 – Polistatic 53 (Free   **–**
State 125) [2001 8m Aug 30] fifth foal: dam, 11f and 1½m winner, sister to Ebor
winner Western Dancer: 25/1, never a threat when eighth of 10 in maiden at Salisbury.
C. A. Horgan

REGAL MISTRESS 3 b.f. Tragic Role (USA) – Regal Salute 68 (Dara Monarch 128) [2001 –: e7g f8g Jan 8] workmanlike filly: little form: has been slowly away: blinkered in 2001. *D. Shaw* —

REGAL SONG (IRE) 5 b.g. Anita's Prince 126 – Song Beam 84 (Song 132) [2001 78§, a63§: 5s 5v* 5s* 6s 5g² 5m 5m 5m f5g⁶ 5.1d 5s⁵ 5m 5v 5d⁴ 5s² 5s³ 5v* 5s Nov 9] useful-looking gelding: fairly useful handicapper: won at Musselburgh in March/April and at Windsor in October: best at 5f/6f: acts on fibresand, probably on good to firm going but revels on soft/heavy: usually blinkered: often races prominently: weak finisher: inconsistent. *T. J. Etherington* — **93 §** **a– §**

REGAL SPLENDOUR (CAN) 8 ch.g. Vice Regent (CAN) – Seattle Princess (USA) (Seattle Slew (USA)) [2001 –§: f12g f8.5g Mar 15] good-topped gelding: temperamental handicapper. *J. W. Mullins* — **– §**

REGAL VISION (IRE) 4 b.g. Emperor Jones (USA) 119 – Shining Eyes (USA) (Mr Prospector (USA)) [2001 51: 11.6g 16.2m 18m Jul 7] leggy gelding: poor maiden handicapper: stays 2¼m: acts on soft and good to firm ground. *C. G. Cox* — **46**

REGAL WOOD (IRE) 2 b.f. (Mar 21) Ridgewood Ben 113 – Regal Destiny (IRE) (Silver Kite (USA) 111) [2001 6s 8d 7d⁴ Nov 17] IR 2,200Y: first foal: dam, Irish maiden, half-sister to useful performer up to 1m Nashcash: well held all starts, including in claimer at Lingfield on debut. *Paul Smith, Belgium* —

REGARDEZ-MOI 4 b.f. Distinctly North (USA) 115 – Tomard (Thatching 131) [2001 56d: f9.4s f7s e10g e12s⁶ 6m 5.3f 7m 8.1s Aug 9] sparely-made filly: has lost her way: tried blinkered. *A. W. Carroll* —

REGATTA POINT (IRE) 3 b.c. Goldmark (USA) 113 – Flashing Raven (IRE) (Maelstrom Lake 118) [2001 97p: 10s⁴ 10.4d² 12f⁵ 10g³ 12m 13.9m 12d Oct 18] lengthy, good-topped colt: useful handicapper: ran well in 2001 when placed in handicaps at York (beaten neck by Canada) in June and Newmarket (1¾ lengths third of 5 to Alphaeus) in July: something possibly amiss final outing: should prove at least as effective at 1½m as 1¼m: acts on soft going, probably on firm: game: sold 60,000 gns. *A. P. Jarvis* — **106**

REGENCY RED (IRE) 3 ch.g. Dolphin Street (FR) 125 – Future Romance (Distant Relative 128) [2001 –: f7g e8g 8.2s⁶ f7g 10f² 10g 12f⁵ Jul 2] poor maiden: probably stays 1½m: acts on firm going: has carried head awkwardly. *S. Mellor* — **37**

REGENT COURT (IRE) 3 gr.f. Marju (IRE) 127 – Silver Singing (USA) 96 (Topsider (USA)) [2001 69: 8g* 10.5m³ 10.4d⁶ 10m⁴ Sep 21] sturdy filly: fair performer: won minor event at Ripon in May: creditable efforts in handicaps after when in frame: stays 1¼m: acts on good to firm going, probably on soft: sold 40,000 gns in December. *T. D. Easterby* — **78**

REGGIE BUCK (USA) 7 b. or br.g. Alleged (USA) 138 – Hello Memphis (USA) (Super Concorde (USA) 128) [2001 37: 11.9g 14.1m Jul 28] leggy, sparely-made gelding: no form on Flat in 2001: tried blinkered: fair winning hurdler. *J. Mackie* —

REHEARSAL HALL (USA) 2 ch.c. (Apr 3) Diesis 133 – Performing Arts 104 (The Minstrel (CAN) 135) [2001 6f* 6m 7.1s² 8m⁴ Sep 6] $300,000Y: quite good-topped colt: seventh foal: brother to useful 1997 2-y-o 6f winner Dance Trick and half-brother to smart 1995 2-y-o 6f winner Woodborough (by Woodman) and 5f (at 2 yrs) to 9f (US Grade 2) winner Performing Magic (by Gone West): dam, 2-y-o 5f/6f winner, third in Irish 1000 Guineas: fairly useful performer: justified favouritism in maiden at Leicester in May: met considerable trouble in Coventry Stakes at Royal Ascot next time: creditable efforts in minor events at Sandown (shied away from rail on bend and carried head awkwardly when beaten ½ length by Cala di Volpe) and Salisbury: stays 1m: acts on firm and soft going: joined N. O'Callaghan in USA. *J. H. M. Gosden* — **90**

REIMS (IRE) 3 b.g. Topanoora 118 – Fairy Folk (IRE) 81 (Fairy King (USA)) [2001 70?: 12m 12.3m f12g 16.2m Jul 23] workmanlike gelding: disappointing maiden: blinkered final start. *T. D. Easterby* —

REINE INDIENNE (IRE) 2 b.f. (Apr 30) College Chapel 122 – Mystic Maid (IRE) 62 (Mujtahid (USA) 118) [2001 6g³ 6.1m 6d Oct 12] 3,000Y, 3,200 2-y-o: small filly: first foal: dam, third once at 5f at 2 yrs, out of half-sister to high-class French 1¼m performer Creator: easily best effort in maidens (modest form) when third at Lingfield. *H. Akbary* — **60**

RELATIVE DELIGHT 3 b.f. Distant Relative 128 – Pasja (IRE) (Posen (USA)) [2001 51: f7s⁵ f11g 8.2s 8.1g f8.5g 8g⁶ 12m⁶ f9.4g 10s 8s 10.1s 8.2s⁶ Nov 5] angular —

filly: modest maiden at 2 yrs: little form in 2001: left R. Hollinshead after ninth start. *John A. Harris*

RELISH THE THOUGHT (IRE) 3 b.f. Sadler's Wells (USA) 132 – Viz (USA) **113** (Kris S (USA)) [2001 104p: 10.4m² 12m³ 12g 12m⁵ Aug 5] big, rangy, attractive filly: smart performer: won listed event at Newbury on only run at 2 yrs: good efforts in 2001 when placed in Musidora Stakes at York (1¾ lengths second to Time Away) and Oaks at Epsom (increasingly edgy beforehand, forged ahead 3f out and, despite becoming unbalanced on undulations, kept on gamely to finish 1½ lengths third to Imagine): disappointing after in Irish Oaks at the Curragh (favourite, again got worked up beforehand) and listed race at Newbury: stayed 1½m: acted on heavy and good to firm going: may have had her share of temperament: reportedly retired. *B. W. Hills*

RELLIM 2 b.f. (Mar 5) Rudimentary (USA) 118 – Tycoon Girl (IRE) 74 (Last Tycoon **70** 131) [2001 5m³ 5g 5.7g p5g² f5s² Dec 21] first foal: dam, 2-y-o 6f winner who was best up to 1m, out of half-sister to smart 1½m performer Pencader: fair maiden: second at Lingfield (blinkered) and Southwell (nursery): headstrong, and will prove best at 5f: acts on polytrack/fibresand, best turf run on good to firm going. *B. J. Meehan*

REMAINS OF THE DAY 2 ch.g. (May 5) Prince Sabo 123 – Pussy Foot 83 (Red **51** Sunset 120) [2001 5s 5g 5d⁶ Oct 9] 26,000Y: strong gelding: half-brother to several winners, including 6-y-o Anstand and fairly useful 1995 2-y-o 5f/6f winner Top Cat (by Be My Chief): dam 5f performer: modest maiden: raced only at 5f on good going or softer. *T. D. Barron*

REMARKABLE 3 ch.f. Wolfhound (USA) 126 – Valika 75 (Valiyar 129) [2001 53: **49** 7g 8m 10.1m⁴ 12f⁶ 12m 16.2g Aug 27] workmanlike filly: poor maiden handicapper: not sure to stay 1½m: blinkered last 2 starts: has looked none too keen. *G. Wragg*

REMEDY 2 gr.f. (May 11) Pivotal 124 – Doctor Bid (USA) (Spectacular Bid (USA)) **68** [2001 8.1s 7g 8.3m⁴ 8s* 7s⁴ 8g⁵ Nov 5] eighth foal: half-sister to useful 1¾m/2m winner On Call (by Alleged), fairly useful 5f (at 2 yrs)/6f winner Doctor's Glory (by Elmaamul), and 1996 2-y-o 7.5f winner Lyrical Bid (by Lyphard): dam unraced from family of very smart sprinters Cassandra Go and Do The Honours: fair performer: won nursery at Pontefract in October: creditable efforts when favourite for similar events after: stays 1m: acts on soft ground: blinkered last 3 starts: has been slowly away: difficult ride, and possibly none too genuine. *Sir Mark Prescott*

REMEMBER STAR 8 ch.m. Don't Forget Me 127 – Star Girl Gay (Lord Gayle **36** (USA) 124) [2001 38: f12g² f12g² e13g* f16g⁵ f16.2g⁵ 16.2m Sep 17] poor handicapper: won selling event at Lingfield in February: stays easy 2m: acts on fibresand/equitrack, firm and soft ground: consistent. *A. D. Smith*

REMINISCENT (IRE) 2 b.c. (Mar 24) Kahyasi 130 – Eliza Orzeszkowa (IRE) 69 **72** (Polish Patriot (USA) 128) [2001 7f Aug 18] IR 7,400Y: rather leggy colt: second foal: half-brother to fairly useful 2000 2-y-o 6f winner Miss Domuch (by Definite Article): dam, Irish maiden who stayed 7f, half-sister to smart French sprinter Export Price: 25/1, one-paced seventh of 17 to Flat Spin in maiden at Newbury: should stay at least 1m. *R. F. Johnson Houghton*

RENAISSANCE LADY (IRE) 5 ch.m. Imp Society (USA) – Easter Morning (FR) **65** (Nice Havrais (USA) 124) [2001 65: 16.2m 17.2f 16.4m* 16.2f 16.2f* 15g⁵ 14.8m² 21m³ 16.2m² 16g 16g Nov 7] small, sparely-made mare: fair handicapper: won at Folkestone and Warwick (fourth course success) in June: effective at 1¾m to 21f: best on good ground or firmer: has been early to post and fitted with net muzzle: best form forcing pace: tough and consistent. *D. W. P. Arbuthnot*

RENATA'S PRINCE (IRE) 8 b.g. Prince Rupert (FR) 121 – Maria Renata (Jaazeiro **45** (USA) 127) [2001 9m 9.9m 7m² 8g 10m⁶ 8.1g 10m f12f⁵ f9.4s³ f12s Dec 27] quite **a39** attractive gelding: poor handicapper in 2001: stays easy 1½m: acts on fibresand, good to firm and good to soft ground: blinkered once. *M. D. I. Usher*

RENDITA (IRE) 5 b.m. Waajib 121 – Rend Rover (FR) (Monseigneur (USA) 127) **42** [2001 48: e8g⁴ f9.4s² f8g f9.4g⁶ f7g² f9.4g³ f7g² e8g⁴ f7g² e8g⁴ f7g* f7g² 7m⁴ f7g 7m **a63 d** f8.5g f8.5g f8.5g f8.5s Dec 26] modest performer on all-weather, poor on turf: won seller at Southwell in May: well held last 6 starts: effective at 7f to 9.4f: acts on fibresand/ equitrack and good to firm ground: usually visored, sometimes blinkered: often slowly away. *D. Haydn Jones*

RENDITION 4 b.f. Polish Precedent (USA) 131 – Rensaler (USA) (Stop The Music **77** (USA)) [2001 95: 7.6m³ May 11] good-topped filly: useful performer at 3 yrs: fair form when third in minor event at Lingfield only run in 2001: stays 7.7f: acts on firm going, probably on good to soft: usually waited with. *W. J. Haggas*

RENEE 3 b.f. Wolfhound (USA) 126 – Montserrat 81 (Aragon 118) [2001 55: 7g 6d – Nov 2] modest form in maidens at 2 yrs: no form in 2001. *M. L. W. Bell*

RENE'S GOLD 2 b.f. (Apr 24) Pyramus (USA) 78 – Balatina 85 (Balidar 133) [2001 – 5g⁵ May 8] 4,000Y: half-sister to several winners, including Irish 1993 2-y-o 6f winner Primo Stampari (by Primo Dominie) and 9.7f winner Aragon Court (by Aragon): dam 5f (including at 2 yrs)/6f winner: 33/1, tailed-off last in maiden at Leicester. *G. Brown*

REN'S MAGIC 3 gr.g. Petong 126 – Bath 76 (Runnett 125) [2001 7m 8.3m 6.9m – 10.1s Aug 31] 13,000Y: sixth living foal: brother to useful 5f (at 2 yrs) to 1¼m winner Thai Morning and half-brother to 7.5f (at 2 yrs) and 1½m winner Scarrots (by Mazilier): dam 7f/1m winner: well held in maidens/handicap. *J. R. Jenkins*

RENZO (IRE) 8 b.g. Alzao (USA) 117 – Watership (USA) (Foolish Pleasure (USA)) **78** § [2001 82: 16m 14s* 15.9m Jul 14] strong gelding: has been hobdayed: fair handicapper: won at Sandown in June, only form in 2001: stays 2m: acts on any going: tried blinkered earlier in career: held up: usually carries head high: inconsistent. *John A. Harris*

REPEAT PERFORMANCE (IRE) 3 b.g. Mujadil (USA) 119 – Encore Une Fois **51** (IRE) 84 (Shirley Heights 130) [2001 71d: f12g⁶ 10f⁵ 11.9f⁵ 12f Jul 2] modest maiden: seems to stay 1½m: acts on firm and good to soft going: usually tongue tied. *W. G. M. Turner*

REPENTANT 3 b.g. Beveled (USA) – Tamandu 40 (Petoski 135) [2001 f8g f8.5g Dec – 11] 1,400 3-y-o: first foal: dam, won seller over hurdles, poor maiden on Flat: soundly beaten in maidens. *D. J. Wintle*

REPERTORY 8 b.g. Anshan 119 – Susie's Baby (Balidar 133) [2001 114: 5.2d³ 5m⁵ **117** 5f⁴ 5g* 5.1m 5m⁴ 5g³ 5s⁵ 5s³ 5v* Oct 28] tall, angular gelding: smart performer: won valuable listed race at the Curragh (by head from Ishiguru) in July and Prix du Petit Couvert at Longchamp (for second year running, by 2½ lengths from Dancing Mystery) in October: also creditable efforts when 3½ lengths fourth to Mozart in Nunthorpe Stakes at York sixth start and 5½ lengths fifth to Imperial Beauty in Prix de l'Abbaye at Longchamp (best of those drawn high) eighth outing: trail-blazing front runner, best at 5f: acts on any going. *M. S. Saunders*

REPLACEMENT PET (IRE) 4 b.f. Petardia 113 – Richardstown Lass (IRE) (Mus- **51** catite 122) [2001 44: 8.2f⁴ 8m⁶ 10m 10.9g 8.1m 8.5g 10.2g⁶ 10v³ 10s 8.3v⁴ p10g⁶ Nov 20] modest maiden: left M. Kettle after ninth start: stays 1¼m: acts on fibresand/polytrack and probably any turf going: tried blinkered/visored: has worn tongue strap. *H. S. Howe*

Richard H. Faught Memorial Stakes, the Curragh—
a strong field for the inaugural running of this listed race;
Repertory holds the late challenge of Ishiguru (far side); Proud Native (No.9) is third

REPRIMAND RASCAL 3 b.g. Reprimand 122 – Summer Eve 63 (Hotfoot 126) –
[2001 8g 8d 8d Aug 19] 500Y: half-brother to a winner in Holland by Chilibang: dam
(maiden) best at 6f: well beaten in seller/maidens. *A. B. Mulholland*

REPTON 6 ch.g. Rock City 120 – Hasty Key (USA) (Key To The Mint (USA)) [2001 **49**
39: 12.4d 18m³ 16.2f f16g* 16g* 16g 15.9d⁵ 17.1d⁴ 16s Oct 30] quite good-topped
gelding: poor handicapper: won at Southwell (apprentices) in July and Thirsk in August:
stays 17f: acts on heavy going, good to firm and fibresand: well held in blinkers earlier in
career: often slowly away/rears at stall: reportedly finished lame final outing. *P. T. Dalton*

REPULSE BAY (IRE) 3 b.c. Barathea (IRE) 127 – Bourbon Topsy 108 (Ile de **84 d**
Bourbon (USA) 133) [2001 84: 10s⁴ 8g 8m³ 9m 10g⁵ 8m⁴ 8m 8.3m² 10.1f 10v 12g Nov
7] big, good-topped colt: has a fluent, rather round action: fairly useful maiden at best: on
downgrade after fourth outing, leaving M. Channon following eighth start: stays 1¼m:
acts on soft and good to firm ground: well held in visor seventh appearance: tends to carry
head awkwardly: usually finds little. *J. S. Goldie*

RESCINDO (IRE) 2 b.c. (Mar 20) Revoque (IRE) 122 – Mystic Dispute (IRE) –
(Magical Strike (USA) 114) [2001 8.3g 7v 6s Nov 10] 55,000Y: second foal: half-brother
to fairly useful 2000 2-y-o 7f/1m winner Specific Sorceror (by Definite Article): dam
unraced half-sister to smart middle-distance performer Trakady: backward, well beaten
in maidens. *N. P. Littmoden*

RESEARCHED (IRE) 2 b.c. (May 24) Danehill (USA) 126 – Sought Out (IRE) 119 – p
(Rainbow Quest (USA) 134) [2001 7d Oct 13] fifth foal: half-brother to 4-y-o Cover Up
and 6-y-o Treasure Chest: dam, won Prix du Cadran, from very good family: weak 8/1,
well held in minor event at Ascot, slowly away, soon off bridle and never a threat: almost
certainly capable of better. *Sir Michael Stoute*

RESEARCHER 2 ch.f. (Feb 27) Cosmonaut – Rest 70 (Dance In Time (CAN)) [2001 **61**
8g 8.2v 8.2s⁶ Oct 30] lengthy, angular filly: has scope: eighth foal: half-sister to 3
winners, including 1989 2-y-o 5f seller winner Premier Girl (by Petong) and a winner up
to 1m in Germany by Hadeer: dam 1½m winner: modest maiden: not sure to stay beyond
1m. *R. M. Beckett*

RESPLENDENT CEE (IRE) 2 ch.c. (Mar 3) Polar Falcon (USA) 126 – Western **104**
Friend (USA) (Gone West (USA)) [2001 6g* 6f³ 6m 6m* 6m* 6g Oct 6] 22,000F,
30,000Y: rangy, quite attractive colt: has scope: fluent mover: fourth foal: brother to
useful German performer up to 1m Wild Woman and half-brother to 5-y-o Western
Command: dam, once-raced sister to smart performer up to 1m in Britain and USA Gold
Land, out of half-sister to high-class miler Soviet Line: useful performer: won minor
events at Windsor in June and August and listed race at Ripon (beat Million Percent by
1¾ lengths) later in August: below form (found little) in Two-Year-Old Trophy at Redcar
final start: should stay 7f: raced only on good ground or firmer: seemed ill at ease on
course at Epsom second start. *P. W. Harris*

RESPLENDENT STAR (IRE) 4 b.g. Northern Baby (CAN) 127 – Whitethroat **79**
(Artaius (USA) 129) [2001 85, a97: e10g² e10s² e10g* e10g² 10g 10f⁴ 10g a10f* a9.7f* **a100**
Dec 21] sturdy, close-coupled gelding: good mover: useful on all-weather, fair on turf:
won minor event at Lingfield (by a length from Hail The Chief) in February: good second
to Sergeant York in listed Winter Derby on same course following month: left P. Harris,
then won minor event at Nad Al Sheba in November and listed race at Jebel Ali (by ½
length from Nadeem) in December: stays 1¼m: acts on fibresand/equitrack/dirt, firm and
soft going: usually blinkered/visored: has tended to hang. *S. Seemar, UAE*

RETIREMENT 2 b.g. (Feb 7) Zilzal (USA) 137 – Adeptation (USA) (Exceller **71**
(USA) 129) [2001 7g f8.5s* f8g⁵ Oct 1] leggy, quite attractive gelding: second foal: dam,
French 1¼m/1½m winner, out of US Grade 1 winner Adept: fair form: won maiden at
Wolverhampton in September: well backed, ran as if something amiss final start (subse-
quently gelded): should stay 1¼m: acts on fibresand. *S. P. C. Woods*

RETSKI 4 b.g. Gabitat 119 – Born To Be 80 (Never So Bold 135) [2001 47: e5g 5.3s **46**
6m 6f³ 5g⁶ 6m³ 6m³ 6g⁴ 7g⁵ Aug 17] workmanlike gelding: poor maiden handicapper:
stays 7f: acts on firm ground. *S. Dow*

RETURN OF AMIN 7 ch.g. Salse (USA) 128 – Ghassanah 73 (Pas de Seul 133) [2001 –
89, a–: 7g 7m 8m f7g⁶ f8g f8g f7g 9.2g⁶ 8f 8.3s Aug 21] one-time useful 6f/7f performer:
little form in 2001: usually blinkered nowadays, has been visored. *D. W. Chapman*

RETURN (USA) 4 b.f. Sadler's Wells (USA) 132 – Slightly Dangerous (USA) 122 **99**
(Roberto (USA) 131) [2001 88P: 10g 12m⁴ 12m Jun 19] sturdy filly: useful performer:

good fourth to Ulundi in minor event at Goodwood (would have finished third but for being hampered) second outing: well held in Duke of Edinburgh Stakes at Royal Ascot only subsequent run: stayed 1½m: acted on soft and good to firm going: retired. *H. R. A. Cecil*

REVEALING   2 ch.f. (Feb 20) Halling (USA) 133 – Rive (USA) (Riverman **106 p** (USA) 131) [2001 8m* Sep 22]

    Revealing still has some way to go if she is to give Henry Cecil a seventh One Thousand Guineas or eighth Oaks victory, but however she fares in those events it will be a surprise if she doesn't win a good race or two at three. An impressive winner of a mile maiden at Newmarket in September on her only start to date, Revealing looks open to a fair amount of improvement and is almost certainly a smart filly in the making.

    Revealing's reputation preceded her and she was sent off at 6/4-on to account for her eleven opponents at Newmarket, seven of whom were also unraced. Two of those with experience had shown at least fair form in maidens on their only starts, Thrasher when second at Goodwood and Platonic, the second favourite, when fourth at Newmarket. In a race in which the pace seemed only steady to halfway, Revealing ran a bit green and was short of room through the early stages, having to be checked on one occasion, but once in the clear she made up her ground in eye-catching style. Joining issue two furlongs out, Revealing quickly put the result beyond doubt when sent about her business and pulled three lengths clear. The next three home, also newcomers, were headed by Sundrenched, with Thrasher and Platonic fifth and sixth. Unfortunately, Revealing, installed as favourite for the Guineas with one firm immediately after the race, returned with slightly sore shins—'nothing serious' according to her trainer—and plans for her to have another run before the end of the season, in the Rockfel Stakes, had to be scrapped.

Mr K. Abdulla's "Revealing"

The subsequent success of Sundrenched in a listed event at Newmarket, however, can only have added to Revealing's reputation.

	Halling (USA) (ch 1991)	Diesis (ch 1980)	Sharpen Up Doubly Sure
Revealing (ch.f. Feb 20, 1999)		Dance Machine (b 1982)	Green Dancer Never A Lady
	Rive (USA) (b 1990)	Riverman (b 1969)	Never Bend River Lady
		Arewehavingfunyet (b 1983)	Sham Just Jazz

The rather leggy, quite attractive Revealing is the fourth foal of Rive, and her third winner. Rive's first foal, Brevity (by Tenby), made remarkable progress at the age of six in the latest season, developing into a useful sprinter; her second, Promote (by Linamix), was a fairly useful two-year-old in France in 1998, winning over a mile. A winner over a mile and a quarter in France at two, Rive ran only twice at three, showing useful form when fourth of six in the Prix Minerve over a mile and a half. Rive is a half-sister to the dam of Mons, the winner of the 1995 Royal Lodge Stakes and subsequently a very smart performer at up to a mile and three quarters. Revealing's grandam Arewehavingfunyet was close to the best of her sex in the United States as a two-year-old, when she won five races, including the Grade 1 Oak Leaf Stakes. She failed to win again as a three-year-old, however. Halling, the sire of Revealing, stayed a mile and a quarter well and that distance should pose no problems for Revealing, who also has good prospects of getting a mile and a half. *H. R. A. Cecil*

REVEILLEZ 2 gr.g. (Apr 10) First Trump 118 – Amalancher (USA) 85 (Alleged (USA) 138) [2001 7m⁶ Aug 13] 20,000Y: half-brother to several winners, including 6f winner Arantxa (by Sharpo) and useful Irish 1½m winner Damancher (by Damister): dam French 2-y-o 1m winner: 10/1, never-dangerous sixth of 13 in maiden at Folkestone: should stay at least 1m: likely to improve. *J. R. Fanshawe* — **63 p**

REVELINO (IRE) 2 b.g. (Apr 16) Revoque (IRE) 122 – Forelino (USA) 62§ (Trempolino (USA) 135) [2001 7g⁵ 8d² 8s² 7s* 8d³ Nov 2] 16,000F, 17,000Y: useful-looking gelding: fifth foal: half-brother to 3 winners, including fairly useful 1½m winner Tough Act (by Be My Chief) and 1¼m/1½m winner Maiella (by Salse): dam 10.6f winner out of half-sister to Derby Italiano winner My Top: fairly useful performer: landed odds in maiden at Catterick in October: creditable third in nursery at Brighton (gelded after): will stay at least 1¼m: raced on good going or softer. *E. A. L. Dunlop* — **82**

REVENGE 5 b.g. Saddlers' Hall (IRE) 126 – Classic Heights (Shirley Heights 130) [2001 66: 21.6s Apr 23] lengthy, quite good-topped gelding: poor mover: fair maiden at 4 yrs: well beaten only Flat run in 2001: blinkered last 4 starts. *C. G. Cox* — **–**

REVERIE 3 b.c. Bishop of Cashel 122 – Space Travel (Dancing Dissident (USA) 119) [2001 50: 6g* 6m⁶ 7d* 7.1v Sep 29] tall, lengthy colt: fair handicapper: won at Redcar in June and Epsom in July: stays 7f: acts on good to soft ground: sold 10,000 gns. *R. Hannon* — **73**

REVIEWER (IRE) 3 b.g. Sadler's Wells (USA) 132 – Clandestina (USA) 98 (Secretariat (USA)) [2001 73: 12f 11.6m⁴ 11.7g* 12m⁶ 11.9d⁶ 12g Nov 7] rangy gelding: fairly useful performer: won maiden handicap at Bath in July: should stay beyond 1½m: acts on soft and good to firm ground: tried blinkered in 2000: held up: carries head awkwardly. *M. Meade* — **80**

REX IS OKAY 5 ch.g. Mazilier (USA) 107 – Cocked Hat Girl 47 (Ballacashtal (CAN)) [2001 77, a70: f6g f7g³ f8g³ f8g⁴ f7g 6.1v f8g⁵ 6.1d* f6g* 7m⁶ 7m 6d f6g⁵ f6g 7m⁵ 6g² 7s² 6v Oct 24] quite good-topped gelding: fair performer on turf, modest on all-weather: won handicaps at Nottingham and Southwell in May: has form at easy 8.5f, probably best at 6f/7f: acts on fibresand and soft going, probably on good to firm: usually leads: usually blinkered, not last 2 starts. *S. R. Bowring* — **77 a61**

RHAETIA (IRE) 2 b.f. (Mar 22) Priolo (USA) 127 – Rainbow Mountain 71 (Rainbow Quest (USA) 134) [2001 7f 7f³ 8m 10v Oct 4] angular filly: third living foal: half-sister to 4-y-o Cornelius: dam, 11.5f winner, out of useful sister to Italian Derby winner My Top: modest maiden: form only when third at Brighton: should stay at least 1m: twice slowly away: sold 5,500 gns, sent to Germany. *E. A. L. Dunlop* — **64**

RHEINBOLD 7 br.g. Never So Bold 135 – Rheinbloom 66 (Rheingold 137) [2001 – f12s f16.2g Feb 22] strong gelding: fair handicapper in 1999: well held both runs since. *Ms A. E. Embiricos*

RHEINPARK 2 ch.g. (Mar 17) Cadeaux Genereux 131 – Marina Park 112 (Local 75 Suitor (USA) 128) [2001 6m⁵ 5g⁴ 5s² 6m² 5m⁴ Sep 30] 24,000Y: well-made gelding: second foal: half-brother to 3-y-o Super Canyon: dam 5f to 7f performer: fair maiden: runner-up at Haydock and Catterick: should prove best at 5f/easy 6f: acts on soft and good to firm ground: gelded after final start. *M. Johnston*

RHETORIC (IRE) 2 b.g. (Mar 21) Desert King (IRE) 129 – Squaw Talk (USA) – p (Gulch (USA)) [2001 7v 7g Nov 5] 160,000Y: quite attractive gelding: second foal: half-brother to a winner in US by Clever Trick: dam, won up to 6f (at 2 yrs)/7f in US, out of half-sister to smart Musidora Stakes and Nassau Stakes winner Optimistic Lass, herself dam of high-class 6f to 1m performer Golden Opinion: green, showed ability when seventh in maidens at Doncaster and Redcar (gelded after): should stay at least 1m: capable of better. *J. H. M. Gosden*

RHODAMINE (IRE) 4 b.g. Mukaddamah (USA) 125 – Persian Empress (IRE) 51 64 (Persian Bold 123) [2001 72: f11g³ f11s⁶ f12g⁴ f16g 10.3s 10d* 10f³ 10.9f⁴ 10.1m⁴ Jun 29] smallish, leggy gelding: has a quick, fluent action: modest handicapper: won at Nottingham in May: stays 1½m, not 2m: acts on fibresand, firm and good to soft going: sometimes starts slowly. *J. L. Eyre*

RHYTHMICALL (IRE) 4 b.g. In The Wings 128 – Rhoman Ruby (IRE) (Rhoman 95 Rule (USA)) [2001 88: 10g 14g² 14.8m Aug 24] tall, unfurnished gelding: useful performer: good second in handicap at Sandown in August: stays 1¾m: acts on good to soft going: has raced freely: possibly none too resolute: sold 5,000 gns. *Mrs A. J. Perrett*

RHYTHM OF LIFE 2 ch.f. (Mar 25) Dr Devious (IRE) 127 – Nashville Blues (IRE) 55 94 (Try My Best (USA) 130) [2001 6.1m⁶ Jul 7] fifth foal: half-sister to 1m (at 2 yrs) and 1¼m seller winner Francesca's Folly (by Efisio) and 5-y-o No Mercy: dam, 7f/1m winner, not one to trust implicitly: 20/1, modest form when strong-finishing close sixth in maiden at Chepstow. *J. W. Hills*

RIBBON OF LIGHT 3 b.g. Spectrum (IRE) 126 – Brush Away (Ahonoora 122) 47 [2001 –p: 8.5s 8s 10.1m 11.5f Jun 13] angular, attractive gelding: poor maiden: tongue tied last 2 starts: sold 11,000 gns in July, then gelded. *B. W. Hills*

RIBEAUVILLE 2 ch.f. (Jan 23) Vettori (IRE) 119 – Juvenilia (IRE) 55 (Masterclass 64 (USA) 116) [2001 5g 6m² Jun 29] big, strong, lengthy filly: first foal: dam third at 7f both starts: better effort in maidens at Newmarket (modest form) when ½-length second of 12 to Sundari: should have stayed at least 7f: dead. *J. A. R. Toller*

RIBERAC 5 b.m. Efisio 120 – Ciboure 74 (Norwick (USA) 125) [2001 103: 10s 8.1v⁴ 110 8s⁶ 8.5m* 8.1m³ 10.1m³ 10m³ 8g* 8g* 8d 8g³ 10d⁴ 8d* 8s Nov 18] sturdy, good-quartered mare: has a round action: smart performer: better than ever in 2001, and won handicaps at Beverley and Goodwood (William Hill Mile, by 3½ lengths under enterprising ride), and listed races at Ascot (by 6 lengths) and Newmarket (beat Smirk 1½ lengths): also ran well when in frame in Sun Chariot Stakes (3¼ lengths third to Independence) and listed race (conceded weight all round, hampered near finish when fourth to Esyou效ffcee) at Newmarket eleventh/twelfth starts: best at 1m/1¼m: acts on any going: sometimes early to post/gives trouble at stalls (has worn blanket for entry), and withdrawn 3 times (once in 2001): usually races prominently/leads: splendidly tough and consistent. *M. Johnston*

RICCARTON 8 b.g. Nomination 125 – Legendary Dancer 90 (Shareef Dancer (USA) – 135) [2001 54: 8.1g 11.6g Jul 23] big gelding: well held on Flat in 2001: blinkered twice. *J. M. Bradley*

William Hill Mile (Handicap), Goodwood—an easy win for the admirable mare Riberac, who makes all under Kevin Darley from Wannabe Around (No.6), Little Amin and Atavus (noseband)

RICHEST VEIN (IRE) 2 b.c. (Mar 9) Ali-Royal (IRE) 127 – Antapoura (IRE) 82 **89**
(Bustino 136) [2001 5g f6g* 6m³ 7.1f² 7.5f⁴ 7g* Aug 4] IR 18,000F, IR 20,000Y: leggy,
close-coupled colt: first foal: dam, Irish 1¾m/2m winner and useful staying hurdler,
half-sister to useful French performer up to 9f Aneysar: fairly useful performer: won
maiden at Southwell in May and nursery at Goodwood (20/1, led final 1f and beat Swing
Wing by ¾ length) in August: should stay 1¼m: acts on fibresand, raced only on good
going or firmer on turf: sent to Czech Republic. *S. P. C. Woods*

RICH GIFT 3 b.f. Cadeaux Genereux 131 – Deep Divide 74 (Nashwan (USA) 135) **99**
[2001 66: 7m² 7.5f² 6g² 6d³ 6s³ 6g⁵ 6d 6s Nov 10] workmanlike filly: useful performer:
best efforts when third to Monnavanna in listed race at Pontefract and fifth to Fantasy
Believer in handicap at Ascot on fourth/sixth starts: well held last 2 outings: probably
stays 7.5f: very best efforts on good/good to soft going: sold 30,000 gns. *J. D. Bethell*

RIDE THE TIGER (IRE) 4 ch.g. Imp Society (USA) – Krisdaline (USA) 98 (Kris **52**
S (USA)) [2001 –, a65: 8.1g 11.8f 10f² 8d f8g 12.6d 10g⁴ 11.6g p10g⁴ Dec 28] modest
handicapper: stays 1¼m: acts on firm going and all-weather. *M. D. I. Usher*

RIDGE AND FURROW (IRE) 3 ch.g. Ridgewood Ben 113 – Ryazana (IRE) 81 **–**
(Fairy King (USA)) [2001 50: 14.1d 10f 10g 12m Jul 31] angular gelding: well held in
2001: left T. Tate after reappearance. *N. Wilson*

RIDGE MANOR (IRE) 2 b.c. (Apr 26) Charnwood Forest (IRE) 125 – Tony's **– p**
Ridge (Indian Ridge 123) [2001 8s Nov 9] useful-looking colt: second foal: dam unraced
half-sister to useful stayer Pedraza: 20/1 and green, well-held tenth of 17 to Zone in
maiden at Doncaster: should improve. *P. W. Harris*

RIDGEWAY (IRE) 6 b.g. Indian Ridge 123 – Regal Promise (Pitskelly 122) [2001 **81 +**
8v 10s 8.5m May 22] tall gelding: lightly-raced handicapper, only fairly useful in 2001:
effective from 1m to 1½m: acts on heavy going. *M. W. Easterby*

RIDGEWAY LAD 3 ch.g. Primo Dominie 121 – Phyliel (USA) 82 (Lyphard (USA) **78**
132) [2001 75: 6s⁴ 5m⁶ 6m⁴ 6m 7.5f² 7m² 7.1f³ 7m 7.5f⁴ 5g 6g Aug 11] good-bodied
gelding: fair maiden handicapper: stays 7.5f: acts on firm and good to soft going.
T. D. Easterby

RIDGEWAY SUNSET (IRE) 2 b.f. (Apr 17) Alhaarth (IRE) 126 – Floralia 81 **61**
(Auction Ring (USA) 123) [2001 7f 8.1g 7m 10v Oct 4] IR 35,000Y: rather leggy filly:
fifth living foal: half-sister to 3 winners around 1m, including Henry Afrika (useful in
Ireland, by Mujadil): dam, 7f and 9f winner, half-sister to 7-y-o Sugarfoot: modest
maiden: well held in nursery final start: should stay 1m: sold 2,000 gns. *M. R. Channon*

RIDGEWOOD BAY (IRE) 4 b.f. Ridgewood Ben 113 – Another Baileys 60 **–**
(Deploy 131) [2001 –, a46: 16.2m Jun 18] probably of little account nowadays. *J. C. Fox*

RIDGEWOOD BELLE (IRE) 3 b.f. Ridgewood Ben 113 – Ring Dem Bells (Simply **–**
Great (FR) 122) [2001 –: 8.3s 10g May 30] well beaten in maidens/claimer: blinkered in
2001. *B. J. Meehan*

RIDICULE 2 b.g. (Feb 23) Piccolo 121 – Mockingbird 64 (Sharpo 132) [2001 5g 6g **60**
6m⁴ 6.1d Sep 21] 11,000F, 34,000Y: tall, lengthy, useful-looking gelding: has scope:
second living foal: dam, 2-y-o 6f winner, half-sister to useful performer up to 2m
Anchor Clever: modest maiden: raced alone in nursery final start (gelded after): stays 6f.
T. D. Easterby

RIDLEY (IRE) 2 ch.c. (Feb 4) Grand Lodge (USA) 125 – Richly Deserved (IRE) **90**
(Kings Lake (USA) 133) [2001 6v² 7s² 6d² 6v² f7g* Dec 14] IR 30,000F, 80,000Y:
sturdy, lengthy colt: has scope: eighth foal: half-brother to 3 winners, including 4-y-o
Kingsdon: dam unraced half-sister to high-class winner up to 1¼m in Britain/USA Star
Pastures: fairly useful performer: runner-up in 4 maidens prior to landing odds in one
when blinkered at Southwell in December by 12 lengths: not sure to stay 1m: acts on
fibresand, raced only on ground softer than good on turf: has started slowly/edged left.
B. J. Meehan

RIFIFI 8 ch.g. Aragon 118 – Bundled Up (USA) (Sharpen Up 127) [2001 76d: f6s² f6g⁵ **–**
f7g⁴ e6g⁴ f6g² f6g³ f8g f6g f6g* f6g³ f5s* f6g³ f6g f6g Oct 20] small, sturdy gelding: poor **a70**
mover: fair performer: left R. Ford after fourth start, Mrs H. Walton after eighth: won
seller at Southwell in July and handicap at Wolverhampton in September: best at 5f (given
bit of a test) to easy 7f: acts on fibresand and equitrack, no recent form on turf: tried
visored/tongue tied: has looked wayward. *R. Wilman*

RIGADOON (IRE)   5 b.g. Be My Chief (USA) 122 – Loucoum (FR) 93 (Iron Duke   **55**
(FR) 122) [2001 63: 16m 16.1m 17.1f³ 18m² 16.2f⁵ 16f³ 16m⁶ 16g⁵ 17.5m³ Sep 21] tall
gelding: modest handicapper: best at 2m+: acts on firm ground, possibly not softer than
good: blinkered: usually races up with pace. *M. W. Easterby*

RIGHT APPROACH   2 b.c. (Apr 6) Machiavellian (USA) 123 – Abbey Strand   **103 P**
(USA) 78 (Shadeed (USA) 135) [2001 7g* 7g² Sep 8]
When the champion jockey says a twice-raced two-year-old could be the
best he has ever sat on, the racing world has to sit up and take notice, and, as a result
of the publicity given to Right Approach, his name will surely be appearing in
plenty of horses-to-follow lists. On the form he has shown so far, Right Approach
isn't even close to matching up to some of the top-class individuals that Kieren
Fallon has partnered, but there's no doubt that he has enormous potential and he
could well come close to living up to Fallon's expectations; in Sir Michael Stoute,
Right Approach has a trainer who is sure to get the best out of him.
Right Approach made his debut in a five-runner minor event run over seven
furlongs at Newmarket in early-August, one of three newcomers in a race for which
Kundooz, impressive in a similar event at Doncaster on his only outing, started
favourite. In a steadily-run contest, Right Approach missed the break and was soon
niggled along at the back of the field, but, after being switched wide, he improved
very strongly to lead inside the final furlong and held on by a neck from another
newcomer, Mamool, the pair pulling three lengths clear. Right Approach was sent
off favourite to follow up in a similar event at Kempton a month later and went very
close to doing so. Once again Right Approach was a little slow leaving the stalls
and took time to find his full stride, but he finished in tremendous style, making up
at least two lengths in the last hundred and fifty yards and failing only by a short
head to peg back Expected Bonus, to whom he was conceding 7 lb. As at Newmarket, the Kempton race wasn't run at a pace strong enough to suit Right
Approach, who will be much more at home over longer distances. Right Approach
is regarded as a Derby horse by Fallon and will almost certainly stay a mile and a
half.

		Mr Prospector	Raise A Native
	Machiavellian (USA)	(b 1970)	Gold Digger
	(b 1987)	Coup de Folie	Halo
Right Approach		(b 1982)	Raise The Standard
(b.c. Apr 6, 1999)		Shadeed	Nijinsky
	Abbey Strand (USA)	(b 1982)	Continual
	(b 1989)	Christchurch	So Blessed
		(b 1973)	Highlight

Machiavellian, the sire of Right Approach, only just got a mile, but is
responsible for plenty who stay much further. They include Right Approach's sister
New Assembly, a useful winner at up to a mile and a quarter in Britain for Stoute in
2000 and successful over a mile and a half in the States in the latest season. Right
Approach is also a half-brother to a couple of useful performers, namely Celtic
Cross (by Selkirk) and Temple Way (by Shirley Heights). The former stayed a mile,
while the latter is best at a mile and three quarters to two miles. Their dam Abbey
Strand has produced one other winner, the fair three-year-old Princes Street (by Sri
Pekan), who is probably best at five and six furlongs. Abbey Strand herself gained
her only success in a mile maiden on the equitrack. She is a half-sister to several
winners, including a couple of smart ones in Church Parade, successful at up to an
extended mile and a quarter, and the middle-distance stayer Castle Rising. The next
dam Christchurch, a fairly useful mile-and-a-half winner, is a half-sister to the One
Thousand Guineas and Prix de Diane winner Highclere, grandam of Nashwan,
Unfuwain and Nayef. This is a family which has proved a very successful one for
the Queen, and Right Approach, a leggy, useful-looking colt and a fluent mover,
looks sure to enhance its reputation still further. What a pleasant coincidence it
would be—and a tremendous boost for racing—if, in Golden Jubilee Year, he could
provide Her Majesty with a first Derby victory. He was available at 25/1 for the race
in the winter ante-post lists. *Sir Michael Stoute*

RIGHT WING (IRE)   7 b.h. In The Wings 128 – Nekhbet 74 (Artaius (USA)   **120**
129) [2001 117: 8s* 9d* 8.1v⁵ 10d⁴ 9d* 8d⁶ Nov 3]

Right Wing has been sent to Australia. Some may hark back to the days
of transportation and conclude that it is an appropriate destination for the horse, a
well-known 'character' who has been called a few rude names in his time. But a
career record of eleven wins from thirty-seven starts and nearly a quarter of a
million pounds in prize money has earned Right Wing his place at stud. He held his
form well and showed his best at the age of seven. 'Has been slowly away/carried
head high/wandered, and best with exaggerated waiting tactics/strong handling'.
This one notation, albeit a lengthy one, from Right Wing's short-style comment in
last year's *Racehorses*, hints that he was not the easiest of rides. Nothing changed
in that respect in 2001, but, although the 1999 Lincoln Handicap remained Right
Wing's biggest pay-day, his last two seasons were his most productive. In 2000 he
took two listed races in Britain and the Prix Andre Baboin at Bordeaux. That French
Group 3, the 'Grand Prix des Provinces', was not an exalted contest, but Right
Wing carried on the good work in 2001 with three more victories, including a
second and rather more prestigious Group 3 event.

Doncaster in March had shown Right Wing to good advantage in 1998,
1999 and 2000, when ringing up one victory and two third places in the Lincoln,
and he again did well in 2001. The difference was that, having proved himself so
thoroughly in the helter skelter of the big handicap, his effectiveness in 2001 was
tested in the five-runner Doncaster Mile. The early stages saw him racing none too
enthusiastically at the back of the field, but he was coaxed along to land his third
listed race by two lengths from Albarahin. These two horses, Albarahin, straight as
a die, and Right Wing, a rather more problematic individual, became a bit of a
double act. They had met twice before, in the Cambridgeshire at Newmarket in
1999 and in a listed race at Goodwood in 2000, Albarahin coming out ahead on
both occasions, and they raced against each other again in their first four races in
2001. Temperamental differences between the two were echoed in often directly
contrasting running styles, and when straight man Albarahin set out to make all in
the six-runner Earl of Sefton Stakes at Newmarket in April, Right Wing again came
through to have the last laugh; for all that they went about their business in such a
different fashion, the pair succeeded in reproducing their Doncaster result to the
pound as Right Wing, conceding 3 lb instead of 2 lb, beat Albarahin by a length and
a quarter. The four horses who followed them home at Newmarket were Fanaar,
Distant Music, Umistim and Katy Nowaitee. In the Group 2 Masai Mile at
Sandown nine days later and Group 3 Scottish Classic at Ayr in July, Right Wing
failed to deliver the punchline and Albarahin finished in front of him, without
winning, after which the two of them went their separate ways. Both tasted further
victory, Right Wing's coming in the listed Newmarket Darley Stakes in October.
Again he got off to a slow start, looking for a time as though he would not warm to
his task, before quickening well to catch three-year-olds Smirk and Lagudin in the

*Weatherbys Earl of Sefton Stakes, Newmarket—better than ever at the age of seven,
the visored Right Wing is produced with a strong burst to master the favourite Albarahin*

last half furlong, overcoming some trouble in running into the bargain. The following month Right Wing was favourite for a similar event at the same track, with his trainer John Dunlop reporting: 'We're putting his retirement on hold, so this is not his swansong.' When Right Wing failed to do a tap, however, in his first race under Kieren Fallon, the trainer was forced to take it all back.

		Sadler's Wings (b 1981)	Northern Dancer
	In The Wings (b 1986)		Fairy Bridge
		High Hawk (b 1980)	Shirley Heights
Right Wing (IRE) (b.h. 1994)			Sunbittern
		Artaius (b 1974)	Round Table
	Nekhbet (b 1981)		Stylish Pattern
		Supreme Lady (b 1965)	Grey Sovereign
			Ulupi's Sister

Right Wing passed through the sale-ring for 35,000 guineas as a foal and 36,000 as a yearling and for his first two seasons was trained by Dick Hern. Right Wing is an unusually speedy sort for a horse by good middle-distance stallion In The Wings, but his dam Nekhbet and grandam Supreme Lady both showed their form as two-year-olds over sprint trips. Supreme Lady won once, whereas Nekhbet was third once before a poor career at three. Right Wing is Nekhbet's seventh foal and four of the others are also winners. They include French ten-and-a-half-furlong listed winner Tarquina (by Niniski) and useful five-furlong to seven-furlong winner Cim Bom Bom (by Dowsing). Nekhbet had a two-year-old called Angel Court (by Shareef Dancer) in training with Michael Bell in 2001. There is plenty of 'black type' further back in the pedigree, the chief provider being Nekhbet's half-brother M-Lolshan, who won the 1978 Irish St Leger and the 1979 Grosser Preis von Baden. One of their half-sisters is the grandam of Vinnie Roe, who won the latest Irish St Leger and Prix Royal-Oak, and another is grandam of the 1999 Ribblesdale winner Fairy Queen.

Right Wing, a smallish horse, was effective at a mile to a mile and a quarter. He ran well on firm ground once as a three-year-old and won on good to firm as a four-year-old, but was afterwards kept to good ground or softer. He first wore a visor in September 1998 and was always equipped with the headgear afterwards. One description of Right Wing in his pre-visor immaturity stuck in the memory of his owner Lord Cadogan: 'One of the unkindest things said about him was by Olivier Peslier, who once remarked that he ran like a snake. He was right then, but now he just puts his head down and goes.' Right Wing established far more fruitful relationships afterwards with Richard Quinn and Pat Eddery. In their hands, his late challenge was a force to reckon with in top handicaps, listed races and Group 3s. He left the stage on a low note, but his career as a whole was a credit to the Dunlop stable. *J. L. Dunlop*

RIGHTY HO 7 b.g. Reprimand 122 – Challanging 95 (Mill Reef (USA) 141) [2001 **49** 48: 10s* 16.2m 11.9g 14.1m 11m* 9.9s⁴ 10.4s Oct 11] tall, leggy gelding: poor performer: won seller at Ripon in April and handicap at Redcar in August: effective at 1¼m to 2m: acts on any going: often visored earlier in career. *W. H. Tinning*

RILEYS ROCKET 2 b.f. (Apr 6) Makbul 104 – Star of Flanders (Puissance 110) – [2001 7.5g Sep 19] leggy filly: first foal: dam unraced: 40/1 and burly, well beaten in maiden at Beverley. *R. Hollinshead*

RIMATARA 5 ch.g. Selkirk (USA) 129 – Humble Pie 92 (Known Fact (USA) 135) **58 d** [2001 44: f8g* f9.4s⁶ f8g² f8g² f8s⁵ f7g* f7g³ f8.5g³ f7g f7g⁴ f8g 7.1m f8.5g f9.4g f7s f8.5s Dec 26] good-topped gelding: modest handicapper: won at Southwell (apprentice race) in January and Wolverhampton in February: off 5½ months before well beaten last 4 starts: free-going sort, probably best at 7f/1m: acts on fibresand: blinkered: races prominently: carries head awkwardly: temperamental. *M. W. Easterby*

RIMBAUD (IRE) 5 b.h. College Chapel 122 – Arcade (Rousillon (USA) 133) [2001 **50** 11.8d⁶ 11.6m 14.1d 16g 11.9s 14.1s³ p13g Nov 13] fourth foal: half-brother to fairly useful Irish 1996 2-y-o 7f winner Fairy Song (by Fairy King), later 1m winner in USA: dam, Irish 5f winner, half-sister to 3-y-o Orientor: fairly useful performer in 1999 for C. O'Brien in Ireland: modest nowadays: probably stays 1¾m: raced mainly on good ground or softer. *I. A. Wood*

RIMFAXI 3 ch.g. Risk Me (FR) 127 – Legal Sound 85 (Legal Eagle 126) [2001 –: f7g – 12m Sep 30] no sign of ability in 3 races: left D. Nicholls/off 8 months prior to final start. *J. M. Jefferson*

RING DANCER 6 b.g. Polar Falcon (USA) 126 – Ring Cycle 64 (Auction Ring 80 § (USA) 123) [2001 81: f6g⁶ 6m 6m 5.2m² 5m⁶ 5m* 6m* 5m² 5.1f² 5.7g³ 6g 5.1g f6g Oct 6] useful-looking gelding: good walker: fairly useful performer: below form after fourth start, though won claimers at Sandown and Folkestone in June: effective at 5f to easy 7f: acts on firm going, good to soft and fibresand: often slowly away, and refused to race second start. *Mrs L. Stubbs*

RINGMOOR DOWN 2 b.f. (Feb 2) Pivotal 124 – Floppie (FR) (Law Society (USA) 81 130) [2001 6g* 6.5g Sep 28] 21,000F, 27,000Y: smallish, strong, angular filly: fourth foal: half-sister to 3-y-o Hiraeth, 5-y-o On Porpoise and Irish 7f winner Still Going On (by Prince Sabo): dam French 1m winner: better for race, fairly useful form when winning maiden at Kempton in September by ½ length from Amber's Bluff, leading over 1f out: something possibly amiss in valuable sales race at Ascot: should stay 1m. *P. J. Makin*

RING OF DESTINY 2 b.c. (Feb 12) Magic Ring (IRE) 115 – Canna (Caerleon 71 (USA) 132) [2001 6.1f⁵ 6.9m² Jul 12] 5,000F, 6,200Y resold 8,000Y: half-brother to several winners, including 5-y-o Stormy Skye and useful German performer up to 1¼m Kasai (by Brief Truce): dam unraced half-sister to Oaks d'Italia winner Ivor's Image: fair form in maidens: ½-length second to Canadian Con at Folkestone: will stay at least 1m. *P. W. Harris*

RINGSIDE JACK 5 b.g. Batshoof 122 – Celestine 62 (Skyliner 117) [2001 76: 10v 73 10s 11s⁴ 10.3m² 10m 10m⁶ 10m³ 10m 12m 10.3d² 10g 10.4d 10v 10d 10g⁴ Nov 5] quite good-topped gelding: fair handicapper: best around 1¼m: acts on heavy and good to firm going: usually visored: none too consistent. *C. W. Fairhurst*

RING THE CHIEF 9 b.g. Chief Singer 131 – Lomond Ring (Lomond (USA) 128) 32 [2001 40: f8g⁴ f7s Feb 9] poor performer: stays 1¼m: acts on fibresand, firm and good to soft ground. *M. D. I. Usher*

RINGWOOD (USA) 3 b.g. Foxhound (USA) 103 – Tewksbury Garden (USA) (Wolf 72 d Power (SAF)) [2001 67: e8g⁴ f7g⁵ 5g³ 5d 6m 6d 7.6m⁶ 8d 6d f8.5g f6s⁴ f7s Dec 18] smallish, useful-looking gelding: fair maiden at best: below form after fifth start, leaving C. Wall before penultimate one: best at 5f/6f: acts on firm going, good to soft and fibresand/equitrack: tried in visor/net muzzle. *J. W. Unett*

RIOJA 6 ch.g. Anshan 119 – Executive Flare (Executive Man 119) [2001 63d: f7g³ f7g 57 f7g p7g p6g³ p7g³ Dec 28] tall, useful-looking gelding: modest handicapper: effective at 6f/7f: acts on good to firm going, soft and fibresand/polytrack. *M. Wigham*

RIO'S DIAMOND 4 b.f. Formidable (USA) 125 – Rio Piedras 86 (Kala Shikari 125) 56 [2001 53, a46: f7g 7g 7d² 8f⁴ 7f⁴ 7.5m 7f² 7m 7g² 7g 8g* 7s⁶ 8.5g 7d⁵ f8g² p7g² Dec 28] small filly: modest handicapper: won at Brighton (apprentices) in August: effective at 7f/ 1m: acts on all-weather, firm and good to soft ground, not on soft/heavy: visored once at 2 yrs: has idled/hung left. *M. J. Ryan*

RIPCORD (IRE) 3 b.g. Diesis 133 – Native Twine 114 (Be My Native (USA) 122) 66 § [2001 63: 8d³ 10m 8.1g 8m Jul 14] big, lengthy, good-topped gelding: fair maiden handicapper: should stay beyond 1m: acts on soft ground: flashes tail/finds little, and one to treat with caution. *J. H. M. Gosden*

RIPSNORTER (IRE) 12 ch.h. Rousillon (USA) 133 – Formulate 119 (Reform 132) – [2001 –: f11g 9f Jul 4] of little account nowadays. *P. D. Purdy*

RISALPUR (IRE) 2 b.c. (Apr 29) Mukaddamah (USA) 125 – Idrak 68 (Young 75 Generation 129) [2001 5m⁵ 5f 5.2m 5m* 5m⁶ Aug 25] 10,500Y: brother to a 2-y-o sprint winner in Italy and half-brother to 3 winners, including 7f winner Marguerite Bay (by Darshaan) and 4-y-o Lucky Heather: dam, 5f winner, from very good middle-distance family: fair performer: won maiden at Windsor in July: reportedly injured in stall final start: likely to prove best at 5f/easy 6f: raced only on going firmer than good: sold 2,500 gns. *Mrs L. Stubbs*

RISE ABOVE (IRE) 7 b.m. Simply Great (FR) 122 – La Tanque (USA) (Last Raise 30 (USA)) [2001 16.2m³ 16.2m⁶ f14.8s Sep 6] poor maiden, lightly raced: stays 2m. *Miss K. M. George*

RISING PASSION (IRE) 3 ch.g. General Monash (USA) 107 – Brazilian Princess –
66 (Absalom 128) [2001 –: f6g f7s 6.1v f5g 6g 8m⁶ f7g 8m Jul 27] sturdy gelding: little
form: tried blinkered: looked none too keen penultimate outing. *D. Nicholls*

RISING SPRAY 10 ch.g. Waajib 121 – Rose Bouquet 78 (General Assembly (USA)) **48 d**
[2001 62d: 13.3g 12m 14.1m³ 14.1m⁶ 14.1m 14.1m⁶ 12m 16.2m Sep 17] quite good-
topped gelding: has a quick action: poor handicapper: stays 1¾m: acts on good to firm
and good to soft going: often visored/blinkered: sometimes slowly away (has seemed
reluctant to race): on downgrade. *Dr J. R. J. Naylor*

RISKER (USA) 2 b.c. (May 18) Gone West (USA) – Trampoli (USA) 115 (Trem- **78**
polino (USA) 135) [2001 7d⁵ 7g⁴ 8m* 8m Sep 30] $100,000Y: quite attractive colt: good
mover: fourth foal: half-brother to fairly useful 10.5f winner (stayed 2m) First Officer (by
Lear Fan), 1¼m/1½m winner in France/USA (including in Group/Graded events),
half-sister to very smart middle-distance performers Roi Normand and Luth Dancer: fair
form: won maiden at Thirsk in September: well held when favourite for nursery final
start: should stay 1¼m: acts on good to firm going. *M. Johnston*

RISK FREE 4 ch.g. Risk Me (FR) 127 – Princess Lily 65 (Blakeney 126) [2001 77, **76**
a91: f6s⁵ f6s e8g* e8g³ e10s f8.5g⁵ f8.5g⁵ f7g 7.6f 8g 8m 7f f12g⁴ f8g f6g* f9.4g 7.6d³ 7g **a92**
7.1g 5.1d⁶ f7g² f6g f6g³ f8g³ p8g² p7g* f6g⁵ f6g⁵ Nov 30] lengthy gelding: fairly useful
on all-weather, fair on turf: won handicap at Lingfield in February, seller at Wolverhampton (final start for N. Littmoden) in August and handicap at Lingfield in November:
effective at 6f to 8.5f: acts on firm going, good to soft and all-weather: usually blinkered/
visored: tough and consistent. *P. D. Evans*

RISKY FLIGHT 7 ch.g. Risk Me (FR) 127 – Stairway To Heaven (IRE) 74 (Gods- **24**
walk (USA) 130) [2001 –: f8g f12g³ f9.4g f16g f11g⁴ May 21] bad maiden: tried
blinkered. *A. Smith*

RISKY GIRL 6 ro.m. Risk Me (FR) 127 – Jove's Voodoo (USA) 74 (Northern Jove –
(CAN)) [2001 11.6v Oct 8] probably of little account nowadays. *H. J. Manners*

RISKY REEF 4 ch.g. Risk Me (FR) 127 – Pas de Reef 49 (Pas de Seul 133) [2001 70: **75**
f7g* f7s* f8g⁴ f7g* f8.5g⁶ 6.1d 7g 7.5s 6g 6v 7v² Oct 27] workmanlike gelding: fairly **a83**
useful handicapper on all-weather, fair on turf: won at Southwell in January and February
(amateurs): probably best at 7f/1m: acts on fibresand and heavy going: has won with/
without visor: sold 11,000 gns. *I. A. Balding*

RISKY REWARD 2 b.f. (May 8) First Trump 118 – Baroness Gymcrak 53§ (Pharly **55**
(FR) 130) [2001 5m 6g³ 6m² 7m 6v⁴ 6d⁶ 6d⁶ Nov 6] strong filly: half-sister to 3-y-o
Windchill and 7f winner Cumbrian Blue (by Weldnaas): dam, ungenerous sprint maiden,
half-sister to smart 1982 2-y-o sprinter Domynsky (later middle-distance stakes winner
in USA): modest maiden: stays 6f: acts on heavy and good to firm going: tried blinkered.
T. D. Easterby

RISOTTO (USA) 2 b.f. (Feb 14) Kris S (USA) – Routilante 96 (Rousillon (USA) **80**
133) [2001 6m² 6m 7g* Sep 14] leggy, unfurnished filly: fifth foal: closely related to
useful 1997 2-y-o 7f winner Amabel (by Silver Hawk) and a winner up to 1½m in USA
by Lear Fan and half-sister to 2 winners, including fairly useful 2000 2-y-o 8.5f winner
Changing Scene (by Theatrical): dam, 2-y-o 6f winner who was probably ungenuine,
later successful in USA: fairly useful form: won maiden at Epsom by neck from unlucky
Atarama, battling on gamely: will stay 1m: went to USA. *I. A. Balding*

RISQUE SERMON 3 b.g. Risk Me (FR) 127 – Sunday Sport Star 96 (Star Appeal **68**
133) [2001 78: 6g 5m⁶ 6m² 6f⁴ 6m 5m⁵ 6g³ 6m³ 7m Aug 25] quite good-topped gelding:
fair handicapper: best at 5f/6f: acts on firm going, well held on softer than good: tongue
tied. *Miss B. Sanders*

RISTRA (USA) 2 b.f. (Jan 30) Kingmambo (USA) 125 – Rhetorical Lass (USA) **82**
(Capote (USA)) [2001 6m² 6m* 5m 7g Oct 6] $100,000Y: angular filly: good mover:
second foal: dam, maiden in USA, half-sister to US Grade 1 9f/1¼m winner Reloy: fairly
useful form: won maiden at Lingfield in May: midfield in Queen Mary Stakes at Royal
Ascot next start: off over 3 months, raced too freely in listed race at Newmarket: should
stay 7f. *J. Noseda*

RISUCCHIO 2 ch.g. (Apr 19) Thatching 131 – Skip To Somerfield 79 (Shavian 125) **69**
[2001 5.1g³ 5.6f 6d 6m Sep 6] close-coupled, unfurnished gelding: second foal: dam
2-y-o 6f winner: extremely coltish, fair form when third in maiden at Nottingham: well
held all 3 starts after (reportedly gelded after next one): edgy and reportedly lost action
third outing. *B. S. Rothwell*

RITA'S ROCK APE 6 b.m. Mon Tresor 113 – Failand 36 (Kala Shikari 125) [2001 **87** 85, a–: 5.1m⁵ 5.3m⁴ 5.1f 5m* 5.1m⁶ 5.1m⁵ 5.5d⁶ 5.2m³ 5.1g² 5g 5g⁶ 5g 5m f5g² f5g **a69** Nov 30] workmanlike mare: fairly useful handicapper on turf, fair on all-weather: won at Salisbury in June: best at 5f: acts on firm going, good to soft and fibresand/equitrack: usually makes running: has reportedly bled from nose, including final start: tough. *R. Brotherton*

RIVAL (IRE) 2 b.c. (May 11) Desert Style (IRE) 121 – Arab Scimetar (IRE) (Sure **79** Blade (USA) 130) [2001 6m³ 6m² Sep 2] IR 14,000Y, 30,000 2-y-o: rather leggy, quite good-topped colt: seventh foal: half-brother to 3 winners, including 5-y-o Mitcham and 1m winner Take Manhattan (both by Hamas): dam unraced: better effort (fair form) when neck second of 23 to Sophies Symphony in maiden at York, always well there: should stay 7f. *P. F. I. Cole*

RIVELLI (IRE) 2 b.f. (Jan 25) Lure (USA) 131 – Kama Tashoof 72 (Mtoto 134) [2001 **66** 7m⁵ 8.1v⁵ Sep 29] 100,000Y: strong filly: second foal: half-sister to 4-y-o Judicious: dam, maiden who stayed 1½m, out of useful winner up to 1m Leipzig: fair form in maidens at Salisbury and Haydock: will probably stay beyond 1m. *P. F. I. Cole*

RIVER BLEST (IRE) 5 b.g. Unblest 117 – Vaal Salmon (IRE) (Salmon Leap (USA) **–** 131) [2001 60: 5v 5m 5d 7.5m 6m 5g 6v f7s Dec 15] tall, angular gelding: modest performer at 4 yrs: little form in 2001 *Mrs A. Duffield*

RIVERBLUE (IRE) 5 b.g. Bluebird (USA) 125 – La Riveraine (USA) 90 (Riverman **77** (USA) 131) [2001 72: f8g⁵ f11s³ f9.4g⁴ f8.5g⁴ 8v⁴ 8.2v* 10s⁶ 10s⁵ f11g 9g⁴ 10.3g 10.3d **a62** 10s Oct 16] rather leggy gelding: fair handicapper on turf, modest on all-weather: won at Nottingham in April: effective at testing 1m to 1½m: acts on heavy going, good to firm and fibresand: tried visored at 3 yrs: sometimes gets behind. *D. J. Wintle*

RIVER BOY (IRE) 5 b.g. River Falls 113 – Natty Gann (IRE) (Mister Majestic 122) **–** [2001 f14.8s Jan 18] of little account nowadays. *G. Brown*

RIVER CANYON (IRE) 5 b.g. College Chapel 122 – Na-Ammah (IRE) 90 **65** (Ela-Mana-Mou 132) [2001 99: 9.2d² 9.9m 10m⁵ Jun 21] workmanlike gelding: useful performer for D. Weld in Ireland at 3/4 yrs (third in Group 3 event at Leopardstown in 1999), sold 3,100 gns after only outing in 2000: fair form in Britain only in claimer on first start: stays 1¼m: acts on heavy ground: blinkered once. *W. Storey*

RIVER ENSIGN 8 br.m. River God (USA) 121 – Ensigns Kit (Saucy Kit 76) [2001 **63 d** 61: f9.4g³ 10v² 12s⁶ 9.7v⁶ 10v f12g⁶ f9.4s f9.4g f9.4s Dec 27] small mare: has stringhalt: modest performer: below form after second start: effective at 9f to bare 1½m: acts on fibresand and heavy going: has been early to post: possibly needs to dominate. *W. M. Brisbourne*

RIVERINA (USA) 3 ch.f. Irish River (FR) 131 – Pattimech (USA) (Nureyev (USA) **88** 131) [2001 7d⁵ 7g* 8.9d* 10.3v p10g Nov 13] IR 140,000Y: fifth foal: half-sister to 1m winner Lamanka Lass (by Woodman) and a winner in US by Cox's Ridge: dam won up to 7f in USA, sister to Grade 1 9f winner Annoconnor and half-sister to Grand Prix de Paris and Melbourne Cup winner At Talaq: fairly useful form: won maiden at Thirsk in May and 27-runner handicap at York in October: ran badly last 2 starts, something seemingly amiss final one: should stay 1¼m: raced only on good going or softer on turf: sold 52,000 gns. *J. L. Dunlop*

RIVER KWAI 4 ch.f. Anshan 119 – Brilliant 75 (Never So Bold 135) [2001 9.9d **–** 11.6m 9.9m Jul 27] first foal: dam 1m to 1¼m winner: tailed off all Flat starts: blinkered final outing. *J. J. Bridger*

RIVER LIGHT (IRE) 3 b.c. Bahri (USA) 125 – Sister Troy (USA) (Far North **56** (CAN) 120) [2001 7d 8s 8.3m⁶ 7.6m 8s f9.4s Dec 18] 37,000F, IR 65,000Y: rather leggy, quite attractive colt: seventh foal: half-brother to 4-y-o Helen Albadou and several winners abroad: dam, sprint winner in USA, half-sister to smart 1980 2-y-o filly Exclusively Raised: modest maiden: disappointing last 3 starts, leaving G. Wragg 5,000 gns after penultimate one: not certain to stay beyond 1m. *J. Cullinan*

RIVER MASTER 2 b.g. (May 9) Most Welcome 131 – River Spey 96 (Mill Reef **65** (USA) 141) [2001 7f 8d 7s⁴ Oct 25] 13,000Y: leggy, rather unfurnished gelding: half-brother to several winners, including smart middle-distance stayer Jahafil and useful 1¼m/1½m winner Mondschein (both by Rainbow Quest) and useful 7f/1m winner Dune River (by Green Desert): dam 2-y-o 7f winner who stayed 1½m: best effort in maidens (fair form) when never-nearer fourth to Thrasher at Brighton: gelded after: should stay at least 1¼m: acts on soft ground. *I. A. Balding*

RIVER NYMPH   3 ch.f. Cadeaux Genereux 131 – La Riveraine (USA) 90 (Riverman   **71**
(USA) 131) [2001 8m 6.9m² 7f³ 7g⁵ f12g Oct 20] leggy, angular filly: third foal: half-
sister to 5-y-o Riverblue and 1m winner Riparian (by Last Tycoon): dam won around
1½m: fair maiden: reportedly finished distressed final start: should be suited by at least
1m: drifted left second outing: sold 800 gns. *Sir Michael Stoute*

RIVER OF FIRE   3 ch.g. Dilum (USA) 115 – Bracey Brook (Gay Fandango (USA)   **58**
132) [2001 60: f7g 10.3s 10.2d³ 10m⁶ 14.1m⁴ 12m⁵ f12g Jul 20] rather unfurnished
gelding: modest performer: barely stays 1¾m: acts on soft and good to firm going (well
beaten on fibresand): visored twice at 2 yrs. *J. M. P. Eustace*

RIVER REINE (IRE)   2 br.f. (Feb 16) Lahib (USA) 129 – Talahari (IRE) (Roi Danzig   **80**
(USA)) [2001 6m⁵ 7.1m² 7.1v* 8d⁵ Oct 19] IR 2,200F, IR 12,000Y: big, good-bodied
filly: third foal: half-sister to temperamental 1m seller winner Sedona (by Namaqualand):
dam lightly raced in Ireland: fairly useful form: won maiden at Haydock in September:
creditable fifth of 24 in nursery at Newmarket final start: should stay 1¼m: acts on good
to firm and heavy going. *B. W. Hills*

RIVERSDALE (IRE)   5 b.g. Elbio 125 – Embustera 73 (Sparkler 130) [2001 –: f8g²   **51**
8s⁶ 8s 8v f8g Dec 17] good-topped gelding: modest maiden handicapper: stays 1m: acts
on good to firm going, soft and fibresand. *J. G. FitzGerald*

RIVER TERN   8 b.g. Puissance 110 – Millaine 69 (Formidable (USA) 125) [2001   **61 d**
72d: 5.2m³ 5g⁶ 5.7g² 5m 5m 5.1g 5s 5m f5g Oct 18] tall gelding: has a high knee action:
modest handicapper: well held after third start: best at 5f/easy 6f: acts on firm and good to
soft going: usually visored/blinkered at 3 yrs: often starts slowly: reportedly bled from
nose fifth outing: held up: difficult ride. *J. M. Bradley*

RIVER TRAIL   3 b.g. Catrail (USA) 123 – River Maiden (USA) (Riverman (USA)   **49**
131) [2001 7g⁴ f6g f7g Nov 23] 8,000Y: third foal: half-brother to Irish 9f winner Zaidaan
(by Ezzoud): dam French 2-y-o 6f winner: poor form in maiden at Thirsk on debut: well
beaten both starts after. *M. Brittain*

RIYADH   3 ch.g. Caerleon (USA) 132 – Ausherra (USA) 106 (Diesis 133) [2001 8s   **95**
e8g² 10s⁵ 11.8f* 14.1d² 14.1g² 15.9m² 14g 13.9m 16m* 14g* Oct 6] lengthy, angular
gelding: poor mover: sixth foal: closely related to 7-y-o Yorkshire and half-brother to
fairly useful 1998 2-y-o 6f/7f winner Asley (by Danehill) and 4-y-o Apache Point: dam,
6f (at 2 yrs) and 11.5f (Lingfield Oaks Trial) winner, sister to Ramruma: useful handicapper: won at Leicester in May, Goodwood in September and Newmarket (by neck from
Compton Commander) in October: stays 2m: acts on equitrack, firm and good to soft
going: blinkered/visored 7 of last 8 starts: tends to hang: sold 75,000 gns, joined M. Pipe.
P. F. I. Cole

RIZERIE (FR)   3 gr.f. Highest Honor (FR) 124 – Riziere (FR) (Groom Dancer (USA)   **98**
128) [2001 91: 7m 10f³ 10.1f 8s Sep 29] strong, close-coupled filly: useful performer:
best effort when 3½ lengths third of 6 to Nafisah in listed event at Newbury in June: well
held in similar company both subsequent starts: stays 1¼m: acts on firm ground: has
swished tail: sold 115,000 gns. *L. M. Cumani*

ROAD TO JUSTICE   2 ch.c. (Mar 22) Danehill Dancer (IRE) 117 – Hopesay 84   **93**
(Warning 136) [2001 6m² 6m⁶ 6m* 6f 6g Oct 6] 14,000F, 22,000Y: strong, quite attractive colt: good walker: first foal: dam maiden who stayed 6f: fairly useful performer: won
maiden at Redcar in September: best effort when seventh to Firebreak in Mill Reef Stakes
at Newbury fourth start: will need to settle to stay 7f: raced only on good going or firmer:
sold 30,000 gns. *J. H. M. Gosden*

ROAMING RONAN (IRE)   3 b.g. Sri Pekan (USA) 117 – Maradata (IRE) 68   **–**
(Shardari 130) [2001 8.1d 11.9g⁴ Aug 11] 30,000Y: smallish, sturdy gelding: has a round
action: first foal: dam, 1¼m and (in France) 11f winner, half-sister to smart stayer Maridpour: well held in maidens at Warwick and Haydock: sold 900 gns. *Jonjo O'Neill*

ROARING TWENTIES   3 ch.f. Halling (USA) 133 – Flower Girl 108 (Pharly (FR)   **81**
130) [2001 7g² 6g² 8.1g* 10.1s⁵ Oct 31] filly: closely related to smart performer up
to 14.6f Eco Friendly (by Sabrehill) and half-sister to 1½m winner Water Flower (by
Environment Friend): dam 6f (including at 2 yrs) winner: fairly useful performer: won
maiden at Sandown in September: stiff task and ran creditably in minor event at Yarmouth final start: stays 1¼m. *M. A. Jarvis*

ROAR OF THE TIGER (USA)   2 ch.c. (Mar 3) Storm Cat (USA) – Mariah's Storm   **98 p**
(USA) 116 (Rahy (USA) 115) [2001 6g* Jun 21] third foal: brother to top-class 1m/1¼m

performer Giant's Causeway and 3-y-o Freud: dam, won several Grade 2/3 events at 1m/
9f in USA, closely related to very smart French middle-distance performer Panoramic:
5/2-on, won 15-runner maiden at Naas on only start by head from Whistle Down (pair 5
lengths clear): sure to improve, provided all is well. *A. P. O'Brien, Ireland*

ROASSI (IRE) 2 ch.f. (Mar 30) Pennekamp (USA) 130 – Virelai 72 (Kris 135) [2001 **53**
7f 7m 6.5g Sep 28] 10,000Y: useful-looking filly: sixth foal: half-sister to 2 winners,
notably useful 7f/1m winner Verzen (by Salse): dam, 1½m winner, out of Free Handicap
winner Lyric Dance: only form (modest) when seventh of 9 in maiden at Brighton second
start: will need to settle to stay 1m. *C. E. Brittain*

ROBANDELA (USA) 4 b.g. Kingmambo (USA) 125 – Yemanja (USA) (Alleged **91**
(USA) 138) [2001 f12g* f12s* f12g⁵ f14g³ f12g³ 12s 13s* 14d⁴ 12d 12m 12g* 12v 12m⁵
14m 11.9g 13.9m 10m* 10.3g 12m* 10v 10v* Nov 8] big, good-topped gelding: reportedly broke pelvis after only 2-y-o start: developed into fairly useful performer: won
maiden at Southwell and handicap at Wolverhampton in January, handicaps at Musselburgh in April and Newmarket in May, apprentice handicap at Leicester and minor event
at Goodwood in September and handicap at Windsor in November: effective at 1¼m/
1½m: acts on fibresand, heavy and good to firm going: blinkered after sixth start: runs the
odd poor race. *M. Johnston*

ROBBER RED 5 b.g. Mon Tresor 113 – Starisk 47 (Risk Me (FR) 127) [2001 –: 8f **–**
7m 7f 7f 10f Jul 4] little form since 1999: tried blinkered/tongue tied. *R. M. Flower*

ROBBIE CAN CAN 2 b.c. (Mar 13) Robellino (USA) 127 – Can Can Lady 82 **66 p**
(Anshan 119) [2001 6d⁵ Oct 12] leggy, useful-looking colt: first foal: dam 6f (at 2 yrs) to
9f winner: 14/1, under 9 lengths fifth of 16 to Pic Up Sticks in maiden at York, slowly
away and not given hard time: should stay at least 1m: should improve. *J. G. Given*

ROBBIES DREAM (IRE) 5 ch.g. Balla Cove 119 – Royal Golden (IRE) (Digamist **–**
(USA) 110) [2001 –, a62: f8g f8g f7g⁶ f8g* f8g⁵ f8g* 8d f8.5g Aug 18] small, sparely- **a64**
made gelding: poor mover: modest handicapper: won twice at Southwell in July: stays
8.5f: acts on fibresand, lightly raced on turf: visored once: tongue tied: has started slowly/
looked none too keen/edged left. *R. M. H. Cowell*

ROBBO 7 b.g. Robellino (USA) 127 – Basha (USA) (Chief's Crown (USA)) [2001 55: **67**
15.8d⁵ 18s* Oct 22] small gelding: useful chaser: fair handicapper on Flat: won at
Pontefract in October: best at 15f+: acts on fibresand and heavy ground: usually blinkered
before 2001. *Mrs M. Reveley*

ROBE CHINOISE 2 b.f. (Mar 15) Robellino (USA) 127 – Kiliniski 119 (Niniski **77**
(USA) 125) [2001 6m 7m 7.5g² 8d Nov 2] rather leggy, useful-looking filly: half-sister to
1½m winner Kilshanny (by Groom Dancer) and a winner in Belgium by Green Desert:
dam 1½m winner (also in frame in Oaks and Yorkshire Oaks) out of half-sister to
Nureyev and dam of Sadler's Wells: easily best effort (fair form) when second in maiden
at Beverley: well held in nursery at Brighton final start, never going well: will be suited
by 1¼m+. *J. L. Dunlop*

ROBELLION 10 b.g. Robellino (USA) 127 – Tickled Trout 70 (Red Alert 127) [2001 **59**
65: 7m⁴ 8.1m f7g Jun 15] sturdy gelding: modest handicapper: stays easy 1¼m: acts on
any turf going, fibresand and equitrack: often visored earlier in career, tried blinkered:
usually held up. *Miss E. C. Lavelle*

ROBELLITA 7 b.g. Robellino (USA) 127 – Miellita 98 (King Emperor (USA)) [2001 **–**
–: 11.9s May 3] probably of little account nowadays. *B. G. Powell*

ROBIN HOOD 4 b.g. Komaite (USA) – Plough Hill (North Briton 67) [2001 60: 5d **47**
5m 5m 5d 5m 5m² 5m 6d³ 6g³ 5m 5s 5m 5g 6v Oct 16] small, sturdy gelding: poor
handicapper: was effective at 5f/6f: acted on heavy going, probably on good to firm: was
often slowly away: reportedly bled from nose penultimate start: dead. *Miss L. A. Perratt*

ROBIN SHARP 3 ch.c. First Trump 118 – Mo Stopher 47 (Sharpo 132) [2001 72: **73**
f7s* f6g³ 7v f7g² 7d p7g f7g⁴ Dec 1] strong colt: fair performer on all-weather: won **a73**
maiden at Wolverhampton in January: should stay 1m: acts on fibresand, no form on turf
in 2001. *W. Jarvis*

ROB LEACH 4 b.g. Robellino (USA) 127 – Arc Empress Jane (IRE) (Rainbow Quest **89**
(USA) 134) [2001 79: 12s³ 12s⁵ 10g² 9.9d² Aug 26] smallish, quite attractive gelding:
has a round action: fairly useful maiden: best effort final start: stays 1½m: acts on soft and
good to firm ground: fairly useful hurdler. *G. L. Moore*

ROBOASTAR (USA) 4 b. or br.g. Green Dancer (USA) 132 – Sweet Alabastar –
(USA) (Gulch (USA)) [2001 76: 12.6m⁵ 12.1g⁶ 11.6m Jul 30] useful-looking gelding:
fair maiden at 3 yrs: well held in 2001. *P. G. Murphy*

ROBZELDA 5 b.g. Robellino (USA) 127 – Zelda (USA) (Sharpen Up 127) [2001 81: 70 §
f8g 10v⁴ 8s³ 10s 9m³ 8f⁶ 10.5g⁴ 12g³ 14f⁴ 15.9m 12m 12.1g³ 10.9m³ 14.1g 11.9s 10.1v⁵
Oct 24] sparely-made gelding: fair handicapper: stayed easy 1¾m: acted on any going:
was sometimes blinkered: was unreliable: dead. *K. A. Ryan*

ROCCIOSO 4 br.g. Pelder (IRE) 125 – Priory Bay 54 (Petong 126) [2001 –: 7m Jun –
12] leggy gelding: little form. *J. C. Fox*

ROCK CONCERT 3 b.f. Bishop of Cashel 122 – Summer Pageant 81 (Chief's 59
Crown (USA)) [2001 –: 10.2d 10m 8d⁵ Jun 17] 12,500F: deep-girthed filly: fourth foal:
half-sister to 5-y-o Join The Parade and a French/Spanish winner around 11f, both by
Elmaamul: dam 1½m winner out of half-sister to Sun Princess and Saddlers' Hall: modest
form: should stay at least 1¼m. *H. Candy*

ROCKERLONG 3 b.f. Deploy 131 – Dancing Rocks 118 (Green Dancer (USA) 132) 112
[2001 94p: 10s⁵ 11.4f* 12f⁵ 12m³ 11.9g³ 14.6m 12d Oct 13] strong, lengthy filly: smart
performer: won listed event at Chester in May by neck from Gay Heroine: very good third
in listed race at Newmarket (beaten 3 lengths by Ranin) and Yorkshire Oaks at York
(beaten 3½ lengths by Super Tassa): took good hold/repeatedly denied run in straight in
Park Hill Stakes at Doncaster penultimate outing: soundly beaten in Princess Royal
Stakes at Ascot final start: stays 1½m, at least when conditions aren't testing: best form
on good ground or firmer (acts on firm): not an easy ride. *G. Wragg*

ROCKING 2 b.c. (May 23) Mazaad 106 – Dalgorian (IRE) (Lancastrian –
126) [2001 8.3v f8g Dec 10] second foal: dam Irish maiden hurdler: well beaten in seller/
maiden. *C. N. Kellett*

ROCK'N COLD (IRE) 3 b.g. Bigstone (IRE) 126 – Unalaska (IRE) 65 (High Estate 55
127) [2001 8s f8g 8v⁴ 10.1m f12g 10m⁶ 10.1g² 10g⁵ 10m 10m⁵ 10.1g⁴ 10s⁶ 10s² 10d⁴
10s² Oct 25] tall, useful-looking gelding: modest maiden handicapper: should stay 1½m:
acts on soft and good to firm going: usually visored/blinkered: tended to wander/look less
than keen eleventh outing: none too consistent. *R. M. H. Cowell*

*Shadwell Stud Cheshire Oaks, Chester—a thrilling finish as Rockerlong lowers the course record; Gay
Heroine (No.2), Elrehaan (striped cap) and Inchiri (No.3) are close behind*

Scottish Equitable Gimcrack Stakes, York—Rock of Gibraltar quickens away impressively from Ho Choi (noseband), Twilight Blues (second right), Waldenburg (star on cap) and Saddad (right)

ROCK OF GIBRALTAR (IRE)   2 b.c. (Mar 8) Danehill (USA) 126 – Offshore   **118**
Boom 96 (Be My Guest (USA) 126) [2001 5s* 6m⁶ 6g* 6g* 7d² 7s* 7d* Oct 20]
The Rock of Gibraltar is solid, imposing and immobile. The colt of that
name is also solid and imposing but far from immobile, as he showed in a splendid
campaign in which he notched a unique double, the Grand Criterium and the
Dewhurst Stakes, and indicated he is a worthy contender for classic honours. Even
before showing his true mettle in the autumn, Rock of Gibraltar proved himself a
force to be reckoned with, winning a maiden at the Curragh in April, the Anheuser
Busch Railway Stakes on the same course in July by two lengths from Hawk Wing
and the Scottish Equitable Gimcrack Stakes at York in August impressively by
three lengths from Ho Choi after blinding his opponents for finishing speed. He
was also none too lucky when sixth in the Coventry Stakes at Royal Ascot, being
one of the worst sufferers in an unsatisfactory race and repeatedly denied a run.
On the strength of this record, Rock of Gibraltar started favourite to beat Dubai
Destination in the Champagne Stakes at Doncaster but the task of beating that colt,
conceding him 4 lb, proved beyond him. Despite being coltish beforehand, Rock of
Gibraltar settled well and made smooth headway to lead two furlongs out before
being made to look positively pedestrian himself this time as Dubai Destination
flew by him to score cosily by a length, the pair clear.
Rock of Gibraltar was flattered by his proximity to the winner that day at
Doncaster, just as his rivals were flattered by their proximity to him at Longchamp
in his next race, the Grand Criterium - Lucien Barriere. The decision taken at the
end of 2000 to reduce the distance of this race to seven furlongs from a mile, and
bring it back by a week, supposedly because French trainers felt seven furlongs was
the perfect distance over which to prepare juveniles for the following year's
Guineas, did nothing to boost the competitiveness of the latest running, or to
increase the participation of French-trained runners. In a less-than-vintage renewal
three of the five contenders were trained abroad—Rock of Gibraltar, his stable-

Grand Criterium - Lucien Barriere, Longchamp—a change in scheduling and a reduction in distance still produce only a small field, but Rock of Gibraltar is a most impressive winner from Bernebeau (No.2), Dobby Road (right) and Shah Jehan

companion Shah Jehan and Imtiyaz, the last two having their first start in a pattern event. That left Bernebeau, runner-up in the Prix La Rochette, and Dobby Road, successful in the Group 3 Prix d'Arenberg over five furlongs, to fly the flag for the home team. Rock of Gibraltar treated them in summary fashion, as he was entitled to. Settled off the pace as usual, he moved readily into contention once in line for home and stretched away to score, eased considerably (as if his jockey might have ridden to the wrong winning post), by three lengths.

Aidan O'Brien's practice of running several horses against each other, particularly in significant two-year-old races, is a tried and trusted one, and sensible too, given the perceived importance of 'black type' as a means of boosting runners' status, plus the strength in depth of the trainer's team. Unquestionably, a number of top juvenile races over the last three years would have been pretty sorry affairs without the O'Brien team. The latest Dewhurst Stakes, sponsored by Darley, was an example, since he fielded four of the eight runners. Ballydoyle's policy is not a case of running batches of horses with only one holding a realistic chance and the others acting as pacemakers or spoilers. Michael Kinane would surely agree, the selection of what to ride in big races clearly proving something of a nightmare on occasions. Kinane partnered the presumed first choice in the Criterium de Saint-Cloud, Royal Lodge Stakes, Coventry Stakes and Killavullan Stakes, as well as both Irish Guineas, only to lose out to a stable companion. O'Brien's second string also won the Racing Post Trophy and another came within a whisker of landing the Dewhurst. Kinane, predictably, was on Rock of Gibraltar at Newmarket. In the absence of Dubai Destination, the horse started at 6/4-on ahead of Acomb Stakes winner Comfy, fellow O'Brien hopes Landseer and Tendulkar, and Somerville Tattersall Stakes victor Where Or When. O'Brien's other runner Shah Jehan, a 4.4 million-dollar yearling incidentally, gave the impression he might have been running as a pacemaker, since he went on, though at not much of a gallop, which led to Rock of Gibraltar refusing to settle. Caught in a pocket when the race began to take shape with under two furlongs left, Rock of Gibraltar managed to get clear and show his customary good acceleration to lead a hundred yards out, but, instead of drawing away, he was all out to hold Landseer and Tendulkar by a short head and a head, the former having had to be switched and make his run from well back. This was the second time, following the Irish Two Thousand Guineas, that O'Brien had trained the first three home in a Group 1 event during the year, and he was to repeat the feat again in the Criterium de Saint-Cloud. Possibly Rock of Gibraltar's run at Longchamp less than a fortnight before, on testing ground, had taken more out of him than his connections realised, although he still looked in excellent shape beforehand. Either way, he deserves credit for landing two of the most prestigious events in the juvenile calendar. Though no horse had won the Grand Criterium and

Darley Dewhurst Stakes, Newmarket—an Aidan O'Brien 1,2,3
as Rock of Gibraltar takes his second Group 1 in under two weeks; he hangs on from Landseer (far side)
and strong-finishing Tendulkar (near side), with Where Or When in fourth

Dewhurst Stakes before Rock of Gibraltar, the change in the Criterium's distance made the double more feasible and makes repetition a distinct possibility. Generally, however, colts are likely to go for one or other of the races, not both, which will probably work to the disadvantage of the French race rather than the Dewhurst, the race with the greater kudos.

Rock of Gibraltar (IRE) (b.c. Mar 8, 1999)	Danehill (USA) (b 1986)	Danzig (b 1977)	Northern Dancer Pas de Nom
		Razyana (b 1981)	His Majesty Spring Adieu
	Offshore Boom (ch 1985)	Be My Guest (ch 1974)	Northern Dancer What A Treat
		Push A Button (b 1980)	Bold Lad River Lady

The one, two, three for O'Brien in the Dewhurst was all the more remarkable considering those three didn't include Hawk Wing, who was promoted to favouritism for the Guineas after the Dewhurst, or the year's top two-year-old, Johannesburg, both also trained by O'Brien. One firm made O'Brien 5/4 to win the Guineas and even if Johannesburg doesn't contest the race—and possibly even if he does—Kinane will have a difficult call, with Hawk Wing and the Dewhurst trio all holding a chance of being in the shake-up. Rock of Gibraltar would not top our list but he is the type to continue giving a good account of himself. His breeding lends confidence to the view that a mile should be within his compass, but he cannot be guaranteed to stay much further. Bred by O'Brien, his wife and his father-in-law, Rock of Gibraltar is by far the best winner out of his dam Offshore Boom, a fairly useful filly who scored over six furlongs and was placed in listed company over seven furlongs as a two-year-old in Ireland. Her five other progeny to have hit the mark, including mile- to mile-and-a-quarter winner Eloquent Way (by the sprinter Dowsing), have not been by stallions as commercial as Danehill.

Sir Alex Ferguson & Mrs John Magnier's "Rock of Gibraltar"

However, having been bought by her current connections for IR 11,000 guineas in 1997, she has produced brothers to Rock of Gibraltar in 2000 and 2001. The grandam Push A Button, a winner at two, produced four other successful foals but her main claim to fame lay in being a half-sister to top-class racehorse and sire Riverman. Rock of Gibraltar, a rather leggy, close-coupled, quite attractive colt, who invariably impresses with his well-being, acts well on soft going; his run in the Coventry Stakes suggests good to firm does not inconvenience him. *A. P. O'Brien, Ireland*

ROCKON ARRY 2 b.g. (Mar 29) Aragon 118 – Rockstine (IRE) 61 (Ballad Rock 122) [2001 f8.5s 6s 5v⁴ p6g⁴ f5f f6s⁶ Dec 26] 6,000 2-y-o: first foal: dam 8.5f/1¼m winner: modest maiden: should stay 7f: acts on polytrack/fibresand, raced only on soft/heavy ground on turf: reportedly had breathing problem second start. *K. Bell* — **50**

ROCK SCENE (IRE) 9 b.g. Scenic 128 – Rockeater 94 (Roan Rocket 128) [2001 53: 10s⁶ 10f 10.3f⁵ 10.9m Aug 27] leggy gelding: poor performer: best around 1¼m: acts on soft going, firm and fibresand: usually held up: sometimes slowly away. *A. Streeter* — **39**

ROCK STEADY 2 b.f. (Jan 31) Puissance 110 – Just A Gem (Superlative 118) [2001 5v³ 5d 5.1f⁶ 5.1f² Jun 6] 3,000Y: heavy-topped filly: first foal: dam unraced sister to Oaks third Pearl Angel: fair maiden: blinkered, beaten ½ length at Chester final start (reportedly destroyed after injuring herself passing post): raced only at 5f: acted on any going. *E. J. Alston* — **65**

ROCKY ISLAND 4 b.g. Rock Hopper 124 – Queen's Eyot 79 (Grundy 137) [2001 –: 14.1v⁵ 13d May 6] close-coupled, workmanlike gelding: poor maiden, lightly raced: probably stays 1¾m: acts on heavy going. *Mrs M. Reveley* — **37**

RODIAK 2 b.g. (Mar 7) Distant Relative 128 – Misty Silks 81 (Scottish Reel 123) [2001 6d⁶ 7v 7s Nov 9] 6,500Y: good-topped gelding: third foal: half-brother to 4-y-o Misty Boy: dam, 1m winner, half-sister to 7-y-o Silk St John: easily best effort in maidens (modest form) when sixth of 16 at York: should stay 1m. *Bob Jones* — **59**

ROFFEY SPINNEY (IRE) 7 ch.g. Masterclass (USA) 116 – Crossed Line (Thatching 131) [2001 53§: 10.1g 12g Aug 23] angular gelding: temperamental performer: well beaten in 2001: blinkered/visored once each. *C. Drew* — **– §**

ROGER ROSS 6 b.g. Touch of Grey 90 – Foggy Dew 45 (Smoggy 115) [2001 51§: e12g⁵ f11s* f12g⁵ f11g f11g f11g² 10m 8m 10g 10g 9.9d f12s p10g Dec 29] small, good-bodied gelding: poor handicapper: won at Southwell in January: stays 11f: acts on good to firm going, soft, fibresand and equitrack: usually blinkered: usually held up: unreliable. *R. M. Flower* — **– §**
a44 §

ROGHAN JOSH 3 b.g. Timeless Times (USA) 99 – Macs Maharanee 85 (Indian King (USA) 128) [2001 –: f5g 6g Jun 3] no form. *P. S. Felgate* — **–**

ROGUE SPIRIT 5 b.g. Petong 126 – Quick Profit 78 (Formidable (USA) 125) [2001 75§: p12g Dec 19] fair handicapper at 4 yrs, though inconsistent: well held only start on Flat in 2001: blinkered once: has reared badly stalls: fair novice hurdler for C. Mann. *R. M. Stronge* — **– §**

ROI DE DANSE 6 ch.g. Komaite (USA) – Princess Lucy 42 (Local Suitor (USA) 128) [2001 –, a52: e10g⁶ e8g⁴ f8.5s* e10g⁵ f8.5g² f9.4g f8.5g 7s f8g⁴ 8.1g f8g Jul 20] lengthy, workmanlike gelding: has a round action: modest performer: won claimer at Wolverhampton in January: effective at 8.5f/easy 1¼m: acts on fibresand and equitrack, no recent form on turf: tried visored earlier in career: usually races up with pace: sold 1,000 gns in December. *M. Quinn* — **–**
a56

ROISIN SPLENDOUR (IRE) 6 ch.m. Inchinor 119 – Oriental Splendour 85 (Runnett 125) [2001 –: e8g e6g⁶ f7s Jan 23] good-topped mare: fair handicapper in 1999: little form since: visored in 2001. *S. Dow* — **–**

ROISTERER 5 ch.g. Rudimentary (USA) 118 – Raffle 82 (Balidar 133) [2001 34: f8g f5g³ f5g f5g⁶ 5m 8m 6m f6g² 5m 6m 8f 7m⁶ 8.3d 5s Aug 21] poor maiden handicapper: best at 5f/6f: acts on soft going, good to firm and fibresand: sometimes blinkered: has started slowly/raced freely. *D. W. Chapman* — **26**
a35

ROJABAA 2 b.g. (Mar 19) Anabaa (USA) 130 – Slava (USA) (Diesis 133) [2001 5s **47** 5g⁶ 5f⁵ 7m Jun 23] 13,500Y: lengthy, rather unfurnished gelding: half-brother to several winners, including 1¾m and 17f winner Monte Calvo (by Shirley Heights) and 6f (at 2 yrs) and 1¼m (in UAE) winner Sava River (by Lycius), both fairly useful: dam, French 11f winner, out of close relative of Soviet Star: poor maiden. *Mrs A. Duffield*

ROKEBY BOWL 9 b.g. Salse (USA) 128 – Rose Bowl (USA) 131 (Habitat 134) **87** [2001 12f 10f 11.6g⁶ Jul 9] small gelding: has had leg trouble: smart performer in 1999: only fairly useful in 2001: stays 13.4f: best form on good going or firmer. *I. A. Balding*

ROLLER 5 b.g. Bluebird (USA) 125 – Tight Spin (High Top 131) [2001 85: e8g³ 8s **58** 8.2s 8.3m 8m 8m 10v⁵ f9.4g 8s⁵ p7g f8g⁶ f9.4g f8.5s⁴ Dec 26] useful-looking gelding: **a55** poor mover: modest handicapper: best at 1m/1¼m: has form on firm going/fibresand, but goes well on softer than good (acts on heavy): sometimes blinkered, including last 6 starts: has run in snatches. *J. M. Bradley*

ROLLY POLLY (IRE) 3 b.f. Mukaddamah (USA) 125 – Rare Sound 69 (Rarity **111** 129) [2001 105: 7d* 8m 5.5g* a7f Dec 29] leggy, sparely-made filly: smart performer: trained in Italy in 2000: won Dubai Duty Free Stakes (Fred Darling) at Newbury in April by ½ length from Fatwa, drifting right under pressure: never-dangerous eighth to Rose Gypsy in Poule d'Essai des Pouliches at Longchamp following month (final outing for H. Cecil): made successful US debut in non-graded handicap at Hollywood in November by 1½ lengths from Twin Set: fair eighth to Affluent in La Brea Stakes at Santa Anita final start, debut on dirt: best up to 7f: acts on firm and good to soft going. *R. J. Frankel, USA*

ROMAHA (IRE) 5 b.h. Storm Bird (CAN) 134 – Eurobird 118 (Ela-Mana-Mou 132) **–** [2001 22.2f Jun 22] 55,000F, IR 8,000 5-y-o: tall, leggy horse: brother to Irish winner up to 1¼m Eurostorm, closely related to Irish 1m winner Golden Cat (by Storm Cat) and half-brother to 2m winner Flocheck (by Hansel), all useful: dam, Irish St Leger winner, half-sister to Prix du Jockey Club winners Bikala and Assert: fairly useful winning form in bumpers: blinkered, tailed off in Queen Alexandra Stakes at Royal Ascot on Flat debut. *S. J. Mahon, Ireland*

ROMAN CANDLE (IRE) 5 b.g. Sabrehill (USA) 120 – Penny Banger (IRE) 74 **–** (Pennine Walk 120) [2001 67: 12m 14.1d 11.9s f9.4g f12g Nov 23] strong, rangy gelding: one-time fair 1½m winner: well held in 2001, leaving G. Gaines after third start. *R. Wilman*

ROMAN CHIEF 2 b.c. (Apr 24) Forzando 122 – Red Cloud (IRE) 61 (Taufan (USA) **47 §** 119) [2001 6m⁶ 6m 5.1g Jul 9] 15,000F, 6,000Y: third foal: dam, maiden who stayed 7f and sometimes looked none too keen, half-sister to 4-y-o Cape Town: poor maiden: virtually refused to race in blinkers second start. *D. Haydn Jones*

ROMAN HIDEAWAY (IRE) 3 b.c. Hernando (FR) 127 – Vaison La Romaine 100 **87 p** (Arctic Tern (USA) 126) [2001 –p: f9.4g* f12g* 14f* f16.2g* 14.1g² Aug 20] big, rather leggy colt: fairly useful handicapper: won at Wolverhampton in June and at Southwell, Haydock and Wolverhampton in July: also good effort final start: will stay beyond 2m: acts on fibresand and firm going: sometimes slowly away: tends to race lazily: remains capable of better, and should win more races. *Sir Mark Prescott*

ROMAN KING (IRE) 6 b.g. Sadler's Wells (USA) 132 – Romantic Feeling 88 **92** (Shirley Heights 130) [2001 87+: 8v 10.1s* 11.9m⁶ 10.1m Jun 9] sturdy gelding: fairly useful handicapper: won at Epsom in April: ran poorly there final start: probably better over 9f/1¼m than 1½m: acts on soft ground, probably on good to firm: has been early to post: raced freely last 2 starts: joined Mrs M. Reveley. *M. Johnston*

ROMANNIE (BEL) 2 b.f. (Feb 28) Piccolo 121 – Green Land (BEL) 72 (Hero's **–** Honor (USA)) [2001 7g 7d Oct 18] 6,500 2-y-o: first foal: dam 1½m to (in France) 15f winner: little form in maiden/seller. *S. C. Williams*

ROMANTIC AFFAIR (IRE) 4 ch.g. Persian Bold 123 – Broken Romance (IRE) **118** (Ela-Mana-Mou 132) [2001 118: 16g³ 16.4m² 20f 14s² 15.9g⁵ Aug 21] leggy, lengthy gelding: smart performer: placed behind Solo Mio in spring in Sagaro Stakes at Newmarket (beaten 2½ lengths) and Bonusprint Stakes (Henry II) at Sandown (best effort, length second): creditable 1½ lengths second to Generic in Prix Maurice de Nieuil at Maisons-Laffitte in July: fair fifth behind Persian Punch in Lonsdale Stakes at York final outing: injured afterwards: effective at 1¾m (given a test) and 2m (gave impression something amiss in Gold Cup over 2½m): acts on heavy and good to firm going: usually held up: has been bandaged fore-joints: genuine. *J. L. Dunlop*

ROMANTIC MYTH 3 b.f. Mind Games 121 – My First Romance 61 (Danehill (USA) 126) [2001 105: 5g 6m⁵ 5m 6g 5m Aug 23] smallish, strong, well-made filly: useful performer: won Queen Mary Stakes at Royal Ascot at 2 yrs: best effort in 2001 when fifth to Volata in listed rated stakes at Haydock: effective at 5f/6f: acts on soft and good to firm going (lashed out in stall when below form on firm). *T. D. Easterby*   **104**

ROMANTIC POET 3 b.g. Cyrano de Bergerac 120 – Lady Quinta (IRE) 59 (Gallic League 119) [2001 66: 6g 8d May 17] second foal: dam 2-y-o 5f winner: fair form in 2 runs at 2 yrs: tongue tied, shaped as if something amiss when tailed off final start in 2001: should stay 6f. *B. R. Millman*   **–**

ROMANY FAIR (IRE) 2 b.g. (Mar 7) Blues Traveller (IRE) 119 – Fantasticus (IRE) 78 (Lycius (USA) 124) [2001 6g 7.1f⁶ 7.1m Jul 6] IR 18,500F, IR 23,000Y: second foal: dam ran 3 times in Ireland at 2 yrs, best effort at 7f: well held in minor events/maiden. *M. L. W. Bell*   **–**

ROMANYLEI (IRE) 4 gr.f. Blues Traveller (IRE) 119 – Krayyalei (IRE) 94 (Krayyan 117) [2001 106: 6d 5g 6d Aug 12] lengthy, sparely-made filly: useful performer: not the force of old in 2001, in listed races at Haydock and the Curragh and Phoenix Sprint Stakes at Leopardstown: stays 6f: has won on good to firm going, best efforts on good or softer. *J. G. Burns, Ireland*   **96**

ROMOH (IRE) 3 ch.c. Caerleon (USA) 132 – Possessive (Posse (USA) 130) [2001 e8g⁶ 10d a8g a12g Dec 16] 165,000F, 155,000Y: angular colt: half-brother to several winners, notably smart Italian/Irish Oaks winner Possessive Dancer (by Shareef Dancer): dam, unraced half-sister to smart performers Long Row (miler) and Colmore Row (sprinter), out of Irish 1000 Guineas winner Front Row: little form: sold from E. Dunlop 2,500 gns after second start: should be suited by 1¼m+. *E. J. Creighton, Spain*   **–**

ROMORA BAY 2 b.f. (Feb 16) Sri Pekan (USA) 117 – Fighting Run (Runnett 125) [2001 5g 6m 5f 6d f7g 7d Oct 18] 3,800Y: half-sister to 7.5f winner Croire (by Lomond) and 2 winners abroad by Royal Academy: dam, maiden, from very good family of Central Park: little form in maidens/sellers. *M. D. I. Usher*   **–**

ROMP IN 2 b.f. (Apr 20) Komaite (USA) – Sizzling Romp 59 (Sizzling Melody 117) [2001 f5g⁶ 5.1d⁴ 6m 5.2m⁶ f5g⁵ f5g f5g Jul 12] 4,000F: first living foal: dam, sprint maiden, half-sister to useful sprinter Jennelle: poor maiden: best form at 5f: acts on good to firm going and fibresand: tried visored: untrustworthy: sold 900 gns. *C. A. Dwyer*   **36 § a49 §**

RONNI PANCAKE 4 b.f. Mujadil (USA) 119 – Funny Choice (IRE) 68 (Commanche Run 133) [2001 56, a–: e10g 9d 9v² Oct 31] leggy filly: modest performer: left J. S. Moore and off course 9 months after first start: stays 1½m: acts on good to firm and heavy ground, well held on fibresand/equitrack. *J. G. Burns, Ireland*   **53**

RONQUISTA D'OR 7 b.g. Ron's Victory (USA) 129 – Gild The Lily 83 (Ile de Bourbon (USA) 133) [2001 43: f11g 11.9m 14.1m Jul 28] no form in 2001: reportedly broke down final start: usually blinkered/visored. *G. A. Ham*   **–**

RON'S PET 6 ch.g. Ron's Victory (USA) 129 – Penny Mint 79 (Mummy's Game 120) [2001 –, a80: f8g² e8g³ e7g e7s e8g f7g² f7f* f8g² 7.1m² 7.1m² 7m* 7.1f⁶ f8g² f8g³ 7m f7g* f7g⁵ f7g* f7g f7g* f7s⁴ Dec 15] tall gelding: fair performer: won claimers at Southwell in March/May and Wolverhampton in September and sellers at Wolverhampton (left T. D. Barron) in November and Southwell (left Andrew Reid) in December: effective at 7f/1m: acts on fibresand/equitrack, good to firm and good to soft going, probably on heavy: blinkered: sometimes tongue tied: has carried head high: races prominently. *P. D. Evans*   **65 a70**

RON'S ROUND 7 ch.g. Ron's Victory (USA) 129 – Magical Spirit 70 (Top Ville 129) [2001 34: f9.4s 10m⁶ Aug 29] rather leggy gelding: poor handicapper: left Miss K. George after first start: was best around 1¼m: acted on firm ground, good to soft, fibresand and equitrack: dead. *A. B. Coogan*   **43**

ROO 4 b.f. Rudimentary (USA) 118 – Shall We Run 59 (Hotfoot 126) [2001 97: 6m 6g⁶ 6m⁶ Jun 12] workmanlike filly: fairly useful performer: best at 5f/6f: acts on firm and soft going: has worn tongue strap: slowly away second start. *R. F. Johnson Houghton*   **89**

ROOFER (IRE) 3 b.f. Barathea (IRE) 127 – Castlerahan (IRE) (Thatching 131) **78**
[2001 80: 8m³ 8g³ 8.1s³ 9.9d⁴ 10.1g³ 10m Sep 21] tall, rather angular filly: fair maiden:
stays 1¼m: acts on soft and good to firm going: tends to carry head awkwardly: found
little final start. *M. R. Channon*

ROOFTOP 5 b.g. Thatching 131 – Top Berry 87 (High Top 131) [2001 60d: 8m 7.1f **–**
7d Oct 3] one-time fair maiden: no form in 2001: often blinkered/visored. *W. Storey*

ROOFTOP ROMANCE 2 ch.f. (Mar 17) Pursuit of Love 124 – Singer On The Roof **–**
62 (Chief Singer 131) [2001 6g Oct 6] angular filly: fifth foal: half-sister to German 9.5f
and 12.5f winner (ungenuine in Britain) Sole Singer (by Slip Anchor) and a 6.5f winner
abroad by Bluebird: dam, 1m winner, half-sister to Prix Saint-Alary winner Air de Rien:
33/1, in rear throughout in maiden at Newmarket: sold 1,000 gns. *I. A. Balding*

ROOKIE 5 b.g. Magic Ring (IRE) 115 – Shot At Love (IRE) 79 (Last Tycoon 131) **–**
[2001 –: e10g f16g 8m 8m f12g Jul 13] of little account nowadays. *M. J. Gingell*

ROOM TO ROOM MAGIC (IRE) 4 ch.f. Casteddu 111 – Bellatrix 45 (Persian **45**
Bold 123) [2001 47: f14g⁴ f12g⁴ 14.1f⁶ f12g⁵ 11.8d⁵ 11.6g⁵ 15m 11.7m³ 11.5g* f14.8s²
Sep 6] leggy filly: poor performer: won seller at Lingfield in August: barely stays 14.8f:
acts on good to firm ground, good to soft and fibresand: usually leads/races prominently.
B. Palling

ROOSTER 6 b.g. Roi Danzig (USA) – Jussoli (Don 128) [2001 10g 12m 16.2m² 16f⁶ **56**
Jul 2] big, strong gelding: unimpressive mover: modest maiden handicapper: stays 2m:
acts on good to firm ground. *D. E. Cantillon*

ROOTLE (FR) 2 gr.f. (Mar 19) Highest Honor (FR) 124 – Delve (IRE) 102 (Shernazar **77**
131) [2001 7g³ Jul 20] big, good-topped filly: has scope: third foal: half-sister to useful
1997 2-y-o 6f winner Deterrent (by Warning): dam, 1¼m winner, half-sister to smart
sprinter Lugana Beach out of half-sister to Mtoto: 33/1, backward and green, close third
of 8 to Kasamba in maiden at Newmarket, staying on. *J. L. Dunlop*

ROPPONGI DANCER 2 b.f. (May 11) Mtoto 134 – Ice Chocolate (USA) 77 **–**
(Icecapade (USA)) [2001 7f 6m 5f 6d 8g Nov 5] small, quite good-topped filly: sister
to 3-y-o Broughtons Motto and half-sister to 3 winners, including 1¼m/1½m winner
Ice Rebel (by Robellino): dam 1m winner at 4 yrs: no form in maidens/nurseries.
Mrs M. Reveley

RORKES DRIFT (IRE) 3 ch.f. Royal Abjar (USA) 121 – Scanno's Choice (IRE) 54 **–**
(Pennine Walk 120) [2001 55: 7m 10m 8.1m Aug 1] workmanlike filly: green, modest
form in 2 runs at 2 yrs: no form in 2001. *T. J. Naughton*

ROSE D'OR (IRE) 2 b.f. (Mar 29) Polish Precedent (USA) 131 – Gold Rose (FR) **65 p**
(Noblequest (FR) 124) [2001 7g Oct 4] unfurnished filly: sixth foal: half-sister to 1m
winner Fairy Star (by Fairy King) and 1994 Grand Criterium winner Goldmark and
French 1997 2-y-o 5.5f winner Gilded Leaf (both by Lyphard): dam, French 10.5f winner,
half-sister to very smart 7f/1m performer Gabina and smart performer around 1¼m
Galetto: 20/1, some late headway when fifteenth of 21 to Millennium Dragon in maiden
at Newmarket: will improve. *J. L. Dunlop*

ROSE GYPSY 3 b.f. Green Desert (USA) 127 – Krisalya 98 (Kris 135) [2001 **114**
90p: 8s² 7g² 8m* 8f 12g Jul 15]
A filly trained in Ireland won the Dubai Poule d'Essai des Pouliches, Rose
Gypsy the first from there to achieve the feat. She caused something of a surprise in
doing so, too, sent off at odds of almost 15/1 in a fifteen-runner field and not really
entitled to start much shorter on her form. A narrow winner of a maiden at Naas on
the second of two outings at two, Rose Gypsy finished second at the Curragh on
both of her starts at three prior to the Pouliches, beaten three lengths by Cool Clarity
in the listed Athasi Stakes at the Curragh just six days before it. The form didn't
quite match up to that shown by most of her rivals at Longchamp, nine home-
trained runners, four from Britain and one from Norway. Favourite at around 2/1
was the French filly Amonita, who had won the Prix Marcel Boussac as a
two-year-old and had split two of the others in the field, Quarter Note and Born
Something, when finishing second in the Prix de la Grotte over the course and
distance on her reappearance. Luck in running played an important part in the

*Dubai Poule d'Essai des Pouliches, Longchamp—Rose Gypsy (No.7) holds on from the
fast-finishing Banks Hill (far side), with Lethals Lady and Tempting Fate (rail) close behind*

Pouliches and Amonita was the worst sufferer, while Banks Hill was one of the
others who didn't enjoy a clear run in the straight. Rose Gypsy, on the other hand,
fared better than most after being held up in rear, switched inside and getting a
good run over a furlong out. Sustaining her effort, Rose Gypsy collared the leader
Tempting Fate well inside the final furlong and held the fast-finishing Banks
Hill by a head. Lethals Lady was the same distance away in third, just ahead of
Tempting Fate, with Amonita fifth, beaten only around two lengths. As with the
five previous winners, Rose Gypsy's victory in the Pouliches turned out to be her
last. Four of those five made their next appearance in the Coronation Stakes at
Royal Ascot, as did Rose Gypsy, but, unlike that quartet, she failed to make the
frame. Rose Gypsy would probably have done so had she reproduced her
Longchamp form, given that the race was won by Banks Hill with Tempting Fate
taking third place and Lethals Lady finishing fourth, though further improvement
from Rose Gypsy would have been required for her to confirm placings with the
progressive winner. Surprisingly, the Irish Oaks was chosen for Rose Gypsy's next
and, as it turned out, final appearance. She stayed a mile well and might have got a
bit further persevered with, but she was hardly equipped to prove effective at a mile
and a half judged on her pedigree. Again held up, as at Ascot, Rose Gypsy never
threatened to take a hand at the Curragh and finished ninth of twelve.

Rose Gypsy, the first daughter of sprinter Green Desert to win a Group 1, is
the seventh foal of Krisalya, a useful performer who gained her sole success for
Geoff Wragg in a four-runner maiden over an extended mile and a quarter at
Chester. Krisalya, the dam of four other winners, including the fairly useful 1994
two-year-old seven-furlong winner Crystal Cavern (by Be My Guest), later
successful in Canada, is from an excellent family. Her dam Sassalya, a half-sister to
the Cumberland Lodge winner Lafontaine out of the good French middle-distance
filly Valya, was a useful winner up to a mile and a quarter in Ireland and has
produced no fewer than thirteen winners, including the smart performers Sally
Rous, Sossus Vlei and The Faraway Tree and the very smart Sasuru, the last-named
winner of the Prix d'Ispahan. Sassalya died at the age of twenty-four after suffering
complications giving birth to what would have been a full brother or sister to
Sasuru. Rose Gypsy has already recouped virtually all of the 115,000 guineas she
fetched as a yearling, and she could prove a money-spinner as a broodmare,

Rose Gypsy (b.f. 1998)	Green Desert (USA) (b 1983)	Danzig (b 1977)	Northern Dancer
			Pas de Nom
		Foreign Courier (b 1979)	Sir Ivor
			Courtly Dee
	Krisalya (b 1986)	Kris (ch 1976)	Sharpen Up
			Doubly Sure
		Sassalya (b 1973)	Sassafras
			Valya

too. A sturdy filly, she gained her first win on good to soft ground but put up easily her best performance on good to firm at Longchamp; her below-par Ascot effort was on firm ground. *A. P. O'Brien, Ireland*

ROSE HILL 5 b.m. Sabrehill (USA) 120 – Petite Rosanna 89 (Ile de Bourbon (USA) 133) [2001 10m May 25] angular mare: modest handicapper, very lightly raced nowadays: stays 1¼m: acts on good to firm ground. *W. Clay* **60**

ROSELYN 3 b.f. Efisio 120 – Ciboure 74 (Norwick (USA) 125) [2001 66: 5.1v⁴ f7g 7.1g 7.1g Jun 7] sparely-made filly: modest maiden: should be suited by at least 7f: acts on heavy and good to firm going. *I. A. Balding* **61**

ROSEMEAD MARY 2 b.f. (Apr 27) Keen 116 – Arasong 76 (Aragon 118) [2001 6g⁵ 8g 8m Sep 20] 500Y: second foal: half-sister to 3-y-o Annie's Song: dam 5f winner (including at 2 yrs): poor maiden: best effort on debut. *M. Dods* **43**

ROSE OF AMERICA 3 ch.f. Brief Truce (USA) 126 – Kilcoy (USA) (Secreto (USA) 128) [2001 58: 7m* 7.9g 7.1m³ 8f² 8m* 8m⁶ 10m 8g² Nov 7] big, strong filly: fairly useful performer: won maiden at Ayr in May and handicap at Newcastle in July: effective at 7f/1m: acts on firm going: free-going sort: has edged right/carried head awkwardly: held up. *Miss L. A. Perratt* **81**

ROSE OF PARADISE (USA) 2 b.f. (Feb 14) Hansel (USA) – Vie En Rose (USA) **61**
(Blushing Groom (FR) 131) [2001 6m⁴ 6m 8.3m Sep 24] $18,000Y: half-sister to several
winners, including winner around 1¼m Arzani (by Shahrastani) and fairly useful 1m/
1¼m winner Marksmanship (by Sharpen Up), later minor stakes winner in USA: dam,
maiden in USA, half-sister to smart French performers up to 1m Vorias and Verria:
modest form when fourth in maiden at Hamilton: folded tamely next start: pulled up lame
final one. *M. Johnston*

ROSE PEEL 3 b.f. Danehill (USA) 126 – Why So Silent (Mill Reef (USA) 141) [2001 **73**
70p: 8.3s* 8.3g May 8] small, close-coupled filly: good walker: fair form, lightly raced:
won maiden at Windsor in April by neck, despite tending to wander: ran poorly in
handicap on same course following month: free-going sort, but should stay 1¼m: raced
only on good ground or softer. *P. W. Harris*

ROSES FLUTTER 2 b.f. (Apr 22) Son Pardo 107 – Silent Scream (IRE) (Lahib **–**
(USA) 129) [2001 6s f5g⁶ Nov 16] 500Y: leggy, quite good-topped filly: second foal:
dam unraced out of half-sister to Derby third Mashkour: well held in maidens. *A. Smith*

ROSES OF SPRING 3 gr.f. Shareef Dancer (USA) 135 – Couleur de Rose (Kalaglow **82**
132) [2001 7.1d 6g⁵ 6m² 6m* 7m 6g⁵ 6m² 6m² 6g² 6m² 5g 6f³ 5g² Oct 4] lengthy filly:
eighth foal: sister to 1992 2-y-o 6f winner Exclusively Yours and half-sister to 2 winners,
including fairly useful 6f/7f winner Rouge (by Rudimentary): dam unraced out of May
Hill winner Exclusively Raised: fairly useful performer: won maiden at Yarmouth in
June: good efforts after when placed in handicaps: effective at 5f/6f: acts on firm ground:
visored (slowly away) eleventh start: often front runner. *R. M. H. Cowell*

ROSE TINTED 2 b.f. (Feb 7) Spectrum (IRE) 126 – Marie La Rose (FR) (Night Shift **69 p**
(USA)) [2001 6m 6.5g Sep 28] 140,000Y: close-coupled, useful-looking filly: third foal:
half-sister to French 2000 2-y-o 1m winner Contemporary Art (by Blushing Flame) and
French winner up to 1½m Danni La Rose (by Lycius): dam French 1¼m winner out of
half-sister to French Group 1 winners Le Nain Jaune, Indian Rose and Vert Amende:
green, fair form when ninth of 21 to Misterah in maiden at Newbury: unfavourably drawn
and never dangerous in valuable sales race at Ascot following month: likely to be suited
by 1m+: should do better. *J. H. M. Gosden*

ROSETTA 4 b.f. Fraam 114 – Starawak 68 (Star Appeal 133) [2001 –: 5.7g⁵ 8f 6.1m⁴ **43 +**
6m⁵ 7m Aug 27] leggy, sparely-made filly: poor maiden: effective at 6f to 1m: acts on
good to firm ground, well held on softer than good: sometimes gets behind. *R. J. Hodges*

ROSEUM 5 b.m. Lahib (USA) 129 – Rose Barton (Pas de Seul 133) [2001 91: 6s 6d **72**
6m² 5m* 7d² 5g* Aug 17] strong, good-quartered mare: fair performer nowadays: won
claimers at Lingfield in July and Catterick in August: best at 5f/6f: acts on good to firm
and heavy going: usually held up (not at Catterick). *R. Guest*

ROSEWOOD BELLE (USA) 3 ch.f. Woodman (USA) 126 – Supreme Excellence **70**
(USA) (Providential 118) [2001 10m⁵ 10.5d³ 12.1g⁵ Sep 13] $60,000F, 700,000 francs Y:
workmanlike filly: ninth foal: half-sister to 3 winners, including US minor stakes winner
up to 13f Glenbarra (by Vice Regent) and 1¼m winner North Russia (by Bering): dam,
minor stakes winner around 1m in USA, half-sister to Arlington Million/Japan Cup
winner Golden Pheasant: best effort in maidens (fair form) on second start: tongue tied:
carries head awkwardly: tail flasher. *W. R. Muir*

ROSHEEN DONN (IRE) 2 b.f. (Mar 21) Revoque (IRE) 122 – Mashoura (Shareef **60 d**
Dancer (USA) 135) [2001 5d² 5m⁴ 5m⁵ 6d 6d 5g p6g⁵ Nov 15] IR 24,000Y: rather leggy
filly: first living foal: dam French 1m winner out of useful sprinter Massorah: modest
maiden: best efforts first 2 starts: may prove best at 5f: has looked difficult ride.
M. Johnston

ROSIE (FR) 3 ch.f. Bering 136 – Scarlet Plume 103 (Warning 136) [2001 76: 12.3v⁴ **67 +**
10m 14.1g Jun 25] useful-looking filly: fair maiden, lightly raced: below form in handicaps in 2001, though met trouble final start: should be well suited by 1¼m+: sold 34,000
gns in July. *J. L. Dunlop*

ROSIE'S POSY 2 b.f. (Mar 31) Suave Dancer (USA) 136 – My Branch 111 (Distant **86 p**
Relative 128) [2001 5.7g* 8d⁵ Nov 3] rather leggy, close-coupled filly: second foal:
half-sister to 3-y-o Future Flight: dam, 5f (at 2 yrs) to 7f winner, also third in Irish 1000
Guineas: fairly useful form: won maiden at Bath in October: fifth to Sundrenched in listed
race at Newmarket, having lot to do when tempo increased and never nearer: should stay
1¼m: capable of better. *B. W. Hills*

ROSIE STARLIGHT (IRE)   3 b.f. Tagula (IRE) 116 – Idrak 68 (Young Generation   **58**
129) [2001 6m 6m⁴ 5f³ 6d 5g³ 5m⁴ 5m⁶ Aug 25] 8,800Y: small filly: seventh foal:
half-sister to several winners, including 1993 2-y-o 6f winner Recaptured Days (by Salse)
and 4-y-o Lucky Heather: dam 5f winner from very good middle-distance family: modest
maiden: stays 6f: acts on firm going, probably on good to soft. *D. Nicholls*

ROSI'S BOY   3 b.c. Caerleon (USA) 132 – Come On Rosi 77 (Valiyar 129) [2001 91:   **109**
10g* 10.4m⁶ 8g³ 8g³ 8d 9d⁴ 8.2s⁴ Nov 5] smallish, well-made colt: useful performer: won
listed event at Newmarket (beat Fair Question a neck) in May: ran well when third to
Aghnoyoh in Prix de la Jonchere at Chantilly (beaten ¾ length) and to Goggles in listed
event at Goodwood (beaten 2 lengths), and when 2¾ lengths fourth to Right Wing in
another listed event at Newmarket (reluctant to go behind stalls) on penultimate start:
effective at 1m/1¼m: acts on good to firm and good to soft going: visored (ran poorly)
fifth outing: held up: possibly temperamental. *J. L. Dunlop*

ROSSELLI (USA)   5 b.g. Puissance 110 – Miss Rossi (Artaius (USA) 129) [2001   **103 d**
104+: 5.1v 5m⁵ 5f 5s⁵ 5.1m 5d⁵ 5d Nov 6] tall, good-topped gelding: suffered suspensory
and sesamoid injuries in 1999: useful performer: generally well below form in 2001 after
fifth to Borders in minor event at Beverley second start: best at 5f: acts on heavy and good
to firm ground: tried blinkered/visored: has had tongue tied: sometimes early to post: not
one to trust. *J. A. Glover*

ROSSEL (USA)   8 b.g. Blushing John (USA) 120 – Northern Aspen (USA) 120   **45**
(Northern Dancer) [2001 16v 13s 14d 12d⁴ 12m 13.1m 9.2g³ 12.1m⁵ 12.4g⁵ 15s 12f 9.2d
12m Aug 22] rangy gelding: poor performer on Flat in 2001: was best at 1½m to 15f:
acted on any going: visored once: dead. *P. Monteith*

Mr Wafic Said's "Rosi's Boy"

ROS THE BOSS (IRE) 2 b.f. (Apr 9) Danehill (USA) 126 – Bella Vitessa (IRE) (Thatching 131) [2001 5.7g 7s Nov 9] 750,000 francs Y: third foal: half-sister to fairly useful 1999 2-y-o 6f winner Bella Bellisimo (by Alzao): dam, no form, half-sister to smart 1½m performer Wind In Her Hair from excellent family: well held in maidens. *G. A. Butler* —

ROSTROPOVICH (IRE) 4 gr.c. Sadler's Wells (USA) 132 – Infamy 123 (Shirley Heights 130) [2001 113: 14g* 22.2f⁴ 14m Sep 15] good-topped colt: smart performer: won listed race at Leopardstown in May by 1½ lengths from Media Puzzle: well held after in Queen Alexandra Stakes at Royal Ascot and Irish St Leger at the Curragh: should be suited by 2m+: raced mainly on good ground or firmer: has been blanketed for stalls entry/worn crossed noseband/tongue strap: visored once at 3 yrs: useful hurdler. *M. F. Morris, Ireland* 113

ROTUMA (IRE) 2 b.g. (Apr 28) Tagula (IRE) 116 – Cross Question (USA) 84 (Alleged (USA) 138) [2001 6f⁴ May 29] 10,000F, 26,000Y: smallish, useful-looking gelding: third foal: dam, Irish 1¼m winner, out of smart winner up to 1¼m Rambushka: fair form when fourth in maiden at Leicester: should stay 1m: sold 6,000 gns, joined M. Dods and gelded. *I. A. Balding* 69

ROUBERIA (IRE) 2 ch.f. (May 15) Alhaarth (IRE) 126 – Robinia (USA) 90 (Roberto (USA) 131) [2001 6g 7s p5g⁵ Nov 24] IR 48,000Y: rather leggy filly: half-sister to several winners, including smart Irish winner up to 1½m/high-class hurdler I'm Supposin (by Posen) and 4-y-o Cayman Sunset: dam 2-y-o 7f winner: modest form in maidens: took good hold second start: not knocked about final one: should stay 1m: capable of better. *G. A. Butler* 64 p

ROUE 3 b.c. Efisio 120 – Ideal Home 104 (Home Guard (USA) 129) [2001 –p: 7d 7g³ 8m⁴ 8m 8m* Jul 7] good-topped colt: good walker: fairly useful handicapper: much improved to win at Leicester final start: lost lot of ground at start and ran as if something amiss time before: stays 1m: yet to race on extremes of going: often tongue tied: sold 4,500 gns in October. *Sir Michael Stoute* 80

ROUGH SEAS (IRE) 2 b.g. (Mar 11) Royal Applause 124 – Hebrides (Gone West (USA)) [2001 5g 5.6f³ 5.1g Jul 9] 29,000F, 60,000Y: compact gelding: first foal: dam unraced granddaughter of very smart performer up to 1m Joking Apart: modest maiden: best effort when third at Doncaster: likely to prove best at 5f/6f: has worn crossed noseband: sold 3,000 gns and gelded. *B. W. Hills* 51

ROUNDTREE (IRE) 2 b.f. (Mar 1) Night Shift (USA) – Island Desert (IRE) 55 (Green Desert (USA) 127) [2001 5d* 5m² 5m³ 6.3d³ 6m⁶ Sep 22] IR 16,000F, IR 39,000Y: smallish, strong filly: good walker: fourth reported foal: half-sister to 1997 2-y-o 5.7f winner Brandon Frank (by Beveled), later winner abroad: dam maiden who stayed 1½m: useful performer: won maiden at Windsor in May: unlucky not to follow up in listed event at Beverley, and beaten less than a length when third of 20 to Queen's Logic in Queen Mary Stakes at Royal Ascot: well below best in valuable sales race at the Curragh and listed event at Ayr (said to have finished lame) last 2 starts: should stay at least 6f: yet to race on extremes of going: swished tail/on toes final outing. *R. Hannon* 98

ROUSING THUNDER 4 b.g. Theatrical 128 – Moss (USA) (Woodman (USA) 126) [2001 86: 10v 10g 10g 10d 12g 10.4m 12g⁴ 13.9d 10.1v Oct 24] leggy, rather unfurnished gelding: fair handicapper: stays 1½m: acts on good to firm going: visored (well held) once. *W. J. Musson* 66

ROUTE BARREE (FR) 3 ch.g. Exit To Nowhere (USA) 122 – Star Des Evees (FR) (Moulin 103) [2001 52p: 10s⁵ 12g⁴ 11.9f² 12f² 12g⁶ 11.9m² 14m⁵ Aug 18] quite attractive gelding: fairly useful maiden: stays 1½m, probably not 1¾m: best efforts on going firmer than good: visored fifth start: carries head awkwardly and has tended to wander. *S. Dow* 83

ROUTE SIXTY SIX (IRE) 5 b.m. Brief Truce (USA) 126 – Lyphards Goddess (IRE) (Lyphard's Special (USA) 122) [2001 70: 8.2v³ 8s⁶ 9g 10.4m 8d⁵ 8g 8d Oct 30] close-coupled mare: fair handicapper: seems best at 1m/9f: acts on any going: blinkered once: weak finisher, waited with. *Jedd O'Keeffe* 65

ROXANNE MILL 3 b.f. Cyrano de Bergerac 120 – It Must Be Millie 66 (Reprimand 122) [2001 76: e6g f5g 5.1d 6s 5d 5m² 5.1m³ 5m⁴ 5.1g³ 5.2d² f5g f5g f5g Dec 14] sturdy filly: fair on turf, modest on all-weather: reportedly finished lame second start: best at 5f: acts on good to firm going, soft and fibresand: reared leaving stall ninth outing: races prominently. *M. D. I. Usher* 71 a61

ROY 6 ch.g. Keen 116 – Billante (USA) (Graustark) [2001 f16.2g Jun 20] rather leggy, –
useful-looking gelding: lightly raced and little form: tried blinkered. *W. Jenks*

ROYAL APPROVAL 2 b.c. (Jan 30) Royal Applause 124 – Inimitable 66 (Polish **70**
Precedent (USA) 131) [2001 7m⁴ 7g 8.2m* Sep 10] 5,000Y: rather leggy, quite attractive
colt: first foal: dam, 1¼m winner who barely stayed 1½m, out of half-sister to Melbourne
Cup winner Jeune: fair form: best effort on debut: got up near finish to win maiden at
Nottingham: should stay 1¼m. *J. L. Dunlop*

ROYAL ARTIST 5 b.g. Royal Academy (USA) 130 – Council Rock 74 (General **95 d**
Assembly (USA)) [2001 96: 6g 7m⁶ 7m² 7m 7g 5.2d 7m f7s Dec 15] workmanlike
gelding: useful performer at best: good second in handicap at Newmarket in June, but
well held after, including in claimers: left W. Haggas 3,200 gns after penultimate start:
stays 8.5f: acts on fibresand, equitrack and firm going, probably on good to soft:
blinkered 4 of last 6 starts: sometimes mulish in preliminaries. *Miss J. F. Craze*

ROYAL AXMINSTER 6 b.g. Alzao (USA) 117 – Number One Spot 71 (Reference **48**
Point 139) [2001 45: 11.8f⁴ 12m² 12m⁵ 12m⁴ 10d 13.1m⁶ Sep 10] useful-looking gelding:
poor maiden handicapper: should stay beyond 1½m: acts on firm going: blinkered (well
held) once. *Mrs P. N. Dutfield*

ROYAL BEAU (IRE) 2 b.f. (Mar 14) Fayruz 116 – Castlelue (IRE) (Tremblant 112) **46**
[2001 f5g 5m⁴ 6g 6m 7m⁴ Jun 23] IR 5,000Y: rather leggy, close-coupled filly: first foal:
dam unraced: poor maiden: fourth in claimer at Thirsk and seller at Redcar: stays 7f.
D. Nicholls

ROYAL BRIGHTEYES 3 b.g. Barbezieux 55 – Royal Hanina (Royal Palace 131) –
[2001 8.2f 8g Jul 18] small gelding: first reported foal: dam unraced: tailed off in maiden
at Nottingham (moved poorly to post) and minor event at Doncaster. *Ronald Thompson*

ROYAL CASCADE (IRE) 7 b.g. River Falls 113 – Relative Stranger (Cragador –
110) [2001 53, a71: f7g⁴ f7g⁴ f7g⁴ f7g² f8g² f8g⁶ f7g⁴ f7g* f7g f8g² f8g⁴ f6g f7g f8.5g³ **a64**
f9.4g⁴ f8.5g f8.5g² f8.5g² f9.4g³ Dec 11] lengthy gelding: modest performer: won minor
event at Southwell in April: effective at 7f to 9.4f: raced mainly on fibresand nowadays:
often blinkered: usually races lazily, and often gets behind early on: largely consistent.
B. A. McMahon

ROYAL CASTLE (IRE) 7 b.g. Caerleon (USA) 132 – Sun Princess 130 (English –
Prince 129) [2001 76: 14.1g Oct 19] sturdy, lengthy gelding: good mover: fair performer
at best: off 15 months, well held only run in 2001: visored final 6-y-o start.
M. H. Tompkins

ROYAL CAVALIER 4 b.g. Prince of Birds (USA) 121 – Gold Belt (IRE) 61 **86**
(Bellypha 130) [2001 77, a84: f8g⁶ 10.3m³ 10f* 10m 10f² 10.5m⁵ 10.3m³ 11.8g⁴ 10.3m **a–**
10d³ 9.9s³ 12m³ 10m* 8d⁴ 12s* f12s Dec 21] sturdy gelding: fairly useful performer: won

Tote Scoop6 November Stakes (Handicap), Doncaster—50/1-shot Royal Cavalier (white sleeves)
gives Reg Hollinshead another success in 2001, during which he celebrated fifty years as a trainer;
Mesmeric (second right) is next with the blinkered Golden Wells and Red Carnation (rail) third and fourth

handicap at Leicester in May, minor event at Nottingham in September and Tote Scoop6 November Handicap at Doncaster (50/1, beat Mesmeric gamely by a head): stays 1½m: acts on fibresand and any turf going: waited with: consistent. *R. Hollinshead*

ROYAL DRAGON (USA)   3 b.c. Danehill (USA) 126 – Carmelized (CAN) (Key To **118** The Mint (USA)) [2001 7.5s* 8m* 10d² 8g* 8d⁶ Aug 19] $280,000F, 250,000Y: third foal: closely related to fairly useful 1¼m winner Abi (by Chief's Crown): dam, won up to 9f in North America, from excellent family of Chief's Crown: very smart performer: progressed well, winning maiden at Cologne at 2 yrs, listed race at Dusseldorf in April, Mehl Mulhens-Rennen at Cologne (by neck from Touch Down) in May and Berlin Brandenburg-Trophy at Hoppegarten (by 1¼ lengths from Golden Silca) in July: also originally awarded Grosser Muller Brot-Preis at Munich (beaten ¾ length by Zollner) in June but winner subsequently reinstated: not discredited when promoted to sixth behind disqualified Proudwings in Prix Jacques le Marois at Deauville final start after making much of running: best at 1m: acts on soft and good to firm ground. *A. Schutz, Germany*

ROYAL EAGLE (GER)   2 ch.c. (Feb 21) Eagle Eyed (USA) 111 – Royal Rivalry **75** (USA) (Sir Ivor 135) [2001 7m² 7m³ 7m² 7.9d⁴ 8d⁴ Oct 25] 18,000Y: fourth foal: closely related to a 1¼m/11f winner in Germany by Polish Precedent: dam, French 11f/1½m winner, half-sister to smart stayer Always Aloof: fair maiden: second at Lingfield and Folkestone: should stay at least 1¼m: wore tongue strap last 2 outings. *L. M. Cumani*

ROYAL EBERSPACHER (IRE)   2 b.f. (Apr 4) Revoque (IRE) 122 – Nicea (IRE) **–** 90 (Dominion 123) [2001 7m 10.2g Oct 1] IR 7,000F, IR 10,000Y: half-sister to useful 1997 2-y-o 7f winner Prose (by Priolo), later winner up to 1m in USA, and 3-y-o Definite Guest: dam Irish 2-y-o 7f winner: well held in maidens. *Mrs P. N. Dutfield*

ROYAL ENCLOSURE (IRE)   3 b.g. Royal Academy (USA) 130 – Hi Bettina 96 **54** (Henbit (USA) 130) [2001 –: f9.4s² f8s f8.5g⁶ f7g⁴ f8g² f9.4g⁴ e8g⁴ f7g 7m 10f⁶ f8g² **a59** 8.2g² 8f⁴ f8g 8g² 8.2m³ 8.1d² 10.1g⁴ 8.1d¹ 10.1g⁴ 8.1g⁴ 10m 5s f9.4g* f8g f9.4s² Dec 27] close-coupled gelding: modest handicapper: left A. Murphy after second start: won at Wolverhampton in December: effective at 1m/1¼m: acts on fibresand/equitrack, firm and good to soft going: effective blinkered/visored or not: tongue tied nowadays: has gone in snatches, and looks a difficult ride. *P. D. Evans*

ROYAL EXPRESSION   9 b.g. Sylvan Express 117 – Edwins' Princess 75 (Owen **55** Dudley 121) [2001 77: f14g f14g f12s Dec 21] tall gelding: fair handicapper in 2000: modest form at 9 yrs only on second start: stays 2¼m: acts on firm ground, soft and fibresand: tried blinkered/visored. *G. M. Moore*

ROYAL GENT   3 b.g. Presidium 124 – Harem Queen 66 (Prince Regent (FR) 129) **–** [2001 –: 11.1m⁵ 10.4g⁵ 12f f12g 16m Aug 22] little form: tried visored. *L. R. James*

ROYAL GLEN (IRE)   3 b.f. Royal Abjar (USA) 121 – Sea Glen (IRE) (Glenstal **–** (USA) 118) [2001 55: 7m 8m 7.1m 8m 8f 8.1d 7.1f 10.4s 10.9v⁵ 11d 10g Nov 5] rather leggy filly: little form in 2001. *H. A. McWilliams*

ROYAL INSULT   4 ch.g. Lion Cavern (USA) 117 – Home Truth 98 (Known Fact **80** (USA) 135) [2001 85: 7f³ 7m 8s 8m² Aug 4] close-coupled gelding: fairly useful handicapper: stays 1m: acts on good to firm going and equitrack: visored (ran creditably) final start. *K. R. Burke*

ROYAL IVY   4 ch.f. Mujtahid (USA) 118 – Royal Climber (Kings Lake (USA) 133) **64** [2001 71: 7m 7.6f 7.6m⁴ 7m 7g² 6m⁴ 7g⁵ 7s⁴ p7g p6g p7g Dec 28] small filly: has a quick **a–** action: modest handicapper: effective at 7f/1m: acts on equitrack and polytrack, very best turf efforts on good ground or firmer: blinkered (below form) last 2 starts. *J. Akehurst*

ROYAL KISS (IRE)   3 b.f. Royal Academy (USA) 130 – Hawajiss 114 (Kris 135) **61** [2001 54: 10s 11.6g 14.1m⁵ 11.9f³ 11.5m⁵ Jun 26] close-coupled, useful-looking filly: has a round action: modest maiden: barely stays easy 1¾m: acts on firm going: tail swisher: sold 50,000 gns in December. *E. A. L. Dunlop*

ROYAL LADY (IRE)   2 b.f. (Mar 16) Royal Academy (USA) 130 – Shahoune **65** (USA) (Blushing Groom (FR) 131) [2001 7d 7d Nov 3] close-coupled, good-topped filly: half-sister to several winners abroad, including smart performer up to 9f in France/USA Bouccaneer (by Hero's Honor) and French 11f winner Silent Lady (by Phantom Breeze): dam French maiden: fair form in maidens at Leicester and Newmarket, not knocked about either time: should stay 1m. *R. Guest*

ROYAL MEASURE   5 b.g. Inchinor 119 – Sveltissima 48 (Dunphy 124) [2001 53: **63** 14.1s² 14.1v* 17.2f 14.1d Oct 3] leggy, angular gelding: modest handicapper: won at Nottingham in May: should stay 2m: acts on heavy going, well beaten on firm. *B. R. Millman*

ROYAL MILLENNIUM (IRE) 3 b.c. Royal Academy (USA) 130 – Galatrix 72 **102** (Be My Guest (USA) 126) [2001 8s³ 7m² 7m* 7.1m² 7.6d³ 7g² 7m Aug 23] rather lengthy, angular colt: unimpressive mover: fifth living foal: half-brother to winner in Sweden by Persian Bold: dam, 1m winner, half-sister to Croco Rouge and to dam of Sleepytime, Ali-Royal (both by Royal Academy) and Taipan: useful performer: landed odds in maiden at Salisbury in June: good second in handicaps at Sandown (short-headed by Lunar Leo) in July and Goodwood (most unfortunate when beaten 1½ lengths by Venturer, repeatedly short of room) in August: ran respectably behind Priors Lodge in listed race at York final outing: better at 7f than further, and may prove effective at 6f: acts on good to firm going, probably on soft. *M. R. Channon*

ROYAL MINSTREL (IRE) 4 ch.g. Be My Guest (USA) 126 – Shanntabariya **90** (IRE) (Shernazar 131) [2001 86§: 16s 14.1g⁶ 14.8m⁵ 10d* 10.1m² 10m* 11.9m* 12s 12d⁵ Oct 18] strong, lengthy gelding: fairly useful handicapper: won at Leicester and Ripon in August and York in September: probably best at 1¼m/1½m: acts on firm and soft going: blinkered once in 2000: tends to carry head high. *M. H. Tompkins*

ROYAL MIRAGE (IRE) 2 ch.f. (Mar 2) Lycius (USA) 124 – Cariellor's Miss (FR) **60** (Cariellor (FR) 125) [2001 7d⁵ f8.5g³ f8.5g⁶ Nov 3] 2,000Y: tall, rather leggy filly: third foal: dam, French 7.5f (at 2 yrs) and 1¼m winner, half-sister to smart French performer up to 7f Wixon: modest form in maidens: third at Wolverhampton: stays 8.5f. *M. L. W. Bell*

ROYAL MUSICAL 3 ch.f. Royal Abjar (USA) 121 – Musical Sally (USA) (The **–** Minstrel (CAN) 135) [2001 39: f11g⁵ 8.1d Aug 9] short-backed filly: poor form on debut at 2 yrs: has shown nothing since. *M. Brittain*

ROYAL PARTNERSHIP (IRE) 5 b.g. Royal Academy (USA) 130 – Go Honey **53** Go (General Assembly (USA)) [2001 63: f12g² f16.2g Feb 22] tall, angular gelding: modest performer: stays 1½m, not 2m: acts on fibresand, good to firm and soft ground: tried visored. *D. L. Williams*

ROYAL PLUM 5 ch.g. Inchinor 119 – Miss Plum 86 (Ardross 134) [2001 –: f12s⁵ **36** f16g f16g 16g⁶ 16m 17.1d Oct 8] fairly useful bumper performer: poor maiden on Flat: should stay beyond 2m: blinkered/visored last 4 starts: has looked reluctant/run in snatches. *Mrs M. Reveley*

ROYAL POPPY 3 b.f. Mind Games 121 – Never So True 52 (Never So Bold 135) **–** [2001 6m 7g 6m Jun 28] lengthy, rather unfurnished filly: second foal: dam 11f winner who stayed 13f: well held in maidens. *H. A. McWilliams*

ROYAL PRODIGY (USA) 2 ch.c. (May 13) Royal Academy (USA) 130 – **77** Prospector's Queen (USA) (Mr Prospector (USA)) [2001 7.9d³ 7d Nov 3] 25,000 2-y-o: rather leggy, close-coupled colt: half-brother to 3 winners in USA, including US Grade 2 8.5f winner Southern Rhythm (by Dixieland Band): dam, won 4 races in USA, half-sister to US Grade 3 2-y-o 1m winner Box Office Gold: fair form when third to Him of Distinction in maiden at York: well held when favourite for similar event at Newmarket: may prove best up to 1m: has worn crossed noseband. *J. Noseda*

ROYAL QUARTERS (IRE) 2 ch.c. (Mar 28) Common Grounds 118 – Queen **93 p** Canute (IRE) (Ahonoora 122) [2001 5g⁴ 6f² 5.7g* Oct 1] 115,000Y: tall, unfurnished colt: fifth foal: half-brother to a 7f/1m winner in Germany by Rudimentary: dam, well beaten, half-sister to useful 6f winner King of The East: fairly useful form: in frame in maidens at Folkestone and Newbury before beating Anne Tudor by 2 lengths in similar event at Bath (edged right): not short of speed, but will probably stay 7f: capable of better. *B. J. Meehan*

ROYAL RACER (FR) 3 b.g. Danehill (USA) 126 – Green Rosy (USA) (Green **78** Dancer (USA) 132) [2001 92: 8v⁵ 10v⁵ 12g 12s p10g Dec 28] 4,200,000 francs Y: ex-French gelding: half-brother to several winners, including smart French/US performer up to 1½m Majorien (by Machiavellian) and smart French 9f (at 2 yrs) to 1½m winner America (by Arazi): dam French 1½m winner: fairly useful form when winning minor event at Chantilly at 2 yrs: below that level in 2001: sold from Mme C. Head-Maarek 14,500 gns before final start: well held in apprentice handicap at Lingfield on British/all-weather debut: should stay at least 1¼m: acts on good to soft ground. *J. R. Best*

ROYAL REBEL   5 b.g. Robellino (USA) 127 – Greenvera (USA) (Riverman   **123** §
(USA) 131) [2001 120: 13.9g⁶ 16.4m 20f* 16g⁶ 15.9g 18d 20v⁴ 16d³ Oct 20]

The fact that the 2001 Gold Cup was rather unfairly labelled as substandard
in some quarters said something about the renewed status of Royal Ascot's main
event. The Gold Cup is twice the race it became at times in the 'eighties and
early-'nineties and its standing is higher now than at any time since the days of
Sagaro, Le Moss and Ardross, who won seven Gold Cups between them in the
period from 1975 to 1982. A fall in the standard of competition and a largely
modest collection of winners resulted in a considerable threat to the Gold Cup's
future in its traditional form. The Jockey Club applied pressure in the early-
'nineties to reduce the distance from two and a half miles to two, even including a
warning that the Gold Cup's Group 1 status might have to be reviewed if no change
was made. The quality of the Gold Cup field had suffered in the post-war era largely
because of a strong prejudice that built up against the Cup races among commercial
breeders, but in the early-'nineties the call for a reduction in the distance of the
Gold Cup and Goodwood Cup was also widely supported by leading trainers. With
Goodwood acceding to Jockey Club pressure to reduce the Goodwood Cup from
two and a half to two in 1991, the Gold Cup was in danger of becoming regarded as
an anachronism.

The Ascot Trustees held out though, and they must be delighted they did.
The turning point came when St Leger winner Moonax and St Leger third Double
Trigger both set out as four-year-olds with the 1995 Gold Cup as their principal
objective. Double Trigger beat Moonax decisively at Royal Ascot and went on to
heighten the profile of the Cup races by landing the stayers' triple crown that year,
beating his year-younger brother Double Eclipse in a memorable race for the
Goodwood Cup and romping home in the Doncaster Cup (which had remained at
two and a quarter miles partly because Doncaster has no suitable place for a
two-mile start). The revival of the Gold Cup continued with the success in 1996 of
St Leger winner Classic Cliche, the first time a classic winner from the previous
season had gone on to victory in the Gold Cup since Ocean Swell in 1945. The
wealth of good older horses available to Godolphin resulted in another of its St
Leger winners, Nedawi, contesting the Gold Cup in 1999, when the race attracted
the largest field in its history. Enzeli's winning performance—with the favourite
Nedawi only fifth—ranked alongside Classic Cliche's as the best in the race for
many years. Kayf Tara's Gold Cup victories in 1998 and 2000 made it three wins in
six years for Godolphin and his overall career record established him as the best
Cup horse since the era of Sagaro, Le Moss and Ardross.

The strengthening of the staying division in recent years has also owed
something to the emergence of a group of geldings—first allowed back into the
Gold Cup in 1986—capable of mounting a realistic challenge for the stayers' title.

*Gold Cup, Royal Ascot—a memorable finish as winner Royal Rebel and Persian Punch (rail) show
tremendous battling qualities; Jardines Lookout, San Sebastian (checks) and Marienbard are next home*

One of them, Celeric, foiled Classic Cliche's bid for a second Gold Cup in 1997. Where would the Gold Cup have been now if geldings had still been excluded? Seven of the twelve runners in the latest edition were geldings and, for the first time, geldings filled the first three places with another gelding, the favourite San Sebastian, taking fourth. San Sebastian had been better than ever in 2000, when successful in the Prix du Cadran, and had come a good second on his reappearance in the Sagaro Stakes (transferred to Newmarket when Ascot was abandoned). The Sagaro winner Solo Mio, who also won the Bonusprint Stakes (Henry II) at Sandown, was the most notable absentee from the Gold Cup field, which also lacked a French challenge and, for that matter, a credible one from Ireland (the only Irish runner Chimes At Midnight started at 33/1). Yorkshire Cup winner Marienbard started second favourite, the only representative of Godolphin, who had also left in Give The Slip and Hatha Anna at the five-day stage. Third favourite was the previous year's Goodwood Cup and Lonsdale winner Royal Rebel, who had been well beaten in both his warm-up races, the Yorkshire Cup (ring rusty, trip barely far enough) and the Henry II (eased once beaten and better than ninth of eleven). Royal Rebel is a hard ride, needing plenty of driving, and, typically, was one of the first off the bridle at both York and Sandown. He seemed best in blinkers or a visor, but wore neither at Royal Ascot for the first time since his reappearance the previous season, Kevin Darley advising after riding him for the first time in the Henry II that the horse might be resenting the headgear. Darley was on Royal Rebel's stable-companion Yavana's Pace in the Gold Cup and, with regular first choice Michael Kinane turning down the ride in favour of San Sebastian, Johnny Murtagh, who had won on Enzeli, was booked for Royal Rebel. Also in the Gold Cup line-up were four others who had finished in front of Royal Rebel in the current season, Romantic Affair, Persian Punch, Mbele and Yorkshire Cup fifth Jardines Lookout, who had filled second, third, fifth and seventh respectively in the Henry II. Another regular in the Cup races Rainbow High, last when joint favourite at Sandown, came into the reckoning judged on the form of his latest victory in the Chester Cup under top weight.

A series of rousing finishes has been another of the ingredients that has helped to restore the popularity of the Gold Cup. The Gold Cup day attendance of 72,589 and the TV audience of around one and a half million (the average viewing figure across the four days of the Royal meeting) were treated to another pulsating encounter, the experience of which had contrasting effects on the two principals. Persian Punch, contesting his fifth Gold Cup, finally did himself justice in the race, being asked to run the finish out of his rivals by stretching the field some way from home. After duelling with Yavana's Pace—the leaders soon having the field spread out—Persian Punch went clear with a mile to go and forged into a six-length lead five furlongs out. Royal Rebel, who had raced in third or fourth all the way, made Murtagh earn his riding fee as he tried to reduce the gap. By the time the leaders straightened for home, Royal Rebel and the smooth-travelling Marienbard had both moved into challenging positions. Soon there were three in line before Marienbard ran out of stamina and was the first to falter. Royal Rebel continued to answer every call from his rider, however, and edged into the lead just inside the two-furlong marker, going about half a length up and seeming to be holding Persian Punch inside the final furlong until a last-ditch rally reduced Royal Rebel's winning margin to a head, both horses showing tremendous battling qualities as the post came just in time for Royal Rebel. The first two were five lengths clear of 25/1-shot Jardines Lookout, who just pipped San Sebastian, with a tired Marienbard a further two lengths back in fifth; the rest, led home by Mbele, came back strung out on the firm ground, except for the 2000 Ebor winner Vicious Circle, who was pulled up in the final straight with a leg injury which led to his being put down. Royal Rebel provided the middle leg of a Gold Cup-day treble for Murtagh, who finished the Royal meeting as leading jockey with five winners. The week also had its tribulations for Murtagh; he collected two extra days' suspension for excessive use of the whip on both Royal Rebel and the Ribblesdale winner Sahara Slew on Gold Cup day, on top of the five incurred on the opening day for irresponsible riding on Mahsusie in the Coventry. The winning owner in the Gold Cup, the British Horseracing Board chairman Peter Savill, must have felt nearly as exhausted as

Royal Rebel after spending most of the week in negotiations over racing's media rights, agreement eventually reached with Go Racing in the early hours of Friday morning after another protracted meeting at Ascot.

The Gold Cup seemed to leave its mark on Royal Rebel, who was well beaten behind Persian Punch in both the Goodwood Cup and the Lonsdale Stakes on his next two outings, slowly away and needing early reminders when visored at York after racing without headgear again at Goodwood. Two more below-form efforts came in the Doncaster Cup (visored, went in snatches) and in the Prix du Cadran (no headgear, no difference). Encouragingly perhaps for Royal Rebel's prospects in the Gold Cup as a six-year-old, he returned to something like his best form on his final outing in the Jockey Club Cup in late-October. On the other hand, however, with headgear left off once more, Royal Rebel again betrayed signs that his long-suspect temperament was more manifest than ever, running in snatches before coming through late to finish third to the three-year-old Capal Garmon and Invermark, beaten half a length and a head, conceding 7 lb to the runner-up and 6 lb more than weight for age to the winner. Royal Rebel showed in the Jockey Club Cup that he has not lost his ability, though the ratio of good efforts to distinctly ordinary ones in the latest season tells its own story and he is clearly not one to rely on.

Royal Rebel (b.g. 1996)	Robellino (USA) (b 1978)	Roberto (b 1969)	Hail To Reason / Bramalea
		Isobelline (b 1971)	Pronto / Isobella
	Greenvera (USA) (ch 1989)	Riverman (b 1969)	Never Bend / River Lady
		Greenway (br 1978)	Targowice / Gracious

Mr P. D. Savill's "Royal Rebel"

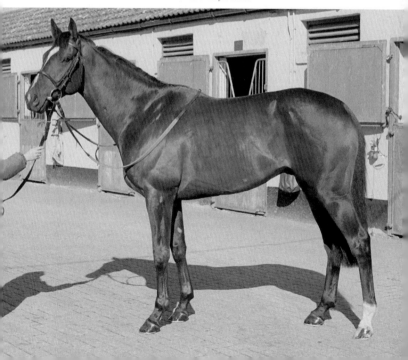

Like most modern-day Cup horses, the good-topped Royal Rebel was not bred to be an out-and-out stayer. His sire Robellino is best known for his milers, including Mister Baileys, who won the Two Thousand Guineas for Royal Rebel's stable, and the Irish One Thousand Guineas winner Classic Park. Royal Rebel's twice-raced dam Greenvera, who has not had another runner to date, is a half-sister to the useful French sprinter Way West, out of the speedy Greenway, one of the fastest two-year-olds of 1980. There is a top-class stayer in the family, though, the Prix de l'Arc de Triomphe, Prix Royal-Oak and Prix du Cadran winner Gold River (by Greenvera's sire Riverman) being a half-sister to Royal Rebel's great grandam Gracious. Royal Rebel acts on firm and good to soft going and is unpredictable with or without blinkers or a visor. *M. Johnston*

ROYAL REPRIMAND (IRE) 6 b.g. Reprimand 122 – Lake Ormond (Kings Lake (USA) 133) [2001 54: 6m 8f² 7.5f 7m⁴ 8m 10.1m 8f² 8m⁴ 7m 8m 7g³ 9m⁶ 8f⁴ 7d 7g⁶ 8d Oct 30] close-coupled, good-topped gelding: modest maiden: effective at 7f to 1¼m: acts on firm and soft going: tried visored: unreliable. *R. E. Barr* **59 §**

ROYAL ROBBIE 3 b.g. Robellino (USA) 127 – Moogie 103 (Young Generation 129) [2001 8g 11.5m May 26] 1,000Y: eighth foal: half-brother to 3 winners, including fairly useful 1996 2-y-o 7f winner Catwalk and 1994 2-y-o 6f winner Mood Swings (both by Shirley Heights): dam 2-y-o 6f winner, later suited by 9f: well held in maiden at Newmarket and seller at Lingfield. *P. Butler* **–**

ROYAL ROMEO 4 ch.g. Timeless Times (USA) 99 – Farinara (Dragonara Palace (USA) 115) [2001 77: f7g f6g² f6s⁴ f6g² f6s⁵ 6v f7g⁴ 7.1d 6m³ May 7] good-bodied gelding: unimpressive mover: fair performer: ran poorly last 2 starts: best at 6f/7f: acts on fibresand, heavy and good to firm going: blinkered sixth and final starts: usually held up: sold 7,400 gns. *T. D. Easterby* **74**

ROYAL SATIN (IRE) 3 b.g. Royal Academy (USA) 130 – Satinette 109 (Shirley Heights 130) [2001 –: 11.6m 11.5m⁶ 11.9g Aug 9] big, rangy gelding: no form: tried blinkered: looks wayward. *N. A. Callaghan* **– §**

ROYAL STORM (IRE) 2 b.c. (Apr 23) Royal Applause 124 – Wakayi 87 (Persian Bold 123) [2001 7g 7m 7g Oct 4] IR 41,000F, IR 50,000Y: quite attractive colt: eighth foal: half-brother to 3 winners, including fairly useful 5f (at 2 yrs) and 7f winner Arruhan (by Mujtahid) and a 6f to 1m winner in Hong Kong by Marju: dam, 2-y-o 5f winner, half-sister to smart sprinter Reesh from very speedy family: fair form in midfield in maidens: likely to prove best up to 7f. *Mrs A. J. Perrett* **72**

ROYAL TARRAGON 5 b.m. Aragon 118 – Lady Philippa (IRE) 77 (Taufan (USA) 119) [2001 –: 10f 10m 10d 7f³ 7d 7.1d 6m 5.3m 6m 6s⁵ 6g 6v f7g Dec 8] quite good-topped mare: poor maiden: stays 7f: acts on firm and soft going: tried blinkered/visored. *W. de Best-Turner* **37**

ROYAL WANDERER (IRE) 3 ch.g. Royal Abjar (USA) 121 – Rose 'n Reason (IRE) (Reasonable (FR) 119) [2001 –: 12v 10.1m⁴ 8m 9f 7.1f⁶ 8f f11g Oct 1] good-topped gelding: well held in varied events. *Mrs A. Duffield* **–**

ROYAL WAVE (IRE) 5 b. or br.g. Polish Precedent (USA) 131 – Mashmoon (USA) 80 (Habitat 134) [2001 55: f9.4g f8s f7g 7.1m⁴ f7g 8m 8d Oct 30] plain, lengthy gelding: poor handicapper: best around 7f: acts on fibresand, best turf efforts on good ground: tried tongue tied. *J. L. Eyre* **34**

ROYAL WINDMILL (IRE) 2 b.g. (Apr 18) Ali-Royal (IRE) 127 – Salarya (FR) (Darshaan 133) [2001 5f³ 6g 5f² 5m³ 7v Oct 27] IR 15,000Y, 31,000 2-y-o: leggy gelding: half-brother to 3 winners in Germany/Scandinavia, including Salad Days (by Diagly-phard), successful up to 15f: dam Swedish 1m/1¼m winner: fair maiden: easily best efforts when placed: should stay at least 1m: acts on firm going. *J. L. Eyre* **74**

ROY MCAVOY (IRE) 3 b.g. Danehill (USA) 126 – Decadence (Vaigly Great 127) [2001 6g f8.5f p10g Dec 29] 16,000Y: half-brother to several winners, including smart 5f performer Mistertopogigo (by Thatching) and fairly useful 5f (including at 2 yrs) to 7f winner Angaar (by Fairy King): dam lightly-raced sister to high-class sprinter Hallgate: well held in maidens. *C. A. Cyzer* **–**

ROYMILLON (GER) 7 b.g. Milesius (USA) – Royal Slope (USA) (His Majesty (USA)) [2001 99d: 18d Oct 20] useful performer at best, winner of 9 races in Germany: lightly raced and little Flat form in Britain: raced mainly around 1¼m: acts on soft ground and sand: has been blinkered, including when successful. *D. J. Wintle* **–**

ROZEL (IRE)   4 ch.f. Wolfhound (USA) 126 – Noirmant (Dominion 123) [2001 97:   **104**
5g⁴ 5m⁵ 5m 5m 5v⁵ 5v Oct 28] lengthy filly: useful performer: good efforts first 4 starts
in 2001, 2¾ lengths seventh to Dietrich in King George Stakes at Goodwood (late
progress after being short of room) and over 4 lengths eighth to Mozart in Nunthorpe
Stakes at York (possibly bit flattered) on third and fourth occasions: raced only at 5f: acts
on soft and good to firm going, below form abroad on heavy last 2 starts. *R. Guest*

RUBY BABE   3 b.f. Aragon 118 – Barrie Baby 86 (Import 127) [2001 40: 6.1v⁴ 6d 5m   **40**
5m 5g Sep 19] tall, unfurnished filly: poor maiden: raced only at 5f/6f: acts on good to
firm and heavy going. *J. J. Quinn*

RUBY LEGEND   3 b.g. Perpendicular 119 – Singing High 87 (Julio Mariner 127)   **52**
[2001 8m³ 9m³ 7m 8d Oct 30] leggy gelding: half-brother to 1m to 1¼m winner Top
Scale (by Tower Walk): dam won at 1m: modest form in maidens first 2 starts: well held
in handicap final outing: should be suited by at least 1¼m. *Mrs M. Reveley*

RUBY ROSE   3 b.f. Red Ransom (USA) – Rose de Reve (IRE) (Persian Heights 129)   **55**
[2001 10m 10s 8f⁵ Jul 4] 52,000Y: rather leggy filly: first foal: dam, won up to 9f in
France (including at 1m at 2 yrs)/USA, half-sister to Irish 1000 Guineas/Irish Oaks
second Kitza and smart 1985 2-y-o 5f performer Marouble: modest form in maidens.
J. R. Fanshawe

RUBY RUBY   3 ch.f. Binary Star (USA) – Runabay (Run The Gantlet (USA)) [2001   **–**
10g 10.9f 10s Sep 24] 500Y: eighth foal: half-sister to winner up to 9f in Italy by Indian
Ridge: dam French maiden: no sign of ability in claimer/sellers. *W. G. M. Turner*

RUBY WEDDING   3 b.f. Blushing Flame (USA) 109 – First Sapphire (Simply Great   **60 p**
(FR) 122) [2001 11.7d⁶ Oct 25] third foal: half-sister to useful 10.2f winner Rolling Stone
(by Northern Amethyst) and 6-y-o First Impression: dam of no account: 33/1, sixth of 19
to Alakananda in maiden at Bath, a little headway from rear not knocked about: should
improve. *Mrs A. J. Perrett*

RUDDER   3 ch.g. Deploy 131 – Wave Dancer 76 (Dance In Time (CAN)) [2001 61:   **79 §**
11.1s² 12g 11.9d⁵ 12m² 16m² 11.7m⁴ 14v f16g f12g Nov 26] big, lengthy gelding: has a   **a– §**
quick action: fair maiden: well held last 3 starts, leaving B. Hills after first of them:
finished lame final outing: stays 2m: acts on soft and good to firm going: tried blinkered:
has carried head awkwardly/raced freely: one to treat with caution. *M. C. Chapman*

RUDE AWAKENING   7 b.g. Rudimentary (USA) 118 – Final Call 79 (Town Crier   **47**
119) [2001 56, a69: f6g* f6g f6s e6s⁶ f5g⁵ f5g³ f6f⁴ 7m 5m 5f 6m 5d f5s f6g Nov 3] sturdy   **a63**
gelding: modest on all-weather, poor on turf: won minor event at Southwell in January:
left C. Fairhurst after penultimate start: best at 5f/6f: acts on fibresand, equitrack, firm
and soft going: occasionally blinkered/visored: usually races prominently: carries head
high: none too consistent. *C. A. Dwyer*

RUDETSKI   4 b.g. Rudimentary (USA) 118 – Butosky 71 (Busted 134) [2001 60:   **60**
9.1m⁶ 10.1m⁶ 9f* 10.9f 8f 9.2g⁴ 10.5g³ 10g 9.9s Sep 25] big, lengthy gelding: modest
handicapper: won at Musselburgh in June: probably stays 11f: acts on any going: has been
early to post/worn crossed noseband/taken fierce hold. *M. Dods*

RUDIK (USA)   4 b. or br.g. Nureyev (USA) 131 – Nervous Baba (USA) (Raja Baba   **93**
(USA)) [2001 102p: 5m 6m 7f 6m 6m 6m 6g 7d 6m⁴ 7g⁶ 6d Oct 13] compact gelding:
fairly useful handicapper: beaten only a length when equal-fourth to Tayif in Silver Cup
at Ayr in September: stays 6f: acts on soft and good to firm going: tongue tied last 4 starts.
D. Nicholls

RUDI'S PET (IRE)   7 ch.g. Don't Forget Me 127 – Pink Fondant (Northfields (USA))   **105**
[2001 118: 5s³ 5m 5m² 5m 6d⁵ 5.1g 5g 5m Sep 11] strong gelding: formerly smart
performer: sold 50,000 gns and well held for S. Shulman in USA final 6-y-o outing:
rejoined former trainer, but only useful in 2001: ½-length second to Vita Spericolata in
minor event at Newmarket prior to 3¼ lengths eighth to Dietrich in King George Stakes
at Goodwood next time: has form at 6f and on soft going, but probably best at 5f on
good or firmer: usually wears blinkers/visor, but effective without: has been early to post/
bandaged in front: very slowly away: usually races prominently: bandaged in front in
2000: none too consistent nowadays. *D. Nicholls*

RUFIJI RIVER   2 b.g. (Apr 8) Hernando (FR) 127 – Jadirah (USA) 68 (Deputy   **61**
Minister (CAN)) [2001 8d⁶ 8g 8.2s Nov 5] 5,000Y: lengthy gelding: fourth living foal:
half-brother to 5f winner Jasmine (by Thatching): dam 1m winner out of half-sister to
Petoski: modest maiden: best effort on debut: should be suited by 1¼m+. *J. L. Dunlop*

RUISSEC (USA)   2 b. or br.f. (Mar 5) Woodman (USA) 126 – Jadana (Pharly (FR)   –
130) [2001 7g 7m Sep 22] $120,000Y: close-coupled filly: closely related/half-sister to
several winners, including US Grade 1 9f/1¼m winner Jade Hunter (by Mr Prospector)
and smart 1m winner L'Ami Louis (by Easy Goer), 5f/6f winner at 2 yrs: dam, won up to
1m in USA, closely related to Dewhurst winner Monteverdi: backward, well held in
minor event/maiden. *J. W. Hills*

RUM CHARGER (IRE)   2 b.f. (Apr 28) Spectrum (IRE) 126 – Park Charger 105   **103**
(Tirol 127) [2001 5m³ 6g² 7m⁵ 6s* Aug 19] IR £28,000Y: compact filly: third foal:
half-sister to fairly useful 1999 2-y-o 6f winner Alpine Park (by Barathea), later winner
abroad, and 3-y-o Stage Presence: dam Irish 1m/1¼m winner: useful form: met trouble
when fifth to Seba in Chesham Stakes at Royal Ascot: impressive 7-length winner of
maiden at the Curragh: will probably stay 1m: acts on soft going. *D. K. Weld, Ireland*

RUM DESTINY (IRE)   2 b.g. (Mar 18) Mujadil (USA) 119 – Ruby River (Red God   **93**
128§) [2001 5.1s 5m* 5g³ 5m⁴ 5m³ 5f* 5.2m 5d* 5g³ 5g 5m 6g Oct 6] IR £28,000Y:
close-coupled, workmanlike gelding: unimpressive mover: brother to 7f winner River-
bird and half-brother to several winners, including useful 1¼m/11f performer Knock
Knock (by Tap On Wood) and fairly useful 1993 2-y-o 5f/6f winner Rohita (by Waajib):
dam ran once: fairly useful performer: won maiden at Musselburgh in May, minor event
at Beverley in July and nursery at Goodwood in August: good length third to Pepperoni
in listed event at York ninth start: will prove best at 5f: acts on firm and good to soft going.
A. Berry

RUMORE CASTAGNA (IRE)   3 ch.g. Great Commotion (USA) 123 – False Spring   –
(IRE) (Petorius 117) [2001 80: 8v 6d 6f 7g 7g f6s Dec 21] rather leggy, workmanlike
gelding: fairly useful at 2 yrs: failed to train on. *S. E. Kettlewell*

RUMPOLD   3 gr.c. Mister Baileys 123 – Southern Psychic (USA) (Alwasmi (USA)   **110 +**
115) [2001 104P: 8g 8d* Sep 14] leggy, useful-looking colt: good walker: smart form:
trained by P. Cole when successful in maiden at Ascot only 2-y-o start: won 1m private
trial at Nad Al Sheba in April by neck from Divine Task with Tobougg third: 9/1, well
held in 2000 Guineas at Newmarket in May: off over 4 months, won minor event at
Doncaster on only subsequent start by 2½ lengths from Caughnawaga, leaving impression idling in front: stays 1m: yet to race on extremes of going. *Saeed bin Suroor*

RUM PUNCH   4 b.c. Shirley Heights 130 – Gentle Persuasion 95 (Bustino 136) [2001   **68**
82: 8s 10s 12.3g⁴ 16.1m 12m Jun 8] big, lengthy colt: fair maiden handicapper: seems to
stay 1½m: acts on good to firm ground: tried tongue tied. *G. M. Moore*

RUNAWAY BRIDE   3 b.f. Bishop of Cashel 122 – Storm Nymph (USA) 78 (Storm   –
Bird (CAN) 134) [2001 40: f8g f6g f7g 10.2d⁶ 7g 7m⁵ Jun 4] no longer of much account.
C. Smith

RUNAWAY STAR   4 ch.f. Superlative 118 – My Greatest Star 93 (Great Nephew 126)   **45**
[2001 45: 8m 10.9g 12g* 12.3g* 12g⁶ Sep 15] workmanlike filly: poor handicapper: won
at Pontefract in July and Ripon in August: will be suited by 1¾m+: best efforts on good/
good to firm going. *W. J. Musson*

RUNNING FOR ME (IRE)   3 ch.f. Eagle Eyed (USA) 111 – Running For You (FR)   –
(Pampabird 124) [2001 –, a60: f6g* f6s⁵ f7g³ f5f⁴ 6.1v⁶ f6g* 6m f6g⁴ 5.5m⁶ f6g⁶ f7g   **a60 d**
f7g f7g f6g f6s Dec 21] leggy filly: modest performer: won claimers at Southwell in
January and June: below form after: stays 6f: acts on fibresand, little form on turf.
R. Hollinshead

RUNNING RED   2 b.c. (Apr 26) Tragic Role (USA) – Rose Mill (Puissance 110)   –
[2001 7s f8g Oct 1] 12,000 2-y-o: second foal: brother to 3-y-o Sholto: dam unraced
daughter of useful sprinter Amber Mill: tailed off in minor events: sent to Portugal.
W. A. O'Gorman

RUNNING TIMES (USA)   4 b.g. Brocco (USA) 124 – Concert Peace (USA) (Hold   **71**
Your Peace (USA)) [2001 63: f12g f11g 16.2m² May 12] good-topped gelding: unimpres-   **a–**
sive mover: but just fair maiden handicapper on Flat: stays 2m: acts on
fibresand, soft and good to firm ground: blinkered once: sold 6,200 gns in August, joined
M. Pipe. *T. D. Easterby*

RUN ON   3 b.c. Runnett 125 – Polar Storm (IRE) 76 (Law Society (USA) 130) [2001   **56**
60: 6f f6g 8.3g 5.2v f6g* f6g⁵ f6g Dec 10] robust colt: sort to carry condition: modest
performer: left B. Meehan after third start: won maiden at Wolverhampton in November:
should stay 7f: acts on fibresand: tongue tied last 4 starts. *D. G. Bridgwater*

RUPERT OF HENTZAU   2 ch.g. (Apr 25) Superpower 113 – Walkonthemoon 58   **38**
(Coquelin (USA) 121) [2001 5.1g⁵ 5m 6g⁵ 7g 6m 6s⁶ 8d 8.3v Nov 8] 3,000Y: small
gelding: first foal: dam 7f winner: poor maiden: left M. Quinn after fifth start: stays 6f:
acts on soft and good to firm ground: tried blinkered: sold 350 gns. *G. M. McCourt*

RUSH ABOUT (IRE)   2 ch.c. (Feb 24) Kris 135 – Rachrush (IRE) (Sadler's Wells   **77 p**
(USA) 132) [2001 8d 7d Nov 3] good-bodied colt: first foal: dam unraced half-sister to
very smart miler Alhijaz: better effort in maidens at Newmarket when eighth of 27 to
Prince Hector second start, still green and not knocked about: should stay 1¼m: bandaged
hind-joints both starts: moved short to post on debut: should improve. *H. R. A. Cecil*

RUSHBY (IRE)   3 b.g. Fayruz 116 – Moira My Girl (Henbit (USA) 130) [2001 73:   **66**
5.3m 5m 5d 5g² 5g Sep 2] close-coupled, well-made gelding: fair maiden: raced only
at 5f: acts on good to firm and good to soft going: edgy type: has been reluctant to post/
hung: refused to enter stalls and withdrawn intended final start: sold 1,700 gns.
Mrs P. N. Dutfield

RUSHCUTTER BAY   8 br.g. Mon Tresor 113 – Llwy Bren (Lidhame 109) [2001 106:   **117 d**
5g* 5m 5m 5m 5s 6d Oct 19] close-coupled gelding: impresses in appearance: smart
performer: career-best effort when winning Palace House Stakes at Newmarket (fourth
win there, beat Cassandra Go by 1½ lengths) in May: well held after, including in King's
Stand Stakes at Royal Ascot and Prix de l'Abbaye de Longchamp: effective at 5f/6f: acts
on firm and good to soft going: effective visored or not: has twice reportedly bled from
nose, including fourth start: tends to wander. *P. L. Gilligan*

RUSH OFF   6 b.g. Robellino (USA) 127 – Arusha (IRE) 84 (Dance of Life (USA))   **–**
[2001 16.2m May 26] little form: dead. *G. H. Yardley*

Treasure Seekers Partnership's "Rushcutter Bay"

RUSSIAN DUNE (IRE) 2 b.g. (May 26) Danehill (USA) 126 – Russian Ribbon **71 p**
(USA) 86 (Nijinsky (CAN) 138) [2001 7s⁶ Oct 16] 120,000Y: quite attractive gelding:
half-brother to several winners, notably smart 5f (at 2 yrs) to 1m winner Bold Russian
(by Persian Bold) and useful performer up to 1¼m in Scandinavia/Ireland True Blue
Victory (by Catrail): dam 1m winner: 16/1, keeping-on sixth of 18 to Cassirer in maiden
at Leicester: wore crossed noseband: subsequently gelded: sure to improve.
E. A. L. Dunlop

RUSSIAN FOX (IRE) 4 ch.g. Foxhound (USA) 103 – La Petruschka (Ballad Rock **66 d**
122) [2001 83: f6g e8g⁴ e8g⁵ f7g⁴ e7g 7m 6m² 6m 5.3f³ 5g 5m 5.3m 5.1g f5g Oct 18]
close-coupled, quite good-topped gelding: fair form at best in 2001: well below par last
4 outings: best at 5f/6f: acts on firm and good to soft going: blinkered last 8 starts: has
folded tamely: tends to race prominently/edge left (has worn near-side pricker): sold
2,000 gns. *R. Hannon*

RUSSIAN RHAPSODY 4 b.f. Cosmonaut – Hannah's Music 85 (Music Boy 124) **100**
[2001 83p: 7.1v⁵ 7.1m 7.1m* 7d* 7g 7s² 7.1s 8.2s* Nov 5] good-topped filly: useful
performer: won minor events at Warwick in June, Epsom in July and Nottingham (beat
Muchea a short head) in November: good second to Bouncing Bowdler in listed event at
Epsom on sixth start: best at 7f/1m: winner on good to firm going, very best efforts on
softer than good: races up with pace. *M. A. Jarvis*

RUSSIAN ROMEO (IRE) 6 b.g. Soviet Lad (USA) – Aotearoa (IRE) (Flash of **67**
Steel 120) [2001 69, a78: f6g* f6s⁵ 6f 6d³ Jul 19] leggy gelding: fairly useful handicapper **a80**
on all-weather, fair on turf: won at Southwell in January: best around 6f: acts on fibresand, good to soft and firm going: visored/blinkered: has shown signs of temperament
(refused to enter stalls once): sent to UAE. *B. A. McMahon*

RUSSIAN WHISPERS (USA) 3 b.g. Red Ransom (USA) – Idle Gossip (USA) **75**
(Lyphard (USA) 132) [2001 89: 6d 6.1f f6f³ 6m 6m² 7f f7g² 7g 7m⁵ a8g⁵ Dec 9] strong **a83**
gelding: poor mover: fairly useful on all-weather, fair on turf: left B. Meehan before final
start: stays easy 7f: acts on fibresand and any turf going: usually blinkered/visored.
C. Bjorling, Spain

RUST EN VREDE 2 b.c. (Apr 19) Royal Applause 124 – Souveniers (Relko 136) **72**
[2001 6m 6.1m⁶ 7d⁴ Oct 3] 11,000Y, 13,000 2-y-o: tall, quite attractive colt: half-brother
to numerous winners, including 1994 2-y-o 5f winner Nazute (by Cyrano de Bergerac)
and 1997 2-y-o 7f winner (stayed 1½m) Simply Gifted (by Simply Great), both fairly
useful: dam third at 1m at 2 yrs (only season to race): fair form in maidens: best effort
when fourth to Barathea Blazer at Newcastle, making running: should stay 1m. *J. L. Eyre*

RUTLAND CHANTRY (USA) 7 b.g. Dixieland Band (USA) – Christchurch (FR) **79**
88 (So Blessed 130) [2001 76: 9.9m⁵ 10v² 11.9d 10.3m 10d² 10g* 10.5s⁴ 12g* 10.5s² 12g
8.9d Oct 13] robust gelding: fair handicapper: won ladies race at Newmarket and amateur

*Moet & Chandon Silver Magnum (Handicap), Epsom—Rutland Chantry (fourth left)
gets a well-judged ride from Italian Christiano Fais to provide trainer Steve Gollings with his
second consecutive winner of the race; The Green Grey (second left), Hibernate (noseband)
and Gold Statuette (rail) are next; the oldest sponsor on the Flat later announced it was
withdrawing support from the amateurs' race after thirty-nine years*

event at Epsom in August: effective at 1¼m/1½m: acts on fibresand, best recent turf form on good going or softer (acts on heavy): tried blinkered: races prominently: tough. *S. Gollings*

RUWAYA (USA) 2 b. or br.f. (Mar 17) Red Ransom (USA) – Upper Class Lady – (USA) (Upper Nile (USA)) [2001 6g 8d⁶ Sep 4] $62,000Y: sixth foal: dam, maiden in USA, half-sister to Prix de Diane winner Lady In Silver: well held in maidens at Windsor (very green) and Yarmouth. *C. E. Brittain*

RYAN'S GOLD (IRE) 3 b.g. Distant View (USA) 126 – Kathleen's Dream (USA) 71 (Last Tycoon 131) [2001 73?: 7s 8.3g² 7m 8m 7m Sep 22] close-coupled gelding: fair maiden: form in 2001 only in handicap at Windsor second start: stays 1m: possibly unsuited by ground firmer than good: tried blinkered: sold 2,200 gns in October. *Mrs A. J. Perrett*

RYAN'S QUEST (IRE) 2 b.f. (May 4) Mukaddamah (USA) 125 – Preponderance 67 (IRE) 85 (Cyrano de Bergerac 120) [2001 5g³ 5m³ 5f² 5f⁵ 5.1s Nov 5] 10,500Y: neat filly: fifth foal: half-sister to 3 winning sprinters, including 5-y-o Guinea Hunter and 4-y-o Hammer And Sickle: dam Irish 2-y-o 5f winner: fair maiden: raced only at 5f: acts on firm ground: looked none too keen penultimate start. *K. R. Burke*

RYDERS STORM (USA) 2 b. or br.c. (Mar 17) Dynaformer (USA) – Justicara 113 94 (Rusticaro (FR) 124) [2001 7m³ 7m* 8g⁴ 8d Oct 13] $25,000Y: strong, angular colt: closely related to a winner around 1m in USA by Kris S and half-brother to several winners abroad, including a US minor stakes winner up to 1¼m by Spend A Buck: dam smart French/US performer up to 9f: fairly useful form: won minor event at Thirsk in July: ran well when 6¼ lengths fourth to Henri Lebasque in listed event at Goodwood: should be suited by 1¼m/1½m: acts on good to firm going, tailed off on good to soft: joined P. Cole. *M. Johnston*

RYEFIELD 6 b.g. Petong 126 – Octavia (Sallust 134) [2001 74: 7.1m² 6d 6m⁵ 7m⁴ 74 6m* 6d 7f⁴ 7f 6d³ 7g 8m 6g² 7.2m 6v 6v 6g Nov 5] small gelding: fair handicapper: won at Ayr in June: effective at 6f to 1m: acts on any going: sometimes slowly away: refused to race once at 5 yrs, seemed reluctant once in 2001: has carried head high: races freely, and held up: none too reliable. *Miss L. A. Perratt*

RYELAND 5 b.m. Presidium 124 – Ewe Lamb 86 (Free State 125) [2001 –: 8m 11.5f – Jul 25] angular mare: lightly raced, and no form. *Mrs P. Sly*

RYKA 6 ch.g. Deploy 131 – Velda 74 (Thatch (USA) 136) [2001 –: 10v 10s 13d May 6] – little form. *W. Clay*

RYMER'S RASCAL 9 b.g. Rymer 121 – City Sound 63 (On Your Mark 125) [2001 77 74: 8.1m 7m 7.5f⁵ f8g 7.1f⁵ 8.5m³ 7.6m⁶ 8m² 7.5m* 7.9m 7.5d⁶ 8g 7d³ Oct 30] sturdy a– gelding: fair handicapper: won at Beverley in August: best at 7f/easy 1m: acts on any going: takes good hold and is waited with. *E. J. Alston*

S

SAABIRR 3 b.c. Polish Precedent (USA) 131 – Safa 109 (Shirley Heights 130) [2001 89 8g 10.2f⁴ 11.5m² 12.3m⁵ 10m² Jul 7] close-coupled, quite attractive colt: fourth living foal: half-brother to smart 1m to 10.5f winner Saafeya (by Sadler's Wells) and 8.5f winner who stayed 1¼m Bayt Alasad (by Lion Cavern): dam, 2-y-o 6f winner who stayed 1½m, sister to Queen's Vase winner Stelvio: fairly useful form: tongue tied, best effort in handicap at Sandown final start, giving impression would have won by a couple of lengths with clear run: reportedly returned lame: stays 1½m: yet to race on ground softer than good: sent to UAE. *A. C. Stewart*

SAAFEND ROCKET (IRE) 3 b.g. Distinctly North (USA) 115 – Simple Annie 68 (Simply Great (FR) 122) [2001 61: e8g* f8.5s* e10g⁵ f8g⁵ e7g f8g⁵ 7.1g⁵ e8g³ 9m 8.1g a77 11.6m 7m³ 6m f8.5g⁴ 7.6m 7g p8g Dec 22] fair handicapper, better on all-weather than turf: won at Lingfield and Wolverhampton in January: below form last 5 starts: stays 8.5f, not 11.6f: acts on fibresand, equitrack and good to firm ground: tried visored (ran creditably)/blinkered (looked wayward): has carried head high. *Andrew Reid*

SAANEN (IRE) 4 b.g. Port Lucaya 118 – Ziffany 68 (Taufan (USA) 119) [2001 65: 9s 65 12.1d² 14.1m² 12m 14.1m 12m Jul 31] lengthy, angular gelding: fair maiden: well below form last 3 starts: stays 1¾m: acts on firm and good to soft going: tried visored: has run in snatches. *Mrs A. Duffield*

*Halliwell Landau Lancashire Oaks, Haydock—Sacred Song is clear of Ranin (left),
All Grain, Miss Lorilaw (stripes) and Moselle (partially hidden)*

SAARYEH   3 b.f. Royal Academy (USA) 130 – Belle Argentine (FR) 113 (Fijar Tango **79**
(FR) 127) [2001 7d 8m³ 8.3g³ 8m* 10.2g⁶ Sep 13] first foal: dam, French 1m winner
(including at 2 yrs) who stayed 10.5f, out of half-sister to high-class French middle-
distance performer Lovely Dancer: fair performer: won maiden at Ascot in July despite
wandering: respectable sixth in handicap at Chepstow final start: probably stayed 1¼m:
acted on good to firm going: visits Josr Algarhoud. *M. P. Tregoning*

SABANA (IRE)   3 b.g. Sri Pekan (USA) 117 – Atyaaf (USA) 48 (Irish River (FR) 131) **74**
[2001 78: 7d 7g 6s 6m* 7m⁶ 6m³ 7f⁶ 7m⁵ 6d³ 8f* 8d Sep 4] quite attractive gelding: fair
performer: won handicap at Yarmouth in June and minor event at Brighton in August:
stays 1m: acts on firm and good to soft going: blinkered (ran poorly in amateur event)
eighth start: sold 14,500 gns. *N. A. Callaghan*

SABIANGO (GER)   3 ch.c. Acatenango (GER) 127 – Spirit of Eagles (USA) (Beau's **120**
Eagle (USA)) [2001 11v⁶ 11g* 11g* 12g² 12d* 12d³ Sep 2] brother to 2 winners in
Germany, including 10.5f to 13f winner Spider, and half-brother to 2 winners there,
notably 5-y-o Silvano: dam, US 6f to 1m winner, sister to US Grade 3 2-y-o 1m winner
Best Pal: very smart performer: won maiden at Hanover only 2-y-o start: successful in
2001 in handicap at Baden-Baden in May, Oppenheim-Union Rennen at Cologne (by ¾
length from Barsetto) in June and Credit Suisse Private Banking Pokal at Cologne (by ½
length from Boreal) in August: also ran creditably when 1¼ lengths second to Anzillero
in Deutschland-Preis at Dusseldorf and 2¾ lengths third to Morshdi in Grosser Preis
von Baden: stays 1½m: acts on good to soft going, though withdrawn from Deutsches
Derby (had been long-standing ante-post favourite) when ground softened appreciably:
reportedly victim of doping on reappearance. *A. Wohler, Germany*

SABO ROSE   3 b.f. Prince Sabo 123 – Crimson Rosella 54 (Polar Falcon (USA) 126) **89**
[2001 84: 7g 7.9g 7m* 7g² 8.1d³ 8m⁵ 7m⁶ 7g⁶ 8d² 8d⁴ Nov 3] quite good-topped filly:
fairly useful handicapper: won at Newmarket in June: generally ran well after: effective
at 7f/1m: acts on good to firm and good to soft going: has started slowly/edged left.
W. J. Haggas

SABRE DANCE   2 ch.g. (Apr 16) Sabrehill (USA) 120 – Anna Karietta 82 (Precocious **62 p**
126) [2001 8s⁶ Nov 9] leggy, unfurnished gelding: half-brother to several winners,
including 6-y-o Premier Baron and 1m winner Frezeliere (by Be My Chief): dam 6f/
7f winner: 20/1, 12¾ lengths sixth to Zone in maiden at Doncaster, running green in
mid-division before keeping on: open to improvement. *H. Candy*

SABREEZE   3 ch.g. Sabrehill (USA) 120 – Zipperti Do 70 (Precocious 126) [2001 **72**
7m⁶ 7m² 7m⁴ 8g 8.1s³ Sep 7] 8,000F: quite good-topped gelding: half-brother to 5f and

7f winner Nobalino (by Sharpo) and 1¼m winner Wonderful Day (by Niniski): dam 1¼m winner: fair maiden: stays 1m, but should be least as effective at 7f: acts on soft and good to firm going. *P. W. Harris*

SABRE LADY   4 ch.f. Sabrehill (USA) 120 – Cal Norma's Lady (IRE) 87 (Lyphard's Special (USA) 122) [2001 82d: 5m⁵ 5m⁶ 5m⁵ 6m 5m 5g⁶ 6m⁵ 6g 5f⁶ 6g Sep 2] leggy, quite good-topped filly: modest form at best in 2001: stays 6f: acts on firm and good to soft going: pulled hard in blinkers fifth start: has left stall very awkwardly: seems wayward and highly strung: on downgrade. *Miss L. A. Perratt*   **62 d**

SABRELINE   2 ch.f. (Feb 4) Sabrehill (USA) 120 – Story Line 98 (In The Wings 128) [2001 f8g⁴ f8s Dec 21] 9,000Y: first foal: dam, 2-y-o 7f winner who stayed 1¾m, out of half-sister to dam of Irish/Yorkshire Oaks winner Pure Grain: modest form in maidens at Southwell: should be suited by 1¼m/1½m. *D. W. P. Arbuthnot*   **58**

SABRESONG   3 ch.f. Sabrehill (USA) 120 – Winsong Melody (Music Maestro 119) [2001 7g 7g 7m 10.1m 8m Jun 22] strong filly: half-sister to several winners, including useful 5f winner El Yasaf (by Sayf El Arab) and 7-y-o Swinging The Blues: dam sprint maiden: well beaten in maidens/handicap/claimer. *C. A. Dwyer*   **–**

SACHIKO   3 b.f. Celtic Swing 138 – Leap of Faith (IRE) 65 (Northiam (USA)) [2001 f8g⁶ f7s³ Jan 27] 1,800Y: third foal: dam 2-y-o 5f/6f winner who stayed 1¼m: modest form in maiden at Wolverhampton second start. *I. A. Wood*   **54**

SACHO (IRE)   8 b.g. Sadler's Wells (USA) 132 – Oh So Sharp 131 (Kris 135) [2001 –: 12v Mar 24] smart form at best: very lightly raced through injuries. *J. L. Harris*   **–**

SACRED SONG (USA)   4 b.f. Diesis 133 – Ruby Ransom (CAN) (Red Ransom (USA)) [2001 114p: 13.3v³ 11.8d³ 11.9d* 11.9g² Aug 22] rather angular filly: unimpressive mover: smart performer, lightly raced: third in listed events at Newbury and Leicester first 2 starts: heavily-backed favourite and looking particularly well, won   **116**

Niarchos Family's "Sacred Song"

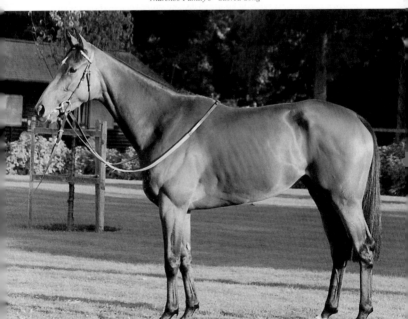

Halliwell Landau Lancashire Oaks at Haydock in July impressively by 4 lengths from Ranin, storming clear 1f out: again favourite, good length second to Super Tassa in Yorkshire Oaks at York (soon off bridle) following month: reportedly picked up a minor chest infection afterwards: should stay 1¾m: best form on good ground or softer (acts on heavy): sometimes swishes tail. *H. R. A. Cecil*

SACREMENTUM (IRE)   6 b.g. Night Shift (USA) – Tantum Ergo 106 (Tanfirion 110) [2001 56, a61: f11g⁴ Mar 13] good-bodied gelding: poor handicapper: barely stays 1½m: acts on firm going, soft and fibresand: tried blinkered: has been slowly away: looks a tricky ride. *A. W. Carroll*   **–**
a38

SADDAD (USA)   2 ch.c. (May 4) Gone West (USA) – Lite Light (USA) (Majestic Light (USA)) [2001 5.2m* 6g⁵ 5g* Sep 15]   **112 p**

There was a time when more often than not the winner of the Flying Childers Stakes would go on to become a force to reckon with in the top sprints, but since Paris House in 1991 only the 1997 winner Land of Dreams has managed to pick up another pattern race after their two-year-old days, taking the King George Stakes. Perhaps Saddad, who made it two wins from three starts when accounting for twelve rivals in good style in the latest edition, will be the one to reverse this recent trend. He certainly has plenty going for him. A strong, lengthy, attractive colt, and a genuine type on the evidence so far, Saddad is in very good hands and looks to have plenty of scope for further improvement.

The majority of the runners in the Polypipe Flying Childers Stakes had already shown useful form, including the favourite Swiss Lake, winner of the listed St Hugh's Stakes at Newbury on her previous start, and Saddad himself, who started second favourite. Impressive when landing the odds in a Yarmouth maiden over five furlongs on his debut in July, Saddad was stepped up both in trip and class on his next start and shaped a fair bit better than his position suggests in finishing fifth of nine to Rock of Gibraltar in the Gimcrack Stakes at York. He was fitted with a crossed noseband but it still didn't stop him taking a strong hold, and his exertions told after he had moved into second approaching the final furlong. The return to the minimum trip at Doncaster proved to be right up Saddad's street. Swiss Lake, as at Newbury, set out to make all, racing under the stand rail, and Saddad tracked her, again racing freely. Produced over two furlongs out, Saddad knuckled down really well, collared Swiss Lake going into the final furlong and forged clear to beat her by a length and three quarters. Berk The Jerk, squeezed out after a furlong and forced to check, finished best to take third, a further length behind. Five furlongs is going to be Saddad's optimum trip for the time being, so the Palace House, Temple, King's Stand and King George Stakes will be among the ideal races for him in the first half of his three-year-old career. In time he may prove equally effective at six

Polypipe Flying Childers Stakes, Doncaster—
Saddad proves well suited by the return to five furlongs; Swiss Lake is second

furlongs, though he will need to learn to conserve his energy much better than he has done so far.

	Gone West (USA) (b 1984)	Mr Prospector (b 1970)	Raise A Native
Saddad (USA)			Gold Digger
(ch.c. May 4, 1999)		Secrettame (ch 1978)	Secretariat
			Tamerett
	Lite Light (USA) (b 1988)	Majestic Light (b 1973)	Majestic Prince
			Irradiate
		Printing Press (b 1981)	In Reality
			Wealth of Nations

Saddad, a 400,000-dollar yearling, is by Gone West, a winner up to nine furlongs and also the sire of Zafonic, out of Lite Light who won four Grade 1 events from a mile to a mile and a quarter, namely the Coaching Club American Oaks, the Kentucky Oaks, the Santa Anita Oaks and the Las Virgenes Stakes. The dam produced two winners from four previous foals, Gaily Egret (by Storm Cat) and Nurey's Thunder (by Nureyev) winning in Japan, including in a Group 3, and in the States respectively. Saddad, raced only on good and good to firm ground, started a bit slowly at both York and Doncaster. *Sir Michael Stoute*

SADDLER'S CREEK (USA) 3 b.c. Sadler's Wells (USA) 132 – Gleeful (USA) **83 +** (Seeking The Gold (USA)) [2001 12m³ 13d* 12m 11.9g 14.6g 12s Oct 7] $200,000Y: strong, rangy colt: first foal: dam, 8.5f winner in USA, out of sister to Caerleon: fairly useful form: won apprentice maiden at Wexford in July by 10 lengths: well beaten in Gordon Stakes at Goodwood next start: acted as pacemaker subsequently: should stay at least 1¾m: acts on good to soft ground. *A. P. O'Brien, Ireland*

SADDLER'S QUEST 4 b.c. Saddlers' Hall (IRE) 126 – Seren Quest 90 (Rainbow **–** Quest (USA) 134) [2001 110: 12s 16g 14v 12d⁴ 14.6s⁴ Nov 9] rather leggy colt: smart form at 3 yrs, winning Derby Trial at Lingfield: later found to have suffered stress fracture of cannon bone: well held in 2001, very slowly away third start: should stay at least 2m: raced only on good going or softer: has worn crossed noseband. *G. A. Butler*

SADEEBAH 6 b.g. Prince Sabo 123 – Adeebah (USA) 94 (Damascus (USA)) [2001 **– §** 10.9d Jul 23] very tall gelding: temperamental maiden handicapper: blinkered once. *M. Todhunter*

SADHAKA 2 b.f. (Mar 10) Slip Anchor 136 – Secretilla (USA) 61 (Secreto (USA) **63 p** 128) [2001 9v⁶ Nov 15] fifth foal: half-sister to 2 winners in Italy, including 5f (at 2 yrs) to 7.5f winner Sarman (by Lion Cavern): dam, 7f winner, out of smart French performer up to 12.5f Satilla: sixth in maiden at Milan: should improve. *L. M. Cumani*

SADIE SADIE 2 b.f. (Apr 14) Primo Dominie 121 – Ann's Pearl (IRE) 81 (Cyrano de **46** Bergerac 120) [2001 6v f6g Oct 18] second foal: dam 5f winner (including at 2 yrs): poor form in maidens. *P. J. Makin*

SADLERS LAW (IRE) 2 b.c. (Mar 9) Sadler's Wells (USA) 132 – Dathiyna (IRE) **– p** (Kris 135) [2001 8d Oct 3] 200,000Y: first foal: dam unraced daughter of very smart 6f/ 7f winner Dafayna, herself half-sister to 2000 Guineas winner Doyoun: 14/1 and green, well held in maiden at Salisbury: probably capable of better. *J. W. Hills*

SADLERS SWING (USA) 5 b.g. Red Ransom (USA) – Noblissima (IRE) 77 **–** (Sadler's Wells (USA) 132) [2001 –: 11.9s 17.2f May 22] leggy gelding: little form: has given trouble/refused to enter stalls. *M. R. Channon*

SADLERS WALTZ (IRE) 4 b.g. In The Wings 128 – Fascination Waltz 83 (Shy **66** Groom (USA)) [2001 –: 12g⁶ 12s 16.2m⁴ 14s 18m 16g Sep 7] fair maiden handicapper: left M. Channon after third start: pulled up final outing: stayed 2m: acted on good to firm ground, probably on soft: dead. *J. J. Sheehan*

SADLERS WINGS (IRE) 3 b.g. In The Wings 128 – Anna Comnena (IRE) 71 **112** (Shareef Dancer (USA) 135) [2001 10d* 14g² 12d* 14m⁵ 10s⁴ 12d³ 10s Oct 29] IR 32,000Y: fifth foal: half-brother to 3 winners, including useful 1¼m winner who stayed 12.5f Abyaan (by Ela-Mana-Mou): dam, maiden who should have stayed 1½m, half-sister to dams of Annus Mirabilis and Annaba: smart performer: won maiden at the Curragh in June and listed race at Leopardstown (by head from Masilia) in August: best effort after when 3 lengths third to Diamond Trim (who rec 6 lb) in listed race at the Curragh penultimate start: better at 1½m than shorter and should prove at least as effective at 1¾m (stiff task in Irish St Leger on second attempt at trip): acts on soft ground. *W. P. Mullins, Ireland*

SAD MAD BAD (USA) 7 b.g. Sunny's Halo (CAN) – Quite Attractive (USA) (Well   –
Decorated (USA)) [2001 17.5m 18s⁵ Oct 22] workmanlike gelding: modest handicapper
in 1999: well held since: blinkered final start: fairly useful chaser. *Mrs M. Reveley*

SAFE SHOT 2 b.g. (Apr 13) Salse (USA) 128 – Optaria 83 (Song 132) [2001 7m 7m⁴   52
8.1g Sep 13] sixth foal: half-brother to 3 winners, notably smart performers Grey Shot
(up to 2m, by Sharrood) and Night Shot (sprinter, by Night Shift): dam 2-y-o 5f winner:
easily best effort (modest form) when fourth to Desert Royal in claimer at Salisbury:
should stay at least 1m: sold 2,000 gns, and gelded. *D. R. C. Elsworth*

SAFE TRIP 2 b.f. (Feb 4) Hector Protector (USA) 124 – Green Charter 77 (Green   77
Desert (USA) 127) [2001 5g⁴ 5.7f⁵ 6m⁴ 7m* 7.5s 8m Sep 10] leggy filly: first foal: dam,
2-y-o 7f winner, granddaughter of Time Charter: fair performer: won nursery at Brighton
in July: well beaten in similar events after, something possibly amiss final start: should
stay 1m. *J. L. Dunlop*

SAFFRON 5 ch.m. Alhijaz 122 – Silver Lodge (Homing 130) [2001 47: 8d⁶ Apr 12]   –
workmanlike mare: poor handicapper at 4 yrs: well held only outing in 2001: tried
blinkered. *D. Shaw*

SAFFRON HEIGHTS 3 b.f. Shirley Heights 130 – Persia (IRE) (Persian Bold 123)   –
[2001 9.9g Sep 19] 46,000Y: second foal: half-sister to 1m winner Queen Zenobia (by
Danehill): dam unraced half-sister to very smart sprinter Sayyaf: 33/1 and tongue tied,
slowly away and always behind in Goodwood maiden. *C. A. Horgan*

SAFI 6 b.g. Generous (IRE) 139 – Jasarah (IRE) 70 (Green Desert (USA) 127) [2001   –
10.5g 8m Jun 18] of little account nowadays. *D. McCain*

SAFINAZ 3 gr.f. Environment Friend 128 – Safidar 83 (Roan Rocket 128) [2001 46:   41
e7g⁴ f9.4g 8.2v 8d f7g⁵ f8g f8.5g⁵ f11s⁶ Dec 21] angular, workmanlike filly: poor maiden
handicapper: left G. Brown after third start: probably stays 8.5f: acts on fibresand/
equitrack, good to firm and good to soft going. *Mrs N. Macauley*

SAFRANINE (IRE) 4 b.f. Dolphin Street (FR) 125 – Webbiana (African Sky 124)   55 d
[2001 –: 6f 8d 10m 7d 5g 6m 5g f6g f6g⁵ f6g p7g Dec 19] rather leggy filly: modest form
at best in 2001 (left J. L. Eyre after sixth start): tried blinkered/visored. *Miss A. Stokell*

SAGACITY (FR) 3 gr.c. Highest Honor (FR) 124 – Saganeca (USA) 120   125
(Sagace (FR) 135) [2001 108p: 10.5v⁴ 12d² 12m 10d³ 10d² 12s³ Oct 7]
        In terms of ability, Sagacity is his namesake, who won the
Yorkshire Cup and Goodwood Cup in 1962 for Cecil Boyd-Rochfort. That is about
as far as any comparison extends. The original Sagacity was a front runner needing
distances of two miles and more to bring out the best in him, whereas the latest
version, a three-year-old French colt, is usually ridden with restraint and has done
all of his racing at up to a mile and a half. Sagacity will stay further, though whether
he'll be given the opportunity to tackle longer distances is another matter. After
leaving his previous form behind when third in the Arc on his final appearance of
the season, a campaign in mile-and-a-half pattern races surely beckons. How he
fares will depend to a great extent on the conditions he encounters. Sagacity will
almost certainly need them to be as testing as those which prevailed at Longchamp
on Arc day if he is to reproduce the high-class form he showed there.
        Sagacity is like his half-brother the 1998 Arc winner Sagamix, in that he
goes particularly well on ground softer than good, something demonstrated very
early in his career. On his two starts at two, Sagacity won a nine-furlong minor
event at Longchamp on good to soft going and the ten-furlong Criterium de
Saint-Cloud on soft ground. Unfortunately for Sagacity's connections, the ground
was on the firm side of good when it came around to his first major engagement as a
three-year-old, in the Prix du Jockey Club at Chantilly in June. In the frame behind
wide-margin winner Maille Pistol in both the Prix Greffulhe and Prix Hocquart on
his first two starts of the season, Sagacity did improve on those performances but
still could finish no higher than ninth at Chantilly. Back on softer ground, Sagacity
continued his progress, gaining places in the Prix Guillaume d'Ornano and the
Prix du Prince d'Orange over a mile and a quarter at Deauville and Longchamp
respectively, despite the distance being on the short side. He was beaten a length by
Masterful on the first occasion and half a length by Equerry, finishing strongly, on
the second. It was no great surprise, therefore, that he should run the race of his life
when facing a stiffer test of stamina in the Arc. Taken wide, Sagacity could never

land a blow but stayed on to snatch third from Golan, finishing a length behind Aquarelliste and seven behind Sakhee. Sagacity's performance, judged strictly on form, merits a rating only 4 lb below that achieved by Sagamix in winning a substandard renewal of the Arc. Sagamix ended his three-year-old career still unbeaten, but failed to win again kept in training for another couple of seasons. It should not be beyond Sagacity to better his half-brother's record in that respect.

			Kenmare	Kalamoun
		Highest Honor (FR)	(gr 1975)	Belle of Ireland
		(gr 1983)	High River	Riverman
Sagacity (FR)			(b 1978)	Hairbrush
(gr.c. 1998)			Sagace	Luthier
		Saganeca (USA)	(b 1980)	Seneca
		(b 1988)	Haglette	Hagley
			(b 1978)	Sucrette

The success enjoyed by Messrs Lagardere and Fabre with the offspring of Saganeca, purchased for 165,000 dollars in 1994, is ongoing. The mare's latest produce to reach the racecourse, Saga d'Ouilly (by Linamix), won a newcomers event for two-year-old fillies at Deauville in October. That made it five winners for Saganeca from her first five foals, which include not only Saga d'Ouilly's full brother Sagamix but her full sister Sage Et Jolie, a smart performer who won the Prix de Malleret. Saganeca herself won the Prix de Royallieu over an extended mile and a half. That was her only victory, though she did finish fourth in the Vermeille and fifth as a four-year-old in the Arc. Sagacity's grandam Haglette was a sprinter who won three races at allowance level in the States, while his great grandam Sucrette was unplaced in each of her three starts. Both mares are well related. Haglette is a half-sister to the Criterium de Maisons-Laffitte winner Round Top, while Sucrette is a half-sister to Irish Derby winner Tambourine and the 1964 King George winner Nasram. The close connection with the Arc goes back a long way in this family, the next dam La Mirambule having finished runner-up in 1952. She also won the Prix Vermeille the same year, not in 1953 as stated in Sagamix's essay in *Racehorses of 1998*. *A. Fabre, France*

SAGE DANCER (USA) 4 b.g. Green Dancer (USA) 132 – Sophonisbe (Wollow 132) [2001 96: 12s 20m 14d⁴ Aug 3] $210,000Y: tall, attractive gelding: half-brother to several winners, notably Irish Derby winner Zagreb (by Theatrical): dam, French listed 11f winner, half-sister to high-class performer (best up to 1¼m) Steinlen: fairly useful performer: best run in 2001 when respectable ninth in Ascot Stakes (Handicap) at Royal Ascot second start: probably stays 2½m: acts on good to firm and good to soft ground: blinkered. *D. K. Weld, Ireland* **85**

SAGITTARIUS 5 b.h. Sadler's Wells (USA) 132 – Ste Nitouche (FR) (Riverman (USA) 131) [2001 11v³ 12g* 13g* 12g² 12g* 12s² 12s² Sep 30] 80,000Y: big, leggy horse: has a quick action: closely related to winner in Italy by Glenstal and half-brother to several winners, including Italian Group 3 1m winner Saint Samba (by Thatch), grandam of 4-y-o Shibuni's Falcon: dam Italian 1¼m winner: made belated debut (only start) at 4 yrs, having suffered serious injury earlier: made into a smart performer in 2001, winning maiden at Krefeld in April, handicap at Ovrevoll in June and listed race at Taby in July, all by wide margins, and minor event at Taby in August: second in Group 3 company other 3 starts, narrowly beaten by Valley Chapel at Klampenborg and Taby, and beaten 1¼ lengths by Nayef in Cumberland Lodge Stakes at Ascot final outing, keeping on gamely: stays 13f: acts on heavy ground. *Rune Haugen, Norway* **117**

SAGUARO 7 b.g. Green Desert (USA) 127 – Badawi (USA) 103 (Diesis 133) [2001 52, a66: f8s⁶ f8.5g f8g⁴ f7g f7g 10.1m 10.5m⁶ 8g 8s f8g² f9.4f⁶ f8s Dec 21] quite attractive gelding: has a quick action: modest performer: stays 9.4f: acts on fibresand and firm going: tried visored: not one to trust implicitly. *K. A. Morgan* **–**
a52

SAHARA ROSE 2 b.f. (Apr 19) Green Desert (USA) 127 – Ruthless Rose (USA) (Conquistador Cielo (USA)) [2001 5d Oct 9] good-topped filly: has scope: sister to a winner up to 1m in Japan, closely related to 2 winners by Danehill (notably 2000 Cheveley Park winner Regal Rose) and half-sister to 2 winners: dam twice-raced half-sister to high-class miler Shaadi: 13/2 and backward, seventh of 11 to Zargus in maiden at Catterick: should do better. *Sir Mark Prescott* **– p**

Ribblesdale Stakes, Royal Ascot—
Sahara Slew shows plenty of improvement on only her third start, catching Nafisah (left) close home;
Marani (right) keeps on willingly for third, with Snowflake and Rockerlong (noseband) next

SAHARA SLEW (USA) 3 b.f. Seattle Slew (USA) – Sahara Sun (USA) (Alysheba 110
(USA)) [2001 10g³ 12d* 12f* Jun 21] tall, leggy, angular filly: third foal: half-sister to
fairly useful Irish 1½m winner Sahara Song (by Woodman) who stayed 1¾m: dam,
French 11f winner, half-sister to very smart 1½m performer Zalazl: won maiden at
Leopardstown in June: smart form when winning Ribblesdale Stakes at Royal Ascot later
in month by head from Nafisah, leading close home under strong handling: suffered
lameness after: would have been suited by 1¾m+: acted on firm and good to soft going:
stud. *J. Oxx, Ireland*

SAHHAR 8 ch.g. Sayf El Arab (USA) 127 – Native Magic 97 (Be My Native (USA) –
122) [2001 –: 10s Apr 28] small gelding: no form on Flat since 1996. *B. D. Leavy*

SAILING SHOES (IRE) 5 b.g. Lahib (USA) 129 – Born To Glamour (Ajdal (USA) 67 §
130) [2001 81: 5g 5g 6d 5m* 5g 5g 5s Sep 27] smallish gelding: fair handicapper: won at
Sandown in July: effective at 5f/6f: acts on any going except possibly heavy: blinkered
third to fifth starts at 4 yrs: tongue tied final start: finds little and can't be trusted.
D. Nicholls

SAILOR JACK (USA) 5 b.g. Green Dancer (USA) 132 – Chateaubrook (USA) –
(Alleged (USA) 138) [2001 f12g f12g Mar 22] modest maiden handicapper in 1999: no
show both Flat runs since: usually blinkered/visored. *D. McCain*

SAINT CIEL (USA) 13 b.g. Skywalker (USA) – Holy Tobin (USA) (J O Tobin –
(USA) 130) [2001 16.2m Sep 17] strong gelding: winning hurdler: poor handicapper on
Flat in 1997: tailed off only run since: tried blinkered/tongue tied. *F. Jordan*

SAINTE JUST (IRE) 2 b.g. (Jan 26) Polish Precedent (USA) 131 – Charlotte Corday 79
105 (Kris 135) [2001 8m⁶ 7d² 8.3v⁵ p8g Nov 20] big, lengthy gelding: has scope: first
foal: dam, 1m winner, sister to useful 1¼m/1½m performer Gai Bulga and half-sister
to 3-y-o Rockerlong and to dam of 3-y-o Superstar Leo: fair performer: won 30-runner
seller at Newmarket (beat Redisham by 3½ lengths, left R. Charlton) in October: better
effort in nurseries after when creditable fifth at Windsor: may prove best at 7f/1m.
W. J. Musson

SAINT GEORGE (IRE) 5 b.g. Unblest 117 – Jumana (Windjammer (USA)) [2001 – §
55?: 11.6m 10m Jun 18] ungenuine maiden. *Miss Z. C. Davison*

SAINT JOHANN (IRE) 2 b.g. (May 3) Ali-Royal (IRE) 127 – Up To You (Sallust 44
134) [2001 5g 6m 5.3m 6g Sep 11] IR 5,000F, IR 4,000Y: half-brother to several winners,
including useful 1990 2-y-o 7f winner Time Line (by Hatim), later multiple winner in
Italy, and fairly useful Irish 7f (at 2 yrs) and 1¼m winner Goldstreet (by Dolphin Street):
dam ran once in Ireland: poor maiden. *G. M. McCourt*

SAKAMOTO 3 b.g. Celtic Swing 138 – Possessive Lady 62 (Dara Monarch 128) –
[2001 47: 7d 8.1v⁶ 8.1g 9m 10m 7.1g f11g 6.1m f6g 8d Nov 2] tall, good-topped gelding:
no longer of much account: tried blinkered/tongue tied. *R. C. Spicer*

SAKHEE (USA)   4 b.c. Bahri (USA) 125 – Thawakib (IRE) 108 (Sadler's Wells   **136**
(USA) 132) [2001 127: 10m* 10.4g* 12s* a10f² Oct 27]

    Whether success genuinely breeds success is a moot point, but the achievements of any consistently successful organisation have an automatic tendency to generate ever-increasing—and often unrealistic—circles of expectation. This applies particularly in business, where every year various companies return figures showing substantial profits which the City promptly interprets as insufficient and disappointing. Sport isn't immune, either, as the Godolphin team might be the first to admit. The latest season did not start well for the Dubai operation, without a winner in Europe until Marienbard in the Yorkshire Cup on May 17th, and, by Royal Ascot, Godolphin's Simon Crisford felt obliged to say this to the media: 'At the moment, you would have to say (Coolmore/Ballydoyle) are doing a lot better than we are, so we've really got to organise ourselves and pick ourselves up to make sure we can compete with them.' He need not have worried. By the end of the season Godolphin had not quite caught up with Aidan O'Brien but its European squad had mustered fourteen Group/Grade 1 victories (not counting Kutub's win in the Singapore Gold Cup), a total second in its eight-year existence only to the eighteen in 1999, and there was an additional one in 2001 from Godolphin's American-based juvenile string. The number of Group 1 winning individuals involved in Europe, seven, was fewer than in 1995, 1998 and 1999, but they included the best three-year-old specialist miler in Noverre, the equal best older miler in Slickly and two outstanding middle-distance performers, Fantastic Light and Sakhee. If that was a bad season, nearly every owner and trainer would be happy to endure a similar one.

    To some extent Sakhee, who proved himself the best horse in training with wide-margin victories in the Juddmonte International and Prix de l'Arc de Triomphe - Lucien Barriere, and then went on to finish second in the Breeders' Cup Classic, was a surprise package. He had shown high-class form with John Dunlop to run Sinndar to a length in the Derby after landing the Sandown Classic Trial and Dante Stakes but had not run again after finishing a lacklustre fourth in the Eclipse Stakes. Reasons given at the time, and through the rest of 2000, included being jarred up behind, marginally lame, having a bruised foot and a throat infection, but Sheikh Hamdan put the record straight in an interview with Channel 4 after the Arc. He said: 'Sakhee broke his knee in the Derby but we didn't discover that until we ran him at Sandown. Richard (Hills) told us that the horse couldn't stride out. When we took him to Dubai we found two chips behind a knee.' The chips were removed but Godolphin bided their time with the colt and he didn't reappear until July, in the listed Steventon Stakes at Newbury. The opposition was strong enough to test him without posing a serious threat to a horse expected to make his presence felt in Group 1 company and Sakhee, who looked in good shape beforehand, disposed of them with the minimum of fuss. After hitting the front over two furlongs out, he passed the post three lengths clear of Aldwych with Frankie Dettori giving him as easy a race as possible.

    The Juddmonte International at York the following month was a different matter. Sakhee started favourite at 7/4, his seven rivals including the first two in the

Juddmonte International Stakes, York—Sakhee produces one of the best performances in thirty runnings of the race, finishing seven lengths ahead of Grandera, Medicean (left), Black Minnaloushe (behind runner-up) and Distant Music (rail)

Eclipse, Medicean (who started at 3/1) and Grandera (7/1), the Irish Two Thousand Guineas and St James's Palace Stakes winner Black Minnaloushe (7/2), Distant Music (9/1), winner of the Group 2 International Stakes at the Curragh in the latest season, and Time Away (16/1) winner of the Musidora Stakes and third in the both the Prix de Diane and Nassau Stakes. It's rare for the International not to produce something newsworthy, be it a top-class winner, a thrilling finish or a major upset, and it certainly provided the first-named on this occasion—Sakhee was a revelation. Frankie Dettori soon had him travelling strongly on the heels of the Ballydoyle pacemaker Darwin and had the confidence to set sail for home in earnest three furlongs out, soon taking an advantage of a couple of lengths and then storming right away inside the final furlong before being allowed to coast home. Sakhee won by seven lengths from Grandera, with Medicean a further length away in third and Black Minnaloushe fourth. The one fly in the ointment when it came to assessing Sakhee's performance was that of Foodbroker Fancy, beaten over eleven lengths in sixth place and appearing to hold down the form; she belatedly more than confirmed that she had shown improved form at York when second in the Sun Chariot Stakes at Newmarket in October. The manner of Sakhee's victory was very similar to that of Royal Anthem, who won the race by a record eight lengths in 1999. Royal Anthem failed to repeat that form on his next outing, trailing in over thirteen lengths behind Daylami in the Irish Champion Stakes, but redeemed himself when finishing second to the same horse in the Breeders' Cup Turf.

Sakhee's next target became the subject of great debate in the media and, presumably, in the Godolphin camp as well. The Dubai Champion Stakes, a race which, together with the Dubai World Cup, seems almost to be an obsession with the Maktoum family, was nominated, for the additional reason that trainer Saeed bin Suroor felt a mile and a quarter, not a mile and a half, was the colt's best trip and that soft going at Longchamp might blunt his speed. Dettori, on the other hand, favoured the Arc from the start, and even though the Champion reportedly remained the principal plan for a time, the decision to run Sakhee in France came at the end of September. The Arc is often the defining race of the middle-distance season in Europe, and, with the Longchamp card now boasting five other Group 1 events, the day is now second to none in the European calendar though it cannot hope to match the international prestige and prize-money of the Breeders' Cup, the attractions of which lured the dual Derby and King George winner Galileo away from the Arc. Perhaps one area in which an improvement might be made to Arc day, and in which imitating the Breeders' Cup doesn't work, is in scheduling the Arc as the penultimate race on the eight-race card at 5.30pm local time. Without any artificial lighting, visibility on a dull day can be bad and poses considerable problems for press photographers, whose images are essential for Longchamp, as well as beneficial for the rest of the racing world. The lateness of the race also hinders reporting of the events by journalists with deadlines to meet, which again works against the race, publicity being vital for any showpiece. Nor does it do much to facilitate racegoers, or anyone else, leaving the track to get transport home, be it within France or abroad. Ideally, the card should start earlier, or the Arc should come midway through the afternoon.

Be that as it may, the notion of using a pacemaker for Sakhee in the Arc, with Equerry and Ekraar among the horses mentioned, was toyed with and discounted, and in testing conditions Sakhee started favourite to beat a field of

Prix de l'Arc de Triomphe - Lucien Barriere, Longchamp—Sakhee is a class apart and has the race won some way out, going on to equal the record winning margin of six lengths; Aquarelliste (fourth left) and Sagacity (far right) stay on past Golan (rail) to take the minor honours

sixteen. As well as Galileo, there was no Fantastic Light, Nayef nor Morshdi, who was injured, but the runners included the two best mile-and-a-half fillies in France, Aquarelliste and Diamilina; the runner-up from 2000, Egyptband; Two Thousand Guineas winner Golan; St Leger winner Milan; the last two winners of the Prix du Jockey Club, Holding Court and Anabaa Blue; and one of the best older horses in France, Hightori. Not a vintage Arc perhaps, but the paying public (the announcement of a record crowd came as a surprise to many regulars) were treated to a vintage performance in a race in which there were few hard-luck stories and no convincing ones. Sakhee had no difficulty travelling strongly, close to the pace, and he moved through readily to lead soon after entering the straight and proceeded to leave the others for dead, passing the post, pushed out, six lengths clear of Aquarelliste, who hadn't enjoyed an entirely smooth passage but still got clear in time to catch Sakhee if good enough. Three-year-old Sagacity, putting up his best performance, was a further length back in third, followed by Golan and Milan. It was the first time in eight years the race had not been won by a three-year-old colt. Few championship races, let alone the Arc, are as good as over so far out or are won by as much as six lengths. Sakhee's margin matched the official ones for Ribot in 1956 and Sea Bird II in 1965, while Helissio's official five in 1996 was actually six, but, whichever way one looks at it, this was a magnificent display by a well-above-average Arc winner.

The Arc tends to take a lot out of a horse, and, although it was advantageous that Sakhee's season hadn't started until July, it hardly boded well for Sakhee's future plans that All Along in 1983 had been the last winner to triumph again during the season. Plenty of others had tried, with Subotica, Saumarez, Trempolino and Dancing Brave all beaten in the Breeders' Cup Turf—Trempolino finished second—and five failing in the Japan Cup, Tony Bin, Carroll House, Urban Sea, Helissio and Montjeu. There seemed no doubt that Sakhee was going to run again; the only issue was in which race. The Champion Stakes remained at the top of the list for a short while, but with Nayef hitting form there was an able substitute for that prize, and a week before Newmarket Sakhee was switched to the Breeders' Cup where his connections had to make another choice, between the Classic and the Turf. Sakhee worked on the main track at Belmont Park and, three days before Breeders' Cup day, was announced as a starter in the Classic, with Fantastic Light going for the Turf. The decision astonished some observers, who believed Sakhee was a near-certainty in the Turf and that Fantastic Light should be running over his perceived best trip of a mile and a quarter in the Classic. Simon Crisford's explanation gave a fascinating insight into how Godolphin works: 'When they travelled over, no decision was made as we wanted to see how they worked, what their actions were like and how they were doing, physically and mentally. The Sheikhs have seen the video footage of the horses working, received feedback from the jockeys and based their decision on the evidence available.' He added: 'Sakhee is a Sheikh Hamdan horse, while Fantastic Light runs under the banner of Sheikh Maktoum's Gainsborough Stud, and Sheikh Mohammed presses the buttons. Collectively they made a decision. It has to be a feeling, but the boss (Sheikh Mohammed) said to me that Fantastic Light could have run second in the Classic whereas Sakhee might win it.' The judgement proved sound and Godolphin almost brought off a remarkable double. Sakhee, along with fellow European challengers Galileo and Black Minnaloushe, had no experience on dirt and faced ten strong but, collectively, far from outstanding North American defenders. In the absence of the retired Point Given and Lido Palace, who wasn't supplemented, the home team was headed by the previous year's winner Tiznow, runaway Jockey Club Gold Cup victor Aptitude, the normally reliable Albert The Great and Macho Uno, winner of the Breeders' Cup Juvenile the year before but mostly out of form since. Sakhee coped with the surface well enough—much better than Galileo—and when he passed Albert The Great rounding the home turn he looked set for success. This time, however, he could not get clear and, although running on strongly, was caught by the doughty Tiznow and beaten a nose; Tiznow had had a neck to spare over Giant's Causeway the year before with Albert The Great three and a half lengths away in fourth. This time Albert The Great finished a place closer and narrowed the gap on the winner to a length and three quarters. Sakhee did not run to his very best, but that's not to belittle his effort or that of the winner, who had experienced training troubles.

Victory at Belmont Park would have put the icing on the cake for Sakhee who was clearly the horse of the year in Europe, despite the achievements of such as Fantastic Light, Galileo and Johannesburg. Sakhee should have the chance to atone in 2002 though, since he stays in training with a campaign including the Dubai World Cup and Breeders' Cup Classic, with unspecified races on turf in Europe in between. This is a real bonus for the sport and for racing fans. In the modern era—and the old one, if the Aga Khan III is a guide, since he retired all five of his Derby winners at the end of their classic campaign—Sakhee might well have been packed off to stud by some owners after the Eclipse, given the level of his form and his injury. Precious few would have decided to keep him in training at five with an Arc under his belt, but Godolphin has a different agenda from most other leading owners, which is why the stable continues landing so many Group 1 races. Besides enjoying seeing horses compete and win in top company, the Maktoums know that having Sakhee running at five should project Godolphin's name across the globe. It will take another exceptional horse to beat him over a mile and a quarter or a mile and a half, whatever the surface.

Sakhee (USA) (b.c. 1997)	Bahri (USA) (b 1992)	Riverman (b 1969)	Never Bend
			River Lady
		Wasnah (b 1987)	Nijinsky
			Highest Trump
	Thawakib (IRE) (b 1990)	Sadler's Wells (b 1981)	Northern Dancer
			Fairy Bridge
		Tobira Celeste (b 1971)	Ribot
			Heavenly Body

Godolphin's "Sakhee"

Campaigning Sakhee for another year may also make sense commercially, as his pedigree is not exceptional for a potential stallion. Bahri always looked as though he would be a better bet to do well as a sire in Europe than in the States and his record, which is far from brilliant, reinforces this, with only two pattern winners so far—the other is Falmouth Stakes winner Alshakr—plus two minor stakes scorers in America. Bahri has not been well patronised, except by the Maktoums, with a total of only sixty-five foals from three crops. His fee for 2002 is 40,000 dollars. On the dam's side, Sakhee is related to a number of good horses, notably King George runner-up Celestial Storm (a half-brother to Sakhee's dam), but none who have made a lasting impact. Sakhee's three-year-old sister Khazayin finished second in two maiden races over a mile and a quarter and her two-year-old half-sister Najayeb (by Silver Hawk) has yet to race. Sakhee's dam Thawakib, successful in the Ribblesdale Stakes, foaled a filly by Red Ransom in 2000, a colt by A P Indy in 2001, is due a foal to Bahri and will then visit Seeking The Gold in 2002. The genuine Sakhee is a strong, good-topped colt who carries plenty of condition and acts on any turf going, as well as on dirt, though it's debatable if he'll ever be risked on firm again—perhaps another reason why he bypassed the Turf at Belmont. He has a splendid turn of foot which he is able to produce after being ridden up with the pace, making him all the more formidable. *Saeed bin Suroor*

SALERNO 2 ch.c. (Mar 11) Mark of Esteem (IRE) 137 – Shamwari (USA) 63 (Shahrastani (USA) 135) [2001 7.1g⁴ 6f⁶ 6v⁵ Oct 26] 19,000F: rather unfurnished colt: fourth foal: half-brother to a winner in South Africa by Bluebird: dam, maiden (stayed 2m), closely related to Derby winner Golden Fleece: fair form in maidens at Sandown and Newbury (2): will stay 1m. *M. P. Tregoning* **71**

SALFORD EXPRESS (IRE) 5 ch.h. Be My Guest (USA) 126 – Summer Fashion 84 (Moorestyle 137) [2001 12s² 12g⁵ May 4] leggy horse: smart performer: won Dante Stakes at York at 3 yrs: missed 2000 reportedly due to leg injury: creditable 3½ lengths second to Lucido in John Porter Stakes at Newbury in April: well-held fifth to Millenary in Jockey Club Stakes at Newmarket only subsequent start: best around 1½m: successful on good to firm ground, best efforts on soft/heavy: often takes strong hold (usually races prominently): sold 25,000 gns in July, resold 14,000 gns in December. *D. R. C. Elsworth* **110**

SALFORD FLYER 5 b.g. Pharly (FR) 130 – Edge of Darkness 62 (Vaigly Great 127) [2001 86: 14.1g 13.9m⁴ 14m⁵ 14.4m⁴ 14s 14.4m⁵ Jul 11] rather sparely-made gelding: fairly useful handicapper: stays 2m: acts on good to firm and good to soft going (has run poorly on fibresand and soft ground): whipped round at flip start once: carries head awkwardly and has flashed tail: held up: sold only 4,200 gns in October. *D. R. C. Elsworth* **83**

SALIM 4 b.g. Salse (USA) 128 – Moviegoer 104 (Pharly (FR) 130) [2001 85: e10g f8.5s³ f8.5s⁵ f8.5g* f9.4g⁵ f8.5g⁶ e8g 10v 7m f8.5g* 8m 8m⁵ 8m f8g f9.4s 8.5g f12g Sep 22] useful-looking gelding: fair performer on all-weather, modest on turf: won minor event in February and handicap in May, both at Wolverhampton: stays easy 1¼m: acts on fibresand, good to firm and good to soft going: tried visored: has raced freely: finds little: sold 3,500 gns, resold 1,500 gns. *C. A. Dwyer* **58 §**
a68 §

SALIM TOTO 3 b.f. Mtoto 134 – Villasanta (Corvaro (USA) 124) [2001 8.3s 8.2d² 9f³ 12m* 12m³ 12m Sep 26] 7,000Y: closely related to 2 winners abroad by Shernazar, including minor US stakes winner, and half-sister to several winners, including 5-y-o Santa Lucia: dam French maiden: fairly useful performer: won handicap at Thirsk in August: will prove best at 1¼m/1½m: acts on good to firm going: may prove best ridden prominently. *J. G. Smyth-Osbourne* **80**

SALIX DANCER 4 b.g. Shareef Dancer (USA) 135 – Willowbank 66 (Gay Fandango (USA) 132) [2001 72: 7s 10g 7m 10g⁶ 12.6f 14.1m 15.8g 16d 17.1d 16v² 16s² Oct 30] tall, angular gelding: has stringhalt: modest maiden handicapper, largely on downgrade: stays 2m: acts on heavy ground. *Pat Mitchell* **61 d**

SALLY TRAFFIC 2 b.f. (Mar 27) River Falls 113 – Yankeedoodledancer (Mashhor Dancer (USA)) [2001 5m 6d 5g 5m 5g f6g Nov 23] small, sturdy filly: sixth living foal: half-sister to 2 winners, notably 3-y-o Vicious Dancer: dam, of little account, out of half-sister to top-class 1m/1¼m performer Wollow: poor maiden: will prove best at 5f. *R. M. Whitaker* **43**

SALOUP 3 b.f. Wolfhound (USA) 126 – Sarcita 111 (Primo Dominie 121) [2001 –p: 7s 6m⁵ 7m Jul 11] angular filly: trained by D. Elsworth only 2-y-o start: poor form in maidens/handicap. *M. R. Channon* **43**

SALSA   3 b.g. Salse (USA) 128 – Lana Turrel (USA) (Trempolino (USA) 135) [2001   **63**
63: f7g 7.1d⁶ 7m² 8.3m 8m 6m 7.5f⁶ 7.1d⁶ 7.1m* 7g Oct 19] leggy gelding: modest
performer: fortunate winner of handicap at Musselburgh in August: best at 7f: acts on
good to firm ground. *M. Dods*

SAL'S GAL   3 b.f. Efisio 120 – Ann's Pearl (IRE) 81 (Cyrano de Bergerac 120) [2001   **73**
f6g³ 6m⁴ 6g³ 6v f6g Oct 18] first foal: dam 5f (including at 2 yrs) winner: fair maiden:
raced only at 6f. *P. J. Makin*

SALSIFY   5 b.g. Salse (USA) 128 – Amaranthus (Shirley Heights 130) [2001 –: 9.9m   **–**
10.2s Aug 9] probably of little account nowadays. *G. A. Ham*

SALSKA   10 b.m. Salse (USA) 128 – Anzeige (GER) (Soderini 123) [2001 62: 16f   **46**
16.2f⁶ 16.5m³ 16f⁶ 15m 18.7m 17.1g Aug 19] strong, lengthy mare: poor handicapper:
will stay beyond 2m: acts on firm and good to soft going: tried visored. *P. L. Clinton*

SALTRIO   3 b.c. Slip Anchor 136 – Hills' Presidium (Presidium 124) [2001 58p: **101 p**
9.9m* 10f* 12s⁴ Sep 30] tall, angular, attractive colt: useful performer: won maiden at
Salisbury (easily) in June and 3-runner minor event at Newbury in July: looked to have
done well physically before good 4 lengths fourth to Hannibal Lad in Betdaq Handicap at
Ascot final start: should stay 1¾m: likely to continue to improve. *J. H. M. Gosden*

SALTWOOD   3 b.f. Mujtahid (USA) 118 – Actualite (Polish Precedent (USA) 131)   **–**
[2001 74: 10g 7m Jun 10] angular filly: fair performer at 2 yrs: well held in 2001.
P. Howling

SALTY JACK (IRE)   7 b.h. Salt Dome (USA) – Play The Queen (IRE) (King of   **92**
Clubs 124) [2001 94: f7g⁴ 8v 8s 8m* 8m* 7m 8m 8s 9g 8d p8g⁴ p7g Dec 29] small horse:
has a round action: fairly useful handicapper: won at Kempton in June and Goodwood in
July: best at 7f/1m: acts on all-weather and any turf going: has good turn of foot, and best
patiently ridden. *D. R. C. Elsworth*

SALUEM   4 b.f. Salse (USA) 128 – Pat Or Else 72 (Alzao (USA) 117) [2001 80+:   **82**
11.7m⁵ 12g² 14.4g 12d* Nov 6] small, workmanlike filly: fairly useful performer: won
maiden at Catterick in November: stays 14.5f: acts on soft and good to firm going.
R. Guest

SALUTE (IRE)   2 b.g. (Feb 11) Muhtarram (USA) 125 – Alasib 93 (Siberian Express   **91**
(USA) 125) [2001 6m* 6m⁴ 7m² 8m* 8g⁵ 6d Oct 19] 8,500Y: lengthy, quite attractive
gelding: third foal: dam, 5f (at 2 yrs) and 6f winner, half-sister to useful sprinter Farhana:
fairly useful performer: won maiden at Windsor in June and valuable nursery at Newcastle in August: ran respectably final start: stays 1m: yet to race on extremes of going:
edgy/nearly unseated leaving stall penultimate outing. *J. M. P. Eustace*

SALVIANO   3 b.g. River Falls 113 – Shiny Kay 65 (Star Appeal 133) [2001 –: 7.1g 12f   **–**
Jul 2] angular gelding: well held in maidens/selling handicap. *N. Tinkler*

SALVIATI (USA)   4 b.g. Lahib (USA) 129 – Mother Courage 67 (Busted 134) [2001   **95**
90: 7g 6m 6m 6d 6m² 6f 6m² 5.5d 6m 6g⁶ 5g* 5g 5.7d* 5.6m Sep 12] sturdy gelding:
useful handicapper: better than ever in 2001, winning at Ascot and Bath (beat Rafters
Music by length) in August: well held in Portland at Doncaster final start: best at 5f/6f:
acts on firm and good to soft ground: waited with. *J. M. Bradley*

SAMADILLA (IRE)   3 b.f. Mujadil (USA) 119 – Samnaun (USA) (Stop The Music   **83**
(USA)) [2001 76: 6s⁶ 6s² 6d 6d⁴ 7.5f 6m⁶ 7.1s⁴ 7.1v⁶ Sep 29] quite attractive filly: fairly
useful handicapper: should stay 1m: acts on any ground. *T. D. Easterby*

SAMAN   2 ch.c. (Apr 9) Samim (USA) 84 – Redspet (Tina's Pet 121) [2001 5g f6g f7g³   **54**
Oct 22] smallish colt: first foal: dam no form: modest maiden: third in seller at Southwell:
stays 7f: acts on fibresand: blinkered all starts. *S. R. Bowring*

SAMARA MIDDLE EAST (FR)   3 b.f. Marju (IRE) 127 – Modelliste (Machia-   **–**
vellian (USA) 123) [2001 87: 9.9m⁸ 8.1g Sep 2] smallish, good-topped filly: fairly useful
form at 2 yrs: well held in listed event at Salisbury (raced too freely) and handicap at
Sandown in 2001. *M. R. Channon*

SAMARARDO   4 b.g. Son Pardo 107 – Kinlet Vision (IRE) 56 (Vision (USA)) [2001   **50**
65: 14.1s 14.1v f16g⁵ 12.4m⁴ 12m 16.4m* 17.2m⁴ 15.4m 16s p13g f16.2g Nov 21] leggy
gelding: modest handicapper: won at Folkestone in July: stays 2m: acts on soft going,
good to firm and fibresand: tried visored: front runner. *N. P. Littmoden*

SAMARA SONG   8 ch.g. Savahra Sound 111 – Hosting (Thatching 131) [2001 66,   **54**
a43: 8.1m⁵ 7.5m 8m 8.5m 7.1m⁶ 8m Aug 25] lengthy gelding: modest handicapper: best   **a–**
at 7f/1m: acts on firm going, good to soft, fibresand and equitrack: tried blinkered/visored

early in career: has been slowly away: looked none too keen final start: best held up. *Ian Williams*

SAMBA BEAT   2 ch.f. (Feb 28) Efisio 120 – Special Beat 65 (Bustino 136) [2001 6m   **56** 7m 6s f6g⁵ f8g² Dec 10] first foal: dam, 17f winner (also fairly useful 2½m winner over hurdles), half-sister to useful 7f winner Cragganmore: modest maiden: second at Southwell: will be suited by at least 1¼m: acts on fibresand. *J. W. Hills*

SAMHARI (USA)   2 ch.c. (Apr 21) Indian Ridge 123 – Cambara 97 (Dancing Brave   **106** (USA) 140) [2001 8.2g³ 7d* 6m⁴ 6g 7v² Oct 26] strong, close-coupled colt: fifth foal: half-brother to UAE 6f winner Afreet (by Kris): dam, 1m winner, half-sister to smart middle-distance performers Pluralisme, Classic Tale and Singletta: useful performer: won maiden at Yarmouth in September: easily best effort when neck second to Rapscallion in Horris Hill Stakes at Newbury, staying on well having been outpaced: should stay at least 1m: acts on heavy going: bit slowly away last 2 starts: hung right penultimate one. *D. R. Loder*

SAMMAL (IRE)   5 b.g. Petardia 113 – Prime Site (IRE) (Burslem 123) [2001 51§,   **– §** a–§: 5m 6m 5g Aug 17] close-coupled gelding: temperamental handicapper: tried visored/blinkered/tongue tied. *D. Nicholls*

SAMMAX (IRE)   2 b. or br.g. (May 9) Mujadil (USA) 119 – Run Bonnie (Runnett   **59** 125) [2001 5.1f 5f 6d⁶ 6m⁵ 6m 5.1f 5d³ 5g Nov 7] IR 16,000Y: neat gelding: half-brother to several winners, including fairly useful 1m winner Tango Two Thousand (by Sri Pekan) and useful Irish 1994 2-y-o 5f winner Soreze (by Gallic League): dam Irish 6f winner: modest maiden: third at Catterick: effective at 5f/6f: acts on good to firm and good to soft ground: often tongue tied. *N. Tinkler*

SAMMY   4 ch.g. Most Welcome 131 – Miss Top Ville (FR) (Top Ville 129) [2001   **–** f9.4g⁶ Mar 24] 3,000Y: eighth foal: brother to 6f (at 2 yrs) to 8.5f winner Welville and 1m to 2m winner Wilcuma, both useful, and half-brother to a winner in Germany by Petong: dam French middle-distance winner: 9/2, tailed-off last in maiden at Wolverhampton (reportedly bled from nose). *M. A. Jarvis*

SAMMY'S SHUFFLE   6 b.g. Touch of Grey 90 – Cabinet Shuffle (Thatching 131)   **52** [2001 55, a65: 9.9d 9.7d 8.5g* p10g p10g² p10g³ Dec 28] modest handicapper: won at   **a64** Epsom in September: effective at testing 1m to easy 1½m: acts on equitrack, polytrack, firm and soft going: blinkered: all 7 wins on undulating tracks. *Jamie Poulton*

SAMSAAM (IRE)   4 b.g. Sadler's Wells (USA) 132 – Azyaa 101 (Kris 135) [2001   **114** 109: 14.1v 16g 13.9g² 15d² 13.4d 14v⁵ Sep 28] strong, well-made gelding: fluent mover: smart performer: good efforts when second to Marienbard (beaten a length) in Yorkshire Cup at York in May and to Generic (beaten short neck) in Prix Kergorlay at Deauville in August: well beaten last 2 starts: stays 2m well: acts on soft ground (well held on heavy), yet to race on firmer than good: usually races prominently: sold only 22,000 gns in December, joined M. Pipe and gelded. *J. L. Dunlop*

SAMSARA   3 ch.g. Pivotal 124 – Fire Lily (Unfuwain (USA) 131) [2001 f11g f8g⁵   **60** 7m³ 10.2f⁶ 8.5d 14.1s f8.5g Sep 8] 20,000Y: third foal: half-brother to useful 11f winner   **a48** who stays 1¾m Hidden Brave (by Bin Ajwaad) and fairly useful 7f (including at 2 yrs) winner Sari (by Faustus): dam no worthwhile form: modest maiden: well held in handicaps final 4 starts: stays 7f: acts on good to firm going: tried blinkered: slowly away/ hung left fourth outing. *P. F. I. Cole*

SAMUM (GER)   4 ch.c. Monsun (GER) 124 – Sacarina (Old Vic 136) [2001 126: 10s   **121** 11m² May 27] tall, good sort: high-class performer at 3 yrs, winning Deutsches Derby at Hamburg and Grosser Preis von Baden: only seventh of 9 in Prix Ganay at Longchamp (found to be running a temperature) in April then neck second to Bonvivant (who rec 7 lb) in Grosser Mercedes-Benz-Preis at Baden-Baden following month: reportedly had bronchial infection afterwards and missed remainder of season: stays 1½m well: has form on good to firm ground, very best effort on soft (also successful on heavy): tends to sweat: hung right for last 2 wins. *A. Schutz, Germany*

SAMWAR   9 b.g. Warning 136 – Samaza (USA) 90 (Arctic Tern (USA) 126) [2001   **–** –, a80d: f5g Oct 18] small, good-bodied gelding: unimpressive mover: one-time useful performer: has finished lame on last 2 starts: blinkered/visored. *Mrs N. Macauley*

SANADJA (IRE)   3 b.f. Slip Anchor 136 – Sanamia (Top Ville 129) [2001 10g³ 12m³   **78** 11.5m² 14g⁶ 11.8s Oct 15] tall, good-topped filly: fifth foal: half-sister to 3 winners, including useful Irish 13f winner Sanaka (by Kahyasi): dam fairly useful Irish 1½m winner: fair maiden: probably stays 1¾m: raced mainly on good/good to firm ground:

visored (well below form) last time: not an easy ride (has flashed tail/carried head awkwardly). *Sir Michael Stoute*

SANAPTA   3 b.f. Elmaamul (USA) 125 – La Domaine 89 (Dominion 123) [2001 –: 8m   –
f8g 8m 10m⁶ 12g Oct 4] little form. *W. R. Muir*

SANDALWOOD (IRE)   3 b.f. Charnwood Forest (IRE) 125 – Miss Java 78 (Persian   –
Bold 123) [2001 6d 7g 8.3d 8d Aug 8] 20,000F, 16,000Y: sixth foal: half-sister to 3
winners, including fairly useful 1m (including at 2 yrs)/1¼m winner Bold Oriental (by
Tirol) and 1994 2-y-o 5f winner Noosa (by Petorius): dam 1m winner who stayed 11.5f:
well beaten in maidens/handicap. *C. F. Wall*

SANDBAGGEDAGAIN   7 b.g. Prince Daniel (USA) – Paircullis (Tower Walk 130)   **66 §**
[2001 75§: 12.4d 16.1m 17.1m 15.9d⁶ 16.1f Sep 10] leggy, shallow-girthed gelding: fair
handicapper: pulled up lame final start: stays 2m: acts on good to firm and good to soft
ground: tried blinkered: often takes strong hold: finds little. *M. W. Easterby*

SANDERSTEAD   2 b.g. (Jan 27) So Factual (USA) 120 – Charnwood Queen 61   **60**
(Cadeaux Genereux 131) [2001 6g⁵ 6d⁶ 6d 6m 7.1s Sep 8] 26,000Y: close-coupled
gelding: has a short, round action: second foal: half-brother to 3-y-o Greenwood: dam, 6f
winner, half-sister to smart 7f/1m winner Sunstreak from family of smart sprinter Superpower: modest maiden: below form, including in nursery, after second start: may prove
best at 5f/6f: tried blinkered. *T. D. Easterby*

SAND HAWK   6 ch.g. Polar Falcon (USA) 126 – Ghassanah 73 (Pas de Seul 133)   –
[2001 65, a78: f7g f6g f7g f7g* f7g³ f7g f7g* f6g 7m f7g⁶ 6d f6g 7.1g f7g⁵ Nov 3]   **a71**
workmanlike gelding: fair performer: won handicap at Wolverhampton in February and
minor event at Southwell in March: probably best around 7f: acts on fibresand, heavy and
good to firm going: blinkered/visored: has been slowly away: usually patiently ridden:
has found little: has bled from nose. *D. Shaw*

SAN DIMAS (USA)   4 gr.g. Distant View (USA) 126 – Chrystophard (USA) (Lypheor   **44**
118) [2001 57: f8g f12g⁴ Sep 8] strong gelding: poor maiden handicapper: probably stays
1½m: acts on firm going and fibresand: tried blinkered. *Andrew Turnell*

SANDLES   3 b.g. Komaite (USA) – Miss Calculate 67 (Mummy's Game 120) [2001   **67**
69: 7d 8g 10m⁵ 8.1f⁴ 8.5f² 8m⁵ 9.9g² 9.9d³ 10.1g³ 10s⁵ f12g⁶ p12g* f9.4f* f12s⁴ Dec 15]
tall, useful-looking gelding: fair performer: won claimers at Lingfield (left S. Williams)
in November and Wolverhampton (edged right, left K. Burke) in December: effective at
1m to easy 1½m: acts on firm going, soft and fibresand/polytrack: bit reluctant leaving
stall tenth start: has worn crossed noseband/tongue strap. *Miss K. M. George*

SANDMASON   4 ch.c. Grand Lodge (USA) 125 – Sandy Island 110 (Mill Reef   **121**
(USA) 141) [2001 105p: 12g² 13.3v² 12f* 12g Jul 10]
Patience and diligence eventually paid dividends with Sandmason. Niggles
and setbacks restricted his appearances on the racecourse—he made only seven in
all spanning a period of almost twenty-two months—but he showed himself
capable of very smart form as a four-year-old, and vindicated the decision to keep
him in training by winning the Hardwicke Stakes at Royal Ascot. Successful in a
maiden at Sandown on his only start at two, Sandmason had been spoken of as a
possible Derby contender after finishing second in listed races at Newmarket and
York in the spring of his three-year-old campaign, but, in the event, he wasn't seen
out after May, his training held up firstly by a reported mucus problem and then
with a problematic hind joint.
Sandmason did not take long as a four-year-old to make his mark, finishing
a good second on his reappearance to St Leger winner Millenary in the Jockey Club
Stakes at Newmarket in May, staying on strongly from behind on his first outing at
a mile and a half and going down by two lengths. A further step up in trip on his
next start, in a listed contest at Newbury, should have suited Sandmason, but he was
again second, unsuited by the steady pace and unable to match the turn of foot
produced by the winner Water Jump, finishing three lengths in arrears this time.
Sandmason lacks a turn of foot and his running at both Newmarket and Newbury
suggested he would probably do better ridden more forcefully to make use of his
stamina. Front-running tactics were adopted in the seven-runner Hardwicke Stakes,
in which, in an average renewal, Sandmason lined up as his stable's longer-priced
runner behind the Coronation Cup runner-up Wellbeing, who started 2/1 favourite

Hardwicke Stakes, Royal Ascot—
Sandmason battles back resolutely to head Zindabad (rail); Mutafaweq is third

with the horse who beat him at Epsom Mutafaweq at 3/1. The smart Lucido, who had shown himself as good as ever when winning the John Porter Stakes at Newbury, came next at 9/2, followed by Adilabad at 8/1 and Zindabad, winner of a listed event at Leicester last time, at 9/1. Sandmason went off relatively unconsidered at 12/1, with only 40/1-shot Rada's Daughter at longer odds. As things turned out, the gallop wasn't strong and stamina played less of a part in Sandmason's victory than sheer guts and determination. Sandmason turned in a thoroughly admirable performance, recovering from a slow start to lead after a couple of furlongs and battling back very gamely, after being headed briefly before the turn and again over a furlong out, to snatch the race from Zindabad. The first two, who had run their best races, were separated by a head at the line with two and a half lengths back to Mutafaweq, conceding 5 lb to the first two; Wellbeing managed only fifth, with Adilabad a place in front of him. The Hardwicke turned out to be the highlight of Sandmason's career. He ran no sort of race next time in the Princess of Wales's Stakes at Newmarket, where he trailed in eighth of nine, dropping away tamely from three furlongs out. No obvious explanation for the performance came to light but Sandmason wasn't seen out again.

Sandmason—so named as he is by Grand Lodge out of Sandy Island—is the tenth and final foal produced by Sandy Island, who was also trained by Cecil and was a smart filly, winning the Pretty Polly Stakes at Newmarket and the Lancashire Oaks at Haydock from five outings as a three-year-old. Like Sandmason, Sandy Island gave the strong impression she would have been suited by further than a mile and a half, but she didn't run again after Haydock. Sandy Island's relatively light racing career is something that has been emulated by all her winning offspring. They have all been trained by Cecil and two of the others were smart performers. Sebastian (by Sadler's Wells) ran four times at a mile and a half in 1995, and, though evidently far from easy to train, progressed well, winning three times and finishing second on his other start, while Sardegna ran five times in the course of three seasons, winning at seven furlongs as a two-year-old in 1989 and at a mile and a quarter the following year. Sardegna is now the dam of the smart Samoa, and the useful Sardonic, both lightly-raced fillies who won at the latter distance for Cecil in 1999 and 1996 respectively. Sandy Island's other winners were both useful. They were Spry (by Suave Dancer), successful over a mile and a half in 1999, and Subterfuge (by Machiavellian), a winning two-year-old over seven furlongs in

Plantation Stud's "Sandmason"

Sandmason (ch.c. 1997)	Grand Lodge (USA) (ch 1991)	Chief's Crown (b 1982)	Danzig
			Six Crowns
		La Papagena (br 1983)	Habitat
			Magic Flute
	Sandy Island (b 1981)	Mill Reef (b 1968)	Never Bend
			Milan Mill
		Sayonara (b 1965)	Birkhahn
			Suleika

1995. Sandy Island herself is very well bred, being a close relation to Derby winner Slip Anchor from a very good German family that descends from Schwarzgold, the winner of the Deutsches Derby in 1940. Sandmason, a tall, close-coupled colt with a quick action, has run his last race in Britain. He was sent to Australia in the winter and, all being well, might continue his racing career there, prior to being retired to stud. Sandmason acted on any going and was a genuine type. *H. R. A. Cecil*

SANDORRA   3 b.f. Emperor Jones (USA) 119 – Oribi 59 (Top Ville 129) [2001 58: 8g **44** 8m 9.9f⁴ 9.9g Aug 15] big, leggy filly: poor maiden: barely stays 1¼m: acts on firm and soft going. *M. Brittain*

SANDOWN ARATINO   3 b.g. Aragon 118 – Cigartino (Cigar 68) [2001 10g f8.5g **–** Nov 17] first foal: dam unraced: no form in maidens (pulled up second start): dead. *J. G. Given*

SANDPOINT   5 b.m. Lugana Beach 116 – Instinction (Never So Bold 135) [2001 44: **52** f6g⁴ 6d² 5m 6m² 5.7g⁵ 5m² 5m f6g f6g Dec 10] modest maiden: left L. G. Cottrell after **a39**

896

sixth start: best at 5f/6f: acts on soft and firm ground: visored once at 4 yrs: usually tongue tied: very slowly away final start. *J. G. Given*

SANDROS BOY 4 b.g. Alhijaz 122 – Bearnaise (IRE) 64 (Cyrano de Bergerac 120) **39**
[2001 43: f9.4g⁶ f12g² f16g⁶ f16.2g⁴ f12g⁵ f14g Mar 13] poor maiden: stays 2m: acts on fibresand, probably on good to firm going: visored. *Mrs N. Macauley*

SANDY GROUND (FR) 6 b.m. Cricket Ball (USA) 124 – Song of Tonga (FR) **42**
(Dancer's Image (USA)) [2001 7s 10m 10d 8f 8m 9f 9.7m 8g 9.9m⁵ 7g⁴ 7.6g 8g Oct 1] half-sister to several winners, including French 1991 2-y-o 6f winner Living Colour (by Zino): dam French 6.5f and 7f winner: won claimer in France at 3 yrs: poor performer nowadays: left Julian Poulton after fifth start: probably stays 1¼m: acts on good to soft and good to firm going: tried blinkered. *J. E. Long*

SANDY LADY (IRE) 2 b.f. (May 5) Desert King (IRE) 129 – Mamma's Too 104 **86**
(Skyliner 117) [2001 5d⁵ 6g² 6d* 7g³ 7m⁴ 7.1s² 7d³ 8d Nov 3] IR 29,000F, IR 58,000Y: tall, close-coupled filly: fourth foal: half-sister to useful 6.5f/7f winner Macina and 7f/1m winner Macarena (both in Germany/by Platini): dam 5f/6f (including at 2 yrs) winner: fairly useful performer: won minor event at Haydock in July: in frame in nurseries/minor event after: should stay 1m: acts on soft and good to firm going: consistent. *R. Hannon*

SANGIOVESE 2 b.c. (Mar 11) Piccolo 121 – Kaprisky (IRE) (Red Sunset 120) [2001 **61**
6g 7m⁵ 7m⁶ 6m 7g Sep 11] 12,000Y: fourth foal: half-brother to 2 winners abroad, including a winner up to 7.5f in Italy by First Trump: dam, German 6f (at 2 yrs)/7f winner, from family of smart sprinter Governor General: modest maiden: tends to race freely, but stays 7f. *B. R. Millman*

SAN GLAMORE MELODY (FR) 7 b.g. Sanglamore (USA) 126 – Lypharitissima **–**
(FR) (Lightning (FR) 129) [2001 –, a54: f8.5g Mar 15] sturdy gelding: has a round action: lightly-raced maiden nowadays: tried visored. *Mrs P. Ford*

SAN MICHEL (IRE) 9 b.g. Scenic 128 – The Top Diesis (USA) (Diesis 133) [2001 **36**
52, a38: f7s³ f7g⁴ f6g f6g⁵ 7m⁶ f7g 6g³ 6m 8.2s Aug 6] sturdy gelding: poor nowadays: **a45**
effective at 6f/7f: acts on fibresand, equitrack, heavy and good to firm going: usually blinkered/visored: has had tongue tied: has been slowly away. *J. L. Eyre*

SANNAAN 3 b.c. Robellino (USA) 127 – Quest For The Best (Rainbow Quest (USA) **77**
134) [2001 54: 10g³ 10.5m⁵ a10f⁴ Nov 15] close-coupled colt: fair maiden: left M. Tregoning and off 5½ months before final outing: will stay 1½m. *D. J. Selvaratnam, UAE*

SAN SEBASTIAN 7 ch.g. Niniski (USA) 125 – Top of The League 85 (High Top **120**
131) [2001 120: 16g² 20f⁴ 16g⁵ 15.9g⁴ 18d 20v³ 16d⁴ 15.5v Oct 28] sturdy gelding: very smart performer: good efforts when in frame in Sagaro Stakes at Newmarket (beaten 1¾ lengths by Solo Mio), Lonsdale Stakes at York (beaten 4 lengths by Persian Punch) and Jockey Club Cup at Newmarket (beaten 2 lengths by Capal Garmon) on first, fourth and seventh appearances: also in frame again, though bit below best, in Gold Cup at Royal Ascot (favourite) and Prix du Cadran at Longchamp second/sixth outings: well beaten in Prix Royal-Oak at Longchamp final start: best at 2m+: acts on any going: usually blinkered/visored but is effective when not: tends to wander. *J. L. Dunlop*

SANTA CATALINA (IRE) 2 br.f. (Mar 7) Tagula (IRE) 116 – Bui-Doi (IRE) 58 **60**
(Dance of Life (USA)) [2001 7m 5g 5.1m Sep 10] IR 5,400Y: third foal: half-sister to 3-y-o Just Murphy: dam, Irish maiden, out of half-sister to US Grade 1 1½m winner Anka Germania: modest maiden: may prove best at 7f/1m: sold 4,000 gns. *I. A. Balding*

SANTA ISOBEL 3 ch.f. Nashwan (USA) 135 – Atlantic Record (Slip Anchor 136) **94 ?**
[2001 70p: 8.1g² 10v* 12m 10.1f⁵ 10.1m Aug 27] lengthy, quite good-topped filly: has a long stride: fairly useful performer: very enterprisingly ridden when winning 5-runner listed event at Newbury in May by head from Nafisah (pair clear): well held after (led until straight and eased once beaten 1½ lengths in Epsom Oaks next time), tailed off long way out final outing: stays 1¼m: acts on heavy going: usually leads. *I. A. Balding*

SANTA LUCIA 5 b.m. Namaqualand (USA) – Villasanta (Corvaro (USA) 124) [2001 **50**
50: 11s⁵ 12.4m³ 10m 12m² 11.9m⁴ Jul 6] tall, workmanlike mare: modest performer: stays 1½m, not 17f: acts on firm and good to soft going, well beaten on fibresand: often forces pace. *M. Dods*

SANTANA (IRE) 3 b.g. Inzar 60 – Annella (IRE) 73 (Glenstal (USA) 118) [2001 67: **–**
f9.4g f6g e8g Feb 24] first foal: dam second at 7f/8.5f and over hurdles: maiden: trained

by J. Burns in Ireland at 2 yrs, fair form only on second of 2 outings: well held in 2001. *M. Wigham*

SANTANDRE 5 ch.g. Democratic (USA) 101 – Smartie Lee 66 (Dominion 123) [2001 54, a76: f8g* f8.5s* f8g² f9.4g⁵ f8.5g² 8.1g 7.5m 7m 8m⁴ 8f³ 8m 8.1g 8s⁵ 7d⁶ f7g⁵ Nov 21] leggy gelding: fair on all-weather, modest on turf: won sellers at Southwell and Wolverhampton in January: barely stays 8.5f: acts on fibresand, soft and firm going: has reportedly broken blood vessel: usually claimer ridden. *R. Hollinshead* **51 a78**

SANTANDRIA 3 b.f. Desert Splendour 97 – California Dreamin (Slip Anchor 136) [2001 –: 6.1v 7s 5.1m Jun 1] seems of little account. *B. N. Doran* **–**

SANTA VIDA (USA) 3 b.f. St Jovite (USA) 135 – Castellina (USA) (Danzig Connection (USA)) [2001 8d 8m³ 10.2m 10m 12.1m⁶ 11.7g³ 12m⁴ 16.2g⁶ Aug 27] first foal: dam, 8.5f winner in USA, half-sister to smart US Grade 1 1¼m winner Chelsey Flower: modest maiden handicapper: may prove best up to 1¾m: acts on good to firm going: raced freely sixth start. *B. W. Hills* **64**

SANTIBURI GIRL 4 b.f. Casteddu 111 – Lake Mistassiu 86 (Tina's Pet 121) [2001 77: e12g 10m 11.6g³ 12m 16.2f 12m 10d⁶ Jul 18] small filly: unimpressive mover: fair performer: ran creditably only on third outing in 2001: stays 1¾m: has won on good to soft going, best form on good or firmer: edgy sort. *J. R. Best* **73**

SANTIBURI LAD (IRE) 4 b.g. Namaqualand (USA) – Suggia (Alzao (USA) 117) [2001 71: 8m⁶ 7m 8m* 12.3m 8m² 8f³ 8.3d* 8m* 9.2s⁴ 7.1m⁶ 7.1f³ f7g f8g⁴ Oct 18] leggy gelding: fair performer: won seller at Ripon and minor events at Hamilton and Redcar in summer: effective at 7f to 9f: acts on fibresand, probably on any turf going: game. *A. Berry* **76**

SANTISIMA TRINIDAD (IRE) 3 b.f. Definite Article 121 – Brazilia 63 (Forzando 122) [2001 45: 8.2v 6m⁵ 7.5m* 7.1m* 7f² 7d³ 7.5m* 7.1d* 8m² 7g⁶ 8d⁵ 7d 7d⁵ Oct 30] lengthy, useful-looking filly: fair performer: won maiden at Beverley and handicaps at Musselburgh, Beverley and Haydock in the summer: effective at 7f/1m: acts on firm and good to soft going: consistent. *T. D. Easterby* **77**

SANTOLINA (USA) 3 b.f. Boundary (USA) 117 – Alamosa (Alydar (USA)) [2001 101: 8g 8.5s⁶ Sep 26] attractive, well-made filly: has a fluent, round action: useful form: won listed race at Kempton at 2 yrs: 8 lengths eighth of 15 to Ameerat in 1000 Guineas at Newmarket (dropped out, hampered then not clear run) in May, final start for J. Gosden: sixth in allowance race at Belmont 4½ months later: should stay 1m: acts on firm and good to soft going: lost action and hung left closing stages third 2-y-o start: best effort patiently ridden. *C. Clement, USA* **99**

SAONE ET LOIRE (FR) 4 b.f. Always Fair (USA) 121 – Saone (USA) (Bering 136) [2001 e8g Mar 19] close-coupled filly: third foal: half-sister to French 1m winner State (by Petit Loup) and French 9.5f winner Salers (by Lead On Time): dam once-raced sister to smart French/US middle-distance stayer Special Price: modest performer in France, second in claimer at Maisons-Laffitte final outing of 2000 (claimed from J. Piednoel 58,000 francs): tailed off in handicap at Lingfield (all-weather debut) only run in 2001: stays 10.5f: acts on soft and good to firm ground: has been blinkered. *M. C. Pipe* **–**

SAORSIE 3 b.g. Emperor Jones (USA) 119 – Exclusive Lottery (Presidium 124) [2001 59: 10g 10m 8.3g³ 7m 8d* 8m⁴ 8.1m 7.1d 9.9d⁵ 11.9s 10d Nov 2] tall, close-coupled gelding: modest handicapper: won apprentice race at Salisbury in June: probably best at 1m: acts on soft ground, probably not firmer than good: has pulled hard/found little: tends to wander: not one to trust. *J. C. Fox* **64 §**

SAPHIR INDIEN 2 b.c. (Feb 8) Bijou d'Inde 127 – Dark Kristal (IRE) 66 (Gorytus (USA) 132) [2001 5f⁶ 5m² 6d* 7g⁶ 6m 6d⁵ Oct 13] 26,000F: good-bodied colt: sixth foal: half-brother to ungenuine 1999 2-y-o 6f winner Risky Gem (by Risk Me): dam, 6f winner, half-sister to dam of Queen Mary winner Risky: fairly useful performer: made all in maiden at Ayr in August: ran in listed races after, creditable efforts at York next and final starts: stays 7f: acts on good to firm and good to soft ground: sold 39,000 gns. *M. Johnston* **89**

SARABANDE 2 ch.f. (Feb 16) Nashwan (USA) 135 – Western Reel (USA) 95 (Gone West (USA)) [2001 7v Oct 26] leggy filly: second living foal: dam, 1m winner, sister to 5f (Queen Mary) to 1m (US Grade 2 event) winner Dance Parade: 10/1 and backward, tenth of 12 to Proven in maiden at Doncaster: should do better. *B. W. Hills* **– p**

SARACEN (IRE)   2 br.c. (Apr 28) Desert King (IRE) 129 – Inanna 105 (Persian Bold   **74**
123) [2001 7d³ Aug 8] IR 200,000Y: closely related to useful 6f (at 2 yrs) to 1¾m (in
France) winner Leonine (by Danehill) and half-brother to several winners, including
useful 1999 2-y-o 5f winner Victory Day (by Fairy King): dam Irish 2-y-o 6f and 1m
winner: 9/4, close last of 3 to Lucayan Legacy in slowly-run minor event at Yarmouth,
seemingly showing fair form: sent to UAE. *Sir Michael Stoute*

SARANAC LAKE (USA)   2 b.f. (May 4) Smart Strike (CAN) 121 – Lake Champlain   **103 p**
108 (Kings Lake (USA) 133) [2001 6g² 7d* 7s* Aug 19] $52,000Y: closely related to
winners in Japan (by Gone West) and USA (by Gulch) and half-sister to 3 winners
abroad: dam, Irish 1m/1¼m performer who later won in USA, half-sister to dam of
Theatrical: useful form: won maiden at Galway in July and Irish National Stud Debutante
Stakes at the Curragh (by head from Quarter Moon, 2 lengths up 1f out) in August: stays
7f: should do better *D. K. Weld, Ireland*

SARANGANI   5 b.g. Polish Precedent (USA) 131 – Height of Folly 81 (Shirley   **97**
Heights 130) [2001 14.1v⁴ 16s 12g 12v 10.1m* 10.1m⁶ 10m³ 11.9m³ 10m* Jul 26] big,
good-topped gelding: reportedly had stifle problem in 2000: useful performer: won minor
event at Yarmouth in May and handicap at Sandown (by neck from Optimate) in July:
effective at 1¼m/1½m: acts on any going: tongue tied last 7 starts: found to be lame
behind fourth start: genuine: sold 9,500 gns. *I. A. Balding*

SARATOV   3 b.g. Rudimentary (USA) 118 – Sarabah (IRE) 83 (Ela-Mana-Mou 132)   **102**
[2001 92: 10.4m* 10m 10f⁶ 9.9g 10.4g 11.9m⁵ Sep 5] big, lengthy, good-topped gelding:
has a round action: useful performer: won valuable handicap at York (by length from
King's Welcome) in May: well held last 3 starts: stays 10.4f: acts on firm ground, looked
none too keen only outing on soft: blinkered (found nothing) final outing. *M. Johnston*

SARAVA (USA)   2 br.c. (Mar 2) Wild Again (USA) – Rhythm of Life (USA) (Deputy   **80**
Minister (CAN)) [2001 7.1s⁴ 7g⁴ 8m a8.5f* a8.5f² Dec 19] $190,000, $250,000 2-y-o:
second foal: brother to a 2000 2-y-o 5.5f winner in USA: dam unraced half-sister to US
Grade 1 9f winner Wilderness Song (by Wild Again): fair form when trained by
B. Meehan in Britain first 3 starts: improved in USA, winning maiden at Churchill Downs
in November and second in allowance race at Turfway Park (blinkered): stays 8.5f: acts
on dirt. *B. Kessinger, jnr, USA*

SARDIS (IRE)   2 b.c. (Apr 10) Priolo (USA) 127 – Punta Gorda (IRE) (Roi Danzig   **67 p**
(USA)) [2001 8d 8d⁵ Oct 25] 8,200F, IR 22,000Y, resold 24,000Y: good-topped colt: first
foal: dam, second at 11f in France, half-sister to useful 7f winner Reported: 33/1, better
effort in maidens (fair form) when fifth to Kaieteur at Bath, tiring and wandering late on:
should stay 1¼m: will probably improve. *Mrs A. J. Perrett*

SAREB (FR)   2 b.f. (Feb 27) Indian Ridge 123 – Prends Ca (IRE) 98 (Reprimand 122)   **–**
[2001 5.1m Aug 24] first foal: dam 6f (including at 2 yrs) to 7.5f winner: eighth of 9 in
maiden at Bath. *R. Hannon*

SARENA PRIDE (IRE)   4 b.f. Persian Bold 123 – Avidal Park 68 (Horage 124)   **74**
[2001 78: e12g⁶ e12g³ e12g⁴ e10g 8.3g* 10m 10g 9f⁶ 9m⁵ 8.3g³ 10m³ 8.3m³ p8g p12g²
Dec 19] leggy filly: fair handicapper: won at Windsor in May: effective at 1m to easy
1½m: acts on equitrack, polytrack, firm and soft going: blinkered: tends to be slowly
away/race freely. *R. J. O'Sullivan*

SARENA SPECIAL   4 b.c. Lucky Guest 109 – Lariston Gale 81 (Pas de Seul 133)   **–**
[2001 72: e7g f7g 6s 8f 8.1g 6m Jul 18] angular colt: one-time fair maiden: has become
disappointing: usually blinkered. *R. J. O'Sullivan*

SARIN   3 b.g. Deploy 131 – Secretilla (USA) 61 (Secreto (USA) 128) [2001 9m 10g⁶   **67**
10g 10d Jun 18] approx. 24,300Y in Italy: fourth foal: half-brother to 2 winners in Italy,
including 5f (at 2 yrs) to 7.5f winner Sarman (by Lion Cavern): dam, 7f winner, out of
smart French performer up to 12.5f Satilla: fair maiden: well held final start: gelded after:
stays 1¼m. *L. M. Cumani*

SARI (USA)   2 gr.f. (Mar 30) Cozzene (USA) – Yamuna (USA) 103 (Forty Niner   **– p**
(USA)) [2001 6g Sep 7] close-coupled filly: fluent mover: first foal: dam, 1m winner,
half-sister to very smart performer in Britain/USA up to 1½m Eltish from very good
family: 33/1, backward and green, hampered leaving stall and not unduly punished when
well held in maiden at Kempton: almost certainly capable of better. *Mrs A. J. Perrett*

SARN   2 b.g. (Apr 20) Atraf 116 – Covent Garden Girl 67 (Sizzling Melody 117) [2001   **70**
5.1f 5d² 5m 6m⁶ 5m 7.1f* 7d f7g 7g* 7.1m 8m 7d⁵ 7m⁶ 8m* 8m⁵ 8m⁵ 8v* 7s 7s f7g   **a–**
Nov 16] 12,000Y, resold 9,500Y, 21,000 2-y-o: smallish, lengthy gelding: third foal: half-

brother to a 5f winner in Belgium by Noble Patriarch: dam 5f winner: fair performer: won nursery at Musselburgh in July, sellers at Catterick in August and Ayr in September, and nursery at Ayr in October: gelded after final start: stays 1m: acts on any turf going, well beaten on fibresand. *A. Bailey*

SARREGO 2 b.g. (May 24) Makbul 104 – Simmie's Special 75 (Precocious 126) **85** [2001 5.1m* 5s³ Oct 20] 1,000F: close-coupled gelding: fourth foal: dam 5f/6f winner: fairly useful form when winning maiden at Nottingham in September: bit below that when third in minor event at Catterick: will prove best at 5f/6f. *R. Hollinshead*

SARTORIAL (IRE) 5 b.g. Elbio 125 – Madam Slaney 92 (Prince Tenderfoot (USA) **115** 126) [2001 107: 6g³ 6g* 6d* 6m² 6m 6d Oct 19] strong gelding: smart performer, lightly raced (has been difficult to train), but better than ever in 2001: won handicap at York (by length from Mister Mal) in June and Prix de Ris-Orangis at Deauville (by head from Danger Over, who gave 4 lb) in July: good efforts when head second to Vision of Night in Jacobs Goldene Peitsche at Baden Baden, and ninth of 17 to Danehurst in well-contested listed race at Newmarket final start: stays 6f: acts on fibresand, good to firm and good to soft going: has been bandaged in front: visored final 4-y-o start: free-going sort. *P. J. Makin*

SARWA 3 ch.f. Timeless Times (USA) 99 – Diebiedale 58 (Dominion 123) [2001 6m **–** Aug 22] first foal: dam, maiden who stayed 1m, half-sister to useful 5f/6f performer Welsh Mist: tailed off in Lingfield maiden, slowly away and soon off bridle. *C. F. Wall*

SASARAM (IRE) 2 ch.c. (Mar 18) Indian Ridge 123 – Flaming June (USA) 69 **73** (Storm Bird (CAN) 134) [2001 7.1s⁶ Jun 16] 24,000F, 190,000Y: second foal: dam, lightly-raced maiden, half-sister to useful performer up to 1¼m Majmu (dam of high-class miler Muhtathir): fair form when sixth of 10 to Imtiyaz in maiden at Sandown, fading after racing freely. *M. P. Tregoning*

SASHA 4 ch.g. Factual (USA) 108 – Twice In Bundoran (IRE) 70 (Bold Arrangement **46** 127) [2001 50: 6s 6d 7m³ 7.5m⁴ 7d⁴ 6f Sep 10] poor maiden: stays 7.5f: acts on soft going, good to firm and fibresand: tried blinkered: has been reluctant stalls. *A. B. Mulholland*

SASHA STAR (IRE) 3 b.g. Namaqualand (USA) – Trojan Relation (Trojan Fen 118) **–** [2001 –: f12g⁵ 14.1d May 11] 10,000 2-y-o: closely related to 11f/1½m winner Lysandros (by Lycius) and half-brother to 2 winners, including fairly useful 6f winner Darren Boy (by Ballad Rock): dam unraced: well held in maidens/handicap. *G. Brown*

SASHAY 3 b.f. Bishop of Cashel 122 – St James's Antigua (IRE) 79 (Law Society **50** (USA) 130) [2001 –: f7g³ f7g f7g 8m 11.5f⁶ 10m² 11.7g⁶ 9.9m⁶ f12g* p13g⁴ Nov 13] **a56** close-coupled filly: modest performer: won maiden handicap at Wolverhampton in August: seems best around 1½m: acts on fibresand/polytrack and good to firm ground. *C. G. Cox*

SASH (IRE) 4 b.f. Sabrehill (USA) 120 – Lady Nash 50 (Nashwan (USA) 135) [2001 **50 §** 58§: e10g e13g⁶ f11g³ f11g f12g⁶ May 19] modest maiden: left S. Dow after fourth start: probably stays 11f: acts on firm going, soft and equitrack (probably on fibresand): has started slowly/flashed tail/found little: usually held up: not to be trusted. *G. M. McCourt*

SASTRA (IRE) 2 ch.f. (Feb 6) Petardia 113 – Come Dancing 48 (Suave Dancer (USA) **42** 136) [2001 5m⁶ 5m 5d Oct 9] IR 14,000Y: smallish filly: first foal: dam, disappointing maiden who should have stayed at least 7f, out of sister to very smart sprinter Primo Dominie: poor maiden: best effort on debut. *J. A. Glover*

SATEEN 4 ch.f. Barathea (IRE) 127 – Souk (IRE) 98 (Ahonoora 122) [2001 56: 6s* **87** 9m² 10g 8g² 8.1g 7g 7d Nov 3] lengthy filly: fairly useful performer: won maiden at Pontefract in May: well held last 3 starts: should stay at least 1¼m: acts on good to firm going, has won on soft: sent to France. *L. M. Cumani*

SATIRE 4 br.f. Terimon 124 – Salchow 116 (Niniski (USA) 125) [2001 53, a–: 8d 13d **36 +** 8d⁵ 12.1d 10s⁴ 14.4d 10.1g 10s 10.1v Oct 24] leggy filly: poor maiden: stays 1¼m: acts on soft ground, well held on fibresand: tried blinkered. *T. J. Etherington*

SATTAM 2 b.c. (Mar 10) Danehill (USA) 126 – Mayaasa (USA) 70 (Lyphard (USA) **75 p** 132) [2001 7v Oct 26] smallish, stocky colt: fourth foal: half-brother to 3-y-o Fatwa, 6-y-o Zaha and useful 6f (at 2 yrs) and 1m winner Hirasah (by Lahib): dam, 1¼m winner, closely related to high-class miler Maroof and to dam of Desert King (by Danehill): 7/2, burly and green, seventh of 12 to Proven in maiden at Doncaster, unable to sustain run and not unduly knocked about: wore crossed noseband: sure to do better. *D. R. Loder*

SATU NUSA   2 b.c. (Feb 6) So Factual (USA) 120 – Tarry 65 (Salse (USA) 128) [2001   **78**
6m⁶ 7d⁴ 7.5g² 6d Oct 19] 6,000Y: neat colt: first foal: dam won at 7f (at 2 yrs) to 1¾m and
over hurdles: fair maiden: in frame at Yarmouth and Beverley (looked difficult ride):
stays 7.5f. *G. C. Bravery*

SATWA BOULEVARD   6 ch.m. Sabrehill (USA) 120 – Winnie Reckless (Local   **44**
Suitor (USA) 128) [2001 39, a46: e10g f7g f9.4g f6g⁵ f7g⁴ e8g⁵ 5.1v⁶ 6s Apr 23] lengthy   **a47**
mare: poor maiden: seems effective at 5f to 1m: acts on fibresand, equitrack and any turf
ground: has had tongue tied. *D. Burchell*

SATYR   3 b.g. Pursuit of Love 124 – Sardonic 105 (Kris 135) [2001 –: 8.3g⁶ 7g³ 8m⁴   **79**
7g² 8m 8.3m² 8m⁵ 8d⁴ Oct 8] quite good-topped gelding: fair maiden: effective at 7f/1m:
acts on good to firm ground: has awkward head carriage: sold 11,000 gns and gelded.
R. Hannon

SAUCE TARTAR   3 ch.f. Salse (USA) 128 – Filly Mignonne (IRE) (Nashwan (USA)   **90**
135) [2001 76: 8m 10m 8m³ 7g* 7g* 8m Jul 31] strong, close-coupled filly: fairly useful
handicapper: won at Newmarket and Leicester in July, making nearly all both times:
should stay 1m: acts on good to firm ground, possibly not on good to soft: blinkered last 3
starts. *N. A. Callaghan*

SAUDIA (USA)   3 b.f. Gone West (USA) – Bint Pasha (USA) 126 (Affirmed (USA))   **83**
[2001 84p: 7d 10.4m 7m Jun 8] tall, leggy, quite good-topped filly: fairly useful
performer, lightly raced: not discredited in Fred Darling Stakes at Newbury and Musidora
Stakes at York first 2 starts in 2001: may prove best around 1m: acts on good to firm and
good to soft going: blinkered (below form in handicap) final start: one to treat with some
caution: sent to USA. *P. F. I. Cole*

SAUTERNE   3 ch.f. Rainbow Quest (USA) 134 – Band (USA) (Northern Dancer)   **98**
[2001 8m⁴ 7.5m* 8m² 10.3m* 10.2m* 9.9m⁴ Aug 15] fourth foal: closely related to
useful 2-y-o winners Applaud (5f/6f in 1995, including Cherry Hinton) and Houston
Time (7f in 1998), both by Rahy, and half-sister to a winner in USA by Seeking The
Gold: dam, maiden, out of high-class sprinter who later won graded stakes up to 9f in
USA Swingtime: useful performer: won maiden at Beverley in June then handicap at
Doncaster and listed race at Chepstow (beat Stay Behind a head) in July: disappointing in
listed race at Salisbury final outing: stays 1¼m: raced only on good to firm ground: races
prominently: difficult at stalls third outing: joined C. Clement in USA. *H. R. A. Cecil*

SAVANNAH BAY   2 ch.c. (Apr 9) In The Wings 128 – High Savannah 77 (Rousillon   **105 p**
(USA) 133) [2001 7g⁶ 7.1m² 7f* 7g³ Oct 5] 45,000F, 92,000Y: good-topped colt: sixth
foal: closely related to smart 1¼m performer Lady In Waiting (by Kylian), 5f/6f winner
at 2 yrs, and half-brother to 2 winners, including 5-y-o Smart Savannah: dam, maiden
who stayed 1½m, half-sister to 2 useful 2-y-o sprinters: useful form: won maiden at
Newmarket in August: good staying-on 2 lengths third to Where Or When in Somerville
Tattersall Stakes at Newmarket: will stay 1¼m: raced on good going or firmer: very much
type to train on well. *B. J. Meehan*

SAVED BY THE BELLE   4 b.f. Emarati (USA) 74 – Belle Danseuse (Bellypha 130)   **–**
[2001 –: 8f 7d 6f 7g 6m Aug 13] no form. *L. A. Dace*

SAVE THE PLANET   4 b.f. Environment Friend 128 – Geoffreys Bird (Master Willie   **39**
129) [2001 53: 8.3m 13d 13g 16f⁴ 13d Aug 15] big, strong, lengthy filly: poor maiden:
stays 2m: acts on firm ground: tried blinkered/visored. *P. Monteith*

SAVE THE POUND (USA)   3 br.g. Northern Flagship (USA) 96 – Key Bid (USA)   **–**
(Key To The Mint (USA)) [2001 –: 12.3v⁶ 8m 6m May 29] little form: tried blinkered.
T. D. Easterby

SAVING LIVES ATSEA (IRE)   3 ch.g. Dolphin Street (FR) 125 – Advantageous   **–**
(Top Ville 129) [2001 49: f9.4s Jan 23] small, sturdy gelding: lightly-raced maiden.
M. H. Tompkins

SAVOIRE VIVRE   4 b.c. Sadler's Wells (USA) 132 – Oh So Sharp 131 (Kris 135)   **–**
[2001 115p: 20v Oct 7] big, strong, deep-bodied colt: smart performer, very lightly raced:
second in Geoffrey Freer Stakes at Newbury at 3 yrs: had further setbacks in 2001, including ligament injury early in year: favourite, pulled up in Prix du Cadran at Longchamp
only start: should stay at least 1¾m: carried head awkwardly/swerved left in front on
debut, raced freely/drifted right at Newbury: clearly difficult to train: has left Godolphin.
Saeed bin Suroor

SAYEDAH (IRE)   3 b.f. Darshaan 133 – Balaabel (USA) 83 (Sadler's Wells (USA)   **105**
132) [2001 105: 8g 12m⁴ 8.1g² 10s³ Oct 6] rather leggy, close-coupled filly: useful
performer: won Rockfel Stakes at Newmarket at 2 yrs: down the field in 1000 Guineas
there on reappearance, subsequently off 3 months: good efforts in listed events last 3
starts, first past post at Longchamp final one (made all, beat Chesnut Bird ¾ length) but
demoted to third after edging left and causing interference: stayed 1½m: acted on soft and
good to firm going: had flashed tail/raced freely: visits Quiet American. *M. P. Tregoning*

SAYEH (IRE)   9 b.g. Fools Holme (USA) – Piffle 87 (Shirley Heights 130) [2001 12g⁶   **71**
12v⁶ May 19] deep-girthed gelding: has a round action: only fair and very lightly raced
on Flat nowadays: unlikely to stay beyond 1½m: yet to race on firm going, acts on any
other turf and dirt: pulls hard, and has worn special bridle: fairly useful hurdler. *P. Bowen*

SAYIT   2 b.c. (Mar 6) Sayaarr (USA) – Wigit (Safawan 118) [2001 7m p8g f8g Nov 30]   **50**
second foal: dam unraced: best effort in maidens (modest form) when eighth at Lingfield
second start. *M. D. I. Usher*

SAYSO   5 b.m. Anshan 119 – Total Sa (IRE) (Gallic League 119) [2001 f8.5g Feb 1]   **–**
well held in maiden/minor event (tongue tied) nearly 2 years apart. *Miss A. Stokell*

SAYYIDNA   2 b.g. (Mar 29) Desert Style (IRE) 121 – Anita's Love (IRE) 53 (Anita's   **–**
Prince 126) [2001 5f 6g Jul 28] IR 16,000Y: rather dipped-backed gelding: fourth foal:
half-brother to 5-y-o Thornaby Girl: dam sprint maiden: well held in maiden/claimer.
R. F. Fisher

SCAFELL   4 b.g. Puissance 110 – One Half Silver (CAN) (Plugged Nickle (USA))   **–**
[2001 62: 6m 5m 7m 7g 12m 8.9m Sep 2] workmanlike gelding: modest performer at 3
yrs: well held in 2001: tried visored/blinkered/tongue tied. *C. Smith*

SCALADO (USA)   2 ch.c. (Jan 31) Mister Baileys 123 – Lady di Pomadora (USA)   **73**
(Danzig Connection (USA)) [2001 6g³ f6g⁵ p8g⁴ Nov 28] \$5,000Y resold 46,000Y:
fourth foal: half-brother to useful 7f (at 2 yrs)/1m winner Trident (by Red Ransom) and a
winner around 11f in France by Exbourne: dam, won up to 9f in USA, from family of
Dancing Brave: fair maiden: in frame twice at Lingfield: will stay 1¼m. *R. Charlton*

SCARLET RIBBONS   2 b.f. (Jan 12) Anabaa (USA) 130 – Scarlet Plume 103   **95**
(Warning 136) [2001 6g* 6d⁵ Nov 2] leggy, workmanlike filly: second foal: dam, 2-y-o
1m (including Italian Group 3) winner, out of Oaks winner Circus Plume: 10/1, won
16-runner maiden at Newmarket in October (when known as Scarlet Ribbon) by 2½
lengths from Pretty Clear: only fifth to Red Liason when favourite for minor event there
4 weeks later: will stay at least 7f. *J. L. Dunlop*

SCARLETT RIBBON   4 b.f. Most Welcome 131 – Scarlett Holly 81 (Red Sunset   **95**
120) [2001 95+: 6g 6g 7.1s³ 7d f7g* Nov 16] quite good-topped filly: useful handicapper: **a104**
best effort when winning at Southwell in November by 3½ lengths from Sharpinch: stays
7f: acts on fibresand, and best turf efforts on soft/good to soft going: free-going sort.
P. J. Makin

SCARPE ROSSE (IRE)   3 b.f. Sadler's Wells (USA) 132 – Red Comes Up (USA)   **88**
(Blushing Groom (FR) 131) [2001 73p: 10.2d* 11.4f 12v Oct 28] lightly-made filly:
fairly useful performer, lightly raced: won maiden at Bath in May: well held after in listed
race at Chester (final start for J. Dunlop) and (after 5-month break) handicap at Galway:
should stay 1½m: acts on good to firm and good to soft going. *C. Collins, Ireland*

SCARROTTOO   3 ch.g. Zilzal (USA) 137 – Bold And Beautiful 105 (Bold Lad (IRE)   **70**
133) [2001 –p: 8.2v 6m⁴ 6f² 6m³ f6g* 7g⁶ 7.1m 6m* 7m* 6.1f² Sep 18] fair performer:
won handicaps at Wolverhampton and Folkestone and minor event at Brighton in July/
August: also looked certain winner when saddle slipped and unseated rider at Musselburgh seventh start: stays 7f: acts on firm ground and fibresand: has won with tongue tied:
reliable. *S. C. Williams*

SCARTEEN SISTER (IRE)   3 ch.f. Eagle Eyed (USA) 111 – Best Swinger (IRE)   **54**
(Ela-Mana-Mou 132) [2001 56: 6.9v 8m f8.5g³ f8.5g⁴ f9.4g⁴ f8.5f³ f11s Dec 21] modest
maiden: stays 9.4f: acts on firm ground and fibresand: visored last 2 starts (wandered first
occasion). *R. M. Beckett*

SCENE (IRE)   6 b.m. Scenic 128 – Avebury Ring (Auction Ring (USA) 123) [2001   **72**
87: f9.4g 8v 8d 10.3m 10v 8.1m 10v4 10d3 10s 12d⁵ 10s⁴ 16.5s⁵ f16g p16g⁶ f16.2g Dec 8]   **a62**
strong mare: fair handicapper: left N. Littmoden after sixth start: seems to stay 2m: acts
on fibresand and probably any turf going: tried visored/blinkered: none too consistent.
J. A. Osborne

SCENIC LADY (IRE)   5 b.m. Scenic 128 – Tu Tu Maori (IRE) (Kings Lake (USA)   **61**
133) [2001 31: 10f² 10g⁵ 11.6g² 14.1m 11.9g* 10m* 12g² 9.9s⁵ 10s³ 11.9s Oct 25]
modest handicapper: won at Brighton (seller) and Lingfield in August: effective at 1¼m
to 1¾m: acts on firm and soft going: blinkered twice as 4-y-o: sometimes slowly away:
often leads. *L. A. Dace*

SCENT AHEAD (USA)   2 b.g. (Apr 12) Foxhound (USA) 103 – Sonseri 95 (Prince   **60**
Tenderfoot (USA) 126) [2001 f5g⁵ f5g⁵ 5.7f⁶ 6m 6.1d f5g Oct 6] 10,000Y: half-brother to
several winners, including 4-y-o Glory Quest and 7f winner Star Goddess (by Northern
Jove), both fairly useful: dam 5f (at 2 yrs)/6f winner who stayed 1m: modest maiden:
below form last 3 starts, blinkered in seller on final one: should stay 6f: acts on fibresand
and firm ground: has worn tongue strap. *Mrs A. J. Bowlby*

SCENTED AIR   4 b.f. Lion Cavern (USA) 117 – Jungle Rose 90 (Shirley Heights   **52**
130) [2001 50?: 7m 8m³ 8g² 8m³ 10g 8f⁴ 8.2s⁴ 8g⁵ 8.3m² 8v f8.5f² f9.4g⁵ f8g⁵ f8.5s⁵
Dec 26] leggy, plain filly: modest maiden handicapper: left Mrs J. Ramsden 1,000 gns
after tenth start: effective at 1m/easy 1¼m: acts on fibresand, firm and soft going: visored
once: looks difficult ride. *P. W. Hiatt*

SCHATZ   3 b.c. General Monash (USA) 107 – Mandalika (USA) (Arctic Tern (USA)   **?**
126) [2001 78p: 5.1s⁴ 6.1v 5m 6.8m⁶ a7g³ a8g* a7g⁴ a7g⁵ Nov 13] quite good-topped
colt: fair form only 2-y-o start: failed to repeat that in maidens for L. Cumani first 2 starts
in 2001: won handicap at Rome in October: stays 1m: acts on sand. *E. Russo, Italy*

SCHEDULE B   3 ch.g. Dancing Spree (USA) – Jolizal 52 (Good Times (ITY)) [2001   **52 d**
53: f7s⁴ 5g f9.4g⁶ 10m 10m Sep 11] close-coupled gelding: modest form: off 6 months
and gelded, below form after reappearance: stays 7f: sold 1,200 gns. *R. Hollinshead*

SCHEHERAZADE   3 b.f. Sadler's Wells (USA) 132 – Impatiente (USA) (Vaguely   **73**
Noble 140) [2001 51p: 8d 10s⁵ 10g 14.1g⁴ 11.9m* Jul 23] strong, well-made filly: fair
handicapper: won at Brighton in July, despite hanging left: stays 1¾m: raced mainly on
good ground or softer: sold 48,000 gns in December. *L. M. Cumani*

SCHEMING   4 br.g. Machiavellian (USA) 123 – Alusha 88 (Soviet Star (USA) 128)   **101**
[2001 79: 10s 12s 10m³ 10.5g⁶ 11.9d⁴ 10f* 10.3f³ 10.5d* 10m² 10g* 10m* Aug 25]
smallish, useful-looking gelding: much improved, and made into a useful handicapper in
2001, winning at Nottingham, Haydock, Ascot and Newmarket in summer: beat Thesis
¾ length on last-named course despite idling in front: better form at 1¼m than 1½m: acts
on firm and good to soft going: waited with: genuine. *W. M. Brisbourne*

SCHOLAR LEO   3 b.g. Greensmith 121 – Clary Sage (Sayf El Arab (USA) 127)   **51**
[2001 f9.4g f8.5g 8v f6g⁴ 6m 5m⁴ 5m f6g⁶ Jun 15] rather leggy, quite good-topped   **a42**
gelding: first foal: dam ran once: modest maiden: stays 6f: blinkered penultimate start:
inconsistent. *C. W. Fairhurst*

SCHOOL DAYS   2 b.f. (Apr 27) Slip Anchor 136 – Cradle of Love (USA) 87   **77**
(Roberto (USA) 131) [2001 8m³ 7.9d Oct 12] angular filly: sister to 6-y-o Captain's Log
and half-sister to 2 winners, including 7-y-o Ivory Dawn: dam, 9f winner, sister to smart
performer up to 1½m Mamaluna: 50/1, shaped well (fair form) when staying-on third to
Revealing in maiden at Newmarket: ninth of 26 in similar event at York: will be well
suited by 1¼m+. *M. L. W. Bell*

SCHUSCHEMIGA   2 ch.f. (Feb 8) Rock City 120 – Bahrain Queen (IRE) (Caerleon   **44**
(USA) 132) [2001 f5g⁴ 5m⁶ 6f f7g Jun 29] 800 2-y-o: sparely-made filly: second foal:
dam, no form on Flat, modest winning hurdler: poor form in sellers. *J. G. Given*

SCIPPIT   2 ch.g. (Jan 31) Unfuwain (USA) 131 – Scierpan (USA) 86 (Sharpen Up 127)   **63 ?**
[2001 7g 6m 5m⁵ Aug 23] 21,000F, 32,000Y: close-coupled gelding: half-brother
to several winners, including French 1m winner Pan Galactic (by Lear Fan) and 6f
(including at 2 yrs) winner Specified (by Known Fact), both useful: dam placed at 5f/6f
at 2 yrs: modest maiden: well held in seller final start: should stay 1m: sold 800 gns.
M. R. Channon

SCISSOR RIDGE   9 ch.g. Indian Ridge 123 – Golden Scissors 76 (Kalaglow 132)   **44**
[2001 58, a65: e7g* e8g⁴ e7g e8g e7g⁶ 7m⁴ 6m 7.6m⁵ 7m 10g 7g 7s 7.1f p7g p7g⁴ Dec 12]   **a62**
sparely-made gelding: modest handicapper on all-weather, poor on turf: won well-
contested event at Lingfield in January: races mainly at 7f/1m nowadays: acts on firm
ground, soft and all-weather: tried blinkered (not since 1996): soon off bridle.
J. J. Bridger

SCONCED (USA) 6 ch.g. Affirmed (USA) – Quaff (USA) 115 (Raise A Cup (USA)) **57 §**
[2001 –: f16.2s f16g⁶ f12s⁶ f16g² f12g* f16g⁵ 16v² 14.1s³ 14.1v³ 12.4d 16.2m 12m²
14m* 16.2f⁴ 12.1m 14.1m 15.8m f12g⁴ f14g 16s f16g f14.8g⁵ f14g⁶ f14g² Dec 17] leggy
gelding: modest handicapper: won at Southwell (apprentices) in March and Musselburgh
in June: effective at 1½m to 2m: acts on fibresand and any turf going: sometimes visored:
tends to run in snatches: unreliable. *M. J. Polglase*

SCORNED (GER) 6 b.g. Selkirk (USA) 129 – Spurned (USA) 91 (Robellino (USA) **103**
127) [2001 14.1m⁶ 12g 13.1m² 12d² 12v* 12s Nov 10] tall, good-looking gelding: smart
performer in 1998, useful form on return in 2001: won handicap at Doncaster in October
by ¾ length from Mana d'Argent: stays 1½m: acts on heavy and good to firm going:
free-going sort, and has worn crossed noseband. *I. A. Balding*

SCOTISH LAW (IRE) 3 ch.g. Case Law 113 – Scotia Rose (Tap On Wood 130) **70**
[2001 70: 8.3s 7.1m³ 9m 8.1g 8m⁴ 10m³ 8.1g³ 7.1g 10.2f Sep 18] close-coupled gelding:
fair handicapper: effective at 1m/1¼m: acts on good to firm going, possibly not on soft:
drifted right penultimate start. *P. R. Chamings*

SCOTMAIL PARK 2 b.g. (May 22) Presidium 124 – Miss Tri Colour 37 (Shavian **54**
125) [2001 6d⁶ 6d³ 6d f6g 8.1s Sep 8] 2,000Y, 6,000 2-y-o: close-coupled gelding: second
foal: dam maiden half-sister to useful performer up to 7f Wantage Park: modest maiden:
third at Haydock: may prove best at 6f/7f: well beaten on fibresand: often slowly away:
gelded after final start. *G. M. Moore*

SCOTTISH KNIGHT 3 b.c. Marju (IRE) 127 – Scottish Eyes (USA) (Green Dancer **61**
(USA) 132) [2001 8m 7f⁶ 8m⁵ 10.1g⁵ 9.9d f9.4g 10s Oct 30] third foal: half-brother to
Irish 1m/9f winner Sunny Slope (by Mujtahid): dam unraced daughter of Coronation
Stakes winner Kesar Queen: modest maiden: left K. Prendergast in Ireland after second
start: unlikely to stay beyond 1¼m: acts on good to soft going, poor effort on fibresand:
slowly away fourth start. *M. R. Bosley*

SCOTTISH RIVER (USA) 2 b.g. (Mar 30) Thunder Gulch (USA) 129 – Overbrook **107**
95 (Storm Cat (USA)) [2001 6d³ 6m⁶ 6g² 7m⁴ 6g 7g Oct 5] $42,000Y: strong gelding:
third foal: closely related to a 2-y-o sprint winner in USA by Gulch: dam, 6f (including at
2 yrs) winner, half-sister to smart performers Hidden Meadow (up to 8.5f) and 6-y-o
Scorned: useful performer: won maiden at Thirsk in June: very good second of 5, beaten
1¼ lengths by Meshaheer, in July Stakes at Newmarket: ran poorly last 2 starts, gelded
after final one: should stay 7f: unraced on extremes of going: often races up with pace.
M. Johnston

SCOTTISH SPICE 4 b.f. Selkirk (USA) 129 – Dilwara (IRE) (Lashkari 128) [2001 **92**
92: 8s 8.3g⁶ 8.3g² 8.3m³ 9m⁶ 9m 8.1s* 8s 7g Oct 6] tall, leggy filly: fairly useful
handicapper: won at Sandown in August: effective at 1m, barely at 1¼m: has form on
good to firm going, possibly best on good or softer: blinkered last 3 starts. *I. A. Balding*

SCOTT'S VIEW 2 b.g. (Feb 5) Selkirk (USA) 129 – Milly of The Vally 93 (Caerleon **71**
(USA) 132) [2001 6g⁵ 7g⁶ 8m² 8v⁶ Oct 16] 21,000Y: first foal: dam, 1½m winner,
half-sister to 3-y-o Bosham Mill out of smart 1½m performer Mill On The Floss: fair
maiden: best effort when second at Thirsk: should be suited by 1¼m/1½m: acts on good
to firm going, well below form on heavy. *M. Johnston*

SCOTTY'S FUTURE (IRE) 3 b.c. Namaqualand (USA) – Persian Empress (IRE) **94 p**
51 (Persian Bold 123) [2001 63p: 8.1g² 8m² 10g² 10m* 10.3m* 10m³ 10f⁴ Sep 22] close-
coupled, quite good-topped colt: fairly useful handicapper: progressed well in 2001,
winning at Ripon in July and Doncaster in August: good efforts after, keeping on well
from poor position when fourth to Albuhera in Courage Best Stakes at Newbury final
one: will prove best at 1m/1¼m: acts on firm ground, shaped quite well on soft/heavy at 2
yrs: held up: sold 65,000 gns in October, joined D. Nicholls: should remain on the
upgrade. *A. C. Stewart*

SCRAMBLE (USA) 3 ch.c. Gulch (USA) – Syzygy (ARG) (Big Play (USA)) [2001 **66**
66p: 8m 8m⁶ 8.2v⁴ f8g f9.4s⁵ Dec 18] long-backed colt: fair maiden on turf, modest **a56**
on all-weather: left J. Gosden 8,000 gns after third start: stays 1m: acts on good to firm
going, probably on heavy: wears tongue strap. *B. Ellison*

SCRAVELS 2 ch.g. (Jan 29) Elmaamul (USA) 125 – Defined Feature (IRE) 91 **63 d**
(Nabeel Dancer (USA) 120) [2001 6.9m 6.9m 8g f8g 7d 8.3v Nov 8] small, workmanlike
gelding: first foal: dam, 2-y-o 5f/6f winner, should have stayed 1m: modest maiden:
showed little, including when blinkered in seller, after third start. *Dr J. D. Scargill*

SCREAMING EAGLE (IRE)   2 b.f. (Mar 8) Sadler's Wells (USA) 132 – Ducking **65 p**
71 (Reprimand 122) [2001 7g 8m 8.3v⁴ Oct 29] 290,000Y: third foal: sister to 3-y-o Silly
Goose and half-sister to useful Irish 1999 2-y-o 7f winner Dance of Love (by Pursuit of
Love): dam, maiden who stayed 1¼m, from good family: fair form in maidens: not given
hard time when fourth at Windsor: will be suited by 1¼m/1½m: should make a better
3-y-o. *J. L. Dunlop*

SCREAMIN' GEORGINA   3 b.f. Muhtarram (USA) 125 – Carrie Kool 69 (Prince **57**
Sabo 123) [2001 64: 6.1d 5m 5m² 5f 5m⁵ 5f⁴ 6g Sep 5] modest performer: best at 5f: acts
on firm going: usually tongue tied: has been reluctant at stalls. *S. C. Williams*

SCURRA   2 b.c. (Mar 24) Spectrum (IRE) 126 – Tamnia 106 (Green Desert (USA) 127) **77**
[2001 6.1m 7.1v³ 7d² Nov 6] second foal: dam, 2-y-o 6f/7f winner, half-sister to smart
middle-distance stayers Azzilfi and Khamaseen: fair maiden: trained by M. Polglase on
debut: placed at Haydock and Catterick: will stay at least 1m. *R. Hollinshead*

SEABORNE   2 b.f. (Apr 14) Slip Anchor 136 – Jezebel Monroe (USA) 98 (Lyphard **62 p**
(USA) 132) [2001 7d Nov 3] leggy, rather unfurnished filly: sixth foal: closely related
to 3-y-o Bel and half-sister to useful French 10.5f to 11.5f winner Leros (by Exit To
Nowhere): dam, 1¼m winner, closely related to 1999 Royal Lodge winner Royal Kingdom and half-sister to dam of 4-y-o Agnes Digital: 20/1, thirteenth of 21 to Maid To
Perfection in maiden at Newmarket, bit slowly away and not knocked about: likely to be
suited by 1½m+: should do better. *R. Charlton*

SEA BUZZARD (IRE)   3 b.g. Bluebird (USA) 125 – Paloma Bay (IRE) 92 (Alzao **–**
(USA) 117) [2001 6.9v 7g 10.2f 7m Jun 7] 35,000Y: first foal: dam, 2-y-o 6f winner
who stayed 1m, out of sister to smart Irish sprinter Rustic Amber: well held in maidens/
handicap. *M. Blanshard*

SEA DANZIG   8 ch.g. Roi Danzig (USA) – Tosara 84 (Main Reef 126) [2001 57§, **49 §**
a80d: e16g⁵ 12g⁴ Aug 17] big, plain gelding: modest handicapper on all-weather, poor on **a62 §**
turf nowadays: stays 1¾m: possibly unsuited by heavy going, acts on any other turf and
fibresand/equitrack: effective blinkered or not: unreliable: sold 450 gns. *J. J. Bridger*

SEA-DEER   12 ch.g. Hadeer 118 – Hi-Tech Girl 98 (Homeboy 114) [2001 73: 6m 7m Jul **–**
24] strong, deep-girthed gelding: formerly fairly useful: well held in 2001. *C. A. Dwyer*

SEA FLEUR   2 b.f. (Apr 11) Botanic (USA) – Sea Fairy 64 (Wollow 132) [2001 5m **55**
5.1s⁶ 5.1d 5.1m Sep 10] 6,000Y: half-sister to several winners, including 5-y-o Ones
Enough and 7f/1m winner Leviathan Mystery (by Elegant Air): dam, 2-y-o 6f winner,
later successful in Spain: easily best effort in maidens (modest form) at Bath on third
start: should stay 6f. *R. Guest*

SEA FLY   3 ch.f. Presidium 124 – Steelock 68 (Lochnager 132) [2001 7s Jul 24] 500Y: **–**
ninth foal: sister to 6-y-o Vice Presidential: dam sprint maiden at 2 yrs: tongue tied, very
slowly away when tailed off in seller at Ayr. *M. A. Barnes*

SEAGULL (IRE)   3 ch.g. Polar Falcon (USA) 126 – Bird of Love 82 (Ela-Mana-Mou **111**
132) [2001 10v* 11.6m* Jun 25] strong gelding: sixth living foal: brother to fairly useful
Irish 7f/1m winner Irina: dam, twice raced, half-sister to smart middle-distance stayer
Water Boatman and useful 6f/7f performer Hill Hopper: won maiden at Newbury in
May by neck from Staging Post, and 3-runner minor event at Windsor by neck from
Tramway, in latter responding gamely and showing smart form: stays 11.6f: stays in
training. *D. R. C. Elsworth*

SEA HAZE   4 ch.g. Emarati (USA) 74 – Unveiled 76 (Sayf El Arab (USA) 127) [2001 **–**
70d: 5.7f 8.5g Oct 20] fair performer at best: no form in 2001: blinkered once. *R. J. Baker*

SEA ISLE   5 ch.m. Selkirk (USA) 129 – Miss Blitz 83 (Formidable (USA) 125) [2001 **36**
–: 7s 7m 6m 5f Jun 13] workmanlike mare: poor maiden handicapper: stays 1m: acts on
good to firm going: blinkered once. *J. Parkes*

SEA JADE (IRE)   2 b.f. (Mar 6) Mujadil (USA) 119 – Mirabiliary (USA) 74 (Crow **–**
(FR) 134) [2001 6m 7m 5m Aug 13] IR 15,000Y, 10,000 2-y-o: workmanlike filly: sister
to 2 winners, notably 4-y-o Sir Ferbet, and half-sister to several winners, including 9f/
1¼m winner Tribal Peace (by Red Sunset): dam 1¼m winner: only a little sign of ability
in maidens/minor event. *J. W. Payne*

SEALED BY FATE (IRE)   6 b.g. Mac's Imp (USA) 116 – Fairy Don (Don 128) **48 +**
[2001 54: f8.5s f6g 5.1v 6s 7.1g 6m 7m 5m⁵ 6m 6m⁵ 7m 6m 6m 8.1d⁶ 5m 5g 5s 6s 5m⁶ **a–**

7m 5d⁴ 7d⁵ 6d 6d 5g Nov 5] big, workmanlike gelding: poor performer: stays easy 7f: acts on fibresand and firm ground, probably not on soft: usually visored/blinkered. *J. S. Wainwright*

SEA MARK 5 gr.g. Warning 136 – Mettlesome (Lomond (USA) 128) [2001 87: 8g **91** 10.4g 8m² 8.1d² 9.1f² 8.1g⁵ 8m 10.3m⁵ 7m⁵ 9g Oct 6] big, rangy gelding: has a round action: carries condition: fairly useful performer: probably stays 1¼m: acts on firm and good to soft going. *C. Grant*

SEA MINSTREL 5 b.m. Sea Raven (IRE) 75 – Give Us A Treat (Cree Song 99) **–** [2001 –: 8m Aug 12] seems of little account nowadays. *J. S. Wainwright*

SEAMSTRESS (IRE) 2 b.f. (Jan 21) Barathea (IRE) 127 – Petite Epaulette 80 (Night **72** Shift (USA)) [2001 7m³ 7.1f* 8.3v⁴ 8s Oct 22] IR 14,000Y: sparely-made filly: fourth foal: sister to fairly useful 2000 2-y-o 5f winner Dress Code and half-sister to fairly useful 2-y-o 5f winners Shalford's Honour (in 1997, by Shalford) and Lady Sarka (in 1999, by Lake Coniston): dam, 5f winner, ran only at 2 yrs: fair form: won maiden at Musselburgh in August: fourth at Windsor, better effort when hanging in nurseries after: stays 1m: acts on any going: sold 9,000 gns, sent to USA. *P. W. Harris*

SEAN'S HONOR (IRE) 3 b.f. Mukaddamah (USA) 125 – Great Land (USA) **59 §** (Friend's Choice (USA)) [2001 54§: e5g⁵ f5g e5g* f5g⁵ f5g⁵ f5f² f6g f6g 5f* 5f 5.3g⁵ **a53 §** 5.1g 7m 6d f5g 5d p5g p5g Dec 4] good-quartered filly: modest performer: won sellers at Lingfield in February and Musselburgh (dead-heated in handicap, first start after leaving C. Kellett) in July: probably best at 5f: acts on fibresand/equitrack, firm and good to soft going: usually visored/tongue tied: tends to look difficult ride, and probably ungenuine. *Miss J. F. Craze*

SEA PLUME 2 b.f. (Apr 17) Slip Anchor 136 – Fine Quill (Unfuwain (USA) 131) **–** [2001 7d Oct 15] 8,000Y: first foal: dam once-raced half-sister to smart performer up to 2m Harbour Dues (by Slip Anchor): 33/1 and edgy, well beaten in maiden at Leicester. *Lady Herries*

SEA PRINCE 2 ch.g. (Mar 19) Bering 136 – Gersey (Generous (IRE) 139) [2001 7m **–** 7d Oct 2] 30,000Y: big, leggy gelding: first foal: dam once-raced half-sister to smart performer up to 1¾m Jahafil: last in maiden at Doncaster and valuable sales race at Newmarket (visored). *I. A. Balding*

SEARCH AND DESTROY (USA) 3 b. or br.g. Sky Classic (CAN) – Hunt The **77** Thimble (USA) 86 (Turn And Count (USA)) [2001 –p: 10g² 13.1f² 11.9f* 9.9m² 12g⁶ Aug 4] big, good-topped gelding: has plenty of scope: easy mover: fair performer: won maiden handicap at Brighton and minor event at Beverley in July: gelded after final start: races freely, but will probably stay 1¾m: acts on firm going. *Sir Mark Prescott*

SEARCH PARTY (FR) 2 b.g. (Apr 6) Efisio 120 – Hunt The Thimble (FR) (Relkino **53** 131) [2001 7.5m⁵ 7m 7.5g 8m 7.5g Sep 19] 90,000 francs Y: rather leggy gelding: sixth foal: half-brother to French 1¾m winner Oh My Goodness (by Hadeer): dam unraced: modest maiden: below form, including in nurseries, after second start: stays 7.5f. *T. D. Easterby*

SEA STAR 3 b.c. Distant Relative 128 – Storm Card (Zalazl (USA) 120) [2001 81p: **91** 8d* 8.2s Nov 5] fairly useful performer: has had only 3 races: off nearly a year prior to winning maiden at Pontefract in October: raced too freely when well below form final outing: stays 1m: raced only on ground softer than good. *H. R. A. Cecil*

SEA STORM (IRE) 3 b.g. Dolphin Street (FR) 125 – Prime Interest (IRE) (Kings **92** Lake (USA) 133) [2001 –: 6s⁴ 7m* 8f⁶ 7m* 7.5f* 7g² 7m⁶ Aug 25] sturdy gelding: fairly useful performer: won maiden at Southwell in May and handicaps at Southwell (made all) and Beverley in July: will probably stay 1m: acts on firm ground, probably on soft. *R. F. Fisher*

SEA TOP 2 gr.g. (Mar 4) Highest Honor (FR) 124 – Anotheranniversary 95 (Emarati **50** (USA) 74) [2001 5s 5g 6m⁵ 7m f5g 5v p5g⁵ f5g Nov 23] 7,000Y: first foal: dam 2-y-o 5f winner: modest maiden: best efforts at 5f: acts on fibresand/polytrack. *J. J. Bridger*

SEATTLE ALLEY (USA) 8 b.g. Seattle Dancer (USA) 119 – Alyanaabi (USA) 74 **–** (Roberto (USA) 131) [2001 f11g⁴ f16.2g Feb 8] good-topped gelding: lightly raced and no form on Flat since 1997: won selling hurdle in November. *D. J. Wintle*

SEATTLE PRINCE (USA) 3 gr.c. Cozzene (USA) – Chicken Slew (USA) (Seattle **86** Slew (USA)) [2001 73: 10m⁶ 11.4g 9.9m* 10.2m² 11.6m 14m³ 14g 12m* 14.4g⁵ 16.2s⁴

14g 14.1g Oct 19] strong, quite attractive colt: fairly useful handicapper: won at Salisbury in June and August: reportedly finished lame final start: stays 2m: acts on soft and good to firm ground: has carried head awkwardly and drifted left under pressure: visored/blinkered last 4 starts. *R. Hannon*

SEA VICTOR   9 b.g. Slip Anchor 136 – Victoriana (USA) (Storm Bird (CAN) 134)   – [2001 f16g Apr 9] sturdy, good-topped gelding: well held only outing since 1997: sometimes visored. *J. L. Harris*

SEA VISTA (USA)   2 gr. or ro.f. (Feb 12) Distant View (USA) 126 – Sarba (USA)   ? (Persepolis (FR) 127) [2001 6f⁵ 8s Oct 25] $95,000F, $150,000Y: leggy, close-coupled filly: third foal: half-sister to 3-y-o Carnoustie: dam, winner up to 2m in France, placed in Prix de Royallieu and Prix Gladiateur: seemed to show ability when last in minor event at Ascot: tongue tied, ran as if something amiss in maiden at Brighton 4 months later: sold 5,500 gns, sent to Germany. *I. A. Balding*

SEA VIXEN   3 ch.f. Machiavellian (USA) 123 – Hill Hopper (IRE) 106 (Danehill   87 (USA) 126) [2001 86p: 8s* f8g Nov 12] fairly useful form in 3 starts: won minor event at Brighton in October by 1½ lengths: raced freely when disappointing in handicap final outing: stays 1m: acts on soft going and fibresand. *Sir Mark Prescott*

SEA YA MAITE   7 b.g. Komaite (USA) – Marina Plata (Julio Mariner 127) [2001 –,   44 a72: f7g⁵ f8g³ f8g³ f8g⁶ f7g f9.4g³ f8.5g⁴ f7g* f7g³ f8.5g* f7g³ f11g f8g* f8g 7.5f⁴ f8g³   a77 8f f8g⁴ f8g 8f² f8.5g³ f8.5g⁴ f9.4f⁴ f8s⁵ Dec 21] tall, rangy gelding: poor mover: fair on all-weather, poor on turf: won minor events at Southwell (2) and Wolverhampton in March/April: stays 8.5f: acts on fibresand and firm going: tried blinkered: has worn tongue strap: sometimes slowly away and tends to run lazily. *S. R. Bowring*

SEBA   2 b.f. (Feb 7) Alzao (USA) 117 – Persian Secret (FR) 101 (Persian Heights 129)   95 [2001 6g* 7m* 7g 8d⁵ Sep 13] smallish, well-made filly: second foal: half-sister to 3-y-o Do The Honours: dam, 6f (at 2 yrs) and 1m (in France) winner, half-sister to Irish 2000 Guineas runner-up Verglas and 5-y-o Cassandra Go: useful performer: won maiden at Newmarket in May and Chesham Stakes at Royal Ascot (by neck from Parasol, overcoming considerable trouble after missing break) in June: creditable efforts in Moyglare Stud Stakes at the Curragh and May Hill Stakes at Doncaster: stays 1m: has worn crossed noseband. *D. R. Loder*

SEBRING   2 ch.c. (Mar 30) Hurricane Sky (AUS) – Carmenoura (IRE) (Carmelite   73 House (IRE) 118) [2001 5d 5d⁵ 6m 6m⁴ 8f⁴ 8m² 7.1m* 8.3v p8g⁶ Nov 20] 13,500Y: close-coupled colt: second foal: dam maiden granddaughter of Irish 1000 Guineas winner Royal Danseuse: fair performer: won nursery at Warwick in September: creditable sixth in similar event at Lingfield: effective at 7f/1m: acts on good to firm going (possibly not heavy) and polytrack. *N. A. Callaghan*

SEBULBA (IRE)   3 b. or br.g. Dolphin Street (FR) 125 – Twilight Calm (IRE) (Hatim   61 d (USA) 121) [2001 75: f8g f7g f8.5g f9.4g f7g⁴ f8g Dec 17] fair performer at 2 yrs: on downgrade: stays 1m: acts on fibresand: blinkered last 3 starts. *J. G. Given*

SECOND AFFAIR (IRE)   4 b.f. Pursuit of Love 124 – Startino 111 (Bustino 136)   85 [2001 80: 10d² 9m² 10.5d 10.1m⁴ 11.8d* Aug 12] angular, workmanlike filly: fairly useful performer: won minor event at Leicester in August: stays 1½m: yet to race on firm going, acts on any other: races prominently: sold 12,000 gns in December. *Jedd O'Keeffe*

SECOND BURST (IRE)   2 b.f. (Mar 2) Sadler's Wells (USA) 132 – Kanmary (FR)   – 117 (Kenmare (FR) 125) [2001 8v Oct 26] strong, rangy, good sort: sister to 1998 Racing Post Trophy winner Commander Collins (later stayed 1½m) and closely related to several winners, notably Breeders' Cup Sprint winner Lit de Justice and very smart 7f winner at 2 yrs who stayed 1½m (third in Derby) Colonel Collins (both by El Gran Senor): dam, won 5f Prix du Bois at 2 yrs, stayed 9f: 6/1, tailed off in maiden at Doncaster: joined R. Gibson in France. *J. H. M. Gosden*

SECOND GENERATION (IRE)   4 ch.g. Cadeaux Genereux 131 – Title Roll (IRE)   – 107 (Tate Gallery (USA) 117) [2001 46: 6s May 3] poor maiden at 3 yrs: well held only outing in 2001: tried blinkered. *D. R. C. Elsworth*

SECOND MINISTER   2 ch.g. (Apr 8) Lion Cavern (USA) 117 – Crime of Passion   79 115 (Dragonara Palace (USA) 115) [2001 5g⁴ 6m⁵ 5m² 6m Sep 2] 22,000Y: big, leggy gelding: half-brother to several winners, including sprinter Master of Passion (by Primo Dominie), useful at 2 yrs: dam, won Cherry Hinton at 2 yrs, didn't train on: fair maiden:

second at Sandown: well held in nursery final start: likely to prove best at 5f/6f: sweating and edgy (not at best) second start. *J. M. P. Eustace*

SECOND PAIGE (IRE) 4 b.g. Nicolotte 118 – My First Paige (IRE) 53 (Runnett 125) [2001 76, a–: 12.3g⁵ 11.6g 14.1m² 14m 14.1d² 14.1d⁴ 13.9d⁶ 11.7d Oct 25] tall gelding: fair handicapper: stays 1¾m: acts on good to firm and good to soft going: blinkered last 4 starts: has found little. *N. A. Graham* **76** **a–**

SECOND STRIKE 3 b.g. Kris 135 – Honeyspike (IRE) 79 (Chief's Crown (USA)) [2001 67: 6.9m⁶ 10g 8f⁵ 9.7g a8g* a8s² Dec 23] fair form in 2 runs at 2 yrs: just modest form in 2001: sold from B. Smart 5,100 gns before winning minor event at Taby in December: may prove best at 7f/1m: acts on dirt: has looked headstrong. *Mrs S. Dysell, Sweden* **60 +**

SECOND TIME AROUND (IRE) 4 b.f. Mukaddamah (USA) 125 – Up The Gates (Captain James 123) [2001 –: f11g f12g f8g f12s f16g Feb 16] little form. *M. C. Chapman* **–**

SECOND VENTURE (IRE) 3 b.g. Petardia 113 – Hilton Gateway (Hello Gorgeous (USA) 128) [2001 76: 6s³ 7.1g 7d Jun 17] good-topped gelding: fair maiden: stays 7f: acts on soft going: gelded after final start. *J. R. Weymes* **73**

SECOND WIND 6 ch.g. Kris 135 – Rimosa's Pet 109 (Petingo 135) [2001 89: 7s 6g 8s 6m 6m⁵ 9d Aug 2] lengthy, workmanlike gelding: unimpressive mover: fair form in 2001: left C. Dwyer after first start: stays 1¼m: acts on any going: often tongue tied: has hung badly right/run well when sweating: often leads: rejoined C. Dwyer. *I. A. Wood* **67**

SECRET ANGEL (USA) 3 gr.f. Colonial Affair (USA) 126 – Petong Secret (Petong 126) [2001 10f⁵ 11.7d p10g Nov 20] $4,500Y: first foal: dam, won in USA, half-sister to smart 7f/1m performer Pasticcio: refused to enter stall on intended debut in July: well beaten in maidens: carried head awkwardly on debut. *G. C. H. Chung* **–**

SECRETARIO 4 b.f. Efisio 120 – Lucidity 67 (Vision (USA)) [2001 45: f12s³ f12g³ f12s⁴ f12s⁴ e16g f14g f11g 13d May 6] small filly: poor maiden: should stay 1¾m: acts on fibresand, probably on equitrack: tried blinkered/visored: has raced freely: usually held up: none too consistent. *J. Hetherton* **45**

SECRET CONQUEST 4 b.f. Secret Appeal – Mohibbah (USA) 86 (Conquistador Cielo (USA)) [2001 73d: 8d 8s 7m⁴ 7m⁶ 8g⁴ 7.5m³ 7f* 7.1f² 7.5m 7g⁶ 7m 7m⁴ 6g 7m⁵ 7.5d f8g Oct 22] strong filly: modest handicapper: won at Doncaster in June: probably best around 7f: has won on good to soft going, best efforts on good or firmer: usually blinkered. *D. W. Barker* **62**

SECRETE CONTRACT 3 b.g. Contract Law (USA) 108 – Secret Account (Blakeney 126) [2001 –: 11s 10.2d 11.6d May 21] workmanlike gelding: well held in maidens/handicap. *G. L. Moore* **–**

SECRET FLUTTER (IRE) 2 b.f. (Jan 28) Entrepreneur 123 – Spend A Rubble (USA) (Spend A Buck (USA)) [2001 8.1v⁴ 8s Oct 16] IR 40,000Y: well-made filly: second foal: dam, French 1¼m winner, half-sister to very smart French 5f/6f winner Kistena: much better effort in maidens (fair form) when fourth to Budoor at Haydock: should stay 1¼m. *J. G. Portman* **73**

SECRETO DREAMS (IRE) 2 b.c. (Feb 15) Distinctly North (USA) 115 – Whittingham Girl 58 (Primo Dominie 121) [2001 5g³ 6m 5d⁴ 6d 6s² Oct 22] 5,000Y: tall, leggy colt: fourth foal: half-brother to 3-y-o Inzacure: dam sprinter: fair maiden: placed at York and Pontefract: will probably stay 7f: acts on soft going. *S. E. Kettlewell* **69**

SECRET PASSION 3 gr.f. Petong 126 – Jamarj 113 (Tyrnavos 129) [2001 59: f9.4g f9.4g² p10g f8.5f Dec 5] modest maiden: trained by P. D'Arcy on reappearance: stays 9.4f: acts on fibresand: blinkered last 3 starts: looks none too resolute. *P. S. McEntee* **57 §**

SECRET SENTIMENT 3 b.f. Mark of Esteem (IRE) 137 – Sahara Baladee (USA) 79 (Shadeed (USA) 135) [2001 –p: 8.1g 11.9m⁵ 14.1m 10d p7g Dec 28] tall, useful-looking filly: modest maiden, lightly raced: sold from E. Dunlop 1,000 gns before final start: should stay 1¼m (refused to settle when tried at 1¾m). *A. B. Coogan* **56**

SECRET SPOOF 2 b.c. (Jan 12) Mind Games 121 – Silver Blessings (Statoblest 120) [2001 5s 5m⁴ 5f⁵ 5m³ 6m* 6m 6d 5g⁵ 6d Oct 12] 22,000Y: sturdy colt: third foal: dam unraced half-sister to smart 5f/6f performer Sylvan Barbarosa: fair performer: won nursery at Redcar in August: ran well in similar event at Newmarket penultimate start: effective at 5f/6f: acts on good to firm going. *T. D. Easterby* **76**

SECRET STYLE   6 b.g. Shirley Heights 130 – Rosie Potts 83 (Shareef Dancer (USA) –
135) [2001 80: f16g f16.2g Jan 6] lengthy, quite good-topped gelding: fairly useful
performer at best: has run only 3 times on Flat since 1999: has won in blinkers.
R. Hollinshead

SECURITE (ARG)   6 ch.h. Southern Halo (USA) – Sesig (ARG) (Cinco Grande   **103**
(USA)) [2001 5v 5.5v a6g* a6g³ a6g* 8g⁵ 6.5g a6g 5.8s 6s a6s⁵ a6s⁴ Dec 30] big,
workmanlike ex-Argentinian horse: useful performer: won minor event at Taby and
handicap at Jagersro in 2000 and minor events at Jagersro and Taby in May: last in
Diadem Stakes at Ascot tenth start: seems best at 6f/7f: acts on dirt, seemingly not on
ground softer than good: forced off track shortly after start at Longchamp first outing.
Diego Lowther, Sweden

SECURITY COUNCIL   3 b.c. Polish Precedent (USA) 131 – Set Fair (USA) (Alleged   –
(USA) 138) [2001 58p: 10g May 12] useful-looking colt: modest form only start at 2 yrs:
saddle reportedly slipped and well held only outing in 2001: sold 800 gns in October, sent
to Holland. *B. W. Hills*

SECURITY TAG (USA)   2 ch.c. (Apr 11) Known Fact (USA) 135 – Secret Angel   **77**
(Halo (USA)) [2001 7.1m⁴ 8.1g⁶ Sep 13] fifth living foal: brother to US 5f (at 2 yrs) to
8.5f winner Satisfy: dam, 1m winner in USA, out of US Grade 1 9f/1¼m winner Ack's
Secret: tongue tied, much better effort in maidens (fair form) when sixth at Chepstow, no
extra final 1f: likely to prove best up to 1m: sold 3,200 gns. *Mrs A. J. Perrett*

SECURON DANCER   3 b.f. Emperor Jones (USA) 119 – Gena Ivor (USA) (Sir Ivor   **49**
135) [2001 60d: 7m 6m 9.7m⁴ 10.1s 7.1g 9.9d Oct 3] tall, workmanlike filly: unimpressive mover: poor maiden handicapper: seems to stay 9.7f: acts on good to firm ground.
R. Rowe

SEEING REALITY (IRE)   2 b.f. (Apr 26) Bin Ajwaad (IRE) 119 – Visage 75   **45**
(Vision (USA)) [2001 5v f5g⁵ 5m 5f May 28] leggy filly: sixth reported foal: half-sister
to 3 winners, including 8-y-o Sotonian: dam, 1¼m winner, daughter of top-class (up to
7f) Be Tuneful: poor maiden: best effort on debut: tried visored: twice slowly away.
P. D. Evans

SEEK   5 br.g. Rainbow Quest (USA) 134 – Souk (IRE) 98 (Ahonoora 122) [2001 99:   –
f11g 12d 12g 13.9m May 16] rather leggy, attractive gelding: useful handicapper at 4 yrs:
well held on Flat in 2001. *J. A. B. Old*

SEEKING SANCTUARY   4 ch.f. Most Welcome 131 – Tjakka (USA) (Little Mis-   –
souri (USA)) [2001 48: f9.4s Jan 18] poor maiden at 3 yrs: well held only 4-y-o outing.
Dr J. D. Scargill

SEEKING THE SUN (IRE)   2 b. or br.g. (Feb 5) Petardia 113 – Femme Savante 89   **90**
(Glenstal (USA) 118) [2001 5m⁶ 6d* 7.1m 6d⁵ Oct 19] useful-looking gelding: second
foal: half-brother to 3-y-o So Sober: dam, 2-y-o 6f winner, half-sister to dam of 3-y-o
Bouncing Bowdler: fairly useful form: won maiden at Haydock in August: best effort
when staying-on fifth of 30 to Major Laugh in sales race at Newmarket: should stay 7f:
failed to handle bend at Warwick third start: gelded after final one. *C. F. Wall*

SEEK THE LIGHT (USA)   4 b.g. Seeking The Gold (USA) – Jolypha (USA) 123   **61**
(Lyphard (USA) 132) [2001 66: e12g² e10g² e12g³ e10g⁴ 10f 10m Jul 11] modest
maiden: ran poorly in sellers last 2 starts: stays 1½m: acts on equitrack: sometimes
blinkered: has found little. *G. L. Moore*

SEEL OF APPROVAL   2 br.c. (Feb 16) Polar Falcon (USA) 126 – Petit Point (IRE)   **68**
78 (Petorius 117) [2001 5.2g 5d 6m⁴ Aug 25] second foal: dam, 6f winner, half-sister to
dams of 4-y-o Kutub, smart sprinter Tropical and very smart miler Shake The Yoke: fair
maiden: should stay 7f. *M. D. I. Usher*

SEEMS SO EASY (USA)   2 b.f. (Feb 18) Palmister (USA) – I'm An Issue (USA)   –
(Cox's Ridge (USA)) [2001 5d Oct 9] smallish, strong filly: fourth foal: half-sister to
6-y-o Nuclear Debate: dam winning sprinter in USA: 7/2 and green, last in maiden at
Catterick. *S. J. Magnier*

SEEYOUF (IRE)   3 b.c. Danehill (USA) 126 – Leipzig 107 (Relkino 131) [2001 7g   **71**
7g³ 9g³ Sep 2] 29,000F, 52,000Y: closely related to fairly useful 10.5f winner Namoodaj
(by Polish Precedent) and half-brother to several winners, including useful miler Pfalz
(by Pharly): dam 6f and 1m winner: fair form in maidens: raced too freely final start: may
prove best at 7f/1m. *E. A. L. Dunlop*

SEFTON LODGE 2 b.c. (Feb 17) Barathea (IRE) 127 – Pine Needle 89 (Kris 135) **– p**
[2001 7f Sep 22] 65,000Y: sturdy, quite attractive colt: second foal: half-brother to 3-y-o
Dumaran: dam, 1m (at 2 yrs) to 1¾m winner, closely related to useful middle-distance
stayer Nibbs Point, herself dam of 6-y-o Border Arrow: 13/2, tailed-off last of 18 in
maiden at Newbury, slowly away and eased after being hampered: seemingly thought
capable of better. *J. Noseda*

SEIGNOSSE (IRE) 3 b.g. College Chapel 122 – How Ya Been (IRE) (Last Tycoon **75**
131) [2001 5.7m³ 5g* 5g³ 5d Oct 12] 3,000F, IR 4,200Y, 10,000 2-y-o: strong, workmanlike gelding: third foal: dam unraced half-sister to smart 1¼m performer Moutahddee:
fair form: won maiden at Beverley in September: very good third in Newmarket handicap
next time: speedy, and will prove best at 5f. *I. A. Balding*

SEIHALI (IRE) 2 b.c. (Mar 28) Alzao (USA) 117 – Edwina (IRE) 63 (Caerleon **87 p**
(USA) 132) [2001 6g⁶ 7s* Oct 3] IR 180,000Y: third foal: half-brother to fairly useful 7f
(in Ireland)/1m winner Your The Lady (by Indian Ridge): dam, maiden, half-sister to
useful sprinter Roger The Butler: much better effort in maidens when winning at Brighton
by ¾ length from Birdie, tending to wander having led going well over 1f out: should stay
1m: slowly away on debut: should make a useful 3-y-o. *A. C. Stewart*

SEL 3 b.f. Salse (USA) 128 – Frog 84 (Akarad (FR) 130) [2001 58: e10g² e10g 10g⁵ **54**
10m 8g⁴ 8m³ 10s⁶ 10s⁴ 10v⁵ p10g Dec 22] modest performer: stays easy 1¼m: acts on
any turf going and equitrack: blinkered: tends to hang/carry head awkwardly: not one to
trust implicitly. *G. L. Moore*

SELECTIVE 2 b.c. (Jan 25) Selkirk (USA) 129 – Portelet 91 (Night Shift (USA)) **86 p**
[2001 7m 8d² Oct 3] 80,000Y: good-bodied colt: second foal: half-brother to 3-y-o
Overspect: dam 5f winner out of half-sister to smart middle-distance stayer Braashee:
better effort in maidens (fairly useful form) when ¾-length second to Diamond Lover at
Newcastle, pulling well clear of remainder: should stay 1¼m: useful prospect, capable of
winning a race or 2. *A. C. Stewart*

SELF PROPELLED (IRE) 3 b.f. Caerleon (USA) 132 – Self Assured (IRE) 97 **56**
(Ahonoora 122) [2001 10g⁴ 10m⁶ Jul 28] third foal: dam, 2-y-o 7f winner and second in
May Hill Stakes, out of half-sister to very smart sprinter Sayyaf: modest form in maidens
at Pontefract (last of 4) and Nottingham: sold 5,000 gns in December. *C. E. Brittain*

SELIANA 5 b.m. Unfuwain (USA) 131 – Anafi 95 (Slip Anchor 136) [2001 86: 16s* **91**
16.2s 18d Oct 20] strong, lengthy mare: fairly useful handicapper: made all at Newbury
in April: off 5 months before folding tamely last 2 starts, including in Cesarewitch: stays
2½m: raced only on good ground or softer: has carried tail awkwardly. *G. Wragg*

SELLINGER'S ROUND (IRE) 5 ch.g. Lucky Guest 109 – Cellophane (Coquelin **–**
(USA) 121) [2001 61d: 7d 11.9m⁵ 10f 7m Jul 23] ex-Irish gelding: disappointing maiden:
tried visored. *Mrs L. C. Jewell*

SELWAN (USA) 2 b.f. (Apr 23) Mt Livermore (USA) – Dubian 120 (High Line 125) **77 p**
[2001 7.5g³ Sep 19] small, quite attractive filly: half-sister to numerous winners, notably
Cheveley Park Stakes and 1000 Guineas winner Sayyedati (by Shadeed), 5-y-o Golden
Snake and smart 7f (at 2 yrs)/1m winner Race Leader (by Gone West): dam 7f (at 2 yrs)
to 1½m winner who was placed in Oaks/Irish Oaks: 6/1, 2 lengths third of 9 to Raison
Garde in maiden at Beverley: will stay 1¼m: wore crossed noseband: joined H-A. Pantall
in France: should improve. *D. R. Loder*

SEMIRAMIS 4 b.f. Darshaan 133 – Sulitelma (USA) 63 (The Minstrel (CAN) 135) **66 §**
[2001 54: f9.4g* f12g² e12s³ f12g Feb 23] fair performer: won maiden at Wolverhampton
in February: stays 1½m: better form on fibresand than equitrack, and acts on good to firm
ground: blinkered/tongue tied in 2001: has reportedly had breathing problem/bled from
nose: needs treating with caution. *Sir Mark Prescott*

SEMPER PARATUS (USA) 2 b.c. (Feb 16) Foxhound (USA) 103 – Bletcha Lass **66**
(AUS) (Bletchingly (AUS)) [2001 6m 6m 7.1f⁵ 7s Oct 5] 12,000Y, 22,000 2-y-o: close-
coupled colt: closely related to a winner in USA by Danzig Connection and half-brother
to several other minor winners in USA: dam, maiden in Australia, out of half-sister to
high-class Middle Park winner Sharpen Up: fair maiden: stays 7f: acts on firm going.
G. C. Bravery

SEMPER SURSUM 5 ch.g. Nicholas Bill 125 – Queen of The Celts (Celtic Cone **–**
116) [2001 f14.8s Sep 6] first foal: dam failed to complete in novice hurdles: no show in
claimer at Wolverhampton. *B. Palling*

SENATOR'S ALIBI 3 b.c. Caerleon (USA) 132 – Salul (Soviet Star (USA) 128) **80**
[2001 65p: f6g² 8m⁶ 8.2s* f8.5g⁴ 8.1s* 8.1v⁶ 10v³ Oct 8] strong colt: fairly useful
performer: won minor event at Nottingham in August and handicap at Haydock in
September: stays 1¼m: acts on heavy going, probably on fibresand: sold 10,000 gns.
Sir Mark Prescott

SEND IT TO PENNY (IRE) 4 b.f. Marju (IRE) 127 – Sparkish (IRE) (Persian Bold **–**
123) [2001 59: 8m 8g 6d Oct 9] big, lengthy filly: poor mover: modest handicapper at 3
yrs: last in 3 outings in 2001: sometimes blinkered. *W. Storey*

SEND ME AN ANGEL (IRE) 4 ch.f. Lycius (USA) 124 – Niamh Cinn Oir (IRE) **–**
(King of Clubs 124) [2001 75: 12.1m 15.9m 12.1m 11.9g 11m 16f 10m f12g f12f Dec 5]
tall, workmanlike filly: fair handicapper at 3 yrs: well held in 2001, including in blinkers.
M. Mullineaux

SENIOR MINISTER 3 b.c. Lion Cavern (USA) 117 – Crime Ofthecentury 80 **102**
(Pharly (FR) 130) [2001 99: 5.2f Sep 22] good-topped, attractive colt: has scope: useful
performer, lightly raced: off 13 months with reported fractured pelvis, creditable 5
lengths seventh to The Trader in listed event at Newbury, only outing at 3 yrs: likely to
prove best at 5f/6f: raced only on ground firmer than good. *J. M. P. Eustace*

SENNEN COVE 2 ch.c. (Mar 24) Bering 136 – Dame Laura (IRE) 100 (Royal **78**
Academy (USA) 130) [2001 7f 6v 6d Oct 18] close-coupled colt: first foal: dam, 5f (at 2
yrs) and 6f winner, out of smart French 1¼m winner Aunty: easily best effort in maidens
(fair form) when seventh of 22 to Hiddendale at Newmarket final start: will probably stay
1m. *H. Morrison*

SENOR MANX TOUCH 2 b.c. (May 17) Magic Ring (IRE) 115 – Inveraven 53 **37**
(Alias Smith (USA)) [2001 6m 6m 7m⁶ 7.5f⁵ 6m Jul 30] 7,400Y: smallish, good-bodied
colt: half-brother to several winners, including useful 1995 2-y-o 1¼m winner Flyfisher
(by Batshoof) and 1993 2-y-o winner around 7f Demi-Plie (by Squill), both later winners
abroad: dam lightly-raced 2-y-o maiden: poor maiden: stays 7.5f: twice reared up in stall.
C. A. Dwyer

SENOR MIRO 3 b.g. Be My Guest (USA) 126 – Classic Moonlight (IRE) (Machia- **76**
vellian (USA) 123) [2001 62: 7m³ 8.3g 7g² Jul 21] leggy, useful-looking gelding: fair
maiden handicapper: stays 7f: yet to race on extremes of going: sometimes races freely:
tongue tied/flashed tail final start. *R. F. Johnson Houghton*

SENSIMELIA (IRE) 3 b.f. Inzar (USA) 112 – In The Papers 87 (Aragon 118) [2001 **68**
58: 8m* 8.3d³ 8.3g² 8.3m⁵ 8.2m* 8.2s² 8m* 7m² Sep 22] leggy, unfurnished filly: fair
performer: won claimers at Ripon in May and Nottingham in July and seller at Thirsk in
September: best at 7f/1m: acts on soft and good to firm going: usually races prominently:
consistent. *G. A. Swinbank*

SENTIMENTAL VALUE (USA) 2 ch.f. (Apr 10) Diesis 133 – Stately Star (USA) **75 p**
(Deputy Minister (CAN)) [2001 7s⁴ Nov 9] rather leggy, quite attractive filly: second
foal: dam US 1m (minor stakes) and 8.5f winner: 13/2, 2¼ lengths fourth to Ballet Score
in maiden at Doncaster, always prominent (carried right late on): open to improvement.
H. R. A. Cecil

SEPTEMBER HARVEST (USA) 5 ch.g. Mujtahid (USA) 118 – Shawgatny **–**
(USA) 83 (Danzig Connection (USA)) [2001 53: f8g³ f8g* f11s f8g³ f8s f9.4g⁵ 8m 10f **a44**
8.5g 8m 12d Sep 25] tall, angular gelding: poor handicapper: won at Southwell in
January: has form at 1½m, effective at 1m: acts on firm going, soft and fibresand: tried
blinkered/visored: tends to get behind. *Mrs S. Lamyman*

SEPT ETOILES (IRE) 2 b.c. (May 5) Machiavellian (USA) 123 – Sueboog (IRE) **–**
109 (Darshaan 133) [2001 7.9d Oct 13] tall, leggy colt: fourth foal: brother to 4-y-o Best
of The Bests and half-brother to fairly useful 1¼m winner Sena Desert (by Green Desert)
and 3-y-o Baratheastar: dam won Fred Darling Stakes and fourth in Oaks: 9/2 and green,
well beaten in maiden at York: wore crossed noseband: coltish and attended by 2
handlers: joined P. Brette in UAE. *D. R. Loder*

SEQUIN (IRE) 2 b.f. (Mar 25) Green Desert (USA) 127 – Sans Escale (USA) (Diesis **80**
133) [2001 6m⁴ 5d⁶ 6g 7g* 7g³ 7d Oct 2] smallish, strong filly: fifth foal: sister to 4-y-o
Escalade and half-sister to useful 1m winner who stayed 1¼m West Escape (by Gone
West): dam, French 11f winner, out of Prix de Diane winner Escaline: fairly useful
performer: won nursery at Folkestone in August: good third in similar event at Epsom:
will stay 1m. *M. A. Jarvis*

Mrs John Magnier's "Sequoyah"

SEQUOYAH (IRE) 3 b.f. Sadler's Wells (USA) 132 – Brigid (USA) (Irish River **113** (FR) 131) [2001 111p: 8g⁴ 8f 12g⁴ 9.9g Aug 4] deep-girthed filly: smart performer: won Moyglare Stud Stakes at the Curragh at 2 yrs: 5½ lengths fourth to Imagine in Irish 1000 Guineas at the Curragh in May: good 1¾ lengths fourth to Lailani in Irish Oaks at the Curragh: tenth in Coronation Stakes at Royal Ascot and last of 7 in Nassau Stakes at Goodwood otherwise: stays 1½m: acts on good to firm going, not discredited on good to soft: sold $1.4m at Keeneland in November. *A. P. O'Brien, Ireland*

SERENGETI BRIDE (USA) 3 ch.f. Lion Cavern (USA) 117 – Island Wedding **91** (USA) 89 (Blushing Groom (FR) 131) [2001 –P: 7d 7g 8m⁵ 10d⁴ 11.8g* 12m* 12g* 12.3m* 14g Oct 6] quite attractive filly: made into fairly useful performer in 2001, winning minor event at Leicester and handicaps at Epsom, Goodwood and Ripon (denied Tiyoun only in last strides) in August/September: stays 1½m, well held at 1¾m: acts on good to firm going. *E. A. L. Dunlop*

SEREN TEG 5 ch.m. Timeless Times (USA) 99 – Hill of Fare (Brigadier Gerard 144) **41** [2001 70d: 6m 5f 6f 5.7g 7g 7f⁵ 5m⁵ Aug 27] quite good-topped mare: unimpressive mover: poor performer nowadays: stays easy 7f: acts on firm going, good to soft (below form both starts on soft), fibresand and equitrack: often blinkered: sometimes sweating/ edgy: has been slowly away. *R. M. Flower*

SERENUS (USA) 8 b.g. Sunshine Forever (USA) – Curl And Set (USA) (Nijinsky **72** (CAN) 138) [2001 77: 12s⁴ Apr 25] leggy gelding: useful jumper: fair handicapper on Flat, lightly raced: probably finds 1½m on sharp side nowadays, and stays 2m: acts on good to firm and heavy going. *N. J. Henderson*

SERGEANT CECIL 2 ch.g. (May 2) King's Signet (USA) 110 – Jadidh 64 (Touch- **69** ing Wood (USA) 127) [2001 8m 10.2g Oct 1] first reported foal: dam, winning staying hurdler (maiden on Flat), half-sister to useful 1m/1¼m performer Refuse To Lose: better effort in maidens (fair form) when seventh to Stage By Stage at Bath second start: shapes as though will stay at least 1½m: reluctant stall on debut. *J. W. Mullins*

SERGEANT'S INN 4 b.g. Sabrehill (USA) 120 – Pink Brief (IRE) 71 (Ela-Mana- Mou 132) [2001 e12g e13g f12g⁶ f16g 8s Apr 16] strong gelding: first foal: dam 7f (at 2 yrs) and 1¼m winner: well held all starts. *Andrew Reid* —

SERGEANT SLIPPER 4 ch.g. Never So Bold 135 – Pretty Scarce (Handsome Sailor 125) [2001 41, a68: f5g f5g f6s f5g f5g f5g⁵ f5g⁴ f5g² f6g 5v* 5v⁶ 5m f5g² f5g 7g 6d f5g 5.2v f5g f5g⁶ Dec 1] workmanlike gelding: modest performer: won claimer at Ripon in April: raced only at 5f/6f: acts on fibresand, good to firm and heavy going: usually visored/blinkered: often claimer ridden: usually slowly away: none too consistent. *C. Smith* **62 a56**

SERGEANT YORK 5 b.g. Be My Chief (USA) 122 – Metaphysique (FR) (Law Society (USA) 130) [2001 84: f8g* f8.5g e10g* a9.5f⁶ 9f³ 8.5f a8.3f a9f Dec 2] big, good-topped gelding: useful performer: successful in handicap at Southwell in February and listed Winter Derby at Lingfield (made all) in March, latter by ½ length from Resplendent Star: mostly well below form afterwards in Pimlico Special (very stiff task, fourth start and final one for T. D. Barron) and allowance races/optional claimers: effective at 1m/easy 1¼m: acts on fibresand/equitrack, heavy and good to firm going: tried visored/blinkered, including final start. *M. W. Dickinson, USA* **100**

SERGEEVNA (IRE) 3 b.f. Barathea (IRE) 127 – Sveltana 82 (Soviet Star (USA) 128) [2001 10m 11.7d Oct 25] IR 52,000F, IR 52,000Y: first foal: dam, 7f winner who probably stayed 1¼m, out of Yorkshire Oaks winner Sally Brown: well held in maidens. *J. G. Portman* —

SERGE LIFAR 3 b.c. Shirley Heights 130 – Ballet 61 (Sharrood (USA) 124) [2001 83p: f12g² 10.2d² 9.9g* 12s³ 11.6g* 10m² 14g 14m² 12d³ Oct 2] angular, quite good-topped colt: useful performer: won handicap at Salisbury in May and minor event at Windsor (beat Isadora by head) in July: good efforts in handicaps at Newmarket last 2 starts, 5-length third to High Pitched final one: stays 1¾m: acts on soft and good to firm going, ran creditably only run on fibresand: sold 50,000 gns. *R. Hannon* **107**

SERIEUX 2 b.c. (Feb 26) Cadeaux Genereux 131 – Seranda (IRE) (Petoski 135) [2001 6m² 6m* 7g⁵ Aug 21] 340,000 francs F, 180,000Y: strong, lengthy, useful-looking colt: fourth foal: half-brother to 3 winners in France, including useful 7f (at 2 yrs) and 1m winner Shine On Me (by Machiavellian) and winner up to 15f Serisio (by Efisio): dam, French 1¼m winner, half-sister to dam of smart French performer up to 11f Shaka: useful form: won maiden at Goodwood in July by 4 lengths from Bishr: favourite, never going with any fluency when fifth to Comfy in listed race at York: should stay 1m. *B. W. Hills* **100**

Bet Direct Winter Derby, Lingfield—one of only two listed races on the all-weather goes to Sergeant York on his final outing before being transferred to the States; later in the year the equitrack surface was replaced by polytrack at a reported cost of £3m

SERIOUS TRUST 8 b.g. Alzao (USA) 117 – Mill Line 71 (Mill Reef (USA) 141) **21**
[2001 f16.2s e16g e13s f12g⁶ 14.1g 16f 16.4m² 12m 16g Sep 5] good-topped gelding: bad
performer nowadays: stays 2m: acts on firm ground, seemingly not soft: tried blinkered/
visored. *Mrs L. C. Jewell*

SEROTONIN 2 b.c. (Feb 19) Barathea (IRE) 127 – Serotina (IRE) 73 (Mtoto 134) **64 p**
[2001 7d Nov 3] 32,000F, IR 180,000Y: angular colt: fifth foal: closely related to a winner
in Germany by Saddlers' Hall and half-brother to 6-y-o Alconleigh and 3-y-o Bajan Blue:
dam 9f winner out of half-sister to very smart miler Waajib: 33/1, not knocked about
when eleventh of 27 to Prince Hector in maiden at Newmarket: should improve.
R. Charlton

SERRA NEGRA 4 b.f. Kris 135 – Congress (IRE) 86 (Dancing Brave (USA) 140) **80**
[2001 83+: 7s 7.1g⁴ 7.1s⁴ 6m 6g 7d Aug 26] leggy filly: fairly useful performer: stays
1m: acts on any ground: ran as though amiss fourth start: blinkered final outing.
W. J. Haggas

SERVICEABLE 3 ch.f. Pursuit of Love 124 – Absaloute Service 96 (Absalom 128) **74**
[2001 75: 6d 8g 8m 8.3m* 8f* 8.5m 8g3 10.3d 7.1v 8d f8.5g Nov 3] workmanlike filly:
fair performer: won minor event at Hamilton and handicap at Ripon in July: stays 1m, at
least when conditions aren't testing: acts on firm and soft going: has been early to post:
played up before start eighth outing: often leads: sold 4,500 gns. *R. M. Whitaker*

SETTLE DOWN 2 b.f. (Apr 22) Reprimand 122 – Russell Creek 80 (Sandy Creek **58**
123) [2001 5v⁴ f5g 5.1s* 7.1f⁶ f7g⁵ 6v f6g f5f Dec 5] 3,100Y: workmanlike filly: good **a48**
walker: sixth foal: half-sister to 1996 2-y-o 5f seller winner Assumpta (by Superpower)
and a winner in Denmark by Valiyar: dam, 1m winner, out of half-sister to very smart 1m/
1¼m performer Jellaby: modest on turf, poor on all-weather: won seller at Nottingham in
April: left M. Easterby after sixth start: stays 7f: acts on heavy going and fibresand: tried
blinkered/visored: has started slowly. *J. D. Czerpak*

SEVEN NO TRUMPS 4 ch.g. Pips Pride 117 – Classic Ring (IRE) 50 (Auction Ring **101**
(USA) 123) [2001 92d: 6v⁶ 6m* 6m* 6m³ 6f⁵ 6g 6g 5.6m² 6m 6d³ 6v* Oct 26] rangy,
good-topped gelding: useful handicapper: won at Doncaster and Goodwood in May, and
at Newbury (beat Now Look Here by ¾ length) in October: also ran well when placed
behind Nice One Clare in Wokingham at Royal Ascot fourth start and behind Smokin
Beau in Portland at Doncaster (beaten a neck) eighth outing: best around 6f: acts on any
going: blinkered once at 3 yrs: edgy sort: tends to carry head high: usually races up with
pace: none too reliable. *B. W. Hills*

SEVEN OF NINE (IRE) 3 b. or br.f. Alzao (USA) 117 – Sharakawa (IRE) (Darshaan **66**
133) [2001 55p: 9.9s⁵ 10m⁶ May 26] fair maiden, raced 3 times: may prove best around
1m. *W. R. Muir*

SEVEN SING (USA) 3 b.f. Machiavellian (USA) 123 – Seven Springs (USA) 114 **–**
(Irish River (FR) 131) [2001 83: 7g Jul 10] leggy filly: fairly useful performer: ran only 4
times: well held only outing in 2001: stayed 6f: acted on firm and good to soft going: stud.
B. W. Hills

SEVEN SPRINGS (IRE) 5 b.g. Unblest 117 – Zaydeen (Sassafras (FR) 135) [2001 **–**
47: f6g⁴ f6s³ f5g* f5g³ f6s* 6g f5g 5m f6g 5d f6g 7f 5g f5g f6g f6g f6g Dec 17] tall, **a59**
workmanlike gelding: modest handicapper: won at Southwell in January/February: best
at 5f/6f: acts on fibresand and any turf going: tried visored: has been early to post/slowly
away. *R. Hollinshead*

SEWMUCH CHARACTER 2 b.g. (Mar 8) Magic Ring (IRE) 115 – Diplomatist **75 §**
69 (Dominion 123) [2001 6m⁵ 6d² 7d² 7d² 6d Oct 12] 15,000Y: big, good-topped gelding:
has scope: third foal: half-brother to 1998 2-y-o 1m winner Top Fit (by Thatching) and
4-y-o Mice Design: dam, 10.5f and 1½m winner, half-sister to smart 7f/1m performer
Norwich: fair maiden: runner-up at Pontefract and twice at Chester: most disappointing
final start: stays 7f: looks untrustworthy. *M. Blanshard*

SEYOOLL (IRE) 3 b.f. Danehill (USA) 126 – Andromaque (USA) 111 (Woodman **78**
(USA) 126) [2001 76: 10s³ 10s³ 11.7m³ Sep 10] leggy filly: third foal: dam 1m winner
and awarded 9f Prix de l'Opera: fair form when placed in maidens, off 4½ months before
10 lengths third to Anticipate at Bath final outing: probably stayed 1½m: acted on soft
and good to firm ground: visits Mtoto. *M. R. Channon*

SHAAM 3 b.g. Charnwood Forest (IRE) 125 – Badawi (USA) 103 (Diesis 133) [2001 **–**
10m 11.9s Sep 30] fourth foal: closely related to useful 1m winner Badagara (by

Warning) and half-brother to 2 winners by Green Desert, including 7-y-o Saguaro: dam 1m and 9f winner: well held in maidens: slowly away on debut. *C. E. Brittain*

SHAAMUL   2 gr.g. (May 16) Elmaamul (USA) 125 – Dangerous Shadow 80 (Absalom   –
128) [2001 f8g f9.4g Dec 8] 2,700Y: fourth foal: dam 2-y-o 5f/6f winner: well beaten in maiden/seller. *K. A. Ryan*

SHAANARA (IRE)   3 b.f. Darshaan 133 – Mochara (Last Fandango 125) [2001 82:   –
10m 8.9d Oct 13] quite good-topped filly: unimpressive mover: fairly useful at 2 yrs: behind in handicaps (very slowly away on reappearance) in 2001. *Andrew Turnell*

SHAANDAR   3 br.c. Darshaan 133 – Moon Parade 73 (Welsh Pageant 132)   **106**
[2001 54P: 11s* 12g³ 14.8g³ Jul 11] tall, useful-looking, rather sparely-made colt: has run only 4 times: impressive winner of maiden at Newbury in April: useful form when third at Newmarket after, in minor event (3¼ lengths behind Terrestrial) and listed race (broke down badly when beaten 5¼ lengths by Arrive): stays 1¾m: raced only on good ground or softer: joined R. White. *J. L. Dunlop*

SHAANMER (IRE)   2 b.c. (Apr 10) Darshaan 133 – Fee des Mers (Alzao (USA)   **109 p**
117) [2001 7.5s* 8m* 8d* Sep 23]   The Derby is the first major target for Shaanmer, the winner of all three of his starts in his first season and installed as favourite for the race with one firm after gaining the last of his victories as a two-year-old in the Group 3 Prix des Chenes at Longchamp in September. The last French-trained winner of the Derby was Empery in 1976, and French challengers at Epsom are unusual these days. In five of the last ten years, including the last two, there has been no French runner in the Derby; and on the five other occasions there has been just a single representative from France, each one of those trained by Andre Fabre, who is also responsible for Shaanmer. If Shaanmer does take up his engagement at Epsom he won't necessarily need to distinguish himself in order to surpass the efforts of his five immediate predecessors. Cloudings achieved the highest placing, tenth, though he did have only twelve opponents. Rainbow Corner, Pennekamp and the latest Breeders' Cup Mile winner Val Royal all finished eleventh, while Sunshack was nineteenth.

Shaanmer is likely to face more opponents in the Derby than he has in all three of his races to date put together, having accounted for five each time in minor events at Deauville and Longchamp, and just three in the Prix des Chenes. Those three, all trained in France, were Caesarion, a well-bred colt who had finished second in a minor event at Chantilly on his only start, Night Bokbel, the winner of a newcomers event at Deauville the previous month, and Existentialiste, a winner of only two of his eight starts and apparently exposed as no more than fairly useful. Shaanmer was sent off at 2/1-on to dispose of them, and he did so without too much fuss. He settled nicely in second as Night Bokbel set a steady pace, was produced

Prix des Chenes, Longchamp—Shaanmer completes a hat-trick and briefly heads the betting on the 2002 Derby; Caesarion (right) and Night Bokbel chase him home

early in the straight and needed only to be pushed along to draw clear after leading a furlong out. At the line Shaanmer had two lengths to spare over the staying-on Caesarion, with the same distance back to Night Bokbel in third. Caesarion upheld the form when a creditable second, beaten a length and a half by Rashbag, in the Group 3 Prix de Conde at Longchamp next time, though, as it stands, the form of the Prix des Chenes is no better than useful and Shaanmer has a lot more improvement to make if he is to reach the level required to win a Derby.

Shaanmer (IRE) (b.c. Apr 10, 1999)	Darshaan (br 1981)		Shirley Heights (b 1975)		Mill Reef
					Hardiemma
			Delsy (br 1972)		Abdos
					Kelty
	Fee des Mers (b 1991)		Alzao (b 1980)		Lyphard
					Lady Rebecca
			Nordica (ch 1983)		Northfields
					Princess Arabella

Not having raced beyond a mile, Shaanmer will also need to show that he has the necessary stamina. At first glance, his pedigree suggests that a mile and a half should pose no problems for him. By the Prix du Jockey Club winner Darshaan, Shaanmer is the third foal of Fee des Mers, who ran her best race when stepped up to a mile and three quarters on the last of her three starts, finishing third of twelve in a minor event at Evry. Fee des Mers's first foal and only other winner to date, Nordican Inch, whose sire Inchinor was just as effective over seven furlongs as a mile, was a useful winner at a mile and at nine furlongs and stayed a mile and a half in France and later won in the States, where she was second in a Grade 1 event. Delving further into the dam's side of Shaanmer's pedigree, there are some worrying elements regarding his prospects of staying a mile and a half. While the grandam Nordica probably stayed a mile and a quarter, she showed better form and gained all her victories at shorter distances, winning three races at a mile in Britain and over six furlongs after being moved to Ireland. The next dam Princess Arabella, though a half-sister to the Oaks winner Fair Salinia, raced only at seven furlongs, over which distance she won a maiden. Sueboog, a half-sister to Fee des Mers and a daughter of Darshaan, finished a respectable fourth in the Oaks, but both her wins came over seven furlongs, including in the Fred Darling Stakes. Sueboog is herself the dam of the Derby fourth Best of The Bests, who went on to show better form at a mile to a mile and a quarter. Shaanmer, who has done his racing so far on ground ranging from good to firm to soft, will certainly stay a mile and a quarter, and more than likely a mile and a half. *A. Fabre, France*

SHAANXI ROMANCE (IRE) 6 b.g. Darshaan 133 – Easy Romance (USA) (Northern Jove (CAN)) [2001 59: 7g f8g f8g 8m 8v f8g Nov 19] tall gelding: modest handicapper at best: no form in 2001: visored. *M. J. Polglase* —

SHAARD (IRE) 3 b.c. Anabaa (USA) 130 – Braari (USA) 97 (Gulch (USA)) [2001 110: 7d⁵ 7g⁴ 8g⁶ a8f³ Dec 27] strong, good-topped colt: useful performer: bit below smart 2-y-o form in 2001, leaving B. Hills after second outing: off 5 months, creditable efforts both starts in UAE, 7½ lengths third to Skoozi in minor event at Nad Al Sheba final one: stays 1m: acts on dirt, raced only on good going or softer on turf: blinkered in Britain: has wandered/found little, and probably suited by waiting tactics. *E. Charpy, UAE* **103**

SHABAAB 3 b.c. Unfuwain (USA) 131 – Kronengold (USA) (Golden Act (USA)) [2001 12d⁵ 12g⁴ 11.5m³ 14m⁵ 14.1g 11.7g⁴ 14.1s a10f⁶ Nov 15] tall colt: third foal: brother to German 10.8f winner Aneefah: dam, German 9f to 11f winner (placed in Group 3 event at 1½m), half-sister to smart German middle-distance performer Komtur: fair maiden handicapper: left M. Channon and off 3 months before final outing: stays 1¾m: acts on good to firm going, probably on good to soft: consistent. *D. J. Selvaratnam, UAE* **73**

SHADALHI 3 ch.f. Alhijaz 122 – Dangerous Shadow 80 (Absalom 128) [2001 43: 7m⁶ 6g Jun 12] sparely-made filly: poor maiden, lightly raced: probably stays 7f. *K. A. Ryan* **40**

SHADOWBLASTER (IRE) 4 b.g. Wolfhound (USA) 126 – Swame (USA) (Jade Hunter (USA)) [2001 79: 10.3m 12s⁵ 14m* 16m⁵ 12m⁵ 14.6f⁵ 13.3m⁶ 12g⁶ 12m 14.1m Sep 6] angular gelding: fairly useful handicapper: won at Haydock in May: below **83**

form last 4 starts: barely stays 2m: acts on soft and good to firm going, probably on firm: tongue tied final outing: tends to carry head bit high: sometimes races freely/finds little. *B. Hanbury*

SHADOW DANCING 2 b.f. (Mar 6) Unfuwain (USA) 131 – Salchow 116 (Niniski (USA) 125) [2001 7g³ 8.1s* 8d³ Sep 13] tall, rather angular filly: has scope: half-sister to several winners, including 11.5f winner Meltemison (by Charmer) and 7.5f winner who stayed 1½m Kalko (by Kalaglow): dam, 2-y-o 7f winner who stayed 1¾m, half-sister to Chester Vase winner Gulland (by Unfuwain): useful form: justified favouritism in maiden at Sandown in August easily by 4 lengths from Light Scent, carrying head bit awkwardly (still seemed green): raced quite freely early on when 3¾ lengths third to Half Glance in May Hill Stakes at Doncaster final start: will be suited by 1¼m/1½m: probably capable of better. *M. P. Tregoning* **96 p**

SHADOW ROLL (IRE) 2 ch.f. (Apr 2) Mark of Esteem (IRE) 137 – Warning Shadows (IRE) 113 (Cadeaux Genereux 131) [2001 6m⁶ 6m³ 7g³ 6.1d⁶ 7f⁵ 7d Oct 2] close-coupled, useful-looking filly: third foal: half-sister to 1m winner Shady Point (by Unfuwain): dam, 7f and 1¼m (Sun Chariot Stakes) winner, also second in Irish 1000 Guineas: fair maiden: 9 lengths third to Muklah in listed event at Newmarket third start: last of 21 in nursery at Newmarket final one: should stay 1m: acts on firm and good to soft ground. *C. E. Brittain* **79**

SHADY DEAL 5 b.g. No Big Deal – Taskalady 47 (Touching Wood (USA) 127) [2001 58, a49: e6g f5g f5g e6s e6g f5g 5.7g 6m³ 5m⁵ 5.1m² 5g 5m 5d³ Nov 6] angular gelding: modest handicapper: left M. Usher after sixth start: best at 5f/6f nowadays: acts on equitrack, soft and firm ground: usually races prominently. *Simon Earle* **54 a–**

SHADY SUSPECT (USA) 6 b.g. Shadeed (USA) 135 – Ann Alleged (USA) (Alleged (USA) 138) [2001 f12g Mar 27] behind in maiden. *M. D. Hammond* **–**

SHAFEEQ (FR) 2 ch.c. (Mar 18) Halling (USA) 133 – Ta Awun (USA) 99 (Housebuster (USA)) [2001 7m³ 8m³ 8s⁴ Oct 16] useful-looking colt: second foal: dam, 1¼m winner, out of half-sister to middle-distance performers Ibn Bey (high class) and Roseate Tern (very smart): fairly useful maiden: third at Leicester and Kempton: should be suited by 1¼m/1½m: acts on good to firm ground, below form on soft. *A. C. Stewart* **83**

SHAFFISHAYES 9 ch.g. Clantime 101 – Mischievous Miss 73 (Niniski (USA) 125) [2001 59: 12.4d 12m⁴ 12m³ 12.3m 12.4m 11.1d 12.3g 11.9g Aug 10] lengthy gelding: modest handicapper: stays 1¾m: acts on fibresand, soft and good to firm going: takes good hold, and usually held up. *Mrs M. Reveley* **54**

SHAGRAAN 2 b.c. (Feb 20) Darshaan 133 – L'Ideale (USA) (Alysheba (USA)) [2001 7f 8d 8d Oct 19] 500,000Y: good-topped colt: has a quick action: second living foal: half-brother to 5-y-o Aegean Dream: dam, ran twice in France, half-sister to high-class French performer up to 1½m Loup Sauvage: fair form, not knocked about, in maidens: will be suited by 1¼m+: type to do well in handicaps. *J. L. Dunlop* **69 p**

SHAHIRAH (USA) 3 b.f. Diesis 133 – Shemaq (USA) 120 (Blushing John (USA) 120) [2001 86: 9m⁴ 10.1m Aug 27] big, lengthy filly: had a round action: fairly useful performer, lightly raced: much better effort in handicaps in 2001 when fourth at Goodwood in August, though not impressing with head carriage and giving odd flick of tail: stayed 9f (on toes, beaten before stamina became issue at 1¼m): acted on good to firm going: visits Sahm. *M. P. Tregoning* **90**

SHAH JEHAN (USA) 2 b.c. (Mar 2) Mr Prospector (USA) – Voodoo Lily (USA) (Baldski (USA)) [2001 6g* 7m² 7s⁴ 7d Oct 20] $4,400,000Y: tall, attractive colt: sixth foal: half-brother to 2 winners in USA, including Lily O'Gold (by Slew O'Gold), winner up to 1m and second in Grade 2 8.5f event at 2 yrs: dam US Grade 3 6f winner: useful form: won maiden at Leopardstown in June: good neck second of 4 to Dress To Thrill in listed race at the Curragh: led until well over 1f out when seventh of 8 to Rock of Gibraltar in Dewhurst Stakes at Newmarket final start: should stay 1m: sent to USA. *A. P. O'Brien, Ireland* **104**

SHAHM (IRE) 2 b.g. (Mar 29) Marju (IRE) 127 – Istibshar (USA) 78 (Mr Prospector (USA)) [2001 6m⁵ 6d 6m² 6g⁵ 7d³ 8d 8v p6g Dec 28] good-topped gelding: third living foal: half-brother to 3-y-o Mostabshir: dam, 6f winner, sister to US Grade 3 8.5f winner Namaqualand from very good family: fair maiden: well held in nurseries last 2 starts (sold from J. Gosden 14,000 gns in between): likely to prove best at 7f/1m: acts on good to firm and good to soft going: visored (wandered) sixth outing, blinkered seventh: often tongue tied: has carried head awkwardly. *B. J. Curley* **74**

917

SHAHZAN HOUSE (IRE) 2 b.c. (Feb 2) Sri Pekan (USA) 117 – Nsx 74 (Roi **75 ?**
Danzig (USA)) [2001 7g 7s Oct 16] sturdy colt: fluent mover: third foal: brother to 4-y-o
Camberley: dam 2-y-o 5f winner: burly, better effort (seemingly fair form) when seventh
of 8 to Expected Bonus in minor event at Kempton on debut. *M. A. Jarvis*

SHAKAKHAN 3 ch.f. Night Shift (USA) – Sea Wedding 72 (Groom Dancer (USA) **87**
128) [2001 82: 8s 10.2m³ 10g⁴ 8.1m 9.1d² 8g* 8.1v f8g⁵ Nov 12] good-topped filly: type
to carry condition: fairly useful handicapper: won at Ayr in August: stays 9f: acts on
fibresand and good to soft going, probably on good to firm: sold 22,000 gns. *B. W. Hills*

SHAKRAN 2 ch.c. (Jan 21) Zafonic (USA) 130 – Myself 110 (Nashwan (USA) 135) **90 p**
[2001 6m³ Jul 28] 76,000F, 170,000Y: good-bodied colt: good walker: second foal:
half-brother to 3-y-o Ghayth: dam, 6f (at 2 yrs) and 7f (Nell Gwyn Stakes) winner, half-
sister to smart 5f to 7f performer Bluebook out of Queen Mary winner Pushy: favourite
but burly, shaped well when narrowly-beaten third of 6 to Far Pavilions on only start in
maiden at Ascot, leading briefly 1f out: useful performer in the making, assuming all is
well. *Sir Michael Stoute*

SHALAMANTIKA (IRE) 2 b.f. (Apr 8) Nashwan (USA) 135 – Sharamana (IRE) **67 p**
110 (Darshaan 133) [2001 7d Oct 15] smallish filly: third foal: dam, French 1¼m/1½m
(Prix Minerve) winner, half-sister to Shergar and Shernazar: 10/1, seventh of 20 to Trojan
Princess in maiden at Leicester, some late headway: will be suited by 1¼m+: should do
better. *Sir Michael Stoute*

SHALBEBLUE (IRE) 4 b.g. Shalford (IRE) 124§ – Alberjas (IRE) (Sure Blade **55**
(USA) 130) [2001 68: f11g* 10.3s⁶ 10.4m 12m⁴ Sep 22] modest **a63**
performer: won apprentices maiden at Southwell in January: stays 1½m: acts on good to
firm going, good to soft and fibresand: usually visored/blinkered. *B. Ellison*

SHALLAT (IRE) 3 b.f. Pennekamp (USA) 130 – Zivania (IRE) 101 (Shernazar 131) **59 ?**
[2001 8d 11.1d³ 12m⁴ May 19] 160,000Y: smallish filly: fifth foal: half-sister to several
winners, including smart performers abroad up to 1½m Ivan Luis (1m winner at 2 yrs, by
Lycius) and Zero Problemo (by Priolo): dam, Irish 2-y-o 1m to 9.5f winner, closely
related to very smart French 9f to 11f performer Muroto: modest form at best in maidens:
visits Lujain. *M. R. Channon*

SHALLUS 2 b.g. (Mar 4) Zamindar (USA) 116 – Wild Truffes (IRE) (Danehill (USA) **59**
126) [2001 5v⁴ f5g³ f5g³ 5.1m Sep 10] 10,000F: leggy gelding: fourth foal: half-brother
to a 6f (including at 2 yrs)/7f winner in Italy by Petong: dam lightly-raced maiden: modest
maiden: off 4 months before well beaten in nursery final start: likely to prove best at 5f.
W. G. M. Turner

SHAMAIEL (IRE) 4 b.f. Lycius (USA) 124 – Pearl Kite (USA) 106§ (Silver Hawk **113**
(USA) 123) [2001 99: 10g² 14m³ 12m⁵ 11m* 14g* 13.4d 14.6m Sep 12] rangy filly:
smart performer: better than ever for new stable in 2001, winning handicap at Newbury
(by 5 lengths from The Glen) and listed event at Goodwood (beat Putra Sandhurst ¾
length) in August: well held last 2 starts, in Park Hill at Doncaster final one: effective at
11f and stays 1¾m: raced mostly on good going or firmer: often held up. *G. A. Butler*

*San Miguel March Stakes, Goodwood—Shamaiel confirms her improvement,
beating Putra Sandhurst (left), Akbar (right), Gallery God (rail) and When In Rome*

SHAMAN 4 b.g. Fraam 114 – Magic Maggie 38 (Beveled (USA)) [2001 72: e12g e10g **72**
9.7v 10d 10m² 10g⁶ 9.7m 10m³ 10m³ 9.9d* 10s p10g⁶ p10g* Dec 22] fluent mover: fair
handicapper: won at Salisbury (apprentices) in October and Lingfield in December: best
around 1¼m: acts on any turf going and equitrack/polytrack: game. *G. L. Moore*

SHAMARCO (IRE) 2 b.f. (Mar 13) Common Grounds 118 – Fanciful (IRE) (Mujta- **54**
hid (USA) 118) [2001 6.1g 6.1m 6m Jul 18] 20,000Y: close-coupled filly: second foal:
half-sister to 3-y-o The Fancy Man: dam ran once at 2 yrs in Ireland: modest maiden:
tongue tied second start: best effort final one. *P. W. Harris*

SHAMOKIN 9 b.g. Green Desert (USA) 127 – Shajan (Kris 135) [2001 31: f8s f8g **–**
Feb 26] workmanlike gelding: lightly-raced maiden: tried visored. *F. Watson*

SHAMPOOED (IRE) 7 b.m. Law Society (USA) 130 – White Caps 71 (Shirley **54**
Heights 130) [2001 51: 16.2m⁶ May 26] lightly raced and modest on Flat nowadays:
blinkered once: fair hurdler/chaser. *R. Dickin*

SHAMROCK CITY (IRE) 4 b.c. Rock City 120 – Actualite (Polish Precedent (USA) **–**
131) [2001 114: 8.9g Mar 24] leggy, useful-looking colt: smart performer at 3 yrs:
reportedly badly struck into when tailed off in Dubai Duty Free at Nad Al Sheba on only
outing in 2001: should stay beyond 1¼m: acts on firm going. *P. Howling*

SHAMSAN (IRE) 4 ch.g. Night Shift (USA) – Awayil (USA) 82 (Woodman (USA) **67**
126) [2001 71: 10m⁵ Jun 24] close-coupled gelding: fair handicapper: stays 1¼m: acts on
fibresand, equitrack, good to firm and soft going: tried blinkered/tongue tied: fair winning
novice hurdler. *P. J. Hobbs*

SHAMWARI SONG 6 b.g. Sizzling Melody 117 – Spark Out (Sparkler 130) [2001 **–**
59, a48: f7g f8g⁴ Dec 17] tall gelding: poor performer in 2001: tried visored/blinkered/ **a44**
tongue tied. *K. A. Ryan*

SHANE 3 ch.g. Aragon 118 – Angel Fire (Nashwan (USA) 135) [2001 6g 5m 6g⁶ 8.5s **52**
Sep 25] leggy, unfurnished gelding: third foal: half-brother to fairly useful 1m winner
Shall We Dance (by Rambo Dancer): dam unraced granddaughter of Arc winner All
Along: modest maiden: should stay 1m. *C. W. Thornton*

SHANGHAI CRAB (USA) 5 b.g. Manila (USA) – Saraa Ree (USA) 102 (Caro 133) **54**
[2001 –: f8g f8g f11s⁶ f12g⁶ Feb 3] big, strong gelding: fair performer at 3 yrs: lightly
raced and modest form at best since: barely stays 11f: acts on fibresand and good to firm
going, probably on good to soft. *J. G. Given*

SHANGHAI LADY 5 b.m. Sabrehill (USA) 120 – Session 80 (Reform 132) [2001 –: **–**
9f 14.1d f12g Oct 23] sturdy mare: one-time fair performer: little form since 1999: has
been tongue tied. *G. A. Butler*

SHANNON FLYER (USA) 3 br.g. Irish River (FR) 131 – Stormeor (CAN) (Lypheor **68**
118) [2001 –: 7m 7.1m⁵ 6m² 6.1m* 7f⁶ 7g p8g⁵ Dec 22] rather leggy, quite good-topped
gelding: fair performer: won 3-runner maiden at Warwick in July: stays easy 1m: acts on
polytrack and firm ground, tailed off on heavy: seems no easy ride. *J. W. Hills*

SHANNON'S DREAM 5 b.m. Anshan 119 – Jenny's Call (Petong 126) [2001 –: **–**
f11g f6g Apr 17] no form. *Mrs Barbara Waring*

SHANOOK 2 ch.c. (Feb 2) Rainbow Quest (USA) 134 – Twafeaj (USA) 110 (Topsider **85 p**
(USA)) [2001 7.2v³ Oct 15] fifth foal: closely related to 4-y-o Inthaar: dam, won
Moyglare Stud Stakes, best around 6f: 12/1 and green, promising 2 lengths third of 13 to
Night Passion in maiden at Ayr, leading 3f out and fading only late on: should stay at least
1m: sure to improve. *M. Johnston*

SHANTY 2 b.f. (Feb 5) Selkirk (USA) 129 – Pippas Song 75 (Reference Point 139) **94 p**
[2001 7m 8d* Oct 3] fourth foal: half-sister to useful 5f to 7f winner Nightbird (by Night
Shift): dam, 1½m winner, half-sister to 3-y-o Rockerlong and to dam of 3-y-o Superstar
Leo: 10/1, stepped up considerably on debut form when winning 17-runner maiden at
Salisbury by short head from Proserpine (pair 14 lengths clear), staying on strongly: will
stay at least 1¼m: should make at least a useful 3-y-o. *B. W. Hills*

SHARAF (IRE) 8 b.g. Sadler's Wells (USA) 132 – Marie de Flandre (FR) 109 (Crystal **53 §**
Palace (FR) 132) [2001 56§: 18m² 21m⁵ 16.4g³ 16g 17.2g Oct 1] lengthy gelding: modest
handicapper, winless since 1998: stays 21f: acts on soft going, good to firm and fibresand:
tried blinkered/visored: not to be trusted. *Mrs A. J. Perrett*

SHARA (IRE) 3 b.f. Kahyasi 130 – Sharamana (IRE) 110 (Darshaan 133) [2001 10g⁴ **75**
11.7d² 12.1g³ 11.6v Oct 8] second foal: dam, French 1¼m/1½m (Prix Minerve) winner,

half-sister to Shergar and Shernazar: fair maiden: stays 1½m: acts on good to soft going. *Sir Michael Stoute*

SHARARAH 2 br.f. (May 1) Machiavellian (USA) 123 – Raknah (IRE) 91 (Night **63 P** Shift (USA)) [2001 6d⁵ Nov 2] fourth foal: closely related to UAE 1m/1¼m winner Murjan (by Lycius) and half-sister to fairly useful 7f to 8.5f winner in Britain/UAE My Pleasure (by Cadeaux Genereux): dam 5f to 7f winner: 33/1, shaped much better than result when 8 lengths fifth of 20 to Feet So Fast in maiden at Newmarket, short of room 2f out before keeping on well under considerate handling: will stay 1m: sure to improve good deal and win races. *E. A. L. Dunlop*

SHARAZAN (IRE) 8 b.g. Akarad (FR) 130 – Sharaniya (USA) 117 (Alleged (USA) **62** 138) [2001 59: 18v⁵ 21.6s³ Apr 23] smallish gelding: modest performer: stays 21.6f: acts on soft and good to firm ground: sometimes blinkered earlier in career, visored once. *O. O'Neill*

SHARED HARMONY (IRE) 3 b.g. Common Grounds 118 – Harmer (IRE) 72 **63 d** (Alzao (USA) 117) [2001 48: 6m² 6d 6m 6m 8f 7s Oct 5] modest maiden: best effort on reappearance: should stay 7f: slowly away last 3 outings. *P. W. Harris*

SHARK GAMES 3 b.f. Mind Games 121 – Sinking (Midyan (USA) 124) [2001 7d 7g⁴ 8s May 18] big, lengthy filly: fourth foal: half-sister to 5f/6f winner Molly Brown (by Rudimentary) and Italian 7f/1m performer Stato King (by Statoblest), both useful: dam unraced: signs of only a little ability in 3 maidens. *R. Hannon*

SHARK (IRE) 8 b.g. Tirol 127 – Gay Appeal 76 (Star Appeal 133) [2001 f11g 10g – 11.8d 16.2s Aug 16] of no account nowadays. *K. A. Morgan*

SHARKS EYES (IRE) 2 br.f. (Feb 17) Marju (IRE) 127 – Dwingeloo (IRE) 83 – (Dancing Dissident (USA) 119) [2001 5s 6g Jun 12] 5,000Y: smallish filly: second foal: dam 2-y-o 5f winner: no form in maidens: lost action and pulled up on debut. *T. D. Easterby*

SHARMY (IRE) 5 b.g. Caerleon (USA) 132 – Petticoat Lane (Ela-Mana-Mou 132) – [2001 107: 8g Sep 15] close-coupled, quite attractive gelding: has a short, unimpressive action: lightly raced: useful at 2 yrs/3 yrs: gelded and off 16 months, well held only Flat outing in 2001. *Ian Williams*

SHAROURA 5 ch.m. Inchinor 119 – Kinkajoo 53 (Precocious 126) [2001 79: 6.1v 8g **66** 5f 6f 5m 5d⁵ 6d 6m 5.1g 6f* f6g⁵ 5.1d⁵ f6g² f6g f5g³ f5s⁵ f5s⁶ Dec 18] angular mare: poor mover: fair handicapper: left D. Nicholls after eighth start: won at Pontefract in September: best at 5f/6f: acts on fibresand, equitrack, firm and soft going: seems effective visored or not: has had tongue tied: has hung right. *J. M. Bradley*

SHARP BELLINE (IRE) 4 b.g. Robellino (USA) 127 – Moon Watch 64 (Night **52 §** Shift (USA)) [2001 61, a67: f12g 16.2m⁴ 16.1m May 24] modest maiden handicapper: stays 2m: acts on good to firm going and fibresand: well beaten in visor/blinkers at 3 yrs: one to treat with caution. *J. L. Harris*

SHARP CITY 2 b.g. (Apr 1) Rock City 120 – Mary Miller 71 (Sharpo 132) [2001 6d **56** 7m 5m⁴ Sep 30] 500 2-y-o: leggy, workmanlike gelding: sixth foal: half-brother to 3 winners abroad, including a sprint winner in Scandinavia by Chilibang: dam maiden who stayed 7f: 100/1, first form (modest) in maidens when 11¾ lengths fourth of 10 to Dominica at Musselburgh, prominent 3f: may prove best at 5f. *A. C. Whillans*

SHARP COMMAND 8 ch.g. Sharpo 132 – Bluish (USA) (Alleged (USA) 138) – [2001 f16.2s Jan 11] good-topped gelding: winning hurdler/chaser: very lightly raced on Flat nowadays. *S. Mellor*

SHARP DECISION 2 ch.f. (Apr 22) Greensmith 121 – Nihaayib (Kris 135) [2001 **67** 5.1m³ 5g³ 5d³ f6g Oct 22] 10,500 2-y-o, resold 3,000 2-y-o: smallish, lengthy, rather dipped-backed filly: fourth foal: half-sister to a winner in Czech Republic by Top Waltz: dam unraced out of half-sister to Shadeed: fair form in maidens: well beaten in nursery final start: should stay at least 6f. *Miss D. A. McHale*

SHARP EDGE BOY 5 gr.g. Mystiko (USA) 124 – Leap Castle (Never So Bold 135) **44** [2001 55, a46: 6s 6f 7m 5.7g 5.7g⁴ 7f Aug 14] good-bodied, close-coupled gelding: poor handicapper: stays 7f: acts on any turf going: tried visored/blinkered/tongue tied: very slowly away third start. *J. M. Bradley*

SHARPE'S LADY 3 b.f. Prince Des Coeurs (USA) – To The Point 96 (Sharpen Up – 127) [2001 7.1s 7m 5.7m f7s Dec 15] half-sister to several winners in Britain/USA, including fairly useful 6f (at 2 yrs) and 1¼m winner Kings Assembly (by Presidium):

dam 2-y-o 5f winner: no sign of ability in maidens: left N. Williams after third start. *Miss K. M. George*

SHARP GOSSIP (IRE)   5 b.g. College Chapel 122 – Idle Gossip (Runnett 125) **70**
[2001 77: f8g⁴ f8g⁵ Jun 21] sparely-made gelding: fair performer: stays 1m: acts on **a73**
fibresand, heavy and good to firm ground: effective blinkered or not. *J. A. R. Toller*

SHARP HAT   7 ch.g. Shavian 125 – Madam Trilby (Grundy 137) [2001 79, a67: e5g* **89**
e5g³ e5g* 5d⁴ 5m⁵ 5m⁵ 5m 5f* 6d 5m 5m 5m 5d 5m* 6m* 5g 5g 5s⁴ 5d³ 5m 6m² 5d* 6d **a82**
5v⁴ f6g f5s⁶ f5s* Dec 18] leggy, angular gelding: fairly useful performer: had a good year,
winning minor events at Lingfield, Beverley and Leicester, and handicaps at Lingfield,
Thirsk, Newcastle and Wolverhampton: best at 5f/easy 6f: acts on any turf going, fibresand and equitrack: well held in blinkers earlier in career: has gone freely, including to
post: effective making running or held up: tough. *D. W. Chapman*

SHARPINCH   3 b.c. Beveled (USA) – Giant Nipper (Nashwan (USA) 135) [2001 **68**
58p: f7g² 6.1d 7f f8g² 7m² 8.5d 8f 8.1f 7s* f7g² f6g f7g⁴ Dec 11] fairly useful on **a88**
all-weather, fair on turf: won handicap at Lingfield in October: ran well next time:
effective at 7f/1m: acts on fibresand, soft and good to firm going: has pulled hard.
P. R. Chamings

SHARP PLAY   6 b.g. Robellino (USA) 127 – Child's Play (USA) (Sharpen Up 127) **106**
[2001 104: 10m⁴ 10g⁵ 10f 10.3f⁵ 10.4m 9.9m 8g Aug 2] smallish, good-topped gelding:
useful handicapper: good fourth to The Whistling Teal in Zetland Gold Cup at Redcar in
May: respectable efforts at best after: best around 1¼m: has won on heavy going, best
efforts on good or firmer: blinkered final start: usually held up: sold 5,500 gns, joined
D. Vienna in USA. *M. Johnston*

SHARP REBUFF   10 b.h. Reprimand 122 – Kukri (Kris 135) [2001 67, a44: 7m May **–**
26] lengthy horse: poor mover: fair handicapper in 2000: well held only outing at 10 yrs:
has been visored. *Mrs L. Stubbs*

SHARP SHUFFLE (IRE)   8 ch.g. Exactly Sharp (USA) 121 – Style (Homing 130) **52**
[2001 66, a60: f8.5g f8.5g f8.5g 8m 8m⁵ 7.1m 8f 8.1g⁶ f8² 8.1g Sep 13] smallish gelding:
unimpressive mover: modest performer: stays 8.5f: acts on fibresand, equitrack, firm and
good to soft going: held up: sometimes slowly away. *Ian Williams*

SHARP SOPRANO   2 b.f. (May 9) Mon Tresor 123 – Gentle Star 77 (Comedy Star **57**
(USA) 121) [2001 6.1m 7m⁶ 5.1m⁶ Sep 10] 3,000Y: half-sister to fairly useful 7f to 1¼m
winner Polish Spirit (by Emarati) and 1988 2-y-o 5f seller winner Tell Me This (by
Goldhills Pride): dam 6f winner: modest maiden: best effort at Bath final start: may prove
best at 5f/6f. *B. R. Millman*

SHARP SPICE   5 b.m. Lugana Beach 116 – Ewar Empress (IRE) 57 (Persian Bold **67**
123) [2001 67: 12m³ 11.9m³ 12g⁴ 13.9d⁵ 12d⁴ f12g⁶ p13g² Dec 29] angular mare: fair **a60**
handicapper: barely stays 1¾m: acts on any turf going and polytrack: tried visored:
sometimes slowly away: seems best held up. *D. J. Coakley*

SHARP STEEL   6 ch.g. Beveled (USA) – Shift Over (USA) 62 (Night Shift (USA)) **43**
[2001 68: f8g* f8g² f8g f8g f8g f8g⁴ 7m⁵ f8g f8g f8g f11g² Nov 30] **a65 d**
leggy, workmanlike gelding: fair at best on all-weather, poor on turf: won seller at
Southwell in January: below form after fifth start: stays 11f: easily best form on fibresand:
tried visored earlier in career. *Miss S. J. Wilton*

SHARVIE   4 b.g. Rock Hopper 124 – Heresheis 69 (Free State 125) [2001 –, a55: f16g² **48**
f16.2s³ f16.2g* f16.2g² f16g⁴ 16g 16d 17.1d f16g⁶ f16.2g³ f16.2g³ f16.2s Dec 18] modest **a58**
handicapper on all-weather, poor on turf: won at Wolverhampton in February: stays 2m:
acts on fibresand/equitrack, yet to race on extremes of going on turf: takes good hold:
reliable. *Mrs Lydia Pearce*

SHASTA   2 b.f. (Feb 15) Shareef Dancer (USA) 135 – Themeda 69 (Sure Blade (USA) **– p**
130) [2001 7g Sep 11] fourth foal: closely related to 4-y-o Odyn Dancer: dam, unreliable
11f winner, half-sister to smart sprinter Cathedral: 40/1 and green, well-held eleventh of
17 in maiden at Lingfield, getting hang of things late on: should be suited by 1¼m+:
likely to improve. *W. R. Muir*

SHATARAH   2 ch.f. (Apr 30) Gulch (USA) – Arjuzah (IRE) 110 (Ahonoora 122) **79 p**
[2001 7m³ Aug 30] fourth foal: closely related to 3-y-o Malhub and half-sister to useful
6f winner (including at 2 yrs) Mutaakkid (by Dayjur): dam 7f winner: 15/2 and green,
considerably handled when 2¾ lengths third of 16 to Brown Eyes in maiden at Salisbury:
should improve. *J. H. M. Gosden*

SHATIN BEAUTY 4 b.f. Mistertopogigo (IRE) 118 – Starisk 47 (Risk Me (FR) 127) **42 §**
[2001 –: 5v 5m⁵ 5d 5m² 5m⁶ 5m 5m 5m 6g 5f⁵ 5g 5g Sep 3] good-topped filly: poor
performer nowadays: best at 5f: acts on firm going: has edged right: inconsistent.
Miss L. A. Perratt

SHATIN DOLLYBIRD (IRE) 3 ch.f. Up And At 'em 109 – Pumpona (USA) –
(Sharpen Up 127) [2001 70: 5m 6m May 30] good-topped filly: fair performer at 2 yrs:
well held in handicaps in 2001: should stay 6f: acts on firm ground, well below form on
good to soft: tends to hang right. *Miss L. A. Perratt*

SHATIN LAD 4 b.g. Timeless Times (USA) 99 – Fauve 71 (Dominion 123) [2001 6g –
Aug 31] last both starts. *Miss L. A. Perratt*

SHATIN PRINCESS (IRE) 2 b.f. (Apr 22) Darnay 117 – Lady Conchita (IRE) **64**
(Whistling Deer 117) [2001 5d 6m⁶ 6m⁴ 5f⁴ 6m 7m³ 5g 6m 6d 5g Nov 7] 10,000
2-y-o: leggy filly: third reported foal: dam well beaten in bumpers/placed in points in
Ireland: modest maiden: best effort in Hamilton nursery eighth start: stays 6f: acts on firm
going: usually races prominently. *Miss L. A. Perratt*

SHATIN VENTURE (IRE) 4 b.g. Lake Coniston (IRE) 131 – Justitia (Dunbeath **84 d**
(USA) 127) [2001 99: 6d 6g 6g 7f⁵ 7f 6s 7d⁵ 7s³ 7.1s 7.2m 6v Oct 16] good-topped
gelding: useful performer at 3 yrs, on downgrade in 2001: stays 7f: acts on any going.
Miss L. A. Perratt

SHAVEN ROCK 4 b.g. Rock City 120 – So Bold (Never So Bold 135) [2001 –: f11g⁵ **38**
f9.4s⁴ f8s Feb 9] poor form in 4 starts: should stay 1m. *K. R. Burke*

SHAW VENTURE 4 ch.g. Whittingham (IRE) 104 – Al Shany 92 (Burslem 123) –
[2001 46, a–: 10d May 16] poor form at 3 yrs: well held only outing in 2001: tried
blinkered. *B. Palling*

SHAYADI (IRE) 4 b.g. Kahyasi 130 – Shayrdia (IRE) 57 (Storm Bird (CAN) 134) **101**
[2001 89: 10s* 10s 10.3m 10.4g 15f² 13.9g Aug 22] leggy, quite attractive gelding: first
foal: dam twice-raced daughter of smart 1m and 1½m winner Shayraz: useful performer:
trained at 3 yrs in Ireland by J. Oxx: won minor event at Pontefract (carried head high/
flashed tail under pressure) in April: probably unlucky when very good length second to
Jack Dawson in handicap at Ayr in June: ran no sort of race in Ebor at York final start:
stays 15f: acts on firm and soft going. *M. Johnston*

SHAYZARA (IRE) 4 b.f. Turtle Island (IRE) 123 – Shayraz 110 (Darshaan 133) –
[2001 12g May 5] lengthy, useful-looking filly: half-sister to 3 winners, including useful
1m/1¼m winner Shaylan (by Primo Dominie) and a winner in Belgium/France around
1½m by Kahyasi: dam, 1m and 1½m winner, half-sister to smart miler Shaikiya: well
held in maiden on Flat debut: fair winning hurdler. *N. J. Henderson*

SHEARWATER 4 b.f. Shareef Dancer (USA) 135 – Sea Ballad (USA) (Bering 136) –
[2001 –: e12g⁶ e13g⁶ Feb 7] well held in 3 maidens: refused to enter stalls on intended
debut. *G. L. Moore*

SHEER BLISS (IRE) 2 b.f. (Feb 20) Sadler's Wells (USA) 132 – Sheer Audacity **86 p**
(Troy 137) [2001 8.2v* 8v Oct 23] leggy, unfurnished filly: closely related to Derby
winner Oath (by Fairy King) and high-class 1m to 1¼m performer Pelder (by Be My
Guest), and half-sister to several winners, including smart 1m to 1¾m winner Sheer
Danzig (by Roi Danzig): dam Italian maiden: won 17-runner maiden at Nottingham in
October by short head from Maimana, short of room before staying on really well to lead
on line: stiff task, well-held seventh in Prix des Reservoirs at Deauville: will be suited by
1¼m/1½m: probably at least a useful prospect. *Sir Mark Prescott*

SHEER DEVIOUS (IRE) 3 ch.g. Dr Devious (IRE) 127 – Peruke (IRE) 102 –
(Thatching 131) [2001 f8g⁶ f8.5g 8s May 18] IR 60,000Y: sturdy gelding: first foal: dam,
Irish 6f winner, half-sister to smart sprinter Carol's Treasure: well held in maidens.
B. W. Hills

SHEER FACE 7 b.g. Midyan (USA) 124 – Rock Face 77 (Ballad Rock 122) [2001 **60**
69: 10f 11.5f⁵ 10m⁶ 10g 10g² 10.2g³ 10m 10m Sep 11] close-coupled gelding: modest
performer: stays 1¼m: yet to race on heavy ground, acts on any other turf going: tried
blinkered: has looked none too genuine. *W. R. Muir*

SHEER FOCUS (IRE) 3 b.g. Eagle Eyed (USA) 111 – Persian Danser (IRE) 69 **65**
(Persian Bold 123) [2001 64: f8.5s⁴ f6s⁶ f8g⁵ 9.9m⁶ 8.1g⁶ 7f 7m⁶ 8g* 8.1m* 8d 8m 8.1s
8.5s⁵ 8d f8.5g⁴ f8.5g⁵ Nov 27] leggy, angular gelding: fair handicapper: won at Pontefract
in July and Warwick in August: probably stays 1¼m: acts on fibresand, soft and good to
firm going: has had tongue tied: often races freely: none too consistent. *E. J. Alston*

SHEER PASSION 3 b.c. Distant Relative 128 – Yldizlar 77 (Star Appeal 133) [2001 –
66: f7g f8.5g 6m 7.1g 8.1f 10g 8.1g Sep 13] good-topped colt: fair maiden at 2 yrs: well
held in 2001, leaving B. Hills after second start: should stay 7f: acts on good to firm
going: has been slowly away: tried visored. *R. Brotherton*

SHEIK'N SWING 2 b.f. (May 10) Celtic Swing 138 – Elegantissima 57 (Polish –
Precedent (USA) 131) [2001 f7g Jul 27] 6,000F, 1,000Y: second foal: dam, maiden who
stayed 1m, out of close relation of Pebbles: 12/1, well beaten in Southwell seller.
W. G. M. Turner

SHEILA BLIGE 2 ch.f. (Apr 5) Zamindar (USA) 116 – Stripanoora (Ahonoora 122) **83**
[2001 5g* 5m 5.2m 5m⁶ 6m 6m Sep 12] 27,000Y: leggy, close-coupled filly: half-sister
to several winners, including smart 1m (at 2 yrs) to 1½m winner Naked Welcome (by
Most Welcome) and fairly useful 1996 2-y-o 5f/6f winner Olympic Spirit (by Puissance):
dam maiden who stayed 1m: fairly useful performer: won maiden at Warwick in May:
best efforts in valuable sales race at Newbury and Molecomb Stakes at Goodwood third/
fourth starts: best form at 5f: raced only on good/good to firm going: reared stall (well
beaten) final outing. *A. Berry*

SHEILAS FANTASY 2 b.c. (Mar 15) So Factual (USA) 120 – Aspen (IRE) 65 **53**
(Scenic 128) [2001 5s 5g⁶ f6g⁴ 6d⁶ 5m⁶ Jul 4] first foal: dam ran twice at 2 yrs: modest
maiden: trained by Mrs L. Jewell third/fourth starts only (visored in sellers both times):
blinkered final one. *Patrick Mooney, Ireland*

SHELL-B-COSMIC 2 ch.f. (Mar 26) Cosmonaut – Shelley Marie 67 (Gunner B –
126) [2001 5m f6g 6g⁶ 7m Jul 24] lengthy filly: first reported foal: dam 2-y-o 5f winner:
little form in sellers. *J. G. Given*

SHEPHERDS REST (IRE) 9 b.g. Accordion – Mandy's Last (Krayyan 117) [2001 –
–: f14g f16g May 21] no form on Flat since 1999: tried visored: won over fences in
October. *S. Mellor*

SHEPPARD'S WATCH 3 b.f. Night Shift (USA) – Sheppard's Cross 88 (Soviet Star **108**
(USA) 128) [2001 99: 7d 7m⁴ 8m* 8.5m* 8g⁶ 7m² 9f⁴ 8f Dec 15] attractive, good-
topped filly: useful performer: won listed races at Goodwood in May and Epsom in June:
beat Lady Miletrian by ½ length on latter course, again displaying good turn of foot:
good neck second to Mauri Moon in listed race at Goodwood in August (final outing for
M. Tregoning): in frame next 2 starts, in Garden City Breeders' Cup Handicap at Belmont
and non-graded stakes at Calder: stays 9f: acts on firm going. *C. Clement, USA*

SHERAZADE 2 ch.f. (Mar 19) Beveled (USA) – Miss Ritz 65 (Robellino (USA) 127) **61**
[2001 6v⁵ 6v 6v⁶ Nov 8] 3,000Y: fourth foal: half-sister to fairly useful 1997 2-y-o 5f
winner Rare Indigo (by Timeless Times): dam 7f winner: modest form in maidens/sales
race: should prove best at 5f/6f: raced only on heavy going. *G. L. Moore*

SHEREKIYA (IRE) 3 b.f. Lycius (USA) 124 – Sheriya (USA) (Green Dancer (USA) **66**
132) [2001 64: 8d Aug 19] fair form on first of 2 starts at 2 yrs: well held only outing in
2001. *Sir Michael Stoute*

SHERIFF 10 b.g. Midyan (USA) 124 – Daisy Warwick (USA) 91 (Sir Gaylord) [2001 **51**
67, a–: 17.2f 17.2g 18m f16g 16g⁵ 18s Oct 22] small, close-coupled gelding: bad mover:
modest handicapper: stays 2¼m: acts on equitrack and any turf going: blinkered once.
J. W. Hills

SHERIFF SONG 3 br.g. Hernando (FR) 127 – Zippy Zoe 46 (Rousillon (USA) 133) **50**
[2001 53: 9.9m 10.1m 10g⁶ 10m⁶ 10m⁵ f11g⁶ Jul 27] leggy, sparely-made gelding:
modest maiden handicapper: stays 1¼m: acts on fibresand and good to firm going, well
held on soft: races freely. *M. W. Easterby*

SHERINGHAM (USA) 4 b.f. Robin Des Pins (USA) 119 – Kimberley (URU) –
(Paradise Bay 110) [2001 80p: 7g May 30] won maiden at Southwell at 3 yrs: well held
only outing in 2001: sent to Bahrain. *P. J. Makin*

SHERVANA 5 b.m. Cigar 68 – Marsdale (Royal Palace 131) [2001 –: 8m May 29] –
quite good-topped mare: behind in maidens/handicap. *C. Drew*

SHERZABAD (IRE) 4 b. or br.g. Doyoun 124 – Sheriya (USA) (Green Dancer **57**
(USA) 132) [2001 –: 10v⁶ 11.8f⁵ 12m 12.6f 10m² 11.5g* 12g³ 11.9m⁵ 10.2f p10g⁶ Nov
28] sturdy, lengthy gelding: modest handicapper: won at Lingfield in August: stays 1½m:
probably acts on any going: visored last 7 starts: tried tongue tied earlier in career: best
held up. *H. J. Collingridge*

923

SHE'S BONNIE (IRE)   4 b.f. Mtoto 134 – Clyde Goddess (IRE) 92 (Scottish Reel   – §
123) [2001 11.8d 10.3f p10g Dec 12] 500 3-y-o: lengthy filly: second foal: half-sister to
5-y-o High Sun: dam 2-y-o 1m winner: no form: virtually refused to race on debut. *W. de
Best-Turner*

SHE'S FLASH (IRE)   2 b.f. (Apr 25) Woodborough (USA) 112 – Beechwood Quest   57
(IRE) 65 (River Falls 113) [2001 5.1f⁴ 5m 5f³ 7g⁶ f8.5s³ 7.5g Sep 19] 3,500Y: rather
unfurnished filly: first foal: dam 2-y-o 5f seller winner: modest maiden: left B. Rothwell
after second start: seems barely to stay 8.5f: acts on fibresand, raced only on good going
or firmer on turf. *G. A. Swinbank*

SHESGOTTOHAVEIT (IRE)   2 b.f. (May 11) Flying Spur (AUS) – Carousel Mall   –
(IRE) (Soughaan (USA) 111) [2001 f8g f7g⁶ Dec 14] IR 3,000Y: half-sister to winner in
Czech Republic by Ilium: dam unraced: well held in maidens at Southwell. *J. A. Glover*

SHE'S SMOKIN   3 b.f. Cigar 68 – Beau Dada (IRE) 66 (Pine Circle (USA)) [2001 f7s   –
f6g f5g 6m 6g f6g Nov 16] sister to 4-y-o Smokin Beau and half-sister to winner in
Sweden by Kylian: dam 6f (at 2 yrs) to 1m winner who stayed 1¼m: little form.
J. Cullinan

SHE WADI WADI   3 b.f. Green Desert (USA) 127 – Great Inquest 80 (Shernazar 131)   61
[2001 50: 7g 8.3g 8f³ 7g² 8d 8m 8.5g Sep 19] useful-looking filly: good walker: modest
maiden handicapper: stays 1m: acts on firm and soft going. *A. C. Stewart*

SHIBBOLETH (USA)   4 b.c. Danzig (USA) – Razyana (USA) 87 (His Majesty   118
(USA)) [2001 116: 7g* 8m 7m* 6m⁵ Jul 12] big, good sort: has a quick, fluent action:
smart performer: off 11 months (reportedly underwent operation for chip on a hind leg)
before winning minor event at Newmarket in May: also successful in Hitchins Criterion
Stakes there (by 1¼ lengths from Reel Buddy) in June: creditable 5 lengths fifth to Mozart
in July Cup on same course on final outing: at least as effective at 6f/7f as at 1m: yet to
race on extremes of going: often tongue tied (wasn't when reportedly swallowing tongue
in Queen Anne Stakes at Royal Ascot second outing): free-going sort: has carried head
awkwardly/flashed tail under pressure/seemed reluctant to post: joined R. Frankel in
USA. *H. R. A. Cecil*

SHIBUNI'S FALCON   4 b.c. Polar Falcon (USA) 126 – Shibuni (Damister (USA)   114
123) [2001 114: 11g 10m⁶ 12m* 12g 12g 10s⁴ 11s⁴ 10d* 10d* Nov 18] approx 3,200Y in
Italy: second foal: dam unraced daughter of Italian Group 3 1m winner Saint Samba:
smart performer: winner of 7 races prior to 2001, notably Premio Guido Berardelli at
Rome at 2 yrs and 2 listed races at Milan at 3 yrs, when also good fourth to Golden
Snake in Gran Premio del Jockey Club at same track: successful in minor event in
June and handicap in October, both at Milan, and Premio Roma (blinkered, beat Monos
2½ lengths) in November: stays 1½m: probably acts on any ground: front runner.
M. Guarnieri, Italy

SHIFTY   2 b.c. (Mar 2) Night Shift (USA) – Crodelle (IRE) (Formidable (USA) 125)   87
[2001 6m² 7f* 7g² 8g 7d Oct 2] 155,000Y: well-made colt: fifth foal: half-brother to 5-y-o
Ela Athena: dam French 9.5f winner: fairly useful performer: won maiden at Lingfield in
July: good second to Dupont in minor event on same course next time: below form last 2
starts: should stay 1m: acts on firm going: joined J. Bethell. *L. M. Cumani*

SHII-TAKE'S GIRL   3 ch.f. Deploy 131 – Super Sally 108 (Superlative 118) [2001   80
72: 10s³ 12d⁴ 9.9m³ 10m* 10d 10g 11m⁶ 10v⁶ Oct 8] angular filly: fairly useful handicapper: made all at Newbury in July: better at 1¼m than 1½m: acts on firm and soft
ground: blinkered third to sixth starts: none too consistent: sold 8,000 gns. *Mrs
A. J. Perrett*

SHINBONE ALLEY   4 b.g. Lake Coniston (IRE) 131 – Villota (Top Ville 129) [2001   – §
82§, a–§: 5s 5s f6g Nov 27] lengthy gelding: fairly useful performer at best: little form in
2001: untrustworthy. *D. W. Chapman*

SHINING OASIS (IRE)   3 b.f. Mujtahid (USA) 118 – Desert Maiden 74§ (Green   73 d
Desert (USA) 127) [2001 73: 8.3g 8.1m⁵ 10m⁴ 10g⁶ 8.3m f9.4s⁶ 12g f9.4g f8g Nov 26]
angular filly: fair performer: generally disappointing in 2001: left P. Cole before final
outing: stays 1m: raced only on good/good to firm ground on turf: blinkered seventh/
eighth starts. *N. Tinkler*

SHINNER   3 b.f. Charnwood Forest (IRE) 125 – Trick (IRE) 76 (Shirley Heights 130)   55
[2001 67, a56: 7g 8.1d³ 8.5f 7g 6g 6d⁴ 7s Oct 16] smallish filly: modest performer: a–
probably stays 1m: acts on good to firm and good to soft going: often races prominently:
none too consistent: sold 5,000 gns. *T. D. Easterby*

SHINY 2 b.f. (Apr 20) Shambo 113 – Abuzz 101 (Absalom 128) [2001 6m⁵ 5f* 5m 6g⁵ Jul 10] tall, useful-looking filly: has scope: eighth foal: sister to 3-y-o Shush and half-sister to several useful winners, including useful 5f/6f winner (including at 2 yrs) World Premier (by Shareef Dancer) and 7-y-o Puzzlement: dam, 5f (at 2 yrs) and 7f winner, half-sister to dam of very smart miler Revoque: fairly useful performer: won listed race at Sandown in May by ¾ length from Maktavish: respectable efforts in Queen Mary Stakes at Royal Ascot and Cherry Hinton Stakes at Newmarket after: should stay at least 7f: raced only on good going or firmer. *C. E. Brittain* **92**

SHIPTON WOOD 3 b.c. Caerleon (USA) 132 – Bolas 118 (Unfuwain (USA) 131) [2001 11s⁶ 11.8m⁴ 14.1m² 14.1m² Jul 14] angular, good-topped colt: third foal: half-brother to 5-y-o Twice: dam, 11f/1½m (including Irish Oaks) winner, out of half-sister to Gold Cup winner Longboat: fairly useful maiden: unlucky when head second at Salisbury final start: likely to stay 2m: sold 16,000 gns in October. *H. R. A. Cecil* **85**

SHIRAZI 3 b.g. Mtoto 134 – Al Shadeedah (USA) 86 (Nureyev (USA) 131) [2001 77: 9s³ 10.2f⁴ 9.9m² 9m* 9d 10.1m* 10.1g 10v Oct 8] strong gelding: fairly useful performer: won maiden at Ripon in July and minor event at Epsom in August: gelded after final start: races freely, but stays 1¼m: acts on soft and good to firm ground. *J. W. Hills* **86**

SHIRLEY COLLINS 2 b.f. (Apr 19) Robellino (USA) 127 – Kisumu (Damister (USA) 123) [2001 6g⁵ 6g 7g⁴ 5g 7s Oct 25] 46,000Y: good-topped filly: fourth foal: half-sister to very smart Italian/US performer up to 1½m Timboroa (by Salse): dam unraced half-sister to very smart 7f/1m performer Efisio and US Grade 1 1¼m winner Mountain Bear: fair maiden: best efforts first 2 starts: may prove best at 5f/6f. *M. L. W. Bell* **65**

SHIRLEY FONG (IRE) 3 b.f. Bluebird (USA) 125 – Decrescendo (IRE) (Polish Precedent (USA) 131) [2001 58: 8m 10m Jun 25] sturdy, compact filly: modest maiden handicapper: stays 1¼m: best form on good ground or firmer. *C. F. Wall* **57**

SHIRLEY NOT 5 gr.g. Paris House 123 – Hollia 72 (Touch Boy 109) [2001 79: 5m³ 5.1f⁴ 5m⁴ 5.1f 5f⁵ 5g⁵ 5g⁴ 5.1g⁴ 5d³ 5g⁴ 5m⁵ 7.5d Sep 25] big, lengthy gelding: fair handicapper: best at 5f: acts on firm going, soft and fibresand: often blinkered/visored in 2000: has run in snatches/looked wayward. *S. Gollings* **71**

SHIRLEY'S SHINE (IRE) 2 b.f. (Apr 25) Sri Pekan (USA) 117 – Encore Une Fois (IRE) 84 (Shirley Heights 130) [2001 7g 8.5m Aug 26] IR 5,000Y, resold 5,000Y: robust, lengthy filly: fourth foal: half-sister to 5-y-o Pluralist: dam, 1½m to 2m winner, out of smart performer up to 7f Guest Performer: better effort in maidens (poor form) when eighth of 17 at Leicester on debut: dead. *S. C. Williams* **46**

SHOAL CREEK (IRE) 4 b.c. Fairy King (USA) – Catalonia Express (USA) (Diesis 133) [2001 112: 10g³ 8d² 7s* Nov 11] good-bodied colt: smart performer: blinkered, won listed race at Leopardstown in November by 4 lengths from Tiger Royal: effective at 7f to 10.4f: acted on good ground or softer: also blinkered/visored final 3 starts in 2000: off 5 months after first start in 2001. *A. P. O'Brien, Ireland* **114**

SHOCKLAND (IRE) 2 b.g. (Apr 30) Zamindar (USA) 116 – Eurythmic 58 (Pharly (FR) 130) [2001 5m⁵ 6m² 6g 6.3d 7d 7m⁴ 7m 6g⁶ 7g⁴ 6.1d⁴ 5g⁶ Sep 2] IR 5,000Y: strong, close-coupled gelding: fourth living foal: half-brother to 3 winners, including 3-y-o I Got Rhythm: dam 1½m winner who stayed 2m: fair maiden: lost form after sixth start: stays 7f: acts on good to firm ground: blinkered final outing: subsequently gelded. *A. Berry* **75 d**

SHOESHINE BOY (IRE) 3 b. or br.g. Prince Sabo 123 – Susie Sunshine (IRE) 81 (Waajib 121) [2001 94: 5.1s⁴ 5s⁶ 5.1f³ 5m* 5g 5f 5g 5g 6g 5s 5v⁵ Oct 29] smallish, strong gelding: useful handicapper: won at Thirsk in May by head from Prince of Blues: below form after: probably best at 5f: acts on any turf going: blinkered once in 2000: wandered/found nothing penultimate start. *B. J. Meehan* **102**

SHOETIME SHADOW 2 ch.g. (Apr 2) Timeless Times (USA) 99 – Willrack Farrier 73 (Lugana Beach 116) [2001 f5g 5.2m⁵ 5m⁵ 6g 6.3s 5v Oct 17] 4,000Y: third foal: brother to 3-y-o Timeless Farrier: dam 2-y-o 5f winner: modest maiden: should stay 6f: acts on good to firm ground. *C. N. Allen* **52**

SHOLAY (IRE) 2 b.c. (Mar 10) Bluebird (USA) 125 – Splicing 82 (Sharpo 132) [2001 5.7g³ 7d² 7g* Nov 5] 60,000Y: lightly-made colt: second foal: half-brother to 3-y-o Pairing: dam, 5f/6f winner, sister to smart sprinter Splice: fairly useful form: second to Eastern Image in minor event at Redcar before landing odds in maiden there by 3½ lengths from Hatalan, quickening clear from over 1f out: not sure to stay 1m. *G. A. Butler* **88**

SHOLOKHOV (IRE) 2 b.c. (Feb 22) Sadler's Wells (USA) 132 – La Meilleure 86 **108** (Lord Gayle (USA) 124) [2001 7g* 7g² 7m³ 8s* Oct 21] brother to 3 winners in Ireland up to 1¼m/11f, including useful pair Irish Summit and Basanta, and closely related/ half-brother to several winners, including useful Irish 7f (at 2 yrs) and 1¼m winner who stays 1¾m Affianced (by Erins Isle): dam Irish 7f/1m winner: useful form: won maiden at the Curragh in July and Gran Criterium at Milan (beat Swing Wing 1½ lengths) in October: placed behind impressive stable-companion Hawk Wing in Futurity Stakes (3 lengths second) and National Stakes (4 lengths third) at the Curragh, setting pace both times: will stay at least 1¼m. *A. P. O'Brien, Ireland*

SHOLTO 3 b.g. Tragic Role (USA) – Rose Mill (Puissance 110) [2001 –: 7m 6.1s* **58** 6m² 6f f5g⁶ Oct 18] close-coupled gelding: modest handicapper: won at Nottingham in August: best at 5f/6f: acts on soft and good to firm ground: blinkered: drifts right. *J. O'Reilly*

SHONTAINE 8 b.g. Pharly (FR) 130 – Hinari Televideo 97 (Caerleon (USA) 132) **–** [2001 34, a50d: f8g⁴ e8g f8s Jan 19] small gelding: poor handicapper in 2001: seemed **a45** best at 1m/9f: was possibly unsuited by heavy going, acted on any other turf and fibre-sand/equitrack: was usually blinkered: had been slowly away: dead. *Mrs L. Stubbs*

SHOOF (USA) 2 b.f. (Mar 24) Dayjur (USA) 137 – Shemaq (USA) 98 (Blushing John **68 p** (USA) 120) [2001 7d⁶ Oct 15] third foal: sister to fairly useful 1999 2-y-o 6f winner Shafaq and half-sister to 3-y-o Shahirah: dam, 7f (at 2 yrs) and 1m winner, out of US Grade 2 9f winner Geraldine's Store, herself half-sister to very smart miler Al Bahathri: 25/1, 5 lengths sixth of 20 to Trojan Princess in maiden at Leicester, no extra final 1f: should improve. *A. C. Stewart*

SHOOT AWAY 3 b.f. Polar Falcon (USA) 126 – Cut Clear 82 (Kris 135) [2001 –: **34** f8.5s³ f8g f8.5g⁴ 10f f8g f9.4g f7g Dec 3] poor maiden: stays 8.5f: acts on fibresand: tongue tied last 2 starts, visored final one. *R. M. H. Cowell*

SHORE VISION 3 b.g. Efisio 120 – South Shore 102 (Caerleon (USA) 132) [2001 **79 +** –p: 7m 7.1m³ 8m³ 8.5g⁴ Jun 15] strong, good-bodied gelding: fair maiden: will stay 1¼m: acts on good to firm ground: gelded after final start. *P. W. Harris*

SHORT CHANGE (IRE) 2 b.g. (Jan 21) Revoque (IRE) 122 – Maafi Esm (Polish **72** Precedent (USA) 131) [2001 7.1s 6.1f² 6.1m² 6f 7m³ 8g⁴ 7s Sep 30] IR 12,000F, 24,000Y: big, lengthy gelding: has plenty of scope: third foal: half-brother to unreliable 7f (at 2 yrs) and 9f (in Belgium) winner Sawbo Lad (by Namaqualand): dam unraced: fair maiden: good fourth in nursery at Doncaster: stays 1m: acts on firm ground: well below form in blinkers (got very worked up) final start, and subsequently gelded. *B. J. Meehan*

SHORT REIGN (IRE) 2 b.f. (Apr 17) Mujadil (USA) 119 – Echoing 93 (Formidable **52** (USA) 125) [2001 f5g³ f5g² 5.2m² f5g² 5f 5.1m⁶ 5m 5g⁶ f5g f6g⁴ Nov 21] 2,500Y: workmanlike filly: half-sister to several winners, including 5-y-o Calcutta and 1½m winner Sommersby (by Vision): dam 2-y-o 5f winner: modest maiden: placed at Yarmouth and 3 times at Southwell: should stay 6f: acts on fibresand and firm going: visored final outing. *C. A. Dwyer*

SHORT RESPITE 2 b.f. (Mar 5) Brief Truce (USA) 126 – Kingdom Princess 69 **77 p** (Forzando 122) [2001 6.1m 7d* Oct 3] 15,000Y: second foal: dam 7f/1m winner: much better effort in maidens (fair form) when beating Alessandro Severo a length at Newcastle, staying on to lead final 1f despite attempting to hang left: will stay 1m: bandaged hind joints both starts: moved poorly to post on debut: should improve further. *M. L. W. Bell*

SHORTS 2 b.f. (Mar 2) Primo Dominie 121 – Gentle Irony 65 (Mazilier (USA) 107) **57** [2001 6g⁶ 6m⁴ 6m 5.1m⁵ f5g² 5.7d 6d³ 6d⁴ f6g f5f f5s Dec 27] 4,600Y: third foal: **a52** half-sister to 6f to 8.5f winner Violent (by Deploy): dam, 7f (including at 2 yrs) to 11f winner, out of half-sister to very smart performer up to 8.5f Forzando: modest maiden: left Andrew Reid after second in seller at Wolverhampton: well held last 3 outings: stays 6f: acts on fibresand, good to firm and good to soft going: visored penultimate start: usually races up with pace. *P. D. Evans*

SHOTACROSS THE BOW (IRE) 4 b.g. Warning 136 – Nordica 99 (Northfields **–** (USA)) [2001 73: 8.1m 12m 10g f9.4g² p8g f9.4g² f9.4g² f9.4g* f8.5s² Dec 27] tall, **a86 +** angular gelding: fairly useful handicapper: progressed late in year, and won at Wolverhampton in December: stays 9.4f: acts on fibresand and firm ground, probably on good to soft: waited with: genuine. *M. Blanshard*

SHOTLEY DANCER 2 ch.f. (Feb 28) Danehill Dancer (IRE) 117 – Hayhurst **60** (Sandhurst Prince 128) [2001 5m³ 5g⁵ 7.5m⁴ 7g³ 6m 8g⁴ 7m Sep 8] 9,000Y: small, unfurnished filly: fluent mover: seventh foal: half-sister to Irish 9f winner River Hopper (by River Falls) and a 7f/1m winner in Italy by Classic Secret: dam, winning hurdler in Ireland, staying maiden on Flat: modest maiden: well below form last 3 starts: may prove best at 6f/7f: raced only on good/good to firm ground. *N. Bycroft*

SHOTSTOPPA (IRE) 3 ch.g. Beveled (USA) – From The Rooftops (IRE) (Thatch- **–** ing 131) [2001 8m 7.1m⁶ f8g 7d Jul 16] 5,000F, 5,000Y: strong gelding: fifth foal: half-brother to 4-y-o On The Trail: dam unraced: little form. *J. L. Eyre*

SHOT TO FAME (USA) 2 b.c. (Jan 26) Quest For Fame 127 – Exocet (USA) **94 p** (Deposit Ticket (USA)) [2001 7.9d* 8v³ Oct 26] 160,000 francs Y: rather leggy, angular colt: first foal: dam, sprint winner in USA, half-sister to 1¾m (7f/1m winner at 2 yrs) Mixsterthetrixster out of half-sister to Prix du Cadran winner Molesnes: beat King Solomon by 5 lengths in 26-runner maiden at York in October: seemingly similar form when last of 3 at odds on for minor event at Newbury: likely to be suited by 1¼m/1½m: should make a useful 3-y-o. *P. W. Harris*

SHOUF AL BADOU (USA) 4 b.g. Sheikh Albadou 128 – Millfit (USA) 62 **74 d** (Blushing Groom (FR) 131) [2001 83, a92: 5s f7g⁴ 6d⁶ 7m 6m f6g⁵ 8m⁶ 7m 6f 6.1v⁶ 6v⁵ f6g f6s⁵ p7g Dec 29] good-bodied gelding: fair performer, on downgrade: left D. Nicholls after sixth start, Mrs J. Ramsden for 6,500 gns after twelfth: best at 6f/7f: acts on heavy going, good to firm and fibresand: blinkered 3 starts prior to final 2. *N. P. Littmoden*

SHOVE HA'PENNY (IRE) 2 b.c. (Apr 24) Night Shift (USA) – Penny Fan 58 **76** (Nomination 125) [2001 5d 5.3s³ 5.3m² f6g⁴ 6g 6f⁴ 7.5s² 7m³ 7g⁴ 8g 10.2g⁵ 8s² 10d³ p8g⁵ Nov 20] workmanlike colt: has scope: fifth foal: half-brother to useful 6f (at 2 yrs) to 1m winner Ffestiniog (by Efisio) and 3-y-o City of London: dam, sprint maiden, closely related to useful sprinter Rivers Rhapsody: fair maiden: made frame 9 times: barely stays 1¼m: acts on polytrack, soft and firm ground: blinkered (ran respectably) sixth start. *N. A. Callaghan*

SHOWDOWN 2 gr.f. (Jan 19) Darshaan 133 – Last Second (IRE) 121 (Alzao (USA) **65 p** 117) [2001 7m³ Jul 30] first foal: dam, 6f (at 2 yrs) to 1¼m (Nassau and Sun Chariot Stakes) winner, half-sister to 3-y-o Alleluia and useful Irish filly up to 1½m Alouette (by Darshaan), herself dam of dual Champion Stakes winner Alborada: 3/1 from 5/1, promising third of 5 to Evening Serenade in maiden at Folkestone, slowly away and keeping on under considerate handling: likely to be suited by 1¼m/1½m: should do better. *Sir Mark Prescott*

SHOWERING 2 b.f. (Feb 6) Danehill (USA) 126 – Bright Spells (USA) (Alleged **– p** (USA) 138) [2001 7s Oct 31] second foal: half-sister to 3-y-o Clearing: dam, fairly useful French 1½m winner, sister to smart performer up to 15.5f Non Partisan from good family: 10/1, eighth of 10 to Miss Corniche in maiden at Yarmouth, not given hard time once fading: should do better. *J. H. M. Gosden*

SHOWING 4 b.g. Owington 123 – Sharanella (Shareef Dancer (USA) 135) [2001 58: **–** f6s f6g 8.5s 7f 6m 5.3f⁶ 6g 7g Sep 11] good-topped, angular gelding: disappointing maiden: left W. Brisbourne after second start: tried blinkered/tongue tied. *B. R. Johnson*

SHOWPIECE 3 b.g. Selkirk (USA) 129 – Hawayah (IRE) 68 (Shareef Dancer (USA) **68** 135) [2001 8d 10.2d 10v² 11.7d⁵ f12g* 11m Nov 26] 25,000F, 500,000 francs Y: lengthy gelding: has scope: fourth foal: brother to French 9f winner Nena Maka (later winner in USA) and half-brother to 7f winner Tee Cee (by Lion Cavern): dam 2-y-o 7f winner out of Nell Gwyn winner Ghariba, herself half-sister to smart middle-distance stayer Braashee: fair performer: sold from Sir Michael Stoute 27,000 gns, then won maiden at Southwell in November, despite looking none too keen (subsequently gelded): should stay beyond 1½m: acts on fibresand, raced only on ground softer than good on turf. *W. J. Haggas*

SHOW THE WAY 3 ch.g. Hernando (FR) 127 – Severine (USA) 65 (Trempolino **49** (USA) 135) [2001 –: f11g 11s 11.8f⁴ 14m⁶ 14.1m 14.1m 14.1s⁶ 17.1g Aug 19] good-topped gelding: poor maiden: seems to stay 1¾m: acts on firm ground. *A. P. Jarvis*

SHOWTIME SHIRLEY 3 ch.f. First Trump 118 – Wollow Maid 73 (Wollow 132) **49** [2001 f8g f8g⁶ f8g 10g 12f* 12f⁵ 12.1m 12.1g f11g Dec 3] 6,500Y: half-sister to several winners, including 7f/1m winner Reverand Thickness (by Prince Sabo) and 5-y-o Pinchaninch: dam 1¼m winner: poor handicapper: won at Musselburgh in June: stays 1½m: acts on firm ground: slowly away third outing: races prominently. *A. Bailey*

SHRIVAR (IRE) 4 b.g. Sri Pekan (USA) 117 – Kriva 69 (Reference Point 139) [2001   **78**
86: 11.7m⁴ 9.9m Jul 31] workmanlike gelding: fairly useful performer at 3 yrs: fair form
in 2001 only on first start: probably stays 1¾m: acts on good to firm and good to soft
ground: usually visored nowadays. *M. R. Channon*

SHUDDER 6 b.g. Distant Relative 128 – Oublier L'Ennui (FR) 79 (Bellman (FR) 123)   **73**
[2001 66: 7s² 6v 6d* 7m³ 7m 6.1m² 5.7g* 6g⁴ 5.7m³ 6v² 5.1d 6v* Nov 8] fair performer:
won claimers at Windsor in May and Bath in August, and handicap at Windsor in November: effective at 5.7f to 7f: acts on heavy and good to firm going: won in visor earlier in
career. *R. J. Hodges*

SHUFFLE 4 b.c. First Trump 118 – Secret Dance (Sadler's Wells (USA) 132) [2001 –:   **–**
f12g⁶ f7g f8g f12g f11g May 21] no form: tried blinkered/visored. *Mrs N. Macauley*

SHUFFLING KID 2 ch.g. (Apr 26) Rock City 120 – Clashfern (Smackover 107)   **92**
[2001 5s* 5.1f² 5f⁶ 5m 5.1m⁵ 5g⁵ 5g 6d⁶ 6v⁵ Oct 27] 2,000Y: tall, leggy gelding: third
foal: dam unraced: fairly useful performer: won minor event at Doncaster in March: best
effort when close fifth to Pepperoni in listed event at York on sixth start: will prove best
at 5f/6f: acts on firm and soft ground: sold 10,000 gns, sent to USA. *B. A. McMahon*

SHUKRAN 2 b.f. (Feb 1) Hamas (IRE) 125§ – Ajeebah (IRE) (Mujtahid (USA) 118)   **99**
[2001 5m* 6f² 6g⁴ 6m⁶ Sep 6] lightly-made filly: first foal: dam, ran 3 times, half-sister
to useful performer up to 10.5f Cape Grace: useful performer: won maiden at Kempton in
June: in frame in minor event at Ascot and Cherry Hinton Stakes at Newmarket (under a
length fourth to Silent Honor) next 2 starts: found little final outing: will probably stay 7f:
raced only on good going or firmer. *R. Hannon*

SHUSH 3 b.g. Shambo 113 – Abuzz 101 (Absalom 128) [2001 86: f7g e5g f7g 8g 7m   **83**
10m⁴ 10.1m⁴ 12.3m⁴ 10.2m³ 12m 10.3d⁴ 10.2g* 8s 10s³ p10g⁴ p12g Dec 19] quite   **a75**
attractive gelding: fairly useful handicapper on turf, fair on all-weather: won at Chepstow in September: best around 1¼m: acts on polytrack, heavy and good to firm going.
C. E. Brittain

SHUWAIB 4 b.c. Polish Precedent (USA) 131 – Ajab Alzamaan (Rainbow Quest   **100**
(USA) 134) [2001 108: 15v 12f Jun 9] tall, quite attractive colt: useful performer: won
listed race at Deauville at 3 yrs: stiffish tasks in 2001, stumbling leaving stalls and failing
to handle home turn in handicap at Epsom second start: likely to stay 2m: acts on heavy
and good to firm going. *M. R. Channon*

SICKNOTE (IRE) 2 b.g. (May 15) Lake Coniston (IRE) 131 – Maellen (River Beauty   **– p**
105) [2001 f8g⁶ Nov 19] 4,500 2-y-o: brother to winner in Czech Republic, closely
related to winner in Hong Kong by Bluebird, and half-brother to several winners,
including 7f winner Hujoom (by Fairy King) and 6f (at 2 yrs) to 1½m winner Lifewatch
Vision (by Vision), both useful: dam Irish 1½m winner: 20/1, sixth in maiden at
Southwell, running on from slow start: should improve. *J. A. Glover*

SIDBURY GIRL 4 b.f. Presidium 124 – Busted Love (Busted 134) [2001 12v³ 10g   **–**
11.6m 12.6f 16v Oct 17] 5,000Y: half-sister to several winners, including 7f and 1¼m
winner Tankersley (by Timeless Times) and 11f/1½m winner Tessajoe (by Clantime),
both fairly useful: dam unraced: little form in varied company. *Miss E. C. Lavelle*

SIENA STAR (IRE) 3 b.g. Brief Truce (USA) 126 – Gooseberry Pie 63 (Green   **73**
Desert (USA) 127) [2001 77: 8m⁵ 8m⁶ 8m⁶ 10.3m⁴ 8m⁵ 8d⁶ 8.5g⁴ 9m* 8m⁴ 8f³ 10s² f11g⁵
p10g² p10g* Dec 22] close-coupled gelding: has a quick action: fair performer: won
claimer at Musselburgh in August and (having been claimed from J. L. Eyre £6,000 after
eleventh start) handicap at Lingfield in December: stays 1¼m: acts on firm going, good
and polytrack, probably on fibresand: has carried head awkwardly/hung right. *P. F. I. Cole*

SIENNA SUNSET (IRE) 2 ch.f. (Apr 28) Spectrum (IRE) 126 – Wasabi (IRE)   **66 p**
(Polar Falcon (USA) 126) [2001 7g⁴ Nov 5] 9,000Y, 19,000 2-y-o: second foal: dam,
unraced half-sister to useful 1¼m winner Tiger Flower: 40/1, 6½ lengths fourth to Sholay
in maiden at Redcar, tracking pace and keeping on: likely to stay 1¼m: should improve.
Mrs H. Dalton

SIFAT 6 b.m. Marju (IRE) 127 – Reine Maid (USA) (Mr Prospector (USA)) [2001 71:   **68**
11.9d⁵ 11.5m² 10m⁴ 10g⁵ 10m⁵ 10.1g⁴ p10g⁶ p10g p13g Dec 29] fair handicapper: **a60**
effective at 1¼m/11.5f: acts on heavy and good to firm going: visored nowadays, has
been blinkered: has looked less than keen, and best
with exaggerated waiting tactics. *J. R. Jenkins*

SIGHTING (IRE) 2 b.c. (Mar 6) Eagle Eyed (USA) 111 – Sandystones 60 (Selkirk   **83**
(USA) 129) [2001 6m⁵ 6g 6.1f⁴ 5m² 5m² 6g⁴ 5d* 6g² 6g 6m Sep 12] IR 5,000F, IR

8,400Y: leggy, angular colt: first foal: dam, maiden (best effort at 9f), half-sister to useful performer up to 10.5f Sonic Boy: fairly useful performer: won nursery at Haydock in August: second 3 times in similar events: well beaten last 2 starts: effective at 5f/6f: acts on firm and good to soft going: blinkered last 7 starts: usually races up with pace: sold 6,000 gns. *R. F. Johnson Houghton*

SIGNED AND DATED (USA) 2 b.c. (May 7) Red Ransom (USA) – Libeccio (NZ) **57** (Danzatore (CAN) 120) [2001 8.2g⁴ 7d 7m 10v 8s Oct 22] $40,000Y: lengthy, good-topped colt: has scope: half-brother to 8.5f winner Hollow Haze (by Woodman): dam unraced daughter of half-sister to Generous and 3-y-o Imagine: modest maiden: ran poorly in nurseries last 2 starts: should stay 1¼m: sold 7,200 gns. *P. F. I. Cole*

SIGN OF THE DRAGON 4 b.g. Sri Pekan (USA) 117 – Tartique Twist (USA) 78 **57** (Arctic Tern (USA) 126) [2001 44: 8v⁴ 8d 7m² 6m⁶ 8f⁴ 8f 6g⁶ 7.1f* 7m 6d 8.3m⁵ 7d Oct 30] modest handicapper: left I. Semple after sixth start: won maiden event at Musselburgh in August: best at 7f/1m: acts on any going: takes good hold: often races prominently: none too consistent. *Miss L. A. Perratt*

SIGN OF THE TIGER 4 b.g. Beveled (USA) – Me Spede (Valiyar 129) [2001 75: **–** f8g 10.1g f7g Sep 8] quite good-topped gelding: fair performer at 3 yrs: well held in 2001. *P. C. Haslam*

SIGY SAM 2 ch.f. (Mar 24) King's Signet (USA) 110 – Hosting (Thatching 131) **58** [2001 5m 5m 5.1g³ 6m⁵ 5.1s 5.1m⁵ Aug 24] fourth living foal: half-sister to 8-y-o Samara Song: dam unraced: modest maiden: effective at 5f/6f: acts on good to firm ground. *R. J. Baker*

SIHAFI (USA) 8 ch.g. Elmaamul (USA) 125 – Kit's Double (USA) (Spring Double) **73** [2001 73: 5v 5v 5m⁵ 5m* 5m⁴ 5m⁴ 5.7f 5m 5f⁴ 5m⁴ 5m Aug 1] tall gelding: fair performer: won minor event at Hamilton in May: races mainly at 5f: acts on firm going, good to soft and fibresand/equitrack: blinkered once at 7 yrs: often apprentice ridden: takes good hold and best covered up. *D. Nicholls*

SIKASSO (USA) 5 b. or br.g. Silver Hawk (USA) 123 – Silken Doll (USA) (Chieftain **82** II) [2001 12v² 9d⁵ 11.1d* 13d* 14g³ 13s⁵ 12.3m⁵ 11.1d² Aug 15] $300,000Y, 11,000 3-y-o: leggy gelding: brother to 9-y-o Juyush and half-brother to several winners in North America, including 1995 champion Canadian 2-y-o filly Silken Cat (by Storm Cat): dam won up to 9f in USA, including minor stakes: fairly useful form in bumpers and on Flat: won maiden and handicap at Hamilton in May: will stay 2m: acts on good to firm and heavy going: game and consistent. *G. A. Swinbank*

SILCABEE 3 b.f. Silca Blanka (IRE) 104 – Shamrock Dancer (IRE) 36 (Dance of Life **–** (USA)) [2001 9g 8.1m 11.9s Sep 30] first foal: dam third at 8.5f: well held in maidens. *A. D. Smith*

SILCA BLANKA (IRE) 9 b.h. Law Society (USA) 130 – Reality 88 (Known Fact **–** (USA) 135) [2001 96, a89: 7d 7g 7s p7g Nov 28] smallish, quite attractive horse: went to stud in 1997: useful handicapper in 2000: well held in 2001. *A. G. Newcombe*

SILENCE AND RAGE 2 b.c. (Mar 9) Green Desert (USA) 127 – Shot At Love (IRE) **59 p** 79 (Last Tycoon 131) [2001 6g 6m 7g 7s* Oct 25] close-coupled, workmanlike colt: third foal: dam 1m winner: modest form: shaped well before saddle slipped penultimate start: won 17-runner nursery at Brighton, racing alone far side: likely to prove best up to 1m: acts on soft ground: probably capable of better still. *C. A. Cyzer*

SILENCE IS GOLDEN 2 ch.f. (Feb 5) Danehill Dancer (IRE) 117 – Silent Girl 75 **77** (Krayyan 117) [2001 5m⁴ 6m³ 6m 6m³ 7m* 7g⁴ 8f* 7d Oct 2] 7,500Y: rather leggy, angular filly: sixth foal: half-sister to winners in Germany (1m/9f, by Law Society) and Hong Kong (up to 1½m, by Shalford): dam, 1m (at 2 yrs) to 1½m winner, half-sister to smart performer up to 1¼m Always Valiant: fair performer: won maiden at Lingfield in July and nursery at Newmarket (sweating) in August: stays 1m: acts on firm going, well held on good to soft: blinkered (below form) once. *B. J. Meehan*

SILENT GIFT 2 b.f. (Feb 13) Brief Truce (USA) 126 – Goodwood Lass (IRE) 71 **62 d** (Alzao (USA) 117) [2001 5g 5.2m 6m⁵ 7.5m* 7.5f⁶ 7m 6d 8d Nov 2] 2,000F, 3,000Y: small, sturdy filly: first foal: dam 7f (at 2 yrs) and 1½m winner: modest performer: won maiden at Beverley in June: showed little after: stays 7.5f: acts on good to firm ground: sold 500 gns. *P. L. Gilligan*

Cherry Hinton Stakes, Newmarket—Silent Honor lands the odds narrowly from Lady High Havens (right); Sundari and Shukran (rail) are next home

SILENT HONOR (IRE) 2 ch.f. (Feb 25) Sunday Silence (USA) – Wood Vine (USA) (Woodman (USA) 126) [2001 6m* 6g* 6m³ Aug 23] smallish, leggy, quite attractive filly: good mover: first foal: dam unraced half-sister to useful French 1½m winner Maeander out of sister to top-class miler Miesque: useful form: started favourite all starts: beat Lady High Havens in maiden (impressively by 4 lengths) in June and Cherry Hinton Stakes (by short head after refusing to settle under restraint) in July, both at Newmarket: conceding weight all round, best effort when 2½ lengths third to Queen's Logic in Lowther Stakes at York, allowed to stride on but headed over 1f out: withdrawn from Cheveley Park Stakes in October due to forecast soft ground: bred to stay at least 1m: has worn crossed noseband/had 2 handlers: rather lacking in physical scope. *D. R. Loder* — **107**

SILENT SEA 2 b.f. (Apr 10) Mistertopogigo (IRE) 118 – Whispering Sea 52 (Bustino 136) [2001 f5g f5g 5f 5f f5g⁵ 5.1g⁶ Jul 9] 1,200Y: sixth living foal: dam twice-raced half-sister to smart performer up to 1m Bahamian Bandit: little form, including in sellers. *J. L. Spearing* — **–**

SILENT SOUND (IRE) 5 b.g. Be My Guest (USA) 126 – Whist Awhile (Caerleon (USA) 132) [2001 59: 10g 9m 11.6m 12g 10m p12g⁶ Nov 20] rather leggy gelding: modest handicapper: effective at 1½m, probably at 1¾m: acts on firm and soft ground, probably on polytrack: usually blinkered at 3 yrs: sometimes very slowly away: needs treating with caution. *Mrs A. J. Perrett* — **52 §**

SILISTRA 2 gr.c. (Feb 21) Sadler's Wells (USA) 132 – Dundel (IRE) 82 (Machiavellian (USA) 123) [2001 8.2s³ Oct 30] 180,000Y: first foal: dam, 7f winner, out of sister to high-class middle-distance stayer High Hawk, herself dam of In The Wings (by Sadler's Wells), and to dams of High-Rise and Infamy: 14/1, 11 lengths third of 13 to odds-on stable-companion Balakheri in maiden at Nottingham, not knocked about when unable to sustain promising run: will be well suited by 1¼m+: sure to improve, and could well prove useful. *Sir Michael Stoute* — **76 P**

SILKEN BRIEF (IRE) 2 b.f. (May 13) Ali-Royal (IRE) 127 – Tiffany's Case (IRE) 65 (Thatching 131) [2001 7d² Nov 3] sturdy filly: fourth foal: half-sister to 3-y-o Golden Brief and 5-y-o Legal Set: dam 1m winner: 20/1, 1¾ lengths second of 21 to Maid To Perfection in maiden at Newmarket, staying on well: sure to improve. *S. P. C. Woods* — **80 p**

SILKEN LADY 5 br.m. Rock Hopper 124 – Silk St James (Pas de Seul 133) [2001 27: f16g⁵ 10.1g⁴ 10.9m Aug 27] little form in 2001. *M. J. Ryan* — **–**

SILKEN TOUCH 3 b.f. Pivotal 124 – Prima Silk 82 (Primo Dominie 121) [2001 53?: 7m p5g f7g Dec 31] no form since debut at 2 yrs: blinkered last 2 starts. *M. J. Ryan* — **–**

SILKEN WINGS (IRE) 3 b.f. Brief Truce (USA) 126 – Winged Victory (IRE) 93 (Dancing Brave (USA) 140) [2001 62: f7g⁴ f6g² 5.3d³ 6m* 6.1m f6g 5.1f f6s² Dec 15] — **70**

unfurnished filly: fair handicapper: made all at Windsor in June: probably best at 6f: acts on fibresand, firm and good to soft ground: has found little. *R. Hollinshead*

SILK LAW (IRE) 3 ch.f. Barathea (IRE) 127 – Jural 108 (Kris 135) [2001 80: 7.6f³ 80 8.1m 8m² 7.1g² 8m 7f⁵ 8m⁴ 7f⁶ f7g Sep 8] compact filly: has a round action: fairly useful performer: below form after fourth start: stays 1m: raced only on good going or firmer on turf, well held only run on fibresand: has raced freely: none too consistent. *A. Berry*

SILK ON SONG (USA) 3 b.g. Hazaam (USA) 113 – Wazeerah (USA) (The Minstrel – (CAN) 135) [2001 –: f7g⁴ f8.5g⁵ f8g⁴ f11g² f12g² 11.5f f12g⁵ f12g⁴ f14.8g f12s Dec 15] a64 modest maiden: left B. Smart after penultimate outing and off 4 months: stays 1½m: acts on fibresand (well held only run on turf): tongue tied penultimate outing: shied away from whip fifth start. *B. J. Llewellyn*

SILK ST JOHN 7 b.g. Damister (USA) 123 – Silk St James (Pas de Seul 133) [2001 82 97, a–: f8g f9.4g f8g 8g 8f⁵ 8.1d 8f⁵ 8m 8.1g⁶ 8g⁴ 8g⁵ 8d² 8.1s 9g⁶ 10g⁴ 8s 8.9d⁵ 8d⁶ a– 10s⁵ 8g* Nov 7] close-coupled gelding: fairly useful handicapper: won at Musselburgh in November: best at 1m/1¼m: acts on fibresand and any turf going: held up. *M. J. Ryan*

SILKY DAWN (IRE) 3 b.f. Night Shift (USA) – Bluffing (IRE) 102 (Darshaan 133) 91 [2001 100p: 7d 8.2d³ 8d* 8g² 8s³ 8.2s Oct 30] good-topped filly: fairly useful performer: won maiden at Salisbury in June: below form last 2 starts: bred to be suited by 1¼m+: raced only on good ground or softer: tongue tied first 3 starts. *H. R. A. Cecil*

SILLA (USA) 3 b.f. Gone West (USA) – Silver Fling (USA) 120 (The Minstrel (CAN) 92 135) [2001 93: 5.1d⁶ 6m 6m 6f Jun 30] big, strong, lengthy filly: fairly useful performer: ran creditably in listed race at Bath and handicap at Newmarket on first/third starts: stays 6f: acts on firm ground, probably on good to soft: sent to USA. *I. A. Balding*

Sheikh Mohammed's "Silent Honor"

SILLY GOOSE (IRE)   3 b.f. Sadler's Wells (USA) 132 – Ducking 71 (Reprimand   **76**
122) [2001 77p: 10.5s⁵ 14.1m⁶ 11.8m³ 10m² 9.9m 10.1g² 11.9s* 11.6v⁵ Oct 8] rather
leggy, quite attractive filly: has a fluent, round action: fair performer: won maiden at
Brighton in September: effective at 1¼m/1½m: acts on soft and good to firm going.
J. L. Dunlop

SILOGUE (IRE)   4 b. or br.g. Distinctly North (USA) 115 – African Bloom (African   **42**
Sky 124) [2001 40: f8g 14.1m⁵ 15.8m² 16.2s 10.9m² Aug 27] small gelding: poor
maiden: stays 15.8f: raced mainly on ground firmer than good on turf. *O. Brennan*

SILVAANI (USA)   3 gr.g. Dumaani (USA) 115 – Ruby Silver (USA) (Silver Hawk   **–**
(USA) 123) [2001 70p: 8g 10g 10m 11.9f Jun 14] workmanlike gelding: little form:
visored/blinkered last 3 starts: gelded after final outing. *Miss Gay Kelleway*

SILVANO (GER)   5 b.h. Lomitas 129 – Spirit of Eagles (USA) (Beau's Eagle   **126**
(USA)) [2001 118: 10g* 12g³ 10m* 10f⁵ 10d* 11f² 10.2g⁴ 10m Dec 16]
          Silvano was the best horse trained in Germany in 2001. Not that he
contested a race in his home country, nor even one in Europe. His eight runs in five
different countries around the world brought him three wins and the equivalent of
more than a million pounds in win prize-money alone. Silvano's earnings from the
latest season moved him into second place behind the 1995 Japan Cup winner
Lando in the list of all-time German prize-money winners. Lando's win in Tokyo
marked the beginning of the now familiar raids by German-trained horses on top
races around the world. Germany has been a relative late-comer compared to
Britain and France in contesting international races on a regular basis but the likes
of Silvano and Proudwings in the latest season are proof of a bolder approach by
German stables. Modest prize-money at home, not to mention an ever-growing

*Arlington Million—a first Grade 1 success in the States for Germany; Silvano (black sleeves) is ready to
pounce on front-running Redatorre, who finishes third; second-placed Hap is hidden behind the winner*

programme of richly-endowed races abroad, is as big an incentive as any for German trainers to campaign their best horses overseas. According to statistics published in Germany's racing newspaper *Sport-Welt*, German-trained horses ran in 214 races abroad in 1997, a figure which had risen to 568 in 2000.

The third of Silvano's wins came in the nineteenth running of the Arlington Million in Chicago in August, British stables having won two of the early editions with Tolomeo in 1983 and Teleprompter in 1985, and French-trained horses Mill Native and Dear Doctor having been successful in 1988 and 1992. Recent seasons had seen home-trained runners dominate as the focus of European attention in the United States had shifted to the Breeders' Cup, and the race was not held in 1998 and 1999 due to temporary closure of the course. A doubling of prize-money and incorporation into the Emirates World Series in 2000 gave more of an incentive for a European challenge. Silvano was joined from Germany in the 2001 Arlington Million by the seven-year-old Caitano, while Compton Bolter and Muakaad were sent from Britain and Ireland respectively. Bienamado, formerly trained in Britain, looked the best of the American horses after a couple of Grade 1 wins in California. However, those wins had come on very firm ground and conditions at Arlington, while no worse than good to soft by European standards, were much softer than the going that usually prevails in American turf races. Silvano enjoyed a perfect run, racing more prominently than usual in a race run at just a fair pace. Although the field was still well bunched at the end of the back straight, it was spread out at the finish. Leading early in the straight, Silvano stayed on strongly to beat second favourite Hap three lengths, with six lengths back to Redattore in third and another four to Caitano in fourth. Favourite Bienamado finished a well-beaten seventh. Silvano was his trainer's first runner in the United States and his jockey's first ride there, and Silvano was also the first German-trained horse to win a Grade 1 race in the States, the victory worth £419,580.

The days are long gone when the Arlington Million was the world's richest race. Silvano had won an even bigger prize earlier in the year when taking the £507,569 Audemars Piguet Queen Elizabeth II Cup at Sha Tin in April. A race with Group 1 status for the first time, it drew most of the best horses in Hong Kong, along with Sobieski, representing Godolphin, Caitano again, and the 1999 winner Jim And Tonic for whom Sha Tin had become something of a home from home. Jim And Tonic had to settle for second place for the second year running however, as Silvano beat him by a length and three quarters, making first run in the straight. A yet more valuable prize was on offer the following month in Singapore for the second running of the Singapore Airlines International Cup at the brand new Kranji racecourse. This time it was Silvano who came off worse with Jim And Tonic as they finished fifth and second respectively behind the British-trained winner Endless Hall. Singapore has established several very valuable races through the year that have attracted interest from Europe, and Silvano had been successful in another of them on his reappearance in March in the £237,369 Singapore Cup. In a field of only six, Silvano beat Caitano again by five and a half lengths in course-record time.

Silvano's best effort in defeat came later in March in the ultra-competitive Dubai Sheema Classic at Nad Al Sheba, where he stayed on well to be beaten two lengths behind Stay Gold and Fantastic Light. Silvano earned more prize-money from his autumn campaign, but he was below form after the Arlington Million. He remained in America to contest the Man o' War Stakes at Belmont, finishing second to With Anticipation after having his heels clipped on the first turn. Then, while most international attention was focused on the Breeders' Cup meeting, Silvano picked up points the same weekend in the World Series in Australia's top weight-for-age race, the Cox Plate. Silvano was not discredited in finishing fourth behind Australia's best horse Northerly and the New Zealand mare Sunline, who was seeking a hat-trick in the race. A return to Sha Tin for the Hong Kong Cup in December saw an anti-climatic end to Silvano's season, and his career, as he finished only eleventh, the only time all year that he failed to pick up any prize-money.

Silvano has been retired to the Gestut Fahrhof at a fee of €7,500. He takes the place there of his sire Lomitas, who has moved to Sheikh Mohammed's Dalham Hall at Newmarket. Also trained by Andreas Wohler, Lomitas was a high-class mile-and-a-half performer who won nine of his twelve starts in Germany before joining Ron McAnally in California, where he was placed in a couple of Grade 2 events. Lomitas made an immediate impact at stud, with his first crop including the top German two-year-old Sumitas, as well as the following year's Deutsches Derby winner Belenus, and Silvano himself.

Silvano (GER) (b.h. 1996)	Lomitas (ch 1988)	Niniski (b 1976)	Nijinsky
			Virginia Hills
		La Colorada (ch 1981)	Surumu
			La Dorada
	Spirit of Eagles (USA) (b 1986)	Beau's Eagle (ch 1976)	Golden Eagle
			Beaufield
		Big Spirit (b 1980)	Big Spruce
			Beautiful Spirit

Silvano's success at Arlington was appropriate given that, unusually for a German horse, he comes from an American family. His dam Spirit of Eagles, a sister to the US Grade 3 mile winner Big Pal, won eleven races up to a mile, all of them claimers at the Arizona track of Turf Paradise. She won at least once in each of her five seasons on the track, her most productive campaign coming as a four-year-old, when she won seven of her twenty-five starts. Her three foals before Silvano included the winners Sirena (by Tejano) and Spider (by Acatenango), the latter successful at up to thirteen furlongs. Two more winners by Acatenango followed on from Silvano, much the better being three-year-old Sabiango. Already a better horse than Silvano was at three, Sabiango had an eventful season. Doped on his reappearance, he then missed the Deutsches Derby (for which he had been ante-post favourite) when the ground turned soft, but proved himself one of the best of his generation in Germany when beating the Deutsches Derby winner Boreal in another Group 1 at Cologne. Spirit of Eagles also has an unraced two-year-old by Sternkonig, named Spirit Queen, and produced a full sister to Silvano in 2001. Neither of the next two dams in Silvano's pedigree saw a racecourse, but great grandam Beautiful Spirit has some rather notable descendants. She is the dam of Beverly Hills Handicap winner Beautiful Melody, grandam of another Grade 1 winner Jeanne Jones (also runner-up in the Breeders' Cup Juvenile Fillies) and, closer to home, fourth dam of the Fillies' Mile winner and Ribblesdale Stakes runner-up Teggiano. Silvano was lightly raced in his early days, winning his only start at two and then missing the second half of his three-year-old season, though not before winning a Group 2 at Cologne and finishing fourth in the Deutsches Derby. Silvano had only four races as a four-year-old, winning another Group 2 at Baden-Baden and giving a hint of his international campaign to come when finishing a close fifth to Daliapour in the Hong Kong Vase. The latter race, and Silvano's win at Sha Tin in the latest season, belied his trainer's view that he was best on a left-handed track, and, while best at a mile and a quarter, he ran some good races in defeat at a mile and a half, notably in Dubai. His best form came on going ranging from good to firm to good to soft. There cannot have been many horses who have clocked up as many air-miles in a single year as Silvano did in the latest season, and the fact that he came back with prize-money from all but one of his races is a tribute to his own toughness, as well as to the skill and enterprise of his connections. *A. Wohler, Germany*

SILVER BAND   2 ch.f. (Mar 5) Zilzal (USA) 137 – Silver Braid (USA) 101 (Miswaki   **72** (USA) 124) [2001 6d⁶ 7.5m 6f⁴ 7d² 6g* 6m² 6m Sep 12] 21,000Y: leggy filly: sixth foal: half-sister to 8-y-o Kass Alhawa, 4-y-o Beading and 3-y-o Intrepidous: dam, 2-y-o 7f winner, later best at 1m: fair performer: won nursery at Catterick in August: best effort when second in similar event at Ripon next time: seems best at 6f: acts on firm and good to soft going: blinkered last 5 starts. *T. D. Easterby*

SILVER BOMBER   2 gr.f. (May 8) Persian Bold 123 – Rich Lass (Broxted 120)   **–** [2001 7.2g 5f Sep 20] leggy, sparely-made filly: half-sister to several winners, including 5-y-o Tayif and useful 1987 2-y-o 6f winner (later winner in Hong Kong) Fortinbras (by Junius): dam maiden: well beaten in maidens. *A. Berry*

SILVER BRACELET   3 b. or br.f. Machiavellian (USA) 123 – Love of Silver (USA)   **85** 110 (Arctic Tern (USA) 126) [2001 e7g⁵ e10s² 8s³ 10.4m 9.7m² 8f⁵ 8g 8.3g* 8.1g 7d 7g⁵   **a92**

8s² 7v p10g⁴ p10g Nov 24] leggy, useful-looking filly: fourth foal: dam 2-y-o 6f/7f (Prestige Stakes) winner who was third in Prix Marcel Boussac: fairly useful performer: won maiden at Windsor in August: also ran well when in frame in listed race at Kempton third start and handicap at Lingfield penultimate outing: best at 1m/1¼m: acted on soft going, equitrack and polytrack: visits Singspiel. *C. E. Brittain*

SILVER BUZZARD (USA)   2 b. or br.c. (Mar 18) Silver Hawk (USA) 123 – Stella-rina (USA) (Pleasant Colony (USA)) [2001 p10g Dec 4] second foal: dam, 7f to 1¾m (minor stakes) winner in North America, half-sister to 7f winner Marcus Maximus out of very smart performer up to 1¼m Star Pastures: 14/1, seventh to Playapart in maiden at Lingfield: should stay 1½m: should do better. *J. W. Hills*   **57 p**

SILVER CHARMER   2 b.f. (Mar 30) Charmer 123 – Sea Dart 55 (Air Trooper 115) [2001 6s⁴ 6m 6g⁴ 5g 6v⁴ Oct 17] 2,000Y: leggy, close-coupled filly: half-sister to 7f winner Needwood Sprite (by Joshua) and 2m winner Needwood Muppet (by Rolfe): dam 11f seller winner: regressed after showing fair form on debut. *H. S. Howe*   **72 d**

SILVER CHARTER (USA)   2 b.g. (Apr 23) Silver Hawk (USA) 123 – Pride of Darby (USA) (Danzig (USA)) [2001 7m* 8g⁶ 8d Oct 19] $250,000Y, 55,000 2-y-o: closely related to 2 winners by Sunshine Forever, including useful 1½m/1¾m winner Bahamian Sunshine, and half-brother to 3 winners in USA: dam, 1m winner in USA, half-sister to Prix du Jockey Club winner Caracolero and to dam of Secreto and Istabraq: overcame greenness and showed fairly useful form to win maiden at Kempton in July, despite hanging markedly left off bridle: soundly beaten in listed event at Goodwood and nursery at Newmarket (subsequently gelded): should be suited by 1¼m+. *G. B. Balding*   **85**

SILVER CHEVALIER (IRE)   3 gr.g. Petong 126 – Princess Eurolink (Be My Guest (USA) 126) [2001 –: 10.2d 12m 7m 8m 8m 10.1g 10s 8d p12g Nov 13] leggy, close-coupled gelding: little form: tried visored/blinkered. *C. N. Allen*   **–**

SILVER CLOUD   3 gr.f. Petong 126 – Pepeke 78 (Mummy's Pet 125) [2001 –: 8v 6g 8m 7.5m 8m 5f 9m⁵ 7.5m Aug 26] sparely-made filly: well held all starts: tried blinkered/visored. *R. E. Barr*   **–**

SILVER GREY LADY (IRE)   3 gr.f. Saddlers' Hall (IRE) 126 – Early Rising (USA) (Grey Dawn II 132) [2001 74p: 10s* 11.5g² 12m 11.9d⁶ 12g Sep 28] rather leggy, quite good-topped filly: useful performer: won maiden at Newbury in April very easily: good neck second to Double Crossed in 3-runner listed race at Lingfield following month, rallying having been badly squeezed 1f out (awarded race on day, winner later re-instated): disappointing after, taking home turn very poorly in Oaks at Epsom (also edgy) next start: stayed 11.5f: acted on soft going: pulled hard penultimate outing, sweating/on toes final one: stud. *J. L. Dunlop*   **101**

SILVER INSTINCT (IRE)   2 gr.g. (Mar 16) Petardia 113 – Aussie Aisle (IRE) (Godswalk (USA) 130) [2001 7g 7.1s⁵ f7g Oct 1] IR 7,800Y: leggy gelding: second living foal: half-brother to 5f seller winner Ma Vielle Pouque (by Fayruz): dam, Irish 1¼m winner, half-sister to useful sprinter Barrys Gamble: poor maiden: visored (well beaten in seller) final start: sold 500 gns, sent to Denmark. *J. L. Eyre*   **49**

SILVER MASCOT   2 gr.g. (Mar 29) Mukaddamah (USA) 125 – Always Lucky 71 (Absalom 128) [2001 f5g⁴ f5g⁵ f5g³ 6m 6g⁵ 5.1f 6v⁵ 7s f6g³ f5g* Dec 17] 8,000Y: first foal: dam, 2-y-o 5f/6f winner, out of sister to very smart sprinter Paris House: fair performer: won at Southwell in December: likely to prove best at 5f/6f: acts on heavy going, good to firm and fibresand. *R. Hollinshead*   **70**

SILVERNUS   3 b.f. Machiavellian (USA) 123 – Agnus (IRE) (In The Wings 128) [2001 11.9m⁵ 10m⁶ 8d Oct 8] 100,000Y: leggy filly: first foal: dam, Belgian 7f (at 2 yrs) and 9f winner, half-sister to smart performer up to 1m Wavy Run: little form in maidens, leaving H. Cecil after debut (moved poorly to post). *S. R. Bowring*   **–**

SILVER PROPHET (IRE)   2 gr.c. (Apr 15) Idris (IRE) 118 – Silver Heart (Yankee Gold 115) [2001 7m³ 8.1s⁴ 7.1g⁵ 8.5g 10.2g Oct 1] half-brother to several winners, including useful Irish 1m/1¼m winner Winning Heart (by Horage) and fairly useful 7f winner Poetry (by Treasure Kay): dam Irish 7f to 9f winner: fair maiden: stays 1¼m: acts on soft going: visored (well held) fourth start: sold 10,500 gns. *K. McAuliffe*   **67**

SILVER SECRET   7 gr.g. Absalom 128 – Secret Dance (Sadler's Wells (USA) 132) [2001 58: 8m 10.5g 12m 10g⁵ 9.9m⁴ 8.5s³ 10.5s 12d Sep 25] well-made gelding: modest handicapper: effective at testing 8.5f to easy 1½m: acts on any going: tried visored/blinkered: usually amateur ridden: lazy. *S. Gollings*   **50**

935

SILVER SHOES 2 b.f. (Mar 6) Woodborough (USA) 112 – Emerald Dream (IRE) 47 **49** (Vision (USA)) [2001 6f 5f⁶ 7m³ 7g³ 7.1f³ 7m⁵ 7d⁴ 7g f8.5s² 7.5g Sep 19] small, good-topped filly: first foal: dam maiden who stayed 1¼m: poor maiden: second at Wolverhampton: should stay 1¼m: acts on firm going, good to soft and fibresand: ran creditably only try in visor. *J. L. Eyre*

SILVER SOCKS 4 gr.g. Petong 126 – Tasmim 63 (Be My Guest (USA) 126) [2001 **72** 52: f11g* f12g* f12g* f12g* f11g² f12g* f12g³ 10.3s² f11g⁶ f11g 12m 10m⁶ 12m Sep 22] quite good-topped gelding: fair handicapper: won at Southwell (twice) and Wolver-hampton (3 times, including amateur/apprentice events), all in February: off 3 months prior to poor efforts last 2 starts: stays 1½m: acts on fibresand and soft ground, probably on good to firm: blinkered: fair winning hurdler. *M. W. Easterby*

SILVER TANGO (IRE) 2 gr.c. (Mar 14) Danehill Dancer (IRE) 117 – Lightning **84** Bug (Prince Bee 128) [2001 5d⁶ 5.1d* 6m⁴ 6s 6d³ 7s³ Oct 16] 8,000Y: leggy colt: third foal: half-brother to fairly useful 1999 2-y-o 6f winner Perugia (by Perugino) and Irish 9f and 11f winner Queen of Fibres (by Scenic): dam, Irish 1½m and 2m winner, from family of Barathea: fairly useful performer: won maiden at Bath in May: good third in minor events at Goodwood and Leicester: stays 7f: acts on soft ground: sold 17,000 gns. *S. Kirk*

SILVER TONGUED 5 b.g. Green Desert (USA) 127 – Love of Silver (USA) 110 **34** (Arctic Tern (USA) 126) [2001 32: f6g f5g⁵ f7s⁴ f7g e7g f5g Feb 1] rather sparely-made gelding: poor maiden: stays 1m: acts on fibresand. *J. M. Bradley*

SILVERWARE (IRE) 5 b.g. Mukaddamah (USA) 125 – Diabola (USA) (Devil's **90** Bag (USA)) [2001 92: 7s³ 8s⁵ 8g 7g⁶ 8m 8g 8g³ 9g 8.5d 8g 8g 10m Sep 15] tall gelding: first foal: dam, French 9f and 11f winner, half-sister to Poule d'Essai des Poulains runner-up Noble Minstrel: fairly useful handicapper: won Irish Cambridgeshire at the Curragh at 4 yrs: well held in Royal Hunt Cup at Royal Ascot fifth start in 2001: effective at 7f to 9f: acts on soft and good to firm going: effective blinkered or not: held up: none too consistent. *P. Hughes, Ireland*

SILVESTER LADY 3 ch.f. Pivotal 124 – Gara Yaka (IRE) 56 (Soviet Star (USA) **108** 128) [2001 11g³ 11s* 11.8d² 10d⁵ 10v Oct 7] 5,600F: ex-German filly: third foal: half-sister to a winner in Japan by Royal Academy: dam twice-raced half-sister to useful German filly (runner-up in Preis der Diana) Quebrada out of US Grade 1 1¼m winner Queen To Conquer: useful performer: won maiden at Frankfurt at 2 yrs and Ostermann-Preis der Diana at Mulheim (by neck from Lilac Queen) in June: failed to repeat latter form, leaving A. Lowe before final start: stays 11f: acts on soft going. *C. Laffon-Parias, France*

SIMA'S GOLD (IRE) 3 b.f. Goldmark (USA) 113 – Mujadil Princess (IRE) (Mujadil **– §** (USA) 119) [2001 48: 6.1m 8m 10m 8m 10m Sep 1] smallish, strong, lengthy filly: poor performer at 2 yrs: little form in 2001: blinkered final start: looks temperamental. *W. R. Muir*

SIMEON 2 b.c. (Apr 25) Lammtarra (USA) 134 – Noble Lily (USA) (Vaguely Noble **95 p** 140) [2001 8.3s² 7m² 8g* 8s* Nov 9] has a round action: eighth foal: brother to useful French winner around 1½m Noctilucent, closely related to 2 winners by Caerleon, notably smart 7f (at 2 yrs) to 14.6f (Park Hill) winner Noble Rose, and half-brother to 1½m winner who stayed 2m Majestic (by Belmez): dam, second at 11f in France, half-sister to US Grade 1 9f winner Talinum: useful form: won maiden at Goodwood in September and minor event at Doncaster (straightforward task, beat Esteemed Master by 5 lengths) in November: should stay at least 1½m: acts on soft and good to firm ground: has awkward head carriage but seems genuine: ridden prominently: should do better still as 3-y-o. *M. Johnston*

SIMIANNA 2 b.f. (Apr 2) Bluegrass Prince (IRE) 110 – Lowrianna (IRE) 50 (Cyrano **90** de Bergerac 120) [2001 5v* 5s² 5s* 5.1f* 5m⁴ 5g⁵ 5m⁴ 5.2m⁶ Aug 17] 1,000Y: unfurn-ished filly: fourth foal: half-sister to 2000 2-y-o 5f seller winner Countess Bankes (by Son Pardo) and 5-y-o Bodfari Anna: dam 2-y-o 5f winner: fairly useful performer: won maiden at Musselburgh in March, minor event at Ripon in April and minor event at Chester in May: about 2½ lengths fourth to Whitbarrow in Molecomb Stakes at Goodwood penultimate start: will stay 6f: acts on any ground: blinkered (ran creditably) final appearance. *A. Berry*

SIMIOLA 2 b.f. (Mar 30) Shaamit (IRE) 127 – Brave Vanessa (USA) 62 (Private **55** Account (USA)) [2001 7d p7g⁴ p7g Dec 22] 600F: fourth foal: dam, 6f winner who stayed 1m, sister to US Grade 2 winner around 1m Topicount: modest maiden: best effort when fourth in claimer at Lingfield, then left I. Wood: will stay at least 1m: acts on polytrack. *G. L. Moore*

SIMLA BIBI   3 ch.f. Indian Ridge 123 – Scandalette (Niniski (USA) 125) [2001 69: 10s 8d 8.2f 7m 10m⁵ 9.7m⁵ 10.1s f12g Nov 23] workmanlike filly: modest maiden handicapper: stays easy 1¼m: acts on good to firm ground and fibresand: tried blinkered: tends to race freely and has carried head awkwardly: sold 11,000 gns. *B. J. Meehan*   **53**

SIMLET   6 b.g. Forzando 122 – Besito 79 (Wassl 125) [2001 –: 16m⁴ 16.2f Jul 17] angular gelding: lightly raced and only modest form on Flat nowadays: probably stays 2m: acts on fibresand, equitrack, firm and soft going: has flashed tail/wandered: often blinkered/visored earlier in career: fair winner over hurdles. *E. W. Tuer*   **62**

SIMON THE POACHER   2 br.g. (Apr 26) Chaddleworth (IRE) 103 – Lady Crusty (Golden Dipper 119) [2001 7s⁵ 7s Oct 16] small, sturdy gelding: sixth foal: dam awarded selling hurdle: tailed-off last in minor events at Ascot and Leicester. *L. P. Grassick*   **–**

SIMPATICH (FR)   3 ch.c. First Trump 118 – Arc Empress Jane (IRE) (Rainbow Quest (USA) 134) [2001 77: 7d 8g 10.1m 11.9d⁶ 11m⁵ Sep 26] strong, angular colt: fair handicapper: may prove best around 1¼m: acts on soft going, probably on good to firm: sent to France. *L. M. Cumani*   **78**

SIMPLE IDEALS (USA)   7 b. or br.g. Woodman (USA) 126 – Comfort And Style 95 (Be My Guest (USA) 126) [2001 58: f14g 14.1s 14.1s⁶ 12.4d 13.9m 14m 14.1m⁶ 14.6f² 16.2f⁵ 15s⁵ 14.4d⁴ 14g⁵ 14m 16.1f³ 16d⁴ 14v⁴ 15.8d³ 14.1g* 13.8d⁶ f16g Nov 12] smallish, workmanlike gelding: has a round action: modest handicapper: won at Redcar in October: effective at 1½m to 2m: acts on any turf going: blinkered twice in 1997: sometimes races freely/hangs: tends to carry head high: usually held up. *Don Enrico Incisa*   **60 a–**

SIMPLY BROKE   3 br.g. Simply Great (FR) 122 – Empty Purse (Pennine Walk 120) [2001 –: 8f Jul 9] sturdy, workmanlike gelding: has a round action: fifth foal: well held in 3 maidens: mulish in paddock second 2-y-o outing: reportedly broke blood vessel last 2 starts. *P. C. Haslam*   **–**

SIMPLY ERIC (IRE)   3 b.g. Simply Great (FR) 122 – Sanjana (GER) (Priamos (GER) 123) [2001 66: 8v⁴ 8.2s⁵ 10.1m 10.5m⁴ 8.5f 9.1d 10m Aug 11] workmanlike gelding: modest maiden handicapper: stays 10.5f: acts on heavy and good to firm going: blinkered final start: sold 900 gns, sent to Denmark. *J. L. Eyre*   **56**

SIMPLY NOBLE   5 b.g. Noble Patriarch 115 – Simply Candy (IRE) 42 (Simply Great (FR) 122) [2001 74: f8g f11g⁵ e16g f12g² f12g⁵ f11g⁶ 10.3f f11g³ May 21] smallish gelding: modest performer: left M. Johnston prior to well held last 2 starts: stays 1½m: acts on fibresand, soft and good to firm going: has worn crossed noseband: often starts slowly: free-going sort. *W. M. Brisbourne*   **63**

SIMPLY REMY   3 ch.g. Chaddleworth (IRE) 103 – Exemplaire (FR) (Polish Precedent (USA) 131) [2001 –: 8.2s f11g³ f12g f12m³ 12g² 12m⁵ 12g⁶ 10m⁵ 10f⁴ Sep 20] lengthy gelding: modest maiden handicapper: effective at 1¼m/1½m: acts on fibresand and firm going: races prominently. *John Berry*   **51**

SIMPLY SENSATIONAL (IRE)   4 ch.c. Cadeaux Genereux 131 – Monaiya (Shareef Dancer (USA) 135) [2001 77: e12g⁴ f8g 10v* May 18] fair performer: won handicap at Newbury in May: stays 1½m: raced only on going softer than good on turf, below form on fibresand/equitrack: has looked weak finisher on occasions. *P. F. I. Cole*   **76**

SIMPLY THE GUEST (IRE)   2 b.c. (Feb 11) Mujadil (USA) 119 – Ned's Contessa (IRE) 48 (Persian Heights 129) [2001 5s 5.1s 5f³ 5g⁴ 5.1g⁴ 5m² 6m⁴ 5.1m² 6f⁶ 6s⁶ 5.1m f6g* f6g³ f6g f6g² f7g⁵ f7g⁶ Dec 10] IR 26,000F: lengthy, useful-looking colt: first foal: dam, 7f winner, half-sister to useful 5f winners Connemara and Presentation (both by Mujadil): fair performer: in frame 6 times before winning claimer at Wolverhampton in October: claimed from M. Channon 11,500 gns after next outing: will prove best at 5f/6f: acts on firm ground and fibresand: tough and reliable. *N. Tinkler*   **72 a68**

SINAMATELLA   2 ch.f. (Mar 24) Lion Cavern (USA) 117 – Regent's Folly (IRE) 101 (Touching Wood (USA) 127) [2001 7g⁵ 7.1f⁴ 6.5g Sep 28] 18,000Y: sturdy, good-bodied filly: fifth foal: half-sister to 3 winners, including 5-y-o Spree Vision and 9f winner Falcon's Fire (by Kalaglow): dam, 2-y-o 7f winner who stayed 14.6f, out of close relative to high-class middle-distance performer Ascot Knight: fair maiden: clearly best effort on debut: should be suited by at least 1m. *C. G. Cox*   **69**

SINCERITY 4 b.f. Selkirk (USA) 129 – Integrity 108 (Reform 132) [2001 75: f8.5g – Feb 6] fair maiden at 3 yrs: well held only run in 2001 (visored). *J. R. Fanshawe*

SING AND DANCE 8 b.m. Rambo Dancer (CAN) 107 – Musical Princess 66 (Cavo **55** Doro 124) [2001 59: 13s 12d² 12m⁶ 12m⁴ 12m⁵ 12m⁴ 13m 12f² 12f³ 12g⁴ 12m⁴ 14m⁴ 12.1g⁶ 10f³ 12m* 12g Nov 7] big, workmanlike mare: modest handicapper: won at Catterick in September: effective at 1¼m to 1¾m: acts on firm and good to soft ground: tried in visor/blinkers (not since 1998): usually held up. *J. R. Weymes*

SING A SONG (IRE) 3 b.f. Blues Traveller (IRE) 119 – Raja Moulana 75 (Raja Baba **73** (USA)) [2001 82: 7.6m 6s 7m 6m f6g 6v⁴ p7g Nov 15] tall, leggy filly: fair form at best in 2001: should stay 7f: acts on soft going, possibly not on firmer than good: sold 5,000 gns. *R. Hannon*

SING FOR FAME (USA) 3 b.f. Quest For Fame 127 – Singing (USA) 91 (The **90** Minstrel (CAN) 135) [2001 9m* 11.7m² 12m 10g Oct 5] smallish, sturdy filly: fourth living foal: half-sister to fairly useful 1¼m winners River's Source (by Irish River) and Gold Disc (by Slew O'Gold), latter also 7f winner at 2 yrs: dam, 7f winner, half-sister to Prince of Wales's Stakes winner Two Timing: fairly useful form: won maiden at Lingfield in June: very good head second to Elsaamri in minor event at Bath next time: well held in handicaps last 2 starts: stayed 11.7f: acted on good to firm going: stud. *Mrs A. J. Perrett*

SING FOR ME (IRE) 6 b. or br.m. Songlines (FR) 121 – Running For You (FR) – (Pampabird 124) [2001 45: f7s⁵ f5s² f6s³ f6g⁶ f5g f5g f6g⁶ f6g⁶ f5g⁶ Mar 27] lengthy, **a47** sparely-made mare: poor performer: stays 7f: acts on good to firm going, soft and fibresand: tried visored: tends to get behind. *R. Hollinshead*

SINGLE CURRENCY 5 b.h. Barathea (IRE) 127 – Kithanga (IRE) 117 (Darshaan – 133) [2001 –: e13g 11.9s 11.9s 11.9f 12m 16.2f Jun 23] strong, angular horse: disappointing maiden handicapper: tried visored/tongue tied: has refused to enter stalls/ given trouble at start. *P. Butler*

SINGLE HONOUR 3 b.f. Mark of Esteem (IRE) 137 – Once Upon A Time 77 (Teen- **90** oso (USA) 135) [2001 93: 8m 10.2m³ 8d⁶ 8.3m* 10d² Nov 2] rather leggy, close-coupled filly: fairly useful performer: won maiden at Windsor in July: stays 1¼m: acts on good to firm and good to soft going: sold 42,000 gns, sent to USA. *R. Hannon*

SINGLE TRACK MIND 3 b.g. Mind Games 121 – Compact Disc (IRE) 48 (Royal **82 d** Academy (USA) 130) [2001 76: 6g 6m⁶ 6m² 6m⁵ 6m² 6f 6m 6m 6m 7s Sep 30] neat, quite attractive gelding: fairly useful performer: below form last 5 starts (reportedly lost action on first occasion, gelded after final one): best at 5f/6f: acts on soft going, good to firm, fibresand and equitrack: visored eighth outing. *N. Hamilton*

SINGSONG 4 b.g. Paris House 123 – Miss Whittingham (IRE) 68 (Fayruz 116) [2001 – 91: f5g f6s 5s 5v 6m 6g Jul 20] small gelding: formerly fairly useful 5f winner: has lost his form. *A. Berry*

SINJAREE 3 b.c. Mark of Esteem (IRE) 137 – Forthwith 104 (Midyan (USA) 124) – [2001 63: 8m 10g Jun 16] leggy, unfurnished colt: second foal: half-brother to smart 1½m to 2m performer Time Zone (by Shirley Heights): dam 7f (at 2 yrs) and 1¼m winner: modest maiden: lightly raced: well held in 2001: should stay 1¼m: sold 800 gns, sent to Holland. *E. A. L. Dunlop*

SIOUXSIE SIOUX 2 b.f. (Mar 31) Pivotal 124 – Tres Sage (Reprimand 122) [2001 **67** 6g³ Jun 8] 28,000Y: tall, leggy, unfurnished filly: second foal: dam, French 1m winner, closely related to smart performer up to 1m Aragon: 3/1, fair form when 4 lengths third of 11 to Parasol in maiden at Haydock, hampered early. *J. G. Given*

SIR ALFRED 2 b.g. (May 10) Royal Academy (USA) 130 – Magnificent Star (USA) **67** 122 (Silver Hawk (USA) 123) [2001 6d⁴ 7m³ 7s Oct 16] fourth living foal: half-brother to fairly useful 1½m winner Profiler (by Capote): dam won Yorkshire Oaks: fair maiden: best effort when third in claimer at Salisbury (then left Sir Mark Prescott): should stay at least 1¼m: tail swisher. *B. R. Millman*

SIR AZZARO (IRE) 2 b.c. (Jan 30) Charnwood Forest (IRE) 125 – Supreme Crown **87** (USA) (Chief's Crown (USA)) [2001 a4.5f³ a4.5f³ 6.3d 8m* 6.3g 5.2m 7d⁶ 8d Aug 18] IR 15,000Y: half-brother to several winners, notably useful performer up to 9f in Britain/ Scandinavia Tough Guy (by Namaqualand): dam unraced daughter of US Grade 1 2-y-o 6f winner Share The Fantasy: fairly useful performer: campaigned in Europe last 6 starts, winning maiden at Bellewstown in July and running respectably in Super Sprint at

Newbury 2 outings later: stays 1m: acts on good to firm going, probably on dirt. *Franck Mourier, USA*

SIR BRASTIAS 2 b.g. (Mar 2) Shaamit (IRE) 127 – Premier Night 102 (Old Vic 136) **64** [2001 7d Nov 3] angular gelding: first foal: dam, 1½m to 2m winner, half-sister to dam of 2-y-o Parasol and 3-y-o Mot Juste: 33/1, soon chased along when never-dangerous twelfth of 27 to Prince Hector in maiden at Newmarket: gelded after: will be suited by 1½m+. *S. Dow*

SIR DESMOND 3 gr.g. Petong 126 – I'm Your Lady 77 (Risk Me (FR) 127) [2001 –: **86** 6.1d 5m³ 6m⁶ 5.1f* 5f* 5m³ 5m² 5.1f⁴ 5g³ 5g 6.1m 5s³ 5g 5d⁴ 5v² Oct 29] workmanlike gelding: fairly useful performer: won maiden at Nottingham and handicap at Mussel-burgh in June: mostly ran well in handicaps after, best efforts on last 2: easily best form at 5f, though should be fully effective at 6f: acts on any going. *R. Guest*

SIR DON (IRE) 2 b.c. (Apr 3) Lake Coniston (IRE) 131 – New Sensitive (Wattlefield **78 +** 117) [2001 5m³ 5g² 5.1m² Sep 10] IR 15,000F, 34,000Y: sparely-made colt: fifth foal: half-brother to 7f winner Anthemion (by Night Shift) and winners abroad by Tom Boat and Eagle Eyed: dam, won 9 times in Belgium, half-sister to very smart sprinter Hever Golf Rose: fair form in maidens: second at Thirsk (raced alone, better than result) and Nottingham: should stay 6f. *J. M. P. Eustace*

SIR EDWARD BURROW (IRE) 3 b.g. Distinctly North (USA) 115 – Alalja (IRE) **52** 95 (Entitled 126) [2001 52: 10m 12.4m⁶ 8.3m 13.1f⁴ 16f³ f14.8g 16m⁶ 16f 13.8m 13.8s Oct 20] modest maiden: stays 2m: very best efforts on ground firmer than good (no show both starts on fibresand): none too consistent: sold 1,500 gns. *R. F. Fisher*

SIR EFFENDI (IRE) 5 ch.g. Nashwan (USA) 135 – Jeema 102 (Thatch (USA) 136) **89** [2001 99: 7m 7.1g³ Jun 8] tall, good-topped gelding: lightly raced: fairly useful form in handicap and minor event in 2001: may prove best at 7f/1m: best efforts on going firmer than good: gelded after final start. *M. P. Tregoning*

SIR FERBET (IRE) 4 b.c. Mujadil (USA) 119 – Mirabiliary (USA) 74 (Crow (FR) **91** 134) [2001 93, a108: 7.6f² 8.3g 8m 8s f7g* 8d Oct 18] strong, lengthy colt: fairly useful performer: below form after first start, including when winning claimer at Wolverhamp-ton in October: best up to 8.5f: acts on fibresand, firm and good to soft ground, possibly not on soft/heavy: sold 10,000 gns. *B. W. Hills*

SIR FRANCIS (IRE) 3 b.g. Common Grounds 118 – Red Note (Rusticaro (FR) 124) **81** [2001 95: 5.1s 6s 5g 5s p7g³ Dec 12] useful-looking gelding: has a round action: fairly useful performer at 2 yrs: best effort in 2001 on final outing: best at 5f/6f: acts on soft ground and polytrack: visored (tailed off) once at 2 yrs: has wandered under pressure. *J. Noseda*

SIR GEORGE TURNER 2 ch.c. (May 2) Nashwan (USA) 135 – Ingozi 91 (Warning **100 p** 136) [2001 7g³ 7g* 7g² 7d* Oct 2] 35,000Y: big, close-coupled colt: fourth foal: half-brother to 3 winners, including 5-y-o Tissifer and 3-y-o Oshiponga: dam, 7f/1m

£400000 Tattersalls Houghton Sales Stakes, Newmarket—
Sir George Turner (left) takes this huge prize by a head from Landseer (right), with Desert Warning third

winner, half-sister to smart 6f/7f performer Inchinor out of smart winner up to 1m Inchmurrin: useful form: won maiden at Leicester in July and 16-runner £400000 Tattersalls Houghton Sales Stakes at Newmarket (by head from Landseer, responding well to lead final 1f) in October: will stay 1¼m: type to make an even better 3-y-o. *M. Johnston*

SIR HAMELIN (IRE)   4 b.g. Hernando (FR) 127 – Georgia Stephens (USA) 64 (The   **66** Minstrel (CAN) 135) [2001 e10g⁴ 10f Jun 14] fairly useful performer at best: won claimer at Maisons-Laffitte at 3 yrs, final start for B. Dutruel: fair form in Britain only on first start: stays 1½m: acts on good to firm and good to soft going, and equitrack: wears blinkers/visor: tongue tied final outing. *M. C. Pipe*

SIR NETBETSPORTS (IRE)   2 b.g. (Apr 23) Dolphin Street (FR) 125 – Bid High   **48** (IRE) (High Estate 127) [2001 5.1s 5s f5g⁶ f6g* 7.1s 7.5g f7g Oct 1] small gelding: second foal: dam unraced: poor performer: won seller at Southwell in May: off 3½ months before well beaten last 3 starts: stays 6f: acts on fibresand: blinkered last 4 outings. *B. S. Rothwell*

SIR NINJA (IRE)   4 b.g. Turtle Island (IRE) 123 – The Poachers Lady (IRE) (Salmon   **91** Leap (USA) 131) [2001 98: f8.5g 8v 8s 10.1s⁵ 10.1m 11.9m 8.1v³ 8g 7.9d² 8.2s 10v³ Nov 8] heavy-bodied gelding: carries plenty of condition: fairly useful handicapper: stays 1¼m: has form on good to firm going, best on softer than good: visored once in 2000: difficult ride: none too consistent. *D. J. S. ffrench Davis*

SIR NORTHERNDANCER (IRE)   2 b.c. (Mar 8) Danehill Dancer (IRE) 117 –   **82** Lady At War (Warning 136) [2001 5m⁶ 6m⁶ 5.1g⁵ 7m² 7g² 7d* 7g⁵ 7s 6d⁵ 6v² p6g³ Nov 28] IR 15,500Y: workmanlike colt: has scope: first foal: dam unraced sister to 5-y-o Weet For Me: fairly useful performer: won nursery at Chester in August: good placed efforts in similar events after: stays 7f: acts on heavy going, good to firm and polytrack: races prominently: reliable. *R. Hannon*

SIR PERSE   5 b.g. Precocious 126 – Anne's Bank (IRE) 77 (Burslem 123) [2001 f11g   **–** e7g Mar 19] modest maiden in 1999: well held in handicaps in 2001: blinkered once at 3 yrs. *Jamie Poulton*

SIR SANDROVITCH (IRE)   5 b.g. Polish Patriot (USA) 128 – Old Downie (Be   **83** My Guest (USA) 126) [2001 79: f5s f5g⁵ f5g³ f6g² 6v 5v f5g⁶ 5m 5m⁴ 5m* 5m³ 5.1f³ 5f   **a75** 6m⁶ 5g* 5f³ 6g 5g 5m 5.1d³ 5d 5m Sep 20] tall gelding: fairly useful handicapper on turf, fair on all-weather: won at Beverley in June and Pontefract in July: best at 5f: acts on firm going, good to soft and fibresand: has worn dropped noseband/gone early to post: sometimes spoils chance at start: tends to pull hard: reportedly lame behind final start. *R. A. Fahey*

SIR WALTER (IRE)   8 b.g. The Bart (USA) 108 – Glenbalda (Kambalda 108) [2001   **37** –: 7.1g² Jul 20] poor performer: lightly raced on Flat nowadays: effective at 7f, barely stays 13f: acts on good to firm going, fibresand and equitrack: tried blinkered/tongue tied: tends to finish weakly. *D. Burchell*

SISAL (IRE)   2 b.f. (Apr 12) Danehill (USA) 126 – Ship's Twine (IRE) 55 (Slip   **84** Anchor 136) [2001 6m f6g* 6f² 6d² 6m³ Aug 13] 22,000Y: fourth foal: dam, maiden who should have stayed 1½m, half-sister to smart 7f to 9f performer Restructure (by Danehill) and very smart 1¼m performer/Champion Hurdle winner Alderbrook: fairly useful performer: won maiden at Wolverhampton in June: placed in nurseries last 2 starts: will need to settle to stay beyond 6f: acts on firm ground, good to soft and fibresand. *M. A. Jarvis*

SISTER IN LAW (FR)   2 b.f. (Mar 23) Distant Relative 128 – Despina (Waajib 121)   **76 p** [2001 5.1m² 5s⁴ Oct 5] first foal: dam, little sign of ability, granddaughter of US Grade 1 8.5f winner Equanimity: better effort in maidens (fair form) when 4 lengths second to Lipstick at Bath: favourite but still green, seemed to flounder when fourth at Lingfield: should stay 6f: probably capable of better. *H. Candy*

SITA (IRE)   3 gr.f. Indian Ridge 123 – Moon Festival 74 (Be My Guest (USA) 126)   **112 ?** [2001 88p: 8s* 10s* 12g 10.3s Nov 9] IR 20,000Y: smallish, strong filly: fourth living foal: closely related to fairly useful Irish 1¾m winner Lunasa (by Don't Forget Me) and half-sister to useful 1m winner Silver Apple (by Danehill): dam, maiden who stayed 1¼m, half-sister to high-class middle-distance performers Moon Madness and Sheriff's Star: smart performer, lightly raced: won maiden at Leopardstown and minor event at Navan (clearly best effort, by 9 lengths from Karsavina, making all) in April, then left K. Prendergast in Ireland and off over 5 months: tailed-off last in listed race at Newmarket then well held in minor event at Doncaster: stays 1¼m: raced only on good going or softer. *J. R. Fanshawe*

SITARA   3 ch.f. Salse (USA) 128 – Souk (IRE) 98 (Ahonoora 122) [2001 57p: 12m² 12f* 14v 11.7d³ 12g⁵ Nov 7] leggy filly: fair performer: won minor event at Musselburgh in September: should stay at least 1¾m: acts on firm going, possibly not on heavy. *L. M. Cumani*   **74**

SITTIN BULL   2 b.c. (May 2) Revoque (IRE) 122 – Taiga 69 (Northfields (USA)) [2001 7s 8.2s p7g Dec 22] 6,200Y: half-brother to several winners, including fairly useful 7f to 9f winner Polonez Prima (by Thatching): dam 1¼m winner: no form in maidens/minor event: left L. Cumani after second start. *T. D. McCarthy*   **–**

SIX BELLS   5 b.m. Gildoran 123 – Strikealightlady (Lighter 111) [2001 e12g p12g Nov 13] only foal: dam fatally injured in a bumper after birth of this foal: modest form at best in bumpers: well held in maidens at Lingfield on Flat 9 months apart. *P. D. Evans*   **–**

SIX HITTER (USA)   2 ch.c. (Mar 10) Boundary (USA) 117 – Granny Kelly (USA) 60 (Irish River (FR) 131) [2001 6f² 6f* 7.5d³ 7.5m* Sep 2] $72,000F: sparely-made colt: fluent mover: first foal: dam, third at 7f at 2 yrs in Ireland, from family of Northern Dancer: fairly useful form: landed odds in minor event at Pontefract (by neck from Goldeva) in July and listed race at Florence (beat Sweet Groom by 4 lengths) in September: stays 7.5f: acts on firm and good to soft going: sent to USA. *P. F. I. Cole*   **88**

SIX PACK (IRE)   3 ch.g. Royal Abjar (USA) 121 – Regal Entrance (Be My Guest (USA) 126) [2001 8v 10m⁴ 10.5d 10.9d 7.1g⁶ 7s² Oct 5] 3,000F, IR 10,000Y, 12,000 2-y-o: tall, good-topped gelding: half-brother to 3 winners, including 1989 2-y-o 6f winner who became ungenuine Rainbow Bridge (by Godswalk) and 1¼m winner Hoochiecoochie Man (by Taufan): dam Irish 7f winner: modest maiden handicapper: should stay 1m: acts on soft ground. *Andrew Turnell*   **56**

SIXTY SECONDS (IRE)   3 b.c. Definite Article 121 – Damemill (IRE) 83 (Danehill (USA) 126) [2001 97p: 10g⁴ 10.4m⁴ 11.9d⁴ 10f⁴ 8g 11m⁴ Aug 17] strong colt: useful performer: creditable efforts in 2001 when fourth in listed races at Newmarket (4 lengths behind Rosi's Boy) and Ascot (beaten 2¾ lengths by Freefourinternet) on first and fourth starts, and in handicap at Newbury (behind Shamaiel, having raced in clear lead) on final one: probably best around 1¼m: acts on firm ground: visored third, fourth and final appearances: flashed tail penultimate outing: possibly not the most straightforward ride: joined D. Oughton in Hong Kong. *J. H. M. Gosden*   **100**

SIZE DOESNT MATTER   3 b.g. Greensmith 121 – Singing Rock (IRE) 67 (Ballad Rock 122) [2001 30: f11g e7g Mar 16] poor form at 2 yrs: well held in 2001. *J. R. Best*   **–**

SKENFRITH   2 b.g. (Apr 14) Atraf 116 – Hobbs Choice 51 (Superpower 113) [2001 5.1g⁶ 5.1s 6s³ 6g⁵ 6m f6g Oct 6] 4,200Y, resold 10,000Y: close-coupled gelding: first foal: dam 6f winner/winning hurdler: modest maiden: stays 6f: acts on good to firm and soft going, well held on fibresand: blinkered last 3 starts. *A. Berry*   **59**

SKIES ARE BLUE   2 b.f. (Mar 3) Unfuwain (USA) 131 – Blue Birds Fly 78 (Rainbow Quest (USA) 134) [2001 7m³ 8.1s³ Aug 19] 220,000Y: fourth foal: half-sister to fairly useful 2-y-o 5f winners For Old Times Sake (in 1996, by Efisio) and Strange Destiny (in 2000, by Mujadil) and Italian 8.5f (at 2 yrs) and 10.5f winner Tenacious Memory (by Ezzoud): dam 1¼m winner: fair form in maidens at Kempton (very slowly away) and Sandown (not knocked about): probably capable of better. *I. A. Balding*   **70 p**

SKIFFLE MAN   5 b.g. Alhijaz 122 – Laundry Maid 89 (Forzando 122) [2001 f12g f16.2g Feb 8] of little account on Flat nowadays. *B. I. Case*   **–**

SKI FOR ME (IRE)   2 ch.f. (Apr 6) Barathea (IRE) 127 – Ski For Gold 76 (Shirley Heights 130) [2001 7d⁴ 8.3v* Oct 29] well-made filly: second foal: dam, 2-y-o 7f winner who may have proved best around 1¾m, half-sister to US Grade 1 1¼m winner Bequest: fair form: 11/8-on, confirmed promise when winning maiden at Windsor by 2 lengths from Yaounde, racing freely but asserting final 1f despite carrying head high: should be suited by 1¼m/1½m: probably capable of better. *J. L. Dunlop*   **78 p**

SKINFLINT   2 b.f. (Mar 20) Emperor Fountain 112 – Bad Payer 72 (Tanfirion 110) [2001 5g f6g f7g Nov 17] unfurnished filly: half-sister to 3 winning sprinters, including 5-y-o AA-Youknownothing: dam 2-y-o 5f winner: poor form in maidens. *C. W. Thornton*   **40**

SKIPPY MAC 2 ch.c. (Mar 10) Presidium 124 – Ski Path (Celtic Cone 116) [2001 5m   **46**
5f⁶ 6m 7m⁴ 8.5m 7m Sep 6] 800Y: leggy colt: first foal: dam bad novice hurdler: poor
maiden. *N. Bycroft*

SKI RUN 5 b.m. Petoski 135 – Cut And Run (Slip Anchor 136) [2001 112: 10.4m⁶   **104**
16.4m 13.9m Jul 14] rather unfurnished mare: smart performer at 4 yrs, useful in 2001:
respectable eighth to Solo Mio in Henry II Stakes at Sandown on second start: last of 7 in
listed rated stakes at York final outing: stays 2m: acts on soft and good to firm going:
waited with. *G. A. Butler*

SKUKUSA 3 b.f. Emarati (USA) 74 – Glensara (Petoski 135) [2001 –: f7g⁶ e6g² e6g⁴   **58**
e7g* e7s² Feb 17] close-coupled filly: modest performer: won claimer at Lingfield in
February: free-going sort, unlikely to stay beyond 7f: acts on equitrack: reportedly mulish
at start penultimate outing. *R. Guest*

SKY DOME (IRE) 8 ch.g. Bluebird (USA) 125 – God Speed Her (Pas de Seul 133)   **71**
[2001 84: 8m³ 9m⁴ 8m 9g 9g 7.1g² 7.6g* 8m⁶ 8m² 9g⁵ p8g p7g² p8g⁴ p7g⁵ Dec 12]
lengthy, leggy gelding: poor mover: fair performer: won minor event at Lingfield in
September: effective at 7f to easy 1¼m: acts on soft going, good to firm and polytrack:
blinkered last 9 starts: has carried head awkwardly/found little. *M. H. Tompkins*

SKYE BLUE (IRE) 4 b.g. Blues Traveller (IRE) 119 – Hitopah (Bustino 136) [2001   **62 §**
71§: 16v³ 11.6g 18m³ 14.1m 16m Aug 28] tall gelding: modest maiden handicapper: left
N. Henderson after second start: stays 2¼m: acts on heavy and good to firm going: has
hung/carried head awkwardly/found little: can't be trusted. *D. W. P. Arbuthnot*

SKYERS A KITE 6 b.m. Deploy 131 – Milady Jade (IRE) (Drumalis 125) [2001 72,   –
a41: 12s Mar 22] small, good-topped mare: fair performer at best: well held only Flat run
in 2001. *Ronald Thompson*

SKYERS FLYER (IRE) 7 b. or br.m. Magical Wonder (USA) 125 – Siwana (IRE)   –
(Dom Racine (FR) 121) [2001 44: e7g Jan 13] probably of little account nowadays.
Ronald Thompson

SKYLARK 4 ch.f. Polar Falcon (USA) 126 – Boozy 111 (Absalom 128) [2001 68:   **73**
5m⁶ 5f⁶ 5m² 5m⁴ 5.1g² 6g⁶ 6g 5g⁵ 5.7m² 5.1g² 6.1d 5s 5.1d 6v Nov 8] leggy filly: fair
maiden handicapper: below form last 4 starts: best at 5f/6f: acts on firm and good to
soft going, below form only run on fibresand: has been slowly away: looks hard ride.
J. L. Spearing

SKYLARKER (USA) 3 b.g. Sky Classic (CAN) – O My Darling (USA) 76 (Mr   **98**
Prospector (USA)) [2001 8d 10m* 11.6m³ 11.9m⁶ Sep 5] tall, rather leggy gelding: fifth
foal: half-brother to useful French 1m (including at 2 yrs) and 1¼m winner Bluebell
Dancer (by Sovereign Dancer): dam, minor sprint winner in USA at 4 yrs, sister to
Preakness winner Tank's Prospect: useful performer: won maiden at Newmarket in June:
good 7½ lengths third to Delius in minor event at Windsor in August: last in handicap at
York final outing: likely to prove best at 1¼m/1½m: yet to race on extremes of going.
C. F. Wall

SLAM BID 4 b.g. First Trump 118 – Nadema (Artaius (USA) 129) [2001 60d: 10m   **– §**
12m⁵ 10f 9m⁶ 8.3d 8m Aug 28] quite good-topped gelding: temperamental maiden: tried
blinkered. *R. E. Barr*

SLANEYSIDE (IRE) 4 ch.g. Project Manager 111 – Erneside (Lomond (USA) 128)   **56**
[2001 70d: 12m³ 12m⁶ 13m Jun 14] modest performer nowadays: stays 1½m: acts on
heavy and good to firm going: tried visored/blinkered: often races prominently. *I. Semple*

SLAPY DAM 9 b.g. Deploy 131 – Key To The River (USA) (Irish River (FR) 131)   **45 §**
[2001 –§: 10m² 11.9f 18m 8.1m 10.2s⁵ 12d 11.8s Oct 16] close-coupled gelding: poor
performer nowadays: stays 1½m: acts on soft and good to firm going: tried visored:
unreliable. *D. Burchell*

SLASHER JACK (IRE) 10 b.g. Alzao (USA) 117 – Sherkraine 98 (Shergar 140)   –
[2001 –: 13.1d⁶ Jul 23] good-bodied gelding: one-time fairly useful winner: lightly raced
nowadays: tried blinkered: winning hurdler. *Mrs D. Thomson*

SLEETING 8 ch.g. Lycius (USA) 124 – Pluvial 90 (Habat 127) [2001 10.2s 12g Aug   –
17] well held in 2 sellers. *J. Gallagher*

SLEW THE RED (USA) 4 b.c. Red Ransom (USA) – Great Lady Slew (USA)   **117**
(Seattle Slew (USA)) [2001 115: 10v 12s* 10g* 10s* 12m³ 12g 12f Oct 27] strong,
close-coupled colt: smart performer: won listed race at Chantilly in May, La Coupe at

Longchamp (by 1½ lengths from Di Moi Oui) in June and Prix Gontaut-Biron at Deau-ville (by length from Mocham Glen) in August: creditable 1¼ lengths third to Hightori in Prix Foy at Longchamp next time and not discredited when eighth to Mutamam in Canadian International at Woodbine penultimate outing: behind in Breeders' Cup Turf at Belmont final start: effective at 1¼m to 12.5f: acts on soft and good to firm going: held up. *A. Fabre, France*

SLICKLY (FR)   5 gr.h. Linamix (FR) 127 – Slipstream Queen (USA) (Conquis-   **128** tador Cielo (USA)) [2001 120: 8.9g⁶ 9g* 8d* 8d* Oct 14]

Slickly has been tried over various distances in his career but it looks as though he has now found his true vocation. He developed into a high-class miler in the latest season, and, along with Medicean, was just about the best in Europe. As a three-year-old with Andre Fabre, Slickly started out as a Derby hope and was reckoned to be a big danger to Montjeu in the Prix du Jockey Club before fourth place at Chantilly put an end to aspirations for him at a mile and a half. In his first season with Godolphin in 2000, Slickly was campaigned exclusively at around a mile and a quarter, winning La Coupe and the Prix Dollar, both at Longchamp. His two defeats that year came after he had raced freely, however, and in his latest campaign he was brought back first to nine furlongs, and then to a mile.

Slickly made his reappearance in the Dubai Duty Free at Nad Al Sheba, where again he failed to settle, pulling hard in a duel for the lead with the top New Zealand mare Sunline, a battle which Slickly finally lost over a furlong out before fading into sixth. A drop back to a mile in a race where he would not be harried for the lead looked the ideal recipe for him next, but, before being found just such an opportunity, Slickly faced a relatively easier task in a minor event over nine furlongs at Sandown in August, making all and landing the odds with little fuss.

Slickly was then sent to Longchamp for the Prix du Moulin, his first outing at a mile since finishing fifth to Sendawar in the same race two years earlier. In his other start over a mile as a three-year-old Slickly had finished second to Dubai Millennium in the Prix Jacques le Marois. Defeat by Sendawar remains the only blot on Slickly's record at Longchamp, where the latest Prix du Moulin saw him record his fifth win at the track. Longchamp's turning mile proved ideal for Slickly's free-running style of racing, and he was soon in a clear lead over the main body of the field headed by two of the British challengers, Olden Times and Danceabout. Allowing his pursuers to close approaching the turn, Dettori asked Slickly to lengthen again in the straight and he never looked in danger of being caught, passing the post with three lengths to spare. Favourite Banks Hill, along with Hawkeye, had been held up in rear and left with too much to do, the pair running on to fill the places without ever looking a threat. Second favourite Vahorimix was another who never got into the race at any stage, following a slow start, and finished sixth behind Olden Times, who dead-heated for fourth with the other British runner Warningford.

The Moulin represented improved form from Slickly, even allowing that some of his rivals had not been seen to best effect. But the opposition which lined up for the Premio Vittori di Capua at Milan the following month was never going to extend Slickly into recording a new career-best effort. Slickly apart, it looked the worst field for a Group 1 in Europe all year, and that was before most of Slickly's main rivals—such as they were—ran poorly. The previous year's German-trained winner Faberger finished a well-beaten fourth, while arguably the best of the Italian

Prix du Moulin de Longchamp—a fifth course success and a career-best performance from Slickly, who makes all to win by three lengths; Banks Hill (white sleeves) stays on for second, ahead of Hawkeye (rail) and Warningford (hooped cap)

runners Crisos Il Monaco all but refused to race. For the record Slickly won easing down by six lengths from Dane Friendly.

In theory at least, the Prix du Moulin and the Premio Vittori di Capua should have drawn similar-quality fields, both being Group 1 contests. In practice however, Italian pattern races, and their Group 1 events in particular, consistently draw substandard fields compared to the rest of Europe. Twenty-five pattern races were run in Italy in 2001 but an inordinate proportion of them, eight (or 32%), carried Group 1 status. There is a notable discrepancy with Germany which has nearly twice as many pattern races, forty-four, but only seven (or 16%) Group 1 contests. What makes the imbalance even more absurd is that Italy has far fewer horses than Germany of Group 1 standard. In 2001, forty-four German horses earned a Timeform rating of at least 110, compared to just nine in Italy. Little wonder then that Italian runners rarely get a look-in in their own Group 1 races—the Vittorio di Capua, for example, was last won by an Italian horse in 1988. The supposed

			Mendez	Bellypha
Slickly (FR)	Linamix (FR)		(gr 1981)	Miss Carina
(gr.h. 1996)	(gr 1987)		Lunadix	Breton
			(gr 1972)	Lutine
			Conquistador Cielo	Mr Prospector
	Slipstream Queen (USA)		(b 1979)	K D Princess
	(b 1990)		Country Queen	Explodent
			(b 1975)	Carrie's Rough

Godolphin's "Slickly"

safeguards ensuring that races are graded according to the strength of field they attract don't seem to be operating, with Italy's Group 1 allocation being clearly over-generous, particularly compared with that of Germany. Germany, for example, has no Group 1 mile race despite a healthy population of good milers, while Italy has a Group 1 mile race but no milers of Group 1 standard.

Slickly's pedigree was discussed in *Racehorses of 2000*. An important update is that his three-year-old half-brother No Slip (by Exit To Nowhere) made a winning debut over a mile at Saint-Cloud for Slickly's former connections before taking the Grade 2 nine-furlong Oak Tree Derby at Santa Anita for Bobby Frankel the day before Slickly won in Milan. Slickly's two-year-old full sister Silamixa, also with Andre Fabre, made a less auspicious start, finishing last at Clairefontaine on her only appearance. Slickly, a tall horse, stays in training in 2002, when he will be attempting to maintain his record of having won pattern races in every season he has raced. The Prix Ganay and Prix d'Ispahan are said to be under consideration for him, and while the Ganay (over an extended ten furlongs) might be a little further than ideal, it would be unwise to rule him out given his record at Longchamp and the likelihood of a small field which he could easily dominate. Slickly has never raced on firm ground but acts on any other. *Saeed bin Suroor*

SLIEVE BLOOM (IRE)   4 b.g. Dancing Dissident (USA) 119 – Full of Sparkle (IRE) (Persian Heights 129) [2001 48: f9.4s⁶ Jan 9] poor maiden at 3 yrs: well held only outing in 2001. *T. G. Mills*   –

SLIP KILLICK   4 b.f. Cosmonaut – Killick 69 (Slip Anchor 136) [2001 61?: f8g f9.4g⁴ f9.4g f8g³ e7g f8f³ f11g 5d² 5d 5m 6d 6m 7m 7.1f 8.1g³ 10.9m 10s f6g f8.5g f6s Dec 15] tall, quite good-topped filly: modest maiden: generally on downgrade in 2001: stays 1m: acts on good to firm ground, good to soft and fibresand: tried visored: has carried head awkwardly/found little. *M. Mullineaux*   **54 d**

SLIPPER ROSE   3 ch.f. Democratic (USA) 101 – Brown Taw 66 (Whistlefield 118) [2001 52: f8g f8.5s⁵ f8s⁴ f7g⁵ f8g f7g 12s⁵ f9.4g May 3] poor performer: stays 1m: acts on heavy going and fibresand: temperament under suspicion. *R. Hollinshead*   **43**

SLIP STREAM (USA)   5 ch.h. Irish River (FR) 131 – Sous Entendu (USA) (Shadeed (USA) 135) [2001 116: 8g⁴ 8.9g⁴ Mar 4] strong, angular horse: fluent mover: smart performer: creditable 3½ lengths fourth to Mahfooth in prestige race at Nad Al Sheba on second of only 2 outings in 2001: stays 9f: acts on any turf going: usually races prominently: visored third 4-y-o start: joined K. McLaughlin in UAE. *Saeed bin Suroor*   **116**

SLOANE   5 ch.g. Machiavellian (USA) 123 – Gussy Marlowe 118 (Final Straw 127) [2001 83: 7.1g² 7s 7f² 7.1m³ 8m³ 7g* 7g Aug 11] big, good-topped gelding: usually looks well: fairly useful handicapper: won at Newcastle in July: probably better at 7f than 1m: acts on firm ground (below form on softer than good). *M. L. W. Bell*   **89**

SLUMBERING (IRE)   5 b.g. Thatching 131 – Bedspread (USA) (Seattle Dancer (USA) 119) [2001 83: f9.4g 8v³ 7s* 7.1g 7.6m⁶ 7g 7d⁴ 7d² 8d⁶ 8d p8g p8g Dec 22] tall gelding: fairly useful handicapper: won at Kempton in April: races mainly over 7f/1m nowadays: has form on firm ground, best efforts on softer than good (acts on heavy): sometimes blinkered earlier in career: has drifted left: withdrawn after bursting out of stall/bolting before intended eleventh outing. *B. A. Pearce*   **87 a–**

SLUPIA (IRE)   2 b.f. (Feb 23) Indian Ridge 123 – Ustka 60 (Lomond (USA) 128) [2001 6g³ Oct 19] quite attractive filly: fifth living foal: sister to 5-y-o Kuster and half-sister to 2 winners, including 7-y-o Travelmate: dam, 7f winner, closely related to useful middle-distance winner Adam Smith and smart middle-distance stayer Braashee: 12/1 and green, length third of 13 to Wish in maiden at Redcar, keeping on well having been soon chased along in rear: should stay at least 1m: sure to improve. *J. H. M. Gosden*   **76 p**

SMALL FRY (IRE)   3 b.f. Tagula (IRE) 116 – Alaroos (IRE) (Persian Bold 123) [2001 57: 6m⁶ f6g 5f 8g Aug 13] modest maiden: no form after reappearance: may prove best at 5f: acts on fibresand and good to firm going. *H. A. McWilliams*   **51 d**

SMALL PRINT   3 b.g. Saddlers' Hall (IRE) 126 – A Nymph Too Far (IRE) 49 (Precocious 126) [2001 10d 10m 10.1g 11.9s⁶ 10d⁵ Oct 15] fifth foal: dam 1m winner: little form: blinkered last 2 starts. *Dr J. D. Scargill*   –

Convergent Systems Avaya Communications Stakes (Handicap), York—Smart Predator improves for the return to five furlongs and records the first of four victories during the year; Smokin Beau finishes second, ahead of Galloway Boy (No.4), Argent Facile (No.11) and Henry Hall (spots)

SMART DANCER (IRE)   3 b.g. Spectrum (IRE) 126 – Plessaya (USA) (Nureyev (USA) 131) [2001 74: 8m 7d 8m² f7g⁶ Jul 13] angular, unfurnished gelding: fair at 2 yrs, only modest in 2001: not sure to stay beyond 1m: acts on firm going, well held on good to soft: sold 2,600 gns. *T. D. Easterby*   **59**

SMARTER CHARTER   8 br.g. Master Willie 129 – Irene's Charter 72 (Persian Bold 123) [2001 63: 12s⁵ 10s⁶ 9.7v⁴ 11s² 10f⁶ 10.1g* 10f 10m⁶ 9.9m⁶ 12f 10.1g 12g 14.1m* 16d 10d 12d 14.1g 10.1v⁶ 12g Nov 7] leggy, lengthy gelding: modest handicapper: won at Yarmouth in June and Redcar in September: effective at 1¼m to 1¾m: acts on any going: held up: ridden by Kristin Stubbs. *Mrs L. Stubbs*   **53**

SMART HOSTESS   2 b. or gr.f. (Jan 27) Most Welcome 131 – She's Smart 88 (Absalom 128) [2001 5g 6v³ Oct 24] heavy-bodied filly: fifth foal: half-sister to 5f/6f winner Rum Lad (by Efisio) and 5-y-o Smart Predator: dam sprinter: better effort in maidens (modest form) when ninth of 18 to Marcus Aurelius at Beverley (moved poorly to post): type to do better as 3-y-o. *J. J. Quinn*   **54 p**

SMART PREDATOR   5 gr.g. Polar Falcon (USA) 126 – She's Smart 88 (Absalom 128) [2001 94: 6s⁵ 6d 5m* 5m 6m 5f* 5m 6g 5g² 5.6m⁶ 5d* 5s³ 5d* 5v² Oct 27] big, lengthy, good-quartered gelding: smart performer: better than ever in 2001, winning handicaps at York and Doncaster in May/July, minor event at Beverley in September and handicap at Newmarket (beat Chookie Heiton by ¾ length) in October: good neck second to Fantasy Believer in handicap at Doncaster final start, ridden with more restraint than usual: has won at 1m, best at 5f nowadays: acts on any ground: very speedy, and usually races prominently: tough and genuine. *J. J. Quinn*   **115**

SMART RIDGE   4 ch.c. Indian Ridge 123 – Guanhumara (Caerleon (USA) 132) [2001 108: 7d⁶ 8s 7g⁵ 6g⁶ 7.1s² 7m⁶ 8g² 9f 8g⁶ 8d Oct 19] smallish, close-coupled colt: has a quick action: useful performer: best efforts in 2001 when second in handicaps at Sandown in June and Ascot (beaten ½ length by Persiano) in August: best at 7f/1m: acts on any going: tends to carry head awkwardly: inconsistent: sent to USA. *Jamie Poulton*   **103 §**

SMART SAVANNAH   5 b.g. Primo Dominie 121 – High Savannah 77 (Rousillon (USA) 133) [2001 –: 8s May 7] big, lengthy gelding: useful handicapper at 3 yrs: well beaten both Flat runs since: has tongue tied: winning hurdler. *E. Stanners*   **–**

SMART SCOT   2 ch.g. (Mar 17) Selkirk (USA) 129 – Amazing Bay 100 (Mazilier (USA) 107) [2001 7g 7m⁴ 6.1g 7m Sep 22] 33,000 2-y-o: leggy, lengthy gelding: has scope: second foal: dam, 2-y-o 5f/6f winner, from family of Nunthorpe winners Lochsong and Lochangel: modest maiden: has shown signs of temperament. *J. G. Given*   **55**

SMASHING TIME (USA)   3 b.f. Smart Strike (CAN) 121 – Broken Peace (USA) (Devil's Bag (USA)) [2001 67: 8g 9m 8m⁴ 8.3m 7d f8g f8g⁵ Dec 10] good-topped filly: fair maiden on turf, modest on all-weather: sold from Mrs A. Perrett 1,500 gns after fifth start: quite free-going sort, and may prove best up to 1m: acts on good to firm going. *M. C. Chapman*   **70 a58**

946

SMILING APPLAUSE 2 b.c. (May 3) Royal Applause 124 – Smilingatstrangers 58 – (Macmillion 110) [2001 8s 8.2s Nov 5] third foal: dam out-and-out stayer: well held in maidens. *Mrs Barbara Waring*

SMIRFYS LINCLON 2 b.g. (Apr 21) Never So Bold 135 – Party Scenes (Most – Welcome 131) [2001 f7g Nov 27] second foal: half-brother to 3-y-o Smirfys Party: dam unraced out of half-sister to very smart 2-y-o 6f winner/US Grade 1 1m winner Forzando: 16/1, slowly away when tailed off in maiden at Wolverhampton. *B. A. McMahon*

SMIRFYS NIGHT 2 b.c. (May 21) Tina's Pet 121 – Nightmare Lady 29 (Celestial – Storm (USA) 132) [2001 5s 6s Sep 27] quite good-topped colt: third foal: dam poor maiden: only a little sign of ability in maidens. *B. A. McMahon*

SMIRFYS PARTY 3 ch.c. Clantime 101 – Party Scenes (Most Welcome 131) [2001 **80** 67: 6.1d² 5.1f² 5.1f⁶ 6d* 6g f7g⁶ 6.1d 7d Oct 13] rather leggy, unfurnished colt: fairly useful handicapper: won at Haydock in July: well below form last 2 starts: effective at 5f/ 6f: acts on fibresand, firm and good to soft going. *B. A. McMahon*

SMIRK 3 ch.c. Selkirk (USA) 129 – Elfin Laughter 76 (Alzao (USA) 117) [2001 87p: **110** 7d* 7m 8m* 7.9m² 9g⁴ 9d² 8d² Nov 3] tall, lengthy colt: made into a smart performer: won maiden in May and handicap in July, both at Newmarket: mostly good efforts after, including 4 lengths fourth to I Cried For You in Cambridgeshire there and second in listed races on same course (beaten length by Right Wing, then 1½ lengths by Riberac) last 2 starts: effective at 1m/9f: acts on heavy and good to firm ground. *D. R. C. Elsworth*

SMITH N ALLAN OILS 2 b.g. (Feb 22) Bahamian Bounty 116 – Grand Splendour **63** 79 (Shirley Heights 130) [2001 6g⁵ 6d³ 7g⁶ 7d⁶ Oct 3] 4,000Y: good-bodied gelding: first foal: dam, 1¼m winner at 4 yrs, granddaughter of Prix Saint-Alary winner Fitnah: modest maiden: third at Hamilton: should stay 7f. *M. Dods*

SMOKER'S FOLLY 2 b.f. (Apr 10) Puissance 110 – Fair Attempt (IRE) (Try My **48** Best (USA) 130) [2001 6d² 7.5g 7d v⁵ Oct 24] 13,000Y: big, leggy filly: fourth foal: half-sister to 3-y-o Fair Princess and 6-y-o Mary Jane: dam unraced: well held after showing poor form when second to Fight Your Corner in slowly-run maiden at Newcastle: should prove best at 5f/6f. *N. Tinkler*

SMOKEY FROM CAPLAW 7 b.g. Sizzling Melody 117 – Mary From Dunlow 49 **53** (Nicholas Bill 125) [2001 –: f7g 8m* 7m* 8f⁴ 6g 6f 8.3m Sep 24] strong, compact gelding: has a round action: modest handicapper: won at Ayr in June and Doncaster in July: stays easy 1m: best form on good going or firmer: blinkered once: has carried head awkwardly. *J. S. Goldie*

SMOKIN BEAU 4 b.g. Cigar 68 – Beau Dada (IRE) 66 (Pine Circle (USA)) [2001 **113** 90, a79: f5g* 5s 5s 5m² 5.1f⁴ 5g 5m* 6g 5.2f 6g* 5g² 5.6m* 6m³ 5g² Oct 4] smallish, robust gelding: smart performer: progressed very well in 2001 and had fine season, winning handicaps at Wolverhampton, Ascot, Goodwood and Doncaster (beat Seven No Trumps by neck in Tote Trifecta Portland) between March/September: good efforts in

Hong Kong Jockey Club Sprint (Handicap), Ascot—
a valuable success for Smokin Beau, who beats Ellens Academy and Lord Kintyre

Tote Trifecta Portland (Handicap), Doncaster—the much improved Smokin Beau holds on well from Seven No Trumps, Guinea Hunter (almost hidden), Brevity (No.6), Eastern Purple (diamonds), Smart Predator (No.8), Candleriggs and Indian Prince

Ayr Gold Cup (¾-length third to Continent) and listed event at Newmarket (neck second to Indian Prince) on last 2 starts: best at 5f/easy 6f: acts on any turf going, fibresand and equitrack: visored twice at 3 yrs: has got upset in stall/been slowly away: has edged right: usually forces pace: tough: a credit to his stable. *J. Cullinan*

SMOOTHIE (IRE)   3 gr.g. Definite Article 121 – Limpopo 49 (Green Desert (USA) **82**
127) [2001 68: e7g* 7.1g⁴ 10.2f* 10g² 10m⁴ 9.9m⁵ Jun 27] close-coupled gelding: unimpressive mover: fairly useful performer: won handicaps at Lingfield in March and Bath in May: gelded after final start: stays 1¼m: possibly unsuited by heavy, acts on any other turf going and on equitrack: consistent. *P. F. I. Cole*

SMOOTH PASSAGE   2 b.g. (Mar 3) Suave Dancer (USA) 136 – Flagship 84 (Rain- **–**
bow Quest (USA) 134) [2001 6f 6g 7.1g Sep 13] 40,000Y: first foal: dam, 1¼m winner, sister to smart 1992 2-y-o 7f winner Yawl, out of Oaks winner Bireme, a very good family: well held in maidens. *M. P. Tregoning*

SMOOTH SAILING   6 gr.g. Beveled (USA) – Sea Farer Lake 74 (Gairloch 122) **83**
[2001 87: 8d 10g 10d³ 10d⁴ 10d⁵ 9.9d 8.1v 8.9d Oct 13] leggy gelding: fairly useful performer: stays 1¼m: probably best on good ground or softer: tried visored/blinkered at 2 yrs: has been slowly away/taken good hold/found little: none too reliable. *K. McAuliffe*

SMUGGLER'S SONG (IRE)   2 b.g. (Feb 13) Dr Devious (IRE) 127 – Liberty Song **90**
(IRE) (Last Tycoon 131) [2001 7m² 7g* 7m Jun 20] IR 65,000Y: close-coupled, workmanlike gelding: third foal: half-brother to fairly useful 2000 2-y-o 6f winner She Rocks (by Spectrum) and 4-y-o Fisher Island: dam, French 1m/11f winner at 4 yrs, granddaughter of Lupe: fairly useful form: landed odds in maiden at Naas in June: not discredited when eighth to Seba in Chesham Stakes at Royal Ascot: should stay 1¼m. *Charles O'Brien, Ireland*

SMYSLOV   3 b.g. Rainbow Quest (USA) 134 – Vlaanderen (IRE) 77 (In The Wings **84**
128) [2001 76: 10.3s 11.8g³ 11.9s 11m 10g⁴ 11.7d Oct 25] strong, lengthy gelding: fairly useful performer: ran creditably in 2001 when in frame: barely stays 1½m: acts on soft and good to firm going: carried head awkwardly penultimate start: sold 26,000 gns, and gelded. *J. L. Dunlop*

SNAILS CASTLE (IRE)   2 b.g. (Mar 10) Danehill (USA) 126 – Bean Island (USA) **75 p**
(Afleet (CAN)) [2001 7g 8g p8g⁴ p10g⁴ Dec 4] big, lengthy, good-topped gelding: second foal: dam, 1m winner in USA, half-sister to smart 1¼m performer Johan Cruyff from very good US family: fair form in maidens at Newmarket and Lingfield: stays 1¼m: probably capable of better. *N. A. Callaghan*

SNAKE GODDESS   3 b.f. Primo Dominie 121 – Shoshone (Be My Chief (USA) 122) **54**
[2001 –: 8.3s 8.1g 12m⁴ 14.1m 11.9s³ f14g Dec 14] workmanlike filly: modest maiden: left H. Morrison 7,000 gns before final start: stays 1½m: acts on soft and good to firm going. *D. W. P. Arbuthnot*

SNAPPY 2 ch.f. (Apr 15) First Trump 118 – Better Still (IRE) (Glenstal (USA) 118) **57**
[2001 5s f5g³ 5s⁵ Apr 23] rather leggy filly: fifth foal: dam little form: modest maiden: should stay 6f. *M. W. Easterby*

SNATCH 4 b.f. Elmaamul (USA) 125 – Tarkhana (IRE) (Dancing Brave (USA) 140) **44**
[2001 56: f12s² e12g f9.4g Feb 13] poor performer: left M. Bell and below form after reappearance: stays 1½m: acts on fibresand and equitrack. *M. Quinn*

SNECK LIFTER 2 b.f. (Mar 4) Zilzal (USA) 137 – Linpac North Moor 69 **63**
(Moorestyle 137) [2001 5s⁵ 5s³ 5.1f 5m⁶ 7.5s³ 8f³ 8m 8m Sep 11] 6,500F: close-coupled filly: poor mover: eighth foal: half-sister to fairly useful 1995 2-y-o 5f/6f winner Benny Glow (by Presidium) and a 9.5f winner in Germany by Elmaamul: dam, 7f/1m winner, half-sister to smart middle-distance performer Linpac West: modest maiden: stays 1m: very best form on soft going: tongue tied last 4 outings. *J. G. Given*

SNIP SNAP 2 b.f. (Jan 31) Revoque (IRE) 122 – Snap Crackle Pop (IRE) 87 **76**
(Statoblest 120) [2001 5.7g² 5.1d² 6m⁶ 6m Sep 12] 26,000Y: first foal: dam, 2-y-o 5f winner, granddaughter of Cheveley Park winner/1000 Guineas runner-up Jacinth: fair form: won maiden at Brighton in August, making virtually all: well held when favourite for nursery at Goodwood final start: should stay 7f: sold 8,000 gns. *Sir Mark Prescott*

SNIZORT (USA) 3 b.g. Bahri (USA) 125 – Ava Singstheblues (USA) (Dixieland **–**
Band (USA)) [2001 73: 10.1d⁶ 11.8f⁶ 12.3m⁶ Jun 10] useful-looking gelding: good mover: fair form on debut at 2 yrs: little form in 2001: blinkered final start: gelded after. *J. D. Bethell*

SNOW BUNTING 3 ch.g. Polar Falcon (USA) 126 – Marl 94 (Lycius (USA) 124) **57 +**
[2001 74: f7g⁵ 8.2m 6g 6g* 7g 7v Oct 26] fair form only 2-y-o start: left R. Charlton after reappearance: modest form when winning maiden at Ayr in August: stays 6f: raced mainly on good/good to firm ground on turf. *Jedd O'Keeffe*

SNOWFIRE 2 b.f. (Mar 27) Machiavellian (USA) 123 – Hill of Snow 80 (Reference **102 p**
Point 139) [2001 7g² 7f² 7g* 7g² Oct 6] strong, close-coupled, good-topped filly: third foal: half-sister to smart Irish 7f (including Moyglare Stud Stakes)/1m winner Preseli (by Caerleon) and 3-y-o Valley of Song: dam, Irish 1¼m winner, out of US Grade 1 8.5f to 1¼m winner White Star Line: useful form: justified favouritism in maiden at Lingfield in September by head from Starfan: gone in coat, best effort when beaten same margin by Protectress in listed event at Newmarket final start, leading over 2f out until final 1f: will stay at least 1¼m: should make a smart 3-y-o. *J. L. Dunlop*

SNOWFLAKE (IRE) 3 b.f. Caerleon (USA) 132 – Ivyanna (IRE) 112 (Reference **105 +**
Point 139) [2001 84: 8m 10g² 12f⁴ 10d 12g 9.9g² 11.9g 10g² Sep 2] 1,000,000 francs Y: leggy filly: good walker: third living foal: dam 1m (at 2 yrs in Ireland) and 1½m (Oaks d'Italia) winner: smart maiden: 3 lengths fourth to Sahara Slew in Ribblesdale Stakes at Royal Ascot: probably flattered when 1½ lengths second to Lailani in Nassau Stakes at Goodwood on sixth outing, all but pinching race under enterprising ride: well held in Yorkshire Oaks at York next time, and beaten 7 lengths when odds-on for maiden at the Curragh final outing: best at 1¼m/1½m: acts on firm going: has worn crossed noseband: made running last 3 starts: sent to USA. *A. P. O'Brien, Ireland*

SNOW LEOPARD (IRE) 2 gr.c. (Mar 5) Highest Honor (FR) 124 – Leopardess **87**
(IRE) 79 (Ela-Mana-Mou 132) [2001 7m 7g³ 7m² 8.1g* 7.9s Oct 11] IR 33,000Y: lengthy colt: third foal: half-brother to Irish 1¼m winner Madamaa (by Alzao): dam, 1¼m winner, half-sister to very smart miler Alflora: fairly useful performer: justified favouritism in maiden at Chepstow in September: well beaten in nursery final start: will stay 1¼m. *J. L. Dunlop*

SNOW PARTRIDGE (USA) 7 ch.g. Arctic Tern (USA) 126 – Lady Sharp (FR) **–**
(Sharpman) [2001 10f May 25] seems of little account nowadays. *N. E. Berry*

SNOW SHOES 2 b.f. (Apr 5) Sri Pekan (USA) 117 – Tundra (IRE) (Common Grounds **77**
118) [2001 6m² 6m⁶ 7m⁶ 6s* 6g Oct 6] 800F, IR 7,500Y: small filly: first foal: dam, ran 3 times, out of half-sister to smart French sprinter Gem Diamond: fair performer: won 21-runner nursery at Leicester in September: edgy, not discredited in similar event at Newmarket final start: should stay 7f: acts on soft going. *D. J. S. Cosgrove*

SNOWSTORM 3 gr.g. Environment Friend 128 – Choral Sundown 81 (Night Shift **116**
(USA)) [2001 97: 12.3f² 11m³ 12f² 12m⁴ 10d 8.9m³ 12g⁶ Oct 5] tall gelding: has a quick action: smart performer: in frame in Chester Vase at Chester (¾-length second to Mr Combustible), listed race at Goodwood, King Edward VII Stakes at Royal Ascot (best

Lord Blyth's "Snowstorm"

effort, went down by 1¼ lengths to Storming Home), Gordon Stakes at Goodwood and listed race at York: stays 1½m: acts on firm going, possibly not on softer than good: usually races prominently: has carried head awkwardly: gelded after final start: sent to Hong Kong. *M. L. W. Bell*

SOAKED   8 b.g. Dowsing (USA) 124 – Water Well 96 (Sadler's Wells (USA) 132) **80** [2001 69: 5m 5m 5m f5g³ 5m³ 5d 5f² 5.5d* 5g² 5.1g* 5g⁴ 5g 5m 5m 5g 5m 5s² 5s² 5d 5g³ 5d 5s Oct 22] workmanlike gelding: fairly useful performer: won handicap at Warwick in July and minor event at Nottingham in August: best around 5f: acts on fibresand, equitrack, firm and soft ground: visored once, blinkered nowadays: has reportedly bled from nose, including fifteenth start: front runner: tough. *D. W. Chapman*

SOARING PHOENIX (USA)   3 b. or br.g. St Jovite (USA) 135 – Pamzig (USA) 91 **60 +** (Danzig (USA)) [2001 –: 7d f8g² 9m⁵ 10m f12g² Jul 2] big, good-topped gelding: fair **a78** maiden on all-weather, modest on turf: stays 1½m: acts on fibresand, best turf effort on good to firm ground: sold 8,000 gns. *B. W. Hills*

SOBA JONES   4 b.g. Emperor Jones (USA) 119 – Soba 127 (Most Secret 119) [2001 **77** 66, a–: 5g* 5m 5m 5d² 5g⁵ 5m 6f* 5.1d⁵ 5d 5d 5s² 5g Nov 5] fair performer: won handicap at Haydock in June and minor event at Catterick in August: best at 5f: acts on fibresand, firm and soft going: effective blinkered or not: has been slowly away: races prominently. *T. D. Easterby*

SOBER AS A JUDGE   4 b.g. Mon Tresor 113 – Flicker Toa Flame (USA) 85 (Empery **44** (USA) 128) [2001 48: f8g⁴ 8m 7m 7f⁴ 8m f6s 7m Sep 22] poor maiden: left J. Pearce after first start: stays 1m: acts on fibresand, equitrack and firm ground: sometimes slowly away: visored last 4 starts. *C. A. Dwyer*

SOBER HILL 3 b.g. Komaite (USA) – Mamoda (Good Times (ITY)) [2001 –: f7s **44** f6s⁴ f7g⁴ f6g³ 6.1v⁵ f6g f8s Dec 21] poor maiden handicapper: stays 7f: acts on fibresand: usually blinkered in 2001. *D. Shaw*

SOBIESKI (IRE) 4 b.c. Polish Precedent (USA) 131 – Game Plan 118 (Darshaan **115** 133) [2001 118: a9f² a10f³ 10m 10s³ Aug 11] well-made colt: smart performer: best efforts at 4 yrs when creditable 1¾ lengths third to Hightori in Maktoum Challenge (Round III) at Nad Al Sheba in March and respectable third to Slew The Red in Prix Gontaut-Biron at Deauville (stays 1½m): acts on dirt and heavy going (possibly unsuited by good to firm): visored (missed break) last 2 starts: has edged right: has left Godolphin. *Saeed bin Suroor*

SOCA 2 ch.f. (Mar 17) So Factual (USA) 120 – Calypso Lady (IRE) 88 (Priolo (USA) **54 d** 127) [2001 5m 6g³ 7g 8.3v f6g Nov 21] first foal: dam, 2-y-o 6f winner who stayed 1m, half-sister to useful German middle-distance performer Last Step: modest maiden: best effort when third in seller at Lingfield: should stay at least 7f. *R. Hannon*

SOCIABLE 2 b.f. (Jan 27) Danehill (USA) 126 – Society Rose 88 (Saddlers' Hall **74 p** (IRE) 126) [2001 6g 7s³ Oct 31] first foal: dam, 2-y-o 7f winner, half-sister to Cheveley Park winner Regal Rose (by Danehill): fair form in maidens at Newmarket (missed break) and Yarmouth (third of 10 to Miss Corniche), not given hard race in either: should stay 1m: capable of better. *W. J. Haggas*

SOCIAL CONTRACT 4 b.g. Emarati (USA) 74 – Just Buy Baileys 69 (Formidable **90** (USA) 125) [2001 90: f7g f7s³ e7g* f7g 8d 7m 7m 7m 7.1g Sep 1] strong, useful-looking gelding: fairly useful handicapper: won at Lingfield in February: below form after: best at 7f/easy 1m: acts on firm going, good to soft, fibresand and equitrack: usually blinkered. *S. Kirk*

SOCIAL HARMONY (IRE) 7 b.g. Polish Precedent (USA) 131 – Latest Chapter **114** (IRE) (Ahonoora 122) [2001 116: 7v² 6f² 6f⁴ 7g³ 6.3g⁵ 5g³ 7d⁶ 6d⁴ 7g 6d Oct 14] smart performer: mostly creditable efforts in 2001, including when third to King Charlemagne (beaten 1½ lengths) in Ballycorus Stakes at Leopardstown in June and to Newpark Lady in valuable handicap at the Curragh in July: well held last 2 starts, though not helped by racing alone final one: effective at 5f to 7f: acts on any turf going: effective blinkered or not: reliable. *D. K. Weld, Ireland*

SOCIALIST (USA) 5 b.g. Hermitage (USA) – Social Missy (USA) (Raised Socially – (USA)) [2001 35: f16.2s Jan 11] probably of little account nowadays. *G. Brown*

SOCIAL ORDER (IRE) 3 b.c. Sadler's Wells (USA) 132 – Aunt Pearl (USA) **72** (Seattle Slew (USA)) [2001 12m 10v⁶ Oct 16] fourth foal: closely related to useful 1998 2-y-o 7f winner Kalidasa and fairly useful 1997 2-y-o 6f/7f winner Social Charter, later Grade 3 8.5f/9.5f winner in North America (both by Nureyev): dam, won up to 7f at 4 yrs in USA, from family of Stravinsky and Dowsing: green when ninth in maiden at Kempton on debut: well held when favourite for similar event on heavy going at Ayr following month: sold 30,000 gns. *J. H. M. Gosden*

SOCIETE GENERALE 2 b.g. (Mar 31) Eagle Eyed (USA) 111 – Canlubang (Muj- – § tahid (USA) 118) [2001 5s 5d May 6] second foal: half-brother to a winner in Sweden by Definite Article: dam no form: looked temperamental in minor event at Doncaster and maiden at Hamilton (blinkered, crashed through rail): one to avoid. *A. Bailey*

SOCIETY KING (IRE) 6 b.g. Fairy King (USA) – Volga (USA) (Riverman (USA) **49 §** 131) [2001 –§: f8s⁴ f8.5g² f7g⁶ f8g f7g Apr 10] lengthy gelding: poor maiden: unlikely to stay beyond 8.5f: acts on fibresand: visored final start: bled from nose/refused to race once: one to treat with caution. *K. R. Burke*

SOCIETY PET 2 b.f. (Feb 26) Runnett 125 – Polar Storm (IRE) 76 (Law Society **57** (USA) 130) [2001 6.1m 5.1f⁴ 6m Aug 15] fourth foal: sister to Irish 9f winner Lawnett and 3-y-o Run On: dam, 6f (at 2 yrs) to 1m winner, half-sister to smart sprinter Polar Bird: modest maiden: raced too freely final outing: should stay 7f: reluctant stall second start: joined D. Bridgwater. *B. J. Meehan*

SOCIETY TIMES (USA) 8 b.g. Imp Society (USA) – Mauna Loa (USA) (Hawaii) – [2001 –: f7g⁴ f8.5s⁵ f9.4g f12g Feb 22] little form. *A. Bailey*

SOCKS 2 b.f. (Apr 4) Sabrehill (USA) 120 – Pink Brief (IRE) 71 (Ela-Mana-Mou 132) – [2001 f5g May 3] 1,800Y: third foal: dam 7f (at 2 yrs) and 1¼m winner: behind in Wolverhampton maiden. *Andrew Reid*

SO DIVINE   3 br.f. So Factual (USA) 120 – Divina Mia 66 (Dowsing (USA) 124)   –
[2001 66: 6g 5g 6d Aug 15] leggy, good-quartered filly: fair performer at 2 yrs: well held
in handicaps in 2001. *M. Johnston*

SOFISIO   4 ch.g. Efisio 120 – Legal Embrace (CAN) 73 (Legal Bid (USA) 120) [2001   –
68, a73: f11g f9.4g^2 f8.5g^4 f9.4g f8g^5 f11g^5 8m f9.4g f11g^6 f12g^2 f12s^6 Dec 15] fair per-   **a70**
former: stays easy 1½m: acts on fibresand, equitrack and firm going: usually blinkered/
tongue tied nowadays. *Miss S. J. Wilton*

SOFT BREEZE   3 ch.f. Zafonic (USA) 130 – Tropical 122 (Green Desert (USA) 127)   **99**
[2001 66: 7d^4 7g^3 7m^3 7f* 7g^6 8m^5 8g* 7.9m 9m 10f^3 9g 10d Oct 18] strong, lengthy filly:
good mover: has a quick action: useful performer: won maiden at Ayr in June and
handicap at Ascot (by 4 lengths from Martin's Sunset) in August: good third to Albuhera
in Courage Best Stakes (Handicap) at Newbury tenth start: stays 1¼m: acts on firm going:
held up. *E. A. L. Dunlop*

SOFTLY (IRE)   2 ch.f. (Apr 29) Grand Lodge (USA) 125 – Decrescendo (IRE)   **70**
(Polish Precedent (USA) 131) [2001 5d 7m^3 7m^3 8m 8d Nov 2] IR 25,000Y: smallish,
sparely-made filly: third foal: dam unraced half-sister to smart 1¼m filly Calando out of
Oaks winner and St Leger second Diminuendo: fair maiden: third at Newbury and
Salisbury: well beaten in nurseries last 2 starts: should stay 1¼m. *M. L. W. Bell*

SOFTLY TREAD (IRE)   3 b.f. Tirol 127 – Second Guess (Ela-Mana-Mou 132)   **111**
[2001 94p: 7v* 8g 7g^2 7d^2 8g^4 Oct 6] strong, well-made filly: has a short, round action:
second reported living foal: dam Irish 1¼m winner: smart performer: won Castlemartin/
La Louviere Studs Gladness Stakes at the Curragh in April by 2 lengths from Social
Harmony: not discredited in Irish 1000 Guineas there following month (final start for
C. Collins in Ireland): creditable efforts when in frame in Britain, in handicap at
Goodwood (neck second to Granny's Pet), listed race at Doncaster (½-length equal
second to Nice One Clare) and Sun Chariot Stakes at Newmarket (4 lengths fourth to

Lael Stable's "Softly Tread"

Independence): better form at 7f than 1m, and may prove effective at 6f: acts on heavy and good to firm going: sent to USA. *J. R. Fanshawe*

SOHAIB (USA) 2 b.c. (Apr 8) Kingmambo (USA) 125 – Fancy Ruler (USA) (Half A **99** Year (USA) 130) [2001 7g² 7m* 7d⁵ 7g⁶ Oct 5] $425,000Y: leggy, attractive colt: first foal: dam, ran twice in USA, out of half-sister to Breeders' Cup Juvenile winner Success Express: useful form: won maiden at Ascot in July: sweating, creditable efforts in Champagne Stakes at Doncaster (went freely in share of lead long way) and Somerville Tattersall Stakes at Newmarket (restrained early, sixth to Where Or When) last 2 starts: should prove at least as effective at 6f as 7f. *B. W. Hills*

SO IT IS 2 b.f. (Feb 18) So Factual (USA) 120 – Big Story 50 (Cadeaux Genereux 131) **47** [2001 5d 6m 5g 6m⁶ 6m 6d f6g f8.5g p6g Dec 22] 5,000Y: small filly: third foal: **a–** half-sister to 1998 2-y-o 6f winner who probably stayed 1¾m Scoop (by Scenic): dam ran twice: poor maiden: stays 6f: acts on good to firm and good to soft ground, well held on fibresand/polytrack. *K. R. Burke*

SOLANZA 2 ch.f. (Apr 15) Bahamian Bounty 116 – Son Et Lumiere (Rainbow Quest **–** (USA) 134) [2001 7d Nov 3] half-sister to several winners, including 3-y-o Sonatina and 13f winner Sound Appeal (by Robellino): dam, poor maiden, out of smart miler Soprano: 25/1, last of 21 in maiden at Newmarket. *Noel T. Chance*

SOLAR COLOURS 3 ch.g. Spectrum (IRE) 126 – Instant Desire (USA) 86 (Northern **61** Dancer) [2001 10m⁶ 9m 12.3m⁶ 14f 18m Jul 7] good-topped gelding: fifth foal: half-brother to several winners, including useful 1m/1¼m winner Monitor (by Machiavellian), and fairly useful out-and-out stayer Speed To Lead (by Darshaan): dam, stayed 1¼m, half-sister to Poule d'Essai des Poulains and Prix Lupin winner Fast Topaze: modest maiden: stayed 1½m: raced only on going firmer than good: blinkered (broke leg) final start: dead. *M. Johnston*

SOLDIER POINT 3 ch.g. Sabrehill (USA) 120 – Reel Foyle (USA) 77 (Irish River **79** (FR) 131) [2001 73: 8v³ 7g⁶ 7.5m² 8m⁶ 7m³ 7d⁵ 7d³ f7g⁶ Nov 16] strong gelding: fair maiden handicapper: best at 7f/1m: acts on good to firm and good to soft ground: hung left sixth start/carried head awkwardly penultimate one. *P. C. Haslam*

SOLITARY 4 b.g. Sanglamore (USA) 126 – Set Fair (USA) (Alleged (USA) 138) **91** [2001 93: 16s 16s² 18.7f 16m 16.2g⁴ 15.9d⁵ 14s 15.9d Sep 26] quite attractive gelding: fairly useful handicapper: stayed 2m: acted on soft and good to firm going: was tried blinkered: dead. *J. G. Given*

SOLLER BAY 4 b.g. Contract Law (USA) 108 – Bichette 66 (Lidhame 109) [2001 **87** 86: 10.5d 10d² 9.2s³ 12g 10g 10v⁴ 8.2s⁵ 8d* 8s Nov 9] fairly useful handicapper: reportedly cracked pelvis final 3-y-o outing: better than ever when winning 30-runner event at Newmarket penultimate start by 1½ lengths from Thihn: effective at 1m/1¼m: acts on heavy going, good to firm and fibresand: often races freely. *K. R. Burke*

SOLLY'S PAL 6 gr.g. Petong 126 – Petriece 64 (Mummy's Pet 125) [2001 59: f7g **–** e7g⁴ f7g* f7g³ 7.1g 7.1m 7g f7s Dec 18] tall, leggy gelding: modest handicapper: won at **a64** Wolverhampton in March: left P. Makin 1,300 gns after penultimate start: best at 6f/7f: acts on fibresand and equitrack, well beaten on turf in 2001: usually visored: sometimes slowly away: carries head awkwardly: not an easy ride. *R. Wilman*

SOLO DANCER 3 ch.f. Sayaarr (USA) – Oiseval (National Trust 89) [2001 9.9s 10v **–** Oct 8] second reported foal: dam unraced: well held in maidens 5 months apart: trained by W. Turner on debut. *Jane Southcombe*

SOLO FLIGHT 4 gr.g. Mtoto 134 – Silver Singer 65 (Pharly (FR) 130) [2001 89: **99** 12d⁴ 12.3f² 12m* 12m⁶ 11.9d 13.9g 14.6d 12d 12d Oct 18] angular, unfurnished gelding: useful handicapper: won at Doncaster in June: often well backed in valuable handicaps after, including when creditable sixth in Duke of Edinburgh Stakes at Royal Ascot and seventh in Old Newton Cup at Haydock and Ebor at York on fourth, fifth and sixth starts: barely stays 1¾m, may well prove as effective at 1¼m as 1½m: acts on firm and soft going: has worn crossed noseband: edgy sort: held up, and has often met trouble. *B. W. Hills*

SOLO MIO (IRE) 7 b.h. Sadler's Wells (USA) 132 – Marie de Flandre (FR) 109 **121** (Crystal Palace (FR) 132) [2001 16g* 16.4m* 16g⁴ Aug 2]

Some scientists' idea of the funniest joke in the world, which took the plaudits on www.laughlab.co.uk in 2001, carries a valuable lesson for form students. The joke goes: Holmes and Watson go camping and pitch their tent under the stars. During the night, Holmes wakes his companion and says 'Watson, look

Bonusprint Stakes (Henry II), Sandown—at the age of seven,
Solo Mio (No.3) confirms himself better than ever; Romantic Affair is second,
ahead of Persian Punch (rail), Life Is Life (partially hidden) and Mbele

up at the stars and tell me what you deduce.' Watson says: 'I see millions of stars, and even if only a few of those have planets, it's quite likely there are some planets like Earth. And if there are a few planets like Earth out there, there might also be life.' Holmes replies: 'Watson, you are an absolute idiot. Somebody has stolen our tent.' Reading between the lines is part-and-parcel of form study, and an endless number of interpretations can be put on a race, but good bets can also be found by looking no further than the obvious and backing horse A to beat horses B and C—just as it did the time before. Take Solo Mio in the Group 3 Bonusprint Stakes (Henry II) at Sandown in May, for example. Solo Mio came into the race fresh from his win in the Group 3 HBLB Sagaro Stakes at Newmarket (the race transferred from Ascot due to waterlogging) earlier in the month, when he had beaten San Sebastian by a length and three quarters with Romantic Affair third and Persian Punch fourth. Solo Mio renewed rivalry with the latter pair at Sandown on not dissimilar terms under similar conditions, yet he started at 7/1, with Romantic Affair 4/1 joint-favourite with the Chester Cup winner Rainbow High, and Persian Punch at 5/1. Not one of the seventeen newspaper tipsters included in the *Racing Post* 'selection box' went for Solo Mio, yet he won again, never far away under Michael Kinane and responding well to pressure to forge ahead close home. Romantic Affair was a length away in second and Persian Punch another head behind in third, making it another decent renewal of the Henry II. In recent seasons the race has been won by the very smart performers Double Trigger, who took the race twice, Persian Punch, successful three times, and Arctic Owl, and the race has been upgraded to Group 2 for 2002.

Solo Mio would have gone very close in the Gold Cup on his Sandown form, but, unfortunately, he was never entered for the race, the Royal Ascot entries having closed a few days before he made his winning reappearance at Newmarket, where, incidentally, he had started at 20/1. Solo Mio had presumably not been with his present stable for long at the time, as he had spent the winter hurdling with Alan King, putting up his best effort when second to the outstanding French-trained novice Baracouda at Fontwell on his last outing in February. Solo Mio had only one more run on the Flat in 2001 after Sandown, again taking on some of the best stayers around but running a bit below form when seven and a half lengths fourth of twelve behind Persian Punch in the Goodwood Cup. Solo Mio looked in fine shape as usual and started favourite this time at 3/1, but he could only plug on as the race took shape, drifting right under pressure.

Cheveley Park Stud's "Solo Mio"

Solo Mio (IRE) (b.h. 1994)	Sadler's Wells (USA) (b 1981)	Northern Dancer (b 1961)	Nearctic
			Natalma
		Fairy Bridge (b 1975)	Bold Reason
			Special
	Marie de Flandre (FR) (b 1980)	Crystal Palace (gr 1974)	Caro
			Hermieres
		Primula (ch 1972)	Petingo
			Valrose II

Solo Mio has a colourful history. He was bought by Wafic Said for 160,000 guineas as a yearling and won a ten-furlong maiden and a twelve-furlong handicap for Barry Hills before being sold for 120,000 guineas at the end of his three-year-old career. He subsequently showed smart form when trained by John Hammond in France, winning the Group 3 Betty Barclay-Rennen over two miles at Baden-Baden in 1998 and again in 1999, when he was also down the field in the Gold Cup. He was returned to Britain for a hurdling career beginning in January 2000, winning twice and finishing sixth in the Royal & SunAlliance Novices' Hurdle at Cheltenham that season. Some of Solo Mio's relatives have been winning hurdlers too, as well as being successful on the Flat, though it is a largely undistinguished family so far as his half-brothers and half-sisters go. Solo Mio's dam Marie de Flandre did start second favourite when well beaten in the Prix de Diane on her debut, and went on to show useful form for Patrick-Louis Biancone, winning over a mile and a quarter. Marie de Flandre is a half-sister to Sakura Reiko, runner-up to Miesque in the Poule d'Essai des Pouliches, and this is also the family of the Prix Royal-Oak winner Top Sunrise. Solo Mio is about the equal of Top Sunrise on his form in 2001. He is a very smart stayer and reportedly remains in training. Untried on extremes of going, Solo Mio has shown smart form on soft ground, though his very best efforts have come on good and good to firm. He was blinkered once on the Flat as a five-year-old and looked none too keen in them over hurdles at Fontwell, but he has done little wrong for his present trainer. A rangy, good-bodied horse, Solo Mio should stay beyond two miles given another chance; presumably, he'll be entered for the Gold Cup in 2002! *Mrs A. J. Perrett*

SOLOMON'S MINE (USA) 2 b.c. (Feb 20) Rahy (USA) 115 – Shes A Sheba (USA) (Alysheba (USA)) [2001 6m⁶ 7m⁶ 6m f7g⁴ 7s³ f8g* 10d f7g f8g f8.5s* Dec 15] $37,000F, $50,000Y: strong colt: third foal: dam, winner up to 9f in USA, half-sister to US Grade 2 9f winner Barkerville and very smart French winner up to 8.5f Air Distingue (dam of Vettori): fair on all-weather, modest on turf: made all in seller at Southwell (left Sir Mark Prescott) in October and minor event at Wolverhampton in December: should stay 1¼m: acts on fibresand and soft going. *M. J. Polglase* **55 a75**

SOLTAAT 2 b.c. (Apr 26) Royal Applause 124 – About Face (Midyan (USA) 124) [2001 7d 7.1m 7s Oct 16] 48,000F, 60,000Y: sturdy colt: easy mover: third foal: half-brother to 3-y-o Indian Giver: dam unraced half-sister to high-class 1m/1¼m performer Bijou d'Inde: well beaten in maidens. *A. C. Stewart* **–**

SOMAYYA 3 b.f. Polar Falcon (USA) 126 – Moonshine Lake 85 (Kris 135) [2001 8.1g² 11.5g* f12g* f12g Oct 18] third foal: half-sister to UAE 7.5f winner Jeryaan (by Fairy King): dam, 1½m winner who stayed 1¾m, sister to smart performer up to 10.5f Moon Cactus (dam of Oaks winner Moonshell): fairly useful performer: won maiden at Lingfield in September and handicap at Wolverhampton (beat Blue Hawk 6 lengths) in October: very disappointing (slowly away and soon off bridle) final outing: will stay 1¾m: acts on fibresand: sold 29,000 gns. *M. P. Tregoning* **94**

SOME DUST 3 ch.g. King's Signet (USA) 110 – Some Dream 53 (Vitiges (FR) 132) [2001 56: e5g⁶ f5g³ e5g³ e6g e6g² f6g² e5g⁵ e5g f6g f6g p7g Nov 15] modest performer: well held last 5 starts: best at 5f/6f: acts on good to firm going, fibresand and equitrack: visored: has hung left: usually races prominently: sold 600 gns. *Andrew Reid* **61**

SOMERS HEATH (IRE) 3 b.f. Definite Article 121 – Glen of Imaal (IRE) (Common Grounds 118) [2001 58: 8.1g 7m 6m 6.1m 7.5f⁴ 7s⁴ 5g 6f 6s Sep 24] angular, workmanlike filly: modest at 2 yrs, only poor in 2001: effective at 5f to 7.5f: acts on firm and soft ground: blinkered (found little) final start: flashed tail leaving stall fourth outing: none too consistent. *T. D. Easterby* **45**

SOMESESSION 4 b.g. Prince Sabo 123 – Session 80 (Reform 132) [2001 76d: 6s³ 5v⁴ f5m⁴ 5m² 5d⁴ 5m⁴ 5m 5d⁴ 5m 5f² 5.5m⁴ 5g 5g f5s⁵ Sep 6] strong, lengthy gelding: fair performer, on downgrade: best form at 5f: acts on firm and good to soft going, probably on heavy and fibresand: usually blinkered/visored: none too resolute. *R. A. Fahey* **68 d**

SOMETHINGABOUTMARY (IRE) 3 b.f. Fayruz 116 – Cut It Fine (USA) (Big Spruce (USA)) [2001 31: 9.9m May 22] small, close-coupled filly: has a round action: poor maiden at 2 yrs: well held only outing in 2001. *J. S. Wainwright* **–**

SOMETHING SPECIAL 3 b.g. Petong 126 – My Dear Watson (Chilibang 120) [2001 11.7d 10.1s 8.1m 10s 11.7d 14.1s Nov 5] 9,500Y: workmanlike gelding: first foal: dam twice-raced half-sister to smart sprinter Sizzling Melody: no form. *H. E. Haynes* **–**

SOME WILL 3 b.g. Handsome Sailor 125 – Bollin Sophie (Efisio 120) [2001 –: f6g 6d* 6m* 7d⁴ 6m⁶ 7g 6g 5.1d f6g Oct 18] tall, lengthy gelding: has a round action: fair handicapper: won at Newcastle and Haydock (apprentice event) in May: badly drawn on 3 occasions afterwards: best around 6f: acts on good to soft and good to firm ground: pulled very hard once at 2 yrs. *T. D. Easterby* **72**

SONATINA 3 b.f. Distant Relative 128 – Son Et Lumiere (Rainbow Quest (USA) 134) [2001 90p: 8m³ 8f⁴ 8g² 8s⁵ Sep 29] strong, lengthy filly: useful performer, quite lightly raced: good efforts when fourth to Independence in listed rated stakes at Ascot and ½-length second to Goggles in listed race at Goodwood: not discredited in listed rated stakes at Ascot final outing: stays 1m: acts on firm going, probably on soft. *J. W. Payne* **103**

SONEAU (IRE)   3 b.c. Ela-Mana-Mou 132 – Acquilata (USA) (Irish River (FR) 131)   **79**
[2001 f11g² Apr 4] 14,000F, 42,000Y: first foal: dam, French maiden, half-sister to smart
1m/1¼m performer Mamouna and to dam of smart stayer Maridpour: ¾-length second to
Jalousie in maiden at Southwell, only outing: dead. *P. F. I. Cole*

SONG 'N DANCE   3 br.f. Dancing Spree (USA) – Don't Smile 76 (Sizzling Melody   **48**
117) [2001 52: e5g² e6s* 5.7g 6m 5.1g⁶ 5f⁴ 5m⁶ Aug 4] poor performer: won seller at
Lingfield in February despite hanging badly right: effective at 5f/easy 6f: acted on firm
going and equitrack: visored once at 2 yrs: was no easy ride: dead. *M. D. I. Usher*

SONIQUE   3 b.f. Shaamit (IRE) 127 – Dolly Bevan 53 (Another Realm 118) [2001 –:   **–**
8s 8.2s Nov 5] leggy filly: tailed off in 3 starts on soft going. *R. C. Spicer*

SONNY JIM   3 b.g. Timeless Times (USA) 99 – Allessa 69 (Alleging (USA) 120)   **56 §**
[2001 7g 8m 8f⁴ 8.1g 8m 10g 12m³ 12g 10.1g Sep 14] 7,000Y: smallish, sturdy gelding:
second foal: dam 1¼m/1½m winner: modest maiden handicapper: stays 1½m: raced only
on good ground or firmer: gave good deal of trouble at start and withdrawn both intended
2-y-o outings: one to treat with caution. *M. D. I. Usher*

SON OF A GUN   7 b.g. Gunner B 126 – Sola Mia 78 (Tolomeo 127) [2001 83: 13.9d   **83**
18d 16.5s Nov 10] workmanlike gelding: fairly useful maiden, lightly raced: off 14
months, good seventh in handicap at York in October: respectable eleventh in Cesarewitch at Newmarket later in month, and shaped better than bare result final outing:
probably stays 2¼m: acts on soft going: has hung left: bandaged in front: fairly useful
bumper winner. *J. Neville*

SON OF FLIGHTY   3 b.g. Then Again 126 – Record Flight (Record Token 128)   **–**
[2001 8.3m 14m⁶ Aug 18] third foal: dam, maiden on Flat, winning hurdler: well held in
maidens at Windsor and Lingfield. *R. J. Hodges*

SON OF SNURGE (FR)   5 b.g. Snurge 130 – Swift Spring (FR) 56 (Bluebird (USA)   **–**
125) [2001 82: 16m 12m 12m 18m 13.8g Aug 7] big, good-topped gelding: one-time
fairly useful performer: well held on return from hurdling in 2001: has been blinkered.
T. P. Tate

SOONA   3 ch.f. Royal Abjar (USA) 121 – Presently 48 (Cadeaux Genereux 131) [2001   **54 §**
64: f9.4g⁴ e8g⁵ 8s 10s⁵ 8m 9m⁵ 10g⁵ 8f 8m⁵ 9.9m 8d⁶ f7g f9.4g f12s⁶ Dec 27] modest
maiden: barely stays 1¼m: acts on good to firm going, fibresand and equitrack: usually
races prominently: inconsistent. *Ronald Thompson*

SOON OR LATE   3 ch.g. Kris 135 – Silky Heights (IRE) 67 (Head For Heights 125)   **–**
[2001 f7g f8g 10.1d⁵ 12.4g⁶ Jul 18] big, workmanlike gelding: second foal: half-brother
to 4-y-o Winged Angel: dam 11f/1½m winner: little form in maidens/handicap. *Miss
J. A. Camacho*

SOOTY TIME   3 ch.g. Timeless Times (USA) 99 – Gymcrak Gem (IRE) 62 (Don't   **52 d**
Forget Me 127) [2001 54: e6g f7g 7s² 7.5m 8d⁴ 7d 7g 7m 6s f7g Oct 23] smallish gelding:
modest performer: well held last 5 starts: barely stays 1m: acts on fibresand, equitrack,
soft and good to firm going: edgy sort: wanders under pressure. *J. S. Moore*

SOPHALA   4 b.f. Magical Wonder (USA) 125 – Fujaiyrah 98 (In Fijar (USA) 121)   **69**
[2001 71: 8.3g⁴ 10m⁵ 11.9s Oct 11] fair handicapper: stays 1½m: acts on heavy and good
to firm ground: has hung right. *C. F. Wall*

SOPHIELU   3 ch.f. Rudimentary (USA) 118 – Aquaglow 84 (Caerleon (USA) 132)   **80**
[2001 76: 7.1d* Apr 24] strong, lengthy filly: fairly useful form: won maiden at
Musselburgh in April: stays 7f: raced only on good/soft ground. *M. Johnston*

SOPHIES SYMPHONY   2 b.f. (Apr 2) Merdon Melody 98 – Gracious Imp (USA)   **78**
(Imp Society (USA)) [2001 6g³ 6g² 6m* 6m² 7d⁴ 7v Oct 27] 3,600Y: workmanlike filly:
first foal: dam no form: fair performer: won maiden at York in September: in frame in
nurseries next 2 starts: stays 7f: acts on good to firm and good to soft ground, possibly not
on heavy. *K. R. Burke*

SOPHISTICAT (USA)   2 b. or br.f. (Jan 25) Storm Cat (USA) – Serena's Song   **105**
(USA) 126 (Rahy (USA) 115) [2001 5m² 6g* 5m² 6g² 6m² 7g³ 6d² a8.5f⁵ Oct 27]   **a109**
$3,400,000Y: big, lengthy, good-topped filly: has a quick action: second foal: half-sister
to North American 5.5f (at 2 yrs) and 6.5f (minor stakes) winner Serena's Tune (by Mr
Prospector): dam multiple Grade 1 winner in USA (also second in Breeders' Cup Juve-
nile Fillies and Breeders' Cup Distaff) and champion US 3-y-o filly: useful performer:
won maiden at Naas in June: placed in Queen Mary Stakes at Royal Ascot, listed race at
Leopardstown, Lowther Stakes at York (1¼ lengths second to Queen's Logic), Moyglare
Stud Stakes at the Curragh (wandered when length third to Quarter Moon) and Cheveley

Mrs John Magnier & Mr M. Tabor's "Sophisticat"

Park Stakes at Newmarket (7 lengths second to Queen's Logic) after: good fifth to Tempera in Breeders' Cup Juvenile Fillies at Belmont: stays 8.5f: acts on dirt, good to soft and good to firm going: visored last 2 starts: has worn crossed noseband. *A. P. O'Brien, Ireland*

SOPHORIFIC (IRE)   2 b.f. (Apr 5) Danehill (USA) 126 – Saucy Maid (IRE) 69   **88** (Sure Blade (USA) 130) [2001 6m³ 6f² 6d* 7.1m² 8m³ 7g⁶ 8s⁴ 9s⁵ Nov 17] IR 110,000Y: well-made filly: third foal: dam, maiden who stayed 1¼m, half-sister to dam of Pilsudski: fairly useful performer: won maiden at Haydock in July: creditable efforts in 4 listed events after, including 1¼ lengths second to Echo River at Sandown: probably stays 9f: acts on firm and soft going. *M. W. Easterby*

SO PRECIOUS (IRE)   4 b.f. Batshoof 122 – Golden Form (Formidable (USA) 125)   **72** [2001 86: 10s 12g 10.5s 12g 12g 11.9s 14.1s p16g f12s⁵ p13g Dec 29] good-topped filly: only fair in 2001, leaving N. Littmoden after second start: stays 1½m: acts on heavy going and fibresand: tried visored. *Ian Williams*

SORBONNE   2 b.g. (Mar 31) College Chapel 122 – French Mist 71 (Mystiko (USA)   **58** 124) [2001 8m Sep 24] 4,000F, 12,000Y: first foal: dam, maiden who stayed 14.6f, half-sister to very smart US performer up to 1¼m Jumron: 16/1 and tongue tied, modest form when ninth of 11 in maiden at Kempton. *B. Hanbury*

SORCEROUS   2 b.c. (Feb 5) Sadler's Wells (USA) 132 – La Papagena (Habitat 134)   **94 P** [2001 8s* Oct 29] 2,000,000Y: half-brother to high-class 1m/1¼m performer Grand Lodge, also Dewhurst winner at 2 yrs, and useful 1m winner Papabile (both by Chief's Crown), and to 11.5f winner Rose Noble (by Vaguely Noble): dam unraced daughter of very smart 5f to 1m winner Magic Flute: 5/4 favourite, won 16-runner maiden at

958

Leopardstown in October by length from In Time's Eye, squeezing thought to lead 1f out and getting comfortably on top despite signs of greenness: will stay at least 1¼m: sure to improve considerably, and will win more races. *A. P. O'Brien, Ireland*

SO ROYAL (USA) 2 ch.f. (Apr 1) Royal Academy (USA) 130 – Exactly So (Caro **78** 133) [2001 8.3m² 8v² 8d f9.4g⁴ Nov 17] $85,000F, $50,000Y: rangy filly: closely related to a winner in USA by Pancho Villa and half-sister to several winners, including 5-y-o Kentucky Bullet and very smart 10.5f Prix Lupin winner Exactly Sharp (by Sharpen Up): dam, French 10.5f winner, later Grade 3 winner in USA: fair maiden: second at Hamilton and Ayr: will stay 1¼m: acts on heavy and good to firm ground. *M. Johnston*

SORRENTO KING 4 ch.g. First Trump 118 – Star Face (African Sky 124) [2001 50: **38** f11g 14.1m⁶ 12m 10f⁶ Jul 2] workmanlike gelding: poor maiden handicapper on Flat: stays easy 1¾m: acts on firm ground: blinkered: sometimes pulls hard. *W. Easterby*

SO SOBER (IRE) 3 b.g. Common Grounds 118 – Femme Savante 89 (Glenstal **78** (USA) 118) [2001 74: f6g² f6g* e6g* f6g 6.1f⁶ f5d⁵ f6g* 5m⁶ 5m 6.1m f6g Oct 18] strong, compact gelding: fair performer: won maiden at Southwell in March, handicap at Lingfield (made all) in April and claimer at Southwell in June: effective at 5f/6f: acts on fibresand, equitrack, soft and firm going: sold 9,500 gns. *C. F. Wall*

SOSUMI 2 b.f. (Feb 11) Be My Chief (USA) 122 – Princess Deya (Be My Guest (USA) **101** 126) [2001 5m⁴ 5s* 5.1m⁶ 6m⁵ 7d⁴ 8d Sep 13] good-topped filly: first foal: dam, seemed reluctant to race when tailed off both starts, half-sister to 5-y-o Compton Admiral and 4-y-o Summoner: useful performer: won maiden at Sandown in June and minor event at Chester (by 1¼ lengths from Kelsey Rose) in July: easily best effort when under 2 lengths fourth to Ya Hajar in Prix du Calvados at Deauville penultimate start: should stay 1m: acts on soft and good to firm going: swished tail throughout preliminaries fourth start. *M. H. Tompkins*

SO TEMPTING 3 b.g. So Factual (USA) 120 – Persuasion 79 (Batshoof 122) [2001 **80** 72: f8g* 8g 7g⁶ 9.2g² 10g 10.3v³ 11m³ 11g Dec 16] tall, rather leggy gelding: fairly useful **a90** performer: won maiden at Southwell in June: sold from J. Fanshawe 6,500 gns after sixth start: stays 11f: acts on heavy and good to firm going and on fibresand: none too consistent. *R. Feligioni, Italy*

SOTONIAN (HOL) 8 br.g. Statoblest 120 – Visage 75 (Vision (USA)) [2001 66: **66 §** f5g* e5g² f5s f5g* 5m⁶ 5g⁵ f5g f5g⁶ 5f 5f² 5g* 5f 5m Sep 26] rather sparely-made gelding: fair performer: won at Wolverhampton in January and February and Catterick in August: best at 5f/easy 6f: acts on firm ground, soft, fibresand and equitrack: tried blinkered earlier in career: reportedly bled from nose once as 6-y-o: often claimer ridden. *P. S. Felgate*

SOUND OF CHEERS 4 br.g. Zilzal (USA) 137 – Martha Stevens (USA) 102 (Super **–** Concorde (USA) 128) [2001 e12g⁶ 7g May 8] no form in Hong Kong for K. Lui at 3 yrs: well held in maiden (tongue tied) and handicap in 2001. *P. W. D'Arcy*

SOUND'S ACE 5 ch.m. Savahra Sound 111 – Ace Girl 58 (Stanford 121§) [2001 54d: **–** f5g Jan 5] probably no longer of any account. *D. Shaw*

SOUND SENSE 3 br.g. So Factual (USA) 120 – Sight'n Sound 63 (Chief Singer 131) **–** [2001 8m 9m 8m Aug 30] first foal: dam, 13f winner, half-sister to smart performers Grey Shot (up to 2m) and Night Shot (sprinter): well beaten in maidens. *D. R. C. Elsworth*

SOUNDS LUCKY 5 b.g. Savahra Sound 111 – Sweet And Lucky (Lucky Wednesday **57** 124) [2001 64d: e6g⁴ f5g f5g e6g f5g⁴ e6g⁵ f5g³ f7g⁵ f6g⁵ f6g* f6g 7m⁵ 6m p5g⁶ f6g⁴ p5g² f5s f6s⁴ Dec 26] leggy gelding: has a round action: modest performer: won amateur events at Wolverhampton (claimer) and Yarmouth (handicap) in May: effective at 5f to 7f: acts on all-weather and good to firm going: effective blinkered/visored or not: has started slowly/swished tail: none too reliable. *N. P. Littmoden*

SOUND THE TRUMPET (IRE) 9 b.g. Fayruz 116 – Red Note (Rusticaro (FR) **–** 124) [2001 40: e8g⁵ e7g Jan 27] rangy gelding: poor form in 2000: well held in 2001: tried blinkered/visored: tongue tied. *R. C. Spicer*

SOUTHERN DANCER 3 b.g. Makbul 104 – Bye-Bye (Superlative 118) [2001 67: **57** 9m⁴ 10m 10.9d⁴ Jul 21] close-coupled gelding: modest maiden: seems to stay 9f: acts on soft and good to firm going. *R. Hollinshead*

SOUTHERN DOMINION 9 ch.g. Dominion 123 – Southern Sky 89 (Comedy Star **–** (USA) 121) [2001 67: f5g f5g f5g* f5g f5g f6g⁶ f5g⁵ 5m⁶ 5m f6g 5g 5g 5g⁶ 5d f5g p5g **a58 d** f5s Dec 27] small gelding: modest at best nowadays: won seller at Wolverhampton in

March: on downgrade after: stays 6f: acts on fibresand, equitrack and any turf going: usually visored/blinkered: usually leads. *Miss J. F. Craze*

SOUTHERN DUNES 5 b.g. Ardkinglass 114 – Leprechaun Lady 57 (Royal Blend – 117) [2001 f11g Jun 15] lightly raced and little form on Flat: tried blinkered. *G. Fierro*

SOUTH LANE 4 br.g. Rock City 120 – Steppey Lane 95 (Tachypous 128) [2001 –: – 10s 11.1d 12.4m Jun 4] of little account. *Don Enrico Incisa*

SOUTH SEA PEARL (IRE) 3 ch.f. Mujtahid (USA) 118 – Rainstone 57 (Rainbow **56 §** Quest (USA) 134) [2001 7f 8g⁶ 8.3m 8m⁵ 10.2g f8.5g⁵ f9.4g f9.4g Nov 21] IR 38,000Y: angular, workmanlike filly: has a round action: fifth foal: sister to 1m winner Yajtahed and half-sister to 2 winners, including useful 1998 2-y-o 5f/6f winner Gipsy Rose Lee (by Marju): dam, placed both starts at 2 yrs (later won in Belgium), half-sister to smart 2-y-o sprinter Magic Ring: modest maiden: stays 8.5f: acts on fibresand, raced only on good ground or firmer on turf: blinkered twice: tends to run in snatches: not one to trust. *B. J. Meehan*

SOVEREIGN STATE (IRE) 4 b.g. Soviet Lad (USA) – Portree 82 (Slip Anchor **51** 136) [2001 77: 8m 7.5m 7g 8g 9.2g⁴ 10.9m Sep 20] small, well-made gelding: modest performer: stays 9f: acts on firm and good to soft ground: visored last 2 starts. *Miss S. E. Hall*

SOVIET FLASH (IRE) 4 b.c. Warning 136 – Mrs Moonlight (Ajdal (USA) 130) **114** [2001 104: 7.9m* 8.5f³ 8m 8g Aug 2] tall, useful-looking colt: smart performer, lightly raced: better than ever when winning listed rated stakes at York in May from unlucky-in-running Tough Speed: beaten a head and the same behind Pulau Tioman and Cauvery when respectable third in Diomed Stakes at Epsom following month, but well held after in Hunt Cup at Royal Ascot and William Hill Mile at Goodwood: likely to prove best up to 1m: acts on firm and good to soft ground. *E. A. L. Dunlop*

SOVIET HERO (IRE) 4 br.g. Soviet Lad (USA) – Tajanama (IRE) 52 (Gorytus – (USA) 132) [2001 5.1f 8.2f⁶ 8.1d 8d f9.4g Aug 18] IR 4,200F: third foal: half-brother to 2 winners in Italy up to 9f by Mukaddamah: dam won at 6.5f at 4 yrs: little sign of ability: looked wayward in blinkers final start. *Miss Gay Kelleway*

SPACE ODYSSEY 2 b.g. (Feb 11) Bin Ajwaad (IRE) 119 – High Stepping (IRE) – (Taufan (USA) 119) [2001 p8g p10g Dec 4] 3,000F, 1,500Y: third foal: brother to 4-y-o Bint Habibi: dam unraced: well beaten in Lingfield maidens: slowly away on debut. *G. C. H. Chung*

SPA GULCH (USA) 3 ch.g. Gulch (USA) – Carezza (USA) (Caro 133) [2001 –: **43** f8.5s³ f8g f11g² f12g⁶ f9.4g⁴ 11.5m⁶ 16m⁶ 10f 8m f9.4g² 12m⁵ 7g Oct 6] smallish, close-coupled gelding: poor maiden: left S. Williams after tenth start: seems effective from 8.5f to 2m: acts on fibresand and good to firm going: tried blinkered (raced freely)/visored: usually tongue tied: sold 1,100 gns, sent to Denmark. *M. E. Sowersby*

SPA LANE 8 ch.g. Presidium 124 – Sleekit 78 (Blakeney 126) [2001 48, a–: 21.6s **48** 16.2m³ 14.1g 16.2f 13.8g 16.2s* 17.1g 16m 12d 17.1d Oct 8] leggy gelding: poor handicapper: won seller at Beverley in August: best at 2m+ nowadays: acts on firm ground, soft (probably on heavy) and fibresand: pulled up reportedly with breathing problem fourth start: usually held up: none too consistent. *Mrs S. Lamyman*

SPANISH BELLS 2 b.c. (Mar 23) Robellino (USA) 127 – Legend of Aragon 67 – (Aragon 118) [2001 6m Jul 27] 19,000F, 25,000Y: first foal: dam 2-y-o 5f winner who stayed 1m: 8/1, well-held seventh of 8 in maiden at Salisbury: sent to UAE. *H. Candy*

SPANISH BUCCANEER 2 b.g. (Apr 27) Forzando 122 – Spanish Heart 86 (King – of Spain 121) [2001 7d Oct 18] smallish, sturdy gelding: sixth foal: half-brother to 3 winners, including 6-y-o Bold King: dam, effective at 7f to 9f, half-sister to smart sprinter Northern Goddess: blinkered, always behind in seller at Newmarket: sold 1,000 gns, sent to Sweden. *J. W. Hills*

SPANISH JOHN (USA) 2 b. or br.c. (Feb 23) Dynaformer (USA) – Esprit d'Escalier **90** (USA) (Diesis 133) [2001 6m* 7.5m* 8s⁶ Sep 23] $35,000Y, resold IR 95,000Y: fourth foal: closely related to 2 winners in USA by Sunshine Forever, notably useful Grade 3 8.5f winner Gastronomical: dam maiden in USA: fairly useful form: won minor event at Kempton (tended to carry head high and wander under pressure) in May and listed race at Milan (by 2¾ lengths from Jeune Dream) in July: well held under much softer conditions in listed race at Milan: should stay at least 1m: acts on good to firm ground. *P. F. I. Cole*

SPANISH SPUR 3 b.c. Indian Ridge 123 – Las Flores (IRE) 102 (Sadler's Wells **88** (USA) 132) [2001 78: 7d 10.2m⁴ 8m* 8m 8m Jul 12] tall colt: fairly useful performer:

won minor event at Newbury in June by 2½ lengths from Silk Law: not discredited in Britannia Handicap at Royal Ascot next time: ran as if something amiss final outing: best at 7f/1m: yet to race on extremes of going: sent to USA. *J. H. M. Gosden*

SPANISH STAR   4 b.g. Hernando (FR) 127 – Desert Girl (Green Desert (USA) 127) **54** [2001 54, a73: f11g² f11g⁴ f11g² f12g* f11g f11g⁶ f12g⁶ f8g f11g⁵ 10f f12g 12m f8g **a70 d** 10.1g⁵ 10m⁴ 8.2s* 9g 8s f8g⁶ f11g³ Dec 3] compact gelding: fair at best on all-weather, modest on turf: won claimer at Southwell (left T. D. Barron) in February and ladies handicap at Nottingham in August: effective at 1m (given a test) to 1½m: acts on fibre-sand and soft going: tried visored: sometimes slowly away. *Mrs N. Macauley*

SPANKINFRANKIE   2 ch.f. (Apr 24) Alhijaz 122 – Rose Ciel (IRE) 80 (Red Sunset **34** 120) [2001 5v⁵ 6f f6g Jun 8] 1,200Y: small filly: fourth foal: half-sister to 5-y-o Xsynna and a 5f winner in Italy by Petong: dam, 7f winner, ran only at 2 yrs: poor form in sellers. *R. A. Fahey*

SPARKLING DOVE   8 ch.m. Lighter 111 – Nimble Dove 62 (Starch Reduced 112) **–** [2001 –: 16v⁶ 17.1s Apr 10] winning hurdler: no show on Flat: blinkered. *C. J. Price*

SPARKLING WATER (USA)   2 br. or b.c. (Apr 9) Woodman (USA) 126 – Shirley **107** Valentine 104 (Shirley Heights 130) [2001 7.1s² 7.5m* 8.2g² 8g² Sep 19] sixth foal: half-brother to smart 1¼m to 1¾m winner Memorise (by Lyphard), 4-y-o Valentine Band and 3-y-o Fully Invested: dam, 1½m winner who stayed 14.6f, sister to top-class 1½m performer Deploy and half-sister to Commander In Chief and Warning: useful performer: landed odds in maiden at Beverley in July: best effort when ¾-length second of 6 to Henri Lebasque in listed event at Goodwood final start: will be suited by 1¼m/1½m: raced prominently last 2 starts. *H. R. A. Cecil*

SPARK OF LIFE   4 b.f. Rainbows For Life (CAN) – Sparkly Girl (IRE) 79 (Danehill **60 §** (USA) 126) [2001 63: 10d 10.1m 11.6g 10.9m² 10m* 11.5m³ 11.5f 10m 9.7d Sep 3] small filly: modest handicapper: won at Lingfield in June: stays 11.5f: acts on firm going, probably on soft: wears blinkers: has proved mulish in preliminaries/flashed tail/hung: often slowly away: unreliable. *T. D. McCarthy*

SPARKY GLENN   3 b.c. Shareef Dancer (USA) 135 – Warthill Girl 70 (Anfield 117) **56 p** [2001 10d 8g 9.9m⁵ 10g 10g 9.7d³ Sep 3] useful-looking colt: sixth foal: dam 2-y-o 6f winner: modest form: left N. Littmoden after second start: best effort, finished well when third in handicap at Folkestone final outing: stays 9.7f: yet to race on extremes of going: capable of better still. *J. Cullinan*

SPARTAK (IRE)   3 b.c. Charnwood Forest (IRE) 125 – Pretext (Polish Precedent **70** (USA) 131) [2001 e7g* a7.5f Dec 6] 30,000F, IR 75,000Y: third foal: half-brother to 4-y-o Cd Flyer: dam, third at 1m in France, half-sister to smart French/US performer at up to 1½m Bon Point: well backed, promising debut to win maiden at Lingfield in January by 1½ lengths: left M. Channon and off over 10 months, behind in handicap at Nad Al Sheba: should stay 1m. *D. J. Selvaratnam, UAE*

SPARTAN FAIR   3 ch.g. Spartan Monarch – Fair Atlanta 73 (Tachypous 128) [2001 **–** 9g⁴ 9.7m 11.9s Sep 30] half-brother to 2 winners, including fairly useful 6f/7f winner Ashgore (by Efisio): dam 1¼m winner: tailed off in maidens. *J. R. Best*

SPARTAN SAILOR   3 b.g. Handsome Sailor 125 – Spartan Native (Native Bazaar **–** 122) [2001 –: 7.1v 8.2s f6s Dec 15] seventh reported foal: dam poor novice hurdler/chaser: tailed off in maidens. *A. Senior*

SPEARHEAD (IRE)   2 b.g. (Apr 12) Elbio 125 – Lake Flyer (USA) (Lomond (USA) **–** 128) [2001 6v Nov 8] IR 5,500F, IR 32,000Y: first foal: dam unraced half-sister to 6-y-o Lear Spear: 33/1, slowly away when last in maiden at Windsor. *M. L. W. Bell*

SPECIAL   3 b.f. Polar Falcon (USA) 126 – Shore Line 107 (High Line 125) [2001 –p: **91** 10.2m⁴ 12m³ 12g² 12m² 14g* 14.4m* 14.6d⁵ Sep 14] quite attractive filly: fairly useful performer: successful in handicaps at Sandown and Newcastle in August: better at 1¾m than shorter and will stay 2m: acts on good to firm and good to soft ground: has wandered under pressure/gone freely. *Sir Michael Stoute*

SPECIAL HERO (IRE)   2 b.c. (Apr 2) Spectrum (IRE) 126 – Royal Heroine 121 **71 p** (Lypheor 118) [2001 6m* Sep 20] IR 20,000Y: tall, long-backed colt: half-brother to several winners, including useful 6f (at 2 yrs)/7f winner who stayed 1¼m Regal Sabre (by Sharpen Up): dam 6f to 9f winner who later won Breeders' Cup Mile: 16/1 and green, won 20-runner maiden at Ayr by 1¼ lengths from Montana Moon, leading 1f out: moved short to post: should stay at least 1m: sure to improve. *K. A. Ryan*

SPECIAL PROMISE (IRE) 4 ch.g. Anjiz (USA) 104 – Woodenitbenice (USA) **49**
(Nasty And Bold (USA)) [2001 –, a78: f11g f16g⁶ f12g⁴ 16v⁶ 13d 16m⁵¹ 17.1m² 14f⁴ **a65**
12.1d 17.1g 15.8m³ f14g Oct 22] strong, lengthy gelding: fair handicapper on
all-weather, poor on turf: left P. Haslam after tenth start: stays 17f: acts on fibresand,
equitrack and firm ground: visored last 2 starts: has been slowly away. *I. Semple*

SPECTINA 3 b.f. Spectrum (IRE) 126 – Catina 102 (Nureyev (USA) 131) [2001 –p: **92**
8.1d² 8g² 8m⁴ 7g² 8m² Aug 30] angular, deep-girthed filly: unimpressive mover: fairly
useful maiden: best effort when second to Stratton in handicap at Yarmouth penultimate
start: may prove best at 7f/1m: acts on good to soft ground: races freely: hung left final
outing. *J. R. Fanshawe*

SPECTRE BROWN 11 b.g. Respect 95 – My Goddess 63 (Palm Track 122) [2001 –: **–**
11.1d May 6] of no account on Flat. *D. A. Nolan*

SPECTROSCOPE (IRE) 2 b.c. (Jan 27) Spectrum (IRE) 126 – Paloma Bay (IRE) **63 p**
92 (Alzao (USA) 117) [2001 7g Aug 10] 36,000F, 310,000Y: quite attractive colt: second
foal: dam, 2-y-o 6f winner who stayed 1m, out of sister to smart Irish sprinter Rustic
Amber: 14/1 and green, eighth of 19 to Grampian in maiden at Newmarket, tending to run
in snatches: should improve. *Jonjo O'Neill*

SPEEDFIT FREE (IRE) 4 b.g. Night Shift (USA) – Dedicated Lady (IRE) 101 **63**
(Pennine Walk 120) [2001 63: f6g* f7g⁶ f7g 6f 6m⁴ 5.1f³ 5.1f 6f⁴ 6g³ 5d 5d 6g 6g f6g⁴
f6g³ f6g f6s³ Dec 15] smallish, well-made gelding: modest handicapper: won at Southwell in March: races mainly at 5f/6f nowadays: acts on fibresand, possibly needs good
going or firmer on turf: twice well held in blinkers: none too consistent. *E. J. Alston*

SPEEDMASTER (GER) 4 b.c. Monsun (GER) 124 – Sarsaparilla (FR) 60 (Shirley **117**
Heights 130) [2001 105: 15.5v⁶ 12v⁵ 15.5m* 15d³ 15.5d⁶ 20v Oct 7] fourth reported foal:
dam German 9f/1¼m winner: smart performer: trained by W. Himmel in Germany in
2000, when made all in Austrian Derby at Freudenau: improved form to win Prix Vicomtesse Vigier at Longchamp in May, beating Polish Summer by 2½ lengths: respectable
efforts after when third to Generic in Prix Kergorlay at Deauville and sixth to Yavana's
Pace in Prix Gladiateur at Longchamp: stays 15.5f (tailed off in Prix du Cadran over
2½m): acts on soft and good to firm going. *F. Doumen, France*

SPEED OF LIGHT (IRE) 3 b.g. Spectrum (IRE) 126 – Phylella (Persian Bold 123) **75**
[2001 65p: 7g³ f9.4g² 8f 7.1d⁶ 10m⁵ 10g⁵ 10m⁴ p12g² f12g* Dec 8] tall, useful-looking **a83**
gelding: fairly useful on all-weather, fair on turf: left W. Muir 7,500 gns after seventh
outing: won maiden at Wolverhampton in December: stays 1½m: acts on good to firm
going and fibresand/polytrack: blinkered (ran creditably) seventh start: reportedly sold to
USA. *Miss D. A. McHale*

SPEED ON 8 b.g. Sharpo 132 – Pretty Poppy 67 (Song 132) [2001 84: 5m 5.1f 5g 5d⁶ **66 §**
5.1g 5g 5g² 5s Sep 24] small, strong gelding: fair handicapper nowadays: barely stays 6f:
acts on firm and soft ground (well held twice on heavy): tried visored: often ridden by
inexperienced apprentice nowadays: inconsistent. *H. Candy*

SPEED QUEEN (IRE) 2 b.f. (Mar 25) Goldmark (USA) 113 – Blues Queen 85 **–**
(Lahib (USA) 129) [2001 5.1m Sep 10] 8,000Y: first foal: dam 2-y-o 6f winner: 33/1 and
ridden by 7-lb claimer, always behind in maiden at Bath. *A. P. Jarvis*

SPEED VENTURE 4 b.g. Owington 123 – Jade Venture 67 (Never So Bold 135) **72**
[2001 75, a–: f14g 10v* 8s⁴ 10.3m 10m⁶ 10s 11.7d Oct 25] sparely-made gelding: fair **a–**
performer: won minor event at Nottingham in April: effective at 1m (given a test) to
1½m: acts on heavy and good to firm going: tongue tied: modest winning hurdler.
J. Mackie

SPEEDY GEE (IRE) 3 b.g. Petardia 113 – Champagne Girl 67 (Robellino (USA) **84**
127) [2001 94: 5s 7.6f 7m 7g 6g Aug 12] strong, good-quartered gelding: fairly useful
performer, though not so good as at 2 yrs: best at 5f/6f: acts on good to firm going, possibly not on soft/heavy: visored (well held) final outing: sold 7,500 gns. *M. R. Channon*

SPEEDY JAMES (IRE) 5 ch.g. Fayruz 116 – Haraabah (USA) 99 (Topsider (USA)) **79**
[2001 –: f6g 5g⁴ 6m⁶ 5f 5m 5g 5.1d 5d 5d Oct 3] strong gelding: good mover: one-time
useful performer: only fair form at best in 2001, though shaped encouragingly in
handicaps last 2 starts: best at 5f: acts on soft and good to firm going: visored once at 3
yrs: reportedly bled from nose final start at 4 yrs: has been early to post and mounted on
track. *D. Nicholls*

SPENCERS WOOD (IRE) 4 b.g. Pips Pride 117 – Ascoli (Skyliner 117) [2001 105: **108** 7g 7g⁶ 7.1d 7g² 7g⁴ 6m* 6d* 6d Nov 18] strong, close-coupled gelding: useful performer: won minor event at Hamilton in September and listed race at the Curragh (by 2 lengths from John Dorans Melody) in October: also ran well in 2001 when in frame at Goodwood in minor event and handicap: best at 6f/7f: yet to race on extremes of ground: has sweated/ got on edge: takes strong hold: often races prominently. *P. J. Makin*

SPETTRO (IRE) 3 b.c. Spectrum (IRE) 126 – Overruled (IRE) 91 (Last Tycoon 131) **82** [2001 106: 10.3f 9d² 10d 10m² Dec 2] quite attractive colt: useful performer at 2 yrs: left P. Cole after reappearance: best efforts in 2001 when second in minor events at Rome and Naples: stays 1¼m: has won on firm ground, best efforts on good or softer (acts on heavy). *L. Camici, Italy*

SPICE ISLAND 3 b.f. Reprimand 122 – Little Emmeline 52 (Emarati (USA) 74) **62** [2001 68: 8.2v² 7s May 19] big, good-topped filly: has scope: fair winner at 2 yrs: modest form in 2001: barely stays testing 1m: acts well on heavy ground. *J. A. Glover*

SPICE OF LIFE 3 b.g. Tagula (IRE) 116 – Lloc 79 (Absalom 128) [2001 6m Sep 8] 51,000Y: first foal: dam, 5f winner (including at 2 yrs), half-sister to July Cup winner Compton Place: showed nothing after slow start in maiden at Thirsk: sold 500 gns. *M. L. W. Bell*

SPINAMIX 2 gr.f. (Jan 16) Spinning World (USA) 130 – Vadsagreya (FR) (Linamix **67** (FR) 127) [2001 7m⁴ 7f 7d 8s Sep 27] 160,000F: strong filly: first foal: dam, French 7f (at 2 yrs) and 1m winner, half-sister to dams of 3-y-o Vahorimix and Breeders' Cup Mile winner Val Royal: fair maiden: well held in nursery final start: should stay at least 1m: acts on firm and good to soft going: joined M. Jarvis. *H. R. A. Cecil*

SPIN A YARN 4 b.g. Wolfhound (USA) 126 – Green Flower (USA) 56 (Fappiano – (USA)) [2001 83: 7.1m 8f 10.3m 12m 8.3s Aug 17] strong gelding: fairly useful performer at best: well held in 2001. *J. G. Given*

SPINDARA (IRE) 3 ch.f. (Apr 7) Spinning World (USA) 130 – Lydara (USA) (Alydar **64** (USA)) [2001 6m 7g 6g 8.3v Oct 8] lengthy, sparely-made filly: fourth foal: half-sister to 7f winner Sporting Lad (by Danzig) and 4-y-o Sporting Ladder: dam winning sprinter in USA from family of Dayjur: modest maiden: well held in nursery final start: should be suited by 7f/1m: slowly away first 2 starts. *P. F. I. Cole*

SPINETAIL RUFOUS (IRE) 3 b.c. Prince of Birds (USA) 121 – Miss Kinabalu 50 **73** (Shirley Heights 130) [2001 61: f6s³ f5g e5g* e5s* e5g² f6g f5s Dec 18] fair performer: won maiden and handicap at Lingfield in February: has form at 6f, but seems best at 5f: acts on fibresand/equitrack: often tongue tied. *D. W. P. Arbuthnot*

SPINEY NORMAN 3 gr.g. Petong 126 – Fairy Ballerina (Fairy King (USA)) [2001 – 7m 8m 7m 8m 7g 10s Oct 3] 3,500Y: rather leggy gelding: sixth foal: half-brother to 6-y-o Aspirant Dancer: dam Irish 2-y-o 7f winner: little sign of ability in maidens/ handicaps: slowly away last 2 starts. *Jamie Poulton*

SPINNER TOY 6 ch.g. Seven Hearts 98 – Priory Bay 54 (Petong 126) [2001 –: 10m – 7m Jun 12] big, lengthy gelding: no form. *J. C. Fox*

SPINNETTE (IRE) 2 b. or br.f. (Apr 1) Spinning World (USA) 130 – Net Worth **93 p** (USA) (Forty Niner (USA)) [2001 8d² Nov 3] rather leggy, lengthy filly: has scope: first living foal: dam, US 8.5f/9f winner, half-sister to US Grade 2 2-y-o 6f winner Bio: 10/1 and green (only newcomer), shaped with plenty of promise when 2½ lengths second of 13 to Sundrenched in listed race at Newmarket, staying on well: will stay 1¼m: useful prospect, sure to win races. *J. Noseda*

SPIPTUNIA 3 ch.f. Blushing Flame (USA) 109 – Comhail (USA) (Nodouble (USA)) – [2001 8.2d May 11] 800Y: fifth foal: half-sister to 3 winners, including 1m winner Polarize (by Polar Falcon): dam ran twice: last in maiden at Nottingham: dead. *Miss J. Feilden*

SPIRIT HOUSE (USA) 3 b.c. Hansel (USA) – Ashwood Angel (USA) (Well – Decorated (USA)) [2001 81p: 12g 14.4m Aug 27] big, angular colt: fair form in 2 minor events at 2 yrs: well held in maiden/handicap in 2001: should stay at least 1m: sold 3,000 gns. *M. Johnston*

SPIRIT OF LIGHT (IRE) 4 b.g. Unblest 117 – Light Thatch (Thatch (USA) 136) – [2001 78§: e8g e8g 9.7v Apr 24] fair maiden handicapper at 3 yrs: well held in 2001: tried visored/blinkered. *B. R. Johnson*

SPIRIT OF LOVE (USA) 6 ch.g. Trempolino (USA) 135 – Dream Mary (USA) **93 d** (Marfa (USA)) [2001 109, a?: f16.2s² f16.2g⁶ 16.1g 16.2m²ᵈ 18.7m⁶ 16.2g 14.1d f14.8s*

17.5m⁴ 16s f16g f16.2g Nov 21] tall, lengthy gelding: has a long stride: one-time smart performer: fairly useful at best in 2001: very much on downgrade after second start, though won claimer at Wolverhampton (left A. Reid) in September: best at 2m+: acts on fibresand, soft and good to firm going: visored once, sometimes blinkered: has wandered/run wide on bends and worn near-side pricker: has worn bandages: usually races prominently. *J. G. Given*

SPIRIT OF SONG (IRE) 3 b.f. Selkirk (USA) 129 – Roxy Music (IRE) 63 (Song – 132) [2001 75: 5.7m 7d 8s Oct 3] fair form first 2 starts at 2 yrs: well held since. *M. R. Channon*

SPIRIT OF TEXAS (IRE) 3 b.g. Namaqualand (USA) – Have A Flutter (Auction 59 Ring (USA) 123) [2001 53: f11g* f12g⁵ 11.6s³ f12g⁴ f14.8g⁵ 12d f12g Oct 18] smallish gelding: modest handicapper: won at Southwell in February: off 4½ months prior to running poorly last 3 starts: stays 1½m: acts on soft going and fibresand: tried blinkered/visored: usually tongue tied. *K. McAuliffe*

SPIRIT'S AWAKENING 2 b.c. (Feb 10) Danzig Connection (USA) – Mo Stopher 60 47 (Sharpo 132) [2001 5g 5.2g⁵ 8d 6v³ Oct 29] third foal: half-brother to 3-y-o Robin Sharp and 6f winner Steppin Out (both by First Trump): dam, maiden, sister to useful sprinter Red Nymph: modest maiden: third in nursery at Windsor: should stay 7f. *J. Akehurst*

SPITFIRE BOB (USA) 2 b.g. (Jan 16) Mister Baileys 123 – Gulf Cyclone (USA) 62 p (Sheikh Albadou 128) [2001 f6s Dec 15] $40,000Y: first foal: dam unraced half-sister to smart miler Sarafan and useful 1m to 1½m winner Hagwah: 20/1 and green, seventh to B Major in maiden at Wolverhampton, late headway after slow start: should improve. *T. D. Barron*

SPLASH OUT AGAIN 3 b.g. River Falls 113 – Kajetana (FR) (Caro 133) [2001 10g 67 8.3m 8g 12g 9.7g 11m² 10d³ Nov 2] 5,000Y: big gelding: half-brother to several winners, notably useful performer up to 1¼m K-Battery (by Gunner B): dam unraced: fair maiden handicapper: stays 11f. *R. J. O'Sullivan*

SPLENDID ROSE 2 b.f. (Feb 9) Prince Sabo 123 – Little Emmeline 52 (Emarati 73 (USA) 74) [2001 5d 6m² 5m² 5g³ 6m² 6m* 6m Aug 13] 10,500Y: first foal: half-sister to 3-y-o Spice Island and 11f winner Preposition (by Then Again): dam 2-y-o 5f winner: fair performer: won maiden at Redcar in July, making virtually all: stays 6f: acts on good to firm going, some promise on good to soft: tends to race freely: hung left when running poorly final start. *R. M. Beckett*

SPLIT THE ACES (IRE) 5 gr.g. Balla Cove 119 – Hazy Lady (Habitat 134) [2001 – 42: 5.7g 6g Aug 23] probably of little account nowadays. *R. J. Hodges*

SPLODGER MAC (IRE) 2 b.c. (Mar 20) Lahib (USA) 129 – Little Love (Warrshan – (USA) 117) [2001 7s Oct 11] IR 3,700Y: sturdy colt: first foal: dam unraced: 100/1, well held in minor event at York. *N. Bycroft*

SPORTING GESTURE 4 ch.g. Safawan 118 – Polly Packer 81 (Reform 132) [2001 80 79: 10v 8s 10s 8m 10.3m 10m* 12m* 12d* 11.9g⁴ 12g³ 12.1m 10g 10g⁵ Nov 5] leggy, unfurnished gelding: has a round action: fairly useful handicapper: fell long way in weights during 5 unplaced runs, then won at Nottingham (9/2), Thirsk (11/10) and Pontefract (7/4) in July/August: stays 1½m: acts on good to firm and good to soft going. *M. W. Easterby*

SPORTING LADDER (USA) 4 b.f. Danzig (USA) – Lydara (USA) (Alydar (USA)) 87 [2001 72: f7g* f7g⁴ a6.5f 8.5f Dec 16] big, lengthy filly: fairly useful handicapper, lightly raced: improved to win at Southwell in March and April: left P. Cole and off 6 months: well held in optional claimers at Woodbine (only outing for R. Attfield in Canada) and Fair Grounds: should stay 1m: acts on fibresand and good to firm going, below form on softer than good. *C. Speckert, USA*

SPORTSDAYSSTROLLER (IRE) 3 b.f. Definite Article 121 – Morning Stroll – (Tower Walk 130) [2001 7m 5.7m f7g Oct 20] half-sister to 2-y-o 5f winners Million At Dawn (in 1993, by Fayruz) and Red Ruffian (in 1991, by Red Sunset), latter useful performer up to 7f in Hong Kong, and a winner in Sweden by Blues Traveller: dam unraced: well held in claimer and maidens. *C. N. Allen*

SPORTS EXPRESS 3 ch.f. Then Again 126 – Lady St Lawrence (USA) 65 (Bering 42 136) [2001 51: f8s 9.2g⁴ 12f Jul 2] workmanlike filly: poor maiden: left W. Haigh after reappearance: should be suited by 1¼m: acts on fibresand and firm ground: drifted left/carried head awkwardly final 2-y-o start. *G. A. Swinbank*

SPOT 4 gr.f. Inchinor 119 – Billie Grey 72 (Chilibang 120) [2001 59d: f6g e8g f8.5g⁴ **46** f9.4g e8g 6m 6m⁶ 6f 6m 8d 7g⁴ 8.2s Nov 5] poor maiden: probably stays 8.5f: acts on good to firm ground and fibresand: tried visored/tongue tied. *Andrew Reid*

SPREE DANCE 2 ch.f. (Feb 9) Dancing Spree (USA) – Irene's Charter 72 (Persian – Bold 123) [2001 8m 8.1v⁶ 10d Nov 3] good-topped filly: half-sister to 3 winners, including useful 7f and 1¼m winner Master Charter (by Master Willie) and 5-y-o Charter Flight: dam 7f to 1¼m winner: signs of just a little ability in maidens/listed race: sent to Spain. *J. G. Given*

SPREE LOVE 3 b.f. Dancing Spree (USA) – Locorotondo (IRE) 83 (Broken Hearted **39** 124) [2001 67: e8g 7m 7m⁴ 8m⁶ 8.1d Aug 9] angular filly: fair maiden at best: poor form in 2001: stays 7f: acts on fibresand and good to firm going. *A. G. Newcombe*

SPREE VISION 5 b.g. Suave Dancer (USA) 136 – Regent's Folly (IRE) 101 **59** (Touching Wood (USA) 127) [2001 64: 12d 13d⁴ 12.1m⁴ 13d 10.9f 12.1m⁴ 10.9d³ 9.1d* 11.1d* 9g² 10g 10v³ 10.1v³ Oct 24] smallish, good-topped gelding: modest handicapper: won at Ayr and Hamilton in August: effective at 9f, barely stays 13f: acts on any going: tried visored: has worn severe noseband. *P. Monteith*

SPRING OAK 3 b.f. Mark of Esteem (IRE) 137 – English Spring (USA) 116 (Grey **113** Dawn II 132) [2001 10.5s* 10.5m⁴ 10d³ 10g³ 10f³ Oct 27] half-sister to several winners, including useful 7f (at 2 yrs) to 11f winner Fragrant Hill (by Shirley Heights), later dam of very smart French performer up to 1½m Fragrant Mix: dam, 1m (including at 2 yrs) to 1¼m winner, from very good US family: smart performer: won Prix Cleopatre at Saint-Cloud in May by 1½ lengths from Epistole: ran well afterwards in Prix de Diane at Chantilly (3¼ lengths fourth to Aquarelliste) and on last 2 starts in E. P. Taylor Stakes at Woodbine (1¾ lengths third to Choc Ice) and Breeders' Cup Filly & Mare Turf at Belmont (7¼ lengths third to impressive Banks Hill, improving wide into turn, then keeping on): will be suited by 1½m: acts on firm and soft going: joined Godolphin. *A. Fabre, France*

SPRING PURSUIT 5 b.g. Rudimentary (USA) 118 – Pursuit of Truth (USA) 69 **90 d** (Irish River (FR) 131) [2001 98d: 14.1v⁶ 12d³ 12s* 12s³ 12v³ 14m 14g 12d⁴ 12g 12g 12g 11.9s 11.9s² 16.5s Nov 10] close-coupled gelding: fairly useful handicapper: won at Epsom in April: good efforts next 2 starts, well below form after: best at 1½m/1¾m, probably on soft/heavy ground: blinkered once at 2 yrs: has been bandaged behind/early to post: usually held up. *R. J. Price*

SPRING SONG 4 b.f. Petong 126 – Naturally Fresh 91 (Thatching 131) [2001 9.9m – Aug 26] big, workmanlike filly: poor maiden at 2 yrs: well held on first run since: tried visored. *M. E. Sowersby*

SPRING SYMPHONY (IRE) 3 b.f. Darshaan 133 – Well Head (IRE) (Sadler's **94** Wells (USA) 132) [2001 63p: 11.9m* 12.3m² Jun 10] useful-looking filly: won maiden at Haydock in May by a head: somewhat unlucky but still good effort when neck second to Tiyoun in handicap at Ripon following month: stayed 1½m: acted on good to firm going: dead. *Sir Michael Stoute*

SPRINGTIME LADY 5 ch.m. Desert Dirham (USA) 108 – Affaire de Coeur 55 – (Imperial Fling (USA) 116) [2001 64: f7g 11.7d 11.9d⁶ May 16] modest performer at 4 yrs: little form in 2001. *J. G. M. O'Shea*

SPRINGTIME SUNRAY (IRE) 2 ch.f. (Apr 19) Gulch (USA) – Youm Jadeed – (IRE) 105 (Sadler's Wells (USA) 132) [2001 7d³ 8s Oct 31] leggy, quite good-topped filly: fourth foal: closely related to a winner in Spain by Machiavellian and half-sister to 1½m winner Youhadyourwarning (by Warning): dam, French 1¼m/1½m performer, sister to dam of Derby runner-up City Honours: only a little sign of ability in Newmarket Challenge Cup and Yarmouth maiden. *E. A. L. Dunlop*

SPRINGWOOD JASMIN (IRE) 3 b.f. Midhish 109 – White Jasmin 53 (Jalmood – (USA) 126) [2001 37: f5g f7g f8g 7m 10g Jun 12] poor maiden at 2 yrs: well held in 2001: should stay 7f (pulled hard over 1¼m): tried blinkered/tongue tied. *D. W. Chapman*

SPRITZERIA 2 b.f. (Feb 9) Bigstone (IRE) 126 – Clincher Club 77 (Polish Patriot **79** (USA) 128) [2001 6m* 7.1f² 7m 6s³ 6g 7s² p7g Nov 13] useful-looking filly: good walker: first foal: dam, 5f (at 2 yrs) and 7.5f winner, out of half-sister to very smart performer up to 7f Tina's Pet: fair performer: won maiden at Pontefract in June: good second in nursery at Brighton penultimate start: should stay 1m: acts on firm and soft going. *W. J. Haggas*

SPUNKIE   8 ch.g. Jupiter Island 126 – Super Sol (Rolfe (USA) 77) [2001 77+: 16.2s – 18d Oct 20] tall, leggy gelding: fairly useful at 6 yrs: well held in 3 starts since. *R. F. Johnson Houghton*

SPUR OF GOLD (IRE)   3 b.f. Flying Spur (AUS) – Tony's Ridge (Indian Ridge – 123) [2001 44: 9d 6m 8m 6m 8v Oct 15] sparely-made filly: poor form on debut at 2 yrs: well held since. *J. S. Wainwright*

SPY KNOLL   7 b.g. Shirley Heights 130 – Garden Pink (FR) (Bellypha 130) [2001 71: – 13.9d 16v⁶ Oct 26] very tall, rangy gelding: one-time fairly useful handicapper: well held in 3 runs since 1999: visored once. *Jamie Poulton*

SPY MASTER   3 b.c. Green Desert (USA) 127 – Obsessive (USA) 102 (Seeking The – Gold (USA)) [2001 82: 7v 6g 6m 5d 5s Sep 27] small, strong colt: fairly useful at 2 yrs for Sir Michael Stoute: well held in 2001, leaving M. Brittain and off 5 months after reappearance: visored/blinkered nowadays: tried tongue tied: has started slowly: best treated with caution. *Miss J. F. Craze*

SQUARE DANCER   5 b.g. Then Again 126 – Cubist (IRE) 71 (Tate Gallery (USA)   **69 d** 117) [2001 74: 6m 7f³ 7f 6d 6g 6g⁴ 6g 6g 6m Aug 22] tall, good-bodied gelding: fair performer: below form after second start: stays easy 7f: acts on fibresand, firm and soft going: tried visored: tends to get on toes, and has given trouble at stalls (has worn crossed noseband/been early to post): sold 1,800 gns. *M. Dods*

SQUIBNOCKET (IRE)   2 b.g. (Feb 10) Charnwood Forest (IRE) 125 – Serenad   **58** Dancer (FR) (Antheus (USA) 122) [2001 7g Jun 19] 5,500F, IR 12,000Y: good-bodied gelding: fourth foal: half-brother to fairly useful Irish 11f winner Brief Dance (by Brief Truce): dam French 10.5f winner: backward, modest form when eighth of 14 in maiden at Thirsk: subsequently gelded. *T. D. Easterby*

SQUIRE TAT (IRE)   3 b.g. Lake Coniston (IRE) 131 – Classic Dilemma (Sandhurst – Prince 128) [2001 63: 5d 10g 8m 6m 7.1d f8g f6s Dec 15] tall, leggy gelding: has a round action: modest maiden at 2 yrs: little form in 2001, leaving R. Fahey after reappearance: best efforts at 6f: blinkered final 3-y-o start. *B. S. Rothwell*

SQUIRREL NUTKIN (IRE)   3 gr.g. Bluebird (USA) 125 – Saltoki 86 (Ballad Rock   **62** 122) [2001 75: f6s² f7g⁴ f6g³ f5g 5m 6f 5f 6m⁶ 7.1f 7m 5g Sep 3] small, strong gelding: fair at 2 yrs, only modest in 2001, leaving B. Hills after fourth start: stays 6f: acts on fibresand, best turf efforts on softer than good: tried blinkered: very slowly away sixth outing. *Jedd O'Keeffe*

SRI GANESHA (IRE)   2 b.f. (Feb 6) Sri Pekan (USA) 117 – Sarabi 64 (Alzao (USA)   **46** 117) [2001 5g f5g⁴ f6g⁵ 6s Aug 31] IR 3,500F, IR 1,000Y, 9,000 2-y-o: first foal: dam 2-y-o 5f winner: poor maiden: should stay 7f. *P. Mitchell*

STADENANZ   2 b.f. (May 8) Rainbow Quest (USA) 134 – Lutoviska (Glenstal (USA)   **– p** 118) [2001 8.5s⁵ Oct 28] half-sister to several winners in Italy, notably smart winner up to 1½m War Declaration (by Persian Bold), later successful in USA: dam useful Italian 7f to 1¼m winner: well-held fifth of 8 in newcomers race at Milan: should do better. *L. M. Cumani*

STAFFORD KING (IRE)   4 b.c. Nicolotte 118 – Opening Day (Day Is Done 115)   **50** [2001 54: e13g⁴ f11g e12g³ 14.1s 11.6m⁶ 12m 12.1s f8.5g p12g f12g⁶ f12g Dec 8] lengthy, workmanlike colt: modest maiden: stays 1½m: acts on soft going, good to firm and fibresand/equitrack: tried visored: often takes good hold. *J. G. M. O'Shea*

STAFFORD PRINCE   4 br.g. Bin Ajwaad (IRE) 119 – Petonellajill 73 (Petong 126)   – [2001 –: 11.7m Aug 24] of little account nowadays. *J. G. M. O'Shea*

STAGE BY STAGE (USA)   2 ch.c. (Apr 2) In The Wings 128 – Lady Thynn (FR)   **101** (Crystal Glitters (USA) 127) [2001 7d² 8.3g² 10.2g* 9v⁵ Oct 21] $65,000F, 160,000Y: fifth foal: half-brother to 2 winners in France, including 7.5f to 1¼m winner Mac Binn (by Pistolet Bleu): dam, French 12.5f winner, half-sister to smart middle-distance performers Lowell and Lady Blessington: useful form: had name changed from On Stage after third start: won maiden at Bath in October: best effort when 4 lengths last of 5 to Rashbag in Prix de Conde at Longchamp later in month, in that position throughout but keeping on: will stay at least 1½m: carried head high second start. *M. L. W. Bell*

STAGE PRESENCE (IRE)   3 ch.f. Selkirk (USA) 129 – Park Charger 105 (Tirol   **85** 127) [2001 78: 7f⁴ 7g² 7g* 7.2g⁶ 7d⁴ 7d p10g⁶ p8g* p10g⁵ Dec 4] good-topped filly: **a95** useful on all-weather, fairly useful on turf: won maiden at Brighton in August and handicap at Lingfield in November: some creditable efforts otherwise, including when fourth to Toffee Nosed in listed event at Ascot in October: stayed easy 1¼m: acted on firm going, good to soft and polytrack: sometimes raced freely/wandered: stud. *B. W. Hills*

STAGING POST (USA) 3 b.c. Pleasant Colony (USA) – Interim 117 (Sadler's **107** Wells (USA) 132) [2001 79p: 10v² 10g* 10g² 12d² 11.9m* Sep 5] quite attractive colt: useful performer: won maiden at Windsor in June and handicap at York (beat Worthily by neck despite almost certainly being unsuited by lack of pace) in September: good second in between in handicaps at Newmarket (to Alphaeus) and Pontefract (to Sporting Gesture): should stay at least 1¾m: acts on heavy and good to firm going: joined R. Frankel in USA. *H. R. A. Cecil*

STAIRWELL 3 b.f. Hernando (FR) 127 – Sliprail (USA) 86 (Our Native (USA)) **57** [2001 10g⁵ 10g 11.7d⁴ 11.7d Oct 25] sixth foal: half-sister to fairly useful Irish 9f winner Super Whizz (by Belmez): dam, 1¼m winner, half-sister to smart Irish miler Thornberry: modest form in maidens: should stay 1½m. *H. Candy*

STALKY 2 ch.f. (Feb 23) Bahamian Bounty 116 – La Noisette (Rock Hopper 124) **56** [2001 f5g⁴ 7m 6g 6g⁶ f5g⁵ f5f* f5g f6s Dec 26] 7,000 2-y-o: leggy, angular filly: second foal: dam unraced half-sister to 8-y-o Repertory: modest performer: won seller at Wolverhampton in December: likely to prove best at 5f/6f: acts on fibresand: refused to enter stall third intended outing. *J. A. Osborne*

STALLONE 4 ch.g. Brief Truce (USA) 126 – Bering Honneur (USA) (Bering 136) **79** [2001 88: 8s 10.1s 8.5m⁵ 10g 10.1m 10m³ 10.3f 10.1m 9m⁵ 10.4d Oct 12] good-bodied gelding: fair handicapper: stays 1¼m: acts on soft and firm ground: tends to start slowly: usually patiently ridden. *D. Nicholls*

STAMFORD HILL 6 ch.g. Jendali (USA) 111 – Laxay 69 (Laxton 105) [2001 –: 10f **–** 10m 10m⁴ 12f 10.5d 10.1m 6m⁵ 8m 17.1g 12m 6s 10.3m 18f 6m 12d 14v 11.9s 14.6s Nov 9] poor winning hurdler: little form on Flat: left M. Sowersby after fourth start. *G. P. Kelly*

STANCE 2 b.c. (Mar 17) Salse (USA) 128 – De Stael (USA) 93 (Nijinsky (CAN) 138) **66 p** [2001 8.2s⁶ Nov 5] half-brother to several winners, notably 9f to 1½m winner in Britain and USA Wandesta (by Nashwan) and French 1½m winner De Quest (by Rainbow Quest), both very smart: dam, 2-y-o 6f winner, sister to Coronation Cup winner Quiet Fling: 2/1, slowly away and very green when 10 lengths sixth of 11 to Star Cross in maiden at Nottingham: sure to improve. *H. R. A. Cecil*

STAND AND STARE (IRE) 2 b.g. (Apr 29) Vettori (IRE) 119 – Premium Gift 63 **52** (Most Welcome 131) [2001 6m 7g 7g 6d⁵ 6s³ 5v Oct 17] 14,500F: angular gelding: second foal: dam 5f winner: modest maiden: best effort when third in claimer at Lingfield: stays 6f: acts on good to soft ground: blinkered last 3 starts: sold 4,200 gns. *M. H. Tompkins*

STANDIFORD GIRL (IRE) 4 b.f. Standiford (USA) – Pennine Girl (IRE) (Pennine **–** Walk 120) [2001 46, a55: f11g Oct 1] sparely-made filly: poor maiden at 3 yrs: well held only start in 2001. *L. A. Dace*

STANDS TO REASON 3 gr.g. Hernando (FR) 127 – Reason To Dance 96 (Damister **85** (USA) 123) [2001 70p: 8d⁴ 10v⁶ 9s* 10m³ 12m Jul 29] tall, close-coupled gelding: unimpressive walker: fairly useful performer: won handicap at Sandown in June: stays 1¼m: acts on soft and good to firm going. *L. G. Cottrell*

STANDS TO REASON (USA) 2 b.f. (Apr 1) Gulch (USA) – Sheer Reason (USA) **80 p** 110 (Danzig (USA)) [2001 6.1v² Oct 4] smallish, quite attractive filly: first foal: dam, French 2-y-o 6f listed winner, daughter of smart 6f (Princess Margaret Stakes) to 1m winner Hiaam from family of Swain and 5-y-o Fantastic Light: 13/2, ½-length second of 11 to Viva Maria in maiden at Nottingham, always prominent: will probably stay 1m: sure to improve. *B. W. Hills*

STANZA (USA) 3 ch.f. Opening Verse (USA) 126 – Raweyah (USA) (Our Native **62** (USA)) [2001 f9.4s⁵ 8.5s⁴ 7s 8m* 10m³ 10m⁵ 10m 8d⁴ 9m 9g 8g⁴ Nov 7] close-coupled filly: half-sister to numerous winners in USA, including 9f minor stakes winner Wild Cataract (by Silver Hawk): dam winner in USA: modest handicapper: won at Musselburgh in May: stays 1¼m: acts on good to firm going, probably on good to soft and fibresand: blinkered eighth to tenth starts: sold 800 gns. *M. Johnston*

STAPLOY 3 b.f. Deploy 131 – Balliasta (Lyphard (USA) 132) [2001 74p: **73** 11.5g² 10d 11.5g³ 10f⁶ Sep 20] good-topped filly: fair maiden, lightly raced: should prove as effective at 1¼m as 1½m: raced mainly on good going or softer: raced freely and found little final start: sold 11,000 gns in December. *B. W. Hills*

STAR ATTRACTION 4 b.f. Rambo Dancer (CAN) 107 – Flying Fascination –
(Flying Tyke 90) [2001 –: f16g f9.4s Jan 18] of little account. *Derrick Morris*

STARBECK (IRE) 3 b.f. Spectrum (IRE) 126 – Tide of Fortune (Soviet Star (USA) **90**
128) [2001 81: 7m 6d⁶ 6f 6g² 6g 6g⁶ 6g Aug 21] unfurnished filly: fairly useful
handicapper: raced mostly at 6f: acts on soft going, probably not firmer than good: has
been slowly away: sold 4,500 gns. *J. D. Bethell*

STAR CAST (IRE) 4 ch.f. In The Wings 128 – Thank One's Stars (Alzao (USA) 117) **82**
[2001 82: 11.7d⁴ 12v⁵ 14.4m² 12g⁵ 12g³ 11.6v Oct 8] small filly: unimpressive mover:
fairly useful handicapper: stays 1¾m: acts on heavy and good to firm going. *R. F. Johnson
Houghton*

STAR CROSS (IRE) 2 b.g. (Apr 5) Ashkalani (IRE) 128 – Solar Star (USA) 93 (Lear **85 p**
Fan (USA) 130) [2001 7v⁴ 8.2s* Nov 5] 20,000Y: strong, useful-looking gelding: has
scope: sixth foal: half-brother to 3 winners, including useful 1999 French 2-y-o 7f winner
Bintalreef (by Diesis) and fairly useful 1m winner Irish Light (by Irish River): dam, 6f
winner at 2 yrs, half-sister to smart US 6f/7f performer Gold Land: 15/8 favourite,
confirmed promise when winning maiden at Nottingham by 3½ lengths from Calamint,
well on top final 1f after tending to race freely: should stay 1¼m: probably a useful
performer in the making. *J. L. Dunlop*

STARDARA (USA) 3 b.f. Theatrical 128 – Lydara (USA) (Alydar (USA)) [2001 55: –
8.3s 12g Aug 25] leggy, lengthy, unfurnished filly: well beaten all 3 starts since debut at 2
yrs: sent to USA. *P. F. I. Cole*

STAR DYNASTY (IRE) 4 b.g. Bering 136 – Siwaayib 97 (Green Desert (USA) 127) **73 +**
[2001 90: 11.5m⁵ Jul 24] angular, close-coupled gelding: fairly useful maiden at 3 yrs:
only fair form only run in 2001: probably stays 11.5f: acts on good to soft going: wore
bandages in 2000 (has reportedly had knee problems): tends to race freely: sold 3,500
gns. *E. A. L. Dunlop*

STAR EXPRESS 2 b.f. (Feb 4) Sadler's Wells (USA) 132 – Vaigly Star 118 (Star **80 p**
Appeal 133) [2001 7g⁴ Sep 11] sister to smart 7f/1m performer in Britain/UAE Yalaie-
tanee, closely related to 1998 2-y-o 1m winner Sabotiere (by Unfuwain) and half-sister to
3 winners, including 1991 Molecomb winner Sahara Star (by Green Desert): dam, best at
6f, half-sister to high-class sprinter Vaigly Great: 9/1, 2¼ lengths fourth of 17 to Snowfire
in maiden at Lingfield, running green after slow start but staying on well: will stay 1m:
sure to improve. *D. R. Loder*

STARFAN (USA) 2 b.f. (Feb 1) Lear Fan (USA) 130 – Willstar (USA) (Nureyev **101**
(USA) 131) [2001 7g² 8s⁴ Oct 7] smallish, strong, lengthy filly: second foal: dam, French
1m winner, sister to useful French 1m/1¼m winner Viviana out of half-sister to dam of
Chief's Crown: useful form: head second to Snowfire in maiden at Lingfield: keeping-on
4 lengths fourth of 9 to Sulk in Prix Marcel Boussac at Longchamp: will stay 1¼m: well
up to winning races. *J. H. M. Gosden*

STARFLEET 3 ch.f. Inchinor 119 – Sunfleet 59 (Red Sunset 120) [2001 66: 7m⁴ f6g⁵ **60**
7.6m 7.1f 9.9d⁴ Oct 3] sparely-made filly: has a quick action: just modest maiden in 2001,
leaving P. Cole after second start: may prove best around 1m: acts on good to firm and
good to soft going. *Mrs P. N. Dutfield*

STAR GLADE 3 b.f. Charnwood Forest (IRE) 125 – Movieland (USA) 109 (Nureyev –
(USA) 131) [2001 –: 8d 11.6g 8.2g Jun 16] big, workmanlike filly: well held, including
in handicaps. *G. Brown*

STAR GUEST (IRE) 2 b.f. (Mar 30) Alhaarth (IRE) 126 – Lady's Vision (IRE) 93 –
(Vision (USA)) [2001 7m 7.5g 7s⁵ Oct 20] IR 20,000Y: angular filly: third foal: half-
sister to Hong Kong 5f to 7f winner Splendid Patrol (by Desert Style): dam, Irish 7f (at 2
yrs) to 11f winner, also won over hurdles: well beaten in maidens: sold 1,000 gns, sent to
Holland. *G. G. Margarson*

STARLIGHT DANCER (IRE) 3 b.f. Muhtarram (USA) 125 – Tintomara (IRE) –
(Niniski (USA) 125) [2001 10g f8g Jun 15] 4,000Y: fourth foal: half-sister to 5-y-o I Tina
and French 1995 2-y-o 7f winner Prowse (by High Estate): dam twice-raced close relative
of smart middle-distance performer Hajade: well held in maidens. *J. G. Portman*

STAR OF NORMANDIE (USA) 2 b.f. (Feb 12) Gulch (USA) – Depaze (USA) **75 p**
(Deputy Minister (CAN)) [2001 6g⁵ 7d⁴ Nov 3] $17,000Y, resold 400,000 francs Y: leggy
filly: fourth foal: dam unraced half-sister to high-class French 1m to 10.5f winner Fast
Topaze: fair form in maidens at Newmarket: fourth of 21 to Maid To Perfection: will stay
1m: capable of better. *J. Noseda*

STAR OF PAKISTAN   2 b.f. (Apr 9) Lugana Beach 116 – Annabel's Baby (IRE) 37 – (Alzao (USA) 117) [2001 6g Sep 5] 1,000 2-y-o: first foal: dam, poor maiden on Flat, winning selling hurdler: 50/1, well held in seller at Lingfield. *G. M. McCourt*

STAR OF WONDER   3 b.f. Celtic Swing 138 – Meant To Be 84 (Morston (FR) 125) – [2001 51: 10.2f 11.4g 11.7g⁵ 12m Aug 13] little form at 3 yrs. *Lady Herries*

STAR OVATION (IRE)   4 ch.g. Fourstars Allstar (USA) 122 – Standing Ovation – (Godswalk (USA) 130) [2001 10d 10d 11.5m Jul 24] IR 25,000Y: half-brother to several winners, including 1989 2-y-o 7f winner Go Holimarine (by Taufan) and French 1½m winner Sinuhe (by Law Society): dam Irish 1½m winner: soundly beaten in maidens in Britain. *Paul Smith, Belgium*

STAR PRINCESS   4 b.f. Up And At 'em 109 – Princess Sharpenup 63 (Lochnager   **58** 132) [2001 79: 6d³ 5.3m 5.1f² 5m 6m⁶ 5m f6g f6g Dec 10] workmanlike filly: modest   **a–** maiden handicapper: left K. Ivory after sixth start: best at 5f: acts on any going: sometimes blinkered/visored: sometimes hangs/looks none too keen. *J. Cullinan*

STAR PROTECTOR (FR)   2 b.c. (Apr 21) Hector Protector (USA) 124 – Frustra-   **83** tion 108 (Salse (USA) 128) [2001 7f 7.2g² 7.2m³ Sep 20] 40,000Y: well-made colt: fluent mover: second living foal: dam, 1¼m winner, half-sister to US Grade 1 9f winner Mister Wonderful: placed in maidens at Ayr: fairly useful form when beaten 2¾ lengths by Legal Approach on second occasion: should stay 1¼m. *J. W. Hills*

STAR RAGE (IRE)   11 b.g. Horage 124 – Star Bound (Crowned Prince (USA) 128)   **81** [2001 90: 16m⁶ 16.1m 16m⁴ 16.4m 16.2f 16m* 16m³ 16.2g² 16g⁴ 16.1f⁴ 17.5m Sep 21] sturdy, angular gelding: fairly useful handicapper: won 21 races on Flat, including 9 in 1994: successful at Southwell in July (reportedly finished lame): probably stayed 2¼m: acted on fibresand, equitrack, firm and good to soft going (well below form on soft): sometimes idled, but seemed effective held up or front running: tough and game, though was often soon off bridle: was also a useful hurdler: reportedly retired. *M. Johnston*

STARRY MARY   3 b.f. Deploy 131 – Darling Splodge (Elegant Air 119) [2001 57:   **61** 10.3s⁶ 11.6s⁴ 11.6g 12.1m³ 14.1m⁵ 10s* 10v⁴ 11.9s Oct 25] close-coupled filly: modest handicapper: won at Brighton in September: effective at 1¼m (given bit of a test) to 1¾m: acts on heavy and good to firm going: sometimes slowly away: consistent. *E. L. James*

STAR SEVENTEEN   3 ch.f. Rock City 120 – Westminster Waltz (Dance In Time   **78** (CAN) [2001 e8g⁶ f8.5g² f8g² 9s⁶ 9m⁶ 11.4g 10g² 10.1s⁴ 10d* f12g* Dec 10] half-sister to several winners, including 5-y-o Calldat Seventeen and 1m/9f winner Seventeens Lucky (by Touch of Grey), both fairly useful: dam race twice: fair performer: won minor event at Nottingham in September and handicap at Southwell in December: stays easy 1½m: acts on good to firm, soft ground and fibresand: usually leads/races prominently: often slowly away earlier in year. *P. W. D'Arcy*

STARS IN HER EYES (IRE)   2 b.f. (Mar 8) Woodman (USA) 126 – Wind In Her   **72** Hair (IRE) 114 (Alzao (USA) 117) [2001 6m⁴ 6m 6m³ 6m³ Sep 12] third foal: half-sister to useful 6f (including at 2 yrs)/7f winner Veil of Avalon (by Thunder Gulch): dam, 1¼m/1½m winner and second in Oaks, from family of Nashwan and Unfuwain: fair maiden: tongue tied, best effort when third in nursery at Goodwood final start: will prove best at 5f/6f. *J. W. Hills*

START OVER (IRE)   2 b.c. (Feb 5) Barathea (IRE) 127 – Carnelly (IRE) 101 (Priolo   **76** (USA) 127) [2001 7m 7v⁴ 7g³ Nov 5] 55,000F/Y: first foal: dam Irish 1½m winner: fair maiden: third at Redcar: likely to be suited by 1¼m/1½m. *E. J. O'Neill*

STAR TRECKER (IRE)   2 b.c. (Apr 8) Spectrum (IRE) 126 – Night Patrol (IRE)   **71** (Night Shift (USA)) [2001 7.9d f8s² Dec 21] IR 21,000Y: small, sturdy colt: first foal: dam ran once: much better effort in maidens when ½-length second of 16 to Redisham at Southwell: should prove better at 1m than shorter. *K. McAuliffe*

STAR TURN (IRE)   7 ch.g. Night Shift (USA) – Ringtail 102 (Auction Ring (USA)   **61** 123) [2001 72, a–: 9g 9d 10g³ 9.9m³ Aug 15] strong gelding: has reportedly suffered knee   **a–** problems: modest handicapper: stays 1¼m: acts on firm and soft going, had form on equitrack/fibresand earlier in career. *R. M. Flower*

STARZAAN (IRE)   2 b.c. (Apr 9) Darshaan 133 – Stellina (IRE) (Caerleon (USA)   **80 p** 132) [2001 8d 8d Oct 19] 220,000Y: tall, rangy colt: on the weak side at 2 yrs: fifth living foal: closely related to smart French performer up to 1½m Sestino (by Shirley Heights) and French 7.5f (at 2 yrs)/1¼m winner Cospicua (by High Estate), and half-brother to

969

French winner up to 12.5f Ravello (by Machiavellian): dam, French 1¼m winner at 2 yrs, from family of Sagaro: better effort in maidens (fairly useful form) when ninth of 20 to Rawyaan at Newmarket on second start: will be suited by 1½m+: should do better. *P. F. I. Cole*

STATE OF CONFUSION (IRE)   2 ch.g. (Apr 6) Great Commotion (USA) 123 –   – Burina (Burslem 123) [2001 f5g 7m f8.5g Oct 9] IR 6,200F, IR 4,000Y, resold IR 4,500Y, 8,500 2-y-o: third reported foal: dam unraced: well held in maidens: dead. *R. M. Beckett*

STATE OPENING   4 ch.f. Absalom 128 – Lightning Legend 71 (Lord Gayle (USA)   – 124) [2001 –: 7.1m 6f 7m 7.1g 8s 8.3v Nov 8] of no account. *Miss Z. C. Davison*

STATEROOM (USA)   3 ch.c. Affirmed (USA) – Sleet (USA) (Summer Squall   85 (USA)) [2001 64p: 8g⁴ 7g 8m* 7f Aug 18] close-coupled, rather unfurnished colt: fairly useful performer, lightly raced: best effort in maiden at Newmarket on reappearance: won similar event at Kempton in July: stays 1m: acts on good to firm going: tongue tied last 2 starts. *J. A. R. Toller*

STATE SHINTO (USA)   5 br.h. Pleasant Colony (USA) – Sha Tha (USA) 118 (Mr   121 Prospector (USA)) [2001 120: a8f* a10f⁴ a9f 11f⁴ 12g Aug 11] tall, good sort: very smart performer: won minor event at Nad Al Sheba in March, beating China Visit (who gave 7 lb) by short head, leading near finish: good 3½ lengths fourth to Captain Steve in Dubai World Cup there later in month (final outing for J. Sadler in UAE): returned to former trainer, well below form in 2 Grade 2 events at Belmont and Sword Dancer Handicap at Saratoga: finds 1m a bare minimum, and stays 10.5f: acts on dirt and heavy going: visored/blinkered. *Saeed bin Suroor*

STATIM   2 b.f. (Mar 21) Marju (IRE) 127 – Rapid Repeat (IRE) 95 (Exactly Sharp   78 p (USA) 121) [2001 7.5g 8.2v 8d² Oct 25] tall, angular filly: has scope: fifth foal: half-sister to 3 winners, including fairly useful 1998 2-y-o 7f winner Subito (by Darshaan) and useful 1½m performer Metronome (by Salse): dam, 2-y-o 7f winner who stayed 1¾m, half-sister to smart French performer up to 1¼m Hello Soso: clearly best effort in maidens (fair form) when beaten ¾ length by Kaieteur at Bath, keeping on well after showing reluctance stall and starting slowly: will be suited by 1¼m/1½m: type to make a fairly useful handicapper at least. *L. M. Cumani*

STATOSILVER   3 b.g. Puissance 110 – Silver Blessings (Statoblest 120) [2001 –: f8g f6g Jun 29] close-coupled gelding: has a round action: well held in maidens/handicap. *Mrs A. Duffield*

STATOYORK   8 b.g. Statoblest 120 – Ultimate Dream 74 (Kafu 120) [2001 70, a–:   59 f6g f5g 5m 5m 5.2m 5d 5g⁴ 5.5d 5g⁵ 5s 5.1g 5v Oct 24] strong gelding: modest handicapper: best at 5f: acts on fibresand, firm and soft going: visored/blinkered last 6 starts: has reportedly bled from nose on several occasions: usually slowly away: has been early to post/upset in stall: best produced late. *D. Shaw*

STATUE GALLERY (IRE)   3 ch.c. Cadeaux Genereux 131 – Kinlochewe 102 (Old   85 Vic 136) [2001 75: 6d⁴ 6.1f* 6s 6m 6g Jul 10] strong, angular colt: fairly useful handicapper: won at Chester in May: below form after: stays 6f: acts on firm and good to soft going. *J. A. R. Toller*

STAY BEHIND   3 ch.f. Elmaamul (USA) 125 – I Will Lead (USA) (Seattle Slew   97 (USA)) [2001 86P: 10g⁴ 9.7m* 10m* 10.2m² 11.9m 10d Oct 18] lengthy, rather unfurnished filly: useful performer: won maiden at Folkestone and minor event at Pontefract (by 1¾ lengths from Prairie Wolf) in June: easily best effort in listed events after when head second to Sauterne at Chepstow: stayed 1¼m: acted on good to firm going: free-going sort: stud. *Mrs A. J. Perrett*

STAY GOLD (JPN)   7 b.h. Sunday Silence (USA) – Golden Sash (USA) (Dictus (FR)   127 126) [2001 120: 12f* 12g* 11f⁴ 12f*ᵈⁱˢ 10d 12f⁴ 12m* Dec 16] second foal: dam, lightly raced in Japan, sister to very good Japanese sprinter/miler Soccer Boy: high-class performer: better than ever at 7 yrs, first past post in Group 2 handicap at Kyoto in January, Dubai Sheema Classic at Nad Al Sheba (swooped late to beat Fantastic Light a nose) in March, Group 2 at Kyoto (disqualified after beating T M Opera O) in October and Hong Kong Vase at Sha Tin in December: gained final success by head from Ekraar, still having plenty to do when hanging inside final 1f but finishing strongly: contested Japan Cup at Tokyo 4 times, best effort when fourth to Jungle Pocket in latest season: effective at 11f to 2m: acted on firm and soft going: had worn blinkers/hood: to stand at Breeders Stallion Station, Japan. *Y. Ikee, Japan*

STEADFAST AND TRUE (USA)   2 b.c. (Apr 14) Danzig (USA) – Always Loyal   **75 +**
(USA) 113 (Zilzal (USA) 137) [2001 6m² May 30] first foal: dam, won Poule d'Essai des
Pouliches and stayed 10.5f, half-sister to top-class French sprinter Anabaa (by Danzig)
and to high-class 1m/1¼m winner in USA/Dubai Key of Luck: weak 11/8-shot, ½-length
second of 4 to Million Percent in minor event at Yarmouth, racing freely in front and worn
down last 50 yds: sent to USA. *D. R. Loder*

STEALTHY TIMES   4 ch.f. Timeless Times (USA) 99 – Stealthy 73 (Kind of Hush   **58**
118) [2001 75d: 6m⁶ 5f 7.1f³ 6g⁶ 7.6m⁶ 6m Aug 11] smallish, sturdy filly: modest handicapper: best at 6f/7f: acts on firm and good to soft going: tends to wander: reportedly in
foal to Bold Edge. *W. M. Brisbourne*

STEAMING HOME (USA)   2 b.f. (Jan 11) Salt Lake (USA) – County Fair (USA)   **96**
(Mr Prospector (USA)) [2001 5m² 5m² 6g* 6g* 6d Oct 2] $52,000Y: small filly: first
foal: dam, ran once in USA, half-sister to US Grade 1 1¼m winner Corporate Report:
useful performer: won maiden in July and nursery race (by 1½ lengths from Minashki) in
September, both at the Curragh: last of 8 in Cheveley Park Stakes at Newmarket: will stay
at least 7f. *D. K. Weld, Ireland*

STEAMROLLER STANLY   8 b.g. Shirley Heights 130 – Miss Demure 106 (Shy   **– §**
Groom (USA)) [2001 –§, a70d: f16g⁵ e16g⁴ f16g⁵ f16g f14g⁵ Jun 8] sturdy gelding: poor   **a42 §**
performer: effective at 1½m to 2m: acts on fibresand and equitrack: sometimes visored/
blinkered: unreliable. *D. W. Chapman*

STEEL BAND   3 b.c. Kris 135 – Quaver (USA) 74 (The Minstrel (CAN) 135) [2001   **93**
89: 7d 9m 9.9m⁴ 11.9d² 12g⁴ 11.9g 10.3g Sep 15] tall, close-coupled colt: fairly useful
handicapper: good 1½ lengths second to Hannibal Lad in Old Newton Cup at Haydock in
July: ran as though something amiss last 2 starts: will prove as effective at 1¼m as 1½m:
yet to race on extremes of going: front runner (has raced too freely): sold 25,000 gns.
H. Candy

STEELY DAN   2 b.g. (Feb 17) Danzig Connection (USA) – No Comebacks 70 (Last   **73**
Tycoon 131) [2001 5s f5g* 5s⁶ 5d* 5.1f⁵ 8m 6.9d⁵ 6m 7g 7s f6g p8g⁶ p6g² p7g² Dec 29]
11,500F, 15,000Y: strong gelding: third foal: half-brother to 4-y-o New Options: dam, 1m
to 1½m winner, out of half-sister to Irish 1000 Guineas winner Katies: fair performer:
won maiden at Southwell in March and minor event at Newmarket in April: second in
nurseries at Lingfield: stays 1m: acts on polytrack/fibresand and good to soft going,
probably on firm: has looked difficult ride. *J. R. Best*

STEENBERG (IRE)   2 ch.c. (Mar 23) Flying Spur (AUS) – Kip's Sister (Cawston's   **96 p**
Clown 113) [2001 6d⁴ 6m² 7g* Aug 11] IR 4,000F, 12,500Y: half-brother to several
winners, including 6f (at 2 yrs) and 1½m winner Charlie's Darling (by Homing): dam
unraced: shaped well in maidens prior to useful form when beating Sir George Turner
by 2½ lengths in minor event at Ascot, travelling smoothly and sweeping through to
lead 2f out: will probably stay 1m: carries head high: probably capable of better still.
M. H. Tompkins

STEINITZ   3 ch.c. Nashwan (USA) 135 – Circe's Isle (Be My Guest (USA) 126) [2001   **87**
80p: 10.3v⁴ 11.8m² 11.7g⁴ 12.4m* 12.3m* 11m⁴ Aug 11] small, angular colt: fine walker:
fluent mover: fairly useful performer: successful in minor event at Newcastle and handicap at Ripon in July: stays 1½m: acts on good to firm going, possibly unsuited by heavy:
usually races prominently: sold 8,000 gns. *J. L. Dunlop*

STEPASTRAY   4 gr.g. Alhijaz 122 – Wandering Stranger 69 (Petong 126) [2001 57:   **54**
11s 12m 14.1m⁴ 12m⁴ 12g 14.1m 9.9f² 9.9m 10.1m 10m 12g⁴ 11m⁴ 9m 12m 12m⁶ Sep
30] tall gelding: modest maiden: barely stays 1¾m: raced mainly on good going or firmer:
visored/blinkered last 5 starts. *R. E. Barr*

STEP BACK (IRE)   8 ch.g. Salt Dome (USA) – Hazy Lady (Habitat 134) [2001 67:   **95**
9f a6g⁴ 5m* 6m 5m⁴ 5f* 6.2d 6s⁵ 5m* 5g* 5m* 5s³ 5v Oct 27] half-brother to fairly
useful 1994 2-y-o 5.7f winner Veuve Hoornaert (by Standaan): dam once-raced sister to
Middle Park winner Steel Heart: unraced on Flat prior to 2000 (well beaten in bumper at
6 yrs): useful handicapper: vastly improved in 2001, winning at Down Royal (twice) and
Tralee in summer and twice at the Curragh in September: below form from flip start at
Doncaster final outing: best at 5f: acts on firm and soft ground (possibly not heavy).
G. Keane, Ireland

STEP ON DEGAS   8 b.m. Superpower 113 – Vivid Impression (Cure The Blues   **52**
(USA)) [2001 –: 7d⁴ 8f May 25] rather leggy mare: modest handicapper: lightly raced last
2 seasons: stays 1m: acts on firm going, soft, fibresand and equitrack: visored twice at 3
yrs. *Mrs A. L. M. King*

STERLING HIGH (IRE) 6 b.g. Mujadil (USA) 119 – Verusa (IRE) (Petorius 117) –
[2001 –, a57: 10m 10f Jun 3] sparely-made gelding: modest performer at best: no form in
2001: tried blinkered: often tongue tied. *J. L. Eyre*

ST EXPEDIT 4 b.c. Sadler's Wells (USA) 132 – Miss Rinjani 83 (Shirley Heights **117**
130) [2001 108: 12s⁴ 13.4f* 12m² 12g Jul 10] big, good-topped colt: smart performer:
won 5-runner Breitling Watches And Waltons of Chester Ormonde Stakes at Chester in
May by 10 lengths from Pairumani Star, making all: ¾-length second to Egyptband in
Grand Prix de Chantilly next outing, despite hanging left: well held in Princess of Wales's
Stakes at Newmarket final start: stays 13.4f: acts on firm and soft going: free-going sort:
probably needs things to go his way. *G. Wragg*

ST GEORGE'S BOY 4 b.g. Inchinor 119 – Deanta In Eirinn (Red Sunset 120) [2001 –
44, a–: 11.9s 11.5m 16m Jun 27] strong gelding: of little account nowadays. *H. Morrison*

ST HELENSFIELD 6 ch.g. Kris 135 – On Credit (FR) (No Pass No Sale 120) [2001 –
96, a–: 12g 18d Oct 20] leggy, angular gelding: useful handicapper at 5 yrs: well held in
2001: tried visored. *M. C. Pipe*

STICKWITHSTERLING (USA) 2 b.c. (Feb 18) Silver Hawk (USA) 123 – Chesa **74 p**
Plana (Niniski (USA) 125) [2001 8d³ 10d⁴ f9.4g² Nov 17] $100,000Y: third foal: half-
brother to French 2000 2-y-o 1m winner Vielle Senlis (by Cryptoclearance): dam, useful
German filly up to 1¾m, sister to 7-y-o San Sebastian: fair form in frame in maidens
at Salisbury, Brighton and Wolverhampton: will be suited by 1½m+: capable of better.
P. F. I. Cole

STILETTO (IRE) 3 b.c. Danehill (USA) 126 – Pinta (IRE) (Ahonoora 122) [2001 **77**
f8.5g e5g³ 6d* 6m² 5.7f⁶ 7d³ 6g⁵ Aug 9] third foal: half-brother to fairly useful 1999
2-y-o 6f winner Teodora (by Fairy King): dam 2-y-o 5f (in Ireland) and 7.5f (Italian listed
race) winner, also 7f winner in Italy at 3 yrs, out of half-sister to high-class 9f/1¼m filly
Timarida: fair performer: won maiden at Brighton in May: stays 7f: acts on good to firm
going, good to soft and equitrack: tried tongue tied: sold 6,200 gns. *J. Noseda*

STILL WATERS 6 b.g. Rainbow Quest (USA) 134 – Krill (Kris 135) [2001 –, a58: –
f8g³ 7.6m 11.5m 10g 8s Sep 30] sturdy gelding: poor handicapper: left I. Wood after first **a48**
start: stays 1m: acts on fibresand, little form on turf. *B. A. Pearce*

STILMEMAITE 3 b.f. Komaite (USA) – Stilvella (Camden Town 125) [2001 49: f6g –
f5g f5.1v 5.1s 6d 6g f7g 7g 6g Aug 31] small, sturdy filly: poor maiden at 2 yrs: little form
in 2001: tried blinkered. *N. Bycroft*

STING LIKE A BEE (IRE) 2 b.c. (Feb 9) Ali-Royal (IRE) 127 – Hidden Agenda **95**
(FR) 55 (Machiavellian (USA) 123) [2001 8d² 7v² Oct 26] rather unfurnished colt: first
foal: dam, maiden who stayed 11f, out of smart 7f/1m winner Ever Genial: useful form
when runner-up in maidens at Newmarket (beaten head by Hathaal) and Doncaster
(beaten ½ length by Proven) in October: may prove best up to 1m: well up to winning a
race. *H. R. A. Cecil*

STIRRED NOT SHAKEN (IRE) 2 b.g. (Mar 31) Revoque (IRE) 122 – Shakey –
(IRE) (Caerleon (USA) 132) [2001 7v Oct 26] tall, leggy, workmanlike gelding: third
foal: dam unraced half-sister to useful Irish 2-y-o 7f winner Rinka Das from family of
very smart middle-distance stayer Seismic Wave: 66/1 and very green, tailed off in
maiden at Doncaster. *Miss L. C. Siddall*

STITCH IN TIME 5 ch.g. Inchinor 119 – Late Matinee 84 (Red Sunset 120) [2001 **56**
51, a68: 10.3s e12g³ f11g* 11.9s 10f² 10.1m² 10f* 10g 10m* 10g² 10m⁵ 9.7m³ 10g⁴ **a69**
9.7d³ 10.9m 10s⁶ f11g f12g* f12g³ f12s⁶ Dec 15] big, leggy gelding: good mover: fair
handicapper on all-weather, modest on turf: won at Southwell, Pontefract (both apprentice events) and Lingfield between April/July and at Southwell in November: effective at
1¼m/easy 1½m: acts on firm going, soft and fibresand/equitrack: effective in visor
(untried in 2001): carries head high/has hung right: usually races prominently: tough.
G. C. Bravery

ST KRISTOPHER 2 ch.g. (Mar 18) Kris 135 – Enlisted (IRE) 83 (Sadler's Wells –
(USA) 132) [2001 7d 8s Nov 9] 8,000Y: lengthy gelding: first foal: dam 1¼m winner:
33/1, signs of a little ability in maidens at Newmarket and Doncaster. *W. J. Musson*

ST MATTHEW (USA) 3 b.g. Lear Fan (USA) 130 – Social Crown (USA) (Chief's **84**
Crown (USA)) [2001 –p: 8.2s* 10.5m 12m⁴ 14g 14.1g³ 15m 16v⁴ Oct 4] good-topped
gelding: has a round action: fairly useful performer: won maiden at Nottingham in April:
best effort in handicaps after when good third on same course in August: ran if something

amiss on fourth and penultimate starts, gelded after final one: barely stays 1¾m: acts on soft and good to firm ground. *J. W. Hills*

ST NICHOLAS 3 b.g. Komaite (USA) – Nikoola Eve 69 (Roscoe Blake 120) [2001 45: 6m f8g⁴ f9.4g Jun 20] good-bodied gelding: poor maiden at 2 yrs: little form in 2001: visored last 2 starts. *D. Shaw* –

STOKESIE 3 b.g. Fumo di Londra (IRE) 108 – Lesley's Fashion 67 (Dominion 123) [2001 87: 7g 6m 6m 5m 5s 5d Oct 12] second foal: dam 1¼m winner: fairly useful 5f performer at 2 yrs: well held in handicaps in 2001, leaving Edward Lynam in Ireland after fourth start. *J. M. Bradley* –

STOLEN HAT 2 b.c. (May 10) Robellino (USA) 127 – Madam Trilby (Grundy 137) [2001 7m⁵ 7g⁶ 6m³ 7g⁵ 7g 6s⁵ Oct 5] smallish, good-topped colt: eighth foal: brother to Norwegian 8.5f winner Bandolero and half-brother to 2 winners, including 7-y-o Sharp Hat: dam, ran once, out of half-sister to Oaks winner Circus Plume: fair maiden: well below form last 3 starts: should stay 1m: acts on good to firm ground: sold 10,000 gns, sent to Sweden. *R. Hannon* **74 d**

STOLI (IRE) 3 ch.g. Spectrum (IRE) 126 – Crystal City (Kris 135) [2001 80p: 7s 7m⁵ 8f 8.1f* 8g Sep 28] smallish, strong gelding: fair performer: won handicap at Chepstow in September: should stay further than 1m: acts on firm going: none too consistent. *P. J. Makin* **78**

STONE CREST (IRE) 3 b.f. Bigstone (IRE) 126 – Hillcrest (IRE) 76 (Thatching 131) [2001 7g⁶ 8.5m⁶ 8d Oct 8] IR 2,400Y: leggy filly: first foal: dam, Irish maiden who stayed 1m, from family of 2000 Guineas winner Shadeed: little form in maidens. *R. A. Fahey* –

STONE DOCK 4 b.g. Bigstone (IRE) 126 – Docklands (USA) (Theatrical 128) [2001 e12g⁵ 10g 10.1g 16d 10s Oct 25] 13,000 3-y-o: third foal: half-brother to smart French 1m/1¼m performer Chelsea Manor (by Grand Lodge) and fairly useful 1m to 1¼m winner Silvertown (by Danehill): dam French 1m and 1¼m winner: well held in maidens/handicaps: sold 800 gns. *P. Mitchell* –

STONEMASON (USA) 2 b.c. (Mar 16) Nureyev (USA) 131 – Sweet Times 60 (Riverman (USA) 131) [2001 6g* 6g³ 6m⁶ 7s* Oct 29] $550,000F, 760,000Y: second foal: dam, maiden sister to Jersey Stakes winner River Deep (also won up to 8.5f in USA), out of close relative to very smart 1¼m performer Zoman: useful form: won maiden at Naas in July and Killavullan Stakes at Leopardstown (by 5 lengths from odds-on stable-companion Temple of Artemis, making all) in October: stays 7f: acts on soft ground. *A. P. O'Brien, Ireland* **106**

STONEY GARNETT 4 b.f. Emarati (USA) 74 – Etourdie (USA) (Arctic Tern (USA) 126) [2001 67: e7s⁴ f7g⁴ e6g³ 7s 6f⁴ 5.7g Jun 16] tall filly: modest on all-weather, poor on turf in 2001: stays 7f: acts on firm going, soft and fibresand: tried blinkered: looks irresolute. *M. S. Saunders* **37 §**
a50 §

STOPPES BROW 9 b.g. Primo Dominie 121 – So Bold (Never So Bold 135) [2001 82: f9.4g⁶ 8s² 8.5s 8m 8m⁶ 8m* 9f⁴ 9d² 8.5m* 7d³ 8m² 9m Sep 12] strong, lengthy gelding: poor mover: fairly useful performer: won handicap at Goodwood in June and claimer at Epsom in August: best at 7f to 9f: acts on fibresand, equitrack, firm and soft going: blinkered, has been visored: sometimes slowly away: held up. *G. L. Moore* **80**

STOP THE TRAFFIC (IRE) 4 b.f. College Chapel 122 – Miss Bagatelle 70 (Mummy's Pet 125) [2001 63d, a66d: f9.4s Jan 20] lengthy filly: one-time fair maiden: well held only outing in 2001: sometimes tongue tied: tried visored. *P. Howling* –

STOPWATCH (IRE) 6 b.g. Lead On Time (USA) 123 – Rose Bonbon (FR) (High Top 131) [2001 –: e12g Jan 31] no recent form on Flat. *Mrs L. C. Jewell* –

STORM CLEAR (IRE) 2 b.c. (Mar 7) Mujadil (USA) 119 – Escape Path (Wolver Hollow 126) [2001 6m⁶ 6m⁶ 6d⁵ Sep 27] 32,000Y: tall, good sort: fifth foal: half-brother to 3 winners, including smart 5f (at 2 yrs) to 7f winner Sergeyev (by Mulhollande) and useful 1999 2-y-o 7f winner Michele Marieschi (by Alzao): dam maiden half-sister to William Hill Futurity winner Sandy Creek: fair maiden: fourth twice at Goodwood: will probably stay 1m. *R. Hannon* **75**

STORM CRY (USA) 6 b.g. Hermitage (USA) – Doonesbury Lady (USA) (Doonesbury (USA)) [2001 –: 8d f8g f8g Dec 17] no show since 1999: tried visored. *M. S. Saunders* –

STORMDANCER (IRE) 4 ch.g. Bluebird (USA) 125 – Unspoiled (Tina's Pet 121) –
[2001 –: 8.2m⁵ 10d Aug 12] good-topped gelding: no recent form. *G. T. Gaines*

STORMEY WONDER (IRE) 2 b.f. (Apr 4) Darnay 117 – Polaregina (FR) (Rex –
Magna (FR) 129) [2001 7d Oct 18] workmanlike filly: half-sister to several winners,
including Irish 7f winner Slip And Slide (by Pennine Walk): dam unraced: 66/1, well
beaten in seller at Newmarket. *J. S. Moore*

STORM FROM HEAVEN (IRE) 3 b. or br.g. Mujadil (USA) 119 – Lady of Man –
85 (So Blessed 130) [2001 50: f8.5s⁶ 7d f8g 12f⁶ 12m Jul 31] neat gelding: modest
maiden at 2 yrs: little show in 2001: dead. *P. C. Haslam*

STORM FROMTHE EAST 6 b.g. Formidable (USA) 125 – Callas Star (Chief –
Singer 131) [2001 –: f8g 7s 8v 7g 7g 7m 7d Aug 7] fairly useful at 3 yrs: generally well
held after, leaving R. Hannon first start in 2001: tried blinkered/tongue tied: dead.
Edward C. Sexton, Ireland

STORMING FOLEY 3 ch.g. Makbul 104 – Cute Dancer (Remainder Man 126§) –
[2001 61: 5m 5g Aug 13] big, strong gelding: modest maiden at 2 yrs: well held in
handicaps in 2001. *W. M. Brisbourne*

STORMING HOME 3 b.c. Machiavellian (USA) 123 – Try To Catch Me (USA) **128**
(Shareef Dancer (USA) 135) [2001 102: 10.1s* 10.4m³ 12f⁵ 12f* 12m⁴ 11.9g² 12m
Sep 16]
　　　'I've been through all this before. . . ,' said Barry Hills. 'There is always
next year. That's the good thing—they run it every year.' If the trainer had been
unable to summon such a stoical response to his Derby fortunes, he would surely be
in the asylum. In the year of foot and mouth, it was also fortunate that his Holy
Grail isn't the Cheltenham Gold Cup or the Champion Hurdle. The Derby is an
immensely hard race to win, of course, but Hills's experience proves in brutal terms
just exactly how hard. From 1971 to 2000, he fielded thirty-two runners in
twenty-three renewals of the classic and was responsible for the runner-up on four
occasions, but never for the winner. Rheingold was beaten a short head in 1972,
Hawaiian Sound by a head in 1978, Glacial Storm by a length and a half in 1988
and Blue Stag by three lengths in 1990. His strongest challenge numerically had
been in the 1979 vintage, in which he sent out three runners that also included his
shortest-priced Derby contender, the Two Thousand Guineas winner Tap On Wood
at 15/2. Tap On Wood finished twelfth, Cracaval eighth and Two of Diamonds
fourteenth.
　　　In the 2001 Derby, Hills was back again, and, theoretically, with a markedly
better chance even than in 1979. He had four runners, in starting-price order
Perfect Sunday at 9/2, Storming Home 14/1, Mr Combustible 20/1 and Chancellor
25/1. This amounted to a quarter of the field and, at combined odds, gave Hills
approximately a 2/1 chance of training the winner. Perfect Sunday had won the
Lingfield Derby Trial, Mr Combustible the Chester Vase and Chancellor the Classic
Trial at Sandown. 'With their form it wouldn't be fair to take them anywhere else,'
said the trainer. 'Winning the Italian Derby [worth nearly £400,000 in 2001]
wouldn't be quite the same, would it ?' To the question he must have been asked
countless times in the Derby build-up, that of which horse was his best Derby
prospect, Hills stressed how hard it was to split them but admitted to a hunch for Mr
Combustible. However, his son Michael, who had to choose between three of the
four for his Derby ride—Perfect Sunday being ridden by the owner's retained rider
Richard Hughes—opted for Storming Home. The sixty-four-year-old trainer was
proved entirely right in the difficulty he had choosing between his team as the four
horses finished fourth, fifth, sixth and tenth, his first three finishers separated by
less than a length. For nine of the twelve furlongs Hills had the first two, in Mr
Combustible and Perfect Sunday, while Storming Home and Chancellor were
tucked away in mid-division. That was before Galileo left them all for dead; Mr
Combustible hung on for fourth as Storming Home ran on to split the early
pacesetters.
　　　Storming Home turned out in the end to be comfortably the best of the
Hills-trained Derby foursome. Although he was the only one not to have won a
significant trial, he had won a race that used to be held in some regard, the Blue

*King Edward VII Stakes, Royal Ascot—a decisive win for the Derby fifth Storming Home;
second place goes to the grey Snowstorm, with Theatre Script (rail) third and Milan (right) fourth*

Riband Trial, now reduced to a conditions event, at Epsom in April, and, more importantly, had been third to Dilshaan, beaten three quarters of a length, in the Dante Stakes at York. Both races suggested that Storming Home was almost guaranteed to be suited by a step up to a mile and a half. The Derby proved it, and it might also have highlighted Storming Home's place in the pecking order more clearly had he not been hampered before the final furlong, after being initially outpaced up the straight. Storming Home's first chance to put things right came just thirteen days later in the King Edward VII Stakes at Royal Ascot. Starting at 9/2, he was second favourite to 13/8-chance Milan, who had also been fifth in a Derby, in his case at Chantilly. With Milan performing below form in fourth at Ascot, Storming Home won the King Edward VII a shade comfortably by a length and a quarter, needing a smooth run to do so, however, as he had to pass six horses once in line for home, eventually squeezing between Snowstorm and Theatre Script to lead just inside the final furlong. A rematch with Galileo in the King George VI and Queen Elizabeth Stakes at Ascot on his next outing still seemed highly ambitious, and Storming Home was sent off at 25/1 but, having gone down by six lengths to the season's top three-year-old at Epsom, Storming Home managed to halve the deficit at Ascot, held up on the inside for much of the way before squeezing through and running on well to finish clear of the remainder. Fourth of twelve in this company was a high-class performance. Sadly, Storming Home failed to reproduce the King George form. One and a half lengths second to Milan in the Great Voltigeur Stakes at York might not sound like a disaster, but some observers blamed Michael Hills that day for giving him too much to do, though to our eyes Storming Home performed with a distinct lack of zest, looking to be going nowhere early in the straight. Last of seven in the Prix Niel was a decidedly worse performance and Storming Home was not seen out again.

   Storming Home's style of running may have left little doubt going into the Derby that he would be suited by a mile and a half, but the issue was not so clear cut on pedigree. Machiavellian, mated with middle-distance mares, gets a lot of offspring that stay a good deal better than he himself did, but Storming Home's dam Try To Catch Me was a miler. She was a useful three-year-old for Criquette Head, notwithstanding a maiden being her sole success. Her sire Shareef Dancer is an obvious stamina influence and her dam's side of the family contains a lot of smart horses. The big name is It's In The Air, Storming Home's grandam, who was champion two-year-old filly in the United States and winner of sixteen races in all from six furlongs to a mile and a quarter, including five Grade 1s. She is also the dam of smart French seven-furlong winner Bitooh. It's In The Air's half-sister

Morning Has Broken is grandam of the Oaks and Irish Derby winner Balanchine and the Derby third Romanov. Before Storming Home, Try To Catch Me produced four foals, three runners and three winners, including the fairly useful middle-distance stayer Follow That Dream (by Darshaan). Storming Home is followed by another Machiavellian colt, True Courage, who has shown fair form in two maidens for Hills.

Storming Home (b.c. 1998)	Machiavellian (USA) (b 1987)	Mr Prospector (b 1970)	Raise A Native	
			Gold Digger	
		Coup de Folie (b 1982)	Halo	
			Raise The Standard	
	Try To Catch Me (USA) (b 1986)	Shareef Dancer (b 1980)	Northern Dancer	
			Sweet Alliance	
		It's In The Air (b 1976)	Mr Prospector	
			A Wind Is Rising	

A leggy, close-coupled colt, Storming Home has a fluent, round action and acts on firm and soft going. He got worked up in the preliminaries at both Epsom and Royal Ascot, which did not adversely affect his performance. At its peak, his performance was high class and a return to that would clearly see him winning more good races. His trainer might not thank us for pointing this out, but on Timeform ratings Storming Home's best form of 2001 was good enough to have won most recent editions of the Derby. *B. W. Hills*

Maktoum Al Maktoum's "Storming Home"

STORM KING (IRE) 3 b.c. Mukaddamah (USA) 125 – Busker (Bustino 136) [2001 –
53: f12g Mar 14] good-topped colt: modest form in 6f maidens at 2 yrs: tailed off only run
in 2001. *J. A. Osborne*

STORM SEEKER 2 b.c. (Feb 27) Rainbow Quest (USA) 134 – Siwaayib 97 (Green **77 p**
Desert (USA) 127) [2001 7g Oct 4] good-topped colt: has scope: fourth foal: brother
to smart 1½m/1¾m winner Rainbow Ways: dam 6f (including at 2 yrs) winner: 20/1,
considerably handled and not clear run when ninth of 21 to Millennium Dragon in
maiden at Newmarket: should be suited by 1¼m/1½m: sure to improve. *B. W. Hills*

STORM SHOWER (IRE) 3 b.g. Catrail (USA) 123 – Crimson Shower 61 (Dowsing –
(USA) 124) [2001 7g Jun 19] good-topped gelding: second foal: half-brother to a winner
abroad by Lion Cavern: dam, 1m winner, half-sister to smart 6f to 1m winner Chipaya:
14/1, slowly away and never a threat in maiden at Thirsk. *E. Stanners*

STORMSWELL 4 ch.f. Persian Bold 123 – Stormswept (USA) 74 (Storm Bird **49**
(CAN) 134) [2001 54: 8.3d 9m⁴ 8f 9.2m⁵ 8f 10m 10f Sep 20] sparely-made filly: poor
handicapper: well held after second start: should stay 1¼m: acts on soft and good to firm
going: sold 1,500 gns. *J. Hetherton*

STORMVILLE (IRE) 4 b.g. Catrail (USA) 123 – Haut Volee (Top Ville 129) [2001 **57**
66: 8m 8g⁶ 7.5m 7d² 8m⁴ 7.5s⁶ 7d f9.4g³ Dec 11] sparely-made gelding: modest maiden
handicapper: barely stays 9.4f: acts on fibresand, good to firm and good to soft ground:
usually races prominently. *M. Brittain*

STORMY CREST (IRE) 3 b.g. Catrail (USA) 123 – Broken Wave 103 (Bustino **69**
136) [2001 –: 7m 8m³ 9.1m* 9.9m² 8.3m 10.9d⁵ 8.5m² 8g Aug 31] sturdy gelding: fair
performer: won maiden at Ayr in May: ran well after when second in handicaps: stayed
easy 1¼m: acted on good to firm going: dead. *John Berry*

STORMY PARKES 2 ch.f. (Mar 28) Zamindar (USA) 116 – Lucky Parkes 108 (Full –
Extent (USA) 113) [2001 5s May 5] second foal: half-sister to 3-y-o Charlie Parkes: dam
prolific 5f winner: favourite, reared as stall opened and unseated in maiden at Haydock.
A. Berry

STORMY RAINBOW 4 b.g. Red Rainbow 105 – Stormy Heights 62 (Golden **75**
Heights 82) [2001 73: 7.1v 7.6f 8d* 8m 7.9m 7d 8g Aug 7] fair handicapper: won at
Leicester in June: below form subsequently, gelded after final start: stays 1m: acts on
fibresand, equitrack and soft ground, probably not on firmer than good. *M. Blanshard*

STORMY SKYE (IRE) 5 b.g. Bluebird (USA) 125 – Canna (Caerleon (USA) 132) **76**
[2001 83: 16s 11.9s² 18d 14.1s* Nov 5] angular gelding: fair performer on Flat: won
minor event (amateurs) at Nottingham in November: stays 2¼m: best efforts on good
going or softer: usually blinkered: tongue tied: has been reluctant stalls: not one to trust
implicitly. *G. L. Moore*

STORMY VOYAGE 3 b.g. Storm Bird (CAN) 134 – Vivid Imagination (USA) **48**
(Raise A Man (USA)) [2001 59: f8s e7g* f7g⁴ e7g⁵ 7s 8m 7.5m⁶ 8.2g⁶ 7m f8g p7g Dec **a67**
28] good-topped gelding: fair performer on all-weather, poor on turf: won handicap at
Lingfield in March: left K. Burke 2,000 gns after ninth start: should stay 1m: acts on
equitrack and good to firm going: tried visored/blinkered: gave trouble at stalls at 2 yrs.
J. M. Bradley

STORNOWAY 3 b.f. Catrail (USA) 123 – Heavenly Waters 64 (Celestial Storm (USA) **66**
132) [2001 64p: f7g² 8f² 9f* 8f⁵ Jun 29] tall, angular filly: left G. Bravery after finishing
runner-up in maiden at Southwell on reappearance in January: won similar event at
Hollywood in May by 2 lengths: respectable fifth in allowance race on same course
following month: stays 9f: acts on heavy going, firm and fibresand. *Kathy Walsh, USA*

STORYTELLER (IRE) 7 b.g. Thatching 131 – Please Believe Me 93 (Try My Best **68**
(USA) 130) [2001 86: 5d 6m 5.1f 5m 5f 6d 5d* 5g 5g 5s Sep 8] quite good-topped
gelding: impresses in appearance: fair handicapper: won at Pontefract in August: best at
stiff 5f/6f: acts on firm and good to soft going: usually visored: has started slowly: usually
held up. *M. Dods*

ST PACOKISE (IRE) 4 b.f. Brief Truce (USA) 126 – Classic Opera (Lomond (USA) **51**
128) [2001 –: 7.1m³ 7m⁴ f8.5g 8f 7.1m⁴ 7g Aug 10] workmanlike filly: modest maiden:
should stay 1m: acts on good to firm ground. *R. J. Smith*

ST PALAIS 3 b.f. (Apr 12) Timeless Times (USA) 99 – Crambella (IRE) 30 (Red –
Sunset 120) [2001 6d 5g 10d Oct 8] leggy, unfurnished filly: first reported foal: dam,
maiden, stayed 1½m: no promise in maidens. *A. Smith*

STRAIGHT AND TRUE 2 b.f. (Mar 17) Lake Coniston (IRE) 131 – Play The Game **58**
70 (Mummy's Game 120) [2001 5g⁴ 6d⁵ Aug 8] 16,000Y: leggy, rather unfurnished filly:
half-sister to several winners, including 4-y-o Labrett and 8-y-o Power Game: dam 2-y-o
5f winner: better effort (modest form) when fourth of 5 to Celestien in minor event at
Doncaster: may prove best at 5f. *A. Berry*

STRAIGHT EIGHT 2 b.g. (Apr 11) Octagonal (NZ) – Kalymnia (GER) (Mondrian –
(GER) 125) [2001 7.1s 7.5g 7d Sep 26] big, lengthy gelding: second foal: dam, German
1½m winner, half-sister to Derby Italiano winner Kallisto: only a little sign of ability in
maidens. *T. D. Easterby*

STRAIT TALKING (FR) 3 b.g. Bering 136 – Servia (Le Marmot (FR) 130) [2001 **72**
8d 8s 8m 9.9m⁵ 8.1f 8g* 8m Sep 6] 350,000 francs Y: rather leggy, close-coupled gelding:
half-brother to numerous winners in France, including useful 1¼m/1½m performer
Creepshow (by Danehill) and 1989 2-y-o 7f winner Serafica (by No Pass No Sale): dam
winner around 1½m in France: fair performer: won handicap at Brighton in August:
should stay 1¼m/1½m: sold 10,000 gns, and gelded. *S. Dow*

STRANDIAM (IRE) 2 b. or br.g. (Apr 8) Darnay 117 – Jack-N-Jilly (IRE) 43 (Anita's **70**
Prince 126) [2001 5s e5g⁵ f5g 5d* 5f⁴ 7m* 7m* 5.8s⁶ Sep 9] IR 5,000Y: first foal: dam,
placed in 5f/6f sellers, ran only at 2 yrs: fair performer: won maiden at Hamilton in May
and sellers at Yarmouth and Redcar (final start for J. S. Moore) in June: stays 7f: acts on
good to firm and good to soft going: visored third outing. *C. Bjorling, Sweden*

STRAND OF GOLD 4 b.g. Lugana Beach 116 – Miss Display 47 (Touch Paper 113) –
[2001 66: f11g f12g Jan 26] quite good-topped gelding: fair maiden at 2 yrs/3 yrs: well
held in handicaps on all-weather last 3 starts: often blinkered at 3 yrs/visored and tongue
tied final outing in 2001. *B. S. Rothwell*

STRAND ONTHE GREEN (IRE) 3 b.g. Ela-Mana-Mou 132 – Fleuretta (USA) **63**
(The Minstrel (CAN) 135) [2001 8m 8m⁴ 9.9d⁵ f12g Oct 18] 30,000Y: third foal: dam,
Irish 2-y-o 6f winner, closely related to US Grade 3 11f winner Helenska from family of
Shareef Dancer: fair maiden: ran poorly in handicap final start (subsequently gelded):
stays 1¼m: acts on good to firm and good to soft going. *T. G. Mills*

STRASBOURG (USA) 4 ch.g. Dehere (USA) 121 – Pixie Erin 110 (Golden Fleece **59 d**
(USA) 133) [2001 99d: f8g 8.5m 7m 8.2s⁵ 8.5s⁵ 9g 7.1g 7.5s a8g a12g Dec 16]
quite good-topped gelding: formerly useful winner: very much on the downgrade: left
N. Tinkler after eighth start: stays 1m: acts on good to firm ground, probably on soft: tried
blinkered/tongue tied. *J. H. Brown, Spain*

STRATHCLYDE (IRE) 2 b.g. (Feb 23) Petong 126 – It's Academic 73 (Royal **50 p**
Academy (USA) 130) [2001 f6s Dec 15] IR 10,000F, IR 26,000Y: third foal: dam 6f/7f
winner: 20/1, eighth of 12 in maiden at Wolverhampton: should do better. *W. Jarvis*

STRATH FILLAN 3 b.f. Dolphin Street (FR) 125 – Adarama (IRE) (Persian Bold **42**
123) [2001 50: 8.2s 10m 12g 9.9g⁵ 9.9m 10m Sep 1] small filly: has a quick action: poor
maiden: stays 1¼m: acts on firm ground. *W. J. Musson*

STRATHSPEY 2 ch.f. (Feb 11) Dancing Spree (USA) – Diebiedale 58 (Dominion –
123) [2001 6d Nov 2] sturdy filly: second foal: dam, maiden who stayed 1m, half-sister
to useful 5f/6f performer Welsh Mist: 50/1, well held in maiden at Newmarket. *C. F. Wall*

STRAT'S QUEST 7 b.m. Nicholas (USA) 111 – Eagle's Quest 62 (Legal Eagle 126) **43 §**
[2001 57, a–: f7g⁵ f7s e8g³ e12g e8g 7s⁴ 6.1v 8.3g f7g f7g⁶ 6d 5v 7d f8g f7g p7g Dec 12] **a39 §**
leggy, sparely-made mare: has a quick action: poor nowadays: stays 1m: acts on fibresand
and equitrack, best turf efforts on ground softer than good: effective visored or not:
inconsistent. *D. W. P. Arbuthnot*

STRATTON (IRE) 4 b.g. Fairy King (USA) – Golden Bloom (Main Reef 126) [2001 **109 +**
68: f8g² f7g* e7g* e7g* e7g⁶ 7m⁴ 10f⁵ 7m 6g 7d* 7g* 7.1g⁴ 7.6g* 7f* 7g* 7d⁴ Oct
20] tall gelding: improved considerably and made into useful performer: won seller at
Southwell and minor event/handicap at Lingfield in January and handicaps at Yarmouth
(2) in August, Lingfield and Newbury in September, and Newmarket (beat Swynford
Welcome very convincingly by 2½ lengths, despite slowish start and edging left) in
October: unlucky when fourth of 27 to Nose The Trade in handicap at Newmarket final
outing: better around 7f than further, and likely to be effective returned to 6f: acts on
firm going, good to soft, fibresand and equitrack: has worn crossed noseband/been taken
steadily to post: has given trouble start/been slowly away: takes good hold and held up:
sold 110,000 gns, joined D. Vienna in USA. *D. E. Cantillon*

STRATUS (FR) 2 b.c. (Apr 10) Septieme Ciel (USA) 123 – Sudden Spirit (FR) **82 p**
(Esprit du Nord (USA) 126) [2001 p5g³ p7g* Dec 22] 400,000 francs Y: half-brother to
several winners abroad, including French 9.5f winner Us Et Coutumes (by Shining Steel):
dam unraced half-sister to Oaks second Sudden Love: better effort at Lingfield (fairly
useful form) when winning minor event by neck from Camp Commander, still green but
staying on to lead close home: will be suited by 1m/1¼m: slowly away both outings, very
much so on debut: useful prospect, should win more races. *G. A. Butler*

STRAVROLE 3 b.g. Tragic Role (USA) – La Stravaganza 74 (Slip Anchor 136) [2001 –
f12g² f11g 16m Jul 5] 500Y: fourth foal: half-brother to 6-y-o Stravsea: dam maiden who
stayed 1¼m: well held in maidens: dead. *R. Hollinshead*

STRAVSEA 6 b.m. Handsome Sailor 125 – La Stravaganza 74 (Slip Anchor 136) [2001 –
–, a65: f6g f8g f8s³ f8g⁶ f8g f8f f7g f8g f8g f7g* f8g² f8g² f8g³ f7g* f7g f8g⁴ **a65**
f8g⁵ f8g² f8g³ f9.4g f7g f8g f8g f7g⁴ f8g⁴ f8g Dec 17] tall, leggy mare: fair handicapper:
raced almost exclusively on fibresand at Southwell nowadays, successful in April and
May: reportedly finished lame final outing: best at 7f/1m: little form on turf: held up.
R. Hollinshead

STRAWBERRY BANK 2 ch.g. (Apr 21) Shaddad (USA) 75 – Precious Girl 76 –
(Precious Metal 106) [2001 5m 6g f5g Jul 5] workmanlike gelding: second foal: half-
brother to 3-y-o Cark: dam 5f/6f winner (including at 2 yrs): no form in claimer/sellers.
D. Moffatt

STRAWBERRY DAWN 3 gr.f. Fayruz 116 – Alasib 93 (Siberian Express (USA) –
125) [2001 52: 8.2d Sep 21] modest form in maiden on debut at 2 yrs: well held only 2
outings since. *N. Hamilton*

STRAWBERRY PATCH (IRE) 2 b.c. (Mar 22) Woodborough (USA) 112 – Okino **85**
(USA) (Strawberry Road (AUS) 128) [2001 5m 5m³ 5m* 6g⁵ 5m 5m* 5m² 5f Sep 4] IR
16,500F, IR 12,000Y: third foal: half-brother to winners by Fit To Fight (in USA) and
Mister Baileys (in Norway): dam won up to 7f in USA: fairly useful performer: made all
in minor event in June and nursery in August, both at Musselburgh: best effort when
second in minor event at Redcar: likely to prove best at 5f: raced only on good going or
firmer. *Miss L. A. Perratt*

STRAWBERRY SANDS 2 b.f. (Mar 5) Lugana Beach 116 – Strawberry Song 87 **74**
(Final Straw 127) [2001 5d 5.1m³ 5.2m 5g⁵ 5.1d* 5.1g² 5.1m⁵ 5.1f⁶ Sep 18] 3,000Y:
small filly: ninth foal: half-sister to fairly useful 1999 2-y-o 5f/6f winner Ebba and 5f
(including at 2 yrs) winner Sans Rivale (both by Elmaamul): dam 1¼m winner: fair
performer: won maiden at Bath in August: creditable efforts in nurseries all 3 starts after:
likely to prove best at 5f: acts on firm and good to soft going: races up with pace:
consistent. *J. G. Portman*

STRAWMAN 4 b.g. Ela-Mana-Mou 132 – Oatfield 69 (Great Nephew 126) [2001 **46**
66?: 14.1v f11g⁵ f12g² f11g 11.8f May 28] useful-looking gelding: poor maiden:
probably stays 1½m: acts on fibresand, soft and good to firm going: tried blinkers.
J. G. Given

*Newmarket Experience Handicap—the vastly improved Stratton leads home his twenty-seven rivals
to gain his eighth success of the year; Swynford Welcome (second left) comes second*

Godolphin's "Street Cry"

STREET CRY (IRE) 3 br.c. Machiavellian (USA) 123 – Helen Street 123 (Troy 137) **121**
[2001 114: a8f* a9f² a9f² Oct 31] brother to useful French 1¼m winner Helsinki and
half-brother to several winners, including useful performer up to 1½m Grecian Slipper
(by Sadler's Wells): dam Irish Oaks winner: very smart performer: trained at 2 yrs by
E. Harty in US, where third behind Macho Uno in Breeders' Cup Juvenile at Churchill
Downs on final start: improved in 2001, winning UAE 2000 Guineas at Nad Al Sheba in
March comfortably by 2 lengths from Noverre and finishing short-head second to
stable-companion Express Tour in UAE Derby on same course later in month: injured an
ankle in April and missed Kentucky Derby: first race for 7 months but odds on, creditable
length second to Evening Attire (who rec 7 lb) in Grade 3 handicap at Aqueduct in
October, forced wide on turns: will stay at least 1¼m: raced only on dirt: visored/
blinkered last 2 outings: has been tongue tied. *Saeed bin Suroor*

STREET INDEX (IRE) 2 br.f. (Feb 3) Dolphin Street (FR) 125 – Casaveha (IRE) **–**
(Persian Bold 123) [2001 6m Aug 25] IR 3,000F, IR 8,000Y: third foal: half-sister to 2
winners, including useful 2000 2-y-o 7f/1m winner Harrier (by Prince of Birds), later
winner abroad: dam unraced from family of Yorkshire Oaks winners Untold and Sally
Brown: 20/1, never-dangerous seventh of 9 in maiden at Newmarket. *Mrs P. N. Dutfield*

STREET LIFE (IRE) 3 ch.g. Dolphin Street (FR) 125 – Wolf Cleugh (IRE) 65 (Last **78**
Tycoon 131) [2001 67p: 8g 7m 8.2m³ 8g⁶ 10v* 10s² Oct 30] tall, unfurnished gelding:
fair handicapper: won at Windsor in October: unlucky not to follow up at Nottingham:
stays 1¼m: acts on heavy going, probably on good to firm. *W. J. Musson*

STREET WALKER (IRE) 5 b.m. Dolphin Street (FR) 125 – Foolish Dame (USA) **–**
(Foolish Pleasure (USA)) [2001 49: 7m 8m Jun 20] rather leggy mare: poor maiden at 4
yrs: well held in 2001: tried visored. *W. Storey*

STRENSALL   4 b.g. Beveled (USA) – Payvashooz 78 (Ballacashtal (CAN)) [2001 –:   **58**
9.2d 5m³ 5.1f⁴ 5m⁵ 6m 5m⁶ 5f 5g² 5g 5m⁵ 5f 5f² 5d 5g 5g⁶ f5g⁶ f5g³ Dec 14] leggy
gelding: modest maiden: best at 5f/6f: acts on firm going and fibresand: sometimes
slowly away. *R. E. Barr*

STRETTON (IRE)   3 br.c. Doyoun 124 – Awayil (USA) 82 (Woodman (USA) 126)   **88**
[2001 70: 10.5s² 10.5d³ 10.3s 7.9g* 9m* 8m 10.3m* 10m⁶ 10.3d³ 10.3g 10.4d⁶ Oct 12]
leggy, close-coupled colt: fairly useful handicapper: won at York and Goodwood in May
and Chester in July: effective at 9f/10.5f: acts on soft and good to firm ground: consistent.
J. D. Bethell

STRICTLY SPEAKING (IRE)   4 b.g. Sri Pekan (USA) 117 – Gaijin 97 (Caerleon   **63**
(USA) 132) [2001 72, a78: f14g⁶ 11.6g⁵ 8.1m 12m 10f⁶ 12.6d³ 12d² 12.1m p12g Nov 20]
tall, quite attractive gelding: modest handicapper: stays 1½m: acts on fibresand, firm and
soft going: tried blinkered: has found little. *P. F. I. Cole*

STRIKE ACCORD (IRE)   7 br.g. Accordion – Ritual Girl (Ballad Rock 122) [2001   **–**
8.2v Mar 28] second foal: dam Irish 11f winner: 50/1, well held in maiden at Nottingham.
I. A. Wood

STRIKE MIDNIGHT (USA)   2 b.g. (Feb 22) Silver Hawk (USA) 123 – Fleur de   **67**
Nuit (USA) (Woodman (USA) 126) [2001 5.2m⁶ Jun 7] $185,000F, 90,000Y: first foal:
dam, US 6f (at 2 yrs) to 9f (Grade 3 event) winner, out of Poule d'Essai des Pouliches
winner Pearl Bracelet: fair form when sixth of 12 in maiden at Newbury: showed some
reluctance at stall. *D. R. C. Elsworth*

STRIKE THE GREEN (USA)   3 b. or br.g. Smart Strike (CAN) 121 – Durrah   **–**
Green 79 (Green Desert (USA) 127) [2001 85: e5g² 6d 6.1f 6g May 14] lengthy gelding: **a82 d**
fairly useful handicapper on all-weather: may prove best around 6f: acts on fibresand and
equitrack, no form on turf: blinkered second and third starts: sold 4,800 gns, sent to
Macau. *B. J. Meehan*

STRIP SEARCH   5 b.m. Bluebird (USA) 125 – Swift Pursuit 57 (Posse (USA) 130)   **–**
[2001 f16g Mar 26] little form: blinkered once. *J. G. Smyth-Osbourne*

STROKE OF SIX (IRE)   2 b.f. (Feb 19) Woodborough (USA) 112 – Angelus Chimes   **75**
80 (Northfields (USA)) [2001 5.1f 6m* 6f⁴ 7g⁴ 5m⁵ 6.9d⁶ 8s² 8.3v⁵ Oct 8] IR 14,000F, IR
8,000Y: close-coupled, useful-looking filly: half-sister to several winners, notably smart
6f (at 2 yrs) and 1¼m winner Revelation (by Thatching): dam Irish 1½m winner at 4 yrs:
fair performer: won maiden at Salisbury in June: beaten head in nursery at Pontefract
penultimate start: should stay 1¼m: acts on firm and soft going. *R. Hannon*

STROMSHOLM (IRE)   5 ch.g. Indian Ridge 123 – Upward Trend 112 (Salmon   **78**
Leap (USA) 131) [2001 75: f8.5s* e8g 8.5s 8.3g* 8.5m⁵ 9g 8m 8.3m³ 8.1s 8m² 8m
p10g p10g Dec 12] unfurnished gelding: fair performer: won maiden at Wolverhampton
in January (then left J. Fanshawe) and handicap at Windsor in July: stays 1¼m: acts on
fibresand/polytrack, good to firm and good to soft going, not on soft: has hung markedly
left: none too consistent. *R. Ingram*

ST ROSE OF LIMA   2 ch.f. (Mar 7) Dr Devious (IRE) 127 – Mayfair 82 (Green   **54**
Desert (USA) 127) [2001 6v p8g⁶ p7g Nov 20] 12,000 2-y-o: first foal: dam, 2-y-o 6f
winner, sister to smart 1991 2-y-o sprinter Magic Ring: modest maiden: best effort on
second start: stays 1m: sold 8,200 gns. *M. R. Channon*

STRUDEL RUSE (IRE)   2 b.f. (Mar 4) Fayruz 116 – Sweet Disorder (IRE) 62   **56**
(Never So Bold 135) [2001 6g³ 6g⁶ 5.7g Oct 1] first foal: dam, 1½m/1¾m winner in
Jersey, half-sister to smart Italian miler Kierkegaard: modest maiden: best effort when
third at Brighton: should stay 7f. *P. W. Harris*

STRUMPET   3 gr.f. Tragic Role (USA) – Fee 111 (Mandamus 120) [2001 75: f7g⁶   **63**
f8g⁴ f8g⁴ 8.5s⁴ 10g⁶ 7f 8.2f⁵ 8.2g⁵ 7m 8g* 8m³ 10d Oct 15] angular, quite good-topped
filly: has a quick action: modest performer: made all in seller at Leicester in July: races
freely and barely stays 1¼m: acts on good to firm going, soft and fibresand: has worn net
muzzle: withdrawn after unseating and bolting to post tenth intended outing: sold 4,100
gns. *P. W. D'Arcy*

STUDIO TIME (USA)   2 b.c. (May 7) Gone West (USA) – Ratings (USA) (Caveat   **88 p**
(USA)) [2001 7d* Oct 19] quite attractive colt: fourth foal: half-sister to US Grade 3 9f
winner Recording (by Danzig): dam US Grade 2 9f winner: 5/2 on, won 3-runner
Newmarket Challenge Cup by neck from Compton Dragon, allowed to dictate and all
out: should stay 1m: should progress. *J. H. M. Gosden*

STUNNING FORCE (IRE)   2 b.c. (Mar 7) Ezzoud (IRE) 126 – New Wind (GER)   **83**
(Windwurf (GER)) [2001 7g² 8.5m² 8.5g* 7s Sep 30] strong, lengthy colt: second foal:
dam, German 6f (at 2 yrs) and 1m winner, half-sister to useful German 1¼m performer
No Dancer: fairly useful form: landed odds in maiden at Epsom in September: ran badly
in nursery at Ascot final start: will be suited by 1¼m/1½m. *M. Johnston*

STUNNING (USA)   3 b.f. Nureyev (USA) 131 – Gorgeous (USA) (Slew O' Gold   **103**
(USA)) [2001 102: 7v* 8g 10m⁵ 7d² 8s 7d Sep 23] close-coupled filly: seventh foal:
half-sister to 7f winner Dreambeach and French 1996 2-y-o 5f winner Sweetheart (both by
Mr Prospector), latter also won in USA: dam, US Grade 1 8.5f/9f winner and second
in Breeders' Cup Distaff, from excellent family: useful performer: won minor event at
Chantilly at 2 yrs and listed race at Longchamp in April: ran well when 4 lengths fifth
to Nadia in Prix Saint-Alary at Longchamp third start and not discredited most other
outings, including when seventh to Ameerat in 1000 Guineas at Newmarket second
start (unable to challenge, reportedly in season afterwards): stays 1¼m, though gave
impression will prove best at shorter: acts on heavy and good to firm ground. *Mme
C. Head-Maarek, France*

STURGEON (IRE)   7 ch.g. Caerleon (USA) 132 – Ridge The Times (USA) 78 (Riva   **–**
Ridge (USA)) [2001 f12g Mar 15] smallish gelding: fair 1¼m winner in 1999: well
beaten only Flat start since (tongue tied): tried visored. *G. Brown*

STUTTER   3 ch.c. Polish Precedent (USA) 131 – Bright Spells 93 (Salse (USA) 128)   **66**
[2001 84: 7m⁴ 6g Oct 19] good-topped colt: fair maiden, lightly raced: probably stays 7f:
yet to race on extremes of going: has raced freely. *W. J. Haggas*

STYLE DANCER (IRE)   7 b.g. Dancing Dissident (USA) 119 – Showing Style (Pas   **83**
de Seul 133) [2001 79, a–: 7g 7.6f⁴ 8g 8.1m³ 8m⁶ 7f³ 7f⁶ 8.5f* 7m 8m² 9d 9.9s 7.9m⁶ 7.1s   **a68**
7d 7d f9.4g⁴ f8.5g³ f8g Dec 14] tall gelding: good mover: fairly useful handicapper on
turf, fair on all-weather: won at Beverley in July: left R. Whitaker after fifteenth start:
effective at 7f to easy 9.4f: unsuited by soft/heavy going, acts on any other turf and
fibresand/equitrack: sometimes blinkered/visored (only once in 2001): reportedly bled
from nose fourteenth start: has pulled hard: usually held up. *T. D. Easterby*

STYLISH CLARE (IRE)   3 b.f. Desert Style (IRE) 121 – Brockley Hill Lass (IRE)   **77**
(Alzao (USA) 117) [2001 7m⁵ 7m 8.3g 6g* 6d 5g 6m Sep 24] workmanlike filly: third
foal: dam ran once at 2 yrs: fair handicapper: won at Windsor in July: may prove best at
6f. *J. W. Payne*

STYLISH FELLA (USA)   3 b.g. Irish River (FR) 131 – Dariela (USA) (Manila   **–**
(USA)) [2001 43: 11.7g 12m 9.9m Aug 25] strong gelding: poor maiden at 2 yrs: little
form in 2001: stays 1m: raced only on good ground or firmer: blinkered then visored last
2 starts. *Ian Williams*

STYLISH WAYS (IRE)   9 b.g. Thatching 131 – Style of Life (USA) (The Minstrel   **54 d**
(CAN) 135) [2001 73: f8g⁶ f8.5s⁴ f8.5g⁴ 7m 6.1v 6v Oct 8] compact gelding: fluent
mover: one-time useful performer: very much on the downgrade: probably stays easy 1m:
acts on any turf going: visored final start: best covered up. *Mrs Lydia Pearce*

SUALAMAR (IRE)   5 b.g. Magical Strike (USA) 114 – Annagh Trust (Jester 119)   **53**
[2001 8f⁴ 8m³ 8d⁴ 10m f12g⁴ Nov 26] workmanlike gelding: fifth living foal: dam Irish
maiden: modest maiden at best: should stay beyond 1m. *G. M. Moore*

SUALDA (IRE)   2 b.c. (Apr 22) Idris (IRE) 118 – Winning Heart 98 (Horage 124)   **69**
[2001 6g⁴ 7f⁴ 7m 8.2m² 8s³ 7.9s 8d 8.3v Nov 8] IR 3,500F, IR 7,000Y: unfurnished colt:
third living foal: half-brother to Italian winner up to 1½m Masonic (by Grand Lodge),
ungenuine performer up to 2m in Britain: dam Irish 1m/1¼m winner: fair maiden: best
efforts first 2 starts: stays 1m: acts on firm going: has worn crossed noseband and tongue
strap. *K. McAuliffe*

SUALTACH (IRE)   8 b.h. Marju (IRE) 127 – Astra Adastra (Mount Hagen (FR) 127)   **61**
[2001 –: f9.4s³ f9.4s² f9.4g f8s³ f9.4g* f9.4g⁴ f8.5g² f9.4g³ f8.5g² f11g f8g³ f8g³ f8g⁶   **a65**
10g³ 10d f8.5g⁵ 10f² 9m⁶ 10m 8.3g 9g 10m f9.4s* f9.4g⁶ f9.4g f8.5g³ f9.4f² f9.4g f9.4s⁶
Dec 27] strong, lengthy horse: has a round action: fair handicapper: left R. Hollinshead
after ninth start: won at Wolverhampton in February and September: effective at 1m/
easy 1¼m: acts on soft going, firm and fibresand: visored once at 3 yrs: usually held up:
sometimes looks none too genuine. *Andrew Reid*

SUAVE FRANKIE   5 ch.g. Suave Dancer (USA) 136 – Francia 59 (Legend of France   **–**
(USA) 124) [2001 –: f16g f16g f12g f7g f11g f11g May 21] smallish, lengthy gelding:

formerly modest maiden: no form in 2001: sometimes blinkered as 3-y-o: has looked difficult ride. *A. Smith*

SUAVE NATIVE (USA) 3 ch.c. Shuailaan (USA) 122 – Courtly Courier (USA) **89 ?** (Raise A Native) [2001 97p: 7m⁴ 7g 7d Oct 20] strong, well-made, attractive colt: reported to have sustained small stress fracture after impressive winning debut in 2000: apparently best effort in 2001 when last of 4 to Surprise Encounter in minor event at Goodwood on return: likely to prove best up to 1m: acts on heavy and good to firm ground: sold 15,000 gns. *A. C. Stewart*

SUAVE PERFORMER 4 b.g. Suave Dancer (USA) 136 – Francia 59 (Legend of **61** France (USA) 124) [2001 55: f8g f12g f9.4g² f12g 9.7v² 9s* 10g⁵ 12m⁶ 9.9f⁶ 10.1d³ 12m 9.9s* 11.9s Oct 11] neat gelding: modest handicapper: won at Redcar (apprentices) in May and Beverley in September: best at 9f/1¼m: has form on fibresand and good to firm going, goes well on soft/heavy. *S. C. Williams*

SUBADAR MAJOR 4 b.g. Komaite (USA) – Rather Gorgeous 37§ (Billion (USA) **43** 120) [2001 –: 13d 14.1m 14.1f⁴ 13.1f* f16.2g⁶ 12.3g 10d Oct 30] big gelding: poor **a–** performer: won apprentice maiden handicap at Ayr in June: stays 1¾m: acts on firm going. *Mrs G. S. Rees*

SUBIACO (GER) 4 b.c. Monsun (GER) 124 – So Sedulous (USA) 102 (The Minstrel **118** (CAN) 135) [2001 111: 10.5s* 12v* 16g² 12g⁴ 12d⁵ Aug 12] second foal: half-brother to useful German 11f winner Satchmo (by Surumu): dam 1m winner: smart performer: won listed race at Dortmund and Walther J. Jacobs-Rennen at Bremen at 3 yrs when also 5 lengths second of 20 to Samum in Deutsches Derby at Hamburg: successful in 2001 in Grosser Preis der Bremer Wirtschaft at Bremen (by 1¾ lengths from Anzillero), Gerling-Preis at Cologne (by 3 lengths from Aeskulap) and Betty Barclay-Rennen at Baden-Baden (by 3 lengths from Tempelwachter) in April/May: respectable efforts in Group 1 events last 2 starts when fourth to Anzillero at Dusseldorf and fifth to Sabiango at Cologne: effective at 10.5f to 2m: acts on heavy going. *A. Schutz, Germany*

SUDDEN FLIGHT 4 b.g. In The Wings 128 – Ma Petite Cherie (USA) 93 **84** (Caro 133) [2001 91: 16s 18.7f 14g⁶ 12g³ 14g³ 14s 11.6v p12g Dec 19] close-coupled gelding: unimpressive mover: fairly useful handicapper: left E. Dunlop before final start: stays 1¾m: acts on good to firm and heavy ground: visored (folded tamely) penultimate outing: has worn crossed noseband/taken good hold: tends to wander/carry head awk-wardly, and is held up. *R. Ingram*

SUDRA 4 b.g. Indian Ridge 123 – Bunting 102 (Shaadi (USA) 126) [2001 78: 7.1d² 7g **73** 8m³ 7.5f* 8m 7f⁶ 8g 7.5m 7m⁶ 7s 7d f8.5g⁶ f8g² f8s² Dec 21] smallish gelding: fair **a66** performer: dead-heated for first place in handicap at Beverley in June: stays easy 8.5f: acts on fibresand and firm going, probably good to soft: no easy ride. *T. D. Barron*

SUE ME (IRE) 9 b. or br.g. Contract Law (USA) 108 – Pink Fondant (Northfields **63** (USA)) [2001 63: f6g² f6s f6s³ f5g* 6s 5m⁴ 6m⁴ f5g 6m 5g⁵ 5m Sep 20] smallish, sturdy **a54** gelding: modest handicapper: won handicap at Southwell in March: effective at 5f/6f: acts on fibresand and any turf going: effective blinkered or not: none too reliable. *D. Nicholls*

SUGAR CUBE TREAT 5 b.m. Lugana Beach 116 – Fair Eleanor (Saritamer (USA) **41** 130) [2001 61d: f6g⁶ 6g 6g 6g⁶ 6s Sep 7] small, close-coupled mare: poor performer: stays easy 7f: acts on good ground or softer: has been early to post/pulled hard. *M. Mullineaux*

SUGARFOOT 7 ch.h. Thatching 131 – Norpella 95 (Northfields (USA)) [2001 116: **114** a9f⁴ a8f 7g² 8s 8m Jun 20] big, good-topped horse: impressed in appearance: smart **a–** performer: won 9 of his 41 races, including 4 good handicaps at York and Park Stakes (in 1999) and Leicestershire Stakes (in 2000), both at Doncaster: easily best effort in 2001 when 1¼ lengths second to Warningford in Leicestershire Stakes (run at Newmarket) in May: was effective at 7f/1m: acted on any turf going, seemingly not on dirt: was most tough and game: to stand at Beechwood Grange Stud, nr York, fee £2,000, Oct 1st. *N. Tinkler*

SUGAR ROLO 3 b.f. Bin Ajwaad (IRE) 119 – Spriolo (Priolo (USA) 127) [2001 47: **–** f8s f8g Jan 29] lengthy, angular filly: poor maiden at 2 yrs: no form in 2001, including in blinkers. *D. Morris*

SUGGESTIVE 3 b.g. Reprimand 122 – Pleasuring 68 (Good Times (ITY)) [2001 7m* **106 p** 7m* May 29] 9,000F, 16,000Y: fourth foal: brother to 5-y-o Swynford Pleasure: dam sprint maiden from very good family: impressive winner of 18-runner maiden at Ling-field by 2 lengths from Independence and minor event at Yarmouth (hardly came off bridle when beating Ratio by 5 lengths, storming clear), both in May: bred to stay 1m, but not short of speed and may prove as effective at 6f: looks capable of holding his own in much stronger company if all is well (missed rest of season after reportedly suffering minor setback). *W. J. Haggas*

SUHAIL (IRE) 5 b.g. Wolfhound (USA) 126 – Sharayif (IRE) (Green Desert (USA) 127) [2001 –: 6m 17.2m 7.1s Aug 9] no longer of much account. *Jane Southcombe* –

SULK (IRE) 2 ch.f. (Feb 15) Selkirk (USA) 129 – Masskana (IRE) (Darshaan 133) [2001 7g⁴ 7f⁵ 7m* 8s* Oct 7] **109**

John Gosden, who had sent out Ryafan to win the Prix Marcel Boussac in 1996, was certainly on the ball when it came to finalising his plans for the latest running of the event. As it became increasingly likely that the ground at Long-champ would turn out very much on the soft side, Gosden decided against sending original entries Cozy Maria and Sundari for the race and instead supplemented both Sulk and Starfan. It proved an inspired switch, as the last-named pair left their maiden-race form well behind and finished first and fourth respectively.

The Prix Marcel Boussac Criterium des Pouliches - Royal Barriere was the third Group 1 race for two-year-old fillies inside nine days, following the Fillies' Mile and the Cheveley Park, and it took less winning than either of those two, the result confirming the general view beforehand that this wasn't a particularly strong renewal. Of the nine runners, four were French-trained and included the favourite Quad's Melody, who had made it two wins from as many starts when scrambling home in the Prix d'Aumale at Chantilly. Aidan O'Brien was represented by Kournakova, well held in a maiden on her only previous outing, and Venus de Milo, the winner of a similar event at the fourth attempt; and the only British challenger, apart from the Gosden fillies, was Ya Hajar, successful in the Prix du Calvados at Deauville on her most recent appearance. All bar one of the field started at longer odds on the pari-mutuel than Sulk and once-raced Starfan, who had been beaten narrowly at Lingfield the previous month. Sulk herself had had three runs, improving to win the third of them without giving any indication that she was capable of following up in Group 1 company. It was by only a short head that Sulk managed to justify favouritism over seven furlongs at Salisbury in September from Proserpine, and, while her performance suggested strongly that the extra furlong at Longchamp would suit her admirably, that alone wasn't enough to consider her a strong contender. There were two other major factors to take into account, however: the ground, which was far more testing than anything Sulk had encountered

Prix Marcel Boussac Criterium des Pouliches - Royal Barriere, Longchamp—
the visored Sulk snatches the spoils near the line from Danseuse d'Etoile; Kournakova is third

previously; and the application of a visor. Together with the step up in trip, they helped bring about a marked improvement in Sulk. Although reportedly something of a nervous sort at home, Sulk had looked to do nothing wrong under pressure at Salisbury, and she certainly couldn't have shown a more willing attitude in the Marcel Boussac, in which she was held up in a well-run race. A fresh strip of ground had been created by the removal of a false running rail immediately before the event, and that's where Sulk weaved her way through to collar Danseuse d'Etoile, who had changed her legs and hung right after sweeping to the front around a furlong out. Sulk's winning margin was a head, the same as Ryafan's, and there were three lengths back to third-placed Kournakova. Mindful that Sakhee was coming up two races later, Sulk's rider Frankie Dettori didn't execute the trademark flying dismount which he normally reserves for Group 1 victories. 'I didn't want to break an ankle an hour before the Arc'.

Sulk (IRE) (ch.f. Feb 15, 1999)	Selkirk (USA) (ch 1988)	Sharpen Up (ch 1969)	Atan Rocchetta
		Annie Edge (ch 1980)	Nebbiolo Friendly Court
	Masskana (IRE) (b 1988)	Darshaan (br 1981)	Shirley Heights Delsy
		Masarika (b 1981)	Thatch Miss Melody

Sulk has a fair bit of improvement still to make before she establishes herself as a major Guineas contender, and proving as successful as Ryafan was at three years looks likely to prove a very tall order indeed. Ryafan showed similar form to Sulk at Longchamp and finished only fourth in the Irish One Thousand Guineas on her return, but she really came into her own later in the season, winning the Falmouth Stakes and Nassau Stakes before completing a five-timer with three further victories in Grade 1 events in the States. Ryafan got a mile and a quarter and Sulk's style of racing suggests that she, too, will stay that trip. Judged on her pedigree it is likely to be far enough for her, though. By the top-class miler Selkirk, Sulk is the fourth foal of the French nine-furlong and mile-and-a-quarter winner Masskana, who didn't get off the mark until she was four and then won twice more the following year. Sulk is Masskana's third winning produce, by far the better of the previous two being the smart performer Wallace (by Royal Academy), who did all of his racing at seven furlongs and a mile. Masskana herself is a daughter of the Poule d'Essai des Pouliches winner Masarika (herself runner-up in the Marcel Boussac) and granddaughter of the smart 1972 two-year-old Miss Melody. Sulk, a rather leggy, useful-looking filly, has already done her owner/breeder proud, and, with such an attractive pedigree plus a Group 1 win under her belt, she will be a prize asset as a broodmare however she fares on the racecourse from now on. *J. H. M. Gosden*

SULTAN GAMAL   3 b.c. Mind Games 121 – Jobiska (Dunbeath (USA) 127) [2001   –
78: 7d⁵ 7g May 4] sturdy, close-coupled colt: won maiden at Haydock on only run at 2 yrs: reportedly operated on to remove chips from knees shortly afterwards: 6¼ lengths fifth of 10 to Proceed With Care in minor event at Newmarket 12 months later: never a threat in competitive handicap at Newmarket following month: likely to prove best around 6f/7f. *B. A. McMahon*

SULU (IRE)   5 b.g. Elbio 125 – Foxy Fairy (IRE) (Fairy King (USA)) [2001 77: 6.1v   –
5v 6m 5m 8g 6m 6f Sep 10] good-topped gelding: fair handicapper at 4 yrs: well held in 2001: blinkered fourth start. *M. W. Easterby*

SUM BABY (IRE)   2 b.g. (May 3) Royal Abjar (USA) 121 – Matsuri (IRE) 89   –
(Darshaan 133) [2001 6m Sep 1] IR 6,500Y: sparely-made gelding: second foal: dam Irish 2-y-o 9f winner: 50/1, tailed off in maiden at Ripon. *D. Nicholls*

SUMMER BOUNTY   5 b.g. Lugana Beach 116 – Tender Moment (IRE) 78 (Caer-   60 §
leon (USA) 132) [2001 58§: 11.6g 10f⁴ 10f 10f³ 8.1g* 10.3m 11.7f* 11.9g f9.4g 10m 10g 10.9m Sep 17] close-coupled gelding: modest performer: won sellers at Warwick (handicap) and Bath in July: probably stays 1½m: acts on good to soft going, firm, fibresand and equitrack: tried blinkered at 4 yrs: has started slowly/virtually refused to race: none too resolute, and inconsistent. *F. Jordan*

SUMMER BREAK (IRE)   4 ch.f. Foxhound (USA) 103 – Out In The Sun (USA) 90   –
(It's Freezing (USA) 122) [2001 83: e10g f11g 12s 11.6g May 8] second foal: dam Irish
9f winner: fairly useful performer in 2000 for A. Mullins: well held on Flat in 2001: stays
1½m: raced mainly on good going or softer on turf (acts on heavy). *S. Dow*

SUMMER CHERRY (USA)   4 b.g. Summer Squall (USA) – Cherryrob (USA)   **58**
(Roberto (USA) 131) [2001 66d: e12g e8g² e10g e7g⁵ e10g* e8g⁴ e8g⁵ e10g² 10f³ 10m
10m⁶ 8.3g 10m p10g* p10g⁴ p10g⁵ Dec 28] leggy gelding: modest handicapper: won at
Lingfield in February and November: effective at 1m/1¼m: acts on equitrack, polytrack,
soft and firm ground: usually tongue tied: sometimes finds little: none too reliable. *Jamie
Poulton*

SUMMERHILL PARKES   3 b.f. Zafonic (USA) 130 – Summerhill Spruce 70 (Wind-   **105**
jammer (USA)) [2001 62: 6m* 6d* 6m 5g Oct 4] strong, lengthy, attractive filly: useful
form: won maiden at Pontefract in May and listed event at Haydock (beat Hot Tin Roof
1¼ lengths, dictating pace and clearly best effort) in June: off 3½ months prior to well
held in Ayr Gold Cup and listed event at Newmarket last 2 starts: will prove best at 5f/6f:
acts on good to soft ground, successful on good to firm. *M. A. Jarvis*

SUMMER JAZZ   4 b.f. Alhijaz 122 – Salvezza (IRE) 97 (Superpower 113) [2001 57:   **34**
f11g 10g 11.6g 11.5m⁴ 11.6m 12.6d Jul 21] poor maiden: stays 11f: acts on fibresand,
probably on soft ground. *P. J. Makin*

SUMMER KEY (IRE)   3 b.f. Doyoun 124 – Summer Silence (USA) (Stop The   –
Music (USA)) [2001 –: 8.3s 10g 7.5m 7m 7m f8.5g f7g f7s Dec 15] small, close-coupled
filly: no form: blinkered once. *R. Guest*

SUMMER SHADES   3 b.f. Green Desert (USA) 127 – Sally Slade 80 (Dowsing   **52**
(USA) 124) [2001 63: 8s⁶ 5g 7s 10m 6.1m³ 6d 6m 6m 8m Sep 10] small, unfurnished
filly: modest maiden handicapper: best at 5f/6f: acts on firm going: sometimes blinkered:
wandered fifth start: sold 800 gns. *C. A. Cyzer*

SUMMER SYMPHONY (IRE)   3 gr.f. Caerleon (USA) 132 – Summer Sonnet   –
(Baillamont (USA) 124) [2001 108p: 8g Oct 6] tall, quite attractive filly: useful form at 2
yrs: off over a year, never dangerous when behind in Sun Chariot Stakes at Newmarket:
bred to stay at least 1¼m: sent to USA. *L. M. Cumani*

SUMMERTIME LEGACY   2 b.f. (Feb 26) Darshaan 133 – Zawaahy (USA) 89 (El   **108 p**
Gran Senor (USA) 136) [2001 8m 8s* 8v* Oct 23] fifth foal: half-sister to 7f and 8.5f
winner Bay of Delights (by Cadeaux Genereaux) and UAE 7f to 11f winner As Friendly
(by Arazi): dam, 1m winner, closely related to Golden Fleece: won minor event at
Saint-Cloud and Prix des Reservoirs at Deauville (by length from Prudence Royale,
leading over 1f out), both in October: will stay at least 1¼m: likely to make a smart 3-y-o.
A. Fabre, France

SUMMER VIEW (USA)   4 ch.g. Distant View (USA) 126 – Miss Summer (Luthier   **108**
126) [2001 114: 8.3g² 10m⁵ 8.2f* Jun 11] tall, good-topped gelding: lightly raced: smart
performer in 2000: 3 lengths second of 5 to Swallow Flight in listed race at Windsor in
May: 40/1-on and wearing tongue tie, won 3-runner minor event at Nottingham final
outing (gelded after): stays 9f, well held over 1¼m: acts on firm and good to soft going:
effective held up or making running: stays in training. *R. Charlton*

SUMMER WINE   2 b.f. (Mar 1) Desert King (IRE) 129 – Generous Lady 98   **77 p**
(Generous (IRE) 139) [2001 7d³ Nov 3] 40,000Y: good-topped filly: first foal: dam, Irish
1½m/1¾m winner, half-sister to smart Italian St Leger winner Jape: 20/1, length third of
21 to Ballet Fame in maiden at Newmarket, tracking leaders and keeping on well: likely
to be suited by 1¼m+: sure to improve. *C. F. Wall*

SUMMONER   4 b.c. Inchinor 119 – Sumoto 101 (Mtoto 134) [2001 113: 10.3m*   **118**
8.9m² 8s* Sep 29]
　　　　　Racing can make fools of people on a regular basis and Ascot's Queen
Elizabeth II Stakes, the most valuable event for milers in Europe, was a race in
which, to use the words of Henrik Ibsen, 'fools are in a terrible, overwhelming
majority all the world over.' One illustration of this is that when betting opened at
the five-day stage, the eventual winner Summoner could be backed at 100/1. He
had been supplemented into the field for £25,000 and was representing Godolphin,
whose racing manager Simon Crisford reported: 'Summoner has been added to the
race as a pacemaker if we need him. Part of the reason we've supplemented him is
that lack of pace really caught out [his stable-companion] Noverre last time. He

wants a truly-run race and Summoner can provide that if needed.' Summoner had not therefore been supplemented because he had shown any revelational improvement that demanded his inclusion after the original entry stage. Neither, for that matter, did he show any major improvement in the Queen Elizabeth II itself either. It was Summoner's best effort, but by only 5 lb on Timeform ratings, and was the lowest-rated winning performance in the event since the race became a Group 1 in 1987; it is necessary to go back a further ten years, to the victory of 20/1-shot Trusted (115), before finding a more lowly-rated winner, in the days when the race was run as a Group 2.

The 2001 Queen Elizabeth II Stakes was a race in which the question of horses making fools of people might properly be directed at seven of the eight participating jockeys. Jamie Spencer was on board the Eclipse and Irish Champion Stakes third Bach, Grant Cooksley on Singapore's top horse Bocelli, Yutaka Take on demoted Prix Jacques le Marois winner Proudwings, Michael Kinane on the Prix du Moulin third Hawkeye, Frankie Dettori on the Sussex Stakes winner Noverre, Richard Hughes on the Two Thousand Guineas runner-up Tamburlaine and Olivier Peslier on the promoted Poule d'Essai des Poulains and Jacques le Marois winner Vahorimix. It was a cosmopolitan and representative line-up, if not a strong one, with Medicean, Black Minnaloushe and Slickly most notable among the absentees and Valentino, No Excuse Needed and Olden Times all withdrawn on the day of the race when rain had turned the ground soft. On form, Summoner deserved to be among the outsiders but he was by no means a no-hoper, his best form, for instance, only 5 lb or 6 lb behind that of Hawkeye and Tamburlaine. Of course it did not sound so good that that pair's form had been in Group 1 events, whereas Summoner's came from a minor event and a listed race the previous summer and a listed race on his start immediately before the Queen Elizabeth. All three performances represented smart form, but Summoner had won only one of the three races, in a career record including only four wins, a two-year-old maiden, two minor events at Doncaster as a three-year-old and a third Doncaster conditions stakes (at 3/1-on, from Down To The Woods) in June as a four-year-old. Summoner was trained by Roger Charlton prior to a sale to Godolphin in August 2000. Off the course for ten months before his Godolphin debut, he followed that third minor event success with a neck second of five to Momentum in a listed event at York in September and was sent off at 33/1 in the Queen Elizabeth, having touched 40/1 in places.

Much more significant for punters than any form considerations, however, was Summoner's designated role as pacemaker. Pacemakers are not supposed to win. But good ones have a fair chance of doing so if the rest of the field takes no notice of them. In the latest Queen Elizabeth II Stakes, the other jockeys were slow to react to what Richard Hills was up to on board Summoner for most of the race. That Summoner was going to make the running could not have been a mystery, but by setting only a fair pace through the early stages Hills seemed to catch his rivals unawares, as, in spite of this, he was still allowed a five-length advantage as the field raced next to the trees on the far rail. When Hills directed Summoner to the inner again four furlongs out to begin the turn for home, he quickened the pace and,

Queen Elizabeth II Stakes, Ascot—pacemaker Summoner pulls off a 33/1-shock from stable-companion Noverre; Hawkeye (second right) comes next, ahead of Bach (rail), the grey Vahorimix, Tamburlaine and Proudwings (right)

with the others still seemingly oblivious to the danger, Summoner stretched his advantage from five lengths to eight. The chase, which it finally became on entering the straight, began much too late and Summoner never looked in danger of being reeled in. Bach and Noverre led the initial pursuers but the deficit began to be eroded significantly only when Summoner began to tire in the final furlong. He had been so far in front that he was still able to hang on by a length and a half from Noverre, with the same distance separating Noverre, Hawkeye and Bach. With the sole exception of Bocelli, all the runners finished within seven lengths of the winner. The chase had not quite been of Keystone Kops proportions, but the race was a farce nevertheless.

Two days before the Queen Elizabeth II, it was reported that Bocelli's jockey Grant Cooksley had 'spent a couple of hours yesterday going through videos of Ascot, and particularly the last six runnings of the Queen Elizabeth.' It would not have made much difference in Bocelli's case, but a study of the last seven runnings of the Queen Elizabeth would have proved a lot more instructive. The 1994 renewal was the one in which Richard Hills made all on Sheikh Hamdan's second string, the 66/1-shot Maroof. The description of that race in *Racehorses of 1994*—'Richard Hills dictated a steady pace from the start until sending Maroof about his business in earnest approaching the home turn. Maroof ran on splendidly in the straight to hold off Barathea by a diminishing length and a quarter . . .'—might have provided a warning. Godolphin had Group 1 victories over a mile in the 1998 and 1999 Lockinge Stakes with supposed pacemakers Cape Cross and Fly To The Stars. 'We use good horses as pacemakers—not 0-75 handicappers,' reflected Simon Crisford, a point that was made most clearly by Summoner, and also by Give The Slip, a horse well capable of pattern-race success himself, who set the pace for his stable-companion Fantastic Light in four consecutive European Group 1s before his second place, doing the job for his own benefit, in the Melbourne Cup. One of the most interesting comments made by Willie Carson in 2001 in his role as BBC racing pundit was in response to Frankie Dettori's observation that the shape of the King George VI and Queen Elizabeth Stakes—one of the races in which Give The Slip acted as pacemaker for Fantastic Light—would depend on how fast Godolphin's pacemaker went. 'Surely you'll be telling him how fast to go,' was Carson's response. The use of pacemakers has become routine for the Godolphin and Ballydoyle camps, but using pacemakers is far from an exact science; sometimes it's hard to understand why they're needed at all. As Carson seemed to intimate, for example, why would Godolphin want an end-to-end gallop in the King George, when Fantastic Light, a horse who had shown fine finishing speed over ten furlongs, was stepping back up in trip? It seemed surprising that the pace set by Give The Slip in the King George and by Summoner in the Queen Elizabeth II Stakes was apparently left to their rider to dictate. When a good-quality pacemaker doesn't turn a race into a thorough test, there's always a chance that he will still be there at the finish, particularly if he is of the quality of some of the pacemakers employed by Godolphin in particular.

In a race which led to some tarnished reputations, the most obvious person to emerge with his reputation enhanced from the Queen Elizabeth was Richard Hills. When he rode Maroof, Hills was second jockey to Sheikh Hamdan. He took over the first retainer when Willie Carson retired in 1996 and in the last four seasons has ridden the winners of thirty-three pattern races, twenty-nine of them on horses in the ownership of Sheikh Hamdan, including with Elnadim, Muhtathir, Mujahid, Almutawakel, Mutafaweq, Lahan, Sakhee, Ekraar, Mutamam, Albarahin and Nayef. It has been a fruitful partnership and 2001 provided a golden autumn. Within twenty-four hours of Summoner's win at Ascot, Hills was riding Mutamam to victory in the Canadian International at Woodbine. Three weeks later Hills was saluting the crowd at Newmarket on board Nayef after the Champion Stakes. Some might say that Hills did not go fast enough early on to fulfil his pacemaking duties adequately in the Queen Elizabeth. Then again, isn't every horse supposed to run on its merits? You can't have it both ways.

In 1994 there was plenty of argument over the true merit of Maroof's performance, in the frustrating knowledge that Maroof would never be put to the test again, being on his way to take up stud duties in New Zealand instead.

Thankfully it should be different with Summoner, who stays in training. There is little argument about the merit of his success at Ascot—he was greatly flattered by the bare result, and his rating takes that into account—so he has plenty to prove in 2002. The Godolphin team did little to talk him up in the immediate aftermath to the Queen Elizabeth, Crisford stating that 'We would have much preferred Noverre to win … Noverre is a much better horse than Summoner but that ground has blunted his turn of foot. Summoner didn't have the credentials of Cape Cross or Fly To The Stars. He'd been pinging coming into the race but, next time round, you'll find that Noverre will beat him easily'. Whether there will be a next time has to be in some doubt, as Crisford also said 'Summoner won't be a pacemaker any more. He gets elevated into the first eleven now.' Summoner's Queen Elizabeth win came over a mile on soft ground, but he also acts on firm and has smart form at a mile and a quarter.

Summoner (b.c. 1997)	Inchinor (ch 1990)	Ahonoora (ch 1975)	Lorenzaccio
			Helen Nicholls
		Inchmurrin (b 1985)	Lomond
			On Show
	Sumoto (b 1990)	Mtoto (b 1983)	Busted
			Amazer
		Soemba (b 1983)	General Assembly
			Seven Seas

A good-bodied, quite attractive colt, Summoner is a half-brother to another surprise Group 1 winner in Compton Admiral (by Suave Dancer), who was the 20/1

Godolphin's "Summoner"

outsider of eight when he got up close home in the 1999 Eclipse. Compton Admiral and Summoner are the second and third winners, out of the dam Sumoto, and they have transformed her standing out of all recognition. Sumoto was sold for 6,500 guineas at the December Sales in 1997, the year of Summoner's birth, and for 920,000 guineas at the December Sales in 2000. After Summoner, Sumoto produced the 1998 filly So Admirable (by Suave Dancer), who has not yet raced, a 2000 colt by Pivotal and a 2001 colt by Inchinor. Sumoto's buyers in 2000 were the Watership Down Stud, and the first stallion they sent her to was Sadler's Wells, to whom she is expecting a foal in 2002. Sumoto, a daughter of the fairly useful nine-furlong winner Soemba, made a striking first impression on the race-course when backed down to 11/10-on for a maiden at Ascot in June as a two-year-old and beating Sayyedati by two lengths. That performance made Sumoto an early favourite for the One Thousand Guineas, but it was Sayyedati who won the classic, while Sumoto, who missed the rest of her juvenile season with a sprained hock and then suffered further setbacks, had a disappointing five-start campaign as a three-year-old that yielded only one win, by a short head in a minor event at Lingfield. Another of Soemba's five winners is Kelimutu, dam of the useful but disappointing filly Whitefoot. Another noteworthy feature of Summoner's pedi-gree is that his fifth dam Miba is also the fourth dam of Summoner's sire Inchinor. It is a close-run thing between Summoner, Orientor and Umistim as Inchinor's best progeny, with Golden Silca not far behind them, and he also sired the 2000 Gimcrack winner Bannister. Inchinor is highly fortunate to have taken a Queen Elizabeth II Stakes and a Gimcrack with horses of Summoner's and Bannister's quality but, you never know, Summoner might yet prove our assessment wrong. A more optimistic view of his record might be that he has had limited opportunities so far for Godolphin and that he finished 2001 on the upgrade. *Saeed bin Suroor*

SUMTHINELSE 4 ch.g. Magic Ring (IRE) 115 – Minne Love 67 (Homeric 133) **a75 d** — [2001 81: f7g f6g⁴ f7g³ f7g 7.6f 7m 7f 7f 6m f6s⁵ 7.1g f8.5g⁵ f7g f7g f8.5g p7g⁵ p7g Dec 28] stocky, good-quartered gelding: unimpressive mover: has reportedly had minor wind operation: fair handicapper: well below form after third start: stays 7f: acts on fibresand and good to firm going, probably not on softer than good: tried blinkered/visored. *N. P. Littmoden*

SUN BIRD (IRE) 3 ch.g. Prince of Birds (USA) 121 – Summer Fashion 84 (Moorestyle **85** 137) [2001 61: 11.1m⁴ 10.9m² 8.3m² 9m² 12.3f* 11m* 12.3m⁴ 10.3d* 12.1m⁶ Sep 24] well-made gelding: fairly useful handicapper: progressed, and won at Ripon in July and Redcar and Chester (beat Dusty Carpet a neck) in August: stays easy 1½m: acts on any turf going: sometimes blinkered/visored: usually races freely: has carried head awk-wardly and wandered. *R. Allan*

SUNDARI (IRE) 2 b.f. (Feb 10) Danehill (USA) 126 – My Ballerina (USA) 94 (Sir **103** Ivor 135) [2001 6m⁵ 6m* 6g³ 8.1g* Sep 2] strong, short-backed filly: seventh living foal: sister to 3-y-o Dane Dancing and half-sister to 2 winners, including fairly useful 7f (at 2 yrs) and 10.5f winner Starry Night (by Sheikh Albadou): dam, 1¼m/1½m winner, from family of US Grade 1 winners up to 1¼m Hatim and Bates Motel: useful form: won maiden at Newmarket (odds on, made all) in June and 3-runner minor event at Sandown (beat Jazan by 1¼ lengths) in September: good ¾-length third to Silent Honor in Cherry Hinton Stakes at Newmarket in between: likely to stay 1¼m. *J. H. M. Gosden*

SUNDAY RAIN (USA) 4 b.g. Summer Squall (USA) – Oxava (FR) 112 (Antheus **– §** (USA) 122) [2001 73§: 18v 12.3f May 10] big, lengthy gelding: fluent mover: fair maiden in 2000: well held on Flat in 2001, looking irresolute: tried blinkered. *Jonjo O'Neill*

SUNDAY SPORT (USA) 2 b.f. (Apr 5) Honour And Glory (USA) 122 – Gold Rule **92** (USA) (Forty Niner (USA)) [2001 5d⁴ 5m⁶ 6m⁴ 5m Aug 2] $45,000F, $75,000Y, $190,000 2-y-o: rangy filly: has scope: third foal: half-sister to a 2-y-o sprint winner in USA by Summer Squall: dam, maiden in USA, out of sister to US 2-y-o Grade 1 winner Contredance: fairly useful maiden: easily best effort when sixth in Queen Mary at Royal Ascot: soundly beaten in Molecomb Stakes at Goodwood final start: should stay 6f. *B. J. Meehan*

SUNDAYS SARAH 3 b.f. Sea Raven (IRE) 75 – Sundays Off (Dubassoff (USA)) — [2001 f8.5g Feb 27] first reported foal: dam unraced: 33/1, tailed off in Wolverhampton seller. *Jedd O'Keeffe*

SUNDIAL 2 ch.f. (Mar 30) Cadeaux Genereux 131 – Ruby Setting 91 (Gorytus (USA) **– p**
132) [2001 7g⁶ Aug 2] tall, lengthy filly: has plenty of scope: sixth foal: half-sister to
winners in Japan by Woodman and Fairy King: dam, 1¼m winner, out of Oaks/St Leger
winner Sun Princess: 20/1 and very green (swished tail persistently in paddock), well-
held sixth in maiden at Goodwood, not unduly knocked about: should do better.
B. W. Hills

SUNDOWN 3 b.f. Polish Precedent (USA) 131 – Ruby Setting 91 (Gorytus (USA) **71**
132) [2001 65p: 7m⁴ 8.3g 10.1m⁵ 8m 7g⁶ f8.5g Nov 3] smallish filly: fair maiden: below
form after third start: likely to prove best up to 1m: yet to race on extremes of going:
blinkered (raced far too freely) fourth outing: sold 6,500 gns. *M. P. Tregoning*

SUNDRENCHED (IRE) 2 ch.f. (Mar 26) Desert King (IRE) 129 – Utr (USA) (Mr **99 p**
Prospector (USA)) [2001 8m² 8d* Nov 3] quite attractive filly: third foal:
half-sister to 3-y-o Bonnard and fairly useful 1¼m/1½m winner Andromedes (by
Sadler's Wells): dam, probably of unsatisfactory temperament, daughter of smart 7f/1m
performer Hasbah: useful form: 3 lengths second to Revealing in maiden at Newmarket
prior to winning listed race there 6 weeks later by 2½ lengths from Spinnette, dictating
pace and quickening clear in good style: likely to be suited by 1¼m/1½m: capable of
better. *W. J. Haggas*

SUNDRIED TOMATO 2 b.g. (Mar 13) Lugana Beach 116 – Little Scarlett 54 **63**
(Mazilier (USA) 107) [2001 5d 6m f6s⁴ p6g³ Dec 28] second foal: dam 8.5f winner:
modest maiden: in frame at Wolverhampton and Lingfield: should stay 7f: acts on
fibresand and polytrack. *P. W. Hiatt*

SUNGIO 3 b.g. Halling (USA) 133 – Time Or Never (FR) (Dowsing (USA) 124) [2001 **70**
64: 10s 8.2v 10.2g² 11.6m³ 12.1s⁶ 12g⁴ 11.9m⁵ 10.9m² Sep 17] fair maiden handicapper:
stays 1½m: acts on soft and good to firm going: blinkered last 3 starts: has swished tail/
hung markedly left/found little. *L. M. Cumani*

SUNLEY SCENT 3 ch.f. Wolfhound (USA) 126 – Brown Velvet 68 (Mansingh **77**
(USA) 120) [2001 68p: 7d 6m² 6.1s⁴ 6m* 6g³ 7m² 6.1m² 7g Sep 14] leggy, lengthy filly:
fair performer: won handicap at Folkestone in August: stays 7f: acts on equitrack and
good to firm ground. *M. R. Channon*

SUNLEY SENSE 5 b.g. Komaite (USA) – Brown Velvet 68 (Mansingh (USA) 120) **91**
[2001 92: 5m 5.1f² 5g⁴ 6m⁴ 5m 5m⁵ 5g 5s* 5g 5g 5g Sep 15] sturdy, workmanlike
gelding: fairly useful handicapper: won at Sandown in August: best at 5f/sharp 6f: acts
on firm and soft ground: visored final 2000 start: sometimes slowly away, usually races
prominently otherwise: none too consistent. *M. R. Channon*

SUNNINGDALE (IRE) 3 gr.f. Indian Ridge 123 – Hayati 94 (Hotfoot 126) [2001 7d **68**
7g⁶ f8g* Nov 30] 16,000F, 32,000Y: leggy gelding: fourth foal: half-brother to very smart 1¼m
(Nassau Stakes) winner Ruby Tiger (by Ahonoora) and half-sister to several winners,
including useful (at 2 yrs) and 7.5f winner Haw't (by Green Desert): dam 7f (at 2 yrs)
and 1¼m winner: fair form in maidens, best effort when winning at Southwell in
November (first run for over 6 months): should stay 1¼m: acts on fibresand: sold 30,000
gns. *M. A. Jarvis*

SUNNY GLENN 3 ch.c. Rock Hopper 124 – La Ballerine 62 (Lafontaine (USA) 117) **114**
[2001 77: 9d² 11.5g⁶ 12f 12g Jul 10] medium-sized, rather leggy colt: unimpressive
mover: smart performer: much improved at 3 yrs: short-head second to Olden Times in
listed race at Newmarket in April: below-form sixth in Derby Trial at Lingfield next time,
but seemed to run very well when ninth to Galileo (beaten only 9½ lengths, though never
a factor) in Derby at Epsom (sweating and edgy): tailed-off last of 9 in Princess of Wales's
Stakes at Newmarket only subsequent outing: stays 1½m: acts on firm and soft going.
N. P. Littmoden

SUNNYSIDE ROYALE (IRE) 2 b.g. (Apr 7) Ali-Royal (IRE) 127 – Kuwah (IRE) **–**
77 (Be My Guest (USA) 126) [2001 7g 7.9m 7.5g Sep 19] 7,500F, 8,000Y: leggy gelding:
fourth foal: half-brother to a 9f winner in Italy by Roi Danzig: dam, Irish 1½m winner,
closely related to 1¼m/1½m performer Suhaad and half-sister to Irish 1m/1¼m
performer Muakaad, both smart: only a little sign of ability in maidens: tongue tied first 2
starts. *M. W. Easterby*

SUNRAY SUPERSTAR 2 b.f. (Mar 17) Nashwan (USA) 135 – Nazoo (IRE) 99 **87 p**
(Nijinsky (CAN) 138) [2001 7d² Oct 15] well-made filly: seventh foal: sister to 3-y-o
Nadia and half-sister to a winner in USA by Hansel: dam, 2-y-o 6f/7f winner, from very
good family: 7/1, shaped well when short-head second of 20 to Opening Ceremony in

maiden at Leicester, finishing strongly having taken while to find full stride: will stay 1¼m: useful prospect, sure to win races. *Sir Michael Stoute*

SUNRIDGE FAIRY (IRE)   2 b.f. (Jan 31) Definite Article 121 – Foxy Fairy (IRE) **42** (Fairy King (USA)) [2001 5s⁵ 5m⁵ 7m 7m f8g⁶ f8g³ f8g⁴ Dec 10] 3,000Y: lengthy filly: **a51** fifth foal: half-sister to 5-y-o Sulu: dam, showed little at 2 yrs in Ireland, half-sister to smart Irish sprinter Fundraiser: modest maiden on all-weather, poor on turf: should stay 1¼m: acts on fibresand. *P. C. Haslam*

SUNRIDGE ROSE   3 b.f. Piccolo 121 – Floral Spark 69 (Forzando 122) [2001 45: **58** f7s³ f7g² f9.4g⁶ f8g⁵ f7g f7g* f8g⁴ e7g f7g 5v* f6g 7m⁵ 7s⁴ f7g⁴ 8f f7g⁴ 6d f7g f7g f7s² **a53** Dec 18] modest performer: claimed from P. Haslam £5,000 after second start: won seller at Southwell (left Mrs N. Macauley) in March and claimer at Folkestone in April: effective at 5f to 7f: acts on fibresand, heavy and good to firm going: tried visored: sometimes slowly away: none too consistent. *Andrew Reid*

SUNRISE GIRL   4 ch.f. King's Signet (USA) 110 – Dawn Ditty 100 (Song 132) [2001 **55** –: 6m² 6d 5.7g² 5f² 5.3f⁵ 5m² 5m⁴ 5.1g⁵ 5m Sep 26] modest maiden handicapper: effective at 5f/6f: acts on firm going: has hung left: usually races prominently. *Mrs P. N. Dutfield*

SUNSET GLOW   4 gr.c. Rainbow Quest (USA) 134 – Oscura (USA) 82 (Caro 133) **–** [2001 –: f12g² f12s* f12g f12g⁴ 11.9s Oct 25] fair performer: won maiden at Southwell **a72** in January: left J. Pearce and off 8 months after next start: stays 1½m: acts on fibresand, probably not on soft going: sold 4,000 gns. *J. Noseda*

SUNSET HARBOUR (IRE)   8 br.m. Prince Sabo 123 – City Link Pet 79 (Tina's Pet **57** 121) [2001 53: f5g³ f5g e5g³ f5g⁶ f5g* f5g⁶ f5g⁴ f5g⁶ Feb 27] tall mare: modest handicapper: won at Wolverhampton in February: effective at 5f/6f: acts on fibresand, equitrack, firm and good to soft going: tried blinkered/visored earlier in career. *J. M. Bradley*

SUNSET (IRE)   3 b.f. Polish Precedent (USA) 131 – Up Anchor (IRE) 114 (Slip **–** Anchor 136) [2001 f9.4g Feb 27] fourth foal: half-sister to useful 7f to 1½m winner Sailing (by Arazi), 1997 2-y-o 7f winner Fleetwood (by Groom Dancer) and smart performer up to 1½m Red Sea (by Barathea), 6f (Coventry Stakes) winner at 2 yrs: dam 1m (at 2 yrs) to 12.5f (St Simon Stakes) winner: weak 9/1-shot, well beaten in Wolverhampton maiden: sold 60,000 gns in December. *P. F. I. Cole*

SUNSETTER (USA)   3 ch.f. Diesis 133 – Hushi (USA) (Riverman (USA) 131) [2001 **89** 94?: 7d⁶ Apr 17] $110,000Y, 250,000Y: lengthy, unfurnished filly: twice raced: fairly useful form in Cheveley Park Stakes (ninth) at 2 yrs and Nell Gwyn Stakes (3½ lengths sixth to Lil's Jessy) at Newmarket, both steadily run, keeping on strongly from poor position in latter: will stay 1m. *G. A. Butler*

SUNSHINE BOY   5 b.g. Cadeaux Genereux 131 – Sahara Baladee (USA) 79 (Shadeed **62** (USA) 135) [2001 f12g³ f16.2g Jul 12] big, rangy, good-topped gelding: has round action: fairly useful handicapper at 3 yrs: modest form at best in 2001: may need 1½m+ nowadays: acts on good to firm going: tried visored: has flashed tail. *G. M. McCourt*

SUNSHINE N'SHOWERS   3 b.f. Spectrum (IRE) 126 – Mainly Dry (The Brianstan **–** 128) [2001 72: 6s 6m 8.2f 8m Jun 24] unfurnished filly: fair form in 2 runs at 2 yrs: well held in 2001. *A. Berry*

SUNSPECKLED   3 ch.f. Salse (USA) 128 – Western Horizon (USA) 58 (Gone West **34** (USA)) [2001 11.9f 14m³ 16.2m⁴ f14.8g 11.7m Aug 24] smallish filly: first foal: dam, maiden who stayed 1¾m, half-sister to smart performer up to 1¾m Ivory Fields out of sister to useful Stewards' Cup winner Repetitious and smart Ribblesdale winner Nanticious: poor maiden: probably stays 2m: withdrawn after refusing to enter stall intended second outing: blinkered (well held) fourth start. *S. Kirk*

SUNSTONE   3 b.f. Caerleon (USA) 132 – Chita Rivera 61 (Chief Singer 131) [2001 **108 §** 59: 10s² 10.4m 12.6m³ 12m⁵ 12f 11.9d 11d² 10.5d* 12.5v Nov 19] leggy, workmanlike filly: useful performer: easily best effort when 4½ lengths fifth of 14 to Imagine in Oaks at Epsom, staying on past tiring rivals: left M. Channon after sixth start: won minor event at Toulouse in November: will stay 1¾m: acts on good to firm and good to soft going: looks a somewhat tricky ride, and not one to trust: sold 30,000 gns. *R. Gibson, France*

SUPERAPPAROS   7 b.g. Superpower 113 – Ayodessa 78 (Lochnager 132) [2001 f6g⁴ **40** f7s f5g⁶ f5g f5g² f5g² f5g⁴ f6g f7g² f6g⁴ f5g³ f7g⁵ f7g f7g 6m⁶ f7g⁵ f6g³ 6m⁴ 6m⁴ 5g 5g **a53** f6g⁵ f5g f6s⁶ f6s² Dec 21] strong, good-topped gelding: seemingly modest maiden on all-weather, poor on turf: effective at 5f to 7f: form only on fibresand and good to firm going: usually blinkered. *S. R. Bowring*

SUPERBIT 9 b.g. Superpower 113 – On A Bit 66 (Mummy's Pet 125) [2001 61, a57: **59** 5m 6.1f³ 6.1m 6d 5.1f 6m 5m³ Aug 27] small, good-bodied gelding: poor mover: modest performer: best at 5f/6f: acts on fibresand and any turf going: tried blinkered/visored. *T. Wall*

SUPER CANYON 3 ch.g. Gulch (USA) – Marina Park 112 (Local Suitor (USA) 128) **66** [2001 6g⁶ 6m 5f* Sep 10] 72,000Y: first foal: dam, effective at 5.5f to 7f, from family of very smart sprinter Greenland Park and Prix Saint-Alary winner Fitnah: fair performer: won maiden at Newcastle in September by 3½ lengths from Strensall: should stay 6f: has been blanketed for stall entry. *P. W. Harris*

SUPERCHIEF 6 b.g. Precocious 126 – Rome Express (Siberian Express (USA) 125) **53** [2001 –, a78: e7g e10g⁴ e8g e8g 10.2g 8g 7g² 8g⁶ 7g p8g p7g p7g* Dec 28] smallish, **a70** sturdy gelding: fair handicapper on all-weather, modest and lightly raced on turf: won at Lingfield (seventh course success) in December: effective at 7f, seems to stay 1¼m: acts on good to firm going and polytrack, went very well on equitrack: blinkered nowadays, has been visored: wears tongue strap: has flashed tail: usually races up with pace. *Miss B. Sanders*

SUPER DECISION 2 ch.f. (Apr 26) Superlative 118 – Kiveton Komet 71 (Precocious **–** 126) [2001 5f Jun 3] 2,000Y: seventh foal: sister to fairly useful 6f winner Mister Superb and half-sister to 1m seller winner Waltz Time (by Rambo Dancer): dam sprinter: 50/1, burly and very green, well held in maiden at Pontefract. *J. J. Quinn*

SUPER DOLPHIN 2 ch.g. (Feb 8) Dolphin Street (FR) 125 – Supergreen (Super- **–** lative 118) [2001 8.3m⁵ Sep 24] seventh reported foal: dam unraced: 33/1, well held in maiden at Hamilton. *T. P. Tate*

SUPER DOMINION 4 ch.c. Superpower 113 – Smartie Lee 66 (Dominion 123) **72** [2001 54, a62: f9.4s f7g⁴ f8.5g⁵ 8.1g 10.9m 6d* 8.5g* 7.5m² 7m 7m 7s 8d² 8d 8.2s* **a64** f9.4g⁶ f8.5g f8.5g⁵ f8g f7s* Dec 18] sturdy, close-coupled colt: fair performer on turf, modest on all-weather: won handicap at Leicester in July, claimer at Beverley in August and handicaps at Nottingham in November and Wolverhampton in December: best form at 7f/1m: acts on fibresand/equitrack, good to firm and soft ground: tongue tied: usually races prominently: none too consistent. *R. Hollinshead*

SUPERFRILLS 8 b.m. Superpower 113 – Pod's Daughter (IRE) 43 (Tender King **46** 123) [2001 46: f5g f6s³ f6g⁴ 6.1v² 5s 6d f6g* 6d 6g 5s 5g 6v f6s Dec 21] small mare: poor handicapper: won at Southwell in July: below form after: effective at 5f/6f: acts on fibresand and any turf going. *Miss L. C. Siddall*

SUPERIOR PREMIUM 7 br.h. Forzando 122 – Devils Dirge 68 (Song 132) [2001 **119** 122: 6d³ 6f 6m⁶ 6m 6.1m⁵ Aug 5] good-topped horse: impressed in appearance: very smart performer at best: won Cork And Orrery Stakes at Royal Ascot in 2000: creditable 1¾ lengths third of 23 to Primo Valentino in listed Abernant Stakes at Newmarket in April: below form after, including fair sixth to Harmonic Way in Cork And Orrery: reportedly suffered joint injury on second time in career final start: was effective at 5f (given bit of test)/6f: probably acted any going: tried blinkered/tongue tied: occasionally got on toes: was normally best coming with late run: was genuine: to stand at Throckmorton Court Stud, Worcestershire, fee £2,000, Oct 1st. *R. A. Fahey*

SUPERLOLA 4 ch.f. Superpower 113 – Polola 42 (Aragon 118) [2001 e8g Feb 21] **–** 800F: half-sister to a winner in Italy (including at 13f) by Sayf El Arab: dam third over 5f at 2 yrs: tailed off in seller. *Mrs P. Townsley*

SUPER SONIC SONIA (IRE) 6 b.m. Tirol 127 – Lunulae (Tumble Wind (USA)) **–** [2001 f7g 9.9m Jul 31] fourth foal: half-sister to fairly useful 7f to 1¼m winner Lunar Mission (by Waajib): dam, Irish 2-y-o 7f winner, also successful over hurdles: fairly useful performer on Flat for M. Brassil in Ireland in 1998: well beaten on belated return: stays 9f: raced mainly on good going or softer (acts on heavy). *K. A. Morgan*

SUPERSTAR LEO (IRE) 3 b.f. College Chapel 122 – Council Rock 74 (General **104** Assembly (USA)) [2001 114: 5f⁶ 5m 5.1m² 6m⁴ 5m Jul 31] small, compact filly: smart performer at 2 yrs, winning 5 times and also excellent second in Prix de l'Abbaye de Longchamp: only useful in 2001, best efforts when 3¼ lengths sixth to Cassandra Go in Temple Stakes at Sandown in May and when 2½ lengths second to Danehurst in listed event at Chester in July: well held in King George Stakes at Goodwood final outing: probably best at 5f: acted on firm and good to soft going: raced prominently: has reportedly been retired. *W. J. Haggas*

Aston Upthorpe Yorkshire Oaks, York—the first Italian-trained winner in Britain
for over a quarter of a century as Super Tassa catches Sacred Song inside the final furlong;
Rockerlong comes third, in front of Karsavina and Zanzibar (white blaze)

SUPER TASSA (IRE) 5 ch.m. Lahib (USA) 129 – Center Moriches (IRE) 74 **118**
(Magical Wonder (USA) 125) [2001 108: 12d² 10v² 14f* 12g³ 12m⁶ 13.5s³ 11.9g*
Aug 22]

'Super, Super, Super Tassa!' No translation of the headline was necessary
to convey the jubilant reaction of Italy's racing press to their first Group 1 success
beyond their borders for thirteen years. Italy's own Group 1 contests regularly fall
prey to British and German stables, so to win a top-level contest in Britain must
have been particularly sweet. Tony Bin's 1988 Arc de Triomphe was the last Group
1 victory abroad by an Italian-trained horse, and it was back in the early 'seventies
that the last Italian-trained horse had won in Britain. That was Brook, who won the
1973 Hungerford Stakes at Newbury and a year later was awarded the Queen Anne
Stakes at Royal Ascot when the first three home were all disqualified. 1960
Champion Stakes winner Marguerite Vernaut was the last Italian-trained winner of
a top-level contest in Britain, though Misil was beaten only a short head by Opera
House in the 1993 Eclipse.

In the absence of the Epsom Oaks principals Imagine, Flight of Fancy and
Relish The Thought, as well as the Irish Oaks winner Lailani, the Aston Upthorpe
Yorkshire Oaks was not so strongly contested as it might have been. The level of
competition still looked tough for Super Tassa though, and not even the booking of
Kevin Darley could prevent her starting the 25/1 outsider in the field of nine. Held
up in rear in the early stages, Super Tassa was switched wide for a run in the
straight, keeping tabs on the favourite Sacred Song, who looked the likely winner
when sweeping into the lead over two furlongs out. But, running on really well,
Super Tassa collared the Lancashire Oaks winner inside the last furlong to win by a
length. Cheshire Oaks winner Rockerlong fared best of the three-year-olds, another
two and a half lengths back in third, ahead of Irish Oaks third Karsavina and the
British-trained Oaks d'Italia winner Zanzibar.

As a two-year-old, Super Tassa was not far behind the best of her generation
in Italy, winning her first two starts and finishing second in the Premio Dormello.
Highlight of her three-year-old campaign was a listed win at Milan, but she made
no show in the Italian classics, finishing down the field in the Guineas and missing
the Oaks altogether. At four, Super Tassa's form stepped up a level, bringing her
victory in the Group 3 Prix Corrida at Saint-Cloud, but in the latest season, prior to
York, her improvement had not reached the level required for Group 1 success. She
did not need to improve to win the Group 2 Premio Carlo d'Alessio at Rome in May
by a neck from London Bank, nor to finish third behind Paolini and Ela Athena
in the Gran Premio di Milano. But after finishing only sixth in the Grand Prix de
Saint-Cloud, Super Tassa came a good third to Abitara in the Prix de Pomone at
Deauville, albeit five lengths behind the runner-up Head In The Clouds, who
re-opposed at York. After Deauville, Super Tassa's preparation for the Yorkshire
Oaks, which had been her target all year, was completed at Newmarket, where she
was boarded with Luca Cumani. Super Tassa's Pisa-based trainer Valfredo Valiani
spent two years as assistant to Cumani.

V. Valiani's "Super Tassa"

Super Tassa (IRE) (ch.m. 1996)	Lahib (USA) (b 1988)	Riverman (b 1969)	Never Bend
			River Lady
		Lady Cutlass (b 1978)	Cutlass
			Generals Sister
	Center Moriches (IRE) (ch 1990)	Magical Wonder (ch 1983)	Storm Bird
			Flama Ardiente
		Tumble Royal (ch 1977)	Tumble Wind
			Royal Nell

The aforementioned Tony Bin proved a bargain buy, sold for only 3,000 guineas as a foal in Ireland. Super Tassa was another, being sold for only 1,800 guineas as a yearling in Ireland (only one of Lahib's thirty-four yearlings who went through the ring in 1997 went for less). The fact that Super Tassa was bought back for 1,600,000 francs at the Arc Sale towards the end of her four-year-old season was some measure of how much her value had appreciated, and that was before she won her Group 1. Super Tassa is her dam Center Moriches' first foal, and her next two to race have both won, Mega Tassa (by Foxhound) successful over an extended mile in Italy and three-year-old Mr Ed (by In The Wings) in a Salisbury handicap over a mile and a quarter. As her lowly yearling price suggests, Super Tassa's pedigree is unexceptional. Her dam won a nine-furlong maiden at Gowran, and her grandam Tumble Royal won a maiden at Down Royal over seven furlongs and a Dundalk handicap over an extended nine furlongs. A strong mare, Super Tassa stayed a mile and three quarters and probably acted on any going. She was retired after the Yorkshire Oaks. *V. Valiani, Italy*

SUPREME ANGEL 6 b.m. Beveled (USA) – Blue Angel (Lord Gayle (USA) 124) **75** [2001 72: f5g⁵ 6s⁴ 5m 5.7m³ 6g 5m 6m* 6f³ f6s* 5s 6.1d⁴ f7g⁴ 6v f6g p6g⁵ Dec 19] **a70** angular mare: fair performer: left M. Muggeridge after second start: won apprentice handicap at Newbury in August and minor event at Wolverhampton in September: probably stays 7f: acts on soft going, good to firm and fibresand/polytrack: effective blinkered (usually is nowadays) or not: has tended to drift left. *E. A. Wheeler*

SUPREME SALUTATION 5 ch.g. Most Welcome 131 – Cardinal Press (Sharrood **78 §** (USA) 124) [2001 80: 7.1d⁵ 7g⁶ 6m 7m² 8.2m³ 7g⁵ 6d⁴ 8.3g⁵ 8.5g² 8m³ 8g³ 8.9d 7d f7g² f7g⁶ f8.5f⁶ f8g⁵ Dec 14] leggy, sparely-made gelding: fair handicapper: best at 7f to 8.5f: acts on fibresand, firm and soft going: blinkered last 2 starts: often gets warm in preliminaries/slowly away/races freely/carries head awkwardly: hard to win with and not to be trusted. *T. D. Barron*

SUPREME SILENCE (IRE) 4 b.g. Bluebird (USA) 125 – Why So Silent (Mill **–** Reef (USA) 141) [2001 57, a65: 14.1g Oct 6] fair handicapper at 3 yrs: well held only outing on Flat in 2001. *Jedd O'Keeffe*

SUPREME TRAVEL 3 b.c. Piccolo 121 – Salinas 65 (Bay Express 132) [2001 –: 7g 7g f8g f9.4s Dec 18] little form. *Mrs Lydia Pearce*

SURAKARTA 3 b.f. Bin Ajwaad (IRE) 119 – Lady of Jakarta (USA) (Procida (USA) **67** 129) [2001 8d⁵ 10.2m Jul 5] second foal: dam, French 1m winner, half-sister to dam of Prix du Jockey Club/Irish Derby winner Dream Well: fair form (but also signs of temperament) on debut when 10 lengths fifth to Silky Dawn in maiden at Salisbury: well held in similar event at Chepstow following month, folding tamely. *J. W. Hills*

SURE QUEST 6 b.m. Sure Blade (USA) 130 – Eagle's Quest 62 (Legal Eagle 126) **63** [2001 66: f11g 11.7d 12s² 11.6g 10m⁵ 11.6g 11.5m 11.6g 11.6m⁵ 10.5v³ f12g* 12d p12g⁵ **a67** Nov 24] close-coupled mare: fair handicapper: won at Wolverhampton in October: best at 1¼m/1½m: acts on fibresand/polytrack and any turf going: visored once in 1999. *D. W. P. Arbuthnot*

SURPRISED 6 b.g. Superpower 113 – Indigo 86 (Primo Dominie 121) [2001 84: 6s **90** 6m* 6f⁴ 6m⁴ 7m Jul 28] big, useful-looking gelding: fairly useful handicapper: won at Hamilton in May: good efforts next 2 starts: has form at 7.5f, but raced mainly at 5f/6f: acts on firm and good to soft going: usually blinkered/visored: has idled, and usually waited with. *R. A. Fahey*

SURPRISE ENCOUNTER 5 ch.g. Cadeaux Genereux 131 – Scandalette (Niniski **110** (USA) 125) [2001 102: 7m* 8m* 7g 8m³ 7m* 7d Oct 20] quite good-topped gelding: smart performer: won handicaps at Doncaster in May and Royal Ascot (Royal Hunt Cup by 2½ lengths from Big Future, storming clear final 1f) in June and 4-runner minor event at Goodwood (got first run in tactical event when beating Granny's Pet by ¾ length) in September: well below form in Challenge Stakes at Newmarket final outing: effective at 7f/1m: easily best form on good ground or firmer: has been early to post: usually held up: genuine. *E. A. L. Dunlop*

Royal Hunt Cup (Handicap), Royal Ascot—Surprise Encounter makes light of a 9-lb rise in his mark, beating Big Future (stand rail) and Muchea

SURPRISE SELECTION   2 b.f. (Apr 21) Be My Chief (USA) 122 – Shamaka 53 – (Kris 135) [2001 7.5m 8m f8g⁶ f6g Oct 18] fourth foal: half-sister to 5-y-o Broke Road and 4-y-o Lou's Wish: dam, lightly-raced maiden, out of close relation to useful Irish miler Chanzi, from very good family: only a little sign of ability in maidens/minor event. *S. R. Bowring*

SUSAN'S DOWRY   5 b.m. Efisio 120 – Adjusting (IRE) (Busted 134) [2001 51: **55 +** f11g* f12g² f12g⁵ f11g² f11g² 10s² f8g 10g 9.9s² 10.1v f12g* f11g² p10g* Dec 19] leggy, **a72** angular mare: has a round action: fair handicapper on all-weather, modest on turf: won at Southwell in January (amateur event) and November, and Lingfield in December: at least as effective at 1¼m as 1½m: acts on heavy going, fibresand and polytrack: reportedly had breathing problem tenth start: best waited with. *Andrew Turnell*

SUSIE'S FLYER (IRE)   4 br.f. Frimaire – Wisdom To Know (Bay Express 132) [2001 **57** –: 5s f6g f5g 5.5d 5m⁴ 6m 5g Aug 7] tall, leggy filly: modest performer: should stay 6f: acts on good to firm and good to soft going. *A. Berry*

SUSIE THE FLOOSIE (IRE)   3 b.f. General Monash (USA) 107 – Cala-Holme – (IRE) (Fools Holme (USA)) [2001 –: 7m 12m 10.5g 15.9d Sep 1] probably of little account. *R. D. Wylie*

SUSSEX LAD   4 b.g. Prince Sabo 123 – Pea Green 98 (Try My Best (USA) 130) [2001 **74** 83: 6m 7.1d⁵ 6g 6m* 6m 5m⁶ 6s 6v 5.1d³ 6v p6g³ p7g Dec 12] strong gelding: fair **a68** handicapper: won apprentice event at Salisbury (for second year running) in August: left Mrs A. Perrett after ninth start: effective at 5f/6f: acts on polytrack/equitrack, good to firm and soft going: has found little. *P. R. Chamings*

SUTTON COMMON (IRE)   4 b.g. Common Grounds 118 – Fadaki Hawaki (USA) **69 §** 60 (Vice Regent (CAN)) [2001 78: 8v 8.5m⁵ 7m⁴ f7g 7.5m 8.5g⁶ 7.5s 8g Oct 6] good-topped gelding: fair handicapper: ran poorly last 2 starts: stays 8.5f: acts on good to soft going, probably on good to firm, well held twice on fibresand: often leads: unreliable. *K. A. Ryan*

SUVRETTA (USA)   2 b.f. (Jan 17) Nureyev (USA) 131 – Naughty Nana (USA) – (Houston (USA)) [2001 6d Aug 26] $300,000Y: second foal: dam, won up to 9f in USA, out of sister to champion US 2-y-o colt Rockhill Native: 5/1, well-held seventh of 8 in maiden at Goodwood: sent to USA. *J. H. M. Gosden*

SWALLOW FLIGHT (IRE)   5 b.h. Bluebird (USA) 125 – Mirage 60 (Red Sunset **120** 120) [2001 124: 8.9g 8.1v² 8.3g* 8s³ 8m² 8g² 8g Oct 4] tall, attractive horse: impresses in appearance: has a quick action: very smart performer: won listed race at Windsor (for second consecutive year) in May by 3 lengths from Summer View: good placed efforts behind Medicean in Juddmonte Lockinge Stakes at Newbury (beaten 2 necks) and Queen Anne Stakes at Royal Ascot (beaten length after meeting trouble) next 2 starts: possibly in need of run after 3-month absence in listed race at Newmarket final start: races mainly at 1m, should be as effective over 1¼m: acts on any going: tough and consistent: sent to UAE. *G. Wragg*

SWALLOW MAGIC (IRE)   3 b.g. Magic Ring (IRE) 115 – Scylla 50 (Rock City – 120) [2001 –: 6.1d May 11] strong, workmanlike gelding: well held in 2 maidens at Nottingham. *P. S. Felgate*

SWANDALE FLYER   9 ch.g. Weldnaas (USA) 112 – Misfire 56 (Gunner B 126) – [2001 28: 12m Jun 26] probably of little account nowadays. *N. Bycroft*

SWAN KNIGHT (USA)   5 b. or br.g. Sadler's Wells (USA) 132 – Shannkara (IRE) **94** (Akarad (FR) 130) [2001 101, a–: 8v⁶ 10.4g a12g⁵ a10.5g² a8g 12d 8d 12f Sep 2] good-topped gelding: fairly useful form in handicaps first 2 Flat starts in 2001 for M. Pipe, sixth of 23 to Nimello in Lincoln at Doncaster on former: best effort after when second in minor event at Mijas: stays easy 1¼m: acts on heavy ground, seemingly on sand (well held on good to firm and equitrack): none too consistent: returned to Britain after final outing, joined R. White. *E. Creighton, Spain*

SWAN LAKE (FR)   5 b.m. Lyphard (USA) 132 – Dame Au Faucon (USA) (Silver – Hawk (USA) 123) [2001 –: f12g f14.8g Feb 3] of little account nowadays. *K. O. Cunningham-Brown*

SWANMORE DELIGHT   3 b.f. Aragon 118 – St Louis Lady 71 (Absalom 128) – § [2001 –§: 7m 6m 8.3g Jul 9] of little account and ungenuine. *J. J. Bridger*

SWANTON ABBOT (IRE)   3 b.g. Charnwood Forest (IRE) 125 – Shaping Up (USA) **56** 89 (Storm Bird (CAN) 134) [2001 70: 7s 8m 7m⁶ 6m⁵ 6m 7g Aug 8] modest maiden: should stay at least 1m: acts on firm going: sold 1,700 gns, sent to Italy. *M. H. Tompkins*

SWEET ANGELINE   4 b.f. Deploy 131 – Fiveofive (IRE) 61 (Fairy King (USA))   **74**
[2001 72: 11.5m⁴ 12m³ 12m 10.1m² 12m⁴ 12g 12d⁴ 10d⁶ Sep 21] smallish filly: fair
performer: stays 1½m: acts on soft and good to firm ground: tried tongue tied.
G. G. Margarson

SWEET APPLAUSE   2 b.f. (Feb 26) Royal Applause 124 – Silver Cape (Kris 135)   **–**
[2001 7.1d 8.2m Sep 10] 11,500Y: first foal: dam, ran twice in USA, out of useful
performer up to 1m Silver Braid: little form in maidens: dead. *A. P. Jarvis*

SWEET BAND (USA)   2 b.c. (Mar 16) Dixieland Band (USA) – Sweetheart (USA)   **94 p**
(Mr Prospector (USA)) [2001 7g³ 7g* Aug 3] $190,000Y: angular, useful-looking colt:
first foal: dam, 5f (at 2 yrs in France) and 7f (in USA) winner, daughter of US Grade 1
8.5f/9f winner Gorgeous from outstanding family of Swain and 5-y-o Fantastic Light:
promising third to Dubai Destination in maiden at Newmarket: landed odds in similar
event at Goodwood by 2½ lengths from Golden Spectrum, quickening on over 1f out:
will stay 1m: useful performer in the making if all is well. *E. A. L. Dunlop*

SWEET BRIAR   2 b.f. (Mar 18) Common Grounds 118 – Pervenche (Latest Model   **49**
115) [2001 6g 6g Sep 7] angular filly: half-sister to 6-y-o Gorse: dam, unplaced in Britain/
USA: poor form in maidens. *H. Candy*

SWEET CHAT (IRE)   3 b.f. Common Grounds 118 – Kaskazi (Dancing Brave   **–**
(USA) 140) [2001 8m 8.1v f8g Nov 30] leggy filly: fifth foal: half-sister to 5-y-o Trinity:
dam, Irish 9f/1¼m winner, out of smart French middle-distance filly Fly Me: little form.
W. Jarvis

SWEET DEIMOS   2 b.f. (Feb 15) Green Desert (USA) 127 – Bint Zamayem (IRE)   **100**
95 (Rainbow Quest (USA) 134) [2001 6g² 6m* 7s³ 7g⁶ 6d⁵ Oct 2] 50,000Y: angular
filly: third foal: half-sister to 3-y-o Queenie: dam, 1¼m winner, half-sister to smart miler
Rouquette: useful performer: won maiden at the Curragh in July: good efforts in Debutante Stakes (1¼ lengths third to Saranac Lake) and Moyglare Stud Stakes, both at the
Curragh, next 2 starts: respectable staying-on fifth to Queen's Logic in Cheveley Park
Stakes at Newmarket (edgy, swished tail in paddock): will stay 1m: acts on soft and good
to firm going. *M. J. Grassick, Ireland*

SWEET EGYPTIAN (FR)   2 b.f. (Apr 15) Snurge 130 – Egyptale (Crystal Glitters   **55**
(USA) 127) [2001 8m 7m 7.9d 8.3v Nov 8] leggy filly: sixth foal: sister to fairly useful
French 1¼m (at 2 yrs) to 13f winner Toutafee, and half-sister to 13f winner Spirit of
The Nile (by Generous) and a winner in France by Linamix: dam, French 10.5f winner,
half-sister to smart dam of 4-y-o Egyptband: modest maiden: blinkered in seller final
start: should be suited by 1¼m+. *P. F. I. Cole*

SWEET ENVIRONMENT   4 gr.f. Environment Friend 128 – Sweets (IRE) (Persian   **–**
Heights 129) [2001 –: 10.2g 8.3v f12g Nov 26] of little account. *D. G. Bridgwater*

SWEET GEORGIA (IRE)   2 ch.f. (Apr 1) Forzando 122 – Woodbury Princess   **–**
(Never So Bold 135) [2001 f5g 5f 5f 6d 6d f7g Oct 1] IR 1,800Y: fourth foal: half-sister
to an 11f winner in Italy by Archway: dam, third at 5f/6f in Ireland, from family of smart
sprinters Blue Persian and Polykratis: little form, mostly in sellers. *L. A. Dace*

SWEET HAVEN   4 b.f. Lugana Beach 116 – Sweet Enough 79 (Caerleon (USA) 132)   **–**
[2001 50: f9.4s⁶ f9.4s f9.4g Feb 17] small filly: modest performer at 3 yrs: well held in
2001: usually visored nowadays. *C. G. Cox*

SWEET KRISTEEN (USA)   2 ch.f. (Jan 8) Candy Stripes (USA) 115 – Aneesati 85   **61**
(Kris 135) [2001 6g⁴ 7s³ Oct 20] $55,000F: workmanlike filly: fourth foal: closely related
to useful 6f winner Epsom Cyclone (by Blushing Groom) and half-sister to useful 1998
2-y-o 6f winner Ras Sheikh (by Sheikh Albadou): dam, 1m winner, out of 1000 Guineas
runner-up Dabaweyaa: green, modest form in maidens at Lingfield and Catterick: should
stay 1m. *J. R. Fanshawe*

SWEET PROSPECT   3 b.f. Shareef Dancer (USA) 135 – Vayavaig 78 (Damister   **97**
(USA) 123) [2001 84: 10.4m³ 10.4d⁴ 8f 8m⁴ 8d⁴ 8.5g* 8s 8.5f³ Oct 26] sturdy filly: useful
handicapper: won at Epsom in September by 2 lengths from Watchkeeper: creditable
third at Belmont final start: effective at 1m/1¼m: acts on firm and good to soft going.
C. F. Wall

SWEET REWARD   6 ch.g. Beveled (USA) – Sweet Revival 41 (Claude Monet   **78 §**
(USA) 121) [2001 75§: 10s* 8g 11.6g⁶ 11.9d 10g 10d 10s Oct 16] leggy, short-backed
gelding: shows knee action: fair handicapper: won at Newbury in April: well held after
third start: stays easy 11.6f: acts on good to firm and heavy going: often looks none too
keen. *J. G. Smyth-Osbourne*

SWEET SINGER 2 b.f. (Feb 6) Hector Protector (USA) 124 – Sweet Contralto 89 **64** (Danehill (USA) 126) [2001 7m f7g* a8g Dec 16] first foal: dam, 7f and 9f winner, sister to smart 1¼m/1½m performer Alriffa: modest form: won seller at Southwell in July by 6 lengths, final start for Sir Mark Prescott: well held in minor event at Mijas nearly 5 months later: should stay at least 1m. *C. Bjorling, Spain*

SWEETSTOCK 3 b.f. Anshan 119 – Stockline (Capricorn Line 111) [2001 8.3m – 12.1g 10.2g Oct 1] fifth living foal: half-sister to 6-y-o April Stock and 1½m to 16.4f winner Chris's Lad (by Thowra): dam soundly beaten: little form in maidens. *G. A. Butler*

SWEET SUPPOSIN (IRE) 10 b.g. Posen (USA) – Go Honey Go (General Assembly – (USA)) [2001 e12g Mar 28] probably of no account nowadays. *C. A. Dwyer*

SWEET TOUCH 2 b.f. (Feb 27) Definite Article 121 – Shirley's Touch (Touching **41** Wood (USA) 127) [2001 7.1g f8.5s⁴ f7g⁶ f8g Dec 10] 2,000F, 1,200Y: fifth foal: half-sister to 5-y-o To The Last Man: dam unraced: poor maiden: fourth at Wolverhampton: should stay 1¼m: acts on fibresand. *M. D. I. Usher*

SWEET VELETA 3 b.f. Cosmonaut – Redgrave Design 77 (Nebbiolo 125) [2001 37: f8s 6g 8g 8m 8m 10f 7.5m 10d Oct 15] small, strong filly: little form in 2001. *R. M. Whitaker*

SWEMBY 4 ch.f. Mizoram (USA) 105 – Equilibrium 67 (Statoblest 120) [2001 –: – 11.5m Jul 11] poor maiden at best: dead. *K. Bell*

SWIFT 7 ch.g. Sharpo 132 – Three Terns (USA) (Arctic Tern (USA) 126) [2001 –, a65: **49** 11.1g 12m⁶ f11g⁴ 12g Oct 4] strong, lengthy gelding: poor mover: modest performer: **a54** reportedly lame final outing: stays 1¾m: acts on fibresand/equitrack and soft going, probably on good to firm: has worn net muzzle: usually held up. *M. J. Polglase*

SWIFT APPRAISAL 2 gr.g. (Feb 17) Slip Anchor 136 – Minsden's Image 78 – (Dancer's Image (USA)) [2001 7s p6g Dec 28] 20,000Y: half-brother to several winners, including 4-y-o Swift Dispersal: dam, out of sister to Busted, stayed 2m: signs of just a little ability in maidens at Yarmouth and Lingfield: slowly away both starts, very much so debut. *S. C. Williams*

SWIFT BABA (USA) 2 b.f. (Apr 5) Deerhound (USA) 64 – Nervous Baba (USA) – (Raja Baba (USA)) [2001 p8g Nov 15] $37,000Y, resold IR 16,000Y, 30,000 2-y-o: closely related to 3 winners in USA by Danzig, notably 1997 2-y-o 7f/8.5f winner Brooklyn Nick, later third in Grade 2 event, and half-sister to several winners, including 4-y-o Rudik: dam US Grade 2 6f winner: well beaten in maiden at Lingfield. *R. Hannon*

SWIFT DISPERSAL 4 gr.f. Shareef Dancer (USA) 135 – Minsden's Image 78 **87** (Dancer's Image (USA)) [2001 86: 8v 6g 7.1m* 8.5m 8m 8.1g 8m 7m 8g 8s³ 8s Nov 3] small, workmanlike filly: fairly useful handicapper: won at Sandown in May: good third to Mowaadah in listed rated stakes at Ascot penultimate start: stays 1m: acts on soft and good to firm going (possibly not heavy or fibresand): blinkered (ran creditably) eighth start. *S. C. Williams*

SWIFTLY 2 ch.f. (Mar 26) Cadeaux Genereux 131 – Run Faster (IRE) (Commanche **73** Run 133) [2001 6m⁴ f5g* 5.1f³ 6.5g f5g Oct 9] 15,000Y: rather leggy, useful-looking filly: sixth foal: half-sister to 5f/6f winner Thats Life (by Mukaddamah) and a 7f (including at 2 yrs) winner in Italy by Running Steps: dam, Italian 1m/9f winner, from family of Salsabil and Marju: fair performer: won maiden at Southwell in June: below form last 2 starts: should stay 6f: acts on fibresand, raced only on good going or firmer on turf. *M. A. Jarvis*

SWIFTMAR 3 b.f. Marju (IRE) 127 – Swift Spring (FR) 56 (Bluebird (USA) 125) **64** [2001 64: 6.9v⁶ 7m 8.1m³ 8.2s³ 8m 8m² 8m f8.5g Oct 20] modest maiden handicapper: rather headstrong, and likely to prove best up to 1m: acts on heavy and good to firm ground. *P. F. I. Cole*

SWIFTWAY 7 ch.g. Anshan 119 – Solemn Occasion (USA) (Secreto (USA) 128) – [2001 50: 17.1d Oct 8] tall, plain gelding: modest handicapper at 6 yrs: well held only start in 2001. *K. W. Hogg, Isle of Man*

SWING ALONG 6 ch.m. Alhijaz 122 – So It Goes 73 (Free State 125) [2001 65, a77: – f11g f9.4g Jan 25] strong mare: fair handicapper in 2000: well held in 2001. *A. B. Coogan*

SWING BAND 3 b.g. Celtic Swing 138 – Inchkeith 72 (Reference Point 139) [2001 **91** 87: 10.2d⁴ 9m 7.1m Jul 7] tall, useful-looking gelding: has plenty of scope: fairly useful performer: creditable fourth in minor event at Bath in May, easily best effort in 2001: seems to stay 1¼m: acts on firm and good to soft ground, possibly unsuited by soft (sweated profusely when tried): visored final outing: sweating/on toes last 2 starts (found little and carried head high first occasion): races prominently. *G. B. Balding*

SWING BAR   8 b.m. Sadeem (USA) 122 – Murex (Royalty 130) [2001 41: 9m 9.7m²   **45** 11.9f⁶ 9.7m² 11.9m⁶ Jul 23] angular, workmanlike mare: poor handicapper: stays 9.7f: acts on firm going, probably on soft. *J. M. Bradley*

SWINGING THE BLUES (IRE)   7 b.g. Bluebird (USA) 125 – Winsong Melody   **51** (Music Maestro 119) [2001 62, a56: f11g⁵ f12g² f12g² f12g³ f12g³ 10.3s 10g 9.9m 10.1m⁵ 12m 10.1g Jul 3] useful-looking gelding: modest handicapper: ran as if something amiss final outing: effective at 1¼m/easy 1½m: acts on soft going, good to firm and fibresand: usually blinkered/visored: tried tongue tied earlier in career: often slowly away: has no easy ride (usually apprentice ridden nowadays). *C. A. Dwyer*

SWING JOB   5 b.m. Ezzoud (IRE) 126 – Leave Her Be (USA) (Known Fact (USA)   **36** 135) [2001 58?, a38: e16g⁶ e13g⁵ e12g⁴ f12g⁴ f12g Feb 17] poor maiden handicapper: stays 1½m: acts on firm going, fibresand and equitrack: tried blinkered. *P. S. McEntee*

SWING OF THE TIDE   4 b.f. Sri Pekan (USA) 117 – Rawya (USA) 80 (Woodman   **75 d** (USA) 126) [2001 e6g f7g f6g 6.1v⁵ 9.2m* 8.3d* 10m² 10.3f³ 9.2m³ 9.2d 9m 9m 10g 9.2g⁶ 10m 10.4s Oct 11] sturdy filly: fair handicapper: won twice at Hamilton in May: well held last 7 starts: effective at 1m/1¼m: acts on firm and good to soft going: has had tongue tied: usually slowly away, markedly so last 4 outings (also unruly in paddock final one): sold 800 gns. *A. Berry*

SWING WING   2 b.c. (Apr 22) In The Wings 128 – Swift Spring (FR) 56 (Bluebird   **105** (USA) 125) [2001 f6g² f6g² f7g⁴ 7g² 8.3s* 8m* 8s² 10v Nov 13] good-topped colt: has a quick, fluent action: fifth foal: half-brother to 5-y-o Son of Snurge and fairly useful but ungenuine 11.5f winner Spring Anchor (by Slip Anchor): dam, 7f winner who seemed to stay 2m, half-sister to smart French performer up to 15.5f Philanthrop: useful performer: won maiden at Hamilton in August and nursery at Bath (edged left) in September: best efforts on last 2 starts, when 1½ lengths second to Sholokhov in Gran Criterium at Milan and equal seventh of 10 to Ballingarry in Criterium de Saint-Cloud: will stay at least 1½m: acts on heavy going, good to firm and fibresand. *P. F. I. Cole*

SWINO   7 b.g. Forzando 122 – St Helena (Monsanto (FR) 121) [2001 59§: 5.3s* 6s   **53 §** 6.1d 6m 6.1f 7.1g Sep 13] leggy gelding: unimpressive mover: modest handicapper: won at Brighton in April: well held after, leaving P. D. Evans before final start (reportedly finished lame): barely stays 7.7f: acts on any turf going and fibresand: usually blinkered/ visored: sometimes slowly away: has carried head awkwardly/looked less than keen: inconsistent, and not to be trusted. *W. M. Brisbourne*

SWISS LAKE (USA)   2 br.f. (Jan 28) Indian Ridge 123 – Blue Iris 105 (Petong 126)   **102 p** [2001 5g* 6m⁶ 5.2m* 5g² Sep 15] $320,000Y: good-topped filly: usually takes the eye: first foal: dam 5f/6f winner, including at 2 yrs: impressive winner of maiden at Sandown in July and listed race at Newbury (by 1½ lengths from Pastel, making all) in August: good 1¾ lengths second to Saddad in Flying Childers Stakes at Doncaster, making most: free-going sort, and will prove best at 5f: edged right when disappointing second start: looks type to train on well and make a smart 3-y-o. *G. A. Butler*

SWORDPLAY   3 ch.g. Kris 135 – Throw Away Line 45 (Cragador 110) [2001 10.2d   **81** 10g⁶ 8m 12f⁵ 11.7g² 12.3m* 13.1d² 11m* 10g f12g 11.6v Oct 29] rangy gelding: has scope: good mover: brother to useful French winner up to 1½m Rebuff and fairly useful 7.5f (at 2 yrs) and 1¼m (in France) winner Wavey and half-brother to 2 winners: dam, winner in USA at 4 yrs, half-sister to champion US filly Go For Wand: fairly useful performer: won minor event at Chester in July and handicap at Goodwood in September: ran poorly last 2 starts: effective at 11f to 13f: acts on good to firm and good to soft ground, below form on fibresand: has raced freely: sold 50,000 gns, joined M. O'Brien in Ireland and gelded. *G. A. Butler*

S W THREE   3 b.f. Slip Anchor 136 – Anna Karietta 82 (Precocious 126) [2001 68:   **76** 11.7f² Jun 27] seventh foal: sister to a useful 7f winner in Germany and half-sister to 3 fairly useful winners, including 6-y-o Premier Baron and 1m winner who stayed 1¼m Frezeliere (by My Chief): dam 6f/7f winner: second in maidens over 10 months apart, beaten ½ length by Harlestone Grey at Bath in June: stays 11.7f. *M. P. Tregoning*

SWYNFORD DREAM   8 b.g. Statoblest 120 – Qualitair Dream 80 (Dreams To   **59** Reality (USA) 113) [2001 64, a–: 5m 5m⁶ 5m 5m⁶ 5f 5m 5m² 5m 5f² 5g³ 6f f5g Oct 18]   **a–** workmanlike gelding: modest handicapper: raced mainly at 5f: acts on firm and good to soft going: has given trouble at start (withdrawn once)/been slowly away: has hung: often races up with pace: none too consistent, and on a long losing run. *J. Hetherton*

SWYNFORD ELEGANCE   4 ch.f. Charmer 123 – Qualitairess 49 (Kampala 120)   **52**
[2001 50: 8s 8.3m 8m⁴ 10.1m² 8.3m³ 8m⁴ 11.1s 8g³ 7.1f² 8.3s 8f* 8.2m⁴ 8.3m* 10v 8d 8g
Nov 7] modest handicapper: won at Musselburgh and Hamilton in September: effective
at 7f to 1¼m: acts on any ground. *J. Hetherton*

SWYNFORD PLEASURE   5 b.m. Reprimand 122 – Pleasuring 68 (Good Times   **72**
(ITY)) [2001 56: 9.1m³ 8.3d⁵ 10m 8m* 7.5m² 8g⁶ 8m* 10.1m* 8.5m³ 10m² 8.5m* 10g⁶   **a–**
8d⁶ 8.1s³ 7.5m³ 9.2g⁵ 7.5s 8d² 8d 8d 8g⁵ Nov 7] angular mare: fair handicapper: better
than ever in 2001, winning at Newmarket (2), Newcastle and Beverley in June/July (first
3 amateur/apprentice events): in-and-out form after: effective at 7.5f to 1¼m: acts on firm
and soft going: tried blinkered (not in 2001): often held up. *J. Hetherton*

SWYNFORD WELCOME   5 b.m. Most Welcome 131 – Qualitair Dream 80   **78**
(Dreams To Reality (USA) 113) [2001 51, a–: f7g 5.3f⁴ 6.1f 7g* 7m 6g* 8.5s⁶ 5.3g*   **a61**
5.3m⁴ 7g² 8m² 6f² 7s* 6g* 7g² 8d 7d 6v 7s⁴ 7d⁵ 7s p7g p7g³ Nov 28] good-topped mare:
fair handicapper on turf, modest on all-weather: had a fine season for new stable: won 4
times at Brighton between July and September, and at Newmarket in October: effective
at 5f to easy 1m: acts on polytrack, firm and soft ground: tried blinkered, better when not:
reformed character. *I. A. Wood*

SYCAMORE LODGE (IRE)   10 ch.g. Thatching 131 – Bell Tower 98 (Lyphard's   **51**
Wish (FR) 124) [2001 52, a–: 6m⁶ 7f 7.1f³ 7.5f⁶ 8.5g Aug 15] strong gelding: modest
performer: races mainly at 7f/1m nowadays: acts on firm and soft going: tried blinkered
earlier in career: usually slowly away/held up. *K. A. Ryan*

SYDENHAM (USA)   3 b.c. A P Indy (USA) 131 – Crystal Shard (USA) (Mr Prospec-   **108**
tor (USA)) [2001 10.2f² 12m 12.3m* 12m 13.3f⁵ 10.3d⁴ Sep 14] $525,000Y: well-made
colt: first foal: dam unraced sister to US Grade 2 7f/8.5f winner Withallprobability: useful
performer: very good 3¾ lengths seventh to Anabaa Blue in Prix du Jockey Club at
Chantilly in June: landed odds in maiden at Ripon later in month: visored, easily best
effort after when 3¼ lengths fourth to Lagudin in minor event at Doncaster final start:
stays 1½m: raced mainly on going firmer than good: led by 2 handlers final outing: joined
Godolphin. *J. H. M. Gosden*

SYLCAN EXPRESS   8 br.g. Sylvan Express 117 – Dercanny (Derek H 97) [2001 10f   **42**
11.8d³ 12.4m 14.1m Aug 11] angular gelding: second foal: dam poor novice hurdler/
chaser: poor maiden: tried visored. *C. N. Kellett*

SYLV   3 b.f. Ridgewood Ben 113 – High Commotion (IRE) 70 (Taufan (USA) 119)   **–**
[2001 9m 8.1s⁶ 8.1g 8g Oct 1] first foal: dam, lightly-raced maiden, out of sister to high-
class 1¼m/1½m performer Master Willie: well held in maidens/handicap. *J. G. Portman*

SYLVA BOUNTY   2 br.g. (Feb 1) Bahamian Bounty 116 – Spriolo (Priolo (USA) 127)   **–**
[2001 5s⁶ 5m⁶ Jun 6] 17,000Y: compact gelding: second foal: dam well beaten on only
start: only a little sign of ability in maiden/minor event. *C. E. Brittain*

SYLVA LEGEND (USA)   5 b.g. Lear Fan (USA) 130 – Likeshot (CAN) (Gun Shot)   **71**
[2001 74, a61: 10d⁶ 12f⁴ 11.6m Aug 13] tall, good-topped gelding: shows plenty of knee   **a–**
action: fair maiden handicapper: stays 1½m: acts on soft and firm going: sometimes
visored/tongue tied: has carried head high. *R. J. Baker*

SYLVAN GIRL (IRE)   3 ch.f. Case Law 113 – Nordic Living (IRE) 53 (Nordico   **71**
(USA)) [2001 75: e8g² f6g* 5.5f* 8.5f⁴ a6.5f² a6.5f⁶ 6.5f a5.5f Nov 28] leggy filly:
fair performer: successful in claimer at Southwell (left C. Allen after) in January and
allowance race at Hollywood in June: claimed $6,250 after final outing: stays easy 1m:
acts on firm going, fibresand, equitrack and dirt. *P. D. Assinesi, USA*

SYLVA PARADISE (IRE)   8 b.g. Dancing Dissident (USA) 119 – Brentsville (USA)   **78**
(Arctic Tern (USA) 126) [2001 78: 5.3s² 6s 5.2m⁵ 5m 5m 5.3m Aug 29] smallish, lengthy
gelding: poor mover: fair handicapper: best at 5f/easy 6f: acts on firm and soft going:
tried blinkered, visored nowadays: none too consistent. *C. E. Brittain*

SYLVA STORM (USA)   3 ch.c. Miswaki (USA) 124 – Sudden Storm Bird (USA)   **73**
(Storm Bird (CAN) 134) [2001 73: f8g* e10g³ 9s 9s 9m⁶ 8m f8⁵ 8m Jul 29] close-coupled   **a87**
colt: fairly useful on all-weather, fair on turf: won maiden at Southwell in January: stays
1¼m: acts on fibresand/equitrack and firm going: tried blinkered: tended to carry head
high first 2 starts. *C. E. Brittain*

SYNERGIE (IRE)   3 ch.f. Exit To Nowhere (USA) 122 – Keepers Dawn (IRE) 103   **–**
(Alzao (USA) 117) [2001 6m 7g 6m⁵ Jul 4] 5,500Y: good-topped filly: first foal: dam
2-y-o 6f winner and second in Fred Darling Stakes: well held in maidens. *E. J. Alston*

SYRAH 5 b.m. Minshaanshu Amad (USA) 91§ – La Domaine 89 (Dominion 123) – [2001 35: 13d 16.1m May 24] probably of no account nowadays. *W. Storey*

SYRIAN FLUTIST 3 ch.f. Shaamit (IRE) 127 – Brave Vanessa (USA) 62 (Private – Account (USA)) [2001 10d 11.5m 12m⁵ Aug 4] 40,000Y: third foal: dam, 6f winner who stayed 1m, sister to US Grade 2 winner/Grade 1-placed performer around 1m Topicount: little form in maidens: tongue tied. *H. Akbary*

SYSTEMATIC 2 b.c. (Jan 31) Rainbow Quest (USA) 134 – Sensation 114 (Soviet **68 p** Star (USA) 128) [2001 8s² 8d³ Oct 3] strong, rangy colt: first foal: dam, 1m (including Falmouth Stakes) winner, out of Breeders' Cup Juvenile Fillies winner Outstandingly: fair form in maidens at Pontefract and Newcastle (still green, 10 lengths third to Diamond Lover): will stay at least 1¼m: should improve. *M. Johnston*

T

TAABEER 3 b.c. Caerleon (USA) 132 – Himmah (USA) 85 (Habitat 134) [2001 94p: – 8.2s Oct 30] angular colt: fairly useful from at 2 yrs: reportedly met with setback in April, and well held only start in 2001: will stay at least 1¼m: raced on good ground or firmer at 2 yrs. *E. A. L. Dunlop*

TABBETINNA BLUE 4 b.f. Interrex (CAN) – True Is Blue (Gabitat 119) [2001 35: – 8m 6m 7m 10.1m 7g Aug 10] leggy, lengthy filly: poor maiden at 3 yrs: well beaten in 2001: tried tongue tied. *J. C. McConnochie*

TABOOR (IRE) 3 b.g. Mujadil (USA) 119 – Christoph's Girl 50 (Efisio 120) [2001 **75** 5d² 5m⁴ 6g³ 6d³ 5g* 5g 5d f6g² Oct 18] 50,000Y: heavy-topped gelding: third foal: brother to fairly useful Irish 5f winner who stays 7f Eveam: dam, Belgian 6f/7f winner, sister to very smart 5f/6f performer Hever Golf Rose: fair performer: won maiden at Leicester in July: effective at 5f/6f: acts on good to soft ground and fibresand. *J. W. Payne*

TACHOMETER (IRE) 7 b.m. Jurado (USA) – Tacheo 64 (Tachypous 128) [2001 – 48: 12g 14.1d 16v Oct 17] of little account nowadays. *H. S. Howe*

TACHYON 3 b.c. Tachyon Park 87 – Raisa Point 60 (Raised Socially (USA)) [2001 – 6g 5g f6g Oct 22] first foal: dam 5f maiden: well beaten in maidens. *P. Howling*

TACTFUL REMARK (USA) 5 ch.h. Lord At War (ARG) – Right Word (USA) **77** (Verbatim (USA)) [2001 107d: 10f 10.1m⁵ 8g 8.2m⁵ Sep 10] strong horse: useful at best, only fair in 2000: stays 10.4f: acts on firm ground, probably not on softer than good: possibly needs to dominate. *J. A. Osborne*

TADEO 8 ch.g. Primo Dominie 121 – Royal Passion 78 (Ahonoora 122) [2001 93d: 6s **94** 6m 5m* 5.1f* 5m³ 6m⁶ 5m² 5m 5f⁵ 5m 5.5d⁵ 5.2m⁵ 5.7d³ 5.7d³ 5.2d 5g Sep 15] small, strong gelding: fairly useful handicapper: won at Thirsk and Bath in May: mostly creditable efforts after: barely stays 6f: acts on firm and soft going: races up with pace: tough. *J. M. Bradley*

TAFFRAIL 3 b.g. Slip Anchor 136 – Tizona (Pharly (FR) 130) [2001 –p: 10s 14.1d* **96 p** 14.1m² 16.2f* 16.2m* 16.2g* 18d Oct 20] lengthy gelding: has scope: made into useful handicapper: won at Nottingham in May, Beverley and Ascot in July, and Beverley again (beat Star Rage by 7 lengths) in August, most readily on last 2 courses: off 10 weeks (bruised foot) and didn't take eye when below form in Cesarewitch at Newmarket final start: acts on firm going, winner on good to soft: should make a smart 4-y-o. *J. L. Dunlop*

TAFFS WELL 8 b.g. Dowsing (USA) 124 – Zahiah 90 (So Blessed 130) [2001 81d: **81** 6.1v 7.1m* 8.3m⁴ 8.1m* 7f 8.1d 8m⁵ 8g 7m³ 7.6d⁵ 9.1m⁶ 8d Oct 3] small gelding: fairly useful handicapper: won at Musselburgh and Haydock in May: below form last 3 starts: seems best at 7f/1m: acts on heavy and good to firm going: held up: sold 3,200 gns. *B. Ellison*

TAFFY DANCER 3 b.g. Emperor Jones (USA) 119 – Ballerina Bay 75 (Myjinski – (USA)) [2001 10.1m⁵ 14g 11.5m Jul 24] 11,000Y: rangy gelding: second foal: half-brother to 6-y-o Wave of Optimism: dam 7f to 11.5f winner: well held in maidens. *H. Morrison*

TAGGERTY (IRE) 3 b.f. Definite Article 121 – Kewaashi (USA) 69 (Storm Bird **60 ?** (CAN) 134) [2001 8d 8s³ 7m 10.2m 9g⁶ f8.5g 7g Oct 6] 1,500Y: workmanlike filly:

second foal: dam lightly-raced maiden: well held all starts, seeming to show modest form on occasions: blinkered final outing. *J. A. Gilbert*

TAHINI 2 b.f. (Jan 22) Mtoto 134 – Sesame 117 (Derrylin 115) [2001 7m 8m Sep 22] **63 p** strong filly: fifth foal: half-sister to fairly useful 1¼m winner Unseeded (by Unfuwain), 6-y-o Double Blade and 1¼m/1½m winner Calendula (by Be My Guest): dam, middle-distance stayer, half-sister to Celeric: green, modest form in maidens at Salisbury and Newmarket: will be suited by 1½m+: capable of better. *J. L. Dunlop*

TAHITIAN STORM (IRE) 2 b.c. (Apr 1) Catrail (USA) 123 – Razana (IRE) 71 **92** (Kahyasi 130) [2001 6m 6m² 6f² 6g* 7.1s* Sep 8] 56,000Y: good-topped colt: has scope: second foal: half-brother to 3-y-o Ovambo: dam, 1¼m winner later successful up to 1½m in France, out of half-sister to Irish St Leger second Rayseka: fairly useful performer: made all in maiden at Yarmouth in August and nursery at Haydock (beat Sandy Lady by 2½ lengths) in September: will stay 1m: acts on firm and soft going. *M. H. Tompkins*

TAHLIL 2 ch.f. (Feb 22) Cadeaux Genereux 131 – Amaniy (USA) 96 (Dayjur (USA) **–** 137) [2001 6m May 26] second foal: dam, 2-y-o 5f/6f winner, half-sister to US Grade 2 7f winner Kayrawan out of Princess Margaret winner Muhbubh: 7/1, eleventh of 14 in maiden at Lingfield, slowly away and not knocked about. *E. A. L. Dunlop*

TAI SIMSEK 3 b.f. Minshaanshu Amad (USA) 91§ – Bedswerver (IRE) (Doulab **49** (USA) 115) [2001 8.3m 9m⁵ 8d⁵ 10.4m Sep 5] second reported foal: dam, lightly-raced maiden, half-sister to smart performers Showbrook (up to 6f) and Smarginato (up to 1¼m): poor maiden: should stay 1¼m. *P. L. Gilligan*

TAJAR (USA) 9 b.g. Slew O' Gold (USA) – Mashaarif (USA) (Mr Prospector (USA)) **42 §** [2001 42§, a52§: e12g f12g 11.9s 11.9s 10.5g 11.9f⁴ 12.3m 13.3f⁴ 16.5m 12.1m² 15m² 14.1d 12m⁵ 16.2m f14g³ f14g f14g⁵ Dec 14] strong, angular gelding: poor performer: stays 15f: acts on equitrack/fibresand, firm and soft going (unraced on heavy): blinkered twice at 5 yrs: tried tongue tied: has been slowly away: normally held up: irresolute. *T. Keddy*

TAKAMAKA BAY (IRE) 4 ch.c. Unfuwain (USA) 131 – Stay Sharpe (USA) **104** (Sharpen Up 127) [2001 84: 10.5g* 10d* 12m* 11.9d Jul 7] sturdy colt: useful performer: in excellent form in June, winning handicap at Haydock, minor event at Leicester and Duke of Edinburgh Stakes (Handicap) at Royal Ascot (beat stable-companion Akbar by short head): favourite, only eighth in Old Newton Cup at Haydock final outing: stays 1½m: seems to act on any ground. *M. Johnston*

TAKAROA 3 b.g. Tagula (IRE) 116 – Mountain Harvest (FR) 64§ (Shirley Heights **77** 130) [2001 84: 8m 10m 10.3m 8g 7.1g 7g² 8.5s* Sep 25] strong gelding: fair handicapper: won at Beverley in September: best around 7f/1m: acts on soft and good to firm ground: visored last 2 starts: gelded after. *I. A. Balding*

TAKE A TURN 6 br.g. Forzando 122 – Honeychurch (USA) 93 (Bering 136) [2001 –: **52** f8.5s⁴ Jan 30] smallish gelding: lightly raced and modest at best nowadays: stays 1¼m: acts on any turf going, fibresand and equitrack: tried blinkered/visored. *M. J. Wilkinson*

Duke of Edinburgh Stakes (Handicap), Royal Ascot—
a 1,2 for trainer Mark Johnston as Takamaka Bay (rail) just holds off Akbar; Gallery God takes third

TAKE FLITE 4 b.g. Cadeaux Genereux 131 – Green Seed (IRE) 78 (Lead On Time **79** (USA) 123) [2001 78: 7s² 7g⁵ 7m⁶ 8m⁶ 7g 7m⁴ 7g⁴ 7.6g 7s³ f8g⁴ Oct 22] angular gelding: fair performer: should stay 1m: acts on fibresand, good to firm and soft ground (possibly not heavy): has worn crossed noseband: consistent: sold 10,000 gns. *W. R. Muir*

TAKEONJON 2 ch.c. (Apr 15) Factual (USA) 108 – Society Girl 73 (Shavian 125) **46** [2001 7.1f 6v f6g Oct 23] first foal: dam, won at 6f (at 2 yrs) to 1¼m, half-sister to 5-y-o Flossy: poor maiden. *J. L. Spearing*

TAKES TUTU (USA) 2 b.g. (Jan 14) Afternoon Deelites (USA) 122 – Lady Affirmed **75** (USA) (Affirmed (USA)) [2001 6m⁶ 6m³ 8f³ 8d⁵ 6d f6g³ p7g² Nov 13] $65,000Y: tall, **a85** useful-looking gelding: second foal: dam US Grade 3 9f winner and second in Grade 1 event: fairly useful maiden on all-weather, fair on turf: good second in nursery at Lingfield: stays 7f, possibly not 1m: acts on fibresand, polytrack and firm ground, probably on good to soft: reluctant stall and slowly away penultimate start. *M. Johnston*

TAKE TO TASK (USA) 3 b. or br.c. Conquistador Cielo (USA) – Tash (USA) **–** (Never Bend) [2001 95: 7m 10.4s⁶ Oct 11] rather leggy, useful-looking colt: useful maiden at 2yrs: reported in April to have been suffering from foot abscesses: well below form in 2001, running as if something amiss on reappearance in May: should stay 1¼m: sold 3,000 gns. *M. Johnston*

TAKHLID (USA) 10 b.h. Nureyev (USA) 131 – Savonnerie (USA) 108 (Irish River **–** (FR) 131) [2001 60, a73: f6g⁶ f7g f7g² f6g Feb 5] strong, compact horse: has won 20 **a62** times, but only modest at best in 2001: stays 8.5f: acts on any turf going, fibresand and equitrack: has twice reportedly finished lame: often races up with pace. *D. W. Chapman*

TALAASH (IRE) 4 b.c. Darshaan 133 – Royal Ballet (IRE) (Sadler's Wells (USA) **100** 132) [2001 110: 12s 16g⁶ 16g 22.2f⁵ 16.1g Jul 11] strong, good sort: good mover: smart performer at 3 yrs: ran only respectably in John Porter Stakes at Newbury and Sagaro Stakes at Newmarket (sixth behind Solo Mio) first 2 starts in 2001: well below even that form after: stays 2m: acts on soft going, probably on firm: sent to UAE. *M. R. Channon*

TALARIA (IRE) 5 ch.m. Petardia 113 – Million At Dawn (IRE) 63 (Fayruz 116) **66** [2001 73: f6g e6g⁵ e7g 5.3s⁶ 6v² 5.7m 6m³ 6d³ 6g 6m⁵ 7m 7.5d f6g 5.2v Oct 26] useful-looking mare: fluent mover: fair performer: left M. Quinn after seventh start: well held last 4 outings: best at 6f: acts on good to firm going, heavy and equitrack: visored once at 4 yrs: sometimes tongue tied: has started slowly: free-going sort: sold 4,500 gns. *W. J. Musson*

TALAT 3 b.f. Missed Flight 123 – Tawnais 80 (Artaius (USA) 129) [2001 –: 8m³ 9m* **55** 10.1m⁵ 10g* 9.7d Sep 3] modest performer: won apprentice handicap at Kempton in June and claimer at Newmarket in August: stays 1¼m, at least when emphasis is on speed: raced mainly on good/good to firm going. *M. J. Ryan*

TALBOT AVENUE 3 b.c. Puissance 110 – Dancing Daughter 79 (Dance In Time **80** (CAN)) [2001 69: 6.1f 5.1f⁵ 6f³ 5.1m⁴ 5m* 5g⁶ 6.1m 5g² Sep 19] compact colt: fairly useful handicapper: made all at Sandown in July: effective at 5f/6f: acts on firm and good to soft going: has edged left: races prominently. *M. Mullineaux*

TALECA SON (IRE) 6 b.g. Conquering Hero (USA) 116 – Lady Taleca (IRE) 49 **42** (Exhibitioner 111) [2001 35, a40: f12g⁶ 10f⁵ Jul 9] smallish gelding: poor maiden: barely stays 1½m: acts on firm going, soft and fibresand: tried blinkered/visored/tongue tied: usually takes good hold. *Mrs L. Williamson*

TALENTS LITTLE GEM 4 b.f. Democratic (USA) 101 – Le Saule d'Or 70 **49** (Sonnen Gold 121) [2001 47, a–: f7f f12g⁵ 10f⁵ 10.2g* 10.2f 12.1s 11.7m⁶ 8m⁴ 10s⁵ Sep **a40** 30] poor handicapper: won at Bath in July: effective at 1m, probably stays 11.7f: acts on firm going, good to soft and fibresand: has been slowly away/reared in stall: blinkered last 2 starts. *A. W. Carroll*

TALENT STAR 4 b.g. Mizoram (USA) 105 – Bells of Longwick 92 (Myjinski **55** (USA)) [2001 50: 6m⁴ 7m⁶ 7.1m 7m⁵ 7.1g f8.5f⁶ Dec 5] modest maiden handicapper: stays 7f: raced only on good/good to firm ground on turf: often slowly away. *A. W. Carroll*

TALIBAN (IRE) 5 b.g. Bigstone (IRE) 126 – Aunt Hester (IRE) 68 (Caerleon (USA) **–** 132) [2001 –: 12s f11g Apr 9] seemingly no longer of any account. *M. W. Easterby*

TALISKER BAY 3 b.c. Clantime 101 – Fabulous Rina (FR) (Fabulous Dancer (USA) **–** 124) [2001 66: 5.1s 5m 5m May 26] leggy colt: modest maiden: well held at 3 yrs: raced only at 5f: visored final outing. *C. Smith*

TALLDARK'N'ANDSOME   2 b.g. (Mar 12) Efisio 120 – Fleur du Val (Valiyar   **77**
129) [2001 5m⁵ 5m 7d³ 7.1m⁴ 7d³ f7g⁴ Oct 23] 6,000Y, 15,000 2-y-o: workmanlike
gelding: fifth foal: brother to 7-y-o Peppiatt: dam unraced half-sister to smart sprinter
Superpower: fair maiden: third at Chester and Newcastle: will probably stay 1m: acts on
good to firm and good to soft ground, well below form on fibresand: gelded after final
start. *N. P. Littmoden*

TAMA (IRE)   2 ch.f. (Mar 5) Indian Ridge 123 – Web of Intrigue 66 (Machiavellian   **58**
(USA) 123) [2001 6m⁶ 5m 7.5m⁶ Aug 25] second foal: dam, lightly-raced maiden who
stayed 7f, half-sister to Yorkshire Oaks winner Catchascatchcan: modest maiden: slowly
away, best effort at Beverley final start: may prove best up to 1m. *Andrew Turnell*

TAMARISK (IRE)   6 b.h. Green Desert (USA) 127 – Sine Labe (USA) (Vaguely   **113**
Noble 140) [2001 6m⁴ 6g² 5m⁶ 6d 6m² 6d Oct 19] sturdy horse: high-class performer
for current trainer in 1998, winner of Sprint Cup at Haydock: went to stud in 1999 but
reportedly had fertility problems: well below best in 3 non-graded races at 5 yrs for
W. E. Walden in USA: smart form in 2001: short-head second to Harmonic Way in listed
race at Windsor in June, then 2½ lengths sixth to Cassandra Go in King's Stand Stakes at
Royal Ascot: below par after (blinkered final outing): winner at 7f, but best at 5f/6f: acts
on firm going, below form on softer than good: has worn crossed noseband: free-going
sort, best allowed to stride on: returned to USA. *R. Charlton*

TAMBURLAINE (IRE)   3 b.c. Royal Academy (USA) 130 – Well Bought (IRE)   **119**
35 (Auction Ring (USA) 123) [2001 114p: 7d⁴ 8g² 8g⁵ 8m 7.3f² 8g² 8d⁴ 8s⁶ Sep 29]

> 'I hold the Fates bound fast in iron chains,
> And with my hand turn Fortune's wheel about,
> And sooner shall the sun fall from his sphere
> Than Tamburlaine be slain or overcome.'

That fourteenth-century Tamburlaine, all-conquering Mongol warrior and
the subject of Christopher Marlowe's play *Tamburlaine The Great*, unfortunately
had little in common with the 2001 version familiar to British racegoers. Upsides
Marlowe's Tamburlaine, who could hardly have breakfast without perpetrating
some bloody slaughter of his enemies, Tamburlaine the three-year-old racehorse
proved rather effete. There have been times when he promised to be a real force at
the top level, but he ended 2001 with a career record of one win from twelve starts
and no wins from eight starts as a three-year-old. For this Tamburlaine there has
been no riding roughshod over continents.

Tamburlaine's sole success so far is in a maiden at Newmarket. He is capable of much better than that would suggest, as shown by his second place in the
Racing Post Trophy and in the Two Thousand Guineas, the striking promise of the
former being confirmed with a fine performance at Newmarket on the first Saturday in May, when he disposed of sixteen opponents but found Golan a length and a
quarter too good. Held up on the outside, he had ten horses to pass three furlongs
out; a furlong and a half later he'd done it smoothly, but Golan had come from
even further back. The two of them showed a fine turn of foot, going clear before
Frenchmans Bay stayed on to finish a neck behind Tamburlaine in third. The
Guineas, however, was easily the highlight of Tamburlaine's season. There had
been a hiccup in his campaign on the way to the classic and he succumbed to a prolonged bout afterwards. The initial disappointment came when Tamburlaine was
7/4 favourite for the Greenham Stakes at Newbury but weakened into fourth of
eight behind Munir after racing far too freely. His performance in that muddling
contest was even more easily forgiven after his show in the Guineas, prior to which
it was striking that the stable seemed to be in little or no doubt that Tamburlaine was
their first string, even though they also fielded the Craven Stakes winner King's
Ironbridge. Tamburlaine was a 12/1-shot at Newmarket. He was 9/4 second favourite in the Irish Two Thousand, but this was where his season began to unravel, and
his finishing effort to be brought into question, fifth to Black Minnaloushe being
well below his Guineas form. Seventh of eleven, beaten just over three lengths, to
Black Minnaloushe in the St James's Palace Stakes at Royal Ascot next time and
fourth of eleven to Tough Speed in the Park Stakes at Doncaster in September were
not too bad, but below expectations all the same. In between, Tamburlaine was
beaten three quarters of a length by the enterprisingly-ridden outsider Atavus in the

Hungerford Stakes at Newbury, and came close to recapturing his Guineas form, the only occasion he really did so, when a length and a half second of six to No Excuse Needed in the Celebration Mile at Goodwood. Excuses were often needed, and the only convincing one was that Tamburlaine had been found to be suffering from a lung infection at Royal Ascot. A 'dirty nose' in December ruled him out of the Hong Kong Mile before he got on the plane, and his next target is a race at the Dubai World Cup meeting in March.

Tamburlaine (IRE) (b.c. 1998)	Royal Academy (USA) (b 1987)	Nijinsky (b 1967)	Northern Dancer / Flaming Page
		Crimson Saint (ch 1969)	Crimson Satan / Bolero Rose
	Well Bought (IRE) (b 1989)	Auction Ring (b 1972)	Bold Bidder / Hooplah
		Knighton House (b 1966)	Pall Mall / Country House

Tamburlaine is a good-topped, attractive colt who will prove best at a mile or seven furlongs. He acts on soft and good to firm going. His pedigree was covered in detail in last year's Annual, a summary being that his dam Well Bought showed poor form, placed twice on the all-weather, but is from a fine family, chiefly associated with the Ballymacoll Stud of Lord Weinstock. Grandam Knighton House is the dam of two pattern winners and the ancestress of many others, including Hellenic. A yearling filly by Danehill out of Well Bought was sold for IR £100,000 at Goffs in October. Tamburlaine, a 110,000-guinea foal, is a fairly typical representative of his sire Royal Academy in terms of distance requirements, as is the 2001 Britannia Stakes winner Analyser, but the stallion also had a smart sprinter in the latest season in Ellens Academy and useful or better middle-distance winners in Lucido, Aquarius, Putra Sandhurst and Torcello. *R. Hannon*

Jeffen Racing's "Tamburlaine"

TAMDALI (IRE)   2 b.g. (Feb 4) Be My Chief (USA) 122 – Tamarzana (IRE) (Lear   **63 p**
Fan (USA) 130) [2001 7.1m Sep 17] smallish, strong gelding: third foal: half-brother to a
winner in Austria by Ezzoud: dam French 7f winner: 8/1, burly and green, seventh of 14
to Krugerrand in maiden at Warwick, getting hang of things late on: unseated beforehand
(reportedly spooked at a rabbit): should do better. *Sir Michael Stoute*

TAMIAMI TRAIL (IRE)   3 ch.c. Indian Ridge 123 – Eurobird 118 (Ela-Mana-Mou   **106**
132) [2001 80: 10.3s* 10.1s² 13.9m⁴ 16.2m 14.8g⁵ Jul 11] sturdy, close-coupled, useful-
looking colt: useful performer: won handicap at Doncaster in March: good efforts after,
5½ lengths fifth to Arrive in listed race at Newmarket final outing: may prove best at
1½m/1¾m: acts on soft and good to firm going. *B. J. Meehan*

TAMILIA (IRE)   3 b.f. Ridgewood Ben 113 – Nellie's Away (IRE) 72 (Magical Strike   **45**
(USA) 114) [2001 47: f7s⁴ f8g e8g⁶ 8.2v⁴ 7m 7f Jun 5] sparely-made filly: poor maiden:
well held after reappearance, leaving D. Arbuthnot after fourth start: should stay at least
1m: acts on fibresand and heavy going. *Mrs L. C. Jewell*

TAMMAM (IRE)   5 b.g. Priolo (USA) 127 – Bristle 96 (Thatch (USA) 136) [2001 91:   –
10.3f 10g 11.5m May 30] angular gelding: fairly useful handicapper at best: has lost his
form: tried blinkered. *Mrs L. Stubbs*

TAM O'SHANTER   7 gr.g. Persian Bold 123 – No More Rosies 74 (Warpath 113)   **37**
[2001 –: 18m 18m 18m 17.2m⁵ Jul 15] angular gelding: poor maiden handicapper: stays
2¼m: acts on good to firm ground. *J. G. M. O'Shea*

TANAJI   2 b.f. (Mar 10) Marju (IRE) 127 – Hamsaat (IRE) 80 (Sadler's Wells (USA)   **77 p**
132) [2001 8m⁴ Sep 22] lengthy filly: third foal: sister to useful 1999 2-y-o 7f winner
Jalad: dam, 1m winner on only start (would have stayed further), sister to very smart 1¼m
performer Batshoof: 16/1, 5 lengths fourth of 12 to Revealing in maiden at Newmarket,
tracking leaders and not given hard time once held: will improve. *B. Hanbury*

TANA MANA (IRE)   2 b.f. (Mar 23) Alzao (USA) 117 – Belle Bijou 61 (Midyan   **46**
(USA) 124) [2001 5m 7.1d 7m Aug 3] IR 20,000Y: smallish filly: first foal: dam, 1¼m
winner who stayed 13f, half-sister to high-class 1m/1¼m performer Bijou d'Inde: poor
maiden: should stay 1¼m. *R. A. Fahey*

TANCHOLO   3 br.f. So Factual (USA) 120 – Tiszta Sharok 81 (Song 132) [2001 7d   –
Apr 20] 13,000Y, 1,600 2-y-o: half-sister to several winners, including Irish 9f/1¼m
winner Petofi (by Petong): dam 2-y-o 5f winner: 50/1, well held in maiden at Newbury.
L. G. Cottrell

TANCRED ARMS   5 b.m. Clantime 101 – Mischievous Miss 73 (Niniski (USA) 125)   **49 §**
[2001 62, a–: f6g f7g* f7g f7s f7g 8m³ 7.1f⁴ f8g 7.5f f7g f6s Dec 21] lengthy mare: poor
performer: won handicap at Southwell in April: barely stays 1m: acts on fibresand and
probably on any turf going: usually visored: has pulled hard: tends to hang: inconsistent.
D. W. Barker

TANCRED MISS   2 b.f. (Apr 14) Presidium 124 – Mischievous Miss 73 (Niniski   **54**
(USA) 125) [2001 5m f6g² 7m 6d f6g f5s⁶ Dec 21] smallish, leggy filly: half-sister to   **a67**
several winners, including 9-y-o Shaffishayes and 6-y-o Tancred Times: dam best at
1¾m/2m: fair maiden on all-weather, modest on turf: best effort when short-headed at
Southwell: stays 6f: acts on fibresand and good to soft going: failed to handle bend at
Catterick third start. *D. W. Barker*

TANCRED TIMES   6 ch.m. Clantime 101 – Mischievous Miss 73 (Niniski (USA)   **73**
125) [2001 65, a50: f6s⁵ f5g⁵ f5g² f5g* f5g* 5s⁵ 5m 6m⁵ 5m f5g* f5g* 5m⁵ 5f 5m²
5m* 6m³ 5g 5g⁴ 5g 5g⁵ 5g 5g* 6m³ 5d⁵ 5m 5s 5d Oct 12] small mare: fair handicapper:
had a fine season, and won at Wolverhampton, Southwell (3), Newcastle (2) and Hamilton between March/September: has won at 7f, better at 5f/easy 6f: acts on firm going,
soft, equitrack and fibresand: well beaten only run in blinkers: front runner: tough and
game. *D. W. Barker*

TANCRED WALK   3 b.f. Clantime 101 – Mischievous Miss 73 (Niniski (USA) 125)   **43**
[2001 –: 5d⁶ 6d⁶ 6g 5f 5d⁴ 6d 5g 5g⁵ Aug 24] smallish filly: poor maiden handicapper:
raced only at 5f/6f: acts on good to firm and good to soft ground: races prominently.
D. W. Barker

TANDAVA (IRE)   3 ch.g. Indian Ridge 123 – Kashka (USA) (The Minstrel (CAN)   **79**
135) [2001 10g* Jul 10] half-brother to several winners, notably smart Irish 1m (at 2 yrs)
to 1¾m winner (also won Yorkshire Oaks, runner-up in Irish St Leger) Key Change (by
Darshaan): dam, French 1½m winner, half-sister to dam of Derby winner Kahyasi: 11/4,
won 4-runner maiden at Pontefract by length from Zoudie (pair well clear), in touch after

slow start, taking long time to respond before leading inside final 1f: will stay at least 1½m: sold 8,000 gns in October, joined I. Semple and gelded. *Sir Michael Stoute*

TAN HILL FAIR (IRE)   2 b.f. (May 3) Woodborough (USA) 112 – Ron's Secret 92   **59** (Efisio 120) [2001 6.1m 7f⁵ 7g 7.1m 8s 7d Oct 18] IR 24,000Y: well-made, smallish filly: second foal: half-sister to 3-y-o Mon Secret: dam 1m/9f winner: modest maiden: should stay 1m: acts on firm ground: sold 2,200 gns. *R. Hannon*

TANTALUS   4 ch.c. Unfuwain (USA) 131 – Water Quest (IRE) (Rainbow Quest   **88** (USA) 134) [2001 100: p12g⁶ p12g f12g Dec 10] sturdy colt: useful performer at 3 yrs: fairly useful form in 2001 only on second start: probably stays 1¾m: acts on polytrack, firm and good to soft going: tongue tied twice in 2000. *J. A. Osborne*

TANTRIC   2 br.g. (Apr 15) Greensmith 121 – Petunia (GER) (Chief Singer 131) [2001   **54** f6g 6g² 6m² 7m⁵ 6m² 6g³ 6d³ f7g* f8g² f7g Oct 22] 2,000Y: first foal: dam unraced: **a60** modest performer: won seller at Southwell in October: claimed from S. Woods after good effort next time: gelded after final start: effective at 7f/1m: acts on fibresand and good to firm going. *J. O'Reilly*

TAP   4 b.g. Emarati (USA) 74 – Pubby 73 (Doctor Wall 107) [2001 85: 7m 7m 9.7d 8.1g   **–** 10s⁵ Oct 25] angular, useful-looking gelding: little form in 2001: blinkered penultimate start: sold 5,200 gns in October, joined D. Nicholls. *Mrs A. J. Perrett*

TAPAGE (IRE)   5 b.g. Great Commotion (USA) 123 – Irena (Bold Lad (IRE) 133)   **77 d** [2001 72: e7g* e7s* e7g* f8g⁵ e7g e7g 8d⁵ 8m 8f 8.5m 8.2m⁶ 7m f9.4g f8.5g f8g p7g Nov 15] fair performer: won handicaps (2) and claimer at Lingfield (left A. Reid after last-named) in February: well below form after: best at 7f/1m: acts on equitrack (not at best on fibresand), firm and soft going: tried blinkered/visored: races prominently. *Mrs N. Macauley*

TAPAU (IRE)   3 b.f. Nicolotte 118 – Urtica (IRE) (Cyrano de Bergerac 120) [2001 68:   **83** e8g⁴ 7g 7g* 6m⁵ 6g* 6f⁴ 7d Oct 13] lengthy filly: fairly useful performer: won minor event at Brighton in August and handicap at Lingfield in September: good seventh in listed event at Ascot final outing: effective at 6f/7f: acts on firm ground, good to soft and equitrack: tends to pull hard: sold 16,000 gns. *D. R. C. Elsworth*

TAP DANCER (IRE)   3 b.g. Sadler's Wells (USA) 132 – Watch Out (USA) (Mr   **64** Prospector (USA)) [2001 81p: 7v⁴ 7g 7m 7m 12d⁵ 9.5d p10g Dec 29] sixth foal: closely related to fairly useful Irish 1998 2-y-o 5f winner Bugatti Reef (by Danzig) and half-brother to 2 winners by Deputy Minister, including useful winner up to 1m in UAE/USA Noraquilon: dam, winning sprinter in USA, sister to dam of Dayjur: maiden: trained by A. O'Brien in Ireland only outing at 2 yrs (best effort): modest form in 2001: sold from J. Gorman in Ireland 3,000 gns, then well held at Lingfield on British debut final outing: stays 7f: acts on heavy going: blinkered second start: has shown wayward tendencies. *B. G. Powell*

TAPIS FILLE (IRE)   2 b.f. (Mar 26) Fayruz 116 – Trubbach (Vitiges (FR) 132) [2001   **56 d** 5f⁵ 6m⁵ 6d 6m f6s f7g f8.5g f8g Oct 18] IR 3,200F, IR 2,600Y, 4,200 2-y-o: seventh reported foal: sister to a 6f/7f winner abroad and half-sister to 1994 2-y-o 6f winner Musical Fantasy (by Gallic League): dam winner in Belgium: disappointing maiden. *R. Ford*

TAPPIT (IRE)   2 b.c. (Mar 16) Mujadil (USA) 119 – Green Life 63 (Green Desert   **76** (USA) 127) [2001 5.3s 5s⁵ 5.3f³ 6m* 6f⁶ 6m 6g 5m⁶ 7g Sep 15] 20,000Y: neat colt: fourth foal: half-brother to a 5f (at 2 yrs) to 6.5f winner in Italy by College Chapel: dam, fourth at 7f in Ireland at 2 yrs, half-sister to Molecomb winner Classic Ruler: fair performer: made all in maiden at Brighton in June: below form last 4 starts: should stay 7f: yet to race on heavy going, acts on any other turf: sold 5,000 gns. *M. R. Channon*

TAP THE STONE (IRE)   2 b.g. (Feb 18) Bigstone (IRE) 126 – Wadeyaa (Green   **56** Desert (USA) 127) [2001 5f⁵ f6g 6d⁵ 6.1g⁶ 6g 7s 7g⁶ Oct 19] 6,500F, IR 16,000Y, 18,000 2-y-o: heavy-topped gelding: first foal: dam unraced sister to smart Scandinavian sprinter Waquaas: modest maiden: stays 7f: acts on firm going, below form on soft/fibresand: visored (ran creditably) final start. *J. S. Wainwright*

TARA GOLD (IRE)   3 b.f. Royal Academy (USA) 130 – Soha (USA) 58 (Dancing   **83** Brave (USA) 140) [2001 78: 8.3d⁵ 10m⁵ 10d⁶ 10.1f* 10m² 12m² 12g⁴ 13.3f Sep 22] leggy filly: fairly useful performer: won maiden at Epsom in July: better form in handicaps next 3 starts: stays 1½m: acts on firm and good to soft going: consistent: sold 34,000 gns. *R. Hannon*

TARANAKI   3 b.c. Delta Dancer – Miss Ticklepenny (Distant Relative 128) [2001   **83** f9.4g⁶ f9.4g³ f8g* 7d² 8.3s 6g³ 7m 6g 6g 5.7d 6g 7.1f* f8g p7g Nov 15] 850Y: rather leggy colt: first foal: dam ran 3 times: fairly useful performer: won maiden at Southwell in April and minor event at Chepstow in September: has won at 1m, probably best at 6f/7f: acts on fibresand, firm and good to soft going: races prominently. *P. D. Cundell*

TARANOG   2 b.g. (Apr 16) Perpendicular 119 – Onemoretime (Timeless Times (USA) 99) [2001 10.2g 8d 8.2s⁶ Nov 5] 2,700Y: first foal: dam little form: well beaten in maidens, though signs of ability in blinkers final start. *B. Palling*   **–**

TARAS EMPEROR (IRE)   3 b.g. Common Grounds 118 – Strike It Rich (FR) (Rheingold 137) [2001 99: 6d 5f 5f 6d 7.5f 7g 7m 5m 5v* 5v* 6d² 5s Nov 9] close-coupled, workmanlike gelding: fair handicapper: won at Ayr and Newcastle in October: stays 6f: best effort on good to firm going, but unbeaten in 4 starts on heavy: reared badly as stall opened final outing. *J. J. Quinn*   **76**

TARASHANI (IRE)   3 ch.g. Primo Dominie 121 – Tarakana (USA) 101 (Shahrastani (USA) 135) [2001 8.2s⁶ 9m 8d⁶ 12.4m⁶ 10.1g Sep 14] sturdy gelding: fourth foal: half-brother to useful Irish 7f/1m winner Tarakan (by Doyoun) and 9f winner Tarabaya (by Warning): dam Irish 9f winner who stayed 1½m: little form, leaving Sir Michael Stoute after second outing: visored last 2 starts. *B. Ellison*   **–**

TARAWAN   5 ch.g. Nashwan (USA) 135 – Soluce 98 (Junius (USA) 124) [2001 81: 10s 8.5m 8m³ 10.2f* 10g 9m² 10.1m⁶ 10.2g⁴ 10.5s⁴ 10f² 12g Sep 28] strong, long-backed gelding: fair handicapper: won amateur event at Bath in June: best at 1m to 10.5f: acts on firm and soft going: tried blinkered, usually visored nowadays: sometimes slowly away/races lazily, but is consistent. *I. A. Balding*   **76**

TARAZONIC   3 ch.f. Zafonic (USA) 130 – Tarasova (USA) (Green Forest (USA) 134) [2001 10m 10f⁵ 10.4m⁴ f12g⁶ f8.5g 10s Oct 30] strong, heavy-bodied filly: half-sister to several winners, including fairly useful 5f/6f winner Galine (by Most Welcome) and useful 1¼m (at 2 yrs) to 2m winner Tarashaan (by Darshaan): dam twice-raced half-sister to top-class French middle-distance colt Le Marmot: modest maiden, left C. Wall after second start: well held in handicaps when blinkered last 3 outings: stays 1¼m: acts on firm going: has refused to enter stall. *J. Balding*   **62 d**

TARBOUSH   4 b.g. Polish Precedent (USA) 131 – Barboukh 95 (Night Shift (USA)) [2001 90: 10g 10.4g 8.3g⁴ 8m⁶ 10g² 10m p10g⁵ p10g⁴ p12g² Dec 12] strong, sturdy gelding: fluent mover: useful handicapper: left H. Cecil 42,000 gns after sixth start: fourth in listed race at Lingfield penultimate start, gelded after final one: stays easy 1¼m: acts on good to firm going and polytrack: often races freely: held up. *N. A. Callaghan*   **95**

TARCOOLA   4 ch.g. Pursuit of Love 124 – Miswaki Belle (USA) 73 (Miswaki (USA) 124) [2001 –: f9.4g f11g f11g³ f8g f12g⁶ 7m 12.6d 10.9m 12s f14.8g⁶ f14.8s⁴ Dec 15] tall, quite attractive gelding: modest maiden handicapper: left M. Johnston after fifth start: probably stays 15f: acts on fibresand, best turf efforts on going softer than good: tried blinkered/visored/tongue tied: often slowly away. *Mrs A. M. Naughton*   **a54 d**

TAR FIH (USA)   3 b. or br.f. Gone West (USA) – Najiya 102 (Nashwan (USA) 135) [2001 77: 8.1v² 8.2f⁶ Jun 11] sparely-made filly: fair maiden, lightly raced: stayed 1m: acted on heavy and good to firm going: tended to wander, and wasn't particularly genuine: visits Aljabr. *J. L. Dunlop*   **75**

TARFSHI   3 b.f. Mtoto 134 – Pass The Peace 116 (Alzao (USA) 117) [2001 93p: 8s 10g² 12m 10.1f* 10m³ 10v Oct 7] lengthy, good-topped filly: useful performer: won listed race at Newcastle in June tenaciously by a head from Balladonia: also ran very well when placed in listed race at Newmarket (beaten short head by Mot Juste) and Blandford Stakes at the Curragh (¾-length third to Dearly): last in Prix de l'Opera at Longchamp final outing: stays 1¼m (seemed not to stay 1½m when seventh in Oaks): acts on firm and soft going. *M. A. Jarvis*   **105**

TARRADALE   7 br.g. Interrex (CAN) – Encore L'Amour (USA) § (Monteverdi 129) [2001 –: e8g³ f9.4s⁶ f9.4g 8s 8s⁶ 10f³ 8m 10m⁴ 10f 10m⁵ 9.1d 11m 10s f11g Nov 30] heavy-topped, plain gelding: poor performer: effective at 1m/1¼m: acts on any turf going, fibresand and equitrack: has hung. *C. B. B. Booth*   **44**

TARRAGONA (IRE)   2 b.f. (Mar 26) Charnwood Forest (IRE) 125 – Limerick Princess (IRE) 68 (Polish Patriot (USA) 128) [2001 f5g 5.1f 6m 5.7m⁵ 5m⁶ 5m⁵ 5m 8.3g 7m Sep 22] 25,000Y: workmanlike filly: good mover: second foal: dam, 5f (at 2 yrs) and 6f winner, closely related to useful 1994 2-y-o sprinter Limerick Belle: modest maiden: not at best after fourth start: likely to prove best at 5f/6f: sold 800 gns. *A. Berry*   **56 d**

TARRY FLYNN (IRE)   7 br.g. Kenmare (FR) 125 – Danzig Lass (USA) (Danzig (USA)) [2001 115: 8s* 8m² 8d³ 8g 7s⁴ 7s Nov 11] tall, leggy gelding: smart performer: **115**

won Thoroughbred County Irish Lincolnshire (Handicap) at the Curragh in April under top weight by ½ length from Montecastillo: below best after, though short-head second to King of Tara in listed race at Leopardstown in May: has won at 9.6f, best at 7f/1m: acts on heavy and good to firm going: best in blinkers. *D. K. Weld, Ireland*

TARSKI 7 ch.g. Polish Precedent (USA) 131 – Illusory 81 (Kings Lake (USA) 133) **53** [2001 53: 10f² 10.2f² 10m⁴ 10g³ 11.6g³ 13.1d⁶ 11.5g⁴ Aug 30] sturdy gelding: modest handicapper: stays 11.6f: acts on good to firm and good to soft going: tried blinkered/ visored: held up: sold 1,700 gns. *W. S. Kittow*

TARXIEN 7 b.g. Kendor (FR) 122 – Tanz (IRE) 79 (Sadler's Wells (USA) 132) [2001 – –: 18d Oct 20] deep-girthed gelding: poor mover: fairly useful handicapper in 1999: well held both Flat runs since, in Cesarewitch in 2001, though made into useful hurdler (completed 6-timer): stays 2m: acts on good to firm and good to soft going, probably on soft: has been tongue tied. *M. C. Pipe*

TASHAWAK (IRE) 2 b.f. (Feb 7) Night Shift (USA) – Dedicated Lady (IRE) 101 **98 p** (Pennine Walk 120) [2001 6m3 6m* 6m* Sep 6] 200,000Y: sturdy filly: sixth foal: sister to 4-y-o Speedfit Free and closely related to smart 7f (at 2 yrs) to 12.5f (Prix de Royallieu) winner Fairy Queen (by Fairy King): dam, Irish 2-y-o 5f/6f winner, out of half-sister to Irish St Leger winner M-Lolshan: won maiden at Goodwood in August and minor event at Salisbury (by neck from Misterah, getting first run) in September: not sure to stay much beyond 6f: should make a smart 3-y-o. *J. L. Dunlop*

TASMANIAN TIGER (USA) 2 ch.c. (Jun 2) Storm Cat (USA) – Hum Along **80 p** (USA) (Fappiano (USA)) [2001 7d³ Oct 14] $6,800,000Y (most expensive yearling sold at public auction in the world in 2000): seventh foal: half-brother to 2 winners in USA by Summer Squall, notably Breeders' Cup Juvenile Fillies winner Storm Song: dam ran twice in USA: 5/4 favourite, 5½ lengths third of 19 to Solid Approach in maiden at the Curragh, leading/prominent until one pace final 1f: likely to do better. *A. P. O'Brien, Ireland*

TASS HEEL (IRE) 2 b.c. (May 9) Danehill (USA) 126 – Mamouna (USA) 113 **60** (Vaguely Noble 140) [2001 7m⁴ 7g 8m⁵ 8d Sep 27] strong, lengthy colt: half-brother to several winners, including fairly useful 2m winner Darter (by Darshaan) and useful Irish 1¼m/1½m winner Mamoura (by Lomond), latter dam of smart Irish middle-distance filly Mouramara: dam, 1m winner, out of half-sister to Poule d'Essai des Pouliches winner Masarika: modest maiden: should stay 1¼m: sold 18,000 gns. *M. R. Channon*

TASSO DANCER 5 gr.m. Dilum (USA) 115 – Dancing Diana 82 (Raga Navarro – (ITY) 119) [2001 40: f11g 10.2f⁵ 7f 8m Jun 22] of little account nowadays. *M. R. Bosley*

TATANTE (IRE) 3 gr.f. Highest Honor (FR) 124 – Tamnia 106 (Green Desert (USA) **53 §** 127) [2001 65p: 6s³ 7.6f Jul 25] modest maiden, lightly raced: virtually refused to race final outing: will stay at least 1m: blinkered last 2 starts: one to avoid: sold 17,000 gns in December. *Sir Mark Prescott*

TATTY THE TANK 3 b.g. Tragic Role (USA) – Springfield Girl (Royal Vulcan 83) **38** [2001 50: 10m³ Jul 11] modest maiden, lightly raced: should stay 1¼m+: well held on fibresand. *M. C. Pipe*

TAW PARK 7 b.g. Inca Chief (USA) – Parklands Belle 73 (Stanford 121§) [2001 57?: **63 d** 10.2f³ 10f 9.9m 9m 8d 8s Sep 24] workmanlike gelding: modest maiden handicapper, on downgrade: stays 1¼m: acts on firm going. *R. J. Baker*

TAXI-FOR-ROBBO (IRE) 4 b.f. Shalford (IRE) 124§ – Miromaid (Simply Great – (FR) 122) [2001 –: f8g 6m 8m 6m 8f 5g 5m 7g 11.9s Oct 11] of little account. *B. W. Murray*

TAYIF 5 gr.g. Taufan (USA) 119 – Rich Lass (Broxted 120) [2001 –: 6v 5s³ 6g 5g 6d* **97** 7f 6s⁴ 6g 7d⁴ 6m* Sep 21] quite good-topped gelding: useful handicapper: revitalised by new stable, and won at York in June and Tote Silver Cup at Ayr (12/1, made up 2 to 3 lengths final 1f to beat Sharp Hat a neck) in September: effective at 6f, barely stays 7f when conditions are testing: acts on soft and good to firm going: tongue tied last 7 starts. *D. Nicholls*

TAYSEER (USA) 7 ch.g. Sheikh Albadou 128 – Millfit (USA) 62 (Blushing Groom **96** (FR) 131) [2001 112: a6f⁵ Mar 1] lightly-made gelding: had a quick action: smart performer in 2000, winning Bunbury Cup at Newmarket and Stewards' Cup at Goodwood and second in Diadem Stakes at Ascot: 7¼ lengths fifth in prestige race at Nad Al Sheba, only outing in 2001: put down after breaking a pastern in workout on same course later in March: winner at 1m, but was best at 6f/7f: acted on fibresand, firm and soft going: was usually held up. *D. Nicholls*

TEA FOR TEXAS 4 ch.f. Weldnaas (USA) 112 – Polly's Teahouse 68 (Shack (USA) **45 §** 118) [2001 51: 6g 7m 8.2f 6d 7f 8f 7.6m³ 8f 7.1m* 7.1m 8m⁵ Aug 22] lengthy filly: poor handicapper: won at Chepstow in July: best around 7f: acts on fibresand, equitrack, firm and good to soft going: tried visored/tongue tied: reportedly had breathing problem sixth outing: unreliable. *P. L. Clinton*

TEAM-MATE (IRE) 3 b.g. Nashwan (USA) 135 – Ustka 60 (Lomond (USA) 128) **82** [2001 8g 9m² 10g⁴ 12m² 11.8s⁴ Oct 15] 50,000Y: fourth living foal: half-brother to 3 winners, including 5-y-o Kuster and 7-y-o Travelmate: dam, 7f winner, closely related to smart middle-distance stayer Braashee: fairly useful maiden: will stay 1¾m: tongue tied last 2 starts: carried head awkwardly and tended to hang in behind penultimate outing: sold 19,000 gns. *J. R. Fanshawe*

TE ANAU 4 b.f. Reprimand 122 – Neenah 107 (Bold Lad (IRE) 133) [2001 –: f8g Feb **–** 23] no form since 2 yrs. *W. J. Musson*

TEARS IN HEAVEN (IRE) 2 ch.f. (Apr 22) Spectrum (IRE) 126 – Dai E Dai **71 ?** (USA) (Seattle Dancer (USA) 119) [2001 7g³ 7.5m 7m⁶ 7m³ 6m² 7m* 7.5m² 8.8m³ 7.5m Dec 19] approx. 13,000Y in Italy: second foal: dam, Italian 2-y-o 7f/1m winner, half-sister to smart miler Pater Noster: fair performer: left M. Bell after third start (well held in claimer at Thirsk, hanging fire under pressure): won minor event at Florence in October: stays 8.8f: raced mainly on good to firm ground. *R. Valeri, Italy*

TECHNICIAN (IRE) 6 ch.g. Archway (IRE) 115 – How It Works (Commanche Run **95** 133) [2001 74: f7g³ f7g⁵ 7.1v 6m* 6m² 6f* 6d⁴ 6f² 6g² 6g* 6m 7g Oct 5] leggy gelding: poor mover: useful handicapper: better than ever in 2001, winning at Thirsk in May, Pontefract in June and York (by neck from Night Flight) in August: best at 6f/7f: acts on soft going, firm and fibresand: blinkered, has been visored: usually races prominently. *E. J. Alston*

TEDBURROW 9 b.g. Dowsing (USA) 124 – Gwiffina 87 (Welsh Saint 126) [2001 **115** 115: a6f 6d⁴ 5g⁴ 6m² 6m 6m* 5.1m 6.1m³ 6s 5d⁴ 6s 6d 6v Oct 26] sturdy, workmanlike gelding: smart performer: won minor event at Haydock in July: ran well otherwise when 2-length fourth to Primo Valentino in listed Abernant Stakes at Newmarket, neck second to Pipalong in Duke of York Stakes at York and close eighth to Danehurst in listed event at Newmarket on second/fourth/penultimate starts: effective at 5f/6f: acts on firm and soft going, probably not on heavy: has won when sweating: successful 4 times at Chester: tough. *E. J. Alston*

TEDJEN 2 br.g. (Feb 12) Overbury (IRE) 116 – Plum Bold 83 (Be My Guest (USA) **–** 126) [2001 7.1f Sep 18] half-brother to several winners, including 1m winner Pomona (by Puissance), who later showed smart form up to 1¼m in USA, and useful Italian sprinter Plumbird (by Statoblest): dam 6f winner: 10/1 and very green, well held in maiden at Chepstow: dead. *P. J. Makin*

Tote (Ayr) Silver Cup (Handicap)—the far side monopolizes the placings as Tayif is galvanized in typical fashion by Kieren Fallon to beat Sharp Hat and Only For Gold (rail); Rudik and Debbie's Warning (No.25) dead-heat for fourth whilst Boanerges is first home on the stand side and sixth overall

TED'S BOY 2 b.g. (May 19) Reprimand 122 – Sylvan Rime (Weldnaas (USA) 112) – [2001 7.1s 8.2d f8g Oct 18] leggy gelding: second reported foal: dam of no account: no sign of ability, including in seller. *J. R. Norton*

TEDSDALE MAC 2 ch.c. (Feb 24) Presidium 124 – Stilvella (Camden Town 125) **68** [2001 6m 7m⁵ 6g⁵ 6m⁵ 6m³ 5d⁶ 6d Oct 12] 1,200Y: close-coupled, quite good-topped colt: sixth foal: half-brother to 1995 2-y-o 5f winner Pathaze (by Totem): dam ran twice at 2 yrs: fair maiden: third at Redcar: stays 6f: yet to race on extremes of going. *N. Bycroft*

TEDSTALE (USA) 3 ch.g. Irish River (FR) 131 – Carefree Kate (USA) (Lyphard **85** (USA) 132) [2001 79: 10s 12m³ 11m³ 12.3m⁵ 8.5f* 8.5m 9g⁵ 8d³ 7m 8d* 8d Nov 3] smallish, sturdy, close-coupled gelding: unimpressive mover: fairly useful handicapper: won at Beverley (tended to hang right) in July and Pontefract in October: gelded after final outing: may prove best at 1m/1¼m: acts on firm and good to soft going: blinkered last 7 starts. *T. D. Easterby*

TEEHEE (IRE) 3 b.g. Anita's Prince 126 – Regal Charmer (Royal And Regal (USA)) **79** [2001 81: 8.2s² 8.2v* 8.2f 8.1m 8g 7d Nov 6] tall, useful-looking gelding: fair performer: won maiden at Nottingham in May: stays 1m well: seems best on ground softer than good: visored final start (subsequently gelded): has carried head awkwardly: front runner. *B. Palling*

TEEJAY'N'AITCH (IRE) 9 b.g. Maelstrom Lake 118 – Middle Verde (USA) – (Sham (USA)) [2001 –: f16.2g 11.1d May 6] no longer of much account. *J. S. Goldie*

TEENAWON (IRE) 3 ch.f. Polar Falcon (USA) 126 – Oasis (Valiyar 129) [2001 48: – 7m 7m Jul 4] poor performer: form only at 6f at 2 yrs. *G. G. Margarson*

TEFI 3 ch.g. Efisio 120 – Masuri Kabisa (USA) 48 (Ascot Knight (CAN) 130) [2001 – 59: 8m 6g 7m 8m 7.1f 7.5m 5g f7g⁴ f9.4g³ f12f³ f14g⁶ f8.5s⁶ Dec 26] smallish gelding: **a51** has a round action: modest maiden: left T. Easterby 1,200 gns after seventh start: probably stays 1¾m: acts on firm going and fibresand: below form in blinkers: has drifted markedly right. *S. R. Bowring*

TEG 3 b.f. Petong 126 – Felinwen (White Mill 76) [2001 7m Aug 24] fifth foal: half- – sister to 2m winner Brynkir (by Batshoof) and 8.5f to 1¼m winner in Italy by Elmaamul: dam claimer: last in claimer at Newmarket on debut. *S. C. Williams*

TELECASTER (IRE) 5 ch.g. Indian Ridge 123 – Monashee (USA) (Sovereign – Dancer (USA)) [2001 82: f6s f5g Feb 8] fairly useful performer at 4 yrs: well held in 2001: blinkered. *C. R. Egerton*

TELEGRAM GIRL 2 b.f. (Mar 27) Magic Ring (IRE) 115 – Lucky Message (USA) – 71 (Phone Trick (USA)) [2001 5m 5m 7.6m 6g f8.5g f7g* f8g⁴ f7s* f8.5s⁵ Dec 27] **a68** 9,000Y: close-coupled filly: third foal: sister to 1998 2-y-o 6f winner Call Me Lucky: dam, 2-y-o 5f winner who stayed 7f and became one to treat with caution, half-sister to useful performer up to 9f Tik Fa: fair performer: won seller at Southwell (final start for J. Smyth-Osbourne) in October and nursery at Wolverhampton in December: stays 1m: acts on fibresand, showed little on turf: visored sixth/seventh starts. *D. Haydn Jones*

TELESTO (USA) 2 b.c. (Apr 16) Mr Prospector (USA) – Aviance 112 (Northfields **84 p** (USA)) [2001 6g⁵ 6g³ Sep 15] rangy colt: has scope: half-brother to several winners, including very smart miler Chimes of Freedom (by Private Account), 3-y-o Denon and to dam of top-class miler Spinning World: dam 2-y-o 6f/7f winner: favourite both starts, better effort (fairly useful form) when length third to Inishowen in minor event at Doncaster: should stay 7f: capable of better. *Sir Michael Stoute*

TELLION 7 b.g. Mystiko (USA) 124 – Salchow 116 (Niniski (USA) 125) [2001 –, – a55: f14g⁶ Jun 8] good-bodied gelding: modest maiden at 6 yrs: well held only outing in 2001: visored. *J. R. Jenkins*

TELORI 3 ch.f. Muhtarram (USA) 125 – Elita (Sharpo 132) [2001 7.1s⁴ 7.1f³ 5g 7s **53** Oct 5] lengthy filly: second foal: dam unraced granddaughter of Molecomb and Lowther Stakes winner Flying Legs: modest maiden: stays 7f: seemed rather reluctant in latter stages on debut. *S. C. Williams*

TEMERAIRE (USA) 6 b.g. Dayjur (USA) 137 – Key Dancer (USA) (Nijinsky (CAN) – 138) [2001 88, a94: e10g³ Jan 31] strong, quite good-topped gelding: fairly useful **a90** performer: creditable third in handicap at Lingfield only run in 2001: effective at 7f, barely stays 1¼m: acts on equitrack, good to firm and good to soft going: visored twice: usually races up with pace. *D. J. S. Cosgrove*

TEMPER TANTRUM   3 b.g. Pursuit of Love 124 – Queenbird 90 (Warning 136)   – [2001 65: 7.9m 10.3d f9.4g Oct 23] fair performer, lightly raced: soundly beaten in handicaps in 2001. *Andrew Reid*

TEMPEST   3 b.c. Zafonic (USA) 130 – Pidona (Baillamont (USA) 124) [2001 112: 8g   **93** 8f⁴ 9f⁶ Aug 6] big, lengthy, attractive colt: smart performer in 2000, best effort when third in Dewhurst Stakes at Newmarket final outing: well below form at 3 yrs, in 2000 Guineas on same course (final start for Sir Michael Stoute), allowance race at Belmont (3¼ lengths fourth) and Grade 2 handicap at Saratoga: bred to stay at least 1m: acts on firm and good to soft going: has pulled hard/flashed tail. *C. Clement, USA*

TEMPLES TIME (IRE)   3 b.f. Distinctly North (USA) 115 – Midnight Patrol   **63 d** (Ashmore (FR) 125) [2001 74: f7g f8.5g⁴ 7m³ 10.2m⁵ 10.9m⁴ 10m 11.5m⁴ f12g⁴ 10.2g⁶ f11g³ 10m³ 11.9m⁵ 8m⁶ 10s⁶ f8.5s Dec 26] angular filly: modest handicapper: left R. Hannon after third start: probably stays 11.5f: acts on soft and good to firm ground, probably on fibresand. *R. Brotherton*

TEMPLE WAY   5 b.g. Shirley Heights 130 – Abbey Strand (USA) 78 (Shadeed (USA)   **99** 135) [2001 100: 14m⁵ 20m 16.2g 14.8m Aug 24] tall, workmanlike gelding: useful handicapper, though ran at least respectably in 2001, including when seventh to Give Notice at Newmarket final outing: best at 1¾m/2m: acts on firm going, possibly not on good to soft: often blinkered/visored: has found little. *R. Charlton*

TEMPRAMENTAL (IRE)   5 ch.m. Midhish 109 – Musical Horn (Music Boy 124)   – [2001 61: 5.7g Jun 16] good-topped mare: modest handicapper at 4 yrs: last in seller only run in 2001: sometimes blinkered/visored earlier in career. *Dr P. Pritchard*

TEMPTING FATE (IRE)   3 b.f. Persian Bold 123 – West of Eden (Crofter (USA)   **113** 124) [2001 102p: a8f³ 8m⁴ 8f³ 8s⁶ Aug 5] strong, close-coupled filly: smart performer: trained by J. Hills at 2 yrs: below form at Nad Al Sheba on reappearance, but good efforts next 2 starts, ¾-length fourth to Rose Gypsy in Poule d'Essai des Pouliches at Longchamp and 2 lengths third to Banks Hill in Coronation Stakes at Royal Ascot: just

Godolphin's "Tempting Fate"

respectable sixth to Ascension in Prix d'Astarte at Deauville: best at 7f/1m: acts on firm and soft ground: tongue tied at Royal Ascot: made running last 3 outings: stays in training. *Saeed bin Suroor*

TEMPUS FUGIT 6 ch.m. Timeless Times (USA) 99 – Kabella (Kabour 80) [2001 **46** f5g³ f5g 5m⁶ 5g 6f⁵ 5f⁵ 5f 5.5m 5m⁵ Aug 27] sturdy mare: has been to stud, and only poor **a48** form on return in 2001: probably stays 6f: acts on firm going, good to soft and fibresand: ran poorly in visor: has been slowly away. *B. R. Millman*

TENAJA TRAIL (USA) 2 ch.c. (Mar 23) Irish River (FR) 131 – Buckeye Gal – p (USA) (Good Counsel (USA)) [2001 8d Oct 2] $250,000Y: big, strong, rangy colt: has plenty of scope: eighth foal: brother to 2 winners, notably very smart French/US 1m to 1½m winner River Bay, and half-brother to 2 winners, including US 9f winner All The Gears (by Gone West): dam, minor stakes winner up to 9f in USA, out of sister to dam of Oh So Sharp: 12/1, burly and very green, well held in maiden at Newmarket, not knocked about: looks type to do fair bit better. *W. J. Haggas*

TENDERFOOT 3 b.f. Be My Chief (USA) 122 – Kelimutu 58 (Top Ville 129) [2001 **61** 54: 11.9m 12m² 12g 12m³ 14.1m* 14.1s 12g Sep 19] sturdy, deep-girthed filly: modest handicapper: won at Redcar in August: stays 1¾m: acts on good to firm going, possibly unsuited by soft: tends to race freely. *Mrs Lydia Pearce*

TENDER TRAP (IRE) 3 b.c. Sadler's Wells (USA) 132 – Shamiyda (USA) 83 (Sir **80** Ivor 135) [2001 66p: 10.3v⁵ 12d⁶ 9.9m² 10d² 10.1m² 10.1s³ Aug 31] useful-looking colt: fairly useful maiden: creditable efforts last 4 starts: should stay at least 1½m: acts on soft and good to firm going: carries head high under pressure. *T. G. Mills*

TENDULKAR (USA) 2 b.c. (Feb 7) Spinning World (USA) 130 – Romanette **114 p** (USA) (Alleged (USA) 138) [2001 5g* 7d³ Oct 20]

While Kumble, rather than Tendulkar, might have been a more appropriate name for a colt by Spinning World, at least the horse in question looks more likely to prove worthy of his sobriquet than many who are named after famous sportsmen and sportswomen. Tendulkar isn't going to reach the heights of the great Indian batsman, who enjoys superstar status in his own country, but it will be a surprise if he doesn't at least make his mark at the top level in the next season. With only two runs under his belt it is already clear that Tendulkar, the horse, is at least a smart performer, and there is every chance he will develop into a high-class one at three.

Tendulkar became Spinning World's first winner as a sire when he landed the odds in a five-furlong maiden at the Curragh in May on his debut, looking the sort who could well run up a sequence. Unfortunately, Tendulkar fractured his pelvis shortly after and, as a result, it was the end of October before he saw a race-course again. Surprisingly, the race chosen for his return was the Group 1 Dewhurst Stakes, which represented a huge step up in class, yet Tendulkar, despite his lack of experience and long lay-off, came very close to winning. One of four O'Brien-trained colts in the eight-runner field, Tendulkar attracted plenty of support at long odds on the morning of the race. He was held up in rear in a race in which the early pace was far from strong and had to be switched around the field to make his effort, so his performance in finishing third is deserving of extra credit. Although others had something of a start in the dash for the line, Tendulkar finished so strongly that he almost pegged back his stable-companions Rock of Gibraltar and Landseer, going down by only a short head and a head.

		Nureyev	Northern Dancer
	Spinning World (USA)	(b 1977)	Special
	(ch 1993)	Imperfect Circle	Riverman
Tendulkar (USA)		(b 1988)	Aviance
(b.c. Feb 7, 1999)		Alleged	Hoist The Flag
	Romanette (USA)	(b 1974)	Princess Pout
	(b or br 1982)	Laughing Bridge	Hilarious
		(b or br 1972)	Brook Bridge

A return to Newmarket for the Two Thousand Guineas is on the cards for Tendulkar, and the step up to a mile will suit him well. Although Spinning World did virtually all of his racing at a mile, he was successful over nine furlongs as a two-year-old and would almost certainly have stayed a mile and a quarter, a distance which should be well within Tendulkar's range. His dam Romanette, a useful performer in the States, won five races at up to eleven furlongs, including the Jersey

TEN

Mrs J. Magnier, Mr M. Tabor and Mrs D. Nagle's "Tendulkar"

Oaks over nine furlongs, from twenty-five starts. She is one of several winners produced by Laughing Bridge, a smart two-year-old in the States in 1974, when she won two graded races at six furlongs and ended the year 8 lb below the top filly Ruffian in the Experimental Free Handicap. Tendulkar, a 200,000-dollar yearling, whose posed portrait was taken very late in the year and doesn't do him full justice, is a half-brother to several winners, including the useful German nine-furlong winner Romanowa (by Topsider) and Blush Rambler (by Blushing Groom). Blush Rambler raced mostly for Sir Michael Stoute and showed smart form at up to a mile and a half, though he never fulfilled the promise of his second in the Grand Criterium at Longchamp on his final two-year-old start. Things should be different with Tendulkar. *A. P. O'Brien, Ireland*

TENERIFE FLYER 3 ch.f. Rock City 120 – Nobleata (Dunbeath (USA) 127) [2001 55: 10g 12m 10m Jun 24] leggy, close-coupled filly: modest maiden at 2 yrs: well held in 2001. *J. R. Norton* —

TENNESSEE (IRE) 4 b.g. Blues Traveller (IRE) 119 – Valiant Friend (USA) (Shahrastani (USA) 135) [2001 –: e12g 8m 10m Jun 18] unfurnished gelding: no form since 2 yrs: tried blinkered. *S. P. C. Woods* —

TENNESSEE MOON 3 b.f. Darshaan 133 – Mrs Moonlight (Ajdal (USA) 130) [2001 7g 8.3d 10m 10m³ 12g Aug 3] rangy filly: has scope: fifth foal: half-sister to 4-y-o Soviet Flash and to a 1m winner in Japan by Machiavellian: dam unraced half-sister to Pushy, Jupiter Island and Precocious: fair maiden: stays 1¼m, probably 1½m: tended to carry head high fourth start: sent to France. *G. Wragg* 73

TENNESSEE WALTZ 3 b.f. Caerleon (USA) 132 – Military Tune (IRE) (Nashwan (USA) 135) [2001 –: 10m³ 10.1m⁶ 10g 10m Aug 22] sturdy filly: modest maiden handicapper: below form after reappearance: should stay 1½m: acts on good to firm going: sold 10,000 gns in December. *E. A. L. Dunlop* 56

Prix de l'Opera - Casino Barriere d'Enghien-Les Bains, Longchamp—a career-best performance from Terre A Terre, who wins from Mot Juste (rail), Rebelline (hoops) and Nadia

TEN PAST SIX 9 ch.g. Kris 135 – Tashinsky (USA) (Nijinsky (CAN) 138) [2001 –: 14.6s⁶ f14g f11g⁶ Nov 30] lengthy, good-quartered gelding: one-time fairly useful winner: well held in 2001: usually blinkered/visored. *M. J. Polglase* —

TENSILE (IRE) 6 b.g. Tenby 125 – Bonnie Isle 115 (Pitcairn 126) [2001 92: 18v 16s⁵ 16m⁵ 16.2g 16v Oct 26] small, sturdy gelding: has a quick action: fairly useful handicapper: well held last 2 starts, leaving M. Pipe and off nearly 5 months before final one: stays 2¼m: acts on soft and good to firm going: usually held up: visored (raced too freely) once: tricky ride, sometimes finds little, and has won only once on Flat. *P. J. Hobbs* **87**

TEOFILIO (IRE) 7 ch.h. Night Shift (USA) – Rivoltade (USA) (Sir Ivor 135) [2001 77: f8g f7g³ p8g⁴ p7g³ p7g f7g⁵ f7s⁵ Dec 15] good-topped horse: fair handicapper: stays 8.5f: acts on all-weather, soft and good to soft going: blinkered: has worn tongue strap: has hung/found little: best held up. *Andrew Reid* **70**

TE QUIERO 3 gr.c. Bering 136 – Ma Lumiere (FR) (Niniski (USA) 125) [2001 69p: 11m 9m⁶ 10.1g² 9.7m² 10.1g⁶ Sep 15] fair maiden: stays 1¼m: acts on soft and good to firm going. *Miss Gay Kelleway* **66**

TE QUIERO (FR) 5 gr.g. Turgeon (USA) 123 – Passerene (FR) (Persepolis (FR) 127) [2001 72: 12s 11.6g 14.4m Jun 6] only modest form in Britain: appears to stay 1¾m: acts on good to soft going, probably on good to firm: sold 900 gns. *P. Mitchell* **51**

TEQUILA 6 b.g. Mystiko (USA) 124 – Black Ivor (USA) (Sir Ivor 135) [2001 8.1g Aug 10] deep-bodied gelding: fairly useful hurdler at 3 yrs: winning hurdler in 1998/9: tailed off when pulled up only run in 2001. *W. Clay* —

TERESA BALBI 2 ch.f. (Mar 31) Master Willie 129 – Pondicherry (USA) 64 (Sir Wimborne (USA) 118) [2001 8v* 8d⁶ Nov 3] quite good-topped filly: fourth living foal: half-sister to 5f and (at 2 yrs) 6f winner Kirsch (by Wolfhound): dam 7f winner: won maiden at Doncaster in October by ½ length from Imoya: similar form when about 6 lengths sixth to Sundrenched in listed race at Newmarket 8 days later: will stay 1¼m. *S. P. C. Woods* **86**

TERFEL 2 ch.c. (Feb 5) Lion Cavern (USA) 117 – Montserrat 81 (Aragon 118) [2001 6m* 7m² 7g³ 7m* 8s⁴ 7s³ Oct 11] quite attractive colt: second foal: dam 5f (at 2 yrs) and 6f winner: fairly useful performer: won minor events at Yarmouth in June and Redcar (odds on) in August: in frame in minor events at Newmarket and York and listed races at Newmarket (1¼ lengths second to Redback) and Milan (4 lengths fourth to Salselon): probably stays 1m: acts on soft and good to firm going. *M. L. W. Bell* **91**

TERN INTERN (IRE) 2 b. or br.g. (Feb 12) Dr Devious (IRE) 127 – Arctic Bird (USA) (Storm Bird (CAN) 134) [2001 7m 8d Aug 26] 4,000 2-y-o: first foal: dam unraced sister to smart Prix Robert Papin winner who stayed 1m Ocean Ridge: better effort in maidens at Yarmouth (modest form) when seventh of 9 on debut. *Miss J. Feilden* **60**

TERRAPIN (IRE) 2 b.f. (Feb 9) Turtle Island (IRE) 123 – Lady Taufan (IRE) (Taufan (USA) 119) [2001 6d⁵ 6m 6f Sep 10] 10,500Y: unfurnished filly: fifth foal: half-sister to useful 1996 2-y-o 6f winner Speedball (by Waajib) and 1997 2-y-o 5f winner Golden Strategy (by Statoblest), later winner abroad: dam, Irish maiden who stayed 9f, sister to useful performer up to 1m Princess Taufan: modest maiden: best effort on debut. *Mrs A. Duffield* **53**

TERRE A TERRE (FR) 4 b.f. Kaldounevees (FR) 118 – Toujours Juste (FR) (Always Fair (USA) 121) [2001 106: 8g² 8v 8g³ 8g⁵ 10d* 10m* 10v* 10m³ Dec 16] smallish, lengthy filly: first foal: dam French 6f winner: smart performer: progressed well in 2001, winning minor event at Bordeaux, valuable listed races at Deauville in August and Longchamp in September, and Prix de l'Opera - Casino Barriere d'Enghien-Les-Bains at Longchamp (by 1½ lengths from Mot Juste after meeting trouble) in October: excellent effort when beaten head and neck behind Agnes Digital and Tobougg in Hong Kong Cup at Sha Tin final start: stays 1¼m: acts on heavy and good to firm going. *E. Libaud, France* **119**

1016

TERRESTRIAL (USA)   3 ch.c. Theatrical 128 – Stellaria (USA) 98 (Roberto (USA)   **109**
131) [2001 91p: 9d⁵ 12g.g* May 5] strong, close-coupled colt: has a fluent, round action:
progressive form in only 3 runs: fifth to Olden Times in listed race at Newmarket in
April, then won minor event there (best effort, confidently ridden to beat Prize Winner ¾
length): reportedly fractured cannon bone later in May and underwent surgery: likely to
prove better around 1½m than shorter: raced only on good/good to soft going: has worn
crossed noseband: stays in training. *J. H. M. Gosden*

TERTULLIAN (IRE)   2 b.c. (May 23) Petorius 117 – Fiddes (IRE) 52 (Alzao (USA)   **77**
117) [2001 7m⁵ 7.9m* 8d³ 8.3v Nov 8] IR 8,500Y: sturdy, good-bodied colt: has scope:
third foal: dam maiden who stayed 7f: fair performer: won maiden at York in September:
very good third of 24 to Bestam in nursery at Newmarket: will stay 1¼m: acts on good to
firm going and good to soft, well held on heavy. *R. Hannon*

TEST THE WATER (IRE)   7 ch.g. Maelstrom Lake 118 – Baliana (CAN) (River-   **57**
man (USA) 131) [2001 –: f11s f9.4s f11g f9.4g³ 8.2v⁵ 8s⁴ 10g⁴ 11.8s 8v² f11g f9.4s Dec   **a43**
27] dipped-backed gelding: poor walker/mover: modest on turf, poor on all-weather:
stays 1¼m: acts on good to firm going, soft and fibresand: sometimes blinkered/visored:
has looked none too keen. *P. Howling*

TEXANNIE   4 b.f. Inchinor 119 – Texanne (BEL) 66§ (Efisio 120) [2001 –: f8g f8g
10s 8s 12m 14.1g Jun 16] leggy filly: maiden, mostly well beaten: tried blinkered.
S. C. Williams

TEXAS GOLD   3 ch.g. Cadeaux Genereux 131 – Star Tulip 99 (Night Shift (USA))   **48 +**
[2001 p6g⁶ f8g f6s⁵ Dec 15] 45,000Y: second foal: half-brother to 4-y-o Indian Sun: dam
6f winner, including at 2 yrs: poor form in maidens: pulled far too hard at 1m. *W. R. Muir*

TEXAS RANGER   3 b.c. Mtoto 134 – Favorable Exchange (USA) (Exceller (USA)   **64**
129) [2001 10g 11.6m 10m³ 14.1m 16.2g³ 12g⁶ 16v³ 16s³ Oct 30] 6,000F, IR 20,000Y:
close-coupled colt: half-brother to several winners, including 4-y-o Total Love and useful
winner up to 15f Shonara's Way (by Slip Anchor): dam French 10.7f to 1½m winner:
modest maiden: stays 2m well: acts on heavy ground: very slowly away/tended to run in
snatches second outing: sold 17,000 gns. *J. W. Hills*

TEYAAR   5 b.g. Polar Falcon (USA) 126 – Music In My Life (IRE) 59 (Law Society   **84 d**
(USA) 130) [2001 84: f5g f6g³ f5s³ f6s² f6s² f6g⁵ f5g² 6v³ 7.1v f6g 6d* 5g 6g 5d 5m 6.1d
6g 6d 5s f6g⁶ f6g⁶ p6g² f5s⁴ Dec 18] strong gelding: fairly useful handicapper: won at
Hamilton in May: below form in second half of season: effective at 5f/6f: acts on heavy
going and fibresand/polytrack, seemingly not good to firm: blinkered once: has hung.
D. Shaw

THAAYER   6 b.g. Wolfhound (USA) 126 – Hamaya (USA) 60 (Mr Prospector (USA))   **–**
[2001 –, a71: f6g⁴ f6s f5g f6g⁶ 6g⁵ f6g³ f6g⁴ f6g² f6g* f6g⁵ f7g² f6g² f7g² f7g⁴ f6g* Dec   **a84**
17] fairly useful handicapper: won at Southwell in October and December: effective at
6f/7f: acts on fibresand, lightly raced on turf nowadays: blinkered once. *I. A. Wood*

THANKS MAX (IRE)   3 b.g. Goldmark (USA) 113 – Almost A Lady (IRE) 70   **72**
(Entitled 126) [2001 63: 8m⁶ 6m 5d³ 5f³ 6f⁶ 7d⁴ 6g* 7.5m 5v Oct 15] strong gelding: fair
handicapper: won at Newcastle in July: effective at 5f to 7f: acts on fibresand, firm and
soft going: unseated before going to post third outing. *Miss L. A. Perratt*

THAQIB (IRE)   2 b.c. (Mar 3) Sadler's Wells (USA) 132 – Temple (Shirley Heights   **71 p**
130) [2001 7g Oct 4] 320,000Y: good-bodied colt: first foal: dam unraced daughter of
very smart performer up to 1m Favoridge from very good family: 16/1 and backward,
chased leaders 5f when thirteenth of 21 to Millennium Dragon in maiden at Newmarket:
will improve. *J. L. Dunlop*

THARI (USA)   4 b. or br.g. Silver Hawk (USA) 123 – Magic Slipper 97 (Habitat 134)   **107**
[2001 109: 10g⁴ 11.6m² 14.6d 12s 12d⁴ Oct 18] strong, sturdy gelding: useful performer:
in-and-out form in 2001, best efforts when 1½ lengths second to Delius in minor event at
Windsor and 3¼ lengths fourth to Mesmeric in handicap at Newmarket final outing:
better at 1½m/1¾m than shorter: acts on good to firm and good to soft going: blinkered
once at 3 yrs: sold 60,000 gns, joined N. Meade in Ireland, and won over hurdles in
December. *B. Hanbury*

THATCHAM (IRE)   5 ch.g. Thatching 131 – Calaloo Sioux (USA) 100 (Our Native   **–**
(USA)) [2001 67, a56: 6m⁶ 6m Jul 4] fair handicapper at 4 yrs: has form at 1¼m, easily
best efforts at 6f: acts on firm, good to soft going and equitrack: tried blinkered at 4 yrs,
pulled up both starts in visor, including when reportedly finishing distressed final outing.
Mrs Lydia Pearce

Mr R. E. Sangster & Mr A. K. Collins' "Theatre Script"

THATCHED COTTAGE   3 b.f. Thatching 131 – Attaproffitt (Batshoof 122) [2001   –
44: 8m Aug 1] well held in maiden/claimer. *B. Palling*

THATCHED (IRE)   11 b.g. Thatching 131 – Shadia (USA) 53 (Naskra (USA)) [2001   **47 +**
54: 9m 8m 7m⁶ 9f⁶ 8f⁴ 9f⁴ 10.1m⁶ 8m 8.5s 11m 8m⁶ 8.9m f11g Nov 30] leggy gelding:
has a quick action: poor performer: effective at 7f to 1¼m: acts on firm going, not at
best on soft/heavy: effective blinkered/visored (not tried since 1996): usually held up.
R. E. Barr

THATCHMASTER (IRE)   10 b.g. Thatching 131 – Key Maneuver (USA) (Key To   **48 d**
Content (USA)) [2001 68: 10f 12m 10m⁴ 11.6g 11.6g Aug 6] tall gelding: winning
handicapper, very much on downgrade: stays easy 1½m: acts on any ground: tongue tied:
usually races prominently. *C. A. Horgan*

THAT MAN AGAIN   9 ch.g. Prince Sabo 123 – Milne's Way 83 (The Noble Player   **75 §**
(USA) 126) [2001 78: 5.3s 5m⁵ 5m 5g 5d* 5m⁶ 5m* 5g 5m³ 5.2f 5m 5.2d Aug 26] robust
gelding: fair handicapper: won at Salisbury in June and Sandown in July: best at 5f/easy
6f: acts on fibresand and equitrack, firm and good to soft ground: visored once, blinkered
nowadays: has found little/edged right: often leads: unreliable. *S. C. Williams*

THATS ALL JAZZ   3 b.f. Prince Sabo 123 – Gate of Heaven 43 (Starry Night (USA))   **58 §**
[2001 41: 8.1v 5m 6m⁶ 6m 5.1g 7.1g* 7.1m² 8.2s 6m⁴ 7s 6s* 7s f7g p7g p6g Dec   **a51 §**
19] workmanlike filly: modest handicapper: left R. Spicer after second start: won at
Chepstow in July and Brighton in September: stays 7f: acts on polytrack, soft and good to
firm going: tried visored: inconsistent. *I. A. Wood*

THAT'S JAZZ   3 b.f. Cool Jazz 116 – Miss Mercy (IRE) 62 (Law Society (USA) 130)   **64**
[2001 67: e8g² e7g² f7g² f6g⁴ 7s 7m³ 7.1m⁴ 6.1m* 6g 6g 6m 6s⁴ Sep 24] smallish, angular
filly: fair performer: won maiden handicap at Chepstow in July: stays 1m: acts on

1018

fibresand, equitrack, soft and good to firm ground: found little third start: sold 9,000 gns. *M. L. W. Bell*

THEATRE LADY (IRE) 3 b.f. King's Theatre (IRE) 128 – Littlepace (Indian King (USA) 128) [2001 75p: 11.1d⁴ 8m⁶ 7m 9.1f³ 8f 12.4g² 8m 10g 7m⁴ 8.1g² 8.1f³ 8.5s⁶ 8g⁴ 10s f8g f8s⁶ f8.5s Dec 26] sturdy filly: fair maiden: left M. Johnston after sixth start: below form after: stays 9f: acts on any turf ground, well held on fibresand: tried visored. *P. D. Evans* **68 d a–**

THEATRE OF LIFE (IRE) 2 b.g. (Apr 23) King's Theatre (IRE) 128 – Miss Iron-wood (Junius (USA) 124) [2001 8s f9.4g Nov 17] IR 5,600F, 5,000Y: sixth foal: half-brother to 3 winners, including 3-y-o Milliken Park: dam maiden half-sister to US Grade 1 winners Anka Germania (1½m) and Mourjane (1¼m): better effort in maidens (modest form) when seventh at Brighton on debut: sold 1,300 gns. *B. J. Meehan* **55**

THEATRE SCRIPT (USA) 3 ch.c. Theatrical 128 – Gossiping (USA) (Chati (USA)) [2001 97p: 10g 12f³ 11.9g Aug 21] big, leggy, lengthy colt: has deal of scope: powerful galloper with round action: impressive maiden winner only run at 2 yrs: bit disappointing in listed event at Newmarket on reappearance (bandaged in front), but showed himself a smart performer when 2 lengths third to Storming Home in King Edward VII Stakes at Royal Ascot: dropped right away when last in Great Voltigeur at York final outing: stays 1½m: raced only on good/good to firm ground: wore crossed noseband at Royal Ascot (edgy) and York: joined S. Bray in USA. *J. H. M. Gosden* **115**

THEATRICAL WALTZ 2 b.f. (May 7) Barathea (IRE) 127 – Fascination Waltz 83 (Shy Groom (USA)) [2001 6m 6g 6f 7s Oct 5] rather leggy filly: shows knee action: third foal: dam 6f winner: little form in maidens/nursery. *J. J. Sheehan* **–**

THEBAN (IRE) 3 b.g. Inzar (USA) 112 – Phoenix Forli (USA) (Forli (ARG)) [2001 61: f7g 8m⁵ 8.3g 7.5m Jun 8] sturdy gelding: poor maiden: probably stays 1m: acts on firm going and fibresand: has raced freely. *D. Nicholls* **–**

THE BARGATE FOX 5 b.g. Magic Ring (IRE) 115 – Hithermoor Lass 75 (Red Alert 127) [2001 50, a62: f11g 11.9s May 3] modest handicapper at 4 yrs: well held in 2001. *R. Brotherton* **–**

THE BEST YET 3 ch.c. King's Signet (USA) 110 – Miss Klew (Never So Bold 135) [2001 62: f8.5g f6g f7g Nov 23] modest form in maidens at 2 yrs: well held in handicaps in 2001, pulling hard last 2 starts: should stay 1m: raced only on fibresand. *A. G. Newcombe* **–**

THE BOLTER 2 b.g. (Mar 18) Puissance 110 – Miami Dolphin 85 (Derrylin 115) [2001 5v 5m 5m 6m 5m³ 5d² 5g 6v Sep 28] unfurnished gelding: half-brother to 2m winner Happy Days (by Primitive Rising): dam won at 5f/6f as 6-y-o: fair maiden: best efforts when placed in claimer at Beverley and nursery at Haydock: should stay 6f: acts on good to soft and good to firm ground. *D. Moffatt* **67**

THE BROKER (IRE) 3 b.g. Rainbows For Life (CAN) – Roberts Pride 62 (Roberto (USA) 131) [2001 –p: f11g⁵ Apr 9] well held in 2 maidens: gelded after. *M. Blanshard* **–**

THE BULL MACABE 4 ch.c. Efisio 120 – Tranquillity 70 (Night Shift (USA)) [2001 58: e5g⁴ e5g⁴ f5g³ e5g 5v f6g⁶ f5g² f5g f5s⁴ Dec 27] fair handicapper: effective at 5f to 7f: acts on fibresand/equitrack, last only turf start in 2001: usually tongue tied: usually races prominently. *Andrew Reid* **69**

THE BUTTERWICK KID 8 ch.g. Interrex (CAN) – Ville Air 85 (Town Crier 119) [2001 73: 12s² f14g* f12g³ 12s f12g Jun 8] workmanlike gelding: fairly useful handi-capper on Flat: won at Southwell in April, despite carrying head awkwardly: effective at 1½m (given good test) and 2½m: acts on fibresand and probably any turf going: sometimes blinkered/visored: best held up: winning jumper. *R. A. Fahey* **81**

THE BYSTANDER (IRE) 3 b.f. Bin Ajwaad (IRE) 119 – Dilwara (IRE) (Lashkari 128) [2001 80p: 7d⁵ 10g 10.4m 7d⁶ Sep 4] close-coupled filly: fairly useful performer, lightly raced: good 3 lengths fifth to Lil's Jessy in Nell Gwyn Stakes at Newmarket in April: well beaten after, in listed event there, Musidora Stakes at York and minor event at Yarmouth: should stay 1¼m: acts on soft going: sometimes mulish paddock/mounted on track/early to post. *N. P. Littmoden* **90**

THE CASTIGATOR 4 b.g. Reprimand 122 – Summer Eve 63 (Hotfoot 126) [2001 –: f8.5s e10g f12g 12v 5.1v 10s 6.1v 7g 7m 7f 7.1g 10m 7m 10m⁶ 12f⁶ 12.4m 6m 8f 6m 9m 8d 9.9m 8f 6.1d 7g 11.9s 7v 8.2s Nov 5] of no account. *R. Bastiman* **–**

THE CHAPLAIN (IRE)   2 ch.c. (Mar 6) College Chapel 122 – Danzig Craft (IRE)   **71 d**
(Roi Danzig (USA)) [2001 5g³ 5g⁶ 6g⁶ 5d 5.1g⁴ 5.1f Sep 18] 4,600F: compact colt: first
foal: dam, unraced, out of half-sister to smart 5f to 7f performer Blue Siren: fair maiden:
bit disappointing after debut: likely to prove best at 5f: edgy/free-going sort: sold 3,800
gns. *R. Hannon*

THE CHOCOLATIER (IRE)   3 b.f. Inzar (USA) 112 – Clover Honey (King of   **80 +**
Clubs 124) [2001 64: 8m 8.2g⁴ 8m* 7m² 8m 8m⁴ 9g 8g⁴ 9.9d* 10d⁴ p10g p10g Dec 12]   **a74**
close-coupled filly: fairly useful handicapper on turf, fair on all-weather: won apprentice
events at Salisbury in July and October: stays 1¼m: acts on fibresand/polytrack, good to
firm and good to soft ground: tends to wander. *P. L. Gilligan*

THE COME BACK KID   4 b.g. Shareef Dancer (USA) 135 – Clockwatch (USA)   **–**
(Alleged (USA) 138) [2001 f8g 8f⁵ 8f 12g Aug 17] workmanlike gelding: modest maiden
at 2 yrs: well beaten in 2001: tongue tied final start. *B. Ellison*

THE COTTONWOOL KID   9 b.g. Blakeney 126 – Relatively Smart 76 (Great   **–**
Nephew 126) [2001 –, a37: f16.2s f16.2g⁶ Feb 22] probably of little account nowadays.
Mrs Merrita Jones

THE COUNT (FR)   2 b.g. (Apr 5) Sillery (USA) 122 – Dear Countess (FR) (Fabulous   **64**
Dancer (USA) 124) [2001 5f⁶ f7g⁴ f8s Dec 21] 180,000 francs Y: leggy gelding: second
foal: dam placed at around 1½m in France: modest maiden: best effort on debut: should
stay at least 1m. *Mrs J. R. Ramsden*

THE DARK LADY   3 b.f. Definite Article 121 – Nuthatch (IRE) 36 (Thatching 131)   **–**
[2001 –: e7g e6s e7g f8.5g f9.4s Dec 15] of no account. *M. D. I. Usher*

THE DOCTOR (IRE)   3 b.c. Dr Devious (IRE) 127 – Night Spell (IRE) 83 (Fairy   **–**
King (USA)) [2001 –: f12g Apr 17] well held in 3 maidens at 2 yrs, and handicap: sent to
Italy. *P. F. I. Cole*

THE DOLPHIN (IRE)   2 b.f. (Mar 30) Dolphin Street (FR) 125 – Saintly Guest   **–**
(What A Guest 119) [2001 7m 8.1g⁵ Aug 27] 10,000Y: half-sister to several winners,
including 11-y-o Benzoe and fairly useful 5f to 7f winner Shalstayholy (by Shalford):
dam lightly raced in France: little form in maidens. *J. G. Portman*

THEEQAR   2 ch.f. (May 6) Greensmith 121 – Shereen (Deploy 131) [2001 f5g f8g   **–**
Dec 10] first foal: dam unraced: well beaten in maidens at Southwell. *K. A. Ryan*

THE FAIRY FLAG (IRE)   3 ch.f. Inchinor 119 – Good Reference (IRE) 84   **60**
(Reference Point 139) [2001 51: 10s 8f* 8m⁵ 8.3d⁵ 9m⁴ 9.2m 11.1d⁵ 9.9g³ 12.1s 10m   **a49**
11.1g² 10m² 10.1g f11g³ 10.9v* 10s³ f12f Dec 5] angular filly: modest on turf, poor on
all-weather: won claimers at Leicester in May and, having left R. Beckett after third start,
Ayr (subsequently left J. Hetherton) in October: stays 11f: acts on any turf going and
fibresand: seemed not to handle course at Epsom: won twice over hurdles in November.
A. Bailey

THE FANCY MAN (IRE)   3 ch.g. Definite Article 121 – Fanciful (IRE) (Mujtahid   **–**
(USA) 118) [2001 61: 10.1f 12g 8.5s 10.4s 10.9v Oct 15] lengthy gelding: modest winner
at 2 yrs: no show in 2001: tried blinkered/visored/tongue tied. *N. Tinkler*

THE FLYER (IRE)   4 b.g. Blues Traveller (IRE) 119 – National Ballet (Shareef   **–**
Dancer (USA) 135) [2001 67: 10.3d Sep 26] leggy, unfurnished gelding: fair maiden at 3
yrs: well held only start on Flat in 2001: blinkered once: won over hurdles in December.
Miss S. J. Wilton

THE FRISKY FARMER   8 b.g. Emarati (USA) 74 – Farceuse (Comedy Star (USA)   **–**
121) [2001 f12g⁶ Jan 26] probably of little account nowadays. *Ian Williams*

THE GAIKWAR (IRE)   2 b.c. (Feb 22) Indian Ridge 123 – Broadmara (IRE) 91   **– p**
(Thatching 131) [2001 7d Nov 3] 56,000Y: lengthy colt: has scope: third foal: half-
brother to 5-y-o Grub Street: dam, Irish 2-y-o 1m winner, out of half-sister to top-class 6f/
7f performer Salieri: 33/1, well held in 27-runner maiden at Newmarket: type to do better.
Mrs A. J. Perrett

THE GAY FOX   7 gr.g. Never So Bold 135 – School Concert 80 (Music Boy 124)   **65 §**
[2001 82: f6g f7g⁶ f6g³ 6v f6g³ e7g 6s 5.1m 6g 7f⁶ 6m² f6g³ 5.7f⁵ 6f f6g⁵ 6f 7.1m 5.7g
5.2v 7d³ f7g⁶ f6g f6g³ p7g² p7g f6s² Dec 26] good-topped gelding: unimpressive mover:
fair performer: left M. Quinn 4,000 gns after eighteenth start: seems best at 6f/easy 7f:
acts on any turf going, fibresand and polytrack: often blinkered/visored/tongue tied: often
slowly away: tends to race lazily: unreliable. *B. G. Powell*

THE GENERALS LADY (IRE)   3 gr.f. General Monash (USA) 107 – Brooks   –
Masquerade (Absalom 128) [2001 –: 6.1d 5m Aug 25] rather sparely-made filly:
unimpressive mover: well held in 4 maidens. *B. S. Rothwell*

THE GIRLS' FILLY   4 b.f. Emperor Jones (USA) 119 – Sioux City (Simply Great   –
(FR) 122) [2001 –, a56: e10g e13g e13g Feb 3] strong filly: modest maiden at 3 yrs: well
held in 2001: tried blinkered/tongue tied. *Miss B. Sanders*

THE GLEN   3 gr.g. Mtoto 134 – Silver Singer 65 (Pharly (FR) 130) [2001 82p: 10d   **91**
10.3f⁵ 10.4g² 10.3f² 10d* 12m 11m² 10.3d⁶ Aug 31] leggy gelding: unimpressive mover:
fairly useful performer: simple task (25/1-on) when winning 4-runner maiden at Ayr in
July: clearly best efforts when 3½ lengths fifth to Dr Greenfield in listed race at Chester
(seemed bit flattered) and 5 lengths second to Shamaiel in handicap at Newbury: should
be suited by 1½m+: acts on firm going, seemingly on good to soft: has been bandaged
near-hind. *B. W. Hills*

THE GOOCH (IRE)   2 br.c. (Feb 5) Idris (IRE) 118 – Malpractice (IRE) (Maledetto   –
(IRE) 103) [2001 7.2v Oct 15] IR 2,000Y: first foal: dam unraced: 100/1, tailed off in
maiden at Ayr. *Miss Lucinda V. Russell*

THE GREEN GREY   7 gr.g. Environment Friend 128 – Pea Green 98 (Try My Best   **74**
(USA) 130) [2001 81, a96: e12g⁶ e12g⁴ e12g³ e10s⁶ e12g 10s 12s 10m 9d 12m 12g²   **a92**
14.4g⁴ 12g 12g Sep 28] big, workmanlike gelding: good mover: fairly useful handicapper
on all-weather, fair on turf: stays 1¾m: acts on equitrack, goes well on good ground or
firmer on turf: visored once at 3 yrs: has been slowly away: generally held up nowadays:
game. *L. Montague Hall*

THE HUNTER (IRE)   2 b.c. (Feb 20) Grand Lodge (USA) 125 – Ring Side (IRE)   **61 p**
(Alzao (USA) 117) [2001 7f Sep 22] 33,000Y: lengthy colt: third foal: dam unraced: 33/1
and backward, ninth of 18 to Al Mohallab in maiden at Newbury, some late headway after
racing freely: moved poorly to post: should do better. *G. C. Bravery*

THE IMPOSTER (IRE)   6 ch.g. Imp Society (USA) – Phoenix Dancer (IRE)   –
(Gorytus (USA) 132) [2001 43, a68: f8g Jun 21] fair performer at 5 yrs: well held only
start in 2001: visored once. *Miss S. J. Wilton*

THE JUDGE   3 b.g. Polish Precedent (USA) 131 – Just Speculation (IRE) 86   **94 p**
(Ahonoora 122) [2001 –p: 7g³ 9.2m* 8.9d³ Oct 13] useful-looking gelding: reportedly
broke his pelvis only 2-y-o start: progressive form: won maiden at Hamilton in
September: shaped like best horse in race when 2¼ lengths third of 27 to Riverina in
handicap at York final start (subsequently gelded): should prove at least as effective at 1m
as 9f: acts on good to firm and good to soft ground: should improve further, and type to
win a good handicap or 2. *P. F. I. Cole*

THE KNAPP   2 b.f. (Mar 24) Zamindar (USA) 116 – Fernlea (USA) (Sir Ivor 135)   –
[2001 5f 5m Jun 4] fifth foal: half-sister to 3-y-o Buddleia and 5-y-o Hopeful Henry:
dam, lightly-raced Irish sprint maiden, second in listed race: tailed off in claimer and
maiden, pulled up lame in latter. *C. Smith*

THE LADY WOULD (IRE)   2 ch.f. (Apr 4) Woodborough (USA) 112 – Kealbra   **38**
Lady (Petong 126) [2001 5.7f 6m 5.7f 5.1g⁶ Aug 7] IR 1,400Y, resold IR 5,000Y: second
foal: half-sister to 3-y-o Vendome: dam, of little account, half-sister to smart 6f/7f
performer Prince Ferdinand: poor maiden: stays 6f. *M. Quinn*

THE LAST CAST   2 ch.g. (Mar 2) Prince of Birds (USA) 121 – Atan's Gem (USA)   **83**
(Sharpen Up 127) [2001 7s⁵ 6v² p8g Nov 28] close-coupled gelding: fourth living foal:
half-brother to an Italian 9.5f to 10.5f winner by Night Shift: dam no form: best effort in
maidens when 1½ lengths second to Dilys at Windsor: gelded after final start: should stay
at least 1m. *C. R. Egerton*

THE LAST MOHICAN   2 b.g. (Apr 26) Common Grounds 118 – Arndilly 75   **59 ?**
(Robellino (USA) 127) [2001 8m 7s Oct 16] 9,000F: small, workmanlike gelding: bad
mover: second foal: half-brother to a winner in Japan by Fairy King: dam 6f (including at
2 yrs) to 1m winner: better effort in maidens (seemingly modest form) when seventh of
10 to Jack The Track at Kempton on debut. *P. Howling*

THE LAST WORD   5 b.g. Cosmonaut – Jolizal 52 (Good Times (ITY)) [2001 –, a49:   **40**
f9.4s⁵ f11s f12s² f12g f11g² f14g f14g³ f12g⁶ 11.7f² f12g Sep 8] compact gelding: poor   **a45**
performer: pulled up lame final start: stays 1¾m: acts on fibresand and firm going.
R. Hollinshead

THE LEATHER WEDGE (IRE) 2 b.c. (Feb 13) Hamas (IRE) 125§ – Wallflower **80**
(Polar Falcon (USA) 126) [2001 5d² 5m² 5m² 5f* 5.1m³ 5m 5g 5.1m Sep 10] 8,500Y:
tall, quite good-topped colt: first foal: dam once-raced half-sister to dam of very smart
sprinter Pivotal: fairly useful performer: made all in maiden at Musselburgh in July: good
third of 5 in minor event at Chester: well beaten last 3 starts: likely to prove best at 5f: acts
on firm and good to soft ground. *A. Berry*

THE LINKS 2 b.g. (Mar 4) Mind Games 121 – Zihuatanejo (Efisio 120) [2001 6m 6g **46**
6d 6.1g 6m 7.1s f6g f8g Oct 18] 18,000Y: leggy, unfurnished gelding: first foal: dam
unraced out of smart winner up to 1m Rare Roberta: poor maiden: below form after fourth
start: left T. Easterby after sixth one: may prove best at 5f/6f: acts on good to firm and
good to soft ground: tried blinkered/tongue tied. *D. W. Chapman*

THE LOOSE SCREW (IRE) 3 b.g. Bigstone (IRE) 126 – Princess of Dance (IRE) **52**
(Dancing Dissident (USA) 119) [2001 –: 5g 5s 5g⁶ 6d³ 6v Oct 16] good-bodied gelding:
modest maiden handicapper: effective at 5f/6f: acts on heavy ground. *J. L. Eyre*

THE MANX TOUCH (IRE) 5 gr.m. Petardia 113 – Chapter And Verse (Dancer's **–**
Image (USA)) [2001 f11g⁴ Feb 2] leggy mare: fair winning handicapper in 1999: well
below best in seller at Southwell in February: stays 11f: acts on soft going and fibresand.
R. Ford

THE MERRY WIDOW (IRE) 3 ch.f. Brief Truce (USA) 126 – Classic Opera **42**
(Lomond (USA) 128) [2001 44: f7g³ f7g* f8g f8g f7g 6d 8.2g 7m 6m⁴ f7g 7.5m Aug 26]
sparely-made filly: poor performer: won seller at Southwell in January: stays 7.5f: acts on
fibresand and good to firm going: usually visored: tried tongue tied: sometimes slowly
away and seems no easy ride. *B. S. Rothwell*

THEME TIME (USA) 5 b.g. Stop The Music (USA) – Ranales (USA) (Majestic Light **39**
(USA)) [2001 10g 8.2f f8g³ 8g Jul 20] poor maiden handicapper: form only when third at
Southwell: stays 1m: acts on fibresand: tongue tied early in career. *H. J. Collingridge*

THE MOG 2 b.g. (Apr 28) Atraf 116 – Safe Secret 50 (Seclude (USA)) [2001 5g 5.7f **48**
5f⁶ 7g 7g f6g f8.5g f5f f7g⁵ f7s* Dec 18] 4,000Y: close-coupled gelding: second foal: **a58**
half-brother to a 5f/6f winner (including at 2 yrs) in Italy by General Monash: dam,
maiden on Flat who seemed to stay 1½m: winning hurdler: modest on all-weather, poor
on turf: left M. Channon 1,100 gns after fifth start: won seller at Wolverhampton: should
stay 1m: acts on fibresand and firm going: blinkered last 5 outings: tongue tied last 3.
S. R. Bowring

THE NAMES BOND 3 b.g. Tragic Role (USA) – Artistic Licence (High Top 131) **58**
[2001 71d: 7v 10s⁵ 12m⁶ 12m³ 11.6m⁵ 10m⁴ Jul 14] tall, leggy gelding: modest handicapper: stays 1½m, at least when conditions aren't testing: acts on firm and good to soft
ground. *Andrew Turnell*

THE NOBLEMAN (USA) 5 b.g. Quiet American (USA) – Furajet (USA) 101 (The **22**
Minstrel (CAN) 135) [2001 32: f16g⁴ f11s f8g Feb 23] strong, lengthy gelding: bad
maiden handicapper: seems to stay 2m: acts on fibresand: tried blinkered/tongue tied.
T. J. Etherington

THE OLD SOLDIER 3 b.g. Magic Ring (IRE) 115 – Grecian Belle 53 (Ilium 121) **54**
[2001 50: 7m 8m 6m⁴ 5m³ Sep 8] tall gelding: modest maiden: should stay 7f: acts on
good to firm going. *A. Dickman*

THE O'MALLEY 4 b.f. Risk Me (FR) 127 – Farrh Nouriya (IRE) (Lomond (USA) **–**
128) [2001 –: f8.5g Nov 17] well held in seller/maiden on fibresand. *M. Mullineaux*

THE PRESIDENT 6 b.g. Yaheeb (USA) 95§ – When The Saints (Bay Express 132) **47**
[2001 11s 13d³ 16m³ 13m 16m⁶ 15.8g³ Aug 17] tall, lengthy gelding: poor maiden
handicapper: stays 2m: acts on firm and soft going: has worn tongue tie: sometimes
slowly away: reared and unseated leaving stall once. *Mrs M. Reveley*

THE PRIEST 4 b.g. College Chapel 122 – Pharazini 72§ (Pharly (FR) 130) [2001 –: **42**
f6g f6s f7g⁶ e6g⁵ f5g⁴ Apr 27] poor maiden: probably stays 7f: acts on fibresand.
J. A. Osborne

THE PRINCE 7 b.g. Machiavellian (USA) 123 – Mohican Girl 112 (Dancing Brave **99**
(USA) 140) [2001 98: f8.5g⁴ f8.5g³ e10g Mar 17] well-made gelding: has a quick action:
useful performer: creditable third to Invader in valuable handicap at Wolverhampton in
March (had won same race previous year): well held final outing: best around 1m: acts on
good to soft going and fibresand, probably on firm: tried visored/blinkered: tongue tied:
sometimes slowly away: needs exaggerated waiting tactics. *Ian Williams*

THE PROSECUTOR 4 b.c. Contract Law (USA) 108 – Elsocko 76 (Swing Easy **–**
(USA) 126) [2001 67, a77: f6g f6s⁵ 7.1g May 7] modest handicapper in 2001: stays 7f: **a62**
acts on fibresand and good to soft ground. *B. A. McMahon*

THERESA GREEN (IRE) 3 b.f. Charnwood Forest (IRE) 125 – In Your Dreams **63**
(IRE) (Suave Dancer (USA) 136) [2001 65: 6m 7m⁵ 6m⁶ Jun 27] compact filly: modest
handicapper: stays 7f: acts on good to firm going, possibly not on softer than good.
Mrs P. N. Dutfield

THERE WITH ME (USA) 4 b.f. Distant View (USA) 126 – Breeze Lass (USA) **–**
(It's Freezing (USA) 122) [2001 63: f7g³ e8g f8.5g⁵ f6g* f6g⁵ Feb 19] poor performer in **a49**
2001: won maiden at Wolverhampton in February: probably stays 1m: acts on fibresand,
raced only on soft going on turf: blinkered last 2 starts. *G. G. Margarson*

THERHEA (IRE) 8 b.g. Pennine Walk 120 – Arab Art (Artaius (USA) 129) [2001 **–**
p7g Dec 19] close-coupled, good-bodied gelding: useful handicapper at 6 yrs: last in
claimer only outing since: twice blinkered. *B. R. Millman*

THE ROBSTER (USA) 4 ch.g. Woodman (USA) 126 – Country Cruise (USA) **–**
(Riverman (USA) 131) [2001 61: f7g⁶ f7g May 14] compact gelding: modest maiden at 3
yrs: little form in 2001: sometimes blinkered. *B. J. Meehan*

THEROSEOFLOUGHREA (IRE) 4 b.f. Lake Coniston (IRE) 131 – Fabulous **–**
Pet (Somethingfabulous (USA)) [2001 58: 9s 7m May 30] half-sister to several winners,
notably 6-y-o Murghem: dam, Irish 1½m winner, half-sister to smart sprinter Orojoya:
modest maiden at best: left J. Hayden in Ireland before soundly beaten in handicaps in
2001: stays 1¼m. *N. Tinkler*

THE ROXBURGH (USA) 4 b. or br.c. Known Fact (USA) 135 – Musical Precedent **62**
(USA) (Seattle Song (USA) 130) [2001 69: 5g⁶ 5g⁴ 6f⁵ 6.5m Dec 22] modest maiden,
lightly raced: sold from J. Toller 3,000 gns before final start: stays 6f. *E. Allegri, Italy*

THESAURUS 2 gr.g. (Feb 5) Most Welcome 131 – Red Embers 64 (Saddlers' Hall **71**
(IRE) 126) [2001 5.2m 6.1m 7m⁶ 7.9s⁵ 6d 8.3v Nov 8] tall gelding: first foal: dam 2-y-o
6f winner who should have stayed beyond 8.5f: fair maiden: best effort in sales race at
Newmarket penultimate start: should stay 1m: acts on good to soft going. *I. A. Wood*

THE SCAFFOLDER 3 b.g. Tachyon Park 87 – Fallal (IRE) 47 (Fayruz 116) [2001 **66 §**
77: f7g⁵ f6g² f6g⁴ f6g² f5g⁴ f5g 5.1s² 5.1f⁴ 6m⁵ 5m⁶ 7d f6g² 6m³ f6g³ f6g² 5.1g 6.1m f6g
f7g³ f6g³ f6g f6s³ f6s⁶ Dec 21] workmanlike gelding: modest maiden: effective at 5f to
7f: acts on fibresand, firm and soft going: tried visored: often slowly away/finds little:
untrustworthy. *Mrs N. Macauley*

THESIS (IRE) 3 ch.c. Definite Article 121 – Chouette 54 (Try My Best (USA) 130) **92 +**
[2001 8m2 8f* 10m2 10.3m³ 8d⁵ Oct 18] 36,000Y: good-topped colt: fourth foal:
half-brother to French 1997 2-y-o 6.5f winner Territory (by Common Grounds): dam
maiden from family of Sayyedati: progressed into fairly useful performer: won maiden at
Leicester in May: ran well after, not clear run when fifth of 30 to Just Nick in handicap at
Newmarket final outing: effective at 1m/1¼m: yet to race on soft/heavy going, acts on
any other. *J. A. Osborne*

THE STUDENT PRINCE 3 b.c. Piccolo 121 – Affaire de Coeur 55 (Imperial Fling **65**
(USA) 116) [2001 8m 10d 8.3m 8.5d 10m 8f³ Aug 14] third reported living foal: dam, 1m
winner, also successful over hurdles: fair maiden: best effort in handicap final start,
despite wandering markedly late on: stays 1m: acts on firm going. *S. Dow*

THE TATLING (IRE) 4 b.g. Perugino (USA) 84 – Aunty Eileen (Ahonoora 122) **103**
[2001 101: 5.2d 6g² 6m Sep 22] lengthy, quite attractive gelding: useful performer: left
M. Bell and off 6 months after first start: good effort in face of stiff task in mid-division in
Ayr Gold Cup final outing: best at 5f/easy 6f: acts on good to firm and good to soft going
(has won on soft): races freely. *D. Nicholls*

THE THIEF 3 b.g. Robellino (USA) 127 – Lady Bankes (IRE) 69 (Alzao (USA) 117) **59**
[2001 7f² f7g Nov 12] 18,000F, 2,800Y: small gelding: first foal: dam, 1¼m winner,
half-sister to smart filly up to 9f in Britain and USA Circle of Gold: modest form when
second in maiden at Ayr on debut: broke down and pulled up 5 months later: dead.
D. W. Barker

THE THIRD CURATE (IRE) 6 b.g. Fairy King (USA) – Lassalia (Sallust 134) **–**
[2001 55: f7g Feb 6] rangy gelding: modest handicapper at 5 yrs, twice landing gamble:
well held only Flat run of 2001: has won in blinkers. *B. J. Curley*

Motability And RAC Rated Stakes (Handicap), York—a smart performance by The Whistling Teal, who has four lengths to spare over Lagudin; Albuhera (rail) is third

THE TRADER (IRE) 3 ch.g. Selkirk (USA) 129 – Snowing 88 (Tate Gallery (USA) **115** 117) [2001 99: 5.1s² 6s⁴ 6s 6m 5g⁶ 7g 5.2f* 5g 5g³ 5m* 5d⁶ 5.2f* 5g³ 5m⁵ Dec 16] sturdy, close-coupled gelding: poor mover: smart performer: better than ever in blinkers last 8 starts, winning handicap at Newbury, minor event at Leicester and listed race at Newbury (beat Eastern Purple ¾ length) in August/September: good efforts last 2 starts when length third to Indian Prince in listed race at Newmarket and 1½ lengths fifth to Falvelon in Hong Kong Sprint at Sha Tin: best at 5f: has form on soft going, very best efforts on good or firmer: very speedy, though usually tracks pace: formerly none too genuine. *M. Blanshard*

THE TUBE (IRE) 3 b.f. Royal Abjar (USA) 121 – Grandeur And Grace (USA) 75 **–** (Septieme Ciel (USA) 123) [2001 –: f9.4s⁵ f7s⁶ 8.2s f7g³ 11.6g⁵ f8g 7.6m 10f⁴ 8g 11.6v f7g Oct 20] signs of ability but little solid form: sold 1,200 gns. *Andrew Reid*

THE WALL 3 b.f. Mistertopogigo (IRE) 118 – Lady Pennington 51 (Blue Cashmere **44** 129) [2001 –: e6g e6g⁵ e5g 8g 7.6m 10f⁶ 5.1f 5.7g⁶ 6m⁶ 5.1g⁴ 5f 5g 5.7m Sep 10] lengthy, workmanlike filly: poor maiden: form only at 5f/6f: acted on firm going, probably on equitrack: dead. *J. A. Gilbert*

THE WALRUS (IRE) 4 b.g. Sri Pekan (USA) 117 – Cathy Garcia (IRE) (Be My **–** Guest (USA) 126) [2001 55, a47: f12g Feb 8] modest maiden at 3 yrs: successful 3 times over hurdles prior to well held only Flat run of 2001. *J. Neville*

THEWHIRLINGDERVISH (IRE) 3 ch.g. Definite Article 121 – Nomadic **80** Dancer (IRE) 52 (Nabeel Dancer (USA) 120) [2001 68: 8m⁴ 10.1m⁶ 12f² 11m² 14f² Jul 5] leggy, lengthy gelding: fair maiden: best effort in handicap final start: stays 1¾m: possibly best on good going or firmer: found little penultimate start. *T. D. Easterby*

THE WHISTLING TEAL 5 b.g. Rudimentary (USA) 118 – Lonely Shore **118** (Blakeney 126) [2001 89: 8s* 8d⁵ 10.3f² 10m* 10f⁵ 10.4g* Aug 22] strong gelding: smart handicapper: much improved performer for new stable in 2001, winning at Pontefract in April, Stanley Racing Zetland Gold Cup (Handicap) at Redcar (beat Pantar by 1¾ lengths) in May and quite valuable event at York (stormed through to beat Lagudin by 4 lengths) in August: unlucky penultimate start: effective at 1m to 10.4f: acts on soft going, firm and fibresand: held up: capable of winning races in better company. *G. Wragg*

THE WIFE 4 b.f. Efisio 120 – Great Steps 88 (Vaigly Great 127) [2001 83: 8g 8.5m **77** 8.1m 8.5m³ 8g² 8m 7.9m 10m⁵ 8g 8m² 8.5g⁴ 7.5d* f7g 7s Oct 20] rather leggy filly: fair handicapper: made all at Beverley in September: poor efforts after (said to have finished distressed penultimate start): effective at 7.5f to 9f: acts on firm and good to soft going: tongue tied last 5 starts: has sweated/got on edge: sold 2,800 gns, sent to Italy. *T. D. Easterby*

THEYAB (USA) 3 b. or br.g. Bahri (USA) 125 – Dish Dash 118 (Bustino 136) [2001 **63** 8d⁶ Apr 21] lightly-made gelding: closely related to useful 1986 2-y-o 7f winner who stayed 1¼m Arrasas (by Irish River) and half-brother to several winners, notably high-class miler Maroof (by Danzig): dam, won Ribblesdale Stakes, grandam of Desert King: 13/2, 6½ lengths sixth in Newbury maiden, only outing, weakening having dictated pace: subsequently gelded: sold 12,000 gns in July. *N. A. Graham*

1024

THIEVING   3 b.g. Common Grounds 118 – Ethical (USA) (Mt Livermore (USA))   –
[2001 e6g f7g Feb 16] 6,000Y: first foal: dam unraced daughter of smart sprinting 2-y-o
Abeer: tailed off in sellers. *J. A. Osborne*

THIHN (IRE)   6 ch.g. Machiavellian (USA) 123 – Hasana (USA) (Private Account   **97**
(USA)) [2001 73: 10v⁶ 9v² 8d* 8.5s* 8.5m² 8.3g³ 8.5m² 8.3m* 8.1g² 8m³ 8g 8.1g⁶ 9m⁴
8s⁵ 9g⁵ 8d² 8d² Nov 3] leggy gelding: useful performer: won handicap at Musselburgh
and minor events at Epsom and Windsor between April and June: ran well in handicaps
after, fifth in Cambridgeshire fifteenth start and excellent second (again at Newmarket)
last 2 starts: has form at 1¼m, very best efforts around 1m: acts on any going: used to
carry head awkwardly: sometimes hangs right: free-going sort, and usually travels very
strongly: effective held up or racing prominently: splendidly tough and consistent.
J. L. Spearing

THIN CLIENT (USA)   2 ch.c. (May 19) Atticus (USA) 121 – Aliata (USA) 89 (Mr   **94**
Prospector (USA)) [2001 6g³ 6g³ 7m² 7m* Aug 23] $27,000Y: ninth foal: half-brother to
3 winners, including US 6f winner Storm Boot (by Storm Cat): dam, 2-y-o 5f/6f winner,
from very good family: fairly useful performer: placed in maidens before winning
nursery at York: stays 7f: raced only on good/good to firm going: sent to USA. *P. F. I. Cole*

THIRN   2 b.g. (Mar 4) Piccolo 121 – Midnight Owl (FR) (Ardross 134) [2001 6d⁵ 7g   **64**
6m⁵ Sep 20] 20,000Y: strong, useful-looking gelding: sixth foal: brother to 3-y-o Floot
and half-brother to 5-y-o Feathertime and Irish 1½m winner Regency Rake (by Ti King):
dam lightly-raced half-sister to smart French middle-distance performer Kathmandu:
modest form in maidens: fifth at York and Ayr (ran in snatches): should stay 7f.
J. D. Bethell

THOLJANAH (IRE)   2 b.c. (May 7) Darshaan 133 – Alkaffeyeh (IRE) (Sadler's   **109 p**
Wells (USA) 132) [2001 7m* 7.1g² 8s² Sep 29]
     The unraced Alkaffeyeh has quickly made her mark at stud. Her first five
foals are all winners, and four of them are well-above-average performers. Kharir
(by Machiavellian), successful in a Yarmouth maiden at two years, has done well
over five and six furlongs in Dubai since; his full brother Mudaa-Eb, now also
racing in Dubai, won over almost nine furlongs there in the latest season, having
been successful at up to a mile and a half in Ireland in 1999; Ta-Lim (by Ela-Mana-
Mou) showed smart form after winning the 1998 March Stakes, including when
fifth in the St Leger and the Doncaster Cup; and Tholjanah got off the mark at the
first time of asking in a maiden at Kempton in July. Tholjanah promises to be the
best of the lot. A late foal who has been brought along steadily, he showed marked
improvement on his debut victory in a maiden at Kempton when second in pattern
races on his two subsequent starts, and is going to continue on the upgrade for some
time to come. On his second appearance, in the Solario Stakes at Sandown,
Tholjanah turned for home last of the ten runners after being one of several who
failed to handle the first bend at all well, and stayed on in very good style to overhaul all but the four-length winner Redback, who made most. The combination of a
longer trip and much more testing ground showed Tholjanah to even better
advantage in the Royal Lodge Stakes at Ascot, where, attended by two handlers, he
became increasingly on edge in the paddock. Sensibly kept in closer touch this

*Ian Wight Happy 50th Birthday Maiden Stakes (Div II), Kempton—a clear-cut debut success for Tholjanah
over (from right to left) Jumeirah Dream, Red Halo and You're An Angel*

time, Tholjanah was tapped for speed two furlongs out then rallied to finish a length and a half behind Mutinyonthebounty.

Tholjanah (IRE) (b.c. May 7, 1999)	Darshaan (br 1981)	Shirley Heights (b 1975)	Mill Reef
			Hardiemma
		Delsy (br 1972)	Abdos
			Kelty
	Alkaffeyeh (IRE) (b 1989)	Sadler's Wells (b 1981)	Northern Dancer
			Fairy Bridge
		Le Melody (ch 1971)	Levmoss
			Arctic Melody

Tholjanah, by the Prix du Jockey Club winner Darshaan, has a pedigree chock-full of stamina. Alkaffeyeh, a sister to the smart mile-and-a-half performer Larrocha, is a half-sister to several other winners, notably the top-class Ardross. Their dam Le Melody, by another Gold Cup winner in Levmoss, was a useful filly who won both her starts, over seven furlongs and a mile and a quarter. The next dam, the Musidora Stakes winner Arctic Melody, also produced the Irish One Thousand Guineas winner Arctique Royale and the Irish Oaks third Racquette. The leggy, angular Tholjanah will come very much into his own when given the opportunity to tackle distances of a mile and a half and more in the next season, and looks just the sort at this stage to develop into a leading contender for the St Leger, or possibly even the Derby before that. *M. P. Tregoning*

THOMAS HENRY (IRE) 5 br.g. Petardia 113 – Hitopah (Bustino 136) [2001 57, a48: f12g e13g e13s⁴ e16g Mar 7] leggy gelding: bad performer: stays 11.5f: acts on equitrack: tried visored. *J. S. Moore*   **– a27**

THORALBY 2 b.g. (Mar 29) Son Pardo 107 – Polish Lady (IRE) 43 (Posen (USA)) [2001 8g 7d f7g Nov 26] lengthy gelding: second foal: dam maiden half-sister to useful but untrustworthy Irish 1¼m/1½m winner Try For Ever: no form, including in seller. *C. W. Fairhurst*   **–**

THORNABY GIRL (IRE) 5 b.m. Fayruz 116 – Anita's Love (IRE) 53 (Anita's Prince 126) [2001 6g f5g Dec 14] fair 5f performer at best: well held both outings since 1999. *Mrs L. B. Normile*   **–**

THORNTOUN CONNECT 2 b.f. (Mar 19) Danzig Connection (USA) – Furry Friend (USA) (Bold Bidder) [2001 5s 5d 6m⁴ 5m³ 5m⁵ 6m³ 7d⁶ 6d 7d 8g 6v Oct 15] sturdy filly: half-sister to 3 winners, including 1990 2-y-o 6f winner Russian Mink (by L'Emigrant) and 1¼m (including at 2 yrs) winner who probably stayed 15f Thorntoun Estate (by Durgam): dam lightly-raced maiden: poor maiden: should stay 7f: acts on good to firm ground. *J. S. Goldie*   **43**

THORNTOUN DANCER 3 b.f. Unfuwain (USA) 131 – Westry (Gone West (USA)) [2001 64: 10.3s 8v 10s 8.3m⁵ 8m 10.9m³ 11.1m² 12f³ 16f 12.1d⁴ 15s 8d 9.2d 9m Aug 23] sparely-made filly: modest maiden: well held final 4 starts: seems best around 1½m: acts on any going: blinkered/visored 4 of last 5 outings. *J. S. Goldie*   **52 d**

THORNTOUN DIVA 3 ch.f. Wolfhound (USA) 126 – Al Guswa 98 (Shernazar 131) [2001 59: 7v 8.2s 6d³ 5m⁴ 6m 6m³ 6m³ 7.1m 5g 6f 7d⁵ 7s⁵ 7g 7d⁶ 8.1d⁵ 8g 10.9m 5v 6v Oct 16] lengthy, unfurnished filly: modest maiden: mostly well held in second half of season: best up to 7f: acts on heavy and good to firm going: effective visored/blinkered or not: has raced freely: has worn tongue strap/crossed noseband. *J. S. Goldie*   **58 d**

THORNTOUN GOLD (IRE) 5 ch.m. Lycius (USA) 124 – Gold Braisim (IRE) 77 (Jareer (USA) 115) [2001 53: 10f⁶ f7g 8m² 10f² 8m⁶ 10g³ 10.2f⁴ 8.1s⁵ 10m 9.7d f9.4s⁵ Dec 27] workmanlike mare: modest handicapper: effective at 1m to 11f: acts on firm and good to soft going (off nearly 4 months before below form on fibresand final start): tried blinkered in 2000. *I. A. Wood*   **55**

THORPENESS (IRE) 2 b.c. (Jan 5) Barathea (IRE) 127 – Brisighella (IRE) (Al Hareb (USA) 123) [2001 7d 8s 8s Oct 31] strong colt: third foal: half-brother to 3-y-o Grove Dancer: dam Italian 5f (at 2 yrs) to 1m winner: only a little sign of ability in maidens. *C. F. Wall*   **–**

THRASHER 2 b.f. (Apr 23) Hector Protector (USA) 124 – Thracian 92 (Green Desert (USA) 127) [2001 7m² 8m⁵ 8.2v⁵ 7s* Oct 25] second foal: dam, 2-y-o 6f/7f winner, half-sister to very smart performers up to 1½m Maysoon, Richard of York and Three   **80**

Tails: fairly useful performer: evens, made all in maiden at Brighton, beating Hoh's Back by ¾ length: stays 1m: acts on soft and good to firm ground. *J. H. M. Gosden*

THREAT 5 br.g. Zafonic (USA) 130 – Prophecy (IRE) 109 (Warning 136) [2001 92: **75** 6v 6m 5m 6m 5f 5m³ 5g⁵ 6m⁴ 7d⁶ 6g 5s³ 5m 5.2d³ 5.3m⁵ 5.1g⁴ 5s 5d 5.2v Oct 26] well-made gelding: has been freeze-fired: fair handicapper: best at 5f/6f: acts on soft going, good to firm and fibresand: tried blinkered/visored: usually tongue tied: has been bandaged in front/worn crossed noseband: sometimes slowly away: bolted before sixteenth start: sold 3,500 gns. *S. C. Williams*

THREE ANGELS (IRE) 6 b.g. Houmayoun (FR) 114 – Mullaghroe (Tarboosh **69** (USA)) [2001 78: 7.1m 7f* 7m³ 7m² 8g⁵ 7g³ Sep 5] robust gelding: fair performer: won claimer at Lingfield (left M. Tompkins) in June: stays 1m: acts on firm going, probably on good to soft: effective visored or not, blinkered last 5 starts. *A. W. Carroll*

THREE BLACK DALES (IRE) 2 b.f. (Apr 13) Alhaarth (IRE) 126 – Annsfield **49** Lady (Red Sunset 120) [2001 6m 6g⁶ 7g⁶ f8.5s⁶ Sep 6] 7,500Y: leggy, lengthy filly: half-sister to several winners, including smart 6f to 1m winner (including at 2 yrs) Pipe Major (by Tirol), 8-y-o Give Me A Ring and useful 1997 2-y-o 5f winner Refined (by Statoblest): dam Irish 1¼m performer: poor maiden: stays 8.5f: acts on fibresand, best turf efforts on good going. *M. Johnston*

THREE CHERRIES 5 ch.m. Formidable (USA) 125 – Mistral's Dancer (Shareef **42** Dancer (USA) 135) [2001 42: f8g f11g f16g 10m⁴ 12m² 12f⁶ 12f 12.4g⁴ 12.4d⁴ 14.1m⁵ **a–** 16.2s 12m Aug 22] lengthy mare: poor maiden: stays 1½m: acts on firm and good to soft going: edgy sort: has refused to race over hurdles. *R. E. Barr*

THREE CLOUDS 4 b.g. Rainbow Quest (USA) 134 – Three Tails 121 (Blakeney **58** 126) [2001 91: 7m 8s 10v 11.9s p16g* p13g Dec 29] half-brother to several winners, including high-class 1¼m/1½m performer Tamure (by Sadler's Wells) and smart but unreliable stayer Three Cheers (by Slip Anchor): dam, untrustworthy winner up to 1½m, from very good family: fairly useful form in minor events at Gowran for J. Oxx in Ireland in 2000: first form in Britain last 2 starts, making all in amateur handicap at Lingfield in December: stays 2m: acts on polytrack: blinkered fourth outing: has raced freely. *G. L. Moore*

THREE DAYS IN MAY 2 b.f. (Mar 28) Cadeaux Genereux 131 – Corn Futures 78 **– p** (Nomination 125) [2001 5s Oct 5] 30,000Y: sixth foal: half-sister to useful 1997 2-y-o 6f winner Crazee Mental (by Magic Ring) and 6f (at 2 yrs)/7f winner Trading Aces (by Be My Chief): dam 2-y-o 6f winner out of half-sister to dam of Wassl: 9/1 and green, in rear throughout in maiden at Lingfield: should do better. *W. J. Haggas*

THREE EAGLES (USA) 4 ch.g. Eagle Eyed (USA) 111 – Tertiary (USA) (Vaguely **52** Noble 140) [2001 f8.5g 12v 10.1d 16.2m* 17.1f⁵ 17.2g 14f 16.2f 10g Aug 11] angular gelding: closely related to 2 winners, including smart performer up to 8.5f Tertian (by Danzig), and half-brother to several winners, including very smart 1m/1¼m performer Kefaah (by Blushing Groom): dam, second at 10.5f in France, sister to high-class filly Nobiliary and half-sister to Lyphard: trained by M. Zilber in France on debut in 2000: modest handicapper: won at Warwick in May: well held after next start: stays 17f: acts on firm ground: blinkered last 6 starts: usually races freely. *A. Bailey*

THREE LEADERS (IRE) 5 ch.g. Up And At 'em 109 – Wolviston (Wolverlife 115) **–** [2001 46: 8m 9f 8m 10.1m 16f Jul 9] workmanlike gelding: little form in 2001: tried blinkered/visored. *W. Storey*

THREE LIONS 4 ch.g. Jupiter Island 126 – Super Sol (Rolfe (USA) 77) [2001 91p: **83** 10m 13.3m 14.8m⁴ 14s 16f⁴ 16v 13.8d* f14g* f14g³ Dec 17] rather leggy gelding: fairly useful handicapper: won at Catterick and Southwell (amateurs) in November: stays 1¾m: acts on fibresand and soft going: free-going sort: races handily. *R. F. Johnson Houghton*

THREE POINTS 4 b.c. Bering 136 – Trazl (IRE) 88 (Zalazl (USA) 120) [2001 119: **119** a6f 7g² 6m² 6m⁴ 6.5d² 6s 7d⁵ Oct 20] leggy, close-coupled colt: smart performer: good efforts in frame in 2001, including length second to Harmonic Way in Cork And Orrery Stakes at Royal Ascot, 4½ lengths fourth to Mozart in July Cup at Newmarket and neck second to King Charlemagne in Prix Maurice de Gheest at Deauville on third to fifth starts: respectable equal-fifth to Munir in Challenge Stakes at Newmarket final outing: has form at 1¼m, best at 6f/7f: acts on firm and good to soft going, below form on dirt, not well drawn on run on soft: tongue tied 3 of last 4 starts: usually races up with pace. *Saeed bin Suroor*

THREEZEDZZ 3 ch.g. Emarati (USA) 74 – Exotic Forest 66 (Dominion 123) [2001 **98** 94: 6d² 5s 6m⁵ 6m 7g⁶ 5m³ 6g 6m Sep 22] tall, useful-looking gelding: useful performer: very good ½-length second of 30 to How Do I Know in handicap at Newmarket on reappearance: failed to go on from that: ran poorly last 2 starts: best at 5f/6f: acts on firm and good to soft going (well below form on soft): blinkered final outing: has worn crossed noseband: edgy type. *J. G. Portman*

THROUGH THE RYE 5 ch.g. Sabrehill (USA) 120 – Baharlilys 67 (Green Dancer **71** (USA) 132) [2001 –: 10.1m⁶ 11.9g² 10m 8m⁴ Jul 4] rangy gelding: good mover: fair performer and lightly raced nowadays: stays easy 1½m: acts on good to firm going, probably on heavy: has had tongue tied: sometimes sweats: races freely: sold 6,500 gns. *W. J. Haggas*

THROWER 10 b.g. Thowra (FR) – Atlantic Line (Capricorn Line 111) [2001 57: 18s **–** 16s f14g Nov 16] sturdy gelding: modest handicapper at 9 yrs: well held in 2001. *W. M. Brisbourne*

THRUST 5 br.g. Prince Sabo 123 – La Piaf (FR) (Fabulous Dancer (USA) 124) [2001 **79 d** 7s⁵ 7m f8g⁶ 8.1v 8.9d 7s Oct 31] lengthy, good-topped gelding: fair maiden: form in 2001 only on first start: stays 7f: acts on soft ground: has raced freely. *W. R. Muir*

THUMAMAH (IRE) 2 b.f. (Mar 1) Charnwood Forest (IRE) 125 – Anam 79 (Persian **64** Bold 123) [2001 6d⁴ 6g 5f³ Sep 20] lengthy, unfurnished filly: has a short action: third foal: sister to French 2000 2-y-o 5.5f winner Farjah and half-sister to useful 7f winner Rayyaan (by Cadeaux Genereux): dam, 7f winner, half-sister to useful 1½m performer Estimraar: modest form in maidens: third at Pontefract: raced only at 5f/6f. *B. Hanbury*

THUMPER (IRE) 3 b.g. Grand Lodge (USA) 125 – Parkeen Princess (He Loves Me **74 d** 120) [2001 8d 8m 7g 8.3v Nov 8] 13,000Y: angular gelding: half-brother to several winners, including 1997 2-y-o 5f/6f winner Phone Alex (by Tirol), later 9f winner in USA and fairly useful 1m/9f winner who stayed 1¼m Transitional (by Dalsaan): dam unraced: fair form first 2 starts: ran as though something amiss both runs after: subsequently gelded. *R. Hannon*

THUNDERBIRD LEGEND (IRE) 2 ch.f. (Apr 8) Common Grounds 118 – **41** Alaroos (IRE) (Persian Bold 123) [2001 5g f5g⁴ 5m 6g⁴ 7g 8g Aug 24] smallish, sturdy filly: fourth living foal: sister to useful 1997 2-y-o 6f winner Arawak Cay and half-sister to 1¼m to 13f winner Persian Conquest (by Don't Forget Me): dam unraced half-sister to dam of US Grade 1 9f winner The Deputy: poor maiden: should stay at least 7f: tried blinkered. *T. D. Easterby*

THUNDER CANYON (USA) 2 b. or br.g. (Feb 26) Gulch (USA) – Naazeq 80 **78** (Nashwan (USA) 135) [2001 8d⁵ 7d⁵ 7v Oct 26] $35,000Y: close-coupled gelding: second foal: closely related to 3-y-o Mostarsil: dam, 10.5f winner, sister to smart performer up to 2½m Shaya: easily best effort in maidens (fair form) when promising fifth of 21 at Newmarket: prominent long way final start (gelded after): bred to stay beyond 1m. *M. Johnston*

THUNDER CAT 2 b.f. (Apr 30) Bin Ajwaad (IRE) 119 – Royal Cat (Royal Academy **–** (USA) 130) [2001 p8g p10g Dec 4] 3,000Y, 1,500 2-y-o: third foal: half-sister to 2000 2-y-o 6f winner Trustthunder (by Selkirk): dam unraced close relation to useful performer up to 2m Life of Riley: only a little sign of ability in Lingfield maidens. *Miss A. M. Newton-Smith*

THUNDERCLAP 2 b. or br.c. (Mar 12) Royal Applause 124 – Gloriana 78 (Formid- **77** able (USA) 125) [2001 6f³ 6m 7m* 6m p8g Nov 20] 10,000Y: second foal: dam, 1m/9f winner who stayed 1½m, also winning hurdler: fair performer: won maiden at Brighton in September by 3½ lengths from First Ordained: well beaten in nursery final start: should stay 1m. *J. W. Hills*

THUNDERED (USA) 3 gr.g. Thunder Gulch (USA) 129 – Lady Lianga (USA) 81 **55** (Secretariat (USA)) [2001 –: 8.2v f12g 8m³ 7.1g⁴ 8m² 9.2s⁴ 7s⁶ Jul 24] workmanlike gelding: modest maiden: left Mrs J. Ramsden after fifth start: probably best at 7f/1m: acts on good to firm ground: tried blinkered. *G. A. Swinbank*

THUNDERGOD 2 b.g. (Feb 26) Torrential (USA) 117 – Reach The Wind (USA) **62** (Relaunch (USA)) [2001 6f 7m 7f³ 7m 8m 8d Sep 27] 21,000F, 32,000Y: sixth foal: half-brother to a 7f winner in Hong Kong by Affirmed and a winner in USA by Gone West: dam, Irish 6f winner (including at 2 yrs), half-sister to useful sprinter Ozone Friendly: modest maiden: third at Lingfield: well held in nurseries after: stays 7f: acts on firm ground. *I. A. Balding*

THUNDERING FALLS (USA) 2 b.f. (Jan 8) Thunder Gulch (USA) 129 – Redwood Falls (IRE) 107 (Dancing Brave (USA) 140) [2001 f6g³ p6g Dec 28] IR 18,000Y: second foal: half-sister to 3-y-o Karpasiana: dam, French 1¼m winner, out of smart French middle-distance stayer Robertet: modest form in maidens at Wolverhampton (slowly away when third to Octennial) and Lingfield (carried head awkwardly/edged left): bred to be suited by 1¼m/1½m. *M. Johnston* **59**

THUNDERING SURF 4 b.c. Lugana Beach 116 – Thunder Bug (USA) 66 (Secreto (USA) 128) [2001 92p: 10g⁴ 10.1m² 10f⁴ 10m² 12m⁶ 12g* 12f³ 12g* 12s³ 12d⁶ 12s Nov 10] big, lengthy colt: has a round action: useful handicapper: won at Ascot in August and Kempton (beat Rajam by 1½ lengths) in September: effective at 1¼m/1½m: acts on any going: has edged right: waited with: consistent. *J. R. Jenkins* **101**

THUNDER KING (USA) 2 b.c. (Mar 21) Thunder Gulch (USA) 129 – Savannah's Honor (USA) 103 (Storm Bird (CAN) 134) [2001 6d⁴ 6m⁵ Sep 1] $12,000Y: deep-girthed colt: seventh foal: half-brother to 2 winners in USA by Blushing John: dam, French 2-y-o 6.5f/7f (Prix du Calvados) winner, later won in USA and third in Grade 1 9f event: burly, modest form in maidens at Haydock and Ripon, prominent long way each time: should stay at least 1m: should do better. *M. Johnston* **60 p**

THUNDERMILL (USA) 3 ch.g. Thunder Gulch (USA) 129 – Specifically (USA) (Sky Classic (CAN)) [2001 74: e10g 9g 8f⁴ 12m⁵ 9.7g* 10g 8.5g 7.5d Dec 29] rangy, useful-looking gelding: fair handicapper: won at Folkestone in August: below form afterwards, sold from T. Mills 2,200 gns before final start: best around 1¼m: acts on firm ground and equitrack: tried visored: has been early to post: front runner. *E. Castelli, Italy* **74**

THUNDER SKY 5 b.g. Zafonic (USA) 130 – Overcast (IRE) 72 (Caerleon (USA) 132) [2001 78: f7s e10g² e10g⁶ e10s f8.5g* f8.5g⁵ f7g f8.5g⁴ 10.3f 7.6f 8.1m 11.9m² 12.1m 10m* 10f⁴ 9.2d* f8g 9f 9.2d² 12.1s 9.2g⁵ 8.3g 8f f7g f8.5g f9.4g f9.4g⁵ Nov 21] lengthy, angular gelding: good mover: fair performer: won handicap at Wolverhampton in March and claimers in June/July: left N. Littmoden and Hamilton in June/July: well held after: effective at 8.5f to easy 1½m: acts on firm going, good to soft, fibresand and equitrack: usually blinkered/visored: has carried head awkwardly/found little: on downgrade. *D. W. Chapman* **77 d**

THWAAB 9 b.g. Dominion 123 – Velvet Habit 89 (Habitat 134) [2001 62: 9m 8m 8m 8m⁵ 8.9m 8m* Sep 6] strong gelding: modest handicapper: won at Salisbury in September: stays 1m: acts on firm and good to soft going: visored last 3 starts, has been blinkered: held up. *F. Watson* **60**

THWAITES SMOOTHIE 2 b.f. (May 24) River Falls 113 – Chilibang Bang 68 (Chilibang 120) [2001 6m⁵ 5f⁶ 5m 6s 7d 8.2s f8.5g f7g Nov 26] small filly: second foal: dam 5f (at 2 yrs) to 7f winner: poor maiden: well held in sellers last 3 starts: stays 7f: acts on firm and good to soft going. *A. Berry* **48**

THWAITES STAR (IRE) 2 b.f. (Apr 26) Petardia 113 – Monterana 99 (Sallust 134) [2001 5m³ 6m 6m⁵ 5s³ 5g 6v f6g 5g f6g f6g p6g Dec 22] leggy, close-coupled filly: half-sister to several winners, including 8-y-o Henry Island and Irish 7f winner Miss Twin Peaks (by Persian Heights): dam 2-y-o 6f/7f winner: modest maiden: disappointing after fourth start: should stay 6f: acts on soft and good to firm ground. *A. Berry* **55 d**

TIBBIE 3 b.f. Slip Anchor 136 – Circe 73 (Main Reef 126) [2001 50p: 8.3s 11.6g 12m⁵ 14.1g 12g² 14.1m⁵ 16.2g⁵ 16f⁵ p13g f12g Nov 23] leggy, unfurnished filly: modest maiden handicapper: stays 2m: acts on firm and soft ground: sometimes pulls hard: sold 800 gns. *R. M. Beckett* **59 a–**

TICCATOO (IRE) 3 br.f. Dolphin Street (FR) 125 – Accountancy Jewel (IRE) 71 (Pennine Walk 120) [2001 55, a60: f6g⁴ f5s³ f5g⁴ Jan 29] useful-looking filly: modest performer: effective at 5f/6f: acts on fibresand and good to firm going. *R. Hollinshead* **59**

TICKER 3 b.g. Timeless Times (USA) 99 – Lady Day (FR) (Lightning (FR) 129) [2001 62: 9d 10.1d* 10m⁵ 10m² 9m³ 10d⁶ 8s⁶ 11.1d⁴ 9.2g³ 8d⁶ 10v Oct 15] smallish gelding: fair performer: won maiden at Newcastle in May: best around 1¼m: acts on good to firm and good to soft ground, possibly not on soft/heavy: sold 11,000 gns. *Denys Smith* **75**

TICKET TO DANCE (IRE) 2 b.f. (Mar 6) Sadler's Wells (USA) 132 – River Missy (USA) (Riverman (USA) 131) [2001 7d Nov 3] closely related to 2 winners, including useful 9f to (in UAE) 1½m winner Lattam (by Lyphard), and half-sister to several **67 p**

winners, including US Grade 2 6f/7f winner Miss Golden Circle (by Crafty Prospector): dam, Irish 1¼m winner on only start, half-sister to Fillies' Mile winner Leap Lively: 15/2, eighth of 21 to Ballet Fame in maiden at Newmarket, racing wide and in mid-field throughout: should stay at least 1¼m: will improve. *J. H. M. Gosden*

TICKIT (IRE) 2 b.c. (Apr 28) Alhaarth (IRE) 126 – Pericolo (IRE) 92 (Kris 135) **57** [2001 7m 6m 6m⁴ 7m⁶ 8m 7m Sep 22] IR 20,000F: sixth foal: half-brother to 3 winners, including 1999 2-y-o 5f winner Nantucket (by Turtle Island) and 1998 2-y-o 6f winner Lady Caroline (by Hamas): dam, third at 7f at 2 yrs on only start, out of half-sister to smart Irish performer up to 1½m Tursanah: modest maiden: below form in nurseries last 3 starts: likely to prove best at 6f/7f: raced only on good to firm going. *M. R. Channon*

TICKLE 3 b.f. Primo Dominie 121 – Funny Choice (IRE) 68 (Commanche Run 133) **83** [2001 84: 6m f7g 7g³ Jul 21] fairly useful handicapper: back to form final outing: stays 7f, not sure to get further: acts on soft going. *P. J. Makin*

TICKOVER 2 b.c. (Feb 21) Overbury (IRE) 116 – Celtic Chimes (Celtic Cone 116) **–** [2001 7m 8g Sep 7] 2,000 2-y-o: smallish colt: third foal: half-brother to 1998 2-y-o 6f seller winner Welsh Assembly (by Presidium): dam, little sign of ability on Flat, won over hurdles: well held in maidens: dead. *G. P. Enright*

TICK TOCK 4 ch.f. Timeless Times (USA) 99 – Aquiletta 67 (Bairn (USA) 126) **68** [2001 55: 5.1f 5d 6m 5.1f 5m⁶ 6m f6g 5g 5g 5m⁴ 5m* 5m* 5.1d⁴ 6s² 5g⁵ 5.2v 5g³ Nov 5] small filly: fair handicapper: won at Thirsk (maiden event) and Ayr (27 ran) in September: effective at 5f/6f: acts on any turf going, well beaten on fibresand: sometimes visored (not for wins in 2001): often races up with pace: withdrawn on veterinary advice final intended outing. *M. Mullineaux*

TIDAL BEACH 2 b.c. (Apr 10) Lugana Beach 116 – Efficacy 62 (Efisio 120) [2001 **53** 6m 6g³ Jul 30] 5,000Y: lengthy colt: first foal: dam 6f winner at 4 yrs: better effort in maidens (modest form) when third at Newcastle, making most: not sure to stay beyond 6f. *C. W. Thornton*

TIE BREAK (IRE) 6 ch.g. Second Set (IRE) 127 – Karayasha (Posse (USA) 130) **40** [2001 f12g 11.9f³ May 23] compact gelding: modest performer at 3 yrs: only poor form in 2001: stays 1½m: acts on good to firm ground and fibresand: tried blinkered at 3 yrs. *R. J. O'Sullivan*

TIGER FEET 2 b.c. (Feb 8) Petong 126 – Selvi (Mummy's Pet 125) [2001 5f³ f5g⁴ **72** 5m⁴ f6g² 5m* 6m f6g p6g f6s Dec 26] 5,000F, 6,800 2-y-o: good-bodied colt: sixth foal: brother to 4-y-o Jailhouse Rocket and half-brother to 3 winners, notably smart 5f/6f winner (including Mill Reef Stakes at 2 yrs) Indian Rocket (by Indian Ridge): dam maiden who was best at 6f: fair performer: second in sales race at Wolverhampton: won nursery at Beverley in August: will prove best at 5f/6f: acts on fibresand, raced only on going firmer than good on turf: races up with pace. *A. Berry*

TIGER GRASS (IRE) 5 gr.g. Ezzoud (IRE) 126 – Rustic Lawn (Rusticaro (FR) 124) **57** [2001 –: f16g² f16g Feb 16] tall, leggy gelding: modest maiden: stays 2m: acts on fibresand, good to firm and good to soft going: tried blinkered. *W. R. Muir*

TIGER PRINCESS 4 b.f. Bin Ajwaad (IRE) 119 – Penny Dip 86 (Cadeaux Genereux **–** 131) [2001 –: 6g 8m 11.8d Jul 19] no sign of ability. *C. N. Kellett*

TIGER ROYAL (IRE) 5 gr.g. Royal Academy (USA) 130 – Lady Redford (Bold **106** Lad (IRE) 133) [2001 108: 5m 6g 6g 6m 6.3g 5g² 5m³ 5s 6d² 7s² Nov 11] second foal: dam once-raced half-sister to dam of Oscar Schindler: useful performer: best effort in Britain when eighth to Yorkies Boy in handicap at York on second start (left D. Nicholls after fifth outing): good placed efforts, including when second in listed race at Leopardstown (beaten 4 lengths by Shoal Creek) final start: stays 7f: has form on good to firm going, very best efforts on good or softer: usually blinkered: usually held up/carries head awkwardly. *D. K. Weld, Ireland*

TIGER TALK 5 ch.g. Sabrehill (USA) 120 – Tebre (USA) 70 (Sir Ivor 135) [2001 –: **–** 12.3s Apr 28] of little account nowadays. *M. E. Sowersby*

TIGHTROPE 6 b.g. Alzao (USA) 117 – Circus Act (Shirley Heights 130) [2001 77: **50** e8g* e10g³ e10g e8g⁶ f8.5g² 8.2v 8f⁵ 8.1g f8g² 8.2s³ f9.4g⁴ f8g⁶ f8g f8g f7g f9.4f **a72** Dec 5] quite good-topped gelding: fair on all-weather, modest on turf: reportedly underwent treatment for fibrillating heart prior to winning seller at Lingfield in January:

left J. Osborne 3,000 gns after tenth start: stays 1¼m: acts on fibresand, equitrack and probably on any turf going: tried visored: has been slowly away: none too consistent. *J. Balding*

TIGHT SQUEEZE   4 br.f. Petoski 135 – Snowline (Bay Express 132) [2001 43:   51
f12g⁵ f12s 10m 9.7m⁵ 10g 12.6f 10d⁵ 11.9g 9.9m² 10m⁴ Aug 22] big, plain filly: modest maiden: best around 1¼m: acts on good to firm going. *P. W. Hiatt*

TIGNE   2 b.g. (Apr 25) Magic Ring (IRE) 105 – Elkie (Most Welcome 131) [2001 f5g⁶   68
5m² 6m* Jul 30] first living foal: dam unraced: fair form: landed odds in seller at Yarmouth (sold to join N. Littmoden 11,000 gns) in July: effective at 5f/6f: sold only 3,000 gns in October. *M. Johnston*

TIGRE BOIS   4 b.g. Mon Tresor 113 – Gentle Star 77 (Comedy Star (USA) 121) [2001   44
7s 10f 7m⁵ 9.9m⁶ 8.1m⁶ 8.1m⁶ 10g 10m⁴ Aug 18] sturdy gelding: poor maiden: stays 1m: acts on good to firm ground. *B. R. Millman*

TIGRELLO   7 ch.g. Efisio 120 – Prejudice 83 (Young Generation 129) [2001 8.1g   53
8.1m 7m⁴ 8d 8m⁴ 8.1g⁵ 8.1m 7d Jul 18] leggy, quite good-topped gelding: modest performer: reportedly finished lame final start: best around 1m: acts on firm and good to soft ground: has been tongue tied. *J. M. Bradley*

TIGRESS (IRE)   2 b.f. (Apr 25) Desert Style (IRE) 121 – Ervedya (IRE) (Doyoun   60
124) [2001 5g³ f5g* 5m⁶ f5g* 6g⁴ 6g 6s⁴ f6s 5.3s³ f5g* 5.2s⁴ 5.1s⁵ f6g³ f5g* f6g³ f5g²   a78
f6g⁶ f5s⁵ f6s³ Dec 26] IR 3,500F, IR 10,000Y: third foal: sister to fairly useful 2000 2-y-o 7f winner Chauntry Gold and half-sister to 4-y-o Cyber Babe: dam ran once: fair on all-weather, modest on turf: won maiden at Southwell in May, then claimer in June and sellers in October (left B. Meehan) and November at Wolverhampton: will prove best at 5f/6f: acts on soft ground and fibresand: sometimes blinkered/visored: usually races prominently: occasionally wanders under pressure. *P. D. Evans*

TIKKUN (IRE)   2 ch. or gr.c. (Apr 15) Grand Lodge (USA) 125 – Moon Festival 74   **100 p**
(Be My Guest (USA) 126) [2001 6m² 6g* Sep 3] IR 260,000Y: fifth living foal: half-brother to useful 1m winner Silver Apple (by Danehill), fairly useful Irish 1¾m winner Lunasa (by Don't Forget Me) and 3-y-o Sita: dam, maiden who stayed 1¼m, half-sister to Sheriff's Star and Moon Madness: shaped well when second of 4 to Carinae in minor event at Newmarket: useful form when beating Elayoon by 7 lengths in maiden at Folkestone 5 weeks later, again racing freely but forging clear from 2f out: bred to stay at least 1¼m: probably a smart performer in the making. *R. Charlton*

TIKOPIA   7 b.g. Saddlers' Hall (IRE) 126 – Shesadelight 67 (Shirley Heights 130)   56
[2001 17.1s 14.1s⁴ 12.3s 12.4d 12m May 25] sturdy gelding: modest handicapper nowadays: stays 1¾m: acts on soft and good to firm ground: tried blinkered/visored: sometimes hangs. *M. E. Sowersby*

TIKRAM   4 ch.g. Lycius (USA) 124 – Black Fighter (USA) 79 (Secretariat (USA))   **89 p**
[2001 86: 10d⁶ 10.1s² 12s⁵ Nov 10] tall, close-coupled gelding: fairly useful form: trained by H. Cecil at 3 yrs: creditable efforts in autumn in handicap at Ascot, minor event at Yarmouth and November Handicap at Doncaster (ran on strongly when fifth to Royal Cavalier): stays 1½m: acts on heavy going: useful hurdler: likely to progress and make his mark in good-class handicaps on return to Flat. *G. L. Moore*

TILLERMAN   5 b.h. In The Wings 128 – Autumn Tint (USA) (Roberto (USA) 131)   **121**
[2001 121: 6m⁴ 6m 7m³ 7.3f⁴ Aug 18] big, strong, good sort: impresses in appearance: very smart performer: best effort in 2001 when beaten a short head and a neck behind Atavus in Tote International Stakes (Handicap) at Ascot on third start, finishing strongly having been switched, unfortunate not to have followed up win in race previous year: creditable efforts in Cork And Orrery Stakes at Royal Ascot (finished full of running after meeting trouble, beaten 3 lengths behind Harmonic Way) and July Cup at Newmarket (eleventh behind Mozart) first 2 starts: probably at least as effective at 6f as 7f/1m: best efforts on good to firm going: usually taken steadily to post: sometimes slowly away: wears crossed noseband, pulls hard and is held up: stays in training. *Mrs A. J. Perrett*

TIMBER LODGE (IRE)   2 ch.g. (Feb 10) Woodborough (USA) 112 – Ornette (IRE)   71
(Bluebird (USA) 125) [2001 5.1d 5g⁴ 5.7f May 22] 8,500F, 9,000Y: third foal: dam unraced daughter of Oaks runner-up Bonnie Isle: best effort in maidens (fair form) when fourth at Windsor: should stay at least 7f. *I. A. Balding*

Tattersalls Musidora Stakes, York—an improved effort from Time Away,
who quickens decisively two furlongs out; Relish The Thought and Heavenly Whisper (right) are next;
finishing fourth is ante-post Oaks favourite Flight of Fancy (left),
whose ride was strongly criticised by her owner's racing manager

TIME AWAY (IRE) 3 b.f. Darshaan 133 – Not Before Time (IRE) (Polish Precedent (USA) 131) [2001 89p: 8s⁵ 10g³ 10.4m* 10.5m³ 12g⁶ 9.9g³ 10.4g Aug 21] strong, good sort with a quick action: smart performer: reportedly chipped a bone in knee on second outing at 2 yrs: won Tattersalls Musidora Stakes at York (quickened smartly to beat Relish The Thought 1¾ lengths) in May: creditable third after to Aquarelliste in Prix de Diane at Chantilly (beaten 2¼ lengths) and to Lailani in Nassau Stakes at Goodwood (beaten 2 lengths, hanging persistently right, seeming ill at ease on course): only seventh in Juddmonte International at York final outing: reportedly had tendon problem after: stayed 1¼m (never really got into it in Irish Oaks over 1½m): acted on good to firm going, possibly not on soft: visits Sadler's Wells. *J. L. Dunlop* **114**

TIME BOMB 4 b.f. Great Commotion (USA) 123 – Play For Time (Comedy Star (USA) 121) [2001 60: 6m 6s 8s⁵ 6v* p7g f7g f8g Dec 10] seemingly fair form when winning maiden at Windsor in October, despite edging left: well held otherwise at 4 yrs: best at 6f: acts well on heavy going: free-going sort. *B. R. Millman* **66 ?**

TIME CAN TELL 7 ch.g. Sylvan Express 117 – Stellaris (Star Appeal 133) [2001 –, a56: f16.2g³ f16.2s⁵ f16.2g⁴ f16g³ f16.2g⁴ f16g f16g f16g f14g⁵ 16.2m³ 16.2f f16.2g⁵ f16g⁴ f14.8g f16.2g Nov 21] big gelding: modest handicapper on all-weather, poor on turf: tried visored/blinkered: has been slowly away. *A. G. Juckes* **42 a55**

TIMECINI 2 ch.f. (Feb 20) Timeless Times (USA) 99 – Veracini (Whittingham (IRE) 104) [2001 6m 6f 5d Oct 9] 3,000Y: small, sturdy filly: first foal: dam unraced: well beaten in maidens. *B. S. Rothwell*

TIME FOR MUSIC (IRE) 4 b.g. Mukaddamah (USA) 125 – Shrewd Girl (USA) 79 (Sagace (FR) 135) [2001 75, a65: 7m 7f* 7m² 6m⁶ 7m³ 7g 7g Aug 17] lengthy, quite attractive gelding: fair performer: won minor event at Brighton in May: probably best at 6f/7f: acts on firm ground and equitrack: tried blinkered: free-going sort. *T. G. Mills* **70**

TIME FOR ONE MORE 2 ch.f. (Apr 5) Timeless Times (USA) 99 – Croft Original (Crofthall 110) [2001 5s 5m 7m⁶ Aug 16] 950Y: seventh foal: half-sister to a winner in Spain by Clantime: dam lightly-raced maiden who was probably ungenuine: no form in maidens: dead. *M. J. Haynes* **–**

TIME FOR THE CLAN 4 ch.g. Clantime 101 – Fyas 52 (Sayf El Arab (USA) 127) [2001 –: e6g f8.5s e10g f12g 12v 5.1v 10s 6.1v 6s 10d 7g 8.1m 6m 7f 7.1g 6m 7m 10m 10.3f⁵ 12.4m 6m 8f 6m 9m 8d 8g 9.9m 9.2g 10.3m 8f 6.1d 7g 11.9s 7v 8.2s Nov 5] of no account. *R. Bastiman* **–**

TIMELESS CHARM 2 b.g. (Mar 30) Timeless Times (USA) 99 – Whittle Rock 91 (Rock City 120) [2001 5.1s⁶ 5g Jun 15] 3,500F, 15,000Y: sturdy gelding: first foal: dam 5f (at 2 yrs) to 7f winner: modest form in maidens: joined A. Bailey, and gelded. *N. Tinkler* **58**

TIMELESS CHICK   4 ch.f. Timeless Times (USA) 99 – Be My Bird 65 (Be My **49**
Chief (USA) 122) [2001 57?, a45: f6g f7g⁵ f7g⁵ f7g⁴ 8s f7g 8m f8g 8g⁵ 8m⁴ 8.1g* 10.9m
8s⁶ Sep 30] quite good-topped filly: has a round action: poor performer: left B. McMahon
after eighth start: won seller at Chepstow in September: stays 1m: acts on good to firm
going and fibresand: often blinkered/visored (not last 5 starts): none too consistent.
J. L. Spearing

TIMELESS FARRIER   3 b.g. Timeless Times (USA) 99 – Willrack Farrier 73 **58**
(Lugana Beach 116) [2001 67: f6g² e6g* e6g² e6g⁵ 5m 5m⁶ Jul 31] fair performer on **a75**
all-weather, modest on turf: won maiden at Lingfield in January: best at 5f/6f: acts on
fibresand, equitrack and good to firm ground: usually blinkered/visored in 2001: has had
tongue tied: races prominently. *B. Smart*

TIMELESS QUEST   4 ch.f. Timeless Times (USA) 99 – Animate (IRE) 62 (Tate **–**
Gallery (USA) 117) [2001 –: f6s f6g Feb 5] seems of little account nowadays. *J. J. Quinn*

TIMELESS QUESTION   2 ch.f. (Apr 19) Timeless Times (USA) 99 – Tarda 63 **48**
(Absalom 128) [2001 5d⁵ f6g Nov 12] smallish, unfurnished filly: third foal: dam, 1m/9f
winner, also successful over hurdles: poor form in maidens at Redcar and (reared leaving
stall) Southwell. *R. M. Whitaker*

TIMELESS TREASURE   2 ch.c. (Apr 17) Timeless Times (USA) 99 – Treasure **–**
Hunt (Hadeer 118) [2001 5m f5g⁵ 5g Aug 19] workmanlike colt: first foal: dam unraced
half-sister to 9-y-o Lago di Varano: only a little sign of ability in maidens/seller.
Miss S. E. Hall

TIME MAITE   3 b.g. Komaite (USA) – Martini Time 90 (Ardoon 124) [2001 76: 6s **–**
5.5d 5g Aug 13] workmanlike gelding: poor mover: fair performer at 2 yrs: well held in
handicaps in 2001. *M. W. Easterby*

Mr R. Barnett's "Time Away"

TIME MARCHES ON   3 b.g. Timeless Times (USA) 99 – Tees Gazette Girl 42   **33**
(Kalaglow 132) [2001 –: f6s f11g⁶ f11g³ 8.2s⁶ 10f* 10g⁶ Jun 12] leggy gelding: poor
performer: won selling handicap at Nottingham in June: should stay 1½m: acts on firm
going, probably on fibresand: carried head awkwardly penultimate start: seemed to lose
action final one. *Mrs M. Reveley*

TIME N TIME AGAIN   3 b.g. Timeless Times (USA) 99 – Primum Tempus 49   **89**
(Primo Dominie 121) [2001 84: 5.1f* 5m⁴ 5f⁶ 5.1m³ 5g 6s 5s Sep 8] leggy, useful-looking
gelding: fairly useful performer: won handicap at Chester in May: below form last 3
starts: probably best at 5f: acts on firm and good to soft ground: races up with pace.
E. J. Alston

TIME PROOF   3 b.g. Clantime 101 – Off Camera (Efisio 120) [2001 41: f7g Apr 10]   **–**
good-topped gelding: poor maiden: may prove best short of 7f. *R. A. Fahey*

TIME ROYAL   2 b.c. (Feb 2) Timeless Times (USA) 99 – Royal Girl 67 (Kafu 120)   **87**
[2001 5v* 5.2d* 5m 5.2m 6g⁴ 6g Oct 6] 5,500Y: strong, good sort: has scope: good
walker: fourth foal: dam 6f/7f winner: fairly useful performer: won maiden at Doncaster
(favourite, idled) in March and minor event at Newbury in April: creditable seventh to
Johannesburg in Norfolk Stakes at Royal Ascot: well below form last 3 starts: should stay
at least 6f: acts on good to firm and heavy ground. *B. A. McMahon*

TIME TEMPTRESS   5 b.m. Timeless Times (USA) 99 – Tangalooma 56 (Hotfoot   **30**
126) [2001 53, a–: 10m 8m 12m³ 12.4g 12f Aug 1] sparely-made mare: poor nowadays: **a–**
stays 1½m: acts on firm and soft going, well held on fibresand: blinkered/visored last 3
starts. *A. Crook*

TIME TO BURN   2 b.f. (Mar 18) Atraf 116 – Into The Fire 74 (Dominion 123) [2001   **50**
5v³ 5v e5g³ Apr 11] 800Y: small, sparely-made filly: half-sister to 3 winners, including
sprinter Down The Middle (by Swing Easy) and miler Cool Fire (by Colmore Row): dam,
stayed 1¼m, winner in Guernsey: best effort (modest form) when third in maiden seller
at Doncaster on debut: should stay 6f: visored final start. *W. G. M. Turner*

TIME TO FLY   8 b.g. Timeless Times (USA) 99 – Dauntless Flight (Golden Mallard   **–**
103) [2001 48, a–: f6g⁵ f6g 5.1v 5m 6m 7m 5m 6m 7m 6s 5d 7d 5g Nov 5] good-bodied
gelding: little form in 2001: usually blinkered. *B. W. Murray*

TIME TO REMEMBER (IRE)   3 b.g. Pennekamp (USA) 130 – Bequeath (USA)   **83**
(Lyphard (USA) 132) [2001 78: 7.9g 6m 7m* Aug 12] big, good-topped gelding: has
plenty of scope: fluent mover: fairly useful performer: won handicap at Redcar in August:
bred to stay 1m: raced only on good/good to firm ground: early to post in 2001: has hung
left: none too tractable until fitted with crossed noseband at Redcar. *T. D. Easterby*

TIME TO TRAVEL (USA)   2 b.c. (May 4) Lear Fan (USA) 130 – Split Sentence   **85 p**
(USA) (Northjet 136) [2001 8m 8d 7s* Oct 20] close-coupled, angular colt: half-brother
to several minor winners in USA: dam 8.5f minor stakes winner in USA: improved with
each outing, winning maiden at Catterick easily by 4 lengths from Ember Days: will stay
1¼m: should make a useful 3-y-o. *P. F. I. Cole*

TIME TO WYN   5 b.g. Timeless Times (USA) 99 – Wyn-Bank 82 (Green God 128)   **50**
[2001 45: 9v⁵ 8s 8s² 8m* 10f 8f 10.1v Oct 24] smallish gelding: modest handicapper:
won apprentice selling event at Ripon in June: effective at 1m to 1¼m: acts on soft and
good to firm going: blinkered/visored last 5 starts. *J. G. FitzGerald*

TIME VALLY   4 ch.f. Timeless Times (USA) 99 – Fort Vally 58 (Belfort (FR) 89)   **65 §**
[2001 74: 7m 8m 7f 7m 8g³ 8g 7m 8m 7m Sep 22] leggy filly: fair performer: stays
easy 1m: acts on firm going: tried visored: usually starts slowly: held up: unreliable.
J. J. Quinn

TIMING   2 b.f. (May 2) Alhaarth (IRE) 126 – Pretty Davis (USA) (Trempolino (USA)   **65**
135) [2001 7.1v⁵ 6s⁴ f7g⁵ f8s⁴ Dec 15] 11,500F, 7,500Y: rather leggy, angular filly:
second foal: half-sister to fairly useful filly Fait Le Jojo (by Pistolet
Bleu): dam 1¼m winner in France: fair form in maidens/claimer: best effort second start:
should be suited by at least 1m: has twice failed stall tests. *T. D. Easterby*

TIMOKO   3 b.f. Dancing Spree (USA) – Encore M'Lady (IRE) 86 (Dancing Dissident   **–**
(USA) 119) [2001 7s 6m 6m Jun 4] smallish filly: first foal: dam, 5f to 7f winner, sister to
smart 5f/6f performer Don't Worry Me: well beaten in maidens/seller. *A. Berry*

TINA BALLERINA   2 ch.f. (Feb 14) Komaite (USA) – Very Bold 57 (Never So Bold   **–**
135) [2001 5s⁵ f5g⁶ 6v⁵ Oct 24] sturdy, close-coupled filly: fourth foal: half-sister to
Italian winner up to 11f Rainbow King (by Puissance): dam 5f winner: little form in
maidens. *W. M. Brisbourne*

TIP

TING (IRE)   4 b.g. Magical Wonder (USA) 125 – Rozmiyn (Caerleon (USA) 132)   **70**
[2001 53: f8g² 8.2s² f8g* 8.1g³ 10m 9f f8g⁶ f8g* f8g⁵ f8g 8.2s² 9.2d⁴ 8s* 8g Oct 6] leggy,
quite good-topped gelding: fair performer: left P. Haslam after first start: won handicaps
at Southwell in April (amateurs) and July, and minor event at Leicester in September:
stays 8.5f: acts on fibresand and soft going, well held on firmer than good. *M. J. Polglase*

TINIAN   3 b.g. Mtoto 134 – Housefull 81 (Habitat 134) [2001 10.3v³ 10s⁴ 10s 11m f12g   **71**
Oct 18] 45,000Y: short-backed gelding: sixth foal: half-brother to 1992 2-y-o 5f winner
Greenlet (by Green Desert) and French 9f winner Dolforwyn (by Caerleon): dam 1m
winner out of 1000 Guineas winner Full Dress II: fair form in maidens first 2 starts: well
held after, including in handicaps: should stay beyond 1¼m: acts on heavy going: raced
freely in visor final start: sold 3,200 gns, sent to Holland. *I. A. Balding*

TINK'S MAN   2 b.c. (Feb 28) Puissance 110 – Expectation (IRE) 59 (Night Shift   **60**
(USA)) [2001 6g 5s f5g⁶ Oct 9] 23,000Y: strong colt: first foal: dam, sprint maiden,
granddaughter of Irish 1000 Guineas winner Front Row: best effort (modest form) when
sixth in minor event at Wolverhampton: may prove best at 5f. *Mrs A. Duffield*

TINSEL MOON (IRE)   4 b.f. River Falls 113 – Fordes Cross (Ya Zaman (USA) 122)   **–**
[2001 95: 10s 10.3s f8g Nov 19] fourth foal: half-sister to 3 winners abroad, including
Italian 9f to 1½m winner Regal Danzig (by Roi Danzig): dam unraced: fairly useful
maiden for C. Collins in Ireland, best effort when fifth in listed race at the Curragh final
3-y-o start: well held in Britain: stays 1¼m: acts on firm and good to soft ground: sold
5,000 gns, joined R. Cowell. *G. B. Balding*

TINSEL WHISTLE   4 b.g. Piccolo 121 – Pewter Lass 56 (Dowsing (USA) 124)   **–**
[2001 69: e6g f7g⁵ f7g Mar 27] leggy, close-coupled gelding: fair performer at 2 yrs: well
held in 2001: tried blinkered. *B. R. Johnson*

TINSTRE (IRE)   3 ch.c. Dolphin Street (FR) 125 – Satin Poppy (Satin Wood 117)   **45**
[2001 –: f8g f7s⁴ e8g⁵ 8.2s 10s 7s 10d⁵ 10m 9m 11.5f 10g 10.9f² 10m Jul 7] small,
sparely-made colt: poor maiden: left Miss J. Doyle after fifth start: stays 11f: acts on firm
and good to soft going: has had tongue tied. *P. W. Hiatt*

TINY TIM (IRE)   3 b.g. Brief Truce (USA) 126 – Nonnita 71 (Welsh Saint 126) [2001   **47**
53: f7g 7d 8f 7m 7m 7m 7.5f³ Jul 17] leggy, sparely-made gelding: poor maiden: likely to
prove best at 7f/1m: form only on good going or firmer. *I. A. Balding*

TIOGA GOLD (IRE)   2 b.g. (Apr 24) Goldmark (USA) 113 – Coffee Bean (Doulab   **63**
(USA) 115) [2001 6s 6g 7g f8g⁵ f8g* Dec 10] 17,000Y: leggy gelding: half-brother to
several winners, including 1m/1¼m winner Java Red and 6f (at 2 yrs) and 11f (in UAE)
winner Grovefair Maiden (both by Red Sunset): dam poor Irish maiden: modest
performer: shaped well a couple of times before winning seller at Southwell: should stay
1¼m: acts on fibresand. *B. J. Meehan*

TIP IT OVER   2 b.g. (Mar 28) Revoque (IRE) 122 – On Tiptoes 107 (Shareef Dancer   **– p**
(USA) 135) [2001 6f 7.1v⁵ 7s Oct 16] big, lengthy, useful-looking gelding: has scope:
sixth foal: half-brother to 3 winners, including useful 6f (at 2 yrs) and 7f winner Caballero
(by Cadeaux Genereux): dam, 5f (including Queen Mary Stakes) winner, from family of
high-class miler Wassl: signs of ability in maidens: gelded after final start: type to make a
better 3-y-o. *J. G. Given*

TIPPERARY SUNSET (IRE)   7 gr.g. Red Sunset 120 – Chapter And Verse   **69**
(Dancer's Image (USA)) [2001 69, a–: 8s 7.1v⁶ 7g 8.5m* 8.1s 7.9m Sep 2] strong, close-   **a–**
coupled gelding: fair handicapper: won at Beverley (third course success) in May:
effective at 7f to 1¼m: acts on any turf going: sometimes blinkered: has been slowly
away/wandered/found little: usually held up. *D. Shaw*

TIP THE SCALES   3 b.g. Dancing Spree (USA) – Keen Melody (USA) 60 (Sharpen   **44**
Up 127) [2001 51: 12m 10.1m 12f 16.2m 15.8m⁵ 16.2s 10m Sep 1] useful-looking
gelding: poor maiden: seems to stay 1¼m: acts on good to firm ground: often visored/
blinkered. *R. M. Whitaker*

TIP TOP   2 b.f. (Jan 29) Mistertopogigo (IRE) 118 – Strawberry Pink 87 (Absalom
128) [2001 6m May 29] strong filly: sixth foal: dam, 2-y-o 5f winner, out of very smart
sprinter Polly Peachum: 25/1, well held in maiden at Redcar. *T. D. Easterby*

TIPTRONIC (IRE)   2 b.c. (May 12) Woodborough (USA) 112 – Snowtop (Thatching   **70**
131) [2001 f8g⁵ f8s³ Dec 21] 16,500F: half-brother to several winners abroad, including
winner around 1m Snow Peak (by Arazi) and 1½m winner Eyrie (by Groom Dancer),
both in France: dam, Irish sprinter, half-sister to William Hill Futurity winner Al Hareb:

1035

better effort in Southwell maidens in December when length third of 16 to Redisham: not sure to stay beyond 1m. *G. C. H. Chung*

TIRANA (IRE) 3 b.g. Brief Truce (USA) 126 – Cloche du Roi (FR) (Fairy King (USA)) [2001 54: f8g f8g f7g* f7g³ 8.1g³ 8.1s 8.5s f8.5g 7g⁶ 8d⁴ Nov 2] angular, workmanlike gelding: modest handicapper: won at Southwell in April: stays 8.5f: acts on fibresand, best turf form on good/good to soft going: usually tongue tied: held up. *D. Shaw*   **55 a60**

TIRARI (IRE) 2 b.f. (Apr 2) Charnwood Forest (IRE) 125 – Desert Victory (Green Desert (USA) 127) [2001 6m 6.1m⁴ 7d p7g² f7g* f8g Dec 3] smallish, useful-looking filly: has a short, round action: third foal: half-sister to a winner in Germany by Barathea: dam, French 7f (at 2 yrs)/1m winner, out of close relative to Irish 1000 Guineas winner Ensconse: fair performer: won seller at Southwell (slowly away, left C. Wall) in November: should stay 1m: acts on good to firm going and fibresand. *R. C. Spicer*   **65**

TIREE 2 ch.f. (Feb 12) Be My Chief (USA) 122 – Madam Zando 51 (Forzando 122) [2001 5m 6.1d Sep 21] 2,000Y: first foal: dam, maiden who stayed 7f, from family of Oaks winner Circus Plume: well beaten in maidens: sold 500 gns. *J. Balding*   **–**

TISHOMINGO 2 ch.g. (Mar 25) Alhijaz 122 – Enchanted Guest (IRE) 74 (Be My Guest (USA) 126) [2001 f6g 5m⁶ 6m 8g* 7.1s 8m⁴ 8m f8g⁵ f8.5g f9.4g² f7s Dec 18] 600F, 1,300Y: strong, close-coupled gelding: first foal: dam 6f winner: modest performer: won claimer at Newcastle in August: left G. M. Moore after eighth start, reportedly had breathing problem next time: stays 9.4f: acts on good to firm going and fibresand: can't be relied upon. *Ronald Thompson*   **61 §**

TISSALY 3 b.f. Pennekamp (USA) 130 – Island Ruler 79 (Ile de Bourbon (USA) 133) [2001 79: 7m⁶ May 29] fair form in minor events/maiden at 2 yrs: well held only outing in 2001: has raced freely, but should stay 1m: sold 800 gns in December. *C. E. Brittain*   **–**

TISSIFER 5 b.g. Polish Precedent (USA) 131 – Ingozi 91 (Warning 136) [2001 104§: 10g² 12g* Oct 4] quite attractive gelding: reportedly fractured cannon bone in 1999: useful nowadays: won 27-runner claimer at Newmarket (joined M. Pipe £20,000 after) in October: stays 1½m: acts on firm and good to soft going: sometimes blinkered: ungenuine: winning hurdler. *M. Johnston*   **98 §**

TITAN 6 b.g. Lion Cavern (USA) 117 – Sutosky 78 (Great Nephew 126) [2001 45§, a–§: 6s 10f 7f Jun 5] good-topped gelding: temperamental handicapper: left M. Muggeridge after first start. *J. S. Moore*   **– §**

TITCHFIELD (USA) 2 b. or br.c. (Feb 24) Mt Livermore (USA) – Morning Colors (USA) (Raise A Native) [2001 7.1m² 8m⁶ Sep 12] $60,000F, $65,000Y: tall, leggy colt: has scope: half-brother to several winners abroad, including 5.5f (at 2 yrs in France) and 9f (in UAE) winner Dawn Aurora (by Night Shift): dam, won up to 1m in USA, closely related/half-sister to Group/Grade 1-winning fillies Flagbird, Runup The Colors and Prospectors Delite: fair form in minor event at Sandown (beaten ½ length by Kriskova) and maiden at York: should stay at least 1m. *P. F. I. Cole*   **77**

TITIAN ANGEL (IRE) 4 ch.f. Brief Truce (USA) 126 – Kuwah (IRE) 77 (Be My Guest (USA) 126) [2001 74: 12v 8.1g 9.9m⁴ 10.2f⁶ 12m⁵ 10m³ 10g² 12g⁵ 14.8m⁴ 10.5s 12g 12g 11.9s⁴ 12d p12g⁵ f12g⁵ f14g⁵ f8.5s Dec 26] angular filly: fair maiden handicapper: lost form after ninth start: stays 14.8f: acts on polytrack and firm ground, seemingly on soft: tried blinkered: often ridden by Mr V. Coogan. *A. B. Coogan*   **74 d**

TITUS BRAMBLE 4 b.g. Puissance 110 – Norska 67 (Northfields (USA)) [2001 58, a–: 11.9s May 3] tall gelding: modest performer at 3 yrs: well held only Flat run in 2001: blinkered once at 2 yrs. *P. C. Ritchens*   **–**

TIYE 6 b.m. Salse (USA) 128 – Kiya (USA) 85 (Dominion 123) [2001 –: e10g Mar 28] lightly-raced maiden: tried blinkered/visored. *D. L. Williams*   **–**

TIYOUN (IRE) 3 b.g. Kahyasi 130 – Taysala (IRE) (Akarad (FR) 130) [2001 86: 10s 12.3f 10.4m 11m* 12.3m* 12f 11.9d 12.3m⁴ 12d³ 12.3m² 12.3m² 12m* 12.1m⁴ 10g Oct 5] leggy gelding: useful handicapper: won at Redcar in May, Ripon in June and Thirsk in September: good fourth to Pulau Pinang under top weight at Hamilton penultimate start: stays 1½m: acts on soft and good to firm (possibly not on firm) going: usually races prominently. *D. W. Barker*   **100**

TIZNOW 4 b.c. Cee's Tizzy (USA) – Cee's Song (USA) (Seattle Song (USA) 130) [2001 133: a8.5f* a9f² a10f* a9f³ a9f³ a10f* Oct 27] top-class colt: reportedly fractured a tibia and unraced at 2 yrs: voted Horse of the Year in USA in 2000: became first to win 2 Breeders' Cup Classics when beating Sakhee by a nose at Belmont in   **133**

October, staying on gamely near finish: successful earlier in year in Grade 2 event at Santa Anita and Santa Anita Handicap (by 5 lengths from Wooden Phone, soon pulling clear in straight with rider sitting motionless): reportedly bled second start and had been off 6 months with reported back problem before fourth outing: stayed 1¼m: blinkered first 5 appearances in 2000: most resolute galloper: to stand at WinStar Farm, Kentucky, fee $30,000. *J. M. Robbins, USA*

T JINOUSKA (USA) 3 gr. or ro.f. Cozzene (USA) – Ocean Jewel (USA) (Alleged **86** (USA) 138) [2001 12.3m³ 12m* 12m Jul 21] IR 75,000Y: lengthy filly: has scope: half-sister to several winners, including useful German performer up to 2m Ocean Sea (by Bering) and US winner up to 9f Dixie Splash (by Dixieland Band), third in Grade 3 8.5f event: dam unraced: won 5-runner maiden at Goodwood in July by 5 lengths: not discredited when ninth to Ranin in listed race at Newmarket only subsequent outing: likely to prove as effective at 1¼m as 1½m: slowly away first 2 outings: sent to USA. *J. H. M. Gosden*

T K O GYM 2 b.g. (Apr 19) Atraf 116 – Pearl Pet 56 (Mummy's Pet 125) [2001 5m⁵ **74** 5f⁵ 6g⁵ 5f³ 5m Aug 26] 3,200F, 13,500Y: smallish, close-coupled gelding: half-brother to several winners, including useful German performer up to 1¼m Signatory (by King's Signet), 7f winner in Britain at 2 yrs, and 6f winner Easy Does It (by Swing Easy): dam maiden who stayed 11f: fair maiden: best effort when third at Musselburgh: should stay 6f. *D. Nicholls*

T M OPERA O (JPN) 5 ch.h. Opera House 131 – Once Wed (USA) (Blushing **128** Groom (FR) 131) [2001 128: 10f⁴ 16f* 11f² 12f* 10d² 12f² 12.5f⁵ Dec 23] high-class performer: world's leading money earner with career total of $16.2m: unbeaten in 8 races in 2000, 5 of them Group 1s, including Japan Cup: less dominant in 2001 but won Tenno Sho (Spring) in April by ½ length from Meisho Doto and awarded Group 2 at Kyoto in October on disqualification of Stay Gold: good second at Tokyo fifth/sixth starts, to Agnes Digital (beaten a length) in Tenno Sho (Autumn) and Jungle Pocket (caught final strides, beaten a neck) in Japan Cup: was effective at 1¼m to 2m: acted on firm and good to soft going: was genuine and consistent: to stand at East Stud, Japan, fee 5m yen. *I. Iwamoto, Japan*

TOBOUGG (IRE) 3 b.c. Barathea (IRE) 127 – Lacovia (USA) 128 (Majestic **125** Light (USA)) [2001 116p: 8g 12f³ 10m⁴ 10d² 10m² Dec 16]

A year is a long time in sport. Defeat at Wembley by Germany in October 2000 dented the England soccer team's chances of World Cup qualification and led to the resignation of their manager. Just over twelve months later, the picture was transformed, England securing automatic qualification and, on the way, Deutschland 1 England 5 in Munich entering football folklore. Shortly after the Wembley defeat, ex-England international Mick Channon saddled unbeaten Tobougg to win the Dewhurst, Britain's most prestigious two-year-old event. As the England football team thrived over the next twelve months under new management, Tobougg's fortunes ebbed and flowed after being transferred to Godolphin. Looking in very good shape after a winter in Dubai and starting 4/1 favourite for the Two Thousand Guineas, Tobougg lost his unbeaten record when ninth of eighteen to Golan, never able to reach a challenging position. Tobougg had finished only third behind Godolphin's two other Guineas runners Rumpold and Divine Task in a private trial at Nad Al Sheba in April and, after his performance at Newmarket, the portents for his three-year-old career were none too encouraging. Tobougg did, in fact, fail to win a race of any sort as a three-year-old, but he went on to show high-class form in top races after the Guineas and may improve again as a four-year-old.

Tobougg was Godolphin's only representative in the Derby. He reportedly worked well at home before Epsom and, ridden by the 'housewives' choice' in the Derby nowadays Frankie Dettori, was backed from 16/1 to 9/1 fifth favourite on the day. Tobougg really took the eye in the paddock and ran very well to finish third to Galileo and Golan, staying on strongly despite drifting left to be beaten three and a half lengths and a neck after being waited with and following the first two through on the outside in the straight. The Eclipse was next for Tobougg and he was provided with a pacemaker to ensure that his now-proven stamina was brought fully into play. Tobougg was dropped right out, however, tactics which seemed hard to fathom at the time, and he never looked like justifying favouritism, his staying-on fourth, less than a length behind the winner Medicean, suggesting a return to a mile and a half would suit him, especially as he was being ridden along from some way out at Sandown. It was October before Tobougg was seen out again, by which time his home work was causing some concern (he had reportedly been tried blinkered on the gallops in an attempt to galvanise him). Dettori passed him over in the Champion Stakes for Best of The Bests and he was easy to back at 11/1 in a field of twelve. Kevin Darley took the mount and rode Tobougg prominently, sending him for home two furlongs out. He held on to the lead until seventy-five yards out, where the favourite Nayef collared him and went on to beat him by three quarters of a length, Tobougg four lengths clear of third-placed Indian Creek. Dettori made the running on Tobougg on his final start, in the Hong Kong Cup over a mile and a quarter at Sha Tin in December. He looked like dropping away when headed over a furlong out but rallied gamely to go down by a head to the Japanese-trained winner Agnes Digital, with French-trained Terre A Terre and British challenger Hawkeye close behind.

Tobougg (IRE) (b.c. 1998)	Barathea (IRE) (b 1990)	Sadler's Wells (b 1981)	Northern Dancer Fairy Bridge
		Brocade (b 1981)	Habitat Canton Silk
	Lacovia (USA) (b 1983)	Majestic Light (b 1973)	Majestic Prince Irradiate
		Hope For All (ch 1975)	Secretariat Hopespringseternal

The pedigree of the rather leggy, good-topped Tobougg was covered fully in *Racehorses of 2000*. His sire, the high-class miler Barathea, is still short of a really big winner as a stallion, though an individual median rating of 80 for his

Godolphin's "Tobougg"

British-raced offspring puts him among the top thirty or so sires. Tobougg's dam Lacovia won the Prix Saint-Alary and the Prix de Diane; she has bred several other winners, none of them better than useful. Tobougg is effective at a mile and a quarter to a mile and a half and acts on firm and good to soft going. *Saeed bin Suroor*

TOCCATA ARIA 3 b.f. Unfuwain (USA) 131 – Distant Music (Darshaan 133) [2001 14g 16.2m 10.2g⁵ Oct 1] 10,000Y: big, good-topped filly: second foal: half-sister to 4-y-o Desert Island Disc: dam unraced granddaughter of high-class French 1m to 1½m performer Dancing Maid: well beaten in Haydock maiden and Queen's Vase at Royal Ascot for S. Knight: modest form in maiden at Bath final start. *J. M. Bradley* **49**

TOEJAM 8 ch.g. Move Off 112 – Cheeky Pigeon (Brave Invader (USA)) [2001 51: 7m 7.5f³ 8m⁵ 8m 8f⁵ 8f³ 9f³ 8m 9.2d³ 10.4m 8m² 8f* 8d 8d 8g f8g⁶ Dec 14] angular gelding: modest performer: won selling handicap at Pontefract in September: best at 7f to 9f: acts on fibresand, firm and good to soft going: tried visored. *R. E. Barr* **56**

TOFFEE NOSED 3 ch.f. Selkirk (USA) 129 – Ever Welcome 58 (Be My Guest (USA) 126) [2001 85: 7d³ 10.4m⁵ 8f² 8f² 7.1g² 7.1m* 6g 7d* 8s Nov 18] tall, unfurnished filly: shows round action: useful performer: won maiden at Warwick in August and listed race at Ascot (by 1¾ lengths from Indaba) in October: effective at 7f, barely stays 10.4f: acts on firm and soft ground: has been bandaged behind: front runner. *B. W. Hills* **97**

TOJONESKI 2 b.c. (Mar 14) Emperor Jones (USA) 119 – Sampower Lady 55 (Rock City 120) [2001 6m 5.1g* 5m* f7g f7g Nov 30] 2,500F, IR 8,500Y: first foal: dam, maiden who should have stayed 7f, out of Cherry Hinton winner Travel On: fair form: won maiden at Chepstow in July and nursery at Lingfield in August: may prove best at 5f/6f. *P. J. Makin* **72**

TOKING N' JOKEN (IRE) 2 b.f. (May 11) Mukaddamah (USA) 125 – We're Joken 62 (Statoblest 120) [2001 5.3m⁴ 5.1m Sep 10] third foal: dam 5f (at 2 yrs)/6f winner: well held in maidens. *W. G. M. Turner* **–**

TOLCEA (IRE) 2 ch.g. (Apr 16) Barathea (IRE) 127 – Mosaique Bleue (Shirley Heights 130) [2001 7d 8.2d 8d Oct 19] IR 60,000Y: heavy-topped gelding: sixth foal: closely related to smart 1¼m/1½m winner Subtle Power (by Sadler's Wells) and half-brother to 3 winners, including 3-y-o Arhaaff: dam unraced half-sister to Prix Saint-Alary winner Muncie and Prix Royal-Oak winner Mersey: burly, never dangerous in maidens: fair form when thirteenth of 20 to Rawyaan at Newmarket final start (subsequently gelded): should be suited by 1¼m/1½m: capable of better, and an interesting type for handicaps. *E. A. L. Dunlop* **66 p**

TOLDYA 4 b.f. Beveled (USA) – Run Amber Run (Run The Gantlet (USA)) [2001 74: e6g⁵ 6g⁶ 5.7m⁴ 6d⁵ 6g 5.1g 6.1d⁵ f6g* 5.2v³ 6v p7g² Dec 12] fair handicapper: won at Wolverhampton in October: left M. Kettle before final start: effective at 5f to 7f: acts on any going and all-weather: effective blinkered, tried once in 2001: has reared/wandered/been slowly away: races prominently. *A. P. Jarvis* **73**

TOLEDO STAR 2 br.c. (Feb 10) Petong 126 – Shafir (IRE) 68 (Shaadi (USA) 126) [2001 6g Sep 15] 21,000Y: leggy, close-coupled colt: third foal: brother to Italian 5f (at 2 yrs) and 7.5f winner El Ciciarela: dam, 2-y-o 5f winner, half-sister to useful miler A La Carte: 66/1 and backward, seemingly modest form when 9 lengths ninth of 10 in minor event at Doncaster, leading over 3f: joined J. Jenkins. *D. Nicholls* **60 ?**

TOLERATION 4 b.f. Petong 126 – Dancing Chimes (London Bells (CAN) 109) [2001 78: 6d 6g⁵ 7g 6d f6g Sep 8] lengthy, unfurnished filly: fair performer: form in 2001 only in handicap at Leicester second start: should stay 7f. *K. O. Cunningham-Brown* **75**

TOLLGATE MELODY 3 b.f. Sabrehill (USA) 120 – Breed Reference (Reference Point 139) [2001 7g 9.9d Sep 27] fourth foal: half-sister to fairly useful 6f/7f winner Jocasta (by Warning) and 10.5f seller winner Home Force (by Chaddleworth): dam placed in France from 1¼m to 14.5f: tailed off in maidens. *R. Rowe* **–**

TOMAMIE 3 b.f. Tina's Pet 121 – Springhead 60 (Komaite (USA)) [2001 –: f6g 8g Jul 25] plain, leggy filly: seems of little account. *J. R. Norton* **–**

TOMANIVI 3 b.f. Caerleon (USA) 132 – Balleta (USA) 87 (Lyphard (USA) 132) [2001 10.1g⁶ Aug 15] sixth foal: half-sister to 3 winners, including smart French/US performer up to 1m Barricade (by Riverman) and useful 1¾m winner War Cabinet (by Rainbow Quest): dam, 1m to 1¼m winner, sister to Dancing Brave and Jolypha: 5/1, showed nothing in Yarmouth maiden: retired. *H. R. A. Cecil* **–**

TOMASINO   3 br.c. Celtic Swing 138 – Bustinetta 89 (Bustino 136) [2001 78p: 12.3v*   **110**
12.3f² 12v³ 12f² 12m³ Aug 1] tall, leggy colt: smart handicapper: won at Ripon in April
in good style: very good placed efforts final 2 starts, in King George V Stakes at Royal
Ascot (½-length second to Beekeeper) and Tote Gold Trophy at Goodwood (2¼ lengths
third to Ovambo), never far away and keeping on gamely both times: reportedly found to
have suffered small fracture of off-fore cannon bone after Goodwood: will stay 1¾m+:
acts on any going. *M. Johnston*

TOM DOUGAL   6 b.g. Ron's Victory (USA) 129 – Fabulous Rina (FR) (Fabulous   **65**
Dancer (USA) 124) [2001 72: 8.2s⁶ 8m⁴ 8m 8m 8d 8.2s f8g* f8.5g Dec 8] leggy, quite
good-topped gelding: fair performer: won amateur handicap at Southwell in November:
stays 9f: acts on fibresand, firm and soft ground: held up. *C. Smith*

TOMENOSO   3 b.g. Teenoso (USA) 135 – Guarded Expression 51 (Siberian Express   **–**
(USA) 125) [2001 –: 8s⁶ 10.9v Oct 15] poor maiden: should stay beyond 1m: raced on
good going or softer/fibresand. *W. G. M. Turner*

TOMILLIE   2 ch.g. (Jan 25) Ventiquattrofogli (IRE) 118 – Royal Comedian 58 (Jester   **70**
119) [2001 6s² 6s² f5g Dec 3] 1,300Y: good-topped gelding: second foal: dam 7f/7.5f
winner: fair form when second in maidens at Pontefract, forcing pace both times: well
held at Southwell, then gelded: should stay 7f. *A. Berry*

TOMMY CARSON   6 b.g. Last Tycoon 131 – Ivory Palm (USA) 93 (Sir Ivor 135)   **53 ?**
[2001 53: 11.9s 10g² 11.5g Aug 30] sturdy gelding: maiden: seemed to show modest
form second start: effective at 1¼m to 1¾m: acts on any going: usually blinkered. *Jamie
Poulton*

TOMMY DOD   2 ch.g. (May 21) Keen 116 – Wyse Folly (Colmore Row 111) [2001 5f   **58**
7.9d 8d Oct 25] good-bodied gelding: first living foal: dam ran twice: modest form on
first 2 starts in maidens: gelded after final appearance: likely to prove best short of 1m.
M. Johnston

TOMMY LORNE   3 b.c. Inchinor 119 – Actress 73 (Known Fact (USA) 135) [2001   **–**
67: 8.2g 9.9g 10d 10s Oct 22] lengthy, useful-looking colt: fair maiden at 2 yrs: well held
in handicaps in 2001. *J. L. Dunlop*

TOMMY SMITH   3 ch.g. Timeless Times (USA) 99 – Superstream (Superpower 113)   **76 §**
[2001 56: 6s⁶ 6s 6m² 5m⁴ 5f² 5m 5f 5f 5f* 6.1s 5g 5m* 6m 5s Sep 27] smallish, sturdy
gelding: fair handicapper: won in large fields at Redcar in July and Beverley in August:
stays 6f: acts on firm going: visored/blinkered last 6 starts: has started slowly/hung:
thoroughly inconsistent. *J. S. Wainwright*

TOMTHEVIC   3 ch.g. Emarati (USA) 74 – Madame Bovary 82 (Ile de Bourbon   **65**
(USA) 133) [2001 79: 6s 5g 5m 6f 5.1f 5m⁶ 5d 5g³ 5m² 5d⁵ 5g⁴ 5m³ 5f 6f 6.1f⁶ 5s Sep 27]
strong-quartered gelding: fair handicapper: best at 5f/easy 6f, possibly on good going or
firmer: visored (well held) thirteenth start: sometimes tongue tied. *J. J. Quinn*

TOM TUN   6 b.g. Bold Arrangement 127 – B Grade 59 (Lucky Wednesday 124) [2001   **95**
84: f5g³ f6s⁶ f5g* f5g² f5g* 6v² 6s* 5m 6f 6g⁵ 6m 5s 5m 6d 6g⁶ f6g³ f7g⁵ Dec 11]
workmanlike gelding: has a round action: useful handicapper: won at Wolverhampton in
February/March and Pontefract in April: effective at 5f to easy 7f: acts on any turf going,
fibresand and equitrack: tongue tied: usually races prominently: tough and game.
Miss J. F. Craze

TOM TYGRYS   2 b.g. (Mar 30) Danzig Connection (USA) – Strath Kitten 36   **–**
(Scottish Reel 123) [2001 7.1s 7g 7m Sep 22] small colt: third foal: dam maiden who
stayed 1¼m: last in minor events/maiden. *P. S. McEntee*

TONG ICE   2 g.r.g. (Mar 17) Petong 126 – Efficacious (IRE) 49 (Efisio 120) [2001 6m   **36**
5m 5m⁶ 5d 5g 8g f8.5g⁶ Nov 27] 9,000Y: first foal: dam maiden who stayed 1½m: poor
maiden: left Miss L. Perratt after fifth start: barely stays 8.5f: acts on fibresand, best turf
effort on good to firm going. *I. Semple*

TONG ROAD   5 gr.g. Petong 126 – Wayzgoose (USA) (Diesis 133) [2001 39: 5d 6m   **44 §**
6m f6g 5f 5m 5f 6m³ 8f⁵ 6m 5g⁴ 6d 5s Aug 21] workmanlike gelding: poor maiden
handicapper: best at 5f/6f: acts on soft and good to firm going, no form on fibresand: tried
blinkered: usually slowly away: inconsistent. *D. W. Chapman*

TONI ALCALA   2 b.g. (Mar 3) Ezzoud (IRE) 126 – Etourdie (USA) (Arctic Tern   **76 d**
(USA) 126) [2001 5v⁶ 5s 5d² 6m² 5m 6f⁵ 7.1f³ 7.1f⁶ f7g 8f⁴ 8m⁶ f8.5g² f9.4g Dec 8]
4,000F, 8,500Y: close-coupled gelding: eighth foal: half-brother to 3 winners, including
4-y-o Stoney Garnett and French winner up to 1½m Easy Gold (by Glint of Gold): dam
unraced: fair maiden: not so good in second half of season as first: will stay 1¼m: acts on

firm going, good to soft and fibresand: edgy type, and has been reluctant stalls/slowly away. *R. F. Fisher*

TONIGHT AT MAMMA'S   2 b.f. (Mar 8) Timeless Times (USA) 99 – Henpot (IRE) 68 (Alzao (USA) 117) [2001 f5g⁶ 5m f5g Jul 2] 2,500Y: fifth foal: half-sister to fairly useful 7f/1m winner Sweet Wilhelmina (by Indian Ridge) and 6-y-o Mamma's Boy: dam won once at 1½m from only 2 starts: well held in sellers/claimer: sold 1,200 gns, sent to Israel. *A. Berry*   –

TONIGHT'S PRIZE (IRE)   7 b.g. Night Shift (USA) – Bestow 76 (Shirley Heights 130) [2001 81: 10g 10g 9m 12m Jun 29] leggy gelding: fairly useful performer at 6 yrs: little form in 2001, and tailed off as if badly amiss final start. *C. F. Wall*   –

TONTO O'REILLY   3 gr.g. Mind Games 121 – Most Uppitty 69 (Absalom 128) [2001 62: 6.1v⁵ 6s 6m 7f 6m Jul 21] useful-looking gelding: has a markedly round action: modest maiden: should prove best up to 7f: acts on heavy ground, probably on good to firm: tongue tied last 3 starts, gelded after final one. *B. Smart*   60

TONY   3 b.g. Marju (IRE) 127 – Present Imperfect 61 (Cadeaux Genereux 131) [2001 –: 8v⁶ 8.2s⁴ f12g⁶ 10.1m 10g Jun 12] big, strong, leggy gelding: little form: often slowly away: blinkered (looked hard ride) final start. *M. W. Easterby*   –

TONY TIE   5 b.g. Ardkinglass 114 – Queen of The Quorn 53 (Governor General 116) [2001 96: 8d 8g 10.4g 10m 8.1d 8.9m⁴ 8m* 7.1f⁵ 7.9m⁴ 7g³ 7.6m² 8.1g³ 8.1s² 8.3g* 8s 8d³ 8d 7s Nov 10] leggy, angular gelding: unimpressive mover: fairly useful handicapper: won at Newcastle in June and Hamilton in September: needs good test at 7f, and stays easy 1¼m: acts on any going: visored once: has idled in front, and often held up: tough and consistent. *J. S. Goldie*   89

TOOTORIAL (IRE)   4 b.c. College Chapel 122 – Touche-A-Tout (IRE) (Royal Academy (USA) 130) [2001 44: f7s e7g³ e8g Mar 28] lightly-raced maiden, modest at best: tongue tied after first start (reportedly had breathing problem). *Mrs L. Stubbs*   62 ?

TOP ACT   5 b.g. Inchinor 119 – Actress 73 (Known Fact (USA) 135) [2001 10s 12.3s 10f 7.5f 10m Jun 21] tall, lengthy gelding: little sign of ability: tried visored. *J. S. Wainwright*   –

TOPAZ   6 b.g. Alhijaz 122 – Daisy Topper (Top Ville 129) [2001 37: f12g⁶ 10.1m 14.1d Aug 8] little form in 2001. *H. J. Collingridge*   –

TOP CRYSTAL (IRE)   3 b.f. Sadler's Wells (USA) 132 – State Crystal (IRE) 114 (High Estate 127) [2001 12m Sep 24] second living foal: sister to fairly useful 1¼m winner True Crystal: dam, 7f (at 2 yrs) and 1½m (Lancashire Oaks) winner, half-sister to smart middle-distance stayer Tchaikovsky (by Sadler's Wells) and 3-y-o Crystal Music: 14/1, well beaten in maiden at Kempton. *H. R. A. Cecil*   –

TOP DIRHAM   3 ch.c. Night Shift (USA) – Miller's Melody 86 (Chief Singer 131) [2001 7d 7.5m* 7m* 8m⁵ Jun 21] 110,000Y: strong, good-topped colt: fifth living foal: half-brother to 3 winners abroad, including useful German 1¼m/1½m performer Metaxas (by Midyan): dam disappointing maiden: progressive form: won maiden at Beverley in May and handicap at Epsom in June, latter despite appearing to handle track none too well: well-backed favourite, ran well when 2½ lengths fifth to Analyser in Britannia Handicap at Royal Ascot final start, drifting left and no extra: will prove best at 7f/1m: acts on good to firm ground: should make a smart colt if all is well. *Sir Michael Stoute*   100 p

TOP FLIGHT QUEEN   2 b.f. (Mar 30) Mark of Esteem (IRE) 137 – Blessed Event 117 (Kings Lake (USA) 133) [2001 5f⁴ 5f⁴ 7.1v 6d⁵ 7s Oct 20] 16,500Y: good-topped filly: half-sister to several winners, including smart 8.5f to 12.5f winner Sacrament (by Shirley Heights) and useful 1997 2-y-o 7f winner Confirmation (by Polar Falcon): dam, 1¼m winner, second in Yorkshire Oaks: fair maiden: good fifth in nursery at Pontefract: bred to stay at least 1m: acts on firm and good to soft going: has been slowly away/flashed tail/worn blanket for stall entry: sold 23,000 gns. *Mrs G. S. Rees*   65

TOPLESS IN TUSCANY   4 b.f. Lugana Beach 116 – Little Scarlett 54 (Mazilier (USA) 107) [2001 50: f6g⁴ e6g f6s f7s² e6g f7g e7g f6g⁴ f6g f7g e6g⁶ Mar 7] poor maiden: stays 7f: acts on fibresand. *P. W. Hiatt*   46

TOPMAN   4 ch.g. Komaite (USA) – Top Yard (Teekay) [2001 –: f12g 15.4v 11.9m May 8] of little account. *A. P. Jones*   –

TOP NOLANS (IRE)   3 ch.g. Topanoora 118 – Lauretta Blue (IRE) (Bluebird (USA) 125) [2001 66: 9.9m 8.3m 7.6g⁶ 6s 7s² p7g 7f g* f8g³ Dec 14] rather sparely-made   63
a59

gelding: fair performer: won maiden at Southwell in November: stays 1m: acts on good to firm going, soft and fibresand: tried visored at 2 yrs. *M. H. Tompkins*

TOP OF THE CHARTS   5 b.g. Salse (USA) 128 – Celebrity 101 (Troy 137) [2001   –
45: e12g f14.8s e16g⁶ Jan 24] quite attractive gelding: little form in 2001: tried visored/
blinkered. *D. L. Williams*

TOP OF THE CLASS (IRE)   4 b.f. Rudimentary (USA) 118 – School Mum (Rep-   **47**
rimand 122) [2001 62: 10m 10.3f³ 8m 10.9d⁵ 9.1d f9.4g* 7d 12.3d f8g⁵ f9.4f f8s⁵ f8.5s
Dec 26] unfurnished filly: has a round action: only poor performer in 2001: won seller at
Wolverhampton in August: stays 9.4f: acts on fibresand, firm and soft going: tried
visored/blinkered, not in 2001. *P. D. Evans*

TOP OF THE PARKES   4 b.f. Mistertopogigo (IRE) 118 – Bella Parkes 83 (Tina's   **42**
Pet 121) [2001 58: f7g⁵ f6s⁶ f7g⁵ Feb 20] modest maiden at 3 yrs: well held in 2001: tried
blinkered. *N. P. Littmoden*

TOPO'S GUEST   3 b.f. Mistertopogigo (IRE) 118 – Arctic Guest (IRE) 71 (Arctic   –
Tern (USA) 126) [2001 51: 8.5f f11g 16g 10m⁶ 13.8m⁵ 11d Oct 30] strong filly: modest
maiden at 2 yrs: little form in 2001: blinkered/visored last 4 starts. *J. G. Given*

TOPPLING   3 b.c. Cadeaux Genereux 131 – Topicality (USA) (Topsider (USA))   **88**
[2001 7.1g⁴ 8.3m* 7.6d 8d Oct 18] smallish, good-bodied colt: third living foal:
half-brother to 4-y-o Border Subject: dam, French 1m winner, sister to smart performer
up to 1m Top Socialite and half-sister to 2000 Guineas second/US Grade 1 1¼m winner
Exbourne: fairly useful form: won maiden at Windsor in June by 2 lengths from Dress
Rehearsal, pulling hard: well held both starts after (played up in stall and veered markedly
right exiting next time): may prove best at 7f/1m: sold 13,000 gns. *Mrs A. J. Perrett*

TOP QUALITY   3 b.f. Simply Great (FR) 122 – Qurrat Al Ain (Wolver Hollow 126)   **53**
[2001 –: 12.4m⁵ 12.4g⁴ 12m⁵ 16g 12.1g Sep 3] tall, workmanlike filly: modest maiden
handicapper: soundly beaten last 3 starts: should be suited by 1¾m+: form only on good
going or firmer. *T. D. Easterby*

Mrs E. M. Stockwell's "Toroca"

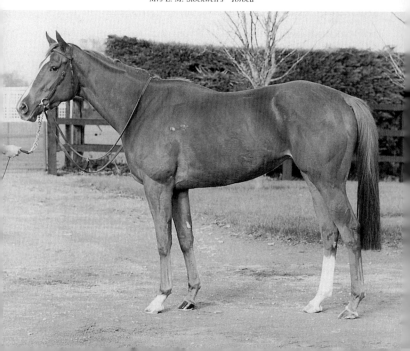

TOPTON (IRE) 7 b.g. Royal Academy (USA) 130 – Circo 77 (High Top 131) [2001 **85** 82, a97: e8g⁴ a8f⁴ a7.5f³ a6g⁴ 6m 7m 8g 7g² 7m* 7m 8f 8m 8g 7m 8g² 7d 7g⁵ 7.1g 7g 8d **a95** p7g p10g p8g⁵ p8g⁵ Dec 28] tall, angular gelding: useful handicapper on all-weather, fairly useful on turf: ran creditably in Dubai second to fourth starts: won at Doncaster in June: best at 7f/1m: acts on firm going, soft, all-weather and dirt: has won in visor, blinkered nowadays: usually held up: none too consistent. *P. Howling*

TOP TREES 3 b.g. Charnwood Forest (IRE) 125 – Low Line 66 (High Line 125) **66 d** [2001 f9.4g³ 11.8m 11m 8.1d⁶ 9.7m 10.1g 8m f9.4s Dec 18] 45,000Y: half-brother to several winners, including fairly useful 1995 2-y-o 7f winner Canons Park (by Keen): dam, lightly-raced maiden, sister to Park Hill winner Quay Line: fair maiden at best: below form after debut: sold out of J. Osborne's stable only 600 gns before final start: may prove best around 1¼m: has been slowly away, markedly so penultimate outing: reluctant to race sixth outing: one to treat with caution. *W. S. Kittow*

TORCELLO (IRE) 3 b.g. Royal Academy (USA) 130 – Vanya (Busted 134) [2001 **108** 10d⁵ 10.3f³ 10v⁴ 10s* 11.9d⁴ 12m 10.3d⁵ 10d⁵ Nov 2] IR 160,000Y: rangy, attractive gelding: fourth foal: half-brother to 3 winners in France, including 1½m and 15f winner Tetravella (by Groom Dancer): dam French 9f/1¼m winner: useful performer: made hard work of landing odds in maiden at Sandown in June: best efforts when third in listed race at Chester (beaten 1¾ lengths by Dr Greenfield), fourth in similar event at Haydock (2½ lengths behind Xtra) on fifth start and fifth in minor event at Doncaster (to Lagudin) penultimate outing: stays 1½m: acts on firm and good to soft going, winner on soft: has wandered/looked hard ride: gelded after final start. *G. Wragg*

TOREADOR (IRE) 2 b.c. (May 7) Danehill (USA) 126 – Purchasepaperchase 104 **98** (Young Generation 129) [2001 7g² 6m² 7g³ 5g 6m* Sep 24] 250,000Y: strong, close-coupled colt: brother to 2 winners, including useful 7f/1m winner Carambola, and half-brother to several others, including Irish 1000 Guineas winner Matiya (by Alzao): dam 1m/1¼m performer: useful performer: 3¼ lengths third to Comfy in listed event at York in August: landed odds in maiden at Listowel: should stay 1m: acts on good/good to firm going: has worn crossed noseband/had 2 handlers. *A. P. O'Brien, Ireland*

TORIGO (USA) 2 b.c. (Feb 12) Distant View (USA) 126 – Our Way (USA) (His **77** Majesty (USA)) [2001 6d⁵ 5m⁵ 7m⁴ 6g⁵ 6m⁵ 6d² f7g³ Nov 17] $23,000Y, 45,000 2-y-o: first foal: dam maiden in USA: fair maiden: best effort when second in nursery at York: was possibly best at 6f: acted on good to soft going: dead. *P. Mitchell*

TORMENTOSO 4 b.g. Catrail (USA) 123 – Chita Rivera 61 (Chief Singer 131) [2001 **–** 47: f8.5g e12g e10g e8g e10g 8.1s Aug 9] of little account nowadays. *A. J. Chamberlain*

TORNADO PRINCE (IRE) 6 ch.g. Caerleon (USA) 132 – Welsh Flame 106 **81 d** (Welsh Pageant 132) [2001 92: 7d 8g 7m⁵ 7m 8f 7m² 7m 10d 8.5s 8m 8s 7d 8s f9.4g Dec 11] quite good-topped gelding: fairly useful handicapper: mostly disappointing in 2001 (reportedly finished lame seventh/eighth starts): sold from Mrs J. Ramsden 8,000 gns after eleventh start (pulled up next one, said to have bled from nose final outing): probably best at 7f/1m: acts on firm and held up: held up. *K. A. Ryan*

TOROCA (USA) 3 ch.f. Nureyev (USA) 131 – Grand Falls (USA) (Ogygian (USA)) **112** [2001 105?: 6s* 8g³ 8g³ 8f⁶ 10d⁵ 8m³ 7m² 8g² 6m² 6s⁵ 7s² 6d⁶ 8s* Oct 21] big, good-topped filly: smart performer: won maiden at the Curragh in April and Premio Sergio Cumani at Milan (beat In The Night 1¼ lengths) in October: several good efforts in between, notably when 2 lengths third to Ameerat in 1000 Guineas at Newmarket, 4 lengths third to Imagine in Irish equivalent at the Curragh and 5 lengths sixth to Banks Hill in Coronation Stakes at Royal Ascot second to fourth starts, and when short-head second to Invincible Spirit in Boland Stakes at the Curragh and 1¾ lengths fifth to Nice One Clare in Diadem Stakes at Ascot ninth/tenth outings: effective at 6f to 1m: acts on firm and soft going: has worn crossed noseband: held up: tough. *A. P. O'Brien, Ireland*

TOROSAY SPRING 3 ch.f. First Trump 118 – Spring Sixpence 60 (Dowsing (USA) **106 p** 124) [2001 5m* 5m³ 6g* 6g² 6g² Sep 28] sturdy, lengthy filly: second reported foal: dam 7f and 1½m winner: progressive form, already useful: won maiden at Doncaster in May and handicaps at Lingfield (impressive) in August and Kempton (beat Cd Flyer a length in 24-runner race) in September: well-backed favourite, hampered more than once when very good ½-length second to Fantasy Believer in well-contested handicap at Ascot final start: will stay 7f: raced only on good/good to firm ground: should make a smart 4-y-o, and type to win a good prize. *J. R. Fanshawe*

TORREALTA 5 b.m. In The Wings 128 – Sea Ring (FR) (Bering 136) [2001 12s 12v² **101** 12v³ 15v³ 15.5s⁶ 10d 14.6m 12v 15.5s² 12.5v Nov 19] small, sturdy mare: poor mover:

first foal: dam, French 8.5f/10.5f winner, out of half-sister to Prix Minerve winner Anitra's Dance: useful performer: successful (for only time) in handicap at Saint-Cloud in 2000: at least creditable efforts in listed races in 2001 when placed at Longchamp and Chantilly second/third starts and at Maisons-Laffitte (beaten 2 lengths by Bosham Mill) penultimate one: effective at 1½m to 15.5f: raced mainly on good or softer going (acts on heavy), below form on good to firm in Park Hill Stakes at Doncaster seventh start. *J. Lesbordes, France*

TORRECILLA 2 b.f. (Feb 28) General Monash (USA) 107 – Mystical Heights (IRE) **68** (High Estate 127) [2001 5.7f³ 5.7f² 6m⁶ 6m* f6g⁵ 6m 5.1f Sep 18] 2,000 2-y-o: first foal: dam unraced out of half-sister to high-class winner up to 1¼m in Britain/USA Star Pastures: fair performer: won maiden at Lingfield in July, making all: below form in nurseries after, pulled up lame final start: stays 6f: acts on fibresand, raced only on ground firmer than good on turf: free-going sort: has looked none too keen. *R. M. Beckett*

TORRENT 6 ch.g. Prince Sabo 123 – Maiden Pool 85 (Sharpen Up 127) [2001 80, **66 §** a77: e5g⁴ e5g² f5g e5g e5g⁵ 5v² 5g 5m³ 5m³ 5m 5m² f5g² 5m 6m⁴ 5d 6m³ 5g⁶ 6m⁵ 5s⁴ **a78 d** 6.1v³ 5g² 6v 5s⁵ 5d² f5g² p5g³ f6g³ f6g² f6s p6g⁵ Dec 29] strong, lengthy gelding: fair performer: on the downgrade in 2001, leaving D. Chapman before final start: best at 5f/6f: acts on any turf going/all-weather: usually blinkered: has worn tongue tie: broke blood vessel twice at 5 yrs: carries head high/has hung right: often doesn't go through with effort. *P. S. McEntee*

TORRENTIAL STORM (USA) 3 b.g. Torrential (USA) 117 – Lady Nitro (USA) **82** (Oh Say (USA)) [2001 10s* 10.1m⁴ 12g 12g 10.4s* Oct 11] $36,000F, $27,000Y: useful-looking gelding: sixth foal: half-brother to several winners in USA, including minor stakes-winning sprinter Sovereign Lady (by Aloha Prospector): dam won up to 7f in USA: fairly useful performer: won maiden at Pontefract in May and claimer at York in October: very best efforts at 1¼m: acts on soft and good to firm going: sold 15,000 gns. *M. A. Jarvis*

TORRID KENTAVR (USA) 4 b.g. Trempolino (USA) 135 – Torrid Tango (USA) **91** (Green Dancer (USA) 132) [2001 92: 10.1s 10v 10g⁵ 12m⁶ 12m* 11.4g* 9.9m⁴ 11m⁶ 12m⁵ 10f Sep 22] close-coupled gelding: fairly useful performer: won at Kempton in June and Sandown (subsequently left T. Mills 30,000 gns) in July: below form after next outing: effective at 1¼m/1½m: acts on firm going, equitrack and fibresand: tried blinkered (not in 2001): tends to race freely. *B. Ellison*

TORY BOY 6 b.g. Deploy 131 – Mukhayyalah (Dancing Brave (USA) 140) [2001 48: **48** 16.2m 16.2f⁶ Jun 27] smallish, lengthy gelding: poor performer: stays 2m: acts on soft going, firm and equitrack/fibresand: sometimes blinkered: has hung left. *Ian Williams*

TOSHIBA TIMES 5 b.g. Persian Bold 123 – Kirkby Belle 44 (Bay Express 132) **–** [2001 –: f7f⁶ 8m Jun 22] of little account. *B. Ellison*

TOSKANO 9 b.g. Salse (USA) 128 – Kukri (Kris 135) [2001 f16.2g Feb 17] probably **–** of little account on Flat nowadays. *D. L. Williams*

TOTAL CARE 4 br.c. Caerleon (USA) 132 – Totality 103 (Dancing Brave (USA) **71** 140) [2001 86: f11g f12g f9.4g⁴ 10v 10g⁶ 12g⁶ 13.3f Sep 22] useful-looking colt: fair **a67** form in handicaps in 2001: tailed off final start (reportedly again suffering from breathing problem): stays 1½m: acts on soft and good to firm going: has worn crossed noseband: tongue tied nowadays. *S. C. Williams*

TOTAL DELIGHT 5 b.g. Mtoto 134 – Shesadelight 67 (Shirley Heights 130) [2001 **78 §** 84§: 11.4g³ 15.9m 14.8m Jul 29] smallish, sturdy gelding: fair handicapper: broke down final start: stayed 1¾m: acted on soft and good to firm going: tried visored/was often tongue tied: wasn't to be trusted: dead. *P. R. Webber*

TOTAL LOVE 4 ch.f. Cadeaux Genereux 131 – Favorable Exchange (USA) **97 d** (Exceller (USA) 129) [2001 97: 6d 5.1d³ 5.1f⁶ 6d 6m 5d 7s 10.3s⁶ p7g Nov 24] smallish, leggy filly: useful performer: best effort good length third to Red Millennium in listed event at Bath in May: below form after: effective at 5f to 1m: acts on good to soft going, probably on good to firm: tongue tied fifth start. *G. A. Butler*

TOTALLY SCOTTISH 5 b.g. Mtoto 134 – Glenfinlass (Lomond (USA) 128) [2001 **–** 49: 12f 9f Jul 22] smallish, quite attractive gelding: little form on Flat in 2001: tried blinkered/tongue tied: winning hurdler. *Mrs M. Reveley*

TOTAL MAGIC 3 ch.c. Pivotal 124 – Inherent Magic (IRE) 95 (Magical Wonder **53** (USA) 125) [2001 53: f6g⁴ 7.1g⁶ 6m 6m³ 7g⁶ 8.1f Sep 18] modest maiden handicapper: probably best at 6f: acts on fibresand, good to firm and good to soft ground: sold 6,000 gns. *I. A. Balding*

TOTAL TURTLE (IRE)   2 b.g. (Mar 23) Turtle Island (IRE) 123 – Chagrin   75
d'Amour (IRE) (Last Tycoon 131) [2001 5g⁴ f6g³ f6g* 7g 7.9s Oct 11] 5,000F, 34,000Y:
big, strong gelding: has scope: third foal: brother to French 1¼m winner Verlaine and
half-brother to fairly useful French 4.5f (at 2 yrs) to 1m winner Nerval (by Common
Grounds): dam, French 7f winner, out of smart French middle-distance performer Fleur
d'Oranger: fair performer: won maiden at Southwell in July: stiffish tasks in nurseries
after, then gelded: should stay at least 1m. *P. F. I. Cole*

TOTEM DANCER   8 b.m. Mtoto 134 – Ballad Opera (Sadler's Wells (USA) 132)   59
[2001 63§: 14.1v 13.9m 14m⁵ 14.1m³ 14.6f³ 13s⁶ 15s* 16m² 17.1g² 16g² 15.9d 16g⁶
16.2m⁴ 14v 17.1d 13.8s Oct 20] lengthy mare: has a short action: modest handicapper:
won at Ayr in July: stays 17f: acts on any going: tried visored: tongue tied nowadays:
tends to run in snatches. *J. L. Eyre*

TOTEM POLE   2 ch.c. (Feb 28) Pivotal 124 – Taza (Persian Bold 123) [2001 6f 6d   71 p
Oct 18] big, good-topped colt: has scope: fourth foal: half-brother to useful 1999 2-y-o 7f
winner who stayed 2m Il Capitano (by Be My Chief): dam, no form, half-sister to very
smart middle-distance performer Apache: better effort in maidens (fair form) when
eleventh of 22 to Hiddendale at Newmarket on second start: will probably stay 1m:
should improve. *B. W. Hills*

TO THE LAST MAN   5 b.g. Warrshan (USA) 117 – Shirley's Touch (Touching   40
Wood (USA) 127) [2001 –: f8g 8.3s⁶ 8f⁴ 9.1v Oct 16] leggy gelding: poor performer: left
G. M. Moore after first start: probably best around 1m: acts on any going: tried visored/
blinkered: has edged right: held up. *T. D. Barron*

TO THE WOODS (IRE)   2 ch.f. (Feb 23) Woodborough (USA) 112 – Iktidar 80   72 +
(Green Desert (USA) 127) [2001 5d³ 5v⁴ 5m* 6f 6g⁶ 7g Aug 11] smallish filly: first foal:
dam, Irish maiden who stayed 1m, out of half-sister to Sheikh Albadou: fair performer:
made all in maiden at Haydock in May: form after only when sixth of 7 to Silent Honor in
Cherry Hinton Stakes at Newmarket (probably flattered): stays 6f: acts on good to firm
going. *N. P. Littmoden*

TOUCH'N'GO   7 b.g. Rainbow Quest (USA) 134 – Mary Martin (Be My Guest (USA)   –
126) [2001 14.1v 10s 12.3s f14g May 14] of little account nowadays. *A. B. Mulholland*

TOUCH OF EBONY (IRE)   2 b.c. (Apr 22) Darshaan 133 – Cormorant Wood 130   64
(Home Guard (USA) 129) [2001 7m⁶ 7m f7g³ p7g Dec 29] half-brother to very smart
middle-distance stayer Rock Hopper (by Shareef Dancer) and useful Irish stayer
Cliveden Gail (by Law Society): dam won Champion Stakes: modest form: left B. Hills
after second start: best effort when never-nearer third to Ridley in maiden at Southwell:
should be suited by 1¼m+. *J. Neville*

TOUCH'N OF FAIRY (IRE)   5 b.h. Fairy King (USA) – Decadence (Vaigly Great   69 +
127) [2001 78+: 6d 6g 5s Nov 9] strong, lengthy horse: fair performer, lightly-raced:
needed race/not knocked about in 2001: may prove best at 5f: raced only on good ground
or softer: tried tongue tied. *J. M. Bradley*

TOUCH OF SPIRIT   2 b.f. (Mar 4) Dancing Spree (USA) – Soft Touch (GER)   50
(Horst-Herbert) [2001 f6g⁵ 6m f7g Jul 27] unfurnished filly: first foal: dam German 7f/
7.5f winner: modest form in maiden at Southwell on debut: well held after, including in
seller. *J. G. Given*

TOUCHY FEELINGS (IRE)   3 b.f. Ashkalani (IRE) 128 – Adjalisa (IRE) 65   58
(Darshaan 133) [2001 63: 7g³ Aug 12] modest form in 3 maidens: should stay at least 1m.
R. Hannon

TOUGH LEADER   7 b.g. Lead On Time (USA) 123 – Al Guswa 98 (Shernazar 131)   95 d
[2001 12.3f 11.9m 11.8g⁶ 10g 12g 16m 16.5s Nov 10] robust gelding: useful performer at
best: trained in 1999 by B. Hanbury, in 2000 by M. Dickinson in USA (won claimer at
Belmont): on the downgrade in handicaps in 2001: stays 1¾m: acts on firm and soft
going, had form on fibresand/equitrack earlier in career: tried blinkered: often tongue
tied. *D. J. S. Cosgrove*

TOUGH LOVE   2 ch.g. (Feb 4) Pursuit of Love 124 – Food of Love 109 (Music Boy   75
124) [2001 6d³ 6s³ 6g* 6g² 6m 6v 6d Oct 12] 22,000Y: strong, lengthy gelding: half-
brother to 5f (including at 2 yrs)/6.5f winner who stayed 8.5f Branston Berry (by Mukaddamah) and 5f (including at 2 yrs) winner Price of Passion (by Dolphin Street), both fairly
useful: dam 5f (including at 2 yrs) winner: fair performer: won maiden at Newcastle in
July: well held last 3 starts (gelded after final one): raced only at 6f: acts on soft ground.
T. D. Easterby

*Bradford & Bingley Rated Stakes (Handicap), York—the very smart Tough Speed (left)
leads close home to win from Smirk (centre) and Duke of Modena*

TOUGH SPEED (USA) 4 b.c. Miswaki (USA) 124 – Nature's Magic (USA) **123**
(Nijinsky (CAN) 138) [2001 100: 7.9m² 8m 7.9m* 8d* 7d 8m Dec 16]

Varying starting times for races taking place at different meetings assists television and the betting shops, but the daily programme does not always run like clockwork. Of all the reasons for races being late off, the instability of a tethered hot-air balloon was among the most unusual in the latest season. The Channel 4 blimp, an unmanned balloon used to provide overhead shots, went out of control and had to be winched in during racing at Doncaster on September 13th. The balloon has been an excellent innovation and has advantages over the use of helicopters and airships, which can cause problems with the horses because of the noise, but on this occasion its technical failure caused a delay of fourteen minutes to the Group 3 GNER White Rose Park Stakes. Fortunately, none of the eleven runners seemed affected by the hold-up and the race produced a good finish between the joint-second favourite Tough Speed and the favourite China Visit. It was Tough Speed's first appearance in pattern company, and in beating China Visit by half a length—edging past him in the last fifty yards—he put up his best performance; the consistent Late Night Out was a further two and a half lengths back in third, with Tamburlaine fourth in a larger field than usual for the race.

Tough Speed has had more than his share of problems—he ran just once at three after a promising three-race two-year-old campaign—and reportedly suffers from sore feet, which mean he has to wear stick-on shoes. He had already rewarded the patience of his connections, and more than paid his way, with a victory on his third start in the latest season in the Bradford & Bingley Rated Stakes, over just short of a mile, at the York August meeting. It was his second appearance at the track as a four-year-old, an eye-catching performance when runner-up to Soviet Flash on his reappearance in May leading to a wholesale ante-post gamble on him for the Royal Hunt Cup. Tough Speed started 3/1 favourite on the day at Royal Ascot, odds which scarcely reflected the utmost competitiveness of the event; the stewards considered his running after he came back ninth of thirty, driven along three furlongs out, but his trainer was unable to offer any explanation and 'in the absence of any other relevant information' they decided not to hold an inquiry. Tough Speed started 5/1 favourite under top weight for the seventeen-runner Bradford & Bingley and put up a smart performance, confidently ridden and quickening impressively once in the clear to lead near the finish, scoring by half a length and a neck from Smirk and Duke of Modena, form which suggested the winner was good enough to win a pattern event. Tough Speed is certainly not short of speed and should prove as effective back at seven furlongs, though he ran well below form tried at the trip in the Challenge Stakes at Newmarket in October. He was switched late to the Challenge after earlier being supplemented for the Champion Stakes on the same day, the change of plan made when the going became good to soft. Tough Speed was also well held on his final outing of the year in the Hong Kong Mile at Sha Tin in December, a race in which China Visit finished third.

Tough Speed (USA) (b.c. 1997)	Miswaki (USA) (ch 1978)	Mr Prospector (b 1970)	Raise A Native
			Gold Digger
		Hopespringseternal (ch 1971)	Buckpasser
			Rose Bower
	Nature's Magic (USA) (b 1992)	Nijinsky (b 1967)	Northern Dancer
			Flaming Page
		Joy Returned (b 1977)	Big Spruce
			Imajoy

Tough Speed is a tall, good sort who has developed well since his two-year-old days, when he was rather unfurnished. He consistently took the eye in the paddock in the latest season and should have another good year as a five-year-old. He stays a mile well but whether he will get a mile and a quarter remains to be seen. His sire Miswaki never won at much beyond a mile, though he has sired winners over a variety of distances. Tough Speed's dam, the maiden Nature's Magic, whose first foal he is, is a half-sister to the dual Grade 3 nine-furlong winner Stalwars and to Joy of Glory, winner of a seven-furlong listed event in France and second in the Group 2 Grosser Preis von Dusseldorf over eight and a half furlongs. Tough Speed has yet to encounter extremes of going. *Sir Michael Stoute*

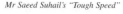

Mr Saeed Suhail's "Tough Speed"

TOUJOURS RIVIERA   11 ch.g. Rainbow Quest (USA) 134 – Miss Beaulieu 106   **52**
(Northfields (USA)) [2001 65: f12g 10f* 8m⁴ 9.2g 11.6g 8g Aug 13] rangy gelding:
modest nowadays: won seller at Pontefract in June: effective at 1m to easy 1½m: acts on
firm going, soft, fibresand and equitrack. *Mrs Lydia Pearce*

TOURVEL   2 b.g. (Jan 24) Bahamian Bounty 116 – Cominna (Dominion 123) [2001   **–**
5.1s f7s f5s Dec 27] 17,500Y: seventh foal: half-brother to 3 winners, including 1994
2-y-o 6f winner Prima Cominna (by Unfuwain) and 5-y-o Forty Forte: dam unraced sister
to very smart sprinter Primo Dominie: well beaten in maiden/sellers: raced too freely
second outing: looked none too keen final one. *N. P. Littmoden*

TOWER OF SONG (IRE)   4 ch.g. Perugino (USA) 84 – New Rochelle (IRE) 65   **–**
(Lafontaine (USA) 117) [2001 65d: f6g f9.4s Jan 9] smallish gelding: has lost his form:
tried blinkered. *D. W. Chapman*

TOWN GOSSIP (IRE)   4 ch.f. Indian Ridge 123 – Only Gossip (USA) (Trempolino   **50**
(USA) 135) [2001 64: f14g 12m 12g 11.9f f11g Dec 3] sturdy filly: modest handicapper:
stays 1¾m: acts on fibresand and good to firm ground. *J. L. Eyre*

TRACE CLIP   3 b.c. Zafonic (USA) 130 – Illusory 81 (Kings Lake (USA) 133) [2001   **103**
6d⁶ 6m³ 5m* 6m⁵ 6m⁴ 6m² 5g² 6g³ 5d³ Oct 18] neat, quite attractive colt: sixth foal:
half-brother to several winners, including useful 7f (also at 2 yrs) winner who stayed
1¼m Sensory (by Selkirk) and fairly useful 1994 2-y-o 5.7f winner Painted Desert (by
Green Desert): dam, 6f winner, sister to smart Lowther Stakes winner Kingscote: useful
performer: won maiden at Doncaster in June: improved form in handicaps after, and good
placed efforts last 4 starts, 2-length third to Smart Predator at Newmarket final one:
headstrong, and should prove better at 5f than 6f: wears tongue strap: usually early to
post: none too resolute. *B. W. Hills*

TRAIKEY (IRE)   9 b.g. Scenic 128 – Swordlestown Miss (USA) (Apalachee (USA)   **–**
137) [2001 –: f8g⁵ f11g 8m 10f Jun 3] one-time useful winner: dead. *Mrs S. Lamyman*

TRAINED BYTHE BEST   3 b.f. Alderbrook 130 – Princess Moodyshoe 72 (Jalmood   **58**
(USA) 126) [2001 7.1g 8m⁵ 7g⁵ 11.9s Oct 3] third foal: half-sister to useful 1999 2-y-o 5f
to 1m winner Misbehave (by Reprimand): dam winner around 1¼m and over hurdles:
modest form in maidens second/third starts: disappointing in amateur handicap on soft
going at Brighton final outing: should be suited by 1¼m+: won over hurdles in December.
M. C. Pipe

TRAMLINE   8 b.g. Shirley Heights 130 – Tramship 110 (High Line 125) [2001 –:   **–**
14.4m 16m Jul 20] strong, lengthy gelding: fair handicapper in 1999: lightly raced and
well held since. *M. Blanshard*

TRAMONTO   2 b.f. (Feb 28) Sri Pekan (USA) 117 – Manhattan Sunset (USA) 76 (El   **91 p**
Gran Senor (USA) 136) [2001 6m 7g⁴ 7.6m* 7s* Oct 16] 34,000Y: well-made filly:
fourth foal: half-sister to a winner in Turkey by Primo Dominie: dam 2-y-o 7f winner who
stayed 1½m: fairly useful form: won maiden at Lingfield in August and minor event at
Leicester (held Red Liason by a neck, having led 2f out) in October: should stay 1m: acts
on soft and good to firm going: capable of better still. *M. P. Tregoning*

TRAMWAY   3 ch.c. Lycius (USA) 124 – Black Fighter (USA) 79 (Secretariat (USA))   **110**
[2001 85p: 10.1m* 10m⁴ 11.6m² 11.9d² Jul 15] tall, close-coupled colt: smart performer:
made all in maiden at Newcastle in May: much improved after, fourth to Potemkin in
listed race at Newmarket, then second in minor event at Windsor (beaten a neck by
Seagull) and listed race at Haydock (length behind Xtra): stays 1½m: acts on good to firm
and good to soft going: sent to Saudi Arabia. *H. R. A. Cecil*

TRANQUIL MOON   3 ch.f. Deploy 131 – Bright Landing 78 (Sun Prince 128) [2001   **64**
e10g 10v p10g² f12s³ p13g* Dec 29] closely related to useful 9f (at 2 yrs) to 2m winner
Upper Strata (by Shirley Heights), dam of Lord of Men, and half-sister to 3 winners,
including 1½m to 2m winner Carnbrea Belle (by Kefaah): dam second at 5f at 2 yrs:
modest form: won handicap at Lingfield in December: stays 13f: acts on fibresand and
polytrack: very slowly away on debut. *D. W. P. Arbuthnot*

TRANSATLANTIC (USA)   3 gr.c. Dumaani (USA) 115 – Viendra (USA) 113   **102**
(Raise A Native) [2001 7g⁵ 7m⁴ 8m⁶ 9g* 10m⁴ 8.1g* 9g Oct 6] $80,000F, IR 16,000Y:
leggy, quite good-topped colt: closely related to useful German winner up to 9.5f Vision
of Spirit (by Chief's Crown) and half-brother to several winners in USA, including useful
performer up to 9f Irish Forever (by Irish River): dam winner in Britain and USA, best at
1¼m: useful performer: much improved when winning handicaps at Kempton in July and
Sandown (by 5 lengths from Red Carnation) in September: well held in Cambridgeshire

at Newmarket final start: stays 9f: raced mainly on good ground or firmer: has worn crossed noseband: free-going sort: waited with. *R. F. Johnson Houghton*

TRANSCENDANTALE (FR)   3 b. or br.f. Apple Tree (FR) 126 – Kataba (FR)   **63**
(Shardari 134) [2001 10m³ 10.2m⁶ 10m³ 10m⁶ 12g 11.5g Sep 11] 130,000 francs Y: fifth foal: half-sister to 2 winners in France, including useful 1m/1¼m winner Subliminal (by Blue Courtier): dam French 2-y-o 4.5f and 1m winner: fair maiden: best form at 1¼m: sold 6,000 gns. *J. H. M. Gosden*

TRANSIT   2 b.c. (Feb 10) Lion Cavern (USA) 117 – Black Fighter (USA) 79   **84 p**
(Secretariat (USA)) [2001 7v³ Oct 26] tall, leggy colt: closely related to several winners, including useful 6f (at 2 yrs) to 9f winner Tracking (by Machiavellian) and 3-y-o Tramway, and half-brother to a winning sprinter in USA by Siberian Express: dam disqualified 1m winner: 5/1 and green, 7½ lengths third of 12 to Foreign Accent in maiden at Doncaster, not knocked about having chased pace for 5f: should improve. *H. R. A. Cecil*

TRAPIO   3 ch.c. Mark of Esteem (IRE) 137 – Pernilla (IRE) 104 (Tate Gallery (USA)   **–**
117) [2001 6g Aug 11] fourth foal: half-brother to 1998 2-y-o 5f winner Paula's Joy (by Danehill) and fairly useful 7f (at 2 yrs and in UAE) winner Hunting Tiger (by Pursuit of Love): dam, Irish 6f/7f performer, half-sister to useful Irish stayer Easy To Please: 33/1 and burly, well held in maiden at Newmarket: dead. *D. Morris*

TRAPPER NORMAN   9 b.g. Mazilier (USA) 107 – Free Skip 68 (Free State 125)   **–**
[2001 –: f11g f7s f7g 7m 7.1d 8.2v Oct 4] of little account nowadays. *R. Wilman*

TRAVELLERS REST   4 b.g. Nomadic Way (USA) 104 – Rest 70 (Dance In Time   **–**
(CAN)) [2001 67?: f11g f12g 10g 10f 6f 8.1g Jul 6] little form in 2001. *J. G. Smyth-Osbourne*

TRAVELLER'S TALE   2 b.g. (Jan 26) Selkirk (USA) 129 – Chere Amie (USA) 75   **62**
(Mr Prospector (USA)) [2001 7.1f⁴ 7g 7.9m⁶ Sep 5] leggy, useful-looking gelding: second foal: dam, French 1¼m winner, closely related to US Grade 2 7f winner Esteemed Friend: modest maiden: best effort when favourite at Musselburgh (veered left) on debut: likely to prove best up to 1m. *P. W. Harris*

TRAVELLING TIMES   2 ch.g. (Apr 16) Timeless Times (USA) 99 – Bollin Sophie   **79**
(Efisio 120) [2001 5s f5g* 5.1m⁴ 6d 6m³ 6m* 6m* 6m Sep 21] strong, leggy gelding: thrived physically: third foal: half-brother to 3-y-o Some Will: dam, little sign of ability, half-sister to smart sprinter Bollin Joanne: fair performer: won maiden at Southwell in May and nurseries at Ripon in August and York (beat Greenhills by length) in September: gelded after final outing: stays 6f: acts on fibresand and good to firm going, possibly not on softer than good: blinkered last 4 starts: usually races prominently. *T. D. Easterby*

TRAVELMATE   7 b.g. Persian Bold 123 – Ustka 60 (Lomond (USA) 128) [2001 –:   **106**
10g² 13.9g Aug 22] lengthy, useful-looking gelding: one-time smart performer, very lightly raced nowadays: returning from tendon injury, 4 lengths second to Albarahin in minor event at Newmarket in August: reportedly suffered another injury in Ebor at York later in month: stays 2m: acts on firm and good to soft going: has wandered and usually held up. *J. R. Fanshawe*

TRAVEL TARDIA (IRE)   3 br.c. Petardia 113 – Annie's Travels (IRE) (Mac's Imp   **92**
(USA) 116) [2001 83p: 6d 5f f6g² f6g² f5s⁵ Dec 15] sturdy, good-bodied colt: fairly useful handicapper: off 5 months before twice good second at Southwell: best at 5f/6f: acts on fibresand and heavy ground: usually races prominently. *I. A. Wood*

TRAVESTY OF LAW (IRE)   4 ch.g. Case Law 113 – Bold As Love (Lomond   **83**
(USA) 128) [2001 90: 5g⁴ 5m 5m² 5.7m 5m⁵ 5m f5g f5s p5g³ Dec 22] smallish, strong,   **a73**
angular gelding: fairly useful performer on turf, fair on all-weather: best at sharp 5f: acts on firm going (below form on softer than good) and polytrack: tried blinkered in 2000. *S. Kirk*

TREASURE CHEST (IRE)   6 b.g. Last Tycoon 131 – Sought Out (IRE) 119   **63**
(Rainbow Quest (USA) 134) [2001 69§: 16.2f* 16.5m² 16.2m³ Jul 27] leggy, angular gelding: fluent mover: modest handicapper: won at Ascot in June: probably stays 2½m: acts on firm and good to soft going: usually visored before 2001: tongue tied earlier in career: sometimes slowly away/hangs: formerly ungenuine. *M. C. Pipe*

TREASURED COIN   3 b.g. Overbury (IRE) 116 – Slip A Coin 63 (Slip Anchor 136)   **–**
[2001 11.7d Oct 25] second foal: dam 9.4f seller winner: 100/1, well held in maiden at Bath on debut. *D. Burchell*

TREASURED GUEST   3 b.g. Rainbow Quest (USA) 134 – Free Guest 125 (Be My   **59**
Guest (USA) 126) [2001 7s 6.9v 8.2v⁶ 10.1m* 10m 10g⁶ Aug 31] tall, leggy gelding:

brother to smart 1m to 1½m winner Freequent and half-brother to several winners, notably Fillies' Mile winner and Oaks second Shamshir (by Kris): dam high-class winner up to 1½m: modest performer: much improved to win handicap at Newcastle in June: failed to progress: likely to be suited by 1½m: acts on good to firm going, probably not on soft/heavy: swished tail in paddock before win: sold 15,000 gns. *L. M. Cumani*

TREASURE TOUCH (IRE) 7 b.g. Treasure Kay 114 – Bally Pourri (IRE) (Law Society (USA) 130) [2001 80, a61: f7g⁶ f7g⁵ 7.1d 5v 5.1d 6m 5.7m 7f 7m 7.6m 6g³ 7m 7d 6g⁶ f8g f7g Nov 23] tall gelding: fair handicapper at best in 2001, on downgrade: effective at 5f (given bit of a test) to 7f: acts on soft going, good to firm and fibresand, possibly not on firm: tried blinkered/tongue tied: often apprentice ridden. *P. D. Evans* **65 d a48**

TREASURE TRAIL 2 b.g. (Mar 23) Millkom 124 – Forever Shineing 62 (Glint of Gold 128) [2001 7m⁶ 8m 7s Oct 16] 10,000F, 11,000Y: good-bodied gelding: third foal: dam, 1½m winner, half-sister to very smart sprinter Crews Hill and to dam of Classic Cliche and My Emma: modest maiden: gelded after final start: should be suited by 1¼m+. *S. Kirk* **60**

TRE COLLINE 2 b.g. (May 8) Efisio 120 – Triple Joy 104 (Most Welcome 131) [2001 7.1g 7.1v⁴ Sep 29] 28,000Y: good-bodied gelding: fourth foal: half-brother to smart 6f (at 2 yrs) and 1m winner Triple Dash (by Nashwan) and 3-y-o Joy of Norway: dam, 6f/7f winner, half-sister to smart middle-distance filly Talented and to dam of 4-y-o Three Points: fair form in maidens: fourth to River Reine at Haydock: gelded after: likely to prove best up to 1m. *S. P. C. Woods* **66**

TREE PIPIT (USA) 2 ch.f. (Apr 22) Woodman (USA) 126 – Skimble (USA) 116 (Lyphard (USA) 132) [2001 7.9d⁴ Oct 13] smallish, well-made filly: fluent mover: fourth foal: closely related to fairly useful 1¼m winner Cloud Hopping (by Mr Prospector) and half-sister to very smart 8.5f to 1¼m winner in Britain/USA Skimming (by Nureyev): dam 6f (at 2 yrs) and 10.4f winner in Britain/USA: 5/1, backward and green, 8½ lengths fourth of 14 to Him of Distinction in maiden at York, taking good hold and carrying head awkwardly once pushed along: should improve. *B. W. Hills* **64 p**

TREE ROOFER 2 b.g. (Mar 31) King's Signet (USA) 110 – Armaiti 78 (Sayf El Arab (USA) 127) [2001 7m 7.1g⁶ 6s Oct 5] 2,600Y, 1,100 2-y-o: fourth foal: dam, 7f winner, half-sister to useful Italian winner up to 11f Dancer Mitral: form in maidens (modest) only when sixth to Dubai Excellence at Chepstow, disputing lead 4f: may prove best up to 7f. *Dr J. R. J. Naylor* **57**

TREETOPS HOTEL (IRE) 2 ch.c. (Apr 10) Grand Lodge (USA) 125 – Rousinette (Rousillon (USA) 133) [2001 6m⁵ 6m³ 6g² 7g⁶ 6d* 6v³ Oct 17] 25,000F, 1,000,000 francs Y: quite attractive colt: seventh foal: half-brother to 3 winners, including Irish 1m winner Renvyle Rose (by Rainbows For Life): dam, twice-raced half-sister to useful performer up to 1½m Rosananti, from family of very smart performer up to 1¾m Sapience: fairly useful handicapper: won 4-runner minor event at Goodwood in September by 1¼ lengths from Addeyll: bred to stay at least 1m: acts on good to soft and good to firm ground. *Mrs A. J. Perrett* **84**

TREMBLEY 4 b.c. Komaite (USA) – Cold Blow 67 (Posse (USA) 130) [2001 6m 6f 6g⁵ 7m 7g 6v⁴ 5v f6g⁶ f6g Dec 10] close-coupled colt: modest maiden, on downgrade: stays 7f: acts on heavy and good to firm going: has been tongue tied. *J. L. Eyre* **59 d**

TREMEZZO 3 b.g. Mind Games 121 – Rosa Van Fleet (Sallust 134) [2001 58: 5.1f 7m 6m⁴ 6.1m 7m⁶ Aug 8] modest maiden: stays 6f: acts on soft and good to firm ground: tried blinkered: won over hurdles in November. *B. R. Millman* **50**

TREMOR 3 ch.g. Zilzal (USA) 137 – Happydrome (Ahonoora 122) [2001 45: f8.5s² e8g⁴ f9.4g⁵ f7g f11g² f9.4g² 9.9m³ 11.5m* 12m Jun 6] modest performer: won seller at Lingfield in May: stays 11.5f: acts on fibresand and good to firm going. *W. R. Muir* **51**

TREVORS SPREE 2 ch.g. (Jan 26) Dancing Spree (USA) – Trevorsninepoints 71 (Jester 119) [2001 5m⁵ 6g⁴ 6.1g 6.1d 7d Oct 18] 1,000F, 3,500Y: leggy, workmanlike gelding: third foal: dam 5f (including at 2 yrs) winner: modest maiden: stays 7f: unraced on extremes of going. *Mrs Lydia Pearce* **60**

TRIBAL PRINCE 4 b.g. Prince Sabo 123 – Tshusick 81 (Dancing Brave (USA) 140) [2001 84: 7g⁶ 8m³ 8.1g 8g⁴ 7d 7d Nov 3] sturdy gelding: fair handicapper: effective at 7f/ 1m: acts on soft and good to firm ground: visored once: usually held up: a tricky ride (has been slowly away). *P. W. Harris* **79**

TRICKS (IRE) 5 b.m. First Trump 118 – Party Line 63 (Never So Bold 135) [2001 58: e10g⁴ e12g f9.4g² Feb 17] poor performer in 2001: stays easy 1¼m: acts on fibresand, equitrack and good to firm ground: tried blinkered. *D. J. Coakley* **40**

TRICKSY (IRE)   3 b.f. Dr Devious (IRE) 127 – Shoof Althahab 63 (Sadler's Wells   –
(USA) 132) [2001 –: f8g f11g² f11g 12f 10m Sep 1] leggy filly: poor maiden at best: **a49**
reportedly had breathing problem when tailed off final 2 starts: stays 11f: acts on
fibresand: tried tongue tied. *Mrs M. Reveley*

TRICKY LADY (IRE)   2 b.f. (Jan 29) Persian Bold 123 – Tropicana (IRE) (Imperial   **55**
Frontier (USA) 112) [2001 8.1s 7.5g 6d⁵ Oct 3] smallish, leggy filly: first foal: dam
unraced half-sister to useful sprinter Harvest Girl and 4-y-o James Stark: modest maiden:
should stay beyond 1m: has given trouble at stalls. *M. Johnston*

TRILLIE   3 b.f. Never So Bold 135 – Trull (Lomond (USA) 128) [2001 86: 6s⁶ 6m 6m   –
8d 6d Oct 3] tall, leggy filly: fairly useful performer at 2 yrs: disappointing in handicaps
in 2001. *C. F. Wall*

TRILLIONAIRE   3 ch.g. Dilum (USA) 115 – Madam Trilby (Grundy 137) [2001 70:   –
8m 5m 7.1g 7g 7m⁶ 8g f8.5g f7g Nov 23] strong, close-coupled gelding: fine mover:
modest maiden at 2 yrs: little form in 2001, leaving D. Nicholls after third start: stays 7f:
acts on firm going, well held on good to soft/fibresand. *D. W. Chapman*

TRILOGY   2 ch.c. (Jan 23) Grand Lodge (USA) 125 – Three More (USA) (Sangla-   **97**
more (USA) 126) [2001 6f 7m³ 7m* 6m³ 7.1g 7g Oct 5] smallish, deep-girthed colt:
second foal: dam unraced half-sister to very smart performer up to 1¼m Kefaah out of
sister to top-class middle-distance performer Nobiliary and half-sister to Lyphard: useful
performer: made all in maiden at Salisbury in July, winning by 5 lengths: below form in
pattern company after, 6¼ lengths fourth to Mister Cosmi in Richmond Stakes at
Goodwood: should stay at least 1m: raced only on good going or firmer: joined R. Frankel
in USA. *J. H. M. Gosden*

TRIMONTIUM (USA)   2 b.g. (Jan 18) Mt Livermore (USA) – Sailing Minstrel   **81**
(USA) (The Minstrel (CAN) 135) [2001 6m³ 6.1d³ 7s³ 8d⁴ Oct 19] $120,000Y, resold
35,000Y: close-coupled gelding: fourth foal: brother to US 8.5f minor stakes winner
Efficient Frontier, closely related to a winner in USA by Rahy and half-brother to smart
US 1m/1¼m performer Navesink (by Irish River): dam, won up to 9f in USA, half-sister
to St Leger fourth Nemain: fairly useful maiden: good fourth of 24 to Bestam in nursery
at Newmarket (subsequently gelded): will stay 1¼m. *J. R. Fanshawe*

TRIMSTONE   4 br.g. Bandmaster (USA) 97 – Klairover 50 (Smackover (107) [2001   **45**
6v f8.5g² f8.5f⁵ Dec 5] 500Y: fourth foal: half-brother to 2 winners, including 6f/7f
winner General Klaire (by Presidium): dam, 5f/6f winner, half-sister to smart sprinter
Bunty Boo: poor form in maidens: stays 8.5f: acts on fibresand. *R. J. Hodges*

TRINITY (IRE)   5 b.h. College Chapel 122 – Kaskazi (Dancing Brave (USA) 140)   **66**
[2001 71: 5g 6g⁶ 5m 6g 6g⁴ 6g* 6.1v Oct 4] close-coupled horse: fair handicapper: won
at Newcastle in August: effective at 5f/6f: acts on firm going: has worn crossed noseband/
tongue tie: sometimes finds little: none too consistent. *M. Brittain*

TRIO   5 b.g. Cyrano de Bergerac 120 – May Light 62 (Midyan (USA) 124) [2001 8.1m   **62 §**
11.5f⁶ 10m 11.5f 10s Oct 25] quite good-topped gelding: modest handicapper: seems to
stay 11.5f: acts on good to firm and good to soft going: difficult ride, best held up: has
refused to race: one to treat with caution. *N. Hamilton*

TRIPHENIA (IRE)   3 b.g. Ashkalani (IRE) 128 – Atsuko (IRE) (Mtoto 134) [2001   **84**
8d³ f11g⁴ 8.5m⁴ 12f Jun 21] IR 65,000Y: lengthy gelding: third foal: half-brother to 1999
2-y-o 5f winner Night Shifter (by Night Shift) and useful Irish 9f winner Atacat (by
Catrail): dam, second at 1m at 2 yrs in Ireland, closely related to very smart French
middle-distance performer Muroto: fairly useful form: won maiden at Southwell in April:
struck into and run best ignored (at Royal Ascot) final outing: should stay 1½m: acts on
fibresand and good to firm ground. *M. L. W. Bell*

TRIPLE BLUE (IRE)   3 ch.c. Bluebird (USA) 125 – Persian Tapestry 70 (Tap On   **93**
Wood 130) [2001 98: 6m 6m 8.1m 6m⁵ 7g 7g Oct 5] strong, smallish colt: useful
performer at 2 yrs: mostly disappointing after reappearance in 2001: probably stays 7f:
acts on any going: sold 6,000 gns. *R. Hannon*

TRIPLE CONCERTO   4 ch.f. Grand Lodge (USA) 125 – On The Bank (IRE) (In   –
The Wings 128) [2001 f12g f12g Jan 15] leggy, unfurnished filly: well held in maidens/
seller: tried blinkered. *B. S. Rothwell*

TRIPLE DECISION (USA)   3 b.f. Torrential (USA) 117 – Triple Kiss 106 (Shareef   –
Dancer (USA) 135) [2001 7d Apr 20] closely related to 5-y-o Gudlage and half-sister to 3
winners, including useful Irish 8.5f to 1¾m winner Rawy (by Rahy): dam Irish 1m winner
who stayed 1¾m: eleventh of 18 to Pearly Gates in Newbury maiden: dead. *B. Hanbury*

TRIPLE GLORY (IRE)   2 b.f. (Feb 18) Goldmark (USA) 113 – Trebles (IRE) (Kenmare (FR) 125) [2001 7m 7m Aug 16] IR 4,000Y: first foal: dam French 1¼m winner: modest form in maidens at Newbury and Salisbury: should stay 1¼m. *Mrs P. N. Dutfield*   **56**

TRIPLEMOON (USA)   2 ch.f. (Apr 26) Trempolino (USA) 135 – Placer Queen (Habitat 134) [2001 6.9m⁴ 6.9m 6m⁵ 7.1m⁴ 7m⁴ 8s³ 10v Oct 4] rather leggy filly: half-sister to several winners, including fairly useful 1994 2-y-o 7f winner Above The Cut (by Topsider) and 7-y-o Beyond Calculation: dam winner up to 1¼m in Canada: fair maiden: in frame in nurseries fourth to sixth starts: should stay 1¼m: acts on soft and good to firm going. *P. W. Harris*   **73**

TRIPLE PLAY (IRE)   2 br.g. (Apr 15) Tagula (IRE) 116 – Shiyra (Darshaan 133) [2001 5d⁴ 5g* 5f³ 6m 5g⁶ 6g³ 6m 6m 6g Oct 6] IR 11,000F, 70,000Y: rather leggy, quite attractive gelding: sixth living foal: brother to useful German 2000 2-y-o 6f/7f winner Tagshira and half-brother to a 5f/6f winner in Italy by Mac's Imp: dam Irish 1m/1¼m winner: fairly useful performer: won maiden at Leicester in May: deteriorated after fourth start: best efforts at 5f: acts on firm going, probably on good to soft: raced too freely in blinkers: sold 6,000 gns. *B. J. Meehan*   **88 d**

TRIPPER (USA)   2 b.f. (Feb 18) Kingmambo (USA) 125 – Summer Trip (USA) 117 (L'Emigrant (USA) 129) [2001 7m 7d⁶ Nov 3] rather leggy, useful-looking filly: sixth foal: closely related to 4-y-o Faraway Look and half-sister to smart 1996 2-y-o 7f winner Musheer (by Known Fact): dam won Prix de Royallieu and stayed 13.5f: much better effort in maidens at Newmarket (fair form) when sixth of 21 to Maid To Perfection, again not given unduly hard time: should stay 1¼m: should make a better 3-y-o. *J. L. Dunlop*   **73 p**

TRIPPITAKA   4 b.f. Ezzoud (IRE) 126 – Bluish (USA) (Alleged (USA) 138) [2001 53: 14.1s 12.4d 14.1m⁵ 16.2m Jun 18] tall, angular filly: modest maiden: stays 1¾m, probably not 2m: acts on good to firm going: blinkered last 2 starts: sent to Holland. *N. A. Graham*   **51**

TRIP THE SWITCH (IRE)   3 b.f. Imperial Frontier (USA) 112 – Brite Mist (IRE) (Shy Groom (USA)) [2001 7g 8.2v 10v Oct 16] IR 2,800Y: fourth foal: dam unraced half-sister to very smart sprinter Cyrano de Bergerac: well beaten in maidens. *B. S. Rothwell*   **–**

TRIUMPHANT RETURN (NZ)   6 br.g. Asti Bay (NZ) – Vaniteux (AUS) (Vain (AUS)) [2001 6g 6g⁵ 5.2f 5g Nov 9] big, lengthy gelding: had good year in Singapore in 2000, completing 4-timer in handicaps: tenth of 11 in listed event at Newbury (beaten 6¼ lengths) penultimate start in 2001, only outing in Britain: stays 7f. *P. Busuttin, Singapore*   **99 ?**

TROJAN GIRL (IRE)   5 b.m. Up And At 'em 109 – Lady-Mumtaz (Martin John) [2001 f6g f5g 7m f7g Jun 15] fair performer in 1999: no form since. *Miss S. J. Wilton*   **–**

TROJAN (IRE)   2 ch.g. (Apr 30) Up And At 'em 109 – Fantasie (FR) (General Assembly (USA)) [2001 7m³ Aug 13] IR 10,000F, IR 62,000Y: brother to 1998 2-y-o 6f/ 7f seller winner Tampa Lady, and half-brother to several winners, including 5f (at 2 yrs) to 1m winner Means Business (by Imp Society): dam second at 7f at 2 yrs in Ireland: 9/2, 5 lengths third of 11 to Welenska in maiden at Folkestone: gelded after: should improve. *S. P. C. Woods*   **69 p**

TROJAN PRINCESS   2 b.f. (Mar 29) Hector Protector (USA) 124 – Robellino Miss (USA) (Robellino (USA) 127) [2001 7f⁶ 7g³ 7d* Oct 15] rather leggy, useful-looking filly: half-sister to several winners, including 1999 2-y-o 7f winner Decision Maid (by Diesis) and 1998 2-y-o 6f winner Chief Rebel (by Chief's Crown), both useful up to 1m: dam, won up to 9f in USA, out of close relative to high-class sprinter Silver Fling: fairly useful form: justified favouritism in 20-runner maiden at Leicester by neck from Fragrant View, always prominent and battling on gamely: should stay 1m: acts on firm and good to soft going: open to progress. *G. Wragg*   **80 p**

TROJAN PRINCE (USA)   3 b. or br.g. Known Fact (USA) 135 – Helen V (USA) (Slewacide (USA)) [2001 73d: 6m 7m Jun 18] useful-looking gelding: fair maiden at 2 yrs: well held in 2001 (reportedly broke blood vessel final start): races freely, and should prove best at 5f/6f: best effort on good to soft ground: edgy sort, has been taken steadily to post: one to treat with some caution. *B. W. Hills*   **– §**

TROJAN WOLF   6 ch.g. Wolfhound (USA) 126 – Trojan Lady (USA) (Irish River (FR) 131) [2001 –§, a82§: f8g⁶ f7f⁵ 8s³ f8g 8m⁶ 8m f8g² f8g* f8g³ 8f f12g f8g f8g* f11g³ f8g Dec 14] strong gelding: fair performer on all-weather, modest on turf nowadays: won claimer in July and seller in November, both at Southwell: probably best at 1m to easy 11f: acts on firm going, soft, fibresand and equitrack: tried visored/tongue tied earlier in career: usually races up with pace: moody, and not to be relied upon. *P. Howling*   **53 §**
   a73 §

TROOPER COLLINS (IRE)   3 b.c. Dolphin Street (FR) 125 – Born To Fly (IRE)   **63**
57 (Last Tycoon 131) [2001 8.1d⁵ 7g⁴ 8d 8.1f⁴ f9.4g Oct 9] IR 11,000F, 25,000Y: fifth
foal: closely related to unreliable (fairly useful at best) 7f/1m winner Blue Flyer (by
Bluebird): dam best at 6f: modest maiden: stays 1m: acts on firm and good to soft ground,
well held on fibresand. *Jonjo O'Neill*

TROP CHERE (IRE)   2 b.f. (Feb 3) Distinctly North (USA) 115 – Break For Tee   **55**
(IRE) 62 (Executive Perk 120) [2001 f5g 5d 6m 6m² 7m⁴ Jun 14] IR 17,000Y: lengthy,
good-topped filly: second foal: sister to useful Irish 9f/1¼m winner Distinguished Cove:
dam, third at 1½m in Ireland, half-sister to dam of high-class performer up to 1½m River
Keen: modest maiden: second in seller at Goodwood: should stay 7f: unraced on
extremes of going: has found little/carried head awkwardly under pressure. *A. P. Jarvis*

TROPICAL RIVER (IRE)   3 b.g. Lahib (USA) 129 – Tropical Dance (USA) 93   **–**
(Thorn Dance (USA) 107) [2001 –: 6d May 21] neat gelding: behind in maidens/claimer.
E. Stanners

TROTTER'S FUTURE   3 b.c. Emperor Jones (USA) 119 – Miss Up N Go (Gorytus   **73**
(USA) 132) [2001 –: e7g⁴ 11.6s 14.1d⁴ 14.1m* 14.1m* 14.1g³ 16.2f⁴ 16.4g² 16.4g* 16g³
16d⁵ f14g Nov 26] close-coupled colt: fair handicapper: won at Redcar in May, Yarmouth
in June and Folkestone (apprentices) in August: left A. Stewart 27,000 gns and off 2
months before final start: stays 2m: acts on firm and good to soft going: held up: has
found less than expected: tends to wander/flash tail, but is consistent. *M. W. Easterby*

TROUBLE   5 b.g. Kris 135 – Ringlet (USA) 58 (Secreto (USA) 128) [2001 –: f9.4s   **49**
f8.5g⁴ f8g³ Feb 2] rangy gelding: poor maiden: stays 8.5f: acts on fibresand. *P. W. Hiatt*

TROUBLE MOUNTAIN (USA)   4 br.g. Mt Livermore (USA) – Trouble Free (USA)   **82**
(Nodouble (USA)) [2001 101: 6.1v 7g 10.4g 8m 6d 7m 7g 10.4m* 12g 10d⁴ 8.9d 8d²
10s Nov 5] small, sparely-made gelding: good mover: has a quick action: fairly useful
handicapper: slipped long way in weights after 8 unplaced efforts, then won apprentice
event at York in September: very good second of 26 to Beauchamp Pilot at Redcar
(forcefully ridden) penultimate start: effective at 1m to 1¼m: acts on firm and good to
soft going. *M. W. Easterby*

TROUBLE NEXT DOOR (IRE)   3 b.g. Persian Bold 123 – Adjacent (IRE) 82   **44**
(Doulab (USA) 115) [2001 44: e8g⁶ f9.4s⁶ 9.9g⁴ 9.9m⁵ 12f 13.1m Sep 10] big, strong,
workmanlike gelding: has markedly round action: poor maiden handicapper: stays 1¼m:
acts on good to firm going. *N. P. Littmoden*

TROUBLESHOOTER   3 b.g. Ezzoud (IRE) 126 – Oublier L'Ennui (FR) 79 (Bellman
(FR) 123) [2001 65: 8v 8d 7g 10d f7g Nov 23] strong, well-made gelding: fair maiden at
2 yrs: well held in 2001: blinkered last 5 starts at 2 yrs, and final 3-y-o outing (tongue
tied). *M. Dods*

TROYS GUEST (IRE)   3 gr.f. Be My Guest (USA) 126 – Troja (Troy 137) [2001 66:   **–**
f11g 12m 10.9m 8.3m Jun 13] sturdy, workmanlike filly: disappointing maiden: has given
trouble at start/left stall awkwardly: headstrong. *E. J. Alston*

TRUDIE   3 b.f. Komaite (USA) – Irish Limerick 89 (Try My Best (USA) 130) [2001   **49**
55: f5s f6g 6g 5g⁴ 5m 6d² f6g* Oct 22] rangy filly: poor performer: left Miss J. Craze
after second start: won maiden at Southwell in October: stays 6f: acts on fibresand and
good to soft ground: has run well when sweating: tried blinkered. *Mrs A. M. Naughton*

TRUE BLADE   3 ch.f. Sabrehill (USA) 120 – Certain Story (Known Fact (USA) 135   **64 d**
[2001 8.1g³ 8f³ 8d 8f⁶ 6g 7m⁵ 5m 7s Oct 16] half-sister to several winners, including
useful 8.5f to 1½m winner Pharly Story and fairly useful 1994 2-y-o 6f winner Noble
Kingdom (by Pharly): dam unraced half-sister to dam of Shaamit: modest maiden:
easily best effort on debut: left G. Butler after fourth start: stays 1m: acts on firm going,
seemingly not on softer than good: sold 1,500 gns. *P. F. I. Cole*

TRUE COURAGE   2 b.c. (Mar 18) Machiavellian (USA) 123 – Try To Catch Me   **76 p**
(USA) (Shareef Dancer (USA) 135) [2001 7m 8d⁶ Oct 2] rather leggy, close-coupled
colt: has a round action: sixth foal: brother to 3-y-o Storming Home and half-brother to 3
winners, including 1½m winner Follow That Dream (by Darshaan) and 11f to 13f winner
Desert Frolic (by Persian Bold), both fairly useful: dam, French 1m winner, out of
champion 2-y-o filly in USA who stayed 1¼m It's In The Air: better effort in maidens
(fair form) when sixth of 21 to Hathaal at Newmarket, travelling strongly until over 1f
out: free-going sort, but bred to stay at least 1¼m: should improve further. *B. W. Hills*

TRUE FANTASY (USA)   3 b.f. Seeking The Gold (USA) – Jood (USA) 87 (Nijinsky   **–**
(CAN) 138) [2001 7d Apr 18] tall, useful-looking filly: fifth foal: closely related to UAE

1053

7f winner Madraar (by Mr Prospector) and 4-y-o Westbound Road and half-sister to 5-y-o Fantastic Light: dam, third at 7f (at 2 yrs) and 1¼m, her only 2 starts, daughter of Canadian Oaks winner Kamar, herself sister to dam of Swain: 14/1, never dangerous and well held in Newmarket maiden: stud. *Sir Michael Stoute*

TRUE LIES 4 ch.f. King's Signet (USA) 110 – Lysithea 63 (Imperial Fling (USA) – 116) [2001 p12g Nov 28] half-sister to 5f (at 2 yrs) and 12.5f winner Lying Eyes (by Interrex): dam 6f seller winner: last in claimer on Flat debut. *W. G. M. Turner*

TRUE NIGHT 4 b.g. Night Shift (USA) – Dead Certain 123§ (Absalom 128) [2001 **94** 80p: 7s 7m 7g 8m⁴ 7.6m² 8m* 8m³ 7d* 8m³ 7m 7g 7d 7f⁶ 9g Oct 6] smallish, attractive gelding: fairly useful handicapper: won at Salisbury in June and Leicester in July: effective at 7f/1m: acts on firm and good to soft going: has worn crossed noseband/been early to post: found little/carried head awkwardly penultimate start: usually held up: sold 17,000 gns in October, joined D. Nicholls. *H. Candy*

TRUE NOTE 3 b.g. So Factual (USA) 120 – Singer On The Roof 62 (Chief Singer **45** 131) [2001 –: f7g f7g f6s⁵ f6g 8.3m 8m⁵ 9m 8.2g 7m 5d f11g 10.9v Oct 15] strong, good-topped gelding: poor maiden: tailed off (reportedly finished distressed) final start: likely to prove best up to 1m: acts on good to firm ground and fibresand: tried tongue tied. *J. Hetherton*

TRUMP APPEAL 3 b.g. First Trump 118 – Appelania 63 (Star Appeal 133) [2001 – 10g 10d⁶ 9m Aug 5] 10,000F: fifth foal: half-brother to 2 winners, including fairly useful 1m (at 2 yrs) to 1½m winner who stayed 2m Domappel (by Domynsky): dam 1m winner: well held in maidens: slowly away on debut. *J. G. Portman*

TRUMPET MAJOR 2 b.c. (May 4) First Trump 118 – Trundley Wood 66 (Wassl **65** 125) [2001 7m 7m⁶ 7m Aug 27] 8,500Y: third foal: half-brother to Italian 5f/6.5f winner Squanto (by Prince Sabo) and a winner in Germany by Deploy: dam 2-y-o 5f winner: easily best effort in maidens (fair form) when sixth to Tholjanah at Kempton: raced only at 7f: dead. *P. Mitchell*

TRUMPINGTON 3 ch.f. First Trump 118 – Brockton Flame 72 (Emarati (USA) 74) **75** [2001 73: 12f 14m⁵ 16.2s⁶ 14g f14g⁵ Oct 22] rather leggy, quite good-topped filly: fair handicapper: stays 1¾m: acts on fibresand, firm and good to soft going: races prominently: sold 10,000 gns. *J. A. R. Toller*

TRUSHAN 3 ch.f. Anshan 119 – Home Truth 98 (Known Fact (USA) 135) [2001 7d **48** 7.5m⁵ May 22] smallish, leggy filly: sixth living foal: half-sister to several winners, including very smart 7f performer Susu (by Machiavellian) and 7-y-o Cadeaux Cher: dam 7f/1m winner: poor form in 2 maidens. *B. W. Hills*

TRUSTED MOLE (IRE) 3 b.g. Eagle Eyed (USA) 111 – Orient Air 74 (Prince Sabo **65** § 123) [2001 68: 10s 8.1g 9.9m* 10m² 10m 10g⁴ 10m 10m* 10m* 10m³ 9.9m³ 12.1s 9.7d **a58** § 10.9m⁴ 10s f12g p12g² p10g Dec 22] deep-girthed gelding: fair performer: won seller at Beverley in May and claimers at Newmarket (left J. Osborne) in June and Leicester in July: effective at 1¼m/easy 1¼m: acts on firm going, good to soft and polytrack (no form on fibresand): all wins in blinkers, has run creditably without: has gone left leaving stall/found little/wandered. *S. Kirk*

TRUST IN PAULA (USA) 3 b.f. Arazi (USA) 135 – Trust In Dixie (USA) **54** (Dixieland Band (USA)) [2001 54: f6g f7g 10m 8m⁶ 8m 10s⁴ f11g⁶ f12s* Dec 27] modest handicapper: visored, won at Wolverhampton in December: stays 1½m: acts on fibresand, soft and good to firm ground. *D. Haydn Jones*

TRUSTTHUNDER 3 ch.f. Selkirk (USA) 129 – Royal Cat (Royal Academy (USA) **68** 130) [2001 87: 7d 6.1f 7m 7f³ 7d⁵ 6m f7g⁵ 6.1f p7g² p7g⁵ f6g p6g³ Dec 29] tall, angular filly: fairly useful at 2 yrs: only fair and inconsistent in 2001: may prove best at 6f/7f: yet to race on heavy, acts on any other turf going and fibresand/polytrack. *N. P. Littmoden*

TRYFAN 2 b.g. (Apr 12) Distant Relative 128 – Sister Sal 74 (Bairn (USA) 126) [2001 **?** 8m⁴ 7d f7g Nov 17] 3,000Y, 4,000 2-y-o: leggy gelding: seventh foal: half-brother to 2-y-o 5f winners Exosal (seller in 1994, by Exodal) and Northern Sal (in 1996, by Aragon): dam 2-y-o 6f winner who later stayed 1¼m: 100/1, appeared to show fair form when fourth of 5 to Bandari in minor event at Ayr (probably flattered): well beaten in maidens: gelded after final start. *A. Bailey*

TRY PARIS (IRE) 5 b.g. Paris House 123 – Try My Rosie 93 (Try My Best (USA) – 130) [2001 38: e12g 11.9m 10d 10.1m 10m 10m Sep 4] good-topped gelding: little form in 2001, leaving H. Collingridge after fourth start: usually visored nowadays. *Mrs L. C. Jewell*

TRYSULL DREAM (IRE) 2 b.f. (May 15) Mujadil (USA) 119 – Emma's Whisper **40**
69 (Kind of Hush 118) [2001 6g 5.2m⁵ 6d Jun 17] fifth reported foal: half-sister to 3
winners abroad, including fairly useful Irish 7f winner Teazel Boy (by Forzando), later
winner up to 9f in Hong Kong: dam, maiden who stayed 1m, half-sister to US Grade 1
1m/1¼m winner In Excess: poor maiden. *C. A. Dwyer*

TSUNAMI 5 b.m. Beveled (USA) – Alvecote Lady 50 (Touching Wood (USA) 127) **30**
[2001 43: f11g⁶ Jan 12] leggy mare: poor maiden, lightly raced nowadays: barely stays
1¾m: acts on fibresand and good to firm going, probably on heavy: has been slowly
away/refused to enter stalls, and was banned from Flat racing from stalls for 6 months
from Mar 22. *P. D. Evans*

TSWALU 4 b.f. Cosmonaut – Madam Taylor 81 (Free State 125) [2001 –: f12g f12g **–**
Feb 8] probably of little account nowadays. *M. Mullineaux*

TUCKER FENCE 2 br.g. (May 6) So Factual (USA) 120 – Daisy Topper (Top Ville **69**
129) [2001 5.1f 5m 5f³ 7m² 6m* 6g 6g⁶ 6.1m* 6m² 6g⁴ 6g f6s² 6m 7d f6g Oct 17] 1,000Y, **a72**
resold 6,000Y: seventh foal: half-brother to fairly useful Irish 7f winner Florida Villas (by
Polar Falcon) and a 5f (including at 2 yrs) to 7f winner in Italy by Beveled: dam unraced
out of half-sister to Royal Lodge winner Robellino: fair performer: won seller at
Newcastle in June and nursery at Chester in August: creditable efforts after when in frame
in nurseries: effective at 6f/7f: acts on fibresand and good to firm going: blinkered/
visored fourth to seventh starts. *A. Berry*

TUDOR WOOD 2 b.c. (Feb 22) Royal Applause 124 – Silent Indulgence (USA) **99 ?**
(Woodman (USA) 126) [2001 6f² 6d 7g⁵ 6d Oct 18] 140,000Y: well-made colt: second
foal: half-brother to fairly useful 2000 2-y-o 6f winner In The Woods (by You And I):
dam placed in USA: 50/1 after 3½-month absence, easily best effort (useful form) when
just over 4 lengths fifth of 9 to Where Or When in Somerville Tattersall Stakes at
Newmarket: ran in maidens otherwise (runner-up at Leicester): free-going sort (has worn
crossed noseband), and will need to settle to stay beyond 7f. *D. J. S. Cosgrove*

TUFAMORE (USA) 5 ch.g. Mt Livermore (USA) – Tufa 78 (Warning 136) [2001 **– §**
58§: 14m f14g Jun 8] temperamental handicapper: no form in 2001: tried blinkered/
visored. *E. W. Tuer*

TUFTY HOPPER 4 b.g. Rock Hopper 124 – Melancolia 77 (Legend of France **62**
(USA) 124) [2001 71, a68: e13g⁴ f12g⁴ f12g* f12g² f12g³ 14.1m 10g 11.6m 14.1d⁵ 12g **a68**
14.1d f12g⁴ f14g³ 15.8d⁶ f14.8g* f16.2g² p16g² f16.2g² f14g⁴ f16.2s⁶ Dec 18] fair
handicapper: won at Wolverhampton in February and November: stays 2m: acts on
all-weather, firm and good to soft going: tried blinkered/visored: held up: carries head
high/often looks none too keen, but generally consistent. *P. Howling*

TUI 6 b.m. Tina's Pet 121 – Curious Feeling (Nishapour (FR) 125) [2001 42: 15g 12.1m⁵ **38**
Jul 27] poor handicapper: stays 1½m: acts on soft and good to firm going, probably on
heavy. *P. Bowen*

TUIGAMALA 10 b.g. Welsh Captain 113 – Nelliellamay (Super Splash (USA) 106) **–**
[2001 –, a39: e8g³ e10g⁵ f8g⁴ f9.4g* e10g² e10g⁵ e10g e10g⁴ Apr 11] good-topped **a47**
gelding: poor performer: won handicap at Wolverhampton in February: stays easy 1¼m:
acts on fibresand, equitrack and firm ground. *R. Ingram*

TUMBLEWEED CHARM (IRE) 2 b.c. (Mar 22) Zafonic (USA) 130 – Vienna **88**
Charm (IRE) 67 (Sadler's Wells (USA) 132) [2001 6f⁶ 6m* 6g 7m Sep 12] 62,000Y:
good-bodied colt: third foal: dam Canadian 7f winner: fairly useful performer: won minor
event at Newbury (made all) in July: well held in Prix Morny at Deauville and minor
event at Doncaster after: free-going sort, and may prove best around 6f. *B. J. Meehan*

TUMBLEWEED RIDGE 8 ch.h. Indian Ridge 123 – Billie Blue 63 (Ballad Rock **107**
122) [2001 115: 7g 7g³ 7g⁴ 7g* 7m⁵ 7.1g* 7s³ 7.3f Sep 21] well-made horse: impresses in
appearance: only useful form in 2001, winning minor event at Chepstow (beat Cd Europe
by neck) in August: ran creditably earlier in year when in frame in minor event at
Newmarket and Prix du Palais-Royal at Longchamp (2¾ lengths fourth to Lunasalt)
second/third starts: best around 7f: best form on good ground or softer in 2001: usually
blinkered/tongue tied: has worn dropped/crossed noseband: usually races prominently:
none too consistent. *B. J. Meehan*

TUMBLEWEED RIVER (IRE) 5 ch.g. Thatching 131 – Daphne Indica (IRE) **–**
(Ballad Rock 122) [2001 81: e7g 7.1v Apr 25] good-topped gelding: fairly useful
performer at 4 yrs: well held in 2001, pulled up final start: blinkered once. *B. J. Meehan*

TUMBLEWEED TENOR (IRE) 3 b.g. Mujadil (USA) 119 – Princess Carmen – (IRE) 61 (Arokar (FR) 124) [2001 74: f6g Apr 14] angular gelding: fair performer at 2 yrs: showed little only run in 2001: stays 7f: acts on fibresand and firm ground. *B. J. Meehan*

TUNNEL OF LOVE 3 ch.f. Mark of Esteem (IRE) 137 – La Dama Bonita (USA) 87 **51** (El Gran Senor (USA) 136) [2001 8.2d⁵ f8g⁵ Nov 30] fourth living foal: half-sister to 2 winners, notably smart winner up to 10.5f in Britain/UAE Conflict (by Warning): dam, 5f (at 2 yrs) and 7f winner, closely related to high-class French sprinter/miler Polar Falcon: better effort in maidens (modest form) when fifth at Nottingham on debut, very free early on: likely to prove as effective at 6f/7f as 1m. *D. W. P. Arbuthnot*

TUNSTALL (USA) 2 b.c. (Feb 18) Bahri (USA) 125 – Princess West (GER) (Gone **74** West (USA)) [2001 7g⁵ 8g⁴ 7m 8d Oct 19] $190,000Y: close-coupled, quite good-topped colt: first foal: dam, German 7.5f winner, half-sister to useful German performer around 1m Page's King: fair form in minor event and maiden at Newmarket first 2 starts: well held after: stays 1m: joined T. Easterby. *L. M. Cumani*

TUPGILL CENTURION 3 b.g. Emperor Jones (USA) 119 – Elisa War (Warning – 136) [2001 44: 10m 8m 11m 11m Jul 28] leggy, angular gelding: poor maiden at 2 yrs: well held in 2001. *S. E. Kettlewell*

TUPGILL FLIGHT (IRE) 3 b.f. Be My Chief (USA) 122 – Wing Partner (IRE) – 83 (In The Wings 128) [2001 –: 10g Jun 12] lengthy, good-quartered filly: little form. *S. E. Kettlewell*

TUPGILL TIPPLE 3 b.f. Emperor Jones (USA) 119 – Highest Baby (FR) (Highest – Honor (FR) 124) [2001 55d: f7g f8g f8.5s 12d 9.5m 6m 9g 10s Nov 1] leggy, workmanlike filly: has a round action: modest form first 3 starts at 2 yrs: well held since, leaving S. Kettlewell after third start in 2001: tried visored. *Patrick Carey, Ireland*

TUPGILL TURBO 3 ch.g. Rudimentary (USA) 118 – Persian Alexandra (Persian – Bold 123) [2001 45: 7v 8m 8f 8m Jul 8] strong, useful-looking gelding: poor maiden at 2 yrs: well held in 2001. *S. E. Kettlewell*

TUPPENCE HA'PENNY 2 gr.f. (Apr 15) Never So Bold 135 – Mummy's Chick 77 **54** (Mummy's Pet 125) [2001 7d 6v Nov 8] unfurnished filly: eighth foal: dam 2-y-o 5f winner: better effort in maidens (modest form) when seventh to Kepler at Windsor final outing: bred to prove best at 5f/6f. *G. G. Margarson*

TURAATH (IRE) 5 b.g. Sadler's Wells (USA) 132 – Diamond Field (USA) 71 (Mr – Prospector (USA)) [2001 89: f9.4g 12g May 6] smallish gelding: fairly useful performer at 4 yrs, on downgrade. *G. M. McCourt*

TURBO (IRE) 2 b.g. (Apr 17) Piccolo 121 – By Arrangement (IRE) 60 (Bold **82** Arrangement 127) [2001 5.1f 6g² 6m³ 7.1d* 7m⁴ 7m 7.1s³ 7d³ 7.9s⁶ 7v Oct 26] 14,500Y: close-coupled gelding: second foal: half-brother to 3-y-o Its Your Bid: dam 1m to 2m winner: fairly useful performer: won maiden at Warwick in July: best efforts after when in frame in nurseries: should stay 1m: acts on soft and good to firm going: visored fourth to sixth starts: gelded after final one. *G. B. Balding*

TURIBIUS 2 b.g. (Mar 22) Puissance 110 – Compact Disc (IRE) 48 (Royal Academy **75** (USA) 130) [2001 6m 6d* 5g² 5.2m 5d 5m⁴ 5g⁴ 6m Sep 12] 8,000Y: quite attractive gelding: second foal: closely related to 3-y-o Single Track Mind: dam, 2-y-o 7f winner, out of half-sister to very smart sprinter Greenland Park: fair performer: won seller at Windsor (then left B. Meehan) in June: respectable fourth in 2 nurseries: will prove best at 5f/easy 6f: unraced on extremes of going: visored last 3 starts: has wandered under pressure. *T. E. Powell*

TURKU 3 b.c. Polar Falcon (USA) 126 – Princess Zepoli 61 (Persepolis (FR) 127) **96** [2001 97: 8.1m 8m* 7f 7.9m⁴ 8g 8.1g² 9.9s 8g² 8.3g 8m 8d p7g f8.5f⁵ f7g p7g Dec 19] lengthy, rather unfurnished colt: useful handicapper: won at Ripon in June: left M. Johnson after eleventh start: stays 1m: acts on fibresand, soft and good to firm going: sometimes makes running. *N. P. Littmoden*

TURNED OUT WELL 4 b.g. Robellino (USA) 127 – In The Shade 89 (Bustino **53** 136) [2001 57: 17.1s 16.2m* f14g² May 25] tall, useful-looking gelding: has a round action: modest handicapper: won at Beverley in May: acts on fibresand, good to firm and good to soft ground: has raced freely. *P. C. Haslam*

TURNING THE TIDE 2 b.c. (Apr 5) Lugana Beach 116 – Robert's Daughter – (Robellino (USA) 127) [2001 f5g f5.1f⁵ 6.1m Sep 17] 1,700Y: first foal: dam ran 3 times at 2 yrs: well held in maidens. *J. M. Bradley*

Phil Bull Trophy Conditions Stakes, Pontefract—at the age of ten, Turnpole continues to more than pay his way; Galleon Beach (far side) is worn down only inside the final furlong, with Bylaw third

TURN OF A CENTURY 3 b.f. Halling (USA) 133 – Colorspin (FR) 118 (High Top **85**
131) [2001 10.5d² 12g* 11.9s Oct 11] rather leggy, good-topped filly: half-sister to 3
winners, notably middle-distance performer Opera House and stayer Kayf Tara, both
top-class performers by Sadler's Wells: dam, won Irish Oaks, half-sister to Bella Colora
and Cezanne: won maiden at Newmarket (wandered/tended to idle) in August: found
little when well held in minor event at York final start: will be suited by 1¾m+.
L. M. Cumani

TURNPOLE (IRE) 10 br.g. Satco (FR) 114 – Mountain Chase (Mount Hagen (FR) **91**
127) [2001 81: 13.9m² 16.2g* 16.1g 18f* 13.9d Oct 13] strong gelding: impresses in
appearance: fairly useful performer: won handicap at Haydock in June and minor event at
Pontefract in September: stays 2½m: acts on firm and good to soft going: has run well
sweating: held up. *Mrs M. Reveley*

TURN TO BLUE 2 b.c. (Apr 19) Bluegrass Prince (IRE) 110 – Alvecote Lady 50 **–**
(Touching Wood (USA) 127) [2001 7m Jun 28] fifth reported foal: half-brother to a
winner up to 1½m in Italy by Risk Me: dam won 1½m seller: behind in maiden at
Salisbury. *J. C. Fox*

TURTLE LOVE (IRE) 2 b.f. (Mar 21) Turtle Island (IRE) 123 – A Little Loving **48**
(He Loves Me 120) [2001 6m f6g³ 7m f7g* f7g² f7g 7g² Aug 17] IR 1,000Y: good-topped **a58**
filly: half-sister to a winner in Italy by King Persian: modest on all-weather, poor on turf: won seller at Southwell in June: runner-up in similar
events there and at Catterick: will stay 1m: acts on fibresand, best turf effort on good
going. *Miss V. Haigh*

TURTLE RECALL (IRE) 2 b.g. (May 2) Turtle Island (IRE) 123 – Nora Yo Ya **–**
(Ahonoora 122) [2001 8.2d 7.9d Oct 13] IR 15,500F, IR 25,000Y: good-topped gelding:
seventh foal: half-brother to 3 winners, including 7f (at 2 yrs) and 1¼m winner Owdbetts
(by High Estate): dam, ran once, from family of very smart 7f/1m winner Gabr: burly,
well held in maidens: gelded after final start. *P. W. Harris*

TURTLE VALLEY (IRE) 5 b.g. Turtle Island (IRE) 123 – Primrose Valley 99 (Mill **97**
Reef (USA) 141) [2001 99, a–: 14.1v* 16s⁶ 16s 18d 16d⁵ 14.6s² Nov 9] small, strong **a–**

gelding: unimpressive mover: useful performer: won minor event at Nottingham in April: creditable second to easy winner Double Honour in minor event at Doncaster final outing: stays 2m: has form on good to firm going, but best on good or softer: blinkered once at 2 yrs: has hung left. *S. Dow*

TUSCAN DREAM 6 b.g. Clantime 101 – Excavator Lady 65 (Most Secret 119) [2001 83, a68: 5s f5g 5.1f³ 5.1m 5m 5m 5.1f² 5f² 5m³ 5.2f⁶ 5g 5g f5g⁵ f5g p5g Dec 22] smallish, sturdy gelding: fairly useful handicapper on turf, fair on all-weather: good efforts when placed in 2001: best at bare 5f: acts on fibresand, races mainly on ground firmer than good on turf: below form tried blinkered: has bolted to post/been taken down early: reared/unseated as stall opened penultimate outing: front runner. *A. Berry* **86 a70**

TUSCAN FLYER 3 b.g. Clantime 101 – Excavator Lady 65 (Most Secret 119) [2001 50: e6g 5m² 5m* 5d 5f³ 5m⁴ 5m⁶ 5m³ 5m⁴ 5g⁵ 5g⁴ f5s f5s Dec 18] deep-bodied gelding: fair handicapper: won at Ayr in May: mostly creditable efforts after: probably best at 5f: acts on firm going, possibly not on fibresand and softer than good: blinkered (ran respectably) seventh start: races up with pace. *A. Berry* **71**

TUSCAN (IRE) 3 b.f. Charnwood Forest (IRE) 125 – Madam Loving 99 (Vaigly Great 127) [2001 60: e5g² f6s e5g⁴ e5s⁴ 7m 6g 6g 6.1f Sep 18] leggy filly: modest performer: below form after reappearance: effective at 5f/6f: acts on good to firm ground and equitrack: tried blinkered/visored: races prominently. *B. G. Powell* **60 d**

TUSCAN TEMPO 2 ch.c. (Mar 18) Perugino (USA) 84 – Fact of Time (Known Fact (USA) 135) [2001 6g 7f 7.1g⁵ Sep 13] 10,000Y: sixth foal: half-brother to 1999 2-y-o 5f/6f winner Sontime (by Son Pardo) and winner Camionneur (by Cyrano de Bergerac): dam unraced: modest maiden: best effort final start: not sure to stay 1m: sold 6,000 gns. *R. Hannon* **62**

TUSCARORA (IRE) 2 b.f. (Jan 8) Revoque (IRE) 122 – Fresh Look (IRE) 64 (Alzao (USA) 117) [2001 5g⁵ 7g 7m³ 7.1m³ 7m f8s⁵ Dec 15] 20,000Y: smallish filly: second foal: dam 11.5f winner: modest maiden: third in claimer at Thirsk and nursery at Musselburgh: has raced freely, but should stay 1m: acts on good to firm going: slowly away 3 times: has looked none too keen. *P. C. Haslam* **62**

TWEED 4 ch.g. Barathea (IRE) 127 – In Perpetuity 90 (Great Nephew 126) [2001 63: 13s 10s Apr 23] good-bodied gelding: type to carry condition: modest maiden at 3 yrs: well held both runs in 2001, including in blinkers. *Jedd O'Keeffe* **–**

TWENTYFOUREVE 2 b.f. (Apr 30) Emperor Jones (USA) 119 – Topwinder (USA) (Topsider (USA)) [2001 7m 8.1v 8d Oct 19] 6,000Y: tall, useful-looking filly: fifth living foal: half-sister to 5f winner Piper's Clan (by Aragon), 7f seller winner (including at 2 yrs) Fast Spin (by Formidable) and 4-y-o Master George: dam ran twice in France: well held in maidens. *G. C. H. Chung* **–**

TWENTY SEVEN (IRE) 2 b.f. (May 10) Efisio 120 – Naked Poser (IRE) 83 (Night Shift (USA)) [2001 5g⁴ 5.2m² 6g* 6m⁶ 6m Sep 12] 21,000Y: smallish, sturdy filly: first foal: dam, 2-y-o 6f winner, half-sister to 5-y-o Damalis: fair performer: won maiden at Leicester in August: last in nursery final start: should stay 7f: raced only on good/good to firm going. *J. A. R. Toller* **75**

TWICE 5 b.g. Rainbow Quest (USA) 134 – Bolas 118 (Unfuwain (USA) 131) [2001 –, a78: e16g² Jan 27] quite good-topped gelding: has reportedly been hobdayed and had tie-back operation: fairly useful handicapper, lightly raced: stays 2m: acts on fibresand and equitrack, had form on turf earlier in career: tongue tied. *G. L. Moore* **– a80**

TWICE BLESSED (IRE) 4 ch.g. Thatching 131 – Fairy Blesse (IRE) (Fairy King (USA)) [2001 –: e8g 7s 8.1m May 29] strong, lengthy gelding: fair winner at 2 yrs: lightly raced since and well held in 2001. *R. Hannon* **–**

TWICE BRIGHT 5 br.g. Precocious 126 – Sweet Helen (No Mercy 126) [2001 10.1g 9.9m Aug 26] half-brother to winning sprinters Grange Farm Lady and Grange Farm Lad (both by Faraway Times): dam ran once: last in maidens. *C. Drew* **–**

TWICE UPON A TIME 2 ch.f. (Apr 15) Primo Dominie 121 – Opuntia (Rousillon (USA) 133) [2001 6g² 6m⁴ 6g⁴ 6.5g 5d² 5.1s³ Nov 5] 36,000Y: good-topped filly: has a quick action: half-sister to several winners, including useful 6f winner (including at 2 yrs) Boomerang Blade (by Sure Blade) and 6-y-o Point of Dispute: dam unraced: fair maiden: best effort when third in nursery at Nottingham: effective at 5f/6f: acts on soft and good to firm ground. *B. Smart* **70**

TWIG N' BERRIES 5 b.g. Rock City 120 – Mardessa 74 (Ardross 134) [2001 12.1d May 18] third foal: dam 1¼m/11f winner: well held in maiden. *M. Mullineaux* **–**

Mrs Susan Roy's "Twilight Blues"

TWILIGHT BLUES (IRE)   2 ch.c. (Feb 23) Bluebird (USA) 125 – Pretty Sharp 64   **101**
(Interrex (CAN)) [2001 5.2m* 6m 6d⁵ 6g³ 6g² 6f³ 7v Oct 26] 140,000Y: good-topped
colt: has scope: first foal: dam, maiden at 2 yrs (best form at 7f), became temperamental:
useful performer: won maiden at Newbury in June: placed in Gimcrack Stakes at York
(3½ lengths third to Rock of Gibraltar), listed race at Kempton (½-length second to
Lipstick) and Mill Reef Stakes at Newbury (2 lengths third to Firebreak): reared and
unseated as stall opened final outing: should stay 7f: acts on firm going, probably on good
to soft. *B. J. Meehan*

TWILIGHT DANCER (IRE)   3 b.f. Sri Pekan (USA) 117 – Manhattan Sunset   **54**
(USA) 76 (El Gran Senor (USA) 136) [2001 54: 10s 10.2f 12m⁶ 12f⁵ 10.1g 10s⁴ f8g   **a–**
Dec 10] useful-looking filly: modest maiden handicapper: left P. Harris 3,700 gns after
penultimate start: stays 1½m: acts on firm ground. *J. M. Bradley*

TWILIGHT HAZE   3 b.g. Darshaan 133 – Hiwaayati (Shadeed (USA) 135) [2001   **76**
74p: f12g* 12.3v³ 14.6m² 12f 11.4g Jul 8] lengthy, good-topped gelding: won maiden at
Wolverhampton in March: ran creditably in handicaps next 2 starts: bit slipped through
mouth and virtually pulled up penultimate outing/reportedly lost action final start: likely
to stay 2m: acts on fibresand, equitrack, heavy and good to firm going: sold 7,000 gns,
and gelded. *E. A. L. Dunlop*

TWILIGHT MISTRESS   3 b.f. Bin Ajwaad (IRE) 119 – By Candlelight (IRE) 84   **83**
(Roi Danzig (USA)) [2001 68: 5f* 5g⁴ 5g 5.1d² f5g⁶ f5g⁴ Dec 8] leggy filly: fairly useful
handicapper: won at Warwick in June: good efforts after, except when hampered third
start: races freely, and will prove best at sharp 5f: acts on fibresand, firm and good to soft
going. *D. W. P. Arbuthnot*

TWILIGHT SONNET 2 b.f. (Feb 18) Exit To Nowhere (USA) 122 – Shawanni 105 **87**
(Shareef Dancer (USA) 135) [2001 6m³ 5m² 5f² 5f* 6d 5g* 5m⁴ Aug 26] close-coupled
filly: second foal: half-sister to 3-y-o Mystic Man: dam, 7f winner at 2 yrs, out of smart
Rockfel Stakes winner and 1000 Guineas third Negligent: fairly useful performer: won
maiden in July and nursery in August, both at Beverley: effective at 5f/6f: acts on firm
going, possibly not on good to soft: has given trouble before start (edgy and walked to
post final appearance): sold 11,000 gns in December. *E. A. L. Dunlop*

TWIN TIME 7 b.m. Syrtos 106 – Carramba (CZE) (Tumble Wind (USA)) [2001 73, **77**
a–: 8m* 7m² 10.2g⁶ 7.1m² Aug 1] quite good-topped mare: fair handicapper: won race at **a–**
Bath (fourth course success) in May: has won at 1¼m, races mainly at 7f/1m nowadays:
acts on firm going, probably on good to soft: has won for apprentice: races up with pace.
J. S. King

TWIST 4 b.g. Suave Dancer (USA) 136 – Reason To Dance 96 (Damister (USA) 123) **53 §**
[2001 65: e10g 11.6g 10d 10f² 10f³ 10m³ 11.7m 10g* Sep 11] leggy gelding: modest
performer: won selling handicap at Lingfield in September: barely stays 1½m: acts on
firm and soft going: tried blinkered/visored: tends to pull hard: not one to trust: sold 7,000
gns. *W. R. Muir*

TWOFORTEN 6 b.g. Robellino (USA) 127 – Grown At Rowan 75 (Gabitat 119) **46 §**
[2001 49§: e12g e16g e13g 10g 12m 7m* 8m 7m⁶ 8m⁵ 10m 9f 7d⁵ 10m 7d 10m 7.6g Sep
5] small, strong gelding: poor performer: won amateur handicap at Lingfield in May:
effective at 7f, probably at 1½m: acts on firm ground, soft and equitrack: sometimes
visored/blinkered: moody and unreliable. *P. Butler*

TWO JACKS (IRE) 4 b.g. Fayruz 116 – Kaya (GER) (Young Generation 129) [2001 **43**
–: 9m f7g 8f 7g⁵ 6m⁶ 6g f6s² Dec 15] workmanlike gelding: modest maiden at best: **a56 ?**
probably stays 7f: acts on fibresand: has had tongue tied. *W. S. Cunningham*

TWO MARKS (USA) 2 ch.f. (May 10) Woodman (USA) 126 – Munnaya (USA) 101 **62 p**
(Nijinsky (CAN) 138) [2001 7g Sep 8] rangy, unfurnished filly: has scope: fluent mover:
fourth foal: half-sister to useful French 1¼m/11f winner Yaya (by Rahy): dam, 11.5f
winner, out of Princess Margaret winner Hiaam from outstanding family of Swain and
5-y-o Fantastic Light: 6/1, eighth of 10 to Distant Valley in minor event at Kempton,
never dangerous after sluggish start: almost certainly capable of better. *Sir Michael Stoute*

TWO RAINBOWS (IRE) 3 b.f. Spectrum (IRE) 126 – Titulata (GER) (Danehill **–**
(USA) 126) [2001 7.1m May 26] IR 12,500F, IR 13,000Y: quite attractive filly: first foal:
dam unraced: behind throughout in maiden at Haydock on debut. *B. A. McMahon*

TWO SOCKS 8 ch.g. Phountzi (USA) 104 – Mrs Feathers 57 (Pyjama Hunt 126) **67**
[2001 73: 12s 13.3g 10m* 12m* 10.1d 12f Aug 1] leggy gelding: fair handicapper: won
at Lingfield (apprentices) in June and Epsom in July: effective at 1¼m (given test)/1½m:
acts on firm going, soft and fibresand: blinkered once at 2 yrs. *J. S. King*

TWO STEP 5 b.m. Mujtahid (USA) 118 – Polka Dancer 93 (Dancing Brave (USA) **55**
140) [2001 50: e8g⁴ e7g* f6g² e7s⁴ e6g³ e6g⁴ 6.1v 6g² 5m⁴ f6g May 19] modest **a60**
handicapper: won at Lingfield in January: best at 6f/7f: acts on fibresand, equitrack and
good to firm going, possibly not on heavy: effective visored or not: tongue tied: has
reportedly broken blood vessel: usually races prominently. *R. M. H. Cowell*

TWO STEPS TO GO (USA) 2 b.g. (Feb 12) Rhythm (USA) – Lyonushka (CAN) **75**
(Private Account (USA)) [2001 5d⁴ 5m³ 7g⁶ 6g² 6m 7g³ 8f⁵ 7m² 7.5g⁶ 6d f8s* Dec 15]
$12,000Y, resold 2,500Y: smallish, sturdy gelding: second foal: dam, useful French 2-y-o
1m winner, from very good family: fair performer: placed in maidens/nursery prior to
winning claimer at Southwell: stays 1m: acts on fibresand and good to firm going,
probably on good to soft: ran respectably only try in blinkers: best efforts when ridden
prominently. *T. D. Barron*

TYBALLA (IRE) 3 b.f. Blues Traveller (IRE) 119 – Mary Mary Mouse (USA) **–**
(Valdez (USA)) [2001 8.2d 8d Oct 8] 1,000Y: well-made filly: eighth foal: half-sister to 3
winners, including fairly useful 1992 2-y-o 7f winner Chevrotain (by Salse), later winner
in UAE: dam unraced: well held in maidens. *M. H. Tompkins*

TYCOON'S LAST 4 b.f. Nalchik (USA) – Royal Tycoon (Tycoon II) [2001 62: 12s* **64**
11.7d 10.3f 14m 12d⁵ 11.9f³ 12.1m² 11.1d⁶ 11.9g* 11.9g 10.5v² 11.9s 13.8s⁵ 12d 10.3s⁵
Nov 9] big, lengthy filly: modest handicapper: won at Kempton in April and Haydock in
August: should stay beyond 1½m: has form on firm going, possibly best on good or softer
(acts on heavy): has been slowly away: none too consistent. *W. M. Brisbourne*

TYLER'S TOAST 5 ch.g. Grand Lodge (USA) 125 – Catawba 98 (Mill Reef (USA) 141) [2001 61, a76: f9.4s² f9.4g* Feb 1] lengthy gelding: fairly useful performer: improved form early in 2001, gaining fourth course success in handicap at Wolverhampton in February: best at 1m/1¼m: acts on fibresand, firm and good to soft going. *S. Dow*   – **a89**

TYPE ONE (IRE) 3 b.g. Bigstone (IRE) 126 – Isca 66 (Caerleon (USA) 132) [2001 70: 5.1s⁶ 5g* 6g* 6m² 6d Jun 16] well-made gelding: fairly useful handicapper: won twice at Windsor in May: good head second to Palanzo in very competitive event at Newmarket next time, drifting left: well below form in William Hill Trophy at York final outing: best at 5f/6f: best form on good/good to firm ground: ridden up with pace of late. *T. G. Mills*   **88**

TYPHOON EIGHT (IRE) 9 b.g. High Estate 127 – Dance Date (IRE) (Sadler's Wells (USA) 132) [2001 13s 8d 9.2d May 6] smallish, sturdy gelding: modest performer in 1999: well held on return in 2001: sometimes blinkered/tongue tied. *I. Semple*   –

TYPHOON GINGER (IRE) 6 ch.m. Archway (IRE) 115 – Pallas Viking (Viking (USA)) [2001 69: 8g 8m 10m² 10.3m⁶ 8m³ 8m* 7.9m* 7.5s⁵ 8d 8.9d² Oct 13] close-coupled mare: fairly useful handicapper: won at Redcar in August and York in September: best at 1m/1¼m: probably acts on any going: sometimes slowly away: tends to wander/find little, and usually held up. *A. B. Mulholland*   **80**

TYPHOON TILLY 4 b.g. Hernando (FR) 127 – Meavy 86 (Kalaglow 132) [2001 79: 12.3f³ 14m⁴ 20m 12m 16m 14.4g Sep 8] quite good-topped gelding: fair handicapper: probably stays 2½m: best efforts on going firmer than good: blinkered last 2 starts. *C. R. Egerton*   **79**

TYPHOON TODD (IRE) 2 ch.c. (May 18) Entrepreneur 123 – Petite Liqueurelle (IRE) (Shernazar 131) [2001 5.2g 7.1s 7m⁴ 7m³ 7m Aug 5] 45,000Y: half-brother to several winners, including useful 5f (at 2 yrs) and 1m winner Caviar Royale (by Royal Academy) and Irish 1½m winner Petite Ville (by Bigstone): dam unraced: fair maiden: third in nursery at Brighton: will stay 1m: acts on good to firm going: has wandered/carried head awkwardly under pressure. *R. Hannon*   **75**

TZAR 2 b.g. (Feb 14) Makbul 104 – Tzarina (USA) (Gallant Romeo (USA)) [2001 5.1f³ 5.6f⁵ f6g⁵ f6g² 5s* 6m⁴ 7.1s f7g² f6g² f6g² 7s³ f6g f6g* f6g⁶ p7g² f6s⁵ Dec 26] 7,200Y: smallish gelding: half-brother to 3 winners, including useful sprinter Mandub (by Topsider) and 1m winner Mary Macblain (by Damister): dam placed in USA: fair performer: won nursery at Haydock in August and (having left B. McMahon after eighth start) claimer at Wolverhampton in November: effective at testing 5f to 7f: acts on firm ground, soft and fibresand/polytrack: reliable. *J. R. Best*   **69 a72**

U

UHOOMAGOO 3 b.g. Namaqualand (USA) – Point of Law (Law Society (USA) 130) [2001 79: f6g⁶ f5s⁴ f7g f7g f8.5g³ f6g 7v f8g⁶ f7g⁶ 6.1f⁴ 6m 7f⁴ 7.5f* 7g³ 7.1d³ 7.5m* 6.1m* 7.1v³ 7d 7v 8s Nov 9] leggy gelding: fairly useful on turf, fair on all-weather: left D. Nicholls after third start: won claimers at Beverley in July/August and handicap at Nottingham in September: below form last 3 starts: best form at 6f to 7.5f: acts on fibresand and any turf going: effective with or without blinkers: tends to wander. *K. A. Ryan*   **81 a68**

ULSHAW 4 ch.g. Salse (USA) 128 – Kintail 76 (Kris 135) [2001 37: f16.2g* f16.2g* 16v⁴ 14.1s⁴ 16.2m³ 18m⁴ 16d* 15.9d³ 15.9d Sep 26] quite good-topped gelding: modest handicapper: won at Wolverhampton (twice) in February, on first occasion in seller, and at Lingfield in July: stays 17f: acts on any turf going and fibresand: visored last 3 starts at 3 yrs: tough. *B. J. Llewellyn*   **54**

ULTIMAJUR (USA) 3 br.c. Dayjur (USA) 137 – Crystal Lady (CAN) (Stop The Music (USA)) [2001 52: f6s f5g 5.1m⁶ 5m f5g⁶ Dec 14] strong, good sort: poor maiden: left J. Hills after reappearance: tried blinkered. *M. D. I. Usher*   **44**

ULTIMATE CHOICE 3 b.g. Petong 126 – Jay Gee Ell 78 (Vaigly Great 127) [2001 53p: 5.2m 6m 5m 6m 7g* 7.1m* 7.6g⁵ 7g² 7s p7g* p7g Dec 28] modest performer: won claimer at Leicester in August and seller at Lingfield (first start after leaving W. Haggas) in December: stays 7f: acts on good to firm going (yet to race on firm) and all-weather: tried visored/tongue tied: none too consistent. *N. P. Littmoden*   **53 a56**

Tote Exacta Stakes (Handicap), Sandown—Ulundi (No.3) shows his versatility by capturing a valuable event on the Flat to add to his success in the Scottish Champion Hurdle; Thundering Surf (No.9) runs on strongly for second with Riberac (rail), Pantar and Invader (right) coming next

ULTRA CALM (IRE) 5 ch.g. Doubletour (USA) – Shyonn (IRE) (Shy Groom (USA)) [2001 –, a68: f12g f9.4g Feb 13] sturdy gelding: one-time fair winner: well held in 2001: tried blinkered/visored. *Miss K. M. George* —

ULUNDI 6 b.g. Rainbow Quest (USA) 134 – Flit (USA) 72 (Lyphard (USA) 132) [2001 102: f12f⁶ 12m* 10m* Jul 6] leggy, useful-looking gelding: useful hurdler, smart performer on Flat: neck winner of minor event at Goodwood (from Hatha Anna, drifting right) in May and Tote Exacta Stakes (Handicap) at Sandown (from Thundering Surf, leading late on having travelled smoothly) in July: effective at 1¼m/easy 1½m: acts on firm and good to soft going, possibly not on soft: has been bandaged in front: waited with. *P. R. Webber* **115**

ULYSSES DAUGHTER (IRE) 4 ch.f. College Chapel 122 – Trysinger (IRE) (Try My Best (USA) 130) [2001 88p: 5m 5m⁶ 6.1d f6g Oct 20] angular filly: fairly useful at 3 yrs: well held in 2001: blinkered final start: usually tongue tied. *G. A. Butler* —

UMBOPA (USA) 3 b.g. Gilded Time (USA) – How Fortunate (CAN) (What Luck (USA)) [2001 –: 8v³ 10.9m⁵ f8.5g² f9.4g f12g⁵ f11g² f12g* f12g³ f12g² f12s⁴ Dec 21] strong, rangy gelding: has scope: fair handicapper: won at Wolverhampton in November: ran creditably after: should stay 1¾m: acts on heavy going, good to firm and fibresand: seems best in blinkers/visor: not an easy ride. *K. R. Burke* **73**

UMISTA (IRE) 2 b.f. (Apr 17) Tagula (IRE) 116 – Nishiki (USA) (Brogan (USA) 110) [2001 5.2m 6m 6f 5.7m 5.2m Aug 15] IR 16,000Y: rather leggy filly: fourth foal: half-sister to 3 winners by Case Law, including 6f (at 2 yrs) and 2m winner Cashiki and 3-y-o Monte Mayor Golf: dam lightly raced on Flat/winning hurdler in Ireland: little form, including in claimer: tried visored. *M. Quinn* —

UMISTIM 4 ch.c. Inchinor 119 – Simply Sooty 78 (Absalom 128) [2001 119: 9d⁵ 8.1v 8s⁵ 8m⁵ 7.3m* 8m* 8d Sep 13] smallish colt: smart performer: good 2½ lengths fifth to Medicean in Queen Anne Stakes at Royal Ascot on fourth start, then won minor event at Newbury in July and listed race at Salisbury (beat Momentum ¾ length) in August: well held in Park Stakes at Doncaster final outing: best at 7f/1m: possibly unsuited by heavy going, acts on any other: ridden prominently for both wins in 2001. *R. Hannon* **115**

UN AUTRE ESPERE 2 b.g. (Apr 2) Golden Heights 82 – Drummer's Dream (IRE) 48 (Drumalis 125) [2001 8.2s Nov 5] second foal: dam 5f winner: 66/1, ran out halfway in maiden at Nottingham. *A. Streeter* —

UNCHAIN MY HEART 5 b.m. Pursuit of Love 124 – Addicted To Love 73 (Touching Wood (USA) 127) [2001 70: 7.1g⁶ 7m⁶ 7m⁶ Sep 4] lengthy, good-bodied mare: modest form in 2001 only on first start: seems best at 7f/1m: acts on equitrack, firm going and probably on soft: usually blinkered/visored: often races prominently. *W. G. M. Turner* **56 a–**

UNCLE CLOCKWISE 4 gr.c. Absalom 128 – Summer Flower 51 (Nomination 125) [2001 7s 6.9v⁵ 7m May 11] lengthy colt: second foal: dam, maiden on Flat (stayed 1½m), winning hurdler: little form in maidens. *Miss Z. C. Davison* —

UNCLE FOLDING (IRE)   3 b.g. Danehill (USA) 126 – Bubbling Danseuse (USA)   – §
(Arctic Tern (USA) 126) [2001 –: 8m 9.2s Jul 13] little form: tried blinkered/tongue tied:
refused to race final start. *Mrs D. Thomson*

UNCLE OBERON   5 b.g. Distant Relative 128 – Fairy Story (IRE) 80 (Persian Bold   – §
123) [2001 46§: f11g f8s f7s 11.9m 10f 8.1d 7.6d Jul 18] tall gelding: temperamental
performer: tried visored/tongue tied. *H. J. Manners*

UNCLE SAM   2 ch.c. (Mar 14) Superpower 113 – Treasure Time (IRE) 65 (Treasure   – §
Kay 114) [2001 f5g 5.1m May 21] 2,400 2-y-o: fourth foal: dam 5f/6f winner: tailed off
in claimer/minor event, looking wayward. *P. D. Evans*

UNDENIABLE   3 b.g. Unfuwain (USA) 131 – Shefoog 90 (Kefaah (USA) 124) [2001   75
64p: 14m* 14.1m⁶ 16m² 14.1s Sep 4] strong, rangy gelding: fair handicapper: won at
Goodwood in June: creditable efforts next 2 starts: will be suited by further than 2m: acts
on good to firm ground: unruly at start final outing: sold 36,000 gns. *J. L. Dunlop*

UNDER CONSTRUCTION (IRE)   3 b.g. Pennekamp (USA) 130 – Madame   70
Nureyev (USA) (Nureyev (USA) 131) [2001 8d² 8m² 9.2m⁴ 8d 10s f8g⁵ f9.4g⁵ f9.4g*
p10g² Dec 29] 8,500Y, 12,000 2-y-o: leggy, quite good-topped gelding: half-brother to
several winners, including US Grade 3 11f winner Miss Universal (by Lycius), earlier
useful at 1m/1¼m in Britain: dam French 2-y-o 6f winner: modest performer: won handicap at Wolverhampton in December: acts on good to firm ground and
fibresand: carried head awkwardly on debut. *M. Johnston*

UNDERCOVER GIRL (IRE)   3 b.f. Barathea (IRE) 127 – Les Trois Lamas (IRE)   49
(Machiavellian (USA) 123) [2001 51: 10m f9.4g⁴ 11.5m 16.4m 12m Aug 13] rather leggy
filly: poor maiden: should stay at least 1¼m. *W. R. Muir*

UNDETERRED   5 ch.g. Zafonic (USA) 130 – Mint Crisp (IRE) 108 (Green Desert   99
(USA) 127) [2001 96: 6s 5m⁶ 5m 6m² 6f* 6g³ 6g 6g 7g 6m 7s 7g Oct 5] deep-girthed
gelding: has a quick action: useful handicapper: won quite valuable event at Newcastle in
June by ½ length from Technician: favourite, fast-finishing close third to Guinea Hunter
in Stewards' Cup at Goodwood in August, despite not clearest of runs: best subsequent
effort when under 4 lengths ninth to Continent in Ayr Gold Cup tenth outing: stays 7f:
acts on firm going, probably on soft: visored/blinkered: tends to be on edge (has been
mounted on course/reluctant to post): tends to get behind and hang. *D. Nicholls*

UNFAITHFUL THOUGHT   2 b. or br.f. (Apr 9) Mind Games 121 – Fleeting Affair   78 p
98 (Hotfoot 126) [2001 7d² Nov 3] IR 18,000Y: rather leggy filly: half-sister to numerous
winners, including 7-y-o Harmony Hall and useful 1¼m/1½m winner Infatuation (by
Music Boy): dam, 1¼m/1½m winner, stayed 2m: 8/1, ½-length second of 21 to Ballet
Fame in maiden at Newmarket, keeping on well after slow start: will stay 1m: should
improve. *P. W. Harris*

UNFORTUNATE   4 ch.f. Komaite (USA) – Honour And Glory 46 (Hotfoot 126)   – §
[2001 55§, a47§: f6g f7s⁴ Jan 23] leggy filly: poor performer: stays 7f: acts on firm   a40 §
ground, good to soft and fibresand: tried blinkered: has wandered: usually starts slowly:
needs treating with caution. *Miss J. F. Craze*

UNICORN STAR (IRE)   4 b.g. Persian Bold 123 – Highland Warning 43 (Warning   36
136) [2001 53: 11.8f 17.1m 12f⁴ 16f 12m⁵ 12g 9.9m⁵ 10.3m 12d Nov 6] tall gelding: poor
maiden: stays 2m: acts on firm and good to soft ground: tried blinkered/visored, including
last 5 starts: carries head high, and takes plenty of riding. *J. S. Wainwright*

UNITED PASSION   4 b.f. Emarati (USA) 74 – Miriam 59 (Forzando 122) [2001 74:   –
f5s p5g⁵ f5s³ Dec 27] fair performer: off 12 months before first start in 2001: speedy, and   a65
races only at 5f: acts on fibresand and polytrack: tongue tied: races up with pace. *D. Shaw*

UNIVERSAL STAR   3 b.f. Unfuwain (USA) 131 – Shirley Superstar 94 (Shirley   74
Heights 130) [2001 12g⁶ 11.5g² 12m⁶ Sep 24] small, quite attractive filly: half-sister to
very smart 1m (at 2 yrs) to 1½m (Oaks) winner Lady Carla (by Caerleon) and 9f winner
Azores (by Polish Precedent): dam, lightly-raced 7f winner (at 2 yrs), out of smart filly up
to 1¾m Odeon: fair form in maidens: will stay further than 1½m. *H. R. A. Cecil*

UNLEASH (USA)   2 ch.c. (Feb 16) Benny The Dip (USA) 127 – Lemhi Go (USA)   85 p
(Lemhi Gold (USA) 123) [2001 7.1g⁴ 8.3s⁴ 7d⁴ f8.5g* Sep 22] strong, close-coupled colt:
fifth foal: half-brother to useful 1¼m winner Abscond (by Unbridled) and a sprint winner
in USA by Summer Squall: dam won 12 times in USA, including Grade 2 1½m event:
fourth in maidens before winning one at Wolverhampton comfortably by 2 lengths from

Figurehead: will be suited by 1¼m/1½m: acts on fibresand, raced only on good going or softer on turf: should make a useful 3-y-o. *Sir Mark Prescott*

UNMASKED   5 ch.m. Safawan 118 – Unveiled 76 (Sayf El Arab (USA) 127) [2001   –
31: 11.1g 12m⁴ f8.5g 12d Nov 6] of little account nowadays. *A. Scott*

UNO MENTE   2 b.f. (Apr 12) Mind Games 121 – One Half Silver (CAN) (Plugged   **59**
Nickle (USA)) [2001 6m⁵ 6.1g⁴ Aug 20] 13,000Y: closely related to 4-y-o Scafell and
half-sister to several winners, including 6-y-o Petarga and fairly useful 8.5f winner
Opulent (by Robellino): dam unraced: modest form in minor event/maiden: will stay at
least 7f. *Mrs P. N. Dutfield*

UNPARALLELED   3 b.f. Primo Dominie 121 – Sharp Chief 71 (Chief Singer 131)   **60 d**
[2001 64: e7g² e6g⁴ e7g 7m 6d p7g p6g Dec 19] modest maiden: disappointing after
reappearance: stays easy 7f: acts on firm going, fibresand and equitrack: sometimes
blinkered: has raced freely/looked far from keen. *G. L. Moore*

UNSHAKABLE (IRE)   2 b.c. (Mar 7) Eagle Eyed (USA) 111 – Pepper And Salt   **87**
(IRE) (Double Schwartz 128) [2001 7.9d⁵ 8s² Nov 9] IR 5,500F, 9,000Y: good-bodied
colt: second foal: dam unraced half-sister to useful performer up to 1¼m Rickenbacker:
shaped with promise in maidens at York (66/1, backward and bandaged behind) and
Doncaster, fairly useful form when 2½ lengths second of 17 to Zone (ran on well despite
wandering) at latter track: shapes as though will stay 1¼m. *Bob Jones*

UNSHAKEN   7 b.h. Environment Friend 128 – Reel Foyle (USA) 77 (Irish River (FR)   **80**
131) [2001 79d: f7g⁶ f6g f7g³ f7g³ 6d 7g* 8f* 8f² 7.1f⁶ 8m 8.1g 7.6d⁴ 8.3g³ 8s f8.5g⁶ Oct   **a58**
9] strong, sturdy horse: fairly useful handicapper on turf, modest on all-weather: won at
Newbury in May and Thirsk in June: effective at 6f to 1m: acts on any turf going and
fibresand: tried blinkered/visored, not since 1999: patiently ridden. *E. J. Alston*

UNSIGNED (USA)   3 b. or br.g. Cozzene (USA) – Striata (USA) (Gone West (USA))   **81**
[2001 76: 9.9m⁶ 12m⁴ 12.3f² 12m 16.2m⁵ 14.4g 12g Oct 4] close-coupled, good-bodied
gelding: fairly useful maiden handicapper: probably stays 2m: acts on firm and soft
ground, possibly not on heavy: sold 11,500 gns. *J. R. Fanshawe*

UNTIDY SON   2 b.g. (Apr 19) Efisio 120 – Reel Foyle (USA) 77 (Irish River (FR) 131)   **66 §**
[2001 5d 5d 6g Jul 11] good-topped, useful-looking gelding: seventh foal: half-brother to
3 winners, including 5-y-o Alastair Smellie and 7-y-o Unshaken: dam, 2-y-o 5f winner,
out of high-class sprinter Abergwaun: coltish, easily best effort (fair form) when close
eighth in maiden at Haydock on second start: twice mulish in preliminaries: soon downed
tools final start: gelded after, then sold 1,200 gns in October. *R. Hannon*

UNVEIL   3 b.f. Rudimentary (USA) 118 – Magical Veil 73 (Majestic Light (USA))   **33**
[2001 46: 10s 6d 7f² 7m Aug 8] leggy filly: poor maiden: best at 6f/7f: acts on fibresand,
soft and firm going. *G. M. McCourt*

UP AND AWAY (GER)   7 b.g. Le Glorieux 127 – Ultima Ratio (FR) (Viceregal   **115**
(CAN)) [2001 107: 8s* 8v* 8g² 8g* 8g³ 8m³ 8m* 8s⁵ 8.5v² 8.5v⁴ Oct 28] half-brother to
a winner in USA by Shelter Half and a winner in Germany by Caerwent: dam won Preis
der Diana: smart performer: better than ever in 2001, winning listed races at Cologne (2)
in April and Hamburg (by ¾ length from Peppercorn) in June and Darley-Oettingen-
Rennen at Baden-Baden (by short head from Touch Down) in August: in frame in several
other pattern races, including neck second to Mahfooth in Prix du Chemin de Fer du Nord
at Chantilly third start: best at around 1m: acts on heavy and good to firm ground: reliable.
Frau E. Mader, Germany

UP FRONT (IRE)   2 b.f. (Apr 26) Up And At 'em 109 – Sable Lake (Thatching 131)   **61**
[2001 f5g 5.1g⁴ 5d 7g⁴ 6g⁵ 7.1m 6d* f7g 6s² 5.7d* 5.1s⁶ f6g⁴ f7g³ p7g f6s² Dec 26] IR
6,000Y: ninth foal: half-sister to 3 winners, including fairly useful Irish 1997 2-y-o 6f/7f
winner Karakorum (by Fairy King) and winner up to 1¼m in Germany by Kings Lake:
dam Irish maiden: modest performer: won sellers at Yarmouth (nursery) in September
and Bath in October: best form around 6f: acts on soft going and fibresand. *A. Berry*

UPHEAVAL (IRE)   2 b.g. (Mar 22) Great Commotion (USA) 123 – Magic Green   **51**
(Magic Mirror 105) [2001 f5g f5g⁵ 5m⁶ 5m 6m 6m⁶ f5g² 5g³ 5m⁴ 5d⁵ Aug 9] IR 5,500F,
10,000Y: good-topped gelding: poor mover: fourth reported living foal: half-brother to
6-y-o Broughton Magic: dam third at 6f in Ireland at 2 yrs: modest maiden: in frame in
seller/nurseries: seems best at 5f: acts on good to firm ground and fibresand: blinkered
last 5 starts: sent to Spain. *M. W. Easterby*

UP IN FLAMES (IRE)   10 br.g. Nashamaa 113 – Bella Lucia (Camden Town 125)   **46 +**
[2001 44, a37: 11.1d⁶ 10f 8f 8m 9.2d⁵ 8.3s² 10g³ 9.9d 10.4s² 10s 10g Nov 5] leggy   **a–**
gelding: poor performer on balance: seemed to run very well ninth start: stays 11f: acts on
firm going, soft and fibresand: tried blinkered: tongue tied: usually held up (sometimes
slowly away): none too reliable. *Mrs G. S. Rees*

UP ON POINTS   3 ch.f. Royal Academy (USA) 130 – Champagne 'n Roses 63 (Chief   **–**
Singer 131) [2001 97p: 6d 8f 7g 7m 7g Oct 6] good-quartered filly: fairly useful winner
at 2 yrs: off over 9 months (reported in April to have been suffering from a viral rash),
well held in 2001. *R. Hannon*

UPPER BULLENS   4 ch.g. Rock City 120 – Monstrosa 70 (Monsanto (FR) 121)   **–**
[2001 –: 12m 10.9f Jun 22] maiden: no form since 2 yrs. *A. Bailey*

UPPER CHAMBER   5 b.g. Presidium 124 – Vanishing Trick 83 (Silly Season 127)   **50 §**
[2001 47§: 5d 5f⁶ 5g⁶ 6m* 5g 6m 5m 6f f5g Nov 23] leggy gelding: modest handicapper:
won ladies seller at Thirsk in August: stays easy 6f: acts on firm going and fibresand:
effective blinkered/visored or not: headstrong and finds little. *J. G. FitzGerald*

UPPITY   6 ch.m. Great Commotion (USA) 123 – Nuit d'Ete (USA) 90 (Super Concorde   **–**
(USA) 128) [2001 –: f7g 9f 8m⁶ 12f Jul 12] IR 2,800Y, resold IR 6,000Y: half-sister to 3
winners, including 9-y-o Hugwity and useful Irish 1m and 1¼m winner Al Guswa (by
Shernazar): dam 2-y-o 5f and 6f winner: little recent form, leaving E. Sexton in Ireland
after final start in 2001 (seller at Wolverhampton). *S. J. Mahon, Ireland*

UPROAR   2 b.g. (Mar 15) Piccolo 121 – Kittycatoo Katango (USA) (Verbatim (USA))   **74**
[2001 f7g 5m² 5f² 6g 6.1d f6g² p5g⁴ Nov 24] 10,000 2-y-o: seventh foal: half-brother to
6f (at 2 yrs) and 1¼m winner Miss Doody (by Gorytus) and 6f (at 2 yrs)/7f winner Mr
Butch (by Aragon): dam Italian 2-y-o 7f listed race winner: fair maiden: runner-up at
Folkestone, Catterick and Wolverhampton: stays 6f: acts on firm ground and fibresand/
polytrack. *R. M. Beckett*

UPSTAGE   3 b.f. Quest For Fame 127 – Pedestal (High Line 125) [2001 8.2d⁶ 10g⁴   **70 d**
10f⁶ 11.6m 8.1m⁵ 9g Oct 19] lengthy, useful-looking filly: seventh foal: half-sister to
1¼m winner Plinth (by Dowsing), fairly useful 7f and (in UAE) 1m winner Diamond
Look (by Dayjur) and useful 7f to 8.5f winner Lionize (by Storm Cat): dam once-raced
half-sister to Precocious and Jupiter Island: fair maiden: well below form after second
start, including in handicaps: stays 1¼m: acts on good to firm and good to soft ground:
tongue tied last 2 outings. *G. C. Bravery*

UPSTREAM   3 b.f. Prince Sabo 123 – Rivers Rhapsody 104 (Dominion 123) [2001   **79**
70: 5g⁴ 5.3f² 5m* 5.1m⁵ 5g 5.2m 5g 5g* Sep 19] fair performer: won maiden at
Folkestone in June and handicap at Goodwood in September: best at 5f: raced mainly on
good going or firmer: sold 23,000 gns, sent to USA. *R. F. Johnson Houghton*

UP TEMPO (IRE)   3 b.c. Flying Spur (AUS) – Musical Essence 65 (Song 132) [2001   **96**
96: 6d 7f6f⁶ 7m⁶ 8.1m⁴ 7.1g⁵ 6d⁴ 6m 6g² 6m Aug 18] useful-looking colt: useful handicapper: good efforts at Ripon last 2 starts, going on strongly when neck second to Pips
Magic, then 2¾ lengths seventh to Antonio Canova in Great St Wilfrid there (slowly
away/seemed to slip leaving stall): effective at 6f to 1m: acts on any going: blinkered
sixth/seventh starts. *T. D. Easterby*

UP THE CLARETS (IRE)   6 b.g. Petardia 113 – Madeira Lady (On Your Mark 125)   **–**
[2001 10.1v Oct 24] very lightly-raced maiden nowadays: blinkered once. *E. J. Alston*

UP THE KYBER   4 b.g. Missed Flight 123 – Najariya (Northfields (USA)) [2001 74:   **63 d**
11.1d² 12m 11.1s 7.1f f8g Nov 26] modest maiden, on downgrade: probably stays 11f:
acts on soft ground: visored once. *A. Crook*

UPTOWN LAD (IRE)   2 b.c. (Mar 5) Definite Article 121 – Shoka (FR) 86 (Kaldoun   **55**
(FR) 122) [2001 6d 5s f6g⁴ Nov 12] 17,500Y: good-bodied colt: sixth foal: half-brother
to 7 winners, including 5-y-o Get Stuck In and 1996 2-y-o 6f seller winner Don't Forget
Shoka (by Don't Forget Me): dam 10.6f winner: modest form: best effort when fourth in
maiden at Southwell, looking hard ride: should stay 7f. *Mrs A. Duffield*

URBAN MYTH   3 b.c. Shaamit (IRE) 127 – Nashville Blues (IRE) 94 (Try My Best   **65**
(USA) 130) [2001 62p: 10g 10g 10.1m⁴ 12.3m⁴ 11.6m f9.4s³ f9.4g² f9.4g f9.4s⁶ Dec 18]
modest maiden: left J. Hills after fifth start: stays 1¼m: acts on good to firm ground and
fibresand: tongue tied last 5 starts: has looked none too keen. *J. W. Unett*

URGENT REPLY (USA)   8 b.g. Green Dancer (USA) 132 – Bowl of Honey (USA)   – §
(Lyphard (USA) 132) [2001 37§: 12.4m 16m 12m⁴ Aug 25] sturdy gelding: little form in
2001: visored once: has worn tongue strap. *B. W. Murray*

URGENT SWIFT   8 ch.g. Beveled (USA) – Good Natured § (Troy 137) [2001 73,   **70**
a76: f16g³ f16g f12s³ f14g* 12s 13.1m⁴ 14.1m⁴ 13.3m⁵ 12m* 14m² 12f² 14.1m² 14.1d
14.1g f14g⁴ f14.8g* f14g² p13g⁵ Dec 29] rangy gelding: fair performer: won claimer at
Southwell in March, apprentice handicap at Epsom in July and claimer at Wolverhampton in December: best at 1½m to 15f: possibly unsuited by soft/heavy going, acts on
any other turf and fibresand/polytrack: blinkered once as 5-y-o: sometimes slowly away:
best held up. *A. P. Jarvis*

URSA MAJOR   7 b.g. Warning 136 – Double Entendre 81 (Dominion 123) [2001 –,   **–**
a89: e12g⁴ e12g⁵ e10s f11g⁴ 7.5m 10.4m 8m p8g⁵ p12g⁶ p10g p12g p10g² Dec 28] small   **a84**
gelding: fairly useful handicapper: stays easy 1½m: acts on all-weather, no form on turf
in 2001: tried blinkered. *C. N. Allen*

USLOOB (IRE)   3 ch.c. Elmaamul (USA) 125 – Rawaabe (USA) 87 (Nureyev (USA)   **70 d**
131) [2001 7.5m³ 7f⁵ 6m⁴ 6.1m² 7.6g 8d 6v Oct 29] strong, good-bodied colt: sixth foal:
half-brother to several winners, including 1997 Horris Hill Stakes winner La-Faah (by
Lahib), 8-y-o Afaan, and 1m winner Dahshah (by Mujtahid): dam, 5f winner, closely
related to smart 5f and 6f (Gimcrack Stakes) winner Doulab: fair maiden: left B. Hills
after fourth start, and no show subsequently: will probably stay 1m: acts on good to firm
going: slowly away penultimate outing. *J. Cullinan*

UTAH (IRE)   7 b.g. High Estate 127 – Easy Romance (USA) (Northern Jove (CAN))   – §
[2001 –§, a51§: f8g f8.5s f8.5g Feb 17] temperamental performer. *A. G. Juckes*

UTHER PENDRAGON (IRE)   6 b.g. Petardia 113 – Mountain Stage (IRE) (Pen-   **–**
nine Walk 120) [2001 7m Sep 4] workmanlike gelding: of little account. *M. Bradstock*

UTMOST (IRE)   3 ch.f. Most Welcome 131 – Bint Alhabib (Nashwan (USA) 135)   **30**
[2001 –: f8g f9.4s⁶ f9.4g³ f8g e10s f11g³ f11g 12g 12f 14.1s Sep 4] poor maiden: seems
to stay 11f: acts on fibresand: usually visored/blinkered. *P. D. Evans*

UZY   5 ch.g. Common Grounds 118 – Loch Clair (IRE) 53 (Lomond (USA) 128) [2001   **44 ?**
–: f8g f7s e7g f12g f5g⁴ 6m⁶ 6m 6m 7.5m f6g Jun 29] lengthy, robust gelding: poor
maiden at best: effective at 5f to 7f: acts on soft going, good to firm and fibresand:
sometimes visored/blinkered: has had tongue tied. *M. J. Polglase*

V

VAHORIMIX (FR)   3 gr.c. Linamix (FR) 127 – Vadsa Honor (FR) 105 (Highest   **120**
Honor (FR) 124) [2001 99: 9v* 8m* 8m⁴ 8d* 8d⁶ 8s⁵ Sep 29]
    Winning one Group 1 race on the disqualification of the first past the post is
a stroke of luck, but winning two, as Vahorimix managed, amounts to scarcely
credible good fortune, considering the colt was some way short of being a tip-top
miler and twice had his limitations ruthlessly exposed. Vahorimix's best two-year-
old form, consisting of a win in a minor event at Longchamp and second place
behind Okawango in the Prix La Rochette, was promising without marking him out
as one to follow in his second season. He started his campaign over nine furlongs, a
trip in keeping with his breeding, in the Prix Matchem at Chantilly in April and had
no difficulty justifying favouritism. It therefore came as something of a surprise
when he spent the rest of the year over a mile, starting with the Dubai Poule d'Essai
des Poulains at Longchamp in May, for which he had to be supplemented. The
money proved well spent as Vahorimix went down by only a head to Noverre after
finishing strongly, having had to be switched when beginning his run. On the
disqualification of the winner in July, for having traces of a cortico steroid in his
system, Vahorimix was promoted to first.
    By that time Vahorimix had another run under his belt, when beaten less
than a length into fourth behind Black Minnaloushe and Noverre in the St James's
Palace Stakes at Royal Ascot, looking ill at ease on the good to firm going and
racing wide throughout. The ground for the Prix du Haras de Fresnay-le-Buffard
Jacques le Marois at Deauville in August was on the soft side of good. Excep-

Dubai Poule d'Essai des Poulains, Longchamp—Vahorimix (right) is awarded the race after Noverre (left) fails a post-race test; Clearing is a close third

tionally, there was only one older runner in a field of nine, the German mare Proudwings, winner of the Falmouth Stakes at Newmarket the previous month. The other three-year-olds included Noverre again, recently successful in the Sussex Stakes, Coronation Stakes winner Banks Hill, smart German miler Royal Dragon and Chichicastenango, dropping back in distance after landing the Grand Prix de Paris. In a rough race, Vahorimix managed to avoid the trouble caused by Proudwings as she hung left in the final furlong, hampering Noverre and Banks Hill among others, and stayed on to be beaten half a length, three quarters of a length ahead of Banks Hill. Proudwings, almost inevitably, was disqualified, leaving Vahorimix a decidedly fortunate winner. On the strength of this run, and despite giving the impression a return to nine furlongs or more would suit him, Vahorimix started second favourite behind Banks Hill in the Prix du Moulin de Longchamp in September but never got into the race after being held up, finishing sixth of eight to Slickly. Vahorimix failed to make any mark in the Queen Elizabeth II Stakes at Ascot later in the month either, coming under strong pressure early in the straight when fifth to the shock winner Summoner.

Prix du Haras de Fresnay-le-Buffard Jacques le Marois, Deauville— Vahorimix (left) benefits from another Group 1 disqualification; this time Proudwings (No.1) is the culprit, placed last after hanging left and hampering Banks Hill (No.8) and Noverre (white face)

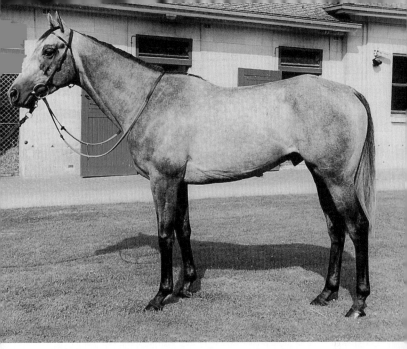

Mr J-L. Lagardere's "Vahorimix"

Vahorimix (FR) (gr.c. 1998)	Linamix (FR) (gr 1987)	Mendez (gr 1981)	Bellypha
			Miss Carina
		Lunadix (gr 1972)	Breton
			Lutine
	Vadsa Honor (FR) (gr 1993)	Highest Honor (gr 1983)	Kenmare
			High River
		Vadsa (b 1979)	Halo
			Rainbow's Edge

Few could have forecast that Vahorimix's sire Linamix, sire also of Slickly and good three-year-old filly Diamilina, would develop into the best sire in France on his retirement in 1990. Although Linamix showed first-rate form to win the Poule d'Essai des Poulains and finish second in three top races afterwards, notably the Champion Stakes, his sire Mendez had not been a noted success, which can be the kiss of death for a prospective stallion. However, the consistent support of owner Jean-Luc Lagardere has reaped great rewards for both, with Linamix siring seven Group 1 scorers, five of whom carried Lagardere's colours with another one bred by him. Oddly, Linamix's success is strictly parochial, with none of his pattern winners having scored in Britain or Ireland. All his progeny have had his grey colouring, which is easily explained because Linamix, by a grey out of a grey and receiving the greying genes from each parent, is a pure breeding grey. This means that whatever colour his offspring may be as youngsters, and whatever colour they are registered as being, they all eventually turn grey. Other stallions with this quality down the years include Al Hattab and Zeddaan. Vahorimix, who starts his stud career alongside Linamix at Haras du Val Henry at a fee of €7,000, and also has a grey dam in Vadsa Honor, may turn out to be another, but there is no certainty about this. Vahorimix is the first foal out of Vadsa Honor, who was successful twice at around a mile and a half, including in a listed event, and foaled two more colts by Linamix in 1999 and 2000. Her dam Vadsa is also grandam of Breeders' Cup Mile winner Val Royal and Vadlawys, who won the Prix Hocquart. There is a fair degree of stamina in the pedigree and Vahorimix would undoubtedly have stayed a mile and a quarter. A lengthy, good-topped colt with more about him than most of his sire's runners, who tend to be light-framed, he was an unimpressive mover who acted on heavy going and might not have stood repeated racing on firm. *A. Fabre, France*

VALDASHO   2 b.f. (Feb 15) Classic Cliche (IRE) 128 – Ma Rivale (Last Tycoon 131)   – [2001 6s 8.2s Nov 5] 2,600Y: sturdy filly: fourth foal: half-sister to fairly useful 6f winner Stand By (by Missed Flight): dam maiden in Belgium: well beaten in maidens. *G. G. Margarson*

VALDERO   4 ch.g. Arazi (USA) 135 – Vale of Truth (USA) (Lyphard's Wish (FR) 124)   **44** [2001 72: f11g 11.6g 11.6m 11.5m 10f Jul 9] smallish, sturdy gelding: fair maiden at 3 yrs: only poor form in 2001: probably stays 11.6f: acts on fibresand, good to firm and good to soft going. *W. R. Muir*

VALDESCO (IRE)   3 ch.g. Bluebird (USA) 125 – Allegheny River (USA) (Lear Fan   **72** (USA) 130) [2001 72: 5m 6m³ 6m 7m³ 8m 6d p7g f7g Dec 1] leggy, quite good-topped   **a67** gelding: fair handicapper: reportedly had breathing problem fifth outing: left Mrs M. Reveley after next one: stays 7f: acts on good to firm going: sometimes slowly away: tried blinkered/visored. *J. L. Eyre*

VALENTINE BAND (USA)   4 b.f. Dixieland Band (USA) – Shirley Valentine 104   **104** (Shirley Heights 130) [2001 104p: 10.4m² 10.1f³ 12m Jul 21] strong, good sort: useful performer, lightly raced: said to have suffered small stress fracture after winning maiden on only run at 3 yrs: placed in listed races at York (2 lengths second to Moselle) in May and Newcastle (¾-length third to Tarfshi) in June: ran as if something amiss final start: stayed 10.4f: acted on firm going: stud in USA. *R. Charlton*

VALENTINES VISION   4 b.g. Distinctly North (USA) 115 – Sharp Anne 74§   – (Belfort (FR) 89) [2001 57: f7g 8s f6g 7v f6g f7g f8g Dec 14] modest performer at 3 yrs: well held in 2001: sometimes visored. *Mrs S. Lamyman*

VALENTINO   4 ch.c. Nureyev (USA) 131 – Divine Danse (FR) 118 (Kris 135) [2001   **118 §** 119: 7f* 8m⁴ 7m³ 7g⁴ 7.3f³ Sep 21] big, leggy, lengthy colt: has a markedly round action: smart performer: won minor event at Leicester in May by 1¾ lengths from Welcome Friend: ran well when 2¼ lengths fourth to Medicean in Queen Anne Stakes at Royal Ascot: only respectable efforts after, third to Shibboleth in Criterion Stakes at Newmarket, fourth to Fath in Lennox Stakes at Goodwood and third to Welcome Friend in listed race at Newbury: subsequently underwent surgery for a soft palate: probably as effective at 7f as 1m: acts on firm and good to soft going: wears crossed noseband/tongue tie: ran poorly when sweating once at 3 yrs: free-going sort: irresolute in finish: sent to Bahrain. *J. H. M. Gosden*

VALE OF LEVEN (IRE)   5 b.g. Fayruz 116 – Speedy Action (Horage 124) [2001   – e8g f12s³ f12g f11g⁵ Feb 2] seems of little account nowadays. *W. G. M. Turner*

VALEUREUX   3 ch.g. Cadeaux Genereux 131 – La Strada (Niniski (USA) 125) [2001   **79 +** –: 8.2v* 10.4g⁵ 7.9d Oct 12] tall gelding: has scope: once raced at 2 yrs: fair form when 100/1-winner of maiden at Nottingham in March by length: very stiff tasks after, in listed race (far from discredited) and handicap, both at York, 5 months apart: probably stays 10.4f: raced only on good ground or softer. *J. Hetherton*

VALFONIC   3 b.g. Zafonic (USA) 130 – Valbra (Dancing Brave (USA) 140) [2001   **71** 9m³ 9.7m* 10v Oct 8] fourth foal: dam, twice-raced sister to useful French performer up to 9f Cheyenne Dream, out of very smart performer up to 1m Interval: won maiden at Folkestone in August: well held in handicap next time: should stay 1¼m: sold 24,000 gns, and gelded. *Mrs A. J. Perrett*

VALJEAN   5 b.g. Alzao (USA) 117 – Escape Path (Wolver Hollow 126) [2001   – 56: f9.4s Jan 18] modest maiden at best in Ireland for J. Murphy: well held on British debut in Wolverhampton claimer: best effort at 9f: raced mainly on going softer than good (acts on heavy): blinkered second 4-y-o start. *D. J. Wintle*

VALLEY CHAPEL (IRE)   5 ch.h. Selkirk (USA) 129 – Valley Springs (Saratoga   **118**
Six (USA)) [2001 113: 10v 12v² 12d³ 9.8m² 12g* 12g 12g* 9s* 12s* Sep 9] smart
performer: winner of all 3 Scandinavian Derbys in 1999: successful in 2000 in 2 listed
races at Ovrevoll and Stockholm Cup International at Taby: won listed race at Ovrevoll
in June, Scandinavian Open Championship at Klampenborg (by ½ length from Sagittarius) and Marit Sveaas Minnelop at Ovrevoll (by ½ length from Martellian) in August
and Stockholm Cup International again at Taby (by head from Sagittarius) in September:
also placed in Prix d'Hedouville at Longchamp and Prix Jean de Chaudenay at Saint-
Cloud second/third starts: stays 1½m: acts on heavy and good to firm ground, below best
on dirt: held up: reliable. *W. Neuroth, Norway*

VALLEY OF DREAMS (IRE)   3 b.f. Fairy King (USA) – Capegulch (USA) (Gulch   **–**
(USA)) [2001 63p: 7m Jun 14] angular filly: modest form in maiden on only outing at 2
yrs: well held in similar event 9 months later. *P. Howling*

VALLEY OF SONG   3 ch.f. Caerleon (USA) 132 – Hill of Snow 80 (Reference Point   **74 p**
139) [2001 9.9d* Sep 27] second foal: sister to smart Irish 7f (at 2 yrs, including Moyglare Stud Stakes)/1m winner who stayed 1¼m Preseli: dam, 1¼m winner who stayed
1½m, out of triple Grade 1 winner White Star Line, a very good family: weak 10/1-shot,
won maiden at Goodwood by 1¼ lengths from Zonergem, seeming very green and off the
bit early, but staying on well to lead over 1f out: will be suited by 1½m: sure to improve.
J. L. Dunlop

VALS RING   3 ch.g. King's Signet (USA) 110 – Factuelle 43 (Known Fact (USA) 135)   **–**
[2001 –: 7s 6g 6f 6f⁵ 6m 6g f6g⁵ 8.2s Aug 6] strong, lengthy gelding: little solid form:
tried tongue tied. *J. Gallagher*

VALUABLE GIFT   4 ch.g. Cadeaux Genereux 131 – Valbra (Dancing Brave (USA)   **54**
140) [2001 8v 5d⁵ 6m 6m 5s Aug 21] 11,000 2-y-o: strong, good-topped gelding: third
foal: dam twice-raced sister to useful French 1m/9f winner Cheyenne Dream out of very
smart filly up to 1m Interval: modest maiden: form only when fifth at Musselburgh in
April: may prove best at 5f/6f. *T. D. Barron*

VANDENBERGHE   2 b.c. (Mar 17) Millkom 124 – Child Star (FR) 58 (Bellypha   **51**
130) [2001 6f 7m 8.1s 8f 7s f7g f8g Dec 3] deep-girthed colt: third foal: half-brother to
4-y-o Lucky Star and 3-y-o Animal Cracker: dam, 14.6f/2m winner on Flat and winning
hurdler, out of half-sister to high-class French miler Mendez: modest maiden: trained by
D. Marks on debut: well held in nurseries last 3 starts: should stay 1¼m. *Mrs Merrita
Jones*

VANDERLIN   2 ch.c. (May 11) Halling (USA) 133 – Massorah (FR) 108 (Habitat 134)   **91**
[2001 5.2g² 7m 6g² Jul 20] 38,000Y: strong colt: half-brother to several winners,
including fairly useful 6f winner Massiba (by Shareef Dancer) and 3-y-o La Yolam: dam
French sprinter: fairly useful maiden: runner-up at Newbury and Pontefract (carried head
awkwardly) when seventh of 11 in Chesham Stakes at Royal Ascot: should
stay 1m. *I. A. Balding*

VAN DE VELDE   2 ch.g. (Feb 24) Alhijaz 122 – Lucky Flinders 77 (Free State 125)   **69**
[2001 6g² 6m³ Sep 22] 17,000Y: seventh foal: brother to 6-y-o Alcayde and half-brother
to 2 winners, notably 3-y-o Pomfret Lad: dam, 1m winner, sister to smart Italian winner
up to 1m Melbury Lad: fair form, staying on, in maidens at Lingfield and Catterick
(slowly away): should stay at least 1m: sold 12,500 gns. *P. F. I. Cole*

VANITY (IRE)   4 b.f. Thatching 131 – Penny Fan 58 (Nomination 125) [2001 –: 6g²   **75**
5m² 5m² 6g⁴ 6d 6v⁴ Oct 29] sparely-made, useful-looking filly: fair maiden: may prove
best at 5f: acts on good to firm ground: slowly away penultimate start. *G. B. Balding*

VANTAGE POINT   5 b.g. Casteddu 111 – Rosie Dickins 59 (Blue Cashmere 129)   **36**
[2001 49: f16.2s f16.2g⁶ 16.2g f16g³ 15.4v⁵ f14g 11.8s 16s⁶ p12g⁵ f14.8s Dec 15]   **a42**
angular gelding: shows knee action: poor performer: effective at 1½m to 2m: acts on
all-weather and any turf going: often races prominently: visored penultimate start.
K. McAuliffe

VASARI (IRE)   7 ch.g. Imperial Frontier (USA) 112 – Why Not Glow (IRE) (Glow   **58 d**
(USA)) [2001 62: e7g⁶ e8g² f9.4g e8g⁶ e10g 6f 8m 7m 6m 5m 7m Jul 24] close-coupled
gelding: modest handicapper: left Jamie Poulton following fifth start and mostly well
held after: stays 1m: acts on good to firm going, heavy and equitrack: tried blinkered/
tongue tied: sold 400 gns in December. *P. Howling*

VEDA'S RAINBOW (IRE)   2 b. or br.f. (Feb 8) Petardia 113 – Sama Veda (IRE) 84   **70 ?**
(Rainbow Quest (USA) 134) [2001 6s 6m 6.9m 7m 7m 7m 6d Oct 18] IR 11,000Y: leggy,

quite good-topped filly: second foal: dam, third at 7f at 2 yrs on only start, out of useful 1m winner Samsova: fair maiden: should stay 1m: blinkered last 3 outings, easily best effort (possibly flattered) on first occasion. *S. Kirk*

VELVET GLADE (USA)   3 b.f. Kris S (USA) – Vailmont (USA) 88 (Diesis 133)   **98**
[2001 84: 7g 7g* 7m 7s⁵ 7d Sep 13] leggy, quite good-topped filly: has a quick action: useful performer: easily best effort when winning handicap at Newmarket (beat Sabo Rose 1¼ lengths) in July: well held in Tote International Handicap and listed events after: raced mainly at 7f: acts on firm going: sent to USA. *I. A. Balding*

VELVET ISLAND (IRE)   3 b.f. Turtle Island (IRE) 123 – Double Grange (IRE)   **75**
(Double Schwartz 128) [2001 53p: 6.1d² 5.1f⁶ 6m³ f6g* 7g 6g f7g³ 7s f8.5g* p10g p8g Nov 24] fair performer: won maiden at Southwell in June and handicap at Wolverhampton in November: stays 8.5f: acts on good to firm going, good to soft, fibresand and polytrack: blinkered (below form) once: sold 32,000 gns. *W. J. Haggas*

VELVET JONES   8 gr.g. Sharrood (USA) 124 – Cradle of Love (USA) 87 (Roberto   –
(USA) 131) [2001 –: 6m 8f 8.5m 12g Aug 23] angular gelding: no longer of much account. *G. F. H. Charles-Jones*

VELVET SLIPPER   3 b.f. Muhtafal (USA) – Magic Slipper 97 (Habitat 134) [2001   **50**
f8g⁵ f7g⁵ e8g 7m² 6m 7.1f⁵ 7s Oct 5] 6,000Y: half-sister to several winners, including 1994 2-y-o 7f winner Muhab (by Lyphard) and 4-y-o Thari, 7f winner at 2 yrs, both useful: dam, 1¼m and 11.5f winner, half-sister to Fairy Footsteps and Light Cavalry: modest maiden handicapper: below form last 3 starts: stays 7f: acts on good to firm going: sold 5,000 gns. *G. C. Bravery*

VENDOME (IRE)   3 b.g. General Monash (USA) 107 – Kealbra Lady (Petong 126)   **80 d**
[2001 87: 5s 5.1f 5m³ 5d 5m 5.1m⁵ f5s⁶ Dec 27] strong gelding: poor mover: fairly useful performer: below form after third start: best at bare 5f: acts on firm and good to soft going: races up with pace. *J. A. Osborne*

VENIKA VITESSE   5 b.g. Puissance 110 – Vilanika (FR) 81 (Top Ville 129) [2001   **50**
72d: f6g f6g⁶ f5g f6g⁵ 5m f7g 6m 6.1f 6m 8f p6g⁶ Dec 19] modest performer nowadays: best at 5f/6f: acts on equitrack and good to firm going, probably on soft: tried blinkered. *T. D. Barron*

VENOSA (IRE)   2 b.f. (Mar 26) Presidium 124 – Breakfast Creek 63 (Hallgate 127)   **41**
[2001 f5g f6g f5g 5m⁵ 6.1d f6g p7g f8.5g Nov 27] 900Y: first foal: dam 2-y-o 5f winner: poor maiden: stays 6f. *D. Haydn Jones*

VENTO DEL ORENO (FR)   4 ch.f. Lando (GER) 128 – Very Sweet (Bellypha 130)   –
[2001 67: f12g⁵ f9.4g Feb 22] smallish filly: fair maiden at 3 yrs: well held in 2001. *Mrs D. Haine*

VENTURER (USA)   3 b.c. Gone West (USA) – Angel In My Heart (FR) 119   **103**
(Rainbow Quest (USA) 134) [2001 8g* 8m* 8f³ 7.3m 7g* 8g 7g Sep 19] $400,000Y: rather leggy, quite attractive colt: first foal: dam, French 1m/1¼m (Prix de Psyche) winner who was later placed in US Grade 1 9f/1¼m events, half-sister to Prix de la Salamandre winner Common Grounds: useful performer: won Newmarket Challenge Whip then twice at Goodwood, in maiden in May and handicap (beat Royal Millennium 1½ lengths) in August: lacklustre efforts last 2 starts: effective at 7f/1m: raced only on good going or firmer: joined E. Charpy in UAE. *J. H. M. Gosden*

VERA TWO   3 ch.f. King's Signet (USA) 110 – Vera's First (IRE) 69 (Exodal (USA))   –
[2001 7m 7m 5m Jul 11] 900F: first foal: dam 2-y-o 7f seller winner: well held in maidens: very slowly away final outing. *G. L. Moore*

VERGIL'S VENTURE   2 b.g. (Mar 16) Alhijaz 122 – Quick Profit 78 (Formidable   **67**
(USA) 125) [2001 6m⁵ 7f³ 7m² 7g² 6g Aug 4] 3,000Y: close-coupled gelding: sixth foal: half-brother to 3 winners, including fairly useful 1996 2-y-o 5f winner Smokey Pete (by Petong) and 5-y-o Rogue Spirit: dam 7f winner: fair maiden: runner-up at Lingfield and Newcastle: stays 7f. *G. C. H. Chung*

VERIDIAN   8 b.g. Green Desert (USA) 127 – Alik (FR) 113 (Targowice (USA) 130)   **84**
[2001 89: 12v 12m 12m⁴ Jul 28] sturdy gelding: fairly useful handicapper: better at 1½m than shorter: acts on soft and good to firm ground: blinkered (ran creditably) final start: seems suited by waiting tactics/strong handling: sold only 6,500 gns. *N. J. Henderson*

VERMILION CREEK   2 b.f. (Mar 15) Makbul 104 – Cloudy Reef 57 (Cragador   **63**
110) [2001 f5g 5.1f⁵ 6m⁵ 6m³ 6m⁵ 6.1d 6d f6g³ f8.5g* f7s Dec 18] close-coupled filly: fourth foal: dam maiden who raced only around 5f: modest performer: won claimer at

Wolverhampton in November: stays 8.5f: acts on good to firm going, good to soft and fibresand: reportedly bled from nose seventh start. *R. Hollinshead*

VERY EXCLUSIVE (USA) 2 b.c. (Mar 7) Royal Academy (USA) 130 – Exclusive Davis (USA) (Our Native (USA)) [2001 p8g p8g Nov 28] 50,000F, 100,000Y: third foal: dam French 7.5f (at 2 yrs) to 1¼m winner: modest form in Lingfield maidens: flashed tail on debut: quite free-going sort. *R. M. H. Cowell* **55**

VICE PRESIDENTIAL 6 ch.g. Presidium 124 – Steelock 68 (Lochnager 132) [2001 62d: f6g* f5g⁴ f6f 5v f6g 6m⁵ f6g f6g f7g f6s Dec 21] big gelding: easy mover: modest performer: won claimer at Southwell (only start for J. Balding) in February: on the downgrade: best at 6f/7f: acts on fibresand, good to firm and heavy going: blinkered final start: has won when sweating: usually races up with pace. *J. A. Glover* **– a62 d**

VICIOUS CIRCLE 7 b.g. Lahib (USA) 129 – Tight Spin (High Top 131) [2001 113: 16g² 20f Jun 21] tall, lengthy, angular gelding: easy mover: smart performer at best: won Ebor Handicap at York and Ritz Club Stakes (Handicap) at Ascot at 5 yrs: 8 lengths second to Lightning Arrow in prestige handicap at Nad Al Sheba in April: put down after sustaining serious injury to off-fore in Gold Cup at Royal Ascot: stayed 1¾m: acted on any going. *L. M. Cumani* **108**

VICIOUS DANCER 3 b.g. Timeless Times (USA) 99 – Yankeedoodledancer (Mashhor Dancer (USA)) [2001 94p: 6m* 6m 7m⁶ 6m 6m⁴ 6g 5g⁵ 5g 5d 6d Oct 13] leggy gelding: useful performer: won valuable handicap at Lingfield in May by head from Blue Reigns: creditable efforts after only when fourth in minor event at Haydock and fifth in handicap at York (beaten 2 lengths behind Jessica's Dream): best at 5f/6f: acts on soft and good to firm going. *R. M. Whitaker* **104**

VICIOUS HERO 2 b.g. (Apr 8) Timeless Times (USA) 99 – Syke Lane 44 (Clantime 101) [2001 5.1g Jun 16] 19,000Y: smallish, good-topped gelding: fourth foal: half-brother to 1m/1¼m winner Complimentary (by Superpower): dam, maiden who stayed 1m, sister to useful sprinter Saint Express: 20/1, backward and very green, tailed off in maiden at Nottingham. *R. M. Whitaker* **–**

VICIOUS KNIGHT 3 b.c. Night Shift (USA) – Myth 89 (Troy 137) [2001 100: 10g 8.1m* Jul 6] robust, good sort: good walker: smart performer, lightly raced: improved to win minor event at Sandown in July by ½ length from Carnival Dancer, going bit freely before leading over 2f out, then hanging right for pressure: will need to settle better to stay beyond 1m: raced only on good/good to firm going: wore crossed noseband at Sandown: stays in training. *L. M. Cumani* **113 +**

VICIOUS LOVER 2 ch.g. (Apr 30) Rudimentary (USA) 118 – Parfait Amour 73 (Clantime 101) [2001 6m 7g 6m 8m* 7.9s 8d Nov 2] strong gelding: fifth foal: dam, 6f (at 2 yrs) to 1m winner, from family of smart 6f/7f performer Branston Abby: modest performer: easily best effort when winning nursery at Musselburgh in September: seems better at 1m than shorter: acts on good to firm ground, possibly not on softer than good. *R. M. Whitaker* **58**

Pentax "Under Any" Conditions Stakes, Sandown—Vicious Knight holds on despite hanging right; Carnival Dancer (right) keeps on strongly for second place, with Mugharreb in third

VICIOUS PRINCE (IRE)   2 b.c. (Mar 9) Sadler's Wells (USA) 132 – Sunny Flower   **75 p**
(FR) (Dom Racine (FR) 121) [2001 7g 8m⁵ 7d Oct 2] 130,000Y: strong, lengthy colt: has
a fluent, round action: half-brother to several winners, notably high-class 1½m performer
Wagon Master (by Rainbow Quest): dam, placed in France, half-sister to dam of Saddlers' Hall (by Sadler's Wells) and Sun Princess: fair form: best effort when tenth of 16 to
Sir George Turner in valuable sales race at Newmarket final start: should be suited by
1¼m+: capable of better. *R. M. Whitaker*

VICIOUS WARRIOR   2 b.g. (Mar 24) Elmaamul (USA) 125 – Ling Lane (Slip   **74**
Anchor 136) [2001 7g⁴ 7g⁵ 7m 8g³ Nov 7] 16,500Y: third foal: half-brother to 5-y-o
Jammie Dodger and 3-y-o Night On The Town: dam, unraced, out of close relation to
Irish Oaks winner Bolas: fair maiden: best effort when third at Musselburgh: should stay
1¼m: slowly away first 2 outings. *R. M. Whitaker*

VICKY SCARLETT   4 gr.f. Missed Flight 123 – Just Greenwich 65 (Chilibang 120)   **–**
[2001 –: 8.2f 7.1g Jul 20] no sign of ability. *P. A. Pritchard*

VICTEDDU   3 b.f. Casteddu 111 – Glint of Victory 96 (Glint of Gold 128) [2001 50:   **74**
7d⁶ 7s May 3] smallish, close-coupled filly: has run only 4 times: fair form when sixth of
28 in maiden at Newmarket on reappearance: reportedly returned lame behind next time:
stays 7f. *M. G. Quinlan*

VICTORIA CROSS (IRE)   3 b.f. Mark of Esteem (IRE) 137 – Glowing With Pride   **101**
114 (Ile de Bourbon (USA) 133) [2001 77P: 7d⁴ 8m 8g⁴ 10.1m⁴ 8d³ Sep 28] tall, leggy
filly: useful performer: won maiden at Newmarket in April impressively: creditable
efforts after, in Poule d'Essai des Pouliches at Longchamp (hampered when trying to
improve from rear when twelfth to Rose Gypsy) and listed races at Ascot, Newcastle
(fourth to Moselle in rated stakes) and Saint-Cloud (3 lengths third to Five Fishes):
probably stays 1¼m: yet to race on extremes of going: races freely: sent to USA.
G. Wragg

VICTORIAN LADY   4 b.f. Old Vic 136 – Semperflorens (Don 128) [2001 –: f11g   **33**
f12g 8.2s⁶ Aug 6] poor maiden: stays 1m: acts on soft going: visored final start.
R. M. H. Cowell

VICTORIET   4 ch.f. Hamas (IRE) 125§ – Wedgewood (USA) (Woodman (USA) 126)   **–**
[2001 52: e8g⁶ 10f 8f 10g Sep 11] little form in 2001: tried blinkered. *N. Hamilton*

VICTORIOUS   5 ch.g. Formidable (USA) 125 – Careful Dancer (Gorytus (USA) 132)   **76**
[2001 76: f7s* f7g* f7g* 8g a8g² a8g a6g* a6s² a6s⁶ a6g* a6s³ Dec 30] strong gelding:
fair performer: has reportedly had wind operation: won 2 sellers at Wolverhampton and
claimer at Southwell in winter for R. Fahey: raced in Sweden after, winning handicaps at
Taby in October (final start for C. Bjorling) and December: effective at 6f/7f: acts on firm
going, good to soft, dirt and fibresand: has had tongue tied: blinkered last 5 starts: has
been slowly away. *Pia Brandt, Sweden*

VICTOR'S CROWN (IRE)   4 b.g. Desert Style (IRE) 121 – Royal Wolff (Prince   **59**
Tenderfoot (USA) 126) [2001 64: 6m² 6f⁴ 6m 6m⁵ 6m⁶ 8.2s 6m² Aug 22] modest maiden:
best around 6f: acts on firm going: blinkered final start: sold 1,200 gns. *M. H. Tompkins*

VICTOR VALENTINE (IRE)   2 ch.c. (Apr 25) Ridgewood Ben 113 – Tarliya   **59**
(IRE) 73 (Doyoun 124) [2001 7m 8g 6v f6g³ f6g² f6g² f6s Dec 15] lengthy colt: poor   **a72**
mover: first foal: dam, third at 1¼m only start in Ireland, half-sister to Irish 1000 Guineas
third Tarwiya: fair maiden on all-weather, best on turf: runner-up at Southwell and
Wolverhampton: should prove best at 5f/6f: acts on fibresand, best turf run on heavy
going. *E. A. Wheeler*

VIEWFORTH   3 b.g. Emarati (USA) 74 – Miriam 59 (Forzando 122) [2001 75: 5d³   **68**
6d 5m³ 5m* 5f⁵ 5f 5d⁶ 5g 5m⁴ 5g⁶ 5g 5m Sep 20] good-bodied gelding: fair performer:
made all in maiden at Musselburgh in June: best at 5f: acts on firm and soft going: usually
races prominently. *Miss L. A. Perratt*

VIEW THE FACTS   2 b.f. (Apr 27) So Factual (USA) 120 – Scenic View (IRE)   **55**
(Scenic 128) [2001 7d 7s 7d Nov 3] third foal: dam unraced granddaughter of Park Hill
winner African Dancer: easily best effort (modest form) when eighth of 14 in maiden at
Brighton second start. *P. L. Gilligan*

VIKING PRINCE   4 b.g. Chilibang 120 – Fire Sprite 83 (Mummy's Game 120) [2001   **–**
–: f7g Jan 4] probably of little account nowadays. *Jamie Poulton*

VILLA CARLOTTA   3 ch.f. Rainbow Quest (USA) 134 – Subya 107 (Night Shift   **110**
(USA)) [2001 83p: 10d³ 12g* 12v* 11.9d³ 11.9d² 10.5d² 10d² 12s* Nov 3] close-

coupled, quite attractive filly: has a round action: progressed into a smart performer: won maiden at Thirsk and handicap at Newbury (never off bridle) in May then listed race at Milan (by 1¼ lengths from Isadora) in November: should stay beyond 1½m: raced only on good going or softer (acts on heavy): held up: reliable: sold 110,000 gns, sent to France. *J. L. Dunlop*

VILLA DEL SOL   2 br.f. (Jan 12) Tagula (IRE) 116 – Admonish 57 (Warning 136)   **86 d**
[2001 5v² 5v² 5s³ 5s* 5m² 5m³ 6m* 6m⁵ 5.1m* 6d* 6d² 5m 6.1m⁴ 6g 6.1d 7.1m 6m p7g f6g f5f³ Dec 5] 8,500Y: leggy, plain filly: first foal: dam second from 2 starts at 6f at 2 yrs: fairly useful performer: won maiden at Haydock in May, seller at York in June and nurseries at Chester and Leicester in July: below form last 7 starts: effective at 5f/6f: acts on good to firm and soft going: usually held up. *A. Bailey*

VILLAGE NATIVE (FR)   8 ch.g. Village Star (FR) 131 – Zedative (FR) 74   **47 d**
(Zeddaan 130) [2001 57: e10g e8g⁵ e8g f9.4g⁴ e8g⁶ e8g e10g 7m 6m⁵ 8.1m 8f⁶ Aug 14] lengthy, angular gelding: poor performer, on downgrade: seems to stay 9.4f: acts on fibresand, equitrack, firm and good to soft going: blinkered nowadays, has been visored. *K. O. Cunningham-Brown*

VILLA ROMANA   4 b.f. Komaite (USA) – Keep Quiet 54 (Reprimand 122) [2001   **–**
53: f7g 7.1m 5m 6m 5.8s Oct 17] strong, lengthy filly: modest performer at 3 yrs: well held in 2001, leaving W. M. Brisbourne after fourth start: tried blinkered/tongue tied. *P. Cluskey, Ireland*

VILLA VIA (IRE)   4 b.f. Night Shift (USA) – Joma Kaanem (Double Form 130)   **–**
[2001 71: f6g f5g f6g Mar 14] smallish, sturdy filly: fair performer at 3 yrs: well held in 2001: tongue tied final start. *Miss J. F. Craze*

VILLE DE PARIS (IRE)   2 b.c. (Feb 17) Common Grounds 118 – Muqaddima (FR)   **69**
(Kaldoun (FR) 122) [2001 6g 7m⁶ 7.9m Sep 5] IR 16,000Y: smallish, sturdy colt: first foal: dam, French 6.5f/1m winner, granddaughter of high-class French 6f/7f performer Proskona from family of Bosra Sham: easily best effort in maidens (fair form) when sixth of 14 at Folkestone: should stay 1m. *R. F. Johnson Houghton*

VINCA   2 b.f. (Mar 30) Aragon 118 – Zamarra 59 (Clantime 101) [2001 5d p5g Nov 13]   **–**
3,000Y: small filly: first foal: dam, lightly raced at 2 yrs, best effort at 5f: well held in maidens: refused to enter stall on intended debut (trained by H. Howe). *A. Berry*

VINCENT   6 b.g. Anshan 119 – Top-Anna (IRE) 71 (Ela-Mana-Mou 132) [2001 43,   **a56**
a68: f14g f16g f14g f12g f16g f14g² f16g² f16.2g⁵ f16.2s³ Dec 18] tall gelding: had   **a56**
screws inserted into fractured leg after final 4-y-o start: modest performer: effective at 1½m to 17f: acts on any turf going/fibresand and equitrack: tends visored/blinkered: tends to hang/carry head high: best with waiting tactics. *John A. Harris*

VINCENTIA   3 ch.f. Komaite (USA) – Vatersay (USA) (Far North (CAN) 120) [2001   **62**
68: 7d 7s³ 7m³ 7m 7m 7m 7s³ 6v² f7g³ f7g Dec 1] sparely-made filly: poor mover: modest maiden: effective 6f/7f: acts on good to firm going, possibly better on softer than good (acts on heavy): has hung right/gone in snatches. *C. Smith*

VINNIE ROE (IRE)   3 b.c. Definite Article 121 – Kayu (Tap On Wood 130)   **126**
[2001 108p: 10s³ 10m⁴ 12f⁴ 12g 14g* 14g* 14m* 15.5v* Oct 28]
    When the Prix Royal-Oak (French St Leger) and the Irish St Leger were opened to older horses—in 1979 and 1983 respectively—European racegoers had to become accustomed to a new type of racehorse, the four-year-old classic winner. In the case of dual Irish St Leger winner Vintage Crop in 1993 and 1994, this even became a six- and seven-year-old classic winner. Neither race is widely regarded nowadays as a classic in the same traditional sense as the Doncaster St Leger, which remains confined to three-year-olds. The Jefferson Smurfit Irish St Leger, in particular, has become almost the exclusive preserve of the older horses. In the latest season it took place on the same day as the St Leger at Doncaster—a puzzling piece of race planning.
    Only two of the eight runners at the Curragh were three-year-olds, in contrast to the first running after the race was opened when two four-year-olds took on eight three-year-olds. Without the four-year-olds, that first open Irish St Leger would have been a very one-sided affair—the two older stayers, the filly Mountain Lodge and Khairpour, were first and third. The latest winner came from the minority age group in the shape of Vinnie Roe, saddled by Vintage Crop's trainer Dermot Weld, whose decision to go to the Curragh rather than Doncaster was apparently

influenced by the wish to see how Vinnie Roe fared against older horses with a tilt at the Melbourne Cup in mind. Vinnie Roe fared very well, putting up a performance that suggested he would have made a race of it with Milan in the St Leger itself. But any ideas about attempting to follow in the footsteps of Vintage Crop, the only winner of the Melbourne Cup trained outside Australasia, were shelved for the time being and Vinnie Roe was sent instead to Longchamp at the end of October for the Prix Royal-Oak. He became the first three-year-old to complete the Irish Leger/Royal-Oak double since Niniski in 1979 (the five-year-old Turgeon won both in 1991). It was only the third time since both races became 'open' that three-year-olds had landed the double, and the first since Authaal and El Cuite both carried Sheikh Mohammed's colours to victory in 1986.

Vinnie Roe showed progressive form as a two-year-old, winning two of his races and looking a smart colt in the making. Creditable efforts in the frame behind Galileo in two of Ireland's spring Derby trials led to Vinnie Roe contesting both the Derby Italiano and the Irish Derby. He finished a staying-on fourth to Morshdi at Rome, a shade unlucky as his rider had to extricate him from a pocket in the straight before beginning his challenge; and he came a respectable seventh—starting at 66/1 and under pressure turning for home—at the Curragh. Dropped in class and stepped up in trip to a mile and three quarters, Vinnie Roe picked up the winning thread in all-aged listed events at Leopardstown in July and the Curragh in August. He beat fellow three-year-old Sadlers Wings by four lengths at Leopardstown, but had to work much harder to reverse form over the longer trip with the Irish Derby fourth Pugin at the Curragh, getting the better of a good battle by a head. These efforts marked Vinnie Roe as a promising young stayer, and he started third favourite for the Irish St Leger, behind the previous year's Doncaster St Leger winner Millenary and the Yorkshire Cup winner Marienbard. He was at shorter odds than Persian Punch, winner of the Goodwood Cup and the Lonsdale Stakes on his last two starts, and Yavana's Pace, runner-up in the last two editions of the Irish Leger and successful on his last two starts, most recently in the Prix Gladiateur. Vinnie Roe stayed on to lead inside the final furlong and kept on strongly to win by two

Jefferson Smurfit Memorial Irish St Leger, the Curragh—Vinnie Roe becomes the first three-year-old winner since 1989; Millenary (rail) is second, Marienbard (right) third and Persian Punch fourth

lengths and two and a half from Millenary and Marienbard, with Persian Punch, who needs more of a test these days, back in fourth; Yavana's Pace was seventh, two places behind Sadlers Wings. Vinnie Roe was the first three-year-old to win the Irish St Leger since the filly Petite Ile in 1989. Since then, only thirty of the ninety-eight runners to contest the race have been from the classic crop and only two of them—Patricia in 1991 and Key Change in 1996, both also fillies—have started favourite.

More three-year-olds contest the Prix Royal-Oak than the Irish St Leger and Vinnie Roe went on to become the sixth to win the race in the twelve runnings from 1990. He was one of four three-year-olds among the thirteen runners in the latest edition and started second favourite behind another from the classic crop, the lightly-raced Godolphin representative Wareed, who had won the Prix Hubert de Chaudenay from the subsequent Jockey Club Cup winner Capal Garmon. Among the older horses were the two best stayers in France, the geldings Germinis and Generic, first and second in the Prix du Cadran last time. Wareed headed a five-strong challenge from Britain which also included Yavana's Pace, and there were also challengers from Germany and Spain. The field was the largest since 1988 and Vinnie Roe's performance in a very good renewal, run at a stronger pace than most French staying events, was as good as any in the race for many a year, probably since Ardross became the first older horse to win the race in 1981. Vinnie Roe improved to lead two furlongs out and kept on well, despite edging right once in front, to win by two and a half lengths and a neck from Generic and Germinis; fifth-placed Yavana's Pace, who did best of those who raced prominently, was the first British-trained finisher, Wareed weakening and finishing last after disputing the lead briefly before the home turn. Vinnie Roe's Irish Leger/Royal-Oak double established him as a high-class stayer who will have a big say in the destination of the major staying events as a four-year-old. He will stay beyond two miles—we'd back him to get the Gold Cup trip—and is effective on going ranging from heavy to good to firm. He was blinkered or visored on his last six starts but showed himself thoroughly reliable, progressing with every run. His usual rider Pat Smullen, by the way, retained his Irish jockeys' title with eighty-one winners, three more than Michael Kinane and Johnny Murtagh.

			Indian Ridge		Ahonoora
	Definite Article		(ch 1985)		Hillbrow
	(b 1992)		Summer Fashion		Moorestyle
Vinnie Roe (IRE)			(b 1985)		My Candy
(b.c. 1998)			Tap On Wood		Sallust
	Kayu		(ch 1976)		Cat O'Mountaine
	(ch 1985)		Ladytown		English Prince
			(ch 1980)		Supreme Lady

The leggy, useful-looking Vinnie Roe is from the first crop of Irish Derby runner-up Definite Article and is easily his best runner to date. Kayu, the unraced dam of Vinnie Roe, is out of the staying-bred mile-and-a-quarter winner Ladytown, a half-sister by Irish Derby winner English Prince to the Irish St Leger winner M-Lolshan. Kayu has bred several other winners, the best of them probably the useful Rich Victim (by Lapierre), twice successful under the name of Mazal in the Queen

Mr Seamus Sheridan's "Vinnie Roe"

Mother's Cup, an important handicap over a mile and a half in Hong Kong, and the fairly useful Irish mile-and-a-half winner Vincitore (by Petorius). *D. K. Weld, Ireland*

VINTAGE PREMIUM　4 b.g. Forzando 122 – Julia Domna (Dominion 123) [2001　**107 d** 107: f8.5g⁴ 8v 8d³ 7.9m⁵ 10.1m⁵ 8m 10m 10.4g 10.3g⁴ 10g³ 9g Oct 6] tall, leggy gelding: useful handicapper at best: good 2-length third to Mastermind in Spring Cup at Newbury on third start: well below that form after fifth start: effective at 1m (given bit of a test) to 10.5f: acts on any turf going and fibresand: visored sixth start: sometimes drifts right. *R. A. Fahey*

VINTAGE ROCK　4 b.g. Rock City 120 – Classical Vintage 80 (Stradavinsky 121)　**–** [2001 9.9m Jun 28] half-brother to 3 winners, including sprinter Simply Sooty (herself dam of 4-y-o Umistim) and irresolute 6f/7f winner Abso (both by Absalom): dam 2-y-o 5f winner: tailed off in maiden at Salisbury (troublesome at stalls). *R. Hannon*

VINTAGE STYLE　2 ch.g. (Mar 28) Piccolo 121 – Gibaltarik (IRE) 68 (Jareer (USA)　**70** 115) [2001 5.2d 5g⁵ 6g 6m 6.1d⁶ 7s⁵ 6d 6v 7g⁴ f6g⁵ p6g* Dec 19] 16,500Y: quite good-topped gelding: third foal: half-brother to useful 1998 2-y-o 5f winner Patriot (by Whittingham): dam, twice-raced 2-y-o 5f winner, half-sister to Mill Reef Stakes winner who stayed 1m Kahir Almaydan: fair performer: won nursery at Lingfield: stays 7f: acts on fibresand, polytrack and soft going: consistent. *R. Hannon*

VIOLENT　3 b.f. Deploy 131 – Gentle Irony 65 (Mazilier (USA) 107) [2001 58, a54:　**54** e7g⁴ e8g e10g⁶ f8.5g³ f8.5g* e8g f8g f7g⁶ 6.1v* 7m² 8m 6s⁶ 7s 8s p7g p10g⁴ Dec 29] small filly: modest performer: won apprentice claimer at Wolverhampton in March and seller at Nottingham in May: left A. Reid after tenth start: needs testing conditions at 6f, barely stays 1¼m: acts on all-weather and any turf going: sometimes visored: has been slowly away: none too consistent. *Jamie Poulton*

VIRBIUS (IRE) 5 ch.g. Wolfhound (USA) 126 – Virelai 72 (Kris 135) [2001 f12g 21.6s Apr 23] deep-girthed gelding: little form: tried blinkered. *R. D. E. Woodhouse* —

VIRGINIAN (FR) 5 b.g. Al Nasr (FR) 126 – Violet Dancer (FR) (Fabulous Dancer (USA) 124) [2001 16m⁴ 16g f12g⁵ f16.2g f16g 14.4d Aug 8] trained in France in 1999 by J. Bertran de Balanda, winning handicap at Clairefontaine: poor form on Flat in Britain: seems to stay 2m: acts on good to firm going and fibresand: blinkered/visored last 5 starts. *A. Crook* **39 a43**

VIRGIN SOLDIER (IRE) 5 ch.g. Waajib 121 – Never Been Chaste (Posse (USA) 130) [2001 102: 12d 11.9m 16m* 13.9m 16.1f 13.9m⁴ 14m 18.7m⁴ 16.2g Aug 11] angular gelding: useful handicapper: won at Kempton in May by neck from Boulevard: ran creditably only once after: stays easy 2¼m: acts on fibresand, equitrack and good to soft going: well held blinkered and visored: has won for amateur: sometimes idles/edges left: usually races prominently: joined G. A. Swinbank, successful over hurdles in December. *M. Johnston* **98**

VIRGOS BAMBINO (IRE) 4 ch.f. Perugino (USA) 84 – Deep In September (IRE) 50 (Common Grounds 118) [2001 f6g May 3] little sign of ability. *R. J. Price* —

VIRTUAL REALITY 10 b.g. Diamond Shoal 130 – Warning Bell 88 (Bustino 136) [2001 82: 7g 8.1m⁵ 9m 8m⁶ 7g⁶ Aug 9] angular gelding: fluent mover: fair performer: well below form last 3 starts in 2001: effective at 1m, barely at 1¼m: acts on firm and good to soft going: tried visored. *J. A. R. Toller* **79 d**

VISION OF NIGHT 5 b.h. Night Shift (USA) – Dreamawhile 85 (Known Fact (USA) 135) [2001 115: 6d 6m⁵ 5f² 5m⁴ 6m 6m* 6m* Aug 29] smallish, strong horse: smart performer: won minor event at Doncaster (by 2½ lengths from Tamarisk) and Jacobs Goldene Peitsche at Baden-Baden (beat Sartorial a head), both in August: also ran well earlier in year in Duke of York Stakes at York (length fifth to Pipalong), Temple Stakes at Sandown (½-length second to Cassandra Go) and King's Stand Stakes at Royal Ascot (2¼ lengths fourth to Cassandra Go): best at 5f/6f: yet to race on heavy going, **115**

Jacobs Goldene Peitsche, Baden-Baden—
a 1,2 for British raiders in Germany's most important sprint for three-year-olds and up;
Vision of Night (near side) heads Sartorial (centre) close home; Call Me Big is a neck away in third

acts on any other: usually waited with: tends to hang left: consistent: stays in training. *J. L. Dunlop*

VISITATION   3 b.f. Bishop of Cashel 122 – Golden Envoy (USA) 68 (Dayjur (USA)   **40** 137) [2001 64: f7g f8g⁴ f7g 10m 6.1d 8.5s f8g f8g f8g f11g³ Dec 17] tall filly: poor nowadays: stays 11f: acts on fibresand and good to firm going: visored/blinkered last 3 starts (slowly away first 2 occasions). *K. A. Ryan*

VISLINK (IRE)   3 br.g. Shalford (IRE) 124§ – Wide Outside (IRE) 50 (Don't Forget   **–** Me 127) [2001 ?: f7g f7g⁵ f12g f14g Dec 14] well-made gelding: poor maiden: races freely and may prove best at 5f/6f: tried blinkered: withdrawn after bolting to post third intended outing. *K. A. Ryan*

VISORHILL (FR)   3 b.c. Danehill (USA) 126 – Visor (USA) (Mr Prospector (USA))   **115** [2001 8g⁵ 8s* 10d² 9.8d⁴ Oct 6] big, lengthy colt: fourth foal: half-brother to 3 winners in France at around 1m/9f by Linamix, notably smart pair Visionary and Visionnaire: dam, minor sprint winner in USA, out of half-sister to Kentucky Derby/Belmont Stakes winner Swale: smart form: won minor event at Deauville in August: plenty more improvement when 2 lengths second to Jim And Tonic in La Coupe de Maisons-Laffitte next time: below that form when only fourth of 5 to Albarahin in Prix Dollar at Longchamp final outing: stays 1¼m: acts on soft going: sent to Hong Kong. *A. Fabre, France*

VISTA CHINO (IRE)   2 b.f. (Apr 6) Perugino (USA) 84 – La Fille de Cirque 49   **45** (Cadeaux Genereux 131) [2001 5.7f⁶ 5.7g Aug 7] 7,500F, 10,000Y: second foal: dam 1m winner: poor form in maidens at Bath. *D. Haydn Jones*

VITA SPERICOLATA (IRE)   4 b.f. Prince Sabo 123 – Ahonita 90 (Ahonoora 122)   **106** [2001 104: 5m² 5f 6m⁴ 6m³ 5m* 6.1m* 6g 5.2f⁴ 5s 5g⁴ 5v Oct 28] lengthy, rather plain filly: useful performer: won minor event at Newmarket in July and listed race at Chester (beat Damalis by 2 lengths) in August: creditable efforts after when fourth in listed events at Newbury (1¾ lengths behind The Trader) and Newmarket (beaten 2¾ lengths by Indian Prince): best at 5f/6f: acts on any going: effective visored or not: sometimes carries head awkwardly/edges left: often makes running. *J. S. Wainwright*

VITELUCY   2 b.f. (Feb 6) Vettori (IRE) 119 – Classic Line 71 (Last Tycoon 131)   **59** [2001 8d 8.3v⁵ Oct 29] 6,000F: first foal: dam, 1¾m winner who stayed 17.5f, from very good family of Salsabil and Marju: better effort in maidens (modest form) when fifth to Ski For Me at Windsor: has raced freely, but should stay at least 1¼m. *I. A. Balding*

VITESSE (IRE)   3 b.f. Royal Academy (USA) 130 – Brentsville (USA) (Arctic Tern   **55** (USA) 126) [2001 61p: 10m 8.1s* 8.1s 8d f11g Nov 12] leggy filly: modest performer: won maiden at Haydock in August, flashing tail: well beaten after: should stay 1¼m: form only on soft ground. *Mrs Lydia Pearce*

VITUS BERING (USA)   4 b. or br.g. Bering 136 – Most Precious (USA) (Nureyev   **73** (USA) 131) [2001 –: 7.1s² 7.1m³ 8m 8.3v p10g Nov 20] fair maiden: form in 2001 only on first 2 starts (reportedly lame final outing): should be suited by 1m+: acts on soft and good to firm ground: tried tongue tied. *S. Kirk*

VIVA MARIA (FR)   2 gr.f. (Feb 8) Kendor (FR) 122 – Tambura (FR) (Kaldoun (FR)   **81 p** 122) [2001 6m⁴ 6.1v* Oct 4] 520,000 francs Y: rather leggy filly: third foal: half-sister to useful French 5.5f (at 2 yrs) and 1m winner Tadorne (by Inchinor): dam useful French 2-y-o 1m winner: fairly useful form: confirmed promise when winning maiden at Nottingham by ½ length from Stands To Reason, making most: will stay 7f: probably capable of better. *J. H. M. Gosden*

VODKA (IRE)   3 b.g. Inzar (USA) 112 – Clear Glade (Vitiges (FR) 132) [2001 46:   **60** f11g² f11g* f12g² 12v* f12g³ f12g Jun 21] big, sturdy gelding: modest performer: won claimer at Southwell (left P. Haslam) in February, minor event at Musselburgh in March and claimer at Southwell in May: should stay beyond 1½m: acts on fibresand and heavy going: usually races prominently: reportedly lost action sixth outing: sold 11,000 gns in July, sent to Kuwait. *J. R. Best*

VODKA QUEEN (IRE)   2 b.f. (Apr 17) Ali-Royal (IRE) 127 – Gentle Guest (IRE)   **–** (Be My Guest (USA) 126) [2001 f6s Dec 26] IR 3,500Y: half-sister to 1m winner who stayed 1½m Freedom Chance (by Lahib) and 3-y-o Engstrum: dam unraced: 14/1, well beaten in claimer at Wolverhampton. *K. R. Burke*

VOICE MAIL   2 b.g. (Apr 18) So Factual (USA) 120 – Wizardry 83 (Shirley Heights   **61** 130) [2001 6m 7.1s 6s Oct 5] half-brother to several winners, including 4-y-o Air Mail: dam, maiden who stayed 1½m, daughter of Jersey Stakes winner Merlin's Charm: modest maiden: likely to prove best up to 1m. *I. A. Balding*

VOICE OF HOPE (IRE)   4 b.g. Magical Strike (USA) 114 – Glendee (Boreen (FR) –
123) [2001 f11s Dec 21] fifth foal: dam unraced: visored, well held in maiden.
Mrs N. Macauley

VOLALI (IRE)   2 b.g. (Apr 28) Ali-Royal (IRE) 127 – Vol de Reve (IRE) (Nordico   **61 d**
(USA)) [2001 5m 5m³ 5g 5g⁶ 6g f7g f7g f6g⁴ f5s⁵ Dec 15] IR 8,000F, IR 6,200Y, 15,000
2-y-o: smallish, useful-looking gelding: third foal: half-brother to a winner up to 6.5f in
Norway by Shalford: dam unraced: modest maiden: mostly disappointing after first 2
starts: left Mrs A. Duffield before penultimate one: probably stays 6f: raced only on good/
good to firm going on turf, probably acts on fibresand: tried blinkered/visored.
M. J. Polglase

VOLATA (IRE)   3 b.g. Flying Spur (AUS) – Musianica 92 (Music Boy 124) [2001   **116**
83p: 8g 6m* 6f* 6m 6g⁶ Aug 11] strong, good-bodied gelding: type to carry condition:
smart performer: won listed rated stakes at Haydock (made all to beat Palanzo by length)
in May and John Smith's Extra Smooth Chipchase Stakes at Newcastle (beat Bahamian
Pirate ¾ length) following month: respectable efforts last 2 starts, in July Cup at Newmarket (eight to Mozart) and valuable conditions event at Ascot (helped force strong pace
when sixth to Orientor): subsequently gelded: should be as effective at 5f as 6f (stiff task
in 2000 Guineas at 1m): raced mainly on going firmer than good (acts on firm ground):
sent to Hong Kong. *M. H. Tompkins*

VOLONTIERS (FR)   6 b.g. Common Grounds 118 – Senlis (USA) 101 (Sensitive   **107 +**
Prince (USA)) [2001 97, a–: 7m² 8f* 7m 7m Jul 12] close-coupled gelding: has a round   **a–**
action: useful handicapper: won at Newbury (beat Red N' Socks 5 lengths) in June:
hampered next time, then didn't get run of race when ninth in Bunbury Cup at Newmarket
final outing: effective at 7f/1m: acts on firm and good to soft going: free-going sort (has
worn crossed noseband), usually held up nowadays. *P. W. Harris*

Mr J. Ellis' "Volata"

VOLTE FACE 3 ch.f. Polar Falcon (USA) 126 – Krameria 72 (Kris 135) [2001 61p: **52 ?**
6g⁵ 6v p6g⁵ f6g Nov 26] lengthy, good-topped filly: modest maiden: appeared to run
creditably in 2001 only on reappearance: raced only at 6f. *S. Kirk*

VOUCHER 2 ch.f. (Mar 31) Polish Precedent (USA) 131 – Superstore (USA) (Blushing **71**
Groom (USA) 131) [2001 7f 6g⁵ Sep 7] rangy filly: has scope: fluent mover: fourth foal:
half-sister to French 1m winner Club Card (by Unfuwain): dam unraced sister to Irish
1000 Guineas winner Al Bahathri: fair form in maidens at Newmarket and Kempton
(favourite), though found little each time: bred to be best up to 1m. *B. W. Hills*

VRUBEL (IRE) 2 ch.g. (Mar 19) Entrepreneur 123 – Renzola (Dragonara Palace **64**
(USA) 115) [2001 6m³ f6g⁴ 6d 6d p8g⁶ p6g⁶ Dec 19] 57,000F, 180,000Y: well-made
gelding: half-brother to several winning sprinters, notably smart 1996 2-y-o 5f/6.5f winner Deadly Dudley (by Great Commotion): dam unraced half-sister to dam of very smart
French performer up to 1½m Millkom: modest maiden: stays 1m: acts on fibresand/poly-
track, best turf effort on good to firm going: gelded after final outing. *N. A. Callaghan*

VUELA-MANA-MOU (IRE) 3 b.g. Goldmark (USA) 113 – Carnival Fugue 58 **–**
(High Top 131) [2001 11.7m 10v Oct 8] 5,000F, 19,500Y: half-brother to several winners,
notably useful 1¼m winner Honey Line (by High Line): dam sprint maiden: well held in
2 maidens: sold 500 gns. *G. A. Butler*

W

WAAFIAH 3 b.f. Anabaa (USA) 130 – First Waltz (FR) 117 (Green Dancer (USA) **57 +**
132) [2001 7m² Aug 4] half-sister to several winners, including 4-y-o Atlantic Rhapsody
and French 1m (including at 2 yrs) winner Gaitero (by Groom Dancer), both useful: dam
won Prix Morny: 7/4, 1½ lengths second to Greek Dream in maiden at Thirsk, headed 2f
out: will stay 1m. *M. Johnston*

WADENHOE (IRE) 4 b.f. Persian Bold 123 – Frill (Henbit (USA) 130) [2001 56d: **–**
8.3g 8f 8m 8f 7f 7g Sep 5] seems of little account nowadays. *M. S. Saunders*

WADI 6 b.g. Green Desert (USA) 127 – Eternal (Kris 135) [2001 73: 12m 12m 10g **67**
11.5f* 12.1s 13.1d 10g 9.7d 12g Sep 15] fair handicapper: won at Lingfield in July: well
held otherwise in 2001: stays 1½m: acts on equitrack, firm and good to soft going: twice
blinkered/tongue tied: has looked less than keen. *Dr J. R. J. Naylor*

WADSWORTH (NZ) 8 br.g. Kirmann 116 – Guard The Gold (NZ) (Imperial Guard **–**
106) [2001 10.3m³ 10m Jun 22] big, lengthy New Zealand-bred gelding: 7f/1m winner in
native country at 5 yrs: little form in minor event/claimer in Britain. *B. P. J. Baugh*

WAFFLES OF AMIN 4 b.g. Owington 123 – Alzianah 102 (Alzao (USA) 117) **60 d**
[2001 75: f8g e6g⁶ e7g f7g f7g 7f 10f 10m⁶ 10.9m 10m 10g 10s⁶ p12g³ Nov 28] small
gelding: modest handicapper, on downgrade: seems to stay easy 1½m: acts on all-
weather, good to firm and good to soft going (well beaten on heavy): tried blinkered.
S. Kirk

WAFF'S FOLLY 6 b.m. Handsome Sailor 125 – Shirl 52 (Shirley Heights 130) [2001 **59**
62: e6g⁵ 6f 5g² 5m⁵ 5.1g 5.1d⁶ Oct 25] sparely-made mare: modest handicapper: best at
5f/6f: acts on firm and good to soft ground. *D. J. S. ffrench Davis*

WAHCHI (IRE) 2 ch.c. (Feb 26) Nashwan (USA) 135 – Nafhaat (USA) 91 (Roberto **97 p**
(USA) 131) [2001 7m 8m* Sep 12] strong, lengthy colt: has scope: closely related to
3-y-o Ranin and half-brother to several winners, including 7f/1m winner Ghalib (by
Soviet Star) and 6.5f (at 2 yrs) and 7f winner Qhazeenah (by Marju), both useful: dam,
1½m winner, out of sister to US Grade 1 1¼m winner Sisterhood: 9/1, confirmed promise
when winning 14-runner maiden at Doncaster by 3 lengths from Yasey, quickening clear
over 2f out: will stay at least 1¼m: should make a smart 3-y-o. *E. A. L. Dunlop*

WAHJ (IRE) 6 ch.g. Indian Ridge 123 – Sabaah (USA) 65 (Nureyev (USA) 131) **104**
[2001 104: f8.5g² 8s⁴ 8m 8f 7f⁵ 7d* 7g 7g³ 7s⁶ Oct 11] sturdy gelding: useful handicapper: won at Chester in August by 3½ lengths from Forever Times: creditable efforts
last 2 starts: races freely, and at least as effective at 7f as easy 8.5f: acts on firm going, soft
and fibresand: tongue tied earlier in career: often makes running. *C. A. Dwyer*

WAIKIKI BEACH (USA) 10 ch.g. Fighting Fit (USA) – Running Melody 86 **– §**
(Rheingold 137) [2001 47§: 11.9s f8g 8.1s Aug 9] lengthy gelding: temperamental
handicapper: tried visored, usually blinkered. *G. L. Moore*

WAIKIKI DANCER (IRE) 3 br.f. General Monash (USA) 107 – Waikiki (GER) **45**
(Zampano (GER)) [2001 48: f8g 8m⁶ 7m⁶ 8m f6g³ 7g Aug 8] workmanlike filly: poor
maiden: best form at 6f: acts on fibresand and firm going: has been slowly away.
B. Palling

WAINAK (USA) 3 b.g. Silver Hawk (USA) 123 – Cask 99 (Be My Chief (USA) 122) **71**
[2001 79: 7m 8.1g 10f⁴ 12d f12g⁴ Oct 18] tall, good-topped gelding: fair handicapper:
stays 1¼m, possibly not 1½m: acts on fibresand, good to firm and good to soft going:
blinkered (ran at least respectably) final outing: has shown signs of temperament.
M. H. Tompkins

WAIT FOR THE WILL (USA) 5 ch.g. Seeking The Gold (USA) – You'd Be **80 d**
Surprised (USA) 117 (Blushing Groom (FR) 131) [2001 91: 12g 12m 12m 12g 12m 14m⁶
12g⁵ 12g Sep 19] tall gelding: fairly useful handicapper at best: on downgrade in 2001:
stays 1¾m: acts on good to firm and good to soft going: usually blinkered/visored: tried
tongue tied: has swished tail/edged left/found little: sold 8,000 gns. *G. L. Moore*

WAKI MUSIC (USA) 3 b.f. Miswaki (USA) 124 – Light Music (USA) (Nijinsky **97**
(CAN) 138) [2001 96: 10.3m³ 10f⁵ 8g³ 7g 6.5f⁵ 8f⁴ 9f³ Nov 10] leggy, angular filly:
useful performer: creditable third in minor events at Doncaster first/third starts, beaten
2¼ lengths by Cornelius in latter: left R. Charlton after next outing: won allowance race
at Santa Anita in October: third in non-graded stakes at Hollywood final start: stays 1¼m:
raced only on good going or firmer: has raced freely: has run well when sweating: reportedly lost action fourth outing. *R. J. Frankel, USA*

WALDENBURG (USA) 2 b.c. (Apr 26) Miswaki (USA) 124 – Erandel (USA) **100 p**
(Danzig (USA)) [2001 6f* 6g⁴ Aug 22] $300,000Y: tall, quite good-topped colt: has
scope: third foal: closely related to US 7f to (minor stakes) 9f winner Runspastum (by
Woodman): dam, winner in USA up to 7f at 4 yrs, sister to US Grade 3 8.5f/9f winner
Lech: 10/1, won maiden at Newbury in June by short head from odds-on Dubai Destination (pair clear): favourite, one-paced when 3¾ lengths fourth of 9 to Rock of Gibraltar
in Gimcrack Stakes at York (bandaged hind joints): should be well suited by 7f/1m:
joined Godolphin: should make a smart 3-y-o. *J. H. M. Gosden*

WALKING AROUND (FR) 3 gr.c. Linamix (FR) 127 – Walk On Air 91 (Cure The **115**
Blues (USA)) [2001 9.8g² 10d* 12m⁴ 15s⁴ Oct 6] brother to smart French 7f (at 2 yrs) and
11f (Prix Noailles) winner Walk On Mix and half-brother to several winners in France:
dam, second at 1m on only start, half-sister to Prix Vermeille winner Walensee: smart
form: won minor events at Saint-Cloud at 2 yrs and Deauville in July: improved effort
when 3¾ lengths fourth to Golan in Prix Niel at Longchamp penultimate start: seemed
not to stay when fourth to Wareed in Prix Hubert de Chaudenay at Longchamp final
outing: stays 1½m: has won on heavy ground, best effort on good to firm. *A. Fabre,*
France

WALTZING WIZARD 2 b.g. (Mar 23) Magic Ring (IRE) 115 – Legendary Dancer **72 d**
90 (Shareef Dancer (USA) 135) [2001 5f³ 5s* 5g⁵ 6m⁶ 6g Sep 7] 7,500F, IR 6,000Y,
15,000 2-y-o: tall, leggy gelding: half-brother to 3 winners, including 2m winner Legend
of Love (by Pursuit of Love) and 1996 2-y-o 5f winner who stayed 1m Legend of Aragon
(by Aragon): dam 1½m winner: fair performer: disappointing after winning maiden at
Hamilton in June: bred to stay 6f: acts on firm and soft ground: tongue tied final start.
A. Berry

WALWORTH STAR 3 ch.g. Clantime 101 – Walworth Lady 54 (Belfort (FR) 89) **50**
[2001 8v³ 8v 10.1d 6m 6m⁵ 7f³ 6m 7m 6d⁶ 5g⁵ 6m 6g f6g⁶ 10d Oct 30] 4,200Y: leggy
gelding: first foal: dam 1¼m/11f winner: modest maiden: effective at 5f to 7f: acts on any
ground: visored (no improvement) tenth start: tongue tied last 5 outings: sold 1,150 gns.
M. Dods

WA-NAAM 3 ch.g. Cadeaux Genereux 131 – Na-Ayim (IRE) 68 (Shirley Heights 130) **77**
[2001 –p: 7g⁴ 9.2m² 10g³ f8.5f* Dec 5] deep-bodied gelding: has a quick action: fair
performer: lightly raced: left E. Dunlop 16,000 gns after reappearance: won maiden at
Wolverhampton in December, idling having gone clear: may prove best at up to 1¼m:
acts on fibresand and good to firm going. *I. Semple*

WANNABE AROUND 3 b.c. Primo Dominie 121 – Noble Peregrine (Lomond **112**
(USA) 128) [2001 90: f7g² 7s³ 8.5s* 9s² 9m* 10.1m⁵ 8m⁴ 8m* 8g² 9s⁴ 8d Sep 13] tall,
leggy colt: smart performer: won maiden at Epsom, handicap at Goodwood and minor
event at Salisbury (beat Bourgainville by 2½ lengths in 5-runner event) between April/
July: very good 3½ lengths second to Riberac in William Hill Mile (Handicap) at Goodwood next time: ran respectably in Marit Sveaas Minnelop at Ovrevoll, but well below

Mr T. G. Mills's "Wannabe Around"

form in Park Stakes at Doncaster last 2 outings: effective at 1m/9f: acts on fibresand, heavy and good to firm going: front runner: game and reliable. *T. G. Mills*

WANNA SHOUT 3 b.f. Missed Flight 123 – Lulu (Polar Falcon (USA) 126) [2001 **57** 70: f6g f6s f6g 7m 7d 6m 6m⁴ 6m 6.1f 5.2v⁵ Oct 26] fair 6f winner at 2 yrs: just modest form in 2001: best at 5f/6f: acts on fibresand, soft and good to firm ground: blinkered/ visored 3 times, looking wayward on second occasion: tried tongue tied: not one to trust implicitly. *R. Dickin*

WANSFORD LADY 5 b.m. Michelozzo (USA) 127 – Marnie's Girl (Crooner 119) **37** [2001 11.6m 11.6g Jul 2] workmanlike mare: poor maiden, lightly raced. *A. W. Carroll*

WARAQA (USA) 2 b.f. (Feb 4) Red Ransom (USA) – Jafn 104 (Sharpo 132) [2001 **76** 5s⁵ 6m⁵ 6.1m² 5.1g³ Aug 3] smallish, good-topped filly: first foal: dam 7f/1m winner: fair maiden: likely to prove best at 5f/6f: acts on good to firm ground: sold 4,000 gns. *B. Hanbury*

WARDEN BELLE 3 b.f. Emperor Jones (USA) 119 – Sing A Rainbow (IRE) 68 **53** (Rainbow Quest (USA) 134) [2001 8.1g 8.1m⁶ 7m 8d f8g Dec 17] 1,700F, 2,200Y: fourth foal: sister to 4-y-o Baytown Rhapsody and half-sister to winner in Holland/Germany by Batshoof: dam, maiden who stayed 1¼m, half-sister to smart middle-distance performer Alriffa: modest maiden: should stay beyond 1m: tongue tied last 4 starts. *J. R. Fanshawe*

WARDEN WARREN 3 b.c. Petong 126 – Silver Spell 54 (Aragon 118) [2001 89: 6d **77 §** 6m 6g 7m* 6g 7m Sep 22] quite attractive colt: fair performer: won claimer at Newmarket in August: stays 7f: acts on good to firm and good to soft going: blinkered last 3 starts (looked ungenuine penultimate one): sold 2,500 gns. *M. A. Jarvis*

*Prix Hubert de Chaudenay - Casino Barriere de Menton, Longchamp—
in torrential rain, Wareed finds plenty to repel Capal Garmon*

WAREED (IRE)   3 b.c. Sadler's Wells (USA) 132 – Truly Special 116 (Caerleon   **118**
(USA) 132) [2001 105p: 11m² 12m⁶ 15s* 15.5v Oct 28] big, rangy, attractive colt: has
plenty of scope: has a round action: smart performer: 1¾ lengths second (drifted right) to
Asian Heights in listed race at Goodwood in May: showed benefit of much stiffer test of
stamina when winning Prix Hubert de Chaudenay - Casino Barriere de Menton at Longchamp in October by 4 lengths from Capal Garmon, making virtually all: disappointing
in Gordon Stakes at Goodwood (sweating, bandaged behind, unimpressive to post) and
Prix Royal-Oak at Longchamp otherwise in 2001: will stay 2m+: acts well on soft
ground: visored in 2001. *Saeed bin Suroor*

WARLINGHAM (IRE)   3 b.g. Catrail (USA) 123 – Tadjnama (USA) (Exceller   –
(USA) 129) [2001 72: 6g 6m 7.6m Jun 26] fair performer at 2 yrs: well held in 2001: takes
good hold, and will prove best at 5f/6f: acts on firm going, good to soft and fibresand:
blinkered (slowly away) second start. *Miss Gay Kelleway*

WARNINGFORD   7 b.h. Warning 136 – Barford Lady 93 (Stanford 121§) [2001 113:   **119**
6d 7g* 8s² 7.3f³ 8d⁴ 7s³ 7d³ Oct 20] lengthy, good-topped horse: smart performer: better
than ever in 2001, winning HBLB Leicestershire Stakes at Newmarket in May by 1¼
lengths from Sugarfoot: good placed efforts in Lockinge Stakes at Newbury (beaten neck
by Medicean) and Prix de la Foret at Longchamp (beaten 2¼ lengths by Mount Abu) on
third and penultimate starts: forced to wait for gaps and finished strongly when length
third to Munir in Challenge Stakes at Newmarket final outing: barely stays testing 1m:
acts on heavy and good to firm going: often visored in 1998: usually held up.
J. R. Fanshawe

WARNING REEF   8 b.g. Warning 136 – Horseshoe Reef 88 (Mill Reef (USA) 141)   **71**
[2001 73: 10.3f⁴ 12.3f 12f³ 11.4g 12m 10.3m³ 12g⁶ 11.9g² 12g 12.1m 12g⁵ 10g Nov 5]
small, workmanlike gelding: poor mover: fair handicapper: best at 1¼m/1½m: acts on
fibresand, firm and soft going (not on heavy): sometimes flashes tail/finds little: best held
up and needs things to go his way, but usually runs his race. *E. J. Alston*

WARRING   7 b.g. Warrshan (USA) 117 – Emerald Ring 74 (Auction Ring (USA) 123)   –
[2001 51, a–: 8f 8.3g 8m 8g Aug 7] sturdy gelding: modest handicapper at 6 yrs: well held
in 2001: has been tongue tied. *M. S. Saunders*

WARRIORS PATH (IRE)   2 b.g. (Feb 27) Namaqualand (USA) – Azinter (IRE)   –
(Magical Strike (USA) 114) [2001 6v Nov 8] IR 6,500F: first foal: dam, Irish bumper
winner, out of half-sister to Oaks winner Blue Wind: 25/1, slowly away and well beaten
in maiden at Windsor (subsequently gelded). *B. G. Powell*

WARRSAN (IRE)   3 b.c. Caerleon (USA) 132 – Lucayan Princess 111 (High Line   **93 p**
125) [2001 10g⁵ 11.5m⁴ 12f⁵ 14m* 13.9m⁶ 13.3f² Sep 22] neat colt: half-brother to
several winners, including very smart 9f to 1½m performer Luso (by Salse), 7f (Nell
Gwyn Stakes) winner who stayed 1½m Cloud Castle (by In The Wings) and 1m to 1½m
performer Needle Gun (by Sure Blade), both smart: dam 2-y-o 7f winner who stayed
1½m: fairly useful form: won handicap at Sandown in July: very good ½-length second
to Mesmeric in similar event at Newbury final start: will stay 2m: acts on firm going, yet
to race on ground softer than good: should make a useful 4-y-o. *C. E. Brittain*

WAR TUNE   5 b.g. Warrshan (USA) 117 – Keen Melody (USA) 60 (Sharpen Up 127)   –
[2001 12v⁵ Apr 7] fifth foal: half-brother to 7-y-o Mutasawwar and 1995 2-y-o 7f winner

Rock Sharp (by Rock City): dam maiden who stayed 1m: well held only outing on Flat. *R. M. Whitaker*

WAR VALOR (USA) 2 b.c. (May 6) Royal Academy (USA) 130 – Western Music (USA) (Lord At War (ARG)) [2001 7m⁴ 6v³ Oct 26] $180,000 2-y-o: rather leggy, useful-looking colt: fourth foal: half-brother to a winner in USA by Farma Way: dam, ran twice in USA, out of half-sister to US Grade 1 winners Time For A Change, Adjudicating and Dispute: better effort in maidens (fairly useful form) when keeping-on third of 17 to Oases at Newbury: will probably stay 1m: has worn crossed noseband: probably capable of better. *J. Nicol* **85 p**

WASEYLA (IRE) 4 b.f. Sri Pekan (USA) 117 – Lady Windley (Baillamont (USA) 124) [2001 66, a61: e12g³ e13g e12g⁶ f16s 12d 11.7d 12.6f³ 15g 10m* 10m 10g³ 9.7d* 10.2f⁶ 10s f11g⁴ f9.4g⁶ Dec 11] modest handicapper: left Julian Poulton after sixth start: won at Windsor in July and Folkestone in September: stays easy 1½m: acts on firm going, good to soft, fibresand and equitrack: tried visored (carried head high/found little) and blinkered: races prominently: unreliable. *Miss E. C. Lavelle* **64 §** **a52 §**

WASHINGTON PINK (IRE) 2 b.g. (May 6) Tagula (IRE) 116 – Little Red Rose (Precocious 126) [2001 6g 7d² 8g⁵ 8f 8m⁵ 8m³ 8.3v³ 7.9s 8s⁴ 8d⁵ 8.3v⁴ Nov 8] strong, close-coupled gelding: has quick action: seventh living foal: half-brother to 3 winners, including fairly useful but ungenuine 1998 2-y-o 6f winner who stayed 1¼m Maple (by Soviet Lad): dam unraced half-sister to smart French performer up to 15.5f Lucky Dream: fair maiden: in frame 5 times, mostly in nurseries: gelded after final start: likely to stay 1¼m: acts on good to firm and heavy ground: consistent. *M. R. Channon* **70**

WASP RANGER (USA) 7 b.g. Red Ransom (USA) – Lady Climber (USA) (Mount Hagen (FR) 127) [2001 86: 12s 14.4m Jun 6] very tall gelding: fairly useful handicapper at 6 yrs: well held in 2001: sometimes blinkered. *G. L. Moore* **–**

WATCHING 4 ch.c. Indian Ridge 123 – Sweeping 104 (Indian King (USA) 128) [2001 117: 5g 5m 6.5d 5.8s³ 5g 6d 7v² Oct 27] neat colt: smart performer at 3 yrs, only useful in 2001: 4 lengths third to El Gran Lode in Taby Open Sprint fifth start: runner-up in minor event at Doncaster final outing: stays 7f: acts on heavy and good to firm going: sold 82,000 gns in October, joined D. Nicholls. *R. Hannon* **100**

WATCHKEEPER (IRE) 3 b.f. Rudimentary (USA) 118 – Third Watch 114 (Slip Anchor 136) [2001 63p: 7g⁶ 8m 7m⁴ 10m³ 10d³ 10g* 10g* 8.5g² 10g Oct 5] quite good-topped filly: fluent mover: fairly useful performer: made all in minor event and handicap at Lingfield in August: effective at 1m to 1¼m: acts on good to firm ground. *J. L. Dunlop* **86**

WATCHWORD 2 ch.f. (Feb 17) Polish Precedent (USA) 131 – Step Aloft 87 (Shirley Heights 130) [2001 7m 7f⁵ 8.1g⁴ 7g² 8d p8g f8s² Dec 15] first foal: dam, 1¼m winner at 4 yrs, half-sister to smart performers up to 1¼m Starlet and Unknown Quantity: fair maiden: second in nursery at Lingfield (left R. Charlton after next outing) and claimer at Southwell: should stay 1¼m: acts on fibresand, well held only start on ground softer than good: tail swisher. *I. A. Wood* **73** **a65**

HBLB Leicestershire Stakes, Newmarket—in a race transferred from Leicester for the second consecutive year, Warningford repeats his success in the 1999 running of the event; Sugarfoot (white colours), Mount Abu and Invincible Spirit (left) make the frame

WATER BABY (IRE) 2 b.g. (May 1) Tagula (IRE) 116 – Flooding (USA) (Irish **74** River (FR) 131) [2001 5m 5m⁴ f5g* Jul 20] 23,000Y: half-brother to several winners, including fairly useful 1998 2-y-o 6f/7f winner Lough Swilly (by Mukaddamah): dam unraced from good US family: fair form: won maiden at Southwell, leading final 1f: should stay 6f. *T. D. Barron*

WATERFORD SPIRIT (IRE) 5 ch.g. Shalford (IRE) 124§ – Rebecca's Girl (IRE) **60 §** (Nashamaa 113) [2001 71d: f6g² f6g f5g² f5g f6f f6g* f5g 5m² f6g f6g 5f 6m 6d³ 5s⁶ f6g Dec 10] big, good-topped gelding: modest handicapper nowadays: won at Southwell in March: left D. Nicholls after penultimate outing: stays 6f: acts on soft going, good to firm and fibresand: tried blinkered/tongue tied at 4 yrs: got very upset in stall second start: unreliable. *G. J. Smith*

WATERFRONT (IRE) 5 b.g. Turtle Island (IRE) 123 – Rising Tide 101 (Red Alert **–** 127) [2001 –: f8.5g f7g f9.4g f6g f12g 12v 5.1v 10s 6s 10d 5m 8.1m 6m 7f 8m 10m 7m 10m 10.1m 6m 7.1d 8g 7g 6m⁶ 5g 7m 8.5g 9.9m⁴ 6s 8m 10.3m 5d 14v 7d 7v f8g Nov 19] little form: tried blinkered/tongue tied. *G. P. Kelly*

WATER JUMP (IRE) 4 b.c. Suave Dancer (USA) 136 – Jolies Eaux 73 (Shirley **122** Heights 130) [2001 102+: 10s⁵ 12.3s* 13.3v* 11.6g* Jun 3]
　　　　Sellers at low-grade courses weren't the only races to be contested on a regular basis by some of the worst horses in training in 2001. Thanks to an appearance money scheme, these slowcoaches could also be found trailing around in selected events at top tracks such as York—which managed to stage two such contests on consecutive days in October—while far superior rivals fought out the finish, their 'efforts' entitling connections to pick up the £300 on offer just for turning up. Prior to June 1st there had been a bonus of £500 for those taking part in classified stakes on the Flat, with minimum rating limits of 0-70, and class B and C conditions stakes. Not surprisingly there was no shortage of takers. On one occasion, at Nottingham in April, useful sprinters Halmahera and Proud Native were both eliminated by ballot after the overnight entry exceeded the limit of eighteen, while a host of no-hopers were allowed to run. BHB chairman Peter Savill, owner of Proud Native, was, understandably, aggrieved. 'The trainers who are abusing the system should know that they are putting the appearance-money scheme—and therefore the VAT scheme for owners—at risk,' said Savill. In November, the BHB acted to stop connections of poor horses taking advantage of the scheme. From now on horses running in qualifying races with a BHB handicap rating of below 45 on the Flat and below 75 over jumps will not be eligible for the appearance payments.
　　　　Plenty of good horses were involved in the types of races mentioned, including two trained by John Dunlop, Lucido and Water Jump. Both were successful, the former in the Doncaster Shield in March and the latter in a lower-profile race at Ripon in April contested by no fewer than twenty horses, thirteen of which started at 100/1 or more. Water Jump himself was the 11/10 favourite, and he gave his supporters little cause for concern, travelling strongly and quickly settling matters in the closing stages. He did not need to step up on the useful form he had shown previously to win in such good style, but further improvement looked assured given he was still a bit short of experience for a four-year-old—Water Jump had run in only seven races prior to Ripon and had won a couple of them, a maiden at Hamilton at two and a handicap at Salisbury at three. Yet just how much Water Jump would improve must have surprised even his trainer. On his next start, Water Jump produced a very smart performance to win a listed race at Newbury, and then matched it when following up in a similar event at Windsor. Water Jump beat the subsequent Hardwicke Stakes winner Sandmason by three lengths in the Grundon Recycle Stakes (Aston Park) at Newbury, showing a good turn of foot in a steadily-run race, and Ela Athena by half a length, the pair clear of four others, in the Berkshire Stakes at Windsor. In the latter, Water Jump needed only to be pushed out after improving to lead a furlong out and was value for another two lengths. Water Jump looked more than capable of adding a Group 3 or Group 2 race, such as the Hardwicke, but, unfortunately, an attack of colic resulted in his missing the remainder of the season. It will be surprising if he doesn't win races in pattern company in 2002 if fully recovered.

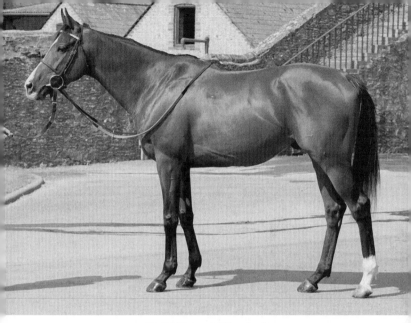

The Earl Cadogan's "Water Jump"

			Nijinsky
	Suave Dancer (USA)	Green Dancer	Green Valley
Water Jump (IRE)	(b 1988)	(b 1972)	Alleged
(b.c. 1997)		Suavite	Guinevere's Folly
		(b 1981)	Mill Reef
	Jolies Eaux	Shirley Heights	Hardiemma
	(b or br 1986)	(b 1975)	Jimmy Reppin
		Joking Apart	Strip The Willow
		(ch 1972)	

Water Jump, very well bought for 14,000 guineas as a yearling, is the fourth foal of Jolies Eaux, a half-sister to the Galtres winners Deadly Serious and Sans Blague but a maiden herself, one who probably stayed a mile and a quarter. All three mares raced for the Queen, as did Water Jump's grandam Joking Apart, a very smart winner at up to a mile, and great grandam Strip The Willow, a lightly-raced maiden. Jolies Eaux has produced two other winners, both fairly useful, namely Slide By (by Aragon) and Becky Simmons (by Mujadil). The former won over seven furlongs in Ireland as a two-year-old, while the latter has won four times at up to six furlongs in Britain, including once in the latest season. Water Jump, a good-topped colt, stays thirteen furlongs and acts on heavy and good to firm going. He does tend to edge left under pressure but seems thoroughly genuine. *J. L. Dunlop*

WATER KING (USA) 2 b.c. (Feb 8) Irish River (FR) 131 – Brookshield Baby (IRE) **76 p** (Sadler's Wells (USA) 132) [2001 7m 7.9d⁵ 7v⁶ Oct 26] IR 115,000Y: useful-looking colt: second foal: dam, French 1½m winner, half-sister to dam of Breeders' Cup Sprint winner Lit de Justice, Racing Post Trophy winner Commander Collins and 2000 Guineas/ Derby third Colonel Collins: fair form in maidens at Newmarket, York (fifth to Him of Distinction) and Doncaster, considerably handled each time: will stay at least 1¼m: should make a better 3-y-o. *E. A. L. Dunlop*

WATERLINER   2 b.f. (Apr 26) Merdon Melody 98 – Double Touch (FR) (Nonoalco   **40**
(USA) 131) [2001 5f 6d f5g f5g⁴ 7g 7g 6d Sep 4] sister to a winning sprinter in Sweden
and half-sister to 3 winners, including 15f winner Lady Madina (by Legend of France):
dam unraced: poor maiden: stays 7f: tried blinkered/visored. *P. D. Evans*

WATER OF LIFE (IRE)   2 b.f. (Mar 26) Dr Devious (IRE) 127 – Simulcast   **78**
(Generous (IRE) 139) [2001 7m 6m⁵ 7s⁴ 6m 7d² Oct 2] 15,000Y: angular, well-made
filly: first foal: dam unraced half-sister to smart French/US performer up to 1¼m
Semillon: fair maiden: good second of 21 in nursery at Newmarket: should stay 1¼m:
acts on soft and good to firm ground: tongue tied last 4 starts. *J. W. Hills*

WATERPARK   3 b.f. Namaqualand (USA) – Willisa 67 (Polar Falcon (USA) 126)   **–**
[2001 75: 6g 7m f5g f5g 6g 6.1v 6d 7g f6g f6g f6g f6g p7g Dec 19] leggy filly: fair winner at
2 yrs: little form in 2001: tried visored. *M. Dods*

WATERSIDE (IRE)   2 b.c. (Apr 6) Lake Coniston (IRE) 131 – Classic Ring (IRE) 50   **96**
(Auction Ring (USA) 123) [2001 5m⁴ 5.2m³ 5m² 5.7m² 5g Sep 15] 16,000Y: strong colt:
has a round action: sixth foal: half-brother to 2 winners, including 4-y-o Seven No
Trumps: dam 2-y-o 7f winner: useful maiden: beaten 1¼ lengths by Johannesburg in
Norfolk Stakes at Royal Ascot third outing: disappointing last 2 starts, pulling too hard
on first occasion: may prove best at bare 5f. *J. W. Hills*

WATKINS   6 ch.g. King's Signet (USA) 110 – Windbound Lass 60 (Crofter (USA)   **34**
124) [2001 f16.2s³ f16.2s⁴ f16g f16.2g Feb 6] poor maiden handicapper: stays 2m: acts on
fibresand and good to firm ground: blinkered once: sometimes tongue tied. *A. T. Murphy*

WATTNO ELJOHN (IRE)   3 b.c. Namaqualand (USA) – Caroline Connors (Fairy   **68**
King (USA)) [2001 68: f8.5s² f7g⁶ 10.3s³ 10s 8.2v 8g³ 8g 7s⁶ 8d 8s f7g³ f8s* Dec 21]   **a62**
good-topped colt: poor mover: fair performer: won claimer at Southwell in December:
stays 1¼m: acts on soft going, good to firm and fibresand: visored last 2 starts: sometimes
edges left under pressure. *D. W. P. Arbuthnot*

WAVE OF OPTIMISM   6 ch.g. Elmaamul (USA) 125 – Ballerina Bay 75 (Myjinski   **103**
(USA)) [2001 93: 16s³ 16.2g⁶ 16.2s* 18d Oct 20] big, raw-boned gelding: useful
handicapper: better than ever when winning at Ascot in September by 1¼ lengths from
Establishment: sweating, only mid-division in Cesarewitch final outing (runner-up in
race in 2000): acts on heavy ground: takes good hold: effective ridden
prominently or held up: has given trouble stalls/been very slowly away. *Mrs Lydia Pearce*

WAVERLEY (IRE)   2 b.c. (Feb 25) Catrail (USA) 123 – Marble Halls (IRE) (Ballad   **84**
Rock 122) [2001 6m⁴ 7g³ 7.5g² 7.9d⁶ 8d⁴ Oct 25] 22,000Y: leggy, quite good-topped colt:
first foal: dam, twice-raced maiden, half-sister to high-class sprinter Hallgate and to dam
of smart sprinter Mistertopogigo: fairly useful maiden: best effort when beaten head by
Ikenga at Beverley (on toes in paddock and mounted in pre-parade ring): stays 7.5f: yet to
race on extremes of going. *H. Morrison*

WAVERLEY ROAD   4 ch.g. Pelder (IRE) 125 – Lillicara (FR) (Caracolero (USA)   **72**
131) [2001 62, a72: f8s 8m⁶ 10.1m⁴ 9m² 8m 9g⁶ 9d* 7.9m 10d³ 11.9s² Oct 11] leggy
gelding: fair handicapper: won at Goodwood in August: effective at 9f to 1½m: acts on
good to firm going, soft and equitrack (well held on fibresand): usually races
prominently: game. *A. P. Jarvis*

WAX LYRICAL   5 b.m. Safawan 118 – Hannah's Music 85 (Music Boy 124) [2001 –:   **76 d**
6g² 6d 6m 7s Oct 31] fair form in 2001 on first start only: stays 6f: acts on good to firm
ground: tried blinkered. *P. J. Makin*

WAXWING   2 b.f. (Mar 16) Efisio 120 – Mountain Bluebird (USA) 79 (Clever Trick   **61**
(USA)) [2001 6m 6g⁴ 7.5f* 7m² 7m* 7m³ f7g² 7m Sep 6] 9,500Y: lengthy, good-bodied
filly: half-sister to several winners, including useful French 7f/1m winner Middleberg (by
Midyan), later successful in USA, and useful stayer Anchor Clever (by Slip Anchor):
dam 1m winner: modest performer: won seller at Beverley (left R. Hannon) and nursery
at Redcar (dictated pace and idled) in July: ran as if something amiss final outing: will
stay 1m: acts on firm going and fibresand: usually races prominently. *N. P. Littmoden*

WAYLAAH   2 b.f. (Apr 13) Common Grounds 108 – Inonder 31 (Belfort (FR) 89)   **60**
[2001 6d 6.1m³ 6m³ 6.1g⁴ 6s⁶ 7s Oct 25] 12,500F, 36,000Y: fifth foal: sister to 3 winners,
including fairly useful 1997 2-y-o 5f to 7.5f winner Chips and 4-y-o Aretino: dam poor
maiden: modest maiden: stays 6f: acts on good to firm and good to soft ground, well held
on soft: visored final start: sold 7,500 gns. *J. L. Dunlop*

WAYYAK (USA) 2 ch.c. (Feb 25) Gold Fever (USA) 119 – My Testarossa (USA) 67
(Black Tie Affair 128) [2001 5.3f⁴ 5f 6m³ 5m 5.1m 5.2s⁵ Oct 31] $12,000F, $90,000Y:
angular colt: first foal: dam, maiden in USA, half-sister to 2 minor stakes winners: fair
maiden: best effort when third at Windsor: should stay 7f: acts on firm going. *J. W. Payne*

WEALTHY STAR (IRE) 6 b.g. Soviet Star (USA) 128 – Catalonda (African Sky –
124) [2001 91+: 8.9m f8g f8g f6g 7.1m Aug 22] rangy gelding: one-time useful
performer: well held in 2001: visored once, often tongue tied. *N. Tinkler*

WEAVER SAM 4 ch.g. Ron's Victory (USA) 129 – Grove Star (Upper Case (USA)) –
[2001 16m 11.9m Jun 1] quite good-topped gelding: no form on Flat. *P. S. McEntee*

WEECANDOO (IRE) 3 b.f. Turtle Island (IRE) 123 – Romantic Air 62 (He Loves 74
Me 120) [2001 8.1s⁴ 9g² 9.9m⁴ 8d⁵ Oct 8] 21,000Y: half-sister to useful 6f/7f performer
(5f winner at 2 yrs) Toocando (by Nordance) and to a winner in Italy by Polish Patriot:
dam ran 3 times (best form at 1m) at 2 yrs: fair maiden: probably stays 1¼m. *C. N. Allen*

WEE JIMMY 5 b.g. Lugana Beach 116 – Cutlass Princess (USA) 41 (Cutlass (USA)) –
[2001 –: f14g Nov 16] of little account. *B. A. McMahon*

WEE NEL 3 ch.f. Imp Society (USA) – Eskimo Nel (IRE) 75 (Shy Groom (USA)) –
[2001 9.7m 11.5g 9.2m 10.1v⁶ Oct 24] first foal: dam, 1¼m/1½m winner, also useful
hurdler: well held in maidens/handicap. *N. P. Littmoden*

WEET-A-MINUTE (IRE) 8 ro.h. Nabeel Dancer (USA) 120 – Ludovica (Bustino 75
136) [2001 95, a102: f9.4f⁵ f9.4f⁵ f8s* f9.4s Dec 26] lengthy horse: covered a mare in 2001:
only fair performer later in year: won claimer at Southwell in December: best at 1m/1¼m:
acts on firm going, soft and fibresand: tried blinkered: sometimes carries head
awkwardly. *R. Hollinshead*

WEET AND SEE 7 b.g. Lochnager 132 – Simply Style (Bairn (USA) 126) [2001 –: –
10v Apr 3] of little account nowadays. *T. Wall*

WEET A ROUND 2 ch.c. (Mar 9) Whittingham (IRE) 104 – Hollia 72 (Touch Boy 79
109) [2001 5d⁴ 5.1f⁵ f5g 6m⁶ 7g³ 7.1g 6d⁵ f7g³ 7v⁵ 7s³ f7g³ f6s³ p7g³ Dec 29] 17,000Y:
big, good-topped colt: half-brother to several winners, including fairly useful 1996 2-y-o
5f winner Fredrik The Fierce (by Puissance) and 5-y-o Shirley Not: dam 2-y-o 5f winner:
fair maiden: likely to prove best at 6f/7f: acts on heavy going and polytrack: consistent.
N. P. Littmoden

WEET A WHILE (IRE) 3 b.g. Lahib (USA) 129 – Takeshi (IRE) 67 (Cadeaux –
Genereux 131) [2001 54: f7g 7.6f Jun 30] sturdy gelding: modest maiden at 2 yrs: well
held in 2 runs in 2001 nearly 6 months apart. *R. Hollinshead*

WEET FOR ME 5 b.h. Warning 136 – Naswara (USA) 88 (Al Nasr (FR) 126) [2001 95
87, a103: f11g* 13.9m 14m 16.2g⁶ 13.9m³ 14m* 16m* 13.9g 14.6s³ p12g³ Nov 15] big a106
horse: useful handicapper, better on all-weather than turf: won at Southwell (beat White
Plains 3½ lengths) in January and at Haydock and Redcar (beat Little John by ½ length
despite wandering) in July, given good front-running ride by N. Callan on each occasion:
below best last 3 starts: stays 2m: yet to race on heavy going, acts on any other turf and
fibresand: usually makes running: genuine. *R. Hollinshead*

WEETMAN'S WEIGH (IRE) 8 b.h. Archway (IRE) 115 – Indian Sand (Indian 64
King (USA) 128) [2001 74, a99: f9.4g⁴ f7g² f8.5s² f8g* f7g² f8g³ f7g* f11g⁶ 7.6f 8m* a71
8m⁴ 7.5f⁵ 10.3f⁶ 7.6m⁴ 7.1d⁵ f8.5g 8m f8.5g⁵ f8g⁶ f9.4g f8g³ f8.5g Dec 1] useful-looking
horse: has stringhalt: only fair at best in 2001, winning claimers at Southwell (apprentices) in February, Wolverhampton in March and Pontefract in May: effective at 7f to
8.5f: acts on firm going, soft and fibresand: tongue tied earlier in career: usually held up
(sometimes hangs left). *R. Hollinshead*

WEET U THERE (IRE) 5 b.g. Forest Wind (USA) 111 – Lady Aladdin (Persian –
Bold 123) [2001 10v Apr 3] sturdy, close-coupled gelding: modest performer at 3 yrs:
well held only Flat run in 2001: tried blinkered. *T. Wall*

WELCH'S DREAM (IRE) 4 b.f. Brief Truce (USA) 126 – Swift Chorus (Music –
Boy 124) [2001 64d: 6m 5f Aug 29] of little account nowadays. *E. J. Alston*

WELCOME EXCHANGE 2 b.f. (Mar 11) Most Welcome 131 – Santarem (USA) –
71 (El Gran Senor (USA) 136) [2001 7m Jul 14] 2,000 2-y-o: fifth foal: half-sister to
fairly useful 1¼m/1½m winner Imani (by Danehill): dam, lightly-raced staying maiden,
half-sister to smart stayer Al Maheb: 66/1, tailed off in maiden at Salisbury. *J. J. Bridger*

Dubai Duty Free Cup, Newbury—a first listed-race win for Welcome Friend; fighting it out for the minor honours are Patsy's Double (centre), Valentino (No.3), the Singapore challenger Bocelli (blinkers), Bouncing Bowdler (black cap, virtually hidden) and Reel Buddy

WELCOME FRIEND (USA) 4 b.c. Kingmambo (USA) 125 – Kingscote 118 (Kings **115 +** Lake (USA) 133) [2001 109+: 7d* 7g 7f² 7.1d⁶ 6d* 6f² 7.3f* 6d Oct 19] well-made, attractive colt: unimpressive mover in slower paces: smart performer: won handicap at Newmarket in April, minor event at Yarmouth (beat Lincoln Dancer comfortably by 5 lengths) in August and listed race at Newbury (beat Patsy's Double by ¾ length) in September: far from discredited when seventh of 17 to Danehurst in listed race at Newmarket final outing: stays 7f: acts on firm and good to soft going: has been bandaged behind: sometimes races freely. *R. Charlton*

WELCOME GIFT 5 b.g. Prince Sabo 123 – Ausonia (Beldale Flutter (USA) 130) **60** [2001 74: f6g f6g f6s f6g² f6g³ f6g f6g p7g⁶ f7s Dec 18] only modest form in 2001: stays 7f: acts on fibresand, raced only on going softer than good on turf: blinkered once. *Mrs L. Stubbs*

WELCOME HEIGHTS 7 b.g. Most Welcome 131 – Mount Ida (USA) 79 (Conquist- **–** ador Cielo (USA)) [2001 49: 7g 10.5s Aug 18] of little account nowadays. *R. C. Spicer*

WELCOME ROSE 2 ch.f. (Apr 26) Most Welcome 131 – Bonica 56 (Rousillon **53** (USA) 133) [2001 6m 5m 7m f6s f8.5g² f8.5g Nov 3] small, sturdy filly: half-sister to several winners, including 7-y-o Bacchus: dam, maiden who should have been suited by 7f+, half-sister to smart performer up to 1m Chipaya: modest maiden: best effort when second in seller at Wolverhampton: will probably stay 1¼m: acts on fibresand, raced only on good to firm going on turf: often slowly away. *P. C. Haslam*

WELCOME SHADE 4 gr.g. Green Desert (USA) 127 – Grey Angel (Kenmare (FR) **–** 125) [2001 54: e10g Jan 13] probably no longer of any account. *L. A. Dace*

WELCOME TO DUE'S (USA) 4 gr.g. Cozzene (USA) – Etoile d'Amore (USA) **–** 81 (The Minstrel (CAN) 135) [2001 f12g 12g⁶ Jul 10] half-brother to several winners, including fairly useful 7f winner Moonlight Saunter (by Woodman) and 7-y-o Forgotten Times: dam twice-raced 7f winner: tailed off both Flat starts. *G. M. Moore*

WELENSKA 2 b.c. (Mar 19) Danzig Connection (USA) – Fairy Story (IRE) 80 **94** (Persian Bold 123) [2001 7m* 7g³ f8g* Oct 1] good-topped colt: fluent mover: third foal: dam, 7f winner (including at 2 yrs), out of half-sister to dam of Shaamit: fairly useful form: won maiden at Folkestone in August and minor event at Southwell (by 1¾ lengths from Lapadar, pair clear) in October: close third to Expected Bonus in minor event at Kempton in between: not certain to stay beyond 1m. *P. F. I. Cole*

WELLBEING 4 b.c. Sadler's Wells (USA) 132 – Charming Life (NZ) (Sir **121** Tristram 115) [2001 121p: 12g⁴ 12m² 12f⁵ Jun 22]

Wellbeing's season comprised three races and spanned only seven weeks, but he came within a whisker of recording his first Group 1 success when going down by a short head to Mutafaweq in the Coronation Cup at Epsom in June. Well-being had looked the sort to make his mark as a four-year-old in good races at middle-distances after progressing well at three, winning four of his five races, including the listed Godolphin Stakes at Newmarket and the Perpetual Stakes (St Simon) at Newbury, both in the autumn, his only defeat coming when a creditable fifth to Sinndar in the Derby. Returned to Epsom for the Coronation Cup, run over the Derby course and distance, Wellbeing just came off worse at the end of a tactical affair, putting in a sustained challenge over the final two furlongs to Mutafaweq, who had been kicked clear off the home turn. Wellbeing's rider Richard Quinn noticeably did not go for his whip (though this is not untypical of him), even when things got very tight close home, perhaps mindful of the fact that Wellbeing had idled in front when winning at Newbury the previous autumn.

Wellbeing's performance at Epsom was as good as any by a Henry Cecil-trained horse all season and was the closest the stable came to landing a Group 1 prize in a conspicuously unsuccessful season by its usual high standards. The statistics must have made particularly grim reading for ten-times champion trainer Cecil, who first took out a licence at the end of 1968 when succeeding to the string of his stepfather Sir Cecil Boyd-Rochfort. Here's just a selection of facts and figures from the latest season: for the first time since 1991, when Midnight Air was disqualified after finishing first past the post in the Fillies' Mile, Cecil failed to have a Group 1 winner; for only the third time in his career, and the first since 1972, Cecil failed to have a single runner in a British classic; and for only the fourth time, and the first since 1973, Cecil failed to make the top ten trainers in the end-of-season list. There were obvious contributing factors to the downturn, including the fact that Cecil trains a smaller string nowadays and that he lost two good horses during the season: Beat Hollow, who met with a couple of minor setbacks and didn't race, and Shibboleth were both transferred to Bobby Frankel in the States. Only time will tell whether Cecil proves able to restore his stable to its former glories but, either way, many racing fans and professionals alike will have been

Plantation Stud's "Wellbeing"

heartened to hear him deny categorically a story in September that he plans to quit the training ranks at the end of the next season. With the likes of promising fillies Half Glance, Protectress and Revealing, as well as St Simon Stakes winner High Pitched, there is plenty to look forward to.

As for Wellbeing, he wasn't at his best on his two other outings, seeming in need of the race on his reappearance in the Jockey Club Stakes at Newmarket in May—in common with many from the stable around that time—and running well below form when turned out fairly quickly after the Coronation Cup on firmer ground than that at Epsom in the Hardwicke Stakes at Royal Ascot. Wellbeing was beaten six and three quarter lengths when fourth of seven to Millenary in the Jockey Club Stakes and over four lengths when fifth of seven to his stable-companion Sandmason when favourite for the Hardwicke, in which he appeared perfectly poised turning for home but couldn't quicken.

Wellbeing (b.c. 1997)	Sadler's Wells (USA) (b 1981)	Northern Dancer (b 1961)	Nearctic
			Natalma
		Fairy Bridge (b 1975)	Bold Reason
			Special
	Charming Life (NZ) (b 1987)	Sir Tristram (b 1971)	Sir Ivor
			Isolt
		Lady Giselle (b 1982)	Nureyev
			Valderna

Wellbeing's pedigree was detailed in *Racehorses of 2000* but it is pertinent to add that two younger half-siblings reached the racecourse in the latest season. The three-year-old Demi Beau (by Dr Devious) won a maiden at Beverley over a mile and a half for William Jarvis before being gelded, and the two-year-old filly Nirvana (by Marju) finished second in a maiden at Redcar for John Dunlop. The big, good-topped Wellbeing, who usually takes the eye in appearance, should stay beyond a mile and a half. He is another who won't be with Cecil in 2002—he'll be in the care of Pascal Bary in France, where connections hope he will have more opportunity to race on good or softer going. Wellbeing showed in the Coronation Cup that he acts on good to firm, but the effects of racing on very firm ground at Royal Ascot reportedly contributed to his missing the rest of the season. It is also probably worth noting that Wellbeing was off the course for three and a half months, reportedly with sore shins, after the Derby, which was run on good ground. *H. R. A. Cecil*

WELL CHOSEN 2 b.c. (Feb 11) Sadler's Wells (USA) 132 – Hawajiss 114 (Kris 135) [2001 7d⁶ Sep 4] third living foal: dam, won May Hill, Musidora and Nassau Stakes, out of Cheveley Park second Canadian Mill: 10/1, shaped very well when sixth of 15 to Samhari in maiden at Yarmouth, going freely close up after slow start and not at all knocked about as principals started to go clear: banned for 30 days, jockey suspended and trainer fined after Jockey Club inquiry: capable of good deal better, and should win races. *E. A. L. Dunlop* **74 P**

WELLCOME INN 7 ch.g. Most Welcome 131 – Mimining 83 (Tower Walk 130) – [2001 –, a46: f12g⁶ f12g f12g f12g Jun 29] big, lengthy gelding: no form in 2001: usually tongue tied. *J. O'Reilly*

WELL HEELED (IRE) 2 b.f. (Mar 12) Woodborough (USA) 112 – Doumayna 79 **43** (Kouban (FR)) [2001 5g May 7] IR 8,000F, IR 9,700Y: half-sister to 1½m winners Foil Stone (by Slip Anchor) and Bondstone (by Miller's Mate), latter useful and stayed 2m: dam, 2m winner, half-sister to Darshaan: poor form when seventh of 15 in maiden at Warwick: sold 7,000 gns in October. *R. M. Beckett*

WE'LL MAKE IT (IRE) 3 b.g. Spectrum (IRE) 126 – Walliser (Niniski (USA) 125) **76** [2001 73: 9.9g² 11.6d⁵ 10m 10.1m⁴ 11.8s⁵ Oct 15] fair maiden handicapper: stays 11.6f: acts on good to firm going, good to soft and equitrack: sometimes blinkered: carries head high. *G. L. Moore*

WELL SPOTTED (IRE) 3 ch.f. Eagle Eyed (USA) 111 – Sand Grouse (USA) – (Arctic Tern (USA) 126) [2001 10.2m 10d f9.4g 11.7m 7m Sep 4] seventh foal: closely related to 1996 2-y-o 1m winner who stayed 1¼m Desert Horizon, later winner abroad, and 7f winner Sandhill (both useful and by Danehill) and half-sister to 2 winners abroad, notably smart French/Spanish performer up to 1m Sand Falcon (by Polar Falcon): dam French 1¼m winner: well held in maidens/sellers. *J. G. Portman*

WELODY 5 ch.g. Weldnaas (USA) 112 – The Boozy News (USA) 44 (L'Emigrant **– §** (USA) 129) [2001 57§, a75d: f8g f12g f8.5g f8.5g³ f8g 8.1g 8s Sep 30] tall, angular **a49 §** gelding: poor performer: stays 8.5f: acts on fibresand, no form on turf in 2001: often blinkered/visored: ungenuine. *G. Prodromou*

WELSH BORDER 3 ch.g. Zafonic (USA) 130 – Welsh Daylight (Welsh Pageant **99** 132) [2001 98p: 10s² 10g 14v Sep 28] rangy gelding: useful performer, lightly raced: good 2½ lengths second to Golden Wells in minor event at Newbury in April: well held after in listed race at Newmarket and minor event at Haydock nearly 5 months apart: should stay 1½m: raced only on good going or softer: sold 26,000 gns, and gelded. *H. R. A. Cecil*

WELSH CHARGER (IRE) 2 b.g. (Apr 12) Up And At 'em 109 – Timissara (USA) **47** (Shahrastani (USA) 135) [2001 5v 5.1s 5m 5m³ 6m⁵ 7g⁴ f5g³ 5d³ 6g 6m Aug 27] IR 5,500Y: small filly: poor walker: has a round action: brother to 2 winners, including useful 1¼m winner Rich Vein, and half-brother to several winners, including fairly useful 1997 2-y-o 7f/1m winner Lift The Offer (by Ballad Rock): dam Irish 1m and 1½m winner: poor maiden: in frame in sellers: may prove best around 6f: acts on fibresand, good to firm and heavy ground: has looked none too keen. *J. J. Quinn*

WELSH DIVA 2 b.f. (Mar 17) Selkirk (USA) 129 – Khubza 86 (Green Desert (USA) **67 p** 127) [2001 8d Oct 19] big, good-bodied filly: fourth foal: sister to smart 6f (at 2 yrs) to 8.5f winner Trans Island and 4-y-o 7f winner Daunted: dam, 7f winner, half-sister to smart performers Barrow Creek (6f to 1m in Germany) and Last Resort (7f): 20/1, burly and green, took strong hold early and not at all knocked about once held when ninth of 20 to Music Club in maiden at Newmarket: sure to improve. *Mrs A. J. Perrett*

WELSH DREAM 4 b.g. Mtoto 134 – Morgannwg (IRE) 86 (Simply Great (FR) 122) **67** [2001 75: 8s 13g 12m⁵ 13d 12.1g f16g³ f16.2s⁴ Dec 18] useful-looking gelding: fair **a58** handicapper on turf, modest on all-weather: stays 2m: unraced on heavy going, acts on any other turf and fibresand. *P. C. Haslam*

WELSH EMPEROR (IRE) 2 b.g. (Apr 3) Emperor Jones (USA) 119 – Simply **96** Times (USA) 64 (Dodge (USA)) [2001 5g³ 5f³ 7g² 7.1f² 6d* 6.1m³ 6g 6g² 6m 5s* Oct 20] 8,500Y: well-grown gelding: second foal: half-brother to 3-y-o Forever Times: dam ran twice at 2 yrs: useful performer: won maiden at Hamilton in July and minor event at Catterick (best effort, beat Marcus Aurelius by 5 lengths) in October: been beaten at 5f/6f: yet to race on heavy going, acts on any other turf: blinkered last 7 starts: has been free to post/ reluctant stalls: seems best with forcing tactics: tough. *T. P. Tate*

WELSH HOLLY (IRE) 2 br.f. (Apr 7) Idris (IRE) 118 – Jane Avril (IRE) 66 **59** (Danehill (USA) 126) [2001 5f⁶ 6m⁴ Sep 6] leggy, workmanlike filly: first reported foal: dam, second at 6f, out of half-sister to Be My Guest: modest form in maidens at Leicester and Redcar over 3 months apart. *M. H. Tompkins*

WELSH LADY 2 b.f. (Feb 19) Magic Ring (IRE) 115 – Little Unknown (Known Fact **49** (USA) 135) [2001 f6g f6g⁶ 6v Nov 8] fourth living foal: dam unraced: poor form in maidens: slowly away final start: should stay 7f. *P. D. Evans*

WELSH MAIN 4 br.g. Zafonic (USA) 130 – Welsh Daylight (Welsh Pageant 132) **101 ?** [2001 105p: 10g May 5] good-topped gelding: useful form, raced only 3 times: won maiden/minor event at 3 yrs: seventh in minor event at Newmarket in May only outing in 2001: raced only around 1¼m: sold 9,000 gns in October, joined S. Magnier and gelded. *H. R. A. Cecil*

WELSH PLOY 4 b.f. Deploy 131 – Safe House 81§ (Lyphard (USA) 132) [2001 74: **–** f8.5g⁵ f12g⁴ e12g² f12g³ e12g³ e12g² 12s⁵ f16.2g⁶ Jun 20] angular, unfurnished filly: **a62** modest performer: stays easy 1½m: acts on heavy going, fibresand and equitrack: tried visored/blinkered at 3 yrs: races prominently. *K. McAuliffe*

WELSH WIND (IRE) 5 b.g. Tenby 125 – Bavaria 80 (Top Ville 129) [2001 97: e10g **94** 8s³ 8s³ 8m 9f 9.7m⁶ 8d³ 8.9m² 8f² 7d* 8d Nov 3] lengthy gelding: fairly useful performer: left B. Powell after ninth start: won handicap at York (beat Slumbering 1½ lengths) in October: effective at 7f (given a test) to 1¼m: acts on firm and good to soft going: tried tongue tied. *M. Wigham*

WELTON ARSENAL 9 b.g. Statoblest 120 – Miller's Gait 74§ (Mill Reef (USA) **64 §** 141) [2001 7.1v 7m² 7m 10.2d 8.2s p7g⁴ p7g* p8g p7g Dec 28] sturdy gelding: modest handicapper: won at Lingfield in November: stays 1m: acts on polytrack, firm and soft ground: tried visored: held up: often finds little, and inconsistent. *K. Bishop*

WENDI'OUSE 3 b.f. Mind Games 121 – Brown's Cay 71 (Formidable (USA) 125) – [2001 5.1s 10s 6f 6d Oct 9] 3,000Y: sturdy filly: closely related to winner in Japan by Puissance and half-sister to several winners, including 1¼m winner Barbary Reef (by Sarab): dam third at 1m at 2 yrs: probably of no account. *M. Mullineaux*

WENSLEY BLUE (IRE) 2 b.g. (May 5) Blues Traveller (IRE) 119 – Almasa 83 **50 p** (Faustus (USA) 118) [2001 6g 6s 7d⁵ f8g Nov 30] 5,200 2-y-o: rangy gelding: third reported foal: half-brother to fairly useful 5f winner Mac's Express (by Mac's Imp): dam, 2-y-o 6f winner, from family of high-class miler Ridgewood Pearl: modest form in maidens: eye-catching fifth at Newcastle (banned for 40 days, jockey suspended, trainer fined) penultimate start, not at all knocked about: stiff task, saddle cloth seemed to come loose final outing: should stay 1m: capable of better. *P. C. Haslam*

WE'RE NOT JOKEN 4 b.f. Foxhound (USA) 103 – We're Joken 62 (Statoblest **34** 120) [2001 47, a–: f5g f7s f5g f5g³ 6m⁶ f5g 6m Aug 22] small filly: poor maiden: best at 5f/6f: acts on good to firm going and fibresand: tried visored. *M. W. Easterby*

WERE NOT STOPPIN 6 b.g. Mystiko (USA) 124 – Power Take Off 109 (Aragon **55** 118) [2001 66: 10v⁶ 8s 7m 8m 10m 9.2m² 9.2g³ 11.9g Aug 10] big, workmanlike gelding: modest handicapper: probably stays 1½m: acts on heavy and good to firm ground. *R. Bastiman*

WESTBOUND ROAD (USA) 4 b.g. Gone West (USA) – Jood (USA) 87 (Nijinsky **96** (CAN) 138) [2001 e10g* Mar 28] fourth foal: closely related to useful UAE 7f to 1½m winner Madraar (by Mr Prospector) and half-brother to 5-y-o Fantastic Light: dam, third at 7f (at 2 yrs) and 1¼m, her only starts, daughter of Canadian Oaks winner Kamar, herself sister to dam of Swain: useful form in 2 starts at Saint-Cloud at 3 yrs: 5/2-on, winning British debut in maiden at Lingfield by 11 lengths from Fly With Me, making all: stays 1½m: acts on equitrack, raced only on soft going on turf: gelded after Lingfield. *D. R. Loder*

WESTCOAST 10 b.g. Handsome Sailor 125 – Pichon (Formidable (USA) 125) [2001 – 16.2m Sep 17] no longer of much account. *M. Tate*

WESTCOURT MAGIC 8 b.g. Emarati (USA) 74 – Magic Milly 60 (Simply Great – (FR) 122) [2001 76d: f5g f5g 5v 5d 5v Oct 24] winning handicapper: has deteriorated considerably: tried blinkered. *M. W. Easterby*

WESTCOURT PEARL 2 b.f. (Mar 27) Emarati (USA) 74 – Carolside 108 (Music **46** Maestro 119) [2001 f5g f5g Apr 17] 4,700Y: resold 4,000Y: half-sister to several winners, including useful 1m/9f winner Eton Lad (by Never So Bold): dam 2-y-o 5f winner who didn't progress: poor form in Southwell maidens. *M. W. Easterby*

WESTENDER (FR) 5 b.g. In The Wings 128 – Trude (GER) (Windwurf (GER)) **99** [2001 103: 12m 11.9d⁶ Jul 7] leggy gelding: useful handicapper: badly hampered in Duke of Edinburgh Stakes at Royal Ascot: respectable sixth in Old Newton Cup at Haydock only other start in 2001: stays 1½m: acts on firm and good to soft going (unraced on softer): visored in 2001: usually held up: useful hurdler. *M. C. Pipe*

WESTERN APPLAUSE 2 b.f. (Feb 11) Royal Applause 124 – Western Sal 75 **76** (Salse (USA) 128) [2001 6g⁴ 6d Oct 18] leggy filly: third foal: half-sister to Italian 1999 2-y-o 7f winner Pemba (by First Trump): dam, 1¼m/1½m winner who stayed 14.8f, half-sister to 2-y-o Redback and 7-y-o Granny's Pet: 33/1, fair form when never-nearer fourth to Scarlet Ribbons in maiden at Newmarket: only mid-field in similar event there later in October: should stay at least 7f. *J. Noseda*

WESTERN BELLE 2 b.f. (Mar 8) Magic Ring (IRE) 115 – Western Horizon (USA) **57** 58 (Gone West (USA)) [2001 6m⁵ 5.3m³ 6m 5m⁶ 7.1g 6s 5v⁵ 5.7d³ p6g f6g⁴ Nov 23] 2,000Y: second foal: dam, maiden who stayed 1¾m, out of sister to Ribblesdale winner Nanticious and Stewards' Cup winner Repetitious, latter dam of Indian Lodge: modest maiden: ended up running in sellers: likely to prove best at 5f/6f: acts on fibresand, good to firm and good to soft ground, well held on good/heavy. *D. Morris*

WESTERN BLUEBIRD (IRE) 3 b.g. Bluebird (USA) 125 – Arrastra 79 (Bustino **64** 136) [2001 8s f7g⁶ 7s 10.2d 8m 10g* 12m² 11.6m³ 14f⁴ 9.9s 14.1d⁶ 11.8s⁴ f14g⁴ f14g⁶ **a68** f12f* Dec 5] 31,000F, 27,000Y: leggy gelding: fourth foal: half-brother to useful 5f (at 2 yrs) to 7f winner Marton Moss (by Polish Patriot): dam, 1¾m winner, also won over hurdles: fair performer: won claimer at Newbury in May and apprentice handicap at Wolverhampton in December: probably best around 1½m: stays 1¾m: acts on fibresand, good to firm and good to soft ground: visored (below form) tenth outing. *H. Morrison*

WESTERN CHIEF (IRE) 7 b.h. Caerleon (USA) 132 – Go Honey Go (General –
Assembly (USA)) [2001 f12g⁶ f16.2g⁶ Feb 22] one-time useful handicapper, very
lightly raced on Flat since 1999: blinkered earlier in career: sometimes tongue tied.
D. L. Williams

WESTERN COMMAND (GER) 5 b.g. Saddlers' Hall (IRE) 126 – Western Friend –
(USA) (Gone West (USA)) [2001 51, a71: f11g⁵ f9.4s³ f9.4s* f9.4g³ f9.4g* f9.4g⁵ f9.4g⁴ **a76 d**
f12g⁶ f9.4g⁴ f8.5g⁶ f11g⁴ f11g f11g f14g f12g f9.4s³ f14g⁵ f12g⁵ f12s² f12s² Dec 27] quite
good-topped gelding: fair handicapper at best on all-weather: won at Wolverhampton in
January/February: mostly below form after: effective at 9.4f (given test) to 2m: acts on
good to firm going and fibresand, below best on equitrack: tried blinkered/visored: takes
good hold. *Mrs N. Macauley*

WESTERN FLAME (USA) 3 b.f. Zafonic (USA) 130 – Samya's Flame 97 (Artaius **64**
(USA) 129) [2001 65: 6g 5.3d 6m² 6m* 5.1g² 5g 5m 5v Oct 15] smallish filly: modest
performer: won maiden at Lingfield in June (carried head awkwardly): well held in
handicaps last 3 starts: stays 6f: acts on soft and good to firm ground: blinkered second
(slowly away) and final outings: sold 40,000 gns. *R. Guest*

WESTERNMOST 3 b.g. Most Welcome 131 – Dakota Girl 55 (Northern State **59**
(USA) 91) [2001 42: f8g 12v² f12g² 12.1m⁴ 14.1m⁴ f12g² 16m 12.4g² f12f³ Aug 29] **a63**
sturdy gelding: modest maiden handicapper: tends to race freely, and at least as effective
around 1½m as 1¾m: acts on fibresand and any turf going: sold 10,000 gns. *T. D. Barron*

WESTERN RIDGE (FR) 4 b.g. Darshaan 133 – Helvellyn (USA) 83 (Gone West **60**
(USA)) [2001 –: f9.4g² e8g⁵ f9.4g⁵ f8g 10.1m 10g 12d f12s Dec 15] close-coupled,
unfurnished gelding: modest maiden: left P. Mitchell 3,000 gns after penultimate start:
should be suited by 1¼m+: acts on fibresand, equitrack and good to soft going, probably
on good to firm. *B. J. Llewellyn*

WESTERN VERSE (USA) 2 b.c. (Feb 3) Gone West (USA) – Reams of Verse **92 p**
(USA) 121 (Nureyev (USA) 131) [2001 6m* 6m Jun 19] small, attractive colt: fluent
mover: first foal: dam, won Fillies' Mile and Oaks, half-sister to high-class 1¼m performer Elmaamul from family of Zafonic (by Gone West): justified favouritism in maiden at
York in May in good style by 1½ lengths from Addeyll: second favourite, well held in
Coventry Stakes at Royal Ascot, later found to have had an infection: will stay at least
1m: should do better if all is well. *H. R. A. Cecil*

WESTFIELD STAR (IRE) 4 b.g. Fourstars Allstar (USA) 122 – Mokaite 55 **73**
(Komaite (USA)) [2001 ?: f6g⁵ f6g⁶ f7g² f6f² f6g f6g* 6m⁶ 7g*⁸ 7m 7g² Aug 17] lengthy
gelding: first foal: dam 2-y-o 7f winner/winning hurdler: fair performer: left M. Hourigan
in Ireland after 3 yrs: won minor event at Southwell in April and handicap at Thirsk in
June: stays 7f: acts on heavy going and fibresand: blinkered once: has looked none too
keen. *T. D. Barron*

WESTGATE FLAME (IRE) 2 ch.g. (Jan 24) Priolo (USA) 127 – Hawksbill Special –
(IRE) (Taufan (USA) 119) [2001 7.9d Oct 12] IR 21,000F, 32,000Y: strong gelding: fifth
foal: half-brother to 3 winning sprinters, including fairly useful Irish 1999 2-y-o 5f
winner Appalachia (by Imperial Frontier) and 3-y-o Zietunzeen: dam unraced daughter
of half-sister to high-class sprinter Sayf El Arab: 66/1, well beaten in maiden at York.
R. A. Fahey

WESTGATE RUN 4 b.f. Emperor Jones (USA) 119 – Glowing Reference **69**
(Reference Point 139) [2001 76: 11.9m 10m 11.9d 12f² 10d⁵ 10.3m 10m 10.4m Sep 5]
close-coupled, sparely-made filly: fair handicapper: ran creditably in 2001 only when
second in July: stays 1½m: acts on firm going, possibly not on softer than good: found
little when visored once. *R. A. Fahey*

WESTLIFE (IRE) 3 b.f. Mind Games 121 – Enchantica 67 (Timeless Times (USA) –
99) [2001 32: e8g Jan 27] lightly-raced maiden. *H. J. Collingridge*

WESTMEAD EMPRESS 2 br.f. (Feb 10) Emperor Jones (USA) 119 – Glossary **78**
(Reference Point 139) [2001 7g 7m⁵ 7g³ 8f² Oct 17] fourth foal: half-sister to 1m winner
Fifth Emerald (by Formidable) and a 5f winner in Greece by Be My Chief: dam unraced
close relation to smart middle-distance filly Valley of Gold: fair maiden: placed at Epsom
(final start for S. Williams) in September and Santa Anita (beaten a head) following
month: stays 1m: raced only on good ground or firmer. *R. B. Hess jnr, USA*

WESTMINSTER CITY (USA) 5 b.g. Alleged (USA) 138 – Promanade Fan **72 d**
(USA) (Timeless Moment (USA)) [2001 58, a73: f11g⁴ f12s⁵ f16.2g⁶ 10.3s 9.7v³ 11.9s
10d² 10.1g 10g f14.8s³ f12s⁶ Dec 26] tall gelding: fair performer at best, on downgrade:

left D. Elsworth after seventh start, Mrs N. Macauley after next outing and Ian Williams after ninth: stays 1½m, probably not 2m: acts on good to firm going, soft and fibresand: sometimes visored/blinkered, not in 2001: tends to get behind: has found little/wandered. *B. J. Llewellyn*

WEST ORDER (USA) 3 ch.c. Gone West (USA) – Irish Order (USA) 102 (Irish **95** River (FR) 131) [2001 104P: 7m 7g³ Oct 6] big, strong, close-coupled colt: has fluent, round action: useful performer: trained in 2000 by R. Hannon: didn't live up to 2-y-o promise after training setbacks early in 2001: last of 18 in Jersey Stakes at Royal Ascot, then only third to May Ball in minor event at Redcar (beaten 3 lengths) 3½ months later: will stay 1m: yet to race on extremes of going. *Saeed bin Suroor*

WETHAAB (USA) 4 b.g. Pleasant Colony (USA) – Binntastic (USA) (Lyphard's **45** Wish (FR) 124) [2001 60: 13s⁵ 12m⁵ 12.3g f14g f11g f12g⁵ 8m f11g³ f14g Dec 14] sturdy, well-made gelding: poor mover: poor performer: left G. M. Moore before penultimate start: stays 1½m: acts on good to firm going and fibresand: tried blinkered/visored/tongue tied. *Mrs A. M. Naughton*

WHALAH (USA) 3 ch.f. Dixieland Band (USA) – Firm Stance (USA) (Affirmed **76** (USA)) [2001 59: 8.1m⁶ 10.1s⁴ 10s* 10d* 10.3s³ Nov 9] angular, workmanlike filly: fair form from 6 runs: won handicaps at Nottingham and Brighton (dictated pace both times) in October/November: good effort final start: stays 1¼m: acts on soft ground: game: sold 30,000 gns. *C. E. Brittain*

WHALE BEACH (USA) 3 b.c. Known Fact (USA) 135 – Zulu Dance (USA) **94 §** (Danzatore (CAN) 120) [2001 93p: 7d 7g 7m 7m³ 8m 7m² 7d⁴ 8m 7s Sep 29] big, quite good-topped colt: fairly useful handicapper: below form last 3 starts: effective at 7f/1m: acts on good to firm and good to soft ground: has worn crossed noseband: usually held up: has been mulish to post, and proved most reluctant final start: unreliable: sold 8,000 gns. *B. W. Hills*

WHALEEF 3 b.c. Darshaan 133 – Wilayif (USA) 75 (Danzig (USA)) [2001 11m* **106** p12g* p10g³ Nov 24] fifth foal: half-brother to 3 winners, including smart French 1999 2-y-o 5f (Prix du Bois) and 5.5f winner Morning Pride (by Machiavellian) and useful performer up to 2m Wilawander (by Nashwan): dam, 7f winner, from outstanding North American family of Fantastic Light and Swain: useful form: won maiden at Goodwood (only run for Saeed bin Suroor, raced freely, swished tail) in June and minor event at Lingfield in November: good 1¾ lengths third to Compton Bolter in listed event at Lingfield final start: effective at 1¼m to 1½m: acts on good to firm going and polytrack. *E. A. L. Dunlop*

WHARFEDALE CYGNET 3 b.f. King's Signet (USA) 110 – Your Care (FR) 42 **25** (Caerwent 123) [2001 37: 8.1m⁴ Jul 5] lengthy filly: poor form in 4 runs, including in seller. *B. G. Powell*

WHASS URRP (IRE) 2 b.c. (Feb 20) Desert King (IRE) 129 – Blue Burgee (USA) **66** (Lyphard's Wish (FR) 124) [2001 6f⁶ 7m Aug 16] IR 30,000Y: second foal: dam, useful French 2-y-o 6f winner (later successful in USA), out of half-sister to top-class French 1½m filly Comtesse de Loir: better effort (fair form) when sixth of 7 in minor event at Newbury: should stay 7f. *R. Hannon*

WHAT A CRACKER 4 b.f. Bustino 136 – Moon Spin 83 (Night Shift (USA)) [2001 **–** –: 11.9m 8m Jun 22] seems of little account. *Miss H. M. Irving*

WHAT-A-DANCER (IRE) 4 b.g. Dancing Dissident (USA) 119 – Cool Gales 85 **88** (Lord Gayle (USA) 124) [2001 55: 8f⁵ 8.3m* 9.2d⁴ 7.5m³ 8m² 7m* 8f⁶ 8g⁶ Oct 6] sparely-made gelding: fairly useful handicapper: won at Hamilton in June and York in September: best form at 7f: raced mainly on going firmer than good: has worn crossed noseband/raced freely: usually held up. *G. A. Swinbank*

WHAT A VIEW 2 b.c. (Feb 20) Sadler's Wells (USA) 132 – Ocean View (USA) 109 **74 p** (Gone West (USA)) [2001 7g 8g³ Sep 7] 400,000Y: quite attractive colt: first foal: dam, US 5.5f (at 2 yrs) and 6.5f winner, placed in Grade 1 events at 8.5f (at 2 yrs) and 9f: better effort in maidens (fair form) when third to Lahooq at Kempton: should stay 1¼m: probably capable of better. *J. L. Dunlop*

WHATSITSNAME 5 br.g. Tragic Role (USA) – Princess Yasmin (USA) (Le **–** Fabuleux 133) [2001 –: 9.2d 9m 13d Jun 20] of little account. *J. L. Eyre*

WHAT'S THE COUNT 5 gr.g. Theatrical Charmer 114 – Yankee Silver (Yankee **–** Gold 115) [2001 f12g 10g May 12] well held in maidens: tried tongue tied. *B. R. Johnson*

WHEATHILL 2 ch.f. (May 25) Magic Ring (IRE) 115 – Hanglands (Bustino 136) **73** [2001 6m⁵ 5m* 6m³ 5s³ 5g 6m 6v Oct 15] half-sister to several winners, including useful

1992 2-y-o 5f/6f winner Zuno Warrior (by Dominion), later winner in USA, and 1m winner who stayed 2m Our Way (by Forzando): dam lightly-raced maiden: fair performer: won maiden at Lingfield in June: creditable efforts in nurseries next 2 starts: will prove best at 5f/6f: acts on soft and good to firm ground: blinkered/visored last 2 starts: sent to USA. *M. P. Tregoning*

WHEN IN ROME 3 b.c. Saddlers' Hall (IRE) 126 – Seasonal Splendour (IRE) 95 **113** (Prince Rupert (FR) 121) [2001 101: 10s³ 10.2d² 11.5g³ 16.2m² 14m* 14.8g 12m⁵ 14g⁵ 14.6g⁴ 14s⁶ Sep 30] close-coupled, quite attractive colt: smart performer: placed in Derby Trial at Lingfield (third to Perfect Sunday) and Queen's Vase at Royal Ascot (neck second to And Beyond) on third/fourth outings, then landed odds in 3-runner maiden at Sandown in July: marginally best effort when 8¾ lengths fourth to Milan in St Leger at Doncaster penultimate start: soundly beaten in German equivalent at Dortmund final outing: finds 1½m on short side, and will stay beyond 2m: acts on soft and good to firm going: game: sent to Saudi Arabia. *C. A. Cyzer*

WHENWILLIEMETHARRY 4 b.f. Sabrehill (USA) 120 – William's Bird (USA) **–** 104 (Master Willie 129) [2001 71d: 8g 8f 6g 12s Oct 20] one-time fair maiden: no form in 2001: left A. Bailey after third start. *M. E. Sowersby*

WHERE ARE YOU 3 b.f. Green Desert (USA) 127 – Dafinah (USA) 89 (Graustark) **65** [2001 8.1d⁴ 7m² 7.1m² 7g⁴ Sep 11] sister to 1m winner El Gahar and half-sister to 2 winners, including useful 1¼m winner who stayed 1½m Alhamad (by Slip Anchor): dam 1¼m and 1½m winner: fair form in maidens: should stay at least 1m: sent to Saudi Arabia. *Sir Michael Stoute*

WHERE EAGLES DARE (USA) 4 b.g. Eagle Eyed (USA) 111 – Velveteen (USA) **55** (Pirateer (USA)) [2001 14.1m⁴ Jul 28] big, useful-looking gelding: modest maiden, very lightly raced nowadays: stays 1¾m: sold 1,200 gns, and gelded. *J. A. Osborne*

WHERE OR WHEN (IRE) 2 ch.c. (Jan 27) Danehill Dancer (IRE) 117 – Future **110** Past (USA) (Super Concorde (USA) 128) [2001 7g* 7m 7m* 7.1g⁴ 7g* 7d⁴ Oct 20] IR

John Humphreys (Turf Accountants) Ltd's "Where Or When"

26,000F, 26,000Y: workmanlike colt: has scope: shows plenty of knee action: half-brother to several winners, including smart performer up to 14.6f All The Way (by Shirley Heights) and useful 1¼m winner who stays 1¾m Just In Time (by Night Shift): dam winner up to 9f in USA: smart performer: won minor events at Ascot in July and Salisbury in August and Somerville Tattersall Stakes at Newmarket (beat Della Francesca by a head) in October: good staying-on fourth, beaten nearly 1½ lengths by Rock of Gibraltar, in Dewhurst Stakes at Newmarket: likely to be suited by 1m/1¼m: unraced on extremes of going: best form on straight tracks: patiently ridden. *T. G. Mills*

WHERE'S JASPER (IRE) 3 ch.g. Common Grounds 118 – Stifen (Burslem 123) **91 d** [2001 90: 6d³ 6m 6d 5f 5g 5s 7.1v Sep 29] unfurnished gelding: fairly useful handicapper: below form after second start: best at 5f/6f: acts on firm and soft going: blinkered fourth to sixth starts: edgy sort: sold 8,000 gns, sent to USA. *K. A. Ryan*

WHERE THE HEART IS 3 ch.g. Efisio 120 – Luminary (Kalaglow 132) [2001 **84** 82?: 7.9g³ 8m² 8f⁴ Jun 22] big, workmanlike gelding: fairly useful performer: stays 1m: acts on good to firm going, probably on firm: joined P. Chapple-Hyam in Hong Kong, where renamed Cellini. *M. H. Tompkins*

WHICH WITCH (IRE) 3 b.f. Alzao (USA) 117 – First Fastnet 64 (Ahonoora 122) **–** [2001 8m⁴ 5f Sep 10] half-sister to 2 winners abroad by Risk Me, including French winner around 1¼m Je Reve: dam 5f winner at 4 yrs: no form in maidens. *M. Johnston*

WHISKAWAY 3 ch.f. Alhijaz 122 – Whirling Words 75 (Sparkler 130) [2001 8d **25** 8.1m³ 10s Sep 24] seventh living foal: half-sister to fairly useful 1996 2-y-o 5f winner Chili Concerto (by Chilibang): dam 1m winner: form only when third in seller. *P. J. Makin*

WHISKY ECHO 2 ch.c. (Feb 17) Dancing Spree (USA) – Stock Pile 39 (Galveston **–** 114) [2001 f8g 8.2s Oct 30] second known foal: dam maiden who stayed 1m: well beaten in sellers. *J. G. Given*

WHISKY NINE 3 b.c. Makbul 104 – Indivisible 56 (Remainder Man 126§) [2001 –p: **84** 6.1d* 6m² 6m⁴ 6g⁵ Aug 17] tall colt: fairly useful form from 5 starts: left M. Jarvis after winning maiden at Nottingham in May: good efforts in handicaps next 2 starts: will be suited by 7f: acts on good to firm and good to soft ground: sent to Singapore. *W. J. Haggas*

WHISPERING RAIN 2 ch.c. (May 24) Young Ern 120 – Bay Meadows Star **–** (Sharpo 132) [2001 f6g f7g Nov 17] 2,000Y: fourth reported foal: dam unreliable maiden who should have stayed 7f: well beaten in claimer and maiden at Wolverhampton. *A. G. Newcombe*

WHISTFILLY 3 b.f. First Trump 118 – Zinzi (Song 132) [2001 8.3d 8m 7m 10g 10m **49** Aug 22] sister to useful 1999 2-y-o 5f winner Mrs P, closely related to 2 winners by Primo Dominie, notably smart sprinter Sarcita, and half-sister to several winners up to 1m: dam Irish 5f winner: poor maiden. *D. R. C. Elsworth*

WHISTLER 4 ch.g. Selkirk (USA) 129 – French Gift 99 (Cadeaux Genereux 131) **90** [2001 98: 5.2d 5.1f⁴ 5m 5g 6m 5g 5m 6g 5v 5s⁶ Nov 9] angular, workmanlike gelding: has a quick action: useful performer at 3 yrs: mostly well held in handicaps after second outing in 2001: effective at 5f/6f: has won on firm ground, but very best efforts on good to soft/soft: tried blinkered: usually races handily. *R. Hannon*

WHISTLING DIXIE (IRE) 5 ch.g. Forest Wind (USA) 111 – Camden's Gift **70** (Camden Town 125) [2001 59: 12m* 13s* 12.1s* 12g³ 12.1m 13.8s³ Oct 20] work-manlike gelding: fair handicapper: won at Southwell and Hamilton (twice, apprentice race on second occasion) in July/August: stays 1¾m: acts on firm and soft going, probably on fibresand: blinkered (below form) 3 times: usually held up: useful hurdler. *Mrs M. Reveley*

WHITBARROW (IRE) 2 b.c. (Feb 25) Royal Abjar (USA) 121 – Danccini (IRE) **103** 78 (Dancing Dissident (USA) 119) [2001 5.1d 5m* 5d* 6f* 5.2m 5m* 6g 5g 7v⁴ Oct 26] IR 32,000Y: strong, good sort: first foal: dam Irish 2-y-o 5f winner: useful performer: won maiden at Lingfield and minor event at Windsor in May, listed race at Epsom in June and Molecomb Stakes at Goodwood (headed only briefly when beating Irony by ½ length) in August: well held in pattern events last 3 starts: best at 5f/easy 6f: acts on firm and good to soft ground: blinkered last 4 starts: races up with pace. *B. R. Millman*

WHITE AMIT 3 b.f. Shaamit (IRE) 127 – White African (Carwhite 127) [2001 –: 7d **–** 8f 8m Jul 29] no form: tried tongue tied: has shown signs of temperament. *J. A. Gilbert*

WHITE BRIDLE (IRE) 2 ch.f. (Feb 23) Singspiel (IRE) 133 – Samira 94 (Rainbow **81** Quest (USA) 134) [2001 7f³ 7g⁵ Jul 20] 400,000Y: well-made filly: has a short, quick action: first foal: dam, Irish 1½m winner, half-sister to smart 1½m filly Cunning: fairly useful form: shaped well when 4¾ lengths third of 4 to Zaeema in maiden at Doncaster: edged left when only fifth of 8 to Kasamba in similar event at Newmarket: should be suited by 1¼m+. *J. L. Dunlop*

WHITE CLIFFS 2 ch.g. (Feb 7) Bluebird (USA) 125 – Preening 62 (Persian Bold **71** 123) [2001 6s 6s 5.1s² Oct 30] strong gelding: half-brother to 1998 2-y-o 5f winner Alpha (by Primo Dominie): dam, 1½m winner, half-sister to smart 7f/1m winner Hadeer: best effort in maidens (fair form) when second to Acorazado at Nottingham: should stay 7f: raced only on soft ground: tongue tied last 2 starts: unseated and ran loose before start/given early reminders second outing: gelded after final one. *W. J. Haggas*

WHITE DOVE (FR) 3 b.f. Beaudelaire (USA) 125 – Hermine And Pearls (FR) **49** (Shirley Heights 130) [2001 10s 8.3g 8.3d 10d 16v⁵ Oct 4] second foal: half-sister to French 11f and 1½m winner Lonesome Dove (by Petit Loup): dam placed up to 1½m in France: poor maiden: well held in handicaps last 2 starts. *R. Dickin*

WHITE EMIR 8 b.g. Emarati (USA) 74 – White African (Carwhite 127) [2001 73: **77** 7g⁶ 7m* 7m² 7m⁵ 7.1g 7f 7d Nov 2] good-quartered gelding: fair handicapper: won at Kempton in June: stays 7.7f: acts on any turf going (below form only outing on fibresand): won in blinkers earlier in career: sometimes wanders under pressure, and best with strong handling/waiting tactics. *L. G. Cottrell*

WHITEFOOT 4 b.f. Be My Chief (USA) 122 – Kelimutu 58 (Top Ville 129) [2001 – 103: 12v 13.4f⁵ 22.2f⁶ 18.7m⁵ 16.2g Aug 11] workmanlike filly: useful performer at best: reportedly had piece of bone removed from fetlock after final 3-y-o start, and well held in 2001: stayed 1½m: acted on good to firm and heavy going: has been covered by Green Desert. *G. A. Butler*

Seasons Holidays' "Whitbarrow"

WHITE LEDGER (IRE) 2 ch.g. (Mar 14) Ali-Royal (IRE) 127 – Boranwood (IRE) **64**
(Exhibitioner 111) [2001 6m 6.1d⁶ f6g⁶ f5g³ f5s⁶ Dec 15] 30,000Y: useful-looking
gelding: fourth foal: half-brother to 3-y-o Ceepio and 1999 2-y-o 5f winner Pegasus Star
(by Lycius): dam, Irish 2-y-o 6f winner, sister to useful Irish sprinter Wicked Folly:
modest maiden: wandered when third at Southwell: should stay 7f: acts on fibresand, yet
to race on extremes on turf. *T. G. Mills*

WHITENEY 2 b.f. (Jan 25) Whittingham (IRE) 104 – Polgwynne 48 (Forzando 122) **–**
[2001 5g May 14] 700Y: first foal: dam 7f winner: 40/1, started slowly and well behind
when falling after 1f in minor event at Windsor. *E. J. O'Neill*

WHITE PLAINS (IRE) 8 b.g. Nordico (USA) – Flying Diva 100 (Chief Singer 131) **–**
[2001 –, a91: f11g² e12g² e12g e10s* f12g³ f9.4g⁵ f12f f11g* f12g² 12m f12g⁶ Jun 8] **a84**
good-bodied gelding: fairly useful performer: won handicap at Lingfield in February and
claimer at Southwell in April: effective at 9.4f to 1½m: acts on fibresand and equitrack (6
of 9 wins at Lingfield): usually tongue tied: sometimes slowly away. *T. D. Barron*

WHITE RABBIT 2 b.f. (Jan 29) Zilzal (USA) 137 – Trick (IRE) 76 (Shirley Heights **91**
130) [2001 6d* 6.1d² 8d 6d³ 8s³ Oct 22] angular, rather unfurnished filly: second foal:
half-sister to 3-y-o Shinner: dam, 1¼m winner, out of half-sister to high-class Flying
Childers/Middle Park winner Hittite Glory: fairly useful performer: won maiden at
Pontefract in August: creditable third in listed events at York (missed break, beaten 4½
lengths by Prism) and Pontefract (9¾ lengths behind Bandari): stays 1m: raced only on
good to soft/soft going: has worn crossed noseband: blanketed for stall entry all starts:
usually bandaged off-hind/hind joints. *T. D. Easterby*

WHITE SETTLER 8 b.g. Polish Patriot (USA) 128 – Oasis (Valiyar 129) [2001 60: **52**
8.1m⁶ 7m³ 8g 8.1g Sep 13] sturdy gelding: modest performer: stays 1m: acts on soft and
good to firm going: blinkered once: normally held up: sold 370 gns. *Miss S. J. Wilton*

WHITE STAG 2 b.g. (Mar 18) King's Signet (USA) 110 – Hibernica (IRE) 69 (Law **55 p**
Society (USA) 130) [2001 6v Nov 8] 1,800Y: first foal: dam, fourth at 1m from 5 starts,
out of half-sister to smart 1984 2-y-o 7f winner (Champagne Stakes) Young Runaway:
20/1, eleventh of 18 to Dilys in maiden at Windsor, soon having plenty to do and not
knocked about: sure to improve. *G. B. Balding*

WHITE STAR LADY 3 ch.f. So Factual (USA) 120 – Cottonwood 80 (Teenoso **48 §**
(USA) 135) [2001 58: 6g 6m 7.1m 7f f7g⁴ 8m 6m f6g⁵ 7.5m* 7m 8m f8g f8.5g Dec 1]
workmanlike filly: poor performer: won claimer at Beverley in August: no form after:
stays 7.5f: acts on firm ground, good to soft and fibresand: tried visored: unreliable.
J. R. Weymes

WHITGIFT ROSE 4 b. or br.f. Polar Falcon (USA) 126 – Celtic Wing (Midyan **–**
(USA) 124) [2001 66: 10g May 4] sparely-made filly: fair maiden at 3 yrs: well held only
run in 2001. *Lady Herries*

WHITLEYGRANGE GIRL 4 b.f. Rudimentary (USA) 118 – Choir's Image 53 **–**
(Lochnager 132) [2001 –: f7g f8s Jan 19] well held in varied company. *J. L. Eyre*

WHIZZ 4 b.f. Salse (USA) 128 – Cut Ahead 85 (Kalaglow 132) [2001 –p: f12g⁶ 10m³ **67**
12d Jun 17] fair maiden, lightly raced: should be suited by 1½m: best effort on good to
firm going. *R. Charlton*

WHIZZ KID 7 b.m. Puissance 110 – Panienka (POL) 70 (Dom Racine (FR) 121) **70**
[2001 77, a57: 5v 5.1d* 5m⁴ 5m 5m 5f 5.1f⁶ f5g 5.1g 6.1v 5.1d 5g⁵ p5g f6g f5g Nov 30] **a–**
tall mare: fair handicapper: won at Bath in May: mostly disappointing after: stays easy 6f:
has form on firm going but probably best on good or softer on turf: sometimes blinkered:
has been reluctant to post/slowly away: held up. *J. M. Bradley*

WHO CARES WINS 5 ch.g. Kris 135 – Anne Bonny 105 (Ajdal (USA) 130) [2001 **77**
77: 16s⁴ 18.7f 20m 16.2f 14.1m Jul 14] rather leggy, quite good-topped gelding: fair
handicapper: stays 2m: acts on firm and soft ground: tried visored/blinkered at 4 yrs.
J. R. Jenkins

WHO GOES THERE 5 ch.m. Wolfhound (USA) 126 – Challanging 95 (Mill Reef **60**
(USA) 141) [2001 63: 8.2s 8.3g⁵ 7.1m 6.9m 7.6f 10m 8.3g³ 7.1g⁵ 7.1m⁵ 8f⁶ 7g⁵ 7.1g
8m Sep 26] modest handicapper: won at Lingfield in August for second year running:
stays 1m: acts on firm and soft going: sometimes slowly away/carries head awkwardly:
none too consistent. *T. M. Jones*

WHO'S ON FIRST (IRE) 2 ch.c. (Jan 26) Common Grounds 118 – Telemania **68**
(IRE) 87 (Mujtahid (USA) 118) [2001 5d⁴ 6s⁴ f6g⁵ Oct 18] 21,000Y: first foal: dam, 2-y-o
6f winner, stayed 1m: fair maiden: stayed 6f: dead. *J. A. Osborne*

WHY ALYS 2 b.f. (Apr 11) Lugana Beach 116 – Classic Times 82 (Dominion 123) **52**
[2001 5f² 5f² 5m⁴ 5d⁶ 5.1g⁴ 5.1f* Sep 18] seventh foal: half-sister to 1994 2-y-o 6f winner
Cedar Girl (by Then Again) and 7f winner Dontdressfordinner (by Tina's Pet): dam, Irish
6f (at 2 yrs) and 1m winner, also successful over hurdles: modest performer: blinkered,
won nursery at Chepstow, always prominent and veering left briefly final 1f: should stay
6f: acts on firm ground. *A. W. Carroll*

WICKED UNCLE 2 b.c. (Feb 28) Distant Relative 128 – The Kings Daughter 79 **81**
(Indian King (USA) 128) [2001 5s 6d 5m³ 5m* 5.1m³ 6f² 6g Aug 25] 6,500F, IR
13,500Y: smallish, sturdy colt: half-brother to several winners, including fairly useful 5f/
6f winner The King's Ransom (by Cadeaux Genereux) and 6f/7f winner King Uno (by Be
My Chief): dam 5f/6f winner: fairly useful performer: won nursery at Doncaster in July:
good efforts in similar events next 2 starts: likely to prove best at 5f/easy 6f: acts on firm
ground: sold 21,000 gns. *R. M. Beckett*

WIGMAN LADY (IRE) 4 b.f. Tenby 125 – Height of Elegance 82 (Shirley Heights **53 d**
130) [2001 –: 13s 9s³ 10d⁵ 12m 16m 11.9f 12g 10s f12g f16g⁵ f14g Nov 26] sparely-made
filly: modest maiden: mostly well held after third start: should stay beyond 1¼m: acts on
soft going, possibly not on firmer than good. *T. J. Etherington*

WIGMO PRINCESS 2 ch.f. (May 7) Factual (USA) 108 – Queen of Shannon (IRE) **54**
76 (Nordico (USA)) [2001 5g⁶ 6m 6g f6g⁴ 5.7d² 7s f6g f7s⁴ Dec 18] 5,000Y: first foal: **a51**
dam 7f/1m winner: modest maiden: in frame in claimer/sellers: stays 7f: acts on fibresand
and good to soft ground. *A. W. Carroll*

WILDERBROOK LAHRI 2 b.g. (Mar 20) Lahib (USA) 129 – Wilsonic 78 **62**
(Damister (USA) 123) [2001 5f 6g³ 6d 7m Sep 6] 9,500Y: fourth foal: half-brother to 3
winners, including 7f to 11f winner Heathyards Sheik (by Alnasr Alwasheek) and 3-y-o
First Steps: dam irresolute maiden who stayed 13f: modest maiden: third at Pontefract:
again not knocked about next time: only ninth in nursery final start: should stay at least
1m. *Mrs J. R. Ramsden*

WILD MUSHROOM 3 ro.g. Norton Challenger 111 – Wild Strawberry 70 (Balla- **–**
cashtal (CAN)) [2001 10v p12g Nov 13] first foal: dam, 6f (at 2 yrs) to 2m winner, also
won over hurdles: well held in maidens: gave trouble at stalls second outing.
Miss B. Sanders

WILD WATER (FR) 3 b.g. Salse (USA) 128 – Dashing Water 87 (Dashing Blade **–**
117) [2001 11.1s 10.2d May 1] tall, useful-looking gelding: has scope: second foal:
half-brother to 1¼m winner Night Diamond (by Night Shift): dam, 2-y-o 7f winner,
half-sister to Nunthorpe winners Lochsong and Lochangel: well held in maidens: gelded
after. *I. A. Balding*

WILEMMGEO 4 b.f. Emarati (USA) 74 – Floral Spark 69 (Forzando 122) [2001 72, **61 §**
a56: f9.4g⁵ f12g f12g 12s 9v 10s 9.7v 8.1g* 7m 8.2f 10f 7.6f f9.4g f8g Dec 17] sturdy **a– §**
filly: modest performer: won apprentice handicap at Warwick in May: ran badly after,
leaving P. D. Evans before penultimate start: effective at 1m to 1¼m: acts on heavy going,
good to firm and fibresand: sometimes visored/blinkered: quirky sort (temporarily
banned from racing on Flat in autumn), and not to be trusted. *Mrs N. Macauley*

WILFRAM 4 b.g. Fraam 114 – Ming Blue 52 (Primo Dominie 121) [2001 71: 8.2s **68**
8.3m 8m 10m⁵ 12m⁵ 12g⁶ 10.1m⁵ 8.3g²ᵈ 9g 8.2g⁶ 8.3g 9g* 10.2d f8.5g⁶ f9.4g⁶ f8g f8.5g **a53**
p10g Dec 22] fair handicapper on turf, modest on all-weather: won at Redcar in October:
seems best at 1m/easy 1¼m: acts on fibresand, polytrack, firm and good to soft ground:
usually blinkered: none too consistent. *J. M. Bradley*

WILLIAM GEORGE (IRE) 2 b.g. (Mar 6) Turtle Island (IRE) 123 – Lady's **68**
Dream 85 (Mazilier (USA) 107) [2001 5m 6g 7m⁴ 7.1g 7.2g 8.1s⁶ 7.1v³ 7.9s 8v Oct 16]
10,000F, 30,000Y: workmanlike gelding: second foal: dam, Irish 7f (at 2 yrs)/1m winner,
out of half-sister to very smart 2-y-o 6f winner/US Grade 1 winner at 1m Forzando: fair
maiden: ran poorly in nurseries last 2 starts: stays 1m: acts on heavy going: sold 3,200
gns. *K. A. Ryan*

WILLIAM'S WELL 7 ch.g. Superpower 113 – Catherines Well 99 (Junius (USA) **74**
124) [2001 85: 6v 6s 5g 6m May 12] useful-looking gelding: fair handicapper: effective
at 5f/6f: acts on firm and soft ground: wears blinkers. *M. W. Easterby*

WILLIE CONQUER 9 ch.g. Master Willie 129 – Maryland Cookie (USA) 101 **75**
(Bold Hour) [2001 79: e12g³ e10g² e10g* e12g⁵ e10s⁵ e10g* 10f 10.3f² 10f* 10g⁴ 10g⁴ **a81**
9.9m* 10.1d* 10g* 8.9m* 9.1m² 10.4s Oct 11] smallish, lengthy, good-bodied gelding:
one-time useful performer: fairly useful on all-weather, fair on turf in 2001: won 16 times

in career, including 2 handicaps at Lingfield and claimers at Brighton (2), Salisbury, Yarmouth and York in 2001: left A. Reid after penultimate start: was effective at 9f to 1¾m: acted on firm going, good to soft and equitrack: was tried tongue tied earlier in career: was usually held up: was tough and reliable: dead. *P. D. Evans*

WILLING   5 b.g. Yaheeb (USA) 95§ – Droskin VII (Damsire Unregistered) [2001   –
10.5d⁶ 12.3m Aug 27] big, strong gelding: tailed off in maidens. *T. J. Etherington*

WILLOUGHBY'S BOY (IRE)   4 b.g. Night Shift (USA) – Andbell (Trojan Fen   **94 d**
118) [2001 91: 8s 7.6f⁵ 8m 7m² 7.6m 7d³ 7g 7.6d 7g 8f⁴ 8d 8d Nov 3] smallish, sturdy
gelding: fairly useful handicapper, on downgrade: effective at 7f/1m: acts on firm and
good to soft going: tried blinkered/tongue tied. *B. Hanbury*

WILLOW MAGIC   4 b.f. Petong 126 – Love Street 62 (Mummy's Pet 125) [2001 61,   –
a50: e7g Jan 13] modest maiden at 3 yrs: well held only start in 2001. *S. Dow*

WILLY BANG BANG   4 b.g. Contract Law (USA) 108 – Megan's Move 66 (Move   –
Off 112) [2001 –: 9m 12.4m Jun 6] seems of little account. *W. Storey*

WILLY WILLY   8 ch.g. Master Willie 129 – Monsoon 66 (Royal Palace 131) [2001   –
11.9g⁶ 12.1m Jul 27] probably of little account nowadays. *D. L. Williams*

WILMING   ch.f. (Mar 18) Komaite (USA) – Ming Blue 52 (Primo Dominie 121)   **35**
[2001 f5g f5g 5.7f 5m 5d 5.3s Oct 3] 900Y: workmanlike filly: fourth foal: half-sister to
4-y-o Wilfram: dam poor maiden on Flat/over hurdles: poor maiden. *J. M. Bradley*

WILSON BLUEBOTTLE (IRE)   2 ch.g. (Apr 26) Priolo (USA) 127 – Mauras   **60**
Pride (IRE) (Cadeaux Genereux 131) [2001 6m⁶ 5m 5m⁶ 7m² 6v 6d 6d 7s Nov 10] IR
7,500Y, 6,000 2-y-o: smallish, strong, lengthy gelding: third foal: half-brother to fairly
useful 2000 2-y-o 1¼m winner Deuce of Trumps (by Desert Style): dam unraced from
family of William Hill Futurity winner Al Hareb: modest maiden: beaten neck in nursery
at Catterick: well held after: should stay 1m: acts on good to firm going, seemingly not on
going softer than good: has hung left. *M. W. Easterby*

WILSON BLYTH   3 b.g. Puissance 110 – Pearls (Mon Tresor 113) [2001 78: 6s² 6s⁶   **78**
6m 6m⁵ 5m 5m 5d⁵ 5g³ 6g⁵ 6g⁶ 5m 5g 6d 5v Oct 24] tall, sparely-made gelding: fair
performer: below form last 4 starts: effective at 5f/6f: acts on firm and soft going:
sometimes gives trouble at stalls/slowly away. *A. Berry*

WIN ALOT   3 b.g. Aragon 118 – Having Fun (Hard Fought 125) [2001 f7g f8g 7s⁶   **58**
9.9m 10.1m 10f 10f Jul 2] sturdy gelding: seventh foal: half-brother to 1m seller winner   **a48**
Mardrew and 2 winners in Italy, all by Rambo Dancer: dam lightly-raced daughter of Prix
Vermeille winner Highest Hopes: modest maiden: should be suited by 1m+: sold 1,300
gns. *J. Hetherton*

WINDCHILL   3 ch.f. Handsome Sailor 125 – Baroness Gymcrak 53§ (Pharly (FR)   **53**
130) [2001 60: 5m 6m⁶ 7m 7g⁵ 6m 7.5m 6f³ Sep 10] small, workmanlike filly: modest
performer: effective at 6f/7f: acts on firm and good to soft going. *T. D. Easterby*

WIND CHIME (IRE)   4 ch.c. Arazi (USA) 135 – Shamisen 86 (Diesis 133) [2001   **70**
75, a64: f9.4s f7g f7g⁴ f8.5g³ f8.5g⁶ f8g³ 8m 7m² 7m* f8g⁶ p7g f8g Dec 17] smallish colt: **a57**
fair handicapper on turf, modest on all-weather: won at Thirsk in June: effective at 7f/
easy 1m: acts on firm going, good to soft and fibresand. *A. G. Newcombe*

WINDMILL LANE   4 b.f. Saddlers' Hall (IRE) 126 – Alpi Dora (Valiyar 129) [2001   –
71, a63: f16g f16s 14d Apr 12] close-coupled filly: modest handicapper at 3 yrs: well held
in 2001: visored once. *B. S. Rothwell*

WINDSHIFT (IRE)   5 b.g. Forest Wind (USA) 111 – Beautyofthepeace (IRE)   **55 §**
(Exactly Sharp (USA) 121) [2001 –§, a84§: f11g⁶ f9.4s* f9.4g⁴ f9.4g f8.5g 8.1g f8g⁴   **a77 §**
10m² 9.9f 10g⁶ p12g f9.4f p10g Dec 22] leggy, workmanlike gelding: fair handicapper
on all-weather, modest on turf: won at Wolverhampton in January: left D. Shaw after
penultimate start: stays 1¼m: acts on fibresand, soft and good to firm going: usually
visored/blinkered: often gets behind/looks none too keen: unreliable. *I. A. Wood*

WINDSOR BOY (IRE)   4 b.c. Mtoto 134 – Fragrant Belle (USA) 90 (Al Nasr (FR)   **95 d**
126) [2001 108: 12s 12g⁵ 12g 11.6m⁴ 13.4d 14.6d Sep 14] lengthy colt: useful performer
at 3 yrs: disappointing in 2001: should stay beyond 1½m: acts on good to firm going,
probably on soft: tried blinkered/tongue tied: sold only 8,000 gns. *P. F. I. Cole*

WINGALONG (IRE)   2 ch.f. (Apr 21) Flying Spur (AUS) – Dutch Queen (Ahonoora   –
122) [2001 5.1v⁶ Apr 3] IR 5,000F, IR 7,000Y: rather leggy, unfurnished filly: half-sister
to several winners, including 3-y-o Le Meridien and 4-y-o Ansellad: dam of little

account: 10/1, backward and green, always behind after slow start in maiden at Nottingham. *T. D. Easterby*

WING COMMANDER   2 b.c. (Apr 9) Royal Applause 124 – Southern Psychic   **97 p**
(USA) (Alwasmi (USA) 115) [2001 6m⁴ 7.2g* 8f² Sep 21] 32,000F, IR 180,000Y: strong,
lengthy colt: has scope: third foal: half-brother to 2 winners, including 3-y-o Rumpold:
dam, sprint winner in USA, out of Kentucky Oaks winner Sun And Snow: fractious in
preliminaries, won maiden at Ayr in August by 3 lengths: 9/1, good 1½ lengths second to
Fight Your Corner, pair clear, in minor event at Newbury, staying on well after travelling
smoothly under restraint until having to be switched: stays 1m: should make a smart 3-y-o
and win more races. *M. L. W. Bell*

WINGED ANGEL   4 ch.g. Prince Sabo 123 – Silky Heights (IRE) 67 (Head For   **53**
Heights 125) [2001 61: 9m⁶ f8g 10.1g 11m f9.4g⁴ Dec 11] modest handicapper: stays
easy 11f: acts on fibresand and firm going, possibly not on softer than good: visored once
at 3 yrs. *Miss J. A. Camacho*

WINGS OF A DOVE   3 b.f. Hernando (FR) 127 – Woodren (USA) 91 (Woodman   **– p**
(USA) 126) [2001 8.2v⁵ Oct 4] first foal: dam, Irish 2m winner, out of half-sister to
Assert, Bikala and Eurobird: 10/1, 12½ lengths fifth to Be Decisive in maiden at Nottingham, keeping on through beaten rivals when short of room and switched 2f out: will be
well suited by 1¼m+: will do better. *G. Wragg*

WINGS OF SOUL (USA)   3 b.c. Thunder Gulch (USA) 129 – Party Cited (USA)   **79**
110 (Alleged (USA) 138) [2001 87p: 10v⁵ 8m² 10.1m 8g 8g 10s 8d Nov 2] tall, good sort:
has plenty of scope: fair maiden: below form after second outing: best at 1m: acts on good
to firm and good to soft going: tried blinkered/tongue tied: none too consistent: sent to
France. *P. F. I. Cole*

WINNING PLEASURE (IRE)   3 b.g. Ashkalani (IRE) 128 – Karamana (Habitat   **73**
134) [2001 63: 7m⁵ 8m³ 7m 7.1m⁴ 8m 6g² 7s 8m⁵ f6g* f6g* f6g⁵ Dec 17] leggy, sparely-   **a84**
made gelding: fairly useful handicapper on all-weather, fair on turf: left A. Jarvis 6,200
gns before winning twice at Southwell in November: effective at 6f to easy 1m: acts on
fibresand, best runs on good/good to firm ground: visored/blinkered last 6 starts.
J. Balding

WINNING VENTURE   4 b.c. Owington 123 – Push A Button (Bold Lad (IRE) 133)   **105**
[2001 108: 7d 7.1s² 7.1d⁵ 7g² 7m² 7g 7g 7.6d 8g³ 7m³ 8d* 7g Oct 5] lengthy, good-topped
colt: unimpressive mover: useful performer: 1½ lengths second to Late Night Out in
listed race at Haydock on second outing: won 4-runner minor event at Goodwood in
September by 2 lengths from Big Future: ran as though something amiss final start: stays
1m: yet to race on heavy going, acts on any other: blinkered once: tongue tied nowadays:
sometimes slowly away: tends to take strong hold (has worn crossed noseband): has
wandered/flashed tail. *S. P. C. Woods*

WINSOME DOLPHIN (IRE)   4 b.g. Dolphin Street (FR) 125 – Wonder Bird (GER)   **–**
(Days At Sea (USA)) [2001 f12s f9.4g⁶ f11g a8.6g⁵ a11.5g Oct 10] 10,000F: third foal:
half-brother to German 11f winner Windfall (by Konigsstuhl): dam German 7f/1m
winner: little form: sold from P. Howling 1,800 gns after third start. *Karl Tuna, Sweden*

WINTER DOLPHIN (IRE)   3 b.f. Dolphin Street (FR) 125 – Winter Tern (USA)   **39**
(Arctic Tern (USA) 126) [2001 58: e7g 7f7g f7g⁶ 8.2s⁴ 8.1v 7d f7g f9.4g Jun 20] poor
performer: probably stays 1m: acts on fibresand and soft ground: has been slowly away:
tried tongue tied: none too consistent. *I. A. Wood*

WINTER JASMINE   3 b.f. Robellino (USA) 127 – Wild Truffes (IRE) (Danehill   **70**
(USA) 126) [2001 68: 6g⁶ 7s⁶ 7m⁴ 8.2f⁴ 8m 8m⁵ Jun 30] sturdy filly: fair maiden: stays
8.2f: acts on firm and soft going: visored penultimate start: sold 7,000 gns, sent to Israel.
B. J. Meehan

WINTERTIDE   5 b.g. Mtoto 134 – Winter Queen 60 (Welsh Pageant 132) [2001 f12g²   **79**
f11g⁵ Apr 28] 30,000 3-y-o: half-brother to several winners, including stayers Safety In
Numbers (smart, by Slip Anchor) and Winter Garden (useful, by Old Vic): dam 13f
winner at 4 yrs in Ireland: useful bumper performer: fair form when head second in
maiden at Wolverhampton on Flat debut: disappointing in similar event at Southwell
following month: likely to prove best at 1½m+. *R. A. Fahey*

WINTZIG   4 b.f. Piccolo 121 – Wrangbrook (Shirley Heights 130) [2001 72, a54: f8g   **–**
f9.4s 9.9s f8.5s⁵ Dec 26] angular filly: one-time fair performer, very much on downgrade.
J. M. Bradley

WISEMAN'S FERRY (USA) 2 ch.c. (Mar 11) Hennessy (USA) 122 – Emmaus **102**
(USA) (Silver Deputy (CAN)) [2001 6f* 5g³ 5m⁶ 6.3g² 6d⁴ 7d⁴ Sep 14] $775,000F,
$300,000Y: good-topped colt: second foal: dam unraced half-sister to smart Irish
performer up to 7f Bernstein and 2 US Grade 3 winners up to 9f: useful performer: won
minor event at Cork in May: 4 lengths second to Johannesburg in Anglesey Stakes at the
Curragh: fourth to same horse in Phoenix Stakes at Leopardstown (beaten 6¾ lengths)
and to Dubai Destination in Champagne Stakes at Doncaster (beaten 5½ lengths): stays
7f: acts on firm and good to soft ground: has worn crossed noseband: sent to USA.
A. P. O'Brien, Ireland

WISH 2 b.f. (Feb 3) Danehill (USA) 126 – Dazzle 116 (Gone West (USA)) [2001 5m² **79**
5m 6g* 6v Oct 27] smallish, sturdy filly: first foal: dam, best at 2 yrs when 5f/6f (Cherry
Hinton) winner, later won at 7f and third in 1000 Guineas and half-sister to dam of 3-y-o
Danehurst (by Danehill): fair performer: won maiden at Redcar in October: well beaten
in listed race final start: stays 6f: acts on good to firm ground. *Sir Michael Stoute*

WISHBONE ALLEY (IRE) 6 b.g. Common Grounds 118 – Dul Dul (USA) **– §**
(Shadeed (USA) 135) [2001 52, a60: 6g² e6g e6g⁶ f5g 6s 5g f8g f7g f6g Dec 17] strong, **a58 d**
close-coupled gelding: modest performer: on downgrade in 2001, leaving M. Dods 800
gns after fifth start: stays 6f: acts on fibresand, equitrack and good to firm going (probably
heavy): usually blinkered/visored: has looked reluctant to race, and carries head high.
R. Wilman

WISHEDHADGONEHOME (IRE) 4 b.f. Archway (IRE) 115 – Yavarro 44 **– §**
(Raga Navarro (ITY) 119) [2001 39§: f9.4s Jan 9] close-coupled filly: temperamental
maiden: often blinkered/visored. *M. Quinn*

WISHFUL THINKER 4 b.g. Prince Sabo 123 – Estonia (Kings Lake (USA) 133) **–**
[2001 53: f12g Jan 26] sturdy gelding: modest performer at 3 yrs: well held only outing in
2001. *N. Tinkler*

WISHINGWELL LADY (IRE) 2 b.f. (May 7) Desert King (IRE) 129 – Friday **–**
Night (USA) (Trempolino (USA) 135) [2001 8g 8s Oct 22] 3,500Y: small filly: second
foal: dam, ran once at 2 yrs, half-sister to smart performer up to 1½m Signorina Cattiva
and very smart stayer El Cuite: tailed off in maiden/listed event. *J. S. Wainwright*

WITH A WILL 7 b.g. Rambo Dancer (CAN) 107 – Henceforth 58 (Full of Hope 125) **72**
[2001 79: 8.5m 10f 8.3d 8.3g⁴ 9g³ 10m⁶ 10m 10.2d p10g Nov 28] good-bodied gelding:
fair handicapper: effective at 1m/easy 1¼m: acts on good to firm and good to soft going,
possibly not soft: often ridden by 7 lb claimer. *H. Candy*

WITHOUT WORDS 3 ch.f. Lion Cavern (USA) 117 – Sans Escale (USA) (Diesis **71 d**
133) [2001 8d⁵ 10s⁴ 8.3d⁴ 7.5m² 7.6m⁴ 7g³ 8f³ f7g 8d Oct 25] good-topped filly: fourth
reported foal: closely related to useful 1m winner who stayed 1¼m West Escape (by Gone
West) and half-sister to 4-y-o Escalade: dam, French 11f winner, daughter of Prix de
Diane winner Escaline: fair maiden: below form after debut: stays 1m: acts on good to
soft ground, probably on good to firm: tried blinkered (raced freely on one occasion): has
been edgy: has raced little: sold 5,000 gns in December. *M. A. Jarvis*

WITH PANACHE 3 b.g. Mtoto 134 – Panache Arabelle (Nashwan (USA) 135) **74**
[2001 12g 10m² 9m 8g 10v 12d Nov 6] 23,000Y: leggy gelding: third foal: half-brother to
smart 7f winner (including at 2 yrs) Maidaan (by Midyan) and fairly useful Irish 1999
2-y-o 6f winner Pissaro (by Green Desert): dam, once-raced half-sister to high-class 1¼m
performer Stagecraft, from family of Opera House and Kayf Tara: form in maidens only
on second start: left J. Noseda after next outing: should stay at least 1½m. *P. Monteith*

WITNESS 2 b.f. (Mar 10) Efisio 120 – Actualite (Polish Precedent (USA) 131) [2001 **63**
6m⁶ 6g 6d³ 5g⁵ 6m 6s Sep 24] good-topped filly: third foal: half-sister to 3-y-o Saltwood
and smart 1m (at 2 yrs) 1¼m winner Shamrock City (by Rock City): dam French 10.5f
winner from family of Old Vic and High Top: modest maiden: should be suited by 7f/1m:
acts on good to firm and good to soft ground. *B. W. Hills*

WITNEY ROYALE (IRE) 3 ch.g. Royal Abjar (USA) 121 – Collected (IRE) **75**
(Taufan (USA) 119) [2001 78: 7g 7m⁵ 8m⁴ 8g⁴ 10d⁵ 8.2m⁶ 8.5d 8m 9m⁶ 10m* 10.2g²
15m² 17.2g Oct 1] fair performer: won seller at Brighton in August: effective at 1¼m,
seemingly at 15f (not at further): yet to race on extremes of going: tried blinkered: has
been slowly away/hung left/seemed reluctant to finish. *J. S. Moore*

WITTABOURGH BLUE (IRE) 2 ch.f. (Apr 11) Bluegrass Prince (IRE) 110 – Sea **–**
Idol (IRE) 65 (Astronef 116) [2001 5.3m⁶ f6g May 21] first foal: dam maiden who stayed
6f: well beaten in maiden/seller. *J. S. Moore*

WODHILL FLORIN   3 ch.f. Dancing Spree (USA) – Muarij (Star Appeal 133)   –
[2001 10m 8m 9.7m 8d Nov 2] fourth reported foal: dam no form: well held in maidens/
handicap. *H. J. Collingridge*

WODHILL FOLLY   4 ch.f. Faustus (USA) 118 – Muarij (Star Appeal 133) [2001 57:   **65**
8m⁴ 8.2m⁶ 12d p12g⁵ Nov 13] fair maiden: should stay 1¼m: acts on good to firm going:
visored final start. *H. J. Collingridge*

WOLF VENTURE   3 ch.g. Wolfhound (USA) 126 – Relatively Sharp 86 (Sharpen   **86**
Up 127) [2001 75: e7g* e8g* 7m 8g* 8f* Jun 27] rather leggy, unfurnished gelding:
fluent mover: fairly useful performer: won maiden in April and handicap in May, both at
Lingfield, and 2 handicaps at Bath in June: best at 7f/1m: acts on equitrack and firm
going, below par on softer than good: sent to Macau. *S. P. C. Woods*

WONDERFUL MAN   5 ch.g. Magical Wonder (USA) 125 – Gleeful 72 (Sayf El   **56 §**
Arab (USA) 127) [2001 56: f11g f8g* f7g 9m 8m⁵ 7.5f 7m Jun 27] compact gelding:
modest handicapper: won at Southwell in April: best at 7f/easy 1m: acts on good to firm
ground and fibresand: unreliable. *R. D. E. Woodhouse*

WONDERGREEN   3 ch.g. Wolfhound (USA) 126 – Tenderetta (Tender King 123)   **58**
[2001 64: 7v 7d² 8m 7m 7.5m* 7.1f² Jun 18] tall, angular gelding: modest performer:
won claimer at Beverley in June: stays 1m: acts on good to firm and good to soft ground:
edgy sort: raced freely/found little fourth start: sent to Macau. *T. D. Easterby*

WONTCOSTALOTBUT   7 b.m. Nicholas Bill 125 – Brave Maiden 63 (Three Legs   **47**
128) [2001 57: 14.1v⁶ 16m 15.9d 17.1d⁵ 16s⁴ Oct 30] smallish, workmanlike mare: poor
handicapper nowadays: stays 17f: acts on heavy going. *M. J. Wilkinson*

WOODBASTWICK CHARM   4 b.g. Charmer 123 – Miss Mint (Music Maestro   –
119) [2001 41: f11g f9.4s e7g⁵ Jan 31] of little account nowadays. *N. P. Littmoden*

WOOD BE KING   2 b.c. (May 1) Prince Sabo 123 – Sylvan Dancer (IRE) 64   –
(Dancing Dissident (USA) 119) [2001 5f 5.1g f7g f7g Dec 14] 2,200Y: smallish colt: first
foal: dam sprint maiden: soundly beaten in maidens. *A. P. James*

WOODBORO KAT (IRE)   2 b.c. (Mar 2) Woodborough (USA) 112 – Kitty Kildare   **54**
(USA) 68 (Seattle Dancer (USA) 119) [2001 7f⁶ Jul 25] IR 25,000F, 21,000Y: first foal:
dam, Irish maiden who stayed 7f, out of sister to smart 7f/1m performer Arjuzah: 20/1,
slowly away and modest form when sixth in maiden at Lingfield. *M. Blanshard*

WOODBORO MINSTREL (IRE)   2 ch.c. (May 13) Woodborough (USA) 112 –   **58**
Quilting 80 (Mummy's Pet 125) [2001 5g f6g² p6g Dec 22] IR 8,000F: half-brother to
several winners, including useful Irish 6f (at 2 yrs) and 7f winner Quintiliani (by
Conquering Hero): dam 5f winner: best effort in sellers (modest form) when second to
Out of This World at Southwell, edging right: should stay 7f: acts on fibresand.
Mrs A. Duffield

WOODBURY   2 b.f. (Apr 30) Woodborough (USA) 112 – Jeewan 82 (Touching Wood   **69**
(USA) 127) [2001 5.3s⁶ 5.1m² 6f 5.7f² 6m⁶ 5m* 6m⁴ 6m⁵ 7d 7s Nov 10] 5,000Y: small
filly: sixth foal: half-sister to 7f to 1¼m winner Harry Browne (by Al Hareb) and 6f
winner Bello Gallico (by Gallic League), later winner abroad: dam 1½m winner: fair
performer: won seller at Windsor (left Mrs P. N. Dutfield) in August: good efforts in
nurseries next 2 starts: seems best at 5f/6f: acts on firm ground, some promise on soft: has
edged right. *M. D. I. Usher*

WOOD COLONY (USA)   3 b.g. Woodman (USA) 126 – Promenade Colony (USA)   **78**
(Pleasant Colony (USA)) [2001 8s⁵ 8.2f 10.5d⁴ 10.5g Aug 10] $125,000F, 55,000Y,
50,000 2-y-o: leggy, workmanlike gelding: moderate mover with a round action: second
foal: dam, won up to 9f in USA, sister to US Grade 2 2-y-o 6f/7f winner Dance Colony
and half-sister to US Grade 1 winners Another Review (9f) and No Review (1¼m): fair
maiden: easily best effort at 1m on soft ground: sold 6,500 gns. *J. L. Dunlop*

WOOD DALLING (USA)   3 b.c. Woodman (USA) 126 – Cloelia (USA) (Lyphard   **89**
(USA) 132) [2001 8d 8g⁴ 8m² 9m* 9.9m² Jul 1] 230,000Y: small, sturdy colt: fourth foal:
closely related to fairly useful Irish 1999 2-y-o 5f winner Finnan (by Mr Prospector) and
half-brother to 2 winners abroad, including useful French 11.5f winner Passinetti (by
Slew O'Gold): dam, French maiden, half-sister to dam of Bosra Sham and Hector
Protector: fairly useful form: won maiden at Ripon in June easily: good 6 lengths second
to Indian Creek in handicap at Goodwood (carried head slightly awkwardly) final start:
stays 1¼m: acts on good to firm going. *H. R. A. Cecil*

WOODFIELD   3 b.g. Zafonic (USA) 130 – Top Society (High Top 131) [2001 84: 8g   **68**
9s 7m⁶ 7g⁵ 7g⁴ 7m⁴ 7.6g² 8g 8d⁴ Oct 25] big, good-bodied gelding: fair maiden: will
prove best at 7f/1m: acts on soft and good to firm ground: races freely: consistent: sold
13,000 gns. *J. W. Hills*

WOODLAND BLAZE (IRE)   2 b.c. (Apr 18) Woodborough (USA) 112 – Alpine   **65**
Sunset (Auction Ring (USA) 123) [2001 5m 6g 5.7g Oct 1] IR 13,000F, IR 13,000Y:
eighth foal: half-brother to fairly useful 1991 2-y-o 5f/6f winner Afif (by Midyan) and 5f
to 1m winner Alpine Johnny (by Salse): dam unraced half-sister to very smart sprinter
Cyrano de Bergerac: easily best effort (fair form) when fifteenth of 29 in sales race at the
Curragh (disputed lead 5f) second start: may prove best at 5f/6f. *C. G. Cox*

WOODLAND PARK (USA)   3 b.g. Woodman (USA) 126 – Yemanja (USA)   **–**
(Alleged (USA) 138) [2001 10s 10s Apr 23] $170,000F, 130,000Y: fifth foal: closely
related to 4-y-o Robandela and half-brother to French 1¼m winner Stone Temple (by
Nureyev): dam, showed signs of ability in 3 starts, half-sister to Hector Protector and
Bosra Sham (both by Woodman): well held in maidens at Brighton (at no stage knocked
about) and Windsor: sold 4,200 gns in July, and gelded. *J. Noseda*

WOODLAND PRINCESS (IRE)   2 br.f. (Mar 15) Woodborough (USA) 112 –   **58**
Lagta 75 (Kris 135) [2001 6d 7.5m 7.5g⁶ Sep 19] IR 3,000Y: half-sister to several
winners, including useful 1¼m/1½m winner who stayed 1¾m Rudagi (by Persian
Bold), later winner abroad, and fairly useful 1m winner La Rochelle (by Salse): dam
1½m/1¾m winner: modest maiden: best effort when sixth at Beverley: should stay 1¼m.
J. L. Eyre

WOODLAND RIVER (USA)   4 ch.g. Irish River (FR) 131 – Wiener Wald (USA)   **89**
(Woodman (USA) 126) [2001 89: 8.1m 8m 8.2g² 7f 8.3m⁴ 7g 8s Oct 25] strong, good
sort: fairly useful handicapper: stays 1m: acts on good to firm going, seemingly not on
softer than good: has been slowly away/found little: has reportedly had breathing problem
(sometimes tongue tied): sold 2,500 gns. *J. R. Fanshawe*

WOODLANDS   4 b.g. Common Grounds 118 – Forest of Arden (Tap On Wood 130)   **61**
[2001 53: 7m 7g 7f 5m⁴ 6f³ 5.7m* 5m 5g 6m 5g 5.3m 6s p7g³ Dec 28] fair performer:
won handicap at Bath in July: stays 7f: acts on firm ground and polytrack: sometimes
slowly away. *S. Dow*

WOODLANDS ENERGY   10 b.m. Risk Me (FR) 127 – Hallowed (Wolver Hollow   **–**
126) [2001 f14.8s f16.2g f16.2g 16f Jun 25] of no account. *P. A. Pritchard*

WOODLAND SPIRIT   2 b.g. (Jan 31) Charnwood Forest (IRE) 125 – Fantastic   **82**
Charm (USA) (Seattle Dancer (USA) 119) [2001 6g 6f 6v² 6v Oct 26] 12,500Y:
good-topped gelding: has scope: fourth foal: half-brother to winners abroad by Barathea
and Arazi: dam, French 1m winner, half-sister to smart performer up to 1½m Germano:
best effort in maidens (fairly useful form) when second of 20 to Overload at Windsor:
gelded after final start: should stay 7f: acts on heavy ground. *D. R. C. Elsworth*

WOODLARK   2 b.c. (Feb 1) Zilzal (USA) 137 – Prima Volta 80 (Primo Dominie 121)   **69**
[2001 5.2m 6m⁵ 7d³ 6g 7.1s⁶ Sep 8] 64,000Y: second foal: half-brother to 3-y-o Bouncing
Bowdler: dam 6f (at 2 yrs) and 9f winner: fair maiden: probably stays 7f: acts on good to
firm and soft ground: tongue tied last 4 starts. *I. A. Balding*

WOODLYON (USA)   2 b.c. (Apr 18) Woodman (USA) 126 – Cloelia (USA)   **59 p**
(Lyphard (USA) 132) [2001 p6g⁶ Dec 28] 90,000Y: brother to 3-y-o Wood Dalling,
closely related to fairly useful Irish 1999 2-y-o 5f winner Finnan (by Mr Prospector) and
half-brother to 2 winners abroad, including useful French 11.5f winner Passinetti (by
Slew O'Gold): dam, French maiden, half-sister to dam of Bosra Sham and Hector
Protector: easy to back, 4½ lengths sixth of 14 to Agincourt Warrior in maiden at
Lingfield, slowly away and green but staying on: sure to improve. *J. Noseda*

WOODSMOKE (IRE)   2 b.g. (Apr 21) Woodborough (USA) 112 – Ma Bella Luna   **81**
76 (Jalmood (USA) 126) [2001 5.2d 5.3m* 5.1m* 5m 5g⁵ 5.2m 5.2m³ 5d⁶ 5.7m³ 5g 5g
f6s p6g Dec 28] IR 3,700F, IR 7,000Y: strong gelding: has a quick action: third foal: dam
1m winner: fairly useful performer: won maiden at Brighton and minor event at Bath in
May: mostly respectable efforts after, leaving R. Hannon after eleventh start: will prove
best at 5f/easy 6f: yet to race on extremes of going on turf, below form on all-weather.
J. S. Moore

WOOD STREET (IRE)   2 b.g. (Mar 19) Eagle Eyed (USA) 111 – San-Catrinia (IRE)   **60**
(Knesset (USA) 105) [2001 7g 8.1s 7.5g⁵ 7s 7v Oct 26] IR 8,500F, 7,000Y, resold 8,500Y:

big, strong gelding: third foal: half-brother to an Italian 6f (at 2 yrs) to 1m winner by Mujadil: dam unraced half-sister to smart stayer Santella Man: modest maiden: well below form in nurseries last 2 starts: gelded after: stays 1m: raced only on good going or softer. *Mrs A. J. Bowlby*

WOODWIND DOWN   4 b.f. Piccolo 121 – Bint El Oumara (Al Nasr (FR) 126)   **52**
[2001 63d: 9.2m² 10.5m Jul 6] sturdy filly: modest maiden: stays 9.3f: acts on equitrack and firm going, seemingly not on softer than good: blinkered once. *M. Todhunter*

WOODYATES   4 b.f. Naheez (USA) 126 – Night Mission (IRE) (Night Shift (USA))   **73**
[2001 57: 11.9s 11.9s 10m³ 12s* 13.3g* 10m² 12m⁴ 12m 10d² 12.1s² 16g³ 16.2s Sep 29] tall filly: fair handicapper: won at Salisbury and Newbury in May: ran badly final outing: stays 2m: acts on soft going, probably on good to firm: tried tongue tied. *D. R. C. Elsworth*

WOODY BATHWICK (IRE)   2 ch.c. (Apr 5) Woodborough (USA) 112 – Sheznice   **74**
(IRE) 58 (Try My Best (USA) 130) [2001 5.1d⁵ 5s⁶ 5m³ 6m 5m⁵ 5m³ 5m 7.1g 6d 5m² 5.7d Oct 25] IR 11,000F, 18,500Y: good-topped, close-coupled colt: has scope: fifth foal: half-brother to 3 winners, including 2m winner Matthias Mystique (by Sharrood) and a 5f winner in Italy by River Falls: dam, ran twice, closely related to smart performer up to 7f Glen Kate: fair maiden: left Dr J. Naylor after seventh start: second at Musselburgh: races freely, and best form at 5f: acts on good to firm going: none too consistent. *E. J. O'Neill*

WOOLFE   4 ch.f. Wolfhound (USA) 126 – Brosna (USA) (Irish River (FR) 131) [2001   **67 d**
75: f7s⁵ 9.2m⁵ 10m 8.3m 8m 9.2d⁴ 10.1g² 8.3s 8f² 9.1m 9.1v 8g Nov 7] strong, lengthy filly: fair maiden, on downgrade: stays 1¼m: acts on firm ground: sometimes visored: left I. Semple after eleventh start. *D. A. Nolan*

WORDS AND DEEDS (USA)   2 ch.g. (Mar 22) Shadeed (USA) 135 – Millfit   **71 p**
(USA) 62 (Blushing Groom (FR) 131) [2001 5m 5m² 5g Aug 13] 26,000F, 53,000Y: strong gelding: sixth foal: half-brother to 3 winners, including 7-y-o Tayseer and fairly useful 9f winner Quiet Millfit (by Quiet American): dam 7f winner: easily best effort in maidens (fair form) when beaten neck at Thirsk: raced on unfavoured part of course and not knocked about final start: should be suited by 6f/7f: remains capable of better. *Mrs J. R. Ramsden*

WORLDLY TREASURE (USA)   4 b. or br.g. Ghazi (USA) – Kitten's First (USA)   **85**
(Lear Fan (USA) 130) [2001 101: 7s 10f 8g 9d 8m 8g⁵ 8d⁵ 12g Oct 24] tall, useful-looking gelding: second living foal: half-brother to a minor stakes winner in USA by Broad Brush: dam, US 2-y-o winner up to 1m, half-sister to very smart US performer up to 1½m Down The Aisle: fairly useful performer: well beaten in Hunt Cup at Royal Ascot fifth outing, veering right under pressure: left D. Weld in Ireland before final start: stays 1¼m: acts on firm and good to soft going: blinkered 3 of last 4 starts: none too consistent. *C. Simon, USA*

WORLD SPINNER   2 b.c. (Feb 2) Indian Ridge 123 – Howaida (IRE) 85 (Night Shift   **61**
(USA)) [2001 7m Jun 30] good-bodied colt: has scope: first foal: dam, 1m winner, half-sister to useful performers up to 1m Himiko and Without Reserve: 10/1 and burly, seventh of 9 to Dubai Status in maiden at Newmarket: dead. *E. A. L. Dunlop*

WORTH A GAMBLE   3 ch.g. So Factual (USA) 120 – The Strid (IRE) 53 (Persian   **52**
Bold 123) [2001 –: 9g 8g⁴ 7s 8.3v³ f9.4g Nov 27] good-topped gelding: modest maiden: stays 1m: acts on heavy going: none too consistent. *H. E. Haynes*

WORTH A RING   3 b.f. Chaddleworth (IRE) 103 – Ring of Pearl (Auction Ring   **–**
(USA) 123) [2001 36: f8g⁵ 10f f12g Jun 21] angular, good-topped filly: little form at 3 yrs. *J. Cullinan*

WORTHILY (USA)   3 b. or br.c. Northern Spur (IRE) 133 – Worth's Girl (USA)   **105**
(Devil's Bag (USA)) [2001 105: 11v³ 10v⁴ 11.5g⁵ 16.2m 14.8g 10.4g 11.9m² 12g⁵ 10g⁶ 10d a10f³ a9.7f⁵ Dec 21] big, leggy colt: useful performer: best efforts at 3 yrs when 7¼ lengths fifth to Perfect Sunday in Derby Trial at Lingfield third start, and neck second to Staging Post in handicap at York: below best after, leaving M. Channon before penultimate appearance: probably stays 2m: acts on heavy and good to firm going: has been edgy/taken good hold. *K. P. McLaughlin, UAE*

WORTH THE RISK   4 b.f. Chaddleworth (IRE) 103 – Bay Risk (Risk Me (FR) 127)   **–**
[2001 43: f12g f11g 12.4g 12g 16.2s Aug 16] lengthy, sparely-made filly: little form in 2001. *Don Enrico Incisa*

WOTAN (IRE) 3 ch.g. Wolfhound (USA) 126 – Triple Tricks (IRE) 70 (Royal Academy (USA) 130) [2001 8.1d⁵ 7.1s⁶ 7.1v⁶ 10s Oct 30] 16,500F, 7,000Y: strong gelding: second foal: half-brother to Swedish winner up to 1m Golden Note (by Efisio): dam, maiden who stayed 1m, out of half-sister to smart sprinter Jester: little form. *R. Curtis* –

WRANGEL (FR) 7 ch.g. Tropular – Swedish Princess (Manado 130) [2001 50: f12g³ f16g Mar 26] little form in 2001. *B. J. Llewellyn* –

<h1 style="text-align:center">X</h1>

XALOC BAY (IRE) 3 br.g. Charnwood Forest (IRE) 125 – Royal Jade 82 (Last Tycoon 131) [2001 73: 6s³ 6s 7m 6g⁶ 6s 7.1m⁵ 6m 6g² 6.1v 6v 7v⁶ f7g* p7g⁵ f6g* f6g³ p6g⁴ p7g⁵ Dec 28] sturdy gelding: poor mover: fair performer: won maiden at Southwell and handicap at Wolverhampton, both in November: effective at 6f/7f: acts on all-weather, soft and good to firm going: tried blinkered, visored nowadays. *K. R. Burke* **71**

XANADU 5 ch.g. Casteddu 111 – Bellatrix 45 (Persian Bold 123) [2001 85: 6v 5s 5d 6d 5m 5g⁵ 6m* 5m⁶ 6f 5f⁵ 5g 5m⁵ 6g 5m 6v Oct 16] big, strong gelding: fair performer in 2001: made all in amateur minor event at Hamilton in June: stays 6f: best on good going or firmer: often slowly away but usually recovers to race up with pace: none too consistent. *Miss L. A. Perratt* **66**

XCEL (IRE) 2 b.c. (Mar 19) Revoque (IRE) 122 – Myran (IRE) 53 (In The Wings 128) [2001 7g 7.1g 7.1v Sep 29] IR 25,000F, IR 70,000Y: first foal: dam, Irish maiden who stayed 1½m, out of half-sister to Middle Park Stakes winner Balla Cove: modest form at best in maidens: should stay 1m: blinkered last 2 starts. *L. M. Cumani* **57**

Mr M. J. Dawson's "Xtra"

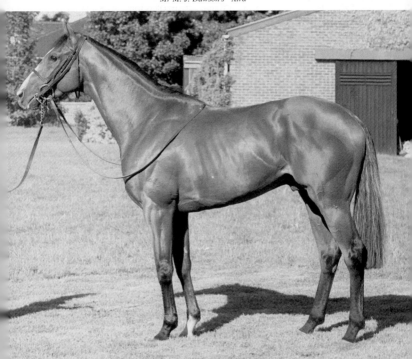

XELLANCE (IRE) 4 b.g. Be My Guest (USA) 126 – Excellent Alibi (USA) **83** (Exceller (USA) 129) [2001 81: 13.9d 16v³ 16g* 16.5s f16g² Nov 19] leggy gelding: **a91** fairly useful handicapper: off 14 months before first start in 2001: won 17-runner Tote Bookmakers Stakes at Musselburgh in November: needs further than 1½m and stays 2¼m: acts on fibresand and any turf going: races prominently. *M. Johnston*

XIBALBA 4 b.g. Zafonic (USA) 130 – Satanic Dance (FR) 80 (Shareef Dancer (USA) **66 d** 135) [2001 70: 9.9m⁶ 10m 11.5g⁵ 10m 8d f9.4f² p10g⁶ f9.4s Dec 27] leggy, angular gelding: fair performer, on downgrade: stays 1¼m: acts on good to soft and good to firm going (lightly raced on fibresand/polytrack): visored once, blinkered last 3 starts. *C. E. Brittain*

XIPE TOTEC 3 ch.g. Pivotal 124 – Northern Bird 86 (Interrex (CAN)) [2001 86: 6d **71** 6m 8.2f⁶ 8m⁶ 8.2m 8g³ 7g 7.5d 8s 7s* Oct 16] strong gelding: fair performer: left R. Fahey after second appearance: not so good as at 2 yrs, but still won selling handicap at Leicester in October: probably stays 1m: acts on firm and soft going: sold 5,200 gns. *C. E. Brittain*

XSYNNA 5 b.g. Cyrano de Bergerac 120 – Rose Ciel (IRE) 80 (Red Sunset 120) [2001 **58 §** –, a66: f6g e6g 5s 7d 5.1m 5.2m 5.3m 6m 5.7g f6g* f6g⁵ 5.7m 5.5d 8m 6m² 7m 6m⁶ f6g **a66 §** 7.1g⁴ 5.1d² 6v f6g f6g Dec 10] tall gelding: unimpressive mover: fair handicapper on all-weather, modest on turf: won at Southwell (final start for J. Gilbert) in June: effective at 5f to 7f: acts on firm going, good to soft and fibresand/equitrack: tried blinkered/ visored: has reportedly bled from nose, including 3 of last 4 outings: unreliable. *M. J. Polglase*

XTRA 3 b.c. Sadler's Wells (USA) 132 – Oriental Mystique 97 (Kris 135) [2001 92p: **113** 11.5g⁴ 12m² 11.9d* 11.9g⁵ Aug 21] well-made colt: smart performer, lightly raced: made all in listed race at Haydock in July, beating Tramway by length: good 5¼ lengths fifth to Milan in Great Voltigeur Stakes at York final outing: will stay at least 1¾m: raced mainly on good ground or softer. *L. M. Cumani*

XTRASENSORY 2 b.f. (May 11) Royal Applause 124 – Song of Hope 103 (Chief **96** Singer 131) [2001 6m* 6m 6m⁵ Aug 23] 50,000Y: quite good-topped filly: half-sister to several winners, including 5f (at 2 yrs) and 7f winner Song of Skye (by Warning) and 7f/ 1m winner Kingdom Princess (by Forzando): dam 2-y-o 5f winner: useful form: won maiden at Goodwood in May by 2½ lengths from Massarra: off 2 months, then better effort in pattern races after when 6¾ lengths fifth to Queen's Logic in Lowther Stakes at York: will stay 7f. *R. Hannon*

Y

YABINT EL SHAM 5 b.m. Sizzling Melody 117 – Dalby Dancer 71 (Bustiki) [2001 **–** 53, a75: f6s* f6s* f5g f5g f6g⁵ Mar 24] leggy, unfurnished mare: modest performer: **a60** won handicap at Wolverhampton and seller at Southwell in January: best at 5f/6f: acts on good to firm going and fibresand: has had tongue tied: pulls hard: sold 1,600 gns. *B. A. McMahon*

YA HABIBI 3 b.g. Selkirk (USA) 129 – Rani (IRE) 102 (Groom Dancer (USA) 128) **67** [2001 10s 10v 10g⁴ Nov 5] tall, quite good-topped gelding: fourth foal: half-brother to a winner in Spain by Sabrehill: dam, 11.5f winner who stayed 1½m well, from family of Oh So Sharp: fair form in maidens: off over 5 months and left L. Cumani prior to third start (best effort, though carried head awkwardly): subsequently gelded: should stay 1½m. *T. D. Easterby*

YA HAJAR 2 b.f. (Feb 26) Lycius (USA) 124 – Shy Lady (FR) 91 (Kaldoun (FR) 122) **106** [2001 6m³ 6m* 7d² 8s⁶ Oct 7] strong, well-grown, close-coupled filly: first foal: dam, German 2-y-o 5f and (listed race) 6f winner, out of half-sister to smart 6f/7f performer Diffident: useful performer: made all in maiden at Ascot in July and Prix du Calvados at Deauville (beat Lady High Havens by 1½ lengths) in August: weakened after helping force pace in Prix Marcel Boussac at Longchamp final start: stays 7f: acts on good to firm and good to soft ground. *M. R. Channon*

YAHESKA (IRE) 4 b.f. Prince of Birds (USA) 121 – How Ya Been (IRE) (Last **–** Tycoon 131) [2001 –: f12g f8g 11.9g 8f 10.2g Aug 27] sparely-made filly: little form: tried blinkered. *J. M. Bradley*

Prix du Conseil de Paris, Longchamp—a fifteenth career success for Yavana's Pace,
who holds off the challenges of Epitre (blinkers) and Foundation Spirit

YALAIL (IRE)   5 b.g. Perugino (USA) 84 – Cristalga 90 (High Top 131) [2001 44: –
f12g e10g 11.9s⁵ 11.9f f14g 12g 12g f14.8s Sep 6] little form in 2001: left G. Prodromou
after fifth start: tried visored/tongue tied. *Miss V. Haigh*

YALLA LARA   2 b.f. (Feb 4) Marju (IRE) 127 – Versami (USA) (Riverman (USA)   – p
131) [2001 5g May 6] first foal: dam, lightly raced in Italy, sister to useful performers
around 1m Underwater and Maze Garden: 12/1, never-dangerous seventh of 8 in minor
event at Salisbury: should do better. *I. A. Balding*

YANUS   3 b.g. Inchinor 119 – Birsay (Bustino 136) [2001 –: 10.1m² 8.3m 14f³ 10s*   **69**
10.9d* 11.9d 10g 11.9s 10.9m 10.9v³ 10s Oct 22] workmanlike gelding: fair handicapper:
won at Ayr in July and August: stays 11f: acts on soft and good to firm ground, probably
on heavy: usually makes running: carried head high penultimate start. *J. S. Goldie*

YAOUNDE (IRE)   2 gr.f. (Jan 27) Barathea (IRE) 127 – Lost Dream (Niniski (USA)   **72**
125) [2001 8m 8.3v² 8g⁶ Nov 7] second foal: dam, ran twice, half-sister to smart 1983
2-y-o sprinter Rocket Alert: 50/1, easily best effort in maidens (fair form) when second to
Ski For Me at Windsor: eased considerably when held final start: will stay 1¼m: acts on
heavy ground. *E. J. O'Neill*

YAQOOTAH (USA)   3 ch.f. Gone West (USA) – Sweet Roberta (USA) (Roberto   **72**
(USA) 131) [2001 70p: 7d 7m³ 6m² 6g³ 5g* Jul 30] fair performer: won maiden at
Newcastle in July: stayed 7f: acted on good to firm going: took good hold/raced
prominently: visits Nashwan. *E. A. L. Dunlop*

YAROB (IRE)   8 ch.g. Unfuwain (USA) 131 – Azyaa 101 (Kris 135) [2001 99: f8g   **90**
f9.4g 7g² 10.3m 8.5m³ 10m 10.3f* 8.5f* 8.1m 10.1d² 8.5m⁶ Aug 15] quite good-topped
gelding: fairly useful nowadays: won claimers at Chester and Epsom in June/July:
effective at 1m (given bit of a test) to 11f: acts on firm going, good to soft and fibresand:
has been edgy/raced freely/folded tamely: often leads, and possibly best on turning track:
none too reliable. *D. Nicholls*

YARROW BRIDGE   2 b.f. (Jan 31) Selkirk (USA) 129 – Both Sides Now (USA)   **75**
(Topsider (USA)) [2001 7.1d 6d 7g⁴ 6.1m* Sep 17] 29,000F: small filly: poor mover:
half-sister to several winners, including useful 1997 2-y-o 6f/7f (Solario Stakes) winner
Little Indian (by Little Missouri) and useful 6f (at 2 yrs) and 1¼m (in UAE) winner
Mukaddar (by Elmaamul): dam placed in USA: fair performer: second favourite, won
maiden at Warwick by 1¼ lengths from Real Ambition, dictating pace: should stay 1m:
acts on good to firm going. *R. Hannon*

YASELDA   2 b.f. (Apr 2) Green Desert (USA) 127 – Pripet (USA) 86 (Alleged (USA)   **82**
138) [2001 6m* Jul 4] rather leggy filly: fifth living foal: sister to useful 1997 2-y-o 5.5f
(Prix Robert Papin)/6f winner who stayed 1¼m Greenlander and half-sister to 1¾m
winner Priluki (by Lycius): dam, 2m winner, sister to 1000 Guineas/Oaks winner Midway

1110

Lady: 11/4 and green, fairly useful form when winning 5-runner maiden at Southwell, leading close home to beat Lillies Bordello a neck: should stay 1m. *C. E. Brittain*

YASEY (JPN) 2 bl.c. (May 16) Sunday Silence (USA) – Millracer (USA) 79 (Le **96** Fabuleux 133) [2001 8m^2 7s^2 Sep 30] $170,000F in Japan: rather leggy, quite attractive colt: easy mover: brother to 3 winners in Japan, including 1994 Group 1 2-y-o 1m winner Fuji Kiseki, and half-brother to several winners: dam, 7f winner in Britain and later successful in USA, out of half-sister to smart 1981 2-y-o sprinter Peterhof: favourite, useful form in maiden at Doncaster and minor event at Ascot: beaten neck by Legal Approach in latter, leading 2f out but drifting left and caught close home: likely to prove best up to 1m: wore crossed noseband both starts. *D. R. Loder*

YAVANA'S PACE (IRE) 9 ch.g. Accordion – Lady In Pace (Burslem 123) [2001 **118** 120: 13.4f^4 15.5m^6 20f 12g^3 11.9s* 15.5d* 14m 12v^2 12v* 15.5v^5 Oct 28] tall, angular gelding: has a markedly round action: smart performer: won minor event at Haydock in August, Prix Gladiateur at Longchamp (beat Woodford Reserve 2½ lengths) in September and Prix du Conseil de Paris at Longchamp (beat Epitre by ½ length) in October: a few creditable efforts otherwise, including when 4 lengths second to Kutub in Preis von Europa at Cologne and fifth to Vinnie Roe in Prix Royal-Oak at Longchamp: effective at 1½m to 15.5f: has form on firm/good to firm going, but needs good or softer nowadays: has proved troublesome before start/been early to post, but is genuine once under way: races prominently. *M. Johnston*

YAZAIN (IRE) 5 b.g. Pips Pride 117 – Trust Sally 65 (Sallust 134) [2001 71: f8g **–** 16m f8.5g 7m Sep 22] disappointing maiden: left G. Prodromou after second start: tried blinkered/tongue tied. *P. S. McEntee*

Mrs Joan Keaney's "Yavana's Pace"

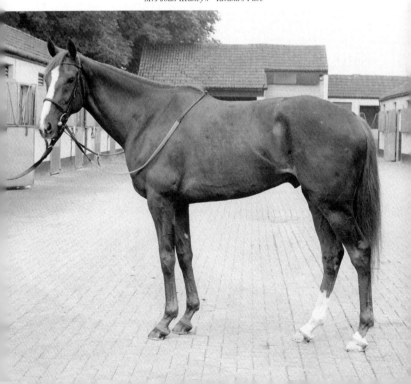

YAZOO RIVER REBEL 2 b.g. (May 20) Sabrehill (USA) 120 – Bidweaya (USA) –
45 (Lear Fan (USA) 130) [2001 8m Sep 8] fourth foal: half-brother to 3-y-o Red River
Rebel: dam, 1m winner at 5/6 yrs, half-sister to Gimcrack winner Chilly Billy: 25/1, tailed
off in maiden at Thirsk. *J. R. Norton*

YEAR TWO THOUSAND 3 b.c. Darshaan 133 – Vingt Et Une (FR) (Sadler's **109**
Wells (USA) 132) [2001 12g² 12m* 16.2m⁴ 14.8g Jul 11] strong, well-made, attractive
colt: first foal: dam, French 1¼m winner, sister to very smart 1m to 1½m performer
Johann Quatz and half-sister to Prix du Jockey Club winner Hernando: useful performer:
won 4-runner maiden at Newmarket (beat Xtra by 4 lengths, edged left/still green) in
June: very good ¾-length fourth to And Beyond in Queen's Vase at Royal Ascot
(wandered having led early in straight) next start, but well held in listed race at
Newmarket final one: stays 2m: raced only on good/good to firm ground: moved poorly
to post at Royal Ascot: stays in training. *H. R. A. Cecil*

YEAST 9 b.g. Salse (USA) 128 – Orient 106 (Bay Express 132) [2001 85: 10g 8g 8m **64**
7.6m² 8m 10m⁶ 8m 8s Sep 24] big, good-bodied gelding: formerly smart, just modest
nowadays: best form at 7f to 1¼m on good going or firmer: has swished tail: possibly
needs to dominate: none too consistent. *W. J. Haggas*

YELLOW SOIL STAR (IRE) 2 b.f. (Jan 24) Perugino (USA) 84 – Standing **48 +**
Ovation (Godswalk (USA) 130) [2001 f5g⁶ 5g f5g⁴ 6f⁴ 5f⁵ 7m f5g 8s Oct 17] IR 4,800Y,
5,000 2-y-o: small filly: half-sister to several winners, including 1989 2-y-o 7f winner Go
Holimarine (by Taufan) and French 1½m winner Sinuhe (by Law Society): dam Irish
1½m winner: poor maiden: left P. D. Evans after seventh start: seems to stay 1m: visored/
blinkered last 4 starts in Britain. *P. P. Corrigan, Ireland*

YELLOW TRUMPET 3 b.f. Petong 126 – Daffodil Fields (Try My Best (USA) –
130) [2001 75: 6g 7f May 23] rather leggy, lengthy filly: fair winner only 2-y-o outing:
well held in 2001: sold 30,000 gns in December. *M. L. W. Bell*

YENALED 4 gr.g. Rambo Dancer (CAN) 107 – Fancy Flight (FR) 74 (Arctic Tern **69**
(USA) 126) [2001 71: 8m² 8.3d 7.1m 8m 9f² 9f² 10.1m⁵ 10.3m² 10s⁵ 10.1g³ 9m 10.1f⁵ **a78 +**
f9.4g³ f8g³ f9.4g³ 8g* f8.5g* f8.5f f9.4s⁴ Dec 27] leggy, sparely-made gelding: fair
handicapper: won at Musselburgh and Wolverhampton in November: stays 1¼m, at least
when conditions aren't testing: acts on fibresand and any turf going: visored (below form)
once: best held up: consistent. *I. Semple*

YERTLE (IRE) 4 b.g. Turtle Island (IRE) 123 – Minatina (IRE) 78 (Ela-Mana-Mou **69**
132) [2001 69d: 13.3g² 14s 14m³ 16m 14.8m⁶ 16.4g* 16g* Sep 5] smallish gelding: fair
handicapper: won at Folkestone in August and Lingfield in September: stays 16.4f: acts
on good to soft ground: refused to race in net muzzle fourth start. *J. A. R. Toller*

YETTI 3 ch.f. Aragon 118 – Willyet (Nicholas Bill 125) [2001 71: 5.1s* 5g² 5d 5m 6g **73**
Jul 23] angular filly: fair performer: sweating and on toes, won maiden at Nottingham in
April: well held last 3 starts: raced only at 5f/6f: yet to race on heavy going, acts on any
other. *H. Candy*

YNYSMON 3 b.g. Mind Games 121 – Florentynna Bay 61 (Aragon 118) [2001 74: **76 §**
5.1f⁵ 6g² 6s 6m⁶ 6f 6m 5g 6d 7v f5g f5g f6g f7s f6s* Dec 21] lengthy, rather unfurnished
gelding: fair performer: sold 900 gns and left A. Berry after tenth start: tongue tied, won
seller at Southwell in December easily: effective at 5f/6f: acts on firm going and
fibresand: blinkered 4 starts prior to final one: edgy sort (has been early/led to post),
and has given trouble in preliminaries: sometimes slowly away: ungenuine. *S. R. Bowring*

YORK CLIFF 3 b.c. Marju (IRE) 127 – Azm (Unfuwain (USA) 131) [2001 89p: 8d* **86**
8m⁴ May 31] good-bodied, quite attractive colt: fairly useful form in 3 starts: won maiden
at Newbury (wore crossed noseband) in April by ½ length: well held in minor event at
Ayr next time: likely to stay 1¼m. *J. H. M. Gosden*

YORKER (USA) 3 b.g. Boundary (USA) 117 – Shallows (USA) (Cox's Ridge **73**
(USA)) [2001 58: f7g* 7s² 8.1m f7g³ f7g f8g² p8g³ Dec 22] strong, lengthy gelding: fairly **a83**
useful on all-weather, fair on turf: won handicap at Southwell in April: off over 4 months
and gelded after fourth start: stays 1m: acts on fibresand, polytrack, soft and good to firm
going. *J. M. P. Eustace*

YORKIE 2 b.g. (Mar 22) Aragon 118 – Light The Way 72 (Nicholas Bill 125) [2001 **70**
7g⁴ 6s⁴ 7m 7m⁶ Sep 22] half-brother to 3 winners by Rambo Dancer, including 4-y-o
Benbyas and fairly useful 6f (including at 2 yrs)/7f winner Carambo: dam 1m seller
winner: fair maiden: stays 7f: acts on soft and good to firm ground: wandered last 2 starts.
I. A. Wood

YORKIES BOY   6 gr.h. Clantime 101 – Slipperose 72 (Persepolis (FR) 127) [2001   **109 §**
102: 6s⁵ 5m⁶ 6g* 6g 7.1d 6f 6m³ 5.7m⁴ 6.8g 6.1m⁶ 6d⁴ 7s⁶ 6m 6m³ 7s 6s Nov 10]
good-bodied horse: useful performer: won handicap at York in May by ¾ length from
Candleriggs: mostly well below form after: effective at 5f to 7f: acts on soft and good to
firm going: tried blinkered: usually races prominently: unreliable. *A. Berry*

YORKSHIRE GREY (IRE)   3 gr.g. Royal Abjar (USA) 121 – Nirvavita (FR)   **68**
(Highest Honor (FR) 124) [2001 7d 7g 7m³ 9m⁶ 7m 7g 8.5m³ 10m⁶ f8.5g⁴ 8s f8g Oct 22]
IR 26,000F, 26,000G: leggy, good-topped gelding: first foal: dam French 1m winner out
of half-sister to very smart French 7f/1m performer Nikos: fair maiden handicapper: stays
8.5f: acts on fibresand and good to firm going: has raced freely, including when blinkered
sixth outing: sold 11,000 gns. *A. C. Stewart*

YORKSHIRE (IRE)   7 ch.g. Generous (IRE) 139 – Ausherra (USA) 106 (Diesis 133)   **113**
[2001 110: 12v² 14.1v² 16.1g* 18.7m⁴ 15.9g 18d 16d⁵ 12s⁵ 15.5s Nov 23] rangy gelding:
smart performer: made all in handicaps at Newmarket (by 4 lengths from Court Shareef)
and Chester in July/August: ran creditably after only when fifth to Capal Garmon in
Jockey Club Cup at Newmarket seventh outing: effective at 1½m (given a test) to 2¾m:
probably acts on any turf going: blinkered once: usually heavily bandaged in front: ran
badly fifth and sixth starts: usually takes good hold and leads. *P. F. I. Cole*

YORK WHINE (IRE)   3 ch.f. Tagula (IRE) 116 – Cwm Deri (IRE) (Alzao (USA)   **61**
117) [2001 62: f7g² f7s* f7g f8g³ f8g f8g f11g⁴ f8g 8f² 7.5m⁴ 8.2f Jun 11] sturdy filly:
modest handicapper: left W. Jarvis before winning at Wolverhampton (apprentices) in
January: broke down final start: stayed 1m: acted on fibresand and firm ground: was tried
visored/blinkered: dead. *M. J. Polglase*

YOU DA MAN (IRE)   4 b.g. Alzao (USA) 117 – Fabled Lifestyle (Kings Lake (USA)   **68**
133) [2001 80§: f9.4g 10s 10g 10g⁴ 10f 11.9d 11.9m 11.6m⁴ Jul 16] well-made gelding:
fair performer: stays easy 1½m: acts on fibresand/equitrack and good to firm going:
blinkered once as 3-y-o: has looked reluctant: probably needs exaggerated waiting
tactics: sold 1,800 gns. *R. Hannon*

YOUNG ALEX (IRE)   3 ch.g. Midhish 109 – Snipe Hunt (IRE) (Stalker 121) [2001   **82**
72: e7g* e6g² f7g⁴ 7m⁴ 8.3m² 8f⁵ 7m⁴ 7m⁴ 7m³ p7g⁵ p7g³ p8g⁴ p7g³ Dec 29] leggy,   **a92**
workmanlike gelding: fairly useful performer: won handicap at Lingfield in February:
best effort in handicap there on final outing: effective at 6f to easy 1m: better form on
equitrack and polytrack than fibresand, and acts on firm going: has been slowly away:
consistent. *K. R. Burke*

YOUNG ANNIE   3 b.f. Young Ern 120 – Snugfit Annie 49 (Midyan (USA) 124) [2001   **–**
7m 7m 7m f7g f8g 10s 10d 14.1s f11g Nov 30] 7,800Y: third reported foal: dam, third in
6f seller, ran only at 2 yrs: of no account. *M. J. Ryan*

YOUNG BIGWIG (IRE)   7 b.g. Anita's Prince 126 – Humble Mission (Shack   **63**
(USA) 118) [2001 62, a59: f6s² f7g* f7g f7g f7g 6g* 6m² 6m³ 6.1f² f6g² 6f 6g⁴ 6m 6v f5g   **a59**
f7g f6g Dec 10] strong, lengthy gelding: modest handicapper nowadays: won at
Wolverhampton in February and Ripon in May: effective at 6f/easy 7f: acts on fibresand,
firm and soft going: usually blinkered: none too consistent. *D. W. Chapman*

YOUNG IBNR (IRE)   6 b.g. Imperial Frontier (USA) 112 – Zalatia 97 (Music Boy   **51**
124) [2001 57: f5g³ 5.1d f5g⁴ f5g 5d 5.7m 5.1g Aug 3] small gelding: modest performer:
best at 5f: acts on fibresand/equitrack, soft and good to firm going: tried blinkered/visored
earlier in career. *B. A. McMahon*

YOUNG LION   2 b.g. (Mar 31) Lion Cavern (USA) 117 – Shimmer 55 (Bustino 136)   **87**
[2001 6m 6m³ 6f 5m* 6g* 7m³ 7g 6g 6v⁶ p7g Nov 13] 10,000Y: useful-looking gelding:
fifth living foal: dam maiden daughter of smart middle-distance performer Light Duty
and from family of Nashwan, Nayef and Unfuwain: fairly useful performer: won maiden
at Lingfield in June and nursery at Pontefract in July: below form last 4 starts, gelded after
final one: should stay 1m: acts on good to firm going. *C. E. Brittain*

YOUNG MAZAAD (IRE)   8 b.g. Mazaad 106 – Lucky Charm (IRE) (Pennine Walk   **–**
120) [2001 –: e8g f8g Jan 26] seems of little account nowadays. *D. C. O'Brien*

YOUNG MONASH (IRE)   3 b.g. General Monash (USA) 107 – Sound Pet (Runnett   **38**
125) [2001 38: 6m 6.1f f6g 5g f6g⁶ f7g Dec 3] plain gelding: poor maiden: stays 6f.
B. S. Rothwell

YOUNG ROSEIN   5 b.m. Distant Relative 128 – Red Rosein 97 (Red Sunset 120)   **74**
[2001 65: 8s 8.3m³ 8f³ 8m* 8.3m³ 7.1f* 7.9m⁵ 8g² 7g 7m³ 7g 7s 7d 7s Nov 10] leggy

mare: fair handicapper: won at Ripon in May and Haydock in July: effective at 7f/1m: acts on any going. *Mrs G. S. Rees*

YOUNG TERN 3 b.g. Young Ern 120 – Turnaway 79 (Runnett 125) [2001 63: f8g⁶ **63** 7m 10m 10.9d⁶ 8g⁶ 8d 8s f8g⁶ f8.5g² f8.5s² Dec 26] smallish gelding: modest maiden handicapper: stays 8.5f: acts on fibresand and good to soft going: blinkered last 2 outings: sometimes starts slowly/pulls hard. *C. G. Cox*

YOUNG-UN 6 b.h. Efisio 120 – Stardyn (Star Appeal 133) [2001 69, a85: f8g³ f7g³ **–** f9.4s* f8.5g³ 8g f8g f8g⁵ p10g f8g p8g Dec 22] quite good-topped horse: fairly useful **a93 d** handicapper: won at Wolverhampton in January: on downgrade after: stays 1¼m: acts on fibresand, well held on polytrack and only turf starts in 2001: tried blinkered/tongue tied: best held up. *M. J. Ryan*

YOU'RE AN ANGEL 2 b.f. (Mar 5) Pursuit of Love 124 – Prima Cominna 86 **70** (Unfuwain (USA) 131) [2001 5.1g⁴ 5.7m 7m⁴ 7s² 7s Oct 5] 10,000Y: second foal: dam, 2-y-o 6f winner, out of sister to very smart sprinter Primo Dominie: fair maiden: second at Epsom: better at 7f than shorter: acts on soft and good to firm ground: found little final start. *R. Hannon*

YOU'RE SPECIAL (USA) 4 b.g. Northern Flagship (USA) 96 – Pillow Mint **84** (USA) (Stage Door Johnny) [2001 94: 18v⁶ 16s² 14s 17.5m 13.9d 14.1s⁴ 16g f16.2f⁴ Dec 5] good-topped, workmanlike gelding: shows knee action: fairly useful performer: neck second to Guard Duty in Queen's Prize at Kempton in April: below form after: should be well suited by further than 2m: acts on heavy going and fibresand, probably not on ground firmer than good: races prominently: visored twice. *P. C. Haslam*

Y TO KMAN (IRE) 3 b.c. Mujadil (USA) 119 – Hazar (IRE) 75 (Thatching 131) **97** [2001 93: 6m³ 6m 6m 6g 6g Sep 8] lengthy, angular colt: useful handicapper: ran well when close third to Vicious Dancer in valuable event at Lingfield in May: well held last 3 starts: effective at 5f/easy 6f: unraced on firm going, acted on any other: dead. *R. Hannon*

Z

ZAAJEL (IRE) 2 b.c. (Mar 10) Nashwan (USA) 135 – Mehthaaf (USA) 121 **90 p** (Nureyev (USA) 131) [2001 7v² Oct 26] sturdy, lengthy colt: fluent mover: fourth foal: brother to fairly useful 1½m winner Raaqi and 3-y-o Najah: dam, 6f (at 2 yrs) and 1m (Irish 1000 Guineas) winner, closely related to high-class sprinter Elnadim and grand-daughter of outstanding broodmare Fall Aspen: 9/2, 5 lengths second of 12 to Foreign Accent in maiden at Doncaster, travelling strongly before running green and edging left as winner asserted: likely to stay 1¼m: useful performer in the making, sure to win races. *J. L. Dunlop*

ZAAJER (USA) 5 ch.g. Silver Hawk (USA) 123 – Crown Quest (USA) (Chief's **–** Crown (USA)) [2001 115: 14.1v⁵ 12s 13.3v⁵ May 19] angular, good-topped gelding: smart performer at 4 yrs: well held in 2001 (gelded after final start). *J. A. B. Old*

ZABAT 2 ch.c. (May 8) Zamindar (USA) 116 – Pluvial 90 (Habat 127) [2001 6f May **–** 29] 30,000Y: close-coupled, useful-looking colt: half-brother to numerous winners, including 4-y-o Awake, smart sprinter Monaassib (by Cadeaux Genereux) and smart 7f/ 1m performer Rain Splash (by Tolomeo): dam sprinter: 11/2, last of 7 in maiden at Leicester: sold 1,800 gns. *M. Johnston*

ZABIONIC (IRE) 4 ch.g. Zafonic (USA) 130 – Scene Galante (FR) (Sicyos (USA) **–** 126) [2001 63: f16g Apr 9] good-topped gelding: modest maiden at 3 yrs: well held only outing in 2001: tried blinkered. *M. E. Sowersby*

ZACCHERA 2 ch.f. (Apr 17) Zamindar (USA) 116 – Palace Street (USA) 103 **70** (Secreto (USA) 128) [2001 6g⁶ 6m 6g Sep 7] smallish foal: fifth foal: half-sister to 3 winners, including 3-y-o Palace Affair and 4-y-o Duke of Modena: dam, 6f/7f winner, from very good US family: fair form in maidens: should stay at least 7f. *G. B. Balding*

ZAEEMA 2 br.f. (Mar 18) Zafonic (USA) 130 – Talented 112 (Bustino 136) [2001 7f* **93 P** Jun 30] fourth foal: dam, 1¼m (including Sun Chariot Stakes) winner who stayed 1½m, half-sister to dam of 4-y-o Three Points out of half-sister to very smart middle-distance performer Richard of York: 5/1-on, won 4-runner maiden at Doncaster by 3¾ lengths from Muklah, dictating steady pace and idling after looking like going clear 3f out: should stay at least 1¼m: said to have recovered from setback, and probably capable of considerable improvement. *D. R. Loder*

ZAFAIR 3 b. or br.f. Zafonic (USA) 130 – Danefair 109 (Danehill (USA) 126) [2001 –
10m Jul 11] first foal: dam, French 1¼m and 1½m (Prix Minerve) winner, half-sister
to smart French performer up to 2m Erudite and granddaughter of high-class 1m/1¼m
performer Cairn Rouge: ninth of 11 in maiden at Kempton on only outing, folding tamely
2f out (swished tail continuously): sold 50,000 gns in December. *R. Charlton*

ZAFFIA 4 b.f. Zilzal (USA) 137 – Zeffirella 88 (Known Fact (USA) 135) [2001 70: –
8.3g 7s 7g May 30] leggy filly: fair maiden at best: well held in 2001. *P. R. Chamings*

ZAFFRANI (IRE) 2 b. or br.f. (Feb 17) Danehill (USA) 126 – Zariysha (IRE) **98**
(Darshaan 133) [2001 6s³ 7d² 7.8f* 6g⁵ 7s⁴ 8d⁴ 7s⁵ 8d⁵ Oct 27] IR 90,000Y: angular,
workmanlike filly: third foal: dam unraced sister to Greenham winner/King Edward VII
second Zayyani: useful performer: won maiden at Dundalk in May: creditable fourth in
Debutante Stakes at the Curragh (beaten nearly 2 lengths by Saranac Lake) and May Hill
Stakes at Doncaster (5 lengths behind Half Glance): stays 1m: acts on firm and soft going:
blinkered fourth start. *David Wachman, Ireland*

ZAFILLY 3 ch.f. Zafonic (USA) 130 – Rifada 103 (Ela-Mana-Mou 132) [2001 –: 10s **53**
11.6s⁵ 10.2d 11.6g² 10.9m⁶ 11.6g 12m Aug 13] tall, sparely-made filly: has a round
action: modest maiden handicapper: well below form last 3 starts: stays 11.6f: acts on soft
ground: has carried head awkwardly: sold 5,000 gns. *G. L. Moore*

ZAFONIUM (USA) 4 ch.c. Zafonic (USA) 130 – Bint Pasha (USA) 126 (Affirmed **100 §**
(USA)) [2001 109§: 10.4m 12g Aug 3] big, lengthy colt: useful performer: respectable
twelfth in John Smith's Cup at York on first outing in 2001: stays 1½m: yet to race on
extremes of going: blinkered twice, found nothing second time: not to be trusted.
P. F. I. Cole

ZAGALETA 4 b.f. Sri Pekan (USA) 117 – Persian Song 45 (Persian Bold 123) [2001 **81**
77: 10v 8.3d³ 10m* 10m 10.5d 10g* Aug 3] quite good-topped filly: fairly useful
handicapper: won at Pontefract in May and Nottingham (amateurs) in August: stays
1¼m: acts on firm and good to soft going: tried tongue tied: often sweating/edgy:
sometimes carries head high. *Andrew Turnell*

ZAHAALIE (USA) 9 ch.g. Zilzal (USA) 137 – Bambee T T (USA) (Better Bee) –
[2001 f16g Jan 12] tailed off only Flat start in 2001. *J. A. Pickering*

ZAHA (IRE) 6 b.h. Lahib (USA) 129 – Mayaasa (USA) 70 (Lyphard (USA) 132) –
[2001 69, a63: 10g 9.9s 10.1v f9.4g Nov 21] leggy horse: little form in 2001: sometimes
visored/blinkered. *Mrs Lydia Pearce*

ZAHEEMAH (USA) 3 b.f. El Prado (IRE) 119 – Port of Silver (USA) (Silver Hawk **96**
(USA) 123) [2001 93: e10g³ f8s* 7d² 8g⁵ 11.4f⁶ 8.5m⁵ Jun 8] strong, good-topped filly:
has a fluent, round action: useful performer: won maiden at Southwell in February:
creditable ¾-length second to Lil's Jessy in Nell Gwyn Stakes at Newmarket in April: at
least respectable efforts after when fifth in Premio Regina Elena at Rome (to Bugia) and
in listed race at Epsom (beaten 3¼ lengths by Sheppard's Watch): best form up to 1m:
acted on fibresand, good to firm and good to soft going: stud. *C. E. Brittain*

ZAHWAH (USA) 3 b.f. Rahy (USA) 115 – Funistrada (USA) (Fappiano (USA)) **105**
[2001 a8f² a8f² a9f² a7f⁴ a8.5f² 8.5f⁵ 9f⁶ Oct 14] $420,000Y, $925,000Y: seventh foal:
half-sister to 3 winners in USA, including minor 7f stakes winner Conte di Savoya (by
Sovereign Dancer), also placed up to 9f in graded stakes: dam, US Grade 2 6f winner
(also second in Grade 1 1m event at 2 yrs), out of half-sister to Breeders' Cup Mile winner
Cozzene: useful performer: trained in 2000 by E. Harty in USA, winning maiden at Bay
Meadows Fair and running well when third in Grade 3 contest at Arlington: creditable
efforts when second in prestige events at Nad Al Sheba first 3 starts in 2001, behind
Muwakleh on first 2 occasions, then beaten 2½ lengths by Laoub in UAE Oaks on last
one: below form on return to USA last 4 starts: stayed 9f: blinkered last 3 starts: tongue
tied second 3-y-o outing: stud. *Saeed bin Suroor*

ZAIDAAN 5 b.h. Ezzoud (IRE) 126 – River Maiden (USA) (Riverman (USA) 131) –
[2001 76: f12g Feb 17] fair form when winning handicap at Dundalk in 1999: well held
only 2 runs since: stays 9f: acts on firm ground. *G. M. McCourt*

ZAKAT (FR) 2 b.g. (Jan 26) Zamindar (USA) 116 – Rose Douceur (FR) (Polish –
Precedent (USA) 131) [2001 7.1g 8.1g Sep 13] 220,000 francs Y: third foal: dam French
1½m winner out of Prix Vermeille winner Indian Rose: well held in maidens. *W. R. Muir*

ZAMAT 5 b.g. Slip Anchor 136 – Khandjar 77 (Kris 135) [2001 49: 11.1d² 12.1d³ 12m⁵ **50**
12.1m⁶ 11.1s⁴ 15s⁴ 14.4d⁵ 13d² 14m² 12.1g² 12m³ Sep 30] modest maiden: stays 15f:
acts on soft and good to firm going. *P. Monteith*

Oaks d'Italia, Milan—a clear-cut success for the Michael Bell-trained Zanzibar, who has seven lengths to spare over a predominantly home contingent led by Rosa di Brema (hooped sleeves)

ZAMINSTAR (IRE)　2 ch.g. (Apr 3) Zamindar (USA) 116 – Guanhumara (Caerleon (USA) 132) [2001 5m 6m 5.2m³ 5g² 6g 7.1g Sep 1] 28,000Y: tall, leggy gelding: has scope: fifth foal: half-brother to 4-y-o Smart Ridge and 3-y-o Moonlight Dancer: dam, maiden, half-sister to Cadeaux Genereux: fair maiden: second in nursery at Sandown: has raced freely, and likely to prove best at 5f/6f: yet to race on extremes of going: gelded after final outing. *A. P. Jarvis*　**68**

ZAMYATINA (IRE)　2 b.f. (Mar 16) Danehill Dancer (IRE) 117 – Miss Pickpocket (IRE) 64 (Petorius 117) [2001 5m² 5.1s² 6g* 6d 5g⁶ 5.1s⁴ p6g⁵ f5g⁵ p6g Dec 28] IR 8,500F, 18,500Y: angular, unfurnished filly: second foal: half-sister to 2000 2-y-o 5f winner Western Hero (by Lake Coniston): dam 2-y-o 5f winner who stayed 7f: fair performer: landed odds in maiden at Brighton in August: creditable efforts in nurseries fifth to eighth starts: likely to prove best at 5f/6f: acts on polytrack, soft and good to firm ground. *R. Hannon*　**76**

ZANANA　2 b.f. (Apr 5) Zafonic (USA) 130 – Divine Quest 81 (Kris 135) [2001 5s² 6m⁵ 7g 6g Oct 19] leggy filly: second foal: half-sister to 3-y-o Ecstatic: dam, 7f winner, sister to smart French sprinter Divine Danse and half-sister to very smart 6f to 1m performer Pursuit of Love: regressed after showing fair form in Sandown maiden on debut: should stay 7f: sold 12,000 gns, sent to Holland. *R. Hannon*　**76 d**

ZANAY　5 b.h. Forzando 122 – Nineteenth of May 86 (Homing 130) [2001 85+, a112: 10m 8f⁵ 10f 8g 7m⁶ Jul 20] tall, useful-looking horse: reportedly had knee-chips removed at 4 yrs: one-time smart performer on all-weather: fairly useful on turf at best in 2001: better at 1¼m than 1m: acts on equitrack, firm and soft going: tried blinkered/tongue tied. *Miss Jacqueline S. Doyle*　**81 a–**

ZANDEED (IRE)　3 b.g. Inchinor 119 – Persian Song 45 (Persian Bold 123) [2001 71: f7g 7.1g 10m 8.1g* 10g* 10.2m* 10.3m* 10g Oct 5] unfurnished gelding: fairly useful performer: won handicaps at Haydock and Chepstow and minor events at Nottingham and Doncaster in June/July: below form after almost 3-month break final start: stays 1¼m: raced only on good going or firmer on turf, well beaten once on fibresand: best in visor: often makes running: sold 15,000 gns. *E. A. L. Dunlop*　**81**

ZANDICULAR　2 b.c. (Feb 14) Forzando 122 – Perdicula (IRE) (Persian Heights 129) [2001 6m⁶ 6m² 6.1d² 6s* 7d³ Oct 19] 15,000F, 54,000Y: good-bodied, sturdy colt: has scope: third foal: dam, German winner around 1¼m at 4 yrs, half-sister to Derby　**89 p**

winner High-Rise: second in maidens prior to winning one at Lingfield in October: 9/1, good 4¼ lengths third to Century City in minor event at Newmarket: will stay at least 1m: should make a useful 3-y-o and win more races. *R. Hannon*

ZANDOMENEGHI (IRE)   2 ch.g. (Mar 25) College Chapel 122 – Fire of London **57**
78 (Shirley Heights 130) [2001 7f 7.1v f6g⁵ 6d 7s Oct 25] 55,000Y: good-topped, workmanlike gelding: has scope: third foal: dam, second at 1¼m, sister to useful winner up to 1¼m Spitfire: modest maiden: will stay 1m: acts on firm going and fibresand: blinkered final start: sold 4,500 gns. *P. F. I. Cole*

ZANDO'S CHARM   3 b.f. Forzando 122 – Silver Charm (Dashing Blade 117) [2001 **–**
60: f8g Jan 8] modest performer at 2 yrs: well held (on fibresand) only outing in 2001: should stay 1m: acts on good to firm going. *J. Akehurst*

ZANOG   2 b.c. (May 7) Forzando 122 – Logarithm (King of Spain 121) [2001 7m 5.1d **–**
5s⁶ f5g p6g Dec 19] 11,000Y: fourth foal: half-brother to unreliable 5f winner General Equation (by Governor General) and 4-y-o Alabama Wurley: dam poor half-sister to smart sprinter Northern Goddess: only a little sign of ability in maidens/nurseries. *Miss Jacqueline S. Doyle*

ZANZIBAR (IRE)   3 b.f. In The Wings 128 – Isle of Spice (USA) 74 (Diesis 133) **113**
[2001 80: 11.8g* 11m* 12m 11.9g⁵ 12m⁶ 10v⁵ 10g Oct 28] sturdy, quite attractive filly: smart performer: successful in May in minor event at Leicester and Oaks d'Italia at Milan (beat Rosa di Brema by 7 lengths): best effort after 5½ lengths sixth to Aquarelliste in Prix Vermeille at Longchamp, slowly into stride and detached for first 4f (appeared not to be striding out properly): stayed 1½m: best efforts on good to firm going: reportedly returned jarred up when last in Oaks at Epsom on third outing: visits Fantastic Light. *M. L. W. Bell*

Mrs G. Rowland Clark & Usk Valley Stud's "Zanzibar"

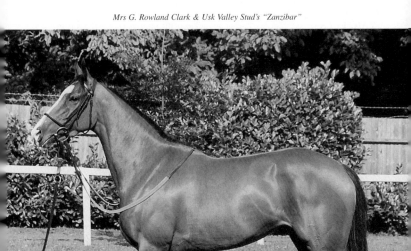

ZARAN 2 gr.f. (Apr 17) Inzar (USA) 112 – African Light 65§ (Kalaglow 132) [2001 **56**
6m⁶ 7m⁵ 6m Aug 1] 7,000Y: half-sister to 3-y-o Reciprocal and several winners abroad:
dam, maiden who stayed 1¼m, daughter of Park Hill winner African Dancer: modest
maiden: stayed 7f: dead. *N. P. Littmoden*

ZARCONIA (IRE) 2 br.f. (Apr 14) Inzar (USA) 112 – Speedy Action (Horage 124) **–**
[2001 5.1s⁶ 6s Nov 10] IR 2,500Y, 1,100 2-y-o: half-sister to 1m winner Bustle'em (by
Burslem) and 5-y-o Vale of Leven: dam Irish 1¼m winner: well held in maidens, shaping
as if something amiss second outing. *Mrs P. Sly*

ZARGUS 2 b.c. (Jan 11) Zamindar (USA) 116 – My First Romance 61 (Danehill **89 p**
(USA) 126) [2001 6m² 5.7g² 5d* Oct 9] 110,000Y: stocky, quite attractive colt: third foal:
half-brother to 3-y-o Romantic Myth and useful 1999 2-y-o 5f winner (later 6f winner in
Sweden) Power Packed (by Puissance): dam ran twice: second in maidens at Goodwood
and Bath before landing odds in one at Catterick by 5 lengths from Philboy, quickening
clear from over 1f out: likely to prove best at 5f/6f: should make a useful 3-y-o and win
more races. *W. R. Muir*

ZARIN (IRE) 3 b.c. Inzar (USA) 112 – Non Dimenticar Me (IRE) 63 (Don't Forget **105 ?**
Me 127) [2001 7v² 7s* 8m May 13] IR 7,000F, 36,000Y: leggy colt: second foal:
half-brother to useful 1999 2-y-o 5f/6f winner Master Fay (by Fayruz): dam 5f winner
who stayed 7f: useful form: nervy beforehand, very easy winner of maiden at Kempton in
April by 7 lengths: stiff task, always behind in Poule d'Essai des Poulains at Longchamp
following month: free-going type, not sure to stay much beyond 1m: joined R. White.
J. L. Dunlop

ZARZA BAY (IRE) 2 b.c. (Apr 29) Hamas (IRE) 125§ – Frill (Henbit (USA) 130) **58**
[2001 5m 6m⁵ 6m f7g⁵ 8m 10v⁵ Oct 4] IR 13,000F, 20,000Y: strong colt: half-brother to
several winners, including fairly useful 11.6f to 17f winner Sudest (by Taufan) and 4-y-o
Wadenhoe: dam, Irish 1½m winner, half-sister to high-class miler Pitcairn: modest
maiden: stays 1¼m: acts on good to firm going, heavy and fibresand. *K. R. Burke*

ZARZELLA 2 b.f. (Jan 18) Makbul 104 – Zarzi (IRE) (Suave Dancer (USA) 136) **–**
[2001 6g⁵ Aug 12] first foal: dam unraced daughter of useful Irish 6f/7f performer
Pernilla: 33/1, last of 5 in Ascot maiden. *M. Wigham*

ZAWRAK (IRE) 2 ch.c. (Feb 25) Zafonic (USA) 130 – Gharam (USA) 108 (Green **58 p**
Dancer (USA) 132) [2001 7s⁶ Sep 24] eighth foal: brother to useful 1997 2-y-o 7f winner
Elshamms and half-brother to several winners by Nashwan, including smart performer
up to 2½m Shaya: dam, 2-y-o 6f winner, fourth in Poule d'Essai des Pouliches and
Ribblesdale Stakes: 16/1, sixth of 10 to Lunar Sovereign in minor event at Leicester,
prominent 5f: should improve. *A. C. Stewart*

ZECHARIAH 5 b.g. Kasakov – Runfawit Pet 41 (Welsh Saint 126) [2001 50d: 8m³ **55**
8m³ 8f 8f³ 8f* 7d* 8g 8f Sep 20] sparely-made gelding: modest performer: won selling
handicaps at Musselburgh in July and Ayr in August: effective at 7f to 8.5f: acts on
fibresand, firm and soft going: has been early to post: usually makes running. *J. L. Eyre*

ZEITLOS 2 b.c. (Apr 20) Timeless Times (USA) 99 – Petitesse 55 (Petong 126) [2001 **62**
5s 5.3m⁴ 6m 5g* 5d 5m 5.1m⁶ 5.1f 6.1d⁴ 6s⁴ 6d 5.7d p6g Dec 19] 5,000F, 4,000Y: small
colt: half-brother to several winners, including 5-y-o Champagne Rider and 3-y-o April
Lee: dam, 5f/6f winner (including at 2 yrs), sister to Paris House: modest performer: won
nursery at Leicester in July: well held last 3 starts, leaving G. Margarson before final one:
effective at 5f/6f: acts on soft and good to firm going: tried blinkered. *R. M. Flower*

ZELENSKY (IRE) 2 b.c. (Jan 22) Danehill Dancer (IRE) 117 – Malt Leaf (IRE) 48 **72**
(Nearly A Nose (USA) 84) [2001 f6g 6d⁶ 6.1g² 6g⁵ Sep 21] IR 6,200F, 16,000Y, 24,000
2-y-o: tall, lengthy, unfurnished colt: second foal: half-brother to Irish 1m winner
Perugino's Malt (by Perugino): dam poor Irish maiden: fair effort when
second to Harry Jake at Nottingham: will stay 7f. *J. A. Osborne*

ZELOSO 3 b.g. Alzao (USA) 117 – Silk Petal 105 (Petorius 117) [2001 82: 8d 9.9m⁴ **81**
10.3m 10m 8.1s⁴ 7d⁶ Aug 26] good-bodied gelding: fairly useful performer: best at 1m/
1¼m: acts on soft and good to firm ground: tried visored in 2000, blinkered final outing
at 3 yrs: sold 4,500 gns, and gelded. *R. Charlton*

ZENDA 2 b.f. (Feb 18) Zamindar (USA) 116 – Hope (IRE) (Dancing Brave (USA) **77 p**
140) [2001 7g² 8v³ Oct 26] good-bodied, attractive filly: easy mover: third foal:
half-sister to smart 7f/1m performer Hopeful Light (by Warning): dam once-raced sister
to Irish Oaks winner Wemyss Bight: fair form in minor event at Kempton (flashed tail)

and maiden at Doncaster (third to Teresa Balbi, travelling strongly long way): not sure to stay beyond 1m: capable of better. *J. H. M. Gosden*

ZENDIUM (IRE)   3 b.g. Earl of Barking (IRE) 119 – Speedy Action (Horage 124)   –
[2001 57: f6g 8v 7d May 7] useful-looking gelding: modest form only run at 2 yrs: well held in 2001. *T. D. Easterby*

ZERO GRAVITY   4 b.g. Cosmonaut – Comfort (Chief Singer 131) [2001 68: 10s 10v   **68 §**
9.9m[6] 12m[3] 14g 13.1d 13.1m 16d Sep 27] big, leggy gelding: fair maiden handicapper: should stay beyond 1½m: acts on soft and good to firm going: not to be trusted (ran out fifth outing). *D. J. S. ffrench Davis*

ZETAGALOPON   3 b.f. Petong 126 – Azola (IRE) 63 (Alzao (USA) 117) [2001 –:   –
f7g e8g[4] e10s[4] f12g[4] f11g 10f f9.4g[4] 11.7m Aug 24] poor maiden: left J. Osborne after   **a38**
seventh start: stays 1½m: acts on fibresand/equitrack, little form on turf: tried blinkered.
C. L. Popham

ZHITOMIR   3 ch.g. Lion Cavern (USA) 117 – Treasure Trove (USA) 62 (The Minstrel   **82**
(CAN) 135) [2001 87: 6m 7m 6m[5] 6m 7m 6m 7s[2] 7g* 7d[4] 7s* 7d Oct 20] strong gelding: fairly useful handicapper: won at Epsom (drifted left) in September and Lingfield in October: stays 7f: acts on soft ground: has run well when edgy/sweating: sometimes slowly away: gelded after final outing. *S. Dow*

ZIBELINE (IRE)   4 b.g. Cadeaux Genereux 131 – Zia (USA) 88 (Shareef Dancer   **94**
(USA) 135) [2001 90: 12v 12m[2] 10f 11.4g[5] 12m[2] 14m[4] 13.3m* 13.9m[4] 13.3f 12s 18d Oct 20] tall, quite attractive gelding: fairly useful handicapper: won at Newbury in August: below form last 3 starts: stays 1¾m when conditions aren't testing: acts on firm going, probably not on softer than good: blinkered last 5 starts: has pulled hard: held up.
B. R. Millman

ZIBET   3 b.f. Kris 135 – Zonda 100 (Fabulous Dancer (USA) 124) [2001 77p: 7g* 8.1s[2]   **90**
7s Sep 29] angular filly: fairly useful form: won maiden at Newmarket in July by 5 lengths: good second to Diamond Max in handicap at Chepstow following month: too free when running poorly in Tote Trifecta Handicap at Ascot final start: stayed 1m: acted on soft going: visits Diktat. *E. A. L. Dunlop*

ZIDAC   9 br.g. Statoblest 120 – Sule Skerry 78 (Scottish Rifle 127) [2001 66, a53: e10g   –
Feb 3] tall gelding: fair performer at 8 yrs: well held only outing in 2001. *P. J. Makin*

ZIETING (IRE)   3 b.g. Zieten (USA) 118 – Ball Cat (FR) (Cricket Ball (USA) 124)   **37**
[2001 55: f9.4s 8.1v 9m[6] 10m[5] 8g 8.1m 11.9g[6] 15.8g 10.9m[3] Aug 27] smallish gelding: poor maiden: left K. Burke after fourth start: stays 11f: acts on firm ground and equitrack.
P. W. Hiatt

ZIETUNZEEN (IRE)   3 b.f. Zieten (USA) 118 – Hawksbill Special (IRE) (Taufan   **85**
(USA) 119) [2001 99: 7g 6m 6d 7g[3] 6.1m[3] 6m[5] 7g 6d 7d[3] 6s[6] 6m 6d[5] Oct 9] lengthy filly: fairly useful performer: below form last 3 starts: stays easy 7f: yet to race on heavy going, probably acts on any other turf: sometimes spoils chance at start. *A. Berry*

ZIETZIG (IRE)   4 b.g. Zieten (USA) 118 – Missing You 89 (Ahonoora 122) [2001   **76 +**
89: 7m 6s 7g 7m[2] 7.6g 6g[4] p7g[6] Dec 19] shallow-girthed gelding: fair handicapper in 2001: left K. Burke before final outing: probably best at 6f/7f: acts on soft and good to firm going, lightly raced on all-weather: has been early to post/raced freely. *T. D. Barron*

ZIG ZIG (IRE)   4 b.g. Perugino (USA) 84 – Queen of Erin (IRE) (King of Clubs 124)   **69**
[2001 72: 8m 10.1m[4] f8g 7.5m 8.5m Jul 31] rather leggy, close-coupled gelding: fair performer: seems to stay 1¼m: acts on fibresand and good to firm going: has been early to post. *Mrs A. Duffield*

ZILARATOR (USA)   5 b.g. Zilzal (USA) 137 – Allegedly (USA) (Sir Ivor 135)   **93**
[2001 103: 12v[6] 18.7f[6] 16.1f 13.9m[5] 18.7m[2] 11.9s* Oct 11] tall, close-coupled gelding: fairly useful performer: won minor event at York (beat Celtic Island by a head) in October, off bridle long way out: effective at testing 1½m, probably stays 18.7f: has form on firm going, all wins on soft/heavy: has looked tricky ride: sold 63,000 gns, joined P. Hobbs. *W. J. Haggas*

ZILCH   3 ch.c. Zilzal (USA) 137 – Bunty Boo 110 (Noalto 120) [2001 100: 6s* 7m 6d[5]   **109**
6g[6] 7d[3] 6s Sep 29] leggy, close-coupled colt: fluent mover: useful performer: won minor event at Newbury in May: best efforts, not beaten far, when fifth to Bahamian Pirate in Phoenix Sprint Stakes at Leopardstown and sixth to Ishiguru in listed race at the Curragh (finished well) third and fourth starts: stays 6f: acts on soft and good to firm ground: rather highly strung: has edged right: held up. *R. Hannon*

1119

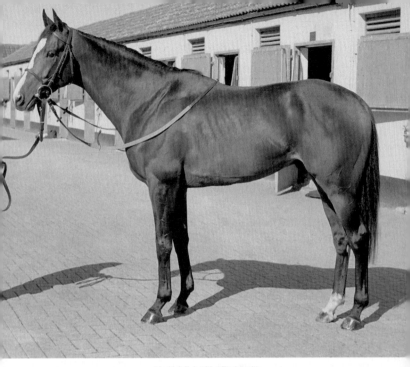

Mr Abdullah Ali's "Zindabad"

ZILKHA 3 gr.f. Petong 126 – Peperonata (IRE) 91 (Cyrano de Bergerac 120) [2001 –: **50**
6f 7m⁶ 8m 8m⁴ 7m 6m 8d Oct 8] leggy filly: modest maiden: best efforts at 7f/1m on good
to firm going: blinkered (very slowly away) penultimate outing. *I. A. Balding*

ZILMAID DANCER 2 b.f. (Jan 31) Zilzal (USA) 137 – Briggsmaid 70 (Elegant Air **55 p**
119) [2001 6m⁴ 6m Jun 12] 13,000Y: good-topped filly: fourth foal: closely related to
5-y-o Kez and half-sister to 2 winners, including 4-y-o Reflex Blue): dam 1½m to 2m
winner: modest form in maidens at Redcar (not knocked about) and Salisbury (forced
wide): should stay 1m: will probably do better. *P. W. Harris*

ZINCALO (USA) 5 gr.g. Zilzal (USA) 137 – Silver Glitz (USA) (Grey Dawn II 132) **48 §**
[2001 64§, a–§: f12g⁴ f16g⁴ e16g³ 15.4v 17.2f⁴ 11.5m f12g 11.6g 14.1m Jul 28] strong
gelding: poor handicapper nowadays: stays 17f: acts on firm ground and fibresand/
equitrack: one to avoid. *C. E. Brittain*

ZINDABAD (FR) 5 b.h. Shirley Heights 130 – Miznah (IRE) 102 (Sadler's Wells **120**
(USA) 132) [2001 117: 10g* 10m⁴ 11.8d* 12f² 12g⁴ 12g⁶ 12m Dec 16] good-topped
horse: fluent mover: very smart performer: better than ever for new stable in 2001, and
beat Mubtaker short head both times when winning minor event at Newmarket in May
and listed race at Leicester in June: ran well after when head second to Sandmason in
Hardwicke Stakes at Royal Ascot and when 1¼ lengths third to Mutamam in Canadian
International at Woodbine (demoted to sixth after edging left) penultimate start: well held
in Hong Kong Vase at Sha Tin final outing: stays 1½m: acts on firm and soft going: races
prominently: game. *M. Johnston*

ZINGING 2 b.c. (Apr 14) Fraam 114 – Hi Hoh (IRE) (Fayruz 116) [2001 5.1v⁴ 5d⁵ 5d* **79 d**
6m⁵ 6f⁴ 5.1f⁵ 5m 6g 5g⁴ 5s 5m⁴ 5.1f⁴ f5g p6g p6g⁴ Dec 28] small, compact colt: first foal:

dam seemed of little account: fair performer: won maiden at Hamilton in May: not so
good after ninth start, leaving M. Channon after twelfth: effective at 5f/easy 6f: acts on
any turf going and polytrack: sometimes finds little. *J. J. Bridger*

ZIPPING (IRE) 2 b.c. (Feb 15) Zafonic (USA) 130 – Zelda (IRE) (Caerleon **118**
(USA) 132) [2001 4.5d² 5g* 5g³ 5.5g* 6g² 6g² Oct 4]

    Act One and Zipping were not so much the A-to-Z of the leading French
two-year-olds, but the A *and* Z—with nothing in between. Just two French-trained
two-year-olds rated 110 or more by Timeform represents a new low after only four
earned a rating of 110 or higher in 2000. As recently as 1995, fifteen French
juveniles made the grade. The dearth of good French two-year-olds will come as
bad news for the French authorities who revamped the French juvenile programme
in 2001, a subject covered in the essay on Act One. The lack of highly-rated French
two-year-olds is not necessarily a reflection of a mediocre crop—only time will tell
if that is the case and Shaanmer in particular looks a good prospect—but it does
confirm the continued reluctance of French trainers to campaign their youngsters in
the top two-year-old events.

    There are five Group 1 races in France restricted to two-year-olds, and in
every one of them in the latest season foreign challengers outnumbered the
French-trained runners. In the Prix Morny there were just four French horses in a
field of eleven, in the Marcel Boussac four out of nine, in the new-style Grand
Criterium two out of five, in the inaugural Criterium International just one out of
six, and in the Criterium de Saint-Cloud three out of ten. All of these races, bar the
Criterium International won by Act One, went abroad, John Gosden's Sulk taking
the Marcel Boussac and the rest going to horses from Aidan O'Brien's stable. The
measly fourteen French-trained two-year-olds contesting these five Group 1 races
represented only nine different stables, those of Beguigne, Collet, Dissaux, Fabre,
Gibson, Guigand, Laffon-Parias, Pease and Smaga. Leading trainers who did not
have a single representative in any of the top two-year-old contests included Pascal
Bary, Criquette Head-Maarek, Jean-Claude Rouget and Alain de Royer-Dupre. The
picture was healthier at a slightly lower level, with French two-year-olds holding

*Prix Robert Papin, Maisons-Laffitte—Zipping is a narrow winner from the John Dunlop-trained
Massarra (No.5), Slap Shot (just coming into picture, right) and Dobby Road (far side)*

on to ten of their fourteen lesser pattern races. In all but the Prix des Chenes and Prix Miesque they faced opposition from abroad.

The strength of Ballydoyle, which won the Prix Morny for the third time in four years, the Grand Criterium for the third time in five years and fielded the first three home in the Criterium de Saint-Cloud, is a major stumbling block for French trainers, but Zipping was one who did take up the challenge, coming up against Ballydoyle's champion two-year-old Johannesburg twice in Group 1 company, chasing him home in the Prix Morny at Deauville and in the Middle Park Stakes at Newmarket. The Morny saw Zipping's best performance. He came from last place, challenging wide and keeping on well to be beaten a length and a half. Johannesburg doubled his advantage over Zipping in the Middle Park but Zipping confirmed himself a smart colt, again held up for a late run and keeping on strongly to pull three lengths clear of the third Doc Holiday without making any impression on the winner.

Zipping's early-season form gave little indication of the improvement he was to show at Deauville. Beaten a neck on his debut at Saint-Cloud, he went on to win a minor event at Maisons-Laffitte in June and then finish a close third at Chantilly in the Prix du Bois, the first juvenile pattern race of the year in France. The pair who beat him at Chantilly, Ziria and Dobby Road, opposed again in the Prix Robert Papin at Maisons-Laffitte in July but the result was very different, with Zipping the winner and Dobby Road and Ziria taking the last two places in a field of five. Once again the finish was close, with Zipping leading well inside the final furlong to hold on by a neck from the British-trained Massarra with the Italian filly Slap Shot a head away third.

Zipping (IRE) (b.c. Feb 15, 1999)	Zafonic (USA) (b 1990)	Gone West (b 1984)	Mr Prospector
			Secrettame
		Zaizafon (ch 1982)	The Minstrel
			Modifa
	Zelda (IRE) (b 1990)	Caerleon (b 1980)	Nijinsky
			Foreseer
		Mill Princess (b 1977)	Mill Reef
			Irish Lass II

Zipping carries the white and dark green hooped colours made famous by Last Tycoon, top-class winner of the King's Stand Stakes and William Hill Sprint Championship before becoming Europe's first winner of the Breeders' Cup Mile. The two are related, Last Tycoon being a half-brother to Zipping's dam Zelda, a winner over six and a half furlongs at Evry. Their dam Mill Princess has been a prolific producer at stud, her offspring also including the smart sprinter Astronef, the Prix du Bois winner The Perfect Life (dam of Gordon Stakes dead-heater Rabah), Side of Paradise, who won a listed race over a mile at Saint-Cloud in the latest season, and the dam of the Poule d'Essai des Pouliches winner Valentine Waltz. The French mile-and-a-quarter winner Mill Princess is a half-sister to a broodmare with an even better record in Irish Bird, responsible for the Prix du Jockey Club winners Assert and Bikala and the Irish St Leger winner Eurobird. Zipping is his dam's fifth foal and third winner in France following the useful five-furlong performer Zelding (by Warning) and the two-year-old seven-furlong winner Aso Rock (by King's Theatre). Zelding's two-year-old campaign also took a similar path to Zipping's, but, after winning the Prix du Bois, she could finish only third in the Robert Papin and seventh in the Morny.

Zipping is unlikely still to be at the top of his generation in France by the end of his three-year-old season. A leggy, quite attractive colt, he did not appeal physically at Newmarket as an obvious type to train on into a better three-year-old, though it should be noted that Last Tycoon was rather lightly built for a sprinter/miler. The way he kept on both at Deauville and Newmarket suggests Zipping should stay further, though a mile could prove beyond him. His first season told us little about his ground requirements as he raced almost exclusively on good going.
R. Collet, France

ZIRIA (IRE) 2 b.f. (Mar 12) Danehill Dancer (IRE) 117 – Surprise Visitor (IRE) (Be **99** My Guest (USA) 126) [2001 4.5g* 5g* 5.5g⁵ 5.5d 6d Oct 2] 27,000Y: rangy, angular filly: has scope: second foal: half-sister to 5f (at 2 yrs) and 7f winner Densim Blue (by

Lake Coniston): dam, lightly-raced French maiden, half-sister to dam of 5-y-o Swallow Flight: useful performer: won newcomers event at Saint-Cloud in May and Prix du Bois at Chantilly (by neck from Dobby Road) in July: 10/1, well held in Cheveley Park Stakes at Newmarket final start: will probably prove best around 5f: raced only on good/good to soft ground. *C. Laffon-Parias, France*

ZOENA 4 ch.f. Emarati (USA) 74 – Exotic Forest 66 (Dominion 123) [2001 58, a67: **66** e6g* f6g⁵ e6g 6m² 6f 6m Jul 12] fair performer: won claimer at Lingfield in January: stays 6f: acts on equitrack, good to firm and good to soft going: races up with pace. *J. G. Portman*

ZOE'S GOLD (USA) 3 b.f. St Jovite (USA) 135 – Six Months Long (USA) **77** (Northern Dancer) [2001 e8g f8.5g² f9.4g* a8.5f⁵ Apr 8] $140,000F: half-sister to numerous winners, notably top-class miler Half A Year (by Riverman) and US 1993 Grade 2 2-y-o 7f winner Winning Pact (by Alydar): dam won up to 1m in USA: fair form: progressed to win maiden at Wolverhampton in February by 1¼ lengths: left J. Noseda: well held in allowance race at Pimlico, only subsequent outing: may stay beyond 9.4f: acts on fibresand. *M. W. Dickinson, USA*

ZOLLNER (GER) 3 b.c. Dashing Blade 117 – Zypern (GER) (Acatenango (GER) **116** 127) [2001 11v⁴ 10g² 10d* 10g* 10s Aug 5] third foal: half-brother to German 7f winner Zyprienne (by Be My Guest): dam German 9.5f and 1¼m winner: smart performer: won maiden at Dortmund (by 10 lengths) at 2 yrs, Grosser Muller Brot-Preis at Munich in June by ¾ length from Royal Dragon (originally demoted for hampering runner-up but later reinstated) and Lotto Hessen-Pokal at Frankfurt in July by length from Salonblue: disappointing behind Kutub in Grosser Dallmayr-Preis at Munich final start: stays 1¼m: has won on heavy ground, though possibly suited by less testing conditions (yet to race on firmer than good). *P. Schiergen, Germany*

ZONE 2 b.c. (Mar 7) Zilzal (USA) 137 – Thea (USA) 95 (Marju (IRE) 127) [2001 8s* **92 p** Nov 9] 72,000Y: strong, good-bodied colt; second foal: dam, 7f winner, granddaughter of Yorkshire Oaks second Light Duty from very good family: 7/4 favourite and looking in fine shape, created good impression when winning 17-runner maiden at Doncaster by 2½ lengths from Unshakable, leading over 2f out and running on strongly: likely to stay 1¼m: seems well regarded, and should make at least a useful 3-y-o. *P. F. I. Cole*

ZONERGEM 3 ch.g. Zafonic (USA) 130 – Anasazi (IRE) (Sadler's Wells (USA) 132) **77** [2001 9.9d² 10v⁶ Oct 8] 3,000 3-y-o: first foal: dam, placed at 9f/1¼m in France, closely related to Dancing Brave and very smart 1¼m/1½m performer Jolypha: 1¼ lengths second to Valley of Song in maiden at Goodwood on debut, making most and rallying despite carrying head awkwardly: well held in similar event at Windsor following month (subsequently gelded). *Lady Herries*

ZORN 2 br.c. (Apr 17) Dilum (USA) 115 – Very Good (Noalto 120) [2001 p8g f7g f7g **45** p7g Dec 29] 6,800F, 1,000Y: third foal: half-brother to 5-y-o Malchik: dam of little account: poor form in maidens/minor event. *P. Howling*

ZORRO 7 gr.g. Touch of Grey 90 – Snow Huntress 80 (Shirley Heights 130) [2001 58: **–** e13g e13s⁵ e13g 11.9s May 3] leggy gelding: lightly-raced handicapper: tried blinkered. *Jamie Poulton*

ZOUDIE 3 b.f. Ezzoud (IRE) 126 – Patsy Western 81 (Precocious 126) [2001 79p: **77** 10g⁵ 11.9m² 10.4d 10f² 10g² 9m³ 10f* Aug 14] close-coupled, rather sparely-made filly: fair performer: won maiden at Brighton in August: stays 1½m: acts on firm and soft going: has edged right under pressure: sold 26,000 gns in December. *J. Noseda*

ZOZARHARRY (IRE) 3 b.c. Nicolotte 118 – Miss Butterfield (Cure The Blues **80** (USA)) [2001 77: 7g⁵ f7g* 7g 7.6m Aug 22] good-topped colt: fairly useful handicapper: **a87** ran for H. Cecil only on reappearance: won at Southwell in June: well held after: stays 7f: acts on fibresand and heavy going: sold 3,500 gns in October. *D. J. S. Cosgrove*

ZSAZSABELLA (IRE) 2 b.f. (Mar 28) Alzao (USA) 117 – Zifta (USA) 82 (Zilzal **66** (USA) 137) [2001 7m⁴ 7d Oct 15] IR 35,000Y: second foal: dam 5f and 7f winner: fair form in maidens at Kempton and Leicester: should stay at least 1m. *J. W. Hills*

ZUCCHERO 5 br.g. Dilum (USA) 115 – Legal Sound 85 (Legal Eagle 126) [2001 91: **99 +** 7m² 7m³ 8f⁶ 8m* 7m Jul 28] big, lengthy gelding: useful handicapper: won quite valuable event at Newbury in July by head from Analyser, getting up close home: mostly creditable efforts otherwise in 2001, not best of runs when ninth of 28 to Atavus in Tote International at Ascot final outing: effective at 7f/1m: yet to race on soft/heavy going, probably acts on any other: often blinkered/visored before 2001: can lead, dropped out last 2 starts: game. *D. W. P. Arbuthnot*

ZUHAIR 8 ch.g. Mujtahid (USA) 118 – Ghzaalh (USA) 87 (Northern Dancer) [2001 **90** 90: 5s 6s 5g 5m 6m⁴ 6m⁵ 5m⁵ 5m 6m³ 5m³ 6m² 5m* 6g 6m 6g 6m 5g⁵ 6m 5s Oct 20] strong gelding: fairly useful handicapper: won at Goodwood (third successive victory in race) in August: ran creditably on several other occasions in 2001, including tenth in Silver Cup at Ayr penultimate start when not clearest of runs: effective at 5f/6f: unsuited by soft/heavy going, acts on any other: well beaten both runs in blinkers: wears bandages: tends to sweat: usually held up: consistent. *D. Nicholls*

ZULFAA (USA) 3 b.f. Bahri (USA) 125 – Haniya (IRE) 92 (Caerleon (USA) 132 **97** [2001 92p: 10.4m⁵ 10.4d⁵ 10m* 9g* 9d⁴ Aug 26] rather leggy, unfurnished filly: useful handicapper: won at Newmarket in June and Ripon in August, given well-judged front-running ride in latter: stayed 10.4f: acted on firm and good to soft going: was genuine: visits Fasliyev. *J. L. Dunlop*

ZUMTOBEL (IRE) 3 b.f. Halling (USA) 133 – Ziggy Belle (USA) (Danzig (USA)) **–** [2001 8g May 6] 20,000Y: workmanlike filly: fourth foal: half-sister to UAE 7f winner Zagreus (by Persian Bold): dam, Irish 1¾m winner, closely related to Grand Criterium winner Treizieme and half-sister to Gold Cup runner-up Eastern Mystic: 14/1 and back-ward, well held in Newmarket maiden. *J. L. Dunlop*

The following unraced horses appeared in ante-post lists for the 2002 classics or had a Group 1 entry at two years, and are included for information purposes:

AKSHAR (IRE) 2 b.c. (Feb 2) Danehill (USA) – Akilara (IRE) 87 (Kahyasi 130) first living foal: dam, 9.6f winner from 2 starts in Ireland, granddaughter of Arc winner Akiyda. *Sir Michael Stoute*

ATTORNEY GENERAL (IRE) 2 b.c. (Apr 5) Sadler's Wells (USA) 132 – Her Ladyship 119 (Polish Precedent (USA) 131) fourth foal: half-brother to useful performer up to 11f Dignify (by Rainbow Quest), 7f/1m winner at 2 yrs: dam, French 10.5f winner (second in Prix de Diane), half-sister to smart performer up to 1¼m Lord of Men. *Sir Michael Stoute*

BEN HUR 2 b.c. (Mar 13) Zafonic (USA) 130 – Gayane 125 (Nureyev (USA) 131) half-brother to 3 winners, including useful 1m winner Maramba (by Rainbow Quest) and fairly useful 6f winner Duel At Dawn (by Nashwan): dam, 6f/7f winner, half-sister to Sun Chariot winner Ristna from family of Oh So Sharp. *J. H. M. Gosden*

DISTINCTION (IRE) 2 b.c. (Mar 20) Danehill (USA) 126 – Ivy Leaf (IRE) 76 (Nureyev (USA) 131) 28,000F, IR 190,000Y: first foal: dam, Irish maiden who stayed 1½m, half-sister to Oaks d'Italia winner Ivyanna. *Sir Michael Stoute*

FUNFAIR 2 b.c. (Jan 28) Singspiel (IRE) 133 – Red Carnival (USA) 109 (Mr Prospector (USA)) lengthy, attractive colt: second foal: half-brother to very smart 1m/1¼m winner Carnival Dancer (by Sadler's Wells): dam, 2-y-o 5f/6f (Cherry Hinton) winner who stayed 1m, sister to smart US Grade 1 2-y-o 8.5f winner Golden Attraction and closely related to high-class US Grade 1 9f winner Cape Town: 5/1 and pick of paddock, withdrawn after refusing to enter stall at Newmarket Nov 2. *Sir Michael Stoute*

INDIGO MAGIC 2 b.c. (Jan 26) Gone West (USA) – Lady Carla 122 (Caerleon (USA) 132) 775,000Y: first foal: dam 1m (at 2 yrs) to 1½m (Oaks) winner. *A. P. O'Brien, Ireland*

JAVA 2 b.f. (Feb 16) Rainbow Quest (USA) 134 – Island Jamboree (USA) (Explodent (USA)) sixth foal: sister to high-class winner up to 1¼m here and in USA Fiji and half-sister to smart 1½m winner Capri (by Generous): dam, won 10 times in USA from 6f to 8.5f, also second in Grade 1 9f event at 5 yrs. *H. R. A. Cecil*

LOVE EXCELLING (FR) 2 b.f. (Mar 25) Polish Precedent (USA) 131 – La Sky (IRE) 107 (Law Society (USA) 130) sixth foal: half-sister to several winners, notably 1¼m and 1½m (Oaks) winner Love Divine (by Diesis): dam, 1¼m winner (probably stayed 1¾m), closely related to Champion Stakes winner Legal Case. *H. R. A. Cecil*

MUTAWAGED (USA) 2 b.c. (Apr 26) Gulch (USA) – Bint Salsabil (USA) 110 (Nashwan (USA) 135) second foal: closely related to 3-y-o Alsaleet: dam, 6f (at 2 yrs, also won 7f Rockfel Stakes) to 1¼m winner, daughter of Salsabil from very good family. *Saeed bin Suroor*

NIGHT SKY   2 ch.f. (Mar 5) Zafonic (USA) 130 – Felucca 94 (Green Desert (USA) 127) third foal: sister to a sprint winner in Scandinavia: dam, 2-y-o 6f winner, half-sister to very smart French/US performer up to 1½m Radevore from family of Al Bahathri. *H. R. A. Cecil*

NOSTRADAMUS (USA)   2 b.c. (Jan 30) Gone West (USA) – Madam North (CAN) (Halo (USA)) closely related to 3 winners abroad, including French 7f winner South Audley (by Gulch) and half-brother to French 1m/9f winner Rubicon (by Irish River): dam unraced sister to Coup de Folie, the dam of Machiavellian, Exit To Nowhere and Coup de Genie. *A. P. O'Brien, Ireland*

OVAL OFFICE   2 ch.f. (Feb 22) Pursuit of Love 124 – Pushy 112 (Sharpen Up 127) half-sister to several winners, including smart performer up to 7f Bluebook (by Secretariat), and useful 7f performer Myself and fairly useful 1¼m winner Nanda (both by Nashwan): dam, 2-y-o 5f (Queen Mary) winner, half-sister to high-class 1½m winner Jupiter Island and high-class 2-y-o 5f/6f winner Precocious. *H. R. A. Cecil*

SCENT OF VICTORY (IRE)   2 b.c. (Apr 22) Polish Precedent (USA) 131 – Dayanata (Shirley Heights 130) 85,000Y: eighth foal: half-brother to several winners, including 6-y-o Courteous and 9-y-o Daryabad: dam unraced sister to Prix du Jockey Club winner Darshaan. *P. F. I. Cole*

SHAMI   2 ch.c. (Jan 30) Rainbow Quest (USA) 134 – Bosra Sham (USA) 132 (Woodman (USA) 126) 1,000,000Y: first foal: dam, won Fillies Mile, 1000 Guineas and Champion Stakes, from excellent family. *Saeed bin Suroor*

SULTANA (USA)   2 ch.f. (Apr 30) Storm Cat (USA) – Sierra Madre (FR) 119 (Baillamont (USA) 124) fourth foal: sister to high-class 7f (Prix de la Salamandre) and 1m (Sussex/Lockinge Stakes) winner Aljabr, and half-sister to 3-y-o Jabaar and useful French 1999 2-y-o 6f winner Makaarem (by Danzig): dam won Prix Marcel Boussac and Prix Vermeille. *Saeed bin Suroor*

TAINWELL   2 ch.c. (May 27) Most Welcome 131 – Mountain Lodge 120 (Blakeney 126) 75,000Y: half-brother to several winners, notably smart Compton Ace (by Pharly), effective at 1½m to 2½m, and 3-y-o Mayville Thunder: dam won Irish St Leger and Cesarewitch. *J. Noseda*

VOLCANIC   2 b.c. (Feb 3) Zafonic (USA) 130 – Ryafan (USA) 121 (Lear Fan (USA) 130) first foal: dam 7f (at 2 yrs) to 1¼m (US Grade 1 event) winner. *J. H. M. Gosden*

ERRATA & ADDENDA

'Racehorses of 1989'

Page 301   The portrait is **not** Executive Perk. (A portrait of the horse appears in *Racehorses of 1988*)

'Racehorses of 1998 and 1999'

Josr Algarhoud (Ire)   in the extended pedigree the third dam is Gay **Apparel**

'Racehorses of 1999'

Aegean Wind   dam **won twice around 1¼m at 4 yrs in Germany**

'Racehorses of 2000'

Bandbox   failed dope test and disqualified from win at Folkestone; race awarded to Double Bounce

Healey (Ire)   final outing was at **York**

Mozart   portrait on page 665 is of **Mediterranean**

PROMISING HORSES

All the British-trained horses (plus those trained by Aidan O'Brien who won the British trainers championship) in *Racehorses of 2001* thought capable of noteworthy improvement are listed below (some horses known to have gone abroad have been omitted).

D. W. P. ARBUTHNOT
Manorson (IRE) 2 ch.c   83p
Mutawaqed (IRE) 3 ch.g   82p

G. B. BALDING
White Stag 2 b.g   55p

I. A. BALDING
Blazing Saddles (IRE) 2 b.c   68p
Borora 2 gr.c   61p
Grande Dame (IRE) 2 b.f   57p
Lochridge 2 ch.f   87p
Passing Glance 2 b.c   94p
Skies Are Blue 2 b.f   70p
Yalla Lara 2 b.f   —p

T. D. BARRON
Exclusive Air (USA) 2 ch.c   65p
Marcus Aurelius (IRE) 2 b.c   85p
Marshall Rooster 2 gr.g   69p
Spitfire Bob (USA) 2 b.g   62p

R. M. BECKETT
Hesperus (IRE) 2 ch.g   —p

M. L. W. BELL
Dusky Warbler 2 br.g   98p
Fluent 2 b.f   64p
Iroquois Chief (USA) 2 b.c   66p
Psychic (IRE) 2 b.f   60P
Short Respite 2 b.f   77p
Wing Commander 2 b.c   97p

J. D. BETHELL
Fittonia (FR) 2 ch.f   65p

M. BLANSHARD
Kingscross 3 ch.g   76p

G. C. BRAVERY
Eric Le Beau (IRE) 2 ch.c   81p
The Hunter (IRE) 2 b.c   61p

C. E. BRITTAIN
Esprit d'Artiste (IRE) 2 ch.c   65p
Haddice (USA) 2 b.c   70p
Halawellfin Hala 2 ch.c   90p
Warrsan (IRE) 3 b.c   93p

M. A. BUCKLEY
Hampton Lucy (IRE) 2 b.f   —p

G. A. BUTLER
Beauchamp Quiz 2 b.f   54p
Common World (USA) 2 ch.c   91p
Compton Dictator 2 b.c   —p
Compton Dragon (USA) 2 ch.c   87P
Goshin's Lad (USA) 2 b.c   67p
Janoueix (IRE) 2 b.c   59p
Playapart (USA) 2 b.c   107p
Purple Haze (IRE) 2 b.f   92p
Rouberia (IRE) 2 ch.f   64p

Stratus (FR) 2 b.c   82p
Swiss Lake (USA) 2 br.f   102p
Beauchamp Pilot 3 ch.g   96p
Conquestadora 3 b.f   92p

N. A. CALLAGHAN
Snails Castle (IRE) 2 b.g   75p

MISS J. A. CAMACHO
Brillano (FR) 2 b.f   75p

H. CANDY
Follow Flanders 2 b.f   74p
Gift Fountain 2 b.f   76p
Last Master 2 b.c   —p
Nivernais 2 b.g   76p
Sabre Dance 2 ch.g   62p
Sister In Law (FR) 2 b.f   76p

D. E. CANTILLON
Piccolezza 2 b.f   75p

H. R. A. CECIL
Bahrqueen (USA) 2 b.f   86p
Burning Sun (USA) 2 b.c   76p
Carib Lady (IRE) 2 b.f   —p
Five Stars 2 ch.f   86p
Half Glance 2 b.f   104p
Handa Island (USA) 2 b.c   85p
Intangible (USA) 2 ch.f   72p
Luluwa (IRE) 2 b.f   83p
Protectress 2 ch.f   103p
Revealing 2 ch.f   106p
Rush About (IRE) 2 ch.c   77p
Sentimental Value (USA) 2 ch.f   75p
Stance 2 b.c   66p
Transit 2 b.c   84p
Western Verse (USA) 2 b.c   92p
Anadonis 3 b.c   81p
Change of Image 3 b.f   65p
High Pitched 3 ch.c   116p

M. R. CHANNON
Harbour House 2 b.g   80p
Lipstick 2 b.f   99p
Live Danger (USA) 2 b.c   54p

R. CHARLTON
Glade Runner (USA) 2 br.f   63p
Seaborne 2 b.f   62p
Serotonin 2 b.c   64p
Tikkun (IRE) 2 ch.c   100p
Bel 3 b.f   83p

D. J. COAKLEY
Cloud Dancer 2 b.f   83p

P. F. I. COLE
Ballybunion (IRE) 2 ch.c   87p
Barman (USA) 2 ch.c   88p
Constable 2 gr.g   83p

Full House (IRE) 2 br.c   84p
Henri Lebasque (IRE) 2 b.c   109p
Jan Brueghel (USA) 2 ch.g   82p
Kepler (USA) 2 ch.c   94P
Long Goodbye (IRE) 2 ch.c   99p
Mr Dinos (IRE) 2 b.c   89p
Orinocovsky (IRE) 2 ch.c   78p
Starzaan (IRE) 2 b.c   80p
Stickwithsterling (USA) 2 b.c   74p
Time To Travel (USA) 2 b.c   85p
Zone 2 b.c   92p
The Judge 3 b.g   94p

A. B. COOGAN
Just Magical 4 b.f   63p

L. G. COTTRELL
Givemethemoonlight 2 ch.f   68p

R. M. H. COWELL
Nassau Night 2 b.g   —p

J. CULLINAN
Sparky Glenn 3 b.c   56p

L. M. CUMANI
Andromache 2 ch.f   66p
Derwent (USA) 2 b.c   90p
Dimple Chad 2 b.c   67p
Gossamer 2 b.f   114p
Ludynosa (USA) 2 b.f   74p
Sadhaka 2 b.f   63p
Stadenanz 2 b.f   —p
Statim 2 b.f   78p

C. A. CYZER
Mist 'n Rain 2 b.f   66p
Silence And Rage 2 b.c   59p

MRS H. DALTON
Sienna Sunset (IRE) 2 ch.f   66p

E. A. L. DUNLOP
Alam (USA) 2 b.c   77P
Answered Promise (FR) 2 gr.g   70p
Baldour (IRE) 2 b.c   87p
Dalal 2 b.f   63p
Fraulein 2 b.f   102p
Havoc 2 b.c   80p
Helloimustbegoing (USA) 2 b.f   76p
King's Envoy (USA) 2 b.g   73p
King's Thought 2 b.c   76P
Luna Moth (USA) 2 b.f   78p
Morning Sky (IRE) 2 b.f   79p
Mubkera (IRE) 2 ch.f   86p
Mulabee (USA) 2 br.c   84p
Munqith (USA) 2 b.c   82p
Russian Dune (IRE) 2 b.g   71p
Shararah 2 br.f   63P
Sweet Band (USA) 2 b.c   94p
Tolcea (IRE) 2 ch.g   66p
Wahchi (IRE) 2 ch.c   97p
Water King (USA) 2 b.c   76p
Well Chosen 2 b.c   74P
Dance On The Top 3 ch.g   93p
Jabaar (USA) 3 gr.c   85p
Pietro Siena (USA) 3 b.c   82p
Rasid (USA) 3 b.g   88p

J. L. DUNLOP
Ajeel (IRE) 2 b.c   67p
Aseelah 2 b.f   72p
Atarama (IRE) 2 b.f   93p
Bestam 2 b.c   103p
Budoor (IRE) 2 b.f   80p
Callisto (IRE) 2 br.f   —p
Contact Dancer (IRE) 2 b.c   56p
Dawn's Sharp Shot (IRE) 2 b.f   68p
Dust Flicker 2 ch.f   63p
Eastern Image (USA) 2 ch.c   96p
Editor In Chief (USA) 2 b.c   86p
Faydah (USA) 2 b.f   72p
Greater Glory (IRE) 2 br.c   70p
Heir To Be 2 b.c   —p
Him of Distinction 2 br.c   93p
In Xanadu (IRE) 2 b.c   72p
I Swear 2 b.c   83p
Karamah 2 b.f   78p
Keetchy (IRE) 2 b.c   76p
Kind of Loving 2 ch.f   63p
King Eider 2 b.g   68p
Mabrum (IRE) 2 b.c   —p
Maid To Perfection 2 b.f   84p
Misck (IRE) 2 ch.f   —p
Nayyel 2 b.c   94p
Nirvana 2 b.f   78p
Old California (IRE) 2 b.c   89p
Persian Lightning (IRE) 2 b.g   73p
Plymsole (USA) 2 ch.f   79p
Ra-Boob (IRE) 2 b.c   55p
Rahwaan (IRE) 2 b.c   78p
Razzle (IRE) 2 b.f   —p
Red Liason (IRE) 2 ch.f   95p
Rose d'Or (IRE) 2 b.f   65p
Screaming Eagle (IRE) 2 b.f   65p
Shagraan 2 b.c   69p
Ski For Me (IRE) 2 ch.f   78p
Snowfire 2 b.f   102p
Star Cross (IRE) 2 b.g   85p
Tahini 2 b.f   63p
Tashawak (IRE) 2 b.f   98p
Thaqib (IRE) 2 b.c   71p
Tripper (USA) 2 b.f   73p
What A View 2 b.c   74p
Zaajel (IRE) 2 b.c   90p
Al Aali 3 b.c   92p
Fallen Star 3 b.f   108p
Harlestone Grey 3 gr.g   101p
Taffrail 3 b.g   96p
Valley of Song 3 ch.f   74p

T. D. EASTERBY
Artie 2 b.g   83p
Bailieborough (IRE) 2 b.c   80p
Bollin Eric 2 b.c   95p
Chapel Orchid 2 b.f   58p
Classic Calvados (FR) 2 b.c   58p
Cumbrian Crystal 2 b.g   69p
Fangio's Quest 2 ch.c   76p
Missing 2 b.f   55p
On The Fairway (IRE) 2 b.f   54p

D. R. C. ELSWORTH
Barry Island 2 b.c   78p
Chapeau 2 ch.f   —p
Grand Aunt Dee (IRE) 2 b.f   64p
Laser Crystal (IRE) 2 b.f   67p

1127

J. M. P. EUSTACE
Agincourt Warrior 2 b.c   70p

R. A. FAHEY
Amused 2 ch.f   63p

J. R. FANSHAWE
Able Baker Charlie (IRE) 2 b.g   73p
Beluga Bay 2 b.g   69p
Calamint 2 gr.g   78p
Cashmere 2 ch.f   69P
Colonnade 2 b.f   51p
Cool Tune 2 b.g   69p
Defining 2 b.g   72p
Exhibitor (USA) 2 b.f   —p
Honey For Money (IRE) 2 b.f   61p
Judge Davidson 2 b.c   90p
Kirtle 2 b.f   81p
Macadamia (IRE) 2 b.f   82p
Miss T 2 b.f   —p
Mythic 2 ch.f   70p
Pious 2 b.f   74p
Polar Ben 2 b.g   86p
Preen 2 b.f   72p
Prins Willem (IRE) 2 b.g   69p
Reveillez 2 gr.g   63p
Torosay Spring 3 ch.f   106p
Johnny Oscar 4 b.g   91p

J. G. GIVEN
Final Faze 2 ch.f   —p
Robbie Can Can 2 b.c   66p
Tip It Over 2 b.g   —p

J. A. GLOVER
Chandris 2 b.g   60p
Red To Violet 2 b.f   77p
Sicknote (IRE) 2 b.g   —p

J. H. M. GOSDEN
Autumn Fantasy (USA) 2 b.c   67p
Ballet Score (IRE) 2 b.f   80p
Camaret 2 b.f   79p
Disco Volante 2 b.f   79p
Drama of Life (USA) 2 ch.f   —p
Epicentre (USA) 2 b.c   89p
Florentine Flutter 2 b.c   72p
Foreign Accent 2 b.c   100p
Imperial Theatre (IRE) 2 b.c   90P
La Paz 2 b.f   70p
Making Waves (IRE) 2 b.f   —p
Mist of Time (IRE) 2 b.f   72p
Moment 2 ch.f   59p
Music Club (USA) 2 b.f   93p
Proven (USA) 2 br.c   96p
Rawyaan 2 b.c   94p
Rhetoric (IRE) 2 b.g   —p
Rose Tinted 2 b.f   69p
Shatarah 2 ch.f   79p
Showering 2 b.f   —p
Slupia (IRE) 2 b.f   76p
Studio Time (USA) 2 b.c   88p
Ticket To Dance (IRE) 2 b.f   67p
Viva Maria (FR) 2 gr.f   81p
Waldenburg (USA) 2 b.c   100p
Zenda 2 b.f   77p
Saltrio 3 b.c   101p

N. A. GRAHAM
Diamond Lover (IRE) 2 ch.c   88p

R. GUEST
Lady Lindsay (IRE) 2 ch.f   82p
Laguna Seca 2 b.f   63p
Madiba 2 b.c   69p

W. J. HAGGAS
Calgarth (IRE) 2 b.f   54p
Sociable 2 b.f   74p
Sundrenched (IRE) 2 ch.f   99p
Tenaja Trail (USA) 2 ch.c   —p
Three Days In May 2 b.f   —p
Kew Green (USA) 3 b.g   78p
Mr Mahoose (USA) 3 b.g   105p
Suggestive 3 b.g   106p

B. HANBURY
Tanaji 2 b.f   77p

R. HANNON
Allenby 2 b.c   89p
Ashton Vale 2 ch.c   65p
Carolina Silk (IRE) 2 b.c   95p
Connor (IRE) 2 ch.c   87p
Cultra (IRE) 2 ch.c   66p
Dechtire (IRE) 2 b.f   —p
Hannon (FR) 2 br.c   61p
Lady Devika 2 b.f   54p
Nysaean (IRE) 2 b.c   83p
Red Halo 2 b.c   75p
Zandicular 2 b.c   89p

P. W. HARRIS
Barathea Blazer 2 b.c   86p
Barolo 2 b.c   77p
Champain Sands (IRE) 2 b.c   70p
Common Thought (IRE) 2 b.g   69p
Cool Storm (IRE) 2 b.f   58p
Palamedes 2 b.c   78p
Ridge Manor (IRE) 2 b.c   —p
Shot To Fame (USA) 2 b.c   94p
Unfaithful Thought 2 b.f   78p
Zilmaid Dancer 2 b.f   55p

P. C. HASLAM
Wensley Blue (IRE) 2 b.g   50p

B. W. HILLS
Alexander Three D (IRE) 2 b.f   101p
Al Mohallab (FR) 2 b.c   97p
Ballet Fame (USA) 2 br.f   79p
Ballet Girl (USA) 2 b.f   70p
Craiova (IRE) 2 b.c   83p
Dear Bridie (IRE) 2 ch.f   66p
Environment Audit 2 ch.c   78p
Far Lane (USA) 2 b.c   70p
Fragrant View (USA) 2 ch.f   79p
Graft 2 b.c   81p
Hills of Gold 2 b.c   103p
Imtihan (IRE) 2 ch.c   —p
Inishowen (IRE) 2 b.c   89p
Lady's Secret (IRE) 2 b.f   88p
Lahberhorn (USA) 2 ch.c   71p
Lakatoi 2 b.f   —p
Popocatepetl (FR) 2 br.f   66p
Rosie's Posy (IRE) 2 b.f   86p
Sarabande 2 ch.f   —p

Shanty 2 b.f 94p
Stands To Reason (USA) 2 b.f 80p
Storm Seeker 2 b.c 77p
Sundial 2 ch.f —p
Totem Pole 2 ch.c 71p
Tree Pipit (USA) 2 ch.f 64p
True Courage 2 b.c 76p
Big Moment 3 ch.g 104p
Faithful Warrior (USA) 3 ch.c 102p

J. W. HILLS
Boundless Prospect (USA) 2 b.c 62p
Danemere (IRE) 2 b.f 79p
Sadlers Law (IRE) 2 b.c —p
Silver Buzzard (USA) 2 b.c 57p
Broadway Score (USA) 3 b.c 80p

R. F. JOHNSON HOUGHTON
Imbibing (IRE) 2 ch.c 83p
Lucky Romance 2 b.f 68p

A. P. JARVIS
Blue Knight (IRE) 2 ch.g 72p

M. A. JARVIS
Andrew Doble 2 ch.c 64p
B Major (IRE) 2 b.g 78p
Celtic Ballet 2 b.f 85p
Cherine (IRE) 2 b.f 60p
Coshocton (USA) 2 b.c 103p
Dryden House (IRE) 2 b.f 70p
Kayseri (IRE) 2 b.c 90p
King Nicholas (USA) 2 b.c —p
Lord Stradbroke (USA) 2 b.g 72p
Loveleaves 2 b.f 84p
Malmand (USA) 2 ch.c 60p
Michael Maher 2 b.c —p
Midnight Parkes 2 b.c 63p
Millennium Dragon 2 b.c 97p
Pinchbeck 2 b.c 61p
Rainbow d'Beaute 2 ch.f —p
Ranville 3 ch.g 102p

W. JARVIS
Jabulani (IRE) 2 b.c 79p
Jasmine Breeze 2 b.f 61p
Nobilissime 2 b.f 73p
Strathclyde (IRE) 2 b.g 50p

B. R. JOHNSON
Frankskips 2 b.g 87p

M. JOHNSTON
Bandari (IRE) 2 b.c 113p
Celtic Style 2 b.c 88p
Decoy 2 b.f —p
Far Pavilions 2 b.c 91p
Fashionable Man (USA) 2 ch.c 93p
Fight Your Corner 2 b.c 114p
Gala Gold 2 b.f 65p
Impavido (IRE) 2 b.c 65p
Legal Approach 2 b.c 100p
Leo's Luckyman (USA) 2 b.c 103p
Love Regardless (USA) 2 b.c 98P
Mazury (USA) 2 b.c 68p
Pyrrhic 2 b.c. 61p
Rajab 2 br.c 94p
Shanook 2 ch.c 85p
Simeon 2 b.c 95p

Sir George Turner 2 ch.c 100p
Systematic 2 b.c 68p
Thunder King (USA) 2 b.c 60p
Desert Deer 3 ch.c 106p

S. KIRK
Out of This World 2 ch.f 59p

W. S. KITTOW
Only For Sue ch.g 62p

D. R. LODER
Activity (IRE) 2 ch.c 76p
Dubai Destination (USA) 2 b.c 119p
Dubai Excellence 2 br.c 89p
Farqad (USA) 2 b.c 101p
Ice And Fire 2 b.g 72p
Kashmor (USA) 2 b.c 78P
Kriskova (USA) 2 b.c 104p
Lahooq 2 b.c 96p
Lunar Sovereign (USA) 2 b.c 95p
Mingora (USA) 2 b.f 89p
Moon Ballad (IRE) 2 ch.c 98p
Pride of Dubai (USA) 2 b.g —p
Sattam 2 b.c 75p
Star Express 2 b.f 80p
Zaeema 2 br.f 93P
Razkalla (USA) 3 b.g 73p

P. J. MAKIN
Greenslades 2 ch.c 82p
Lady Alruna (IRE) 2 ch.f 76p
Liberty Royal 2 b.c 83p
Canterloupe (IRE) 3 b.f 94p
Rare Quality 3 b.f —p

G. M. MCCOURT
Dragon Flyer (IRE) 2 b.f 85p

B. J. MEEHAN
Daimajin (IRE) 2 b.g 74p
Hiddendale (IRE) 2 br.f 90p
Kaieteur (USA) 2 b.c 93p
Mariinsky 2 gr.c 100p
Oases 2 ch.g 92p
Royal Quarters (IRE) 2 ch.c 93p
Savannah Bay 2 ch.c 105p

T. G. MILLS
Fools Rush In (IRE) 2 b.c 87p
Olivia Grace 3 ch.f 103p

G. L. MOORE
Tikram 4 ch.g 89p

H. MORRISON
Chalfont (IRE) 2 b.f 71p

W. R. MUIR
Shasta 2 b.f —p
Zargus 2 b.c 89p

W. J. MUSSON
Feet So Fast 2 ch.g 89p

D. NICHOLLS
Magical Myth 2 b.f 50p
Continent 4 ch.g 111p

J. NICOL
War Valor (USA) 2 b.c 85p

J. NOSEDA
All Business 2 b.f 79p
Andromeda (IRE) 2 b.f 68p
Just James 2 b.c 84p
King Creole 2 b.c 70p
Mellow Park (IRE) 2 b.f 73p
Naughty Nell 2 b.f 69p
Sefton Lodge 2 b.c —p
Spinnette (IRE) 2 b.f 93p
Star of Normandie (USA) 2 b.f 75p
Woodlyon (USA) 2 b.c 59p
Burning Impulse 3 b.c 93p
Master McGrath (IRE) 3 b.c 75p

A. P. O'BRIEN, IRELAND
Ballingarry (IRE) 2 b.c 114p
Canberra (IRE) 2 b.c 99p
Century City (IRE) 2 b.c 96p
Della Francesca (USA) 2 b.c 110p
Hawk Wing (USA) 2 b.c 116p
High Chaparral (IRE) 2 b.c 115p
High Sierra (IRE) 2 b.c 100p
Kournakova (IRE) 2 b.f 102p
Maryinsky (IRE) 2 b.f 107p
On The Nile (IRE) 2 b.f 103p
Quarter Moon (IRE) 2 b.f 106p
Roar of The Tiger (USA) 2 ch.c 98p
Sorcerous 2 b.c 94P
Tasmanian Tiger (USA) 2 ch.c 80p
Tendulkar (USA) 2 b.c 114p

JONJO O'NEILL
Spectroscope (IRE) 2 b.c 63p

J. A. OSBORNE
Hatter's Lad (IRE) 2 b.c 86p
King David 2 b.c 58p
Red Wine 2 b.g 75p

J. W. PAYNE
Ezz Elkheil 2 b.c 85p
Jawwala (USA) 2 b.f 84p

MRS LYDIA PEARCE
Copperfields Lass 2 b.f 51p

MRS A. J. PERRETT
Ashkelon 2 ch.c 86p
Chivite (IRE) 2 b.c 67p
Commanding 2 ch.c 80p
Dawn Invasion (IRE) 2 b.c 88p
Desert Alchemy (IRE) 2 b.f 80p
Dolores 2 b.f 87p
Forest Ridge 2 b.g —p
Indian Solitaire (IRE) 2 b.c 91p
It's The Limit (USA) 2 b.c —p
Kaparolo (USA) 2 ch.c 73p
Mark It 2 b.g —p
Opening Ceremony (USA) 2 br.f 87p
Prince Hector 2 ch.c 86p
Sardis 2 b.c 67p
Sari (USA) 2 gr.f —p
The Gaikwar (IRE) 2 b.c —p
Welsh Diva 2 b.f 67p
Ruby Wedding 3 b.f 60p

SIR MARK PRESCOTT
Affaire d'Amour 2 ch.f 50p
Albanova 2 gr.f 75P
Arachine 2 ch.g —p
Blue Mantle (IRE) 2 ch.f —p
Chivalry 2 b.g 61p
Coalition 2 b.c 54p
Dafne 2 ch.f —p
Denmark (IRE) 2 b.c 81p
Froglet 2 b.f 58p
I Do 2 ch.f 81p
Inglis Drever 2 b.c 65p
Parachute 2 ch.g 62p
Sahara Rose 2 b.f —p
Sheer Bliss (IRE) 2 b.f 86p
Showdown 2 gr.f 65p
Unleash (USA) 2 ch.c 85p
Foreign Affairs 3 ch.c 117p
Roman Hideaway (IRE) 3 b.c 87p

J. J. QUINN
Smart Hostess 2 b.f 54p

MRS J. R. RAMSDEN
Lingo (IRE) 2 b.g 53p
Words And Deeds (USA) 2 ch.g 71p

MRS M. REVELEY
Junkanoo 5 ch.g 66p
My Line 4 b.g 58p

K. A. RYAN
Dundonald 2 ch.g —p
Special Hero (IRE) 2 b.c 71p

B. SMART
Friday's Takings 2 ch.c 57p

A. C. STEWART
Adaleel 2 b.c —p
Amber's Bluff 2 b.c 80p
Garw Valley 2 b.f 62p
Mubaah 2 ch.c 64p
Seihali (IRE) 2 b.c 87p
Selective 2 b.c 86p
Shoof (USA) 2 b.f 68p
Zawrak (IRE) 2 ch.c 58p
Island Light 3 b.g 85p
Scotty's Future (IRE) 3 b.c 94p

SIR MICHAEL STOUTE
Aglow 2 b.f 90p
Alasha (IRE) 2 ch.f 89p
Balakheri (IRE) 2 b.c 96p
Bragadino 2 b.c 104p
Carafe 2 b.f 77p
Cassirer (IRE) 2 ch.c 89p
Comfy (USA) 2 b.c 107p
Constitute (USA) 2 b.f —p
Courtesy (USA) 2 b.f 76p
Eternelle 2 b.f —p
First Charter 2 b.c 94p
First of Many 2 b.f 83p
Gallant Boy (IRE) 2 ch.c 84p
Gamut (IRE) 2 b.c 83P
Grain of Gold 2 b.f 57p
Hathaal (IRE) 2 b.c 95p
Highest (IRE) 2 b.c 98p
Islington (IRE) 2 b.f 100p

King of Happiness (USA) 2 ch.c   105p
Kirov 2 b.f   72p
L'Affaire Monique 2 b.f   73p
Leadership 2 b.c   84p
Light Scent (USA) 2 ch.c   93p
Lishtar (IRE) 2 b.g   79p
Marakash (IRE) 2 b.c   77p
Mount Street (IRE) 2 b.f   82P
Outlaw 2 b.c   —p
Princely Venture (IRE) 2 ch.c   82P
Rabwah (USA) 2 ch.f   66p
Researched (IRE) 2 b.c   —p
Right Approach 2 b.c   103P
Saddad (USA) 2 ch.c   112p
Shakran 2 ch.c   90p
Shalamantika (IRE) 2 b.f   67p
Silistra 2 gr.c   76P
Sunray Superstar 2 b.f   87p
Tamdali (IRE) 2 b.g   63p
Telesto (USA) 2 b.c   84p
Two Marks (USA) 2 ch.f   62p
Alexius (IRE) 3 b.c   120p
Artillery (IRE) 3 b.c   109p
Carnival Dancer 3 b.c   123p
Top Dirham 3 ch.c   100p

Miss Pinkerton 2 b.f   81p
Monturani (IRE) 2 b.f   77P
Northern Desert (IRE) 2 b.c   76p
Trojan Princess 2 b.f   80p
Halland 3 ch.c   108p
Wings of A Dove 3 b.f   —p

SAEED BIN SUROOR
Mount Joy 2 br.c   102p
Equerry (USA) 3 b.c   119p

J. A. R. TOLLER
Pinjarra 2 b.f   —p

M. H. TOMPKINS
Steenberg (IRE) 2 ch.c   96p

M. P. TREGONING
Arzamas 2 b.f   74p
Curate (USA) 2 ch.c   —p
Elayoon (USA) 2 b.f   76p
Esloob (USA) 2 b.f   104p
Proserpine 2 b.f   95p
Shadow Dancing 2 b.f   96p
Tholjanah (IRE) 2 b.c   109p
Tramonto 2 b.f   91p

ANDREW TURNELL
Jelani (IRE) 2 b.c   98p

C. F. WALL
Arbie (CAN) 2 b.g   59p
Cayman Sound 2 b.f   54p
Czarina Waltz 2 b.f   66p
Escenica (IRE) 2 b.f   76p
Locomotive 2 b.g   65p
Summer Wine 2 b.f   77p

R. M. WHITAKER
Vicious Prince (IRE) 2 b.c   75p

S. P. C. WOODS
Acorazado (IRE) 2 b.g   79p
Fortune Island (IRE) 2 b.c   76p
Silken Brief (IRE) 2 b.f   80p
Trojan (IRE) 2 ch.g   69p

G. WRAGG
Frosty Welcome (USA) 2 gr.f   67p
Miss Corniche 2 b.f   81p
Miss Croisette 2 ch.f   60p

SELECTED BIG RACES 2001

Prize money for racing abroad has been converted to £ sterling at the exchange rate current at the time of the race. The figures are correct to the nearest £. The Timeform ratings (TR) recorded by the principals in each race appear on the last line.

NAD AL SHEBA Saturday, Mar 24   Turf course: GOOD, Dirt track: FAST

1   **Dubai Sheema Classic (Gr 2) (4yo+)** £836,571   1½m (Turf)

STAY GOLD (JPN) *YIkee,Japan* 7-8-11 YTake (6)	33/1		1
FANTASTIC LIGHT (USA) *SaeedbinSuroor,UAE* 5-8-11 (t) LDettori (9)	7/4f	ns	2
SILVANO (GER) *AWohler,Germany* 5-8-11 ASuborics (5)	9/1	2	3
Endless Hall *LMCumani,GB* 5-8-11 JPSpencer (13)	10/1	2½	4
Give The Slip *SaeedbinSuroor,UAE* 4-8-11 DFlores (3)	14/1	1¼	5
Caitano *ASchutz,Germany* 7-8-11 (b) AStarke (1)	16/1	1¼	6
Daliapour (IRE) *IWallan,HongKong* 5-8-11 JMurtagh (7)	5/1	2½	7
Mutafaweq (USA) *SaeedbinSuroor,UAE* 5-8-11 RHills (14)	7/1	1¼	8
Island House (IRE) *GWragg,GB* 5-8-11 DHolland (12)	33/1	sh	9
Inchlonaig *ECharpy,UAE* 4-8-11 SSanders (4)	28/1	1	10
Crimson Quest (IRE) *JBarton,SaudiArabia* 4-8-11 CMcCarron (16)	33/1	nk	11
Kutub (IRE) *SaeedbinSuroor,UAE* 4-8-11 (v) JBailey (2)	40/1	hd	12
Indigenous (IRE) *IWallan,HongKong* 8-8-11 (t) WCMarwing (15)	20/1	1½	13
Miletrian (IRE) *MRChannon,GB* 4-8-7 CraigWilliams (8)	25/1	hd	14
Catella (GER) *PSchiergen,Germany* 5-8-7 JQuinn (11)	16/1	½	15
Murghem (IRE) *MJohnston,GB* 6-8-11 KFallon (10)	33/1	3	16

Shadai Race Horse Co. Ltd 16ran 2m28.23   TR: 127/127/124/120/121/117

2   **Dubai Duty Free (Gr 2) (4yo+)** £836,571   1m195y (Turf)

JIM AND TONIC (FR) *FDoumen,France* 7-9-0 GMosse (8)	5/1		1
FAIRY KING PRAWN (AUS) *IWallan,HongKong* 6-9-0 RFradd (10)	5/1	nk	2
SUNLINE (NZ) *TMcKee,NewZealand* 6-8-10 GChilds (9)	7/4f	½	3
Golden Silca *MRChannon,GB* 5-8-10 CraigWilliams (14)	16/1	2¼	4
Arkadian Hero (USA) *LMCumani,GB* 6-9-0 JPSpencer (3)	14/1	1¼	5
Slickly (FR) *SaeedbinSuroor,UAE* 5-9-0 LDettori (12)	12/1	1½	6
Prolix *SRAl-Shaibani,SaudiArabia* 6-9-0 SMadrid (2)	28/1	½	7
Swallow Flight (IRE) *GWragg,GB* 5-9-0 DHolland (1)	25/1	nk	8
Eagle Cafe (USA) *FKojima,Japan* 4-9-0 (h) YTake (5)	40/1	2	9
Mahfooth (USA) *SaeedbinSuroor,UAE* 4-9-0 RHills (4)	12/1	¾	10
Ladies Din (USA) *JCCanani,USA* 6-9-0 (b+t) CMcCarron (1)	25/1	7	11
Happy Diamond (USA) *SaeedbinSuroor,UAE* 4-9-0 DFlores (15)	25/1	4½	12
Sumitas (GER) *PSchiergen,Germany* 5-9-0 OPeslier (7)	16/1	7½	13
Shamrock City (IRE) *PHowling,GB* 4-9-0 KFallon (13)	33/1	dist	14
Crisos Il Monaco (IRE) *LCamici,Italy* 6-9-0 (h) ODoleuze (11)	40/1	rtr	

Mr J. D. Martin 15ran 1m47.83   TR: 124/123/119/115/116/112

3   **Dubai World Cup (Gr 1) (4yo+)** £2,509,714   1¼m (Dirt)

CAPTAIN STEVE (USA) *RBaffert,USA* 4-9-0 (t) JBailey (11)	7/4jf		1
TO THE VICTORY (JPN) *YIkee,Japan* 5-8-10 YTake (5)	25/1	3	2
HIGHTORI (FR) *PHDemercastel,France* 4-9-0 (ec) GMosse (8)	8/1	½	3
State Shinto (USA) *JDSadler,UAE* 5-9-0 (b) TEDurcan (9)	25/1	sh	4
Sei Mi (ARG) *JBarton,SaudiArabia* 5-9-0 CMcCarron (12)	66/1	1½	5
Aptitude (USA) *RJFrankel,USA* 4-9-0 GaryStevens (4)	5/1	1	6
Ekraar (USA) *SaeedbinSuroor,UAE* 4-9-0 (v+t) RHills (3)	12/1	1¾	7
Best of The Bests (IRE) *SaeedbinSuroor,UAE* 4-9-0 LDettori (10)	7/4jf	4	8
Regular Member (JPN) *SYamamoto,Japan* 4-9-0 MMatsunaga (6)	50/1	ns	9
Broche (USA) *SaeedbinSuroor,UAE* 4-9-0 (v) DFlores (2)	22/1	hd	10
Aristotle (IRE) *MPThwaites,Malaysia* 4-9-0 (b+t) JSaimee (7)	40/1	6	11
Early Warning (USA) *SRAl-Shaibani,SaudiArabia* 6-9-0 SMadrid (1)	40/1	2	12

Mr Michael E. Pegram 12ran 2m00.40   TR: 127+/118/122/121/118/117

SHA TIN Sunday, Apr 22   GOOD to FIRM

4   **Audemars Piguet Queen Elizabeth II Cup (Gr 1) (3yo+)** £507,569   1¼m

1	SILVANO (GER) *AWohler,Germany* 5-9-0 ASuborics	62/10		1
2	JIM AND TONIC (FR) *FDoumen,France* 7-9-0 GMosse	13/10f	1¾	2
1	INDIGENOUS (IRE) *IWallan,HongKong* 8-9-0 WCMarwing	41/1	1½	3
	Electronic Unicorn (USA) *PFYiu,HongKong* 5-9-0 (b) FCoetzee	37/1	2½	4
	Oriental Express (IRE) *IWallan,HongKong* 8-9-0 (b) DHarrison	100/1	¾	5

1132

1	Daliapour (IRE) *IWAllan,HongKong* 5-9-0 JFEgan	24/1	hd 6
	Helene Vitality (NZ) *DAHayes,HongKong* 5-9-0 (b) SDye	13/1	1¾ 7
1	Caitano *ASchutz,Germany* 7-9-0 (b) AStarke	49/1	3¾ 8
	Housemaster (IRE) *IWAllan,HongKong* 5-9-0 ESaint-Martin	73/1	½ 9
	Industrial Pioneer (IRE) *PCKan,HongKong* 4-9-0 RFradd	18/10	1½ 10
	Idol (NZ) *DOughton,HongKong* 5-9-0 DWhyte	33/1	2¼ 11
	Sobieski (IRE) *SaeedbinSuroor,UAE* 4-9-0 (v) LDettori	20/1	5¾ 12
	Emission (AUS) *CIBrown,Australia* 4-9-0 ELegrix	100/1	6¼ 13

Stiftung Gestut Fahrhof 13ran 2m03.10   TR: 126/122+/119/114/112/112

LONGCHAMP Sunday, Apr 29   SOFT

5   Prix Ganay (Gr 1) (4yo+) £47,665   1¼m

GOLDEN SNAKE (USA) *JLDunlop,GB* 5-9-2 PatEddery	10/1	1
EGYPTBAND (USA) *MmeCHead-Maarek,France* 4-8-13 ODoleuze	11/10f	3 2
WITH THE FLOW (USA) *MmeCHead-Maarek,France* 6-9-2 (b) OPeslier	156/10	3 3
Little Rock *SirMichaelStoute,GB* 5-9-2 KFallon	271/10	hd 4
Di Moi Oui *PBary,France* 4-8-13 TThulliez	219/10	nk 5
Earlene (IRE) *H-APantall,France* 4-8-13 GMosse	47/10	½ 6
Samum (GER) *ASchutz,Germany* 4-9-2 AStarke	31/10	1½ 7
Boismorand (FR) *M-FMathet,France* 5-8-13 DBoeuf	267/10	10 8
Burning Sunset *DSepulchre,France* 4-8-13 TJarnet	179/10	6 9

The National Stud 9ran 2m16.70   TR: 123/117/114/113/111/110

NEWMARKET Friday, May 4   GOOD (Rowley Mile Course)

6   Sagitta Jockey Club Stks (Gr 2) (4yo+) £34,800   1½m

MILLENARY *JLDunlop* 4-9-0 PatEddery (1)	11/4	1
SANDMASON *HRACecil* 4-8-9 WRyan (6)	14/1	2 2
HOLDING COURT *MAJarvis* 4-9-0 PRobinson (7)	12/1	3 3
Wellbeing *HRACecil* 4-8-9 TQuinn (2)	9/4f	1¾ 4
Salford Express *DRCElsworth* 5-8-9 RHughes (4)	10/1	5 5
Boreas *LMCumani* 6-8-9 JPSpencer (5)	13/2	6 6
Air Marshall (IRE) *SirMichaelStoute* 4-8-12 KFallon (3)	6/1	dist 7

Mr L. Neil Jones 7ran 2m32.67   TR: 124/116/116/108

NEWMARKET Saturday, May 5   GOOD (Rowley Mile Course)

7   Sagitta 2000 Guineas Stks (Gr 1) (3yo c+f) £174,000   1m

GOLAN (IRE) *SirMichaelStoute* 3-9-0 KFallon (19)	11/1	1
TAMBURLAINE (IRE) *RHannon* 3-9-0 RHughes (12)	12/1	1¼ 2
FRENCHMANS BAY (FR) *RCharlton* 3-9-0 PatEddery (14)	14/1	nk 3
Minardi (USA) *APO'Brien,Ireland* 3-9-0 MJKinane (8)	5/1	3 4
Red Carpet *MLWBell* 3-9-0 MFenton (11)	20/1	sh 5
Munir *BWHills* 3-9-0 RHills (7)	8/1	hd 6
Mayville Thunder *GAButler* 3-9-0 JPSpencer (17)	66/1	¾ 7
Nayef (USA) *MPTregoning* 3-9-0 WSupple (16)	10/1	¾ 8
Tobougg (IRE) *SaeedbinSuroor* 3-9-0 LDettori (6)	4/1f	nk 9
King's Ironbridge (IRE) *RHannon* 3-9-0 DaneO'Neill (18)	16/1	nk 10
Volata (IRE) *MHTompkins* 3-9-0 TEDurcan (10)	100/1	1¾ 11
Patsy's Double *MBlanshard* 3-9-0 TQuinn (1)	66/1	2½ 12
Darwin (IRE) *APO'Brien,Ireland* 3-9-0 PaulScallan (5)	100/1	¾ 13
Rumpold *SaeedbinSuroor* 3-9-0 JCarroll (9)	9/1	nk 14
Imperial Dancer *MRChannon* 3-9-0 SDrowne (2)	50/1	1¼ 15
Divine Task (USA) *SaeedbinSuroor* 3-9-0 KDarley (15)	16/1	2½ 16
Tempest *SirMichaelStoute* 3-9-0 JMurtagh (3)	20/1	sh 17
Heretic *JRFanshawe* 3-9-0 MHills (13)	50/1	sh 18

Lord Weinstock 18ran 1m37.48   TR: 122+/119/118/111+/111+/111

NEWMARKET Sunday, May 6   GOOD (Rowley Mile Course)

8   Sagitta 1000 Guineas Stks (Gr 1) (3yo f) £174,000   1m

AMEERAT *MAJarvis* 3-9-0 PRobinson (10)	11/1	1
MUWAKLEH *SaeedbinSuroor* 3-9-0 LDettori (12)	13/2	nk 2
TOROCA (USA) *APO'Brien,Ireland* 3-9-0 MJKinane (7)	10/1	1¾ 3
Crystal Music (USA) *JHMGosden* 3-9-0 RHughes (8)	5/1	1 4
Enthused (USA) *SirMichaelStoute* 3-9-0 JMurtagh (9)	6/1	1½ 5
Arhaaff (IRE) *MRChannon* 3-9-0 CraigWilliams (3)	25/1	2½ 6
Stunning (USA) *MmeCHead-Maarek,France* 3-9-0 ODoleuze (4)	9/1	1 7
Santolina (USA) *JHMGosden* 3-9-0 JFortune (6)	20/1	sh 8
Autumnal (IRE) *BJMeehan* 3-9-0 BDoyle (15)	50/1	1½ 9
Peaceful Paradise *JWHills* 3-9-0 MHills (14)	50/1	nk 10

1133

Mameha *CEBrittain* 3-9-0 BMarcus (13) .... 100/1 ½ 11
Sayedah (IRE) *MPTregoning* 3-9-0 RHills (12) 20/1 2½ 12
Karasta (IRE) *SirMichaelStoute* 3-9-0 KFallon (5) 9/2f 1½ 13
Ashlinn (IRE) *RHannon* 3-9-0 DaneO'Neill (1) .... 100/1 ¾ 14
Dora Carrington (IRE) *PWHarris* 3-9-0 JReid (2) .... 12/1 ½ 15

Sheikh Ahmed Al Maktoum 15ran 1m38.36   TR: 116/115/111/109/107/101

KRANJI Saturday, May 12   FIRM

9   **Singapore Airlines International Cup (Gr 1) (3yo+) £687,023**   1¼m

 1   ENDLESS HALL *LMCumani,GB* 5-9-0 JPSpencer.................................. 84/10   1
 4   JIM AND TONIC (FR) *FDoumen,France* 7-9-0 GMosse .... 24/10f   ¾ 2
 5   WITH THE FLOW (USA) *MmeCHead-Maarek,France* 6-9-0 (b)   sh 3
      ODoleuze 17/1
     Hill of Grace (NZ) *R&WPriscott,NewZealand* 5-8-11 (b) CBrown........... 15/1   1¾ 4
 4   Silvano (GER) *AWohler,Germany* 5-9-0 ASuborics .... 26/10   ½ 5
     Our Aristotle (IRE) *MPThwaites,Malaysia* 4-9-0 (b) OChavez.............. 9/1   1¾ 6
     Carry The Flag *MKent,Singapore* 6-9-0 PPayne .... 168/10   ¾ 7
     Lazy Lode (ARG) *REMandella,USA* 7-9-0 LPincay 54/10   4¼ 8
     Tapildo (NZ) *LLaxon,Singapore* 4-8-5 EWilkinson 172/10   1¾ 9
     Kim Angel (AUS) *JMeagher,Singapore* 5-8-11 (b) LDittman .... 152/10   ns 10

Il Paralupo 10ran 2m00.80   TR: 121/119+//119?/113/115/112

LONGCHAMP Sunday, May 13   GOOD to FIRM

10   **Dubai Poule d'Essai des Poulains (Gr 1) (3yo c) £94,967**   1m
     Order as they passed the post: Noverre was disqualified after failing a dope test

     NOVERRE (USA) *SaeedbinSuroor,GB* 3-9-2 LDettori 19/2   1
     VAHORIMIX (FR) *AFabre,France* 3-9-2 CSoumillon.............................. 64/10   hd 2
     CLEARING (USA) *JHMGosden,GB* 3-9-2 RHughes.............................. 61/10   hd 3
     Denon (USA) *JEPease,France* 3-9-2 TJarnet 9/2   1½ 4
     Okawango (USA) *MmeCHead-Maarek,France* 3-9-2 ODoleuze 36/10   1 5
     Keltos (FR) *CLaffon-Parias,France* 3-9-2 DBoeuf 3/1f   1 6
     Black Minnaloushe (USA) *APO'Brien,Ireland* 3-9-2 JPSpencer............. 74/10   ¾ 7
     King's County (IRE) *APO'Brien,Ireland* 3-9-2 (v) MJKinane .... 74/10   nk 8
     Modigliani (USA) *APO'Brien,Ireland* 3-9-2 PaulScallan .... 74/10   ½ 9
     Greengroom (FR) *CLaffon-Parias,France* 3-9-2 TThulliez...................... 36/10   5 10
     Zarin (IRE) *JLDunlop,GB* 3-9-2 TQuinn 263/10   4 11
     Watteau (IRE) *DSepulchre,France* 3-9-2 OPeslier 29/1   1½ 12

Mr J-L. Lagardere 12ran 1m35.40   TR: 120/120/119/115/113/110

11   **Dubai Poule d'Essai des Pouliches (Gr 1) (3yo f) £94,967**   1m
     ROSE GYPSY *APO'Brien,Ireland* 3-9-0 MJKinane 147/10   1
     BANKS HILL *AFabre,France* 3-9-0 OPeslier .... 33/10   hd 2
     LETHALS LADY *RCollet,France* 3-9-0 SPasquier .... 78/1   hd 3
     Tempting Fate (IRE) *SaeedbinSuroor,GB* 3-9-0 LDettori .... 48/10   ½ 4
     Amonita *PBary,France* 3-9-0 TJarnet 22/10f   1½ 5
     Choc Ice (IRE) *RCollet,France* 3-9-0 GMosse 188/10   3 6
     Calista *JEPease,France* 3-9-0 TGillet .... 104/10   sn 7
     Rolly Polly (IRE) *HRACecil,GB* 3-9-0 TQuinn .... 79/10   ¾ 8
     Quarter Note (USA) *H-APantall,France* 3-9-0 YTake.......................... 48/10   nk 9
     Lil's Jessy (IRE) *JNoseda,GB* 3-9-0 PatEddery .... 27/1   nk 10
     Born Something (IRE) *MmeCHead-Maarek,France* 3-9-0 ODoleuze....... 152/10   sn 11
     Victoria Cross (IRE) *GWragg,GB* 3-9-0 DHolland 267/10   1 12
     Hope Town (FR) *HVandePoele,France* 3-9-0 AMalenfant 449/10   1 13
     Featherquest *MmeCHead-Maarek,France* 3-9-0 PBruneau.................... 152/10   nk 14
     Chiquette *WNeuroth,Norway* 3-9-0 FSanchez 92/1   6 15

Mrs John Magnier & Mr M. Tabor 15ran 1m36.70   TR: 114/114+/113/112/108+

YORK Thursday, May 17   GOOD

12   **Duke of York Victor Chandler Stks (Gr 3) (3yo+) £36,000**   6f
     PIPALONG (IRE) *TDEasterby* 5-9-6 KDarley (8)................................. 14/1   1
     TEDBURROW *EJAlston* 9-9-1 TEDurcan (10) .... 14/1   nk 2
     ASTONISHED *MrsJRRamsden* 5-9-1 KFallon (4) .... 6/1   ½ 3
     Bertolini (USA) *SaeedbinSuroor* 5-9-1 (v) LDettori (1) .... 11/4f   nk 4
     Vision of Night *JLDunlop* 5-9-1 PatEddery (2)................................. 12/1   sh 5
     Munjiz (IRE) *BWHills* 5-9-1 RHills (12).. 10/1   sh 6
     Now Look Here *BAMcMahon* 5-9-1 TQuinn (9) 12/1   1¼ 7
     Bahamian Pirate (USA) *DNicholls* 6-9-1 AlexGreaves (7)................... 12/1   ¾ 8
     Misraah (IRE) *SirMichaelStoute* 4-9-1 FNorton (6)............................. 14/1   nk 9

Harmonic Way *RCharlton* 6-9-1 MJKinane (5) 9/1 1¾ 10
Hot Tin Roof *TDEasterby* 5-8-12 JFortune (13) .... 16/1 ¾ 11
Eastern Purple (IRE) *KARyan* 6-9-5 JCarroll (11) 33/1 1¾ 12
Doctor Spin (IRE) *RFJohnsonHoughton* 5-9-1 JReid (14) .... 25/1 ½ 13
Ho Leng (IRE) *MissLAPerratt* 6-9-1 RWinston (15) 33/1 5 14

Mr T. H. Bennett 14ran 1m11.20   TR: 121/115/114/114/114/113

NEWBURY Saturday, May 19   SOFT

13 Juddmonte Lockinge Stks (Gr 1) (4yo+) £87,000   1m

    MEDICEAN *SirMichaelStoute* 4-9-0 KFallon (5) 3/1   1
    WARNINGFORD *JRFanshawe* 7-9-0 PatEddery (6) .... 9/1   nk 2
  2 SWALLOW FLIGHT (IRE) *GWragg* 5-9-0 LDettori (8) .... 7/4f   nk 3
    Danceabout *GWragg* 4-8-11 JMurtagh (7) 8/1   3 4
    Umistim *RHannon* 4-9-0 DaneO'Neill (2) 12/1   1½ 5
  2 Arkadian Hero (USA) *LMCumani* 6-9-0 JPSpencer (4) .... 7/1   hd 6
    Sugarfoot *NTinkler* 7-9-0 JReid (1) 10/1 2½ 7

Cheveley Park Stud 7ran 1m45.39   TR: 120+/119/119/109

LONGCHAMP Sunday, May 20   GOOD to FIRM

14 Prix d'Ispahan (Gr 1) (4yo+) £47,037   1m1f55y

    OBSERVATORY (USA) *JHMGosden,GB* 4-9-2 RHughes 11/10f   1
  3 HIGHTORI (FR) *PHDemercastel,France* 4-9-2 GMosse .... 6/4   sh 2
  3 EKRAAR (USA) *SaeedbinSuroor,GB* 4-9-2 (b) LDettori 42/10   3 3
    Tikzane (FR) *MBoutin,France* 4-9-2 DHolland 143/10   2½ 4
    Golani (IRE) *ELellouche,France* 4-9-2 DBoeuf 99/10   6 5

Mr K. Abdulla 5ran 1m51.00   TR: 122+/122+/115/109

CURRAGH Saturday, May 26   GOOD

15 Entenmann's Irish 2000 Guineas (Gr 1) (3yo c+f) £98,965   1m

10 BLACK MINNALOUSHE (USA) *APO'Brien* 3-9-0 JMurtagh 20/1   1
    MOZART (IRE) *APO'Brien* 3-9-0 (t) JAHeffernan 20/1   2 2
  7 MINARDI (IRE) *APO'Brien* 3-9-0 MJKinane .... 2/1f   ¾ 3
    Maumee (IRE) *DKWeld* 3-9-0 (b) PJSmullen 40/1   3½ 4
  7 Tamburlaine (IRE) *RHannon,GB* 3-9-0 RHughes 9/4   1½ 5
    Mugharreb (USA) *BHanbury,GB* 3-9-0 RHills 9/2   3½ 6
    Freud (USA) *APO'Brien* 3-9-0 (b+t) JPSpencer .... 9/1   ½ 7
    Dr Brendler (USA) *JCHayden* 3-9-0 FMBerry 20/1   1½ 8
    Arch Stanton (IRE) *WPMullins* 3-9-0 NGMcCullagh 200/1   3½ 9
    Amicable (IRE) *BWHills,GB* 3-9-0 MHills .... 16/1   ¾ 10
    Cruiskeen Lawn (IRE) *CCollins* 3-9-0 PShanahan 100/1   4 11
    Cashel Bay (USA) *LukeComer* 3-9-0 (b) WJSmith 200/1   20 12

Mrs John Magnier 12ran 1m41.40   TR: 122/117/116/108/104

CURRAGH Sunday, May 27   GOOD

16 Tattersalls Gold Cup (Gr 1) (4yo+) £96,875   1¼m110y

  1 FANTASTIC LIGHT (USA) *SaeedbinSuroor,GB* 5-9-0 (t) LDettori 5/4f   1
  5 GOLDEN SNAKE (USA) *JLDunlop,GB* 5-9-0 PatEddery .... 7/1   nk 2
    KALANISI (IRE) *SirMichaelStoute,GB* 5-9-0 KFallon 7/4   3 3
  1 Give The Slip *SaeedbinSuroor,GB* 4-9-0 RHills 25/1   1 4
    Bach (IRE) *APO'Brien* 4-9-0 MJKinane 20/1   7 5
    Muakaad *DKWeld* 4-9-0 (b+t) PJSmullen 7/1   13 6

Godolphin 6ran 2m13.40   TR: 128/127/122/121

17 Entenmann's Irish 1000 Guineas (Gr 1) (3yo f) £98,965   1m

    IMAGINE (IRE) *APO'Brien* 3-9-0 JAHeffernan 16/1   1
  8 CRYSTAL MUSIC (USA) *JHMGosden,GB* 3-9-0 LDettori 9/2f   2 2
  8 TOROCA (USA) *APO'Brien* 3-9-0 MJKinane 11/2   2 3
    Sequoyah (IRE) *APO'Brien* 3-9-0 JPSpencer 14/1   1½ 4
    Rebelline (IRE) *KevinPrendergast* 3-9-0 DPMcDonogh .... 8/1   sh 5
  8 Karasta (IRE) *SirMichaelStoute,GB* 3-9-0 KFallon .... 8/1   nk 6
    Softly Tread (IRE) *CCollins* 3-9-0 PShanahan 11/1   3 7
    Scarlet Velvet (USA) *JOxx* 3-9-0 JMurtagh .... 10/1   ½ 8
    Cool Clarity (IRE) *DKWeld* 3-9-0 PJSmullen .... 6/1   sh 9
    Coney Kitty (IRE) *DHanley* 3-9-0 PatEddery 33/1   1¼ 10
    Katherine Seymour *MJGrassick* 3-9-0 EAhern .... 16/1   ¾ 11
    Dance Till Dawn (IRE) *MrsJohnHarrington* 3-9-0 FMBerry 25/1   3 12
    Speirbhean (IRE) *JSBolger* 3-9-0 KJManning .... 12/1   nk 13
    Bonheur (IRE) *APO'Brien* 3-9-0 CO'Donoghue 100/1   2 14
    Mala Mala (IRE) *TStack* 3-9-0 WMLordan 20/1   2½ 15

Love Me True (USA) *APO'Brien* 3-9-0 PaulScallan .... 100/1 ¾ 16
Mrs John Magnier 16ran 1m41.10   TR: 119/114/110/106/106/106

SANDOWN Monday, May 28   GOOD to FIRM

18   **Bonusprint Stks (Henry II) (Gr 3) (4yo+)** £24,000   2m78y

SOLO MIO (IRE) *MrsAJPerrett* 7-9-1 MJKinane (2) 7/1   1
ROMANTIC AFFAIR (IRE) *JLDunlop* 4-8-10 TQuinn (10) 4/1jf   1 2
PERSIAN PUNCH (IRE) *DRCElsworth* 8-9-3 KFallon (6) .... 5/1   hd 3
Life Is Life (FR) *MAJarvis* 5-8-9 PRobinson (11) .... 20/1   hd 4
Mbele *WRMuir* 4-8-10 MartinDwyer (9) 33/1   1½ 5
Churlish Charm *RHannon* 6-8-12 (v) JFortune (5) 16/1   5 6
Jardines Lookout (IRE) *APJarvis* 4-8-10 YTake (7) 20/1   1¾ 7
Ski Run *GAButler* 5-8-9 LDettori (1) .... 6/1   ¾ 8
Royal Rebel *MJohnston* 5-9-3 (v) KDarley (4) 8/1   2½ 9
  1   Miletrian (IRE) *MRChannon* 4-8-12 CraigWilliams (3) 25/1   1 10
Rainbow High *BWHills* 6-8-12 RHughes (8) 4/1jf   23 11
Cheveley Park Stud 11ran 3m37.43   TR: 121/118/122/114+//116/110

CHANTILLY Sunday, Jun 3   GOOD to FIRM

19   **Prix du Jockey Club (Gr 1) (3yo c+f)** £367,647   1½m

ANABAA BLUE *CLerner,France* 3-9-2 CSoumillon................................. 86/10   1
CHICHICASTENANGO (FR) *PHDemercastel,France* 3-9-2 AJunk .... 184/10   ½ 2
GRANDERA (IRE) *JRFanshawe,GB* 3-9-2 MHills .... 313/10   sh 3
  10   Okawango (USA) *MmeCHead-Maarek,France* 3-9-2 ODoleuze .... 138/10   ¾ 4
Milan *APO'Brien,Ireland* 3-9-2 MJKinane .... 68/10   ¾ 5
Foundation Spirit (FR) *FDoumen,France* 3-9-2 DBonilla .... 40/1   hd 6
Sydenham (USA) *JHMGosden,GB* 3-9-2 RHughes 114/10   1½ 7
Maille Pistol (FR) *J-CRouget,France* 3-9-2 J-RDubosc .... 15/10f   nk 8
Sagacity (FR) *AFabre,France* 3-9-2 OPeslier .... 113/10   sn 9
Marichal (FR) *RLitt,France* 3-9-2 PSogorb .... 204/10   nk 10
Sensible (FR) *PBary,France* 3-9-2 TJarnet 88/10   4½ 11
Musha Merr (IRE) *SaeedbinSuroor,GB* 3-9-2 (v) JPSpencer .... 114/10   ¾ 12
Doctorate (FR) *DSmaga,France* 3-9-2 DBoeuf 144/10   1½ 13
Art Contemporain (FR) *J-CRouget,France* 3-9-2 GMosse .... 216/10   sh 14
Mr C. Mimouni 14ran 2m27.90   TR: 118/117/117/115/114/114

EPSOM DOWNS Friday, Jun 8   GOOD to FIRM

20   **Vodafone Coronation Cup (Gr 1) (4yo+)** £150,000   1½m10y

  1   MUTAFAWEQ (USA) *SaeedbinSuroor* 5-9-0 LDettori (1) 11/2   1
  6   WELLBEING *HRACecil* 4-9-0 TQuinn (2) .... 7/2   sh 2
  6   MILLENARY *JLDunlop* 4-9-0 PatEddery (5) 6/4f   4 3
 14   Ekraar (USA) *SaeedbinSuroor* 4-9-0 (t) RHills (6) .... 9/1   sh 4
Petrushka (IRE) *SirMichaelStoute* 4-8-11 KFallon (4)................................. 7/2   6 5
Chimes At Midnight (USA) *LukeComer,Ireland* 4-9-0 (b) JCarroll (3) 66/1   3 6
Godolphin 6ran 2m36.05   TR: 120/121/115/115/102

21   **Vodafone Oaks (Gr 1) (3yo f)** £211,700   1½m10y

 17   IMAGINE (IRE) *APO'Brien,Ireland* 3-9-0 MJKinane (10).......................... 3/1f   1
FLIGHT OF FANCY *SirMichaelStoute* 3-9-0 KFallon (13)....................... 10/3   1¼ 2
RELISH THE THOUGHT (IRE) *BWHills* 3-9-0 MHills (6)...................... 10/1   hd 3
Mot Juste *EALDunlop* 3-9-0 RHughes (1)... 11/1   3 4
Sunstone *MRChannon* 3-9-0 CraigWilliams (9)...................................... 100/1   sh 5
Gay Heroine *SirMichaelStoute* 3-9-0 JMurtagh (12)............................... 12/1   1¾ 6
Tarfshi *MAJarvis* 3-9-0 PRobinson (11) 10/1   4 7
Silver Grey Lady (IRE) *JLDunlop* 3-9-0 PatEddery (14) 14/1   4 8
  8   Mameha *CEBrittain* 3-9-0 BMarcus (5) .... 100/1   hd 9
Foodbroker Fancy (IRE) *DRCElsworth* 3-9-0 DaneO'Neill (7) .... 20/1   nk 10
Santa Isobel *IABalding* 3-9-0 KDarley (4)... 33/1   14 11
Candice (IRE) *EALDunlop* 3-9-0 TQuinn (2)... 20/1   2 12
Najah (IRE) *SaeedbinSuroor* 3-9-0 LDettori (8) 16/1   1½ 13
Zanzibar (IRE) *MLWBell* 3-9-0 MFenton (3).. 9/1   1½ 14
Mrs John Magnier & Mrs David Nagle 14ran 2m36.70   TR: 115/113+//113/108/108/105

EPSOM DOWNS Saturday, Jun 9   FIRM

22   **Vodafone Derby Stks (Gr 1) (3yo c+f)** £580,000   1½m10y

GALILEO (IRE) *APO'Brien,Ireland* 3-9-0 MJKinane (10)....................... 11/4jf   1
  7   GOLAN (IRE) *SirMichaelStoute* 3-9-0 PatEddery (6)............................... 11/4jf   3½ 2
  7   TOBOUGG (IRE) *SaeedbinSuroor* 3-9-0 LDettori (11) .... 9/1   nk 3
Mr Combustible (IRE) *BWHills* 3-9-0 RHills (8)..................................... 20/1   1¾ 4
Storming Home *BWHills* 3-9-0 MHills (1).. 14/1   ½ 5

Perfect Sunday (USA) *BWHills* 3-9-0 RHughes (9).. 9/2 nk 6
Dilshaan *SirMichaelStoute* 3-9-0 JMurtagh (4) 5/1 1¾ 7
Putra Sandhurst (IRE) *MAJarvis* 3-9-0 PRobinson (3) 16/1 1 8
Sunny Glenn *NPLittmoden* 3-9-0 JWeaver (12) .... 150/1 nk 9
Chancellor (IRE) *BWHills* 3-9-0 TQuinn (5)... 25/1 6 10
King Carew (IRE) *MRChannon* 3-9-0 CraigWilliams (2).............................. 200/1 1¾ 11
15 Cashel Bay (USA) *LukeComer,Ireland* 3-9-0 (b) JCarroll (7) 300/1 1½ 12

Mrs John Magnier & Mr M. Tabor 12ran 2m33.27
TR: 132+/125/125/121/120+/120/117/115/114

CHANTILLY Sunday, Jun 10   GOOD to FIRM

23   Prix de Diane Hermes (Gr 1) (3yo f) £154,968   1¼m110y

AQUARELLISTE (FR) *ELellouche,France* 3-9-0 DBoeuf 18/10f 1
NADIA *CLaffon-Parias,France* 3-9-0 LDettori 62/10 1½ 2
TIME AWAY (IRE) *JLDunlop,GB* 3-9-0 PatEddery .... 49/10 ¾ 3
Spring Oak *AFabre,France* 3-9-0 OPeslier 8/1 1 4
Mare Nostrum *PBary,France* 3-9-0 TJarnet .... 62/10 sn 5
11 Choc Ice (IRE) *RCollet,France* 3-9-0 SPasquier.. 35/1 nk 6
8 Arhaaff (IRE) *MRChannon,GB* 3-9-0 CraigWilliams .... 65/1 ¾ 7
Zghorta (USA) *J-CRouget,France* 3-9-0 J-RDubosc 41/1 2 8
Snataka (FR) *MBoutin,France* 3-9-0 DHolland.. 41/1 ¾ 9
Light Ballet *AFabre,France* 3-9-0 RHughes .... 31/1 sn 10
Baldwina (FR) *FRohaut,France* 3-9-0 GMosse 89/10 2 11
Epistole (IRE) *H-APantall,France* 3-9-0 CSoumillon................................. 21/2 4 12

Mr Daniel Wildenstein 12ran 2m09.50   TR: 118/116/114/112/111/111

ASCOT Tuesday, Jun 19   GOOD to FIRM

24   Queen Anne Stks (Gr 2) (3yo+) £72,000   1m (Str.)

13 MEDICEAN *SirMichaelStoute* 4-9-7 KFallon (8) 11/2 1
13 SWALLOW FLIGHT (IRE) *GWragg* 5-9-2 DHolland (1) 11/2 1 2
13 ARKADIAN HERO (USA) *LMCumani* 6-9-2 JPSpencer (10) .... 10/1 nk 3
Valentino *JHMGosden* 4-9-2 (t) JFortune (3).. 11/2 1 4
Umistim *RHannon* 4-9-2 DaneO'Neill (9) .... 33/1 nk 5
Mull of Kintyre (USA) *APO'Brien,Ireland* 4-9-2 MJKinane (5).................. 16/1 5¼ 6
2 Golden Silca *MRChannon* 5-8-13 SDrowne (6)...................................... 16/1 ½ 7
Shibboleth (USA) *HRACecil* 4-9-2 TQuinn (7)....................................... 11/4f 1½ 8
Fanaar *JNoseda* 4-9-2 JMurtagh (2) 40/1 3 9
Island Sands (IRE) *DRLoder* 5-9-2 LDettori (4)...................................... 13/2 12 10

Cheveley Park Stud 10ran 1m40.46   TR: 127+/120+/119/117+/116?

25   King's Stand Stks (Gr 2) (3yo+) £81,000   5f

CASSANDRA GO (IRE) *GWragg* 5-8-13 MRoberts (5) 8/1 1
MISTY EYED (IRE) *MrsPNDufield* 3-8-7 KDarley (3) 50/1 1¼ 2
FUNNY VALENTINE (IRE) *TGMills* 3-8-10 TQuinn (12) 100/1 1 3
12 Vision of Night *JLDunlop* 5-9-2 PatEddery (7).. 16/1 hd 4
12 Bertolini (USA) *SaeedbinSuroor* 3-8-7 (v) LDettori (8) .... 14/1 hd 5
Tamarisk (IRE) *RCharlton* 6-9-2 JReid (16) .... 14/1 nk 6
Nuclear Debate (USA) *JEHammond,France* 6-9-5 GMosse (1)................... 11/4f hd 7
Ellens Lad (IRE) *WJMusson* 7-9-2 OPeslier (19) .... 33/1 ½ 8
Danehurst *SirMarkPrescott* 3-8-7 GDuffield (9) .... 10/1 sh 9
Ishiguru (USA) *APO'Brien,Ireland* 3-8-10 JPSpencer (17)....................... 20/1 hd 10
Dietrich (USA) *APO'Brien,Ireland* 3-8-7 MJKinane (2) .... 10/1 hd 11
Imperial Beauty (USA) *JEHammond,France* 5-8-13 YTake (14) .... 20/1 nk 12
12 Astonished *MrsJRRamsden* 5-9-2 KFallon (10)...................................... 10/1 1 13
Superstar Leo (IRE) *WJHaggas* 3-8-7 MHills (13) 20/1 1 14
Compton Banker (IRE) *GAButler* 4-9-2 (b) JFortune (21) 66/1 1 15
Kier Park (IRE) *MAJarvis* 4-9-2 PRobinson (20) .... 12/1 hd 16
Rushcutter Bay *PLGilligan* 8-9-2 (v) JMurtagh (11) .... 25/1 nk 17
Rudi's Pet (IRE) *DNicholls* 7-9-2 AlexGreaves (4) .... 25/1 nk 18
Dananeyev (FR) *CLaffon-Parias,France* 5-9-2 DBoeuf (15) 14/1 1¾ 19
Awake *NPLittmoden* 4-9-2 RHughes (6) 150/1 3 20
Dancing Mystery *EAWheeler* 7-9-2 SCarson (18) .... 100/1 ½ 21
Travesty of Law (IRE) *SKirk* 4-9-2 MTebbutt (22)................................... 100/1 2 22

Mr Trevor C. Stewart 22ran 1m00.49   TR: 119/112/112/115+/114/113/116

26   St James's Palace Stks (Gr 1) (3yo c) £156,600   1m (Rnd)

15 BLACK MINNALOUSHE (USA) *APO'Brien,Ireland* 3-9-0
JMurtagh (1) 8/1 1
10 NOVERRE (USA) *SaeedbinSuroor* 3-9-0 (t) LDettori (5) .... 9/2f nk 2
OLDEN TIMES *JLDunlop* 3-9-0 GMosse (6) .... 16/1 hd 3
10 Vahorimix (FR) *AFabre,France* 3-9-0 OPeslier (3) .... 6/1 ½ 4

1137

No Excuse Needed *SirMichaelStoute* 3-9-0 KFallon (4) 12/1 1¼ 5
10 Keltos (FR) *CLaffon-Parias,France* 3-9-0 DBoeuf (8) .... 33/1 hd 6
15 Tamburlaine (IRE) *RHannon* 3-9-0 JFortune (9) 10/1 1 7
15 Minardi (USA) *APO'Brien,Ireland* 3-9-0 MJKinane (10) 5/1 3¾ 8
Malhub (USA) *JHMGosden* 3-9-0 (t) RHills (2) 15/2 2 9
Dandoun *JLDunlop* 3-9-0 PatEddery (7) 11/2 3 10
7 Darwin (IRE) *APO'Brien,Ireland* 3-9-0 PaulScallan (11) 150/1 12 11
Mrs John Magnier & Mr M. Tabor 11ran 1m41.37 TR: 122+/121/121/120/117+/116/114

ASCOT Wednesday, Jun 20 GOOD to FIRM

27 Prince of Wales's Stks (Gr 1) (4yo+) £145,000 1¼m

16 FANTASTIC LIGHT (USA) *SaeedbinSuroor* 5-9-0 (t) LDettori (8) 10/3 1
16 KALANISI (IRE) *SirMichaelStoute* 5-9-0 KFallon (1) 2/1f 2½ 2
14 HIGHTORI (FR) *PHDemercastel,France* 4-9-0 GMosse (5) .... 7/1 ¾ 3
14 Observatory (USA) *JHMGosden* 4-9-0 RHughes (6) 4/1 1¼ 4
16 Give The Slip *SaeedbinSuroor* 4-9-0 RHills (4) 25/1 3 5
9 Endless Hall *LMCumani* 5-9-0 JPSpencer (2) .... 10/1 hd 6
16 Bach (IRE) *APO'Brien,Ireland* 4-9-0 MJKinane (3) 33/1 4 7
Border Arrow *IABalding* 6-9-0 (v) KDarley (7) 25/1 2½ 8
Compton Bolter (IRE) *GAButler* 4-9-0 JFortune (9) 50/1 3 9
Godolphin 9ran 2m04.60 TR: 134/129/127/125/119/118

ASCOT Thursday, Jun 21 Race 28: FIRM, Race 29: GOOD to FIRM

28 Gold Cup (Gr 1) (4yo+) £121,800 2½m

18 ROYAL REBEL *MJohnston* 5-9-2 JMurtagh (10) 8/1 1
18 PERSIAN PUNCH (IRE) *DRCElsworth* 8-9-2 TQuinn (3) .... 10/1 hd 2
18 JARDINES LOOKOUT (IRE) *APJarvis* 4-9-0 JFortune (1) 25/1 5 3
San Sebastian *JLDunlop* 7-9-2 (b) MJKinane (8) .... 3/1f sh 4
Marienbard (IRE) *SaeedbinSuroor* 4-9-0 (v) LDettori (9) 4/1 2 5
18 Mbele *WRMuir* 4-9-0 MartinDwyer (7) 10/1 9 6
18 Rainbow High *BWHills* 6-9-2 RHughes (4) 11/1 5 7
20 Chimes At Midnight (USA) *LukeComer,Ireland* 4-9-0 (b) PRobinson (2) .... 33/1 dist 8
18 Romantic Affair (IRE) *JLDunlop* 4-9-0 PatEddery (6) 10/1 5 9
Kuwait Trooper (USA) *GAButler* 4-9-0 KFallon (11) 14/1 4 10
Yavana's Pace (IRE) *MJohnston* 9-9-2 KDarley (12) .... 25/1 dist 11
Vicious Circle *LMCumani* 7-9-2 JPSpencer (5) .... 20/1 pu
Mr P. D. Savill 12ran 4m18.92 TR: 123/123/119/117/117

29 Cork And Orrery Stks (Gr 2) (3yo+) £72,000 6f

12 HARMONIC WAY *RCharlton* 6-9-0 SDrowne (1) 10/1 1
THREE POINTS *SaeedbinSuroor* 4-9-0 LDettori (2) 6/1f 1 2
15 FREUD (USA) *APO'Brien,Ireland* 3-8-7 (t) JPSpencer (9) 25/1 1½ 3
Tillerman *MrsAJPerrett* 5-9-0 RHughes (14) .... 10/1 ½ 4
12 Misraah (IRE) *SirMichaelStoute* 4-9-0 KFallon (15) 10/1 1¼ 5
Superior Premium *RAFahey* 7-9-4 JMurtagh (6) 11/1 1½ 6
10 Modigliani (USA) *APO'Brien,Ireland* 3-8-7 GDuffield (4) 25/1 4 7
12 Pipalong (IRE) *TDEasterby* 5-9-3 KDarley (8) .... 10/1 ½ 8
Invincible Spirit (IRE) *JLDunlop* 4-9-0 PatEddery (19) .... 10/1 nk 9
12 Eastern Purple (IRE) *KARyan* 6-9-0 FLynch (16) .... 33/1 nk 10
12 Bahamian Pirate (USA) *DNicholls* 6-9-0 ANicholls (10) .... 33/1 nk 11
Orientor *JSGoldie* 3-8-7 JFortune (17) .... 25/1 ½ 12
12 Tedburrow *EJAlston* 9-9-0 TEDurcan (18) 20/1 1¾ 13
Juniper (USA) *APO'Brien,Ireland* 3-8-7 MJKinane (20) 14/1 3¾ 14
12 Munjiz (IRE) *BWHills* 5-9-0 RHills (12) .... 16/1 hd 15
Fath (USA) *MPTregoning* 4-9-0 WSupple (21) .... 20/1 nk 16
Vicious Dancer *RMWhitaker* 3-8-7 JQuinn (3) .... 66/1 ¾ 17
Lots of Magic *RHannon* 5-9-0 (t) DaneO'Neill (11) 66/1 1¼ 18
Baaridd *MAJarvis* 3-8-7 PRobinson (13) .... 33/1 ½ 19
Primo Valentino (IRE) *PWHarris* 4-9-0 TQuinn (5) 8/1 2½ 20
Bouncing Bowdler *MJohnston* 3-8-11 MHills (7) 40/1 30 21
Mrs Alexandra J. Chandris 21ran 1m13.45 TR: 121/119/113/114+/110+/110

ASCOT Friday, Jun 22 FIRM

30 Hardwicke Stks (Gr 2) (4yo+) £81,000 1½m

6 SANDMASON *HRACecil* 4-8-9 WRyan (1) 12/1 1
ZINDABAD (FR) *MJohnston* 5-8-9 KDarley (8) .... 9/1 hd 2
20 MUTAFAWEQ (USA) *SaeedbinSuroor* 5-9-0 LDettori (7) 3/1 2½ 3
Adilabad (USA) *SirMichaelStoute* 4-8-9 KFallon (2) 8/1 1½ 4
20 Wellbeing *HRACecil* 4-8-9 TQuinn (6) .... 2/1f sh 5
Lucido (IRE) *JLDunlop* 5-8-9 PatEddery (5) .... 9/2 ½ 6

Rada's Daughter *IABalding* 5-8-6 MHills (4)... 40/1   15 7
Plantation Stud 7ran 2m29.59   TR: 121/120/120/113/113/111

31   Coronation Stks (Gr 1) (3yo f) £156,600   1m (Rnd)

11	BANKS HILL *AFabre,France* 3-9-0 OPeslier (4) 4/1jf	1
17	CRYSTAL MUSIC (USA) *JHMGosden* 3-9-0 RHughes (12) 4/1jf	1½ 2
11	TEMPTING FATE (IRE) *SaeedbinSuroor* 3-9-0 (t) LDettori (2) 12/1	½ 3
11	Lethals Lady *RCollet,France* 3-9-0 DBoeuf (5)............................ 25/1	nk 4
8	Ameerat *MAJarvis* 3-9-0 PRobinson (9)... 5/1	1¼ 5
17	Toroca (USA) *APO'Brien,Ireland* 3-9-0 JMurtagh (6)................... 12/1	1½ 6
	Monnavanna (IRE) *GWragg* 3-9-0 DHolland (3) 11/1	½ 7
8	Enthused (USA) *SirMichaelStoute* 3-9-0 KFallon (14).................. 8/1	½ 8
	Lady Miletrian (IRE) *MRChannon* 3-9-0 CraigWilliams (8)............ 66/1	nk 9
17	Sequoyah (IRE) *APO'Brien,Ireland* 3-9-0 JPSpencer (13) 11/1	2 10
11	Rose Gypsy *APO'Brien,Ireland* 3-9-0 MJKinane (7)..................... 8/1	nk 11
11	Lil's Jessy (IRE) *JNoseda* 3-9-0 PatEddery (10)........................... 33/1	1 12
	Lurina (IRE) *JHMGosden* 3-9-0 RHavlin (1).............................. 40/1	12 13

Mr K. Abdulla 13ran 1m39.61   TR: 118+/114/113/113/110/109+

CURRAGH Sunday, Jul 1   GOOD

32   Budweiser Irish Derby (Gr 1) (3yo c+f) £392,973   1½m

22	GALILEO (IRE) *APO'Brien* 3-9-0 MJKinane 4/11f	1
	MORSHDI *MAJarvis,GB* 3-9-0 PRobinson 20/1	4 2
22	GOLAN (IRE) *SirMichaelStoute,GB* 3-9-0 KFallon....................... 4/1	4 3
	Pugin (IRE) *JOxx* 3-9-0 NGMcCullagh.................................... 100/1	½ 4
	Exaltation (IRE) *JOxx* 3-9-0 LDettori 8/1	2 5
22	Mr Combustible (IRE) *BWHills,GB* 3-9-0 RHills 20/1	hd 6
	Vinnie Roe (IRE) *DKWeld* 3-9-0 (b) PJSmullen 66/1	1¼ 7
	Ice Dancer (IRE) *APO'Brien* 3-9-0 PaulScallan 66/1	4 8
	Pebble Island (USA) *APO'Brien* 3-9-0 JAHeffernan..................... 25/1	5 9
15	Dr Brendler (USA) *JCHayden* 3-9-0 FMBerry 150/1	6 10
22	Cashel Bay (USA) *LukeComer* 3-9-0 (b) WJSmith 500/1	3½ 11
	March King (IRE) *TStack* 3-9-0 PShanahan 100/1	5 12

Mrs John Magnier & Mr M. Tabor 12ran 2m27.10   TR: 130+/123/116/115/112/111

SAINT-CLOUD Sunday, Jul 1   GOOD to FIRM

33   Grand Prix de Saint-Cloud (Gr 1) (3yo+) £110,803   1½m

	MIRIO (FR) *J-MdeChoubersky,France* 4-9-8 CSoumillon 148/10	1
22	PERFECT SUNDAY (USA) *BWHills,GB* 3-8-9 PatEddery 34/10	1½ 2
5	EGYPTBAND (USA) *MmeCHead-Maarek,France* 4-9-5 ODoleuze........... 3/5jf	nk 3
	Acceleration (FR) *MissVDissaux,France* 4-9-5 SPasquier 175/10	6 4
	Dano-Mast *FPoulsen,Denmark* 5-9-8 MLarsen.............................. 61/10	1½ 5
	Super Tassa (IRE) *VValiani,Italy* 5-9-5 TThulliez 232/10	1½ 6
	Nolt (FR) *JLesbordes,France* 3-8-9 GMosse 202/10	nk 7
	Roman Saddle (IRE) *CLaffon-Parias,France* 3-8-9 DBoeuf 3/5jf	6 8
	Beyond The Waves (USA) *JEPease,France* 4-9-5 YTake 263/10	15 9

Mr E. Soderberg 9ran 2m29.30   TR: 124/120/117/107

SANDOWN Saturday, Jul 7   GOOD to FIRM

34   Coral Eurobet Eclipse Stks (Gr 1) (3yo+) £200,100   1¼m7y

24	MEDICEAN *SirMichaelStoute* 4-9-7 KFallon (7) 7/2	1
19	GRANDERA (IRE) *JRFanshawe* 4-9-7 MHills (1) 8/1	½ 2
27	BACH (IRE) *APO'Brien,Ireland* 4-9-7 JReid (2) 20/1	nk 3
22	Tobougg (IRE) *SaeedbinSuroor* 3-8-10 LDettori (5)..................... 9/4f	hd 4
26	Black Minnaloushe (USA) *APO'Brien,Ireland* 3-8-10 MJKinane (6)............. 5/2	hd 5
3	Broche (USA) *SaeedbinSuroor* 4-9-7 (v) DO'Donohoe (9)............ 50/1	15 6
26	Darwin (IRE) *APO'Brien,Ireland* 3-8-10 PaulScallan (4)............... 150/1	3 7
27	Endless Hall *LMCumani* 5-9-7 JPSpencer (8) 8/1	5 8

Cheveley Park Stud 8ran 2m04.65   TR: 123+/120/121/119+/119+

NEWMARKET Thursday, Jul 12   GOOD to FIRM (July Course)

35   Darley July Cup (Gr 1) (3yo+) £133,400   6f

15	MOZART (IRE) *APO'Brien,Ireland* 3-8-13 MJKinane (19) 4/1f	1
25	CASSANDRA GO (IRE) *GWragg* 5-9-2 MRoberts (18) 7/1	3½ 2
29	MISRAAH (IRE) *SirMichaelStoute* 4-9-5 RHills (7) 14/1	1 3
29	Three Points *SaeedbinSuroor* 4-9-5 (t) LDettori (20)..................... 8/1	sh 4
24	Shibboleth (USA) *HRACecil* 4-9-5 (t) TQuinn (10)...................... 11/2	½ 5
	Mount Abu (IRE) *JHMGosden* 4-9-5 JFortune (9) 25/1	sh 6
25	Ishiguru (USA) *APO'Brien,Ireland* 3-8-13 JMurtagh (8) 50/1	1½ 7
7	Volata (IRE) *MHTompkins* 3-8-13 TEDurcan (11)........................ 20/1	½ 8

1139

29	Tillerman *MrsAJPerrett* 5-9-5 RHughes (14)	10/1	sh 9
29	Freud (USA) *APO'Brien,Ireland* 3-8-13 JPSpencer (6)	16/1	1½ 10
29	Harmonic Way *RCharlton* 6-9-5 SDrowne (15)	10/1	hd 11
25	Vision of Night *JLDunlop* 5-9-5 PatEddery (4)	25/1	1 12
29	Pipalong (IRE) *TDEasterby* 5-9-2 KDarley (1)	11/1	1¼ 13
	Gorse *HCandy* 6-9-5 JReid (5)	50/1	2½ 14
29	Superior Premium *RAFahey* 7-9-5 SSanders (7)	40/1	1¼ 15
	Lincoln Dancer (IRE) *MAJarvis* 4-9-5 PRobinson (12)	20/1	3½ 16
29	Primo Valentino (IRE) *PWHarris* 4-9-5 WSupple (2)	33/1	nk 17
31	Enthused (USA) *SirMichaelStoute* 3-8-10 KFallon (3)	25/1	9 18

Mr M. Tabor & Mrs John Magnier 18ran 1m09.86   TR: 131/119/119+/119/117/117+

CURRAGH Sunday, Jul 15   GOOD

36   Kildangan Stud Irish Oaks (Gr 1) (3yo f) £97,442   1½m

	LAILANI *EALDunlop,GB* 3-9-0 LDettori (1)	5/1	1
21	MOT JUSTE *EALDunlop,GB* 3-9-0 RHughes (12)	8/1	nk 2
	KARSAVINA (IRE) *APO'Brien* 3-9-0 MJKinane (7)	9/1	1 3
31	Sequoyah (IRE) *APO'Brien* 3-9-0 JMurtagh (10)	10/1	½ 4
	Lime Gardens *MJGrassick* 3-9-0 EAhern (11)	16/1	nk 5
23	Time Away (IRE) *JLDunlop,GB* 3-9-0 PatEddery (9)	11/2	2½ 6
17	Rebelline (IRE) *KevinPrendergast* 3-9-0 DPMcDonogh (4)	11/2	2 7
	Chamela Bay (IRE) *APO'Brien* 3-9-0 PaulScallan (3)	66/1	sh 8
31	Rose Gypsy (IRE) *APO'Brien* 3-9-0 JAHeffernan (6)	25/1	1½ 9
21	Relish The Thought (IRE) *BWHills,GB* 3-9-0 MHills (2)	4/1f	¾ 10
	Fantasy Royale (USA) *APO'Brien* 3-9-0 PJSmullen (8)	100/1	¾ 11
	Snowflake (IRE) *APO'Brien* 3-9-0 CO'Donoghue (5)	33/1	5 12

Maktoum Al Maktoum 12ran 2m30.50   TR: 116+/115/114/113/112+/108

AYR Monday, Jul 16   GOOD to SOFT

37   Sodexho Prestige Scottish Classic (Gr 3) (3yo+) £20,300   1¼m

	CARNIVAL DANCER *SirMichaelStoute* 3-8-6 KFallon (4)	11/4	1
	ALBARAHIN (USA) *MPTregoning* 6-9-2 RHills (2)	11/4	3 2
1	ISLAND HOUSE (IRE) *GWragg* 5-9-5 DHolland (3)	5/2f	¾ 3
	Right Wing (IRE) *JLDunlop* 7-9-5 (v) PatEddery (6)	4/1	¾ 4
	Flossy *CWThornton* 5-8-13 ACulhane (5)	20/1	13¾ 5
	Rathkenny (IRE) *JGGiven* 3-8-6 KDarley (1)	66/1	13 6

Cheveley Park Stud 6ran 2m10.61   TR: 121+/116/118/117+/107

ASCOT Saturday, Jul 28   GOOD to FIRM

38   King George VI and Queen Elizabeth Diamond Stks (Gr 1) (3yo+) £435,000   1½m

32	GALILEO (IRE) *APO'Brien,Ireland* 3-8-9 MJKinane (7)	1/2f	1
27	FANTASTIC LIGHT (USA) *SaeedbinSuroor* 5-9-7 (t) LDettori (3)	7/2	2 2
27	HIGHTORI (FR) *PHDemercastel,France* 4-9-7 GMosse (8)	22/1	1 3
22	Storming Home *BWHills* 3-8-9 MHills (10)	25/1	sh 4
20	Millenary *JLDunlop* 4-9-7 KFallon (2)	25/1	3 5
16	Golden Snake (USA) *JLDunlop* 5-9-7 PatEddery (5)	25/1	8 6
19	Anabaa Blue *CLerner,France* 3-8-9 CSoumillon (9)	18/1	1½ 7
32	Morshdi *MAJarvis* 3-8-9 PRobinson (4)	25/1	sh 8
	Mutamam *ACStewart* 6-9-7 RHills (12)	20/1	2 9
28	Chimes At Midnight (USA) *LukeComer,Ireland* 4-9-7 (b) WSmith (4)	200/1	2½ 10
27	Give The Slip *SaeedbinSuroor* 4-9-7 DO'Donohoe (6)	66/1	2½ 11
32	Ice Dancer (IRE) *APO'Brien,Ireland* 3-8-9 PaulScallan (11)	200/1	7 12

Mrs John Magnier & Mr M. Tabor 12ran 2m27.71   TR: 134/130+/128+/128/123+

GOODWOOD Wednesday, Aug 1   GOOD to FIRM

39   Champagne Lanson Sussex Stks (Gr 1) (3yo+) £159,500   1m

26	NOVERRE (USA) *SaeedbinSuroor* 3-9-0 (t) LDettori (11)	9/2	1
26	NO EXCUSE NEEDED *SirMichaelStoute* 3-9-0 KFallon (10)	7/2	2 2
34	BLACK MINNALOUSHE (USA) *APO'Brien,Ireland* 3-9-0 MJKinane (7)	3/1f	1½ 3
26	Olden Times *JLDunlop* 3-9-0 PatEddery (4)	9/1	¾ 4
	Distant Music (USA) *BWHills* 4-9-7 RHughes (8)	11/2	nk 5
	Cape Town (IRE) *RHannon* 4-9-7 DaneO'Neill (9)	14/1	1¼ 6
34	Bach (IRE) *APO'Brien,Ireland* 4-9-7 JMurtagh (5)	9/1	hd 7
31	Ameerat *MAJarvis* 3-8-11 PRobinson (3)	16/1	3½ 8
24	Golden Silca *MRChannon* 5-9-4 SDrowne (1)	50/1	6 9
34	Darwin (IRE) *APO'Brien,Ireland* 3-9-0 PaulScallan (2)	150/1	9 10

Godolphin 10ran 1m37.12   TR: 125/121/116/115/115+

GOODWOOD Thursday, Aug 2   GOOD

40   JPMorgan Private Bank Goodwood Cup (Gr 2) (3yo+) £52,200   2m

28	PERSIAN PUNCH (IRE) *DRCElsworth* 8-9-5 TQuinn (1)	6/1	1
	DOUBLE HONOUR (FR) *MJohnston* 3-8-1 GDuffield (4)	9/1	1½ 2
28	RAINBOW HIGH *BWHills* 6-9-2 MHills (7)	14/1	3 3
18	Solo Mio (IRE) *MrsAJPerrett* 7-9-2 MJKinane (3)	3/1f	3 4
28	San Sebastian *JLDunlop* 7-9-7 (b) LDettori (11)	13/2	3½ 5
28	Royal Rebel *MJohnston* 5-9-7 JMurtagh (10)	7/1	5 6
	Bosham Mill *GWragg* 3-8-6 DHolland (12)	20/1	nk 7
18	Life Is Life (FR) *MAJarvis* 5-8-13 PRobinson (9)	8/1	nk 8
28	Jardines Lookout (IRE) *APJarvis* 4-9-2 JFortune (13)	14/1	4 9
18	Miletrian (IRE) *MRChannon* 4-9-2 MRoberts (2)	50/1	16 10
28	Mbele *WRMuir* 4-9-2 (b) MartinDwyer (6)	20/1	nk 11
	Pairumani Star (IRE) *JLDunlop* 6-9-2 PatEddery (8)	16/1	7 12

Mr J. C. Smith 12ran 3m27.09   TR: 124/120/116/112/113

LEOPARDSTOWN Sunday, Aug 12   GOOD to SOFT

41   Independent Waterford Wedgwood Phoenix Stks (Gr 1) (2yo c+f) £99,567   6f

	JOHANNESBURG (USA) *APO'Brien* 2-9-0 MJKinane (7)	2/5f	1
	MISS BEABEA (IRE) *KevinPrendergast* 2-8-11 WSupple (9)	25/1	5 2
	AGNETHA (GER) *DKWeld* 2-8-11 PJSmullen (5)	10/1	1½ 3
	Wiseman's Ferry (USA) *APO'Brien* 2-9-0 JAHeffernan (4)	12/1	nk 4
	Twilight Blues (IRE) *BJMeehan,GB* 2-9-0 BDoyle (3)	12/1	1½ 5
	High Society (IRE) *EdwardLynam* 2-8-11 JMurtagh (6)	12/1	hd 6
	Minashki (IRE) *HRogers* 2-9-0 EAhern (11)	10/1	¾h 7
	Highdown (IRE) *MRChannon,GB* 2-9-0 FMBerry (8)	12/1	1½ 8
	Line Rider (USA) *APO'Brien* 2-9-0 PaulScallan (10)	20/1	2 9
	Maskaya (IRE) *JGBurns* 2-8-11 DPMcDonogh (2)	25/1	1½ 10
	Cherry Falls (IRE) *KevinPrendergast* 2-8-11 PShanahan (1)	20/1	7 11

Mr M. Tabor 11ran 1m13.20   TR: 119+/102/98/100/96/93

DEAUVILLE Sunday, Aug 12   GOOD to SOFT

42   Prix Maurice de Gheest (Gr 1) (3yo+) £47,215   6f110y

	KING CHARLEMAGNE (USA) *APO'Brien,Ireland* 3-8-12 JPSpencer	4/5jf	1
35	THREE POINTS *SaeedbinSuroor,GB* 4-9-2 PatEddery	31/10	nk 2
25	KIER PARK (IRE) *MAJarvis,GB* 4-9-2 PRobinson	39/1	2 3
35	Mount Abu (IRE) *JHMGosden,GB* 4-9-2 OPeslier	82/10	2 4
	Danger Over *PBary,France* 4-9-2 TThulliez	7/1	¾ 5
26	Minardi (USA) *APO'Brien,Ireland* 3-8-12 FSanchez	4/5jf	sn 6
	Watching *RHannon,GB* 4-9-2 TJarnet	49/1	½ 7
12	Hot Tin Roof (IRE) *TDEasterby,GB* 5-8-13 GMosse	108/10	1½ 8
	Tertullian (USA) *PSchiergen,Germany* 6-9-2 FMinarik	12/1	6 9

Mr M. Tabor & Mrs John Magnier 9ran 1m17.66   TR: 120/119/114/110

NEWBURY Saturday, Aug 18   FIRM

43   Stan James Geoffrey Freer Stks (Gr 2) (3yo+) £35,700   1m5f61y

32	MR COMBUSTIBLE (IRE) *BWHills* 3-8-6 MHills (2)	9/4	1
38	MILLENARY *JLDunlop* 4-9-9 PatEddery (1)	5/6f	2½ 2
28	KUWAIT TROOPER (USA) *GAButler* 4-9-3 (b) DHolland (4)	25/1	3½ 3
	Dalampour (IRE) *SirMichaelStoute* 4-9-3 JPSpencer (5)	8/1	½ 4
19	Sydenham (USA) *JHMGosden,USA* 3-8-7 LDettori (3)	10/1	dist 5

Mr R. A. N. Bonnycastle 5ran 2m46.31   TR: 121/123+/112/111

ARLINGTON Saturday, Aug 18   GOOD to SOFT

44   Arlington Million (Gr 1) (3yo+) £419,580   1¼m

9	SILVANO (GER) *AWohler,Germany* 5-9-0 ASuborics	63/10	1
	HAP (USA) *WIMott,USA* 5-9-0 JBailey	36/10	3 2
	REDATTORE (BRZ) *REMandella,USA* 6-9-0 ASolis	117/10	6 3
4	Caitano *ASchutz,Germany* 7-9-0 (b) KDesormeaux	66/1	4 4
	White Heart *NDDrysdale,USA* 6-9-0 GaryStevens	87/10	3 5
16	Muakaad *DKWeld,Ireland* 4-9-0 PJSmullen	16/1	½ 6
	Bienamado (USA) *JPGonzalez,USA* 5-9-0 CMcCarron	15/10f	4 7
	Senure (USA) *RJFrankel,USA* 5-9-0 RobbieDavis	8/1	1 8
	Takarian (IRE) *CBGreely,USA* 6-9-0 CNakatani	51/1	5½ 9
	Quiet Resolve (USA) *MRFrostad,Canada* 6-9-0 TKabel	22/1	nk 10
27	Compton Bolter (IRE) *GAButler,GB* 4-9-0 MFenton	102/1	ns 11
	Make No Mistake (IRE) *BKessinger,jnr,USA* 6-9-0 RAlbarado	33/1	1 12

Stiftung Gestut Fahrhof 12ran 2m02.64   TR: 126/120/108/100

DEAUVILLE Sunday, Aug 19   GOOD to SOFT

45 Prix du Haras de Fresnay-le-Buffard Jacques le Marois (Gr 1) 1m
(3yo+ c+f) £143,541

Order as they passed the post: Proudwings was disqualified and placed last for causing interference

	PROUDWINGS (GER) *RSuerland,Germany* 5-9-1 CSoumillon	15/1		1
26	VAHORIMIX (FR) *AFabre,France* 3-8-13 OPeslier	33/10	½	2
31	BANKS HILL *AFabre,France* 3-8-10 RHughes	23/10	¾	3
39	Noverre (USA) *SaeedbinSuroor,GB* 3-8-13 LDettori	9/5f	sh	4
19	Chichicastenango (FR) *PHDemercastel,France* 3-8-13 AJunk	74/10	¾	5
	Bonnard (IRE) *APO'Brien,Ireland* 3-8-13 JPSpencer	27/1	sh	6
	Royal Dragon (USA) *ASchutz,Germany* 3-8-13 AStarke	184/10	ns	7
11	Amonita *PBary,France* 3-8-10 TJarnet	19/1	½	8
31	Lethals Lady *RCollet,France* 3-8-10 DBoeuf	41/1	1½	9

Mr J-L. Lagardere 9ran 1m38.80   TR: 116+/118+/113+/116+/114/114

YORK Tuesday, Aug 21   GOOD

46 Weatherbys Insurance Lonsdale Stks (Gr 3) (3yo+) £58,000 1m7f195y

40	PERSIAN PUNCH (IRE) *DRCElsworth* 8-9-6 TQuinn (7)	10/3f		1
40	JARDINES LOOKOUT (IRE) *APJarvis* 4-9-1 MJKinane (1)	16/1	hd	2
	QAATEF (IRE) *SirMichaelStoute* 3-8-1 (v) WSupple (5)	7/1	3	3
40	San Sebastian *JLDunlop* 7-9-8 LDettori (2)	10/1	1	4
28	Romantic Affair (IRE) *JLDunlop* 4-9-1 PatEddery (3)	5/1	1½	5
40	Rainbow High *BWHills* 6-9-1 RHughes (8)	6/1	2½	6
40	Royal Rebel *MJohnston* 5-9-8 (v) JMurtagh (9)	9/1	3½	7
	Capal Garmon (IRE) *JHMGosden* 3-8-1 FNorton (10)	25/1	6	8
	Miss Lorilaw (FR) *JWHills* 4-8-12 MHills (4)	50/1	13	9
	Yorkshire (IRE) *PFICole* 7-9-1 JFortune (6)	15/2	dist	10

Mr J. C. Smith 10ran 3m23.47   TR: 124/119/115/120/112+

47 Juddmonte International Stks (Gr 1) (3yo+) £261,000 1¼m85y

	SAKHEE (USA) *SaeedbinSuroor* 3-8-11 LDettori (5)	7/4f		1
34	GRANDERA (IRE) *JRFanshawe* 3-8-11 MHills (9)	7/1	7	2
34	MEDICEAN *SirMichaelStoute* 4-9-5 KFallon (8)	3/1	1	3
39	Black Minnaloushe (USA) *APO'Brien,Ireland* 3-8-11 MJKinane (1)	7/2	1¼	4
39	Distant Music (USA) *BWHills* 4-9-5 RHughes (6)	9/1	½	5
21	Foodbroker Fancy (IRE) *DRCElsworth* 3-8-8 TQuinn (2)	33/1	1½	6
36	Time Away (IRE) *JLDunlop* 3-8-8 PatEddery (4)	16/1	3	7
39	Darwin (IRE) *APO'Brien,Ireland* 3-8-11 PaulScallan (3)	200/1	28	8

Godolphin 8ran 2m08.27   TR: 136/121/120/116/116/109

48 Great Voltigeur Stks (Gr 2) (3yo c+g) £87,000 1m3f195y

19	MILAN *APO'Brien,Ireland* 3-8-9 MJKinane (8)	6/1		1
38	STORMING HOME *BWHills* 3-8-12 MHills (3)	1/1f	1½	2
	DEMOPHILOS *MrsAJPerrett* 3-8-9 TQuinn (5)	9/1	nk	3
	Beekeeper *SirMichaelStoute* 3-8-9 KFallon (7)	13/2	1¾	4
	Xtra *LMCumani* 3-8-9 JPSpencer (4)	11/1	1¾	5
	Hill Country (IRE) *JHMGosden* 3-8-9 LDettori (1)	25/1	8	6
	Halawan (IRE) *SirMichaelStoute* 3-8-9 JMurtagh (6)	14/1	13	7
	Saddler's Creek (USA) *APO'Brien,Ireland* 3-8-9 PaulScallan (2)	50/1	25	8
	Theatre Script (USA) *JHMGosden* 3-8-9 JFortune (9)	8/1	2½	9

Mr M. Tabor & Mrs John Magnier 9ran 2m29.32   TR: 122+/122+/119/116/113

YORK Wednesday, Aug 22   GOOD

49 Aston Upthorpe Yorkshire Oaks (Gr 1) (3yo+ f+m) £145,000 1m3f195y

33	SUPER TASSA (IRE) *VValiani,Italy* 5-9-4 KDarley (7)	25/1		1
	SACRED SONG (USA) *HRACecil* 4-9-4 TQuinn (8)	2/1f	1	2
	ROCKERLONG *GWragg* 3-8-8 DHolland (5)	20/1	2½	3
36	Karsavina (IRE) *APO'Brien,Ireland* 3-8-8 MJKinane (9)	6/1	2½	4
21	Zanzibar (IRE) *MLWBell* 3-8-8 KFallon (1)	14/1	1½	5
	Nafisah (IRE) *BHanbury* 3-8-8 RHills (2)	14/1	3	6
36	Snowflake (IRE) *APO'Brien,Ireland* 3-8-8 JPSpencer (6)	12/1	3½	7
36	Mot Juste *EALDunlop* 3-8-8 LDettori (4)	5/2	¾	8
36	Head In The Clouds (IRE) *JLDunlop* 3-8-8 PatEddery (3)	8/1	3	9

Mr V. Valiani 9ran 2m30.17   TR: 118/116/112/108/106+

YORK Thursday, Aug 23   GOOD to FIRM

50 Victor Chandler Nunthorpe Stks (Gr 1) (2yo+) £107,300 5f

35	MOZART (IRE) *APO'Brien,Ireland* 3-9-7 MJKinane (4)	4/9f		1
25	NUCLEAR DEBATE (USA) *JEHammond,France* 6-9-9 GMosse (8)	5/1	2	2

BISHOPS COURT *MrsJRRamsden* 7-9-9 KFallon (3) .... 20/1 ¾ 3
Repertory *MSSaunders* 8-9-9 DSweeney (1) .... 33/1 ¾ 4
42 Kier Park (IRE) *MAJarvis* 4-9-9 PRobinson (7) .... 25/1 hd 5
25 Misty Eyed (IRE) *MrsPNDutfield* 3-9-4 PaulEddery (6) .... 25/1 ½ 6
35 Pipalong (IRE) *TDEasterby* 5-9-6 KDarley (2) .... 12/1 ½ 7
Rozel (IRE) *RGuest* 4-9-6 SSanders (5) .... 150/1 nk 8
35 Harmonic Way *RCharlton* 6-9-9 RHughes (11) .... 16/1 ½ 9
Romantic Myth *TDEasterby* 3-9-4 JPSpencer (10) 50/1 6 10
Mr M. Tabor & Mrs John Magnier 10ran 57.27secs   TR: 126+/119+/117/114/114

DEAUVILLE Sunday, Aug 26   GOOD
51   **Prix Morny Casinos Barriere (Gr 1) (2yo c+f)** £77,445   6f
41 JOHANNESBURG (USA) *APO'Brien,Ireland* 2-9-0 MJKinane 3/5jf   1
ZIPPING (IRE) *RCollet,France* 2-9-0 DBonilla 18/1 1½ 2
MESHAHEER (USA) *DRLoder,GB* 2-9-0 LDettori 63/10 1½ 3
Firebreak *IABalding,GB* 2-9-0 MartinDwyer 172/10 1½ 4
War Zone (USA) *AFabre,France* 2-9-0 OPeslier .... 34/10 ½ 5
Sforza (FR) *XGuigand,France* 2-9-0 CSoumillon 30/1 1½ 6
Berk The Jerk (IRE) *PWD'Arcy,GB* 2-9-0 PatEddery 95/1 1½ 7
Whitbarrow (IRE) *BRMillman,GB* 2-9-0 (b) GMosse 148/10 4 8
Tumbleweed Charm (IRE) *BJMeehan,GB* 2-9-0 BDoyle .... 57/1 nk 9
Dulce de Leche (USA) *RGibson,France* 2-9-0 DBoeuf 34/1 4 10
Line Rider (USA) *APO'Brien,Ireland* 2-9-0 PaulScallan 3/5jf 11
Mr M. Tabor & Mrs John Magnier 11ran 1m10.40   TR: 117+/113+/108+/104+/102+/98

52   **Prix de Meautry Royal Barriere (Gr 3) (3yo+)** £21,298   6f
DO THE HONOURS (IRE) *H-APantall,France* 3-8-8 LDettori 26/10f   1
29 INVINCIBLE SPIRIT (IRE) *JLDunlop,GB* 4-9-1 PatEddery 5/1 3 2
42 HOT TIN ROOF (IRE) *TDEasterby,GB* 5-8-11 MRoberts 146/10 1½ 3
42 Danger Over *PBary,France* 4-9-1 TThulliez .... 28/10 sh 4
Gaelic Dream (FR) *JBertrandeBalanda,France* 4-8-11 TGillet .... 117/10 ¾ 5
35 Freud (USA) *APO'Brien,Ireland* 3-8-11 MJKinane 96/10 1 6
Silver Desert (USA) *JEPease,France* 4-9-1 AJunk 20/1 1½ 7
Lunasalt (IRE) *AFabre,France* 3-9-2 OPeslier .... 52/10 nk 8
Season's Greetings (IRE) *CLaffon-Parias,France* 3-8-8 GMosse .... 14/1 hd 9
Sheikh Mohammed 9ran 1m09.50   TR: 102+/115/107/111/105/105

BADEN-BADEN Sunday, Sep 2   GOOD to SOFT
53   **UAE Grosser Preis von Baden (Gr 1) (3yo+)** £322,581   1½m
38 MORSHDI *MAJarvis,GB* 3-8-9 PRobinson 9/2   1
BOREAL (GER) *PSchiergen,Germany* 3-8-9 JReid 26/10 1¼ 2
SABIANGO (GER) *AWohler,Germany* 3-8-9 ASuborics 2/1f 1½ 3
Paolini (GER) *AWohler,Germany* 4-9-6 ABoschert .... 8/1 ¾ 4
Passimo (GER) *GKussatz,Germany* 4-9-6 LHammer-Hansen 24/1 2 5
Aeskulap (GER) *HBlume,Germany* 4-9-6 AStarke .... 171/10 ½ 6
Krombacher (GER) *PRau,Germany* 3-8-9 TMundry 102/10 2 7
Near Honor (GER) *TGibson,Germany* 3-8-9 JBojko 302/10 2 8
Bonvivant (GER) *HHorwart,Germany* 4-9-6 JPalik .... 31/1 ¾ 9
Foreman (GER) *CVonDerRecke,Germany* 3-8-9 FMinarik 60/1 1¾ 10
Onaldo (GER) *CVonDerRecke,Germany* 3-8-9 JAQuinn .... 55/1 ½ 11
5 Earlene (USA) *H-APantall,France* 4-9-2 TThulliez .... 131/10 nk 12
Darley Stud Management, Inc 12ran 2m31.27   TR: 123/121/118/119/116/115

HAYDOCK Saturday, Sep 8   SOFT
54   **Stanley Leisure Sprint Cup (Gr 1) (3yo+)** £87,000   6f
50 NUCLEAR DEBATE (USA) *JEHammond,France* 6-9-0 GMosse (9) 11/2   1
42 MOUNT ABU (IRE) *JHMGosden* 4-9-0 JFortune (10) 15/2 3 2
MONKSTON POINT (IRE) *DWPArbuthnot* 5-9-0 (v) JDSmith (6) .... 25/1 ¾ 3
24 Mull of Kintyre (USA) *APO'Brien,Ireland* 4-9-0 JReid (7) .... 16/1 hd 4
29 Orientor *JSGoldie* 3-8-12 WRyan (12) 11/1 3½ 5
50 Kier Park (IRE) *MAJarvis* 4-9-0 TQuinn (11) 8/1 2½ 6
50 Pipalong (IRE) *TDEasterby* 5-8-11 KDarley (13) 7/2f 1½ 7
50 Harmonic Way *RCharlton* 6-9-0 SDrowne (3) 20/1 3 8
42 Minardi (USA) *APO'Brien,Ireland* 3-8-12 GDuffield (4) 8/1 3 9
42 Three Points *SaeedbinSuroor* 4-9-0 (t) PatEddery (5) 5/1 1 10
35 Lincoln Dancer (IRE) *MAJarvis* 4-9-0 MHills (8) 20/1 1¼ 11
29 Tedburrow *EJAlston* 9-9-0 WSupple (2) .... 33/1 ½ 12
Mr J. R. Chester 12ran 1m15.39   TR: 124+/116/114/114/105

KEMPTON Saturday, Sep 8   GOOD
55   **Milcars September Stks (Gr 3) (3yo+)** £21,000   1½m
38 MUTAMAM *ACStewart* 6-9-8 PRobinson (2) 4/6f   1

1143

```
  33   PERFECT SUNDAY (USA) BWHills 3-8-11 RHughes (4)............................   3/1     1½ 2
       DELIUS (USA) SirMichaelStoute 4-9-3 KFallon (1) .............................   9/2      2  3
       King O' The Mana (IRE) RHannon 4-9-3 DaneO'Neill (3) .........................  20/1    13  4
       Mr Hamdan Al Maktoum 4ran 2m35.68                            TR: 122/118+/111
```

LEOPARDSTOWN Saturday, Sep 8   GOOD

56   Ireland The Food Island Irish Champion Stks (Gr 1) (3yo+) £378,373   1¼m

```
  38   FANTASTIC LIGHT (USA) SaeedbinSuroor,GB 5-9-4 (t) LDettori (2).........   9/4      1
  38   GALILEO (IRE) APO'Brien 3-9-4 MJKinane (4) ....................................   4/11f   hd 2
  39   BACH (IRE) APO'Brien 4-9-4 JAHeffernan (7) ....................................  20/1     6  3
  38   Give The Slip SaeedbinSuroor,GB 4-9-4 RHills (3)...............................  50/1     4  4
  38   Ice Dancer (IRE) APO'Brien 3-8-11 PaulScallan (1) .............................. 200/1    6  5
       Siringas (IRE) JSBolger 3-8-8 (b+t) KJManning (5) .............................. 66/1     4  6
  38   Chimes At Midnight (USA) LukeComer 4-9-4 (b) JMurtagh (6) ............... 150/1     8  7
       Godolphin 7ran 2m01.80                                       TR: 134/133/121/113
```

LONGCHAMP Sunday, Sep 9   GOOD to SOFT

57   Prix du Moulin de Longchamp (Gr 1) (3yo+) £85,960   1m

```
   2   SLICKLY (FR) SaeedbinSuroor,GB 5-9-2 LDettori..................................   43/10     1
  45   BANKS HILL AFabre,France 3-8-8 RHughes ......................................    6/4f     3  2
       HAWKEYE (IRE) APO'Brien,Ireland 3-8-11 MJKinane .......................  109/10    1½ 3
  13   Warningford JRFanshawe,GB 7-9-2 KFallon......................................    30/1     ½  4
  39   Olden Times JLDunlop,GB 3-8-11 PatEddery..................................     66/10    dh 4
  45   Vahorimix AFabre,France 3-8-11 OPeslier ........................................   2/1     1½ 6
  45   Lethals Lady RCollet,France 3-8-8 DBoeuf ...................................... 328/10    hd 7
  13   Danceabout GWragg,GB 4-8-12 (v) DHolland ...................................   44/1     ¾  8
       Godolphin 8ran 1m39.00                      TR: 128/118+/118+/117/117/114
```

GOODWOOD Wednesday, Sep 12   GOOD to FIRM

58   Select Stks (Gr 3) (3yo+) £26,200   1m1f192y

```
   7   NAYEF (USA) MPTregoning 3-8-10 RHills (2) ...................................   8/13f     1
       ASKHAM (USA) LMCumani 3-8-7 JPSpencer (1) .............................   13/8     6  2
       PREMIER PRIZE DRCElsworth 4-8-11 DaneO'Neill (3)..........................   9/1     1½ 3
       Mr Hamdan Al Maktoum 3ran 2m06.33                           TR: 126/111/105
```

DONCASTER Thursday, Sep 13   GOOD to SOFT

59   GNER White Rose Park Stks (Gr 3) (3yo+) £24,000   1m (Rnd)

```
       TOUGH SPEED (USA) SirMichaelStoute 4-9-0 KFallon (4) .......................   6/1      1
       CHINA VISIT (USA) SaeedbinSuroor 4-9-0 LDettori (7).......................   10/3f    ½  2
       LATE NIGHT OUT WJarvis 6-9-0 MTebbutt (6)..................................   10/1     2½ 3
  26   Tamburlaine (IRE) RHannon 3-8-9 JFortune (3).................................   6/1     1¼ 4
       Duck Row (USA) JARToller 6-9-0 SWhitworth (2)..............................  25/1     4  5
  47   Distant Music (USA) BWHills 4-9-6 RHughes (8) .............................   8/1     nk 6
  24   Umistim RHannon 4-9-0 DaneO'Neill (1) .........................................   8/1     1½ 7
       Riberac MJohnston 5-8-11 KDarley (11).........................................   8/1     4  8
       Rosi's Boy JLDunlop 3-8-9 (v) MJKinane (10) ...................................  33/1     4  9
  29   Fath (USA) MPTregoning 4-9-4 RHills (9)........................................  12/1     4 10
       Wannabe Around TGMills 3-8-9 TQuinn (5) ...................................  25/1    11 11
       Mr Saeed Suhail 11ran 1m39.8                                 TR: 123/122/116/113
```

DONCASTER Friday, Sep 14   GOOD to SOFT

60   Rothmans Royals Champagne Stks (Gr 2) (2yo c+g) £60,000   7f

```
       DUBAI DESTINATION (USA) DRLoder 2-8-10 LDettori (1)....................   3/1      1
       ROCK OF GIBRALTAR (IRE) APO'Brien,Ireland 2-9-0                          1  2
          MJKinane (5) ............................................................................  11/10f
       LEO'S LUCKYMAN (USA) MJohnston 2-8-10 KDarley (9) ....................   9/1     4  3
  41   Wiseman's Ferry (USA) APO'Brien,Ireland 2-8-10 JPSpencer (7)..............   8/1     ½  4
       Sohaib (USA) BWHills 2-8-10 RHills (8) .......................................   8/1     3  5
       Amour Sans Fin (FR) BJMeehan 2-8-10 BDoyle (2)............................  50/1     2  6
       Great View (IRE) BJMeehan 2-8-10 PatEddery (4)............................  50/1    12  7
       Ice And Fire DRLoder 2-8-10 WRyan (6)........................................  50/1    13  8
       Sheikh Mohammed 8ran 1m26.45                   TR: 116+/117+/103/102/95
```

DONCASTER Saturday, Sep 15   GOOD

61   Rothmans Royals St Leger Stks (Gr 1) (3yo c+f) £222,000   1¾m132y

```
  48   MILAN APO'Brien,Ireland 3-9-0 MJKinane (7) ..................................  13/8f     1
  48   DEMOPHILOS MrsAJPerrett 3-9-0 TQuinn (4) ................................   10/1     5  2
  43   MR COMBUSTIBLE (IRE) BWHills 3-9-0 MHills (3)............................   3/1     3  3
       When In Rome CACyzer 3-9-0 NCallan (6)......................................  50/1     ¾  4
```

32	Pugin (IRE) *JOxx,Ireland* 3-9-0 JMurtagh (11)	7/1	5 5
	Alunissage (USA) *SaeedbinSuroor* 3-9-0 (v) TEDurcan (9)	16/1	nk 6
	And Beyond (IRE) *MJohnston* 3-9-0 KDarley (10)	10/1	3 7
	Life Match (FR) *APO'Brien,Ireland* 3-9-0 JFortune (1)	200/1	dist 8
48	Saddler's Creek (USA) *APO'Brien,Ireland* 3-9-0 PaulScallan (5)	200/1	22 9
	Mediterranean *APO'Brien,Ireland* 3-9-0 JPSpencer (8)	7/1	pu

Mr M. Tabor & Mrs John Magnier 10ran 3m05.16 TR: 126+/119/115/113/106/106

CURRAGH Saturday, Sep 15 GOOD to FIRM

62 Jefferson Smurfit Memorial Irish St Leger (Gr 1) (3yo+) £103,110 1¾m

32	VINNIE ROE (IRE) *DKWeld* 3-8-12 (b) PJSmullen (1)	5/1	1
43	MILLENARY *JLDunlop,GB* 4-9-9 PatEddery (3)	9/4f	2 2
28	MARIENBARD (IRE) *SaeedbinSuroor,GB* 4-9-9 (b) LDettori (5)	5/2	2½ 3
46	Persian Punch (IRE) *DRCElsworth,GB* 8-9-9 RHughes (4)	6/1	1½ 4
	Sadlers Wings (IRE) *WPMullins* 3-8-12 PShanahan (2)	12/1	10 5
56	Chimes At Midnight (USA) *LukeComer* 4-9-9 JAHeffernan (7)	66/1	1½ 6
28	Yavana's Pace (IRE) *MJohnston,GB* 9-9-9 JFanning (8)	8/1	6 7
	Rostropovich (IRE) *MFMorris* 4-9-9 (t) DJCasey (6)	33/1	10 8

Mr Seamus Sheridan 8ran 2m58.40 TR: 126/123+/119/117+

CURRAGH Sunday, Sep 16 GOOD to FIRM

63 Aga Khan Studs National Stks (Gr 1) (2yo) £116,535 7f

	HAWK WING (USA) *APO'Brien* 2-9-0 MJKinane (5)	8/15f	1
	NAHEEF (IRE) *DRLoder,GB* 2-9-0 LDettori (7)	9/4	2½ 2
	SHOLOKHOV (IRE) *APO'Brien* 2-9-0 PaulScallan (6)	12/1	1½ 3
	Monarchoftheglen (USA) *APO'Brien* 2-9-0 (b) JAHeffernan (1)	12/1	4 4
	Funfair Wane *MRChannon,GB* 2-9-0 SDrowne (3)	10/1	2 5
	Chief Mosconomo *TMWalsh* 2-9-0 JMurtagh (4)	33/1	7 6
	Schiller (IRE) *TStack* 2-9-0 PJSmullen (2)	14/1	nk 7

Mrs John Magnier 7ran 1m21.95 TR: 116/109/105/93

LONGCHAMP Sunday, Sep 16 GOOD to FIRM
All Hand Times

64 Prix Niel - Casino Barriere d'Enghien-Les-Bains (Gr 2) (3yo c+f) £37,700 1½m

32	GOLAN (IRE) *SirMichaelStoute,GB* 3-9-2 KFallon	13/10f	1
38	ANABAA BLUE *CLerner,France* 3-9-2 CSoumillon	52/10	¾ 2
45	CHICHICASTENANGO (FR) *PHDemercastel,France* 3-9-2 AJunk	44/10	2 3
	Walking Around (FR) *AFabre,France* 3-9-2 OPeslier	87/10	1 4
	Sangreal (NZ) *AFabre,France* 3-8-10 TGillet	17/1	nk 5
	King of Tara (IRE) *FDoumen,France* 3-9-2 TThulliez	13/1	2½ 6
48	Storming Home *BWHills,GB* 3-9-2 MHills	38/10	nk 7

Lord Weinstock 7ran 2m25.88 TR: 121+/120/117/115/112

65 Prix Vermeille - Hermitage Barriere (Gr 1) (3yo f) £75,401 1½m

23	AQUARELLISTE (FR) *ELellouche,France* 3-9-0 DBoeuf (1)	8/5f	1
	DIAMILINA (FR) *AFabre,France* 3-9-0 OPeslier (6)	17/10	sn 2
23	MARE NOSTRUM *PBary,France* 3-9-0 TJarnet (4)	131/10	2½ 3
49	Mot Juste *EALDunlop,GB* 3-9-0 RHughes (3)	143/10	2 4
49	Karsavina (IRE) *APO'Brien,Ireland* 3-9-0 JPSpencer (7)	233/10	sh 5
49	Zanzibar (IRE) *MLWBell,GB* 3-9-0 KFallon (12)	45/1	¾ 6
23	Nadia *CLaffon-Parias,France* 3-9-0 GMosse (5)	68/10	sn 7
23	Baldwina (FR) *FRohaut,France* 3-9-0 YTake (8)	44/1	2 8
	Inchiri *GAButler,GB* 3-9-0 FNorton (9)	58/1	¾ 9
	Nalani (FR) *H-APantall,France* 3-9-0 TThulliez (10)	256/10	4 10
36	Lime Gardens *MJGrassick,Ireland* 3-9-0 EAhern (11)	39/1	1½ 11
	Reine Zao (FR) *JdeRoualle,France* 3-9-0 CSoumillon (2)	21/1	nk 12

Mr Daniel Wildenstein 12ran 2m27.95 TR: 122/121/117/114/114/113

MAISONS-LAFFITTE Tuesday, Sep 18 GOOD to SOFT

66 La Coupe de Maisons-Laffitte (Gr 3) (3yo+) £21,013 1¼m

9	JIM AND TONIC (FR) *FDoumen,France* 7-9-3 TThulliez	7/10f	1
	VISORHILL (FR) *AFabre,France* 3-8-6 OPeslier	52/10	2 2
	CAZOULIAS (FR) *MmeNRossio,France* 4-8-11 AJunk	237/10	¾ 3
	Cherbon (FR) *ELibaud,France* 4-8-11 (b) CSoumillon	79/10	½ 4
	Mocham Glen (FR) *JEHammond,France* 4-8-11 YTake	54/10	sh 5
37	Island House (IRE) *GWragg,GB* 5-9-1 DHolland	56/10	2½ 6
	Goustranville (FR) *AKleinkorres,Germany* 5-8-11 MTimpelan	24/1	6 7

Mr J. D. Martin 7ran 2m05.50 TR: 124/115/112/111/111/110

NEWBURY Saturday, Sep 22   FIRM

67   Dubai Arc Trial (L) (3yo+) £29,750   1m3f5y

47	GRANDERA (IRE) *JRFanshawe* 3-8-9 MHills (4)	5/6f	1
	MUBTAKER (USA) *MPTregoning* 4-9-2 WSupple (5)	11/4	1½ 2
44	COMPTON BOLTER (IRE) *GAButler* 4-9-2 GMosse (1)	7/1	3½ 3
40	Miletrian (IRE) *MRChannon* 4-8-11 SDrowne (3)	25/1	1¾ 4
22	Chancellor (IRE) *BWHills* 3-8-12 KFallon (2)	7/1	4 5

Lael Stable & Mrs V. Shelton 5ran 2m16.54   TR: 124/121/115/107

COLOGNE Sunday, Sep 23   HEAVY

68   Deutsche Post Euro Express Preis von Europa (Gr 1) (3yo+) £96,154   1½m

1	KUTUB (IRE) *SaeedbinSuroor,GB* 4-9-6 (v) LDettori	24/10	1
62	YAVANA'S PACE (IRE) *MJohnston,GB* 9-9-6 DHolland	99/10	4 2
	NOROIT (GER) *WFigge,Germany* 3-8-10 CCzachary	178/10	½ 3
53	Aeskulap (GER) *HBlume,Germany* 4-9-6 AStarke	181/10	1¾ 4
	Hale Bopp (GER) *FrauEMader,Germany* 4-9-6 LHammer-Hansen	478/10	11 5
	Tareno (GER) *PSchiergen,Germany* 3-8-10 JAQuinn	82/10	3½ 6
	Network (GER) *ASchutz,Germany* 4-9-6 WNewnes	395/10	4 7
53	Near Honor (GER) *TGibson,Germany* 4-9-6 JBojko	25/1	¾ 8
	Kombinacja (POL) *BMazurek,Poland* 3-8-6 EZachariew	262/10	¾ 9
	Albaran (GER) *MsCErichsen,Norway* 8-9-6 EAhern	546/10	3 10
	Bor (RUS) *ATschugujewez,Russia* 3-8-10 VMelekhov	39/1	½ 11
53	Bonvivant (GER) *HHorwart,Germany* 4-9-6 MJKinane	433/10	6 12
	Barsetto (IRE) *PLautner,Germany* 3-8-10 ASuborics	139/10	2½ 13
53	Boreal (GER) *PSchiergen,Germany* 3-8-10 JReid	14/10f	f

Godolphin 14ran 2m38.21   TR: 123/118/116/115

ASCOT Saturday, Sep 29   SOFT

69   Meon Valley Stud Fillies' Mile (Gr 1) (2yo f) £116,000   1m (Rnd)

	GOSSAMER *LMCumani* 2-8-10 JPSpencer (8)	4/5f	1
	MARYINSKY (IRE) *APO'Brien,Ireland* 2-8-10 MJKinane (6)	12/1	2½ 2
	ESLOOB (USA) *MPTregoning* 2-8-10 RHills (2)	14/1	1¼ 3
	Half Glance *HRACecil* 2-8-10 TQuinn (1)	5/2	nk 4
	Fraulein *EALDunlop* 2-8-10 LDettori (4)	11/1	¾ 5
	Moon Safari (USA) *APO'Brien,Ireland* 2-8-10 JMurtagh (5)	50/1	nk 6
	Reefs Sis *EJAlston* 2-8-10 MFenton (3)	100/1	7 7

Gerald W. Leigh - CancerBACUP 7ran 1m46.40   TR: 112+/107/104/104/102/101

70   Betdaq Diadem Stks (Gr 2) (3yo+) £60,000   6f

	NICE ONE CLARE (IRE) *JWPayne* 5-8-11 JMurtagh (7)	6/1	1
54	ORIENTOR *JSGoldie* 3-8-12 KFallon (11)	8/1	nk 2
29	BAHAMIAN PIRATE (USA) *DNicholls* 6-9-0 DHolland (15)	12/1	sh 3
54	Pipalong (IRE) *TDEasterby* 5-9-3 KDarley (10)	12/1	sh 4
31	Toroca (USA) *APO'Brien,Ireland* 3-8-9 MJKinane (14)	7/1	1½ 5
54	Mount Abu (IRE) *JHMGosden* 4-9-0 JFortune (16)	10/3f	¾ 6
52	Hot Tin Roof (IRE) *TDEasterby* 5-8-11 OPeslier (9)	14/1	hd 7
29	Munjiz (IRE) *BWHills* 5-9-0 MHills (20)	25/1	hd 8
54	Tedburrow *EJAlston* 9-9-0 MFenton (12)	25/1	3½ 9
54	Harmonic Way *RCharlton* 6-9-4 SDrowne (2)	14/1	1 10
52	Freud (USA) *APO'Brien,Ireland* 3-8-12 JPSpencer (4)	16/1	sh 11
	Zilch *RHannon* 3-8-12 DaneO'Neill (3)	40/1	1 12
54	Monkston Point (IRE) *DWPArbuthnot* 5-9-0 (v) TQuinn (13)	10/1	3 13
	Atavus (IRE) *GGMargarson* 4-9-0 JMackay (6)	16/1	nk 14
	Securite (ARG) *DiegoLowther,Sweden* 6-9-0 CLopez (1)	100/1	1¾ 15

Oremsa Partnership 15ran 1m17.60   TR: 116+/118/118+/121/111/112

71   Queen Elizabeth II Stks (Gr 1) (3yo+) £188,500   1m (Rnd)

	SUMMONER *SaeedbinSuroor* 4-9-1 RHills (7)	33/1	1
45	NOVERRE (USA) *SaeedbinSuroor* 3-8-11 (t) LDettori (8)	2/1f	1½ 2
57	HAWKEYE (IRE) *APO'Brien,Ireland* 3-8-11 MJKinane (1)	13/2	1½ 3
56	Bach (IRE) *APO'Brien,Ireland* 4-9-1 JPSpencer (6)	6/1	1½ 4
57	Vahorimix (FR) *AFabre,France* 3-8-11 OPeslier (11)	4/1	1 5
59	Tamburlaine (IRE) *RHannon* 3-8-11 RHughes (9)	16/1	1 6
45	Proudwings (GER) *RSuerland,Germany* 5-8-12 JVTake (5)	9/2	hd 7
	Bocelli (NZ) *PBusuttin,Singapore* 5-9-1 (b) GCooksley (3)	20/1	4 8

Godolphin 8ran 1m44.54   TR: 118/115+/112+/109+/107+/105+

BELMONT PARK Saturday, Sep 29   GOOD

72   Flower Bowl Invitational (Gr 1) (3yo+ f+m) £308,219   1¼m

36	LAILANI *EALDunlop,GB* 3-8-6 JBailey	245/100	1

ENGLAND'S LEGEND (FR) *CClement,USA* 4-8-11 CNakatani .... 11/10f   ¾ 2
STARINE (FR) *RJFrankel,USA* 4-8-8 (b) JVelazquez .... 245/100   ¾ 3
Chaste (USA) *FSSchulhofer,USA* 5-8-6 EPrado 30/1   3¼ 4
Babae (CHI) *FAAlexander,USA* 5-8-6 (b) JChavez 17/1   4½ 5
Tweedside (USA) *TAPletcher,USA* 3-8-6 RMigliore .... 32/1   pu
Maktoum Al Maktoum 6ran 2m01.88   TR: 122/119/115/106

ASCOT Sunday, Sep 30   SOFT

73   **Royal Court Theatre Cumberland Lodge Stks (Gr 3) (3yo+)** £32,400   1½m

58 NAYEF (USA) *MPTregoning* 3-8-9 WSupple (6)...................................... 8/13f   1
    SAGITTARIUS *RuneHaugen,Norway* 5-9-0 FernandoDiaz (3) 12/1   1¼ 2
6 BOREAS *LMCumani* 6-9-0 LDettori (1).. 7/2   1 3
    Love Everlasting *MJohnston* 3-8-3 RFfrench (5)................................... 12/1   7 4
37 Flossy *CWThornton* 5-8-11 RWinston (4) 25/1   6 5
67 Compton Bolter (IRE) *GAButler* 4-9-0 DHolland (8)............................. 12/1   11 6
    Herodotus *CEBrittain* 3-8-6 PRobinson (7)... 33/1   dist 7
Mr Hamdan Al Maktoum 7ran 2m39.70   TR: 123+/117/116+/104

WOODBINE Sunday, Sep 30   GOOD

74   **Canadian International Stks (Gr 1) (3yo+)** £393,013   1½m

    Order as they passed the post: Zindabad was demoted to sixth for causing
    interference to Falcon Flight; Daliapour was demoted to 7th for causing
    interference on the first turn

55 MUTAMAM *ACStewart,GB* 6-9-0 RHills.. 425/100   1
53 PAOLINI (GER) *AWohler,Germany* 4-9-0 ASuborics................................... 99/10   ½ 2
30 ZINDABAD (FR) *MJohnston,GB* 5-9-0 KDarley................................... 148/10   ¾ 3
4 Daliapour (IRE) *SirMichaelStoute,GB* 4-9-0 JMurtagh............................. 75/10   ½ 4
    Lodge Hill (CAN) *PEngland,Canada* 4-9-0 RDosRamos 49/1   1 5
    Strut The Stage (USA) *MRFrostad,Canada* 3-8-6 (b) TKabel .... 265/100f   ¾ 6
    Falcon Flight (FR) *DJBurkeII,USA* 5-9-0 RDouglas........................... 9/1   dh 6
    Slew The Red (USA) *AFabre,France* 4-9-0 OPeslier.......................... 93/10   2¼ 8
    Dawson's Legacy (USA) *MDoyle,Canada* 6-9-0 ERamsammy................... 80/1   1¾ 9
    Slew Valley (USA) *MWDickinson,USA* 4-9-0 MPino................................. 65/10   ¾ 10
    Williams News (USA) *TAmoss,USA* 6-9-0 DClark .... 91/10   ¾ 11
    River Boat (CAN) *FHuarte,Canada* 6-9-0 (b) SCallaghan.................... 106/1   6½ 12
Mr Hamdan Al Maktoum 12ran 2m28.46   TR: 122/121/120/119/117/117/116+

NEWMARKET Tuesday, Oct 2   GOOD to SOFT (Rowley Mile Course)

75   **Shadwell Stud Cheveley Park Stks (Gr 1) (2yo f)** £87,000   6f

    QUEEN'S LOGIC (IRE) *MRChannon* 2-8-11 SDrowne (3) 10/11f   1
    SOPHISTICAT (USA) *APO'Brien,Ireland* 2-8-11 (v) MJKinane (12) 11/4   7 2
    GOOD GIRL (IRE) *TDEasterby* 2-8-11 WSupple (13)................................ 12/1   2 3
    Lahinch (IRE) *APO'Brien,Ireland* 2-8-11 PaulScallan (11).................... 33/1   ¾ 4
    Sweet Deimos *MJGrassick,Ireland* 2-8-11 EAhern (1)........................... 16/1   ½ 5
    Massarra *JLDunlop* 2-8-11 PatEddery (2) 20/1   2 6
    Ziria (IRE) *CLaffon-Parias,France* 2-8-11 GMosse (5).......................... 25/1   ¾ 7
    Steaming Home (USA) *DKWeld,Ireland* 2-8-11 PJSmullen (6)...................... 7/1   1¾ 8
Mr Jaber Abdullah 8ran 1m12.34   TR: 125/105/100/98/96/91

NEWMARKET Thursday, Oct 4   GOOD (Rowley Mile Course)

76   **Middle Park Stks (Gr 1) (2yo c)** £87,000   6f

51 JOHANNESBURG (USA) *APO'Brien,Ireland* 2-8-11 MJKinane (4).......... 3/10f   1
51 ZIPPING (IRE) *RCollet,France* 2-8-11 DBonilla (3)................................... 13/2   3 2
    DOC HOLIDAY (IRE) *BJMeehan* 2-8-11 BDoyle (8) 40/1   3 3
    Farqad (USA) *DRLoder* 2-8-11 LDettori (7)... 13/2   ¾ 4
    Mr Toad (IRE) *JAOsborne* 2-8-11 (t) RHughes (2) 50/1   5 5
51 Line Rider (USA) *APO'Brien,Ireland* 2-8-11 PaulScallan (6)................... 100/1   ¾ 6
    Official Flame (USA) *DRLoder* 2-8-11 (v) JPSpencer (1)............................. 20/1   1½ 7
Mr M. Tabor & Mrs John Magnier 7ran 1m11.73   TR: 121+/112+/104/101/87

LONGCHAMP Saturday, Oct 6   SOFT
    Hand Times

77   **Prix du Rond-Point - Casino Barriere La Rochelle (Gr 2) (3yo+)** £37,771   1m

59 CHINA VISIT (USA) *SaeedbinSuroor,GB* 4-9-1 LDettori (7) 21/10   1
66 JIM AND TONIC (FR) *FDoumen,France* 7-9-3 TThulliez (3)...................... 1/1f   1 2
    LUGNY (FR) *PVandePoele,France* 3-8-11 DBonilla (1) 22/1   4 3
    Ethelinda *H-APantall,France* 4-8-11 GMosse (4)................................... 89/10   nk 4
    Domedriver (IRE) *PBary,France* 3-8-11 TJarnet (6) 67/10   1½ 5

15 Maumee (IRE) *DKWeld,Ireland* 3-8-11 (b) OPeslier (2) 15/2 15 6
Godolphin 6ran 1m43.85 TR: 122/122+/111/107/108

LONGCHAMP Sunday, Oct 7 Races 78 and 79: HEAVY, Remainder: SOFT
A false running rail was removed before the Marcel Boussac, creating a fresh strip of ground. Hand Times

78 Prix du Cadran - Casino Barriere de Cannes Croisette (Gr 1) (4yo+) £47,215 2½m

GERMINIS (FR) *PChevillard,France* 7-9-2 RJanneau (1) 119/10 1
GENERIC (FR) *J-PGallorini,France* 6-9-2 AJunk (3) 23/10 6 2
46 SAN SEBASTIAN *JLDunlop,GB* 7-9-2 (v) DBonilla (9) 36/10 4 3
46 Royal Rebel *MJohnston,GB* 5-9-2 MJKinane (11) 56/10 8 4
Roli Abi (FR) *FBelmont,France* 6-9-2 GMosse (2) 255/10 1 5
London Bank *BGrizzetti,Italy* 5-9-2 MDemuro (4) 36/10 15 6
Overtop (IRE) *ADepau,Italy,GB* 6-9-2 (b) ADepau (5) 241/10 2½ 7
Speedmaster (GER) *FDoumen,France* 4-9-2 TThulliez (8) 208/10 dist 8
Savoire Vivre *SaeedbinSuroor,GB* 4-9-2 LDettori (6) 22/10f pu
Mr R. Sallet 9ran 4m46.31 TR: 121/116/112/103/102

79 Prix de l'Abbaye de Longchamp - Majestic Barriere (Gr 1) (2yo+) £47,215 5f

25 IMPERIAL BEAUTY (USA) *JEHammond,France* 5-9-8 YTake (1) 38/10 1
70 BAHAMIAN PIRATE (USA) *DNicholls,GB* 6-9-11 TJarnet (5) 22/1 ½ 2
70 PIPALONG (IRE) *TDEasterby,GB* 5-9-8 KDarley (3) 20/1 2½ 3
29 Eastern Purple (IRE) *KARyan,GB* 6-9-11 (b) DHolland (2) 53/1 2 4
50 Repertory *MSSaunders,GB* 8-9-11 DSweeney (13) 36/1 ½ 5
52 Do The Honours (IRE) *H-APantall,France* 3-9-8 LDettori (6) 26/10 ¾ 6
25 Dietrich (USA) *APO'Brien,Ireland* 3-9-8 JPSpencer (8) 38/10 ½ 7
54 Nuclear Debate (USA) *JEHammond,France* 6-9-11 GMosse (11) 2/1f ½ 8
Prince Cyrano *SCWilliams,GB* 2-8-7 GCarter (4) 51/1 ¾ 9
Final Exam (IRE) *DKWeld,Ireland* 4-9-11 (b) PJSmullen (7) 50/1 2½ 10
25 Danehurst *SirMarkPrescott,GB* 3-9-8 GDuffield (10) 11/1 2 11
Indian Spark *JSGoldie,GB* 7-9-11 KFallon (12) 53/1 2 12
Ivory's Joy *KTIvory,GB* 6-9-8 OPeslier (15) 56/1 nk 13
25 Rushcutter Bay *PLGilligan,GB* 8-9-11 (v) SSanders (14) 97/1 ¾ 14
8 Autumnal (IRE) *BJMeehan,GB* 3-9-8 FNorton (9) 150/1 2 15
35 Ishiguru (USA) *APO'Brien,Ireland* 3-9-11 MJKinane (19) 38/10 3 16
25 Dananeyev (FR) *CLaffon-Parias,France* 5-9-11 ODoleuze (16) 32/1 5 17
54 Kier Park (IRE) *MAJarvis,GB* 4-9-11 PRobinson (18) 77/1 2 18
Aramus (CHI) *FCastro,Sweden* 4-9-11 FDiaz (17) 22/1 1 19
Mrs John Magnier 19ran 58.88secs TR: 118/120/112/110/109+/105

80 Prix Marcel Boussac Criterium des Pouliches - Royal Barriere (Gr 1) (2yo f) 1m
£75,543

SULK (IRE) *JHMGosden,GB* 2-8-11 (v) LDettori (5) 113/10 1
DANSEUSE D'ETOILE (FR) *RGibson,France* 2-8-11 OPeslier (6) 69/10 hd 2
KOURNAKOVA (IRE) *APO'Brien,Ireland* 2-8-11 JPSpencer (9) 63/10 3 3
Starfan (USA) *JHMGosden,GB* 2-8-11 KFallon (1) 153/10 ½ 4
Sue Generoos (IRE) *CLaffon-Parias,France* 2-8-11 GMosse (3) 39/10 2 5
Ya Hajar *MRChannon,GB* 2-8-11 SDrowne (8) 7/2 2½ 6
Quad's Melody (IRE) *J-MBeguigne,France* 2-8-11 TJarnet (4) 2/1f 5 7
Guana (FR) *CLaffon-Parias,France* 2-8-11 DBoeuf (2) 178/10 10 8
Venus de Milo (USA) *APO'Brien,Ireland* 2-8-11 MJKinane (7) 63/10 2 9
Mr James Wigan 9ran 1m41.95 TR: 109/109/102/101/97

81 Grand Criterium - Lucien Barriere (Gr 1) (2yo c+f) £118,036 7f

60 ROCK OF GIBRALTAR (IRE) *APO'Brien,Ireland* 2-9-0 1
MJKinane (1) 4/5jf
BERNEBEAU (FR) *AFabre,France* 2-9-0 OPeslier (3) 21/10 3 2
DOBBY ROAD (FR) *MissVDissaux,France* 2-9-0 AJunk (2) 15/2 1½ 3
Shah Jehan (USA) *APO'Brien,Ireland* 2-9-0 JPSpencer (4) 4/5jf 2½ 4
Imtiyaz (USA) *DRLoder,GB* 2-9-0 (v) LDettori (5) 37/10 4 5
Sir Alex Ferguson & Mrs John Magnier 5ran 1m22.98 TR: 110+/102+/98/91

82 Prix de l'Arc de Triomphe - Lucien Barriere (Gr 1) (3yo+ c+f) £566,572 1½m

47 SAKHEE (USA) *SaeedbinSuroor,GB* 4-9-5 LDettori (15) 22/10f 1
65 AQUARELLISTE (FR) *ELellouche,France* 3-8-8 DBoeuf (4) 9/2 6 2
19 SAGACITY (FR) *AFabre,France* 3-8-11 YTake (11) 21/2 1 3
64 Golan (IRE) *SirMichaelStoute,GB* 3-8-11 KFallon (6) 76/10 sh 4
61 Milan *APO'Brien,Ireland* 3-8-11 MJKinane (1) 48/10 1 5
5 Little Rock *SirMichaelStoute,GB* 5-9-5 JPSpencer (16) 105/1 1½ 6
38 Hightori (FR) *PHDemercastel,France* 4-9-5 GMosse (9) 93/10 ½ 7
33 Egyptband (USA) *MmeCHead-Maarek,France* 4-9-2 ODoleuze (10) 18/1 3 8
64 Anabaa Blue *CLerner,France* 3-8-11 CSoumillon (17) 112/10 2½ 9

```
        Foreign Affairs SirMarkPrescott,GB 3-8-11 GDuffield (13) ........................ 42/1      4 10
 65  Diamilina (FR) AFabre,France 3-8-8 OPeslier (3) ................................... 21/2      5 11
     Honorifique (FR) RodolpheCollet,France 4-9-2 TGillet (12)...................... 94/1      ½ 12
     Anzillero (GER) DRichardson,Germany 4-9-5 KWoodburn (8)................ 101/1      1 13
     Idaho Quest H-APantall,France 4-9-5 TThulliez (2) ............................... 88/1      5 14
  6  Holding Court MAJarvis,GB 4-9-5 (b) PRobinson (7).............................. 23/1     nk 15
 61  Saddler's Creek (USA) APO'Brien,Ireland 3-8-11 PaulScallan (14) ......... 48/10     20 16
 62  Chimes At Midnight (USA) LukeComer,Ireland 4-9-5 (b)                         dist 17
       WJSmith (5)....................................................................... 200/1
     Godolphin 17ran 2m35.87                      TR: 135+/123/125/125/123+/121/120
```

LONGCHAMP Sunday, Oct 14   SOFT

83   Prix de la Foret (Gr 1) (3yo+) £47,304   7f

```
 70  MOUNT ABU (IRE) JHMGosden,GB 4-9-2 JFortune ........................ 167/10       1
 77  CHINA VISIT (USA) SaeedbinSuroor,GB 4-9-2 JPSpencer ...................... 8/5f      2  2
 57  WARNINGFORD JRFanshawe,GB 4-9-2 KFallon................................. 5/1      sn  3
     Nicobar IABalding,GB 4-9-2 MartinDwyer.......................................... 41/1      2  4
 45  Amonita PBary,France 3-8-10 TJarnet.................................................. 34/10     hd  5
 54  Mull of Kintyre (USA) APO'Brien,Ireland 4-9-2 KDarley ................... 97/10      2  6
 10  Greengroom (FR) CLaffon-Parias,France 3-9-0 TThulliez ...................... 19/1     1½  7
 57  Lethals Lady RCollet,France 3-8-10 DBoeuf.......................................... 19/1     sh  8
     Deep Sleep (USA) AFabre,France 4-9-2 OPeslier.................................... 63/10    1½  9
     El Gran Lode (ARG) DiegoLowther,Sweden 4-9-2 FDiaz ...................... 56/1      1 10
     Waquaas MrsENordling,Sweden 5-9-2 GNordling .................................. 42/1     10 11
     Gary Seidler & Andy J. Smith 11ran 1m22.90            TR: 123/118/117/111/108
```

NEWMARKET Saturday, Oct 20   GOOD to SOFT (Rowley Mile Course)

84   Darley Dewhurst Stks (Gr 1) (2yo c+f) £116,000   7f

```
 81  ROCK OF GIBRALTAR (IRE) APO'Brien,Ireland 2-9-0
       MJKinane (3) ................................................................................. 4/6f      1
     LANDSEER APO'Brien,Ireland 2-9-0 JPSpencer (8) ....................... 13/2      sh  2
     TENDULKAR (USA) APO'Brien,Ireland 2-9-0 JMurtagh (2) ............ 8/1      hd  3
     Where Or When (IRE) TGMills 2-9-0 TQuinn (5) ........................... 14/1    1¼  4
     Comfy (USA) SirMichaelStoute 2-9-0 KFallon (1)........................... 5/1    1½  5
     Parasol (IRE) MRChannon 2-9-0 SDrowne (6).................................. 20/1     hd  6
 81  Shah Jehan (USA) APO'Brien,Ireland 2-9-0 KDarley (4)................. 66/1    1¼  7
     Prince Tulum (USA) NPLittmoden 2-9-0 JMurtagh (7) ................... 200/1     10  8
     Sir Alex Ferguson & Mrs John Magnier 8ran 1m28.70TR: 114+/114+/113+/110/107/107
```

85   Dubai Champion Stks (Gr 1) (3yo+) £259,840   1¼m

```
 73  NAYEF (USA) MPTregoning 3-8-11 RHills (1) ................................... 3/1f      1
 34  TOBOUGG (IRE) SaeedbinSuroor 3-8-11 KDarley (2) ....................... 11/1     ¾  2
     INDIAN CREEK DRCElsworth 3-8-11 TQuinn (6) ........................... 66/1      4  3
 71  Hawkeye (IRE) APO'Brien,Ireland 3-8-11 MJKinane (12).................. 7/1     nk  4
 37  Carnival Dancer SirMichaelStoute 3-8-11 OPeslier (13)..................... 4/1    1¼  5
 59  Distant Music (USA) BWHills 4-9-2 MHills (4) ................................. 25/1     ½  6
  3  Best of The Bests (IRE) SaeedbinSuroor 4-9-2 (t) LDettori (9)............ 9/1      3  7
 36  Rebelline (IRE) KPrendergast,Ireland 3-8-8 DPMcDonogh (7)............ 16/1      2  8
 37  Albarahin (USA) MPTregoning 6-9-2 WSupple (10).......................... 14/1      5  9
     Beckett (IRE) APO'Brien,Ireland 3-8-11 JMurtagh (5) ..................... 12/1      3 10
 67  Chancellor (IRE) BWHills 3-8-11 PatEddery (11) ............................. 25/1    1¾ 11
 39  No Excuse Needed SirMichaelStoute 3-8-11 KFallon (3)...................... 10/1      8 12
     Mr Hamdan Al Maktoum 12ran 2m07.72              TR: 126+/125/117/116/114/113+
```

MAISONS-LAFFITTE Thursday, Oct 25   HEAVY

86   Criterium de Maisons-Laffitte (Gr 2) (2yo) £66,603   6f

```
     CAPTAIN RIO RMWhitaker,GB 2-9-0 TJarnet............................... 5/2f      1
 51  WAR ZONE (USA) AFabre,France 2-9-0 OPeslier ......................... 10/3      8  2
     PERREXA (FR) DSmaga,France 2-8-11 DBoeuf ........................... 81/10     ¾  3
     Hothaifah FHead,France 2-9-0 DBonilla .......................................... 12/1    1½  4
 41  Highdown (IRE) MRChannon,GB 2-9-0 SDrowne ......................... 18/1    1½  5
     Loupy Glitters (FR) PHDemercastel,France 2-8-11 AJunk................ 82/10     ½  6
 76  Doc Holiday (IRE) BJMeehan,GB 2-9-0 BDoyle ........................... 42/10      4  7
     Slap Shot (IRE) LRiccardi,Italy 2-8-11 TGillet.............................. 20/1      3  8
 51  Sforza (FR) XGuigand,France 2-9-0 PMarion ................................ 50/1      2  9
     Dimaro (GER) HBlume,Germany 2-9-0 LHammer-Hansen.............. 17/1      2 10
     Mister Cavern GColella,Italy 2-9-0 TThulliez ............................... 27/1      11
     Mr D. Samuel 11ran 1m14.30                       TR: 122/107/102/101/97
```

DONCASTER Saturday, Oct 27   HEAVY

87   Racing Post Trophy (Gr 1) (2yo c+f) £114,000   1m (Str.)

```
     HIGH CHAPARRAL (IRE) APO'Brien,Ireland 2-9-0 KDarley (3)............... 9/2      1
```

CASTLE GANDOLFO (USA) *APO'Brien,Ireland* 2-9-0 GDuffield (5) ..... 8/13f ¾ 2
REDBACK *RHannon* 2-9-0 JFortune (1).. 12/1 5 3
Mount Joy *SaeedbinSuroor* 2-9-0 DHolland (4)... 6/1 3 4
Camp David (USA) *APO'Brien,Ireland* 2-9-0 SDrowne (6) 20/1 1¼ 5
Mr Sandancer *JGGiven* 2-9-0 MFenton (2)... 66/1 dist 6

Mr M. Tabor & Mrs John Magnier 6ran 1m45.39   TR: 115/113/103/97

BELMONT PARK Saturday, Oct 27   Turf course: FIRM, Dirt track: FAST

88   **Breeders' Cup Mile (Gr 1) (3yo+)** £411,667   1m (Turf)

       VAL ROYAL (FR) *JCCanani,USA* 5-9-0 JValdivia (12) 51/10 1
       FORBIDDEN APPLE (USA) *CClement,USA* 6-9-0 JSantos (1)................ 82/10 1¾ 2
   71 BACH (IRE) *APO'Brien,Ireland* 4-9-0 MJKinane (4)............................ 335/10 ¾ 3
       Irish Prize (USA) *NDDrysdale,USA* 5-9-0 GaryStevens (13)................. 5/1 1½ 4
       Navesink (USA) *AEGoldberg,USA* 3-8-11 EPrado (2) .... 17/1 nk 5
       Brahms (USA) *WEWalden,USA* 4-9-0 (b) ASolis (10) .... 124/10 nk 6
   71 Noverre (USA) *SaeedbinSuroor,GB* 3-8-11 LDettori (3) .... 41/10f nk 7
       Sarafan (USA) *NDDrysdale,USA* 4-9-0 (b) VEspinoza (9) 27/1 1 8
       City Zip (USA) *LindaRice,USA* 3-8-11 (b) JChavez (6) .... 32/1 nk 9
       Express Tour (USA) *SaeedbinSuroor,GB* 3-8-11 JVelazquez (7)......... 21/1 2¼ 10
       Affirmed Success (USA) *RESchosberg,USA* 7-9-0 JBailey (8) 54/10 2¼ 11
       Balto Star (USA) *TAPletcher,USA* 3-8-11 PDay (5).......................... 81/10 1¾ 12

Mr David S. Milch 12ran 1m32.05   TR: 127/123/121/117/117/116/115

89   **Breeders' Cup Filly & Mare Turf (Gr 1) (3yo+ f+m)** £501,945   1¼m (Turf)

   57 BANKS HILL *AFabre,France* 3-8-9 OPeslier (5) 6/1 1
       SPOOK EXPRESS (SAF) *TJSkiffington,USA* 7-8-11 MESmith (1).......... 137/10 5½ 2
   23 SPRING OAK *AFabre,France* 3-8-9 LDettori (11) 37/1 1¾ 3
       Solvig (USA) *CANafzger,USA* 4-8-11 PDay (8)................................. 34/1 nk 4
       Volga (IRE) *CClement,USA* 3-8-9 JSantos (6) .... 132/10 nk 5
       Kalypso Karie (IRE) *NDDrysdale,USA* 4-8-11 GaryStevens (7) 188/10 1 6
   31 Crystal Music (USA) *JHMGosden,GB* 3-8-9 CMcCarron (9) .... 35/1 nk 7
   72 Lailani *EALDunlop,GB* 3-8-9 JBailey (12).................................... 275/100 1¼ 8
   72 Chaste (USA) *FSSchulhofer,USA* 5-8-11 EPrado (4) .... 79/1 nk 9
   72 Starine (FR) *RJFrankel,USA* 4-8-11 (b) JVelazquez (10) 54/10 2¾ 10
   72 England's Legend (USA) *CClement,USA* 4-8-11 CNakatani (2) 265/100f 2 11
   65 Mot Juste *EALDunlop,GB* 3-8-9 MJKinane (3)............................... 21/1 7 12

Mr K. Abdulla 12ran 2m00.36   TR: 128/114/113/109/112/106

90   **Bessemer Trust Breeders' Cup Juvenile (Gr 1) (2yo c+g)** £361,111   1m110y (Dirt)

   76 JOHANNESBURG (USA) *APO'Brien,Ireland* 2-8-10 MJKinane (3)......... 72/10 1
       REPENT (USA) *KGMcPeek,USA* 2-8-10 (b) AD'Amico (10)................ 42/1 1¼ 2
       SIPHONIC (USA) *DEHofmans,USA* 2-8-10 JBailey (1) 93/10 1¼ 3
       Publication (USA) *TKnight,USA* 2-8-10 (b) MESmith (6) .... 103/1 ¾ 4
       Officer (USA) *RBaffert,USA* 2-8-10 (b) VEspinoza (2).................... 75/100f 2 5
       French Assault (USA) *JKDesormeaux,USA* 2-8-10 (b) KDesormeaux (7) ... 62/1 hd 6
       Came Home (USA) *JPGonzalez,USA* 2-8-10 CMcCarron (11).......... 5/1 hd 7
       Saarland (USA) *CMcGaugheyIII,USA* 2-8-10 JVelazquez (9)........... 22/1 nk 8
       Ibn Al Haitham *EHarty,USA* 2-8-10 DFlores (8) 94/1 6½ 9
       It'sallinthechase (USA) *WLBrown,USA* 2-8-10 RDWilliams (12) 147/1 2¼ 10
       Jump Start (USA) *DWLukas,USA* 2-8-10 (b) PDay (5)................ 123/10 1¾ 11
       Essence of Dubai (USA) *EHarty,USA* 2-8-10 (b) ASolis (4)................ 33/1 4 12

Mr M. Tabor & Mrs John Magnier 12ran 1m42.27   TR: 122+/120/118/117/114/114

91   **Breeders' Cup Turf (Gr 1) (3yo+)** £772,778   1½m (Turf)

   56 FANTASTIC LIGHT (USA) *SaeedbinSuroor,GB* 5-9-0 (t) LDettori (2)..... 14/10f 1
   82 MILAN *APO'Brien,Ireland* 3-8-9 MJKinane (12) .... 75/10 ¾ 2
       TIMBOROA *RJFrankel,USA* 5-9-0 EPrado (8) 83/10 5¾ 3
       Blazing Fury (USA) *JJToner,USA* 3-8-9 (b) CNakatani (3)..................... 52/1 ¾ 4
   44 Hap (USA) *WIMott,USA* 5-9-0 JBailey (11)................................ 56/10 3¼ 5
       Chorwon (USA) *HRWiggins,USA* 8-9-0 JKCourt (4)......................... 59/1 2 6
       With Anticipation (USA) *JESheppard,USA* 6-9-0 (b) PDay (1) .... 395/100 ½ 7
   74 Lodge Hill (CAN) *PEngland,Canada* 4-9-0 JVelazquez (6).............. 57/1 1 8
   74 Slew The Red (USA) *AFabre,France* 4-9-0 OPeslier (7) 58/1 5½ 9
   44 Quiet Resolve (USA) *MRFrostad,Canada* 6-9-0 RAlbarado (9) 39/1 4¾ 10
   74 Mutamam *ACStewart,GB* 6-9-0 RHills (10)................................. 113/10 18 11

Godolphin 11ran 2m24.36   TR: 128+/129/116/117/109

92   **Breeders' Cup Classic (Gr 1) (3yo+)** £1,444,445   1¼m (Dirt)

       TIZNOW (USA) *JMRobbins,USA* 4-9-0 CMcCarron (10) 69/10 1
   82 SAKHEE (USA) *SaeedbinSuroor,GB* 4-9-0 LDettori (6) .... 48/10 ns 2
       ALBERT THE GREAT (USA) *NPZito,USA* 4-9-0 JChavez (9)................ 13/1 1¾ 3
       Macho Uno (USA) *JFOrseno,USA* 3-8-10 (b) GaryStevens (7)............... 195/10 2¾ 4

Guided Tour (USA) *NMO'Callaghan,USA* 5-9-0 (b) LMelancon (2) 182/10   1¼ 5
56 Galileo (IRE) *APO'Brien,Ireland* 4-9-0 MJKinane (5) 335/100   2 6
    Include (USA) *GDelp,USA* 4-9-0 (b) JVelazquez (4).................................. 105/10   ½ 7
3 Aptitude (USA) *RJFrankel,USA* 4-9-0 (b) JBailey (12) 235/100f   1½ 8
    Gander (USA) *JPTerranovaII,USA* 5-9-0 (b) VEspinoza (8)................... 81/1   nk 9
47 Black Minnaloushe (USA) *APO'Brien,Ireland* 3-8-10 JMurtagh (3) .... 51/1   nk 10
    A Fleets Dancer (USA) *RAttfield,Canada* 4-9-0 (b) RLandry (11) 146/1   1 11
    Orientate (USA) *DWLukas,USA* 3-8-10 PDay (1).. 34/1   19 12
    Freedom Crest (USA) *RBaltas,USA* 5-9-0 KDesormeaux (13).................... 69/1   3¼ 13
Cee's Stable 13ran 2m00.62   TR: 130+/130+/127/124/120/118

LONGCHAMP Sunday, Oct 28   HEAVY
93   **Prix Royal-Oak (Gr 1) (3yo+)** £38,059   1m7f110y
62 VINNIE ROE (IRE) *DKWeld,Ireland* 3-8-9 (b) PJSmullen 37/10   1
78 GENERIC (FR) *J-PGallorini,France* 6-9-4 AJunk 98/10   2½ 2
78 GERMINIS (FR) *PChevillard,France* 7-9-4 RJanneau................................. 43/10   nk 3
    Le Tintoret (IRE) *YdeNicolay,France* 8-9-4 CSoumillon 41/1   2½ 4
68 Yavana's Pace (IRE) *MJohnston,GB* 9-9-4 DHolland 114/10   1½ 5
    Bonnet Rouge (FR) *ELellouche,France* 4-9-4 DBoeuf 171/10   15 6
78 San Sebastian *JLDunlop,GB* 7-9-4 (b) ODoleuze .... 50/1   ¾ 7
    Epitre (FR) *AFabre,France* 4-9-4 (b) OPeslier...................................... 115/10   6 8
40 Double Honour (FR) *MJohnston,GB* 3-8-9 GDuffield 39/1   1 9
    Duke d'Alba (GER) *WFigge,Germany* 4-9-4 TJarnet................................... 96/1   10 10
    Persian Ruler *FBedouret,Spain* 6-9-4 JHorcajada.................................... 55/1   11
    Fair Question (IRE) *JLDunlop,GB* 3-8-9 DBonilla.. 21/1   12
    Wareed (IRE) *SaeedbinSuroor,GB* 3-8-9 (v) LDettori........................... 18/10f   13
Mr Seamus Sheridan 13ran 3m37.80   TR: 126/121/121/118?/117

SAINT-CLOUD Saturday, Nov 3   SOFT
94   **Criterium International (Gr 1) (2yo c+f)** £75,974   1m
    ACT ONE *JEPease,France* 2-9-0 TGillet.. 24/10   1
84 LANDSEER *APO'Brien,Ireland* 2-9-0 MJKinane .... 3/5cpf   ½ 2
    GUYS AND DOLLS *PFICole,GB* 2-9-0 CSoumillon .... 32/10   ¾ 3
    Mutinyonthebounty *APO'Brien,Ireland* 2-9-0 JMurtagh........................... 3/5cpf   1½ 4
    Diaghilev (IRE) *APO'Brien,Ireland* 2-9-0 TJarnet...................................... 3/5cpf   4 5
    Halawellfin Hala *CEBrittain,GB* 2-9-0 BDoyle 172/10   6 6
Mr Gerald Leigh 6ran 1m47.10   TR: 116/115/113/110/102

FLEMINGTON Tuesday, Nov 6   GOOD to SOFT
95   **Tooheys New Melbourne Cup (Gr 1) (3yo+)** £859,375   2m
    ETHEREAL (NZ) *SLaxon,NewZealand* 4-8-3 SSeamer................................... 9/1   1
56 GIVE THE SLIP *SaeedbinSuroor,GB* 4-8-3 RHills .... 30/1   ¾ 2
62 PERSIAN PUNCH (IRE) *DRCElsworth,GB* 8-9-1 TQuinn 12/1   6 3
    Karasi (IRE) *DHall,Australia* 6-7-12 (b) GBoss...................................... 25/1   ¾ 4
    Maythehorsebewithu (NZ) *MMoroney,NewZealand* 5-7-12 JPatton .... 12/1   nk 5
    Rain Gauge (AUS) *GHanlon,Australia* 4-7-5 KMcEvoy .... 8/1   ns 6
62 Marienbard (IRE) *SaeedbinSuroor,GB* 4-8-9 (b) LDettori.......................... 16/1   ¾ 7
    Sky Heights (NZ) *CAlderson,Australia* 6-8-13 (b) DMOliver....................... 5/1f   hd 8
    Reenact (AUS) *JDenham,Australia* 4-8-0 LCassidy 80/1   1½ 9
    Prophet's Kiss (AUS) *RQuinton,Australia* 6-7-12 BYork 60/1   1¾ 10
    Inaflury (NZ) *CIBrown,Australia* 6-8-3 BPrebble.................................... 30/1   1¼ 11
    Mr Prudent (AUS) *GHanlon,Australia* 7-8-4 (b) CraigWilliams................. 50/1   3½ 12
44 Caitano *ASchutz,Germany* 7-8-9 (b) JMurtagh.. 50/1   1 13
    Celestial Show (AUS) *LMorton,Australia* 6-7-10 RMcLeod...................... 16/1   2 14
    Rum (AUS) *DLawson,Australia* 4-7-11 CMunce.. 16/1   2¼ 15
    Freemason (AUS) *JHawkes,Australia* 5-8-6 DGauci .... 40/1   ¾ 16
    Spirit of Westbury (NZ) *CIBrown,Australia* 6-7-12 SDye......................... 12/1   1¼ 17
    Yippyio (AUS) *ADenham,Australia* 8-8-8 DBeadman............................... 16/1   6 18
    Big Pat (AUS) *PTulloch,Australia* 4-8-0 PMertens.................................. 12/1   5½ 19
    Pasta Express (AUS) *PCave,Australia* 7-8-4 DNikolic............................. 70/1   3 20
9 Hill of Grace (NZ) *R&WPriscott,NewZealand* 5-8-3 (b) CoreyBrown .... 16/1   ur
    Curata Storm (AUS) *JHawkes,Australia* 4-8-8 (b) GChilds .... 60/1   pu
P. J. & P. M. Vela 22ran 3m21.08   TR: 119+/121/120/102/102/101

SAINT-CLOUD Tuesday, Nov 13   HEAVY
96   **Criterium de Saint-Cloud (Gr 1) (2yo c+f)** £37,383   1¼m
    BALLINGARRY (IRE) *APO'Brien,Ireland* 2-9-0 JPSpencer 7/10cpf   1
87 CASTLE GANDOLFO (USA) *APO'Brien,Ireland* 2-9-0 MJKinane....... 7/10cpf   1 2
    BLACK SAM BELLAMY (IRE) *APO'Brien,Ireland* 2-9-0
      JAHeffernan 7/10cpf   1 3

Banyu Dewi (GER) *MHofer,Germany* 2-8-11 ASuborics 27/1   3 4
Martaline *AFabre,France* 2-9-0 OPeslier .... 71/10 nk 5
Special Kaldoun (IRE) *DSmaga,France* 2-9-0 DBoeuf .... 48/10 hd 6
Swing Wing *PFICole,GB* 2-9-0 CSoumillon .... 10/1 sn 7
Agog (IRE) *JEPease,France* 2-9-0 TGillet .... 44/10 dh 7
Angelus Sunset (USA) *BJMeehan,GB* 2-9-0 PatEddery .... 40/1 ¾ 9
Master In Law (IRE) *GCBravery,GB* 2-9-0 JWeaver 52/1 15 10

Mrs John Magnier 10ran 2m24.60   TR: 110+/109+/107+/100/102/102

TOKYO Sunday, Nov 25 FIRM

97 **Japan Cup (Gr 1) (3yo+)** £1,443,897   1½m

      JUNGLE POCKET (JPN) *SWatanabe,Japan* 3-8-10 OPeslier................... 32/10   1
      T M OPERA O (JPN) *IIwamoto,Japan* 5-9-0 RWada....................... 18/10f nk 2
      NARITA TOP ROAD (JPN) *HYamaji,Japan* 5-9-0 KWatanabe.............. 134/10 3½ 3
  1 Stay Gold (JPN) *YIkee,Japan* 7-9-0 (b) YTake .... 71/10 nk 4
      Meisho Doto (IRE) *IYasuda,Japan* 5-9-0 YYasuda .... 39/10 ¾ 5
 82 Golan (IRE) *SirMichaelStoute,GB* 3-8-10 JMurtagh........................... 23/1 ns 6
  4 Indigenous (IRE) *IWAllan,HongKong* 8-9-0 WCMarwing................... 114/1 ½ 7
 44 White Heart *NDDrysdale,USA* 5-9-0 GaryStevens 62/1 1¼ 8
 91 With Anticipation (USA) *JESheppard,USA* 6-9-0 (b) MEbina............ 22/1 3 9
      American Boss (USA) *FTago,Japan* 6-9-0 TEda 117/1 1 10
      Daiwa Texas (JPN) *SMasuzawa,Japan* 8-9-0 (b) YShibata 140/1 2 11
      Cagney (BRZ) *REMandella,USA* 4-9-0 MESmith........................... 25/1 2½ 12
 74 Paolini (GER) *AWohler,Germany* 4-9-0 ASuborics .... 17/1 ns 13
  3 To The Victory (JPN) *YIkee,Japan* 5-8-10 HShii .... 33/1 dist 14
 91 Timboroa *RJFrankel,USA* 5-9-0 JBailey 25/1 2½ 15

Mr Y. Saito 15ran 2m23.80   TR: 131/128/122/122/120/122/119/117

SHA TIN Sunday, Dec 16 GOOD to FIRM

98 **Hong Kong Vase (Gr 1) (3yo+)** £716,845   1½m

 97 STAY GOLD (JPN) *YIkee,Japan* 7-9-0 (h+ec) YTake (14)................... 105/100f   1
 20 EKRAAR (USA) *SaeedbinSuroor,GB* 4-9-0 (v+t) LDettori (12)............. 10/1 hd 2
 97 INDIGENOUS (IRE) *IWAllan,HongKong* 8-9-0 (t) DWhyte (7) 16/1 6¾ 3
 19 Foundation Spirit (FR) *FDoumen,France* 3-8-10 TThulliez (10)........... 37/1 1¼ 4
  4 Helene Vitality (NZ) *DAHayes,HongKong* 5-9-0 (b) BMarcus (5) .... 37/1 sh 5
 74 Daliapour (IRE) *SirMichaelStoute,GB* 5-9-0 JMurtagh (8).................. 41/10 2¼ 6
 97 White Heart *NDDrysdale,USA* 5-9-0 (t) GaryStevens (2)................... 12/1 sh 7
  9 Tapildo (NZ) *LLaxon,Singapore* 4-8-11 EWilkinson (13)................... 64/1 1¼ 8
 95 Caitano (GER) *ASchutz,Germany* 7-9-0 (b) OPeslier (3) 25/1 3¾ 9
 74 Zindabad (FR) *MJohnston,GB* 5-9-0 KDarley (6)........................... 9/1 nk 10
      Rainbow And Gold (USA) *PCKan,HongKong* 4-9-0 GMosse (4) 13/1 3¾ 11
      Survey General (IRE) *JMoore,HongKong* 5-9-0 (b) ESaint-Martin (4) 100/1 5¼ 12
  4 Oriental Express (IRE) *IWAllan,HongKong* 8-9-0 (b) FCoetzee (1)........ 56/1 4¼ 13
      Litigado (ARG) *ATMillard,HongKong* 4-9-0 AMarcus (11)................. 54/1 2¾ 14

Shadai Race Horse Co. Ltd 14ran 2m27.80   TR: 126+/125/115/114/113

99 **Hong Kong Mile (Gr 1) (3yo+)** £716,845   1m

      EISHIN PRESTON (USA) *SKitahashi,Japan* 4-9-0 (h+t) YFukunaga (13) . 24/1   1
  4 ELECTRONIC UNICORN (USA) *JSize,HongKong* 5-9-0 (b) RFradd (4) . 37/10 3¼ 2
 83 CHINA VISIT (USA) *SaeedbinSuroor,GB* 4-9-0 LDettori (9)................ 12/1 ¾ 3
 88 Forbidden Apple (USA) *CClement,USA* 6-9-0 (t) CNakatani (9).......... 44/10 ½ 4
      Shogun Lodge (AUS) *RThomsen,Australia* 5-9-0 SDye (7) .... 14/1 nk 5
      Red Pepper *PCKan,HongKong* 4-9-0 GMosse (6) .... 46/1 hd 6
      Charming City (AUS) *DAHayes,HongKong* 5-9-0 (b+t) BMarcus (8)....... 79/1 ½ 7
      Show A Heart (AUS) *BMiller,Australia* 4-9-0 (t) GBoss (10)................ 91/1 sh 8
 71 Proudwings (GER) *RSuerland,Germany* 5-8-11 YTake (12) .... 41/1 hd 9
      Super Molly (USA) *DAHayes,HongKong* 4-9-0 DMOliver (2)............. 66/1 ¾ 10
 59 Tough Speed (USA) *SirMichaelStoute,GB* 4-9-0 JMurtagh (3) 48/1 2½ 11
      Red Sun (ARG) *ASCruz,HongKong* 4-9-0 (t) FCoetzee (11)............... 55/1 ½ 12
 83 Mount Abu (IRE) *JHMGosden,GB* 4-9-0 JFortune (14).................... 98/1 hd 13
      Zenno El Cid (IRE) *KFujisawa,Japan* 4-9-0 OPeslier (5) 1/1f 3¼ 14

Mr T. Hirai 14ran 1m34.80   TR: 125/117/115/114/113/113

100 **Hong Kong Cup (Gr 1) (3yo+)** £913,978   1¼m

      AGNES DIGITAL (USA) *TShirai,Japan* 4-9-0 HShii (12) 295/100   1
 85 TOBOUGG (IRE) *SaeedbinSuroor,GB* 3-8-11 LDettori (8) .... 14/10f hd 2
      TERRE A TERRE (FR) *ELibaud,France* 4-9-0 CSoumillon (13)............. 34/1 nk 3
 85 Hawkeye (IRE) *MAJarvis,GB* 3-8-11 GaryStevens (4)................... 16/1 ½ 4
 77 Jim And Tonic (FR) *FDoumen,France* 7-9-0 TThulliez (5) 62/10 1 5
      Saddle Up (IND) *LLaxon,Singapore* 6-9-0 OPeslier (10) 70/1 1¼ 6
      Peak Power (IRE) *DHill,HongKong* 5-9-0 (b) RFradd (1) 39/1 1¼ 7

71	Bocelli (NZ) *PBusuttin,Singapore* 5-9-0 (b) GCooksley (2)	98/1	½ 8
23	Choc Ice (IRE) *RCollet,France* 3-8-8 JMurtagh (3)	97/1	sh 9
	Momentum (AUS) *DAHayes,HongKong* 5-9-0 SDye (7)	50/1	nk 10
44	Silvano (GER) *AWohler,Germany* 5-9-0 ASuborics (14)	87/10	2¾ 11
	Monards (AUS) *JMoore,HongKong* 5-9-0 (b) ESaint-Martin (11)	98/1	nk 12
4	Housemaster (IRE) *IWAllan,HongKong* 5-9-0 FCoetzee (6)	69/1	1¾ 13
88	Bach (IRE) *APO'Brien,Ireland* 4-9-0 MJKinane (9)	71/10	1½ 14

Mr Takao Watanabe 14ran 2m02.80   TR: 123+/124+/119/122/119/117

INDEX TO SELECTED BIG RACES

THE TIMEFORM 'TOP HORSES ABROAD'

This review of the year covers the major racing countries outside Britain. It includes Timeform Ratings for the top two-year-olds, three-year-olds and older horses. Horses not rated highly enough to be included in the main lists but which finished in the first three in a European pattern race or, in the section on North America, won a Grade 1 during the season are included below the cut-off line. Fillies and mares are denoted by (f); * denotes the horse was trained for only a part of the season in the country concerned. Overseas customers wishing to keep in touch with Timeform's coverage of racing through the year can subscribe to Computer Timeform, Timeform Perspective or our internet site (http://www.timeform.com) for reports on all the important races. It is now possible to obtain up-to-date Timeform commentaries (including many not published in the weekly Timeform Black Book), undertake progeny research and access daily form guides on the internet site.

IRELAND Any review of Irish racing in 2001 must begin with the outstanding achievements of Aidan O'Brien. After missing out on classic success in 2000, he took seven such races in Britain, Ireland and France, with the Derby, Oaks and St Leger in Britain playing a big part in making him the first Irish trainer to become champion in Britain since Vincent O'Brien in 1977. His haul of Group or Grade 1 races by the end of the season totalled twenty-three. Derby winner **Galileo** was the best three-year-old in Europe, a position he cemented with further successes in the Irish Derby and King George VI and Queen Elizabeth Diamond Stakes. Losing his unbeaten record to Fantastic Light in the Irish Champion Stakes, a candidate for the race of the season, hardly diminished his standing and defeat on dirt in the Breeders' Cup Classic should not detract from his achievements on turf in Europe. In **Milan**, Ballydoyle had a formidable second string for the top middle-distance races. Seemingly short of classic standard in the first half of the season, Milan developed into a high-class colt with wins in the Great Voltigeur and St Leger (in which Ebor winner **Mediterranean** was injured) and a good second in the Breeders' Cup Turf. The third of O'Brien's British classic winners was **Imagine**, whose Oaks victory followed her success in the Irish 1000 Guineas. Stable-companions **Black Minnaloushe**, **Mozart** and **Minardi** filled the first three places in the Irish 2000 Guineas. Black Minnaloushe went on to win the St James's Palace Stakes but it was Mozart who proved best of that trio, developing into a top-class performer over five and six furlongs following success in the Jersey Stakes with clear-cut victories in the July Cup and Nunthorpe. Another who did well over shorter trips was **King Charlemagne**, who was unbeaten for the year in a couple of Group 3 events in Ireland over seven furlongs and the Prix Maurice de Gheest at Deauville. Desmond Stakes winner **Hawkeye** and the Prix Jean Prat runner-up **King of Tara** both showed smart form for Aidan O'Brien before joining Michael Jarvis and Francois Doumen respectively during the year.

The Irish St Leger, won by **Vinnie Roe**, was one classic that did not fall to the O'Brien stable. The Dermot Weld-trained colt made into a high-class stayer after finishing down the field in the Irish Derby, winning listed races from **Sadlers Wings** and **Pugin** before the Irish St Leger and then completing a four-timer in the Prix Royal-Oak at Longchamp. He looks a good prospect for the Cup races in 2002. Several of Ireland's leading three-year-old fillies also ran well outside Ireland. **Sahara Slew** took the Ribblesdale Stakes at Royal Ascot with subsequent Prix Minerve winner **Lime Gardens** down the field. **Rebelline** was another Irish-trained filly to run her best race in France, finishing third in the Prix de l'Opera having earlier won the Pretty Polly Stakes at the Curragh. **Golden Apples** ran her final race in Ireland when third in the Pretty Polly before going on to Grade 1 success in the USA with Ben Cecil. Apart from Imagine, Ballydoyle housed some other smart fillies, including **Dietrich**, Irish Oaks third **Karsavina** and **Toroca**, who was third in the 1000 Guineas at both Newmarket and the Curragh. The stable's other classic winner was the Poule d'Essai des Pouliches winner **Rose Gypsy**.

But it was the two-year-old scene that Aidan O'Brien again dominated to the greatest extent. Of the ten European Group 1 juvenile events open to colts, only the Criterium

International at Saint-Cloud escaped his grasp. **Johannesburg** was the stable's outstanding two-year-old, unbeaten in seven starts, including the Phoenix Stakes, Prix Morny and Middle Park Stakes before putting himself at the head of the Kentucky Derby betting, as well as the 2000 Guineas market, with victory in the Breeders' Cup Juvenile. Should connections elect to go to Churchill Downs instead, they have at least two other worthy contenders for Newmarket. **Hawk Wing** was not seen outside Ireland but put up impressive performances to win both the Futurity Stakes and the National Stakes. His only defeat came earlier on in the Railway Stakes at the hands of **Rock of Gibraltar**, who went on to win the Gimcrack, Grand Criterium and Dewhurst Stakes. In the Dewhurst, Rock of Gibraltar prevailed in a three-way photo with stable-companions **Landseer** (earlier successful in the Coventry Stakes) and the twice-raced **Tendulkar**. Remarkably, another clean sweep for the stable occurred in the Criterium de Saint-Cloud, won by **Ballingarry** from the Beresford Stakes winner **Castle Gandolfo** and Galileo's maiden brother **Black Sam Bellamy**. Castle Gandolfo had finished second on his previous outing to one of the yard's best middle-distance prospects, **High Chaparral**, in the Racing Post Trophy. Other colts who showed plenty of ability were the Royal Lodge winner **Mutinyonthebounty**, Gran Criterium winner **Sholokhov** and the promising Somerville Tattersall Stakes runner-up **Della Francesca**. The Leopardstown maiden winner Sorcerous looks one of the best prospects among the stable's darker horses.

As usual the two-year-old fillies at Ballydoyle were less dominant but still made their mark. Best of them was the 3.4 million dollar daughter of champion US filly Serena's Song, **Sophisticat**. Placed in the Queen Mary, Lowther, Moyglare Stud and Cheveley Park Stakes, she ran just about her best race when fifth in the Breeders' Cup Juvenile Fillies. She does look quite exposed, however, and others with more scope for improvement at three are the Moyglare Stud Stakes winner **Quarter Moon** and the Fillies' Mile runner-up **Maryinsky**, both by Sadler's Wells. Also by Sadler's Wells (and out of dams who are half-sisters), the Marcel Boussac third **Kournakova** and the Leopardstown listed winner **On The Nile** are also potentially smart three-year-old prospects. Elsewhere, Dermot Weld has a couple of useful fillies with the potential to improve further; **Saranac Lake** beat Quarter Moon in the Debutante Stakes, while **Dress To Thrill** finished second to the same O'Brien filly in the Moyglare Stud Stakes.

The older horses in Ireland were no better than smart for the most part. Best of them was the Royal Whip winner **Bach**, who also finished third in the Eclipse Stakes, Irish Champion Stakes and Breeders' Cup Mile. The Royal Whip runner-up **Jammaal** and the Meld Stakes winner **Muakaad** proved reliable mile and a quarter performers for the Weld stable, though the latter broke a leg on the gallops towards the end of the year. Geldings **Final Exam** and **Social Harmony** also performed well in sprints for the same stable. Two of the best staying performances from older horses came from the first two in the listed Saval Beg Stakes, in which **Rostropovich** (in receipt of weight) beat **Media Puzzle**. Older handicappers put up some notable efforts, none more so than **D'Anjou**, who won the valuable Tote Exacta Handicap over seven furlongs at Leopardstown. **Caumshinaun** made rapid progress in handicaps before retiring to the paddocks after a listed win at Cork while seven-year-old **Tarry Flynn** showed he was as good as ever when carrying top weight to victory in the Irish Lincolnshire from subsequent Concorde Stakes winner **Montecastillo**.

Two-Year-Olds

127	Johannesburg	106	Camp David	101	Monarchoftheglen
118	Rock of Gibraltar	106	Stonemason	101	Moon Safari (f)
116p	Hawk Wing	104p	Dress To Thrill (f)	100p	High Sierra
115p	High Chaparral	104	Lahinch (f)	100	Sweet Deimos (f)
115	Landseer	104	Shah Jehan		
114p	Ballingarry	103p	On The Nile (f)	98	Agnetha (f)
114p	Tendulkar	103p	Saranac Lake (f)	97	High Society (f)
113	Castle Gandolfo	103+	*Stage Call	96	Lady Digby (f)
112	Mutinyonthebounty	103	Brooklyn	95	Temple of Artemis
111	Black Sam Bellamy	103	Rum Charger (f)	90	Easy Sunshine (f)
110p	Della Francesca	102p	Kournakova (f)	87	Ulysses
109	Sophisticat (f)	102	Bringontheclowns		
108	Sholokhov	102	Diaghilev		
107p	Maryinsky (f)	102	Miss Beabea (f)	**Three-Year-Olds**	
106p	Quarter Moon (f)	102	Wiseman's Ferry	134	Galileo
		101	*Daneleta (f)	131	Mozart
				129	Milan

126	Vinnie Roe	107	Dearly (f)	116	D'Anjou
123	Black Minnaloushe	107	Gaelic Queen (f)	116	Media Puzzle
122	*Hawkeye	107	Hans Anderson	115	Final Exam
120	King Charlemagne	107	King's County	115	Jammaal
119	Imagine (f)	106	Adonesque (f)	115	Tarry Flynn
116	*King of Tara	106	Alegranza (f)	114	Caumshinaun (f)
116	Minardi	106	Chamela Bay (f)	114	Mull of Kintyre
115	Dietrich (f)	106	Derivative	114	Shoal Creek
115	*Golden Apples (f)	106	Freud	114	Social Harmony
115	Pugin	106	Modigliani	113	One Won One
114	Bonnard	106	Tender Cove	113	Rostropovich
114	Karsavina (f)	105+	Snowflake (f)	113?	Montecastillo
114	Mediterranean	105	Deeply (f)	112	Mutakarrim
114	Rose Gypsy (f)	105	Juniper	111	Common Kris
113	Avorado	105	Lethal Agenda	110	Osprey Ridge
113	Beckett	104	Kalamunda (f)	110	Pine Dance
113	Lime Gardens (f)	103	Coney Kitty (f)	109	Masilia (f)
113	Sequoyah (f)	103	Crimphill (f)	108	Free To Speak
112+	Ishiguro	103	Henry Afrika	108	Provosky
112	Exaltation	103	Julie Jalouse (f)	108	Scottish Memories
112	Ice Dancer	103	Right Honorable	108§	Chimes At Midnight
112	Rebelline (f)	103	Scarlet Velvet (f)	106	Tiger Royal
112	Sadlers Wings	103?	Josh's Pearl (f)	105	Masnada (f)
112	Toroca (f)	102	Alexander Express (f)	105	Moving On Up
112?	*Sita (f)	102	Chill Seeking (f)	104	Molomo (f)
111	Diamond Trim (f)	102	El Bueno	104d	Rush Brook
111	*Softly Tread (f)	102	Rayyana (f)	103	Anna Elise (f)
111	Speirbhean (f)	102	Reina Blanca (f)	102	Mr Houdini
110	Chiming (f)	101	Galanta	102	Tarakan
110	One More Round	101	Katherine Seymour (f)	101	Citizen Edward
110	Pebble Island	101	*Translucid	101	Conormara
110	Sahara Slew (f)	101?	Frosty Wind	101	Golovin
109	Affianced (f)	100	La Stellina (f)	101	Newpark Lady (f)
109	Cool Clarity (f)	100	March King	101	Vatirisk
109	Just Special (f)	100	Moonbi Ridge (f)	101d	Berenica (f)
109	Siringas (f)	100	*Saffron Dancer (f)	100	Ancelin (f)
109	Taraza (f)	100?	Lady of Kildare (f)	100	Doonaree
108	*Darasim			100	Sheer Tenby
108	Magic Cove (f)		**Older Horses**		
108	Maumee	121	Bach	96	Pillars of Society (f)
108	Saying Grace (f)	118	Muakaad	92	Miracle Ridge

FRANCE   For the second year running, fillies came to the fore among the three-year-olds in France. **Banks Hill** showed smart form at a mile in her European campaign, winning the Prix de Sandringham and the Coronation Stakes and finishing second in the Poule d'Essai des Pouliches, Prix Jacques le Marois and Prix du Moulin. Things did not go her way in each of those defeats, particularly in the Pouliches, but when stepped up to a mile and a quarter for the Breeders' Cup Filly & Mare Turf she was a revelation, putting up a high-class performance with the easiest win on the card. Little wonder that she will be kept in training at four, when a meeting with Aquarelliste will be one to look forward to. **Aquarelliste** dominated the fillies' middle-distance races, winning the Prix de Diane from the Prix Saint-Alary winner **Nadia**, and the Prix Vermeille from **Diamilina** (winner of the Prix de Malleret and Prix de la Nonette) and the Saint-Alary runner-up **Mare Nostrum**. She ended her season with second place in the Prix de l'Arc de Triomphe, a final runner in the race for France's most successful owner-breeder of recent decades, Daniel Wildenstein, who died later in October. Aquarelliste had been one of more than forty horses transferred by Wildenstein from Andre Fabre to Elie Lellouche earlier in the year.

Banks Hill was not the only French-trained filly to excel herself across the Atlantic. **Choc Ice** led home a clean sweep for France in the E. P. Taylor Stakes at Woodbine when beating **Volga** and **Spring Oak**, respective winners of the Prix de Royaumont and Prix Cleopatre. The latter pair went on to finish fifth and third behind Banks Hill at Belmont. Another of the leading fillies **Do The Honours** progressed from handicap company in the Provinces to winning the Prix de Meautry, and this very smart sprinter has now joined

Godolphin. Another good sprinter to have left a French stable in 2001 was **Iron Mask**, who was transferred to the States, having won the very valuable Singapore Airlines KrisFlyer Sprint at Kranji in May.

Defeat in a couple of trials for the Prix du Jockey Club and the big race itself was an inauspicious start to **Sagacity**'s season, but he gradually found his form, putting up a high-class performance to take third place in the Prix de l'Arc de Triomphe. The Prix du Jockey Club winner **Anabaa Blue** finished down the field in the Arc and has to be considered a substandard winner of the French Derby. **Chichicastenango** had to miss the Arc but performed consistently in top company, running second to Anabaa Blue at Chantilly between wins over the same rival in the Prix Lupin and over subsequent US Grade 1 winner **Mizzen Mast** in a disappointing field for the Grand Prix de Paris. The front-running **Maille Pistol** started favourite for the Prix du Jockey Club following wide-margin victories in the Prix Greffulhe and Prix Hocquart, but he disappointed subsequently and will be going hurdling in 2002.

Vahorimix was the best miler among the three-year-old colts and had the unusual distinction of being awarded both the Poule d'Essai des Poulains and the Prix Jacques le Marois following the disqualifications of Noverre and then Proudwings. **Denon**, **Okawango** and **Keltos** were promoted to third, fourth and fifth respectively in the Poulains. Denon ended up winning the Hollywood Derby for Bobby Frankel late in the year but Okawango, the leading French two-year-old of 2000, failed to win, though he did run a creditable fourth in the Prix du Jockey Club. Keltos started the surprise favourite in the Poulains on his pattern-race debut, and after finishing sixth in the St James's Palace Stakes, came back in the autumn to win the Prix Perth. Another who did well over a mile was the ex-German colt **Aghnoyoh**, who won the Prix de la Jonchere at Chantilly and a Group 2 at Cologne. Finally, among the three-year-olds, the progressive **Poussin**, who won a listed race at Deauville on his final start, looks capable of making his mark in better company in 2002.

Hightori was France's top older horse, a position he earned more through his defeats than his wins in Group 3 company in Dubai early in the year and in the Prix Foy (against **Idaho Quest** and **Slew The Red**) in September. In between he was placed in the Dubai World Cup, Prix d'Ispahan, Prince of Wales's Stakes and King George VI and Queen Elizabeth Diamond Stakes, but defeat in the Arc prefaced his sale to Saudi Arabia. **Nuclear Debate** was another who was sold abroad before the end of the year but he had earlier proved himself still one of the best sprinters in Europe with victory in the Sprint Cup at Haydock. He was one of several who took advantage of the Prix de l'Abbaye being open to geldings for the first time, but the race was won instead by his stable-companion the mare **Imperial Beauty**, only the second occasion since 1978 that the race had gone to a French-trained horse.

Course regular **Mirio** sprang a surprise against the previous season's Arc runner-up **Egyptband** in the Grand Prix de Saint-Cloud on his debut in pattern company but missed the remainder of the season. Egyptband never recaptured her best form despite a win in the Grand Prix de Chantilly. An injury sustained when third at Saint-Cloud disrupted her Arc preparation and she never threatened at Longchamp in October. Seven-year-old **Jim And Tonic** returned as good as ever though, winning a thrilling Dubai Duty Free at Nad Al Sheba and the Coupe de Maisons-Laffitte later in the year, with second places in Hong Kong and Singapore in between. A couple of new names emerged at the top of the staying division, though neither six-year-old **Generic** nor seven-year-old **Germinis** were hardly in the first flush of youth. Off the course for over two years with leg problems earlier in his career, Generic made up for lost time with seven wins in a busy campaign which included successes in the Prix Maurice de Nieuil and Prix Kergorlay. He met his match in the Prix du Cadran in the form of the much-improved Germinis. Generic turned the tables when they met again, filling the places in the Prix Royal-Oak. The ex-German colt **Speedmaster** was the other stayer of note, winning the Prix Vicomtesse Vigier in May, but he finished behind Generic on the three occasions they met. The most progressive older filly was **Terre A Terre**, who followed a win over younger rivals in the Prix de l'Opera with an excellent close third in the Hong Kong Cup at Sha Tin, with Jim And Tonic and Choc Ice among those behind her.

The French two-year-old calendar underwent some important changes which were previewed here in *Racehorses of 2000* and are covered again in the essay on the only French juvenile to win a Group 1, **Act One**. The alterations failed miserably to boost French participation in the top two-year-old events, a topic discussed in the essay on the other leading two-year-old **Zipping**, winner of the Prix Robert Papin and runner-up in the Morny and Middle Park. The Criterium International winner Act One looks a fine middle-distance prospect, as does the Prix des Chenes winner **Shaanmer**, who is also unbeaten in three starts. The runner-up in the Prix des Chenes, **Caesarion**, went on to finish second to **Rashbag** in the Prix de Conde. Pick of the fillies were the Marcel Boussac runner-up **Danseuse d'Etoile** and **Summertime Legacy**, who won the Prix des Reservoirs from **Prudence Royale**. Unbeaten listed winners **Medecis** and **Firth of Lorne** are a couple more names worth looking out for in pattern company in 2002.

The coverage–or lack of it–of French racing on British television in recent years has given a whole new meaning to the phrase 'channel hopping'. Viewers in Britain were particularly poorly served in that regard by both the BBC and Channel 4 in 2001. The BBC's existing agreement with France Galop ended when rights to the televising of racing in France were taken over early in the year by Trans World International. The asking price by the new holders was more than the BBC was willing to pay and consequently the French Guineas were not covered. Although Channel 4 stepped in to cover racing in France for the rest of the year from May, it was too late to alter their schedules to cover either the Prix du Jockey Club or the Prix de Diane in June and they could only guarantee live broadcasting of the Arc weekend. Therefore Deauville's big races (an eventful Jacques le Marois and the clash between Johannesburg and Meshaheer in the Prix Morny) also went untelevised and the Arc trials were only shown as recordings in a highlights programme. That left Channel 4's Arc weekend coverage (the first time it had covered the meeting since 1994) as the only live French racing on terrestrial television during the whole year. According to Channel 4, its audience peaked at 1.7 million for their Arc coverage compared to viewing figures of 1.3 million for the BBC's coverage the year before. However, the fact that there was a British-trained favourite (Sakhee) in 2001, compared with no British runners at all in the 2000 Arc, surely had some influence on those figures.

At the end of the year it was all change once more with the announcement that the BBC had won back their rights to televise French racing as part of a five-year deal. A deciding factor had apparently been Channel 4's inability to commit itself to covering other important races outside the Arc meeting. Speaking for France Galop, Louis Romanet said he hoped that a deal could also be struck with SIS to allow coverage of French racing in betting shops 'but we will not be giving away French racing. We know what it did for the British bookmakers' profits this year; and we want a fair price.' That was a reference to temporary SIS coverage of foreign racing, including from France, when British racing was hit badly during the height of the foot and mouth crisis in the spring. Ladbrokes reported in March that 'the foreign racing has proven surprisingly popular. In fact on one of the recent Sundays turnover actually rose 13%—and that with no UK or Irish horse-racing.' BOLA director-general Tom Kelly also stressed the importance to bookmakers of television coverage of foreign racing. 'Televised racing is always preferable to non-televised racing, no matter where it's coming from. You would turn over more on a race that's televised than a race that isn't. That's especially the case when it's a race from overseas.' With the vast majority of French Group 1 races drawing runners from Britain and/or Ireland, and considering that other top-class sporting events in France and the rest of Europe are regularly broadcast live, racing fans in Britain have a good case for expecting a better service than has been provided lately.

Two-Year-Olds					
118	Zipping	106	Melody Blue (f)	103	Ana Marie (f)
116p	Act One	106	Prudence Royale (f)	102p	Agog
109p	Danseuse d'Etoile (f)	106	Rouvres	102p	Restless Rixa (f)
109p	Shaanmer	106	Tau Ceti	102p	Without Connexion
108p	Summertime Legacy (f)	105	Bernebeau	102	Contemporary (f)
108	Rashbag	105	Caesarion	102	Dulce de Leche
107	Quad's Melody (f)	105	Hothaifah	102	Glia (f)
107	War Zone	104p	Firth of Lorne (f)	102	Great Deal
		104p	Medecis	102	Kifissos

102 Kithira (f)
102 Martaline
102 Perrexa (f)
102 Pont d'Or
102 Special Kaldoun
102 Urgele (f)
101 Bashful (f)
101 Dobby Road
101 Loup Masque
101 Night Bokbel
101 Westcliffe
100 Extinguisher
100 Goto
100 Mariensky (f)
100 On Reflection
100 Sky Quest

99 Ziria (f)
97 Porlezza (f)

Three-Year-Olds
128 Banks Hill (f)
125 Sagacity
123 Aquarelliste (f)
121 Diamilina (f)
121 Do The Honours (f)
120 Anabaa Blue
120 Vahorimix
119 Chichicastenango
118 *Denon
117 *Iron Mask
117 Maille Pistol
117 Mare Nostrum (f)
117 *Mizzen Mast
116 Aghnoyoh
116 Keltos
116 Nadia (f)
115 Choc Ice (f)
115 Okawango
115 Poussin
115 Visorhill
115 Walking Around
114 Foundation Spirit
114 Homeland
114 *Tarzan Cry
113 Lethals Lady (f)
113 Spring Oak (f)
112 Amonita (f)
112 Domedriver
112 Greengroom
112 Kouroun
112 Moon Queen (f)
112 Panis
112 Sangreal
112 Stardan
112 *Volga (f)
111 Amiwain
111 Baldwina (f)
111 Lugny
111 Lunasalt
111 *No Slip
111 Pushkin
111 Shamdara (f)
111 Sharbayan
111 Street Shaana (f)
110 *Ing Ing (f)
110 Kentucky Rose (f)
110 Roman Saddle

110 Swedish Shave
110 Zanapour
109 Abajo
109 *Art Contemporain
109 Danella (f)
109 Khaliyna (f)
109 Luna Kya (f)
109 Magic Mission (f)
109 Marichal
109 Miss Gazon (f)
109 Prove (f)
109 Quarter Note (f)
109 Sensible
108 Ange Gabriel
108 Califet
108 Calista (f)
108 Chesnut Bird (f)
108 Doctorate
108 Maximum Security
108 Messoeurs (f)
107 Chronos
107 Epistole (f)
107 Fascinating Mix
107 Five Fishes (f)
107 Go Got
107 Luna Sacra (f)
107 Marque Royale (f)
107 Reine Zao (f)
107 Shawara (f)
107 Tailfeather
106 Belfortain
106 Blue Inside
106 First Fleet (f)
106 Jomana (f)
106 Kadence
106 Mister Pacha Pacha
106 Mon Legionnaire
106 Nolt
106 Red Snake
106 Sahaat
106 Season's Greetings (f)
106 Snataka (f)
106 Spanish Don
106 Zghorta (f)
106 Zuleika Dobson (f)
105 Bellona (f)
105 Born Something (f)
105 Chercheuse (f)
105 Favourite Son
105 High Hope
105 Inventing Paradise (f)
105 Light Ballet (f)
105 Marchand Volant
105 Northern Blue (f)
105 Strawberry Blonde (f)
105 Whitton Court

104 Gris de Fer
103 Alta Lena (f)
103 Side of Paradise (f)
102 Balthazar
99 *Cap Amiral
99 Cybergenic
98 Pescia (f)

Older Horses
129 Hightori
126 *Nuclear Debate

124 Jim And Tonic
124 Mirio
121 Generic
121 Germinis
119 Terre A Terre (f)
118 Danger Over
118 Idaho Quest
118 Imperial Beauty (f)
117 Egyptband (f)
117 First Magnitude
117 Slew The Red
117 Speedmaster
115 Bleu d'Altair
115 Epitre
114 Bonnet Rouge
114 Dananeyev
114 Deep Sleep
114 Polish Summer
114 Ultimately Lucky
114 With The Flow
113 Golani
113 Mont Rocher
113 Riddlesdown
112 Cazoulias
112 Folie Danse (f)
112 Magna Graecia (f)
112 Woodford Reserve
111 Cherbon
111 Di Moi Oui (f)
111 Earlene (f)
111 Kappa King
111 Mocham Glen
111 Si Symphonie (f)
110 Double Heart
110 Ethelinda (f)
109 Boismorand (f)
109 Cayoke
109 Cheshire
109 Dionello
109 Execute
109 Honorifique (f)
109 Le Tintoret
109 Roli Abi
109 Self Defense
109 Tikzane
108 Al Namix
108 Burning Sunset (f)
108 Miliana (f)
108 *Snetterton
108 Special Discount
108 Tajoun
108 Turbo Jet
108d *Ben Ewar
107 Acceleration (f)
107 Bedawin
107 Beyond The Waves (f)
107 Gaelic Dream (f)
107 Ladonia
107 *Laveron
107 Mon Pote Le Gitan
107 Ponte Brolla (f)
107 Texalina (f)
107 Zanskar
107§ Berine's Son
106 Catchacoma
106 Cut Quartz
106 Jewel King

106	Le Nomade	105	Cyllarus	105	Percent Premium
106	Original Cast	105	Darakiyla (f)	105	Reallier
106	Silver Desert	105	Dear Girl (f)	105	Skipping
106	*Special Ring	105	Fine And Mellow (f)		
106	Turbotiere (f)	105	*Jafar	103	*La Cibeles (f)
106	Vellano	105	Oro Bering (f)		

GERMANY   German trainers have been much more willing to campaign their horses abroad in recent years and in 2001 German horses were more successful than ever, not just elsewhere in Europe, but globally. Valuable prizes in the USA, Japan, Hong Kong and Singapore all came their way, as well as races in Britain, France, Italy and Turkey and the equivalent of the Derby in Austria, Switzerland, Slovakia and the Netherlands. Germany's best horse in 2001, **Silvano**, was also the best example of this international approach, as he was campaigned exclusively outside Europe, becoming the first German-trained winner of a Grade 1 race in the USA when winning the Arlington Million and retiring as Germany's second-highest all-time money-earner following other valuable wins in Singapore and Hong Kong. **Proudwings** also made history on her travels when becoming the first German-bred winner of a British Group race in the Falmouth Stakes. She also won the Prix du Muguet at Saint-Cloud and a valuable race in Japan, and was disqualified after passing the post first in the Prix Jacques le Marois. The greatest traveller of all from Germany is **Caitano**, who has now raced in ten countries outside his homeland, and although he has little to show for it in terms of wins in recent seasons, he is still among Germany's leading older horses at the age of seven.

Domestically, honours were spread quite evenly among the older horses. The best horse in Germany in 2000, **Samum**, was restricted to just two outings, finishing seventh in the Prix Ganay before going down to **Bonvivant** in the Grosser Mercedes-Benz-Preis at Baden-Baden, but will be in training again at five. Silvano's stable-companion **Paolini** ran well abroad too, winning two Group 1 races in Italy in the first half of the year and running second in the Canadian International after a fourth place in the Grosser Preis von Baden. With Morshdi winning the Grosser Preis von Baden and Kutub taking two more Group 1 races back to Britain, the WGZ Bank-Deutschlandpreis winner **Anzillero** was the only German older horse to win a local Group 1. The 1999 Deutsches Derby winner **Belenus** returned after missing his four-year-old season and showed he retains his ability with third place in the Credit Suisse Private Banking Pokal at Cologne ahead of **Passimo** in fourth and **Subiaco** in fifth. Subiaco had won three pattern races earlier in the year,

Credit Suisse Private Banking Pokal, Cologne—Sabiango holds off Deutsches Derby winner Boreal (right) with 1999 Deutsches Derby winner Belenus (blinkered) in third

Deutsche Post Euro Express Preis von Europa, Cologne—Deutsches Derby winner Boreal takes a heavy fall on the first bend; the race was won by Godolphin's Kutub from Yavana's Pace

including the Gerling-Preis at Cologne from **Aeskulap** and the two-mile Betty Barclay Rennen. Aeskulap had several of the above-named horses behind him in the Hansa-Preis at Hamburg but sixth place in the Grosser Preis von Baden and fourth in the Preis von Europa at Cologne is a better reflection of his place in the pecking order.

Among the three-year-olds, **Boreal** and **Sabiango** stood out as the pair who dominated the classic generation. Silvano's brother Sabiango was withdrawn from the Deutsches Derby after heavy rain changed the going. A victim of doping on his reappearance, Sabiango had cemented his position as Derby favourite with a defeat of **Barsetto** and Boreal in the Oppenheim-Union-Rennen. In Sabiango's absence, Boreal took the Deutsches Derby ahead of **Lierac** and **Near Honor**. When the pair eventually met again in the Credit Suisse Private Banking Pokal, Sabiango beat Boreal half a length but the positions were reversed when they filled the places behind Morshdi in the Grosser Preis von Baden. The same pair should be leading contenders for the big middle-distance prizes again in 2002. **Noroit** did not contest the Derby but developed into one of the better three-year-old colts with a win in a Group 2 at Frankfurt and third place in the Europa-Preis, a race in which Boreal started favourite but fell early on. **Zollner** also missed the Derby despite winning one of the main trials, the Grosser Muller Brot-Preis at Munich; kept to a mile and a quarter instead, he followed up in a Group 3 at Frankfurt.

Proudwings was just one of several smart milers. **Banyumanik** was not the most consistent of them, but he put up marginally the best performance to win the Jaguar-Meile at Cologne in July when reliable yardsticks **Up And Away** and **Peppercorn** finished third and fourth respectively. This pair met numerous times throughout the year, Up And Away winning the Oettingen-Rennen at Baden-Baden and Peppercorn a couple of Group 3 races at Dusseldorf in October. **El Lute** also put up a smart effort, his career best, to win the Emirates-Mile at Baden-Baden in May. Best of the three-year-old milers was **Royal Dragon**, who won the Mehl-Mulhens-Rennen (2000 Guineas) from **Touch Down** and the Berlin Brandenburg-Trophy. Germany's sprinters made little show in their own Group races, though three-year-old **Call Me Big** showed smart form to win a listed race at Dortmund and **Herve Leger** seemed to excel himself with second place in the Premio Omenoni at Milan. With the exception of Proudwings, **Abitara**, whose wins included the Prix de Pomone at Deauville, was the only older filly or mare of note. The three-year-old fillies were a substandard group and neither of the classic winners, **Dakhla Oasis** (Henkel-Rennen) nor **Silvester Lady** (Preis der Diana), made a name for herself subsequently.

Traditionally Germany's top two-year-old race, the Preis des Winterfavoriten went to Peppercorn's brother **Peppershot**, but it did not look a strong renewal. The winner had earlier been beaten convincingly in a maiden by **Next Desert** (a seven-length winner of a national listed race on his other start) and had also finished second to **Orfisio** in a national listed race at Krefeld. The Maurice-Lacroix Trophy winner **Flying Dash** put up the best performance by a German two-year-old when second to Firebreak in the Prix de

Cabourg at Deauville but has since been sold to the USA. The Premio Dormello winner **Kazzia**, Germany's top two-year-old filly, has also been sold and has joined Godolphin. Another filly, **Narooma**, was unbeaten in three starts and looks an interesting prospect for 2002; she completed her hat-trick in the Preis der Winterkonigin (a Group 3 for the first time) at the expense of **Banyu Dewi**, who went on to finish fourth in the Criterium de Saint-Cloud.

Two-Year-Olds

108	Flying Dash
107p	Next Desert
106p	Orfisio
105p	Kazzia (f)
105	Peppershot
103p	Narooma (f)
103	Stolzing
101	Classic Law
100	Banyu Dewi (f)
100	Ingeburg (f)
100	Sergeant Pepper
99	Dimaro
97	Davignon
97	Medina (f)
94	Barsac
93	Gondoro

Three-Year-Olds

121	Boreal
120	Sabiango
118	Royal Dragon
116	Noroit (Ger)
116	Zollner
114	Call Me Big
113	Pryor
112	Denaro
112	Lierac
112	Limerick Boy
112	Touch Down
111	Krombacher
111	Monos
111	Near Honor
109	Goethe
109	Peu A Peu (f)
108	Barsetto
108	Ingolf
108	Lilac Queen (f)
108	Saldenschwinge (f)
108	*Silvester Lady (f)
108	Street Poker

108	Syrakus
107	Dakhla Oasis (f)
107	Iberus
107	Irish Man
107	Maitre Levy
107	Nouvelle Fortune (f)
107	Saitensohn
106	Blue Baloo
106	Blush Damask (f)
106	Boana (f)
106	Denice (f)
106	Guns 'n Roses
106	Lavendel
106	Onaldo
106	Salonblue (f)
105	Bedford Set (f)
105	Bergum
105	Just Time
105	Orebano
105	Scapolo
105	Tareno
104	El Royal
103	Tomster
99	Sherekan
98	Stingray

Older Horses

126	Silvano
121	Paolini
121	Samum
120	Anzillero
119	Banyumanik
119	Belenus
118	Proudwings (f)
118	Subiaco
117	Caitano
116	Passimo
115	Aeskulap
115	Bonvivant
115	El Lute
115	Peppercorn (Ger)
115	Up And Away
114+	King's Boy

114	Abitara (f)
114	Pardus
114	*Sumitas
114?	Herve Leger
113	Faberger
112	Duke d'Alba
112	Well Made
111	Acamani
111	Bernardon
111	Chagall
111	Diamante
110	Aboard
110	Tertullian
110	War Blade
109	Barrow Creek
109	Fruhtau
109	Terek
108	Arc Royal (Ger)
108	Karakal
108	National Academy
108	Nicara (f)
108	Noel
108	Sambakonig
108	Sunderland
108	Sword Local
108	Tempelwachter
107	Luca
107	Network
107	Well Minded (f)
106	Bedford Forrest
106	Hale Bopp
106	Just Heavens Gate (f)
106	Montalban
106	Wild Seed
105	Huambo
105	Kaka
105	Kalatos
105	Montestefano
105	Pearlmix (f)
105	Royal Hussar
102	Macina (f)

ITALY   In 2001 Italy could boast its best horse for a number of seasons, the Yorkshire Oaks winner **Super Tassa**, who became the first Italian-trained horse to win a Group 1 outside Italy since Tony Bin, the 1988 Prix de l'Arc de Triomphe winner. Her York success was the first by an Italian-trained horse in Britain since the early 'seventies. Otherwise there was little cheer for Italian horses, and it remains hard to see how the European Pattern Committee can justify an Italian programme that has eight Group 1 races but very few local horses worthy of contesting, let alone winning, such a race. The only domestic Group 1 won by an Italian horse was a substandard Premio Roma won by **Shibuni's Falcon**, the previous season's leading three-year-old. **Caluki** had claims to being the top Italian miler judged on his second place to Nicobar in the Premio Emilio Turati but the rest of his performances fell well below that level. Premio Umbria winner **Nil**, **Indian Mary**, who won Group 3 races at Rome and Naples, and the first two in a listed race at Milan (with Indian Mary and Nil behind them), **Distinctly Dancer** and **Development**, were the leading sprinters.

Distinctly Dancer was also one of the best three-year-olds, along with **Falbrav** and **Giovane Imperatore**. Falbrav ran second in the Derby Italiano, in which Giovane Imperatore failed to stay, but the latter proved much more effective at a mile, winning the Premio Parioli in the spring (from 200/1-shot **L'Erede**) and the Premio Ribot from five-year-old **Dane Friendly** in November. Falbrav came out on top again in another clash with Giovane Imperatore in a valuable ten-furlong restricted event late in the year. The Premio Regina Elena winner **Bugia** made little show afterwards, and, with the Italian fillies being soundly beaten behind Zanzibar in the Oaks, it was **Canasita** who put up the best performance by an Italian three-year-old filly in winning a listed race at Deauville in August.

Salselon was the top two-year-old on the strength of his defeat of older horses in the Premio Chiusura; he had earlier beaten **Nordhal** and the subsequent Premio Guido Berardelli winner **Fisich** in a listed race at Milan. **Slap Shot** was the best two-year-old filly, finishing a close third in the Prix Robert Papin before winning a couple of listed sprints at Rome in the autumn.

Two-Year-Olds					
104	Salselon	107	Canasita (f)	110	Development
99	Nordhal	106	Prophet Island	109	Embody
99	Slap Shot (f)	105	Cincischiando (f)	108	Dane Friendly
98	Clefairy (f)	105	Montesino	108	Midyan Call
98	Sopran Woodbird	105	Morena Park (f)	108	Mon Alexandrino
97p	Bhanumat	105	Sopran Glaumix	107	Doowaley
97	Fisich			107	Dream Chief
97	Rosa delle Alpi (f)	104	Bugia (f)	107	Fairy Charm
96	Mister Cavern	104	Low Pivot	107	London Bank
95	Far Hope (f)	104	Sorella Luce (f)	106	As You Like
95	Muk Muka	103	Rosa di Brema (f)	106	Fay Breeze
		102	*Love Roi (f)	106	Fingle Fangle
89	Goblin	102	Strategic Tactics (f)	106	Onice Nero
		100	Miss Meltemi (f)	106	Slaney Squire
		99	Baranja (f)	106	Sopran Montanelli
				105	Albano
Three-Year-Olds		**Older Horses**		105	Cameron
112	Falbrav	118	Super Tassa (f)	105	Czar
112	Giovane Imperatore	114	Caluki	105	Fascino
111	Distinctly Dancer	114	Shibuni's Falcon	105	In The Night (f)
108	L'Erede	112	Nil	105	Masaniella (f)
107	Altieri	111	Indian Mary (f)		

SCANDINAVIA   The quality of racing in Scandinavia is improving steadily, and, in **Valley Chapel**, **Sagittarius** and **Dano-Mast**, the Scandinavians had a trio of smart middle-distance performers capable of making their mark further afield as well as on home turf. Only a length covered the trio when they finished clear, in that order, in the Scandinavian Open Championship at Klampenborg in August, and the result was the same, though just heads separated them, when they took the first three places in the Stockholm Cup International at Taby, again finishing clear. Valley Chapel had been placed in a couple of Group races in France in the spring, including when finishing third to Dano-Mast, Denmark's best horse, in the Prix Jean de Chaudenay at Saint-Cloud. Between his wins at Klampenborg and Taby, Valley Chapel also won Europe's most valuable Group 3 race, the Marit Sveaas Minnelop (one of two races in Norway promoted from listed level for the first time) over nine furlongs at Ovrevoll, from **Martellian** and **Jaunty Jack**. The Sadler's Wells five-year-old Sagittarius has had a chequered career. Unraced in France due to injury in his early days, he had had only one race (as a four-year-old) prior to the latest season but made rapid progress, winning his first three races by wide margins and winding up his campaign by running Nayef to a length and a quarter in the Cumberland Lodge Stakes at Ascot.

Albaran was no match for the big three but showed he retained his ability at the age of eight by finishing second in Hamburg's Hansa-Preis for the second year running. Nine-year-old **Stato One** beat a below-par Valley Chapel in a listed race at Taby in June. The promotion of Ovrevoll's Polar Million Cup over an extended six furlongs gives Scandinavia's sprinters a second opportunity at Group 3 level to go with the Taby Open Sprint Championship. **Waquaas** established himself as the top sprinter with victory at

Ovrevoll (he also won three listed races during the year) but failed in an attempt to win the Taby race for the second year running. The Open Sprint went instead to **El Gran Lode** from another South American import **Aramus**. Stable-companions **Shawdon** and **Terroir** were campaigned extensively in Germany, where both won listed sprints.

Three-Year-Old					
101	In The Woods (f)	113	Waquaas	108	Pistachio
		112	Albaran	108	Prime Match
		111	El Gran Lode	108	Rex
Older Horses		111	Stato One	107	Rolo Tomasi
118	Valley Chapel	110	Aramus	107	Tough Guy
117	Dano-Mast	110	Jaunty Jack	105	Hangover Square
117	Sagittarius	110	Shawdon	105	Parthe
113	Martellian	110	Terroir	105	Tragic Love

UNITED ARAB EMIRATES   The latest Dubai World Cup meeting was the richest and most international yet, with nearly sixty horses from fifteen countries outside the UAE contesting the six races. Unlike the Breeders' Cup (now grandly billed as the 'World Thoroughbred Championships'), whose international element relies almost solely on competition between North America and Europe, the Dubai World Cup meeting has a truly global draw, with the likes of Japan, Australia, New Zealand, Brazil and Argentina all represented in 2001, as well as Europe and the USA. The Breeders' Cup may still have the edge in terms of quality but the Dubai World Cup meeting is gaining ground; three of the supporting races, the Dubai Duty Free, Dubai Sheema Classic and Dubai Golden Shaheen have all been raised to Group 1 status for 2002, alongside the Dubai World Cup itself, in recognition of the quality of fields those races are now attracting. The other two races on the card, the UAE Derby and the Godolphin Mile, have been upped to Group 2, with an all-Group 1 card the ultimate aim and surely not too far away. Over the 2001/2 UAE season as a whole, there will be thirty major designated races in the calendar, the majority listed or prestige events. All three rounds of the Maktoum Challenge will be Group races in 2002 and the UAE 2000 Guineas has also been upgraded to Group 3.

The extension of the programme for three-year-olds was the main development in the UAE calendar in 2001. The first running of the UAE 2000 Guineas went to Godolphin's **Street Cry** from stable-companion Noverre, who had a bigger part to play in some of Europe's top mile events later in the season. A hot favourite to follow up in the UAE Derby, Street Cry was touched off by one of his stable's six other representatives, **Express Tour**, in the world's richest Derby. Godolphin likewise dominated the fillies' classics, with **Muwakleh** taking the UAE 1000 Guineas and **Laoub**, third on her debut in that event, winning the UAE Oaks. Apart from the Derby, which drew an international line-up, the other three-year-old races had the look of Godolphin private trials, and unless European trainers take up the challenge, those events (all run on dirt) are likely to remain rather uncompetitive for the money on offer.

Racing in the UAE caters principally for older horses, however, and there is plenty of strength in depth in that division. **Fantastic Light**'s narrow defeat by Japan's Stay Gold

Dubai Golden Shaheen, Nad Al Sheba—
a 1,2 for the United States as Caller One wins from Men's Exclusive

Dubai Sheema Classic, Nad Al Sheba—
Japanese-trained Stay Gold (white bridle) catches Fantastic Light near the line

in a high-quality Dubai Sheema Classic wasn't quite so good as the form he showed later in the year, but was still the best performance by a Dubai-based horse. In the Dubai World Cup itself, Godolphin's three representatives made little show, the most disappointing being joint-favourite **Best of The Bests**, who had earlier given a sound beating to **Sobieski** in Round II of the Maktoum Challenge. **China Visit** had taken Round I of the series over a mile before filling fourth place behind **Festival of Light**, **Curule** and **Conflict** in the Godolphin Mile. A maiden at the start of the year, Festival of Light was unbeaten in three starts in the UAE but was not seen out again. **Skoozi** was well beaten in the Godolphin Mile when still with his Australian stable, but beat Conflict in a conditions race in December on his debut for his new trainer in Dubai. **Headhunter** was another to put up a smart performance in December, winning a prestige race at Abu Dhabi. **State Shinto** had beaten China Visit in a conditions race before running an excellent fourth in the World Cup, while **Broche**, well held in the same race, had earlier shown smart form when second to World Cup third Hightori in Round III of the Maktoum Challenge.

Give The Slip, fifth in the Sheema Classic, spent much of the year pacemaking for Fantastic Light, but he had got his head in front in February in the Group 3 Dubai City of Gold. **Inchlonaig** finished third, with **All The Way** and **Alva Glen**, who both won prestige races during the season, further back. Over shorter distances on turf, **Mahfooth** put up one of the best performances when winning the Jebel Hatta over just short of nine furlongs, in which **Slip Stream** finished fourth giving weight. A prestige race in 2001, it becomes a Group 3 in 2002, serving as a trial for the Duty Free over the same course and distance. Mahfooth finished down the field in the Duty Free, as did **Happy Diamond**, who won a handicap in February at the chief expense of Inchlonaig. None of the sprinters stood out on form, but two of the best were **Mutamayyaz**, a prestige winner on turf early in the year who returned in good form in handicaps on dirt at the start of the new season, and the ex-Australian horse **Flight Pattern**, who won a listed race on dirt at Jebel Ali.

The performances reviewed here are those that took place in the calendar year 2001. Horses which were trained and raced in the UAE but showed significantly better form elsewhere are not included in the list below.

Three-Year-Olds					
121	*Express Tour	116	*Curule	111	Rhythm Band
121	*Street Cry	116	Happy Diamond	111	Sheer Hamas
115	*Muwakleh (f)	116	Slip Stream	110	Bahamian Bandit
110	*Laoub (f)	115	All The Way	110	Jaydoom
105	*Qawaqeb	115	*Conflict	109	Jila
105	*Zahwah (f)	115	*Headhunter	109	Strahan
		115	*Sobieski	108	Glad Master
Older Horses		114	Alva Glen	108	Jalaab
134	*Fantastic Light	114	Lightning Arrow	108	Razik
122	*Best of The Bests	114	Pacino	108	Zoning
122	*China Visit	114	River's Curtain	107	Altichiero
121	*Give The Slip	112	Flight Pattern	107	Dubai Two Thousand
121	*State Shinto	112	Inchlonaig	107	Meadaaar
118	Festival of Light	112	Maidaan	107	River Times
117	*Broche	112	Mutamayyaz	106	Caballero
117	*Mahfooth	112	Superiority	106	Moonis
117	*Skoozi	112	Swiss Law	106	Siege
		111	Elghani		

NORTH AMERICA   The emergence of **Point Given** as the best American three-year-old in recent years was the highlight of 2001, a year which was otherwise distinguished by the lack of an outstanding performer in any of the various turf and dirt divisions Stateside.

But even Point Given's excellent campaign was halted by a tendon injury to his near-fore suffered in his Travers Stakes triumph in late-August, in which he scored his fifth Grade 1 victory of the year—and fourth in succession—those last four coming in races with a gross value of $1 million each. Point Given's premature retirement prevented the Bob Baffert-trained son of Thunder Gulch from being tested by his elders. It also marked the second successive year in which none of the Triple Crown principals was around to try the older generation in the big autumn contests. The gruelling regime which is annually set the American classic generation never fails to take its toll, and it will continue to do so as long as trainers persist in giving their charges four or five preps for

Belmont Stakes, Belmont Park—
Point Given has already taken the lead on his way to a twelve-and-a-quarter-length victory

the Kentucky Derby after abbreviated winter vacations (more can be found on this subject in the essay on Johannesburg).

Point Given is a case in point. His juvenile campaign had begun in August 2000 in a Del Mar maiden and ended with a victory in the Hollywood Futurity in December. Just three months later he returned to action with a victory in the Grade 2 San Felipe Stakes over an extended mile, and he remained in training until his injury.

A five-and-a-half-length rout of five inferior rivals in the Santa Anita Derby prompted his supporters to back Point Given down to 9/5 favouritism for the Kentucky Derby, and while he was taking the unusual route (for a non-Godolphin-trained horse) of just two preps for the Run for the Roses, lack of condition had nothing to do with his fifth-place finish behind Florida Derby winner and Wood Memorial runner-up **Monarchos**, who pulled clear to a four-and-three-quarter-length win over the 55/1-shot **Invisible Ink** in the second fastest time for the race, behind only that of Secretariat.

Monarchos was probably flattered by his seemingly easy victory, especially in that Point Given simply failed to fire that day, the only time his considerable ability deserted him in thirteen career starts. Point Given's subsequent classic triumphs over **A P Valentine** in both the Preakness Stakes and the Belmont Stakes, the latter by an ever-widening twelve and a quarter lengths over a distance on dirt of a mile and a half (an anachronism in North America these days), virtually assured him the three-year-old championship. With two-thirds of the Triple Crown on his side of the scoreboard, Point Given was emulating his sire Thunder Gulch, who had succeeded in the Kentucky Derby and the Belmont for Michael Tabor in 1995. However, Point Given had to fight hard for a half-length win at the expense of much inferior competition in the Haskell Invitational Handicap over an inadequate nine furlongs in early-August. That effort could not be redeemed by his having conceded between 5 lb and 10 lb to his rivals. Under most European handicapping guidelines, Point Given might have been asked to give away at least 12 lb to his next best rival.

*Travers Stakes, Saratoga—Point Given takes over
from E Dubai (right) to register his sixth success of the year*

With Monarchos, Invisible Ink, Wood Memorial and Swaps Stakes winner **Congaree**, and Blue Grass Stakes winner **Millennium Wind** all sidelined by midsummer, it was left to Godolphin's **E Dubai** to challenge Point Given in the Travers Stakes, Saratoga's so-called 'Midsummer Derby'. A Mr Prospector colt with plenty of speed, E Dubai had avoided the rigours of the Triple Crown, instead posting two very easy front-running victories at Nad Al Sheba and Belmont Park, on the latter course making all in the Grade 2 Dwyer Stakes in July over an extended mile. Although E Dubai found the mile and a quarter of the Travers an absolute maximum, he was simply not good enough to trouble Point Given, who breezed by him approaching the furlong pole on his way to a convincing three-and-a-half-length victory. E Dubai subsequently failed to justify odds-on favouritism in the Super Derby over the same trip, his stamina stretched by the muddy conditions when beaten by **Outofthebox**. Meanwhile E Dubai's Godolphin teammates **Express Tour** and **Street Cry**, one, two in the UAE Derby in March, will be back for a four-year-old campaign. After his narrow Nad Al Sheba failure, Street Cry did not run again until finishing runner-up to the 65/1-shot **Evening Attire** in the Grade 3 Discovery Handicap. Express Tour, eighth in the Kentucky Derby, has the makings of a fine miler on dirt if his win in the Grade 2 Jerome Handicap against three-year-olds proves a more reliable indicator than his lacklustre tenth in the Breeders' Cup Mile on turf. 2000 juvenile champion **Macho Uno**, sidelined until late-July, made a move towards the top of the three-year-old standings with his victory in the Grade 3 Pennsylvania Derby in September and may yet prove to be one of 2002's better older horses following his good fourth in the Breeders' Cup Classic, the best effort by one of his own generation in America's definitive race.

If Point Given gave nothing else a chance in the race for three-year-old colt honours, the contest for the three-year-old filly championship was a relay race. **Golden Ballet** was first out of the blocks. The daughter of the Nijinsky stallion Moscow Ballet hardly put a foot wrong all year, but her season was curtailed by an injury to a suspensory ligament in May. She began with three straight front-running victories, including the Las Virgenes Stakes and the Santa Anita Oaks, and by mid-March she looked much the best among her own age and sex, having already beaten subsequent Grade 1 winners **Affluent** (three times) and **Flute**, plus subsequent Grade 2 winner **Two Item Limit**. Trainer Jenine Sahadi sent Golden Ballet east for the Ashland Stakes at Keeneland; horses from southern California, where the dirt tracks are shallow and favour speed, are not infrequently hindered by the deeper tracks in the eastern half of the country. While Golden Ballet acquitted herself well in the Ashland's extended mile, she couldn't hold off the Michael Dickinson-trained **Fleet Renee**. Six weeks later at Hollywood Park Golden Ballet made all in the Grade 2 Railbird Stakes, but soon afterwards fell victim to injury.

But the baton was picked up by Flute, the Seattle Slew filly who spearheaded a remarkable season in America for Khalid Abdulla's Juddmonte Farms and their Brooklyn-born trainer Bobby Frankel. Flute beat Fleet Renee into fourth in the Kentucky Oaks over nine furlongs at Churchill Downs. After a brief break, there followed a bloodless win in a minor event at Saratoga which served as the perfect preparation for a front-running victory of her own in the mile-and-a-quarter Alabama Stakes at the same upstate New York track. But Flute did not win again in 2001, as she eventually made way for **Exogenous**, whose Alabama second had been preceded by a similar placing behind **Tweedside** in the Coaching Club American Oaks, the fillies' equivalent of the Belmont Stakes. A daughter of Unbridled, Exogenous put up one of the best performances of the year by a three-year-old filly when she beat Two Item Limit and Fleet Renee in the nine-furlong Gazelle Handicap at Belmont in September. She then slightly bettered that effort with a length-and-a-quarter defeat of Flute (with **Spain** a head further back in third) in the Beldame Stakes, a course and distance pair against older fillies for the Breeders' Cup Distaff. Exogenous looked ready to claim her championship when disaster struck. Spooked by the crowd as she was about to step on to the track for the Distaff, she suddenly reared over backwards, landing on her head while somehow getting a hind leg entangled in a fence. It took ten minutes before handlers could free her and she was eventually vanned off. There were brief hopes for her recovery, but a few days later she was put down, providing a chilling reminder of the death of Go For Wand in the 1990 Breeders' Cup Distaff on the same track. Exogenous had accomplished just enough to maintain a championship edge over Flute and eventual Distaff winner **Unbridled Elaine**, who came late to pip the previous year's winner Spain on the line.

Of the other three-year-old fillies, **Xtra Heat** had a tremendous year. She won nine of her thirteen starts at six and seven furlongs and split Squirtle Squirt and Caller One in the Breeders' Cup Sprint. **Victory Ride** followed a narrow loss to **Forest Secrets** in the Acorn Stakes in June by making it three wins from four starts with an emphatic success over Xtra Heat in the seven-furlong Test Stakes at Saratoga, albeit in receipt of 7lb from the runner-up. Victory Ride was ruled out for the season shortly afterwards with an injury but the daughter of Seeking The Gold will return in 2002.

Banks Hill put up a high-class performance when cruising to a five-and-a-half length rout of Spook Express with Spring Oak, **Lailani**, **England's Legend** and **Starine** (all of them Group or Graded race winners) in the Breeders' Cup Filly & Mare Turf. Her performance was the best in North America by a filly of any age on any surface in 2001. One who might have given Banks Hill something more to do in the Filly & Mare Turf was no longer around by the time of the Breeders' Cup. **Astra**, a four-length winner of the ten-furlong Beverly Hills Handicap over **Happyanunoit**, suffered a setback when last behind England's Legend in Arlington's Beverly D Stakes in August. When England's Legend improved on her Grade 2 New York Handicap victory with a stunningly easy seven-and-three-quarter length win in the Beverly D, she appeared to have the filly and mare turf division at her mercy. A front runner trained by New York-based European import master Christophe Clement, England's Legend couldn't quite stave off the British-trained Lailani in the Flower Bowl Invitational. But neither of them was prepared for Banks Hill in the Filly & Mare Turf. That all three were based or formerly based in Europe is a typical state of affairs in American turf racing these days.

None of America's older fillies or mares on dirt was in quite the same league as Banks Hill. Like the three-year-olds, they took turns beating each other all year. **Gourmet Girl** and **Lazy Slusan** both won a pair of Grade 1s, while four others, **Critical Eye**, **Pompeii**, **Serra Lake** and the Argentine-bred **Miss Linda**, each took a single Grade 1. Gourmet Girl gained victories over Lazy Slusan in the Apple Blossom Handicap at Oaklawn and in the Vanity Handicap at Hollywood in the first half of the year. **Tranquility Lake** subsequently defeated Gourmet Girl in the Grade 2 Clement L. Hirsch Handicap over an extended mile. Tranquility Lake's run had been preceded by a pair of seconds to Happyanunoit and **Janet** in Grade 1 turf events and was followed by a length defeat at the hands of Janet, again, in the Yellow Ribbon Stakes over a mile and a quarter. However, the California-based Tranquility Lake could not get the hang of the deep Belmont Park dirt track on Breeders' Cup day, trailing in a distant ninth in the Distaff. It was defending Breeders' Cup Distaff champion Spain who put up the best performances among the older fillies on dirt. Despite a string of five consecutive losses coming into the Distaff, she returned to her best at Belmont, opening up a two-length lead in mid-straight and holding Unbridled Elaine until two strides from the line. Two Item Limit came third with **Atelier**, who put up her best effort at long odds, close up in fourth. Another of the best older fillies on dirt was **Go Go**, who did not contest a Grade 1 but won four races at Grade 3/2 level.

The older horse division, or handicap division as it is often referred to in America, was just as much of a toss-up as the filly and mare divisions. By virtue of his dramatic victory over Giant's Causeway in the 2000 Breeders' Cup Classic, **Tiznow** was the pre-season favourite to carry all before him, and the obscurely-bred son of Cee's Tizzy out of Cee's Song obliged at stingy odds of 3/10 against ordinary opposition in the Grade 2 San Fernando Breeders' Cup Stakes two weeks into the New Year. But in the Strub Stakes, a Grade 2 nine-furlong race restricted to four-year-olds, he was unable to give the unheralded **Wooden Phone** 6 lb in a surprising two-length defeat. Tiznow took his revenge on Wooden Phone in the $1 million mile-and-a-quarter Santa Anita Handicap in March, giving his rival 5 lb and a five-length beating. Those who felt that the Strub's distance was a furlong too short for him had their judgement confirmed later in the autumn when Tiznow finished third behind some good horses in both the Woodward Stakes at Belmont and the Goodwood Handicap at Santa Anita. The Woodward proved to be one of the season's most informative races. **Lido Palace**, the Chilean three-year-old champion who couldn't cope with Express Tour and Street Cry in the UAE Derby, had impressed with his victory in the Whitney Handicap in August, beating **Albert The Great**. Those two were

1172

challenged by Tiznow in the Woodward, in which Albert The Great was the beneficiary of a 9-lb turnaround in the weights with Lido Palace. But the last-named, also from the stable of Bobby Frankel, proved to be another one of the increasing number of good-class South American imports to the United States. Lido Palace came late to take the measure of Albert The Great by a length as Tiznow, probably in need of the race following a six-month absence since the Santa Anita Handicap, was a one-paced third. **Captain Steve** began the year in the sort of form which had seen him finish third in the previous season's Breeders' Cup Classic, but some disappointing performances in the summer led to his retirement and ruled him out of a rematch with Tiznow in the Classic. Earlier, he had put up a top-class effort to defeat Albert The Great (the pair clear) in the Donn Handicap at Gulfstream, and had then become America's third winner of the Dubai World Cup, in which the other US runner, **Aptitude**, finished sixth.

Aptitude proved yet another ace from the Frankel stable. Always highly thought of since his seconds in the 2000 Kentucky Derby and Belmont Stakes, the son of A P Indy had earned his Grade 1 laurels in June when placed first in the Hollywood Gold Cup through the disqualification of dual Grade 2 winner **Futural**. Aptitude put up a powerful performance in the Grade 2 Saratoga Breeders' Cup Handicap. Then, in the Jockey Club Gold Cup, the pre-eminent prep for the Breeders' Cup Classic, he turned in a career-best effort with a ten-length rout of the former British-trained Generous Rosi. Aptitude looked so strong going into the Breeders' Cup Classic that Frankel did not even consider sending Juddmonte's **Skimming** east for the season finale. In August, the Nureyev five-year-old had taken his second successive Pacific Classic in his usual front-running fashion, but the previous autumn he had failed twice on Belmont's deeper surface. And so, after splitting **Freedom Crest** and Tiznow in the Goodwood, Skimming was put away for the winter. Aptitude, however, was not up to the challenge of either Tiznow or Sakhee in the Classic, in which he was a well-beaten eighth. Tiznow had redeemed himself with another gallant performance in the Classic, just getting the better of Sakhee, who was several pounds below his best turf form. Sadly, a rematch in the Dubai World Cup will not materialize as Tiznow was retired to WinStar, the former Vinery, in Midway, Kentucky. Third in the Classic was Albert The Great, who put his only poor effort of the year, in the Jockey Club Gold Cup, firmly behind him.

The top six Timeform-rated turf horses in America were all either trained in Europe or European imports. **Fantastic Light**, like Daylami and Swain before him, was even better at five than he had been at four, capping a fine season with victory over **Milan** in the Breeders' Cup Turf to clinch a second Emirates World Series Racing Championship. Yet there are still lingering doubts as to Godolphin's decision to send Fantastic Light for the Turf and Sakhee for the Classic. **Silvano** gave German racing a boost with his rather easy victory over **Hap** in the Arlington Million, while **Mutamam** beat fellow Europeans **Paolini**, **Zindabad** and **Daliapour** in the Canadian International. **Bienamado**, formerly trained by Peter Chapple-Hyam, failed in his only attempt on dirt when ninth to Tiznow in the Santa Anita Handicap. Returned to turf, he took the San Juan Capistrano Handicap, at nearly one and three quarter miles America's longest graded race (from the ex-French

Breeders' Cup Classic, Belmont Park—Tiznow (No.10) wins the race for the second time after a good battle with Sakhee; Albert The Great (rail) improves one place on his effort the previous year

Breeders' Cup Mile, Belmont Park—ex-European Val Royal takes the measure of Forbidden Apple (rail); third-placed Bach fares best of the overseas challengers

Persianlux (rated 115) and the ex-British **Blueprint**), and the mile and a quarter Charles Whittingham Stakes (from the ex-British **Senure** and the ex-Italian Turf Classic winner **Timboroa**). But Bienamado could not cope with the good to soft ground in the Arlington Million in which he weakened into seventh, suffering a minor injury. After a prolonged effort to get him back to the races, he was ultimately retired. **Val Royal**, formerly with Andre Fabre in France, produced the best effort by an American-trained horse on turf with his stunning win over **Forbidden Apple**, **Bach** and **Irish Prize** in the Breeders' Cup Mile. A high-class performer, Val Royal has been plagued throughout his career with nagging injuries. A trip to Sha Tin for the Hong Kong Mile had to be cancelled by trainer Julio Canani when the horse suffered a quarter crack in his last work prior to departure, but he will return in 2002. Other notable turf performers included **With Anticipation**, demoted a place after beating Senure by a head in the United Nations Handicap, then successful in the Sword Dancer Invitational, from **King Cugat**, and the Man o' War Stakes under a good ride by just over two lengths from Silvano.

After swooping to victory in the Dubai Golden Shaheen, **Caller One** found home-grown competition a little tougher upon his return to America, managing only a Grade 3 victory in five attempts. He was a game third in the Breeders' Cup Sprint, beaten narrowly by **Squirtle Squirt** and Xtra Heat, with defending champion **Kona Gold** a disappointing seventh, another West Coaster, perhaps, unsuited by Belmont Park. Squirtle Squirt, who was also successful in the King's Bishop Stakes, against his own age group, was the top three-year-old sprinter. It was closer for the title of best older sprinter, though,

*Breeders' Cup Juvenile Fillies, Belmont Park—
a 1,2 for Godolphin's American operation, Tempera winning from Imperial Gesture*

Kona Gold being dominant in the first half of the year with wins which included the newly-upgraded San Carlos Handicap at Santa Anita and a Grade 2 at Del Mar from Caller One. **Swept Overboard**, who came from well off the pace to win the Ancient Title Breeders' Cup Handicap from Kona Gold, **Left Bank**, who beat Squirtle Squirt in the Vosburgh Stakes over seven furlongs, and **Delaware Township** were fourth, fifth and sixth respectively in a strongly-contested Breeders' Cup Sprint. Delaware Township had earlier won the Forego Handicap from Left Bank and put up another very smart performance with a three-length win in the Frank J de Francis Memorial Dash at Laurel, where Xtra Heat, Kona Gold and Caller One were some way below form. **El Corredor** finished only twelfth when second favourite for the Breeders' Cup Sprint, but had earlier won two Grade 2s, the first of them from Swept Overboard.

Among two-year-olds, the supremacy of **Johannesburg** on both sides of the Atlantic is probably not entirely reflected in his margins of victory, such was the relative ease with which he went past **Officer** and company in the Breeders' Cup Juvenile. Officer, whose five-race undefeated streak came to an ignominious end that day, was surprisingly tried a week later in a race restricted to California-breds, after which he deserved to be stripped of whatever rank he held when losing to **Yougottawanna**. Even Bob Baffert has admitted that Officer will probably not be tried beyond a mile at three. Though Johannesburg has been installed as the favourite for the Kentucky Derby, there are reservations about his ability to stay one and a quarter miles. Moreover, Aidan O'Brien may find it difficult to find suitable prep races for a testing event like the Kentucky Derby, which is thought by Americans to be impossible to win with just a single run beforehand. Juvenile runner-up **Repent** and third-placed **Siphonic** might be wiser Kentucky Derby ante-post wagers. Repent, by Preakness winner Louis Quatorze, followed his visit to Belmont Park with a weight-giving victory in the Grade 2 Kentucky Jockey Club Stakes and has plenty of scope. Siphonic, the six-length winner of the Grade 2 Lane's End Breeders' Futurity Stakes prior to fading into third at Belmont, later impressed when successful in the Hollywood Futurity by three and a half lengths. **Saarland**, only eighth in the Juvenile, showed himself more effective at longer distances when he came from far back to land the nine-furlong Grade 2 Remsen Stakes at Aqueduct in November. An impeccably-bred son of Kentucky Derby winner Unbridled and Breeders' Cup Distaff runner-up Versailles Treaty trained by Shug McGaughey, he is a towering individual in the mould of Point Given.

Godolphin will be trying the Kentucky Derby for the fourth time in 2002. Their best Eoin Harty-trained two-year-old colt of 2001 was Grade 2 Norfolk Stakes winner **Essence of Dubai**. Plum last in the Breeders' Cup Juvenile, he may lack what is required for the Run for the Roses, so Godolphin may have to hope for an as yet unknown horse to emerge as their Kentucky Derby hope. There was, however, no question about the class of their two-year-old fillies. With **Tempera** and **Imperial Gesture** running one, two in the Breeders' Cup Juvenile Fillies, Godolphin is poised to pick up where Exogenous, Flute and Fleet Renee left off. Amongst the other two-year-old fillies **Habibti** and Frizette Stakes winner **You** were disappointing in the Breeders' Cup, but the former had Tempera back in third when winning the Del Mar Debutante in August and rallied to get the better of You by a head in the Hollywood Starlet in December. However, Godolphin and everyone else must beware of **Bella Bellucci**. Third in the Juvenile Fillies following her victory in the Grade 2 Astarita Stakes, she is a sister to the redoubtable Kurofune, winner of the Japan Cup Dirt. Owned by Michael Tabor and trained by Neil Drysdale, Bella Bellucci should play a leading role amongst the three-year-old fillies in 2002. *Text for North America kindly supplied by Alan Shuback of Daily Racing Form*

European-trained horses who showed or reproduced their best form in North America are included in this list	121	Siphonic	114	French Assault
	120	Officer	114	Who Loves Aleyna (f)
	120	Repent	113p	Saarland
	117	Publication	113	Buster's Daydream
† commentary in *Racehorses of 2001*	117	Tempera (f)	113	Cashier's Dream (f)
	116	Came Home	113	Jump Start
	116	Habibti (f)	113	Fonz's
Two-Year-Olds	116	You (f)	113	Leelanau
	115	Imperial Gesture (f)	113	Mayakovsky
127 †Johannesburg	115	Tali'sluckybusride (f)	113	Touch Love (f)

112	Essence of Dubai	
112	Forest Heiress (f)	
112	Heavyweight Champ	
112	Jeremiah Jack	
112	Kamsack	
112	Nokoma	
112	Smok'n Frolic (f)	
111p	Bella Bellucci (f)	
110	Changeintheweather	
109	Beltera (f)	
109	El Soprano	
109	Harlan's Holiday	
109	Labamta Babe	
109	Listen Here	
109	†Sophisticat (f)	
108	Georgia's Storm (f)	
108	Ibn Al Haitham	
108	Lotta Rhythm (f)	
108	Miesque's Approval	
108	Popular	
108	Request For Parole	
108	Silent Fred	
108	Sunray Spirit	
108	Take Charge Lady (f)	
108	Yougottawanna	

DIRT

Three-Year-Olds

134	†Point Given
129	Monarchos
126	Exogenous (f)
125	Squirtle Squirt
124	Flute (f)
124	Macho Uno
124	Unbridled Elaine (f)
123	Fleet Renee (f)
122	A P Valentine
122	Congaree
122	†E Dubai
122	Golden Ballet (f)
122	Invisible Ink
122	Millennium Wind
121	†Express Tour
121	†Street Cry
121	Two Item Limit (f)
121	Xtra Heat (f)
120	Balto Star
120	Dollar Bill
120	Tweedside (f)
119	Starrer (f)
119	Victory Ride (f)
118	Evening Attire
118	Nasty Storm (f)
118	Songandaprayer
118	Outofthebox
117	Crafty C.T.

117	Forest Secrets (f)
117	†Mizzen Mast
115	Scorpion

Older Horses

133	†Tiznow
130	†Captain Steve
129	Lido Palace
128	Aptitude
127	Albert The Great
125	Kona Gold
124	Caller One
124	Delaware Township
124	Skimming
123	El Corredor
123	Futural
123	Spain (f)
123	Swept Overboard
122	Left Bank
121	Guided Tour
121	Include
120	Atelier (f)
120	Big Jag
120	Five Star Day
120	Go Go (f)
120	Miss Linda (f)
120	Tranquility Lake (f)
120	Wooden Phone
119	Freedom Crest
119	Gourmet Girl (f)
119	Heritage of Gold (f)
119	Jostle (f)
119	Peeping Tom
118	Apple of Kent (f)
118	Bet On Sunshine
118	Big Bambu (f)
118	Critical Eye (f)
118	Lazy Slusan (f)
118	Men's Exclusive
118	Pompeii (f)
117	Broken Vow
117	Dat You Miz Blue (f)
117	Dream Supreme (f)
117	Feverish (f)
117	Lu Ravi (f)
117	Nany's Sweep (f)
117	Secret Status (f)
117	Serra Lake (f)
117	Sir Bear
117	Smile Again
117	Traditionally
116	Exciting Story
115	Lovellon (f)

112	Shine Again (f)

TURF

Three-Year-Olds

129	†Milan
128	†Banks Hill (f)
122	†Lailani (f)
119	Strut The Stage
118	†Denon
117	Blazing Fury
117	Navesink
117	Startac
116	Affluent (f)
115	†Choc Ice (f)
115	†Golden Apples (f)
114	Voodoo Dancer (f)

Older Horses

134	†Fantastic Light
127	Val Royal
126	†Silvano
124	Bienamado
123	Forbidden Apple
123	With Anticipation
122	King Cugat
122	†Mutamam
121	†Bach
121	England's Legend (f)
121	Irish Prize
121	†Paolini
121	Timboroa
120	Astra (f)
120	Hap
120	Hawksley Hill
120	Janet (f)
120	Quiet Resolve
120	Senure
120	Super Quercus
120	†Zindabad
119	†Daliapour
119	Gaviola (f)
119	Morluc
119	Perfect Sting (f)
118	Affirmed Success
118	Brahms
118	El Cielo
118	Redatorre
118	Starine (f)
117	Blueprint
117	Bonapartiste
117	Ciro
117	Colstar (f)
117	Falcon Flight
117	Happyanunoit (f)
117	Lodge Hill
117	Touch of The Blues
117	White Heart
116	Numerous Times
115	Subtle Power

JAPAN   After some successful visits in recent seasons, Japanese horses were absent from Europe in 2001 but still made a significant impact on the international stage. Japan's participants in the Dubai World Cup had cut little ice previously but their top older mare **To The Victory** made a bold bid to make all in the latest running, before finding only America's Captain Steve (purchased to stand at stud in Japan at the end of the year) too strong. Earlier on the same card, seven-year-old **Stay Gold** had succeeded in pulling off a shock win in the Dubai Sheema Classic by a nose from Fantastic Light in a very strong field. Stay Gold narrowly deprived Godolphin of another big prize late in the year when

Japan Cup, Tokyo—Jungle Pocket (No.6) stays on well to catch the previous year's winner T M Opera O

gaining another dramatic last-stride victory in the Hong Kong Vase, this time at the expense of Ekraar. Stay Gold's win in the Vase was part of Japan's most successful foreign raid to date, as it initiated a Group 1 treble at the Hong Kong International meeting, completed by **Eishin Preston** in the Mile and **Agnes Digital** in the Cup.

Domestically, Japan boasted a strong crop of three-year-olds headed by Horse of the Year **Jungle Pocket**. The winner of the Tokyo Yushun (Derby) from **Dantsu Flame**, Jungle Pocket later put up a top-class performance under Olivier Peslier to defeat the previous year's winner **T M Opera O** by a neck in the Japan Cup. Jungle Pocket is reportedly set for a possible European campaign in 2002. **Kurofune** was another top-class colt from the three-year-old crop and he too looked set to make his mark outside Japan before he was found to have suffered a tendon injury in the Japan Cup Dirt. Already a Group 1 winner on turf in the spring in the NHK Mile Cup, it was not until switched to dirt that he showed his full powers, winning a Group 3 event by nine lengths and then the Japan Cup Dirt by seven. The second running of the Japan Cup Dirt attracted a much stronger international field than the inaugural contest, but Japanese horses dominated, with **Wing Arrow** (the 2000 winner), **Miracle Opera** and **Nobo True** (winner of the other Group 1 on dirt, the February Stakes) filling the frame. Another good three-year-old to emerge by the end of the year was **Manhattan Cafe**. The winner of the Kikuka Sho (St Leger), in which Jungle Pocket finished only fourth, Manhattan Cafe didn't contest the Japan Cup but defeated several top older horses in the Arima Kinen in December. He looks like making into a leading Japan Cup contender in 2002. Manhattan Cafe is by Japan's outstanding sire Sunday Silence, as is the Satsuki Sho (2000 Guineas) winner **Agnes Tachyon**. Unbeaten in five starts, Agnes Tachyon was building himself the reputation of a potential champion, but after defeating Dantsu Flame and Jungle Pocket in the Guineas, he was retired to stud with a tendon injury, syndicated at a value of US $15m.

The three-year-old fillies were headed by a trio who proved hard to split. **T M Ocean** took the Oka Sho (1000 Guineas) and had several from that race behind her again when finishing third in the Yushun Himba (Oaks) behind **Lady Pastel** and **Rosebud**. The same fillies filled the first three places when they met again in the Shuka Sho over ten furlongs in October, though this time they finished in reverse order. A third meeting between them, against older fillies in the Queen Elizabeth II Commemorative Cup, failed to make the pecking order any clearer; in a blanket finish, Rosebud took second, Lady Pastel fourth and T M Ocean fifth behind older mare To The Victory. T M Ocean was the only one of the trio to take on males, finishing a creditable sixth in the Arima Kinen in December.

Among the older horses, T M Opera O showed he retained all his ability from his remarkable unbeaten campaign as a four-year-old. But as we pointed out here last year, his superiority over his rivals was only a slender one, and he enjoyed nothing like the

Japan Cup Dirt, Tokyo—home-trained Kurofune trounces his field

same dominance in 2001. His only Group 1 success this time round came in the two-mile Tenno Sho (Spring) with a defeat of his long-suffering chief rival **Meisho Doto**. After several near-misses, Meisho Doto finally turned the tables on T M Opera O in the eleven-furlong Takarazuka Kinen in June (**Hot Secret** third) and additionally pipped him for fourth place in the Arima Kinen. T M Opera O emerged the better in their two other exchanges, in the Japan Cup (Meisho Doto finished fifth) and when both were placed behind Agnes Digital in the ten-furlong Tenno Sho (Autumn). T M Opera O retired to stud having consolidated his position as the world record prize-money winner. His career earnings of more than US $16m leaves him well clear of second-placed Cigar, who retired with earnings just short of US $10m.

Agnes Digital's defeat of the then top older horses in Japan in October, and his subsequent victory in Hong Kong, points to his being a leading contender for the Dubai World Cup —he's done most of his winning on dirt. Stay Gold saved his best performances for Dubai and Hong Kong but ran some creditable races at home. He took fourth place in both the Takarazuka Kinen and the Japan Cup (his best placing in four attempts at the race) and was disqualified after beating T M Opera O in a Group 2 at Kyoto in October. Other performances of note came from **Narita Top Road**, third in the Japan Cup, and the Arima Kinen runner-up **American Boss**. As well as her fine second in the Dubai World Cup and her defeat of the top three-year-old fillies mentioned above, To The Victory showed plenty of versatility, with third place in both the February Stakes (over a mile on dirt) and the Arima Kinen (over an extended twelve furlongs on turf).

Unlike in Europe, where sprinters and milers tend to specialise in separate divisions, the same horses tend to contest both the top sprint and mile events in Japan. **Trot Star** came out on top in both the Group 1 sprints, lifting the Takamatsunomiya Kinen in the spring from **Black Hawk** and the Sprinters Stakes in the autumn narrowly from Mejiro

Darling (rated 114) and **Daitaku Yamato**. Trot Star finished down the field in both his Group 1 attempts at a mile, however. Black Hawk went on to win the Yasuda Kinen from **Breaktime** and **Meisho Odo**, but he had been retired by the time of the Mile Championship in November won by **Zenno El Cid** from Eishin Preston and **Taiki Treasure**. Zenno El Cid started hot favourite to confirm that form with Eishin Preston in the Hong Kong Mile but ran poorly, leaving Eishin Preston to run out the easiest of the Japanese winners at Sha Tin.

Three-year-olds

131	Jungle Pocket	128	T M Opera O	118	Nobo True
130	Kurofune	127	Stay Gold	118	To The Victory (f)
124	Manhattan Cafe	125	Eishin Preston	117	Admire Boss
121	Agnes Tachyon	123	Meisho Doto	117	Daitaku Riva
118	Dantsu Flame	122	Narita Top Road	117	Daiwa Texas
117	Grass Eiko O	122	Trot Star	117	Meisho Odo
117	Meiner Despot	121	Black Hawk	117	Symboli Sword
117	Shinko Calido	121	Hot Secret	116	Checkmate
117	T M Ocean (f)	120	American Boss	116	Johnkaranotegami
116	Air Eminem	120	Matikane Kinnohosi	116	Magnaten
116	Rosebud (f)	120	Zenno El Cid	116	Mikki Dance
115	Agnes Gold	119	Agnes Flight	116	Rosado
115	Lady Pastel (f)	119	Breaktime	116	Sky And Ryu
115	Rikiai Taikan	119	Wing Arrow	116	Taiki Treasure
115	Sunrise Pegasus	118	Daitaku Yamato	116	Tokai Oza
115	Tenzan Seiza	118	Eagle Cafe	115	Air Shakur
		118	Ibuki Government	115	Joten Brave
Older Horses		118	Kris The Brave		
130	Agnes Digital	118	Maquereau		
		118	Miracle Opera		

HONG KONG Although he wasn't able to compete at the Hong Kong International meeting **Fairy King Prawn** retained his title of 'best horse trained in Hong Kong' in 2001 with a string of good performances at home and abroad. He won four races in all, namely the Stewards' Cup and Sprint Trophy in January, the Chairman's Sprint Prize in

Hong Kong Vase, Sha Tin—Stay Gold (stripes) gains his
second very valuable win of the year outside Japan, catching Ekraar on the line

Hong Kong Cup, Sha Tin—another big win for Japan as Agnes Digital narrowly beats Tobougg (far side), with Terre A Terre and Hawkeye third and fourth

April and the National Day Cup in October, and very nearly won the Dubai Duty Free on the Dubai World Cup card, too, nailed on the line by Jim And Tonic after coming from well back to lead briefly inside the last. A disagreement over the carrying out of riding orders following that defeat led to a split between trainer Ivan Allan and regular jockey Robbie Fradd, the rider being replaced by Weichong Marwing in his subsequent races. Unfortunately, Fairy King Prawn sustained an injury to his off-fore in the autumn and was ruled out for the rest of the season after undergoing surgery.

Fairy King Prawn's absence meant that the flag bearer for Hong Kong at its International meeting was the much improved **Electronic Unicorn**. He started second favourite for the Mile having won the National Panasonic Cup and the Chevalier Cup easily for his new trainer John Size, in his first year training in Hong Kong, but he wasn't quite able to reproduce his best form and went down by just over three lengths to the Japanese raider Eishin Preston. With Fairy King Prawn sidelined, he'll continue to take all the beating in Hong Kong.

Like Electronic Unicorn, **All Thrills Too** did Hong Kong proud at the International meeting by finishing a close third behind Falvelon and Morluc in the Hong Kong Sprint. It has been a rapid rise to the top for All Thrills Too who won on his debut at the International meeting twelve months earlier.

Indigenous showed that there is still life in the old legs yet with a good third behind Stay Gold and Ekraar in the Hong Kong Vase, albeit six lengths adrift. He had another tough season racing all over the world where the highlights include a seventh place in the Japan Cup. Again, he didn't manage to get his head in front at home, but was a good third behind Silvano in the Queen Elizabeth II Cup.

The Hong Kong Cup attracted few domestic runners with **Peak Power** faring best in finishing seventh behind Agnes Digital. As well as Peak Power, the Mile sixth and Champions Mile winner **Red Pepper**, and the TVB Cup winner **Billion Win** both showed smart form during the year, as did the milers **Charming City** and **New Trumps**. **Oriental Express** isn't the force of old, but he won his first race since 1999 when defeating Rainbow And Gold in the Champions & Chater Cup.

127	Fairy King Prawn	114	Billion Win	113	New Trumps
124	Electronic Unicorn	114	Red Pepper	112	Charming City
119	Indigenous	114?	Peak Power	112	Oriental Express
118	All Thrills Too	113	Best of The Best	110	Cliffhanger

AUSTRALIA AND NEW ZEALAND   The year was highlighted by the rise of a new star on the Australian racing scene—the tough West Australian gelding **Northerly**, who

1180

began his assault on the Eastern States top performers with a high-class display in the Group 1 Australian Cup over ten furlongs in March. From that point, many awaited eagerly the clash with last year's champion mare **Sunline** in the Cox Plate at Moonee Valley over an extended ten furlongs in October. Northerly was a late-comer to racing and did the majority of his racing in 2001, competing eleven times for seven wins, four of which were at Group 1 level. Apart from the Australian Cup, Northerly also won the Underwood Stakes (9f), Caulfield Stakes (1¼m) and the Cox Plate. Regarded as the weight-for-age championship of Australia, the Cox Plate developed into a titanic struggle between Northerly, Sunline and the three-year-old **Viscount** with the first-named prevailing on the post, becoming the highest-rated horse in Australia for the year. The aftermath of the Cox Plate was nearly as exciting as the race itself with Northerly having to withstand objections from connections of both the placed horses.

The champion mare in 2000 Sunline had a mixed year, winning four races from nine starts, her defeats including a gallant third in the Dubai Duty Free (8.5f) behind Jim And Tonic. Clearly, she lost her dominance in weight-for-age races, failing to win at Group 1 level in Australia, but some of her better performances during the year included wins in the Group 1 NZ Waikato Draught Sprint (7f), Group 2 Futurity Stakes (7f) and Group 2 Turnbull Stakes (1¼m). Other older horses to rank highly were **Sky Heights** and **Shogun Lodge**. The evergreen gelding Sky Heights was plagued by injuries during the year which hampered his performances, but he still managed wins in the Group 3 AJC St Leger Stakes (13f), Group 2 Doomben Labor Day Stakes (1¼m) and the Group 2 Sandown Classic (1½m). Sky Heights, carrying top weight, was also just beaten in the Group 1 Caulfield Cup (1½m)—a race he won back in 1999 as a four-year-old. Shogun Lodge notched his ninth Group 1 placing when an unlucky second to Northerly in the Caulfield Stakes which says much about the luck this horse had during the year. The son of Grand Lodge did,

Carlton Draught Cox Plate, Moonee Valley—
Australia's top weight-for-age race and the blinkered Northerly denies Sunline a hat-trick

however, have some high points, including wins in the Group 1 Queen Elizabeth Stakes (1¼m) at Randwick and Group 2 Hollindale Cup (9f) at the Gold Coast. He was also runner-up in the Group 1 Doomben Cup (1¼m) and Group 1 AJC Doncaster Handicap (1m).

History was made in the Group 1 Melbourne Cup (2m) when New Zealand mare **Ethereal** completed the Caulfield and Melbourne Cup double. The four-year-old Rhythm mare won the Group 1 Queensland Oaks (1½m) earlier in the year and then was specifically trained for the big Cups. She came into the Group 1 Caulfield Cup (1½m) on a relatively light staying preparation but managed to get home in a photo finish. Her win in the Melbourne Cup was much more comprehensive, overpowering the Godolphin representative Give The Slip, who looked to have the race safely in his keeping at the two-furlong mark. In winning both Group 1 staying classics, Ethereal became the first mare since Let's Elope in 1991 and just the eleventh horse ever to take the double. Ethereal's trainer Sheila Laxon (wife of Laurie, now based in Singapore) also became the first woman trainer to prepare a Melbourne Cup winner as well as to train the Cup double. A possible European campaign culminating in the Prix de l'Arc de Triomphe could be on the agenda for Ethereal in 2002.

Univeral Prince and **Assertive Lad** were the leading four-year-olds. Universal Prince (a close relative of 1994 Victoria Derby winner Blevic) scored a breathtaking win in the Group 1 AJC Australian Derby (1½m), unleashing a devastating burst of acceleration at the two-furlong mark to win by nearly four lengths. The Derby win followed an equally sensational effort in the Group 1 Canterbury Guineas (9.5f), in which he staged an amazing last-to-first victory. Universal Prince raced without luck in Melbourne in the Spring but did push both Sunline and Northerly to close finishes in the Turnbull Stakes (1¼m) and Underwood Stakes (9f) respectively. Assertive Lad was out for most of the year with injury, but there is no doubting his ability. He scored his second Group 1 win over the Randwick mile with an outstanding win in the AJC Doncaster Handicap. The win also gave his trainer Gai Waterhouse her fifth win in the race in the last nine years.

The Australian turf was fortunate to have an above-average group of three-year-olds in 2001. **Lonhro** and **Viscount** earned equal-top rating with some fine performances, but

Tooheys New Melbourne Cup, Flemington—Caulfield Cup winner Ethereal gets up to beat Godolphin's Give The Slip (far side)

North Boy, **Viking Ruler**, **Ha Ha**, **Magical Miss**, **Ustinov**, and **Mistegic** all earned high ratings. Lonhro provided former champion racehorse, now sire, Octagonal, with his first Group 1 winner when he took the Caulfield Guineas (1m) in outstanding fashion. On good to soft ground, Lonhro came from near the tail of the field in the straight to overpower his high-quality rivals. Many believe the 2001 Caulfield Guineas field was one of the best, if not *the* best, ever to contest the 120-year-old classic, with Ustinov (Seeking The Gold—Let's Elope) and Nureyev colt **Pure Theatre** filling the placings. Lonhro raced nine times during 2001 for seven wins and ended the year as the winner of his last five races. Stablemate Vincent was assessed equal to him following three Group 1 wins for the year. He was successful in the AJC Champagne Stakes (1m), AJC Sires Produce Stakes (7f) and George Main Stakes (1m). He failed in the Caulfield Guineas after suffering interference mid-race, but redeemed himself with a game third in the Cox Plate after receiving severe interference close to the winning post. The highest rated three-year-old filly was the Bart Cummings-trained Magical Miss, a latecomer who won both the Group 1 One Thousand Guineas and Group 1 VRC Oaks (12.5f). By Danehill, Magical Miss provided champion trainer Bart Cummings with his fifth One Thousand Guineas and his eighth VRC Oaks winner. The leading sprinting three year-old filly was the Gai Waterhouse-trained Ha Ha, also by Danehill, who won the Group 1 Golden Slipper Stakes (6f) in April. Gai Waterhouse, not only became the first woman to train a Slipper winner, but also the first to be responsible for the first three home in the 45-year race history. The best staying effort by a three-year-old was by **Amalfi** in winning the Group 1 Victoria Derby (12.5f). The Carnegie colt, under the skilful guidance of champion rider Damien Oliver, showed great courage to claim the Derby in a photo after a battle over the last furlong and a half. The depth of three-year-olds coming through should ensure a very high-quality group of older horses in 2002.

From the limited number of two-year-olds seen there were some very encouraging performances. The Royal Academy colt **Bel Esprit** earned the honour of the highest-rated juvenile with two impressive wins from as many starts. Bel Esprit's better effort was in the Group 2 Maribyrnong Plate (5f) in the Spring carnival. Other two-year-olds who were not extended in their wins were **Snowland** and **Bardego**. Both have scope to improve their ratings considerably. Two unbeaten juvenile fillies who looked outstanding prospects were **Calaway Gal** and **Innovation Girl**. The Queenslander Calaway Gal won four from four by a total of almost twenty-three lengths while Innovation Girl won three from three and a combined winning margin of over ten lengths.

On the international scene, apart from Sunline's Dubai effort, classy sprinter **Falvelon** defended his title successfully in the Group 2 Hong Kong Sprint. Earlier in the year he had won the Group 1 Doomben Ten Thousand in Australia over a short seven furlongs his best effort all season. There was also considerable interest in overseas horses racing in Australia during the Spring carnival. The German-trained Arlington Million winner Silvano was a gallant fourth in the Cox Plate, while Godolphin had to be content with another second in the Melbourne Cup with the aforementioned Give The Slip. Godolphin did, however, have some success, with Hatha Anna winning the Group 2 Queen Elizabeth Stakes (12.5f) on the final day of the Carnival. It was certainly another excellent year for Australian and New Zealand racing.

Ratings and text for Australia and New Zealand are supplied courtesy of Gary Crispe (www.racingandsports.com.au). The ages listed below are as at 31st December 2001.

Two-Year-Olds

117p	Bel Esprit
116p	Calaway Gal (f)
114p	Innovation Girl (f)
114p	Snowland
113p	Bardego (f)
113	Brief Embrace (f)
112	Sir Breakfast
112	Victory Vein (f)
112	Wyndam Glory

Three-Year-Olds

123	Lonhro
123	Viscount
122	Mistegic
122	Ustinov
122	Viking Ruler
121	Magic Albert
120	Excellerator
120	Magical Miss (f)
120	North Boy
119	Pure Theatre
118	Chong Tong
118	Ha Ha
118	Red Hannigan
118	Royal Code
117	Amalfi
117	Royal Courtship
116	Dash For Cash
116	King of Prussia
115	Deprave
115	Fair Embrace (f)
115	Leica Guv
115	Moon Dragon (f)
115	Newquay
115	Portsmouth

115	Regal Kiss (f)	115	Gillespie	119	Landsighting
115	True Jewels (f)	115	Kootoomootoo	118	Chattanooga
		115	Mannington (f)	118	El Mirada
Four-Year-Olds		115	Pembleton	118	Zonda
124	Assertive Lad	115	Rose Archway (f)	117	Camena (f)
124	Universal Prince	115	Tempest Morn (f)	117	Crawl
121	Century Kid			117	Hire
121	Show A Heart	**Older Horses**		117	Native Jazz
120	De Gaulle Lane	128	Northerly	117	Referral
120	Ethereal (f)	125	Shogun Lodge	117	Sports
120	Keeper	125	Sky Heights	117	Toledo
119	Desert Sky	124	Sunline (f)	117	Yippyio
119	Mr Murphy	122	Mr Innocent	116	Fritz
119	Zariz	120	Cent Home	116	Giovana (f)
118	Regal Shot	120	Falvelon	115	Black Bean
117	Belle du Jour (f)	120	Go Flash Go	115	Brave Prince
116	Bush Padre	120	Inaflury (f)	115	Emission
116	Phoenix Park	120	Kaapstad Way	115	Make Mine Magic
116	Tit For Taat	120	King Keitel	115	Pleasure Giver
115	Diamond Dane	120	Le Zagaletta	115	Tiger's Eye
		120	Tie The Knot		

THE 2001 TIMEFORM IRISH HANDICAP

† indicates horse with commentary or essay in *Racehorses of 2001*

Two-Year-Olds

61	Achates
88	Addeyll†
77	Addo†
98	Agnetha
77	Agoodred
92p	Ahsanabad
50	Ahshado
82	Akrabad
—	Albarino
86	Alexander Ballet
59	Ali Bava
71	Ali Shuffle
74	Allheartnoroses
—	All Native
75	All Pop
97	Alluring Park
87	Almost Famous
80	Alserna
75p	Alstemeria
72	American Isle
79	Anarchy
92p	Ancestor
62	Angel's Folly
79	Anima Mundi†
94	Annie Daly
—	Anniemah
80	Anticline
—	Aoibhneas
80	Approaching Storm
90p	Aqualina
81	Ardara
80	Ario
98	Arkaga
55	Arwean
45	Assuring Ways
—	Audreys Light
81	Avoir du Cran
77	Awholelotagold
64	Ayman
56	Babble On
54	Babylonia
79	Bahrain Pearl
—	Ballina Belle
114p	Ballingarry†
—	Barrack Buster
84	Barriance
86	Barring Order
73	Bartra Rock
73	Batool
73	Baxter Point
86	Beau Cheval
64	Beaumont Style
69	Be Charismatic
—	Beeper's Lodge
74	Begonia
84	Bella Bella
94	Bella Chica†
—	Bellaficient
48	Ben's Guest
81	Be Patient
78	Bev Who
67	Black Pagoda
67	Black Turtle
64	Bluebell Line
69	Bold Doll
—	Boningale
61	Boom Or Bust†
65	Bothar Rua
78	Bought Direct
84	Bounce Back
89p	Bowmans Crossing
58	Brave Harvey
76	Brest†
—	Brief Breezer
102	Bright And Clear†
102	Bringontheclowns
—	Brook Hill Girl
103	Brooklyn
63	Bubble N Squeak
—	Bushido
62	Caishill
89	Calamella
106	Camp David†
99p	Canberra†
57	Carrig On Bannow
71	Casadei
75	Casa Que Canta
72	Casta Diva†
113	Castle Gandolfo†
—	Catch The Swallow
82	Cat Five
58	Catwalk's Flyer
—	Celtic Blaze
74	Ceol Na Sraide
82	Ceremonious
66	Chapel Story
—	Charente Walk
81	Cherry Falls
76	Chief Mosconomo
—	Chief Odin
94	Church Cross
83	Ciara's Delight
—	Cidreigneys Girl
42	Cifonelli
—	Classe Spectre
—	Class Reunion
56	Clew Bay
80	Clochette
79p	Clouseau
—	Coldstream Lass
88	Colourfast
71	Commoya
71	Contrarian
70	Cool Ballerina
76	Coral Son
—	Cotton Lady
67	Countess Marengo
82	Court Ruling
85p	Creekview
89	Crooked Wood
—	Crystal Light
81	Dancing
—	Dancing At Boulta
101	Daneleta
85	Dangerous Years
65	Darita
63	Dashing Home
75	Dash of Grey
110p	Della Francesca†
—	Deoraoicht
71	Derhaam
64	Desert Kite
72	Desperado
63	Devious Daughter
81	Dexileos
102	Diaghilev†
—	Dilly Stars
48	Dolphins View
—	Dont Talk Shop
76	Double Royal
104p	Dress To Thrill†
—	Dromadaire
—	Dromhall Dancer
61	Dubai Bound
—	Due Diligence
61	Eagle Sep
90	Easy Sunshine
63p	Ebaraya
43	Ebika
51	Echo Beach
88	Egyptian
68	Elbowroom
78p	Elegant Cat
57	Elva Express
63	Emily's Song
66	Emlagher
80	Emma O
—	Ennistown Lady
74	Ensenada
—	Erinella
—	Euro Ace
60	Europaea
76	Evora
—	Ex Ante
54	Fabula
49	Fairland
87	Fashion Guide
87	Fearn Royal
55	Feeling Free
—	Feichead Ghra
58	Feile Na Ndeise
62	Fille d'Argent†
53	Filmgame
65	Final Case
76	Fingal Nights
57	Finians Dale
78	Fionns Folly
—	Firando
80	Fortune
48	Foxhollow Lady
—	Frankie Dori
75	Frank Mor†
78p	Fresh As A Rose
57	Friendly Intent
101	Funfair Wane†
55	Gallant Intent
—	Galoretta
62	Gan Eagla
74	Gaoth Na Mara
67	Gazebo Blue
76	Gilded Vanity
—	Giveherthehay
—	Given To Fly
80	Glandore

–	Glow Lady Glow	
63	Golden Cross	
83	Golden Glow	
56	Goldrand	
–	Golly Gosh	
–	Good Golly Miss	
90	Goodwin Sands	
–	Go On My Beauty	
72	Goula	
87	Gravy Train	
86p	Great Divide	
–	Grimaldi	
66	Guillemot	
–	Hacienda Playa	
79	Hanorla	
77	Hasina	
89p	Hathlool	
116p	Hawk Wing†	
–	Hazy Isle	
52	Hereforagoodtime	
76	Here Goes	
73	Hiawatha	
89p	Hidden Dragon	
51	Hidden Genius	
115p	High Chaparral†	
100	Highdown†	
78	High Maintenance	
100p	High Sierra†	
97	High Society	
92	Hot Trotter†	
–	Howsabouty	
72	Hurry Purr	
–	Huxley	
73	Hymn of The Dawn	
79p	Ilios	
66	Illegal†	
94§	Indy Rose†	
78	In His Time	
59	In Other Words	
77	In Theory	
92p	In Time's Eye	
–	Irish Silver	
78p	Irresistible Jewel	
90	Jakeal	
92	Jassas	
80p	Jazz Beat	
76	Jimjonpaddal†	
127	Johannesburg†	
65	Just A Carat†	
67	Just A Country Boy	
68	Kaneshiro	
85	Kasparov†	
–	Katies Pearl	
79	Keen Look	
95	Keepers Hill†	
–	Kentucky Sport	
–	Kerkira	
–	Kerry Way	
80	Khaisara	
–	Kiddo's Dream	
79p	Kiltubber	
65	King of The Skies	
102p	Kournakova†	
–	Kufstein	
–	Kyalami	
96	Lady Digby	
75	Lady Esther	
59	Lady Kia	
104	Lahinch†	
66	Lakeland	

75	Landofheartsdesire	
115	Landseer†	
70	Langkawi Bay	
87	Laoch Na Mara	
78	La Pieta	
–	Lash One	
67	Later On	
–	Latin Crystal	
–	Leeside Legend	
73	Leinster Mills	
–§	Le Moineau	
103p	Leo's Luckyman†	
79	Lets Try It	
61	Libras Child	
97	Line Rider†	
83	Lines of Battle	
79	Literary Lover	
59	Little Alex	
–	Little Perfect	
81	Little Rort	
61	Lolita's Gold	
66	Long Journey	
96	Lord Merlin†	
–	Love All	
–	Lovejoy	
73	Lowlander	
–	Lucagene	
75	Luck Happy	
–	Lucky Guess	
94	Luminous Beauty	
55	Mac Han	
49	Macha Rua	
92	Madame Cerito	
49	Madame Royale	
80p	Madeira Mist	
87	Magnitudo	
97	Mahsusie†	
51	Mainly Mine	
–	Majesty's Dancer	
76	Major Title	
–	Manchester	
69	Man From Artemus	
85p	Marannatha	
81	Margarula	
67	Marie Gracia	
99	Marionnaud	
54	Market Minstrel	
72	Markino	
–	Mark The Begining	
50	Marlita Bay	
83	Martin Gunne	
107p	Maryinsky†	
–	Mary Leadbeater	
83	Masani	
91	Maskaya	
91	Master Papa	
78	Master's Melody	
46	Mean Oiche	
–	Mellisina	
76	Memphis Raines	
62	Millers Weir	
96	Million Percent†	
86	Millstreet	
76	Milton Star	
81	Minamala	
95	Minashki†	
98	Minatonic	
70	Minaun Heights	
92	Mine Host†	
72	Mirassou	

72	Mirela
77	Mirpour
102	Miss Beabea
69	Miss Grimm
–	Miss Heartbeat
76	Miss Koen
–	Miss Odlum
64	Misstwosteps
54	Mivec
91	Moayed
56	Modern Goddess
73	Molly Ellen
101	Monarchoftheglen†
77	Monash Prince†
68	Montara
74	Moondarra
101	Moon Safari†
–	Moorhall
66	Morning
80	Mottsey
62	Mrs Beatty
68	Ms Mary C
87	Mughas
–	Mulberry Walk
77p	Munda Nai
62	Mutineer
112	Mutinyonthebounty†
–	Mystical Magic
109	Naheef†
80	Nathan Jones
74	Nazimabad
–	Neckar Valley
–	Needtoknow
67	Neminos
66	Newcorr
54	Newlands Gold
66	Newtown Dancer
75	Niallon
80	No Apologies
67	Nomination Blues
–	No Truce
88	Nutley King
70	Nutley Queen
94	Ocean Sound†
74	Octomone
73	Oileann Oir
–	Olivers Army
59	One Flag
–	Onefortheboys
103p	On The Nile†
53	Orphan King
92	Osterhase
–	Paal Lady
–	Padre Nostro
95	Paris Express
91	Partytime†
42	Pastry Cake
58	Patricias Party
76p	Paula Smith
54	Peace Angel
73p	Peach Sorbet
55	Pearl Egg
74p	Penny Poor
46	Perfect Sky
–	Perry's Island
–	Persian Chieftan
–	Perugino Lodge
–	Petite Petasse
–	Phantom Act
50	Phantom Turtle

99 Exceptional Paddy	122 Hawkeye†	77 Ladylishandra
74 Factice Royal	58 Headford Lad	67 Lady Marian
– Fading With Music	105 Heavenly Whisper†	– Lady Natuschka
– Failte	55 Heidelberg Castle	100? Lady of Kildare†
76 Fair McLain	– Helldorado Days	58 Lady of The Chase
57 Fair Replacement	103 Henry Afrika	– Lady Rainbow
– Fanfire	60 High Blade†	84 Lady Semillon
96 Fantasy Royale	– High Flight	86 La Golondrina
77 Faolchu	– Holy Ground	122 Lailani†
76§ Favourable Bounce	112 Ice Dancer†	66 Lambay Island†
55 Feadog	119 Imagine†	84 Langkawi Island
62 Feel The Pride	73 Imperial Eye	84d Lanquani
– Feet of Fire	? Incite	100 La Stellina
59d Feet of Flame	116 Independence†	– Last Rolo
43 Finians Flite	– Indiana Colony	94 Last Tango
– Firoza	– In Ernest	97 Last Theatre
87 First Breeze	83 Inishmot Lady	57 Latin Quarter Lad
79 Flinders Street	– Instants	60 Lauras Theme
88 Florida Villas	– Interstate	– Lavender Island
51 Fluttery Dancer	80 In The Dusk	80d Lavish Spirit
92 Flying Knight	96 Irish Empire	87 Leaffoney
56 Foreal	112+ Ishiguru†	70 Leeside
78 Forest Leaf†	79 I-Timad	– Le-Monde
– Formula Venetta	60 It's A Gimme	86 Leopard Spot
68 Fortfield	75d Jaykay Lady	74 Le Petite Fleur
75 Fosse	– Jemapel	105 Lethal Agenda
77 Frametti	– Jensen	85+ Life Match†
60d Frank's Lady	108 Jentzen†	91 Like A Dream
92 French Smile	– Jerez	78d Lily Dale
– Freshfromthecreeks	56 Jewel Note	113 Lime Gardens†
106 Freud†	68 Jimmy Jinks	– Lisa's Girl
101? Frosty Wind	90+ John Dorans Melody	– Little Sovereign
36 Fungi Street	103? Josh's Pearl	42 Little White Face
107 Gaelic Queen	103 Julie Jalouse	93 Longueville Legend
101 Galanta	58 Jumbo Romance	75 Lorli
134 Galileo†	– Junior Doctor	66d Los Monteros
72 Galtip Flyer	105 Juniper†	– Lough Cara
– Garymore	– Just Riva	55 Lough Currane
– Gaysian	109 Just Special	– Love And Desire
77 Georgia Peach	61 Kahrena	99? Love Me True
86 Gerobies Girl	104 Kalamunda	37 Lucky Grace
– Ginger Wine	107 Karasta†	– Lucky Three
77 Giocomo	114 Karsavina†	59 Lucy Liu
96 Give A Whistle	62 Kathandori	94 Lunardi
51 Givre†	101 Katherine Seymour	– Macedon Princess
75 Glass Note	53 Katonka	83 Madamaa
44 Glenhaven Lady	46 Kennedys Music	– Maddenstown House
76 Global Explorer	76 Kesh Kumay	75 Mad Madam Mym
59 Glympse	66? Khaysar†	–§ Maggies Mare
125 Golan†	93 Khetaam	108 Magic Cove
115 Golden Apples†	– Kilpatrick River	84d Magzaa†
– Golden Mistress	– Kimash	69 Maiskaya
– Golden Puff	120 King Charlemagne†	56 Majeda
115 Golden Wells†	116 King of Tara†	95 Mala Mala
– Gold Prospector	107 King's County	76 Mambo Jambo
73 Go On Q P R	– Kings Feature	75+ Mar Blue
75 Gormans Best	74 King's Opera	– Marcato
95d Gotarapofahames	89 Kingsridge	100 March King
54 Grandmette	68 Kiruna†	– Marcovina†
61 Grass	– Kissimmee Girl	86 Marefonic
66 Gravieres	65 Knockatotaun	78 Marko Jadeo
– Great Manoeuvre	– Knockkerra Boy	85 Mark One†
86 Grisham	– Kono	75 Marsh Harrier
64 Gulch King	91 Kropotkin	85 Masakala
84 Gwapa	– Lady Anne	70? Massimo
– Gypsy Lee	– Lady Atina	– Master Glow
64d Haalim†	– Ladybedaisy	74 Material Lady
– Handsome Knight	56 Lady Birdseye	108 Maumee
107 Hans Anderson†	60 Lady Killeen	65 Maxerial
55 Haveasession	– Lady Le Droff	85 Mayara

114	Mediterranean†	71	Osteria	68	Safe Route
–	Meemon	84	Ostjessy	100	Saffron Dancer
–	Melindsey	–	Out of The Common	110	Sahara Slew†
98	Merchant of Venice	82	Pakiefromathleague	–	Samawi
79	Meritocracy	77	Panchita	81	San Marco
–	Merlins Trail	–	Paraphet	–	Saraho'byrne
63	Mexican Miss	85	Paris In The Fall	88	Sarayah
63	Mighty Mist	–	Paris Sweet	–	Say But Little
129	Milan†	84	Pasteur	108	Saying Grace
78	Milkat	71	Patrizio	103	Scarlet Velvet
65	Millenium Dancer	86	Peace Keeping	88	Scarpe Rosse†
–	Millenium Love	68	Peace Within†	85	Scolardy
79	Millennium Lilly	110	Pebble Island	61	Scottish Knight†
116	Minardi†	96	Per Amore	77	Scottish Minstrel
36	Mind Over Matter†	66	Perfect Trip	71	Send Him On
79	Mirs Style	92	Perigee Moon	75	Sephora
73d	Mise Rafturai	67	Persian Bliss	113	Sequoyah†
–	Missing A Bit	58	Pertemps Thatcher†	87	Serov
64	Missing You Too	–	Pet Shadow	74	Seychelles
–	Miss Sandy Claws	64	Phantom Lake	–	Shalamina
65?	Miss Troy	70	Pigeon Top	–	Sharp Act
–	Mizen Star	63	Plant A Smacker	62	Sharply's Gift
106	Modigliani†	96	Polite Reply	76	Sheer Dane
–	Mollies Tale	–	Popiplu	46	She'll Be Grand
93	Monty Wolley	–	Poppy Lewis	–	Shenkara
91	Mood Indigo	83	Princess Button	79	Sherry Spinner
100	Moonbi Ridge	47	Princess Galina	–§	Shes My Baby
78	Moore's Law	94	Princess Nutley	–	She's No Blonde
67	Morissett	–	Princess Pud	84	She's Our Girl
123	Morshdi†	92	Private Ben	–	Shimla
115	Mot Juste†	80	Pro Dancer	–	Shiraz Dancer
–	Mountain Shadows	–	Profitable Lady	73	Shirzadiyan
–	Move Over Tiney	–	Prospect Hill	–	Sicily Flyer
86	Moyeala	115	Pugin†	91	Silver Dagger
131	Mozart†	78	Queens Wharf	84	Silver Risks
121	Mr Combustible†	67	Quit The Pack	89	Silver Skates
82	Mr Mister	–	Rachames	109	Siringas
76	Mr Shoeshine	81	Rainbow Royale	112?	Sita†
62	Mrs Pertemps	–	Rainbows Pride	–	Sitoco
117	Mugharreb†	–	Rambling Rampage	–	Skin And Hair
53	Mujavail	74	Rasana	87	Sky To Sea
94	Musadaf	–	Ratatoe	–	Sky View
69	Muskerry Sportsman	–	Ratholm Kate	44	Slaney Boy
71d	Myfavouriteman	102	Rayyana	–	Slieverue
–	My Jenny	–	Rc's Grandaughter	76	Smile From Heaven
93	Naahil	–	Rebel Hero	79	Snake Mountain
110	Najah†	112	Rebelline†	105+	Snowflake†
–	Napeta	54+	Received Wisdom	62	Socrates
78	National Honour	99	Red Bartsia	65	Sodfahh
82	Nebulae	99	Red Millennium†	111	Softly Tread†
–	Netsuk	83	Reilly Mac	88d	Solar At'em
–	Never Give Up Hope	102	Reina Blanca	74	Sondheim
80	Newhall	113	Relish The Thought†	–	So Saintly
–	New Lodge Express	–	Remember The Time	111	Speirbhean
71	Nijinsky Dancer	–	Repentance	66	Spraoi
–	Nimosflyer	–	Rick	83d	Spurn
–	Noble Chamike	103	Right Honorable	–	Squire James
76d	No Frontier	72	River Days	91	Standing Applause
88	Nonchalant	76	Riyal Dream	95	Starlight Venture
92	Northern Rock	75	Room To Room Value	56	Starry Lady
93	Northfields Dancer†	–	Rosalia	–	Stokesie†
88	Norway†	114	Rose Gypsy†	–	Storm Cavern
59	Notlackinginstyle	–	Rosganna	71	Stovash
92	Okey Dorey	81	Royal Jubilee	–	Stracomer Thalia
110	One More Round	–	Royal Tribute	60	Stracomer Urania
–	Only One Left	58	Rubioso	73	Street Player
99	Only The Lonely	67	Rugged Man	–	Striking Sound
93	On The Razz	83+	Saddler's Creek†	73	Sudden Interest
90	Oriental Ben	99	Sadima	48	Sullivan's Cascade
53	Orinoco	112	Sadlers Wings†	79	Summer Stock

Older Horses

70	Eymir	–	Goldenhalo	64	Impressive Way†
78	Ezbek	81	Golden Hop	64	Impulsif
–	Fair And Lively	–	Golden Pamela	–	Indalo Grey
58	Fairy House	–	Golden Retriever	–	Independence Hall†
–	Fantastic Dance	127	Golden Snake†	56	Indian Desert
134	Fantastic Light†	–	Golden Storm	–	Indian Drive†
43	Fashions Dante	–	Golden Vision	112	Indian Spark†
82	Fast And Furious†	79	Goldnecu	–	Indimaaj
–	Fast Break	–	Goldstreet	49	Indy Carr
27	Fast Friend	101	Golovin	112	Inglenook†
84	Fearsome Factor	49	Go My Dream	–	Inner Peace
36	Feelin' Looser	–§	Gonemoggelease	?	Inourhearts
–	Fenton's Warrior	–	Gorgeous Georgina	–	Insan Magic
–	Fernwood Lady	70	Goss	84	Intensity
32	Festive Isle	73	Gossie Madera	56§	In The Gods
–	Filoli Gardens	–	Gothic Revival	74	Inver Gold†
115	Final Exam†	55	Grafton Style	115	Invincible Spirit†
–	Final Trial	–	Grange Leader	–	Ira Hayes
–	Fionas Dance VI	–	Grannys Handbag	76	Irish Lady
–	Firey Senorita	92	Grassland Star	48	Irresistible Force
66	First Draw	52	Great Days	–	Ishkasullus
92	First Son	81	Great Guns	–	Island Diva
66	Five of Hearts	–§	Great Melody	–	Italian Counsel†
–	Flagship Queen	57	Grecian Myth	–	Its The Boss
–	Flash of Speed	–	Greenhue	–	Its Time For A Win
–	Flaunt	75	Gregorian	62	I'vehadit
57	Flitwick	–	Greyskies	55	Ivorela
64	Flying Boat	77	Grianan Realta	107d	Ivory's Joy†
38	Flying Chance	99	Grinkov	69	Izmir
–	Flying Dolphin	34	Gruff Gott	97	Jacks Estate
62	Forest Chief	79	Hadath	–	Jalouise
–	Forever Relic	63?	Half Barrell	115	Jammaal†
86	Forrestfield	71§	Handsome Bop	67	Jasmin d'Oudairies
31	Fort Apache	64	Hang'em High	–	Joe Cullen
–	Four Aces	71	Hanger Straight	69	John Magical
54	Francies Fancy	40	Ha-Pa	–	Johnny's Band
90	Francis Bay	–	Harak	69	Joking Rebuff
108	Free To Speak	99	Hariya	–	Jordans Pride
69	French Style	49	Harlenog	33	Joy's Darling
59	Freya	68	Harry's Game	–	Justbuttercup
85	Fruit Defendu	75	Hat Or Halo	79	Just Our Job
48	Furnitureville	73	Have Merci	89	Just Wondering
62	Fustanella	–	Hawadeth	–	Kadir
–	Gallaher's Sister	63	Headfort Rose†	71	Kadoun
57	Gallileo Strike	67§	Heart of The Ocean	129	Kalanisi†
94	Gamekeeper	79	Heemanela	79§	Kaldan Khan
§§	Garrick	–	Heffo's Army	60+	Kalingalinga†
64	Gateway	–	Helena John	65	Karakam
–	Gaudi	80	Helen Bach	48	Kariyadan
76	Gemini Guest	–	Hennessy Feeds	73	Kate Emily
–	General Cloney	34	Highway One Eleven	74	Keeping The Faith
–	Genghis Khan	66	Hill Society	–	Keith Woods
67	Geodalus	63	Hill Style	–	Kelly's Isle
54	Geraldo	74	Hobart Frisbey	29	Kenny's Pet
57	Gers Gold	99	Holy Orders†	61	Kerry Isle
–	Ger's Royale	–	Home Port	30	Kevins View
86	Gift Token	74	Homer	85	Khairambar
51	Gincell Lady	54§	Homestead	50	Kharshani
–	Ginger Lily	40	Honeyschoice	–	Khazaika
59	Girl Wonder	–	Hot Bunny	–	Kickham's Princess
121	Give The Slip†	89	Hot Stuff	50	Kilbride King
61	Glacial Queen	–	Houston Time	–	Kilcarrig House
55	Glastonbury	65	Hunters Bar	61	Kilcash Castle
–	Glenbar	–	Hyelord	73d	Kilcullen Lad
78	Glens Music	56	Iftatah	37	Killadoon
–	Gloating	49	I Have To Go	–	Kilmeade Prince
48	Go Girl Go	–	Illusion's Best	62	Kilmoney Gamble
91	Gold Chaser	45	Illusions Tom	65	Kimberley
–	Golden Angel	–	I'm Happy	–	King of Ireland
90d	Golden Fact†	–	Imminent	70	King of Peace

65	Kiptanui	52	Making A Break	–	Moonridge
–	Kissangel	–	Malakal	79	Moon Shot
72	Knife Edge	–	Malian Project	95	Moratorium
–	Knockalassa	–	Mallaca Hill	74	Morning Breeze
44	Knockdromin Lady	–	Mallon	37	Morning Georgie
–	Knock Na Garm Lad	–	Man of Courage	82	Moscow Express
78	Knysna Lily	–	Ma Petite Rouge	–	Moscow Maid
–	Koko Nor	53	Marabeesh	77	Moscow Retreat
73	Kramer	–	Maradan	107	Moselle†
42	Kudrow	72	Marakiya	58	Most Gifted
–	Ladies View	119	Marienbard†	–	Mostovio
75§	Lady Ellen-M	86	Markskeepingfaith	33	Mountain Rocket
34	Lady Monilousha	–	Martanza	62	Mountain Star
55	Lady of Bilston	–	Masalarian	105	Moving On Up
–	Ladys Choice	–	Masarkal	102	Mr Houdini
–	Lady's Heart	109	Masilia†	–	Mr Perfect
77	Lake Millstatt	105	Masnada	118	Muakaad†
83	Land of Promise	112	Mastermind†	–	Mullawn Dancer
59	Larifaari	–	Max Time	114	Mull of Kintyre†
–	La Shalak	–	May Contessa	113	Munjiz†
–	Lashing Night†	–	Maydaymayday	108	Murghem†
38	Latino Bay†	–	McCracken	83	Murrayfield
43	Laura Aisling	–	Me And My Girl	52	Muscovite Marble
66	Laurier Rose	116	Media Puzzle†	47	Music Time
53	Lavadores	66§	Meigiu	112	Mutakarrim†
84	Lawz	39	Melody's Castle	60	My Delilah
40	Lee's Lodge	–	Menawa	50	Mykon Gold
37	Lefty Fugerri	–	Mesri	–	My Ramona
53§	Lichen	51	Messrs Maguire	60	Mysilverriverfeale
58	Liffeydale	–	Metal Detector	–	Mythological
76	Lily's Choice	68d	Mighty Pip†	39	My Wakashan
–	Lilywhite	59d	Mighty Rebel	–	Na Huille Ban
65	Limestone Lad	41	Mighty Term	–	Nailer
85	Lindissima	–	Milesville	–	Nama
70	Lions Den	124	Millenary†	79	Namibia
–	Lisalee Lady	–	Millenium Belle	76	Natalie Know's
–	Liscannor Bay	–	Millennium Prince	62	Native Endurance
59	Lisselan Fairways	–	Millennium Summit	–	Native Kin
–	Little Apache	40	Millie's Lily	–	Native Lucy
–	Little Bittydancer	56	Mill Lane Flyer	65§	Near Dunleer
?	Little Miss Muffet	80	Miltonfield	–	Neglected
–	Little Misstrouble	67	Minnie Kc	–	Nellie Gannon
–	Little Rachel	–	Mi Picasso	37	Nero's Dancer
63	Little Sean	92d	Miracle Ridge	–	Nessus
–	Lk's Chance	–	Mira	101	Newpark Lady†
48	Load And Lock	62	Miskilette	–	Newtown Breeze
70	Lord Edwards Army	–	Misniuil	45	Nick The Butler
55	Love Academy	–	Miss Egypt	–	Night Shadow
69	Lucky Bet	–	Miss Grapette	59	Nipitinthebud
–	Lucky Gem	33	Miss Information	–	Nopolo
57	Lucky Kandahar	60	Miss Lauren Dee	–	Nordic Oak
55	Lucky Loreley	59	Miss Pavlova	60	Northern Mill
47	Lucky Me	41	Miss Singer	69	Not A Sound
–	Lucky Player	–	Mister Boreen	–	Oakley Lad
35	Ludgrove	–	Mister Chippy	–	Off You Go
48	Luferton Lane	–	Mister Dolphin	–	Often's Girl
50	Luna Fleur	87	Mist of Magic	59	Ogan Hill
–	Lys Treasure	–	Misty Moments	–	Oileanach
75	Macabeo	–	Mitigate	74	Ojay
76d	Macintosh Man	67	M N L Duchess	–	Okay
–	Madame Vela	–	Moigh Endeavour	33	Omy Dancer
47	Maghas†	61	Moll Hackabout	54	One For The Money
–	Magical Emma	99d	Molly-O	113	One Won One†
–	Magical Lady	104	Molomo†	97?	On The Ridge
–§	Magical Mick	–	Mona Day	68	On Your Marks
–	Magic Risks	–	Monitor	49	Opaque
–	Main Man Paul	113?	Montecastillo†	70	Orchestral Strings
56	Majariyya	94	Montpelier Street	–	Ortelius
62	Majestic Mariner	67	Monty's Fancy	110	Osprey Ridge
–	Major Ballaby	–	Moondigua	–	Otto

–	Ourbus	85	Quest For A Star	–	Sahara Cheetah
–	Our Luck	85	Quest For Peace	74	Sail With The Wind
51	Owen Roe	48§	Quick Date	–	Saint-Declan
–	Padamul	–	Quiet Millfit	–	Saintly Sow'n'sow
–	Pagan Streams	82	Quinstars	52	Sakina
–	Palace Road	77	Quintus	54	Salsicaia
51	Palace Storm	–	Quinze	74	Samasakhan
63	Palacio	70	Rachael's Delight	–	Sammagefromtenesse
65	Palouse	–	Radunsky	69	Sanaka
–	Pancho Villa	81	Rainbow Melody	56	Sandymount Alice
–	Paris Jester	70	Rainbow Realm	–	Sarah
64	Park Leader	–	Rainswept	–	Sarahs Crusader
70	Pas Possible	70	Raise A Storm	60	Sardakaan
–	Passionate Pilgrim	–	Ramaphosa	90	Sarraaf
79	Patriot Games	95	Rapid Deployment	115	Sartorial†
75	Patsy Veale	77	Rashay	–	Sarwani
62	Pavla	–	Rashers Dasher	32	Scanlons Lass
82	Peaceful Sarah†	–	Rathbaun	60	Schwartzhalle
96	Peace In Ireland	–	Rathbawn Prince	–	Scopeful
72	Peace Leader	–	Rathnally Star	108	Scottish Memories
–	Peace of Mind	66	Really Chuffed	58	Sea Fisher
72	Peak Viewing	–	Red Setter	57	Sea Hymn
–	Pearl Lady	–	Red Tonic	57d	Sea Leopard
81	Penny Rich	52d	Red Venus	–	Second Nature
–	Penybont	39	Regal Dancer	62	Secret Promise
67	Penzita	–	Reggae Rhythm	20	Seeking Destiny
57	Persian Isle	35	Reken	67§	Segaview
–	Persian Life	51	Reminiscer	–	Sergeant Bill
124	Persian Punch†	117	Repertory†	–	Sevarine
71	Peru Genie†	69	Reptar	–	Shabob
61	Perugino Lady	–	Rhythm And Style	–	Shakieyl
41	Peru Girl	–	Rice's Hill	–	Shalgo
74	Peruvian Athlete	70	Richie Rich	55§	Shamartini
–	Petasus	–	Ridgewood Gem	–	Shanko
83	Petersham	68	Ridyan	–	Shantonagh
–	Petite Galerie	94	Right Job	69	Shareef Khan
61	Petite Ville	64	Rightontime	–	Sharon's Magic
–	Petno	–	Risky Whisky	80	Sharpaten
–	Piercetown Lad	47§	River Hopper	–	Sharp 'n' Shady
–	Pilgrim Star	–	River Tempest	100	Sheer Tenby
96	Pillars of Society	–	Robergerie	–	Sherbourne Guest
110	Pine Dance	98?	Rocamadoura	–	Shereevagh
96	Pipisflying	96	Romanylei†	91	She's Our Mare
54d	Pip'n Judy	53	Ronni Pancake†	114	Shoal Creek†
61	Planet Clare	59§	Rooftop Protest	34	Shoeless Joe
?	Polar Challenge	62	Roseau	37	Shvera
68	Polish Legion	63§	Rossmill Native	81	Siamsa
–	Political Animal	–	Rossmore Rosie	–§	Side Winding
82	Pollardsfield	113	Rostropovich†	58	Silent Native
70	Pollster	–	Roundstone	73	Silver Spray
68	Port Lush	–	Royal Albert	90	Silverware†
–	Portobello Express	73	Royal Barathea	–	Sir Foley
62	Powerswood	61	Royal Bart	–	Sirs Delight
–	Praia Grande	48	Royal Mark	32	Sir True Blue
64	Precious Love	62	Royal Midyan	57	Sister Christian
–	Prince Hussar	93d	Royal South	–	Skin Deep
–	Prince Robert	49	Royals Special	–	Skyline
–	Private Peace	35	Royal Suzy	72	Slightly Swift
90	Promising Lady	50	Rua Lass	–	Slippy Helen
108	Proud Native†	67	Rubenco	–	Smooth Sand
–	Provincial Lady	78	Rumours Abound	80	Snob Wells
108	Provosky	67	Rumson Way	–	Snugfit Rosie
112	Pulau Tioman†	78	Rupununi	114	Social Harmony†
–	Pure Gin	104d	Rush Brook	69	Society Blue
71	Purty Dancer	72§	Russian Comrade	46	Society Friend
79	Quadco	–	Rusticano	–	Sockittothem
94	Quality Team	89	Sabrinsky	69	Softly Softly
58	Queen For A Day	–	Saddle Mountain	63	Soldiered Again
–	Queen of Fibres	–	Saddler's Bay	–	Somegirlsdo
64	Queen Sarabi	85	Sage Dancer†		

INDEX TO PHOTOGRAPHS

PORTRAITS & SNAPSHOTS

Malhub	3 b.c Kingmambo – Arjuzah	*John Crofts*	604
Man O'Mystery	4 b.g Diesis – Eurostorm	*Clare Williams*	607
Masilia	4 b.f Kahyasi – Masmouda	*Peter Mooney*	616
Medicean	4 ch.c Machiavellian – Mystic Goddess	*John Crofts*	626
Milan	3 b.c Sadler's Wells – Kithanga	*Peter Mooney*	636
Mirio	4 ch.c Priolo – Mira Monte	*Bertrand*	645
Mister Cosmi	2 b.c Royal Applause – Degree	*John Crofts*	653
Morshdi	3 b.c Slip Anchor – Reem Albaraari	*John Crofts*	667
Mot Juste	3 b.f Mtoto – Bunting	*John Crofts*	669
Mount Abu	4 b.c Foxhound – Twany Angel	*John Crofts*	671
Mozart	3 b.c Danehill – Victoria Cross	*Caroline Norris*	676
Mr Combustible	3 b.c Hernando – Warg	*John Crofts*	679
Mubtaker	4 ch.c Silver Hawk – Gazayil	*John Crofts*	683
Mugharreb	3 b.c Gone West – Marling	*Clare Williams*	685
Munjiz	5 b.h Marju – Absaar	*John Crofts*	688
Murghem	6 b.h Common Grounds – Fabulous Pet	*John Crofts*	689
Mutamam	6 b.h Darshaan – Petal Girl	*John Crofts*	694
Nadia	3 ch.f Nashwan – Nazoo	*Bertrand*	702
Nayef	3 b.c Gulch – Height of Fashion	*John Crofts*	709
Nicobar	4 b.c Indian Ridge – Duchess of Alba	*John Crofts*	716
Noverre	3 b.c Rahy – Danseur Fabuleux	*John Crofts*	730
Olden Times	3 b.c Darshaan – Garah	*John Crofts*	739
Orientor	3 b.c Inchinor – Orient	*Alec Russell*	746
Parasol	2 br.c Halling – Bunting	*Clare Williams*	756
Pawn Broker	4 ch.c Selkirk – Dime Bag	*John Crofts*	761
Perfect Sunday	3 b.c Quest For Fame – Sunday Bazaar	*John Crofts*	767
Persiano	6 ch.g Efisio – Persiandale	*Clare Williams*	768
Priors Lodge	3 br.c Grand Lodge – Addaya	*Clare Williams*	798
Protectress	2 ch.f Hector Protector – Quota	*Clare Williams*	801
Pugin	3 b.c Darshaan – Gothic Dream	*Peter Mooney*	806
Quarter Moon	2 b.f Sadler's Wells – Jude	*Tim Hannan*	811
Queen's Logic	2 ch.f Grand Lodge – Lagrion	*Clare Williams*	817
Rainbow High	6 b.h Rainbow Quest – Imaginary	*John Crofts*	823
Ranin	3 b.f Unfuwain – Nafhaat	*John Crofts*	827
Revealing	2 ch.f Halling – Rive	*Clare Williams*	843
Rock of Gibraltar	2 b.c Danehill – Offshore Boom	*Peter Mooney*	858
Rose Gypsy	3 b.f Green Desert – Krisalya	*Peter Mooney*	864
Rosi's Boy	3 b.c Caerleon – Come On Rosi	*John Crofts*	866
Royal Rebel	5 b.g Robellino – Greenvera	*John Crofts*	873
Rushcutter Bay	8 br.g Mon Tresor – Llwy Bren	*Clare Williams*	877
Sacred Song	4 b.f Diesis – Ruby Ransom	*Clare Williams*	881
Sakhee	4 b.c Bahri – Thawakib	*John Crofts*	890
Sandmason	4 ch.c Grand Lodge – Sandy Island	*Clare Williams*	896
Sequoyah	3 b.f Sadler's Wells – Brigid	*Peter Mooney*	912
Silent Honor	2 ch.f Sunday Silence – Wood Vine	*John Crofts*	931
Slickly	5 gr.h Linamix – Slipstream Queen	*John Crofts*	944
Snowstorm	3 gr.g Environment Friend – Choral Sundown	*Clare Williams*	950
Softly Tread	3 b.f Tirol – Second Guess	*Clare Williams*	952
Solo Mio	7 b.h Sadler's Wells – Marie de Flandre	*John Crofts*	955
Sophisticat	2 b.f Storm Cat – Serena's Song	*Peter Mooney*	958
Storming Home	3 b.c Machiavellian – Try To Catch Me	*John Crofts*	976
Street Cry	3 br.c Machiavellian – Helen Street	*John Crofts*	980
Summoner	4 b.c Inchinor – Sumoto	*John Crofts*	989
Super Tassa	5 ch.m Lahib – Center Moriches	*Clare Williams*	995
Tamburlaine	3 b.c Royal Academy – Well Bought	*Clare Williams*	1006
Tempting Fate	3 b.f Persian Bold – West of Eden	*John Crofts*	1013
Tendulkar	2 b.c Spinning World – Romanette	*Peter Mooney*	1015
Theatre Script	3 ch.c Theatrical – Gossiping	*John Crofts*	1018
Time Away	3 b.f Darshaan – Not Before Time	*John Crofts*	1033
Tobougg	3 b.c Barathea – Lacovia	*John Crofts*	1038
Toroca	3 ch.f Nureyev – Grand Falls	*Peter Mooney*	1042
Tough Speed	4 b.c Miswaki – Nature's Magic	*John Crofts*	1047
Twilight Blues	2 ch.c Bluebird – Pretty Sharp	*Clare Williams*	1059
Vahorimix	3 gr.c Linamix – Vadsa Honor	*Bertrand*	1068
Vinnie Roe	3 b.c Definite Article – Kayu	*Caroline Norris*	1077
Volata	3 b.g Flying Spur – Musianica	*Clare Williams*	1080
Wannabe Around	3 b.c Primo Dominie – Noble Peregrine	*Clare Williams*	1083

RACE PHOTOGRAPHS

Dubai Duty Free Mill Reef Stakes (Newbury)	*Ed Byrne*	341
Dubai Poule d'Essai des Poulains (Longchamp)	*Ed Byrne*	1067
Dubai Poule d'Essai des Pouliches (Longchamp)	*John Crofts*	863
Dubai World Cup (Nad Al Sheba)	*George Selwyn*	171
Duke of Edinburgh Stakes (Handicap) (Royal Ascot)	*John Crofts*	1003
Duke of York Victor Chandler Stakes (York)	*Ed Byrne*	779
EDS Handicap (Epsom)	*John Crofts*	138
Ed Weetman Haulage And Storage Lincoln Trial Stakes (Handicap) (Wolverhampton)	*Alec Russell*	483
Entenmann's Irish 1000 Guineas (the Curragh)	*Ed Byrne*	466
Entenmann's Irish 2000 Guineas (the Curragh)	*Caroline Norris*	129
Falmouth Stakes (Newmarket)	*John Crofts*	803
Ford Solario Stakes (Sandown)	*W. Everitt*	833
Foster's Lager Northumberland Plate (Handicap) (Newcastle)	*Alec Russell*	78
Foster's Silver Cup Rated Stakes (Handicap) (York)	*Alec Russell*	37
£400000 Tattersalls Houghton Sales Stakes (Newmarket)	*John Crofts*	939
Gerrard Richmond Stakes (Goodwood)	*Ed Byrne*	652
GNER Doncaster Cup (Doncaster)	*John Crofts*	48
Godolphin Mile (Nad Al Sheba)	*Ed Byrne*	336
Goffs International Stakes (the Curragh)	*Caroline Norris*	266
Gold Cup (Royal Ascot)	*Ed Byrne*	871
Grand Criterium - Lucien Barriere (Longchamp)	*Bertrand*	856
Grand Prix de Saint-Cloud (Saint-Cloud)	*John Crofts*	644
Great Voltigeur Stakes (York)	*Alec Russell*	634
Hackney Empire Royal Lodge Stakes (Ascot)	*Alec Russell*	696
Halliwell Landau Lancashire Oaks (Haydock)	*Alec Russell*	880
Hardwicke Stakes (Royal Ascot)	*Alec Russell*	895
HBLB Leicestershire Stakes (Newmarket)	*John Crofts*	1085
Heathorns Bookmakers Gordon Richards Stakes (Sandown)	*John Crofts*	489
Hong Kong Jockey Club Sprint (Handicap) (Ascot)	*George Selwyn*	947
Ian Wight Happy 50th Birthday Maiden Stakes (Div II) (Kempton)	*Ed Byrne*	1025
IAWS Curragh Cup (the Curragh)	*Caroline Norris*	199
Independent Waterford Wedgwood Phoenix Stakes (Leopardstown)	*Caroline Norris*	506
Ireland The Food Island Irish Champion Stakes (Leopardstown)	*Ed Byrne*	327
Jacobs Goldene Peitsche (Baden-Baden)	*Frank Nolting*	1078
Jefferson Smurfit Memorial Irish St Leger (the Curragh)	*Peter Mooney*	1075
Jersey Stakes (Royal Ascot)	*John Crofts*	673
Jockey Club Cup (Newmarket)	*Alec Russell*	164
John Porter Stakes (Newbury)	*John Crofts*	589
John Smith's Cup (Handicap) (York)	*Bill Selwyn*	354
Joy UK Conditions Guaranteed Sweepstakes (Doncaster)	*George Selwyn*	552
JPMorgan Private Bank Goodwood Cup (Goodwood)	*John Crofts*	770
JRA Nakayama Rous Stakes (Newmarket)	*John Crofts*	477
Juddmonte Grand Prix de Paris (Longchamp)	*John Crofts*	198
Juddmonte International Stakes (York)	*George Selwyn*	887
Juddmonte Lockinge Stakes (Newbury)	*John Crofts*	623
Kildangan Stud Irish Oaks (the Curragh)	*Ed Byrne*	553
King Edward VII Stakes (Royal Ascot)	*John Crofts*	975
King George Stakes (Goodwood)	*John Crofts*	261
King George V Stakes (Handicap) (Royal Ascot)	*John Crofts*	116
King George VI and Queen Elizabeth Diamond Stakes (Ascot)	*John Crofts*	377
King's Stand Stakes (Ascot)	*George Selwyn*	179
Ladbrokes Bunbury Cup (Handicap) (Newmarket)	*George Selwyn*	88
Melrose Rated Stakes (Handicap) (York)	*Ed Byrne*	83
Meon Valley Stud Fillies' Mile (Ascot)	*John Crofts*	406
Merewood Homes Yorkshire Cup (York)	*John Crofts*	611
Middle Park Stakes (Newmarket)	*John Crofts*	508
Millennium And Copthorne Shergar Cup Stayers (Rated Stakes Handicap) (Ascot)	*W. Everitt*	662
Moet & Chandon Silver Magnum (Handicap) (Epsom)	*Ed Byrne*	878
Motability And RAC Rated Stakes (Handicap) (York)	*Alec Russell*	1024
Moyglare Stud Stakes (the Curragh)	*Caroline Norris*	810
Newmarket Experience Handicap (Newmarket)	*Ed Byrne*	979
NGK Spark Plugs Abernant Stakes (Newmarket)	*Ed Byrne*	792
Norfolk Stakes (Royal Ascot)	*John Crofts*	505

1200

Oaks d'Italia (Milan)	*Perrucci*	1116
Owen Brown Rockfel Stakes (Newmarket)	*John Crofts*	267
Paradime Acomb Stakes (York)	*John Crofts*	212
Pentax "Under Any" Conditions Stakes (Sandown)	*Ed Byrne*	1072
Peterhouse Group Rated Stakes (Handicap) (York)	*Ed Byrne*	455
Peugeot Gordon Stakes (Goodwood)	*John Crofts*	43
Peugeot Lowther Stakes (York)	*Alec Russell*	813
Peugeot Sun Chariot Stakes (Newmarket)	*Ed Byrne*	474
Phil Bull Trophy Conditions Stakes (Pontefract)	*Keith Robinson*	1057
Phoenix Sprint Stakes (Leopardstown)	*Peter Mooney*	98
Polypipe Flying Childers Stakes (Doncaster)	*Alec Russell*	882
Porcelanosa Sprint Stakes (Sandown)	*George Selwyn*	647
Prince of Wales's Stakes (Royal Ascot)	*Alec Russell*	325
Princess Margaret Stakes (Ascot)	*Alec Russell*	566
Princess of Wales's Pearl And Coutts Stakes (Newmarket)	*John Crofts*	693
Prix de Diane Hermes (Chantilly)	*John Crofts*	74
Prix de l'Abbaye de Longchamp – Majestic Barriere (Longchamp)	*John Crofts*	470
Prix de la Foret (Longchamp)	*John Crofts*	670
Prix de l'Arc de Triomphe – Lucien Barriere (Longchamp)	*Ed Byrne*	888
Prix de l'Opera – Casino Barriere d'Enghien-Les Bains (Longchamp)	*John Crofts*	1016
Prix de Malleret (Saint-Cloud)	*John Crofts*	257
Prix de Meautry Royal Barriere (Deauville)	*Ed Byrne*	274
Prix de Ranelagh (Longchamp)	*John Crofts*	259
Prix des Chenes (Longchamp)	*Ed Byrne*	915
Prix d'Ispahan (Longchamp)	*John Crofts*	734
Prix Dollar Fouquet's Barriere (Longchamp)	*Bertrand*	41
Prix du Cadran – Casino Barriere de Cannes Croisette (Longchamp)	*Bertrand*	386
Prix du Conseil de Paris (Longchamp)	*Bertrand*	1110
Prix du Haras de Fresnay-le-Buffard Jacques le Marois (Deauville)	*George Selwyn*	1067
Prix du Jockey Club (Chantilly)	*George Selwyn*	62
Prix du Moulin de Longchamp (Longchamp)	*Ed Byrne*	943
Prix du Prince d'Orange (Longchamp)	*John Crofts*	308
Prix du Rond-Point – Casino Barriere La Rochelle (Longchamp)	*John Crofts*	201
Prix Foy – Gray d'Albion Barriere (Longchamp)	*Ed Byrne*	450
Prix Ganay (Longchamp)	*John Crofts*	400
Prix Guillaume d'Ornano (Deauville)	*Bertrand*	618
Prix Hubert de Chaudenay – Casino Barriere de Menton (Longchamp)	*John Crofts*	1084
Prix Jean Prat (Chantilly)	*Ed Byrne*	738
Prix Kergorlay (Deauville)	*George Selwyn*	384
Prix La Rochette Royal Thalasso Barriere (Longchamp)	*John Crofts*	419
Prix Lupin (Longchamp)	*John Crofts*	197
Prix Marcel Boussac Criterium des Pouliches – Royal Barriere (Longchamp)	*Bertrand*	984
Prix Maurice de Gheest (Deauville)	*John Crofts*	531
Prix Morny Casinos Barriere (Deauville)	*John Crofts*	507
Prix Niel – Casino Barriere d'Enghien-Les-Bains (Longchamp)	*George Selwyn*	395
Prix Robert Papin (Maisons-Laffitte)	*Bertrand*	1121
Prix Royal-Oak (Longchamp)	*Bertrand*	1076
Prix Saint-Alary (Longchamp)	*Bertrand*	701
Prix Vermeille – Hermitage Barriere(Longchamp)	*Ed Byrne*	75
Queen Alexandra Stakes (Royal Ascot)	*John Crofts*	570
Queen Anne Stakes (Royal Ascot)	*John Crofts*	624
Queen Elizabeth II Stakes (Ascot)	*John Crofts*	987
Queen Mother's Cup (Ladies) Handicap (York)	*Alec Russell*	442
Queen's Vase (Royal Ascot)	*George Selwyn*	66
Racecourse Video Services Maiden Stakes (Newcastle)	*John Grossick*	586
Racing Post Trophy (Doncaster)	*John Crofts*	444
Randombet.com Lincoln (Handicap) (Doncaster)	*Alec Russell*	719
Ribblesdale Stakes (Royal Ascot)	*John Crofts*	886
Richard H. Faught Memorial Stakes (the Curragh)	*John Crofts*	841
Riggs Bank Rated Stakes (Handicap) (Ascot)	*George Selwyn*	501
Rothmans Royals Champagne Stakes (Doncaster)	*Ed Byrne*	283
Rothmans Royals May Hill Stakes (Doncaster)	*Alec Russell*	422

Rothmans Royals Park Hill Stakes (Doncaster)	*Alec Russell*	826
Rothmans Royals St Leger Stakes (Doncaster)	*John Crofts*	635
Royal Hunt Cup (Handicap) (Royal Ascot)	*Alec Russell*	996
Ruinart Champagne Stakes (Hackwood) (Newbury)	*Bill Selwyn*	485
Sagitta Jockey Club Stakes (Newmarket)	*John Crofts*	639
Sagitta 1000 Guineas Stakes (Newmarket)	*George Selwyn*	57
Sagitta 2000 Guineas Stakes (Newmarket)	*Ed Byrne*	393
San Miguel March Stakes (Goodwood)	*John Crofts*	918
Scottish Equitable Gimcrack Stakes (York)	*Alec Russell*	856
Shadwell Stud Cheshire Oaks (Chester)	*Ed Byrne*	855
Shadwell Stud Cheveley Park Stakes (Newmarket)	*John Crofts*	814
Singapore Airlines International Cup (Kranji)	*Associated Press*	304
Sodexho Prestige Scottish Classic (Ayr)	*Alec Russell*	174
Stan James Geoffrey Freer Stakes (Newbury)	*Bill Selwyn*	678
Stanley Leisure Sprint Cup (Haydock)	*Alec Russell*	732
St James's Palace Stakes (Royal Ascot)	*George Selwyn*	130
Tattersalls Breeders Stakes (the Curragh)	*Peter Mooney*	117
Tattersalls Gold Cup (the Curragh)	*Peter Mooney*	324
Tattersalls Musidora Stakes (York)	*John Crofts*	1032
The Mail On Sunday Mile Final (Handicap) (Ascot)	*John Crofts*	420
timeform.com Silver Salver (Handicap) (Newmarket)	*Ed Byrne*	91
TNT July Stakes (Newmarket)	*Ed Byrne*	630
Tom McGee Autumn Stakes (Ascot)	*John Crofts*	338
Tote (Ayr) Gold Cup (Handicap) (Ayr)	*Alec Russell*	217
Tote (Ayr) Silver Cup (Handicap) (Ayr)	*Alec Russell*	1011
Tote Bookmakers Silver Tankard Stakes (Pontefract)	*Alec Russell*	105
Tote Cesarewitch (Handicap) (Newmarket)	*John Crofts*	267
Tote Chester Cup (Handicap) (Chester)	*George Selwyn*	822
Tote Ebor (Handicap) (York)	*Alec Russell*	627
Tote Exacta Stakes (Handicap) (Ascot)	*John Crofts*	236
Tote Exacta Stakes (Handicap) (Sandown)	*Ed Byrne*	1062
Tote Gold Trophy Stakes (Handicap) (Goodwood)	*Ed Byrne*	750
Tote International Stakes (Handicap) (Ascot)	*John Crofts*	89
Tote Scoop6 Cambridgeshire (Handicap) (Newmarket)	*Ed Byrne*	462
Tote Scoop6 November Stakes (Handicap) (Doncaster)	*Bill Selwyn*	868
Tote Ten To Follow Rated Stakes (Handicap) (Newbury)	*John Crofts*	658
Tote Trifecta Portland (Handicap) (Doncaster)	*Alec Russell*	948
Tote Trifecta Stakes (Handicap) (Ascot)	*Alec Russell*	279
Tripleprint Temple Stakes (Sandown)	*W. Everitt*	178
£200000 St Leger Yearling Stakes (Doncaster)	*Alec Russell*	27
UAE Derby (Nad Al Sheba)	*Ed Byrne*	317
UAE Grosser Preis von Baden (Baden-Baden)	*Frank Sorge*	666
Victor Chandler Challenge Stakes (Newmarket)	*John Crofts*	688
Victor Chandler European Free Handicap (Newmarket)	*Ed Byrne*	206
Victor Chandler Lupe Stakes (Goodwood)	*Ed Byrne*	353
Victor Chandler Nunthorpe Stakes (York)	*Ed Byrne*	675
Vodafone Coronation Cup (Epsom)	*John Crofts*	691
Vodafone 'Dash' Rated Stakes (Handicap) (Epsom)	*John Crofts*	127
Vodafone Derby Stakes (Epsom)	*George Selwyn*	372
Vodafone Derby Stakes (Epsom)	*Ed Byrne*	374
Vodafone Derby Stakes (Epsom)	*John Crofts*	375
Vodafone Diomed Stakes (Epsom)	*Ed Byrne*	807
Vodafone Horris Hill Stakes (Newbury)	*John Crofts*	828
Vodafone Nassau Stakes (Goodwood)	*John Crofts*	554
Vodafone Oaks (Epsom)	*Ed Byrne*	467
Vodafone Stewards' Cup (Handicap) (Goodwood)	*John Crofts*	418
Watership Down Stud Sales Race (Ascot)	*Ed Byrne*	594
Weatherbys Earl of Sefton Stakes (Newmarket)	*John Crofts*	848
Weatherbys Insurance Lonsdale Stakes (York)	*John Crofts*	771
Weatherbys Super Sprint (Newbury)	*Ed Byrne*	404
William Hill Great St Wilfrid Stakes (Handicap) (Ripon)	*Alec Russell*	71
William Hill Mile (Handicap) (Goodwood)	*John Crofts*	845
William Hill Trophy (Handicap) (York)	*Alec Russell*	745
Willmott Dixon Cornwallis Stakes (Ascot)	*John Crofts*	271
Windsor Castle Stakes (Royal Ascot)	*Bill Selwyn*	487
Wokingham Stakes (Handicap) (Royal Ascot)	*Alec Russell*	714

COMPTON PLACE

chesnut 1994 by INDIAN RIDGE - NOSEY by Nebbiolo

CHAMPION EUROPEAN 3-Y-O SPRINTER

First crop yearlings made
130,000 gns, 120,000 gns, 80,000 gns, etc.

Foal Median of
17,500 gns in 2001

FIRST RUNNERS IN 2002

Standing at:
Whitsbury Manor Stud
Fee: £3,500 October 1st

C. Oakshott,
Whitsbury Manor Stud,
Fordingbridge, SP6 3QP
Telephone: 01725 - 518254
Fax: 01725 - 518503

Enquiries to:
LONDON THOROUGHBRED
SERVICES LTD.,
Biddlesgate Farm, Nr Cranborne,
Dorset BH21 5RS.
Telephone: 01725 - 517711.
Fax: 01725 - 517833.
email: lts@lts-uk.com
Website: www.lts-uk.com

FIRST TRUMP

chesnut 1991 by PRIMO DOMINIE - VALIKA by Valiyar

A LEADING BRITISH SIRE OF 2-Y-O.s

MRS P	- Flying Childers Stakes **Gr.2**
MEDIA MOGUL	- Will Rogers Stakes **Gr.3**
	2nd July Stakes **Gr.3**
TWO CLUBS	- Doncaster Stakes **LR**

57% Winners to Runners from his first 3 crops
and sire of **34 individual 2-Y-O winners**

FORZANDO

bay 1981 by FORMIDABLE - PRINCELY MAID by King's Troop

MULTIPLE GROUP WINNER

Won 12 races including Metropolitan H'cap **Gr.1**
and **5 consecutive races as a 2-year-old**

Year After Year Sire of Top, Consistent, Sound 2-Year-Olds
EASYCALL, GREAT DEEDS, HIGH PREMIUM,
MISTERIOSO, PHILIDOR, POOL MUSIC,
PURE FORMALITY, SUPERIOR PREMIUM,
UP AND AT'EM, etc.

55% Winners to Runners

GENEROUS

chesnut 1988 by CAERLEON - DOFF THE DERBY by Master Derby

TIMEFORM's EUROPEAN CHAMPION OF THE DECADE

Group 1 Winner at 2
European Champion at 3 - Timeform Rated 139

From his first 4 European crops sire of:-

27 Black Type Winners inc. **15** Group Winners
14% Black Type Winners to Foals
19% Black Type Performers to Foals

INCHINOR

chesnut 1990 by AHONOORA - INCHMURRIN by Lomond

THE GROUP ONE SIRE

SUMMONER	Queen Elizabeth II Stakes **Gr.1 in 2001**
BANNISTER	Gimcrack Stakes **Gr.2 at 2**
GOLDEN SILCA	Mill Reef Stakes **Gr.2 at 2**
	Desmond Stakes **Gr.3**, Victress Stakes **LR**
	2nd Irish 1000 Gns and Coronation S **Gr.1**
PALANCA	Premio Primi Passi **Gr.3 at 2**
UMISTIM	Horris Hill Stakes **Gr.3 at 2**, Craven Stakes **Gr.3**

IMPERIAL MEASURE - NORDICAN INCH - SHAWDON - SOSSUS VLEI

Standing at: **Woodland Stud**
Fee: £10,000 October 1st

Woodland Stud, Snailwell Road,
Newmarket, Suffolk CB8 7DJ.
Telephone: Newmarket
01638 - 663081.
Fax: 01638 - 663036.
email: lts@lts-uk.com
Website: www.lts-uk.com

Enquiries to:
**LONDON THOROUGHBRED
SERVICES LTD.,**
Biddlesgate Farm, Nr Cranborne,
Dorset BH21 5RS.
Telephone: 01725 - 517711.
Fax: 01725 - 517833.
email: lts@lts-uk.com
Website: www.lts-uk.com

LTS

MUTAMAM

bay 1995 by DARSHAAN - PETAL GIRL by Caerleon

DARSHAAN'S MOST PROLIFIC PATTERN WINNER

Winner of 7 Group Races and Group 1 placed at 2 viz:-

Canadian International **Gr.1**
Princess of Wales's Stakes **Gr.2**
September Stakes **Gr.3** (twice)
Rose of Lancaster Stakes **Gr.3**
Select Stakes **Gr.3**
Cumberland Lodge Stakes **Gr.3**
3rd Racing Post Trophy **Gr.1** *at 2*

> Jt **CHAMPION**
> in Canada 2001

PURSUIT OF LOVE

bay 1989 by GROOM DANCER - DANCE QUEST by Green Dancer

CHAMPION BRITISH-BASED SIRE IN 2001

(active sires, races won worldwide)

DUAL CHAMPION SIRE OF 2-Y-O.s
with **60 INDIVIDUAL 2-Y-O WINNERS**

64% WINNERS TO RUNNERS

ROBELLINO
bay 1979 by ROBERTO - ISOBELLINE by Pronto

IN 2001
Sire of **ROYAL REBEL (Gr.1)**,
REBELLINE (Gr.2) PULAU TIOMAN (Gr.3)
RAPSCALLION (Gr.3 at 2)

Sire of Classic Winners:
CLASSIC PARK - Airlie/Coolmore Irish 1000 Gns **Gr.1**
ROBERTICO - German Derby **Gr.1**
MISTER BAILEYS 2000 Gns **Gr.1**

Standing at:
Littleton Stud
Fee: £6,000 October 1st

Littleton Stud,
Winchester,
Hants. S022 6QX.
Telephone: 01962 - 880210
Fax: 01962 - 882290

LTS

Enquiries to:
LONDON THOROUGHBRED
SERVICES LTD.,
Biddlesgate Farm, Nr Cranborne,
Dorset BH21 5RS.
Telephone: 01725 - 517711.
Fax: 01725 - 517833.
email: lts@lts-uk.com
Website: www.lts-uk.com

SELKIRK LANWADES

chesnut 1988 by SHARPEN UP - ANNIE EDGE by Nebbiolo

CHAMPION EUROPEAN MILER 1991 AND 1992
CHAMPION SIRE OF 2-Y-O's IN GB & IRE 2001
(% winners to runners, minimum 20 runners)

SULK	Prix Marcel Boussac **Gr.1 at 2 in 2001**
FIELD OF HOPE	Prix de la Foret **Gr.1**
SQUEAK	Beverly Hills H'cap **Gr.1**, Matriarch Stakes **Gr.1**
WINCE	1000 Guineas **Gr.1**
INDEPENDENCE	Sun Chariot Stakes **Gr.2 in 2001**
COUNTRY GARDEN	Honeymoon H'cap **Gr.2**
KIRKWALL	Prix Eugene Adam **Gr.2**, Keeneland Turf Mile **Gr.2**
SIGN OF HOPE	Oak Tree Derby **Gr.2**
TRANS ISLAND	Prix du Rond Point **Gr.2**, Diomed Stakes **Gr.3**
HARBOUR ISLAND	Prix de Cabourg **Gr.3**
HIDDEN MEADOW	Prix du Palais-Royal **Gr.3**

Standing at: **Lanwades Stud**
Fee: £30,000 October 1st

Kirsten Rausing,
Lanwades Stud, Moulton,
Suffolk, CB8 8QS.
Telephone: 01638 - 750222.
Fax: 01638 - 751186.
email: lanwades@msn.com
Website: www.lanwades.com

Enquiries to:
**LONDON THOROUGHBRED
SERVICES LTD.,**
Biddlesgate Farm,
Nr Cranborne, Dorset BH21 5RS.
Telephone: 01725 - 517711.
Fax: 01725 - 517833.
email: lts@lts-uk.com
Website: www.lts-uk.com

LTS

SUPERIOR PREMIUM

brown 1994 by FORZANDO - DEVIL'S DIRGE by Song

GROUP 2 WINNING SON OF A LEADING 2-Y-O SIRE

Winner of Cork & Orrery Stakes **Gr.2**
at Royal Ascot
and
Vodafone Stewards Cup
at Goodwood

Retires to Stud in 2002

Standing at:
Throckmorton Court Stud
Fee: £2,000 October 1st

Peter Balding,
Throckmorton Court Stud,
Pershore,
Worcestershire WR10 2JX
Telephone: 01386 - 462559
Fax: 01386 - 462566

Enquiries to:
LONDON THOROUGHBRED
SERVICES LTD.,
Biddlesgate Farm, Nr Cranborne,
Dorset BH21 5RS.
Telephone: 01725 - 517711
Fax: 01725 - 517833
email: lts@lts-uk.com
Website: www.lts-uk.com

LTS

TIMEFORM RACELINE
with Jim McGrath

'Timeform Raceline aims to provide an insight into the day's racing as I see it, and to give members the opportunity to back what I'll be backing'

Timeform managing director Jim McGrath is widely regarded as one of the best form-book experts in the country. The points system Jim uses for account bets on *Timeform Raceline* gives members an idea of the strength behind the selections and suits all pockets.

In his preview of each day's racing—available by 10.30 a.m. on a standard-rate number—Jim goes through a number of races, highlighting all the horses worthy of note. These can offer extra betting opportunities, but the profit figures quoted refer to the account bets alone.

TIMEFORM RACELINE SUMMARISED

- A daily preview of the best of the day's racing
- Account bets with advised stakes (in points), given at the start of each message
- Pointers and advice about other horses and races
- Occasional ante-post wagers and bets in big races overseas
- Message available by 10.30 a.m. and often much earlier

2002 FLAT SUBSCRIPTION RATES
Any individual calendar month ONLY £129
(apply March-October 2002; rates for longer subscriptions on request)

19 Timeform House, Halifax, West Yorkshire HX1 1XE
Tel: 01422 330540 Fax: 01422 398017

AGE, WEIGHT & DISTANCE TABLE

Timeform's scale of weight-for-age for the flat

Dist	Age	July 1-16	17-31	Aug 1-16	17-31	Sept 1-16	17-30	Oct 1-16	17-31	Nov 1-16	17-30	Dec 1-16	17-31
5f	4	10-0	10-0	10-0	10-0	10-0	10-0	10-0	10-0	10-0	10-0	10-0	10-0
	3	9-11	9-12	9-12	9-12	9-13	9-13	9-13	9-13	10-0	10-0	10-0	10-0
	2	8—8	8—9	8-10	8-11	8-12	8-13	9—0	9—1	9—2	9—2	9—3	9—4
6f	4	10-0	10-0	10-0	10-0	10-0	10-0	10-0	10-0	10-0	10-0	10-0	10-0
	3	9-10	9-10	9-11	9-11	9-12	9-12	9-12	9-13	9-13	9-13	9-13	10-0
	2	8—5	8—6	8—7	8—8	8—9	8-10	8-11	8-12	8-13	9—0	9—1	9—2
7f	4	10-0	10-0	10-0	10-0	10-0	10-0	10-0	10-0	10-0	10-0	10-0	10-0
	3	9—9	9—9	9-10	9-10	9-11	9-11	9-11	9-12	9-12	9-12	9-13	9-13
	2	8—2	8—3	8—4	8—5	8—6	8—7	8—9	8-10	8-11	8-12	8-13	9—0
1m	4	10-0	10-0	10-0	10-0	10-0	10-0	10-0	10-0	10-0	10-0	10-0	10-0
	3	9—7	9—8	9—8	9—9	9—9	9-10	9-10	9-11	9-11	9-12	9-12	9-12
	2			8—2	8—3	8—4	8—5	8—6	8—7	8—8	8—9	8-10	8-11
9f	4	10-0	10-0	10-0	10-0	10-0	10-0	10-0	10-0	10-0	10-0	10-0	10-0
	3	9—6	9—7	9—7	9—8	9—8	9—9	9—9	9-10	9-10	9-11	9-11	9-12
	2					8—1	8—3	8—4	8—5	8—6	8—7	8—8	8—9
1¼m	4	10-0	10-0	10-0	10-0	10-0	10-0	10-0	10-0	10-0	10-0	10-0	10-0
	3	9—5	9—5	9—6	9—7	9—7	9—8	9—8	9—9	9—9	9-10	9-10	9-11
	2					8—0		8—1	8—2	8—4	8—5	8—6	8—7
11f	4	10-0	10-0	10-0	10-0	10-0	10-0	10-0	10-0	10-0	10-0	10-0	10-0
	3	9—3	9—4	9—5	9—5	9—6	9—7	9—7	9—8	9—8	9—9	9—9	9-10
1½m	4	10-0	10-0	10-0	10-0	10-0	10-0	10-0	10-0	10-0	10-0	10-0	10-0
	3	9—2	9—2	9—3	9—4	9—5	9—5	9—6	9—7	9—7	9—8	9—9	9—9
13f	4	9-13	9-13	10-0	10-0	10-0	10-0	10-0	10-0	10-0	10-0	10-0	10-0
	3	9—0	9—1	9—2	9—3	9—4	9—4	9—5	9—6	9—6	9—7	9—8	9—8
1¾m	4	9-13	9-13	9-13	10-0	10-0	10-0	10-0	10-0	10-0	10-0	10-0	10-0
	3	8-13	9—0	9—1	9—2	9—3	9—3	9—4	9—5	9—5	9—6	9—7	9—7
15f	4	9-12	9-13	9-13	9-13	9-13	10-0	10-0	10-0	10-0	10-0	10-0	10-0
	3	8-12	8-13	9—0	9—1	9—1	9—2	9—3	9—4	9—4	9—5	9—6	9—6
2m	4	9-12	9-12	9-13	9-13	9-13	9-13	10-0	10-0	10-0	10-0	10-0	10-0
	3	8-10	8-11	8-12	8-13	9—0	9—1	9—2	9—3	9—3	9—4	9—5	9—5
2¼m	4	9-11	9-12	9-12	9-12	9-13	9-13	9-13	9-13	10-0	10-0	10-0	10-0
	3	8—8	8—9	8-10	8-11	8-12	8-13	9—0	9—1	9—2	9—2	9—3	9—3
2½m	4	9-10	9-11	9-11	9-12	9-12	9-12	9-13	9-13	9-13	9-13	10-0	10-0
	3	8—6	8—7	8—8	8—9	8-10	8-11	8-12	8-13	9—0	9—1	9—2	9—3

For 5-y-o's and older, use 10-0 in all cases
Race distances in the above tables are shown only at 1 furlong intervals.
For races over odd distances, the nearest distance shown in the table should be used:
thus for races of 1m to 1m 109 yards, use the table weights for 1m;
for 1m 110 yards to 1m 219 yards use the 9f table

**The age, weight and distance table covering January to June
appears on the end paper at the front of the book**